Concordance to the Poetical Works of John Dryden

CONCORDANCE
to the Poetical Works of
JOHN DRYDEN

Edited by

GUY MONTGOMERY

Assisted by

MARY JACKMAN *and* HELEN S. AGOA

Preface by Josephine Miles

UNIVERSITY OF CALIFORNIA PRESS

Berkeley and Los Angeles

1957

UNIVERSITY OF CALIFORNIA PRESS
Berkeley and Los Angeles

CAMBRIDGE UNIVERSITY PRESS
London, England

PREFACE

This Concordance had the form, at Professor Guy Montgomery's death in 1951, of 240,000 alphabetized cards, based on the Cambridge Edition of the Poetical Works of John Dryden, edited by George Rapall Noyes, 1920, revised and enlarged in 1950. (The Houghton-Mifflin Co., Boston.)

Three problems were primary: the bulk of the work, the cost of publication, the difficulty of accurate checking by assistants unfamiliar with the material. The decision to use IBM machines as an aid in checking helped solve the other problems in turn. Quotations could not be handled by machines, and their omission reduced bulk, while IBM printing made possible a photolith process to minimize publication costs.

The process was this: IBM cards were punched for word, poem symbol, and line number, following the order of Professor Montgomery's cards. The resulting listing was corrected, and the cards were then sorted by machine into poem and line order, so that proof could be read in text-order. After correction and return to alphabetical order, the final listing was made, the columns pasted three to a page on specially ruled sheets, and the pages then delivered to the Press for photolithography.

All poems in the main text have been included, but not those in the appendices. All prose passages, including stage directions, are omitted.

Use of machines makes cross references and homographic distinctions impractical, and also necessitates replacement of letters represented by an apostrophe in Dryden's work, like watery for wat'ry. The one exception is see'st. Possessive apostrophes and accents have been added by hand.

Listing is strictly alphabetical, with an example of punctuation as follows: field, field's, fields, fields' A word appearing more than once in a single line is listed only once. Words in phrases like King Arthur, Covent Garden, King's House, posse poetarum, are listed separately as single words Abbreviations are spelled out in full (with the exception of Mr., which occurs twice.) Greek and Polish words are transliterated into Roman letters. All variant spellings have been retained, and such odd usages as beats for beads, VP2, 9; rear for rare, BP, 98; descents for dissents, G2, 710; and the occasional salvage for savage, negromancer for necromancer. Three apparent misprints in the text may be noted: astonomical for astronomical, UDH 42; bewixt for betwixt, P5, 229; and erom for from, AE3, 169.

The following omitted words include all those omitted by other Concordances, with the exceptions of scarce and something, and with the addition of certain terms for consistency's sake, such as upper in addition to up: a, about, above, adown, after, afterward, afterwards, again, against, ah, alas, all, along, also, although, am and other forms of to be, amid, amidst, among, amongst, an, and, another, any, anywhere, around, as, at, aught, away, awhile, ay, aye, backward, because, before, behind, below, beneath, beside, besides, between, betwixt, beyond, both, but, by, can and other forms, did and other forms of do, down, downward, downwards, each, e'en, e'er, either, else, elsewhere, 'em, ere, even, ever, every, everywhere, for, forth, fro, from, 'gainst, had and other forms of have, he and other forms, hence, henceforth, henceforward, her and other forms, here, hereafter, heretofore, hether, hither, hitherto, how, however, I and other forms, if, indeed, into, inward, inwardly, it and other forms, i'th', least, less, lessen and other forms, lest, let and other forms, like (adjec-

tive, noun, adverb), lo, many, may and other forms, mid, midst, more, most, must, nay, naught, ne'er, neither, never, nevertheless, no, none, nor, not, now, nowhere, O, o', o'er, of, off, oft, often, oh, on, once, one, only, onward, onwards, or, o'th', other, others, other's, others', our and other forms, out, outward, over, own, quite, round (adverb and preposition), 's, said and other forms, same, shall and other forms, she, should and other forms, since, sith, so, soever, some, somewhat, somewhere, still, such, t', 't, th', than, that, that's, the, thee, their and other forms, then, thence, there, therefore, there's, these, thether, thine and other forms, this, thither, thitherward, tho', those, though, thro', through, throughout, thus, till, 'tis, to, too, toward, towardly, towards, 'twas, twixt, under, underneath, until, unto, up, upper, uppermost, upon, upward, upwards, us and other forms of we, very, well, what, whatever, whatsoever, when, whenas, whence, whenever, where, whereas, wherein, whereof, wheresoever, wherever, whether, which, whichever, whichsoever, while, whilst, whither, who and other forms, why, with, withal, within, without, would and other forms, yes, yet, you and other forms, and Dryden's own special contractions: b', 'bove, 'it, t'other, 'ts, w'

The following normally excluded terms are included in their special noun, verb, or adjective forms only: after, art, being, can, down, even, like, may, might, mine, must, own, round, still, till, well, will.

Of the roughly 208,000 word occurrences listed in this Concordance after the 32,000 omissions, about 33,000, or one-sixth of the total, consist of a few repeated adjectives, nouns, and verbs ranging in use from 400 to 1,100 times apiece. The 57 words so used by Dryden are as follows: arms, bear, blood, care, come, day, death, eye, fair, fall, fate, fear, fire, fight, find, first, fly, foe, force, friend, full, give, go, God, good, ground, hand, head, heaven, high, king, know, lie, last, leave, live, long, love, make, man, mind, name, new, night, place, please, power, rise, rest, see, stand, take, think, time, war, way, youth. (As love includes both noun and verb, so think includes thought; youth, young; and so on.) A comparative study of a similar number of major terms in the Spenser, Donne, Milton, and Pope Concordances shows that Dryden shares 33 terms with Spenser, 30 with Milton, 29 each with Donne and Pope. The words care, fate, fight, foe, force, ground, and war are his alone; the words arms, bear, blood, fear, fly, full, high, king, night, place, please, power, rest, stand, he shares with Spenser or Milton or both. With Donne and Pope he shares fire and lie, new and name; with Pope alone, friend, head, mind, and rise. The rest are terms generally shared by all. Dryden's major vocabulary is clearly an heroic one; not only his translation but his satire makes rich use of it. His own characteristic words are terms of deliberation: care, fate, friend, head, and mind. He is one of the few leading poets for whom a Concordance has been lacking, and now that it is available we may hope to discern more precisely his contributions to poetic tradition.

Special debts must be acknowledged to many: to Mrs. Guy Montgomery; to President Robert Gordon Sproul and the Faculty Research Committee, who helped finance the work on the volume; to Professors Douglas Chrétien of the Department of Speech and Francis Carmody of the Department of French; to Professors Willard Farnham, James D. Hart, and the late George R. Potter, chairmen of the Department of English; to the Editors of the new edition of Dryden at the University of California at Los Angeles; to Mr. John Goetz of the University Press; to

many under the guidance of Mr. Gordon Morrison and Mr. Boyd Judd at the Computer Laboratory, especially Shirley Rice, Odette Carothers, and Penny Gee; to Professor Lester A. Hubbard who assisted Professor Montgomery; and finally to the volume's present assistant editors, Mary Jackman and Helen S. Agoa, without whom it could never have been completed.

Josephine Miles

Berkeley, January, 1957

The following is an alphabetical list of the symbols used in this Concordance to designate titles in the poems of Dryden. The titles which here accompany the symbols are taken from the Table of Contents in the Cambridge Edition of the Poetical Works of John Dryden, 1950. (The Houghton Mifflin Co., Boston.) For example, AA designates the poem Absalom and Achitophel, SAA designates the poem The Second Part of Absalom and Achitophel. The page numbers indicate the pages in this Edition on which the poems begin. Under each word in the Concordance, the order of the symbols is chronological, following the order of sequence in the Noyes text.

Word	Ref	No.
À	WB	340
AARON	HAP	187
	BR	297
AARON'S	AA	525
	SAA	1024
ABANDON	AE2	472
	KT3	287
	CI	527
ABANDONED	EAZ	37
	BR	126
	BR	288
	AE1	841
	AE2	90
	AE2	762
	AE2	769
	AE2	915
	AE3	793
	AE4	281
	AE10	1216
	AE11	399
	AE11	1072
	KT3	764
	B	277
ABANDONING	AM	895
	HAP	1612
	J10	153
	MC	67
	AE2	1015
	AE12	723
ABAS	AE1	173
	AE3	371
	AE10	249
	AE10	605
	M12	423
ABASED	B	285
ABASHED	HIF	767
ABATE	L2	38
	M1	688
	AE9	838
ABATED	AE9	687
	M15	345
ABATES	G1	463
ABBETHDIN	AA	188
ABBETHDIN'S	SAA	1014
ABBEY	C	44
ABDAEL	SAA	967
	SAA	968
	SAA	974
ABDICATED	M15	275
ABED	PT	38
	PD	19
	HAP	2319
	J6	585
	J16	70
	WB	128
ABELLA	AE7	1020
ABETTORS	HAP	1647
ABHOR	HS	43
	AA	187
	EPC	25
	SAA	786
	HAP	843
	HAP	2000
	BR	342
	J3	105
	M13	178
	G1	337
	AE5	886
ABHORRED	ELN	15
	AA	619
	MO	6
	HAP	1752
	HAP	2359
	AE1	101
	AE2	782
	AE7	856
	AE11	391
	AE11	1228
	M10	2
	M15	433
	CI	215
ABHORREST	AE5	902
ABHORRING	AA	290
	HAP	195
	EL	85
ABHORS	EAZ	18
	M1	648
	G3	748
	C	283
	WB	148
ABIDE	HAP	1928
	J3	456
	M13	122
	G2	365
	G4	607
	AE8	662
ABIDE	AE8	800
	AE10	1147
	KT2	158
	KT2	208
	KT3	615
	M8	108
	CAM	139
	C	301
	C	311
	C	342
	FL	324
	M15	362
ABIDES	G1	270
	G4	261
	KT1	389
ABJECT	VP7	58
	HIF	228
	HIF	347
	AU	24
ABLE	AM	187
	EDGA	34
	TA	73
	HAP	1002
	HAP	1004
	J6	572
	J10	236
	M9	119
	M15	2
	G3	120
	AE4	27
	WB	337
ABLER	ENH	37
	ERL	10
ABLEST	AE8	725
ABOARD	P5	196
	AE5	1000
	C	345
	AU	357
	CI	267
	PWR	9
ABODE	AM	1113
	AA	736
	SAA	796
	HAP	1279
	HAP	2505
	HAP	2553
	BR	179
	M1	221
	M1	777
	VP2	70
	VP6	22
	G1	20
	G1	268
	G1	450
	G3	68
	G4	427
	G4	456
	G4	557
	G4	611
	G4	644
	AE1	858
	AE2	26
	AE2	38
	AE3	126
	AE3	136
	AE3	220
	AE3	277
	AE3	941
	AE4	545
	AE5	994
	AE6	14
	AE6	82
	AE6	160
	AE6	897
	AE6	1108
	AE7	94
	AE7	842
	AE11	794
	KT2	528
	KT3	374
	KT3	391
	TJD	178
	B	703
	HIF	147
	HIF	275
	M11	4
	M11	268
	M15	30
	M15	563
	P2	112
	M1	215
	M1	378
	M13	207
	G3	636
	G4	512
	G4	529
ABODES	AE1	91
	AE1	492
	AE1	736
	AE2	337
	AE2	393
	AE2	473
	AE2	1073
	AE3	151
	AE3	618
	AE4	874
	AE4	964
	AE6	510
	AE6	761
	AE6	911
	AE6	1007
	AE7	165
	AE7	315
	AE7	329
	AE7	696
	AE8	54
	AE9	342
	AE10	8
	AE11	1153
	AE12	284
	AF	144
	HIF	330
	C	604
ABOLISH	G3	836
ABOLISHED	M1	491
ABORTION	CM	46
	J6	485
ABOUND	AM	1130
	L4	33
	HAP	2241
	EL	103
	J3	109
	J6	462
	J10	313
	GK	98
	VP7	71
	VP10	63
	G2	15
	G2	130
	G2	250
	G2	449
	G2	472
	G2	665
	G3	690
	AE5	996
	AE9	215
	OAL	261
	OAL	289
	OAL	692
	TJD	125
	C	166
	C	465
ABOUNDING	TA	309
	C	147
ABOUNDS	G1	387
	G2	733
	OAL	55
ABREAST	AE2	270
	AE11	598
	KT3	933
	M11	165
ABROACH	AE1	273
ABROAD	AR	6
	AR	79
	AR	298
	VHH	7
	AM	2
	AM	92
	AM	598
	AM	682
	ET	3
	RA	25
	PCG1	38
	PM	18
	ENH	30
	PRH	4
	OE	41
	PD	55
	EC	26
	L2	67
	L3	279
	L4	263
	HH	6
	HAP	839
	HAP	1003
	HAP	1468
	HAP	1848
	HAP	1883
	BR	75
	J1	46
	J3	406
	J3	434

Word	Ref	No.
ABROAD	J3	479
	J6	222
	J6	434
	J6	521
	J6	627
	EHC	38
	VP6	85
	VP9	89
	G2	240
	G2	417
	G2	712
	G2	748
	G3	581
	G3	635
	G4	234
	AE1	602
	AE4	428
	AE6	395
	AE12	873
	DO	99
	KT1	441
	KT3	560
	M8	35
	BP	49
	C	224
	M11	295
	AU	344
	WB	229
	ETP	41
	PMK	22
ABROGATE	SAA	218
ABRUPTLY	AE4	562
ABSALOM	AA	566
	AA	683
	AA	927
	SAA	19
	SAA	119
	SAA	347
	SAA	430
	SAA	507
	SAA	871
	SAA	998
	SAA	1044
ABSOLOM'S	AA	478
	AA	970
	SAA	841
	SAA	908
ABSALON	AA	18
	AA	221
	SAA	885
ABSENCE	AR	21
	HP	150
	SAA	592
	SAA	825
	SKA6	17
	SLT1	14
	VP7	63
	AE1	910
	KT1	405
	TH	45
	M11	22
	M11	62
	M11	189
ABSENT	HS	93
	VHH	32
	AM	436
	HP	162
	SAA	720
	L3	156
	L3	308
	L4	15
	T18	69
	T27	41
	HAP	900
	HAP	912
	BR	289
	STS2	9
	J1	185
	EHC	33
	VP3	116
	VP6	80
	VP7	20
	G3	361
	AE1	301
	AE1	894
	AE4	119
	AE7	385
	AE9	217
	AE9	247
	AE9	298
	AE9	491
	AE10	132
	AE10	933
	AE11	742
	AE12	162
	OAL	140
ABSENT	DO	157
	KT1	390
	KT3	141
	M8	347
	M11	423
	FL	438
	M12	6
ABSOLUTE	AM	1073
	E	12
	MF	6
	SAA	215
	HAP	978
	J6	215
	J6	297
	J10	125
	AE1	316
	AE4	155
	KT1	471
	C	508
ABSOLUTELY	AM	194
ABSOLVE	LC	60
	J3	247
	M15	56
ABSOLVED	HAP	488
ABSOLVES	AE6	585
ABSTAIN	HAP	2573
	G1	493
	AE6	369
	OAL	467
	HIF	580
	M15	101
ABSTAINED	VP5	38
ABSTEMIOUS	M15	486
ABSTINENCE	HAP	363
	HAP	2275
	GP	11
ABSTRACTEDLY	RL	138
ABSURD	OAE1	9
	C	341
ABUNDANCE	AM	184
	PTC	10
	EWR	17
ABUNDANT	MO	11
	AS	81
ABUSE	A	3
	EUF	27
	SAA	448
	J16	42
ABUSED	CI	453
	PMQ	36
	ECD	6
	HAP	472
	HAP	2399
ABUSING	B	105
ABYSS	DA	59
	AK	11
	HAP	66
	HAP	1205
	BR	226
	J10	233
	M1	20
	VP1	109
	G1	646
	AE3	281
	AE4	33
	AE6	803
	M11	205
	M15	82
	AE5	392
ACARNANIAN	M8	56
ACASTUS	AE11	1197
ACCA	G4	641
ACCENT	M1	709
	GP	16
	AE6	77
	AE8	491
	CI	116
ACCENTS	P5	20
	VP3	113
	G2	243
	AE1	567
	AE4	10
	AE7	269
	AE7	500
	AE11	385
	AE12	87
	AE12	1318
	B	748
	M11	12
ACCEPT	EEL	35
	PMQW	8
	HAP	1084
	HAP	1253
	HAP	2426
	TA	304
	VP5	137
ACCEPT	AE3	628
	AE5	643
	AE5	704
	AE8	479
	AE11	838
	KT3	306
	M8	213
	CAM	327
ACCEPTED	WB	110
	KT3	366
	G2	145
ACCEPTING	MS	23
ACCEPTS	KT2	162
	AE8	960
ACCESS	AA	191
	AE6	340
	AE7	210
	OAL	397
ACCESSARY	AE4	543
ACCESSION	AU	461
ACCIDENT	RL	30
ACCIDENTS	BR	182
	KT1	29
ACCLAIM	HIF	35
	HIF	521
ACCLAIMS	KT3	525
ACCLAMATIONS	MF	132
	AE5	142
	OAL	194
	KT2	601
ACCOMMODATION	PW	11
ACCOMPANIED	AA	29
ACCOMPANIES	AA	129
ACCOMPLICE	OE	59
	J3	361
	P3	81
	CAM	279
	GP	59
ACCOMPLICES	J6	714
ACCOMPLISH	AE2	956
	DO	38
ACCOMPLISHED	HAP	1839
	HAP	2551
	VP3	84
	AE8	703
	OAL	368
	WB	56
ACCOMPLISHMENT	P2	88
ACCOMPLISHMENTS	J6	268
ACCORD	VP7	13
	G2	715
	AE9	919
	AE12	626
	OAL	552
	OAL	691
	DO	79
	KT2	387
	KT2	424
	KT3	1127
	BP	124
	HIF	27
	M11	105
	CI	214
	CI	306
ACCORDING	PMQW	20
	PRH	33
	RL	318
	P5	21
	AE5	129
	KT3	744
	KT3	929
	C	20
	C	76
	FL	469
	WB	123
	M15	244
	GP	46
ACCORDS	SEL2	13
ACCOSTED	AE8	221
	WB	292
ACCOSTS	AE5	506
ACCOUNT	AA	628
	L3	208
	HAP	1893
	J1	176
	J3	241
	J6	622
	J10	19
	G4	626
	AE12	54
	WB	138
ACCOUNTED	AA	652
	C	162
ACCOUNTS	SCG3	20
ACCOUTERED	P3	163
ACCRUE	RL	178

Word	Ref	No.
ACCRUE	L3	29
ACCRUING	J16	2
ACCURSED	EL	170
	M1	178
ACCURST	AM	145
	BR	354
	M1	204
	M9	143
	G2	331
	KT1	391
	BP	145
	CAM	294
	HIF	137
ACCUSATION	EPC	11
	AM	529
ACCUSE	ML	45
	AA	486
	AA	606
	AA	622
	AA	719
	MF	150
	SAA	239
	HAP	807
	J3	95
	J6	714
	J10	141
	P3	30
	AE2	1011
	AE4	285
	OAL	764
	MM	29
	AU	323
ACCUSED	EMQ	8
	TA	261
	HAP	473
	HAP	1041
	HAP	1529
	J6	378
	M9	83
	G4	205
	G4	754
	AE2	106
	MM	17
	B	295
	AU	82
	AU	480
ACCUSER	P1	164
	B	278
ACCUSERS'	SAA	41
ACCUSERS	HAP	1041
ACCUSING	HAP	2475
	VP5	35
	KT2	87
ACCUSTOMED	AE4	629
	DO	57
ACERRA	G2	307
ACESTA	AE5	941
ACESTES	AE1	775
	AE1	784
	AE5	44
	AE5	78
	AE5	95
	AE5	396
	AE5	513
	AE5	556
	AE5	603
	AE5	662
	AE5	685
	AE5	699
	AE5	932
ACESTES'	AE1	271
	AE1	800
	AE5	141
	AE5	941
ACHAEMENIDES	AE3	805
	AE3	906
ACHAIAN	M15	446
ACHATES	AM	689
	AE1	173
	AE1	245
	AE1	265
	AE1	432
	AE1	814
	AE1	911
	AE1	925
	AE1	976
	AE3	686
	AE6	53
	AE6	237
	AE8	610
	AE8	688
	AE8	773
	AE10	459
	AE12	567
ACHATES'	AE10	478
	AE12	677
ACHE	OE	14
	J10	48
	G4	172
ACHELOÜS	BP	1
ACHERON	AE6	161
	AE6	410
ACHÈS	UDH	82
	J6	751
ACHIEVE	AE11	22
ACHIEVED	MC	31
	KT3	307
	HIF	392
	M12	224
	M12	256
ACHIEVEMENTS	M1	614
	AE11	114
	AE11	264
	KT3	344
	KT3	932
ACHILLEAN	AE6	1153
ACHILLES	RH	68
	J1	247
	J3	443
	J10	400
	HI	63
	HI	74
	VP4	44
	G3	144
	AE1	643
	AE1	655
	AE1	664
	AE1	676
	AE1	1055
	AE2	38
	AE5	1051
	AE6	136
	AE9	1002
	AE10	819
	AE11	410
	AE11	624
	AE11	674
	OAL	10
	OAL	19
	OAL	778
	HIF	79
	HIF	126
	HIF	223
	HIF	411
	M12	102
	M12	130
	M12	194
	M12	226
	M12	227
	M12	244
	M12	264
	M12	489
	M12	769
	M12	801
	M12	818
	AU	42
	AU	207
	AU	208
	AU	213
	AU	214
	AU	262
	AU	442
	AU	463
ACHILLES'	DA	177
	AE3	417
	AE12	527
	M8	58
	AU	43
	AU	423
ACHING	PC2	21
	SAA	632
	AT	118
	C	236
ACHITOPHEL	AA	150
	AA	200
	AA	220
	AA	491
	AA	566
	AA	741
	PPC	25
	SAA	17
	SAA	104
	SAA	124
	SAA	184
	SAA	206
	SAA	436
	SAA	510
	SAA	912
	SAA	1001
	SAA	1016
	SAA	1044
ACHITOPHEL'S	AA	929
ACHITOPHELS	SAA	155
ACIS	M13	1
	M13	176
	M13	184
	M13	197
	M13	205
	M13	212
	M13	214
	M13	230
	M13	231
ACIS'	M13	64
ACKNOWLEDGE	AE5	887
	AE8	179
ACKNOWLEDGED	KT3	306
	B	743
ACKNOWLEDGMENT	HAP	426
ACKNOWLEDGMENTS	HAP	1340
ACMON	AE10	188
ACMON'S	AE10	192
A-COCK-HORSE	PSH	9
ACOETES	AE11	45
	AE11	123
ACONITE	G2	209
ACONTEUS	AE11	914
	AE11	918
ACORNS	J6	15
	M1	137
	G2	101
	G4	119
ACQUAINTANCE	PCB	14
ACQUAINTED	B	458
ACQUIRED	A	11
	GK	144
ACQUITS	HAP	484
ACRES	L3	193
	GE	33
	J3	239
	G1	194
	G4	189
	AE6	807
ACRON	AE10	1014
	AE10	1027
ACROSS	TA	193
	G1	141
	G1	657
	AE11	958
	KT1	42
	KT1	223
	KT3	213
	M11	40
	WB	401
ACROSTIC	MF	206
ACT	HS	12
	RH	24
	EWG	14
	AM	698
	PT	33
	EMQW	9
	PM	6
	PLN	43
	POE	36
	PLG	34
	PUO3	8
	PUO4	15
	EUF	1
	PLB	50
	MD	16
	MF	59
	EC	4
	L4	120
	L4	238
	TA	268
	HAP	1437
	HAP	2174
	EL	226
	EL	290
	EL	331
	J3	286
	J6	103
	J10	257
	P3	116
	P6	74
	HI	164
	AE9	385
	AE10	59
	AE10	1125
	AE12	717
	OAL	692
	DO	128
	KT2	647
	M8	17
	M8	143
	M8	204
	B	646
	HIF	107
	HIF	300

Word	Ref	Line
ACT	C	537
	M12	110
	M12	228
	AU	102
	AU	259
	AU	273
	AU	328
	W8	77
	M15	277
	CI	470
	ETP	30
	PMK	36
	EMKG	28
	EMKG	39
ACTAEON	KT1	258
	KT2	627
ACTED	EKK	5
	J6	441
	AE2	147
	MG	34
ACTIAN	AE3	363
	AE8	935
ACTING	ETL	30
	PCG1	18
	J6	108
ACTION	AR	34
	AR	106
	AR	161
	AM	686
	PMQ	4
	EAZ	5
	HP	210
	PUO3	28
	PUO3	35
	AA	723
	J6	433
	J6	447
	J6	454
	J10	542
	J16	30
	J16	76
	MC	59
	GK	167
	GK	172
	AE3	372
	AE7	66
	AE8	203
	AE9	238
	AE11	186
	AE12	389
	MM	33
	M8	91
	BP	171
	HIF	395
	HIF	561
	TH	126
	M11	331
	M12	257
	AU	192
	AU	204
	AU	581
	GP	16
ACTIONS	AR	88
	SMA	77
	LCA	21
	AM	461
	ML	12
	ML	23
	EPF	7
	AA	638
	SAA	751
	HAP	2443
	PKA	30
	P6	110
	AE4	15
	AE5	886
	AE7	964
	AE11	188
	AE11	1162
	TJD	205
	C	338
	C	525
	M11	337
	M11	444
	AU	163
	AU	278
	W8	137
ACTIUM	AE8	897
ACTIVE	AR	111
	LC	105
	L4	279
	H9	29
	EL	114
	VP6	50
	G1	190
	AE6	984
ACTIVE	AE6	1110
	AE7	222
	TJD	58
	M8	61
	W8	478
	CI	230
ACTOR	PMS	26
	PMS	27
	P5	12
	AE9	665
	AE12	146
	AE12	149
ACTOR'S	PKK	4
	J10	341
ACTORS	ET	8
	PAR	1
	PUO4	1
	MF	76
	PMS	30
	J6	517
	G2	526
	ESK	8
ACTRESS	ETL	9
	EMQW	29
ACTRESSES	ETP	40
ACTS	HS	36
	HS	39
	HS	126
	AR	179
	PW	18
	SAA	1011
	EAA	19
	EL	121
	EL	289
	PSH	8
	J6	379
	P1	20
	AE1	849
	AE3	655
	AE4	3
	AE6	767
	AE8	382
	AE8	415
	AE10	556
	AE11	345
	KT2	495
	B	59
	TH	226
	FL	563
	W8	2
	M15	187
	M15	720
	CI	7
	CI	28
	CI	35
ACTUAL	MD	222
	HAP	339
ACTUATES	M15	244
AD	GE	14
ADAGE	P1	57
ADAM	AR	114
	AA	771
	PPC	13
	HAP	309
	OD	28
	GK	23
ADAMANT	OAL	744
	KT1	473
	KT2	554
	KT3	628
ADAMANTINE	L4	90
	TA	491
	AE6	745
ADAM-WITS	AA	51
ADD	JH	10
	SMA	67
	AM	629
	AA	777
	L3	86
	T18	83
	HAP	1585
	HAP	1588
	BR	315
	J1	221
	J3	248
	J3	503
	J6	669
	J10	67
	J10	332
	P1	67
	P6	185
	M1	5
	M13	167
	GK	175
	GK	179
	G1	60
ADD	G2	213
	G3	180
	G3	687
	AE2	863
	AE5	135
	AE7	761
	AE8	546
	AE8	794
	AE11	259
	AE11	537
	OAL	205
	OAL	266
	OAE2	81
	KT3	174
	M8	330
	M12	532
	M15	262
ADDED	SEL3	12
	ER	5
	MO	12
	AK	64
	HAP	1355
	OD	29
	P1	181
	GK	37
	G1	197
	G3	765
	AE4	74
	AE8	358
	AE8	400
	AE8	570
	AE8	687
	AE9	613
	AE9	1027
	AE10	227
	AE11	997
	AE12	747
	AF	165
	AF	175
	KT1	6
	KT2	16
	KT2	496
	KT3	305
	M11	145
	M12	83
	M12	452
	M12	509
	M15	40
ADDING	SMA	22
	M1	288
	M11	375
ADDITION	HP	54
ADDLE	PDS	24
ADDLE-PATE	PLT	28
ADDLE-PATED	SAA	402
ADDRESS	AE1	1028
	AU	496
	PMK	4
ADDRESSED	TA	40
	AE1	95
	AE4	691
	AE5	1019
	AE6	87
	AE6	905
	AE7	83
	AE10	594
	AE10	637
	AE10	648
	AE10	1119
	AE11	1152
	OAL	641
	KT2	63
	KT2	470
	KT3	191
	KT3	249
	M8	113
	BP	167
	HIF	24
	HIF	504
	HIF	520
	TH	390
	M11	245
	M12	795
	CI	420
ADDRESSES	PW	20
	LS	13
ADDRESSING	EC	8
ADDS	RH	8
	AM	752
	P2	70
	P6	34
	M1	46
	M9	87
	G1	420
	AE2	199
	AE5	1070

Word	Ref	No.
ADDS	AE7	717
	AE9	980
	AE11	341
	AE11	1053
	AE12	370
	OAL	278
	BP	55
	M10	39
	M12	288
	M12	789
	M15	538
	CI	30
ADIEU	ECG1	21
	PM	12
	J3	363
	VP1	112
	VP3	123
	VP10	91
	AE2	871
	AE3	637
	AE9	643
	M8	357
	BP	188
	C	256
	C	345
	TH	348
	CI	194
ADJOINING	AK	93
	OAL	94
	KT2	633
ADJOURN	P5	89
	AE7	182
ADJOURNED	KT3	188
ADJUDGED	WB	312
ADJURE	AE9	343
	AE12	88
	B	734
ADJURED	AE2	210
	CAM	166
ADJURES	AE10	650
	CAM	208
ADJURING	P3	179
ADMINISTERED	CI	548
ADMINISTERS	AU	554
	M15	113
ADMIRABLY	P1	216
ADMIRAL	AM	241
	AM	765
	BR	328
ADMIRALS	AM	745
ADMIRATION	HP	19
	J6	842
	BP	2
	M12	232
	M15	87
ADMIRE	JH	13
	RH	21
	RH	87
	PIE	23
	PW	19
	PUO1	37
	PNH	16
	SAA	626
	AK	118
	HAP	1682
	PKA	19
	EL	100
	ODA	78
	J10	555
	VP1	13
	G1	150
	G2	731
	AE6	1162
	AE6	1197
	AE8	683
	OAL	566
	AF	34
	M8	207
	CI	145
	ESK	10
ADMIRED	DC	20
	LCA	45
	PRL	20
	SAA	630
	HAP	543
	OD	37
	J10	432
	P1	60
	P6	16
	GK	143
	DHP	12
	AE1	636
	AE1	868
	AE6	552
	AE6	1213
	AE7	531
ADMIRED	AE10	627
	TH	386
	FL	190
	GP	130
	CI	220
ADMIRES	LC	131
	ODA	72
	J6	96
	M1	964
	VP3	136
	G1	55
	G2	116
	AE1	999
	AE8	821
	AE8	829
	AE8	976
	AE10	352
	M10	11
ADMIRING	AM	644
	POE	8
	AA	686
	MF	132
	J6	493
	M1	981
	HI	27
	G4	535
	BP	2
ADMISSION	AE1	732
	AE7	268
	AE7	301
	AE7	317
	AE9	305
ADMIT	RH	33
	SMA	66
	PRL	23
	AM	503
	E	19
	DA	180
	D	36
	SAA	257
	EDGA	27
	HAP	122
	HAP	2123
	G2	226
	G2	644
	AE1	175
	AE2	63
	AE2	304
	AE8	232
	AE9	984
	AE12	858
	TJD	37
ADMITS	E	11
	MF	23
	SAA	774
	G2	437
	AE4	276
	AE4	313
	KT3	469
	CAM	295
ADMITTED	SMA	111
	DA	92
	RL	325
	L4	175
	ODA	74
	G2	109
	AE1	988
	AE2	249
	M8	306
ADMONISHED	HAP	2588
	VP6	7
	AE1	495
	M11	445
ADO	PMQ	43
	EWGR	27
	P3	16
	M1	947
	C	12
ADONIS	AT	112
	VP10	26
	OAL	81
	OAL	577
	KT3	147
ADOPTED	AR	70
	MD	144
	AK	6
	BR	148
	P6	129
ADOPTING	J6	307
ADOPTION	PUO4	29
ADOPTS	GK	138
ADORATION	L4	172
	VCS	38
	KT3	491
ADORE	VHH	53
	SCG2	15
ADORE	SCG3	18
	ESF	27
	HP	101
	SDG	3
	OE	19
	H29	20
	FS3	6
	STS1	14
	EKA	32
	J3	243
	J6	68
	J6	260
	M1	434
	M13	170
	G1	471
	G4	307
	G4	563
	G4	783
	AE1	385
	AE1	985
	AE3	25
	AE3	105
	AE3	518
	AE3	555
	AE3	649
	AE3	914
	AE4	302
	AE4	319
	AE4	494
	KT3	293
	M8	115
	M10	19
	FL	532
	M12	15
ADORED	AA	536
	EC	39
	TA	68
	OD	37
	M1	506
	M1	954
	M1	1044
	M9	163
	HI	171
	G2	670
	AE2	207
	AE2	949
	AE3	345
	AE6	12
	AE6	1213
	AE12	265
	DO	53
	KT2	116
	M8	115
	B	641
	M10	12
	CAM	245
	HIF	604
	TH	157
	FL	190
	ETP	24
ADORES	PKA	17
	J6	199
	G2	703
	G4	792
	AE3	473
	AE5	974
	M10	12
	M11	183
ADORING	EMK	19
	HAP	2347
	SFL	20
	AE7	185
ADORN	UDH	63
	HS	25
	SMA	124
	AM	702
	PAR	4
	AA	880
	RL	81
	AT	41
	L1	38
	T18	47
	T18	51
	T18	67
	TA	73
	AK	75
	HAP	1089
	EMI	2
	BR	142
	BR	209
	LS	17
	J3	143
	J3	281
	J6	34
	J6	75
	J6	114

ADORN	J6	502	ADULTERATE	JH	25	ADVANCE	AS	9		
	J10	98		AK	63	ADVANCED	AM	254		
	P5	61		J3	32		AA	865		
	M1	91	ADULTERER	HAP	823		SAA	48		
	M1	605		J6	147		SAA	1036		
	M1	757		J6	597		ER	4		
	M1	766		J6	736		P1	196		
	M13	227		OAE2	52		GK	35		
	MC	70		M12	806		VP6	44		
	VP4	33		WB	488		AE5	98		
	VP5	47	ADULTERER'S	J1	87		AE6	260		
	VP7	85	ADULTERERS	HAP	2507		AE10	319		
	VP9	65		J6	32		AE10	634		
	G2	198		J6	306		AE12	453		
	G2	536		J10	485		M8	236		
	G3	17	ADULTERESS	AE1	917		TH	300		
	G3	248		AE11	414		M11	166		
	AE2	326	ADULTEROUS	AE10	141		FL	202		
	AE4	287		OAL	377		FL	307		
	AE4	501	ADULTERY	HAP	354		CI	216		
	AE5	83		ETS	11	ADVANCEMENT	SAA	243		
	AE6	312		AE6	831	ADVANCES	PDS	32		
	AE6	1059	ADUST	C	156		STS3	25		
	AE6	1235	ADVANCE	EIE	13		EL	101		
	AE7	952		EWGR	48	ADVANCING	AM	264		
	AE9	924		PNH	44		MO	12		
	AE10	210		ENH	15		STS3	5		
	AE10	993		EOE	19		G1	291		
	AE11	98		PSF	45		G2	115		
	AE11	120		PUO5	1		G3	648		
	OAL	340		ELB	37		AE2	602		
	KT2	419		MF	145		AE5	152		
	KT2	608		SAA	261		AE5	183		
	KT3	104		PDG	3		AE5	204		
	KT3	396		PDG	28		AE9	505		
	KT3	737		EDGA	23		AE10	428		
	M10	46		RL	371		AE10	579		
	M11	64		ER	38		AE10	912		
	M11	313		HAP	214		AE11	906		
	FL	500		HAP	293		AE12	188		
	FL	556		J3	73		AE12	663		
	M12	240		J6	422		AE12	849		
	M15	657		J6	784		CI	147		
	AS	20		J10	330	ADVANTAGE	PTL	24		
ADORNED	UMR	3		J16	57		PTS	13		
	AA	831		M13	35		AE2	167		
	T18	2		HI	99		AE3	897		
	T23	29		VP5	115		AE10	389		
	HAP	1211		G1	490		AE10	1033		
	SKA2	11		G1	537		AE11	517		
	ODA	35		G2	67		KT1	462		
	J10	516		G3	299		KT3	387		
	P3	70		G4	690		KT3	571		
	MC	24		AE1	383		HIF	195		
	AE5	95		AE2	274		M12	194		
	AE5	407		AE4	381		AU	41		
	AE5	727		AE5	652		M15	175		
	AE5	748		AE5	723	ADVANTAGES	KT1	583		
	AE7	1073		AE6	367	ADVENTURE	KT1	351		
	AE8	48		AE8	593		KT1	399		
	AE10	902		AE8	879		FL	463		
	AE12	255		AE9	49		FL	605		
	DO	1		AE9	221	ADVENTURED	FL	474		
	KT1	549		AE9	876	ADVENTURERS	AR	305		
	KT2	449		AE9	1068	ADVENTURES	SAA	1051		
	KT3	68		AE10	338		HAP	561		
	KT3	208		AE10	644		J6	89		
	HIF	49		AE10	804		AE4	110		
	HIF	172		AE10	1072		BP	180		
	HIF	811		AE11	1035	ADVENTUROUS	HAP	2207		
	C	456		AE11	1214		G4	4		
	TH	3		AE12	395	ADVERSARIES	HAP	2163		
	FL	426		AE12	1142	ADVERSE	AM	473		
	FL	516		AE12	1327		AM	745		
	M12	548		OAL	282		P1	84		
	M15	446		OAL	424		AE8	313		
	CI	212		OAL	564		AE8	826		
ADORNS	SAA	1126		OAL	648		AE10	716		
	L1	12		OAL	813		AE12	549		
	BR	144		DO	24		AE12	1044		
	M1	1075		KT1	348		KT2	206		
	G1	541		KT2	194		KT3	589		
	G2	438		KT2	412		FL	286		
	AE3	683		KT2	490		AU	290		
	AE4	83		KT3	456		AS	4		
	OAL	394		KT3	618	ADVERSITIES	AR	97		
	DO	27		B	560	ADVERSITY	HAP	444		
	M15	192		HIF	227		HAP	1342		
	M15	292		TH	24		C	399		
	CI	32		M12	142	ADVICE	AA	477		
ADRASTUS	AE6	648		M12	411		PLB	6		
ADRIEL	AA	877		AU	176		PLB	8		
ADRIFT	SAA	849		WB	394		MD	48		
	M11	27		M15	684		MD	57		
	M11	448		CI	588		MD	66		
ADULT	M15	309		EMKG	12		SAA	224		

Word	Ref	No.	Word	Ref	No.	Word	Ref	No.
ADVICE	RL	144	AENEAS	AE6	51	AETOLIAN	AE11	348
	HAP	696		AE6	234		AE12	528
	HAP	1771		AE6	250	AFAR	VHH	30
	HAP	1817		AE6	257		AM	417
	HAP	1941		AE6	331		E	23
	HAP	2394		AE6	358		AA	734
	PDS	17		AE6	929		SAA	195
	PTS	26		AE6	964		H29	8
	EL	249		AE6	1044		H29	31
	J6	339		AE6	1188		H2	24
	J6	640		AE6	1243		TA	169
	J10	512		AE7	162		HAP	503
	P3	6		AE8	17		HAP	1469
	P5	250		AE8	92		ODA	13
	AE1	554		AE8	99		J6	491
	AE3	85		AE8	115		J10	267
	AE4	414		AE8	152		HI	152
	AE7	133		AE8	166		VP2	95
	AE10	110		AE8	499		VP10	67
	AE12	42		AE8	608		G1	518
	OAL	439		AE8	701		G1	638
	OAL	480		AE8	773		G2	382
	OAE2	68		AE8	802		G3	367
	C	164		AE9	9		G3	391
	C	556		AE9	112		G3	570
	C	797		AE9	317		G3	640
	TH	44		AE10	36		G4	446
	WB	243		AE10	232		G4	500
ADVISE	SAA	592		AE10	235		G4	809
	AE10	98		AE10	243		AE2	397
	AE12	856		AE10	429		AE4	437
	OAL	438		AE10	448		AE4	593
ADVISED	POE	25		AE10	814		AE5	568
	SAA	183		AE10	901		AE5	761
	J1	255		AE10	933		AE6	885
	AE7	224		AE10	1146		AE6	1089
	AE11	452		AE10	1172		AE6	1103
	C	767		AE10	1251		AE7	719
ADVISING	J1	22		AE10	1252		AE7	763
ADVOCATE	P3	139		AE10	1268		AE7	969
AEACIAN	AE2	359		AE10	1289		AE7	1010
AEACIDES	OAL	780		AE11	54		AE7	1024
AEACUS	AU	35		AE11	357		AE8	3
	AU	39		AE11	447		AE8	252
AEAS	M1	788		AE11	625		AE8	333
AEGAEAN	AE3	99		AE11	683		AE8	901
	AE12	545		AE11	1311		AE8	909
AEGAEON	AE10	791		AE12	252		AE9	677
	HIF	556		AE12	264		AE9	1090
AEGEUS	KT3	877		AE12	469		AE10	208
	KT3	943		AE12	665		AE10	316
AEGLE	VP6	32		AE12	701		AE10	480
AEGON	VP5	114		AE12	713		AE10	794
AEGON'S	VP3	2		AE12	734		AE10	1005
AENEAN	AE8	449		AE12	950		AE10	1089
	AE12	793		AE12	1079		AE10	1245
AENEANS	AE10	182		AE12	1150		AE11	11
AENEAS	RH	61		AE12	1284		AE11	800
	RH	67		M15	662		AE11	966
	DA	27	AENEAS'	AE7	4		AE11	1005
	DA	212		AE10	1180		AE11	1215
	HAP	2061		AE12	652		AE12	515
	BR	128	AENEIAN	AE3	131		AE12	530
	AE1	255	AENOS	AE3	28		AE12	770
	AE1	304	AEOLIAN	J10	293		AE12	817
	AE1	353		AE8	598		AE12	1034
	AE1	420	AEOLUS	AE1	79		AE12	1246
	AE1	521		AE1	97		AE12	1256
	AE1	611		AE5	1034		OAL	626
	AE1	632		AE10	53		KT1	537
	AE1	717	AËRIAL	L4	18		KT2	179
	AE1	767		L4	62		KT2	180
	AE1	872		G4	2		KT2	532
	AE1	874		AE7	129		KT3	50
	AE1	909		AE8	288		KT3	507
	AE1	1010	AESARIS	M15	31		M8	208
	AE3	373		M15	70		HIF	236
	AE4	144	AESCHYLUS	PO	5		TH	100
	AE4	166	AESCULAPIAN	AE7	1057		TH	133
	AE4	203	AESOP	HAP	1300		M11	447
	AE4	476	AESOP'S	EAA	1		FL	209
	AE4	568		HAP	620		STP	7
	AE4	676		KT1	342	AFEARD	C	136
	AE5	36	AETHON	AE11	131	AFFABLE	C	75
	AE5	57	AETION	HI	66	AFFAIR	AE4	162
	AE5	98	AETION'S	HI	34		AE9	306
	AE5	340	AETNA	G4	253		AE11	509
	AE5	556		AE3	727		CI	443
	AE5	564		AE3	747	AFFAIRS	HP	153
	AE5	631		AE3	885		SAA	723
	AE5	646		AE8	554		GE	38
	AE5	883		M15	509		P4	2
	AE5	1007	AETNAEAN	AE12	141		P4	31
	AE5	1038	AETNA'S	J1	12		G1	62
	AE5	1049		G1	636		G4	260
	AE5	1058	AETNAS	AM	335		AE1	927

Word	Code	No.
AFFAIRS	AE2	469
	AE9	1
	AE11	635
	OAL	401
	B	191
AFFECT	AM	1091
	E	17
	SAA	37
	L4	34
	EAA	15
	AE6	787
	OAL	529
	OAL	670
	WB	298
AFFECTATION	HH	10
	HAP	397
AFFECTATIONS	J6	275
AFFECTED	HP	15
	HAP	1373
	HAP	2585
	J6	9
	J6	265
	P1	152
AFFECTING	AA	178
	G4	441
	G4	816
AFFECTION	DA	4
	HAP	180
	HAP	435
	AE6	34
	AE9	365
	M11	492
	AU	296
AFFECTIONS	J6	317
	KT3	830
AFFECTS	AA	473
	G1	56
	AF	40
	AF	45
	KT3	1074
	HIF	406
	WB	280
AFFIANCED	AE8	157
AFFIRM	RL	306
	HAP	652
AFFIRMED	AA	111
AFFLICT	OAL	149
	B	729
	M11	1
	M12	29
AFFLICTED	AR	221
	AM	1038
	EL	46
	KT1	59
	HIF	502
	HIF	623
	AS	82
	AS	91
AFFLICTIONS	AR	83
	AR	96
AFFORD	AM	346
	AM	360
	PA	15
	ELN	16
	ML	7
	PAL	40
	CM	19
	HP	151
	AA	455
	H2	80
	TA	5
	EAA	19
	HAP	1247
	HAP	1267
	EL	348
	OD	38
	J3	185
	J3	380
	J3	501
	J6	852
	P6	19
	M1	704
	M13	134
	G2	284
	G2	716
	G4	195
	G4	211
	AE4	174
	AE4	552
	AE5	999
	AE6	370
	AE6	1211
	AE10	1172
	AE11	649
	AE12	190
	AE12	792
AFFORD	AE12	1139
	OAL	267
	OAL	510
	OAL	689
	DO	136
	TJD	203
	M8	116
	BP	101
	CAM	312
	CAM	323
	M15	106
	M15	432
AFFORDED	AE1	889
	AE4	942
AFFORDS	AA	674
	MF	83
	ER	18
	HAP	137
	HAP	2249
	HAP	2544
	J6	279
	P1	34
	M1	905
	VP3	81
	G1	683
	G3	455
	OAL	29
	OAL	60
	OAL	439
	M11	433
	AU	352
	PWR	32
AFFRIGHT	LC	137
	AA	71
	H3	22
	HI	146
	G1	654
	G3	792
	G3	822
	G4	588
	AE2	489
	AE2	1004
	AE2	1024
	AE3	762
	AE4	11
	AE4	273
	AE6	1184
	AE7	23
	AE8	397
	AE8	738
	AE9	213
	AE9	975
	AE12	603
	OAL	629
	AU	382
	M15	701
	GP	64
AFFRIGHTED	L2	52
	TA	141
	J3	425
	M1	877
	M13	203
	G4	340
	AE7	1068
	OAL	620
	M15	223
AFFRONT	ECD	5
	OE	51
	HIF	292
	HIF	319
	HIF	687
AFFRONTED	AE12	785
	C	643
AFFRONTING	HIF	243
AFFRONTS	AA	666
	AA	951
	J3	222
	AE9	170
	HIF	140
AFIELD	VP2	38
AFLOAT	AE4	574
	B	675
AFOOT	EAL	10
AFORE	EMKG	19
AFRAID	AR	243
	AM	960
	PWGR	5
	PC1	14
	J16	4
	P5	270
	OAL	882
	M10	31
	CAM	324
	HIF	790
	C	592
	TH	368
AFRAID	TH	373
AFRESH	AE2	364
	KT3	639
AFRIC	AM	692
	ECD	19
	J6	119
	J10	236
	G3	52
	AE4	315
	AE6	464
	AE6	1082
	AE1	324
AFTER		
AFTER-ACCEPTION	HAP	660
AFTER-AGES	EAZ	30
AFTER-KISS	PEL	10
AFTER-MALICE	HAP	2367
AFTERNOON	HAP	1890
	P1	275
	C	497
AFTER-STORMS	SMA	91
AFTERTHOUGHT	KT2	484
AFTERTIMES	PUF	23
	HAP	672
AGAG'S	AA	676
AGAMEMNON	AE1	642
	AE7	1002
AGAMEMNON'S	J6	856
	AE6	659
AGATE	J6	226
AGE	HS	31
	HS	36
	AR	23
	AR	28
	AR	53
	AR	111
	AR	320
	RH	83
	LC	148
	LCA	48
	PRL	7
	AM	631
	AM	643
	PA	15
	STL	23
	PCG1	19
	PCG1	28
	ECG1	20
	ECG2	2
	ECG2	22
	ECG2	34
	PUO1	11
	PNH	21
	ENH	15
	EUO2	8
	EUO2	19
	PAZ	17
	EAZ	32
	EAL	25
	EMK	4
	PTW	1
	POE	11
	PTC	7
	PTC	19
	PLG	13
	PLG	34
	DA	162
	DA	173
	UMR	8
	EMP	3
	EMP	8
	EPF	13
	PSF	18
	ETG	4
	PR	3
	PUO3	1
	PUO3	12
	PUO4	38
	PUO5	28
	PUF	24
	AA	166
	AA	236
	AA	267
	AA	941
	PLB	2
	PLB	30
	MD	159
	MD	261
	MD	293
	MD	320
	SAA	375
	SAA	510
	SAA	960
	SAA	991
	SAA	1027
	PK	8
	PDG	21

Headword	Code	Number
AGE	EDGA	39
	RL	136
	RL	337
	RL	388
	ER	20
	MO	12
	L3	161
	L3	255
	TA	13
	TA	306
	PAA	2
	AK	63
	HH	14
	HAP	790
	HAP	879
	HAP	1106
	HAP	1127
	HAP	1208
	HAP	1689
	HAP	1993
	HAP	2229
	HAP	2312
	HAP	2528
	BR	18
	ETS	29
	PMS	30
	EKA	39
	SKA3	13
	SKA6	26
	EL	220
	EL	295
	EL	361
	EL	368
	OD	4
	MS	31
	J1	129
	J1	133
	J1	143
	J1	220
	J3	42
	J3	48
	J3	306
	J6	35
	J6	37
	J6	460
	J6	642
	J6	839
	J10	73
	J10	119
	J10	305
	J10	316
	J10	384
	J10	388
	J10	399
	J10	410
	P1	21
	P3	67
	P4	30
	P5	47
	P6	10
	M1	113
	M1	146
	M1	160
	M1	273
	M9	68
	M9	77
	PLT	6
	PLT	35
	MC	2
	MC	11
	MC	24
	MC	28
	MC	66
	GK	59
	GK	117
	GK	146
	GK	175
	VP4	5
	VP6	64
	VP8	38
	G1	673
	G2	185
	G2	668
	G2	792
	G3	111
	G3	152
	G3	161
	G4	813
	AE1	386
	AE1	397
	AE1	852
	AE1	949
	AE2	458
	AE2	696
	AE2	702
	AE2	728
AGE	AE2	736
	AE2	864
	AE3	933
	AE4	699
	AE4	899
	AE5	531
	AE5	553
	AE5	572
	AE5	583
	AE5	663
	AE5	742
	AE5	849
	AE6	169
	AE6	386
	AE6	900
	AE6	1081
	AE7	490
	AE7	658
	AE8	433
	AE8	669
	AE9	286
	AE9	374
	AE9	390
	AE9	396
	AE9	832
	AE10	1150
	AE11	387
	AE12	71
	AE12	647
	OAL	9
	OAL	69
	OAL	852
	MG	4
	MG	15
	MM	1
	MM	14
	B	428
	CAM	173
	CAM	207
	M11	235
	DO	119
	KT3	82
	KT3	387
	KT3	568
	KT3	1078
	TJD	4
	TJD	61
	M8	372
	B	51
	B	325
	B	436
	B	567
	CAM	192
	HIF	46
	HIF	388
	M12	234
	M12	252
	M12	258
	M12	482
	WB	67
	WB	236
	WB	366
	WB	491
	M15	137
	M15	312
	M15	346
	M15	358
	M15	400
	ETP	3
	ETP	37
	SMP	25
	SMP	37
	SMP	41
	SMP	46
	SMP	90
	SMP	96
	ESK	20
	EMKG	39
AGED	UDH	73
	AM	55
	DA	115
	MF	7
	T18	78
	HI	164
	G4	564
	AE4	920
	AE7	224
	AE8	409
	AE8	767
	AE10	871
	AE12	582
AGENT	AA	373
	SAA	240
AGENTS	SAA	273
	C	538
	C	542
AGE'S	EMW	9
	AE11	41
	AE12	91
	KT2	457
AGES	UDH	82
	AR	105
	PAZ	21
	STC	11
	AA	151
	MF	159
	RL	80
	RL	129
	RL	141
	RL	180
	RL	273
	L3	32
	L3	175
	L4	224
	H2	7
	HAP	110
	HAP	807
	HAP	875
	HAP	927
	HAP	1157
	HAP	1202
	HAP	1785
	EMI	1
	BR	38
	BR	144
	SSH	12
	J3	489
	GK	180
	VP4	63
	G2	290
	G2	405
	G3	81
	AE9	98
	AE11	1229
	OAL	879
	DO	26
	DO	86
	TJD	203
	M8	365
AGGRAVATES	AE11	341
AGGRAVATING	AE7	796
AGGRESSOR	AE9	1039
AGGRESSOR'S	G4	345
AGHAST	KT3	362
	HIF	305
	C	99
	J3	350
	M1	471
	AE2	1050
	AE7	640
	AE8	941
	AE9	149
	KT3	283
	C	712
	TH	277
	CI	343
AGIS	AE10	1063
AGITATED	AR	273
AGNUS	FL	172
	FL	188
	FL	511
AGO	PA	1
	SM1	2
	PKK	1
	PSF	23
	AT	61
	ER	46
	L3	321
	AF	155
	KT2	381
	WB	162
	PWR	38
A-GOD'S	P1	39
AGOG	J6	587
AGONIZING	HAP	1581
	J6	564
	AE11	1192
AGONY	KT1	449
	C	757
AGRAGAS	AE3	924
AGREE	LC	37
	SCG1	19
	DA	137
	DA	201
	PUF	20
	ELB	32
	MD	276
	SAA	808
	PK	13
	RL	329
	L3	18
	STS2	3

Word	Ref	Num	Word	Ref	Num	Word	Ref	Num
AGREE	STS2	9	AID	AE6	283	AIM	AE2	557
	J3	53		AE6	502		AE5	673
	J3	161		AE7	898		AE7	692
	M1	41		AE7	942		AE8	338
	M9	136		AE7	1002		AE10	480
	VP2	75		AE7	1033		AE12	712
	G2	361		AE8	14		M12	799
	AE10	1232		AE8	76	AIMED	HAP	7
	KT3	848		AE8	107		HAP	1609
	HIF	521		AE8	489		AE9	552
	C	546		AE8	494		AE9	1013
	WB	491		AE8	607		AE10	1277
	SMP	64		AE8	621		AE12	411
AGREED	PSF	41		AE8	707		AE12	787
	EUF	31		AE9	135		AE12	1332
	SAA	279		AE10	47		BP	36
	HAP	1012		AE10	57		M12	170
	HAP	2428		AE10	109		M12	649
	AE2	177		AE10	491	AIMEST	P4	35
	AE11	492		AE10	622		OAL	500
	AE12	476		AE10	857	AIMING	EWGR	33
	KT1	377		AE10	861		PK	14
	WB	82		AE10	1228		J10	361
	WB	118		AE11	351		G3	340
AGREEING	RL	142		AE11	660		AE5	568
AGREES	PK	4		AE11	717		AE5	638
	RL	151		AE11	730		AE6	251
	AE1	821		AE11	807		M8	146
AGREO	AT	71		AE11	888	AIMS	J10	184
	AT	72		AE12	233		AE1	185
AGRIPPA	AE8	903		AE12	559		AE6	654
AGRIPPINA'S	J6	812		AE12	597		AE12	462
AGROUND	G3	807		AE12	793		AE12	1058
	AE7	273		AE12	961	AIR	HS	63
	AE10	418		AE12	1081		SMA	102
	AU	6		AE12	1104		DC	11
AGUE	SEL4	19		AE12	1124		VHH	56
	L4	14		AE12	1131		AM	85
	C	182		AE12	1323		AM	91
AGUES	KT3	403		OAL	29		AM	222
AGYLLINA	AE8	628		KT2	654		AM	406
AHAZ'	HAP	1832		KT3	286		AM	430
AHEAD	AE5	206		KT3	323		AM	878
	AE5	1087		KT3	640		PM	25
AID	AM	165		KT3	765		SCD2	3
	AM	616		KT3	1070		DA	129
	SLN	5		M8	116		PSF	34
	EAL	30		M8	128		SAA	26
	CM	61		M8	172		PK	4
	HP	235		CAM	171		L1	3
	AA	282		CAM	213		L1	20
	AA	288		CAM	361		L3	282
	AA	399		HIF	64		T23	97
	AA	718		HIF	352		T27	107
	AA	853		HIF	525		H3	49
	MF	158		HIF	548		HAP	298
	SAA	25		HIF	563		HAP	1259
	SAA	122		HIF	688		HAP	1568
	SAA	229		HIF	702		HAP	1743
	SAA	671		HIF	791		HAP	1845
	SAA	951		C	247		HAP	1863
	SAA	966		TH	101		HAP	1913
	L1	32		TH	128		HAP	1930
	NS	13		TH	281		ODA	70
	HAP	248		AU	49		J1	46
	HAP	468		AU	77		J1	186
	HAP	816		AU	95		J3	499
	HAP	1878		AU	97		J6	627
	J3	275		AU	485		J16	50
	M1	375		AU	601		P4	37
	M9	122		M15	47		P5	178
	M9	164		CI	548		P6	2
	M9	210		CI	586		M1	18
	VCS	1	AIDING	AE5	357		M1	19
	VP10	12	AIDS	PLB	16		M1	27
	VP10	18		SAA	676		M1	28
	G1	241		SKA6	12		M1	34
	G4	480		G4	465		M1	60
	G4	569		AE2	712		M1	95
	AE1	878		AE4	599		M1	152
	AE2	19		AE5	262		M1	232
	AE2	217		AE7	990		M1	478
	AE2	227		AE8	908		M1	817
	AE2	284		AE12	622		M1	928
	AE2	463		TJD	138		M1	979
	AE2	542	AIGNAN	GE	73		M1	1049
	AE2	696	AIM	JH	15		M13	26
	AE2	873		AM	994		VP1	80
	AE3	30		SEL4	8		VP1	109
	AE3	556		MD	50		VP4	62
	AE3	775		MD	315		VP6	50
	AE4	63		SAA	754		G1	359
	AE5	196		EDG	5		G1	557
	AE5	975		L3	206		G1	634
	AE6	140		M1	615		G2	67
	AE6	173		AE2	79		G2	456

Headword	Code	No.
AIR	G2	499
	G2	589
	G2	596
	G3	172
	G3	234
	G3	378
	G3	431
	G3	439
	G3	468
	G3	502
	G3	635
	G3	651
	G3	721
	G4	21
	G4	29
	G4	90
	G4	103
	G4	249
	G4	375
	G4	424
	G4	441
	G4	666
	G4	699
	G4	723
	AE1	88
	AE1	123
	AE1	196
	AE1	309
	AE1	436
	AE1	770
	AE2	156
	AE2	292
	AE2	338
	AE2	941
	AE2	1031
	AE2	1075
	AE3	190
	AE3	463
	AE3	571
	AE3	673
	AE3	787
	AE3	883
	AE4	15
	AE4	42
	AE4	713
	AE4	728
	AE4	796
	AE4	821
	AE4	1009
	AE5	500
	AE5	839
	AE5	962
	AE5	1120
	AE6	20
	AE6	118
	AE6	148
	AE6	260
	AE6	353
	AE6	409
	AE6	593
	AE6	757
	AE6	987
	AE6	1008
	AE6	1031
	AE6	1115
	AE7	314
	AE7	554
	AE7	773
	AE8	41
	AE8	255
	AE8	350
	AE8	560
	AE9	230
	AE9	419
	AE9	636
	AE9	762
	AE9	886
	AE9	898
	AE9	1006
	AE10	115
	AE10	278
	AE10	458
	AE10	484
	AE10	615
	AE10	813
	AE10	900
	AE10	911
	AE10	1282
	AE11	840
	AE11	850
	AE11	869
	AE11	1066
	AE11	1166
	AE11	1250
	AE12	268
	AE12	549
AIR	AE12	553
	AE12	876
	AE12	923
	AE12	1096
	AE12	1227
	AE12	1283
	ETO	2
	DO	102
	KT1	206
	KT1	210
	KT1	414
	KT1	452
	KT1	547
	KT2	351
	KT2	405
	KT2	519
	KT2	547
	KT3	404
	KT3	1028
	KT3	1106
	TJD	116
	M8	37
	M8	163
	M8	186
	M8	363
	M8	401
	BP	13
	CAM	194
	HIF	131
	C	464
	TH	266
	TH	335
	M11	37
	M11	222
	M11	251
	M11	280
	M11	350
	M11	382
	M11	476
	FL	17
	FL	30
	FL	36
	FL	42
	FL	147
	FL	318
	FL	380
	M12	81
	M12	332
	M12	685
	M12	745
	M12	749
	AU	589
	WB	218
	WB	532
	M15	333
	M15	370
	M15	377
	M15	383
	M15	451
	M15	513
	M15	516
	M15	521
	M15	522
	M15	609
	M15	616
	M15	621
	M15	623
	M15	671
	M15	699
	M15	704
	CI	153
AIRY	CM	16
	L3	72
	TA	366
	HAP	464
	BR	154
	EL	91
	M1	625
	M1	921
	M13	51
	G1	553
	G1	559
	G4	86
	AE1	79
	AE1	114
	AE1	255
	AE2	567
	AE4	360
	AE4	638
	AE5	789
	AE5	969
	AE6	280
	AE6	343
	AE6	422
	AE6	541
	AE6	654
AIRY	AE6	873
	AE6	958
	AE6	1025
	AE6	1192
	AE7	98
	AE7	396
	AE12	384
	C	158
	FL	482
	WB	12
	M15	139
	M15	538
AJACES	HI	94
AJAX	GK	78
	AE2	563
	HIF	208
	HIF	218
	M12	829
	AU	26
	AU	40
	AU	154
	AU	244
	AU	266
	AU	315
	AU	337
	AU	349
	AU	396
	AU	427
	AU	451
	AU	497
	AU	502
	AU	519
	AU	531
	AU	544
	AU	546
	AU	601
ALABAND	J3	126
ALABASTER	KT2	464
	CI	90
ALACRITY	AM	771
ALAEAN	AE6	784
ALAND	AE1	161
	AE10	405
ALARM	G4	27
	G4	92
	AE3	313
	AE4	805
	AE5	870
	AE11	688
	AE11	719
	AE12	599
	C	595
	TH	95
	TH	264
	TH	314
	M12	89
ALARMED	AE1	936
	AE10	282
	B	721
ALARMS	PLB	41
	SAA	264
	SAA	567
	SAA	653
	EDGA	17
	SSC	28
	G1	686
	G2	238
	G4	100
	G4	358
	G4	801
	AE1	407
	AE2	401
	AE2	423
	AE6	245
	AE6	1182
	AE7	64
	AE7	304
	AE7	855
	AE8	574
	AE8	716
	AE8	750
	AE8	921
	AE9	261
	AE12	912
	OAL	236
	C	637
	AU	340
	CI	399
ALASTOR	AU	401
ALBA	AE1	368
	AE5	778
	AE6	1039
	AE6	1046
	AE12	1201
ALBAN	AE1	9
	AE6	1035

Word	Code	No.
ALBAN	AE9	525
ALBANO	AE12	206
ALBANO S	AE12	205
ALBA'S	AE9	525
ALBEMARLE	AM	349
	AM	415
	AM	466
	AM	764
ALBION	AR	251
	TJD	158
ALBULA	AE8	439
ALBUMAZAR	PA	7
ALBUNEA'S	AE7	124
ALBURNIAN	G3	235
ALCANDER	AE9	1032
	AU	402
ALCANOR	AE9	915
	AE10	469
ALCATHOÜS	AE10	1052
ALCHYMIST	PA	8
ALCIBIADES	P4	6
ALCIDES	H3	50
	TA	447
	BR	55
	VP7	84
	AE5	546
	AE6	533
	AE7	916
	AE8	269
	AE8	285
	AE8	478
	AE10	446
	AE10	649
	AE10	655
	M12	712
	M12	736
	M12	743
	M15	16
ALCIDES'	AE10	1106
	M12	428
	AU	71
ALCIMEDON	VP3	56
ALCINOÜS'	G2	126
ALCIPPE	VP7	19
ALCON'S	VP5	13
ALCORAN	HAP	381
	HAP	708
ALCUMENA'S	M15	62
ALCYONE	M11	17
	M11	188
	M11	215
	M11	225
	M11	232
	M11	262
	M11	397
	M11	431
	M11	494
ALDER	VP6	91
	VP8	73
	G1	207
	G2	633
	KT3	962
ALDERMAN	PTC	28
ALDERS	G2	156
	M13	69
	VP10	108
ALE	PCG1	16
	PAL	33
	PCB	29
	MF	121
	SKA4	24
	PSH	28
	WB	38
ALECTO	AE7	451
	AE10	60
ALECTO'S	AE7	622
ALEHOUSE	PAR	3
ALEMONIDES	M15	61
ALEMON'S	M15	27
ALETHES	AE1	172
	AE9	325
	AE9	412
ALEXANDER	UDH	17
	HS	120
	GK	97
ALEXANDERED	C	660
ALEXANDER'S	J10	273
ALEXIS	SM2	1
	SM2	15
	SM2	17
	VP2	2
	VP2	5
	VP2	78
	VP2	93
	VP7	77
ALGA	AR	119

Word	Code	No.
ALGEBRA	RL	239
ALGERINE	HAP	1642
ALIEN	MF	163
	VP8	62
	VP8	68
	G2	117
	AE1	890
	AA	434
ALIENATE	HIF	702
ALIENATED	AE2	229
ALIGHT	AE2	554
	AE6	281
	AE7	99
	AE11	1042
	AE12	604
	FL	304
ALIGHTING	AE6	22
	AE10	1060
ALIKE	ELN	13
	SAA	301
	SAA	427
	SAA	886
	SAA	894
	RL	47
	MO	6
	GE	5
	HH	31
	HAP	242
	HAP	360
	HAP	2540
	PDS	15
	J3	292
	J6	90
	J10	314
	P1	128
	M1	324
	M1	604
	M13	14
	VP7	3
	G3	188
	AE5	404
	AE5	576
	AE9	1010
	AE11	446
	AE12	771
	AE12	997
	AE12	1144
	AE12	1228
	OAL	39
	KT1	339
	KT2	347
	KT3	25
	KT3	491
	B	504
	B	510
	BP	38
	FL	247
	M12	269
	AU	134
ALIVE	AM	537
	PCG2	24
	DA	171
	EPF	6
	MD	7
	L3	63
	TA	299
	HAP	1926
	HAP	2450
	J16	81
	M1	572
	HI	195
	GK	45
	AE3	401
	AE6	889
	AE9	473
	AE10	632
	AE10	955
	AE10	1013
	AE12	58
	KT1	151
	M12	478
	M15	200
	M15	395
	M15	650
	EWR	20
ALL-ATONING	AA	179
ALLAY	SMA	95
	EMP	5
	EAA	11
	HAP	320
	M1	630
	G4	131
	G4	155
	AE1	94
	AE6	990

Word	Code	No.
ALLAY	MM	47
ALLAYED	HP	234
	AE1	276
	AS	57
ALL-DISPENSING	HAP	2140
ALLEGE	B	545
ALLEGIANCE	SAA	381
ALLEN	AM	685
ALLEY	MF	47
ALL-FORGIVING	TA	257
ALL-GOOD	AM	1131
ALLIA	AE7	993
	OAL	468
ALLIANCE	HAP	2106
	AE4	152
	AE7	323
	AE7	361
	AE7	438
	AE7	769
	AE9	815
	AE10	161
	AE11	196
	AE11	251
	AE11	353
	AE11	452
	AE11	540
	MM	35
ALLIANCES	HP	55
ALLIED	AM	650
	PUO4	4
	AA	24
	AA	163
	SAA	993
	MO	3
	AE9	364
	C	60
	AU	238
	AS	72
ALLIES	HAP	2369
	HAP	2399
	G3	549
	AE4	65
	AE8	8
	AE8	27
	AE10	608
ALL-MAKING	KT3	1035
ALL-MATURING	AM	559
ALLOTTED	AA	252
	KT3	280
ALLOW	AM	1176
	PT	22
	PAL	20
	SAA	1059
	HAP	414
	HAP	1645
	HAP	1991
	HAP	2139
	J3	487
	J6	389
	P5	277
	M1	133
	M1	525
	PLT	12
	PLT	23
	G2	263
	G3	255
	G3	284
	G4	465
	AE3	641
	AE4	310
	AE5	985
	AE6	859
	OAL	523
	M8	303
	BP	130
	HIF	464
	M11	65
	M12	525
	ESK	25
ALLOWED	PTL	17
	PCG1	40
	PNH	28
	EAZ	40
	ML	49
	PC2	31
	AA	224
	AA	777
	PLB	50
	MD	141
	SAA	161
	SAA	572
	SAA	604
	HAP	707
	HAP	827
	HAP	1617
	HAP	1700

Word	Code	Num
ALLOWED	HAP	2493
	EL	276
	OD	16
	J3	288
	J6	170
	J10	448
	M13	213
	VP3	36
	G2	120
	AE11	201
	KT2	447
	KT3	512
	M8	117
	B	193
	B	478
	HIF	392
	HIF	412
	M12	786
ALLOWING	ECG2	16
ALLOWS	SCG3	6
	MD	39
	HAP	1090
	AE3	589
	AE5	611
	AE6	630
ALLOY	HS	98
ALL-POWERFUL	AE4	392
	AE4	595
	AE7	602
ALL-RIGHTEOUS	RL	60
ALL-SEEING	AE12	266
	KT3	1035
ALL-SUFFICIENT	EL	75
ALLUDED	HAP	1660
ALLURE	PPC	26
	HAP	1662
	HAP	1680
	OAL	345
	AU	182
ALLURED	L4	183
	HAP	379
	HAP	1492
	AE8	271
	B	603
	CI	146
ALLUREMENT	L4	130
ALLUREMENTS	SAA	1008
ALLURER	PP	11
ALLURES	HAP	1278
	G3	533
ALLURING	L4	3
	AK	94
	HAP	2332
	P4	115
	M1	177
	M1	679
	G3	332
	G4	88
	AE8	489
ALLUSION	HAP	1425
	GK	93
ALLUSIONS	BR	54
ALLWAYS	EPN	2
ALLY	HAP	2191
ALMAIN	GE	33
ALMANAC	J6	743
ALMEYDA	EDS	14
ALMIGHTY	AR	262
	PIE	1
	AM	1117
	AA	1026
	MD	91
	T18	84
	TA	287
	HAP	1071
	HAP	1228
	HAP	2492
	J10	469
	M1	232
	M1	832
	VCS	15
	VCS	35
	G2	440
	G4	245
	AE1	308
	AE2	937
	AE7	572
	AE10	7
	AE10	868
	B	505
	M10	63
	GP	39
ALMIGHTY'S	AA	645
ALMON	AE7	741
	AE7	793
ALMONDS	SAA	429

Word	Code	Num
ALMONDS	G1	272
ALMOST	PWGR	26
	PAL	9
	PLG	19
	HP	77
	MF	103
	SAA	603
	SAA	730
	SAA	1098
	TA	84
	TA	104
	TA	314
	TA	385
	HAP	1933
	ETS	1
	EL	86
	EL	310
	OD	37
	J10	93
	P6	43
	GK	19
	AE5	423
	AE5	426
	AE6	1195
	AE9	754
	AE9	854
	B	24
	GP	11
	EMKG	27
ALMS	PNH	39
	EOE	25
	HAP	1399
	HAP	1400
	HAP	2238
	BR	272
	EL	28
	EL	63
	J1	179
	J6	700
	J10	130
	P1	176
ALOFT	AM	199
	AM	605
	H29	58
	AK	174
	HAP	854
	HAP	1111
	HAP	2326
	J1	26
	J1	83
	J10	561
	M1	109
	M1	407
	VP8	144
	VP9	36
	G1	434
	G1	549
	G1	580
	G3	14
	G3	171
	G3	288
	G3	313
	G4	84
	AE1	123
	AE1	145
	AE1	308
	AE2	314
	AE2	644
	AE3	178
	AE3	571
	AE3	706
	AE3	739
	AE4	375
	AE4	821
	AE5	331
	AE5	567
	AE5	683
	AE5	728
	AE6	183
	AE6	295
	AE6	412
	AE6	794
	AE7	192
	AE7	373
	AE7	647
	AE8	977
	AE9	590
	AE9	744
	AE9	751
	AE9	860
	AE10	278
	AE10	344
	AE10	903
	AE10	1080
	AE10	1282
	AE11	658

Word	Code	Num
ALOFT	AE11	869
	AE11	1050
	AE12	693
	AE12	846
	AE12	1328
	AE12	1374
	AF	3
	KT2	187
	KT3	49
	KT3	557
	C	158
	FL	189
	FL	591
	M12	87
	CI	370
ALONE	UDH	93
	HS	21
	AR	96
	AR	99
	AR	234
	AR	308
	AR	320
	RH	38
	SMA	32
	SMA	58
	SMA	69
	SMA	84
	SMA	118
	PWG	53
	EIE	22
	AM	9
	AM	66
	AM	107
	AM	153
	AM	175
	AM	186
	AM	267
	AM	399
	AM	1059
	PWGR	3
	SEL3	3
	STL	9
	SCG2	14
	SCG2	17
	SCG3	17
	EMQW	9
	SM2	10
	ELN	11
	PUO2	18
	POE	30
	EOE	1
	PCB	19
	PLG	3
	CM	48
	HP	83
	HP	177
	DA	78
	ETG	14
	AA	28
	AA	297
	AA	702
	AA	716
	AA	792
	AA	886
	MD	3
	MD	208
	MD	278
	MF	15
	MF	17
	SAA	676
	EDGA	6
	RL	176
	RL	193
	RL	203
	RL	342
	RL	362
	RL	444
	OE	13
	DOD	3
	DOD	15
	L1	44
	L4	50
	T18	22
	T18	31
	H29	65
	FS4	7
	PAA	22
	EAA	21
	AK	135
	AK	148
	HH	20
	HAP	25
	HAP	70
	HAP	385
	HAP	513
	HAP	684

Word	Ref	Num
ALONE	HAP	724
	HAP	810
	HAP	926
	HAP	1009
	HAP	1018
	HAP	1726
	HAP	1812
	HAP	1860
	HAP	1888
	HAP	1902
	HAP	1903
	HAP	2030
	HAP	2043
	HAP	2238
	BR	196
	PDS	13
	ELW	1
	EL	105
	OD	43
	J1	136
	J3	85
	J3	93
	J3	109
	J3	416
	J6	571
	J6	630
	J6	655
	J6	792
	J6	859
	J10	152
	J10	543
	J16	34
	J16	83
	P5	189
	M1	172
	M1	321
	M1	373
	M1	674
	M1	746
	M1	793
	M1	802
	M1	808
	M9	58
	M9	72
	M9	83
	M13	114
	M13	118
	M13	170
	M13	211
	HI	20
	HI	33
	HI	82
	PLT	10
	ELT	31
	GK	179
	DHP	30
	VP2	3
	VP3	114
	VP9	60
	VP10	22
	VP10	76
	G1	178
	G1	309
	G1	632
	G2	390
	G2	515
	G2	597
	G3	108
	G3	161
	G3	405
	G4	59
	G4	136
	G4	224
	G4	315
	G4	563
	G4	672
	G4	738
	G4	743
	G4	750
	AE1	42
	AE1	99
	AE1	392
	AE1	426
	AE1	533
	AE1	693
	AE1	837
	AE1	937
	AE2	180
	AE2	388
	AE2	770
	AE2	776
	AE4	118
	AE4	465
	AE4	610
	AE4	661
	AE4	677
ALONE	AE4	689
	AE4	768
	AE4	783
	AE5	290
	AE5	490
	AE5	795
	AE5	907
	AE5	916
	AE5	922
	AE5	1066
	AE5	1094
	AE6	82
	AE6	470
	AE6	1173
	AE7	546
	AE7	547
	AE7	654
	AE7	893
	AE7	975
	AE7	1062
	AE8	588
	AE8	705
	AE8	810
	AE9	5
	AE9	153
	AE9	170
	AE9	256
	AE9	391
	AE9	571
	AE9	587
	AE9	641
	AE9	703
	AE10	274
	AE10	420
	AE10	658
	AE10	741
	AE10	858
	AE10	980
	AE10	1272
	AE11	175
	AE11	336
	AE11	474
	AE11	570
	AE11	579
	AE11	580
	AE11	667
	AE11	671
	AE11	679
	AE11	763
	AE11	1148
	AE12	92
	AE12	222
	AE12	478
	AE12	685
	AE12	948
	AE12	1008
	AE12	1179
	OAL	60
	OAL	429
	OAL	562
	OAL	788
	MM	37
	MM	48
	DO	88
	DO	116
	DO	157
	KT1	61
	KT1	242
	KT1	280
	KT1	343
	KT1	533
	KT2	75
	KT2	154
	KT2	170
	KT2	323
	KT2	502
	KT3	8
	KT3	734
	KT3	797
	KT3	806
	KT3	1074
	TJD	29
	TJD	152
	M8	250
	B	9
	B	139
	B	167
	B	192
	B	248
	B	368
	B	463
	B	486
	B	493
	B	520
	B	531
	B	566
ALONE	B	600
	BP	67
	BP	81
	BP	143
	BP	154
	CAM	1
	CAM	21
	CAM	31
	CAM	39
	CAM	135
	CAM	243
	HIF	37
	HIF	177
	HIF	178
	HIF	226
	HIF	238
	HIF	267
	HIF	303
	HIF	739
	C	65
	C	220
	C	342
	TH	14
	TH	39
	TH	76
	TH	320
	M11	43
	M11	163
	M11	488
	FL	58
	FL	140
	FL	142
	FL	490
	M12	6
	M12	25
	M12	235
	M12	322
	M12	537
	M12	607
	M12	659
	M12	730
	M12	794
	AU	142
	AU	149
	AU	417
	AU	486
	AU	540
	AU	593
	WB	195
	M15	147
	M15	186
	M15	340
	GP	64
	GP	66
	CI	138
	CI	183
	CI	286
	CI	293
	CI	348
	CI	392
	CI	448
	CI	471
	CI	505
	CI	615
	STP	2
	STP	15
	PMK	25
ALOOF	HAP	306
	HAP	2543
	GK	83
	G3	706
	AE2	400
	AE3	547
	AE5	215
	AE5	1132
	AE9	678
	AE10	1006
	AE11	1128
	AE12	900
	AE12	965
	M8	108
	M8	183
	HIF	339
	HIF	422
ALOUD	AM	46
	SCD1	23
	HP	146
	MD	14
	L3	149
	T18	28
	T23	20
	TA	99
	HAP	468
	HAP	2510
	J1	152
	P3	14

ALOUD	P5	18	ALREADY	VP3	172	ALTAR		AE12	441
	AE2	53		VP9	81			AE12	451
	AE3	828		G1	674			KT2	460
	AE3	882		G4	734			KT3	180
	AE4	968		AE1	553			KT3	210
	AE5	18		AE1	610			KT3	248
	AE5	105		AE1	977			KT3	252
	AE5	858		AE1	997			KT3	294
	AE6	68		AE2	139			KT3	347
	AE6	329		AE2	171			HIF	613
	AE6	525		AE2	383			M11	255
	AE7	191		AE3	638			M12	14
	AE7	532		AE4	1			M12	210
	AE7	542		AE4	518			M12	351
	AE7	700		AE5	504			M12	362
	AE7	797		AE5	679			M12	366
	AE8	10		AE6	1031			M12	367
	AE8	693		AE6	1061	ALTAR'S		AE4	321
	AE8	734		AE6	1087			HIF	602
	AE9	41		AE7	756			M12	367
	AE9	510		AE9	894	ALTARS		MF	112
	AE9	875		AE10	664			MF	207
	AE9	994		AE10	835			SAA	541
	AE10	621		AE10	1259			SAA	1006
	AE10	916		AE11	28			L4	242
	AE10	1038		AE11	637			HAP	581
	AE10	1094		AE12	322			HAP	1631
	AE11	697		AE12	619			HAP	2284
	AE11	1040		AE12	977			J1	171
	AE12	325		AE12	1107			J3	356
	AE12	471		OAL	229			J10	547
	AE12	702		OAL	240			P6	100
	AE12	1005		OAL	241			M1	335
	OAL	557		OAL	547			M1	505
	KT1	89		OAE1	17			VP5	102
	KT1	236		DO	40			VP8	89
	KT2	350		KT3	122			VP8	154
	KT3	496		KT3	1121			G1	192
	M8	223		B	574			G1	462
	M8	285		B	697			G2	545
	M8	294		HIF	318			G3	7
	M8	352		HIF	365			G3	733
	HIF	210		C	425			G3	739
	HIF	289		TH	85			G4	396
	M11	173		TH	210			G4	545
	M11	325		TH	324			G4	782
	AU	103		FL	609			G4	793
ALOW	G3	171		M12	47			AE1	75
	CI	370		M12	511			AE1	157
ALPHESIBOEUS	VP5	115		M12	609			AE1	460
ALPHEÜS	AE3	910		AU	360			AE1	489
ALPINE	AE6	1140		CI	254			AE1	578
	AE8	877		CI	279			AE2	209
	AE10	18		CI	378			AE2	707
ALPS	HS	119		CI	394			AE2	1039
	J10	243		CI	538			AE3	89
	J10	271	ALSUS	AE12	461			AE3	161
	VP10	71	ALTAR	AR	119			AE3	301
	G1	640		DA	121			AE3	390
	G3	718		ER	65			AE4	86
ALREADY	SMA	79		BR	79			AE4	209
	LC	129		BR	180			AE4	289
	AM	509		J6	462			AE4	298
	AM	669		J6	512			AE4	736
	AM	1169		J6	717			AE4	971
	AM	1173		J10	414			AE5	66
	AM	1209		M9	164			AE5	119
	AA	442		M9	183			AE5	836
	MD	139		VP1	10			AE5	859
	SAA	962		VP8	104			AE5	1009
	EDG	35		G2	524			AE7	1047
	TA	18		AE1	482			AE8	246
	TA	473		AE2	294			AE8	377
	PAA	18		AE2	576			AE8	720
	AK	173		AE2	684			AE8	952
	HAP	337		AE2	701			AE8	956
	HAP	1182		AE2	900			AE9	548
	HAP	1693		AE2	31			AE9	794
	HAP	1799		AE3	31			AE11	72
	HAP	1877		AE3	35			AE12	180
	HAP	2574		AE3	430			AE12	256
	BR	80		AE4	76			AE12	285
	BR	169		AE4	81			AE12	300
	OD	15		AE4	750			AE12	425
	J3	328		AE6	189			AE12	479
	J6	39		AE6	360			AE12	722
	J6	486		AE7	110			AE12	1219
	J10	133		AE8	116			OAE2	31
	P3	35		AE8	142			BP	170
	P3	192		AE8	359			M10	60
	M1	269		AE8	447			HIF	63
	M1	342		AE8	849			HIF	440
	M1	448		AE8	956			M11	242
	M1	969		AE9	859			M12	302
	M13	42		AE12	293	ALTAR-WISE		AE6	259
	MC	66		AE12	332	ALTER		B	418

Word	Ref	No.	Word	Ref	No.	Word	Ref	No.
ALTER	PTC	15	AMAIN	CI	341	AMBIENT	AE6	93
ALTERED	AA	290	AMALEK	BR	296		ETO	2
	SAA	335	AMANTUM	PPC	19		M15	573
	HAP	1373	AMARYLLIS	AT	1	AMBIGUOUS	AE2	131
	M1	881		AT	87		AE6	150
	G1	567		VP1	6		OAL	640
	AE2	229		VP1	40		M15	498
	AE5	888		VP2	16	AMBIGUOUSLY	OAL	557
	AE7	27		VP2	74	AMBITION	EAL	22
	AE11	388		VP8	109		PUO4	33
	AE12	473		VP8	155		AA	198
	AF	85		VP9	26		AA	304
	AF	89	AMASENE	AE7	947		AA	479
	KT1	562		AE11	825		MD	30
	KT2	85	AMASTRUS	AE11	997		SAA	259
	WB	360	AMATA	AE7	482		SAA	292
	M15	239		AE7	560		SAA	453
	M15	388		AE9	996		SAA	866
	CI	206	AMATA'S	AE7	488		FS4	14
	CI	226		AE7	565		HAP	1366
	CI	366		AE7	804		G2	734
ALTERING	AA	415		AE12	89		AE7	80
	KT3	880		AE12	97		AE11	525
ALTERNATE	TA	135	AMAZE	G4	123		MM	29
	EL	125		AE1	991		KT3	809
	VP7	25		AE5	3		HIF	551
	G1	107		AE5	840		C	36
	AE1	302		AE5	850	AMBITION'S	SAA	120
	AE5	752		AE11	215		SAA	672
	AE6	181	AMAZED	AM	249	AMBITIOUS	HS	86
	DO	153		AM	978		AR	9
	KT2	652		SAA	610		PNH	21
	KT3	882		HAP	534		AA	309
	B	246		HAP	971		AA	927
	M15	614		HAP	1286		MD	315
ALTERNATIVE	HIF	204		HAP	1897		SAA	22
ALTERS	VP10	92		M1	518		SAA	832
	WB	433		VP1	48		RL	411
	M15	276		VP10	31		H3	35
ALTHAEA'S	M8	281		G1	666		AK	91
ALTHEA	M8	243		AE2	154		HAP	1151
ALTITUDE	UDH	40		AE2	280		EL	284
	EL	269		AE2	508		J1	39
ALWAYS	EWGR	10		AE2	720		J3	299
	PC1	6		AE2	933		J10	271
	ML	37		AE2	1083		P1	56
	POE	26		AE3	40		P4	29
	PCB	3		AE4	564		M1	1088
	ETG	9		AE9	62		AE2	699
	ETG	25		AE9	559		AE6	796
	AA	547		AE11	181		AE7	795
	AA	603		AE12	1258		AE7	1017
	AA	724		AE12	1329		AE11	1145
	AA	748		OAL	141		OAL	828
	AA	781		AF	130		OAE1	18
	AA	832		KT1	236		KT3	175
	AA	833		M8	238		CAM	29
	MD	90		B	163		C	668
	MF	186		B	633		AU	449
	SAA	244		B	691	AMBITIOUSLY	AM	443
	SAA	811		CAM	268		MF	86
	SAA	954		M11	116		L2	12
	SAA	1109		M12	232	AMBROSIAL	G4	2
	L4	189		M12	661		AE1	559
	H29	55	AMAZEMENT	TA	50		HIF	712
	TA	45		TA	496	AMBROSIAN	AE12	616
	PAA	34		G4	497	AMBUSCADE	AE6	698
	PAA	39		AE2	300	AMBUSH	AM	450
	HAP	1432		KT3	302		PKA	28
	HAP	2208		M8	238		AE11	782
	ETS	27		B	238		AE11	804
	MS	4		CAM	312		AE11	1151
	J10	385	AMAZING	TA	19		OAL	263
	P3	154		AE9	704		B	265
	AE5	581		M15	612	AMBUSHED	AM	718
	C	357	AMAZON	L4	150		AE11	1293
	CI	27		AE11	666		KT1	493
AMAIN	SCD2	17		AE11	858		AU	339
	HAP	1914	AMAZONIAN	J6	365		CI	268
	SKA1	5		J6	523	AMELLUS	G4	392
	P2	91		AE1	689	AMEN	MF	144
	G1	155		AE5	408		HAP	1964
	G1	513	AMAZONS	AM	195	AMENANE	M15	428
	G3	149		AE11	975	AMENDED	TA	505
	AE5	43		KT1	17		CI	234
	AE5	258	AMBASSADOR	AE8	190	AMENDS	AR	218
	AE5	609		GP	6		PWGR	21
	AE9	718	AMBER	EL	157		HP	32
	AE11	658		J6	744		PLB	43
	KT3	836		VP8	74		EPC	2
	KT3	994		M10	44		SKA6	23
	M8	99		M15	477		J16	17
	B	683	AMBER-COLORED	KT3	72		AES	368
	TH	118	AMBIENT	PUF	19		WB	364
	FL	383		M1	242		WB	365
	M12	417		AE1	813		CI	430

Word	Ref	No.
AMES-ACE	P3	94
AMIEL	AA	899
AMIEL'S	AA	899
AMINEAN	G2	138
AMISS	AR	209
	PA	42
	HP	91
	T27	78
	WB	508
	WB	523
AMITERNIAN	AE7	983
AMITY	AE5	435
	AE5	706
AMMON	M15	467
AMMON'S	AE4	288
AMMUNITION	AM	409
AMNON'S	AA	39
AMOMUM	CAM	16
	M15	583
AMOROUS	EUO	17
	L4	2
	L4	119
	FS1	3
	SKA2	24
	VP1	77
	G2	302
	G3	417
	G3	434
	KT3	116
	KT3	900
	B	34
	WB	51
AMOUNT	J1	177
AMOUR	PEL	14
AMPHION	J6	251
	VP2	29
AMPHITHEATER	KT2	444
AMPHITRITE	AR	246
AMPHRYSIAN	G3	3
AMPHRYSOS	M1	787
AMPHYX	M12	602
AMPLE	AM	615
	HP	65
	HAP	2546
	M1	49
	M13	164
	G3	97
	G3	515
	G3	525
	AE3	215
	AE5	471
	AE5	498
	AE5	597
	AE5	638
	AE6	907
	AE6	1008
	AE7	358
	AE7	910
	AE7	1018
	AE8	367
	AE8	825
	AE8	946
	AE9	302
	AE9	989
	AE9	1094
	AE10	584
	AE10	716
	AE11	179
	AE11	504
	AE11	752
	AE12	198
	AE12	558
	OAL	328
	DO	48
	KT3	53
	HIF	69
	M12	330
	M15	261
AMPLER	AK	112
	P6	18
	AU	176
AMPLY	CI	436
AMRI	SAA	1013
	SAA	1017
AMSANCTUS	AE7	778
AMULETS	VP7	38
AMYCIAN	AE5	493
AMYCLA	AE10	790
AMYCUS	AE1	306
	AE9	1042
	AE12	739
	M12	342
	M12	357
AMYDON	J3	127
AMYNTA	DOD	3
	FS2	1
AMYNTA'S	T23	87
AMYNTAS	SEL3	3
	ODA	18
	ODA	34
	ODA	68
	ODA	81
	R	1
	VP2	43
	VP2	49
	VP3	100
	VP3	109
	VP5	10
	VP10	55
	VP10	57
	VP10	62
ANAGNIA	AE7	947
ANAGRAM	MF	204
ANAK	HAP	2436
ANARCHY	PA	17
	PO	11
	AA	172
	MD	122
	HAP	980
ANASTASIA'S	AS	13
ANATOMY	PUO1	25
ANCAEUS	M8	61
	M8	165
	M8	177
	M8	183
	M8	352
ANCESTORS	AR	47
	DC	2
	PA	3
	ER	47
	L4	227
	HAP	1204
	J3	489
	J10	403
	J16	50
	P6	139
	AE3	128
	AE11	391
	KT3	1090
	C	635
	AU	227
	WB	392
	WB	453
ANCESTORS'	AE6	1154
ANCESTRY	AE1	885
	AE3	146
	AE10	271
	AE11	82
	TH	151
ANCHEMOLUS	AE10	543
ANCHISES	EL	197
	AE1	875
	AE2	860
	AE2	935
	AE3	13
	AE3	343
	AE3	688
	AE3	733
	AE3	802
	AE5	72
	AE5	76
	AE5	992
	AE6	441
	AE6	909
	AE6	921
	AE6	978
	AE6	1229
	AE6	1240
	AE7	166
	AE7	180
	AE7	336
	AE8	207
	AE8	217
ANCHISES'	AE4	506
	AE5	40
	AE5	100
	AE5	134
	AE5	796
	AE6	191
	AE9	888
	AE12	1354
	M15	646
ANCHOR	AM	247
	AM	706
	BR	329
	AE6	946
	AE10	328
	OAL	291
	M15	443
ANCHORS	AM	709
	M1	405
	AE1	240
ANCHORS	AE3	358
	AE4	602
	AE4	825
	AE5	1011
	AE6	3
	AE8	653
	AE9	140
	HIF	597
	M11	443
	M15	407
	CI	612
ANCIENT	UDH	2
	HS	30
	AR	93
	LC	11
	LCA	33
	PMQ	49
	ECD	9
	EUO2	23
	POE	27
	HP	58
	PSF	12
	AA	801
	AA	844
	AA	900
	D	31
	MF	66
	MF	87
	SAA	388
	SAA	989
	RL	135
	RL	336
	PD	24
	ER	75
	H29	1
	H2	36
	TA	515
	AK	120
	HAP	62
	HAP	347
	HAP	397
	HAP	471
	HAP	807
	HAP	996
	HAP	1093
	HAP	1154
	HAP	1163
	HAP	1371
	HAP	1875
	HAP	2065
	J3	1
	J6	31
	J6	239
	J6	301
	J6	371
	P5	1
	M1	566
	M1	769
	ELT	11
	VP3	17
	VP6	103
	G2	66
	G2	244
	G2	787
	G3	347
	G3	514
	G4	90
	G4	407
	G4	491
	AE1	20
	AE1	27
	AE1	517
	AE1	1039
	AE2	395
	AE2	490
	AE2	612
	AE3	111
	AE3	129
	AE3	609
	AE3	647
	AE4	338
	AE4	962
	AE5	46
	AE5	598
	AE5	706
	AE5	784
	AE6	261
	AE6	1214
	AE7	54
	AE7	102
	AE7	189
	AE7	245
	AE7	296
	AE7	516
	AE7	891
	AE8	172

Word	Ref	No.
ANCIENT	AE8	415
	AE8	625
	AE8	654
	AE10	289
	AE11	6
	AE11	289
	AE11	642
	AE12	342
	AE12	1102
	AE12	1209
	MG	7
	MG	36
	DO	2
	KT1	35
	KT1	129
	KT1	363
	KT2	71
	TJD	50
	BP	191
	C	209
	TH	3
	FL	155
	WB	16
	WB	435
	M15	416
ANCIENTS	RH	94
	RL	436
ANCUS	L3	237
	L3	238
	TA	466
	AE6	1115
ANDRÉ'S	MF	53
ANDREW'S	PTP	39
	EMKG	10
ANDROGEOS	AE2	500
	AE2	514
ANDROGEOS'	AE2	529
	AE6	26
ANDROMACHE	HI	2
	AE3	384
ANEW	AA	805
	MD	316
	SAA	315
	RL	168
	L3	30
	VP8	70
	AE1	1008
	AE12	380
	AE12	1368
	DO	137
	KT2	355
	KT3	519
	KT3	593
	B	28
	CAM	213
	M15	665
ANGEL	AM	893
	AA	853
	T23	36
	TA	208
	TA	387
	HAP	893
	HAP	1229
	SSC	53
	BR	45
	BR	155
	EL	57
	AF	170
	AF	180
	DO	32
	DO	131
	C	602
	C	650
	FL	158
ANGELO	ML	52
ANGEL'S	KT1	401
	SAA	56
ANGELS	SMA	68
	AM	62
	AM	453
	AA	273
	MD	20
	PRH	38
	SAA	61
	FS3	9
	TA	371
	AK	61
	HAP	2591
	BR	3
	BR	227
	EL	120
	ODA	78
	KT1	198
ANGELS'	AA	310
	TA	419
	BR	320

Word	Ref	No.
ANGELS'	EL	128
ANGER	SMA	92
	SMM2	22
	SEL4	13
	SEL4	21
	SSC	27
	J1	121
	P4	62
	M1	1005
	M1	1054
	GK	84
	G4	777
	AE2	559
	AE2	728
	AE5	224
	AE9	70
	AE10	557
	AE10	865
	AE11	1046
	AE12	1206
	KT2	563
	HIF	593
	M12	789
	CI	356
ANGITIAN	AE7	1041
ANGLE	M13	210
	AE12	755
ANGLER	AR	171
	OAL	50
ANGRY	AR	100
	AM	92
	AM	478
	AM	1115
	SCG2	3
	PTC	40
	CM	92
	MD	190
	L4	113
	HAP	1564
	HAP	1968
	OD	40
	J3	37
	P1	246
	M1	129
	M1	608
	VP9	8
	G1	448
	G2	208
	G4	101
	G4	246
	G4	590
	AE1	60
	AE1	159
	AE1	187
	AE1	219
	AE1	870
	AE3	488
	AE4	506
	AE4	558
	AE7	772
	AE8	565
	AE10	612
	AE12	500
	AE12	1230
	OAL	503
	KT1	356
	KT2	88
	KT2	202
	KT2	657
	M8	333
	AU	299
	AU	457
	M15	95
	M15	119
ANGUISH	SKK	12
	STC	11
	CM	104
	MD	53
	SDG	1
	HAP	146
	HAP	1776
	SKA2	24
	SSH	6
	VP6	80
	AE4	937
	AE5	849
	AE10	1187
	AE10	1247
	AE12	875
	KT1	253
	B	744
	CAM	325
	HIF	488
ANIEN	AE7	945
ANIGROS	M15	432
ANIMAL	SAA	434

Word	Ref	No.
ANIMAL	M15	513
	EDG	43
ANIMALS	M1	557
	G4	224
	M15	281
ANIMATE	ML	41
	T18	57
	OAL	133
ANIMATED	GK	20
	AE2	466
	AE6	983
	M8	161
	M12	341
ANIMATING	M1	202
	KT3	1043
	G4	527
ANIO	AE3	106
ANIUS	AE1	464
ANKLES	AE8	602
	OAL	36
ANNA	AE4	11
	AE4	601
	AE4	632
	AE4	722
ANNABEL	AA	34
ANNALS	SAA	534
	TA	333
	AE1	514
ANNEALED	MFL	12
ANNEXED	HAP	1059
ANNIVERSE	BR	29
ANNOY	KT3	1111
ANNUAL	PUO1	3
	BR	325
	J16	62
	P6	56
	M1	150
	M1	173
	VP5	104
	VP5	117
	VP5	125
	G1	286
	G1	305
	G1	462
	AE1	363
	AE3	368
	AE5	65
	AE5	785
	AE5	993
	AE6	108
	AE8	233
	AE8	357
	AE8	798
	AE9	858
	OAL	80
	KT1	604
	TJD	150
	CI	438
ANODYNES	HAP	1376
ANOINT	AA	430
	AE6	315
ANOINTED	AR	80
	AM	1143
	AA	130
	AA	584
	MF	63
	SAA	146
	SAA	503
	TA	63
	HAP	1601
	J6	230
ANOINTING	AA	265
ANOINTS	SMA	59
	P2	64
	G4	599
ANON	H29	58
	VP3	151
ANSWER	HAP	649
	HAP	794
	HAP	804
	HAP	1300
	HAP	1615
	HAP	2028
	J3	305
	J3	464
	J3	468
	J6	330
	J6	515
	P6	4
	M1	1064
	VP7	4
	VP10	10
	G1	274
	G4	765
	AE2	160
	AE3	120

Word	Ref	No.
ANSWER	AE3	126
	AE5	502
	AE6	713
	AE7	365
	AE8	789
	AE10	823
	AE11	191
	AE11	679
	AE12	1176
	OAL	253
	OAL	548
	OAE2	20
	HIF	696
	M12	280
	WB	94
	WB	112
	WB	221
	WB	265
	WB	296
ANSWERED	CM	97
	HP	159
	HAP	1964
	HAP	2059
	HAP	2120
	P1	85
	HI	16
	AE2	378
	AE3	139
	AE3	803
	AE7	545
	AE8	204
	KT3	573
	CAM	119
	HIF	151
	HIF	196
	HIF	259
	HIF	324
	C	260
	TH	160
	FL	405
	WB	123
	WB	273
	CI	70
ANSWEREST	M1	905
ANSWERING	AM	1183
	RL	131
	L4	281
	HAP	491
ANSWERS	SMA	130
	PCD	14
	AA	422
	J6	717
	J6	759
	AE2	507
	AE6	474
	AE7	147
	OAL	550
	M12	328
	AU	513
ANT	J6	477
	G1	271
	G1	522
ANTAEUS	AE10	783
ANTANDROS	AE3	7
ANT-BORN	HIF	270
ANTECHAMBERS	AE4	189
ANTEMNAE	AE7	872
ANTENOR	AE1	332
	AU	325
ANTENOR'S	AE6	652
ANTEROS	KT3	1144
ANTEUS	AE12	654
ANTHEUS	AE1	257
	AE1	719
ANTHORES	AE10	1104
	AE10	1105
ANTIC	MD	1
	VP5	116
	G1	666
	G2	649
	AE9	351
	M12	330
ANTICHRIST	PCB	11
	PLB	27
	HAP	852
ANTICIPATE	AE10	16
ANTICIPATES	L3	232
ANTIDOTE	J6	860
	G2	177
ANTIGENES	VP5	139
ANTIMACHUS	M12	611
ANTIOCHUS	J3	167
ANTIPATHY/	HAP	177
ANTIPHATES	AE9	944
ANTIQUARY'S	UDH	84
ANTIQUATED	EAL	24
ANTIQUATED	P1	147
ANTIQUE	L4	230
	HAP	1782
	AE1	904
	AE12	1300
ANTIQUITIES	M15	15
ANTIQUITY	J6	839
ANTISSA	M15	438
ANTLERS	AE7	669
	M12	377
ANTONIUS	AE8	907
ANTONY	KT2	607
ANTRONIUS	AE10	1067
ANTS	AE4	582
	OAL	104
ANUBIS	AE8	927
ANVILS	G4	253
	J6	569
	J10	96
	AE6	858
	AE8	561
	AE8	592
ANXIETY	L3	115
ANXIOUS	AM	322
	AM	421
	CM	42
	RL	36
	L3	267
	L4	47
	L4	114
	H2	55
	J10	457
	J10	526
	P1	1
	M1	262
	M1	853
	HI	137
	G3	110
	AE1	15
	AE1	424
	AE1	927
	AE2	136
	AE4	1
	AE4	411
	AE4	799
	AE4	905
	AE5	269
	AE5	1068
	AE6	390
	AE6	454
	AE6	589
	AE7	343
	AE8	30
	AE8	486
	AE8	533
	AE9	3
	AE9	1107
	AE10	218
	AE11	362
	AE11	830
	AE12	336
	AE12	904
	AE12	1164
	OAL	410
	KT3	1075
	TJD	2
	B	296
	HIF	459
	TH	361
	M11	186
	FL	98
	AU	468
	WB	119
	M15	33
	CI	347
ANXIOUSLY	H29	44
	AE4	88
ANXUR	AE10	763
ANXUR'S	AE10	761
ANYTHING	PWG	45
	HP	26
	HP	86
	SAA	479
	SAA	529
	HAP	2219
	OAL	179
	OAL	669
	WB	187
AONIAN	VP10	16
APACE	PWGR	23
	SCD1	17
	TA	49
	HAP	372
	HAP	1874
	AE2	659
	OAE2	67
APACE	M8	258
	C	427
	M15	347
A-PADDING	PPC	29
APART	PDG	42
	HAP	658
	M13	130
	G4	240
	AE8	889
	AE11	526
	HIF	675
	HIF	729
	C	67
APARTMENT	PWG	29
	PWG	41
	AE7	480
	B	120
	M11	354
APARTMENTS	AE2	675
APE	HAP	39
	PKA	16
	J10	311
APELLES'	GK	97
APENNINE	P1	185
	AE12	1021
	M11	333
	WB	225
APES	M12	460
APHAREUS	M12	436
APHIDAS	AE9	950
APHIDNUS	M1	786
APIDANUS	J3	123
APING	C	460
APOCRYPHA	PTP	33
APOCRYPHAL	AA	665
APOLLO	EUO2	30
	VP4	12
	VP6	5
	VP10	31
	G1	320
	AE3	163
	AE4	204
	AE6	87
	AE6	113
	AE7	329
	AE8	935
	AE9	873
	AE11	1165
	HIF	111
	HIF	625
	HIF	809
	M12	788
	AU	611
APOLLO'S	EIE	24
	ER	65
	P1	96
	M1	633
	AE2	429
	AE3	430
	AE8	176
	AE8	959
	AE10	250
	AE10	747
	AE12	578
	AE12	750
	KT2	632
	HIF	513
APOPLEX	BR	239
	J1	217
APOSTATE	PLG	8
	SAA	371
	SAA	391
	HAP	151
	HAP	961
APOSTLE	UDH	23
	RL	199
	GP	128
APOSTLES	HAP	817
	HAP	879
	HAP	896
	HAP	933
	HAP	923
APOSTLES'	EL	39
APOSTOLIC	HAP	743
	HAP	1151
	HAP	1185
APOTHECARIES'	C	407
APOTHECARY	TJD	104
	C	168
APPARENT	BR	125
	AE12	329
APPARITIONS	PWR	7
APPEACH	KT1	300
APPEAL	SMA	84
	PC2	29
	RL	59

Word	Ref	No.	Word	Ref	No.	Word	Ref	No.
APPEAL	RL	95	APPEAR	AE1	217	APPEARED	EL	68
	RL	314		AE1	556		J6	22
	HAP	769		AE1	645		M1	120
	HAP	941		AE2	134		M13	218
	HAP	1044		AE2	138		VP1	54
APPEALS	RL	149		AE2	571		AE1	824
	HAP	107		AE2	662		AE2	20
APPEAR	UDH	33		AE2	713		AE2	416
	AR	247		AE2	802		AE3	779
	RH	18		AE2	843		AE4	510
	SMA	31		AE2	897		AE5	243
	LC	1		AE2	958		AE5	874
	LC	112		AE3	312		AE6	944
	AM	213		AE3	858		AE7	895
	AM	327		AE3	351		AE8	49
	AM	678		AE4	436		AE10	904
	AM	739		AE4	682		AE11	14
	AM	745		AE5	167		OAL	325
	AM	875		AE5	152		OAL	706
	EWGR	28		AE5	883		KT1	547
	PMM	3		AE6	136		KT2	203
	ET	1		AE6	596		KT2	444
	PEL	32		AE6	1001		KT2	541
	STL	23		AE6	1049		KT3	82
	ECG1	28		AE6	1058		KT3	948
	PCG2	5		AE7	933		M8	154
	PM	21		AE7	990		B	303
	PLN	31		AE8	697		C	230
	ENH	33		AE8	883		C	243
	PUO2	23		AE9	32		FL	174
	EUO2	26		AE9	193		FL	338
	ML	2		AE9	328		M12	46
	EMW	7		AE9	675		M12	172
	PUO3	29		AE9	923		AU	58
	PUF	7		AE10	232		WB	272
	AA	656		AE10	614		CI	273
	PRH	38		AE10	748	APPEARING	AM	672
	MF	80		AE10	908		PKA	46
	SAA	304		AE10	1077		AE7	591
	SAA	455		AE11	49	APPEARS	EIE	18
	RL	73		AE11	115		AM	208
	AT	21		AE11	657		AM	417
	AT	87		AE12	245		AM	949
	ER	27		AE12	601		PCG2	13
	ER	34		AE12	663		AA	817
	L1	14		AE12	872		PLB	28
	L1	31		OAL	173		SAA	280
	NS	23		OAL	610		SAA	302
	TA	137		OAE2	52		RL	234
	TA	287		DO	80		L2	50
	AK	111		DO	140		L3	142
	AK	116		KT1	152		L4	15
	AK	133		KT1	598		T18	42
	GE	26		KT2	89		TA	506
	HAP	161		KT3	937		HAP	661
	HAP	672		M8	141		ETS	21
	HAP	1879		M8	244		J3	294
	HAP	2313		B	679		J6	97
	BR	182		M11	131		J6	322
	BR	287		M11	176		J6	489
	STS3	19		M11	371		J6	598
	LS	1		M11	406		J10	4
	EL	30		FL	7		M1	448
	EL	58		FL	487		M1	461
	MS	11		M12	513		M1	785
	J3	213		M15	297		M1	835
	J6	56		M15	323		GK	106
	J6	79		M15	392		GK	109
	J10	50		M15	542		EHC	26
	J16	41		M15	559		VP5	69
	J16	46		PTP	37		VP6	91
	J16	73		STP	1		VP10	20
	P1	82		SMP	72		G1	575
	P1	219		PMK	20		G3	504
	P1	254	APPEARANCE	AM	442		G3	533
	P4	102		AM	462		G3	716
	P4	128		TA	477		G3	750
	P5	78		HAP	157		G4	145
	M1	148		M1	76		G4	525
	M1	289		C	780		AE1	134
	M1	427		FL	246		AE1	221
	M1	467	APPEARED	SMA	8		AE1	234
	VP1	34		AM	629		AE1	486
	VP3	60		PEL	23		AE2	352
	VP4	63		CM	109		AE2	499
	VP7	62		PRH	22		AE2	1047
	VP7	69		MF	106		AE2	1048
	G2	122		EC	3		AE3	19
	G2	460		L3	159		AE3	99
	G2	513		TA	128		AE3	355
	G2	672		TA	356		AE3	405
	G3	34		HAP	263		AE3	441
	G3	569		HAP	894		AE3	723
	G3	840		HAP	1619		AE3	842
	G4	71		HAP	1852		AE3	900
	G4	338		SSC	53		AE4	194

Word	Code	No.	Word	Code	No.	Word	Code	No.
APPEARS	AE4	506	APPETITE	PMQ	42	APPLIES	PUO1	22
	AE4	676		L2	20	APPLY	UDH	95
	AE4	693		L3	214		PUF	7
	AE4	721		L4	58		P1	57
	AE4	803		T27	88		OAL	686
	AE5	385		H2	74		KT3	137
	AE5	448		P3	228		AU	552
	AE5	486		AE2	479		AU	604
	AE5	721		OAL	506	APPOINT	PW	5
	AE6	32		B	179	APPOINTED	SAA	528
	AE6	269		B	344		HAP	922
	AE6	582		B	570		HAP	960
	AE6	668		BP	108		HAP	2432
	AE6	929		M15	255		VP4	15
	AE6	1029	APPETITES	PAA	14		AE1	358
	AE6	1043		J6	549		AE2	437
	AE6	1103		G3	277		AE2	1086
	AE7	129		G4	288		AE3	480
	AE7	795		KT2	220		AE5	150
	AE7	924		B	445		AE5	413
	AE7	957	APPLAUD	SAA	114		AE5	755
	AE8	738		SAA	1095		AE6	28
	AE8	841		P1	47		AE11	31
	AE9	21		AE10	1041		AE11	117
	AE9	44		OAL	711		AE12	1168
	AE9	416		AF	146		OAL	478
	AE9	637		M8	205		KT2	177
	AE10	41	APPLAUDING	AE5	293		KT2	215
	AE10	199		AE5	440		KT2	235
	AE10	255		AE9	61		KT3	4
	AE10	299	APPLAUSE	HS	6		KT3	637
	AE10	1156		LCA	14		KT3	887
	AE11	51		LCA	51		KT3	1037
	AE11	327		AM	274		B	100
	AE11	367		PUO2	35		BP	178
	AE11	529		HP	126		C	429
	AE11	628		EPF	10		TH	246
	AE11	724		PUO4	10		CI	569
	AE11	753		AA	295	APPOINTMENT	B	260
	AE11	907		SAA	808	APPOINTS	AE3	156
	AE12	186		SAA	889		AE5	989
	AE12	255		L3	203		KT1	554
	AE12	330		HAP	2386		KT3	406
	AE12	335		P1	76		C	292
	AE12	373		P1	89	APPREHEND	AR	311
	AE12	671		G2	733	APPREHENSION	TA	343
	AE12	1085		AE2	795	APPRENTISHIP	AE8	681
	KT1	524		AE5	294	APPROACH	VHH	48
	KT2	216		AE5	726		AM	385
	KT2	222		AE6	251		STL	4
	KT3	594		AE10	147		PRH	6
	KT3	673		AE10	1134		SAA	306
	KT3	854		AF	107		SAA	626
	KT3	922		KT2	322		SAA	795
	M8	24		KT3	525		HAP	530
	B	668		KT3	665		J6	231
	CAM	386		KT3	739		P4	66
	C	240		M8	156		P6	145
	M11	157		AU	589		GK	16
	M11	228	APPLAUSES	P4	112		VP1	16
	M11	356		G3	294		VP1	67
	M11	377		AE5	199		G3	428
	FL	511		AE5	489		AE1	989
	FL	586	APPLE	AT	94		AE3	832
	WB	157		G2	595		AE6	1087
	M15	285		G4	212		AE7	217
	CI	582		OAL	521		AE7	858
APPEASE	SAA	593		OAL	772		AE8	170
	SAA	781	APPLES	M13	72		AE8	291
	J6	542		VP1	51		AE8	873
	PPS	14		VP3	97		AE9	42
	P2	55		G1	368		AE9	81
	P3	44		G2	97		AE9	304
	VP9	8		G2	117		AE11	700
	VP10	87		G2	126		AE11	898
	G4	775		G4	201		AE12	128
	G4	787		OAL	855		AE12	328
	AE2	798		BP	113		AE12	842
	AE3	157	APPLICATIONS	L4	25		OAL	555
	AE3	691	APPLIED	TA	161		DO	60
	AE8	81		HAP	584		KT1	43
	CAM	179		HAP	917		KT2	179
	HIF	641		HAP	1149		KT3	804
	M11	31		HAP	2405		M8	206
	AU	294		AE1	121		HIF	559
	M15	190		AE7	49		M11	312
APPEASED	RL	133		AE7	1080		AU	136
	M1	1026		AE10	1311		CI	146
	AE1	300		AE11	1247	APPROACHED	AM	93
	AE1	1011		B	689		AM	373
	AE4	941		HIF	291		AM	465
	AE6	554		HIF	814		TA	90
	KT1	268		M12	497		BR	253
	HIF	535		M12	574		M9	159
	HIF	653		AU	261		AE3	784
APPENDIX	AA	671		WB	376		AE6	616

Word	Ref	No.	Word	Ref	No.	Word	Ref	No.
APPROACHED	AE6	864	ARBITRARY	AA	212	ARCITE	KT1	271
	AE6	937		AA	330		KT1	275
	AE9	94		AA	701		KT1	282
	AE9	535		AA	762		KT1	285
	AE11	1248		MD	78		KT1	305
	AE12	18		MD	142		KT1	311
	KT2	241		MD	249		KT1	367
	KT3	1		MD	314		KT1	373
	KT3	209		PDG	34		KT1	381
	M10	61		PDG	36		KT1	442
	HIF	637		TA	62		KT1	509
	M12	208		HAP	266		KT1	518
	M12	512		BR	341		KT1	555
	CI	452		J10	23		KT1	566
APPROACHES	PMQ	13		G4	162		KT1	599
	M1	195		AE1	93		KT2	1
	M9	30		AE6	1122		KT2	34
	G3	195		AE8	438		KT2	43
	AE2	399		AE8	631		KT2	75
	AE2	896		OAE1	6		KT2	85
	AE4	613		B	601		KT2	102
	AE5	589		HIF	342		KT2	127
	AE6	524	ARBOR	AE3	300		KT2	141
	AE12	598		FL	60		KT2	169
APPROACHETH	AR	253		FL	203		KT2	171
APPROACHING	AR	251		FL	308		KT2	202
	AM	1083		FL	427		KT2	242
	CM	90		FL	436		KT2	274
	SAA	66	ARBORS	VP9	56		KT2	294
	SAA	871	ARBUTE	G2	96		KT2	356
	L4	10	ARCADIA	AE5	391		KT2	427
	TA	56	ARCADIAN	P3	15		KT3	19
	PP	2		VP2	55		KT3	62
	M1	286		VP4	71		KT3	292
	G3	767		VP7	35		KT3	362
	AE2	853		VP10	48		KT3	368
	AE4	926		VP10	80		KT3	558
	AE5	968		G1	21		KT3	661
	AE8	4		G4	404		KT3	664
	AE8	713		AE8	70		KT3	667
	AE8	873		AE8	137		KT3	684
	AE9	1020		AE8	187		KT3	749
	AE11	806		AE8	212		KT3	770
	AE11	1314		AE8	612		KT3	852
	AE12	224		AE8	704		KT3	911
	KT3	862		AE8	722		KT3	1102
	M8	272		AE8	775	ARCITE'S	KT1	370
	B	208		AE9	9		KT1	501
	B	745		AE10	337		KT3	177
	TH	105		AE10	504		KT3	640
	FL	148		AE10	635		KT3	648
	FL	328		AE11	139		KT3	722
APPROBATION	AE5	400		AE11	210		KT3	993
APPROVE	HS	79		AE11	608		KT3	1126
	AA	981		AE12	350	ARCTOPHYLAX	CAM	264
	HAP	2000		AE12	409	ARCTURUS	G1	102
	EH	9		AE12	421		G1	295
	VP10	105		AE12	791	ARDEA	AE7	873
	AE8	67		AE12	807	ARDEAN	AE9	493
	WB	77		M15	497		AE11	704
APPROVED	PMQ	37	ARCADIANS	VP7	3	ARDEANS	AE7	604
	KT3	23		AE8	463	ARDEA'S	AE7	576
APRICOT	PR	26		AE9	186		AE9	995
APRIL	FL	315		AE10	555	ARDENT	L4	10
APT	MM	14		AE10	683		L4	47
	DO	121		AE10	704		G4	151
	WB	163		AE11	1214		AE2	277
	M15	669		M1	953		AE2	645
APTLY	OAL	403		G3	4		AE5	845
APTNESS	AM	564	ARCADIA'S	M1	820		AE9	255
	EL	218		G3	601		AE9	952
APULIAN	P1	115	ARCADY	AE9	790		AE10	388
	AE11	1004	ARCENS	AU	234		AE11	1144
APULIAN'S	H2	62	ARCESIUS	AU	233		AE12	112
AQUADUCTS	J3	31	ARCESIUS'	J10	213		AF	70
AQUILINE	KT3	74	ARCH	AE5	791		KT1	283
AQUIN	PO	25		AE6	857		M8	212
AQUINUM	J3	498		M11	265		M10	73
ARAB	J1	196	ARCHANGEL	CI	343		CAM	109
ARABIA	J6	599	ARCH-ATTESTOR	AA	640		HIF	306
	G2	161	ARCHER	M8	156		C	69
	G2	190	ARCHER'S	AE5	688		TH	121
	M15	584	ARCHERS	G2	174		CI	164
ARABIAN	AR	270		AE5	647	ARDOR	HP	80
	HAP	378		AE5	652		L4	216
	AE7	837		AE9	895		M9	150
	CAM	317	ARCHES	G2	36		AE7	957
	AE8	909		AE6	797		AE9	237
ARABIANS	G2	321		AE12	692		AE9	617
ARABLE	G2	653		AE12	675		AE10	975
ARABY	CAM	15	ARCHETIUS	UDH	30		AE11	233
ARAR'S	VP1	81	ARCHIMEDES'	AE7	1033		AE11	1076
ARAUNAH'S	BR	176	ARCHIPPUS	AR	165		AE12	420
ARAXES	AE8	970	ARCHITECT	HIF	812		AE12	720
ARBACES	PC1	12	ARCITE	KT1	155		DO	109
ARBITER	E	24		KT1	237		KT1	119

Word	Ref	Num	Word	Ref	Num	Word	Ref	Num
ARDOR	KT2	432	ARISE	HS	122	ARM	DA	131
	AU	424		T23	71		DA	212
ARDUA	AE7	576		H29	90		AA	203
AREOS	M12	430		HAP	477		H29	86
ARETHUSA	VP10	1		HAP	888		TA	82
	G4	486		HAP	1847		TA	479
	G4	498		SSC	7		PKA	10
	AE3	912		PSH	19		J1	245
ARETHUSIAN	AK	68		P4	119		AE1	140
ARGENT	HAP	1488		M1	773		AE3	314
	KT1	109		GK	16		AE4	834
ARGITIS	G2	142		EHC	35		AE4	849
ARGIVE	AE6	659		VP7	18		AE5	522
	AE7	521		VP9	63		AE5	550
	AE7	933		G1	263		AE5	621
	M15	235		G1	348		AE6	801
ARGIVES	AE7	574		G1	431		AE7	604
	AE7	1085		G1	501		AE7	782
	M12	28		G2	19		AE7	1013
ARGO	VP4	42		G2	114		AE8	391
ARGOLIC	AE2	597		G2	591		AE8	878
ARGONAUTS	VP6	66		G3	173		AE9	43
ARGOS	HI	128		G3	247		AE10	109
	VP6	71		G3	739		AE10	342
	G1	308		G4	83		AE10	473
	G3	192		AE1	1043		AE10	674
	AE1	24		AE2	421		AE10	762
	AE1	917		AE2	826		AE11	437
	AE2	257		AE4	505		AE11	689
	AE2	446		AE4	817		AE11	994
	AE6	1151		AE5	27		AE12	27
	AE7	396		AE5	268		AE12	80
	AE10	1105		AE5	292		AE12	403
	AE10	1110		AE5	454		AE12	1004
	AE11	378		AE5	844		AE12	1160
	HIF	368		AE5	869		AE12	1338
	M15	27		AE5	910		AE12	1374
ARGOS'	M15	422		AE5	1016		KT3	409
ARGUE	HAP	847		AE6	215		M8	187
	PDS	4		AE6	344		M11	282
ARGUED	OAL	836		AE6	755		M12	155
	M15	100		AE6	1221		AU	175
ARGUES	HAP	2162		AE6	1237		WB	533
	AE4	17		AE7	849	ARMADOES	AM	54
ARGUMENT	SAA	649		AE8	23	ARMED	AR	33
	HAP	782		AE8	94		AM	114
	HAP	1494		AE9	909		AM	322
	HAP	1691		AE9	966		AM	579
	HAP	1965		AE10	370		AM	1066
	P4	22		AE10	566		PCB	29
	M10	88		AE12	855		H3	15
	AU	308		AE12	909		TA	98
	AU	462		AF	132		AK	97
ARGUMENTS	PC2	18		KT1	553		HAP	266
	AA	214		KT3	980		HAP	936
	AA	379		C	233		HAP	1995
	MF	62		C	248		J6	456
	SAA	35		TH	267		HI	68
	HAP	963		M12	692		G1	220
	M9	24		WB	293		G1	374
	KT3	1138		CI	333		G2	195
	M11	59	ARISES	AE7	782		G2	233
	AU	192		FL	492		AE1	431
	WB	535	ARISING	L3	310		AE2	441
	M15	100		AE4	558		AE2	665
ARGUS	M1	857		M11	283		AE2	698
	M1	858	ARISTAEUS	G4	451		AE2	913
	M1	938		G4	503		AE3	677
	M1	999	ARISTOPHANES	P1	251		AE4	360
ARGUS'	AE8	455	ARISTOTLE	PO	27		AE5	88
	KT1	552		RL	74		AE5	719
ARGYRIPA	AE11	377	ARISTOTLE'S	DC	8		AE5	1068
ARIADNE	OAL	594	ARIUS	RL	220		AE6	178
ARICIA	P6	131		RL	346		AE6	269
	AE7	1045		EC	3		AE6	565
ARIES	C	448		HAP	722		AE7	705
	C	679	ARK	SMA	4		AE7	764
ARIGHT	VP5	23		AM	374		AE7	933
	AE3	866		PW	21		AE8	850
	AE5	32		EMW	9		AE9	85
	AE5	171		PUF	1		AE9	212
	AE9	546		PUF	11		AE9	414
	AE12	281		AA	302		AE9	913
	KT2	423		AA	520		AE9	921
	KT3	1088		AA	804		AE9	1102
	B	541		SAA	657		AE10	85
	HIF	756		SAA	1005		AE10	209
	C	144		AK	126		AE10	293
	M11	449		HAP	191		AE10	974
	M12	803		BR	286		AE11	163
	WB	8		BR	289		AE11	1286
	WB	233		DO	71		AE12	187
	WB	265		ESK	17		AE12	450
ARION	MF	43		AS	56		OAL	225
	VP8	77	ARLEQUIN	EUO	16		KT2	192
ARISBA	AE9	350	ARM	EEL	14		KT2	195

Word	Ref	No.
ARMED	KT2	583
	KT3	35
	KT3	91
	KT3	489
	KT3	519
	KT3	558
	KT3	635
	CAM	91
	HIF	20
	HIF	452
	HIF	516
	TH	147
	TH	273
	FL	275
	FL	577
	M12	121
	M12	594
	M12	815
	AU	379
	M15	28
	GP	17
	CI	283
ARMEDA	S	1
	A	1
ARMENIA	G3	46
	OAL	258
ARMENIAN	J6	710
ARMIES	AM	940
	PAL	2
	J6	547
	G1	639
	AE6	647
	AE7	890
	AE10	502
	AE10	609
	AE11	405
	AE11	1170
	AE11	1309
	AE11	1317
	AE12	2
	AE12	424
	AE12	673
	AE12	1012
ARMING	G3	398
	OAL	777
ARMIPOTENT	KT2	545
	KT3	293
ARMOR	J6	362
	J10	209
	AE2	997
	AE2	1018
	AE3	396
	AE6	682
	AE6	1114
	AE6	1134
	AE6	1189
	AE8	899
	AE9	555
	AE9	615
	AE9	791
	AE9	931
	AE9	990
	AE10	249
	AE10	434
	AE10	992
	AE10	1097
	AE10	1160
	AE11	669
	AE11	675
	AE12	449
	AE12	689
	AE12	935
	AE12	1019
	KT2	173
	KT3	26
	KT3	446
	KT3	606
	FL	256
	FL	528
	M12	179
	M12	823
ARMOR-BEARER	AE9	442
ARMORER	KT2	598
ARMORERS	KT3	459
ARMPITS	OAL	587
ARMS	HS	67
	HS	78
	HS	111
	AR	4
	AR	116
	AR	322
	LC	54
	DC	8
	VHH	28
	VHH	34
	AM	132

Word	Ref	No.
ARMS	AM	597
	PCG1	44
	SM2	2
	EUO	2
	PCB	10
	CM	66
	CM	137
	HP	94
	HP	247
	DA	104
	DA	166
	EMW	3
	PR	37
	AA	286
	AA	294
	AA	316
	AA	463
	AA	719
	AA	720
	AA	841
	PLB	42
	MD	290
	SAA	127
	SAA	151
	SAA	152
	SAA	265
	SAA	538
	SAA	566
	SAA	801
	SAA	815
	SAA	862
	SAA	884
	SAA	888
	SAA	1099
	SAA	1124
	EDGA	18
	RL	81
	RL	156
	AT	44
	L2	54
	L3	4
	L3	78
	T18	89
	T27	126
	H29	42
	FS1	10
	TA	59
	TA	193
	TA	459
	TA	472
	HAP	273
	HAP	1171
	HAP	1212
	HAP	1637
	HAP	2024
	SSC	26
	BR	81
	BR	209
	LS	16
	J3	143
	J3	290
	J6	158
	J6	237
	J6	355
	J6	408
	J16	4
	P1	187
	P3	81
	P6	99
	P6	109
	M1	17
	M1	314
	M1	613
	M1	650
	M1	744
	M1	748
	M1	900
	M1	976
	M1	1022
	M1	1058
	M1	1074
	HI	31
	HI	110
	HI	142
	HI	155
	HI	159
	HI	172
	MC	4
	VP1	16
	VP2	59
	VP3	111
	VP6	23
	VP7	42
	VP8	94
	VP8	100
	VP8	106

Word	Ref	No.
ARMS	VP8	110
	VP8	120
	VP8	128
	VP8	134
	VP8	146
	VP8	152
	VP8	160
	G1	239
	G1	639
	G1	670
	G1	679
	G1	685
	G2	237
	G2	408
	G2	621
	G3	290
	G3	298
	G3	514
	G3	537
	G4	6
	G4	108
	G4	251
	G4	359
	G4	725
	G4	811
	AE1	1
	AE1	169
	AE1	216
	AE1	338
	AE1	406
	AE1	686
	AE1	694
	AE1	963
	AE1	1002
	AE1	1052
	AE2	25
	AE2	112
	AE2	319
	AE2	402
	AE2	424
	AE2	455
	AE2	465
	AE2	514
	AE2	524
	AE2	528
	AE2	548
	AE2	574
	AE2	610
	AE2	626
	AE2	632
	AE2	640
	AE2	695
	AE2	711
	AE2	830
	AE2	836
	AE2	888
	AE2	906
	AE2	922
	AE2	1077
	AE2	1086
	AE3	47
	AE3	70
	AE3	373
	AE3	419
	AE3	514
	AE3	591
	AE3	604
	AE4	125
	AE4	577
	AE4	715
	AE4	717
	AE4	881
	AE4	900
	AE4	903
	AE4	985
	AE5	146
	AE5	488
	AE5	499
	AE5	554
	AE5	558
	AE5	564
	AE5	567
	AE5	644
	AE5	882
	AE6	136
	AE6	224
	AE6	246
	AE6	249
	AE6	312
	AE6	395
	AE6	527
	AE6	544
	AE6	660
	AE6	668
	AE6	694
	AE6	702

ARMS		ARMS		ARMS	
AE6	886	AE10	362	OAL	230
AE6	930	AE10	368	OAL	237
AE6	950	AE10	388	OAL	630
AE6	1045	AE10	395	OAE1	10
AE6	1058	AE10	444	OAE2	8
AE6	1142	AE10	525	OAE2	43
AE6	1183	AE10	578	OAE2	50
AE6	1218	AE10	597	OAE2	76
AE7	65	AE10	681	AF	8
AE7	144	AE10	749	DO	6
AE7	305	AE10	755	DO	9
AE7	428	AE10	764	KT1	3
AE7	610	AE10	769	KT1	147
AE7	619	AE10	787	KT1	157
AE7	635	AE10	792	KT1	223
AE7	642	AE10	902	KT1	238
AE7	651	AE10	967	KT1	290
AE7	657	AE10	973	KT1	367
AE7	807	AE10	1173	KT1	608
AE7	856	AE10	1190	KT2	30
AE7	866	AE10	1228	KT2	153
AE7	871	AE10	1312	KT2	156
AE7	890	AE11	9	KT2	176
AE7	922	AE11	13	KT2	198
AE7	949	AE11	29	KT2	256
AE7	958	AE11	113	KT2	308
AE7	988	AE11	126	KT2	413
AE7	1030	AE11	172	KT2	613
AE7	1072	AE11	175	KT2	666
AE7	1099	AE11	187	KT3	17
AE8	154	AE11	235	KT3	24
AE8	191	AE11	298	KT3	46
AE8	507	AE11	390	KT3	67
AE8	512	AE11	397	KT3	96
AE8	522	AE11	426	KT3	107
AE8	527	AE11	429	KT3	177
AE8	536	AE11	482	KT3	296
AE8	573	AE11	532	KT3	311
AE8	581	AE11	568	KT3	318
AE8	593	AE11	613	KT3	323
AE8	621	AE11	636	KT3	331
AE8	642	AE11	700	KT3	344
AE8	649	AE11	708	KT3	355
AE8	656	AE11	729	KT3	370
AE8	658	AE11	733	KT3	450
AE8	659	AE11	812	KT3	497
AE8	697	AE11	845	KT3	670
AE8	707	AE11	881	KT3	708
AE8	710	AE11	890	KT3	725
AE8	717	AE11	900	KT3	740
AE8	751	AE11	943	KT3	800
AE8	767	AE11	968	KT3	858
AE8	777	AE11	977	TJD	155
AE8	785	AE11	1005	M8	139
AE8	808	AE11	1098	M8	353
AE8	818	AE11	1100	M8	390
AE8	846	AE11	1132	B	158
AE8	946	AE11	1225	B	230
AE8	963	AE11	1238	B	434
AE9	32	AE12	20	BP	175
AE9	52	AE12	35	BP	184
AE9	58	AE12	65	CAM	157
AE9	134	AE12	137	CAM	344
AE9	185	AE12	165	CAM	378
AE9	194	AE12	172	HIF	188
AE9	197	AE12	190	HIF	340
AE9	205	AE12	251	HIF	355
AE9	260	AE12	271	HIF	392
AE9	302	AE12	280	HIF	447
AE9	331	AE12	323	HIF	506
AE9	358	AE12	342	C	638
AE9	482	AE12	412	C	740
AE9	511	AE12	466	TH	3
AE9	539	AE12	474	TH	155
AE9	735	AE12	490	TH	289
AE9	782	AE12	556	M11	381
AE9	795	AE12	630	M11	382
AE9	833	AE12	636	M11	408
AE9	874	AE12	651	M11	483
AE9	891	AE12	676	FL	42
AE9	899	AE12	684	FL	215
AE9	907	AE12	707	FL	233
AE9	960	AE12	824	FL	240
AE9	1029	AE12	829	FL	257
AE9	1047	AE12	839	FL	311
AE9	1053	AE12	848	FL	316
AE9	1084	AE12	913	FL	519
AE10	14	AE12	951	FL	544
AE10	31	AE12	1104	M12	118
AE10	41	AE12	1172	M12	181
AE10	57	AE12	1263	M12	201
AE10	122	AE12	1310	M12	205
AE10	135	AE12	1320	M12	222
AE10	244	AE12	1341	M12	256
AE10	248	AE12	1347	M12	291
AE10	266	AE12	1376	M12	337

Word	Ref	Num
ARMS	M12	341
	M12	373
	M12	395
	M12	445
	M12	473
	M12	564
	M12	576
	M12	616
	M12	722
	M12	826
	AU	18
	AU	31
	AU	43
	AU	47
	AU	55
	AU	58
	AU	154
	AU	169
	AU	193
	AU	195
	AU	206
	AU	286
	AU	287
	AU	321
	AU	332
	AU	337
	AU	339
	AU	343
	AU	394
	AU	423
	AU	443
	AU	450
	AU	459
	AU	506
	AU	585
	WB	347
	M15	352
	M15	555
	GP	110
	CI	155
	CI	302
	CI	308
	CI	407
	CI	528
	CI	548
	STP	17
	SMP	47
	SMP	48
	AS	65
ARMY	AM	972
	HAP	13
	AE6	431
	AE6	962
	AE7	105
	AE7	970
	AE7	975
	AE8	803
	AE8	861
	AE10	242
	AE11	262
	AE11	667
	AE12	351
	AE12	427
	AE12	1028
	OAL	154
	KT1	13
	KT1	20
	KT3	8
	KT3	672
	HIF	2
ARMY'S	J10	286
	J16	56
ARNON	SAA	1079
AROD	SAA	535
AROMATIC	AM	116
AROSE	HS	141
	HAP	15
	HAP	902
	HAP	920
	HAP	1370
	HAP	1790
	HAP	1903
	HAP	1916
	M13	221
	MC	46
	VP6	56
	VP10	30
	AE2	931
	AE3	134
	AE3	150
	AE3	902
	AE4	245
	AE4	823
	AE5	997
	AE7	9
	AE8	46

Word	Ref	Num
AROSE	AE9	737
	KT1	181
	KT1	208
	KT2	39
	KT3	358
	KT3	381
	KT3	438
	KT3	484
	KT3	1020
	BP	53
	HIF	84
	HIF	107
	HIF	362
	HIF	531
	C	257
	M11	98
	FL	67
	FL	415
	M12	54
	AU	193
	AU	199
	M15	92
	M15	573
	CI	560
AROW	FL	249
	FL	345
ARRAIGN	J1	258
	MM	18
	TH	355
	AU	347
	PTP	47
ARRAIGNED	J6	643
	CI	16
ARRANT	EMQW	13
	J6	69
ARRAS	G2	648
	AE9	482
ARRAY	AM	263
	L2	48
	TA	509
	AE1	441
	AE5	719
	AE8	786
	AE10	521
	AE11	114
	AE11	614
	AE11	1313
	KT1	14
	KT1	38
	KT1	78
	KT1	181
	KT1	572
	KT2	501
	KT3	61
	KT3	101
	KT3	531
	KT3	595
	KT3	977
	KT3	1013
	M11	353
	FL	35
	FL	217
	FL	241
	FL	390
	FL	397
ARRAYED	SAA	1120
	AE1	444
	AE11	107
	KT2	643
	KT3	911
	M10	49
	FL	247
	FL	353
	FL	442
	M12	45
	VP5	91
ARRAYS	SAA	303
ARREARS	KT3	680
ARREST	HAP	1114
	AE12	1147
	C	115
	C	253
	TH	181
ARRESTED	TA	82
ARRESTS	HAP	1568
	AE10	772
ARRIVAL	SAA	805
ARRIVE	SAA	762
	ER	53
	MO	8
	L3	42
	J10	468
	AE9	472
	KT3	1079
	WB	258
	EWR	19

Word	Ref	Num
ARRIVED	ECG2	23
	SCD1	9
	DA	160
	TA	60
	HAP	255
	HAP	1234
	EL	133
	M13	34
	VP10	39
	G4	535
	AE2	858
	AE2	992
	AE3	561
	AE3	929
	AE6	862
	AE8	267
	AE8	441
	AE11	267
	MFL	25
	KT1	577
	KT3	543
	M8	88
	B	147
	HIF	513
	C	214
	AU	317
	WB	191
	M15	12
ARRIVES	ER	37
	HI	181
	AE10	826
	AE11	1034
ARRIVING	SAA	795
	M1	1010
	AE4	382
	M1	206
ARROGANT	PIE	24
ARROGANTLY	MF	172
ARROGATING	L4	5
ARROW	NS	25
	G2	172
	G3	306
	AE5	665
	AE5	672
	AE5	689
	AE5	713
	AE7	693
	AE7	742
	AE11	884
	AE11	1250
	AE12	482
	AE12	1240
	OAE1	26
	M8	153
	C	694
	M12	799
	CI	157
ARROW'S	BP	149
ARROWS	DA	169
	M1	591
	G4	445
	G4	617
	AE1	267
	AE5	409
	AE5	651
	AE6	1096
	AE8	936
	AE9	906
	AE10	197
	AE10	208
	AE12	847
	KT2	523
	KT3	268
	KT3	282
	HIF	70
	HIF	76
	M12	793
	AU	71
	AU	495
	AE7	287
ARROWS'	MF	181
ARSE	SAA	482
ARSENIC	UDH	7
ART	UDH	26
	RH	1
	RH	6
	RH	19
	RH	55
	DC	37
	PWG	24
	LCA	3
	AM	617
	PMQ	13
	PT	6
	PA	34
	PLN	42

Word	Ref	No.
ART	PCD	31
	PUO1	29
	EUO	25
	EUO2	16
	EAZ	12
	ML	35
	PO	1
	PSF	47
	AA	559
	AA	825
	MD	6
	MD	72
	MF	176
	MF	217
	SAA	77
	SAA	639
	RL	358
	PD	35
	ER	19
	ER	34
	ER	56
	TA	72
	TA	113
	TA	151
	TA	160
	TA	177
	TA	184
	TA	242
	TA	392
	AK	71
	AK	123
	HH	20
	HAP	1840
	HAP	1935
	HAP	2090
	SSC	42
	PP	1
	PMS	9
	EL	154
	EL	159
	PSH	37
	J1	95
	J3	205
	J6	38
	J6	723
	J6	734
	J6	756
	J10	205
	J10	489
	P1	134
	P1	183
	P4	86
	P6	11
	M9	45
	M9	119
	MC	10
	GK	28
	GK	35
	GK	41
	GK	45
	GK	64
	GK	97
	GK	140
	GK	174
	G2	74
	G3	819
	G4	403
	G4	416
	G4	635
	AE1	946
	AE1	949
	AE4	89
	AE4	711
	AE5	328
	AE5	472
	AE5	576
	AE5	688
	AE5	780
	AE6	25
	AE6	48
	AE6	63
	AE7	259
	AE7	262
	AE7	1039
	AE7	1061
	AE7	1070
	AE8	502
	AE8	526
	AE8	814
	AE9	353
	AE9	706
	AE9	896
	AE11	581
	AE12	43
	AE12	577
	AE12	591
ART	AE12	596
	AE12	597
	AE12	621
	AE12	1320
	OAL	4
	OAL	14
	OAL	42
	OAL	302
	OAL	476
	OAL	496
	OAL	757
	OAL	801
	MM	3
	MM	46
	KT1	416
	KT2	437
	KT2	657
	KT3	420
	KT3	754
	KT3	767
	M10	8
	M10	17
	CAM	377
	HIF	811
	C	452
	C	696
	M11	175
	M11	375
	FL	434
	M12	424
	M12	529
	AU	541
	CI	129
	EMKG	37
ARTFUL	DA	108
	T18	10
	H29	6
	VP7	33
	G2	48
	AE6	876
	AE8	587
	AE10	692
	C	623
ARTFULLY	AE4	150
	TH	260
ARTHUR	WB	1
	WB	69
	PTP	27
ARTHUR'S	FL	542
	WB	46
	WB	351
	WB	409
ARTICLES	GE	37
	HAP	988
ARTIFICER	EL	222
	AE8	526
	C	776
ARTIFICERS	AA	1011
	OAL	740
	M15	590
ARTIFICIAL	B	213
ARTILLERY	BR	206
	M1	351
	M15	569
	GP	38
ARTIQUE	GE	6
ARTIST	AE6	43
ARTIST'S	HS	94
ARTISTS	AR	125
	AE1	637
	KT2	453
ARTLESS	TA	55
	P5	149
ART'S	RL	246
	AE12	633
ARTS	TJD	81
	UDH	31
	HS	9
	HS	127
	AR	48
	AR	77
	AR	212
	AR	322
	LC	105
	AM	1
	AM	675
	AM	1184
	EAZ	20
	CM	50
	HP	138
	PUO4	34
	AA	228
	AA	289
	AA	402
	AA	443
	AA	498
ARTS	AA	692
	AA	873
	AA	1010
	MD	257
	MD	291
	D	3
	MF	178
	SAA	37
	SAA	167
	SAA	198
	SAA	327
	SAA	950
	RL	81
	RL	140
	OE	23
	ER	2
	L3	251
	TA	255
	TA	338
	TA	348
	TA	383
	HAP	96
	HAP	2218
	HAP	2333
	HAP	2397
	HAP	2449
	HAP	2560
	BR	209
	PTS	42
	J3	39
	J3	143
	J6	192
	J6	411
	J6	770
	J6	860
	P4	93
	M1	489
	GK	57
	GK	89
	VP6	107
	VP7	39
	G1	189
	G1	203
	G1	217
	G2	244
	G4	6
	G4	178
	G4	597
	G4	648
	G4	812
	AE1	185
	AE2	57
	AE2	116
	AE2	145
	AE2	203
	AE2	260
	AE4	125
	AE4	426
	AE4	599
	AE4	634
	AE4	699
	AE6	900
	AE6	1177
	AE7	144
	AE7	428
	AE7	541
	AE7	1051
	AE8	422
	AE11	1057
	AE11	1121
	AE12	390
	AE12	584
	AE12	707
	OAL	3
	OAL	17
	OAL	26
	OAL	528
	OAL	668
	AF	166
	AF	176
	KT2	453
	KT3	327
	C	92
	TH	3
	TH	397
	M15	716
	CI	32
	CI	213
	ESK	12
ARTS'	AM	646
	AE1	637
ARTURIUS	J3	52
	J3	346
	J3	359
ARUNCI	AE7	283
ARUNS	AE11	1121

Word	Ref	Line
ARUNS	AE11	1179
	AE11	1237
ARUSPEX	J6	519
ASAPH	SAA	1039
	SAA	1042
	SAA	1048
	SAA	1058
	SAA	1064
ASAPH'S	SAA	938
ASCANIUS	DA	166
	MF	108
	AE1	364
	AE1	930
	AE1	951
	AE1	969
	AE2	813
	AE2	984
	AE3	437
	AE4	120
	AE4	200
	AE4	223
	AE4	399
	AE4	508
	AE5	96
	AE5	716
	AE5	745
	AE5	777
	AE5	870
	AE5	880
	AE7	158
	AE7	664
	AE7	691
	AE8	64
	AE9	307
	AE9	338
	AE9	340
	AE9	394
	AE9	417
	AE9	663
	AE9	802
	AE9	851
	AE9	871
	AE9	889
	AE10	73
	AE10	335
	AE10	852
	AE11	88
	AE12	253
	AE12	277
	AE12	568
	DO	162
ASCEND	HS	112
	AM	259
	AA	15
	AA	351
	AA	876
	AA	908
	RL	156
	HAP	2134
	HAP	2150
	G2	401
	AE1	129
	AE1	395
	AE2	654
	AE3	108
	AE3	379
	AE3	651
	AE3	715
	AE4	709
	AE6	185
	AE8	874
	AE9	45
	AE10	574
	AF	23
	KT3	248
	BP	146
	HIF	49
	HIF	543
	HIF	578
	C	708
	M15	366
	M15	527
	CI	574
	CI	580
ASCENDANT	J6	565
	P5	66
ASCENDANT'S	PWG	25
ASCENDED	M1	32
	AE7	288
	C	47
	FL	425
ASCENDING	G2	419
	G2	754
	AE3	271
	AE5	692
	AE6	1065
ASCENDING	HIF	669
	M11	125
ASCENDS	RH	105
	RL	9
	TA	429
	HAP	1070
	EL	151
	VP1	118
	AE1	698
	AE2	417
	AE5	987
	AE6	11
	AE7	227
	AE7	715
	AE8	644
	AE10	928
	AE12	605
	AE12	1056
	M10	71
	M12	17
ASCENT	HI	92
	AE1	580
	AE2	605
	AE10	924
	AE12	1089
	B	102
	M11	322
	AU	526
ASCENTS	AE11	777
ASCRAEAN	VP6	98
	G2	246
ASCRIBE	M15	187
ASCRIBED	HAP	253
	HAP	2532
	EL	104
	CAM	113
ASCRIBING	L4	180
ASDRUBAL	C	707
ASH	VP7	91
	VP7	95
	G2	93
	G2	99
	AE2	846
	AE9	1003
	AE10	1087
	AE11	206
	AE11	987
	AE12	148
	KT3	513
	M12	457
ASHAMED	VHH	32
	AM	270
	PWGR	19
	TA	277
	AE11	939
	AE12	903
	KT2	657
	KT3	855
	M10	16
	M12	702
	AU	356
	CI	198
ASHEN	G2	492
	M12	496
ASHES	HS	145
	AM	1023
	AM	1151
	DA	206
	OD	18
	J10	235
	P6	82
	VP6	100
	VP8	147
	VP8	154
	G1	118
	G2	424
	AE2	759
	AE3	4
	AE4	709
	AE5	62
	AE5	107
	AE6	265
	AE7	408
	AE11	323
	AE12	832
	AE12	1103
	BP	49
	CI	227
A-SHIPBOARD	P5	211
ASHORE	DA	91
	L5	2
	H29	104
	P6	68
	AE2	505
	AE3	103
	AE5	53
ASHORE	AE10	402
	AE10	419
	AE12	1172
	HIF	600
	M11	462
ASH'S	G2	157
ASIA	HP	206
	G2	238
	AE1	532
	AE2	760
	M12	8
ASIAN	AM	205
	AM	372
	G3	47
	AE3	627
	AE7	305
	AE7	968
ASIA'S	AA	428
ASIDE	AA	479
	RL	276
	RL	305
	L2	26
	TA	214
	GE	64
	HAP	87
	HAP	364
	HAP	477
	HAP	678
	HAP	819
	HAP	1047
	HAP	1595
	HAP	2404
	P2	8
	P6	104
	M1	338
	M1	752
	G3	249
	G3	664
	AE1	965
	AE2	512
	AE5	594
	AE7	580
	AE8	579
	AE8	583
	AE10	458
	AE10	843
	OAE2	9
	KT1	40
	KT3	363
	KT3	451
	KT3	687
	M8	106
	B	565
	BP	25
	CAM	168
	CAM	193
	M11	351
	FL	102
	M12	324
	M12	485
	M12	685
	AU	247
	M15	275
	GP	115
ASIUM	AE10	247
ASIUS	AE10	188
ASK	PWG	2
	AM	998
	EMM	14
	PAR	14
	ELN	16
	AT	45
	HAP	1451
	HAP	1536
	HAP	1601
	HAP	1835
	HAP	2329
	EDS	33
	J6	146
	J6	397
	J6	630
	J10	85
	J10	110
	J10	252
	J10	296
	J10	302
	J10	348
	P5	96
	P5	210
	P6	149
	P6	162
	M1	331
	M13	11
	M13	123
	SFL	1
	GK	74

Word	Code	No.	Word	Code	No.	Word	Code	No.
ASK	VP3	32	ASPIRE	AA	307	ASSEMBLED	WB	268
	G3	478		AT	73	ASSEMBLIES	AA	884
	AE3	860		H3	38		J3	54
	AE4	626		HAP	317		P1	13
	AE6	836		P2	87		AE7	339
	AE7	357		P6	141		OAL	55
	AE8	228		M1	348	ASSEMBLING	G4	802
	AE10	414		VP9	46	ASSEMBLY	M1	216
	AE10	1299		G2	730		KT3	1018
	AE12	285		G4	554		FL	154
	OAL	812		AE1	747		FL	307
	KT1	280		AE2	1031	ASSENT	HAP	1692
	KT2	371		DO	122		M1	326
	KT3	159		KT3	367		KT3	1121
	KT3	356	ASPIRED	SAA	356	ASSENTING	VP5	99
	CAM	203		HAP	967	ASSENTS	AE5	511
	M12	277		VP1	43	ASSERT	AM	53
	AU	585		AE8	19		AA	341
	WB	244		AU	389		HAP	1097
	WB	247	ASPIRES	RL	163		BR	60
ASKALON	SAA	1075		J6	297		M1	1065
ASKANT	HIF	224		G2	420		HI	161
ASKED	EEL	25		AE11	318		AE6	997
	AA	642		WB	285		AE8	860
	TA	262	ASPIRING	J6	723		AE11	568
	HAP	523		M1	660		AE12	27
	HAP	737		G1	167		AE12	651
	HAP	2194		G2	301		AE12	1140
	J10	398		G2	686		OAL	227
	M1	894		G3	824		KT2	390
	M1	949		KT2	284		TJD	184
	HI	12		FL	317		HIF	262
	VP10	30	ASS	PMM	6		HIF	686
	AE1	1052		ESF	4	ASSERTED	HS	85
	AE6	437		MD	145		EMW	3
	AE6	456		L3	52		TA	514
	AE6	755		J3	171		HAP	118
	AE6	964		P3	15		AE4	18
	AE6	1192		P5	137	ASSERTERS	DC	21
	AE8	189		G1	367	ASSERTING	AE6	1124
	AE8	494		OAL	610	ASSERTIONS	HAP	1493
	AE10	221	ASSAIL	AR	118	ASSERTS	HAP	1069
	KT1	239		AM	879		G4	811
	CAM	118		HAP	2477		AE7	818
	CAM	159		AE3	895		AE12	851
	CAM	252		AE12	708		AU	46
	M11	306		M8	276	ASSES,	EUO	17
	M12	243	ASSAILANTS	SAA	835	ASSES'	SAA	395
	AU	540	ASSAILED	TA	101		PAA	18
	WB	86		M1	848		J6	605
	WB	120		AE6	941		HIF	558
	WB	305		AE10	429	ASSESSOR	AE6	583
ASKING	PCG2	28		AE10	443	ASSESSORS	G3	463
	KT3	481		AE12	740	ASSIDUOUS	HP	198
	M11	307		OAE2	10	ASSIGN	RL	164
ASKS	EAL	13		KT2	119		AE1	378
	M1	815		TH	374		AE5	965
	ELT	29		TH	394		AE11	197
	G2	321		AU	296		AE11	501
	AU	183	ASSAILS	AE8	904		OAL	786
	AU	582		AE10	1061	ASSIGNED	PUO2	1
ASLANT	M12	755	ASSARACI	AE10	188		HAP	643
ASLEEP	AM	808	ASSARACUS	AE6	883		M1	53
	AM	862	ASSASSINATING	KT2	567		M9	8
	SMM1	10	ASSAULT	SAA	775		G1	326
	SCG1	35		G4	345		G3	206
	SCG2	10		AE2	595		AE1	858
	DA	57		AE2	630		AE3	10
	SAA	622		AE6	578		AE3	136
	SAA	1082		AE7	605		AE3	332
	HAP	1305		AE10	169		AE3	693
	EL	314		AE12	418		AE5	23
	P3	60		C	777		AE5	43
	P3	98		M11	146		AE11	243
	M1	991		FL	392		KT3	1034
	J6	449	ASSAULTED	M1	181		TH	323
	AE3	827	ASSAULTING	AE2	535		M11	419
	AE5	1102	ASSAULTS	PMQ	14		FL	264
	AE8	40		G3	576		WB	112
	OAL	635		AE9	1036		CI	423
	TH	220	ASSAY	T27	45		CI	569
	AU	335	ASSAYED	HS	47	ASSIGNS	G2	158
	SMP	65		HAP	2090		AE8	964
ASPECT	AM	70		G4	725	ASSIST	AA	286
	KT1	247		AE5	122		SAA	1134
	KT3	167		AE6	49		L1	39
	KT3	471		AE10	968		T18	11
	GP	12		AE11	1121		TA	194
ASPECTS	BR	149		M11	12		J3	270
ASPERSIONS	AU	477	ASSAYS	P4	68		J3	502
ASPIRE	JH	7	ASSEMBLE	AE7	702		M9	40
	AM	859		KT1	456		M9	118
	SMQ	15	ASSEMBLED	AE8	1		VP7	28
	PFD	21		KT2	428		G4	9
	PUO1	36		KT2	633		G4	659
	PUO2	36		HIF	83		AE3	508

Word	Code	No.	Word	Code	No.	Word	Code	No.
ASSIST	AE5	92	ASSURED	KT2	135	ATHENS	KT1	553
	AE5	307		KT2	301		231	577
	AE10	652		B	67		KT3	102
	AE10	1095		AU	541		KT3	428
	KT1	133		M15	489		KT3	530
	KT1	309	ASSURES	L4	10		KT3	865
	KT2	390		BR	117		KT3	1007
	HIF	262	ASSYRIAN	L4	99	ATHIRST	P1	115
ASSISTANCE	AM	160		G2	652		G3	213
	SKA6	10		OAL	81	ATHOS	J10	281
	P6	73	ASTERN	AE1	152		AE12	1020
	M9	138	ASTON	MF	48		M11	203
	AE2	310	ASTONISHED	J6	673	ATHWART	AE1	692
	AE2	391		G4	728		AE5	360
	AE8	615		AE2	512		AE8	195
	WB	113		AE2	1050		AE10	563
ASSISTANTS	AE9	393		AE3	229		AE11	1094
	TH	306		AE3	397		AE12	1321
ASSISTED	HAP	667		AE5	543	ATINAS,	AE12	808
	KT2	13		AE6	754	ATINAS'	AE12	961
ASSISTING	SAA	934		AE9	970	ATINIAN	AE7	871
	RL	262		AE11	1034	ATLANTIC	J10	237
	AE2	255		AE12	1331	ATLAS	TA	29
	AE4	748	ASTRAEA,	G2	671		TA	35
ASSISTS	AE3	158	ASTRAEA'S	G1	298		AE1	1039
	AE5	283	ASTRAY	AM	791		AE4	362
	AE10	1183		AM	1057		AE4	364
ASSIZES	AK	182		EWGR	7		AE4	696
ASSOCIATE	AE1	844		HAP	720		AE6	1085
ASSOCIATING	HAP	2107		J10	166		AE8	180
ASSOCIATION	PDG	14		VCS	28		AE8	181
ASSOCIATIONS	SAA	270		OAL	56		M15	216
ASSOCIATORS	PK	5	ASTRIDE	J1	31	ATLAS'	AE8	185
ASS'S	P1	240	ASTROLABE	UDH	45	ATOM	MFL	6
	WB	158	ASTROLOGER	PA	8	ATOMS	RH	31
	WB	198		EEL	10		PUO1	33
	PTP	50	ASTROLOGERS	J6	720		L3	19
ASSUAGE	AA	942	ASTROLOGIC	J6	727		L3	112
	L4	198	ASTROLOGUE	EEL	16		L3	117
	HAP	1376	ASTRONOMER	EL	265		L4	222
	VP8	39	ASTRONOMER'S	HAP	1893		HAP	1809
	G2	791	ASTRONOMICAL	UDH	42		SSC	4
	G4	651	ASTUR	AE10	261		BR	154
	AE2	140	ASTYANAX	HI	42		J6	20
	AE5	1021		AE2	623		M1	35
	AE7	1036		AE3	632		M1	576
	KT3	727	ASTYLOS	M12	424		DO	113
	WB	235	ASUNDER	HP	201		WB	422
ASSUAGED	M12	216		AF	125	ATOMS'	RL	18
ASSUME	E	2		KT3	627	ATONE	SMA	57
	MD	230	ASYLAS	AE9	775		ECG2	9
	RL	317		AE9	777		RL	89
	RL	358		AE10	255		AK	67
	G4	587		AE11	925		GE	3
	AE1	461	ASYLUS	G3	238		BR	188
	AE1	929	ATALANTA,	M8	65		G1	674
	AE1	960	ATALANTA'S	KT2	636		AE2	164
	AE6	371	ATE	AE10	1079		AE3	45
	HIF	686	ATHAMAN	M15	469		AE5	917
ASSUMED	HAP	12	ATHAMAS	AE2	342		AE5	1067
	BR	339	ATHANASIUS	HAP	54		AE7	823
	M1	229	ATHEIST	HAP	1545		AE12	1009
	M1	553	ATHEISTS	PCD	22	ATONED	G4	798
	M13	26		HAP	39		AE1	382
	AE1	975		HAP	2033		HIF	149
	AE8	631		HAP	2506	ATONEMENT	BR	167
	AE12	344		PUO1	2	ATONES	J6	695
	AE12	1135	ATHENIAN	EOE	7	ATONING	AE4	911
	B	376		ER	9	ATREUS	AE8	172
	HIF	410		M1	425		AE9	817
ASSUMES	BR	117		G4	668		HIF	25
	AE12	492		KT1	20	ATREUS'	OAL	370
	AE12	689		KT1	38	ATRIDES	OAL	376
	AF	39		KT1	374		HIF	8
	AF	44		KT1	574		HIF	196
	HIF	197		KT2	277		HIF	360
	M11	352		KT2	302		HIF	403
	M15	248		KT3	484		HIF	436
ASSUMING	M1	1049		KT3	546	ATRIP	M11	93
	AU	420		KT3	1010	ATTACK	AE9	14
ASSUMPTION	P5	122		M12	480		AE9	942
ASSURANCE	LCA	35	ATHENIANS	EUO2	22	ATTACKED	HAP	1117
	TA	203		P4	17	ATTAIN	DA	173
	TA	403	ATHENS	POE	1		L3	315
	ODA	24		PO	7		AE12	1123
	KT2	478		PUO4	38		TJD	77
ASSURE	LC	79		MD	95	ATTAINED	AE6	644
	EOE	29		J10	201		AE6	850
	PUF	23		P4	4	ATTAINTS	BR	174
	AA	577		P6	88	ATTEMPT	AR	29
	RL	6		G2	525		AR	147
	EL	309		AE6	27		AM	883
	HIF	206		KT1	5		PSF	43
	C	23		KT1	106		SAA	861
ASSURED	HAP	1961		KT1	164		SAA	884
	G1	284		KT1	457		P1	131

Word	Code	No.
ATTEMPT	P5	140
	MC	55
	GK	81
	G3	13
	G4	594
	AE1	189
	AE9	138
	AE9	310
	AE9	400
	AE9	539
	AE9	857
	AE10	652
	AE12	241
	AE12	1291
	OAL	306
	OAL	441
	KT2	130
	B	238
	CAM	98
	HIF	293
	HIF	758
	C	624
	M12	184
ATTEMPTED	M1	256
ATTEMPTS	PWGR	6
	AA	228
	TA	168
	J3	188
	G4	636
	AE1	942
	AE2	216
	AE4	20
	AE6	631
	AE10	1150
	AE11	866
	AE12	1152
	AM	328
	AM	568
	AM	810
ATTEND	PMQ	16
	ECG1	36
	HP	254
	DA	119
	DA	206
	EPF	7
	AA	16
	SAA	977
	TA	367
	GE	41
	HAP	908
	HAP	1858
	HAP	2133
	HAP	2149
	BR	19
	J1	28
	J1	50
	J3	436
	J6	607
	J10	422
	J16	65
	P2	4
	VCS	35
	VP9	80
	G1	422
	G1	473
	G2	462
	G4	85
	G4	374
	AE1	262
	AE1	592
	AE1	897
	AE2	613
	AE2	838
	AE3	119
	AE3	213
	AE4	163
	AE4	229
	AE4	470
	AE4	778
	AE4	877
	AE5	380
	AE5	440
	AE6	225
	AE6	511
	AE6	655
	AE7	170
	AE8	69
	AE8	609
	AE9	46
	AE9	50
	AE9	263
	AE9	368
	AE10	847
	AE11	3
	AE11	193
	AE11	708
ATTEND (cont.)	AE11	722
	AE11	982
	AE12	646
	AE12	655
	OAL	304
	OAL	650
	DO	96
	KT1	358
	KT1	398
	KT3	61
	KT3	90
	KT3	465
	KT3	785
	KT3	1002
	B	59
	HIF	48
	HIF	57
	HIF	670
	TH	317
	FL	476
	M12	518
	CI	556
	ESK	9
ATTENDANCE	HAP	1530
	HAP	1534
	HAP	2256
	B	194
	WB	133
ATTENDANT	EL	51
	GK	27
ATTENDANTS	SAA	791
	L4	168
	EL	3
	AE1	982
	AE4	954
	AE5	133
	AE11	48
	AE11	1177
ATTENDANTS'	TA	67
ATTENDED	J6	687
	HI	4
	G2	636
	G3	37
	G3	491
	AE2	788
	AE3	445
	AE11	1002
	AE12	822
	KT1	575
	KT3	192
	KT3	719
	TJD	50
	CI	92
ATTENDING	SAA	608
	J6	220
	G4	539
	AE1	791
	OAL	245
	OAL	632
	KT1	589
	B	218
	B	225
	FL	54
	FL	197
ATTENDS	MF	169
	L3	304
	FS2	16
	HAP	2224
	SKA6	24
	J1	178
	J10	261
	M1	610
	AE1	300
	AE1	432
	AE2	89
	AE2	579
	AE3	868
	AE4	326
	AE6	1141
	AE7	790
	AE10	892
	AE10	1045
	AE11	123
	AE11	143
	AE11	218
	AE11	304
	AE11	1124
	AE11	1187
	AE12	96
	B	713
	HIF	273
	C	314
	CI	562
	WB	310
ATTENT ATTENTION	VP3	79
ATTENTION	AE5	634
	OAL	303
	AU	202
ATTENTIVE	ENH	18
	G4	695
	AE2	1
	AE5	477
	AE10	159
	KT3	272
	KT3	1023
	CAM	9
ATTENTIVELY	AE11	384
ATTENUATE	L4	270
ATTEST	AE4	514
	AE5	1050
	AE8	456
	AE12	301
	HIF	65
ATTESTING	AE10	173
ATTESTS	AE6	444
	AE12	851
ATTIRE	J10	497
	AE1	916
	AE2	532
	AE6	417
	AE6	1163
	AE7	111
	AE9	361
	AE12	182
	KT1	111
	KT1	539
	KT3	70
	B	349
	FL	159
	FL	185
	FL	416
	FL	507
	GP	5
	CI	211
ATTIRED	J3	296
	KT2	228
	FL	348
ATTIRES	KT3	454
ATTRACT	EL	169
	G4	328
ATTRACTION	HAP	1664
ATTRIBUTE	AA	328
	MD	92
	BR	334
	BP	7
	C	281
ATTRIBUTES	BR	353
ATYS	P1	182
	P1	203
AUBURN	AE5	741
	KT3	924
	M12	545
AUCTION	J6	360
AUCTORITY	HAP	453
	HAP	480
	HAP	835
	HAP	848
AUDACIOUS	MD	221
	H3	53
	TA	71
	J6	454
	J10	545
	M1	197
	M9	197
	G4	642
	G4	645
	AE1	188
	AE6	793
	AE10	42
	AE11	1185
	M8	176
AUDIENCE	VHH	57
	ENH	31
	PTC	36
	PLG	18
	MS	12
	P1	41
	P1	72
	M1	779
	G2	533
	AE2	663
	AE7	267
	AE11	381
	KT3	1023
	BP	1
	M12	229
	M12	243
	AU	201
	M15	98
	GP	20
	ESK	8

Word	Ref	No.
AUFIDUS	AE11	626
AUGMENT	AA	350
	T18	84
	HAP	1912
	M1	388
	G1	456
	AE1	773
	AE4	675
	AE9	662
	AE10	305
	OAL	599
	M8	358
	C	735
	M11	45
	M11	112
AUGMENTED	ER	60
	M13	229
	AE2	1083
	M11	142
AUGMENTS	M13	186
	AE7	289
	AE7	796
	AE12	599
	B	548
	C1	356
AUGUR	J6	710
	M13	41
	AE7	102
	AE8	654
	AE11	1085
	AE12	678
	HIF	155
	M12	424
AUGURIES	HAP	1735
	AE3	121
	AE5	10
AUGURS	AE5	690
	AE12	46
	HIF	104
AUGURS'	AE12	390
AUGURY	M1	532
	HI	98
	AE1	543
	AE7	356
AUGUST	AM	1177
	AE1	825
AUGUSTA	MF	64
	MF	65
AUGUSTUS	MF	3
	AE6	1079
AUGUSTUS'	AR	321
AULESTES	AE12	437
AULETES	AE10	296
AULIS	M12	12
	AU	289
	AU	316
AUNUS	AE11	1034
AURORA	G1	340
	G1	595
	AE4	839
	AE8	505
	KT1	186
AURUNCAN	AE7	1087
	AE12	146
AURUNCANS	AE7	1005
	AE11	487
AURUNCI	AE10	490
AUSONIA	AE7	56
	AE8	14
AUSONIAN	AE1	156
	AE3	613
	AE4	347
	AE4	400
	AE6	94
	AE7	370
	AE7	655
	AE7	762
	AE7	770
	AE7	861
	AE7	889
	AE10	82
	AE10	494
	AE11	87
	AE11	246
	AE11	337
	AE11	386
	AE12	266
	AE12	277
	AE12	388
	AE12	852
	AE12	1010
	AE12	1030
	AE12	1209
AUSONIANS	AE8	435
AUSPEX	J10	517
AUSPICE	AM	1150
AUSPICE	BR	50
	AE3	647
	OAL	30
AUSPICES	AE3	464
	AE3	481
AUSPICIOUS	AM	77
	AM	657
	AA	230
	ER	66
	L1	56
	H3	1
	TA	373
	AK	42
	HAP	2134
	BR	17
	BR	321
	J1	175
	P2	1
	VP4	13
	VP4	72
	AE1	1023
	AE2	523
	AE3	607
	AE6	109
	AE6	168
	AE6	283
	AE6	735
	AE6	1063
	AE8	355
	AE9	8
	AE11	47
	AE11	187
	MG	1
	HIF	324
	AS	73
AUSPICIOUSLY	B	177
AUSTER	M1	81
AUSTERE	G2	779
AUSTIN	C	524
AUTHENTIC	HS	8
	PUO1	46
	HAP	2132
	HIF	471
AUTHOR	PWGR	14
	PA	31
	EEL	27
	PCG2	7
	EM	23
	PLN	40
	PAZ	1
	EAL	9
	PKK	13
	PO	18
	HP	216
	ETG	1
	AA	132
	MD	76
	RL	236
	RL	253
	PD	11
	EC	22
	L3	254
	HAP	1629
	HAP	1949
	HAP	2454
	PMS	4
	EL	180
	MS	27
	PSH	39
	J1	96
	P1	73
	M1	878
	EHC	33
	AE2	124
	AE5	154
	AE7	75
	AE8	401
	AE10	213
	AE11	531
	AE12	194
	AE12	252
	M8	198
	HIF	725
	C	209
	C	516
	C	819
	M12	6
	M12	700
	EWR	9
AUTHORITY	SAA	380
	SAA	779
	RL	351
	HAP	121
	C	199
AUTHORITY'S	RL	339
AUTHORIZE	AR	178
AUTHORIZED	RL	373
AUTHORIZES	OAL	742
AUTHOR'S	RH	72
	PWG	42
	ELB	6
	MF	156
	RL	228
	HH	15
	HH	22
	P1	255
AUTHORS	DC	39
	PA	15
	PCG1	29
	PNH	40
	PUO2	19
	EUF	24
	MF	100
	SAA	552
	EC	5
	ER	55
	TA	339
	HAP	174
	HAP	806
	HAP	825
	P1	29
	P1	110
	P1	147
	EHC	8
	G4	549
	C	1
	C	567
	AU	323
AUTHORS'	EUO	34
AUTOMEDON	AE2	649
AUTUMN	UDH	78
	PAL	37
	H2	29
	M1	148
	G1	171
	G1	419
	G2	9
	G2	752
	G4	212
	AE6	428
	M15	185
	M15	312
AUTUMNAL	J6	668
	M13	112
	G2	435
	G3	723
	AE6	421
	OAL	68
	M8	5
	BP	92
AUXILIARY	M1	376
AVAIL	CM	17
	SAA	244
	G1	599
	AE4	90
	AE12	707
	AE12	1340
	OAL	839
	KT3	333
	HIF	754
	C	630
	M12	665
AVAILED	AE10	444
	AE11	1224
	M11	60
	AU	543
AVAILING	AE12	793
	OAL	143
AVAILS	AM	993
	M1	706
	VP3	115
	G3	784
	AU	183
	AU	416
AVARICE	AM	148
	H2	57
	EL	85
	J1	134
	J3	25
	J3	69
	J10	16
	J10	226
	P5	191
	P5	226
	M1	165
	AE8	434
	MM	29
AVAUNT	WB	331
	L4	44
AVENGE	J10	268
	M1	197
	AE4	877

Word	Ref	No.
AVENGE	B	279
	HIF	542
	M12	8
AVENGER	AE4	901
	AE8	300
	TH	334
	M12	355
AVENGING	DA	47
	DA	67
	SAA	72
	L3	231
	BR	155
	M1	304
	VP6	65
	G1	549
	AE2	822
	AE2	879
	AE3	757
	AE4	34
	AE6	711
	AE6	762
	AE6	844
	AE6	1117
	AE8	266
	AE8	570
	AE12	480
	M8	4
	CAM	92
	CAM	313
	HIF	143
	TH	334
	WB	95
AVENTINE	AE7	920
AVENTINUS	AE7	907
AVER	EH	5
AVERNIAN	AE4	742
AVERNUS	AE3	562
	AE6	347
AVERNUS'	G2	226
AVERSE	AA	326
	P3	86
	G4	289
	G4	749
	AE2	227
	AE5	620
	AE7	807
	AE7	904
	AE8	277
	AE9	920
	AE10	44
	AE11	882
	AE12	230
	OAL	239
	M8	79
	B	21
	B	215
	HIF	571
AVERSION	M13	12
AVERT	POE	13
	HAP	2166
	J6	668
	P5	274
	G2	239
	AE2	196
	AE3	48
	AE3	345
	AE6	494
	AE9	88
	AE12	731
	KT3	242
	HIF	624
AVERTS	AE10	666
	AE11	1104
	M8	341
AVOID	SAA	756
	J3	448
	VP9	39
	G4	579
	AE3	586
	AE5	886
	AE7	259
	AE11	449
	HIF	39
	FL	458
AVOIDING	SAA	483
	HAP	1328
	AE2	585
	AE3	640
	AE4	795
	M11	4
AVOIDS	L4	32
	OAL	446
AVOW	AM	545
	AE2	183
	AE12	1161
	OAL	314
AVOW	B	456
AVOWED	B	402
AWAKE	SCG2	10
	SAA	682
	L3	114
	L3	265
	HAP	1207
	BR	317
	EL	314
	J3	221
	J6	48
	P3	8
	M1	947
	M9	41
	G1	464
	AE2	348
	AE4	183
	AE4	768
	AE9	971
	AE10	324
	HIF	587
	C	245
	C	248
	M11	319
	M11	383
	CI	181
	SMP	66
AWAKED	G3	792
	AF	129
	B	233
	HIF	652
	TH	365
AWAKENED	KT1	555
AWAKES	G1	395
	G1	464
	AE10	386
	CI	29
AWAKING	CI	175
AWARD	PA	45
	HAP	953
	AE5	455
	AE6	581
	KT2	403
	KT2	429
	KT3	615
	TJD	8
	AU	585
	WB	207
AWARDED	MN	5
AWE	HS	73
	DC	26
	SEL3	14
	SAA	217
	H2	16
	TA	61
	HAP	549
	J10	521
	P1	236
	P5	128
	P5	272
	GK	74
	G4	307
	AE1	324
	AE6	551
	AE8	464
	AE8	700
	AE9	458
	AE10	627
	AE11	542
	TH	217
	GP	26
	PTP	32
AWED	AM	4
	AM	90
	AM	684
	PAZ	15
	SAA	10
	EC	25
	L2	54
	L3	7
	HAP	840
	EL	178
	J3	478
	G2	711
	AE5	1027
	AE8	662
	DO	57
	FL	206
AWFUL	AM	58
	AM	377
	AM	1102
	PTC	2
	AA	937
	D	8
	D	35
	SAA	791
AWFUL	T23	8
	TA	481
	HAP	530
	HAP	1674
	HAP	2084
	HAP	2335
	BR	106
	P1	190
	P4	16
	M1	235
	M1	811
	M9	173
	M9	193
	VP6	47
	G2	398
	G4	530
	AE1	26
	AE1	70
	AE1	179
	AE1	225
	AE1	314
	AE1	938
	AE2	582
	AE3	477
	AE4	213
	AE4	354
	AE5	354
	AE6	86
	AE6	764
	AE6	1173
	AE7	236
	AE8	218
	AE9	108
	AE10	154
	AE11	626
	AE12	1155
	AF	3
	KT2	352
	KT3	78
	KT3	493
	KT3	1020
	HIF	20
	HIF	80
	HIF	282
	HIF	466
	HIF	516
	HIF	617
	HIF	676
	GP	2
	CI	164
	CI	174
AWFULLY	VHH	18
	HAP	304
	BR	74
AWKWARD	PC1	7
	HAP	2216
	J6	661
	WB	228
AWKWARDLY	OAL	355
AWLESS	AE5	505
AWRY	AE10	477
	OAL	452
AX	HAP	439
	J10	50
	AE2	656
	AE2	660
	AE2	848
	AE5	404
	AE6	263
	AE6	1119
	AE7	868
	AE11	1029
	AE12	314
	AE12	464
	KT3	480
	M8	86
	M8	166
	M12	811
AXES	G1	215
	G3	560
	AE7	236
	AE7	253
	AE11	205
	KT3	906
AXIOMS	MD	246
AXLE	J3	411
AXLES	AE5	1073
	AE10	154
AXLETREE	M1	346
	G3	291
AXLETREES	AE8	572
AX'S	AE11	967
AZURE	AR	247
	T27	124
	HAP	1223
	G4	560

AZURE	AE5	1072	BACK	PLG	10	BACK	AE10	1233		
	AE8	47		HP	144		AE11	74		
	AE12	1281		DA	116		AE11	93		
				PUO5	18		AE11	179		
				PUF	6		AE11	702		
				AA	1025		AE11	733		
				EPC	1		AE11	865		
				SAA	344		AE11	936		
B'S	HAP	2432		SAA	1068		AE11	1006		
BAALISH	SAA	543		L3	245		AE12	1274		
BAAL'S	SAA	659		T27	98		OAL	235		
BABE	AM	32		TA	114		OAL	536		
	CM	71		HAP	767		OAE2	23		
	CM	78		HAP	1560		DO	95		
	CM	101		HAP	2011		KT1	9		
	CM	125		BR	4		KT1	236		
	DA	151		J1	56		KT2	189		
	L5	2		J3	38		KT2	522		
	MN	5		J3	68		KT2	648		
	BR	104		J6	189		KT3	51		
	BR	164		J6	613		KT3	474		
	BR	212		J10	58		M8	24		
	EL	214		J10	302		M8	112		
	J6	769		J10	358		M8	195		
	M9	43		J10	455		B	647		
	HI	38		J10	477		M10	27		
	HI	154		J16	84		HIF	30		
	AE4	475		P1	113		HIF	629		
	AE8	383		P1	144		C	671		
	AE11	818		P3	26		C	722		
	KT2	590		P4	68		C	747		
	M8	260		P4	127		C	763		
	CAM	374		P5	200		TH	183		
	CAM	382		P5	207		TH	191		
	CAM	386		P6	67		TH	287		
	M15	335		P6	77		TH	297		
BABEL	HAP	1042		M1	313		TH	302		
BABES	AM	1031		M1	868		M12	171		
	AA	243		M13	205		M12	417		
	PRH	31		SFL	8		M12	465		
	VP8	65		HI	131		M12	534		
	AE1	374		HI	147		M12	582		
	AE6	576		HI	191		AU	103		
	AE9	193		DHP	19		AU	120		
	CAM	367		VP2	97		AU	374		
	PMK	33		VP3	44		AU	508		
BABYLON	PLB	28		G1	142		WB	58		
BABY-TOYS	P2	126		G3	186		M15	609		
BACCHANALIAN	AE4	436		G3	409		CI	83		
	AE10	54		G3	555		CI	273		
BACCHANALS	HAP	387		G3	577		CI	340		
	G2	693		G3	646		CI	357		
	AE11	1086		G3	650		CI	598		
BACCHUS	L4	158		G4	69		PTP	50		
	VP5	45		G4	160		SMP	15		
	VP5	124		G4	716		ESK	19		
	VP7	86		AE1	446	BACKED	G3	126		
	G1	9		AE2	741	BACKS	AM	1008		
	G1	81		AE2	901		PP	33		
	G1	246		AE2	982		M1	517		
	G2	5		AE3	903		G1	531		
	G2	51		AE3	820		AE1	158		
	G2	371		AE4	197		AE1	720		
	G2	529		AE4	363		AE4	587		
	G2	542		AE5	3		AE5	167		
	G2	772		AE5	114		AE5	729		
	G4	156		AE5	356		AE11	802		
	AE1	1026		AE5	498		AE11	922		
	AE4	78		AE5	684		AE11	930		
	AE5	101		AE6	166		HIF	239		
	AE6	1097		AE6	1106		M11	171		
	AE7	542		AE8	119	BACON	DC	23		
	AE7	544		AE8	130		BP	62		
	AE7	801		AE8	294		C	34		
	OAL	264		AE8	308	BACTRIA	G2	189		
	OAL	217		AE8	732	BACTRIANS	AE8	909		
	OAL	590		AE8	839	BAD	EIE	10		
	AF	47		AE9	152		PMQW	8		
	AF	48		AE9	279		PTC	34		
	AF	54		AE9	531		AA	44		
	KT3	99		AE9	554		AA	78		
BACCHUS'	G2	524		AE9	588		AA	109		
	AF	56		AE9	972		AA	335		
	AF	61		AE9	1065		AA	583		
BACHELOR	J6	55		AE9	1070		SAA	416		
	WB	48		AE9	1079		RL	61		
BACK	SMA	62		AE10	93		RL	382		
	AM	231		AE10	373		RL	399		
	AM	476		AE10	422		HH	15		
	AM	528		AE10	426		HAP	407		
	AM	896		AE10	640		HAP	1801		
	AM	928		AE10	705		HAP	1893		
	EMM	11		AE10	729		HAP	2310		
	EUO	37		AE10	771		EL	368		
	ESF	29		AE10	932		EL	369		
				AE10	1032		J10	161		

BAD	J10	442	BAIT	OAL	51	BALMY	T27	128
	J16	43		TJD	33		HAP	277
	P1	207		M8	71		M1	74
	M1	151	BAITED	PTP	4		VP2	101
	M1	382	BAITING	C	215		G2	447
	M9	156	BAITS	HAP	2332		AE3	202
	HI	178		P5	160		AE4	758
	HI	181		G1	214		AE6	961
	PLT	19		G2	705		AE12	72
	GK	80		M15	703		B	197
	G1	382		J3	6		FL	29
	G3	264	BAJAE	AE9	961	BALSAM	J6	861
	AE3	656	BAJAN			BALTIC	AM	123
	AE5	701	BAKE	G1	99	BAND	PUO4	32
	AE9	373		G2	354		AA	577
	AE11	432	BAKED	SAA	928		AA	906
	OAL	513		G2	754		AA	914
	KT1	306		G4	618		MD	177
	KT1	481	BAKING	KT2	534		MD	240
	KT3	700	BALAAM	AA	574		MF	51
	KT3	750	BALAK	SAA	396		SAA	937
	KT3	761	BALANCE	AA	76		P6	59
	KT3	1087		AA	886		M9	142
	TJD	32		RL	124		VP7	46
	B	496		HAP	1195		G2	377
	BP	135		HAP	1894		AE2	500
	HIF	746		BR	361		AE3	819
	HIF	775		J10	234		AE4	124
	C	399		P5	62		AE4	868
	C	515		G1	46		AE5	384
	C	556		G1	298		AE5	501
	C	683		G2	635		AE5	822
	C	787		AE8	765		AE7	155
	TH	169		B	362		AE7	255
	M11	454	BALANCED	AM	38		AE7	648
	AU	118		AE10	399		AE7	943
	AU	292	BALANCES	MD	118		AE7	981
	WB	66	BALD	J10	318		AE7	973
	WB	67		M13	158		AE8	69
	WB	416	BALDPATE	J6	688		AE8	685
	SMP	19	BALEARIC	G1	415		AE8	728
BADE	AM	1083	BALEFUL	VP9	39		AE9	52
	PUO5	25		G2	158		AE10	1301
	HAP	531		G2	349		AE11	704
	P3	174		G4	688		AE11	785
	P3	185		AE3	91		AE11	905
	M1	45		AE4	732		AE11	1080
	M9	22		AE4	745		AE12	350
	VP6	5		AE6	294		AE12	358
	G1	202		AE6	311		AE12	396
	G4	769		AE7	493		AE12	408
	AE2	169		AE7	721		AE12	791
	AE2	236		AE12	1265		AF	136
	AE3	799		KT1	247		KT3	832
	AE10	363	BALK	SAA	850		M8	204
	OAL	130		RL	212		C	728
	KT3	660		OAL	71		TH	310
	KT3	722	BALKED	PWGR	25		FL	339
	B	614	BALKS	M15	488		FL	358
	B	705	BALL	AM	53		FL	364
	CAM	121		AM	113		FL	397
	HIF	437		AM	596		FL	444
	FL	421		AM	750		M12	347
	WB	257		PM	33		M12	610
	WB	271		MF	120		AU	359
BADGES	P6	76		RL	16		AU	500
BAFFLE	SAA	848		TA	33		CI	403
BAFFLED	ECD	6		AK	143		CI	514
	MD	142		J6	418	BANDED	KT2	521
	BR	124		M1	7	BANDIED	AE4	650
	J6	179		M1	61	BANDS	PUO1	40
	AE5	523		M13	164		PC2	33
	AE7	898		VP6	52		AA	149
	AE8	18		M15	287		AA	339
	HIF	241		AA	440		L4	200
	C	134		PO	2		L4	294
BAG	MD	296	BALLAD	G4	285		HAP	1869
	L4	83	BALLADS	L2	29		HAP	2068
BAGGAGE	P5	206	BALLAST	L4	108		BR	296
BAGGING	VP2	53	BALLS	AE6	584		EKA	27
BAGNIOS	PMK	10		AE7	951		ELW	5
BAGPIPE	MD	35		KT2	493		M1	183
BAGS	J3	358		KT3	41		M13	5
	VP9	40	BALM	UГH	96		VP6	28
	G3	493		AM	11		G1	430
	G3	607		STL	10		AE2	76
	M15	552		T18	76		AE2	223
BAIAN	OAL	291		T18	78		AE2	294
BAIL	J1	54		NS	27		AE2	545
	WB	111		TA	294		AE2	581
BAIT	AM	456		BR	90		AE2	832
	SEL4	22		G2	165		AE2	974
	AA	754	BALMS	M11	311		AE3	81
	J6	52	BALMY	LC	75		AE4	208
	PPS	16		AM	389		AE4	444
	AE6	571		L1	51		AE4	579
				T18	35			

BANDS	AE4	831
	AE5	354
	AE5	669
	AE6	1184
	AE7	140
	AE7	1085
	AE8	219
	AE8	374
	AE8	383
	AE9	183
	AE12	388
	AE12	469
	AE12	826
	AE12	965
	AF	125
	KT1	296
	KT3	462
	B	16
	CAM	90
	HIF	132
	HIF	202
	HIF	382
	HIF	553
	HIF	611
	FL	531
	M12	447
	CI	571
BANE	SAA	485
	G3	731
	G3	817
	AE2	779
	AE6	1160
	KT3	575
	B	707
	WB	489
BANEFUL	AM	793
	VP3	124
	VP8	136
BANISH	HAP	1201
	HAP	2045
	G4	769
BANISHED	HS	62
	AR	79
	AA	59
	AA	700
	D	6
	PDG	5
	DOD	7
	HAP	155
	HAP	2171
	HAP	2362
	BR	36
	LS	8
	J1	210
	J3	23
	J3	210
	J6	637
	J6	728
	J10	259
	M1	144
	VP1	81
	VP4	16
	AE1	7
	AE1	342
	AE1	398
	AE1	1065
	AE4	313
	AE5	67
	AE5	822
	AE7	316
	AE8	18
	AE8	53
	AE8	69
	AE8	426
	AE8	858
	AE10	40
	AE11	419
	KT1	385
	KT1	510
	KT1	517
	KT3	508
	C	604
	AU	235
	ETP	5
BANISHMENT	AR	60
	LC	18
	SAA	176
	TA	267
	J1	112
	J6	607
	J6	722
	VP1	3
	AE10	1212
	KT1	384
	CI	76
	AS	76

BANK	DOD	1
	HAP	149
	M1	590
	VP6	78
	G4	664
	AE8	270
	AE10	421
	AE11	628
	AE12	1085
	FL	132
BANKERS	AM	944
	PNH	14
BANKERS'	PCG2	10
BANKRUPT	PMQ	58
	AA	168
	SAA	281
BANKS	DA	1
	MD	70
	SAA	225
	SAA	313
	T18	40
	HAP	2125
	HAP	2154
	M1	47
	M1	879
	M1	880
	M1	1010
	M9	37
	VP3	146
	VP7	16
	VP7	73
	VP9	12
	G2	15
	G2	573
	G3	825
	G4	31
	G4	453
	G4	764
	G4	810
	AE1	699
	AE4	825
	AE5	158
	AE5	268
	AE5	865
	AE5	983
	AE6	505
	AE7	919
	AE8	43
	AE8	318
	AE8	810
	AE9	924
	AE10	92
	AE11	825
	AE12	499
	OAL	701
	HIF	430
	M11	28
	M11	73
	M11	474
	M15	638
BANNER	FL	231
BANNERS	KT1	108
	KT3	342
	KT3	560
	KT3	564
	FL	234
BANQUET	HAP	1323
	BP	117
	FL	432
	FL	453
BANQUETS	J10	557
BANQUIER-LIKE	EEL	34
BANTAM'S	GK	54
BAPTISMAL	BR	188
BAPTIST	HAP	43
BAPTIZED	BR	191
BAR	SEL1	10
	SM1	14
	PAZ	27
	EPC	16
	MD	70
	SAA	583
	SAA	773
	L3	259
	TA	103
	PDS	2
	PKA	11
	J3	470
	J6	341
	J10	452
	P1	159
	M9	139
	G1	600
	AE6	1171
	AE7	859
	OAL	525

BAR	AU	13
	WB	310
BARBADOES	MF	140
BARBARE	EAZ	25
BARBARIAN	AE2	730
	AE8	908
	CI	125
BARBARIANS	VP1	97
	G3	588
BARBARITY	ER	23
	HAP	1952
BARBAROUS	PTC	7
	HP	12
	PUO3	29
	ER	11
	L1	41
	HAP	2075
	J3	115
	VP9	22
	AE1	761
	AE2	551
	AE9	621
	AE9	767
	KT3	65
	B	570
BARBAROUSLY	SAA	760
	J10	164
	M15	134
BARBED	FL	217
BARBER	J10	357
	OAL	583
BARBER'S	J6	490
BARBERS	J6	431
	P4	91
	MF	67
BARBICAN	AE4	60
BARCAEAN	AE4	909
BARCE	MF	213
BARD	P6	21
	VP6	46
	DO	1
BARDS	AE6	346
BARE	AM	224
	AM	243
	PFD	2
	PAR	3
	PM	23
	EM	13
	PNH	4
	PUO3	21
	SAA	401
	PDG	20
	L2	27
	T18	33
	T27	91
	HAP	1493
	HAP	1906
	HAP	2027
	HAP	2256
	HAP	2577
	PP	44
	ETS	9
	J6	328
	J6	400
	J6	631
	J6	652
	J6	678
	P1	135
	P6	64
	M1	638
	M1	669
	M1	870
	HI	10
	VP1	108
	G2	271
	G3	209
	AE1	65
	AE1	437
	AE1	880
	AE2	109
	AE2	306
	AE2	753
	AE2	874
	AE3	665
	AE3	773
	AE4	751
	AE5	479
	AE6	268
	AE8	254
	AE8	307
	AE9	732
	AE9	915
	AE10	201
	AE11	739
	AE11	954

Headword	Ref	Num
BARE	AE11	964
	AE12	470
	OAL	571
	OAL	597
	OAE2	61
	AF	82
	KT2	515
	KT2	530
	KT2	539
	KT2	569
	KT3	91
	KT3	916
	M8	68
	HIF	21
	HIF	517
	M11	381
	FL	388
	M12	574
	AU	64
	M15	319
	M15	452
	GP	51
	CI	101
BARED	G2	39
	AE6	801
	AE11	6
	KT3	970
	CAM	165
	AU	410
BAREFACED	AM	515
	HAP	1412
	ETP	32
BAREFOOT	J6	231
BAREHEADED	KT3	689
BARELY	HAP	804
	HAP	2288
	PKA	11
	EL	370
	GK	45
	VP3	157
	AE2	744
BARES	AE1	488
	AE5	561
BARGAIN	AR	137
	EKK	2
	T27	64
	PDS	36
	PKA	36
	ESH	35
	J1	61
	J6	390
	OAL	481
	WB	524
	CI	298
BARGAINS	EKK	21
	MF	181
	PP	46
BARGE	MF	39
BARGES	G4	412
BARING	AE6	603
BARK	SAA	849
	SAA	1125
	SAA	1084
	TA	396
	TA	397
	HAP	1464
	VP5	18
	VP8	156
	VP10	109
	G2	363
	AE1	162
	TJD	101
	M8	110
	BP	187
	CAM	359
	CAM	368
	CAM	385
	CI	272
BARKED	VP3	25
BARKING	OE	39
	HAP	192
	HAP	2340
	J6	541
	J10	419
	VP6	108
	AE6	535
	OAL	375
BARKS	L3	217
	H29	31
	VP6	90
	VP10	96
	G2	534
	G4	48
	G4	284
	AE8	927
	BP	51

Headword	Ref	Num
BARLEY	P4	71
BARLEY-WATER	PLG	25
BARMY	G3	585
BARN	C	740
BARNS	HAP	1402
	SKA4	2
	G1	74
	G2	748
	G3	216
	M8	34
	M8	35
BARONS	KT3	94
BARRED	AM	107
	DA	154
	AA	768
	J3	476
	P1	211
	G3	420
	AE1	321
	AE2	652
BARREL	P4	67
BARREL-BELLIED	G3	126
BARREN	AR	219
	AR	220
	AA	297
	AA	438
	AA	987
	SAA	944
	SAA	1056
	RL	32
	L1	23
	L4	240
	L4	259
	T27	118
	AK	109
	J6	771
	J10	318
	M9	145
	GK	85
	GK	99
	G1	100
	G1	104
	G1	123
	G1	277
	G2	68
	G2	75
	G2	80
	G2	131
	G2	249
	G4	189
	AE1	871
	AE4	58
	AE4	892
	AE5	67
	AE5	817
	AE6	359
	AE7	1031
	OAL	510
	KT3	158
	HIF	455
	HIF	487
	M15	411
	CI	132
BARRENNESS	L4	247
BARRIER	AE5	415
	AE12	1301
	KT3	518
	KT3	559
	KT3	585
BARRIERS	HAP	2122
	G1	307
	TJD	176
	L4	90
BARS	HAP	98
	HAP	480
	HAP	1972
	J16	76
	G2	719
	AE1	404
	AE2	659
	AE2	673
	AE2	674
	AE5	473
	AE7	253
	AE8	298
	AE9	1022
	AE10	732
	AE10	738
	KT1	230
	KT2	414
	M12	66
BARTER	PCG1	28
	PK	22
BARTERED	G1	370
BARTERING	MD	32
	P5	72

Headword	Ref	Num
BARZILLAI	AA	817
	AA	818
	AA	856
BASE	AM	8
	AM	784
	HP	25
	HP	39
	DA	86
	PSF	10
	PR	14
	AA	636
	AA	806
	MD	9
	HAP	1412
	HAP	2035
	J3	44
	J6	149
	J10	88
	J10	121
	P1	48
	P1	245
	P4	127
	M1	630
	M1	1053
	MC	17
	VP4	9
	VP4	62
	AE2	829
	AE4	441
	AE4	529
	AE4	949
	AE5	413
	AE9	159
	AE10	1092
	AE11	572
	AE12	21
	AE12	486
	AE12	984
	KT2	139
	KT2	574
	B	522
	B	528
	B	546
	HIF	190
	M12	806
	AU	359
	WB	415
	WB	468
	PWR	31
BASE-BEGOTTEN	AE9	945
BASELY	EKK	10
	TA	490
	M1	690
	AE6	710
	AE6	833
	AU	11
BASENESS	AE2	891
	B	547
	AU	66
BASER	HAP	446
	GP	86
BASEST	PNH	33
	HAP	1630
BASHFUL	PR	1
	HAP	2109
	OAL	881
	CAM	278
BASHFULNESS	OAL	685
BASILUS	J10	352
BASIS	EAA	33
	AE6	260
BASK	HAP	1361
	P4	77
	G1	544
BASKED	AE7	48
BASKET	J3	24
	J6	703
BASKETS	P1	137
	VP10	103
	G1	359
BASKET-WORKS	T18	55
BASKING	M1	590
	G3	473
	G4	39
	AE5	169
	C	574
BASS	P5	279
BASSARIS	P1	195
BASSES	MF	46
BASTARD	EC	28
	HAP	854
	EDS	13
	G2	113
	G4	149
	AE9	733
	WB	397

Word	Source	Line
BASTARDS	EKK	15
	J10	405
BASTINADOED	SAA	344
BAT	EDG	42
BATAVIA	AR	217
	TA	478
BATAVIAN	AM	533
	AM	804
BATE	P6	36
	M1	688
	PWR	40
BATES	PAL	11
BATH	T23	102
	T23	103
	J1	216
	J6	492
	J6	598
	P3	183
	P3	187
	C	570
	PMK	10
BATHE	AM	1182
	AE4	982
	AE7	422
	-AE12	620
BATHED	G3	344
	AE2	353
	AE6	611
	AE7	48
	AE7	681
	AE7	752
	AE9	821
	AE11	990
	KT1	448
	KT2	199
	M8	241
	B	708
	BP	75
	CAM	216
	M12	551
BATHES	P3	198
BATHING	T18	60
	AK	87
	J6	546
	M15	533
BATHING-SHEETS	J3	421
BATHS	OAL	291
BATHSHEBA'S	AA	710
BATHURST	EUO2	17
BATS	HAP	1925
BATTALIA	AE4	582
BATTALIONS	G2	374
BATTEN	PD	53
	P5	74
BATTENING	HAP	390
	G2	113
BATTER	AA	918
	SAA	465
	AE2	61
BATTERED	AM	242
	AM	509
	AM	765
	ETG	23
	TA	169
	J6	152
	J10	377
	G3	189
	G3	646
	AE2	554
	AE5	549
	AE9	1093
	KT3	766
	TJD	149
	HIF	799
	M12	401
	M12	471
	AU	189
BATTERIES	ENH	20
BATTERING	SAA	558
	KT3	448
	M11	140
BATTERING-ENGINES	AE12	1337
BATTERING-RAMS	AE12	1027
BATTERY	HAP	626
	C	777
BATTLE	AM	84
	AM	571
	AM	732
	EDG	9
	T18	95
	HAP	955
	HAP	1963
	HAP	2110
	PSH	17
	J10	258
	J10	329
BATTLE	G2	382
	G3	387
	G4	104
	G4	111
	G4	359
	AE1	685
	AE2	979
	AE4	886
	AE5	939
	AE6	650
	AE7	251
	AE7	791
	AE7	923
	AE7	959
	AE7	1030
	AE9	33
	AE9	63
	AE9	319
	AE10	253
	AE10	346
	AE10	709
	AE11	111
	AE11	154
	AE11	295
	AE11	317
	AE11	394
	AE11	687
	AE11	1315
	AE12	352
	AE12	453
	AE12	518
	AE12	634
	AE12	750
	AE12	809
	OAE1	10
	AF	138
	KT1	79
	KT1	128
	KT2	204
	KT2	234
	KT2	243
	KT3	91
	KT3	444
	KT3	502
	KT3	639
	KT3	1080
	TJD	167
	C	393
	M11	39
	FL	453
	FL	549
	M12	766
	GP	116
BATTLEMENT	AE2	606
BATTLEMENTS	M1	348
	G1	376
	HIF	795
BATTLE-ROYAL	HAP	689
BATTLES	HS	51
	SMA	108
	AM	742
	S	9
	A	9
	J10	248
	P6	111
	VP6	4
	G2	766
	AE2	39
	AE4	865
	AE7	60
	AE10	515
	AE12	500
	AF	67
BATULUM	AE7	1020
BAUBLE	PTW	19
	HH	7
BAUBLES	P1	222
BAUCIS	BP	32
	BP	46
	BP	85
	BP	176
	BP	181
	BP	183
BAUCIS'	BP	97
BAVIUS	VP3	140
BAWD	PPC	8
	-OE	42
	HAP	2153
	J6	337
BAWDIER	PD	64
BAWDRY	P1	46
BAWDS	OAL	426
	ETP	15
BAWDS'	SAA	303
BAWDY	J3	84
	J6	281
BAWDY	J6	424
	OAL	75
	OAL	881
BAWDYHOUSE	J6	628
BAWL	J1	194
	J10	342
	J16	33
	AE8	474
BAWLED	RL	405
BAWLING	HP	200
	J6	654
	G2	719
	AE10	448
	KT2	574
BAWLS	J1	15
BAY	SMA	114
	AM	683
	P6	19
	G2	25
	G3	128
	G3	620
	AE1	228
	AE2	29
	AE3	723
	AE3	905
	AE6	946
	AE6	1245
	AE9	740
	AE10	1138
	KT3	64
	CI	377
BAYED	TH	279
BAYES	EAL	17
BAYS	JH	10
	HS	25
	RH	52
	PUO1	44
	PTC	6
	VP3	96
	VP4	67
	VP7	38
	VP7	85
	VP7	90
	VP8	116
	AE4	212
	AE12	584
	M15	66
BEACH	AR	278
	PFD	2
	AA	272
	AE4	578
	AE11	932
BEADS	C	601
	WB	45
BEAGLE'S	C	120
BEAGLES	KT2	644
	TJD	52
BEAK	AM	588
	J10	68
	AE5	263
	AE6	809
	AE11	1114
	KT3	477
	M12	740
BEAKS	G4	107
	AE7	254
	AE8	896
	M8	401
BEAM	UDH	44
	D	37
	T23	91
	EL	351
	G1	251
	AE9	750
	AE12	688
	AE12	881
	AE12	1054
	M8	284
	BP	72
	CAM	144
	C	93
	C	426
	C	506
BEAMS	SMA	13
	LC	88
	AM	394
	AM	1011
	SCD1	7
	MD	13
	MF	21
	SAA	119
	SAA	1117
	RL	1
	L2	67
	TA	221
	TA	347

BEAMS	HAP	505
	HAP	1851
	EL	81
	M1	1076
	H1	39
	VP5	96
	G1	469
	G1	542
	G1	591
	G4	420
	AE1	629
	AE1	1016
	AE2	609
	AE2	629
	AE3	206
	AE4	513
	AE4	840
	AE6	992
	AE7	670
	AE8	37
	AE9	705
	AE9	887
	AE12	247
	AE12	978
	KT2	39
	KT3	218
	C	576
	FL	373
	FL	438
	WB	10
	GP	36
	CI	120
	AS	13
	AS	28
BEAMY	G3	625
	AE1	260
	AE8	825
	AE8	901
	AE10	1020
	AE12	444
	AE12	641
	AE12	1093
	KT3	480
	AU	175
BEAN	G1	317
BEANS	J3	460
	P3	107
	G1	304
BEAR	RH	17
	LC	66
	AM	15
	AM	215
	AM	288
	AM	762
	AM	824
	AM	1190
	PMQ	48
	SCG3	7
	S	11
	EAZ	22
	ML	23
	CM	136
	CM	144
	HP	25
	HP	137
	HP	215
	DA	36
	DA	68
	DA	81
	DA	209
	AA	435
	AA	948
	AA	962
	MD	84
	SAA	997
	EDG	16
	RL	57
	RL	100
	ER	55
	L1	30
	L3	27
	L3	45
	L4	168
	T18	17
	T23	85
	T27	42
	T27	54
	H29	95
	H2	91
	NS	26
	TA	197
	PAA	14
	AK	81
	GE	27
	HAP	35
	HAP	156

BEAR	HAP	189
	HAP	293
	HAP	447
	HAP	462
	HAP	466
	HAP	1086
	HAP	1258
	HAP	1487
	HAP	1811
	HAP	1929
	HAP	2049
	HAP	2227
	HAP	2326
	BR	18
	BR	265
	EDS	13
	PP	48
	SKA6	6
	EL	136
	EL	210
	EL	352
	EL	357
	PSH	3
	J3	58
	J3	108
	J3	309
	J3	315
	J3	403
	J3	455
	J3	469
	J6	131
	J6	162
	J6	258
	J6	293
	J6	363
	J6	671
	J6	766
	P1	5
	P1	84
	P1	210
	P2	7
	P2	129
	P4	87
	P5	71
	P5	218
	P6	76
	M1	66
	M1	172
	M1	384
	M1	395
	M1	468
	M1	555
	M1	920
	M1	1050
	M9	19
	M9	28
	M9	202
	M13	155
	M13	81
	M13	92
	M13	97
	M13	118
	M13	173
	M13	176
	SFL	2
	H1	106
	GK	88
	GK	156
	VP3	113
	VP4	29
	VP4	48
	VP5	43
	VP5	106
	VP8	147
	VP9	9
	VP9	36
	VP9	88
	G1	109
	G1	112
	G2	46
	G2	76
	G2	97
	G2	123
	G2	195
	G2	205
	G2	468
	G2	595
	G2	752
	G3	32
	G3	81
	G3	88
	G3	167
	G3	268
	G3	291
	G3	385
	G3	589

BEAR	G3	614
	G4	20
	G4	286
	G4	298
	G4	448
	AE1	108
	AE1	144
	AE1	195
	AE1	265
	AE1	281
	AE1	354
	AE1	451
	AE1	463
	AE1	534
	AE1	674
	AE1	910
	AE2	122
	AE2	411
	AE2	526
	AE2	549
	AE2	583
	AE2	976
	AE2	991
	AE2	1055
	AE3	499
	AE3	524
	AE3	547
	AE3	735
	AE3	789
	AE4	353
	AE4	587
	AE4	606
	AE4	920
	AE4	1007
	AE5	49
	AE5	151
	AE5	172
	AE5	213
	AE5	217
	AE5	518
	AE5	548
	AE5	568
	AE5	866
	AE5	929
	AE6	518
	AE6	531
	AE6	592
	AE6	690
	AE6	1006
	AE6	1057
	AE6	1234
	AE7	29
	AE7	325
	AE7	373
	AE7	508
	AE7	552
	AE7	602
	AE7	637
	AE7	772
	AE7	791
	AE7	801
	AE7	821
	AE7	840
	AE7	1013
	AE8	158
	AE8	169
	AE8	380
	AE8	884
	AE9	225
	AE9	278
	AE9	302
	AE9	387
	AE9	568
	AE9	574
	AE9	666
	AE9	671
	AE9	683
	AE9	820
	AE9	1001
	AE9	1070
	AE10	46
	AE10	233
	AE10	248
	AE10	344
	AE10	404
	AE10	426
	AE10	597
	AE10	684
	AE10	699
	AE10	705
	AE10	809
	AE10	865
	AE10	944
	AE10	1198
	AE11	93
	AE11	179

BEAR	AE11	263
	AE11	272
	AE11	505
	AE11	889
	AE11	1182
	AE11	1199
	AE11	1261
	AE11	1266
	AE12	183
	AE12	246
	AE12	274
	AE12	315
	AE12	346
	AE12	845
	AE12	875
	AE12	940
	AE12	1046
	AE12	1206
	AE12	1273
	OAL	539
	KT1	87
	KT1	250
	KT2	167
	KT2	182
	KT2	624
	KT3	57
	KT3	352
	KT3	467
	KT3	885
	TJD	122
	M8	318
	B	647
	BP	175
	CAM	55
	CAM	67
	CAM	92
	CAM	123
	HIF	208
	HIF	239
	HIF	349
	HIF	414
	HIF	695
	HIF	746
	C	784
	M11	35
	M11	49
	M11	368
	FL	515
	FL	525
	FL	542
	M12	111
	M12	279
	M12	457
	M12	479
	AU	224
	AU	396
	AU	456
	AU	530
	WB	408
	M15	79
	M15	170
	GP	82
	CI	242
	CI	592
	CI	610
	ETP	36
	SMP	10
BEARD	J1	33
	J6	23
	J6	156
	J6	490
	J6	575
	J10	321
	J10	397
	P1	272
	P2	58
	P4	10
	M1	359
	M13	28
	EHC	6
	VP8	49
	G3	562
	AE2	362
	AE3	776
	AE4	368
	AE6	415
	AE6	1105
	AE10	1193
	AE12	454
	AE12	893
	OAL	582
	OAL	585
	KT3	40
	KT3	83
	KT3	351
	KT3	475

BEARD	B	304
	C	137
	M11	356
	M11	405
	M12	379
	M12	475
	M12	526
BEARDED	HAP	225
	J6	484
	P2	89
	P3	236
	M1	140
	M1	370
	M13	162
	G1	113
	G1	424
	G2	746
	AE1	240
	AE7	1101
	OAL	446
	HIF	440
	M11	299
BEARDLESS	ETG	1
	MD	28
	MC	36
	AE7	531
	AE9	875
	AE9	1014
	AE10	1106
	AE10	450
	M12	406
	EMKG	40
BEARDS	J16	49
	P2	105
	G3	485
	M8	32
BEARER	P6	103
	DO	74
	B	634
BEAREST	AE6	1146
BEARING	PR	22
	M9	52
	G1	273
	G2	107
	AE12	1013
	GP	44
	EK	30
BEARNS	M12	438
BEAR'S	AR	255
BEARS	PWG	41
	AM	235
	PCG2	17
	PAR	22
	ENH	30
	PAZ	24
	MD	3
	PRH	4
	PRH	11
	MF	15
	EK	24
	RL	113
	RL	173
	AT	33
	L4	220
	H9	26
	H29	59
	HAP	1298
	HAP	1598
	HAP	1599
	J1	216
	J3	136
	P3	6
	M1	450
	M1	313
	M13	20
	M13	151
	GK	108
	VP3	164
	G1	85
	G1	335
	G2	44
	G2	98
	G2	126
	G2	142
	G3	96
	G3	140
	G3	534
	G3	542
	G3	577
	G4	532
	AE1	133
	AE1	972
	AE2	679
	AE3	439
	AE3	676
	AE3	843

BEARS	AE4	120
	AE4	632
	AE4	648
	AE4	707
	AE5	288
	AE5	333
	AE5	487
	AE5	1095
	AE6	210
	AE6	296
	AE6	419
	AE6	1044
	AE6	1104
	AE7	20
	AE7	539
	AE7	576
	AE7	754
	AE8	483
	AE8	977
	AE9	630
	AE9	860
	AE9	1041
	AE10	298
	AE10	755
	AE10	771
	AE11	751
	AE11	829
	AE11	856
	AE11	1106
	AE12	89
	AE12	256
	AE12	432
	AE12	672
	AE12	706
	OAL	210
	OAL	324
	KT1	67
	KT1	73
	KT3	557
	KT3	861
	CAM	19
	CAM	253
	HIF	80
	M11	142
	FL	510
	FL	580
	M12	184
	M12	203
	M12	502
	M12	681
	M12	738
	M12	477
	M15	119
	M15	559
	M15	569
	M15	584
	M15	615
BEAR'S-FOOT	VP3	67
	G4	185
	G4	204
BEARSKIN	KT3	51
BEAST	PIE	9
	AM	383
	EUO	26
	PO	24
	PPC	9
	MD	120
	L5	9
	HAP	35
	HAP	54
	HAP	162
	HAP	285
	HAP	309
	HAP	330
	HAP	401
	HAP	569
	HAP	802
	HAP	2307
	EDS	19
	P3	57
	G4	428
	AE2	309
	AE4	228
	AE5	640
	AE6	37
	AE7	673
	AE7	687
	AE7	708
	AE8	258
	AE11	856
	AE12	12
	KT1	477
	KT2	531
	KT2	634
	M8	106
	M8	117

BEAST

Code	No.
M8	125
M8	172
M8	175
M8	211
CAM	42
C	114
C	593
M11	278
M12	294
M12	531
M12	554
M12	582
M12	634
M15	206
M15	242
M15	259
M15	337
M15	677
CI	233
SMP	87
SMP	93
AS	31

BEASTS

Code	No.
AM	1029
PUF	29
PLB	15
SAA	1
SAA	423
EDG	42
L1	18
L3	51
L3	69
L4	196
HAP	155
HAP	245
HAP	1261
HAP	1298
HAP	1520
J6	5
J10	484
M1	94
M1	280
M1	334
M1	636
VP3	70
VP6	44
G1	211
G1	450
G2	445
G2	465
G2	665
G2	786
G3	588
G3	724
G4	327
G4	588
G4	637
G4	758
AE1	426
AE1	1042
AE3	194
AE4	217
AE4	293
AE4	796
AE6	355
AE6	986
AE7	552
AE8	42
AE8	281
AE8	372
AE9	520
AE10	781
AE12	259
AE12	319
KT1	484
KT2	223
KT2	506
KT2	642
KT3	100
KT3	247
KT3	970
KT3	1048
HIF	382
C	152
C	585
M11	333
M12	478
M12	736
M15	115
M15	123
M15	148
CI	141

BEAT

Code	No.
AR	197
LC	144
AM	243
AM	880
PMQ	18

BEAT

Code	No.
PMM	8
CM	41
CM	108
SAA	897
L3	306
T18	11
T23	83
T23	97
HAP	253
SSC	29
SKA1	4
J6	662
J6	675
P2	96
P3	215
VP9	58
G1	136
G2	789
G3	301
G4	87
AE1	673
AE3	398
AE7	994
AE8	736
AE11	52
AE11	1268
AE12	236
AE12	1259
OAL	54
OAL	602
AF	50
KT1	44
KT1	523
KT3	872
KT3	996
KT3	1067
M8	367
M8	381
B	290
C	125
M11	140
M11	380
M12	81
M12	426
SMP	58
SMP	62

BEATEN

Code	No.
AM	779
ETC	4
AA	103
J6	616
J16	14
G3	459
AE4	365
AE8	592
AE9	1093
AE10	421
AE11	559
AE11	602
MG	12
HIF	565
HIF	656
HIF	790
M11	393
M12	379
WB	230

BEATING

Code	No.
AM	426
H3	19
PAA	8
J3	470
J6	569
M1	418
M9	189
VP9	88
VP10	29
G2	153
AE4	650
AE5	414
AE8	562
AE9	788
AE11	1180
AE11	1253
OAL	361
M10	74
FL	408

BEATS

Code	No.
SMM2	18
L4	123
BR	260
J6	620
J6	621
J6	622
VP2	9
G1	307
G1	424
G4	299
AE4	967
AE5	678

BEATS

Code	No.
AE7	700
AE11	128
AE12	879
AE12	1249
M8	101
M12	186

BEAU

Code	No.
PKA	17
J3	120
J10	456
P4	42
OAL	807

BEAUS

Code	No.
PTP-	4
PDS	35
PWR	19

BEAUSHIP

Code	No.
EHC	27

BEAUTEOUS

Code	No.
RH	8
AM	1184
ML	49
EAL	28
SAA	1066
AT	6
L4	3
T18	8
T18	48
AK	37
AK	150
HAP	2236
BR	316
EL	171
ODA	60
J3	33
J10	492
M1	843
M9	54
M9	66
M13	144
VP6	107
VP10	65
G1	329
G2	423
G3	339
G4	499
AE1	206
AE1	544
AE1	697
AE1	830
AE1	991
AE3	535
AE3	912
AE4	81
AE5	372
AE5	741
AE5	756
AE6	537
AE7	83
AE9	147
AE9	579
AE10	199
AE11	567
AE11	1236
AE12	29
AE12	101
AE12	125
AE12	1259
OAL	283
OAL	340
OAL	352
OAL	677
KT1	9
KT1	460
KT2	32
KT2	284
KT2	324
KT3	593
KT3	661
KT3	664
KT3	771
KT3	1015
KT3	1120
M10	50
CAM	386
TH	107
FL	38
CI	271
AS	25
AS	59

BEAUTIES

Code	No.
RH	77
EWG	10
VHH	50
AM	196
AM	1102
PMQ	9
PCG2	6
EAZ	16
HP	40
PR	20

Word	Ref	No.
BEAUTIES	D	32
	SAA	619
	AT	9
	T18	43
	FS3	5
	BR	13
	PP	39
	LS	1
	ODA	40
	P6	6
	M1	677
	MC	16
	MC	28
	GK	114
	GK	181
	AE8	524
	AE12	37
	OAL	63
	OAL	68
	OAL	280
	DO	5
	TJD	199
	M8	76
	C	410
BEAUTIES'	T18	72
BEAUTIFUL	RH	32
	AA	18
	L1	31
	BR	310
	AE8	786
BEAUTIFY	AS	8
BEAUTY	UDH	3
	UDH	32
	RH	44
	LC	6
	LC	10
	LCA	22
	LCA	38
	LCA	44
	LCA	47
	EIE	27
	VHH	40
	AM	1203
	PT	17
	ECG1	1
	PMQW	19
	E	9
	E	12
	ML	54
	EMK	17
	HP	167
	HP	171
	AA	22
	AA	723
	D	2
	D	9
	EDGA	17
	L4	163
	T27	54
	FS1	2
	FS3	16
	AK	135
	AK	141
	AK	156
	BR	309
	PTS	35
	SKA5	15
	MS	9
	J6	147
	J6	258
	J10	449
	J10	479
	M1	658
	M13	229
	PLT	55
	GK	109
	VP2	20
	VP10	27
	G2	673
	G3	128
	AE4	202
	AE5	387
	AE5	449
	AE7	658
	AE10	614
	OAL	250
	OAL	327
	OAL	705
	DO	8
	DO	31
	DO	69
	DO	153
	KT1	277
	KT1	403
	KT2	377
	KT2	398
BEAUTY	KT2	480
	KT2	507
	KT3	817
	M8	228
	CAM	28
	CAM	254
	C	82
	FL	82
	FL	177
	FL	184
	FL	376
	FL	592
	M12	265
	M12	309
	M12	542
	WB	505
	WB	529
	CI	2
	CI	41
	CI	55
	CI	158
	CI	176
	CI	434
	HP	116
BEAUTY'S	T27	10
	VP5	140
	AF	11
	HIF	169
BEAUX	EKA	2
	EKA	34
	ESH	12
	PLT	8
	PLT	38
	EHC	25
	C	624
BEAVER	J10	212
	G1	87
BECALMED	AM	393
	TA	28
BECAME	AM	623
	AM	670
	SCG1	7
	ECD	15
	AA	89
	SAA	912
	HAP	1822
	EL	11
	J10	478
	P5	110
	MC	40
	AE3	3
	AE4	49
	AE5	738
	AE5	805
	AE10	59
	OAL	152
	OAL	600
	OAL	873
	KT2	624
	TH	12
	AS	75
BECKONED	EL	319
BECKONING	EAA	24
BECKONS	AE10	1181
BECOME	UDH	69
	RH	70
	DC	58
	EWG	12
	EWGR	44
	PAL	32
	EAL	14
	DA	48
	D	26
	SAA	734
	HAP	1274
	HAP	2562
	PSH	17
	J3	149
	J6	46
	J6	275
	P1	62
	P1	201
	P4	118
	P5	113
	M1	672
	HI	185
	VP7	58
	G2	517
	AE1	376
	AE4	775
	AE9	686
	AE12	3
	OAL	603
	OAL	604
	KT3	132
	B	181
BECOME	B	659
	TH	240
	M11	172
	AU	179
	WB	349
	WB	526
	M15	340
	M15	552
	M15	576
	M15	683
	GP	99
BECOMES	PA	12
	PUO3	19
	AA	382
	J3	124
	M9	200
	EHC	21
	AE12	32
	AE12	234
	OAL	574
	OAL	825
	KT3	866
	HIF	788
	TH	208
	M15	634
BECOMEST	HIF	757
BECOMING	ODA	55
	P5	178
	M1	213
	AE1	707
	AE11	770
	AE12	1154
	KT3	1017
	M8	353
	GP	28
BED	UDH	98
	AR	19
	SMA	113
	SMA	123
	AM	554
	AM	927
	SCD1	13
	CM	94
	DA	92
	DA	113
	AA	15
	AA	829
	SAA	308
	SAA	341
	SAA	861
	SAA	1108
	T18	6
	T18	15
	T18	21
	T27	64
	T27	67
	T27	125
	H29	57
	TA	513
	HAP	181
	HAP	393
	HAP	1460
	BR	13
	ODA	5
	J3	267
	J3	332
	J6	6
	J6	67
	J6	76
	J6	86
	J6	126
	J6	186
	J6	213
	J6	374
	J6	545
	J6	703
	J6	769
	J10	518
	P2	127
	P5	77
	M1	566
	M1	577
	M1	648
	M1	660
	M1	802
	M1	870
	M1	908
	M1	982
	M1	1004
	M1	1023
	M9	31
	M9	49
	M9	146
	HI	52
	VP4	77
	VP10	27

Word	Ref	No.
BED	G1	43
	G2	400
	G2	762
	G3	553
	G3	813
	G4	498
	G4	525
	AE1	41
	AE1	247
	AE1	474
	AE1	974
	AE1	979
	AE2	462
	AE2	1062
	AE3	383
	AE3	412
	AE3	424
	AE3	913
	AE4	118
	AE4	159
	AE4	176
	AE4	276
	AE4	313
	AE4	458
	AE4	472
	AE4	539
	AE4	567
	AE4	716
	AE4	735
	AE4	839
	AE4	932
	AE4	989
	AE6	695
	AE6	849
	AE6	1209
	AE7	81
	AE7	350
	AE7	502
	AE7	640
	AE7	1050
	AE8	98
	AE8	239
	AE8	320
	AE8	482
	AE8	488
	AE8	541
	AE8	548
	AE8	601
	AE8	771
	AE9	152
	AE9	449
	AE9	610
	AE10	544
	AE11	2
	AE11	240
	AE11	405
	AE11	416
	AE12	221
	AE12	1193
	OAL	144
	OAL	849
	KT2	43
	KT2	284
	KT2	400
	KT3	714
	KT3	1147
	M8	262
	M8	386
	B	207
	B	231
	B	711
	BP	77
	M10	4
	M10	51
	M10	97
	CAM	29
	CAM	153
	CAM	198
	CAM	221
	CAM	242
	CAM	282
	CAM	304
	HIF	48
	C	26
	C	75
	C	218
	C	227
	C	307
	C	495
	C	711
	TH	73
	TH	363
	TH	370
	M11	87
	M11	252
	M11	292

Word	Ref	No.
BED	M11	346
	M11	355
	FL	20
	FL	34
	FL	378
	M12	266
	M12	668
	WB	331
	WB	342
	WB	542
	M15	286
	M15	593
	M15	622
BEDDING	G3	465
	KT2	159
	KT2	172
BEDE	C	374
BEDEW	T18	77
	AE6	949
	AE11	292
BEDEWED	M8	325
BEDEWS	AE9	449
BEDFELLOW	L4	158
	J6	47
	J6	188
BEDIGHT	MD	285
BEDLAM	L4	139
BEDLOE	HAP	2013
BEDS	HS	76
	AM	712
	ETL	12
	L2	39
	HAP	1498
	J6	18
	J6	33
	P1	98
	M1	96
	M1	157
	G1	645
	G2	727
	G4	181
	G4	278
	AE2	685
	AE3	298
	AE4	301
	AE6	312
	AE6	818
	AE6	914
	WB	31
BEDTIME	J3	441
BEE	AT	29
	PTS	1
	G1	5
	G4	259
BEECH	G1	254
	G2	21
	G2	98
	AE9	518
	KT3	962
BEECHEN	VP1	1
	VP2	3
	VP3	55
	G4	817
	BP	72
	BP	104
	BP	122
BEECH'S	VP5	18
BEEF	PAA	15
BEEF'S	AE8	243
BEER	PMS	36
	G3	585
	SAA	70
	HAP	2259
BEERSHEBA	SMA	56
BEES	AM	574
	AM	909
	SAA	563
	SAA	1061
	AK	50
	HAP	2580
	VP1	72
	VP1	73
	VP5	121
	VP7	18
	VP10	44
	G2	294
	G2	610
	G2	634
	G3	688
	G4	10
	G4	39
	G4	47
	G4	59
	G4	169
	G4	220
	G4	225

Word	Ref	No.
BEES	G4	257
	G4	286
	G4	322
	G4	344
	G4	440
	G4	452
	G4	774
	G4	801
	G4	808
	AE1	599
	AE2	35
	AE6	959
	AE7	97
	AE12	862
	OAL	105
	C	740
	FL	218
	M15	110
	M15	542
	EWR	23
BEESTINGS	VP3	42
	G3	283
BEET	P3	232
BEETLE	HAP	321
	J3	154
BEFALL	L3	95
	AE1	639
	AE7	275
	AE12	302
	OAE2	87
	KT1	482
	HIF	161
BEFALLS	G2	712
BEFELL	AE2	964
	HAP	1715
	AE2	16
	KT1	517
	KT1	581
	C	303
	C	363
	C	579
	WB	46
BEFIT	SAA	318
BEFITS	H29	40
BEFOAMS	M8	27
BEFOREHAND	PMQ	24
	VP3	74
BEFRIEND	DOD	26
	HAP	2231
	J16	5
	AE2	839
	AE3	214
	AE11	176
BEFRIENDS	AE10	398
BEG	AM	1156
	EWGR	38
	PUO1	19
	PNH	18
	PUO2	20
	EKK	1
	EK	27
	EK	35
	L3	148
	T23	41
	FS4	4
	FS4	8
	HAP	1532
	J1	185
	J3	472
	J10	130
	J16	17
	P6	77
	M1	654
	DHP	16
	VP1	85
	VP5	140
	AE1	958
	AE2	882
	AE3	582
	AE3	788
	AE4	457
	AE7	313
	AE8	14
	AE8	159
	AE8	502
	AE9	299
	AE9	305
	AE10	73
	AE10	840
	AE10	881
	AE11	152
	AE11	165
	AE11	558
	AE12	1191
	AE12	1357
	OAL	743

Word	Ref	No.
BEG	KT1	64
	B	378
	B	739
	BP	173
	HIF	672
BEGAN	AM	178
	AM	923
	PWGR	11
	PWGR	17
	EWGR	15
	PT	35
	SEL3	7
	SEL3	23
	ECG1	23
	PUO1	24
	PKK	11
	PUF	4
	AA	52
	AA	108
	AA	1028
	MD	29
	SAA	2
	SAA	74
	PDG	46
	RL	388
	MO	2
	TA	313
	TA	447
	EAA	26
	GE	78
	HH	1
	HAP	61
	HAP	A11
	HAP	196
	HAP	275
	HAP	280
	HAP	380
	HAP	572
	HAP	980
	HAP	1179
	HAP	1498
	HAP	1685
	HAP	1701
	HAP	1731
	HAP	1733
	HAP	1890
	HAP	1907
	HAP	1912
	HAP	1936
	HAP	2103
	HAP	2587
	SSC	2
	SSC	12
	SSC	56
	OD	11
	OD	32
	J6	163
	J6	239
	P3	26
	P3	175
	M1	111
	M1	152
	M1	561
	M1	944
	M1	950
	M1	967
	M1	968
	M1	989
	M1	1028
	M9	198
	M13	8
	HI	61
	GK	28
	GK	38
	GK	50
	DHP	15
	VP8	57
	G2	525
	AE1	13
	AE1	734
	AE1	869
	AE2	2
	AE2	366
	AE2	807
	AE2	944
	AE2	1052
	AE2	1089
	AE3	12
	AE3	458
	AE3	782
	AE4	388
	AE4	440
	AE4	518
	AE4	958
	AE5	112
	AE5	160
BEGAN	AE5	809
	AE5	1097
	AE6	366
	AE6	506
	AE6	564
	AE6	609
	AE6	672
	AE7	34
	AE7	58
	AE7	113
	AE7	269
	AE7	298
	AE7	500
	AE7	544
	AE7	590
	AE8	213
	AE8	370
	AE9	6
	AE10	7
	AE10	140
	AE10	322
	AE10	656
	AE10	839
	AE10	845
	AE10	855
	AE11	20
	AE11	58
	AE11	164
	AE11	186
	AE11	370
	AE11	524
	AE11	809
	AE11	868
	AE12	18
	AE12	323
	AE12	345
	AE12	838
	OAL	111
	OAL	792
	AF	25
	AF	88
	AF	92
	KT1	56
	KT1	93
	KT1	240
	KT1	307
	KT1	360
	KT1	546
	KT2	142
	KT2	236
	KT2	251
	KT2	312
	KT2	513
	KT3	83
	KT3	121
	KT3	271
	KT3	295
	KT3	365
	KT3	433
	KT3	436
	KT3	793
	KT3	1073
	TJD	74
	M8	289
	M8	347
	B	305
	B	306
	B	501
	B	510
	BP	12
	BP	90
	CAM	41
	CAM	110
	CAM	217
	CAM	338
	HIF	366
	C	88
	C	427
	C	445
	TH	264
	TH	382
	TH	399
	M11	91
	M11	101
	M11	455
	FL	178
	FL	291
	FL	364
	FL	373
	M12	314
	M12	530
	M12	619
	M12	661
	WB	260
	WB	278
	M15	145
BEGAN	M15	185
	M15	308
	M15	324
	M15	399
	CI	123
	CI	468
	STP	25
BEGET	AR	206
	LC	149
	SEL4	16
	HAP	2464
	BR	328
	J10	172
	M1	203
	G3	842
	AE6	1040
	TH	153
BEGETS	HAP	519
	SKA6	9
	WB	415
	M15	553
	M15	615
BEGETTER	J16	84
BEGETTER'S	WB	417
BEGETTERS	AA	425
BEGETTING	WB	164
BEGGAR	J10	33
	P1	177
	P4	129
	WB	471
BEGGARED	AA	561
BEGGAR'S	HAP	1396
	P6	33
BEGGARS	SAA	513
	PDG	6
BEGGED	SMA	131
	ML	20
	CM	102
	T23	27
	TA	271
	J1	74
	J3	344
	J6	49
	J10	425
	J10	431
	M1	843
	M1	1018
	M1	1069
	VP2	56
	HIF	727
	M11	415
	GP	131
BEGGING	J1	177
	J1	183
	OAL	477
BEGIN	JH	13
	HS	17
	RH	14
	AM	624
	PM	22
	PM	36
	PLN	2
	PR	9
	AA	1
	SAA	775
	PAA	44
	HAP	2314
	ETS	12
	ETS	26
	EL	297
	SSH	10
	J3	176
	J6	30
	J6	160
	J6	447
	J6	466
	J6	848
	P1	29
	P2	59
	P5	97
	P5	170
	M1	543
	M1	582
	VP1	38
	VP3	73
	VP4	1
	VP4	72
	VP5	13
	VP5	16
	VP8	30
	VP8	35
	VP8	45
	VP8	52
	VP8	59
	VP8	63
	VP8	69

Word	Ref	No.
BEGIN	VP8	79
	G1	318
	G1	489
	G3	265
	G4	442
	AE1	365
	AE3	187
	AE3	658
	AE4	367
	AE4	408
	AE5	990
	AE8	683
	AE9	308
	AE9	696
	AE9	1000
	AE11	1043
	AE12	1035
	OAL	166
	OAL	170
	OAL	440
	OAL	465
	OAL	498
	OAL	690
	OAL	804
	OAL	808
	OAL	861
	DO	111
	KT3	1040
	BP	185
	CAM	133
	HIF	461
	HIF	677
	WB	456
	M15	151
	M15	330
	M15	390
	M15	685
	CI	181
	ETP	38
	SMP	23
	SMP	26
	SMP	91
	SMP	97
BEGINNER	PWGR	25
BEGINNERS	EMKG	42
BEGINNING	AM	76
	SAA	377
	EL	15
	AE9	881
	AE10	440
	AF	101
	M8	10
	B	475
	M10	79
	CI	102
BEGINNINGS	AM	618
	HAP	2559
	AE4	252
	AE9	396
BEGINS	EWGR	21
	SCD2	9
	AA	729
	PLB	45
	EDGA	39
	L3	286
	HAP	338
	BR	40
	J6	376
	P3	13
	DHP	6
	VP3	90
	VP8	156
	G4	271
	G4	422
	G4	436
	AE4	360
	AE4	654
	AE7	736
	AE10	155
	AE11	137
	OAL	696
	KT3	759
	KT3	1067
	C	397
	M15	377
	M15	382
	M15	587
	M15	604
	M15	637
	B	569
	CI	636
BEGOT	AM	697
	PDG	2
	L3	172
	HAP	355
	HAP	1179
BEGOT	HAP	1458
	J1	231
	J10	373
	M1	695
	M1	1080
	AE7	976
	AE8	262
	AU	40
BEGOTTEN	M15	580
BEGS	ET	12
	ECG1	37
	SCD1	21
	EAL	21
	ELB	5
	J3	427
	J6	700
	J10	260
	P5	255
	AE4	112
	AE12	576
	OAL	481
	OAL	800
	M11	318
	M15	687
BEGUILE	LC	140
	SMM2	22
	MD	194
	RL	91
	HAP	559
	BR	360
	OAL	715
	KT2	33
	KT2	132
BEGUILED	J10	353
	P1	233
	AE2	519
	AE4	122
	AE8	411
BEGUILES	BR	115
	EL	214
BEGUN	AR	292
	SMA	60
	LC	153
	PRL	10
	AM	71
	AM	96
	AM	497
	AA	517
	L3	176
	HH	42
	HAP	350
	J6	20
	J10	5
	VP4	7
	G2	436
	G4	555
	G4	673
	AE1	600
	AE3	414
	AE4	133
	AE4	454
	AE5	815
	AE6	364
	AE6	978
	AE7	756
	AE7	766
	AE7	887
	AE8	487
	AE8	719
	AE9	95
	AE9	231
	AE11	462
	AE12	643
	KT3	777
	TJD	65
	B	177
	B	474
	CAM	291
	HIF	7
	HIF	499
	HIF	796
	C	573
	FL	368
	M12	248
	AU	200
	AU	332
	M15	38
	M15	93
	CI	413
	CI	488
	STP	34
	SMP	16
BEHALF	M1	1021
	AE9	104
BEHAVIOR	HAP	2448
	ELT	23
	KT1	455
BEHAVIOR	FL	400
BEHELD	AR	61
	AR	195
	AM	197
	AM	408
	AM	1110
	SCD2	23
	EPF	21
	PUO3	29
	T27	130
	HAP	529
	HAP	2292
	J3	12
	J10	53
	J10	427
	P6	22
	M1	208
	M1	439
	M1	471
	M1	474
	M1	800
	M1	884
	M13	147
	HI	30
	HI	44
	HI	80
	GK	1
	VP3	159
	VP10	39
	G3	165
	AE1	632
	AE2	681
	AE2	708
	AE3	285
	AE3	395
	AE3	708
	AE3	818
	AE5	45
	AE6	435
	AE6	885
	AE6	1188
	AE7	40
	AE7	297
	AE7	397
	AE8	93
	AE8	131
	AE8	326
	AE9	211
	AE9	977
	AE10	709
	AE10	710
	AE10	1089
	AE10	1165
	AE11	375
	AE11	604
	AE11	806
	AE11	1144
	AE12	204
	AE12	660
	AE12	928
	AE12	1146
	AE12	1256
	OAL	330
	KT1	4
	KT1	219
	KT1	562
	KT2	376
	KT2	659
	KT3	659
	KT3	972
	M8	78
	B	56
	CAM	267
	C	116
	C	446
	C	708
	C	720
	C	772
	TH	43
	FL	294
	FL	336
	M12	306
	M12	310
	M12	493
	M12	695
	AU	398
	AU	482
	M15	235
BEHOLD	AR	251
	AR	263
	AM	25
	AM	661
	AM	777
	AM	965
	AM	1001
	AM	1115

Word	Code	Num	Word	Code	Num	Word	Code	Num
BEHOLD	AM	1159	BEHOLD	AE7	165	BELCHING	AE7	1074
	AM	1185		AE7	364	BELDAM	WB	261
	PNH	5		AE7	383		WB	291
	EAZ	38		AE7	634	BELDAME	AT	77
	PTC	13		AE7	636		CAM	164
	PCB	41		AE7	755		CAM	206
	DA	43		AE8	225		CAM	250
	AA	B68		AE8	353	BELEAGUERED	J10	347
	AA	700		AE8	508		M1	193
	MD	55		AE8	813	BELEAGUERS	AE5	587
	D	15		AE8	869	BELGIAN	HS	116
	AT	17		AE9	328		AM	16
	AT	56		AE9	429		AM	266
	L2	1		AE9	487		AM	288
	L2	5		AE9	1048		AM	336
	T18	64		AE10	947		AM	369
	H9	1		AE10	1198		AM	773
	H9	3		AE11	274		AM	825
	TA	510		AE12	380		AM	917
	AK	172		AE12	1179		AM	1195
	HAP	1089		AF	136		G3	317
	HAP	1092		AF	143	BELGIANS	AM	233
	HAP	1120		DO	7		AM	309
	HAP	1218		KT1	277		AM	325
	HAP	2170		KT1	515		AM	669
	HAP	2172		KT2	356		AM	725
	BR	74		KT2	366		AM	761
	BR	84		KT2	422		AM	787
	BR	176		KT2	537	BELGIANS'	AM	753
	SKA1	7		KT3	11	BELIAL	AA	598
	OD	35		KT3	64		AA	1016
	ODA	66		KT3	267		SAA	287
	ODA	70		KT3	441	BELIDES	J6	854
	SSH	3		KT3	450	BELIE	HI	109
	J1	34		KT3	532	BELIED	HAP	1431
	J1	85		KT3	935		AE10	907
	J1	117		KT3	1141		AE10	1066
	J3	101		BP	161		OAL	86
	J3	121		CAM	11		AF	28
	J3	430		CAM	80		CI	54
	J6	359		HIF	308		HP	119
	J6	365		HIF	376	BELIEF	AA	651
	J10	334		HIF	761		RL	185
	P3	223		C	53		HAP	111
	P4	113		TH	198		HAP	430
	P6	32		TH	261		J3	160
	M1	146		TH	294		AE2	78
	M1	399		TH	316		AE11	557
	M13	106		FL	256		OAL	694
	M13	127		FL	482		LMC	6
	M13	224		FL	506		B	586
	HI	79		FL	546		C	198
	VP1	71		M12	595		C	369
	VP1	104		WB	91		M12	700
	VP5	102		WB	498	BELIEFS	HAP	689
	VP8	16		SMP	5	BELIES	T23	36
	G2	32		AS	63		AE5	843
	G3	42		J10	285		AE12	943
	G3	594	BEHOLDER	CM	5	BELIEVE	SCG1	25
	G3	711	BEHOLDEST	DA	71		HP	42
	G4	139	BEHOLDS	AM	1129		HP	89
	G4	395		L1	6		HP	220
	G4	437		J6	533		HP	225
	G4	799		M1	110		SSF	4
	AE1	153		VP5	89		AA	250
	AE1	352		G4	536		AA	727
	AE1	544		AE1	999		PPC	12
	AE1	830		AE2	1062		MD	135
	AE1	923		AE5	537		SAA	100
	AE2	84		AE8	29		SAA	530
	AE2	371		AE10	574		SAA	654
	AE2	471		AE10	1018		SDG	12
	AE2	269		AE12	1030		RL	304
	AE2	543		KT1	515		RL	432
	AE2	718		M11	136		RL	433
	AE2	905		M15	196		EC	32
	AE2	1083	BEING	L3	26		EC	33
	AE3	502		L3	167		TA	503
	AE3	613		BR	352		EAA	31
	AE3	676		AE10	1206		HAP	68
	AE4	532		KT3	1045		HAP	80
	AE5	143		B	644		HAP	92
	AE5	335		FL	468		HAP	118
	AE5	344		WB	421		HAP	182
	AE5	845	BEINGS	AM	662		HAP	608
	AE5	880		HAP	325		HAP	615
	AE5	1056		AE6	924		HAP	1684
	AE6	16		M12	355		HAP	1846
	AE6	70	BELATES				HAP	2178
	AE6	210	BELAY	AE9	515		HAP	2189
	AE6	656	BELCH	M15	510		BR	284
	AE6	933	BELCHED	J6	15		STS2	5
	AE6	1077		AE8	263		J3	165
	AE6	1089	BELCHING	J3	186		J10	156
	AE6	1130		P3	200		P5	118
	AE7	103		G3	373		P5	234
				AE3	828			

Word	Ref	Num	Word	Ref	Num	Word	Ref	Num
BELIEVE	VCS	31	BELLOWING	AE6	35	BEMOAN	VP10	21
	VP8	157		AE6	743		AE5	796
	AE5	300		AE7	783		AE12	1180
	AE5	1106		AE9	861	BEMOANS	AE7	699
	AE8	613		AE9	912		AU	66
	AE10	1126		AE10	151	BEN	PWG	48
	AE11	622	BELLOWINGS	AE2	295		PA	11
	OAL	34		AE8	282		PNH	46
	OAL	305	BELLOWS	J10	92		PC1	11
	OAL	508		P5	13		G2	220
	OAL	720		G4	248		AE10	294
	OAL	847		AE8	590	BENAIAH'S	SAA	819
	KT3	846		AE8	532	BENCH	PM	23
	M10	29		AE12	160		HAP	2027
	M10	87		AF	156		PP	44
	CAM	6		KT3	759		P1	266
	CAM	10	BELLS	AM	576		WB	309
	HIF	372		PLN	1	BENCHED	FL	66
	C	205		PO	18	BENCHES	PW	14
	C	342		HAP	368		ENH	9
	C	561		G4	276		PLG	8
	C	796		AE6	961		EDGA	9
	M12	233	BELLY	HAP	161		PSH	8
	AU	408		PMS	5		J3	258
	WB	359		J10	477		G2	732
	WB	459		P1	108		AE5	1090
	M15	535		M13	181	BEND	J3	29
	EWR	14		G3	650		J3	452
BELIEVED	PT	26		AE2	67		J6	251
	HP	171		AE5	362		J6	542
	HP	130		AE10	303		P3	40
	SAA	759		C	11		P3	117
	RL	216		M12	523		M1	107
	RL	355		M12	647		VP9	41
	EC	33	BELLYING	HIF	654		VP9	79
	EAA	24	BELLY-PIECE	HAP	1461		VP10	85
	HAP	880	BELONG	ETC	15		G1	311
	HAP	895		SAA	1023		G3	285
	HAP	2222		J6	270		G4	86
	BR	250		J10	316		AE2	937
	J6	726		PPS	7		AE2	972
	M1	1042		P5	121		AE3	378
	AE2	166		HI	187		AE3	713
	AE2	325		VP3	85		AE3	714
	AE3	249		AE4	263		AE4	230
	AE6	936		AE9	825		AE4	640
	AE7	148		OAL	106		AE5	87
	KT3	1150		OAL	398		AE5	664
	B	259		KT1	586		AE7	221
	B	275	BELONGED	J10	252		AE7	937
	BP	4		AE1	934		AE9	776
	CAM	297	BELONGING	HIF	668		AE9	826
	HIF	328	BELONGS	L3	317		AE9	905
	C	336		P5	1		AE11	1311
	C	505		VP3	91		AE12	547
	C	554		AE8	705		AE12	837
	TH	413		AE10	1047		AE12	1187
	M12	486		OAE2	17		OAL	23
	AU	61		KT1	101		AM	891
BELIEVER	EC	41		HIF	309		L2	13
BELIEVES	RL	322		M12	281		T18	40
	J6	720	BELOVED	UDH	94		T18	54
	M1	677		AA	328		HAP	336
	M10	22		AA	522		HAP	2230
	WB	470		DOD	9		HIF	394
BELIEVING	AA	117		ER	73		KT3	478
	AA	540		TA	404		KT3	606
	T27	85		HAP	1090		M15	104
	STS2	6		M1	954	BENDED	BR	7
BELINUS	C	636		AE1	23		M12	140
BELL	SCD2	16		AE11	808	BENDING	J3	337
	PCB	19		AE12	217		J10	302
	C	45		KT1	592		P1	193
	GP	43		TH	405		VP7	16
BELLIES	J3	278		M11	17		VP8	56
	G4	183		M12	538		VP10	103
	AE2	273	BELT	J6	361		G1	254
	AE5	913		P4	104		G2	7
BELLIES-FULL	PDG	12		AE1	692		G2	599
BELLONA	AE7	444		AE5	410		G2	620
	AE8	933		AE9	407		G2	629
BELLONA'S	J6	657		AE10	691		G3	267
BELLOW	P5	279		AE10	692		G3	512
	AE6	366		AE10	702		AE1	430
BELLOWING	MD	268		AE12	413		AE2	982
	BR	243		AE12	1365		AE3	701
	M1	911		CAM	272		AE8	839
	M13	199		SMP	3		AE9	303
	HI	75	BELTMEN	J16	75		AE10	640
	G1	443	BELUS	AE1	879		AE11	688
	G1	636		AE1	1019		AE11	835
	G3	338	BELY	AR	198		KT2	184
	AE3	124		M11	330		M8	96
	AE3	762	BELZEBUB	AA	1016		B	687
	AE3	814	BEMOAN	SAA	198		CAM	362
	AE3	884		L3	49		M11	266

Word	Ref	No.
BENDING	FL	196
	M12	744
BENDS	MF	192
	M1	370
	M1	611
	M1	1092
	M9	85
	G2	774
	G3	311
	AE1	717
	AE3	838
	AE4	597
	AE5	194
	AE5	855
	AE6	1240
	AE9	587
	AE10	417
	AE10	824
	AE11	1123
	AE12	700
	MM	45
	HIF	111
BENEDICITE	WB	374
BENEDICTION	EMM	2
BENEFICE	PTC	24
	C	646
	GP	126
BENEFICENT	HAP	249
BENEFICES	HAP	1469
BENEFIT	AM	1107
	AA	537
	MD	140
	HAP	298
	HAP	2124
	CAM	314
BENEFITS	PA	37
	BR	62
	J16	55
	AE1	284
BENIGHTED	AM	642
	EL	57
	DO	43
BENIGHTING	UDH	50
BENIGNLY	TA	223
BENJAMIN	HAP	1217
BEN-JOCHANAN	SAA	353
BENT	AM	484
	AM	793
	EM	17
	EOE	5
	PCB	7
	AA	257
	AA	499
	AA	917
	SAA	526
	SAA	811
	L4	216
	TA	177
	TA	273
	TA	325
	HAP	41
	HAP	1085
	HAP	1693
	HAP	1747
	HAP	2441
	J3	68
	J10	175
	J10	228
	P1	2
	P4	1
	P5	53
	M1	115
	M1	351
	M1	509
	M1	549
	M1	714
	M1	971
	M9	113
	HI	93
	G1	296
	G4	127
	G4	740
	AE1	525
	AE1	752
	AE1	798
	AE2	79
	AE3	52
	AE3	509
	AE5	373
	AE5	567
	AE5	679
	AE6	438
	AE7	692
	AE9	511
	AE9	804
	AE10	384
BENT	AE10	500
	AE10	925
	AE10	1103
	AE11	970
	AE11	1173
	AE11	1236
	AE12	1308
	OAL	64
	OAE1	25
	KT1	287
	KT1	574
	KT2	539
	KT2	544
	KT3	268
	KT3	292
	KT3	383
	KT3	489
	KT3	621
	KT3	695
	B	160
	B	364
	B	375
	B	439
	M10	80
	CAM	139
	CAM	316
	HIF	73
	HIF	427
	C	488
	TH	274
	M11	35
	FL	361
	M12	357
	M12	449
	AU	463
	WB	493
	M15	7
	CI	45
	CI	267
	CI	377
	CI	476
	CI	599
	ESK	23
BENTING	HAP	2577
BENUMBED	H9	6
	M1	742
	G4	378
	B	749
BENUMBING	J6	800
BENUMBS	AE9	632
BEQUEATH	UDH	10
	T18	70
	HI	58
	G2	185
	AE4	43
	AE11	883
	AE11	1254
	AE11	1291
	KT3	781
	FL	326
	M15	57
BEQUEATHED	AR	12
	TA	228
	HAP	947
	AE9	492
BEQUEATHING	ESH	31
BEQUEATHS	PLT	47
BEREAVE	SEL4	2
	STS1	3
	AE6	354
BERECYNTHIAN	P1	182
	AE9	132
BEREFT	AR	229
	AM	117
	DA	8
	AA	567
	SAA	93
	HAP	816
	BR	307
	J1	229
	J6	42
	J6	303
	J10	360
	P6	127
	HI	63
	AE2	999
	AE2	1016
	AE4	466
	AE4	478
	AE6	482
	AE9	806
	AE9	997
	AE10	473
	AE10	743
	AE12	1124
	KT1	527
BEREFT	KT3	520
	M12	349
	AU	97
	AU	485
BERENICE'S	J6	227
BERGAMOTES	G2	127
BERKELEY	AM	267
BEROE	G4	481
	AE5	805
	AE5	843
	AE5	848
BERRIES	M1	136
	VP6	35
	VP7	75
	G1	411
	G2	123
	G2	255
	G2	601
	AE3	855
	OAL	103
BESEECHING	AM	528
BESEEMS	B	170
BESET	AM	721
	AA	280
	L3	302
	L4	132
	HAP	1904
	J10	34
	J10	485
	AE2	1029
	AE4	808
	AE8	642
BESETS	AM	806
BESHREW	C	795
BESIEGE	AR	301
	AM	108
	J1	182
	AE4	60
	AE6	399
BESIEGED	BR	56
	AE3	791
	AE7	481
	AE10	853
	KT1	19
	KT1	80
	TJD	153
BESMEAR	AE3	364
	AE11	1033
	AE12	466
BESMEARED	T23	108
	M1	580
	G2	530
	AE3	777
	AE5	178
	AE5	433
	AE10	1029
	AE11	14
	AE11	130
	KT3	1000
	C	244
	M12	378
BESMEARS	AE12	893
	CI	608
BESOTTED	SAA	28
	M8	229
BESOUGHT	AE2	238
	KT1	92
BESPAKE	AE12	210
BESPATTERED	EPC	2
BESPEAK	P4	17
BESPEAKEST	P1	102
BESPEAKING	AA	695
BESPEAKS	AE5	477
	KT3	497
	M15	4
BESPOKE	HAP	1272
	ODA	30
	M1	235
	AE1	313
	AE5	58
	AE5	105
	AE7	501
	AE8	96
	AE8	167
	AE8	476
	AE9	154
	AE9	875
	HIF	108
	HIF	307
	HIF	448
	HIF	490
	HIF	603
	M11	256
	M11	360
	M12	771
	AU	273

BESPOKE	M15	29	BEST	HAP	1677	BEST	AU	243
BESPREAD	T18	7		HAP	2203		AU	422
	KT2	572		HAP	2402		AU	492
BESPRINKLES	AE9	449		HAP	2415		WB	113
BESS'S	PLB	18		PTS	35		WB	122
BESSUS	ML	8		PTS	39		WB	246
BEST	UDH	90		EJG	1		WB	290
	UDH	107		EL	59		WB	492
	HS	5		EL	113		WB	494
	RH	54		EL	212		WB	516
	SMA	54		EL	372		GP	24
	AM	659		J1	24		CI	131
	AM	660		J1	17		EMKG	24
	EWGR	2		J3	358		PWR	32
	PT	12		J6	150	BEST-BELOVED	HAP	1217
	PA	5		J10	84	BESTIAL	HAP	167
	PA	6		M1	441		M12	314
	PCG1	19		M1	476	BESTIR	PEL	3
	ECG2	1		M1	677	BESTIUS	P6	84
	SCG3	8		M13	136	BEST-LOVED	HS	32
	SM2	2		MC	15		AM	614
	PUO1	8		GK	62	BESTOW	LCA	20
	ENH	35		GK	67		PSF	4
	EUO2	8		GK	80		SAA	1060
	EAZ	35		GK	168		L1	44
	PC1	5		VP3	36		T23	77
	ML	12		VP5	143		ODA	80
	EAL	14		VP7	30		J10	52
	EAL	18		VP8	136		J10	453
	PKK	1		VP9	7		J10	559
	POE	10		G1	120		P1	175
	PTC	34		G1	379		P5	132
	PCB	12		G2	145		VCS	27
	HP	43		G2	355		HI	158
	HP	128		G2	434		GK	154
	HP	186		G3	691		VP1	98
	DA	159		G4	136		VP2	24
	ETG	17		AE1	780		VP8	131
	PR	26		AE7	380		G3	453
	AA	44		AE8	168		G3	494
	AA	61		AE8	725		AE3	505
	AA	356		AE9	335		AE3	861
	AA	478		AE9	379		AE4	897
	AA	495		AE9	703		AE6	322
	AA	571		AE9	777		AE6	1226
	AA	679		AE11	60		AE9	279
	AA	875		AE11	535		AE9	337
	PLB	48		AE12	76		AE10	687
	ELB	5		AE12	79		AE10	1176
	MD	61		OAL	47		AE11	35
	MD	104		OAL	132		AE11	324
	MD	139		OAL	243		AE11	543
	MD	250		OAL	313		AE12	579
	PRH	23		OAL	439		KT2	275
	D	46		OAL	825		TJD	75
	MF	167		MG	16		CAM	332
	SAA	53		MM	51		CAM	377
	SAA	90		DO	11		M11	287
	SAA	318		KT1	32		AU	181
	SAA	501		KT2	157		WB	388
	SAA	635		KT2	404		CI	489
	SAA	810		KT3	20		AS	51
	EDG	29		KT3	132		AS	54
	EDGA	31		KT3	206	BESTOWED	T27	69
	RL	32		KT3	241		HAP	1533
	RL	44		KT3	278		BR	31
	RL	132		KT3	741		ETS	20
	RL	198		KT3	780		OD	15
	RL	329		KT3	850		VP1	7
	RL	339		KT3	1000		G4	221
	RL	401		KT3	1084		AE1	40
	OE	23		KT3	1089		AE2	524
	ER	23		TJD	115		AE5	404
	L3	265		B	94		AE5	476
	L3	308		B	495		AE5	993
	L4	277		B	616		AE7	377
	T27	118		B	637		AE8	116
	H3	8		B	648		AE9	489
	H9	31		BP	48		AE11	300
	TA	36		BP	60		AE12	143
	TA	197		BP	101		AE12	529
	TA	267		M10	50		DO	135
	TA	355		CAM	107		KT2	660
	TA	404		CAM	A19		KT3	112
	TA	405		HIF	247		M8	377
	TA	484		HIF	398		B	503
	AK	79		HIF	510		C	540
	HAP	148		HIF	775		M15	103
	HAP	408		C	209		M15	619
	HAP	842		C	565		CI	496
	HAP	849		C	690	BESTOWS	AR	309
	HAP	884		TH	45		AM	488
	HAP	977		M11	309		G4	393
	HAP	1012		M11	328		AE2	656
	HAP	1019		M12	773		AE4	54
	HAP	1484		AU	56		AE5	80

BESTOWS	AE5	327	BETRAYED	HP	191	BETTER	PK	21		
	AE9	8		DA	86		PDG	10		
	HIF	192		AA	275		RL	7		
	M11	184		AA	366		RL	227		
	CI	149		MD	72		RL	229		
BESTRIDE	ECD	14		SAA	845		RL	301		
	CAM	43		SAA	873		AT	60		
BESTRIDES	AE2	834		PD	25		ER	74		
	M11	108		MO	18		L3	238		
BESTRODE	AE1	441		L4	98		L4	128		
	AE9	873		HAP	49		T27	37		
	AE10	683		HAP	469		T27	79		
	AE10	818		HAP	2057		T27	106		
	AE11	1003		HAP	2472		H3	11		
	KT3	66		STS3	11		H2	7		
BET	PKA	25		SKA6	19		TA	164		
	PKA	39		J1	49		HH	29		
BETAKE	AR	161		J1	70		HAP	133		
	T18	21		J6	62		HAP	431		
BETHLEM'S	P5	212		M1	181		HAP	504		
BETHOUGHT	HAP	384		M1	828		HAP	589		
	HIF	668		M13	197		HAP	707		
BETIDE	H9	11		VP6	88		HAP	824		
	AE9	373		VP10	13		HAP	850		
	C	737		G2	343		HAP	1596		
BETIDES	KT1	249		G4	487		HAP	1624		
BETIMES	JH	19		G4	703		HAP	1632		
	SCG3	10		AE1	658		HAP	1738		
	TA	458		AE1	1059		HAP	1800		
	HAP	1737		AE2	244		HAP	2250		
	BR	1		AE4	19		HAP	2312		
	PTS	40		AE4	848		EDS	32		
	G1	63		AE5	1107		PP	8		
	G1	165		AE6	470		STS2	8		
	G3	251		AE6	688		EKA	37		
	G3	261		AE8	157		EL	27		
	G3	296		AE9	507		EL	99		
	KT2	45		AE10	1151		EL	249		
BETOOK	HAP	2590		AE12	213		ODA	62		
BETRAY	HS	35		OAL	369		J3	162		
	AR	315		OAL	520		J3	180		
	AM	452		OAL	790		J3	274		
	AM	676		KT2	510		J6	47		
	SMQ	6		M8	75		J6	207		
	AA	329		B	90		J6	299		
	AA	714		B	249		J6	740		
	MD	191		B	404		J10	466		
	MD	313		B	462		J16	6		
	MF	152		B	482		J16	85		
	SAA	258		CAM	33		P2	31		
	SAA	740		TH	139		P2	123		
	SAA	771		AU	50		P4	66		
	SAA	825		AU	78		P5	50		
	SAA	856		AU	98		P6	167		
	SAA	894		AU	270		HI	56		
	SAA	1009		CI	353		MC	71		
	PDG	40	BETRAYS	MD	43		VP3	78		
	L4	84		HAP	747		VP6	28		
	L4	176	BETROTHED	AE10	1015		VP7	65		
	H2	51	BETS	PKA	27		G1	127		
	HAP	2221		PKA	34		G1	383		
	STS2	6		OAL	195		G2	55		
	J3	93	BETTER	UDH	29		G2	87		
	J6	415		UDH	102		G3	768		
	J10	129		AR	231		G3	732		
	J10	141		RH	4		G4	142		
	M1	845		PWG	54		G4	149		
	M9	160		LCA	41		AE1	290		
	SLT2	10		EMM	3		AE2	57		
	G1	574		PTL	21		AE2	72		
	G2	650		PCG1	21		AE2	239		
	G4	426		ECG1	40		AE2	248		
	G4	593		PAR	24		AE2	984		
	AE1	453		EMQW	16		AE2	999		
	AE2	78		SCD1	8		AE3	49		
	AE2	211		PUO1	19		AE3	590		
	AE2	573		PNH	11		AE3	647		
	AE7	293		EUO2	12		AE4	140		
	AE9	191		ML	22		AE4	325		
	AE9	476		PAL	35		AE4	623		
	AE11	1130		PKK	15		AE4	710		
	AE12	65		PCB	33		AE4	947		
	OAL	408		PCB	35		AE5	201		
	OAL	449		HP	148		AE5	552		
	OAL	659		HP	259		AE5	1080		
	OAL	726		UMR	6		AE6	736		
	KT1	288		PSF	30		AE6	824		
	KT2	510		PR	31		AE6	882		
	B	243		PUF	12		AE6	1081		
	CAM	290		AA	76		AE6	1168		
	CAM	378		AA	416		AE6	1171		
	M11	29		AA	430		AE8	622		
	WB	182		AA	630		AE9	227		
BETRAYED	LC	76		AA	885		AE9	776		
	DC	2		D	24		AE10	90		
	CM	62		SAA	391		AE10	582		

Word	Ref	No.
BETTER	AE10	674
	AE10	772
	AE10	1035
	AE11	266
	AE11	465
	AE12	450
	OAL	148
	OAL	426
	OAL	442
	MG	7
	MG	37
	DO	6
	DO	144
	KT1	250
	KT1	423
	KT2	158
	KT2	161
	KT2	163
	KT2	454
	KT3	469
	KT3	738
	KT3	853
	KT3	890
	KT3	886
	KT3	1087
	TJD	33
	TJD	92
	TJD	99
	TJD	122
	M8	181
	M8	305
	B	604
	B	667
	B	421
	B	448
	BP	9
	BP	148
	CAM	33
	CAM	55
	CAM	72
	CAM	233
	HIF	170
	HIF	227
	HIF	255
	C	193
	C	324
	C	375
	C	505
	C	549
	C	556
	C	804
	TH	180
	TH	148
	TH	229
	FL	575
	M12	67
	M12	283
	M12	717
	M12	724
	M12	798
	AU	59
	AU	213
	AU	240
	AU	415
	AU	542
	AU	544
	WB	54
	WB	126
	WB	145
	WB	414
	WB	420
	WB	544
	M15	289
	CI	201
	CI	237
	CI	253
	CI	315
	ETP	37
	STP	34
	SMP	20
	SMP	21
	SMP	65
	PMK	38
	AS	29
	PWR	37
BETTERED	G1	109
BETTERS	EMQ	7
	J3	180
	J6	214
BEVERAGE	G1	170
	G2	294
	G3	790
	KT2	15
	M15	499
BEVY	M12	304
BEWAIL	L3	239

Word	Ref	No.
BEWAIL	OAL	380
BEWAILED	AE6	318
	C	705
BEWAILS	AE1	146
BEWARE	AA	1005
	T23	87
	AT	5
	T27	24
	H3	48
	SSH	7
	J1	243
	J6	741
	J6	823
	J6	824
	P3	34
	P3	185
	VP3	145
	VP9	30
	G3	189
	G4	595
	AE10	226
	OAL	184
	OAL	444
	OAL	582
	OAL	663
	OAL	751
	OAL	859
	OAL	860
	TJD	32
	HIF	740
	C	178
	C	812
	TH	425
	WB	99
BEWARED	C	799
BEWILDERED	RL	189
	L2	11
	FL	611
BEWITCH	HAP	2020
	VP7	40
	OAL	504
BEWITCHED	AM	690
	VP3	158
BEZALIEL	SAA	941
	SAA	947
BIANOR'S	VP9	82
	M12	465
BIAS	MD	63
	MF	189
BIASED	AA	79
BIB-CRAVAT	PNH	27
BIBLE	RL	377
	RL	408
BIBLIS	OAL	319
BID	PWG	12
	EWG	15
	PMM	15
	PTL	19
	ECG1	21
	SCG1	25
	SLN	14
	SCD1	8
	PCB	6
	HP	155
	HP	172
	HP	246
	PSF	5
	T27	119
	NS	25
	HAP	1520
	J3	141
	J3	233
	J3	363
	VP4	57
	AE3	307
	AE4	348
	AE5	1103
	AE11	1200
	OAL	615
	OAE2	34
	C	601
	C	762
	M11	117
	M11	258
	M11	317
BIDDEN	T27	122
BIDDER	ESH	28
BIDDEST	P4	119
BIDE	AM	714
	HIF	339
BIDING	RL	338
BIDS	PR	1
	RL	198
	H9	17
	MS	25
	EH	31

Word	Ref	No.
BIDS	J3	219
	J3	456
	J6	624
	P4	72
	M1	302
	M1	451
	GK	79
	AE3	197
	AE3	348
	AE4	417
	AE5	616
	AE5	828
	AE9	307
	AE11	369
	OAL	551
	WB	45
BIER	J1	109
	P3	211
	AE6	317
	AE11	95
	AE11	98
	KT3	908
	KT3	916
	KT3	938
	M8	245
	C	167
BIERS	J10	386
BIG	AM	868
	ENH	7
	PCB	28
	MF	41
	HAP	505
	J6	12
	J6	250
	P1	266
	P2	10
	AE2	312
	AE10	194
	AE10	996
	AE11	134
	KT1	585
BIG-BONED	KT3	45
BIG-CORNED	AM	595
BIGLY	J10	164
BIGNESS	EL	264
BIGOTRY	HAP	142
BILANDERS	HAP	128
BILBO	PP	23
BILBO-GALLANTS	EDGA	5
BILE	C	147
BILKED	MF	104
BILL	EEL	31
	PR	15
	L3	145
	HAP	1932
	HAP	2244
	OAL	488
	MG	22
	TJD	72
	TJD	114
	C	51
	C	86
	M11	275
	M11	478
	M11	494
	M15	589
BILLETS-DOUX	EKA	1
BILLING	VP3	105
	M15	570
BILLOW	AM	610
	AE10	1086
	M11	200
	M11	226
	M11	369
BILLOWS	AR	9
	LC	141
	AM	516
	AM	938
	SCD2	12
	DA	43
	DA	185
	SAA	728
	SAA	983
	H3	19
	H29	95
	M1	446
	M13	93
	VP5	130
	G1	458
	G1	493
	G2	153
	G2	220
	G3	406
	G4	284
	G4	605
	G4	766

BILLOWS	AE1	127
	AE1	148
	AE1	177
	AE1	193
	AE1	721
	AE2	275
	AE2	569
	AE3	179
	AE3	258
	AE3	375
	AE3	731
	AE3	873
	AE3	883
	AE5	159
	AE5	165
	AE5	185
	AE5	208
	AE5	252
	AE5	1017
	AE5	1033
	AE6	636
	AE7	45
	AE7	417
	AE7	738
	AE7	994
	AE7	1103
	AE8	898
	AE9	147
	AE9	967
	AE10	284
	AE10	301
	AE10	408
	AE11	976
	AE12	545
	M11	52
	M11	128
	M11	139
	M11	165
BILLS	EEL	35
	PAR	7
	ELN	1
	SAA	254
	HAP	474
	HAP	2277
	J3	279
	J10	351
	C	170
BIND	AM	589
	AM	720
	AM	1051
	AM	1074
	E	32
	AA	277
	AA	414
	AA	771
	MF	64
	EC	31
	HAP	1096
	PTS	10
	P5	141
	M1	52
	M9	142
	M9	185
	VP4	20
	VP6	29
	VP6	39
	VP8	89
	VP8	103
	G1	322
	G1	480
	G4	574
	G4	584
	AE1	239
	AE1	437
	AE4	603
	AE4	914
	AE5	306
	AE8	366
	AE8	970
	AE12	1193
	OAL	35
	KT1	184
	KT2	62
	B	420
	BP	185
	CAM	50
	C	76
BINDING	MD	84
BINDS	M1	355
	M1	639
	M1	1025
	G1	430
	G2	25
	G2	222
	G4	633
	AE1	81

BINDS	AE1	113
	AE4	213
	AE4	350
	AE6	417
	AE8	905
	KT1	297
	C	511
	C	531
BIRD	PIE	9
	AM	348
	CM	100
	H2	78
	HAP	1756
	HAP	2300
	HAP	2307
	HAP	2408
	BR	275
	J6	241
	M13	36
	G2	433
	AE1	546
	AE5	332
	AE5	676
	AE6	343
	AE7	264
	AE9	762
	AE11	1114
	AE12	373
	AE12	385
	AE12	397
	AE12	1247
	OAL	445
	C	469
	M11	474
	M12	203
	M12	692
	M12	738
	M15	567
	G4	57
BIRDLIME	RH	3
BIRDS	SIE	6
	AM	44
	SAA	423
	EDG	42
	L1	16
	L3	69
	L4	196
	H2	43
	TA	380
	HAP	1224
	HAP	1715
	HAP	1722
	HAP	1898
	HAP	1944
	HAP	2244
	HAP	2250
	HAP	2269
	HAP	2285
	HAP	2358
	HAP	2505
	HAP	2533
	HAP	2538
	HAP	2545
	BR	172
	M1	95
	M9	103
	M13	136
	M13	160
	SFL	3
	VP3	83
	VP5	94
	G1	211
	G1	234
	G1	365
	G1	635
	G2	291
	G2	444
	G3	814
	G4	16
	G4	168
	G4	681
	AE3	12
	AE3	302
	AE3	341
	AE6	282
	AE6	987
	AE7	47
	AE8	41
	AE8	600
	AE10	781
	AE11	420
	AE11	696
	AE12	1265
	OAL	30
	OAL	308
	KT3	137

BIRDS	KT3	969
	C	91
	C	458
	C	585
	TH	61
	M11	333
	M11	490
	FL	46
	FL	318
	M12	20
	M12	30
	M12	699
	AU	74
	M15	139
	M15	536
	M15	699
	G1	569
	G2	84
BIRDS'	UDH	22
BIRTH	AR	131
	AR	288
	AM	174
	AM	851
	AM	866
	AM	1135
	EOE	13
	AA	364
	AA	369
	AA	482
	AA	636
	AA	900
	MF	148
	SAA	999
	SAA	1004
	RL	174
	RL	258
	ER	52
	L2	43
	L3	3
	L5	6
	AK	39
	AK	44
	AK	55
	HAP	297
	HAP	2224
	BR	122
	J1	35
	J1	160
	J6	1
	J6	19
	P5	59
	P6	133
	M1	6
	M1	179
	M1	331
	M1	512
	M1	558
	M1	571
	GK	89
	VP1	60
	VP4	12
	VP6	62
	VP8	62
	VP8	68
	VP10	53
	G1	5
	G1	16
	G1	127
	G1	196
	G1	373
	G1	668
	G2	13
	G2	70
	G2	365
	G2	462
	G2	781
	AE1	373
	AE1	453
	AE1	509
	AE1	853
	AE2	99
	AE3	128
	AE3	653
	AE4	3
	AE4	18
	AE4	258
	AE5	391
	AE5	1046
	AE6	804
	AE7	73
	AE7	286
	AE7	390
	AE7	1001
	AE8	171
	AE8	419
	AE9	730

Word	Ref	No.	Word	Ref	No.	Word	Ref	No.
BLAMES	AE12	895	BLAZE	OD	51	BLEEDING	M15	631
	AE12	1099		J1	237	BLEEDS	G3	759
	C1	355		M9	186		OAL	517
BLANCH	AE12	60		AE1	252	BLEMISH	TJD	31
BLANDISHMENT	J6	285		AE2	778	BLEMISHED	AM	784
	AE1	944		AE2	944	BLEND	HS	72
BLANDISHMENTS	AA	488		AE5	4	BLENDED	L4	219
	MD	258		AE5	695		GK	33
	M1	651		AE6	790		AE6	584
	KT3	317		AE6	1207		FL	347
	M10	54		AE8	785		WB	433
	CAM	209		AE11	216	BLESS	AR	72
	M12	542		AE11	294		AM	204
BLANK	EL	296		AE11	318		AM	560
	OD	9		KT3	182		AA	241
BLANKETS	MF	42		KT3	253		AA	378
BLASPHEME	SAA	466		M8	361		AA	728
	BR	280		BP	53		MF	139
BLASPHEMED	HAP	2457		M11	160		SAA	62
	AE5	223		FL	415		SAA	384
	AE8	10		WB	411		DOD	20
BLASPHEMERS	HAP	218		AS	27		L4	243
BLASPHEMING	C	517	BLAZED	AE3	380		L4	256
BLASPHEMY	HAP	56		AE4	428		T18	81
	MM	12		AE12	977		H29	76
BLAST	UDH	77		KT3	92		HAP	1537
	AM	448	BLAZING	H3	41		HAP	1881
	EAZ	33		HAP	1675		BR	84
	PC1	4		J3	12		J3	7
	ML	1		M1	349		J3	438
	CM	13		AE4	815		P2	127
	SAA	488		AE4	965		M9	146
	SAA	1041		AE7	1076		VP4	57
	H2	45		AE9	692		VP4	77
	HAP	1158		AE9	987		VP7	81
	BR	228		AE10	366		G1	45
	EL	5		AE12	451		G1	475
	J6	668		M12	389		G2	657
	M1	455		M12	800		G4	729
	M9	184	BLEACH	AE6	1003		AE1	566
	GK	88	BLEAK	ENH	29		AE1	1023
	VP2	84		G3	543		AE4	177
	VP7	37		AE2	762		AE4	475
	VP10	113		AE8	254		AE8	758
	G2	620	BLEAKY	HAP	1906		AE11	61
	G3	311		G3	489		AE11	872
	AE1	154	BLEAR	J6	155		AE12	291
	AE1	186		P3	85		AE12	1194
	AE2	1080	BLEAR-EYED	HAP	1088		DO	85
	AE3	520		J10	203		KT2	300
	AE3	569		P1	150		KT2	430
	AE5	968	BLEAT	VP4	55		KT3	1154
	AE6	126	BLEATING	T18	69		TJD	45
	AE6	484		M1	311		HIF	172
	AE6	817		H1	75		WB	30
	AE7	721		VP7	73		M15	715
	AE8	337		G3	491		C1	469
	AE10	301		G4	629		AS	56
	AE10	570		AE1	897		PWR	6
	AE11	919		AE7	749	BLESSE	MHD	8
	KT2	533		AE9	72	BLESSED	HS	67
	KT2	550		AE9	766		AR	129
	KT3	361		OAL	874		AR	153
	KT3	465	BLEATS	G3	826		AR	240
	KT3	592	BLED	HS	46		AM	1085
	M8	30		M1	997		TA	359
	CAM	177		M10	60		HAP	181
	FL	8	BLEED	STL	12		HAP	284
	FL	580		AA	715		HAP	1618
BLASTED	AM	992		AA	1011		HAP	1790
	MD	260		SAA	40		VP10	27
	H3	45		SAA	787		AE3	608
	VP1	25		SAA	900		AE8	950
	G2	425		J6	774		DO	74
	AE2	879		VP1	10		KT3	1143
	AE3	756		AE1	482		B	300
BLASTING	HAP	224		AE9	858		M10	97
	G1	224		KT2	366		M15	22
	KT3	404		TJD	56		GP	105
BLASTS	DA	185		M8	288	BLESSES	VP3	92
	L5	13	BLEEDING	DA	33		AS	38
	HAP	1734		SAA	705	BLESSING	HS	38
	P1	195		TA	295		SMA	63
	G1	325		BR	78		SMA	117
	G1	487		EL	13		VHH	51
	G2	158		G2	165		AM	1040
	AE3	191		AE1	579		SEL2	13
	AE7	575		AE4	90		ETC	27
	FL	375		AE6	603		STC	1
	AU	290		AE7	695		STC	3
BLATANT	HAP	802		AE9	595		STC	9
BLAZE	AM	897		AE11	541		SSF	7
	AM	922		AE11	1054		AA	276
	AK	144		AE12	564		SAA	30
	HAP	67		AE12	925		SAA	477
	HAP	1222		M11	415		SAA	508

BLESSING

SAA	1023
SDG	4
SDG	10
L1	44
L3	213
L3	308
L3	309
T18	6
FS4	11
TA	316
HAP	1451
BR	23
BR	64
BR	247
BR	277
BR	291
STS1	9
SKA3	15
SKA6	30
OD	48
J6	790
J10	305
GK	74
GK	96
G1	248
AE3	410
AE9	384
OAL	647
DO	97
KT1	440
KT3	1153
TJD	41
AS	29
AS	49
CI	506
AR	141

BLESSING'S
BLESSINGS

AR	137
PUF	26
SMA	41
SMA	71
SAA	645
SAA	1071
RL	51
L3	85
L3	127
L3	132
TA	297
TA	397
BR	270
VP1	7
G1	36
G2	8
AF	56
AF	61
KT1	430
HS	147
AR	1
AR	296
AR	317
AM	801
AM	1113
SMM2	3
SMM2	29
SMM2	30
PUO2	15
HP	96
HP	166
EMW	13
AA	43
AA	165
AA	350
AA	484
AA	553
MD	251
MF	8
SAA	282
SAA	991
SAA	993
RL	45
RL	133
RL	294
AT	114
L1	11
L2	36
T18	49
FS1	1
TA	251
TA	385
TA	422
TA	503
AK	2
AK	54
HAP	1273
HAP	1591
HAP	1945
SSC	58

BLEST (beside HS 147)

BLEST

BR	168
BR	186
STS1	1
STS3	8
EL	120
EL	292
J10	118
J10	390
J10	408
J10	431
P1	74
P2	112
M1	76
M1	215
M9	74
SLT1	1
SLT2	11
G1	55
G4	555
AE2	393
AE3	619
AE3	941
AE4	830
AE5	72
AE5	807
AE5	959
AE5	994
AE6	1228
AE7	69
AE7	77
AE7	179
AE10	8
OAL	842
DO	146
KT1	319
KT3	161
KT3	355
KT3	799
TJD	1
TJD	45
TJD	178
M8	5
M8	12
B	8
B	9
CAM	19
HIF	157
HIF	330
HIF	618
TH	6
FL	151
AU	208
M15	189
GP	7
CI	47
CI	261
CI	346
CI	436
STP	23

BLEW

AR	243
ESF	26
T27	127
HAP	1750
HAP	1798
M1	166
KT3	818
CAM	250

BLIGHT

BR	72
KT2	59

BLIGHTED

AE3	193

BLIGHTS

G4	468

BLIND

AR	45
AR	95
AM	731
AM	987
SMM2	1
PFD	17
SCD2	21
HP	100
AA	537
SAA	106
SAA	140
SAA	750
L2	11
L4	136
TA	498
HAP	697
HAP	824
HAP	1697
HAP	1838
J6	785
P1	110
M1	607
VP1	23
G1	266
AE2	59

BLIND

AE2	71
AE2	620
AE4	95
AE4	307
AE4	426
AE8	248
AE9	688
AE9	1024
AE10	698
AE11	804
AE11	1148
AE11	1283
KT1	235
KT1	437
KT2	354
KT2	549
TJD	104
M8	348
B	112
B	126
B	224
B	308
B	593
B	465
HIF	477
C	644
M12	378
WB	162
M15	332
M15	420
CI	324

BLINDED

AE1	480
AE2	320

BLINDER
BLINDFOLD

AE8	248
HAP	324
C	802

BLINDING
BLINDLY

AE12	657
AM	140
AM	797
PCG2	22
RL	23
J10	541
P5	244
VP6	52
AE2	535
AE4	312
CAM	281
CI	373
CI	491

BLINDS

AA	304
KT2	354
M11	196
CI	466

BLISS

AR	210
PEL	9
SEL3	23
SCG1	16
SM2	8
SLN	13
SSF	14
RL	35
L4	31
L4	192
T23	78
T27	3
H9	32
AK	10
HAP	148
HAP	387
HAP	1662
HAP	2484
BR	151
STS1	7
STS1	12
STS3	24
EL	250
EL	309
SSH	11
J6	279
J6	483
M9	130
M13	13
SLT1	4
G2	759
G3	109
OAL	366
OAL	754
OAL	813
KT1	68
KT2	1
KT3	130
KT3	794
KT3	799
KT3	1143
B	164
B	292

BLISS	B	452	BLOOD	HAP	277	BLOOD	AE5	469
	M10	75		HAP	280		AE5	527
	M10	99		HAP	350		AE5	551
	C	412		HAP	373		AE5	626
	C	420		HAP	421		AE5	964
	C	468		HAP	425		AE6	133
	C	472		HAP	428		AE6	356
	FL	120		HAP	435		AE6	492
	WB	507		HAP	1152		AE6	611
	WB	537		HAP	1321		AE6	896
BLISSES	DOD	17		HAP	1437		AE6	1035
BLISSFUL	HAP	158		HAP	1558		AE6	1057
	EL	183		HAP	1591		AE6	1129
	EL	209		HAP	1658		AE6	1146
	AE1	972		HAP	1762		AE7	60
	AE6	871		HAP	1980		AE7	422
	AE6	920		HAP	2271		AE7	438
	AE6	1202		HAP	2574		AE7	443
	AF	26		BR	160		AE7	469
	KT1	402		BR	213		AE7	476
	C	687		BR	218		AE7	517
BLISTERS	UDH	57		BR	274		AE7	596
	G3	840		OD	30		AE7	643
BLOAT	PC1	25		J1	62		AE7	744
BLOATED	J3	64		J1	153		AE7	752
	G2	268		J,3	446		AE7	756
	G4	800		J6	158		AE7	760
BLOBBER	L4	160		J6	238		AE7	822
	J3	154		J6	439		AE7	914
BLOCK	AE2	448		J6	806		AE7	992
BLOCKHEAD	PTS	14		J10	220		AE7	1067
	SKA4	11		J10	344		AE8	176
	SKA4	14		J10	465		AE8	634
	SKA4	17		P1	118		AE8	656
	EHC	20		P1	205		AE8	668
BLOCKHEADS	MD	47		M1	201		AE8	713
	PTS	15		M1	202		AE8	795
	P3	152		M1	207		AE8	855
BLOCKS	PCG1	20		M1	548		AE8	932
	SAA	406		M9	5		AE9	223
BLOOD	HS	48		M13	32		AE9	447
	AR	11		M13	216		AE9	470
	AR	34		GK	142		AE9	476
	DC	29		VP8	65		AE9	555
	PIE	10		G1	653		AE9	607
	AM	5		G1	661		AE9	633
	AM	1052		G1	674		AE9	949
	PMQ	29		G2	685		AE9	1017
	EWGR	18		G3	155		AE9	1024
	PM	16		G3	239		AE10	187
	A	7		G3	704		AE10	461
	PCD	16		G3	728		AE10	494
	EAZ	4		G3	773		AE10	577
	PC2	24		G4	19		AE10	586
	EAL	8		G4	435		AE10	680
	EKK	15		G4	776		AE10	776
	PCB	3		AE1	220		AE10	801
	PLG	7		AE1	268		AE10	873
	CM	1		AE1	440		AE10	1029
	HP	58		AE1	669		AE10	1057
	DA	200		AE1	883		AE10	1118
	UMR	1		AE2	140		AE10	1164
	EPF	9		AE2	162		AE10	1184
	PUF	21		AE2	164		AE11	14
	AA	11		AE2	174		AE11	38
	AA	96		AE2	482		AE11	118
	AA	136		AE2	492		AE11	130
	AA	294		AE2	764		AE11	234
	AA	314		AE2	684		AE11	334
	AA	326		AE2	749		AE11	527
	AA	641		AE2	756		AE11	590
	AA	947		AE2	792		AE11	641
	PLB	26		AE2	865		AE11	748
	MD	149		AE2	898		AE11	920
	MF	175		AE2	906		AE11	942
	SAA	149		AE2	979		AE11	960
	SAA	594		AE3	41		AE11	963
	SAA	680		AE3	60		AE11	990
	SAA	708		AE3	63		AE11	1033
	SAA	766		AE3	66		AE11	1068
	SAA	970		AE3	67		AE11	1176
	EDG	31		AE3	87		AE11	1218
	RL	88		AE3	93		AE12	49
	AT	35		AE3	817		AE12	81
	ER	45		AE3	822		AE12	123
	L4	214		AE3	871		AE12	342
	L4	241		AE4	293		AE12	409
	L4	270		AE4	303		AE12	466
	T23	108		AE4	523		AE12	472
	T27	94		AE4	659		AE12	512
	T27	113		AE4	901		AE12	624
	PAA	12		AE4	953		AE12	662
	AK	26		AE4	987		AE12	680
	HAP	13		AE5	51		AE12	724
	HAP	15		AE5	163		AE12	748
	HAP	134		AE5	429		AE12	776

Word	Ref	No.
BLOOD	AE12	1050
	AE12	1209
	AE12	1216
	AE12	1254
	AE12	1309
	AE12	1376
	OAL	271
	OAL	404
	AF	79
	DO	29
	DO	68
	DO	136
	KT1	19
	KT1	145
	KT1	468
	KT2	96
	KT2	127
	KT2	189
	KT2	199
	KT2	317
	KT2	329
	KT2	572
	KT2	583
	KT3	138
	KT3	348
	KT3	499
	KT3	527
	KT3	604
	KT3	629
	KT3	706
	KT3	753
	KT3	824
	KT3	989
	TJD	89
	TJD	110
	TJD	159
	M8	22
	M8	39
	M8	119
	M8	154
	M8	178
	M8	195
	M8	209
	M8	241
	M8	286
	M8	298
	M8	309
	B	6
	B	49
	B	343
	B	422
	B	428
	B	489
	B	504
	B	512
	B	546
	B	570
	B	605
	CAM	72
	CAM	116
	CAM	343
	HIF	62
	HIF	175
	HIF	294
	HIF	424
	C	58
	C	143
	C	156
	C	244
	C	404
	C	484
	TH	114
	TH	213
	TH	271
	TH	369
	FL	11
	M12	23
	M12	41
	M12	95
	M12	152
	M12	174
	M12	182
	M12	309
	M12	335
	M12	378
	M12	388
	M12	511
	M12	566
	M12	793
	AU	29
	AU	240
	AU	249
	AU	294
	AU	305
	AU	328
	AU	361
BLOOD	AU	415
	AU	608
	AU	609
	WB	91
	WB	382
	WB	402
	WB	439
	M15	101
	M15	114
	M15	120
	M15	202
	M15	631
	M15	685
	M15	710
	GP	111
	CI	41
	CI	603
	ETP	29
	STP	24
	AS	40
BLOODIER	ET	9
BLOODILY	ESH	1
BLOODLESS	HAP	1565
	AE2	739
	AE11	651
	M11	480
BLOODSHOT	M15	285
BLOODY	AM	220
	EM	17
	SCD2	3
	SCD2	24
	PAR	7
	DA	122
	AA	1014
	SAA	770
	EDGA	16
	PD	59
	HAP	35
	HAP	1368
	HAP	1675
	HAP	1952
	HAP	1986
	HAP	2365
	J3	67
	J3	399
	J6	857
	J10	268
	J10	297
	M1	161
	M13	21
	HI	7
	VP6	4
	G1	412
	AE1	142
	AE1	360
	AE1	488
	AE1	685
	AE2	222
	AE2	277
	AE2	353
	AE2	753
	AE3	39
	AE7	485
	AE7	633
	AE7	769
	AE7	839
	AE10	659
	AE10	682
	AE10	1200
	AE10	1234
	AE11	75
	AE11	237
	AE11	607
	AE11	976
	AE11	1315
	AE12	57
	AE12	1012
	OAL	360
	OAL	473
	KT1	144
	KT3	561
	TJD	114
	B	594
	HIF	201
	HIF	665
	M12	172
	M12	359
	AU	17
	M15	132
	M15	138
	M15	145
	M15	161
BLOODY-BONES	P5	24
BLOODY-MINDED	PRL	15
BLOOM	PC1	19
	SAA	992
BLOOM	SAA	1120
	T27	10
	NS	1
	G4	211
	AE10	450
	AE11	41
	KT3	83
	HIF	47
	HIF	169
	WB	532
	AS	51
BLOOMED	M12	526
BLOOMING	HP	40
	SAA	562
	T23	61
	AK	149
	J3	191
	SLT2	13
	MC	31
	G2	99
	AE3	440
	AE4	43
	AE5	386
	AE5	449
	AE7	78
	AE7	658
	AE12	37
	AE12	578
	OAL	64
	OAE1	24
	AF	10
	MG	15
	B	51
	CAM	159
	AS	59
BLOOMS	G1	273
	G4	269
	FL	14
	FL	105
BLOOMY	BR	13
	AE9	276
	FL	343
BLOSSOM	PC1	4
	BR	18
BLOSSOMED	ETG	7
BLOSSOMS	SMA	30
	HAP	1847
	VP3	83
	VP7	69
	KT1	172
	KT2	59
	AU	470
BLOT	PUO4	19
	HAP	1457
	AE11	592
	AE12	984
	BP	85
BLOTS	HAP	995
	AE1	1008
	AE2	291
	WB	144
BLOTTED	AE6	671
	AE10	1215
	KT2	90
BLOW	AR	243
	LCA	34
	PRL	14
	VHH	19
	AM	882
	AM	1215
	SCD2	18
	PAZ	33
	ML	39
	ETG	5
	AA	57
	AA	800
	OE	33
	OE	46
	L3	44
	L3	232
	L4	279
	T23	106
	H9	16
	TA	6
	TA	89
	TA	148
	TA	406
	TA	436
	TA	478
	AK	155
	HAP	898
	HAP	1734
	HAP	2355
	SKA5	10
	J1	11
	J1	224

BLOW	J3	406	BLOWS	AM	477	BLUSH	SCG1	21
	J3	420		AM	526		PM	8
	J10	416		AM	977		DA	118
	P5	14		AM	1015		AA	435
	M1	44		CM	87		HAP	1457
	M13	62		AA	744		P1	231
	VP1	26		L4	202		P3	57
	VP3	83		H29	97		VP4	34
	VP8	66		H2	45		VP10	25
	G1	580		HAP	324		G2	601
	G3	365		M1	444		AE11	83
	G3	549		M1	723		AE12	101
	G3	827		G1	454		DO	3
	G4	251		G2	268		DO	154
	AE1	150		G2	429		CAM	112
	AE1	329		G2	447		FL	615
	AE2	140		G3	175		M12	796
	AE2	184		G3	646		WB	289
	AE2	555		G4	249		CI	474
	AE2	806		AE2	655		EMKG	24
	AE2	1012		AE5	500	BLUSHED	SEL3	9
	AE4	605		AE5	568		J10	465
	AE5	137		AE5	577		M1	1054
	AE5	574		AE5	613		VP6	2
	AE5	594		AE7	534		AE7	36
	AE9	681		AE8	562		KT3	1135
	AE9	1013		AE8	590		M8	155
	AE9	1039		AE9	1092		CAM	122
	AE10	540		AE9	1101	BLUSHES	AM	475
	AE10	558		AE12	738		SLN	3
	AE10	662		AE12	1038		PR	6
	AE10	726		KT3	612		HAP	1129
	AE10	753		KT3	623		HAP	2108
	AE10	761		M8	266		M1	649
	AE10	1133		BP	52		CAM	199
	AE11	438		M11	392	BLUSHING	SCD1	12
	AE11	1029		M12	178		HP	84
	AE11	1181		M12	329		SKA2	10
	AE12	456		M12	644		M13	108
	AE12	462		AU	370		VP3	96
	AE12	532		CI	104		VP5	22
	AE12	714		CI	341		VP9	65
	AE12	774	BLUBBERED	CM	108		AE6	671
	AE12	1058		VP3	35		AE8	94
	AE12	1330		M11	392		OAL	144
	AE12	1373	BLUE	SMA	100		KT1	187
	OAL	621		PR	25		M8	76
	OAL	859		L4	103		CAM	108
	AF	156		J3	282		AU	277
	KT2	243		J10	331		CI	308
	KT3	555		P6	77	BLUSHT	MHD	3
	KT3	644		M13	230	BLUSTER	AE1	202
	M8	175		VP1	82	BLUSTERING	H29	100
	M8	239		VP2	67		M1	67
	M8	158		G1	546		G2	152
	M8	381		G1	607		AE6	484
	CAM	194		G4	476		AE12	542
	TH	27		G4	712		KT3	678
	M11	91		AE2	291		CI	403
	M11	204		AE2	513	BOAR	AT	113
	M12	49		AE3	91		H2	48
	M12	359		AE5	114		HAP	43
	M12	394		DO	44		HAP	156
	M12	434		KT3	74		HAP	293
	M12	485		HIF	552		J1	31
	M12	518		C	52		P1	137
	M12	585		C	457		M1	416
	CI	372		FL	551		M13	135
	CI	601		WB	434		VP2	83
BLOWN	HS	85	BLUECAP	PUO3	8		VP7	41
	AM	85	BLUE-EYED	HI	19		VP10	89
	AM	867		AE2	243		G3	397
	STL	7		HIF	310		G4	589
	AA	278		M12	208		AE1	448
	MD	27	BLUES	G4	268		AE4	229
	OE	5	BLUFF	HAP	2438		AE6	1095
	T27	13		OAL	827		AE7	424
	PMS	18	BLUISH	AE3	684		AE10	1000
	EL	6	BLUNDERING	SAA	413		M8	3
	G3	217		PK	31		M8	18
	AE1	640	BLUNDERS	KT1	435		M8	99
	AE3	457	BLUNT	AM	500		M8	121
	AE7	37		P1	210		M8	171
	AE7	739		M1	630		M8	190
	AE8	175		AE6	992	BOARD	AM	518
	AE11	209		WB	285		SCD2	17
	AE12	548	BLUNTED	HAP	1979		PAL	39
	AE12	761		M1	14		AA	618
	AE12	883		M1	632		HAP	1248
	KT1	594		G2	413		HAP	2254
	KT3	363		AE7	868		PDS	2
	WB	2		AE8	572		J1	210
	M15	460		M12	183		J3	144
	CI	229		M12	643		J6	143
BLOWS	AR	104	BLUNTLY	M9	9		J6	213
	AM	59	BLUNTNESS	HAP	2221		J6	565

Word	Ref	No.	Word	Ref	No.	Word	Ref	No.
BOARD	P3	76	BOAST	OAL	845	BODIES	EL	237
	VP4	77		MG	37		EL	252
	G4	196		KT3	884		J3	417
	AE3	596		TJD	140		J10	298
	AE4	800		M8	235		M1	1
	AE5	207		CAM	16		M1	573
	AE7	683		HIF	196		M9	143
	AE10	651		HIF	267		VP6	90
	AE11	512		HIF	436		G1	660
	OAL	268		M12	622		G3	214
	OAE2	6		M12	782		G3	713
	OAE2	31		AU	153		G4	124
	BP	87		AU	380		G4	183
	BP	99		AU	433		G4	275
	BP	125	BOASTED	MF	189		G4	785
	HIF	215		AK	74		AE1	143
	HIF	433		HAP	2384		AE1	268
	HIF	802		J1	95		AE2	283
	C	75		M1	1052		AE2	351
	M12	312		G4	460		AE2	792
	M12	356		AE4	305		AE3	821
BOARDED	J10	211		AE5	521		AE4	757
BOARD-WAGES	J1	142		AE9	733		AE5	567
BOAR'S	M8	195		AE10	763		AE5	763
BOARS	J1	212		AE11	80		AE5	1054
	VP5	119		AE12	391		AE6	409
	G3	387		M8	173		AE6	530
	G3	625		C	468		AE6	591
	AE1	896	BOASTER	VP3	73		AE6	785
	AE7	20		AE5	530		AE6	924
	AE11	303		AE9	869		AE6	967
	KT2	204		AE11	1064		AE6	1137
	KT2	589		AE11	1240		AE8	199
	M12	423		M12	631		AE9	197
BOAR-SPEAR	M8	110		AU	353		AE9	480
BOAST	LC	5		AU	416		AE10	462
	DC	46	BOASTFUL	AM	546		AE11	152
	PWG	47		HAP	154		AE11	156
	AM	223	BOASTING	AM	460		AE11	942
	AM	671		EMK	20		AE11	1020
	AM	1194		T27	81		AE12	320
	AM	1206		AK	120		AE12	724
	PMQ	26		AE7	838		AE12	775
	EMQW	7		AE12	776		AE12	1025
	ECD	9		AU	523		KT1	84
	PUO2	30	BOASTS	AM	755		KT1	128
	CM	27		SAA	960		KT3	434
	HP	52		L3	55		KT3	568
	HP	57		BR	147		KT3	596
	HP	218		M1	1048		B	702
	HP	242		VP8	141		BP	186
	DA	207		G1	149		CAM	294
	PUO4	1		G2	651		M11	430
	AA	162		AE1	775		FL	483
	AA	829		AE7	654		M15	102
	MD	194		AE11	533		M15	320
	SAA	1001		M12	806		M15	366
	ER	41		AU	427		M15	395
	L3	252	BOAT	MF	49		M15	480
	T18	31		J1	123	BODING	MN	2
	T18	43		M1	402		HAP	1774
	T27	3		G4	285		J10	202
	HAP	431		AE6	530		M9	156
	HAP	1947	BOATMAN	AE6	433		G1	654
	BR	309		AE6	447		G3	410
	ETS	16		AE6	522		AE4	671
	ODA	21	BOAT'S	G1	290		AE4	949
	PSH	24	BOATS	AM	627		AE7	96
	J3	211		G1	355		AE12	115
	J3	342		AE10	403		AE12	907
	J6	147	BOATSMEN	M15	449		AE12	1247
	J6	255	BOB	J6	588		OAL	464
	J10	14	BOBBING	P1	37		KT3	263
	J10	479	BODE	PAL	4		HIF	156
	P3	54	BODES	G1	577		C	424
	P4	40		G1	608		M12	16
	P6	108		C	111	BODY	UDH	27
	VP5	20		C	399		UDH	36
	VP6	27	BODIES	AR	59		UDH	98
	VP8	10		SMA	78		AR	164
	G2	307		SMA	120		AM	253
	G2	341		LC	149		AM	947
	G2	757		AM	211		S	14
	G3	351		AM	224		A	13
	AE1	202		AM	1016		CM	141
	AE2	250		PMM	12		AA	157
	AE2	794		MD	253		AA	167
	AE5	634		L2	42		PPC	17
	AE5	688		L3	2		AT	55
	AE6	1212		L3	18		L2	23
	AE8	752		L3	22		L3	61
	AE9	230		L4	78		L3	108
	AE9	1058		L4	296		L3	256
	AE10	100		H2	94		L4	138
	AE12	486		HAP	101		H2	83
	OAL	29		HAP	320		TA	116

BODY			BODY			BOLD		
	HAP	94		M8	386		AM	638
	HAP	97		B	712		AM	746
	HAP	103		M10	30		AM	831
	HAP	421		CAM	95		AM	890
	HAP	714		CAM	127		AM	916
	HAP	1757		CAM	198		AM	967
	EL	375		CAM	309		PT	21
	J3	87		C	54		PA	19
	J10	280		C	110		PTL	12
	J10	419		C	115		ECG2	18
	J10	549		C	165		PMQW	13
	P2	74		C	180		PCD	28
	P3	114		C	279		SCD2	5
	P3	214		TH	196		EAZ	22
	P4	77		M11	87		PKK	13
	P6	81		M11	220		PTC	14
	M1	23		M11	381		CM	79
	M1	529		M11	459		AA	102
	M1	589		M11	480		AA	153
	M1	743		FL	467		AA	205
	M13	155		M12	133		AA	367
	VP5	27		M12	201		AA	514
	VP10	72		M12	230		MD	66
	G2	404		M12	237		MD	214
	G3	120		M12	488		SAA	155
	G4	140		M12	648		SAA	292
	G4	151		M12	660		SAA	835
	G4	429		AU	558		SAA	860
	G4	541		WB	208		EDG	6
	AE1	679		WB	318		RL	312
	AE2	357		M15	227		PD	15
	AE2	874		M15	673		EC	19
	AE3	58		M15	681		L2	54
	AE3	234		CI	59		H3	38
	AE3	758		CI	100		H9	9
	AE3	831		CI	212		TA	477
	AE4	35		STP	27		AK	123
	AE4	912		ESK	29		AK	127
	AE4	934	BODY'S	DC	30		HAP	301
	AE5	117		M1	547		HAP	903
	AE5	194	BOEOTIAN	M1	425		HAP	1165
	AE5	360	BOG	PTP	27		HAP	1381
	AE5	479	BOGLAND	PP	31		HAP	1493
	AE5	561	BOGS	J3	482		HAP	1527
	AE5	584		J10	75		HAP	1723
	AE6	231		M1	823		SKA1	12
	AE6	256		G3	653		ESH	19
	AE6	314		M15	411		ESH	29
	AE6	318	BOIL	AA	136		J1	111
	AE6	683		L4	86		J1	228
	AE6	864		L4	123		J1	245
	AE6	1224		G1	280		J3	188
	AE7	681		G3	373		J6	12
	AE7	729		G3	684		J6	83
	AE7	745		G4	399		J6	136
	AE8	47		G4	436		J6	561
	AE8	294		AE1	296		P1	191
	AE9	278		AE3	754		P1	236
	AE9	411	BOILED	SAA	928		P1	247
	AE9	496		AE12	6		P2	122
	AE9	556		HIF	285		M1	179
	AE9	651	BOILING	AA	38		M1	629
	AE9	746		HAP	1556		M1	1061
	AE9	837		J6	806		HI	97
	AE9	960		P3	238		MC	57
	AE10	521		G1	443		GK	79
	AE10	563		AE1	153		G1	60
	AE10	681		AE8	557		G2	506
	AE10	687		AE9	1024		G3	177
	AE10	705		AE11	234		G4	585
	AE10	992		AE12	969		G4	817
	AE10	1176		KT2	329		AE1	173
	AE10	1305		BP	106		AE1	189
	AE11	75		HIF	360		AE1	749
	AE11	90		C	147		AE2	340
	AE11	97		AU	5		AE2	449
	AE11	632		M15	313		AE2	477
	AE11	889	BOILS	HAP	1115		AE2	603
	AE11	895		J1	67		AE2	988
	AE11	904		M1	299		AE3	21
	AE11	1102		G1	393		AE3	222
	AE11	1206		AE9	237		AE5	219
	AE12	28	BOISTEROUS	MC	10		AE6	254
	AE12	413		AE7	724		AE7	613
	AE12	445		B	159		AE8	10
	AE12	458		AU	551		AE8	435
	AE12	781	BOLA	AE6	1051		AE9	3
	AE12	1356	BOLD	HS	50		AE9	29
	OAL	502		HS	82		AE9	112
	OAL	571		AR	29		AE9	137
	OAL	607		AR	37		AE9	310
	KT3	782		RH	69		AE9	400
	KT3	909		AM	214		AE9	450
	KT3	978		AM	310		AE9	456
	TJD	187		AM	373		AE9	481
	TJD	209					AE9	708

BOLD	AE9	771	BONDAGE	KT1	394	BOOKS	PLT	27		
	AE9	915		KT1	502		PTP	19		
	AE9	930		KT3	1009	BOOM	ML	32		
	AE9	985	BONDMEN	P5	101	BOON	EKK	1		
	AE9	1039	BONDS	AR	152		G4	753		
	AE9	1050		E	15		KT3	187		
	AE10	187		AA	387		HIF	672		
	AE10	224		MD	259		WB	104		
	AE10	398		VP1	41		WB	301		
	AE10	453		AE2	184	BOOR	ECD	6		
	AE10	490		AE5	435	BOOT	J3	332		
	AE10	813		KT1	251	BOOTED	J16	18		
	AE11	70		KT1	266	BOOTH'S	AR	145		
	AE11	512		KT1	384	BOOTLESS	WB	109		
	AE11	689		KT1	386	BOOTS	SAA	266		
	AE11	974		KT2	107		PP	23		
	AE12	1139		KT2	477		J6	362		
	OAL	275		TJD	193		G4	458		
	OAL	688		HIF	33	BOOTY	AM	830		
	KT3	292		HIF	794		CI	293		
	M8	50		WB	136	BORACHIO	P5	216		
	M8	61	BONE	AE10	194	BORDERED	AT	52		
	M8	189		AE10	536		FL	90		
	B	134		AE10	584	BORDERING	VP1	71		
	B	286		KT1	342		AE5	140		
	CAM	274		C	766		AE12	106		
	HIF	127		M12	384	BORDERS	HAP	1240		
	HIF	465	BONES	DA	174		AE7	47		
	C	129		SAA	338		AE10	495		
	M12	292		AK	184		AE10	827		
	M12	342		J3	414		AE11	827		
	M12	463		P3	96		KT2	532		
	AU	298		M1	517		BP	78		
	AU	318		M1	529		FL	344		
	AU	548		M1	550		M15	595		
	WB	278		VP3	157	BORE	AR	116		
	CI	36		G1	667		AR	208		
	CI	536		G3	697		RH	40		
	PTP	32		G4	436		RH	57		
	ETP	40		AE3	821		AM	99		
BOLDER	SEL3	21		AE5	40		AM	363		
	HP	250		AE5	562		AM	484		
	J6	395		AE5	1029		AM	518		
	M11	108		AE5	1127		AM	596		
BOLDEST	AE10	1064		AE6	450		AM	771		
	M12	610		AE7	5		AM	822		
BOLDLY	HS	121		AE8	515		PC1	16		
	LC	69		AE11	324		CM	79		
	EWG	16		AE12	60		AA	13		
	AM	872		KT1	585		AA	90		
	PMQ	54		KT3	606		AA	520		
	SEL1	7		CAM	342		MD	317		
	EUO	37		M15	72		MF	58		
	SAA	414	BONNY	PUO3	8		RL	129		
	SAA	972	BOOBY	PSH	10		ER	2		
	SAA	1132	BOOK	VP3	34		T27	1		
	P2	13		AA	654		T27	76		
	G2	456		RL	125		T27	105		
	AE3	799		RL	139		TA	37		
	OAL	162		RL	146		TA	355		
	B	386		RL	172		TA	374		
	PWR	36		RL	234		PAA	6		
BOLDNESS	RH	12		RL	264		EAA	25		
	PWG	8		RL	364		AK	126		
	HP	19		RL	389		HAP	131		
BOLE	M1	748		RL	400		HAP	394		
	VP7	54		TA	491		HAP	447		
	G2	110		AK	181		HAP	626		
	CAM	362		HH	39		HAP	1232		
BOLES	VP10	108		HAP	855		HAP	1599		
BOLOGNA'S	HS	63		BR	227		BR	139		
BOLT	M1	632		BR	107		BR	235		
	AE6	802		EL	292		EL	176		
	C	523		OD	1		EL	205		
	M12	738		P1	20		ODA	53		
BOLTED	T23	31		P1	257		ODA	55		
	KT3	361		P3	16		MS	10		
	KT3	970		C	479		J1	133		
BOLTS	AA	67		FL	615		J10	409		
	HAP	98		WB	157		P1	145		
	M1	200		GP	43		M1	962		
	G1	447		EMKG	35		G1	652		
	AE1	63		AS	43		G2	97		
	AE1	404	BOOK-LEARNED	PPC	20		G2	566		
	AE3	770		SKA4	18		G3	143		
	AE4	307		J6	561		G3	557		
	AE7	844		P3	152		AE1	4		
	AE8	465	BOOKS	DC	42		AE1	162		
BOND	AA	175		PUO5	22		AE1	446		
	HAP	1024		SAA	961		AE1	874		
	AE3	78		TA	190		AE1	921		
	KT1	331		AK	79		AE1	984		
	B	411		HAP	680		AE2	48		
BONDAGE	SAA	714		EH	5		AE2	363		
	J6	293		J3	338		AE2	989		
	HI	134		J3	357		AE3	180		

BORE	AE3	354	BORE	FL	251	BORN	P1	236
	AE3	371		FL	267		P3	25
	AE3	660		FL	270		P4	13
	AE3	824		FL	355		P4	40
	AE3	833		M12	55		P4	62
	AE4	197		M12	237		P5	62
	AE4	860		M12	366		P6	41
	AE5	50		M12	433		M1	555
	AE5	154		M12	465		M1	603
	AE5	158		M12	743		M1	690
	AE5	339		M12	768		M9	6
	AE5	548		AU	79		M9	14
	AE5	624		AU	443		M13	2
	AE5	648		AU	510		HI	108
	AE5	729		M15	77		MC	60
	AE5	740		M15	606		MC	71
	AE6	19		M15	631		GK	56
	AE6	169		GP	7		G1	95
	AE6	305		GP	25		G1	226
	AE6	332		CI	269		G2	573
	AE6	433		CI	319		G4	142
	AE6	463		CI	375		G4	463
	AE6	486		ETP	9		AE3	225
	AE6	690	BOREAN	AE10	487		AE4	286
	AE7	235	BOREAS	HAP	1914		AE4	500
	AE7	338		M1	79		AE6	576
	AE7	511		M1	442		AE6	710
	AE7	922		G1	135		AE6	736
	AE7	1045		G2	429		AE6	882
	AE7	1054		G3	309		AE6	1036
	AE8	183		G3	549		AE6	1040
	AE8	440		AE1	147		AE6	1055
	AE8	641		AE3	369		AE6	1060
	AE8	770		AE12	542		AE6	1081
	AE9	153	BORED	J1	159		AE7	283
	AE9	379		AE2	357		AE7	308
	AE9	1104		AE3	871		AE7	330
	AE10	250		AE9	588		AE7	386
	AE10	270		AE11	17		AE7	519
	AE10	294		M12	181		AE7	992
	AE10	317		AU	189		AE7	1002
	AE10	532		CI	604		AE9	261
	AE10	902	BORING	G3	438		AE10	209
	AE10	923	BORN	GP	95		AE10	437
	AE10	1270		HS	27		AE10	758
	AE11	55		AR	237		AE10	996
	AE11	212		RH	105		AE11	814
	AE11	299		SMA	99		AE11	1038
	AE11	832		LCA	26		AE12	45
	AE11	1094		AM	698		AE12	195
	AE11	1118		AM	704		AE12	409
	AE11	1235		EM	6		AE12	1032
	AE12	145		ECD	5		AE12	1225
	AE12	310		EOE	16		AE12	1272
	AE12	439		CM	72		OAL	11
	AE12	522		CM	130		OAL	222
	AE12	560		DA	40		OAL	491
	AE12	748		DA	177		MM	42
	AE12	780		AA	26		DO	29
	AE12	946		AA	103		KT1	226
	AE12	1000		AA	172		KT1	289
	AE12	1069		AA	539		KT1	307
	AE12	1339		AA	954		KT2	338
	OAL	365		AA	963		KT2	396
	OAL	379		MF	89		KT2	609
	OAL	632		RL	80		KT3	80
	DO	43		RL	141		KT3	738
	DO	70		RL	327		KT3	883
	KT1	100		ER	55		TJD	202
	KT1	115		L1	4		B	322
	KT1	550		L1	37		B	510
	KT2	5		L3	64		B	557
	KT2	196		L3	238		B	473
	KT2	522		T27	79		M10	99
	KT2	647		H2	7		CAM	62
	KT3	49		AK	27		CAM	374
	KT3	53		AK	47		C	194
	KT3	88		AK	76		C	562
	KT3	193		AK	88		TH	125
	KT3	714		HAP	601		M12	241
	KT3	918		EMI	1		M12	262
	KT3	930		BR	9		M15	170
	KT3	938		BR	118		M15	177
	KT3	945		BR	143		M15	390
	M8	349		BR	208		M15	656
	BP	35		J1	159		CI	50
	CAM	13		J3	142		CI	497
	CAM	47		J3	150		AS	21
	CAM	383		J6	18		PWR	41
	TH	297		J6	35	BORNE	HS	2
	TH	355		J6	115		LC	114
	M11	199		J6	125		AM	225
	M11	203		J6	769		AM	493
	FL	172		J10	202		PEL	27
	FL	189		J10	486		HP	160
	FL	198		P1	139		DA	116

BORNE

DA	146
MF	215
H29	62
TA	104
TA	421
J1	46
J1	100
J1	219
J3	389
J3	408
J6	743
J6	847
J10	183
J10	210
M1	402
M13	182
VP6	25
VP8	144
G1	434
G2	269
G3	47
G3	172
G4	373
G4	761
AE1	615
AE2	406
AE2	503
AE2	567
AE2	590
AE3	103
AE3	420
AE3	571
AE5	519
AE6	213
AE6	313
AE6	484
AE7	393
AE7	716
AE7	819
AE7	967
AE8	53
AE8	122
AE8	715
AE9	401
AE9	588
AE10	246
AE10	710
AE10	945
AE10	1219
AE11	10
AE11	97
AE11	119
AE11	136
AE11	313
AE11	395
AE11	915
AE11	1168
AE12	321
AE12	860
AE12	992
KT2	174
KT3	627
KT3	1123
M8	385
HIF	191
C	86
C	704
C	723
M11	83
FL	408
AU	70

BORROW

PEL	34
RL	51
J6	470
P5	92
G1	96
OAL	494
STP	33

BORROWED

HS	25
EEL	8
CM	52
HP	47
RL	1
H3	49
AK	76
HAP	50
HAP	504
HAP	1155
J3	45
J6	103
P1	168
M1	1053
AE1	565
AE2	574
AE3	765
KT2	133
KT2	280
KT2	650
AU	265
AS	5

BOSOM

AM	99
AM	142
DA	203
SAA	911
T27	91
AK	77
J3	91
P5	49
M13	64
G1	65
G2	448
G3	557
G4	19
G4	299
AE1	65
AE1	488
AE1	1007
AE3	130
AE3	544
AE3	664
AE4	120
AE4	240
AE4	854
AE6	611
AE8	946
AE9	369
AE9	595
AE10	1159
AE10	1193
AE11	55
AE12	535
AE12	1206
AE12	1375
OAL	597
OAL	861
OAE2	45
KT1	429
KT1	556
KT2	86
M8	237
M10	78
HIF	285
M11	305
M12	116
M12	574
WB	199
CI	101
CI	104
CI	105
AE10	61
KT1	150
M8	390

BOSOMS

SAA	485

BOTCHED

BOTCHES HAP 1115
BOTCHING J3 407
BOTTLED PCB 29
BOTTLES PD 27
BOTTOM RH 14

AK	111
OD	36
P3	55
G4	557
G4	618
AE1	1037
AE2	379
AE5	662
AE6	419
AE7	645
AE7	740
AE11	583
AE11	1220
AE12	624
AE12	969
KT3	955
M8	95
HIF	503
C	352
M11	129
SIE	6
PC1	14
AT	24

BOUGH

VP1	25
G2	164
G4	806
AE6	210
AE6	296
AE6	303
AE6	549
AE6	860
AE6	866
AE10	1189
FL	44

BOUGH

BOUGHS

FL	105
SMA	132
DA	107
T18	71
M1	413
M1	744
M1	766
M13	72
M13	118
VP1	1
VP1	116
VP5	61
VP7	90
G1	235
G2	26
G2	114
G2	401
G2	507
G2	519
G2	596
G2	752
G4	394
G4	429
AE2	702
AE4	641
AE5	176
AE5	860
AE6	311
AE6	958
AE7	326
AE11	6
BP	55
BP	195
CAM	344
CAM	365
FL	282
FL	319
M12	297
M15	587

BOUGHT

DC	7
E	21
DA	126
SAA	21
TA	402
TA	490
HAP	1534
HAP	1772
BR	179
J3	124
J6	39
J6	482
HI	112
VP1	44
VP2	44
G1	184
G4	573
AE1	507
AE2	162
AE2	163
AE4	309
AE7	438
AE7	596
AE11	38
AE11	334
AE11	354
AE11	396
AE11	651
DO	68
KT3	411
KT3	1153
TJD	140
TJD	159
HIF	244
EDGA	35
T23	96
PSH	4

BOUNCE

AE11	1283

BOUNCED
BOUNCING
BOUND

KT1	556
EWR	27
DC	17
PWG	57
PRL	21
AM	465
AM	821
PEL	7
PAZ	9
AA	54
AA	923
MD	236
SAA	367
SAA	665
EDG	9
AT	51
MO	24
L1	18
L4	282

BOUND		
	H9	5
	H29	5
	TA	120
	AK	189
	HAP	438
	HAP	1024
	HAP	1242
	HAP	2100
	HAP	2247
	J10	291
	P1	198
	P5	169
	M1	69
	M1	223
	M1	426
	VP2	69
	VP2	76
	VP6	37
	G2	576
	G3	137
	G3	181
	G3	302
	G4	585
	AE1	69
	AE1	392
	AE1	405
	AE2	85
	AE2	208
	AE3	107
	AE4	57
	AE4	218
	AE4	365
	AE4	449
	AE5	12
	AE5	93
	AE5	354
	AE5	1002
	AE6	839
	AE6	903
	AE7	137
	AE7	145
	AE7	183
	AE7	272
	AE7	294
	AE7	587
	AE7	1111
	AE8	296
	AE8	345
	AE8	378
	AE10	1059
	AE11	574
	AE11	659
	AE11	835
	AE11	862
	AE11	898
	AE11	931
	AE11	949
	AE11	1067
	AE11	1143
	AE12	22
	AE12	306
	AE12	413
	AE12	512
	AE12	1300
	OAL	299
	AF	7
	KT1	298
	KT1	309
	KT1	392
	KT1	486
	KT2	19
	KT2	128
	KT2	370
	KT3	58
	KT3	517
	KT3	614
	KT3	651
	KT3	1028
	M8	66
	M8	355
	B	233
	B	643
	BP	31
	BP	166
	HIF	257
	HIF	550
	C	158
	C	370
	C	493
	C	545
	C	550
	C	569
	M11	394
	FL	231
	FL	551
	FL	578

BOUND		
	M12	47
	M12	58
	AU	129
	WB	234
	WB	256
	WB	328
	M15	339
	CI	251
	STP	24
	PWR	4
	PWR	26

BOUNDED		
	LC	34
	LC	89
	L2	25
	HAP	31
	HAP	205
	GK	147
	VP6	54
	AE7	307
	CAM	197
	C	747
	M12	637

BOUNDING		
	M1	47
	VP6	54
	AE8	300
	AE10	809
	AE12	175
	KT3	702
	M11	52
	M11	141

BOUNDLESS		
	AR	299
	DC	26
	MD	134
	SAA	1019
	RL	188
	L1	25
	H3	33
	BR	341
	J16	80
	M13	16
	AE4	484
	HIF	115
	C	282

BOUNDS		
	LC	31
	SCG2	8
	AA	164
	MD	239
	SAA	42
	SAA	762
	HAP	2547
	EL	76
	EL	241
	EL	280
	J16	60
	J16	61
	P5	88
	M1	464
	M1	719
	M9	3
	GK	41
	VP2	102
	VP7	32
	G1	193
	G4	686
	AE1	378
	AE3	917
	AE4	98
	AE5	616
	AE6	200
	AE6	742
	AE8	617
	AE9	744
	AE10	657
	AE12	799
	AF	164
	AF	174
	KT3	809
	KT3	1032
	HIF	390
	TH	242
	AU	71
	M15	639
	AA	872
	AA	893
	MD	168
	L3	127
	L5	17
	H2	29
	TA	336
	HAP	2246
	BR	266
	EL	86
	J6	25
	P2	20
	P6	36
	VP8	138

BOUNTEOUS		

BOUNTEOUS		
	G1	248
	G2	13
	G2	371
	G3	280
	G3	498
	AE1	115
	AE3	594
	AE3	623
	AE11	536
	B	48

BOUNTEOUSLY	CI	489
BOUNTIES'	SAA	63
BOUNTIFUL	AM	693
	HAP	2468
	P5	158
	ODA	28

BOUNTY	RH	80
	AM	182
	AM	615
	AM	1145
	PMM	15
	J3	7
	M9	140
	AE5	464
	AE6	901
	AE6	902
	AF	81
	WB	447
	AS	84
	AS	92

BOUT	EM	21
	PC2	12
	J6	369
	OAL	102
	OAE2	61

BOUTS	J3	226
	J10	354

BOW	HS	74
	PMQ	15
	EUO	27
	ESF	27
	SAA	191
	HAP	415
	EKA	2
	LS	10
	J6	251
	P3	117
	M1	611
	M1	699
	M1	962
	VP3	18
	VP10	85
	G1	249
	G1	415
	G2	35
	G2	173
	G2	774
	G2	629
	G3	536
	G3	770
	AE1	264
	AE1	439
	AE1	966
	AE3	701
	AE5	87
	AE5	118
	AE5	679
	AE5	688
	AE5	787
	AE5	855
	AE7	221
	AE7	692
	AE8	224
	AE8	967
	AE9	690
	AE9	776
	AE9	804
	AE9	826
	AE9	865
	AE9	900
	AE10	1070
	AE11	859
	AE11	883
	AE11	970
	AE11	1138
	AE11	1244
	AE11	1251
	AE11	1266
	AE12	580
	AE12	1187
	AE12	1240
	OAL	239
	OAE1	25
	KT2	232
	KT2	522
	KT2	647

Word	Ref	No.
BOW	KT3	268
	KT3	935
	KT3	953
	M8	73
	M8	152
	B	85
	CAM	379
	HIF	58
	HIF	70
	HIF	73
	HIF	111
	HIF	616
	HIF	626
	M11	266
	M11	322
	FL	357
	FL	471
	M12	428
	M12	744
	SMP	26
BOWED	AK	104
	M1	875
	MC	39
	AE9	863
	KT2	346
	KT3	689
	M8	293
	HIF	677
	FL	191
	M12	107
	AU	587
BOWELS	AM	316
	CM	105
	CM	106
	M13	181
	AE2	26
	AE2	442
	AE3	751
	AE7	694
	AE10	1104
	AE11	1115
	OAL	375
	M8	177
	M8	291
	CAM	296
	TH	191
	M12	521
	M15	126
	M15	472
	M15	542
	G4	425
	G4	800
BOWER	AT	29
	HAP	158
	STS3	2
	VP2	70
	VP9	83
	G4	472
	AE11	100
	B	216
	B	298
	HIF	172
	C	504
	FL	78
	FL	122
	FL	404
	FL	425
	FL	427
	FL	436
BOWERS	G2	702
	SAA	880
	G4	75
	AE1	583
	AE1	955
	AE8	132
	AE10	79
	AE10	134
	HIF	26
	FL	500
BOWING	AA	689
	AE11	186
BOWL	J6	805
	J10	38
	P2	6
	P3	203
	P6	36
	P6	113
	VP7	47
	G3	446
	AE1	1017
	AE1	1019
	AE1	1035
	AE4	745
	AE8	367
	AE9	353
	AE12	619
BOWL	KT3	945
	HIF	784
	HIF	802
	M12	437
	M12	444
BOWLS	AR	188
	PAL	33
	L2	31
	T18	18
	PDS	21
	P1	65
	P5	264
	M13	131
	VP3	55
	VP5	106
	VP5	107
	G1	405
	G2	725
	G4	544
	G4	547
	AE1	898
	AE1	1013
	AE2	1039
	AE3	93
	AE3	292
	AE3	455
	AE5	102
	AE5	121
	AE5	350
	AE6	355
	AE7	196
	AE8	235
	AE8	242
	AE9	208
	AE11	1084
	AE12	430
	OAL	634
	KT2	506
	KT3	989
	BP	104
	BP	122
	C	33
	M12	216
	M12	339
	M12	762
	WB	21
	CI	568
BOWS	PMQ	21
	G3	48
	G4	445
	AE1	463
	AE5	664
	AE5	647
	AE9	905
	AE10	248
	HIF	706
	FL	542
	FL	544
	M12	788
BOWSTRING	AE11	1249
BOWSY	J10	288
	J16	72
BOWYER	HIF	138
	HIF	648
BOX	UDH	54
	ETG	20
	EUF	33
	EDG	19
	PD	50
	T18	76
	PAA	37
	PTS	11
	PKA	12
	MS	13
	J6	97
	P3	95
	P5	76
	G2	630
	OAL	516
	KT3	963
	C	750
	M15	59
BOXEN	G2	613
	KT1	531
	M11	10
BOXES	EMM	11
	PW	15
	PLN	32
	EDGA	13
	PSH	10
	PT	30
	ETG	4
	ELB	3
	MF	61
	EDG	18
	L4	220
BOY	T18	36
	T18	87
	T23	11
	ODA	20
	J1	84
	J1	119
	J6	47
	J6	486
	J6	497
	J6	778
	J6	787
	J10	180
	J10	342
	J10	456
	J10	473
	J10	491
	P3	91
	P3	118
	P3	178
	P4	34
	P5	43
	P6	165
	M1	612
	M9	57
	M9	66
	M9	120
	M13	10
	M13	179
	HI	142
	HI	151
	VP3	19
	VP4	13
	VP4	72
	VP5	83
	G3	9
	AE1	665
	AE1	913
	AE1	954
	AE1	960
	AE1	991
	AE1	999
	AE2	109
	AE4	864
	AE5	333
	AE5	386
	AE5	734
	AE5	738
	AE8	213
	AE8	758
	AE9	484
	AE9	540
	AE9	892
	AE10	83
	AE10	105
	AE10	199
	OAL	211
	OAL	217
	OAE1	6
	OAE1	24
	OAE2	36
	M8	75
	M10	99
	CAM	386
	C	336
	TH	155
	EWR	27
BOYLE	DC	27
BOY'S	L4	3
	AE1	960
	C	369
BOYS	ENH	32
	EKK	17
	EDG	6
	EDG	17
	L3	77
	L4	202
	L4	261
	HAP	1453
	PTS	11
	SKA4	3
	SKA4	4
	SKA4	9
	J6	254
	J6	431
	J10	272
	J10	355
	J10	446
	P2	127
	PLT	43
	VP3	144
	VP6	37
	VP8	42
	AE1	373
	AE2	282
	AE2	312
	AE5	773

BOYS	AE6	424	BRANCHES	VP8	56	BRANDS	AE12	870
	AE7	218		VP9	41		AE12	952
	AE7	1104		VP9	79		KT3	259
	AE9	821		G1	273		CAM	92
	AE10	452		G2	394		AU	62
	HIF	644		G2	412	BRANDY	PD	27
	C	204		G2	504	BRASS	AR	198
	EMKG	40		G2	554		PSF	9
BRACE	J3	226		G2	565		AA	633
	KT3	55		G2	599		HAP	2033
BRACHMAN	J6	759		G4	64		J10	95
BRACKISH	M15	437		AE2	326		P2	74
BRADWARDIN	C	524		AE4	641		P2	101
BRAG	VP3	76		AE6	212		P2	107
BRAGGING	C	134		AE6	300		P5	154
BRAIDED	KT1	184		AE7	184		M1	147
BRAIN	AR	166		AE7	937		VP5	138
	AR	201		AE8	169		G2	646
	AT	119		AE11	150		G4	89
	BR	208		AE12	312		AE5	352
	J6	797		MM	8		AE6	245
	J10	219		KT2	538		AE6	797
	PPS	3		TH	79		AE6	852
	P4	34		FL	104		AE6	1169
	G2	674		FL	283		AE8	35
	AE4	854		FL	515		AE8	585
	AE9	800		M12	33		AE10	677
	C	334	BRANCHING	M1	881		AE10	1113
	TH	366		VP7	86		AE11	734
	AU	553		G2	21		AE11	1135
	M15	483		AE1	261		AE12	138
BRAINPAN	AE9	562		FL	42		AE12	315
BRAINS	E	25		M12	375		KT1	473
	PLG	20	BRAND	SMA	79		M12	67
	AA	334		ECG2	19		GP	86
	AA	621		HP	230		SMP	45
	MD	266		MF	177	BRAT	P6	33
	HAP	1015		RL	57	BRAVE	RH	49
	PDS	24		TA	118		SMA	39
	J6	422		HAP	401		VHH	22
	J6	807		BR	177		VHH	41
	AE2	55		M1	342		AM	168
	AE5	549		M13	39		AM	299
	AE9	1017		M13	42		AM	404
	AE10	586		P4	27		AM	417
	AE11	1033		AE3	833		AM	474
	AE12	466		AE7	445		AM	693
	M12	335		AE7	704		SEL1	16
	M12	401		AE9	83		PFD	15
	M12	587		AE9	713		SCD2	2
	STP	26		AE10	581		SCD2	24
BRAKE	J1	63		AE11	592		EAZ	22
	VP8	97		AE11	1078		PAL	21
	G4	664		AE12	451		AA	18
	AE2	510		M8	259		AA	821
	AE2	642		M8	265		AA	887
	AE11	1305		M8	292		AA	967
	KT1	495		M8	341		MD	129
	B	113		M8	342		MD	179
	B	145		B	84		SAA	358
BRAKES	AE11	777		M12	380		SAA	810
	KT2	68		M12	413		SAA	967
	TH	112	BRANDED	PUO3	31		SAA	1051
BRAMBLE	M1	136		AE11	1228		TA	206
	G3	490		AE12	983		HAP	1392
BRAMBLES	G1	227	BRANDING	G3	251		PDS	7
	G1	365	BRANDISH	OAL	787		J10	289
	G2	559	BRANDISHED	M1	182		J10	396
	G3	678		AE2	235		J16	47
	AE8	855		AE2	278		P1	60
	KT2	68		AE6	406		P1	184
	B	114		AE9	60		HI	1
	TH	104		AE10	1082		HI	72
BRAN	HAP	2279		AE12	147		G2	495
	P3	227		TH	283		AE1	14
	G3	201		M8	105		AE1	305
	C	523		M8	144		AE1	623
BRANCH	AT	23	BRANDISHES	J1	251		AE2	467
	J16	79		AE2	648		AE4	20
	AE5	1111		AE5	364		AE5	339
	AE6	284		AE6	772		AE5	531
	AE6	328	BRANDISHING	EOE	19		AE5	982
	AE7	99		G3	666		AE6	458
	AE8	153		AE5	728		AE6	679
	AE12	609		AE10	920		AE7	905
	HIF	349		AE12	1328		AE8	656
	FL	188	BRANDS	CM	121		AE9	216
	AS	61		AE1	215		AE9	333
BRANCHES	PT	2		AE4	852		AE9	401
	CM	80		AE5	830		AE9	693
	H2	21		AE5	836		AE9	778
	AK	4		AE5	859		AE9	944
	HAP	440		AE7	17		AE9	1051
	M1	468		AE7	731		AE10	245
	M13	158		AE9	138			
	VP7	41		AE12	429			

Headword	Ref	Loc
BRAVE	AE10	266
	AE10	268
	AE10	1056
	AE10	1297
	AE11	446
	AE11	554
	AE11	665
	AE11	784
	AE12	31
	AE12	932
	AF	13
	AF	14
	AF	15
	AF	17
	AF	18
	AF	19
	KT3	697
	KT3	739
	HIF	393
	TH	5
	TH	384
	FL	549
	M12	292
	M12	612
	M12	757
	AU	149
	AU	439
	AU	547
	PWR	41
BRAVELY	HS	122
	EPF	19
	SAA	998
	J10	442
	AE9	58
	AE11	650
BRAVER	AM	680
	HIF	375
BRAVES	PW	22
	PM	2
	AE3	102
	AE7	809
	AE10	769
	OAL	115
BRAVEST	AA	356
	AE1	139
BRAVING	AM	455
BRAWL	J3	445
BRAWLING	HIF	700
BRAWLS	J6	48
	J6	373
	J16	21
BRAWN	J1	56
	G2	173
	AE5	562
	KT3	479
	AU	553
BRAWNY	AM	567
	ECG1	9
	PP	33
	J10	14
	P5	276
	P6	181
	G1	290
	G2	80
	G2	408
	G3	127
	G4	248
	G4	779
	AE1	588
	AE4	195
	AE4	363
	AE5	498
	AE6	361
	AE10	280
	AE10	1085
	AE11	735
	AE11	1134
	OAL	630
	B	262
	FL	544
	M12	350
	M12	535
BRAWNY-BUILT	HAP	2439
BRAY	J3	171
	G3	575
BRAYED	EUO	17
BRAYS	P1	50
	P3	14
BRAZEN	OE	27
	P3	73
	M1	160
	G1	648
	G2	790
	G3	44
	G3	558
	AE1	405
BRAZEN	AE1	628
	AE1	629
	AE1	630
	AE1	631
	AE2	658
	AE2	745
	AE3	371
	AE4	744
	AE5	188
	AE5	259
	AE6	313
	AE6	326
	AE6	775
	AE7	733
	AE7	844
	AE7	858
	AE7	1023
	AE8	896
	AE9	669
	AE10	467
	AE10	1189
	AE11	15
	AE11	669
	AE12	501
	AE12	789
	OAL	738
	HIF	587
	C	750
BRAZEN-FACED	J3	133
BRAZEN-FOOTED	AE6	1094
BREACH	AM	984
	AA	915
	HAP	474
	AE2	306
	AE2	661
	AE8	844
	AE12	852
	AE12	1009
	OAL	531
	M11	148
BREACHES	BR	90
BREAD	AM	1144
	PFD	5
	SAA	351
	T27	109
	HAP	117
	HAP	417
	HAP	714
	HAP	1401
	HAP	1490
	HAP	1516
	HAP	2290
	BR	65
	EL	17
	J3	245
	J3	340
	J6	704
	J6	823
	J10	425
	P1	48
	P1	117
	P3	227
	M9	16
	VP1	85
	AE1	981
	AE7	152
	AE8	547
	AE9	827
	AE12	755
	TJD	47
	C	8
	C	33
	C	386
	M15	132
	M15	691
	AS	85
BREADTH	HAP	1481
	G3	515
	AE5	114
	AE5	314
	M8	207
	B	610
BREAK	RH	90
	PWGR	10
	EWGR	32
	EEL	35
	PAR	8
	EM	27
	DA	20
	AA	287
	AA	387
	AA	605
	SAA	828
	AT	42
	L4	133
	L4	279
BREAK	T18	24
	FS3	9
	EAA	20
	HAP	145
	HAP	336
	HAP	1015
	HAP	1411
	BR	243
	EKA	20
	EL	358
	EL	368
	J3	411
	J3	433
	J10	165
	P1	266
	P2	33
	P5	243
	P5	245
	M1	483
	ELT	11
	VP8	150
	G1	153
	G2	412
	G2	553
	G2	583
	G3	186
	G3	265
	G3	506
	G4	334
	G4	351
	G4	591
	G4	666
	AE1	813
	AE2	442
	AE2	806
	AE2	1079
	AE3	680
	AE3	731
	AE4	37
	AE5	765
	AE6	1125
	AE6	1220
	AE7	850
	AE9	144
	AE9	681
	AE9	826
	AE11	424
	AE11	716
	AE11	731
	AE12	232
	AE12	306
	AE12	898
	AE12	1337
	OAL	466
	OAL	672
	AF	125
	DO	121
	KT1	94
	KT1	288
	KT1	296
	KT1	331
	KT1	338
	KT1	347
	KT1	513
	KT1	546
	KT3	606
	CAM	58
	CAM	85
	CAM	359
	HIF	33
	HIF	794
	C	257
	C	308
	C	397
	C	491
	C	733
	TH	404
	M11	291
	M11	471
	FL	473
	WB	258
	WB	324
	PTP	50
	STP	20
	PMK	36
BREAKEST	GE	36
BREAKFAST	AT	125
BREAKING	PKA	45
	ODA	66
	J6	586
	P1	133
	AE1	177
	AE7	783
	AE8	692
	AE11	712
	C1	373

BREAKS	AM	853
	AM	874
	HP	201
	J3	396
	J6	586
	P3	2
	P5	17
	M1	1038
	VP8	97
	G4	528
	AE2	294
	AE2	295
	AE4	969
	AE8	808
	AE9	1081
	AE10	422
	AE11	228
	AE11	1080
	AE12	572
	AE12	701
	KT1	177
	KT3	1069
	HIF	416
	M11	227
	M15	332
BREAST	UDH	108
	HS	102
	AR	57
	SMA	75
	VHH	5
	AM	37
	AM	952
	AM	1118
	SEL3	15
	SCG2	8
	SM2	3
	S	15
	PAZ	14
	CM	20
	CM	43
	CM	143
	CM	144
	AA	934
	MD	74
	MD	322
	PRH	29
	MF	137
	SAA	123
	SAA	585
	SAA	621
	SAA	841
	SAA	1129
	SAA	1102
	L1	10
	L1	49
	L3	75
	L3	80
	L3	198
	L3	266
	L3	274
	L3	310
	T18	89
	T23	83
	NS	4
	TA	276
	AK	84
	HAP	258
	HAP	1250
	HAP	1556
	HAP	2172
	HAP	2432
	HAP	2536
	BR	210
	STS1	2
	STS3	5
	EL	246
	EL	362
	ODA	43
	J3	99
	J3	357
	J6	134
	J6	151
	J6	354
	J6	631
	P1	256
	P5	39
	P5	187
	M1	99
	M1	119
	M1	633
	M1	668
	M1	675
	M1	853
	M1	906
	M1	1077
	M9	91

BREAST	HI	38
	HI	174
	SLT1	2
	GK	79
	VP6	70
	VP7	29
	VP10	51
	G1	451
	G3	333
	G3	347
	G4	502
	AE1	681
	AE1	692
	AE1	706
	AE1	863
	AE1	962
	AE1	1005
	AE2	379
	AE3	499
	AE4	13
	AE4	296
	AE4	368
	AE4	591
	AE4	631
	AE4	690
	AE4	789
	AE4	799
	AE4	846
	AE4	967
	AE5	180
	AE5	236
	AE5	498
	AE5	597
	AE5	607
	AE5	1133
	AE6	75
	AE6	122
	AE6	150
	AE6	237
	AE6	454
	AE6	603
	AE6	810
	AE6	907
	AE7	343
	AE7	472
	AE7	482
	AE7	525
	AE7	565
	AE7	639
	AE7	700
	AE7	723
	AE8	218
	AE8	353
	AE8	941
	AE9	237
	AE9	391
	AE9	437
	AE9	453
	AE9	581
	AE9	947
	AE9	954
	AE9	989
	AE10	304
	AE10	319
	AE10	542
	AE10	600
	AE10	655
	AE10	848
	AE10	1037
	AE10	1085
	AE10	1154
	AE10	1250
	AE11	128
	AE11	183
	AE11	583
	AE11	645
	AE11	733
	AE11	771
	AE11	964
	AE11	1021
	AE11	1071
	AE11	1115
	AE11	1190
	AE11	1208
	AE11	1220
	AE11	1249
	AE11	1300
	AE12	6
	AE12	90
	AE12	111
	AE12	153
	AE12	236
	AE12	459
	AE12	879
	AE12	969

BREAST	AE12	1165
	AE12	1259
	AE12	1298
	OAL	79
	OAL	332
	OAL	602
	OAE1	30
	OAE2	44
	AF	31
	AF	115
	AF	122
	DO	122
	KT1	178
	KT1	523
	KT2	515
	KT3	213
	KT3	240
	KT3	277
	KT3	712
	KT3	751
	KT3	763
	KT3	857
	KT3	1021
	M8	269
	B	58
	B	124
	B	290
	B	371
	B	486
	B	595
	B	615
	B	631
	B	734
	B	746
	M10	23
	M10	25
	M10	74
	M10	80
	CAM	38
	CAM	165
	CAM	215
	HIF	119
	HIF	153
	HIF	503
	C	113
	C	453
	TH	33
	TH	184
	TH	341
	M11	380
	M11	393
	FL	25
	M12	161
	M12	197
	M12	289
	M12	321
	M12	329
	M12	419
	M12	475
	M12	637
	M12	656
	AU	149
	AU	410
	AU	506
	AU	604
	CI	155
	CI	189
	CI	218
	CI	604
BREAST-HIGH	C	575
BREASTPLATE	KT3	28
BREASTS	AR	48
	AM	903
	EUO2	24
	CM	108
	MD	267
	L2	63
	T27	91
	J6	177
	SLT2	8
	G1	563
	AE1	673
	AE8	736
	AE11	52
	AE11	292
	OAL	18
	KT1	44
	KT2	206
	KT3	872
	M8	367
	M8	381
	CAM	347
	HIF	10
	M11	74
	CI	576
BREATH	AR	244

BREATH		
AM	526
AM	918
SEL3	6
STL	11
SCG3	23
SM2	18
CM	110
SAA	618
AT	124
L1	51
L3	112
L3	234
L3	262
T23	79
T23	95
H29	32
TA	64
TA	213
TA	284
HAP	800
SSC	52
BR	256
EL	237
EL	307
J1	127
J1	216
P3	111
P3	171
M1	44
M1	355
M1	455
P3	186
VP2	46
VP4	64
VP8	29
G2	186
G2	448
G2	463
G2	789
G3	756
G4	328
G4	699
AE2	615
AE2	872
AE3	673
AE4	486
AE4	753
AE4	876
AE4	925
AE4	983
AE5	573
AE5	611
AE5	946
AE6	277
AE6	618
AE6	769
AE6	955
AE6	977
AE6	986
AE7	493
AE7	717
AE7	744
AE7	785
AE7	1059
AE8	941
AE9	437
AE9	558
AE10	157
AE10	448
AE10	663
AE10	795
AE10	839
AE10	1042
AE10	1295
AE11	156
AE11	1202
AE12	87
AE12	930
AE12	1316
AE12	1356
OAL	586
AF	53
KT1	153
KT1	557
KT2	261
KT3	618
KT3	798
KT3	709
KT3	1038
KT3	1070
M8	326
M8	363
B	162
B	382
B	738
B	749

BREATH		
BP	52
CAM	143
CAM	154
CAM	194
HIF	493
C	96
C	755
TH	330
M11	31
M11	226
M11	280
M11	369
M11	398
FL	96
FL	327
FL	375
FL	380
M12	409
M12	680
AU	111
AU	337
WB	186
M15	333
M15	459
M15	693
ERL	7
BREATHE		
SMM2	18
SAA	1121
EDG	31
J6	65
P1	80
G2	193
G3	700
G4	424
AE3	357
AE3	692
AE4	42
AE6	593
AE6	1008
AE6	1137
AE8	350
AE10	615
KT1	209
BREATHED		
AR	11
AM	479
AM	1163
HAP	1930
BR	133
M1	478
M1	979
G4	602
AE1	829
AE6	170
AE7	387
AE12	176
AE12	959
KT2	579
BP	89
M12	443
BREATHES		
L1	21
M1	731
G1	342
AE2	805
AE5	962
AE7	643
AE11	920
KT3	16
C	618
BREATHING		
HS	48
SM2	12
TA	27
P3	200
M1	310
G2	646
G3	55
AE1	201
AE6	245
AE6	1169
AE7	37
AE8	532
AE9	788
AE9	886
AF	158
KT3	755
KT3	762
B	117
FL	16
FL	357
M15	132
BREATHINGS	G1	131
BREATHING-TIME	HAP	1571
BREATHLESS	HI	36
	LC	131
	AA	1022
	T23	70
	VP5	27

BREATHLESS		
AE4	969
AE5	330
AE6	227
AE6	318
AE7	412
AE8	347
AE10	705
AE11	75
AE11	90
AE11	249
AE11	889
KT1	84
BP	176
C	280
TH	196
TH	329
AU	406
M12	378
M15	329
BREATHS		
SAA	1095
BRED		
AR	16
AM	858
PWGR	1
ECD	10
PCB	31
PCB	35
AA	871
PPC	15
MF	75
RL	65
RL	226
PD	20
AK	77
HAP	180
HAP	1246
HAP	1684
BR	210
J3	330
J6	119
J6	125
J6	244
J6	373
J10	373
P1	54
P1	139
P1	203
P3	101
P4	4
P5	50
M1	134
M1	501
M9	78
VP3	134
VP8	60
G2	101
G2	200
G2	778
G3	317
G3	339
G3	441
G3	647
G3	770
AE5	395
AE5	741
AE7	673
AE7	891
AE7	903
AE9	261
AE9	793
AE10	266
AE10	721
AE10	1000
KT1	139
B	439
CAM	305
C	92
C	141
C	150
AU	136
M15	172
BREECHES	J6	103
	J6	575
BREED	HS	144
	ENH	38
	EKK	14
	PTW	24
	AA	530
	ELB	40
	L4	223
	L4	266
	HAP	18
	HAP	208
	HAP	838
	HAP	2244
	ETS	32
	PSH	14

BREED	M1	561
	VP1	9
	VP3	133
	G2	205
	G3	76
	G3	107
	G3	186
	G3	192
	G3	225
	G3	260
	G3	593
	G3	617
	G3	633
	G4	79
	AE5	746
	AE6	1038
	AE7	386
	M8	21
	HIF	572
	AU	46
	WB	415
	PMK	35
BREEDING	PAR	16
	PAR	26
	HAP	2271
	HAP	2442
	J6	269
	J16	38
	B	310
BREEDS	AR	236
	MD	254
	EC	28
	L1	4
	HAP	226
	P4	95
	M1	368
	G1	89
	G3	85
BREERS	TH	104
BREEZE	DC	11
	AM	711
	H29	39
	G3	239
	G3	521
	AE5	997
	AE6	954
	AE7	9
	M11	91
	FL	327
BREEZES	H3	5
	VP2	99
	G1	618
	G2	58
BRENNUS	C	636
BRETHREN	PUO3	5
	MD	300
	HAP	185
	HAP	710
	HAP	1214
	SSC	18
	M1	67
	DHP	27
	AE8	562
	AE10	453
	AE10	813
	AE11	294
	AE12	738
	OAL	223
	M8	222
	M8	245
	M12	728
	M15	115
	GP	131
	AS	95
BREW	HS	100
	AR	269
BREWED	AA	114
	B	706
BREWS	G1	578
	AE12	615
BRIAREUS	AE6	401
	HIF	554
BRIBE	ML	4
	HP	122
	ELB	20
	SAA	1072
	RL	86
	AT	96
	HAP	1356
	HAP	1534
	HAP	2010
	HAP	2092
	PDS	31
	EL	30
	J1	53
	J3	99

BRIBE	J6	229
	J6	466
	P2	57
	P2	84
	M1	629
	PLT	33
	G3	602
	AE10	598
	OAL	400
	TJD	112
	HIF	353
	AU	483
	M15	186
BRIBED	HS	124
	PWG	5
	VHH	25
	AA	709
	SAA	294
	SAA	689
	SAA	749
	H2	16
	TA	102
	PAA	6
	ODA	52
	J6	509
	J6	697
	P1	102
	G4	731
	AE5	450
	AE12	49
BRIBES	PWG	45
	J6	332
	J10	72
	J10	469
	P2	125
	P5	75
	P5	257
	G2	704
	G4	573
	AE6	833
	AE12	1274
	OAL	472
	KT2	324
	M10	36
	HIF	276
BRIBING	AE5	1034
BRICK-BUILT	J10	277
BRIDAL	J10	516
	M1	908
	VP8	41
	AE4	176
	AE4	716
	M11	87
	M15	594
	CI	449
BRIDE	AR	17
	AR	232
	SMA	124
	AM	603
	SCD1	12
	CM	117
	AA	6
	AA	34
	SAA	994
	T18	8
	T18	22
	T18	80
	T27	1
	H2	62
	HAP	1872
	HAP	2070
	EH	18
	J3	84
	J6	37
	J6	69
	J6	76
	J6	578
	M1	642
	G2	441
	G4	661
	G4	696
	G4	714
	G4	762
	G4	788
	AE2	1065
	AE3	423
	AE6	537
	AE7	539
	AE7	596
	AE9	808
	AE10	121
	AE10	142
	AE10	918
	AE10	1017
	AE11	170
	AE11	333

BRIDE	AE11	539
	AE11	554
	AE11	716
	AE11	724
	AE11	872
	AE12	29
	AE12	51
	AE12	125
	AE12	1174
	OAL	146
	OAL	635
	OAE2	10
	AF	10
	KT3	2
	KT3	274
	KT3	664
	KT3	771
	KT3	927
	KT3	1145
	M8	80
	B	24
	B	46
	B	407
	B	743
	M10	53
	CAM	44
	M12	302
	M12	311
	M12	325
	WB	342
	WB	371
	WB	377
	M15	719
	CI	271
	CI	280
	CI	308
	CI	317
	CI	434
	CI	519
	AS	25
	AS	54
	AS	70
BRIDEGROOM	PEL	2
	SCD1	12
	SCD1	17
	T18	12
	T18	80
	T27	132
	EL	328
	J3	191
	AE10	121
	AE12	1174
	OAE2	10
	KT3	1145
	B	743
	M12	298
	WB	342
	WB	377
	CI	562
	AS	70
BRIDEGROOM'S	SCD1	2
	OAL	79
	OAL	635
BRIDEGROOMS	AE10	695
BRIDE'S	SCD1	2
BRIDES	M9	148
	AE10	693
	CI	540
	CI	585
	CI	632
BRIDGE	AM	889
	L3	243
	J6	45
	J10	284
	G3	124
	AE8	864
	AE8	970
BRIDGES	AM	983
	EKA	17
	G4	38
	AE9	214
	AE10	403
	AE12	979
BRIDLE	AE5	1070
	KT1	46
BRIDLES	P1	198
	G3	181
	G3	393
	AE8	226
BRIEF	M1	380
	AE3	404
BRIEFLY	HAP	2181
	M1	272
	AE1	789
	AE2	15
	AE4	907

Word	Code	Num
BRIEFLY	AE8	204
	KT3	1003
BRIEFS	J6	343
BRIER	FL	74
BRIGHT	UDH	44
	JH	10
	AR	288
	LC	86
	LCA	25
	AM	69
	SMM1	6
	SCG1	8
	SCD1	7
	DA	25
	EPF	16
	AA	248
	PRH	10
	SAA	110
	SAA	932
	SAA	995
	SAA	1068
	RL	9
	ER	36
	AK	134
	AK	145
	AK	176
	HAP	502
	SSC	51
	BR	132
	PP	39
	SKA2	7
	LS	1
	EL	144
	P3	70
	M13	68
	HI	157
	VP5	49
	G1	71
	G1	311
	G1	320
	G4	546
	AE1	825
	AE2	419
	AE2	800
	AE3	163
	AE3	205
	AE3	677
	AE4	512
	AE5	138
	AE7	10
	AE7	733
	AE8	370
	AE8	692
	AE8	710
	AE8	825
	AE8	899
	AE9	32
	AE9	931
	AE10	249
	AE10	456
	AE10	769
	AE11	669
	KT2	39
	KT2	297
	KT2	313
	KT2	523
	KT3	250
	KT3	266
	KT3	363
	KT3	931
	KT3	949
	M8	361
	B	5
	M11	228
	M11	300
	FL	272
	M12	262
	M12	304
	M12	363
	M12	694
	WB	411
	M15	289
	GP	139
	STP	13
	AS	13
BRIGHTEN	T18	47
BRIGHTER	RL	12
	BR	9
BRIGHTEST	AK	116
	G3	128
	M12	773
BRIGHTNESS	BR	312
	J6	598
BRILLANT	GP	139
BRIM	PLN	32
	P3	64
BRIM	C	802
BRIMFUL	G2	332
	B	681
BRIM-FULL	AM	16
BRIMMER	AE1	1037
BRIMMERS	L3	99
	J6	420
	J6	421
BRIMMING	VP3	43
	CI	568
BRIMS	PCG1	13
	G1	394
	AE7	646
	AE7	911
	AE7	1081
	AE8	367
BRIMSTONE	VP8	116
BRINDED	VP3	40
	C	14
BRINDICE	SCD2	6
BRINE	J10	46
	P6	46
	AE1	253
	AE5	203
	AE5	1014
	KT2	515
BRING	UDH	4
	UDH	99
	HS	26
	AR	221
	SMA	30
	SMA	90
	PIE	26
	VHH	39
	AM	54
	AM	72
	AM	98
	AM	347
	AM	476
	AM	559
	AM	616
	AM	790
	AM	970
	PMQ	56
	PMM	16
	PCG1	27
	SCD1	8
	SCG2	6
	PUO2	19
	PUO2	28
	ML	38
	PTC	18
	DA	163
	DA	168
	PUO3	23
	PUO5	19
	PUF	8
	AA	59
	AA	283
	AA	429
	AA	511
	AA	585
	AA	811
	AA	852
	AA	951
	PLB	6
	MD	189
	D	45
	SAA	171
	SAA	250
	SAA	260
	SAA	613
	SAA	676
	SAA	725
	SAA	1068
	PK	41
	PD	19
	L2	67
	L3	23
	L4	112
	PAA	30
	HAP	644
	HAP	1959
	HAP	2060
	HAP	2072
	HAP	2188
	BR	24
	PDS	30
	PP	31
	SKA6	10
	ODA	62
	J3	352
	J6	449
	J6	683
	J6	740
	PPS	18
BRING	P1	160
	P1	186
	P2	31
	P2	112
	P3	189
	P6	123
	M1	790
	M1	912
	VCS	11
	HI	131
	HI	163
	VP2	61
	VP2	83
	VP2	97
	VP3	38
	VP3	87
	VP4	22
	VP5	19
	VP8	89
	VP9	75
	VP10	1
	G1	13
	G1	172
	G2	54
	G2	593
	G3	16
	G3	71
	G3	605
	G3	714
	G4	160
	G4	786
	AE1	806
	AE1	913
	AE1	931
	AE2	75
	AE4	609
	AE4	818
	AE4	852
	AE4	911
	AE4	982
	AE6	1105
	AE6	1222
	AE7	362
	AE7	675
	AE8	151
	AE8	159
	AE8	723
	AE8	754
	AE9	96
	AE10	1233
	AE11	349
	AE11	380
	AE11	433
	AE12	400
	AE12	1268
	OAL	154
	OAL	235
	OAL	734
	DO	95
	KT1	472
	KT2	409
	KT2	665
	B	132
	B	362
	HIF	31
	HIF	137
	HIF	450
	HIF	467
	HIF	471
	HIF	572
	HIF	600
	HIF	647
	C	12
	C	184
	M12	60
	AU	362
	AU	508
	M15	109
	M15	221
	M15	416
	M15	543
	AS	49
	AS	60
	PWR	32
BRINGING	GE	4
	M9	13
BRINGS	SMA	53
	AM	597
	ET	11
	ESF	29
	PAL	8
	HP	175
	EPC	1
	EPC	11
	PRH	37
	D	13

Word	Code	No.
BRINGS	PD	49
	L3	155
	L4	185
	HAP	176
	HAP	1092
	HAP	1463
	J1	138
	J6	189
	J10	368
	M1	357
	VP6	9
	AE4	253
	AE7	445
	AE7	898
	AE7	959
	AE8	808
	AE8	857
	AE8	907
	AE11	1256
	AE12	615
	OAL	276
	M12	342
	M12	820
	WB	481
	M15	565
BRINK	AM	979
	M13	221
	VP1	81
	VP5	36
	G3	22
	AE10	713
	OAL	598
	WB	193
BRINKS	P3	147
BRINY	H3	17
	M13	45
	VP2	32
	VP10	7
	G4	339
	G4	619
	AE1	175
	AE1	232
	AE2	233
	AE3	18
	AE5	186
	AE5	236
	AE10	279
	AE10	307
	OAL	599
	KT1	448
	M11	156
	M11	358
BRISEIS	HIF	202
	HIF	281
	HIF	482
BRISK	PCG1	26
	ECG1	12
	PAR	6
	EM	21
	ESF	11
	L4	282
	HAP	1723
	SLT2	15
	OAL	266
BRISTLED	HAP	43
	G3	397
	G3	624
	AE7	20
	AE10	1008
	AE11	303
	M8	24
	M8	195
BRISTLES	P3	235
	AE2	1051
	KT2	205
	M8	217
	AE3	69
	AE5	365
	OAL	752
BRISTLING	M13	156
	AE6	565
	TH	146
BRISTLY	G2	98
	G4	589
	AE12	454
BRITAIN	AM	88
	AM	256
	AM	298
	AM	643
	PTC	12
	ER	24
	ER	42
	TA	376
	TA	471
	HAP	154
	BR	9
BRITAIN	BR	147
	DO	43
	WB	13
	ESK	6
BRITAIN'S	AM	78
	EAA	33
BRITISH	HS	82
	AR	246
	DC	26
	AM	124
	AM	704
	AM	716
	AM	733
	AM	1206
	ETC	5
	EPF	19
	ER	27
	ER	46
	TA	9
	TA	512
	HAP	289
	HAP	1129
	HAP	1303
	BR	89
	PDS	7
	J10	22
	DO	2
	KT3	16
	TJD	151
BRITON	PTP	32
BRITONS	EAZ	22
	POE	24
	PTC	1
	SKA1	12
	VP1	89
	G3	39
BRITTLE	L3	85
	EL	171
	M13	86
	G1	430
BROACH	P4	67
	G2	547
BROACHERS	HIF	638
BROAD	AM	991
	AM	1123
	PCG1	4
	PAR	7
	PPC	7
	L2	61
	BR	118
	P4	104
	M1	413
	M9	41
	M13	39
	G3	92
	G3	631
	AE4	306
	AE6	260
	AE6	1086
	AE7	913
	AE9	407
	AE9	1014
	AE10	1199
	AE11	1006
	AE11	1070
	AE12	464
	OAL	433
	OAL	672
	KT3	41
	KT3	955
	M8	105
	HIF	60
	M11	74
	FL	234
	FL	238
	M12	129
	AU	115
	M15	157
	M15	192
	M15	589
	CI	18
	CI	125
BROAD-BACKED	HAP	2439
BROAD-BRIMMED	PCG1	10
BROADER	AM	929
	C	121
	FL	14
	G3	126
BROADLY		
BROAD-SHOULDERED	KT3	46
BROADSIDE	SCD2	19
BROADSIDES	EDG	7
BROAD-SPEAKING	PWR	26
BROAD-WAY	HAP	1523
	P3	110
BROIL	AE1	297
	AE5	137
BROILED	AE8	243
	M12	214
BROILING	AE6	362
BROILS	HS	141
	PUF	31
	MD	318
	SAA	570
	SAA	705
	SAA	717
	G4	92
	AE1	380
BROKE	AM	955
	AM	1019
	AA	175
	AA	588
	MD	259
	D	4
	SAA	226
	SAA	731
	SAA	925
	T23	27
	AK	145
	HAP	1222
	J10	174
	M1	142
	M1	234
	M1	158
	M13	80
	VP1	41
	VP3	18
	G3	406
	G4	713
	AE1	231
	AE1	832
	AE1	935
	AE2	184
	AE2	403
	AE3	78
	AE3	530
	AE5	267
	AE6	148
	AE6	833
	AE7	110
	AE8	166
	AE8	297
	AE8	864
	AE9	330
	AE9	592
	AE9	694
	AE9	886
	AE10	331
	AE10	739
	AE10	853
	AE11	185
	AE12	53
	KT2	289
	KT3	807
	HIF	403
	HIF	425
	HIF	723
	C	769
	C	783
	M11	386
	FL	296
	FL	522
	M12	463
	M12	649
	M15	183
BROKEN	AM	259
	AM	430
	PNH	14
	DA	60
	PUO3	34
	EUF	6
	PDG	9
	L3	141
	L5	13
	TA	489
	AK	121
	HAP	50
	HAP	1844
	HAP	2089
	LS	10
	J3	431
	J10	331
	J10	358
	P1	47
	P1	70
	P3	227
	P5	233
	M1	183
	VP10	46
	G3	319
	G3	651
	G4	379
	G4	429

BROKEN	G4	800
	AE2	44
	AE2	143
	AE2	674
	AE3	404
	AE3	821
	AE5	252
	AE5	765
	AE7	254
	AE8	572
	AE9	556
	AE9	1050
	AE9	1081
	AE10	424
	AE10	679
	AE10	1029
	AE11	333
	AE11	743
	AE11	1073
	AE12	2
	AE12	479
	AE12	679
	AE12	804
	AE12	1009
	KT2	472
	KT3	612
	M12	75
	M12	483
	M15	200
BROMINGAM	PSF	11
BROMUS	M12	612
BROOD	SAA	982
	RL	419
	HAP	176
	HAP	1907
	BR	237
	M1	206
	VP4	28
	G1	197
	G3	629
	G4	18
	G4	79
	G4	149
	AE4	902
	AE6	299
	AE7	759
	AE7	799
	AE8	115
	AE9	819
	TJD	109
	B	257
	M12	22
	M12	308
	M15	119
	M15	564
BROODED	AM	100
	G2	473
	AE4	799
BROODING	PRH	2
	H3	45
	HAP	1878
	G1	339
	G2	729
	AE4	762
	AE6	827
	AE12	1226
	M11	495
	M12	83
BROODS	J6	787
	G1	148
	WB	469
BROOK	PR	18
	MF	130
	SAA	901
	BR	243
	J3	387
	M1	499
	M1	736
	M1	799
	VP3	151
	G3	72
	AE9	25
	OAL	50
	OAL	214
	OAL	447
	M12	355
BROOKS	AK	110
	HAP	1852
	M1	377
	M1	789
	M1	823
	VP8	147
	G1	174
	G1	213
	G2	15
	G4	31

BROOKS	M15	156
BROOM	G2	18
	G2	608
BROTEAS	M12	369
BROTHEL	J10	377
BROTHEL-HOUSE	J6	173
BROTHEL-HOUSES	MF	70
BROTHELS	OAL	37
	WB	62
BROTHER	DC	28
	PWG	34
	AM	1011
	PMQ	45
	PO	21
	AA	353
	AA	437
	AA	469
	AA	750
	SAA	258
	SAA	306
	SAA	430
	EDG	37
	AT	36
	TA	36
	TA	76
	TA	93
	TA	279
	AK	165
	HAP	1003
	HAP	2005
	EDS	9
	EDS	17
	J6	117
	J10	381
	P3	208
	P6	49
	M1	375
	HI	96
	PLT	12
	G2	778
	AE1	473
	AE2	563
	AE2	682
	AE3	887
	AE5	548
	AE5	659
	AE5	680
	AE6	182
	AE7	931
	AE8	173
	AE9	123
	AE9	977
	AE10	174
	AE10	195
	AE10	470
	AE10	475
	AE10	846
	AE10	847
	AE10	1106
	AE11	404
	AE12	228
	AE12	698
	AE12	925
	OAL	321
	OAL	860
	KT1	290
	KT1	308
	KT1	366
	KT1	477
	KT2	193
	M8	150
	M8	389
	HIF	24
	HIF	241
	HIF	379
	HIF	520
	HIF	552
	C	232
	M12	772
	AU	70
	AU	309
	M15	337
	M15	678
	PTP	5
BROTHER-ANGELS	AK	44
BROTHERHOOD	EK	24
	HAP	1979
BROTHER'S	CM	23
	DA	34
	DA	122
	TA	58
	TA	460
	ODA	79
	J6	229
	VP6	89
	AE1	470

BROTHER'S	AE1	481
	AE1	942
	AE12	688
	AE12	984
	AE12	1184
	AE12	1275
	M8	241
	M8	288
	CAM	89
	M12	338
	M15	259
	CI	449
BROTHERS	PWG	49
	PC1	21
	PC2	19
	ML	8
	HP	208
	HI	62
	HI	72
	HI	83
	HI	120
	G2	735
	SAA	611
	SAA	708
	AE2	141
	AE7	930
	AE9	171
	AE9	943
	AE10	187
	AE10	487
	AE11	610
	AE12	408
	AE12	749
	M8	334
	M8	337
	M8	354
	C	211
	M12	4
	M12	760
	WB	310
	CI	208
	CI	515
	PMK	17
BROTHERS'	SAA	708
	TA	249
	J6	237
	AE6	824
	M8	296
BROTHS	UDH	86
BROUGHT	UDH	77
	JH	6
	AR	70
	AR	90
	SMA	57
	SMA	118
	LC	77
	EWG	11
	VHH	28
	AM	95
	AM	127
	AM	247
	AM	586
	AM	694
	AM	1145
	PMQ	2
	EMQ	6
	EMM	11
	PCG1	25
	SCG1	3
	PUO2	11
	E	22
	HP	7
	HP	103
	DA	95
	PUO5	18
	PUF	6
	AA	212
	PLB	32
	SAA	51
	SAA	512
	SAA	1016
	EDGA	24
	PMS	8
	RL	321
	RL	363
	RL	415
	ER	8
	TA	292
	TA	397
	TA	437
	HAP	532
	HAP	934
	HAP	1625
	HAP	1763
	HAP	2277
	HAP	2296

BROUGHT	HAP	2447	BROUGHT	AU	223	BROWS	FL	578
	BR	22		AU	474		M12	471
	EKA	4		WB	60		M15	192
	ODA	33		WB	476	BROWSE	T27	87
	ODA	75		M15	712		M1	412
	J1	239		PTP	2		M1	942
	J3	267		ETP	6		VP2	92
	J3	407		SMP	88		VP3	128
	J6	196		SMP	94		VP10	9
	J6	197	BROUGHTEST	AM	1047		VP10	44
	J6	247		HIF	554		G2	602
	J6	772	BROW	LC	143		G2	517
	J10	208		AM	1174		G3	471
	J16	52		SAA	880		G3	489
	P1	225		SAA	976		G3	498
	P3	159		J3	178		M15	118
	P6	87		P1	143	BROWSED	VP10	114
	M1	585		P5	184	BROWSING	VP1	107
	M9	54		P6	34		VP2	38
	HI	32		M1	362		VP8	48
	GK	135		M1	524		AT	2
	VP1	45		VP1	107	BRUCE	MF	93
	VP5	37		G1	159		MF	212
	VP8	137		G1	609	BRUISE	M1	406
	G2	545		AE1	255	BRUISED	L4	26
	G3	303		AE1	430		G4	194
	G3	765		AE3	515		G4	425
	G4	450		AE3	862		AE5	362
	G4	644		AE4	914		KT3	712
	AE1	917		AE5	306	BRUISES	AM	1051
	AE1	977		AE6	918		KT3	727
	AE1	1038		AE7	195	BRUISING	M8	381
	AE2	160		KT2	544	BRUSH	G4	15
	AE2	239		M8	84		AE4	838
	AE2	623		B	497		AE5	203
	AE2	103		HIF	463		AE5	1017
	AE2	393		M11	200		OAL	176
	AE2	463		FL	186		OAL	177
	AE2	818		FL	401		OAL	752
	AE2	1038		FL	521		CI	613
	AE2	1085		M12	517	BRUSHED	T18	16
	AE3	155	BROWN	SCG1	11		T23	99
	AE3	211		PAL	33		HAP	521
	AE3	248		HAP	1231		AE10	279
	AE3	624		P5	215		KT1	194
	AE5	352		VP10	57		M11	301
	AE5	356		G4	477		CI	229
	AE5	473		AE7	41	BRUSHING	AE5	188
	AE5	778		AE8	560		FL	30
	AE6	166		AE12	1226		CI	30
	AE6	349		OAL	829	BRUSHWOOD	BP	54
	AE6	468		KT2	27	BRUSHWOOD-HELPSRL		269
	AE6	658		C	33	BRUTAL	PUF	29
	AE6	714		TH	92		AA	1019
	AE7	251		M11	301		L1	45
	AE7	439		WB	212		M1	308
	AE7	975		M15	315		GK	56
	AE8	222	BROWS	MF	110		VP9	23
	AE8	265		MF	135		AE2	729
	AE8	427		MO	24		AE7	27
	AE8	974		AT	41		AE8	249
	AE9	939		HAP	1089		AE8	273
	AE10	247		PP	36		OAL	366
	AE10	1166		LS	17		TH	126
	AE11	61		J3	154		M12	308
	AE11	105		J6	114		M12	321
	AE11	638		J6	162		AU	565
	AE12	609		M9	186		AU	592
	AE12	1032		MC	41		WB	72
	OAL	218		VP6	35		M15	675
	DO	69		VP7	38		CI	123
	KT1	9		VP7	85		CI	140
	KT2	17		VP10	37		CI	192
	KT2	174		G1	590		CI	218
	KT2	361		G2	25		CI	225
	KT2	562		G3	50	BRUTE	WB	435
	KT3	4		AE2	932		CI	67
	TJD	41		AE4	213	BRUTES	HAP	236
	TJD	54		AE5	93		HAP	252
	B	79		AE5	177		HAP	1308
	B	269		AE5	612		HAP	1309
	B	705		AE6	1198		KT3	742
	CAM	255		AE7	183		HIF	267
	CAM	310		AE7	896		M12	676
	HIF	105		AE8	905		M15	145
	HIF	171		AE9	98	BRUTIDIUS	J10	134
	HIF	482		AE9	861	BRUTTIAN	P6	61
	HIF	508		AE9	1093	BRUTUS	P5	121
	HIF	594		OAL	328		AE6	1118
	C	557		OAL	340	BUBBIES	T27	92
	C	600		OAE1	33		OAE2	46
	M11	440		AF	7	BUBBLE	PAA	28
	M11	459		MG	6		P3	64
	FL	99		KT1	287		AF	100
	AU	34		KT2	62	BUBBLE'S	J3	206
	AU	133		HIF	257	BUBBLES	AA	139

Word	Code	No.
BUBBLES	L4	111
	G1	538
	G3	400
BUBBLING	VP1	54
	AE7	645
	AE8	102
	AE12	1283
	M12	388
BUCK	PCD	3
BUCKETS	AM	914
	J3	323
	AE5	897
	KT2	82
	EMKG	13
BUCKLE	J6	37
	M8	66
BUCKLER	AA	206
	AE2	299
	AE2	530
	AE2	833
	AE7	256
	AE9	987
	AE10	466
	AE10	827
	AE10	1114
	AE10	1130
	AE10	1273
	AE11	15
	AE12	714
	KT3	456
	FL	270
	M12	119
	M12	180
	M12	186
	M12	196
	M12	820
	AU	115
	M15	236
BUCKLERS	AE2	605
	AE3	314
	AE7	949
	AE7	998
	AE7	1013
	AE7	1023
	AE11	300
	AE12	1038
	KT3	30
	KT3	343
BUCKLES	L4	100
	AE11	1143
BUCKLING	AE3	877
BUCKS	GE	75
BUD	G2	103
	OAL	585
BUDDING	VP6	76
	G2	765
	G3	501
	AE7	679
BUDS	PT	4
	L1	14
	ODA	41
	VP3	125
	G2	107
	G2	456
	FL	8
BUFF	RH	74
	ENH	32
	J10	308
	J16	75
BUFFALOES	G2	518
	G3	794
BUFFETS	M12	187
BUFFOON	PLN	24
	AA	550
	HAP	39
BUFFOONRY	MS	5
BUFFOONS	ETP	13
BUG	OAL	882
	PWR	23
BUGBEAR	L3	1
	L3	180
BUGBEARS	L2	64
BUGGARY	SAA	437
BUGLE	OAE1	14
BUILD	HS	14
	PFD	30
	PUO1	32
	PNH	20
	PNH	35
	AA	532
	SAA	916
	SAA	1115
	HAP	1948
	J3	362
	J6	645
	G4	47
BUILD	G4	262
	G4	296
	G4	417
	AE1	361
	AE1	368
	AE1	588
	AE1	625
	AE1	737
	AE3	9
	AE3	217
	AE3	333
	AE3	652
	AE5	940
	AE7	172
	AE7	315
	AE8	65
	AE11	197
	AE11	493
	AE11	497
	AE12	539
	TJD	149
	M15	587
	KT3	961
BUILDER	MC	13
BUILDERS	HAP	124
BUILDING	AE2	829
	AE5	778
	AE8	625
	KT3	769
	M12	39
BUILDINGS	AM	858
BUILDS	HAP	2543
	G1	265
	AE3	513
	AE4	308
BUILT	AM	237
	AM	616
	ML	12
	DA	13
	SAA	113
	RL	83
	RL	431
	HAP	494
	HAP	1161
	HAP	2250
	J10	547
	M1	398
	HI	118
	VP2	89
	G2	68
	G3	59
	AE1	6
	AE2	316
	AE3	151
	AE6	22
	AE7	229
	AE7	571
	AE8	310
	AE9	180
	AE9	705
	KT1	72
	KT1	203
	KT2	448
	KT3	568
	FL	79
	M12	67
	M12	668
	M15	73
BULGED	AE1	167
BULK	AR	156
	PC1	26
	MF	195
	SAA	462
	SAA	479
	L3	192
	T23	92
	M1	588
	M13	151
	M13	229
	G1	166
	G2	80
	G3	782
	AE3	865
	AE5	113
	AE5	155
	AE5	495
	AE9	959
	AE10	442
	AE10	443
	AE11	268
	AE12	327
	M8	132
	BP	158
	M12	829
	AU	413
	AU	532
BULKIEST	AE11	1020
	M12	615
BULKS	AM	280
	OE	22
BULKY	ESF	19
	J1	6
	G2	404
BULL	AR	121
	ER	67
	T27	115
	J10	98
	P3	73
	M9	36
	M9	109
	M13	193
	VP3	134
	G1	307
	G3	327
	G3	329
	G3	346
	AE3	31
	AE3	162
	AE3	163
	AE5	308
	AE5	483
	AE5	505
	AE5	539
	AE5	637
	AE8	391
	AE9	957
	AE10	639
	AE10	677
	AE10	1114
	AE12	159
	OAL	21
	OAL	315
	OAL	325
	OAL	339
	OAL	365
	OAL	367
	ETO	1
	CAM	43
	C	215
	M12	128
	M12	137
	P5	42
BULLA		
BULLETS	AM	239
	AM	581
	S	9
BULL-FACED	AA	581
BULLIES	PSF	41
	PD	59
	J6	414
BULLION	G3	85
BULLOCK	P2	86
BULLOCK'S	AE11	1183
	KT3	629
	M13	81
BULLOCKS	AE6	58
	AE6	348
BULL'S	G3	96
	G3	99
	G4	532
	AE1	508
	AE7	954
	M12	510
	T27	88
	VP3	154
BULLS	VP5	48
	G2	193
	G4	779
	G4	794
	AE5	103
	AE6	361
	AE8	350
	AE11	302
	AE12	1042
	KT3	47
	KT3	140
	M8	20
	M8	41
	HIF	440
	C	157
BULLY	PAL	10
	J3	445
BULRUSH	M8	97
BULWARKS	AE9	46
	AE9	673
BUM	MF	101
BUMASTUS	G2	146
BUMPERS	GE	46
BUMPKIN	J3	295
	P5	177
BUMPS	J16	15
	WB	194
BUMS	J6	433

BUNCH	AE7	246	BURN	AE1	61	BURNISHED	AE5	730		
BUNCHES	M13	108		AE1	399		AE9	488		
	G2	7		AE2	253		KT2	546		
BUNGLER	ML	53		AE2	257		KT3	48		
BUNGLERS	PUO4	24		AE2	273		KT3	342		
	EWR	15		AE3	192		KT3	936		
BUNGLING	HAP	142		AE3	301		BP	57		
BUNHILL	MF	97		AE4	850		C	54		
BUOY	AA	821		AE5	878		C	701		
BUR	VP7	60		AE5	917	BURNS	SCG3	15		
BURBON	AM	803		AE5	1037		SLN	16		
BURDEN	LC	44		AE7	446		PLB	39		
	E	6		AE7	624		MD	109		
	HP	164		AE9	138		L4	88		
	L3	137		AE11	72		J3	351		
	L3	274		AE11	110		J10	381		
	L3	278		AE11	347		M1	310		
	HAP	189		AE12	1048		M1	663		
	P5	207		KT2	117		M1	667		
	M9	53		KT2	190		M1	965		
	AE11	96		KT3	903		M9	86		
	OAL	21		M8	291		M9	150		
	KT2	654		M8	387		SLT1	25		
	KT3	1039	BURNED	EL	183		G2	519		
	CAM	322		M1	304		G3	159		
	FL	198		AE4	296		G3	333		
	FL	367		AE5	606		G3	428		
	M12	466		AE7	1074		AE2	419		
	M12	680		AE11	442		AE2	644		
	M12	688		DO	126		AE4	854		
	M15	611		KT1	126		AE4	918		
	CI	357		KT1	138		AE6	351		
BURDENED	AM	565		KT2	116		AE7	997		
	VP9	40		KT3	903		AE7	1076		
	G2	566		B	58		OAL	27		
BURGHERS	MD	180		HIF	37		M8	30		
BURGUNDIAN	PW	13		HIF	333		M11	160		
BURGUNDY	PDS	21		HIF	360	BURNT	SMA	80		
BURIAL	AE6	684		HIF	637		HP	233		
	M11	221		C	713		AA	97		
BURIED	POE	36		M15	581		AA	624		
	T23	86	BURNING	LC	20		SAA	547		
	HAP	1918		AM	407		BR	178		
	P3	192		AM	696		J3	362		
	M1	488		AM	882		M13	24		
	G1	71		AM	1027		AE2	780		
	G1	148		AM	1034		KT2	588		
	G2	35		EOE	34		KT3	349		
	G2	446		L3	223		FL	386		
	G2	729		L4	12	BURS	VP5	58		
	G3	547		J6	681		G1	227		
	G3	568		P5	14		G3	591		
	AE3	58		M1	1092	BURST	MD	296		
	AE6	447		VP2	12		MF	138		
	AE9	562		VP10	97		L4	83		
	AE9	725		G3	63		T23	96		
	AE10	537		G3	390		TA	26		
	AE10	1159		G3	626		HAP	551		
	AE11	313		G3	675		HAP	2375		
	FL	386		AE1	68		P1	26		
BURIS	M15	447		AE2	1020		G4	444		
BURLESQUE	EIE	15		AE2	1039		AE3	256		
BURLY	J6	250		AE3	211		AE9	912		
	P2	49		AE3	753		FL	13		
	M13	54		AE5	906		WB	183		
BURN	VHH	36		AE6	742		M15	96		
	AM	332		AE6	839	BURSTS	G1	74		
	AM	820		AE7	308		HIF	120		
	SEL4	9		AE7	335	BURTHEN	J6	573		
	CM	141		AE7	704		M1	370		
	DA	25		AE7	731		G3	90		
	T23	24		AE8	346		G3	216		
	T23	63		AE11	305		G3	557		
	SKA4	19		AE12	108		G3	577		
	SKA4	20		AE12	870		AE1	605		
	SKA4	21		KT1	465		AE4	587		
	SKA4	22		KT3	250		AE4	860		
	SKA4	23		KT3	985		AE6	166		
	J3	91		KT3	990		AE8	380		
	J3	328		M8	251		AE9	1104		
	J3	346		M8	275		AE12	387		
	P6	81		M8	317	BURTHENS	AA	952		
	L3	69		M8	363		G4	298		
	M1	349		M10	24	BURY	P3	194		
	M1	354		M12	380		M1	488		
	M9	97		M12	400		G1	302		
	M13	185	BURNISH	PC1	21		BP	174		
	VP8	116		M9	199		M12	670		
	VP8	118	BURNISHED	L2	31	BUSH	J10	32		
	VP8	126		HAP	390		VP4	30		
	G1	114		HAP	1852		G2	600		
	G1	123		P2	99		KT3	351		
	G2	271		HI	152		VP3	83		
	G2	564		G3	650	BUSHES	G3	591		
	G2	724		G4	422		FL	447		
	G4	469		AE3	677	BUSHY	M13	162		

Word	Code	No.
BUSHY	VP3	128
	AE2	510
BUSILY	AM	785
BUSINESS	PIE	17
	PTL	13
	E	20
	ETG	16
	AR	89
	LC	46
	EIE	20
	EAZ	9
	AA	565
	AA	614
	MF	9
	L1	45
	L3	164
	L4	285
	H29	10
	H29	52
	H2	4
	H2	59
	BR	10
	PDS	12
	PMS	35
	PKA	13
	EL	112
	EL	262
	J3	75
	J3	237
	J6	799
	J6	830
	J16	41
	P1	274
	P2	48
	P4	21
	P4	76
	P6	27
	HI	7
	EHC	23
	VP3	11
	VP3	80
	VP10	53
	G1	31
	G2	640
	G4	644
	G4	646
	AE4	272
	AE6	528
	AE6	658
	AE8	151
	AE9	1047
	AE10	1262
	OAL	428
	OAL	537
	OAE2	86
	KT3	340
	TH	67
	M12	630
	WB	528
	CI	222
	CI	408
	ESK	12
	ESK	26
BUSIRIS'	G3	7
BUSKINED	KT2	646
	M8	68
	SMP	29
BUSKINS	MF	79
	J6	829
	VP7	46
	AE1	464
	AE8	601
BUSTLE	L3	23
BUSY	AR	106
	AM	257
	AM	913
	HP	36
	PUO5	13
	AA	126
	MD	186
	SAA	310
	SAA	1123
	H29	19
	HAP	1460
	HAP	1823
	EL	291
	J3	423
	VP1	73
	G4	26
	G4	257
	AE1	585
	AE1	598
	AE1	614
	AE4	102
	KT3	444
	BP	97

Word	Code	No.
BUSY	CAM	54
	M12	66
BUTCHER	J6	857
	G3	737
	KT2	598
	M15	687
BUTCHERED	M13	22
BUTCHER'S	PLB	22
	HAP	625
BUTCHERS	PMQ	31
	EAZ	27
BUTES	AE5	493
	AE11	1019
	AE11	1021
	AE12	540
BUTES'	AE9	888
BUTHROTUS'	AE3	379
BUTLER	C	387
BUTT	HAP	2053
	PMS	35
BUTTER	PP	28
BUTTERFLIES	M15	552
BUTTERFLY	C	580
BUTTING	AT	5
	VP3	135
	VP9	30
BUTTONS	PAR	8
BUTTRESS	AA	802
BUTTRESSES	J3	315
BUTTS	G2	773
	AE9	861
	J6	16
	G2	441
	AE5	1017
	AE7	543
	KT2	519
	M15	609
	CI	613
BUY	HS	84
	EMK	19
	EUF	21
	AA	396
	AA	897
	SAA	575
	RL	240
	T27	106
	ESH	35
	EH	26
	J1	203
	J6	106
	J6	300
	P1	242
	AE4	889
	AE9	279
	AE11	434
	OAL	483
	OAL	512
	HIF	17
	HIF	513
	C	8
	FL	558
	CI	305
	PWR	33
BUYER	MD	192
BUYS	PIE	16
	EMK	22
	ELB	24
	HAP	1519
	J6	290
	J6	730
	J6	795
	J10	494
	P6	83
BUZZ	PCB	25
	RL	418
	AT	29
BUZZARD	HAP	322
	HAP	2415
	HAP	2429
	HAP	2434
	HAP	2494
	HAP	2519
	HAP	2567
BUZZARD'S	HAP	2193
BUZZING	AA	210
	SAA	336
	G4	279
	G4	801
	ML	12
BY-ENDS		
BY-PATH	HAP	697
BYRSA	AE1	507
BY-STREET	PW	3
BY-STROKE	PEL	17

Word	Code	No.
CABALLER	AE11	514
CABALS	SAA	523
CABIN	P5	214
CABINET	UDH	64
	J6	383
CABLE	AE2	341
CABLES	G1	614
	AE1	128
	AE2	309
	AE3	841
	AE3	875
	AE5	983
	AE8	872
CACKLE	ELB	2
CACKLED	C	718
CACKLING	AM	330
CACUS	AE8	258
	AE8	273
	AE8	321
	AE8	405
CADENCE	PNH	46
	ER	17
	MO	16
CADMUS	KT2	93
	KT2	95
CADMUS'	KT2	95
CAEAN	G1	17
CAECULUS	AE10	757
CAEDICUS	AE9	489
	AE10	1052
CAENEUS	AE6	608
	AE9	778
	AE9	779
	M8	53
	HIF	377
	M12	236
	M12	238
	M12	247
	M12	287
	M12	609
	M12	624
	M12	632
	M12	653
	M12	680
CAENIS	M12	261
	M12	262
	M12	287
	M12	624
CAERE	AE8	627
	AE10	264
CAESAR	UDH	70
	SMA	84
	AM	352
	ECD	22
	EPC	24
	TA	175
	TA	176
	HAP	1354
	HAP	1393
	HAP	1403
	J10	108
	J10	110
	P6	98
	M1	260
	M1	263
	G1	38
	G1	59
	G1	628
	G1	629
	G1	672
	G1	677
	G2	237
	G3	23
	G3	31
	G3	57
	G3	61
	G4	314
	G4	809
	AE1	390
	AE6	1075
	AE6	1078
	AE8	899
	AE8	958
	OAL	198
	OAL	231
	FL	555
CAESAR-LIKE	AM	698
CAESAR'S	SMA	104
	AM	762
	EAL	22
	HAP	1354
	J6	186
	J6	811
	J10	139
	J10	513
	P6	113

Word	Ref	No.
CAESAR'S	M1	6
	M1	759
	VP9	64
	G3	42
	G3	50
	G3	80
	G3	82
	OAL	212
	KT2	605
	FL	556
CAESINIA	J6	194
CAESONIA	J6	803
CAGE	DO	118
CAGES	M10	42
CAICUS	AE1	258
	AE9	39
	M12	151
	M15	427
CAIN	PUO3	31
	SAA	389
	HAP	279
CAIUS	J6	803
CAJETA	AE7	3
CAJETA'S	AE6	1245
CAKE	P2	135
	P3	107
	AE4	749
	KT2	534
CAKES	J16	62
	VP7	47
	G1	418
	G2	544
	AE2	182
	AE5	975
	AE7	152
	AE7	157
	HIF	614
	HIF	628
CALABRIAN	P2	117
	M15	476
CALABRIA'S	G3	647
CALCHAS	AE2	135
	AE2	168
	AE2	236
	AE2	242
	HIF	101
	HIF	102
	M12	25
CALCULATE	HAP	1180
CALDRON	AE7	644
CALDRONS	P3	238
	G1	280
	G3	558
	AE1	296
	AE3	596
	AE5	352
	AE6	313
CALEB	AA	574
CALEDON	HAP	1297
CALEDONIAN	HAP	14
	KT2	634
CALENDAR	KT2	90
	AS	8
CALES'	AE7	1008
CALF	AA	66
	T27	115
	P1	196
	G3	259
	G3	284
	G4	789
	C	730
	M15	686
CALISTO	KT2	623
CALKING-IRON	AM	583
CALL	LC	127
	SIE	16
	AM	55
	AM	510
	AM	1018
	PA	18
	PAR	7
	A	1
	A	3
	PLN	6
	PUO1	35
	ESF	15
	PAL	10
	EAL	20
	EAL	30
	HP	64
	PR	14
	EUF	3
	AA	116
	AA	398
	AA	421
	AA	664
CALL	AA	676
	AA	947
	AA	955
	PLB	46
	MD	157
	MD	261
	PRH	20
	MF	47
	SAA	15
	SAA	397
	SAA	430
	SAA	564
	PD	6
	PD	16
	PD	62
	EC	16
	MO	2
	L3	121
	L3	312
	T23	83
	T27	74
	H29	66
	HAP	143
	HAP	987
	HAP	1172
	HAP	1173
	HAP	1421
	HAP	1439
	HAP	1878
	HAP	1909
	HAP	2064
	HAP	2302
	HAP	2417
	HAP	2497
	EL	20
	EL	146
	EL	156
	J1	193
	J3	175
	J6	370
	J6	393
	J6	419
	J6	494
	J10	305
	J16	35
	P3	52
	P5	162
	M1	227
	M1	448
	M1	867
	M13	130
	HI	42
	HI	133
	MC	50
	VP3	116
	VP6	122
	VP8	142
	G1	155
	G1	479
	G1	481
	G3	238
	G3	501
	G4	9
	G4	99
	AE1	201
	AE1	377
	AE1	388
	AE1	459
	AE1	586
	AE1	735
	AE2	891
	AE2	909
	AE2	1046
	AE3	28
	AE3	83
	AE3	289
	AE3	340
	AE3	652
	AE4	554
	AE4	708
	AE4	909
	AE5	273
	AE5	941
	AE5	1000
	AE7	180
	AE7	282
	AE8	214
	AE8	543
	AE9	649
	AE11	467
	AE11	708
	AE12	957
	AE12	1199
	OAL	258
	OAL	259
	OAL	678
CALL	OAL	713
	KT2	286
	KT2	473
	KT3	117
	KT3	1104
	B	348
	B	397
	B	493
	BP	37
	CAM	361
	HIF	138
	C	275
	C	429
	C	444
	C	529
	C	763
	TH	234
	TH	402
	M11	34
	M11	336
	M11	445
	FL	12
	M12	337
	WB	423
	M15	189
	M15	362
	M15	392
	GP	129
	CI	547
	STP	29
CALLED	SMA	14
	AM	46
	AM	768
	AM	898
	S	5
	EUO	22
	PTC	31
	PCB	23
	PO	28
	HP	153
	DA	109
	AA	40
	AA	86
	AA	263
	ELB	19
	MD	171
	MF	4
	SAA	396
	PK	14
	PK	24
	PK	26
	AT	10
	L4	156
	H2	99
	AK	10
	AK	130
	GE	67
	HAP	359
	HAP	594
	HAP	673
	HAP	1740
	HAP	1788
	HAP	1834
	PP	47
	PKA	21
	J3	270
	J6	2
	J6	149
	J6	197
	J6	333
	J6	615
	J6	641
	J10	61
	J16	67
	P1	159
	M1	214
	M1	703
	M1	921
	M9	60
	VP1	36
	VP6	100
	G3	409
	G3	603
	G4	392
	G4	480
	G4	673
	AE1	157
	AE1	287
	AE1	365
	AE1	507
	AE1	521
	AE1	751
	AE1	1034
	AE2	168
	AE3	221
	AE3	224

Word	Ref	Num
CALLED	AE3	909
	AE4	249
	AE5	57
	AE5	132
	AE5	216
	AE5	715
	AE6	525
	AE6	597
	AE6	681
	AE6	1108
	AE7	3
	AE7	93
	AE7	285
	AE7	1064
	AE8	149
	AE8	429
	AE8	444
	AE8	446
	AE8	628
	AE9	152
	AE9	264
	AE9	525
	AE10	459
	AE10	1225
	AE10	1251
	AE11	158
	AE11	491
	AE11	807
	AE11	821
	AE12	206
	AE12	559
	AE12	1229
	KT1	590
	KT2	212
	KT2	282
	KT2	654
	KT3	319
	KT3	685
	KT3	1016
	M8	82
	M8	354
	B	51
	B	206
	M10	101
	CAM	19
	CAM	86
	HIF	448
	HIF	555
	C	14
	C	345
	M11	325
	M11	368
	M11	369
	FL	509
	FL	535
	FL	552
	AU	95
	AU	103
	WB	82
	M15	74
	M15	237
	M15	249
	M15	251
	CI	67
	CI	176
	CI	433
	AS	31
CALLEST	J6	312
	AE3	632
CALLING	ETL	16
	J3	316
	P4	45
	G4	205
	AE4	968
	AE5	720
	AE12	1100
CALLIOPE	AE9	696
CALLOUS	P3	61
CALLOW	AM	428
	ELB	6
	PAA	19
	J1	33
	VP8	57
	G1	562
	G2	292
	G4	22
	AE5	279
	AE8	213
	M12	19
CALLS	MF	203
	SAA	425
	SAA	737
	SAA	914
	EC	22
	ER	31
	L4	179

Word	Ref	Num
CALLS	T18	32
	HAP	84
	HAP	1620
	HAP	2510
	PP	21
	J1	152
	J6	50
	J6	816
	M1	377
	M9	46
	VP4	60
	G2	772
	G3	73
	G3	442
	G4	28
	G4	318
	G4	508
	AE1	353
	AE1	876
	AE2	310
	AE2	455
	AE3	433
	AE3	785
	AE4	326
	AE4	415
	AE5	833
	AE5	931
	AE5	1084
	AE6	704
	AE7	817
	AE8	72
	AE8	706
	AE9	41
	AE9	615
	AE9	622
	AE9	695
	AE9	1036
	AE10	621
	AE10	916
	AE11	377
	AE11	598
	AE11	678
	AE11	699
	AE11	720
	AE11	1085
	AE12	686
	AE12	702
	AE12	821
	AE12	877
	AE12	1017
	OAL	590
	OAL	760
	KT1	84
	TJD	120
	B	326
	B	522
	M10	53
	M11	181
	M11	285
CALM	AM	163
	SEL3	1
	AA	161
	SAA	1081
	H9	18
	TA	285
	HAP	2098
	AE3	165
	AE9	999
	MFL	32
	HIF	311
	AU	290
	ESK	13
CALMED	EAZ	7
	AE6	519
CALMER	HS	71
	AE4	623
CALMNESS	RH	10
	SMA	91
	MD	255
CALMS	G1	568
	SMP	72
	TJD	182
	M11	497
	M12	13
CALVED	G3	249
CALVES	HAP	580
	VP3	41
	G3	743
	G4	629
	AE5	1009
CALVIN	HAP	181
	HAP	688
	HAP	1524
CALVINIST	HAP	1027
CALVIN'S	HAP	401
CALYDON	AE7	424

Word	Ref	Num
CALYDON	M8	364
CALYDONIAN	M8	77
CALYDONIANS	M8	1
CAMARINE	AE3	920
CAMBRIA	HAP	171
CAME	HS	55
	HS	133
	AR	28
	AR	76
	AR	87
	LC	72
	LCA	48
	PIE	6
	AM	445
	AM	1013
	AM	1062
	AM	1105
	PEL	25
	SEL3	22
	SCG1	5
	EM	27
	CM	21
	AA	744
	PRH	25
	MF	33
	SAA	544
	SAA	1116
	PD	33
	T27	116
	TA	114
	TA	153
	TA	370
	AK	23
	GE	18
	HAP	190
	HAP	388
	HAP	789
	HAP	1901
	HAP	1902
	HAP	1903
	HAP	2209
	HAP	2354
	HAP	2433
	BR	4
	EL	46
	EL	74
	EL	131
	EL	200
	J10	105
	P3	90
	M1	160
	M1	786
	M1	788
	M1	880
	M1	930
	M1	1094
	M9	9
	HI	28
	HI	37
	HI	192
	GK	20
	GK	40
	DHP	10
	VP1	37
	VP5	32
	VP6	32
	VP10	28
	VP10	31
	VP10	37
	G2	235
	G4	507
	AE1	517
	AE1	729
	AE1	756
	AE1	877
	AE1	919
	AE2	278
	AE2	378
	AE2	446
	AE2	756
	AE2	902
	AE3	109
	AE3	148
	AE3	226
	AE3	443
	AE3	756
	AE3	801
	AE3	804
	AE4	72
	AE4	512
	AE4	953
	AE5	138
	AE5	421
	AE5	442
	AE5	617
	AE5	626

Word	Ref	Number
CAME	AE5	631
	AE5	1057
	AE6	21
	AE6	53
	AE6	73
	AE6	79
	AE6	186
	AE6	368
	AE6	422
	AE6	534
	AE7	72
	AE7	225
	AE7	685
	AE7	705
	AE7	930
	AE7	973
	AE7	984
	AE7	1000
	AE7	1094
	AE8	21
	AE8	172
	AE8	180
	AE8	300
	AE8	425
	AE8	431
	AE8	435
	AE9	378
	AE9	771
	AE9	786
	AE9	789
	AE9	801
	AE10	192
	AE10	394
	AE10	479
	AE10	539
	AE10	555
	AE10	577
	AE10	600
	AE10	609
	AE10	712
	AE10	875
	AE10	1014
	AE10	1050
	AE10	1252
	AE10	1284
	AE10	1298
	AE10	1313
	AE11	61
	AE11	167
	AE11	383
	AE11	393
	AE11	958
	AE11	989
	AE11	1294
	AE12	357
	AE12	405
	AE12	483
	AE12	945
	AE12	1215
	AE12	1283
	AE12	1369
	AE12	1377
	OAL	97
	OAL	616
	AF	161
	AF	171
	DO	75
	KT1	10
	KT1	345
	KT1	358
	KT1	440
	KT1	577
	KT1	606
	KT2	281
	KT2	320
	KT2	455
	KT2	555
	KT3	22
	KT3	39
	KT3	62
	KT3	441
	KT3	640
	KT3	710
	KT3	776
	KT3	836
	KT3	949
	KT3	1016
	TJD	183
	TJD	208
	M8	50
	M8	65
	M8	227
	M8	255
	B	68
	B	155
	B	206
CAME	B	297
	B	407
	B	721
	BP	23
	M10	57
	CAM	280
	CAM	306
	CAM	364
	HIF	17
	HIF	539
	HIF	748
	C	277
	C	444
	TH	115
	TH	133
	TH	235
	TH	269
	TH	251
	TH	272
	TH	362
	TH	376
	M11	242
	M11	307
	FL	195
	FL	241
	FL	250
	FL	275
	FL	567
	M12	295
	M12	298
	M12	305
	M12	384
	M12	395
	M12	588
	AU	47
	AU	51
	AU	133
	AU	145
	AU	267
	AU	467
	WB	219
	WB	266
	M15	13
	M15	37
	M15	60
	M15	163
	M15	401
	GP	89
	CI	332
	AS·	17
	AS	98
CAMEL	AA	952
	J10	455
CAMELOTS	G3	487
CAMEL'S	P5	200
CAMERS	AE10	786
	AE10	788
CAMERTUS'	AE12	341
CAMEST	CM	63
CAMILLA	AE7	1094
	AE11	758
	AE11	809
	AE11	821
	AE11	843
	AE11	885
	AE11	962
	AE11	1018
	AE11	1170
	AE11	1218
	AE11	1242
	AE11	1295
CAMILLA'S	AE11	905
	AE11	1288
CAMILLUS	TA	267
	J16	20
	G2	235
	AE6	1132
CAMP	AM	201
	J16	3
	P6	97
	G3	366
	G3	540
	G4	100
	G4	358
	AE2	36
	AE2	131
	AE2	628
	AE7	193
	AE9	10
	AE9	64
	AE9	193
	AE9	247
	AE9	300
	AE9	500
	AE9	602
	AE9	1057
CAMP	AE9	1067
	AE10	4
	AE10	37
	AE10	215
	AE10	219
	AE10	335
	AE10	365
	AE10	367
	AE10	853
	AE11	148
	AE11	610
	AE11	684
	AE12	251
	AE12	525
	AE12	603
	AE12	656
	KT1	137
	HIF	16
	HIF	78
	HIF	90
	HIF	456
	HIF	480
	HIF	531
	HIF	564
	HIF	662
	AU	366
CAMPAIGNS	DO	67
	EKA	13
CAMPANIA	J10	434
	AE7	1018
CAMPANIAN	G2	305
	G3	789
CAMPS	SAA	1107
	ER	68
	P6	108
	VP10	68
	G2	720
	AE8	662
	AE12	645
CAN	VP6	26
CANAAN	AS	93
CANAANITE	MD	178
CANAAN'S	SAA	879
	SAA	944
	TJD	133
CANCEL	AA	181
	HAP	2136
	M1	269
CANCELED	J1	101
CANDIA	CI	639
CANDIAN	EPF	8
	CI	629
CANDID	M15	60
CANDIDATE	AK	22
CANDIDATES	ML	17
CANDLELIGHT	C	26
CANDLE'S	J3	453
CANDLES	PRL	14
	J3	475
CANDOR	PAL	20
CANDY	PD	26
	CI	326
CANE	B	79
CANES	M1	978
CANISTERS	VP2	61
	AE1	981
	AE6	1222
	AE8	241
	BP	115
CANKERED	D	39
	HAP	1365
CANNON	VHH	30
	TA	170
	TA	512
	AM	90
	AM	103
	AM	105
	AM	365
	AM	411
	AM	421
	POE	25
	HAP	635
CANNONS	AM	329
CANNONS'	AR	227
	AM	495
	AM	594
CANON	RL	288
CANON-LAWS	HAP	1760
CANONS	HAP	668
CANOPIES	L2	39
	P1	98
CANOPY	HAP	1861
	M1	8
	M1	870
CANS	J10	97
CANT	AA	521

CANT	PPC	18	CAPTIVE	AE5	677	CARE	AM	807
	SAA	1029		AE6	595		AM	950
	HAP	2502		AE7	253		AM	965
	J6	267		AE7	918		AM	1019
	PTP	39		AE8	865		AM	1037
CANTING	AA	575		AE9	540		AM	1049
	ELB	21		AE11	1101		PMQ	7
	MD	17		KT1	167		SMM1	4
	MD	275		KT1	202		PFD	13
	MN	8		KT1	371		PM	24
	J3	80		KT1	507		EM	4
	C	146		KT1	511		SCD1	14
	PTP	49		KT2	3		PUO1	25
CANTING-COAT	HAP	1526		KT3	616		PUO2	7
CANTLETS	M12	180		HIF	44		EUO2	15
CANVAS	AM	434		HIF	141		PAZ	35
	AM	511		HIF	207		PAL	19
	AM	569		HIF	450		EMK	2
	GK	20		HIF	469		PKK	9
	GK	32		HIF	540		PKK	14
	G1	347		C	705		CM	140
	AE4	602		C	755		HP	157
	AE3	177		WB	208		DA	5
	AE3	272		WB	448		DA	10
	AE6	418		CI	415		DA	187
	AE10	374		CI	479		PUO3	20
	HIF	654	CAPTIVED	STS1	16		AA	12
CAP	PTW	19	CAPTIVES	HS	114		AA	393
	PRH	25		LCA	38		AA	892
CAPABLE	HP	91		FS1	15		AA	961
	AE5	9		J10	429		AA	997
CAPACIOUS	M1	99		G4	21		MD	26
	M1	529		AE1	82		MD	231
	AE3	746		AE3	819		SAA	56
CAPANEUS	KT1	76		AE11	116		SAA	326
CAP-A-PE	KT3	489		OAL	143		SAA	578
CAPARISON	AE9	485		KT1	265		SAA	882
	KT3	29		KT3	518		SAA	952
CAPARISONED	AE7	382	CAPTIVITY	AE3	418		PK	2
CAPE	AM	1214		KT1	242		EK	2
	AE3	918	CAPUAN	AE10	213		EK	36
	AE6	335	CAPYS	AE1	257		EK	41
CAPERING	J6	91		AE2	46		RL	136
	EMKG	11		AE6	1042		RL	236
CAPES	M15	67		AE10	213		RL	262
CAPHAREAN	AE11	403	CAPYS'	AE9	782		RL	413
CAPITAL	SAA	450	CAR	EL	339		OE	20
CAPITOL	J10	99		G1	210		L1	46
	AE6	1148		G3	316		L3	82
	AE6	1186		G3	795		L3	294
	KT2	604		G4	560		L3	303
CAPITOL'S	AE9	599		AE5	1072		L4	14
CAPONED	J6	487		AE6	1098		L4	127
CAPON'S	PUO3	18		AE11	982		H9	12
CAPPADOCIAN	P6	182		AE12	433		H29	10
CAPRI	AE7	1016		AE12	496		H2	12
CAPRICORN	HAP	1892		AE12	506		H2	35
	G2	437		AE12	527		H2	55
	KT3	390		AE12	531		H2	60
CAPS	P5	119		AE12	975		TA	225
	AE8	881		KT1	110		TA	296
CAPTAIN	RH	49		KT2	594		HAP	901
	MF	105		KT3	48		HAP	1158
	HAP	169		KT3	556		HAP	1335
	HAP	2486		M12	102		HAP	1352
	P3	148		M12	176		HAP	1398
	P5	278		M15	567		HAP	1452
	VP9	5	CARBUNCLES	G3	841		HAP	1773
	AE5	216	CARCASS	PAL	3		HAP	1823
	AE5	587		L3	67		HAP	2154
	AE7	50		J3	414		HAP	2422
	AE9	700		G3	414		BR	1
	AU	561		AE2	739		PP	21
CAPTAINS	AE3	604		AE2	763		STS3	17
	AE9	203		AE6	255		EKA	34
	AE11	312	CARCASSES	G3	807		SKA5	6
	AE11	1259		AE2	536		SKA6	7
CAPTIVE	AM	723		M12	100		EL	211
	PLN	12	CARD	SAA	382		EL	214
	PC2	33		M12	629		EL	291
	SAA	569	CARDED	G4	476		EL	374
	SAA	895	CARDINALS	PO	22		ODA	12
	SAA	1005	CARDS	ENH	40		PSH	16
	HAP	19		MD	234		EH	30
	PP	31	CARE	HS	61		J1	150
	J10	214		AR	141		J1	200
	P6	106		AR	193		J3	423
	M1	239		RH	30		J3	497
	M1	867		SMA	11		J6	416
	HI	77		LC	96		J6	643
	AE2	76		LC	117		J6	786
	AE2	81		SIE	9		J6	822
	AE2	96		AM	351		J16	62
	AE2	788		AM	425		P1	12
	AE2	1043		AM	565		P1	94
	AE3	382		AM	657		P2	47

Word	Code	No.
CARE	P2	106
	P4	8
	P4	35
	P4	91
	P5	85
	P5	159
	P5	177
	P6	29
	P6	125
	M1	130
	M1	263
	M1	339
	M1	556
	M1	856
	M1	986
	M9	56
	M9	81
	M9	93
	M13	25
	H I	102
	EHC	7
	VP1	113
	VP2	17
	VP2	59
	VP2	107
	VP3	91
	VP4	4
	VP7	20
	VP7	49
	VP10	33
	VP10	62
	VP10	75
	G1	3
	G1	21
	G1	188
	G1	231
	G1	309
	G1	352
	G1	562
	G2	6
	G2	45
	G2	270
	G2	350
	G2	358
	G2	561
	G2	688
	G3	113
	G3	190
	G3	208
	G3	224
	G3	267
	G3	327
	G3	451
	G3	463
	G3	467
	G3	478
	G3	590
	G3	776
	G4	160
	G4	193
	G4	200
	G4	257
	G4	363
	G4	402
	G4	596
	G4	791
	AE1	282
	AE1	300
	AE1	326
	AE1	421
	AE1	524
	AE1	535
	AE1	909
	AE1	934
	AE1	1008
	AE2	110
	AE2	148
	AE2	229
	AE2	816
	AE2	839
	AE2	875
	AE2	964
	AE2	1015
	AE2	1074
	AE3	22
	AE3	75
	AE3	214
	AE3	572
	AE3	610
	AE3	868
	AE4	9
	AE4	87
	AE4	99
	AE4	161
	AE4	291
	AE4	416
CARE	AE4	572
	AE4	700
	AE4	712
	AE4	909
	AE4	919
	AE5	279
	AE5	371
	AE5	1008
	AE5	1049
	AE5	1099
	AE5	1121
	AE6	158
	AE6	286
	AE6	481
	AE6	890
	AE6	927
	AE6	1233
	AE7	91
	AE7	176
	AE7	516
	AE7	617
	AE7	620
	AE7	677
	AE7	706
	AE7	741
	AE7	789
	AE7	863
	AE7	1063
	AE8	28
	AE8	84
	AE8	110
	AE8	420
	AE8	708
	AE9	47
	AE9	136
	AE9	218
	AE9	232
	AE9	294
	AE9	361
	AE9	370
	AE9	417
	AE9	651
	AE9	983
	AE10	29
	AE10	73
	AE10	200
	AE10	247
	AE10	361
	AE10	457
	AE10	1227
	AE11	47
	AE11	80
	AE11	143
	AE11	239
	AE11	308
	AE11	350
	AE11	399
	AE11	449
	AE11	470
	AE11	502
	AE11	788
	AE11	1126
	AE12	71
	AE12	76
	AE12	234
	AE12	260
	AE12	286
	AE12	610
	AE12	646
	AE12	922
	AE12	1164
	AE12	1226
	AE12	1235
	OAL	114
	OAL	272
	OAL	410
	OAL	576
	OAL	861
	AF	111
	AF	118
	DO	158
	KT1	159
	KT1	302
	KT1	412
	KT1	474
	KT2	35
	KT2	192
	KT2	484
	KT3	143
	KT3	164
	KT3	307
	KT3	315
	KT3	403
	KT3	426
	KT3	574
	KT3	681
CARE	KT3	858
	KT3	886
	TJD	121
	TJD	148
	M8	263
	B	11
	B	90
	B	178
	B	199
	B	381
	B	414
	B	463
	B	467
	B	565
	B	611
	B	623
	B	645
	B	712
	BP	61
	BP	97
	BP	198
	CAM	160
	HIF	108
	HIF	222
	HIF	263
	HIF	277
	HIF	402
	HIF	501
	HIF	572
	HIF	607
	HIF	704
	HIF	729
	C	102
	C	195
	C	623
	TH	34
	TH	81
	TH	162
	TH	240
	TH	254
	TH	417
	M11	116
	M11	208
	M11	214
	M11	236
	M11	312
	FL	31
	FL	98
	M12	21
	M12	489
	M12	544
	M12	798
	AU	261
	AU	449
	AU	472
	AU	553
	AU	569
	WB	517
	M15	10
	M15	608
	GP	68
	CI	61
	CI	70
	CI	77
	CI	99
	CI	129
	CI	176
	CI	264
	CI	337
	CI	419
	CI	499
	CI	509
	CI	535
	SMP	68
	SMP	74
CARED	HAP	2054
	CI	483
CAREER	PTL	20
	BR	269
	G1	306
	AE11	915
	AE12	786
	KT3	512
	FL	573
CAREERS	AA	909
CAREFUL	AM	49
	AM	133
	AM	395
	AM	593
	AA	80
	AA	934
	SAA	920
	PD	30
	HAP	391
	HAP	582
	HAP	1868

CAREFUL	SKA6	15	CARES	KT3	750	CARTHAGE	AE10	17
	P3	97		TJD	2		AE10	82
	P6	158		TJD	67		TJD	166
	M1	495		TJD	75	CARTHAGINIAN	L3	248
	M1	832		CAM	125		J6	248
	ELT	35		CAM	180		AE1	807
	G1	522		HIF	668		C	706
	G4	314		C	424	CARTRAGE	AM	596
	G4	473		TH	63	CART'S	G1	244
	AE1	894		FL	24	CARVED	VP3	67
	AE2	189		M12	217		AE7	241
	AE3	676		ESK	28		AE10	233
	AE5	949		AS	64		M10	7
	AE10	310	CARESSED	OAL	333	CARVER	M10	18
	AE10	406	CAREST	P6	125	CARVERS	KT2	455
	AE10	1093	CARGO	PWR	5	CARVING	VP3	59
	AE10	1195	CARIANS	AE8	965		OAL	648
	AE11	304	CARMENTA	AE8	448	CARVINGS	KT2	468
	KT2	21	CARMENTAL	AE8	446	CASE	SEL3	18
	CAM	182	CARNAL	J6	693		ECG1	17
	M11	185	CAROL	KT2	491		PW	5
	WB	500	CAROLED	KT1	197		AA	455
CARELESS	SCG1	9	CAROLINA'S	PK	5		EK	2
	PCB	15	CAROUSELS	AE5	777		PD	21
	AA	708	CARPATHIAN	G4	557		J6	386
	SAA	922	CARPENTERS	AM	567		J6	503
	L2	35	CARPET	H29	27		J6	862
	HAP	253	CARPET-GROUND	VP1	115		J10	523
	HAP	2477	CARPETS	MF	98		G3	204
	VP8	125		AE1	902		EHC	16
	G1	465	CARRHAE'S	AE7	839		AE11	835
	G2	769	CARRIAGE	HP	16		MFL	16
	G3	5		SAA	912		KT1	438
	G3	366		PD	44		KT3	282
	G4	504		EKA	26		B	453
	AE4	96		J3	409		C	289
	AE5	226		J10	30		TH	298
	AE5	430		ELT	16		TH	314
	AE9	591		CI	224		M11	453
	AE9	423	CARRIED	LC	117		AE12	315
	AE12	818		PUO5	18	CASED	KT3	534
	KT2	500		HAP	1820	CASEMENTS	EDG	25
CARELESSLY	RL	259		AE5	629	CASES	AE5	982
CARES	SMA	97		AE12	362	CASHIER	PEL	24
	SMA	109		OAL	554	CASHIERED	P6	38
	LC	43		B	178	CASK	EDS	34
	SIE	3		CAM	305	CASKET	AE11	819
	VHH	5		C	269	CASMILLA	AE7	988
	AM	551		EL	62	CASPERIA	AE6	1088
	E	21		J3	84	CASPIAN	OAL	258
	STC	5		J6	256	CASQUE	AE5	629
	SAA	870	CARRIER	RL	367		AE11	738
	L2	22	CARRIERS	G4	13	CASQUES	AE5	727
	L2	51	CARRIES	L4	252		AE7	1025
	L3	136		PKA	32	CASSANDRA	AE2	323
	L3	272	CARRION	SAA	473		AE2	544
	T23	15		AT	127		AE3	244
	EL	63		J10	323		AE3	249
	EL	361		P3	118		AE5	828
	J6	737		G3	832		AE10	102
	J10	79	CARRY	RH	37		CI	435
	J16	75		PNH	13		CI	439
	P1	1		HAP	1125		CI	510
	P1	22		BR	138	CASSANDRA'S	AE2	462
	P4	30		PDS	20	CASSIA	P2	114
	P5	135		VP6	120		P6	83
	M1	269		G2	238		VP2	66
	M1	292		AE7	210		G4	430
	MC	66		AE11	234		M15	592
	VP5	71	CARS	AE7	220	CASSOCK	HAP	1526
	VP7	11	CART	PO	2	CAST	UDH	106
	VP9	69		PO	20		HS	91
	G1	61		PLB	34		AR	124
	G1	422		GE	31		VHH	17
	G2	759		J3	18		AM	79
	G4	78		C	253		AM	203
	G4	489		C	268		AM	1117
	AE1	15		C	272		EMM	15
	AE2	351		C	278		PMQW	11
	AE3	201	CARTED	PUO3	7		EM	32
	AE3	934	CARTER	C	291		PAZ	21
	AE4	1	CARTHAGE	AM	17		CM	14
	AE4	807		AM	198		DA	91
	AE4	916		ECD	22		PSF	15
	AE6	238		DA	21		AA	805
	AE6	385		DA	165		PLB	31
	AE6	519		J10	425		MD	18
	AE6	640		AE1	23		MD	33
	AE6	699		AE1	30		MD	118
	AE6	1017		AE1	468		MD	316
	AE11	3		AE1	506		PRH	16
	AE11	875		AE4	147		EK	12
	AE11	1087		AE4	322		RL	146
	AE12	708		AE4	329		RL	283
	AE12	756		AE4	963		EC	18
	AE12	968		AE6	1160		MO	4

Word	Ref	No.
CAST	L3	54
	L3	78
	L3	230
	T23	98
	TA	199
	TA	221
	TA	256
	TA	432
	HAP	455
	HAP	1175
	HAP	1359
	PDS	3
	EL	141
	J3	196
	J3	241
	J3	337
	J10	243
	P1	101
	M1	106
	M1	530
	M1	535
	M1	735
	M1	892
	M1	1014
	M1	1022
	M1	1068
	M9	186
	M13	199
	SFL	8
	HI	8
	GK	22
	VP4	72
	VP5	41
	VP5	50
	VP8	147
	VP8	148
	G2	353
	G3	174
	G3	312
	G3	664
	G4	131
	G4	708
	AE1	155
	AE1	187
	AE1	755
	AE1	871
	AE2	91
	AE2	231
	AE2	547
	AE2	601
	AE2	778
	AE2	819
	AE2	1061
	AE3	236
	AE3	262
	AE3	358
	AE3	403
	AE3	780
	AE3	830
	AE3	857
	AE4	322
	AE4	917
	AE4	934
	AE5	309
	AE5	820
	AE5	861
	AE5	1014
	AE6	30
	AE6	49
	AE6	255
	AE6	273
	AE6	568
	AE6	939
	AE7	213
	AE7	273
	AE7	629
	AE8	37
	AE8	412
	AE8	565
	AE8	802
	AE9	351
	AE9	528
	AE10	76
	AE10	215
	AE10	829
	AE10	942
	AE10	1110
	AE11	217
	AE11	315
	AE11	918
	AE11	950
	AE11	1081
	AE12	457
	AE12	871
	AE12	1347
	OAE2	62

Word	Ref	No.
CAST	MG	9
	DO	90
	KT1	40
	KT1	69
	KT1	213
	KT1	229
	KT2	334
	KT2	546
	KT3	451
	KT3	476
	KT3	602
	KT3	693
	KT3	702
	KT3	958
	KT3	986
	M8	346
	B	43
	B	328
	B	498
	B	565
	B	572
	CAM	176
	HIF	439
	HIF	484
	HIF	489
	HIF	628
	C	278
	C	333
	C	424
	C	489
	C	579
	C	678
	TH	172
	TH	285
	M11	303
	M11	387
	M11	410
	M11	446
	M11	467
	FL	102
	FL	259
	FL	335
	M12	50
	M12	361
	M12	487
	AU	194
	AU	264
	WB	51
	WB	457
	WB	530
	M15	55
	M15	196
	M15	334
	M15	491
	M15	512
	CI	281
	CI	291
	CI	415
	CI	622
	PMK	29
CASTING	HAP	1766
	M1	650
	M1	747
	G1	213
	AE2	643
	AE5	3
	AE9	544
	AE9	626
	AE12	1364
	C	449
CASTLE	AE2	221
	AE5	588
	KT3	447
	C	50
CASTLE'S	KT1	218
CASTOR	P5	198
	AE10	191
	M12	533
CASTORS	AM	97
CASTS	AM	541
	ESF	28
	T23	13
	J6	622
	J10	215
	P3	224
	AE11	702
	WB	434
	M15	265
CASTUS	FL	172
	FL	188
	FL	511
CASUAL	HAP	1816
	AE10	558
	AE12	1364
CASUALLY	RH	31
CASUALTY	AE4	998

Word	Ref	No.
CAT	ELT	34
CATAMITE	P4	85
	VP3	10
CATARRHS	UDH	82
CATASTROPHE	EH	1
CATCALLS	PTP	40
CATCH	AM	716
	PK	23
	HAP	593
	P1	157
	M1	346
	M1	666
	AE4	983
	AE7	706
	MG	14
	KT3	327
	M11	94
	M11	222
CATCHES	AE2	418
	KT3	182
	M15	597
CATCHING	AE10	569
	AE11	110
	C	801
	M15	525
CATEGORY	PTP	48
CATERPILLARS	AE3	192
CATERWAUL	PD	61
CATES	HAP	1293
	AE5	54
CAT-EYED	L4	147
CATHARIN	ETL	30
CATHERINE	HAP	1503
CATHOLIC	AR	102
	NS	15
CATILINE	AE8	886
CATILLUS	AE7	932
	AE11	705
	AE11	951
CATO	UDH	70
	LCA	11
	AM	691
	ECD	19
	P3	87
	AE6	1156
	C	162
	C	196
	C	203
CATO'S	AE8	890
	C	204
	LCA	9
CATOS	E	13
CATS	EUO	18
	EUO	26
	EPC	3
CATTLE	PTW	23
	PSH	18
	P3	2
	M13	125
	VP5	38
	VP6	122
	VP10	9
	G2	205
	G2	303
	G2	512
	G3	240
	G3	515
	G3	566
	G3	590
	G3	724
	G3	828
	AE2	680
	AE11	488
	C	13
	CI	77
	PMK	37
CAUCASIAN	G2	618
CAUCASUS	WB	409
CAUGHT	RH	28
	AA	657
	AA	739
	HAP	1926
	J3	313
	J6	395
	J6	834
	P1	226
	VP3	148
	G4	571
	AE1	249
	AE2	1039
	AE5	68
	AE5	437
	AE7	111
	AE8	329
	AE9	716
	AE11	1056

CAUGHT	OAL	95
	OAL	822
	OAL	865
	KT2	36
	KT2	382
	KT2	591
	KT3	328
	M10	18
	C	670
	M12	385
	M12	386
	AU	53
	AU	475
	WB	347
CAUL	AE4	198
	AE7	1111
	AE11	110
	M11	394
CAULONIAN	AE3	726
CAULS	HIF	632
CAUSE	HS	43
	HS	89
	AR	266
	AR	315
	SMA	10
	SMA	81
	LC	50
	LCA	13
	LCA	27
	EIE	11
	AM	34
	PUO1	26
	ETC	7
	HP	68
	HP	118
	HP	236
	HP	241
	DA	48
	DA	66
	DA	211
	EMW	4
	EPF	12
	PUO5	13
	AA	82
	AA	89
	AA	107
	AA	206
	AA	296
	AA	320
	AA	475
	AA	608
	AA	700
	AA	875
	AA	970
	MD	141
	MD	156
	MD	199
	MD	200
	MD	270
	SAA	107
	SAA	248
	SAA	266
	SAA	289
	SAA	317
	SAA	364
	SAA	856
	SAA	890
	SAA	966
	SAA	1027
	EDG	2
	EDG	8
	EDG	43
	RL	13
	RL	150
	EC	24
	L3	146
	L3	268
	L3	273
	L3	295
	HAP	357
	HAP	489
	HAP	567
	HAP	814
	HAP	944
	HAP	952
	HAP	1065
	HAP	1412
	HAP	1421
	HAP	1610
	HAP	1620
	HAP	1695
	HAP	1713
	HAP	1963
	HAP	2054
	HAP	2110
	HAP	2161

CAUSE	HAP	2247
	HAP	2354
	HAP	2385
	HAP	2519
	PDS	29
	STS1	10
	SKA6	12
	OD	42
	J1	73
	J6	133
	J6	341
	J10	74
	J10	442
	J16	18
	J16	23
	J16	32
	J16	77
	P1	90
	P3	141
	M1	121
	M1	627
	M1	823
	M1	1013
	SFL	1
	G1	92
	G2	683
	G2	699
	G3	763
	G4	570
	G4	770
	G4	811
	AE1	42
	AE1	419
	AE1	479
	AE1	714
	AE1	766
	AE1	1045
	AE2	113
	AE2	378
	AE2	796
	AE3	51
	AE3	763
	AE4	273
	AE4	595
	AE5	5
	AE5	446
	AE6	141
	AE6	579
	AE6	620
	AE6	964
	AE6	1126
	AE6	1152
	AE6	1211
	AE7	671
	AE8	523
	AE9	172
	AE9	289
	AE10	139
	AE10	148
	AE10	220
	AE10	351
	AE11	155
	AE11	172
	AE11	332
	AE11	344
	AE11	383
	AE11	548
	AE11	665
	AE11	1287
	AE12	68
	AE12	877
	OAL	87
	OAL	91
	OAL	227
	OAL	229
	OAL	777
	OAL	833
	AF	108
	KT1	332
	KT2	155
	KT2	258
	KT2	323
	KT2	336
	KT3	539
	KT3	666
	KT3	676
	KT3	740
	KT3	1012
	KT3	1024
	KT3	1041
	TJD	10
	TJD	190
	M8	3
	M8	248
	B	691
	CAM	57

CAUSE	CAM	148
	HIF	9
	HIF	164
	HIF	463
	C	782
	TH	419
	TH	149
	TH	230
	TH	245
	M11	61
	M11	395
	M12	42
	M12	718
	M12	821
	M12	833
	AU	8
	AU	49
	AU	114
	AU	126
	AU	220
	AU	248
	AU	257
	AU	306
	AU	321
	AU	344
	AU	590
	WB	238
	WB	308
	WB	375
	M15	9
	M15	51
	M15	90
	CI	301
	CI	480
	CI	633
CAUSED	SEL3	17
	SKK	12
	P6	1
	VP10	55
	AE3	529
	AE5	471
	AE7	119
	AE10	548
	AE10	603
	AF	111
	AF	118
	KT1	253
	KT2	99
	KT3	775
	CAM	160
	M12	48
	AU	68
	AU	206
	CI	176
CAUSELESS	HAP	1977
	G4	501
	AE10	894
	AE11	162
CAUSES	SEL2	4
	TA	110
	J1	28
	J3	493
	J16	66
	M9	139
	G3	670
	AE1	11
	AE1	36
	AE1	573
	AE5	1030
	AE7	768
	KT2	12
	B	491
	HIF	106
	CI	206
CAUTION	AR	181
	AM	727
	SAA	304
	G4	593
	G4	703
	AE11	231
CAUTIOUS	J3	448
	J6	463
	M1	852
	ELT	16
	AE8	200
	AE11	513
	B	90
CAUTIOUSLY	AE5	214
	KT1	606
CAVALCADE	SMA	37
	J10	70
	KT3	540
CAVALCANTI	TH	152
CAVALIER	ET	15
CAVALIERS	EUF	5
CAVE	DA	95

Word	Ref	No.
CAVE	J6	3
	J6	85
	M1	777
	M1	793
	M13	63
	VP5	7
	AE1	78
	AE3	564
	AE3	810
	AE4	174
	AE4	242
	AE6	14
	AE6	62
	AE6	128
	AE6	149
	AE6	235
	AE6	338
	AE6	573
	AE8	278
	AE8	284
	AE8	835
	B	103
	B	146
	B	181
	B	252
	M11	301
	M12	318
	M12	557
	M15	524
CAVERN	VP8	98
	AE4	240
	AE5	278
	AE8	322
	B	121
	B	139
	B	261
	M11	269
CAVERN'S	AE3	568
	AE8	305
CAVERNS	L3	223
	M1	280
	M13	25
	G1	268
	G3	233
	G4	520
	AE1	199
	AE3	55
	AE3	850
	AE3	886
	AE5	885
	AE7	22
	AE10	1143
	M15	454
CAVE'S	M12	296
CAVES	AA	55
	PRH	3
	HAP	196
	HAP	1745
	J3	31
	M1	156
	M1	378
	M13	122
	VP10	77
	G3	578
	G4	223
	G4	620
	AE3	844
	AE8	554
	M11	30
	M15	122
	M15	519
CAWS	AM	347
CEASE	HS	83
	AR	312
	RH	65
	SMA	121
	LC	106
	LC	152
	DC	25
	SCG1	33
	HP	111
	DA	51
	AA	854
	MD	115
	SAA	723
	SAA	727
	EDGA	4
	L1	41
	H9	17
	AK	13
	AK	34
	HH	41
	HAP	1681
	HAP	1977
	J6	571
	P6	101
CEASE	M1	1031
	DHP	7
	VP8	78
	VP8	86
	VP9	91
	G1	292
	G1	319
	G1	487
	G2	745
	AE1	396
	AE1	416
	AE2	638
	AE4	70
	AE4	139
	AE4	888
	AE5	615
	AE5	889
	AE6	98
	AE6	1162
	AE7	757
	AE8	58
	AE8	82
	AE8	847
	AE10	22
	AE11	562
	AE11	1015
	AE12	171
	AE12	278
	AE12	473
	AE12	1005
	AE12	1175
	OAL	149
	OAL	340
	KT1	102
	KT1	408
	KT2	254
	KT3	234
	KT3	393
	KT3	617
	KT3	660
	CAM	80
	CAM	300
	HIF	149
	HIF	316
	HIF	608
	HIF	624
	C	763
	C	804
	TH	135
	M11	62
	M11	92
	M12	72
CEASED	M1	1008
	DHP	10
	AE1	267
	AE1	1036
	AE6	153
	AE9	143
	AE9	325
	AE11	461
	AE12	623
	KT3	357
	M8	13
	CAM	222
	HIF	403
	HIF	689
	TH	382
	FL	394
	M12	49
	AU	441
	AU	587
	M15	625
	CI	455
	AA	725
	VP1	52
	KT2	94
CEASES	CAM	80
CEASING	AU	587
CECILIA	SSC	51
	AF	161
	AF	171
	C	632
CECROPIAN	G4	390
CEDAR	HAP	1998
	P1	82
	G3	626
	AE1	629
	AE7	17
	AE7	241
CEDARS	EL	93
	G2	623
CEILING	J1	89
	AE8	39
	AE12	145
CELADON	M12	348
CELAENO	AE3	322
CELAENO	AE3	469
	AE3	938
CELEBRATE	J3	286
	J3	400
	G1	466
	AE5	65
	AE5	783
	AE8	231
	FL	488
CELEBRATED	HAP	1627
CELEBRATES	OAL	460
	DO	93
CELESTIAL	UDH	38
	JH	8
	SMA	23
	AA	306
	MF	40
	RL	105
	AT	109
	T18	46
	AK	13
	AK	38
	SSC	20
	BR	65
	M1	3
	VP4	59
	G1	206
	AE1	117
	AE1	453
	AE1	462
	AE1	873
	AE2	876
	AE3	5
	AE4	139
	AE4	288
	AE4	822
	AE6	286
	AE7	53
	AE7	388
	AE10	1101
	AE11	877
	AE12	639
	AE12	1151
	OAL	213
	MFL	2
	KT1	318
	B	521
	HIF	308
	HIF	679
	CI	166
CELESTIALS	AE10	159
CELIA	SM2	6
	STS1	1
	STS1	13
CELIMENA	SEL4	1
CELL	ELN	10
	CM	49
	SAA	924
	HAP	1235
	J6	181
	G1	522
	G4	43
	AE7	619
	AE7	635
	AE7	785
	KT3	1068
	KT3	760
	ESK	11
CELLAR	J3	466
CELLARS	AA	618
CELLS	AM	909
	HAP	1824
	G4	90
	G4	240
	G4	277
	G4	523
	AE1	603
	AE4	584
	C	741
CELTIC	HAP	235
CEMENTED	HAP	1876
CENOTAPH	M12	3
CENSE	AE8	377
CENSED	M12	362
CENSER	AE6	1104
CENSERS	AE1	985
	AE11	727
CENSING	HAP	2047
CENSOR	PMQ	26
	P1	267
	P3	51
CENSORIOUS	P4	101
CENSURE	EIE	14
	PCG2	12
	ML	1
	SAA	1057

Word	Code	Num	Word	Code	Num	Word	Code	Num
CENSURE	RL	452	CERES'	CAM	245	CHAINS	P5	180
	HAP	481	CERRIAL	FL	230		G4	633
	HAP	1296		FL	284		AE1	405
	HAP	1527	CERTAIN	DA	183		AE4	130
CENSURED	PA	4		PUF	16		AE4	705
CENSURES	EWG	21		RL	280		AE5	730
	EEL	2		RL	343		AE6	753
	PTL	9		RL	385		AE6	1153
	PC1	3		PD	32		AE7	632
	PLG	18		L4	54		AE8	296
	P1	11		HAP	643		AE8	866
	HAP	990		HAP	1897		AE8	876
	CI	5		EDS	25		AE10	18
CENTAUR	EUO	16		ESH	12		KT1	245
	AE5	161		J6	505		KT1	265
	AE5	203		J10	135		KT1	513
	AE5	205		P3	115		KT2	4
	AE5	237		P5	115		M8	90
	AE5	265		M1	21		CAM	58
	AE5	284		G1	483		HIF	550
	AE5	367		G1	620		M15	80
	AE10	280		G4	228	CHAIR	PCB	40
	OAL	12		AE3	147		CM	75
	M12	358		AE8	89		PLB	36
	M12	442		AE9	113		MD	87
	M12	463		AE9	982		SAA	1134
	M12	506		AE10	891		HAP	587
	M12	601		AE10	1149		HAP	781
CENTAUR'S	M12	498		AE11	551		HAP	2026
CENTAURS	AE6	399		OAL	53		J1	47
	AE7	422		OAL	454		J1	187
	AE7	934		OAL	661		J3	230
	AE8	390		DO	23		J3	270
	OAE2	8		KT1	433		J6	470
	M12	325		KT3	1032		AE6	841
	M12	657		TJD	173		AE7	266
	M15	435		B	142		AE10	807
CENTAURS'	J1	14		C	43		AE11	506
	G2	637		C	146		AE11	723
CENTAURY	G4	390		M11	263		OAL	554
	C	190		CI	371		KT3	56
CENTER	HS	134	CERTAINLY	HAP	926		B	209
	LC	156	CERTAINTY	HAP	1056		HIF	457
	RL	37		M1	481		WB	84
	P3	56		KT3	849		M15	339
	AE1	616		AU	576	CHAIRMAN'S	J3	396
	AE6	780	CERTITUDE	HAP	540	CHAIRS	AM	252
	AE7	781	CESSATION	G1	109		HAP	1016
	AE7	1060	CETHEGUS	J10	440		MM	25
	AE11	474		AE12	746	CHALDEANS	J6	715
	M15	367	CEYLON	AM	12	CHALICES	M12	343
CENTERED	HIF	226	CEYX	M11	19	CHALK	P5	79
CENTRAL	HAP	1102		M11	72		GK	29
CENTURIES	AR	293		M11	188		G2	295
	RL	347		M11	316	CHALLENGE	PA	39
	HAP	1950		M11	378		PTW	21
	KT2	217		M11	398		VP3	85
	KT3	1060		M11	400		VP8	77
	HIF	365		M11	406		G4	125
	M15	586		M11	421		AE1	1035
CENTURY	HAP	349		M11	422		AE4	456
	BR	49		M11	431		AE5	542
	M12	260	CHAERONEAN	EP	1		AE6	254
CEPHISUS'	M1	499	CHAFED	J6	744		AE10	1254
CERANOS	AU	401		AE4	986		WB	483
CERAUNIAN	AE3	660		AE5	691	CHALLENGED	KT2	178
CERBERUS	AE6	564		M8	121		KT3	581
CEREMONIAL	J10	57	CHAFF	PCG1	42		AU	140
	B	700		HAP	113	CHALLENGER	TA	200
CEREMONIES	HAP	599		BR	235		AE5	512
	EL	261		G1	279		AE5	554
	J3	259		G1	505		KT2	178
	AE3	154		G3	217		KT3	580
	KT3	199		C	821	CHALLENGES	G3	305
CEREMONY	PA	21	CHAFFER	GP	70		KT3	631
CERES	L4	157	CHAFFERS	EH	24	CHALYBE	AE7	589
	P4	66	CHAFING	M10	85	CHAMBER	EPC	16
	VP5	124	CHAIN	AA	596		AK	95
	G1	9		L4	135		HAP	1480
	G1	57		SKA3	2		J6	111
	G1	81		J10	307		CAM	280
	G1	139		P5	233		C	217
	G1	219		P5	251		ETP	26
	G1	479		AE7	19	CHAMBERLAIN	KT1	582
	G1	481		AE7	494	CHAMBERMAID	PSH	32
	AE2	970		AE10	331		J6	615
	AE4	78		KT2	289	CHAMBERS	G4	60
	OAE1	14		KT3	1025	CHAMELEON	HAP	2082
	DO	65		KT3	1030		M15	616
	TJD	46		HIF	141	CHAMP	AE3	713
	M8	7		GP	19		AE7	384
	CAM	238	CHAINED	AE3	599	CHAMPED	KT3	458
CERES'	J6	71	CHAINS	FS1	6	CHAMPIAN	TJD	51
	G1	462		HAP	19	CHAMPION	AA	293
	AE2	1007		J3	476		SAA	220
	AE6	652		J6	728		HAP	638

Word	Ref	Num
CHAMPION	HAP	1541
	HI	113
	AE2	368
	AE5	481
	AE5	517
	AE5	631
	AE6	254
	AE10	454
	AE10	759
	AE10	1039
	AE11	87
	AE11	953
	AE12	1294
	KT3	156
	KT3	357
	KT3	676
	HIF	393
	FL	334
	AU	142
	AU	523
CHAMPION'S	AE11	129
	AE12	366
	AE12	938
	AE12	1015
	AU	193
CHAMPIONS	AM	224
	AM	746
	SAA	249
	HAP	2385
	VP7	25
	AE12	727
	AE12	1031
	KT2	420
	KT2	435
	KT3	9
	KT3	112
	FL	411
	AU	85
CHAMPIONS'	AE12	327
	AE12	1055
	KT3	343
CHAMPS	HAP	1594
	AE4	193
CHANCE	RH	30
	DC	37
	LCA	21
	ECG2	8
	PFD	7
	PUO1	23
	PUO1	34
	PCB	12
	SAA	141
	SAA	919
	SAA	1074
	RL	19
	L3	19
	L3	187
	T23	100
	HAP	172
	HAP	323
	HAP	1344
	HAP	2145
	HAP	2262
	BR	100
	J3	74
	J3	438
	J6	785
	P1	85
	P1	86
	P4	9
	P6	158
	M13	34
	M13	195
	HI	98
	PLT	15
	VP2	52
	AE1	518
	AE1	717
	AE2	103
	AE3	388
	AE4	307
	AE5	262
	AE5	653
	AE6	717
	AE8	248
	AE8	273
	AE9	50
	AE9	222
	AE9	272
	AE9	359
	AE10	922
	AE10	1048
	AE10	1071
	AE11	29
	AE11	1034
	AE12	33

Word	Ref	Num
CHANCE	AE12	70
	AE12	96
	AE12	302
	AE12	646
	AE12	1040
	AE12	1056
	AE12	1118
	AE12	1144
	OAL	425
	OAL	565
	OAL	649
	OAL	671
	OAL	789
	AF	86
	AF	90
	KT1	67
	KT1	278
	KT1	325
	KT1	349
	KT1	561
	KT2	11
	KT2	137
	KT2	212
	KT2	216
	KT2	411
	KT3	162
	B	462
	B	559
	B	562
	C	601
	FL	124
	FL	524
	M12	27
	M12	316
	M12	410
	M12	429
	WB	221
	WB	421
	WB	423
	WB	504
	CI	86
	CI	444
	AS	7
CHANCED	G4	188
	AE10	559
	KT1	40
	KT1	358
	M12	673
CHANCELS	HAP	1725
CHANCERY	HH	13
CHANCES	AE9	272
CHANGE	UDH	65
	AR	129
	LC	150
	AM	944
	AM	1129
	EWGR	41
	EWGR	46
	PAL	32
	HP	188
	PSF	17
	PSF	29
	PSF	30
	PSF	33
	PSF	34
	EUF	3
	EUF	15
	AA	219
	AA	330
	AA	798
	AA	805
	SAA	21
	SAA	156
	L3	275
	L5	14
	TA	146
	PAA	30
	PAA	31
	HAP	607
	HAP	622
	HAP	1057
	HAP	1239
	HAP	1518
	HAP	1525
	HAP	1614
	HAP	1657
	HAP	1696
	HAP	1709
	HAP	1731
	HAP	1801
	HAP	1932
	HAP	2083
	HAP	2459
	BR	39
	PP	20
	SSH	1

Word	Ref	Num
CHANGE	J3	347
	J6	40
	J6	57
	J6	316
	J10	144
	J10	413
	J10	454
	P1	243
	P6	1
	P6	120
	M1	740
	M9	120
	SFL	16
	EHC	35
	VP1	79
	VP8	70
	VP9	70
	G1	120
	G1	519
	G1	588
	G1	626
	G2	72
	G2	102
	G3	412
	G3	816
	G4	370
	AE1	949
	AE2	526
	AE3	219
	AE7	120
	AE7	263
	AE9	117
	AE9	832
	AE10	9
	AE10	887
	AE11	389
	AE12	105
	AE12	339
	AE12	356
	AE12	897
	OAL	391
	OAL	878
	KT1	240
	KT1	384
	KT1	569
	KT2	80
	KT2	83
	KT2	629
	KT3	1047
	CAM	344
	TH	34
	TH	377
	M11	132
	M12	248
	M12	283
	M12	628
	M12	734
	WB	366
	WB	544
	M15	320
	M15	467
	M15	480
	M15	625
	M15	641
	M15	672
	GP	124
	CI	395
	ETP	35
CHANGED	AR	158
	PFD	9
	EUF	11
	PPC	12
	SAA	361
	EK	14
	PDG	13
	AT	12
	AT	18
	L3	168
	PAA	42
	AK	127
	HH	25
	HAP	392
	HAP	565
	HAP	607
	HAP	629
	ODA	32
	J1	37
	J10	120
	M1	1
	M9	3
	M13	231
	VP1	39
	VP8	96
	AE1	542
	AE2	153
	AE5	808

Word	Ref	No.	Word	Ref	No.	Word	Ref	No.
CHARIOTEER	AE12	1326	CHARMED	SAA	908	CHARMS	AE2	804
	KT2	593		HAP	265		AE4	704
	AU	547		PTS	38		AE4	719
CHARIOTEERS	AA	908		J6	95		AE8	491
	G3	166		VP6	99		AE8	521
CHARIOTS	AA	730		AE3	153		AE8	535
	SAA	193		AE6	574		AE8	766
	J1	241		HIF	170		AE8	711
	J10	283		C	603		AE8	807
	M1	600		FL	370		AE10	763
	G3	28		M15	98		AE12	896
	G3	180		GP	18		OAL	343
	G3	286		GP	21		OAE2	7
	AE3	712	CHARMER	SSF	20		DO	8
	AE6	885	CHARMING	SCG1	15		KT1	232
	AE6	890		HP	88		KT1	262
	AE7	253		AA	34		KT2	505
	AE9	425		AA	485		KT3	178
	OAL	5		DOD	14		KT3	317
	OAL	158		AK	25		KT3	332
	OAL	173		SKA2	2		KT3	369
CHARITIES	HAP	1542		OD	3		KT3	726
	HAP	1547		OD	42		KT3	801
	MFL	30		J10	256		B	157
	GP	132		M1	697		B	435
CHARITY	AM	1094		VP5	70		CAM	175
	PCG1	23		AE1	107		FL	606
	PFD	10		AE4	407		M15	356
	RL	198		AE7	899		M15	490
	RL	212		AE10	862		M15	491
	RL	224		KT1	521		CI	260
	GE	23		KT3	789		STP	20
	HH	25		HIF	512	CHARON	AE6	413
	HAP	363		HIF	741		AE6	447
	HAP	700		FL	49	CHAROPES	AU	403
	HAP	904		FL	157	CHART	HAP	1143
	HAP	1221		WB	532	CHARTER	SAA	12
	HAP	1399		CI	97		PK	24
	HAP	1404	CHARMS	RH	8		PAA	45
	HAP	1714		DC	7		MD	196
	BR	158		AM	943	CHARTER'S	AM	1175
	BR	301		PCG1	45	CHARWORK	AT	73
	EL	60		E	20	CHARYBDIS	AE3	537
	EL	90		HP	93		AE3	734
	EL	117		HP	101		AE11	407
	EL	152		DA	114	CHARYBDIS'	AE3	899
	EL	193		D	35	CHASE	AM	382
	EL	294		SAA	20		AM	811
	ESH	10		SAA	27		HAP	963
	P1	178		SAA	167		ODA	4
	P6	74		SAA	809		J10	224
	MC	50		SAA	887		M1	315
	B	318		SAA	1022		M1	634
	C	648		SAA	1100		M1	730
	GP	4		AT	43		M1	813
CHARLEMAGNE	C	502		AT	75		VCS	26
	FL	543		L1	56		HI	81
CHARLES	AR	19		FS1	9		VP10	80
	AR	49		FS3	8		VP10	89
	AR	111		TA	56		G3	551
	AR	120		TA	151		G3	623
	AR	143		TA	302		AE3	643
	AR	231		TA	471		AE4	201
	AR	240		AK	149		AE4	222
	RH	90		HAP	1389		AE5	775
	RH	93		HAP	2019		AE7	414
	RH	105		BR	108		AE8	423
	LC	154		STS1	16		AE9	941
	AM	163		SKA2	22		AE11	824
	AM	170		LS	15		AE11	925
	AM	324		ODA	35		AE11	1004
	ER	29		MS	10		AE11	1013
	TA	19		PSH	40		AE11	1027
	TA	241		SSH	3		AE11	1125
	TA	369		J6	191		AE12	9
	TA	416		J6	236		AE12	1080
	MC	6		J6	407		AE12	1091
	GK	100		P3	70		AE12	1108
CHARM	LCA	46		M1	651		OAL	99
	ENH	3		M1	803		DO	89
	EOE	32		GK	2		KT2	223
	SSF	19		VP3	112		KT2	236
	MF	153		VP8	93		KT2	630
	SAA	118		VP8	96		KT3	247
	EDGA	25		VP8	99		TJD	51
	VP2	20		VP8	105		TJD	88
	VP7	55		VP8	109		TH	120
	AE6	567		VP8	119		TH	261
	B	59		VP8	127		SMP	32
	M11	216		VP8	133		SMP	87
CHARMED	AR	190		VP8	145		SMP	93
	AM	607		VP8	151	CHASED	AR	135
	AM	1199		VP8	159		AM	169
	SEL1	1		G3	332		SAA	800
	AA	708		AE1	700		HAP	5
	SAA	607		AE1	1003		HAP	55

CHASED	HAP	235	CHEAP	ECG2	11	CHEEK	SAA	75
	HAP	2453		PNH	9		J10	309
	VP2	93		EAZ	36		P1	40
	J3	482		ML	7		P4	90
	AE4	7		RL	90		G1	596
	AE5	55		RL	397		AE7	585
	AE10	360		SKA2	12		OAL	274
	AE10	785		J6	44		OAE2	44
	AE10	917		J6	438		B	299
	AE10	1216		AE12	903		HIF	458
	KT1	186		CI	288		CI	152
	TJD	56	CHEAPER	AM	340	CHEEKS	AM	958
	TJD	70		L2	36		CM	27
	C	749		J6	756		CM	108
CHASE-GUNS	AM	326	CHEAPEST	HAP	375		L4	121
CHASERS'	SAA	839		OAL	509		T23	19
CHASES	AE11	1148	CHEAPLY	PMQ	27		J3	420
CHASING	AE5	329		DA	202		J6	156
	TJD	70		SAA	685		J6	187
CHASMS	AR	108		PAA	29		J6	604
CHASSI'S	TH	58		J3	281		J6	665
CHASTE	SMA	119		DO	68		P3	237
	VHH	24	CHEAT	LC	68		M13	29
	AM	134		PMQW	4		VP10	32
	EUO2	29		PCD	11		VP10	40
	HP	1		EMK	23		G1	607
	AA	618		EKK	9		G4	506
	D	17		EKK	10		AE1	992
	L3	77		HP	226		AE2	1090
	L4	290		PSF	25		AE5	606
	T18	60		AA	436		AE9	231
	T27	25		AA	592		AE9	633
	H2	58		AA	748		AE9	1014
	ESH	18		MD	36		AE9	1099
	J6	197		MD	43		AE11	1008
	J6	236		MD	198		AE11	1194
	J6	398		SAA	283		AE12	102
	J10	459		PDG	10		AE12	335
	J10	501		RL	143		AE12	886
	VP4	11		OE	44		OAL	827
	G2	762		HAP	1688		AF	70
	AE1	455		SKA4	10		DO	151
	AE5	963		ESH	33		KT3	872
	AE6	758		J6	689		M8	270
	AE7	1056		P3	32		M8	271
	AE8	884		P4	108		CAM	115
	OAL	704		P6	169		M11	10
	OAL	851		M9	65		M11	392
	DO	158		M9	115		M11	405
	KT2	466		G2	656		M11	465
	KT2	618		G4	587		FL	420
	KT3	203		G4	647		M12	354
	KT3	214		AE1	957		M12	404
	KT3	246		AE11	1038		M12	741
	C	79		OAL	285	CHEER	PMM	16
	WB	64		OAL	523		SCD2	5
	WB	141		OAL	727		PNH	8
	CI	6		OAL	729		PAL	35
CHASTELY	TA	312		OAL	742		PLB	33
CHASTISE	PDG	26		M10	17		PRH	1
	HIF	451		C	484		T23	11
CHASTISED	AM	668	CHEATED	SAA	114		HAP	1731
	AM	1089		RL	393		HAP	1881
	SAA	346		PD	40		BR	15
	AU	342		HAP	2019		PMS	34
CHASTITY	DA	101		SKA4	10		J3	279
	ESH	15		J10	217		J6	102
	J6	2		M1	963		J10	336
	J6	22		KT2	131		P6	36
	J6	90	CHEATEST	P4	108		P6	167
	J6	258	CHEATING	PSF	25		VP5	107
	KT3	158		OAL	729		G3	584
	FL	509	CHEATS	AR	252		G4	556
	WB	492		PPC	5		G4	768
CHAT	HAP	561		PD	40		AE1	299
	HAP	2197		L4	67		AE1	899
	PP	45		L4	185		AE1	1026
	BP	71		HAP	1447		AE2	93
	M12	221		PKA	31		AE2	624
	PMK	15		EKA	26		AE5	485
CHATTELS	EK	36		J6	332		AE8	236
CHATTER	P3	204		P4	56		AE8	693
CHATTERING	PPS	13		AE6	35		AE9	1107
	OAL	30		OAL	511		AE12	169
	AE7	265	CHECK	AM	344		OAL	490
	TH	146		AM	794		KT1	240
CHAUCER	DO	11		PC1	7		KT2	83
	DO	32		BR	269		KT3	721
CHAW	MD	147	CHECKED	SAA	797		M8	246
	M15	132		VP6	5		M8	247
CHAWED	C	485		AE5	202		B	615
CHAWS	PDG	14		AF	72		HIF	779
	VP6	78	CHECKING	CI	170		C	32
	VP7	60	CHEEK	SEL3	20		C	193
CHEAP	LC	123		PC1	8		C	788
	EEL	33		PLB	33		TH	327

CHEER	FL	396	CHERUB	AM	1082	CHIEF	AE9	115		
	FL	604	CHERUBIN	DO	156		AE9	298		
	WB	203	CHERUBS	ODA	68		AE9	712		
	CI	395	CHEST	AM	830		AE9	756		
CHEERED	AE2	738		J3	338		AE10	182		
	AE5	229		J10	17		AE10	220		
	AE5	244		G3	127		AE10	310		
	AE8	50		AE11	752		AE10	339		
	KT1	212		AE11	1134		AE10	352		
	KT1	548		M12	358		AE10	443		
	KT3	875		M12	535		AE10	618		
	TH	123	CHESTNUT	G2	20		AE10	644		
	M12	108		G2	98		AE10	804		
	M12	173	CHESTNUTS	M13	116		AE10	830		
	AU	342		VP1	114		AE10	910		
	WB	510		VP2	73		AE10	949		
	GP	75		VP7	74		AE10	1060		
	CI	292	CHESTS	AE10	805		AE10	1138		
CHEERFUL	AR	226		AE12	136		AE11	3		
	AM	469	CHEW	J3	473		AE11	141		
	D	27		CI	17		AE11	183		
	L1	14	CHEWED	OAE2	42		AE11	283		
	L3	257	CHIAN	VP5	109		AE11	554		
	L4	101		G2	140		AE11	788		
	H2	93	CHICK	PLG	27		AE12	342		
	HAP	1223		CAM	47		AE12	631		
	BR	149		C	80		AE12	1108		
	PDS	5	CHICKEN-HEARTED	PSF	41		AE12	1327		
	ODA	31	CHICKENS	HAP	2423		AE12	1346		
	P2	6		HAP	2518		OAL	527		
	M1	1081	CHIDE	L3	163		MG	7		
	VP5	90		HAP	2052		MG	30		
	VP7	70		VP5	132		KT1	3		
	G1	201		AE3	579		KT1	135		
	G1	463		AE4	670		KT3	484		
	G2	198		AE6	732		KT3	520		
	G2	258	CHIDES	M1	646		KT3	577		
	G2	267		AE4	507		KT3	666		
	G2	300		AE6	724		KT3	926		
	G2	771		AE11	1074		M8	2		
	G3	77	CHIDING	M12	73		M8	77		
	G3	318	CHIEF	AM	85		M8	210		
	G3	579		PO	26		M8	255		
	AE1	52		AA	220		HIF	83		
	AE1	252		AA	294		HIF	487		
	AE1	276		AA	564		TH	2		
	AE1	422		AA	902		TH	259		
	AE1	1014		AA	914		FL	236		
	AE3	238		MD	28		FL	514		
	AE3	687		SAA	856		M12	168		
	AE4	169		SAA	975		M12	184		
	AE5	708		RL	184		M12	215		
	AE5	927		L3	248		M12	814		
	AE5	1085		TA	269		AU	424		
	AE6	194		HAP	308		WB	121		
	AE6	891		HAP	1190		WB	270		
	AE7	181		HAP	1698	CHIEFLY	SAA	721		
	AE7	195		ETS	5		HAP	2365		
	AE7	353		J6	631		G1	30		
	AE8	408		J10	35	CHIEFS	HS	41		
	AE8	599		J10	380		AM	185		
	AE8	721		P1	42		AM	254		
	AE9	209		P1	142		AA	543		
	AE11	23		HI	92		MD	179		
	AE11	1193		G3	24		MD	308		
	KT1	169		AE1	135		PRH	34		
	BP	53		AE1	172		SAA	39		
	M10	71		AE1	275		SAA	823		
	TH	407		AE1	824		SAA	935		
	FL	349		AE3	290		SAA	972		
	FL	415		AE4	101		HAP	688		
	GP	129		AE4	272		VP4	42		
	CI	546		AE4	330		G4	133		
CHEERFULLY	AM	306		AE5	24		AE1	883		
	TA	212		AE5	370		AE2	37		
CHEERLESS	DOD	4		AE5	484		AE4	415		
	ODA	11		AE5	509		AE6	649		
CHEERLY	G3	539		AE5	714		AE6	659		
CHEERS	AM	967		AE5	733		AE6	815		
	M1	1078		AE6	155		AE7	153		
	AE5	1007		AE6	404		AE7	606		
	AE10	604		AE6	453		AE7	889		
	AE10	759		AE6	543		AE8	849		
CHEESE	M13	132		AE6	574		AE9	204		
	VP1	45		AE6	885		AE9	1048		
CHEESE-CAKE	ETL	20		AE6	1063		AE10	784		
CHELIDONIAN	HAP	1788		AE7	203		AE11	19		
CHERISH	J16	93		AE7	255		AE11	119		
	AE1	383		AE7	372		AE11	262		
	M8	383		AE7	676		AE11	663		
CHERISHED	PFD	16		AE7	727		AE11	1258		
	SAA	63		AE8	42		AE12	169		
	AE7	677		AE8	158		AE12	488		
	M12	830		AE8	239		AE12	727		
CHERRY	G2	24		AE8	664		AE12	821		
CHERSIDAMAS	AU	404		AE9	92		AE12	1142		

CHIEFS	AE12	1357
	KT3	8
	KT3	544
	KT3	719
	KT3	731
	KT3	964
	M8	92
	M8	126
	HIF	19
	HIF	185
	HIF	343
	HIF	515
	M11	341
	FL	310
	FL	534
	FL	576
	M12	833
	AU	1
	AU	375
	AU	429
	AU	569
	M15	656
CHILD	UDH	25
	RH	30
	CM	49
	L4	219
	AK	70
	HAP	1600
	HAP	1686
	HAP	1946
	BR	220
	BR	255
	OD	12
	ODA	36
	J6	822
	P4	42
	HI	25
	HI	37
	HI	172
	GK	143
	G3	265
	AE1	876
	AE2	954
	AE4	121
	AE11	834
	OAL	8
	B	355
	CAM	191
	CAM	234
	CAM	370
	C	365
	C	370
	M11	42
	M12	598
	EWR	27
CHILDBED	J6	766
CHILDBIRTH	T27	50
	M9	9
CHILDHOOD	J10	363
	G2	500
	AE9	260
	OAL	212
	KT1	361
CHILDISH	P5	40
	P5	269
	AE5	717
	M15	304
CHILDLESS	J3	221
	J3	359
CHILDREN	AM	134
	AM	202
	EOE	15
	PSF	35
	EUF	33
	L2	59
	L2	63
	L3	84
	H2	66
	HAP	2002
	EL	193
	EL	231
	EL	235
	EL	349
	J6	121
	J6	252
	J10	322
	J10	373
	M1	613
	VP9	68
	G2	743
	G2	760
	G4	293
	G4	683
	G4	742
	AE2	281
	AE3	132

CHILDREN	AE5	750
	AE6	1225
CHILDREN'S	SMA	136
	HAP	1332
	VP9	68
	AE1	1001
	AE3	132
	AE6	1126
	AE6	1144
	AE8	547
	AE10	739
	B	309
	M15	690
CHILD'S	PTW	21
	RL	395
CHILL	GE	1
	G1	135
	AE5	527
	AE8	668
	AE12	662
CHILLED	G2	470
CHILLING	G3	168
CHILLNESS	AE12	1254
	KT2	188
CHILLS	AE9	975
CHIMAERA	AE6	403
	AE7	1074
CHIMAERA'S	AE5	155
CHIMAERAS	AR	159
CHIME	PMQ	5
	VP9	72
	G4	252
	CI	34
	AE8	594
CHIMERAS	C	341
CHIMES	P1	183
CHIMING	PLN	2
	L4	16
CHIMNEY	M1	404
	VP6	115
	G3	633
	G4	434
CHIMNEY'S	AE4	673
CHIMNEYS	HAP	1725
CHIN	JH	14
	ECD	16
	AA	648
	J6	155
	M13	8
	VP1	39
	VP8	57
	G3	89
	AE4	366
	AE6	414
	AE8	214
	AE12	465
	HIF	678
	M11	305
	M12	198
	M12	357
CHINA	GE	22
	J6	226
CHINE	P1	45
	P1	185
	G3	137
	G3	197
	G3	746
	AE8	243
	AE10	535
	M8	217
	BP	62
CHINK	SAA	460
	P3	2
	M13	220
CHINKING	P2	21
CHINKS	J3	318
	G1	130
	G2	477
	G3	656
	G4	54
CHINKY	G4	63
CHINS	AE9	844
CHIPS	KT3	974
	M8	266
	BP	54
CHIROMANCERS'	J6	756
CHIRON	J3	337
	OAL	13
CHIRPING	AE8	600
CHISEL	M1	543
CHIVALRY	HI	186
	KT1	101
	KT1	120
	KT3	10
	KT3	96
	TH	8

CHIVALRY	FL	539
CHLOE	R	1
	R	15
	R	19
CHLOREUS	AE11	1131
CHLORIS	SFL	5
	SFL	7
	SFL	19
CHLORIS'S	ETC	20
CHOCOLATE	EKA	19
CHOICE	HS	8
	AR	82
	LC	16
	AM	173
	HP	106
	HP	132
	AA	981
	PRH	43
	HAP	408
	HAP	1338
	HAP	2183
	EL	253
	PSH	31
	EH	9
	J10	122
	J10	513
	P5	21
	M9	71
	DHP	31
	VP5	9
	VP8	37
	VP8	46
	VP10	74
	G1	287
	G2	370
	G3	117
	AE1	592
	AE2	986
	AE4	493
	AE8	177
	AE8	657
	AE9	234
	AE10	111
	AE10	963
	AE12	955
	AE12	985
	OAL	47
	OAL	99
	OAL	108
	OAL	202
	MM	32
	KT1	327
	KT1	328
	KT3	5
	B	53
	B	409
	B	466
	B	478
	B	485
	B	509
	B	534
	CAM	30
	C	527
	C	532
	AU	270
	AU	317
	AU	432
	M15	5
	GP	123
	CI	438
CHOICEST	SMA	54
CHOIR	SMA	49
	AM	914
	AM	1081
	AM	1102
	L4	153
	T18	5
	TA	371
	AK	38
	AK	193
	BR	321
	LS	1
	ODA	79
	J6	687
	DHP	23
	VP9	47
	G1	473
	G4	340
	G4	546
	AE1	702
	AE2	395
	AE5	312
	AE6	892
	AE8	379
	AE10	312
	AE10	322

CHOIR	AF	21
	KT1	41
	KT2	313
	HIF	808
	FL	51
	FL	150
	FL	169
	FL	184
	WB	215
CHOIRS	SSC	47
	EL	127
	J6	457
	AE2	313
	AE5	1078
	AE9	132
	WB	32
CHOISE	MHD	7
CHOKE	J1	69
	VP5	56
	P1	53
	P5	8
	G4	335
	AE3	190
	AE8	716
	AE11	1276
	CAM	143
	M12	672
CHOKED	AR	278
	MF	103
	L3	71
	T27	109
	J10	298
	G1	225
	G3	746
	AE2	288
	AE5	1057
	AE8	317
	AE8	638
	AE11	287
	AE12	1255
	B	114
	B	146
	B	276
	TH	104
	M12	409
	CI	227
CHOKES	G1	182
	M15	518
CHOKING	MD	47
CHOLER	AE12	1208
	OAL	415
	C	147
	C	150
	C	156
	C	174
	C	181
CHOLERIC	PRL	31
	AA	647
CHOÖN	AU	404
CHOOSE	SMA	135
	SMA	127
	EWG	15
	LCA	12
	SIE	11
	AM	56
	AM	179
	PTL	23
	PLG	24
	PC1	6
	AA	827
	AA	979
	EPC	26
	MF	205
	SAA	902
	AT	95
	TA	331
	HAP	40
	HAP	128
	SKA5	3
	LS	2
	SSH	2
	J3	46
	J6	58
	J6	87
	J10	162
	P5	7
	P5	226
	P6	133
	M9	103
	G1	38
	G1	372
	G2	311
	G2	368
	G3	80
	G3	185
	AE1	590

CHOOSE	AE4	151
	AE4	419
	AE6	58
	AE8	611
	AE11	494
	OAL	108
	OAL	134
	OAL	279
	OAL	480
	KT1	304
	KT2	157
	KT3	160
	KT3	242
	KT3	791
	KT3	1088
	B	326
	B	360
	CAM	31
	CAM	104
	WB	463
	WB	483
	WB	496
	WB	513
CHOOSES	PUO4	38
	AE8	110
CHOOSING	EL	254
	J6	559
CHOOSING-TRIBES	SAA	550
CHOP	MD	227
CHOPPED	HAP	629
	HIF	631
CHORISTER	HAP	1729
CHORISTERS	TA	366
	TH	61
CHOSE	LC	15
	DC	52
	LCA	10
	AM	462
	AM	300
	AM	1082
	PA	5
	AA	417
	AA	594
	AA	885
	AA	886
	SAA	342
	SAA	371
	RL	453
	PD	22
	TA	233
	HAP	441
	HAP	883
	HAP	2280
	PTS	35
	EL	254
	J3	2
	J3	104
	P2	38
	M1	293
	M13	51
	VP7	25
	G2	780
	AE3	149
	AE5	665
	AE6	250
	AE6	677
	AE6	862
	AE7	380
	AE7	453
	AE7	1097
	AE9	300
	AE10	1107
	AE11	91
	AE11	850
	AE11	1150
	AE11	1245
	OAE1	26
	AF	73
	B	611
	M10	3
	C	224
	TH	41
	FL	604
	FL	617
	M12	160
	WB	449
	CI	71
	CI	242
	AS	63
CHOSEN	PUO3	24
	AA	88
	SAA	16
	SAA	379
	SAA	697
	TA	428
	HAP	705

CHOSEN	HAP	965
	BR	296
	EL	207
	PSH	29
	G1	285
	AE4	77
	AE5	954
	AE5	988
	AE6	114
	AE7	648
	AE7	943
	AE8	722
	AE10	306
	AE10	1191
	AE11	781
	AE11	884
	MM	31
	KT1	322
	KT2	419
	M8	44
	B	592
	HIF	217
	HIF	430
	M11	343
	FL	311
	FL	334
	CI	266
	CI	547
	AS	101
CHOUGHS	HAP	2545
CHOUSED	SAA	553
	PAA	27
CHRIST	RL	312
	HAP	704
	HAP	871
CHRISTENED	PTC	20
	PSF	26
CHRISTIAN	EDG	16
	RL	130
	RL	222
	RL	280
	RL	322
	HAP	691
	HAP	1146
	HAP	1352
	HAP	1645
	PDS	23
	EDS	9
	FL	536
CHRISTIAN'S	TA	502
	HAP	2165
CHRISTIANS	EK	30
	NS	13
	EL	39
CHRISTMAS-DAY	PC1	19
CHROMIS	AE11	1000
	M12	451
CHROMIUS	AU	401
CHRONICLE	M12	711
CHRONICLERS	PLB	19
CHRONICLES	AR	106
CHRONOS	SMP	1
	SMP	17
CHRONOS'	KT3	426
CHRYSA	HIF	59
	HIF	618
	AU	283
CHRYSA'S	HIF	596
CHRYSEIS	HIF	433
	HIF	511
	HIF	512
CHRYSES	HIF	17
	HIF	614
CHRYSIPPUS	P6	186
CHTHONIUS	M12	593
CHU	PLN	35
CHUCK	C	430
CHUCKED	C	441
CHUCKLE	T27	69
CHURCH	AR	21
	SMA	47
	AM	148
	PTC	32
	AA	649
	AA	930
	D	40
	SAA	393
	SAA	386
	RL	275
	RL	281
	RL	282
	RL	319
	RL	354
	RL	357
	RL	360
	RL	376

Word	Ref	No.	Word	Ref	No.	Word	Ref	No.
CHURCH	RL	438	CICERO	RL	79	CIRCUS	OAL	190
	RL	445	CIDER	G3	585		M12	138
	HAP	42	CILICIA'S	HI	32	CIRQUE	AE5	720
	HAP	198	CILLA	HIF	59	CISSEUS	AE5	705
	HAP	360		HIF	617		AE10	442
	HAP	398		AU	282		AE12	790
	HAP	431	CIMBRIAN	J10	429	CITADEL	AE1	588
	HAP	469	CIMINIA	AE7	960		AE2	1033
	HAP	480	CIMMERIANS	M11	268		AU	527
	HAP	491	CINDERS	M1	350	CITADELS	L5	15
	HAP	585	CINNAMON	CAM	16	CITE	WB	271
	HAP	656		M15	592	CITED	AE1	28
	HAP	662	CINNA'S	VP9	46	CITES	HAP	821
	HAP	678	CINYRAS	AE10	267	CITESSES	PAA	43
	HAP	835		CAM	2	CITHAERON	G3	73
	HAP	848		CAM	68	CITHERON	KT2	498
	HAP	867		CAM	102	CITIES	PUO2	10
	HAP	872		CAM	145		M1	410
	HAP	926		CAM	292		GK	132
	HAP	930		CAM	308		VP2	89
	HAP	936	CIONS	G2	92		VP4	39
	HAP	988	CIPSEUS	CI	244		G1	687
	HAP	1011		CI	245		G2	213
	HAP	1018	CIRCE	VP8	96		G2	246
	HAP	1026		AE7	260		G3	47
	HAP	1036		AE7	13		G4	225
	HAP	1055		AE7	388		G4	296
	HAP	1066	CIRCEAN	KT2	505		AE1	361
	HAP	1069	CIRCE'S	AE3	495		AE1	774
	HAP	1101		AE7	12		AE3	98
	HAP	1160		AE7	24		AE3	144
	HAP	1188		AE7	1091		AE3	533
	HAP	1196	CIRCLE	PT	20		AE4	56
	HAP	1211		PUO5	4		AE4	251
	HAP	1218		AA	838		AE7	177
	HAP	1499		GE	27		AE7	861
	HAP	1935		HAP	698		AE7	871
	HAP	1947		G1	571		AE11	442
	HAP	2038		G2	556		AE12	35
	HAP	2089		AE5	61		TH	1
	HAP	2355		AE5	146		AU	458
	HAP	2555		KT2	626		M15	446
	BR	19		KT3	647	CITIZEN	PKK	14
	BR	78		TJD	65		J3	5
	BR	295		B	77		J3	150
	EH	20		HIF	675		J16	11
	EH	21		CI	340	CITIZENS	PD	5
	J3	467	CIRCLED	AE10	203		HAP	167
	J6	628	CIRCLES	AR	299		J3	323
	AE2	1034		RL	36		J16	38
	C	621		L3	176		P5	105
	M15	610		VP4	8		G4	20
	GP	92		G4	767		G4	295
	CI	81		AE5	776		G4	336
	CI	424		FL	169		AE11	469
	CI	564		M12	412		AE12	844
CHURCH-BEGOT	HAP	1756		M15	549	CITRON	P1	98
CHURCH-BELIEVING	HAP	1756	CIRCLING	DC	29		G2	726
CHURCHES	AM	283		BR	306	CITRONS	G2	175
	EWGR	34		G4	689	CITS	PW	23
	PLN	1		AE1	832		PUO1	37
	HAP	683		AE6	595		EUF	6
	HAP	1025		AE6	655		PAA	43
	HAP	1475		AE7	496		PKA	25
CHURCHMEN	AM	1092		AE11	1117		EKA	2
	GP	92		AE12	306	CITY	AM	614
CHURCH-MILITANT	PLB	51		DO	84		AM	651
CHURCH'S	LC	14		FL	190		AM	911
	ETC	27	CIRCUIT	M1	456		AM	964
	HAP	398		G1	35		AM	1159
	HAP	622		AE1	551		AM	1170
	HAP	660		AE5	754		PFD	20
	HAP	1177		AE8	304		PM	26
	C	77		AE9	701		PM	39
CHURCH-TRADITION	HAP	780		AE11	210		EM	32
CHURL	EOE	19	CIRCUITS	AE1	370		EKK	8
	HAP	2465	CIRCULAR	HS	18		PCB	9
	G4	744		KT2	442		PLG	5
	WB	438	CIRCULARLY	AM	5		DA	126
	M15	160	CIRCUMCISED	EC	45		PUO4	11
CHURLISH	AE4	783	CIRCUMFERENCE	M1	461		AA	593
CHURLS	AE7	672		HAP	661		AA	619
	AE7	702		KT2	441		ELB	26
	KT3	408	CIRCUMSCRIBED	DC	34		SAA	290
	C	762		EAZ	5		EDGA	3
	GP	46		AA	54		L3	287
CHURNED	P1	206		M1	69		H29	41
	HIF	361	CIRCUMSTANCES	AA	209		PKA	45
CHURNING	G3	400		C	364		EKA	23
	AE7	633	CIRCUMVENT	AE2	80		J3	314
CHURNS	M1	309		AE8	272		J3	348
	AE10	1025		C	487		J3	483
	M8	27	CIRCUMVENTED	AA	754		J6	45
CHYMIC	AM	1169		AU	314		P1	224
CHYMIST	AA	550	CIRCUS	P4	95		G4	272
CHYMISTS	AR	162		OAL	159		G4	282

Word	Code	No.
CITY	G4	335
	G4	350
	AE1	377
	AE1	467
	AE1	805
	AE2	7
	AE2	256
	AE2	263
	AE2	316
	AE2	490
	AE3	28
	AE3	359
	AE3	446
	AE3	453
	AE3	505
	AE3	513
	AE3	652
	AE4	64
	AE4	138
	AE4	184
	AE4	332
	AE4	435
	AE4	940
	AE5	156
	AE5	984
	AE7	194
	AE7	577
	AE7	600
	AE8	138
	AE8	410
	AE8	734
	AE9	630
	AE10	289
	AE10	401
	AE11	40
	AE11	197
	AE11	377
	AE11	685
	AE11	778
	AE11	1311
	AE12	364
	AE12	817
	AE12	837
	KT1	82
	KT1	122
	KT1	160
	KT2	23
	KT2	93
	KT2	586
	M10	101
	HIF	507
	C	743
	M11	172
	M12	777
	M15	610
	M15	657
CITY-CUCKOLD	OE	45
CITY'S	J10	438
CITY-TREATS	PSF	4
CIVET	EL	156
CIVIL	HS	141
	AM	315
	AM	1051
	AM	1103
	PMQ	37
	PMQ	38
	PWGR	18
	PEL	7
	ETL	5
	PAR	21
	EMQW	25
	PM	3
	PCD	15
	PUF	31
	EUF	34
	EAL	8
	PCB	36
	AA	74
	PLB	25
	MD	113
	MD	300
	D	41
	SAA	139
	SAA	794
	EDGA	8
	OE	57
	T27	56
	HAP	484
	HAP	569
	HAP	732
	PDS	9
	PDS	13
	STS2	7
	EKA	28
	J3	305
	P5	210
CIVIL	VP1	99
	G4	95
	AE7	568
	AE8	428
	DO	64
	KT1	333
	TJD	3
	HIF	772
	ESK	19
	PWR	19
CIVILITIES	CI	134
	HAP	1372
CIVILITY	ECD	12
	EAZ	29
	MS	21
CIVILIZE	HS	68
CIVILIZED	AR	48
CIVILLY	ETS	14
	PC2	25
	HAP	1290
CLAD	D	27
	MF	33
	P1	68
	P3	51
	P6	107
	P6	175
	M1	367
	M1	936
	M1	959
	G4	482
	AE7	552
	AE8	606
	AE9	30
	AE9	205
	AE9	361
	AE9	615
	AE12	1371
	KT1	221
	FL	252
	FL	265
	FL	354
CLAIM	HS	16
	HS	83
	AR	287
	RH	66
	DC	16
	DC	21
	AM	3
	AM	443
	AM	672
	PA	33
	PUO2	21
	HP	115
	SAA	33
	SAA	207
	SAA	287
	SAA	974
	RL	172
	RL	190
	RL	363
	HAP	294
	HAP	480
	HAP	770
	HAP	809
	HAP	1070
	HAP	1165
	HAP	1309
	HAP	1418
	HAP	1447
	HAP	2066
	HAP	2264
	PSH	26
	J3	266
	PPS	6
	P5	116
	P5	261
	M1	614
	M9	61
	VP5	78
	G3	346
	AE1	462
	AE1	649
	AE1	873
	AE2	195
	AE3	100
	AE4	489
	AE5	464
	AE5	1047
	AE6	824
	AE6	1145
	AE6	1164
	AE8	74
	AE8	173
	AE9	398
	AE10	495
	AE11	1161
CLAIM	DO	107
	KT1	314
	KT2	136
	KT2	417
	M8	226
	HIF	167
	TH	151
	M12	826
	AU	43
	AU	231
	AU	240
	AU	246
	AU	545
	AU	567
	AU	598
	WB	283
	WB	304
	CI	296
CLAIMED	AA	483
	SAA	660
	SAA	990
	SAA	1014
	RL	395
	AK	98
	J16	55
	AE6	456
	AE7	286
	AE8	20
	B	512
CLAIMER	SAA	870
CLAIMING	B	18
CLAIMS	PEL	30
	MD	84
	HAP	1462
	M1	1048
	AE1	509
	AE5	505
	AE5	1046
	AE6	208
	AE11	1198
	AE12	278
	M15	371
CLAMMY	AT	122
	G2	338
	G3	750
	G3	842
	G4	58
	G4	236
	AE3	233
	AE7	641
	C	124
CLAMOR	AE2	455
	AE4	962
	AE7	803
	AE9	301
	AE10	1012
	KT3	997
	M12	570
CLAMOROUS	MD	306
	SAA	584
	SAA	147
	SAA	833
	P3	14
	G1	533
	AE2	926
	AE12	382
	M11	31
CLAMORS	CM	58
	AA	995
	H2	14
	M1	273
	M1	327
	G1	234
	AE1	787
	AE2	175
	AE2	421
	AE2	593
	AE5	197
	AE5	295
	AE7	531
	AE7	794
	AE9	661
	AE9	904
	AE11	223
	AE11	824
	AE12	407
	AE12	681
	AE12	855
	AE12	909
	AE12	1060
	KT1	447
	KT3	262
	KT3	437
	KT3	550
	M8	103
	HIF	697

Word	Ref	Num		Word	Ref	Num		Word	Ref	Num
CLAN	HAP	522		CLAWS	M15	547		CLEARED	TA	358
CLANGOR	SSC	25			M15	589			M1	524
	AE5	149		CLAY	AA	158			M13	219
	AE5	182			ER	74			AE2	415
	AE7	870			TA	65			AE3	50
	AE9	668			HAP	270			KT2	514
	KT3	582			HAP	318			KT3	971
CLANGORS	G4	99			HAP	1876			HIF	463
	AE2	421			OD	33			M12	103
CLANIUS	G2	308			J3	337			CI	231
CLANKING	AE4	226			P3	38		CLEARER	M1	84
CLANKS	G1	638			GK	23		CLEAREST	HAP	139
CLANS	AE10	120			VP8	111		CLEARING	G1	623
CLAP	VHH	57			G1	259			AE5	355
	PCG1	6			G2	250		CLEARLY	RL	443
	PAR	20			G2	482		CLEARNESS	AR	208
	PC1	8			G4	63			HAP	914
	PC2	25			AE6	411		CLEARS	SAA	259
	PUO4	12			AE8	133			G3	310
	HH	7			AE9	645			AE1	348
	HAP	2302			MFL	6			AE4	692
	J3	264		CLEAN	AA	189			AE5	720
	J6	757			L4	291			AE6	556
	P1	10			MS	16		CLEAVE	G2	338
	M9	185			G2	299			G3	560
	AE1	550			OAL	181			AE3	18
	AE7	966			OAL	578			AE4	328
	PWR	9			BP	76			AE6	266
CLAPPED	EDGA	20			BP	104			AE7	966
	HAP	164			M12	529			AE11	208
	AE9	785			ETP	46			M12	693
	C	46			EMKG	10		CLEAVES	ODA	70
	C	429			PWR	35			M1	313
	C	666		CLEANER	T27	95			G2	484
CLAPPING	AE5	678		CLEANSE	J3	57			AE1	413
CLAPS	EMQ	10			J3	318			AE5	279
	AE11	1116			AE2	978			AE7	569
	AE11	1186			AE4	987			AE8	646
CLARET	PCB	28			AE12	840			AE9	1014
	PMS	5			CAM	20			AE11	225
CLARIAN	M11	3		CLEANSED	BR	191			AE12	465
CLAROS	M1	693			AE6	1007			M12	586
CLARUS	AE10	190		CLEAR	AR	246			M15	617
CLASH	AE8	699			PRL	13		CLEFT	AM	1086
	AE11	691			AM	393			PPS	1
	AE11	983			SEL3	1			M13	220
	AE12	1038			STL	24			VP10	16
	AE12	1053			PM	5			KT3	647
CLASHED	KT3	370			HP	14			CI	600
CLASHING	G1	205			SAA	908		CLEMENCY	AA	943
	G3	292			RL	72			SAA	9
	G3	341			RL	167			TA	260
	AE1	246			RL	298			AE1	740
	AE2	318			RL	299			AE11	151
	AE2	402			RL	335			KT1	72
	AE2	455			RL	451			KT3	500
	AE5	569			H29	28			PTC	27
	AE6	6			AK	110		CLENCH	AE1	145
	AE12	428			HAP	558		CLENCHED	M1	363
	AE12	501			HAP	673			AE7	709
	M11	39			HAP	874			AE11	1009
CLASP	G2	506			HAP	957			KT2	557
	G4	376			HAP	1942		CLERGY	PAZ	27
	AE4	199			OD	32			RL	371
CLASPED	AE10	727			OD	35			HAP	348
	AE11	1092			PSH	1			HAP	1546
CLASPING	H2	18			ESH	21			HAP	1672
	NS	8			J3	157			HAP	2366
	NS	19			J6	553			M15	165
	NS	30			J16	22		CLERGYMEN	J6	661
	AE7	100			P1	262		CLERGY-WEAPON	HAP	992
	M11	382			P2	3		CLERK	C	645
CLASS	HAP	189			P5	117		CLERKS	HAP	781
CLATTER	AE11	691			M1	218			C	509
CLATTERED	AE8	6			G1	397		CLEW	VP4	57
CLATTERING	EAZ	23			G3	468			AE6	42
	J3	13			AE1	207		CLIENT	J16	33
	AE3	294			AE2	617		CLIENT'S	J3	392
	AE3	312			AE2	803			P3	141
	AE5	278			AE3	121		CLIENTS	HH	43
	AE7	1084			AE5	166			J1	146
	AE9	960			AE6	979			J1	200
	KT3	446			AE9	864			AE6	826
	KT3	996			AE10	623			OAL	97
CLAUDIAN	AE7	976			OAL	611		CLIFF	J1	125
	AE7	977			KT1	197			J6	846
CLAUSE	EC	10			KT2	84			M1	402
CLAUSUS	AE7	973			KT2	559			M1	430
	AE10	479			KT3	248			VP8	84
CLAWS	EDG	44			B	255			G2	157
	HAP	199			B	275			G3	458
	HAP	267			BP	15			AE2	413
	HAP	300			C	642			AE3	322
	G1	50			FL	112			AE5	47
	AE3	284			FL	194			AE5	233
	AE3	305		CLEARED	D	23			AE11	725

CLIFFORD	EH	5	CLITORIAN	M15	485	CLOSE	G4	700
CLIFFS	AR	251	CLITUMNUS	G2	201		G4	742
	VP1	105	CLOAK	J1	36		AE3	297
	G3	430		J3	294		AE3	666
	AE3	703		GP	37		AE4	267
	AE5	1125	CLOAKS	J3	202		AE4	757
	AE6	489		FL	242		AE4	983
	AE7	985		FL	266		AE5	212
	AE11	422	CLOANTHUS	AE1	719		AE5	646
	C1	627		AE1	864		AE5	699
CLIFTS	SAA	983		AE5	162		AE5	759
	P6	17		AE5	201		AE5	1002
CLIMATE	PFD	5		AE5	219		AE6	1135
	MD	252		AE5	303		AE7	22
	BR	307		AE5	319		AE7	703
	GK	138	CLOCK	EEL	20		AE7	991
	G2	204		C	44		AE8	589
CLIMATES	AM	95	CLOD	G1	154		AE8	740
	PAZ	33	CLODS	G1	139		AE8	767
	ML	40		G2	354		AE9	50
	TA	362		G2	553		AE9	80
	M1	58		G2	583		AE9	202
	GK	128		M15	183		AE9	316
	AE4	697	CLOELIA	AE8	866		AE9	647
CLIMB	LC	148	CLOG	AA	615		AE11	131
	EIE	15		EH	18		AE11	514
	RL	77	CLOGGED	DA	112		AE11	924
	HAP	1829		M1	153		AE11	1279
	J1	110		AE4	952		AE12	642
	J10	271		AE5	232		OAL	163
	M1	943		KT3	710		OAL	483
	HI	5		CAM	259		OAL	791
	VP1	104	CLOISTERED	HAP	2316		AF	83
	VP10	71	CLOISTERS	KT2	571		KT1	149
	G3	195	CLOMB	AE8	288		KT3	357
	G3	427	CLONIUS	AE9	780		KT3	537
	AE1	580		AE10	1061		KT3	624
	AE2	255	CLORINDA	SKA2	6		KT3	1092
	AE7	647		SKA2	9		M8	198
CLIMBING	AM	988	CLOSE	HS	80		B	56
	L3	79		AR	179		B	714
	H2	23		SMA	42		BP	138
	HAP	798		AM	102		CAM	124
	G2	760		AM	327		CAM	309
CLIMBS	J6	583		AM	497		HIF	663
	M1	402		AM	518		HIF	725
	AE1	255		AM	673		HIF	746
	AE2	413		AM	778		C	368
	AE5	233		AM	779		TH	103
	M15	284		AM	809		TH	280
CLIME	DC	14		EMM	6		TH	317
	VHH	44		SEL3	20		M11	88
	AM	845		ELN	10		M11	97
	HAP	1127		SCD1	19		FL	128
	HAP	2446		DA	105		FL	197
	EL	363		EPF	21		FL	366
	J10	240		AA	152		M12	177
	VP10	93		MF	64		WB	79
	AE1	575		ER	14		WB	144
	AE3	200		L4	119		M15	455
	AE6	975		T18	89		GP	60
	AE7	891		T27	107		C1	566
	AE8	55		NS	6		C1	593
	DO	87		NS	11		ETP	26
	CAM	12		NS	17	CLOSED	AR	150
	CAM	21		NS	22		HAP	1635
	CAM	62		NS	28		HAP	2400
	AS	14		NS	33		BR	90
	AS	77		FS2	16		J6	814
CLIMES	SMA	89		TA	237		M1	1001
	H3	52		AK	181		G3	513
	GE	5		HAP	164		G4	632
	HAP	1548		HAP	1524		AE4	359
	HAP	1738		HAP	1902		AE4	379
	VP1	85		HAP	2585		AE4	992
	G1	321		PP	4		AE5	1113
	G2	175		EL	313		AE8	297
	G4	751		J1	186		AE10	310
	AE12	1032		J3	90		AE11	108
CLINCHES	MF	83		J3	318		AE11	834
CLING	L4	191		J6	385		AE11	905
CLINGING	L2	51		J6	464		AE12	666
	G2	495		P5	58		AE12	1034
CLINGS	AE4	645		M1	559		AE12	1078
CLIO	TA	327		M1	946		AE12	1083
	G4	481		DHP	5		AE12	1312
	OAL	31		G1	642		KT2	578
CLIP	MD	229		G2	108		KT3	576
	G4	161		G2	331		KT3	583
	OAL	671		G2	372		B	596
CLIPPED	PKA	3		G3	223		B	715
	P5	281		G3	573		C	239
	EHC	32		G4	110		TH	210
	TH	54		G4	381		FL	377
CLIPS	AM	344		G4	417		FL	465
	AE12	261		G4	435		M12	567

CLOSED	M15	126	CLOUD	P5	17	CLOUDS	AE2	841		
	M15	519		G4	83		AE3	257		
	GP	109		G4	803		AE3	269		
CLOSELY	AM	231		AE1	726		AE3	766		
	L4	40		AE1	813		AE3	892		
	L4	71		AE1	822		AE4	231		
	J1	7		AE1	832		AE4	361		
	AE3	70		AE2	834		AE4	381		
	AE4	180		AE3	728		AE4	403		
	AE4	645		AE3	748		AE5	574		
	AE11	969		AE4	170		AE5	914		
	B	211		AE5	15		AE5	1033		
	B	461		AE5	19		AE6	382		
	FL	70		AE5	1060		AE7	99		
CLOSE-PENT	AM	869		AE7	192		AE7	740		
CLOSER	SCG3	30		AE7	647		AE8	141		
	AE5	221		AE7	1083		AE8	263		
	AE7	1012		AE8	692		AE8	336		
	AE10	1119		AE8	783		AE8	808		
	KT3	509		AE8	826		AE9	20		
	M12	508		AE9	37		AE9	42		
	M12	641		AE9	131		AE9	912		
CLOSET	J6	335		AE9	873		AE10	157		
	AE2	621		AE10	126		AE10	896		
	M10	37		AE10	917		AE10	1088		
CLOSING	SSC	15		AE10	936		AE11	870		
	G3	661		AE11	888		AE11	895		
	G3	762		AE12	83		AE11	1269		
	AE1	545		AE12	383		AE12	16		
	AE12	628		AE12	657		AE12	428		
	KT3	840		AE12	1146		AE12	615		
	BP	190		AE12	1221		AE12	848		
CLOTH	AM	826		KT3	587		AE12	1022		
	PCG1	16		KT3	863		AE12	1180		
	J3	199		B	338		AE12	1244		
	J16	69		M11	231		KT2	540		
	P6	175		M12	790		B	684		
	G4	482		WB	539		CAM	273		
	KT3	67	CLOUD-BEGOTTEN	M12	294		HIF	300		
	KT3	910	CLOUD-BORN	AE7	934		HIF	441		
	C	20		AE8	390		TH	336		
	FL	242	CLOUD-COMPELLER	HIF	695		M11	39		
	FL	259	CLOUD-COMPELLING	HIF	544		M11	122		
	CI	14	CLOUD-DISPELLING	M1	356		M11	136		
CLOTHE	VP8	57	CLOUDS	UDH	50		FL	317		
	G1	417		AR	5		FL	383		
	AE1	900		AR	294		M15	96		
	AE2	981		AM	368	CLOUDY	SCG1	11		
	AE3	12		AM	438		AA	233		
	FL	9		AM	992		H29	28		
	GP	51		AM	1063		HAP	565		
CLOTHED	AK	187		PKK	3		G3	310		
	BR	123		AA	851		M1	524		
	EL	22		PRH	33		M1	774		
	EL	330		SAA	565		AE3	355		
	J3	145		SAA	897		AE4	692		
	G2	257		SAA	933		AE8	568		
	G2	300		SAA	1117		AE9	313		
	VP3	82		L1	7	CLOVEN	J10	213		
	AE6	1137		H29	90		G2	32		
	KT1	572		HAP	1612		AE4	729		
	KT3	29		ODA	6		AE7	711		
	FL	483		ODA	15		HIF	636		
	FL	502		ODA	33	CLOVER	G1	304		
	WB	457		M1	64		G3	232		
	M15	171		M1	83		G3	605		
	M15	664		M1	364	CLOVES	GE	21		
	GP	6		M1	369	CLOWN	ECG1	9		
CLOTHES	PRL	22		M1	429		T27	37		
	PA	10		M1	443		HAP	1703		
	PAR	3		M1	482		HAP	1923		
	EMQw	13		VP5	89		J3	119		
	T27	97		VP6	57		J16	51		
	T27	106		VP6	58		PPS	10		
	J3	175		VP7	18		G3	774		
	J3	347		VP9	87		OAL	758		
	J6	470		G1	438		HIF	801		
	J10	496		G1	445		CI	116		
	P3	12		G1	511		CI	159		
	AE3	777		G1	576	CLOWNISH	J3	290		
	AE5	232		G1	590		AE7	701		
	AE6	490		G1	623		OAE2	39		
	OAL	579		G1	630		CI	56		
	KT2	159		G2	297	CLOWNS	PSH	28		
	TH	109		G3	139		M1	371		
CLOTHING	AU	73		G3	173		G1	473		
CLOTTED	DA	72		G3	551		AE7	724		
	G3	773		G3	740		AE7	791		
	AE10	1184		G3	815		AE10	430		
	KT3	753		G4	443		KT3	463		
CLOTTERED	AE2	749		G4	614		CI	200		
	KT2	577		AE1	348	CLOYED	AE3	424		
	M8	178		AE1	547		B	184		
CLOUD	TA	10		AE1	571		VP9	38		
	ODA	66		AE1	613	CLOYING	H29	16		
	J6	169		AE2	826	CLOYS	L3	309		

CLUB	EMM	10	COAST	G2	308	COAT	C	20
	EEL	7		G4	42		FL	233
	SAA	528		AE1	44	COATS	AM	590
	EDGA	30		AE1	321		PCG1	45
	AE7	705		AE1	423		PLN	29
	M12	462		AE1	458		J3	407
	M12	471		AE1	520		J6	367
	M15	28		AE1	722		C1	576
CLUBBED	HAP	1810		AE1	792	COAX	OAE2	88
CLUBS	ELB	26		AE1	835	COBBLED	P4	127
	AE7	731		AE1	1062	COBBLER	J3	462
CLUE	LC	71		AE3	19	COBBLERS	PDS	40
	J10	394		AE3	47		C	328
	KT3	169		AE3	168	COB'S	ECG2	6
CLUENTIUS	AE5	163		AE3	377	COCK	EMQW	4
CLUES	AR	155		AE3	435		T18	92
CLUMSY	SAA	502		AE3	494		J3	158
CLUNG	AE7	100		AE3	509		G1	395
CLUSIUM	AE10	923		AE3	528		C	41
CLUSTER	G4	805		AE3	548		C	43
	AE7	101		AE3	613		C	55
CLUSTERED	VP4	34		AE3	932		C	106
CLUSTERING	H2	31		AE4	205		C	139
	AK	50		AE4	347		C	552
	G2	6		AE5	1039		C	577
CLUSTERS	M13	107		AE5	1125		C	583
	VP3	58		AE6	21		C	643
	G1	598		AE6	95		C	651
CLUTTER	EK	15		AE6	131		C	703
CLYMENE	M1	1070		AE6	448		C	755
	G4	488		AE6	413		C	795
CLYTEMNESTRA'S	HIF	169		AE6	483		C	804
CLYTEMNESTRAS	J6	855		AE6	492		C	814
CLYTIUS	AE9	1044		AE6	499		M11	274
	AE10	450		AE6	515	COCKLE	AA	195
COACH	EAL	10		AE6	941		TA	355
	PSH	5		AE7	14	COCKLOFTS	J3	329
	J3	448		AE7	29	COCKS	EEL	15
	PMK	16		AE7	172		ESF	9
COACHED	PUO3	7		AE8	17	COCKWOOD	MF	640
COACHES	PW	17		AE8	753	COCLES	AE8	864
COACH'S	PTP	42		AE8	947	COCYTUS	G4	686
COAGULATED	M15	327		AE9	161		AE6	201
COAL	GK	29		AE9	1106		AE6	412
	HAP	1631		AE10	338	CODE	HAP	1760
	KT1	465		AE10	406	CODRUS	J3	332
COAL-BLACK	AE3	165		AE11	87		J3	342
	TH	120		AE11	403		J3	343
	M12	536		MG	38		VP5	15
COALS	AM	1025		KT3	298		VP7	29
	PAL	34		M8	317		VP7	30
	AE6	324		B	255		VP7	36
	AE11	1158		CAM	15	CODRUS'	J1	2
	KT3	257		M15	440	COEUR	C	698
	BP	50		C1	628	COEVAL	M8	87
	C	34		ESK	18	COFFEE	EIE	19
COAN	P5	198	COASTED	SAA	1020	COFFEE-HOUSE	EIE	4
COARSE	ECG2	5	COASTING	AM	635	COFFEE-HOUSES	PDG	46
	AA	677		AE6	1245	COFFER	J6	61
	SAA	494		M15	69	COG	P3	92
	HAP	1244	COASTS	AM	98	COGNIZANCE	J16	24
	HAP	1322		AM	805	COIN	AM	632
	J3	282		HP	103		PSF	11
	P3	107		DA	183		AA	679
	P3	226		SAA	1071		MD	144
	G2	293		HAP	230		SAA	543
	AE6	993		M1	38		T27	111
	AE6	1163		AE1	333		EAA	8
	KT1	572		AE1	774		HAP	1166
	BP	48		AE1	807		HAP	1449
	BP	80		AE2	56		BR	303
	PMK	3		AE4	450		PKA	4
	PWR	35		AE7	200		OAL	486
COARSELY	MF	33		AE7	271		GP	83
COARSER	EL	260		AE8	552	COINED	PLT	28
	KT3	169		AE8	652		AE1	484
COAST	LCA	6		AE9	285	COINS	HAP	278
	AM	8		AE10	76	COITION	G3	376
	AM	131		AE11	421	COLANDER	G2	328
	AM	669	COAT	EAL	9		M12	588
	AM	714		L4	103	COLCHOS	HAP	232
	AM	1208		HAP	1192	COLD	AR	100
	HP	212		HAP	1987		AR	135
	DA	127		J3	450		AM	99
	L4	77		J10	209		AM	459
	HAP	129		J10	209		PFD	3
	HAP	1134		P1	260		SLN	8
	PSH	1		P4	56		ENH	29
	P6	16		AE3	598		DA	37
	P6	63		AE5	339		DA	206
	M1	401		AE5	561		AA	574
	M13	33		AE9	958		PRH	1
	VP8	9		AE10	1161		D	37
	G2	64		AE11	9		L3	73
	G2	160		AE12	1341		L4	14
	G2	272		KT3	26			

COLD	L4	170	COLEWORTS	C	580	COLT	G3	118
	H9	7	COLIC	M15	455		G3	323
	H2	71	COLL	C	728		AE9	826
	TA	440	COLLAR	G3	266		ETP	42
	TA	476	COLLARS	PP	33	COLUMBUS	DC	9
	AK	86		KT3	59	COLUMN	AA	956
	GE	3		FL	238	COLUMNS	AK	121
	HAP	904	COLLATERAL	AA	352		AE1	596
	HAP	1724	COLLATIAN	AE6	1052		AE2	631
	SSC	8	COLLATINE	MD	317		AE4	292
	ETS	24	COLLEAGUE	J3	220		AE6	745
	EL	109	COLLECTED	OD	53		BP	160
	J1	253		G3	363	COMB	PCG2	15
	J6	135		AE5	28		J6	638
	J6	789		AE10	578		P1	35
	P3	217		AE10	1091		G4	235
	P3	226		B	240		C	49
	P6	14		TH	98	COMBAT	VHH	25
	M1	23		J1	132		AM	218
	M1	59	COLLECTION	SAA	325		AM	270
	M1	66	COLLEGE	GE	48		AM	315
	M1	742		HAP	2580		AM	679
	M1	999		P5	212		PCG1	45
	M9	148		FL	218		G4	128
	M13	84	COLLEGES	AA	872		G4	319
	M13	105		PD	35		AE1	664
	PLT	26		EMKG	6		AE2	452
	VP1	88	COLLIDE	M15	522		AE2	486
	VP3	125	COLLISION	M15	506		AE3	315
	VP7	7	COLLOPS	HIF	633		AE5	89
	VP7	72	COLON	J10	490		AE5	341
	VP10	23	COLONEL'S	J1	91		AE5	490
	VP10	82	COLONIES	HAP	206		AE7	1075
	G1	73		HAP	1131		AE9	683
	G1	102		HAP	1883		AE9	768
	G1	153		EL	6		AE9	908
	G1	301		M1	95		AE9	1080
	G1	350		PWR	15		AE11	1045
	G1	509	COLONY	AM	936		AE12	20
	G2	347		G4	28		AE12	95
	G2	365		AE1	21		AE12	686
	G2	430		AE1	468		AE12	728
	G2	436		AE4	981		AE12	1005
	G2	618		AE7	244		AE12	1052
	G3	466		AE8	75		AE12	1117
	G3	488		M15	13		KT2	399
	G3	542	COLOR	ML	3		KT2	666
	G3	579		CM	27		KT3	485
	G3	584		L4	57		KT3	510
	G3	586		M13	230		HIF	474
	G4	49		G1	610		AU	428
	G4	202		G2	248	COMBATANTS	AE5	615
	G4	230		G2	346		OAL	89
	G4	378		G3	93		KT2	254
	AE7	641		G3	127		KT3	588
	AE7	991		AE4	418	COMBATED	G3	61
	AE7	945		AE6	72	COMBATS	AM	496
	AE8	183		AE11	1194		SAA	1027
	AE9	67		OAL	618	COMBED	M1	671
	AE9	632		OAL	832		M13	27
	AE9	645		KT1	173		AE7	680
	AE9	654		C	117		M12	545
	AE9	822		TH	94	COMBINATION	MD	205
	AE9	975		M11	132	COMBINE	DA	178
	AE11	451		M12	536		EPF	13
	AE11	986		M15	617		AK	41
	AE12	744	COLORED	AA	745		G4	241
	AE12	1309		GK	52		AE1	497
	KT1	466	COLORS	HS	95		AE1	606
	KT1	478		AR	125		AE1	1025
	KT2	124		RH	75		AE8	674
	KT2	528		AM	288		KT3	1115
	KT2	626		PMQ	7		STP	18
	KT3	403		PMQ	18	COMBINED	L3	33
	B	428		SCD2	3		HAP	654
	B	690		PR	19		HAP	1191
	B	746		PUO4	23		HAP	2548
	M10	26		HAP	868		J6	818
	TH	167		HAP	2337		AE1	42
	M11	9		M1	367		AE8	508
	AU	72		GK	33		AE10	143
	M15	468		GK	66		KT3	816
	M15	532		GK	178	COMBS	AM	578
	M15	696		VP4	51		G4	208
	AS	10		VP8	102		G4	262
COLDER	AM	827		G1	604		G4	355
	ML	40		AE4	1004		AE12	135
	AE12	349		AE5	117		OAL	414
	M15	487		AE9	613	COMBUSTIBLE	WB	413
COLDLY	HAP	1350		AE12	103	COME	UDH	39
	J10	506		KT2	499		AR	148
COLDNESS	G2	469		KT3	561		LC	42
COLDS	KT3	298		FL	350		PWG	5
COLEMAN	ELN	3		FL	430		PIE	3
COLEWORTS	BP	58	COLOURED	ETO	3		AM	126
	C	496	COLT	PD	56		AM	231

COME			COME			COME		
	AM	329		SKA4	4		AE2	611
	AM	681		SKA4	9		AE3	103
	AM	747		SKA6	26		AE3	752
	AM	990		ELW	6		AE4	555
	AM	1016		ELW	5		AE4	913
	AM	1186		EL	44		AE4	976
	PMQ	17		EL	54		AE5	133
	PWGR	23		EL	328		AE6	68
	EWGR	17		EL	285		AE6	1063
	PEL	19		ODA	10		AE7	194
	EEL	13		PSH	33		AE7	276
	EEL	32		ESH	26		AE7	300
	SEL4	30		J1	157		AE7	371
	ETL	3		J3	113		AE7	505
	ETL	12		J3	382		AE7	977
	PAR	19		J3	431		AE7	991
	PM	10		J3	470		AE8	89
	PM	26		J3	482		AE8	190
	PM	29		J3	502		AE8	622
	PM	35		J6	74		AE9	104
	SLN	4		J6	100		AE9	125
	SLN	5		J6	221		AE9	760
	PLN	27		J6	600		AE9	1083
	SCD1	1		J6	717		AE10	15
	SCD1	16		J10	138		AE10	19
	PUO1	11		J10	226		AE10	522
	PUO1	17		J16	50		AE10	700
	EUO	3		P1	43		AE10	821
	EUO	22		P2	10		AE11	237
	ENH	23		P2	91		AE11	364
	EAZ	28		P2	134		AE11	658
	POE	34		P3	145		AE11	902
	ETC	8		P6	74		AE11	1068
	PCB	13		P6	88		AE11	1269
	CM	55		P6	96		AE11	1297
	CM	57		M1	298		AE12	713
	HP	10		M1	366		AE12	905
	HP	56		M1	740		OAL	200
	HP	90		M13	146		OAL	242
	HP	107		VCS	3		OAL	437
	DA	38		VCS	4		OAL	509
	DA	110		VCS	11		OAE2	15
	DA	149		HI	162		OAE2	16
	EPF	23		PLT	14		OAE2	75
	PSF	10		PLT	31		KT1	366
	PSF	25		PLT	44		KT1	426
	ETG	18		MC	1		KT2	29
	PR	2		MC	15		KT2	94
	PUO4	29		GK	103		KT2	155
	PUO5	16		EHC	4		KT2	497
	PLB	47		VP1	30		KT3	21
	D	25		VP1	37		KT3	463
	MF	100		VP2	35		KT3	635
	MF	112		VP2	59		KT3	681
	SAA	330		VP3	66		TJD	7
	SAA	360		VP3	77		M8	295
	SAA	458		VP3	154		B	206
	PDG	16		VP3	100		B	433
	OE	11		VP3	120		B	639
	DOD	25		VP5	59		BP	179
	PD	37		VP7	55		HIF	29
	L3	39		VP7	56		HIF	103
	L3	47		VP8	25		HIF	311
	L3	166		VP9	3		HIF	452
	L3	169		VP9	50		HIF	469
	T23	62		VP9	57		HIF	708
	H29	9		VP10	63		C	202
	H29	15		G1	26		C	241
	H29	16		G1	418		C	304
	H29	21		G1	439		C	312
	H29	60		G2	11		C	334
	H2	67		G2	17		C	467
	TA	85		G2	43		C	597
	TA	216		G2	286		C	805
	PAA	18		G3	15		TH	251
	EAA	2		G3	71		M11	165
	AK	170		G3	79		M11	240
	GE	13		G3	110		FL	12
	HAP	404		G3	151		FL	215
	HAP	638		G3	157		M12	639
	HAP	1467		G3	491		WB	362
	HAP	1589		G4	110		M15	330
	HAP	1667		G4	264		M15	643
	HAP	1785		G4	566		CI	258
	HAP	2046		G4	649		PTP	35
	HAP	2063		AE1	9		SMP	61
	HAP	2507		AE1	29	COMEDIAN	J3	170
	HAP	2528		AE1	283	COMEDIANS	PCG1	19
	HAP	2577		AE1	744	COMEDY	EWGR	36
	SSC	31		AE1	952		PMM	11
	BR	93		AE2	69		PA	1
	PKA	23		AE2	181		ECG2	5
	SKA1	1		AE2	397		ECG2	7
	SKA1	2		AE2	437		PKK	7
	SKA1	3		AE2	501		EPC	29
	SKA4	3		AE2	505		G2	525

Word	Ref	No.
COMELY	T18	5
	AE11	646
	AE12	236
	C	626
	KT1	407
	CI	99
COMER	ECG2	11
	L3	162
COMERS	J10	378
	KT3	467
COMES	HS	107
	SMA	26
	PWG	2
	EWG	24
	AM	269
	PWGR	8
	EWGR	22
	SEL2	9
	ECG1	19
	ECG2	28
	SCD1	17
	SCD2	20
	EAZ	32
	PC2	24
	EKK	16
	DA	111
	DA	112
	PSF	36
	PR	6
	AA	274
	AA	360
	AA	969
	SAA	395
	PK	21
	OE	3
	PD	1
	EC	36
	L3	157
	H3	47
	HAP	606
	HAP	1533
	HAP	2552
	BR	17
	PP	12
	PKA	14
	SKA2	6
	SKA2	9
	ODA	79
	EH	21
	J6	525
	J6	551
	P4	71
	SFL	19
	GK	9
	VP8	159
	VP8	160
	VP9	93
	G1	301
	G2	755
	AE4	635
	AE5	242
	AE6	70
	AE6	1147
	AE9	471
	AE9	762
	AE9	910
	AE9	963
	AE10	680
	AE10	1140
	AE10	1283
	AE12	1239
	OAL	174
	OAL	471
	OAL	478
	AF	49
	AF	53
	KT1	336
	KT2	185
	KT2	213
	HIF	354
	C	794
	M11	120
	WB	395
	WB	401
	M15	623
	GP	120
	CI	392
	SMP	22
	SMP	77
COMEST	RL	72
	M9	145
	HIF	308
COMET	UDH	65
	EUF	12
	J6	533
COMETES'	M12	396
COMET-EYES	J10	514
COMET-LAWS	HAP	1675
COMETS	AM	64
	AM	1162
	AA	636
	G1	658
	AE10	380
COMFORT	AM	1038
	CM	65
	EL	351
	HI	11
	HI	58
	AE2	1016
	AE6	513
	AE9	388
	KT1	99
	B	341
	CAM	183
	M11	81
	M11	399
COMFORTER	BR	24
COMFORTS	KT3	730
COMIC	EWGR	1
	MF	198
	GE	76
	CI	24
COMING	AM	454
	TA	89
	ELT	17
	J10	416
	VP1	26
	G2	561
	G4	230
	AE10	220
	AE12	1330
	DO	80
	M8	239
	B	98
	M11	285
	M12	49
	CI	372
	ETP	37
COMMAND	HS	121
	AR	300
	SMA	99
	VHH	22
	AM	694
	AM	734
	AM	841
	E	9
	ML	53
	HP	219
	DA	14
	DA	153
	AA	9
	AA	94
	AA	299
	AA	437
	AA	775
	MD	241
	MF	205
	SAA	29
	SAA	943
	ER	57
	H3	28
	H9	15
	TA	110
	TA	228
	TA	394
	HAP	851
	HAP	867
	HAP	892
	ETS	8
	EL	220
	J1	91
	J6	680
	J10	125
	P3	38
	P4	15
	P5	53
	P5	183
	P5	194
	P6	3
	P6	163
	M1	255
	M1	386
	M1	519
	M1	527
	M1	809
	SFL	14
	VCS	16
	GK	104
	GK	126
	VP5	9
	G3	24
	G3	735
COMMAND	G4	163
	G4	649
	AE1	114
	AE1	191
	AE1	260
	AE1	316
	AE1	408
	AE1	808
	AE2	3
	AE2	1087
	AE3	20
	AE3	143
	AE3	374
	AE4	155
	AE4	327
	AE4	336
	AE4	349
	AE4	394
	AE4	406
	AE4	447
	AE4	481
	AE4	516
	AE4	542
	AE4	867
	AE4	890
	AE6	103
	AE6	219
	AE6	546
	AE6	555
	AE6	1072
	AE7	50
	AE7	154
	AE7	300
	AE7	327
	AE7	360
	AE7	381
	AE7	612
	AE7	663
	AE7	681
	AE7	758
	AE7	890
	AE8	168
	AE8	196
	AE8	444
	AE8	500
	AE8	526
	AE8	597
	AE8	615
	AE8	636
	AE8	651
	AE8	684
	AE9	51
	AE9	117
	AE9	142
	AE9	204
	AE9	920
	AE9	969
	AE10	67
	AE10	156
	AE10	260
	AE10	410
	AE11	68
	AE11	167
	AE11	195
	AE11	283
	AE11	372
	AE11	446
	AE11	490
	AE11	703
	AE11	786
	AE11	860
	AE12	36
	AE12	289
	AE12	678
	AE12	824
	AE12	1175
	AE12	1184
	AE12	1213
	OAL	336
	OAL	788
	DO	57
	DO	94
	KT1	551
	KT2	453
	KT2	655
	KT3	412
	KT3	506
	KT3	833
	KT3	1083
	KT3	1139
	M8	11
	B	596
	B	740
	BP	39
	CAM	201
	HIF	22

COMMON

P 1	119
P 1	218
P 4	45
P 5	164
P 6	41
M 1	171
M 1	478
M 1	1045
M 1	1073
M 9	21
M 9	60
M 13	114
G K	40
V P 2	106
V P 3	47
V P 4	30
V P 7	89
G 1	195
G 2	600
G 4	102
G 4	225
G 4	226
G 4	227
G 4	270
G 4	366
G 4	475
G 4	654
G 4	698
AE 1	276
AE 1	750
AE 1	785
AE 2	493
AE 2	758
AE 2	779
AE 2	714
AE 2	715
AE 2	1074
AE 3	202
AE 3	787
AE 4	145
AE 4	156
AE 4	240
AE 4	767
AE 4	796
AE 4	977
AE 5	176
AE 5	249
AE 5	401
AE 5	940
AE 6	618
AE 6	982
AE 7	314
AE 8	15
AE 8	26
AE 8	186
AE 8	364
AE 9	218
AE 9	233
AE 9	295
AE 9	347
AE 10	2
AE 11	153
AE 11	315
AE 11	329
AE 11	492
AE 11	522
AE 11	758
AE 11	728
AE 11	1286
AE 12	181
AE 12	1212
AE 12	1300
OAL	71
OAL	122
OAL	657
OAL	658
MM	11
KT 1	33
KT 1	42
KT 1	292
KT 1	332
KT 3	468
KT 3	575
KT 3	798
KT 3	1029
T J D	53
T J D	121
T J D	190
M 8	93
B	181
B	385
B	479
B	502
B	552
B	755
B P	44

COMMON

B P	127
H I F	23
H I F	129
H I F	179
H I F	245
H I F	346
H I F	519
H I F	541
H I F	745
C	66
C	253
T H	153
T H	190
T H	219
M 11	384
M 11	429
M 11	432
F L	327
M 12	42
M 12	244
M 12	554
M 12	733
M 12	783
A U	114
A U	205
A U	220
A U	304
A U	344
A U	465
A U	575
W B	62
W B	71
M 15	57
M 15	97
C I	168
C I	517
P T P	3
E W R	20

COMMONERS G 2 733
COMMONLY J 6 325
COMMONS

H S	106
V H H	46
M D	234
M D	311
H A P	1322
H A P	2286
J 6	817
M 1	224
G 4	309
M 11	342

COMMONWEAL HAP 234
COMMONWEALTH

E C D	11
A A	292
E L B	9
S A A	925
OAL	114

COMMONWEALTHS A A 84
COMMONWEALTH'S-MAN'S E L B 20
COMMONWEALTH'S-MEN A A 571
COMMUNICATE

E L	251
W B	165

COMMUNICATES A U 377
COMMUNION

H A P	419
H A P	1010
H A P	1027
H A P	1193

COMPACTED AE6 980
COMPANION

A M	69
P A L	14
S A A	1068
H A P	169
J 3	462
J 6	172
AE 2	111
AE 5	604
AE 6	237
AE 9	369
AE 11	818
AE 12	1275
KT 3	146
OAL	849

COMPANION'S D A 91
COMPANIONS

D A	170
H A P	1344
P 5	45
M 13	143
V P 2	54
G 4	772
AE 1	496
AE 1	523
AE 2	390
AE 3	210
AE 3	579
AE 10	514
AE 11	34
AE 11	420

COMPANIONS

AE 11	974
KT 1	362
F L	46

COMPANY

E W G R	20
E T L	26
P A R	24
E S F	10
A A	605
R L	407
H A P	28
H A P	550
J 1	250
J 16	37
M 1	888
V P 1	70
AE 4	235
OAL	655
OAL	673
OAE 2	60
M 11	428
A U	76
A U	376

COMPARE

R L	126
T 18	34
H A P	1567
E L	99
M 1	726
M 9	72
V P 3	39
V P 5	12
V P 7	90
G 4	256
M 10	8
A U	157
A U	158

COMPARED

A T	48
J 6	44
J 6	625
V P 1	34
V P 5	24
B	528
E T P	30
E P	4

COMPASS

A M	634
A A	175
M D	274
S A A	668
R L	247
S S C	14
E L	37
J 6	500
J 6	761
P 2	84
M 1	61
M 9	114
G 2	550
G 2	784
AE 3	449
AE 3	614
AE 5	221
AE 5	275
AE 6	272
AE 6	1196
AE 10	694
AE 11	778
KT 1	374
KT 2	456
KT 3	1152
B	138

COMPASSED

H H	28
M 1	859
M 9	174
V P 4	39
AE 2	515
AE 3	276
AE 6	327
AE 8	303
AE 9	1072
AE 11	376
H I F	72
A U	515

COMPASSION

AE 1	764
AE 4	443
AE 8	105
AE 12	941
AE 12	1363
OAL	832
KT 1	269
KT 2	342
M 8	335
F L	393

COMPASSIONATE AE12 949
COMPASSIONATING AA 694
COMPEL HAP 85
AE5 1022
COMPELLED L 4 200

Word	Ref	No.	Word	Ref	No.	Word	Ref	No.
COMPELLED	AE2	17	COMPLETE	CAM	291	CONCEAL	OAL	762
	AE2	331		HIF	667		OAL	820
	AE6	1016		AU	392		OAE2	54
	OAL	147	COMPLEXION	OAL	825		AF	109
	OAL	805		C	141		AF	116
	KT3	654		C	177		KT3	199
	KT3	720	COMPLEXIONS	HS	100		CAM	199
	TJD	142		KT3	422		TH	396
	FL	301	COMPLIED	AE11	715		M11	7
	WB	191		CI	365		AU	52
COMPELS	AT	1	COMPLIES	SAA	593		WB	196
COMPENDIOUS	PMQ	34		G4	631	CONCEALED	AA	688
	PDG	19	COMPLIMENT	EM	18		RL	207
COMPLAIN	CM	53		PCD	4		L4	223
	HP	11		GE	39		HAP	51
	HP	37		HAP	42		HAP	68
	DA	32		HAP	2452		HAP	1629
	AA	722		M1	715		BR	199
	SAA	651		BP	136		P1	58
	SAA	699	COMPLIMENTS	OAE2	69		P1	227
	L3	124	COMPLY	SAA	586		G1	630
	L3	153		SAA	673		G4	604
	FS2	2		HAP	2129		AE1	292
	TA	425		J3	78		AE1	483
	HAP	1379		AE4	153		AE1	613
	HAP	1504		KT3	1139		AE2	31
	SKA6	2		WB	306		AE2	661
	J1	77	COMPLYING	R	21		AE3	617
	J1	248		WB	354		AE3	937
	J3	177	COMPORT	M11	41		AE4	662
	J10	401	COMPOSE	AR	15		AE4	725
	M1	56		EM	4		AE6	549
	M1	493		AE4	731		KT1	606
	M9	144		AE6	500		KT2	67
	VP1	78		AE6	538		KT2	516
	VP8	29		AE10	23		M8	146
	VP8	33		AE10	290		B	55
	VP9	21		OAL	342		B	612
	G3	510		OAL	623		B	737
	AE3	702		KT3	382		BP	24
	AE4	478		KT3	434		CAM	251
	AE4	508		HIF	323		HIF	445
	AE4	531		HIF	363		C	496
	AE7	792	COMPOSED	SAA	796		TH	110
	AE8	283		EL	154		TH	408
	OAL	141		J3	169		WB	159
	OAL	486		M1	267		M15	211
	OAL	843		GK	168		M15	703
	OAE2	22		G1	568		ETP	21
	MM	17		AE5	562	CONCEALS	HAP	2488
	KT1	252		AE6	450		BR	158
	KT1	421		KT3	721		P3	83
	KT2	117		M8	388		AE8	101
	KT3	151		B	208		HIF	501
	KT3	393		B	502	CONCEIT	P1	241
	HIF	210		B	712	CONCEIVE	L4	277
	C	693		FL	351		L4	285
	C	697		CI	99		HAP	119
COMPLAINED	J3	339		CI	309		HAP	315
	OAE1	25	COMPOSING	TJD	17		J6	123
	C	262	COMPOSS	C	269	CONCEIVED	BR	249
COMPLAINING	SSC	33	COMPOSURE	RH	6		AE7	390
	SKA5	9	COMPOUND	PPC	16		AE10	802
	B	692		SAA	666	CONCEIVES	PIE	26
	WB	375		SAA	858	CONCEPTION	L4	236
COMPLAINS	ELB	35		HAP	144		G3	441
	AA	446		HAP	1654		M1	575
	J10	358		ELW	8	CONCERN	RL	450
	VP6	114		J6	634		HI	123
	OAL	387		PMK	38		G2	709
COMPLAINT	DA	137	COMPOUNDS	C	327		C	809
	STS1	10	COMPREHEND	RL	39	CONCERNED	PA	41
	M1	276	COMPREHENDS	EL	147		RL	26
	KT2	583	COMPRESSED	HAP	352		M1	236
	HIF	544		AE3	701		AE3	135
COMPLAINTS	AR	177		AE12	214		AE8	549
	DA	143		M11	494		AE10	1078
	HAP	1378	COMPRISED	AE2	84		AE10	1195
	J3	481		KT3	825		AE11	1172
	VP8	88	COMPUTATION	PMK	40		CI	429
	VP10	49	COMPUTE	CI	13	CONCERNMENT	L4	269
	AE1	568	COMPUTES	M11	233	CONCERNS	VHH	9
	AE4	649	COMPUTING	AE6	936		HAP	1746
	AE10	146	CONCAVE	B	80		HAP	1955
	KT2	475		M15	458		PSH	23
	KT3	901		SMQ	14		AE9	371
	M11	436		MD	39		AE12	77
	CI	349	CONCEAL	SAA	952	CONCERT	FL	370
COMPLAISANCE	PEL	8		HAP	2108	CONCESSIONS	AA	925
COMPLETE	HAP	1318		EL	269	CONCHS	M10	39
	EL	289		P2	14		HS	17
	M1	4		P4	104	CONCLUDE	PWG	42
	M9	209		AE3	487		PTL	2
	GK	173		AE6	209		ECD	21
	AE7	757		AE6	768		HP	213
	AE12	937		OAL	335		AA	105

Word	Code	No.	Word	Code	No.	Word	Code	No.
CONCLUDE	SAA	186	CONDENSE	G1	566	CONFESS	AM	339
	RL	220		G4	239		PWGR	21
	L4	235		AE1	602		PT	21
	HAP	641	CONDENSED	L4	248		PCG1	17
	BR	2		L4	251		PMQW	7
	BR	267		VP6	57		PAZ	7
	HI	61		AE10	900		EAZ	11
	G1	577	CONDENSING	M15	384		HP	61
	G2	316	CONDITION	EDG	29		EUF	20
	AE2	912		PAA	41		AA	240
	AE9	659		HAP	1059		MD	156
	AE11	640		KT1	593		MD	206
	KT1	542		B	546		SAA	634
	KT2	418		WB	499		SAA	663
	KT2	479		ERL	9		SDG	13
	KT3	1118	CONDITIONAL	C	530		L1	17
	B	336	CONDITIONS	SAA	256		TA	185
	C	160		SAA	665		TA	344
	WB	452		HAP	1078		HAP	1045
	M15	670		AE4	889		BR	123
	CI	468		AE11	354		G3	49
	STP	22		AE12	23		AE4	29
CONCLUDED	HAP	108		AE12	85		AE4	316
	HAP	1780		AE12	1271		AE6	768
	AE7	59		KT1	372		AE10	102
	AE11	194		PWR	8		AE12	348
	AE11	453	CONDOLE	J3	352		OAL	216
	OAL	411		M1	790		OAL	287
CONCLUDES	EUO2	8	CONDUCT	AM	189		OAL	644
	SAA	604		AM	481		OAL	765
	PD	45		HP	211		KT1	262
	M1	353		AA	894		M8	389
	AE12	874		SAA	813		CAM	328
	KT3	521		SAA	821		HIF	356
	WB	519		TA	164		C	780
CONCLUDING	HAP	2536		HAP	976		AU	23
	AE3	944		HAP	1887		AU	124
	C	658		J10	4		AU	418
CONCLUSION	EC	1		G2	692		AU	565
CONCLUSIONS	EDS	24		G3	35	CONFESSED	AR	241
CONCOCTED	J1	62		G4	510		AM	87
CONCORD	HAP	2194		G4	576		AM	546
	J1	173		AE3	650		PTC	2
	G4	308		AE4	67		HP	127
	AE1	1025		AE6	162		EPC	30
	AE3	654		AE6	276		MD	73
	TJD	17		AE6	927		MD	81
	M8	51		AE8	667		SAA	801
	ESK	16		AE8	682		SAA	842
CONCORD'S	OAL	74		AE9	371		SAA	966
CONCOURSE	AK	125		AE10	105		TA	123
	AE1	585		AE12	569		TA	279
	AE6	437		B	369		TA	454
	OAL	202		B	677		HAP	99
	M11	120		HIF	29		M1	233
CONCUBINE	AA	6		AU	542		G1	452
CONCUR	M9	131		AU	582		AE1	436
CONCURRED	HAP	1755		AU	591		AE2	803
CONCURRENT	RL	147		WB	512		AE3	125
	KT3	818	CONDUCTED	J1	199		AE5	701
CONCURRING	J6	113		J3	86		AE8	291
	AE2	266		GK	134		AE9	572
CONDEMN	EWG	21		AE6	173		AE10	175
	SAA	183		AE8	166		AE10	269
	HAP	725		AE9	307		KT3	80
	HAP	1974		CI	86		TJD	162
	VP4	71	CONDUCTING	FL	457		CAM	216
	P5	157	CONDUCTOR	HAP	1697		CAM	251
	VP5	126	CONDUCTS	AE6	717		HIF	303
	MM	40		AE6	917		C	454
CONDEMNED	LCA	52	CONDUIT-GATE	J3	19		TH	406
	PRL	27	CONDUITS	AR	167		TH	410
	EIE	10	CONFEDERATE	M1	323		M12	150
	PMQW	6		KT1	80		M12	794
	CM	106	CONFEDERATES	AE9	29		WB	289
	SAA	769		AE11	649		CI	290
	RL	205		WB	430		CI	320
	T23	48	CONFER	AR	93	CONFESSES	J6	834
	HAP	334		AR	139	CONFESSING	ETC	28
	HAP	1157		HAP	1048		EPC	32
	J1	76		HAP	2425		HAP	270
	J10	115		AE9	249		M12	543
	P2	46		KT3	166		AE7	163
	VP1	93		KT3	1129		AE11	1018
	VP8	46		AU	165		CI	594
	AE4	36	CONFERENCE	HP	252	CONFESSION	PWGR	24
	AE4	44		AE10	855		HAP	425
	AE6	579	CONFERRED	HS	140		HAP	2470
	AE9	270		AE5	447		C	294
	KT1	161		AE5	453	CONFESSIONS	HAP	364
	KT1	387	CONFERS	SAA	1012	CONFESSOR	EPC	26
	B	379	CONFESS	RH	68		HAP	1505
	TH	200		RH	88		WB	169
	AU	114		PIE	18		AS	74
	M15	47		AM	75	CONFIDE	SMA	86
CONDEMNS	C	163		AM	168		AE10	879

Word	Ref	Num	Word	Ref	Num	Word	Ref	Num
CONFIDENCE	EIE	5	CONFOUND	CAM	88	CONQUERED	AM	196
	HP	161		C	753		AM	358
	RL	292	CONFOUNDED	ETL	1		AM	540
	J10	15	CONFOUNDING	HAP	1815		AM	1209
	AE5	1047	CONFOUNDS	KT3	808		PUO2	6
	AE6	706	CONFRONT	HAP	1616		EOE	20
	AE10	816	CONFRONTED	C	291		DA	168
	OAL	306	CONFRONTS	AE5	637		TA	113
	OAL	686	CONFUSED	HAP	1042		TA	207
CONFIDENT	HS	99		M1	22		EL	275
	PWG	8		M13	192		J1	34
	HAP	2442		AE2	497		P3	104
	B	91		AE11	944		P6	108
CONFIDENTLY	M9	201		AE11	1180		GK	19
CONFIDENTS	J3	104		AE11	1261		G2	782
CONFIDING	J6	425		AE12	910		G3	16
CONFINE	AK	91		AE12	1124		AE3	216
	J16	20		KT3	438		AE4	315
	P6	186		M12	73		AE4	339
	M9	26	CONFUSEDLY	SAA	927		AE6	46
	G3	53	CONFUSIO	C	418		AE6	1149
	G3	219	CONFUSION	SAA	75		AE7	374
	G4	164		EC	2		AE7	917
CONFINED	SCG2	20		L3	5		AE8	745
	EMW	10		G3	830		AE9	97
	AA	4		AE1	126		AE9	355
	AA	999		AE9	978		AE9	486
	EPC	20		AE11	689		AE9	883
	RL	176		AE12	889		AE10	1238
	L3	173		TH	311		AE10	1304
	H3	36		M11	111		AE11	37
	TA	334		CI	586		AE11	122
	HAP	230	CONFUSIONS	EDS	23		AE11	154
	HAP	403	CONFUTE	RL	220		AE11	308
	HAP	896	CONGEAL	AE2	765		AE11	472
	EL	271		KT2	540		AE12	648
	EL	280		M11	178		AE12	1160
	J10	274	CONGEALED	TA	3		OAL	218
	J10	548		G3	568		OAL	245
	P1	52		AE3	41		OAL	251
	M1	127		KT2	577		OAL	795
	GK	124	CONGEALS	G4	50		KT1	8
	VP1	89		AE12	1309		KT1	116
	AE1	31		C	156		KT1	124
	AE1	91		M15	621		KT1	136
	AE1	199	CONGEE	PLB	25		KT2	452
	AE6	996	CONGENIAL	G4	332		KT3	99
	AE7	27	CONGLOBATE	UDH	35		KT3	915
	AE7	829	CONGRATULATE	TA	126		KT3	1009
	AE8	528		M1	783		M12	250
	MFL	29	CONGRATULATES	KT3	730		M12	490
	B	394	CONGREGATED	M1	45		M12	662
	TH	55	CONGRESS	AE10	616		AU	279
	M11	331	CONGREVE	MC	26		M15	17
	M15	455	CONJOINED	HAP	2446		M15	618
	CI	73		FL	131		M15	659
	CI	202		M12	323		M15	667
	ESK	6		W8	425		CI	306
	ESK	28	CONJUGAL	M11	492		CI	326
CONFINEMENT	BR	243	CONJUNCTION	EOE	30	CONQUERING	AM	805
	AE2	339		SAA	934		PSF	31
CONFINES	EM	6		L4	284		DA	164
	G4	706	CONJURE	OAL	884		SAA	892
	AE6	956	CONJURED	SAA	137		ER	7
	AE6	1228	CONJURER	J3	137		ER	47
	AE7	579	CONJURING	PTL	16		FSI	9
	KT3	120		P3	157		TA	511
	M11	154	CONNING	VP9	48		BR	81
CONFINING	M12	58	CONNIVING	OE	47		J1	196
CONFIRM	SAA	767	CONON	VP3	61		MC	4
	SAA	864	CONQUER	HS	87		VP5	135
	RL	150		AR	84		G4	811
	AE2	939		M1	623		AE1	35
	AE3	270		HI	23		AE1	388
	AE11	779		AM	350		AE1	881
	BP	193		ECD	2		AE3	373
CONFIRMED	HP	132		DA	14		AE5	354
	EMW	4		AA	125		AE5	484
	MF	18		AE1	277		AE6	1157
	EL	226		AE5	300		AE6	1183
	M1	993		AE6	103		AE8	511
	B	377		AE7	593		AE9	350
	HIF	245		AE8	511		AE9	493
	C	266		AE9	1071		AE9	601
	CI	243		AE10	66		AE10	1041
CONFIRMS	RL	338		AE10	358		AE11	1255
	CAM	213		AE10	500		AE12	698
	CAM	237		AE11	172		AE12	1329
CONFORM	HAP	1521		AE11	762		DO	36
CONFORMED	ECG2	2		KT3	324		KT1	553
CONFORMS	HAP	1472		HIF	321		KT3	668
CONFOUND	G1	678		M12	28		KT3	737
	AE5	660		AU	533		KT3	964
	AE7	474		CI	267		M8	210
	AE12	435	CONQUERED	UDH	18		HIF	194
	AE12	1322		HS	93		HIF	355

CONQUERING
HIF	625
M11	170
M12	609
M15	445
M15	618

CONQUEROR
PA	13
AE5	319
AE8	478
AE12	1160
M12	402

CONQUEROR'S
AA	515
J10	210
AE11	1017
PNH	41

CONQUERORS
AK	96
BR	339
PP	29

CONQUERS
VP10	99
AE7	106
TJD	13

CONQUEST
SMA	40
DC	46
VHH	8
VHH	36
AM	76
AM	547
AA	456
MD	143
SAA	274
SAA	886
SAA	962
FS3	7
TA	490
AK	147
P3	126
G3	53
G4	640
AE2	237
AE2	517
AE2	794
AE8	19
AE9	243
AE9	429
AE9	499
AE10	66
AE10	717
AE10	1238
AE10	1259
AE12	1358
OAL	11
KT2	161
KT2	600
KT3	164
KT3	312
KT3	338
KT3	395
KT3	657
KT3	1099
KT3	1142
M8	244
HIF	30
M11	201
M12	731
AU	137
AU	534
GP	115
CI	288
CI	301
CI	398

CONQUESTS
HS	55
HS	109
VHH	43
AM	320
SAA	685
M1	623
AE6	1064
DO	20

CONS
CONSCIENCE
P1	179
AR	190
EPC	1
SAA	160
SAA	284
SAA	311
SAA	317
SAA	367
SAA	632
SAA	660
RL	205
L4	112
HAP	478
HAP	479
HAP	976
HAP	1501
HAP	1942
HAP	2042
HAP	2079

CONSCIENCE
HAP	2080
HAP	2085
HAP	2087
HAP	2103
HAP	2107
HAP	2112
HAP	2117
HAP	2119
HAP	2151
HAP	2509
BR	190
EDS	16
PKA	44
J3	247
P1	15
M1	122
OAL	728
KT3	774
TH	314

CONSCIONABLE
CONSCIOUS
J10	500
AR	245
LC	95
AM	97
AM	759
PUO2	25
ML	11
CM	56
HP	143
DA	112
AA	21
SAA	806
SAA	875
AT	7
L3	231
HAP	1068
HAP	1381
EL	100
J3	90
J6	377
M1	99
M9	58
VP8	23
VP8	83
G3	210
AE1	851
AE4	244
AE4	754
AE4	932
AE5	607
AE6	767
AE8	520
AE8	670
AE8	701
AE9	336
AE9	386
AE10	960
AE10	1248
AE11	1185
AE12	331
AE12	971
KT1	576
KT3	219
KT3	898
B	151
B	231
B	720
CAM	185
CAM	212
TH	202
TH	373
FL	142
M12	825
AU	22
CI	191

CONSECRATE
MF	127
VP8	108
AE1	625

CONSECRATED
HAP	53
HAP	2276
J3	309

CONSECRATES
EPF	24
AA	736

CONSENT
EMQ	4
EMQ	9
CM	40
AA	978
AA	1026
SAA	130
SAA	431
SAA	1003
T27	3
TA	268
HAP	487
HAP	2266
J10	525
P5	163

CONSENT
M1	656
AE3	251
AE10	49
AE11	66
AE11	490
AE11	672
AE12	1194
OAL	430
OAE2	81
KT3	873
KT3	1006
B	22
B	420
B	440
C	534
TH	49
TH	416
TH	423
AU	310
WB	82

CONSENTED
SLN	2
AA	774

CONSENTING
AA	313
P4	117
M9	130

CONSENTS
HP	2
AE4	180
AE12	1220

CONSEQUENCE
PCG2	8
HP	153
AA	135
RL	399
EL	212
EL	333
M1	833
B	620

CONSEQUENTLY
CONSIDER
ECG2	27
RL	275
L3	175
L3	237
ESH	27
B	446
B	447

CONSIDERED
VHH	33
EWGR	35
L3	88
G2	350

CONSIDERING
AA	459
HAP	256
HAP	569
J1	255
M8	252
B	470
CAM	137
HIF	689
M12	143
WB	510

CONSIDERS
EM	16
J6	632

CONSIGNED
G4	734
MFL	3

CONSIGNS
CONSISTORY
CONSISTS
CONSOLED
CONSONANTS
CONSORT
AE6	335
HAP	1074
TA	495
J10	191
HAP	958
H2	42
HAP	179
M1	983
HI	190
AE2	967
AE7	426
M10	4
HIF	730
M11	214
SAA	618
M1	847

CONSORT'S
CONSORTS
CONSPICUOUS
AU	375
G3	25
AE2	640
AE6	878
AE8	776
AE10	492
AE11	20
AE11	1010
KT1	598
KT3	50
KT3	487
M8	143
B	538

CONSPIRACY
MD	209
TA	407

CONSPIRE
HP	232
DA	116
PUF	33
SAA	591

Word	Ref	No.
CONSPIRE	RL	143
	L4	216
	HAP	185
	BR	25
	BR	154
	BR	320
	J10	303
	M9	117
	M9	127
	VP2	13
	G1	389
	AE2	473
	AE2	734
	AE2	895
	AE2	960
	AE3	483
	AE8	531
	AE10	978
	AE12	952
	FL	151
CONSPIRED	J10	438
	G4	757
	AE1	389
	AE8	492
	AE9	706
	HIF	552
CONSPIRES	HP	180
	AE12	1040
CONSPIRING	M1	259
CONSTANCY	LC	124
	AM	1157
	EMK	3
	SAA	813
	HAP	436
CONSTANT	AM	1215
	HP	38
	SAA	639
	OE	35
	SKA6	28
	SKA6	29
	EL	61
	J6	122
	C	414
	TH	15
	WB	151
	WB	315
	GP	129
CONSTANTINE	EC	7
	BR	81
	BR	88
CONSTANTINOPLE	MD	104
CONSTELLATION	UDH	66
	EL	148
	M1	862
CONSTITUTION	GE	7
	HAP	1257
	P6	13
CONSTITUTIONS	L4	258
CONSTRAIN	AR	131
	PRH	40
	HAP	454
	BR	300
	G2	430
	AE6	223
	AE6	540
	KT2	384
	C	536
	M15	484
	M15	700
CONSTRAINED	AM	1133
	AA	472
	MD	160
	HAP	1610
	EL	277
	G3	554
	AE6	478
	AE7	264
	AE8	223
	AE9	158
	AE11	457
	TJD	153
	C	535
	CI	86
CONSTRAINS	AA	450
	J6	801
	G1	132
	G4	634
	AE1	963
	KT1	469
	M11	30
	CI	390
CONSTRUE	HAP	139
CONSTRUED	AA	38
	HAP	482
CONSUBSTAN-TIATING	HAP	1026
CONSUL	EL	277
CONSUL	J10	191
	MC	36
	AE6	1129
	AE6	1163
	AE7	847
CONSUL'S	VP4	4
CONSULS	EOE	8
	AE6	1120
	TJD	182
CONSULSHIP	VP4	14
	G2	138
CONSULT	MD	232
	TA	190
	HAP	2402
	J6	336
	HIF	91
CONSULTED	RL	396
	J6	745
CONSULTING	J6	745
CONSULTS	J6	734
	AE7	131
	HIF	426
	AU	556
CONSUME	AM	981
	M1	1077
	M9	99
	AE2	790
	AE5	827
	AE5	1026
	B	62
CONSUMED	HP	231
	AE2	773
	AE5	983
	AE7	577
	AE8	566
	HIF	47
	M12	815
	WB	204
	M15	228
	M15	529
CONSUMES	SCG3	15
	VP8	112
	G3	844
	AE2	440
	M15	597
	M15	598
CONSUMING	AM	1064
	M1	667
	AE4	142
	KT2	638
CONSUMPTION	HS	45
CONSUMPTIVE	L4	155
CONTAGION	AM	973
	BR	233
	G3	710
	AE9	716
	AE10	568
	M8	348
	HIF	15
	HIF	137
	ESK	14
CONTAGIOUS	G3	814
CONTAIN	SAA	42
	RL	368
	HAP	101
	HAP	139
	HAP	193
	HAP	668
	HAP	681
	HAP	912
	HAP	925
	HAP	1283
	HAP	2504
	BR	205
	EL	208
	EL	245
	J1	45
	J3	492
	J10	236
	P1	2
	P2	90
	VP2	25
	G4	97
	AE7	145
	AE11	519
	AE11	295
	AE12	295
	AU	4
	AU	160
	M15	374
	PTP	48
CONTAINED	RL	166
	RL	294
	J3	338
	M1	464
	AE5	658
CONTAINED	OAL	201
	M15	644
CONTAINS	HP	178
	AA	445
	RL	214
	VP3	160
	G2	784
	G4	305
	AE3	62
	AE5	40
	AE11	667
	M12	817
	AE12	803
	M11	429
CONTEMN	PUO4	14
	AA	381
	SAA	11
	HAP	711
	GK	80
	G2	183
	M8	45
	M12	125
CONTEMNED	HP	134
	J10	43
	VP8	47
	AE1	478
CONTEMNING	H29	100
CONTEMNS	AM	457
	J1	74
	G3	395
CONTEMPLATING	M15	350
CONTEMPLATION	AA	73
CONTEMPORARIES	MC	32
CONTEMPT	AM	143
	HAP	216
	HAP	1287
	PLT	46
	AE11	36
	C	319
CONTEND	LCA	20
	AM	336
	AA	945
	MD	310
	SAA	160
	L2	12
	T18	41
	T18	56
	HAP	717
	M1	25
	GK	119
	VP2	40
	VP4	70
	VP7	98
	VP8	75
	G2	192
	G2	406
	G3	286
	AE5	86
	AE5	622
	AE6	874
	AE7	410
	AE8	845
	AE10	17
	AE10	32
	AE11	175
	AE11	557
	AE12	1262
	KT3	5
	CAM	29
	HIF	345
	HIF	393
	HIF	479
	AU	9
	AU	28
	GP	96
CONTENDED	HAP	956
	AE10	464
	AE11	650
	MG	8
	KT2	314
CONTENDING	CM	13
	PLB	37
	SAA	596
	ER	50
	H3	18
	G2	528
	G2	707
	G4	121
	AE2	566
	AE5	647
	AE10	496
	DO	15
	KT1	342
	KT3	275
	KT3	488
	TJD	7

Word	Code	Num
CONTENDING	M12	821
CONTENDS	HAP	411
	G2	137
	AE12	857
	AU	256
CONTENT	AR	27
	AR	297
	RH	48
	EWGR	47
	EMQW	15
	S	5
	ELN	11
	PUO2	17
	EUO2	4
	CM	39
	HP	125
	DA	189
	AA	92
	AA	192
	AA	246
	AA	1007
	MD	184
	RL	29
	RL	381
	L3	152
	H29	86
	PAA	9
	AK	89
	AK	129
	AK	154
	HH	27
	HAP	285
	HAP	405
	HAP	1251
	HAP	2143
	HAP	2567
	PP	19
	ETS	18
	J3	363
	J6	78
	J6	128
	J10	549
	P2	101
	M1	134
	M1	374
	M13	166
	ELT	25
	VP2	36
	G2	580
	G2	592
	G4	308
	AE3	797
	AE3	807
	AE5	412
	AE7	536
	AE9	596
	AE11	260
	OAL	386
	MM	7
	M8	396
	HIF	339
	C	29
	TH	69
	M11	36
	M11	477
	AU	389
	WB	466
	WB	494
	WB	525
	M15	6
	AS	52
CONTENTED	AM	332
	HP	113
	AT	44
	J3	36
	AE3	324
	AE9	689
	AE9	875
	AE11	875
	MM	41
	GP	49
CONTENTION	HIF	316
	C	804
	FL	435
CONTENTIOUS	H2	14
CONTENTS	SMQ	2
CONTEST	KT2	571
	M8	268
	CI	555
CONTIGUOUSLY	M1	30
CONTINENCE	J6	574
CONTINENT	HS	113
	HAP	207
	HAP	2167
	J10	282
	M1	74

Word	Code	Num
CONTINENT	AE3	510
	OAL	58
	CAM	317
	M15	439
CONTINGENT	AA	757
	DO	140
CONTINGENCY	TA	494
CONTINUE	AM	1079
	MD	108
	PLT	18
	AE4	68
	B	445
	B	476
	CAM	121
	C	573
	FL	572
	FL	573
	WB	403
	M15	399
	CI	106
CONTINUED	SMA	13
	PWG	38
	MF	145
	SAA	76
	G1	350
	G3	527
	G4	736
	AE2	366
	AE4	794
	AE6	667
	AE8	243
	AE12	465
	KT1	344
	KT3	998
	M8	140
	HIF	806
	C	306
	FL	369
	M12	581
	WB	538
CONTINUES	EK	14
	HAP	1685
	M9	27
CONTRACT	HAP	658
	HAP	665
	VP7	61
	G1	91
	AE5	22
	GP	86
CONTRACTED	M1	151
	M9	76
	G3	729
	AE2	598
	AE10	1301
	AE12	1247
	KT2	276
	M8	152
	GP	60
	ESK	4
CONTRACTS	AA	450
	G1	50
	M11	79
CONTRADICTING	HAP	412
CONTRIBUTE	PR	34
	WB	501
CONTRIBUTES	HP	227
CONTRIVANCE	PRL	13
CONTRIVE	HP	81
	G4	55
	G4	237
	G4	311
CONTRIVED	AA	204
	SAA	239
	G4	419
	AE4	972
	AE6	539
	AE7	537
	B	148
	B	212
	B	461
	C	491
	TH	260
CONTRIVER	HIF	725
CONTRIVES	PFD	22
	SAA	800
CONTROL	AA	468
	AA	807
	AA	993
	FSI	7
	HAP	499
	HAP	1366
	HAP	1706
	HAP	2473
	HAP	2513
	BR	214
	ODA	54

Word	Code	Num
CONTROL	PSH	20
	J3	202
	J10	37
	P5	46
	P5	120
	P5	128
	P6	120
	M1	934
	VCS	22
	AE6	124
	AE9	837
	AE9	962
	KT1	140
	B	374
	CAM	94
	HIF	129
	HIF	341
	AU	302
	M15	668
CONTROLLED	HAP	1288
	HAP	1652
	P1	235
	AE12	554
	HIF	199
CONTROLLER	AE2	1057
	WB	460
CONTROLLING	HIF	407
CONTROLS	G1	564
	AE1	938
	AE9	109
CONTROVERSIES	HAP	775
CONTROVERTED	HAP	1168
CONVENIENCE	PNH	4
	HAP	2234
	J3	368
CONVENIENT	PW	15
	MD	56
	AT	58
	G1	258
	OAL	651
	FL	133
CONVENTICLE	MD	284
	PD	64
CONVENTICLES	SAA	301
	HAP	313
CONVERSATION	ECG2	4
	ECG2	26
	TA	337
	B	200
CONVERSE	EWG	20
	EUO2	29
	P5	56
CONVERSION	HAP	1655
CONVERT	SAA	624
	CAM	342
CONVERTED	PRL	4
	AE7	261
CONVERTING	G3	731
CONVERT'S	HAP	1655
CONVERTS	AA	127
	HAP	1476
	HAP	1489
	HAP	1515
	HAP	1519
	HAP	1667
	M1	550
	AE4	660
	M15	473
CONVEX	J10	214
CONVEY	LC	84
	VHH	26
	S	13
	A	13
	CM	78
	MF	122
	FS2	7
	J1	138
	J3	147
	J6	414
	J10	238
	P3	95
	GK	180
	G2	393
	G4	385
	AE2	405
	AE2	903
	AE2	1037
	AE2	1094
	AE4	147
	AE4	584
	AE5	963
	AE6	113
	AE8	406
	AE9	602
	AE11	285
	OAL	532

CONVEY	OAL	660	COOLER	M1	805	CORN	HAP	225		
	B	703		AE7	498		HAP	2294		
	C	250	COOLING	DC	11		SKA4	1		
	C	818		H29	39		P3	236		
	M15	41		H2	26		M1	140		
CONVEYANCES	RL	384		G3	21		M1	403		
CONVEYED	LC	75		FL	419		M1	370		
	MD	83	COOLNESS	VP2	8		VP5	48		
	SAA	846		G1	386		VP5	56		
	SAA	924		M15	514		VP8	115		
	HAP	1127	COOPED	J10	154		VP8	143		
	HAP	2471		J10	274		VP9	66		
	J1	48		AE2	33		VP10	113		
	VP2	52		AE9	812		G1	2		
	G4	745	COOTS	G1	497		G1	10		
	AE3	941		BP	22		G1	96		
	AE6	703	COPE	J6	168		G1	103		
	AE8	274		M13	179		G1	225		
	AE11	311		M15	352		G1	241		
	MG	25	COPIED	PT	19		G1	359		
	KT1	158		EAL	25		G2	446		
	KT2	64		MD	22		G2	339		
	KT3	714		SAA	958		G2	610		
	KT3	858		G3	205		G4	468		
	KT3	940		KT2	610		AE1	253		
	B	89	COPIER'S	RL	249		AE2	407		
	B	116	COPIES	UDH	101		AE3	193		
	B	741		RL	279		AE4	584		
	M10	97		RL	287		AE8	104		
	M11	257		MF	160		OAL	621		
	FL	601	COPIEST	MG	40		OAE1	13		
	AU	515	COPPER	JH	25		M8	31		
	WB	12		PUO3	16		C	85		
	CI	617		PP	33		C	821		
CONVEYS	J3	111		M15	401		M15	103		
	AE6	530	COPSE	B	141		M15	118		
	AE7	894	COPSES	G1	249		M15	582		
CONVICT	SAA	39	COPY	ER	37		CI	77		
	SAA	787		EDS	25		AS	96		
	CAM	228		EL	300		AS	99		
CONVICTED	L3	146		MS	27	CORN-DEVOURING	G1	270		
CONVINCE	SAA	380		MS	31	CORNEILLE	MM	34		
	RL	148		VP2	40	CORNEILLE'S	PMQ	6		
	GE	74		AE8	683		EOE	6		
	B	312		MG	40	CORNEL	G2	44		
CONVINCED	SEL3	11		M10	10		AE5	728		
	SAA	97	CORAH	AA	632		AE9	948		
	G4	640		AA	676		AE12	406		
	M10	90		SAA	48		KT3	270		
	AU	481		SAA	79		KT3	934		
CONVOY	AE1	802		SAA	86		FL	271		
CONVULSIONS	BR	242		HAP	185	CORNELIA	J6	245		
CONVULSIVE	HAP	1581	CORAH'S	AA	668	CORNELS	M1	136		
	AE6	74		AA	680		M13	112		
	CAM	369		SAA	78		G2	628		
	M15	517		SAA	537		AE3	33		
COOK	PMM	13	CORAL	G4	521		AE3	855		
	J3	137		KT2	465		BP	92		
	J6	765		M15	622	CORNERS	AR	295		
	KT2	591	CORAL-RED	C	49		AK	185		
COOKE	EDG	24	CORANUS	J16	86		AE9	720		
COOKS	RH	81	CORAS	AE7	932	CORNETS	J10	340		
	AA	620		AE11	903	CORNS	C	441		
COOL	PUO2	4	CORBULO	J3	404	CORNY	HAP	2253		
	AA	621	CORD	AM	483	COROEBUS	AE2	461		
	L2	35		AM	569		AE2	519		
	J3	501		AM	720		AE2	549		
	J6	849		T23	43		AE2	575		
	M13	47		J6	144	CORONATION	MD	85		
	VP2	99		AE4	834		MF	95		
	VP9	55		AE5	675		HAP	271		
	G2	661		M12	346	CORONET	HAP	2368		
	G3	231	CORDED	SSC	17		KT3	53		
	G3	507	CORDIAL	SDG	9		FL	168		
	G3	521		EL	42	CORONETS	AR	30		
	G3	699		G2	177	CORPORATIONS	HAP	2248		
	G4	31	CORDIALS	PLG	23	CORPOREAL	L2	24		
	G4	216		HAP	1389		B	656		
	G4	582	CORE	G3	692	CORPS	HAP	23		
	AE7	690	CORINNA	OE	9		HAP	1931		
	AE7	816	CORINTH	AE6	1149		J1	109		
	AE8	810	CORINTHIAN	MC	18		AE7	793		
	AE11	748		G2	646		AE8	715		
	OAL	73	CORITUM	AE7	286		AE10	800		
	KT1	189	CORITUS	AE10	1014		AE11	312		
	HIF	388	CORK	PMS	10		AE11	594		
	M11	287		AE7	1025		HIF	355		
	FL	85		AE9	833		CI	607		
	FL	323		AE11	833	CORPSE	UDH	66		
	M12	296	CORMORANT	BP	22		PLB	37		
	CI	94	CORMORANTS	G1	495		L3	196		
COOLED	AA	903		AE5	169		T23	81		
	M15	524	CORN	UDH	79		J10	139		
COOLER	MD	237		T18	50		AE1	677		
	VP5	7		H2	9		AE2	871		
	HAP	511		TA	355		AE3	59		

Word	Ref	No.
CORPSE	AE5	1136
	AE6	500
	AE9	649
	AE9	653
	AE10	683
	AE10	1205
	AE11	39
	AE11	45
	AE11	107
	AE11	123
	AE11	226
	AE11	1219
	AE12	934
	KT2	584
	KT3	911
	KT3	940
	M8	383
	B	740
	C	250
	C	251
	M11	448
	M11	452
	M11	464
CORRECT	PUO1	21
	PAZ	12
	G1	39
	C	404
CORRECTED	AE2	506
CORRECTS	J6	585
	AE10	321
CORRESPONDENT	M1	53
CORRODING	J10	244
CORRUPT	RL	265
	RL	287
	L3	103
	J3	99
	M1	243
	AE3	191
	M8	382
	M15	360
CORRUPTED	PLG	12
	MD	170
	SAA	464
	OD	32
	J1	118
	P3	199
	P6	83
	G2	719
	OAL	426
	M15	228
	M15	576
CORRUPTION	RL	298
	M15	540
CORRUPTIONS	HAP	1173
CORRUPTLESS	M15	595
CORRUPTS	KT3	754
	KT3	1051
	WB	416
CORSE	AE10	690
CORSLET	AE8	823
	AE10	678
	AE10	1158
	AE11	17
	AE12	153
CORSLETS	KT2	197
CORYCIAN	G4	188
CORYDON	VP2	1
	VP2	47
	VP2	77
	VP2	93
	VP2	105
	VP7	26
	VP7	99
	VP7	100
CORYDON'S	VP5	134
CORYNAEUS	AE6	327
	AE12	450
CORYTHUS	M12	403
	M12	404
COSA	AE10	247
COSSUS	J3	302
	AE6	1157
COST	AR	114
	PMQ	27
	PMM	4
	ECG1	31
	S	12
	A	12
	PLN	8
	EUO	9
	PKK	4
	ETC	10
	PLG	31
	PUF	31
	AA	392
	AA	506
COST	EDG	1
	AT	32
	TA	401
	HAP	1203
	EDS	30
	ELW	3
	EL	154
	OD	15
	ESH	36
	J1	115
	J3	124
	J3	278
	J6	819
	J10	503
	P4	58
	P6	45
	M1	290
	M9	13
	G4	402
	AE1	905
	AE5	327
	AE9	609
	AE10	1211
	AE11	103
	AE11	349
	AE11	435
	AE11	502
	AE11	597
	OAL	492
	OAL	793
	KT1	19
	KT1	33
	KT2	660
	KT3	483
	TJD	10
	M8	234
	HIF	283
	HIF	567
	HIF	749
	HIF	778
	TH	254
	M12	97
	AU	177
	CI	70
	SMP	68
	DA	50
	L2	29
COSTLY	L4	107
	H29	12
	H2	77
	P2	11
	P3	43
	P4	91
	G2	214
	G2	653
	AE1	887
	AE3	279
	AE6	22
	AE9	177
	AE9	353
	KT1	157
	KT2	491
	KT3	936
	M8	308
	B	660
	BP	79
	C	21
	FL	223
	FL	239
	M15	597
COSTS	T27	51
	TA	438
	HH	26
	HH	27
	J3	66
	J3	381
	AE10	686
	OAL	473
COT	BP	154
	BP	160
COTE	G3	472
COTES	VP1	18
	VP2	37
COTS	VP2	36
	G3	719
	AE2	680
	AE4	236
	AE8	135
COTTAGE	HAP	1247
	G2	690
	BP	101
	C	3
	C	614
COTTAGES	VP1	118
	G3	525
COTTONED	PC2	28
COUCH	PM	37
	EKA	17
	AE2	2
	AE3	233
	AE4	934
	AE4	944
	AE8	550
	AE11	851
	AE11	906
	KT2	225
	CAM	246
COUCHED	HAP	1294
	G3	706
	G4	741
	AE2	298
	AE8	488
	AE10	814
COUCHEES	HAP	516
COUCHES	G2	726
	AE1	989
COUGHS	L4	155
	G3	746
COUNCIL	CM	76
	AA	931
	RL	290
	HAP	662
	HAP	666
	HAP	728
	HAP	753
	HAP	942
	HAP	1072
	HAP	1740
	BR	26
	PDS	2
	M1	214
	AE3	891
	AE8	200
	AE9	247
	AE9	293
	AE9	297
	AE10	2
	AE11	363
	AE11	468
	AE11	512
	AE11	587
	AE11	713
	KT1	301
	KT1	308
	HIF	81
	HIF	367
	HIF	425
	HIF	662
	HIF	699
	HIF	730
	AU	332
	AU	367
COUNCILS	POE	28
	RL	255
	HAP	398
	HAP	469
	HAP	653
	HAP	673
	HAP	678
	HAP	741
	J3	21
COUNSEL	AE1	355
	MD	75
	MD	56
	SAA	223
	SAA	484
	SAA	512
	HAP	449
	HAP	492
	HAP	1818
	EDS	17
	J6	110
	J6	463
	J6	643
	J10	512
	J10	535
	P3	175
	M9	181
	AE2	1016
	AE4	163
	AE5	952
	AE6	206
	AE7	122
	AE7	816
	AE8	651
	AE10	227
	OAL	429
	OAL	451
	OAE2	13
	KT3	1021
	CAM	212
	HIF	737

COUNSEL	HIF	776	COUNTRY	EL	5	COUNTRY	CI	78
	C	557		EL	259		CI	116
	AU	491		PSH	27		CI	159
	WB	178		J1	107		CI	184
	WB	189		J3	62		CI	200
	WB	235		J3	213		CI	399
	WB	277		J3	281		PMK	6
COUNSELED	HAP	1605		J3	295		PMK	21
	EL	327		J3	312		AS	78
	J10	422		J3	365		PWR	34
	HIF	290		J3	499	COUNTRYMEN	PAR	19
	C	367		J6	97		PTW	25
	TH	237		J6	244		AA	698
	AU	62		J6	585		HAP	866
COUNSELOR	AR	94		J10	49		AE2	54
COUNSELORS	OAL	90		P1	136		AE3	808
COUNSEL'S	SAA	228		P1	264	COUNTRY'S	RH	98
COUNSELS	HS	79		P3	42		SMA	122
	LC	77		P3	136		VHH	5
	AM	38		P4	52		AM	746
	AA	152		M1	936		AA	232
	AA	212		HI	79		FS1	10
	HAP	939		VP1	34		HAP	1138
	HAP	2393		VP1	45		EJG	2
	J3	94		VP1	96		EJG	8
	P4	18		VP2	36		G4	106
	AE1	928		VP2	39		G4	811
	AE2	113		VP7	47		AE2	368
	AE4	600		VP9	10		AE6	895
	AE8	31		VP10	37		AE6	1128
	HIF	385		G1	482		AE11	1287
	AU	501		G2	229		OAL	225
	WB	152		G2	307		KT1	224
COUNT	EEL	30		G2	527		KT2	99
	EC	31		G2	660		B	556
	J1	123		G2	690		M12	698
	J10	391		G2	735	COUNTS	P1	269
	J10	551		G2	741	COUPLE	HAP	1873
	AE12	351		AE1	423		STS2	11
COUNTED	P5	260		AE1	509		EL	183
	VP6	122		AE1	745		M1	495
	AU	400		AE2	100		AE9	292
	WB	141		AE2	139		BP	133
COUNTENANCE	EUO	19		AE2	363		WB	343
	HS	73		AE2	427		WB	540
	CM	63		AE2	952	COUPLED	PW	21
	PAA	23		AE2	974		AE8	637
	HAP	565		AE2	1017	COURAGE	AR	56
	BR	132		AE3	362		SMA	106
	AE9	999		AE4	277		LCA	33
	KT3	705		AE4	908		VHH	3
	KT3	917		AE5	54		AM	189
	B	629		AE5	823		AM	217
	EMKG	34		AE5	974		AM	249
COUNTERBALANCE	AM	48		AE6	845		AM	304
COUNTERBUFFED	CI	342		AE6	1144		AM	456
COUNTERFEIT	PEL	9		AE6	1182		AM	482
	MD	9		AE7	120		AM	531
COUNTERFEITED	J6	613		AE7	250		AM	539
	KT3	721		AE7	448		AM	679
COUNTERS	EKK	20		AE7	672		AM	694
COUNTER-TIDES	TA	147		AE7	686		AM	782
COUNTRIES	AR	76		AE7	942		AM	1154
	DA	124		AE8	11		PA	39
	AA	484		AE8	472		PMQW	16
	RL	129		AE8	925		HP	242
	G2	162		AE9	326		EPF	12
	G2	722		AE9	341		AA	357
	KT1	6		AE9	1061		SAA	466
COUNTRY	VHH	34		AE10	221		L3	82
	VHH	50		AE11	325		HAP	1337
	AM	850		AE11	418		BR	214
	AM	976		AE11	492		ESH	19
	EWGR	34		AE12	400		J6	396
	EMM	1		OAL	226		P1	19
	PA	25		KT1	138		HI	109
	ENH	4		KT2	29		VP3	53
	PO	2		TJD	1		G3	325
	HP	7		TJD	120		G3	185
	HP	205		TJD	128		G3	161
	PUO3	32		TJD	171		G4	98
	PUO5	15		B	556		AE1	282
	MD	198		BP	96		AE1	538
	SAA	349		BP	117		AE1	633
	SAA	1113		BP	129		AE2	226
	EK	46		BP	156		AE2	427
	RL	240		CAM	63		AE2	496
	L3	277		CAM	77		AE2	615
	L3	285		TH	57		AE2	835
	H29	12		WB	39		AE3	338
	H2	3		WB	58		AE5	250
	H2	95		M15	10		AE5	478
	NS	13		M15	34		AE5	956
	TA	266		M15	665		AE6	371
	AK	99		GP	46		AE6	1183
	HAP	1293		CI	73		AE7	712

COURAGE	AE8	682
	AE9	662
	AE9	974
	AE9	1046
	AE9	1054
	AE9	1077
	AE10	368
	AE10	386
	AE10	502
	AE10	860
	AE10	1229
	AE11	986
	AE11	1040
	AE12	2
	AE12	166
	AE12	349
	AE12	371
	AE12	422
	AE12	1040
	AE12	1291
	KT1	454
	CAM	283
	HIF	367
	C	433
	M11	175
	M12	108
	M12	238
	M12	701
	AU	157
	AU	405
	AU	591
	WB	341
	CI	432
	CI	500
	CI	526
COURAGES	AM	301
	AM	370
	AE5	244
COURSE	JH	12
	LC	153
	AM	522
	PMQ	50
	AA	549
	AA	949
	AA	1020
	MD	85
	SAA	186
	SAA	202
	SAA	213
	SAA	610
	SAA	964
	SAA	1062
	SAA	1119
	L3	275
	H29	56
	TA	135
	HAP	753
	HAP	1114
	HAP	1187
	HAP	2402
	BR	170
	STS2	7
	OD	34
	P3	1
	P3	196
	P5	250
	P6	144
	M1	150
	M1	160
	M1	719
	M1	771
	M1	971
	M1	1092
	M13	223
	VP4	6
	VP8	70
	VP10	15
	G1	59
	G1	76
	G1	553
	G1	671
	G2	793
	G3	170
	G3	316
	G3	412
	G4	533
	AE1	59
	AE1	103
	AE1	504
	AE1	525
	AE1	754
	AE1	779
	AE1	798
	AE2	274
	AE2	678
	AE3	200

COURSE	AE3	262
	AE3	351
	AE3	368
	AE3	378
	AE3	468
	AE3	472
	AE3	482
	AE3	509
	AE3	581
	AE3	587
	AE3	660
	AE3	674
	AE3	907
	AE3	943
	AE4	409
	AE4	938
	AE5	31
	AE5	42
	AE5	381
	AE6	290
	AE6	464
	AE6	476
	AE6	798
	AE7	30
	AE7	42
	AE7	206
	AE7	271
	AE7	293
	AE7	935
	AE8	11
	AE8	123
	AE8	375
	AE9	324
	AE9	612
	AE9	816
	AE9	1007
	AE10	326
	AE10	348
	AE10	410
	AE10	453
	AE10	471
	AE10	675
	AE10	808
	AE10	1101
	AE10	1115
	AE11	140
	AE11	456
	AE11	910
	AE11	1123
	AE12	384
	AE12	546
	AE12	554
	AE12	697
	AE12	767
	AE12	794
	AE12	1019
	AE12	1105
	AE12	1315
	OAL	472
	OAL	749
	DO	24
	KT2	184
	KT2	611
	KT3	397
	KT3	637
	TJD	150
	B	360
	B	517
	B	655
	BP	112
	M11	95
	FL	2
	AU	352
	M15	272
	M15	416
	CI	371
	SMP	31
	KT3	56
COURSED		
COURSER	G3	130
	G3	289
	G3	327
	AE1	442
	AE4	190
	AE4	223
	AE8	730
	AE9	357
	AE10	1225
	AE10	1241
	AE11	744
	AE12	436
	AE12	519
	AE12	541
	OAL	710
	KT3	64
	KT3	457
	KT3	609

COURSER	TH	215
	M12	533
COURSER's	G1	16
	G3	116
	AE1	620
	AE9	150
	AE11	1041
	OAL	158
	KT1	46
COURSERS	J1	92
	G1	690
	G3	27
	G3	84
	G3	143
	G4	560
	AE1	211
	AE2	355
	AE2	567
	AE5	190
	AE5	747
	AE6	793
	AE6	886
	AE7	220
	AE7	386
	AE7	1067
	AE8	227
	AE8	789
	AE9	534
	AE10	508
	AE10	803
	AE11	898
	AE11	909
	AE11	915
	AE11	1024
	AE12	127
	AE12	175
	AE12	249
	AE12	490
	AE12	503
	AE12	554
	AE12	902
	OAL	372
	KT3	590
	FL	211
	FL	221
	FL	297
	M15	668
COURSERS'	KT3	448
COURT	AR	281
	SMA	111
	LC	138
	EIE	4
	VHH	47
	ET	6
	PM	39
	EM	31
	PCD	2
	EUO2	9
	E	1
	ML	18
	PCB	23
	PO	8
	HP	146
	HP	182
	HP	203
	AA	127
	AA	563
	AA	683
	AA	739
	AA	825
	AA	921
	D	2
	SAA	48
	SAA	180
	SAA	515
	SAA	517
	SAA	1008
	EK	46
	AT	37
	EC	7
	ER	68
	T18	4
	H2	15
	HH	13
	HAP	515
	HAP	1430
	HAP	1454
	HAP	1530
	STS3	24
	LS	13
	J3	40
	J3	117
	J3	242
	J6	88
	J10	147
	J10	260

COURT	M1	121	COURTIER	PRH	23	COVERING	AA	272
	M1	225		EL	325		DOD	2
	M1	782	COURTIER'S	AA	825		HAP	354
	M13	101		HAP	42		VP1	116
	HI	14	COURTIERS	PKA	25		AE7	1025
	HI	16		EUF	7		AE9	314
	VP9	94		KT1	346		AE11	851
	G2	721		B	47		AE11	1008
	G3	196	COURT-INFORMER	AA	719		M11	147
	G4	535	COURTING	M10	29		M11	294
	AE1	953	COURTLY	SAA	639		FL	73
	AE2	113		FL	399		WB	80
	AE2	121		WB	48	COVERINGS	AE1	630
	AE2	653		CI	224		AE1	693
	AE2	1033	COURT'S	GE	63		M10	52
	AE3	387	COURTS	AM	823	COVERLET	BP	79
	AE4	166		PUO2	9	COVERS	PRH	2
	AE4	190		EUO2	5		J1	8
	AE4	270		ML	24		J3	339
	AE4	283		EUF	7		J6	789
	AE4	348		AA	144		M1	8
	AE4	433		AA	188		KT1	336
	AE4	712		MF	72		BP	153
	AE4	728		SAA	272	COVERT	AM	102
	AE4	776		L3	204		PRH	11
	AE4	958		EKA	27		H29	35
	AE5	446		J6	52		MN	11
	AE5	451		J6	199		M1	724
	AE6	140		VP3	4		VP7	12
	AE7	81		VP6	84		G1	496
	AE7	206		G2	704		G4	11
	AE7	529		AE2	721		G4	624
	AE7	808		AE12	692		G4	664
	AE8	210		OAL	66		AE2	334
	AE8	321		DO	149		AE6	262
	AE8	472		FL	565		AE6	1036
	AE8	647		M12	77		AE7	703
	AE11	344		WB	61		AE8	144
	AE11	454		ETP	11		AE9	569
	AE12	17	COURTSHIP	LC	5		AE10	1142
	OAL	170		M1	970		KT2	22
	OAL	350		MC	29		KT2	230
	OAL	683		OAL	792		KT2	584
	DO	61		TH	15		B	716
	KT1	303		PWR	16		C	4
	KT1	577	COUSIN	P3	52	COVERTS	AM	382
	KT1	594	COVENANT	AA	767		AE4	235
	KT2	499		MD	211	COVET	AA	798
	KT3	1015		SAA	226		AE6	977
	TJD	128		PDG	2	COVETOUS	AA	309
	TJD	186		PDG	11		L3	150
	B	27	COVENANTING	AR	101		P6	141
	B	43	COVENANTS	SAA	268		AE6	491
	B	82		G4	713		AE10	1207
	B	318	COVENT	EKK	22		B	330
	B	523		EKA	4		M11	186
	B	529		PWR	4		M15	160
	HIF	582	COVER	AM	954	COW	OE	29
	HIF	716		T27	107		M1	835
	HIF	766		HAP	1911		M1	867
	C	328		P4	52		G1	518
	C	662		HI	117		G3	87
	TH	55		G1	152		G3	101
	M11	42		G2	31		G3	283
	M11	94		G2	697		G3	328
	M11	292		AE4	170		OAL	315
	M11	315	COVERED	AM	451		OAL	352
	FL	469		PCG1	14		OAL	365
	AU	319		CM	80		OAL	367
	WB	60		L3	192		OAL	738
	WB	245		AK	190		C	730
	WB	258		HAP	1773	COWARD	SCD2	14
	WB	266		J3	258		TA	476
	WB	293		M1	283		HAP	2218
	WB	341		M9	65		AE5	953
	WB	351		VP3	157		AE9	1055
	WB	409		G1	175		AE10	752
	CI	42		G2	475		AE10	916
	CI	632		G3	798		AE11	592
	ETP	5		G4	609		AE11	1055
	ETP	18		AE4	578		AE11	1230
COURTED	HS	130		AE4	592		AE12	83
	LC	12		AE4	814		AE12	984
	AM	4		AE6	317		C	133
	AM	193		AE10	295		AU	79
	AE10	450		AE10	374		AU	55
COURTEOUS	TH	347		AE11	594		AU	117
	FL	496		AE11	833		CI	36
COURTESANS	AM	881		AE11	1135	COWARDICE	HAP	1773
COURTESIES	HAP	2463		AE12	661		KT3	734
COURTESY	PAR	15		KT3	194		FL	574
	PM	35		KT3	910		AU	96
	HAP	2417		KT3	932	COWARDS	AM	403
	KT1	594		KT3	950		SEL1	15
	FL	409		B	213		HAP	1818
	WB	228		FL	276		AE4	315

Word	Ref	No.
COWARDS	AE9	811
	AE11	1079
	CI	409
COWARDS'	G4	98
	AE9	157
COWERING	AA	515
	C	463
COWERS	AE12	1329
COWLEY	ETG	7
COWS	T27	9
	M9	99
	VP9	40
	G2	147
	G2	518
	OAL	329
	C	14
	M15	18
COWS'	G4	14
COX	EMKG	23
COXCOMB	EAL	3
	HP	18
	C	134
COXCOMBS	PLN	10
	PTP	14
COY	HS	30
	T27	24
	EMKG	24
COYNESS	H9	36
COYSTREL	HAP	2413
COZENAGE	HAP	830
COZENED	AR	61
	PIE	17
	ELN	13
	HP	47
	PR	10
	PPC	13
	PAA	26
	C	798
	AU	265
CRAB	G2	43
	MG	38
	M15	547
CRABBED	RL	235
CRABS	G4	67
CRACK	AT	65
	J6	107
	J10	230
	AE1	128
CRACKED	AA	500
	P5	268
	G1	262
CRACKERS	PMS	17
CRACKLE	AE12	762
CRACKLED	AE7	112
CRACKLES	J10	94
	VP8	117
	G1	125
	G2	419
CRACKLING	AM	897
	G3	563
	G4	521
	G4	591
	AE2	407
	AE2	958
	AE3	821
	AE5	582
	AE5	865
	AE7	644
	AE12	455
	KT3	956
	M8	102
	HIF	628
	M12	389
CRACKNELS	J3	310
CRACKS	AM	951
CRADLE	AM	32
	AM	852
	CM	132
	TA	451
	BR	43
	P2	61
	VP4	27
	G4	530
	AE9	819
	OAL	216
	M15	608
	M15	642
CRAFT	SAA	848
	HAP	818
	BR	115
	J6	466
CRAFTY	AM	881
	PRH	13
	J6	329
	P1	228
	M1	930

Word	Ref	No.
CRAFTY	OAL	90
	CAM	247
CRAG	AE12	995
CRAGGY	AE3	322
	AE4	219
	AE6	489
	AE7	985
	AE10	507
	L2	19
	L3	131
	HAP	2423
	J10	363
	H9	6
CRAMMED	G3	729
CRAMPED	P6	51
CRAMS	MD	305
CRANE	J3	155
	G1	179
	G1	516
	AE11	870
CRANES	G1	413
	AE10	370
CRANNIES	G1	263
	G4	56
	AE1	237
	M12	65
CRANNY	PEL	18
	G3	645
CRANTOR	M12	494
CRANTOR'S	M12	488
CRASHING	AE12	464
CRASSI	OAL	208
CRATHIS	M15	475
CRATINUS	P1	247
CRAVE	AA	383
	AA	988
	L3	110
	FS4	9
	AE6	159
	AE7	301
	AE11	381
	KT3	794
	BP	169
CRAVEN	AM	347
CRAVES	L2	21
	J6	219
	J6	595
	M1	375
CRAVING	OAL	480
	BR	275
	ESH	23
	J6	794
	P4	55
	P5	159
	G3	207
	OAL	475
CRAWL	HAP	1910
	J6	678
	M1	465
	M15	552
	M15	564
	PMK	22
CRAWLING	RL	419
CRAWLS	AE5	363
CRAZY	HAP	1445
	KT3	768
CREAKED	J6	33
CREAKING	OE	39
	J3	157
	VP2	13
	G3	510
	M11	291
	M11	478
CREAM	VP1	114
	BP	96
CREATE	AR	14
	SMA	70
	AM	185
	AA	65
	AA	222
	SAA	589
	SAA	694
	SAA	875
	PK	17
	HH	41
	HAP	2489
	BR	26
	J6	547
	VP4	43
	G4	295
	G4	462
	DO	61
	KT1	485
	KT3	769
	PTC	8
CREATED	HAP	249

Word	Ref	No.
CREATED	J3	34
	P6	6
	M1	584
	G4	324
	C	446
	M12	56
CREATES	RL	419
	SKA6	1
	KT1	415
CREATING	EL	77
	GK	114
CREATION	AK	126
	HAP	254
	M1	107
	M1	131
	G2	460
	G2	468
	G3	722
	KT3	1029
	GP	105
CREATOR	OD	25
	P3	131
	VCS	1
	KT3	129
CREATOR'S	AM	659
	HAP	1077
CREATURE	SSC	57
	SSF	3
	SDG	15
	SDG	17
	RL	64
	OE	35
	PD	54
	HAP	328
	HAP	402
	STS1	5
	PKA	19
	SKA2	14
	SKA3	6
	J1	213
	P5	243
	M1	97
	M1	476
	M1	1082
	M9	17
	VP2	85
	G3	375
	AE3	201
	AE7	695
	AE12	1087
	OAL	354
	KT1	488
	C	461
	WB	531
	M15	170
	M15	331
CREATURES	AM	437
	ETL	8
	PW	21
	RL	86
	RL	92
	ETS	4
	M1	568
	M1	582
	G4	437
	AE9	294
	KT1	475
	CAM	49
	M12	666
	M15	540
	M15	707
	M15	188
CREATURES'	HAP	109
CREDIBILITY	ELN	18
CREDIT	HP	243
	SAA	379
	SAA	748
	PAA	26
	HAP	2564
	EDS	12
	J3	242
	J6	715
	J6	839
	AE2	96
	AE2	260
	AE11	344
	CAM	8
	AU	409
CREDULITY	C	811
	M12	84
CREDULOUS	SAA	846
CREED	POE	28
	SAA	278
	RL	214
	RL	283
	RL	434

Word	Ref	No.
CREED	HAP	147
	HAP	1148
CREEK	H29	103
CREEKS	AE1	809
CREEP	RH	9
	SMA	114
	AM	1128
	SMM1	7
	MF	197
	AT	122
	T18	19
	HAP	128
	PKA	8
	M1	990
	VP4	36
	G4	182
	AE6	961
	AU	122
CREEPING	AM	987
	VP9	56
	AE4	238
	AE10	727
	KT1	45
	B	748
	HIF	46
CREEPS	AM	527
	PTL	14
	J10	344
	AE2	698
	AE8	668
	KT1	468
	KT3	1072
	M11	284
	M15	316
	M15	348
CREMONA'S	VP9	34
CRENAEUS	M12	432
CREON	KT1	81
	KT1	104
	KT1	124
	KT1	135
CREON'S	KT1	159
CREPT	AM	869
	PT	10
	T23	95
	J10	192
	AE12	1254
	CI	89
	PTP	28
CRESCENT	G1	576
	AE6	383
CRESCENTS	AM	500
CREST	HAP	164
	HAP	2301
	G3	641
	G3	648
	AE2	513
	AE2	530
	AE3	601
	AE7	1073
	AE8	577
	AE9	33
	AE9	55
	AE9	206
	AE9	358
	AE9	498
	AE9	990
	AE9	1094
	AE10	377
	AE10	903
	AE10	992
	AE10	1080
	AE11	14
	AE11	135
	AE11	738
	AE11	1110
	AE11	1207
	AE12	154
	AE12	548
	KT3	584
CRESTED	J6	361
	HI	189
	AE2	641
	AE6	565
	AE8	822
	KT3	452
	C	469
CRESTS	AM	264
	AE2	272
	AE2	288
	AE2	557
	AE6	1059
	AE9	923
CRETAN	VP6	68
	G4	223
	AE3	181
CRETAN	AE4	208
	AE5	371
	AE5	769
	AE6	18
	AE6	34
	AE12	610
	OAL	329
	OAL	350
	KT1	116
	AU	547
CRETANS	CI	633
CRETA'S	HIF	219
CRETE	BR	207
	J1	82
	M9	1
	M9	2
	M9	107
	G2	787
	AE3	141
	AE3	159
	AE3	167
	AE3	178
	AE3	220
	AE3	228
	AE3	241
	AE6	28
	AE6	32
	OAL	335
CRETEUS	AE9	1045
CREÜSA	AM	268
	DA	85
	AE2	813
	AE2	916
	AE2	986
	AE2	1002
	AE2	1046
	AE2	1048
	AE2	1067
	AE9	399
	AE2	1045
CREÜSA'S		
CREVAT	ESF	23
CREW	PLG	7
	SAA	103
	SAA	523
	SAA	900
	H3	40
	H2	92
	TA	464
	MN	8
	HAP	235
	HAP	450
	HAP	965
	HAP	1217
	J6	143
	J6	350
	J6	493
	P1	194
	P3	206
	PLT	17
	GK	171
	DHP	10
	VP1	111
	G1	227
	G1	290
	G3	35
	G4	14
	G4	149
	AE1	162
	AE1	293
	AE1	687
	AE1	786
	AE2	788
	AE2	870
	AE2	1085
	AE3	14
	AE3	608
	AE3	687
	AE4	603
	AE4	783
	AE5	23
	AE5	176
	AE5	237
	AE5	247
	AE5	272
	AE5	323
	AE5	938
	AE5	1085
	AE6	3
	AE6	94
	AE6	327
	AE6	445
	AE6	458
	AE7	547
	AE7	724
	AE8	390
	AE8	725
CREW	AE9	724
	AE10	185
	AE11	400
	AE11	576
	AE11	720
	AE11	953
	AE11	1020
	AE12	402
	AE12	411
	AE12	517
	OAL	131
	AF	142
	KT1	98
	KT3	305
	KT3	468
	M8	44
	M8	160
	CAM	118
	HIF	217
	C	344
	C	353
	C	726
	TH	347
	M11	72
	FL	612
	M12	368
	AU	326
	AU	390
	CI	193
	CI	286
	CI	390
	CI	548
	CI	612
	AS	101
CRIED	SCG1	27
	SM2	8
	SM2	14
	PLN	39
	SKK	2
	CM	83
	CM	101
	DA	110
	D	16
	MF	13
	MF	144
	EDG	23
	AT	96
	NS	12
	HAP	16
	ODA	14
	ODA	30
	J10	117
	M1	680
	M1	737
	M1	898
	M13	205
	VP3	26
	VP6	38
	VP10	41
	G4	455
	G4	653
	G4	763
	AE2	53
	AE2	323
	AE2	547
	AE2	710
	AE2	996
	AE3	711
	AE5	18
	AE5	224
	AE5	901
	AE5	970
	AE5	1119
	AE6	81
	AE6	369
	AE7	542
	AE7	546
	AE9	509
	AE9	529
	AE9	571
	AE9	1054
	AE10	943
	AE10	1148
	AE11	1239
	AE12	149
	AE12	559
	KT1	236
	KT1	450
	KT3	578
	KT3	663
	M8	79
	M8	168
	M8	181
	M8	233
	M8	352
	B	237

CRIED	B	690	CRIES	AE5	216	CRIME	J1	111		
	HIF	570		AE5	286		J6	161		
	C	98		AE5	336		J6	313		
	C	271		AE5	451		J6	409		
	C	583		AE5	511		J6	617		
	C	736		AE5	670		J6	693		
	TH	101		AE5	798		J10	24		
	TH	116		AE6	68		J10	398		
	TH	274		AE6	316		P2	52		
	M11	383		AE6	427		P3	30		
	M12	111		AE6	436		M1	130		
	M12	276		AE6	576		M1	197		
	M12	321		AE6	754		M1	648		
	M12	363		AE6	842		VP6	112		
	M12	372		AE7	642		VP9	34		
	M12	406		AE7	700		G2	546		
	M12	427		AE7	819		G3	709		
	M12	441		AE7	853		AE2	211		
	M12	494		AE9	565		AE2	797		
	M12	644		AE10	1038		AE3	796		
	M12	652		AE10	1094		AE4	250		
	M12	698		AE10	1201		AE4	998		
	AU	95		AE10	1287		AE6	706		
	AU	7		AE11	697		AE6	765		
	AU	359		AE11	982		AE6	1010		
	WB	58		AE11	1040		AE9	174		
	WB	311		AE11	1055		AE9	575		
	WB	347		AE12	391		AE10	129		
CRIER	J1	152		AE12	446		AE11	253		
	WB	271		AE12	471		AE11	714		
CRIES	AM	432		AE12	630		AE12	241		
	AM	905		AE12	905		AE12	242		
	AM	1095		AE12	908		AE12	834		
	SCD1	23		AE12	1005		MM	20		
	CM	55		AE12	1051		MM	38		
	CM	59		AE12	1097		KT2	97		
	CM	86		AE12	1251		KT2	108		
	SAA	289		AE12	1260		KT2	293		
	SAA	307		AE12	1368		KT3	821		
	RL	43		OAL	133		M8	297		
	L3	152		AF	131		B	42		
	L5	7		DO	75		B	259		
	H29	9		KT1	131		B	279		
	TA	67		KT2	341		B	359		
	TA	146		KT2	583		B	451		
	HAP	468		KT3	484		B	522		
	HAP	2510		KT3	920		B	548		
	SSC	31		KT3	997		B	593		
	BR	323		KT3	1070		CAM	11		
	PKA	22		M8	286		CAM	20		
	J1	6		M8	366		CAM	37		
	J1	157		B	373		CAM	63		
	J3	259		CAM	145		CAM	148		
	J3	458		HIF	501		CAM	210		
	J6	251		C	699		CAM	247		
	J6	368		TH	268		CAM	266		
	J6	379		M11	121		CAM	285		
	J6	388		M11	395		CAM	295		
	J6	837		M11	465		CAM	305		
	J10	132		M11	481		CAM	311		
	J10	249		M12	569		HIF	560		
	J16	44		M15	335		C	286		
	P3	11		M15	690		C	373		
	P3	123		CI	611		C	498		
	P3	150	CRIME	UDH	12		C	775		
	P4	44		AR	80		TH	295		
	P5	195		EWG	18		M12	315		
	M1	274		CM	22		AU	62		
	HI	140		CM	48		AU	225		
	VP5	90		CM	125		AU	298		
	VP6	66		CM	129		AU	464		
	VP9	6		HP	50		AU	486		
	VP10	33		HP	142		WB	458		
	G1	533		HP	195		CI	354		
	G1	692		HP	216		CI	480		
	G3	77		HP	239		ETP	28		
	G3	619		DA	176		SMP	38		
	G3	622		AA	328		SMP	42		
	G4	510		AA	342		AS	75		
	AE1	128		AA	460	CRIME'S	HP	216		
	AE1	733		AA	597	CRIMES	AR	189		
	AE1	787		AA	834		AR	315		
	AE1	897		MD	237		SMA	20		
	AE1	1014		SAA	441		SMA	87		
	AE2	398		SAA	734		SMA	90		
	AE2	402		SAA	860		LC	60		
	AE2	422		PD	14		LC	92		
	AE2	667		L4	176		LC	119		
	AE2	724		HAP	481		PUO2	18		
	AE2	926		HAP	1179		CM	114		
	AE2	1053		HAP	1647		DA	89		
	AE3	442		HAP	1988		AA	181		
	AE4	266		HAP	2136		AA	204		
	AE4	955		EL	170		AA	663		
	AE4	960		EL	364		AA	790		
	AE5	197		OD	43		MD	208		

Word	Ref	No.
CRIMES	MD	273
	MD	282
	SAA	17
	SAA	65
	SAA	504
	SAA	686
	SAA	785
	SAA	875
	SAA	883
	SAA	1128
	EDG	8
	RL	53
	RL	100
	H3	53
	TA	263
	HH	17
	HAP	1927
	HAP	2475
	HAP	2509
	BR	38
	BR	156
	BR	290
	BR	294
	J1	70
	J1	114
	J1	221
	J3	90
	J6	377
	J6	397
	J6	671
	J6	842
	J6	848
	J10	44
	J10	105
	J10	143
	P1	167
	P1	224
	P3	65
	P4	27
	M1	271
	M1	323
	VP4	17
	G1	675
	G1	680
	G4	654
	G4	657
	G4	773
	AE1	11
	AE2	106
	AE2	133
	AE6	583
	AE6	756
	AE6	853
	AE6	854
	AE7	796
	AE7	1054
	AE8	452
	AE8	633
	AE11	335
	AE11	518
	OAL	382
	M8	299
	HIF	309
	HIF	478
	GP	35
	CI	475
	CI	625
	SMP	18
CRIMINAL	CAM	287
	CAM	311
	WB	271
CRIMINALS	J3	491
	C	290
CRIMSON	HAP	1240
	M1	998
	AE5	1055
	AE9	55
	AE9	469
	AE9	990
	AE10	1117
	AE10	1312
	AE11	135
	AE12	101
	AE12	1084
	KT2	465
	M12	151
CRINISUS	AE5	52
CRIPPLÈ	MD	272
CRIPPLED	P5	79
CRIPPLES	AE8	345
	ML	44
CRISIS	AR	178
CRISPINUS	J1	35
CRITIC	PMQ	25
	PMQ	46
	POE	11
CRITIC	PLB	6
	PLB	12
	PLT	47
	PTP	4
CRITIC-DAME	J6	562
CRITIC'S	PMQ	28
CRITICS	EWG	4
	PIE	1
	PTL	3
	PCG2	2
	PCG2	7
	ECG2	13
	ECG2	31
	ENH	8
	PAL	1
	PKK	24
	ETC	1
	EUF	25
	PLB	2
	PLB	3
	PLB	11
	PLT	45
	PLT	52
	GK	81
CROAK	HAP	1770
CROAKING	MD	305
	VP9	18
	PAL	4
	P1	71
	VP1	26
	G1	558
CROAKS	G1	521
CROATIAN	MD	240
CROCODILE	M9	38
CROESUS	J10	20
	C	389
CROESUS'	J10	421
CRONE	P2	74
	CAM	247
	WB	264
	WB	315
	WB	333
	WB	374
CRONES	WB	126
CROOK	AT	111
CROOKED	AA	152
	MD	257
	SAA	701
	J3	113
	J10	476
	P1	194
	P5	52
	M1	173
	M1	450
	M1	994
	M1	1030
	M13	28
	VP2	97
	G1	220
	G1	243
	G1	250
	G1	684
	G2	508
	G2	739
	G3	227
	G3	771
	G4	183
	AE3	311
	AE3	358
	AE4	825
	AE5	333
	AE6	809
	AE7	200
	AE7	243
	AE7	715
	AE7	1012
	AE8	595
	AE9	140
	AE9	763
	AE10	300
	AE11	1107
	HIF	474
	HIF	660
	M15	547
	M15	589
	CI	281
	CI	389
CROP	TA	374
	PAA	8
	J1	133
	P6	32
	VP1	105
	VP5	55
	VP10	9
	G1	72
	G1	226
CROP	G1	248
	G1	313
	G1	440
	G2	195
	G2	503
	G2	747
	G3	490
	G3	707
	AE3	34
	AE12	455
	OAL	394
	KT3	354
	M15	158
	M15	179
	ETP	10
CROPPED	M1	408
	VP2	64
	VP3	15
	AE3	709
	AE11	100
	M15	164
CROPS	HAP	2253
	HAP	2285
	G1	150
	G1	237
	G1	275
	G4	433
CROSIER	HAP	395
CROSLET	AE7	877
CROSS	AR	19
	AR	237
	AM	624
	AM	675
	AM	838
	AM	931
	DA	198
	PUO5	18
	RL	160
	HAP	1595
	HAP	2241
	EH	21
	J6	780
	G1	328
	G3	229
	AE2	917
	AE4	228
	AE5	436
	AE6	449
	AE6	508
	AE9	165
	AE9	516
	AE10	559
	AE11	494
	AE12	384
	DO	110
	KT2	240
	C	299
	C	686
	C	722
	M12	13
	WB	31
CROSS-BARRED	J10	478
CROSSED	HS	121
	AR	24
	AR	73
	L4	90
	ODA	16
	M1	281
	AE1	445
	AE1	527
	AE2	1023
	AE4	378
	AE6	911
	TH	131
	CI	441
CROSSES	AM	220
CROSSGRAINED	MD	146
CROSSING	G2	527
CROTCHES	BP	160
CROTCHETS	OAL	864
CROTON	M15	20
	M15	72
	M15	11
	M15	74
CROUCH	TA	480
CROUCHING	AM	2
CROW	AM	345
	HAP	2364
	P3	118
	G1	533
	C	582
CROWD	AM	999
	EAZ	41
	PC2	32
	ML	19
	ML	50

CROWD		
	CM	82
	HP	145
	AA	68
	AA	203
	AA	225
	AA	359
	AA	686
	AA	727
	AA	765
	AA	778
	PLB	51
	MD	82
	MD	91
	MD	142
	MD	314
	PRH	16
	PRH	32
	SAA	24
	SAA	114
	SAA	162
	SAA	191
	SAA	246
	SAA	247
	SAA	573
	SAA	605
	SAA	653
	SAA	666
	SAA	729
	SAA	765
	SAA	781
	SAA	1031
	EC	18
	L3	204
	T18	27
	TA	97
	TA	320
	HAP	220
	HAP	373
	HAP	507
	HAP	826
	HAP	1216
	HAP	1698
	HAP	1897
	HAP	2495
	EL	277
	J1	154
	J1	242
	J3	115
	J3	287
	J3	303
	J3	393
	J3	412
	J10	116
	P1	13
	P1	61
	P1	233
	P4	108
	P4	124
	P5	255
	GK	83
	VP3	37
	G3	42
	G3	579
	G4	114
	G4	316
	G4	680
	AE1	213
	AE1	708
	AE2	52
	AE2	346
	AE2	640
	AE3	888
	AE4	601
	AE4	969
	AE5	195
	AE5	234
	AE5	418
	AE5	440
	AE5	445
	AE5	477
	AE5	511
	AE5	537
	AE5	721
	AE5	793
	AE5	808
	AE5	867
	AE5	1078
	AE6	256
	AE6	330
	AE6	422
	AE6	457
	AE7	82
	AE7	535
	AE8	9
	AE8	646
	AE8	735

CROWD		
	AE8	782
	AE9	462
	AE9	509
	AE9	586
	AE9	874
	AE9	985
	AE9	1025
	AE10	125
	AE10	204
	AE10	620
	AE10	749
	AE10	1079
	AE11	19
	AE11	365
	AE11	572
	AE11	698
	AE11	1292
	AE12	324
	AE12	461
	AE12	586
	AE12	701
	OAL	194
	OAL	561
	OAL	682
	OAE2	70
	AF	34
	KT3	78
	KT3	438
	KT3	497
	KT3	551
	KT3	690
	KT3	891
	B	53
	B	194
	B	479
	B	551
	CAM	103
	CAM	244
	TH	285
	M11	174
	M11	326
	FL	190
	M12	325
	M15	87
	GP	135
	CI	605
	CI	614
	EMKG	14
CROWDED	AR	220
	AM	216
	POE	7
	L3	74
	HAP	2345
	MS	12
	J10	17
	J10	146
	J10	227
	VP6	43
	G1	74
	G1	476
	G2	394
	G2	748
	AE5	142
	DO	60
	KT3	920
	M10	38
	AU	320
	AU	365
CROWDING	ESK	5
	VHH	47
	VP4	63
	AE6	965
	AE9	720
	AE12	656
	AE12	823
	OAL	164
	KT3	463
CROWD'S	CI	411
	SAA	694
	SAA	782
	SAA	808
	SAA	855
	HAP	1952
CROWDS	AR	276
	LC	1
	PLN	33
	DA	22
	AA	184
	AA	211
	AA	787
	AA	897
	AA	996
	AA	1018
	MD	2
	MD	99
	MD	290

CROWDS		
	PRH	7
	SAA	7
	SAA	147
	SAA	148
	SAA	584
	SAA	718
	SAA	1140
	RL	417
	FS3	3
	HAP	1531
	BR	87
	EL	68
	J10	52
	J10	350
	M1	120
	SFL	20
	EHC	3
	G4	372
	AE1	712
	AE2	652
	AE4	269
	AE6	1196
	AE8	962
	AE9	606
	AE11	1274
	AE12	988
	KT3	447
	KT3	737
	TJD	50
	CAM	29
	M12	78
	M12	658
CROWING	T18	92
	HAP	2316
	C	40
	C	43
	C	429
	C	454
	M11	274
CROWN	JH	10
	HS	26
	AR	39
	AR	52
	AR	258
	RH	50
	SMA	46
	SMA	47
	SMA	128
	LC	64
	PUO1	40
	PO	26
	HP	61
	DA	92
	DA	136
	DA	163
	AA	11
	AA	24
	AA	58
	AA	192
	AA	207
	AA	434
	AA	474
	AA	685
	AA	927
	MD	216
	SAA	110
	SAA	125
	SAA	143
	SAA	188
	SAA	812
	SAA	884
	SAA	951
	SAA	970
	SAA	973
	SAA	1026
	SAA	1040
	SAA	1060
	SAA	1116
	PDG	41
	SDG	23
	SDG	28
	PD	50
	H3	54
	TA	317
	EAA	6
	AK	139
	GE	69
	HAP	202
	HAP	1059
	HAP	1081
	HAP	1109
	HAP	1386
	HAP	1999
	HAP	2121
	PMS	22
	ESH	36

Word	Code	Ref
CRUEL	AE2	468
	AE2	848
	AE2	1028
	AE3	860
	AE4	653
	AE4	888
	AE4	952
	AE5	812
	AE6	491
	AE6	687
	AE6	788
	AE6	809
	AE7	473
	AE7	506
	AE8	492
	AE8	924
	AE9	271
	AE9	568
	AE9	641
	AE10	1236
	AE12	732
	OAL	13
	OAL	77
	KT1	104
	KT2	234
	B	569
	B	611
	B	754
	CAM	58
	C	283
	TH	82
	M11	392
	M11	425
	FL	493
CRUELTY	PCD	29
	AA	480
	RL	88
	TA	243
	HAP	1983
	J6	158
	M13	32
	AE4	470
	KT2	269
	B	665
	TH	171
CRUISE	L4	77
	AE3	492
CRUMBLE	VP8	115
	G2	337
CRUMBLING	SSC	60
	J10	232
	G1	139
	G2	280
	G2	295
	M15	410
CRUMPED	EWR	8
CRUPPER	KT3	622
CRUSE	PTW	9
	HAP	2294
	AS	87
CRUSH	AR	174
	L3	186
	J3	393
	J3	412
	J6	348
	M13	212
	AE1	389
	AE2	608
	AE6	747
CRUSHED	T23	107
	J10	63
	J10	171
	G1	511
	AE5	360
	AE9	686
	AE9	774
	AE11	1274
	AE12	779
	KT3	415
	KT3	417
	M12	396
	M12	457
	M12	522
CRUSHES	AE12	496
CRUST	T27	109
	J6	604
CRUSTED	M1	568
	G2	488
CRUSTUMERIAN	AE7	873
CRUTCH	SAA	409
CRUTCHES	G2	493
CRY	EIE	23
	AM	437
	EWGR	18
	PMQW	1
	SCD2	7
CRY	PNH	46
	EAZ	23
	ESF	9
	PC2	14
	EMK	2
	PTW	17
	PSF	8
	ETG	15
	AA	291
	AA	521
	AA	783
	PLB	40
	PLB	41
	PLB	47
	MD	103
	MF	76
	SAA	104
	SAA	429
	SAA	542
	SAA	695
	SAA	1137
	PDG	30
	EDG	19
	AT	102
	EC	29
	L3	101
	HAP	280
	HAP	368
	HAP	595
	HAP	2044
	HAP	2309
	HAP	2330
	HAP	2434
	BR	55
	BR	79
	PMS	26
	EKA	8
	SKA1	12
	PSH	4
	ESH	3
	J1	175
	J1	249
	J3	174
	J3	323
	J6	376
	J6	448
	J10	102
	J10	114
	J16	26
	P1	8
	P1	61
	P1	78
	P1	162
	P2	43
	P3	28
	P5	146
	M1	328
	M13	130
	M13	199
	G3	241
	AE1	448
	AE2	300
	AE2	882
	AE3	178
	AE3	293
	AE3	403
	AE3	882
	AE4	218
	AE6	664
	AE7	866
	AE8	652
	AE9	767
	AE11	51
	AE11	219
	AE11	692
	AE11	927
	AE11	944
	AE11	1281
	AE11	1298
	AE12	1257
	AE12	1316
	OAL	739
	OAL	746
	OAE2	50
	KT1	43
	KT1	253
	KT2	229
	KT3	371
	KT3	439
	KT3	528
	KT3	715
	KT3	873
	M8	346
	CAM	112
	C	231
	C	253
CRY	C	288
	C	714
	C	718
	C	724
	C	763
	M11	101
	M11	173
	M11	279
	FL	211
	WB	71
	PTP	7
	SMP	20
	SMP	21
	SMP	34
	SMP	36
CRYEST	L3	83
CRYING	HAP	1409
	R	3
	R	7
	R	15
	R	19
	G1	495
	G1	526
	G4	500
	AE5	808
	AE9	649
	KT1	45
	CAM	370
CRYSTAL	AM	1121
	PUO2	14
	J3	35
	J3	370
	M13	30
	M13	68
	VP2	83
	VP5	61
	VP5	74
	G2	276
	G2	690
	G3	779
	G4	515
	AE1	238
	AE4	912
	AE6	915
	AE7	1082
	AE9	26
	MFL	16
	KT2	240
	KT2	541
	M15	449
	CI	89
CRYSTALS	J6	225
CUBBED	P5	214
CUBIT-BONE	M12	463
CUBITS	G3	548
CUBS	M13	138
	M15	559
CUCKOLD	PEL	35
	EM	30
	PCB	9
	J1	88
	J6	524
	OAL	652
	OAL	680
	OAE2	34
	OAE2	80
CUCKOLD-FOOL	J6	381
CUCKOLDIZING	SAA	339
CUCKOLD-LIKE	PCD	12
CUCKOLD-MAKER	OE	62
CUCKOLD'S	J6	61
	J6	202
	OAL	777
CUCKOLDS	ENH	36
	ETS	17
	J10	484
	J10	528
CUCKOW	HAP	1853
	KT2	489
CUCUMERS	G4	182
CUD	VP6	78
	CI	17
CUDDEN	CI	179
CUDGELLED	T27	63
CUDGELS	J3	455
	KT3	463
CUFF	AM	348
	AE11	422
	AE12	384
CUFFED	HAP	2518
	M12	741
CUIRASS	AE12	445
	M12	115
CUISHES	AE7	877
	AE8	828
	AE11	735

Word	Ref	No.	Word	Ref	No.	Word	Ref	No.
CUISHES	AE12	637	CUPIDS	D	4	CURIOUS	G2	632
CULL	MF	165		T18	62		AE1	906
	T27	114	CUPPING	KT3	755		AE8	412
CULLED	VP8	138	CUPS	J10	288		AE9	348
	M8	7		P3	201		OAL	49
	BP	61		OAL	636		DO	160
CULLIES	EMK	20		OAE2	9		B	87
	ETC	8	CUR	J6	544		M15	15
CULLS	ESF	17		G3	536	CURL	J6	638
	G1	287		KT1	345		M1	672
	G4	793	CURATE	GP	67		OAL	570
	AE4	743	CURATES	RL	240		MFL	33
CULLY	MF	153	CURB	AA	340		FL	31
CULPRIT	WB	273		RL	447	CURLED	AE5	998
CULPRITS	ELB	17		T23	26		AE7	737
CULTIVATE	PUO1	13		DO	110		AF	32
	PAZ	31		KT1	486		M12	33
	J3	372		HIF	416	CURLING	AM	938
	J6	271		HIF	760		L1	53
	G2	50		GP	10		J6	38
	G2	571	CURBED	SEL3	10		M9	195
	M15	8		HAP	238		VP1	118
	CI	213		AE9	150		VP5	8
CULTIVATED	EL	213		AE10	90		VP5	44
	MC	11		AE10	356		G3	62
	G2	160		M8	47		G3	648
	G2	642		B	639		G4	432
	G4	193	CURBING	RL	160		AE1	827
CULTURE	G1	78	CURBS	G1	692		AE3	271
CULVERIN	SCD2	10		AE1	80		AE3	699
CULVERINS	SCD2	16		AE5	527		AE5	2
CUM	C	90	CURDLED	M12	589		AE6	351
CUMAE	J3	320	CURDS	M13	76		AE6	1100
	J3	3		VP1	114		AE7	626
	AE3	561		BP	96		AE9	314
CUMAEAN	HAP	1783	CURE	LC	68		AE10	321
	AE6	21		SEL4	19		AE12	456
CUMAN	AE6	2		STL	10		KT3	181
CUMBER	AU	184		ECD	18		KT3	318
CUMBERED	AM	942		RL	120	CURLS	ENH	7
	AE5	232		RL	122		J6	645
	AE6	490		L3	268		AE5	115
CUMBROUS	KT3	708		L4	92		AE5	363
	GP	37		HH	35		AE7	1111
CUNNING	PD	44		HAP	1119		HIF	302
	L4	181		EL	39		HIF	712
	J3	209		P3	125		M12	545
	J6	332		M1	706	CURRENT	MD	80
	J10	52		SFL	12		BR	159
	G3	245		SLT1	16		G1	290
	AE11	780		VP2	100		M8	277
	AE11	1051		G2	186		M15	435
	OAL	762		G3	603	CURRENTS	AE3	493
	OAL	880		G3	699	CURRIER	G3	833
	AU	53		G4	570	CURS	HAP	194
CUP	HAP	1252		AE1	949		C	763
	J6	552		AE4	90	CURSE	PCG1	26
	J10	40		AE7	1040		EMK	13
	P5	217		AE12	622		CM	106
	AE3	688		AE12	632		PSF	29
	OAL	277		OAL	302		PUF	2
	OAL	646		OAL	586		AA	108
	OAE2	33		KT1	478		AA	331
	B	687		KT2	110		AA	584
	HIF	801		KT2	270		AA	590
CUPAVO	AE10	268		KT3	726		AA	605
	AE10	279		TJD	94		AA	809
CUPBOARDS	J3	281		B	589		AA	932
CUPBOARD'S	J3	334		CAM	101		MD	169
CUPENTUS	AE12	792		CAM	175		MD	187
CUPID	SMM2	11		CAM	227		MD	262
	DA	33		C	24		PRH	10
	T18	28		C	237		SAA	320
	T27	26		TH	46		SAA	688
	T27	115		GP	127		SAA	883
	NS	23		STP	28		DOD	19
	AK	87		ERL	9		PD	29
	GE	18	CURED	HH	33		HAP	1603
	ETS	5		MC	8		HAP	2349
	SKA5	5		G1	128		STS1	3
	SSH	13		G1	285		J3	14
	M1	608		AE10	452		J3	385
	AE1	929		KT1	159		J6	72
	AE1	975		AU	280		J6	540
	OAL	7		M15	490		J6	558
	OAL	19	CURELESS	KT1	244		J6	577
	OAE1	4	CURES	DC	42		J10	323
	CAM	22		T27	52		J10	369
	CAM	379		HAP	1479		P4	62
CUPID'S	DA	169		HAP	2405		P5	274
	L4	288		AE7	979		M1	915
	T23	7	CURIOUS	RH	26		M1	1063
	OAL	1		RH	83		M9	97
	OAL	40		PLG	4		PLT	47
	OAL	267		T18	7		G1	288
CUPIDS	VHH	45		VP3	59		G3	243

Word	Code	No.
CYNTHIA'S	AE11	1215
	AE11	1244
	KT3	191
	M8	4
CYNTHIAS	J6	10
CYNTHUS,	AE4	210
CYNTHUS'	AE1	699
CYPRESS	SKK	1
	SKK	14
	T27	86
	T27	103
	GK	34
	VP5	61
	G1	25
	G2	121
	G2	624
	AE2	970
	AE3	91
	AE3	894
	AE4	731
	AE6	310
CYPRESSES	VP1	35
CYPRIAN	SKA5	4
	VP7	87
	AE10	78
	AE10	133
	AE12	813
	KT1	261
	CI	46
	CI	268
CYPRIANS	CI	412
CYPRIOTS	M10	58
CYPRUS	ETP	23
	AE1	880
CYRENE	G4	456
	G4	500
	G4	509
CYRUS	AM	1158
CYTHERA	AE1	956
	AE10	78
	AE10	133
CYTHERON	KT3	145
CYTORUS	G2	612
CZARS	HAP	2572
DA	PLN	35
DAD	PD	31
	T27	55
DADDY	SMM1	10
DAEDALUS	J3	45
	M9	118
	AE6	18
DAEMON	HAP	1608
	AE5	1120
DAGGER	J6	863
	KT2	566
DAFFODIL	VP2	65
DAFFODILS	VP8	73
DAILY	EIE	9
	AM	1144
	PEL	19
	PLN	13
	PAL	31
	DA	28
	PUF	17
	AA	249
	SAA	351
	RL	421
	AT	74
	PAA	35
	AK	78
	HAP	915
	HAP	1401
	HAP	1532
	HAP	2233
	HAP	2389
	BR	271
	PDS	45
	EL	14
	J3	316
	J10	386
	P3	1
	P5	177
	M13	132
	HI	93
	HI	102
	G1	231
	G1	571
	G2	552
	G2	740
	G4	193

Word	Code	No.
DAILY	AE1	484
	AE3	11
	AE6	182
	AE8	546
	AE8	565
	AE9	294
	AE9	612
	AE9	652
	AE10	877
	AE10	1227
	OAL	492
	OAL	829
	KT1	403
	KT2	353
	B	190
	CAM	102
	TH	176
	TH	177
	TH	201
	AU	293
	M15	172
	M15	320
	M15	631
	AS	85
DAINTIES	H2	72
	M13	133
DAINTY	P3	229
DAIRIES	VP2	25
DAIRY	H2	70
	VP3	43
	WB	19
DAIRYMAID	J6	764
	PWGR	6
	WB	20
DAISIES	FL	360
	FL	530
DAISY	FL	363
	FL	367
	FL	368
	G3	77
	C	649
DALES	ELT	7
DALINDA'S	J10	557
DALLIANCE	EDG	20
DALLY	HAP	1651
DAM	M13	139
	VP3	171
	G3	86
	G3	249
	AE3	504
	AE7	674
	AE8	838
	AE9	766
	CAM	46
	M12	23
	P5	107
DAMA	P5	111
	J6	126
DAMASK	AE11	736
DAMASKED	AE12	107
DAME	EUF	35
	GE	17
	HAP	353
	HAP	573
	HAP	635
	HAP	760
	HAP	788
	HAP	966
	HAP	1243
	HAP	1499
	HAP	1716
	HAP	1787
	HAP	2080
	HAP	2109
	HAP	2196
	HAP	2589
	SSC	41
	J6	625
	J10	492
	J10	510
	M1	1023
	HI	29
	GK	111
	J6	636
	AE1	996
	AE2	1069
	AE4	318
	AE5	51
	AE5	408
	AE5	806
	AE6	54
	AE7	70
	AE7	686
	AE7	1095
	AE8	448
	OAL	96

Word	Code	No.
DAME	KT1	9
	M8	77
	M8	261
	B	120
	B	133
	B	619
	B	586
	B	722
	CAM	279
	HIF	168
	HIF	540
	HIF	602
	HIF	747
	C	68
	C	97
	C	113
	C	136
	C	463
	TH.	9
	TH	101
	TH	143
	TH	249
	TH	252
	TH	269
	TH	329
	TH	344
	TH	353
	TH.	358
	M11	306
	FL	334
	FL	410
	FL	480
	FL	533
	FL	597
	AU	268
	CI	95
	CI	481
DAMES	J6	8
	J6	416
	J10	406
	AE1	670
	AE2	705
	AE4	436
	AE5	937
	AE5	1036
	AE6	696
	AE7	340
	AE7	559
	AE8	842
	AE10	61
	AE12	884
	OAL	136
	OAL	385
	OAL	608
	OAL	612
	OAL	613
	DO	161
	KT1	41
	KT1	134
	HIF	726
	C	568
	C	572
	C	700
	TH	387
	FL	362
	FL	369
	FL	399
	FL	559
DAMME	EEL	20
	PCG2	20
	P3	152
DAMN	EWG	4
	PRL	32
	EIE	20
	EIE	23
	PMQ	58
	PLN	4
	PC1	24
	PKK	25
	POE	14
	POE	34
	EOE	14
	AA	575
	AA	773
	PLB	44
	MD	300
	RL	379
	OE	54
	HAP	1527
	P1	9
	PLT	14
	PLT	16
	PLT	20
	KT3	851
	WB	101
	PTP	5

Word	Ref	No.
DAMN	ERL	4
	EWR	12
DAMNATION	ETC	2
	EDGA	28
	HAP	1033
	HAP	1203
	WB	327
DAMNATION'S	HAP	721
DAMNED	PMQ	46
	ET	12
	ETL	1
	ETL	17
	PCG1	35
	PLN	39
	EAZ	19
	EKK	13
	ETG	10
	PLB	2
	ELB	35
	EPC	32
	PK	24
	EDG	39
	EDGA	24
	RL	223
	EC	25
	EC	37
	L3	219
	HAP	832
	BR	352
	MS	20
	ESH	24
	J10	132
	SLT1	26
	EHC	19
	EHC	20
	VP3	141
	G4	690
	AE5	961
	AE8	886
	C	170
	TH	165
	TH	358
	PWR	6
	EWR	1
DAMNING	PMQ	50
	ET	2
	POE	23
	ETC	14
	HAP	703
	PDS	6
	PLT	19
DAMNS	PLN	4
	PAZ	4
	J6	559
	PLT	50
	MM	2
DAMOETAS	VP2	46
	VP3	85
	VP5	113
DAMON	SEL4	8
	SKK	2
	DOD	9
	DOD	13
	DOD	15
	DOD	27
	ODA	3
	ODA	19
	ODA	20
	ODA	66
	VP3	32
	VP8	21
	VP8	50
	VP8	81
DAMON'S	VP3	24
DAMP	AE6	85
	KT3	797
DAMPNESS	HAP	1802
DAMPS	SMA	14
	AM	1116
	MF	135
	M1	774
	KT1	210
	B	117
DAMS	M1	384
	VP1	32
	VP3	8
	VP3	50
	VP3	158
	VP7	22
	G3	610
	AE1	897
	AE2	679
	AE9	73
DAMSEL	M1	635
	M1	678
	ELT	11

Word	Ref	No.
DAMSEL	VP3	5
	AE11	1255
	OAL	48
	OAL	414
	OAL	440
	HIF	36
	HIF	141
	TH	224
	FL	346
	WB	49
	EMKG	12
DAMSEL'S	WB	71
DAMSELS	B	201
	B	218
	B	717
	C	719
DAN	HAP	2259
DANAE	OE	27
	AE7	572
DANCE	PWG	39
	PRL	16
	PIE	12
	EIE	14
	AM	891
	AM	990
	ETL	12
	EAZ	15
	PSF	32
	RL	18
	L3	20
	T23	102
	PAA	16
	HAP	215
	J6	423
	J6	662
	P3	225
	P5	178
	VP5	92
	VP5	116
	G1	538
	G4	691
	AE1	123
	AE1	701
	AE2	313
	AE2	959
	AE4	375
	AE6	366
	AE7	548
	AE8	380
	AE8	880
	AE9	849
	AE9	927
	AE10	301
	OAL	281
	DO	25
	KT2	491
	KT3	115
	FL	11
	FL	208
	FL	333
	FL	488
	WB	7
	M15	94
	CI	568
	EMKG	13
	AS	10
DANCED	DC	13
	VP6	45
	AE7	114
	BP	125
	FL	175
	FL	192
	FL	201
	FL	308
	FL	454
	FL	612
	WB	4
DANCER	J3	139
	OAL	566
DANCES	PRL	11
	H29	82
	G1	482
	G2	541
	G3	135
	AE4	207
	AE6	696
	AE7	802
	AE7	1113
	AE9	842
	OAL	128
	PLG	10
DANCING	J6	91
	J6	418
	J6	432
	VP3	70
	G1	506

Word	Ref	No.
DANCING	AE6	302
	AE8	893
	AE9	22
	OAL	668
	KT2	55
	C	28
	TH	80
	FL	201
	WB	217
	SMP	39
	SMP	43
	EMKG	9
DANDLES	P2	67
DANES	DC	45
	AM	165
DANES'	AE8	971
DANGER	LCA	37
	AM	179
	AM	246
	AM	267
	AM	435
	AM	901
	S	10
	HP	167
	DA	76
	AA	160
	AA	511
	AA	924
	SAA	102
	SAA	597
	SAA	615
	SAA	853
	SAA	1028
	SAA	1109
	RL	425
	HAP	4
	HAP	586
	HAP	1346
	HAP	1793
	HAP	2038
	J3	447
	M9	46
	G4	122
	AE1	542
	AE2	993
	AE2	1021
	AE3	275
	AE5	520
	AE6	156
	AE6	488
	AE7	1099
	AE8	15
	AE8	99
	AE8	250
	AE8	397
	AE9	59
	AE9	218
	AE9	383
	AE9	622
	AE9	903
	AE10	74
	AE10	186
	AE10	619
	AE10	1195
	AE11	681
	AE11	699
	AE11	765
	AE11	963
	AE11	1286
	AE12	600
	OAL	431
	DO	111
	M8	45
	M8	92
	B	99
	TH	95
	M11	50
	M11	105
	FL	392
	FL	517
	WB	42
	WB	248
	WB	507
	CI	347
	CI	508
	PMK	35
DANGEROUS	RH	12
	AM	177
	PUO2	9
	PUO3	22
	AM	450
	AM	1210
	AA	135
	SAA	202
	SAA	539
	SAA	587

DANGEROUS	HAP	798
	HAP	1311
	J1	256
	J10	510
	P3	187
	OAL	499
	AE4	622
	AE5	1124
	AE7	14
	B	600
	C	566
	AU	507
	PMK	19
DANGER'S	SAA	172
DANGERS	AR	306
	AM	42
	DA	55
	SAA	578
	SAA	654
	SAA	724
	L2	17
	L3	302
	H2	13
	TA	450
	HAP	1329
	HAP	1776
	HAP	1904
	HAP	2390
	PP	40
	J3	321
	J3	429
	J6	127
	J10	485
	M1	477
	M1	807
	HI	85
	HI	103
	HI	112
	VP3	118
	G2	95
	G4	696
	AE3	471
	AE3	485
	AE5	937
	AE5	955
	AE5	1004
	AE6	129
	AE6	164
	AE6	1101
	AE7	274
	AE7	599
	AE8	499
	AE8	709
	AE11	235
	AE11	450
	AE12	753
	HIF	380
	C	411
	M12	224
	AU	383
	GP	65
DANGLING	PNH	27
	M13	153
	J3	333
	M12	379
	M12	521
DANIEL	MN	6
	C	380
DANISH	DC	56
DAN'S	SAA	70
DANTE'S	ER	19
DAPHNE	M1	609
	KT2	631
DAPHNIS	T27	74
	VP2	34
	VP3	18
	VP5	28
	VP5	40
	VP5	43
	VP5	45
	VP5	50
	VP5	51
	VP5	60
	VP5	63
	VP5	65
	VP5	80
	VP5	81
	VP5	86
	VP5	95
	VP7	5
	VP7	9
	VP8	92
	VP8	94
	VP8	100
	VP8	106
	VP8	110

DAPHNIS	VP8	113
	VP8	118
	VP8	120
	VP8	126
	VP8	128
	VP8	132
	VP8	146
	VP8	152
	VP8	159
	VP9	62
DAPPLED	M9	36
	G3	128
DARDAN	AE1	884
	AE2	597
	AE4	146
	AE5	51
	AE5	698
	AE5	902
	AE5	1036
	AE6	90
	AE6	1035
	AE7	340
	AE7	1040
	AE10	902
	M15	637
DARDANIAN	AE3	387
	AE5	59
	AE5	633
DARDANUS	AE3	225
	AE7	283
	AE7	330
	AE8	178
DARE	RH	33
	SMA	81
	AM	108
	AM	284
	AM	385
	AM	1211
	SMQ	15
	PA	29
	SEL1	7
	PTL	12
	ETL	23
	PAR	13
	PMQw	14
	PMQw	15
	EM	7
	SLN	9
	ENH	30
	PUO2	23
	PTW	29
	PCB	32
	HP	102
	HP	185
	AA	625
	AA	814
	PPC	7
	MD	199
	RL	290
	DOD	10
	T27	22
	H29	41
	FS2	2
	FS2	8
	TA	200
	EAA	13
	EAA	14
	HAP	302
	HAP	650
	HAP	757
	HAP	1064
	HAP	1285
	HAP	1464
	HAP	2219
	BR	203
	PMS	13
	SKA1	1
	SKA1	2
	LS	15
	OD	11
	ESH	20
	EH	25
	J1	96
	J1	111
	J1	257
	J6	73
	J16	11
	P1	105
	P1	117
	M1	227
	MC	57
	GK	148
	VP3	38
	VP5	11
	VP6	6
	VP9	46

DARE	G2	457
	G3	184
	G4	280
	AE1	461
	AE1	747
	AE2	99
	AE2	485
	AE3	54
	AE3	325
	AE3	899
	AE4	448
	AE5	478
	AE5	555
	AE5	835
	AE5	938
	AE5	954
	AE6	157
	AE6	246
	AE6	828
	AE6	1217
	AE7	561
	AE8	200
	AE8	479
	AE8	680
	AE9	58
	AE9	110
	AE9	688
	AE9	813
	AE9	1077
	AE10	28
	AE10	50
	AE10	390
	AE10	910
	AE11	525
	AE11	741
	AE11	762
	AE11	780
	AE11	1047
	AE11	1082
	AE12	645
	AE12	820
	AE12	1103
	AE12	1290
	MM	40
	DO	101
	KT3	508
	HIF	41
	HIF	420
	HIF	791
	C	169
	C	181
	C	816
	AU	240
	AU	383
	GP	121
	PWR	36
DARED	AM	780
	AA	263
	AA	584
	AA	915
	H2	16
	M1	259
	G1	550
	G4	677
	AE2	303
	AE2	846
	AE6	627
	AE6	786
	AE6	850
	AE11	645
	KT2	563
	KT3	309
	HIF	346
	C	395
	M15	36
	CI	482
DARES	SMA	106
	AM	876
	PM	23
	PAZ	19
	ML	28
	PKK	13
	HP	3
	MF	80
	SAA	308
	SAA	840
	AT	69
	HAP	2479
	BR	121
	EL	363
	J1	91
	J6	557
	J10	556
	J16	41
	P1	246
	P6	46

Word	Ref	Num
DARES	VP3	33
	G1	625
	G2	448
	G3	418
	AE1	694
	AE5	483
	AE5	486
	AE5	490
	AE5	496
	AE5	502
	AE5	507
	AE5	508
	AE5	541
	AE5	586
	AE5	593
	AE5	624
	AE5	981
	AE6	449
	AE8	928
	AE9	745
	AE9	862
	AE9	1085
	AE10	1004
	AE11	342
	AE11	569
	AE11	596
	AE11	603
	AE11	1035
	AE11	1181
	AE12	540
	OAL	275
	OAL	717
	KT2	7
	KT2	257
	HIF	139
	AU	9
	CI	173
	CI	556
DARES'		
DAREST	AE5	642
	JH	7
	DA	56
	SAA	490
	RL	93
	P1	57
	P6	117
	AE12	233
	KT1	299
	KT2	130
	C	135
	C	136
	CI	528
DARING	AM	1101
	AM	1115
	AA	159
	AA	1008
	SAA	863
	H3	30
	BR	283
	J6	127
	HI	49
	G4	111
	AE2	520
	AE5	262
	AE9	5
	AE9	769
	OAL	141
	HIF	762
	AU	81
	WB	477
	CI	364
	CI	473
DARIUS	AF	75
DARK	AR	96
	RH	85
	DC	31
	AM	283
	AM	799
	AM	908
	AM	1166
	ENH	28
	CM	49
	AA	301
	SAA	518
	SAA	588
	SAA	931
	RL	386
	L2	60
	L3	37
	H9	33
	H29	46
	HAP	190
	HAP	323
	HAP	795
	HAP	1898
	BR	129
	BR	226

Word	Ref	Num
DARK	M1	20
	M1	283
	M1	525
	HI	73
	VP6	22
	G2	682
	G4	354
	G4	529
	G4	611
	G4	644
	G4	675
	G4	803
	AE1	81
	AE1	91
	AE2	26
	AE2	337
	AE2	987
	AE3	126
	AE3	262
	AE3	303
	AE3	564
	AE3	810
	AE4	33
	AE4	611
	AE4	679
	AE4	874
	AE4	921
	AE6	101
	AE6	147
	AE6	160
	AE6	510
	AE6	718
	AE6	911
	AE6	996
	AE7	452
	AE9	38
	AE9	342
	OAL	286
	KT2	485
	KT2	652
	KT3	252
	KT3	402
	KT3	797
	TJD	100
	B	338
	CAM	282
	C	604
	M11	194
	M11	268
	AU	160
	AU	513
	M15	212
	GP	65
	PMK	7
DARKEN	G3	598
DARKENED	AE11	1270
	ESK	1
DARKENS	G4	84
DARKER	AM	701
DARKEST	WB	408
DARKLING	AE7	24
	KT3	589
	TH	372
	M11	347
	AU	398
	WB	7
DARKLY	HAP	917
	AE7	894
DARKNESS	AM	1013
	PRH	2
	HAP	66
	BR	120
	J6	180
	G1	503
	G1	446
	AE1	204
	AE3	265
	AE8	781
	AE9	521
	KT3	119
	M11	158
	M11	196
	M15	224
	M15	278
	CI	119
DARKSOME	L2	67
	J3	367
	J10	306
DARLING	AA	232
	AA	433
	AA	960
	SAA	233
	AT	10
	EC	29
	HAP	1584
	BR	334

Word	Ref	Num
DARLING	J6	508
	P1	241
	P3	82
	P4	85
	G4	503
	AE3	73
	AE7	486
	AE10	124
	B	122
	C	281
	WB	132
	AS	54
DARNEL	VP5	56
	G1	229
DART	AM	480
	SMM2	3
	DA	34
	L4	1
	L4	75
	L4	288
	T27	26
	M1	699
	HI	80
	G3	403
	AE1	145
	AE1	475
	AE1	690
	AE4	99
	AE6	90
	AE7	487
	AE7	868
	AE7	1040
	AE7	1060
	AE8	967
	AE9	60
	AE9	226
	AE9	546
	AE9	789
	AE9	946
	AE9	953
	AE9	954
	AE10	378
	AE10	448
	AE10	595
	AE10	600
	AE10	826
	AE10	1005
	AE10	1070
	AE10	1264
	AE11	866
	AE11	957
	AE11	1251
	AE12	572
	AE12	590
	AE12	711
	AE12	1188
	OAL	196
	KT1	272
	KT2	111
	KT2	187
	M8	55
	M8	73
	M8	191
	M8	200
	B	69
	CAM	23
	M12	125
	M12	439
	M12	450
	M12	560
	M12	572
	M12	594
	M12	786
	CI	189
DARTED	P2	50
DARTING	M1	54
	G4	618
	AE5	317
	AE7	628
DARTS	AM	1067
	D	4
	L1	19
	T23	7
	J10	267
	J10	514
	G2	233
	G3	571
	AE1	431
	AE2	989
	AE4	186
	AE5	403
	AE5	761
	AE7	222
	AE7	252
	AE8	334
	AE8	565

Word	Code	No.	Word	Code	No.	Word	Code	No.
DARTS	AE9	44	DAUGHTER	M1	801	DAUNTLESS	TA	274
	AE9	635		M1	886		EL	362
	AE9	658		M9	73		P3	87
	AE9	690		M9	109		HI	48
	AE9	726		M9	162		GK	79
	AE9	1043		AE1	350		G3	125
	AE9	1090		AE1	921		AE2	988
	AE10	198		AE3	425		AE5	478
	AE10	369		AE7	13		AE5	605
	AE10	455		AE7	79		AE8	146
	AE10	981		AE7	367		AE9	328
	AE10	1012		AE7	460		AE10	1090
	AE10	1137		AE8	185		AE12	772
	AE10	1147		AE10	43		AU	582
	AE10	1273		AE11	855		CI	577
	AE11	300		AE12	884	DAUNUS	AE12	1354
	AE11	910		AE12	1244	DAVID	AR	79
	AE11	1001		OAL	322		LC	53
	AE11	1290		OAL	374		AA	14
	AE12	428		MFL	35		AA	31
	AE12	1002		DO	151		AA	42
	AE12	1027		KT3	393		AA	59
	OAL	25		KT3	677		AA	196
	OAL	875		B	8		AA	262
	KT3	220		B	122		AA	288
	M8	162		B	285		AA	345
	HIF	143		B	427		AA	407
	M12	659		CAM	43		AA	433
	CI	623		CAM	117		AA	507
DASH	SIE	15		CAM	300		AA	512
	AE5	189		HIF	538		AA	811
	M11	122		HIF	605		AA	888
DASHED	SEL3	8		TH	248		AA	937
	SEL3	16		FL	471		AA	1030
	AA	114		FL	480		PPC	25
	SAA	414		FL	533		SAA	214
	G1	457		M12	123		SAA	488
	AE1	160		AS	74		SAA	592
	AE1	757	DAUGHTER'S	ODA	51		SAA	902
	AE3	820		J3	267		SAA	906
	AE5	1053		J6	330		SAA	1116
	AE12	453		J6	340		SAA	1139
	AE12	513		M1	784		BR	179
	CAM	56		AE6	1141		MM	4
	M12	382		AE6	1142		GP	23
DASHES	AE3	543		AE7	346	DAVID'S	AA	77
	AE11	456		AE12	69		AA	93
DASHING	SAA	918		B	190		AA	291
	AE3	878		B	207		AA	333
DASTARD	AM	345		B	291		AA	368
	AE5	508		B	298		AA	467
	AE5	938		B	635		AA	749
	AE9	62		B	735		AA	865
	AE9	183		HIF	18		AA	880
	AE9	759		HIF	33		AA	970
	AE10	125		HIF	514		SAA	9
	AE11	603		M11	498		SAA	36
	AE12	380		AU	294		SAA	54
	HIF	335		AU	305		SAA	143
DASTARD'S	AE10	1032		CI	299		SAA	252
DASTARDS	AE12	683	DAUGHTERS	SAA	1076		SAA	253
DATE	SMA	40		EL	202		SAA	257
	AM	1175		J6	372		SAA	294
	UMR	5		J10	407		SAA	306
	AA	847		J10	445		SAA	403
	SAA	867		HI	17		SAA	430
	SAA	963		VP2	63		SAA	506
	L3	148		AE1	107		SAA	543
	H3	47		AE1	206		SAA	585
	BR	137		AE9	119		SAA	725
	ETS	21		AE10	128		SAA	799
	AE8	528		AE12	1225		SAA	804
	AE9	110		OAL	78		SAA	890
	AE9	276		CAM	4		SAA	936
	AE9	881		CAM	60		SAA	966
	AE12	798		CAM	67		SAA	994
	FL	546		C	11		SAA	1010
DATED	HAP	1821		C	717		SAA	1089
DATES	D	34		ETP	8		SAA	1129
	P6	89	DAUGHTERS'	AE6	849		HAP	2027
	BP	114	DAUNCE	HAP	170'1		BR	178
DAUB	PUO4	24	DAUNIAN	AE9	17	DAWN	DOD	4
	J6	594		AE10	339		GK	143
DAUBED	J16	94		AE10	618		AE3	159
DAUBER	ML	51		AE10	910		AE7	176
	J10	254		AE11	511		KT2	164
DAUBING	HAP	2344		AE12	706		C	95
DAUBS	L4	167		AE12	1099		TH	399
DAUBY	AM	589		AE12	1137		M11	355
	G4	54	DAUNIAN'S	AE11	1300		FL	611
DAUCIAN	AE10	545	DAUNT	PMQW	16		CI	174
DAUGHTER	AM	602	DAUNTED	HAP	2335	DAWNING	AA	236
	T18	8		M1	1055		G1	68
	J3	190		HI	148		AE9	329
	J6	333		AE5	541		AE9	477
	J6	700	DAUNTLESS	AA	354		OAL	65

DAWNING	KT3	436	DAY	HAP	1859	DAY	G1	622
	HIF	651		HAP	1886		G2	143
	C	248		HAP	1896		G2	278
DAWNINGS	AE6	145		BR	5		G2	379
DAWNS	AE9	611		BR	128		G3	318
DAWS	HAP	2545		BR	135		G3	528
	PPS	18		BR	141		G3	788
DAY	AR	136		BR	144		G3	793
	AR	169		BR	291		G4	132
	AR	284		BR	302		G4	266
	SMA	31		BR	312		G4	273
	SMA	36		BR	315		G4	281
	SMA	40		BR	319		G4	431
	PWQ	11		BR	326		G4	577
	PRL	17		PDS	17		G4	673
	PIE	3		PTS	38		AE1	204
	VHH	13		PKA	20		AE1	307
	VHH	21		SKA2	7		AE1	422
	VHH	31		EL	18		AE1	454
	AM	135		EL	77		AE1	516
	AM	271		EL	116		AE1	823
	AM	396		EL	186		AE1	1016
	AM	476		EL	216		AE1	1025
	AM	500		EL	276		AE2	181
	AM	514		EL	323		AE2	327
	AM	556		EL	330		AE2	437
	AM	561		ODA	3		AE2	1079
	AM	574		ODA	9		AE2	1090
	AM	597		ODA	16		AE3	245
	AM	670		ODA	41		AE3	265
	AM	783		ESH	1		AE3	768
	AM	789		ESH	36		AE4	8
	AM	807		SSH	11		AE4	78
	AM	913		EH	4		AE4	107
	AM	949		J1	4		AE4	268
	EWGR	5		J1	37		AE4	563
	PMM	1		J3	146		AE4	677
	PT	3		J3	181		AE4	766
	PA	20		J6	326		AE4	842
	EEL	34		J6	376		AE5	56
	SEL2	2		J6	469		AE5	63
	SEL4	4		J6	610		AE5	64
	SCG2	24		J6	614		AE5	84
	PAR	7		J6	687		AE5	138
	SLN	3		J6	781		AE5	718
	SLN	10		J6	836		AE6	192
	PCD	25		J10	343		AE6	233
	ECD	3		J10	354		AE6	712
	SCD1	1		J10	451		AE6	725
	SCD1	3		J10	457		AE6	750
	SCD1	9		J10	526		AE6	937
	PUO1	2		J16	67		AE6	952
	PUO1	7		J16	63		AE6	992
	PUO1	9		P1	133		AE6	1202
	EUO	19		P1	179		AE7	178
	PNH	5		P1	274		AE7	197
	PAZ	3		P2	30		AE7	436
	PC1	10		P2	33		AE7	579
	PAL	7		P3	24		AE7	647
	PAL	21		P4	53		AE7	685
	STC	5		P4	64		AE8	34
	PO	13		P5	92		AE8	39
	ETG	1		P5	264		AE8	79
	EUF	18		P6	101		AE8	94
	AA	131		P6	130		AE8	117
	AA	236		M1	664		AE8	127
	AA	910		M1	831		AE8	137
	MD	16		M1	865		AE8	231
	PRH	6		M1	1091		AE8	329
	D	10		M9	141		AE8	348
	D	22		M9	153		AE8	355
	MF	24		M9	159		AE8	403
	MF	37		M9	206		AE8	781
	RL	7		HI	7		AE8	798
	AT	45		HI	72		AE9	8
	L2	67		HI	116		AE9	21
	L3	84		HI	178		AE9	192
	L4	108		ELT	19		AE9	209
	T18	24		EHC	13		AE9	455
	T27	47		EHC	15		AE9	477
	TA	424		VP2	53		AE9	611
	PAA	20		VP3	41		AE9	802
	AK	139		VP3	50		AE9	823
	HH	31		VP3	118		AE9	1023
	HH	37		VP5	26		AE10	359
	HAP	89		VP6	27		AE10	390
	HAP	271		VP8	25		AE10	606
	HAP	608		VP9	86		AE10	703
	HAP	841		VP9	92		AE10	708
	HAP	1091		G1	395		AE10	710
	HAP	1361		G1	400		AE10	733
	HAP	1431		G1	466		AE10	1233
	HAP	1565		G1	573		AE10	1235
	HAP	1741		G1	583		AE11	287
	HAP	1754		G1	593		AE11	1160
	HAP	1832		G1	602		AE12	151

DAY			DAY			DAYS		
	AE12	176		C	465		AM	1045
	AE12	248		C	491		AM	1109
	AE12	647		C	506		SMM2	7
	AE12	726		C	620		PKK	1
	AE12	831		C	689		PSF	13
	AE12	1010		C	698		AA	246
	OAL	213		C	735		AA	520
	OAL	242		TH	85		AA	629
	OAL	248		TH	208		AA	815
	OAL	249		TH	246		MD	18
	OAL	282		TH	251		SAA	74
	OAL	373		TH	376		SAA	1106
	OAL	457		M11	98		EK	17
	OAL	464		M11	275		L3	60
	OAL	470		M11	300		TA	108
	OAL	473		M11	311		TA	179
	OAL	478		M11	355		TA	202
	MFL	5		FL	15		GE	38
	MFL	30		FL	36		HAP	1800
	DO	43		FL	71		BR	298
	DO	66		FL	224		PP	8
	KT1	77		FL	299		PMS	10
	KT1	121		FL	372		SKA6	15
	KT1	137		FL	439		J1	191
	KT1	147		FL	451		J3	15
	KT1	168		FL	458		J6	150
	KT1	174		FL	469		J6	740
	KT1	180		FL	488		J10	182
	KT1	189		FL	611		P3	174
	KT1	212		M12	70		P3	175
	KT1	331		M12	204		P5	95
	KT1	344		M12	551		P5	55
	KT1	375		M12	556		M1	151
	KT1	391		M12	602		M9	83
	KT1	430		M12	710		GK	163
	KT1	505		AU	11		DHP	29
	KT1	546		AU	20		VP1	30
	KT1	571		AU	158		G1	46
	KT2	25		AU	163		G1	299
	KT2	33		AU	435		G1	371
	KT2	37		WB	101		G1	420
	KT2	51		WB	107		G2	244
	KT2	83		WB	112		G2	664
	KT2	89		WB	205		G2	684
	KT2	173		WB	258		G3	82
	KT2	216		WB	336		G4	815
	KT2	225		M15	37		AE1	1046
	KT2	277		M15	283		AE2	173
	KT2	368		M15	294		AE3	267
	KT2	407		M15	467		AE3	456
	KT2	435		M15	499		AE3	849
	KT2	493		M15	625		AE4	278
	KT3	1		GP	72		AE4	330
	KT3	81		CI	119		AE4	906
	KT3	118		CI	128		AE5	82
	KT3	121		CI	174		AE5	995
	KT3	124		CI	177		AE7	14
	KT3	187		CI	373		AE8	678
	KT3	346		CI	408		AE8	953
	KT3	425		CI	416		AE11	201
	KT3	431		CI	446		AE12	78
	KT3	436		CI	452		AE12	1302
	KT3	543		CI	539		OAL	467
	KT3	592		CI	545		OAL	770
	KT3	679		PTP	45		KT1	1
	KT3	882		STP	33		KT3	732
	KT3	1149		SMP	27		B	3
	B	56		SMP	77		HIF	77
	B	57		SMP	81		HIF	78
	B	118		AS	7		HIF	577
	B	195		AS	29		HIF	584
	B	643		AS	67		HIF	667
	B	334		EWR	11		C	1
	B	725	DAY-DREAMS	L3	266		C	91
	M10	57	DAYLIGHT	PRH	13		TH	162
	HIF	50		L2	61		M11	495
	HIF	249		HAP	2173		AU	397
	HIF	647		BR	118		WB	1
	HIF	651		M1	822		ESK	23
	HIF	796		G1	398		AS	42
	C	25		OAL	283		AS	47
	C	70		C	427		G2	520
	C	79		AS	2	DAYS'	UDH	50
	C	88	DAY'S	AM	560	DAYSPRING	HP	77
	C	129		RL	9	DAZZLE	LC	99
	C	186		ODA	33	DAZZLED	AA	686
	C	215		J6	622		AE10	376
	C	248		VP7	63	DAZZLING	SAA	119
	C	257		G3	508		KT3	450
	C	308	DAYS	AA	123	DE	EH	6
	C	313		AR	26		C	698
	C	338		RH	51	DEAD	AM	283
	C	348		PRL	5		AM	740
	C	397		AM	424		PMQ	7
	C	438		AM	471		PA	28
	C	450		AM	1009		PA	32

DEAD		
	ECG2	12
	PM	20
	SM1	7
	PUO2	19
	PAZ	19
	EOE	24
	CM	124
	CM	141
	DA	102
	DA	174
	EPF	6
	AA	57
	PD	48
	L3	27
	L3	39
	L3	59
	L3	63
	L3	237
	L3	249
	L3	319
	T23	10
	T23	78
	T23	101
	TA	21
	TA	339
	AK	187
	HAP	1441
	HAP	1544
	HAP	1602
	HAP	2227
	SSC	7
	SSC	62
	PP	50
	ELW	10
	OD	9
	MS	27
	J1	258
	J3	58
	J3	87
	J3	284
	J6	283
	J16	48
	P2	24
	P3	210
	P5	216
	P6	85
	P6	179
	M1	795
	SFL	21
	HI	138
	HI	195
	ELT	2
	VP3	141
	G1	383
	G2	39
	G3	810
	G4	372
	G4	452
	AE1	303
	AE1	486
	AE1	1009
	AE2	350
	AE2	529
	AE2	618
	AE2	1053
	AE4	757
	AE4	798
	AE4	908
	AE4	945
	AE4	1006
	AE5	785
	AE5	944
	AE6	170
	AE6	229
	AE6	307
	AE6	330
	AE6	379
	AE6	497
	AE7	1059
	AE8	636
	AE9	606
	AE9	640
	AE9	723
	AE9	1028
	AE9	1052
	AE10	563
	AE10	475
	AE10	632
	AE10	710
	AE10	986
	AE10	1165
	AE10	1234
	AE11	8
	AE11	34
	AE11	114
	AE11	122

DEAD		
	AE11	218
	AE11	276
	AE11	285
	AE11	291
	AE11	309
	AE11	423
	AE12	448
	AE12	498
	AE12	511
	AF	129
	KT1	87
	KT1	140
	KT1	151
	KT1	277
	KT1	491
	KT2	93
	KT2	399
	KT3	178
	KT3	704
	KT3	895
	KT3	1102
	M8	296
	CAM	331
	HIF	16
	HIF	530
	HIF	583
	HIF	630
	C	229
	C	272
	TH	358
	M11	220
	M11	253
	M11	483
	M11	486
	FL	593
	M12	2
	M12	147
	M12	200
	AU	112
	AU	287
	AU	290
	WB	424
	M15	395
	M15	576
DEAD-BORN	EWR	9
DEADLIER	EWR	22
DEADLIEST	PTP	23
	L4	23
DEADLY	HAP	229
	HAP	2220
	AM	239
	L3	232
	T27	50
	HAP	2370
	J6	773
	J6	835
	J10	39
	P3	220
	M1	700
	M1	774
	G2	178
	G3	447
	G4	130
	G4	663
	G4	687
	AE4	954
	AE5	639
	AE6	344
	AE8	586
	AE9	553
	AE9	723
	AE10	828
	AE11	1001
	AE11	1100
	AE11	1137
	AE12	462
	AE12	787
	AE12	1235
	AE12	1328
	AE12	1373
	KT1	239
	KT2	122
	KT2	363
	KT2	523
	B	706
	CAM	355
	HIF	73
	HIF	96
	C	94
	C	732
	TH	145
	M11	9
	M15	433
	M15	500
DEADNESS	AE12	335
DEAF	AR	177

DEAF		
	HAP	2382
	P5	239
	P6	65
	M1	776
	M13	93
	AE2	470
	AE6	512
	AE6	636
	AE7	853
	AE11	352
	AE11	1173
	KT1	538
	KT2	346
	M8	221
	B	228
	M11	34
	M12	72
	M15	686
	M15	688
DEAFENS	AE5	445
DEAFS	CM	86
	AE7	130
DEAL	MD	226
	HAP	1265
	P3	211
	AE8	555
	KT2	597
	HIF	96
	CI	425
DEALING	EAA	4
	EAA	5
DEALINGS	OAL	725
DEALS	P4	69
	VP5	95
	G1	447
	AE2	655
	AE5	500
	KT3	612
	M8	107
	PTP	41
DEALT	J10	189
	J1	147
	AE1	275
	AE5	577
	AE8	465
	AE10	1071
	AE11	913
	KT3	222
	M12	98
	M12	602
	AS	92
DEAR	DC	6
	PMM	4
	PIE	16
	PAR	6
	PW	9
	SM2	8
	SM2	14
	A	12
	PAZ	30
	ESF	31
	PC2	22
	PLG	10
	CM	68
	HP	68
	DA	50
	DA	205
	PUO5	15
	AA	356
	AA	700
	SAA	296
	SAA	1066
	EDG	11
	AT	20
	PD	54
	L3	77
	TA	41
	TA	94
	TA	224
	HH	26
	HAP	591
	HAP	1576
	PKA	16
	J3	278
	J3	301
	J3	364
	J3	381
	J6	229
	J6	290
	J6	482
	J6	508
	J6	730
	P3	208
	M1	290
	M1	795
	R	5

Headword	Ref	No.	Headword	Ref	No.	Headword	Ref	No.
DEAR	R	11	DEATH	ETL	7	DEATH	J10	524
	R	17		STL	12		J10	531
	H I	31		SCG3	24		J10	550
	VP3	103		SCG3	27		P3	112
	VP3	123		S	8		P3	187
	G4	672		PC2	34		P5	222
	AE2	890		SKK	3		P5	224
	AE2	962		SKK	16		M1	180
	AE2	983		PCB	35		M1	291
	AE3	933		CM	8		M1	617
	AE4	439		CM	<22		M1	912
	AE4	936		CM	61		M1	997
	AE5	64		CM	109		M1	1019
	AE5	947		HP	69		M9	43
	AE6	932		DA	1		H I	59
	AE6	948		DA	47		SLT1	16
	AE7	438		DA	58		VP5	40
	AE7	560		DA	65		G2	790
	AE9	341		DA	78		G3	727
	AE9	609		DA	103		G3	763
	AE9	651		DA	197		G3	767
	AE9	1045		DA	211		G3	828
	AE10	234		EPF	13		G4	310
	AE10	686		EPF	20		G4	331
	AE10	1205		PSF	44		AE1	134
	AE10	1211		AA	456		AE2	128
	AE11	240		AA	1011		AE2	108
	AE11	1222		MF	115		AE2	141
	OAL	705		SAA	189		AE2	190
	OAL	718		SAA	1085		AE2	424
	OAL	849		EDG	32		AE2	450
	OAE2	27		AT	16		AE2	478
	KT1	382		AT	125		AE2	484
	KT1	610		DOD	25		AE2	499
	KT3	323		L1	52		AE2	586
	M8	306		L2	49		AE2	588
	B	13		L3	1		AE2	616
	B	647		L3	44		AE2	636
	M10	74		L3	46		AE2	637
	CAM	145		L3	50		AE2	727
	HIF	528		L3	55		AE2	733
	C	101		L3	65		AE2	873
	C	358		L3	68		AE2	883
	C	455		L3	93		AE2	889
	WB	13		L3	106		AE2	896
	STP	4		L3	111		AE2	912
	AS	40		L3	115		AE2	920
	PWR	13		L3	159		AE2	965
DEAR-BOUGHT	EKK	12		L3	235		AE2	1019
	J1	61		L3	236		AE3	416
	AE4	793		L3	246		AE3	431
	KT1	430		L3	258		AE3	792
DEARER	CM	68		L3	263		AE3	796
	HP	221		L3	300		AE3	861
	DA	205		L3	316		AE4	246
	PUO4	35		T23	80		AE4	359
	AA	502		T23	94		AE4	445
	OE	18		T27	34		AE4	556
	M11	468		H3	22		AE4	631
	AE4	42		H3	46		AE4	656
	AE4	444		FS2	16		AE4	664
	AE6	496		TA	66		AE4	689
DEAREST	AE4	11		TA	106		AE4	732
	AE7	468		TA	165		AE4	754
	AE7	505		TA	189		AE4	877
	AE10	393		TA	196		AE4	926
	AE12	930		TA	201		AE4	946
DEAR-GAINED	SAA	685		TA	214		AE4	974
DEARLY	SAA	21		TA	285		AE4	982
	TA	402		TA	408		AE4	994
	HAP	1583		HAP	8		AE5	9
	M1	1071		HAP	442		AE5	538
	HI	112		HAP	578		AE5	641
	G1	556		HAP	1919		AE5	796
	G3	480		BR	231		AE5	947
	AE8	714		STS3	19		AE5	1134
	AE11	396		EL	173		AE6	26
	KT3	1153		EL	236		AE6	278
	HIF	244		EL	308		AE6	388
	HIF	319		EL	315		AE6	619
DEARTH	PT	29		EL	333		AE6	770
	EUF	12		OD	27		AE6	890
	HAP	227		ODA	48		AE6	976
	PKA	1		SSH	14		AE6	998
	C	385		SSH	15		AE6	1124
	AS	90		J1	112		AE7	637
DEATH	UDH	68		J1	217		AE7	826
	UDH	7		J1	235		AE7	1056
	UDH	9		J6	11		AE8	405
	HS	141		J6	42		AE8	455
	AM	480		J6	192		AE8	578
	AM	515		J6	308		AE8	659
	AM	748		J6	498		AE8	751
	AM	847		J10	179		AE8	763
	AM	1176		J10	264		AE8	942
	EMQ	11		J10	279		AE9	557

Word	Ref	No.	Word	Ref	No.	Word	Ref	No.
DEBAUCH	TJD	73	DECEIVE	SAA	173	DECKS	HIF	650
	CAM	95		SAA	653	DECLAIM	AA	601
	HIF	647		STS1	5		SAA	753
DEBAUCHED	RH	48		SLT2	12		AE11	591
	EUO	12		VP8	158		AE11	699
	PR	4		G3	190	DECLAIMING	MF	213
	AA	47		G4	648		J1	20
	AA	312		AE1	564		J1	65
	PLB	2		AE4	973	DECLARE	AM	659
	MD	153		AE9	385		MD	114
	J3	190		AE12	921		HAP	96
	WB	68		OAL	657		HAP	752
	ETP	8		AU	409		HAP	780
DEBAUCHES	PSF	17	DECEIVED	AM	334		HAP	996
DEBENTURES	PLT	3		RL	439		HAP	1166
DEBONAIR	C	72		HH	24		HAP	1257
DEBT	LCA	49		HAP	2223		HAP	1492
	EOE	25		HAP	832		PSH	20
	D	23		GK	12		ESH	9
	SAA	551		VP10	102		J10	299
	M1	270		AE2	1009		P2	39
	VP3	32		AE2	1078		M1	272
	AE4	484		AE6	665		G1	547
	AE11	76		AE6	937		G1	611
	WB	304		AE12	1073		G3	452
DEBTORS	J16	63		B	544		AE1	1061
DECAY	PEL	21		TH	34		AE2	228
	AA	157	DECEIVERS	SAA	691		AE3	68
	MF	1	DECEIVERS'	SAA	747		AE3	464
	SAA	855	DECEMBER	G1	301		AE4	16
	L3	165	DECEMBER'S	G2	519		AE5	828
	L4	297	DECENCE	AE10	96		AE5	1048
	T23	59	DECENCIES	P3	135		AE6	1158
	HAP	1183		B	701		AE7	55
	HAP	1875	DECENCY	OAE2	17		AE7	836
	HAP	2566		B	19		AE8	15
	M1	248	DECENT	PTC	32		AE10	244
	VP9	73		EDGA	7		AE12	55
	G1	158		HAP	396		OAL	313
	G2	83		HAP	2056		OAL	319
	G3	714		J6	359		OAE2	21
	G3	115		G4	373		C	101
	G4	369		OAL	810		AU	511
	AE5	695		OAL	839		WB	85
	AE6	991		CI	99		M15	231
	AE8	670		EWR	4	DECLARED	AA	767
	OAL	541	DECENTLY	AM	352		RL	60
	MG	36		J3	368		TA	20
	KT1	256		P1	163		HAP	972
	KT3	1030		M15	611		HAP	1078
	M8	359	DECIDE	AM	172		J10	480
	M11	310		AM	262		P5	43
	FL	581		MD	95		G1	32
	WB	412		PDG	22		AE3	592
	M15	314		T23	43		AE5	337
	M15	402		HAP	728		AE10	222
	M15	626		HAP	769		DO	41
DECAYED	LC	9		HAP	777		KT1	103
	SM1	4		HAP	920		KT2	353
	PUO3	12		HAP	942		KT3	773
	L3	26		HAP	960		KT3	1023
	L3	256		HAP	1037		B	239
	L4	97		AE5	174		BP	9
	L4	155		AE10	495		BP	140
	J10	370		AE11	597		C	317
	GK	44		AE12	124		M15	44
	G2	436		KT1	496		CI	516
	AE2	226		KT2	209	DECLARES	J16	82
	AE2	695		KT3	1		P2	93
	FL	595		KT3	380		ELT	31
	M12	253		CI	537		G1	620
	AS	58	DECIDES	AE1	716		G1	626
DECAYING	SEL4	12		AE10	549		G3	421
DECAYS	EMK	7	DECIDING	J10	258		G4	488
	SAA	736	DECII	G2	235		AE7	847
	KT3	1061		AE6	1131		AE12	853
DECEASE	HS	136	DECISION	HAP	1514		AU	492
DECEIT	LC	67	DECK	AM	395	DECLARING	OAL	389
	EMK	22		SAA	1127	DECLINE	J3	447
	HP	227		HAP	1091		M1	687
	P3	33		G4	173		M13	85
	M9	64		AE5	227		AE3	76
	AE1	956		AE5	243	DECLINED	HAP	1081
	AE11	1039		AE5	1012		HAP	1445
	OAL	741		AE6	556		HAP	1799
	M10	18		M10	45		J10	181
	AU	18	DECKED	HIF	634		M1	752
DECEITFUL	OAL	507		FL	92		G2	325
	OAL	730	DECKS	AM	233		AE11	1316
DECEITS	OE	8		AM	278		AE12	718
	AE2	259		AM	609		AE12	967
DECEIVE	AM	272		TA	317		KT3	638
	HP	41		M13	161		CI	368
	HP	192		G1	83	DECLINES	VP8	44
	SSF	9		G2	702		G2	435
	PPC	11		AE11	307		MG	17

Word	Ref	No.
DECLINES	AE4	107
DECLINING	LC	87
	AA	267
	H2	28
	G1	421
	G4	273
	AE2	374
	AE11	1208
	KT1	504
	AE3	670
	AE8	678
	AE9	638
	HIF	806
DECOCTIONS	PLG	25
DECORATIONS	M12	120
DECORUM	EEL	19
	ESF	29
DECREASE	PUF	5
	M1	1030
	G3	780
	KT3	586
DECREASED	HAP	2564
	AE6	154
	AS	88
DECREASES	HAP	1407
	PP	10
DECREE	AM	1073
	EMM	10
	PA	45
	PUO1	7
	AA	361
	AA	758
	SAA	582
	TA	80
	TA	182
	TA	241
	TA	322
	TA	417
	TA	493
	GE	34
	HAP	2066
	M1	607
	M1	922
	M9	45
	M13	126
	VP1	93
	G1	289
	G1	336
	G4	701
	AE1	355
	AE2	324
	AE2	1058
	AE3	460
	AE3	921
	AE4	492
	AE4	997
	AE5	1042
	AE6	358
	AE6	1220
	AE7	434
	AE7	847
	AE8	500
	AE9	128
	AE9	334
	AE10	100
	AE10	131
	AE10	168
	AE11	879
	AE12	117
	AE12	241
	AE12	1177
	OAL	284
	DO	133
	KT1	330
	KT2	96
	KT2	267
	KT3	493
	KT3	501
	B	492
	B	563
	B	575
	B	597
	HIF	35
	HIF	218
	HIF	242
	C	677
	TH	167
	TH	226
	M12	759
	AU	209
	AU	274
	AU	479
	AU	585
DECREED	AM	77
	AA	1010
	SAA	899
DECREED	SAA	976
	HAP	2371
	HAP	2547
	BR	29
	ESH	7
	M1	598
	VP1	62
	G3	257
	G4	333
	AE1	331
	AE2	866
	AE2	867
	AE5	405
	AE6	680
	AE6	692
	AE7	76
	AE7	349
	AE7	385
	AE12	827
	KT2	306
	KT3	238
	KT3	574
	KT3	1008
	KT3	1104
	M8	46
	M8	287
	M8	398
	B	655
	B	755
	HIF	571
	C	394
	C	522
	TH	181
	M12	26
	AU	307
	M15	666
	CI	252
	CI	475
DECREES	L4	237
	H29	46
	HAP	654
	HAP	988
	HAP	2579
	M1	779
	VP10	92
	G1	183
	G2	718
	G3	7
	AE3	328
	AE4	422
	AE4	656
	AE6	92
	AE8	762
	KT1	471
	KT2	210
	KT3	272
	TJD	14
	C	510
	AU	513
	M15	201
DECREPID	AE5	531
	AE6	169
DECREPIT	MD	293
	L3	151
	B	567
DECRIED	PTC	34
	AA	110
	MD	154
DECRY	PTL	4
	HAP	813
DECUMBITURE	J6	752
DEDALUS	H3	48
DEDICATE	PLG	3
	AE2	246
DEDICATED	AE11	839
DEDICATIONS	MF	170
DEDUCE	HAP	178
DEDUCED	M1	6
DEED	HP	33
	AA	641
	AA	770
	L4	286
	T27	114
	HAP	991
	HAP	2359
	J1	87
	J6	833
	J6	863
	M1	597
	AE1	483
	AE4	413
	AE4	733
	AE6	679
	AE11	1185
	AE11	1246
	AE12	1140
DEED	KT2	307
	KT2	339
	TJD	57
	M8	374
	B	392
	B	754
	HIF	545
	C	246
	C	521
	AU	118
	WB	502
	CI	474
	CI	521
	CI	637
DEEDS	AM	698
	AM	702
	AA	675
	HAP	1616
	ETS	21
	EL	40
	EL	60
	EL	115
	J1	138
	VP8	12
	G4	130
	G4	243
	AE1	608
	AE2	747
	AE4	543
	AE5	1048
	AE6	1110
	AE7	473
	AE8	844
	AE9	273
	DO	9
	KT1	49
	KT3	10
	B	569
	B	395
	C	283
	TH	389
	FL	519
	FL	539
	FL	571
	M12	222
	M12	240
	M12	327
	AU	19
	AU	192
	AU	227
	AU	339
	AU	395
DEEM	UDH	12
	SAA	81
	VP1	8
	G2	434
	AE1	303
	AE5	70
	AE12	322
	AU	153
DEEMED	HAP	2102
	J6	716
	M1	264
	G4	198
	AE3	241
	KT1	146
	KT1	310
	KT2	436
	B	585
	TH	170
	M12	691
	AU	139
	AU	224
DEEMING	AE2	993
DEEMS	HAP	2535
	AE10	741
	B	485
DEEP	HS	128
	AR	23
	RH	10
	PRL	17
	AM	33
	AM	239
	AM	292
	AM	363
	AM	611
	AM	718
	AM	865
	AM	927
	AM	1146
	HP	217
	DA	58
	AA	135
	AA	394
	SAA	607
	SAA	609

Headword	Ref	No.
DEEP	SAA	621
	SAA	680
	SAA	731
	SAA	847
	SAA	1081
	RL	34
	RL	76
	T23	4
	T23	52
	H3	25
	H3	33
	H2	13
	HH	17
	HAP	115
	HAP	130
	HAP	256
	HAP	1205
	EL	92
	OD	35
	J6	127
	J6	151
	P3	59
	P4	34
	P5	278
	M1	409
	M1	415
	M1	777
	M13	207
	HI	130
	VP1	109
	VP3	147
	VP4	38
	G1	451
	G1	214
	G2	95
	G2	111
	G2	227
	G2	353
	G2	395
	G2	511
	G3	127
	G3	548
	G3	682
	G3	697
	G4	65
	G4	183
	G4	187
	G4	235
	G4	343
	G4	512
	G4	568
	AE1	38
	AE1	65
	AE1	125
	AE1	153
	AE1	167
	AE1	209
	AE1	433
	AE1	595
	AE2	48
	AE2	569
	AE3	27
	AE3	428
	AE3	681
	AE3	881
	AE4	558
	AE4	647
	AE4	950
	AE5	215
	AE5	775
	AE5	1103
	AE5	1124
	AE6	14
	AE6	73
	AE6	199
	AE6	277
	AE6	338
	AE6	391
	AE6	410
	AE6	475
	AE6	781
	AE6	803
	AE6	1016
	AE7	88
	AE7	488
	AE8	41
	AE8	100
	AE8	257
	AE8	364
	AE8	553
	AE8	690
	AE9	148
	AE9	567
	AE9	964
	AE10	94
	AE10	297
DEEP	AE10	315
	AE10	587
	AE10	1088
	AE10	1159
	AE10	1213
	AE11	127
	AE11	790
	AE12	1118
	AE12	1224
	AE12	1282
	AE12	1360
	AE12	1375
	OAL	174
	KT1	273
	KT1	587
	KT3	625
	KT3	644
	KT3	1021
	M8	130
	B	136
	B	150
	CAM	249
	HIF	110
	HIF	498
	HIF	585
	HIF	672
	C	3
	C	122
	TH	163
	TH	342
	TH	398
	M11	159
	M11	269
	M12	217
	M12	656
	CI	87
	CI	415
DEEP-CUT	AM	726
DEEP-DINTED	AE7	585
DEEPER	AK	112
	VP6	48
	G2	31
	TH	92
	M11	197
	CI	64
	PTP	38
	EWR	18
DEEPEST	AA	528
	OAL	193
	TH	77
	CI	344
DEEPLY	AM	396
	L3	295
	HAP	1374
	P5	39
	M1	906
	G3	610
	G3	754
	AE1	512
	AE10	537
	AE11	1176
	M8	195
DEEP-MOUTH	G1	212
DEEP-MOUTHED	AE12	1085
DEEP-ROOTED	G3	689
DEER	M1	592
	M13	135
	G3	623
	VP2	37
	KT2	622
DEFACE	AK	161
	GK	48
	G2	724
	AE1	30
	AE1	741
	AE6	673
	AE10	137
	M15	251
DEFACED	HP	14
	AK	122
DEFAMATION	J1	244
DEFAMATIONS	P4	99
DEFAME	HAP	808
	HAP	1497
	HAP	1551
	AE10	1214
DEFEAT	AM	369
	SAA	886
	J10	334
	G4	52
	AE2	537
	AE11	638
	AE11	764
	C	760
	AU	28
DEFEATED	VP3	27
DEFECT	EWGR	4
DEFECTS	L4	138
	L4	188
	P1	110
	TJD	200
DEFENCE	MF	116
	MF	155
DEFEND	PWG	57
	AM	1097
	DA	136
	EPF	6
	AA	998
	T27	27
	HAP	482
	BR	240
	J6	387
	J16	41
	P3	91
	M9	43
	M9	181
	MC	72
	VP7	68
	VP9	22
	G1	597
	G1	671
	G3	22
	G3	495
	G3	515
	AE1	804
	AE2	456
	AE2	596
	AE2	614
	AE8	14
	AE8	846
	AE9	411
	AE9	839
	AE10	33
	AE10	170
	AE10	198
	AE10	1272
	AE12	67
	AE12	914
	AE12	956
	OAL	725
	OAL	858
	MM	9
	M8	172
	CAM	36
	HIF	480
	C	131
	AU	10
	AU	102
	AU	440
	AU	487
	AU	518
	M15	534
	M15	696
	CI	621
	CI	634
	PWR	22
DEFENDANT	PMQ	12
	EK	16
DEFENDANTS	J6	342
	AE2	676
DEFENDED	P3	140
	AE2	388
	FL	71
	M12	580
	CI	88
DEFENDENDO	EDG	12
DEFENDER	AA	318
DEFENDERS	AE9	721
	M12	777
DEFENDING	TA	95
DEFENDS	HI	43
	HI	121
	AE6	340
	AE9	1067
	AE11	1023
	AE12	961
	TJD	147
	M12	503
DEFENSE	SMA	110
	LCA	29
	EOE	26
	AA	102
	AA	464
	AA	904
	SAA	255
	SAA	271
	SAA	574
	MD	51
	MD	139
	MD	161
	MD	211
	TA	483

DEFENSE	AK	99
	HAP	348
	HAP	495
	HAP	676
	HAP	727
	HAP	862
	HAP	870
	HAP	2477
	PRH	11
	EDGA	14
	PKA	5
	PTS	15
	EL	369
	PSH	19
	J10	137
	P1	161
	P6	51
	VCS	17
	HI	86
	AE2	93
	AE2	370
	AE2	592
	AE2	626
	AE4	383
	AE4	487
	AE5	343
	AE5	794
	AE5	1046
	AE7	613
	AE9	10
	AE9	215
	AE9	676
	AE9	721
	AE9	1037
	AE10	37
	AE10	434
	AE10	770
	AE11	443
	AE11	1113
	AE11	481
	AE12	481
	KT1	333
	KT3	30
	B	70
	B	267
	B	280
	B	453
	M10	9
	HIF	88
	HIF	685
	HIF	762
	TH	289
	FL	548
	FL	606
	M12	91
	M12	134
	M12	181
	M12	714
	AU	222
	WB	73
	CI	402
	CI	589
	EMKG	25
DEFENSELESS	AA	761
	G3	678
	G3	811
	AE6	709
DEFENSIVE	SEL1	12
	PR	37
	AE9	679
DEFER	BR	47
	AE7	436
	OAL	463
	B	254
DEFERENCE	AE12	1163
	GP	137
DEFERRED	SMA	7
	AT	54
	TA	106
	AE4	473
	AE9	306
	KT1	130
	M12	428
	CI	361
DEFIANCE	AM	219
	AA	205
	AE7	643
DEFICIENCE	MM	53
DEFIED	AM	235
	SAA	503
	SAA	1008
	M13	17
	G4	111
	AE1	280
	AE1	663
	AE9	810

DEFIED	AE10	433
	AE10	794
	AE10	1064
	AF	71
	TH	149
	M12	512
	M12	736
	CI	275
DEFIES	HAP	938
	J10	378
	P1	97
	G2	773
	AE1	643
	AE5	531
	AE11	1049
	CI	348
	P1	155
DEFILE	P6	90
	G2	653
DEFILED	AE2	471
	M1	504
	M1	872
DEFILING	AE3	295
DEFINE	HAP	94
DEFINED	P5	123
DEFLOWER	PR	7
DEFORM	TA	11
	AE5	17
	AE12	1173
DEFORMED	AT	18
	HAP	162
	HAP	409
	J10	308
	J10	473
	M13	157
	VP2	31
	VP6	108
	VP7	60
	G2	534
	AE3	865
	AE12	506
	KT2	536
	KT3	871
	WB	497
	AS	2
DEFORMITIES	OAL	285
	KT2	617
DEFORMITY	L4	142
	P4	49
DEFORMS	AE2	376
	AE12	894
	M8	371
	CAM	21
DEFRAUD	AA	245
	MD	196
	SAA	1096
	HAP	1999
	HAP	2041
	J10	390
	P1	24
	AE4	342
	AE6	826
	OAL	639
DEFRAUDED	HAP	1406
	M1	371
	M9	146
	G3	425
	AE4	509
DEFRAUDEST	VP3	8
DEFRAUDS	P4	63
	G3	158
DEFRAY	A	7
DEFT	HIF	805
DEFY	ET	6
	MD	300
	MF	78
	RL	241
	H9	19
	AK	74
	HAP	1016
	HAP	1337
	J10	550
	G4	319
	AE4	448
	AE6	786
	AE8	816
	AE8	926
	AE10	1261
	KT2	147
	KT3	580
	C	406
DEFYING	ETC	26
	PK	37
	AE7	897
DEGENERATE	HH	16
	HAP	2243

DEGENERATE	J3	38
	J10	121
	M1	273
	VP4	9
	G1	289
	G2	325
	AE4	17
	AE4	389
	AE5	980
	AE5	1003
	AE8	433
	B	353
	M12	797
	AU	359
	WB	415
	CI	53
	B	528
DEGRADATION	GE	68
DEGRADED	WB	438
DEGRADES	H29	79
DEGREE	ECG2	23
	AA	658
	SAA	355
	SAA	510
	RL	406
	T27	76
	H2	1
	GE	1
	GE	72
	HAP	1153
	EL	162
	OD	54
	J3	291
	J6	505
	J10	157
	J10	338
	P3	50
	P3	130
	P5	107
	P6	43
	P6	138
	M9	73
	GK	12
	GK	145
	G2	578
	G4	258
	AE7	74
	AE9	832
	AE10	875
	OAL	1
	OAL	654
	AF	94
	DO	148
	KT1	591
	KT2	283
	KT2	401
	KT2	446
	KT3	9
	KT3	95
	KT3	541
	KT3	929
	KT3	1047
	B	284
	B	319
	HIF	283
	C	682
	TH	10
	FL	41
	AU	232
	WB	380
	WB	419
	GP	52
	GP	96
DEGREES	AR	126
	AM	1137
	PWGR	13
	SEL4	14
	EAZ	7
	MD	231
	PD	57
	TA	23
	TA	108
	TA	455
	EL	9
	EL	195
	M1	454
	M1	465
	M1	540
	M13	48
	GK	35
	GK	70
	VP6	53
	G2	206
	AE4	421
	AE5	158
	AE5	378

DEGREES	AE6	291	DELAY	J3	387	DELIBERATE	J6	643
	AE7	498		J6	444		B	467
	AE10	6		J16	68	DELICATES	G3	278
	AE11	1205		P5	90	DELICIOUS	HAP	2423
	AE12	973		M1	994		P4	36
	OAL	549		M9	154		C	19
	KT2	445		M9	200	DELIGHT	AR	280
	KT3	108		M13	102		RH	41
	KT3	1059		VP8	24		SMA	26
	M8	365		VP8	153		SMA	107
	B	503		G1	152		PMQ	41
	C	47		G3	72		PMQ	53
	C	448		G4	272		SMQ	13
	TH	36		AE1	815		PEL	31
	M15	155		AE2	502		SEL4	23
	M15	338		AE2	950		PCG2	29
	M15	380		AE3	548		SCG3	3
	M15	682		AE3	579		PAR	6
	CI	147		AE4	507		EUO	13
	CI	332		AE4	622		EAZ	17
	PTP	16		AE4	626		ESF	31
	EMKG	6		AE4	818		PC1	7
DEIDAMIA	OAL	770		AE4	824		PLG	1
DEIFIED	VP5	66		AE5	509		CM	6
DEIGNED	C	442		AE5	978		HP	244
	WB	461		AE6	81		ETG	16
DEIOPEIA	G4	483		AE6	336		PR	34
	AE1	110		AE6	574		PUO4	16
DEÏPHOBE	AE6	55		AE6	724		AA	318
DEÏPHOBUS	AE2	417		AE7	437		AA	841
	AE6	666		AE8	147		SAA	478
	AE6	731		AE8	232		PK	28
DEIST	RL	42		AE10	228		AT	39
	RL	115		AE10	427		L1	1
	RL	168		AE10	715		L1	22
DEITIES	AA	120		AE10	1271		L2	3
	HAP	2340		AE12	575		L2	21
	ETS	5		AE12	826		L3	160
	M1	738		AE12	987		L3	215
	M1	780		OAL	214		L4	57
	M1	954		OAL	818		L4	107
	G1	7		KT1	105		L4	286
	G1	668		KT3	188		T18	26
	AE2	836		TJD	79		T27	46
	AE6	844		B	155		HAP	2439
	AE6	1062		B	295		BR	109
	AE9	340		BP	68		PP	13
	AE10	354		BP	71		J6	71
	OAL	172		CAM	289		J6	166
	KT1	470		CAM	348		J6	290
	BP	24		C	176		J6	742
	FL	520		TH	232		P4	123
DEITY	TA	454		TH	416		P5	100
	HAP	250		M11	14		M1	717
	HAP	281		FL	574		M1	818
	HAP	969		M12	10		HI	110
	HAP	1083		M12	113		GK	55
	BR	350		M12	205		DHP	8
	LS	14		AU	466		VP3	115
	J6	68		STP	31		VP4	3
	J6	506	DELAYED	ML	21		VP4	74
	J6	695		AA	940		VP5	65
	P2	20		D	29		VP5	119
	M1	290		SAA	1119		VP5	129
	M1	634		H29	4		VP9	59
	M9	47		AE11	444		VP10	88
	VP1	7		OAL	428		G2	390
	AE1	562		B	15		G2	613
	AE2	822		C	371		G2	762
	AF	35		M11	442		G3	132
	AF	36		M12	106		G3	210
	M8	12		CI	207		AE1	968
	M12	803	DELAYS	AM	29		AE1	1050
DEJECTED	SAA	929		SAA	735		AE2	35
	VP10	45		TA	389		AE2	732
	AE3	92		HAP	2390		AE4	272
	AE3	413		BR	276		AE4	474
	AE6	1191		SFL	2		AE5	381
	AE10	185		VP3	73		AE6	52
	AE11	529		G2	683		AE6	657
	AE12	333		AE1	1045		AE7	233
	AE12	1176		AE6	1167		AE7	1107
	KT3	673		AE7	541		AE8	215
DEKKER	MF	87		AE9	290		AE8	759
DELAY	AR	170		AE12	19		AE8	820
	AM	309		M11	72		AE9	102
	AM	674		M12	29		AE9	232
	ECG1	25	DELEGATED	PUO1	15		AE9	621
	S	7	DELIA	VP3	102		AE9	840
	SCD1	21		VP7	43		AE9	1047
	UMR	7	DELIAN	AE3	108		AE10	576
	L4	24		AE3	170		AE11	973
	HAP	1753		AE3	208		AE11	1087
	HAP	1793		AE3	219		OAL	69
	HAP	1819		AE4	544		OAL	199
	HAP	2424	DELIBERATE	J6	311		KT2	466

Word	Ref	No.
DELIGHT	KT3	88
	KT3	430
	KT3	881
	TJD	20
	B	11
	B	173
	B	189
	B	220
	B	229
	B	553
	B	569
	C	415
	C	439
	C	465
	C	687
	TH	62
	FL	48
	FL	64
	FL	76
	FL	94
	FL	336
	M12	220
	WB	149
	M15	124
	M15	204
	CI	16
	CI	78
	CI	110
	CI	567
	ESK	25
	EMKG	15
DELIGHTFUL	AE12	105
DELIGHTS	SAA	1104
	RL	233
	H9	23
	H29	79
	GE	51
	HAP	378
	PP	37
	PTS	38
	SKA2	12
	J3	289
	J6	690
	M9	146
	VP7	87
	AE4	178
	AE4	278
	AE7	454
	KT3	204
	B	416
	FL	562
DELIVER	PA	22
	AE12	956
DELIVERANCE	PLN	11
	AE2	965
DELIVERED	AE3	416
	AE5	398
	CAM	293
DELIVERS	CAM	369
	M15	75
DELL	C	3
DELOS	AE3	198
	AE4	206
DELPHIAN	J6	718
	VP6	117
	AE4	496
	OAL	29
DELPHIC	HAP	1485
DELPHOS	M1	693
	M11	4
DELUDE	SCG2	12
	AA	1021
	M1	956
	M9	45
	AE1	485
	AE4	975
	AE6	507
	AE7	464
	OAL	556
DELUDED	LC	115
	DA	84
	AA	683
	L4	61
	VP6	30
	VP8	134
	G4	461
	AE3	242
	AE3	490
	AE5	596
	AE7	598
	AE10	914
	AE11	1028
	AU	345
DELUDES	DA	161
	M12	400
DELUDING	AE3	644
DELUDING	AE6	691
	AE6	1238
DELUGE	SMA	1
	SAA	797
	EL	362
	J6	412
	M1	353
	M1	483
	AE1	175
	AE4	234
	AE7	310
	AE10	35
	AE12	953
	KT1	336
	FL	216
DELUGES	AE2	408
DELUGE-VOMIT	J6	554
DELUSION	HAP	2019
	AE10	937
DELVE	G1	258
DELVING	G2	357
DEMAINS	AK	103
DEMAND	HAP	650
	HAP	2070
	HP	252
	J1	225
	J16	28
	P6	143
	AE3	803
	AE5	502
	AE7	126
	AE7	803
	AE9	110
	AE9	249
	AE10	108
	AE11	149
	AE11	278
	AE11	553
	AE11	670
	AE11	679
	AE11	1017
	AE12	389
	OAL	209
	KT1	53
	HIF	449
	HIF	469
	AU	287
	AU	324
	WB	94
	WB	249
	WB	265
	WB	300
DEMANDED	FL	602
	AU	23
	GP	107
DEMANDING	GK	21
	G3	383
DEMANDS	P2	74
	VP6	36
	G1	533
	G3	696
	AE3	139
	AE3	796
	AE5	304
	AE5	512
	AE6	83
	AE10	837
	AE12	1101
	M11	395
	M8	327
DEMERIT	AE3	792
DEMERITS	TA	313
DEMIGODS	M1	249
	AE9	879
DEMI-LANCES	AA	227
DEMOCRACY	HAP	211
DEMOCRITUS	EUF	23
	L3	255
	J10	47
	J10	73
DEMODOCUS	AE10	580
DEMOGORGON	FL	493
DEMOLEON	M12	479
DEMOLEÜS	AE5	339
	AE5	347
DEMOLISH	HAP	2508
	G3	640
DEMOLISHED	J16	17
	M1	199
	G1	378
	AE2	607
	M11	335
	M11	347
DEMON	KT3	847
DEMONSTRATIVE	AE11	999
DEMOPHOÖN		
DEMOSTHENES	J10	185
DEMUR	J3	228
DEMURE	PPC	27
	EKA	26
DEMURELY	PW	12
DEN	KT2	565
	AM	718
	HAP	1641
	M13	47
	G3	385
	AE1	280
	AE3	541
	AE3	809
	AE6	562
	AE8	256
	AE8	276
	AE8	351
	AE8	405
	AE11	407
	AE11	852
	B	119
DENIAL	SEL2	9
	P5	193
	C	292
DENIALS	AM	884
DENIED	AR	19
	AR	224
	VHH	10
	SCG1	26
	SCG3	26
	A	2
	HP	179
	AA	5
	AA	33
	AA	111
	SAA	817
	SAA	960
	RL	48
	OE	20
	L4	56
	AK	142
	GE	65
	HAP	633
	HAP	990
	HAP	1536
	HAP	2058
	M1	907
	VP5	141
	G1	222
	AE4	776
	AE5	772
	AE5	971
	AE11	159
	AE11	169
	AE12	50
	AE12	226
	OAL	145
	B	73
	B	387
	BP	147
	CAM	169
	CAM	218
	HIF	14
	HIF	412
	HIF	450
	M11	435
	M12	269
	M12	277
	CI	197
DENIES	HP	2
	L4	49
	HAP	666
	VP3	32
	G1	80
	G1	241
	AE3	228
	AE10	889
	AE11	605
	KT1	83
	CAM	22
	CAM	53
	CAM	173
	AU	218
	M15	528
	CI	628
DENIZENED	J3	130
DENIZENS	AE10	8
DENMARK	AM	108
	AM	166
	AM	827
DENOTE	PWG	27
	HAP	1782
DENOTING	AE4	732
DENOUNCE	AE6	1090
	AE12	120
	M11	100

Word	Code	No.	Word	Code	No.	Word	Code	No.
DENOUNCED	TA	196	DEPEND	KT1	302	DEPTH	G2	399
	AE3	939		KT3	1044		G2	474
DENS	MD	192		TJD	94		G3	495
	G3	624		WB	506		G4	325
	AE4	217	DEPENDED	KT2	201		G4	457
	M12	478	DEPENDENCE	EL	18		AE6	344
DENTS	C	50		J3	212		AE6	729
DENY	AR	131		G4	806		AE6	834
	SMQ	12	DEPENDENCES	AK	95		AE8	293
	SEL2	10	DEPENDENT	M1	780		B	610
	SCG1	16	DEPENDING	AA	225		CAM	264
	MD	311		BR	271		M11	137
	SAA	587		J10	147		CI	486
	SAA	631		AE1	1015		AS	20
	L1	55	DEPENDS	AA	255	DEPTHS	AR	303
	L4	238		SAA	246		SMA	112
	T23	12		SAA	276		AM	452
	HAP	709		SAA	514		PUO4	18
	HAP	847		RL	442		AA	742
	J3	246		HAP	2420		SAA	44
	J3	377		J1	179		J10	187
	J10	506		AE4	113		M1	167
	J10	510		AE4	368		G2	678
	J16	64		AE12	93		G4	690
	M1	1081		AE12	948		AE5	189
	AE4	607		AE12	1110		M15	84
	AE4	621		OAL	813		M15	261
	AE7	432		KT2	219	DERCENNUS	AE11	1234
	AE8	653		HIF	122	DERIDE	M12	650
	AE9	280		WB	87	DERIVATION	PO	29
	AE10	1237		WB	99	DERIVE	HAP	184
	AE11	153	DEPILATION	P4	84		HAP	640
	AE12	1317	DEPLORE	AM	295		BR	345
	OAL	385		AM	1140		P6	137
	KT3	175		TA	194		M1	555
	B	412		M1	371		AE3	128
	B	392		HI	195		AE3	146
	B	735		GK	85		AE3	653
	HIF	692		VP5	40		KT3	1044
	FL	27		VP8	26		HIF	399
	M12	720		G3	413		WB	391
	WB	305		G4	670	DERIVED	HS	21
	M15	431		AE6	241		EUO2	22
DENYEST	DA	192		AE6	316		RL	258
DENYING	SKK	13		AE8	499		ER	46
	CM	39		AE11	258		TA	316
	R	9		OAE2	57		HAP	789
	R	13		OAE2	78		J1	227
DEPART	UDH	8		KT1	95		G2	531
	AM	1200		KT1	442		G2	781
	PO	19		BP	155		G4	511
	SSH	15	DEPLORED	G4	753		AE3	241
	J3	17		AE3	622		AE7	519
	J16	30		AE5	1134		AE8	73
	M1	515		AE7	1056		AE8	432
	GK	42		AE10	707		M15	203
	G3	818		AE11	58		M15	655
	AE10	1163		KT3	1105	DERIVES	AE10	288
	OAL	766		M12	2		AE10	874
	OAE2	69	DEPONENT'S	SAA	88		AU	35
	KT2	405	DEPOPULATED	AE11	565	DESART	SCG2	20
	HIF	703	DEPOSE	AA	418		PFD	4
	HIF	810		AA	980		PAZ	36
	M11	55		SAA	581		SAA	838
	M12	126		MC	45		J3	10
	WB	410	DEPOSED	HS	78		J6	82
	M15	34		HAP	758		M1	472
	CI	171		J10	127		M1	505
DEPARTED	ETL	4		P5	48		VP5	41
	PTC	22		MC	42		G1	94
	PUO3	5		GP	108		G1	534
	AA	859	DEPRESS	B	560		G3	379
	P3	208	DEPRESSED	AA	896		G3	389
	MC	73		EL	361		G3	624
DEPARTING	AM	541		AE5	181		G4	147
	TA	213	DEPRIVE	HAP	231		AE1	762
	BR	12		M15	199		AE2	7
	EL	370	DEPRIVED	AA	94		AE2	1033
	M1	78		EL	237		AE4	679
	G2	672		J10	533		AE5	794
	G4	382		AE3	865		AE8	255
	AE8	741		AE6	228		AE10	958
	AE9	381		AE6	446		AE11	852
	AE9	642		AE10	695		BP	153
	KT2	431		M8	304		M15	412
	M15	22		AU	85	DESARTS	AM	176
	AS	3		CI	398		D	5
DEPARTURE	DA	155		CI	416		J6	682
	J3	494	DEPTH	SMA	5		VP8	60
	HIF	332		AA	467		VP10	74
DEPEND	EAZ	13		H29	47		G3	527
	AA	872		SSC	40		G4	672
	HAP	774		J3	276		AE1	533
	J16	66		J10	12		TJD	47
	M9	180		J10	285	DESCEND	AM	52
	G3	563		G1	258		AM	889

Word	Code	Num
DESCEND	MD	262
	HAP	1607
	BR	20
	J10	178
	P1	9
	M1	275
	M1	314
	VCS	13
	MC	75
	G1	310
	G1	388
	G1	437
	G1	598
	AE1	238
	AE1	553
	AE3	522
	AE3	545
	AE3	560
	AE3	659
	AE3	740
	AE4	33
	AE4	904
	AE5	612
	AE6	183
	AE6	916
	AE6	1172
	AE7	399
	AE8	162
	AE8	594
	AE11	1307
	AE12	1038
	KT3	218
	KT3	605
	M8	361
	CAM	340
	C	793
	TH	318
	WB	485
	M15	279
	M15	410
	CI	596
DESCENDANT	TJD	195
DESCENDANTS	AS	45
DESCENDED	LCA	42
	H29	1
	M1	124
	MC	43
	AE1	340
	AE1	865
	AE4	16
	AE5	945
	AE8	369
	AE9	591
	AE10	535
	AE11	112
	KT3	1130
	HIF	298
	C	506
	AU	227
	AU	232
	WB	368
	WB	378
	CI	185
DESCENDING	RL	107
	ER	57
	FS1	5
	HAP	1241
	EL	325
	J10	430
	M1	534
	M1	964
	M9	209
	GK	69
	G2	94
	G4	804
	AE1	152
	AE2	314
	AE2	408
	AE2	856
	AE3	181
	AE4	237
	AE4	580
	AE5	45
	AE5	594
	AE5	639
	AE6	280
	AE6	693
	AE6	1099
	AE7	710
	AE7	935
	AE9	67
	AE9	1013
	AE10	327
	AE10	375
	AE10	1157
	AE11	802
DESCENDING	AE12	444
	B	6
	B	111
	HIF	600
	FL	165
	M12	90
	M12	585
	WB	407
	WB	441
	CI	154
	CI	601
DESCENDS	SMA	63
	AM	487
	RL	351
	HAP	345
	EL	153
	P4	46
	M1	369
	VP4	10
	VP7	83
	VP8	95
	G1	318
	G1	605
	G1	546
	G2	440
	G3	89
	AE1	414
	AE1	560
	AE3	256
	AE3	444
	AE3	867
	AE4	369
	AE4	598
	AE5	193
	AE5	331
	AE5	791
	AE5	896
	AE5	913
	AE5	1092
	AE6	415
	AE6	729
	AE6	1140
	AE7	142
	AE7	299
	AE9	911
	AE10	56
	AE10	898
	AE11	740
	AE11	757
	AE11	893
	AE11	1021
	AE12	561
	AE12	1057
	OAE2	6
	M11	151
	M11	168
	M11	219
	M11	267
	FL	5
	WB	436
	M15	383
DESCENT	AR	256
	AA	100
	AA	256
	AA	366
	SAA	812
	RL	344
	TA	311
	HAP	1152
	PSH	22
	M1	833
	AE1	526
	AE4	329
	AE6	187
	AE6	193
	AE6	339
	AE7	84
	AE8	931
	KT3	1050
	AE10	289
	AE10	385
	B	150
	B	512
	B	350
	AU	405
	WB	404
	CI	598
DESCENTS	LC	140
	G2	710
	WB	403
DESCRIBE	AM	747
	PUO3	25
	TA	50
	HAP	310
	HAP	1355
	GK	112
DESCRIBE	G4	220
	AE6	1171
	M8	380
DESCRIBED	AE6	45
DESCRIBING	J3	156
DESCRIED	SSF	13
	MD	207
	HAP	93
	AE2	627
	AE3	231
	AE4	148
	AE4	844
	AE9	564
	AE11	686
	C	354
	ESK	3
DESCRIES	M11	447
DESCRIPTION	P1	135
DESCRY	HAP	59
	G1	539
	AE2	997
	AE3	684
	AE9	987
	AE12	525
	KT1	231
	C	653
DESERT	AM	989
	ECG1	3
	ML	21
	DA	88
	AA	560
	MD	169
	SAA	640
	SAA	989
	J16	93
	MC	50
	AE1	851
	AE2	195
	AE4	837
	AE7	399
	AE7	504
	AE9	334
	OAL	758
	AF	8
	MM	16
	KT2	306
	AU	240
	AU	257
	AU	567
DESERTED	AE2	36
	AE2	771
	AE2	1007
	AE3	850
	AF	80
DESERTER	AE12	21
DESERTERS	G4	91
	AE6	832
DESERTERS'	PR	15
DESERTING	AE10	949
	KT3	411
DESERTS	LCA	14
	AE8	361
	AE10	719
	AE12	1063
	MM	52
	KT3	740
DESERVE	PCB	5
	HP	9
	EMW	11
	PUO3	35
	L4	180
	HAP	2042
	HAP	2201
	PSH	12
	J10	253
	P1	213
	M9	93
	VP4	4
	VP5	143
	AE10	632
	AE11	340
	KT1	64
	KT1	395
	KT2	262
	KT2	395
	KT3	307
	TJD	5
	CAM	329
	M15	176
	CI	500
DESERVED	AM	121
	EUO2	19
	HP	23
	DA	74
	DA	79
	EPF	10

DESERVED	AA	186	DESIGN	AE12	362	DESIGNED	AE8	31		
	MD	54		AE12	422		AE8	210		
	PMS	31		OAL	458		AE10	10		
	SAA	814		OAE2	23		AE10	224		
	P1	88		MM	39		AE10	756		
	VP3	168		KT1	25		AE11	261		
	AE2	588		KT1	297		AE12	259		
	AE6	1124		KT2	29		AE12	405		
	AE10	193		M8	164		AE12	440		
	AE10	685		CAM	83		AE12	820		
	AE10	944		TH	232		AE12	897		
	AE10	1032		TH	342		OAL	126		
	AE11	45		AU	564		OAL	242		
	AE11	248		M15	43		OAL	679		
	AE12	1349		CI	263		OAL	729		
	KT2	362		CI	530		OAE1	3		
	KT3	1124	DESIGNED	AR	151		KT2	641		
	B	556		RH	74		KT3	895		
	CAM	27		SMA	98		TJD	14		
	HIF	496		PWG	37		B	86		
	C	803		AM	238		B	125		
	TH	170		AM	342		B	209		
	WB	288		AM	562		B	468		
	M15	49		AM	607		B	321		
	CI	314		AM	613		B	608		
DESERVES	SAA	323		AM	817		B	667		
	PD	12		AM	823		B	730		
	H2	34		AM	948		CAM	97		
	J1	112		AM	1197		HIF	442		
	M1	321		PNH	4		TH	291		
	VP4	74		ESF	23		TH	427		
	VP7	64		DA	15		FL	617		
	G4	136		AA	413		M12	256		
	AE9	276		AA	848		AU	312		
	OAL	754		MD	17		AU	387		
	AF	15		MF	26		AU	519		
	AF	19		MF	86		GP	92		
	KT2	300		RL	365		CI	40		
	KT2	404		FS3	7		CI	59		
	M8	313		TA	246		CI	212		
	CAM	66		TA	499		AS	80		
	HIF	566		AK	106	DESIGNING	AR	31		
DESERVEST	DA	47		AK	146		AM	673		
	VP2	48		HAP	538	DESIGNMENT	HS	96		
DESERVING	TA	405		HAP	591	DESIGNS	LC	85		
	LS	15		HAP	897		AM	28		
	G2	744		HAP	1424		AM	33		
	AE5	457		HAP	1758		AM	137		
	AE12	1234		HAP	1843		HP	3		
	KT3	823		HAP	1998		AA	152		
	B	417		HAP	2365		AA	279		
	B	536		HAP	2387		SAA	122		
	C	609		BR	102		SAA	54		
DESIGN	HS	37		PTS	32		EDGA	23		
	EM	28		SKA6	27		J10	118		
	POE	10		ODA	3		G2	622		
	DA	65		J6	796		AE1	928		
	EPF	14		J10	5		AE4	344		
	AA	67		J10	264		AE5	984		
	AA	494		P3	128		AE7	211		
	SAA	267		P5	143		AE9	13		
	SAA	668		M1	84		AE9	56		
	SAA	904		M1	98		AE10	339		
	EK	3		M1	659		AE11	790		
	RL	331		SFL	23		HIF	753		
	EC	25		VP3	104	DESIRE	AM	886		
	TA	434		VP8	135		SMM2	14		
	HAP	115		G2	607		SMM2	30		
	HAP	2338		G3	118		SEL3	10		
	MS	30		G3	178		SEL4	25		
	J10	132		G4	141		STL	2		
	P1	227		AE1	26		SCG1	14		
	P6	118		AE1	591		SCG3	13		
	M9	131		AE1	651		S	10		
	GK	62		AE1	951		A	10		
	GK	65		AE2	47		SLN	9		
	GK	148		AE2	62		EMK	8		
	GK	173		AE2	70		EOE	33		
	VP5	102		AE2	521		HP	99		
	VP6	37		AE2	711		HP	251		
	G3	604		AE3	328		AA	232		
	AE1	104		AE3	557		AA	305		
	AE1	109		AE3	616		AA	344		
	AE1	594		AE4	418		AA	372		
	AE1	744		AE4	723		MF	158		
	AE2	191		AE4	792		OE	6		
	AE2	920		AE4	930		AT	10		
	AE4	832		AE5	401		L3	107		
	AE5	857		AE5	596		L4	2		
	AE7	400		AE6	240		L4	9		
	AE8	367		AE6	261		L4	52		
	AE8	621		AE6	272		L4	73		
	AE9	187		AE6	539		L4	195		
	AE9	697		AE6	684		T27	75		
	AE9	709		AE6	973		HAP	519		
	AE10	1299		AE8	23		HAP	1289		

DESIRE		
EDS	3
STS3	13
EKA	23
EL	29
J6	809
J10	10
J10	304
J10	542
J10	554
J16	87
P2	88
P3	134
P5	36
M1	608
M1	627
M1	631
M1	644
M1	667
M9	88
M9	100
M9	118
M9	128
M13	12
M13	23
SLT1	3
VP2	14
VP8	122
G2	688
AE1	220
AE1	350
AE1	480
AE1	746
AE1	816
AE2	14
AE2	477
AE3	85
AE4	93
AE4	297
AE4	787
AE5	382
AE5	951
AE5	1005
AE6	600
AE6	592
AE6	994
AE7	376
AE8	514
AE8	529
AE8	538
AE8	666
AE9	75
AE9	236
AE9	1024
AE10	577
AE10	979
AE11	566
AE12	77
AE12	108
AE12	472
OAL	368
AF	160
KT1	317
KT1	323
KT1	423
KT1	540
KT1	559
KT2	321
KT3	223
KT3	234
KT3	700
KT3	776
KT3	819
TJD	129
B	134
B	234
B	311
B	329
B	400
BP	121
BP	164
M10	70
CAM	128
CAM	234
CAM	287
HIF	33
HIF	589
C	185
TH	32
FL	50
WB	56
WB	97
WB	240
WB	279
WB	301
CI	137
CI	170

DESIRE		
CI	234
CI	440

DESIRED		
AR	53
PRL	1
PRL	19
T23	39
HAP	1253
HAP	1884
BR	251
BR	225
M9	109
AE1	811
AE1	1057
AE4	141
AE4	568
AE5	138
AE6	131
AE6	970
AE7	295
AE7	323
AE11	374
AE11	1167
AE12	392
AE12	898
KT1	209
KT1	320
B	20
B	600
CAM	266
CAM	308
HIF	101
TH	387
FL	472
M12	55
WB	275
WB	313

DESIRES		
CM	145
AA	55
AA	81
SAA	201
L2	19
L2	25
T18	82
L3	157
T23	51
HAP	72
HAP	1970
EKA	16
SKA2	1
LS	9
J1	130
J6	318
J10	7
P1	2
P5	249
M1	659
M1	965
M1	1077
M9	80
M9	125
M9	136
HI	9
VP3	137
VP8	92
G4	702
AE4	153
AE5	979
AE7	432
AE10	90
AE11	316
AE12	1207
AE12	1220
OAL	67
OAL	265
OAL	645
OAL	743
OAL	763
KT1	316
KT1	487
KT2	475
KT3	900
B	245
B	432
B	455
B	651
M10	12
CAM	66
CAM	174
CAM	388
C	130
TH	50
AU	376

DESIRING		
SDG	22
SDG	27
J6	177
M1	800

DESIRING		
VP8	160
AE8	812

DESIST		
AE2	1054
AE12	1012

DESISTED		
AE8	306

DESISTS		
AE10	1152

DESK		
SAA	356
MM	25
M1	470

DESOLATE		
M1	513

DESOLATED		
DESOLATION	SAA	69
HAP	1917

DESPAIR		
AR	23
AM	355
AM	776
AM	1005
AM	1039
EWGR	37
SCG3	10
S	4
A	4
EUO2	31
PAZ	16
CM	63
CM	139
PUO5	21
OE	6
L4	126
T23	4
T23	46
FS1	3
TA	189
PAA	13
HAP	1184
BR	126
BR	231
SKA5	8
SKA6	8
J1	201
M1	419
M9	82
M9	87
SFL	9
VP5	33
VP8	37
G3	420
G3	818
G4	724
AE1	771
AE2	17
AE2	476
AE2	487
AE2	496
AE2	550
AE2	772
AE2	887
AE2	1014
AE3	428
AE4	297
AE4	771
AE4	772
AE4	795
AE4	845
AE4	966
AE4	999
AE8	330
AE8	690
AE9	567
AE9	585
AE9	740
AE9	976
AE10	1248
AE11	127
AE11	1212
AE11	1285
AE12	505
AE12	868
AE12	887
AE12	1282
OAL	139
OAL	320
MG	21
KT1	413
KT1	453
KT1	461
KT1	466
KT1	522
KT2	170
KT2	485
KT3	405
B	380
B	624
CAM	161
TH	163
M11	115
M11	209

DESPAIR	M12	684	DESTINED	AE2	178	DESTROY	AE10	55		
	C1	62		AE2	280		AE10	82		
	C1	338		AE2	806		AE10	112		
	C1	527		AE3	468		AF	147		
DESPAIRED	AU	346		AE4	336		AF	151		
DESPAIRERS	AM	968		AE4	509		KT1	51		
DESPAIRING	AM	441		AE4	747		KT2	223		
	SCD1	24		AE5	1066		B	188		
	M1	735		AE5	1093		HIF	266		
	VP8	1		AE6	30		HIF	750		
	VP8	6		AE6	232		C	499		
	AE2	699		AE6	337		M15	698		
	AE4	445		AE6	552		EWR	28		
	AE6	835		AE7	165	DESTROYED	PNH	14		
	AE12	1137		AE8	957		CM	130		
	WB	209		AE10	885		SAA	153		
	C1	398		AE11	254		SAA	641		
DESPAIRS	CAM	130		AE12	1246		SAA	760		
	M11	177		AE12	1334		SAA	1113		
DESPERATE	SEL2	1		TH	137		RL	30		
	SAA	874		TH	288		AK	159		
	HAP	2405		M11	193		BR	261		
	P1	234		WB	318		J3	486		
	PLT	3		C1	434		M1	243		
	G1	613		C1	550		AE4	863		
	AE2	469	DESTINIES	SMA	130		AE4	980		
	AE9	541		HAP	1786		AE5	811		
	AE11	831		G4	716		DO	64		
	KT2	87		AE6	69		KT2	642		
	TH	372		AE10	524		KT3	757		
	TH	381	DESTINY	AR	63		KT3	766		
	AU	581		LC	95		M12	38		
DESPERATION	SSC	38		EWG	23		M12	783		
DESPICABLY	BR	219		AM	798		AU	32		
DESPISE	LCA	17		AA	21		M15	148		
	E	25		AA	481		M15	388		
	ML	45		SAA	1072	DESTROYEST	M15	180		
	HP	71		SAA	1093	DESTROYING	AF	102		
	HP	220		AK	154		M15	135		
	AA	672		HAP	583	DESTROYS	AM	835		
	MD	225		HAP	1885		HP	200		
	OE	35		OD	1		AA	711		
	L2	56		ODA	54		H9	27		
	HAP	1279		HI	182		H2	56		
	HAP	2163		G1	564		HAP	2388		
	SKA3	12		AE2	17		SKA6	11		
	P5	160		AE2	43		J6	534		
	M13	171		AE2	921		P1	270		
	VP2	85		AE2	1003		VP3	155		
	VP10	25		AE4	154		G2	79		
	AE7	325		AE6	973		G2	423		
	OAL	392		AE9	992		AE9	461		
	OAL	568		AE10	590		B	686		
	HIF	166		KT1	227		M15	264		
DESPISED	PWG	58		KT1	249		SMP	75		
	SMM2	20		KT2	11	DESTRUCTION	AM	1020		
	EUO	31		KT2	402		PO	27		
	T23	6		KT3	1037		J3	416		
	HAP	405		M8	260		J10	225		
	HAP	1358		M11	440		P5	244		
	AE11	400		WB	87		G3	386		
	B	324	DESTITUTE	P6	64		G3	660		
	TH	161		AE6	233		AE2	312		
	GP	88		AE12	1314		AE2	525		
DESPITE	AA	539		M15	47		AE2	818		
	HAP	1364	DESTROY	AR	44		AE5	892		
	BR	64		RH	34		AE5	1063		
	AE4	845		AM	112		AE7	439		
	KT2	150		AM	160		AE7	637		
	B	24		AM	275		AE8	643		
	B	198		AM	464		AE11	393		
	KT2	361		AM	792		AE12	672		
	HIF	207		PNH	53		AE12	769		
	HIF	279		PUF	30		AE12	1242		
	C	765		AA	532		KT2	569		
	WB	335		AA	764		TJD	108		
	C1	359		MD	113		HIF	105		
DESPOIL	SAA	685		SDG	9		TH	228		
DESPOILED	HI	66		H29	75		M12	31		
	AE4	577		TA	408		AU	69		
	KT3	725		HAP	158	DESTRUCTIVE	AM	814		
	M11	353		HAP	238		HAP	360		
DESPONDING	BR	258		BR	351		HAP	2534		
	G3	819		M1	382		J6	407		
	AE12	331		M9	94		AE3	74		
DESPOTIC	B	599		VP1	15		AE11	552		
DESSERT	P1	100		G3	220		AE11	616		
	TH	263		G4	468		M8	211		
DESSERTS	J6	289		AE2	409	DETAIN	DA	42		
DESTINED	SMA	122		AE3	316		AA	244		
	SCD1	5		AE5	831		AE4	548		
	AA	348		AE5	876		AE5	849		
	L4	252		AE6	89		AE11	269		
	G2	351		AE7	607		AE11	577		
	AE1	6		AE8	510		OAL	802		
	AE1	779		AE9	168		HIF	165		

Word	Code	No.
DETAINED	AE9	194
	AE12	1133
	C	607
	M12	13
	AU	291
	AU	469
	CI	297
DETAINEST	HIF	202
DETAINS	AE1	944
DETECT	SAA	1033
DETERMINE	C	525
DETERMINED	AE3	136
	AE4	733
	AE12	1091
	M12	832
	M15	560
DETERMINES	AE1	714
DETEST	HAP	1065
	EH	18
	CAM	37
DETESTED	CM	120
	AE3	353
	AE12	1200
	B	588
	DO	128
	M8	319
DETESTING	AM	804
DETHRONE	MD	199
DETRACTION	HAP	1552
DEUCALION	M1	431
	M1	473
	M1	524
	G1	93
DEUCALION'S	J1	123
DEUCE	PMS	3
DEVEST	HAP	187
DEVIATE	HAP	751
DEVIATES	MF	20
DEVICE	FL	268
DEVICES	AE2	526
	KT3	92
DEVIL	PIE	2
	EEL	21
	SEL4	29
	ETL	6
	PCG1	6
	EAL	5
	EKK	4
	PCB	42
	PLG	11
	AA	80
	AA	133
	AA	538
	AA	558
	PLB	32
	PLB	45
	PRH	22
	SAA	370
	SAA	499
	PDG	8
	EDG	28
	OE	43
	OE	58
	PMS	36
	EH	17
	J6	592
	P2	26
	ELT	4
	EHC	4
	OAE2	32
	C	481
	C	518
	C	561
	TH	427
	WB	262
	WB	373
	EMKG	43
DEVILISH	ESH	14
	J3	278
DEVIL'S	J6	624
	PMK	19
DEVILS	PLN	7
	SAA	399
	SAA	465
	EC	18
	C	157
DEVIOUS	AE2	987
	AE7	540
DEVISE	AA	50
	AA	653
	HAP	2370
	M9	157
	TH	17
	M12	79
DEVOID	AK	131
	AE1	796

Word	Code	No.
DEVOID	M11	338
DEVOLVED	RL	110
DEVOTE	AE4	1006
	AE11	678
DEVOTED	SAA	996
	AE2	132
	AE4	749
	AE5	908
	AE6	1131
	AE11	275
	AE12	355
	KT3	221
	M8	19
	CAM	294
	HIF	72
	C	688
	TH	124
	M12	44
	AU	505
DEVOTION	RL	417
	AK	167
	HAP	1835
	HAP	2282
	ETS	24
	EL	106
	ESH	25
	J6	677
	M1	497
	AE8	80
	AE8	248
	AE8	737
	OAL	174
	KT1	319
	KT3	951
	BP	126
	M10	58
	ETP	26
DEVOTIONS	J6	493
	G1	461
	AE8	798
	M11	253
DEVOUR	MD	274
	SAA	742
	SAA	1084
	L3	51
	L3	59
	HAP	159
	SSC	60
	BR	53
	P5	223
	VP3	6
	G3	424
	G4	357
	AE6	323
	AE7	156
	AE7	159
	AE7	1107
	KT3	449
	HIF	121
	HIF	343
	M15	133
	M15	154
DEVOURED	J3	340
	VP6	110
	AE1	1003
	AE7	303
	M12	22
DEVOURING	AM	871
	MD	305
	G2	645
	AE1	651
	AE3	192
	AE6	93
	AE12	1278
	KT3	985
	WB	545
	M15	358
DEVOURS	G2	278
	AE5	504
	AE6	363
	AE6	571
	TJD	61
DEVOUT	ETL	24
	HAP	1789
	P2	32
	G2	538
	MG	14
	KT3	373
	C	211
DEVOUTER	AR	187
DEVOUTLY	EMQW	28
	PSF	38
	EKA	26
	P5	275
	M9	50
	AE5	223

Word	Code	No.
DEVOUTLY	AE10	876
	OAL	712
	B	641
	HIF	56
	CI	169
DEW	SMA	23
	SMA	64
	AM	10
	SMQ	8
	SAA	979
	SAA	1061
	TA	380
	AK	51
	SKA2	11
	OD	26
	ODA	7
	VP1	110
	VP5	121
	VP8	20
	VP8	55
	G1	384
	G2	278
	G4	15
	G4	236
	AE5	1111
	AE6	328
	AE6	959
	KT1	194
	KT3	259
	TJD	47
	FL	29
	FL	92
	FL	109
	AU	212
	M15	376
	M15	377
	M15	383
	M15	384
	M15	585
DEWDROPS	HAP	1256
DEWED	KT3	923
DEWLAP	G3	89
DEWLAPS	G3	344
	AE12	1050
DEWS	AM	1030
	DOD	5
	T18	14
	HAP	1236
	VP10	43
	VP10	112
	G1	531
	G2	297
	G2	478
	G3	506
	G3	508
	G3	520
	G3	842
	G4	2
	G4	269
	G4	578
	AE3	743
	AE3	769
	AE8	484
	AE8	780
	AE12	616
	KT2	42
	HIF	712
DEWY	T18	66
	G2	294
	AE4	8
	AE7	982
	AE7	946
	AE11	306
DEXTEROUS	AA	904
	SAA	851
	G3	570
DEXTEROUSLY	P3	93
DEXTROUS	J6	638
DIADEM	AA	346
	AA	382
	BR	313
	G1	311
	AE10	203
	OAL	346
	AS	41
DIAL	HAP	1832
DIALOGUE	MC	20
DIALOGUES	J6	424
DIAMOND	L4	100
	HAP	1099
	AE5	411
	M8	66
	PPC	35
	KT3	54
DIAMONDS	FL	164
	FL	245

DIAN	M8	120	DIE	SCG1	26	DIE	KT1	281
	CI	93		SCG3	25		KT1	304
DIANA	T18	60		SM2	10		KT1	351
	T27	25		SM2	15		KT1	461
	T27	27		SM2	18		KT2	114
	T27	52		SLN	20		KT2	130
	AE1	700		SCD2	13		KT2	135
	AE6	59		PUO2	27		KT2	263
	AE7	1056		PC2	15		KT2	298
	KT2	618		EMK	1		KT2	308
	M8	171		PCB	37		KT3	770
	M8	172		AA	425		KT3	788
	FL	509		AA	1009		KT3	790
DIANA'S	AK	87		SAA	438		KT3	793
	J10	449		SAA	498		KT3	805
	M1	655		RL	421		KT3	883
	HI	80		AT	16		KT3	1056
	G4	486		AT	17		KT3	1084
	AE1	455		AT	44		KT3	1089
	AE3	894		AT	54		TJD	112
	AE3	915		AT	127		TJD	168
	AE7	1047		L3	2		M8	350
	AE11	812		L3	64		B	326
	AE11	968		L3	238		B	383
	AE11	1225		T27	35		B	579
	KT2	637		NS	13		B	584
	M8	13		FS2	2		B	626
	M8	302		FS4	18		CAM	141
	AU	295		TA	413		CAM	146
DIANAS	AE4	741		HAP	8		CAM	147
DIAN'S	OAL	295		HAP	82		CAM	231
DIAPASON	SSC	15		HAP	1204		CAM	335
DICE	PD	38		HAP	1312		C	232
	J1	135		HAP	2310		C	254
	P1	275		SSC	62		C	715
	P3	92		EDS	32		C	765
	SCD2	19		STS2	1		TH	26
	AE9	452		SKA6	6		TH	28
	KT1	400		ESH	2		TH	170
	C	754		ESH	4		TH	176
DICITUR	PO	4		ESH	6		TH	207
DICTATE	E	14		ESH	9		TH	401
	AE12	1162		SSH	4		M11	53
DICTATES	RL	208		J3	376		M11	423
	DA	197		J6	301		M12	810
	HIF	388		J6	309		AU	508
DICTATOR	TJD	183		J10	115		AU	603
DICTATOR'S	P1	143		J10	513		WB	72
DICTYS	M12	452		J10	551		WB	78
	M12	455		M1	652		M15	392
DIDO	RH	62		M9	20		CI	267
	DA	7		SFL	10		CI	519
	DA	110		HI	57	DIED	UDH	67
	DA	210		HS	129		HS	129
	AE1	469		VP2	6		ETL	30
	AE1	624		VP4	28		SCG1	28
	AE1	697		VP10	66		SM2	13
	AE1	707		G4	127		SM2	19
	AE1	944		G4	320		SM2	20
	AE1	1004		AE1	857		DA	211
	AE4	94		AE2	80		AA	552
	AE4	130		AE2	92		D	19
	AE4	142		AE2	178		SAA	1074
	AE4	144		AE2	301		SAA	1078
	AE4	459		AE2	424		AT	112
	AE4	555		AE2	483		L3	321
	AE4	591		AE2	594		TA	202
	AE4	768		AE2	748		TA	240
	AE4	921		AE2	862		AK	162
	AE4	988		AE2	880		HAP	421
	AE5	6		AE2	888		EL	15
	AE6	610		AE3	417		EL	305
	AE9	354		AE3	797		EL	335
	AE11	106		AE4	609		OD	24
DIDO'S	PAL	9		AE4	812		J10	408
	J6	564		AE4	944		J10	418
	AE1	474		AE5	298		J10	432
	AE4	274		AE6	471		J10	443
	AE4	385		AE6	579		VCS	37
	AE4	554		AE8	764		VP3	20
	AE4	876		AE9	933		AE1	138
	AE5	746		AE10	189		AE2	589
DIDYMAON	AE5	472		AE10	1048		AE2	947
DIE	UDH	1		AE10	1238		AE4	600
	UDH	74		AE10	1262		AE4	997
	UDH	87		AE10	1297		AE8	639
	PRL	16		AE11	154		AE9	1026
	AM	116		AE11	172		AE11	85
	AM	352		AE11	254		AE12	728
	AM	401		AE11	762		AE12	882
	AM	982		AE12	606		KT1	363
	SMQ	4		AE12	986		KT2	628
	ET	15		AE12	1272		KT3	892
	ETL	15		AE12	1318		M8	184
	ETL	18		OAL	740		M8	324
	SCG1	22		KT1	162		M8	353
				KT1	267			

Word	Ref	Loc
DIED	B	750
	C	392
	TH	168
	TH	182
	TH	309
	M11	13
	M12	442
	M12	576
	AU	480
	WB	181
	M15	162
	CI	364
DIES	UDH	80
	PC1	26
	EMK	5
	MF	202
	RL	11
	L3	320
	SKA5	8
	EL	1
	J1	66
	J6	313
	J6	707
	M1	423
	M1	709
	PLT	34
	GK	70
	EHC	36
	G3	772
	G4	425
	AE9	950
	AE10	1110
	TH	40
	M12	568
	M15	175
	M15	229
	M15	239
	M15	599
	M15	688
DIEST	OAL	419
DIET	EWGR	13
	OE	25
	PAA	14
	HAP	979
	HAP	1244
	BR	273
	AE9	828
	C	23
DIFFER	AE3	657
DIFFERED	POE	5
DIFFERENCE	PLN	3
	PR	32
	EAL	5
	ELB	31
	RL	348
	HAP	888
	HAP	920
	J6	856
	ELT	26
	EHC	14
	VP3	167
	MG	39
	AE9	832
	KT2	209
	KT3	382
	M8	169
	M8	234
	B	284
	B	472
	B	511
	CAM	378
	HIF	283
DIFFERENT	LC	38
	AM	237
	MF	209
	L4	226
	HAP	462
	HAP	753
	HAP	1014
	HAP	2083
	J3	32
	P5	68
	P6	40
	M1	626
	M9	115
	VP1	17
	G2	120
	G2	182
	G3	51
	AE2	574
	AE3	639
	AE5	576
	AE5	774
	AE6	726
	AE10	14
	AE12	761
DIFFERENT	AE12	769
	OAL	869
	OAL	879
	KT2	525
	KT3	95
	KT3	422
	KT3	1047
	CAM	261
	FL	535
	AU	15
	M15	366
	CI	341
	CI	465
DIFFERING	AA	493
	MF	162
	SAA	278
	HAP	281
	HAP	410
	HAP	687
	HAP	837
	HAP	950
	MC	24
	G2	309
	G3	51
	G3	830
	AE5	601
	AE7	447
	AE11	696
	DO	152
	KT3	745
DIFFICULT	AU	458
	SAA	302
	L4	132
	G2	347
	AE8	534
	M11	61
	AU	306
DIFFICULTIES	TA	456
DIFFICULTY	CI	508
DIFFIDE	AE11	636
DIFFIDES	M1	532
DIFFUSE	HAP	1131
	ODA	31
	VP1	1
	AE7	374
	M12	67
DIFFUSED	HAP	662
	HAP	1124
	GP	3
DIFFUSIVE	AM	209
	EL	153
	M1	91
DIG	AE10	378
	P1	237
	G2	312
	G2	352
	G2	564
	AE1	589
DIGEST	PT	11
	PLG	23
	J6	289
	M1	871
	HIF	118
DIGESTED	M1	560
DIGESTION	EDS	16
DIGESTIVE	AR	89
DIGESTIVES	C	189
DIGESTS	AM	555
DIGGED	M1	175
	G2	87
	AE6	810
	AE1	619
DIGGING	HAP	1181
DIGITS	EK	22
DIGNIFIED	AA	570
DIGNITY	MD	232
	HAP	1758
	AE6	1109
	B	301
	WB	379
	CI	461
	G3	398
	AE12	163
DIGS	EL	216
DILATED	KT3	1066
DILATES	P5	204
DILEMMA	AM	861
DILIGENCE	HAP	391
	G3	116
	G3	494
	G4	244
	AE1	609
	AE1	926
	AE5	1085
	OAL	435
	CAM	173
DILIGENCE	WB	478
	CI	255
DILIGENT	AM	22
	AM	673
	EL	63
	RL	1
DIM	HAP	1446
	P1	262
	HIF	376
DIMENSIONS	J10	278
DIMINISHED	AA	274
	AE12	1106
	HIF	386
DIMINUTION	GE	8
DIMLY	AM	1164
DIMNESS	DO	106
DIMPLED	AM	376
	L4	122
	AE7	43
	M12	53
	CI	152
	M12	77
DIN	AE9	845
DINDYMUS	PDS	21
DINE	P3	79
	P3	180
	P6	44
	P6	119
	G4	400
	AE1	254
	AE1	298
	AE1	902
	BP	108
DINING	EEL	20
DINNER	J10	286
	AE1	294
	AE3	298
DINT	HH	12
	HAP	1494
	MC	4
	G2	385
	G3	576
	AE6	1113
	M10	32
	M10	82
	M12	116
	AU	188
	AU	308
DIOMED	AU	164
	AU	168
DIOMEDE	J1	80
	HI	97
	AE1	659
	AE1	1054
	AE2	218
	AE2	261
	AE8	13
	AE10	41
	AE10	818
	AE11	351
	AE11	376
	AE11	473
	AE11	625
	AE11	660
	M12	824
	AU	101
	AU	376
DIONAEAN	AE3	29
DIONYSIUS	HAP	2554
DIORES	AE5	389
	AE5	422
	AE5	442
	AE5	451
	AE12	741
DIP	HAP	1864
	P6	46
	P6	160
	AE8	122
DIPHILUS	J3	203
DIPPED	AM	1122
	PKK	2
	B	6
	PPC	17
	J3	90
	J3	461
	J10	135
	P2	38
	AE5	1111
	AE6	328
	AE6	1096
	OAL	443
DIPS	P2	63
	AE8	931
DIRAE	AE12	1229
DIRE	AM	422
	AM	517

Word	Code	No.	Word	Code	No.	Word	Code	No.
DIRE	AM	849	DIRECT	HAP	1023	DISBAND	PLB	16
	AM	973		G1	8		HAP	868
	AM	990		AE3	200		J16	29
	AM	1162		AE3	468	DISBANDED	CI	618
	PAL	4		AE3	587	DISBELIEVING	PO	16
	CM	124		AE9	546	DISCARD	HS	32
	AA	373		AE10	595	DISCARDS	PLB	12
	AA	669		AE11	140	DISCERN	EAZ	39
	AA	1011		KT2	616		DA	22
	SAA	137		B	704		PUO4	8
	SAA	276		TH	229		SAA	640
	HAP	1619		M11	195		P3	100
	HAP	2015		M11	247		P5	88
	HAP	2534		WB	297		VP9	45
	BR	152	DIRECTED	AE6	90		VP9	82
	ODA	47		AE10	482		MM	13
	J6	666		AE11	1171		BP	120
	J6	831		B	535	DISCERNED	RH	89
	J10	158		M12	636		AM	289
	P1	217	DIRECTING	M13	196		HAP	1239
	M1	293		AE10	208		HAP	2443
	M1	351		AU	552	DISCERNING	AA	189
	M1	519	DIRECTLY	M1	54		SAA	116
	M1	587		TH	274		GE	80
	M1	607		FL	442		HAP	2031
	M1	1060		CI	272	DISCHARGE	EPF	3
	M9	45	DIRECTOR	HAP	70		L4	20
	PLT	45	DIRECTS	AM	969		HAP	1591
	VP1	22		SAA	839		EL	247
	VP1	99		P3	109		J3	428
	G1	53		AE3	482		M1	68
	G1	640		AE7	206		M1	344
	G3	7		AE8	647		AE12	242
	G3	151		AE10	477		M8	376
	G3	446		M12	803		B	688
	G3	710	DIREFUL	G2	178	DISCHARGED	RH	64
	G3	716		AE2	124		LCA	50
	AE1	1005		C	685		H2	4
	AE1	490	DIRGE	SSC	36		P5	18
	AE1	396		B	694		AE12	759
	AE2	25		C	696		TH	64
	AE2	158	DIRT	RH	14	DISCHARGES	HAP	1611
	AE2	171		PCG1	31	DISCIPLES	HAP	687
	AE2	266	DIRTY	PSH	6	DISCIPLINE	UDH	11
	AE2	322	DISABLED	HAP	300		ELN	8
	AE2	341		AE7	277		HAP	396
	AE2	843		KT3	613		HAP	1031
	AE2	900		M12	748		HAP	1592
	AE2	979		CI	551		G2	74
	AE3	277	DISABLES	ECG1	34		G2	387
	AE3	354	DISADVANTAGE	EHC	18		G2	509
	AE3	469		AE12	329		G3	323
	AE3	823	DISAGREE	PUO5	11		AE9	475
	AE3	938		RL	440	DISCIPLINED	AE11	70
	AE4	655		HAP	646	DISCIPLINING	HAP	2321
	AE4	661		HAP	683	DISCLAIM	J6	356
	AE4	724		HAP	979		G2	509
	AE4	811		HAP	1025		AE2	99
	AE4	881		HAP	2195		AE9	264
	AE4	930		FL	531	DISCLAIMED	KT3	284
	AE5	3	DISAGREEING	RL	279	DISCLAIMS	AA	370
	AE5	10	DISALLOWED	HAP	741		AE4	624
	AE5	689		HAP	761		AE7	818
	AE5	1095	DISAPPEAR	PRH	9	DISCLOSE	AM	866
	AE6	202		RL	8		SAA	50
	AE6	513		L1	8		SAA	57
	AE6	628		T18	44		SAA	981
	AE6	674		G1	348		RL	101
	AE6	749		WB	25		HAP	2113
	AE6	761		GP	40		J6	709
	AE7	87	DISAPPEARED	OD	23		M9	53
	AE7	121		G1	658		VP6	55
	AE7	302	DISAPPROVED	CI	441		G2	23
	AE7	310	DISARM	E	32		G2	104
	AE7	452		SAA	742		G2	182
	AE7	693	DISARMED	HAP	300		G2	334
	AE7	758		AE1	665		G2	446
	AE7	842		AE7	411		G3	38
	AE10	590		AE12	1064		G3	633
	AE10	573	DISARRAY	KT3	304		G4	6
	AE10	703	DISASTERS	PK	40		AE1	125
	AE10	1202		EK	25		AE1	373
	AE11	853		AE1	646		AE3	133
	AE12	506	DISASTROUS	SAA	919		AE5	933
	AE12	878		L4	125		AE8	349
	AE12	1238		AE1	997		KT2	654
	CAM	11		AE2	14		CAM	210
	HIF	2		AE4	269		CAM	367
	HIF	137		AE4	916		HIF	532
	HIF	319		AE6	468		M11	159
	C	109		AE11	236	DISCLOSED	HAP	940
	M12	24	DISAVOW	AM	547		M13	222
	M15	204		HAP	723		G1	646
DIRECT	AA	991	DISAVOWED	HAP	400		G2	244
	RL	117		AE7	798		AE7	197
	EAA	16	DISBAND	EKK	1		OAL	796

Word	Code	No.
DISCLOSED	KT1	549
	B	630
	CI	128
DISCLOSES	SMQ	7
DISCOLOR	J6	781
DISCOLORED	G3	110
	AE8	433
	AE9	966
	KT3	1149
DISCOLORING	KT2	488
DISCOMPOSE	HAP	2524
	AE10	163
	OAL	838
	MFL	33
DISCOMPOSED	G1	568
	AE4	924
	KT3	758
DISCONSOLATE	FL	389
DISCONTENT	EEL	24
	HAP	524
	HAP	567
	HAP	1413
	AE1	54
	AE6	235
	KT2	581
	M8	220
	HIF	720
	FL	98
	WB	115
	WB	177
DISCONTENTED	AR	314
	J3	30
DISCORD	SMA	57
	SMA	121
	PUO3	1
	D	43
	D	44
	D	45
	SAA	794
	L1	41
	HAP	941
	BR	184
	M1	578
	VP1	99
	AE4	139
	AE7	473
	AE7	757
	AE7	766
	AE8	932
	KT3	234
	HIF	774
DISCORDANT	AE8	910
	CAM	260
DISCORDS	D	41
	D	42
	EDGA	4
	HAP	902
	HAP	1037
	M1	26
DISCOURAGED	AE4	883
DISCOURSE	RL	71
	RL	454
	PD	28
	HAP	1572
	J6	686
	M1	944
	AE1	1054
	OAL	166
	TH	352
	FL	432
	M12	220
	M15	396
DISCOURSED	M15	89
DISCOURSING	AE6	1239
	AE8	471
DISCOVER	DC	40
	LCA	2
	SEL2	3
	SCG2	22
	SLN	3
	SLN	15
	RL	4
	DOD	10
	FS4	15
	SKA2	21
	SKA2	27
	SKA3	4
	M1	445
	AE1	424
DISCOVERED	EMQ	3
	CM	34
	RL	179
	RL	423
	HAP	1923
	VP3	27
	AE4	181
DISCOVERED	AE6	9
	AE6	485
	KT2	126
	B	236
	HIF	445
	AU	269
DISCOVERIES	AM	640
	SAA	45
	G3	460
DISCOVERING	EDS	7
DISCOVERS	L4	186
	SSC	34
	AE3	159
DISCOVERY	HAP	1215
DISCREET	HP	38
	C	72
DISDAIN	AM	197
	AM	246
	AM	383
	AM	786
	AM	1207
	SCG1	33
	PNH	8
	PNH	37
	PAZ	18
	HP	12
	DA	147
	SSF	20
	AA	517
	SAA	522
	SAA	1006
	ER	56
	L3	149
	L3	262
	L4	126
	T23	46
	H9	23
	FS3	15
	HAP	471
	HAP	1284
	HAP	1364
	HAP	1701
	J3	43
	J10	254
	P1	267
	M1	303
	M1	631
	M13	87
	M13	185
	SLT1	14
	VP2	78
	VP6	11
	G3	323
	G3	602
	G4	96
	AE2	559
	AE5	295
	AE5	513
	AE5	607
	AE7	261
	AE7	462
	AE7	483
	AE7	896
	AE7	1058
	AE9	75
	AE10	510
	AE10	1030
	AE10	1081
	AE10	1291
	AE11	1046
	AE11	1071
	AE11	1210
	AE12	508
	AE12	550
	AE12	1138
	OAL	550
	KT1	311
	KT2	168
	HIF	591
	HIF	625
	KT3	330
	M8	15
	HIF	321
	HIF	332
	HIF	358
	TH	160
	TH	202
	TH	385
	M12	178
	AU	3
	AU	596
	M15	445
DISDAINED	AM	350
	DA	138
	AA	202
	TA	277
DISDAINED	HAP	544
	HAP	28
	HAP	2181
	SAA	44
	M1	957
	M13	174
	VP5	39
	G4	755
	AE1	39
	AE4	295
	AE7	1017
	TH	16
	TH	29
	TH	139
	TH	392
	CI	287
DISDAINFUL	T23	10
	SSC	41
	J1	242
	G2	223
	AE4	677
	AE10	1313
	AE12	1377
DISDAINFULLY	AE6	633
DISDAINING	AM	307
	PUO2	34
	SAA	518
	SAA	837
	SKA5	11
	AE12	74
	TH	392
DISDAINS	AA	368
	HAP	1566
	HAP	2173
	VP6	83
	G3	163
	AE7	611
	AE9	1064
	AE10	984
	AE11	873
	AE12	683
	HIF	415
	M15	425
	CI	300
DISEASE	UDH	9
	UDH	48
	PLG	21
	PLG	22
	AA	334
	AA	756
	AA	810
	AA	926
	SAA	32
	SAA	782
	AT	71
	L3	292
	L4	129
	TA	22
	TA	168
	PAA	30
	AK	163
	HH	33
	HAP	1167
	BR	231
	J6	753
	J16	31
	P3	121
	G3	752
	DO	112
	CAM	178
	C	169
	TH	37
	M11	132
DISEASED	PUO1	23
	P3	202
DISEASES	EL	48
	J3	382
	P3	214
	G3	151
	G3	712
	G3	822
	G4	452
	AE6	386
	AE12	1235
DISEMBOGUE	HAP	1134
DISEMBOGUES	AE1	335
DISEMBOGUING	M9	167
DISEMBROILED	M1	29
DISENCUMBERED	AA	850
DISENGAGE	AE2	594
	M12	481
DISGORGE	AE5	236
DISGRACE	PTC	25
	CM	119
	PUO3	31
	SAA	1086

Word	Ref	No.
DISGRACE	AA	155
	AA	669
	HAP	1115
	ODA	33
	J6	179
	J16	16
	P1	217
	P5	236
	M1	1060
	GK	53
	VP5	58
	G4	143
	AE2	375
	AE2	1070
	AE3	544
	AE5	257
	AE6	674
	AE6	1154
	AE7	317
	AE10	965
	AE12	811
	AE12	889
	AE12	933
	OAL	601
	OAL	826
	KT1	268
	KT1	457
	KT2	287
	KT2	573
	KT3	321
	TJD	201
	HIF	591
	C	411
	TH	202
	TH	373
	M12	432
	WB	369
	CI	55
DISGRACED	PWG	25
	AA	97
	HAP	400
	J3	210
	J6	726
	AE11	82
	KT3	733
	C	645
DISGUISE	AA	740
	MD	37
	SAA	158
	HAP	2037
	EL	53
	P4	102
	M1	884
	SLT2	7
	AE1	993
	AE4	425
	AE8	811
	AE9	839
	OAL	286
	KT1	568
	KT1	575
	B	348
	BP	23
	AU	262
	WB	130
DISGUISED	RH	81
	SAA	543
	ER	34
	HAP	81
	BR	190
	J6	453
	M1	277
	AE2	83
	AE9	628
	OAL	779
	MG	27
	KT1	264
DISGUISES	AA	443
DISH	PMM	1
	PA	39
	H29	24
	H2	77
	P2	80
	M1	300
DISHEIR	HAP	1999
DISHERIT	J1	56
DISHERITED	KT3	968
DISHES	RH	81
	J1	145
	J1	208
	P3	229
	AE1	987
DISHEVELED	M1	670
	M9	162
	G4	478
	AE1	557
DISHEVELED	AE2	544
	AE7	111
	AE7	802
	AE11	50
	OAL	596
	TH	108
DISHONEST	AA	72
	HAP	1119
	AE6	668
	AE11	84
	AE11	646
DISHONOR	HP	207
	AE10	1297
	KT3	1129
DISHONORABLE	AE11	1160
DISHONORED	M1	468
	AE12	314
	HIF	683
	M15	318
DISIMBOGUED	M1	49
DISINCHANTED	MD	180
DISINCUMBERED	LC	54
DISINHERIT	P6	117
DISINTERESSED	RL	335
DISJOIN	H2	20
	VP4	49
	AE5	759
	B	739
DISJOINED	L3	9
	P3	113
	VP1	90
	AE5	420
	B	738
	M11	420
DISJOINS	G3	775
DISJOINTED	P3	202
	AE9	964
	C	327
	M11	27
DISK	AE3	837
	M15	284
DISLIKE	MD	225
	AE10	148
DISLODGE	M15	259
DISLODGED	KT2	239
DISLODGING	J10	335
DISMAL	AM	101
	A	13
	SKK	1
	SKK	14
	PD	61
	L3	183
	M1	472
	AE2	181
	AE3	323
	AE3	470
	AE3	810
	AE4	957
	AE8	691
	AE10	711
	AE12	908
	AE12	1224
	M12	353
DISMANTLED	C	734
DISMAY	FL	517
DISMAYED	SAA	929
	SAA	965
	AE2	158
	AE12	488
	HIF	559
	C	584
	TH	346
	AU	367
DISMEMBERED	AE1	144
	AE9	654
	AE10	552
DISMISS	AM	222
	PUF	11
	J1	201
	VP7	10
	G4	277
	AE1	282
	AE1	350
	AE1	783
	AE1	790
	AE2	199
	AE8	705
	AE11	630
	AE12	477
	KT3	271
	CI	313
	CI	427
DISMISSED	MS	21
	J6	237
	M1	351
	M1	931
DISMISSED	HI	152
	AE2	97
	AE6	330
	AE6	1241
	AE10	74
	AE11	713
	KT1	134
	B	300
	HIF	524
	M12	199
	CI	393
DISMISSION	HAP	346
DISMOUNTED	FL	305
DISMOUNTING	TH	141
DISMOUNTS	AE11	1047
DISOBEDIENCE	HAP	485
	B	750
DISOBEDIENT	AA	881
	G2	507
DISOBEY	HAP	1434
	OAL	24
	HIF	777
	C	80
DISOBEYED	AM	1087
	TA	234
	M12	37
	M15	40
DISOBLIGE	PLN	21
DISORDER	G2	86
DISORDERED	AM	725
	HP	79
	HAP	166
	AE2	825
	AE11	225
	AE11	710
	AE12	1067
	AE12	1306
DISOWN	PRL	29
	HAP	642
	HAP	1060
	HAP	2469
	AE6	670
	AE6	824
DISOWNED	CI	242
DISOWNING	AM	803
DISOWNS	CAM	23
DISPARAGED	WB	381
DISPATCH	AA	191
	J1	188
DISPATCHED	J1	148
	AE1	911
	AE7	155
	AE7	223
	TJD	86
	B	649
	B	658
	HIF	277
	M11	343
	M12	360
	AU	386
DISPATCHING	J6	835
DISPEL	SAA	1117
	L2	65
	HAP	1231
	AE3	140
	AE10	157
DISPELLED	AR	295
	M9	41
	AE1	204
	AE3	769
	AE9	886
	AE11	281
	AE11	320
	TH	336
	TH	407
DISPELS	M1	830
	AE8	781
DISPENSATION	C	64
DISPENSE	AR	167
	LC	26
	LC	27
	PTC	21
	MD	140
	MD	269
	PRH	13
	SAA	45
	SAA	254
	T27	120
	EL	211
	VCS	18
	G3	561
	AE1	603
	AE1	1043
	HIF	351
	AE10	883
	C	274

Word	Ref	No.
DISPENSE	M15	86
	AS	28
DISPENSED	SMA	23
	RL	55
	B	508
	B	552
DISPENSES	AE1	713
DISPENSING	D	36
	AE8	890
DISPEOPLED	HAP	2167
	M1	333
DISPERSE	SAA	933
	J10	230
	AE1	106
	AE3	574
	AE6	118
	AE8	784
DISPERSED	OD	50
	AE1	182
	AE1	757
	AE2	560
	AE4	173
	AE4	235
	AE5	885
	AE8	427
	AE9	423
	AE9	448
	M11	251
	CI	286
	CI	609
DISPERSES	AE1	315
DISPLACE	HAP	853
DISPLAY	DA	203
	AM	255
	ECD	19
	MF	207
	L1	36
	L2	66
	HAP	1360
	HAP	1857
	J3	421
	P6	17
	M9	21
	G1	399
	G1	465
	G2	378
	G2	394
	AE1	1015
	AE2	1089
	AE3	320
	AE5	1084
	AE12	725
	OAL	479
	DO	153
	TH	245
	M11	148
	M11	274
	M11	341
	FL	14
	AU	513
DISPLAYED	AM	1085
	AT	9
	L1	13
	J10	251
	P3	17
	M1	177
	M1	285
	HI	39
	AE3	369
	AE3	568
	AE6	818
	AE7	8
	AE7	66
	AE7	775
	AE10	270
	AE12	1347
	KT2	585
	KT2	614
	KT3	560
	M8	74
	M11	295
	FL	232
DISPLAYS	AA	731
	MD	13
	AK	166
	J6	262
	G2	769
	G3	40
	AE1	415
	AE4	103
	AE4	164
	AE6	395
	AE7	470
	AE7	734
DISPLEASE	HP	129
	AA	333
DISPLEASE	M12	706
	WB	502
DISPLEASED	HP	37
	EMQw	27
	HAP	2352
	AE1	178
	KT3	264
	FL	395
DISPLEASURE	AM	1059
DISPOSE	HS	67
	E	31
	HAP	884
	HAP	2105
	ESH	11
	J10	148
	P5	127
	G3	768
	G4	214
	AE1	119
	AE1	277
	AE1	1044
	AE6	325
	KT3	162
	KT3	356
	KT3	485
	KT3	1093
	B	564
	HIF	115
	WB	462
	WB	495
	AS	65
DISPOSED	LC	39
	T27	21
	J10	126
	M9	79
	AE1	504
	KT2	664
	B	390
	B	508
	B	571
DISPOSING	AE1	316
	AE6	1175
	KT3	391
DISPOSSESSED	AR	182
	SAA	398
	HAP	2028
	HAP	2500
	AE7	483
	M15	241
DISPROVE	J6	205
	KT1	314
DISPUTANTS	EAL	1
DISPUTE	E	11
	PUO3	17
	MD	91
	D	45
	MF	5
	SAA	204
	RL	221
	HAP	932
	HAP	2147
	AE10	612
	AE11	173
	AE12	80
	HIF	417
	C	507
	C	543
	WB	98
	GP	122
DISPUTED	HP	116
DISPUTES	RL	448
	HAP	636
	HAP	670
	HAP	774
	AE5	454
DISPUTING	EWG	22
	EL	107
DISQUISITIONS	RL	431
DISSECTED	P1	224
DISSEIZED	HAP	2005
DISSEMBLE	AR	307
	HP	147
	HP	149
	OAL	312
DISSEMBLED	AM	452
	HP	75
	AA	283
	AA	940
	SAA	749
	SAA	830
	TA	132
	J3	59
	M1	830
	VP4	51
	G4	636
	AE1	960
DISSEMBLED	AE5	826
	AE8	875
	AE11	629
	M12	739
	WB	80
DISSEMBLERS	ETG	10
DISSEMBLING	AA	448
	T27	32
	J3	134
	AE4	692
	AE5	1104
	AE12	340
	B	243
	C	794
	TH	398
	AU	464
	CI	311
DISSENSION	HAP	694
	AE10	22
DISSENSIONS	HAP	1039
	HIF	265
DISSENT	HAP	783
DISSENTERS	HAP	840
DISSENTING	AA	607
	SAA	217
	AE12	855
DISSEVER	STS1	17
DISSEVERED	M1	996
DISSIPATES	AE9	743
DISSOLUTE	P3	58
DISSOLVE	SAA	262
	H9	7
	J6	11
	G1	66
	AE2	819
	AE4	996
	AE8	736
DISSOLVED	AA	780
	SAA	774
	BR	129
	BR	311
	P3	114
	VP6	58
	G4	51
	G4	723
	AE1	823
	AE4	281
	AE4	556
	AE4	1009
	B	250
	B	411
	HIF	426
	M11	346
	CI	550
DISSOLVES	SAA	1080
	RL	11
	L4	82
	L4	249
	G4	310
	TJD	207
DISSOLVING	HAP	2566
	P5	77
	AE8	522
DISSUADED	M12	425
DISTAFF	AE8	545
	OAL	783
	OAL	797
	C	729
DISTAFFS	G4	475
DISTAIN	AE1	268
DISTAINED	AE2	757
	AE10	1312
	AE11	56
	AE12	1376
DISTAINS	M8	178
DISTANCE	AM	377
	AM	749
	AA	449
	HAP	1040
	HAP	1073
	EL	269
	GK	39
	GK	171
	AE1	581
	AE2	590
	AE3	395
	AE3	617
	AE3	707
	AE6	434
	AE9	717
	AE10	645
	AE10	671
	AE10	1012
	AE10	1137
	AE11	910
	AE11	946

Word	Ref	No.
DISTANCE	AE11	1310
	KT2	184
	KT3	188
	KT3	635
	CAM	75
	HIF	676
	HIF	721
	TH	279
	M11	77
	M11	138
	M11	449
	FL	41
	M12	76
DISTANCES	AE9	201
DISTANT	AR	196
	VHH	31
	VHH	49
	AM	225
	AM	282
	AM	444
	HP	7
	AA	236
	MF	97
	TA	504
	MN	12
	HAP	1131
	HAP	1620
	HAP	1659
	EM1	1
	PP	6
	EL	6
	EL	40
	EL	196
	J3	283
	J6	600
	P3	71
	M1	56
	M1	123
	VP8	144
	G2	36
	G2	710
	G3	392
	G3	571
	AE3	269
	AE3	884
	AE4	374
	AE5	235
	AE5	417
	AE6	781
	AE7	742
	AE8	334
	AE9	1
	AE9	38
	AE9	690
	AE10	967
	AE10	1181
	AE11	1137
	AE11	1248
	AE12	905
	KT1	538
	B	153
	CAM	14
	TH	53
	M11	448
	M15	417
	CI	169
	CI	382
	CI	623
	ESK	2
	BR	138
DISTEMPER	TA	158
DISTEMPERED	AR	112
	D	39
	AE4	854
	HIF	370
DISTEND	VP9	40
	G3	197
	G4	267
	KT3	763
	C	293
DISTENDED	G3	483
	AE9	71
	AE9	1075
	AE11	212
	M15	109
DISTENDS	G1	130
	G3	757
	CAM	355
DISTIL	L4	12
	M1	360
	VP3	139
	VP8	74
	VP10	112
	AE3	61
	HIF	712
DISTILLED	T18	76
DISTILLED	AK	51
	AE2	233
	AE3	39
	KT3	674
	B	623
	CAM	371
	HIF	364
DISTILLING	AE12	743
DISTILS	VP6	92
DISTINCT	AE2	402
DISTINCTION	PUO4	7
	J6	417
	M1	420
	M1	961
	M13	140
	AE3	264
	AE3	267
	AE10	550
	KT1	335
	KT3	570
DISTINCTIONS	J10	313
DISTINCTIVE	HAP	2556
DISTINCTLY	AR	165
	EL	279
	J6	583
	M1	228
	M9	42
DISTINGUISH	AA	743
	L3	61
	FS3	4
	FS3	6
	HAP	257
	J3	303
	P5	153
	G2	345
	G3	251
	CI	141
DISTINGUISHED	PTC	3
	MD	155
	SAA	765
	J10	265
	P2	2
	M1	87
	M1	963
	G1	194
	G2	336
	G4	137
	G4	523
	AE3	175
	AE3	532
	AE4	923
	AE5	324
	AE5	538
	AE5	758
	AE6	880
	AE10	204
	AE10	536
	AE11	1142
	B	511
	C	153
	TH	106
	FL	430
	CI	96
DISTINGUISHING	CI	211
DISTORTED	TA	69
	AE3	889
	AE8	578
	MM	12
DISTRACT	AE4	13
DISTRACTED	AM	1015
	PLG	13
	SAA	925
	ODA	12
	M13	191
	AE2	550
	AE4	97
	AE4	681
	AE4	956
	AE7	526
	AE8	33
	AE11	215
	AE11	720
	AE12	871
	C	719
	TH	321
	TH	370
DISTRACTION	TA	61
	AE12	889
	AU	52
DISTRACTS	OAL	108
DISTRESS	AM	1046
	AA	888
	AA	998
	HAP	1776
	P3	180
	M9	168
DISTRESS	AE1	303
	AE6	287
	AE9	299
	AE11	800
	AE11	831
	AE12	1171
	C	781
DISTRESSED	DA	93
	SAA	809
	HAP	2171
	AE1	182
	AE1	531
	AE1	888
	AE1	1063
	AE7	126
	AE9	390
	AE10	335
	AE10	599
	TH	101
	TH	268
	GP	63
	CI	321
DISTRIBUTED	RL	47
DISTRICT	HAP	2547
DISTRUST	HAP	2161
	AE8	524
	OAL	694
	CAM	193
	CI	191
DISTURB	AA	799
	RL	448
	L3	98
	L3	202
	L3	236
	H2	11
	FS1	2
	EL	112
	J1	190
	J6	541
	VP7	11
	G4	279
	AE1	356
	AE4	13
	AE4	559
	AE4	760
	CAM	51
	HIF	697
	C	566
	M11	277
	WB	527
	CI	165
DISTURBED	HAP	1177
	HAP	1327
	J6	134
	M1	22
	M13	9
	AE1	754
	AE4	798
	AE5	943
	CAM	187
	C	104
	M11	302
DISTURBS	L3	187
	G2	714
	G4	502
	AE4	674
	AE5	445
	HIF	774
DISUNITES	HIF	371
DISUSE	AA	620
DISUSED	AE2	695
	AE6	1112
	AE12	864
	B	140
	B	519
	C	458
DITCH	G3	228
	AE9	673
	AE9	769
	C	38
	PMK	19
DITCHES	J10	76
	VP3	171
	G1	512
	G2	511
	G4	687
	AE1	591
	AE11	590
DIT-IL	EEL	15
DITTANY	AE12	609
DITTY	AT	121
	VP9	53
DIVE	PAL	26
	RL	77
	G1	337
	G1	530

Word	Code	Number
DIVE	AE4	375
	AE9	146
DIVED	PUO3	13
	AE8	320
DIVERSIFIED	AE4	386
DIVERT	PUO2	2
	AA	949
	SAA	578
	TA	389
	TA	499
	HI	183
	AE1	59
DIVERTED	AE2	927
	M15	417
DIVERTS	AE5	31
	AE11	144
	B	517
DIVES	M15	420
DIVIDE	HS	100
	VHH	9
	AM	264
	AM	550
	AM	940
	HP	178
	AA	164
	SAA	895
	SAA	955
	L4	202
	H3	29
	HAP	332
	HAP	768
	HAP	1348
	HAP	1473
	OD	46
	EL	188
	EL	306
	EL	356
	J1	191
	HI	27
	G4	514
	G4	606
	AE2	51
	AE2	270
	AE2	288
	AE2	447
	AE3	189
	AE3	491
	AE3	705
	AE3	740
	AE3	877
	AE4	771
	AE5	135
	AE5	195
	AE5	482
	AE5	323
	AE5	918
	AE5	1079
	AE7	198
	AE7	1091
	AE8	36
	AE8	186
	AE8	318
	AE8	584
	AE8	893
	AE9	21
	AE9	218
	AE9	315
	AE9	365
	AE9	601
	AE10	120
	AE11	681
	AE12	135
	AE12	303
	AE12	1061
	AF	168
	AF	178
	MM	27
	KT3	544
	KT3	831
	M8	107
	M8	283
	HIF	380
	HIF	656
	M11	418
	FL	288
DIVIDED	AR	2
	CM	82
	ER	52
	L3	16
	HAP	498
	J1	147
	M1	103
	M1	359
	G4	94
	AE2	973
DIVIDEND	HIF	189
DIVIDEND	AU	167
DIVIDES	AM	213
	AA	235
	H2	60
	HAP	1348
	PKA	24
	J6	328
	J10	240
	G1	299
	G1	321
	G1	335
	G1	688
	AE1	715
	AE3	530
	AE4	834
	AE5	474
	AE5	757
	AE6	726
	AE8	933
	AE9	1018
	AE10	13
	AE10	304
	AE10	320
	AE10	550
	AE10	620
	KT3	559
	CAM	368
	M12	586
DIVINATION	HS	75
DIVINE	UDH	104
	JH	9
	JH	12
	AM	1172
	SEL1	2
	EPF	15
	EUF	9
	AA	807
	AA	838
	SAA	637
	RL	152
	RL	165
	RL	238
	RL	330
	T18	37
	TA	363
	EAA	7
	AK	14
	AK	160
	GE	31
	HAP	10
	HAP	114
	HAP	253
	HAP	358
	HAP	1466
	HAP	1573
	HAP	1728
	EKA	30
	J1	171
	J10	39
	J10	196
	P2	98
	P2	130
	P3	179
	M1	286
	M1	552
	HI	118
	GK	72
	GK	102
	GK	149
	VP3	56
	VP3	165
	VP5	49
	VP5	80
	VP5	113
	VP5	123
	VP7	44
	G1	9
	G1	361
	G1	471
	G2	136
	G4	548
	AE1	7
	AE1	322
	AE1	341
	AE1	394
	AE1	478
	AE1	627
	AE1	826
	AE1	994
	AE1	1017
	AE2	316
	AE3	479
	AE3	689
	AE4	299
	AE4	302
	AE5	59
DIVINE	AE5	622
	AE5	722
	AE5	856
	AE5	1112
	AE6	190
	AE6	908
	AE6	1077
	AE6	1188
	AE7	90
	AE7	555
	AE8	242
	AE8	355
	AE8	454
	AE8	700
	AE8	707
	AE8	833
	AE9	19
	AE9	118
	AE9	181
	AE9	880
	AE10	840
	AE10	876
	AE12	195
	AE12	251
	AE12	281
	AE12	475
	AE12	633
	AE12	1022
	AE12	1150
	OAL	228
	OAL	233
	AF	161
	AF	171
	DO	12
	DO	30
	KT3	128
	KT3	161
	KT3	264
	KT3	945
	M8	116
	BP	170
	M10	62
	CAM	85
	HIF	272
	HIF	756
	C	572
	C	635
	FL	83
	FL	262
	M12	39
	M12	264
	AU	230
	M15	77
	GP	136
	CI	4
	CI	168
	ETP	24
DIVINED	CM	90
	G1	635
	AE5	6
	AE6	239
	AE7	348
	AE7	830
	AE8	923
	AE10	1201
	KT3	483
	B	85
	CAM	186
	HIF	532
	C	138
	TH	350
	M12	607
DIVINELY	ODA	67
	AE6	875
	AE8	973
DIVINER	JH	20
	AA	19
	SAA	1103
DIVINERESS	HAP	1784
DIVINERS'	AA	238
DIVINES	AE10	893
	KT1	496
	KT3	846
DIVING	ESF	27
	J3	110
DIVINING	AE6	54
	AE6	1242
	AE7	257
	HIF	463
DIVINITY	HAP	151
	BR	56
	J6	701
DIVISIBLE	HAP	319
DIVISION	KT2	596
DIVISIONS	G4	309
	SAA	691

Word	Ref	No.	Word	Ref	No.	Word	Ref	No.
DIVISIONS	EDGA	4	DOGMAS	P3	102	DOMINION	AM	796
DIVORCED	J6	319	DOGS	EUO	26		CM	14
DIVORCING	HAP	1499		EAZ	19		AA	526
DIVULGED	CM	95		OE	39		MF	141
	HAP	2474		L4	201		J6	297
	J1	218		HAP	222		G2	402
	AE2	119		J6	711		AE1	384
	AE3	147		VP3	102		WB	283
	AE7	148		VP6	108	DOMINIONS	AM	1114
DOCTOR	HAP	977		G1	212		D	33
	J6	333		G1	635		G4	675
	J10	350		G3	572		AE4	290
	P3	124		G3	616		AE6	379
	P3	173		AE3	536		OAE1	17
	P3	194		AE3	546		KT2	652
	TJD	93		AE4	187	DON	HS	90
	PTP	53		AE5	336	DONOR'S	J1	182
DOCTORAL	RL	406		AE6	367	DONORS	HAP	1030
DOCTOR'S	C	170		AE8	605	DONS	EIE	21
DOCTORS	PAA	13		AE9	646	DONYSA	AE3	172
	HAP	657		M8	90	DOOM	RL	206
	HAP	687		M8	107		RL	215
	HAP	1000		HIF	5		RL	303
	TJD	71		HIF	75		SMA	127
	TJD	114		C	731		PWG	6
	C	405		TH	123		AM	827
	C	507		TH	180		AM	1014
DOCTORS'	ERL	10		TH	273		AM	1076
DOCTRINE	RH	33		M11	276		AM	1188
	MD	111	DOG-STAR	AA	334		PMQ	16
	RL	148		G2	484		EMM	14
	RL	158		G4	615		SCD1	15
	RL	329	DOLE	EL	20		PUO1	7
	HAP	484		ODA	28		D	24
	HAP	725		J1	147		SAA	176
	HAP	751		J1	184		SAA	506
	HAP	767		P3	211		SAA	1073
	HAP	1007	DOLEFUL	AT	121		L3	170
	HAP	1031		AE2	882		L5	8
	HAP	1126		AE11	219		TA	83
	HAP	1433		AE12	909		TA	113
	BR	284		M8	346		TA	212
	ETS	28		B	227		HAP	2527
	P5	277		C	231		BR	92
	BP	10		C	714		J1	235
	C	73		C	732		J10	191
	GP	80	DOLES	P5	102		M1	259
DOCTRINES	HAP	216		J3	400		M9	20
	HAP	873	DOLON	AE12	522		HI	182
	HAP	913	DOLOPEIAN	M12	490		VP4	76
	HAP	1161	DOLPHIN	P1	184		G3	111
	HAP	1163		AE3	546		G4	565
	HAP	2328		AE5	153		AE1	38
DODDERED	P5	80		AE5	203		AE1	326
	VP9	12		AE5	206		AE2	438
	AE2	702		AE5	282		AE2	908
	KT3	905		AE5	299		AE5	828
DODGING	HAP	825	DOLPHIN'S	AE5	237		AE6	716
DODONA	AE5	352	DOLPHINS	M1	411		AE7	372
DODONAEAN	AE3	596		J10	21		AE7	506
DODONIAN	G1	221		AE5	775		AE8	442
DOE	M1	681		AE8	893		AE8	855
	G1	416		AE9	145		AE9	126
	G3	803	DOLT	PD	55		AE10	16
DOEG	SAA	408		ETP	41		AE10	449
	SAA	412	DOMAINS	AE9	363		AE11	42
	SAA	492	DOME	SMA	61		AE11	236
	SAA	494		DA	109		OAL	739
	SAA	509		AA	868		KT1	266
DOFFS	J16	71		G3	24		KT2	95
	P4	56		AE4	667		KT2	268
DOG	AM	522		KT2	462		KT2	300
	ETL	1		KT2	524		KT2	307
	SAA	440		KT2	580		KT2	378
	L3	222	DOMES	AE8	955		KT2	496
	HAP	193	DOMESTIC	AM	551		TJD	8
	J3	15		AM	1189		TJD	78
	J6	541		PUO4	26		M8	336
	M9	36		SAA	717		HIF	51
	G1	308		L4	294		HIF	125
	G2	520		TA	321		HIF	453
	G3	745		HAP	864		HIF	707
	G4	692		HAP	2289		C	677
	AE6	540		HAP	2533		TH	290
	AE8	927		J6	686		TH	355
	M8	191		P4	60		AU	583
	C	728		AE2	761		M15	195
	EWR	29		AE3	169		CI	254
DOG-FOXES	VP3	143		KT3	1149	DOOMED	AM	80
DOGGEREL	EIE	16		BP	172		AT	79
	PKK	3	DOMINATING	C	161		L3	300
	SAA	411	DOMINEER	J3	130		HAP	8
	J10	189	DOMINEERS	G1	229		J6	309
	P1	186	DOMINION	HS	37		J10	268
	PTP	23		DC	45		AE1	997
DOGHOLE	J3	367		AM	174		AE2	301

DOOMED	AE4	718	
	AE4	997	
	AE5	1136	
	AE6	840	
	AE7	328	
	AE8	501	
	AE8	763	
	AE10	89	
	AE10	617	
	AE11	398	
	AE11	1121	
	AE12	798	
	KT1	162	
	KT1	412	
	KT1	491	
	KT3	274	
	KT3	770	
	TJD	192	
	M8	171	
	B	575	
	C	715	
	TH	169	
	TH	177	
	AU	480	
	WB	72	
DOOMING	AE6	512	
DOOMS	MD	97	
	AE6	585	
	AE6	1124	
	AE11	878	
	KT3	522	
DOOMSDAY	FL	485	
DOOR	SMM1	2	
	SMM1	7	
	SCG2	5	
	ML	19	
	CM	83	
	SAA	445	
	L3	285	
	L4	174	
	T23	96	
	HAP	701	
	HAP	1540	
	HAP	2153	
	BR	253	
	PDS	26	
	EL	32	
	SSH	13	
	J1	147	
	J1	199	
	J3	216	
	J3	476	
	J6	321	
	J6	335	
	J10	111	
	J10	263	
	J10	378	
	P5	186	
	M1	284	
	M1	384	
	G4	400	
	AE2	666	
	AE3	370	
	AE4	687	
	AE6	399	
	AE6	704	
	AE6	774	
	AE6	864	
	AE7	481	
	AE8	261	
	AE8	294	
	AE8	295	
	AE8	477	
	AE9	1008	
	OAE2	77	
	KT2	551	
	KT2	552	
	TJD	36	
	B	110	
	B	152	
	B	222	
	B	229	
	BP	42	
	CAM	154	
	CAM	281	
	C	225	
	C	431	
	M11	290	
	FL	9	
	WB	120	
	M15	419	
	CI	562	
	ETP	31	
	PMK	29	
DOORKEEPERS	PUO3	14	
DOORS	AM	579	

DOORS	OE	39	
	T23	31	
	T23	67	
	HAP	2046	
	HAP	2504	
	J6	75	
	J6	249	
	J6	616	
	J6	783	
	J10	98	
	P1	211	
	P5	239	
	M1	225	
	M9	184	
	G4	334	
	AE1	631	
	AE2	431	
	AE2	657	
	AE6	40	
	AE6	65	
	AE6	126	
	AE8	348	
	KT3	359	
	BP	27	
DOP	EUF	2	
DORIC	MC	17	
	VP6	2	
DORIMANT	MF	152	
DORIS	AE3	100	
DORP	HAP	1905	
DORYCLUS'	AE5	806	
DORYLAS	M12	509	
DOSE	ETC	12	
	P2	26	
	G3	764	
DOTAGE	PCD	5	
DOTARD	J10	330	
	J10	358	
	P5	258	
	AE5	227	
	HIF	39	
DOTARD'S	J6	814	
DOTARDS	EUO	27	
	P1	156	
DOTE	SMM2	14	
	L4	142	
	AE7	618	
	AE7	634	
	HAP	1446	
DOTED	J6	96	
DOTES	L4	179	
DOTING	VP8	70	
	B	567	
DOTINGLY	J6	62	
DOTIS	AE9	119	
DOUBLE	AR	214	
	AM	488	
	AM	495	
	PM	17	
	AA	511	
	MD	49	
	MF	217	
	SAA	307	
	SAA	367	
	SAA	496	
	SAA	1023	
	EK	40	
	AT	13	
	L4	233	
	TA	360	
	AK	160	
	HAP	402	
	HAP	1622	
	HAP	2401	
	SSC	29	
	SKA1	4	
	J6	174	
	J6	423	
	J10	240	
	P3	21	
	P6	183	
	P6	184	
	M1	180	
	M1	721	
	VP6	105	
	G2	236	
	G3	50	
	G3	89	
	G3	137	
	G4	179	
	AE1	232	
	AE1	923	
	AE2	128	
	AE2	659	
	AE3	176	
	AE3	240	

DOUBLE	AE3	657	
	AE4	682	
	AE6	296	
	AE6	399	
	AE6	1160	
	AE7	245	
	AE7	789	
	AE8	365	
	AE8	737	
	AE9	774	
	AE9	958	
	AE10	369	
	AE11	3	
	AE12	298	
	AE12	12	
	KT1	463	
	KT3	35	
	TJD	27	
	TJD	112	
	M8	51	
	M8	219	
	M8	279	
	M8	328	
	B	680	
	CAM	18	
	CAM	263	
	C	155	
	C	789	
	TH	367	
	M11	158	
	M12	467	
	M12	541	
	M12	615	
	M12	811	
	M15	495	
	M15	613	
	GP	100	
	CI	20	
	CI	177	
	CI	448	
	CI	562	
	AS	101	
DOUBLE-BITING	KT3	480	
	M8	166	
DOUBLED	AM	181	
	AM	1214	
	AA	95	
	G1	223	
	G4	70	
	AE7	196	
	AE11	959	
	AE12	672	
	AE12	1343	
	HIF	688	
	AS	99	
DOUBLE-EDGED	HAP	1486	
DOUBLE-ENTENDRES	PLT	23	
DOUBLE-FORMED	M12	337	
DOUBLE-FRONTED	AE12	299	
DOUBLES	AE9	748	
	SMP	34	
	SMP	36	
DOUBLE-TONGUED	AE1	933	
	AU	385	
DOUBLING	AM	474	
	M1	455	
	MC	23	
	AE3	918	
	KT2	243	
	FL	547	
	M15	69	
DOUBLY	AM	488	
	AM	700	
	PUO5	24	
	TA	398	
	AE2	288	
	AE4	945	
	AE7	845	
	AE12	853	
	CAM	61	
DOUBT	PRL	13	
	AM	855	
	EWGR	21	
	EOE	28	
	HP	40	
	HP	174	
	HP	192	
	HP	238	
	DA	89	
	DA	155	
	PUO4	13	
	AA	473	
	AA	1018	
	MD	95	
	SAA	97	
	EK	17	

DOUBT
EK 39
T27 19
EAA 26
HAP 1087
HAP 1512
BR 119
EL 297
J10 132
P4 21
M1 1069
M1 1084
ELT 33
G2 604
G3 453
AE4 154
AE4 866
AE6 131
AE6 1101
AE7 430
AE11 596
OAL 211
OAL 384
OAE2 53
MG 13
KT3 810
B 563
BP 15
HIF 589
HIF 747
C 358
M11 488
FL 9
FL 559
M12 671
AU 509
WB 205
CI 125

DOUBTED
HP 171
EDG 2
AE8 130
TH 26
M15 37
CI 115

DOUBTFUL
AR 71
RH 89
SMA 134
VHH 15
AM 272
AA 281
AA 408
SAA 163
SAA 566
SAA 936
RL 6
RL 435
L4 117
TA 116
TA 117
TA 485
HAP 410
HAP 644
HAP 670
HAP 950
HAP 2206
BR 270
M1 783
M1 796
M9 64
M13 8
VP5 26
G1 493
G2 379
G3 750
G4 128
AE1 5
AE1 301
AE1 725
AE2 42
AE2 507
AE3 120
AE3 242
AE3 266
AE4 413
AE4 865
AE5 127
AE5 918
AE5 1055
AE6 36
AE6 381
AE6 613
AE6 614
AE6 1127
AE9 48
AE9 273
AE9 506
AE10 498

DOUBTFUL
AE10 963
AE10 1090
AE12 65
OAL 425
OAL 627
DO 4
DO 34
TJD 168
M8 269
B 67
M11 273
M12 158
M12 690
WB 507
M15 648

DOUBTFULLY
AE2 228
CI 205

DOUBTING
HAP 1855
M8 240

DOUBTLESS
PKA 8

DOUBTS
PMQW 18
MD 210
SAA 124
SAA 848
SAA 911
RL 285
HAP 78
HAP 477
HAP 888
HAP 920
HAP 2389
J6 138
J10 37
M1 533
M1 725
AE1 791
AE3 477
AE9 1064
AE12 956
KT2 485
M8 274
TH 391
M12 144

DOUGHTY
PD 59
PP 40

DOVE
PUF 5
PUF 9
EK 24
L4 148
HAP 2550
AE5 276
AE5 650
AE5 674
AE11 1066
DO 70
DO 99
M15 570
PTP 3
AS 60

DOVE-HOUSE
HAP 2381

DOVER'S
AR 276

DOVES
HAP 2240
HAP 2273
HAP 2500
HAP 2529
HAP 2561
M1 683
AE2 706
AE6 280
OAL 135

DOWAGER
C 5

DOWDIES
L4 142

DOWDY
PCG2 30

DOWER
J6 200
HI 32
HI 33
AE4 147
AE11 567
CM 118
DA 163

DOWN
JH 13
AR 109
J3 308
J6 126
M13 8
M13 75
VP8 57
AE8 213
AE9 231

DOWNCAST
CM 35
T27 130
G4 506
AE1 788
AE8 689
AE11 724
OAL 764

DOWNCAST
AF 84
KT2 651
CAM 162
M12 824
EMKG 34

DOWNFALL
PTW 2
SAA 591
AT 56
C 714
TH 350

DOWNHILL
HAP 372
M15 348

DOWN-LOOKED
KT2 489

DOWNRIGHT
PK 20
J6 441
OAL 759
M12 644
M15 177
PTP 29

DOWNS
VP5 1

DOWNY
AM 712
J1 241
VP2 72
AE4 762
AE8 550
M12 404

DOWRY
G1 44

DOZED
VP6 21

DOZEN
PMM 8
EKA 1

DOZY
P3 9

DRABS
ELB 32
P1 275

DRAG
SAA 714
J6 308
VP1 19
AE3 407
AE3 849
AE6 1153
AE8 351
KT1 412
SMP 84

DRAGGED
CM 132
J10 100
G2 545
G4 716
AE1 667
AE2 355
AE2 544
AE2 748
AE2 877
AE8 276
AE10 744
AE10 1129
AE12 155
KT2 4
TH 162
M12 521
M12 522
M12 779
AU 54

DRAGGING
J10 384
AE6 753

DRAGON
BR 52
G1 295
G1 334
G4 592

DRAGON'S
AE4 701
AF 28

DRAGONS
C 152
M11 333

DRAGS
AM 724
P5 233
G1 214
G1 523
G3 644
AE10 772
EMKG 13

DRAIN
SAA 332
PLB 52
J6 480
VP2 53
VP7 22
G1 282
G3 610
AE1 374
OAL 475
M8 93
BP 69

DRAINED
PTC 9
SAA 312
DOD 24
TA 342
HAP 2259
J6 51
P5 95

Word	Code	Number
DRAINED	AE6	1005
	M12	590
DRAINS	HS	107
	J1	140
	VP3	155
	G1	169
	M11	288
	M15	583
DRAKE	GE	20
DRAM	AU	557
DRAMA	MS	20
DRAMATIC	EWGR	1
DRANCES	AE11	183
	AE11	199
	AE11	341
	AE11	510
	AE11	585
	AE11	631
	AE11	680
	AE12	939
DRANK	HAP	534
	BR	153
	M1	872
	AE1	1050
	AE7	744
	AE9	555
	M8	195
	HIF	807
DRAUGHT	UDH	69
	AM	611
	PUO4	22
	L3	103
	L3	314
	L4	111
	T23	52
	AK	107
	HAP	534
	HAP	1418
	HAP	2342
	BR	153
	EL	263
	J1	238
	J6	773
	J6	835
	J10	37
	P3	182
	GK	9
	G2	178
	AE5	236
	AE7	181
	OAL	265
	KT2	18
	TJD	93
	B	706
	M12	440
	M15	500
DRAUGHTS	PAL	33
	HAP	1132
	GK	148
	G3	447
	AE1	1050
	AE6	572
	AE6	1017
	AE8	364
	KT3	728
	TJD	116
	M12	217
	M15	432
DRAW	UDH	68
	HS	18
	HS	75
	HS	97
	AR	5
	AR	155
	SMA	33
	DC	25
	AM	663
	AM	737
	AM	740
	AM	748
	AM	779
	PT	8
	SEL3	6
	SEL3	7
	PCG2	10
	EUO	2
	ML	54
	EOE	4
	PUO5	9
	PUF	4
	AA	407
	AA	457
	AA	581
	AA	928
	AA	1002
	PLB	36
DRAW	SAA	234
	SAA	272
	SAA	606
	SAA	678
	SAA	783
	SAA	883
	RL	134
	PD	13
	TA	328
	HH	8
	PP	27
	PTS	29
	EL	333
	EL	365
	MS	30
	J1	97
	J10	310
	P1	222
	P3	186
	P5	23
	P5	247
	P6	94
	GK	157
	G2	717
	G3	227
	G3	239
	G3	439
	G3	795
	G4	699
	AE1	1036
	AE3	26
	AE4	338
	AE5	10
	AE5	219
	AE6	521
	AE7	391
	AE8	760
	AE9	219
	AE10	114
	AE10	125
	AE10	168
	AE10	955
	AE10	1070
	AE11	152
	AE12	574
	AE12	614
	OAL	785
	KT1	26
	KT1	193
	KT1	580
	KT2	344
	KT3	48
	M8	343
	B	117
	HIF	131
	C	464
	C	474
	C	755
	TH	230
	M12	371
	M12	478
	M12	583
	AU	212
	AU	498
	WB	530
	M15	182
	M15	333
	M15	658
	GP	31
	PTP	40
	EMKG	17
DRAWEST	P3	111
	KT1	452
DRAWING	AE4	833
	HIF	598
DRAWN	UDH	49
	PWG	11
	EWGR	18
	EM	7
	EUF	13
	AA	227
	AA	302
	MF	160
	SAA	275
	SAA	390
	HAP	211
	HAP	865
	HAP	984
	HAP	1186
	HAP	1884
	HAP	2346
	BR	36
	EDS	3
	EL	142
	J10	225
	J10	269
DRAWN	P3	49
	M1	906
	VP8	95
	G2	174
	G3	508
	G4	104
	G4	540
	AE5	654
	AE5	756
	AE6	479
	AE6	1098
	AE6	1118
	AE7	756
	AE8	786
	AE9	435
	AE9	567
	AE9	936
	AE11	708
	AE11	897
	AE11	1049
	AE11	1308
	OAL	244
	OAL	617
	OAL	876
	LMC	3
	DO	33
	KT1	110
	KT2	499
	KT2	571
	KT2	619
	KT3	954
	B	211
	HIF	641
	TH	249
	FL	286
	M12	360
	M12	562
	CI	406
DRAWS	AM	143
	AM	953
	PUO1	27
	HP	175
	EPF	11
	AA	449
	SAA	288
	SAA	316
	HAP	2246
	MS	12
	P3	140
	P4	68
	M1	36
	M1	626
	HI	116
	G3	800
	G4	249
	G4	611
	G4	812
	AE1	764
	AE1	770
	AE3	542
	AE4	356
	AE5	163
	AE5	458
	AE5	581
	AE5	988
	AE5	1092
	AE6	965
	AE7	212
	AE7	585
	AE8	725
	AE8	889
	AE10	352
	AE11	683
	AE11	1191
	AE11	665
	AE12	665
	OAL	21
	OAL	832
	KT2	204
	TJD	116
	B	356
	CAM	149
	M11	265
	AU	229
	M15	567
	M15	588
	HS	118
	AM	841
	ETC	7
DREAD	SAA	149
	SAA	675
	SAA	756
	L2	59
	L3	248
	TA	478
	HAP	1674

DREAD	J 1	52	DREAM	PPS	1	DREAMT	AE 5	830	
	P 3	79		P 2	103		AE 9	454	
	G 2	587		P 4	74		KT 1	546	
	AE 2	207		P 6	22		KT 2	35	
	AE 3	477		VP 1	76		KT 3	435	
	AE 5	937		AE 2	1079		B	237	
	AE 6	86		AE 4	820		C	113	
	AE 6	844		AE 7	591		C	230	
	AE 8	319		AE 7	602		C	243	
	AE 8	762		AE 8	60		C	320	
	AE 10	156		AE 8	92		C	392	
	AE 11	626		DO	134		C	685	
	AE 12	1177		KT 1	546		TH	364	
	AE 12	1296		C	94	DREARY	AE 6	378	
	KT 3	506		C	109		AE 6	413	
	C	296		C	154		AE 9	121	
	M 12	418		C	161		M 8	317	
	AU	135		C	238	DREGS	AA	227	
DREADED	AM	241		C	240		L 3	314	
DREADFUL	AR	3		C	266		HAP	211	
	AM	90		C	268		BR	153	
	AM	226		C	308		J 6	480	
	AM	261		C	362		P 6	37	
	AM	514		C	366		M 1	86	
	AM	897		C	382		G 1	394	
	CM	9		C	384		G 4	541	
	DA	97		C	388		AE 6	1005	
	AT	56		C	395		AE 11	243	
	L 1	46		C	399		C	472	
	L 2	46		C	425	DRENCH	T 23	50	
	L 3	7		C	505		G 2	11	
	HAP	797		C	554		G 3	680	
	HAP	1917		C	685		G 3	760	
	SSC	59		M 11	260		G 4	174	
	EL	5		M 11	313	DRENCHED	L 3	70	
	ESH	30		FL	121		EH	33	
	J 1	237		AU	345		J 1	238	
	J 3	430		AU	348		J 3	327	
	J 6	60		M 15	29		P 3	59	
	M 13	61		M 15	38		VP 3	172	
	HI	7		M 15	224		AE 8	957	
	G 3	341	DREAMED	HAP	539		AE 9	311	
	G 3	792	DREAMER	C	316		AE 10	1161	
	G 4	130	DREAMING	AA	529		AE 12	1242	
	AE 1	403		HAP	341	DRENCHING	SAA	1118	
	AE 2	160	DREAMS	SMA	43	DREPANUM'S	AE 3	930	
	AE 2	269		AM	275	DRESS	EWG	17	
	AE 2	842		AM	281		PCG 1	18	
	AE 2	1025		EMQW	23		PMQW	8	
	AE 3	57		EMQW	24		ENH	14	
	AE 3	851		SAA	120		EDGA	25	
	AE 3	882		SAA	623		AK	136	
	AE 3	891		L 3	180		HH	10	
	AE 5	266		HAP	1806		HAP	1302	
	AE 6	29		EL	311		PP	16	
	AE 6	775		J 3	100		EL	327	
	AE 7	763		J 3	386		J 3	123	
	AE 8	569		J 6	706		EHC	30	
	AE 10	909		J 10	154		VP 2	70	
	KT 2	245		P 2	92		G 2	548	
	TH	294		P 3	83		AE 1	436	
	TH	380		P 3	158		AE 3	298	
	M 11	334		VP 8	158		AE 4	317	
	M 11	385		G 3	792		AE 10	1226	
	PWR	7		AE 3	230		AE 11	100	
DREADS	L 3	186		AE 4	11		OAL	288	
	J 10	38		AE 4	506		OAL	570	
	AE 2	780		AE 4	676		OAL	588	
	AE 2	781		AE 5	1095		OAL	838	
	C 1	352		AE 6	397		KT 2	500	
DREAM	DC	18		AE 6	952		KT 3	983	
	SMM 2	17		AE 8	78		M 12	578	
	SCG 1	30		AE 10	909	DRESSED	AR	58	
	SCG 1	34		HIF	93		LCA	46	
	SCG 2	12		C	138		SCD 1	7	
	DA	28		C	140		SAA	880	
	EUF	10		C	150		SAA	992	
	AA	52		C	158		L 1	9	
	AA	239		C	198		L 2	37	
	D	24		C	201		T 23	22	
	SAA	232		C	205		TA	121	
	SAA	1045		C	210		PTS	24	
	L 4	63		C	238		J 1	208	
	MN	2		C	324		J 1	212	
	AK	85		C	325		J 6	588	
	HAP	1745		C	336		J 10	518	
	HAP	1774		C	340		P 3	58	
	HAP	1810		C	357		P 5	25	
	BR	100		C	379		M 1	301	
	BR	279		TH	221		M 1	632	
	EL	312		TH	367		GK	68	
	EL	316		M 11	301		VP 5	44	
	M 9	172		M 11	339		G 2	87	
	M 13	150	DREAMT	HP	230		G 3	734	
	VP 8	158		TA	15		AE 2	528	
	J 6	676		EKA	21		AE 4	753	

Word	Code	Num
DRESSED	AE7	379
	AE7	928
	AE8	835
	MG	29
	KT1	181
	KT2	488
	BP	61
	M10	49
	FL	173
	FL	228
	FL	341
	FL	530
	M12	544
	WB	19
	M15	237
	CI	208
	CI	540
DRESSER	J6	615
	C	17
DRESSERS	J6	630
DRESSING	RH	82
	PD	50
	G2	587
	FL	35
DREW	UDH	65
	HS	60
	AR	82
	AM	41
	AM	62
	AM	361
	AM	422
	PCD	16
	POE	8
	CM	110
	SAA	373
	SAA	1018
	PAA	12
	NS	24
	MN	3
	AK	106
	HAP	541
	HAP	578
	HAP	1290
	HAP	1560
	HAP	1735
	HAP	2208
	HAP	2336
	PTS	34
	EL	37
	OD	25
	J10	395
	P1	205
	M1	994
	M9	27
	M9	69
	M13	37
	AE1	620
	AE1	676
	AE1	681
	AE1	768
	AE1	1005
	AE2	220
	AE2	460
	AE2	900
	AE3	757
	AE4	786
	AE4	925
	AE4	1004
	AE5	227
	AE5	248
	AE5	497
	AE5	692
	AE5	838
	AE5	881
	AE6	793
	AE7	72
	AE7	232
	AE8	294
	AE9	407
	AE9	437
	AE9	758
	AE9	853
	AE9	1028
	AE9	1038
	AE10	475
	AE10	668
	AE10	671
	AE10	803
	AE10	995
	AE10	1049
	AE10	1057
	AE10	1119
	AE10	1200
	AE11	857
	AE11	923
	AE11	951

Word	Code	Num
DREW	AE11	992
	AE11	1220
	AE11	1249
	AE12	711
	AE12	1001
	AE12	1280
	AF	170
	AF	180
	KT1	38
	KT1	193
	KT1	587
	KT2	86
	KT2	655
	M8	119
	M8	232
	M8	343
	M8	356
	B	144
	B	722
	BP	44
	BP	64
	M10	39
	CAM	166
	CAM	220
	CAM	313
	HIF	302
	HIF	794
	C	96
	C	255
	TH	191
	TH	303
	M11	73
	FL	80
	FL	108
	FL	147
	FL	235
	FL	262
	FL	380
	M12	7
	M12	175
	M12	416
	M12	728
	AU	211
	AU	341
	AU	374
	AU	387
	GP	20
DRIBBLING	PC2	24
	PK	32
	G3	158
DRIBLET	TA	424
DRIBS	PLB	22
	OAL	492
DRIED	VP3	152
	DO	100
	M8	274
	BP	76
	CAM	114
	FL	29
	FL	416
DRIES	SMA	15
	VP3	149
	KT2	42
	M8	251
DRIFT	AM	622
DRIFTS	AE12	132
DRINK	AR	186
	PCG1	16
	PAL	33
	PTW	25
	DA	200
	PSF	26
	AA	107
	ELB	32
	MD	235
	SAA	424
	SAA	478
	SAA	482
	SAA	553
	OE	32
	AT	74
	L3	106
	L4	53
	L4	64
	L4	269
	T23	50
	H2	26
	HAP	1424
	HAP	2245
	J3	280
	J6	827
	P1	275
	P3	177
	P4	34
	P6	38
	M13	132

Word	Code	Num
DRINK	DHP	8
	VP1	82
	VP5	37
	G2	12
	G2	725
	G3	21
	G3	703
	G4	46
	AE1	662
	AE6	1016
	AE8	855
	AE9	454
	AE11	243
	OAL	661
	OAE2	34
	OAE2	36
	KT1	527
	M15	413
DRINKING	PSF	38
	AA	551
	SAA	395
	PD	36
	HAP	526
	P3	187
	G3	200
	OAL	662
	AF	55
	AF	57
	AF	62
	KT2	650
	SMP	39
	SMP	43
DRINKS	PCB	4
	DA	200
	J6	144
	J6	556
	P3	182
	P3	198
	P4	60
	G1	524
	G4	180
	OAL	646
	M15	494
DRIP	G2	547
DRIPPING	G2	259
DRIVE	AR	137
	AM	266
	AM	582
	AM	912
	AM	956
	AM	1039
	AM	1083
	AM	1120
	AM	1148
	PNH	38
	ENH	18
	PKK	27
	POE	21
	DA	186
	PLB	14
	SAA	761
	MO	7
	L2	49
	L3	94
	H2	71
	HAP	2358
	EL	94
	P1	79
	P3	98
	M1	600
	M1	941
	M9	124
	HI	177
	VP1	18
	VP1	31
	VP2	38
	VP3	150
	VP8	25
	G1	293
	G1	396
	G1	619
	G3	27
	G3	240
	G3	583
	G3	629
	G4	12
	G4	227
	G4	241
	AE1	606
	AE1	745
	AE1	763
	AE3	326
	AE4	35
	AE7	220
	AE7	832
	AE7	950

Word	Code	No.	Word	Code	No.	Word	Code	No.
DRIVE	AE10	119	DRIVES	M12	401	DROPPING	AE6	490
	AE10	369		M15	286		AE9	629
	AE10	957	DRIVING	EM	26		KT2	42
	AE10	1012		HAP	698		M11	358
	AE10	1137		M13	96		M11	405
	AE11	801		G1	301		FL	389
	AE12	966		G3	564		M12	395
	AE12	1027		AE1	89	DROPS	LC	128
	KT3	635		AE1	656		AM	588
	B	172		AE2	959		PT	14
	C	741		AE6	1015		SEL4	26
	GP	31		AE9	1099		SEL4	28
DRIVEL	J10	320		AE10	600		PC2	24
DRIVELING	J6	814		AE12	103		L4	12
DRIVEN	PW	1		AE12	405		L4	117
	AA	1025		AE12	600		L4	252
	PRH	34		AE12	905		L4	298
	BR	239		OAL	616		BR	188
	M1	27	DRIZZLING	G1	593		PP	12
	M1	145	DRIZZLY	G3	475		J1	253
	M1	154	DROLLS	HH	7		J6	178
	M1	345	DRONE	T18	21		G2	279
	M1	406		PTS	2		G2	333
	M1	444	DRONES	ML	45		G3	750
	M13	96		P3	154		AE3	39
	G1	125		G4	242		AE4	742
	G1	367		G4	356		AE4	913
	G1	435		AE1	607		AE5	640
	G2	151		OAL	722		AE7	641
	G2	422	DRONING	G4	89		AE9	27
	G3	349	DROOP	SMA	28		AE9	1098
	G3	807		CI	526		AE11	1207
	G4	72	DROOPED	D	3		AE12	386
	G4	605		FL	376		AE12	1310
	G4	681	DROOPING	AM	896		OAL	48
	AE1	503		T23	11		KT1	63
	AE1	537		TA	121		M8	341
	AE1	546		TA	348		CAM	114
	AE1	799		G3	783		CAM	353
	AE2	706		G4	556		M11	345
	AE2	1030		G4	768		AU	212
	AE3	539		AE1	899		M15	325
	AE3	932		AE4	988	DROPSY	P3	122
	AE5	69		AE5	244		P5	273
	AE6	140		AE8	727	DROPSY-BELLY	P3	190
	AE6	715		AE10	1192	DROSS	HAP	2033
	AE7	575		AE11	53		AK	35
	AE7	1067		AE11	1178		PTS	34
	AE8	70		AE11	1208		AE2	821
	AE8	441		KT1	548	DROSSY	HAP	319
	AE8	882		B	698		P1	254
	AE8	943		M12	752	DROUGHT	AM	437
	AE9	578		M15	646		L4	63
	AE10	620		AS	11		G1	147
	AE11	398	DROP	PCB	14	DROUGHTY	G1	546
	AE11	565		PMS	5	DROVE	SCD1	6
	AE11	930		EPN	1		D	1
	AE11	988		J1	249		AT	104
	AE11	1263		J3	207		J1	93
	AE12	1172		M1	405		J10	199
	OAL	372		M1	419		M1	868
	KT3	188		M15	58		M1	917
	BP	73		SMP	8		M1	937
	CAM	264		AE3	62		AE1	45
	M11	462		AE11	643		AE1	147
	FL	589		AE11	1265		AE3	903
	M12	590		AE12	1029		AE5	672
	CI	373		OAE2	66		AE5	1052
	CI	393		KT3	1066		AE6	434
DRIVER	AE5	192		CAM	384		AE6	663
DRIVER'S	AE12	911		C	124		AE7	44
DRIVES	MD	80		M11	155		AE7	917
	SAA	799		M15	585		AE8	269
	H29	34	DROPPED	RL	67		AE8	340
	M1	631		HAP	344		AE9	554
	M1	1007		HAP	1332		AE9	586
	G1	602		VP6	24		AE9	717
	G3	822		AE6	3		AE10	761
	AE1	348		AE6	50		AE11	946
	AE2	828		AE8	881		AE12	445
	AE4	357		OAL	493		AE12	736
	AE4	361		KT1	449		AE12	973
	AE5	610		KT2	314		AE12	1119
	AE6	725		KT3	259		AE12	1375
	AE7	907		HIF	597		OAL	82
	AE9	445		WB	228		KT3	693
	AE10	827	DROPPEST	CM	143		M8	29
	AE10	897	DROPPING	PFD	3		M8	130
	AE11	1080		BR	150		FL	3
	AE12	493		J10	321		FL	221
	AE12	544		VP10	23		M12	408
	AE12	668		G1	513		M12	450
	AE12	695		G3	46		M12	655
	M8	277		G3	652		M12	755
	FL	495		AE1	251		WB	219
	M12	76		AE5	233		WB	262

Word	Ref	No.
DROVE	M15	17
	M15	99
	CI	298
	CI	369
DROVER	J3	383
DROVES	MD	47
	J6	219
	AE6	1015
DROWN	AR	237
	AR	303
	EWG	24
	AM	1031
	L4	153
	H29	61
	HAP	1787
	J1	250
	M1	354
	VP10	38
	G1	440
	AE1	61
	AE4	806
	TJD	177
	M15	430
DROWNED	SMA	1
	SMA	5
	SMA	56
	DC	18
	HAP	1205
	ODA	46
	J10	13
	J10	62
	J10	88
	J10	187
	P5	265
	VP6	66
	AE4	323
	AE6	254
	AE8	591
	AE11	125
	AE11	819
	AE12	906
	LMC	9
	KT1	536
	KT2	20
	CAM	249
	C	159
	M11	104
	M11	424
	M12	217
	M12	390
	M12	570
	M12	715
	M15	448
DROWNING	EUF	1
	AE1	762
DROWNS	HI	167
DROWSY	T18	21
	TA	470
	J3	386
	M1	990
	G4	634
	AE4	824
	AE5	1090
	HIF	810
	C	317
	M11	269
	CI	232
DRUDGE	EAL	26
	OE	48
	J6	46
	J6	496
	J10	495
	P4	74
	G4	234
	KT1	580
	M15	177
DRUDGERY	PEL	6
	SAA	357
DRUDGES	G3	158
	PCG1	34
	J6	306
	J10	349
	GK	148
DRUDGING	PC8	3
	HAP	371
	PDS	45
	EH	12
	G1	367
	G2	560
DRUG	EUO	32
	PDG	17
	J10	39
DRUGGET	PUO3	16
	MF	33
	MF	214
DRUGGETS	PNH	9

Word	Ref	No.
DRUGS	PTW	6
	P5	71
	G2	653
	AE6	568
DRUIDS	LC	25
DRUM	PMQ	18
	TA	475
	SSC	30
	SKA1	4
	M1	129
	M12	640
	SMP	58
	SMP	62
DRUMS	SCD2	15
	H2	11
	G2	789
	AE11	293
	AF	50
DRUNK	ENH	24
	CM	60
	AA	312
	PD	59
	L3	203
	L4	104
	GE	50
	HAP	2257
	HAP	2386
	PSH	30
	J1	75
	J3	457
	J10	286
	P3	198
	PLT	44
	VP1	43
	G3	479
	G3	727
	G3	838
	G4	77
	AE2	792
	AE3	826
	AE5	1111
	AE9	424
	AE11	942
	AE11	1176
	AE12	563
	M11	155
	M12	23
	M12	436
	CI	408
	SMP	56
DRUNKARD	J3	440
	HIF	335
DRUNKARDS	UDH	85
DRUNKEN	SAA	384
	J3	65
	J6	416
	P3	111
	P6	22
	VP6	23
	G1	170
	OAL	279
	OAL	612
	OAL	613
	OAL	663
	KT1	432
	HIF	810
	M15	430
	M15	488
	CI	609
DRUNKENNESS	OAL	670
	OAL	675
DRUSIAN	AE6	1132
DRUSUS	J3	386
DRY	AM	918
	SMM2	10
	SAA	338
	SAA	1079
	EDG	32
	PD	24
	L3	94
	GE	25
	HAP	1560
	HAP	1804
	SSC	8
	J10	179
	J16	42
	M1	665
	VP7	78
	G1	146
	G1	303
	G2	34
	G2	132
	G3	242
	G3	728
	G3	758
	G4	40

Word	Ref	No.
DRY	G4	148
	G4	389
	G4	542
	G4	578
	G4	616
	AE1	253
	AE1	983
	AE2	482
	AE4	706
	AE9	715
	AE10	383
	OAL	731
	KT1	524
	KT3	1065
	M8	351
	B	388
	BP	114
	CAM	167
	C	38
	C	177
	M11	179
	M12	386
	CI	26
	AS	46
DRYADS	AE3	45
	KT3	967
DRYAS	M8	59
	HIF	377
	M12	403
	M12	410
	M12	413
	M12	429
DRYLY	J1	113
	G4	477
DRYMO	J6	833
DRYMON'S	AE10	480
DRYOPS	PAA	39
DU	PSF	7
DUB	PTP	53
DUBBED	BR	122
DUBIOUS	M1	430
	G1	172
	G3	458
	AE5	425
	AE8	37
	AE10	899
DUCKING	P2	33
DUCK-LEGGED	J6	649
DUCKS	C	736
DUCKTILE	AE6	211
	AE7	878
DUE	SMA	47
	SMA	117
	EPC	24
	SAA	755
	SAA	1054
	EDG	28
	L3	227
	L4	217
	T18	72
	EAA	21
	HAP	236
	HAP	486
	HAP	923
	HAP	1000
	HAP	1354
	HAP	2261
	BR	113
	BR	335
	EL	104
	EL	159
	J6	266
	J6	595
	J6	842
	P1	99
	P3	207
	M1	268
	M1	615
	GK	120
	VP10	5
	G1	461
	G2	590
	G4	275
	G4	655
	AE1	344
	AE2	784
	AE3	162
	AE3	551
	AE3	792
	AE5	73
	AE5	462
	AE5	762
	AE6	446
	AE8	360
	AE8	798
	AE9	883

Word	Code	Num
DUE	AE10	624
	AE10	645
	AE10	1304
	AE11	34
	AE11	63
	AE11	445
	AE11	578
	AE12	32
	AE12	1151
	AE12	1154
	OAE2	80
	AF	141
	MM	16
	DO	55
	DO	58
	KT1	175
	KT2	273
	KT2	296
	KT3	179
	KT3	956
	KT3	988
	M8	159
	M8	233
	M8	296
	M8	307
	M8	338
	B	405
	B	693
	HIF	315
	M10	58
	TH	86
	TH	301
	FL	41
	FL	363
	FL	467
	FL	489
	FL	541
	M12	428
	M12	758
	AU	68
	AU	74
	AU	285
	AU	419
	AU	470
	WB	89
	CI	52
	CI	296
	CI	494
	HIF	421
DUEL	PWGR	12
DUELISTS	PCG1	41
DUELS	EDG	8
DUES	DA	102
	SAA	953
	AE3	721
	AE5	785
	AE6	229
	AE9	280
	AE9	398
	AE12	318
	M8	243
	GP	47
DUG	AE9	73
	B	103
DUGS	M13	127
	VP3	9
	VP4	25
	VP8	61
	G2	147
	AE8	837
	AE11	856
	M15	431
DUKE	VHH	21
	AM	197
	AM	217
	AM	255
	D	46
	TA	71
	GE	73
	WB	437
DUKES	KT3	94
DULL	RH	21
	RH	92
	PRL	19
	AM	480
	EWGR	37
	EEL	20
	SEL1	12
	SEL4	11
	SEL4	23
	ETL	17
	PCG1	8
	PCG1	25
	PCG1	35
	PCG1	42
	PCG2	27
DULL	ECG2	4
	PW	19
	EM	3
	PLN	2
	ENH	18
	PAZ	28
	ETC	12
	PCB	31
	AA	440
	ELB	17
	MF	166
	SAA	47
	SAA	402
	SAA	497
	SAA	477
	SAA	521
	SAA	530
	SAA	964
	PK	33
	PDG	8
	OE	37
	OE	54
	MO	21
	TA	303
	GE	28
	HAP	1659
	HAP	2309
	PKA	1
	ESH	24
	J10	57
	J10	467
	P5	278
	PLT	52
	EHC	19
	G3	72
	G3	221
	OAL	214
	OAL	653
	OAL	769
	OAE2	84
	FL	574
	AU	396
	AU	452
	CI	53
	PTP	30
DULLER	AR	289
	ECG1	25
	EUF	22
DULLY	PCG1	35
	EUF	27
DULNESS	PCG1	17
	PKK	4
	PTC	23
	PTC	25
	PTC	32
	AA	573
	MF	16
	MF	63
	MF	90
	MF	111
	MF	115
	MF	136
	MF	158
	MF	190
	EHC	21
	OAL	759
DULY	M13	131
	J1	61
	J6	593
	C	10
	GP	72
DUMB	AM	411
	EUO	21
	ML	31
	CM	58
	EK	9
	T23	28
	FS2	5
	TA	1
	AK	103
	HAP	600
	HAP	601
	HAP	775
	J3	464
	J6	101
	J6	718
	J10	56
	GK	3
	DHP	12
	G1	644
	G2	744
	G3	60
	G3	722
	AE2	174
	AE2	1050
	AE6	83
DUMB	OAL	139
	KT2	192
	KT2	309
	TH	91
	M11	281
	M11	436
	WB	162
DUMBNESS	CM	36
DUMFOUNDING	PP	47
DUMPLIN	SKA4	19
	SKA4	22
DUN	G3	129
DUNCE	MF	31
	HAP	1759
	VP3	36
DUNCES	UDH	14
	PUO1	30
DUNG	SAA	327
	G1	119
	G2	475
	C	252
	C	269
	C	279
DUNGEON	AE6	996
	AE8	299
	KT1	246
	KT1	267
	KT3	402
	TJD	192
	C	112
	CI	415
DUNGEON'S	AE6	834
DUNGEONS	HAP	1132
	J1	112
DUNGHILL	SAA	504
	EL	82
	C	139
DUNKIRK	HS	118
DURABLE	EL	227
DURANCE	KT1	162
DURING	ETC	21
	AA	597
	HAP	496
	G3	475
	G3	723
	AE11	201
	WB	325
DURST	AR	146
	AR	197
	AM	414
	AM	714
	EMQ	1
	PT	20
	PA	44
	PCG2	1
	PM	7
	PM	8
	PLN	21
	PUO1	9
	HP	59
	EMW	2
	PUO3	33
	AA	418
	AA	606
	AA	849
	RL	223
	RL	346
	AK	123
	HH	4
	HAP	530
	HAP	553
	HAP	1374
	HAP	2102
	BR	201
	EL	99
	OD	20
	ODA	54
	P1	25
	P4	83
	M1	354
	M1	1060
	EHC	4
	VP2	49
	AE3	881
	AE4	452
	AE6	502
	AE6	673
	AE9	177
	AE9	573
	AE11	945
	AE12	1162
	DO	122
	KT3	79
	CAM	235
	HIF	461
	HIF	532

Word	Ref	No.
DURST	HIF	560
	HIF	677
	HIF	765
	C	483
	TH	355
	FL	563
	M12	416
	AU	10
	AU	28
	AU	104
	AU	302
	AU	347
	WB	165
	M15	138
	GP	68
	CI	165
	CI	181
	CI	359
	CI	482
DUSK	KT3	77
DUSKY	VP2	22
	G1	609
	AE3	663
	AE6	382
	AE6	395
	AE6	614
	AE7	569
	AE9	20
	AE12	685
	FL	219
	WB	434
	CI	231
DUST	AM	1094
	AM	1159
	PT	3
	MF	180
	SAA	337
	TA	480
	HAP	2455
	PSH	28
	J3	412
	P1	270
	P6	100
	G2	337
	G3	272
	G4	131
	G4	148
	AE2	357
	AE2	826
	AE4	494
	AE4	618
	AE5	366
	AE6	323
	AE9	1099
	AE10	543
	AE10	1203
	AE11	431
	AE11	1269
	AE12	155
	AE12	513
	AE12	600
	AE12	657
	AE12	894
	OAL	175
	KT3	871
	M8	128
	M8	371
	M8	388
	M12	505
	M15	602
DUSTY	HP	244
	MF	100
	TA	469
	J10	55
	HI	85
	G3	179
	AE1	669
	AE1	689
	AE4	221
	AE7	219
	AE7	599
	AE7	950
	AE8	783
	AE9	37
	AE11	863
	KT3	341
DUTCH	EIE	20
	AM	74
	AM	87
	AM	165
	AM	213
	AM	261
	AM	275
	AM	349
	AM	423
	AM	445

Word	Ref	No.
DUTCH	AM	453
	AM	481
	AM	546
	AM	666
	AM	713
	AM	767
	PCD	6
	ECD	7
	EUO	1
	EOE	16
	GE	51
	J3	402
	P5	281
	G3	587
	OAL	589
DUTCHMAN	ML	32
DUTCHMEN	PCD	33
DUTCHMEN'S	PCD	16
DUTEOUS	RH	93
	AE9	901
	MFL	35
	WB	133
DUTIES	P5	185
DUTIFUL	L4	290
DUTY	HS	13
	AR	146
	SMA	69
	AM	191
	AM	579
	AM	964
	AM	1088
	AA	106
	AA	502
	AA	746
	AA	803
	AA	923
	MD	189
	PRH	19
	SAA	132
	SAA	828
	SAA	997
	EK	40
	PDG	36
	TA	236
	HAP	2085
	HAP	2556
	SKA5	13
	EL	178
	P4	15
	M1	861
	M1	1037
	AE1	113
	AE1	926
	AE2	386
	AE5	970
	AE6	934
	AE6	942
	AE10	1182
	AE11	574
	DO	165
	KT2	368
	KT2	370
	KT3	230
	KT3	1154
	M8	307
	B	719
	B	753
	BP	131
	J6	649
	TH	104
	AM	701
	PFD	26
	SAA	418
	SAA	1043
	RL	374
	T18	62
	HAP	103
	SSC	21
	M1	222
	VP1	81
	VP6	2
	AE2	136
	AE6	385
	AE8	462
	AE11	145
	LMC	1
	KT1	418
	HIF	26
DWARF	FL	135
DWARFISH	M12	606
DWELL	AU	259
	AU	282
	WB	151
	M15	122
	M15	256
	M15	454

Word	Ref	No.
DWELL	GP	29
	ESK	12
DWELLERS	AM	905
DWELLING	HAP	1274
	SKA5	3
	EL	259
	M1	33
	G3	628
	AE2	952
DWELLINGS	AM	1072
	M1	396
	G3	805
	AE1	590
	AE3	189
DWELLS	RH	5
	P4	59
	M1	249
	G4	524
	AE6	41
	KT3	746
	M11	269
	M11	281
	M15	369
DWELT	EUO2	24
	M9	5
	M15	77
	CI	156
DWINDLE	EDGA	38
DWINDLED	MF	182
	TJD	91
DWINDLES	HAP	619
	PTS	23
DYE	J6	648
	AR	36
	HAP	2083
	J1	36
	P2	116
	M1	367
	AE3	43
	AE5	148
	AE8	920
	AE11	1136
	AE12	123
	M11	130
	M11	197
	M15	280
	M15	477
	SMP	56
	SAA	680
	G2	651
	AE4	951
	AE8	932
DYED	AE9	469
	AE10	494
	AE11	960
	AE12	193
	KT1	114
	TH	144
	M12	511
DYES	VP6	35
	MFL	20
	KT3	604
DYING	LCA	52
	AM	271
	PAL	5
	SKK	2
	SKK	15
	CM	62
	DA	6
	SSF	23
	AA	111
	SAA	1094
	PK	38
	DOD	22
	T23	66
	FS2	8
	FS3	18
	TA	205
	TA	221
	TA	272
	HAP	24
	HAP	948
	SSC	34
	BR	161
	ODA	43
	SSH	16
	J10	190
	P3	87
	P6	157
	M13	207
	R	5
	R	11
	R	17
	R	23
	VP2	46
	VP5	14

Word	Ref	No.
DYING	VP8	29
	VP8	85
	G3	413
	G3	772
	G3	826
	G4	382
	G4	656
	G4	661
	AE1	248
	AE4	753
	AE4	876
	AE4	893
	AE4	1005
	AE7	2
	AE9	492
	AE9	593
	AE9	606
	AE9	647
	AE9	723
	AE9	746
	AE10	653
	AE10	952
	AE10	1042
	AE10	1116
	AE10	1301
	AE11	647
	AE11	941
	AE11	1178
	AE11	1189
	AE11	1204
	AE12	86
	AE12	781
	AE12	930
	AE12	1067
	AE12	1367
	OAL	693
	OAE1	12
	MG	6
	KT3	800
	KT3	1097
	M8	343
	B	738
	CAM	155
	HIF	666
	C	79
	FL	378
	GP	93
	EWR	16
DYKES	G1	441
DYMAS	AE2	459
	AE2	531
	AE2	579
EAGER	HS	3
	AR	280
	AM	269
	AM	419
	AM	1120
	SEL4	24
	HP	77
	RL	221
	L4	8
	L4	45
	L4	282
	NS	5
	TA	112
	HAP	1076
	HAP	1718
	HAP	2479
	J1	120
	J6	167
	M1	713
	M1	1089
	HI	30
	G2	645
	G4	157
	AE1	424
	AE3	109
	AE3	182
	AE4	984
	AE5	8
	AE5	47
	AE5	196
	AE5	263
	AE5	330
	AE5	427
	AE5	603
	AE5	681
	AE6	53
	AE6	407
	AE7	691

Word	Ref	No.
EAGER	AE7	883
	AE8	288
	AE8	535
	AE8	584
	AE9	74
	AE9	238
	AE9	305
	AE9	476
	AE9	742
	AE10	531
	AE10	642
	AE10	921
	AE10	1003
	AE12	389
	AE12	417
	AE12	435
	AE12	575
	AE12	1091
	OAE2	38
	KT1	283
	KT2	248
	M8	91
	B	184
	BP	108
	M12	82
	M12	200
	AU	4
	AU	131
	AU	430
EAGERLY	B	20
	C	507
EAGERNESS	AM	343
EAGLE	HS	4
	AM	425
	J10	67
	VP9	17
	AE1	66
	AE9	600
	AE11	1105
	KT3	89
	TH	318
	M12	739
	M15	570
EAGLE-EYED	P4	48
EAGLE'S	KT3	477
	M8	54
EAGLES	PUO2	37
	HAP	733
	AE7	839
	OAL	135
EAGLET	JH	11
	BR	121
	TA	134
EAGRE	SAA	563
EANED	AR	7
EAR	EEL	5
	PC2	26
	DA	82
	PPC	2
	MD	31
	SAA	832
	ER	18
	T27	16
	TA	48
	HAP	1263
	HAP	2165
	HAP	2294
	HAP	2393
	J3	207
	J6	588
	J6	699
	J10	337
	J10	340
	P1	6
	P1	37
	P2	42
	P4	125
	P5	139
	P6	95
	M1	709
	G1	252
	G1	257
	AE1	218
	AE4	527
	AE9	551
	AE9	863
	AE10	1278
	AE11	947
	AE12	41
	OAE2	28
	M8	153
	BP	139
	HIF	527
	HIF	727
	HIF	737
	C	606

Word	Ref	No.
EAR	TH	106
	FL	113
	FL	196
	FL	370
	M12	453
	M12	587
	AU	293
EARL	WB	437
EARLIER	AE11	467
EARLIEST	VP8	18
EARL-MARSHAL	KT3	531
EARLY	HS	28
	AR	73
	AR	211
	LC	5
	AM	557
	AM	950
	PAR	12
	E	26
	EAZ	33
	UMR	6
	EPF	8
	ETG	5
	AA	23
	AA	585
	MD	26
	SAA	326
	SAA	965
	RL	136
	MO	11
	H9	25
	TA	454
	MN	4
	AK	28
	HAP	1531
	HAP	2204
	BR	111
	BR	165
	EL	215
	EL	324
	ODA	5
	J6	1
	J6	428
	P3	106
	P5	256
	M1	75
	M1	457
	HI	110
	MC	55
	MC	56
	GK	139
	G1	68
	G1	97
	G1	249
	G1	621
	G2	350
	G2	644
	G3	117
	G3	265
	G3	545
	AE4	572
	AE4	9
	AE4	184
	AE4	802
	AE4	840
	AE5	871
	AE6	1214
	AE8	541
	AE8	683
	AE9	614
	AE9	795
	AE10	517
	AE10	1171
	AE11	636
	OAL	218
	KT1	360
	KT1	533
	KT2	225
	KT3	125
	KT3	191
	KT3	435
	KT3	440
	KT3	1099
	B	623
	HIF	4
	M12	729
	CI	432
	PTP	45
	AS	24
EARN	AE8	547
	AE9	827
EARNED	SAA	369
	AE12	755
	TJD	88
EARNEST	AE1	540
	KT1	284

Headword	Ref	No.
EARTH	AE12	803
	AE12	934
	AE12	967
	AE12	998
	AE12	1126
	AE12	1133
	AE12	1178
	AE12	1278
	AE12	1293
	AE12	1303
	AE12	1346
	AF	71
	AF	82
	DO	71
	DO	83
	KT1	248
	KT1	414
	KT2	211
	KT2	351
	KT3	136
	KT3	216
	KT3	233
	KT3	535
	KT3	684
	KT3	699
	KT3	823
	KT3	1025
	KT3	1028
	TJD	209
	M8	194
	M8	207
	M8	366
	BP	13
	C	649
	C	748
	TH	206
	TH	334
	M11	37
	M11	339
	FL	93
	M12	57
	M12	162
	M12	482
	M12	523
	M12	675
	M12	737
	AU	130
	AU	455
	WB	218
	WB	387
	M15	26
	M15	93
	M15	111
	M15	129
	M15	215
	M15	373
	M15	376
	M15	385
	M15	403
	M15	420
	M15	442
	M15	470
	M15	527
	M15	528
	M15	548
	M15	620
	M15	659
	M15	660
	M15	671
	M15	699
	GP	7
	CI	44
	CI	122
	AS	91
EARTHEN	PUO5	5
	J3	334
	G2	536
	BP	100
EARTHENWARE	J3	280
	P2	107
	BP	99
EARTHLY	AR	257
	LC	94
	DC	48
	EMW	6
	HAP	11
	EL	82
	J6	685
	M1	61
	M1	262
	G4	541
	AE7	914
	AE12	1157
	KT3	902
	FL	483
	GP	98
EARTHQUAKE	AE3	529
	TH	91
	M12	689
EARTHQUAKES	J6	847
	BR	242
	G1	640
	M15	416
EARTH'S	LC	110
	SAA	889
	BR	237
	AE6	980
	M15	513
EARTHY	AA	637
	M1	108
	VCS	20
	AE6	990
	KT3	402
EASE	AR	105
	AR	159
	SMA	97
	LC	52
	AM	36
	AM	118
	AM	592
	AM	668
	AM	1037
	EWGR	38
	ECG1	6
	SCG1	35
	EMQW	24
	EAL	19
	EOE	17
	HP	130
	DA	189
	AA	27
	AA	47
	AA	168
	AA	691
	AA	708
	AA	755
	ELB	13
	MD	231
	MD	236
	SAA	31
	SAA	594
	SAA	641
	OE	3
	RL	268
	AT	8
	L3	108
	L3	291
	L4	263
	H2	59
	FS1	11
	GE	36
	HAP	201
	HAP	365
	HAP	568
	HAP	1159
	HAP	1378
	HAP	1482
	HAP	1579
	HAP	1617
	HAP	1680
	HAP	1814
	HAP	1834
	HAP	2039
	HAP	2324
	HAP	2331
	EKA	13
	SKA6	14
	EL	58
	EL	223
	EH	22
	J1	98
	J1	204
	J3	8
	J3	214
	J3	390
	J3	484
	J6	64
	J6	130
	J6	405
	J6	541
	J6	689
	J10	557
	P3	45
	P4	97
	P5	221
	P5	104
	P5	92
	P6	171
	M1	943
	M9	75
	M13	188
	R	6
EASE	R	12
	R	18
	MC	23
	VP1	5
	VP6	20
	VP7	93
	VP9	90
	VP10	86
	G1	184
	G1	408
	G2	298
	G2	336
	G2	580
	G2	632
	G2	750
	G2	794
	G3	779
	G4	137
	G4	197
	AE1	298
	AE2	142
	AE2	797
	AE3	104
	AE3	498
	AE3	934
	AE4	73
	AE4	281
	AE4	331
	AE4	769
	AE5	936
	AE6	221
	AE6	304
	AE7	127
	AE7	170
	AE7	497
	AE7	601
	AE7	862
	AE9	137
	AE9	264
	AE9	655
	AE11	611
	AE11	1012
	AE11	1065
	AE12	71
	AE12	614
	OAL	631
	KT1	54
	KT1	416
	KT2	47
	KT2	158
	KT2	359
	KT2	372
	KT3	688
	KT3	745
	TJD	67
	B	34
	B	210
	B	437
	BP	120
	HIF	342
	HIF	642
	C	226
	C	559
	C	711
	TH	38
	TH	44
	M11	498
	FL	88
	FL	294
	FL	324
	FL	407
	FL	562
	AU	250
	WB	145
	WB	501
	WB	518
	WB	527
	M15	113
	M15	282
	CI	210
	CI	223
	CI	550
EASED	EEL	12
	L2	42
	M1	497
	M9	63
	R	24
	HI	176
	G2	759
	AE1	326
	AE3	207
	AE4	10
	AE4	937
	AE6	489
	AE8	264
	B	606

EASED	WB	199	EASY	G2	641	EBBS	M15	263		
EASES	G3	486		G2	655	EBON	AT	41		
EASIER	RH	41		G2	663		G1	85		
	VHH	11		G3	122		G2	163		
	HAP	1496		G3	268		M11	293		
	HAP	2311		G3	303	EBUSUS	AE12	452		
	J16	77		G4	161	ECHION	M8	57		
	VP2	108		G4	392		M8	109		
EASILY	PMM	5		G4	704	ECHO	J3	173		
	PMQw	12		G4	778		VP10	11		
EAST	HS	50		OAL	384		VP10	77		
	AR	306		OAL	397		G3	78		
	VHH	54		OAL	504		AE3	886		
	AM	917		AE2	259		AE4	643		
	AM	1187		AE2	331		AE5	293		
	AA	731		AE2	517		AE5	489		
	HAP	1122		AE4	309		SMP	34		
	M1	457		AE4	800		SMP	36		
	G1	509		AE5	1091	ECHOED	DA	97		
	AE1	126		AE6	193		AE1	1048		
	AE2	567		AE6	916		AE8	316		
	AE3	700		AE8	124		KT1	90		
	AE9	877		AE9	243		FL	117		
	OAL	205		AE9	686		M12	647		
	KT3	545		AE10	790	ECHOES	MF	47		
	KT3	566		AE11	95		TA	320		
	M11	98		AE11	714		HAP	2185		
	M11	123		AE12	903		P1	200		
EASTER	ETL	20		OAL	9		M1	458		
	PKK	18		OAL	715		G4	668		
EASTERN	AM	10		KT2	225		AE11	52		
	AM	100		KT3	697		M8	102		
	AM	408		TJD	97		C	747		
	AM	1213		B	268	ECHOING	M12	69		
	HAP	379		B	460		PAA	37		
	HAP	1093		CAM	249		HI	194		
	ODA	7		HIF	293	ECLIPSE	SAA	931		
	M1	75		TH	426		HAP	1180		
	M1	1085		M12	731		J6	602		
	G2	463		GP	134		DO	105		
	G2	620		CI	305		KT3	591		
	AE1	392	EAT	AA	107	ECLIPSED	AM	359		
	AE6	1142		SAA	424		T18	42		
	AE8	908		SAA	482		HAP	1895		
	AF	10		HAP	1424		MFL	13		
	KT2	458		HAP	2257	ECLIPSES	G2	680		
	KT3	133		J3	280		AE1	1041		
	FL	165		J6	104	ECONOMY	EL	76		
	WB	321		J6	826	ECSTASIES	AR	228		
EASTWARD	KT2	448		P1	117	ECSTASY	J6	92		
EASY	HS	29		P3	28		FL	120		
	AR	63		P3	228	EDDIES	AM	376		
	AR	92		AE7	169		AE6	411		
	PIE	22		AE9	824		AE11	459		
	STL	12		OAL	543	EDDY	AE3	542		
	EM	4		OAE2	2	EDDY-WINDS	G1	505		
	E	15		C	193	EDEN	PUF	27		
	HP	173		FL	421		SAA	1055		
	SSF	9		M15	206		TJD	96		
	AA	180		M15	361	EDENBOROUGH	PUO3	7		
	AA	191	EATEN	P5	275	EDEN'S	D	6		
	AA	215		G3	674		GK	90		
	AA	325		C	766	EDGE	AM	500		
	AA	696	EATING	J1	201		DA	199		
	AA	958		HIF	643		AE6	992		
	AA	894	EATS	AM	946		AE11	967		
	D	21		PCB	4		KT3	502		
	OE	25		J3	237		M8	138		
	OE	31		J6	144	EDGED	G4	24		
	RL	96		P1	69		AE8	826		
	L3	34		P4	60		FL	166		
	L3	187		P4	73	EDGES	M8	96		
	H2	54		G3	843	EDGING	AT	52		
	TA	281		AE5	893	EDICT	HAP	2541		
	HAP	269		M15	692	EDICTS	AR	316		
	HAP	1230	EBB	EUO	33	EDIFICE	OAL	74		
	HAP	1370		H29	54	EDIFIED	OE	19		
	HAP	1419		TA	139		GP	133		
	HAP	1693		TA	149	EDMOND-BERRY	PLB	20		
	HAP	1972		TJD	174	EDUCATE	AM	580		
	STS2	12	EBBED	AE2	225		G4	79		
	STS3	9	EBBING	HS	129	EDUCATION	HAP	1683		
	SKA3	2		AA	226	EDWARD	BR	134		
	J3	128		L4	84		MC	45		
	J3	370		T27	94		MC	46		
	J10	45		M1	566	EDWARD'S	BR	142		
	P3	39		AE6	154	EDWARDS	AM	322		
	HI	99		AE8	749		AE7	318		
	MC	20		AE9	36	EFFACE	EL	227		
	VP2	15		AE10	426	EFFACED	AR	130		
	VP7	66		KT3	119	EFFECT	A	10		
	G1	117		AS	97		AA	303		
	G1	539		AM	645		SAA	169		
	G2	283	EBBS	PK	1		L3	154		
	G2	345		PP	12		HAP	157		
	G2	604		MFL	32		HAP	1671		

Word	Code	No.
EFFECT	HAP	1812
	HAP	2516
	J10	332
	AE8	60
	AE12	633
	KT3	427
	KT3	767
	KT3	1026
	B	730
	HIF	412
	C	810
	TH	230
	M12	639
	AU	229
	AU	351
	WB	202
EFFECTS	AA	427
	AA	1003
	RL	54
	RL	164
	HAP	210
	HAP	1619
	HAP	2380
	HAP	2534
	J10	90
	VP1	99
	G2	366
	G2	699
	AE2	130
	AE4	811
	AE5	1031
	AE12	878
	HIF	2
	M15	493
	M15	498
	AS	33
EFFIMINATE	P1	172
	OAL	572
EFFIMINATED	P6	87
EFFORT	J10	414
	AE12	1311
EFFORTS	AE9	1101
	B	724
EFFUSION	HIF	175
EGERIAN	AE7	1045
	AE7	1064
EGG	C	35
	C	466
EGGS	PMM	8
	HAP	1877
	J6	667
	G1	523
	G3	633
	G3	668
	BP	97
EGGSHELL	P5	268
EGLANTINE	FL	72
	FL	96
	FL	130
EGYPT	AA	283
	AA	705
	SAA	231
	SAA	571
	SAA	677
	SAA	1004
	HAP	2099
	M9	165
	G1	317
	G4	306
	AE11	406
	OAL	731
EGYPTIAN	PA	30
	EUO	27
	AA	118
	RL	213
	HAP	1110
	HAP	2339
	J10	439
	M1	1040
	G2	167
	AE8	912
	M8	20
	C	384
	AS	91
	AM	367
EGYPTIAN'S	AM	183
EGYPTIANS	AE8	937
EGYPT'S	SAA	671
	SAA	692
	SAA	711
	SAA	749
	SAA	1077
	G4	410
EIGHT	BR	102
	J6	323
	G1	251

Word	Code	No.
EIGHT	M12	20
EIGHTH	HAP	1497
EJECT	AE11	932
EJECTS	M11	110
ELATED	AE5	272
ELBOW	M11	345
ELBOWS	J3	395
ELDER	PWG	49
	ECG1	14
	PC1	17
	SAA	548
	HAP	809
	P1	22
	AE9	730
	KT1	324
	B	704
ELDERS	AA	404
	SAA	256
ELDERSHIP	KT1	309
ELDEST	AA	458
	AA	831
	EK	10
	EL	212
	ODA	51
	AE1	921
	AE7	741
	C1	50
ELEAN	AM	223
	G1	89
	G3	315
	EH	3
ELEANOR	EL	10
ELEANORA'S	HAP	2515
ELECT	AE1	593
	AE12	1155
ELECTING	SAA	553
ELECTION	SAA	1136
	HAP	981
	B	410
ELECTORS	GE	48
	PSH	30
ELECTRA	AE8	179
	AE8	180
ELECTRA'S	AE1	41
ELECTS	AE10	400
ELEGIES	UDH	92
	J1	3
	P1	95
ELEGY	DA	2
	DO	129
ELEMENT	AM	841
	ELB	27
	SAA	1121
	AE1	753
	AE5	898
	DO	115
ELEMENTAL	G1	612
ELEMENTS	AM	646
	SAA	1081
	AE11	238
	M15	362
	M15	394
	G3	41
	AM	235
ELEPHANT	J10	255
	AE3	595
ELEPHANTS	AR	36
	J10	241
	M8	28
	J1	60
ELEVEN	J10	182
ELF	C	655
	WB	3
ELFS	SAA	985
ELIAB	SAA	986
ELIS	AE6	792
	M12	725
ELISA	DO	162
ELISA'S	RH	59
	RH	65
ELIZA	AE4	146
ELIZABETH	T27	35
ELIZA'S	AE1	932
	AE4	485
	AE4	968
	VP3	161
ELLS	T27	20
ELM	AE6	395
ELMS	HI	71
	VP1	78
	VP5	4
	VP10	96
	G1	4
	G1	249
	G2	24
	G2	100

Word	Code	No.
ELMS	G2	120
	G2	302
	G2	453
	G2	626
	G2	496
	G2	506
	G3	580
	G4	213
ELOCUTION	P5	19
	AU	110
ELOQUENCE	AA	869
	SAA	1022
	RL	333
	L1	57
	J10	12
	J10	187
	VCS	19
	OAL	92
	OAL	524
	OAL	527
	M12	246
	AU	221
	AU	364
	AU	592
	GP	17
ELOQUENT	RH	60
	GK	107
ELORUS	AE3	917
ELUDE	M12	140
ELVES	HAP	214
	WB	34
ELYSIAN	SAA	624
	AE5	962
	AE6	545
	AE6	1008
	AE6	1228
ELYSIUM	FL	145
ELYSIUM'S	G1	55
EMANATION	MFL	10
EMATHIAN	G1	659
EMBALMED	KT3	978
EMBARK	G2	57
	AE4	787
EMBARKED	AE2	332
	AE6	1244
EMBASSADORS	PUO1	16
	AE7	401
	AE11	181
EMBASSY	HAP	2427
	GK	54
	AE7	650
	AE11	350
	AU	318
EMBATTLED	G4	4
	G4	446
	AE7	729
	C	50
EMBELLISH	G3	456
EMBELLISHED	J3	34
EMBELLISHES	ER	61
EMBERS	AE3	749
	AE5	973
	AE8	542
	HIF	119
EMBEZZLED	P6	150
EMBITTERS	HIF	775
EMBLEM	SAA	336
	HAP	2350
	BR	32
	KT3	915
	TJD	63
	P3	74
	FL	283
	FL	545
EMBODIED	AE4	582
	AE7	974
	M9	193
EMBOLDENED	AE9	740
	FL	12
EMBOSSED	J1	114
	VP3	60
	AE1	904
	AE6	25
	AE8	831
	AE9	349
	AE11	104
	AE11	296
	KT3	65
	AU	178
	AK	173
EMBRACE	HAP	273
	HAP	1213
	HAP	1372
	PKA	16
	J3	116
	J6	168

EMBRACE	J6	385	EMBRACES	AE5	1002	EMPIRE	AM	372
	J6	501		AE6	948		AM	630
	M1	30		AE6	1135		AM	797
	M1	589		AE7	363		ECD	17
	M1	635		AE8	514		HP	135
	M1	732		AE8	638		DA	12
	M1	752		OAL	886		DA	132
	M1	812		M12	33		AA	371
	M1	975		M12	645		AA	411
	M13	86	EMBRACING	AR	174		AA	703
	HI	31		SAA	602		AA	963
	G2	60		G2	302		MF	4
	G2	389		AE1	1205		MF	133
	AE1	565		M12	576		ER	28
	AE2	670	EMBROIDERED	J3	450		AK	88
	AE2	929		J10	58		HAP	277
	AE3	130		AE1	674		SAA	27
	AE3	416		AE4	384		SAA	120
	AE3	451		AE5	148		SAA	151
	AE3	644		AE8	225		SAA	743
	AE4	885		AE8	777		SAA	1114
	AE5	48		AE9	841		L3	6
	AE5	699		KT3	37		FS4	12
	AE5	971		M10	48		BR	33
	AE6	806	EMBROIL	AA	501		M1	100
	AE6	932	EMBROILED	RL	266		M1	237
	AE6	1143		AE7	568		MC	6
	AE7	764	EMBRUE	AE12	1003		G1	53
	AE7	884	EMBRUED	AE3	66		G2	782
	AE8	740		AE12	679		G4	93
	AE8	761		TH	114		G4	141
	AE9	269	EMBRYO	M15	329		AE1	26
	AE12	222	EMERALD	L4	101		AE1	119
	AE12	419	EMERALDS	KT3	69		AE1	198
	AE12	642		FL	162		AE1	378
	OAL	436	EMERGES	M15	278		AE1	391
	OAE2	25	EMERGING	HIF	672		AE1	736
	OAE2	43	EMETRIUS	KT3	63		AE2	5
	B	160		KT3	640		AE2	28
	CAM	309	EMILIA	KT1	10		AE2	74
	HIF	52		KT1	170		AE2	215
	HIF	562		KT1	206		AE3	117
	HIF	588		KT1	394		AE3	149
	M11	381		KT3	161		AE4	64
	M11	407	EMILIA'S	KT1	560		AE4	778
	FL	43		KT1	582		AE6	626
	FL	400		KT3	332		AE6	742
	CI	6		KT3	1140		AE7	204
	CI	585	EMILY	DO	33		AE7	346
EMBRACED	HS	89		DO	39		AE7	411
	AA	118		KT1	180		AE8	431
	HAP	560		KT1	232		AE8	436
	M9	164		KT1	271		AE8	497
	VP5	32		KT1	389		AE8	528
	AE1	861		KT1	441		AE8	614
	AE1	1035		KT1	459		AE10	81
	AE2	716		KT1	521		AE11	442
	AE2	918		KT1	590		KT2	321
	AE3	609		KT2	32		TH	350
	AE3	798		KT2	113		M11	498
	AE4	717		KT2	129	EMPIRE'S	AR	48
	AE4	933		KT2	136	EMPIRES	BR	76
	AE4	985		KT2	228		J6	317
	AE8	165		KT2	284		G1	626
	AE8	485		KT2	297		M15	626
	AE8	817		KT2	397	EMPIRIC	LC	67
	AE11	67		KT2	432		DC	7
	AE11	665		KT3	190	EMPIRIC-LIKE	PUO1	22
	OAL	850		KT3	312	EMPLOY	SMA	49
	KT1	46		KT3	539		SMA	67
	KT1	238		KT3	547		PT	29
	KT3	107		KT3	661		HP	182
	KT3	804		KT3	694		HP	247
	TJD	142		KT3	716		DA	166
	TJD	205		KT3	775		PUF	29
	B	230		KT3	789		AA	553
	M10	30		KT3	841		SAA	529
	CAM	157		KT3	874		SAA	829
	HIF	678		KT3	926		SAA	1069
	TH	419		KT3	949		L4	9
	M11	483		KT3	1015		J6	786
	FL	311		KT3	1120		M1	381
	M12	273		KT3	1125		M1	613
	M12	576	EMISSARIES	AA	210		M9	56
	WB	537	EMISSARY	HAP	2391		VP2	107
	CI	282	EMISSION	HAP	647		G2	551
EMBRACES	AM	465	EMMETS	SAA	920		G3	58
	CM	40	EMONIDES	AE10	747		G4	78
	AA	710	EMPALAMOS	M8	127		AE1	72
	DOD	21	EMPEROR	PUO3	19		AE1	840
	J10	504	EMPIRE	HS	88		AE2	40
	M9	148		AR	70		AE3	315
	M13	100		AR	298		AE4	616
	G4	721		SMA	93		AE5	833
	AE1	1001		SMA	100		AE7	176
	AE2	1078		AM	33		AE7	336

Word	Ref	No.
EMPLOY	AE9	539
	AE11	429
	AE11	579
	OAE1	23
	OAE2	35
	OAE2	73
	M8	162
	B	175
	M12	166
	M12	218
	M12	307
	AU	73
	AU	496
	M15	697
	CI	626
	AS	64
EMPLOYED	AM	573
	SAA	125
	SAA	152
	SAA	642
	RL	232
	HAP	2237
	PSH	40
	J3	485
	J6	859
	HI	185
	G2	749
	G4	261
	AE4	545
	AE4	634
	AE10	981
	AE11	350
	AE12	1320
	DO	99
	KT1	605
	TJD	132
	B	294
	HIF	793
	C	590
	FL	138
	M12	39
	M12	153
	M12	776
	M12	445
	AU	31
	AU	220
	AU	315
	AU	344
	WB	356
	M15	147
	M15	389
	CI	70
EMPLOYMENTS	J1	191
EMPLOYS	LC	108
	AM	362
	CM	3
	EK	38
	EL	123
	J1	17
	M1	636
	G4	748
	AE1	695
	AE5	949
	AE9	11
	AE9	460
	DO	158
	HIF	143
	M11	188
	M11	238
EMPORIUM	AM	1205
	MD	167
EMPRESS	AM	845
	CM	51
	MF	94
	P6	102
EMPTIED	L3	138
	J1	136
	M9	158
	BP	123
	HIF	803
	AS	56
	AS	87
EMPTIES	HIF	144
EMPTINESS	LC	42
	TA	401
EMPTY	LC	22
	LCA	17
	AM	1144
	SEL4	6
	PNH	36
	PC2	21
	MF	69
	AT	47
	AT	48
	L3	120
	T27	5
EMPTY	HAP	1913
	PP	43
	EL	243
	J1	187
	J6	358
	J10	28
	J10	209
	P1	33
	P1	94
	P4	38
	P4	120
	P6	85
	M1	83
	M1	663
	M1	715
	M1	909
	VP1	47
	VP3	153
	VP6	26
	G1	279
	G1	665
	G2	428
	G3	125
	G3	271
	G3	677
	G4	158
	G4	284
	G4	364
	G4	377
	G4	405
	G4	493
	G4	516
	G4	710
	AE1	88
	AE1	202
	AE1	652
	AE2	721
	AE2	1079
	AE3	16
	AE4	319
	AE5	13
	AE5	500
	AE6	57
	AE6	118
	AE6	397
	AE6	403
	AE6	408
	AE6	654
	AE6	802
	AE6	952
	AE7	529
	AE8	64
	AE9	281
	AE9	658
	AE9	736
	AE10	126
	AE10	630
	AE10	833
	AE10	911
	AE10	985
	AE11	1166
	AE12	83
	AE12	207
	AE12	692
	AE12	900
	AE12	966
	AE12	1180
	AE12	1287
	OAL	845
	MG	21
	AF	100
	M8	37
	M8	174
	M8	235
	B	416
	C	163
	M11	28
	M11	243
	M11	382
	M12	81
	M12	444
	M12	523
	M12	622
	M12	742
	AU	250
	AU	520
	WB	22
	WB	390
	M15	223
	M15	252
	M15	370
	M15	632
	CI	313
	CI	323
	AM	1113
	GK	80
EMPYREAN		
EMULATE		
EMULATE	AE1	1016
	AE8	480
	AE10	395
	C	650
EMULATED	AE12	523
EMULATING	AE4	835
	AE6	789
EMULATION	SMA	75
	TA	162
	GK	142
	CI	558
EMULOUS	HAP	1284
	AE10	518
EN	ET	15
ENAMORED	J6	435
	M1	634
ENCELADUS	AE3	755
ENCHAINED	VP1	56
ENCHANT	AA	423
	EMKG	16
ENCHANTED	PT	18
	PAZ	10
	RL	28
	FL	149
ENCHANTING	J10	336
	VP2	19
	AE6	178
	FL	49
ENCHANTMENT	SAA	909
ENCHASE	J10	40
	G2	725
ENCHASED	AE1	831
	AE10	205
ENCLINED	AA	326
	PRH	32
ENCLOSE	AE2	572
ENCLOSED	J6	27
	HI	71
	G3	567
	KT1	167
	KT1	205
	KT2	440
	KT2	463
	KT2	663
	B	80
	C	37
	C	252
ENCLOSURE	HAP	577
	G3	801
ENCOMPASS	MO	25
	AE2	702
	HIF	89
ENCOMPASSED	HAP	576
	VP3	70
	G4	474
	AE2	400
	AE3	503
	BP	16
ENCOMPASSES	G4	688
ENCOUNTER	G4	125
	AE8	918
	AE10	593
	AE10	759
	M11	122
ENCOUNTERED	AE12	786
ENCOUNTERING	AE12	439
	AE12	711
	M12	423
	AU	333
ENCOUNTERS	PC1	25
ENCOURAGE	G3	201
	G4	123
	AE11	621
	OAE2	65
ENCOURAGED	HAP	532
	HAP	2331
	AE3	803
	AE5	943
	AE11	789
ENCOURAGER	TA	383
ENCOURAGES	AE11	1074
ENCOURAGING	AA	335
	WB	38
ENCREASE	AR	16
	FS2	13
	HAP	369
	HAP	1039
	HAP	1682
	HAP	2503
	HAP	2542
	HAP	2559
	P6	183
	HI	136
	G3	753
	AE12	276
	OAL	265

ENCREASE	OAL	816
ENCREASED	HAP	18
	HAP	197
	HAP	284
	HAP	2232
	BR	166
ENCREASES	HAP	520
	G3	481
ENCREASING	HAP	2407
	BR	156
	BR	230
	J3	42
ENCROACH	PMK	15
ENCROACHING	HAP	885
	G3	824
ENCUMBERED	J16	68
	KT2	265
	B	267
END	HS	47
	AR	194
	RH	42
	RH	95
	LC	70
	AM	23
	AM	816
	PWGR	10
	SM1	11
	PTW	28
	DA	120
	EUF	34
	AA	352
	AA	946
	MF	141
	SAA	159
	PK	20
	RL	314
	RL	38
	AT	121
	DOD	25
	L3	136
	L3	233
	L4	203
	T23	45
	TA	414
	HH	29
	HAP	61
	HAP	116
	HAP	491
	HAP	775
	HAP	941
	HAP	980
	HAP	2314
	HAP	2583
	SSH	10
	J3	453
	J6	733
	J10	42
	J10	179
	J10	256
	J10	402
	J10	423
	P3	115
	P3	129
	P3	189
	P3	212
	P5	235
	P5	211
	P6	187
	P1	26
	P1	914
	VP10	100
	G4	175
	AE1	331
	AE2	14
	AE2	202
	AE2	837
	AE2	1064
	AE3	118
	AE3	199
	AE3	466
	AE3	506
	AE3	546
	AE3	658
	AE4	916
	AE6	98
	AE6	468
	AE6	917
	AE7	171
	AE7	411
	AE7	825
	AE8	57
	AE9	184
	AE9	198
	AE9	479
	AE10	176
	AE12	61
END	AE12	68
	AE12	838
	AE12	1168
	OAL	248
	OAL	527
	OAL	820
	DO	142
	KT1	413
	KT1	554
	KT3	258
	KT3	637
	KT3	804
	KT3	888
	KT3	1003
	KT3	1040
	KT3	1101
	HIF	772
	C	112
	C	184
	C	471
	C	709
	TH	222
	FL	59
	FL	224
	M12	31
	M12	799
	ETP	34
	ESK	10
	PMK	27
ENDANGERED	AA	750
ENDEAR	PM	34
ENDEARMENTS	L4	282
ENDEAVOR	SEL4	17
	HAP	2073
	STS1	15
	SSH	1
	AE2	518
	AE12	1321
	TH	30
ENDEAVORED	GK	144
	B	459
ENDEAVORING	L4	137
	HAP	2401
	J10	332
	CI	247
ENDEAVORS	HS	147
	PUO4	27
	RL	25
	RL	38
	L2	13
	VP8	153
	G1	60
	G2	592
	TJD	81
ENDED	PRL	10
	AM	561
	SSF	19
	L3	176
	J1	193
	AE1	307
	AE4	140
	AE5	476
	AE5	623
	AE6	365
	AE9	1023
	AE11	155
	OAL	862
	KT2	251
	KT3	179
	B	113
	HIF	797
	TH	57
	FL	134
	FL	453
	M12	581
	AE6	609
	AF	101
ENDING	HAP	1310
ENDITE	BP	95
ENDIVE	PUF	14
ENDLESS	RL	36
	RL	215
	L3	106
	L4	58
	L4	161
	HAP	146
	HAP	963
	EL	294
	ODA	46
	ODA	80
	J6	373
	J6	525
	M1	57
	M1	82
	VCS	34
	SLT1	24
ENDLESS	G1	218
	AE1	15
	AE1	54
	AE1	380
	AE2	175
	AE3	931
	AE4	36
	AE4	134
	AE4	992
	AE5	824
	AE6	600
	AE6	1042
	AE7	319
	AE7	592
	AE9	110
	AE10	38
	AE10	162
	AE10	944
	AE12	468
	AE12	1206
	LMC	10
	KT1	508
	AU	331
ENDLONG	KT3	691
ENDOW	OAL	625
ENDOWED	AE7	442
	WB	158
ENDOWMENTS	SAA	1016
	EL	270
ENDS	SMA	98
	SKK	3
	SKK	16
	AA	494
	AA	740
	AA	806
	G3	90
	G4	273
	PLB	45
	MD	274
	SAA	113
	SAA	247
	SAA	511
	EDGA	40
	RL	131
	HAP	115
	HAP	1347
	HAP	2550
	EDS	21
	P3	100
	M13	49
	VP4	9
	G1	319
	G2	33
	G2	560
	AE4	114
	AE5	792
	AE7	175
	AE9	650
	AE10	304
	AE11	1022
	AE12	562
	AE12	635
	KT3	386
	KT3	524
	TJD	65
	BP	1
	HIF	227
	WB	435
	WB	442
ENDUE	AE8	747
ENDUED	AA	883
	HAP	18
	HAP	1728
	ODA	63
	PPS	13
	M13	180
	G4	323
	OAL	668
	KT3	14
	KT3	334
	M8	400
	B	424
	M12	739
	AU	448
	M15	120
	M15	466
	M15	555
ENDURE	AM	665
	ML	9
	SAA	866
	EAA	12
	HAP	1337
	SKA6	21
	J10	104
	SFL	11
	AE1	277

Word	Ref	No.
ENDURE	AE1	289
	AE9	91
	AE10	699
	AE10	1240
	AE11	760
	KT1	479
	KT2	109
	KT2	176
	C	128
ENDURED	RL	271
	HAP	1180
	AE1	174
	AE3	421
	KT1	543
ENDURES	LMC	7
	KT2	148
ENDYMION	AT	114
	J10	491
ENEMIES	EEL	28
	PM	21
	HP	237
	AA	91
	AA	104
	AA	711
	HAP	2400
	M1	385
	AE1	106
	AE10	528
	AE11	1117
	AE11	1312
	OAL	227
ENEMY	VHH	4
	AA	186
	TA	183
	HAP	1422
	G3	361
	AE3	169
	AE8	815
	AE9	238
	AE12	162
	AE12	1104
	AE12	1305
	KT2	103
	KT2	185
ENERGY	M1	104
	VCS	14
	G2	77
	AE10	26
ENERVATE	GK	50
ENERVATES	G4	290
ENFLAME	SAA	1031
ENFLAMING	SAA	838
ENFORCE	KT3	155
ENFRANCHISEMENT	P5	104
ENGAGE	LCA	47
	PCB	32
	AA	266
	AA	1018
	SAA	511
	SAA	648
	SAA	720
	SAA	860
	SAA	959
	SAA	1028
	SAA	1112
	L4	79
	SKA6	3
	J6	352
	P5	27
	G3	341
	G3	418
	G3	625
	AE2	457
	AE7	61
	AE8	530
	AE8	895
	AE9	688
	AE11	338
	EMKG	20
ENGAGED	AE11	482
	AE12	1182
ENGAGES	G3	573
ENGENDER	M1	64
ENGENDERED	MD	174
	SAA	922
ENGINE	RH	22
	G3	374
	AE2	60
	AE2	345
	AE7	530
	AE9	191
	M8	123
ENGINEERS	PMQ	11
ENGINE-HAND	P4	86
ENGINE'S	AE11	919
ENGINES	AM	915
ENGINES	EUO	22
	EOE	12
	AA	917
	AE5	544
	KT1	587
	C	293
ENGLAND	AM	789
	AM	791
	PCD	25
	PNH	48
	PUF	18
	MD	123
	PDG	29
	ER	48
	EMI	2
	SKA4	25
	SKA4	26
	SKA4	27
	SKA4	28
	SKA4	29
	EHC	35
	DO	93
	ETP	34
ENGLAND'S	AR	230
	PAA	26
	TJD	152
	FL	548
ENGLISH	HS	115
	AR	216
	DC	22
	DC	34
	PWG	52
	PWG	53
	PWG	58
	PWG	59
	EWG	16
	VHH	25
	AM	106
	AM	131
	AM	147
	AM	169
	AM	273
	AM	301
	AM	336
	AM	340
	AM	401
	AM	423
	AM	572
	AM	638
	AM	677
	AM	714
	AM	757
	AM	778
	AM	781
	AM	801
	AM	825
	AM	840
	PMQ	2
	EEL	11
	PCG1	39
	PAR	20
	PCD	16
	PCD	32
	ECD	21
	EUO	28
	PNH	40
	PAZ	39
	EAZ	20
	PTW	24
	PO	9
	PSF	34
	PUO3	9
	PUO3	28
	EUF	28
	MD	2
	ER	60
	ER	77
	TA	301
	TA	505
	GE	52
	EH	4
	MC	10
	C	744
	PWR	39
	PCD	5
	BR	41
	PP	20
ENGLISHMEN	J3	205
ENGROSS	SAA	286
ENGROSSED	M1	525
ENIGMA	M1	787
ENIPEUS	G4	525
ENJOINED	AE3	914
	AE6	172
	AE6	1002
	KT1	31
ENJOINED	KT3	496
	KT3	904
	B	591
	C	77
ENJOY	AR	43
	SIE	8
	AM	110
	AM	158
	AA	554
	AA	763
	ELB	4
	SAA	940
	SDG	16
	SDG	18
	SDG	19
	L4	52
	T18	33
	H29	50
	H29	81
	TA	409
	HAP	237
	HAP	1676
	BR	352
	J1	120
	J6	46
	J6	498
	J10	492
	P6	29
	M1	252
	M9	119
	M9	133
	VP2	8
	VP9	68
	G1	403
	G3	153
	G3	474
	AE2	866
	AE3	437
	AE3	645
	AE4	890
	AE5	255
	AE6	883
	AE7	182
	AE7	502
	AE7	595
	AE11	416
	AE11	580
	AE12	539
	OAL	424
	OAL	812
	KT3	801
	TJD	159
	CAM	234
	C	761
	FL	569
	M15	357
	CI	625
ENJOYED	CM	129
	SAA	126
	SAA	1114
	RL	29
	RL	233
	AT	105
	L3	128
	L3	153
	T27	2
	HAP	20
	M1	818
	G2	750
	G2	787
	KT1	223
	TJD	4
	B	183
	B	736
	C	576
	FL	139
	FL	323
	AU	219
ENJOYING	AF	104
	KT3	1096
ENJOYMENT	OAL	512
ENJOYS	EUO2	19
	AA	913
	EL	122
	J1	76
	J16	91
	M9	211
	G2	660
	AE4	318
	TJD	4
	CI	640
ENLARGE	AR	244
	AM	1108
	HAP	665
	HAP	869
	G3	524

Word	Source	Ref
ENLARGE	BP	115
ENLARGED	HAP	1339
	M1	151
	AF	164
	AF	174
ENLIGHTEN	AE4	242
	WB	411
	AE2	823
ENLIGHTENS	CI	466
ENLIVENED	JH	9
	M15	646
ENLIVENER	WB	427
ENMITIES	HAP	2429
ENMITY	HAP	30
ENNIUS	P6	16
	P6	26
ENNOBLED	M12	112
	AU	28
ENNOBLES	AA	641
	AU	237
ENNOMUS	AU	403
ENORMOUS	P1	249
	AE6	570
	AE6	785
	AE12	1303
	M12	487
ENOUGH	SMA	10
	AM	1065
	PMM	11
	PA	2
	ECG1	18
	PCG2	11
	EMQW	1
	EM	23
	PLN	41
	PUO1	42
	PC1	27
	PKK	16
	PKK	18
	PCB	20
	HP	256
	DA	78
	DA	94
	PUF	32
	PDG	31
	RL	409
	AT	126
	PD	18
	AK	14
	HH	15
	HAP	1147
	HAP	1271
	HAP	1477
	BR	152
	BR	165
	BR	166
	BR	169
	PP	17
	EL	239
	EL	358
	J1	141
	J10	169
	J16	91
	P3	46
	P5	115
	P5	26
	M13	211
	GK	25
	GK	117
	G2	742
	AE2	72
	AE2	385
	AE2	386
	AE2	868
	AE4	483
	AE9	174
	AE9	176
	AE9	250
	AE11	563
	OAL	535
	KT1	396
	KT3	874
	TJD	158
	B	324
	BP	65
	BP	157
	C	8
	C	567
	TH	402
	AU	104
	PTP	50
ENOW	PKK	25
	PR	17
	EDG	35
ENQUIRE	AM	785
	MD	164
ENQUIRE	SAA	546
	RL	388
	HAP	1444
	P1	154
	AE2	159
	AE2	691
	AE6	69
	OAL	167
	OAL	251
ENQUIRED	HAP	2354
	M1	839
	VP7	9
	AE1	1051
	AE10	238
	AE10	1196
	B	695
	CAM	106
	WB	121
	M15	12
ENQUIRES	J6	731
	J6	764
	M1	1056
	AE6	766
	AE8	414
ENQUIRING	C	259
	M12	88
	WB	256
ENQUIRY	DO	112
ENRAGED	G3	388
ENRICH	B	554
ENRICHED	RH	43
	SAA	548
	ER	9
	AE1	626
	AE4	293
ENROLLED	KT1	601
ENSIGNS	AE1	687
	AE7	869
	AE10	272
	AE11	32
	OAL	207
	HIF	20
	HIF	516
ENSLAVE	SAA	219
	L4	95
	AE6	572
ENSLAVED	AA	523
	M15	667
ENSNARE	SAA	865
ENSTALLS	SAA	913
ENSUE	HAP	485
	EH	32
	M1	901
	AE1	131
	AE6	1139
	AE9	61
	AE9	621
	AE10	1048
	AE11	1095
	AE11	1221
	AE12	477
	KT3	304
	KT3	505
	HIF	113
	GP	124
ENSUED	J1	127
	M1	140
	AE1	479
	AE2	129
	AE3	57
	AE11	1211
	M12	387
	AU	198
	L4	85
ENSUES	WB	147
	CI	633
ENSUING	M9	159
	G1	112
	AE10	342
	AE10	363
	AE12	173
	KT1	121
	KT3	118
	B	239
	B	260
	FL	440
ENSURER	HAP	148
ENT	DC	32
ENTAIL	SAA	770
ENTAILED	TA	310
	GP	114
ENTANGLE	M1	413
ENTANGLED	L4	81
ENTELLUS	AE5	515
	AE5	525
	AE5	545
ENTELLUS	AE5	560
	AE5	583
	AE5	592
	AE5	595
ENTELLUS'	AE5	616
ENTER	PD	59
	J16	59
	AE1	886
	AE2	690
	AE6	17
	DO	112
	M11	169
	AU	573
	CI	577
ENTERED	AR	183
	AM	251
	PWGR	9
	L3	285
	HAP	1892
	EL	261
	J1	256
	J10	277
	M1	284
	AE4	515
	AE4	950
	KT3	103
	BP	42
	FL	25
	KT1	106
	M12	409
	M12	498
	AU	319
	AU	606
ENTERING	AM	516
	HAP	1269
	J6	536
	AE1	52
	AE1	612
	AE1	733
	AE2	653
	AE2	693
	AE3	206
	KT3	558
	CAM	154
	HIF	460
	HIF	596
	M11	300
	M12	78
	CI	549
ENTERPRISE	AE4	930
	AE6	944
	AE7	660
	AE8	24
	AE12	526
	KT1	576
	KT3	2
	AU	301
	CI	364
ENTERPRIZED	J6	454
ENTERS	DA	204
	HAP	1278
	AE1	1010
	AE2	315
	AE4	737
	AE5	444
	AE12	464
	KT3	562
ENTERTAIN	AR	248
	PFD	28
	SAA	623
	HAP	292
	HAP	1311
	EL	52
	P6	174
	VP1	2
	AE1	845
	AE3	876
	AE10	886
	FL	15
	M12	229
ENTERTAINED	AE3	452
	KT1	602
	B	437
	M15	20
ENTERTAINMENT	PCB	30
	BP	118
ENTERTAINS	CI	563
ENTHRONED	SAA	663
ENTHUSIASMS	JH	18
ENTHUSIAST	AF	163
	AF	173
ENTHUSIASTIC	AA	530
ENTICING	G3	337
ENTIRE	EAZ	4
	HAP	989
	HAP	1099

Word	Ref	No.	Word	Ref	No.	Word	Ref	No.
ENTIRE	G3	115	ENVIOUS	AE12	867	EPITHET	J10	459
	AE1	351		AE12	1274	EPITOME	AA	546
ENTIRELY	EL	189		KT3	792		AE3	449
	AE11	1296		KT3	1100	EPOCHES	AR	108
ENTITLED	AE1	341		CAM	41	EPSOM	MF	42
ENTRAILS	J3	83		CAM	176		MF	164
	J6	514		HIF	573	EPULON	AE12	675
	J6	709		M15	358	EQUAL	LC	134
	P2	80		GP	106		AM	185
	M1	175	ENVIOUSLY	PNH	23		AM	501
	G1	94	ENVOY	VHH	49		AM	535
	G1	449		GE	50		PTL	10
	G1	637		AU	318		EMQW	7
	G2	269	ENVOYS	AE11	369		DA	34
	G2	546	ENVY	LC	119		HP	8
	G3	738		LC	121		AA	116
	AE1	297		ECG2	17		MD	118
	AE3	749		SCG2	21		MF	53
	AE4	88		PUO2	7		SAA	263
	AE4	524		ML	14		SAA	869
	AE5	137		ML	16		RL	124
	AE5	309		ML	31		ER	75
	AE5	1014		HP	126		L4	163
	AE6	362		MD	309		L4	216
	AE6	812		D	19		TA	138
	AE8	142		MF	174		TA	314
	AE8	243		MF	57		AK	164
	AE10	257		SAA	933		HAP	136
	AE12	320		SAA	1003		HAP	732
	HIF	439		T23	78		HAP	1308
	TH	185		HAP	551		HAP	1323
	TH	304		HAP	811		HAP	1562
	TH	325		HAP	1364		HAP	1946
	M12	211		HAP	1412		HAP	2567
	M15	200		HAP	2506		BR	347
ENTRANCE	HAP	937		SKA5	6		BR	359
	EL	173		ODA	25		ELW	5
	J3	307		P3	138		EL	183
	J10	180		MC	34		ODA	20
	M1	285		GK	82		ODA	63
	AE2	444		VP1	13		ODA	64
	AE3	568		G1	237		J1	18
	AE4	881		G3	60		J6	296
	AE6	124		G4	243		J6	763
	AE7	227		AE1	37		J10	81
	AE7	780		AE1	184		P1	122
	AE9	517		AE1	608		P1	248
	AE11	24		AE5	461		P4	23
	AE11	614		AE6	253		P6	8
	AE11	1276		AE7	473		M1	844
	B	264		AE9	254		M1	1046
	M12	170		OAE2	78		M9	61
	M12	297		MG	2		M9	81
ENTRANCED	TA	471		MM	34		M9	150
	KT3	713		KT1	51		M13	69
ENTRENCHED	HAP	938		KT1	57		VCS	38
ENTRIES	AE6	65		KT1	349		MC	16
	M12	63		KT3	746		GK	52
ENTRUSTED	J6	822		M8	160		VP3	44
ENTRY	AR	264		CAM	56		VP3	169
	AE6	71		CAM	375		VP5	138
	KT2	548		C	440		G1	510
	B	146		C	762		G2	304
	M11	286		M11	170		G2	384
ENTWINE	AE1	995		M12	831		G2	393
ENURED	G3	268	ENVYEST	HIF	253		G3	188
ENVELOPS	KT3	587	ENVYING	B	17		G3	301
ENVENOMED	AE7	489	ENVY'S	SAA	1041		G3	477
ENVIED	AR	26	EPAPHUS	M1	1042		G3	478
	J10	85		M1	1047		G4	431
	G2	180		M1	1058		AE1	269
	AE5	710	EPEÜS	AE2	345		AE1	274
	AE5	786	EPHEMERIS	C	451		AE1	475
	AE11	417	EPHOD	SAA	358		AE1	715
	OAL	331		HAP	187		AE1	773
	KT2	635	EPHYRE	G4	485		AE2	767
	KT3	11	EPIC	AM	687		AE3	427
	KT3	321		J1	247		AE3	655
	M8	222		PTP	41		AE3	669
	M15	144	EPICTETUS	AK	82		AE3	900
ENVIES	AM	158	EPICURUS	RL	22		AE4	534
	J10	361		L3	259		AE4	590
	G2	713	EPIDAURUS	G3	75		AE5	81
	AE9	896	EPIGRAMS	JH	21		AE5	151
ENVIOUS	AM	190	EPILOGUE	EMM	6		AE5	187
	AM	840		ETL	2		AE5	204
	SAA	913		EWR	2		AE5	302
	SAA	1072	EPIRIAN	G3	192		AE5	326
	T23	19		AE3	510		AE5	387
	HAP	1419	EPIRUS	G1	89		AE5	419
	P6	35	EPIRUS'	AE3	377		AE5	466
	VP5	51	EPISCOPACY'S	HAP	859		AE5	475
	VP7	37	EPISTLES	HP	1		AE5	558
	AE6	467		HAP	907		AE5	564
	AE6	475		J6	384		AE5	575
	AE7	397	EPITAPH	ETL	27		AE5	742

EQUAL	AE5	855
	AE5	1016
	AE5	1079
	AE6	238
	AE6	373
	AE6	989
	AE6	1134
	AE6	1190
	AE6	1210
	AE7	654
	AE7	735
	AE7	751
	AE8	25
	AE8	192
	AE8	593
	AE8	765
	AE8	896
	AE9	15
	AE9	77
	AE9	134
	AE9	333
	AE9	560
	AE9	727
	AE9	896
	AE9	935
	AE9	1019
	AE10	166
	AE10	472
	AE10	497
	AE10	518
	AE10	525
	AE10	610
	AE10	614
	AE10	1036
	AE10	1071
	AE11	47
	AE11	175
	AE11	190
	AE11	267
	AE11	268
	AE11	446
	AE11	482
	AE11	500
	AE11	653
	AE11	788
	AE11	935
	AE11	1043
	AE12	283
	AE12	422
	AE12	741
	AE12	805
	AE12	917
	AE12	1041
	AE12	1217
	OAL	237
	OAL	328
	OAL	654
	DO	19
	KT1	147
	KT1	349
	KT2	198
	KT2	247
	KT2	401
	KT2	413
	KT2	432
	KT2	526
	KT3	336
	KT3	537
	KT3	568
	KT3	626
	KT3	743
	KT3	885
	M8	193
	M8	260
	B	471
	B	508
	BP	39
	HIF	256
	HIF	286
	HIF	314
	HIF	375
	HIF	509
	C	209
	C	683
	C	696
	TH	13
	TH	67
	M11	50
	M11	56
	FL	42
	FL	254
	FL	289
	FL	298
	FL	547
	M12	291
	M12	531

EQUAL	M12	554
	M12	819
	M12	830
	AU	105
	AU	155
	AU	424
	AU	447
	M15	292
	M15	706
	CI	439
	CI	558
EQUALED	AE6	640
	AE11	652
	MM	32
	M12	608
EQUALLY	AM	192
	HAP	2540
	BR	209
	STS2	12
	EL	108
	G1	389
	AE6	1045
	OAL	721
EQUAL-PERFECT	HS	20
EQUALS	PFD	24
	RL	230
	T18	38
	HAP	456
	HAP	1044
	AE5	719
	AE5	872
	B	636
	CI	217
EQUICOLAE	AE7	1028
EQUICOLUS	AE9	931
EQUINOX	C	447
EQUINOXES	HAP	1798
EQUIP	EHC	34
EQUIPAGE	EAL	4
	PKA	47
	J6	546
	J10	496
	KT3	569
	FL	273
EQUIPPED	PR	36
	CI	265
EQUIPS	M11	67
EQUITY	HAP	2359
EQUIVALENT	HIF	181
EQUIVOCATE	HAP	617
ERA	J6	30
ERASINUS	M15	420
ERATO	AE7	52
EREBUS	AE4	739
ERECT	UDH	107
	PO	12
	AA	633
	HAP	394
	M13	69
	G3	666
	AE2	392
	AE3	185
	AE4	138
	AE4	713
	AE12	1142
ERECTED	L4	88
	TA	124
	AK	127
	M1	109
	M1	121
	M1	1036
	G1	499
	AE1	488
	AE5	487
	AE12	292
	M8	25
	M11	28
	CI	159
ERECTING	J10	155
ERECTS	MF	74
	SAA	324
	AE3	813
	AE10	1008
	AE11	1110
	AE12	14
ERETIAN	AE7	981
ERGENNA'S	P2	54
ERICETES	AE10	1056
ERICHTHONIUS	G3	177
ERINGOES	J6	419
ERIPHYLE	AE6	602
ERITHACIS	AT	82
ERMINE	FL	258
	M12	553
EROS	KT3	1144
ERR	PC1	6

ERR	AA	782
	MD	86
	MD	99
	HAP	475
	HAP	633
	HAP	1047
	HAP	1050
	AE2	814
	AE10	894
	C	452
ERRAND	EL	339
	P6	154
	AE3	323
	AE9	512
	HIF	748
	AU	384
ERRANT	M1	298
ERRED	B	412
ERRING	HAP	65
	HAP	1204
	G1	604
	G3	9
	AE1	1044
	AE6	45
	AE8	338
	AE12	1119
ERROR	DC	38
	SAA	1052
	SAA	1140
	MO	17
	HAP	1156
	G3	769
	AE3	240
	AE4	25
	AE5	772
	AE5	887
	AE10	548
	OAL	287
	M12	83
	AU	181
	CI	58
	CI	237
ERRORS	EEL	38
	PTL	4
	ECG2	20
	PAL	25
	AA	799
	RL	248
	RL	265
	L2	58
	HAP	936
	HAP	1060
	HAP	1103
	HAP	1176
	HAP	2138
	AE5	456
	AE6	715
	AE5	580
ERRS	AE5	581
	AE6	1095
	AE9	950
ERYMANTHUS	AE5	600
ERYMANTHUS'	AE5	521
ERYX	AE5	535
	AE5	548
	AE5	643
	AE5	990
	AE12	1020
ERYX'	AE5	1009
ESAU'S	AA	982
ESCAPE	PFD	1
	SAA	320
	T23	21
	T27	3
	AE2	381
	AE9	116
	AE11	1275
ESCAPED	ML	13
	EDGA	19
	TA	406
	G1	407
	AE1	758
	AE6	129
	AE7	312
	AE10	607
	M12	705
	CI	378
ESCAPES	J6	730
ESDRAS	RL	291
ESPIED	M1	590
	AE6	739
	AE9	251
	AE11	1238
ESPIES	M11	76
ESPOUSE	HP	241
	AA	107

Word	Src	No.
ESPOUSE	SAA	317
	HAP	2091
	HAP	2111
	M1	754
ESPOUSED	AA	320
	M9	75
	AE11	359
ESPY	HAP	2522
	FL	87
	FL	124
ESSAY	AM	558
	HP	140
	ER	31
	HAP	200
	VP7	42
	AE11	236
	HIF	75
	C	458
	M11	485
	WB	241
	M15	145
	CI	407
ESSAYED	TA	162
	TA	171
	AE3	880
	TH	271
	M12	105
	CI	195
ESSAYS	PC1	24
	TA	155
	P3	8
	KT3	123
	M15	336
ESSENCE	MD	20
	MD	92
	M15	583
EST	C	418
ESTABLISHED	DA	132
	AA	993
	HAP	985
	HAP	1694
	AE7	474
	AE10	516
ESTATE	AR	55
	PWG	47
	AM	359
	SCG3	9
	PNH	25
	AA	562
	AA	698
	RL	391
	L4	96
	T27	57
	TA	399
	HAP	946
	HAP	956
	HAP	1643
	HAP	2210
	J1	139
	J3	242
	J3	260
	J3	435
	J6	53
	J6	471
	J6	651
	J6	707
	P2	24
	P3	132
	P3	193
	P6	94
	P6	180
	PLT	37
	AE11	560
	AF	78
	KT1	69
	KT1	484
	KT1	570
	KT2	98
	B	50
	TH	42
	M11	180
	AU	126
	WB	461
ESTATES	J1	209
	WB	393
ESTEEM	UDH	11
	SAA	637
	HAP	1335
	J6	725
	AE6	1161
	KT1	608
	B	481
ESTEEMED	M1	263
	M9	7
	AE8	88
	KT1	592
ESTIAN	BR	216
ESTRANGE	AA	290
ESTRANGED	HAP	337
	HAP	564
ET	PO	4
ETERNAL	LC	84
	AM	1081
	PTC	4
	AA	376
	MD	94
	SAA	55
	RL	104
	RL	193
	RL	214
	L1	48
	L3	103
	L3	111
	L3	182
	L3	191
	L3	195
	L3	267
	L3	298
	L3	317
	H3	32
	TA	113
	AK	15
	HAP	80
	HAP	117
	HAP	494
	HAP	723
	HAP	880
	HAP	1082
	HAP	1199
	BR	24
	BR	92
	EL	292
	EL	309
	J1	15
	J10	320
	P2	29
	VCS	30
	VCS	39
	HI	60
	VP10	71
	G1	631
	G1	641
	G2	636
	AE6	495
	AE6	626
	AE6	774
	AE6	841
	AE7	460
	AE8	561
	AE10	26
	KT1	405
	KT1	470
	KT2	554
	KT3	350
	KT3	1031
	C	514
	C	519
	TH	138
	TH	290
	M15	364
	GP	29
	AS	43
ETERNALLY	TA	85
ETERNITY	UDH	105
	RL	20
	L3	252
	HAP	1313
	AE12	1273
ETESIAN	H3	6
	DO	46
ETHER	M1	85
	AE6	870
	AE6	1012
	WB	433
	M15	290
ETHERAGE	MC	29
	MF	184
	MS	28
ETHEREAL	G1	657
	TA	90
	HAP	389
	HAP	2303
	BR	146
	ODA	72
	M1	28
	M1	52
	M1	104
	M1	560
	M13	17
	G3	56
	G4	322
	G4	706
ETHEREAL	AE5	60
	AE6	494
	AE6	988
	AE7	387
	AE8	51
	AE8	928
	AE12	175
	AE12	273
	DO	21
	KT3	399
	KT3	1050
	M15	596
	J10	102
ETHIOP	G4	413
ETHIOPIAN	AE4	697
	M15	483
ETHIOPIA'S	J10	240
ETHIOP'S	J6	777
ETHIOPS	HIF	585
ETHIOPS'	G2	168
ETHNIC	AA	517
ETNA	M13	187
	M13	201
ETNA'S	M13	35
ETRURIA	AE7	897
ETRURIAN	G2	779
	AE10	337
	AE11	67
	AE11	1078
EUBOEAN	AE11	404
EUMEDES	AE12	520
EUMELUS	AE5	866
EUMENIUS	AE11	987
EUNUCH	AM	157
	MD	23
	J6	657
	AE12	154
EUNUCH-LOVE	J1	95
EUNUCHS	J1	29
	J6	483
	AE9	847
	OAL	573
EUPHORBUS	P6	24
	M15	232
EUPHRATES	G1	685
	AE8	968
	OAL	255
EUPHRATES'	G4	810
EUPOLIS	P1	246
EUREKA	RL	43
EUROPA	OAL	364
EUROPE	UDH	22
	HS	85
	G3	52
	AE1	532
	AE7	145
	TJD	158
EUROPEAN	AE7	305
EUROTAS	CI	94
EUROTAS'	T18	40
	AE1	699
EURUS	J10	292
	M1	73
	G2	152
	AE1	159
	AE1	186
	FL	8
EURYALUS	AE5	385
	AE5	386
	AE5	421
	AE5	434
	AE5	439
	AE5	448
	AE9	228
	AE9	229
	AE9	253
	AE9	288
	AE9	372
	AE9	460
	AE9	481
	AE9	507
	AE9	637
EURYBATES	HIF	446
EURYDICE	G4	763
	G4	764
EURYPYLUS	AE2	159
	AU	545
EURYSTHEUS	G3	8
EURYSTHEUS'	AE8	388
EURYTION	AE5	679
	AE5	710
	OAL	665
	M8	57
EURYTION'S	AE5	658
	AE10	692
EURYTUS	M12	314

Word	Ref	No.
EURYTUS	M12	321
EUSEBIUS	EC	5
EUXINE	P5	197
EVADE	MD	206
	HAP	1067
	AE10	87
EVADNE	AE6	606
EVAGRUS	M12	403
	M12	405
EVANDER	AE8	70
	AE8	202
	AE8	245
	AE8	365
	AE8	472
	AE8	740
	AE10	218
	AE10	718
	AE11	40
EVANDER'S	AE8	135
	AE8	599
	AE10	649
	AE10	1108
	AE11	93
	AE11	223
	AE12	276
EVANDRIAN	AE10	592
EVAS	AE10	994
EVE	PPC	13
	EL	170
	GK	91
EVEN	SEL3	1
	G1	621
EVENING	EEL	21
	T18	14
	T18	25
	TA	156
	HAP	511
	HAP	322
	HAP	2293
	ESH	26
	VP9	29
	G1	548
	G3	521
	G3	613
	G4	13
	G4	276
	G4	628
	AE8	106
	AE8	370
	KT3	349
	C	303
	M15	468
EVENINGS	SMA	101
EVENSONG	WB	45
EVENT	PWG	7
	PAL	4
	AA	935
	AA	1018
	TA	109
	MN	2
	HAP	887
	J10	299
	AE1	725
	AE2	158
	AE2	171
	AE2	266
	AE3	71
	AE5	690
	AE6	101
	AE6	131
	AE8	702
	AE9	400
	AE10	1202
	AE11	483
	AE12	489
	AE12	1046
	AE12	1148
	KT3	1019
	TJD	154
	M8	193
	B	720
	CAM	9
	CAM	275
	HIF	91
	HIF	157
	C	377
	TH	319
	M11	46
	M11	263
	AU	433
	AU	492
	WB	116
	CI	477
EVENTS	TA	216
	P2	103
	AE1	285

Word	Ref	No.
EVENTS	AE4	865
	AE5	925
	AE10	236
	AE11	432
	AE11	662
	AE12	271
	C	206
	FL	295
EVER-ANSWERED	AM	1095
EVER-ANXIOUS	L3	199
EVER-CHANGING	MD	24
	L3	165
EVER-CRAVING	L3	212
EVERLASTING	L3	300
	T23	84
	HAP	1274
	AE10	1051
EVER-LOYAL	TA	229
EVER-TRUSTY	AE11	808
EVER-WANTING	AA	407
EVERYONE	P4	48
EVERYTHING	HP	180
	AA	548
	J3	71
	OAL	83
EVIDENCE	AA	661
	AA	678
	SAA	46
	SAA	91
	J1	49
	J3	200
	J10	106
	J16	44
	J16	53
	M15	46
EVIDENCES	PMK	30
EVIDENCING	SAA	74
EVIL	EKK	3
	SAA	498
	HAP	598
	J6	591
	P2	25
	P5	88
	M9	96
	G3	843
	HIF	40
	C	264
EVIL-MINDED	HAP	1261
EVILS	BR	93
	AE11	656
EVINCE	HAP	805
EVINCED	HAP	762
EVION	P1	199
	P1	200
EVOE	AE7	544
	AE7	545
EWE	G4	789
	AE3	164
	AE4	77
	C	14
EWES	M9	101
	M13	128
	VP1	69
	VP3	7
	VP3	130
	G2	751
	AE6	59
EXACT	DA	102
	MD	49
	BR	51
	ODA	65
	AE5	187
	AE9	397
	KT3	1132
	M8	334
EXACTEST	PMQ	3
EXACTLY	J3	140
	AE12	1055
	BP	87
EXACTS	AE8	162
EXADIUS	M12	372
EXALTED	AM	872
	EMW	13
	MD	55
	ER	27
	TA	129
	ETS	20
	M1	97
	GK	149
	G3	476
	G4	77
	AE6	1078
	AE7	1078
	AE9	141
	B	29
	B	285

Word	Ref	No.
EXALTED	B	496
	C	179
	C	387
	C	679
	FL	2
	M15	683
EXALTS	AA	711
	AE10	62
	OAL	273
	CI	41
EXAMINED	EMK	10
	P3	157
	PUO4	18
EXAMPLE	HS	146
	AR	207
	AR	317
	ET	17
	CM	124
	HP	46
	HP	213
	AA	267
	AA	870
	SAA	1009
	ER	36
	HH	42
	HAP	443
	HAP	1976
	HAP	2310
	EDS	20
	EDS	25
	ETS	12
	J6	205
	J6	850
	G3	716
	AE2	552
	AE3	738
	AE5	94
	AE10	58
	AE10	604
	AE11	1288
	AE12	644
	OAL	513
	OAL	717
	C	356
	C	818
	TH	425
	M12	676
	AU	354
	WB	66
	CI	480
EXAMPLES	ETP	7
	EM	7
	EPF	7
	AA	1001
	SAA	388
	AK	78
	HAP	1306
	BR	301
	EKA	14
	M1	494
	PLT	50
	GK	140
	G2	669
	G3	264
	G4	321
	OAL	853
EXCEED	LC	55
	AA	994
	B	32
EXCEEDED	HAP	2231
EXCEEDING	PT	32
	PAR	15
	AA	651
	EKA	22
EXCEEDS	EL	265
EXCEL	AM	963
	PFD	25
	EAZ	34
	PTC	38
	PUO4	28
	AA	660
	MF	55
	SAA	1015
	ER	38
	EAA	29
	SKA5	15
	J10	539
	MC	16
	VP5	75
	AE9	702
	LMC	2
	DO	5
	FL	208
	FL	478
EXCELLED	HAP	2095
	EL	205

Word	Ref	No.	Word	Ref	No.	Word	Ref	No.
EXCELLED	M1	147	EXCLUDED	PMQ	31	EXERCISE	AE4	124
	VP5	67		L4	170		AE6	873
	AE10	318		PTS	37		AE8	423
	AE11	448		AE11	1280		AE10	252
	KT1	3		KT3	332		C	27
	TH	8		HIF	178		TJD	94
	FL	519		FL	143		M8	37
	FL	539		AU	57		M8	384
	M12	238	EXCLUDES	HAP	2124		AU	503
	CI	51	EXCLUDING	B	725		M15	359
EXCELLENCE	PTL	15	EXCLUSION	HAP	978		CI	220
	GE	56	EXCLUSIVE	SAA	254	EXERCISED	EUF	25
	GE	58	EXCORIATION	PAA	4		AA	237
	KT3	1097	EXCREMENT	PDG	14		J10	553
	AU	185		MS	8		TA	430
EXCELLENCY'S	GE	54		P2	66		P3	173
EXCELLENT	EDG	30	EXCREMENTS	J3	70		G1	232
EXCELLING	SKA5	1	EXCURSIONS	PC1	13		AE7	713
	M1	147		G4	283		AE9	69
	AE12	1217		M11	475		AE9	805
	B	540	EXCUSE	PIE	14		KT1	597
	HIF	377		EEL	25		KT3	837
	M12	541		EEL	38		B	434
	CI	136		ETL	22		B	605
	CI	167		ECG1	38		WB	451
EXCELS	RH	6		ECG2	20		M10	6
	J6	351		ENH	16		M12	631
	B	646		HP	50		CI	62
EXCEPT	LC	42		PPC	18	EXERCISES	AE12	591
	PRL	25		L4	140	EXERT	L4	223
	PRL	30		AK	66		M1	89
	EWGR	24		HAP	556		VP8	151
	ECG2	8		EDS	10		G2	596
	PAZ	34		J6	542		AE5	246
	SAA	870		J16	43		AU	304
	AE9	296		AE4	565	EXERTED	EL	165
	KT2	108		AE4	440	EXERTS	AE8	778
	BP	3		AE11	451		AE11	1103
	CAM	30		OAL	673	EXHALATIONS	AM	65
	CAM	31		KT3	786	EXHALED	OD	25
	TH	387		B	345		EL	303
	EWR	22		B	385		G4	710
EXCEPTED	PMQ	29		AU	236		FL	96
	HIF	419		AU	102	EXHALES	GP	33
EXCEPTING	HAP	1921		CI	23	EXHALING	G2	297
	P5	129		ERL	3	EXHAUSTED	SMA	21
	M8	397	EXCUSED	SAA	121		SAA	1038
EXCEPTIONS	P4	25		PTS	14		BR	331
EXCEPTS	HAP	815		KT2	339		J3	486
EXCESS	AR	186		C	638		J6	476
	AM	249		CI	238		J10	168
	PNH	23	EXCUSES	L4	178		G3	484
	SAA	31		TA	244		AE9	1085
	SDG	11		VP9	77		AE11	564
	L4	37		AE12	19		M12	255
	L4	82		ERL	7		M15	511
	HAP	1765	EXCUSING	BP	129	EXHIBIT	J3	66
	EL	88	EXECRABLE	AE3	86	EXHORT	AE3	184
	M13	14		AE5	1037		OAL	236
	G2	570		AE7	408	EXHORTATION	M1	381
	TJD	74		AE8	632	EXHORTS	AE11	788
	CI	8	EXECRABLY	P1	207	EXILE	AR	75
	CI	238	EXECUTE	AM	470		LC	17
EXCESSES	AA	37		PRL	28		AM	630
EXCESSIVE	G2	469		AE7	462		AM	1046
EXCHANGE	PCB	24		AE8	645		AM	1158
	HAP	2145		AU	564		AA	264
	J6	852	EXECUTED	B	576		AA	823
	VP5	137	EXECUTES	KT2	211		D	1
	AE12	79	EXECUTION	PR	6		SAA	599
	HIF	205		AE9	479		TA	236
EXCHANGING	J10	218	EXEMPT	AR	30		TA	265
EXCHEQUERS	AA	894		AE7	287		TA	421
EXCISE	PCG1	36		AE9	359		HAP	20
	J3	57		AE12	1270		BR	91
EXCITE	SAA	107	EXEMPTED	BP	143		J1	76
	G3	362	EXEMPTION	HAP	1644		J6	725
	G4	98	EXEMPTS	L3	44		J10	424
	AE9	1062	EXEQUIES	B	661		M1	190
	AU	371	EXERCISE	MD	233		G2	736
EXCITES	SSC	26		T18	41		AE1	531
	AE4	900		BR	268		AE1	847
	AE12	819		EL	120		AE2	864
EXCITING	M11	326		EL	225		AE4	537
	CI	137		ODA	61		AE5	818
EXCLAIM	AE11	336		J6	350		AE5	824
EXCLAIMING	AE5	444		HI	184		AE11	398
	OAL	598		G1	143		AU	86
EXCLUDE	LC	50		G1	186		CI	638
	SAA	112		G2	489	EXILED	AR	42
	SAA	764		G2	501		RH	50
	G2	512		G3	356		MD	319
	AE1	236		G4	108		HAP	1220
	AE12	858		AE1	18		HAP	1336
	TJD	37		AE1	599		HAP	2072
	M12	66		AE3	365		BR	67

Word	Ref	No.	Word	Ref	No.	Word	Ref	No.
EXILED	AE1	3	EXPEDIENTS	AA	455	EXPERIMENT	CI	503
	AE1	877		HAP	846	EXPERT	AM	685
	AE2	1085		HAP	2218		HAP	576
	AE3	168		AE4	412		G2	174
	AE6	94	EXPEL	PDG	21		AE8	967
	AE7	175		L2	49	EXPIATE	AR	275
	AE7	415		FS1	11		RL	85
	AE10	138		HAP	2048		J6	668
	AE10	1216		M1	538	EXPIATION	EDGA	27
	KT1	503		AE6	825	EXPIRE	UDH	74
	CI	218		AE7	465		AM	846
EXILE'S	AR	310		KT3	761		AM	1024
EXILES	VP1	91		M8	152		A	9
	AE6	105		M15	257		SAA	888
	AS	84		M15	485		L4	74
EXISTENCE	HAP	645		M15	681		L5	3
EXORCISE	WB	31	EXPELLED	HAP	852		OD	50
EXPANDED	M1	217		HAP	2317		EL	302
	M1	392		J3	28		G1	129
	AE11	1255		G1	233		G1	205
	M15	376		AE1	3		G1	636
	M15	368		AE1	517		G4	254
EXPANDING	EPF	17		AE1	633		AE2	878
EXPECT	PRL	9		AE3	168		AE4	918
	AM	210		AE4	883		AE6	734
	PT	33		AE7	296		AE10	723
	PW	22		AE8	155		AE11	303
	PMQW	11		AE8	193		AE11	609
	PC1	4		AE11	409		AE11	1278
	ETC	3		AE12	801		AE12	16
	AA	345		AU	608		KT1	560
	RL	118	EXPELS	L3	310		KT3	829
	RL	452	EXPENSE	A	8		KT3	1051
	HAP	1754		PLN	5		M8	121
	PTS	30		PNH	19		BP	50
	P1	213		PTW	15		WB	239
	P2	86		SAA	679		M15	510
	G1	313		PD	4		M15	530
	G1	580		HAP	772	EXPIRED	AM	85
	AE2	241		EL	304		SAA	747
	AE2	391		J1	102		SAA	1092
	AE2	481		P6	50		BR	252
	AE3	199		P6	86		EL	317
	AE9	318		P6	116		J6	180
	AE11	277		MC	68		J10	433
	OAL	811		KT2	439		OAL	544
	M8	34		KT2	484		KT3	747
	C	754		TJD	11		B	26
	WB	302		B	103		M12	556
	PWR	14		TH	51		CI	455
EXPECTATION	HP	65		TH	64		CI	639
	L3	7		TH	241	EXPIRES	AM	750
	HAP	1833		TH	253		SKA2	3
	B	217		M12	95		AE2	725
EXPECTATIONS	AE2	144		AU	361		AE6	1005
EXPECTED	ELN	1		M15	631		AE8	335
	PNH	3		CI	401		AE10	795
	J10	368	EXPENSES	PP	4		AE11	286
	AE2	369	EXPENSIVE	PAZ	38		AE11	1209
	AE5	414		AA	394		AE12	455
	AE6	932		AA	587		KT3	182
	AE8	264	EXPERIENCE	AM	459		M8	203
	AE8	52		PAZ	1		B	652
	AE8	706		CM	33		M15	227
	DO	54		AA	891	EXPIRING	UDH	6
	B	148		MD	189		AR	285
	B	621		SAA	89		SDG	21
	M12	92		SAA	659		SDG	26
	CI	270		SAA	704		T23	109
	CI	563		OE	34		TA	117
EXPECTING	AR	132		HAP	2093		M1	596
	PFD	4		G2	29		AE10	881
	SAA	567		G4	450		AE11	1182
	SAA	727		AE3	733		TH	195
	L4	199		AE5	942	EXPLAIN	HAP	603
	J10	362		AE11	69		HAP	876
	M13	110		OAL	33		HAP	926
	AE1	634		OAL	293		HAP	2141
	AE1	861		OAL	862		AE3	484
	AE6	835		KT3	385		AE11	476
	AE7	394		B	431	EXPLAINED	RL	293
	B	292		C	208		RL	414
	B	333		C	469		AE5	399
	CAM	282		EWR	26		KT2	392
	HIF	717	EXPERIENCED	AR	23		B	137
	AU	201		G3	187		B	632
	CI	205		G4	259	EXPLAINING	CI	19
EXPECTINGLY	J6	176		AE5	924	EXPLAINS	HAP	1014
EXPECTS	P1	51		AE8	198	EXPLICATE	RL	289
	AE11	342		AE9	308	EXPLOITS	J1	13
	M11	179		BP	11		AU	160
	WB	20		HIF	388	EXPLORE	AM	553
	CI	554	EXPERIMENT	HAP	2034		AM	594
EXPEDIENT	SAA	589		M1	293		HAP	133
	KT3	424		G2	327		M1	125
	TH	45		M15	539		VP4	41

Word	Code	Number
EXPLORE	G1	203
	G2	47
	G2	57
	AE1	808
	AE2	49
	AE2	1022
	AE3	156
	AE7	199
	AE9	213
	KT2	197
	HIF	93
	M15	9
EXPLORED	MN	4
	B	134
	M10	33
EXPLORES	AE8	32
	AE11	1099
	M8	201
EXPLORING	CAM	280
EXPORT	HAP	1136
EXPOSE	HP	204
	AA	324
	AA	465
	SAA	190
	SAA	982
	EK	19
	HAP	1546
	HAP	2462
	J6	129
	J16	36
	P4	83
	P5	26
	G2	448
	AE1	539
	AE2	924
	M11	57
EXPOSED	ESF	5
	CM	88
	AA	701
	MD	76
	SAA	595
	L3	73
	L4	170
	L5	5
	HAP	1305
	HAP	1636
	HAP	1930
	HAP	2338
	J6	26
	J6	783
	M1	712
	G2	354
	G3	646
	AE1	16
	AE1	65
	AE2	30
	AE2	586
	AE4	466
	AE4	713
	AE4	728
	AE4	862
	AE6	561
	AE8	255
	AE9	255
	AE9	656
	AE9	982
	AE10	37
	AE10	220
	AE10	403
	AE10	781
	AE11	956
	AE12	347
	AF	82
	B	722
	B	742
	CAM	311
	CAM	385
	AU	64
	AU	149
	AU	329
	M15	451
EXPOSES	HP	36
EXPOSITION	RL	332
EXPOUND	RL	336
	RL	367
	RL	410
	HAP	618
	HAP	765
	HAP	999
	HAP	1004
EXPOUNDED	MN	1
	RL	378
EXPOUNDING	HAP	475
EXPOUNDS	AE10	257
	AE12	170
EXPRESS	AR	71
EXPRESS	RH	3
	SIE	6
	ECG1	39
	PUO3	20
	AA	997
	L1	16
	TA	248
	AK	129
	HAP	1325
	HAP	1777
	HL	233
	P3	74
	P6	96
	MC	76
	VP1	32
	G2	532
	AE4	477
	AE11	189
	M12	71
	KT3	778
	AU	613
	EWR	15
EXPRESSED	RH	59
	EMP	6
	AA	62
	PRH	28
	SAA	124
	SAA	500
	RL	199
	L4	157
	TA	122
	TA	283
	AK	83
	AK	86
	HAP	36
	HAP	2487
	J10	519
	P2	1
	P5	38
	M1	907
	GK	169
	GK	174
	VP6	96
	VP6	111
	VP10	52
	G3	12
	AE1	96
	AE1	680
	AE2	380
	AE3	943
	AE4	515
	AE5	475
	AE5	1134
	AE6	151
	AE8	689
	AE8	949
	AE10	693
	AE11	584
	OAL	755
	KT2	469
	KT2	633
	M8	6
	B	645
	BP	43
	HIF	11
	M11	327
	M12	317
	GP	104
	CI	95
EXPRESSES	LMC	5
EXPRESSING	SMA	68
	SEL2	15
	SSF	6
	P6	11
	M1	207
	GK	17
	M11	313
EXPRESSION	TH	384
	B	367
EXPRESSIONS	CM	103
	PPC	26
	AE2	1010
EXQUISITE	B	426
EXTEMPORE	P3	120
EXTEND	RL	195
	HAP	659
	HAP	1542
	HAP	2104
	HAP	2238
	PKA	34
	EL	240
	M1	744
	M9	25
	VP10	108
	G1	309
	G1	670
EXTEND	G2	374
	G3	514
	G4	177
	AE1	587
	AE1	683
	AE6	901
	AE6	1083
	AE9	877
	AE11	1308
	DO	20
	M15	657
EXTENDED	AA	234
	AT	108
	HAP	14
	HAP	272
	J1	134
	J10	397
	VP1	106
	G4	427
	AE3	919
	AE5	438
	AE5	1114
	AE6	242
	AE6	432
	AE6	868
	AE9	624
	AE9	868
	AE10	1258
	AE11	27
	AE12	414
	KT2	639
	M12	505
	M12	530
	M15	154
	M15	657
EXTENDING	M11	332
EXTENDS	PUO2	39
	L1	25
	HAP	1403
	J3	235
	J6	655
	P1	265
	P3	122
	P6	173
	M1	51
	M1	913
	VP1	117
	VP10	79
	G2	561
	AE6	341
	AE7	143
	AU	87
	M15	459
EXTENT	AA	46
	TA	314
	HAP	136
	HAP	1077
	M1	454
	G3	531
	AE5	566
	KT1	203
	FL	316
EXTENUATES	M15	379
EXTENUATING	L4	144
EXTERNAL	B	524
EXTINCT	KT3	279
EXTINGUISH	BR	215
	M9	121
EXTINGUISHED	LS	10
	AE4	869
	AE8	354
	KT1	179
	KT3	251
	KT3	255
	TJD	59
	EWR	24
EXTINGUISHER	AM	1123
EXTINGUISHES	M15	488
EXTOL	G4	315
	AE11	620
	CAM	15
EXTOLLED	KT2	429
	WB	150
EXTORTED	ML	26
	SAA	293
EXTORTING	SAA	280
EXTRACTED	AE12	616
EXTRAVAGANT	P4	43
EXTRAVAGANTLY	M9	111
EXTREME	RL	427
	H29	55
	HAP	1328
	EL	84
	P4	75
EXTREMELY	OAL	501
EXTREMES	AA	110

Word	Ref	Num
EXTREMES	AA	556
	MD	99
	MD	248
	TA	137
	HAP	843
	HAP	2525
	EL	109
	P3	234
	M1	58
	G1	324
	G3	168
	G4	52
	AE2	484
	KT3	1116
	B	185
	CI	458
	ESK	30
EXTREMEST	SAA	590
	SAA	602
	TA	173
	T23	49
	EL	12
	EL	41
	M1	737
	G2	160
	G2	389
	KT1	404
EXTREMITIES	J6	478
	CI	277
EXTREMITY	PNH	26
	AA	159
EXUBERANT	G1	282
EXULT	G1	570
EXULTING	AE7	753
	AE10	927
	AE10	769
	AE11	741
	AE12	509
	AE12	1018
	HIF	713
EXULTS	KT2	426
	CI	322
	CI	396
EYE	LC	31
	LC	115
	AM	104
	AM	231
	AM	342
	AM	1117
	EWGR	3
	PUO2	25
	E	8
	DA	70
	AA	989
	AA	1008
	MF	25
	SAA	116
	SAA	1031
	AT	22
	AT	86
	EC	30
	L3	185
	L4	184
	T23	68
	T23	98
	T23	104
	AK	122
	HAP	29
	HAP	58
	HAP	533
	HAP	1419
	BR	77
	STS2	2
	EL	201
	EL	341
	J3	173
	J3	183
	J6	78
	J6	751
	PPS	17
	P1	125
	P4	116
	M1	961
	M13	31
	M13	39
	M13	163
	M13	166
	SFL	8
	G1	140
	G3	631
	AE2	91
	AE3	834
	AE3	871
	AE4	442
	AE5	585
	AE6	35

Word	Ref	Num
EYE	AE9	988
	AE10	585
	AE11	1036
	AE11	1070
	OAL	49
	OAL	124
	OAL	482
	OAL	745
	DO	156
	KT1	40
	KT1	254
	KT1	584
	KT3	570
	KT3	693
	B	142
	HIF	60
	HIF	753
	C	413
	C	579
	TH	96
	TH	315
	FL	86
	FL	102
	M12	377
	WB	51
	WB	530
	M15	285
	GP	106
EYEBALL	AE3	833
EYEBALLS	HAP	795
	P3	204
	AE9	557
	AE12	15
	KT1	526
	M8	22
	M8	122
	M12	352
	M12	379
EYEBROW	OAE2	21
EYEBROWS	VP8	49
	KT3	44
EYEING	EWGR	20
EYELIDS	AM	900
	T18	16
EYES	UDH	91
	JH	24
	AR	61
	AR	150
	AR	180
	AR	229
	AR	291
	RH	89
	SMA	33
	SMA	42
	LC	13
	LC	99
	DC	20
	AM	49
	AM	285
	AM	322
	AM	444
	AM	528
	AM	543
	AM	690
	AM	747
	AM	840
	AM	1022
	AM	1028
	AM	1093
	AM	1130
	AM	1192
	SMQ	6
	SMQ	13
	SMM2	10
	SMM2	30
	SEL2	4
	SEL2	10
	SEL2	14
	SCG1	14
	SCG2	11
	PMQW	21
	S	4
	ECD	20
	SCD1	2
	SCD1	24
	POE	8
	PTC	2
	CM	7
	CM	35
	CM	60
	HP	1
	HP	77
	HP	100
	HP	115
	HP	123
	HP	143

Word	Ref	Num
EYES	DA	22
	EPF	21
	PUF	9
	AA	189
	AA	442
	AA	646
	AA	687
	AA	717
	AA	739
	PLB	21
	MD	36
	MD	89
	MD	222
	SAA	166
	SAA	745
	SAA	838
	SAA	842
	SAA	908
	AT	41
	AT	123
	L1	50
	L4	38
	L4	67
	L4	119
	T18	46
	T18	62
	T23	14
	T23	18
	T23	33
	T23	72
	T23	87
	T27	130
	H2	40
	FS1	13
	FS2	16
	FS3	2
	TA	70
	TA	123
	TA	199
	TA	237
	TA	275
	AK	151
	HAP	166
	HAP	265
	HAP	1176
	HAP	1207
	HAP	1238
	HAP	1846
	HAP	1902
	HAP	2019
	HAP	2291
	HAP	2501
	BR	111
	BR	133
	BR	203
	PP	50
	PTS	31
	SKA2	15
	SKA2	26
	SKA3	11
	EL	13
	EL	135
	EL	169
	EL	352
	ODA	11
	ODA	80
	SSH	3
	J1	89
	J3	59
	J3	101
	J3	168
	J6	99
	J6	155
	J6	177
	J6	210
	J6	221
	J6	332
	J6	380
	J6	508
	J6	814
	J10	46
	J10	321
	J10	360
	J10	532
	J16	14
	P2	53
	P3	10
	P3	85
	P3	240
	P4	101
	P4	113
	P5	161
	M1	109
	M1	318
	M1	360
	M1	673

EYES	M8	365
	B	31
	B	43
	B	63
	B	87
	B	197
	B	205
	B	235
	B	274
	B	309
	B	388
	B	532
	B	595
	B	617
	B	634
	B	662
	B	673
	B	681
	B	698
	B	725
	BP	151
	BP	155
	M10	73
	M10	94
	CAM	74
	CAM	109
	CAM	125
	CAM	162
	CAM	168
	CAM	176
	CAM	223
	HIF	153
	HIF	223
	HIF	304
	HIF	306
	HIF	376
	HIF	484
	HIF	512
	HIF	616
	HIF	721
	HIF	741
	C	116
	C	122
	C	239
	C	247
	C	449
	C	628
	C	667
	C	800
	TH	19
	TH	39
	TH	121
	M11	11
	M11	75
	M11	82
	M11	88
	M11	179
	M11	231
	M11	319
	M11	356
	M11	387
	M11	446
	FL	48
	FL	179
	FL	377
	M12	236
	M12	265
	M12	310
	M12	493
	M12	683
	M12	824
	AU	5
	AU	105
	AU	141
	AU	211
	AU	265
	AU	452
	AU	482
	WB	142
	WB	294
	M15	211
	M15	303
	M15	355
	GP	3
	CI	57
	CI	107
	CI	154
	CI	160
	CI	174
	CI	177
	CI	188
	CI	192
	CI	320
	AS	13
EYESIGHT	KT2	354
	P1	262

EYRY	AM	427
	HAP	2410
FABARIS	AE7	989
FABII	AE6	1164
FABIUS	TA	388
	MC	35
FABLE	RH	84
	EAA	1
	HAP	620
	HAP	2583
	J6	832
	PLT	29
	C	810
	M12	584
	AU	99
	WB	153
FABLED	M13	171
FABLE-MAKERS	GE	32
FABLE'S	L3	218
FABLES	AE11	622
	FL	601
	M15	226
FABRIC	AM	1097
	MF	25
	MF	66
	HAP	2235
	EL	89
	G4	263
	AE2	19
	AE2	45
	AE2	58
	AE2	311
	KT2	450
	KT3	757
	KT3	957
FABRICIUS	AE6	1162
	WB	450
FABRIC'S	AE6	310
FABRICS	AA	801
FACE	JH	16
	AR	158
	RH	8
	RH	76
	AM	247
	AM	292
	AM	956
	AM	1127
	AM	1192
	PA	24
	PA	20
	SEL1	1
	SEL3	20
	PCG2	16
	PCG2	30
	SCD1	18
	EAL	26
	EAL	14
	PCB	15
	PCB	27
	HP	15
	HP	40
	HP	93
	HP	170
	HP	243
	DA	69
	PUO3	32
	AA	30
	AA	649
	AA	1006
	PPC	29
	MD	10
	MD	23
	D	6
	MF	111
	EK	19
	RL	210
	PD	22
	L3	32
	L3	257
	L4	3
	L4	162
	L4	213
	L4	227
	L4	229
	T18	38
	T23	36
	T23	76
	T27	29
	T27	94
	T27	129

FACE	H3	42
	FS3	7
	TA	50
	TA	68
	TA	122
	TA	205
	AK	102
	AK	137
	AK	150
	AK	172
	HAP	33
	HAP	161
	HAP	370
	HAP	528
	HAP	1039
	HAP	1116
	HAP	1212
	HAP	1373
	HAP	1455
	HAP	1493
	HAP	2334
	HAP	2349
	HAP	2557
	BR	105
	BR	116
	BR	130
	BR	229
	PDS	6
	ETS	17
	PKA	17
	EKA	31
	EL	197
	EL	267
	ODA	11
	ODA	32
	EH	24
	EH	27
	J1	150
	J1	196
	J1	252
	J3	47
	J3	51
	J3	117
	J3	182
	J3	303
	J3	425
	J6	148
	J6	154
	J6	202
	J6	209
	J6	511
	J6	524
	J6	593
	J6	602
	J6	609
	J6	621
	J6	636
	J10	56
	J10	103
	J10	120
	J10	252
	J10	312
	J10	381
	J10	465
	J10	515
	J16	17
	P1	111
	P1	230
	P4	32
	P5	13
	M1	9
	M1	313
	M1	319
	M1	447
	M1	553
	M1	564
	M1	672
	M1	822
	M1	1059
	M9	66
	M9	192
	M9	206
	M13	144
	M13	146
	M13	153
	M13	162
	SFL	14
	HI	148
	GK	34
	GK	75
	GK	115
	VP2	19
	VP4	13
	VP9	7
	G1	259
	G1	436

Word	Ref	No.	Word	Ref	No.	Word	Ref	No.
FACE	G1	520	FACE	OAL	600	FACES	GK	53
	G1	579		OAL	677		AE3	231
	G1	590		OAL	702		AE3	282
	G1	604		OAL	831		AE3	520
	G2	540		OAL	869		AE6	319
	G3	96		OAE2	26		AE9	627
	G3	550		AF	52		AE12	506
	G4	138		MFL	7		OAL	188
	G4	144		DO	32		CI	594
	G4	345		DO	155	FACETIOUS	PP	46
	G4	532		KT1	261	FACING	KT3	995
	AE1	133		KT1	263	FACT	POE	35
	AE1	347		KT1	401		EL	332
	AE1	829		KT1	465		J6	834
	AE1	866		KT1	530		M9	58
	AE1	929		KT2	51		G1	632
	AE1	960		KT2	126		AE2	795
	AE1	975		KT2	178		AE6	1127
	AE2	376		KT2	318		AE9	90
	AE2	817		KT2	542		AE9	572
	AE3	260		KT3	40		AE11	1161
	AE3	441		KT3	76		M8	335
	AE3	540		KT3	706		B	387
	AE3	543		KT3	865		HIF	95
	AE3	669		KT3	921		C	289
	AE3	672		KT3	1021		M12	373
	AE3	778		M8	74		M12	584
	AE4	108		M8	229		AU	487
	AE4	477		M8	273		PWR	38
	AE4	684		B	377	FACTION	HS	142
	AE4	721		B	539		AR	22
	AE4	923		B	673		AA	489
	AE5	17		BP	119		AA	514
	AE5	468		M10	13		AA	568
	AE5	698		CAM	92		AA	919
	AE5	744		CAM	219		AA	973
	AE5	752		CAM	308		ELB	19
	AE5	805		CAM	375		ELB	20
	AE5	843		HIF	693		ELB	24
	AE5	846		HIF	720		D	18
	AE5	1075		C	291		D	41
	AE5	1104		C	410		SAA	10
	AE6	72		TH	111		SAA	498
	AE6	156		TH	119		SAA	515
	AE6	406		TH	260		SAA	570
	AE6	648		TH	297		SAA	806
	AE6	661		M11	26		SAA	893
	AE6	667		M11	81		SAA	907
	AE6	933		M11	303		SAA	914
	AE6	949		M11	404		SAA	965
	AE6	1001		FL	179		SAA	1136
	AE6	1170		FL	183		PK	1
	AE6	1191		FL	191		H29	41
	AE7	37		M12	329		TA	318
	AE7	245		M12	349		TA	390
	AE7	456		M12	431		TA	407
	AE7	584		M12	540		HAP	904
	AE7	627		M12	551		BR	195
	AE7	902		M12	567		AE10	20
	AE7	1109		M12	741		FL	396
	AE8	203		AU	203	FACTIONS	PWG	5
	AE8	290		WB	54		AA	140
	AE8	397		WB	126		ELB	30
	AE8	578		WB	367		MD	154
	AE8	637		M15	248		MD	318
	AE8	741		M15	289		G4	94
	AE9	230		M15	294		AE11	478
	AE9	639		M15	317	FACTIOUS	AA	68
	AE9	792		M15	355		AR	313
	AE9	991		M15	402		PLG	5
	AE9	1018		M15	461		AA	180
	AE10	186		GP	4		AA	606
	AE10	201		GP	13		AA	1018
	AE10	482		GP	103		ELB	12
	AE10	635		CI	54		MD	291
	AE10	989		CI	97		D	1
	AE10	1034		CI	109		SAA	181
	AE10	1132		CI	143		SAA	217
	AE11	134		CI	166		SAA	362
	AE11	307		CI	186		SAA	377
	AE11	529		EMKG	37		SAA	631
	AE11	783		PWR	29		SAA	1029
	AE11	912		HAP	734		PK	13
	AE11	926	FACED	AE9	57		HAP	1304
	AE11	1033		ETO	1		HAP	2531
	AE12	101	FACES	PCG2	5		AE11	347
	AE12	348		EMQW	16		AE11	454
	AE12	453		EDG	26		AE11	512
	AE12	784		HAP	812		KT3	472
	AE12	890		HAP	2282	FACTOR	AR	78
	AE12	946		SSC	19	FACTORS	OAL	659
	OAL	62		SKA3	13	FACTS	AE9	702
	OAL	137		PSH	10	FACULTIES	HAP	87
	OAL	288		J3	64		J10	370
	OAL	435		P2	105		B	507
	OAL	479		PLT	26	FADE	HS	58

FADE	AE12	104
FADED	KT1	531
	M11	10
FADES	UDH	79
	T23	57
FADING	SIE	1
	EUO2	2
	AE4	341
	AE9	117
	FL	376
FADUS	AE9	463
FAECES	M1	580
FAGOTED	SAA	419
FAGOTS	AE9	769
FAIL	UDH	91
	AM	707
	PMQ	33
	ENH	38
	EAL	1
	POE	13
	ETC	3
	PLG	30
	PR	11
	AA	723
	MD	289
	SAA	245
	SAA	274
	SAA	891
	PDG	18
	PDG	45
	L3	206
	HH	43
	HAP	149
	HAP	1195
	HAP	1933
	HAP	2332
	BR	356
	PTS	42
	J1	53
	J6	863
	J10	359
	J10	470
	P4	24
	P5	140
	M1	989
	M1	1002
	VP3	42
	G3	107
	G3	483
	AE9	405
	AE9	659
	AE12	151
	OAL	837
	KT1	480
	KT3	756
	B	582
	HIF	755
	AU	501
	CI	263
	PMK	12
	PMK	28
	EWR	3
FAILED	PCG1	2
	ECG1	37
	EUO	21
	EAZ	10
	AA	134
	AA	655
	SAA	538
	SAA	1136
	RL	251
	RL	272
	HAP	1333
	HAP	1943
	HAP	2255
	HAP	2499
	PMS	28
	AE7	816
	AE11	230
	KT2	120
	KT3	669
	M8	112
	M8	133
	M8	189
	CAM	233
	AU	591
FAILING	SAA	865
	DOD	23
	VP1	21
	DO	145
	KT1	351
	M8	357
FAILINGS	ELB	14
	SAA	388
	P1	261
FAILS	ENH	3

FAILS	PTW	9
	PSF	2
	ETG	25
	HAP	1436
	HAP	1547
	HAP	1664
	J1	58
	M1	707
	VP2	27
	AE3	338
	AE12	368
	B	75
	M10	83
	M11	175
	WB	131
	WB	431
	CI	464
FAIN	AM	110
	PR	10
	PLB	13
	T27	16
	TA	274
	HAP	636
	HAP	1443
	HAP	2297
	BR	122
	SKA6	3
	M1	307
	M1	873
	B	360
	CAM	76
	CAM	133
	M11	411
FAINT	FL	52
	AM	279
	AM	884
	PEL	10
	ETG	24
	PUO4	23
	EPC	17
	MF	19
	SDG	8
	L4	178
	TA	155
	TA	247
	HAP	1372
	J6	334
	M1	850
	VP8	123
	VP9	77
	G3	129
	G3	204
	AE6	383
	AE9	1096
	AE11	993
	KT1	152
	KT1	255
	CAM	284
	SMP	83
FAINTER	SEL2	9
	SAA	931
	AE11	693
FAINTING	AA	374
	AA	842
	MD	270
	SAA	1037
	H29	34
	HAP	966
	SKA1	9
	EL	42
	P3	201
	AE1	653
	AE2	360
	AE4	566
	AE4	989
	AE8	922
	AE9	473
	AE10	185
	AE10	976
	AE10	1120
	AE10	1,188
	AE10	1223
	AE12	488
	AE12	1122
	KT3	305
	FL	301
	CAM	157
	AU	342
FAINTLY	AR	243
	AM	525
	SEL1	11
	SCG1	24
	PKA	43
	AE2	745
	AE5	627
	AE9	241

FAINTLY	AE10	1043
	M8	344
	CI	320
FAINTS	BR	173
	AE3	399
	M12	563
	M12	687
FAINTY	G2	431
	FL	381
FAIR	HS	39
	HS	96
	AR	17
	AR	147
	RH	29
	SMA	37
	PWG	9
	VHH	23
	VHH	41
	AM	41
	AM	456
	SMM1	1
	SEL1	1
	SCG1	11
	SCG1	15
	SCG2	7
	PFD	15
	S	1
	EAL	21
	PKK	16
	HP	45
	HP	71
	HP	166
	HP	193
	EMP	1
	PSF	43
	ETG	9
	PR	13
	AA	298
	AA	432
	AA	463
	D	17
	D	35
	MF	64
	MF	65
	SAA	912
	PK	29
	EDG	19
	RL	394
	OE	37
	AT	31
	AT	114
	ER	23
	L4	13
	L4	41
	L4	116
	L4	164
	T18	1
	T18	35
	T18	63
	T23	3
	T23	96
	H29	69
	NS	1
	FS1	4
	FS3	1
	HAP	389
	HAP	586
	HAP	946
	HAP	956
	HAP	961
	HAP	1121
	HAP	1273
	HAP	1741
	HAP	1750
	HAP	1866
	HAP	2070
	HAP	2145
	HAP	2202
	HAP	2448
	SSC	41
	BR	107
	PDS	29
	PDS	37
	PP	50
	ETS	10
	ETS	19
	PTS	29
	STS2	1
	STS3	1
	STS3	21
	SKA2	9
	SKA2	23
	ELW	1
	LS	7
	LS	12
	LS	18

FAIR	EL	97	FAIR	AE5	1064	FAIR	KT3	595
	PSH	22		AE6	213		KT3	677
	PSH	23		AE6	1037		KT3	859
	SSH	7		AE7	71		KT3	1127
	EH	6		AE7	107		TJD	31
	EH	31		AE7	141		M8	46
	J1	115		AE7	224		M8	65
	J1	161		AE7	577		M8	75
	J6	85		AE7	664		M8	80
	J6	208		AE7	930		M8	156
	J6	235		AE7	1044		M8	213
	J6	256		AE7	1077		B	8
	J6	455		AE7	1094		B	30
	J6	492		AE8	183		B	100
	J6	757		AE8	184		B	190
	J10	315		AE8	274		B	200
	J10	445		AE8	486		B	217
	J10	453		AE9	360		M10	7
	J10	459		AE9	451		M10	65
	J16	53		AE9	546		M10	69
	P3	193		AE9	582		CAM	375
	P4	19		AE9	792		HIF	146
	M1	727		AE10	261		HIF	215
	M1	801		AE10	787		C	71
	M1	838		AE10	995		C	624
	M1	840		AE10	1107		C	651
	M1	857		AE10	1159		C	704
	M1	953		AE11	56		C	813
	M1	987		AE11	103		TH	11
	M1	1075		AE11	121		TH	35
	M9	71		AE11	154		TH	82
	M9	133		AE11	539		TH	414
	M9	150		AE11	554		TH	426
	M9	165		AE11	905		TH	428
	M9	171		AE12	39		M11	223
	M13	43		AE12	220		M11	406
	M13	144		AE12	291		FL	128
	M13	173		AE12	1042		FL	154
	SFL	7		OAL	16		FL	155
	SFL	11		OAL	103		FL	170
	HI	2		OAL	162		FL	307
	HI	41		OAL	185		FL	402
	HI	175		OAL	287		FL	463
	PLT	51		OAL	347		FL	480
	MC	18		OAL	412		FL	533
	GK	105		OAL	415		FL	573
	VP2	2		OAL	436		FL	582
	VP2	18		OAL	510		FL	605
	VP2	65		OAL	577		M12	44
	VP2	108		OAL	594		M12	261
	VP3	19		OAL	618		M12	278
	VP3	100		OAL	664		M12	293
	VP3	126		OAL	698		M12	313
	VP7	27		OAL	702		M12	383
	VP7	52		OAL	727		M12	539
	VP8	36		OAL	752		M12	564
	VP10	58		OAL	768		M12	811
	G1	353		OAL	773		WB	73
	G1	548		OAL	779		WB	84
	G1	558		OAL	826		WB	110
	G2	68		OAL	832		WB	289
	G2	188		OAL	858		WB	436
	G3	11		OAE2	4		WB	484
	G3	202		OAE2	62		WB	503
	G3	333		AF	15		WB	526
	G3	647		AF	19		WB	531
	G4	451		AF	30		M15	478
	G4	477		AF	48		GP	69
	G4	722		AF	54		CI	39
	G4	760		AF	110		CI	52
	G4	781		AF	117		CI	78
	G4	796		ETO	1		CI	152
	AE1	51		DO	10		CI	175
	AE1	371		DO	74		CI	243
	AE1	452		DO	97		CI	245
	AE1	474		DO	123		CI	256
	AE1	576		DO	162		CI	420
	AE1	838		DO	164		CI	500
	AE1	874		KT1	10		CI	524
	AE1	1007		KT1	145		CI	544
	AE2	143		KT1	171		STP	14
	AE2	462		KT1	182		PMK	9
	AE2	543		KT1	459		PMK	23
	AE3	384		KT1	581		AS	5
	AE3	429		KT2	113	FAIRBORNE'S	EPF	4
	AE3	528		KT2	150	FAIRER	SAA	1055
	AE4	175		KT2	164		T27	4
	AE4	204		KT2	374		AK	36
	AE4	334		KT3	14		HAP	1648
	AE4	483		KT3	55		HAP	1754
	AE4	516		KT3	75		M13	72
	AE5	372		KT3	142		AE8	730
	AE5	376		KT3	327		AE9	230
	AE5	529		KT3	475		MFL	27
	AE5	745		KT3	510		KT1	170
	AE5	791		KT3	532		TH	35

FAIREST	MHD	5	FAITH	HAP	150	FAITHFUL	AA	914
	T23	2		HAP	376		AT	15
	T23	3		HAP	406		ER	69
	H2	32		HAP	464		FS4	16
	TA	317		HAP	541		HAP	422
	HAP	328		HAP	607		HAP	423
	HAP	450		HAP	614		HAP	962
	HAP	981		HAP	745		SKA6	31
	SKA5	1		HAP	752		R	10
	ESH	28		HAP	878		R	14
	M1	606		HAP	881		G2	762
	GK	1		HAP	894		G3	616
	VP1	24		HAP	899		AE1	173
	VP5	67		HAP	997		AE2	967
	VP6	33		HAP	1024		AE5	624
	VP7	91		HAP	1104		AE6	42
	G4	794		HAP	1166		AE6	111
	AE1	110		HAP	1175		AE7	820
	AE7	380		HAP	1185		AE8	615
	AE12	376		HAP	1336		AE11	737
	OAL	243		HAP	2239		AE11	893
	OAL	284		HAP	2326		AE12	140
	OAL	326		BR	246		OAL	451
	DO	13		EKA	14		OAL	853
	DO	14		EL	151		KT3	240
	KT2	54		ESH	28		KT3	835
	KT3	114		J1	173		KT3	1123
	KT3	132		M1	190		M8	90
	TH	11		ELT	15		B	594
	M15	190		ELT	36		B	699
FAIRIES	PK	35		VP8	26		BP	189
FAIRLY	PWGR	20		G2	452		CAM	150
	PAA	10		AE1	345		HIF	75
	HAP	1654		AE1	398		M11	185
	HAP	2190		AE1	940		M11	256
	P2	23		AE2	194		AU	90
	P6	148		AE2	214		AU	92
	VP3	30		AE2	415		WB	357
	KT3	579		AE3	81		M15	354
	C	302		AE3	551	FAITHFULLY	CM	145
	AU	481		AE4	37	FAITHLESS	VHH	2
	WB	522		AE4	456		HP	6
	PMK	29		AE4	857		SAA	1088
FAIRS	MD	5		AE5	1105		M1	826
FAIRY	HAP	212		AE5	1122		AE2	29
	FL	57		AE5	1135		AE3	75
	FL	79		AE6	470		AE4	535
	FL	141		AE6	833		AE4	551
	FL	481		AE6	1214		AE4	715
	FL	494		AE7	322		AE4	869
	FL	500		AE8	189		AE7	507
	WB	3		AE8	197		AE9	169
	WB	20		AE8	714		AE12	480
	WB	32		AE8	844		KT2	319
FAITH	AM	146		AE9	91	FAITH'S	AA	318
	AM	191		AE9	344	FAITHS	RL	156
	AM	1092		AE9	368	FALCHION	HIF	295
	SMQ	12		AE9	397	FALCON	AM	342
	PA	25		AE10	141		HAP	2414
	ETL	13		AE11	47		AE11	1065
	EMQW	3		AE11	80	FALCONS	M1	683
	PCD	18		AE12	852	FALERNIAN	G2	137
	EMK	7		OAL	151	FALISCANS	AE7	959
	POE	19		OAL	844	FALL	UDH	37
	HP	188		LMC	9		RH	13
	DA	114		KT1	100		SMA	64
	EMW	9		KT1	288		LC	128
	ETG	14		KT1	302		SIE	13
	EUF	32		KT2	152		AM	115
	EAL	7		KT2	165		AM	512
	MD	93		KT3	807		AM	848
	SAA	583		KT3	849		SMQ	8
	SAA	656		CAM	237		SMQ	16
	PK	34		HIF	112		SMM2	24
	EDG	2		HIF	127		EEL	40
	EDG	24		HIF	328		SEL4	26
	RL	69		HIF	705		SEL4	28
	RL	130		HIF	732		PCG1	36
	RL	219		C	767		PFD	16
	RL	280		TH	219		PM	38
	RL	300		FL	523		A	6
	RL	308		FL	552		PLN	28
	RL	431		M12	259		PCD	13
	RL	442		AU	493		PCD	23
	T27	73		WB	247		SCD2	20
	TA	502		WB	302		ENH	22
	PAA	9		WB	324		EAL	21
	EAA	25		CI	249		POE	23
	EAA	31		CI	353		DA	73
	HAP	79		PMK	9		DA	116
	HAP	85		PMK	33		PSF	38
	HAP	106		EMKG	20		AA	680
	HAP	120	FAITHFUL	EMK	1		AA	774
	HAP	122		PTC	37		AA	793
	HAP	142		HP	196		AA	801
	HAP	148		AA	397		AA	956

Word	Ref	No.
FALL	PLB	26
	PLB	37
	MD	260
	MF	21
	SAA	197
	SAA	236
	SAA	517
	SAA	565
	SAA	904
	SAA	940
	SAA	1011
	PD	51
	TA	146
	AK	66
	GE	77
	HAP	607
	HAP	1514
	HAP	1826
	HAP	2300
	BR	76
	BR	337
	PKA	30
	EJG	8
	EL	21
	EL	28
	EL	167
	J3	312
	J6	89
	J6	493
	J10	172
	J10	232
	J10	351
	P1	129
	P3	228
	P4	72
	P6	155
	M1	260
	M1	325
	M1	398
	M1	446
	M1	466
	M1	686
	M1	773
	M1	1028
	SFL	20
	HI	116
	GK	16
	VP6	51
	G1	502
	G3	114
	G3	372
	G3	815
	G3	829
	G4	116
	G4	201
	G4	263
	G4	337
	G4	368
	AE1	248
	AE1	389
	AE1	460
	AE2	70
	AE2	179
	AE2	384
	AE2	465
	AE2	475
	AE2	494
	AE2	575
	AE2	633
	AE2	851
	AE2	892
	AE2	910
	AE3	196
	AE3	339
	AE4	709
	AE4	891
	AE5	234
	AE5	467
	AE5	907
	AE6	817
	AE7	406
	AE8	82
	AE9	175
	AE9	219
	AE9	274
	AE9	464
	AE9	721
	AE9	780
	AE9	906
	AE9	964
	AE9	1032
	AE10	89
	AE10	165
	AE10	617
	AE11	27
	AE11	109
FALL	AE11	207
	AE11	549
	AE11	659
	AE11	996
	AE11	1035
	AE11	1284
	AE12	67
	AE12	274
	AE12	764
	AE12	915
	AE12	998
	OAL	130
	OAL	421
	OAL	735
	KT1	63
	KT1	335
	KT1	427
	KT2	186
	KT2	605
	KT3	354
	KT3	417
	KT3	624
	M8	133
	M8	301
	M8	321
	B	343
	B	393
	CAM	137
	CAM	363
	HIF	240
	HIF	562
	HIF	782
	C	475
	C	689
	C	748
	TH	404
	M11	94
	M12	150
	M12	405
	M12	432
	M12	458
	M12	564
	M12	754
	M12	775
	AU	168
	AU	275
	AU	421
	WB	508
	M15	666
	CI	582
	PMK	34
FALLACIES	HAP	651
FALLACIOUS	M13	84
	AE2	116
	AE11	1060
	WB	383
FALLEN	AM	453
	AM	600
	PAR	10
	PNH	3
	HAP	450
	HAP	2311
	P3	113
	AE4	871
	AE5	604
	AE9	724
	AF	77
	AF	78
	KT3	596
	KT3	609
FALLIBLE	HAP	1045
FALLING	UDH	33
	AM	352
	AM	743
	AM	951
	AM	1036
	T23	74
	T23	107
	HAP	2582
	J3	317
	J6	382
	J10	411
	M1	137
	M1	997
	M13	67
	VP7	50
	VP7	75
	G1	617
	G2	101
	G2	585
	G2	755
	G4	454
	AE2	608
	AE3	504
	AE4	20
	AE4	116
FALLING	AE4	462
	AE4	642
	AE4	696
	AE5	463
	AE5	466
	AE5	694
	AE6	573
	AE6	930
	AE6	949
	AE7	859
	AE8	726
	AE10	800
	AE10	1109
	AE11	942
	AE12	1310
	KT3	127
	KT3	310
	KT3	733
	KT3	869
	M8	94
	CAM	114
	CAM	208
	M11	153
	M11	226
	FL	586
	M12	334
	M12	575
	M12	640
	AU	577
	M15	409
	CI	312
	EMKG	21
FALLINGS	HAP	1397
FALLOW	G1	119
	G1	682
	G3	623
FALLOWS	G2	739
FALLS	SAA	738
	H2	84
	TA	118
	HAP	439
	HAP	2315
	BR	65
	J3	321
	J10	416
	P2	51
	P5	80
	M9	167
	G3	772
	AE1	223
	AE1	238
	AE2	490
	AE2	789
	AE2	855
	AE3	272
	AE3	399
	AE3	784
	AE5	599
	AE7	698
	AE7	741
	AE9	199
	AE9	685
	AE9	759
	AE10	681
	AE10	991
	AE10	1036
	AE11	226
	AE11	1031
	AE12	678
	AE12	812
	AE12	1336
	OAL	606
	KT2	594
	KT3	864
	M8	132
	M8	177
	M8	203
	M11	175
	M11	202
	FL	580
	M12	94
	M12	334
	M12	472
FALSE	AR	152
	SMA	6
	AM	451
	AM	717
	ECG1	11
	SCG2	27
	SCG3	11
	SLN	19
	EKK	4
	DA	65
	DA	83
	PUO4	23
	AA	83

FALSE	AA	150
	AA	173
	AA	929
	PPC	5
	PPC	25
	MF	165
	MF	171
	MD	286
	SAA	320
	SAA	549
	SAA	784
	SAA	826
	SAA	1044
	EDGA	26
	SDG	14
	RL	384
	L4	186
	TA	435
	HH	41
	HAP	53
	HAP	74
	HAP	1008
	HAP	2220
	HAP	2394
	HAP	2499
	PP	15
	ETS	25
	EKA	34
	STS2	3
	STS2	4
	J6	122
	J10	71
	J10	165
	P1	132
	P2	96
	P3	96
	P5	104
	P5	131
	SLT1	22
	VP3	147
	VP10	34
	G3	441
	AE1	1001
	AE2	197
	AE2	219
	AE2	263
	AE4	449
	AE4	522
	AE4	551
	AE4	693
	AE4	943
	AE4	948
	AE7	514
	AE11	619
	AE12	369
	KT1	35
	KT1	305
	KT2	127
	KT2	133
	KT2	134
	KT3	575
	B	91
	B	547
	C	502
	C	581
	C	589
	C	595
	C	670
	M11	29
	M11	399
	M12	173
	AU	340
	AU	482
FALSEHOOD	SAA	955
	HAP	1200
	SAA	751
	M1	854
	OAL	718
FALSEHOODS	PCD	29
FALSELY	AM	671
	DA	60
	J3	76
	M13	41
	VP8	27
FALSIFIED	AE9	1095
FALSTAFF	PUO3	10
FALSTAFF-FAT	PC1	23
FALTERING	AE3	68
	AE3	400
	AE4	106
	AE12	1318
	KT3	786
	CAM	218
	TH	309
	M11	13
FAME	UDH	75

FAME	HS	5
	HS	53
	HS	18
	HS	85
	HS	129
	RH	103
	SMA	76
	LC	79
	DC	22
	DC	34
	LCA	17
	LCA	18
	VHH	40
	AM	42
	AM	189
	AM	274
	AM	458
	AM	638
	AM	701
	AM	784
	AM	1183
	ECG1	5
	ECG1	11
	ECG1	13
	PCG2	3
	ECG2	11
	ECG2	33
	A	11
	PUO1	27
	PUO1	36
	PNH	17
	PUO2	22
	ML	5
	PAL	19
	PTC	18
	PTC	39
	HP	14
	HP	114
	HP	164
	HP	204
	DA	101
	DA	208
	AA	40
	AA	178
	AA	186
	AA	201
	AA	309
	AA	358
	AA	420
	AA	708
	AA	733
	AA	847
	MD	232
	MF	85
	MF	94
	MF	96
	MF	128
	MF	171
	MF	203
	SAA	194
	SAA	487
	SAA	873
	SAA	942
	SAA	959
	SAA	973
	SAA	1050
	SAA	1064
	SAA	1099
	SAA	1115
	EDGA	19
	ER	60
	L4	98
	TA	44
	TA	330
	TA	489
	HAP	1145
	HAP	1578
	HAP	1584
	HAP	1630
	HAP	1699
	HAP	1879
	HAP	2480
	HAP	2488
	BR	192
	BR	204
	BR	230
	PTS	30
	ETS	14
	EL	9
	EL	40
	J1	108
	J6	80
	J6	129
	J6	146
	J6	538
	J10	217

FAME	J10	224
	J10	252
	J10	299
	P1	81
	P2	3
	P2	15
	M1	597
	M1	601
	M1	622
	M1	1073
	M9	1
	VCS	34
	HI	166
	MC	39
	MC	64
	MC	74
	GK	135
	GK	180
	DHP	11
	G2	192
	G3	14
	G3	52
	G4	126
	G4	736
	AE1	339
	AE1	391
	AE1	522
	AE1	640
	AE1	648
	AE1	750
	AE1	795
	AE1	872
	AE2	104
	AE2	115
	AE2	119
	AE2	386
	AE2	734
	AE3	141
	AE3	147
	AE3	223
	AE3	380
	AE3	724
	AE3	910
	AE4	73
	AE4	252
	AE4	263
	AE4	280
	AE4	325
	AE4	342
	AE4	431
	AE4	465
	AE4	561
	AE5	140
	AE5	398
	AE5	407
	AE5	443
	AE5	465
	AE5	524
	AE5	526
	AE5	632
	AE5	659
	AE5	736
	AE5	981
	AE6	20
	AE6	334
	AE6	519
	AE6	533
	AE6	815
	AE6	884
	AE6	1042
	AE6	1053
	AE7	1
	AE7	143
	AE7	149
	AE7	374
	AE7	466
	AE7	571
	AE7	659
	AE7	777
	AE7	894
	AE7	939
	AE7	983
	AE8	65
	AE8	162
	AE8	178
	AE8	184
	AE8	450
	AE8	734
	AE8	977
	AE9	91
	AE9	265
	AE9	368
	AE9	598
	AE9	630
	AE9	700
	AE9	795

Word	Ref	No.
FAME	AE9	876
	AE9	902
	AE9	1060
	AE10	214
	AE10	395
	AE10	517
	AE10	711
	AE10	940
	AE10	960
	AE10	1066
	AE11	188
	AE11	209
	AE11	211
	AE11	345
	AE11	412
	AE11	566
	AE11	676
	AE11	774
	AE11	1162
	AE12	356
	AE12	206
	AE12	484
	AE12	523
	AE12	730
	AE12	883
	AE12	984
	AE12	1014
	AE12	1066
	DO	17
	DO	56
	KT1	1
	KT1	60
	KT1	147
	KT1	605
	KT2	321
	KT2	454
	KT3	18
	KT3	159
	KT3	734
	KT3	1091
	TJD	209
	M8	64
	B	119
	B	408
	B	515
	HIF	278
	HIF	380
	HIF	493
	M11	370
	FL	303
	FL	534
	FL	616
	M12	61
	M12	87
	M12	202
	M12	224
	M12	239
	M12	274
	M12	278
	M12	605
	M12	719
	M12	798
	M12	806
	AU	87
	AU	296
	AU	361
	AU	371
	WB	2
	WB	405
	M15	75
	M15	434
	M15	531
	M15	635
	CI	40
	CI	459
	EP	3
FAMED	AM	73
	AM	214
	AM	371
	AM	686
	AM	1205
	PUO5	1
	HAP	800
	HAP	1626
	BR	139
	J1	13
	J1	27
	M9	107
	VP8	77
	G2	227
	G3	76
	G3	141
	AE1	875
	AE1	917
	AE2	344
	AE3	171
FAMED	AE6	544
	AE6	675
	AE6	1150
	AE7	1043
	AE7	1044
	AE10	271
	AE10	445
	AE10	1104
	AE12	587
	AE12	676
	KT1	156
	M8	48
	HIF	367
	C	377
	M11	4
	CI	224
FAME'S	HAP	1529
	P1	88
	G4	408
FAMILIAR	AM	648
	AA	691
	TA	219
	HAP	1722
	EL	320
	J1	9
	P5	31
	M1	883
	G3	632
	AE7	697
	OAL	532
	KT1	359
	FL	443
	M15	86
FAMILIARLY	EL	132
	C	608
FAMILIES	SMA	93
	MF	93
	L4	226
	J6	784
	AE12	39
FAMILY	UDH	2
	PTW	22
	L4	127
	L4	261
	T27	80
	H2	66
	HAP	252
	HAP	1945
	HAP	2302
	BR	166
	EL	345
	ODA	44
	ODA	58
	J3	189
	J3	210
	P3	143
	P6	181
	M13	168
	G4	304
	G4	349
	AE2	881
	AE7	75
	AE7	291
	KT3	423
	C	151
	C	615
	C	730
	TH	244
	AS	22
FAMINE	PFD	4
	D	25
	H3	42
	HAP	305
	HAP	1219
	EL	74
	G4	452
	AE3	335
	AE3	470
	AE3	507
	AE7	169
	AE7	174
	AE8	862
	AE10	383
	AS	93
FAMINE-PINED	G4	362
FAMINE'S	AE6	387
FAMISHED	PNH	38
	SAA	350
	L1	50
	HAP	161
	HAP	285
	M1	313
	G3	64
	G3	205
	G4	349
	AE4	108
FAMISHED	AE9	456
	AE9	639
	AE10	1024
	KT3	630
	CAM	81
	TH	39
	TH	270
	M15	530
	GP	51
FAMOUS	AR	98
	AM	773
	HP	54
	BR	194
	J6	491
	P3	48
	G3	191
	C	639
	WB	156
FAN	EDGA	16
	L4	51
	H29	39
	EH	27
	PLT	26
	G1	246
	AE4	4
	PWR	29
FANATIC	RH	52
	AM	890
	MD	59
	HAP	1949
	POE	31
	HAP	865
FANCIES	RH	13
	RH	26
	ETG	5
	M1	661
	AE2	50
	KT3	473
	CAM	299
	C	145
FANCIFUL	L2	62
FANCY	JH	6
	AR	160
	PMQ	39
	PT	37
	PTL	17
	SCG1	32
	SCG1	31
	EAZ	13
	SAA	623
	HAP	1810
	J3	166
	J6	157
	P5	268
	AE8	60
	AE10	915
	AE12	1313
	B	465
	CAM	64
	HIF	209
	C	323
	C	325
	C	488
	C	757
	TH	72
	FL	37
FANE	HI	15
	VP6	102
	AE1	402
	AE1	671
	AE1	698
	AE1	733
	AE7	589
	AE12	750
	OAL	74
	OAL	295
	KT2	608
	KT2	633
	KT3	126
	KT3	191
	KT3	341
	M8	13
	M15	235
FANES	AE2	326
	AE5	996
	KT2	659
FANG	M8	130
FANGS	HAP	202
	AE2	283
	TH	114
	M15	149
FANNED	DC	11
	T23	24
	J1	38
	KT2	519
	KT3	364

FANNED	HIF	333	FAR	EL	204	FAR	AE8	784
FANNING	OAL	188		EL	258		AE8	841
	M11	348		EL	263		AE8	885
	CI	104		J1	229		AE9	37
	CI	105		J3	4		AE9	417
	CI	106		J3	235		AE9	501
FANS	C	770		J6	565		AE9	667
	SMP	6		J6	710		AE9	747
FANTASTIC	OE	9		J10	466		AE9	796
	M11	296		J16	26		AE9	991
FANTASTICAL	KT2	486		P1	79		AE10	3
FAR	AR	3		P1	258		AE10	36
	AR	196		P2	25		AE10	376
	RH	91		M1	226		AE10	441
	SMA	82		M1	718		AE10	602
	EWG	22		M1	1051		AE10	638
	VHH	43		M1	1085		AE10	702
	AM	18		M9	135		AE10	780
	AM	25		M13	19		AE10	883
	AM	127		M13	66		AE10	938
	AM	241		M13	82		AE10	1105
	AM	289		M13	195		AE10	1138
	AM	313		SLT1	23		AE10	1201
	AM	413		VP1	17		AE11	188
	AM	719		VP1	87		AE11	234
	AM	743		VP5	88		AE11	599
	AM	951		VP9	82		AE11	900
	AM	990		G1	87		AE11	918
	AM	1101		G1	324		AE11	932
	AM	1197		G1	416		AE11	1131
	STL	5		G2	1		AE11	1179
	PFD	23		G2	215		AE11	1248
	PFD	25		G2	709		AE11	1310
	PMQW	10		G3	29		AE12	130
	PM	26		G3	130		AE12	516
	EM	11		G3	306		AE12	659
	S	11		G3	332		AE12	706
	ENH	18		G3	419		AE12	965
	PUO2	38		G3	449		AE12	990
	POE	21		G3	550		AE12	1123
	EOE	22		G3	757		AE12	1239
	HP	160		G4	14		OAL	35
	AA	133		G4	17		OAL	56
	AA	259		G4	283		OAL	59
	AA	533		G4	562		OAL	148
	AA	697		G4	629		OAL	196
	AA	699		AE1	19		OAL	299
	AA	803		AE1	44		OAL	401
	AA	863		AE1	358		OAE1	31
	AA	943		AE1	467		KT1	26
	EPC	15		AE1	505		KT1	286
	MD	69		AE1	754		KT1	437
	D	18		AE1	996		KT2	25
	MF	140		AE2	53		KT2	319
	SAA	163		AE2	119		KT2	376
	SAA	248		AE2	413		KT2	384
	SAA	557		AE3	32		KT2	413
	SAA	730		AE3	73		KT2	547
	SAA	740		AE3	490		KT2	568
	SAA	831		AE3	510		KT3	5
	SAA	840		AE3	536		KT3	236
	SAA	1107		AE3	613		KT3	627
	SAA	1119		AE3	684		KT3	638
	RL	194		AE3	729		KT3	859
	RL	224		AE3	774		TJD	198
	RL	398		AE3	780		M8	3
	AT	22		AE3	789		M8	180
	AT	69		AE3	853		B	50
	L2	5		AE3	889		B	301
	L3	238		AE3	920		BP	21
	L3	260		AE4	202		BP	30
	T23	3		AE4	646		CAM	14
	TA	246		AE4	720		CAM	283
	AK	56		AE4	948		HIF	52
	AK	174		AE5	32		HIF	344
	GE	16		AE5	164		C	212
	GE	20		AE5	420		C	354
	HAP	150		AE5	783		C	599
	HAP	312		AE6	39		C	706
	HAP	529		AE6	92		TH	119
	HAP	783		AE6	96		M11	99
	HAP	1134		AE6	123		M11	244
	HAP	1351		AE6	368		M11	475
	HAP	1456		AE6	596		FL	126
	HAP	1496		AE6	610		FL	320
	HAP	1542		AE7	82		M12	75
	HAP	1850		AE7	216		M12	138
	HAP	1886		AE7	371		M12	507
	HAP	1957		AE7	499		M12	530
	HAP	2094		AE7	508		M12	780
	HAP	2342		AE7	567		M12	800
	BR	222		AE8	131		WB	224
	PDS	24		AE8	149		M15	291
	PMS	6		AE8	217		M15	406
	PKA	32		AE8	624		M15	419
	EL	93		AE8	799		CI	331

Word	Ref	No.
FAR	CI	501
	ETP	1
	ESK	3
	PWR	37
FARCE	EWGR	42
	EEL	18
	PCG1	35
	PCG1	38
	ESF	3
	PTC	21
	PLG	24
	PLG	34
	MF	182
	EK	8
	PAA	18
	GE	75
	MS	7
	J6	791
	C	340
	PTP	46
	EWR	6
	EWR	7
FARCE-LOVERS	PSH	31
FARCES	PLN	20
	ESH	24
FAR-DECEIVING	AE1	1070
FARE	AM	349
	HAP	1247
	HAP	1408
	HAP	1825
	HAP	2293
	HAP	2423
	HAP	2575
	J3	428
	P4	36
	P6	39
	VP1	114
	VP5	39
	VP7	47
	G2	667
	G3	232
	G3	503
	G4	194
	AE3	279
	AE4	701
	AE7	155
	BP	96
	BP	129
FARED	J1	144
	AE12	1319
	KT2	202
	M8	129
	M12	136
FARES	AR	228
	P4	74
	AE7	534
	AE9	1078
	AE12	159
	AE12	15
	M8	281
FAREWELL	AR	221
	ETL	25
	S	1
	SSF	1
	SSF	2
	MO	1
	MO	22
	T23	47
	T23	53
	T23	110
	HAP	1578
	EJG	7
	J3	497
	VP1	102
	VP8	82
	G4	718
	AE2	1072
	AE5	967
	AE9	387
	AE11	146
	AE11	1202
	KT1	418
	KT1	419
	KT3	281
	KT3	800
	KT3	994
	BP	189
	CAM	145
	TH	205
	M11	70
FAR-FETCHED	HS	123
FAR-LABORING	SAA	563
FARM	HAP	2287
	HAP	2352
	HAP	2418
	HAP	2539
FARM	VP1	64
	VP9	4
	CI	73
	CI	202
FARMED	J3	57
FARMER	H2	89
	G1	405
	G1	427
FARMER'S	M15	159
	M15	303
FARMERS	T27	76
	WB	30
FARMOST	AE6	62
	B	264
FARMS	HAP	2362
FARRE	MHD	8
FARROWED	J6	257
FAR-SHOOTING	AE10	1253
	HIF	32
	HIF	276
FARTHER	LC	36
	LC	130
	EIE	14
	AM	1112
	PT	37
	SM1	10
	AA	491
	SAA	443
	RL	117
	AT	69
	HAP	69
	HAP	123
	HAP	282
	HAP	791
	HAP	1421
	HAP	2088
	EMI	5
	ODA	64
	J1	221
	J16	13
	P1	265
	P5	119
	P6	137
	G4	731
	AE2	922
	AE3	617
	AE3	639
	AE3	790
	AE3	881
	AE4	720
	AE6	292
	AE6	448
	AE6	644
	AE6	836
	AE6	859
	AE8	193
	AE9	1106
	AE10	886
	AE11	76
	AE11	160
	AE11	826
	AE11	845
	AE11	1035
	AE11	1181
	AE12	1149
	AE12	1286
	KT1	297
	KT1	298
	KT2	293
	TJD	26
	B	715
	CAM	211
	C	225
	TH	24
	TH	56
	TH	382
	M11	433
	FL	335
	FL	502
	M12	142
	AU	191
	AU	579
	WB	101
FARTHERED	OAL	428
FARTHEST	AR	295
	AR	306
	ML	27
	BR	6
	J6	606
	G2	238
	G2	272
FARTHING	EKK	21
	ELB	21
	P4	57
	P5	108
FARTHINGS	J3	428
FARTHINGS	EUF	21
	J6	705
FASCES	AR	249
	AM	199
	TA	517
	G1	42
FASCINATING	BR	203
FASHION	PMM	13
	PA	10
	PCG2	25
	ECD	10
	EUO	31
	PKK	17
	EUF	29
	PLB	40
	PK	1
	RL	254
	EDS	1
	PP	34
	ETS	6
	J6	269
	P1	120
FASHIONABLE	J1	106
	M10	45
FASHIONED	PA	9
	HP	245
	AE6	63
	CI	219
FASHIONS	EWGR	46
	PDG	4
	L4	107
	J6	414
FAST	JH	17
	SIE	5
	AM	721
	AM	973
	SM2	13
	PLN	19
	EAZ	32
	ML	30
	EAL	12
	PTW	24
	PSF	11
	SAA	1034
	SAA	1063
	SAA	1117
	L4	291
	T23	24
	FS2	13
	HAP	698
	HAP	1246
	HAP	1520
	HAP	1882
	HAP	2312
	SKA6	26
	EL	185
	J6	198
	J10	502
	P3	145
	VP9	1
	G3	506
	G4	584
	AE3	827
	AE5	201
	AE5	285
	AE5	970
	AE8	299
	AE9	719
	AE10	537
	AE11	1061
	AE12	1128
	KT3	863
	KT3	985
	B	165
	B	171
	HIF	599
	C	95
	M12	483
	M12	579
	AU	357
	M15	504
	GP	9
	CI	216
	CI	416
	SMP	65
	PMK	1
	PMK	34
FASTEN	HH	17
	HAP	2411
	AE2	308
FASTENED	MD	151
	HAP	202
	M1	742
	M1	925
	G1	251
	AE5	676

FASTENED	AE5	1108	FATAL	MD	75	FATAL	AE10	140
	AE7	1011		SAA	9		AE10	461
	AE10	922		SAA	71		AE10	542
	AE11	846		SAA	170		AE10	665
	AE11	865		SAA	228		AE10	675
	AE12	882		SAA	487		AE10	693
	KT3	633		SAA	688		AE10	702
	M8	148		AT	99		AE10	821
	M8	153		T23	93		AE10	826
	BP	185		TA	78		AE10	848
	HIF	301		TA	148		AE10	870
	TH	114		TA	406		AE10	996
	M12	469		TA	480		AE10	1045
FASTENING	L4	39		BR	97		AE10	1075
	M1	732		ODA	49		AE10	1289
	AE11	1107		J6	747		AE11	209
	TH	143		J10	409		AE11	256
	M12	312		J10	515		AE11	450
FASTENS	TJD	80		M1	995		AE11	593
FASTER	SLN	14		M9	160		AE11	724
	AA	786		M13	195		AE11	810
	MD	54		HI	65		AE11	966
	SAA	360		HI	72		AE11	1250
	GE	79		HI	116		AE12	96
	M1	417		HI	124		AE12	410
	AE2	225		HI	180		AE12	678
	WB	222		VP1	28		AE12	726
FASTING	AA	629		VP8	53		AE12	883
	RL	414		G1	594		AE12	916
	OE	12		G3	412		AE12	1144
	J10	368		AE1	106		AE12	1335
	P6	101		AE1	197		AE12	1366
	TH	37		AE1	504		DO	31
FASTNESS	AE9	940		AE1	1060		KT1	17
FASTS	HAP	364		AE2	47		KT1	77
	HAP	2322		AE2	16		KT1	272
	P5	267		AE2	107		KT1	440
FAT	PCD	3		AE2	184		KT2	212
	PTC	24		AE2	208		KT2	636
	PUO3	10		AE2	220		KT3	1063
	PK	33		AE2	230		M8	130
	H2	81		AE2	294		M8	255
	AK	64		AE2	311		M8	292
	HAP	45		AE2	345		B	626
	HAP	377		AE2	382		CAM	290
	HAP	1466		AE2	437		HIF	575
	PP	27		AE2	442		C	313
	J1	47		AE2	555		C	371
	J3	397		AE2	585		C	395
	J6	15		AE2	671		TH	182
	J6	419		AE2	1003		TH	275
	J6	596		AE2	1012		TH	299
	J6	696		AE4	24		TH	376
	J10	76		AE4	99		TH	404
	P2	80		AE4	428		M11	7
	P2	111		AE4	727		M12	93
	P3	140		AE4	733		M12	250
	P5	278		AE4	927		M12	632
	P6	101		AE4	938		M12	804
	P6	182		AE4	956		AU	277
	M1	567		AE4	979		AU	435
	VP8	74		AE4	1008		AU	516
	VP8	91		AE5	682		AU	588
	G1	470		AE5	792		AU	604
	G2	122		AE5	832		M15	191
	G2	196		AE5	853		CI	388
	G2	280		AE5	879		CI	452
	G2	305		AE5	1094	FATALLY	AM	45
	G3	220		AE6	218		J10	11
	G3	687		AE6	265		J10	196
	AE1	895		AE6	276		M9	79
	AE3	286		AE6	423		AE2	521
	AE5	321		AE6	477		AE3	470
	AE5	1009		AE6	548		AE12	788
	AE6	322		AE6	675		OAE1	27
	AE7	947		AE6	693	FATE	MHD	7
	AE8	142		AE6	866		HS	67
	AE9	87		AE7	167		HS	118
	AE9	794		AE7	174		AR	13
	AE10	210		AE7	442		AR	42
	AE11	1085		AE7	693		AR	51
	KT3	347		AE7	790		AR	56
	M8	9		AE7	993		AR	204
	M15	127		AE8	111		AR	321
	M15	528		AE8	630		SMA	119
FATAL	LC	59		AE8	768		SMA	133
	DC	54		AE8	823		LC	16
	VHH	4		AE8	939		LC	25
	AM	96		AE9	172		LC	97
	AM	699		AE9	422		LC	124
	AM	866		AE9	445		LC	133
	CM	1		AE9	467		LC	132
	CM	118		AE9	564		SIE	5
	HP	239		AE9	701		AM	81
	AA	146		AE9	1044		AM	140
	AA	812		AE10	111		AM	187

FATE				FATE				FATED					

FATE

AE7	346
AE7	368
AE7	349
AE7	420
AE7	605
AE7	617
AE7	819
AE7	823
AE7	1041
AE7	1063
AE8	20
AE8	55
AE8	440
AE8	492
AE8	527
AE8	654
AE8	676
AE8	756
AE8	832
AE8	912
AE8	924
AE9	112
AE9	155
AE9	168
AE9	180
AE9	277
AE9	365
AE9	368
AE9	382
AE9	439
AE9	782
AE9	942
AE9	1000
AE9	1010
AE9	1020
AE10	10
AE10	51
AE10	77
AE10	100
AE10	145
AE10	164
AE10	181
AE10	236
AE10	466
AE10	477
AE10	533
AE10	550
AE10	565
AE10	615
AE10	631
AE10	698
AE10	883
AE10	1058
AE10	1068
AE10	1219
AE10	1308
AE10	1237
AE10	1261
AE11	86
AE11	161
AE11	168
AE11	243
AE11	247
AE11	272
AE11	356
AE11	477
AE11	551
AE11	561
AE11	731
AE11	878
AE11	1241
AE12	8
AE12	62
AE12	229
AE12	238
AE12	331
AE12	366
AE12	424
AE12	440
AE12	751
AE12	799
AE12	867
AE12	960
AE12	1011
AE12	1032
AE12	1055
AE12	1118
AE12	1234
AE12	1270
AF	76
DO	90
KT1	86
KT1	95
KT1	244
KT1	328
KT1	351

FATE

KT1	381
KT1	421
KT1	483
KT1	554
KT2	64
KT2	87
KT2	113
KT2	209
KT2	411
KT3	162
KT3	356
KT3	636
KT3	791
KT3	798
KT3	822
KT3	861
KT3	868
KT3	879
TJD	35
TJD	80
M8	167
M8	303
M8	350
M8	353
B	49
B	187
B	224
B	228
B	328
B	359
B	382
B	401
B	470
B	581
B	621
B	673
B	745
B	757
BP	156
CAM	70
HIF	408
HIF	709
HIF	761
C	246
C	676
TH	29
TH	41
TH	139
TH	200
TH	323
TH	414
M11	48
M11	179
M11	193
M11	232
M11	370
M11	384
M11	491
M12	46
M12	230
M12	242
M12	340
M12	493
M12	525
M12	726
M12	731
M12	769
M12	785
AU	74
AU	117
AU	125
AU	209
AU	495
WB	81
WB	460
M15	56
M15	220
M15	503
M15	648
CI	252
CI	325
PTP	1
EWR	23
HAP	8

FATED

AE1	622
AE2	71
AE3	317
AE5	853
AE7	575
AE7	956
AE8	507
AE8	711
AE8	808
AE9	185
AE10	343
AE10	435

FATED

AE10	919
AE11	675
AE12	1069
M12	235
M12	660

FATE'S

GE	34
HAP	2066
EL	292
J10	394
VP1	93
G1	289
G1	336
AE3	921
AE4	492
AE5	1042
AE6	92
AE6	358
AE6	1220
AE8	168
AE8	442
AE8	500
AE9	126
AE12	927

FATES

AM	762
AA	834
SAA	1096
L3	318
J3	436
M1	347
M13	213
HI	122
VP4	56
G3	738
G4	659
AE1	328
AE1	351
AE1	417
AE1	780
AE2	248
AE2	468
AE2	1056
AE2	1064
AE3	14
AE3	133
AE3	215
AE3	435
AE3	483
AE3	487
AE3	565
AE4	878
AE5	920
AE5	925
AE5	966
AE6	158
AE6	370
AE6	736
AE6	859
AE6	927
AE6	1092
AE7	131
AE7	375
AE7	405
AE7	434
AE7	807
AE7	904
AE9	164
AE9	920
AE10	44
AE10	168
AE10	171
AE10	230
AE10	587
AE10	887
AE10	962
AE10	1155
AE11	176
AE11	197
AE11	1231
AE11	1300
AE12	170
AE12	899
AE12	981
AE12	1148
AE12	1168
AE12	1191
OAL	786
DO	40
KT1	398
KT1	414
KT2	609
KT3	169
M8	80
B	655
HIF	74
HIF	571
TH	186

FATES	TH	190	FATHER	AE2	905	FATHER	WB	455
	AU	261		AE2	962		M15	550
	AU	574		AE2	975		M15	677
	CI	423		AE2	983		GP	100
	STP	18		AE2	995		CI	69
FATES'	AE7	636		AE3	14		CI	203
	B	492		AE3	83		CI	236
FATHER	SMA	94		AE3	137		CI	245
	LC	57		AE3	197		CI	316
	AM	136		AE3	711		AS	41
	AM	291		AE3	757		AS	95
	AM	925		AE3	806	FATHER'S	AR	52
	AM	1141		AE3	933		AR	258
	PTW	32		AE4	860		CM	93
	CM	6		AE5	470		CM	146
	CM	74		AE6	175		DA	174
	CM	111		AE6	974		AA	381
	CM	113		AE6	1021		AA	420
	CM	118		AE6	1129		AA	774
	AA	20		AE6	1140		AA	830
	AA	36		AE7	70		AA	536
	AA	317		AE7	122		MF	116
	AA	349		AE7	440		MF	142
	AA	429		AE7	675		MF	217
	AA	462		AE7	708		SAA	128
	AA	707		AE7	328		SAA	385
	AA	942		AE7	947		SAA	857
	MD	100		AE8	46		SAA	968
	PRH	29		AE8	98		SAA	995
	MF	173		AE8	206		L4	214
	SAA	174		AE8	296		L4	231
	SAA	392		AE8	559		TA	368
	PD	22		AE8	755		TA	460
	PD	28		AE9	223		AK	79
	PD	47		AE9	260		HAP	1984
	T27	68		AE9	330		BR	45
	T27	80		AE9	339		BR	112
	AK	26		AE9	403		EPN	4
	HAP	737		AE9	547		ODA	29
	HAP	1071		AE9	793		J1	92
	HAP	1590		AE10	71		J3	82
	BR	45		AE10	76		J6	82
	BR	215		AE10	196		J6	247
	EDS	8		AE10	445		J10	504
	EDS	11		AE10	625		P6	126
	ODA	53		AE10	1128		P6	157
	J3	118		AE10	1135		M1	186
	J6	112		AE10	1185		M1	189
	J6	777		AE11	65		M1	799
	J10	401		AE11	77		M1	880
	J16	81		AE11	634		M1	1093
	P3	65		AE11	676		M9	24
	P3	90		AE11	815		M9	55
	P6	136		AE12	524		VCS	8
	P6	151		AE12	1021		VCS	35
	M1	229		AE12	1069		HI	88
	M1	337		AE12	1352		HI	113
	M1	489		OAL	77		HI	167
	M1	646		OAL	150		VP3	46
	M1	655		OAL	224		G2	761
	M1	891		OAL	231		G3	162
	M1	898		OAL	321		G4	814
	M1	1066		DO	56		AE1	67
	M9	59		M8	58		AE1	878
	M9	69		M8	369		AE2	368
	M9	101		B	121		AE2	387
	M13	167		B	313		AE2	650
	VCS	33		B	355		AE2	733
	HI	43		B	363		AE2	766
	HI	65		B	379		AE2	899
	HI	146		B	422		AE2	924
	MC	43		B	441		AE2	1026
	VP3	89		B	537		AE4	121
	VP3	148		B	582		AE4	477
	VP4	16		B	615		AE4	618
	VP4	52		B	665		AE5	62
	VP7	8		CAM	43		AE5	105
	G1	444		CAM	68		AE5	128
	G1	669		CAM	109		AE5	132
	G2	5		CAM	183		AE5	945
	G3	681		CAM	195		AE5	1075
	G4	481		CAM	302		AE6	48
	G4	550		HIF	685		AE6	163
	AE1	90		C	619		AE7	17
	AE1	111		C	645		AE7	573
	AE1	221		TH	248		AE7	910
	AE1	346		TH	421		AE7	1055
	AE1	476		M11	185		AE7	1070
	AE1	879		M11	213		AE8	336
	AE1	951		M12	245		AE8	609
	AE2	109		M12	502		AE8	758
	AE2	284		M12	708		AE9	893
	AE2	672		M12	723		AE10	589
	AE2	747		AU	297		AE10	728
	AE2	812		WB	400		AE10	742
	AE2	890		WB	418		AE10	871

Word	Ref	No.
FATHER'S	AE10	973
	AE10	1066
	AE10	1121
	AE11	46
	AE11	516
	AE11	543
	AE12	69
	AE12	523
	AE12	758
	AE12	1192
	OAL	210
	OAL	219
	OAL	220
	OAL	379
	TJD	42
	M11	42
	M11	63
	DO	167
	B	27
	B	31
	B	193
	B	645
	CAM	87
	CAM	184
	HIF	610
	C	194
	C	650
	C	702
	TH	244
	M12	489
	AU	46
	WB	396
	WB	405
	M15	601
	M15	607
	CI	61
	CI	129
	CI	201
	AS	39
FATHERS	UDH	88
	HS	124
	AM	252
	AM	793
	AM	1048
	AM	1090
	ECD	4
	PNH	42
	ESF	21
	PSF	33
	AA	720
	MD	112
	MD	127
	SAA	710
	RL	336
	RL	440
	L4	239
	HAP	398
	HAP	470
	HAP	820
	HAP	833
	HAP	1701
	HAP	1761
	J6	73
	P1	64
	P1	150
	G2	780
	AE1	9
	AE5	723
	AE6	320
	AE9	309
	AE12	76
	AE12	360
	TJD	88
	CAM	4
	TH	153
	FL	155
	WB	440
FATHERS'	EKK	17
	SAA	709
	L4	105
	G1	410
	AE6	426
	AE8	176
	AE10	395
	AE11	643
FATHOM	AA	742
	RL	41
	P4	28
	KT3	955
	EMKG	28
FATHOMED	SAA	1020
FATHOMS	PUO4	18
FATIGUE	HAP	1258
FATIGUES	GE	41
FATNESS	G2	547
	G2	757

Word	Ref	No.
FATNESS	AE8	104
FATTED	P1	137
	G4	789
	AE8	851
	HIF	630
FATTEN	PAZ	28
	G1	661
	HIF	424
FATTENED	MD	172
	P2	87
	P3	61
	AE12	321
	M15	127
FATTENING	VP6	6
	G1	23
	G1	119
	G2	256
	G3	232
	G3	617
	AE10	1001
FATTENS	J3	112
	G4	534
	AE8	86
	M15	295
	M15	423
FATTER	G2	335
FAUCHION	AE2	753
	AE6	333
	AE9	1089
	AE10	553
	AE10	668
	AE10	746
	AE10	801
	AE10	1119
	AE11	737
	AE12	140
	AE12	142
	OAL	787
	M8	232
	HIF	423
	M12	641
	M12	642
	AU	597
FAUCHIONS	AE7	881
	AE11	299
	KT2	244
	KT2	599
	KT3	602
	KT3	625
	TH	283
FAULCHION	M1	994
FAULT	UDH	60
	PMQ	52
	EMQ	8
	PA	42
	PTL	21
	PAL	23
	HP	51
	J6	396
	J6	635
	P1	259
	G4	704
	AE1	62
	AE2	587
	AE2	817
	AE9	572
	AE10	271
	AE11	174
	AE11	252
	OAL	379
	OAL	674
	MM	37
	KT3	736
	KT3	1125
	B	385
	B	492
	M11	16
	AU	224
	AU	465
	WB	364
FAULTLESS	ECG2	5
	AA	783
	HAP	542
	J10	454
	M1	836
	G3	710
	AE6	673
	MFL	9
	DO	114
FAULTS	HS	33
	PIE	14
	EMQ	6
	PTL	11
	PTL	25
	ECG2	19
	EM	15

Word	Ref	No.
FAULTS	PUO1	20
	PUO2	25
	PUO2	29
	AA	35
	PPC	14
	EPC	25
	SAA	175
	L4	140
	TA	263
	HAP	333
	J6	264
	P1	117
	P4	49
	M13	97
	PLT	48
	MM	9
	MM	18
	B	281
	B	309
	TH	410
	WB	144
	CI	236
FAUNS	VP6	44
	G1	11
	AE8	418
FAUNUS	M13	2
	AE7	70
	AE7	72
	AE7	122
	AE7	348
	AE12	1113
	AE12	1125
	AE12	1126
FAUNUS'	AE7	291
FAVOR	LCA	7
	LCA	51
	ET	12
	SCG1	20
	ETG	9
	AA	343
	PPC	30
	SAA	1011
	J10	118
	M9	63
	ELT	22
	AE1	735
	AE3	794
	AE4	66
	AE5	448
	AE8	623
	AE10	21
	AE10	148
	AE10	1303
	AE11	837
	KT1	600
	KT2	28
	KT3	482
	KT3	671
	B	7
	B	364
	C	807
	TH	19
	M12	705
	WB	294
	CI	572
FAVORABLE	HIF	527
FAVORED	M12	54
	EC	24
	AE1	522
	AE2	112
	AE2	336
	AE2	426
	AE3	619
	AE5	196
	AE6	221
	AE7	85
	AE7	730
	AE8	24
	AE8	646
	AE11	1039
	AE12	226
	KT1	429
	KT3	287
	CAM	315
	HIF	82
	HIF	109
	HIF	299
	M15	65
	CI	440
FAVORING	AE5	292
	KT3	472
FAVORITE	LC	91
	MD	4
	HAP	1636
	EKA	41
	SKA5	5

Word	Ref	Num
FAVORITE	J3	307
	J6	497
	AE4	610
	AE7	486
	AE10	98
	B	91
FAVORITES	HS	31
FAVORS	LC	93
	ECG1	2
	PNH	12
	ENH	11
	EUO2	13
	EAZ	36
	EDG	20
	HAP	445
	BR	337
	PSH	24
	J6	529
	J6	792
	AE4	484
	AE9	13
	AE10	170
	AE10	1017
	AE11	192
	OAL	171
	OAL	187
	KT3	166
FAWN	PCD	6
	AE4	526
FAWNING	PLB	7
	PRH	22
	G3	745
	G4	741
	AE2	263
	AE6	1115
	AE8	394
	AE8	838
FAWNS	M1	250
	FL	195
FEAR	AR	8
	AR	180
	AR	306
	AR	310
	SMA	105
	LC	143
	LCA	37
	PIE	2
	VHH	32
	AM	177
	AM	494
	AM	520
	AM	907
	AM	1138
	AM	1148
	AM	1214
	SEL3	7
	SEL3	11
	PTL	21
	PFD	3
	EM	10
	ELN	12
	SLN	1
	EUO	1
	PNH	7
	EUO2	27
	PC1	2
	PC2	25
	ML	1
	ML	24
	POE	13
	ETC	9
	PCB	11
	CM	58
	CM	74
	CM	94
	HP	26
	HP	39
	HP	174
	HP	177
	HP	181
	HP	234
	DA	6
	DA	41
	DA	130
	AA	178
	AA	401
	AA	420
	AA	468
	AA	937
	AA	947
	AA	1004
	EPC	18
	PRH	39
	MF	46
	SAA	76
	SAA	99

Word	Ref	Num
FEAR	SAA	105
	SAA	249
	SAA	612
	SAA	716
	SAA	772
	SAA	907
	PDG	33
	EDGA	23
	RL	452
	ER	76
	L1	7
	L3	46
	L3	187
	L3	232
	L5	13
	T23	73
	T23	79
	T27	20
	H29	49
	H29	92
	NS	25
	TA	34
	TA	53
	TA	136
	TA	198
	TA	481
	AK	80
	AK	118
	AK	131
	AK	170
	HAP	307
	HAP	531
	HAP	630
	HAP	1067
	HAP	1145
	HAP	1254
	HAP	1264
	HAP	1314
	HAP	1345
	HAP	1696
	HAP	1713
	HAP	1768
	HAP	1789
	HAP	1802
	HAP	1812
	HAP	1817
	HAP	1900
	HAP	2103
	HAP	2154
	HAP	2164
	HAP	2394
	HAP	2406
	HAP	2445
	HAP	2472
	BR	270
	BR	288
	EDS	1
	PTS	9
	STS3	32
	STS3	38
	PKA	20
	EL	23
	EL	297
	ESH	3
	EH	34
	J1	108
	J1	186
	J3	206
	J3	208
	J3	321
	J3	349
	J6	132
	J6	514
	J6	698
	J10	39
	J10	78
	J10	534
	J16	13
	P1	18
	P1	83
	P3	95
	P5	185
	P5	269
	P6	93
	P6	120
	M1	65
	M1	116
	M1	233
	M1	261
	M1	338
	M1	345
	M1	530
	M1	710
	M1	728
	M1	848

Word	Ref	Num
FEAR	M9	44
	M9	163
	M9	190
	M13	98
	M13	172
	HI	24
	HI	107
	ELT	5
	ELT	18
	ELT	20
	DHP	18
	EHC	3
	VP1	70
	VP3	78
	VP5	94
	VP7	10
	VP7	72
	VP9	87
	G1	256
	G1	427
	G1	452
	G1	459
	G1	692
	G2	433
	G2	585
	G2	711
	G3	49
	G3	62
	G3	124
	G3	168
	G3	218
	G3	622
	G4	497
	G4	501
	G4	509
	G4	769
	AE1	90
	AE1	240
	AE1	498
	AE1	633
	AE1	758
	AE2	97
	AE2	147
	AE2	265
	AE2	403
	AE2	445
	AE2	480
	AE2	516
	AE2	539
	AE2	599
	AE2	727
	AE2	765
	AE2	824
	AE2	990
	AE2	995
	AE2	1050
	AE2	1068
	AE3	41
	AE3	140
	AE3	874
	AE3	895
	AE4	17
	AE4	304
	AE4	434
	AE4	404
	AE4	526
	AE4	681
	AE4	823
	AE5	181
	AE5	520
	AE5	526
	AE5	537
	AE5	559
	AE5	852
	AE5	853
	AE5	884
	AE5	1064
	AE6	85
	AE6	387
	AE6	405
	AE6	561
	AE6	994
	AE7	363
	AE7	611
	AE7	616
	AE7	696
	AE7	722
	AE7	800
	AE7	841
	AE7	932
	AE8	57
	AE8	145
	AE8	235
	AE8	290
	AE8	395
	AE8	459

Word	Ref	Num	Word	Ref	Num	Word	Ref	Num
FEAR	AE8	705	FEAR	AU	368	FEARFUL	AE3	808
	AE8	942		WB	42		AE4	172
	AE9	104		WB	161		AE4	566
	AE9	164		WB	186		AE4	583
	AE9	188		WB	257		AE5	669
	AE9	329		M15	141		AE5	1008
	AE9	466		M15	313		AE8	735
	AE9	522		GP	32		AE9	763
	AE9	687		CI	164		AE10	416
	AE9	818		CI	173		AE10	941
	AE9	978		CI	306		AE11	692
	AE10	13		CI	396		AE12	1083
	AE10	83		CI	594		OAL	623
	AE10	145		PTP	2		M8	107
	AE10	283		PTP	32		HIF	462
	AE10	602	FEARED	AM	453		C	138
	AE10	631		AM	926		FL	473
	AE10	785		PNH	51		M12	24
	AE10	806		ESF	33		M12	433
	AE10	815		HP	83		AU	426
	AE10	864		HP	170		WB	116
	AE10	913		T23	8		M15	219
	AE10	1182		H3	18	FEARING	HAP	2332
	AE10	1255		TA	18		G3	147
	AE10	1261		TA	129		AE1	178
	AE11	25		HAP	4		AE2	1019
	AE11	522		HAP	168		AE3	44
	AE11	526		HAP	265		AE5	215
	AE11	545		HAP	497		M10	5
	AE11	914		HAP	550		C	495
	AE11	928		HAP	1260	FEARLESS	AA	449
	AE11	1077		HAP	1888		G2	701
	AE11	1180		BR	344		AE5	24
	AE11	1283		BR	348		AE12	960
	AE12	664		EL	65		M12	512
	AE12	687		EL	186		AU	318
	AE12	871		J3	195	FEARS	AM	206
	AE12	889		J6	27		PMQ	8
	AE12	1095		P1	223		SEL3	17
	AE12	1124		M1	798		ECG1	4
	AE12	1075		M1	855		ECG1	33
	AE12	1258		M13	148		PCG2	7
	AE12	1285		VP6	75		PCG2	8
	AE12	1331		G1	631		ECG2	29
	OAL	137		AE1	33		SCD1	16
	OAL	515		AE1	933		EAZ	15
	OAL	606		AE2	166		EAZ	42
	OAE1	20		AE2	736		CM	98
	OAE2	51		AE3	727		HP	248
	KT1	23		AE4	726		DA	112
	KT2	59		AE5	214		AA	211
	KT2	219		AE6	940		AA	397
	KT2	563		AE7	843		AA	469
	KT3	271		AE9	1034		MF	65
	KT3	722		AE12	84		SAA	875
	M8	135		KT2	25		SAA	561
	B	90		KT2	70		SAA	579
	B	166		KT3	264		SAA	649
	BP	2		KT3	379		SAA	650
	M10	92		M8	350		SAA	671
	CAM	195		B	720		SAA	759
	HIF	260		M10	33		SAA	1053
	HIF	413		CAM	289		PK	17
	HIF	693		C	348		OE	5
	HIF	764		C	481		PD	17
	C	106		C	737		L2	22
	C	110		TH	319		L2	49
	C	156		TH	371		L2	51
	C	194		TH	415		L2	61
	C	411		FL	137		T27	49
	C	551		AU	522		H2	13
	C	758		M15	506		HAP	452
	C	789		GP	76		HAP	1709
	C	801		CI	114		HAP	2356
	TH	97		CI	192		HAP	2499
	TH	326	FEAREST	CAM	90		BR	360
	TH	338	FEARFUL	AM	281		SKA6	17
	TH	374		AM	303		ODA	24
	TH	375		AM	521		PSH	40
	TH	393		AM	967		J3	312
	TH	394		EEL	9		J6	272
	M11	32		HP	143		J10	3
	M11	51		L3	185		J10	79
	M11	62		H2	53		P1	129
	M11	143		HAP	528		P1	239
	M11	414		HAP	825		P3	75
	FL	8		J10	29		P3	80
	FL	206		M1	719		P3	235
	M12	86		M1	916		P4	57
	M12	417		HI	144		P6	44
	AU	52		G3	418		M1	1039
	AU	103		G3	803		M9	153
	AU	110		AE1	128		HI	177
	AU	112		AE2	158		PLT	31
	AU	124		AE2	669		VP3	5
	AU	134		AE3	71		G2	706

Word	Ref	No.
FEARS	G3	95
	AE1	302
	AE1	350
	AE1	356
	AE1	790
	AE2	32
	AE2	199
	AE2	498
	AE3	49
	AE3	82
	AE3	338
	AE3	356
	AE3	801
	AE3	901
	AE4	430
	AE4	507
	AE4	675
	AE5	195
	AE5	701
	AE5	752
	AE5	1018
	AE6	444
	AE6	1092
	AE7	767
	AE7	796
	AE8	25
	AE8	247
	AE8	533
	AE8	570
	AE8	737
	AE8	765
	AE9	267
	AE9	392
	AE9	635
	AE9	662
	AE9	743
	AE10	40
	AE10	894
	AE11	619
	AE11	629
	AE11	828
	AE11	1263
	AE12	324
	AE12	477
	AE12	705
	AE12	1061
	AE12	1232
	OAL	552
	KT2	58
	KT3	289
	CAM	300
	C	321
	TH	407
	M11	24
	M11	45
	M11	46
	M11	47
	M11	178
	M11	460
	FL	524
	AU	414
	CI	313
	CI	356
	CI	374
FEAST	PR	31
	AA	619
	L3	130
	T27	123
	HAP	1304
	HAP	2582
	BR	28
	BR	277
	EL	319
	J1	206
	J1	213
	J6	71
	J6	288
	J6	320
	P5	11
	P5	26
	M1	137
	M1	302
	VP5	111
	VP6	112
	G4	22
	G4	543
	AE1	117
	AE1	273
	AE1	893
	AE1	961
	AE1	988
	AE3	289
	AE4	301
	AE5	149
	AE6	811
	AE7	180
FEAST	AE8	145
	AE8	233
	AE8	246
	AE8	405
	AE11	1084
	OAL	666
	AF	1
	KT1	22
	KT2	491
	KT3	114
	KT3	732
	BP	90
	BP	126
	M10	57
	CAM	238
	HIF	640
	HIF	768
	HIF	774
	HIF	806
	C	216
	TH	71
	TH	185
	TH	253
	TH	262
	TH	278
	TH	340
	TH	364
	FL	423
	M12	208
	M12	214
	M12	295
	M12	316
	WB	21
	WB	339
	M15	113
	M15	207
	CI	421
	CI	446
	CI	541
	CI	566
	CI	578
FEASTED	SMA	36
	PMQw	21
	J1	146
	AE8	480
FEASTING	AE6	891
FEASTS	EWGR	15
	PFD	11
	PAL	31
	PCB	41
	H2	86
	J3	286
	J3	377
	P1	64
	P1	137
	M13	21
	G1	363
	G3	787
	AE1	901
	AE3	453
	AE4	107
	AE5	141
	AE5	995
	AE6	819
	AE7	196
	AE9	210
	OAL	261
	KT2	505
	KT3	105
	BP	81
	M12	340
	M15	124
	M15	134
	M15	145
	M15	151
FEAT	PCD	12
	L4	272
	J6	94
	P5	259
	OAL	430
	HAP	2505
	J6	86
FEATHER	VHH	53
	AM	440
	T18	93
	HAP	1730
	HAP	1787
	HAP	2568
	M1	617
	G2	172
	AE5	409
	AE5	661
	AE5	668
	AE5	689
FEATHERED	AE9	866
FEATHERED	AE11	958
	AE12	847
	KT3	222
	M8	402
	HIF	74
	C	70
	C	437
	C	770
	M11	483
	M12	746
	M15	571
FEATHERS	SMA	28
	HP	48
	M13	160
	G1	507
	AE11	1068
	M12	694
	M15	534
	M15	702
FEATLY	WB	216
FEATS	HAP	2315
	HI	186
	AE9	874
	KT1	3
	KT1	17
	TH	8
FEATURE	DOD	14
	L4	57
	T23	20
	AK	124
	J10	314
	AE10	547
	M12	349
FEATURES	ML	53
	UMR	3
	L4	213
	L4	219
	ODA	29
	M9	194
	AE2	376
	AE3	633
	AE4	477
	AE5	744
	AE7	902
	AE8	206
	AE11	738
	MFL	7
	KT1	563
	B	539
	C	612
	M11	362
	M11	404
	M12	540
	CI	54
	CI	97
FED	AM	870
	AM	1142
	PFD	27
	PC1	27
	PCB	30
	DA	91
	AA	626
	SAA	340
	SAA	350
	SAA	545
	AT	3
	TA	379
	AK	78
	HAP	2
	HAP	53
	HAP	2233
	HAP	2258
	HAP	2289
	EL	22
	J3	341
	J3	462
	P1	49
	P1	116
	P3	239
	P5	215
	P6	165
	P6	182
	M1	135
	M1	661
	M1	869
	M1	909
	M13	53
	VP5	54
	VP7	10
	VP8	61
	VP9	28
	VP10	26
	G2	100
	G3	609
	G3	693
	G3	812

FED

G4	223
G4	360
AE1	250
AE1	263
AE1	652
AE2	932
AE3	754
AE4	2
AE4	289
AE4	538
AE5	123
AE5	552
AE6	291
AE7	107
AE7	153
AE7	159
AE7	378
AE7	674
AE7	919
AE8	97
AE8	806
AE8	840
AE9	474
AE9	639
AE9	828
AE10	915
AE10	1001
AE11	855
AE12	109
OAL	337
OAL	519
AF	81
KT1	88
KT3	900
HIF	663
TH	192
M15	131
M15	137
M15	173
M15	300
M15	616
M15	692
GP	136
AS	84

FEE

PCD	4
SAA	322
J16	33
TJD	93

FEEBLE

AM	892
PTC	19
SAA	409
TA	72
PKA	13
J10	315
J10	330
J10	412
M1	619
VP1	17
G1	163
G1	421
G2	490
G4	376
G4	720
AE2	473
AE2	697
AE2	742
AE2	919
AE4	227
AE4	860
AE5	936
AE6	427
AE6	664
AE8	616
AE9	178
AE9	953
AE10	185
AE10	771
AE11	124
AE11	475
AE11	693
AE12	534
KT1	152
KT3	371
KT3	715
KT3	787
FL	589
AU	134
AU	246
MF	197

FEEBLY

SMP	84

FEED

AM	840
AM	934
SMQ	1
AA	687
ER	67
L4	19

FEED

T27	88
H9	8
HAP	1219
HAP	2245
HAP	2546
BR	66
J3	239
J3	345
J6	232
J10	47
P1	49
P4	125
P6	172
M1	369
M1	865
VP1	63
VP3	46
VP4	26
VP5	1
VP5	121
VP6	5
VP6	60
VP7	21
G2	260
G2	486
G2	744
G3	198
G3	247
G3	258
G3	277
G3	319
G3	471
G3	518
G3	592
G3	616
AE3	292
AE3	336
AE6	7
AE6	56
AE6	960
AE7	668
AE9	772
AE10	887
AE11	315
KT1	401
KT3	959
TJD	49
TJD	178
M8	20
CAM	81
M15	118
M15	258
M15	417
GP	51
CI	565

FEEDING

AM	1126
M1	668
VP7	65
G1	165
G1	488
G2	303
G3	347
G3	528

FEEDS

AE2	1063
AM	29
AA	247
SAA	60
SAA	1110
L1	50
HAP	1406
HAP	1726
BR	275
VP2	42
G2	442
G2	715
G3	358
G3	767
AE1	706
AE4	86
AE4	91
AE4	108
AE6	983
AE7	548
AE12	263
OAL	278
KT3	345
KT3	1068
BP	51
TH	39
TH	40
M11	82
M15	303
M15	525
M15	528
M15	691

FEEL

UDH	6

FEEL

AR	130
RH	20
RH	35
RH	40
LC	131
SEL2	11
AT	53
AT	120
L4	194
L3	12
L3	16
L3	28
L3	45
L3	57
T23	78
J6	545
J10	90
P1	88
P3	40
P3	170
P3	216
VP9	73
G3	64
G3	272
G3	326
G4	694
AE4	225
AE5	532
AE5	968
AE6	265
AE9	833
AE10	1212
AE12	56
AE12	1156
KT3	154
KT3	779
KT3	804
B	329
C	125
C	421
TH	87
STP	24

FEELING
FEELS

AE2	1019
AM	719
MD	266
L3	43
L3	63
L4	1
P3	75
M1	1093
G1	448
G3	397
AE8	516
AE9	972
OAL	196
OAL	697
KT1	489
KT3	399
KT3	1076
M8	279
M10	22
M10	89
CAM	286
C	287
TH	325
M15	227

FEES

J6	705
P3	124
P3	140
C	170

FEET

AM	688
SCG1	6
SCG2	4
SCG3	22
PUO1	43
EPC	14
MF	53
MF	54
SAA	24
AT	100
T18	11
T23	97
FS3	3
HAP	268
HAP	382
PMS	7
PSH	4
PSH	6
J1	168
J6	678
P3	216
P5	24
M1	728
M1	741
M1	1036
M13	191

Word	Code	No.
FEET	VCS	28
	VP7	6
	VP7	52
	G2	133
	G2	314
	G3	92
	G4	320
	AE2	298
	AE2	308
	AE2	356
	AE2	632
	AE2	726
	AE2	972
	AE2	994
	AE3	854
	AE4	256
	AE4	351
	AE5	739
	AE5	771
	AE7	100
	AE7	1103
	AE8	253
	AE8	292
	AE8	313
	AE8	351
	AE8	394
	AE8	602
	AE9	520
	AE9	747
	AE9	758
	AE10	397
	AE10	520
	AE10	986
	AE10	1281
	AE11	601
	AE11	624
	AE11	641
	AE11	1061
	AE12	658
	AE12	1037
	AE12	1289
	OAL	142
	OAL	189
	OAL	581
	OAL	597
	OAL	619
	OAL	662
	OAL	703
	OAE1	3
	DO	53
	KT1	46
	KT1	448
	KT2	61
	KT2	644
	KT3	448
	KT3	457
	KT3	704
	M8	135
	M8	148
	BP	75
	BP	78
	BP	125
	BP	147
	BP	185
	CAM	208
	CAM	339
	C	52
	M11	462
	FL	57
	FL	222
	FL	416
	M12	535
	AU	131
	AU	357
	M15	337
	M15	350
	M15	554
	CI	291
FEIGN	RH	19
	OE	21
	L4	31
	L4	189
	H9	36
	J1	185
	P6	146
	SLT2	4
	G2	66
	KT2	657
FEIGNED	EEL	16
	PAZ	3
	ML	34
	HP	16
	HP	121
	EAA	3
	HAP	546
	J6	352
FEIGNED	J6	440
	J6	828
	AE2	21
	AE4	742
	AE6	695
	AE7	463
	AE7	542
	OAL	676
	OAL	699
	B	302
	AU	52
	AU	60
FEIGNING	CM	65
	EKA	5
FEIGNS	M9	155
	AE4	271
	OAL	358
FELICITY	AR	107
	E	28
	P3	72
	KT3	884
	WB	135
FELL	PT	14
	PEL	26
	ECG1	36
	SCG1	10
	EM	28
	EPF	19
	PUF	32
	AA	565
	ELB	34
	MF	56
	MF	216
	SAA	15
	SAA	419
	OE	12
	MO	9
	T23	107
	TA	35
	HAP	344
	HAP	574
	HAP	902
	HAP	1236
	HAP	1364
	HAP	1640
	HAP	2262
	SSC	19
	BR	234
	P3	98
	P3	168
	M1	397
	M1	539
	M1	996
	GK	92
	VP6	51
	G1	346
	G1	629
	G1	648
	G3	737
	AE1	198
	AE2	120
	AE2	500
	AE2	688
	AE2	758
	AE2	1003
	AE3	125
	AE3	757
	AE4	726
	AE4	989
	AE5	428
	AE5	433
	AE5	597
	AE5	1116
	AE5	1118
	AE6	8
	AE6	46
	AE6	153
	AE6	249
	AE6	465
	AE6	478
	AE6	678
	AE9	175
	AE9	494
	AE9	579
	AE9	595
	AE9	737
	AE9	953
	AE9	1044
	AE10	431
	AE10	437
	AE10	580
	AE10	661
	AE10	741
	AE10	752
	AE10	986
	AE10	1180
FELL	AE11	174
	AE11	204
	AE11	252
	AE11	310
	AE11	415
	AE11	646
	AE11	959
	AE12	440
	AE12	727
	AE12	746
	AE12	780
	AE12	796
	AE12	932
	OAL	377
	OAL	381
	OAL	665
	KT1	77
	KT1	124
	KT1	183
	KT2	202
	KT2	246
	KT2	429
	KT2	476
	KT2	581
	KT3	255
	KT3	260
	KT3	417
	KT3	907
	M8	149
	M8	248
	M8	331
	BP	128
	HIF	796
	C	372
	TH	164
	TH	206
	TH	299
	M11	71
	M12	348
	M12	378
	M12	430
	M12	451
	M12	575
	M12	600
	M12	614
	M12	705
	M12	753
	M12	805
	FL	463
	AU	260
	AU	283
	AU	478
	M15	92
	M15	234
	CI	343
	CI	412
FELLED	AE4	576
	AE6	267
	AE9	93
	AE11	1156
	AE12	1116
	KT3	646
	KT3	975
FELLOW	PC2	15
	RL	86
	PKA	19
	EL	291
	P2	30
	G3	775
	AE2	310
	AE10	1179
	OAE2	22
	KT1	364
	KT1	475
	C	116
	C	222
	C	227
	C	258
	C	320
	C	354
	M12	427
	M12	594
	M12	676
	AU	44
	AU	108
FELLOW-CITIZENS	STA	420
FELLOW-DROVER	J3	383
FELLOW-FEELING	AA	608
FELLOW-GROOM	G2	773
FELLOW-MARES	M9	100
FELLOW-NYMPHS	M1	883
	G4	665
FELLOW-ROGUE	J16	28
FELLOW'S	P3	7
	KT1	294

FELLOWS	PIE	24	FEMALE	AE9	843	FERN	AE9	519		
	AM	988		AE11	984		KT2	238		
	PUO5	14		AE11	1083	FERNY	HAP	555		
	PDS	19		AE11	1163		AE11	1305		
	J3	61		AE11	1195	FERONIA	AE8	747		
	M1	887		AE11	1272	FERONIA'S	AE7	961		
	M1	952		AE12	1042	FERRIED	AE6	440		
	G4	217		MFL	34	FERRIES	AE6	448		
	AE2	349		KT1	20	FERRYBOAT	P4	57		
	AE5	229		KT2	383	FERRYMAN	G4	730		
	AE9	41		KT3	139	FERRYMAN'S	J3	425		
	AE9	1029		KT3	230	FERTILE	AR	201		
	AE11	298		B	403		SAA	944		
	M8	168		B	685		G2	370		
	FL	608		TH	310		G2	739		
	M12	398		TH	428		G2	248		
	AU	271		FL	154	FERTILITY	FS4	5		
	AU	504		M12	544	FERVENT	TA	39		
	CI	23		M12	809	FERVOR	AE1	961		
FELLOWS'				M12	318	FESCENNIAN	AE7	962		
	HAP	248		AU	239	FESCUES	PSH	38		
	J3	418		AU	271	FESTERED	MD	151		
	OAL	857		WB	83	FESTERING	HAP	939		
	M8	128		WB	124	FESTIVAL	SAA	913		
	M11	170		WB	268	FESTIVALS	M1	757		
	M15	101		WB	492		AE6	108		
	M15	127	FEMALE'S	AE12	159	FETCH	AR	217		
FELLOWSHIP	HAP	544	FEMALES	L4	232		AE11	870		
	KT2	168		L4	273	FETCHED	G3	757		
	AU	379		M9	104	FETLOCKS	AE5	739		
FELLOW-SUBJECTS	HAP	2496		G3	104		AE12	512		
FELLOW-SUFFERER	HAP	563		G3	208	FETTER	SAA	428		
FELLOW-TYRANT	AE8	859		G3	225		EDS	31		
FELON	AK	157		G3	247	FETTERED	L1	54		
	AE6	803		AE11	746		P5	180		
	KT2	560	FEMALES'	G3	416		AE4	130		
	C	727	FEN	AE10	263		AE6	1176		
	TH	272		WB	189		KT1	448		
FELONIOUS	MF	201	FENCE	PUF	27	FETTERS	PAZ	9		
FELON-MINDS	HAP	2464		SAA	776		SAA	272		
FELONS	TJD	57		PDG	32		H9	5		
FELT	AR	3		RL	267		J3	485		
	AM	200		HAP	885		J6	198		
	HP	48		M1	128		P5	126		
	L3	3		VP1	71		G4	574		
	NS	2		VP3	28		G4	596		
	HAP	1980		VP7	38		AE1	94		
	EL	12		G1	364		AE2	198		
	J10	48		G2	224		AE6	535		
	M9	80		G2	483		KT2	7		
	M13	23		G2	575		KT2	357		
	VP6	76		G3	343		CI	416		
	AE1	806		G3	802	FEVER	SEL4	20		
	AE2	764		C	494		C	183		
	AE2	850		FL	89		L4	13		
	AE2	1013		J10	76		J10	435		
	AE5	1129		M1	157		G1	162		
	AE11	563		VP7	7	FEVERED	TH	369		
	AE11	1252		G1	153	FEVERISH	KT2	57		
	AE12	1362		G2	511		DC	11		
	OAL	203		AE7	844		AM	1112		
	KT1	234		AE9	79		L3	311		
	KT1	386		DO	155		VP5	73		
	KT2	123		B	150		G3	168		
	KT2	330		CI	223	FEVER'S	L2	38		
	KT2	383	FENCER	J6	114		J10	345		
	KT3	221	FENCERS	EUF	30	FEVERS	AE3	196		
	KT3	901	FENCES	H3	32		PLG	20		
	B	371		H2	35		AA	136		
	B	745		HAP	296		H3	43		
	M10	81		VP3	138		G3	697		
	CAM	116		G1	193	FEW	LC	89		
	TH	211		AE9	457		LCA	45		
	M12	97		KT1	334		SIE	3		
	CI	5	FENCING	HAP	605		AM	867		
	SMP	80		J6	157		AM	1069		
	AS	93		AE11	1103		AM	1071		
FEMALE	EMQW	19		G3	466		EWGR	23		
	EKK	18	FEND	VP10	38		PA	4		
	EPC	21	FENNEL	HAP	209		PA	5		
	OE	8	FENNY	AE3	921		EM	10		
	L4	106	FENS	G3	657		PLN	44		
	L4	199	FERETRIAN	HS	77		EAZ	34		
	T27	32		J10	208		PC2	30		
	HAP	2440		AE6	1187		PLG	1		
	PP	29	FERMENT	AA	140		PO	11		
	PP	51		MD	270		EMW	11		
	J6	568		HAP	318		AA	485		
	P1	153		P1	256		AA	696		
	M1	554		G4	436		AA	782		
	M9	67	FERMENTED	M15	326		AA	813		
	M9	104	FERMENTING	G2	10		AA	959		
	M9	110	FERN	AT	31		PLB	31		
	G4	795		P4	98		MD	180		
	AE4	599		G2	262		MD	245		
	AE7	545		G3	466		SAA	713		
	AE7	1051								

FEW	RL	12	FIELD	AM	448	FIELD	AE11	360
	RL	326		AM	542		AE11	447
	RL	432		HP	65		AE11	471
	AT	98		HP	244		AE11	513
	ER	73		SAA	662		AE11	602
	EAA	13		SAA	708		AE11	650
	HAP	1408		SAA	770		AE11	655
	HAP	1657		SAA	801		AE11	674
	HAP	1899		SAA	836		AE11	683
	HAP	1910		SAA	1056		AE11	690
	HAP	2147		SAA	1088		AE11	776
	HAP	2201		SAA	1089		AE11	908
	BR	91		H2	9		AE11	937
	BR	337		TA	359		AE11	979
	BR	348		TA	469		AE11	1049
	EKA	14		MN	12		AE11	1164
	EL	26		HAP	731		AE11	1216
	EL	254		HAP	955		AE11	1232
	OD	8		HAP	1395		AE11	1257
	J3	47		HAP	1488		AE11	1296
	J3	325		BR	262		AE12	1
	J3	338		PDS	12		AE12	208
	J6	72		SKA2	5		AE12	274
	J6	73		J1	226		AE12	502
	J10	1		J10	329		AE12	520
	J10	178		M1	427		AE12	566
	J10	221		M13	194		AE12	638
	J10	224		HI	22		AE12	648
	P5	68		HI	109		AE12	673
	PLT	31		VP7	64		AE12	656
	ELT	20		VP7	79		AE12	682
	ELT	24		G1	162		AE12	709
	VP6	61		G1	114		AE12	720
	VP10	4		G1	170		AE12	730
	G4	189		G1	182		AE12	753
	AE1	758		G1	228		AE12	772
	AE2	348		G1	234		AE12	872
	AE2	473		G1	240		AE12	1034
	AE2	676		G1	265		AE12	1075
	AE3	252		G1	364		AE12	1264
	AE3	484		G1	426		OAL	394
	AE5	982		G2	271		OAL	781
	AE6	196		G2	273		OAL	796
	AE6	1007		G2	378		MG	8
	AE8	685		G2	383		KT1	25
	AE9	244		G2	430		KT1	109
	AE9	520		G2	745		KT2	258
	AE9	604		G3	307		KT3	50
	AE10	24		G4	260		KT3	93
	AE10	184		G4	759		KT3	159
	AE10	268		AE1	360		KT3	310
	AE11	1275		AE1	654		KT3	446
	AE12	684		AE2	915		KT3	508
	KT1	436		AE3	286		KT3	579
	KT2	662		AE3	709		KT3	582
	KT3	469		AE4	882		KT3	596
	KT3	1079		AE5	13		KT3	600
	TJD	203		AE5	191		KT3	655
	M11	208		AE5	489		KT3	714
	AU	260		AE5	536		KT3	719
	AU	325		AE5	645		KT3	915
	WB	483		AE6	133		M8	25
	M15	325		AE6	244		HIF	355
	M15	464		AE6	1206		HIF	479
	CI	410		AE6	1216		HIF	575
	CI	547		AE7	173		FL	90
FEWER	PA	4		AE7	875		FL	276
	EMW	12		AE7	909		FL	295
	G3	711		AE7	950		FL	297
	AE9	461		AE7	1097		FL	302
	OAL	62		AE8	816		FL	335
	KT2	662		AE8	930		FL	385
	C	462		AE8	938		FL	537
FIAT	RL	155		AE9	77		M12	597
FIBERS	AE3	38		AE9	259		M12	802
FIBROUS	M12	447		AE9	362		M12	812
FICKLE	PSF	6		AE9	736		AU	1
	AA	785		AE9	813		AU	51
	L4	116		AE9	1065		AU	121
	STS2	3		AE10	261		AU	144
	STS2	4		AE10	378		AU	188
	AE10	226		AE10	433		AU	196
	FL	524		AE10	501		AU	253
FICTION	AK	123		AE10	612		AU	277
	HAP	752		AE10	616		AU	334
FICTITIOUS	TA	330		AE10	623		AU	399
	M15	224		AE10	704		AU	411
FIDDLER	AA	550		AE10	708		AU	434
FIDENA	AE6	1050		AE10	751		AU	455
FIE	EDG	24		AE10	767		M15	181
	T27	28		AE10	821		M15	207
	OAL	749		AE10	1073		CI	289
	C	126		AE10	1134	FIELD'S	J6	679
FIEF	AK	98		AE10	1197	FIELDS	RH	66
FIELD	HS	80		AE10	1266		AM	1029
	DC	54		AE11	317		AM	1136

FIELDS

AA	23
SAA	624
ER	70
L1	47
T18	50
T27	58
H2	81
EAA	13
HAP	212
HAP	313
HAP	1913
HAP	2542
ODA	9
P1	138
P3	236
P6	31
M1	138
M1	60
M1	85
M1	306
M1	393
M1	426
M1	565
M1	663
M1	702
M1	704
M1	820
M1	865
M13	134
VP1	4
VP1	67
VP1	98
VP1	103
VP2	95
VP3	82
VP4	33
VP5	48
VP5	52
VP5	55
VP5	118
VP6	113
VP8	144
VP10	67
G1	7
G1	22
G1	58
G1	193
G1	204
G1	225
G1	578
G1	661
G1	682
G2	76
G2	189
G2	198
G2	255
G2	284
G2	305
G2	370
G2	446
G2	464
G2	541
G2	616
G2	687
G2	754
G3	1
G3	386
G3	546
G3	660
G3	726
G4	103
G4	114
G4	173
G4	234
G4	807
AE1	142
AE1	196
AE2	480
AE2	791
AE3	16
AE3	22
AE3	514
AE3	534
AE3	643
AE3	922
AE6	596
AE6	644
AE6	869
AE6	896
AE6	919
AE6	1008
AE6	1111
AE7	63
AE7	593
AE7	732
AE7	835

FIELDS

AE7	946
AE7	997
AE7	1048
AE7	1083
AE7	1101
AE8	5
AE8	12
AE8	86
AE8	200
AE8	680
AE8	713
AE8	797
AE8	920
AE8	954
AE9	40
AE9	49
AE9	830
AE10	4
AE10	29
AE10	119
AE10	210
AE10	265
AE10	666
AE10	800
AE10	954
AE10	998
AE10	1040
AE11	216
AE11	237
AE11	311
AE11	639
AE11	706
AE11	901
AE11	941
AE11	984
AE11	1254
AE11	1309
AE11	1312
AE12	57
AE12	188
AE12	360
AE12	423
AE12	563
AE12	610
AE12	645
AE12	670
AE12	1301
OAE1	13
MM	22
KT1	156
KT2	72
KT2	240
KT3	60
KT3	997
TJD	44
TJD	92
TJD	116
M8	19
M8	42
CAM	316
CAM	323
HIF	345
HIF	424
M11	40
M11	299
FL	6
FL	219
FL	479
FL	553
M12	104
M12	569
AU	17
M15	18
M15	305
M15	408
M15	423
M15	430
M15	543
M15	653
CI	400

FIELDS'
FIEND

VP5	65
MD	81
HAP	2049
HAP	2351
J1	52
AE7	693
AE7	702
AE7	775
AE12	1263
KT2	577
TH	193
TH	215
TH	224
TH	377
WB	329

FIEND'S

TH	264

FIENDS

AM	545
AM	991
AA	145
BR	122
J6	848
JE4	875
AE6	730
AE7	132
AE10	57
WB	40

FIERCE

AM	262
AM	753
AM	879
SM2	4
PAZ	9
CM	87
DA	38
DA	177
PR	3
SAA	719
SAA	821
SAA	841
SAA	921
SAA	1049
SAA	1090
L4	9
H3	42
HAP	452
HAP	2414
J6	442
J6	816
PPS	14
P1	190
P1	209
M1	79
M1	240
M1	442
M13	23
M13	91
HI	97
VP2	14
VP5	43
G1	627
G1	690
G2	238
G3	239
G3	416
G4	741
AE1	147
AE1	159
AE1	360
AE1	643
AE1	655
AE1	1055
AE2	649
AE2	677
AE3	20
AE3	167
AE3	280
AE3	335
AE3	513
AE3	584
AE3	716
AE4	57
AE5	192
AE5	364
AE6	137
AE6	245
AE6	1207
AE7	304
AE7	458
AE7	836
AE7	932
AE7	1005
AE7	1098
AE8	6
AE8	9
AE8	74
AE8	300
AE8	452
AE8	918
AE9	563
AE9	616
AE9	938
AE9	986
AE10	249
AE10	356
AE10	442
AE10	454
AE10	577
AE10	605
AE10	671
AE10	717
AE10	751
AE10	860
AE10	899

FIERCE	AE10	979	FIERY	AE12	503	FIGHT	HI	111
	AE10	1291		AF	28		GK	56
	AE11	25		KT2	45		GK	78
	AE11	625		KT2	111		G2	766
	AE11	700		KT2	249		G3	49
	AE11	768		TJD	58		G3	94
	AE11	918		M8	47		G3	133
	AE11	972		FL	255		G3	143
	AE11	980		M12	109		G3	338
	AE11	1144		M12	408		G3	364
	AE12	530		M12	412		G3	573
	AE12	739		AU	394		G4	99
	AE12	784		CI	328		G4	115
	AE12	950	FIFTEEN	NS	1		G4	133
	AE12	961		SLT2	16		AE1	677
	OAL	10		C	47		AE2	497
	DO	126	FIFTH	PWG	35		AE2	508
	KT2	111		HP	60		AE2	562
	KT2	242		EPN	4		AE2	577
	KT2	327		J10	257		AE2	589
	KT3	81		J10	362		AE2	888
	KT3	580		P6	23		AE2	911
	KT3	631		G1	372		AE3	309
	M8	59		KT3	168		AE4	53
	M8	75	FIFTH-RATE	PCG2	4		AE5	520
	M8	103	FIFTY	L3	219		AE5	542
	HIF	182		AE1	984		AE5	535
	HIF	456		AE2	685		AE5	558
	FL	221		AE10	693		AE5	605
	M12	22		AE10	795		AE5	623
	M12	226		OAL	78		AE6	676
	M12	227	FIFTY-ONE	GE	4		AE6	786
	M12	380	FIFTY-THREE	GE	2		AE6	1185
	M12	405	FIG	J10	228		AE7	655
	AU	3		P1	54		AE7	731
	M15	524		HI	92		AE7	753
	CI	36	FIGHT	AR	100		AE7	935
	CI	239		PRL	16		AE7	953
	CI	284		AM	109		AE7	1012
	CI	597		AM	167		AE7	1024
FIERCELY	HS	88		AM	221		AE8	746
	T23	16		AM	237		AE8	900
	M9	86		AM	300		AE8	906
	M13	10		AM	391		AE8	913
	VP10	109		AM	407		AE8	940
	G1	157		AM	433		AE9	77
	G3	764		AM	458		AE9	226
	KT2	142		AM	477		AE9	239
	TH	150		AM	482		AE9	429
FIERCENESS	M9	67		AM	497		AE9	615
FIERCER	AM	105		AM	501		AE9	679
	HAP	153		AM	537		AE9	688
	G3	805		AM	544		AE9	830
	TH	12		AM	557		AE9	862
	FL	374		AM	599		AE9	902
FIERY	AM	275		AM	689		AE9	937
	AM	330		AM	738		AE9	941
	AM	365		AM	748		AE9	1046
	AA	156		AM	753		AE9	1063
	L4	1		AM	766		AE9	1079
	H3	43		AM	778		AE10	342
	HAP	227		SEL1	6		AE10	357
	HAP	180		SEL4	21		AE10	363
	BR	20		PCG1	41		AE10	372
	BR	267		PMQW	15		AE10	431
	EL	339		PM	7		AE10	493
	G1	157		ECD	1		AE10	508
	G1	447		SCD2	6		AE10	604
	G1	579		EUO	14		AE10	623
	G1	605		EAZ	18		AE10	637
	G3	130		EMK	26		AE10	659
	AE1	249		HP	245		AE10	665
	AE1	661		EPF	18		AE10	722
	AE3	754		PUF	22		AE10	757
	AE5	190		AA	1016		AE10	826
	AE5	745		AA	1022		AE10	845
	AE5	916		EDG	9		AE10	860
	AE6	6		EDG	17		AE10	870
	AE6	742		ER	50		AE10	899
	AE6	793		L2	47		AE10	941
	AE7	491		HAP	267		AE10	953
	AE7	646		HAP	459		AE10	977
	AE8	129		HAP	687		AE10	1014
	AE8	596		HAP	858		AE10	1036
	AE8	854		HAP	954		AE10	1064
	AE9	53		HAP	1471		AE10	1119
	AE9	150		HAP	1496		AE10	1127
	AE9	714		HAP	1562		AE10	1274
	AE10	416		HAP	1612		AE11	231
	AE10	804		HAP	2206		AE11	299
	AE11	216		HAP	2581		AE11	342
	AE11	748		J3	440		AE11	435
	AE11	948		J6	176		AE11	440
	AE11	1097		J16	4		AE11	533
	AE12	158		M13	179		AE11	549
	AE12	372		HI	54		AE11	569

Word	Ref	Num
FIGHT	AE11	600
	AE11	604
	AE11	670
	AE11	733
	AE11	882
	AE11	944
	AE11	974
	AE11	978
	AE11	1043
	AE11	1070
	AE11	1076
	AE11	1088
	AE11	1127
	AE11	1212
	AE12	4
	AE12	26
	AE12	67
	AE12	111
	AE12	116
	AE12	121
	AE12	160
	AE12	166
	AE12	191
	AE12	231
	AE12	275
	AE12	280
	AE12	323
	AE12	331
	AE12	347
	AE12	389
	AE12	477
	AE12	518
	AE12	575
	AE12	638
	AE12	680
	AE12	700
	AE12	718
	AE12	732
	AE12	741
	AE12	805
	AE12	814
	AE12	821
	AE12	903
	AE12	913
	AE12	920
	AE12	983
	AE12	1007
	AE12	1018
	AE12	1024
	AE12	1031
	AE12	1042
	AE12	1182
	AE12	1190
	AE12	1289
	OAL	155
	OAL	198
	OAL	219
	OAL	228
	OAL	240
	OAL	296
	MG	10
	DO	108
	KT1	17
	KT1	116
	KT1	344
	KT2	186
	KT2	258
	KT2	317
	KT2	322
	KT2	376
	KT2	410
	KT2	413
	KT2	422
	KT2	588
	KT3	15
	KT3	23
	KT3	301
	KT3	323
	KT3	395
	KT3	435
	KT3	506
	KT3	510
	KT3	515
	KT3	519
	KT3	523
	KT3	593
	KT3	601
	KT3	618
	KT3	648
	KT3	659
	KT3	930
	KT3	1142
	TJD	161
	M8	183
	HIF	201
	HIF	240
FIGHT	HIF	248
	HIF	261
	HIF	299
	HIF	337
	HIF	341
	HIF	475
	HIF	580
	HIF	666
	C	135
	TH	284
	M11	162
	FL	303
	FL	310
	FL	451
	M12	93
	M12	142
	M12	177
	M12	339
	M12	416
	M12	422
	M12	425
	M12	605
	M12	641
	M12	791
	AU	16
	AU	48
	AU	58
	AU	80
	AU	140
	AU	183
	AU	189
	AU	373
	AU	430
	AU	501
	AU	538
	AU	555
	AU	556
	M15	234
	CI	278
	CI	284
	CI	397
	CI	551
	CI	533
	CI	559
	CI	606
FIGHTING	HS	47
	AM	333
	AM	705
	AM	981
	EMQw	5
	E	22
	AA	828
	MD	296
	L1	47
	EKA	13
	J3	454
	M1	575
	VP6	4
	VP10	67
	AE2	422
	AE2	673
	AE6	896
	AE6	1111
	AE6	1216
	AE7	63
	AE7	593
	AE7	835
	AE7	875
	AE8	680
	AE9	874
	AE10	125
	AE10	708
	AE11	1219
	AE12	360
	AE12	436
	AE12	684
	AF	102
	KT2	208
	KT3	503
	FL	553
	M12	431
	AU	562
FIGHTS	AM	207
	SCD2	673
	PAL	7
	PAL	13
	PP	38
	J3	454
	J6	352
	J16	85
	J16	88
	P1	131
	HI	129
	AE1	907
	AE2	450
	AE8	713
FIGHTS	AE8	859
	AE11	237
	AE11	1110
	OAL	192
	TJD	141
	AU	21
	AU	87
	AU	562
FIGS	J3	148
	BP	114
FIGURE	RH	74
	HAP	623
	HAP	1483
	HAP	2336
	EL	272
	J6	578
	GK	116
	VP1	84
	VP8	111
	G1	250
	G2	381
	G2	593
	G2	629
	AE1	682
	AE2	114
	AE6	673
	KT2	469
	M11	260
	M11	402
	M12	35
	M15	238
	M15	246
	M15	363
	M15	399
	M15	560
FIGURED	AK	132
	J6	364
	P2	94
	AE5	704
	AE8	943
	MFL	16
FIGURES	PD	36
	L4	226
	J10	19
	P1	161
	GK	172
	GK	177
	VP3	60
	G2	646
	AE1	907
	AE5	351
	AE8	973
	OAL	872
	KT2	525
	KT2	614
	BP	103
	M12	331
	M15	265
	M15	386
	M15	675
FILCH	HAP	2297
FILE	ESF	14
	AA	817
	CI	406
FILED	CI	219
FILES	J10	19
	G2	375
	G2	423
	G2	579
	KT3	460
	TJD	105
FILIAL	AA	419
	MF	136
	SAA	123
	SAA	150
	M1	651
	AE5	970
	AE6	544
	AE6	942
	AE9	395
	AE10	1167
FILL	JH	8
	SMA	4
	VHH	47
	AM	711
	PLN	32
	PTC	18
	HP	205
	PR	17
	PUO5	10
	MF	170
	L3	214
	L3	221
	L3	312
	L4	54
	L4	59

Headword	Ref	No.
FILL	H3	5
	AK	38
	HAP	1019
	HAP	1391
	HAP	2505
	BR	327
	EJG	3
	J1	98
	J1	132
	M1	216
	M1	328
	M1	379
	PLT	44
	VP3	138
	VP10	114
	G1	259
	G2	313
	G3	522
	G3	607
	G4	294
	G4	493
	AE1	646
	AE2	675
	AE5	142
	AE6	880
	AE6	1034
	AE6	1206
	AE7	23
	AE7	53
	AE7	626
	AE7	794
	AE8	363
	AE8	975
	AE9	388
	AE9	673
	AE11	618
	AE12	1232
	MG	21
	DO	167
	KT3	523
	KT3	920
	B	416
	BP	123
	HIF	716
	M12	441
	M15	3
	M15	115
	M15	643
	CI	330
FILLED	UDH	32
	AM	1144
	SMM2	8
	PCG2	23
	CM	52
	HP	63
	MD	10
	L4	261
	HAP	45
	HAP	522
	ODA	15
	P3	5
	P5	34
	M1	792
	M13	106
	M13	163
	VP6	72
	G1	441
	G2	62
	G2	256
	G2	332
	G3	103
	G3	150
	G3	283
	G3	720
	AE1	369
	AE1	733
	AE2	277
	AE2	491
	AE2	667
	AE2	766
	AE2	1029
	AE3	454
	AE3	836
	AE5	61
	AE5	524
	AE5	1054
	AE6	423
	AE6	989
	AE7	749
	AE8	281
	AE9	99
	AE9	104
	AE9	212
	AE9	603
	AE9	769
	AE9	978
FILLED	AE9	1095
	AE10	34
	AE11	222
	AE11	374
	AE11	454
	AE11	489
	AE11	653
	AE12	603
	OAL	20
	OAL	368
	OAL	410
	OAL	864
	KT1	60
	KT2	650
	KT3	466
	KT3	946
	BP	74
	BP	124
	HIF	78
	HIF	153
	HIF	644
	HIF	801
	C	773
	TH	102
	TH	121
	FL	95
	M12	32
	M12	77
	M12	239
	M12	345
	M12	444
	M12	719
	M12	817
	WB	1
	WB	385
	M15	633
	AS	96
FILLET	M1	639
	AE3	475
	AE4	213
	AE7	495
	AE11	862
	M15	192
FILLETS	VP8	90
	VP8	102
	VP8	107
	G2	675
	AE2	182
	AE2	208
	AE2	291
	AE3	91
	AE3	107
	AE3	232
	AE4	914
	AE5	483
	AE6	903
	AE7	563
	AE7	587
	AE10	748
	HIF	640
FILLS	PUO3	11
	AA	210
	MF	25
	L5	7
	BR	87
	M1	93
	VP1	6
	HI	193
	J1	47
	G1	429
	G1	512
	G2	538
	G2	740
	G3	654
	G4	547
	G4	747
	AE2	292
	AE2	926
	AE4	266
	AE4	274
	AE4	507
	AE5	451
	AE6	360
	AE6	573
	AE7	527
	AE7	698
	AE7	910
	AE7	1083
	AE8	331
	AE9	82
	AE9	636
	AE10	1024
	AE10	1242
	AE11	861
	AE12	197
	AE12	724
FILLS	AE12	812
	AE12	888
	AE12	1096
	OAL	277
	OAE2	33
	KT3	997
	TJD	65
	M8	26
	M10	37
	M12	569
	M15	671
	CI	586
FILMS	AE2	820
FILMY	AM	720
	M1	743
	G1	543
	M15	551
FILTH	AK	69
	J6	184
	G3	835
	AE3	777
	AE5	433
	AE6	999
	AE9	629
	AE12	893
	OAL	584
	C	252
FILTHINESS	UDH	54
FILTHY	EAZ	24
	PPC	9
	T27	99
	P1	50
	P3	172
	AE3	305
FINAL	AE9	173
	TJD	8
FIND	AR	96
	AR	213
	AR	260
	AR	291
	SMA	107
	LC	36
	LC	45
	LC	57
	PWG	36
	PRL	36
	AM	118
	AM	139
	AM	184
	AM	240
	AM	564
	AM	721
	AM	803
	AM	820
	AM	821
	AM	1196
	AM	1212
	PMQ	52
	PWGR	3
	PT	33
	PT	38
	PTL	25
	PCG1	16
	ECG1	24
	SCG2	4
	SCG2	13
	PMQW	9
	PMQW	19
	S	2
	S	7
	ELN	2
	PCD	11
	PCD	17
	PUO1	38
	EUO	9
	PNH	3
	ENH	37
	EUO2	3
	EUO2	22
	EUO2	31
	PC2	12
	PAL	23
	EKK	4
	EKK	7
	EOE	15
	HP	5
	HP	206
	DA	16
	ETG	9
	ETG	21
	PUO5	8
	PUO5	12
	PUO5	16
	PUO5	25
	AA	185
	AA	359

FINDS	AE11	355	FINISHED	VP8	8	FIRE	BR	156
	AE11	1037		G1	428		SKA5	10
	OAL	862		G4	674		EL	301
	KT1	382		G4	790		OD	51
	KT2	213		AE1	881		J1	180
	KT2	333		AE4	938		J1	203
	M8	138		AE5	111		J1	236
	C	180		AE6	721		J3	12
	M11	133		AE8	129		J3	175
	FL	494		AE12	841		J3	234
	CI	464		B	655		J3	349
FINE	EWGR	33		FL	303		J3	361
	PEL	21		M12	519		J3	420
	PNH	44		M15	185		J6	184
	EMP	5	FINISHING	G1	603		J6	808
	EK	17	FINITE	RL	40		J6	816
	EDG	13		HAP	105		J10	92
	EDG	32	FIN-LIKE	AM	628		J10	397
	RL	102	FINNY	M1	96		P2	110
	RL	106		VP5	120		M1	32
	GE	61		G4	560		M1	34
	HAP	1767		G4	621		M1	101
	PDS	45		AE1	211		M1	347
	PTS	43		AE5	1069		M1	490
	ETS	4	FINS	TA	142		M1	505
	J1	74		M1	413		M1	567
	J1	191	FIR	AM	571		M1	668
	J3	299		G2	94		M9	87
	J6	217		AE6	309		M9	99
	J6	592		KT3	959		M13	24
	J10	346	FIRE	JH	8		M13	91
	J10	412		SMA	108		VCS	9
	P1	56		LC	19		VCS	21
	P1	100		AM	606		SLT1	24
	P1	171		AM	848		SLT1	25
	G4	542		AM	857		GK	25
	AE11	1222		AM	866		VP1	14
	DO	120		AM	877		VP2	105
FINELY	P1	163		AM	888		VP5	112
FINES	J10	383		AM	891		VP8	111
FINEST	AM	824		AM	904		VP8	112
	AE9	352		AM	916		VP8	116
	KT3	170		AM	921		G1	128
FINGER	PUO4	19		AM	929		G1	201
	HAP	1118		AM	942		G1	206
	HAP	1985		AM	977		G1	365
	J6	227		AM	993		G1	390
	P2	63		AM	1025		G1	637
	P5	170		AM	1083		G2	415
	P5	172		AM	1104		G2	771
FINGERS	AM	135		AM	1110		G3	103
	J1	40		AM	1153		G3	139
	J6	282		AM	1163		G3	251
	P1	61		SMM2	13		G3	579
	P1	113		SMM2	29		G3	727
	P3	19		SEL3	12		G4	247
	P5	79		STL	4		G4	255
	P6	46		SCG1	13		G4	553
	M1	675		SCG3	14		G4	636
	M1	1033		PFD	18		AE1	246
	G2	338		PFD	22		AE1	297
	G4	172		S	9		AE1	879
	AE6	879		SLN	8		AE1	947
	AE10	553		SLN	16		AE2	361
	OAL	703		PNH	14		AE2	396
	OAE2	30		PNH	52		AE2	406
	AF	22		ML	42		AE2	440
	M10	47		EMK	9		AE2	474
	M10	80		PLG	7		AE2	478
	M10	81		CM	122		AE2	689
	CAM	344		HP	233		AE2	692
FINICAL	OAL	578		EUF	14		AE2	856
FINISH	AM	232		AA	233		AE2	879
	ESF	14		AA	308		AE2	934
	MD	19		AA	625		AE2	961
	AT	16		PLB	24		AE2	1030
	AK	155		MD	188		AE4	289
	GE	78		MF	173		AE4	296
	HAP	2147		SAA	72		AE4	4
	BR	40		SAA	547		AE4	91
	OD	12		SAA	596		AE4	718
	J10	270		EDGA	35		AE4	863
	M1	1019		AT	11		AE4	902
	AE2	468		L1	17		AE4	917
	AE9	128		L1	33		AE4	963
	AE12	899		L2	38		AE5	6
	AE12	1011		L3	284		AE5	116
	TH	164		L4	51		AE5	838
	CI	263		L4	154		AE5	896
FINISHED	ER	31		H3	39		AE5	950
	HAP	1925		H29	39		AE6	319
	J1	8		H2	64		AE6	321
	J10	448		FS4	5		AE6	416
	M1	741		AK	143		AE6	601
	GK	116		HAP	208		AE6	972
	VP4	6		HAP	251		AE7	53

FIRE		
	AE7	107
	AE7	112
	AE7	387
	AE7	448
	AE7	607
	AE7	628
	AE7	863
	AE7	899
	AE7	940
	AE7	956
	AE7	1076
	AE8	160
	AE8	263
	AE8	510
	AE8	516
	AE8	532
	AE8	559
	AE8	567
	AE8	582
	AE8	590
	AE8	644
	AE8	648
	AE8	745
	AE9	169
	AE9	718
	AE9	1031
	AE10	84
	AE10	127
	AE10	137
	AE10	513
	AE10	724
	AE10	996
	AE11	110
	AE11	302
	AE11	568
	AE11	1299
	AE12	15
	AE12	109
	AE12	141
	AE12	183
	AE12	319
	AE12	429
	AE12	762
	AE12	953
	AE12	976
	AE12	1039
	OAL	278
	OAL	332
	OAL	404
	DO	124
	KT1	112
	KT1	324
	KT1	414
	KT2	591
	KT3	71
	KT3	194
	KT3	236
	KT3	250
	KT3	279
	KT3	335
	KT3	368
	KT3	699
	KT3	818
	KT3	828
	KT3	950
	KT3	985
	KT3	993
	KT3	1028
	KT3	1050
	M8	22
	M8	122
	M8	329
	B	58
	B	61
	B	84
	BP	51
	BP	56
	BP	70
	BP	98
	M10	71
	CAM	116
	HIF	153
	HIF	333
	HIF	602
	HIF	637
	C	463
	FL	380
	FL	414
	FL	415
	M12	211
	M12	382
	AU	425
	AU	594
	WB	55
	WB	408
	WB	427

FIRE		
	M15	108
	M15	368
	M15	371
	M15	382
	M15	509
	M15	522
	M15	525
	M15	529
	M15	651
	CI	146
	CI	227
	CI	235
	CI	439
	SMP	49
FIREBALLS	AE8	919
FIREBRANDS	AE2	654
	AE4	815
	AE9	770
	AE10	197
	AE12	845
FIRE-CHARGED	SAA	565
FIRED	AM	66
	AA	685
	SAA	842
	EDG	7
	BR	223
	J3	446
	PPS	4
	P1	248
	M1	716
	M1	1072
	M9	110
	GK	142
	G2	470
	G2	673
	G3	185
	G3	434
	G4	756
	AE2	427
	AE2	550
	AE4	142
	AE5	513
	AE5	607
	AE5	691
	AE6	1230
	AE7	80
	AE7	483
	AE7	499
	AE8	218
	AE9	86
	AE9	616
	AE9	934
	AE9	974
	AE10	39
	AE10	1011
	AE10	1136
	AE10	1154
	AE11	1288
	AE12	415
	AE12	521
	AE12	578
	AE12	701
	AE12	717
	AF	150
	AF	154
	KT1	464
	KT3	980
	KT3	1145
	M8	15
	B	217
	M10	23
	CAM	254
	HIF	294
	HIF	551
	M12	309
	M12	386
	CI	132
	CI	534
	CI	558
	AR	214
	AR	290
	AM	336
	AM	408
	AM	752
	AM	814
	AM	981
	AM	1125
	AM	1178
	HP	187
	DA	25
	DA	80
	DA	148
	RL	4
	OE	24
FIRES	T18	83
	T23	18

FIRES		
	T23	52
	H9	8
	HAP	73
	HAP	858
	EL	183
	LS	10
	J3	321
	J6	296
	J6	537
	J10	220
	M1	55
	M1	62
	M1	1076
	M9	79
	VP7	70
	VP8	91
	VP8	99
	VP8	126
	VP8	150
	G1	123
	G1	282
	G1	454
	G2	421
	G3	159
	G3	347
	G4	323
	AE1	132
	AE1	399
	AE1	741
	AE1	1043
	AE2	454
	AE2	790
	AE2	904
	AE3	301
	AE4	242
	AE4	868
	AE4	971
	AE5	11
	AE5	137
	AE5	835
	AE5	859
	AE5	889
	AE5	973
	AE6	1004
	AE7	117
	AE7	409
	AE7	446
	AE7	566
	AE7	667
	AE7	881
	AE8	336
	AE8	554
	AE8	720
	AE8	822
	AE9	83
	AE9	131
	AE9	192
	AE9	201
	AE9	209
	AE9	239
	AE9	242
	AE9	312
	AE9	473
	AE9	988
	AE10	91
	AE10	113
	AE10	181
	AE10	330
	AE10	378
	AE10	568
	AE10	796
	AE11	285
	AE11	290
	AE11	317
	AE11	321
	AE11	653
	AE11	1071
	AE12	443
	AE12	454
	AE12	771
	AE12	840
	OAL	593
	OAL	644
	OAL	762
	MM	16
	KT1	83
	KT3	181
	KT3	210
	KT3	350
	KT3	901
	M8	344
	B	128
	B	246
	B	431
	B	444
	B	486

Word	Ref	No.
FIRES	CAM	389
	HIF	78
	C	710
	M11	126
	M11	159
	M12	302
	M12	363
	M15	228
	M15	516
	CI	41
FIRE-SHIPS	AM	327
FIREWORKS	SAA	451
	HAP	1229
FIRKIN	PP	28
FIRM	RH	15
	SAA	244
	SAA	813
	SAA	953
	SAA	988
	TA	493
	HAP	1435
	HAP	1668
	EL	18
	MC	17
	G3	121
	AE1	355
	AE4	652
	AE7	356
	AE7	729
	AE8	108
	AE10	357
	AE12	113
	TJD	126
	M10	82
	CAM	341
	FL	280
	FL	523
FIRMAMENT	AA	1027
	EL	338
	M1	198
	M1	231
	AE3	766
	KT3	524
FIRMAMENTAL	AM	1122
FIRMED	AE7	434
FIRMER	RL	42
FIRMLY	HAP	2069
	AE7	376
	B	726
	M15	507
FIRMNESS	AM	594
FIRS	VP7	71
	AE6	264
	AE9	85
	AE9	99
	AE9	917
	AE11	207
	AE11	489
	KT3	905
FIRST	JH	18
	HS	42
	HS	116
	HS	137
	AR	7
	AR	20
	AR	91
	AR	174
	AR	187
	AR	190
	RH	93
	RH	103
	SMA	3
	SMA	93
	LC	76
	LC	93
	DC	9
	PWG	25
	LCA	43
	PRL	3
	PRL	8
	EIE	13
	VHH	52
	AM	49
	AM	73
	AM	84
	AM	99
	AM	147
	AM	179
	AM	196
	AM	203
	AM	293
	AM	302
	AM	372
	AM	439
	AM	444
	AM	475
FIRST	AM	561
	AM	565
	AM	619
	AM	623
	AM	632
	AM	643
	AM	665
	AM	672
	AM	690
	AM	791
	AM	802
	AM	855
	AM	858
	AM	867
	AM	880
	AM	933
	AM	969
	AM	983
	AM	1062
	AM	1135
	PWGR	6
	SMM2	30
	PT	5
	PT	16
	PEL	1
	PEL	25
	EEL	3
	SEL1	9
	STL	4
	PCG1	1
	ECG1	13
	ECG2	11
	PFD	3
	SM1	8
	PCD	3
	PUO1	14
	PUO1	24
	EUO	7
	ENH	10
	EUO2	24
	PAZ	22
	PC1	11
	PC1	16
	PC1	18
	PC1	23
	ML	4
	EMK	13
	EMK	14
	PKK	11
	PKK	13
	POE	28
	POE	36
	PTC	8
	ETC	4
	PO	1
	PO	6
	PO	20
	CM	34
	CM	48
	HP	45
	HP	60
	HP	119
	HP	217
	DA	84
	DA	95
	PSF	26
	PSF	28
	PSF	42
	ETG	4
	PR	19
	PR	22
	PUO5	23
	PUF	1
	PUF	6
	PUF	30
	AA	140
	AA	150
	AA	257
	AA	406
	AA	544
	AA	817
	AA	1019
	PLB	20
	MD	26
	MD	164
	MD	198
	MD	212
	MD	225
	PRH	8
	PRH	18
	PRH	39
	SAA	86
	SAA	137
	SAA	138
	SAA	183
FIRST	SAA	266
	SAA	280
	SAA	377
	SAA	684
	SAA	757
	SAA	826
	SAA	941
	SAA	974
	SAA	1109
	EK	1
	EK	48
	PDG	4
	EDGA	33
	EDGA	37
	RL	14
	RL	68
	RL	102
	RL	217
	RL	137
	RL	155
	RL	342
	RL	358
	PD	29
	PD	33
	PD	51
	PD	57
	EC	33
	ER	3
	ER	6
	ER	13
	ER	48
	ER	70
	ER	71
	L1	16
	L3	112
	L4	6
	L4	38
	L4	112
	L5	6
	T23	34
	T23	38
	T23	67
	T27	92
	T27	86
	T27	100
	T27	101
	T27	129
	H3	13
	H3	17
	TA	13
	TA	53
	TA	100
	TA	173
	TA	434
	TA	449
	TA	452
	PAA	24
	MN	7
	AK	19
	AK	30
	AK	60
	AK	159
	AK	188
	HH	1
	HAP	47
	HAP	54
	HAP	106
	HAP	137
	HAP	151
	HAP	173
	HAP	180
	HAP	200
	HAP	210
	HAP	262
	HAP	278
	HAP	280
	HAP	459
	HAP	469
	HAP	484
	HAP	501
	HAP	518
	HAP	526
	HAP	539
	HAP	552
	HAP	640
	HAP	722
	HAP	741
	HAP	879
	HAP	881
	HAP	892
	HAP	911
	HAP	1174
	HAP	1259
	HAP	1293
	HAP	1631
	HAP	1871

FIRST		
AE9	932
AE9	944
AE9	1005
AE9	1050
AE10	5
AE10	10
AE10	150
AE10	342
AE10	429
AE10	433
AE10	485
AE10	533
AE10	578
AE10	605
AE10	646
AE10	671
AE10	708
AE10	1027
AE10	1048
AE10	1093
AE10	1203
AE10	1263
AE11	5
AE11	26
AE11	39
AE11	57
AE11	185
AE11	256
AE11	380
AE11	587
AE11	614
AE11	727
AE11	841
AE11	866
AE11	916
AE11	951
AE11	987
AE11	1091
AE11	1152
AE11	1155
AE11	1292
AE12	113
AE12	324
AE12	345
AE12	594
AE12	601
AE12	628
AE12	629
AE12	734
AE12	739
AE12	820
AE12	919
AE12	920
AE12	1004
AE12	1068
AE12	1125
AE12	1333
OAL	41
OAL	156
OAL	512
OAL	305
OAL	307
OAL	313
OAL	319
OAL	396
OAL	422
OAL	436
OAL	646
OAL	738
OAL	804
OAL	806
OAL	813
OAL	815
AF	55
MG	29
MM	23
MM	53
DO	1
DO	148
KT1	8
KT1	31
KT1	56
KT1	143
KT1	306
KT1	307
KT1	314
KT1	316
KT1	321
KT1	325
KT1	330
KT1	392
KT1	582
KT1	601
KT2	12
KT2	54
KT2	89

FIRST		
KT2	163
KT2	270
KT2	272
KT2	276
KT2	333
KT2	379
KT2	440
KT2	513
KT2	527
KT3	113
KT3	234
KT3	377
KT3	433
KT3	501
KT3	659
KT3	716
KT3	821
KT3	973
KT3	1018
KT3	1022
KT3	1032
KT3	1066
KT3	1076
KT3	1080
TJD	21
TJD	24
TJD	73
TJD	80
TJD	99
TJD	114
M8	109
M8	157
M8	194
M8	242
M8	265
M8	281
B	68
B	158
B	318
B	320
B	402
B	410
B	468
B	474
B	510
B	529
B	534
B	537
B	544
B	576
B	675
B	707
B	712
B	749
BP	43
BP	90
M10	37
M10	61
CAM	95
CAM	241
CAM	267
CAM	270
CAM	315
HIF	49
HIF	112
HIF	183
HIF	248
HIF	305
HIF	397
HIF	425
HIF	461
HIF	645
HIF	696
HIF	738
C	33
C	436
C	446
C	509
C	513
C	516
C	522
C	531
C	540
C	557
C	704
C	726
C	789
TH	222
TH	269
M11	76
M11	100
FL	7
FL	555
FL	572
FL	601
M12	22

FIRST		
	M12	29
	M12	42
	M12	99
	M12	111
	M12	154
	M12	216
	M12	245
	M12	320
	M12	339
	M12	404
	M12	699
	M12	815
	AU	34
	AU	58
	AU	82
	AU	120
	AU	253
	AU	333
	AU	387
	WB	206
	WB	256
	WB	273
	WB	299
	WB	406
	WB	449
	WB	530
	WB	538
	M15	12
	M15	56
	M15	99
	M15	144
	M15	188
	M15	285
	M15	299
	M15	344
	M15	368
	M15	554
	M15	588
	M15	597
	CI	10
	CI	33
	CI	39
	CI	114
	CI	118
	CI	124
	CI	139
	CI	148
	CI	163
	CI	195
	CI	207
	CI	338
	CI	411
	CI	413
	CI	491
	CI	494
	CI	534
	CI	571
	PTP	31
	ETP	4
	ETP	8
	ETP	22
	ETP	38
	AS	53
FIRST-BEGOTTEN	TJD	42
FIRSTLING	ER	64
FIRSTLINGS	VP1	9
	TJD	55
FISH	AM	924
	SAA	315
	EDG	40
	H2	75
	P1	83
	P3	145
	P5	197
	M1	96
	VP1	80
	VP5	120
	G3	654
	G3	812
	AE10	304
	OAL	51
	OAL	446
	OAL	875
	WB	436
	M15	141
	M15	703
FISHER	GP	101
	AT	57
FISHERY	J3	58
FISHES	SMA	112
	AM	619
	MF	49
	AE8	41
	M15	406
FISHING	BP	22
FISHY	AE4	373

Word	Code	Number
FIST	AM	341
	J16	45
	M1	363
	AE7	709
	KT2	489
	KT3	88
FISTS	RL	404
FIT	UDH	83
	HS	80
	AR	199
	EIE	13
	EIE	26
	AM	26
	AM	664
	AM	1104
	SEL4	19
	PTL	7
	ETL	21
	PCG1	36
	PUO1	45
	EUO	5
	PUO2	3
	PAZ	25
	PAL	14
	POE	19
	HP	22
	HP	46
	AA	152
	AA	221
	AA	525
	AA	696
	AA	765
	AA	869
	AA	907
	MF	11
	SAA	479
	SAA	525
	SAA	804
	SDG	23
	SDG	28
	AT	49
	L3	290
	H29	23
	PAA	20
	HAP	975
	PP	38
	PSH	27
	J1	198
	J3	192
	J6	324
	J10	77
	P2	54
	P2	71
	P5	8
	M1	100
	M9	24
	VP3	114
	G1	250
	G2	303
	G2	311
	G2	323
	G3	497
	G4	154
	AE1	193
	AE2	523
	AE6	261
	AE7	316
	AE7	453
	AE8	672
	OAL	279
	OAL	402
	OAL	411
	OAL	684
	OAE1	26
	OAE2	39
	MM	47
	TJD	123
	M8	298
	B	109
	B	599
	HIF	220
	HIF	738
	AU	318
	WB	167
	WB	200
	M15	352
FITLY	AS	71
FITS	EUF	1
	LC	83
	L3	98
	HAP	2388
	J6	564
	G1	447
	AE2	648
	AE3	565
	AE5	894

Word	Code	Number
FITS	AE6	383
	AE8	110
	AE8	784
	KT3	617
	M8	360
	HIF	804
	M11	133
	FL	586
	M12	687
	M15	517
	CI	330
FITTED	AM	599
	AM	616
	UMR	6
	AA	177
	SAA	227
	T23	93
	EL	27
	EL	256
	AE11	792
FITTER	LC	59
	HAP	2351
	EDS	20
	G2	280
	AE11	713
	AE12	447
	KT1	130
FITTEST	RL	454
FITTING	KT3	894
FIVE	PCG1	2
	PC2	22
	PLB	50
	PLB	54
	MD	18
	MF	149
	TA	108
	TA	179
	BR	184
	PDS	44
	EL	24
	J1	161
	J6	323
	P4	95
	M1	52
	M1	53
	M1	1033
	G1	322
	AE2	173
	AE5	129
	AE7	749
	AE7	871
	AE10	293
	HIF	638
	M12	610
	AU	404
	M15	586
FIX	EMP	5
	AA	803
	MF	177
	SAA	240
	SAA	683
	SAA	1073
	RL	37
	HAP	835
	HAP	848
	HAP	1795
	HAP	2495
	J3	449
	M1	576
	G3	697
	G4	347
	AE3	118
	AE4	705
	AE5	822
	AE6	104
	AE6	860
	AE6	1039
	AE6	1073
	AE7	1105
	AE9	565
	AE10	51
	AE11	1100
	AE12	199
	OAL	687
FIXED	UDH	35
	AM	543
	AM	1078
	SAA	218
	SAA	773
	SAA	792
	L3	298
	TA	317
	AK	8
	HAP	1238
	EL	230
	EL	253

Word	Code	Number
FIXED	M1	23
	M1	751
	M1	1074
	M13	87
	G1	209
	G2	588
	G4	126
	AE1	310
	AE1	338
	AE1	351
	AE1	696
	AE1	866
	AE1	1044
	AE2	79
	AE2	613
	AE2	880
	AE3	50
	AE3	101
	AE3	149
	AE3	370
	AE3	859
	AE4	28
	AE4	413
	AE4	647
	AE4	812
	AE5	2
	AE5	170
	AE5	668
	AE5	1109
	AE6	465
	AE6	634
	AE6	841
	AE6	866
	AE6	887
	AE6	913
	AE7	342
	AE7	488
	AE7	523
	AE7	743
	AE7	753
	AE7	768
	AE8	315
	AE9	599
	AE9	948
	AE9	1008
	AE10	237
	AE10	328
	AE10	353
	AE10	790
	AE10	1037
	AE10	1088
	AE10	1104
	AE11	13
	AE11	121
	AE11	768
	AE12	946
	AE12	954
	AE12	983
	AE12	1025
	AE12	1331
	OAL	270
	KT1	271
	KT3	241
	M8	188
	M8	194
	B	384
	B	470
	B	579
	B	621
	B	634
	CAM	109
	CAM	141
	HIF	76
	HIF	224
	HIF	254
	TH	400
	M11	48
	FL	50
	FL	179
	M12	91
	M12	517
	M12	746
	AU	141
	AU	317
	AU	607
	M15	407
	CI	109
	CI	120
	CI	172
	CI	188
	CI	485
	CI	559
FIXES	M1	644
FIXING	J3	3
	AE11	1036
	AE12	112

Word	Code	No.	Word	Code	No.	Word	Code	No.
FLABBY	G3	780	FLAME	AE11	573	FLAMES	AE2	844
FLAG	AM	605		AE12	263		AE2	857
	HAP	1803		AE12	936		AE2	958
FLAGGING	AM	512		OAL	41		AE2	1029
	AE3	694		OAL	203		AE3	236
	AE3	744		OAL	315		AE3	728
	C1	330		OAL	643		AE3	750
FLAGGY	M1	358		OAL	809		AE4	34
	G4	40		KT2	592		AE4	948
FLAGON	P3	181		KT3	182		AE5	66
	P6	38		KT3	237		AE5	692
	AE9	244		KT3	254		AE5	811
FLAGS	AR	225		KT3	818		AE5	869
	J10	251		KT3	986		AE5	906
	AE7	801		M8	78		AE5	915
	AE10	362		M8	256		AE5	1037
FLAGSTAFFS	AM	220		M8	262		AE6	7
FLAIL	MF	89		B	471		AE6	323
	PDG	19		B	514		AE7	109
	G1	245		CAM	250		AE7	644
FLAILS	M8	37		CAM	270		AE7	1074
FLAKES	G4	254		C	180		AE8	343
	AE3	750		C	462		AE8	354
	AE8	263		M11	63		AE8	558
	AE12	1039		M11	241		AE8	901
FLAMBEAU	AE11	214		FL	261		AE9	87
	AF	147		FL	374		AE10	377
	AF	151		M12	382		AE10	569
FLAMBEAUX	J3	450		M12	554		AE10	574
FLAME	AM	276		AU	146		AE11	305
	AM	1064		AU	372		AE11	1158
	AM	1107		WB	410		AE11	1289
	AM	1169		M15	224		AE12	300
	SMQ	1		M15	379		AE12	321
	SEL4	9		M15	580		AE12	760
	SCG3	28		M15	596		AE12	847
	HP	89		AS	18		AE12	951
	DA	26	FLAMED	KT2	244		AE12	977
	AA	98	FLAMES	AR	20		AE12	1181
	SAA	545		AR	204		AE12	1369
	SAA	1113		SMA	52		OAL	278
	SDG	21		LC	6		OAL	544
	SDG	26		AM	336		DO	126
	AT	13		AM	815		KT1	179
	ER	36		AM	868		KT3	186
	L4	19		AM	882		KT3	248
	FS4	17		AM	919		KT3	363
	TA	39		AM	932		KT3	367
	TA	117		AM	936		KT3	812
	AK	84		AM	961		KT3	902
	OD	50		AM	978		KT3	959
	M9	81		AM	1006		KT3	980
	M9	104		AM	1033		KT3	991
	VP5	134		AM	1087		M8	121
	VP6	50		AM	1089		M8	289
	VP10	30		AM	1101		M8	385
	G2	193		AM	1120		M8	387
	G2	418		AM	1124		M8	347
	G3	379		SEL3	12		M8	358
	G3	443		SCG1	5		BP	53
	G3	835		CM	23		M10	71
	AE1	67		HP	176		HIF	120
	AE1	247		EPF	17		HIF	628
	AE1	920		OE	5		C	151
	AE1	997		L3	51		TH	121
	AE2	279		L4	88		CI	239
	AE2	430		T23	64		CI	565
	AE2	931		T27	127		C	699
	AE3	634		J3	322		C	708
	AE4	2		J3	233		M15	512
	AE4	31		J3	406		M15	527
	AE4	53		J10	94	FLAMING	AM	368
	AE4	74		J10	411		AM	1082
	AE4	555		P2	87		HP	230
	AE4	858		P3	239		TA	31
	AE4	871		M1	200		HAP	1241
	AE5	862		M1	304		BR	177
	AE5	894		M1	666		M1	342
	AE6	363		M9	92		M13	39
	AE6	403		M13	187		M13	42
	AE6	598		VP10	106		G2	422
	AE6	981		G1	124		G3	841
	AE6	989		G3	739		G4	617
	AE7	448		G4	254		AE2	156
	AE7	704		G4	554		AE2	272
	AE7	1047		G4	591		AE2	654
	AE8	570		AE2	47		AE3	204
	AE8	644		AE2	209		AE3	758
	AE8	956		AE2	253		AE3	833
	AE9	88		AE2	382		AE4	833
	AE9	772		AE2	418		AE4	852
	AE9	794		AE2	444		AE5	248
	AE10	72		AE2	583		AE5	830
	AE11	109		AE2	773		AE5	838
	AE11	118		AE2	778		AE5	859
	AE11	315		AE2	786		AE5	951

FLAMING	AE6	803
	AE6	1207
	AE7	117
	AE7	556
	AE7	733
	AE7	1060
	AE8	373
	AE8	825
	AE9	33
	AE9	83
	AE9	713
	AE10	127
	AE10	795
	AE10	814
	AE10	1156
	AE12	176
	AE12	256
	M8	342
	M12	363
	M12	391
	AU	12
FLANDERS	AM	31
	ENH	29
	ESH	20
FLANK	AE9	922
FLANKED	AM	102
FLANKS	G3	780
	AE4	225
	TH	271
FLAPS	AE12	1253
FLASH	SAA	1041
	AE8	39
	AE8	518
	AE10	796
	AE11	900
	AE12	15
	AF	135
	M11	124
FLASHED	TA	138
	G1	656
	AE6	660
	AE8	694
	KT3	81
	FL	385
FLASHES	J1	252
	G4	712
FLASHING	G1	446
	AE1	132
	AE4	242
	AE10	382
	AE12	1369
	KT3	699
	TH	121
	M11	159
FLASHY	P1	243
FLAT	PEL	26
	EPC	32
	HAP	415
	BR	262
	P1	183
	P3	157
	GK	53
	AE9	1093
	AE11	477
FLAT-NOSE	L4	159
FLATS	AM	450
	AM	731
FLATTED	AE10	158
	AE10	989
	AE12	670
	M11	131
FLATTER	HP	128
	PRH	18
	L4	129
	HAP	1531
	J6	272
	OAL	501
	CI	474
FLATTERED	SAA	910
	J10	82
	HAP	2457
	AE2	534
	AE6	474
	M12	173
FLATTERER	WB	486
FLATTERERS	J10	324
	C	812
FLATTEREST	MD	293
FLATTERIES	J3	151
	OAL	700
FLATTERING	LC	1
	SAA	20
	SAA	120
	J3	131
	J10	71
	J10	155

FLATTERING	P1	105
	P1	244
	P4	124
	M1	661
	M1	1020
	G1	283
	G3	269
	AE5	1135
	OAL	309
	CAM	299
	C	590
	C	661
	C	799
	M11	240
	GP	118
FLATTERS	L4	47
	HAP	508
	BR	115
	WB	132
FLATTERY	HP	224
	AA	304
	RL	398
	TA	435
	J3	184
	J3	160
	P1	116
	VP9	45
	G4	573
	M10	35
	C	475
	C	654
	M11	399
	WB	130
FLAUNTING	HAP	1430
	J3	297
	J6	589
FLAVINIAN	AE7	962
FLAVOR	G2	83
	G2	129
FLAVOROUS	G2	326
FLAW	TA	31
	HAP	986
	P3	36
	AE3	529
	AE8	325
	AE9	722
	AE9	970
FLAWED	G3	558
FLAWS	AA	802
	RL	344
FLAX	P5	198
	G1	114
	M8	258
FLAY	J6	327
FLAYED	HIF	630
FLEAS	PAL	29
FLECKED	VP2	55
	G3	93
FLECKNOE	MF	3
	MF	85
	MF	173
FLED	DC	54
	PFD	6
	SM1	7
	PUO5	9
	AA	857
	AA	858
	L3	40
	T23	9
	TA	350
	HAP	582
	HAP	2317
	HAP	2446
	BR	288
	LS	7
	EL	48
	J3	331
	J6	118
	J10	424
	M1	307
	M1	565
	M1	678
	M1	710
	M1	812
	M1	882
	M9	48
	M13	203
	G4	451
	AE1	470
	AE2	184
	AE2	209
	AE2	280
	AE2	431
	AE3	167
	AE3	411
	AE4	277

FLED	AE4	536
	AE4	770
	AE4	956
	AE5	682
	AE6	661
	AE7	573
	AE8	425
	AE9	718
	AE10	330
	AE10	562
	AE10	785
	AE10	914
	AE10	987
	AE11	241
	AE11	980
	AE12	664
	AE12	1071
	AE12	1075
	AE12	1108
	KT2	293
	KT2	349
	KT2	575
	KT3	839
	M8	145
	M8	322
	B	197
	CAM	314
	HIF	55
	TH	94
	TH	123
	TH	344
	M11	321
	FL	100
	FL	376
	FL	441
	M12	148
	M12	163
	M12	201
	M12	417
	M12	418
	M12	432
	AU	11
	AU	97
	AU	439
	CI	409
	SMP	52
FLEECE	AA	129
	J1	14
	VP3	149
	VP4	54
	G3	479
	G3	676
	AU	34
	M15	171
	M15	319
FLEECES	G1	21
	G3	600
	AE4	666
	AE7	135
FLEECY	J6	223
	G1	417
	G2	170
	G2	270
	G3	837
	M15	91
FLEET	AR	223
	AR	300
	AM	61
	AM	93
	AM	213
	AM	266
	AM	273
	AM	277
	AM	313
	AM	323
	AM	333
	AM	337
	AM	442
	AM	473
	AM	485
	AM	534
	AM	549
	AM	670
	AM	686
	AM	761
	AM	773
	AM	804
	AM	1203
	PM	5
	SAA	1126
	L4	62
	J10	409
	P3	148
	VP6	109
	G1	347
	AE1	50

FLEET	AE1	182
	AE1	242
	AE1	428
	AE1	499
	AE1	529
	AE1	541
	AE1	801
	AE1	817
	AE2	31
	AE3	9
	AE3	158
	AE3	259
	AE3	517
	AE3	738
	AE3	929
	AE4	71
	AE4	416
	AE4	541
	AE4	574
	AE4	616
	AE4	784
	AE4	850
	AE5	45
	AE5	69
	AE5	794
	AE5	827
	AE5	917
	AE5	951
	AE5	1037
	AE5	1047
	AE5	1065
	AE5	1122
	AE7	56
	AE7	329
	AE7	615
	AE8	918
	AE9	89
	AE10	55
	AE10	373
	FL	221
	M12	13
	M12	90
	AU	8
	AU	146
	AU	152
	AU	291
	AU	418
	AU	425
	SMP	31
FLEETER	M13	95
	AE9	756
FLEETEST	PSF	15
FLEETING	TA	114
	G4	594
	G4	722
	AE2	1073
FLEETNESS	AE12	133
FLEETS	DC	26
	AM	227
	AM	814
	SAA	620
	AE5	878
	AE8	895
	AE10	127
FLESH	UDH	57
	EWGR	14
	PM	16
	EAL	8
	EKK	15
	AA	96
	AA	627
	MD	226
	SAA	300
	EDG	40
	T27	113
	AK	187
	HAP	134
	HAP	373
	HAP	425
	HAP	428
	HAP	1658
	HAP	2268
	HAP	2422
	ESH	7
	ESH	8
	M1	299
	GK	111
	G3	767
	G3	834
	AE3	773
	AE3	826
	AE6	1020
	AE6	1170
	AE11	56
	DO	136
	B	422

FLESH	B	503
	BP	69
	M10	21
	M10	82
	C	58
	C	485
	C	577
	TH	213
	M12	182
	M15	99
	M15	152
FLESHED	PC1	9
	AU	137
FLESHY	M15	131
FLETCHER	PWG	48
	PT	6
	PT	9
	PT	18
	EUO	31
	PC1	11
	MF	79
	MF	183
FLETCHER'S	PUO2	21
	MC	20
	MC	23
FLEW	HS	52
	AM	508
	AM	796
	D	18
	SAA	128
	RL	222
	TA	379
	HAP	1889
	J6	28
	P1	206
	M13	36
	HI	31
	HI	36
	G2	466
	AE1	823
	AE2	65
	AE2	551
	AE2	743
	AE3	337
	AE5	416
	AE5	432
	AE5	667
	AE5	691
	AE5	875
	AE6	792
	AE6	958
	AE7	149
	AE7	193
	AE7	524
	AE7	725
	AE7	1101
	AE8	872
	AE9	53
	AE9	462
	AE9	570
	AE9	799
	AE9	897
	AE10	350
	AE10	466
	AE10	481
	AE10	802
	AE10	936
	AE10	1100
	AE11	843
	AE11	1250
	AE12	410
	AE12	1002
	AE12	1321
	AE12	1335
	KT1	97
	KT1	113
	KT3	251
	KT3	258
	KT3	361
	KT3	703
	TJD	46
	M8	120
	M8	125
	M8	186
	B	161
	HIF	70
	C	426
	M11	74
	M12	20
	M12	169
	M12	212
	M12	367
	M12	410
	M12	496
	M12	527
	M12	660

FLEW	WB	222
FLEXIBLE	G3	263
FLICKERING	KT3	123
	M11	484
FLIES	AR	6
	DC	35
	AM	218
	AM	344
	AM	430
	AM	1180
	EUO	2
	PAZ	10
	CM	85
	DA	10
	AA	261
	OE	36
	H3	37
	H2	39
	TA	49
	HAP	113
	HAP	1608
	HAP	1641
	HAP	1746
	PKA	28
	SKA3	16
	ODA	70
	J3	351
	J10	259
	J10	329
	M1	190
	M1	442
	M1	708
	EHC	37
	VP3	99
	VP10	34
	G1	262
	G1	551
	G1	554
	G1	549
	G3	313
	G4	74
	AE1	412
	AE1	574
	AE1	939
	AE1	969
	AE2	294
	AE2	450
	AE2	514
	AE2	633
	AE2	720
	AE3	261
	AE3	707
	AE4	97
	AE4	232
	AE4	283
	AE4	352
	AE4	362
	AE4	377
	AE4	533
	AE4	686
	AE5	278
	AE5	316
	AE5	579
	AE5	677
	AE5	911
	AE5	1124
	AE7	133
	AE7	530
	AE7	538
	AE7	661
	AE7	753
	AE7	787
	AE8	517
	AE9	18
	AE9	313
	AE9	446
	AE9	559
	AE9	566
	AE9	600
	AE9	865
	AE9	908
	AE9	965
	AE9	1030
	AE9	1041
	AE10	567
	AE10	570
	AE10	896
	AE11	625
	AE11	821
	AE11	840
	AE11	1027
	AE11	1179
	AE11	1185
	AE11	1194
	AE12	81
	AE12	157

FLIES	AE12	509
	AE12	544
	AE12	692
	AE12	704
	AE12	1044
	AE12	1062
	AE12	1064
	AE12	1099
	AE12	1242
	AE12	1252
	OAL	272
	KT3	564
	M8	124
	BP	137
	CAM	272
	C	801
	M11	264
	M11	312
	M15	240
	M15	252
	M15	371
	M15	378
	CI	146
	CI	334
	CI	609
	AR	270
FLIGHT	DC	36
	AM	484
	AM	768
	AM	780
	PC1	11
	HP	199
	DA	11
	AA	854
	AA	860
	SAA	897
	SAA	939
	AK	34
	HAP	268
	HAP	1224
	HAP	1613
	HAP	1620
	HAP	1740
	HAP	1747
	HAP	2570
	EL	134
	P2	109
	M1	77
	M1	624
	M1	734
	M1	817
	M1	829
	M1	968
	M1	1008
	G1	499
	G2	671
	G2	685
	G3	14
	G3	351
	G3	434
	G3	572
	G4	34
	G4	85
	G4	166
	G4	287
	G4	614
	G4	682
	G4	726
	G4	803
	AE1	496
	AE1	1061
	AE2	236
	AE2	381
	AE2	509
	AE2	860
	AE2	1000
	AE3	683
	AE4	172
	AE4	261
	AE4	371
	AE4	402
	AE4	548
	AE4	578
	AE4	622
	AE4	687
	AE4	473
	AE4	488
	AE4	802
	AE4	820
	AE4	828
	AE4	949
	AE4	1003
	AE5	281
	AE5	336
	AE5	885
	AE5	969

FLIGHT	AE5	1061
	AE5	1091
	AE6	280
	AE6	289
	AE6	295
	AE6	343
	AE6	430
	AE6	628
	AE7	31
	AE7	98
	AE7	396
	AE7	479
	AE8	287
	AE8	310
	AE8	560
	AE8	647
	AE8	936
	AE9	16
	AE9	92
	AE9	103
	AE9	189
	AE9	513
	AE9	739
	AE9	886
	AE9	976
	AE9	998
	AE9	1078
	AE10	183
	AE10	278
	AE10	284
	AE10	509
	AE10	519
	AE10	831
	AE10	961
	AE10	976
	AE10	1128
	AE11	534
	AE11	601
	AE11	826
	AE11	881
	AE11	894
	AE11	922
	AE11	925
	AE11	1075
	AE11	1236
	AE11	1261
	AE12	133
	AE12	379
	AE12	699
	AE12	864
	AE12	938
	AE12	1064
	AE12	1243
	AE12	1267
	AE12	1288
	OAL	30
	OAL	241
	OAL	246
	OAL	267
	OAL	619
	OAL	620
	KT2	14
	KT2	28
	KT2	67
	KT3	57
	TJD	160
	M8	125
	B	106
	B	515
	BP	146
	BP	149
	CAM	315
	HIF	40
	HIF	67
	HIF	88
	HIF	586
	HIF	796
	C	416
	C	721
	C	771
	TH	113
	TH	181
	TH	212
	TH	274
	TH	375
	M11	347
	M11	476
	FL	301
	FL	441
	M12	338
	M12	606
	M12	704
	M12	750
	M12	790
	M12	804
	AU	184

FLIGHT	AU	350
	AU	374
	WB	12
	M15	41
	M15	254
	M15	538
	M15	605
	M15	702
	CI	274
	CI	398
	CI	522
	CI	552
	SMP	6
FLIGHTS	AA	656
	G4	445
	AE3	464
	AE4	254
	AE10	197
FLING	SAA	140
	AE9	1090
	AE11	866
FLINGS	L4	43
	M8	197
FLINT	AT	90
FLINTS	G1	205
	AE1	246
	AE6	6
	FL	414
	M15	521
FLINTY	J3	433
	G2	250
	G3	357
	AE8	307
FLIT	AE12	1227
	M8	401
FLITS	G1	543
	M15	671
FLITTING	AE2	292
	AE4	397
	AE5	676
	AE6	117
	AE6	419
	AE6	642
	AE6	951
	AE9	419
	AE10	484
	M11	315
	M11	349
FLIX	AM	526
	M1	723
FLOAT	AM	815
	J1	124
	M1	393
	G1	364
	G1	442
	G4	284
	AE2	492
	AE5	234
	AE8	713
FLOATED	BR	171
	AE3	101
	AE6	485
	BP	152
	M15	504
FLOATING	AM	228
	AM	604
	AM	623
	DA	186
	VP6	25
	G1	507
	G2	275
	G3	414
	AE1	169
	AE5	13
	AE5	271
	AE5	1122
	AE6	1208
	AE8	28
	AE8	917
	AE9	106
	AE9	471
	AE10	424
	KT3	466
	M11	211
	M11	447
	M11	495
FLOATS	AA	137
	MF	50
	MF	186
	G1	512
	G4	37
	AE10	211
	AE11	459
	C	148
	M15	412
	CI	608

FLOCK	ETC	6	FLOOD	S	13	FLOOD	AE8	423
	AA	129		DA	199		AE8	439
	AA	432		AA	137		AE8	468
	SAA	379		AA	820		AE8	585
	SAA	697		SAA	619		AE8	716
	SAA	742		SAA	774		AE8	864
	T18	93		SAA	816		AE9	26
	T27	67		SAA	924		AE9	122
	H29	34		L1	19		AE9	446
	H2	88		T23	32		AE9	471
	TA	428		H3	17		AE9	625
	HAP	284		HAP	523		AE9	820
	HAP	389		HAP	844		AE9	1103
	HAP	900		HAP	849		AE10	19
	HAP	962		HAP	1320		AE10	173
	HAP	2569		HAP	2097		AE10	279
	M1	311		BR	159		AE10	312
	VP1	103		J1	124		AE10	421
	VP3	46		J6	671		AE10	847
	VP3	148		M1	422		AE10	968
	VP3	152		M1	580		AE10	1084
	VP5	16		M1	792		AE10	1117
	VP5	67		M1	801		AE10	1186
	VP7	8		M1	971		AE11	457
	VP7	64		M13	45		AE11	500
	VP7	68		M13	89		AE11	747
	VP10	26		M13	182		AE11	826
	G1	683		M13	183		AE11	1297
	G3	29		M13	217		AE12	59
	G3	598		M13	224		AE12	100
	G3	710		HI	41		AE12	144
	AE2	706		MC	5		AE12	215
	AE3	11		VP2	32		AE12	499
	AE3	864		VP2	63		AE12	693
	GP	72		VP6	33		OAL	599
	AS	82		VP6	118		KT2	240
FLOCK'S	G3	681		VP8	4		KT3	1028
FLOCKS	PAL	1		G1	198		B	186
	L5	9		G1	293		B	366
	T27	58		G1	418		B	682
	H2	69		G1	524		M11	120
	AK	108		G1	529		M11	471
	HAP	221		G2	275		M12	151
	HAP	720		G2	690		M12	334
	HAP	882		G3	123		M12	387
	HAP	1880		G3	213		M15	31
	HAP	2128		G3	228		M15	71
	J6	217		G3	287		M15	475
	P2	85		G3	330		M15	487
	M1	395		G3	427		CI	89
	M13	52		G3	748		CI	604
	M13	120		G3	772	FLOODS	AR	134
	VP1	63		G3	791		L3	70
	VP2	42		G4	385		AK	112
	VP3	92		G4	457		HAP	2155
	VP3	156		G4	617		SKA6	18
	VP5	1		AE1	158		ODA	46
	VP6	6		AE1	221		J6	537
	VP8	20		AE1	442		P1	200
	G1	525		AE1	662		M1	355
	G1	165		AE2	406		M1	377
	G1	488		AE2	493		M1	385
	G1	594		AE2	677		M1	396
	G2	199		AE2	791		VP3	171
	G2	270		AE2	961		VP5	29
	G2	521		AE3	394		VP5	120
	G2	609		AE3	501		VP7	92
	G3	21		AE3	561		VP7	96
	G3	452		AE4	372		VP8	77
	G3	503		AE5	221		G1	155
	G3	526		AE5	52		G1	492
	G3	545		AE5	110		G1	578
	G3	720		AE5	251		G1	637
	G4	327		AE5	625		G1	649
	G4	568		AE6	134		G3	4
	G4	621		AE6	161		G3	779
	G4	626		AE6	423		G4	76
	G4	628		AE6	524		G4	86
	G4	681		AE6	742		G4	444
	G4	807		AE6	957		G4	522
	AE2	412		AE6	966		G4	530
	AE4	763		AE6	1016		G4	750
	AE7	749		AE7	47		AE4	98
	AE7	971		AE7	477		AE4	760
	AE8	797		AE7	782		AE4	861
	AE9	458		AE7	993		AE5	1032
	TJD	55		AE7	1068		AE5	1054
	M8	402		AE7	1082		AE6	9
	FL	320		AE8	28		AE6	429
	M15	423		AE8	46		AE6	442
FLOOD	SMA	5		AE8	96		AE6	508
	AM	393		AE8	120		AE6	594
	AM	606		AE8	143		AE7	695
	AM	627		AE8	311		AE7	1042
	AM	735		AE8	317		AE8	87
	AM	1189		AE8	363		AE8	103

Word	Ref	Num	Word	Ref	Num	Word	Ref	Num
FLOODS	AE11	695	FLOW	G4	38	FLOWERS	KT1	222
	AE12	272		AE2	81		KT2	56
	OAL	732		AE3	753		KT3	104
	B	304		AE9	36		KT3	136
	WB	389		AE12	1216		KT3	533
	M15	409		OAL	271		CAM	17
FLOOR	AM	1030		OAL	854		TH	258
	L3	194		AF	88		M11	339
	L4	173		AF	92		FL	6
	J6	554		KT1	93		FL	75
	P6	57		M8	271		FL	220
	VP6	25		M11	282		FL	347
	G1	258		WB	389		FL	376
	G1	278		M15	290		FL	385
	G3	742	FLOWED	CM	98		AS	69
	AE3	810		AK	110	FLOWERY	L1	23
	AE5	432		G3	146		P1	138
	M8	370		AE2	225		M13	68
	B	109		KT3	924		VP1	11
	B	221		M8	67		VP1	105
	M10	51	FLOWER	AA	297		VP2	84
	C	226		SAA	993		VP6	78
	M12	365		T27	117		VP10	44
	WB	27		ODA	41		VP10	64
	CI	608		VP3	164		G1	18
FLOORING	G1	262		G3	501		G2	201
	G4	237		G4	391		G2	661
	G4	418		G4	395		G3	4
FLOORS	J3	193		AE8	656		G3	779
	J3	328		AE9	582		G4	177
	G1	476		AE11	91		G4	300
FLORA	FL	561		AE11	99		G4	433
FLORENCE	FL	342		AF	11		AE1	599
FLOUNDERING	AE10	1285		KT1	120		AE1	974
	AE12	541		KT3	6		AE2	1063
	KT3	610		KT3	1078		AE3	286
	CI	64		KT3	1097		AE3	709
FLOUNDERS	HAP	1595		BP	96		AE5	71
FLOUR	HAP	2279		M10	43		AE5	99
	AE7	157		FL	109		AE6	888
FLOURISH	PTW	25		FL	123		AE6	921
	HAP	234		FL	424		AE7	919
	HAP	1496		FL	448		KT1	171
	HAP	1847		FL	532		FL	360
	J6	349		FL	570		M15	118
	MM	49		FL	587		M15	193
	AU	14		FL	603	FLOWING	AA	786
	M15	626		AU	609		T18	18
FLOURISHED	RH	52	FLOWERED	AE4	196		T18	2
	PUO1	1		FL	342		TA	14
	PKK	4	FLOWERETS	M15	304		M1	605
	ETG	7	FLOWERING	G1	272		M1	639
	ETS	22		G4	45		M1	711
	AE3	601	FLOWERS	SEL3	2		M13	159
	AE8	628		AR	132		VP7	88
	HIF	374		AR	287		G2	681
FLOURISHES	P1	170		SMA	30		AE1	558
	AE10	911		LC	138		AE4	198
	M8	166		SCG1	6		AE6	878
FLOURISHING	MF	7		SCG1	7		AE6	981
	CAM	181		MF	165		AE7	553
FLOUT	P1	211		SAA	562		AE7	563
FLOW	HS	109		SAA	1061		AE11	862
	AR	299		L1	9		AE12	135
	LC	29		L2	37		AE12	1259
	VHH	20		L4	173		OAL	636
	AM	5		T18	7		M11	458
	AM	292		HAP	1847		M12	64
	AM	516		P5	262		M12	537
	AM	645		M1	138		M12	547
	STL	23		SFL	2		M12	761
	PAL	25		VP1	72	FLOWN	HS	10
	DA	199		VP3	144		PUO5	3
	AA	894		VP4	27		J3	417
	MF	91		VP9	54		P6	153
	MF	185		G1	464		M9	1
	SAA	879		G2	183	FLOWS	SMA	111
	RL	341		G4	15		AA	869
	ER	45		G4	54		RL	332
	L3	99		G4	76		L4	99
	L4	281		G4	165		HAP	289
	TA	3		G4	196		M13	50
	TA	149		G4	209		G2	201
	HAP	505		G4	268		G2	477
	HAP	1852		G4	293		G4	65
	J1	223		G4	364		G4	527
	P1	120		G4	428		AE3	903
	P6	33		AE1	918		AE7	201
	M1	45		AE1	995		AE8	85
	M1	85		AE3	625		AE8	891
	M1	361		AE4	83		AE9	447
	VP1	99		AE6	1224		AE9	928
	G1	160		AE11	1142		AE11	750
	G2	216		AE12	612		OAL	256
	G3	43		DO	160		MFL	32
	G3	139		KT1	195		M15	263

Word	Source	No.
FLUENT	HAP	2448
	J3	133
FLUNG	AE2	1077
	AE10	988
	KT3	302
FLUSH	AE12	104
FLUSHED	J6	551
	P1	66
	VP10	32
	AF	51
	M12	402
FLUSHING	P3	237
	G1	579
FLUSTERED	PMS	19
FLUTE	SSC	33
	VP8	30
	VP8	35
	VP8	45
	VP8	52
	VP8	59
	VP8	63
	VP8	69
	VP8	79
	VP8	86
	AE9	848
	AF	158
FLUTES	FL	364
FLUTTER	OAE1	22
FLUTTERING	EK	13
	HAP	1743
	HAP	2251
	J1	84
	AE2	743
	AE5	650
	AE6	291
	AE7	130
	M12	23
FLUTTERS	AE5	280
	AE5	669
	AE12	1253
	OAL	268
FLUX	M15	266
FLUXING	PMK	21
FLY	HS	4
	AR	38
	AR	294
	SMA	52
	AM	114
	AM	350
	AM	720
	AM	770
	AM	984
	AM	1004
	SMM1	8
	SLN	10
	SLN	14
	SCD2	14
	PUO2	26
	DA	69
	MD	121
	MF	129
	SAA	1032
	L4	245
	AK	184
	HAP	7
	HAP	104
	HAP	756
	HAP	812
	HAP	865
	HAP	993
	HAP	1017
	HAP	1033
	HAP	1360
	HAP	1767
	HAP	1803
	HAP	1855
	HAP	1907
	HAP	1975
	HAP	2411
	SKA1	11
	J1	83
	J3	46
	J3	322
	J6	355
	J10	505
	P1	197
	P5	156
	M1	689
	M1	812
	HI	181
	VP7	77
	G1	559
	G1	618
	G3	171
	G3	183
	G4	126
FLY	G4	289
	G4	332
	G4	442
	AE1	27
	AE1	89
	AE1	215
	AE1	258
	AE1	563
	AE2	658
	AE2	707
	AE2	1056
	AE3	64
	AE3	179
	AE3	273
	AE3	294
	AE3	353
	AE3	375
	AE3	490
	AE3	749
	AE3	840
	AE3	883
	AE3	892
	AE4	329
	AE4	407
	AE4	441
	AE4	453
	AE4	469
	AE4	620
	AE4	813
	AE5	651
	AE5	931
	AE5	1017
	AE5	1075
	AE6	18
	AE6	952
	AE7	126
	AE7	264
	AE7	456
	AE7	858
	AE7	869
	AE8	330
	AE8	919
	AE9	86
	AE9	158
	AE9	768
	AE9	932
	AE9	991
	AE9	1020
	AE9	1103
	AE10	27
	AE10	272
	AE10	586
	AE10	913
	AE10	950
	AE10	954
	AE10	1142
	AE11	420
	AE11	752
	AE11	895
	AE11	928
	AE11	1025
	AE11	1037
	AE11	1083
	AE11	1199
	AE11	1259
	AE11	1270
	AE12	382
	AE12	427
	AE12	497
	AE12	503
	AE12	682
	AE12	847
	AE12	1039
	AE12	1256
	OAL	136
	OAL	818
	KT2	25
	KT2	532
	KT3	135
	M8	129
	B	131
	B	677
	HIF	269
	C	164
	C	586
	C	740
	TH	177
	M11	38
	M11	52
	M11	102
	M11	272
	M11	296
	FL	219
	M12	376
	AU	132
FLY	GP	39
	CI	624
	STP	17
	SMP	53
	SMP	57
FLY-BLOWN	RL	419
FLYING	LC	114
	AM	434
	AM	612
	AM	775
	AM	1063
	PMQ	18
	SM2	5
	HP	94
	PK	39
	SSH	15
	ODA	4
	P5	222
	M1	686
	M1	727
	M1	925
	M13	37
	M13	95
	VP2	12
	VP2	37
	G1	246
	G1	347
	G1	392
	G1	416
	G1	435
	G1	450
	G2	58
	G2	292
	G3	170
	G3	237
	G3	316
	G3	623
	G3	804
	G4	726
	AE1	147
	AE2	275
	AE3	166
	AE3	643
	AE4	351
	AE4	265
	AE4	784
	AE4	826
	AE4	983
	AE5	56
	AE5	283
	AE5	764
	AE5	819
	AE6	95
	AE6	293
	AE6	720
	AE6	879
	AE7	743
	AE7	1103
	AE8	948
	AE9	226
	AE9	635
	AE10	560
	AE10	595
	AE10	645
	AE10	726
	AE10	823
	AE10	921
	AE10	1031
	AE10	1070
	AE11	684
	AE11	866
	AE11	912
	AE11	957
	AE11	1011
	AE11	1061
	AE11	1097
	AE11	1254
	AE12	83
	AE12	461
	AE12	718
	AE12	788
	AE12	902
	AE12	944
	AE12	1099
	AE12	1123
	OAL	196
	OAL	239
	OAL	240
	AF	22
	KT2	67
	KT2	622
	CAM	319
	TH	333
	M11	84
	M11	85
	M11	265

Word	Ref	Num
FLYING	M11	370
	M12	439
	M12	560
	M12	743
	M15	269
	CI	626
FOAL	J6	804
	AE4	746
FOAM	AA	141
	L4	73
	HAP	44
	J6	802
	P3	240
	M1	309
	G3	175
	AE3	829
	AE4	193
	AE7	633
	AE7	737
	AE9	1017
	AE10	305
	AE11	459
	M8	197
	M8	203
	HIF	361
	M12	335
FOAMED	L3	244
	KT3	458
FOAMING	AT	78
	G3	314
	AE1	127
	AE2	677
	AE5	164
	AE6	80
	AE6	153
	AE6	1095
	AE6	1219
	AE7	384
	AE8	892
	AE10	246
FOAMS	J1	8
	AE9	563
FOAMY	DA	43
	G3	773
	G4	589
	AE3	179
	AE3	258
	AE5	1070
	AE8	898
	AE12	765
	AE12	945
	HIF	657
	STP	6
FOB	J1	136
FOBBED	EKK	6
FODDER	VP3	8
	G3	331
	AE7	675
FODDERED	G3	464
FODDERING	G3	606
FOE	LC	22
	LC	130
	AM	159
	AM	164
	AM	236
	AM	290
	AM	308
	AM	362
	AM	366
	AM	373
	AM	541
	AM	678
	AM	758
	AM	784
	AM	803
	AM	837
	AM	947
	AM	976
	AM	1156
	EEL	6
	SEL1	13
	HP	10
	DA	64
	EPF	5
	AA	404
	MD	68
	MD	73
	MF	113
	SAA	1093
	OE	45
	L4	48
	H29	43
	TA	480
	HAP	153
	HAP	296
	HAP	734

Word	Ref	Num
FOE	HAP	966
	HAP	1563
	HAP	1611
	HAP	2409
	PDS	8
	PDS	11
	SAA	427
	J10	139
	J10	214
	M1	240
	M1	680
	VCS	26
	HI	69
	HI	91
	MC	74
	G2	776
	G3	140
	G3	184
	G3	348
	G3	366
	G3	540
	G3	643
	G3	805
	G4	111
	G4	123
	AE1	62
	AE1	362
	AE1	672
	AE1	884
	AE2	82
	AE2	96
	AE2	138
	AE2	440
	AE2	608
	AE2	617
	AE2	835
	AE2	910
	AE4	126
	AE4	453
	AE4	614
	AE4	778
	AE4	851
	AE5	592
	AE5	608
	AE5	630
	AE5	636
	AE6	1216
	AE7	1001
	AE7	1011
	AE8	171
	AE8	298
	AE9	57
	AE9	241
	AE9	278
	AE9	311
	AE9	433
	AE9	478
	AE9	769
	AE9	805
	AE9	1096
	AE10	365
	AE10	369
	AE10	388
	AE10	526
	AE10	533
	AE10	643
	AE10	661
	AE10	771
	AE10	933
	AE10	1064
	AE10	1120
	AE10	1132
	AE10	1236
	AE11	8
	AE11	184
	AE11	295
	AE11	342
	AE11	468
	AE11	478
	AE11	569
	AE11	589
	AE11	639
	AE11	670
	AE11	1028
	AE11	1111
	AE11	1137
	AE11	1182
	AE11	1290
	AE12	152
	AE12	353
	AE12	381
	AE12	418
	AE12	463
	AE12	533
	AE12	558
	AE12	702

Word	Ref	Num
FOE	AE12	962
	AE12	1059
	AE12	1082
	AE12	1088
	AE12	1091
	AE12	1285
	AE12	1329
	OAL	297
	OAE2	56
	KT2	69
	KT2	98
	KT2	140
	KT2	172
	KT2	193
	KT2	271
	KT2	274
	KT2	294
	KT2	363
	KT3	33
	KT3	158
	KT3	344
	KT3	521
	KT3	645
	KT3	806
	M8	136
	M8	144
	M8	176
	B	173
	B	224
	B	659
	HIF	232
	HIF	260
	HIF	264
	HIF	369
	C	395
	C	586
	C	681
	C	689
	TH	28
	TH	178
	TH	316
	TH	411
	FL	100
	M12	92
	M12	109
	M12	166
	M12	193
	M12	373
	M12	675
	M12	704
	M12	722
	M12	743
	AU	115
	AU	123
	AU	182
	AU	333
	AU	340
	AU	414
	AU	594
	WB	450
	CI	275
	PTP	3
FOE'S	HAP	1643
FOES	AR	118
	LCA	31
	VHH	7
	VHH	12
	AM	119
	AM	144
	AM	250
	AM	302
	AM	323
	AM	464
	AM	737
	AM	919
	AM	1080
	E	32
	ML	28
	EAL	29
	DA	85
	DA	168
	EPF	22
	AA	280
	AA	323
	AA	357
	AA	449
	AA	466
	AA	611
	AA	664
	AA	743
	AA	814
	AA	845
	AA	1017
	PLB	14
	MD	275
	SAA	129

Word	Ref	No.
FOES	SAA	490
	SAA	506
	SAA	508
	SAA	580
	SAA	653
	SAA	707
	SAA	746
	SAA	830
	SAA	1057
	SAA	1089
	EDGA	17
	RL	190
	TA	127
	TA	323
	TA	460
	HH	11
	HAP	16
	HAP	290
	HAP	452
	HAP	508
	HAP	864
	HAP	885
	HAP	938
	HAP	1266
	HAP	1371
	HAP	1429
	HAP	1545
	HAP	1559
	HAP	1997
	HAP	2106
	HAP	2114
	HAP	2220
	HAP	2336
	HAP	2370
	HAP	2461
	HAP	2466
	SSC	31
	BR	288
	PP	29
	SKA1	2
	P1	258
	M1	31
	PLT	41
	G1	233
	G1	264
	G2	380
	G3	51
	G3	769
	G4	17
	G4	319
	G4	362
	G4	446
	AE1	524
	AE1	693
	AE1	792
	AE2	9
	AE2	59
	AE2	90
	AE2	338
	AE2	383
	AE2	426
	AE2	444
	AE2	475
	AE2	601
	AE2	693
	AE2	720
	AE2	856
	AE2	857
	AE2	873
	AE2	904
	AE2	996
	AE2	1029
	AE3	312
	AE3	511
	AE3	781
	AE3	791
	AE4	55
	AE4	808
	AE4	880
	AE4	963
	AE5	508
	AE5	939
	AE6	678
	AE6	1133
	AE6	1143
	AE7	404
	AE7	600
	AE7	652
	AE7	923
	AE8	29
	AE8	53
	AE8	156
	AE8	192
	AE8	744
	AE8	904
	AE9	46
FOES	AE9	77
	AE9	149
	AE9	211
	AE9	221
	AE9	301
	AE9	319
	AE9	421
	AE9	461
	AE9	536
	AE9	618
	AE9	738
	AE9	746
	AE9	749
	AE9	940
	AE9	1033
	AE9	1081
	AE10	64
	AE10	131
	AE10	178
	AE10	336
	AE10	346
	AE10	464
	AE10	511
	AE10	576
	AE10	709
	AE10	716
	AE10	760
	AE10	899
	AE10	960
	AE10	1026
	AE10	1304
	AE11	70
	AE11	111
	AE11	154
	AE11	202
	AE11	257
	AE11	484
	AE11	599
	AE11	621
	AE11	700
	AE11	800
	AE11	810
	AE11	817
	AE11	823
	AE11	844
	AE11	849
	AE11	880
	AE11	927
	AE11	1083
	AE11	1089
	AE11	1127
	AE11	1219
	AE11	1263
	AE11	1280
	AE11	1296
	AE11	1304
	AE12	396
	AE12	494
	AE12	521
	AE12	538
	AE12	601
	AE12	602
	AE12	697
	AE12	835
	AE12	858
	AE12	869
	AE12	901
	AE12	954
	AE12	988
	AE12	1129
	AE12	1171
	AE12	1182
	OAL	858
	AF	68
	MM	5
	KT1	84
	KT1	143
	KT3	611
	TJD	9
	TJD	131
	TJD	142
	M8	124
	B	598
	HIF	56
	HIF	480
	HIF	563
	FL	301
	FL	400
	M12	147
	M12	291
	M12	398
	AU	170
	AU	194
	AU	323
	AU	379
	AU	417
FOES	AU	529
	M15	630
	CI	282
	CI	290
	CI	410
	CI	515
	CI	533
FOES'	AE3	416
FOGGY	AE4	365
FOGS	MF	24
	MF	110
	J10	76
	M1	358
	M1	775
	M1	824
	G3	551
FOGUE	AR	203
FOIL	UDH	56
	JH	26
	EMQ	11
	TA	166
	G2	776
	AE10	206
	AE11	780
	KT3	1001
	GP	140
FOILED	SAA	491
	SAA	866
	L4	218
	MC	32
	AE7	429
	KT3	676
	KT3	741
FOILS	L4	218
FOIN	KT2	196
FOIST	HAP	1450
FOLD	SAA	698
	H2	69
	HAP	285
	HAP	302
	HAP	885
	J6	788
	M9	101
	VP1	21
	VP2	52
	VP3	124
	VP3	152
	VP4	52
	VP7	8
	VP7	50
	VP7	73
	G1	199
	G2	649
	G3	465
	G3	541
	G3	595
	G3	671
	G3	712
	G3	802
	AE2	287
	AE5	770
	AE8	575
	AE9	66
	AE9	457
	AE9	986
	AE10	1114
	M8	40
FOLDED	AM	222
	AM	824
	AT	31
	T18	89
	T27	126
	M13	122
	G4	506
	AE10	677
	KT3	31
FOLDING	G4	725
	AE11	1279
	FL	450
FOLD'S	G3	618
FOLDS	AM	1131
	H29	61
	P2	90
	M1	395
	M13	129
	VP1	44
	VP2	25
	G1	488
	G3	530
	AE2	412
	AE2	1063
	AE5	538
	AE7	496
	AE10	1019
	TJD	56
	M11	109

FOLIAGE	AE1	918
	AE1	995
FOLLIES	PLN	27
	PUO1	20
	PSF	17
	J10	44
	P5	22
	P5	81
	P5	166
	GK	158
FOLLOW	SIE	5
	AM	60
	AM	534
	PM	36
	ESF	21
	PAL	5
	CM	134
	HP	70
	HP	238
	DA	140
	AA	511
	MD	71
	AT	65
	L3	170
	HAP	365
	HAP	1657
	EDS	29
	EL	313
	J6	137
	J10	114
	P5	156
	M1	680
	VP2	94
	G1	275
	G3	282
	G4	113
	G4	408
	AE2	951
	AE3	119
	AE4	850
	AE5	764
	AE8	783
	AE9	24
	AE9	415
	AE10	362
	AE10	961
	AE11	23
	AE11	1025
	OAL	560
	OAL	591
	OAE2	77
	KT3	698
	B	416
	BP	144
	HIF	261
	HIF	299
	C	322
	TH	123
	TH	177
	FL	458
FOLLOWED	CM	38
	DA	88
	DA	123
	EPF	22
	AA	583
	EPC	27
	PPC	23
	RL	208
	EC	9
	ER	21
	HAP	74
	HAP	1490
	HAP	1516
	HAP	2018
	EDS	20
	J3	63
	M1	887
	M9	191
	M13	53
	M13	208
	G4	700
	AE2	52
	AE2	183
	AE2	577
	AE3	212
	AE3	839
	AE5	99
	AE5	733
	AE6	642
	AE7	892
	AE7	982
	AE9	382
	AE9	724
	AE9	753
	AE10	243
	AE10	268
FOLLOWED	AE10	751
	KT2	231
	KT3	357
	TJD	154
	HIF	236
	HIF	428
	TH	118
	TH	333
	M11	84
	WB	10
	GP	130
FOLLOWER'S	G3	174
FOLLOWERS	SAA	1097
	AE5	245
	AE10	1198
	AE12	507
	AE5	1039
FOLLOWING	AM	366
	PUO2	3
	SAA	972
	HAP	788
	HAP	927
	M1	140
	G1	573
	G3	451
	G3	669
	G4	1
	G4	649
	AE1	976
	AE3	864
	AE5	55
	AE5	237
	AE5	1088
	AE6	221
	AE7	574
	AE8	117
	AE12	456
	AE12	1086
	OAL	690
	KT3	540
	CI	270
	CI	288
	M11	169
FOLLOWS	SAA	443
	J3	393
	G1	552
	AE6	1115
	AE8	775
	AE8	912
	AE10	261
	AE11	998
	AE12	81
	AE12	626
	C	297
FOLLY	PLN	7
	ESF	19
	PNH	34
	PUO4	11
	AA	116
	AA	259
	MF	154
	SAA	33
	HAP	1310
	HAP	2403
	B	402
	C	562
	C	774
	CI	4
	CI	5
	CI	225
FOMENT	AA	284
	G3	685
	AE12	368
	AE12	1208
	KT3	727
FOMENTED	AA	926
FOMENTEST	B	444
FOMENTS	AE12	622
FOND	AR	159
	HP	190
	ECG1	16
	AA	425
	SAA	21
	L3	107
	L3	301
	HAP	2483
	J6	720
	J10	444
	P2	71
	P5	131
	P5	243
	M9	69
	M9	125
	AE9	484
	AE9	902
FOND	AE11	1145
	B	313
	B	329
	C	811
FONDLY	HAP	2400
	STS3	24
	B	189
	B	441
FONDNESS	PTL	5
	CAM	232
FONDS	AE1	962
FONT	GE	65
	BR	191
FOOD	AR	173
	SMA	78
	DC	30
	SCG3	14
	PCB	20
	CM	28
	PR	29
	PUF	17
	AA	121
	AA	626
	MD	235
	RL	420
	OE	24
	AT	34
	L1	18
	L3	196
	L4	269
	L5	12
	H2	95
	PAA	11
	HAP	135
	HAP	221
	HAP	390
	HAP	522
	HAP	2270
	HAP	2297
	HAP	2518
	HAP	2573
	BR	212
	BR	214
	J1	154
	J1	180
	J6	15
	J6	824
	J10	368
	M1	134
	M1	423
	M1	871
	M13	116
	VP8	5
	G1	238
	G1	410
	G1	525
	G1	530
	G1	561
	G2	295
	G2	277
	G2	609
	G2	641
	G3	196
	G3	212
	G3	322
	G3	335
	G3	703
	G3	743
	G3	747
	G3	790
	G4	386
	AE1	250
	AE1	661
	AE2	481
	AE3	816
	AE3	856
	AE4	373
	AE4	538
	AE5	123
	AE6	813
	AE7	683
	AE8	243
	AE8	424
	AE8	479
	AE8	856
	AE9	824
	AE10	782
	AE12	694
	OAL	841
	KT2	172
	KT3	347
	KT3	631
	KT3	908
	KT3	991
	TJD	88

Word	Ref	No.
FOOD	M8	345
	CAM	166
	C	142
	TH	214
	TH	270
	M12	220
	AU	73
	M15	102
	M15	174
	M15	203
	M15	529
	M15	695
	M15	709
	GP	136
	EWR	7
FOODFUL	G1	204
	G3	726
	AE6	805
FOOD'S	M15	144
FOOL	EWGR	26
	EWGR	42
	PLN	41
	EAZ	1
	ESF	7
	ESF	14
	ESF	34
	DA	30
	PCB	6
	EMK	15
	EAL	3
	AA	968
	EPC	27
	MD	186
	SAA	363
	SAA	463
	PK	33
	L3	54
	L3	137
	L3	150
	L3	177
	L4	135
	L4	179
	HH	6
	HAP	143
	HAP	1794
	J3	256
	J6	581
	J10	14
	J10	157
	J10	271
	P1	7
	P1	56
	P2	86
	P3	33
	P3	50
	P3	84
	P3	153
	P3	188
	P3	212
	P5	176
	P5	204
	ELT	10
	ELT	12
	GK	157
	EHC	39
	VP1	29
	VP3	21
	AE4	151
	AE4	540
	AE6	796
	AE8	923
	AE9	756
	AE9	983
	AE9	992
	AE10	111
	AE11	1055
	OAL	363
	OAL	652
	KT2	148
	KT3	326
	KT3	678
	CAM	53
	C	133
	C	203
	C	814
	AU	462
	AU	475
	WB	148
	CI	73
	CI	107
	CI	182
	CI	243
	CI	466
	PTP	21
	PTP	19
	SMP	16
FOOL-BANE	ETC	10
FOOLED	PAA	29
FOOLING	PLN	43
FOOLISH	SM1	1
	PSF	36
	AA	58
	AA	753
	L3	219
	L3	271
	HAP	1853
	HAP	2562
	MS	3
	J1	84
	P1	158
	OAL	807
	C	145
	PMK	39
FOOLISHLY	MD	246
FOOLS	EWGR	19
	PMM	1
	PEL	16
	PLN	6
	PLN	14
	PLN	23
	PLN	28
	PNH	25
	ESF	1
	ML	22
	EAL	6
	PTW	3
	PTW	12
	PTW	15
	ETC	5
	ETC	20
	PUO4	9
	AA	115
	AA	125
	AA	247
	AA	561
	MD	101
	MD	112
	MD	288
	MF	155
	SAA	409
	SAA	513
	PK	35
	EDG	20
	EDGA	35
	PD	6
	PD	16
	EC	16
	MO	6
	L2	12
	L3	97
	T27	44
	H29	20
	PAA	33
	HAP	2401
	PTS	43
	PSH	21
	PSH	24
	PSH	41
	PSH	42
	J1	19
	J3	73
	J3	116
	J3	128
	J10	205
	J10	561
	P1	10
	P1	208
	EHC	35
	G2	730
	G2	731
	AE6	588
	OAL	530
	MM	10
	KT2	371
	KT2	379
	C	764
	WB	140
	WB	143
	PTP	12
	SMP	67
	SMP	71
FOOL-TRAPS	PKA	27
FOOT	PM	25
	PAA	36
	HAP	1790
	J3	255
	J3	451
	J3	465
	J6	366
	P1	114
	P1	270
	M1	685
FOOT	M1	896
	G1	251
	G3	700
	AE3	7
	AE3	747
	AE4	520
	AE4	751
	AE5	167
	AE5	437
	AE5	676
	AE6	1217
	AE7	953
	AE7	1083
	AE9	504
	AE10	503
	AE10	509
	AE10	527
	AE10	637
	AE10	690
	AE10	825
	AE10	1037
	AE10	1061
	AE11	290
	AE11	781
	AE11	1045
	AE12	518
	AE12	533
	AE12	740
	AE12	842
	AE12	1082
	OAE1	5
	OAE2	18
	KT2	200
	KT3	515
	KT3	601
	KT3	624
	M8	47
	M8	210
	B	263
	BP	84
	C	442
	FL	340
	M12	177
	M12	356
	M12	503
	GP	64
FOOTBALL	KT3	611
FOOTED	FL	204
FOOTING	AM	68
	G2	33
	AE2	511
	WB	216
FOOTMAN'S	J1	142
FOOTSTEPS	HAP	215
	HAP	1849
	BR	73
	VP2	12
	VP4	37
	VP6	82
	AE6	284
	AE8	275
	AE12	629
	M8	89
	M11	412
FOOTSTOOL	HIF	562
FOOTSTOOLS	OAL	189
FOP	EMQ	4
	ETL	21
	ECG1	12
	PMQW	3
	PLN	9
	PLN	25
	PLN	30
	EAL	3
	EAL	12
	PUO4	11
	EPC	13
	PD	18
	PAA	7
	HH	9
	EKA	24
	P4	43
	EHC	34
	OAL	570
	PTP	15
FOP-CORNER	PM	3
	ENH	17
FOPLING	ESF	7
	ESF	15
	MF	153
FOPLINGS	PSH	20
FOPPISH	J10	51
FOPS	PMM	5
	PCG2	19
	PLN	17
	PNH	44

FOPS			FORBIDS			FORCE		
FOPS	ESF	13	FORBIDS	AE4	106	FORCE	AE1	94
	PAL	27		AE6	594		AE1	99
	PTW	6		CAM	45		AE1	401
	ETC	11	FORBORE	AA	37		AE1	411
	SAA	521	FORBORNE	OE	49		AE1	517
	PDS	35		AE10	1151		AE1	573
	PKA	31		KT1	29		AE1	606
	EKA	2	FORCE	UDH	89		AE1	694
	ESH	16		LC	108		AE1	942
	P1	188		AM	362		AE1	1055
	PTP	7		AM	369		AE1	745
	PTP	15		AM	385		AE1	792
FORAGE	PKK	21		AM	537		AE2	62
	SAA	920		AM	879		AE2	135
	G4	233		EMQW	7		AE2	201
	G4	283		ENH	20		AE2	275
	G4	365		E	8		AE2	441
	AE4	585		E	10		AE2	527
	AE8	12		EOE	4		AE2	563
	AU	343		HP	27		AE2	651
FORBADE	G3	740		HP	182		AE2	673
	TH	134		PUF	29		AE2	852
	M12	394		AA	122		AE3	316
	M15	34		AA	382		AE3	369
FORBEAR	EK	35		AA	471		AE3	675
	TA	71		AA	842		AE3	694
	AK	168		AA	950		AE3	752
	EKA	8		AA	1021		AE4	186
	LS	13		MD	73		AE4	353
	J1	43		MD	84		AE4	785
	J3	15		MD	120		AE5	30
	J3	229		MD	221		AE5	283
	P1	27		MD	314		AE5	503
	P5	140		SAA	133		AE5	532
	P6	35		SAA	779		AE5	591
	SAA	478		SAA	933		AE5	608
	SAA	606		SAA	1096		AE5	621
	AE6	732		PK	36		AE5	1059
	AE9	135		RL	338		AE6	123
	AE9	852		RL	255		AE6	138
	AE10	630		RL	154		AE6	391
	AE10	1262		AT	32		AE6	405
	AE12	1163		MO	18		AE6	537
	AE12	1264		L4	28		AE6	539
	OAL	307		L4	76		AE6	746
	OAL	620		T23	7		AE6	787
	OAE2	12		T23	89		AE6	799
	KT1	24		T27	2		AE6	1218
	KT3	133		H29	59		AE7	43
	HIF	317		FS1	6		AE7	322
	C	396		TA	104		AE7	331
	C	408		TA	138		AE7	487
	M12	599		HAP	452		AE7	639
	GP	137		HAP	610		AE7	646
	ERL	4		HAP	692		AE7	652
FORBEARANCE	SAA	729		HAP	739		AE7	808
FORBEARS	G1	106		HAP	754		AE8	12
	AE4	720		HAP	967		AE8	124
FORBID	AE1	741		HAP	1016		AE8	193
	DA	68		HAP	1113		AE8	222
	OE	53		HAP	1416		AE8	266
	HAP	1206		HAP	2164		AE8	272
	HAP	1963		EMI	5		AE8	385
	M1	520		BR	300		AE8	582
	AE4	155		BR	332		AE8	645
	AE10	615		BR	349		AE8	711
	TJD	97		BR	351		AE8	858
	M11	117		J6	282		AE9	77
	M11	230		J6	499		AE9	183
FORBIDDEN	AR	188		J6	794		AE9	540
	H3	37		P2	65		AE9	578
	HAP	2364		M1	32		AE9	739
	PDS	42		M1	165		AE9	772
	P6	691		M1	416		AE9	815
	AE2	247		M1	772		AE9	901
	AE3	615		M1	818		AE9	918
	AE6	505		M1	1093		AE9	957
	AE6	526		M13	23		AE9	1005
	AE6	759		MC	4		AE9	1010
	AE7	780		MC	23		AE9	1031
	AE8	301		VP8	152		AE9	1037
	AE10	626		G1	60		AE9	1087
	AE11	746		G1	205		AE10	18
	AE11	880		G1	249		AE10	119
	TJD	76		G1	435		AE10	347
	BP	151		G1	554		AE10	369
	CAM	65		G1	693		AE10	412
	C	494		G3	169		AE10	454
FORBIDS	EL	114		G3	191		AE10	472
	SAA	722		G3	222		AE10	497
	HAP	67		G3	411		AE10	505
	HAP	304		G3	426		AE10	513
	HAP	2122		G4	241		AE10	647
	P5	209		G4	584		AE10	667
	G1	184		AE1	58		AE10	689
	AE3	488		AE1	72		AE10	832

Headword	Code	No.
FORCE	AE10	859
	AE10	1065
	AE10	1099
	AE10	1102
	AE10	1116
	AE10	1120
	AE10	1275
	AE11	189
	AE11	436
	AE11	455
	AE11	480
	AE11	545
	AE11	579
	AE11	705
	AE11	780
	AE11	842
	AE11	897
	AE11	902
	AE11	919
	AE11	983
	AE12	52
	AE12	86
	AE12	147
	AE12	151
	AE12	214
	AE12	279
	AE12	304
	AE12	381
	AE12	385
	AE12	547
	AE12	766
	AE12	795
	AE12	837
	AE12	927
	AE12	986
	AE12	1018
	AE12	1106
	AE12	1120
	AE12	1223
	AE12	1314
	AE12	1320
	OAL	26
	OAL	146
	OAL	230
	OAL	674
	OAL	750
	OAL	760
	OAL	802
	OAE2	10
	DO	109
	KT1	8
	KT1	414
	KT2	146
	KT2	213
	KT2	246
	KT2	288
	KT2	414
	KT2	610
	KT3	305
	KT3	334
	KT3	481
	KT3	607
	KT3	620
	KT3	646
	KT3	650
	KT3	742
	TJD	151
	TJD	187
	M8	184
	M8	193
	M8	279
	B	61
	B	518
	HIF	73
	HIF	123
	HIF	188
	HIF	248
	HIF	293
	HIF	304
	HIF	378
	HIF	396
	HIF	400
	HIF	495
	HIF	506
	HIF	657
	HIF	791
	C	590
	M11	119
	M11	142
	M11	161
	FL	302
	M12	105
	M12	159
	M12	179
	M12	273
	M12	289
FORCE	M12	313
	M12	402
	M12	481
	M12	497
	M12	665
	M12	672
	AU	146
	AU	447
	AU	463
	AU	529
	AU	557
	AU	592
	AU	607
	WB	56
	WB	306
	M15	241
	M15	357
	M15	397
	CI	262
	CI	263
	CI	285
	CI	303
	CI	310
	CI	378
	CI	452
	CI	457
	CI	476
	CI	521
	STP	20
	EMKG	2
FORCED	AR	50
	AR	38
	AR	75
	LC	12
	AM	174
	AM	413
	AM	428
	AM	756
	AM	982
	PT	29
	ECG1	36
	PFD	6
	EAZ	6
	ML	26
	CM	37
	HP	21
	PUO5	30
	AA	897
	AA	1000
	MD	216
	SAA	258
	SAA	835
	RL	333
	L3	210
	T27	63
	H3	50
	TA	152
	TA	268
	HH	17
	HAP	7
	HAP	1013
	HAP	1372
	HAP	1975
	HAP	2445
	J1	202
	J6	520
	J10	505
	M1	608
	M1	841
	M1	1062
	M13	193
	GK	157
	VP1	4
	G3	681
	AE1	1
	AE2	1021
	AE3	259
	AE3	278
	AE3	418
	AE4	225
	AE4	517
	AE5	1038
	AE6	429
	AE6	532
	AE6	623
	AE6	677
	AE7	169
	AE7	279
	AE7	292
	AE7	409
	AE7	859
	AE7	921
	AE8	671
	AE9	561
	AE9	867
	AE10	39
FORCED	AE10	419
	AE10	538
	AE10	752
	AE10	945
	AE10	1158
	AE11	602
	AE11	611
	AE11	614
	AE11	715
	AE11	815
	AE12	398
	AE12	566
	AE12	688
	AE12	717
	AE12	1273
	OAL	763
	OAL	766
	OAL	814
	OAE2	59
	DO	113
	DO	123
	KT1	387
	KT2	101
	KT2	588
	M8	83
	B	198
	B	306
	B	415
	B	474
	B	659
	HIF	479
	HIF	485
	HIF	691
	C	221
	C	294
	C	528
	C	539
	C	791
	TH	368
	M12	704
	AU	51
	AU	304
	AU	426
	AU	435
	AU	511
	GP	31
	CI	340
	CI	388
FORCEFUL	G3	374
	AE2	65
	AE5	666
	KT2	11
FORCES	AM	986
	AA	375
	G2	598
	AE2	346
	AE4	572
	AE5	595
	AE9	14
	AE9	676
	AE10	231
	AE11	683
	AE12	189
FORCING	AE6	487
	AE10	530
FORD	M1	500
	VP7	14
	AE9	324
	AE10	407
	OAL	499
	M11	373
FORDS	AE7	1007
FOREARMS	MD	68
	AE6	1233
FOREBODE	C	201
FOREBODES	HI	114
	AE3	470
FOREBODING	L5	7
	AE3	938
	AE8	655
	AE10	1202
FOREBORE	AE4	521
FORECAST	G1	352
	TH	262
FOREDOOMED	MD	286
	AE1	286
	AE3	330
	AE6	222
	AE12	1151
	KT3	636
FOREFATHER	BR	139
FOREFATHER'S	AE12	943
FOREFATHERS	PTC	39
	HAP	603
	HAP	2309
	J1	144

Word	Ref	No.
FOREFATHERS	J 10	124
FOREFATHERS'	SAA	701
FOREFEND	C	183
FOREFINGER	OAE2	26
FOREGO	AA	58
	RL	429
	VP4	46
	VP10	70
	VP10	94
	AE11	1042
	AE11	1265
	AE12	399
	C	558
	M15	384
FOREGOING	L4	122
FOREHEAD	J10	318
	J16	15
	P2	64
	M9	33
	M13	163
	D	35
	AT	31
	T23	17
	HAP	565
	J6	804
	G3	97
	G4	526
	AE3	834
	AE4	256
	AE4	746
	AE5	638
	AE10	203
	AE10	295
	AE10	485
	AE11	53
	OAL	272
	KT3	53
	C	121
	CI	152
	SMP	30
FOREHEADS	L3	100
	T27	128
	H29	28
	VP6	76
	AE3	892
	AE12	261
	FL	170
	FL	274
	FL	277
	DA	124
	HS	109
	AR	118
	AM	1080
	PFD	25
FOREIGN	PTW	23
	PTC	11
	HP	205
	AA	23
	AA	177
	AA	282
	AA	659
	AA	709
	AA	890
	MD	319
	MF	158
	SAA	37
	SAA	227
	EC	24
	L4	102
	H2	75
	FS1	6
	TA	321
	AK	69
	HAP	404
	HAP	1879
	HAP	2322
	BR	332
	EJG	2
	J1	205
	J3	112
	J6	33
	J6	412
	J10	260
	P6	111
	HI	127
	VP4	47
	G1	180
	G2	42
	G2	191
	G2	218
	G2	598
	G2	654
	G2	722
	G3	17
	G3	349
	AE1	646
FOREIGN	AE1	792
	AE3	6
	AE3	169
	AE3	710
	AE4	391
	AE4	450
	AE4	502
	AE4	503
	AE5	1039
	AE6	142
	AE6	846
	AE6	1133
	AE7	103
	AE7	142
	AE7	168
	AE7	225
	AE7	349
	AE7	371
	AE7	446
	AE7	517
	AE7	518
	AE7	597
	AE7	799
	AE8	661
	AE8	675
	AE9	645
	AE10	103
	AE10	115
	AE10	231
	AE10	1240
	AE11	356
	AE11	1254
	AE12	47
	AE12	359
	AE12	396
	AE12	803
	OAL	203
	OAE1	18
	MG	22
	MM	50
	DO	59
	KT1	6
	KT3	969
	TJD	138
	TJD	165
	M8	226
	CAM	76
	FL	86
	AU	44
	WB	12
	M15	652
	CI	249
	CI	617
	PWR	2
FOREIGNER	EAZ	24
	AE7	514
	OAL	733
FOREIGNERS	DA	16
	J3	123
	AE12	1213
FOREKNEW	HIF	103
	M11	413
	M12	25
FORE-KNOW	BR	71
FOREKNOW	C	526
FOREKNOWING	C	527
FOREKNOWN	C	531
FORELAID	AE9	537
FORELAY	AE11	781
FORELAYS	KT1	493
FOREMAN	EKA	25
FOREMEN	PPC	27
FOREMOST	AM	81
	AM	250
	AM	741
	ENH	9
	PAZ	18
	AK	141
	AK	189
	HAP	2355
	EL	283
	HI	111
	AE2	655
	AE5	253
	AE5	405
	AE8	744
	AE11	411
	AE11	588
	AE11	985
	KT2	273
	M8	49
	HIF	197
	HIF	337
	TH	7
	M11	162
	FL	268
FOREMOST	FL	537
	FL	538
	M12	805
FORESAW	AM	713
	HAP	886
	AE8	709
	TJD	40
	C	513
	C	539
FORESEE	AM	795
	AM	1075
	G1	573
	AA	757
	EL	187
	HI	48
	HI	57
	HI	122
	MC	71
	G4	348
	C	389
	C	398
FORESEEING	HAP	1943
	M1	833
	AE9	47
	M12	608
FORESEEN	TA	5
	TA	84
	AE4	446
	AE6	1087
	HIF	124
	HIF	462
	M12	809
FORESEES	G1	516
	G1	536
	AE12	669
	C	509
	AU	554
FORESEIZE	SAA	976
FORESHEW	AR	322
	AE1	621
	AE7	351
FORESHEWS	EUF	15
	KT3	280
FORESHOW	J3	79
	MD	287
	AE2	956
	C	205
FORESHOWED	AE8	712
	M12	40
FORESHOWN	AE5	923
FORESHOWS	AE3	482
	AE8	906
FORESIGHT	AM	1076
	TA	85
	G4	565
	KT2	221
	C	510
FORESLOW	M12	524
FORESLOWED	D	15
	BR	169
FOREST	L1	24
	HAP	2
	HAP	555
	M1	769
	VP6	79
	VP6	81
	G1	212
	G1	222
	G1	618
	G2	288
	G3	230
	G3	312
	G3	342
	G4	74
	G4	682
	AE1	445
	AE2	411
	AE3	337
	AE6	265
	AE6	277
	AE6	638
	AE7	153
	AE8	451
	AE8	796
	AE9	518
	AE9	524
	AE10	567
	AE10	570
	AE10	1001
	AE11	1305
	AE12	1023
	KT2	23
	KT2	207
	KT2	530
	KT3	970
	M8	84

FORKY	G1	656
	G2	492
	G3	666
	AE2	648
	AE4	232
	AE4	306
	AE5	911
	AE6	791
	AE8	518
	AE8	694
	AE8	913
	AE10	794
	AE11	1112
	M11	124
	CI	334
FORLORN	ENH	10
	AR	55
	P6	64
	HI	127
	AE5	357
	KT1	410
	HIF	525
	AU	485
FORM	AM	972
	CM	74
	AA	531
	D	15
	SAA	214
	SAA	219
	RL	19
	L1	50
	L4	57
	T23	5
	H3	22
	FS3	13
	TA	109
	TA	391
	AK	116
	GE	59
	HAP	36
	HAP	263
	HAP	446
	HAP	628
	HAP	1455
	HAP	2256
	OD	53
	ODA	22
	EL	55
	J6	343
	J10	77
	J10	458
	J10	481
	J10	522
	M1	21
	M1	111
	M1	541
	M1	564
	M1	740
	M1	952
	M9	72
	VP4	32
	G2	423
	G4	104
	G4	448
	G4	606
	G4	639
	AE1	39
	AE1	958
	AE1	975
	AE3	633
	AE5	722
	AE5	756
	AE5	804
	AE5	1096
	AE6	578
	AE6	671
	AE6	1077
	AE6	1188
	AE7	263
	AE7	582
	AE7	625
	AE8	520
	AE8	811
	AE9	672
	AE9	888
	AE11	501
	AE12	340
	AE12	1013
	AE12	1135
	AE12	1251
	OAL	369
	OAL	601
	AF	28
	KT2	442
	KT2	526
	KT2	612

FORM	KT3	593
	M10	86
	CAM	252
	CAM	334
	CAM	376
	M11	229
	M11	260
	M11	262
	M11	313
	M11	352
	M12	306
	M12	349
	M12	524
	M12	525
	M12	734
	M15	250
	M15	251
	M15	384
	M15	467
	M15	562
	CI	191
FORMA	HAP	2055
FORMAL	MD	44
	MF	169
	J10	56
	OAL	90
	CI	316
FORMAL'S	MF	168
FORMED	AA	67
	AA	692
	AA	741
	AA	905
	MD	24
	MF	75
	SAA	3
	SAA	889
	RL	326
	ER	74
	T18	71
	TA	433
	TA	463
	AK	30
	HAP	2440
	SKA3	7
	J1	213
	J10	95
	P4	31
	P5	54
	M1	41
	M1	100
	M1	568
	M1	985
	VP9	83
	G3	305
	AE1	235
	AE1	827
	AE4	440
	AE5	731
	AE8	840
	AE9	16
	AE10	840
	AE11	792
	AE12	842
	MFL	8
	KT1	263
	KT2	311
	KT3	1067
	TJD	123
	B	506
	BP	56
	M12	548
	WB	413
	M15	44
	M15	328
	M15	591
	CI	33
	CI	44
	CI	571
FORMER	HS	41
	AR	275
	LC	10
	LC	146
	PRL	5
	AM	320
	AM	482
	PNH	52
	PUO3	14
	AA	123
	SAA	313
	PD	25
	L3	20
	L3	175
	L3	306
	H2	101
	HAP	110
	HAP	623

FORMER	HAP	628
	HAP	744
	HAP	1380
	HAP	1993
	HAP	2315
	HAP	2400
	HAP	2575
	EMI	6
	BR	89
	BR	244
	J6	398
	J6	840
	M1	551
	M1	1027
	M1	1039
	HI	137
	HI	165
	VP1	63
	G2	315
	G3	68
	G3	153
	G3	160
	G4	790
	AE1	329
	AE1	1008
	AE2	146
	AE2	1022
	AE3	389
	AE4	31
	AE4	804
	AE5	173
	AE6	705
	AE6	1019
	AE6	1195
	AE8	583
	AE8	612
	AE9	464
	AE9	532
	AE10	471
	AE10	813
	AE10	932
	AE11	345
	AE11	992
	OAL	593
	AF	81
	AF	164
	AF	174
	MFL	26
	DO	25
	KT2	101
	KT3	467
	KT3	812
	KT3	1126
	M8	300
	B	4
	B	36
	B	130
	B	733
	M10	86
	C	337
	C	359
	TH	293
	TH	343
	M11	90
	FL	466
	M12	594
	M12	715
	M12	820
	M15	236
	M15	274
	M15	350
	M15	600
	CI	246
	CI	248
	CI	428
	PTP	22
	ESK	20
FORMERLY	PMQW	10
	M15	391
	M15	393
FORMIDABLE	MD	272
	J1	5
	J6	646
	AE6	778
	AE8	22
	AE10	283
	AU	88
FORMIDABLY	TA	512
FORMING	AA	564
	TA	440
	AK	124
	EL	221
	P3	41
	AE6	50
	AE8	532
	AE8	582

Word	Ref	No.
FORMING	CI	61
FORMS	E	17
	DA	58
	SAA	1103
	GE	36
	HAP	599
	HAP	2322
	HAP	2421
	SKA6	19
	J6	513
	M1	1
	M1	93
	M1	558
	VP6	55
	VP10	36
	G2	120
	G4	329
	G4	587
	G4	595
	AE1	134
	AE1	230
	AE2	843
	AE5	766
	AE6	389
	AE6	398
	AE6	409
	AE6	439
	AE6	837
	AE7	471
	AE7	457
	AE9	117
	AE10	272
	AE10	333
	AE12	1290
	OAL	872
	KT2	12
	KT3	485
	KT3	1030
	KT3	1033
	KT3	1040
	KT3	1051
	BP	8
	C	331
	M11	298
	FL	157
	FL	478
	WB	274
	M15	230
	M15	297
	M15	398
	M15	402
	M15	675
FORNICATION	ETP	30
FORSAKE	AM	935
	AM	1152
	AA	755
	SAA	878
	SAA	979
	PDG	38
	OE	61
	T27	94
	H29	16
	HAP	71
	HAP	834
	HAP	868
	HAP	2045
	SKA5	4
	J6	765
	J10	324
	M1	460
	M13	194
	HI	109
	VP9	50
	G1	308
	G1	495
	G1	525
	G2	291
	G3	743
	G4	218
	AE2	811
	AE3	252
	AE3	681
	AE4	348
	AE4	433
	AE4	778
	AE6	429
	AE6	555
	AE7	551
	AE9	141
	AE10	833
	AE10	918
	AE12	77
	AE12	308
	AE12	656
	AE12	1315
	OAL	841
FORSAKE	KT2	101
	HIF	565
	C	504
	TH	71
	M11	20
	M11	32
	M11	428
	AU	190
	WB	32
	M15	674
	CI	82
	CI	330
	CI	457
FORSAKEN	AM	1070
	SLN	21
	DA	86
	MD	79
	D	3
	VP1	18
	VP7	94
	VP10	76
	G1	562
	AE2	768
	AE3	809
	AE4	848
	AE9	390
	AE10	308
	AE12	965
	OAL	595
	OAL	603
	DO	95
	KT3	1065
	B	199
	M11	86
	AU	106
	AU	366
FORSAKES	AA	683
	SAA	598
	PLT	5
	G1	522
	G3	335
	G3	385
	G3	776
	AE3	398
	AE5	276
	AE9	633
	AE10	106
	AE11	1204
	OAL	350
	CAM	283
	M11	352
	M15	426
FORSAKING	VP1	83
	AE3	722
	AE9	1060
	KT3	555
FORSEE	EMM	13
FORSEES	KT2	211
FORSHEWED	AT	68
FORSOOK	JH	11
	LC	20
	PR	19
	SAA	365
	TA	188
	M1	164
	M1	308
	M9	192
	VP5	52
	G1	645
	AE1	421
	AE3	77
	AE3	424
	AE3	744
	AE5	1123
	AE6	622
	AE6	591
	AE8	92
	AE9	285
	AE10	935
	AE10	1162
	AE11	533
	OAL	618
	KT2	225
	KT3	257
	CAM	244
	TH	278
	AU	93
	AU	106
	M15	10
	M15	32
	GP	126
	EMKG	38
FORSOOTH	EDG	16
FORSWEAR	SAA	296
	EWR	29
FORSWEARING	OAE2	88
FORSWORE	MD	152
	MF	57
FORSWORN	DA	145
	AT	15
	J3	244
	AE4	522
	AE8	714
	OAL	717
	KT1	313
	KT2	129
FORT	AE2	53
	AE3	185
	M11	140
	CI	553
FORTHRIGHT	AE12	1076
	KT2	237
FORTIFIED	PMQ	10
	L2	9
	B	377
FORTIFIES	HAP	1691
FORTIFY	G4	262
	AE9	391
	KT2	189
	AU	246
FORTITUDE	HI	166
	WB	479
FORTRESS	TA	167
FORTS	AM	226
	G2	215
FORTUNATE	J10	402
	SKA1	15
	VP1	64
	VP5	77
	KT1	96
	AU	494
FORTUNATELY	AA	51
FORTUNE	HS	22
	HS	29
	HS	53
	HS	91
	AR	68
	AR	95
	RH	44
	RH	106
	LC	129
	LC	95
	PWG	12
	PIE	23
	VHH	38
	AM	75
	AM	298
	AM	413
	AM	530
	EMM	15
	SEL1	5
	PUO1	27
	CM	123
	CM	57
	DA	120
	DA	172
	ETG	2
	AA	256
	AA	263
	AA	843
	AA	849
	MD	46
	SAA	859
	SAA	988
	EDG	20
	RL	59
	AT	61
	L4	98
	H29	73
	HAP	1430
	HAP	1535
	HAP	1713
	HAP	2135
	HAP	2209
	HAP	2453
	BR	67
	BR	142
	BR	358
	EDS	36
	PMS	12
	EL	27
	J3	72
	J6	480
	J6	786
	J10	82
	J10	114
	J10	190
	J10	536
	J10	560
	P6	92
	P6	132
	P6	147

Word	Code	No.
FORTUNE	P6	163
	M1	607
	MC	71
	VP1	13
	VP3	137
	VP7	6
	VP9	13
	G2	379
	G2	385
	G2	701
	G4	132
	G4	304
	AE1	301
	AE1	329
	AE1	522
	AE1	621
	AE1	636
	AE1	764
	AE1	794
	AE1	858
	AE2	28
	AE2	112
	AE2	224
	AE2	426
	AE2	497
	AE2	518
	AE2	522
	AE2	767
	AE2	893
	AE2	895
	AE2	1066
	AE3	140
	AE3	212
	AE3	638
	AE3	799
	AE3	869
	AE4	153
	AE4	239
	AE4	790
	AE4	942
	AE5	301
	AE5	455
	AE5	466
	AE5	467
	AE5	784
	AE5	820
	AE5	930
	AE6	144
	AE6	712
	AE6	1234
	AE7	730
	AE7	751
	AE8	24
	AE8	623
	AE8	676
	AE8	977
	AE8	906
	AE9	280
	AE9	343
	AE9	373
	AE10	4
	AE10	165
	AE10	169
	AE10	226
	AE10	387
	AE10	398
	AE10	501
	AE10	647
	AE10	699
	AE10	859
	AE10	1300
	AE11	59
	AE11	241
	AE11	440
	AE11	637
	AE11	657
	AE11	1039
	AE11	1216
	AE12	226
	AE12	240
	AE12	304
	AE12	730
	AE12	867
	AE12	913
	AE12	982
	AE12	1041
	AE12	1350
	OAL	188
	OAE2	78
	OAE2	87
	MG	9
	KT1	12
	KT1	75
	KT1	348
	KT1	400
	KT1	408
FORTUNE	KT1	421
	KT1	483
	KT1	517
	KT2	36
	KT2	64
	KT3	1
	KT3	301
	KT3	389
	KT3	579
	KT3	655
	KT3	666
	KT3	698
	KT3	736
	KT3	792
	KT3	1093
	KT3	1124
	B	60
	B	374
	B	492
	B	521
	B	560
	CAM	181
	C	753
	C	761
	TH	6
	TH	46
	TH	239
	FL	26
	FL	550
	M12	270
	M12	480
	M12	724
	AU	512
	WB	210
	M15	253
	M15	649
	CI	48
	CI	392
	CI	425
	CI	436
	CI	440
	CI	518
FORTUNE'S	AR	103
	RH	25
	AM	193
	AM	797
	AM	852
	SCD2	21
	AA	199
	SAA	1111
	L2	43
	H9	22
	H29	51
	H29	97
	HAP	445
	J3	61
	J10	118
	J10	434
	P1	259
	M9	63
	M9	74
	AE2	101
	AE2	102
	AE5	456
	AE8	442
	OAL	687
	B	7
FORTUNES	AU	432
	PUO2	16
	PAZ	26
	SAA	311
	J6	704
	J6	763
	VP1	28
	AE1	868
	AE3	656
	AE4	398
	AE4	462
	AE5	966
	AE9	392
	AE10	272
	AE11	561
	FL	295
	CI	514
FORTY	ECG1	19
	PTW	28
	AA	629
	PLB	42
	PLB	54
	BR	68
FORTY-EIGHT	PLG	17
FORTY-ONE	PLG	16
FORULI	AE7	989
FORWARD	AR	145
	AM	920
	CM	72
FORWARD	ETG	8
	SAA	959
	BR	7
	P4	1
	GK	40
	AE6	453
	AE6	643
	AE6	1032
	AE9	672
	AE9	892
	AE10	350
	AE10	522
	AE10	1285
	AE11	690
	AE11	899
	AE11	1188
	AE12	416
	KT3	703
	M8	167
	CAM	291
	C	334
	M12	328
	CI	388
	CI	594
FORWARDS	J3	496
	CI	340
FOSTER	VP4	59
	AE7	708
	AE8	838
	AE12	1127
FOSTERED	AE7	940
FOSTERING	G1	9
FOSTERS	G2	443
FOUGHT	HS	47
	HS	53
	HS	122
	VHH	12
	VHH	29
	VHH	37
	AM	161
	AM	314
	AM	354
	AM	424
	AM	696
	AM	703
	EWGR	17
	EMW	4
	MD	127
	HAP	626
	MC	3
	AE5	773
	AE5	1058
	AE6	165
	AE7	57
	AE7	250
	AE7	1098
	AE9	938
	AE9	1046
	AE10	1299
	AE11	37
	AE11	650
	AE11	956
	OAL	217
	OAL	795
	AF	67
	KT1	147
	KT2	208
	KT2	235
	KT3	652
	KT3	719
	KT3	899
	TJD	158
	M8	47
	FL	479
	M12	103
	AU	143
	AU	398
	AU	424
	AU	433
	CI	292
FOUL	UDH	48
	SAA	121
	SAA	464
	H29	69
	HAP	1768
	J1	71
	J6	188
	J10	103
	J10	182
	J10	455
	P5	217
	M13	159
	G2	515
	G3	712
	AE2	747
	AE3	277

FOUL	AE3	283
	AE3	536
	AE4	530
	AE6	417
	AE6	605
	AE6	831
	AE8	260
	AE9	851
	AE10	1217
	AE11	130
	AE11	416
	AE11	1068
	OAL	82
	OAL	580
	KT2	573
	KT3	1106
	M12	333
	AU	322
	AU	477
	WB	333
	WB	337
	GP	85
	ETP	30
FOULER	M13	157
	M11	129
	WB	224
FOULNESS	J10	316
	AE7	582
FOUND	AR	54
	RH	55
	SMA	2
	SMA	55
	LC	73
	DC	10
	DC	47
	LCA	41
	AM	6
	AM	101
	AM	188
	AM	467
	AM	548
	EWGR	23
	PMM	14
	SM2	4
	EOE	2
	EOE	11
	PTC	8
	PTC	15
	CM	26
	CM	33
	CM	107
	HP	46
	AA	53
	AA	78
	AA	373
	AA	451
	AA	526
	AA	561
	AA	843
	AA	1024
	PPC	18
	MD	46
	MD	75
	MF	3
	SAA	155
	SAA	292
	SAA	728
	SAA	896
	SAA	1107
	PDG	35
	RL	14
	RL	27
	RL	34
	RL	43
	RL	74
	RL	104
	RL	253
	RL	281
	RL	366
	RL	390
	RL	409
	L3	169
	L3	307
	L4	263
	T27	40
	H9	37
	TA	281
	TA	445
	HAP	313
	HAP	432
	HAP	745
	HAP	1008
	HAP	1470
	HAP	1508
	HAP	1610
	HAP	1623

FOUND	HAP	1624
	HAP	1649
	HAP	1781
	HAP	1905
	HAP	1916
	HAP	2014
	HAP	2088
	HAP	2235
	HAP	2363
	BR	73
	PDS	43
	PMS	31
	EL	102
	EL	173
	EL	207
	EL	321
	EL	329
	ODA	5
	SSH	16
	J3	345
	J3	467
	J6	81
	J6	194
	J6	399
	J6	413
	J6	446
	J6	461
	J6	633
	J10	12
	J10	81
	J10	201
	J10	278
	J10	292
	J10	314
	P1	93
	P1	231
	P2	110
	P3	36
	P5	79
	P5	104
	M1	42
	M1	210
	M1	278
	M1	391
	M1	617
	M1	741
	M1	748
	M1	823
	M1	904
	M1	903
	M9	114
	M13	138
	M13	148
	R	1
	HI	3
	MC	17
	GK	33
	GK	97
	VP2	52
	VP3	107
	VP6	20
	VP6	22
	G1	76
	G1	122
	G1	192
	G1	208
	G1	211
	G1	314
	G1	338
	G2	29
	G2	49
	G2	253
	G2	480
	G2	483
	G2	574
	G2	586
	G3	692
	G3	701
	G3	810
	G3	831
	G4	59
	G4	192
	G4	206
	G4	355
	G4	392
	G4	398
	G4	416
	G4	744
	AE1	619
	AE1	736
	AE1	814
	AE2	507
	AE2	517
	AE2	755
	AE2	770
	AE2	779

FOUND	AE3	185
	AE3	240
	AE3	264
	AE3	665
	AE3	711
	AE3	879
	AE3	910
	AE4	322
	AE4	382
	AE4	698
	AE4	743
	AE4	795
	AE4	800
	AE4	991
	AE5	100
	AE5	656
	AE5	1129
	AE6	42
	AE6	47
	AE6	95
	AE6	241
	AE6	263
	AE6	284
	AE6	602
	AE6	562
	AE6	666
	AE6	683
	AE6	736
	AE6	788
	AE6	881
	AE6	1051
	AE7	63
	AE7	93
	AE7	204
	AE7	295
	AE7	567
	AE7	815
	AE7	921
	AE7	940
	AE8	44
	AE8	111
	AE8	285
	AE8	343
	AE8	561
	AE9	5
	AE9	423
	AE9	467
	AE9	605
	AE9	738
	AE9	782
	AE9	947
	AE9	1034
	AE10	42
	AE10	801
	AE10	917
	AE10	937
	AE10	1058
	AE11	247
	AE11	610
	AE11	1091
	AE12	339
	AE12	412
	AE12	447
	AE12	485
	AE12	573
	AE12	629
	AE12	734
	AE12	1084
	AE12	1221
	AE12	1323
	OAL	63
	OAL	262
	OAL	300
	OAL	574
	OAL	607
	OAL	793
	MFL	31
	DO	114
	KT1	142
	KT1	258
	KT1	272
	KT1	373
	KT2	129
	KT2	264
	KT2	276
	KT2	535
	KT3	264
	KT3	382
	KT3	415
	KT3	567
	KT3	597
	KT3	896
	TJD	62
	TJD	97
	TJD	101
	TJD	126

FOUND
M8 139
B 47
B 88
B 112
B 129
B 146
B 204
B 307
B 435
B 535
B 644
B 663
BP 29
BP 165
M10 93
CAM 117
CAM 248
CAM 297
HIF 2
HIF 155
HIF 334
HIF 675
C 5
C 218
C 223
C 258
C 268
C 279
C 436
C 441
C 466
TH 19
TH 35
TH 130
M11 15
M11 412
FL 28
FL 93
FL 127
FL 144
FL 322
FL 463
FL 492
M12 10
M12 105
M12 170
M12 181
M12 194
M12 353
M12 373
M12 413
M12 724
M12 792
AU 90
AU 108
AU 111
AU 267
AU 605
WB 178
WB 290
WB 534
M15 69
M15 406
M15 447
CI 69
CI 114
CI 126
CI 138
CI 479
CI 501
EMKG 8
AS 85

FOUNDATION
DA 39
HAP 464
HAP 757
EL 95
AE2 828
AE9 599
CAM 341

FOUNDATIONS
EL 92
AM 577
AM 1179
AA 805
H29 63
HAP 1160
HAP 1184
J6 846
M1 16
VCS 2
G1 455
G4 235
AE1 595
AE2 5
AE2 845
AE3 27
AE3 496

FOUNDATIONS
AE4 28
AE4 647
AE8 315
C 678

FOUNDED
HAP 47
AE1 336
AE2 217
AE6 884

FOUNDER
HAP 1881
G1 24
AE1 376
AE1 908
AE7 938
AE7 1061
AE8 72
AE8 178
AE8 416
AE12 1203
M10 101

FOUNDERED
SAA 98
EMKG 18

FOUNDER'S
AE8 470
M15 12

FOUNDERS
PFD 12
L3 251
PTP 29

FOUNDERS'
FOUNDLING
AM 1094
J6 782
P6 134

FOUNDRESS
EL 51
AE1 622

FOUNT
OD 32
VCS 9
G4 524
AE8 100
KT2 502
TJD 26
M12 549
CI 91

FOUNTAIN
L4 110
HAP 849
HAP 1199
J3 33
M1 501
AE7 124
M12 550
M15 267
M15 270
CI 90

FOUNTAIN'S
SAA 798
HAP 1417

FOUNTAINS
HS 112
SKK 5
SAA 1062
SAA 1079
J3 501
M13 84
VP5 61
VP7 67
VP10 64
G1 173
AE7 720
AE12 272
OAL 292
WB 389
M15 414
M15 415

FOUNTS
J3 22
G3 684
AE4 367
CAM 167

FOUR
UDH 21
AM 1109
AM 1110
POE 28
EUF 21
MD 19
SAA 448
EDGA 14
TA 202
AK 185
HAP 586
EKA 4
P3 174
M1 1037
VP5 102
G1 349
G1 581
G1 690
G2 363
G3 99
G3 178
G3 299
G4 419
G4 420
G4 779

FOUR
G4 781
G4 782
G4 793
G4 794
G4 795
AE1 137
AE2 318
AE3 709
AE5 151
AE5 916
AE6 348
AE6 793
AE8 274
AE8 854
AE10 291
AE10 721
AE10 803
AE12 246
DO 117
KT3 47
M15 297
M15 337
M15 365
M15 366
PMK 1

FOUR-FOOT
FOUR-FOOTED
L4 273
M12 425
M12 604

FOURTH
AM 802
HAP 1150
HAP 1153
P3 177
P6 138
G1 83
G3 508
AE3 268
AE10 875
KT3 976
M11 109
SMA 115
AM 338

FOWL
HAP 2537
P3 145
VP9 16
AE4 763
AE7 971
AE12 374
AE12 380
KT2 532
BP 135
TH 316

FOWLER
OAL 52
FOWLER'S
OAL 444
FOWLS
HAP 1879
M1 418
G1 527
G4 327
AE6 429
AE9 646
HAP 190
HAP 466
TJD 54

FOX
C 480
C 587
C 724
C 749
C 814
GP 74
SMP 31
PRH 12
G3 589
C 747

FOXES
FOX'S
FRAGMENT
M13 211
AE9 773
AE12 991
M11 211
M12 461

FRAGMENTS
AE12 1074
FRAGRANT
SMA 60
ML 39
L1 9
T23 57
H29 7
P4 78
P6 91
HI 174
VP4 23
G2 183
G4 44
G4 244
G4 350
AE1 609
KT3 976
AE6 315
AE6 1222
AE12 156

Word	Code	Num		Word	Code	Num		Word	Code	Num
FRAGRANT	KT2	62		FRAMES	AR	160		FRAUGHT	VP1	72
	M10	43			AA	690			AE1	76
	CAM	17		FRANCE	UDH	20			AE1	392
	FL	74			HS	86			AE1	913
	CI	565			AR	14			AE2	1086
FRAIL	PR	12			AR	310			HIF	276
	RL	52			AM	27			HIF	595
	RL	185			AM	155			CI	11
	TA	399			AM	165			ETP	5
	AE10	1206			AM	166		FRAY	EAZ	22
	OAL	391			AM	795			PAL	22
	B	403			AM	827			SAA	840
	WB	153			AM	838			EDGA	16
FRAILITIES	PIE	15			AM	1202			HH	32
	PWGR	21			EWGR	47			PTS	27
	VCS	22			PM	5			G4	130
FRAILTY	AR	208			PNH	45			AE12	431
	EM	13			ENH	21			M12	435
	HAP	332			EOE	20			M12	709
	HAP	448			PCB	11		FREAKS	AA	552
	J6	691			PSF	33		FRECKLED	L4	148
	AE4	29			PSF	46			ETO	1
	B	342			PUO5	2			KT3	475
	B	385			ELB	38		FRECKLES	KT3	76
	PWR	40			PDG	4		FREE	AR	39
FRAISCHEUR	SMA	102			PDG	29			AR	304
FRAME	UDH	38			EDGA	24			LC	120
	AM	848			PAA	25			DC	21
	PCD	22			PAA	32			LCA	38
	AA	310			PAA	34			VHH	3
	AA	962			HAP	173			PMQ	50
	MD	316			J6	527			PTL	9
	RL	107			TJD	155			ECG2	24
	RL	155			TH	52			PM	3
	RL	360		FRANCHISE	HAP	2541			ECD	11
	L2	24		FRANK	PWGR	24			PUO1	8
	L3	9			EDG	4			PUO2	7
	L3	18		FRANKINCENSE	P1	83			DA	184
	TA	115			VP8	91			PUO4	30
	TA	244			G2	164			PUF	22
	AK	37		FRANTIC	AM	111			AA	35
	AK	123			L4	40			AA	51
	HAP	1085			HAP	138			AA	69
	HAP	2230			SSC	39			AA	202
	SSC	2			J6	64			AA	574
	SSC	12			G3	420			AA	609
	EL	73			AE3	565			AA	627
	J10	253			AE4	434			AA	850
	P3	113			AE7	800			MD	176
	P5	67			AE9	983			PRH	44
	GK	21		FRATERNITY	AK	54			SAA	416
	GK	110		FRAUD	AM	148			SAA	877
	VP4	61			AM	668			SAA	909
	VP6	49			AA	124			PK	14
	G2	214			SAA	915			RL	298
	AE1	49			M1	165			RL	316
	AE2	246			M9	63			RL	408
	AE2	377			VP4	37			L3	11
	AE3	182			VP6	36			L3	82
	AE3	635			VP6	87			T27	3
	AE3	835			G1	678			H2	5
	AE4	486			AE1	401			FS1	1
	AE4	556			AE1	942			TA	412
	AE4	565			AE2	62			TA	495
	AE5	552			AE2	527			MN	13
	AE6	22			AE4	148			HAP	249
	AE6	402			AE4	427			HAP	334
	AE6	980			AE8	272			HAP	479
	AE7	630			AE8	285			HAP	857
	AE8	181			AE8	862			HAP	1096
	AE8	569			AE10	119			HAP	1103
	AE12	290			AE11	792			HAP	1192
	AF	162			OAL	726			HAP	2539
	AF	172			OAL	856			BR	210
	MFL	9			KT3	575			PKA	31
	DO	114			AU	46			EL	63
	DO	137		FRAUDFUL	VP6	30			EL	116
	KT2	546			G4	648			EL	228
	KT2	554			AE2	203			J3	26
	KT3	760			AE12	43			J3	164
	TJD	207		FRAUDS	MD	59			J3	187
	B	505			SAA	1033			J3	273
	M10	86			G4	575			J6	234
	C	461			AE2	49			J6	451
	FL	333			AE2	416			J6	746
	FL	596			AE6	391			P1	236
	WB	427			AE6	539			P3	214
	M15	597			AE7	662			P5	47
FRAMED	MD	65			AE7	767			P5	106
	MD	164			AE9	818			P5	130
	SDG	15		FRAUGHT	SMA	26			P5	135
	SDG	17			AM	93			P5	163
	AK	95			SAA	947			P5	174
	AE2	345			RL	244			P5	180
	KT2	483			RL	326			P5	212
FRAME'S	L3	165			TA	398			P6	27

Word	Code	No.
FREE	P6	75
	M1	527
	M1	923
	M9	178
	VCS	5
	PLT	52
	SLT1	17
	GK	137
	VP3	156
	VP9	43
	G1	47
	G1	196
	G2	110
	G2	577
	G2	640
	G2	686
	G3	95
	G3	467
	G4	357
	G4	424
	AE1	313
	AE1	409
	AE1	542
	AE2	206
	AE2	560
	AE2	619
	AE2	652
	AE3	168
	AE3	347
	AE3	559
	AE3	901
	AE4	491
	AE4	794
	AE4	995
	AE5	906
	AE5	964
	AE6	182
	AE6	888
	AE6	1176
	AE8	77
	AE9	127
	AE9	540
	AE9	831
	AE9	929
	AE10	440
	AE10	484
	AE11	496
	AE11	593
	AE12	43
	AE12	116
	AE12	1010
	AE12	1117
	AE12	1120
	OAL	397
	OAL	407
	OAL	587
	KT1	327
	KT1	440
	KT1	507
	KT1	514
	KT2	8
	KT2	107
	KT2	134
	KT2	338
	KT2	405
	KT3	353
	KT3	653
	KT3	682
	KT3	1036
	KT3	1106
	KT3	1122
	KT3	1126
	TJD	48
	TJD	188
	TJD	194
	B	401
	B	685
	CAM	47
	CAM	177
	CAM	368
	HIF	36
	HIF	390
	HIF	522
	HIF	611
	C	129
	C	512
	C	527
	C	538
	C	542
	C	548
	C	550
	C	560
	C	577
	TH	70
	FL	392
	FL	523

Word	Code	No.
FREE	M12	230
	AU	75
	AU	241
	AU	295
	AU	413
	AU	490
	WB	40
	WB	81
	WB	95
	WB	136
	WB	424
	M15	651
	M15	667
	M15	699
	GP	16
	GP	45
	CI	9
	CI	460
	SMP	38
	SMP	42
	DC	3
	PTW	26
	MD	130
	BR	300
	J3	223
	HIF	415
	LC	107
	AM	39
	AM	1166
	SCG2	28
	EAZ	4
	AA	194
	AA	716
	SAA	39
	SAA	788
	RL	205
	L4	7
	MN	8
	HAP	146
	HAP	203
	HAP	860
	BR	263
	P5	182
	P5	240
	P5	251
	G2	207
	G3	835
	AE6	1095
	AE10	74
	AE11	615
	AE11	743
	AE11	1303
	AE12	988
	AE12	1141
	KT1	378
	KT1	426
	KT1	444
	KT1	491
	KT2	137
	KT2	337
	KT2	338
	KT2	357
	KT3	519
	KT3	1009
	KT3	1103
	M8	373
	B	656
	M10	92
	AU	117
	CI	285
	HIF	553
	J1	156
	AR	43
	AR	152
	AM	6
	SMM2	20
	CM	107
	HP	151
	MD	124
	MD	251
	SAA	32
	SAA	740
	SAA	754
	SAA	771
	PK	22
	PDG	30
	L4	134
	T23	16
	TA	299
	TA	300
	TA	301
	PAA	27
	EJG	2
	J1	229
	J10	122
	J16	28
	P5	100

FREE-BORN
FREEBORN

FREED

FREEDEST
FREEDMAN
FREEDOM

Word	Code	No.
FREEDOM	P5	123
	P5	133
	P5	168
	P5	179
	VP1	37
	VP1	43
	AE11	1291
	KT1	370
	KT1	386
	KT1	388
	KT1	439
	KT1	453
	B	600
	C	540
	AR	138
	EWG	14
	PMQw	7
	SAA	1012
	HAP	624
	HAP	1249
	EL	44
	J10	559
	P5	29
	P5	127
	P5	220
	P6	57
	M1	134
	VP3	29
	AE2	94
	AE8	533
	KT2	391
	B	411
	AU	226
	GP	42
	P5	110
	HS	113
	AE9	734
	AE7	788
	AE11	1206
	VP10	93
	M1	355
	GP	32
	VP1	86
	G1	135
	G3	468
	G4	738
	AE12	499
	KT1	469
	KT2	547
	KT3	297
	AR	234
	P5	197
	J6	242
	J10	63
	M13	128
	G1	163
	G2	196
	G2	599
	AE2	963
	AE6	556
	AE11	837
	B	231
	M11	203
	M12	367
	SMP	8
	AM	818
	AE6	419
	AM	170
	AM	684
	PMQ	2
	EEL	11
	EEL	14
	EEL	28
	PCG1	37
	PCG1	38
	PAR	6
	PAR	14
	EUO	2
	EUO	7
	PNH	48
	ENH	40
	EAZ	18
	EAZ	29
	ESF	22
	PTW	14
	PCB	29
	PSF	29
	MD	202
	ER	24
	L4	107
	GE	37
	HAP	1028
	HAP	1416
	HAP	1467
	PSH	16

FREELY

FREEMAN
FREEMEN

FREES

FREEZE
FREEZES

FREEZING

FREIGHT

FREIGHTED
FREIGHTS
FRENCH

Word	Code	No.
FRENCH	EH	3
	OAL	589
	PWR	9
FRENCHMAN	C	745
FRENCHMAN'S	HS	89
FRENCHMEN	PNH	38
FRENZY	SAA	101
	SAA	721
	VP2	103
	VP10	88
	AE2	423
	M12	320
FREQUENT	AM	1165
	AM	1069
	SAA	527
	AK	100
	HAP	914
	HAP	1237
	HAP	1319
	J1	109
	J3	223
	J3	376
	G1	143
	G2	444
	G3	831
	AE2	491
	AE7	369
	AE12	393
	KT3	246
	CAM	307
	TH	65
FREQUENTLY	OAL	659
FREQUENTS	G4	582
FRESH	HS	26
	HS	130
	SMA	8
	LC	98
	DC	14
	AM	406
	AM	597
	AM	883
	PEL	12
	PEL	31
	AA	248
	AA	375
	MD	271
	SAA	706
	AT	4
	L3	100
	L3	162
	HAP	1845
	J1	103
	J6	16
	J6	598
	M1	918
	G4	365
	AE5	1016
	AE6	462
	AE6	611
	AE7	727
	AE8	209
	AE8	280
	AE9	1082
	AE11	361
	AE11	648
	OAL	154
	KT1	172
	KT1	182
	KT1	222
	KT3	75
	KT3	86
	B	30
	C	289
	C	464
	TH	187
	TH	210
	TH	343
	FL	40
	FL	96
	FL	160
	FL	336
	FL	582
	M12	64
	AU	131
	WB	542
	M15	301
FRESHER	AM	875
	BP	197
	FL	67
	M12	257
FRESHNESS	FL	568
FRETS	AE10	1008
	KT1	446
FRETTED	AA	157
FRIAR	ELN	4
	EDS	4
FRIARS	WB	28
FRIDAY	KT2	84
	C	685
	C	697
	TH	207
	TH	246
	TH	376
FRIED	VP2	14
FRIEND	JH	4
	LC	130
	DC	33
	AM	334
	AM	463
	AM	467
	AM	468
	PWGR	9
	SEL1	13
	STL	14
	PMQw	4
	EM	30
	SM1	9
	EAZ	14
	HP	157
	HP	237
	HP	255
	DA	205
	PR	23
	AA	738
	AA	873
	AA	877
	AA	888
	EPC	10
	MD	68
	MD	309
	SAA	427
	SAA	636
	SAA	1010
	RL	157
	RL	228
	RL	398
	EC	38
	ER	69
	MO	10
	L3	137
	L4	263
	T27	25
	H29	9
	TA	77
	TA	279
	HH	18
	HAP	332
	HAP	563
	HAP	718
	HAP	744
	HAP	818
	HAP	1541
	PMS	4
	PMS	24
	PKA	35
	ELW	2
	EL	45
	EL	161
	EL	241
	EL	319
	ODA	60
	J1	49
	J3	1
	J3	17
	J3	30
	J3	40
	J3	101
	J3	153
	J3	199
	J3	443
	J3	500
	J6	142
	J10	372
	J16	34
	J16	40
	J16	43
	P1	101
	P1	102
	P1	230
	P1	242
	P3	82
	P3	136
	P3	165
	P3	188
	P5	30
	P5	152
	P5	173
	P5	210
	P5	234
	P6	1
	P6	61
FRIEND	P6	96
	P6	161
	M1	940
	MC	73
	GK	128
	VP1	7
	VP9	94
	VP10	18
	VP10	101
	AE1	552
	AE1	644
	AE1	682
	AE2	487
	AE3	59
	AE3	109
	AE3	553
	AE3	609
	AE4	72
	AE4	975
	AE4	976
	AE5	441
	AE5	457
	AE5	619
	AE5	932
	AE5	952
	AE5	1098
	AE6	184
	AE6	226
	AE6	240
	AE6	334
	AE6	467
	AE6	656
	AE6	829
	AE7	515
	AE7	605
	AE8	163
	AE8	208
	AE8	610
	AE8	615
	AE8	741
	AE9	228
	AE9	255
	AE9	262
	AE9	304
	AE9	369
	AE9	410
	AE9	428
	AE9	478
	AE9	524
	AE9	528
	AE9	536
	AE9	576
	AE9	619
	AE9	752
	AE10	169
	AE10	599
	AE10	686
	AE10	1106
	AE11	4
	AE11	39
	AE11	88
	AE11	194
	AE11	250
	AE11	536
	AE11	556
	AE11	661
	AE11	994
	AE12	69
	AE12	930
	AE12	1371
	OAL	434
	OAL	651
	OAL	676
	OAL	821
	OAL	823
	OAL	846
	OAL	859
	OAL	861
	AF	83
	MG	1
	MM	1
	MM	55
	KT1	12
	KT1	87
	KT1	238
	KT1	301
	KT1	322
	KT1	359
	KT1	369
	KT1	377
	KT1	397
	KT2	13
	KT3	653
	KT3	925
	KT3	1098
	KT3	1105

FRIEND	B	149
	B	379
	B	660
	HIF	260
	HIF	372
	HIF	771
	C	130
	C	230
	C	240
	C	243
	C	257
	C	319
	C	592
	C	779
	TH	71
	AU	93
	AU	101
	AU	108
	AU	145
	AU	439
	AU	517
	AU	540
	AU	543
	WB	357
	WB	486
	M15	678
	CI	479
	CI	518
	CI	631
	PMK	14
FRIENDLESS	DA	123
FRIENDLY	DA	128
	AM	586
	T23	43
	H29	102
	HAP	1268
	HAP	1327
	HAP	1903
	HAP	1941
	EL	246
	J6	180
	J6	739
	P5	59
	M1	578
	VP5	107
	G2	265
	G4	33
	G4	210
	G4	544
	AE1	382
	AE1	537
	AE1	783
	AE1	803
	AE1	842
	AE1	1026
	AE2	199
	AE3	103
	AE3	456
	AE3	592
	AE3	897
	AE3	940
	AE5	71
	AE5	768
	AE6	622
	AE8	211
	AE8	234
	AE8	647
	AE8	849
	AE9	268
	AE9	285
	AE9	538
	AE10	1148
	AE12	178
	AE12	411
	KT1	248
	KT2	27
	KT3	720
	M8	204
	B	624
	B	677
	C	761
	M11	157
	M11	221
	FL	454
	FL	497
	WB	524
FRIEND'S	PMQ	51
	PMS	23
	EL	259
	VP8	88
	AE5	942
	AE7	363
	C	615
FRIENDS	VHH	32
	AM	144
	AM	160

FRIENDS	AM	1018
	AM	1054
	PM	17
	PM	21
	PM	26
	E	32
	PTW	10
	CM	19
	HP	31
	AA	280
	AA	357
	AA	397
	AA	466
	AA	606
	AA	682
	AA	711
	AA	743
	AA	813
	AA	995
	AA	142
	PLB	12
	PLB	44
	PLB	48
	MD	275
	MD	309
	PRH	24
	MF	171
	SAA	277
	SAA	515
	SAA	746
	SAA	829
	SAA	1113
	L3	81
	L3	84
	L3	92
	H3	8
	TA	126
	TA	191
	PAA	23
	GE	72
	HAP	996
	HAP	410
	HAP	1348
	HAP	1405
	HAP	1569
	HAP	1975
	HAP	2114
	HAP	2170
	HAP	2220
	HAP	2421
	HAP	2495
	EDS	13
	EDS	22
	EL	257
	PSH	3
	J3	214
	J3	373
	J3	413
	J6	146
	J6	656
	J10	72
	J10	398
	P3	32
	P3	178
	P5	134
	P5	236
	HI	62
	VP8	96
	VP9	10
	G1	405
	G4	123
	G4	374
	AE1	301
	AE1	431
	AE1	542
	AE1	605
	AE1	718
	AE1	726
	AE1	771
	AE1	785
	AE1	817
	AE1	861
	AE1	894
	AE2	90
	AE2	188
	AE2	369
	AE2	418
	AE2	425
	AE2	502
	AE2	522
	AE2	555
	AE2	580
	AE2	771
	AE2	787
	AE2	798
	AE2	1007

FRIENDS	AE2	1009
	AE2	1082
	AE3	11
	AE3	307
	AE3	446
	AE3	452
	AE3	602
	AE3	839
	AE4	616
	AE4	863
	AE4	886
	AE5	53
	AE5	245
	AE5	624
	AE5	873
	AE5	879
	AE5	887
	AE5	976
	AE5	1002
	AE5	1008
	AE6	322
	AE6	455
	AE6	1135
	AE6	1142
	AE7	228
	AE7	468
	AE8	76
	AE8	645
	AE9	42
	AE9	182
	AE9	588
	AE9	597
	AE9	649
	AE9	981
	AE9	1049
	AE10	130
	AE10	386
	AE10	416
	AE10	511
	AE10	621
	AE10	713
	AE10	960
	AE10	976
	AE10	1181
	AE11	21
	AE11	124
	AE11	180
	AE11	217
	AE11	256
	AE11	261
	AE11	271
	AE11	285
	AE11	305
	AE11	484
	AE11	621
	AE11	739
	AE11	1188
	AE11	1219
	AE11	1254
	AE11	1280
	AE12	290
	AE12	395
	AE12	498
	AE12	507
	AE12	576
	AE12	601
	AE12	602
	AE12	858
	AE12	916
	AE12	949
	AE12	1180
	AE12	1356
	KT1	354
	KT1	605
	KT2	412
	KT3	1091
	M8	158
	HIF	228
	HIF	274
	C	211
	TH	43
	TH	64
	TH	234
	TH	245
	TH	247
	TH	417
	M11	184
	M12	323
	AU	88
	CI	244
	CI	266
	CI	288
	CI	441
	CI	555
	CI	563
	EMKG	16

FROWNING	AE10	300	FRUITFUL	J6	256	FRUITS	P1	56		
	OAL	356		J10	238		M13	106		
	KT3	238		J16	59		M13	117		
	C	309		M1	133		VP7	75		
FROWNS	LC	49		M1	158		G1	34		
	PMQW	11		M1	426		G1	82		
	AE5	931		M1	578		G1	594		
	AE6	144		M1	820		G2	76		
	OAL	469		M9	165		G2	83		
FROWSY	ETO	2		VP1	103		G2	325		
FROZE	AM	1138		VP4	40		G2	591		
	KT2	540		VP5	55		G2	715		
	KT3	839		G1	2		G2	752		
	M15	313		G1	151		G2	758		
FROZEN	CM	98		G1	195		AE7	153		
	PRH	7		G1	236		AE11	26		
	HAP	1918		G1	283		AE11	80		
	M1	80		G1	302		CAM	241		
	VP8	99		G2	196		TH	263		
	VP10	71		G2	197		M11	339		
	G1	65		G2	241		M15	107		
	G3	547		G2	257	FRUSTRATE	AE9	187		
	G3	562		G2	441		M8	164		
	G4	750		G2	575		TH	193		
	AE7	307		G2	626	FRUSTRATES	M12	484		
	FL	416		G4	173	FRY	AM	811		
	AS	14		G4	410		EKK	18		
FRUGAL	AA	622		G4	534		H29	33		
	AA	892		AE1	103		J3	378		
	AA	893		AE1	525		J6	660		
	L4	105		AE1	623		P1	221		
	J3	373		AE1	749		M1	619		
	J6	402		AE3	141		G3	215		
	P5	58		AE3	222		AE3	196		
	P6	44		AE3	534		AE12	765		
	G1	5		AE3	917		M8	347		
	G1	592		AE6	812	FRYING	VP7	79		
	G2	777		AE7	173		M12	388		
	G4	17		AE7	472	FUCINE	AE7	1042		
	G4	194		AE7	989	FUDDLED	J6	420		
	AE9	828		AE7	1048		OAE2	67		
FRUGALLY	AE8	547		AE8	104	FUEL	DC	30		
	CI	447		AE8	619		SMQ	10		
FRUIT	AR	170		AE9	362		T18	83		
	AM	43		AE10	211		T23	24		
	PC1	4		AE11	488		P3	239		
	STC	10		AE12	360		M9	87		
	HP	25		OAL	290		AE2	478		
	AA	202		MM	42		OAL	278		
	AA	250		TJD	44		KT3	907		
	SAA	752		CAM	1		M8	342		
	RL	415		HIF	234		WB	412		
	H2	32		AU	609		M15	523		
	HAP	24		M15	325		M15	530		
	HAP	361		CI	495	FUGITIVE	AM	1089		
	BR	15		ETP	9		VP6	85		
	EL	203		PMK	10		G3	109		
	J6	771	FRUITFULNESS	M10	97		AE2	89		
	M13	112		CI	132		AE4	294		
	VCS	27	FRUITION	SMA	70	FUGITIVES	G4	159		
	VP1	50	FRUITLESS	AR	103		AE1	742		
	VP1	101		AM	362		AE1	846		
	VP6	88		MF	148		AE10	69		
	VP8	72		SAA	641		AE10	92		
	VP9	68		L3	293	FULFIL	CM	145		
	G1	222		J1	200		HAP	1076		
	G2	79		P3	120		BR	16		
	G2	115		P5	95		AE1	113		
	G2	177		P6	65		AE2	823		
	G3	57		M1	668		AE4	894		
	G4	214		M9	99		AE6	10		
	AE4	704		VP8	126		KT1	487		
	AE12	536		G3	694		C	73		
	KT1	451		G3	776		AU	67		
	TH	198		AE1	72	FULFILLED	AA	836		
	M15	137		AE2	148		AE3	334		
	M15	197		AE2	837		AE3	368		
FRUITFUL	DC	12		AE2	1081		AE7	754		
	PTC	12		AE3	443		HIF	365		
	AA	332		AE4	99		TH	190		
	AA	829		AE8	343		WB	303		
	MD	168		AE9	540		M15	25		
	D	5		AE12	1190		M15	586		
	ER	1		KT1	344	FULFILS	J6	351		
	L4	256		M8	384	FULL	SMA	70		
	L4	257		TH	162		SMA	66		
	L4	276		M11	208		EIE	1		
	T18	81	FRUITLESSLY	AE6	239		EIE	22		
	TA	351	FRUITS	AM	692		AM	449		
	AK	109		ECD	19		AM	900		
	HAP	17		PAL	40		AM	1022		
	HAP	209		PD	46		AM	1126		
	HAP	2098		MO	19		EEL	24		
	EL	194		AK	19		PTL	17		
	ODA	61		J6	26		PTL	20		
	J6	235		J6	162		STL	19		

Word	Code	Num
FUNERAL	AE9	279
	AE10	724
	AE11	33
	AE11	78
	AE11	92
	AE11	98
	AE11	118
	AE11	180
	AE11	203
	AE11	214
	AE11	261
	AE11	285
	AE11	361
	AE11	573
	AE12	1267
	KT1	48
	KT1	83
	KT3	894
	KT3	925
	KT3	950
	KT3	999
	M8	289
	M8	385
	M8	387
	B	628
	B	661
	CAM	276
	HIF	78
	TH	364
	M11	481
	M15	593
	M15	594
FUNERALS	AM	1069
	CM	140
	DA	100
	AE2	373
	AE2	491
	AE2	863
	AE5	492
	AE11	132
	KT1	133
	M8	300
	M11	181
FUR	P3	172
FURBISHED	FL	258
	TA	467
	HAP	1876
	AE8	573
	KT3	446
FURIES	DA	100
	CM	121
	SAA	139
	L3	222
	TA	458
	M1	1006
	VP9	9
	G1	373
	G3	63
	G4	693
	G4	756
	AE4	687
	AE4	875
	AE6	509
	AE6	820
	AE7	456
	AE7	627
	AE8	888
	AE11	1299
	AF	132
	M8	294
	STP	19
FURIES'	AE3	329
	AE6	392
FURIOUS	PFD	19
	T23	88
	HAP	46
	HAP	351
	HAP	692
	BR	222
	J10	484
	M13	190
	VP5	33
	G1	606
	G3	419
	AE4	769
	AE4	810
	AE4	845
	AE4	921
	AE4	928
	AE4	966
	AE6	126
	AE7	450
	AE7	725
	AE7	820
	AE7	843
	AE7	1052

Word	Code	Num
FURIOUS	AE9	75
	AE10	570
	AE11	902
	AF	146
	KT3	607
	KT3	693
	HIF	223
	TH	285
	TH	369
	M12	361
	CI	285
FURIOUSLY	M1	708
FURL	AM	221
	G1	513
	AE3	698
	M11	103
FURLED	HIF	598
FURLS	SAA	837
FURNACE	L4	88
	G4	381
	AE8	586
FURNACES	AE6	416
FURNISH	PFD	11
	T18	82
	PP	36
	J1	213
	J6	344
	AE9	707
	AE12	694
	KT3	409
FURNISHED	AA	692
	T27	66
	T27	127
	HAP	2431
	OD	15
	M1	137
	AE4	264
	AE9	412
	KT3	25
	TH	131
FURNISHES	M10	37
FURNITURE	J1	115
	P3	43
	FL	223
FURRED	VP6	90
FURRIER	EHC	29
FURROW	G3	274
	G3	777
	G3	797
	AE10	413
FURROWED	L4	283
	M1	447
	G1	141
	G1	168
	G1	204
	G1	240
	G2	30
	G3	656
	AE7	584
	AU	411
	M15	317
FURROWS	MD	23
	SKA3	13
	J3	47
	P1	140
	M1	158
	G1	97
	G1	153
	G1	664
	G2	353
	G2	396
	G2	591
	G3	220
	G3	256
	AE1	53
	AE9	835
FURRY	HAP	267
	HAP	1319
	G3	589
FURS	ENH	30
	M12	552
FURTHER	LCA	37
	AK	143
	AE2	187
	HIF	765
	WB	345
	WB	494
	M15	262
FURTHERED	UDH	26
FURY	AM	920
	PMQ	14
	PMQ	30
	SCD1	18
	AA	399
	AA	451
	AA	916

Word	Code	Num
FURY	AA	1005
	EDGA	37
	RL	222
	AT	99
	HAP	1320
	HAP	1593
	SSC	39
	J1	14
	J6	41
	J10	90
	P3	237
	M1	68
	M1	311
	M1	325
	M1	829
	M1	1072
	HI	24
	VP6	70
	G3	106
	G3	765
	G4	714
	AE1	55
	AE1	76
	AE1	91
	AE1	99
	AE1	155
	AE1	216
	AE1	223
	AE1	405
	AE2	54
	AE2	180
	AE2	562
	AE3	539
	AE4	74
	AE4	296
	AE4	644
	AE4	853
	AE5	192
	AE5	606
	AE5	619
	AE5	579
	AE5	862
	AE5	879
	AE5	889
	AE5	907
	AE5	1036
	AE6	78
	AE6	97
	AE6	153
	AE6	554
	AE6	771
	AE7	412
	AE7	453
	AE7	477
	AE7	485
	AE7	534
	AE7	550
	AE7	565
	AE7	580
	AE7	661
	AE7	667
	AE7	707
	AE7	739
	AE7	752
	AE7	767
	AE7	787
	AE7	1076
	AE8	82
	AE9	462
	AE9	577
	AE9	1025
	AE10	802
	AE10	1154
	AE11	347
	AE11	988
	AE11	1000
	AE12	6
	AE12	167
	AE12	508
	AE12	701
	AE12	1252
	AE12	1321
	OAL	422
	KT2	190
	M8	270
	M8	395
	B	486
	CAM	24
	CAM	174
	HIF	37
	HIF	68
	HIF	153
	HIF	333
	HIF	795
	TH	130
	TH	301

FURY	TH	422	FUTURE	OAL	513	GAIN	J6	714
	M11	74		DO	41		J6	841
	M11	118		DO	91		J10	141
	M12	115		DO	143		J10	526
	M12	169		DO	167		J10	546
	M12	337		KT3	435		PPS	16
	WB	260		KT3	845		P1	48
	WB	360		KT3	1095		P2	84
FURZES	G1	346		M8	62		P6	145
	OAL	855		M8	141		M9	16
FURZY	SAA	921		CAM	381		M9	125
FUSTIAN	ENH	31		HIF	477		SLT2	3
	PK	31		C	206		GK	5
	P1	32		TH	223		EHC	15
	P1	146		M12	214		VP1	43
	P1	207		WB	514		VP3	165
	P5	9		M15	220		VP4	38
	PLT	21		M15	648		G1	369
	PTP	22		CI	127		G1	500
FUTURE	AR	90		CI	324		G4	231
	SMA	72		ESK	24		G4	357
	DC	24	FUTURITY	AE6	101		G4	378
	AM	204					AE1	375
	HP	211					AE1	732
	DA	172					AE1	953
	AA	420					AE2	793
	AA	654					AE3	486
	AA	771					AE4	347
	AA	979	GABBLE	VP9	47		AE4	695
	MF	75	GABBLING	AE7	972		AE5	253
	MF	133	GABIAN	AE6	1050		AE5	298
	MF	159	GABIN	AE7	258		AE5	439
	SAA	93	GABINE	AE7	944		AE5	921
	SAA	316	GAD	EAZ	26		AE5	1065
	SAA	651	GADDERS	EKK	19		AE6	547
	SAA	893	GADDING	PPC	28		AE7	319
	RL	23		M1	1007		AE8	422
	RL	58		G3	240		AE9	289
	L3	178	GAETULIAN	AE4	56		AE9	376
	L3	298	GAETULIA'S	AE5	67		AE9	495
	L4	243	GAGE	AM	79		AE9	538
	L5	8	GAGS	G3	611		AE10	530
	H29	46	GAIN	HS	84		AE10	652
	TA	57		AR	202		AE10	869
	TA	96		LC	81		AE10	967
	TA	449		LCA	13		AE11	339
	HAP	1696		AM	45		AE12	705
	HAP	1709		AM	196		OAL	42
	HAP	2145		AM	320		OAL	91
	HAP	2361		AM	340		OAL	355
	HAP	2592		AM	652		OAL	396
	BR	114		AM	763		OAL	502
	BR	145		AM	861		OAL	517
	BR	182		AM	998		OAL	757
	EL	42		PM	18		OAL	856
	EL	198		SM1	15		KT1	581
	J1	220		EMK	11		KT2	416
	J6	719		HP	20		KT3	334
	J10	544		HP	27		TJD	141
	P5	260		HP	70		B	603
	GK	163		DA	122		HIF	320
	GK	180		AA	296		C	82
	G1	312		AA	329		C	298
	G2	582		AA	488		C	322
	G3	715		AA	588		C	402
	G4	80		MD	34		TH	159
	G4	238		SAA	658		TH	417
	AE1	278		SAA	978		AU	25
	AE1	597		RL	145		AU	56
	AE1	621		RL	275		AU	216
	AE1	709		L3	23		AU	314
	AE2	389		L3	316		M15	666
	AE3	133		L4	134		ETP	14
	AE3	585		H9	24	GAINED	AR	98
	AE4	332		H29	93		VHH	8
	AE4	341		TA	377		ECG1	6
	AE4	397		TA	490		ESF	25
	AE4	583		HAP	1141		HP	122
	AE4	899		HAP	1285		AA	404
	AE5	981		HAP	1396		AA	471
	AE6	519		HAP	1480		SAA	313
	AE6	924		HAP	1492		TA	409
	AE6	969		HAP	1521		HAP	1821
	AE6	1201		HAP	1669		HAP	1922
	AE6	1231		HAP	1692		HAP	2051
	AE7	131		HAP	2153		J16	82
	AE7	182		HAP	2246		P5	94
	AE7	345		BR	301		M9	116
	AE7	894		PTS	5		MC	12
	AE8	654		STS3	13		G3	276
	AE8	832		EL	355		AE2	259
	AE8	942		MS	8		AE5	400
	AE10	517		J3	60		AE6	1245
	AE10	587		J3	128		AE8	149
	AE11	1162		J3	245		AE8	422
	AE12	166		J6	713		AE9	350

Headword	Ref	No.
GAINED	AE9	429
	AE10	1033
	AE11	263
	AE11	845
	AE12	360
	OAL	547
	OAL	753
	OAL	772
	KT1	383
	KT3	312
	KT3	679
	KT3	772
	KT3	1121
	B	2
	HIF	178
	HIF	186
	HIF	200
	TH	15
	TH	47
	M11	201
	FL	554
	AU	590
	WB	522
	CI	87
	CI	444
	CI	504
	PMK	6
	PMK	41
GAINEST	AU	565
GAINFUL	HS	45
	RL	371
	H2	12
	HAP	2040
GAINING	AR	10
	ER	42
	M1	725
GAINS	PA	14
	SAA	369
	PK	26
	L4	105
	HAP	124
	PP	6
	ODA	71
	J1	60
	J1	68
	J3	160
	J6	685
	J6	704
	J6	727
	J16	91
	P3	72
	P3	141
	M1	305
	VP3	6
	VP7	24
	G1	74
	AE2	410
	AE5	862
	AE11	825
	AE12	491
	AE12	1089
	AE12	1092
	OAL	566
	OAL	660
	OAL	753
	MG	32
	KT1	495
	KT2	366
	KT2	597
	M11	164
	M12	685
	CI	13
	CI	301
GAIT	G3	95
	G3	122
GALAESUS	G4	187
GALATEA	M13	66
	M13	80
	M13	146
	M13	206
	VP7	52
	VP9	50
GALATEA'S	VP1	41
GALAXY	HS	56
GALBA	AR	69
GALBANEAN	G4	383
GALBANUM	G3	627
GALE	AM	308
	MD	80
	H29	101
	HAP	467
	HAP	1390
	HAP	1750
	AE3	897
	AE5	999
	AE5	1098
GALE	DO	46
	M8	277
	HIF	654
	C	305
	C	346
	M11	98
	M12	54
GALEN	C	140
GALES	AR	65
	SAA	617
	L1	15
	H3	6
	PP	41
	AE3	96
	AE3	456
	AE3	580
	AE3	607
	AE3	621
	AE3	694
	AE3	916
	AE4	808
	AE5	1016
	AE7	31
	AE8	903
	AE8	940
	AE10	970
	HIF	594
	M11	83
	M11	94
	AU	316
	M15	64
	CI	329
GALESUS	AE7	746
	CI	66
GALL	CI	242
	MF	199
	OE	26
	HAP	2241
	J6	261
	G4	446
	AE7	1011
	AE9	689
	AE11	1290
	HIF	162
	C	148
GALLA	J1	189
GALLANT	EWG	1
	AM	601
	PWGR	14
	PEL	12
	ECG2	34
	PMQW	18
	EM	22
	ELB	10
	EKA	41
	J6	150
	E	19
GALLANTRY	EWG	19
GALLANTS	EIE	2
	PMM	14
	EMM	13
	ET	1
	PEL	22
	PEL	34
	ETL	11
	PW	1
	PW	18
	PMQW	5
	PCD	1
	ESF	6
	PTW	1
	PR	1
	PUO4	11
	PK	29
	PKA	46
	EKA	24
	ESH	25
	ESH	35
	EH	7
	EHC	26
	OAL	392
	TH	282
	EMKG	32
	EWR	26
GALLED	AM	589
	RL	404
	HAP	1425
	AE11	1137
GALLERIES	PD	58
	J3	265
	AE2	721
GALLERY	EK	12
	AE2	620
	J10	211
GALLEY	AE1	151
	AE5	202
GALLEY	AE5	264
	AE5	315
	AE5	356
	AE5	369
	AE5	648
	AE10	928
	HIF	659
	C	533
	M11	82
	M11	83
GALLEY'S	AE2	335
	AE5	242
GALLEYS	AE3	254
	AE3	386
	AE3	699
	AE3	741
	AE4	575
	AE4	851
	AE5	85
	AE5	151
	AE5	839
	AE6	1246
	AE8	109
	AE10	313
	AE11	497
	M12	55
	AU	6
GALLIC	HAP	1975
	H29	42
	GE	74
	C	501
	G3	148
GALLOPED		
GALLOWS	SAA	439
	P5	186
GALLOWS-FREE	SAA	431
GALLS	G4	389
GALLUS	J16	1
	VP6	93
	VP10	5
	VP10	8
	VP10	13
	VP10	18
	VP10	41
	VP10	105
	VP10	106
GAMBOLED	WB	4
GAMBOLS	KT3	100
GAME	EWG	1
	ML	6
	ELB	6
	MD	43
	MD	234
	SAA	275
	FS4	19
	TA	164
	HAP	127
	HAP	1498
	J6	357
	J6	467
	J10	477
	M9	105
	VP10	90
	AE1	66
	AE4	167
	AE5	522
	AE5	777
	AE5	781
	AE7	691
	OAL	53
	OAL	202
	OAL	316
	KT3	226
	TJD	58
	TH	377
	AU	172
	PWR	19
GAMES	M1	598
	VP2	94
	G3	29
	AE3	363
	AE5	65
	AE5	77
	AE5	90
	AE5	150
	AE5	319
	AE5	481
	AE5	714
	AE6	108
	AE7	339
	AE8	841
	KT3	999
GAMESOME	AE10	1019
GAMESTER	PAZ	23
	OAL	516
GAMESTERS	PRL	31
	PMQ	58

GATHERED	M13	111
	VP6	52
	G1	266
	G1	511
	G3	444
	G4	55
	G4	148
	G4	200
	AE4	752
	AE8	914
	AE11	301
	AE11	1143
	KT3	706
	B	257
	BP	88
	CAM	339
	FL	418
	M12	751
	M15	462
	CI	120
	CI	614
GATHERING	AM	713
	PCG1	31
	L4	24
	ODA	15
	VP9	87
	AE4	231
	AE5	19
	AE5	793
	AE6	487
	AE8	337
	AE9	719
	AE11	459
	AE11	712
	AE11	1028
	AE11	1193
	AE12	325
	AE12	513
	M8	135
	FL	383
	M15	295
	CI	605
GATHERS	LC	65
	ESF	19
	EL	4
	P3	147
	M1	730
	G3	693
	AE2	568
	AE3	573
	M15	338
GATH'S	SAA	1076
GAUDRY	PNH	11
GAUDS	AM	822
GAUDY	SMA	29
	AM	206
	PW	23
	PM	28
	EAL	9
	AA	297
	L2	37
	HAP	1360
	HAP	1718
	J6	587
	J10	229
	M1	1003
	AE8	911
	AE9	484
	KT3	454
	FL	106
	GP	89
GAUFRIDE	C	693
GAUL	TA	478
GAULISH	AE6	1185
GAULS	J3	350
	AE8	873
	MM	40
	TJD	183
GAULS'	AE8	873
GAUNT	HAP	161
	G3	320
	G4	144
	TH	113
GAUNTLET	J16	36
	AE5	488
	AE5	581
	AE5	623
GAUNTLET-FIGHT	AE5	479
GAUNTLETS	AE5	88
	AE5	534
	AE5	535
	AE5	546
	AE5	557
	AE5	569
	AE5	645
	AE11	120

GAUNTLETS	KT3	1001
GAVE	UDH	25
	DC	32
	VHH	10
	AM	1010
	PT	7
	ECG1	35
	S	4
	S	11
	EUO	18
	PUO2	22
	POE	2
	PTC	10
	CM	61
	DA	212
	EMW	14
	AA	432
	AA	580
	AA	658
	AA	769
	AA	1026
	EPC	24
	MD	57
	RL	378
	RL	406
	EC	26
	L4	44
	H29	85
	AK	124
	HH	36
	HAP	30
	HAP	527
	HAP	1604
	HAP	1800
	HAP	1840
	HAP	2052
	HAP	2190
	HAP	2233
	HAP	2492
	HAP	2495
	BR	135
	BR	326
	ETS	18
	EL	29
	EL	30
	EL	217
	EL	281
	OD	38
	OD	39
	ODA	24
	ODA	39
	J6	13
	J6	803
	P5	168
	M1	44
	M1	136
	M1	179
	M1	655
	M1	710
	M1	866
	M1	891
	M13	60
	M13	213
	HI	40
	MC	63
	GK	31
	VP1	11
	VP2	46
	VP3	94
	VP3	2
	G1	10
	G1	373
	G2	792
	G3	423
	G4	398
	G4	567
	G4	712
	G4	765
	AE1	170
	AE1	337
	AE1	349
	AE1	476
	AE1	622
	AE1	822
	AE1	853
	AE2	214
	AE2	727
	AE3	126
	AE3	593
	AE3	680
	AE4	37
	AE4	241
	AE4	456
	AE4	525
	AE4	655
	AE5	689

GAVE	AE5	705
	AE6	760
	AE7	268
	AE7	423
	AE8	223
	AE8	277
	AE8	316
	AE8	627
	AE8	710
	AE9	103
	AE9	354
	AE9	410
	AE9	564
	AE10	12
	AE10	265
	AE10	334
	AE10	410
	AE10	1112
	AE10	1154
	AE11	59
	AE11	89
	AE11	142
	AE11	260
	AE12	87
	AE12	223
	OAL	129
	OAL	331
	OAL	515
	OAE1	6
	DO	18
	DO	44
	KT1	230
	KT1	257
	KT1	295
	KT1	506
	KT2	147
	KT3	183
	KT3	364
	KT3	495
	KT3	626
	KT3	988
	KT3	1001
	KT3	1136
	KT3	1140
	TJD	38
	M8	118
	B	22
	B	160
	B	357
	B	422
	B	444
	M10	70
	CAM	24
	CAM	388
	HIF	496
	HIF	527
	HIF	610
	C	22
	C	198
	C	436
	C	439
	C	583
	C	637
	FL	598
	FL	606
	M12	700
	AU	214
	WB	66
	WB	75
	WB	302
	WB	421
	GP	132
	GP	133
	CI	497
	CI	498
	CI	499
	ERL	6
	PMK	21
	AS	89
GAVEST	B	423
GAY	STL	2
	PCG1	26
	PM	28
	PUO1	37
	ESF	11
	TA	371
	KT1	540
	WB	49
GAZE	AM	154
	AM	924
	SMQ	13
	BR	104
	AE1	990
	AE5	851
	AE6	1197
GAZED	AM	251

Word	Code	No.
GAZED	SAA	560
	SAA	611
	HAP	535
	GK	3
	AE1	635
	AE4	925
	AE8	820
	AE11	182
	AE12	108
	AF	110
	AF	117
	KT2	247
	M11	411
	FL	65
GAZES	AE9	78
GAZETTES	PLG	5
GAZING	AE5	334
	AE5	497
	AE6	256
	AE8	696
	AE9	563
	AE12	844
	KT1	562
	M8	212
	CI	171
	ESK	9
GEAR	WB	24
	PTP	36
GEARS	MD	60
GEESE	G1	179
	C	740
	M11	276
GEHAZI	SAA	549
GELA	AE3	923
GELDER	J6	487
GELDING	J6	659
	P5	270
GELOAN	AE3	922
GELONS	G3	703
GELT	J10	473
GEM	TA	317
	BR	314
	J1	41
	AE10	204
GEMS	UDH	63
	J6	502
	J10	39
	G2	105
	G2	455
	G2	513
	G2	725
	AE1	924
	AE1	1017
	AE4	386
	OAL	340
	B	609
	FL	13
	M15	621
GENERAL	AR	1
	AM	56
	AM	289
	AM	395
	AM	401
	AM	418
	AM	489
	AM	1014
	ET	4
	EPF	19
	AA	60
	AA	244
	AA	291
	AA	296
	AA	413
	MD	313
	RL	50
	RL	170
	RL	335
	TA	20
	HAP	653
	HAP	1742
	HAP	2434
	J6	444
	J16	26
	P1	81
	P4	25
	M1	214
	M1	233
	AE2	300
	AE5	400
	AE5	801
	AE7	866
	AE9	47
	AE9	337
	AE11	544
	AE11	766
	AE12	634

Word	Code	No.
GENERAL	AE12	823
	KT1	334
	KT1	599
	KT2	378
	KT3	528
	KT3	1006
	TH	310
	FL	18
	AU	590
	WB	427
GENERAL'S	AM	537
	EPF	20
	J16	92
	AU	293
GENERALS	ER	57
GENERALS'	AM	689
	AM	762
GENERATION	SAA	375
GENEROUS	AR	273
	VHH	36
	AM	41
	AA	423
	SAA	945
	SAA	1085
	ER	45
	MO	19
	T18	18
	T18	86
	H29	3
	AK	168
	HAP	2175
	HAP	1561
	EL	223
	GK	110
	GK	142
	VP5	109
	G2	2
	G2	83
	G2	176
	G2	263
	G3	83
	G3	119
	G3	199
	G3	289
	G3	350
	G3	617
	G3	761
	G4	399
	AE1	271
	AE1	850
	AE1	898
	AE5	131
	AE5	322
	AE6	976
	AE7	249
	AE8	198
	AE9	237
	AE9	292
	AE10	1136
	AE12	263
	AE12	415
	DO	37
	KT1	117
	KT2	188
	KT3	335
	KT3	443
	TJD	75
	TJD	107
	TJD	188
	M8	39
	HIF	644
	TH	4
	TH	29
	WB	455
	M15	106
	CI	630
	AS	96
GENEROUSLY	AM	355
GENEURA	WB	73
	WB	289
GENEVA	TA	354
	HAP	173
GENIAL	L1	17
	L4	222
	L4	272
	H9	8
	HAP	2441
	BR	13
	J6	76
	J10	518
	M1	577
	VP5	111
	G1	135
	G1	403
	G2	439
	G2	455

Word	Code	No.
GENIAL	G3	221
	G3	429
	G4	292
	AE6	819
	AE7	180
	AE10	651
	OAL	144
	OAL	639
	KT3	129
	B	711
	BP	77
	HIF	646
GENITURE	RH	104
GENIUS	HS	139
	RH	35
	DC	55
	AM	1127
	ECG2	2
	PUO4	25
	MF	203
	TA	470
	AK	142
	PMS	29
	ODA	23
	P1	166
	P2	5
	P4	63
	P5	220
	P6	169
	MC	13
	MC	60
	GK	65
	GK	135
	GK	147
	G1	5
	G1	80
	G2	16
	G2	50
	G3	71
	G3	259
	AE5	127
	AE7	185
	AE8	622
	C	312
	TH	229
	ESK	15
GENS	EAZ	25
GENTILES	RL	200
GENTLE	SIE	16
	PWGR	6
	SLN	4
	HP	229
	UMR	1
	MF	81
	MF	151
	MF	197
	SAA	6
	SAA	903
	SAA	700
	T18	19
	H3	5
	H29	56
	H2	40
	FS2	1
	FS4	5
	TA	171
	TA	286
	HAP	2379
	HAP	2583
	SKA5	9
	SKA6	10
	EL	242
	EL	311
	P1	128
	P1	165
	P5	21
	M1	889
	M1	971
	VP1	74
	G1	282
	G2	263
	G4	380
	AE1	465
	AE1	932
	AE2	1062
	AE3	501
	AE3	694
	AE4	91
	AE4	760
	AE5	168
	AE5	997
	AE6	954
	AE7	9
	AE8	120
	AE10	1229
	AE12	414

GENTLE	AE12	589	GET	OAL	514	GHOSTS	J6	371
	KT1	178		B	166		VP8	142
	KT1	593		C	343		G4	677
	KT2	34		AU	357		AE4	36
	KT2	66		PTP	46		AE4	47
	KT2	224		PMK	12		AE4	356
	KT2	332	GETTING	EC	12		AE4	709
	KT3	499	GETS	PEL	16		AE4	939
	B	49		EEL	22		AE5	960
	BP	98		ECG1	10		AE6	376
	C	55		HH	31		AE6	419
	C	595		J1	246		AE6	439
	M11	282		J6	520		AE6	445
	FL	10		J6	729		AE6	541
	FL	393		P3	198		AE6	555
	M12	108		AE5	206		AE6	655
GENTLEMAN	EUF	37	GETTEST	H9	24		AE6	752
	PLB	29	GEWGAW	PSF	36		AE8	327
	HAP	1703		J10	61		AE10	908
GENTLEMEN	EWG	16	GEWGAWS	P3	28		AE10	1179
	PMQ	47	GHASTLY	L3	159		AE11	1017
	PA	3		H3	40		AF	138
	PA	41		TA	58		M8	306
	ETL	3		G4	146		M8	338
	ETL	25		AE3	772		TH	379
	PLN	22		AE4	925	GIANT	HS	138
	ENH	2		AE6	648		AM	506
	AA	645		AE9	620		RL	80
	EK	45		OAL	836		M1	238
	PD	1		AF	136		M13	40
	EC	13		KT3	971		M13	51
	WB	380		CAM	223		M13	180
GENTLER	SAA	73		C	231		MC	5
GENTLEWOMAN	HAP	570		M11	359		AE3	827
GENTLY	AR	109	GHOST	RH	63		AE3	863
	RH	9		ETL	4		AE3	878
	AM	1216		EOE	32		AE5	571
	STL	8		PTC	2		AE8	268
	HAP	345		PTC	40		AE8	353
	P1	232		CM	138		AE9	1015
	VP5	132		DA	70		AE9	943
	AE1	972		DA	104		AE10	432
	AE2	931		ER	59		AE11	610
	AE9	1106		L3	181		M11	202
	AE12	136		J3	424		AU	413
	OAL	181		AE1	486	GIANT-BROOD	HAP	1107
	OAE2	26		AE2	352	GIANTESS	J6	647
	DO	47		AE2	1052	GIANT'S	L3	194
	BP	74		AE3	56	GIANTS	HAP	1841
GENUINE	MF	23		AE3	89		M1	193
	SAA	784		AE3	402	GIANTS'	TA	104
	RL	332		AE4	506	GIBBONS	P3	126
	P2	132		AE4	558		TJD	82
GEOMANTIC	KT2	614		AE4	683	GIBBOUS	AE8	308
GEOMETRICIAN	J3	138		AE5	105	GIBE	J3	248
GEOMETRY	P1	269		AE5	132	GIBEONITES	HAP	1843
GEORGE	SCD2	7		AE5	949	GIBES	PMS	24
	MF	151		AE5	1028	GIBLET	P6	172
	GE	80		AE6	26	GIDDY	SCD2	21
	P5	215		AE6	227		AA	216
GERMAN	AM	146		AE6	498		SAA	118
	GE	17		AE6	516		L3	204
	HAP	49		AE6	605		H29	48
	HAP	1415		AE6	473		HAP	1718
	VP1	82		AE6	685		J6	139
	G1	638		AE6	771		J10	101
GERMANS	P6	106		AE6	776		P3	98
GERYON	AE6	402		AE6	943		AE2	50
	AE7	917		AE7	6		KT1	67
	AE8	267		AE6	1200		KT1	228
GESTURE	M11	329		AE8	890		KT1	483
	M11	376		AE9	1001		M8	202
GESTURES	AA	690		AE10	723		B	559
	M11	402		AE10	688		TH	93
GET	AM	524		AE11	1002		M11	198
	EWGR	27		AE12	1275		CI	339
	SMM2	20		KT3	781	GIFT	UDH	24
	SEL1	14		KT3	988		AR	140
	PM	7		KT3	1110		AR	308
	PC1	26		M8	288		HP	72
	ML	18		B	704		DA	201
	AA	510		TH	256		L1	20
	EK	1		TH	345		T23	42
	PDG	31		TH	362		AK	57
	AT	93		M11	364		HAP	631
	AT	125		M11	373		HAP	2105
	PAA	46		UDH	88		HAP	2267
	EDS	13		HAP	1505		BR	316
	EDS	33	GHOSTLY	J6	690		EL	76
	ETS	32		AM	321		J6	735
	PSH	30	GHOSTS	AM	739		P2	128
	J1	21		AM	889		P6	147
	J1	75		ET	7		M1	852
	J3	93		AK	133		M1	846
	J3	151		HAP	1808		M9	51
	OAL	116		J1	12		M9	140

GIFT		
	VCS	19
	GK	73
	VP2	50
	VP2	58
	VP3	19
	VP9	37
	AE1	271
	AE2	253
	AE2	902
	AE3	202
	AE3	787
	AE4	385
	AE4	767
	AE5	311
	AE5	344
	AE5	461
	AE5	510
	AE5	644
	AE5	746
	AE6	553
	AE6	1225
	AE6	1226
	AE8	819
	AE9	295
	AE9	347
	AE9	410
	AE9	494
	AE10	1302
	KT2	292
	M8	218
	M8	231
	B	614
	B	668
	HIF	353
	M12	131
	M12	284
	M12	290
	AU	25
	AU	451
	WB	170
	M15	713
	CI	48
	CI	505
GIFTED	RL	405
GIFTS	UDH	33
	UDH	47
	STL	15
	CM	117
	UMR	5
	AA	377
	L1	38
	T23	6
	HAP	1022
	HAP	1358
	HAP	2454
	ODA	26
	J6	54
	P5	160
	M9	202
	HI	158
	VCS	18
	VP2	24
	VP2	78
	G1	14
	G1	462
	G2	635
	G3	32
	G4	1
	AE1	626
	AE1	913
	AE1	977
	AE1	990
	AE3	390
	AE3	557
	AE3	593
	AE3	626
	AE4	152
	AE5	66
	AE5	79
	AE5	134
	AE5	144
	AE5	475
	AE5	700
	AE5	712
	AE5	993
	AE6	323
	AE6	1205
	AE9	333
	AE12	1268
	OAL	400
	OAL	504
	KT1	134
	KT3	112
	M8	6
	B	48
	BP	196

GIFTS		
	M10	36
	HIF	18
	HIF	36
	HIF	216
	HIF	429
	HIF	514
	HIF	522
	HIF	613
	TH	6
	TH	15
	M12	365
	WB	495
	CI	490
GIG	PTS	21
	J6	433
GIGANTIC	BR	237
	J3	404
	J6	13
	P6	106
	G1	667
	AE4	255
	AE5	493
	AE6	785
	AE6	806
	AE7	913
	AE8	437
	AE9	951
	KT3	481
GILBERT	DC	25
GILBOAH'S	SAA	979
GILD	UDH	46
	SAA	915
	HAP	1231
	SKA2	4
	G1	503
	AE7	188
	AE12	121
	CI	546
GILDED	PPS	16
	AE1	1015
	AE2	611
	AE5	483
	AE5	729
	AE8	777
	AE11	1135
	AE11	1140
	M10	59
	M15	193
GILDS	P2	89
	AE4	165
	AE6	285
	OAL	280
GILT	EAL	10
	EK	44
	J6	66
GIRD	AE2	907
	AE5	410
GIRDLE	J6	809
	AE6	417
GIRDLE-BELT	AE9	488
GIRDLES	G1	322
GIRDS	HAP	207
GIRES	M8	202
GIRL	PCG1	21
	ELB	4
	T18	37
	T18	87
	J6	244
	J6	637
	P4	115
	OAL	883
	WB	39
	WB	51
	PWR	34
GIRLS	J10	447
	P2	127
	M9	13
	OAL	822
GIRT	G4	482
	AE4	752
	AE6	750
	AE7	258
	AE12	140
	AE12	1181
	AE12	1228
GIVE	UDH	86
	UDH	101
	HS	132
	AR	138
	AR	262
	RH	63
	SMA	24
	LC	2
	LC	68
	DC	43
	PWG	6

GIVE		
	LCA	15
	PRL	14
	PIE	4
	VHH	14
	AM	36
	AM	74
	AM	86
	AM	384
	AM	614
	AM	811
	AM	1079
	PMQ	42
	SMQ	11
	SEL2	10
	SCG2	18
	SCG3	10
	SCG3	27
	EMQW	15
	EMQW	23
	SM1	12
	SM1	15
	PLN	15
	SCD2	19
	PNH	22
	PNH	40
	EAZ	37
	PC2	23
	PTW	16
	EOE	25
	CM	65
	HP	185
	HP	234
	DA	139
	DA	192
	DA	194
	EUF	36
	AA	389
	AA	713
	AA	759
	AA	791
	AA	976
	PLB	10
	EPC	18
	MD	125
	MD	235
	SAA	131
	SAA	386
	SAA	451
	SAA	574
	SAA	670
	SAA	677
	SAA	950
	SAA	1075
	EK	28
	EDG	19
	EDG	28
	EDGA	17
	EDGA	35
	OE	7
	AT	27
	ER	35
	L3	102
	L3	127
	L3	130
	L3	144
	T18	25
	T18	85
	T23	42
	T27	110
	H29	21
	FS2	9
	FS4	2
	FS4	10
	FS4	19
	TA	272
	TA	503
	TA	339
	PAA	17
	PAA	28
	EAA	2
	GE	55
	HAP	650
	HAP	1128
	HAP	1316
	HAP	1587
	HAP	2266
	HAP	2421
	BR	42
	BR	50
	BR	106
	BR	175
	STS3	33
	STS3	34
	PMS	24
	SKA2	14
	SKA6	30

GIVE

EL	70
EL	106
EL	352
MS	25
ESH	19
ESH	23
ESH	27
ESH	31
ESH	33
J1	162
J3	43
J3	302
J3	356
J3	373
J6	300
J6	315
J6	481
J6	489
J6	735
J6	758
J10	128
J10	436
J10	512
P1	18
P1	99
P2	15
P2	85
P2	105
P2	125
P3	126
P3	144
P4	22
P4	88
P4	112
P4	127
P5	136
P5	220
P6	122
M1	252
M1	452
M1	652
M1	1091
M13	213
SFL	12
VCS	32
HI	27
HI	178
PLT	54
ELT	29
MC	63
GK	130
GK	155
GK	181
VP9	9
G1	44
G1	196
G1	625
G2	677
G3	62
G4	275
AE1	325
AE1	417
AE1	912
AE2	784
AE2	871
AE2	889
AE2	901
AE2	1053
AE3	114
AE3	189
AE4	569
AE5	456
AE5	707
AE6	102
AE6	347
AE6	828
AE6	1210
AE7	178
AE7	514
AE7	461
AE7	553
AE7	880
AE7	936
AE8	123
AE8	197
AE9	196
AE9	336
AE9	551
AE9	597
AE9	618
AE9	685
AE10	70
AE10	93
AE10	110
AE10	117
AE10	422

GIVE

AE10	596
AE10	871
AE10	891
AE10	1007
AE10	1035
AE10	1206
AE11	165
AE11	278
AE11	523
AE11	539
AE11	558
AE11	1159
AE12	63
AE12	153
AE12	1350
AE12	1356
OAL	69
OAL	232
OAL	241
OAL	422
OAL	509
OAL	514
OAL	573
OAL	661
OAL	748
AF	53
AF	141
MM	11
MM	13
KT1	569
KT2	295
KT2	387
KT3	2
KT3	151
KT3	792
KT3	1045
KT3	1054
KT3	1113
KT3	1136
TJD	130
TJD	135
TJD	187
M8	169
M8	260
M8	312
B	330
B	398
B	637
BP	8
BP	188
M10	67
CAM	171
CAM	173
CAM	263
CAM	334
CAM	379
HIF	28
HIF	150
HIF	186
HIF	205
HIF	250
HIF	315
HIF	470
HIF	609
HIF	681
HIF	702
HIF	737
TH	49
TH	69
TH	128
TH	137
TH	292
M11	128
M11	399
M12	258
M12	282
AU	120
AU	186
AU	586
WB	101
WB	138
WB	249
WB	420
M15	172
M15	431
M15	705
M15	718
GP	113
CI	491
ERL	5
EMKG	6

GIVEN

AS	89
HS	40
EMQ	4
S	16
EMW	15

GIVEN

RL	46
RL	94
AM	151
AA	300
AA	380
AA	964
PLB	35
SAA	466
SAA	484
PK	37
PDG	12
L3	174
TA	227
TA	272
AK	19
HAP	251
HAP	376
HAP	1585
HAP	2185
SSC	52
BR	165
BR	184
LS	4
EL	25
EL	87
EL	326
ODA	36
ODA	48
J1	150
J1	59
J6	291
J6	715
J6	813
P2	135
P5	66
VP5	125
G1	325
AE1	98
AE1	828
AE3	220
AE4	332
AE5	474
AE5	306
AE5	621
AE5	1066
AE6	214
AE6	933
AE7	883
AE7	1040
AE8	4
AE8	707
AE9	165
AE10	124
AE10	370
AE11	593
AE11	601
AE12	196
AE12	1108
AE12	1169
OAE2	82
KT2	291
KT3	437
KT3	679
M8	329
B	562
HIF	245
HIF	350
HIF	409
HIF	541
C	276
M12	734
WB	446
M15	50
CI	249

GIVER

EMK	23
HP	72
BR	316
VP2	58

GIVER'S

AE3	630
M8	219
M8	231

GIVERS

HAP	1358
G2	267

GIVES

RH	51
EIE	22
AM	668
AM	1171
PCG2	3
PNH	32
PAL	6
PCB	42
CM	118
HP	65
HP	151
PR	33
AA	362

GIVES	AA	346
	AA	437
	AA	461
	AA	713
	EPC	7
	MD	40
	MF	198
	SAA	632
	SAA	942
	RL	337
	MO	13
	L3	168
	L4	219
	HAP	664
	HAP	1405
	HAP	1713
	HAP	2040
	BR	293
	BR	343
	SKA6	8
	J3	5
	J3	238
	J3	253
	J3	358
	J3	289
	J6	174
	J6	339
	J6	396
	J6	439
	J6	640
	J6	790
	P1	51
	M1	455
	M1	779
	SLT1	25
	GK	65
	VP10	47
	AE1	151
	AE1	899
	AE2	390
	AE5	182
	AE5	460
	AE5	835
	AE6	1120
	AE7	50
	AE8	33
	AE8	812
	AE9	895
	AE9	1092
	AE11	1031
	AE11	1167
	AE12	1373
	OAL	190
	OAL	274
	OAL	508
	KT1	422
	KT2	354
	KT3	1043
	KT3	1086
	TJD	107
	CAM	53
	HIF	699
	C	403
	M11	68
	M12	89
	M12	192
	WB	479
	WB	486
	M15	557
	M15	561
	M15	621
	AS	30
GIVEST	MD	265
GIVING	PUO4	16
	OD	21
	TJD	39
	AS	100
GIZZARDS	HAP	2253
GLAD	HS	83
	AM	183
	AM	290
	AM	418
	AM	441
	PAL	28
	AA	238
	PRH	38
	SAA	792
	SAA	805
	EC	10
	TA	496
	HAP	1635
	G2	529
	G4	813
	AE1	912
	AE2	939
	AE3	227

GLAD	AE3	251
	AE4	223
	AE5	133
	AE8	352
	AE10	1118
	AE10	1252
	AE11	431
	AE11	767
	AE11	1085
	AE12	371
	OAL	204
	KT3	1094
	M8	218
	B	616
	HIF	34
	HIF	405
	HIF	611
	C	29
	FL	6
	M12	290
	M12	807
	WB	465
GLADDED	KT3	432
	KT3	723
GLADDER	KT3	145
GLADE	PMM	10
	G3	516
GLADES	AK	115
	HAP	1863
GLADIATORS	J6	353
	P6	115
GLADLY	J6	55
	AE11	165
	AE11	251
	AE11	279
GLADNESS	AM	1137
	TA	122
	HAP	21
GLADSOME	AE6	655
GLANCE	MS	24
	P3	224
	P4	117
	M13	196
	AE1	187
	AE1	710
	AE3	890
	AE11	702
	AE12	1364
	KT1	257
	KT1	279
	B	68
	B	389
	M12	26
	T23	10
GLANCES	J1	242
	OAL	645
	B	56
GLANCING	AE2	293
	AE5	674
	AE10	478
	AE10	670
	AE10	1102
	M8	107
GLARE	KT2	546
	M8	22
	M11	302
GLARED	KT1	356
	KT3	42
	M8	105
GLARES	AE5	365
	AE8	322
GLARING	AM	64
	T23	14
	HAP	29
	P3	1
	M13	31
	GK	43
	G3	658
	AE2	231
	AE8	39
GLASS	RH	78
	AM	211
	PWGR	10
	PCG1	27
	EAL	13
	HP	81
	SAA	529
	RL	301
	PDS	20
	EL	139
	J6	635
	M13	147
	SLT1	22
	VP2	33
	AE8	128
	OAL	342

GLASS	MFL	12
	M15	354
	CI	327
	ESK	1
GLASSES	H2	51
GLASS−LIKE	AR	208
GLASSY	AE5	998
	AE10	297
GLAUCUS	AE6	651
	AE12	517
GLEAM	AE2	799
	AE8	125
	KT2	245
	WB	434
GLEAMING	KT3	602
GLEAMS	CI	588
GLEAMY	WB	214
GLEAN	PDG	38
	HAP	1397
GLEANED	AE6	663
	CI	289
GLEANINGS	MG	37
GLEANS	PD	41
	G4	267
	AE12	901
GLEBE	L4	30
	M1	569
	M1	719
	VP4	50
	G1	97
	G1	274
	G2	321
	G2	552
	G3	255
	G3	260
	G3	785
GLIDE	SMA	112
	AM	626
	HAP	1863
	EL	242
	M1	242
	M1	411
	VP5	62
	VP5	131
	VP10	7
	G2	211
	G2	225
	G2	662
	G4	679
	AE1	232
	AE5	112
	AE7	51
	AE8	124
	OAL	292
	M15	548
	ESK	4
GLIDED	KT2	124
GLIDES	AM	491
	AA	258
	AA	693
	G1	334
	G3	645
	AE5	1125
	AE7	493
	AE7	1092
	AE8	968
	CAM	380
	M11	347
GLIDING	PMM	10
	P4	115
	VP9	25
	AE2	1075
	AE5	793
	AE6	376
	AE6	957
	B	68
GLIMMERING	PRH	8
	RL	5
	G1	391
	G4	707
	AE6	367
	MG	35
	KT1	231
	B	116
	CI	113
GLIMPSE	HAP	74
	VP1	57
	AE2	1027
	AE12	705
	HIF	681
GLIMPSES	EL	281
GLITTER	VP8	72
	AE11	901
GLITTERED	AE8	144
	AE11	11
	AE12	1365

Word	Ref	No.
GLITTERED	KT1	113
GLITTERING	AM	394
	AT	96
	HAP	1851
	HAP	795
	M1	182
	G2	705
	G2	725
	G4	151
	AE2	640
	AE2	913
	AE3	310
	AE4	386
	AE5	881
	AE6	285
	AE6	297
	AE6	301
	AE6	312
	AE6	790
	AE6	1189
	AE8	36
	AE8	698
	AE8	894
	AE9	22
	AE9	495
	AE9	791
	AE10	379
	AE10	581
	AE10	749
	AE10	1244
	AE11	669
	AE11	1132
	AE12	139
	AE12	193
	AE12	782
	AF	145
	KT3	450
	KT3	602
	C	54
	M11	128
	FL	259
	M12	305
	AU	171
	AU	320
	WB	383
GLITTERS	HAP	787
	G2	383
GLOBE	SAA	460
	L3	194
	OD	51
	J6	760
	J10	276
	M1	350
	G1	330
	G1	605
	AE3	836
	AE9	160
	M15	295
	CI	120
GLOBE'S	AM	653
GLOCESTER S	AR	235
GLOOM	AE6	466
GLOOMY	AM	513
	AM	954
	DA	105
	MD	284
	D	22
	SAA	526
	MO	25
	L3	223
	HAP	30
	ODA	1
	M13	47
	VP5	26
	G2	614
	G3	516
	G4	145
	AE2	841
	AE2	1001
	AE4	173
	AE6	208
	AE6	273
	AE6	340
	AE6	372
	AE6	550
	AE6	861
	AE6	1191
	AE7	51
	AE8	793
	KT2	581
	KT3	43
	KT3	218
	B	270
	HIF	460
	HIF	765
	M11	270
GLOOMY	M11	292
GLORIES	UDH	37
	SMA	20
	AM	416
	AM	544
	AA	248
	AA	731
	MF	110
	SAA	500
	SAA	958
	SAA	978
	SAA	1004
	TA	96
	EL	353
	VP2	62
	G1	504
	AE1	10
	AE1	41
	AE7	114
	AE11	511
	DO	91
	B	488
	C	709
	M12	710
	WB	442
	ESK	21
GLORIFIED	HAP	94
	VCS	36
GLORIOUS	HS	110
	SMA	11
	SMA	43
	LC	153
	VHH	13
	AM	70
	PAR	2
	PM	30
	E	6
	E	29
	EMK	17
	AA	260
	AA	598
	MF	37
	SAA	192
	SAA	935
	SAA	940
	TA	223
	TA	369
	HAP	1064
	HAP	2592
	BR	11
	EL	281
	P3	162
	P6	110
	M9	32
	M9	174
	M13	165
	VP4	12
	VP5	50
	G1	582
	G4	395
	AE1	923
	AE3	214
	AE4	939
	AE5	344
	AE6	677
	AE6	971
	AE7	383
	AE8	225
	AE9	494
	AE11	258
	OAL	247
	KT1	212
	KT2	457
	KT3	935
	B	337
	FL	256
	AU	194
	AS	17
GLORIOUSLY	AM	1168
GLORY	SMA	67
	VHH	56
	AM	1194
	EWGR	28
	PEL	25
	EPF	18
	EUF	28
	AA	307
	EC	7
	HAP	67
	HAP	77
	EL	210
	EL	274
	J10	256
	HI	135
	G1	444
	AE2	644
GLORY	AE4	340
	AE4	396
	AE5	724
	AE6	735
	AE6	1210
	AE9	258
	AE9	842
	AE10	1179
	AE11	1156
	AE12	1017
	MG	32
	LMC	10
	KT3	267
	HIF	681
	M12	121
GLOSS	PR	24
	SAA	784
	HAP	891
GLOSSED	P5	167
GLOSSES	MM	14
GLOSSING	HIF	203
GLOSSY	M13	113
	VP2	72
	KT3	52
GLOVE	KT3	36
GLOVES	PC2	27
	AE5	538
	KT3	912
GLOW	L3	100
	HAP	1850
	P1	256
	P3	237
	M1	152
	G1	579
	AE6	297
	AE8	554
	KT1	112
	M8	270
GLOWING	T27	129
	HAP	795
	VP10	32
	G1	605
	AE5	606
	AE8	595
	AF	70
	KT1	467
	C	122
GLOWS	M1	649
	GK	110
	G1	323
	AE8	914
	AE11	1046
	AE12	106
	M15	623
	J6	596
	G4	55
	M15	700
	B	641
GLUE	AM	577
GLUED	G1	511
GLUEY	AE2	534
GLUT	AE4	631
	AE10	873
	B	595
GLUTTED	MD	128
	AE7	413
	AE9	479
	AE11	615
	HIF	99
GLUTTING	AE7	1055
GLUTTON	RL	33
	HAP	2275
	P4	58
	P5	73
	G1	179
	AE3	823
	M15	255
GLUTTONS	HAP	2298
	G4	166
GNASHED	G4	653
	AE3	872
	AE8	303
GNASHING	AE9	69
	HIF	361
GNAWED	AE11	647
GNAWING	HAP	1364
	HIF	663
GNAWS	AE5	1029
	P5	232
GNOSIAN	AE5	403
GNOSSIAN	M9	3
	G1	311
	G1	415
	AE3	157
	AE8	224
	AE11	1138

GO			GO			GO		
	J H	19		J 3	116		M 8	305
	H S	128		J 3	141		B	168
	H S	148		J 3	296		B	670
	A R	65		J 6	252		C A M	201
	A R	126		J 6	308		C A M	203
	L C	21		J 6	582		C A M	204
	L C	30		J 6	614		H I F	259
	P W G	10		J 6	652		H I F	705
	V H H	50		J 6	734		T H	410
	A M	7		J 6	748		M 11	49
	A M	125		J 10	87		M 11	417
	A M	204		J 10	130		M 12	372
	A M	234		J 10	271		M 12	629
	A M	306		J 10	479		A U	128
	A M	368		P 1	65		A U	522
	A M	379		P 3	26		M 15	30
	A M	647		P 4	18		M 15	35
	A M	653		P 4	40		P T P	45
	A M	732		P 5	196		S T P	17
	A M	797		P 5	205		S T P	29
	A M	801		P 5	241		E R L	5
	A M	945		P 5	264		P M K	39
	A M	1213		P 6	177		E M K G	20
	E W G R	7		M 1	1053		E W R	25
	S M M 1	5		M 1	1086	GOAD	G 1	70
	E T	6		H I	90	GOADED	L 1	22
	P C G 1	31		P L T	30	GOADS	J 3	488
	P C G 2	19		G K	105		A E 9	834
	S C G 2	3		V P 10	84	GOAL	A A	835
	P A R	15		G 1	474		M O	7
	P M Q W	10		G 3	529		L 4	194
	S M 2	14		G 3	590		G K	86
	S C D 1	13		G 3	804		G 3	27
	P U O 1	12		G 3	828		G 3	165
	P U O 2	9		G 4	122		A E 5	86
	E S F	13		A E 1	671		A E 5	417
	E M K	16		A E 2	533		A E 5	426
	P T C	28		A E 2	746		A E 5	441
	P L G	10		A E 2	865		A E 11	244
	P L G	29		A E 2	887		B	657
	P O	15		A E 2	957		M 15	669
	P O	25		A E 3	127		S M P	5
	H P	29		A E 3	250	GOAT	A T	80
	H P	57		A E 3	292		M 1	592
	H P	154		A E 3	618		M 13	135
	D A	143		A E 4	328		V P 3	24
	D A	144		A E 4	548		V P 3	30
	D A	184		A E 4	549		G 2	523
	E T G	15		A E 4	615		G 2	544
	P U O 3	21		A E 4	777		G 3	481
	A A	133		A E 4	847		A E 10	1019
	P L B	47		A E 4	909		O A L	587
	E P C	15		A E 4	938		C A M	46
	P R H	3		A E 5	958		M 15	163
	S A A	617		A E 6	182		M 15	164
	S A A	625		A E 6	920	GOATS	A T	2
	S A A	849		A E 7	196		T 27	87
	S A A	925		A E 7	209		M 1	934
	P D G	20		A E 7	598		M 1	941
	R L	340		A E 7	620		V P 1	17
	P D	5		A E 8	223		V P 1	104
	L 3	99		A E 8	562		V P 2	38
	T 18	23		A E 9	208		V P 3	13
	T 23	47		A E 9	432		V P 4	25
	T 23	49		A E 9	510		V P 7	2
	T 27	9		A E 9	845		V P 9	41
	T 27	23		A E 9	846		V P 10	44
	T 27	30		A E 9	847		V P 10	114
	H 3	26		A E 9	869		G 2	271
	F S 1	16		A E 10	445		G 2	518
	F S 2	1		A E 10	525		G 2	530
	A K	193		A E 10	762		G 3	452
	G E	16		A E 11	271		G 3	469
	H A P	525		A E 11	279		G 3	477
	H A P	1415		A E 11	288		A E 3	287
	H A P	1744		A E 11	858		A E 4	218
	H A P	1828		A E 11	1242		A E 12	613
	H A P	2214		A E 12	119		K T 2	60
	E M I	5		A E 12	151		H I F	62
	B R	167		A E 12	352		H I F	440
	P D S	37		A E 12	981		M 15	117
	P P	25		A E 12	1274		M 15	460
	P P	29		A E 12	1372		M 15	695
	P T S	39		O A L	72		S M P	32
	P K A	2		O A L	272	GOATS'	G 4	14
	P K A	7		O A L	363	GOBLET	A E 1	1030
	E L	50		O A L	561		A E 1	1038
	E L	322		O A L	681		A E 4	82
	O D A	64		L M C	6		A E 5	704
	P S H	13		L M C	8		A E 9	426
	E S H	7		K T 1	553		B	609
	E S H	20		K T 1	558		M 12	330
	J 1	220		K T 2	139	GOBLETS	V P 5	108
	J 1	240		K T 3	852		G 2	266
	J 3	80		K T 3	873		G 2	771
	J 3	86		K T 3	906		G 3	584

GOBLETS		AE5	131	GOD		HAP	1208	GOD		
		AE5	310			HAP	1280		G4	558
		AE7	181			HAP	1281		G4	562
		AE8	363			HAP	1458		G4	586
		AE9	347			HAP	1537		G4	610
		HIF	644			HAP	1596		G4	632
GOBLIN		ETL	10			HAP	1848		G4	643
GOBLINS		L3	181			HAP	2233		G4	646
		WB	25			HAP	2250		G4	653
GOD		SMA	126			HAP	2320		AE1	112
		DC	16			HAP	2349		AE1	121
		LCA	42			HAP	2360		AE1	184
		AM	563			HAP	2387		AE1	208
		AM	658			HAP	2434		AE1	414
		AM	1045			HAP	2506		AE1	965
		AM	1095			SSC	21		AE1	1000
		AM	1115			BR	75		AE1	1005
		PCD	19			BR	99		AE1	1026
		PUO2	27			BR	160		AE2	998
		E	4			BR	180		AE3	47
		E	9			BR	207		AE3	112
		CM	119			BR	238		AE3	125
		DA	153			BR	293		AE3	135
		DA	154			BR	289		AE3	198
		AA	48			BR	303		AE3	208
		AA	307			BR	348		AE3	219
		AA	376			LS	9		AE3	478
		AA	418			EL	180		AE3	940
		AA	429			EL	192		AE4	78
		AA	536			EL	342		AE4	92
		AA	558			J1	169		AE4	326
		AA	580			J3	304		AE4	360
		AA	586			J6	83		AE4	369
		AA	645			J6	410		AE4	388
		AA	735			J6	676		AE4	402
		AA	758			J10	294		AE4	437
		AA	963			P1	73		AE4	544
		AA	988			P2	55		AE4	637
		PLB	40			P2	84		AE4	803
		PLB	45			P4	110		AE4	827
		PLB	47			P6	145		AE5	522
		MD	19			M1	25		AE5	680
		MD	127			M1	40		AE5	837
		MD	214			M1	84		AE5	950
		MD	215			M1	102		AE5	992
		MD	269			M1	233		AE5	1091
		MD	276			M1	289		AE5	1097
		MD	279			M1	591		AE5	1110
		PRH	20			M1	660		AE5	1115
		MF	137			M1	667		AE5	1123
		SAA	361			M1	684		AE6	15
		SAA	467			M1	713		AE6	55
		SAA	492			M1	714		AE6	70
		SAA	702			M1	727		AE6	79
		SAA	748			M1	753		AE6	83
		SAA	795			M1	778		AE6	121
		RL	41			M1	815		AE6	150
		RL	44			M1	841		AE6	154
		RL	48			M1	924		AE6	243
		RL	63			M1	930		A.E6	396
		RL	84			M1	943		AE6	414
		RL	96			M1	970		AE6	471
		RL	107			M1	974		AE6	550
		RL	133			M1	992		AE6	898
		RL	153			M1	1017		AE6	1015
		RL	260			M1	1043		AE6	1060
		RL	296			M9	38		AE7	95
		RL	312			SFL	13		AE7	289
		RL	375			VP1	8		AE7	298
		AT	28			VP1	59		AE7	516
		AT	78			VP3	95		AE7	543
		ER	6			VP4	71		AE7	843
		L3	104			VP4	77		AE7	915
		T18	9			VP5	100		AE7	928
		T18	18			VP6	23		AE7	1071
		T23	103			VP6	30		AE7	1081
		T27	18			VP6	39		AE8	49
		T27	49			VP6	104		AE8	85
		T27	122			VP6	117		AE8	251
		H9	12			VP8	33		AE8	265
		H29	45			VP8	51		AE8	339
		H2	38			VP10	87		AE8	364
		TA	449			G1	19		AE8	376
		EAA	9			G1	448		AE8	397
		EAA	24			G2	11		AE8	461
		AK	56			G2	535		AE8	480
		AK	181			G2	692		AE8	540
		HAP	59			G2	778		AE8	868
		HAP	64			G2	791		AE8	943
		HAP	80			G3	59		AE9	24
		HAP	118			G3	143		AE9	123
		HAP	203			G3	601		AE9	453
		HAP	219			G4	167		AE9	856
		HAP	972			G4	246		AE9	895
		HAP	1141			G4	324		AE9	973
		HAP	1198			G4	449		AE9	1011

GOLD			GOLD			GOLDEN		
AM	874		AE6	211		P5	42
AM	943		AE6	218		M1	113
AM	1003		AE6	304		M1	962
AM	1172		AE6	827		M9	124
AM	1187		AE6	833		VP4	10
PA	12		AE6	846		VP6	64
PNH	6		AE6	1081		VP6	88
EAZ	39		AE7	384		G1	113
EMK	16		AE7	572		G1	306
EMP	5		AE7	878		G1	399
AA	103		AE8	226		G1	430
AA	405		AE8	458		G1	440
AA	596		AE8	576		G2	135
AA	709		AE8	585		G2	188
MD	32		AE8	733		G2	266
SAA	293		AE8	824		G2	432
SAA	539		AE8	830		G2	466
SAA	543		AE8	870		G2	728
SAA	749		AE8	875		G2	792
RL	238		AE8	877		G4	71
AT	97		AE9	55		G4	153
L2	55		AE9	352		G4	208
T27	111		AE9	408		G4	279
EAA	12		AE9	488		G4	385
HAP	787		AE9	958		G4	531
HAP	1219		AE10	205		G4	813
HAP	1289		AE10	434		AE1	605
HAP	1443		AE10	691		AE1	626
HAP	1484		AE10	732		AE1	692
HAP	1852		AE11	104		AE1	915
HAP	2011		AE11	387		AE1	918
HAP	2030		AE11	508		AE1	935
HAP	2035		AE11	736		AE1	979
BR	313		AE11	1141		AE1	1013
PTS	34		AE11	1147		AE1	1017
SKA1	8		AE12	193		AE1	1039
OD	36		AE12	637		AE2	1039
J1	169		MM	45		AE3	455
J3	97		KT1	602		AE3	625
J3	102		KT3	48		AE4	82
J3	122		KT3	65		AE4	193
J3	358		KT3	69		AE4	196
J6	290		KT3	449		AE4	197
J6	413		KT3	475		AE4	198
J10	494		KT3	874		AE4	199
P2	91		KT3	910		AE4	213
P2	95		KT3	936		AE4	350
P2	99		B	609		AE4	704
P2	105		B	636		AE5	310
P2	109		B	714		AE5	410
P2	123		BP	57		AE5	459
P3	222		BP	162		AE5	748
P4	114		HIF	18		AE6	296
P5	154		HIF	166		AE6	551
M1	147		HIF	257		AE6	727
M1	178		C	54		AE6	818
M1	181		C	254		AE6	860
M1	628		FL	186		AE6	959
M13	107		FL	242		AE6	1070
HI	78		FL	257		AE7	192
GK	98		FL	259		AE7	335
VP4	36		FL	507		AE7	338
VP4	53		M12	331		AE7	383
VP7	51		AU	178		AE7	1111
G1	200		AU	180		AE8	432
G2	228		WB	469		AE8	488
G2	650		M15	477		AE8	876
G2	734		GP	70		AE8	891
G3	41		GP	82		AE9	131
G4	50	GOLDEN	AM	631		AE9	873
G4	140		AM	821		AE9	1092
G4	396		STL	15		AE10	212
G4	482		PFD	27		AE10	250
AE1	479		SCD1	3		AE10	379
AE1	678		PUO4	6		AE10	697
AE1	831		AA	66		AE10	1269
AE1	904		AA	202		AE11	110
AE1	905		MD	8		AE11	862
AE1	924		OE	28		AE11	1139
AE1	1036		AT	94		AE11	1143
AE2	687		ER	20		AE11	1174
AE2	738		L2	28		AE11	1211
AE3	80		L2	39		AE12	138
AE3	73		H9	25		AE12	247
AE3	595		H2	44		AE12	1365
AE3	599		TA	13		OAL	772
AE3	677		AK	51		AF	123
AE4	384		AK	178		KT1	215
AE5	114		PTS	2		KT3	58
AE5	147		ODA	73		KT3	458
AE5	326		J1	14		KT3	647
AE5	345		J1	129		KT3	534
AE5	704		J6	198		KT3	945
AE5	730		J10	68		KT3	1025
AE6	17		P1	98		M10	68
AE6	49		P2	119		HIF	58

Entry	Code	Num		Entry	Code	Num		Entry	Code	Num
GOLDEN	HIF	359		GOOD	PWG	32		GOOD	PD	53
	HIF	508			LCA	27			EC	20
	M11	128			PRL	6			EC	26
	M11	394			EIE	10			ER	18
	FL	256			AM	141			L3	237
	FL	261			AM	152			L4	275
	FL	528			AM	180			T27	59
	FL	576			AM	379			T27	77
	M12	526			AM	968			T27	81
	M12	527			AM	971			TA	220
	M12	694			AM	1050			TA	222
	AU	34			AM	1054			TA	499
	AU	83			AM	1067			PAA	40
	M15	137			PMQ	28			PAA	44
	M15	400			PMQ	47			AK	25
	GP	19			ET	1			HAP	78
	EWR	23			PEL	20			HAP	330
GOLDFINCH	FL	106			SEL4	3			HAP	357
	FL	445			PTL	2			HAP	406
GOLIAH'S	HAP	1172			PCG1	33			HAP	560
GONE	UDH	94			PAR	26			HAP	706
	PEL	5			PW	9			HAP	736
	ETL	27			PW	11			HAP	846
	SCG2	11			EMQW	11			HAP	850
	PM	2			EMQW	15			HAP	1242
	PM	7			EM	29			HAP	1383
	PM	20			ELN	20			HAP	1436
	PAL	6			PNH	48			HAP	1659
	HP	176			EAZ	3			HAP	1796
	EMP	9			PC1	18			HAP	1818
	PUO3	7			PAL	17			HAP	1858
	D	7			PAL	39			HAP	1969
	SAA	163			PKK	16			HAP	2132
	RL	175			PKK	26			HAP	2135
	DOD	9			EKK	16			HAP	2200
	L3	27			PTC	34			HAP	2201
	L3	175			PCB	4			HAP	2313
	L3	254			PLG	6			HAP	2327
	L4	178			HP	64			HAP	2382
	HAP	74			HP	173			BR	23
	HAP	384			EMW	2			BR	59
	HAP	1351			PR	27			BR	93
	PDS	14			PUF	16			BR	219
	PP	41			AA	82			BR	273
	PTS	1			AA	255			PDS	17
	EJG	3			AA	120			PDS	19
	J3	218			AA	293			PDS	31
	J6	410			AA	319			PDS	32
	J6	624			AA	325			EDS	22
	J16	73			AA	376			EDS	26
	P2	25			AA	413			PTS	24
	P2	93			AA	421			ETS	12
	P5	9			AA	504			ETS	21
	P5	94			AA	506			PKA	23
	P5	231			AA	508			EKA	39
	P6	154			AA	605			EL	153
	P6	179			AA	640			EL	180
	M1	745			AA	749			EL	249
	SFL	5			AA	812			OD	29
	SFL	7			AA	856			MS	22
	HI	3			AA	950			ESH	24
	HI	13			AA	973			ESH	35
	HI	18			ELB	38			J1	57
	HI	21			PPC	32			J3	253
	GK	122			MD	62			J3	438
	VP9	6			MD	123			J6	86
	G4	460			MD	150			J6	163
	G4	742			PRH	23			J6	203
	AE2	56			PRH	43			J6	428
	AE2	151			MF	60			J6	430
	AE2	771			SAA	35			J10	2
	AE2	918			SAA	107			J10	102
	AE4	117			SAA	154			J10	161
	AE9	9			SAA	209			J10	221
	AE11	244			SAA	285			J10	301
	AE11	1303			SAA	416			J10	502
	OAL	602			SAA	488			J16	38
	KT1	444			SAA	777			J16	5
	KT2	357			PK	6			J16	39
	KT3	834			PK	28			P1	119
	B	173			PK	30			P1	148
	B	201			EK	30			P2	15
	B	331			EK	47			P2	43
	C	260			EDG	40			P3	100
	M11	18			RL	26			P3	175
	M11	233			RL	29			P4	36
	M11	400			RL	44			P4	39
	WB	437			RL	61			P5	88
	M15	526			RL	122			P5	112
	CI	616			RL	221			P5	153
GOOD	UDH	10			RL	382			P6	104
	JH	3			RL	396			M1	115
	JH	7			RL	399			M1	144
	AR	26			AT	86			M1	151
	SMA	74			PD	7			M1	656
	SMA	77			PD	36			M9	6

GOOD		
	HI	181
	PLT	15
	PLT	17
	PLT	54
	ELT	1
	ELT	21
	ELT	23
	ELT	25
	GK	136
	GK	160
	VP1	99
	VP3	10
	VP3	54
	VP5	81
	VP5	101
	VP6	32
	VP8	157
	VP9	9
	VP9	93
	G1	382
	G1	660
	G2	167
	G2	301
	G2	321
	G2	791
	G3	680
	G3	768
	G4	217
	AE1	245
	AE1	278
	AE1	521
	AE1	784
	AE1	800
	AE1	909
	AE2	173
	AE2	525
	AE2	789
	AE2	860
	AE2	948
	AE3	238
	AE3	481
	AE3	656
	AE3	802
	AE4	568
	AE5	710
	AE5	834
	AE5	1007
	AE6	331
	AE6	895
	AE6	1128
	AE7	247
	AE7	747
	AE8	679
	AE9	373
	AE9	412
	AE10	872
	AE10	1254
	AE11	432
	AE11	544
	AE11	656
	AE11	711
	AE12	469
	AE12	1350
	OAL	248
	OAL	401
	OAL	435
	OAL	470
	AF	75
	AF	106
	MM	38
	MM	55
	DO	140
	KT1	292
	KT1	438
	KT1	481
	KT2	128
	KT2	220
	KT2	310
	KT3	142
	KT3	384
	KT3	526
	KT3	761
	KT3	825
	KT3	881
	KT3	1112
	TJD	7
	TJD	53
	TJD	135
	TJD	198
	M8	174
	B	98
	B	185
	B	331
	B	367
	B	496
	B	509

GOOD		
	B	513
	B	552
	BP	63
	BP	82
	BP	198
	CAM	172
	CAM	222
	HIF	129
	HIF	173
	HIF	525
	HIF	779
	HIF	783
	C	57
	C	281
	C	366
	C	405
	C	512
	C	538
	C	550
	C	612
	C	680
	C	683
	C	791
	TH	230
	FL	497
	FL	575
	FL	588
	AU	30
	AU	97
	AU	118
	AU	129
	AU	304
	AU	545
	AU	603
	WB	105
	WB	235
	WB	237
	WB	346
	WB	383
	WB	403
	WB	416
	WB	473
	WB	483
	WB	514
	WB	526
	M15	20
	GP	66
	CI	163
	ETP	12
	SMP	52
	PWR	22
	PWR	24
GOOD-FELLOWSHIP	SAA	527
GOODLY	AM	601
	AA	687
	MF	25
	SAA	461
	L4	157
	HAP	2435
	HAP	2570
	EL	196
	P6	102
	M13	74
	VP6	52
	G2	612
	AE1	373
	AE1	548
	AE5	350
	AE5	563
	AE8	216
	AE12	408
	KT3	64
	FL	37
	FL	66
	FL	104
	FL	240
	WB	198
	CI	50
	AR	256
	AR	265
	AR	267
	LC	59
	AA	386
	RL	194
	HAP	2095
	EL	88
	EL	229
	J10	539
	AE1	848
	AE7	279
	AE9	376
	AE10	879
	KT1	62
	C	782
	WB	242
GOOD-NIGHT	L3	96

GOODNESS

GOODS		
	EK	36
	J3	18
	J6	703
	J10	26
	M9	74
	AE1	169
	WB	317
GOOSE	J6	696
	VP9	47
	AE8	871
	BP	130
GORDIAN	HAP	2116
GORE	SCD2	12
	AA	1014
	SAA	709
	M1	596
	G3	344
	G3	741
	G3	759
	G3	838
	G4	406
	AE2	362
	AE3	53
	AE3	811
	AE4	987
	AE5	103
	AE5	433
	AE5	549
	AE6	1096
	AE6	1144
	AE7	923
	AE7	1055
	AE8	260
	AE9	957
	AE9	629
	AE9	1105
	AE10	1025
	AE11	56
	AE12	59
	AE12	513
	AE12	743
	KT2	577
	M12	100
	CI	607
GORED	AE12	1050
GORES	AE11	1115
GORGE	M8	397
	B	570
	M15	136
GORGED	L3	160
	P1	66
	AE3	826
	AE9	424
GORGEOUS	G4	120
GORGET	AE11	1022
GORGONIAN	AE7	476
GORGON'S	AE8	577
GORGONS	AE6	402
GORING	AE4	226
	AE11	1054
	AE12	161
	KT2	250
	M12	510
GOSPEL	HAP	724
	HAP	1509
	GP	30
GOSPEL-LIBERTY	HAP	987
GOSPEL-PHRASE	MD	191
GOSPEL'S	HAP	1174
GOSPEL-SOUND	HAP	1124
GOSSAMER	G1	543
GOSSIP	J6	587
GOSSIPS	HAP	2197
GOT	AM	535
	PA	7
	PCG1	9
	ECG1	3
	PTW	32
	DA	40
	PSF	47
	AA	20
	AA	171
	ELB	36
	SAA	89
	SAA	95
	SAA	363
	PDG	2
	HAP	356
	HAP	1914
	PSH	9
	EH	4
	P3	230
	PLT	37
	VP1	46
	G1	406
	AE5	222

GOT	OAL	754	GOWNS	OAL	36	GRACE	P4	70		
	KT2	200	GRABBLE	PD	60		M1	605		
	BP	58		PMK	16		M1	671		
	CAM	383	GRACCHI	AE6	1158		M1	759		
	HIF	188	GRACE	JH	15		M9	67		
	ETP	16		RH	7		M9	193		
	EMKG	4		SMA	31		M9	207		
GOTH	ER	16		AM	963		M13	161		
GOTHS	HAP	2508		PWGR	24		VCS	13		
	GK	47		SMM2	26		MC	19		
GOTTEN	J6	778		PT	27		MC	70		
GOURMANDS	HAP	2263		PA	23		GK	32		
GOUT	UDH	81		SEL1	3		GK	179		
	J6	520		PCG2	15		EHC	6		
	C	28		SCG1	13		EHC	10		
GOUTS	G3	467		PFD	30		EHC	17		
GOUTY	MD	182		PAR	11		VP3	121		
	P5	78		ECD	7		VP4	14		
GOVERN	AA	48		PNH	32		VP5	49		
	LS	2		PC1	28		VP6	59		
	HI	160		EAL	23		VP6	104		
	OAL	9		PCB	13		G2	229		
	KT2	143		PCB	42		G2	541		
GOVERNED	AR	112		DA	98		G3	18		
	SMA	94		UMR	3		AE1	40		
	AA	216		PUO4	26		AE1	116		
	MF	4		PUO5	25		AE1	688		
	KT1	483		AA	29		AE1	742		
	WB	546		AA	46		AE1	828		
	EMKG	38		AA	526		AE1	867		
GOVERNMENT	RH	54		AA	580		AE1	930		
	AA	93		AA	643		AE1	958		
	AA	141		AA	648		AE1	1032		
	AA	500		AA	831		AE4	200		
	AA	528		AA	865		AE4	301		
	AA	590		AA	972		AE5	79		
	AA	793		AA	1007		AE5	84		
	AA	918		MD	22		AE5	96		
	AA	977		PRH	30		AE5	145		
	MD	83		D	13		AE5	387		
	MD	125		MF	110		AE5	718		
	L3	202		SAA	50		AE5	724		
	TA	209		SAA	299		AE5	751		
	AK	90		SAA	319		AE5	1076		
	AK	104		SAA	397		AE6	65		
	HAP	2426		SAA	744		AE6	196		
	J3	44		SAA	857		AE6	647		
	J3	88		SAA	947		AE6	882		
	J10	27		SAA	1013		AE6	1181		
	P4	2		RL	412		AE6	1187		
	G4	310		L4	4		AE7	901		
	AE1	800		L4	151		AE7	1108		
	AE10	290		TA	69		AE8	204		
	DO	37		TA	203		AE8	400		
	BP	20		AK	136		AE8	506		
	CI	616		AK	149		AE8	976		
	ETP	12		GE	75		AE9	19		
	EWR	6		HAP	47		AE9	389		
GOVERNOR	CI	616		HAP	136		AE10	66		
GOVERNS	PAZ	25		HAP	162		AE10	706		
	AA	317		HAP	371		AE10	869		
	KT1	415		HAP	420		AE10	1035		
GOWN	AR	35		HAP	667		AE11	325		
	ECG1	10		HAP	1199		AE11	740		
	PTC	29		HAP	1211		AE11	769		
	AA	193		HAP	1252		AE11	1032		
	MD	306		HAP	1454		AE12	131		
	SAA	401		HAP	1570		AE12	743		
	ER	71		HAP	2096		AE12	1370		
	HAP	1387		HAP	2187		OAL	653		
	J1	22		HAP	2335		OAL	678		
	J3	120		HAP	2399		OAL	830		
	J3	166		HAP	2493		AF	51		
	J3	202		HAP	2523		MG	7		
	J3	252		HAP	2544		MFL	8		
	J3	284		HAP	2555		KT1	65		
	J6	621		BR	131		KT1	260		
	J10	148		BR	271		KT1	395		
	J16	71		PDS	27		KT1	596		
	P1	36		EDS	35		KT2	269		
	P5	20		PP	42		KT2	275		
	G3	25		PMS	34		KT2	327		
	AE1	560		EL	372		KT2	391		
	AE1	385		OD	53		KT2	394		
	AE4	752		ODA	51		KT2	413		
	AE6	750		ODA	63		KT2	526		
	AE7	258		ODA	76		KT2	625		
	OAL	90		J6	153		KT3	66		
	OAL	596		J6	201		KT3	383		
	KT2	566		J6	603		KT3	500		
	BP	82		J10	149		KT3	743		
	WB	37		J10	311		KT3	949		
GOWNED	FL	161		J10	405		KT3	1020		
GOWNMEN'S	SAA	956		J10	464		KT3	1129		
GOWNS	HS	78		J10	514		M8	66		
	PMQW	10		P1	229		B	29		

Word	Src	No.	Word	Src	No.	Word	Src	No.
GRACE	B	32	GRACE'S	UDH	7	GRAIN	G1	180
	B	497	GRACES	UDH	31		G1	219
	B	608		ER	18		G1	224
	BP	118		L1	38		G1	266
	CAM	374		T18	49		G1	275
	HIF	172		FS3	13		G1	283
	HIF	493		SKA3	10		G1	287
	HIF	612		LS	8		G1	300
	HIF	694		OD	4		G1	345
	HIF	749		P3	70		G1	360
	C	282		DO	150		G1	370
	M11	403		KT2	55		G1	399
	FL	157		CI	490		G1	594
	FL	178	GRACING	HI	129		G2	241
	FL	182	GRACIOUS	AM	1058		G3	797
	FL	313		ET	16		AE4	588
	FL	399		AA	319		AE7	1101
	FL	588		TA	21		KT3	963
	FL	598		TA	81		CAM	241
	M12	295		TA	220		HIF	775
	M12	304		TA	418		C	436
	M12	616		AK	56		FL	91
	M12	698		HAP	64		CI	502
	AU	204		HAP	1596	GRAINS	ECG2	16
	AU	228		HAP	2078		ELB	36
	AU	572		HAP	2272		HAP	836
	WB	33		HAP	2541		OAL	175
	WB	88		BR	160	GRAMERCY	C	195
	WB	400		EL	1	GRAMMAR	PUO1	31
	WB	447		J3	304		J6	583
	WB	454		M1	514		P1	133
	GP	3		HI	158	GRANARIES	HAP	1402
	GP	102		VP5	99	GRAND	EAL	20
	CI	7		AE1	710		PAA	39
	CI	43		AE1	732		GE	38
	CI	98		AE1	836	GRANDAM	J10	311
	CI	144		AE1	1027		P2	60
	PWR	28		AE4	62		AE9	94
GRACED	ETG	3		AE8	108	GRANDAME	PPC	13
	SAA	968		AE9	863		HAP	1443
	SAA	1047		OAL	155		WB	225
	J3	334		KT1	72		WB	312
	P5	253		KT2	430		WB	402
	M9	34		KT3	183	GRANDAME'S	T23	38
	AE1	862		KT3	271	GRANDAM'S	P6	128
	AE5	712		KT3	526	GRANDCHILD	CM	99
	AE6	900		KT3	696	GRANDEUR	HS	21
	AE7	1077		KT3	1113	GRANDISON	LCA	24
	AE8	952		B	2	GRANDSIRE	UDH	103
	AE10	1244		BP	139		AR	98
	AE11	8		HIF	731		CM	84
	AE11	266		FL	406		P6	136
	KT2	601		FL	471		M9	62
	KT3	108		WB	77		AE2	624
	KT3	548		WB	309		AE5	735
	B	319	GRACIOUSLY	TA	245		AE6	1056
	BP	162		HAP	1272		AE9	4
	M10	47		P1	72		DO	56
	HIF	438		VP1	62		TJD	98
	HIF	682	GRADUAL	M1	506		TJD	188
	C	611	GRAECIA	AE2	254		CAM	383
	TH	348	GRAFF	ESF	12		M12	733
	FL	169		VP1	100		WB	402
	FL	245		G2	41	GRANDSIRE'S	L4	220
	FL	576		G2	103		AE1	375
GRACEFUL	RH	24		AE6	1028		AE2	624
	AA	723	GRAFFS	G2	71		AE5	718
	T18	63		G2	96		AE12	522
	ODA	22	GRAFT	VP9	67		KT3	420
	J3	164	GRAFTED	G2	100		BP	20
	GK	104		G4	214	GRANDSIRES	AE7	242
	AE1	561	GRAFTS	H2	22		AE12	1198
	AE1	701	GRAIN	AM	1136		M15	674
	AE5	731		PUO5	15	GRANDSIRES'	G4	305
	AE5	732		SAA	333	GRANDSON	AE2	432
	AE5	780		SAA	561	GRANDSONS	T18	85
	AE7	84		EC	19		G4	305
	AE7	1072		TA	375	GRANT	PIE	20
	AE11	186		HAP	2276		EMQW	2
	AE11	755		HAP	2296		EMQW	19
	KT2	643		BR	164		SLN	11
	KT3	73		BR	260		HP	196
	KT3	115		EL	207		AA	795
	B	57		J1	202		AA	988
	HIF	107		P2	116		PRH	30
	FL	506		M1	371		SAA	587
	CI	223		M1	393		SAA	663
GRACEFULLY	E	16		M13	88		SAA	687
	AE4	21		VP3	64		SAA	767
GRACELESS	HAP	54		VP3	129		SAA	891
	HAP	356		VP5	53		RL	186
	M1	291		G1	28		RL	360
	G1	228		G1	109		L4	162
	AE2	775		G1	148		T23	66
	AE8	329		G1	156		HAP	612
	TH	132		G1	167			

GRANT	HAP	624
	HAP	773
	HAP	961
	HAP	1046
	HAP	1052
	HAP	1510
	HAP	2111
	HAP	2160
	BR	2
	PDS	23
	STS1	7
	J6	238
	J6	261
	J6	840
	J10	166
	J10	301
	J10	537
	P1	5
	P1	89
	P2	29
	P2	81
	P3	220
	P5	123
	P6	151
	M9	134
	HI	159
	SLT1	4
	GK	120
	GK	179
	G1	63
	AE2	210
	AE4	48
	AE4	630
	AE7	434
	AE9	7
	AE9	96
	AE9	114
	AE10	882
	AE10	890
	AE11	479
	OAL	743
	KT1	323
	KT1	346
	KT2	259
	KT3	155
	KT3	176
	KT3	234
	TJD	188
	B	37
	B	412
	B	434
	B	543
	M10	64
	CAM	105
	HIF	589
	HIF	692
	AU	472
	WB	92
	WB	295
	WB	301
	WB	496
	M15	398
	PMK	33
GRANTED	HAP	2058
	HAP	2430
	BR	248
	J10	177
	AE3	331
	AE11	192
	AE12	392
	KT1	211
	KT2	365
	KT3	187
	KT3	375
	KT3	378
	BP	196
	HIF	528
	CI	210
GRANTING	HP	121
	RL	111
	HAP	1051
	STS3	12
	PMS	6
	AE11	1165
	KT3	377
	M10	70
GRANTS	AA	383
	AA	385
	SDG	4
	L5	17
	HAP	1569
	P6	14
	AE4	310
	AE11	160
GRAPE	G2	129
	G2	132

GRAPE	G2	136
	BP	127
GRAPES	PAL	38
	H2	31
	M13	77
	M13	107
	VP3	58
	VP4	34
	VP5	47
	VP9	65
	G2	6
	G2	84
	G2	263
	G2	325
	G2	585
	G4	388
	G4	805
	M8	39
	BP	114
GRAPPLE	SCD2	17
GRAPPLED	TA	452
GRAPPLES	CI	281
GRAPPLING	AM	335
	KT3	57
GRASP	L4	61
	HAP	105
	AE9	71
GRASPED	J10	168
	KT3	843
	AU	272
GRASPS	AE4	354
	AE6	1076
	AE8	342
	M11	211
GRASS	AM	491
	L2	34
	T27	130
	H2	37
	HAP	225
	ODA	2
	M1	408
	M1	891
	VP3	8
	VP3	82
	VP4	36
	VP7	82
	G1	83
	G2	257
	G2	300
	G2	339
	G2	450
	G3	232
	G3	336
	G3	501
	G3	532
	G3	546
	G3	605
	G3	707
	G3	726
	G4	24
	G4	616
	AE2	647
	AE3	193
	AE3	310
	AE5	116
	AE8	280
	AE12	180
	OAL	336
	KT1	114
	C	563
	FL	7
	FL	40
	FL	67
	FL	69
	FL	91
	WB	6
	M15	173
	CI	89
GRASSHOPPER	OAL	307
GRASSHOPPERS	G3	510
GRASSY	AM	1030
	VP5	39
	G2	529
	AE1	298
	AE5	136
	AE5	432
	AE6	281
	AE9	207
GRATE	AE12	41
	B	227
GRATEFUL	SMA	49
	EWG	12
	SAA	341
	SAA	1060
	PD	11
	ER	65

GRATEFUL	H29	22
	HAP	562
	HAP	2232
	SKA5	14
	J6	457
	M1	767
	M13	74
	VP3	129
	VP5	3
	VP5	122
	G3	507
	AE3	184
	AE4	174
	AE4	897
	AE5	311
	AE5	369
	AE6	106
	AE7	765
	AE8	84
	AE8	250
	AE8	402
	AE9	337
	AE9	548
	AE10	235
	AE10	549
	AE12	214
	AE12	1372
	OAL	799
	KT3	348
	KT3	1132
	BP	89
	HIF	546
	HIF	561
	M12	212
	AU	448
	AU	570
	CI	502
	EP	2
GRATEFULLY	G2	744
	G3	154
GRATIFIED	HAP	366
	T27	121
	HIF	680
	FL	349
GRATIFY	PLT	6
	AE1	953
	AE5	686
	KT1	369
	TJD	129
	B	737
	HIF	369
	C	490
	TH	28
GRATIS	OAL	514
GRATITUDE	HAP	1351
	HAP	2464
	P6	114
	VP1	83
	VP6	96
	VP9	37
	AE4	781
	AE7	318
	DO	128
	M8	6
GRATULATE	CAM	12
GRATULATES	CAM	257
	M12	27
GRAVE	HS	90
	AM	402
	SEL4	18
	PW	12
	E	17
	PTC	31
	CM	134
	AA	987
	PLB	19
	MD	44
	SAA	359
	L3	109
	L3	304
	T23	81
	GE	9
	HAP	1453
	HAP	2402
	PDS	28
	J1	219
	J6	640
	J10	233
	J10	390
	J16	48
	P1	75
	P3	6
	P6	93
	G4	259
	AE1	719
	AE1	217

Word	Ref	No.		Word	Ref	No.		Word	Ref	No.
GRAVE	AE4	39		GREAT	AR	321		GREAT	HAP	82
	AE4	670			RH	17			HAP	144
	AE4	897			RH	39			HAP	908
	AE6	500			RH	68			HAP	1306
	AE8	456			RH	90			HAP	1361
	AE10	296			SMA	12			HAP	1567
	AE10	1306			SMA	97			HAP	1840
	AE11	259			LC	17			HAP	1985
	AE12	582			LC	24			HAP	2004
	AE12	1353			LC	63			HAP	2344
	OAL	96			DC	28			HAP	2433
	KT3	795			EWG	18			HAP	2463
	TJD	83			LCA	21			HAP	2513
	BP	194			LCA	23			SSC	57
	HIF	426			EIE	21			BR	23
	TH	167			AM	45			BR	48
	WB	318			AM	189			BR	58
GRAVED	MD	143			AM	274			BR	86
	HAP	893			AM	298			BR	128
	AE6	39			AM	321			BR	146
	AE8	930			AM	416			BR	301
	AU	458			AM	552			BR	316
GRAVEL	OD	36			AM	558			BR	324
	G2	293			AM	658			BR	333
	G2	476			AM	698			BR	340
	G4	286			AM	847			PMS	28
GRAVELY	EM	3			AM	874			PKA	42
	PLN	6			AM	1177			EL	1
	J6	760			AM	1212			EL	53
GRAVEN	AE1	38			PMQ	21			EL	97
GRAVER	OAL	70			EMQ	15			EL	288
GRAVER'S	MD	25			PMM	2			EL	359
GRAVES	HAP	1225			SMM2	6			OD	25
	AE4	356			EEL	17			ODA	23
	AE6	450			PCG1	29			J1	114
	AE6	456			ECG1	39			J1	158
	HIF	99			PFD	23			J1	199
GRAVISCA	AE10	253			PNH	23			J1	232
	AE10	263			PUO2	14			J1	245
GRAVITY	EWGR	44			PUO2	21			J3	101
	ER	26			EAZ	5			J3	131
	J10	51			ML	23			J6	130
	AE6	1156			PTC	39			J6	259
	BP	12			PCB	24			J6	769
GRAY	AR	26			PLG	33			J6	840
	G2	17			CM	42			J6	842
	G3	127			HP	55			J10	75
	AE9	839			HP	67			J10	94
	KT2	38			HP	167			J10	124
	M15	282			HP	240			J10	156
	M15	315			DA	157			J10	173
GRAYBEARD	ETG	13			EPF	7			J10	221
GRAYBEARDS	UDH	81			EPF	14			J10	234
	EMKG	38			AA	144			J10	421
GRAZE	VP1	11			AA	163			P1	189
	VP3	146			AA	650			P1	210
	G1	18			AA	901			P2	19
	G2	271			MD	16			P2	129
	G2	275			MD	64			P3	65
	G4	568			MD	167			P3	102
	G4	780			MD	185			P3	129
	AE1	262			MD	272			P4	5
	AE3	286			D	8			P4	31
	AE6	888			MF	30			P6	5
	AE8	270			MF	79			P6	136
	AE11	488			SAA	314			M1	703
GRAZED	VP7	2			SAA	461			M1	726
	AE10	669			EK	26			M9	18
GRAZES	AE10	1020			PDG	27			M9	163
GRAZIER'S	J1	164			EDG	3			SFL	13
GRAZING	G2	199			RL	20			HI	43
	G3	529			RL	91			HI	159
	G3	720			RL	131			MC	22
	AE7	685			RL	199			GK	139
	M15	18			RL	416			VP1	33
GREASE	J6	55			ER	57			VP1	36
	J6	594			L3	121			VP3	89
	P2	86			L3	204			VP4	5
	AE6	417			L3	237			VP4	39
GREASED	P3	139			H29	13			VP4	44
GREASY	J3	252			H29	14			VP7	23
	J6	743			H29	28			VP7	84
	P5	217			TA	29			VP8	7
	OAE2	41			TA	103			VP10	39
GREAT	UDH	17			TA	222			G1	275
	UDH	67			TA	233			G2	5
	UDH	71			TA	315			G2	235
	UDH	75			TA	382			G2	242
	UDH	103			TA	383			G2	462
	HS	22			TA	456			G2	669
	HS	146			EAA	15			G3	91
	AR	38			EAA	16			G4	256
	AR	49			EAA	21			G4	310
	AR	98			AK	78			G4	549
	AR	235			GE	44			G4	655
	AR	250			GE	61			G4	814

GREAT		
	AE1	142
	AE1	471
	AE1	708
	AE1	772
	AE1	872
	AE2	3
	AE2	804
	AE2	1057
	AE3	555
	AE4	203
	AE4	252
	AE4	300
	AE5	76
	AE5	100
	AE5	134
	AE5	141
	AE5	161
	AE5	556
	AE5	803
	AE6	87
	AE6	191
	AE6	196
	AE6	247
	AE6	286
	AE6	531
	AE6	1047
	AE6	1055
	AE6	1156
	AE6	1165
	AE6	1180
	AE6	1190
	AE6	1205
	AE6	1211
	AE7	4
	AE7	180
	AE7	297
	AE7	425
	AE7	955
	AE7	1047
	AE8	160
	AE8	217
	AE8	401
	AE8	926
	AE8	958
	AE9	4
	AE9	127
	AE9	317
	AE9	340
	AE9	352
	AE9	389
	AE9	396
	AE9	410
	AE9	857
	AE10	196
	AE10	243
	AE10	354
	AE10	431
	AE10	432
	AE10	446
	AE10	516
	AE10	616
	AE10	652
	AE10	787
	AE10	1067
	AE10	1170
	AE10	1180
	AE10	1253
	AE11	145
	AE11	198
	AE11	258
	AE11	263
	AE11	376
	AE11	509
	AE11	628
	AE11	661
	AE11	838
	AE11	1018
	AE11	1288
	AE12	343
	AE12	709
	AE12	797
	AE12	943
	AE12	1020
	AE12	1072
	OAL	231
	OAL	431
	AF	75
	MM	55
	DO	140
	KT1	58
	KT1	352
	KT1	600
	KT3	68
	KT3	531
	KT3	1026
	TJD	119

GREAT		
	TJD	129
	M8	58
	M8	198
	M8	299
	CAM	329
	HIF	8
	HIF	367
	HIF	378
	C	377
	FL	276
	FL	471
	M12	228
	M12	428
	M12	722
	M12	723
	M12	818
	AU	17
	AU	23
	AU	35
	AU	89
	AU	207
	AU	208
	AU	219
	AU	245
	AU	279
	AU	446
	AU	464
	AU	473
	WB	149
	WB	398
	WB	417
	WB	440
	WB	460
	M15	662
	GP	25
	GP	110
	CI	471
	CI	503
	ETP	7
	ESK	6
	AS	23
	AS	36
GREATER	UDH	97
	HS	24
	RH	97
	SMA	17
	SMA	50
	LC	126
	AM	71
	AM	188
	AM	339
	ECG1	4
	ECG2	32
	PAZ	19
	HP	132
	AA	20
	MF	34
	MF	80
	MF	142
	SAA	172
	RL	39
	L3	246
	TA	165
	TA	341
	AK	144
	HAP	52
	HAP	659
	HAP	1646
	HAP	1664
	HAP	1666
	HAP	2132
	HAP	2243
	PMS	29
	SKA6	30
	EL	71
	EL	113
	EL	285
	J1	162
	J3	8
	J3	124
	J3	214
	J3	442
	J10	173
	M1	222
	M1	326
	M9	85
	M13	13
	HI	33
	HI	96
	MC	46
	GK	122
	VP7	11
	G1	336
	G2	191
	G2	236
	G2	242

GREATER		
	AE1	281
	AE2	261
	AE2	264
	AE3	17
	AE3	345
	AE3	474
	AE3	481
	AE4	772
	AE6	76
	AE6	130
	AE6	184
	AE6	187
	AE7	67
	AE9	137
	AE10	617
	AE10	1054
	AE11	22
	AE11	537
	AE12	343
	AE12	635
	AE12	963
	AE12	1017
	AE12	1140
	AE12	1219
	OAL	231
	KT1	338
	KT1	437
	KT1	512
	KT1	595
	KT3	66
	KT3	152
	KT3	688
	KT3	792
	KT3	869
	TJD	141
	M8	299
	B	603
	HIF	213
	HIF	333
	HIF	378
	C	625
	C	711
	TH	393
	M11	214
	FL	182
	M12	781
	M12	827
	AU	168
	AU	245
	AU	389
	AU	456
	AU	563
	M15	654
	AS	100
GREATEST	SMA	34
	PWG	40
	EWG	10
	PUO2	31
	DA	149
	SAA	951
	J1	169
	J6	560
	J6	735
	AE3	937
	AE6	1165
	AE7	297
	AE9	335
GREAT-GRANDSIRE'S	AE8	73
GREATLY	AM	846
	AE11	762
GREATNESS	LC	3
	LC	38
	LC	137
	AA	222
	AA	372
	AA	485
	TA	45
	TA	56
	TA	94
	EL	262
	J10	539
	P1	202
	G1	62
	AE7	978
	AE11	558
	B	395
	B	583
	AU	89
GRECIAN	LCA	40
	AM	83
	EUO2	24
	POE	1
	HP	233
	DA	148
	ER	4
	ER	8

GRECIAN	T18	34	GRECIANS	AE2	1091	GREEDY	B	175
	HH	1		AE4	615		HIF	511
	J3	106		AE6	165		TH	194
	J6	267		AE6	698	GREEK	UDH	76
	J10	198		AE11	393		HS	50
	HI	106		AE11	623		AM	254
	HI	115		AE11	980		PTC	9
	HI	129		OAL	775		PTC	38
	G3	12		KT3	937		MD	161
	G3	141		HIF	250		EC	5
	AE1	61		HIF	352		AK	32
	AE1	139		HIF	496		HAP	2468
	AE1	332		HIF	620		J3	140
	AE1	387		M12	7		J3	338
	AE1	684		M12	95		J6	269
	AE1	883		AU	153		J6	272
	AE1	1059	GRECIANS'	AE3	3		J6	273
	AE2	145		KT3	1006		J6	277
	AE2	164		HIF	515		J6	561
	AE2	216		HIF	749		AE2	76
	AE2	416	GREECE	UDH	20		AE2	138
	AE2	430		PUO1	1		AE3	779
	AE2	439		POE	2		AE3	790
	AE2	524		POE	22		OAL	884
	AE2	536		EOE	4		HIF	229
	AE2	628		EOE	13		AU	135
	AE2	790		HP	207	GREEKS	BR	335
	AE2	832		RL	81		J3	109
	AE2	989		ER	26		J3	151
	AE2	1069		ER	52		J3	243
	AE3	70		T18	53		J6	24
	AE3	367		AK	120		HI	23
	AE3	420		HAP	1301		HI	53
	AE3	511		EMI	2		AE2	18
	AE3	648		J1	13		AE2	69
	AE3	720		J3	107		AE2	83
	AE3	819		J3	170		AE2	108
	AE3	837		J6	268		AE2	200
	AE5	68		J10	281		AE2	211
	AE5	412		GK	37		AE2	360
	AE5	810		GK	46		AE2	471
	AE6	146		G1	55		AE2	533
	AE6	346		G3	16		AE2	596
	AE6	688		G3	29		AE2	635
	AE6	792		AE1	35		AE2	675
	AE6	1149		AE2	31		AE2	1028
	AE8	16		AE2	100		AE3	373
	AE8	171		AE2	238		AE5	661
	AE8	492		AE2	779		AE6	1152
	AE8	795		AE3	382		AE8	168
	AE9	171		AE3	911		AE8	179
	AE9	193		AE10	143		AE10	87
	AE10	462		OAL	777		AE10	607
	AE11	375		KT1	103		AE11	412
	AE12	525		HIF	241		AE11	441
	AE12	796		HIF	371		KT2	633
	AF	138		HIF	626		HIF	137
	KT1	120		HIF	687		HIF	194
	HIF	105		HIF	702		HIF	35
	HIF	185		M12	27		HIF	65
	HIF	168		AU	33		HIF	77
	HIF	2		AU	288		HIF	521
	HIF	19		AU	436		HIF	530
	HIF	25		EP	3		HIF	537
	HIF	475	GREEDILY	A	11		HIF	666
	M12	55		P4	114		M12	101
	M12	90	GREEDY	JH	24		M12	207
	M12	98		AM	445		M12	291
	M12	805		AM	829		M12	791
	M12	813		MD	274	GREEN	AM	1136
	M12	833		H29	92		PC1	3
	AU	6		P5	69		PTC	4
	AU	62		M1	174		PR	3
	AU	375		VP2	91		PR	26
	AU	500		VP4	46		PR	30
	AU	569		G1	72		PUO4	37
GRECIAN'S	HI	179		G1	429		D	27
	AE6	91		G2	100		NS	2
GRECIANS	ER	5		G2	521		AK	5
	J3	160		G2	756		HAP	213
	J3	196		G3	222		HAP	2149
	J3	202		AE1	1003		OD	4
	P6	87		AE2	534		LS	3
	G3	238		AE2	814		J3	34
	AE1	653		AE3	538		J3	48
	AE2	36		AE5	417		J6	321
	AE2	56		AE6	5		J10	385
	AE2	148		AE6	323		M1	604
	AE2	161		AE6	569		M1	766
	AE2	332		AE8	414		VP1	24
	AE2	501		AE8	819		VP2	7
	AE2	556		AE10	1022		VP7	82
	AE2	561		AE11	1173		G1	425
	AE2	690		AE12	448		G1	465
	AE2	814		AE12	1017		G2	25
	AE2	1035		KT3	449		G2	167

GREEN

G2	198
G2	300
G2	426
G2	612
G2	619
G2	769
G3	232
G3	235
G3	263
G4	181
G4	185
G4	414
G4	496
G4	652
AE1	234
AE1	576
AE3	172
AE3	390
AE4	48
AE4	212
AE4	577
AE4	732
AE5	145
AE5	547
AE5	731
AE5	860
AE5	893
AE6	297
AE6	421
AE6	874
AE7	195
AE8	854
AE9	396
AE11	102
AE11	286
OAL	32
KT1	114
KT1	171
KT1	221
KT2	53
KT2	228
KT2	516
KT2	518
KT2	643
KT3	86
KT3	215
KT3	259
KT3	898
KT3	957
TJD	167
M8	38
BP	91
BP	182
M10	43
HIF	349
FL	11
FL	45
FL	62
FL	67
FL	75
FL	132
FL	170
FL	230
FL	243
FL	274
FL	278
FL	342
FL	349
FL	354
FL	396
FL	421
FL	430
FL	456
FL	500
FL	529
FL	559
FL	568
FL	586
AU	610
WB	4
WB	36
M15	302
SMP	54
SMP	56
EWR	8

GREENS

L1	14
G1	192
G4	364
AE3	35
AE8	835
AE11	98
KT2	62
KT2	619
KT3	975

GREENSWARD

G3	507
AE3	291

GREENWOOD

AE8	128
AE8	791
CI	80

GREET

SAA	628
HAP	1880
P3	51
M1	76
G1	560
AE3	227
AE6	5
AE11	280
AE12	119

GREETING

EIE	2
KT2	191

GREETS

KT2	191

GREW

DC	6
AM	12
AM	43
AM	794
AM	1137
PT	18
SEL3	21
PCG1	13
PCG1	14
CM	28
AA	88
SAA	2
SAA	101
SAA	236
SAA	314
RL	387
TA	219
MN	6
HAP	564
HAP	904
HAP	1164
ETS	23
ETS	24
EL	19
EL	195
EL	225
OD	40
J10	509
M1	540
M1	733
M9	78
M9	194
GK	36
VP8	54
G1	111
G3	723
AE2	18
AE2	701
AE3	33
AE7	682
AE8	308
AE8	385
AE9	1004
AE11	814
AF	66
BP	187
M10	84
M11	99
FL	81
AU	609
AS	100

GREYHOUND

P5	232
M1	718

GREYHOUNDS

G3	804
KT3	55

GRIDELIN

FL	343

GRIEF

UDH	89
AM	836
AM	959
AM	1041
AM	1140
S	1
A	1
PLN	42
CM	103
CM	129
CM	136
AA	445
AA	917
SAA	1070
SAA	1102
L3	11
L3	60
L3	66
L3	89
L4	47
T23	28
FS2	5
TA	1
TA	8
TA	23

GRIEF

TA	55
TA	62
TA	74
TA	76
TA	159
TA	273
TA	416
HAP	21
BR	239
EL	184
EL	356
ODA	42
ODA	55
J3	159
M1	497
M1	895
M1	913
M9	21
M9	85
HI	175
VP10	5
VP10	41
VP10	48
G4	537
AE1	276
AE1	657
AE2	123
AE2	1052
AE4	43
AE4	569
AE4	627
AE4	688
AE5	485
AE6	43
AE6	48
AE6	627
AE6	995
AE8	43
AE8	689
AE9	1048
AE10	275
AE10	510
AE10	557
AE10	706
AE10	866
AE10	1121
AE10	1247
AE11	93
AE11	142
AE11	227
AE11	529
AE12	75
AE12	224
AE12	235
AE12	607
AE12	614
AE12	876
AE12	1138
AE12	1165
KT1	52
KT1	54
KT1	63
KT1	90
KT1	242
KT1	416
KT1	569
KT3	149
KT3	854
KT3	869
KT3	875
KT3	1095
KT3	1105
KT3	1116
M8	249
B	303
B	686
B	695
B	701
B	724
CAM	162
CAM	190
CAM	225
CAM	312
HIF	488
HIF	581
TH	136
M11	23
M11	178
M11	379
M11	426
M11	433
M12	572
M12	701
AU	364
AU	437
AU	595

Word	Ref	No.
GRIEF	AU	613
	WB	235
	CI	450
GRIEFS	RH	59
	CM	31
	J10	385
	G4	673
	AE1	649
	M11	396
GRIESLY	KT1	150
GRIEVANCE	ELB	35
	SAA	31
	SAA	877
	SAA	906
	J6	539
GRIEVANCES	AA	747
	MD	224
	EK	46
GRIEVE	AM	966
	SMQ	5
	A	12
	AA	416
	EL	67
	EL	350
	J3	172
	AE6	1211
	AE11	1227
	OAL	707
	KT3	788
	KT3	886
GRIEVED	EIE	9
	AM	39
	SAA	615
	AT	14
	TA	84
	HAP	2299
	ODA	49
	MC	32
	J3	1
	AE1	681
	AE5	1133
	AE10	1166
	AE11	83
	OAL	775
	M8	350
	B	258
	B	293
	HIF	81
	HIF	789
	CI	525
GRIEVES	AE5	461
	M11	189
	KT3	675
GRIEVING	AE4	993
	AE6	238
	AE12	990
	HIF	34
	M12	493
GRIFFONS	VP8	38
GRIM	PWG	26
	AM	515
	HAP	1495
	J3	425
	VP9	5
	G3	145
	G4	146
	G4	532
	AE6	564
	AE9	765
	OAL	629
	KT2	579
	TH	113
GRIMACE	PLN	38
	EUO	12
	HH	10
GRIMACES	PSH	9
GRIN	MD	240
	J6	372
	M1	319
	M13	40
	AE6	779
	AE7	927
GRIND	HAP	2041
	P6	57
	AE1	254
	AE2	283
	AE3	336
	AE7	868
	CI	622
GRINDED	G1	360
GRINDERS	J10	365
	P1	226
	HIF	361
	M15	360
GRINDING	CM	54
	M9	52

Word	Ref	No.
GRINDS	P3	139
	G3	398
	G3	766
	AE3	823
	M8	137
GRINEUS	M12	361
	M12	376
GRINNED	HAP	29
	HAP	632
	AE11	1008
GRINNING	PM	18
	AE6	569
	AE7	786
	CI	180
GRINS	J6	94
	P1	50
	M1	287
	AE9	68
	AE9	1074
	AE10	1022
GRIPE	L4	75
	AE5	180
	AE6	479
	AE11	1092
	M10	25
	M10	34
GRIPED	TH	271
	WB	190
GRIPES	PCD	2
	AE1	66
	AE2	605
	AE12	640
GRIPING	H2	5
	AE6	303
	HIF	184
	WB	469
GRISLY	T23	76
	TA	200
	J6	153
	G4	145
	AE2	499
	AE6	542
	AE10	1193
	AE11	54
	AE12	1342
	KT3	594
	M8	245
	C	255
	TH	197
	TH	283
	TH	345
GROAN	AR	21
	PCG1	22
	SAA	199
	TA	283
	ODA	45
	J6	445
	G2	599
	G3	216
	G3	353
	G3	776
	AE2	435
	AE3	56
	AE5	801
	KT3	152
	KT3	358
	M8	343
	B	639
	C	103
	MD	34
	RL	87
	CAM	222
	C	95
	M11	379
	TH	266
	AE3	872
	B	290
GROANING	AA	663
	HI	132
	G3	291
	AE2	379
	AE5	1133
	AE11	205
	AE11	226
	AE11	583
	CAM	365
	AR	235
GROANS	SKK	8
	EDGA	40
	TA	67
	HAP	36
	HAP	2501
	G1	70
	G3	754
	G4	253
	AE1	681

Word	Ref	No.
GROANS	AE2	69
	AE2	319
	AE2	853
	AE3	730
	AE3	762
	AE4	651
	AE4	960
	AE5	208
	AE6	73
	AE6	316
	AE6	427
	AE6	557
	AE6	752
	AE6	1206
	AE7	20
	AE7	698
	AE8	592
	AE10	952
	AE11	693
	AE11	941
	AE11	1032
	AE12	504
	AE12	606
	AE12	1344
	KT1	91
	KT2	207
	KT3	920
	M8	366
	M11	436
	AU	65
	CI	611
GROAT	C	10
	C	181
GROATS	PSF	11
GROIN	AE10	828
	M8	176
GROINS	G3	440
GROOM	P5	107
	VP3	155
	G2	773
	G4	627
	KT3	444
	J10	262
	AE12	134
	M8	41
	CI	540
GROOMS	CAM	281
	RL	23
GROPE	AE8	341
	M15	421
GROPED	AM	728
GROPES	AM	929
GROSS	MD	43
	SAA	87
	SAA	115
	RL	265
	RL	322
	OE	25
	HAP	314
	HAP	1985
	HAP	2521
	J6	857
	P3	61
	AE6	990
	AU	338
	WB	130
	M15	383
	CI	135
	CI	145
	CI	231
	AS	34
GROSSER	HAP	1809
	M1	28
	M1	63
	C	329
	CI	499
GROSSLY	PUO4	17
	AA	782
	J3	159
GROSSNESS	AA	619
GROT	HAP	1783
	J1	10
	VP1	106
	AE1	235
	AE8	592
	B	112
	B	264
GROTESQUE	HAP	2338
GROTS	G2	661
GROTTO	VP5	26
GROTTOES	VP9	55
GROTTOS	AT	7
GROUND	AR	131
	AR	197
	RH	56
	SMA	6

GROUND		
SMA	14
SMA	62
LC	102
DC	34
SIE	15
AM	388
AM	527
AM	987
AM	992
AM	1132
PT	2
PTL	23
PAZ	10
EOE	12
HP	165
HP	217
DA	126
PUF	2
AA	374
AA	452
AA	1025
PLB	26
D	27
SAA	837
SAA	857
SAA	1108
RL	28
RL	42
RL	280
L2	41
L3	306
L4	283
T18	77
T18	11
H3	45
H9	6
H29	33
H2	85
AK	179
AK	190
HAP	223
HAP	575
HAP	744
HAP	764
HAP	771
HAP	1506
HAP	1733
HAP	1807
HAP	1906
HAP	1918
HAP	1981
HAP	2016
HAP	2159
HAP	2364
BR	242
BR	260
SKA1	9
ODA	7
J3	110
J3	371
J3	374
J3	466
J6	82
J10	250
J10	293
P1	220
P1	237
P2	22
P2	111
P5	80
M1	172
M1	366
M1	389
M1	579
M1	730
M1	742
M1	929
M13	139
HI	71
VP1	16
VP3	108
VP3	147
VP4	28
VP4	40
VP5	58
VP5	91
VP6	19
VP6	58
VP6	82
VP7	75
VP8	90
VP8	97
VP9	54
VP10	64
G1	28
G1	75

GROUND		
G1	81
G1	83
G1	99
G1	119
G1	123
G1	191
G1	219
G1	241
G1	261
G1	265
G1	315
G1	339
G1	442
G1	468
G1	506
G2	16
G2	30
G2	50
G2	87
G2	131
G2	155
G2	249
G2	254
G2	263
G2	317
G2	334
G2	347
G2	352
G2	373
G2	392
G2	399
G2	429
G2	450
G2	473
G2	476
G2	484
G2	512
G2	564
G2	575
G2	666
G2	716
G2	757
G3	98
G3	138
G3	398
G3	454
G3	507
G3	657
G3	693
G3	702
G3	749
G3	811
G3	820
G4	60
G4	68
G4	88
G4	117
G4	174
G4	191
G4	207
G4	391
G4	415
G4	472
G4	689
AE1	123
AE1	177
AE1	252
AE1	507
AE1	549
AE1	590
AE1	618
AE1	669
AE1	1031
AE2	230
AE2	234
AE2	516
AE2	703
AE2	757
AE3	12
AE3	39
AE3	52
AE3	122
AE3	291
AE3	502
AE3	615
AE3	664
AE3	710
AE3	741
AE3	831
AE3	854
AE3	911
AE4	192
AE4	219
AE4	293
AE4	642

GROUND		
AE4	738
AE4	742
AE4	762
AE5	58
AE5	101
AE5	362
AE5	120
AE5	378
AE5	583
AE5	588
AE5	641
AE5	683
AE5	1130
AE6	94
AE6	285
AE6	308
AE6	634
AE6	684
AE6	888
AE6	1023
AE6	1052
AE6	1228
AE6	1246
AE7	342
AE7	449
AE7	999
AE7	1005
AE8	112
AE8	149
AE8	238
AE8	257
AE8	304
AE8	324
AE8	466
AE8	473
AE8	485
AE8	493
AE8	769
AE8	790
AE8	801
AE8	888
AE9	162
AE9	202
AE9	207
AE9	243
AE9	449
AE9	527
AE9	580
AE9	607
AE9	645
AE9	723
AE9	868
AE9	906
AE9	913
AE9	959
AE9	1003
AE9	1016
AE9	1073
AE10	413
AE10	485
AE10	565
AE10	682
AE10	762
AE10	829
AE10	850
AE10	906
AE10	938
AE10	991
AE10	1028
AE10	1033
AE10	1060
AE10	1072
AE10	1183
AE10	1200
AE10	1222
AE11	7
AE11	53
AE11	90
AE11	126
AE11	138
AE11	206
AE11	292
AE11	528
AE11	611
AE11	647
AE11	796
AE11	846
AE11	863
AE11	899
AE11	934
AE11	950
AE11	959
AE11	969
AE11	990
AE11	1068
AE11	1268

GROUND		
	AE12	307
	AE12	414
	AE12	552
	AE12	658
	AE12	735
	AE12	740
	AE12	775
	AE12	928
	AE12	997
	AE12	1003
	AE12	1052
	AE12	1078
	AE12	1092
	AE12	1117
	AE12	1301
	AE12	1343
	OAL	180
	OAL	290
	OAL	606
	OAL	867
	KT1	113
	KT1	149
	KT1	215
	KT1	374
	KT1	446
	KT2	86
	KT2	200
	KT2	277
	KT2	419
	KT2	440
	KT2	534
	KT3	16
	KT3	365
	KT3	414
	KT3	457
	KT3	516
	KT3	598
	KT3	604
	KT3	650
	KT3	707
	KT3	897
	KT3	971
	KT3	981
	M8	27
	M8	38
	M8	67
	M8	89
	M8	95
	M8	101
	M8	149
	M8	178
	M8	191
	M8	391
	B	111
	B	130
	BP	15
	BP	30
	BP	59
	BP	158
	CAM	338
	CAM	363
	CAM	373
	HIF	72
	HIF	359
	HIF	798
	C	6
	C	16
	C	85
	C	164
	C	217
	C	269
	C	278
	C	435
	C	442
	C	494
	C	570
	C	618
	TH	91
	TH	129
	TH	144
	TH	196
	TH	209
	TH	266
	TH	329
	M11	79
	M11	411
	M11	439
	FL	6
	FL	92
	FL	145
	FL	149
	FL	182
	FL	261
	FL	287
	FL	418
	FL	580

GROUND		
	M12	87
	M12	140
	M12	180
	M12	187
	M12	195
	M12	352
	M12	446
	M12	474
	M12	502
	M12	521
	M12	563
	M12	723
	M12	755
	AU	138
	AU	406
	WB	6
	WB	185
	WB	216
	WB	255
	M15	70
	M15	338
	M15	407
	M15	446
	M15	453
	CI	57
	CI	384
	CI	502
	SMP	82
	PWR	3
GROUND-IVY	C	191
GROUNDLESS	AA	995
	SAA	724
	HAP	2356
GROUNDLESSLY	SAA	699
GROUNDS	J16	59
	P4	7
	M1	463
	VP1	63
	VP1	67
	VP2	71
	G1	132
	G1	141
	G1	194
	G3	349
	AE7	687
	AE8	619
	AE11	746
	OAL	54
	CI	132
GROUNDWORK	M1	220
GROUT	G4	239
GROVE	VHH	55
	HP	87
	DA	105
	SAA	1041
	SAA	1105
	AT	7
	T27	86
	T27	102
	J1	11
	J3	28
	P1	135
	M1	807
	M13	154
	VP2	7
	VP2	73
	VP2	87
	VP3	70
	VP6	14
	VP6	72
	VP8	31
	VP8	121
	VP10	10
	G2	444
	G3	336
	G3	516
	G4	798
	AE2	945
	AE3	393
	AE3	894
	AE4	663
	AE6	16
	AE6	159
	AE6	206
	AE6	273
	AE6	340
	AE6	369
	AE6	545
	AE6	639
	AE6	954
	AE7	961
	AE7	1064
	AE8	139
	AE8	166
	AE8	270
	AE8	794

GROVE		
	AE9	100
	AE9	102
	AE9	553
	AE9	793
	AE9	858
	AE10	1009
	KT2	48
	KT2	49
	KT2	63
	KT2	77
	KT2	145
	KT2	152
	KT3	898
	KT3	906
	KT3	1147
	TH	60
	TH	78
	TH	92
	TH	103
	TH	205
	TH	255
	FL	37
	FL	117
	FL	135
	FL	153
	FL	213
	FL	501
	M12	689
	CI	87
GROVELING	P2	111
	G3	13
	AE4	989
	AE5	366
	AE6	995
	AE11	127
	AE11	1064
	KT1	90
	KT3	598
	B	321
GROVELS	AE10	991
GROVES	AR	270
	DC	14
	AM	346
	SKA5	4
	VP1	6
	VP7	87
	VP8	82
	G1	644
	G2	3
	G2	613
	G2	663
	G3	235
	G3	288
	G3	312
	AE1	234
	AE1	972
	AE3	8
	AE5	329
	AE5	994
	AE6	914
	AE6	1038
	AE7	1045
	AE9	545
	AE10	274
	AE10	588
	AE11	205
	KT1	532
	KT2	53
	KT3	140
	FL	195
	M12	679
GROW	HS	24
	HS	76
	AR	18
	SMA	132
	AM	24
	AM	466
	AM	504
	AM	618
	AM	658
	AM	913
	AM	997
	EWGR	13
	EWGR	19
	PT	9
	SEL1	15
	PCG1	30
	ECG1	16
	SCG2	25
	EMQW	6
	PLN	17
	EUO2	6
	PC1	20
	PC1	29
	ML	40
	EKK	19

Word	Code	No.
GROW	PTW	6
	CM	31
	PSF	24
	AA	249
	MD	165
	MD	247
	PRH	6
	PK	1
	H29	90
	TA	7
	HAP	444
	HAP	841
	HAP	1165
	BR	72
	BR	237
	PDS	24
	PP	14
	J3	131
	J6	213
	J6	264
	J6	855
	P3	161
	M1	701
	HI	159
	VP4	45
	VP10	79
	G2	14
	G2	77
	G2	131
	G2	154
	G2	163
	G2	396
	G2	589
	G3	322
	G3	591
	G4	181
	AE7	624
	AE12	963
	OAL	222
	OAL	549
	OAL	622
	OAL	855
	OAL	880
	TJD	23
	BP	158
	C	172
	C	192
	M11	286
	M15	396
	M15	540
	ETP	43
	PMK	32
	EMKG	42
	AS	69
GROWING	AR	176
	AR	278
	P6	72
	M13	123
	VP7	40
	G3	336
	AE1	469
	AE2	590
	AE4	577
	AE6	810
	AE6	811
	AE7	682
	AE8	16
	AE8	709
	AE10	1214
	HIF	349
	M15	1
GROWLING	EPC	4
	EK	15
GROWN	JH	3
	AM	1
	AM	935
	PAR	6
	EMQW	10
	PM	1
	PNH	9
	PNH	43
	PLG	17
	PLG	19
	PSF	37
	AA	146
	AA	200
	AA	710
	SAA	9
	EK	25
	PDG	8
	L3	135
	PAA	21
	BR	207
	PKA	29
	J3	65
	J6	64
GROWN	J6	84
	J6	101
	J6	488
	J6	858
	J10	121
	P3	22
	P5	83
	M13	115
	VCS	24
	G3	60
	G3	782
	AE5	225
	AE10	1271
	M10	100
	M15	425
	M15	604
	CI	65
	CI	158
	PTP	51
GROWS	AM	111
	AM	304
	AM	337
	AM	420
	AM	573
	AM	911
	PWGR	10
	SCD2	9
	SCD2	21
	E	5
	PAZ	8
	ESF	20
	EAL	5
	EAL	12
	PSF	39
	PUO5	15
	AA	813
	SAA	932
	RL	10
	RL	159
	L4	24
	HAP	1936
	BR	82
	J3	495
	J6	139
	J6	584
	M1	316
	M1	454
	M1	743
	M1	769
	VP9	73
	G2	24
	G2	82
	G2	105
	G2	109
	G2	113
	G2	181
	G2	210
	G2	404
	G4	66
	G4	391
	AE4	252
	AE4	255
	AE10	303
	AE12	599
	KT3	1060
	KT3	1087
	BP	192
	CAM	354
	M11	118
	M15	302
	M15	309
GROWTH	AR	322
	PWG	52
	ECD	17
	PAZ	32
	SAA	675
	SAA	692
	EAA	28
	AK	147
	M13	58
	M13	227
	G1	317
	G2	2
	G2	140
	G2	340
	G2	504
	G2	510
	G2	605
	G3	320
	G4	204
	AE1	621
	AE6	785
	AE7	88
	OAL	66
	ETP	19
	PWR	15
GRUB	HAP	382
GRUBBLE	OAE2	72
GRUBS	G2	289
	G4	440
	M15	563
GRUDGE	PC1	28
	AA	186
	SAA	206
	SAA	682
	BR	126
	AE4	343
	AE11	251
	KT1	58
	KT3	1101
	HIF	250
	GP	47
GRUDGED	VP2	50
	MD	308
	HAP	1429
	HAP	2295
	G1	677
	AE5	296
	AE11	63
	AE11	510
	AE12	222
	B	176
	P6	170
GRUDGES	KT3	1073
GRUDGING	MD	58
	BR	62
	G1	140
	G1	186
	G1	315
	AE5	685
	TJD	130
GRUDGINGLY	HAP	2257
GRUFFLY	KT2	613
GRUMBLING	P6	121
GRUNT	PLN	12
	ELB	36
	C	732
GRUNTING	M8	26
GRUNTS	EDGA	40
	AE7	20
	KT2	207
GRUTCH	SAA	661
GUARD	HS	120
	AR	181
	LCA	30
	AM	410
	PW	2
	HP	169
	AA	990
	MF	105
	SAA	79
	SAA	133
	SAA	564
	SAA	696
	SAA	1000
	OE	38
	TA	17
	HAP	296
	HAP	2432
	BR	34
	BR	44
	BR	286
	SSH	13
	J6	366
	M1	122
	HI	100
	G1	33
	AE1	792
	AE1	802
	AE2	953
	AE2	1035
	AE4	589
	AE4	687
	AE6	405
	AE6	567
	AE6	777
	AE8	868
	AE9	200
	AE9	234
	AE9	292
	AE9	304
	AE9	431
	AE9	943
	AE10	583
	AE11	707
	AE11	766
	AE12	177
	KT2	73
	KT3	462
	KT3	526
	B	241
	B	262

Word	Code	Num
GUARD	B	287
	CAM	150
	HIF	293
	C	367
	M12	92
	M12	137
	M12	207
	M12	516
	CI	405
	CI	572
GUARDED	AE8	606
	FL	345
GUARDIAN	AM	157
	AM	893
	AA	233
	AA	853
	AA	735
	SAA	56
	SAA	571
	SAA	1126
	H2	85
	TA	387
	J6	410
	J10	466
	M1	762
	M1	917
	VP5	52
	G1	670
	G4	169
	AE4	873
	AE5	128
	AE7	845
	AE8	797
	AE9	545
	AE12	1113
	HIF	315
	AU	516
GUARDIANS	RH	47
	SAA	698
	J1	68
	J10	353
	AE2	221
GUARDS	AM	957
	PLB	13
	PLB	14
	SAA	307
	L3	247
	H2	35
	J10	25
	P4	122
	P5	276
	M9	104
	M9	127
	G4	110
	AE1	698
	AE2	330
	AE2	613
	AE2	673
	AE2	674
	AE3	514
	AE4	195
	AE5	335
	AE8	645
	AE9	221
	KT3	486
	KT3	552
	TJD	36
	B	591
	B	602
	AU	524
	WB	492
GUERRE	EH	6
GUESS	AM	1033
	PCG2	22
	EAZ	12
	CM	104
	HP	253
	PK	20
	HAP	1370
	HAP	1766
	HAP	2558
	PP	1
	PTS	22
	OD	19
	OD	20
	EH	15
	J3	135
	J10	483
	P6	138
	KT3	984
	CAM	190
	WB	233
GUESSED	RL	22
	RL	252
	NS	3
	EL	268

Word	Code	Num
GUESSED	ODA	19
GUESSES	EKA	6
	TJD	82
GUEST	DA	160
	T27	65
	T27	122
	HAP	1243
	HAP	1272
	HAP	1311
	HAP	1722
	HAP	2357
	HAP	2589
	BR	27
	BR	278
	EL	320
	ODA	72
	J1	151
	J1	207
	M1	185
	VP5	86
	VP6	95
	G4	544
	AE1	116
	AE1	811
	AE1	886
	AE1	892
	AE1	979
	AE1	1004
	AE1	1012
	AE1	1058
	AE3	290
	AE3	942
	AE4	14
	AE4	105
	AE4	117
	AE4	277
	AE4	467
	AE4	715
	AE5	123
	AE6	142
	AE6	462
	AE6	1242
	AE7	365
	AE7	385
	AE7	484
	AE7	509
	AE7	651
	AE7	929
	AE8	163
	AE8	245
	AE8	455
	AE8	476
	AE8	606
	AE8	688
	AE8	731
	AE10	649
	AE11	158
	AE11	633
	OAL	736
	OAE2	3
	MG	30
	MM	50
	DO	73
	KT1	369
	B	154
	B	332
	BP	44
	HIF	674
	C	260
	C	611
	TH	70
	TH	275
	TH	277
	FL	424
	WB	20
	WB	219
	M15	20
	CI	542
GUESTS	PFD	12
	EUO2	25
	HP	191
	PAL	32
	SAA	927
	EL	52
	EL	53
	J3	401
	J6	549
	M13	22
	VP5	107
	G1	228
	AE1	410
	OAL	734
	KT3	106
	BP	75
	HIF	804
	TH	251

Word	Code	Num
GUESTS	TH	346
	M12	215
	M15	133
GUIDE	LC	26
	AM	230
	AM	365
	AM	461
	AM	552
	AM	583
	AM	1046
	POE	1
	AA	254
	AA	380
	RL	7
	RL	225
	RL	277
	RL	284
	L2	7
	HAP	65
	HAP	88
	HAP	122
	HAP	133
	HAP	147
	HAP	365
	HAP	478
	HAP	541
	HAP	652
	HAP	679
	HAP	872
	HAP	919
	HAP	921
	HAP	943
	HAP	962
	HAP	1022
	HAP	1038
	HAP	1046
	HAP	1051
	HAP	1056
	HAP	1058
	HAP	1255
	HAP	1717
	P2	21
	P3	133
	P4	2
	M1	808
	M1	1091
	M13	56
	VCS	29
	G1	35
	G1	59
	G2	495
	G3	287
	G4	697
	G4	780
	AE2	50
	AE2	340
	AE2	523
	AE2	774
	AE2	946
	AE3	263
	AE3	361
	AE3	866
	AE5	171
	AE6	168
	AE6	482
	AE6	437
	AE6	644
	AE6	755
	AE6	1148
	AE6	1192
	AE8	663
	AE8	866
	AE9	252
	AE9	317
	AE9	502
	OAL	34
	OAL	560
	OAL	627
	DO	37
	KT1	12
	KT2	61
	KT3	473
	CAM	192
	C	208
	WB	8
	WB	230
	WB	259
	M15	1
	CI	198
	CI	518
GUIDED	AA	903
	AE2	335
	AU	378
GUIDELESS	AR	12
	AE4	679
GUIDES	AM	432

Word	Ref	No.	Word	Ref	No.	Word	Ref	No.	Word	Ref	No.
GUIDES	EUO2	16	GUILTY	L3	226	GUST	AE7	736	HA	SEL3	8
	MD	203		L4	112		OAL	856		SEL3	16
	H9	35		T23	54		KT3	231		SEL3	24
	HAP	471		HAP	814		CAM	263		EAZ	25
	HAP	675		HAP	1225		FL	139		SMP	13
	G1	320		BR	294		M15	202	HABERDASHER'S	EKA	25
	G3	457		J1	252	GUSTS	AE5	19	HABIT	HS	142
	G4	560		J6	458	GUT	J1	207		PLN	38
	G4	613		J6	833		J10	26		AT	110
	AE1	210		J10	111	GUTS	J3	460		BR	39
	AE4	223		P3	83		P6	39		EL	228
	AE4	239		VP4	17	GUTTER	EK	16		M9	66
	AE5	758		G1	550	GUTTERED	G4	418		AE1	435
	AE5	1072		G2	544	GUTTERING	AE3	871		AE3	778
	AE6	283		G2	727		AE5	261		AE5	469
	AE6	727		AE2	212	GUTTERS	EUO	18		AE7	226
	AE7	693		AE4	519		J3	318		AE7	1108
	AE9	577		AE4	789		J6	155		AE8	963
	OAL	4		AE5	307	GUTTLES	P6	51		AE9	891
	M12	771		AE6	390	GUZZLING	J10	392		AE12	341
	M15	372		AE6	541	GYAS	AE1	306		AE12	1210
GUIDING	AR	291		AE6	585		AE1	864		KT1	264
GUIDO	TH	152		AE6	771		AE5	155		M11	330
GUILE	HAP	52		AE12	1236		AE5	200		M12	578
	AE2	201		MFL	18		AE5	209		AU	264
GUILEFUL	G1	413		KT1	427		AE5	223	HABITABLE	RL	175
	AE1	1000		KT3	815		AE5	239		J10	1
	AE10	935		B	752		AE5	288		G1	327
	AE12	524		CAM	197		AE10	441	HABITATION	OAL	351
	M15	141		CAM	263	GYAS'	AE12	677	HABITATIONS	HAP	2252
GUILT	AR	180		CAM	314	GYGES	AE9	1026	HABITS	PRL	11
	AR	275		C	287	GYLIPPUS'	AE12	410		PIE	5
	SMA	86		AU	36	GYPSY	J6	699		L5	14
	ML	11		AU	472	GYVES	M8	150		HAP	1288
	CM	42	GUINEA	AM	690					J3	291
	CM	62		AM	821					P5	166
	CM	127		PM	15					AE12	1198
	DA	78		PCD	9					M8	142
	AA	185		EK	44					M8	368
	PRH	19		PKA	49					FL	247
	SAA	114		EKA	33					M15	155
	SAA	135	GUISARDS	PDG	2					M15	682
	SAA	148	GUISCARD	B	51					M15	683
	SAA	248		B	77				HABITUAL	AE6	1011
	SAA	277		B	97				HABITUDE	L4	293
	SAA	876		B	216				HABITUDES	TA	340
	TA	263		B	225				HACKNEY	J10	375
	HAP	49		B	263				HAEMON	AE9	932
	HAP	2057		B	465					AE10	189
	J6	396		B	534				HAEMONIAN	VP6	46
	J10	24		B	574				HAEMUS'	G2	694
	M1	211		B	591				HAG	ETG	13
	M1	323	GUISCARD'S	B	398					HAP	2021
	VP6	73	GULF	AE3	899					J6	276
	AE2	134		AE6	780					WB	224
	AE2	784	GULL	PDG	7					WB	312
	AE2	978	GULLED	AR	33						
	AE3	44		PCD	17						
	AE7	822		AA	965						
	AE9	181		KT3	392						
	AE10	1214	GULP	M11	222						
	CAM	123		M12	685						
	CAM	259	GUM	J6	599						
	TH	321		G4	236						
	AU	467	GUMMY	P3	10						
	AU	473		VP6	92						
GUILTLESS	DC	13		G2	190						
	DA	152	GUMS	EL	301						
	PLB	26		J10	319						
	RL	87		P5	173						
	TA	45		AE8	884						
	HAP	1978		KT3	194						
	J10	554		M15	584						
	J6	194		AM	752						
	J6	663	GUN-ROOM	SCD2	9						
	J10	89	GUNS	AM	219						
	M1	132		AM	364						
	AE2	975		AM	390						
	AE7	1055		AM	412						
	AE9	573		AM	478						
	AE10	892		AM	609						
	KT1	479		AA	131						
	KT3	353	GUNS'	SCD2	11						
	C	715	GUSH	AE9	1017						
	M12	726	GUSHED	AE3	43						
	AU	189		AE9	580						
	M15	113		AE10	1117						
GUILTY	SMA	18		AE10	1199						
	LC	76	GUSHING	T23	108						
	EEL	39		M1	388						
	PC1	15		AE4	40						
	ETC	27		KT3	923						
	CM	36		AM	985						
	DA	104	GUST	AA	20						
	SAA	38		OE	17						
	SAA	900		J6	74						

HAG	WB	319
HAGGARD	T23	33
	HAP	166
	HAP	2410
	G4	370
	AE2	86
	AE7	557
	AE10	942
HAGGARDLY	J6	601
HAH	J6	368
HAIL	MO	22
	T18	80
	T23	84
	BR	35
	BR	259
	G1	600
	G2	241
	G2	454
	AE4	171
	AE5	106
	AE5	613
	AE7	164
	AE8	400
	AE9	910
	AE10	1140
	AE11	146
	AE11	291
	KT2	541
	KT3	994
	FL	321
	FL	384
	M12	638
	M12	698
	WB	536
	PMK	17
HAILSTONES	PRH	34
	HAP	1915
	G4	118
HAIR	SCG1	10
	PM	11
	ESF	28
	CM	64
	CM	135
	DA	72
	L4	227
	L4	228
	T18	2
	H29	7
	J3	308
	J6	38
	J6	434
	J6	632
	J16	49
	P1	35
	P1	272
	P3	235
	P4	89
	P4	92
	P5	247
	M1	639
	M1	670
	M1	711
	M1	731
	M1	744
	M1	1028
	M9	162
	M9	195
	M13	27
	M13	156
	VP5	34
	VP7	88
	VP10	61
	G1	556
	G3	486
	G4	371
	G4	478
	AE1	438
	AE1	557
	AE1	667
	AE1	673
	AE2	182
	AE2	362
	AE2	544
	AE2	754
	AE2	765
	AE2	934
	AE2	1051
	AE3	40
	AE3	69
	AE3	92
	AE3	232
	AE4	198
	AE4	212
	AE4	405
	AE4	737
	AE4	752
HAIR	AE4	846
	AE4	967
	AE4	1000
	AE4	1008
	AE5	224
	AE5	841
	AE6	74
	AE6	351
	AE6	565
	AE7	90
	AE7	111
	AE7	548
	AE7	553
	AE7	563
	AE7	587
	AE7	802
	AE7	1110
	AE8	875
	AE9	635
	AE10	202
	AE10	277
	AE11	50
	AE11	109
	AE11	128
	AE11	862
	AE11	955
	AE12	155
	AE12	184
	AE12	236
	AE12	261
	AE12	314
	AE12	548
	AE12	885
	AE12	1228
	AE12	1255
	AE12	1259
	OAL	35
	OAL	138
	OAL	256
	OAL	374
	OAL	414
	OAL	570
	OAL	583
	OAL	596
	OAL	827
	OAL	838
	AF	134
	ETO	3
	KT1	183
	KT1	523
	KT2	50
	KT2	577
	KT3	44
	KT3	52
	KT3	207
	KT3	351
	KT3	871
	M8	69
	M8	368
	CAM	93
	CAM	224
	HIF	58
	HIF	301
	TH	108
	TH	146
	M11	394
	M11	405
	M11	466
	FL	351
	M12	312
	M12	385
	M12	391
	M12	545
	M15	318
	M15	477
	CI	151
HAIRS	AR	26
	M1	312
	VP1	39
	G3	751
	AE7	496
	AE9	890
	AE12	894
	C	119
	M11	358
	M12	618
HAIRY	G2	559
	G3	477
	AE10	302
	OAE2	44
HALCYON	AR	236
HALCYON'S	G3	523
HALCYONS	HS	144
	G1	544
HALE	P3	219
	P4	105
HALESUS	AE7	1000
	AE10	490
	AE10	577
	M12	616
HALESUS'	AE10	587
	AE10	596
HALF	UDH	103
	AM	485
	AM	995
	AM	1016
	AM	1119
	AM	1209
	PMQ	19
	PWGR	5
	PTL	11
	PNH	14
	PC1	1
	PTW	20
	CM	39
	HP	2
	PR	26
	EUF	5
	AA	313
	AA	830
	ELB	24
	PPC	12
	PPC	16
	PPC	25
	PRH	2
	SAA	30
	SAA	126
	SAA	1070
	SAA	1102
	PD	50
	EC	17
	L3	258
	L3	264
	H3	47
	TA	54
	TA	83
	TA	139
	PAA	38
	HH	23
	HH	35
	HAP	10
	HAP	141
	HAP	340
	HAP	433
	HAP	557
	HAP	1042
	HAP	1210
	HAP	2487
	BR	3
	BR	83
	PMS	22
	EKA	33
	ELW	7
	EL	201
	ESH	36
	J3	226
	J6	241
	J6	808
	J10	415
	J10	540
	PPS	10
	P2	82
	P3	8
	P3	125
	P3	199
	P6	130
	M1	572
	M1	708
	M9	63
	M13	90
	HI	123
	PLT	15
	PLT	40
	VP2	104
	VP6	26
	VP9	81
	VP10	65
	G1	50
	G2	521
	AE3	432
	AE4	551
	AE5	191
	AE5	242
	AE5	419
	AE5	983
	AE5	1102
	AE5	1089
	AE6	721
	AE6	853
	AE6	854
	AE8	129
	AE8	258

HALF	AE8	342
	AE8	517
	AE8	522
	AE8	674
	AE9	160
	AE9	799
	AE10	193
	AE10	309
	AE11	1165
	OAE2	11
	LMC	5
	KT2	559
	KT2	578
	KT3	21
	KT3	217
	KT3	372
	KT3	597
	M8	341
	CAM	265
	CAM	349
	HIF	295
	TH	85
	TH	194
	TH	428
	M11	95
	FL	82
	M12	294
	M12	336
	M12	669
	AU	112
	WB	15
	WB	227
	CI	83
	ERL	6
HALF-ANIMATED	HAP	314
HALF-BROILED	AE12	426
HALF-BROTHER	AE6	388
HALF-CAUGHT	M1	841
HALF-CLOTHED	AM	902
HALF-CONTENTED	AE12	904
HALF-CROWN	PM	24
	EMK	24
	PUO3	9
HALF-DISDAINING	AE8	863
HALF-NAKED	AM	902
HALF-OPENED	G1	595
	AE8	544
HALFPENCE	P4	56
HALF-READ	HAP	1703
HALF-SURPRISED	G3	147
HALF-THREATENING	AE8	863
HALF-TIRED	EEL	12
HALF-UNBURNED	AE12	426
HALF-UNSATISFIED	PNH	2
HALF-UNWILLING	H9	34
HALFWAY	HAP	344
	HAP	349
	HAP	384
	HAP	1108
HALF-WITS	PAL	29
HALIUS	AE9	1032
	AU	402
HALL	CM	75
	MF	48
	HAP	2240
	HAP	2299
	PKA	9
	J1	193
	J6	101
	J16	32
	AE1	84
	AE1	202
	AE1	1020
	AE3	454
	AE7	929
	AE8	473
	AE10	2
	AE11	363
	AE11	587
	OAL	86
	KT3	416
	KT3	469
	KT3	918
	HIF	715
	C	17
	C	407
	C	430
	C	443
	C	747
	M11	335
	M12	336
	WB	270
	CI	581
	CI	607
HALLOWED	SMA	62
	AM	914

HALLOWED	HAP	2266
	VP5	102
	AE1	399
	AE2	684
	AE2	970
	AE4	742
	AE5	40
	AE5	101
	AE12	1248
	KT3	197
	CAM	296
	WB	33
	AS	45
HALLS	AE1	901
	AE2	663
	WB	30
HALTER	J6	43
	J6	729
HALTING	MD	320
	SAA	735
	KT3	613
HALVES	SAA	366
	EL	190
HALYS	AE9	1030
HAMBURG	AM	569
HAMLETS	KT1	138
HAMMER	J10	91
	AE7	875
HAMMERS	J6	569
	G2	788
	G4	252
	AE8	555
	AE8	594
	KT3	460
HAMMON'S	J6	717
HAMSTRINGED	AE9	1026
	AE10	991
HAND	JH	5
	HS	59
	AR	10
	AR	92
	AM	34
	AM	156
	AM	583
	AM	585
	AM	700
	AM	930
	AM	1058
	PA	36
	SEL2	7
	SEL3	15
	SCD1	22
	PC1	6
	ML	54
	ML	6
	EKK	2
	CM	3
	CM	56
	HP	80
	HP	139
	HP	257
	AA	80
	AA	595
	AA	844
	PRH	25
	PRH	37
	MF	52
	MF	108
	MF	120
	MF	129
	SAA	145
	SAA	476
	SAA	778
	EDG	11
	EDG	17
	RL	246
	RL	268
	RL	400
	OE	52
	AT	33
	ER	58
	ER	66
	T18	5
	L5	18
	T27	93
	TA	111
	TA	229
	TA	232
	TA	379
	TA	395
	TA	516
	PAA	36
	AK	124
	AK	130
	HH	7
	HAP	127

HAND	HAP	186
	HAP	832
	HAP	866
	HAP	893
	HAP	1094
	HAP	1403
	HAP	1783
	HAP	1995
	BR	178
	BR	257
	BR	360
	EDS	5
	PTS	11
	ETS	7
	STS3	5
	EL	221
	J3	183
	J3	224
	J3	230
	J6	824
	J10	188
	J10	267
	J10	310
	J10	343
	J10	391
	P3	39
	P3	103
	P3	203
	P3	218
	P4	16
	P4	23
	P5	54
	P5	148
	P6	4
	P6	48
	P6	60
	P6	164
	M1	256
	M1	265
	M1	343
	M1	450
	M1	577
	M1	811
	M1	926
	M9	141
	M13	38
	M13	104
	M13	111
	VCS	15
	VCS	25
	HI	46
	HI	65
	GK	105
	GK	115
	GK	137
	GK	177
	VP3	66
	VP6	93
	VP7	21
	G1	402
	G2	63
	G2	344
	G2	502
	G2	641
	G2	764
	G3	280
	G3	294
	G3	498
	G3	604
	G3	691
	G3	736
	G3	798
	G4	169
	G4	513
	AE1	115
	AE1	314
	AE1	439
	AE1	683
	AE1	862
	AE2	302
	AE2	387
	AE2	432
	AE2	605
	AE2	742
	AE2	753
	AE2	806
	AE2	914
	AE2	966
	AE2	984
	AE3	532
	AE3	802
	AE3	818
	AE3	832
	AE4	194
	AE4	354
	AE4	455

Word	Code	No.	Word	Code	No.	Word	Code	No.
HAND	AE4	891	HAND	AE12	483	HAND	M11	211
	AE5	50		AE12	485		M11	254
	AE5	250		AE12	492		M11	318
	AE5	314		AE12	515		FL	188
	AE5	491		AE12	538		FL	267
	AE5	494		AE12	577		FL	340
	AE5	585		AE12	639		FL	359
	AE5	609		AE12	647		FL	398
	AE5	897		AE12	677		FL	443
	AE6	90		AE12	710		FL	511
	AE6	189		AE12	758		FL	515
	AE6	220		AE12	770		M12	93
	AE6	361		AE12	790		M12	146
	AE6	504		AE12	915		M12	165
	AE6	674		AE12	1036		M12	328
	AE6	947		AE12	1065		M12	346
	AE6	1104		AE12	1073		M12	381
	AE7	86		AE12	1128		M12	437
	AE7	256		AE12	1229		M12	469
	AE7	444		AE12	1361		M12	504
	AE7	470		OAL	160		M12	516
	AE7	637		OAL	176		M12	517
	AE7	682		OAL	210		M12	560
	AE7	710		OAL	361		M12	566
	AE8	153		OAL	337		M12	609
	AE8	165		OAL	417		M12	655
	AE8	169		OAL	565		M12	809
	AE8	525		OAL	648		AU	179
	AE8	637		OAL	783		AU	272
	AE8	738		OAL	787		AU	286
	AE8	850		OAE2	6		AU	360
	AE9	82		OAE2	22		AU	406
	AE9	85		OAE2	28		AU	458
	AE9	111		OAE2	45		AU	588
	AE9	386		OAE2	56		AU	594
	AE9	633		AF	72		WB	95
	AE9	712		AF	137		WB	217
	AE9	752		LMC	8		WB	250
	AE9	780		DO	48		WB	514
	AE9	785		DO	59		M15	326
	AE9	787		KT1	192		M15	387
	AE9	937		KT1	354		GP	62
	AE9	1031		KT1	416		CI	197
	AE10	231		KT1	550		CI	237
	AE10	320		KT1	584		CI	404
	AE10	463		KT2	146		CI	456
	AE10	470		KT2	460		PMK	16
	AE10	472		KT2	511	HANDED	DHP	25
	AE10	492		KT2	656	HANDERS	RL	361
	AE10	551		KT3	400	HANDICRAFTS	G1	189
	AE10	582		KT3	494	HANDLE	J6	154
	AE10	624		KT3	507		VP5	138
	AE10	714		KT3	707		OAE2	30
	AE10	720		KT3	802		BP	73
	AE10	745		KT3	843		CI	599
	AE10	772		KT3	899	HANDLES	J6	144
	AE10	797		KT3	1140		VP3	67
	AE10	904		TJD	176	HANDLING	J6	744
	AE10	929		M8	10		J10	488
	AE10	1061		M8	73		G2	335
	AE10	1069		M8	192	HANDMAID	AM	617
	AE10	1095		M8	198		T27	112
	AE10	1168		M8	205		AE3	423
	AE10	1180		M8	267	HANDMAIDS	J6	629
	AE10	1192		M8	291		AE1	984
	AE10	1302		M8	340		AE9	360
	AE11	150		B	79	HANDMILLS	G1	370
	AE11	214		B	322	HANDS	LC	65
	AE11	277		B	508		PIE	29
	AE11	338		B	628		AM	573
	AE11	379		M10	78		AM	1131
	AE11	429		CAM	200		EEL	36
	AE11	445		CAM	279		SCG1	12
	AE11	499		CAM	366		SM2	3
	AE11	552		HIF	21		PCD	1
	AE11	593		HIF	42		PUO1	41
	AE11	606		HIF	80		ENH	21
	AE11	673		HIF	230		PC2	34
	AE11	678		HIF	280		CM	7
	AE11	800		HIF	291		CM	96
	AE11	861		HIF	301		CM	112
	AE11	885		HIF	395		CM	122
	AE11	891		HIF	433		HP	163
	AE11	904		HIF	458		HP	173
	AE11	995		HIF	470		DA	108
	AE11	1009		HIF	474		DA	125
	AE11	1079		HIF	517		DA	146
	AE12	20		HIF	678		EPF	9
	AE12	147		HIF	763		AA	64
	AE12	152		HIF	780		AA	189
	AE12	250		HIF	786		AA	340
	AE12	311		C	124		AA	728
	AE12	418		C	172		AA	982
	AE12	450		C	729		MD	182
	AE12	457		M11	77		MD	197
	AE12	478		M11	78		SAA	680

HANDS			HANDS			HANDS		
L4	38		AE4	82		KT3	912	
L4	60		AE4	138		M8	165	
L4	69		AE4	209		M8	333	
L4	72		AE4	306		B	6	
L4	101		AE4	618		B	654	
L4	276		AE4	749		B	713	
T18	10		AE4	940		BP	124	
T18	11		AE4	953		BP	128	
H29	6		AE5	303		M10	32	
TA	363		AE5	334		M10	85	
TA	453		AE5	353		CAM	91	
AK	139		AE5	469		CAM	206	
HAP	272		AE5	536		HIF	133	
HAP	494		AE5	544		HIF	247	
HAP	1164		AE5	592		HIF	381	
HAP	1357		AE5	649		HIF	554	
HAP	1640		AE5	829		HIF	610	
HAP	1868		AE5	837		HIF	615	
HAP	2290		AE5	858		HIF	635	
BR	273		AE5	900		HIF	684	
BR	297		AE5	934		TH	111	
PDS	18		AE5	1013		TH	122	
ODA	12		AE5	1108		TH	175	
PSH	4		AE5	1119		M11	221	
J3	325		AE6	50		M11	390	
J6	401		AE6	106		M11	467	
J6	511		AE6	401		FL	83	
J6	678		AE6	432		FL	281	
J6	778		AE6	858		M12	39	
J10	88		AE7	325		M12	364	
J10	363		AE7	475		M12	448	
J16	64		AE8	220		M12	499	
P2	73		AE8	373		M12	774	
P3	149		AE8	384		AU	7	
P3	216		AE8	389		AU	12	
P5	24		AE8	564		AU	327	
P5	200		AE8	587		AU	551	
P6	159		AE8	594		AU	552	
M1	182		AE8	611		AU	607	
M1	694		AE8	823		WB	451	
M1	874		AE8	884		M15	350	
M1	890		AE9	17		CI	155	
M1	1032		AE9	27		CI	336	
M9	50		AE9	181		CI	401	
HI	91		AE9	182		ERL	10	
HI	118		AE9	344	HANDSOME	EWG	17	
HI	171		AE9	853		T27	65	
GK	26		AE9	856		J10	501	
VP6	29		AE9	980		WB	129	
VP6	37		AE10	192	HANDY	J3	422	
VP9	83		AE10	282		BP	61	
G1	25		AE10	393	HANG	UDH	84	
G1	292		AE10	520		SEL4	9	
G1	429		AE10	526		SCD2	3	
G2	408		AE10	617		PSF	7	
G2	415		AE10	692		EUF	32	
G2	632		AE10	793		AA	859	
G3	62		AE10	836		PK	42	
G3	68		AE10	942		EDG	38	
G3	695		AE10	981		L2	28	
G4	506		AE10	1204		T23	59	
G4	658		AE10	1242		T27	23	
G4	720		AE11	100		T27	83	
AE1	136		AE11	106		HAP	1675	
AE1	144		AE11	115		HAP	2011	
AE1	207		AE11	120		J6	321	
AE1	690		AE11	726		J16	15	
AE1	724		AE11	1189		P1	171	
AE1	826		AE11	1272		P3	78	
AE1	982		AE12	292		P5	10	
AE2	198		AE12	333		P6	109	
AE2	206		AE12	470		M13	153	
AE2	222		AE12	572		VP1	109	
AE2	252		AE12	588		VP7	34	
AE2	255		AE12	618		G3	565	
AE2	290		AE12	625		AE4	714	
AE2	316		AE12	633		AE7	679	
AE2	439		AE12	636		OAL	876	
AE2	546		AE12	850		PMK	32	
AE2	582		AE12	880	HANGED	SAA	435	
AE2	630		AE12	978		SAA	499	
AE2	872		AE12	1029		EDG	25	
AE2	936		AE12	1116		AT	97	
AE2	948		AE12	1157	HANGING	SAA	433	
AE2	975		AE12	1289		EDG	32	
AE2	1042		OAL	14		L4	160	
AE3	60		OAE2	12		HAP	1931	
AE3	111		KT1	44		P3	78	
AE3	178		KT1	91		J6	187	
AE3	235		KT1	295		J10	103	
AE3	284		KT1	588		J10	212	
AE3	314		KT2	522		M1	775	
AE3	344		KT3	213		G3	749	
AE3	629		KT3	409		AE2	709	
AE3	646		KT3	460		C	388	
AE3	797		KT3	463		J10	59	

HANGINGS	AE1	900
HANGMEN	L3	229
	PRL	27
HANGS	SAA	559
	EDG	37
	L3	290
	J10	309
	M1	649
	G3	783
	AE7	926
	AE8	961
	AE9	1019
HANNIBAL	MF	112
	J6	249
	J6	404
	J10	234
	MC	38
	MG	10
	TJD	165
HAP	ODA	62
HAPLESS	L5	6
	M9	20
	G2	273
	AE3	72
	AE3	392
	AE4	23
	AE5	427
	AE6	47
	AE10	1169
	HIF	792
HAPPED	M8	147
	C	93
	TH	72
	WB	209
HAPPEN	S	15
	DA	75
	EMW	8
	KT1	430
HAPPENED	HAP	1837
	HAP	2558
	AE7	96
	AE10	561
	KT1	207
	KT1	545
	KT2	217
	B	195
	WB	49
	C	213
	M11	2
	CI	79
HAPPENS	KT3	885
	WB	504
HAPPIER	AM	1165
	CM	123
	RL	80
	TA	362
	HAP	2135
	HAP	2150
	M1	58
	AE2	391
	AE3	6
	AE3	117
	AE3	629
	AE6	300
	AE6	430
	AE6	882
	AE7	906
	AE9	523
	AE9	981
	AE10	64
	AE12	646
	TJD	67
	CAM	49
	M11	419
	M15	653
HAPPIEST	SAA	623
	HAP	2237
HAPPILY	LCA	4
	T23	51
	TA	12
	AS	15
HAPPINESS	RH	23
	SMA	35
	SMA	72
	SMA	136
	LCA	8
	LCA	40
	SIE	7
	SMM2	12
	EUO2	9
	AA	201
	SAA	4
	RL	27
	TA	497
	SKA6	25
	HI	137

HAPPINESS	G2	658
	KT1	436
HAPPY	UDH	41
	MHD	7
	AR	318
	AR	320
	RH	104
	SMA	31
	LC	2
	LC	74
	LC	120
	LC	135
	DC	14
	LCA	1
	LCA	16
	AM	149
	AM	296
	AM	397
	SMQ	15
	SCG1	2
	SCG2	17
	SCG3	5
	ENH	19
	EUO2	1
	E	27
	EAZ	12
	STC	14
	HP	141
	AA	481
	MD	123
	MD	162
	PRH	8
	PRH	44
	SAA	845
	SAA	975
	SAA	1065
	EC	1
	L4	239
	T18	27
	T18	12
	T27	120
	H29	65
	H2	1
	H2	22
	H2	86
	FS1	1
	TA	211
	TA	291
	TA	372
	AK	12
	AK	107
	HAP	197
	HAP	291
	HAP	375
	HAP	2298
	BR	143
	PP	41
	PKA	5
	SKA3	1
	EL	8
	EL	188
	EL	340
	SSH	9
	J1	99
	J3	262
	J3	472
	J3	489
	J6	291
	J10	423
	J10	427
	J16	6
	P2	28
	M1	126
	M1	803
	M1	909
	M9	141
	M9	152
	M9	188
	M9	209
	GK	90
	VP1	5
	VP1	16
	VP1	98
	VP3	169
	VP4	56
	VP6	69
	VP6	86
	VP7	16
	VP8	44
	G1	82
	G1	150
	G2	115
	G2	166
	G2	204
	G2	405
	G2	639

HAPPY	G2	698
	G2	702
	G3	720
	AE1	59
	AE1	111
	AE1	137
	AE1	241
	AE1	336
	AE1	356
	AE1	610
	AE1	852
	AE2	1061
	AE3	385
	AE3	415
	AE3	466
	AE3	489
	AE3	588
	AE3	610
	AE3	618
	AE3	638
	AE3	650
	AE3	695
	AE3	858
	AE4	451
	AE4	517
	AE5	69
	AE5	327
	AE6	209
	AE6	290
	AE6	871
	AE6	908
	AE6	913
	AE6	923
	AE6	937
	AE6	1009
	AE7	31
	AE7	172
	AE7	202
	AE7	301
	AE8	55
	AE8	443
	AE8	889
	AE8	906
	AE9	23
	AE9	345
	AE9	597
	AE10	163
	AE10	181
	AE10	352
	AE11	29
	AE11	240
	AE11	1275
	OAL	678
	AF	12
	AF	16
	MM	43
	DO	87
	DO	164
	KT1	165
	KT1	398
	KT1	451
	KT2	403
	KT2	411
	KT3	1092
	KT3	1101
	KT3	1110
	TJD	133
	M8	79
	M8	303
	M8	352
	B	10
	B	336
	BP	33
	M10	6
	CAM	3
	CAM	15
	CAM	21
	CAM	60
	CAM	221
	CAM	331
	HIF	171
	HIF	29
	HIF	60
	HIF	234
	C	758
	M11	181
	FL	470
	M12	27
	AU	316
	WB	467
	M15	715
	GP	109
	CI	640
	AS	71
	PWR	10
HARANGUE	P1	170

Word	Ref	No.	Word	Ref	No.	Word	Ref	No.
HARANGUE	AE9	616	HARD	VP9	15	HARDENED	TH	184
HARANGUERS	AA	509		VP10	92		M12	462
	AE11	698		G1	95		M12	637
HARASS	G3	214		G1	183		M15	472
HARBINGER	UDH	5		G2	92		M15	623
	PUF	10		G2	232	HARDENING	TA	440
	AK	194		G2	570		G3	356
	DO	62		G3	8	HARDENS	VP8	111
	KT3	109		G3	69		G3	402
HARBINGERS	AM	953		G3	640		M15	629
	GP	39		G4	118	HARDER	AA	96
HARBOR	DA	93		G4	172		GE	62
	HAP	2249		G4	466		J1	43
	G3	530		G4	574		J6	123
	G4	176		AE1	368		M13	80
	G4	609		AE1	764		M13	88
	AE1	241		AE2	1002		KT1	486
	AE1	530		AE2	1059		B	351
	AE3	695		AE3	418		AU	311
	AE4	575		AE3	869	HARDEST	AE2	9
	OAL	53		AE4	530	HARDHEAD	HAP	1015
	KT2	238		AE4	889	HARD-HEARTED	PRL	4
	BP	27		AE6	204	HARDLY	AR	85
HARBORED	HAP	1748		AE6	935		PWG	50
	M1	185		AE7	1031		ECG1	27
	M1	853		AE8	681		PM	26
	AE11	183		AE8	762		TA	197
	AE12	1287		AE8	879		GE	77
	HIF	443		AE9	91		HAP	517
HARBORS	AE4	810		AE9	280		HAP	1579
HARD	HS	30		AE9	753		BR	240
	AR	163		AE9	1097		EL	333
	LC	123		AE10	112		J10	525
	DC	8		AE10	114		P3	186
	PIE	26		AE11	238		P6	46
	AM	105		AE11	354		M1	871
	EMQ	9		AE11	659		AE5	231
	EWGR	2		AE12	85		AE6	612
	EWGR	35		AE12	526		AE8	299
	PFD	5		AE12	940		AE9	828
	PW	1		AE12	982		AE10	336
	PMQW	7		AE12	1039		AE12	1303
	PAZ	2		AE12	1271		OAL	61
	ML	18		OAL	371		OAE2	12
	ML	53		OAL	425		KT1	154
	EOE	7		OAL	540		KT2	365
	HP	168		OAL	542		KT3	772
	PR	38		OAL	543		TJD	21
	AA	125		OAL	752		TH	249
	AA	862		OAL	864		M12	392
	AA	895		MM	1	HARD-MOUTHED	M15	668
	MD	36		KT1	242	HARDNESS	AT	40
	MD	107		KT1	372		G4	155
	SAA	134		KT1	512	HARDSHIP	H3	34
	SAA	439		KT3	963		J6	134
	SAA	665		B	139		G2	667
	SAA	743		BP	18	HARDSHIPS	G1	404
	SAA	939		M10	31		AE1	289
	SAA	986		M10	78		HAP	2204
	EDG	25		M10	79	HARDY	SAA	609
	RL	215		HIF	292		AE10	286
	AT	66		HIF	454		KT1	18
	L2	41		HIF	727		HIF	3
	L3	284		TH	49		C	132
	L4	130		TH	401		M15	628
	L4	296		M12	162	HARE	AM	521
	T27	42		M12	722		H2	53
	TA	80		AU	209		HAP	37
	TA	265		AU	301		M1	719
	HAP	428		AU	503		M13	135
	HAP	444		WB	74		G1	414
	HAP	814		WB	117		GE9	761
	HAP	2130		WB	241		TJD	62
	HAP	2293		M15	649	HARES	EMQ	11
	HAP	2376		GP	34		G3	623
	HAP	2558		PTP	11		M15	140
	BR	285		ERL	6	HARK	SIE	13
	PDS	38	HARDEN	HAP	1484		SCD2	11
	ETS	28	HARDENED	DA	37		SSC	31
	EKA	32		AA	145		VP8	155
	EL	155		H3	14		AF	127
	EL	225		AK	157		STP	5
	EH	32		HAP	2334	HARKENED	AE3	878
	J1	43		J3	480	HARLEQUINS	ESF	3
	J6	128		J6	401	HARLOT	OE	33
	J10	292		J10	552		HAP	2020
	P1	5		M1	556		J6	175
	P1	23		G1	255		P3	223
	P1	87		AE4	636		L4	187
	M1	24		AE4	524		AE5	1104
	M1	162		AE9	822	HARLOT'S	PMS	22
	M1	1070		AE9	911		P5	189
	M9	27		B	734	HARLOTS	L4	284
	ELT	8		M10	25		J3	115
	VP5	141		CAM	345		ETP	15
	VP8	114		HIF	160	HARM	SMA	115

HARM	HAP	2419	HARVEST	AM	446	HASTE	G3	595
	J1	246		HP	254		AE1	294
	KT3	205		MD	292		AE1	724
	C	596		SAA	456		AE1	860
HARMAN	AM	695		SAA	686		AE1	911
HARMED	AM	488		AT	72		AE2	285
HARMFUL	G1	115		AT	73		AE2	342
	G2	521		TA	360		AE2	837
	G3	281		HAP	1396		AE2	838
HARMLESS	ETL	6		HAP	1937		AE2	839
	SCG1	28		BR	162		AE2	870
	HP	48		BR	163		AE2	907
	EUF	30		BR	261		AE2	962
	MF	84		P2	89		AE2	996
	T18	24		P6	58		AE3	109
	H2	54		M13	152		AE3	182
	HH	11		VP1	68		AE3	235
	HAP	286		VP2	10		AE3	359
	HAP	537		G1	1		AE3	736
	SKA6	20		G1	277		AE3	840
	P1	217		G1	315		AE3	875
	G2	656		G1	433		AE4	259
	G2	766		G2	286		AE4	424
	AE5	121		G2	746		AE4	614
	AE5	762		G2	753		AE4	813
	M12	172		G3	311		AE4	825
	M15	688		AE7	734		AE4	837
HARMONIOUS	MF	51		AE7	1021		AE4	851
	TA	371		AE12	964		AE4	928
	VP10	75		OAL	511		AE4	984
	G1	569		KT2	359		AE5	202
	AE6	879		B	442		AE5	419
	MFL	8		CAM	243		AE5	427
HARMONIZED	CI	34		M15	544		AE5	603
HARMONY	SMA4	49	HARVEST-HOME	SKA4	5		AE5	681
	LC	116		SKA4	6		AE5	827
	D	44		SKA4	7		AE5	860
	PAA	38		SKA4	8		AE5	873
	AK	60		P4	64		AE6	57
	SSC	1	HARVESTS	VP4	33		AE6	855
	SSC	11		G1	115		AE7	450
	SSC	13		G1	149		AE7	604
	DHP	20		G2	197		AE7	725
	KT3	1118		G4	337		AE8	288
HARMS	AM	488		AE7	996		AE8	300
	HAP	2361		AE10	210		AE8	584
	AE11	425		CAM	18		AE9	2
	AE11	531	HARVEY'S	DC	31		AE9	150
HARNESS	AE6	888	HASTE	HS	1		AE9	290
	BR	173		HS	51		AE9	513
	M1	924		AR	277		AE9	523
	G3	422		AR	282		AE10	16
	KT3	445		SMA	17		AE10	326
HARP	EOE	7		SMA	42		AE10	531
	AA	196		SIE	2		AE10	927
	AA	439		AM	201		AE11	710
	P5	137		AM	305		AE11	830
	P6	3		AM	725		AE11	881
	G4	670		AM	942		AE11	1091
	AE12	580		EMM	5		AE11	1148
	OAE1	20		EEL	38		AE12	238
	HIF	808		ETL	25		AE12	401
	M12	218		SM2	11		AE12	417
HARPALYCE	AE1	441		PLN	17		AE12	425
HARPALYCUS	AE11	999		SLN	10		AE12	636
HARPIES	HAP	2254		PCD	32		AE12	1068
	J1	181		EUO	2		AE12	1119
	AE3	294		DA	75		OAL	127
	AE3	277		SAA	926		OAE2	61
	AE3	326		AT	95		KT1	237
	AE3	340		L3	79		KT1	516
	CI	581		L3	101		KT2	617
HARPONS	OAL	875		L3	258		KT2	665
HARPS	EUF	32		T27	131		KT3	605
	L2	32		H29	3		KT3	775
	BR	320		H29	10		KT3	1003
	J3	113		H29	15		B	164
HARRIES	AM	321		TA	82		B	229
HARROWS	G1	138		TA	126		BP	147
	G1	233		TA	433		CAM	156
	G2	588		HAP	1718		CAM	380
	AE9	829		HAP	1889		HIF	448
HARRY	AM	695		SKA6	25		TH	420
	AM	802		EL	288		M11	258
	EH	14		ESH	17		FL	577
	GP	109		J3	103		M12	200
HARSH	AA	646		J6	667		AU	186
	MO	16		J10	138		WB	55
	TA	241		P3	12		CI	596
	P1	151		M1	921		PTP	43
	P5	184		M9	152	HASTEN	SAA	408
	GP	18		M13	77		HAP	2563
HARSHER	J3	158		VP4	12		J10	420
HARSHLY	KT3	360		VP5	31		G4	246
HART	AE5	329		VP8	109		AE4	656
	KT2	230		G1	293		AE9	248

Word	Ref	No.
HASTEN	AE9	1049
	AE11	1177
	CI	408
HASTENED	HI	151
	AE10	276
	AE10	1255
	AE12	68
	CAM	266
HASTENING	AM	742
	G4	176
	AE10	1289
	AE11	1312
	OAL	796
	CI	284
	CI	552
HASTENS	G3	242
	AE6	258
	AE12	431
	AE12	588
	AE12	608
	AE12	1079
	M11	237
HASTES	AM	257
	AM	433
	J6	627
	AE6	337
	AE11	790
HASTILY	AM	902
HASTING	AE8	164
	AE12	999
HASTINGS	UDH	1
	UDH	102
	UDH	77
HASTY	AR	134
	AR	169
	SM2	4
	CM	72
	TA	55
	G1	174
	G3	159
	G4	85
	AE4	473
	AE4	823
	AE6	430
	AE9	630
	KT2	262
	M8	262
	B	466
	CI	194
HAT	PCG1	5
	PCG1	10
	PCG1	12
	PCG1	15
	ESF	26
	M1	925
	KT1	549
HATCH	AM	1151
HATCHED	AM	792
	P1	204
	G2	458
	CAM	48
HATCHES	SCD2	18
	AE10	926
	M11	146
HATCHET	PKA	17
	AE7	709
	M15	184
HATCHING	KT3	1069
	TH	341
	M11	499
HATE	SMA	134
	AM	162
	PMQ	38
	PCG2	8
	EAZ	20
	PTC	30
	DA	50
	DA	123
	DA	151
	AA	173
	AA	223
	AA	401
	AA	538
	AA	593
	AA	929
	PLB	5
	MD	76
	MD	316
	D	39
	SAA	724
	SAA	758
	SAA	905
	AT	79
	AT	19
	TA	132
	TA	450

Word	Ref	No.
HATE	HAP	36
	HAP	325
	HAP	359
	HAP	1262
	HAP	1331
	HAP	1939
	HAP	2001
	HAP	2420
	HAP	2490
	EKA	13
	EH	31
	J3	106
	J3	349
	J6	582
	J6	656
	J10	85
	J10	554
	M1	692
	HI	67
	VP6	106
	G4	471
	AE1	2
	AE1	12
	AE1	470
	AE1	498
	AE2	129
	AE2	213
	AE4	463
	AE4	654
	AE4	810
	AE4	856
	AE4	895
	AE4	904
	AE5	784
	AE5	1023
	AE6	137
	AE6	1138
	AE7	62
	AE7	421
	AE7	469
	AE7	672
	AE7	768
	AE7	1052
	AE8	326
	AE8	388
	AE8	655
	AE10	21
	AE10	162
	AE10	293
	AE10	979
	AE10	1010
	AE10	1218
	AE10	1307
	AE11	155
	AE11	184
	AE11	430
	AE12	5
	AE12	423
	AE12	1233
	KT1	353
	KT2	88
	KT2	94
	KT2	218
	KT3	228
	KT3	503
	B	132
	B	667
	CAM	26
	HIF	117
	HIF	97
	HIF	232
	HIF	346
	C	468
	C	744
	TH	30
	TH	199
	TH	396
	TH	424
	M12	341
	M12	718
	AU	81
	WB	80
HATED	T23	6
	HAP	168
	AE3	843
	AE7	404
	AE7	788
	AE9	991
	AE10	413
	AE10	1221
	OAL	333
	OAL	389
	KT2	69
	CAM	147
	TH	14
	M15	79

Word	Ref	No.
HATEFUL	AR	312
	HAP	170
	AE6	637
	AE7	397
	AE10	1302
	AE11	806
	KT1	214
	KT3	410
	KT3	656
	TH	313
	M12	479
	WB	473
HATES	EAL	9
	M1	643
	VP3	140
	AE7	455
HATFIELD	EUF	21
HATING	PUO2	35
	AA	512
HATRED	PWG	4
	AA	586
	MD	29
	M1	205
	AE4	631
	AE5	1030
	AE7	475
	KT2	180
	KT3	814
HATS	PCG1	42
	ENH	13
HATTERED	HAP	371
HAUBERKS	KT3	603
HAUGHTILY	T23	5
HAUGHTY	AM	233
	PUO1	30
	EOE	17
	HP	57
	AA	331
	AA	843
	AA	951
	L3	242
	T23	63
	HAP	160
	HAP	1580
	BR	287
	J6	246
	J10	175
	J10	289
	P1	197
	P6	131
	M1	1049
	VP2	16
	G3	641
	G4	109
	AE1	2
	AE1	43
	AE1	380
	AE1	688
	AE3	419
	AE3	558
	AE4	320
	AE4	597
	AE4	614
	AE4	880
	AE5	254
	AE5	486
	AE5	1024
	AE7	62
	AE7	402
	AE7	622
	AE8	58
	AE8	508
	AE8	816
	AE9	435
	AE10	70
	AE10	629
	AE10	915
	AE10	986
	AE10	1030
	AE11	523
	AE11	546
	AE12	8
	AE12	550
	AE12	1268
	AE12	1366
	KT1	312
	HIF	414
	HIF	539
	TH	11
	TH	156
	TH	349
	M12	278
	CI	275
	HIF	38
HAUL	G1	614
	AE2	309

HAUL	AE2	321	HEAD	MD	182	HEAD	VP2	64
	AE4	851		MF	74		VP3	135
HAULED	AE2	751		MF	127		VP8	103
	AE3	186		MF	134		VP8	148
	AE10	591		SAA	309		VP9	30
	AU	6		SAA	645		G1	230
HAULING	HIF	659		SAA	798		G1	252
HAULSERS	AE1	239		SAA	806		G1	357
	AE3	349		SAA	862		G1	425
	AE5	1011		RL	13		G2	40
	AE9	144		OE	14		G2	409
	AE10	930		AT	5		G2	492
	HIF	599		AT	118		G2	498
HAUNT	ET	8		EC	36		G2	559
	SAA	301		ER	4		G2	619
	L3	267		L3	58		G3	340
	G1	12		L3	236		G3	408
	G1	528		T18	65		G3	552
	G3	379		T18	67		G3	644
	AE4	559		H29	58		G3	648
	AE4	764		H2	21		G3	692
	AE7	47		H2	29		G3	709
	BP	21		TA	47		G4	421
	WB	490		TA	111		G4	453
	M15	543		TA	349		G4	499
HAUNTED	TH	255		TA	514		G4	601
HAUNTER	KT3	215		PAA	36		G4	760
	M12	476		HAP	170		G4	766
HAUNTING	AM	1023		HAP	260		AE1	179
	AE10	908		HAP	392		AE1	620
HAUNTS	HAP	1862		HAP	398		AE1	973
	HAP	2418		HAP	583		AE2	132
	VP8	83		HAP	1188		AE2	208
	AE4	270		HAP	1271		AE2	219
	AE12	1248		HAP	1417		AE2	289
	OAL	53		HAP	1675		AE2	930
	WB	41		HAP	1790		AE2	971
HAUTBOYS,	AF	53		HAP	2318		AE3	475
HAUTBOYS'	FL	358		HAP	2404		AE3	718
HAVEN'S	C	302		SSC	5		AE3	813
HAWK	HAP	1746		BR	264		AE4	268
	HAP	2410		ODA	43		AE4	364
	HAP	2417		J3	26		AE4	520
	AE11	1109		J3	60		AE4	646
	AE12	382		J3	268		AE4	988
HAWKS	AE12	693		J3	334		AE4	1005
HAWTHORN	FL	282		J3	463		AE5	15
HAWTHORNS	PC1	19		J3	396		AE5	95
HAY	SKA4	1		J6	7		AE5	166
	J3	24		J6	70		AE5	231
	J6	703		J6	139		AE5	267
HAYCOCK	WB	44		J6	417		AE5	320
HAYNES	PLN	45		J6	586		AE5	396
	EH	20		J6	630		AE5	487
	ETP	47		J6	645		AE5	499
HAZARD	AM	112		J6	657		AE5	553
	SAA	263		J6	694		AE5	628
	RL	444		J6	801		AE5	672
	M1	238		J10	62		AE5	732
	AE5	981		J10	96		AE5	881
	AE9	233		J10	188		AE5	908
	AE10	411		J10	439		AE5	1066
	AE11	774		P1	55		AE6	396
	OAL	134		P1	159		AE6	486
	C	553		P1	193		AE6	703
HAZARDS	HP	74		P1	197		AE6	894
	TA	315		P1	204		AE6	1059
	G1	178		P2	23		AE6	1104
	AE1	285		P2	39		AE6	1199
	AE2	1088		P3	9		AE7	114
	AE4	818		P3	78		AE7	248
	AE8	387		P4	89		AE7	353
	AE9	273		P5	49		AE7	402
HAZEL	VP7	88		P5	245		AE7	495
	VP7	90		P6	146		AE7	556
	G2	96		P6	166		AE7	594
	G2	410		M1	231		AE7	631
	G2	547		M1	360		AE7	788
HAZELS	VP5	4		M1	502		AE7	855
	G2	92		M1	515		AE7	952
HEAD	RH	25		M1	649		AE7	1034
	SMA	46		M1	768		AE7	1110
	SMA	59		M1	858		AE8	48
	DC	53		M1	875		AE8	181
	PIE	11		M1	881		AE8	286
	AM	620		M1	925		AE8	311
	AM	872		M1	966		AE8	371
	AM	925		M1	996		AE8	577
	AM	1056		M1	1005		AE8	635
	PA	36		M9	32		AE8	661
	SCG1	8		M13	64		AE8	763
	SM2	3		M13	152		AE8	773
	ML	36		M13	204		AE8	778
	AA	348		HI	144		AE8	839
	AA	489		HI	149		AE8	852
	MD	181		VP1	116		AE8	902

HEAD	AE9	151
	AE9	274
	AE9	402
	AE9	436
	AE9	446
	AE9	584
	AE9	671
	AE9	798
	AE9	860
	AE9	885
	AE9	1041
	AE10	172
	AE10	201
	AE10	551
	AE10	581
	AE10	775
	AE10	843
	AE10	903
	AE10	993
	AE10	1088
	AE10	1192
	AE10	1203
	AE10	1233
	AE10	1243
	AE10	1285
	AE10	1290
	AE11	1
	AE11	108
	AE11	275
	AE11	358
	AE11	364
	AE11	627
	AE11	751
	AE11	865
	AE11	954
	AE11	1008
	AE11	1062
	AE11	1139
	AE11	1208
	AE12	139
	AE12	154
	AE12	442
	AE12	449
	AE12	470
	AE12	563
	AE12	715
	AE12	789
	AE12	1022
	AE12	1093
	AE12	1281
	AE12	1294
	OAL	330
	AF	128
	KT1	196
	KT1	376
	KT1	547
	KT1	552
	KT2	278
	KT2	342
	KT2	348
	KT2	517
	KT2	549
	KT2	602
	KT2	615
	KT3	41
	KT3	208
	KT3	610
	KT3	621
	KT3	703
	KT3	912
	M8	68
	M8	216
	B	208
	B	688
	B	698
	BP	5
	M10	56
	CAM	199
	CAM	214
	CAM	349
	CAM	373
	HIF	21
	HIF	395
	HIF	478
	HIF	498
	HIF	517
	HIF	664
	HIF	669
	HIF	710
	HIF	798
	HIF	814
	C	273
	C	496
	C	710
	TH	93
	TH	107

HEAD	TH	124
	M11	227
	M11	296
	M11	304
	M11	345
	M11	487
	FL	73
	FL	253
	FL	317
	FL	346
	FL	377
	FL	584
	FL	591
	M12	162
	M12	375
	M12	396
	M12	399
	M12	504
	M12	510
	M12	532
	M12	586
	AU	173
	AU	505
	AU	552
	WB	193
	WB	267
	WB	284
	WB	332
	M15	39
	M15	299
	M15	425
	M15	496
	M15	568
	CI	577
	CI	601
	CI	606
	ETP	18
HEADED	AA	519
	HAP	1924
	FL	272
HEADGEAR	T27	99
HEADING	SAA	597
HEADLESS	AE2	763
	KT2	537
HEADLONG	CM	132
	MD	122
	J6	845
	J10	86
	J10	247
	G1	293
	G1	502
	G3	140
	G4	116
	AE1	166
	AE2	632
	AE2	773
	AE2	1020
	AE3	795
	AE4	837
	AE5	597
	AE5	610
	AE5	1052
	AE5	1118
	AE6	465
	AE6	663
	AE6	725
	AE8	8
	AE9	586
	AE10	807
	AE10	1283
	AE11	801
	AE11	1091
	AE11	1262
	AE12	434
	AE12	999
	KT1	69
	M8	132
	HIF	781
	C	741
	M11	472
	M12	176
	M12	456
	J10	331
HEADPIECE	AE7	884
	G1	164
HEAD'S	AM	260
HEADS	AM	994
	ENH	33
	PUO5	10
	AA	542
	SAA	278
	SAA	858
	SAA	890
	T23	59
	HAP	1002
	HAP	1004

HEADS	HAP	1080
	ESH	18
	J3	433
	J3	388
	J3	403
	J6	25
	J6	435
	P5	274
	M1	89
	M1	399
	M1	483
	G3	819
	G4	740
	AE1	261
	AE1	702
	AE2	192
	AE2	315
	AE3	256
	AE3	891
	AE4	381
	AE5	568
	AE6	4
	AE6	816
	AE6	903
	AE6	1247
	AE7	208
	AE8	261
	AE8	362
	AE8	378
	AE8	399
	AE8	934
	AE9	619
	AE9	686
	AE9	725
	AE9	923
	AE9	925
	AE9	1055
	AE10	569
	AE11	668
	AE11	917
	AE12	128
	AE12	182
	AE12	375
	AE12	743
	AE12	808
	KT3	91
	M8	105
	CAM	91
	FL	167
	FL	229
	FL	290
HEADSTRONG	AA	45
	J10	541
	AE10	1058
HEADY	PAA	17
	AE8	249
HEAL	T27	27
	HAP	224
	HAP	939
	P4	103
	M1	705
	AE10	1213
	KT3	728
	M12	154
	ESK	24
HEALED	SAA	796
	HIF	799
HEALING	DC	41
	TA	294
	BR	90
	P3	181
	AE12	584
	AE12	609
HEALS	M15	462
HEALTH	AA	756
	PLB	44
	MD	295
	L2	14
	L4	33
	H2	55
	TA	41
	GE	49
	HAP	1252
	PDS	19
	EL	308
	J6	334
	J10	549
	P3	126
	P6	113
	G2	771
	G4	367
	AE3	437
	AE12	627
	OAL	837
	DO	130
	KT3	749

Word	Ref	No.
HEALTH	TJD	92
	TJD	117
	B	34
	CAM	182
	C	23
	FL	23
HEALTHFUL	AR	173
	J10	303
	OAL	294
HEALTHFULLY	UDH	14
HEALTHS	L3	99
HEAP	AM	978
	SAA	1091
	L3	118
	SSC	3
	EL	31
	J3	415
	J10	302
	P3	222
	P6	187
	G2	320
	G2	481
	G3	548
	AE2	825
	AE6	678
	AE8	347
	AE11	315
	KT1	85
	KT1	141
	KT3	174
	TH	312
	M12	673
HEAPED	AA	951
	SAA	949
	SKA4	2
	G3	829
	AE1	981
	AE4	729
	AE5	147
	M8	35
	CI	607
HEAPING	AA	591
HEAPS	VHH	47
	AM	113
	AA	277
	SAA	645
	J10	17
	VP8	4
	G1	457
	G2	255
	G4	117
	G4	515
	G4	605
	AE2	608
	AE5	1057
	AE7	745
	AE8	253
	AE8	467
	AE8	745
	AE9	906
	AE10	346
	AE10	709
	AE10	953
	AE11	606
	AE11	943
	AE12	775
	OAL	109
	KT3	368
	M8	266
	HIF	16
	HIF	530
	M11	174
	M12	157
HEAPY	VP7	70
	G2	713
HEAR	AR	17
	PWG	1
	AM	59
	AM	286
	AM	744
	PMQ	45
	SEL2	16
	SEL3	4
	PAR	16
	PM	6
	PM	12
	PM	29
	EM	8
	A	11
	ELN	5
	E	23
	POE	14
	PCB	18
	CM	93
	HP	147
	HP	214
HEAR	AA	938
	PPC	1
	EK	28
	OE	39
	AT	88
	AT	117
	ER	59
	L2	2
	T23	65
	T27	21
	T27	43
	T27	55
	T27	102
	H29	94
	FS3	10
	FS3	11
	TA	192
	TA	271
	AK	16
	AK	188
	HAP	972
	HAP	1075
	HAP	2185
	PP	45
	EKA	8
	OD	46
	J1	1
	J1	194
	J3	16
	J3	348
	J6	161
	J6	211
	J6	463
	J6	526
	J6	768
	J10	393
	J10	473
	J10	528
	J16	23
	P1	146
	P1	162
	P2	8
	P2	46
	P2	72
	P3	165
	P4	3
	P4	124
	P5	130
	P5	203
	P6	121
	M1	531
	M1	970
	M1	1063
	M9	10
	HI	140
	VP3	114
	VP5	25
	VP5	42
	VP5	85
	VP5	126
	VP8	33
	G1	63
	G2	676
	G3	33
	G3	292
	G4	9
	G4	740
	AE1	513
	AE1	1057
	AE2	9
	AE2	83
	AE2	401
	AE2	842
	AE2	909
	AE2	940
	AE2	994
	AE3	139
	AE3	311
	AE3	550
	AE3	729
	AE3	853
	AE3	887
	AE4	109
	AE4	112
	AE4	424
	AE4	437
	AE4	550
	AE5	868
	AE6	84
	AE6	520
	AE7	33
	AE7	603
	AE7	763
	AE7	870
	AE8	696
	AE8	755
HEAR	AE9	245
	AE9	851
	AE9	900
	AE10	354
	AE10	683
	AE10	841
	AE10	844
	AE11	157
	AE11	483
	AE11	730
	AE12	40
	AE12	274
	AE12	298
	AE12	825
	AE12	1130
	OAL	704
	OAL	713
	DO	59
	KT1	198
	KT2	403
	KT3	272
	KT3	493
	KT3	805
	BP	1
	CAM	6
	CAM	8
	CAM	205
	CAM	258
	CAM	327
	HIF	64
	HIF	619
	HIF	666
	HIF	738
	C	87
	C	651
	M11	34
	M11	170
	FL	52
	FL	146
	FL	195
	FL	321
	FL	371
	FL	428
	M12	82
	M12	227
	M12	622
	AU	104
	AU	109
	CI	545
	CI	611
HEARD	HS	118
	VHH	30
	AM	412
	AM	421
	AM	1081
	AM	1092
	EEL	23
	ELN	18
	EUO	17
	CM	71
	CM	84
	EPC	9
	PPC	22
	MF	211
	SAA	440
	SAA	791
	EDG	23
	RL	191
	RL	321
	AT	112
	T23	109
	NS	3
	TA	16
	TA	42
	TA	105
	AK	49
	HAP	737
	HAP	895
	HAP	971
	HAP	1079
	HAP	1362
	HAP	1392
	HAP	1794
	HAP	1853
	HAP	2076
	HAP	2430
	SSC	6
	SSC	53
	SSC	61
	BR	1
	PDS	32
	PKA	41
	EL	40
	EL	324
	ODA	45
	J1	155

HEARD			HEARD			HEARSE		
	J3	477		BP	10		A	16
	J6	207		BP	139		AA	859
	J6	515		CAM	122		G4	374
	J16	78		CAM	365		AE6	230
	P1	39		HIF	497		AE11	97
	P3	102		HIF	619		AE11	113
	P3	134		HIF	625		M8	325
	P3	173		HIF	764	HEART	RH	2
	P4	9		C	98		SMA	33
	M1	129		C	318		SMA	104
	M1	278		C	344		LC	44
	M1	457		C	366		LC	81
	M1	708		C	601		AM	550
	M1	1020		C	622		AM	752
	M1	1088		C	664		AM	759
	M9	42		C	718		AM	1130
	M9	175		C	736		AM	1138
	M9	185		TH	100		SMQ	2
	M13	62		TH	298		SMQ	10
	HI	26		M11	250		SMM2	4
	DHP	23		M11	348		SMM2	9
	VP1	62		FL	47		SMM2	18
	VP6	47		FL	148		SMM2	23
	VP9	59		FL	210		SMM2	26
	G1	638		FL	337		SEL1	7
	G1	643		M12	75		SEL4	1
	G2	719		M12	80		SEL4	9
	G3	563		M12	247		STL	8
	G4	379		M12	697		SCG1	13
	G4	473		M12	708		SCG2	8
	G4	656		AU	104		SLN	16
	AE1	27		AU	111		PCD	32
	AE1	176		AU	143		ML	36
	AE1	450		AU	205		CM	41
	AE1	518		AU	482		CM	116
	AE1	793		WB	173		HP	136
	AE2	319		WB	334		HP	258
	AE2	325		WB	509		DA	30
	AE2	453		M15	43		DA	33
	AE2	737		M15	88		DA	87
	AE4	294		M15	463		PUF	33
	AE4	321		M15	481		AA	7
	AE4	420		GP	80		AA	436
	AE4	511		CI	331		AA	826
	AE4	593	HEARED	M1	121		PLB	23
	AE4	669	HEARER	AE4	113		PLB	33
	AE4	671	HEARERS	MS	18		EPC	8
	AE5	213	HEAREST	ODA	67		MD	181
	AE5	295		P6	96		MF	201
	AE5	313		AE4	808		AT	13
	AE5	446	HEARING	RL	445		AT	113
	AE5	516		J16	74		EC	39
	AE5	951		VP5	42		L4	2
	AE6	253		AE2	927		L4	12
	AE6	752		M8	247		L4	76
	AE7	18		HIF	67		L4	289
	AE7	306		M11	34		T23	36
	AE7	969		B	312		T23	30
	AE8	283		FL	138		T23	63
	AE8	557	HEARKEN	G4	693		T27	27
	AE8	695		AE2	405		T27	111
	AE8	788		AE4	874		H3	14
	AE9	132		C	474		FS1	3
	AE9	305	HEARKENED	HAP	901		FS4	2
	AE10	276	HEARKENS	G4	564		TA	130
	AE10	654	HEARS	PAZ	15		TA	239
	AE10	1201		DA	111		TA	274
	AE11	384		BR	79		AK	130
	AE11	941		J6	98		HAP	7
	AE11	1165		J6	336		HAP	260
	AE11	1252		G2	709		HAP	338
	AE12	338		G3	130		HAP	1942
	AE12	586		G4	494		HAP	2092
	AE12	664		G4	521		EDS	1
	AE12	687		G4	538		EKA	33
	AE12	856		AE1	714		SKA6	3
	AE12	930		AE1	584		EL	169
	AE12	1015		AE2	1046		EL	190
	OAL	89		AE4	119		EL	192
	DO	45		AE4	429		EL	248
	KT1	237		AE4	649		EL	259
	KT2	77		AE4	966		EL	358
	KT2	141		AE6	583		ODA	56
	KT2	272		AE6	765		SSH	1
	KT2	341		AE6	1091		J3	206
	KT2	573		AE9	533		J10	462
	KT3	84		AE11	1314		P1	99
	KT3	439		OAL	450		P2	96
	KT3	443		AF	38		P3	60
	KT3	529		AF	43		P3	87
	B	156		KT1	535		P3	170
	B	260		KT1	537		P3	218
	B	286		KT2	183		P3	225
	B	293		M15	194		P4	85
	B	368		M15	195		P4	106
	B	626	HEARSAY	HAP	1517		P5	30

HEART	
P5	33
P5	243
P5	245
P5	275
M1	700
M1	750
M1	848
M9	189
M13	187
H1	6
H1	48
H1	81
G1	108
G3	166
G3	404
G4	497
AE1	38
AE1	291
AE1	474
AE1	850
AE1	947
AE1	1008
AE2	755
AE4	5
AE4	28
AE4	90
AE4	100
AE4	482
AE4	613
AE4	636
AE4	652
AE4	771
AE4	810
AE4	830
AE5	918
AE6	674
AE7	263
AE7	488
AE7	503
AE8	33
AE8	503
AE9	354
AE9	788
AE9	947
AE10	94
AE10	467
AE10	596
AE10	678
AE10	890
AE10	1162
AE11	582
AE11	1180
AE11	1252
AE12	42
AE12	578
AE12	669
AE12	737
AE12	794
OAL	149
OAL	203
OAL	341
OAL	355
OAL	361
OAL	407
OAL	500
OAL	534
OAL	744
OAL	767
KT1	94
KT1	154
KT1	234
KT1	273
KT1	528
KT1	556
KT2	112
KT2	119
KT2	124
KT2	189
KT3	147
KT3	316
KT3	335
KT3	432
KT3	753
KT3	779
KT3	903
KT3	1067
TJD	38
M8	54
M8	78
M8	182
M8	201
B	18
B	54
B	70
B	76
B	364

HEART	
B	372
B	594
B	612
B	630
B	636
B	641
B	653
B	690
B	692
B	699
B	708
B	714
B	721
B	731
B	746
CAM	22
HIF	135
HIF	285
HIF	663
C	29
C	68
C	81
C	101
C	125
C	137
C	236
C	433
C	584
C	617
C	695
TH	68
TH	159
TH	184
TH	191
TH	241
TH	302
TH	325
TH	351
TH	374
M11	9
M11	54
M11	240
M11	248
M11	415
FL	18
M12	561
M12	573
M12	636
AU	124
AU	296
AU	605
WB	115
WB	510
M15	33
CI	130
CI	170
CI	157
STP	27
PC1	9

HEARTENED
HEARTH

H9	8
H2	93
VP7	70
G2	770
G3	580
G3	632
AE2	701
AE7	697
AE8	542
M8	253
M8	266
BP	49
BP	62
M12	380

HEARTHS

AM	1128
HAP	2074
G3	559
AE8	54

HEARTLESS

AM	512
AE7	958

HEART'S
HEARTS

C	559
AR	211
AM	304
AM	441
EAZ	21
PC2	21
HP	226
ETG	12
PPC	35
AA	290
AA	444
AA	497
AA	693
AA	743
PLB	39
MD	256
D	44

HEARTS	
SAA	168
SAA	517
SAA	530
SAA	634
T23	8
FS2	11
TA	384
HAP	2398
PP	30
EL	13
J6	102
M9	142
M9	143
SFL	14
VCS	10
VCS	21
G2	234
AE1	579
AE2	117
AE2	144
AE2	259
AE4	596
AE5	414
AE6	994
AE7	1031
AE8	199
AE8	220
AE9	657
AE9	975
AE11	480
AE11	1058
AE12	773
AE12	1061
KT2	384
KT3	219
KT3	746
M8	161
HIF	144
HIF	76
C	733
TH	4
TH	295
M12	265
ESK	14
PMK	6

HEARTY

PAL	33
PSF	1
EDG	6
EC	23
PAA	15
HAP	1248
BP	43
BP	119

HEAT

AR	136
AR	214
LC	88
LC	128
AM	9
AM	459
SEL4	26
SEL4	28
ENH	12
ETG	25
L4	65
L4	200
TA	440
EAA	4
HAP	254
EL	110
J3	177
J3	378
J6	363
P3	217
M1	3
M1	202
M1	560
M1	573
M1	582
M13	105
VP1	88
VP2	14
VP3	152
G1	132
G1	135
G1	477
G2	365
G2	436
G2	520
G3	474
G3	509
G3	512
G3	698
G4	32
G4	51
G4	217
G4	581

HEAT	AE3	195
	AE3	397
	AE3	769
	AE6	960
	AE7	690
	AE10	54
	OAL	607
	KT3	1066
	B	195
	B	202
	B	653
	FL	10
	FL	315
	FL	323
	FL	378
	FL	417
	FL	422
	FL	445
	M15	311
	GP	32
HEATED	AE9	799
HEATH	G2	249
HEATHEN	PO	15
	AA	98
	SAA	390
	ETS	2
	KT3	369
	C	819
HEATHENS	RL	73
	RL	147
	KT3	852
HEATHPOUT	H2	78
HEATHS	HAP	555
	WB	4
	M15	140
HEATHY	AE8	787
HEATS	SMA	75
	AA	334
	L4	206
	M1	152
	VP2	10
	VP2	99
	VP7	68
	G1	262
	G1	275
	G1	484
	G2	469
	G3	246
	G3	659
	G3	723
	AE1	236
	OAL	72
	M8	362
	HIF	370
HEAVE	STL	8
	L3	209
	L4	191
	L4	278
	L4	284
	SSC	5
	J10	229
	SLT2	8
	VP10	109
	AE5	270
	AE8	324
	AE12	1316
	KT2	551
	M12	682
	M15	704
HEAVED	AM	730
	CM	43
	T23	89
	M1	750
	AE6	75
	AE8	315
	AE10	281
	AE10	534
	AE11	584
	AE12	1304
	DO	49
	KT1	154
	M8	267
	M12	366
	M12	460
	M15	457
HEAVEN	UDH	51
	JH	15
	HS	7
	HS	21
	HS	38
	HS	59
	HS	105
	AR	13
	AR	38
	AR	40
	AR	59

HEAVEN	AR	73
	AR	137
	AR	144
	AR	185
	AR	196
	AR	238
	AR	318
	SMA	23
	SMA	36
	SMA	85
	LC	36
	LC	55
	LCA	26
	AM	63
	AM	75
	AM	79
	AM	87
	AM	142
	AM	171
	AM	203
	AM	300
	AM	539
	AM	560
	AM	561
	AM	710
	AM	834
	AM	849
	AM	1091
	AM	1104
	AM	1113
	AM	1176
	SMM2	25
	EUO	5
	PAZ	29
	EAL	26
	EMK	4
	PKK	9
	PKK	26
	PTW	1
	POE	13
	DA	68
	UMR	7
	EMW	10
	EMW	16
	EPF	16
	PUF	2
	AA	44
	AA	197
	AA	252
	AA	320
	AA	422
	AA	672
	AA	832
	AA	848
	AA	860
	AA	936
	AA	985
	AA	1000
	PLB	52
	MD	137
	MD	190
	MD	21
	MD	280
	MD	283
	MD	285
	MD	305
	PRH	40
	SAA	5
	SAA	62
	SAA	470
	SAA	474
	SAA	744
	SAA	773
	SAA	940
	EDG	34
	RL	323
	RL	47
	RL	62
	RL	67
	RL	122
	RL	120
	RL	140
	RL	149
	RL	186
	RL	438
	DOD	2
	EC	45
	L1	11
	L1	36
	L3	5
	L3	13
	L4	245
	H3	39
	H29	71
	TA	9
	TA	80

HEAVEN	TA	83
	TA	99
	TA	103
	TA	226
	TA	237
	TA	415
	TA	436
	TA	491
	PAA	20
	EAA	7
	AK	146
	AK	22
	AK	40
	AK	53
	AK	67
	AK	163
	AK	194
	HAP	1861
	HAP	145
	HAP	150
	HAP	217
	HAP	252
	HAP	322
	HAP	343
	HAP	377
	HAP	387
	HAP	638
	HAP	918
	HAP	1085
	HAP	1108
	HAP	1238
	HAP	1574
	HAP	1662
	HAP	1710
	HAP	1738
	HAP	1827
	HAP	1963
	HAP	2166
	HAP	2225
	HAP	2232
	HAP	2447
	HAP	2576
	HAP	2590
	SSC	54
	BR	1
	BR	36
	BR	41
	BR	73
	BR	92
	BR	150
	BR	166
	BR	181
	BR	193
	BR	206
	BR	229
	BR	240
	BR	268
	BR	305
	PTS	34
	ETS	9
	PKA	40
	EKA	9
	SKA2	13
	SKA6	30
	EL	25
	EL	31
	EL	33
	EL	58
	EL	75
	EL	90
	EL	113
	EL	124
	EL	130
	EL	189
	EL	288
	EL	306
	EL	316
	EL	324
	OD	11
	OD	20
	ODA	20
	ODA	39
	J3	141
	J6	518
	J6	685
	J6	716
	J6	735
	J10	76
	J10	104
	J10	264
	J10	408
	J10	436
	J16	35
	P2	7
	P2	29
	P2	68

HEAVEN	P5	61
	P5	205
	M1	28
	M1	84
	M1	155
	M1	191
	M1	193
	M1	226
	M1	251
	M1	255
	M1	264
	M1	283
	M1	346
	M1	348
	M1	373
	M1	445
	M1	493
	M1	520
	M1	581
	M1	870
	M1	1015
	M1	1074
	M9	10
	M9	19
	M9	94
	M9	134
	M9	135
	M13	15
	M13	165
	VCS	16
	SLT1	5
	MC	62
	GK	160
	VP1	99
	VP2	100
	VP3	91
	VP3	113
	VP3	114
	VP3	160
	VP4	10
	VP4	61
	VP4	64
	VP5	86
	VP8	29
	VP8	95
	VP8	157
	VP9	22
	VP10	94
	VP10	98
	G1	47
	G1	51
	G1	208
	G1	236
	G1	324
	G1	332
	G1	341
	G1	436
	G1	461
	G1	519
	G1	602
	G1	616
	G1	676
	G2	401
	G2	462
	G2	622
	G2	678
	G3	581
	G3	696
	G4	1
	G4	9
	G4	223
	G4	325
	G4	507
	G4	602
	G4	814
	AE1	13
	AE1	25
	AE1	55
	AE1	71
	AE1	89
	AE1	97
	AE1	130
	AE1	183
	AE1	341
	AE1	353
	AE1	381
	AE1	393
	AE1	412
	AE1	504
	AE1	526
	AE1	536
	AE1	855
	AE1	889
	AE1	806
	AE1	1029
	AE2	70

HEAVEN	AE2	126
	AE2	205
	AE2	453
	AE2	547
	AE2	579
	AE2	700
	AE2	731
	AE2	866
	AE2	867
	AE2	875
	AE2	879
	AE2	936
	AE2	946
	AE2	951
	AE3	1
	AE3	84
	AE3	156
	AE3	235
	AE3	260
	AE3	280
	AE3	325
	AE3	344
	AE3	460
	AE3	540
	AE3	589
	AE3	636
	AE3	672
	AE3	739
	AE4	54
	AE4	62
	AE4	393
	AE4	491
	AE4	543
	AE4	654
	AE4	936
	AE5	24
	AE5	59
	AE5	70
	AE5	834
	AE5	900
	AE5	913
	AE5	923
	AE5	949
	AE5	1109
	AE6	102
	AE6	168
	AE6	476
	AE6	514
	AE6	593
	AE6	620
	AE6	692
	AE6	723
	AE6	787
	AE6	800
	AE6	805
	AE6	869
	AE6	980
	AE6	992
	AE6	1065
	AE7	76
	AE7	104
	AE7	368
	AE7	432
	AE7	433
	AE7	824
	AE7	897
	AE8	316
	AE8	401
	AE8	697
	AE8	706
	AE8	742
	AE8	779
	AE8	881
	AE8	931
	AE9	19
	AE9	27
	AE9	97
	AE9	109
	AE9	161
	AE9	670
	AE9	722
	AE9	880
	AE9	925
	AE10	1
	AE10	49
	AE10	63
	AE10	103
	AE10	129
	AE10	175
	AE10	256
	AE10	276
	AE10	353
	AE10	498
	AE10	648
	AE10	791
	AE10	942

HEAVEN	AE10	1075
	AE10	1110
	AE10	1144
	AE10	1204
	AE11	5
	AE11	239
	AE11	287
	AE11	307
	AE11	318
	AE11	358
	AE11	399
	AE11	912
	AE11	1152
	AE11	1272
	AE12	67
	AE12	117
	AE12	170
	AE12	204
	AE12	223
	AE12	268
	AE12	294
	AE12	308
	AE12	348
	AE12	798
	AE12	850
	AE12	923
	AE12	982
	AE12	1147
	AE12	1229
	AE12	1237
	AE12	1296
	OAL	62
	OAL	242
	OAL	625
	OAL	732
	AF	71
	MM	3
	MFL	2
	MFL	17
	MFL	24
	DO	24
	DO	86
	DO	116
	DO	135
	KT1	243
	KT1	263
	KT1	389
	KT1	415
	KT2	81
	KT2	87
	KT2	103
	KT2	143
	KT2	154
	KT2	211
	KT2	292
	KT2	318
	KT2	351
	KT2	423
	KT2	540
	KT3	216
	KT3	233
	KT3	423
	KT3	432
	KT3	439
	KT3	526
	KT3	670
	KT3	684
	KT3	790
	KT3	810
	KT3	826
	KT3	1152
	TJD	22
	TJD	40
	TJD	47
	TJD	208
	M8	6
	M8	366
	M8	398
	B	125
	B	215
	B	325
	B	364
	B	663
	B	666
	B	680
	BP	3
	BP	199
	CAM	178
	CAM	179
	CAM	265
	CAM	271
	HIF	161
	HIF	243
	HIF	268
	HIF	555
	HIF	573

HEAVEN

HIF	578
HIF	582
HIF	586
HIF	709
HIF	772
C	9
C	101
C	126
C	176
C	281
C	288
C	473
C	509
C	538
C	610
C	649
C	700
C	748
C	787
TH	116
TH	117
TH	226
TH	231
TH	281
TH	291
M11	65
M11	368
FL	156
FL	371
FL	590
M12	26
M12	57
M12	213
M12	343
AU	67
AU	118
AU	205
AU	218
AU	589
WB	163
WB	386
WB	447
WB	459
WB	542
M15	49
M15	81
M15	120
M15	186
M15	280
M15	366
M15	655
M15	660
M15	715
GP	27
GP	82
CI	122
CI	344
CI	469
CI	537
PMK	33
AS	24
AS	30

HEAVEN-BEGOT	M1	1065
HEAVEN-BORN	HAP	150
	AK	34
	AE9	263
HEAVEN-HIGH	M8	204
HEAVENLY	AR	257
	LC	149
	AM	1081
	CM	19
	EMW	5
	AA	308
	AA	664
	AA	773
	AA	869
	SAA	15
	RL	258
	AT	28
	L1	50
	T18	61
	T23	5
	H3	52
	TA	30
	AK	57
	AK	137
	HAP	543
	HAP	1089
	HAP	1221
	HAP	1727
	SSC	1
	SSC	11
	SSC	46
	EL	204
	EL	348
	P2	110

HEAVENLY

M1	91
M1	101
M1	330
M1	567
M1	673
M1	698
M1	952
VCS	10
DHP	6
DHP	23
VP1	27
VP1	60
VP2	18
VP4	68
VP5	69
VP9	26
G1	563
G2	1
G2	615
G3	146
G4	323
AE1	17
AE1	313
AE1	672
AE1	849
AE2	233
AE2	800
AE3	611
AE4	512
AE4	547
AE5	804
AE5	846
AE6	197
AE6	997
AE7	186
AE7	386
AE7	914
AE8	811
AE8	831
AE9	900
AE12	591
AE12	618
OAL	601
AF	24
MFL	7
B	514
BP	7
BP	199
HIF	26
HIF	526
HIF	781
C	634
M11	229
FL	52
FL	113
M12	306
AU	451
AU	530
WB	531
M15	216

HEAVEN-RAVISHED	UDH	94
HEAVEN'S	UDH	33
	AR	147
	LC	84
	LC	94
	AM	118
	AM	639
	ESF	2
	DA	47
	EMP	6
	AA	7
	AA	265
	AA	361
	AA	584
	PRH	21
	SAA	68
	SAA	446
	SAA	736
	SAA	889
	SAA	1089
	RL	91
	RL	262
	RL	331
	RL	423
	RL	121
	RL	136
	L3	73
	TA	432
	TA	353
	TA	486
	AK	15
	HAP	121
	HAP	1234
	HAP	2096
	HAP	2183
	HAP	2265

HEAVEN'S

BR	353
BR	355
EL	267
P2	12
P5	163
M1	8
M1	217
MC	68
VP10	36
G2	363
G2	458
G2	473
G3	631
G4	459
AE2	542
AE2	470
AE3	480
AE4	997
AE5	968
AE6	443
AE6	546
AE6	716
AE6	746
AE7	191
AE7	612
AE7	857
AE8	444
AE10	154
AE11	31
AE11	167
AE11	470
AE11	471
AE11	879
AE12	226
AE12	1205
DO	85
DO	153
KT3	272
KT3	1133
B	493
BP	13
HIF	80
HIF	325
HIF	711
HIF	795
C	544
TH	167
TH	322
M11	335
FL	322
AU	209
AU	274
AU	455
AU	513
WB	113
M15	89
GP	38
CI	359

HEAVENS	UDH	30
	RH	40
	SMA	90
	AM	9
	AA	973
	D	26
	MF	139
	H29	33
	HAP	1384
	EL	94
	M13	176
	VP6	124
	G1	485
	G3	652
	G3	814
	AE2	328
	AE2	587
	AE3	760
	AE4	550
	AE4	754
	AE4	840
	AE5	14
	AE6	1085
	AE7	416
	AE9	130
	AE9	863
	AE9	872
	AE10	14
	AE11	437
	AE12	121
	KT2	610
	M8	79
	M11	153
	AU	129
	AS	62
	PWR	22
HEAVENS'	AK	9
HEAVES	G3	756

Word	Ref	No.
HEAVES	AE1	210
	AE2	829
	AE5	573
	AE8	941
	M12	393
	M12	684
HEAVIER	PCG1	26
	G2	310
	G2	343
	AE10	1190
	AE12	1079
HEAVINESS	B	204
HEAVING	HAP	1391
	J6	177
	J6	511
	G3	166
	AE4	482
	AE5	236
	AE9	437
	AE10	1162
	AF	156
	KT1	556
	B	746
	M15	457
	CI	155
HEAVINGS	BR	245
	J6	50
HEAVY	AM	900
	PCG1	31
	EOE	11
	PSF	22
	AA	505
	ELB	18
	MD	45
	SAA	406
	PK	39
	AT	33
	AT	123
	HAP	1606
	ODA	10
	J10	61
	J10	369
	P3	66
	P5	177
	M1	24
	M1	361
	M9	28
	M13	46
	HI	6
	GK	58
	VP6	21
	G1	433
	G2	197
	G2	320
	G2	685
	G3	537
	G4	153
	G4	265
	G4	583
	AE1	501
	AE2	609
	AE2	709
	AE3	595
	AE4	990
	AE5	361
	AE5	540
	AE5	583
	AE5	597
	AE5	1116
	AE6	19
	AE6	396
	AE6	701
	AE7	698
	AE8	297
	AE8	555
	AE9	464
	AE9	521
	AE9	584
	AE9	926
	AE9	955
	AE9	979
	AE9	1089
	AE11	836
	AE11	1294
	AE12	468
	AE12	669
	AE12	1312
	KT3	33
	KT3	181
	KT3	400
	KT3	624
	KT3	753
	HIF	780
	C	247
	C	696
	C	720

Word	Ref	No.
HEAVY	TH	339
	M12	119
	M12	583
	M12	754
	AU	38
	AU	312
	AU	502
	WB	115
	WB	203
	M15	215
	M15	347
	M15	385
	M15	484
	M15	496
	CI	53
	CI	228
	EMKG	13
HEAVY-LADEN	G2	287
HEBESUS	AE9	463
HEBREW	AA	128
	AA	440
	MD	161
	RL	243
	PTP	24
HEBREW'S	SAA	970
HEBRON	AA	59
	SAA	328
	SAA	352
	SAA	793
	SAA	803
HEBRONITE	SAA	320
	SAA	330
	SAA	348
HEBRONITISH	SAA	333
HEBRON'S	SAA	1065
HEBRUS	G4	761
	AE10	986
HEBRUS'	AE12	499
HECATE	AE4	740
	AE4	874
	AE6	352
	AE6	368
	AE6	760
HECATOMB	P2	135
	HIF	601
HECATOMBS	HIF	136
	HIF	438
HECTOR	HP	246
	J10	404
	HI	1
	HI	26
	HI	40
	HI	44
	HI	82
	HI	101
	HI	108
	HI	151
	HI	195
	AE1	141
	AE1	677
	AE1	1051
	AE2	358
	AE2	712
	AE2	713
	AE2	739
	AE3	392
	AE3	411
	AE3	441
	AE6	247
	AE6	249
	KT3	870
	HIF	354
	C	391
	M12	4
	M12	104
	M12	106
	M12	721
	M12	778
	M12	808
	AU	133
	AU	136
	AU	284
	AU	385
	AU	428
	AU	434
	HI	59
	HI	133
HECTOR'S	AE2	352
	AE2	415
	AE2	622
	AE3	402
	AE3	408
	AE3	411
	AE3	631
	AE5	245
	AE5	492

Word	Ref	No.
HECTOR'S	AE9	194
	AE11	445
	AE11	624
	AE12	652
	OAL	502
	OAL	786
	KT3	870
	M12	93
	M12	597
	AU	12
	AU	285
HECTORS	PMQ	22
	PAL	22
	GE	47
HECUBA	HP	208
	AE2	704
HEDGE	SAA	1110
	VP8	55
	C	492
	FL	73
	FL	86
HEDGES	M1	665
	VP3	15
	G2	511
	G2	610
	FL	413
HEED	AE2	968
	AE3	327
HEEDLESS	AM	1057
	PPS	9
	AE12	1116
	B	232
HEEDS	M1	938
HEEL	HIF	794
HEELS	J3	394
	P3	209
	P6	146
	M1	926
	G3	362
	G4	663
	VP3	135
	AE5	432
	AE9	448
	AE11	1253
	C	288
	M12	472
	M15	496
HE-GOAT'S	J3	463
HEIFER	J6	66
	M1	843
	M1	851
	M1	889
	M1	1034
	VP3	40
	VP3	72
	VP3	133
	VP8	121
	G3	339
	AE4	83
	AE6	359
	AE8	283
	OAL	333
	OAL	345
	M12	210
HEIFERS	VP7	13
	G4	781
	G4	795
	M10	59
	AE12	1045
HEIGH	EMQ	14
HEIGHT	LC	140
	AM	111
	AM	331
	EEL	41
	SEL4	25
	ECG2	10
	ECG2	15
	DA	21
	EPF	17
	AA	273
	AA	855
	AA	962
	SAA	65
	SAA	101
	SAA	453
	RL	246
	ER	22
	H9	1
	TA	29
	HAP	1739
	HAP	2436
	SSC	40
	STS3	31
	EL	264
	J3	430
	J10	170

HEIGHT	M1	424	HEIR	M1	490	HELD	B	28
	M1	625		M9	12		B	78
	M1	918		HI	34		BP	128
	M13	69		AE4	398		CAM	283
	G1	243		AE9	492		CAM	309
	VP5	24		AE12	45		HIF	22
	G2	172		AE12	1205		HIF	518
	G2	315		DO	145		HIF	528
	G2	602		TJD	43		HIF	658
	G2	686		M8	264		HIF	727
	G3	371		M8	321		C	541
	G3	435		C	615		TH	7
	G3	799		C	641		TH	122
	AE1	699		AU	206		M11	55
	AE2	20		AU	233		M11	255
	AE2	553		M15	601		FL	268
	AE2	629		CI	49		FL	282
	AE2	861		CI	211		FL	300
	AE3	271		PMK	12		FL	520
	AE3	697	HEIRED	AE7	79		FL	538
	AE4	370	HEIRESS	SAA	991		M12	33
	AE4	673	HEIRS	AA	758		M12	196
	AE5	600		MD	319		M12	645
	AE6	907		SAA	281		AU	327
	AE7	395		SAA	770		AU	531
	AE7	934		TA	310		WB	13
	AE8	288		HAP	950		WB	61
	AE8	935		HAP	1093		WB	186
	AE9	93		J6	112		M15	72
	AE9	705		J6	307		CI	416
	AE9	916		J10	353		TA	395
	AE10	327		J10	543	HELDEST	T18	48
	AE10	432		J16	83	HELEN	T18	52
	AE10	629		AE4	904		T18	62
	AE10	758		AE7	367		T27	4
	AE10	1283		AE7	597		VP4	43
	AE11	1069		AE9	882		AE2	775
	AE11	1237	HELD	VHH	16		AE7	511
	AE12	173		AA	206		OAL	773
	AE12	205		AA	628		AF	150
	AE12	822		SAA	12		AF	154
	AE12	1043		SAA	118		M15	354
	KT1	218		SAA	946	HELENOR	AE9	728
	KT1	504		TA	204		AE9	730
	KT2	447		TA	224	HELEN'S	ER	61
	KT3	1089		TA	274		T18	75
	M8	362		HAP	893		T18	79
	M8	359		HAP	1727		AE1	916
	B	115		HAP	2018		AE2	817
	BP	145		ETS	7		AE3	425
	BP	158		J3	27		AE6	689
	HIF	68		J6	403	HELENUS	AE3	381
	M12	456		AE1	750		AE3	426
	M15	215		AE2	276		AE3	432
	CI	344		AE2	330		AE3	487
	CI	428		AE2	622		AE3	551
HEIGHTENED	SMA	64		AE2	744		AE3	719
	AE12	489		AE2	753		AE3	898
HEIGHTENING	TA	255		AE2	806		AE3	914
HEIGHTH	STS3	37		AE2	928		M15	645
	AE4	128		AE3	223		M15	662
HEIGHTS	PT	9		AE4	321	HELICE	M15	447
	SAA	196		AE5	48	HELICON	JH	20
	SAA	957		AE5	62		P5	10
	L2	8		AE6	234		AE7	888
	AE2	773		AE7	710		M8	377
	AE3	379		AE7	834	HELICONIAN	PPS	2
	AE6	1140		AE8	153	HELL	ETL	10
HEIR	AR	52		AE8	373		PKK	9
	LC	61		AE9	1045		MD	280
	AA	436		AE10	366		SAA	352
	AA	441		AE10	583		EDG	34
	AA	975		AE10	855		OE	43
	MD	217		AE10	1138		L2	64
	SAA	165		AE11	438		L3	184
	SAA	255		AE12	86		L3	189
	SAA	579		AE12	557		L3	219
	SAA	764		AE12	710		L3	235
	SAA	793		AE12	800		H3	50
	PDG	21		AE12	1071		HAP	343
	HAP	1336		OAL	611		M1	145
	HAP	1353		KT1	44		M1	176
	HAP	2008		KT1	66		M1	245
	BR	17		KT1	610		SLT1	5
	BR	125		KT2	461		DHP	16
	J3	82		KT2	517		DHP	22
	J3	262		KT2	626		VP10	98
	J3	269		KT3	455		G1	52
	J6	54		KT3	843		G1	646
	J10	376		KT3	914		G4	690
	P2	40		KT3	934		G4	705
	P2	68		KT3	976		AE3	740
	P6	78		KT3	1007		AE4	243
	P6	124		M8	148		AE5	132
	P6	129		M8	292		AE6	160
	P6	142		B	13		AE6	192

HELL	AE6	353
	AE6	356
	AE6	384
	AE7	433
	AE7	771
	AE7	786
	AE10	49
	AE10	57
	AE12	296
	AE12	1267
	KT1	364
	KT1	390
	KT2	81
	KT2	475
	KT3	233
	M8	307
	B	679
	TH	165
	TH	228
	M11	137
	GP	27
	CI	344
HELLEBORE	P3	123
	P4	34
	P5	144
	G3	689
HELLE'S	G1	297
HELLHOUNDS	TH	142
	TH	213
	TH	332
HELLISH	AE3	308
	AE7	625
	TH	394
HELL'S	AA	373
	SAA	240
	M1	245
	G2	402
	AE3	281
HELM	SAA	202
	J10	213
	HI	152
	HI	189
	AE3	600
	AE5	229
	AE5	485
	AE5	1132
	AE6	478
	AE7	832
	AE8	822
	AE9	55
	AE9	206
	AE9	413
	AE9	497
	AE9	507
	AE9	1041
	AE9	1092
	AE9	1097
	AE10	269
	AE10	744
	AE10	1244
	AE11	1007
	AE11	1030
	AE11	1139
	AE12	139
	AE12	716
	AE12	789
	AE12	1059
	KT3	455
	KT3	687
	FL	268
	M12	119
	M12	198
	M12	620
	AU	171
HELMET	AE5	412
	AE5	654
	AE5	881
	AE9	608
	AE10	456
	AE10	989
	AE10	1189
	AE11	1022
	AE12	643
	AE12	562
	KT3	36
	KT3	584
	KT3	643
HELMETS	G1	665
	AE7	252
	AE7	875
	AE12	1039
HELMS	AE2	554
	AE9	839
	AE9	907
	AE11	120
	AE11	296

HELMS	KT3	603
HELON'S	SAA	1003
HELOPS	M12	452
	M12	453
HELOTS	AR	205
HELP	PIE	27
	AM	993
	SCD1	23
	ESF	13
	EAL	26
	PO	29
	CM	19
	HP	223
	AA	540
	MD	137
	MD	305
	SAA	98
	PAA	45
	HH	30
	HAP	470
	HAP	559
	HAP	1378
	HAP	1391
	HAP	1414
	J3	230
	J3	311
	J6	774
	P2	12
	P6	64
	M1	376
	M1	552
	M1	737
	M1	1015
	M13	205
	M13	206
	VCS	22
	VP9	88
	G3	696
	G4	650
	AE11	717
	KT1	238
	KT1	265
	KT1	411
	KT2	154
	KT3	707
	KT3	826
	TJD	30
	TJD	81
	M8	114
	B	40
	B	459
	CAM	75
	C	99
	C	232
	C	233
	C	241
	C	793
	FL	497
	WB	241
HELPED	PUO5	20
	OE	30
	TH	192
	AU	114
HELPFUL	AM	971
	AE8	525
HELPING	AE5	1119
	AE9	752
	AE10	470
HELPLESS	LC	20
	AM	519
	AM	904
	DA	134
	EK	34
	L5	4
	TA	191
	GE	24
	HAP	1909
	J3	276
	HI	51
	VP1	42
	G3	496
	AE1	683
	AE2	704
	AE2	812
	AE7	723
	AE11	950
	AE11	1278
	AE12	859
	KT1	92
	KT3	1071
	B	419
	HIF	53
	TH	311
	M11	174
	M15	301
	M15	335

HELPLESS	CI	622
HELPS	UDH	86
	CM	73
	MD	68
	RL	180
	M1	416
	OAL	592
HELVETIAN	HAP	178
HELYMUS	AE5	94
	AE5	394
	AE5	422
	AE5	442
	M12	611
HEMISPHERE	UDH	46
	LC	33
	RL	9
	AS	1
HEMMED	AE4	55
HEN	EWGR	11
	CAM	47
	C	80
HENBANE	HAP	2375
HENCHMEN	FL	264
HENPECKED	VP3	49
HENRY'S	HAP	1497
	HAP	1614
	HAP	1616
HEPTARCHY	KT3	291
HERACLITUS	EUF	23
HERALD	AE4	510
	AE5	318
	AE12	118
	KT3	524
	KT3	572
HERALDRY	J6	239
HERALD'S	P3	47
	HIF	470
HERALDS	HAP	348
	HAP	1450
	KT1	146
	KT3	494
	KT3	578
	KT3	663
	KT3	683
	HIF	447
	HIF	539
	M11	100
	FL	251
HERB	DO	134
	BP	89
HERBAGE	HAP	213
	VP7	61
	VP10	113
	G2	275
	G3	606
	G3	791
	G4	578
HERBLESS	SAA	1108
HERBS	CM	45
	J6	770
	P4	44
	P6	45
	P6	91
	M1	701
	M1	869
	VP4	23
	G1	158
	G2	792
	G3	198
	G3	358
	G3	505
	AE2	645
	AE3	856
	AE7	26
	AE7	262
	AE7	1039
	AE7	1057
	AE12	620
	CAM	373
	C	15
	C	171
	FL	418
	M15	105
	M15	491
	M15	582
HERCULEAN	G2	18
	AE5	550
	AE10	444
	M12	473
HERCULES	RH	39
	TA	35
	J1	81
	J3	156
	J10	556
	P2	19
	AE3	724

HERCULES	AE6	1093
	AE7	912
	AE7	924
	AE8	140
	AE8	266
	AE8	382
	AE8	719
	AE10	648
	OAL	215
	M8	398
	M12	707
	M12	740
	M12	758
	AU	32
	M15	28
	M15	352
	M15	434
HERD	HS	138
	AM	59
	EMQ	13
	ESF	34
	AA	533
	SAA	519
	AT	105
	T27	9
	T27	131
	TA	141
	HAP	264
	HAP	498
	HAP	549
	HAP	554
	J6	576
	J6	660
	J10	265
	M1	840
	M1	910
	M1	934
	VP2	29
	VP3	155
	VP6	74
	VP8	48
	VP8	5
	VP9	28
	G3	253
	G4	793
	AE11	1014
	AE12	1045
	OAL	326
	OAL	331
	OAL	338
HERDED	AM	1029
HERDING	B	479
HERDS	EC	9
	L4	196
	L5	9
	T27	114
	H2	24
	AK	108
	HAP	391
	J10	353
	P2	85
	M1	94
	VP4	26
	VP5	37
	VP5	48
	VP6	69
	G1	18
	G1	652
	G2	199
	G2	270
	G3	112
	G3	451
	G3	486
	G3	545
	G3	565
	G3	568
	G3	828
	G4	327
	AE3	286
	AE3	845
	AE4	221
	AE4	763
	AE7	21
	AE7	749
	AE7	918
	AE8	269
	AE11	257
	AE11	302
	AE11	1186
HERDSMAN	J3	119
	G4	625
	AE8	279
	KT2	181
HERDSMEN	G2	770
HEREDITARY	M1	110
	VP4	32

HEREDITARY	AE11	389
HERESIES	HAP	1157
	HAP	1165
HERESY	HAP	356
	HAP	1172
	HAP	1193
HERETICS	RL	223
	HAP	726
	HAP	1106
HERILUS	AE8	746
HERMAPHRODITE	PR	35
HERMES	M1	932
	M1	951
	M1	988
	G1	460
	AE4	350
	AE4	545
	AE4	820
	KT1	547
	BP	23
	AU	237
HERMINIUS	AE11	952
HERMIONE	OAL	850
HERMIT	AM	1042
HERMIT'S	HAP	1271
HERMO	STP	11
	STP	13
HERMON	SAA	58
HERMUS	G2	188
	AE7	996
HERNICUS	AE7	946
HERO	VHH	1
	PAL	10
	HP	21
	PUO3	17
	MD	26
	SAA	613
	SAA	617
	SAA	625
	SAA	720
	SAA	969
	SAA	1103
	EC	1
	TA	53
	TA	276
	HAP	2459
	BR	58
	BR	140
	PSH	34
	J10	255
	AE1	812
	AE1	1000
	AE2	343
	AE4	119
	AE4	336
	AE4	648
	AE5	48
	AE5	170
	AE5	373
	AE5	399
	AE5	543
	AE5	899
	AE5	1012
	AE5	1129
	AE6	349
	AE6	435
	AE6	612
	AE6	641
	AE6	739
	AE6	910
	AE6	1165
	AE6	1227
	AE7	151
	AE7	183
	AE7	258
	AE7	1003
	AE8	279
	AE8	312
	AE8	333
	AE8	389
	AE8	581
	AE9	17
	AE9	263
	AE9	1038
	AE10	217
	AE10	712
	AE10	737
	AE10	799
	AE10	843
	AE11	105
	AE11	160
	AE11	260
	AE11	338
	AE12	585
	AE12	636
	AE12	706

HERO	AE12	729
	AE12	744
	AE12	849
	AE12	1014
	AE12	1132
	AE12	1333
	OAL	11
	OAL	217
	OAL	791
	AF	4
	KT1	18
	M8	346
	HIF	3
	HIF	100
	HIF	284
	HIF	336
	M11	166
	M12	136
	M12	164
	M12	173
	M12	332
	M12	469
	AU	264
	AU	433
	AU	474
	M15	22
	PWR	39
HEROD'S	P5	264
HEROES	LCA	33
	AM	195
	AM	245
	PAZ	28
	HP	53
	HP	244
	EPC	15
	MF	75
	SAA	629
	T18	31
	TA	432
	TA	435
	PAA	6
	PP	25
	EL	199
	P1	131
	GK	170
	VP4	19
	G3	56
	AE1	144
	AE2	317
	AE7	892
	AE11	528
	AE12	768
	M8	88
	M12	98
	EP	4
HEROES'	GK	119
	AE6	425
HEROIC	UDH	104
	HS	51
	HS	105
	AM	461
	EMQw	6
	ML	31
	PUO3	15
	TA	128
	EL	147
	J3	341
	VP4	31
	G4	290
	AE6	875
	AE6	881
	AE8	867
	AE9	366
	AE10	1123
	AE11	985
HEROICALLY	SAA	417
HEROINE	B	376
HEROINES	AK	140
HERON	AE11	870
HERONS	G1	498
HERO'S	UDH	40
	SAA	1066
	TA	327
	TA	457
	HAP	10
	BR	335
	G4	684
	AE1	163
	AE1	681
	AE4	3
	AE5	353
	AE5	918
	AE5	1083
	AE6	1193
	AE7	688
	AE8	356

HERO'S	AE8	975
	AE10	727
	AE11	445
	AE11	582
	AE12	142
	M12	636
	AU	55
	AU	251
HERRING	EDG	40
HERRINGMAN	MF	105
HERRINGS	PCD	9
HESIOD	OAL	32
HESPERIA	AE1	748
	AE3	221
HESPERIAN	VP8	72
	AE4	700
HESPERIA'S	AE7	5
HESPERUS	G3	504
HEW	HAP	1998
	AE1	596
	AE2	629
	AE9	433
	AE10	520
	KT1	588
HEWED	AE6	63
	AE8	296
	AE10	582
	KT2	555
	KT3	603
	B	423
	CAM	134
	AU	189
HEWN	AE4	524
	AE10	313
HEWS	AE2	659
	AE10	716
	AE11	967
HEXAMETERS	OAE1	31
HEYWOOD	MF	29
	MF	102
HEZEKIAH'S	TA	106
HIBERNIA	DO	53
HID	RH	76
	ECG1	10
	DA	150
	RL	187
	H29	45
	HAP	793
	HAP	1896
	BR	235
	ETS	15
	J6	594
	J10	283
	VP6	90
	AE2	185
	AE3	663
	AE3	704
	AE6	41
	AE6	638
	AE7	855
	AE12	1293
	OAL	286
	KT2	68
	KT2	566
	KT3	942
	M10	17
	CAM	199
	FL	447
	FL	584
	AU	115
	WB	336
	M15	84
	CI	160
HIDDEN	RH	22
	H2	43
	HAP	1262
	EL	164
	P2	22
	G1	267
	G1	627
	AE1	156
	AE1	246
	AE1	494
	AE2	49
	AE2	338
	AE4	148
	AE6	1092
	OAL	252
	OAL	836
	HIF	734
	AU	84
	M15	9
HIDE	SMA	92
	LC	68
	AM	330
	AM	783

HIDE	EMQ	6
	SLN	7
	SCD1	11
	ELB	14
	PPC	14
	EPC	3
	L4	182
	T18	43
	T23	82
	H3	14
	TA	133
	HAP	1147
	HAP	1256
	HAP	1271
	HAP	2173
	HAP	2569
	EH	27
	J3	51
	M1	312
	M13	121
	VP5	61
	VP8	81
	G2	634
	G3	152
	G3	751
	AE1	447
	AE1	508
	AE2	24
	AE2	134
	AE2	981
	AE3	310
	AE4	366
	AE5	72
	AE5	460
	AE7	582
	AE7	680
	AE7	780
	AE7	925
	AE7	954
	AE7	1090
	AE8	240
	AE8	604
	AE8	732
	AE9	411
	AE9	1055
	AE10	1008
	AE11	738
	AE11	864
	AE11	912
	AE11	1006
	AE11	1183
	OAL	528
	MFL	18
	B	40
	B	459
	HIF	745
	M12	438
	WB	179
	M15	521
	M15	541
	M15	547
HIDEOUS	EPC	4
	TA	391
	HAP	2336
	AE3	293
	AE7	456
	AE7	625
	KT2	537
HIDES	RH	19
	AM	142
	AM	851
	PLB	9
	H9	37
	BR	204
	J3	97
	J6	5
	J10	241
	G2	648
	G3	833
	G4	381
	AE1	428
	AE3	536
	AE3	544
	AE3	760
	AE4	240
	AE5	539
	AE6	13
	AE6	396
	AE6	894
	AE7	208
	AE7	788
	AE8	483
	AE8	948
	AE9	957
	AE10	677
	AE10	1088

HIDES	AE10	1114
	AE11	627
	AE11	1053
	AE12	1022
	KT3	31
	M12	128
	M12	579
	M15	130
HIDING	B	633
HIE	SMP	28
HIERA	AE9	915
HIERARCHY	HAP	864
	HAP	1080
HIES	VP3	98
	M10	72
	CAM	256
HIEW	MHD	1
HIGH	HS	109
	HS	112
	HS	147
	AR	195
	RH	11
	SMA	38
	SMA	51
	LC	15
	PRL	12
	EIE	18
	AM	252
	AM	486
	AM	639
	AM	694
	AM	712
	AM	846
	AM	1186
	EEL	31
	PTL	3
	STL	19
	ECG1	21
	ECG2	23
	PFD	28
	ML	30
	EMK	18
	CM	75
	DA	43
	AA	148
	AA	160
	AA	306
	AA	482
	AA	500
	AA	634
	AA	642
	AA	684
	AA	813
	AA	896
	MF	107
	SAA	60
	SAA	179
	SAA	334
	SAA	557
	SAA	558
	SAA	820
	SAA	1014
	SAA	1127
	RL	3
	RL	209
	RL	222
	AT	23
	AT	57
	AT	109
	PD	38
	L3	186
	L4	275
	T18	73
	T23	105
	H29	17
	H29	29
	H29	53
	TA	353
	AK	45
	GE	72
	HAP	345
	HAP	1021
	HAP	1082
	HAP	1797
	HAP	1929
	HAP	2253
	HAP	2265
	HAP	2301
	HAP	2424
	HAP	2553
	SSC	6
	SSC	61
	BR	54
	BR	80
	BR	234
	EL	91

HIGH	EL	340
	J 1	116
	J 1	173
	J 1	241
	J 3	279
	J 3	410
	J 6	91
	J 6	154
	J 6	505
	J 6	659
	J 6	700
	J 10	53
	J 10	67
	J 10	214
	J 10	246
	J 10	252
	J 10	428
	J 10	496
	J 16	94
	PPS	16
	P 1	40
	P 1	108
	P 1	196
	P 1	219
	P 3	77
	P 4	28
	P 5	42
	P 5	75
	P 6	114
	P 6	171
	M 1	8
	M 1	32
	M 1	83
	M 1	208
	M 1	399
	M 1	430
	M 1	438
	M 1	809
	M 1	819
	M 9	35
	M 9	50
	M 9	147
	M 13	225
	VCS	13
	H I	149
	MC	53
	GK	145
	DHP	23
	VP 3	80
	VP 6	27
	VP 7	31
	VP 8	55
	VP 8	84
	G 1	139
	G 1	155
	G 1	298
	G 1	453
	G 1	485
	G 1	606
	G 1	655
	G 2	140
	G 2	258
	G 2	401
	G 2	537
	G 2	647
	G 2	694
	G 2	783
	G 3	41
	G 3	75
	G 3	319
	G 3	681
	G 3	829
	G 4	116
	G 4	459
	G 4	559
	AE 1	17
	AE 1	84
	AE 1	224
	AE 1	406
	AE 1	656
	AE 1	711
	AE 1	956
	AE 1	981
	AE 1	979
	AE 2	205
	AE 2	384
	AE 2	647
	AE 2	850
	AE 2	958
	AE 2	971
	AE 2	557
	AE 2	595
	AE 2	611
	AE 3	194
	AE 3	322
	AE 3	376

HIGH	AE 3	748
	AE 3	891
	AE 4	34
	AE 4	134
	AE 4	646
	AE 4	729
	AE 5	113
	AE 5	147
	AE 5	225
	AE 5	379
	AE 5	592
	AE 5	957
	AE 5	1012
	AE 5	1072
	AE 6	23
	AE 6	486
	AE 6	651
	AE 6	697
	AE 6	744
	AE 6	800
	AE 6	816
	AE 6	860
	AE 6	1067
	AE 6	1204
	AE 7	84
	AE 7	181
	AE 7	191
	AE 7	243
	AE 7	266
	AE 7	378
	AE 7	556
	AE 7	631
	AE 7	670
	AE 7	857
	AE 7	965
	AE 7	1000
	AE 7	1021
	AE 7	1058
	AE 7	1072
	AE 8	71
	AE 8	152
	AE 8	174
	AE 8	325
	AE 8	361
	AE 8	363
	AE 8	373
	AE 8	553
	AE 8	625
	AE 8	695
	AE 8	712
	AE 8	867
	AE 8	961
	AE 9	349
	AE 9	436
	AE 9	620
	AE 9	697
	AE 9	714
	AE 9	1013
	AE 9	1102
	AE 10	90
	AE 10	299
	AE 10	366
	AE 10	643
	AE 10	699
	AE 10	1156
	AE 10	1290
	AE 11	11
	AE 11	207
	AE 11	372
	AE 11	438
	AE 11	595
	AE 11	635
	AE 11	723
	AE 11	751
	AE 11	795
	AE 11	893
	AE 11	1105
	AE 11	1153
	AE 11	1215
	AE 11	1232
	AE 11	1289
	AE 12	128
	AE 12	434
	AE 12	550
	AE 12	764
	AE 12	784
	AE 12	800
	AE 12	824
	AE 12	952
	AE 12	1038
	AE 12	1085
	AE 12	1304
	OAL	617
	AF	20
	AF	78
	AF	143

HIGH	MFL	21
	KT 1	37
	KT 1	44
	KT 1	69
	KT 1	115
	KT 1	600
	KT 2	81
	KT 2	283
	KT 2	543
	KT 2	549
	KT 2	612
	KT 3	9
	KT 3	342
	KT 3	438
	KT 3	493
	KT 3	532
	KT 3	546
	KT 3	660
	KT 3	929
	KT 3	951
	KT 3	976
	KT 3	1014
	KT 3	1026
	M 8	11
	M 8	291
	B	50
	B	485
	BP	62
	CAM	57
	CAM	206
	HIF	549
	C	38
	C	49
	C	489
	C	543
	C	656
	C	666
	C	701
	TH	10
	TH	120
	TH	284
	TH	316
	M 11	135
	M 11	335
	FL	167
	FL	194
	FL	374
	M 12	178
	M 12	262
	M 12	344
	M 12	814
	AU	582
	WB	52
	WB	61
	WB	380
	M 15	236
	M 15	284
	M 15	288
	M 15	368
	M 15	409
	M 15	468
	GP	19
	GP	96
	GP	109
HIGH-DESIGNING	AK	132
HIGHER	LC	30
	E I E	15
	AM	260
	SMQ	16
	ECG 2	21
	PFD	20
	PUO 2	37
	AA	482
	MD	165
	SAA	356
	RL	77
	RL	437
	OE	5
	H 9	2
	TA	125
	TA	461
	HAP	1606
	HAP	184
	HAP	316
	HAP	1525
	SSC	51
	PKA	7
	EL	101
	J 3	362
	J 10	18
	M 13	11
	MC	18
	AE 7	1075
	AE 8	238
	OAL	277
	KT 1	597

Word	Ref	No.
HIGHER	B	28
	FL	174
	WB	389
HIGHEST	HS	10
	HS	126
	SMA	16
	PMM	4
	ECG1	8
	EMQW	18
	HP	128
	OE	15
	J1	223
	AE4	750
	OAL	652
	B	186
	HIF	549
	FL	514
HIGH-FLYER	PMS	15
HIGH-FLYING	EPC	6
	G4	162
HIGH-MOUNTED	BR	5
HIGHNESS	VHH	21
HIGH-RAISED	AM	233
	AM	1166
HIGH-SHOED	P5	147
HIGHT	PCB	24
	PUO3	9
	MF	67
	C	41
HILL	SMA	3
	LC	139
	M1	942
	VP1	117
	G3	65
	AE2	1094
	AE3	715
	AE3	758
	AE6	11
	AE6	916
	AE6	920
	AE9	251
	AE10	355
	AE11	488
	AE12	207
	AE12	659
	HIF	711
	M12	456
	M15	451
	M15	458
HILLOCK	AE3	32
HILLOCKS	G2	260
HILL'S	AE6	64
HILLS	AM	449
	PUF	3
	SAA	979
	HAP	1850
	M1	194
	M1	420
	VP5	40
	VP6	46
	VP10	49
	G1	331
	G1	467
	G2	95
	G2	215
	G2	369
	G2	373
	G2	409
	G2	539
	G2	783
	G3	76
	G3	77
	G3	427
	G3	490
	G3	575
	G3	825
	AE3	123
	AE3	663
	AE3	685
	AE4	216
	AE4	237
	AE4	438
	AE5	198
	AE7	1091
	AE8	407
	AE8	427
	AE8	793
	AE11	791
	AE11	852
	AE12	1345
	C	649
HILLS'	G3	435
HILLY	H2	23
	M1	918
	G2	249
	G2	481

Word	Ref	No.
HILLY	G2	619
	G2	694
	G3	548
	G3	702
	G3	799
	AE7	1005
	AE8	624
	AE10	641
	AE11	1232
	AE11	1301
HILT	AE12	1065
HILTS	AE10	746
HIMELLA'S	AE7	987
HIND	T27	39
	HAP	1
	HAP	286
	HAP	302
	HAP	326
	HAP	327
	HAP	528
	HAP	537
	HAP	552
	HAP	557
	HAP	562
	HAP	590
	HAP	616
	HAP	642
	HAP	744
	HAP	877
	HAP	1235
	HAP	1293
	HAP	1310
	HAP	1324
	HAP	1438
	HAP	1512
	HAP	1670
	HAP	1933
	HAP	2141
	HAP	2181
	HAP	2583
	P4	61
	M9	102
	M13	95
	VP4	49
	VP8	39
	G1	278
	G1	479
	G2	560
	G3	418
	G3	637
	AE4	96
	AE6	1094
	AE10	1141
	AE12	669
	KT1	573
	M12	51
HINDER	PEL	31
	SM1	16
	AA	1008
	EDG	10
	L4	239
	HAP	1461
	HAP	1803
	P2	82
	P6	116
	VP10	82
	G1	673
	AE5	822
	AE10	138
	AE10	385
	M15	556
	SMP	18
HINDERANCE	AE10	606
HINDERED	AM	530
	KT2	358
	B	744
	CAM	69
	C	28
	LC	142
HINDERS	E	5
	M9	128
	PAZ	22
HINDMOST	P5	98
	G3	175
	KT1	294
HINDRANCE	AM	445
HINDS	HAP	2213
	HAP	2278
	P6	90
	M1	395
	VP2	10
	VP8	33
	G1	652
	G2	357
	AE2	847
	M8	36

Word	Ref	No.
HINDS	G2	415
HINGE	KT2	551
HINGES	AE1	631
	AE2	658
	AE6	775
	AE7	858
	AE9	979
	M11	291
HINT	J3	253
	MFL	26
HINTED	HAP	1709
	B	125
	M8	59
	M12	475
	J6	116
	J10	349
HIPPOCOÖN	AE5	655
HIPPOCOÖN'S	AE5	666
HIPPODAME	G3	11
	M12	293
HIPPODAMIA'S	OAE2	7
HIPPOLYTA	KT1	21
	KT2	227
HIPPOLYTUS	AE7	1043
	AE7	1049
	AE7	1063
	OAL	381
	OAL	576
HIPPOMANES	G3	443
HIPPOMENES	AT	91
HIPPOPLACUS	HI	35
HIPS	M8	140
HIRE	PSF	44
	AT	74
	TA	377
	PSH	5
	J3	56
	J3	71
	J3	367
	J6	667
	J10	498
	AE12	527
	KT1	579
	KT2	454
	WB	249
	WB	302
	EMKG	6
HIRED	EPC	10
	SAA	357
	HAP	862
	J3	22
	AE2	42
HIRELING	AA	922
	J3	224
	P3	207
HIRELINGS	SAA	318
HIRES	PD	46
	J3	70
	J6	619
	AE10	539
HISBON	M13	61
HISS	G4	592
	AE7	911
	AF	134
	M15	577
HISSED	MS	20
	AE9	789
	AE12	715
	M12	390
HISSES	AE9	866
	AE11	1108
	KT2	112
HISSING	AM	390
	TA	453
	TA	464
	J6	806
	J10	92
	J10	267
	G1	269
	G3	642
	G3	658
	G4	250
	AE1	67
	AE2	65
	AE2	279
	AE2	647
	AE5	627
	AE5	915
	AE6	393
	AE6	822
	AE8	399
	AE8	591
	AE8	888
	AE9	138
	AE9	553
	AE10	481

Word	Ref	Num
HISSING	AE10	1080
	AE10	1100
	AE11	820
	AE12	144
	AE12	309
	AE12	604
	AE12	1228
	KT3	222
	KT3	991
	M8	186
	CAM	93
	M12	409
HISSINGS	AE7	458
	AE7	626
	AE8	556
HISTORIAN'S	KT2	436
HISTORY	RL	353
	J6	580
	GK	153
HIT	EWGR	2
	PEL	18
	PLN	20
	PUO1	34
	EDGA	12
	EDGA	33
	HAP	995
	HAP	1838
	AE9	523
	WB	144
HITS	OE	47
	ELT	29
HITTING	EAZ	9
HIVE	AM	910
	G4	13
	G4	56
	G4	92
	G4	238
	G4	242
	G4	312
	G4	384
	AE1	607
	EWR	24
HIVES	G4	59
	G4	63
	G4	81
	G4	158
	G4	364
	G4	373
	G4	377
	G4	405
	OAL	105
HO	VP3	1
	VP9	1
	AE1	443
HOARD	L4	22
	HAP	1402
	G4	231
	TJD	117
HOARDED	M15	460
HOARINESS	M1	316
HOARSE	PAA	38
	J1	2
	J6	500
	VP1	25
	VP8	76
	VP9	51
	VP9	73
	G4	100
	AE1	201
	AE7	972
	AE11	719
	CI	331
HOARSELY	AE11	137
	TH	279
HOARSENESS	VP10	110
HOARSE-RESOUNDING	HIF	54
HOARY	MF	106
	H9	1
	H2	46
	HAP	1270
	G2	168
	G2	356
	G3	485
	G4	766
	AE2	754
	AE3	107
	AE4	743
	AE4	914
	AE5	841
	AE6	414
	AE6	1105
	AE7	587
	AE7	1034
	AE9	342
	AE9	890
	AE10	277
HOARY	AE10	1203
	AE11	128
	KT3	871
	M8	371
	CAM	224
	HIF	21
	HIF	517
	FL	584
HOBBLING	ER	13
HOBBY-HORSES	EUO	14
HOBBY'S	AM	780
HOBNAILED	J3	398
	J16	37
HOGS	PLN	12
	ELB	36
	C	730
HOIGH	SKA4	25
	SKA4	28
HOIST	P3	211
	AE3	606
	AE3	896
	AE8	653
	M11	93
HOISTED	HP	199
	AE2	32
	AE5	228
HOISTING-LEVERS	AE2	307
HOISTS	AE8	939
HOLD	PRL	23
	AM	216
	AM	829
	ETL	1
	HP	94
	MD	65
	MD	234
	SAA	154
	SAA	189
	SAA	538
	SAA	750
	EDG	14
	RL	311
	AT	96
	L4	169
	L4	291
	T27	13
	T27	119
	H9	20
	HAP	63
	HAP	1057
	HAP	1380
	HAP	1442
	HAP	1576
	HAP	1653
	HAP	2010
	HAP	2034
	HAP	2141
	BR	207
	BR	297
	BR	361
	ETS	25
	PMS	10
	EL	108
	J10	150
	J10	393
	ESH	30
	P2	104
	P3	177
	P4	12
	P4	23
	P4	38
	P5	122
	P6	60
	M1	58
	M1	874
	M1	1062
	M13	83
	VCS	25
	GK	129
	VP3	117
	G2	431
	G2	505
	G3	24
	G3	487
	G3	620
	G4	552
	G4	586
	AE1	119
	AE1	324
	AE1	553
	AE2	604
	AE2	975
	AE3	81
	AE5	276
	AE5	297
	AE6	303
	AE7	202
HOLD	AE7	560
	AE7	834
	AE7	1023
	AE8	227
	AE8	259
	AE8	301
	AE8	823
	AE9	380
	AE9	814
	AE9	821
	AE10	590
	AE10	872
	AE10	1168
	AE11	1146
	AE12	534
	AE12	553
	AE12	1006
	AE12	1128
	OAL	399
	OAL	687
	OAL	705
	OAL	879
	OAE2	31
	DO	143
	KT3	474
	M8	334
	B	610
	B	713
	HIF	184
	HIF	691
	C	219
	C	478
	C	508
	TH	117
	M11	209
	AU	173
	WB	104
	WB	145
	WB	155
	M15	365
	CI	282
	CI	557
HOLDING	EDG	33
	EDG	36
	HI	142
	AE10	473
	FL	449
	PMK	15
HOLDS	DA	197
	MD	214
	SAA	518
	L4	204
	HAP	1094
	HAP	2153
	J1	55
	J6	776
	J10	280
	M1	927
	G2	398
	AE2	827
	AE4	82
	AE4	480
	AE4	750
	AE5	303
	AE5	654
	AE6	1030
	AE10	311
	AE10	811
	AE12	1094
	OAL	361
	KT2	107
	KT2	364
	KT3	732
	KT3	823
	KT3	1030
	CAM	206
	GP	100
	AS	40
HOLE	P1	237
	G1	267
	G2	313
	G3	810
HOLES	AE2	357
HOLIDAY	PEL	22
	PLG	32
	MD	17
	AK	55
	HAP	1854
	P6	167
	P6	168
	FL	486
	CI	79
HOLIDAYS	J3	65
	J3	282
	J10	131
	P5	259

Word	Ref	No.	Word	Ref	No.	Word	Ref	No.
HOME	VHH	8	HOME	AE11	1164	HOMER	C	202
	AM	2		AE11	1277		M12	818
	AM	128		OAL	96	HOMER'S	PTC	40
	AM	508		OAL	235		ER	52
	AM	534		OAL	460		HAP	2438
	AM	550		OAL	672		GK	63
	AM	724		OAE2	76	HOMES	AM	1017
	AM	816		KT1	11		VP1	94
	AM	1017		KT1	365		G2	736
	EWGR	43		KT1	427		AE3	279
	PEL	20		KT1	433		AE7	296
	PEL	33		TJD	9		KT3	748
	EEL	33		M8	35	HOMESPUN	P6	175
	PCG1	38		CAM	256	HOMESTEAD	H29	62
	PW	3		HIF	30		C	13
	PM	9		HIF	52		C	39
	PM	27		HIF	255	HOMEWARD	T27	133
	EM	19		TH	352		J3	452
	PUO1	16		M11	239		VP4	25
	DA	168		AU	34		G1	296
	UMR	7		AU	59		G3	577
	MD	106		AU	344		G4	12
	SAA	331		AU	362		AE7	967
	SAA	346		AU	530		HIF	87
	SAA	459		WB	207		TH	231
	SAA	997		M15	544		FL	610
	OE	12		CI	199	HOMICIDE	HAP	1553
	PD	56		CI	640		HIF	354
	ER	8		ETP	42	HOMINIS	C	418
	L4	253	HOME-BORN	G1	668	HOMO	J6	394
	L4	262	HOME-BRED	HAP	1133	HONEST	HP	226
	T27	9		G2	657		PSF	24
	T27	85	HOMELIER	L4	166		AA	105
	H2	68	HOMELY	PNH	8		AA	507
	AK	171		ENH	2		ELB	15
	HAP	405		PAL	34		MD	61
	HAP	840		AA	101		SAA	530
	HAP	862		AT	110		RL	317
	HAP	1468		PD	46		L4	287
	HAP	1481		L4	289		T27	17
	HAP	1590		T23	81		T27	61
	HAP	2578		H29	24		HAP	1250
	BR	88		HAP	1248		HAP	1271
	PP	31		HAP	1302		HAP	2172
	PKA	33		HAP	2199		HAP	2221
	EL	45		PMS	34		HAP	2444
	J1	10		EH	12		EH	14
	J1	199		J3	119		J1	233
	J3	345		J3	285		J3	51
	J3	483		J6	6		J3	94
	J6	222		J10	38		J3	337
	J6	522		P1	252		J6	133
	J6	601		P3	107		J16	25
	J6	748		P6	39		J16	50
	J10	259		P6	91		P1	252
	J10	508		M1	156		M9	5
	P1	29		VP1	42		ELT	35
	P1	141		VP2	78		VP3	29
	P5	73		G1	410		G2	540
	P6	112		G2	648		G4	138
	M1	1006		G2	667		AE10	556
	HI	3		G2	766		AF	52
	HI	163		G2	780		KT3	100
	HI	183		G3	282		M8	351
	HI	192		G3	790		B	712
	ELT	19		G4	196		C	797
	VP1	4		AE1	583		AU	408
	VP1	31		AE4	236		WB	465
	VP2	71		AE4	380		PMK	4
	VP3	65		AE5	54	HONESTY	PCD	34
	VP3	119		AE7	155		SAA	84
	VP6	86		AE7	928		HAP	1133
	G1	369		AE8	133		HAP	1457
	G2	240		AE8	234		HAP	2226
	G2	287		AE8	458		PLT	41
	G2	712		AE8	479	HONEY	SAA	879
	G2	717		AE8	718		OE	26
	G3	16		AE8	771		L3	70
	G3	152		OAL	121		H2	27
	G3	331		OAE2	60		EKA	34
	G3	492		BP	30		J6	261
	G4	41		HIF	51		M1	143
	G4	197		HIF	800		VP3	139
	G4	228		C	32		VP4	35
	G4	234		FL	616		G1	472
	G4	261		WB	453		G2	610
	G4	265		WB	490		G2	634
	G4	628		ER	76		G4	2
	AE2	153	HOMER	L3	253		G4	82
	AE2	481		HAP	2115		G4	239
	AE2	858		J6	563		G4	258
	AE6	1132		P6	25		G4	299
	AE8	55		GK	99		G4	312
	AE8	441		VP8	16		G4	337
	AE10	523		MG	40		G4	384
	AE10	780		DO	3		AE4	702

Word	Code	Num
HONEY	AE6	567
	OAL	854
	KT2	16
	KT3	946
	KT3	989
	HIF	364
	M15	110
	M15	544
HONEY-BAG	PTS	7
HONEYCOMB	BP	116
HONEYCOMBS	G4	153
HONEYMOON	PEL	5
HONEYSUCKLES	G4	87
HONOR	UDH	2
	AR	74
	RH	97
	DC	32
	PWG	57
	VHH	10
	AM	42
	AM	179
	AM	754
	ECG2	21
	SCG3	6
	SCG3	26
	PM	18
	S	5
	A	2
	A	4
	ECD	12
	PNH	17
	EMK	16
	HP	17
	HP	69
	DA	8
	EMW	8
	PSF	3
	AA	165
	AA	312
	AA	818
	AA	835
	AA	844
	SAA	822
	SAA	957
	ER	70
	L2	15
	TA	44
	EAA	32
	HAP	1580
	HAP	1695
	HAP	2174
	BR	133
	PP	21
	PKA	48
	SKA4	25
	SKA4	28
	J6	644
	J6	727
	J10	206
	J10	220
	P2	3
	M1	755
	M1	784
	M1	1048
	M1	1067
	VCS	34
	HI	107
	G2	537
	G3	365
	G4	106
	G4	320
	G4	544
	AE1	857
	AE2	428
	AE2	793
	AE4	247
	AE4	275
	AE4	288
	AE4	346
	AE4	466
	AE5	382
	AE5	523
	AE6	832
	AE6	1041
	AE6	1102
	AE6	1128
	AE6	1212
	AE7	94
	AE7	118
	AE7	319
	AE8	233
	AE9	59
	AE9	199
	AE9	736
	AE9	1060
	AE10	940

Word	Code	Num
HONOR	AE11	397
	AE11	578
	AE11	598
	AE11	759
	AE11	961
	AE11	1244
	AE12	4
	AE12	53
	AE12	89
	AE12	355
	AE12	853
	AE12	917
	AE12	932
	AE12	1155
	OAL	199
	AF	100
	KT1	11
	KT1	190
	KT1	287
	KT1	300
	KT1	608
	KT2	171
	KT2	279
	KT2	288
	KT2	393
	KT3	106
	KT3	159
	KT3	196
	KT3	338
	KT3	503
	KT3	515
	KT3	742
	KT3	825
	KT3	895
	KT3	952
	KT3	1089
	KT3	1102
	M8	13
	M8	82
	B	319
	B	405
	BP	199
	HIF	278
	HIF	621
	C	131
	C	572
	TH	7
	FL	174
	FL	193
	FL	538
	FL	563
	M12	603
	M12	813
	AU	155
	AU	248
	AU	421
	AU	479
	WB	176
	WB	184
	WB	390
	WB	394
	WB	435
	SMP	47
	SMP	48
HONORABLE	HAP	1338
	G3	176
	AE6	246
	AE7	251
	M8	92
	WB	63
HONORABLY	AE11	130
HONORED	AR	94
	PT	3
	AA	833
	SAA	1065
	AE3	611
	AE4	665
	AE4	699
	AE5	325
	AE5	992
	AE12	1129
	KT1	368
	KT3	299
	M8	224
	HIF	621
	C	594
	AU	156
	TH	10
	TH	158
	TH	244
	TH	259
	TH	319
	TH	342
HONORING	AE5	700
HONOR'S	PTS	38
	FL	573

Word	Code	Num
HONOR'S	AU	248
HONORS	EIE	17
	PAZ	18
	AA	880
	MF	134
	SAA	873
	FS4	1
	H29	64
	H29	1326
	H29	1387
	H29	1565
	HAP	350
	BR	47
	BR	264
	ETS	18
	J1	110
	J1	162
	J10	148
	M1	768
	GK	120
	VP4	58
	VP5	122
	VP5	123
	VP5	125
	G1	27
	G2	146
	G2	559
	G3	24
	G3	312
	G3	462
	AE1	462
	AE2	851
	AE3	237
	AE5	73
	AE5	126
	AE5	657
	AE5	737
	AE6	110
	AE6	456
	AE6	680
	AE7	879
	AE8	360
	AE10	172
	AE10	519
	AE11	78
	AE11	259
	AE12	648
	MG	8
	KT3	731
	HIF	688
	HIF	710
	FL	489
	FL	554
	AU	25
	AU	56
HOODED	HAP	2318
HOODS	AM	1124
	J3	282
	AE12	184
	FL	163
HOOF	M12	426
HOOFS	AR	197
	M1	1032
	G3	136
	AE6	796
	AE8	790
	AE10	1281
	AE11	1267
	AE12	164
	KT3	535
	M12	502
HOOK	AR	172
	PDG	20
	M1	933
	VP3	150
	VP4	50
	AE7	248
	OAL	51
	OAL	446
	OAL	876
HOOKED	HIF	247
HOOKS	G1	214
	G2	577
	M15	141
	M15	703
HOOPS	J1	45
HOOT	AE12	938
HOOTED	HAP	2319
HOOTING	VP8	75
	SMP	33
	SMP	35
HOPE	JH	17
	AR	29
	AR	67
	RH	51
	LC	4

HOPE	LCA	8
	PRL	36
	AM	292
	AM	351
	AM	968
	EWGR	48
	SEL1	9
	SEL1	14
	PCG1	7
	PCG1	18
	SCG3	12
	PM	32
	ELN	12
	PCD	31
	PCD	33
	PUO1	42
	ENH	34
	SKK	13
	EOE	33
	STC	14
	HP	20
	HP	86
	DA	3
	PUO5	25
	AA	295
	AA	831
	ELB	14
	PPC	1
	MD	79
	MF	109
	SAA	112
	PK	40
	RL	198
	RL	277
	OE	50
	DOD	7
	L3	291
	L4	47
	TA	136
	HAP	875
	HAP	1510
	HAP	1538
	HAP	1661
	HAP	1677
	HAP	1827
	HAP	1966
	EL	152
	PSH	1
	J1	91
	J1	118
	J6	63
	J6	326
	J6	337
	J16	25
	P4	6
	P5	205
	P6	72
	M1	276
	M1	530
	M1	850
	M9	26
	M9	82
	M9	125
	M9	126
	HI	143
	PLT	19
	SLT1	15
	EHC	33
	VP1	21
	VP1	58
	G1	247
	G1	312
	G3	168
	G3	715
	G4	152
	AE1	330
	AE1	319
	AE2	237
	AE2	433
	AE2	889
	AE2	1016
	AE2	1027
	AE4	75
	AE4	441
	AE4	623
	AE4	692
	AE5	181
	AE5	436
	AE5	852
	AE5	853
	AE5	921
	AE5	1045
	AE5	1082
	AE6	146
	AE8	271
	AE9	391

HOPE	AE9	530
	AE9	997
	AE9	1009
	AE9	1055
	AE10	13
	AE10	200
	AE10	363
	AE10	368
	AE10	631
	AE10	1298
	AE12	90
	AE12	254
	AE12	1349
	OAL	537
	OAL	852
	KT1	36
	KT1	70
	KT1	411
	KT2	7
	KT2	139
	KT2	219
	KT2	481
	KT3	773
	B	11
	M10	73
	HIF	734
	C	298
	C	591
	C	723
	TH	382
	TH	399
	M11	171
	M11	387
	M11	411
	FL	616
	WB	18
	WB	220
	WB	231
	M15	159
	M15	178
	M15	303
	M15	544
	CI	443
	CI	527
	ETP	37
	PMK	1
	EMKG	8
	PWR	10
HOPED	AR	185
	AM	725
	TA	42
	HAP	568
	HAP	2192
	EL	43
	AE4	334
	AE4	488
	AE11	157
	M8	321
	TH	32
	TH	413
	AU	25
	WB	306
HOPEFUL	PWGR	26
	PTW	1
	MF	61
	SAA	291
	PD	20
	PAA	19
	PMS	1
	P1	214
HOPELESS	SCG3	9
	S	10
	A	10
	T23	4
	T23	9
	SSC	35
	PPS	9
	P3	64
	M9	121
	VP1	42
	VP10	8
	VP10	90
	G4	724
	AE3	339
	AE10	183
	AE11	161
	KT1	340
	KT2	2
HOPES	UDH	78
	SMA	69
	PWG	44
	PTL	9
	ECG1	18
	ECG1	24
	SCG3	3
	PFD	27

HOPES	PLN	41
	HP	107
	HP	254
	ETG	23
	PR	7
	PUO4	33
	PUF	16
	AA	266
	AA	487
	AA	684
	MD	274
	SAA	19
	SAA	23
	SAA	203
	SAA	316
	SAA	857
	SAA	869
	SAA	891
	OE	5
	OE	62
	L4	187
	H2	16
	TA	400
	TA	408
	HH	41
	HAP	1718
	HAP	1800
	HAP	2149
	BR	261
	BR	299
	BR	360
	PP	8
	PP	11
	PSH	39
	J1	201
	J10	3
	J10	184
	P1	129
	P4	101
	M1	661
	M1	909
	M9	86
	M9	153
	M9	180
	M9	188
	G1	90
	G1	574
	G2	706
	G3	133
	G3	669
	G4	710
	AE1	302
	AE1	672
	AE2	187
	AE2	216
	AE2	226
	AE2	249
	AE2	519
	AE2	534
	AE2	685
	AE2	922
	AE3	360
	AE3	440
	AE3	491
	AE3	859
	AE4	344
	AE5	195
	AE5	238
	AE5	752
	AE5	878
	AE5	1068
	AE6	507
	AE6	937
	AE6	1210
	AE8	188
	AE8	761
	AE8	765
	AE9	739
	AE9	752
	AE10	63
	AE10	606
	AE10	887
	AE10	915
	AE11	71
	AE11	473
	AE11	474
	AE12	58
	AE12	958
	AE12	1061
	AE12	1149
	AE12	1287
	OAL	506
	OAL	517
	OAL	830
	DO	147
	KT1	510

Word	Ref	No.
HOPES	KT1	511
	KT2	182
	KT3	289
	B	67
	B	237
	CAM	65
	CAM	69
	HIF	664
	M11	29
	M11	218
	FL	461
	AU	151
	AU	575
	CI	323
HOPEST	L3	268
	P2	83
HOPING	HAP	1375
HOPKINS	PTP	35
HOPPED	PC1	13
	FL	107
HOPPING	AE6	293
	HIF	769
	FL	47
	FL	443
HORACE	PO	5
	ER	39
	HH	14
	J1	78
	P1	228
	C	634
HORIZON	KT2	40
HORN	M13	226
	G1	524
	G2	268
	G3	761
	AE6	1236
	AE6	1237
	AE7	715
	OAE1	14
	M10	98
HORNED	AE8	103
	OAL	347
HORNET'S	C	566
HORNETS	C	155
	M15	546
HORNPIPE	AE11	1086
HORNS	OE	61
	T27	62
	HAP	5
	HAP	266
	ODA	4
	J6	66
	P1	194
	M1	14
	M1	1030
	M9	33
	M9	185
	M13	226
	VP6	76
	VP10	82
	G1	306
	G1	542
	G1	582
	G2	545
	G2	765
	G3	341
	G3	360
	G3	569
	G4	409
	G4	422
	G4	531
	AE3	847
	AE4	84
	AE4	169
	AE4	183
	AE4	321
	AE5	483
	AE5	506
	AE6	350
	AE7	665
	AE7	679
	AE7	1078
	AE9	854
	AE11	1248
	AE12	161
	AE12	262
	AE12	1044
	OAL	264
	OAL	328
	KT2	229
	KT2	622
	KT3	195
	M10	59
	CAM	320
	C	752
	M12	140

Word	Ref	No.
HORNS	M12	375
	M12	510
	M12	514
	WB	11
	M15	193
	M15	293
	M15	643
	ETP	10
	SMP	27
HORNY	RL	404
	G3	92
	G3	136
	G4	172
	AE6	796
	AE7	709
	AE8	790
	M8	401
	M11	275
HOROSCOPE	AK	42
	J10	202
	P5	60
	KT1	245
HORRIBLE	AE4	260
	AE8	331
	AE9	1074
	AE11	458
HORRIBLY	AE11	900
HORRID	AR	7
	PP	22
	J3	121
	VP10	36
	AE1	163
	AE2	235
	AE3	814
	AE6	133
	AE6	400
	AE6	853
	AE7	527
	AE7	929
	AE9	519
	AE11	1036
	AF	127
HORROR	LC	137
	AM	284
	PUO1	6
	L3	179
	L3	231
	TA	51
	HAP	1231
	HAP	1900
	M1	357
	G1	451
	AE2	765
	AE2	1024
	AE2	1076
	AE3	36
	AE3	69
	AE5	17
	AE7	23
	AE7	41
	AE8	462
	AE8	794
	AE9	134
	AE10	635
	AE12	1255
	KT2	549
	BP	10
	CAM	5
	CAM	224
	CAM	286
	C	236
	C	366
	C	604
	C	718
	C	731
	TH	93
	TH	295
	TH	312
	TH	339
	WB	211
HORRORS	J3	426
	AE2	382
	AM	387
HORSE	ECG2	6
	EKK	22
	MD	119
	SAA	495
	PDS	42
	P2	200
	P2	794
	G3	189
	G3	223
	G3	315
	G3	747
	AE2	63
	AE2	321

Word	Ref	No.
HORSE	AE2	337
	AE2	442
	AE2	540
	AE2	564
	AE4	187
	AE6	693
	AE6	1219
	AE7	933
	AE8	684
	AE9	56
	AE9	204
	AE9	502
	AE9	504
	AE9	515
	AE10	262
	AE10	492
	AE10	504
	AE10	1058
	AE10	1276
	AE10	1284
	AE11	91
	AE11	139
	AE11	290
	AE11	706
	AE11	776
	AE11	783
	AE11	896
	AE11	903
	AE11	911
	AE11	1042
	AE11	1048
	AE11	1052
	AE11	1093
	AE12	739
	OAL	22
	OAL	167
	OAL	539
	OAE2	11
	KT3	65
	KT3	443
	KT3	608
	CAM	44
	FL	296
	M12	392
	M12	666
	WB	222
	WB	259
	WB	262
	EMKG	18
HORSEBACK	J1	31
	AE5	718
HORSED	AE9	30
HORSEHAIR	AE10	1245
HORSEMAN	KT3	608
	TH	362
	AE7	903
	M15	340
	AA	730
HORSEMEN	SAA	193
	G4	103
	AE8	772
	AE10	337
HORSE'S	P3	54
	AE2	308
	AE4	225
	AE11	947
	AE11	1062
	KT2	48
	M12	532
HORSES	ENH	29
	HAP	690
	HAP	860
	PDS	41
	J3	496
	J10	89
	G3	178
	G3	829
	AE1	666
	AE3	604
	AE6	889
	AE7	378
	AE7	1053
	AE8	806
	AE9	444
	AE10	824
	AE11	113
	AE11	943
	AE11	1262
	AE11	1267
	AE11	1314
	AE12	433
	AE12	510
	AE12	527
	AE12	696
	OAL	244
	KT3	29

HORSES	M8	142	HOSTESS	HAP	1268	HOTLY	M1	714
HORSES'	AR	197	HOSTILE	AM	918	HOT-MOUTHED	MD	119
	G3	76		AA	138	HOTTER	AE12	599
	G3	704		MF	172		OAL	383
	AE11	917		VP1	16	HOTTEST	KT3	901
	AE12	548		AE1	668	HOUND	VP8	39
	FL	290		AE2	493		AE12	1085
	KT3	535		AE2	843		M8	190
HORTA	AE7	990		AE2	998	HOUND'S	P5	278
HOSE	PP	30		AE3	520	HOUNDS	H2	49
HOSPITABLE	LCA	6		AE4	345		HAP	5
	AM	1198		AE4	807		HAP	578
	PAR	21		AE4	891		ODA	4
	HP	4		AE4	898		VP10	82
	AA	737		AE5	68		G3	74
	AA	867		AE5	878		G3	622
	HAP	1291		AE6	138		AE4	183
	HAP	2461		AE9	52		AE7	665
	J3	114		AE9	586		AE7	688
	G3	530		AE9	997		AE9	742
	AE1	765		AE10	413		AE10	1003
	AE1	843		AE10	1118		KT1	88
	AE1	1021		AE11	130		KT1	342
	AE3	23		AE12	484		KT2	229
	AE4	68		AE12	485		KT2	236
	AE5	34		AE12	664		KT2	629
	AE7	281		AE12	717		C	339
	AE9	491		AE12	1172		C	752
	AE10	68		AE12	1296		TH	185
	AE10	651		AF	145		TH	192
	AE10	720		KT1	215		TH	270
	BP	29		KT2	126		TH	279
	C	783		HIF	424		TH	394
	M15	19		M11	149		M15	701
	CI	634		M12	131		SMP	27
HOSPITAL	UDH	83		AU	319	HOUR	AR	147
	J10	306		AU	525		PWG	11
HOSPITALITY	EUO2	23		CI	271		AM	533
	J10	507		CI	383		SMM2	1
	M1	184		G3	556		SCG2	25
HOST	AM	716	HOSTRY	AM	734		STC	7
	AA	529	HOSTS	EAL	29		CM	21
	MF	41		BR	146		ETG	19
	SAA	690		AE1	332		AA	553
	HAP	93		AE2	441		AA	613
	HAP	1079		AE6	832		ELB	2
	M13	21		AE7	655		ELB	29
	G2	195		AE9	134		MD	137
	G4	41		AE11	940		SAA	170
	AE1	45		AE11	1315		SAA	641
	AE2	236		AE12	804		SAA	932
	AE3	812		BP	118		SAA	1083
	AE5	633		C	264		OE	21
	AE5	976		FL	318		L4	23
	AE6	228	HOT	AM	12		T27	116
	AE6	447		AM	901		H9	20
	AE7	28		PW	13		H9	32
	AE7	734		SLN	8		H29	50
	AE7	898		SCD2	9		H29	72
	AE8	18		EUO	8		HAP	509
	AE8	193		E	25		HAP	558
	AE8	948		ML	38		HAP	566
	AE9	44		ETG	21		HAP	578
	AE9	229		AA	489		HAP	628
	AE9	423		AA	519		HAP	2187
	AE9	1059		AA	621		HAP	2563
	AE9	1107		MD	238		SSC	59
	AE10	179		SAA	392		EDS	26
	AE10	337		PD	43		STS3	4
	AE10	1287		T27	15		EL	329
	AE11	1171		HAP	904		PSH	41
	AE12	350		SSC	8		J3	212
	KT1	20		EL	109		J6	199
	KT1	31		J6	419		J6	750
	KT1	80		J10	345		J10	177
	KT1	120		J10	542		J10	343
	KT3	587		J16	71		J10	431
	TJD	49		P5	71		J16	6
	BP	77		M1	23		P5	222
	HIF	82		M1	59		M1	296
	HIF	197		M9	100		M1	946
	HIF	401		G2	161		M9	152
	HIF	437		G2	475		HI	124
	HIF	623		AE2	595		HI	180
	HIF	750		AE3	749		MC	1
	C	259		AE4	131		VP1	28
	C	291		AE5	973		VP3	7
	TH	347		AE12	156		VP8	11
	M11	163		AE12	436		VP9	84
	FL	150		KT2	475		VP10	107
	FL	276		KT3	236		G2	267
	M12	621		C	177		G3	425
	AU	85		PMK	11		G3	444
	AU	140	HOT-BRAINED	PDG	3		G3	508
	AU	214	HOTCHPOTCH	J3	415		AE1	283
	AU	381	HOTLY	HAP	2244		AE1	1023

HOUR

AE2	323
AE2	437
AE2	878
AE4	245
AE5	811
AE5	833
AE5	1100
AE6	770
AE6	1075
AE7	25
AE7	182
AE7	714
AE8	549
AE8	630
AE9	13
AE9	167
AE9	318
AE9	644
AE10	696
AE10	821
AE11	31
AE12	1169
OAL	459
MFL	31
DO	92
KT2	215
KT3	290
KT3	681
KT3	791
KT3	1096
B	147
B	215
B	297
B	580
B	621
BP	173
BP	179
HIF	7
HIF	171
HIF	318
HIF	529
HIF	646
HIF	792
C	220
C	450
C	454
C	503
C	684
TH	73
FL	27
FL	298
FL	435
FL	569
M12	770
AU	148
WB	93
WB	355
M15	269
M15	643
CI	569
SMP	73
AS	73

HOURLY

AM	1186
EUO2	10
L4	68
TA	86
STS2	1
EL	322
J6	481
P1	130
AE4	87
AE4	671
KT1	352
M11	234

HOURS

PWG	39
SLN	12
AA	166
MD	279
RL	230
RL	232
L3	187
HAP	2237
HAP	2304
SKA6	16
EL	117
J3	442
J6	263
VP7	57
G1	396
G1	463
G3	583
G4	748
AE4	419
AE6	720
AE9	125
OAL	639

HOURS

MFL	16
DO	159
DO	163
KT2	55
KT2	198
KT2	483
KT3	1036
TJD	60
B	192
B	296
B	438
C	44
M11	419
FL	566
WB	137
CI	327
PTP	41
ESK	25
ESK	28

HOUSE

AR	183
PWG	26
PWG	35
PWG	36
AM	888
EWGR	24
EEL	24
PAR	1
PW	5
PW	23
EMQW	19
PNH	1
PNH	52
ENH	2
ENH	27
ENH	33
HP	178
PUO3	3
AA	735
ELB	7
SAA	544
OE	53
T27	65
T27	66
T27	85
H29	62
HAP	347
HAP	494
HAP	1326
HAP	2234
HAP	2249
HAP	2287
HAP	2503
PKA	20
EL	46
EL	344
J3	379
J3	194
J6	120
J6	617
J10	461
P2	28
P2	50
HI	190
PLT	44
ELT	34
VP7	21
G1	351
G2	566
G3	535
AE1	490
AE2	667
AE2	814
AE2	884
AE2	904
AE2	926
AE2	1026
AE2	1029
AE3	131
AE4	959
AE5	524
AE6	1235
AE7	237
AE7	490
AE7	568
AE7	659
AE7	698
AE8	358
AE8	498
AE8	643
AE10	731
AE12	758
AE12	1173
DO	57
KT2	594
KT3	110
KT3	126

HOUSE

TJD	203
BP	29
CAM	181
HIF	716
HIF	811
C	611
C	723
C	725
TH	68
M11	258
M11	267
M11	290
M12	638
WB	85
WB	281
WB	408
M15	19
GP	61
CI	201
AS	60

HOUSED

PAZ	34
HAP	1807
HAP	1834
HAP	2240
AE4	380
AE10	1143
M15	676

HOUSEHOLD

AM	1127
SAA	707
SAA	990
L3	76
H2	60
HAP	1764
HAP	2074
J1	180
J10	385
P5	43
P6	169
M1	397
M13	133
G2	724
G2	742
G3	535
AE1	491
AE1	523
AE2	703
AE7	164
AE7	687
AE7	697
AE8	721
AE9	341
KT2	567
M8	301
HIF	51
HIF	172
HIF	752
M15	691

HOUSEHOLDS
HOUSE-RENT
HOUSE'S

AM	552
J3	277
PCG1	1
PNH	49
J3	312
M8	321

HOUSES

AM	951
ECG1	30
EMQW	26
EDGA	1
HAP	1875
J1	161
J3	11
J3	56
J6	224
J6	400
J6	746
J10	7
M1	154
M1	156
M1	397
VP1	94
G1	460
G1	652
G2	623
G2	724
G3	634
AE2	492
AE2	1038
AE3	185
AE10	392
AE12	870
KT3	941
J3	430
AE12	203

HOUSES'

T27	77

HOUSEWIFE

BP	82

HOUSEWIFERY

P6	104

HOUSEWIVES

AE8	541

Word	Code	Num
HOUSING	KT3	410
HOUSS	M12	582
HOUTED	AE5	358
HOVELS	SKA4	2
HOVER	PAL	1
	AE6	657
	KT3	783
HOVERED	AE10	91
	M12	21
HOVERING	SAA	559
	TA	117
	J6	404
	G2	729
	G3	438
	AE5	15
	AE6	1198
	AE10	1050
	AE11	358
	AE11	421
HOVERS	VP6	116
	B	676
HOWL	HAP	552
	J10	419
	AE4	438
	AE9	849
HOWLED	G1	653
HOWLING	DA	97
	M1	307
	G1	635
	G3	417
	AE4	244
	AE6	367
	AE7	21
	KT1	132
	KT3	968
HOWLINGS	HAP	301
	KT3	920
HOWLS	VP8	140
	AE7	527
	AE8	331
	AE9	68
HUBBARD	HAP	1302
HUDDLED	PUO1	33
	AA	171
	G1	353
	OAE2	61
HUDDLING	EMM	2
HUDIBRAS	HAP	1541
HUE	HAP	543
	HAP	2082
	J6	780
	M1	470
	M13	108
	VP2	68
	VP10	40
	G1	608
	G4	150
	G4	370
	AE3	814
	AE5	130
	AE8	512
	KT1	114
	KT1	173
	KT1	531
	KT1	563
	KT2	85
	KT2	180
	KT2	485
	KT3	75
	KT3	260
	M10	40
	C	153
	C	288
	M11	10
	M11	264
	FL	234
	M12	526
	AU	610
	WB	433
	M15	60
	M15	382
	STP	10
HUFF	EMQW	2
	ETC	25
	PCB	29
HUFFING	PMQW	15
	J10	257
HUG	PW	9
	L4	135
	AE2	707
	OAE2	5
	M8	390
HUGE	AM	266
	AM	498
	AM	810
	EL	31
HUGE	J1	5
	J3	403
	J6	226
	J6	456
	G1	160
	G1	525
	G2	97
	G3	567
	G4	153
	G4	254
	AE2	608
	AE3	852
	AE6	267
	AE7	745
	AE7	951
	AE8	335
	AE8	398
	AE10	346
	AE10	507
	M12	180
HUGGED	HI	155
	CI	367
HUGS	AE1	962
	OAL	483
HUGUENOTS	HAP	711
HUGY	AE5	113
HULLABABILAH	PLN	35
HULLS	AM	239
HUM	PCB	25
HUMAN	SIE	3
	AM	143
	AM	1177
	EWGR	14
	ETL	8
	PFD	7
	PUO2	8
	PTC	2
	HP	125
	AA	255
	AA	609
	AA	653
	AA	807
	MD	226
	MF	1
	SAA	433
	RL	107
	RL	118
	RL	149
	RL	186
	L3	102
	L5	4
	T23	8
	T23	35
	T23	89
	H29	45
	TA	399
	HAP	10
	HAP	123
	HAP	255
	HAP	358
	HAP	490
	HAP	1580
	SSC	43
	OD	41
	PPS	12
	P1	20
	P2	130
	M1	277
	M1	302
	M1	308
	M1	331
	M1	510
	M1	541
	M13	130
	VP5	98
	G1	188
	G1	201
	G1	361
	G1	451
	G2	617
	G2	697
	G4	465
	G4	604
	G4	641
	AE1	18
	AE1	311
	AE1	393
	AE1	478
	AE1	765
	AE2	402
	AE3	281
	AE3	543
	AE3	797
	AE3	812
	AE3	826
	AE4	547
HUMAN	AE4	596
	AE4	998
	AE5	897
	AE6	41
	AE6	209
	AE6	374
	AE7	454
	AE8	260
	AE9	520
	AE9	805
	AE10	1076
	AE10	1178
	AE11	793
	AE11	836
	AE11	891
	AE12	59
	AE12	475
	AE12	483
	AE12	485
	AE12	1124
	AE12	1157
	OAL	228
	OAL	349
	MFL	29
	KT1	331
	KT2	384
	KT3	879
	TJD	63
	TJD	77
	TJD	207
	B	540
	M10	41
	CAM	38
	CAM	85
	HIF	76
	HIF	525
	C	540
	C	675
	M11	279
	M11	313
	M11	332
	FL	483
	AU	485
	M15	47
	M15	211
	M15	298
	CI	167
	CI	233
HUMANITY	TA	350
HUMAN-KIND	J10	265
HUMANKIND	AM	137
	AM	664
	PWGR	4
	PUO1	15
	MD	278
	RL	26
	RL	55
	RL	131
	AT	33
	L1	1
	L2	10
	HAP	239
	HAP	878
	EL	366
	J1	130
	J10	74
	P3	129
	P5	100
	P5	151
	M1	433
	VCS	4
	G1	327
	AE1	426
	AE6	76
	AE7	26
	AE8	972
	AE10	225
	AE10	383
	AE10	1306
	OAL	18
	KT1	410
	KT1	474
	KT2	531
	TJD	102
	B	618
	CI	323
	SMP	12
HUMBLE	AR	307
	LC	133
	EIE	6
	AM	234
	AM	1062
	AM	1152
	PW	10
	PNH	15
	ML	47

Word	Code	Num
HUMBLE	MF	180
	AA	325
	SAA	354
	L4	172
	H2	2
	TA	336
	GE	66
	HAP	1271
	HAP	1633
	BR	299
	ETS	8
	PKA	6
	EL	96
	EL	360
	J6	581
	P2	101
	P6	133
	M1	1018
	VP6	9
	G2	608
	AE1	456
	AE3	151
	AE8	502
	OAL	418
	OAL	798
	MFL	21
	B	65
	C	79
	M11	476
	FL	596
	WB	387
	WB	515
	M15	426
HUMBLED	G1	452
HUMBLY	HIF	623
	PMQ	16
	EWGR	38
	PFD	29
	EM	32
	EOE	28
	HP	125
	PUO3	34
	PLB	6
	EK	47
	RL	101
	HAP	405
	BR	104
	P5	254
	AE3	340
	AE4	614
	AE8	968
	FL	474
HUMID	L4	75
	VP10	20
	G3	597
	AE4	505
	M11	75
HUMILITY	HAP	1508
	HAP	1623
	EL	96
	MM	28
HUMMING	AM	911
	AE6	959
	WB	38
HUMOR	EWG	7
	PRL	35
	PMQ	6
	EWGR	5
	PCG1	42
	ECG2	3
	ECD	17
	PNH	46
	PKK	6
	PTC	21
	AA	62
	AA	138
	PK	33
	OE	9
	PAA	30
	G3	730
	OAL	47
	OAL	470
	HIF	783
	C	161
HUMORING	AE12	345
HUMORISTS	MF	92
HUMOROUS	SAA	212
HUMORS	AR	176
	EUO	13
	MF	188
	M1	548
	G1	129
	C	27
	C	143
	C	153
	C	166

Word	Code	Num
HUNDRED	AM	705
	AM	994
	EAZ	31
	PSF	23
	J3	401
	J3	402
	J10	392
	P5	2
	P5	36
	P5	37
	P5	219
	P5	280
	P6	115
	M1	859
	M1	1000
	M13	58
	G2	62
	G3	27
	AE1	370
	AE1	578
	AE1	896
	AE2	683
	AE3	144
	AE3	843
	AE4	287
	AE4	289
	AE4	740
	AE6	65
	AE6	126
	AE6	401
	AE6	451
	AE6	851
	AE6	1071
	AE7	134
	AE7	205
	AE7	230
	AE7	378
	AE7	750
	AE7	911
	AE7	1080
	AE8	684
	AE8	951
	AE9	204
	AE9	502
	AE10	251
	AE10	253
	AE10	264
	AE10	293
	AE10	296
	AE10	793
	AE11	503
	OAL	491
	KT2	409
	KT3	22
	KT3	61
	KT3	90
	M8	375
	M8	376
	HIF	554
	C	70
	FL	324
	SMP	2
HUNDREDS	J1	140
HUNG	AM	578
	AM	1167
	EDG	34
	T18	73
	HAP	1080
	ODA	2
	J3	333
	J6	242
	J10	209
	PPS	16
	P5	42
	M1	926
	VP1	51
	VP6	27
	VP6	124
	VP10	20
	G1	214
	G1	298
	G2	537
	G3	597
	G4	61
	AE1	439
	AE1	667
	AE1	1001
	AE2	156
	AE2	687
	AE2	984
	AE2	1078
	AE4	265
	AE4	387
	AE4	665
	AE5	15
	AE5	628

Word	Code	Num
HUNG	AE5	730
	AE6	23
	AE6	839
	AE6	1003
	AE7	101
	AE7	252
	AE7	1103
	AE8	113
	AE8	261
	AE8	311
	AE8	837
	AE8	887
	AE8	902
	AE9	550
	AE10	202
	AE10	1130
	AE11	11
	AE11	16
	AE12	553
	AE12	555
	AE12	1114
	KT2	602
	KT3	32
	KT3	44
	KT3	52
	KT3	359
	KT3	342
	KT3	1025
	B	684
	BP	62
	BP	73
	BP	196
	M10	42
	TH	308
	M11	12
	FL	377
	M12	344
	M12	379
	M12	552
	M12	747
	M12	752
	M15	236
	CI	83
HUNGARY	HAP	954
HUNGER	AR	100
	PFD	6
	AT	126
	L4	55
	HAP	307
	HAP	520
	J6	403
	J6	550
	PPS	14
	G2	791
	G3	388
	AE1	300
	AE1	1011
	AE3	80
	AE3	292
	AE6	571
	AE6	813
	AE8	244
	AE9	68
	AE9	456
	KT1	478
	KT2	144
	HIF	641
	C	22
	C	254
	TH	87
	M12	216
	AU	72
	M15	162
	M15	258
HUNGER-STARVED	EL	47
HUNGRY	AM	1007
	MF	164
	J1	148
	J3	111
	J3	140
	J3	279
	J3	402
	PPS	17
	VP8	5
	VP8	140
	G1	199
	G2	518
	G4	18
	AE1	479
	AE2	479
	AE3	294
	AE4	538
	AE7	155
	AE7	668
	AE10	1018
	KT3	991

Word	Ref	No.
HUNGRY	B	332
	HIF	99
	TH	185
	TH	328
	GP	74
HUNKS	ESH	29
HUNT	PRH	4
	HAP	27
	G1	414
	AE6	959
	KT2	230
	TJD	92
	TH	379
HUNTED	AM	97
	EMQ	9
	ESF	34
	T23	13
	M1	958
	AE9	753
	AE11	849
	KT2	182
	M12	556
HUNTER	HAP	283
	AE7	1054
	AE11	1003
	AE11	1013
	KT2	589
	TH	280
	TH	332
	SMP	34
	SMP	36
HUNTERS,	AA	454
HUNTERS'	SAA	833
HUNTING	M1	636
	VP7	44
	AE7	665
	AE7	1029
	AE9	322
	KT2	634
	TH	427
HUNTINGS	KT2	641
HUNTRESS	T27	112
	AE1	435
	AE9	224
	KT2	628
	KT3	269
	M8	151
HUNTS	J1	31
	G3	78
	G3	384
	KT3	139
	M15	243
HUNTSMAN	G3	570
	AE7	903
	AE9	1042
	OAL	52
HUNTSMEN	AM	381
	HAP	576
	AE4	168
	AE4	185
	AE5	395
	AE9	742
	AE10	1003
HUR	BR	297
HURDLES	G1	245
HURLED	RH	31
	L3	5
	L5	1
	G1	93
	AE1	120
	AE1	166
	AE10	583
	AE10	912
	AE12	309
	M12	357
HURLS	AE12	1235
HURRICANE	TA	24
HURRIED	AR	51
	AR	215
	TA	151
	AK	62
	EL	278
	J6	845
	AE1	16
	AE1	154
	AE1	666
	AE2	591
	AE7	819
	AE11	42
	AE12	859
	M8	310
HURRIES	AM	854
	J6	629
	J10	86
HURRY	AE11	935
HURRYING	AE12	1067
HURT	HS	44
	EDGA	31
	HAP	2517
	VP4	50
	AE2	720
	AE7	1101
	AE9	783
	KT1	254
	KT1	275
	M10	32
	M15	434
HURTFUL	J10	9
	J10	84
	G2	410
	CAM	176
HURTLESS	AE9	1101
HURTS	L4	41
	G1	514
	OAL	458
	KT3	728
	KT3	1109
HUSBAND	AM	133
	HP	106
	HP	176
	DA	142
	EPC	26
	ELB	10
	SAA	90
	OE	37
	OE	60
	T27	40
	T27	77
	J1	86
	J6	120
	J6	299
	J6	328
	J6	331
	J6	510
	J6	557
	J6	612
	J6	692
	J6	748
	J6	795
	M1	187
	M1	647
	M1	826
	M1	910
	M9	57
	M9	128
	HI	95
	VP6	74
	G1	351
	G1	389
	G2	302
	G3	253
	G3	595
	G4	669
	AE4	479
	AE6	1141
	AE6	1142
	AE7	501
	AE7	511
	AE8	488
	AE8	513
	OAL	624
	OAL	650
	OAL	651
	OAL	679
	OAE2	1
	OAE2	63
	KT3	1128
	BP	58
	CAM	48
	C	6
	C	130
	C	607
	C	707
	M11	76
	M11	363
	WB	182
	WB	197
	WB	280
	WB	515
	WB	520
HUSBAND-FOOL	WB	139
HUSBANDMAN	TA	356
	G2	506
	G2	549
	M15	184
HUSBANDMEN	G2	480
HUSBANDRY	AA	508
	HAP	224
	MC	8
	G3	262
HUSBAND'S	PEL	30
	HP	240
HUSBAND'S	DA	102
	DA	141
	L4	264
	ETS	13
	ELW	3
	J1	105
	J6	7
	J6	586
	J6	595
	J6	651
	J6	851
	M9	45
	HI	88
	HI	134
	AE2	710
	AE3	389
	AE4	490
	AE4	668
	AE7	490
	HIF	736
	HIF	789
	C	81
	M11	54
	M11	89
	M11	364
	M11	464
	WB	176
	PMK	14
HUSBANDS	AM	109
	PEL	7
	EM	19
	AA	572
	L4	291
	GE	11
	HAP	1869
	J6	323
	J10	487
	G2	578
	AE6	424
	OAL	392
	WB	140
	WB	542
HUSBANDS'	J6	237
	KT1	132
	WB	152
HUSH	AE1	218
HUSHAI	AA	888
HUSHED	VHH	17
	AM	1116
	VP9	79
	AE9	245
	AE10	158
	AE11	371
	KT3	1020
	M12	53
	STP	16
HUSHES	M11	497
HUSKS	P3	107
	G1	283
HUSKY	G1	315
HUSWIFES	J6	6
HUSWIFING	C	9
HUTS	AE1	583
HUZZA	PLB	35
HUZZAED	EDG	7
HYACINTHS	VP2	22
	VP2	67
	VP3	96
HYADES	H3	20
HYADS	G1	210
	AE3	675
	AU	456
HYAENA	M15	613
HYARBA	AE4	471
HYARBA'S	AE4	283
	AE4	775
HYARBAS	DA	139
	AE4	51
HYBLA	VP7	53
HYBLA-DROPS	AA	697
HYBLAEAN	SAA	1123
HYDASPES	AE10	1053
HYDRA	AA	541
	TA	464
	AE6	400
	AE6	778
	AE7	910
HYDRA-EMPIRE	SAA	896
HYDRA-LIKE	AM	993
HYLAS	J1	249
	VP6	66
	VP8	156
	G3	9
HYLLUS	AE12	784
HYLONOME	M12	539
	M12	540

Word	Ref	No.
HYMEN	T18	94
	M9	147
	M9	208
	AE4	179
	AE7	769
	KT3	1146
	M12	301
HYMEN'S	M9	142
	M9	151
HYMN	MF	41
HYMNS	C	606
	FS3	10
	AK	14
	AK	61
	EL	121
	ODA	67
	GK	90
	G2	535
	G2	594
	KT3	369
	HIF	648
	GP	21
HYPANIS	G4	527
	AE2	459
	AE2	580
	M15	436
HYPERBOREAN	KT3	297
	M15	532
HYPOCRISY	PRH	17
	KT2	564
HYPOCRITE	HIF	442
	C	499
HYPOCRITES	MF	92
	SAA	827
HYPOCRITIC	MD	38
HYPSIPYLE	HP	190
HYRCANIAN	AE4	525
HYRCANIANS	AE7	836
HYRTACUS	AE9	223
IAMBICS	MF	204
IANTHE	M9	71
	M9	120
	M9	150
IAPIS	AE12	577
	AE12	628
IASIUS	AE3	225
IBERIAN	AR	17
	AM	29
	VP4	42
ICARIUS	CAM	270
ICARUS	AE6	47
ICE	SLN	8
	AA	199
	SAA	1110
	J6	675
	M1	153
	M13	78
	G1	418
	G3	554
	G3	559
	G4	203
	AE4	368
	OAL	423
ICELOS	M11	335
ICICLES	VP10	73
	G3	563
	G3	675
ICY	H9	5
	AE9	632
IDA	AE2	1089
	AE3	145
	AE9	781
	AE10	233
	AE10	234
	AU	499
IDAEAN	VP2	87
	G4	57
	AE1	875
	AE2	945
	AE3	153
	AE7	189
	M12	689
IDAEUS	AE6	653
	AE9	665
IDALIAN	AE1	955
	KT2	498
	KT3	1147
IDA'S	AE2	861
	AE3	7
	AE3	393

Word	Ref	No.
IDA'S	AE5	329
	AE5	600
	AE9	93
	AE9	98
	AE9	849
	AE9	916
	AE10	313
	AE10	327
	AE10	355
	OAL	325
IDAS	M8	52
IDEA	L4	15
	GK	2
	AE6	1106
	DO	11
IDEAS	UDH	100
	HS	103
	RH	28
	AM	41
	AM	663
	AE4	14
IDES	KT2	604
IDIOM	MM	49
IDIOT	GK	159
	CI	112
IDIOTS	MD	2
	L3	105
	C	798
IDLE	AM	156
	AM	457
	AM	965
	RL	127
	L3	60
	HAP	1792
	HAP	2396
	G1	121
	G2	49
	G2	290
	G3	696
	G4	377
	AE8	60
	KT2	484
	B	437
	HIF	42
	HIF	381
	C	320
	C	568
	M12	650
	M15	222
IDLENESS	KT2	501
	M10	5
	FL	565
IDLY	L3	124
	G4	158
	AE4	387
	AE7	522
	HS	84
IDOL	AA	64
	MD	7
	SAA	221
	SAA	662
	G4	307
	B	31
	M10	11
	HIF	166
IDOLATER	HAP	2521
IDOLATRY	HAP	1205
	HAP	415
	ETS	3
IDOLS	MD	105
	SAA	545
	G1	648
IDOMENEUS	AE3	167
	AE3	513
	AE11	408
IDUMAEAN	AM	11
	G2	166
IDUME	G1	86
IDUME'S	G3	18
IGAD	PAR	21
IGNOBLE	AM	999
	AK	17
	HAP	1558
	PDS	8
	J10	557
	M1	334
	G2	84
	G3	152
	AE1	213
	AE1	261
	AE2	539
	AE9	462
	AE10	519
	AE11	534
	AE11	572
	AE11	1080

Word	Ref	No.
IGNOBLE	AE12	1359
	M11	342
	M12	797
IGNOBLER	GK	171
	AE5	397
IGNOBLEST	HAP	1630
IGNOBLY	AE10	954
IGNOMINIOUS	G3	351
IGNOMINOUS	J10	441
IGNOMINY	AE6	1123
	KT3	321
IGNORAMUS	PDG	43
	PDG	44
	EDGA	38
IGNORANCE	DC	38
	PUO1	35
	ENH	16
	ML	15
	PUO4	14
	MF	146
	RL	197
	RL	306
	RL	370
	RL	428
	ER	16
	HAP	324
	M1	692
	AE8	249
	AE11	30
IGNORANT	UDH	14
	L3	292
	J6	719
	M1	885
	AE1	410
	AE4	137
	AE9	382
	AE10	36
	OAL	883
ILIA	AE1	371
ILIADS	P1	93
	P1	244
ILIAN	AE1	138
	AE2	74
ILION	HI	5
ILIONEUS	AE1	172
	AE1	734
	AE1	786
	AE1	862
	AE7	290
	AE9	664
	AE9	771
ILION'S	HI	41
ILIUM	HP	233
	MD	67
	AE2	436
	AE2	599
	AE2	780
	AE2	845
	AE2	869
	AE3	150
	AE3	16
	AE5	986
	AE6	141
	AE10	462
	C	699
	AU	275
	M15	647
ILIUM'S	AE3	4
ILL	AR	177
	RH	47
	RH	70
	PWG	32
	PWG	37
	EWG	9
	LCA	7
	PRL	26
	AM	141
	AM	151
	AM	280
	AM	855
	AM	1053
	PMQ	35
	EWGR	31
	ET	3
	ET	17
	PCG2	1
	ECG2	29
	EMQw	22
	EMQw	23
	ECD	7
	ECD	8
	ECD	15
	ML	11
	HP	112
	DA	30
	PR	14

Headword	Code	No.
ILL	PUO3	35
	AA	81
	AA	92
	AA	182
	AA	313
	AA	327
	AA	753
	AA	982
	AA	1004
	MD	65
	MD	133
	MD	159
	PRH	43
	SAA	183
	RL	424
	L3	135
	L3	146
	L3	289
	H29	78
	TA	49
	HAP	339
	HAP	408
	HAP	1288
	HAP	1368
	HAP	1598
	HAP	1614
	HAP	1628
	HAP	1696
	HAP	1812
	HAP	1970
	HAP	2132
	HAP	2563
	BR	190
	BR	203
	BR	230
	EL	174
	ODA	9
	J3	480
	J6	636
	J6	845
	J10	534
	P2	36
	P3	100
	P3	195
	P5	153
	P5	166
	M1	177
	M1	324
	M1	977
	VP3	75
	VP3	142
	VP3	159
	VP7	39
	G3	245
	G3	794
	AE1	1056
	AE2	533
	AE3	481
	AE3	509
	AE3	939
	AE4	252
	AE7	713
	AE7	806
	AE8	309
	AE8	679
	AE8	912
	AE10	505
	AE10	696
	AE11	391
	AE12	877
	AE12	1257
	OAL	469
	OAE2	61
	MG	34
	DO	132
	KT1	244
	KT1	285
	KT2	220
	KT2	516
	KT3	261
	KT3	386
	KT3	422
	KT3	861
	KT3	881
	B	185
	B	509
	B	605
	M10	5
	CAM	94
	CAM	167
	CAM	228
	CAM	262
	HIF	155
	HIF	529
	C	27
	C	262
ILL	C	512
	C	538
	C	786
	TH	230
	M11	120
	FL	407
	FL	607
	AU	68
	AU	54
	AU	179
	WB	514
	M15	155
	M15	682
	M15	683
	CI	14
	CI	186
	CI	392
	ERL	5
ILL-BAKED	P3	36
ILL-BODING	AE9	644
ILL-BRED	HP	13
ILL-DISSEMBLED	G2	650
ILLEGAL	PLB	14
ILL-EXTINGUISHED	AE10	91
ILL-FATED	HAP	1886
ILL-GOTTEN	MD	307
	H29	93
ILLITERATE	PUO1	22
ILL-MANNERED	HIF	269
ILL-NATURE	SAA	422
ILL-NATURED	HH	30
	CAM	50
ILL-OMENED	T23	68
	TA	48
	AE4	245
	AE10	476
	KT1	50
	B	215
	HIF	7
ILL-PAID	HIF	255
ILL-PAIRED	WB	343
ILL-PAVED	ENH	28
ILL-PLEASED	PEL	11
ILL-REWARDED	TH	198
ILLS	LC	126
	PAR	5
	PUO2	17
	AA	923
	SAA	239
	SAA	716
	H3	40
	L4	126
	HAP	198
	HAP	1608
	HAP	2405
	BR	152
	BR	182
	J6	34
	J6	136
	J6	406
	J6	840
	J10	480
	SLT1	12
	VP3	126
	G2	738
	G3	497
	G3	713
	G3	831
	AE1	281
	AE6	130
	AE6	850
	AE7	471
	AE7	537
	AE8	640
	AE11	242
	AE11	548
	KT1	478
	KT2	592
	B	328
	HIF	92
	HIF	113
	HIF	161
	HIF	533
	HIF	725
	TH	338
	ESK	24
ILL-TIMED	CAM	163
ILLUMINATIONS	P5	263
ILLUMINED	CI	122
ILLUSTRIOUS	D	12
	SAA	184
	SAA	937
	SAA	941
	SAA	975
	SAA	999
	J10	216
ILLUSTRIOUS	HI	154
	HI	174
	VP5	50
	G2	213
	G2	242
	AE1	883
	AE1	907
	AE6	925
	AE6	1194
	AE8	507
	AE9	876
	DO	7
	KT3	948
	B	340
ILL-WRITTEN	ECG2	9
ILLYRIAN	VP8	9
	AE1	333
ILUS	AE6	883
	AE10	560
ILVA	AE10	253
IMAGE	AM	212
	EMP	6
	AA	10
	AA	32
	MF	15
	L4	220
	T23	104
	TA	63
	TA	66
	EAA	8
	AK	107
	AK	130
	HAP	250
	BR	30
	PKA	16
	EL	139
	EL	230
	J6	694
	M1	106
	GK	101
	VP8	101
	AE1	133
	AE1	859
	AE2	220
	AE2	230
	AE2	766
	AE4	121
	AE4	735
	AE4	917
	AE6	171
	AE9	395
	AE10	1166
	AF	33
	KT3	241
	TJD	25
	M8	332
	M10	94
	C	546
	C	547
	C	548
	TH	380
	M12	317
	AU	516
	GP	84
	GP	104
	CI	233
IMAGERY	AE9	348
	KT2	468
IMAGES	ML	49
	AA	792
	L4	18
	J3	356
	P6	66
	G2	536
	G4	70
	G4	588
	AE2	707
	M11	297
	M11	334
IMAGINARY	L3	89
IMAGINATION	PCG2	26
	ENH	6
	C	489
IMAGINE	EMQw	14
	CM	2
	AA	756
	OD	55
	GK	12
	AE10	642
IMAGINED	AM	276
	AA	790
	SAA	135
	L3	188
	L4	65
	AE7	619
	AE7	635

Word	Ref	No.
IMAGINED	CAM	40
IMBALMED	L3	71
IMBATTLED	M12	619
IMBIBED	G2	478
IMBIBES	AE5	118
	M15	514
IMBIBING	G2	298
IMBITTERED	HIF	494
IMBRACE	M1	239
IMBRACED	RL	181
	OE	17
	AE10	366
IMBRACUS	AE12	516
IMBREUS	M12	430
IMBROIDERED	AE10	1161
IMBROIDERY	L4	103
IMBROWN	GK	178
IMBRUE	EPF	9
IMITATE	PWG	46
	PNH	26
	BR	346
	G4	590
	AE6	799
	AS	23
IMITATED	GK	29
	VP6	72
	AE5	336
	AE10	905
	AE11	1290
	AE12	1136
	M11	328
IMITATES	PT	12
	ECG2	29
	G4	101
	AE11	757
	M11	479
	M15	337
	M15	690
IMITATING	PLN	45
	M1	816
	M13	107
	GK	18
	OAL	877
	KT3	26
	M10	41
IMITATION	PUO3	21
IMITATIVE	G2	282
	KT2	527
IMMATURE	AE10	22
IMMATURELY	UDH	1
IMMEDIATE	MD	223
	AE5	436
IMMENSE	TA	33
	M13	16
	AE10	26
	AE12	1120
	M12	17
IMMERSED	TH	89
IMMODERATE	AA	847
	AK	147
	J10	176
	VP10	41
	G2	483
IMMORAL	J10	499
IMMORTAL	HS	11
	RH	57
	LC	155
	AM	1099
	AA	197
	AA	855
	MF	12
	RL	273
	L1	35
	L3	247
	L3	254
	AK	5
	HAP	1
	HAP	12
	HAP	2101
	HAP	2117
	EL	135
	EL	203
	MS	29
	P1	73
	M1	139
	M1	205
	M1	764
	VCS	34
	EHC	36
	VP9	37
	G4	303
	G4	408
	G4	457
	AE1	346
	AE1	379
	AE2	396
IMMORTAL	AE4	343
	AE6	534
	AE6	813
	AE6	1068
	AE7	1
	AE8	382
	AE9	21
	AE9	598
	AE9	838
	AE10	162
	AE10	334
	AE10	347
	AE10	861
	AE10	1124
	AE11	427
	AE12	143
	AE12	254
	AE12	340
	AE12	356
	AE12	1202
	AE12	1271
	AE12	1277
	DO	17
	KT3	340
	M8	64
	HIF	109
	C	200
	M12	772
	AU	79
	AU	568
	M15	252
	AS	27
IMMORTALITY	TA	420
	BR	349
	M1	915
	FL	557
IMMORTALIZE	M12	202
IMMORTALIZED	SAA	938
IMMOVABLE	M13	87
	AE12	1025
IMMUNITIES	GK	130
IMMUNITY	HAP	1060
IMMURED	KT2	3
IMMUTABLE	AM	1078
	TA	493
IMPAIR	G3	112
	M8	362
IMPAIRED	DO	108
IMPAIRS	KT3	749
IMPALED	J1	235
	M8	24
	LC	43
IMPART	AM	619
	SMM2	25
	PT	5
	CM	115
	HP	259
	AA	8
	FS4	1
	HAP	259
	HAP	1377
	EL	249
	P1	101
	P2	42
	P5	29
	M9	188
	GK	139
	G4	404
	AE2	95
	AE3	49
	AE5	779
IMPARTIAL	SAA	789
	HAP	2544
	G2	384
	AE10	633
	KT2	422
IMPARTS	AA	377
	M1	380
	AE2	204
	AE6	196
	AE12	391
IMPASSIBLE	HAP	95
	M12	126
IMPASSIVE	AE6	409
	M12	650
IMPATIENCE	J1	85
IMPATIENT	AM	699
	AA	155
	AA	684
	MD	241
	L4	7
	HAP	1594
	J6	444
	M1	642
	M1	718
	M1	1004
IMPATIENT	G3	164
	G3	324
	G3	659
	G4	702
	AE1	82
	AE1	727
	AE4	297
	AE4	434
	AE6	120
	AE6	1076
	AE10	1271
	AE11	948
	AE12	575
	AE12	811
	M8	197
	M8	232
	B	149
	CAM	255
	HIF	284
	M12	136
	CI	512
IMPATIENTLY	AE4	227
IMPEACH	SAA	758
IMPEACHED	SAA	54
IMPED	G4	439
IMPEL	CI	411
IMPELLED	AM	919
	AE10	349
	CAM	138
	HIF	657
	M11	145
IMPELS	G3	316
	M15	271
IMPENDING	L3	186
	TA	478
	HAP	2406
	BR	157
	G1	536
	AE3	347
	AE5	636
	AE11	450
	AE12	1332
	AU	117
IMPENETRABLE	TA	442
	J10	337
	AE6	199
	AE8	506
	AE10	344
	AE10	764
	AE10	1267
IMPENITENCE	AA	145
IMPENITENTLY	BR	285
IMPERFECT	AM	555
	PCG2	22
	L4	42
	HAP	83
	BR	350
	EL	263
	EL	298
	J3	378
	M1	542
	M1	571
	M1	709
	G3	667
	KT3	1046
	TH	309
	W8	426
IMPERFECTIONS	PUO2	28
	P4	47
IMPERIAL	SMA	96
	AM	948
	AA	22
	MF	98
	SAA	732
	SDG	23
	SDG	28
	H3	54
	TA	290
	TA	317
	TA	455
	HAP	1998
	HAP	2522
	HAP	2553
	BR	212
	EL	267
	J6	164
	J10	67
	M1	802
	VP1	29
	G2	458
	G3	377
	G3	795
	AE1	80
	AE1	176
	AE2	335
	AE2	490

Word	Ref	No.
IMPERIAL	AE2	830
	AE3	142
	AE3	31
	AE3	791
	AE4	129
	AE4	161
	AE4	401
	AE5	781
	AE5	1027
	AE6	443
	AE6	1064
	AE6	1177
	AE7	978
	AE8	450
	AE8	671
	AE9	124
	AE9	1007
	AE10	62
	AE10	153
	AE11	1114
	AE12	373
	AE12	1145
	OAL	211
	AF	5
	DO	161
	KT3	692
	B	493
	HIF	28
	HIF	297
	HIF	406
	C	713
	AU	302
	M15	640
IMPERIOUS	HAP	2131
	J6	303
	AE2	1069
	AE5	1020
	AE7	857
	KT2	255
	M8	280
	HIF	468
	HIF	764
	TH	134
	TH	426
IMPERTINENCE	P4	44
IMPERVIOUS	HAP	98
	AE8	259
IMPETUOUS	L3	211
	L4	195
	H29	59
	TA	120
	M1	369
	M1	772
	G1	173
	G1	484
	G1	578
	G2	633
	G3	313
	G4	25
	G4	444
	AE5	1127
	AE9	554
	AE9	957
	AE10	506
	AE10	1158
	AE11	690
	AE12	493
	AE12	671
	AE12	989
	M8	106
	M8	280
	HIF	285
	HIF	760
	M11	167
	CI	241
IMPETUOUSLY	M1	717
IMPIETY	BP	142
IMPIOUS	AR	200
	DA	146
	EMW	1
	AA	498
	MD	77
	MD	246
	MD	290
	MD	310
	SAA	141
	SAA	888
	RL	127
	TA	415
	AK	59
	HAP	56
	J1	68
	J6	713
	M1	162
	M1	206
	G1	631
IMPIOUS	G1	679
	G3	769
	AE1	396
	AE2	218
	AE2	582
	AE2	976
	AE3	81
	AE3	325
	AE4	431
	AE4	711
	AE5	858
	AE5	960
	AE7	714
	AE7	1052
	AE8	635
	AE10	544
	AE12	54
	AE12	396
	AE12	425
	AE12	474
	OAL	227
	KT1	81
	M8	17
	M8	287
	M8	319
	M8	345
	M8	374
	BP	5
	CAM	27
	CAM	33
	CAM	64
	CAM	79
	CAM	83
	CAM	186
	CAM	205
	C	259
	TH	226
	AU	328
	M15	125
	M15	187
IMPLACABLE	CI	470
	AA	173
IMPLANTED	P5	142
IMPLEAD	J1	257
IMPLIED	J6	390
IMPLORE	SMA	126
	PT	27
	HP	223
	PLB	30
	L1	57
	HAP	1539
	HAP	1570
	HAP	2078
	PDS	27
	J6	517
	M1	435
	M1	967
	M1	973
	G4	569
	G4	649
	AE1	740
	AE3	198
	AE3	556
	AE3	774
	AE4	66
	AE5	802
	AE5	1040
	AE7	792
	AE8	189
	AE8	495
	AE11	546
	KT1	65
IMPLORED	HAP	1401
	BR	247
	J1	125
	M1	507
	M9	164
	AE2	948
	AE3	689
	AE4	299
	AE6	274
	KT2	327
	KT3	128
	M10	62
	M11	244
	M12	492
IMPLORES	AE3	474
	AE5	286
	AE5	975
	AE7	699
	M11	182
IMPLORING	PDS	9
	TH	281
IMPLOY	AA	531
	SAA	627
	SAA	792
IMPLOY	L4	35
IMPLOYED	T23	15
	G3	244
IMPLOYS	AA	712
IMPLY	C	814
	FL	544
IMPORT	L4	265
IMPORTANCE	L4	271
	OAE2	14
IMPORTANT	AM	262
	RL	314
	AE9	306
	AE11	383
	KT1	322
	KT3	2
IMPORTED	AS	16
IMPORTUNATE	CAM	202
IMPORTUNE	EDS	35
IMPORTUNED	G1	57
	HIF	759
IMPOSE	AR	152
	PTL	8
	PNH	24
	AA	975
	SAA	49
	SAA	343
	RL	102
	HAP	2281
	AE1	361
	AE2	78
	AE4	339
	AE6	1151
IMPOSED	SAA	99
	HAP	2281
	J10	436
	G1	92
	AE1	93
	AE12	1273
	C	204
IMPOSES	HAP	1686
IMPOSING	AE6	846
IMPOSITION	GE	62
IMPOSSIBLE	M9	113
	M13	83
	MC	65
	WB	365
	WB	475
IMPOST	EWGR	40
IMPOSTURE	HAP	2017
IMPOTENCE	PEL	24
	PCG1	22
	J1	131
	KT3	817
IMPOTENT	ECG1	16
	J6	84
	J6	166
	J6	844
	P4	107
	P6	69
	GK	84
	AE4	435
	AE9	70
	AE12	875
	HIF	723
	CI	366
	CI	461
IMPOVERISHED	AR	218
	AA	94
IMPOWERED	J16	81
	AE11	200
IMPRECATIONS	AE8	852
IMPREGNABLE	TA	168
IMPREGNANT	M1	203
IMPREGNATE	L4	244
	G3	440
IMPRESSED	M1	21
	AE7	638
	M8	210
	M10	24
	M12	753
	GP	82
	CI	232
IMPRESSION	LC	145
	AA	257
	L4	295
	EL	224
	AE2	117
	KT2	330
	TH	221
	M15	248
	CI	139
IMPRESSIONS	EL	238
	P5	63
IMPRIMATUR	HAP	1550
IMPRINT	HS	73
IMPRINTED	AE4	5

Word	Ref	No.
INCREASE	CI	356
	AS	55
INCREASED	VHH	55
	PTW	22
	CM	55
	L5	10
	HAP	1518
	HAP	1900
	EL	69
	AE8	292
	AE8	399
	AE9	549
	AE10	214
	AE11	868
	B	57
	BP	127
	BP	158
	HIF	372
	FL	444
	M12	468
	M12	701
	M12	754
	AU	110
	AS	86
	AS	101
INCREASES	L3	311
	M1	466
INCREASING	AM	493
	ODA	58
	M1	711
	G1	356
	AE10	35
	AE12	337
	CAM	94
INCROACH	AE11	931
INCROACHING	G2	512
	OAL	185
	BP	190
INCUBUS	WB	41
INCUMBENT	AE12	543
	AE12	1132
	M15	596
INCUMBERED	SAA	1133
	G2	569
	AE10	1129
	AE10	1286
	AE12	385
	AE12	1121
INCURABLE	AE11	1079
INCURS	AE3	640
INCURSIONS	M11	471
INDANGERED	PWG	43
	AE5	1047
	AE7	653
	AE9	297
INDE	KT3	63
INDEARS	AR	86
INDEAVOR	PWGR	27
INDENTED	J6	151
	G2	522
INDENTS	J3	399
INDEPENDENT	PDG	41
	HAP	35
INDIA	AM	93
	MD	105
	M1	1093
	G1	85
	G2	163
	G4	306
	AE6	1082
	OAL	218
	M15	618
INDIAN	HS	92
	AM	626
	PUO3	19
	RL	179
	TA	24
	TA	361
	HAP	231
	HAP	442
	HAP	1134
	HAP	2482
	G2	171
	G2	189
	G3	42
	G4	616
	AE1	687
	AE6	1097
	AE7	837
	AE12	105
	KT2	555
	M8	28
	WB	225
	PWR	15
INDIANS	PIE	1
	PCG1	28
INDIANS	PUO3	21
	G2	239
	AE8	937
INDICT	PSF	20
	SAA	450
INDICTMENT	RL	204
INDIES	AR	308
	SMA	123
	LC	73
	AM	108
	AM	1171
	ECD	20
	J6	600
	P5	70
	KT3	99
INDIFFERENCE	EM	6
	SKA6	8
INDIFFERENT	EAZ	35
INDIGENCE	WB	481
INDIGESTED	L3	133
	M1	10
	AE3	829
	AE8	254
	C	142
INDIGNATION	SAA	842
	HAP	1556
	SSC	39
	J1	67
	P1	248
	M1	234
	AE10	94
	AE10	1136
INDIGNANT	B	315
	HIF	655
	M12	478
INDIGNITIES	AA	673
INDISTINCT	FL	112
INDITE	PLB	19
	J1	121
	J6	344
	P5	12
INDITED	HAP	892
INDITING	SAA	394
	PDS	45
	EKA	12
	PLT	36
INDIVIDUAL	L3	26
	OD	48
INDIVIDUALS	KT3	1056
INDOWING	J6	290
INDUCE	VP9	22
INDUCED	M1	943
	G4	321
	C	299
INDUCEMENTS	HAP	1245
INDUCTION	EHC	13
INDUED	AA	972
	M1	202
	MC	10
	AE12	1227
	C	462
	M11	264
INDULGE	PC1	24
	AA	898
	J10	529
	P2	5
	P2	44
	P5	74
	P5	220
	G1	408
	G2	388
	G2	390
	G2	500
	G3	320
	AE2	1054
	HIF	581
	HIF	646
INDULGED	PAL	38
	RL	157
	HI	175
	VP8	58
	AE1	735
	B	455
	B	509
	HIF	488
	M11	33
	M11	300
	CI	240
	AR	240
INDULGENCE	SAA	8
	SAA	726
	OE	52
	HAP	2105
	EL	179
	G2	473
	DO	85
INDULGENCE	B	356
INDULGENT	HP	184
	AA	31
	SAA	1087
	L5	10
	HAP	451
	HAP	2576
	J6	786
	J10	435
	P2	79
	P4	63
	M9	56
	VP10	94
	G1	148
	AE1	347
	AE2	126
	AE4	491
	AE5	470
	AE5	936
	AE6	88
	AE8	708
	OAL	593
	B	663
INDULGING	AA	675
	G2	604
	G3	107
	B	245
INDURE	GE	16
INDUSTRIOUS	SAA	535
	HAP	1143
	G3	208
	G4	53
	TJD	53
INDUSTRY	AM	793
	MF	148
	GK	85
	G1	188
	G2	48
	G2	617
	AE5	591
INEVITABLE	TA	195
	J10	531
	AE2	694
	AE12	231
	KT1	232
	C	676
	M12	744
INEXHAUSTED	TA	259
	AK	28
INEXORABLE	G3	111
	G4	678
	AE10	1237
	AE11	1198
	AE12	1263
	TH	252
INFALLIBILITY	RL	286
	RL	251
	HAP	637
INFALLIBLE	PCB	40
	RL	387
	AT	63
	HAP	611
INFALLIBLY	HAP	765
INFAMOUS	M1	280
	M1	282
	AE5	1126
INFAMOUSLY	J6	229
INFAMY	SAA	41
	HAP	1338
	HAP	1577
	J1	74
	M1	1057
	AE10	944
	KT2	574
	WB	443
INFANCY	SAA	376
	TA	448
	TA	457
	HAP	81
	ODA	37
	P3	26
	AE7	4
	MG	18
	KT1	360
	M15	299
INFANT	AM	871
	AM	1035
	CM	83
	CM	88
	CM	126
	CM	138
	MF	77
	AT	34
	ER	2
	TA	459
	HAP	59

Word	Code	Number
INFANT	HAP	1895
	BR	22
	BR	55
	BR	110
	BR	149
	BR	201
	BR	321
	EL	214
	J1	174
	J3	290
	P1	21
	HI	4
	HI	144
	HI	174
	VP4	24
	VP4	73
	G2	109
	G2	498
	AE8	384
	AE11	822
	AE11	847
	OAL	215
	KT2	520
	M8	324
	BP	51
	CAM	354
	M15	600
	M15	643
	SMP	46
INFANTRY	AE2	651
INFANT'S	BR	183
	J10	270
	VP4	76
INFANTS	EIE	7
	AM	428
	AM	904
	J6	13
	J6	712
	J6	767
	AE2	189
	AE7	723
	AE9	820
INFANTS'	AM	203
INFECT	AM	206
	PLG	20
	MD	198
	SAA	1034
	G3	712
	AE2	733
	AE10	569
	C	143
INFECTED	EUO	4
	EAZ	29
	AA	788
	AE1	253
	AE7	499
	KT3	260
	M15	500
INFECTING	AR	113
	P6	91
INFECTION	PC2	20
	MD	176
	G3	723
	B	694
	M15	291
	ETP	4
INFECTIOUS	AE12	757
	KT2	313
INFECTS	MD	295
	H29	32
	G3	671
	AE3	195
	AE6	345
INFEEBLED	MM	44
INFER	EOE	17
	RL	356
	RL	361
	L3	35
	HAP	929
	HAP	2520
INFERENCE	HAP	1670
INFERIOR	DA	180
	HAP	252
	J6	660
	P2	100
	M1	350
	GK	118
	AE1	905
	AE5	1076
	AE8	571
	AE10	5
	AE11	119
	AE11	447
	KT2	292
	M8	214
INFERIORS	HAP	2369

Word	Code	Number
INFERNAL	CM	122
	L3	224
	HAP	495
	HAP	1113
	VCS	26
	G4	679
	G4	691
	G4	730
	AE4	684
	AE4	1007
	AE6	200
	AE6	394
	AE6	509
	AE6	719
	AE6	807
	AE7	451
	AE7	582
	AE7	636
	AE7	671
	AE7	718
	AE7	787
	AE8	396
	AE10	1079
	KT2	482
	CAM	24
	CAM	90
	C	603
	TH	189
	TH	300
	TH	345
	EWR	10
INFERRED	HAP	648
	HAP	2269
INFERS	AA	980
	HAP	2154
INFEST	J6	738
	G1	199
	G4	358
	AE3	512
	AE12	397
INFESTED	L3	4
	HAP	173
INFESTING	AE8	75
INFIDELIUM	GE	14
INFIDELS	PO	17
INFINITE	RL	114
	J10	313
	BP	13
INFINITELY	TA	181
INFINITY	RL	40
	RL	93
	HAP	105
INFIRM	M15	307
INFIXED	AE11	1176
	KT1	273
	TH	349
INFLAME	HS	42
	VCS	21
	VP9	77
	AE9	170
	AE10	557
INFLAMED	G3	404
	G3	659
	G4	96
	G4	728
	AE4	131
	AE6	525
	AE11	582
	AE11	1299
	AE12	638
	KT1	317
	CAM	22
	M12	265
	CI	3
INFLAMES	G4	577
	AE7	459
	AE10	60
	AE10	416
	AE12	473
	CI	28
INFLATED	C	750
INFLICT	AE6	674
INFLICTED	AE6	514
INFLICTS	G1	142
	M12	414
	UDH	36
	HS	71
	SMA	15
	LC	28
	AM	72
	SAA	688
	L1	30
	L1	37
	MS	3
	M1	1081
	VP5	96

Word	Code	Number
INFLUENCE	VP9	67
	G4	326
	AE1	797
	AE1	1044
	AU	263
	AS	29
INFLUENCED	J3	67
INFOLD	AE2	906
	AE6	807
	AE8	732
	AE11	735
	AE12	636
INFORCE	AE11	784
INFORCED	HIF	231
INFORM	MF	66
	PK	2
	AE6	1169
	AE8	15
INFORMED	EM	1
	AA	890
	RL	68
	HAP	2081
	OAL	733
	C	585
	WB	264
	CI	63
INFORMERS	AE4	270
INFORMING	HAP	251
	M1	490
INFORMS	GE	2
INFRINGE	AE12	279
INFRINGED	HAP	2530
	AE12	919
INFUSE	LCA	51
	P3	22
	G3	446
	G4	384
	AE1	964
	AE8	514
	AF	74
	WB	400
INFUSED	AA	842
	ER	74
	NS	27
	J3	209
	J6	805
	G3	761
	J10	464
	AE6	984
	AE8	537
	AE12	594
	MM	3
INFUSING	VP4	65
	L1	40
	G4	600
INGAGE	EWGR	25
	PLN	10
	PUO4	37
	MD	291
	MD	318
	ER	75
	G1	509
	G1	672
	AE7	659
	AE9	397
	AE9	935
	AE10	505
	AE12	1040
	M11	37
	M12	559
	AU	14
INGAGED	AM	25
	AM	313
	AE7	416
	AE9	1033
INGENDERED	SAA	558
INGENDERS	C	149
INGENIOUS	PIE	9
	B	74
	C	499
	M15	698
INGLORIOUS	SAA	598
	SAA	1074
	SAA	1078
	ER	56
	TA	490
	HAP	1566
	J10	329
	G1	682
	G2	689
	AE4	331
	AE9	159
	AE10	75
	AE10	779
	AE11	41
	AE11	1164

Word	Ref	No.
INGLORIOUS	AE11	1230
	AE12	358
	AF	140
	FL	564
INGLORIOUSLY	AA	246
INGOTS	AE5	147
	AE10	732
	AE10	738
INGRAFT	GK	113
	AU	44
INGRATITUDE	EL	182
INGRAVED	T18	75
	AE9	353
	AE12	1114
INGREDIENTS	P2	114
	DO	117
INGROSS	HIF	252
INHABIT	J3	314
	VP5	120
	AE6	597
	FL	99
INHABITANTS	AA	85
	VP1	79
	G2	229
	G3	702
	AE1	738
	AE3	463
	AE7	1008
	AE8	795
	TH	4
INHABITED	RL	177
INHABITS	VP9	52
INHANCE	L4	140
INHANCED	GK	36
INHERENT	MD	114
INHERIT	SAA	804
	J6	779
	AU	253
INHERITANCE	LCA	22
	HAP	294
	HAP	2146
	HAP	2263
	J16	58
	WB	395
	WB	446
INHOSPITABLE	AE5	817
INHUMAN	M1	211
	M13	21
	M13	188
	VP8	67
	G2	788
	G4	467
	AE1	280
	AE1	760
	AE2	671
	AE2	899
	AE6	515
INIMITABLE	AE6	799
INISKELLING	PWR	41
INITIATE	PD	28
INJECT	L4	8
INJECTED	L4	253
INJOINED	SAA	603
INJOY	PUF	26
INJUNCTION	WB	172
INJURED	AM	788
	HP	222
	SSF	3
	AA	40
	MD	158
	SAA	335
	SAA	617
	SAA	625
	T23	104
	TA	269
	HAP	335
	HAP	1637
	M1	1004
	G1	553
	AE1	41
	AE2	196
	AE2	239
	AE2	344
	AE2	781
	AE4	554
	AE4	756
	AE4	867
	AE5	9
	AE6	1056
	AE11	405
	AE12	479
	AE12	722
	OAL	415
	KT1	53
	KT3	807
	M8	338
INJURED	HIF	66
	HIF	140
	HIF	278
	HIF	542
	AU	288
	AU	309
	CI	481
INJURIES	PCD	13
	AA	933
	BR	282
	AE7	797
	FL	590
INJURIOUS	AM	666
INJURY	HAP	1383
INJUSTICE	SAA	763
	AE4	531
	CI	472
INK	ETC	22
	SAA	483
	EDGA	20
	P3	21
INLAID	AE10	691
INLARGE	HAP	2181
	GK	135
	AE4	262
	AE12	574
INLARGED	M1	366
	M15	458
	CI	35
INLETS	M15	516
INLY	AE5	567
	AE5	1133
	AE11	147
	KT1	119
INMATE	AK	20
	G2	41
	M15	256
INMATES	HAP	2292
	AE11	496
INMOST	L4	193
	TA	4
	AE4	611
	KT1	276
	TH	302
INN	KT3	888
	C	216
INNATE	HAP	177
	HAP	453
	AE1	220
	GP	17
INNAVIGABLE	AE6	161
	AE6	205
	AE9	122
INNOCENCE	LCA	30
	PT	17
	CM	126
	HP	96
	PUF	10
	PUF	28
	PRH	12
	AK	70
	ODA	76
	P1	233
	M1	1084
	M9	20
	G4	745
	AE2	195
	AE7	818
	AE8	456
	AE12	851
	OAL	882
	B	386
	FL	505
	FL	607
	M15	60
	M15	169
	AS	39
	AS	75
INNOCENT	EMP	1
	NS	2
	HAP	3
	HAP	1994
	PMS	14
	J6	309
	G2	738
INNOCENTLY	HP	158
	L2	36
	KT3	98
	PWR	28
INNOVATES	M15	277
INNOVATING	M15	387
INNOVATION	AA	800
INNUENDO	EKA	28
INNUMERABLE	TA	97
	L4	126
INOCULATE	G2	103
INOFFENSIVE	MF	200
INQUIRE	PWG	12
	M1	878
INQUIRES	M1	189
INQUISITION	HAP	2377
INQUISITIVE	H29	44
	J16	88
	FL	459
INQUISITOR	AE6	582
	AU	36
INRAGED	AM	886
	AE4	257
	AE9	1080
	M12	501
	M12	657
INROADS	SAA	923
	AK	100
INROLLED	T18	63
	KT3	12
INSATIATE	HAP	153
	J6	50
	AE1	998
	AE2	142
	HIF	253
INSCRIBE	P5	102
	OAL	40
INSCRIBED	AM	774
	HAP	1781
	J1	197
	J10	197
	VP3	164
	VP6	13
	AE1	669
	AE3	566
	AE6	23
	M8	393
	B	757
	AU	612
INSCRIPTION	DA	209
	T23	85
	M9	203
	VP5	64
INSCRIPTIONS	PCD	27
	J10	227
	AE11	121
INSECT	SAA	336
	B	321
INSECTS	HAP	1864
	G3	236
INSENSIBLE	G4	369
	AE4	324
	KT1	256
INSENSIBLY	GK	44
INSERTED	G2	108
INSHRINED	HIF	300
INSIDIOUS	M15	700
INSINUATING	P1	229
INSIPID	PTC	30
	J3	153
INSLAVED	J10	129
	C	384
	CI	413
INSNARED	L4	134
INSOLENCE	SAA	729
	G2	42
	AE1	189
	AE5	505
	AE11	542
	HIF	414
INSOLENT	AE2	732
	P1	263
	HIF	335
INSOLENTLY	HI	133
	TA	319
INSPECT	M15	201
INSPECTED	G3	738
INSPECTION	J6	712
INSPIRATION	PO	30
	AA	524
	SAA	1024
	P4	26
	KT2	433
INSPIRE	SCG1	12
	HP	250
	MD	166
	SAA	177
	SAA	618
	RL	389
	L1	32
	T18	58
	FS4	6
	TA	115
	TA	476
	HAP	1633
	M1	3
	M1	102

Word	Ref	No.	Word	Ref	No.	Word	Ref	No.
INTENT	FL	146	INTERMITTING	AE12	75	INTRUDING	J1	151
	M12	82	INTERMIXED	VP5	4		AE7	651
	M12	484	INTERPOSE	MF	163		M11	110
	M15	558		J6	740	INTRUST	J10	536
	CI	485		M9	154	INTRUSTED	B	551
INTENTION	P1	169		AE1	759		HIF	434
INTENTS	L3	319		KT2	386		HIF	483
INTERCEDE	TA	88		TJD	79		M15	158
INTERCEPT	AM	230	INTERPOSED	HAP	1181		GP	57
	AA	705		HAP	2390		CI	502
	GK	88		G3	394	INTUITION	HS	102
	AE2	248	INTERPOSING	AE1	535	INUNDATIONS	HAP	2155
	AE2	509		CI	359	INURED	AR	87
	AE4	687	INTERPRET	RL	362		H3	35
	HIF	40		RL	292		HAP	2204
	FL	220		HAP	381		J6	355
	AU	186		HAP	856		G1	185
	M15	159	INTERPRETATION	HAP	1001		G2	667
	M15	702	INTERPRETED	HAP	763		G3	291
INTERCEPTED	AE10	565		HAP	998		AE4	629
	B	118		B	72		AE6	157
INTERCEPTS	KT2	595	INTERPRETER	UDH	20		AE7	1009
	M8	33		HAP	463		AE9	822
INTERDICTED	J10	263		HAP	930		AE10	461
	HIF	41		HAP	1049		B	452
	M15	203	INTERPRETERS	HAP	682		B	605
INTEREST	HS	13		HIF	465		BP	35
	HS	66	INTERPRETS	RL	310		CI	603
	AR	16		J6	706	INURNED	J10	406
	AR	286		AE10	256	INVADE	AR	192
	AR	296	INTERRED	AE6	334		LCA	32
	RH	98		KT1	129		AM	159
	PWG	5	INTERRUPT	OAL	373		AM	864
	AM	150	INTERSPERSED	M12	618		AM	1006
	AM	191	INTERUPTING	L3	25		AM	1202
	PCD	19	INTERVAL	AR	4		PMQ	49
	EMK	12		MF	22		PMM	9
	AA	68		EL	348		SEL1	7
	AA	287		AE4	627		PCG2	9
	AA	501		AE9	179		DA	132
	AA	724		DO	90		AA	706
	MD	88	INTERVALS	AM	955		MD	71
	MD	89		TA	159		SAA	13
	SAA	100		G2	386		SAA	146
	SAA	200		G2	759		SAA	650
	SAA	208	INTERVIEW	AE6	630		SAA	684
	SAA	238	INTERWOVEN	G3	39		SAA	919
	SAA	241	INTESTATE	J1	217		AT	30
	SAA	243	INTESTINE	SAA	706		PD	60
	SAA	644		M1	26		L3	255
	SAA	737		G4	92		H3	31
	RL	275		M11	113		H9	15
	H29	11	INTHRAL	HAP	2496		J6	32
	HAP	437	INTHRALLED	KT3	320		P5	238
	HAP	547	INTIMATE	HAP	1778		M1	80
	HAP	630	INTIRE	SAA	128		M1	180
	HAP	810		RL	298		M13	105
	HAP	951		RL	299		SFL	15
	HAP	1366	INTOLERABLE	TA	174		G1	165
	HAP	1521		J6	264		G1	180
	HAP	1678		AE10	468		G1	216
	HAP	1688		KT3	81		G2	42
	HAP	1691		M12	682		G2	508
	HAP	2118	INTOMB	M1	739		G2	569
	HAP	2119		AE9	105		G2	632
	HAP	2360	INTOMBED	G2	485		G2	721
	HAP	2443		AE6	426		G3	642
	HAP	2548		B	756		G3	661
	BR	190	INTOMBS	G2	728		G4	584
	J6	339	INTRANCED	SM2	16		G4	643
	G1	62		FL	119		G4	702
	AE2	13	INTREAT	AE2	882		AE1	250
	AE4	608	INTREATS	CAM	208		AE2	285
	AE5	249	INTRENCH	PAR	13		AE2	347
	AE7	804		HAP	2160		AE3	288
	AE8	26	INTRENCHED	AE9	443		AE3	534
	AE11	562		AE11	1317		AE3	730
	OAL	444	INTREPID	TA	206		AE4	584
	OAL	719		G4	122		AE4	789
	MM	29		AE8	837		AE5	191
	B	542		AE10	196		AE6	1065
	HIF	174	INTRICATE	HAP	957		AE7	156
	HIF	195		AE9	519		AE7	670
	HIF	371	INTRIGUE	SAA	87		AE12	869
	C	63	INTRIGUES	HS	80		KT3	519
	AU	296		PRL	17		TJD	131
	WB	180		EDS	7		BP	190
INTERESTS	RL	160		J3	90		HIF	159
	RL	250		J6	528		FL	411
	HAP	2571		HIF	746		M12	677
INTERFERING	RL	18	INTRIGUING	SAA	521		CI	360
INTERIOR	M15	83	INTRODUCE	AA	122	INVADED	VP6	28
INTERLINING	J1	103	INTRODUCED	AE11	380		AE1	880
INTERLOPE	MD	41	INTRUDING	HAP	1465		AE11	935
INTERLOPING	PTS	17		HAP	2063		B	157
INTERLUDES	C	325		HAP	2357		AU	390

INVADED	M15	149
	CI	585
INVADER	AE9	1087
INVADERS	SKA1	16
	AE10	1005
INVADES	AR	7
	PAZ	14
	H2	55
	HAP	1107
	P1	45
	VP10	110
	G2	224
	G4	495
	AE1	481
	AE4	805
	AE6	202
	AE6	598
	AE7	139
	AE7	565
	AE9	444
	AE12	720
	AE12	862
	AE12	951
	M8	30
	CAM	347
	TH	106
	M12	475
	AU	170
	PTP	34
INVADING	HAP	296
	AE5	1109
	AE8	328
	AE9	742
	AE10	388
	M11	165
INVASION	AE7	764
	AE11	441
INVECTIVE	SAA	447
INVEIGHED	VP8	22
	B	483
INVENOMED	AE9	1043
	M12	804
	CI	189
INVENT	AM	632
	EEL	25
	PKK	18
	PF	188
	L3	139
	TA	178
	HAP	1414
	M1	949
	G3	243
	G4	733
	AE4	69
	OAL	257
INVENTED	AA	131
	L3	251
	PAA	24
	P1	187
	AE2	133
	GP	118
	CI	33
INVENTING	EDS	29
	AE10	774
	WB	154
INVENTION	ER	54
	M1	697
	AE2	521
	B	129
INVENTIVE	AE2	219
	B	75
INVENTOR	G1	23
INVENTRESS	AF	162
	AF	172
INVENTS	L4	177
	AE7	662
INVERT	SFL	4
INVERTED	G3	45
	AE9	835
	M12	189
INVERTS	H2	46
INVEST	HAP	1066
	AE9	205
	AE11	734
	M12	638
INVESTED	AE2	593
	AE11	812
INVESTS	AE2	695
	AE12	951
	CAM	346
INVETERATE	HAP	508
	BR	39
	J6	406
	J10	462
	AE6	1000
INVIDIOUS	AE11	518
INVIDIOUS	M8	13
INVIGORATES	OAL	273
INVINCIBLE	RL	197
INVIOLABLE	H3	31
	M1	245
	AE2	207
	AE6	1215
	AE7	512
	AE10	173
	DO	78
	KT3	832
	M12	133
INVIOLABLY	EL	253
	HIF	112
INVIOLATE	TA	486
	AE10	1175
	KT3	352
	J3	417
INVISIBLE	FL	406
INVITATION	AM	104
INVITE	AM	170
	SAA	985
	HAP	1242
	VP1	74
	G2	663
	G2	764
	G3	5
	G3	21
	G4	33
	G4	165
	G4	386
	AE2	12
	AE3	96
	AE3	581
	AE4	116
	AE4	604
	AE4	670
	AE4	809
	AE5	382
	AE8	600
	AE9	919
	AE11	1084
	TH	243
	TH	248
	CI	568
INVITED	J1	207
	J3	401
	AE3	290
	OAE2	3
	MG	30
	B	154
	BP	83
	TH	251
	M12	215
	M12	295
	M12	558
INVITES	HAP	2568
	M1	805
	G1	405
	AE1	601
	AE3	110
	AE4	497
	AE6	61
	AE6	705
	AE9	848
	OAL	316
	OAL	591
	M10	54
INVITING	EDG	22
	VP7	66
	G1	476
	BP	45
INVOKE	H2	38
	P2	12
	M1	336
	M1	496
	G1	145
	G4	546
	AE1	1021
	AE1	579
	AE3	94
	AE4	85
	AE4	604
	AE4	978
	AE6	81
	AE7	354
	AE8	364
	AE8	368
	AE10	1096
	OAL	638
	HIF	130
	CI	564
INVOKED	TA	385
	M1	1013
	G1	236
	G4	762
INVOKED	AE4	876
	AE5	680
	AE5	904
	AE6	330
	AE7	656
	AE9	856
	AE11	462
	AE11	837
	AE12	1131
	OAL	503
	M8	294
	HIF	56
	HIF	615
INVOKES	AE1	136
	AE4	738
	AE8	489
	AE8	940
	AE9	18
	AE12	721
	OAL	140
	M11	213
INVOKING	M9	151
	G1	475
	AE6	352
	AE12	931
INVOLVE	SAA	263
	G3	223
	AE1	105
	AE2	820
	AE2	884
	AE3	519
	AE8	141
	AE9	87
	AE12	866
	HIF	441
	HIF	632
INVOLVED	SAA	524
	L1	54
	M1	324
	M1	816
	G1	445
	G4	545
	G4	614
	G4	718
	AE1	15
	AE2	474
	AE3	766
	AE4	173
	AE4	403
	AE4	921
	AE4	965
	AE5	771
	AE6	152
	AE7	65
	AE7	109
	AE8	26
	AE8	372
	AE10	896
	AE11	162
	AE12	615
	AE12	923
	AE12	976
	AE12	1180
	KT2	95
	M12	790
INVOLVES	AE1	129
	AE1	571
	AE3	257
	AE5	28
	AE6	382
	AE6	1199
	AE11	1318
	CAM	273
INVOLVING	L4	133
	G2	421
	AE6	1066
INVULNERABLE	HAP	2478
IO	J6	680
	M1	795
	M1	897
	M1	1027
	AE7	559
	AE7	1077
	AE10	1040
	OAL	364
	M12	301
	VP2	80
IOLAS	VP3	120
	AE11	951
	AE12	796
	M8	60
IONIA	H2	79
IONIAN	P6	62
	G2	153
	AE3	276
	AE3	881

Word	Code	No.	Word	Code	No.	Word	Code	No.
IONIAN	M15	64	IRON	AE12	156	ISRAEL	AA	753
IOPAS	AE1	1038		AE12	467		AA	846
IO'S	OE	29		AE12	964		SAA	28
	J6	680		KT1	110		SAA	199
	M1	835		KT2	557		SAA	227
	G3	244		KT3	296		SAA	230
IPHIGENE	CI	175		KT3	359		SAA	746
	CI	248		KT3	837		SAA	800
	CI	258		B	110		SAA	1002
	CI	296		M12	390		SAA	1129
	CI	307	IRON-HEADED	G2	233		HAP	19
	CI	349	IRRADIATIONS	UDH	106		HAP	182
	CI	414	IRREMEABLE	AE6	575		BR	285
	CI	510	IRRESOLUTE	CAM	105		TJD	49
IPHIGENIA	M12	44		CAM	140	ISRAELITE	AA	722
	CI	419	IRREVOCABLE	HI	182	ISRAELITES	AA	492
IPHIS	M9	3		AE2	438		SAA	117
	M9	60		AE7	119	ISRAEL'S	AA	7
	M9	62		AE9	126		AA	24
	M9	72		KT3	256		AA	188
	M9	85		HIF	707		AA	664
	M9	149		TH	173		AA	906
	M9	178	ISCHIA	AE9	968		MD	177
	M9	191	ISGRIM'S	HAP	449		SAA	65
	M9	204	ISHBAN	SAA	280		SAA	329
	M9	205		SAA	282		SAA	588
IPH'ITUS	AE2	457		SAA	284		SAA	675
IPHITUS	AE2	591	ISHBOSHETH	AA	58		SAA	800
IRE	G4	96	ISIS	P5	272		SAA	1010
	HIF	145		M1	1050		SAA	1018
IREFUL	KT2	582		M9	32		SAA	1116
IRELAND	HS	65		M9	163		SAA	1139
	MF	139		M9	186	ISSACHAR	AA	738
	ER	41	ISIS'	J6	628	ISSUE	UDH	105
	ER	48		OAL	84		AA	351
	PSH	13	ISLAND	HS	54		AA	639
IRELAND'S	DO	92		PCB	31		AA	829
IRIS	STS2	1		ER	43		MF	8
	STS2	10		AE1	229		MF	160
	STS3	1		AE3	99		HAP	944
	STS3	21		AE3	495		EL	246
	M1	368		AE3	843		J6	785
	AE4	995	ISLE	HS	139		J16	77
	AE5	118		PT	18		M1	215
	AE5	791		ELB	30		M1	909
	AE9	2		MD	167		M9	90
	AE9	19		MD	248		G4	104
	AE9	1086		MD	289		G4	802
	AE10	54		TA	351		AE1	1060
	AE10	110		HAP	2097		AE2	34
	M11	256		BR	148		AE2	1074
IRISH	AM	625		BR	204		AE3	570
	PCB	19		BR	330		AE4	184
	PUO3	28		BR	361		AE6	66
	MF	202		SKA5	1		AE7	77
	PSH	18		J10	154		AE7	604
	PMK	37		M9	166		AE8	693
IRKSOME	AE6	1018		GK	134		AE9	813
IRON	PCG1	27		G3	9		AE10	40
	AT	123		G4	410		AE10	151
	H3	15		AE2	27		AE11	598
	TA	70		AE3	141		AE12	564
	HAP	1937		AE3	173		AE12	1167
	J1	45		AE3	760		AE12	1205
	J3	476		AE3	909		AE12	1323
	J3	486		AE5	62		KT3	221
	J6	34		AE5	524		M8	311
	HI	139		AE7	23		B	110
	GK	57		AE7	1017		HIF	681
	VP2	67		AE8	551		HIF	749
	VP4	9		AE10	254		M15	456
	VP9	15		DO	55		CI	47
	G1	220		DO	85	ISSUED	J10	133
	G1	232		DO	96		M13	216
	G1	630		KT3	17		AE4	668
	G2	61		BP	154		AE10	849
	G2	195		AU	64		AE12	251
	G2	299		CI	42		AE12	653
	G2	487		CI	628		KT2	550
	G4	717	ISLES	LC	135		M8	48
	AE1	404		SKA5	1		B	136
	AE2	26		AE3	174		FL	153
	AE5	88		AE3	276		FL	228
	AE5	270		M15	439	ISSUES	AM	722
	AE5	540		M15	505		AM	1052
	AE5	1095	ISMARUS	G2	51		PTC	19
	AE6	392		AE10	207		SAA	917
	AE6	779		AE10	488		M1	79
	AE6	852	ISOTTA	FL	526		G4	529
	AE6	857	ISRAEL	VHH	29		AE1	403
	AE8	296		AM	367		AE7	695
	AE8	934		AA	69		AE7	843
	AE9	467		AA	177		AE7	860
	AE10	676		AA	295		AE11	1302
	AE10	1270		AA	327		KT3	506
	AE11	1009		AA	432		FL	19

Word	Code	Num
ISSUES	M12	756
	C I	335
ISSUING	HAP	264
	M1	779
	AE2	69
	AE5	574
	AE7	726
	AE8	834
	AE9	415
	AE9	789
	AE9	936
	AE10	680
	AE12	186
	AE12	866
	KT2	474
	KT3	269
	KT3	630
	KT3	1072
	TJD	110
	TH	108
	TH	144
	TH	307
	FL	215
	M12	78
	M12	588
	C I	405
ISTER	G3	544
ITALIA	AE1	751
	AE3	224
ITALIAN	EUO	11
	PUO5	1
	HAP	2061
	P5	72
	G2	128
	AE3	330
	AE3	331
	AE3	494
	AE3	527
	AE3	584
	AE3	661
	AE6	5
	AE6	472
	AE6	1027
	AE9	948
	AE10	88
	AE11	663
	AE11	886
	AE12	45
	M15	76
	M15	442
ITALIANS	PAA	24
	AE5	956
	AE9	708
	AE11	973
	AE12	282
	AE12	378
	AE12	448
	AE12	915
ITALUS	AE7	244
ITALY	UDH	20
	PCB	36
	ER	15
	HAP	291
	EMI	2
	J3	112
	J3	283
	J10	247
	G2	192
	AE1	57
	AE1	103
	AE1	319
	AE1	359
	AE1	525
	AE1	779
	AE3	228
	AE3	246
	AE3	468
	AE3	491
	AE3	560
	AE3	643
	AE3	685
	AE3	687
	AE3	884
	AE5	25
	AE5	109
	AE5	819
	AE5	921
	AE7	65
	AE7	435
	AE7	465
	AE7	777
	AE8	155
	AE8	501
	AE9	355
	AE10	50
	AE10	101

Word	Code	Num
ITALY	AE10	1107
	AE11	495
	AE11	769
ITALY'S	VP10	94
	AE7	653
ITCH	EUO	10
	PLG	4
	HAP	2021
	J6	525
	J6	762
	J10	206
	PMK	18
ITCHES	AT	86
	J6	752
ITCHING	RL	410
	P4	125
ITHACA	AE3	804
ITHACA'S	AE3	353
ITHACUS	AE2	142
	AE2	176
	HIF	219
	AU	169
ITYS	AE9	780
	MG	29
IÜLUS	AE1	365
	AE1	782
	AE1	967
	AE5	741
	AE10	728
	M15	658
	AE1	910
	AE2	930
IÜLUS'	M1	230
	G1	85
IVORY	G3	10
	AE1	830
	AE4	567
	AE6	1236
	AE6	1238
	AE6	1241
	AE9	409
	AE10	205
	AE11	506
	AE12	105
	M10	7
	M10	28
	M10	67
	WB	533
IVY	AT	51
	MO	24
	HAP	1270
	J6	75
	PPS	7
	P1	198
	VP3	58
	VP4	22
	VP5	44
	VP7	36
	VP8	17
	G2	349
	G4	185
	AE7	549
IVY-CHAPLET	AT	30
IXION	G4	694
	AE6	814
IXION'S	G3	66
	BP	3
	M12	292
	M12	667
JACK	PO	12
	EDG	30
	PP	23
	P5	217
	C	742
	PMK	41
JACKALS	AM	327
JACK-PUDDING	PA	38
JACOB	TJD	43
	AS	93
JACOB'S	AA	982
	SAA	16
	HAP	792
	GK	96
	EMKG	11
	ETG	23
	J10	375
	EMKG	1
JADE	ESK	29
JADED	EKK	10
JADES	OAL	880

Word	Code	Num
JAIL	AM	877
	J3	491
	KT1	217
	AE1	200
JAILER		
JAILER'S	KT1	209
JAKES	J3	70
JAMAICA	PSH	15
JAMBEUX	KT3	35
JAMES	TA	128
	TA	398
	TA	470
	MN	10
	HAP	1227
	HAP	1567
	BR	49
	BR	140
	BR	295
JANE	EH	5
JANICULA'S	AE8	469
JANUS	J6	506
	MC	7
	AE1	402
	AE7	245
	AE7	845
	AE12	299
	SMP	17
JANUS-LIKE	P1	111
JAPONIAN	HAP	1144
JAR	PM	4
	MD	306
	L4	258
	G4	94
	AE9	466
	HIF	773
JARRING	DA	137
	MD	197
	HAP	686
	HAP	889
	SSC	4
	P3	37
	M1	12
	DHP	21
	VP4	20
	AE11	454
	AE11	694
	AE12	732
	AE12	907
	KT3	360
	KT3	554
	KT3	1027
	KT3	1118
	B	227
	ESK	13
JARRINGS	AE10	162
JARS	PUO5	5
	H2	27
	AE1	271
	AE1	898
	KT2	418
	M12	339
JASON	AT	116
	M8	48
	M8	111
	M8	189
	AU	33
JASON'S	HP	224
JAUNDICE	HAP	1367
	J6	732
	KT2	487
	B	542
JAUNTY	PEL	19
	SLT2	15
JAVELIN	P5	6
	AE2	742
	AE5	50
	AE7	552
	AE7	1112
	AE8	148
	AE9	559
	AE9	777
	AE10	1111
	AE11	861
	AE11	994
	AE11	1169
	AE11	1189
	AE12	11
	AE12	410
	AE12	531
	AE12	736
	M8	111
	M8	120
	M8	185
	M12	165
	M12	562
	M12	595
	AU	272

Word	Code	No.
JAVELINS	G2	628
	AE7	922
	AE8	919
	AE9	711
	AE9	1028
	AE9	1095
	AE10	1005
	AE10	1243
	AE11	912
	AE11	966
	AE12	417
	AE12	710
JAW	J10	309
JAWS	AM	812
	AM	1007
	L3	51
	HAP	300
	HAP	1292
	J10	365
	P3	200
	M1	319
	M1	1031
	VP7	61
	G2	226
	G3	762
	AE2	279
	AE3	541
	AE5	582
	AE5	1070
	AE6	384
	AE6	569
	AE6	779
	AE7	586
	AE7	786
	AE7	927
	AE10	1022
	AE11	1007
	AE12	1096
	OAL	22
	KT2	205
	C	756
	TH	271
	M12	354
	AU	125
JEALOUS	SMA	81
	PWG	7
	SMM1	9
	SCG2	25
	SM1	13
	AA	442
	AA	989
	SAA	166
	SAA	174
	SAA	251
	SAA	670
	EK	41
	OE	7
	OE	43
	SSC	38
	SKA6	17
	J3	101
	J6	61
	J6	379
	J10	142
	M1	819
	M1	850
	M1	1021
	M9	128
	G3	148
	G3	243
	AE4	426
	AE7	395
	AE12	110
	AE12	1048
	OAL	412
	KT2	92
	KT3	623
	M8	15
	HIF	116
	HIF	703
	HIF	721
JEALOUSIES	AR	213
	AA	211
	AA	397
	PK	17
	HAP	2158
	HAP	2356
JEALOUSY	HP	165
	L4	118
	HAP	1367
	HAP	1382
	SKA5	7
	M1	847
	SLT1	7
	SLT1	9
	SLT1	10
JEALOUSY	SLT1	18
	SLT1	19
	SLT1	20
	SLT1	28
	SLT1	29
	AE12	972
	KT1	464
	KT1	501
	KT2	487
	KT3	1150
	B	129
	FL	524
	WB	489
JEBUS	AA	90
JEBUSITE	AA	213
	AA	286
	AA	338
	AA	538
JEBUSITE'S	BR	179
JEBUSITES	AA	86
	AA	118
	AA	133
	AA	398
	AA	518
	AA	706
	SAA	38
	SAA	540
	SAA	786
JEBUSITIC	AA	663
	SAA	652
JEER	P1	261
JEHOSAPHAT	AK	180
JEHU	MD	119
	HAP	692
JERUSALEM	AA	85
	AA	333
	AA	602
	AA	866
	AA	932
	SAA	12
	SAA	305
	SAA	1131
JERUSALEM'S	SAA	72
	SAA	324
JEST	PIE	21
	EWGR	32
	PCG1	1
	ECG2	6
	PAR	18
	POE	21
	AA	562
	HH	5
	HAP	1549
	PTS	25
	J1	219
	J3	251
	P1	79
	P4	100
	GK	163
	OAL	672
	OAL	696
	HIF	769
	ERL	1
JESTERS	SAA	521
JESTING	KT1	284
	KT1	285
JESTS	EEL	7
	P1	47
JESUIT	MD	201
JESUITS	HAP	617
JET	AE10	206
	C	51
	M12	536
	G3	136
JETTY	PPC	12
JEW	SAA	354
	SAA	471
	EDG	27
	HAP	184
	HAP	693
	C	745
	UDH	56
	EAA	5
	EAA	6
	P1	37
	OAL	341
JEWEL	HS	26
	SMA	124
JEWELS	J6	588
	J10	497
	AE7	112
	OAL	288
	KT3	986
	FL	167
	FL	237
JEWESS	J6	699
JEWISH	AA	104
	AA	503
	SAA	374
	RL	250
	OAL	82
	OAL	466
JEWS	AM	1157
	EEL	4
	AA	45
	AA	61
	AA	126
	AA	216
	AA	282
	AA	338
	AA	417
	AA	592
	AA	607
	AA	623
	AA	627
	SAA	14
	SAA	217
	SAA	631
	SAA	657
	SAA	689
	HAP	889
	HAP	972
	BR	66
	EL	118
	J3	23
	P5	267
	P6	83
	FL	536
JIG	PTS	20
JILT	ECG1	8
	OE	7
	OAL	553
JILTED	J6	530
JILTING	OE	33
JOAN	PO	22
	EH	12
JOB	PRH	24
	ODA	57
	GP	107
	PTP	25
	PTP	27
JOCUNDLY	T27	133
JOG	MG	23
	PTP	26
JOHN	ETC	26
	PUO3	10
	MF	36
	PAA	3
JOIN	HS	39
	PIE	27
	AM	167
	AM	227
	AM	1195
	PA	32
	PLN	11
	EAL	28
	CM	142
	HP	181
	AA	68
	AA	493
	AA	678
	SAA	266
	SAA	779
	EK	4
	EDGA	29
	L4	71
	L4	258
	L4	267
	FS2	3
	HH	21
	HAP	412
	HAP	419
	HAP	660
	HAP	1032
	HAP	1971
	HAP	2064
	BR	45
	ELW	5
	P1	228
	M1	495
	M13	5
	MC	37
	GK	66
	GK	172
	VP2	41
	VP3	142
	VP5	79
	VP5	114
	VP8	38
	G1	13
	G1	379
	G3	52

Word	Code	No.
JOIN	G3	203
	G3	788
	G4	156
	G4	713
	G4	720
	AE1	382
	AE1	712
	AE1	724
	AE1	803
	AE1	986
	AE2	346
	AE2	563
	AE3	77
	AE3,	111
	AE4	143
	AE4	158
	AE4	209
	AE5	556
	AE5	767
	AE5	827
	AE6	1027
	AE6	1135
	AE7	86
	AE7	369
	AE7	440
	AE7	769
	AE8	8
	AE8	219
	AE8	611
	AE8	620
	AE8	656
	AE9	186
	AE9	214
	AE9	708
	AE9	842
	AE9	1063
	AE10	119
	AE10	160
	AE10	622
	AE11	198
	AE11	663
	AE11	728
	AE11	773
	AE11	1214
	AE12	189
	AE12	806
	AE12	979
	OAL	231
	OAL	673
	KT2	30
	KT3	589
	KT3	1116
	M8	163
	M8	214
	C	177
	TH	379
	M11	431
	FL	152
	M15	165
	CI	449
	STP	19
JOINED	HS	6
	LC	32
	LC	35
	LC	58
	LCA	23
	PLN	42
	CM	21
	AA	509
	AA	891
	MD	16
	MD	210
	MD	211
	EDGA	1
	HAP	746
	HAP	1010
	HAP	1193
	EMI	6
	STS2	12
	J10	458
	P1	123
	M1	477
	M1	573
	M1	658
	M1	984
	M9	75
	M13	184
	VP8	102
	G3	177
	G3	270
	AE1	541
	AE2	39
	AE2	620
	AE2	715
	AE3	24
	AE3	427

Word	Code	No.
JOINED	AE3	747
	AE5	390
	AE5	402
	AE5	717
	AE5	942
	AE5	1069
	AE8	165
	AE9	257
	AE9	491
	AE9	854
	AE10	190
	AE11	262
	AE11	1315
	AE12	178
	AE12	284
	AE12	518
	AE12	732
	AE12	1066
	KT1	454
	KT3	390
	KT3	639
	KT3	1120
	M8	50
	B	546
	B	702
	M10	92
	CAM	60
	CAM	115
	CAM	294
	CAM	318
	HIF	662
	C	82
	C	265
	C	820
	FL	431
	M12	85
	M12	249
	M12	499
	M12	567
	M12	774
	AU	539
	AU	557
	WB	79
	M15	507
	GP	123
	CI	52
	CI	60
	CI	514
	CI	544
	CI	570
	STP	27
JOINING	EMQW	26
JOINS	EWG	19
	HAP	1984
	M9	105
	G1	460
	G2	306
	G2	382
	AE4	203
	AE10	229
	AE10	253
	AE11	789
JOINT	AR	322
	EMQ	9
	G1	672
	AE4	153
	AE6	314
	AE10	669
	AE11	537
	BP	168
	M12	414
JOINTED	AE2	66
	AE6	19
	AE11	1100
	AE12	412
	AE12	1019
JOINTLY	HS	148
	AE9	665
JOINTS	P4	78
	P5	78
	VP2	45
	G3	297
	G4	600
	AE3	816
	AE9	1040
	KT3	407
	C	293
	T27	57
JOINTURE		
JOINTURE-CHIMNEYS	HAP	1872
JOLLILY	P6	102
JOLLITY	AE2	327
JOLLY	MD	279
	H2	87
	HAP	380
	HAP	2285
	P6	49

Word	Code	No.
JOLLY	M1	937
	VP3	146
	VP7	1
	VP7	86
	G2	9
	G2	535
	AE1	293
	AE5	395
	AE9	208
	OAL	590
	AF	49
	KT2	224
	FL	19
	FL	205
	FL	339
	WB	5
	CI	546
JONAS	AA	581
JONSON	PT	6
	PT	10
	PA	5
	ECG2	3
	ECG2	15
	PUO1	9
	EUO	31
	MF	80
	MF	175
	MC	22
JONSON'S	PMQ	6
	PUO2	21
	MF	172
	PMS	28
JORDAN	SAA	980
	SAA	1079
JORDAN'S	AA	270
	AA	820
JOSEPH	MN	1
	HAP	1214
	HAP	1218
	HAP	1220
	C	383
	AS	94
	AS	100
JOSEPH'S	D	24
JOSHUA'S	AM	472
	HAP	1832
JOTHAM	AA	882
JOTHRAN	SAA	811
JOURNEY	AM	987
	HP	152
	J6	747
	J10	481
	P6	130
	M1	1089
	AE2	862
	KT1	574
	M11	21
	M11	350
	WB	263
	M15	11
JOURNEY'S	AM	835
	AE6	917
	KT3	888
JOURNEYS	DC	35
JOURNEYWORK	ETC	18
JOVE	HS	77
	AR	40
	AR	38
	AR	100
	RH	62
	RH	94
	PWG	28
	AM	155
	AM	1166
	PUO2	37
	E	10
	CM	11
	CM	18
	HP	56
	HP	60
	OE	28
	ER	73
	T18	9
	T18	32
	T18	80
	T18	84
	H3	2
	BR	60
	BR	207
	PDS	15
	ETS	8
	ETS	12
	ETS	18
	ETS	31
	J6	23
	J6	84

JOVE

Ref	No.
J6	739
J10	301
J10	208
P2	17
P2	36
P2	45
P2	72
P5	203
P5	64
M1	145
M1	196
M1	213
M1	264
M1	294
M1	374
M1	382
M1	763
M1	800
M1	808
M1	826
M1	839
M1	844
M1	854
M1	920
M1	1015
M1	1020
M1	1043
M13	150
M13	171
HI	19
HI	156
VP3	90
VP3	91
VP4	59
VP7	83
VP9	37
G1	197
G1	376
G2	22
G2	144
G2	440
G3	55
G3	57
G4	221
G4	491
AE1	58
AE1	63
AE1	71
AE1	277
AE1	286
AE1	308
AE1	345
AE1	381
AE1	546
AE1	1021
AE2	835
AE2	937
AE3	158
AE3	228
AE3	290
AE3	328
AE3	361
AE3	483
AE3	755
AE3	893
AE4	34
AE4	154
AE4	300
AE4	392
AE4	423
AE4	532
AE4	512
AE4	571
AE4	878
AE4	915
AE5	25
AE5	332
AE5	901
AE5	979
AE5	1024
AE6	186
AE6	207
AE6	382
AE6	543
AE6	789
AE6	1187
AE7	179
AE7	189
AE7	299
AE7	423
AE7	432
AE7	433
AE7	772
AE7	920
AE7	1065
AE7	1058

JOVE

Ref	No.
AE8	140
AE8	425
AE8	463
AE8	527
AE8	565
AE8	754
AE9	156
AE9	659
AE9	855
AE9	863
AE9	1086
AE10	1
AE10	51
AE10	59
AE10	65
AE10	616
AE10	633
AE10	656
AE10	792
AE10	943
AE10	1047
AE10	1253
AE11	1069
AE12	213
AE12	220
AE12	373
AE12	731
AE12	827
AE12	1054
AE12	1145
AE12	1230
AE12	1268
AE12	1296
OAL	85
OAL	714
OAL	814
OAL	815
AF	25
KT2	149
KT3	146
KT3	379
TJD	163
BP	23
BP	138
BP	167
HIF	6
HIF	32
HIF	93
HIF	108
HIF	262
HIF	297
HIF	350
HIF	492
HIF	544
HIF	558
HIF	582
HIF	669
HIF	693
HIF	705
HIF	722
HIF	725
HIF	755
HIF	771
C	470
C	793
M12	76
M12	15
M12	772
M12	738
AU	7
AU	40
AU	145
AU	230
AU	231
AU	345
AU	348
AU	417
WB	164
M15	95
M15	569
CI	628
SMA	129
LC	101

JOVE'S

Ref	No.
T18	8
H3	54
TA	455
BR	208
J10	58
J10	414
P2	42
M1	802
VP6	65
G2	397
G3	795
AE1	941
AE2	438

JOVE'S

Ref	No.
AE2	879
AE3	31
AE3	142
AE4	481
AE4	545
AE5	1020
AE5	1042
AE8	400
AE8	500
AE8	849
AE9	128
AE9	762
AE9	969
AE10	974
OAL	706
DO	133
KT3	670
M8	29
HIF	11
HIF	732
HIF	753
HIF	791
AU	594
CI	628

JOVIAL

Ref	No.
G3	582
HIF	774

JOWL

Ref	No.
PLB	33

JOY

Ref	No.
AR	215
AR	244
AR	274
SMA	4
SMA	50
SMA	68
SMA	70
LC	122
SIE	1
AM	273
AM	1001
AM	1130
AM	1139
SMM2	6
SEL2	12
SEL2	15
SEL2	16
S	1
PUO2	5
PUO2	19
CM	72
HP	131
HP	183
AA	31
AA	244
AA	688
AA	734
MF	60
SAA	195
SAA	628
SAA	791
SAA	824
SAA	830
SAA	1070
SDG	11
L4	10
L4	36
L4	82
H29	73
TA	159
AK	40
HAP	2190
BR	106
SKA2	16
SKA2	20
EL	184
EL	293
ODA	21
J6	485
M1	953
M1	1088
M9	49
M13	6
M13	9
HI	36
HI	150
MC	35
G1	560
G2	532
G3	221
G4	77
AE1	550
AE1	706
AE1	998
AE2	368
AE3	134
AE3	181
AE3	447
AE5	73

JOY	AE5	987	JOYS	SMA	22	JUDAS	SAA	323		
	AE5	1062		AM	440		PDG	39		
	AE6	5		AM	467		HAP	2009		
	AE6	972		AM	551		ETO	3		
	AE6	995		AM	723	JUDEA	SAA	797		
	AE7	178		AM	833	JUDGE	SMA	72		
	AE7	869		SM1	11		AM	1049		
	AE8	414		CM	41		PWG	4		
	AE8	975		HP	201		PWG	24		
	AE9	23		EPC	3		PWG	35		
	AE9	330		MF	71		EWG	14		
	AE11	279		AT	47		EWG	20		
	AE11	378		DOD	8		LCA	39		
	AE12	167		DOD	24		EIE	16		
	OAL	248		L3	76		EWGR	4		
	OAE2	74		L3	102		PTL	6		
	OAE2	81		L3	133		PTL	11		
	AF	146		L3	161		ECG2	31		
	DO	148		L3	307		EAZ	43		
	KT1	52		L4	33		PC1	29		
	KT2	222		L4	42		EAL	27		
	KT2	426		L4	50		PTC	28		
	KT2	481		L4	194		ETC	8		
	KT3	188		L4	262		PLG	17		
	KT3	686		T18	81		PUO4	15		
	KT3	886		T27	5		PUO4	22		
	KT3	1099		T27	45		PUO4	28		
	KT3	1112		T27	121		AA	187		
	KT3	1117		H9	25		AA	665		
	M8	155		H9	38		AA	765		
	B	65		H29	70		AA	875		
	B	98		H2	30		SAA	746		
	B	176		H2	54		SAA	752		
	B	187		TA	292		EDGA	16		
	CAM	259		HAP	1575		RL	357		
	HIF	265		HAP	1658		PD	2		
	C	83		BR	181		L3	178		
	C	87		BR	291		HAP	486		
	C	471		ETS	15		HAP	827		
	TH	166		SKA2	16		HAP	960		
	FL	18		SKA2	20		HAP	1012		
	FL	29		SKA3	8		HAP	1029		
	FL	95		SKA3	17		HAP	1030		
	M12	173		SKA6	12		HAP	1162		
	M12	300		SKA6	18		HAP	1517		
	M12	306		EL	348		HAP	1528		
	M12	397		J3	501		HAP	1574		
	WB	533		J6	298		HAP	1655		
	CI	544		P2	4		HAP	1678		
	SMP	81		M1	643		HAP	1700		
	AS	26		M1	637		BR	127		
	AS	30		M9	127		PDS	1		
	AS	62		VCS	4		PSH	37		
JOYED	DC	50		VP8	43		J1	178		
	T23	16		G2	9		J6	311		
	P1	142		G2	584		J16	18		
	B	617		G2	635		J16	44		
	CAM	258		G3	376		J16	71		
JOYFUL	AR	154		G4	749		P5	154		
	AR	233		AE1	1026		P5	114		
	SMA	61		AE4	45		M1	120		
	AM	286		AE4	80		M1	1070		
	AA	271		AE5	1083		M13	126		
	SAA	833		AE6	691		VP3	75		
	TA	119		AE10	451		VP5	23		
	PAA	43		AE10	1206		VP5	136		
	ODA	78		AE11	1180		AE5	690		
	VP4	63		AE12	1276		AE7	376		
	G3	577		OAL	66		AE9	310		
	AE1	724		OAL	126		AE10	861		
	AE1	861		OAL	573		OAL	773		
	AE2	339		AF	24		DO	34		
	AE3	359		AF	55		KT1	516		
	AE3	686		KT1	418		KT2	260		
	AE4	209		KT1	463		KT2	267		
	AE5	91		KT3	289		KT2	304		
	AE7	50		B	25		KT2	423		
	AE7	193		B	36		KT3	658		
	AE7	398		B	450		B	278		
	AE8	702		B	477		B	541		
	AE8	727		M11	189		M11	449		
	OAL	133		M11	240		AU	242		
	OAL	359		M12	84		AU	307		
	OAL	775		M12	275		WB	334		
JOYFULLY	AM	769		GP	27		CI	144		
JOYLESS	HAP	1916		CI	323		CI	158		
	ODA	1	JUBAL	SSC	17		CI	159		
	G3	336	JUBILEE	KT3	105	JUDGED	AM	51		
	AF	84	JUBILEES	SAA	1047		AM	749		
JOYOUS	L1	16	JUDAH	SAA	568		RL	24		
	G2	444	JUDAH'S	J6	230		TA	324		
	G4	485		SAA	683		MN	3		
	AE7	15		SAA	1026		VP2	34		
	KT2	40		SAA	1063		AE6	579		
JOYS	AR	25		SAA	321		OAL	283		
	SMA	11	JUDAS	SAA	322		KT2	336		

Word	Code	No.
JUST	MD	56
	MD	77
	MF	56
	MF	81
	MF	128
	SAA	336
	SAA	639
	SAA	813
	SAA	954
	SAA	1022
	SAA	1052
	SAA	1054
	SAA	1060
	EK	16
	EDG	34
	EDG	42
	RL	99
	RL	447
	L2	59
	L3	48
	L3	145
	L4	73
	L4	258
	H2	85
	TA	40
	TA	23
	TA	336
	TA	423
	EAA	31
	HAP	294
	HAP	344
	HAP	1382
	HAP	1395
	HAP	1907
	HAP	1990
	HAP	2009
	HAP	2156
	HAP	2178
	HAP	2210
	HAP	2213
	HAP	2306
	HAP	2526
	BR	5
	BR	342
	PMS	22
	PKA	6
	EKA	14
	EL	181
	EL	223
	EL	368
	ODA	34
	ODA	41
	MS	4
	MS	23
	MS	30
	ESH	32
	J3	17
	J3	43
	J6	367
	J6	536
	J10	314
	J10	345
	P1	255
	P2	15
	P2	52
	P3	43
	P3	166
	P5	280
	P5	47
	M1	285
	M1	321
	M1	464
	M1	732
	M1	799
	M1	975
	M9	141
	MC	67
	GK	13
	GK	164
	VP5	136
	G1	660
	G2	106
	G2	513
	G2	642
	G2	768
	G4	430
	G4	626
	G4	660
	AE1	14
	AE1	393
	AE1	539
	AE1	766
	AE2	137
	AE2	578
	AE2	731
	AE2	744
JUST	AE2	796
	AE2	823
	AE2	988
	AE3	725
	AE4	619
	AE5	91
	AE5	378
	AE5	513
	AE5	564
	AE5	719
	AE5	951
	AE6	384
	AE6	569
	AE6	585
	AE6	843
	AE6	956
	AE6	1032
	AE6	1203
	AE7	432
	AE7	462
	AE7	959
	AE7	1058
	AE8	80
	AE8	523
	AE8	621
	AE8	648
	AE8	658
	AE8	945
	AE9	1062
	AE9	1079
	AE10	118
	AE10	148
	AE10	536
	AE10	625
	AE10	669
	AE10	1011
	AE10	1124
	AE10	1277
	AE11	159
	AE11	211
	AE11	340
	AE11	547
	AE11	712
	AE11	1034
	AE12	413
	AE12	736
	AE12	1008
	AE12	1095
	AE12	1158
	AE12	1174
	AE12	1361
	OAL	132
	OAL	549
	OAL	725
	OAL	773
	OAE2	74
	DO	47
	KT1	64
	KT1	104
	KT1	497
	KT3	83
	KT3	527
	KT3	576
	KT3	699
	KT3	793
	KT3	862
	KT3	1105
	TJD	7
	TJD	66
	M8	346
	M8	362
	B	313
	BP	164
	CAM	382
	HIF	64
	HIF	300
	HIF	326
	HIF	446
	HIF	544
	C	8
	C	95
	C	187
	C	214
	C	519
	TH	136
	TH	203
	TH	263
	TH	393
	M11	409
	FL	199
	FL	533
	M12	10
	M12	376
	M12	526
	M12	633
JUST	AU	39
	AU	167
	AU	444
	WB	295
	WB	375
	M15	324
	M15	637
	M15	708
	CI	140
	CI	378
	PTP	25
	EMKG	35
JUSTER	DA	44
	HP	165
	AA	486
	HAP	1410
	AE1	767
	AE11	359
	AE12	280
	AE12	529
JUSTEST	M15	26
JUSTICE	AR	266
	LC	49
	LCA	15
	DA	62
	AA	322
	AA	595
	AA	773
	AA	1002
	MD	141
	MD	152
	SAA	257
	SAA	272
	SAA	733
	SAA	789
	SAA	1137
	RL	49
	RL	57
	RL	95
	RL	106
	HAP	993
	HAP	1075
	HAP	2161
	BR	334
	BR	338
	BR	355
	J3	478
	J6	28
	M1	191
	M1	270
	AE4	536
	AE5	475
	AE5	445
	AE6	711
	AE6	1045
	AE11	189
	KT1	480
	KT2	271
	B	106
	B	359
	B	361
	B	393
	B	494
	B	549
	C	273
	C	286
	C	295
	TH	138
	TH	313
	TH	322
	AU	487
	WB	270
	M15	178
	CI	454
JUSTIFIED	AA	524
	MD	208
	J6	590
	KT3	822
	B	281
	B	386
	B	409
	M15	150
JUSTIFIES	B	487
	GP	120
JUSTIFY	MF	156
	AK	97
	KT3	811
	HIF	453
	M12	324
	AU	348
	CI	521
JUSTING	KT3	431
JUSTLE	AM	908
	MD	312
	KT1	346
JUSTLED	HAP	1898

Word	Ref	No.	Word	Ref	No.	Word	Ref	No.
JUSTLED	AE8	916	KEEN	KT3	268	KEEP	AE6	777
	HIF	286		M12	642		AE8	99
JUSTLES	HAP	2480	KEEN-EDGED	KT3	914		AE8	548
	J1	156	KEENER	KT3	502		AE9	51
	J3	395	KEENNESS	AE12	143		AE9	200
JUSTLING	SAA	928	KEEP	AM	110		AE9	678
	AE4	639		PMQ	43		AE9	902
	KT3	590		SEL3	14		AE10	401
JUSTLY	AR	311		ECG1	8		AE10	493
	RH	64		ECG1	11		AE10	1006
	SMA	47		PAR	24		AE10	1013
	DC	16		PW	17		AE12	58
	LCA	50		PLN	29		AE12	1210
	PNH	29		PCD	10		OAL	427
	E	12		PNH	46		OAL	451
	CM	11		PKK	15		OAL	453
	HP	106		EKK	3		DO	20
	HP	211		EKK	12		DO	141
	EMP	8		PTW	26		KT1	176
	PUO4	20		STC	4		KT1	202
	AA	348		PLQ	32		KT1	338
	MD	118		HP	17		KT2	155
	ER	72		EPF	1		KT2	163
	L4	215		PSF	27		KT2	304
	T18	11		AA	225		KT3	220
	HAP	1047		AA	390		TJD	166
	HAP	1381		MF	72		M8	41
	HAP	1641		SAA	682		CAM	97
	BR	359		EDGA	5		HIF	402
	OD	42		EDGA	25		HIF	584
	J10	333		RL	35		C	368
	P3	134		RL	264		C	607
	P6	11		RL	379		M11	290
	M1	12		EC	30		M11	319
	M1	855		L3	181		M11	428
	MC	26		L3	299		FL	24
	VP8	46		T18	79		AU	262
	AE2	213		T27	14		WB	107
	AE2	301		T27	34		WB	328
	AE4	508		T27	66		GP	101
	AE5	707		H29	87		CI	304
	AE6	1118		H2	83		SMP	63
	AE7	912		TA	431		EWR	30
	AE9	398		PAA	23	KEEPER	PCD	4
	AE9	585		PAA	36		M1	875
	AE12	562		AK	182		M1	923
	OAL	665		HAP	129		M1	995
	OAL	741		HAP	1215		AE3	287
	KT1	310		HAP	1304		AE6	574
	B	525		HAP	1989		AE7	1079
	B	750		BR	46		AE12	1044
	B	751		BR	321		KT2	17
	BP	142		EKA	38	KEEPER'S	M1	946
	CAM	328		EL	83		M1	989
	HIF	150		EL	169	KEEPERS	J6	465
	C	779		EL	313		AE11	743
	AU	106		ESH	34	KEEPING	PAL	15
	AU	374		SSH	14		ETC	7
JUSTS	FL	291		J1	117		GE	57
	FL	412		J1	163		J3	94
JUTTED	DO	52		J3	240		AE6	1190
JUTTING	AE1	231		J3	317		HIF	663
JUTURNA	AE10	618		J3	379	KEEPS	DC	32
	AE12	336		J6	464		PWGR	2
	AE12	663		J6	465		PCG2	27
	AE12	687		J6	549		EUF	16
	AE12	705		J16	63		SAA	305
	AE12	1134		P1	156		SAA	321
	AE12	1162		P5	73		SAA	456
	AE12	1183		M1	861		H29	57
	AE12	1238		M13	143		EL	375
	AE12	1256		H1	74		J1	73
				SLT2	3		J6	48
				GK	58		J10	496
				VP3	2		G1	107
				VP3	96		AE6	749
				VP3	119		AE11	1128
KAI	J6	278		VP7	67		OAL	490
KEEL	SCD2	22		VP10	96		TJD	209
	VP4	47		G2	276		HIF	141
	AE10	412		G3	209		TH	110
	DO	49		G3	321		CI	42
	CI	389		G3	463		P4	90
KEELS	AM	726		G3	615	KEMBEST	JH	2
	G2	625		G4	567	KEN	RH	91
	AE5	895		AE1	403		AM	443
KEEN	MF	204		AE1	955		AM	635
	SAA	1033		AE2	952		AE4	844
	G3	210		AE3	327		M11	446
	AE8	824		AE3	666	KENELM	C	360
	AE9	582		AE3	845	KENITES'	SAA	943
	AE9	1018		AE4	219	KENNEL	HAP	204
	AE10	379		AE5	585	KENNEST	AK	174
	AE12	314		AE5	1108	KENULPH	C	360
	KT2	523		AE6	389	KEPT	LC	98
				AE6	476		AM	128

KEPT	AM	156
	AM	537
	AM	635
	EEL	9
	PCG2	24
	ECG2	12
	CM	58
	DA	90
	DA	156
	MF	53
	SAA	217
	SAA	225
	RL	372
	OE	10
	OE	27
	EC	11
	T18	4
	TA	1
	TA	215
	TA	296
	TA	326
	TA	486
	AK	55
	HAP	600
	BR	199
	EDS	17
	EL	329
	OD	20
	J1	92
	M1	919
	M1	947
	ELT	32
	MC	68
	GK	45
	VP1	50
	VP1	53
	G4	664
	AE2	972
	AE2	986
	AE7	91
	AE7	589
	AE7	1062
	AE8	472
	AE9	589
	AE10	96
	AE10	237
	AE10	471
	AE10	675
	OAL	442
	KT3	310
	KT3	943
	M8	263
	B	16
	B	55
	B	133
	B	629
	B	693
	B	726
	C	227
	FL	181
	M12	3
	M12	206
	M12	437
	AU	334
	WB	14
	GP	83
	CI	182
	PTP	28
	SMP	66
	AS	44
KERCHIEF	WB	245
KERN	AM	625
KERNS	DO	58
KERVE	G2	632
KERVED	J6	495
KETCH	EDG	30
	PMK	41
KETCHES	PAA	3
KETTLE	BP	56
	BP	106
KETTLES	G1	393
KEY	AM	921
	SAA	446
	J6	464
	B	133
	B	156
	B	182
	B	294
	CI	614
KEYS	HAP	1094
	AE7	246
KICK	OE	42
	T27	47
	J3	465
KICKED	SAA	348
	T27	63

KICKED	VP9	7
KICKS	HAP	1196
KID	ER	64
	M13	70
	ELT	19
	VP2	92
	M15	688
KIDNEY	G1	317
KIDS	AT	81
	M1	408
	M13	130
	VP1	32
	VP2	51
	VP3	128
	VP3	150
	VP9	8
	VP9	85
	G1	295
	G2	765
	G3	491
	G3	610
	AE9	909
KILDERKIN	MF	196
KILL	EIE	25
	AM	524
	ETL	19
	MD	100
	FS1	16
	HAP	1944
	J3	68
	J3	481
	J6	314
	J6	732
	J6	820
	J10	158
	J10	324
	J16	80
	M1	923
	HI	84
	VP10	113
	AE2	449
	AE2	676
	AE6	1185
	AE9	824
	AE10	180
	AE11	1130
	AE12	606
	AE12	798
	AE12	963
	KT2	270
	KT2	272
	KT2	299
	KT2	415
	TJD	71
	TJD	113
	TH	194
	WB	76
	M15	116
	M15	153
	M15	707
KILLED	AM	84
	PCG1	3
	PCG2	24
	T23	86
	G1	225
	G4	758
	AE9	604
	AE9	977
	AE9	1042
	AE10	709
	AE10	1055
	AE11	1295
	AE12	515
	AE12	674
	AE12	729
	AE12	752
	MG	29
	HIF	77
KILLS	PWGR	12
	SDG	11
	J10	350
	AE6	361
	AE9	442
	KT1	278
	PTP	43
KIMBO	VP3	67
KIN	HAP	1448
	HAP	1764
	EDS	6
	P2	60
	P6	127
	M1	30
	OAL	860
	KT2	108
	TH	421
	AU	43

KIN	AU	244
	M15	678
KIND	AR	63
	AR	185
	SMA	13
	SMA	85
	LC	13
	PRL	23
	PIE	14
	AM	182
	AM	347
	AM	433
	PMQ	47
	PEL	35
	ETL	3
	ETL	13
	SCG2	19
	PW	2
	EMQW	18
	S	13
	A	16
	SLN	11
	ENH	36
	PUO2	15
	PUO2	30
	EUO2	32
	ESF	12
	PC2	14
	PAL	13
	PKK	26
	SKK	3
	SKK	16
	DA	94
	PSF	1
	ETG	10
	PUO4	27
	PUO5	26
	AA	3
	AA	360
	AA	424
	AA	572
	AA	694
	AA	1001
	EPC	19
	PRH	13
	SAA	413
	SAA	934
	SAA	961
	SAA	1096
	EDG	32
	EDG	42
	RL	67
	RL	352
	OE	8
	OE	35
	DOD	12
	EC	41
	ER	13
	L1	5
	L2	44
	L3	54
	L3	213
	L4	20
	L4	188
	L4	233
	L4	273
	T23	74
	H3	4
	H9	36
	H29	81
	FS2	6
	TA	220
	TA	336
	AK	38
	HH	37
	HAP	1759
	HAP	23
	HAP	37
	HAP	178
	HAP	229
	HAP	249
	HAP	271
	HAP	287
	HAP	328
	HAP	402
	HAP	703
	HAP	839
	HAP	1212
	HAP	1422
	HAP	1841
	HAP	2059
	HAP	2243
	HAP	2249
	HAP	2261
	HAP	2275
	HAP	2353

Word	Ref	No.
KIND	HAP	2366
	HAP	2409
	HAP	2526
	BR	41
	BR	103
	PDS	39
	ETS	19
	PMS	34
	PKA	19
	EKA	17
	SKA2	24
	SKA5	11
	SKA6	28
	SKA6	29
	SKA6	31
	ELW	1
	EL	194
	EL	201
	EL	223
	EL	239
	OD	6
	ODA	23
	MS	4
	MS	21
	SSH	8
	EH	23
	J6	43
	J6	122
	J6	280
	J6	648
	P2	132
	P3	170
	P6	103
	M1	72
	M1	97
	M1	475
	M1	511
	M1	538
	M1	570
	M1	574
	M9	54
	M9	135
	ELT	14
	MC	72
	GK	1
	VP3	14
	VP8	136
	VP9	49
	G1	95
	G2	71
	G2	134
	G2	232
	G2	326
	G2	336
	G2	606
	G3	119
	G3	154
	G3	199
	G3	207
	G3	332
	G3	375
	G3	433
	G3	496
	G3	636
	G4	17
	G4	53
	G4	142
	G4	363
	G4	401
	AE1	25
	AE1	887
	AE3	23
	AE3	138
	AE3	315
	AE4	17
	AE4	459
	AE5	154
	AE5	932
	AE6	43
	AE6	262
	AE6	997
	AE8	105
	AE8	509
	AE9	642
	AE9	752
	AE10	63
	AE10	144
	AE10	191
	AE10	387
	AE10	743
	OAL	38
	OAL	349
	OAL	413
	OAL	480
	OAL	593
	OAL	730
KIND	OAL	811
	OAE2	63
	MFL	23
	MFL	35
	DO	145
	KT1	92
	KT2	319
	KT2	324
	KT2	642
	KT3	499
	KT3	1055
	TJD	75
	M8	12
	B	322
	B	342
	B	353
	B	361
	B	403
	B	425
	B	441
	B	483
	B	520
	B	665
	BP	118
	CAM	49
	CAM	55
	CAM	61
	CAM	114
	CAM	183
	CAM	293
	CAM	344
	HIF	546
	C	75
	C	139
	C	264
	C	555
	C	643
	C	794
	TH	12
	TH	125
	TH	322
	TH	348
	TH	428
	M11	332
	M11	496
	FL	154
	FL	159
	FL	265
	FL	279
	FL	356
	FL	468
	FL	496
	FL	594
	FL	618
	M12	314
	M12	538
	M12	625
	AU	600
	WB	90
	WB	118
	WB	124
	WB	134
	WB	385
	WB	397
	WB	426
	M15	107
	M15	160
	M15	244
	M15	258
	M15	546
	M15	557
	M15	571
	M15	613
	GP	46
	CI	27
	CI	136
	CI	140
	CI	497
	PTP	18
	PTP	14
	ESK	14
	PMK	13
	PMK	6
	EWR	13
KINDER	SCG1	31
	TA	251
	VP9	32
	WB	540
KINDER-HEARTED	PUO3	6
KINDEST	PC2	23
KINDLE	L1	33
	M1	90
	M1	666
	M1	1077
	VP8	150
	AE1	43
KINDLE	AE4	815
	AE5	239
	AE6	245
	AE7	469
	AE7	489
	AE12	239
	AF	160
	CAM	66
	C	751
	AU	372
	M15	469
	SMP	50
KINDLED	T18	13
	AK	175
	HAP	1631
	J6	809
	M1	213
	G1	123
	AE3	764
	AE4	74
	AE6	7
	AE7	1075
	AE9	85
	AE11	288
	AE11	1158
	KT1	465
	M8	293
	B	246
	B	506
	HIF	68
	AU	3
	AU	295
	CI	567
KINDLES	G1	343
	G3	170
	G4	326
	AE2	92
	AE7	535
KINDLING	AM	477
	HP	187
	AE5	693
	AE9	772
	KT3	210
	M15	523
KINDLY	AR	136
	AM	9
	AM	1134
	AT	26
	L1	27
	L3	99
	L4	25
	L4	198
	L4	254
	L4	266
	TA	265
	TA	347
	STS3	21
	STS3	22
	STS3	28
	STS3	29
	EL	81
	J6	18
	J10	532
	M1	561
	M1	645
	VP7	83
	VP9	66
	G1	29
	G2	443
	G2	449
	G3	103
	G3	411
	G3	731
	AE1	372
	AE1	570
	AE2	12
	AE3	11
	AE4	528
	OAL	734
	KT1	178
	CAM	166
	TH	404
	AU	212
	M15	311
	SMP	74
	AS	69
KINDNESS	RH	68
	LC	88
	LC	125
	PLN	15
	EUO2	25
	AA	427
	AA	468
	L4	294
	HAP	1346
	HAP	1373

KINDNESS	HAP	1379
	HAP	2186
	HAP	2462
	SKA6	12
	J16	9
	P6	60
	AE4	443
	AE11	813
	AE12	49
	OAE2	41
	KT3	1151
	B	733
	M11	18
	WB	80
	PTP	52
KINDRED	CM	17
	HP	223
	AA	370
	AA	852
	T27	78
	HAP	275
	HAP	546
	HAP	968
	J10	382
	M1	477
	M1	789
	HI	84
	G1	54
	G2	707
	G3	411
	G4	546
	AE3	63
	AE3	654
	AE5	820
	AE6	829
	AE7	288
	AE7	469
	AE7	684
	AE8	173
	AE12	49
	AF	95
	DO	19
	KT3	548
	KT3	819
	TJD	201
	CAM	72
	HIF	489
	AU	247
	CI	637
KINDS	HAP	1301
	HAP	2195
	HAP	2540
	M13	114
	G1	78
	G2	46
	G2	68
	G2	118
	G2	149
	AE11	696
	C	586
	M12	633
KINE	EUF	10
	VP1	11
	G1	3
	G2	763
	AE8	274
	OAL	395
	M8	8
	M15	109
KING	HS	28
	AR	39
	AR	99
	AR	222
	SMA	32
	SMA	94
	SMA	116
	SMA	125
	LC	34
	AM	4
	AM	37
	AM	56
	AM	70
	AM	77
	AM	614
	AM	792
	AM	894
	AM	949
	AM	960
	AM	972
	AM	1010
	AM	1040
	AM	1129
	ET	9
	SCG2	15
	PFD	26
	EOE	8

KING	CM	76
	CM	107
	DA	164
	EMW	11
	EMW	12
	EMW	13
	PUO3	24
	PUO5	20
	PUF	34
	AA	48
	AA	60
	AA	213
	AA	263
	AA	284
	AA	358
	AA	418
	AA	430
	AA	512
	AA	586
	AA	604
	AA	611
	AA	749
	AA	812
	AA	853
	AA	924
	AA	942
	AA	952
	AA	979
	AA	977
	PLB	7
	PLB	40
	MD	11
	MD	190
	MD	196
	MD	228
	D	46
	MF	36
	MF	118
	MF	119
	SAA	141
	SAA	172
	SAA	237
	SAA	251
	SAA	261
	SAA	430
	SAA	488
	SAA	500
	SAA	506
	SAA	517
	SAA	614
	SAA	616
	SAA	635
	SAA	675
	SAA	692
	SAA	726
	SAA	906
	PDG	24
	RL	97
	EC	10
	EC	23
	L3	242
	T18	87
	TA	146
	TA	239
	TA	257
	EAA	9
	AK	128
	GE	37
	GE	46
	HAP	57
	HAP	432
	HAP	1537
	HAP	1602
	HAP	1960
	HAP	2061
	HAP	2102
	HAP	2189
	HAP	2434
	HAP	2492
	BR	23
	EL	71
	J10	113
	J10	388
	J10	472
	P1	240
	P2	69
	P3	67
	P6	122
	M1	208
	M1	695
	M1	804
	VP4	24
	G1	649
	G2	140
	G2	458
	G2	660

KING	G4	113
	G4	134
	G4	223
	G4	307
	G4	313
	G4	459
	G4	678
	G4	787
	AE1	93
	AE1	97
	AE1	314
	AE1	526
	AE1	775
	AE1	807
	AE2	76
	AE2	197
	AE2	203
	AE2	214
	AE2	594
	AE2	627
	AE2	762
	AE3	106
	AE4	283
	AE5	80
	AE5	735
	AE5	747
	AE5	949
	AE5	987
	AE6	179
	AE6	800
	AE6	1040
	AE6	1106
	AE6	1185
	AE7	74
	AE7	148
	AE7	227
	AE7	291
	AE7	299
	AE7	361
	AE7	385
	AE7	597
	AE7	608
	AE7	676
	AE7	792
	AE7	852
	AE7	941
	AE7	964
	AE7	1033
	AE8	103
	AE8	138
	AE8	157
	AE8	246
	AE8	476
	AE8	649
	AE8	667
	AE8	704
	AE8	722
	AE8	731
	AE8	755
	AE8	863
	AE9	97
	AE9	438
	AE9	503
	AE9	526
	AE9	732
	AE9	796
	AE9	1061
	AE10	317
	AE10	372
	AE10	630
	AE10	854
	AE10	923
	AE10	978
	AE10	1041
	AE10	1046
	AE11	157
	AE11	169
	AE11	194
	AE11	283
	AE11	327
	AE11	381
	AE11	411
	AE11	434
	AE11	462
	AE11	519
	AE11	1235
	AE12	18
	AE12	30
	AE12	171
	AE12	212
	AE12	226
	AE12	268
	AE12	287
	AE12	293
	AE12	390
	AE12	401

Word	Ref	No.
KING	AE12	437
	AE12	561
	AE12	777
	AE12	859
	AE12	955
	AE12	1030
	OAL	116
	OAL	155
	OAL	735
	OAL	733
	AF	66
	AF	147
	AF	151
	KT1	59
	KT2	327
	KT2	392
	KT2	410
	KT2	430
	KT3	39
	KT3	63
	KT3	97
	KT3	475
	KT3	497
	KT3	536
	KT3	544
	KT3	574
	KT3	652
	KT3	717
	KT3	729
	KT3	893
	KT3	1020
	KT3	1082
	TJD	160
	TJD	171
	TJD	191
	B	363
	CAM	248
	HIF	3
	HIF	13
	HIF	32
	HIF	37
	HIF	91
	HIF	100
	HIF	134
	HIF	138
	HIF	152
	HIF	219
	HIF	224
	HIF	257
	HIF	320
	HIF	389
	HIF	397
	HIF	429
	HIF	451
	HIF	468
	HIF	472
	HIF	495
	HIF	539
	HIF	566
	HIF	601
	HIF	605
	HIF	648
	HIF	683
	C	57
	C	360
	C	381
	M12	124
	M12	491
	M12	827
	M12	830
	AU	39
	AU	297
	AU	304
	AU	345
	AU	369
	AU	429
	AU	504
	AU	547
	AU	556
	WB	3
	WB	46
	WB	65
	WB	75
	WB	157
	WB	188
	WB	197
	WB	351
	WB	386
	WB	409
	M15	1
	M15	234
	GP	113
	CI	301
KINGDOM	AR	12
	AM	1048
	CM	16
KINGDOM	MF	122
	MF	143
	SAA	738
	PDG	42
	HAP	275
	AE2	566
	AE2	787
	AE2	1065
	AE3	431
	AE4	145
	AE4	549
	AE5	1046
	AE7	359
	AE8	135
	AE8	212
	AE8	617
	M8	321
	GP	90
KINGDOM'S	SAA	773
KINGDOMS	AR	78
	SMA	127
	SAA	852
	TA	146
	HAP	26
	VP1	96
	G3	354
	AE1	114
	AE1	288
	AE6	1088
	AE8	848
	KT2	322
KINGLY	AM	383
	AA	226
	AA	483
	MD	83
	MD	204
	T18	36
	TA	218
	HAP	2175
	HAP	2536
	AE2	141
	AE7	344
	AE8	606
	KT3	80
	HIF	341
KING'S	SMA	88
	LC	98
	PT	24
	AA	464
	ELB	7
	SAA	271
	J10	113
	G4	106
	AE2	621
	AE7	512
	AE7	852
	AE8	159
	AE9	363
	AE9	920
	AE11	157
	B	553
	M11	352
	KT3	615
	AU	393
	ESK	27
KINGS	SMA	54
	SMA	120
	LC	80
	DC	48
	AM	47
	AM	320
	AM	358
	AM	563
	PUO1	45
	ML	10
	PLG	15
	HP	53
	PSF	4
	AA	24
	AA	84
	AA	290
	AA	388
	AA	410
	AA	505
	AA	580
	AA	615
	AA	727
	AA	764
	AA	766
	AA	768
	AA	775
	AA	783
	AA	792
	AA	795
	AA	872
	AA	897
KINGS	AA	953
	AA	997
	PLB	16
	PLB	53
	MD	135
	MD	202
	MD	204
	MD	316
	PRH	27
	SAA	5
	SAA	161
	TA	404
	EAA	12
	EAA	15
	EAA	18
	HAP	177
	HAP	220
	HAP	271
	HAP	1093
	HAP	1464
	HAP	2182
	HAP	2532
	BR	219
	BR	339
	BR	345
	EJG	4
	EL	181
	EL	257
	J3	490
	J6	25
	P1	127
	P6	108
	GK	155
	VP3	164
	VP6	4
	G4	4
	G4	162
	G4	294
	AE1	643
	AE2	563
	AE2	682
	AE6	1040
	AE6	1117
	AE7	54
	AE7	234
	AE7	250
	AE7	827
	AE8	173
	AE8	415
	AE8	437
	AE8	848
	AE8	858
	AE8	908
	AE11	312
	AE11	535
	AE12	245
	AE12	315
	OAL	251
	OAL	723
	KT2	214
	KT2	322
	KT3	94
	KT3	107
	KT3	889
	TJD	136
	B	551
	B	558
	B	597
	B	601
	HIF	83
	HIF	263
	HIF	394
	HIF	407
	C	328
	TH	66
	M11	341
	FL	240
	M12	821
	WB	61
	WB	164
	WB	321
	M15	275
	PTP	52
KINGS'	ECD	18
	HAP	357
	HAP	1970
	KT3	414
KINGSHIP	AA	396
KINSMAN	SAA	636
	AE2	111
	AE2	120
	AE7	515
	KT1	290
	KT1	397
	KT2	151
	KT3	947

KINSMAN	KT3	1107
	M15	63
KINSMAN'S	AU	58
KINSMEN	AA	147
	AE12	66
	KT1	146
	KT1	167
KISS	SEL3	23
	SM2	7
	MF	181
	OE	18
	AT	46
	AT	83
	L3	79
	L4	191
	T23	11
	T23	77
	T27	4
	T27	6
	T27	9
	T27	19
	T27	31
	T27	47
	H9	34
	STS3	6
	STS3	21
	STS3	26
	STS3	28
	STS3	30
	J6	484
	J6	503
	J6	650
	R	5
	R	6
	R	11
	R	12
	R	17
	R	18
	G2	760
	AE1	349
	AE2	670
	AE9	383
	AE9	642
	AE11	1202
	OAL	747
	OAL	751
	OAL	753
	OAL	755
	OAE2	5
	OAE2	47
	OAE2	65
	OAE2	72
	OAE2	83
	M8	386
	M10	24
	M10	26
	M10	76
	M10	93
	CAM	82
	M11	70
	M11	443
	M11	485
	M11	488
	WB	524
KISSED	T27	8
	M1	507
	HI	155
	R	22
	R	23
	R	24
	AE4	944
	B	299
	B	690
	M10	29
KISSES	CM	26
	HP	27
	PPC	6
	AT	11
	AT	48
	DOD	16
	L4	41
	L4	160
	L4	174
	T23	79
	T27	5
	J6	74
	J6	596
	VP2	44
	VP5	139
	AE1	963
	AE2	929
	OAL	483
	OAL	748
	OAE2	79
	M8	394
	B	161

KISSES	M10	75
	CAM	115
	M12	568
	WB	536
KISSING	HP	156
	PPC	30
	T23	34
	T27	7
	NS	6
	NS	10
	NS	11
	NS	17
	NS	21
	NS	22
	NS	28
	NS	32
	NS	33
	AE12	643
KITCHEN	AA	621
	J10	97
	P4	59
	C	463
KITCHENS	J3	402
KITE	P4	52
KNACK	MD	193
	RL	386
	J3	54
KNARES	KT2	536
KNAVE	PCD	2
	MD	58
	MD	186
	HAP	143
	EKA	18
	VP3	22
KNAVE'S	C	814
	C	661
KNAVES	C	797
	ET	3
	ML	22
	PTW	6
	SAA	367
	EC	19
	MO	6
	J3	54
	J6	450
	P1	10
	P4	61
	P6	181
	GK	160
KNEADED	HAP	274
	B	504
KNEE	VP3	101
	OAL	185
KNEE-FRINGE	PNH	27
KNEEL	M13	170
	AE12	834
KNEELED	WB	192
KNEELING	J6	494
	KT3	213
	B	300
KNEELS	PSF	5
	AE8	504
	AE10	1241
KNEES	HAP	41
	HAP	2346
	BR	252
	M1	1012
	AE1	437
	AE2	918
	AE3	52
	AE3	784
	AE3	798
	AE10	727
	AE12	458
	AE12	1081
	AE12	1308
	KT2	429
	KT3	34
	KT3	127
	CAM	103
	CAM	284
	HIF	562
	HIF	588
	HIF	678
	M12	197
	M12	467
KNELL	SCD2	15
	PTC	22
KNELLER	GK	7
KNEW	HS	87
	HS	98
	AR	141
	AR	242
	LC	61
	AM	481
	AM	540

KNEW	AM	636
	AM	674
	AM	767
	EEL	6
	SEL3	17
	SCG1	29
	PLN	34
	PUO1	1
	E	26
	PO	7
	CM	31
	EPF	8
	PUF	31
	AA	70
	AA	214
	AA	224
	AA	535
	AA	827
	AA	1031
	MD	123
	SAA	44
	SAA	470
	SAA	1017
	RL	82
	RL	261
	OE	9
	PD	25
	EC	40
	T23	7
	TA	46
	TA	288
	TA	342
	TA	376
	EAA	22
	HAP	4
	HAP	1301
	HAP	1439
	HAP	1557
	HAP	1736
	HAP	2312
	EL	36
	EL	97
	EL	99
	EL	130
	EL	215
	ODA	25
	J10	167
	J10	423
	P6	86
	M1	114
	M1	500
	M1	854
	M1	884
	M9	80
	M13	99
	GK	42
	G2	639
	G4	213
	AE1	156
	AE1	184
	AE1	686
	AE1	934
	AE2	459
	AE2	1006
	AE3	231
	AE3	781
	AE5	7
	AE6	282
	AE6	457
	AE6	466
	AE6	612
	AE6	670
	AE6	902
	AE6	1093
	AE7	614
	AE8	420
	AE8	461
	AE9	565
	AE9	608
	AE9	776
	AE9	627
	AE10	349
	AE10	460
	AE11	232
	AE12	756
	AE12	918
	AE12	920
	AE12	1177
	AE12	1246
	AE12	1257
	AE12	1306
	MFL	32
	DO	87
	KT1	216
	KT1	444
	KT1	564

Word	Src	No.
KNEW	KT2	69
	KT2	118
	KT2	141
	KT2	179
	KT2	248
	KT2	375
	KT3	187
	KT3	263
	B	143
	B	168
	B	182
	B	236
	B	404
	B	450
	B	691
	M10	69
	CAM	32
	CAM	104
	CAM	211
	C	21
	C	30
	C	48
	C	608
	C	817
	TH	221
	TH	297
	TH	397
	TH	415
	M11	80
	M11	195
	M11	402
	M11	450
	FL	381
	M12	40
	AU	313
	AU	261
	WB	109
	WB	165
	WB	179
	WB	206
	WB	218
	M15	463
	GP	98
	GP	123
	CI	168
	CI	204
	CI	409
	CI	458
	CI	482
KNIFE	HAP	625
	HAP	1981
	J3	458
	J6	43
	J6	857
	P3	80
	G2	413
	G2	502
	G2	563
	G3	741
	M12	47
	M15	198
	M15	686
KNIGHT	ESF	16
	HAP	2207
	PKA	9
	G4	105
	AE10	603
	DO	35
	KT1	18
	KT1	207
	KT1	310
	KT1	371
	KT1	407
	KT1	517
	KT2	3
	KT2	66
	KT2	151
	KT2	224
	KT2	248
	KT2	279
	KT2	411
	KT2	421
	KT3	13
	KT3	110
	KT3	156
	KT3	396
	KT3	643
	KT3	649
	KT3	679
	KT3	682
	KT3	687
	KT3	702
	KT3	735
	KT3	823
	KT3	918
	KT3	932

Word	Src	No.
KNIGHT	KT3	1123
	KT3	1136
	KT3	1141
	HIF	3
	C	128
	C	134
	C	414
	C	688
	C	705
	TH	133
	TH	119
	TH	189
	TH	328
	TH	360
	FL	264
	FL	270
	FL	311
	FL	325
	FL	410
	FL	429
	FL	503
	M12	480
	M12	601
	M12	650
	M12	795
	AU	277
	WB	47
	WB	60
	WB	69
	WB	86
	WB	108
	WB	203
	WB	228
	WB	234
	WB	237
	WB	253
	WB	264
	WB	272
	WB	288
	WB	296
	WB	305
	WB	312
	WB	334
	WB	369
	WB	509
	PTP	53
KNIGHT-ERRANT	EUF	35
KNIGHTHOOD	KT1	100
	KT2	425
	KT3	10
KNIGHTLY	KT2	260
	KT3	485
	TH	389
	FL	233
	FL	571
	WB	299
KNIGHT'S	KT3	868
KNIGHTS	PD	10
	PP	40
	PTS	29
	J1	176
	KT1	100
	KT1	142
	KT1	202
	KT2	208
	KT2	234
	KT2	391
	KT2	395
	KT2	409
	KT2	430
	KT2	666
	KT3	22
	KT3	61
	KT3	90
	KT3	113
	KT3	275
	KT3	453
	KT3	488
	KT3	497
	KT3	514
	KT3	522
	KT3	601
	FL	254
	FL	277
	FL	324
	FL	339
	FL	348
	FL	362
	FL	369
	FL	381
	FL	387
	FL	399
	FL	479
	FL	516
	FL	522
	FL	529

Word	Src	No.
KNIGHTS	FL	536
	FL	542
	FL	561
	FL	564
	WB	352
KNIT	T27	51
	VP8	107
	G3	297
	AE12	1080
KNITS	G1	133
KNIVES	ETC	22
	AE6	354
	KT2	571
KNOBS	VP5	138
KNOCK	PA	23
	PO	13
	P5	33
	AE10	418
	AE11	917
	B	226
	CAM	284
	HIF	587
KNOCKED	TA	99
	P2	23
	M1	407
	G4	425
	AE3	741
	BP	27
	M11	305
	M12	162
	WB	120
KNOCKING	AE6	1091
	AE12	1308
	B	155
KNOCKS	PK	20
	PKA	11
	AE5	1129
	M12	350
	M15	419
KNOT	EEL	5
	ESF	23
	T23	75
	T23	92
	HAP	2116
	G2	105
	AE4	80
	AE8	345
	M8	70
KNOTS	J6	502
	P5	78
	VP8	107
	VP8	108
	G2	110
	AE1	437
	AE2	290
	KT2	536
	KT3	470
KNOTTED	M13	82
	VP4	35
	AE8	286
	AE9	955
	AE9	1004
KNOTTY	VP5	58
	AE7	705
	AE11	832
	M8	97
KNOW	JH	25
	AR	142
	AR	298
	SMA	71
	LC	143
	SIE	11
	AM	556
	AM	655
	AM	660
	AM	782
	AM	787
	AM	799
	SMQ	5
	PWGR	28
	ET	14
	PCG2	18
	SCG3	16
	PMQW	4
	PCD	27
	ENH	40
	PUO2	10
	PUO2	18
	PUO2	34
	EUO2	5
	EUO2	12
	EUO2	17
	ML	51
	PAL	30
	EKK	15

KNOW			KNOW			KNOW		
	EOE	33		J 16	75		OAL	52
	PCB	34		P 1	54		OAL	319
	CM	32		P 1	87		OAL	462
	CM	38		P 3	55		OAL	477
	CM	113		P 4	12		OAL	555
	CM	115		P 4	17		OAL	641
	HP	163		P 4	50		OAL	782
	DA	21		P 4	82		OAL	792
	DA	99		P 4	106		MG	26
	DA	176		P 4	107		MFL	25
	DA	183		P 5	133		KT 1	431
	DA	195		P 5	65		KT 1	496
	PSF	22		P 5	31		KT 2	70
	PUO5	22		P 6	54		KT 2	148
	AA	132		P 6	115		KT 2	150
	AA	417		P 6	135		KT 2	289
	ELB	39		M 1	219		KT 2	293
	PPC	20		M 1	254		KT 2	297
	MD	107		M 1	420		KT 2	362
	MD	120		M 1	614		KT 2	380
	MD	288		M 1	702		KT 3	224
	PRH	31		M 1	961		KT 3	853
	SAA	453		M 1	1087		TJD	76
	SAA	659		M 9	47		B	223
	SAA	1075		M 9	123		B	676
	EK	32		PLT	22		CAM	165
	RL	78		PLT	24		CAM	195
	RL	261		GK	82		CAM	202
	RL	373		DHP	20		HIF	110
	RL	430		DHP	31		HIF	254
	OE	34		VP 2	23		HIF	469
	AT	62		VP 3	11		HIF	556
	AT	117		VP 3	46		HIF	734
	PD	37		VP 8	60		HIF	744
	PD	44		VP 9	63		HIF	792
	EC	5		VP 10	78		C	113
	L 3	52		G 1	344		C	171
	L 3	137		G 1	676		C	396
	L 3	294		G 2	162		C	469
	L 3	313		G 2	309		C	562
	L 4	206		G 2	347		C	585
	T 23	55		G 2	395		TH	151
	T 23	62		G 2	677		M 11	41
	T 27	38		G 3	86		M 11	45
	T 27	71		G 3	183		FL	101
	T 27	80		G 3	226		FL	459
	H 29	44		G 3	530		FL	472
	TA	76		G 4	86		FL	480
	TA	251		G 4	188		FL	502
	TA	329		AE 1	357		FL	598
	TA	401		AE 1	465		M 12	721
	TA	479		AE 1	503		WB	237
	PAA	23		AE 2	14		WB	330
	EAA	17		AE 2	95		WB	382
	AK	47		AE 2	139		WB	482
	GE	52		AE 3	135		WB	486
	HAP	218		AE 3	333		M 15	7
	HAP	325		AE 4	125		M 15	539
	HAP	416		AE 4	191		C I	142
	HAP	426		AE 4	560		C I	371
	HAP	621		AE 4	613		C I	395
	HAP	1183		AE 4	898		PTP	47
	HAP	1405		AE 4	1001		EMKG	39
	HAP	1433		AE 5	635		EWR	2
	HAP	1449		AE 5	965		EWR	26
	HAP	1596		AE 5	1107	KNOWEST	DA	55
	HAP	1746		AE 6	225		AK	171
	HAP	1958		AE 6	529		P 4	23
	HAP	2117		AE 6	657		M 1	691
	HAP	2354		AE 6	691		G 4	645
	HAP	2418		AE 6	836		AE 1	941
	BR	322		AE 6	872		AE 3	459
	PDS	16		AE 6	980		AE 12	1150
	PTS	32		AE 6	1106		OAL	253
	PMS	3		AE 6	1200		KT 3	148
	PMS	12		AE 7	131		KT 3	154
	PMS	26		AE 7	505		KT 3	227
	PKA	40		AE 7	518		TH	148
	EKA	18		AE 7	893		KT 1	326
	EKA	24		AE 8	170		CAM	147
	EKA	37		AE 8	660		HIF	505
	EL	54		AE 9	136		HIF	697
	EL	142		AE 9	324		M 11	361
	EL	266		AE 9	729		C I	531
	ESH	8		AE 9	825	KNOWING	EWGR	36
	J 1	13		AE 9	850		EMM	3
	J 3	195		AE 9	899		EUO2	32
	J 3	413		AE 10	316		PC 2	30
	J 6	207		AE 10	698		CM	25
	J 6	527		AE 10	1177		CM	53
	J 6	610		AE 10	1307		UMR	7
	J 6	733		AE 11	435		SAA	412
	J 6	737		AE 11	556		RL	388
	J 6	763		AE 12	1266		J 6	216
	J 10	2		AE 12	1349		J 10	2
	J 10	356		OAL	5		PLT	25

KNOWING	AE10	131
	B	718
	CAM	225
	M11	463
KNOWINGLY	OAL	254
KNOWLEDGE	UDH	100
	RH	45
	DC	24
	LCA	28
	AM	142
	PWGR	13
	PWGR	17
	PUO1	24
	PUO2	38
	SAA	87
	RL	374
	RL	412
	TA	338
	TA	345
	HAP	276
	AE12	1161
	TJD	96
	HIF	738
	CI	128
KNOWN	AR	103
	EIE	3
	EIE	9
	AM	74
	AM	306
	AM	634
	AM	856
	AM	957
	EWGR	6
	PCG1	21
	PUO1	10
	EUO	34
	PNH	11
	ML	21
	POE	15
	PCB	39
	AA	184
	AA	589
	AA	840
	EPC	10
	MF	85
	MF	141
	MF	159
	SAA	205
	RL	171
	RL	177
	RL	181
	RL	192
	RL	202
	RL	343
	RL	369
	RL	443
	ER	70
	MO	1
	L3	128
	L3	293
	TA	91
	TA	22
	EAA	5
	HAP	1626
	HAP	1725
	HAP	2207
	HAP	2253
	HAP	2484
	HAP	2485
	BR	206
	STS1	8
	ODA	77
	J1	152
	J3	64
	J3	283
	J6	150
	J6	173
	J6	192
	J6	337
	J6	453
	J6	750
	J10	544
	J16	58
	M1	228
	M1	1066
	GK	41
	VP3	102
	VP6	16
	G2	48
	G2	210
	G2	699
	G4	751
	G4	770
	AE1	472
	AE1	561
	AE1	641
KNOWN	AE1	646
	AE1	703
	AE1	872
	AE2	57
	AE2	621
	AE3	141
	AE3	728
	AE4	47
	AE4	793
	AE5	76
	AE5	736
	AE6	671
	AE7	550
	AE7	686
	AE7	696
	AE7	777
	AE8	791
	AE11	603
	AE12	218
	AE12	328
	AE12	342
	AE12	437
	AE12	592
	AE12	613
	AE12	651
	AE12	884
	OAL	334
	DO	56
	KT1	159
	KT1	367
	KT1	393
	KT1	593
	KT2	398
	KT3	7
	KT3	268
	KT3	300
	KT3	878
	TJD	6
	B	121
	B	229
	B	324
	B	369
	B	416
	B	462
	HIF	307
	C	66
	C	80
	C	294
	FL	78
	FL	499
	FL	504
	M12	40
	M12	89
	M12	234
	M12	247
	M12	370
	AU	29
	AU	235
	WB	201
	WB	440
	CI	115
	CI	184
	CI	225
	CI	395
	CI	432
KNOWS	PRL	21
	AM	57
	AM	418
	AM	608
	SCG2	23
	PUO1	41
	HP	258
	PR	11
	PUO4	20
	AA	657
	ELB	23
	SAA	141
	SAA	443
	SAA	586
	SAA	646
	SAA	677
	EK	43
	RL	194
	RL	196
	L3	65
	L4	37
	T27	18
	H2	12
	AK	146
	HAP	2250
	HAP	2470
	J3	140
	J6	479
	J6	534
	J6	583
	J6	737
KNOWS	J10	372
	J10	374
	P1	136
	P5	246
	M1	645
	M13	124
	ELT	4
	G2	656
	G3	442
	G4	569
	AE4	818
	AE11	841
	AE12	240
	OAL	51
	OAL	69
	OAL	183
	OAL	341
	OAL	378
	OAL	398
	OAL	450
	OAE1	29
	KT1	422
	KT1	433
	KT1	434
	KT3	330
	B	364
	M10	19
	M10	20
	CAM	131
	CAM	211
	M11	117
	M11	463
	AU	329
	M15	262
	M15	572
	EWR	2
LA	WB	340
LABEO	P1	244
LABEO'S	P1	8
	P1	93
LABICANS	AE7	1088
LABOR	UDH	12
	LC	107
	AM	282
	AM	560
	AM	1009
	CM	53
	AA	898
	AA	912
	MF	166
	SAA	985
	T23	90
	HAP	772
	SKA1	7
	J6	401
	P1	149
	P5	57
	M1	734
	M9	16
	GK	151
	VP1	101
	VP10	2
	G1	117
	G1	218
	G1	223
	G1	240
	G1	372
	G2	85
	G2	214
	G2	286
	G2	548
	G2	560
	G2	570
	G2	666
	G2	740
	G3	304
	G3	639
	G3	688
	G4	82
	AE1	49
	AE1	368
	AE1	587
	AE1	601
	AE1	709
	AE2	837
	AE3	357
	AE3	646
	AE3	940
	AE4	104
	AE6	195

Word	Code	Num	Word	Code	Num	Word	Code	Num
LABOR	AE6	223	LABORING	G4	265	LABORS	AE3	506
	AE6	270		G4	401		AE3	931
	AE7	461		G4	808		AE4	124
	AE7	887		AE1	54		AE4	766
	AE8	527		AE2	410		AE5	800
	AE8	546		AE2	847		AE6	1018
	AE9	652		AE4	12		AE6	1093
	AE9	827		AE4	838		AE7	171
	AE9	1088		AE4	996		AE8	251
	AE10	425		AE5	157		AE8	381
	AE11	193		AE5	246		AE8	496
	AE11	720		AE5	260		AE8	598
	AE12	178		AE5	927		AE12	271
	AE12	863		AE6	75		AE12	379
	OAE2	73		AE6	121		AE12	658
	KT2	556		AE6	150		AE12	726
	KT3	337		AE7	788		AE12	1313
	M11	109		AE8	421		M8	215
	FL	579		AE9	360		HIF	249
	M12	30		AE10	404		M11	311
	M12	783		AE10	1141		M12	204
	AU	17		AE10	1249		M12	217
	CI	69		AE11	771		AU	571
	CI	338		AE12	971		M15	50
LABORED	LCA	3		AE12	1148		M15	197
	AM	1050		KT1	573	LABYRINTH	L3	270
	ECG2	8		KT2	561		HAP	403
	PTW	3		KT3	591		AE5	769
	L3	210		KT3	893	LABYRINTHS	AM	1027
	HAP	1394		TJD	102	LACE	PUO3	16
	EL	222		M8	254		J16	94
	MS	20		B	124		AE7	883
	M1	159		CAM	136	LACED	PUO3	22
	M13	202		CAM	360		HI	189
	VP8	14		HIF	652		AE10	1243
	G2	414		M12	371		KT3	455
	G4	207		M15	180	LACEDAEMON	T18	53
	G4	235		M15	455	LACES	AE9	498
	G4	253		CI	387	LACHESIS	J3	49
	AE3	187	LABORIOUS	PAZ	4	LACINIAN	AE3	725
	AE4	570		TA	242	LACKEY	ECG1	9
	AE6	858		J10	60	LACKEYS	PAR	12
	AE8	814		M1	4		EK	21
	AE8	974		M1	556		J3	449
	AE12	142		HI	132	LADDER	HAP	792
	HIF	811		G1	95		HAP	799
	AU	450		G1	266	LADDER'S	EMKG	12
	M15	105		G2	232	LADDERS	AM	916
	CI	478		G2	322		AE2	603
LABORER	AM	13		G3	538		AE9	674
	G2	37		G4	34		AE9	695
	M15	207		G4	242		AE12	845
LABORER'S	VP9	83		AE1	607	LADE	AM	1008
LABORING	AR	5		AE6	63		M13	72
	LC	46		KT3	1143	LADED	G2	752
	AM	574	LABORS	AR	173	LADEN	M13	118
	AM	1173		LC	147		G2	114
	PT	6		DA	157		G2	716
	SAA	935		MD	321		G4	41
	L2	7		MF	107		G4	265
	L2	45		SAA	159		AE1	501
	H9	4		SAA	536		AE1	952
	TA	150		SAA	1135		AE2	504
	TA	192		L3	136	LADES	AE12	517
	TA	283		L4	66	LADIES	LC	11
	PAA	1		GE	29		PWG	9
	HH	23		HAP	899		EWG	19
	HAP	671		J3	134		EIE	2
	HAP	1233		J3	189		EIE	24
	PTS	1		P1	107		ETL	5
	J1	81		P4	33		ECG2	25
	J3	91		P5	4		PMQW	12
	J6	477		M1	372		PMQW	19
	J6	572		HI	22		ENH	27
	P1	34		G1	140		ESF	8
	P1	204		G1	440		PSF	42
	M1	395		G2	679		ETG	1
	M9	40		G2	745		PR	18
	VP1	74		G3	65		PPC	1
	VP3	63		G3	110		PK	29
	VP4	49		G3	156		EDGA	15
	VP4	60		G3	188		EDGA	21
	VP6	75		G3	289		EDGA	33
	G1	177		G3	304		PD	10
	G1	351		G3	746		GE	24
	G1	362		G4	52		PDS	26
	G1	402		G4	175		PTS	27
	G1	479		AE1	4		ETS	2
	G1	652		AE1	331		ETS	24
	G1	662		AE1	1040		J1	183
	G2	185		AE2	290		J6	130
	G3	102		AE2	372		J10	508
	G3	273		AE2	1059		P2	69
	G3	757		AE3	30		HI	105
	G3	796		AE3	118		PLT	24
	G4	191		AE3	218		KT1	127

LADIES	KT3	549
	C	478
	FL	214
	FL	309
	FL	328
	FL	339
	FL	341
	FL	355
	FL	379
	FL	387
	FL	417
	FL	429
	FL	525
	FL	530
	FL	564
	WB	77
	WB	215
	WB	222
	PMK	9
LADIES'	ESF	31
	KT1	23
	FL	350
	CI	1
	CI	419
LADING	PWR	11
LADON	AE10	580
	M15	497
LADON'S	M1	971
LADY	PWG	36
	SMM1	1
	PAR	17
	ENH	5
	EAZ	14
	EAL	24
	EK	43
	AT	92
	HAP	572
	HAP	715
	J1	104
	J6	97
	J6	438
	J6	505
	AE4	420
	AE11	1178
	KT1	316
	B	156
	C	610
	FL	168
	FL	176
	FL	325
	FL	365
	FL	423
	FL	424
	FL	448
	FL	456
	FL	464
	FL	502
	FL	508
	WB	278
	WB	511
	PMK	23
LADY-HAND	J1	39
LADY-LIKE	HAP	1258
LADY'S	EK	10
	EK	42
	ETS	14
	J6	495
	J6	769
	J10	532
	OAL	42
	OAL	404
	KT1	303
	KT2	325
	KT2	394
	KT3	36
	C	127
	TH	19
	TH	282
	PWR	28
LADYSHIP	PD	8
	EKA	16
	J1	189
LAERTES	M8	61
	AU	233
LAERTES'	M12	828
	AU	119
LAETAMUR	MD	15
LAG	G3	708
	HIF	337
	FL	494
	SMP	83
LAGAEAN	G2	132
LAGGING	AM	338
	HAP	2578
	M1	788
	HI	25
LAGGING	HI	37
	VP8	25
	AE4	589
LAGS	ML	43
	J6	182
	AE5	256
	AE5	239
	AE12	379
LAGUS	AE10	533
LAID	HS	92
	RH	75
	AM	862
	AM	1061
	AM	1094
	PEL	3
	SEL3	5
	SEL3	20
	ELN	8
	EUO	24
	HP	217
	EUF	20
	MD	201
	SAA	201
	SAA	230
	SAA	476
	SAA	920
	SAA	1118
	AT	8
	AT	106
	EC	40
	L2	35
	L4	278
	TA	172
	TA	235
	EAA	33
	HH	36
	HAP	581
	HAP	1047
	HAP	1282
	HAP	1825
	HAP	1877
	HAP	2284
	EL	41
	EL	70
	OD	13
	J3	45
	J6	4
	J10	95
	J10	250
	P3	16
	P5	214
	P6	172
	M1	176
	M1	1012
	M13	57
	VCS	2
	HI	38
	VP2	7
	VP3	57
	G1	378
	G2	523
	G3	739
	G4	685
	G4	773
	AE1	266
	AE2	752
	AE3	31
	AE3	160
	AE3	567
	AE4	567
	AE6	189
	AE6	700
	AE6	838
	AE7	136
	AE7	580
	AE8	43
	AE8	482
	AE8	770
	AE8	836
	AE9	778
	AE9	797
	AE10	441
	AE10	543
	AE10	563
	AE10	590
	AE10	676
	AE10	924
	AE10	1053
	AE11	310
	AE11	477
	AE11	892
	AE11	986
	AE11	1056
	AE11	1064
	AE11	1094
	AE12	979
LAID	AE12	1346
	OAL	647
	OAL	791
	OAL	797
	MFL	1
	KT1	149
	KT1	202
	KT1	552
	KT2	65
	KT2	165
	KT2	509
	KT2	584
	KT3	210
	KT3	687
	KT3	713
	KT3	910
	KT3	973
	KT3	1071
	M8	127
	M8	300
	M8	308
	B	461
	B	740
	BP	25
	BP	81
	M10	44
	CAM	188
	HIF	63
	C	6
	C	251
	C	671
	TH	90
	TH	155
	TH	167
	FL	420
	M12	210
	AU	247
	AU	406
	WB	193
	WB	386
	CI	91
	GP	115
	PTP	38
	PMK	30
LAIN	PMK	23
LAIR	HAP	555
	G3	233
	G3	471
LAITY	M15	165
LAKE	AA	137
	SAA	980
	H3	51
	H2	73
	HAP	179
	J3	424
	J6	556
	M1	245
	M1	439
	G2	222
	G4	35
	AE2	185
	AE3	497
	AE3	921
	AE6	294
	AE6	341
	AE6	347
	AE6	205
	AE6	503
	AE6	521
	AE6	911
	AE6	968
	AE6	1088
	AE7	719
	AE7	778
	AE7	787
	AE7	960
	AE8	399
	AE9	121
	AE12	211
	AE12	309
	AE12	754
	AE12	1185
	OAL	716
	BP	21
	BP	152
	C	477
	C	739
	TH	315
	WB	195
	M15	448
	M15	501
	M15	533
	M15	556
LAKES	L3	223
	L4	65
	M1	46

LAKES		
	G2	219
	G2	661
	G3	63
	G3	653
	G3	725
	G4	520
	AE3	753
	AE7	968
	AE12	216
	AE12	374
	AE12	1097
	M15	411
	M15	483
LAMB		
	AR	122
	AA	576
	H2	84
	M1	682
	VP4	55
	VP8	71
	AE5	1010
	AE6	356
	AE9	765
	AE12	257
	OAL	874
LAMBENT		
	MF	111
	AK	84
	HAP	1230
	AE2	931
	AE7	114
LAMBKINS		
	M13	129
LAMBS		
	SAA	563
	T18	69
	VP1	31
	VP2	26
	VP3	9
	VP3	51
	VP3	159
	VP7	21
	VP7	50
	G1	470
	G1	570
	G4	629
	AE1	896
	AE9	72
	OAL	135
	C	485
LAMBSKINS		
	T27	98
LAME		
	SAA	405
	M1	571
	RL	287
	BR	350
	EL	47
	J10	476
	P1	32
	GK	39
	BP	84
	HIF	812
LAMED		
	C	644
LAMELY		
	RH	73
	EL	142
LAMENT		
	M1	784
	AA	486
	L3	67
	L3	151
	AM	82
	A	5
	PUO5	17
	DHP	28
	VP5	28
	AE2	108
	AE4	887
	AE6	601
	AE11	330
	AE12	366
	KT3	868
LAMENTABLE		
	P1	69
	AE2	724
	M11	479
	CI	611
LAMENTED		
	EPF	23
	J10	44
	AE6	650
	AE9	766
	AE11	44
	AE11	1222
	TH	298
LAMENTING		
	M13	189
LAMENTS		
	HI	193
	HI	194
	VP3	69
	G4	666
	G4	743
	AE2	398
	AE2	667
	AE2	886
	AE4	960

LAMENTS		
	AE5	1001
	AE6	436
	AE6	757
	AE9	636
	AE11	291
	AE11	361
	KT3	654
	TH	102
	TH	267
	TH	281
	M11	180
	M12	766
LAMP		
	RL	12
	AK	82
	M13	165
	VP9	64
	AE2	942
	AE8	543
LAMPOON	EPC	9
LAMPOONERS	PLT	52
LAMPOONING	EUF	26
LAMPOONS	PTS	19
LAMPS		
	J6	187
	P5	262
	M1	673
	G1	537
	AE1	1015
	AE2	205
	AE12	308
LAMUS	AE9	450
LAMYRUS	AE9	450
LANCE	EUO	15
	J10	331
	AE2	235
	AE2	722
	AE4	306
	AE7	549
	AE9	226
	AE9	797
	AE9	835
	AE9	955
	AE9	1003
	AE10	477
	AE10	563
	AE10	645
	AE10	770
	AE10	805
	AE10	1029
	AE10	1038
	AE11	135
	AE11	436
	AE11	731
	AE11	832
	AE11	952
	AE11	1265
	AE12	80
	AE12	146
	AE12	403
	AE12	495
	AE12	555
	AE12	585
	AE12	640
	AE12	679
	AE12	1119
	AE12	1143
	AE12	1328
	AE12	1339
	OAL	788
	KT1	115
	KT2	138
	KT2	195
	KT3	455
	KT3	617
	KT3	934
	M8	134
	M8	180
	M8	188
	FL	281
	M12	110
	M12	113
	M12	143
	M12	146
	M12	175
	M12	504
	M12	507
	M12	603
	M12	620
	M12	636
	M12	811
	AU	175
LANCED	KT3	709
LANCES	HI	106
	AE2	73
	AE2	989
	AE3	66
	AE6	887

LANCES		
	AE6	1048
	AE10	1009
	AE11	16
	AE11	138
	AE11	301
	AE12	199
	KT3	583
	KT3	987
	M8	144
	FL	292
LAND		
	HS	49
	HS	68
	HS	117
	AR	253
	AR	254
	AR	277
	AR	301
	RH	91
	SMA	80
	DC	52
	VHH	43
	AM	26
	AM	36
	AM	39
	AM	318
	AM	403
	AM	451
	AM	635
	AM	648
	AM	806
	AM	1060
	AM	1080
	EWGR	39
	PFD	1
	PAR	21
	HP	218
	HP	221
	HP	231
	DA	10
	DA	13
	DA	154
	PUF	27
	AA	10
	AA	95
	AA	199
	AA	235
	AA	271
	AA	300
	AA	438
	AA	543
	AA	732
	AA	840
	AA	916
	ELB	33
	MD	172
	MD	178
	MD	258
	PRH	36
	MF	206
	SAA	30
	SAA	203
	SAA	221
	SAA	329
	SAA	599
	SAA	688
	SAA	712
	SAA	944
	SAA	1128
	PK	7
	L1	9
	L1	41
	L3	4
	H3	10
	H3	29
	TA	147
	TA	300
	TA	396
	TA	428
	TA	488
	MN	10
	HAP	129
	HAP	982
	HAP	1112
	HAP	2008
	HAP	2062
	HAP	2126
	HAP	2157
	HAP	2206
	BR	15
	BR	191
	BR	331
	EJG	3
	J1	92
	J1	206
	J3	125
	J6	825

LANGUAGE	HAP	2115
	MS	16
	J6	269
	M1	893
	GK	68
	GK	125
	AE12	1197
	KT1	312
	KT2	574
	KT3	778
	M15	86
LANGUAGES	UDH	18
	UDH	31
LANGUID	J3	378
LANGUISH	PAR	23
	S	7
	A	7
	SKK	10
	STC	13
	SDG	2
	SKA1	10
	SKA2	25
	SSH	5
	M13	101
	SFL	10
	G4	369
	AE12	78
	KT1	461
	M8	359
	CAM	161
LANGUISHED	SCG1	14
	M9	82
	GK	44
	AE2	226
	AE5	552
	AE8	771
	AE10	1013
	AE11	1212
LANGUISHES	G3	156
	G3	334
	AE10	405
LANGUISHEST	OAL	419
LANGUISHING	NS	12
	STS2	2
	P1	193
	M1	1014
	KT1	213
LANK	P2	93
	VP3	154
	G2	342
LAOCOON	AE2	52
	AE2	267
	AE2	281
	AE2	301
LAODAMIA	AE6	606
LAOMEDON	G1	675
	AE4	782
LAP	CM	4
	CM	79
	DA	198
	P5	189
	AE1	971
	AE8	537
	OAL	175
	OAL	178
	KT3	1071
	CAM	189
	CAM	197
	M15	373
LAPDOG	J6	853
LAPITHAE	G3	180
LAPITHAEAN	M12	299
	M12	347
	M12	368
LAPLAND	EUO	24
LAPS	J6	788
LAPWING	VP6	113
LARBOARD	AE3	526
	AE3	737
LARD	MF	164
	BP	107
	HIF	632
LARDED	HIF	63
LARDS	P1	170
LARES	AM	1128
	P3	44
LARGE	HS	102
	RH	47
	SMA	61
	LC	62
	AM	980
	PCG1	11
	PCG1	14
	CM	77
	UMR	4
	AA	365

LARGE	AA	826
	MD	40
	MD	173
	MF	8
	MF	195
	SAA	94
	SAA	287
	SAA	989
	RL	172
	L4	150
	TA	309
	AK	103
	HAP	273
	HAP	898
	HAP	1825
	HAP	2503
	HAP	2559
	BR	86
	EL	256
	EL	273
	J1	133
	J1	227
	J3	56
	J6	257
	J6	659
	J10	99
	P2	85
	P5	41
	P6	123
	P6	181
	M1	67
	M1	454
	M1	588
	M1	1030
	GK	170
	G1	161
	G1	170
	G1	275
	G2	7
	G2	60
	G2	141
	G2	181
	G2	285
	G2	306
	G2	341
	G2	442
	G2	570
	G3	91
	G3	226
	G4	415
	G4	531
	G4	604
	G4	805
	G4	806
	AE1	1050
	AE1	1058
	AE2	299
	AE2	686
	AE3	143
	AE3	603
	AE3	810
	AE3	836
	AE3	923
	AE4	368
	AE5	863
	AE6	806
	AE6	1017
	AE7	239
	AE8	586
	AE9	140
	AE9	347
	AE9	363
	AE9	955
	AE10	25
	AE10	193
	AE10	432
	AE10	719
	AE11	68
	AE11	1048
	OAE1	17
	KT1	203
	KT1	452
	KT1	607
	KT2	266
	KT2	439
	KT3	45
	KT3	70
	M8	21
	M8	375
	BP	66
	BP	157
	HIF	195
	C	657
	TH	51
	TH	66
	FL	232

LARGE	FL	426
	M15	428
	ESK	3
	AS	86
LARGE-LIMBED	HAP	1842
LARGELY	SAA	949
	HAP	1120
	HAP	1405
	HAP	1500
	HAP	2212
	HAP	2245
	EL	25
	J3	238
	P4	51
	M13	151
	G2	374
	G3	482
	OAL	712
	KT1	602
	B	733
	HIF	185
LARGENESS	G2	147
LARGER	AM	1180
	AA	826
	PAA	8
	HAP	1621
	HAP	1663
	P6	32
	M1	31
	M9	25
	M9	191
	AE2	1049
	AE3	614
	AE5	275
	AE7	66
	AE7	518
	AE11	778
	OAL	394
	KT1	217
	M8	20
	FL	498
	AS	86
LARGESS	RL	364
	J1	149
	P6	118
	AE5	401
LARGEST	G1	287
LARINA	AE11	972
LARIS	AE10	546
LARIS'	AE10	551
LARIUS	G2	219
LARK	DHP	1
	KT2	37
	KT3	122
	C	428
LARKS	AM	780
	H2	52
	AK	192
LASCIVIOUS	P4	116
	M1	612
	M10	1
LASH	AR	117
	PAA	4
	P1	24
	P5	22
	G3	169
	G3	324
	AE4	226
	AE4	589
	AE5	193
	AE7	532
	AE10	824
	AE10	1282
	KT2	196
LASHED	AM	1088
	H3	46
	P1	224
	AE5	185
	AE6	753
	AE12	14
	AE12	511
	FL	495
LASHING	HAP	692
	J1	104
	G3	63
	AE12	1266
	M11	139
	M12	472
LASS	AT	82
	G3	335
LASSES	SKA1	15
	OAL	300
LAST	UDH	105
	JH	18
	AR	227
	LC	91

Word	Code	No.
LATELY	MO	1
	TA	91
	TA	201
	P5	164
	M1	440
	VP5	18
	AE1	443
	AE2	463
	AE10	788
	AE12	367
	BP	111
	TH	354
LATENT	L4	225
	HAP	279
	EL	80
	M9	198
	G1	128
	FL	414
	AU	172
LATER	G2	134
	AE3	223
	AE8	549
LATE-REPENTING	AE6	632
LATEST	HS	133
	AM	351
	AT	124
	BR	318
	VP8	18
LATH	G4	168
LATIAN	PDS	15
	AE1	6
	AE1	44
	AE1	798
	AE3	247
	AE3	651
	AE4	337
	AE4	625
	AE4	497
	AE4	879
	AE5	737
	AE5	1043
	AE5	1065
	AE6	103
	AE6	464
	AE6	1232
	AE7	69
	AE7	85
	AE7	103
	AE7	125
	AE7	140
	AE7	206
	AE7	218
	AE7	328
	AE7	373
	AE7	443
	AE7	464
	AE7	479
	AE7	284
	AE7	559
	AE7	608
	AE7	649
	AE7	676
	AE7	716
	AE7	759
	AE7	908
	AE8	7
	AE8	17
	AE8	156
	AE8	618
	AE8	717
	AE8	815
	AE9	44
	AE9	115
	AE9	166
	AE9	362
	AE9	646
	AE9	973
	AE10	12
	AE10	45
	AE10	61
	AE10	161
	AE10	338
	AE10	546
	AE10	666
	AE10	789
	AE10	947
	AE10	999
	AE11	79
	AE11	112
	AE11	122
	AE11	161
	AE11	168
	AE11	192
	AE11	344
	AE11	363
	AE11	507
LATIAN	AE11	550
	AE11	785
	AE11	903
	AE11	1285
	AE12	93
	AE12	123
	AE12	171
	AE12	209
	AE12	220
	AE12	227
	AE12	293
	AE12	315
	AE12	537
	AE12	563
	AE12	676
	AE12	777
	AE12	831
	AE12	1357
LATIANS	AE7	278
	AE7	601
	AE8	74
	AE9	928
	AE10	99
	AE10	112
	AE10	376
	AE11	202
	AE11	308
	AE11	316
	AE11	449
	AE12	26
	AE12	60
	AE12	364
LATIN	PTC	9
	PO	3
	PPC	19
	PPC	21
	PD	34
	AK	32
	HAP	2068
	J6	561
	AE5	779
	AE10	505
	AE11	921
	AE12	187
	AE12	809
	AE12	1006
	C	419
LATINE	AE7	992
	AE12	419
LATINS	TA	469
	AE5	778
	AE7	202
	AE11	463
	AE11	485
	AE11	730
	AE11	882
	AE11	938
	AE11	1095
	AE11	1120
	AE12	1
	AE12	661
	AE12	682
	AE12	868
	AE12	938
	AE12	1196
	AE12	1344
LATINS'	AE12	1113
LATINUS	AE7	68
	AE7	74
	AE7	92
	AE7	121
	AE7	133
	AE7	267
	AE7	341
	AE7	391
	AE9	526
	AE11	355
	AE11	711
	AE12	93
	AE12	246
	AE12	287
	AE12	431
	AE12	891
LATITUDE	AA	675
	HAP	1454
	HAP	1477
LATIUM	AE1	286
	AE1	343
	AE3	248
	AE7	54
	AE7	145
	AE7	292
	AE7	312
	AE7	834
	AE8	429
	AE11	527
LATIUM	AE11	1235
	AE12	1201
	AE12	1214
LATIUM'S	AE2	1061
LATMOS'	AT	115
LATONA	T18	81
	J10	449
	AE1	705
LATONA'S	G3	9
	AE12	298
	HIF	11
LATONIAN	AE11	805
LATREUS	M12	615
LATTER	HAP	110
	HAP	1907
	M9	29
	M13	112
	AE2	11
	AE5	690
	AE11	993
	MFL	74
	KT3	1079
	B	3
	C	471
	CI	429
LAUDABLE	HAP	2175
LAUFELLA	J6	436
LAUGH	AM	1136
	PCG1	6
	PCG1	8
	PCG1	43
	PAR	8
	PNH	39
	MD	147
	MF	76
	L4	169
	H9	35
	HH	30
	HH	39
	HAP	1444
	PTS	25
	MS	6
	J3	170
	J6	369
	J6	830
	J10	74
	P5	22
	P5	279
	EHC	26
	AE9	208
	OAL	615
	DO	84
	CI	112
	CI	180
	SMP	20
	SMP	21
	SMP	22
	PWR	37
LAUGHED	AR	116
	SEL3	24
	AA	563
	MD	145
	HH	4
	J10	44
	P1	230
	VP3	14
	AE5	235
	KT2	40
	KT3	669
	KT3	671
	KT3	866
	BP	4
	HIF	807
LAUGHING	HAP	1549
	P3	197
	R	15
	R	19
	G2	462
	OAE1	4
	KT2	582
	HIF	785
	PTP	14
	SMP	40
	SMP	44
LAUGHS	SAA	717
	H29	48
	J6	791
	J10	79
	P6	50
	VP7	76
	KT2	149
	KT3	136
	KT3	329
	M15	304
LAUGHTER	J6	679
	J10	45

LAUGHTER	J10	101	LAURELS	VP8	17	LAW	SAA	741
	P3	34		AE3	123		SAA	784
	G2	533		AE7	908		RL	135
	OAL	274		AE12	762		RL	170
	HIF	804		KT1	164		RL	200
LAUNCELOT	C	477		KT3	964		RL	201
LAUNCH	HAP	130		AE6	1157		RL	203
	G3	691		MG	5		T27	59
	AE3	97		TJD	165		H2	14
	AE9	140		B	497		TA	62
	AE12	1036		FL	278		MN	13
	M11	68	LAURENTIAN	AE7	70		HH	9
LAUNCHED	SAA	43		AE8	97		HAP	262
	AE2	361	LAURENTINE	AE12	209		HAP	887
	AE9	552	LAURENTUM	AE7	93		HAP	2005
	AE12	531		AE11	149		HAP	2228
	AE12	847		AE12	38		HAP	2260
	TH	301		AE12	936		HAP	2361
	M12	161	LAURENTUM'S	AE8	2		HAP	2380
LAUNCHING	AE6	801		AE10	948		EL	334
LAUNCHING-KNIFE	G3	695	LAUSUS	AE7	899		J1	87
LAUND	KT2	235		AE10	601		J3	266
	KT3	898		AE10	613		J6	567
LAUREAT	FL	455		AE10	993		J6	779
LAUREATS	PA	35		AE10	1098		J10	375
LAUREL	SAA	1041		AE10	1121		J10	522
	J10	428		AE10	1148		J16	76
	M1	603		AE10	1165		J16	82
	M1	745		AE10	1194		P5	129
	GK	99		AE10	1236		M1	118
	MC	41		AE10	1258		M1	119
	MC	54		AE10	1310		MC	36
	VP2	75	LAUSUS'	AE10	619		G2	719
	VP8	119	LAVE	HI	41		G4	226
	VP10	19		G1	531		G4	709
	G1	411		AE5	208		AE1	325
	G2	181	LAVED	AE12	1050		AE2	727
	G2	183	LAVEERING	AR	65		AE4	339
	AE2	701	LAVES	AM	610		AE6	439
	AE2	717		AE3	871		AE6	837
	AE3	106		AE10	1086		AE10	46
	AE5	145		M11	109		AE10	115
	AE5	306	LAVINIA	HAP	2070		AE11	558
	AE5	320		AE6	1037		MG	3
	AE5	709		AE7	107		KT1	326
	AE5	727		AE7	141		KT1	327
	AE6	893		AE11	357		KT2	305
	AE7	95		AE11	539		KT2	345
	AE7	101		AE12	38		KT3	1054
	MG	15		AE12	51		B	164
	KT3	86		AE12	100		B	277
	KT3	396		AE12	885		B	443
	KT3	913	LAVINIAN	AE1	352		B	517
	HIF	22		AE7	652		HIF	399
	HIF	518	LAVINIA'S	AE7	86		HIF	408
	FL	127		AE7	350		C	292
	FL	130		AE7	502		TH	219
	FL	171		AE9	996		WB	350
	FL	193		AE12	291		GP	30
	FL	263	LAVINIUM	AE1	367		CI	454
	FL	284	LAVISH	AA	385	LAWFUL	DA	111
	FL	312		MD	125		AA	201
	FL	401		L5	18		AA	351
	FL	411		TA	333		AA	516
	FL	441		P6	50		AA	918
	FL	464		VP7	76		AA	1031
	FL	503		G1	423		AA	1024
	FL	516		MM	7		PLB	1
	FL	528		C	456		MD	60
	FL	541		M15	112		MD	115
	FL	553	LAVISHLY	ODA	26		SAA	726
	FL	555		M15	305		SAA	764
	FL	579	LAW	VHH	14		PDG	21
LAURELED	SAA	938		AM	86		HAP	455
	P6	97		AM	661		HAP	499
	FL	534		PMQ	30		HAP	654
LAUREL'S	AE7	89		PT	7		HAP	853
	AE7	95		PNH	22		HAP	1187
LAURELS	HS	58		EMW	14		HAP	1353
	HS	130		AA	5		HAP	1642
	AR	58		AA	37		HAP	1777
	RH	57		AA	408		J6	286
	LCA	15		AA	458		G4	134
	EUO2	6		AA	582		G4	511
	HP	133		AA	966		AE4	489
	DA	168		AA	991		AE8	659
	SAA	816		AA	992		AE10	15
	SAA	880		AA	1003		AE10	118
	MO	24		AA	1006		AE12	1169
	AK	32		MD	148		B	450
	PP	36		SAA	38		HIF	752
	LS	17		SAA	216		C	56
	J10	11		SAA	235		WB	354
	J10	98		SAA	273		M15	153
	MC	75		SAA	438	LAWFULLY	EKK	9
	VP6	118		SAA	677		HAP	1458

LAWLESS	AR	46
	AM	850
	AA	337
	MD	273
	SAA	683
	SAA	923
	PK	23
	HAP	361
	G2	509
	G2	637
	G4	661
	AE3	422
	AE4	323
	AE6	1145
	AE7	773
	AE10	140
	AE12	213
	OAL	136
	TJD	186
	B	105
	B	497
	HIF	410
	AU	326
	CI	298
LAWN	SCG1	9
	HAP	983
	AE1	445
	AE4	98
	KT2	572
	KT2	620
	TH	74
LAWNS	HAP	2
	VP10	12
	G2	272
LAWS	AR	267
	SMA	82
	LC	26
	LC	49
	LCA	28
	EIE	12
	AM	36
	EUO2	27
	E	14
	POE	2
	HP	67
	DA	47
	AA	54
	AA	207
	AA	319
	AA	476
	AA	609
	AA	610
	AA	628
	AA	666
	AA	701
	AA	763
	AA	764
	AA	807
	AA	874
	AA	969
	ELB	22
	MD	140
	MD	157
	MD	269
	SAA	218
	SAA	237
	SAA	343
	SAA	754
	SAA	787
	SAA	1019
	EK	3
	RL	151
	RL	165
	EC	23
	L3	202
	L3	296
	EAA	18
	HAP	200
	HAP	244
	HAP	286
	HAP	295
	HAP	358
	HAP	376
	HAP	474
	HAP	490
	HAP	664
	HAP	890
	HAP	985
	HAP	993
	HAP	1291
	HAP	1411
	HAP	1637
	HAP	1645
	HAP	1694
	HAP	1829
	HAP	1927

LAWS	HAP	1952
	HAP	1973
	HAP	2000
	HAP	2075
	HAP	2123
	HAP	2130
	HAP	2160
	HAP	2248
	HAP	2511
	PDS	40
	EDS	19
	J1	72
	J6	852
	J10	394
	J10	488
	J10	507
	J16	19
	P2	130
	SFL	16
	G1	49
	G1	91
	G1	361
	G2	698
	AE1	361
	AE1	401
	AE1	418
	AE1	478
	AE1	592
	AE1	713
	AE1	761
	AE1	765
	AE2	183
	AE2	737
	AE3	189
	AE3	460
	AE4	596
	AE5	989
	AE5	1071
	AE6	578
	AE6	847
	AE6	1107
	AE6	1125
	AE6	1151
	AE8	420
	AE8	428
	AE8	890
	AE10	292
	AE12	284
	AE12	475
	AE12	1195
	OAL	165
	OAL	228
	OAL	303
	OAL	739
	OAL	776
	OAE1	8
	KT1	329
	KT1	331
	KT1	333
	KT1	337
	KT1	486
	KT2	257
	KT2	337
	KT2	425
	KT3	1008
	KT3	1074
	TJD	11
	TJD	173
	TJD	191
	B	418
	B	483
	CAM	36
	CAM	41
	CAM	50
	CAM	56
	CAM	59
	HIF	163
	HIF	351
	C	274
	C	783
	M12	43
	M12	832
	AU	113
	AU	248
	AU	322
	WB	274
	WB	307
	M15	8
	M15	34
	M15	52
	M15	89
	M15	125
	M15	150
	M15	718
	CI	300
	CI	525

LAWS	CI	634
LAWSON	AM	80
	AM	81
LAWYER	RL	383
	J6	110
	J6	345
LAWYERS	HH	43
	HAP	1871
	HAP	2531
	J1	194
	AE8	474
	OAL	93
LAXATIFE	KT3	765
LAXATIVE	C	186
LAXATIVES	C	165
	C	400
LAY	UDH	90
	HS	103
	AR	78
	AR	150
	LC	96
	SIE	9
	AM	33
	AM	42
	AM	90
	AM	103
	AM	253
	AM	267
	AM	450
	AM	509
	AM	522
	AM	554
	AM	577
	AM	716
	AM	839
	AM	975
	AM	983
	AM	1059
	AM	1216
	PMQ	7
	PMQ	55
	PWGR	15
	EWGR	40
	SEL3	9
	EM	19
	SM2	1
	S	14
	ECD	20
	POE	29
	EOE	3
	PCB	38
	CM	77
	CM	88
	DA	198
	PUO5	21
	AA	428
	MD	74
	MF	99
	MF	102
	SAA	33
	SAA	189
	SAA	330
	SAA	400
	SAA	445
	SAA	538
	SAA	712
	SAA	867
	RL	403
	AT	64
	AT	66
	AT	124
	L1	35
	L3	7
	L3	117
	L3	137
	L3	278
	T27	36
	T27	98
	T27	100
	T27	126
	H9	20
	NS	2
	TA	63
	TA	352
	TA	451
	AK	93
	AK	99
	HAP	13
	HAP	158
	HAP	580
	HAP	625
	HAP	719
	HAP	992
	HAP	1061
	HAP	1831
	HAP	1919

LAY		
	HAP	2321
	HAP	2368
	SSC	4
	PDS	10
	PTS	4
	PTS	7
	PKA	28
	EL	164
	EL	329
	J3	23
	J3	148
	J3	336
	J3	420
	J6	175
	J6	644
	J10	234
	PPS	11
	P1	164
	P1	178
	P1	261
	P3	218
	M1	246
	M1	338
	M1	618
	M1	720
	VCS	25
	HI	145
	DHP	6
	VP3	24
	VP3	40
	VP3	53
	VP3	111
	VP5	25
	VP9	26
	VP9	85
	G1	462
	G2	481
	G2	695
	G2	727
	G4	64
	G4	235
	AE1	32
	AE1	37
	AE1	75
	AE1	494
	AE1	595
	AE2	30
	AE2	36
	AE2	185
	AE2	532
	AE2	917
	AE3	4
	AE3	27
	AE3	666
	AE3	827
	AE3	834
	AE4	765
	AE4	983
	AE5	431
	AE5	438
	AE5	790
	AE5	1113
	AE6	112
	AE6	231
	AE6	242
	AE6	318
	AE6	490
	AE6	868
	AE6	1145
	AE7	276
	AE7	408
	AE7	482
	AE7	578
	AE7	702
	AE8	112
	AE8	381
	AE8	394
	AE8	429
	AE8	537
	AE8	551
	AE9	421
	AE9	435
	AE9	486
	AE9	562
	AE9	868
	AE10	537
	AE10	773
	AE10	835
	AE10	1159
	AE10	1190
	AE10	1310
	AE11	44
	AE11	473
	AE11	732
	AE11	804
	AE11	1234

LAY		
	AE12	443
	AE12	971
	AE12	1103
	AE12	1219
	OAL	674
	OAL	685
	OAL	807
	OAE1	7
	KT1	41
	KT1	545
	KT2	23
	KT2	238
	KT2	578
	KT3	294
	KT3	318
	KT3	571
	KT3	704
	KT3	842
	KT3	907
	KT3	978
	M8	224
	M8	253
	M8	386
	B	108
	B	141
	B	210
	B	242
	B	250
	B	265
	B	292
	B	523
	CAM	150
	CAM	200
	CAM	282
	CAM	193
	HIF	16
	HIF	456
	HIF	530
	HIF	815
	C	125
	C	167
	C	181
	C	220
	C	258
	C	307
	C	574
	C	581
	C	756
	TH	327
	TH	329
	M11	209
	M11	294
	FL	20
	FL	55
	FL	70
	FL	134
	FL	360
	FL	378
	M12	163
	M12	192
	M12	436
	M12	474
	M12	505
	AU	98
	AU	116
	AU	514
	WB	346
	WB	537
	CI	227
	CI	268
	SMP	14
	PMK	21
	EWR	28
	EPN	2
LAYD		
LAYING	AA	507
	OAL	187
	OAL	189
LAYMAN'S	RL	317
LAYMEN	RL	372
	RL	381
LAYMEN'S	B	95
LAY-PREFERMENT	HAP	2262
LAYS	PUO1	43
	PUO4	19
	AA	439
	D	30
	SAA	287
	H2	43
	TA	381
	SSC	55
	PKA	11
	EL	128
	J3	469
	J6	436
	P3	18
	M1	300

LAYS		
	M1	446
	PLT	1
	DHP	30
	VP4	66
	VP5	14
	VP5	77
	VP9	44
	G1	482
	G2	542
	G4	818
	AE1	974
	AE5	609
	AE5	1009
	AE7	15
	AE9	1097
	AE12	1054
	OAL	263
	OAL	635
	KT3	137
	BP	46
	M10	78
	M11	351
	AU	598
	M15	611
	CI	358
LAZINESS	J6	411
LAZY	AA	201
	AR	105
	L1	15
	L3	264
	P3	9
	P3	84
	P4	75
	P5	73
	P5	91
	P5	190
	M1	362
	G1	313
	G1	402
	G4	242
	G4	356
	AE1	607
	AE6	977
	AE8	574
	AE12	361
	AE12	1254
	OAL	722
	CAM	265
	M11	272
	M11	344
	SMP	52
LE	PAA	39
LEAD	PA	12
	ECD	3
	RL	196
	OE	54
	SSC	48
	BR	70
	EH	7
	J6	658
	J10	99
	M1	630
	VP4	18
	G2	689
	G2	696
	G3	123
	G3	271
	G3	511
	G3	518
	G4	580
	AE1	602
	AE2	966
	AE4	62
	AE4	471
	AE4	493
	AE4	831
	AE5	205
	AE5	510
	AE5	540
	AE5	719
	AE6	163
	AE6	284
	AE6	876
	AE6	1038
	AE7	802
	AE7	951
	AE8	660
	AE9	799
	AE10	357
	AE10	399
	AE11	365
	AE11	704
	AE12	395
	OAL	96
	OAL	219
	OAL	432

Word	Code	No.	Word	Code	No.	Word	Code	No.
LEAD	OAL	724	LEAF	FL	504	LEAP	L4	199
	KT2	55		FL	557		T27	89
	BP	144		FL	585		HAP	302
	CI	531		FL	603		HAP	1621
	CI	564		FL	604		SSC	9
	CI	568		M13	158		J6	45
LEADEN	ELB	21	LEAFLESS	AE11	13		P1	157
	KT3	381		AU	500		M9	116
LEADENHALL	PCB	10	LEAFS	G2	498		VP10	83
LEADER	VHH	35		AE3	566		G3	211
	AM	773		AE3	567		G3	228
	HAP	964		AE3	571		G3	328
	J10	437		AE6	297		G3	681
	G3	526		AE12	611		G3	802
	AE1	641		AE12	612		AE1	244
	AE2	487		FL	540		AE6	36
	AE5	175	LEAFY	VP7	67		AE8	318
	AE5	379		G2	408		AE9	729
	AE6	458		G2	504		AE10	405
	AE8	16		G4	64		AE12	491
	AE8	205		G4	75		OAL	331
	AE8	729		G4	204		TH	369
	AE9	602		AE2	851		STP	25
	AE11	754		AE3	35		PMK	18
	AE11	1075		AE7	184		PMK	19
	AE11	1257		AE9	925		AS	10
LEADER'S	AM	274		AE10	571	LEAPED	UMR	8
	AE1	751		M15	452		G4	767
	AE2	552	LEAGUE	PDG	1		AE2	234
	AE3	224		HAP	2069		AE2	773
	AE9	59		EDS	10		AE9	1102
	AE9	505		AE4	898	LEAPEST	MD	94
LEADERS	AR	31		AE8	228	LEAPING	G4	498
	HAP	694		AE11	246		AE8	879
	HAP	2499		AE11	333		AE10	636
	AE1	265		AE11	540		AE12	532
	AE5	324		AE12	367		AE12	740
	AE5	732		AE12	898		AE12	987
	AE8	774	LEAGUE'S	AR	101		OAL	628
	AE10	242	LEAGUES	DA	131		M10	89
	AE10	610		G1	688	LEAPINGS	L4	274
	AE11	122		AE4	158	LEAPS	AM	886
	M12	97		AE12	733		VP8	160
LEADING	AM	791	LEAK	P3	35		G3	657
	SAA	197		C	350		AE9	751
	SAA	382	LEAKED	L3	129		M12	176
	PAA	22	LEAKS	AM	572		M12	485
	AE3	864	LEAKY	RL	35		M15	555
	AE5	161		L3	220	LEAPT	RL	19
	AE7	1071		L4	20		G2	530
LEADS	AM	474		J3	432		AE12	552
	PLB	21		G4	735		C	494
	H2	3		AE6	557		M12	456
	HAP	720		M11	107		M12	465
	HAP	2129		WB	155	LEARN	JH	22
	VP9	2	LEAN	AR	154		AR	210
	G3	317		PC1	22		AM	627
	G4	518		PUO3	10		HP	98
	AE1	502		EUF	10		DA	193
	AE1	689		MF	191		EMW	8
	AE1	701		L4	155		MF	76
	AE3	250		HAP	376		MF	147
	AE3	446		HAP	1369		SAA	345
	AE4	101		VP1	109		SAA	389
	AE4	201		G1	316		EDGA	5
	AE5	1088		G2	293		RL	436
	AE6	957		G3	209		RL	449
	AE6	1021		G4	371		PD	34
	AE7	444		AE3	284		HAP	567
	AE7	548		OAL	511		HAP	1648
	AE7	942		HIF	632		MS	30
	AE8	457	LEAN-CHAPPED	PMK	22		MS	31
	AE8	900	LEANDER'S	EWG	23		J6	580
	AE9	24	LEANED	WB	226		J10	75
	AE9	31	LEANING	AM	654		J10	205
	AE10	232		L4	276		P3	86
	AE10	296		HAP	927		P3	99
	AE10	427		M1	1012		P3	127
	AE10	490		AE8	311		P3	136
	AE11	794		KT3	442		P3	138
	AE11	925		KT3	617		P5	87
	AE12	665		M8	134		SLT2	9
	AE12	809		CI	111		G2	150
	OAE2	76	LEANS	AA	79		G2	493
	KT3	698		MD	63		AE1	891
	TJD	1		G4	695		AE3	51
	FL	19		AE4	414		AE3	199
	FL	334		AE6	1032		AE5	635
LEAF	AT	66		M1	230		AE5	966
	AT	68	LEANT	AE10	1188		AE6	844
	HAP	1781	LEAP	AM	980		AE7	199
	HAP	1929		AM	1003		AE7	611
	AE6	397		SAA	406		AE8	680
	HIF	349		OE	30		AE12	224
	C	191		AT	58		AE12	644
	FL	423		L3	20		OAL	2

LEARN	OAL	452
	OAL	524
	OAE1	16
	MM	14
	KT2	249
	M8	234
	HIF	283
	HIF	568
	HIF	740
	C	92
	C	471
	C	598
	C	812
	WB	103
	WB	122
	M15	8
	CI	206
	CI	505
	PWR	29
LEARNED	UDH	39
	UDH	8
	UDH	71
	DC	33
	PWG	34
	AM	135
	PUO1	24
	EUO2	17
	POE	11
	PO	7
	PUO3	27
	PUO4	3
	AA	106
	PDG	15
	RL	243
	RL	386
	PD	36
	T18	59
	TA	344
	AK	195
	HAP	802
	HAP	2115
	HAP	2444
	HAP	2502
	J1	184
	P1	52
	P6	21
	GK	92
	G2	45
	G3	818
	OAL	531
	AE5	779
	OAL	886
	AF	156
	MFL	24
	DO	111
	KT1	200
	KT2	384
	TJD	71
	TJD	111
	AU	453
	CI	216
LEARNING	UDH	3
	UDH	32
	PUO1	1
	EUO2	21
	PO	23
	PUO4	1
	AA	871
	AA	883
	MF	177
	SAA	817
	RL	244
	RL	372
	RL	326
	L2	9
	HAP	1762
	PMS	28
	P1	56
	P3	45
	EHC	6
	EHC	9
	OAL	883
	WB	35
LEARNING'S	UDH	28
LEARNS	PAA	35
LEARNT	SMA	109
	MD	59
	SAA	643
	SAA	672
	J6	24
	J6	267
	M15	85
LEASE	AT	72
	M15	603
LEASH	P5	232
LEATHER	PDS	40

LEATHER	B	144
LEATHERN	J10	312
	AE7	951
	AE7	1011
	KT3	30
	B	159
	B	225
LEAVE	AR	106
	LC	22
	PIE	29
	AM	161
	AM	270
	SMM1	10
	PA	26
	SEL4	3
	SEL4	5
	ECG1	13
	SM2	10
	PLN	15
	ENH	22
	PAL	27
	HP	148
	HP	168
	HP	193
	HP	202
	HP	207
	DA	141
	DA	144
	DA	187
	PSF	38
	SSF	11
	PR	12
	PUF	15
	AA	169
	AA	459
	AA	979
	ELB	5
	MD	233
	MF	205
	SAA	187
	SAA	396
	SAA	451
	SAA	984
	EK	28
	EK	34
	EK	36
	PDG	33
	RL	296
	OE	4
	OE	47
	AT	27
	L3	161
	L3	280
	L4	295
	T18	22
	T18	23
	T27	60
	T27	91
	H29	10
	H29	12
	H2	97
	TA	152
	PAA	10
	PAA	28
	GE	53
	HAP	132
	HAP	314
	HAP	799
	HAP	423
	HAP	527
	HAP	1147
	HAP	2052
	HAP	2189
	HAP	2279
	HAP	2327
	BR	168
	EDS	24
	PP	18
	PP	25
	STS1	6
	STS1	15
	PKA	44
	ESH	15
	ESH	21
	ESH	24
	SSH	2
	J3	44
	J3	125
	J6	124
	J6	302
	J10	537
	P4	28
	P5	150
	P6	148
	M1	71
	PLT	53

LEAVE	ELT	12
	VP2	35
	VP2	47
	VP7	78
	VP9	57
	G1	20
	G1	54
	G1	498
	G2	606
	G3	815
	G4	132
	G4	347
	G4	428
	G4	516
	G4	647
	G4	785
	AE1	497
	AE1	731
	AE2	150
	AE2	485
	AE2	786
	AE2	811
	AE2	874
	AE3	15
	AE3	86
	AE3	98
	AE3	170
	AE3	279
	AE3	296
	AE3	319
	AE3	386
	AE3	577
	AE4	67
	AE4	517
	AE4	491
	AE4	837
	AE5	415
	AE5	456
	AE5	559
	AE5	953
	AE5	1039
	AE6	214
	AE6	510
	AE6	1136
	AE7	51
	AE7	358
	AE7	774
	AE7	820
	AE8	189
	AE8	541
	AE9	240
	AE9	384
	AE9	483
	AE9	500
	AE9	641
	AE10	44
	AE10	70
	AE10	87
	AE10	399
	AE10	739
	AE10	882
	AE10	951
	AE11	152
	AE11	179
	AE11	195
	AE11	382
	AE11	523
	AE11	593
	AE11	1226
	AE11	1280
	AE12	1
	AE12	566
	AE12	814
	AE12	821
	AE12	1169
	OAL	402
	OAL	572
	OAE2	64
	KT1	87
	KT1	209
	KT2	157
	KT2	239
	KT2	430
	KT2	665
	KT3	747
	KT3	771
	KT3	1065
	KT3	1093
	B	365
	B	578
	B	664
	BP	145
	CAM	171
	CAM	357
	HIF	234
	HIF	435

Word	Ref	Num	Word	Ref	Num	Word	Ref	Num
LEAVE	HIF	652	LEAVES	AE5	440	LED	SAA	439
	C	821		AE5	683		SAA	755
	TH	69		AE6	117		RL	12
	TH	137		AE6	211		AT	4
	TH	395		AE6	302		L2	58
	M11	19		AE6	428		L3	250
	M11	230		AE8	483		T18	5
	M11	416		AE8	601		TA	469
	M12	630		AE10	212		HH	42
	AU	26		AE10	401		HAP	720
	AU	360		AE11	98		HAP	860
	AU	365		AE11	1048		HAP	1306
	WB	114		AE11	1301		HAP	2445
	WB	496		AE12	423		PKA	19
	M15	30		AE12	494		J1	28
	M15	321		AE12	742		J1	70
	M15	215		AE12	1016		J6	66
	GP	107		OAL	119		J6	546
	CI	525		OAL	621		J10	429
	STP	26		DO	4		J10	541
	SMP	9		KT1	531		P1	158
	ERL	10		KT2	42		P1	199
	EWR	29		KT2	115		P5	69
LEAVENED	AE2	182		TJD	15		P5	244
	AE4	749		M8	30		M1	503
LEAVES	LC	48		BP	51		M1	716
	LC	110		BP	60		HI	53
	LC	103		BP	182		HI	78
	AM	244		CAM	153		HI	126
	CM	87		HIF	714		VP6	94
	AA	259		TH	88		VP7	6
	AA	343		TH	265		VP8	54
	AA	851		M11	266		VP8	64
	RL	308		M11	298		VP8	104
	OE	32		FL	44		VP9	29
	L4	118		FL	80		G2	491
	HH	28		FL	279		G2	777
	HAP	407		FL	578		G3	470
	HAP	478		M12	626		G4	222
	HAP	1734		WB	416		AE1	528
	HAP	2456		M15	65		AE1	892
	OD	8		M15	248		AE2	432
	J1	77		M15	307		AE2	461
	J6	5		M15	551		AE2	621
	J6	545		PTP	34		AE2	1090
	P2	48	LEAVEST	MD	174		AE3	476
	M1	412		L3	93		AE3	912
	M1	744		TA	290		AE4	312
	M1	869		HI	51		AE4	566
	M9	49	LEAVING	VHH	44		AE4	797
	PLT	35		AM	3		AE5	94
	PLT	36		PTL	9		AE5	321
	PLT	41		SAA	350		AE5	734
	PLT	43		PD	31		AE5	742
	PLT	45		SSH	11		AE5	870
	VP1	115		G2	736		AE5	882
	VP3	82		G3	667		AE6	230
	VP5	59		AE3	252		AE6	293
	G1	200		AE9	256		AE6	378
	G1	276		AE11	242		AE6	696
	G1	340		OAL	782		AE6	710
	G1	394		B	499		AE6	761
	G1	506		M15	18		AE6	918
	G1	517		CI	199		AE6	1227
	G1	597	LEAVY	L1	24		AE7	80
	G2	39		G1	491		AE7	244
	G2	97		FL	316		AE7	892
	G2	116		FL	512		AE7	904
	G2	385		M12	18		AE7	918
	G2	419	LECHER	PCB	7		AE7	933
	G2	438		J1	117		AE7	973
	G2	515		J6	57		AE7	979
	G2	554		M1	832		AE7	1003
	G2	568		G3	148		AE7	1027
	G2	621		G3	399		AE7	1032
	G2	626	LECHERS	UDH	85		AE7	1095
	G3	242	LECHERY	AA	472		AE8	9
	G3	278		J3	188		AE8	177
	G3	306		J6	437		AE8	278
	G3	334	LECTURE	EH	10		AE8	372
	G3	358		J6	374		AE8	481
	G3	546		P1	63		AE8	779
	G3	646	LECTURES	P3	105		AE8	801
	G3	657	LED	SMA	45		AE8	805
	G3	777		LC	154		AE8	851
	G4	195		AM	371		AE9	859
	G4	236		AM	704		AE9	1053
	G4	293		AM	943		AE10	285
	G4	394		PWGR	7		AE10	722
	AE1	247		PT	37		AE10	784
	AE1	431		EM	2		AE10	951
	AE3	639		ECD	1		AE11	113
	AE4	204		AA	55		AE11	132
	AE4	642		AA	311		AE11	255
	AE4	706		AA	527		AE11	290
	AE5	279		AA	870		AE11	404

Word	Code	Num
LED	AE11	854
	AE11	979
	AE12	754
	OAL	143
	AF	148
	AF	152
	KT2	548
	KT3	97
	KT3	614
	KT3	616
	B	268
	B	465
	B	480
	M10	59
	CAM	28
	HIF	485
	HIF	603
	C	7
	TH	72
	FL	37
	FL	60
	FL	252
	M12	267
	M12	351
	WB	5
	WB	210
	WB	541
	M15	301
	M15	424
	CI	199
LEDA'S	HP	45
	AE1	919
	M8	46
	M8	141
LEDGE	AE1	428
LEE	AM	509
	B	317
LEECH	P4	103
	G3	245
	AE12	621
	TJD	79
LEECHES	AR	175
	G3	818
LEECHES'	KT3	750
LEECH-LIKE	MD	149
LEEKS	J3	459
LEER	KT2	564
	C	482
	WB	39
LEERING	VP3	13
	ETO	1
LEES	AR	272
	SEL4	13
	J10	286
	G1	281
	BP	93
LEFT	UDH	48
	UDH	93
	SMA	6
	LC	59
	LC	62
	AM	119
	AM	232
	AM	583
	AM	700
	AM	904
	AM	919
	AM	1210
	PFD	15
	EM	14
	EUO	10
	EAL	2
	PKK	25
	PKK	28
	DA	7
	DA	85
	PUO5	14
	AA	400
	AA	568
	AA	761
	AA	858
	AA	989
	MF	129
	MF	214
	SAA	94
	SAA	291
	PK	11
	L3	46
	L3	120
	L3	287
	TA	241
	TA	282
	TA	413
	AK	37
	GE	34
	HAP	228

Word	Code	Num
LEFT	HAP	817
	HAP	826
	HAP	1208
	HAP	1573
	HAP	1770
	HAP	1849
	HAP	2008
	HAP	2259
	HAP	2278
	SSC	49
	BR	14
	BR	308
	PTS	34
	PKA	48
	EL	239
	EL	336
	EL	346
	OD	28
	ODA	81
	EH	19
	J1	20
	J1	141
	J1	230
	J3	49
	J3	201
	J3	214
	J3	224
	J6	43
	J6	117
	J6	120
	J6	304
	J10	69
	J10	361
	P1	202
	P2	97
	P5	41
	P5	48
	P5	125
	P5	127
	P6	126
	P6	151
	P6	161
	P6	180
	M1	67
	M1	223
	M1	336
	M1	432
	M1	476
	M1	487
	M13	712
	M13	139
	SFL	9
	HI	62
	DHP	22
	EHC	39
	VP1	20
	VP1	26
	VP2	86
	VP8	129
	G1	324
	G4	331
	G4	487
	G4	724
	AE1	3
	AE1	51
	AE1	161
	AE1	272
	AE1	500
	AE1	691
	AE1	728
	AE1	863
	AE2	121
	AE2	133
	AE2	224
	AE2	605
	AE2	689
	AE2	754
	AE2	940
	AE2	1017
	AE3	367
	AE3	537
	AE3	809
	AE3	901
	AE4	126
	AE4	469
	AE4	474
	AE4	599
	AE4	479
	AE4	734
	AE4	839
	AE4	862
	AE4	908
	AE4	929
	AE5	425
	AE5	733
	AE5	848

Word	Code	Num
LEFT	AE5	1080
	AE6	695
	AE6	728
	AE6	739
	AE6	1011
	AE7	2
	AE7	711
	AE7	776
	AE7	832
	AE7	953
	AE7	1014
	AE8	25
	AE8	145
	AE8	312
	AE8	804
	AE8	856
	AE8	878
	AE9	10
	AE9	302
	AE9	529
	AE9	556
	AE9	624
	AE9	655
	AE9	739
	AE9	864
	AE9	889
	AE9	921
	AE9	940
	AE9	998
	AE10	37
	AE10	101
	AE10	237
	AE10	320
	AE10	474
	AE10	508
	AE10	529
	AE10	690
	AE10	744
	AE10	825
	AE10	1015
	AE11	2
	AE11	15
	AE11	171
	AE11	799
	AE11	1023
	AE12	244
	AE12	457
	AE12	484
	AE12	710
	AE12	990
	AE12	1149
	OAL	549
	AF	26
	ETO	3
	DO	17
	KT1	34
	KT1	107
	KT1	139
	KT2	43
	KT2	326
	KT2	402
	KT2	646
	KT3	170
	KT3	252
	KT3	255
	KT3	426
	KT3	944
	KT3	995
	TJD	131
	TJD	163
	M8	125
	B	36
	B	38
	B	167
	B	222
	B	302
	B	345
	B	456
	B	581
	B	586
	M10	34
	CAM	304
	CAM	307
	CAM	319
	HIF	508
	HIF	590
	C	640
	TH	73
	TH	196
	M11	86
	M11	187
	M11	364
	M11	442
	FL	309
	M12	170
	M12	348

Word	Ref	No.
LEFT	M12	464
	M12	500
	M12	832
	AU	92
	AU	78
	AU	76
	AU	63
	AU	176
	AU	484
	WB	76
	WB	164
	WB	205
	WB	446
	GP	23
	GP	93
	CI	431
	CI	535
	CI	615
	SMP	82
	ERL	3
	PMK	18
	PMK	10
	AS	77
LEFT-HAND	HAP	353
LEG	OAE2	55
	BP	86
	BP	148
LEGACIES	J1	59
	P6	153
LEGACY	LC	62
	AA	438
	MD	261
	J6	302
	PLT	53
	AE10	1263
LEGATES	M1	297
	AE11	348
LEGATOR'S	HAP	947
LEGEND	STS2	11
	J6	838
	J10	287
	G4	407
	C	476
	CI	40
LEGENDS	PT	25
	AE6	346
	BP	6
	C	335
	C	361
	C	569
LEGGS	ETO	3
LEGION	AR	182
	ESF	18
	AE9	503
	AE12	187
LEGIONS	AA	852
	SAA	133
	SAA	557
	SAA	1035
	L2	6
	L2	47
	L3	245
	G2	378
	AE9	212
LEGISLATORS	HH	8
	PDS	28
LEGITIMATELY	TA	456
LEGS	EMQW	22
	L3	78
	T18	17
	HAP	163
	HAP	586
	J3	333
	J3	399
	J10	359
	J16	34
	M1	315
	M1	712
	VP7	46
	G4	376
	G4	439
	AE5	628
	KT2	646
	KT3	34
	M8	68
	BP	138
	CAM	339
	HIF	640
	C	52
	C	460
	C	644
	FL	551
	M12	537
	M15	339
	M15	555
	M15	558

Word	Ref	No.
LEISURE	ECG1	35
	E	27
	AA	612
	EK	48
	AK	53
	J1	166
	G2	82
	OAL	422
	DO	96
	KT3	151
	M8	81
	B	435
	B	468
	CAM	158
	C	375
	M15	565
	CI	380
	PTP	41
LEISURELY	AM	727
LELEX	M8	57
	BP	11
LEMAN	HAP	179
LEMNIAN	AE8	597
	AE9	1011
	AE12	165
	HIF	798
LEMNOS	AU	484
LEND	JH	3
	EM	29
	J3	230
	P5	112
	P6	73
	M9	210
	AE1	218
	AE6	504
	AE6	828
	AE7	533
	AE9	182
	AE9	309
	AE11	660
	AE11	730
	AE12	227
	OAL	303
	OAL	495
	DO	98
	TJD	187
	TJD	191
	M8	171
	M11	157
	AU	107
	M15	660
	M15	695
LENDEST	TJD	196
LENDS	P1	19
	AE3	832
	AE5	192
LENGTH	AR	199
	RH	53
	LC	12
	LC	23
	AM	53
	AM	422
	AM	611
	AM	745
	AM	835
	AM	897
	AM	935
	AM	1117
	PWGR	8
	SM2	14
	AA	89
	AA	793
	AA	1002
	AA	1025
	MF	9
	MF	138
	RL	134
	L3	316
	L4	297
	HAP	659
	STS3	5
	OD	34
	ODA	50
	J3	409
	J6	28
	J6	180
	J6	551
	J6	623
	J6	679
	J10	237
	J10	301
	J10	387
	J10	395
	P2	70
	M1	234
	M1	469

Word	Ref	No.
LENGTH	M1	524
	M1	815
	M1	849
	M1	903
	M1	986
	M1	991
	M1	1010
	M1	1011
	M1	1042
	M9	198
	M13	54
	MC	11
	MC	15
	GK	59
	VP1	37
	VP1	92
	VP5	30
	G1	662
	G2	147
	G2	211
	G2	261
	G2	290
	G2	342
	G2	405
	G2	420
	G2	496
	G2	576
	G3	98
	G3	273
	G3	528
	G3	643
	G3	717
	G3	827
	G4	330
	G4	415
	G4	443
	G4	641
	G4	656
	G4	696
	G4	757
	AE1	49
	AE1	72
	AE1	310
	AE1	336
	AE1	382
	AE1	486
	AE1	520
	AE1	560
	AE1	1056
	AE2	97
	AE2	311
	AE2	372
	AE2	620
	AE2	659
	AE2	1046
	AE2	1059
	AE3	50
	AE3	180
	AE3	274
	AE3	319
	AE3	355
	AE3	400
	AE3	444
	AE3	486
	AE3	559
	AE3	929
	AE4	194
	AE4	212
	AE4	283
	AE4	439
	AE4	482
	AE4	571
	AE4	654
	AE4	888
	AE5	242
	AE5	280
	AE5	1114
	AE6	2
	AE6	21
	AE6	95
	AE6	153
	AE6	415
	AE6	452
	AE6	560
	AE6	938
	AE6	1009
	AE6	1246
	AE7	217
	AE7	295
	AE7	311
	AE7	318
	AE7	353
	AE7	413
	AE7	429
	AE8	82
	AE8	223

Word	Ref	Num
LENGTH	AE8	760
	AE8	847
	AE8	878
	AE9	78
	AE9	90
	AE9	125
	AE9	207
	AE9	527
	AE9	543
	AE9	935
	AE9	1102
	AE10	15
	AE10	766
	AE10	852
	AE10	891
	AE10	972
	AE10	1028
	AE10	1162
	AE10	1275
	AE11	267
	AE11	825
	AE11	939
	AE11	955
	AE11	1028
	AE11	1241
	AE12	18
	AE12	392
	AE12	537
	AE12	1092
	AE12	1280
	OAL	102
	OAL	541
	OAL	544
	OAL	733
	OAE2	73
	AF	114
	AF	121
	AF	165
	AF	175
	MG	33
	DO	22
	DO	26
	KT1	27
	KT1	68
	KT1	183
	KT1	358
	KT1	506
	KT3	182
	KT3	370
	KT3	398
	KT3	351
	KT3	434
	KT3	511
	KT3	636
	KT3	650
	KT3	715
	KT3	747
	KT3	1022
	KT3	1069
	M8	244
	M8	287
	B	19
	B	64
	B	477
	B	697
	CAM	232
	CAM	290
	CAM	320
	CAM	381
	HIF	55
	HIF	445
	HIF	531
	HIF	798
	C	237
	C	626
	TH	25
	TH	48
	M11	60
	M11	306
	M11	496
	FL	110
	FL	122
	FL	153
	FL	300
	M12	652
	M12	683
	M12	737
	M12	763
	AU	267
	AU	335
	WB	510
	M15	529
	M15	558
	CI	175
	CI	198
	CI	609
LENGTH	PMK	1
LENGTHEN	TA	209
	BR	318
	VP2	98
	G1	691
	M11	426
LENGTHENED	AR	136
	HAP	1569
	BR	8
	AE9	809
	AE10	880
	KT1	506
	KT2	24
	BP	184
	AS	6
LENGTHENING	AA	269
	AE10	869
LENIFY	AE12	594
LENITIVES	AA	926
	EDG	29
LENT	AM	1011
	EEL	5
	PKK	19
	AA	203
	AA	365
	MD	82
	RL	6
	TA	108
	HAP	1263
	HAP	1676
	VP8	66
	AE4	527
	AE6	44
	AE6	723
	AE9	863
	AE11	65
	OAE2	82
	KT3	696
	HIF	268
	C	9
	C	482
	FL	196
LENTEN	HAP	1321
LENTILS	G1	316
LEOPARDS	KT3	97
LEO'S	GK	98
LERNAEAN	AE6	1096
LERNA'S	M1	813
	AE8	399
	AE12	754
LESBIAN	G2	129
LESBIAS	J6	10
LESBOS	AU	281
LESSON	TA	402
	P1	179
	WB	276
LESSONS	HAP	905
	CI	215
LETHAEAN	G4	786
	AE6	1016
LETHARGY	TA	2
LETHE	AE5	1111
	AE6	957
	M11	282
LETHE'S	AE6	968
LETTER	AR	268
	CM	1
	HP	63
	RL	366
	J10	109
	J16	7
	P5	129
	AE11	820
	OAL	518
	OAL	520
	OAL	528
	OAL	531
	OAE2	23
	B	137
LETTER-BEARING	OE	42
LETTERS	PA	47
	SAA	448
	HAP	910
	J6	201
	J6	329
	P6	97
	OAL	498
	OAL	642
	AU	612
	PTP	9.
LEUCADIAN	M15	440
LEUCASPIS	AE6	457
LEUCATE'S	AE3	355
	AE8	898
LEUCIPPUS	M8	55
LEVÉ	M1	1086
LEVEE	J6	428
LEVÉES	HAP	516
	J10	146
	J3	217
	G4	316
LEVEL	EWGR	3
	PUO2	33
	PAL	27
	PKA	6
	J10	237
	J10	250
	P1	125
	AE8	493
	AE9	708
	AE11	797
	AE12	775
	AE12	832
	KT2	440
	B	142
	B	221
	BP	152
	M15	410
	M15	453
	PTP	27
LEVELED	AM	664
	HAP	46
	HAP	635
	PMS	16
	M1	421
	M12	723
LEVELING	PTS	12
LEVELS	G2	774
	B	283
LEVER	M12	400
LEVERS	AE8	298
LEVI	SAA	400
LEVIATHANS	AM	810
LEVIED	SAA	229
LEVI'S	HAP	2261
LEVITE	AA	644
	SAA	89
	SAA	355
LEVITES	AA	519
LEWD	PWGR	15
	EUO	12
	PAL	12
	PLB	29
	EPC	9
	MD	299
	MF	71
	SAA	478
	J1	44
	J3	192
	J6	63
	J6	454
	J10	377
	P4	120
	P5	81
	P5	136
	P5	237
	AE10	543
	AE11	1087
	OAE2	6
	WB	488
	PTP	8
LEWDER	PUO3	26
	P4	86
LEWDLY	J6	418
LEWDNESS	MD	37
	PD	58
	MS	17
	ETP	5
	ETP	28
LEWIS	AM	169
LEYS	VP3	15
LIABLE	EL	334
	KT1	476
	AU	534
	CI	454
LIBATIONS	AE1	1031
	HIF	645
LIBEL	PLG	6
	SAA	1030
	HAP	2343
	PTS	19
	GK	163
LIBELS	ML	9
	EDGA	19
	EDGA	29
	EDGA	37
	HAP	1459
LIBEL-SPAWNING	SAA	520
LIBERAL	HS	9
	PD	55
	T27	108
	HAP	1546

Word	Ref	No.
LIBERAL	G4	543
	M8	11
	C	92
	C	132
	CI	35
	CI	213
LIBERALLY	PMQ	39
LIBERTIES	PUF	21
	AA	704
LIBERTY	AR	46
	PT	22
	AA	52
	AA	292
	AA	316
	AA	341
	RL	317
	HAP	519
	J3	471
	P3	91
	P5	44
	P5	118
	P5	131
	VP1	38
	VP1	57
	OAL	728
	KT1	371
	KT1	511
	KT2	5
	KT2	275
	KT2	291
	TJD	193
	B	509
	HIF	18
	HIF	464
	HIF	514
	C	386
	C	536
	CI	529
LIBRA	C	682
LIBYA	G3	390
LIBYAN	AM	381
	DA	183
	VP1	88
	VP5	42
	VP9	30
	VP10	97
	G1	331
	G2	151
	G3	524
	AE1	227
	AE1	310
	AE1	414
	AE1	465
	AE1	510
	AE1	520
	AE1	533
	AE1	781
	AE1	835
	AE4	52
	AE4	150
	AE4	251
	AE4	311
	AE4	395
	AE4	379
	AE4	464
	AE4	501
	AE4	901
	AE5	49
	AE5	1032
	AE6	941
	AE7	994
	AE12	9
LIBYA'S	VP5	41
LICE	G3	842
LICENSE	PA	34
	SAA	15
	HAP	1551
	HAP	2530
	J1	233
	AE3	593
	HIF	410
	HIF	699
	M15	154
LICENTIOUS	SAA	762
	G3	275
LICHAS	AE10	437
LICINIUS	J1	165
LICK	TA	480
	G3	698
	AE3	750
	KT3	991
LICKED	HAP	1292
	M1	892
	AE2	279
	AE8	840
	M8	344

Word	Ref	No.
LICKS	AM	525
	M1	722
	KT2	42
	M15	561
LICTORS	J3	219
	J10	49
	P1	145
	AE7	235
LICYMNIA	AE9	732
LID	B	612
	B	629
	HIF	785
	CI	161
LIDS	M1	860
	M1	990
	VP3	58
	AE4	992
	AE12	468
	OAL	746
LIE	AR	132
	SMA	56
	AM	102
	AM	278
	AM	392
	AM	403
	AM	519
	AM	718
	AM	780
	AM	808
	AM	809
	AM	1029
	AM	1114
	AM	1119
	PEL	4
	SCG3	22
	PAR	23
	SM2	16
	PTW	13
	PCB	17
	PLG	31
	HP	177
	DA	162
	PPC	15
	MF	128
	SAA	115
	SAA	632
	SAA	819
	RL	143
	OE	13
	OE	22
	AT	103
	DOD	22
	L3	72
	L3	195
	L3	314
	L4	81
	L4	223
	T27	107
	AK	121
	GE	24
	HAP	80
	HAP	333
	HAP	1261
	HAP	1559
	HAP	2219
	HAP	2308
	HAP	2416
	BR	78
	EL	79
	EL	95
	J3	76
	J3	247
	J3	275
	J3	409
	J6	354
	J6	838
	J16	52
	P3	4
	P5	202
	P6	69
	M1	16
	M1	62
	M1	194
	M1	276
	M1	439
	M1	841
	M1	1080
	M9	148
	M13	129
	SLT2	10
	GK	49
	VP2	21
	VP10	51
	G1	625
	G1	682
	G2	737

Word	Ref	No.
LIE	G3	473
	G3	630
	G3	830
	G4	39
	G4	118
	AE1	141
	AE1	252
	AE2	102
	AE2	298
	AE2	558
	AE3	303
	AE3	419
	AE3	569
	AE4	36
	AE4	127
	AE4	647
	AE4	730
	AE4	892
	AE5	146
	AE5	169
	AE5	1090
	AE5	1136
	AE6	784
	AE6	818
	AE6	914
	AE6	1054
	AE7	124
	AE7	177
	AE7	309
	AE7	606
	AE7	988
	AE8	61
	AE8	253
	AE8	765
	AE9	243
	AE9	427
	AE9	459
	AE10	149
	AE10	158
	AE10	778
	AE10	779
	AE10	953
	AE10	1143
	AE11	641
	AE11	771
	AE11	850
	AE11	943
	AE11	1317
	AE12	832
	AE12	1293
	MM	11
	KT1	85
	KT1	161
	KT1	245
	KT1	266
	KT3	328
	KT3	598
	KT3	919
	KT3	1064
	TJD	192
	B	212
	B	316
	BP	83
	BP	194
	CAM	243
	HIF	440
	C	224
	C	481
	C	815
	M12	778
	AU	100
	AU	123
	AU	385
	M15	281
	EWR	29
LIED	P5	109
	AE6	474
LIEGE	WB	278
	WB	293
LIES	AM	298
	AM	526
	EWGR	3
	ETL	29
	CM	4
	DA	150
	DA	210
	PUO4	21
	AA	114
	AA	652
	EPC	14
	MD	88
	MF	201
	SAA	188
	SAA	243
	SAA	252
	SAA	907

LIES

PDG	20
RL	273
L1	49
L2	57
L3	39
L3	109
L3	189
L3	297
L4	151
L5	3
T23	86
T27	57
H2	37
FS2	15
AK	152
HAP	1044
HAP	1493
HAP	1563
HAP	1949
HAP	2162
BR	110
BR	124
ETS	28
SKA2	23
J3	55
J3	152
J6	176
J6	438
J6	495
J6	535
J6	594
J10	45
J10	531
P1	58
P1	75
P1	92
P3	208
P5	5
M1	221
M1	421
M1	999
M9	158
HI	92
HI	179
ELT	5
EHC	30
VP2	104
VP3	14
VP3	33
VP3	167
VP10	24
G1	98
G1	550
G1	587
G2	424
G3	357
G3	547
G3	813
G4	247
G4	603
G4	638
G4	778
AE1	228
AE1	420
AE2	27
AE2	306
AE2	762
AE2	825
AE3	143
AE3	617
AE3	700
AE3	704
AE3	909
AE4	58
AE4	271
AE5	34
AE6	160
AE6	195
AE6	227
AE6	780
AE6	909
AE6	1238
AE7	570
AE7	746
AE7	778
AE8	347
AE8	563
AE8	861
AE8	956
AE9	79
AE9	339
AE9	431
AE9	441
AE9	599
AE9	646
AE10	523

LIES

AE10	884
AE10	1023
AE10	1029
AE10	1039
AE10	1258
AE11	25
AE11	99
AE11	127
AE11	226
AE11	624
AE11	791
AE11	822
AE11	990
AE11	1060
AE12	561
AE12	934
OAL	295
OAL	343
OAL	433
OAL	492
AF	82
KT1	494
KT2	478
KT2	534
KT3	165
KT3	753
M8	207
M8	364
M8	370
BP	6
BP	138
BP	152
M10	74
HIF	159
C	163
C	238
C	272
C	776
C	799
TH	186
M11	462
M11	480
M12	80
WB	129
M15	334
M15	373
M15	598
M15	670
M15	686
UDH	62
UDH	68
UDH	75
AR	11
AR	54
AR	317
SMA	2
PWG	27
PWG	31
LCA	52
SIE	3
AM	416
AM	1040
PWGR	15
SCG3	26
PUO2	8
EKK	5
STC	1
STC	3
PCB	3
CM	67
CM	133
HP	170
DA	8
DA	83
DA	141
DA	196
EPF	13
AA	43
AA	168
AA	457
AA	465
AA	479
AA	667
AA	749
AA	858
AA	1015
SAA	54
SAA	55
SAA	143
SAA	505
SAA	595
SAA	769
SAA	948
SAA	1091
RL	132
OE	54

LIFE

LIFE

AT	92
EC	27
L1	52
L2	11
L2	16
L2	58
L3	21
L3	38
L3	47
L3	56
L3	85
L3	91
L3	102
L3	120
L3	126
L3	131
L3	135
L3	144
L3	158
L3	173
L3	201
L3	235
L3	263
L3	270
L3	301
L3	303
L3	311
L3	314
L3	315
L4	95
L4	115
L4	149
L4	243
T23	44
H29	80
H2	3
H2	59
TA	91
TA	101
TA	155
TA	186
TA	285
AK	79
AK	156
AK	187
HH	2
HAP	78
HAP	137
HAP	441
HAP	624
HAP	1655
HAP	1982
HAP	2237
HAP	2331
HAP	2363
BR	246
BR	354
BR	357
EDS	31
ETS	26
STS3	20
ELW	8
EL	8
EL	114
EL	271
EL	280
EL	315
OD	10
ODA	50
EH	7
J3	231
J6	40
J6	57
J6	235
J6	310
J6	441
J6	559
J6	644
J6	851
J10	4
J10	301
J10	426
J10	503
J10	526
J10	553
P2	59
P3	116
P3	135
P4	74
P5	136
P5	223
M1	186
M1	481
M1	486
M1	556
SFL	22

Headword	Ref	No.
LIFE	HI	54
	HI	63
	HI	132
	HI	180
	SLT1	1
	GK	18
	GK	154
	VP2	106
	VP4	18
	G2	501
	G2	656
	G2	689
	G2	777
	G2	780
	G3	844
	G4	301
	G4	465
	G4	657
	G4	757
	AE1	15
	AE1	249
	AE1	481
	AE1	641
	AE1	837
	AE1	942
	AE2	476
	AE2	586
	AE2	769
	AE2	866
	AE2	877
	AE2	924
	AE2	964
	AE2	1049
	AE3	407
	AE3	437
	AE3	612
	AE3	793
	AE4	492
	AE4	797
	AE4	996
	AE4	1009
	AE4	44
	AE4	335
	AE5	683
	AE5	981
	AE6	181
	AE6	355
	AE6	462
	AE6	468
	AE6	589
	AE6	688
	AE6	969
	AE6	986
	AE6	1038
	AE7	1057
	AE8	760
	AE9	264
	AE9	269
	AE9	275
	AE9	385
	AE9	541
	AE9	598
	AE9	656
	AE9	806
	AE9	831
	AE10	334
	AE10	440
	AE10	486
	AE10	657
	AE10	729
	AE10	734
	AE10	766
	AE10	837
	AE10	841
	AE10	869
	AE10	891
	AE10	939
	AE10	1076
	AE10	1162
	AE10	1209
	AE10	1232
	AE10	1299
	AE11	243
	AE11	414
	AE11	417
	AE11	574
	AE11	849
	AE11	854
	AE11	1090
	AE11	1101
	AE11	1149
	AE11	1225
	AE12	79
	AE12	84
	AE12	92
	AE12	97
LIFE	AE12	355
	AE12	635
	AE12	754
	AE12	1056
	AE12	1109
	AE12	1184
	AE12	1261
	AE12	1270
	AE12	1277
	AE12	1357
	OAL	376
	LMC	7
	KT1	152
	KT1	267
	KT1	380
	KT1	412
	KT1	419
	KT1	428
	KT1	490
	KT1	509
	KT1	521
	KT2	31
	KT2	253
	KT2	265
	KT2	291
	KT2	292
	KT2	295
	KT2	372
	KT2	469
	KT3	18
	KT3	143
	KT3	223
	KT3	340
	KT3	505
	KT3	520
	KT3	722
	KT3	764
	KT3	773
	KT3	810
	KT3	814
	KT3	829
	KT3	838
	KT3	1043
	KT3	1073
	KT3	1092
	KT3	1108
	KT3	1148
	TJD	1
	TJD	63
	TJD	87
	TJD	99
	M8	328
	M8	372
	B	13
	B	277
	B	327
	B	330
	B	334
	B	357
	B	380
	B	391
	B	400
	B	448
	B	506
	B	572
	B	587
	B	651
	BP	134
	BP	140
	BP	171
	M10	1
	CAM	86
	CAM	161
	CAM	324
	CAM	330
	CAM	357
	CAM	385
	HIF	44
	HIF	115
	HIF	420
	HIF	494
	HIF	736
	HIF	758
	C	7
	C	55
	C	112
	C	361
	C	367
	C	553
	C	707
	TH	42
	TH	157
	TH	163
	TH	164
	TH	176
	TH	179
LIFE	TH	187
	TH	394
	M11	20
	M11	56
	M11	65
	M11	362
	M11	426
	M11	456
	M11	468
	FL	9
	FL	585
	M12	251
	AU	120
	AU	468
	WB	86
	WB	92
	WB	99
	WB	147
	WB	239
	WB	243
	WB	251
	WB	288
	WB	303
	WB	325
	WB	353
	WB	489
	WB	499
	WB	512
	WB	528
	WB	539
	M15	54
	M15	135
	M15	199
	M15	229
	M15	298
	M15	582
	M15	586
	M15	603
	M15	687
	M15	705
	M15	709
	GP	79
	GP	87
	CI	134
	CI	417
	CI	484
	CI	511
	CI	535
LIFEBLOOD	AE10	486
LIFELESS	L3	10
	M1	11
	M1	572
	VP5	32
	VP8	81
	AE1	679
	AE1	682
	AE6	493
	AE10	687
	AE12	742
	KT1	88
	KT3	255
	KT3	909
LIFE'S	DC	30
	AE9	369
LIFT	AM	584
	AM	910
	CM	20
	HAP	1111
	J1	26
	M9	147
	VP2	49
	G2	498
	G2	694
	AE3	235
	AE9	925
	AE10	1183
	AE12	1304
	OAE2	59
	HIF	230
	HIF	763
	M11	137
LIFTED	AM	156
	AM	1131
	AA	728
	RL	209
	BR	80
	P2	73
	P4	16
	J3	183
	J10	192
	G1	506
	G4	251
	AE1	136
	AE1	611
	AE2	205
	AE2	454

LIFTED	AE5	334	LIGHT	EL	77	LIGHT	AE6	342
	AE5	499		EL	135		AE6	367
	AE5	673		EL	145		AE6	381
	AE6	217		EL	200		AE6	494
	AE9	856		ODA	31		AE6	593
	AE10	282		J1	40		AE6	615
	AE10	1132		J1	236		AE6	625
	AE10	1156		J3	12		AE6	1030
	AE10	1204		J3	92		AE6	1137
	AE12	403		J6	401		AE7	11
	OAE2	21		J6	427		AE7	17
	M12	395		J10	105		AE7	671
	M12	516		J16	3		AE7	776
	AU	128		P1	78		AE7	1010
	AU	327		P5	171		AE7	1013
LIFTING	AE3	344		M1	19		AE7	1025
LIFTS	RH	12		M1	24		AE8	35
	AM	994		M1	78		AE8	229
	H29	58		M1	85		AE8	322
	M9	50		M1	91		AE8	545
	G4	499		M1	171		AE8	826
	AE8	821		M1	585		AE9	130
	AE9	17		M1	660		AE9	190
	AE11	1050		M1	831		AE9	614
	KT2	187		M1	1000		AE9	737
	M8	340		M1	1079		AE10	248
	FL	591		M1	1095		AE10	341
LIGEA	G4	484		M9	30		AE10	636
LIGER	AE9	775		M9	54		AE10	660
	AE9	776		M9	160		AE10	695
	AE10	810		M9	171		AE10	736
	AE10	811		VCS	7		AE10	1221
	AE10	816		SLT1	25		AE10	1273
	AE10	822		GK	14		AE11	282
	AE10	835		GK	41		AE11	287
LIGHT	HS	90		GK	42		AE11	307
	HS	95		GK	69		AE11	319
	AR	96		VP10	51		AE11	776
	AR	149		G1	124		AE12	120
	AR	289		G1	342		AE12	174
	RH	90		G1	385		AE12	552
	LC	48		G1	504		AE12	1224
	DC	4		G1	537		OAL	186
	DC	35		G1	592		OAL	287
	LCA	26		G1	615		OAL	626
	PRL	14		G1	625		OAL	628
	PIE	14		G1	630		AF	149
	AM	72		G2	310		AF	153
	AM	239		G2	316		MFL	13
	AM	503		G2	466		KT1	122
	AM	513		G2	633		KT1	187
	AM	559		G2	687		KT1	208
	AM	1012		G3	308		KT1	230
	AM	1088		G3	613		KT1	235
	PAL	29		G3	824		KT2	4
	CM	52		G4	114		KT2	26
	CM	121		G4	274		KT2	552
	HP	119		G4	354		KT2	650
	DA	26		G4	613		KT3	28
	AA	212		G4	676		KT3	120
	AA	274		G4	698		KT3	151
	MD	9		G4	706		KT3	189
	RL	5		G4	804		KT3	218
	RL	11		AE1	132		KT3	251
	RL	69		AE2	328		KT3	256
	RL	183		AE2	335		KT3	265
	RL	209		AE2	367		KT3	364
	ER	35		AE2	416		KT3	602
	L1	6		AE2	420		KT3	950
	L1	11		AE2	799		KT3	972
	L2	29		AE2	803		KT3	999
	L4	186		AE2	1079		B	84
	T18	93		AE3	206		B	116
	H2	52		AE3	268		B	136
	TA	156		AE3	406		B	207
	TA	377		AE3	662		B	211
	AK	81		AE3	682		B	289
	AK	85		AE3	765		B	538
	AK	177		AE4	115		B	723
	HAP	31		AE4	164		M10	95
	HAP	66		AE4	359		CAM	153
	HAP	98		AE4	654		CAM	269
	HAP	113		AE4	743		CAM	310
	HAP	501		AE4	840		HIF	57
	HAP	1223		AE4	990		HIF	714
	HAP	1230		AE4	1004		HIF	746
	HAP	1821		AE5	33		HIF	806
	HAP	2308		AE5	56		C	103
	HAP	2587		AE5	83		C	261
	BR	63		AE5	85		C	284
	BR	83		AE5	139		C	329
	BR	120		AE5	886		C	433
	BR	133		AE5	968		C	449
	BR	263		AE5	1092		TH	247
	PMS	17		AE6	162		TH	335
	EL	17		AE6	198		TH	336

Word	Ref	No.
LIGHT	TH	407
	M11	64
	M11	138
	M11	157
	M11	302
	FL	484
	FL	494
	M12	345
	M12	747
	AU	129
	AU	276
	AU	523
	WB	7
	WB	214
	WB	217
	WB	239
	WB	441
	M15	83
	M15	217
	M15	278
	M15	292
	M15	496
	GP	140
	CI	117
	CI	146
	CI	545
	STP	14
	SMP	79
	AS	5
	AS	14
	AS	36
LIGHTED	J3	453
	M1	13
	VP9	64
	M11	390
	FL	438
LIGHTEN	CI	498
	SMP	15
LIGHTENED	AM	922
	EL	81
	AE11	216
	AE12	387
	DO	49
	FL	297
LIGHTENS	M15	606
LIGHTER	M1	62
	G1	434
	G2	344
	AE9	972
	M11	202
	FL	45
LIGHTEST	L4	296
	AK	190
LIGHT-FOOT	AE11	807
LIGHTING	TA	341
	AE5	1096
	KT2	49
LIGHTLY	RH	37
	P1	75
	G1	101
	G1	425
	AE5	348
	AE12	532
	KT1	97
	FL	57
	FL	292
LIGHTNESS	M1	34
LIGHTNING	AM	448
	AM	834
	EUO	23
	E	8
	DA	73
	HAP	223
	M1	198
	M13	172
	G1	377
	G4	712
	AE2	633
	AE2	943
	AE4	232
	AE5	911
	AE6	783
	AE8	694
	AE10	794
	AE12	950
	KT2	244
	M8	100
	FL	385
	CI	334
LIGHTNING'S	AE11	919
LIGHTNINGS	G1	656
	AE4	306
	AE6	791
	AE8	518
	M11	40
	M11	124
LIGHTNINGS	M11	160
	GP	38
LIGHTS	AM	63
	AM	113
	AM	1165
	TA	341
	HAP	74
	VP8	40
	G1	341
	AE4	372
	AE6	982
	AE6	1086
	AE8	341
	AE8	349
	AE8	779
	AE9	209
	AE10	382
	AE10	1281
	AE11	756
	HIF	370
	M11	60
	WB	55
	M15	242
LIGHTSOME	M11	271
	FL	4
LIGURIAN	P6	14
	AE11	1038
	AE11	1057
LIGURIANS	G2	232
LIKE	PWG	2
	EWG	8
	AM	832
	PMQ	35
	PCG1	33
	PAR	14
	EAL	16
	EOE	22
	HP	72
	PLB	48
	HAP	2270
	HAP	2279
	PKA	15
	J3	2
	PLT	21
	PLT	33
	EHC	14
	EHC	25
	VP9	44
	OAL	170
	C	400
	CI	141
	CI	143
	PA	10
LIKED	PCG1	24
	ELN	15
	PD	22
	HAP	1771
	DO	137
	CAM	119
	WB	53
	WB	54
	CI	237
	EWR	1
LIKELIEST	OAL	54
LIKELY	RL	437
LIKENESS	MF	194
	L4	210
	L4	225
	L4	230
	L4	231
	GK	26
	GK	67
	GK	106
	GK	107
	AE4	122
	M10	67
	C	60
LIKES	EAZ	14
	EAL	16
	PUO4	17
	EKA	40
	OAL	170
	CI	148
LIKEWISE	RH	104
LIKING	TA	153
	J10	515
	L3	156
	OAL	566
	CI	142
LILBURNE	ETC	26
LILIES	AM	576
	T23	59
	M13	67
	VP2	21
	VP2	61
	VP10	38
LILIES	G4	195
	AE6	960
	AE6	1222
	AE12	107
	M12	546
LILLY	EMM	13
	EUF	14
LILY	UDH	58
	AR	18
	SAA	58
	ETS	7
	KT1	171
	KT1	192
LILYBAEAN	AE3	927
LILY'S	AR	18
LILY-WHITE	KT3	89
LIMB	UDH	37
	PCG2	17
	EAZ	27
	PTW	30
	AA	392
	SAA	944
	L4	217
	J10	346
	G3	120
	KT2	123
	M10	33
	C	657
LIMBECS	AM	51
	AM	663
LIMBER	EM	5
	J10	328
LIMBOS	SAA	94
LIMBS	CM	44
	CM	141
	HP	245
	MF	99
	AT	8
	L1	53
	L2	35
	L3	50
	L4	70
	L4	190
	HAP	1282
	BR	255
	J3	414
	J6	152
	J6	347
	J6	677
	J10	96
	J10	275
	J10	317
	P3	9
	P3	202
	P5	192
	M1	571
	M1	960
	M13	155
	M13	162
	M13	180
	M13	182
	GK	60
	VP5	32
	VP8	81
	VP9	85
	VP1Q	60
	VP10	73
	G1	465
	G2	12
	G2	442
	G2	727
	G2	769
	G2	775
	G3	91
	G3	146
	G3	356
	G3	678
	G3	683
	G3	685
	G3	698
	G3	729
	G3	844
	G4	97
	G4	278
	G4	584
	G4	634
	G4	759
	AE1	296
	AE2	233
	AE2	283
	AE2	331
	AE2	695
	AE2	1019
	AE3	68
	AE3	104
	AE3	234

Word	Code	No.		Word	Code	No.		Word	Code	No.
LIMBS	AE3	364		LINDEN	BP	192		LINE	AE12	807
	AE3	398		LINE	JH	4			DO	31
	AE3	756			HS	121			OAL	232
	AE3	777			RH	17			OAL	487
	AE3	783			AM	15			KT1	159
	AE3	811			AM	225			TJD	195
	AE3	823			AM	647			KT1	404
	AE4	862			ECG2	14			KT3	172
	AE4	920			E	29			B	523
	AE5	479			POE	9			B	528
	AE5	570			DA	177			CAM	84
	AE5	598			AA	352			C	636
	AE5	804			AA	839			M11	432
	AE5	1114			MF	167			FL	38
	AE6	19			SAA	449			FL	129
	AE6	75			RL	34			AU	41
	AE6	315			RL	153			AU	229
	AE6	493			MO	16			AU	236
	AE6	572			L4	268			WB	406
	AE6	667			T18	36			WB	437
	AE6	701			H29	1		LINE-A	GE	21
	AE6	806			TA	290		LINEAGE	M13	214
	AE6	864			TA	362			G3	252
	AE6	873			HAP	9			G4	507
	AE6	977			HAP	397			AE1	775
	AE6	990			HAP	659			AE1	873
	AE6	996			HAP	1450			AE3	138
	AE7	492			HAP	1465			AE3	800
	AE7	581			HAP	1727			AE5	41
	AE7	641			HAP	1947			AE6	186
	AE7	865			HAP	2063			AE6	534
	AE7	913			BR	46			AE6	543
	AE8	669			BR	89			AE8	172
	AE8	732			BR	332			AE10	269
	AE8	771			EL	83			AE10	874
	AE8	840			J1	104			AE10	1057
	AE8	856			J16	21			AE12	248
	AE9	632			P1	44			OAL	221
	AE9	1016			P1	185			KT1	289
	AE10	432			P5	52			M8	227
	AE10	1188			P6	26			M15	233
	AE10	1223			M1	334			M15	656
	AE11	891			HI	119		LINEAL	HAP	1187
	AE12	137			GK	61			HAP	2202
	AE12	783			G4	303			MC	44
	AE12	570			G4	549		LINEAMENT	AK	102
	AE12	1122			AE1	8			EL	140
	AE12	1315			AE1	111			GK	106
	MFL	8			AE1	323		LINED	PLN	27
	KT1	88			AE1	340			G4	54
	KT3	45			AE1	379			PC2	27
	KT3	345			AE1	383			HAP	179
	KT3	708			AE1	1019			J6	384
	KT3	903			AE1	1024			P3	182
	B	144			AE2	317			AE12	203
	BP	45			AE2	1066			BP	105
	HIF	5			AE3	26		LINEN	PUO3	22
	TH	111			AE4	145			SAA	358
	M11	295			AE4	157			T27	96
	M11	311			AE4	338			M1	1041
	AU	489			AE5	183			AE7	492
	M15	21			AE5	204			AE10	1113
	M15	243			AE5	652			AE11	1141
	M15	550			AE5	712			AE12	184
	M15	565			AE5	723			CAM	239
	CI	52			AE5	756			M11	393
	CI	99			AE5	760			M12	45
LIME	G1	211			AE5	768			PWR	35
LIMES	PR	28			AE5	966		LINES	AM	748
	G2	630			AE6	191			TA	68
	G4	209			AE6	1028			HAP	2337
LIMIT	TJD	173			AE6	1078			BR	105
LIMITED	LC	35			AE6	1132			J6	757
	EIE	12			AE7	298			J6	861
	AA	299			AE7	370			P1	81
	M1	170			AE7	441			P1	201
LIMITS	AR	298			AE7	520			P1	253
	SAA	70			AE7	770			P1	254
	HAP	2104			AE8	198			MC	76
	BR	8			AE8	205			G2	389
	EL	244			AE8	675			AE3	654
	M1	1009			AE8	834			AE7	212
	G1	328			AE8	907			AE9	14
LIMPED	ER	14			AE9	623			AE9	50
LIMPID	RL	341			AE9	881			AE9	57
	HAP	1186			AE10	81			AE9	183
LIMPING	H3	46			AE10	118			AE9	936
	HAP	2018			AE10	161			AE10	32
	BP	86			AE11	906			AE10	340
	BP	134			AE11	1213			OAL	546
	HIF	768			AE11	1308			C	65
	HIF	805			AE12	188			FL	286
	M12	421			AE12	194			AU	341
LINDEN	G1	255			AE12	252			M15	704
	KT3	963			AE12	363		LINGER	DHP	29
	BP	18			AE12	421		LINGERED	M15	43

Word	Ref	No.
LINGEREST	AE12	1153
LINGERING	L4	92
	T23	44
	TA	482
	J6	182
	M9	83
	VP8	94
	VP8	100
	VP8	128
	VP8	134
	VP8	146
	VP8	151
	AE2	877
	AE4	345
	AE4	395
	AE4	994
	AE6	304
	AE7	630
	AE8	639
	AE10	1153
	AE11	273
	AE11	306
	AE12	168
	AE12	1141
	KT1	162
	KT2	33
	CAM	289
	TH	40
	TH	175
	M11	442
	M15	361
LINGUIST	UDH	15
LINK	SAA	461
	L4	203
	KT3	1029
LINKED	CAM	279
LINKS	L1	54
	L4	292
	AE8	297
LINNET	DHP	1
LINNETS	G3	522
LINSEED	G1	302
LINSTOCKS	AM	750
LINUS	VP4	67
	VP6	96
LION	HS	115
	AR	118
	AM	382
	AA	447
	SAA	834
	SAA	1026
	H29	29
	HAP	41
	HAP	289
	HAP	304
	HAP	335
	HAP	351
	HAP	531
	HAP	579
	HAP	1264
	HAP	1519
	HAP	1561
	HAP	1969
	HAP	2084
	M1	415
	M1	681
	G3	381
	AE4	230
	AE9	456
	AE9	1073
	AE10	638
	AE10	1018
	AE12	9
	OAL	874
	KT2	203
	KT3	43
	KT3	138
	KT3	630
	B	242
	C	698
	M11	141
LIONESS	HAP	1303
	VP2	91
LION'S	SAA	568
	HAP	1315
	HAP	1430
	HAP	1530
	G2	208
	G4	590
	AE2	981
	AE5	460
	AE7	925
	AE8	240
	AE8	732
	AE9	411
	KT3	410

Word	Ref	No.
LION'S	M8	54
	M12	579
	M15	119
LIONS	AM	288
	AM	328
	VP4	26
	VP5	42
	AE3	155
	AE7	19
	AE10	233
	KT1	356
	KT3	98
LIONS'	KT2	345
LIP	ENH	4
	STS2	2
	VP3	35
	VP3	57
LIPARE	AE8	552
LIPS	SCG1	12
	AT	21
	L1	51
	L4	60
	L4	160
	L4	169
	T23	77
	T27	6
	J3	154
	J6	382
	J10	102
	J10	362
	P1	206
	P2	64
	P3	156
	P3	240
	M1	309
	M1	674
	M1	751
	M1	984
	AE2	807
	AE4	983
	AE9	6
	AE11	857
	OAL	647
	OAE2	38
	KT3	75
	B	642
	BP	190
	M10	24
	M10	26
	M10	75
	M10	92
	M11	484
	M12	567
	CI	150
	EWR	7
LIQUID	L1	24
	HAP	1852
	ODA	70
	P1	184
	M1	60
	M1	85
	M1	928
	VP4	36
	G1	200
	G1	557
	G2	753
	G3	378
	G4	21
	G4	50
	G4	240
	G4	515
	G4	601
	AE1	125
	AE1	198
	AE1	223
	AE1	603
	AE3	571
	AE3	753
	AE4	361
	AE4	838
	AE5	274
	AE5	305
	AE5	667
	AE6	757
	AE7	97
	AE7	966
	AE8	128
	AE8	930
	AE9	121
	AE9	160
	AE9	636
	AE11	749
	AE11	1108
	AE12	681
	OAL	642
	DO	22

Word	Ref	No.
LIQUID	KT1	468
	HIF	435
	C	739
	FL	318
	M12	693
	M15	511
LIQUOR	SEL4	12
	L3	220
	PAA	17
	GE	25
	G4	208
	AE11	857
	AE12	616
	OAL	635
	BP	101
	M15	431
LIQUORED	SAA	460
LIQUORISH	WB	319
LIQUORS	L4	281
LIRIS	AE11	991
LISP	AA	243
	J6	267
LISPING	L4	151
LIST	SAA	1013
	J16	46
	P5	124
	G4	305
	AE5	980
	AE12	178
	AE12	1013
	AE12	1077
	C	582
LISTED	SAA	1088
	SAA	1089
	AE5	536
	AE8	686
	AE12	196
	AE12	1052
	AE12	1107
	KT2	258
	FL	479
LISTEN	AE6	629
	AE9	72
	CAM	9
LISTENED	AE2	842
	AE3	673
	C	664
	FL	51
	FL	132
LISTENING	POE	8
	AA	211
	L1	42
	T23	14
	HAP	1263
	SSC	18
	M1	459
	DHP	9
	VP8	3
	G4	680
	AE1	218
	AE3	942
	AE4	265
	AE4	527
	AE9	253
	AE9	533
	AE10	156
	AF	34
	KT2	77
	KT3	497
	B	293
	TH	88
	M12	243
LISTENS	AM	431
LISTLESS	G1	313
	G4	378
	AE8	669
LISTLESSLY	G3	707
LISTS	AM	154
	AM	747
	J1	256
	AE5	152
	AE5	486
	KT2	410
	KT2	440
	KT2	663
	KT3	11
	KT3	125
	KT3	543
	KT3	663
	KT3	674
	KT3	683
LITERAL	HAP	428
LITERALLY	HAP	1401
LITIGIOUS	PAZ	27
	J6	341
	G1	194

LITIGIOUS	AE8	473
	OAL	95
	TJD	11
LITTER	HAP	172
	J6	257
	G1	545
	KT3	713
LITTERED	C	226
LITTERS	J1	182
	J3	389
	J6	427
	AE8	882
LITTLE	UDH	59
	EIE	7
	AM	134
	AM	280
	AM	313
	AM	337
	AM	436
	AM	548
	AM	724
	AM	909
	AM	955
	AM	1128
	PMQ	22
	ETL	6
	PCG1	32
	ECG1	5
	PUO2	13
	PAL	13
	PAL	29
	PKK	21
	PO	29
	CM	99
	DA	51
	PR	28
	AA	506
	AA	534
	MD	61
	MF	49
	MF	78
	SAA	176
	SAA	311
	SAA	372
	SAA	876
	EK	32
	RL	30
	RL	288
	RL	318
	RL	416
	MO	1
	L2	18
	L2	24
	L2	45
	L3	78
	L3	263
	L4	149
	L4	287
	H29	85
	H29	103
	TA	377
	AK	13
	HAP	1295
	HAP	1449
	HAP	1555
	HAP	1615
	HAP	1757
	HAP	1762
	HAP	1800
	HAP	1811
	HAP	2139
	HAP	2217
	HAP	2297
	BR	204
	BR	276
	STS3	17
	PKA	26
	EL	310
	OD	31
	J3	19
	J3	149
	J6	516
	J10	21
	J10	344
	P1	34
	P1	95
	P1	222
	P4	67
	P6	125
	P6	155
	P6	156
	M1	431
	M1	552
	M1	726
	M1	748
	M1	1032

LITTLE	M1	1086
	M9	14
	M9	18
	M13	219
	ELT	33
	MC	54
	EHC	6
	EHC	11
	VP1	46
	VP2	79
	VP7	49
	G2	760
	G3	207
	G3	399
	G4	5
	G4	191
	G4	199
	G4	256
	G4	295
	G4	703
	AE1	1004
	AE2	966
	AE3	239
	AE3	359
	AE4	54
	AE4	309
	AE4	540
	AE5	1026
	AE6	723
	AE7	414
	AE7	533
	AE7	678
	AE8	734
	AE10	880
	AE11	858
	AE11	1058
	AE12	803
	OAL	431
	OAL	488
	OAL	588
	OAL	703
	OAL	756
	OAL	845
	KT1	191
	KT1	229
	KT1	581
	KT2	35
	KT2	66
	KT2	644
	KT3	252
	KT3	705
	KT3	842
	KT3	1067
	TJD	12
	TJD	35
	M8	325
	B	27
	B	84
	B	89
	B	223
	B	341
	B	372
	B	414
	B	571
	B	658
	BP	34
	BP	42
	BP	57
	BP	66
	BP	115
	BP	157
	HIF	251
	HIF	252
	HIF	682
	C	9
	C	219
	C	276
	C	655
	TH	47
	TH	359
	TH	363
	M11	482
	FL	31
	FL	587
	FL	615
	M12	307
	M12	817
	M15	328
	M15	554
	AU	380
	WB	3
	WB	341
	GP	50
	GP	125
	CI	443
	CI	627

LITTLE	ERL	2
	EMKG	7
LIVE	UDH	82
	UDH	85
	UDH	87
	UDH	102
	HS	130
	AR	60
	AR	205
	AR	263
	LC	80
	LCA	16
	EIE	27
	AM	356
	DC	25
	DC	44
	AM	687
	AM	1001
	AM	1149
	ECG1	19
	PLN	16
	ECD	22
	PNH	18
	PNH	39
	PAZ	20
	PAL	30
	EMK	4
	EOE	26
	PCB	12
	CM	66
	CM	68
	HP	180
	HP	113
	DA	66
	DA	167
	DA	172
	AA	957
	SAA	411
	SAA	483
	SAA	331
	SAA	338
	SAA	361
	MD	236
	AT	45
	L3	41
	L3	58
	L3	101
	L3	128
	L3	143
	L3	275
	L4	164
	T23	41
	H2	98
	FS2	10
	TA	340
	TA	383
	TA	384
	TA	385
	TA	386
	GE	1
	HAP	299
	HAP	651
	HAP	1588
	HAP	1867
	SSC	62
	BR	69
	STS3	31
	STS3	37
	EJG	5
	EL	377
	ODA	57
	ESH	34
	SSH	4
	SSH	16
	J3	9
	J3	52
	J3	179
	J3	355
	J3	484
	J6	475
	J6	736
	J16	94
	P3	57
	P3	194
	P5	41
	P5	120
	P5	128
	P5	221
	P5	224
	P6	56
	P6	59
	P6	160
	M1	251
	M1	492
	M1	652
	HI	159

LIVE

MC	69
GK	38
GK	121
GK	131
GK	154
GK	165
DHP	29
VP2	36
VP2	86
VP10	66
G2	90
G3	108
G4	226
G4	309
AE1	290
AE2	587
AE2	813
AE2	890
AE3	406
AE3	654
AE4	478
AE4	609
AE4	655
AE4	947
AE5	29
AE6	591
AE6	895
AE6	914
AE7	960
AE7	1006
AE9	277
AE9	598
AE9	840
AE10	75
AE10	116
AE10	1207
AE10	1220
AE11	166
AE11	273
AE12	64
AE12	98
AE12	1349
OAL	722
MM	23
KT1	387
KT1	570
KT3	223
KT3	793
KT3	803
KT3	850
KT3	853
KT3	1055
KT3	1096
KT3	1114
TJD	45
M8	311
M8	315
B	329
B	357
B	399
B	648
BP	174
M10	3
CAM	236
CAM	335
HIF	682
C	185
M11	53
M12	259
M12	323
WB	421
M15	128
M15	706
ETP	11
PMK	33

LIVED

UDH	43
UDH	75
RH	47
ETL	29
HP	109
EUF	4
MD	149
RL	209
DOD	15
DOD	18
H29	68
H2	7
TA	12
TA	239
TA	380
TA	409
HH	16
HAP	2203
HAP	2212
EL	16
EL	55

LIVED

EL	175
J10	389
J10	410
J10	419
M1	440
AE5	947
AE7	1065
AE8	268
AE10	1231
AE11	86
AE11	253
DO	32
DO	34
KT2	1
KT1	165
KT1	607
KT3	966
TJD	71
B	14
B	334
B	652
BP	32
BP	33
HIF	375
C	1
C	39
C	559
TH	17
TH	66
TH	70
M11	420
FL	519
FL	562
M12	729
WB	64
WB	461
M15	599
GP	9
CI	46

LIVELY

HAP	2326
GK	66
AE3	634
KT2	228
GP	104
CI	568
STP	25

LIVER

L3	190
G3	404
AE6	810
AE6	811

LIVERIES

J10	387
KT2	53
KT3	454
FL	159
FL	353
FL	504

LIVERY

EL	330
J1	142
J3	295
G3	665
KT1	221
FL	265

LIVES

LC	52
PT	2
ETC	21
PCB	2
AA	345
AA	462
SAA	61
SAA	741
EK	29
EDG	35
HAP	403
HAP	1553
BR	284
BR	292
BR	344
EDS	36
EL	26
J3	4
J3	237
J6	340
J6	653
J10	153
J10	380
J16	90
P3	25
M1	725
M9	178
HI	164
GK	10
EHC	38
G2	139
G2	406
G3	653
G4	82

LIVES

G4	365
AE1	770
AE2	517
AE4	782
AE5	225
AE5	1066
AE6	583
AE6	897
AE6	909
AE8	747
AE11	1291
OAL	724
KT2	1
KT2	387
KT3	883
KT3	1077
TJD	108
CAM	52
CAM	183
C	168
TH	287
M12	780
M12	782
M12	818
AU	36
AU	75
AU	491
WB	480
WB	541
WB	545
CI	294
EP	4
EP	6

LIVEST

P3	120
P5	224
KT1	452
M8	326

LIVID

T23	77
G1	607
AE4	923
AE5	16
AE8	263
AE12	335
KT1	467
M8	382
M10	34

LIVING

AM	1069
PMQ	9
PA	28
PA	32
PUO2	23
PTC	20
SSF	24
EUF	7
PPC	6
MD	193
OE	48
L1	26
L1	28
L3	45
L3	66
L3	91
T27	84
HAP	872
HAP	919
HAP	962
HAP	1472
HAP	1544
HAP	1631
SSC	62
BR	161
BR	180
BR	298
ELW	10
EJG	7
MS	27
J1	257
J3	35
J6	326
J10	245
J10	383
P5	124
M1	106
M1	387
M1	501
M13	103
M13	181
M13	209
HI	130
GK	111
GK	151
VP3	140
G1	342
G2	34
G2	193
G2	661

LIVING	G3	470	LOAD	AE2	963	LOATHES	M8	372	
	G3	684		AE2	983	LOATHING	AM	1028	
	G4	23		AE4	688		L3	156	
	AE1	78		AE5	360		AE4	563	
	AE1	237		AE5	609		AE6	589	
	AE1	1009		AE6	120		M10	1	
	AE2	476		AE8	264		CAM	324	
	AE2	618		AE8	375		TH	163	
	AE2	978		AE8	563	LOATHSOME	CM	28	
	AE3	62		AE9	483		DA	196	
	AE3	406		AE9	926		T23	44	
	AE4	798		AE9	1097		HAP	522	
	AE4	913		AE10	608		G3	832	
	AE5	328		AE10	1240		G3	842	
	AE5	651		AE11	335		AE3	296	
	AE5	962		AE11	518		AE3	306	
	AE6	33		AE12	781		AE3	849	
	AE6	231		AE12	1308		KT1	267	
	AE6	324		KT1	142		KT1	412	
	AE6	497		KT2	265		TJD	192	
	AE6	530		M8	34		B	723	
	AE6	714		BP	48		C	112	
	AE6	863		CAM	368		WB	498	
	AE6	1213		HIF	813		CI	484	
	AE8	257		C	671	LOAVES	HAP	1518	
	AE8	295		M12	366		AE8	241	
	AE8	542		M15	104	LOBES	L3	190	
	AE8	636		M15	606	LOCK	SAA	446	
	AE9	640		CI	228		L4	72	
	AE9	1052		CI	358		J6	464	
	AE10	722		CI	583		AE5	265	
	AE10	742		PTP	50	LOCKED	AE1	92	
	AE10	1174		SMP	12		M8	263	
	AE11	35	LOADED	AA	596		BP	28	
	AE11	276		SAA	926	LOCKING	B	222	
	AE12	183		HAP	1397	LOCKS	AA	261	
	AE12	216		G4	13		J3	121	
	AE12	272		AE2	698		J3	309	
	AE12	498		AE2	1094		M1	605	
	AE12	781		AE3	73		M1	765	
	KT3	198		AE5	347		M9	195	
	KT3	930		AE6	1132		M13	152	
	M8	122		AE9	319		G3	562	
	M8	392		AE10	85		G4	476	
	BP	50		AE11	72		AE1	827	
	M10	14		AE11	120		AE3	107	
	CAM	330		AE12	1057		AE4	317	
	CAM	368		HIF	63		AE4	685	
	C	612		AU	442		AE7	485	
	TH	358		WB	424		AE8	780	
	M11	367		M15	695		AE10	1184	
	M11	403	LOADEN	G1	369		OAE2	77	
	M11	421		G3	486		KT1	539	
	FL	593		AE2	431		KT3	72	
	AU	286		AE4	581		KT3	924	
	WB	318		AE11	208		M8	371	
	M15	174	LOADS	AA	933		M12	389	
	M15	333		MF	103		M12	469	
	M15	414		J3	397		M12	527	
	M15	415		G1	82		WB	159	
	M15	540		AE1	92		WB	197	
	M15	559		AE1	903		M15	315	
	M15	575		AE3	66		M15	422	
	GP	78		AE3	626	LOCRIANS	AE3	512	
	GP	93		AE5	540	LOCUST	PKK	28	
	PWR	23		AE9	28	LOCUSTS	SAA	711	
LIZARD	J3	375		AE11	859		VP2	13	
	VP2	7		HIF	494		VP5	121	
	G4	16		M12	677	LODGE	HAP	2252	
LIZARDS	G4	352		HAP	1663		G2	748	
LOAD	AM	818	LOADSTONE	DC	25		G3	832	
	AA	505	LOADSTONES	J6	400		G4	11	
	AA	673	LOAM	PUF	17		G4	352	
	SAA	36	LOATHE	MD	131		AE2	45	
	SAA	400		SAA	700		AE3	850	
	L3	135		J6	263		AE12	1164	
	L3	280		J10	322		KT3	110	
	L4	242		G4	158	LODGED	VHH	5	
	T18	17		AE3	406		PUOS	4	
	TA	331		AE12	1190		L3	274	
	HAP	811		KT3	227		HAP	639	
	HAP	1545		CAM	161		J6	126	
	J3	405	LOATHED	E	25		M1	253	
	J10	553		J6	116		M1	871	
	M9	28		M1	635		G3	675	
	VP6	21		AE2	877		G4	59	
	VP6	86		AE8	638		OAL	790	
	VP9	90		AE12	85		B	110	
	G1	119		M8	345		B	632	
	G1	273		CI	72		B	660	
	G2	7	LOATHES	J10	495		CAM	38	
	G2	747		AE4	407		ETP	7	
	G3	580		AE4	655		PMK	27	
	G4	543		AE12	876	LODGES	M15	242	
	AE2	25		KT1	527	LODGING	AM	1018	
	AE2	854		KT3	138		PW	4	

LODGING
- PW 8
- T27 65
- HAP 1770
- HAP 1905
- G2 399
- AE3 665
- AE11 633
- C 222
- FL 319

LODGINGS
- HAP 2431
- G4 64
- G4 81
- AE7 686

LOFTIER VP4 1

LOFTINESS EMI 3

LOFTY
- JH 12
- EIE 6
- AM 260
- AA 516
- AK 114
- HAP 1757
- EL 93
- J3 389
- P5 28
- M1 429
- GK 68
- GK 121
- VP1 35
- VP1 78
- VP6 59
- VP6 60
- VP8 14
- VP10 19
- G1 439
- G1 650
- G2 606
- G2 643
- G2 691
- G3 70
- G3 125
- G3 461
- G3 778
- G4 209
- AE1 612
- AE1 631
- AE1 703
- AE2 2
- AE2 247
- AE2 629
- AE3 4
- AE3 123
- AE3 370
- AE3 924
- AE4 102
- AE4 147
- AE4 190
- AE4 215
- AE4 261
- AE4 268
- AE4 713
- AE4 940
- AE5 44
- AE6 25
- AE6 308
- AE6 335
- AE6 740
- AE7 216
- AE7 578
- AE7 779
- AE7 872
- AE10 30
- AE10 364
- AE10 731
- AE10 812
- AE10 948
- AE10 1292
- AE11 461
- AE11 756
- AE11 982
- AE11 1055
- AE11 1271
- AE12 491
- AE12 531
- AE12 760
- AE12 825
- AE12 1346
- AF 34
- MM 25
- KT1 97
- KT3 229
- KT3 495
- KT3 953
- M8 364
- BP 41
- C 390
- TH 20

LOFTY (continued)
- M11 135
- FL 285
- FL 304
- M12 62
- M12 176
- CI 574

LOG
- AM 621
- M8 253
- M8 263

LOGIC J6 580

LOGICIAN HAP 1495

LOGS H9 7

LOIN AE10 536

LOINS AA 262
- MF 125
- L4 20
- L4 104
- L4 275
- T18 86
- HAP 279
- HAP 1985
- G4 458
- AE8 180
- AS 101

LOITER AE2 503
- AE2 743
- P6 171
- G2 726

LOLL AM 525
- P1 114
- G4 741
- AE8 838

LOLLING ENH 9
- L4 201
- J1 98
- J3 145
- J6 405
- AE5 122
- AE8 394

LOLLS J1 204
- P2 47

LOMBARD AM 944
- GK 61

LONDON AR 233
- AM 601
- AM 845
- PUO1 29
- PUO4 17
- PUO5 11
- MD 167
- PDG 41
- C 742
- ETP 9

LONELY SCG1 17
- RL 2
- HAP 1235
- J3 29
- P1 30
- G2 444
- G3 384
- AE2 664
- AE4 44
- AE4 667
- AE4 797
- AE7 619
- AE7 635
- AE10 588
- AE12 1153
- B 289
- C 3
- TH 74
- WB 211
- M15 122

LONG AR 21
- AR 212
- SMA 74
- LC 12
- PWG 31
- PWG 39
- LCA 3
- LCA 5
- EIE 26
- AM 1
- AM 17
- AM 24
- AM 37
- AM 133
- AM 193
- AM 263
- AM 309
- AM 421
- AM 470
- AM 492
- AM 574
- AM 641
- AM 677

LONG (continued)
- AM 761
- AM 899
- AM 934
- AM 1043
- AM 1097
- AM 1133
- AM 1149
- PA 1
- PEL 27
- ETL 26
- ECG1 11
- ECG1 34
- SCG1 16
- PM 14
- SM1 2
- SM1 5
- SLN 1
- SCD1 3
- PUO1 10
- PUO1 16
- PNH 1
- ENH 28
- ML 21
- PKK 1
- PTW 3
- STC 11
- PLG 22
- CM 30
- CM 33
- CM 137
- HP 152
- HP 163
- HP 177
- HP 179
- DA 157
- DA 195
- EMP 4
- SSF 8
- ETG 7
- PUO3 12
- PUO5 26
- PUF 34
- AA 63
- AA 204
- AA 244
- AA 301
- AA 542
- AA 548
- AA 620
- AA 648
- AA 819
- AA 902
- AA 934
- AA 939
- AA 1025
- AA 1029
- PLB 17
- PPC 2
- MD 21
- MD 108
- MD 131
- MD 276
- MF 4
- MF 87
- MF 136
- SAA 116
- SAA 166
- SAA 283
- SAA 315
- SAA 725
- SAA 794
- SAA 866
- SAA 909
- SAA 966
- SAA 987
- SAA 1111
- SAA 1112
- RL 344
- RL 387
- RL 393
- OE 49
- AT 61
- ER 46
- L3 31
- L3 96
- L3 176
- L3 320
- L4 115
- L4 223
- L4 293
- T23 25
- T23 39
- T23 51
- H29 2
- FS3 12
- TA 1

LONG			LONG			LONG		
TA	43			VP2	105			AE7	277
TA	159		VP3	105		AE7	295
TA	311		VP3	123		AE7	427
TA	507		VP4	75		AE7	813
TA	421		VP5	84		AE7	922
TA	430		VP6	24		AE7	965
TA	431		VP6	30		AE8	52
TA	471		G1	122		AE8	182
TA	481		G1	251		AE8	209
PAA	35		G1	256		AE8	232
HAP	73		G1	474		AE8	264
HAP	182		G1	504		AE8	372
HAP	462		G1	676		AE8	443
HAP	601		G2	124		AE8	525
HAP	605		G2	352		AE8	628
HAP	626		G2	423		AE8	791
HAP	636		G2	793		AE8	877
HAP	772		G3	91		AE9	102
HAP	905		G3	538		AE9	612
HAP	1180		G3	563		AE9	683
HAP	1200		G4	34		AE10	387
HAP	1238		G4	128		AE10	501
HAP	1258		G4	147		AE10	853
HAP	1578		G4	305		AE10	919
HAP	1586		G4	478		AE10	1222
HAP	1615		G4	711		AE10	1231
HAP	1694		AE1	4		AE10	1232
HAP	1729		AE1	10		AE10	1256
HAP	1889		AE1	28		AE11	114
HAP	1988		AE1	36		AE11	141
HAP	2062		AE1	46		AE11	184
HAP	2093		AE1	228		AE11	253
HAP	2250		AE1	457		AE11	373
HAP	2367		AE1	483		AE11	443
HAP	2496		AE1	493		AE11	510
HAP	2531		AE1	671		AE12	185
HAP	2573		AE1	815		AE12	218
BR	36		AE1	984		AE12	267
BR	47		AE1	1000		AE12	361
BR	276		AE1	1060		AE12	392
EDS	30		AE2	33		AE12	719
PP	17		AE2	95		AE12	753
PP	32		AE2	148		AE12	777
STS3	3		AE2	339		AE12	898
STS3	20		AE2	369		OAL	43
PMS	10		AE2	392		OAL	145
PKA	10		AE2	482		OAL	582
SKA4	18		AE2	502		OAL	840
EL	225		AE2	871		AF	155
EL	114		AE2	876		MG	8
EL	320		AE2	972		DO	98
EL	8		AE2	1043		KT1	16
ODA	61		AE2	1058		KT1	71
J1	4		AE3	137		KT1	165
J3	155		AE3	366		KT1	367
J3	212		AE3	387		KT2	3
J3	221		AE3	491		KT2	20
J6	100		AE3	533		KT2	198
J6	311		AE3	579		KT2	266
J6	520		AE3	659		KT2	368
J6	573		AE3	925		KT2	381
J6	800		AE4	222		KT2	418
J10	60		AE4	279		KT2	548
J10	120		AE4	345		KT3	46
J10	227		AE4	414		KT3	52
J10	239		AE4	697		KT3	188
J10	287		AE5	133		KT3	385
J10	306		AE5	473		KT3	453
J10	383		AE5	508		KT3	523
J10	390		AE5	550		KT3	833
J10	426		AE5	594		KT3	896
J16	49		AE5	599		KT3	1003
P1	170		AE5	1126		KT3	1005
P3	50		AE6	105		KT3	1033
P5	55		AE6	131		KT3	1050
P5	85		AE6	511		KT3	1123
M1	4		AE6	572		KT3	1154
M1	296		AE6	657		TJD	11
M1	372		AE6	676		TJD	20
M1	418		AE6	724		M8	268
M1	523		AE6	868		M8	278
M1	537		AE6	932		M8	283
M1	589		AE6	945		M8	356
M1	595		AE6	968		B	7
M1	734		AE6	970		B	16
M1	760		AE6	1014		B	63
M1	1033		AE6	1024		B	87
M9	39		AE6	1079		B	123
M9	195		AE6	1122		B	133
SFL	2		AE7	68		B	148
HI	15		AE7	88		B	183
SLT2	16		AE7	101		B	250
GK	3		AE7	171		B	292
GK	57		AE7	239		B	334
DHP	21		AE7	257		B	469
VP1	50		AE7	260		B	710

LONG	B	736
	BP	33
	CAM	139
	CAM	220
	CAM	239
	CAM	242
	CAM	316
	HIF	374
	HIF	727
	C	170
	C	256
	C	301
	C	304
	C	333
	C	371
	C	487
	C	594
	TH	47
	TH	99
	TH	162
	TH	174
	TH	186
	TH	217
	TH	221
	TH	232
	TH	267
	M11	14
	M11	21
	M11	70
	FL	43
	FL	54
	FL	132
	FL	165
	FL	209
	FL	223
	M12	29
	M12	63
	M12	205
	M12	236
	M12	480
	M12	494
	M12	715
	M12	743
	M12	768
	AU	50
	AU	227
	AU	335
	AU	361
	AU	466
	AU	490
	AU	571
	WB	133
	WB	159
	WB	162
	WB	257
	WB	378
	WB	441
	WB	509
	WB	537
	M15	555
	M15	630
	CI	111
	CI	156
	CI	197
	CI	207
	CI	270
	CI	315
	CI	478
	ESK	17
	EMKG	26
	AS	45
	PWR	38
LONGA	AE1	368
LONG-ABANDONED	G1	238
LONG-ATTENDING	KT3	1146
LONG-CHARMED	SAA	745
LONG-CONTRACTED	AE6	999
LONGED	AE1	813
	AE8	219
	DO	149
	CI	160
LONGER	UDH	51
	JH	23
	AR	230
	AR	252
	DC	46
	AM	414
	AM	538
	AM	885
	AM	1201
	PM	4
	PCD	17
	PNH	17
	ML	34
	PKK	9
	PTW	23

LONGER	PO	14
	CM	27
	AA	412
	D	9
	SAA	20
	TA	190
	TA	426
	EAA	25
	HAP	1682
	HAP	1855
	HAP	2454
	BR	137
	ETS	25
	STS3	6
	STS3	7
	STS3	14
	STS3	15
	ELW	8
	EL	213
	PSH	24
	J3	477
	P2	106
	M1	88
	M1	196
	M1	212
	M1	335
	M1	416
	M1	467
	M1	563
	M1	920
	M1	1050
	VP2	95
	VP5	53
	VP5	93
	G2	139
	G3	117
	G4	721
	AE1	534
	AE1	910
	AE2	176
	AE2	403
	AE3	95
	AE3	398
	AE4	248
	AE4	521
	AE4	548
	AE4	759
	AE5	424
	AE8	497
	AE8	641
	AE8	928
	AE9	276
	AE9	688
	AE9	1088
	AE11	202
	AE11	542
	AE12	116
	OAL	208
	OAL	246
	KT2	125
	M8	387
	M8	399
	B	41
	B	302
	M10	77
	M11	80
	FL	380
	M12	184
	M12	411
	M12	416
	M12	750
	AU	490
	WB	11
	WB	437
	GP	84
	GP	119
	PTP	26
	EMKG	2
LONGEST	DC	1
	AA	948
	L3	315
	BR	10
	BR	319
	J10	389
	TH	41
LONG-EXPERIENCED	CAM	192
LONG-FORGOTTEN	D	30
	TA	468
LONG-GROWING	LCA	49
LONGING	AM	932
	AM	1192
	DA	28
	PUF	3
	AA	232
	PRH	7
	AT	22

LONGING	L4	67
	BR	15
	J10	510
	P4	113
	VP2	59
	VP6	87
	VP8	94
	VP8	100
	VP8	106
	VP8	110
	VP8	120
	VP8	128
	VP8	146
	VP8	152
	G3	203
	G3	425
	G4	698
	G4	707
	G4	729
	AE2	144
	AE2	1082
	AE3	429
	AE3	857
	AE6	163
	AE6	948
	AE7	1106
	AE8	663
	AE9	331
	AE10	730
	AE10	973
	AE11	62
	B	156
	HIF	444
	FL	462
	M11	469
	WB	190
	WB	200
LONGINGLY	MD	63
	AE9	487
LONG-INVETERATE	TA	127
LONG-LABORING	DO	71
LONG-LIVED	TJD	88
LONG-LOOKED-FOR	J16	67
LONG-LOST	PUO5	12
	HAP	1213
LONG-LOVED	PAZ	8
LONG-PLIGHTED	G1	688
LONG-RIBBED	P1	185
LONGS	SMA	40
	HAP	1870
	J6	53
	J16	88
	M1	1090
	AE1	724
	AE4	109
	AE4	407
	AE8	827
	M12	291
LONG-SUFFERING	AR	265
	HAP	1570
LONGVIL	MF	212
LOOK	JH	16
	RH	69
	SMA	38
	LC	13
	AM	285
	AM	447
	AM	1020
	ETL	11
	PFD	2
	PW	20
	PMQW	6
	ELN	21
	ENH	7
	ENH	30
	POE	17
	HP	144
	PCB	28
	AA	694
	AA	1007
	MD	18
	D	19
	RL	101
	RL	138
	RL	302
	OE	47
	AT	26
	AT	27
	L2	10
	L3	31
	T23	11
	T23	33
	T27	101
	H2	92
	TA	124
	TA	324

Word	Code	No.
LOOK	TA	496
	AK	127
	AK	174
	HAP	1507
	HAP	1869
	HAP	2351
	BR	63
	BR	106
	SKA2	25
	EL	140
	EL	291
	EL	346
	ODA	47
	MS	24
	SSH	8
	J3	118
	J3	204
	J3	213
	J3	350
	J6	295
	J6	647
	J10	1
	J10	21
	J10	164
	J10	215
	P1	19
	P3	176
	P3	186
	P3	195
	P4	15
	P5	161
	M1	473
	M1	735
	M1	800
	M1	892
	M1	1020
	M9	201
	PLT	24
	ELT	29
	GK	11
	GK	75
	VP1	40
	VP3	156
	VP8	148
	G1	237
	G3	87
	G4	711
	AE1	312
	AE2	812
	AE2	830
	AE3	776
	AE4	527
	AE4	601
	AE6	76
	AE6	217
	AE6	1047
	AE7	1106
	AE9	432
	AE9	544
	AE9	643
	AE10	166
	AE11	385
	AE12	341
	AE12	975
	OAL	356
	ETO	1
	KT1	259
	KT1	271
	KT1	357
	KT1	562
	KT2	122
	KT2	263
	KT2	348
	KT2	432
	KT3	566
	KT3	593
	KT3	490
	B	388
	B	627
	BP	146
	BP	163
	CAM	223
	HIF	98
	HIF	306
	HIF	489
	HIF	767
	C	231
	C	266
	TH	285
	M11	359
	M11	363
	M11	410
	FL	405
	M12	361
	M12	528
	AU	105
LOOK	AU	180
	AU	201
	AU	271
	AU	300
	M15	217
	GP	25
	CI	309
	STP	1
	ESK	19
	EMKG	34
	AS	35
LOOKED	AM	322
	PKK	2
	PUO5	19
	SAA	969
	T23	97
	TA	58
	TA	207
	HAP	41
	HAP	513
	HAP	1241
	HAP	2101
	HAP	2223
	EL	197
	EL	338
	P1	230
	P3	77
	M1	877
	GK	64
	G4	602
	AE1	425
	AE2	770
	AE2	842
	AE4	843
	AE5	16
	AE5	357
	AE6	420
	AE6	633
	AE8	130
	AE12	109
	AF	112
	AF	113
	AF	119
	AF	120
	KT1	218
	KT1	239
	KT2	248
	KT2	340
	KT2	613
	KT3	43
	M8	135
	B	180
	B	535
	BP	183
	M10	27
	C	482
	TH	193
	TH	341
	TH	359
	FL	57
	FL	94
	M12	145
	M12	374
	M12	388
	M12	433
	AU	200
	WB	531
	CI	58
	SMP	51
LOOKEST	P3	195
LOOKING	JH	24
	AA	71
	HAP	968
	EL	342
	J3	38
	J6	443
	P3	154
	M13	43
	HI	147
	HI	191
	AE1	580
	AE2	995
	AE6	739
	AE8	93
	AE10	373
	AE10	984
	OAL	100
	KT2	241
	KT2	565
	KT3	418
	CAM	110
	C	303
	TH	39
	TH	40
	FL	122
LOOKING-GLASS	J3	181
LOOKS	SMA	8
	AM	528
	AM	557
	PMQW	15
	PC1	22
	ETC	2
	CM	110
	DA	71
	AA	442
	AA	690
	AA	848
	SAA	948
	PDG	8
	EDGA	3
	L3	185
	L3	234
	TA	189
	TA	443
	HAP	2228
	HAP	2337
	BR	113
	PDS	5
	EKA	30
	J1	63
	J6	601
	J10	532
	M1	109
	M1	1049
	M9	193
	M13	30
	M13	196
	GK	111
	VP7	63
	G1	518
	G2	612
	G3	334
	G3	337
	G4	143
	G4	371
	AE1	704
	AE2	644
	AE2	805
	AE2	1069
	AE3	284
	AE3	889
	AE4	5
	AE4	21
	AE4	316
	AE7	581
	AE7	625
	AE8	663
	AE8	941
	AE9	638
	AE9	751
	AE11	99
	AE11	1278
	AE12	1325
	OAL	342
	OAL	831
	OAE2	19
	AF	84
	KT1	528
	KT3	721
	KT3	478
	M8	272
	B	72
	M10	76
	HIF	460
	M11	135
	M11	192
	M11	460
	M15	687
	PTP	18
	AS	26
	AS	30
LOOM	AM	607
	AM	722
	AM	825
	ER	27
	T18	56
	H29	27
	HI	128
	HI	184
	G1	392
	AE7	16
	AE7	1096
	HIF	50
	HIF	170
	M11	238
	M15	551
LOON	C	589
LOOPHOLE	HAP	718
LOOPHOLES	AE9	711
LOOSE	AR	151
	HP	1
	AA	909

LOOSE	L4	203	LORD	AM	1077	LORD	AE11	514
	T23	75		PM	1		AE11	950
	H29	21		PKK	10		AE12	52
	HL	368		EKK	19		AE12	219
	J3	120		PTW	12		AE12	535
	P5	126		HP	150		AE12	783
	P5	223		DA	121		AE12	912
	M1	183		PR	16		AE12	1047
	M1	383		PUF	30		AE12	1063
	VP6	38		AA	219		OAL	353
	G1	592		AA	657		OAL	511
	G2	281		AA	762		OAL	655
	G2	374		AA	1031		OAE2	5
	G3	820		MD	144		OAE2	32
	G4	470		MD	259		DO	37
	G4	586		SAA	82		DO	54
	AE1	94		SAA	1140		DO	125
	AE1	438		PDG	23		DO	147
	AE2	198		RL	9		KT1	5
	AE3	349		H29	40		KT1	343
	AE4	752		TA	515		KT1	511
	AE7	563		HAP	543		KT2	360
	AE7	854		HAP	1997		KT2	388
	AE12	502		HAP	2255		KT2	595
	OAL	37		HAP	2576		KT3	240
	OAL	596		PDS	1		KT3	395
	KT1	185		BR	174		KT3	498
	KT2	501		PMS	12		KT3	522
	KT3	56		PKA	9		KT3	1128
	FL	35		EKA	8		TJD	18
	FL	562		EL	54		B	26
LOOSE-BODIED	ECG1	10		EL	176		B	651
LOOSED	PTL	19		EL	349		CAM	244
	MD	65		J1	49		C	144
	SAA	1049		J1	160		C	193
	HAP	602		J1	211		C	443
	P5	252		J3	145		C	591
	M1	357		J3	186		C	608
	M1	442		J3	218		C	647
	AE4	1009		J3	374		C	779
	AE9	140		J3	451		M11	8
	AE10	330		J6	116		M11	16
	KT1	166		J6	137		M11	239
	HIF	691		J6	145		M11	246
	TH	117		J6	160		M11	367
	AU	128		J6	195		M11	374
LOOSELY	SCG1	9		J6	214		M11	388
	J10	212		J6	817		M11	398
	P3	58		J6	853		M12	820
	P5	125		J10	102		AU	190
	VP2	69		J10	343		AU	147
	AE4	931		P5	183		AU	600
	OAL	581		P5	187		WB	270
	MM	15		P5	195		WB	359
	KT3	207		P5	209		WB	382
	CI	15		P5	227		WB	452
LOOSEN	G2	488		M1	652		GP	55
LOOSENED	DA	9		M1	705		CI	46
	H2	83		M1	843		EMKG	29
	H2	91		HI	9	LORDED	L3	242
	M1	516		HI	83	LORD-LIKE	HIF	342
	GK	21		HI	127	LORDLY	AA	454
	G3	307		ELT	8		AE1	260
	AE1	171		VP8	134		AE9	1073
	AE1	224		G2	285		AE12	12
	AE1	665		G2	384		KT3	631
	AE5	363		G2	787	LORD'S	SAA	66
	AE5	863		G3	380		SAA	503
	AE5	1071		G4	189		HAP	2512
	AE10	422		AE1	195		J3	319
	AE10	834		AE1	487		P1	145
	AE12	696		AE1	660		AE10	1286
	AE12	993		AE1	767		DO	157
LOOSEST	SAA	1125		AE2	708	LORDS	AM	35
LOP	PAL	28		AE2	781		AA	570
	PDG	32		AE2	1054		AA	795
	G2	507		AE3	409		MD	309
LOPPED	M1	247		AE3	444		HAP	2498
	G1	235		AE3	623		J1	32
	G2	565		AE3	868		J1	183
	AE6	668		AE4	146		J6	14
	AE10	551		AE4	175		J6	746
	AE12	563		AE4	553		G2	733
LOPS	G1	521		AE4	941		AE1	978
LOQUACIOUS	G3	654		AE6	542		AE1	1028
	AE12	694		AE6	705		AE4	52
	HIF	700		AE7	394		AE6	846
	M15	553		AE7	505		AE6	1122
LORD	UDH	61		AE7	513		AE11	337
	AR	233		AE8	496		AE12	359
	PWG	25		AE9	444		KT1	79
	PWG	41		AE10	324		KT1	128
	SIE	10		AE10	864		KT3	549
	VHH	26		AE10	1239		C	715
	AM	124		AE11	132		FL	273
	AM	1073		AE11	271		FL	328

LORDS	FL	525
	AU	205
	CI	587
	PMK	32
LORDSHIP	J1	204
	PLT	4
LORDSHIPS	HAP	2202
	J1	158
	J10	356
LORE	MF	124
	G4	564
LOSE	AR	271
	SMA	128
	AM	128
	AM	340
	EWGR	46
	PTL	23
	STL	11
	ECG1	4
	SCG1	23
	PR	2
	PDG	29
	AT	92
	AT	101
	T23	51
	H29	98
	PKA	43
	PKA	46
	J3	1
	J6	130
	J6	771
	J10	524
	P1	68
	M1	715
	G2	73
	G2	146
	G4	715
	AE3	607
	AE4	695
	AE9	541
	AE11	1090
	AE12	355
	OAL	91
	OAL	420
	OAL	754
	MG	10
	MFL	5
	KT1	441
	KT2	301
	KT3	789
	KT3	798
	B	41
	B	382
	HIF	387
	M11	456
	M12	251
	AU	47
	AU	217
	WB	308
	WB	472
	M15	382
	M15	437
	M15	693
	GP	45
	CI	444
	CI	483
	CI	504
	CI	635
	PMK	35
	AS	66
LOSER	HAP	2052
LOSER'S	AE5	485
LOSERS	CI	523
LOSES	AM	68
	J6	216
	J10	511
	AE9	1068
	AE9	1076
	OAL	517
LOSING	PAZ	23
	TA	164
	HAP	509
	OAL	515
	OAL	516
	AU	27
LOSS	AM	45
	AM	339
	AM	840
	PNH	16
	EPF	23
	PUO5	17
	AA	90
	MD	238
	SAA	88
	RL	323
	NS	5

LOSS	NS	16
	NS	27
	TA	195
	HAP	1576
	HAP	1594
	HAP	2363
	PDS	4
	PP	48
	PKA	40
	EL	11
	J6	490
	J10	369
	P1	107
	P3	62
	M1	790
	M13	1
	HI	107
	VP1	22
	VP6	89
	G3	164
	G4	670
	AE2	121
	AE2	1014
	AE3	439
	AE3	578
	AE5	1131
	AE10	274
	OAL	290
	OAL	568
	KT1	224
	KT1	519
	KT1	542
	KT3	734
	KT3	860
	HIF	187
	HIF	194
	HIF	253
	HIF	321
	C	354
	M15	666
LOSSES	PP	9
	EL	355
	J3	360
	M1	794
	AE1	785
	AE11	652
LOST	MHD	4
	AR	10
	AR	23
	AR	74
	AR	85
	AR	105
	AR	136
	AR	202
	AR	231
	SMA	53
	LC	6
	DC	45
	PRL	32
	AM	6
	AM	121
	AM	268
	AM	630
	AM	1009
	AM	1153
	AM	1196
	EWGR	8
	ECG1	6
	ECG1	32
	PUO1	4
	EAL	23
	PKK	3
	CM	28
	CM	137
	HP	51
	HP	213
	HP	236
	DA	4
	DA	5
	DA	64
	DA	103
	DA	208
	SSF	22
	PUO5	8
	PUF	29
	AA	95
	AA	830
	AA	971
	MD	139
	D	11
	SAA	78
	SAA	363
	SAA	462
	SAA	875
	SAA	1002

LOST	SAA	1097
	EDG	2
	RL	115
	RL	231
	RL	278
	RL	288
	ER	42
	L2	13
	L3	13
	L3	168
	L3	251
	L4	78
	L4	89
	T18	42
	T23	69
	FS3	14
	TA	18
	TA	205
	PAA	2
	PAA	46
	HAP	772
	HAP	1133
	HAP	1202
	HAP	1313
	HAP	1335
	HAP	1818
	BR	83
	BR	310
	BR	311
	BR	314
	PTS	9
	ELW	4
	ODA	17
	J1	73
	J1	116
	J1	139
	J3	212
	J3	343
	J6	146
	J6	254
	J6	801
	J10	15
	J10	188
	J10	334
	J10	511
	P3	72
	P5	151
	P6	62
	M1	49
	M1	331
	M1	400
	M1	487
	M1	904
	M13	32
	M13	43
	M13	217
	VCS	37
	HI	87
	MC	12
	GK	81
	VP3	31
	VP6	63
	G2	83
	G2	273
	G2	342
	G3	352
	G3	448
	G4	401
	G4	657
	G4	732
	AE1	167
	AE1	319
	AE2	249
	AE2	1002
	AE2	1005
	AE2	1067
	AE2	1092
	AE3	376
	AE3	409
	AE3	412
	AE3	612
	AE3	632
	AE3	933
	AE4	275
	AE4	324
	AE4	346
	AE5	823
	AE5	1038
	AE5	1126
	AE6	412
	AE6	482
	AE6	495
	AE6	457
	AE6	1106
	AE6	1213
	AE7	839

Word	Ref	No.
LOST	AE7	897
	AE8	79
	AE8	614
	AE9	160
	AE9	419
	AE9	608
	AE9	954
	AE10	420
	AE10	660
	AE10	1210
	AE10	1259
	AE11	88
	AE11	350
	AE11	406
	AE11	414
	AE11	420
	AE11	1001
	AE11	1059
	AE11	1257
	AE12	1159
	AE12	1215
	OAL	493
	OAL	844
	DO	147
	KT1	79
	KT2	5
	KT2	31
	KT2	194
	KT2	575
	KT2	607
	KT3	256
	KT3	424
	KT3	588
	KT3	676
	KT3	680
	KT3	849
	KT3	1109
	KT3	1142
	TJD	100
	M8	305
	B	4
	B	119
	BP	152
	CAM	269
	CAM	350
	HIF	402
	HIF	568
	HIF	779
	C	127
	C	707
	TH	84
	TH	428
	M11	81
	M11	97
	M11	180
	M11	251
	M11	363
	M11	398
	M11	403
	FL	299
	M12	716
	M12	783
	AU	86
	AU	213
	WB	59
	M15	107
	M15	166
	M15	246
	M15	466
	M15	550
	M15	650
	CI	69
	CI	348
	CI	414
	CI	430
	CI	627
	PMK	40
LOT	PWG	42
	HP	110
	SAA	743
	L3	49
	H2	84
	GK	123
	DHP	28
	G3	257
	AE1	197
	AE2	267
	AE3	189
	AE3	335
	AE5	685
	AE5	703
	AE6	30
	AE9	356
	AE10	739
	AE11	339
	OAL	735

Word	Ref	No.
LOT	KT2	402
	KT3	243
	HIF	189
	HIF	245
	HIF	421
	C	182
	C	388
LOTES	G2	120
LOTH	SLN	3
	PAZ	31
	PR	20
	AA	313
	FS3	12
	HAP	1380
	BR	123
	P3	86
	G2	503
	AE4	711
	AE6	768
	AE9	481
	AE10	1163
	HIF	298
	C	74
	C	167
	M12	38
	WB	182
LOTOS	T.18	71
LOTS	AE1	716
	AE3	830
	AE4	544
	AE5	174
	AE5	654
	AE5	985
	AE6	681
	AE9	219
	AE10	168
	AU	141
	AU	382
LOTTERY	EUF	5
	H29	80
LOUD	HS	6
	HS	140
	AR	123
	SMA	35
	AM	219
	AM	274
	AM	347
	AM	383
	AM	430
	AM	478
	ENH	7
	ESF	9
	CM	93
	HP	228
	DA	52
	AA	646
	PLB	35
	PRH	17
	MF	132
	SAA	830
	SAA	1095
	EK	7
	EK	23
	EC	17
	TA	319
	HAP	1964
	HAP	2451
	HAP	2483
	SSC	25
	EL	64
	ODA	67
	J10	117
	J10	527
	P1	76
	P4	112
	M1	276
	M9	4
	M13	201
	HI	193
	HI	194
	GK	84
	G2	533
	G3	294
	G4	358
	G4	484
	G4	666
	AE1	131
	AE1	214
	AE2	295
	AE2	398
	AE2	401
	AE2	639
	AE2	667
	AE2	831
	AE2	886
	AE3	403

Word	Ref	No.
LOUD	AE3	550
	AE3	577
	AE4	251
	AE4	282
	AE4	649
	AE4	955
	AE5	199
	AE5	444
	AE5	489
	AE5	912
	AE5	1001
	AE6	757
	AE6	636
	AE7	64
	AE7	725
	AE7	850
	AE7	855
	AE8	556
	AE8	574
	AE8	716
	AE8	921
	AE9	621
	AE9	636
	AE9	695
	AE10	367
	AE10	1148
	AE10	1251
	AE10	1252
	AE11	205
	AE11	223
	AE11	291
	AE11	1095
	AE12	542
	AE12	681
	AE12	1051
	OAL	236
	OAE2	69
	AF	107
	DO	75
	KT2	573
	KT3	85
	KT3	262
	KT3	525
	KT3	550
	M8	156
	HIF	35
	HIF	521
	HIF	804
	C	40
	C	637
	C	743
	TH	102
	TH	267
	TH	277
	TH	281
	M11	139
	M11	180
	M11	385
	M12	61
	M12	518
	AU	589
	CI	399
	CI	611
LOUD-BUZZING	G3	239
LOUDER	EDGA	35
	TA	475
	J3	171
	M13	18
	AE2	401
	AE2	634
	AE5	216
	AF	124
	C	699
	C	706
	M11	395
LOUDEST	MD	35
	SAA	397
	RL	405
	HAP	280
	PTP	6
LOUDLY	SAA	753
	RL	315
	P3	7
	P3	52
	P3	73
	P3	241
	P3	343
	AE2	123
	AE3	380
	AE5	235
	AE5	574
	AE7	633
	AE11	1239
	AE11	1281
	AE12	1368
	KT2	78

LOUDLY	KT3	578
	C	361
	M11	464
	AU	359
	AU	369
LOUDNESS	PC2	26
LOUSY	J16	95
	P5	215
LOUVRE	M1	227
LOVE	UDH	97
	HS	72
	HS	86
	AR	20
	RH	93
	SMA	121
	SMA	122
	SMA	134
	LC	4
	LC	10
	LC	89
	LC	82
	LC	146
	PWG	4
	PWG	55
	EIE	26
	VHH	6
	VHH	10
	AM	112
	AM	181
	AM	193
	AM	429
	AM	962
	EMQ	16
	SMQ	3
	SMQ	9
	SMQ	12
	SMQ	14
	PWGR	5
	SMM1	5
	SMM1	8
	SMM2	1
	SMM2	6
	SMM2	26
	PT	11
	PA	30
	SEL2	5
	SEL4	11
	SEL4	16
	SEL4	21
	ETL	18
	STL	1
	STL	5
	STL	13
	STL	19
	PCG1	8
	ECG1	18
	ECG1	34
	ECG2	7
	ECG2	21
	SCG1	2
	SCG1	3
	SCG1	6
	SCG1	12
	SCG1	17
	SCG1	19
	SCG2	9
	SCG2	22
	SCG2	27
	SCG3	27
	PW	8
	SM1	6
	SM1	10
	SM2	9
	S	4
	S	7
	PLN	37
	SLN	1
	SLN	12
	SLN	15
	SLN	17
	PCD	12
	PCD	25
	SCD1	4
	SCD1	18
	EUO	17
	ENH	20
	E	5
	EAZ	16
	PC2	17
	ML	34
	EAL	23
	EMK	5
	EMK	8
	EMK	15
	SKK	13
	PTC	21

LOVE	STC	3
	STC	4
	PCB	18
	PLG	29
	CM	24
	CM	31
	CM	35
	CM	70
	CM	139
	HP	18
	HP	37
	HP	43
	HP	73
	HP	76
	HP	88
	HP	98
	HP	104
	HP	112
	HP	138
	HP	150
	HP	174
	HP	196
	HP	200
	HP	227
	DA	8
	DA	32
	DA	49
	DA	54
	DA	106
	DA	118
	DA	135
	DA	176
	DA	180
	DA	192
	DA	196
	DA	204
	SSF	8
	SSF	11
	SSF	16
	SSF	21
	ETG	11
	ETG	16
	PUO4	3
	PUF	10
	AA	26
	AA	223
	AA	300
	AA	423
	AA	426
	AA	488
	AA	679
	AA	746
	AA	880
	PLB	5
	PPC	5
	EPC	3
	EPC	7
	MD	183
	D	2
	D	7
	D	9
	D	31
	D	42
	D	46
	MF	179
	SAA	880
	SAA	1038
	SAA	1106
	PK	32
	EK	17
	PDG	26
	EDG	26
	EDG	31
	EDGA	22
	EDGA	30
	SDG	5
	SDG	6
	SDG	7
	OE	2
	OE	4
	OE	25
	AT	1
	AT	6
	AT	19
	AT	32
	AT	62
	AT	68
	AT	79
	AT	90
	AT	98
	AT	105
	AT	108
	AT	116
	AT	119
	AT	127
	DOD	23

LOVE	DOD	27
	PD	42
	L1	2
	L1	27
	L1	48
	L1	54
	L3	197
	L4	10
	L4	18
	L4	26
	L4	35
	L4	45
	L4	50
	L4	56
	L4	60
	L4	67
	L4	81
	L4	92
	L4	124
	L4	146
	L4	147
	L4	189
	L4	201
	L4	206
	L4	238
	L4	272
	L4	292
	T18	81
	T23	1
	T23	18
	T23	22
	T23	29
	T23	40
	T23	44
	T23	50
	T23	63
	T23	82
	T23	86
	T23	88
	T23	111
	T23	103
	T27	84
	T27	103
	T27	120
	T27	122
	H3	1
	H9	10
	H9	23
	H2	56
	H2	100
	FS2	10
	FS2	12
	FS3	14
	FS4	5
	FS4	9
	FS4	13
	TA	132
	TA	228
	TA	244
	TA	260
	AK	54
	AK	61
	AK	83
	HH	32
	HAP	386
	HAP	547
	HAP	901
	HAP	1228
	HAP	1325
	HAP	1414
	HAP	1971
	HAP	2001
	HAP	2138
	HAP	2193
	HAP	2472
	SSC	45
	BR	151
	BR	348
	EDS	7
	EDS	27
	EDS	33
	PP	17
	PP	31
	ETS	6
	ETS	15
	STS1	6
	STS1	18
	STS2	1
	STS2	9
	STS2	11
	STS3	12
	STS3	14
	STS3	31
	STS3	37
	EKA	13
	EKA	29

LOVE			LOVE			LOVE		
	AF	114		B	74		CI	4
	AF	121		B	82		CI	24
	MG	3		B	124		CI	27
	DO	6		B	128		CI	31
	DO	164		B	130		CI	33
	KT1	8		B	149		CI	41
	KT1	12		B	175		CI	72
	KT1	243		B	183		CI	110
	KT1	281		B	219		CI	124
	KT1	294		B	236		CI	125
	KT1	303		B	281		CI	126
	KT1	307		B	311		CI	131
	KT1	315		B	354		CI	133
	KT1	320		B	369		CI	145
	KT1	326		B	396		CI	163
	KT1	328		B	398		CI	300
	KT1	332		B	435		CI	303
	KT1	334		B	457		CI	315
	KT1	336		B	473		CI	345
	KT1	349		B	526		CI	351
	KT1	350		B	589		CI	358
	KT1	360		B	646		CI	222
	KT1	398		B	732		CI	229
	KT1	501		B	736		CI	230
	KT1	510		BP	34		CI	260
	KT1	513		BP	39		CI	262
	KT1	540		M10	36		CI	293
	KT2	5		CAM	23		CI	299
	KT2	8		CAM	27		CI	429
	KT2	78		CAM	33		CI	430
	KT2	110		CAM	59		CI	459
	KT2	111		CAM	67		CI	464
	KT2	130		CAM	80		CI	484
	KT2	144		CAM	175		CI	498
	KT2	146		CAM	186		CI	514
	KT2	148		CAM	187		CI	518
	KT2	153		CAM	191		CI	528
	KT2	166		CAM	235		CI	529
	KT2	170		CAM	250		CI	534
	KT2	204		CAM	298		CI	640
	KT2	218		CAM	388		ETP	39
	KT2	291		HIF	97		STP	1
	KT2	297		HIF	167		STP	21
	KT2	323		HIF	593		SMP	73
	KT2	339		HIF	726		SMP	81
	KT2	350		C	69		ESK	16
	KT2	360		C	101		EMKG	41
	KT2	364		C	127		PWR	14
	KT2	367		C	135		EWR	16
	KT2	373		C	176	LOVE-AFFAIRS	GE	10
	KT2	375		C	188	LOVED	HS	43
	KT2	404		C	647		SMA	117
	KT2	416		C	691		LC	25
	KT2	459		TH	24		AM	961
	KT2	504		TH	33		ECG1	40
	KT2	508		TH	38		SCG1	30
	KT2	520		TH	54		SM1	5
	KT2	607		TH	61		SM1	6
	KT2	632		TH	69		SM2	2
	KT3	17		TH	84		S	2
	KT3	37		TH	87		SKK	4
	KT3	87		TH	179		SKK	17
	KT3	96		TH	224		PTC	1
	KT3	116		TH	238		CM	24
	KT3	129		TH	256		CM	25
	KT3	137		TH	299		DA	24
	KT3	156		TH	389		AA	41
	KT3	168		TH	396		AA	429
	KT3	226		TH	424		AA	431
	KT3	230		M11	22		AA	600
	KT3	237		M11	62		EPC	30
	KT3	276		M11	377		DOD	18
	KT3	280		M11	485		EC	37
	KT3	316		FL	4		TA	221
	KT3	326		FL	25		HAP	34
	KT3	329		FL	332		HAP	265
	KT3	376		FL	522		HAP	497
	KT3	431		M12	269		HAP	1502
	KT3	668		M12	293		HAP	2094
	KT3	676		M12	543		ELW	10
	KT3	780		M12	698		EL	177
	KT3	795		M12	773		OD	37
	KT3	808		M12	830		J3	89
	KT3	809		AU	313		J6	597
	KT3	831		WB	78		J10	540
	KT3	897		WB	246		P2	75
	KT3	903		WB	290		P4	4
	KT3	1025		WB	322		M1	488
	KT3	1029		WB	327		M1	1071
	KT3	1123		WB	452		M9	7
	KT3	1154		WB	488		M9	82
	TJD	5		WB	538		M13	10
	M8	71		M15	485		R	16
	M8	273		GP	32		R	20
	M8	322		GP	47		VP2	2
	B	55		CI	1		G1	20

LOVED

G2	717
G4	373
AE4	39
AE4	964
AE5	947
AE5	1049
AE6	468
AE7	57
AE7	260
AE8	758
AE9	269
AE9	405
AE9	438
AE9	444
AE9	637
AE10	273
AE10	324
AE11	418
AE11	811
AE12	159
OAL	322
OAL	637
OAL	695
KT1	165
KT1	316
KT1	362
KT1	519
KT2	528
KT3	10
KT3	786
KT3	816
KT3	827
TJD	6
TJD	120
B	29
B	189
B	339
B	354
B	355
B	396
B	618
B	630
B	650
HIF	52
HIF	485
HIF	807
C	594
TH	9
TH	16
TH	156
TH	158
TH	384
M11	6
M11	56
M11	398
M12	273
M12	494
M12	555
WB	69
WB	122
WB	130
WB	359
M15	86
GP	29
GP	31
GP	130
CI	57
CI	235
CI	241
CI	245
CI	253
CI	439
CI	442

LOVE-INVENTIONS OAE2 57

LOVEIT MF 152

LOVELIER
L4	4
M13	148
CAM	387

LOVELY
L4	70
ODA	42
M1	835
M9	211
M13	1
M13	66
M13	194
HI	190
GK	111
VP2	59
VP3	111
VP4	13
VP8	110
VP8	120
G4	696
AE3	425
AE5	372
AE5	394

LOVELY (continued)
AE5	734
AE5	744
AE6	542
AE10	25
AE10	201
AE11	99
AE12	212
AE12	235
OAL	138
OAL	300
AF	9
AF	105
M10	99
CAM	374
M12	303
AM	898

LOVER
SEL2	1
SEL3	14
SCG3	1
SLN	7
SLN	16
HP	51
EPC	13
AT	69
DOD	11
L4	37
L4	171
T23	9
FS4	16
HAP	1871
SKA2	22
SKA3	1
J6	160
M1	629
M1	804
M9	116
M13	4
M13	51
SFL	9
SLT2	2
VP8	37
G3	384
G4	657
G4	708
G4	724
AE4	410
AE4	429
AE4	695
AE9	568
AE9	594
AE12	69
AE12	108
OAL	54
OAL	124
OAL	146
OAL	191
OAL	343
OAL	348
OAL	457
OAL	475
OAL	692
OAL	802
OAL	821
OAL	823
OAL	830
OAE1	12
KT1	507
KT3	314
B	149
B	236
B	295
M10	95
CAM	118
TH	178
M12	288
M12	668
CI	345
CI	355
CI	285
CI	481
PMK	11

LOVER'S
L4	58
M13	26
SLT1	2
SLT1	15
VP6	87
VP8	51
G3	603
AE4	442
AE4	1005
AE6	35
AE7	444
AE12	41
OAL	409
OAL	567
OAL	676

LOVER'S (continued)
KT2	323
KT2	355
KT2	383
KT2	475
KT3	857
KT3	861
B	23
B	612
TH	44
M12	573

LOVERS
AR	211
PRL	34
VHH	50
AM	109
PEL	19
PTL	12
STL	7
STL	11
ECG1	14
SCG1	2
SCG1	18
PW	22
EMK	1
STC	11
SAA	1127
L4	31
L4	139
L4	205
T23	110
FS2	8
HAP	1378
SSC	35
J1	128
J6	448
M1	619
VP8	157
G4	705
AE6	597
OAL	136
OAL	161
KT2	80
KT2	319
KT2	379
KT2	400
KT2	497
KT2	510
KT3	1155
B	132
CI	593
SMP	89
SMP	95

LOVERS'
PW	6
VP8	2
KT2	149
B	6

LOVE'S
SMM2	12
SMM2	29
STL	4
CM	139
DA	36
MF	122
MF	143
SDG	23
SDG	28
PD	46
H9	23
HAP	2439
J6	141
VP3	115
G3	403
AE1	997
AE8	486
AE8	926
AE9	277
OAL	6
OAL	16
OAL	297
KT1	329
KT1	404
KT1	405
KT2	373
KT2	478
KT3	832
EWR	13
EIE	17

LOVES
AM	595
A	4
HP	181
HP	235
DA	19
PUO4	34
AA	198
AA	469
MF	71
OE	31
OE	54

Headword	Ref	No.
LOVES	ER	61
	SKA5	2
	J3	89
	J6	228
	J6	296
	J6	437
	J6	529
	P6	9
	M1	606
	M1	684
	M1	747
	VP1	5
	VP2	42
	VP3	92
	VP3	93
	VP3	136
	VP6	80
	VP7	86
	VP7	89
	VP8	83
	VP10	60
	G2	52
	G2	155
	G3	352
	G4	818
	AE1	971
	AE4	93
	AE4	178
	AE4	324
	AE6	607
	OAL	595
	OAL	688
	KT1	179
	KT2	497
	KT3	14
	KT3	141
	KT3	241
	KT3	278
	KT3	828
	B	177
	CAM	377
	HIF	314
	M10	20
	CI	43
LOVE-SICK	M1	705
	M9	149
	VP9	53
	AE4	420
LOVESICK	GE	24
	VP3	103
LOVESOME	L1	31
LOVEST	KT1	404
	B	616
LOVE-TRICK	EDGA	24
LOVING	HP	50
	HP	148
	T27	71
	SKA6	27
	EH	33
	AE6	44
	AE8	222
	B	339
	M12	543
	WB	326
	WB	354
LOW	EIE	18
	AM	839
	AM	1061
	AM	1094
	AM	1132
	AM	1154
	AM	1183
	SMQ	16
	ECG2	4
	PUO1	43
	EUO	33
	AA	689
	AA	895
	PRH	17
	SAA	191
	SAA	230
	SAA	355
	SAA	1121
	RL	372
	PD	38
	H29	53
	H2	1
	TA	250
	HAP	2159
	BR	239
	EL	95
	J3	494
	P1	228
	P2	11
	P5	107
	VP2	98
LOW	G2	155
	G2	402
	G3	321
	G3	454
	G3	519
	AE5	194
	AE6	295
	AE6	780
	AE7	1078
	AE10	699
	AE11	638
	AE11	732
	AE12	713
	AE12	1346
	OAL	737
	KT1	536
	KT1	570
	KT2	81
	KT3	294
	KT3	489
	KT3	554
	KT3	689
	B	343
	B	684
	FL	329
	WB	461
	WB	481
	GP	109
	PTP	8
LOWED	M1	876
	M1	1016
	AE8	474
LOWER	SMM2	24
	RL	77
	HAP	344
	G2	400
	AE6	37
	AE11	489
	B	109
LOWERED	AR	224
	HIF	394
LOWERING	ETC	2
	G1	423
	M1	362
	G3	87
	KT2	544
	M8	272
	HIF	720
	TH	395
LOWEST	HAP	793
	J3	328
	G2	558
	B	558
	CI	426
LOW-HUNG	KT3	863
LOWING	M1	907
	VP4	26
	VP7	13
	G2	199
	G2	764
	G4	629
	AE8	269
	OAL	315
LOWINGS	M1	1039
	VP6	72
	G3	826
LOW-LAID	AM	610
LOWLANDS	M1	824
LOWLY	AA	865
	HAP	1269
	M1	516
	VP4	2
	VP5	98
	VP6	12
	VP10	20
	G1	517
	G2	369
	G2	606
	AE1	312
	AE1	734
	AE3	413
	AE7	1092
	AE8	132
	AE8	481
	AE8	601
	KT3	214
	KT3	229
	B	485
	FL	405
	FL	618
	J6	400
LOW-ROOFED	AR	24
LOYAL	SMA	106
	AM	614
	AM	685
	ECD	21
LOYAL	PUO5	27
	AA	314
	AA	876
	AA	905
	MD	51
	MD	181
	MD	258
	PRH	15
	SAA	297
	SAA	812
	SAA	1025
	SAA	1135
	EC	17
	HAP	1335
	HAP	2185
	BR	233
	J10	138
	J10	407
	AE6	607
	AE11	521
	C	790
LOYALLY	EAA	29
LOYALTY	AM	1153
	EMW	9
	PUOS	12
	AA	62
	AA	358
	AA	871
	ELB	8
	MD	239
	D	7
	SAA	963
	SAA	1015
	TA	505
	HAP	596
	HAP	1385
	HAP	2384
	VP8	130
LUBBER	ECD	14
LUBBERS	PK	39
	HAP	1844
LUBRIC	AK	63
LUCAGUS	AE10	810
	AE10	812
	AE10	824
LUCETIUS	AE9	771
LUCID	MF	22
LUCIFER	MD	21
	SAA	197
	VP8	25
	M11	228
LUCILIUS	J1	27
	J1	251
	P1	223
LUCINA	CM	61
	T27	52
	VP4	11
	CAM	364
LUCINA'S	HAP	1878
	G4	480
	KT2	654
	CAM	361
LUCK	PWG	32
	AT	86
	PSF	1
	HAP	589
	HAP	1859
	EKA	20
	OAL	388
	WB	420
LUCKIER	SAA	868
LUCKILY	J10	5
LUCKLESS	J10	177
	M1	296
	VP8	81
	AE3	25
	AE11	299
	KT1	498
LUCKY	AM	533
	AA	253
	AT	65
	T18	29
	HAP	1838
	HAP	2224
	J6	751
	J16	3
	P2	69
	P3	93
	G1	371
	AE9	320
	AE9	454
	AE9	455
	AE9	1023
	AE11	1150
	AE12	1056
	OAL	457

LUCKY	M12	518	LUST	J6	445	LUXURY	J1	37
	CI	478		J10	176		J6	399
LUCRE	HAP	796		J10	333		P1	67
	P5	69		P4	120		P6	85
	P5	193		P5	252		AE4	279
	P6	177		P6	173		KT2	480
	G2	717		G2	637		B	436
	AE3	81		G3	221		M15	112
	AE6	826		G4	290	LYAEUS	M8	7
LUCRETIAN	PUO1	32		G4	661	LYCAEAN	G3	3
LUCRETIA'S	J10	452		AE2	1070	LYCAEUM	PUO1	14
LUCRINE	H2	73		AE3	421	LYCAEUS	M1	964
	G2	222		AE4	281		VP10	23
LUCY	AS	5		AE10	140		G4	780
LUDGATE	PCB	10		AE10	451	LYCAON	M1	282
LUFF	AE5	22		AE10	544		AE9	408
LUG	PD	62		AE12	213	LYCAON'S	M1	211
	J16	78		OAL	317		M1	256
	P1	272		OAL	383		AE10	1057
LUGGAGE	HAP	2327		OAL	408	LYCAS	AE10	783
LUGGED	PTP	4		OAL	848	LYCIAN	AE1	162
LUGGING	EK	31		KT2	479		AE4	205
LUKEWARM	AE2	756		CAM	262		AE4	544
LULL	L1	42		M15	718		AE6	458
LULLABY	P3	29		CI	192		AE7	997
LULLED	AM	392	LUSTER	JH	10		AE7	1113
	DA	52		AM	1196		AE8	224
	AE1	971		BR	314		AE10	191
	AE7	862		AE5	139		AE10	1063
	AE8	40		DO	103		AE11	1138
	CAM	189		TJD	196		AE12	517
	TH	63		B	4		AE12	749
LUMBER	PKK	8		HIF	387		M12	162
	SAA	545		M11	403		AU	399
	PK	41	LUSTFUL	J6	83	LYCIANS	T27	74
	J3	325		J6	409	LYCIDAS	VP7	93
	G3	229		M1	956		VP9	2
LUMP	AA	172		M1	974		M12	430
	L3	10		AE4	323	LYCORIAS	G4	479
	TA	65		AE6	831	LYCORIS	VP10	3
	M1	11		M12	310		VP10	34
	G4	50	LUSTRATION	J6	683	LYCOTAS	M12	474
	M15	385		P2	62	LYCTIAN	VP5	114
	M15	559	LUSTRATIONS	RL	128	LYCURGUS	AE3	20
LUMPISH	P4	119		BR	189		KT3	39
	C	461	LUSTS	RL	158		KT3	60
LUMPS	HAP	314		BR	281		KT3	652
	M10	44		J10	152	LYCUS	G4	524
LUNA	P6	21		J10	500		AE1	306
LUNACY	AA	788	LUSTY	SCD2	5		AE9	728
LUNAR	AM	656		PC2	13		AE9	747
	M9	185		L4	199		M12	451
	AE1	691		T27	89		M15	418
LUNATICS	SAA	780		SKA6	9	LYDIA	AE10	209
LUNGED	J10	92		J6	448	LYDIAN	G2	139
LUNGS	AR	245		P1	44		G4	547
	G2	61		G3	104		AE4	317
	G2	186		AE12	1047		AE8	626
	G3	756		OAL	146		AE8	656
	AE6	852		CAM	45		AE9	732
	AE9	788		M11	72		AF	97
	AE9	949		WB	47	LYGDUS	M9	10
	AE10	497	LUTE	MF	35		M9	27
	KT3	759		MF	44	LYING	SKK	1
	M12	501		MF	58		SKK	14
	M15	514		MF	210		EPC	5
LUPERCI	AE8	880		T18	10		HAP	1816
LUPINES	G1	111		SSC	36		J10	231
LUPUS	P1	225		J6	501		R	1
LURCH	EH	19		OAE1	1		AE2	734
LURE	AA	928		KT2	517		AE8	277
	EK	12		FL	359		AE12	369
LURK	PMS	9	LUTHER	HAP	380		OAL	335
	VP3	58		HAP	688		C	569
LURKED	HAP	52		HAP	713		C	660
	AE2	776		HAP	1935	LYING'S	P5	109
	OAL	779	LUXURIANT	G1	166	LYNCESTIS	M15	493
LURKING	G1	206		G2	340	LYNCEUS	AE9	1035
	G4	352		G2	503		M8	54
	AE5	890		G2	568	LYNX	P1	199
	AE6	218		AE11	749		M15	619
	C	662	LUXURIOUS	L4	115	LYNXES	VP8	3
	M12	792		J1	211		G3	415
	AU	50		J6	411	LYNX'S	AE1	447
LUSCIOUS	T27	14		J10	474	LYONS	PKA	32
	G1	470		P3	212		J1	65
LUST	AA	19		VP4	52	LYRCAEAN	M1	814
	HAP	352		AE7	601	LYRE	MO	5
	BR	341	LUXURIOUSLY	J3	341		T18	57
	J6	73		G3	788		AK	45
	J6	108	LUXURY	AM	862		SSC	50
	J6	132		PAZ	30		J6	501
	J6	172		SAA	312		P6	9
	J6	193		L4	102		M1	697
	J6	421		HAP	362		DHP	27
	J6	441		HAP	1409		VP3	69

LYRE	VP4	69
	AE1	1039
	AE6	178
	OAL	15
	AF	22
	AF	123
	AF	159
	DO	2
	HIF	809
	C	634
	FL	152
	GP	24
LYRNESSIAN	M12	149
LYRNESSUS	AE12	800
LYRNESUS	AU	283
LYSIMACHUS	CI	437
	CI	450
	CI	536
MACAREUS	M12	605
MACBETH	EUO	30
MACE	M1	389
	M1	446
	AE2	828
	KT3	33
MACEDON	DO	133
MACEDONIAN	M12	620
MACEDONS	TJD	161
MACES	KT3	523
	KT3	605
MACHINE	AE2	25
MACHINES	EUO	22
	PNH	36
	PNH	48
	PNH	53
	EOE	10
MACHINING	PKK	8
	OAL	120
MACKEREL	HAP	1750
MACROBIUS	C	376
MACS	PUO3	29
MAD	SEL1	9
	PTL	19
	ETL	1
	AA	336
	AA	912
	MD	286
	SAA	7
	SAA	417
	SAA	776
	EC	9
	T27	30
	HAP	1784
	ETS	1
	SKA1	7
	J6	64
	J6	658
	J6	807
	J10	224
	P1	208
	P3	242
	P4	14
	P5	213
	M1	195
	M13	192
	M13	193
	VP3	52
	G2	718
	G3	745
	AE1	214
	AE2	122
	AE2	320
	AE2	1010
	AE3	249
	AE3	563
	AE4	297
	AE4	683
	AE5	857
	AE6	34
	AE6	54
	AE8	880
	AE9	993
	AE10	102
	AE10	110
	AE10	806
	AE11	426
	AE12	337
	AE12	875
	OAL	508
	KT1	339
	KT2	144
MAD	CAM	101
	CAM	128
	C	330
	M12	319
	M12	635
	M15	490
MADAM	LCA	50
	HAP	822
	EKA	9
	EKA	30
	J1	58
	C	105
	C	195
	C	205
	C	419
	C	574
	FL	475
	WB	370
	EMKG	23
	EMKG	29
MAD-BRAINED	HAP	845
MADDER	P3	243
	M9	112
MADDING	J6	688
	AE7	539
	AE9	666
MADE	UDH	62
	HS	22
	HS	24
	HS	51
	HS	78
	HS	86
	HS	113
	HS	124
	AR	76
	AR	81
	AR	103
	AR	114
	AR	191
	AR	194
	AR	217
	AR	269
	AR	271
	AR	279
	SMA	121
	LC	91
	DC	4
	LCA	31
	PRL	27
	AM	64
	AM	179
	AM	290
	AM	345
	AM	826
	AM	957
	AM	1096
	AM	1099
	PA	11
	EEL	29
	SEL1	16
	PCG1	39
	SCG1	2
	SCG1	18
	SCG1	30
	MD	60
	MD	70
	EMQW	30
	PM	16
	EM	22
	SM1	2
	SM1	8
	PLN	20
	PLN	40
	ECD	2
	PUO1	28
	PNH	12
	PUO2	29
	E	1
	E	26
	PC1	13
	ML	44
	EMK	12
	EMK	13
	EMK	15
	PTW	14
	CM	42
	HP	18
	HP	32
	HP	73
	HP	76
	HP	124
	HP	141
	DA	122
	DA	131
	DA	202
	DA	204
MADE	PSF	43
	ETG	22
	PUO3	17
	PUO4	30
	AA	2
	AA	21
	AA	34
	AA	58
	AA	64
	AA	68
	AA	312
	AA	371
	AA	402
	AA	410
	AA	576
	AA	610
	AA	627
	AA	634
	AA	666
	AA	672
	AA	704
	AA	751
	AA	768
	AA	928
	AA	945
	PRH	23
	MF	63
	MF	118
	MF	157
	MF	179
	SAA	1
	SAA	77
	SAA	97
	SAA	147
	SAA	199
	SAA	231
	SAA	233
	SAA	237
	SAA	249
	SAA	268
	SAA	277
	SAA	285
	SAA	297
	SAA	353
	SAA	362
	SAA	372
	SAA	388
	SAA	413
	SAA	427
	SAA	469
	SAA	474
	SAA	492
	SAA	547
	SAA	649
	SAA	821
	SAA	874
	SAA	900
	SAA	923
	SAA	994
	PK	12
	PK	34
	PDG	34
	EDGA	34
	RL	45
	RL	112
	RL	157
	RL	248
	RL	324
	RL	384
	RL	402
	RL	451
	AT	127
	DOD	6
	ER	6
	ER	19
	MO	17
	L3	25
	L3	252
	L3	258
	L4	96
	T18	43
	T23	70
	T27	52
	T27	97
	H3	48
	H9	2
	H9	13
	H29	5
	H29	64
	FS2	11
	TA	46
	TA	126
	TA	155
	TA	289
	TA	434
	TA	435

MADE			MADE			MADE		
	EAA	7		VP3	56		OAL	117
	EAA	34		VP3	61		OAL	146
	AK	2		VP5	4		OAL	197
	AK	58		VP5	84		OAL	365
	AK	100		VP5	111		OAL	441
	AK	133		VP6	97		OAL	531
	GE	26		VP8	111		OAL	738
	GE	73		VP9	42		OAL	824
	GE	75		G1	16		OAE1	30
	HAP	48		G1	215		MG	26
	HAP	140		G2	79		MFL	4
	HAP	188		G2	84		DO	15
	HAP	192		G2	615		DO	120
	HAP	247		G2	630		KT1	191
	HAP	351		G3	259		KT1	201
	HAP	437		G3	838		KT1	326
	HAP	491		G4	5		KT1	355
	HAP	515		G4	216		KT1	370
	HAP	556		AE1	21		KT1	458
	HAP	689		AE1	269		KT1	576
	HAP	797		AE1	482		KT2	163
	HAP	921		AE1	556		KT2	335
	HAP	1137		AE1	568		KT2	479
	HAP	1229		AE1	627		KT2	591
	HAP	1342		AE1	827		KT3	123
	HAP	1628		AE1	880		KT3	266
	HAP	1792		AE1	901		KT3	518
	HAP	1866		AE2	7		KT3	822
	HAP	1973		AE2	21		KT3	951
	HAP	2003		AE2	38		TJD	25
	HAP	2017		AE2	77		TJD	56
	HAP	2034		AE2	114		TJD	73
	HAP	2106		AE2	117		TJD	95
	HAP	2239		AE2	216		TJD	145
	HAP	2263		AE2	306		TJD	182
	HAP	2283		AE2	360		B	24
	HAP	2385		AE2	541		B	107
	HAP	2494		AE2	661		B	158
	BR	122		AE2	750		B	164
	BR	132		AE3	300		B	420
	BR	342		AE3	404		B	513
	ETS	4		AE3	535		B	542
	SKA6	20		AE3	638		B	668
	EL	24		AE4	20		B	724
	EL	168		AE4	248		M10	32
	EL	169		AE4	790		M10	81
	EL	226		AE4	1002		M10	91
	OD	14		AE5	358		M10	96
	MS	17		AE5	443		CAM	42
	ESH	2		AE5	674		CAM	212
	J1	102		AE6	177		CAM	225
	J6	228		AE6	604		HIF	5
	J6	233		AE6	697		HIF	126
	J6	531		AE6	819		HIF	599
	J6	811		AE6	847		HIF	751
	J10	10		AE7	264		C	18
	J10	72		AE7	290		C	64
	J10	96		AE7	364		C	115
	J10	177		AE7	613		C	373
	J10	290		AE7	618		C	470
	J10	376		AE7	634		C	492
	J10	402		AE7	798		C	538
	J10	449		AE8	108		C	546
	J10	475		AE8	156		C	558
	P1	73		AE8	284		C	658
	P1	197		AE8	299		C	673
	P1	234		AE8	453		C	684
	P2	74		AE8	744		C	703
	P3	128		AE8	814		TH	80
	P3	164		AE9	190		TH	171
	P5	105		AE9	408		TH	305
	P5	114		AE9	480		TH	314
	M1	41		AE9	495		TH	412
	M1	150		AE9	650		M11	5
	M1	179		AE9	698		M11	350
	M1	282		AE9	1103		M11	453
	M1	713		AE10	111		FL	68
	M1	933		AE10	692		FL	84
	M1	1073		AE10	765		FL	104
	M9	48		AE10	900		FL	197
	M9	187		AE10	1059		FL	203
	M13	21		AE10	1278		FL	246
	M13	59		AE11	200		FL	258
	M13	103		AE11	251		FL	329
	M13	201		AE11	386		FL	362
	SFL	13		AE11	443		FL	412
	SFL	18		AE11	570		FL	419
	HI	26		AE12	35		FL	424
	HI	77		AE12	215		FL	469
	PLT	40		AE12	429		FL	518
	MC	36		AE12	735		FL	594
	MC	55		AE12	1152		FL	600
	VP1	55		AE12	1176		M12	65
	VP2	4		AE12	1222		M12	296
	VP2	100		AE12	1294		M12	622
	VP3	31		AE12	1321		M12	656

Word	Code	No.
MADE	M12	679
	M12	714
	AU	16
	AU	162
	AU	225
	AU	358
	AU	534
	WB	15
	WB	25
	WB	62
	WB	121
	WB	292
	WB	364
	M15	50
	M15	52
	GP	11
	CI	36
	CI	60
	CI	72
	CI	124
	CI	125
	CI	139
	CI	208
	CI	230
	CI	362
	CI	397
	CI	461
	CI	260
	CI	590
	PTP	53
	AS	9
MADEST	KT3	144
MADLY	SAA	4
	SAA	716
	SAA	771
	HAP	1810
	AE5	230
	AE6	794
	AE12	416
MADMAN	AA	553
	AT	85
	P5	174
	G1	613
	MM	9
MADMAN'S		
MADMEN	J10	66
	PTL	6
	ETC	22
	PK	6
	RL	31
	AE7	821
	KT2	322
	KT2	366
MADMEN'S		
MADNESS	P3	158
	AR	22
	SM1	13
	PLG	14
	AA	163
	AA	789
	AA	813
	ELB	28
	MD	271
	SAA	18
	TA	416
	BR	223
	BR	224
	EDS	27
	PMS	19
	J1	139
	PPS	4
	P5	251
	M1	1008
	M9	88
	VP6	68
	G2	538
	G3	367
	G3	773
	G4	642
	AE2	808
	AE2	1044
	AE2	55
	AE3	576
	AE4	211
	AE5	622
	AE5	876
	AE7	748
	AE7	814
	AE9	816
	AE10	1247
	AE11	388
	AE12	887
	AE12	972
	AF	69
	KT1	522
	KT2	582
	M10	19
	CAM	101

Word	Code	No.
MADNESS	CAM	227
	AU	60
	AU	80
	AU	596
	HIF	363
	TH	9
	M12	572
	M15	484
MAE'ANDER'S	DA	1
MAECENAS	G1	6
	G2	54
	G3	69
	G4	3
MAECENAS-LIKE		
MAENALIAN	J1	99
	VP8	30
	VP8	35
	VP8	45
	VP8	52
	VP8	59
	VP8	63
	VP8	69
	VP8	79
	VP8	86
	VP10	21
MAENALUS	M1	279
	VP8	31
MAENAS	P1	198
	P1	203
MAEON'S	AE10	466
MAEOTIAN	G3	543
	AE6	1088
MAEVIA	J1	30
MAEVIUS	J10	194
	VP3	141
MAGAZINE	J6	360
	M9	158
	B	625
MAGAZINES	L2	9
	EL	73
	G4	232
MAGAZINS	AM	1084
MAGGOT'S	M15	564
MAGGOTS	RL	420
	EHC	37
MAGI	HAP	1117
MAGIC	PT	19
	PT	23
	PT	32
	EUO	25
	L4	246
	AK	133
	HAP	232
	HAP	1111
	J6	794
	VP3	158
	VP6	107
	VP8	88
	VP8	135
	G3	446
	AE4	355
	AE4	699
	AE7	262
	AE7	1039
	AE10	763
	WB	367
	M15	536
MAGICIANS	HAP	2015
MAGISTRATE	AA	594
	HAP	489
	J3	294
	P1	264
	CI	438
	CI	453
	CI	463
MAGISTRATES	AA	624
	J10	52
	J10	123
	C	274
MAGNATUM	J1	231
MAGNETS	HAP	1662
MAGNIFICENCE	PFD	22
	PNH	20
	G3	456
	TH	65
	KT2	438
	KT2	664
	TH	254
MAGNIFICENT	TA	52
	AE9	408
MAGNIFIED	KT2	335
MAGUS	EUO	30
	AE10	725
	EC	40
	HAP	702
MAHOMET	M1	922
MAIA	G1	310

Word	Code	No.
MAIA	AE8	183
	AE8	184
MAID	SCG1	23
	SCG1	28
	SLN	6
	PC1	15
	HP	96
	HP	190
	PUO3	13
	EUF	21
	AT	107
	PD	24
	L4	4
	L4	156
	T27	10
	T27	116
	T27	118
	T27	129
	NS	12
	STS3	9
	J6	63
	J6	79
	J6	637
	P5	271
	M1	653
	M9	83
	M9	88
	M9	121
	M9	169
	M9	200
	M9	205
	M9	211
	HI	4
	VP3	111
	VP6	87
	VP6	107
	VP8	23
	VP10	14
	G1	48
	G1	555
	G3	413
	G4	479
	G4	486
	G4	683
	G4	772
	AE1	436
	AE1	476
	AE2	243
	AE2	305
	AE2	464
	AE3	415
	AE3	576
	AE6	13
	AE6	44
	AE6	100
	AE6	731
	AE7	83
	AE7	442
	AE7	671
	AE11	729
	AE11	808
	AE11	839
	AE11	889
	AE11	985
	AE11	1036
	AE11	1055
	AE11	1122
	AE11	1144
	AE11	1215
	AE11	1222
	AE11	1294
	AE12	212
	OAL	396
	OAL	424
	OAL	426
	OAL	429
	OAL	437
	OAL	521
	OAL	789
	OAL	881
	MFL	2
	KT2	314
	KT2	615
	KT3	209
	KT3	244
	KT3	249
	KT3	261
	KT3	287
	KT3	979
	KT3	1017
	M8	76
	B	16
	B	66
	B	91
	M10	7
	M10	14

MAID	M10	32	MAIDS	WB	128	MAIN	AE7	399
	M10	67		WB	282		AE7	416
	CAM	32		WB	542		AE7	574
	CAM	83	MAIL	PCG1	45		AE7	738
	CAM	108		AE3	598		AE7	994
	CAM	162		AE5	339		AE7	1091
	CAM	189		AE9	958		AE8	895
	CAM	227		AE12	1341		AE8	916
	HIF	44		KT3	27		AE9	33
	HIF	171		CI	576		AE9	145
	HIF	272	MAIMED	AM	338		AE9	910
	HIF	324		AM	568		AE10	52
	TH	20		RL	279		AE10	151
	TH	107		J3	88		AE10	158
	TH	127		M12	423		AE10	307
	TH	140		M12	464		AE10	332
	TH	156	MAIN	HS	82		AE10	529
	TH	166		AR	122		AE10	966
	TH	280		AR	249		AE11	395
	TH	291		AM	78		AE11	607
	TH	333		AM	199		AE12	294
	TH	405		AM	248		AE12	543
	M11	256		AM	318		DO	110
	FL	510		AM	338		KT3	1081
	FL	598		AM	376		HIF	235
	M12	44		AM	506		HIF	439
	M12	208		AM	947		C	299
	M12	261		DA	56		C	749
	M12	628		PUF	27		TH	53
	AU	516		MF	140		M11	33
	WB	252		SAA	624		M11	77
	WB	287		L1	24		M11	156
	WB	387		L3	4		M11	206
	CI	92		L3	242		M11	212
	CI	196		H3	21		M11	366
	CI	256		H3	31		M12	733
	AS	59		H29	96		M12	765
	AS	65		TA	488		CI	331
	AS	66		TA	517		CI	386
MAIDEN	AM	1185		HAP	1788		AS	61
	EMQ	2		HAP	600	MAINLAND	M15	440
	MD	153		HAP	2406	MAINMAST	AM	518
	T18	23		J10	237	MAINSHEET	M11	102
	T18	72		J10	297	MAINTAIN	AM	50
	NS	26		P6	62		AM	521
	AE1	694		P6	158		AM	976
	AE11	978		M1	419		PCG2	25
	AE11	1050		M1	792		PM	19
	OAL	297		GK	173		PC2	32
	KT1	190		VP4	61		HP	69
	KT3	192		G1	39		PLB	53
	KT3	565		G1	438		MD	242
	CAM	113		G1	494		MF	115
	CAM	298		G1	577		SAA	104
	AU	187		VP8	84		SAA	972
MAIDENHEAD	PWGR	2		G2	681		OE	24
	PR	2		G3	410		TA	231
	T27	34		G3	519		EAA	27
MAIDENS	M9	123		G4	533		HAP	715
	OAL	200		G4	559		HAP	725
	M8	367		AE1	47		HAP	889
	TH	418		AE1	53		HAP	951
	M12	538		AE1	100		HAP	1176
MAID'S	EDS	23		AE1	107		HAP	1478
MAIDS	PRL	34		AE1	179		HAP	1695
	T18	63		AE1	192		HAP	2121
	T18	70		AE1	206		EJG	1
	STS3	26		AE1	781		J1	158
	EKA	6		AE1	819		J1	228
	J6	468		AE2	164		J6	396
	P2	126		AE2	240		MC	64
	HI	184		AE3	96		G4	128
	HI	194		AE3	99		AE2	451
	VP6	71		AE3	257		AE2	885
	G2	693		AE3	276		AE2	923
	AE2	665		AE3	485		AE3	325
	AE4	566		AE3	795		AE4	222
	AE6	424		AE3	877		AE6	892
	AE8	543		AE4	182		AE7	561
	AE8	865		AE4	452		AE9	937
	AE9	147		AE4	549		AE10	899
	AE11	329		AE4	836		AE11	174
	AE11	971		AE5	186		AE12	772
	AE11	982		AE5	210		OAL	224
	OAL	404		AE5	217		OAL	275
	OAL	705		AE5	309		KT1	300
	OAL	715		AE5	920		KT2	166
	KT1	335		AE5	1004		B	599
	KT3	219		AE5	1034		C	201
	KT3	867		AE5	1044		C	509
	B	153		AE5	1107		M12	327
	B	300		AE5	1118		M12	416
	B	691		AE6	987		AU	15
	M11	389		AE7	18		CI	303
	WB	42		AE7	40	MAINTAINED	SMA	77
	WB	64		AE7	51		AM	616

MAINTAINED	AA	374	MAKE	AM	207	MAKE	SAA	690
	L3	302		AM	210		SAA	772
	TA	218		AM	402		PDG	25
	TA	299		AM	640		PDG	27
	HAP	1428		AM	831		PDG	41
	J6	544		AM	834		EDG	26
	M1	139		AM	1150		EDGA	6
	M1	958		AM	1211		RL	98
	AE4	291		PMQ	13		RL	239
	TJD	58		EWGR	9		RL	243
	B	301		EWGR	12		RL	345
	C	65		EWGR	29		RL	423
	M15	128		EWGR	33		RL	434
	CI	401		EWGR	35		OE	6
MAINTAINS	MD	86		EMM	5		OE	22
	SAA	601		SMM1	1		AT	38
	AT	13		PA	2		AT	93
	H2	42		PA	16		PD	6
	M1	641		PA	30		PD	7
	G2	70		PA	37		PD	61
	AE1	225		SEL1	11		PD	64
	AE9	1073		PTL	25		L3	22
	AE10	812		ETL	18		L3	101
	M15	345		ETL	25		L3	204
MAINTOP	AM	286		PCG2	28		L4	146
MAJESTIC	RL	152		PFD	12		L4	227
	TA	70		PFD	17		L4	266
	TA	204		PAR	18		T18	36
	AK	9		PW	16		T27	30
	AK	119		PMQW	5		T27	59
	BR	105		PMQW	22		T27	61
	GK	75		EMQW	20		T27	69
	VP4	15		EMQW	25		T27	92
	P6	12		PM	4		T27	99
	G4	526		PCD	7		H29	3
	G4	684		PUO1	33		H29	10
	AE1	10		PUO1	45		H29	15
	AE1	225		PNH	10		FS1	15
	AE1	704		PUO2	35		TA	185
	AE4	15		E	15		TA	487
	AE4	191		EAZ	34		AK	20
	AE5	847		ML	39		GE	50
	AE6	425		ML	47		HH	19
	AE6	1175		PKK	19		HAP	10
	AE8	464		PCB	37		HAP	103
	MG	36		PCB	38		HAP	140
	KT1	260		PLG	18		HAP	348
	FL	176		PLG	26		HAP	383
	M12	285		CM	46		HAP	673
	WB	192		HP	114		HAP	694
MAJESTICALLY	G3	821		HP	155		HAP	828
	AE3	205		HP	195		HAP	865
	AE9	35		HP	237		HAP	995
	AE11	368		DA	75		HAP	1333
MAJESTY	HS	72		PSF	44		HAP	1436
	MF	26		ETG	13		HAP	1476
	MF	106		PR	8		HAP	1584
	SAA	59		PUO4	7		HAP	1638
	RL	337		AA	288		HAP	1648
	ER	12		AA	410		HAP	1720
	AK	138		AA	503		HAP	1976
	HAP	394		AA	582		HAP	1989
	HAP	1092		AA	671		HAP	2225
	EMI	4		AA	715		HAP	2325
	BR	201		AA	722		HAP	2396
	J1	170		AA	758		HAP	2399
	J10	54		AA	795		HAP	2440
	J10	68		AA	994		HAP	2498
	M9	173		AA	1001		HAP	2570
	AE1	71		PLB	43		EMI	6
	AE1	180		ELB	5		BR	41
	AE1	838		ELB	22		BR	98
	AE9	95		EPC	2		BR	181
	AE12	1202		EPC	10		BR	206
	OAL	123		EPC	17		BR	291
	B	686		MD	93		BR	309
MAJOR	HAP	1820		MD	146		BR	350
MAKE	UDH	8		MD	161		PDS	32
	UDH	39		MD	163		EDS	9
	UDH	99		MD	200		EDS	25
	JH	22		MD	272		EDS	27
	MHD	8		PRH	21		EDS	36
	HS	44		AA	938		PTS	39
	AR	162		MF	19		PTS	43
	RH	36		MF	22		STS3	8
	RH	42		MF	132		STS3	25
	RH	56		MF	152		PKA	23
	SMA	50		MF	193		EKA	6
	SMA	84		SAA	19		EKA	14
	DC	44		SAA	35		EL	284
	EWG	2		SAA	90		EL	334
	EWG	18		SAA	274		EL	377
	AM	35		SAA	382		ODA	27
	AM	74		SAA	406		MS	6
	AM	152		SAA	465		PSH	7
	AM	176		SAA	480		PSH	22

MAKE		
	PSH	41
	PSH	42
	ESH	21
	EH	28
	EH	34
	J1	25
	J1	96
	J1	237
	J1	240
	J3	16
	J3	153
	J3	307
	J3	388
	J3	390
	J6	83
	J6	105
	J6	224
	J6	302
	J6	427
	J6	443
	J6	504
	J6	757
	J6	771
	J6	774
	J6	783
	J6	802
	J10	78
	J10	123
	J10	281
	J10	342
	J10	454
	J16	43
	J16	81
	P1	84
	P1	100
	P1	112
	P1	173
	P1	181
	P2	15
	P2	68
	P2	71
	P2	117
	P3	12
	P3	71
	P3	232
	P5	84
	P5	174
	P5	196
	P5	201
	P5	211
	P5	224
	P6	119
	P6	170
	M1	195
	M1	244
	M1	490
	M1	629
	M1	782
	M1	836
	M1	1066
	M9	119
	M13	4
	M13	93
	M13	169
	SFL	6
	VCS	6
	VCS	30
	PLT	24
	PLT	48
	SLT2	2
	GK	131
	EHC	37
	VP3	45
	VP3	71
	VP4	4
	VP5	6
	VP5	110
	VP6	32
	VP8	91
	VP9	51
	G1	117
	G1	152
	G1	268
	G2	88
	G2	106
	G2	111
	G2	221
	G2	391
	G2	553
	G3	196
	G3	266
	G3	274
	G3	293
	G3	415
	G3	460
	G3	574

MAKE		
	G4	31
	G4	36
	G4	38
	G4	49
	G4	80
	G4	121
	G4	283
	G4	294
	G4	803
	G4	806
	AE1	111
	AE1	227
	AE2	93
	AE2	102
	AE2	134
	AE2	281
	AE2	297
	AE2	434
	AE2	493
	AE2	507
	AE2	626
	AE2	821
	AE2	870
	AE2	1026
	AE3	171
	AE3	631
	AE3	904
	AE5	43
	AE5	307
	AE5	751
	AE5	754
	AE6	346
	AE6	600
	AE6	843
	AE6	897
	AE6	1174
	AE8	76
	AE8	338
	AE8	679
	AE9	236
	AE9	345
	AE9	485
	AE9	548
	AE9	870
	AE10	351
	AE10	391
	AE10	1254
	AE11	85
	AE11	317
	AE11	421
	AE11	449
	AE12	23
	AE12	79
	AE12	769
	AE12	1005
	AE12	1117
	OAL	47
	OAL	178
	OAL	194
	OAL	204
	OAL	416
	OAL	441
	OAL	508
	OAL	535
	OAL	571
	OAL	683
	OAL	717
	OAL	747
	OAL	818
	OAL	882
	OAE1	2
	OAE2	20
	OAE2	60
	OAE2	84
	DO	29
	DO	114
	KT1	79
	KT1	196
	KT2	415
	KT2	557
	KT3	161
	KT3	235
	KT3	240
	KT3	247
	KT3	324
	KT3	570
	KT3	606
	KT3	1085
	KT3	1094
	TJD	106
	TJD	206
	M8	174
	B	365
	B	367
	B	390
	B	648

MAKE		
	BP	136
	M10	65
	CAM	44
	CAM	48
	CAM	55
	CAM	84
	HIF	27
	HIF	181
	HIF	195
	HIF	649
	HIF	783
	C	61
	C	102
	C	176
	C	359
	C	401
	C	542
	C	649
	C	788
	TH	221
	TH	383
	M11	139
	M11	158
	M11	263
	FL	11
	FL	32
	FL	226
	M12	311
	M12	319
	M12	628
	AU	30
	AU	167
	AU	225
	WB	229
	WB	341
	WB	380
	WB	455
	M15	30
	M15	156
	M15	395
	M15	405
	M15	680
	M15	684
	CI	183
	CI	407
	PTP	15
	ETP	40
	ETP	46
	STP	28
MAKER	PD	16
	TA	443
	PAA	10
	HAP	82
	HAP	2557
	EL	129
	MFL	27
MAKER'S	FL	617
	AM	662
	AM	1098
	AA	10
	RL	210
	PTS	33
	EL	159
	P6	8
	MM	6
	C	548
	GP	103
	CI	233
MAKERS	PUO2	29
	HAP	2000
MAKES	UDH	89
	AR	107
	RH	80
	LC	142
	VHH	54
	AM	180
	AM	618
	AM	651
	AM	667
	AM	760
	AM	842
	AM	878
	AM	968
	AM	1123
	PMM	6
	SMM2	18
	SEL1	4
	SEL1	15
	PTL	2
	PCG1	43
	ECG1	2
	SCG2	24
	SCG2	25
	PUO1	46
	PNH	33
	ML	28

Headword	Ref	No.
MAKES	PR	32
	PUO4	12
	AA	209
	AA	726
	AA	798
	ELB	19
	MD	126
	PRH	44
	D	44
	MF	191
	SAA	446
	EDGA	13
	SDG	8
	RL	106
	EC	35
	ER	72
	L3	56
	L3	167
	L3	235
	L4	178
	H9	9
	H29	80
	H2	53
	TA	477
	PAA	8
	HAP	502
	HAP	1411
	HAP	1957
	HAP	2132
	HAP	2538
	BR	58
	BR	195
	ETS	1
	STS3	19
	PMS	15
	SKA2	7
	SKA6	7
	SKA6	23
	J1	87
	J1	160
	J1	218
	J3	469
	J6	135
	J6	203
	J6	299
	J6	374
	J6	417
	J6	793
	J10	444
	J10	490
	P2	53
	P2	62
	P2	115
	P4	70
	M1	47
	M1	537
	M1	575
	M1	777
	M1	896
	M1	915
	M9	150
	VP5	26
	VP6	115
	G1	1
	G1	130
	G1	137
	G2	70
	G3	386
	G3	395
	G3	571
	G3	649
	G3	844
	G4	414
	G4	431
	G4	504
	G4	557
	AE4	80
	AE4	104
	AE4	543
	AE6	14
	AE6	1069
	AE7	707
	AE8	724
	AE9	722
	AE9	835
	AE9	1101
	AE10	770
	AE11	1026
	AE12	10
	AE12	1093
	OAL	33
	OAL	85
	OAL	271
	OAL	351
	OAL	448
	KT1	334
MAKES	KT1	445
	KT1	532
	KT2	213
	KT3	581
	KT3	1053
	KT3	1082
	TJD	5
	TJD	141
	M8	164
	B	330
	B	477
	CAM	39
	CAM	40
	CAM	63
	CAM	132
	CAM	284
	C	161
	C	325
	C	378
	C	402
	TH	185
	M11	163
	AU	24
	WB	32
	WB	482
	M15	68
	M15	474
	M15	518
	CI	12
	CI	18
	AS	69
MAKEST	AE4	390
MAKING	JH	15
	AR	282
	PCG1	1
	PLN	25
	ESF	2
	MD	21
	RL	17
	RL	390
	PSH	9
	SAA	475
	M13	169
	G3	694
	AE10	621
	AE10	938
	BP	14
	CAM	52
	STP	8
MALADY	TA	185
	HAP	1363
	KT2	110
	WB	175
	ETP	17
MALCONTENTS	AA	492
MALE	L4	232
	PP	29
	J6	459
	M9	110
	G3	106
	G3	224
	G3	420
	AE7	77
MALEAN	AE5	251
MALECONTENTS	HAP	1956
MALEFACTOR	ET	14
	J6	543
	G2	523
MALE-HARLOT	J1	119
MALES	L4	196
	L4	274
	M9	103
MALICE	LC	125
	AM	1161
	PTL	3
	ELN	9
	AA	622
	MD	52
	SAA	580
	TA	177
	HAP	238
	HAP	891
	HAP	1295
	HAP	1365
	HAP	1463
	HAP	1606
	HAP	1934
	HAP	1936
	HAP	2350
	PTS	24
	PMS	13
	J10	193
	J10	434
	P1	79
	AE2	105
	AE2	130
MALICE	AE3	703
	AE5	1021
	AE7	536
	AE11	581
	B	241
	B	666
	HIF	444
	CI	11
MALICIOUS	AR	212
	ECG2	18
	SAA	828
	H29	73
	AK	43
	HAP	1343
	VP7	39
	KT3	791
	KT3	1100
	B	188
	BP	133
MALICIOUSLY	EKA	36
MALIGNANT	TA	500
	HAP	2291
	MS	2
	G1	181
	AE5	851
	AE6	381
	AE7	628
	OAE2	84
	DO	113
	B	116
MALIGNER	AE11	544
MALKIN	C	729
MALL	PM	25
	J6	88
MALLET	AM	584
MALLOWS	H2	82
MALLY	EDG	21
	C	14
MAM	PD	31
	T27	55
MAMAMOUCHI	EMQW	30
	PLN	30
	PLN	37
MAMMON	SAA	286
MAN	LC	85
	PIE	28
	SIE	10
	AM	496
	PMQ	37
	PWGR	12
	PWGR	18
	EWGR	16
	EWGR	21
	EWGR	25
	EWGR	30
	PMM	1
	PT	34
	PT	36
	ET	13
	PA	39
	PA	48
	PEL	20
	ECG1	24
	PCG2	4
	PCG2	14
	PLN	16
	SCD2	6
	SCD2	13
	PUO1	25
	PUO2	13
	EAZ	42
	ESF	5
	ESF	18
	ESF	33
	PC1	10
	PC1	23
	PAL	21
	PAL	28
	EAL	11
	EAL	26
	EMK	5
	PKK	13
	PKK	19
	PCB	1
	PCB	27
	HP	78
	HP	173
	DA	86
	DA	133
	DA	144
	PSF	7
	SSF	4
	PUF	6
	PUF	13
	AA	3
	AA	545

MAN		MAN		MAN	
AA	558	J6	312	AE7	747
AA	700	J6	356	AE8	202
AA	887	J6	370	AE8	214
AA	1005	J6	428	AE9	5
ELB	23	J6	567	AE9	43
PPC	5	J10	418	AE9	623
EPC	6	J10	468	AE9	887
EPC	12	J10	157	AE9	1057
MD	8	J16	2	AE10	98
MD	28	J16	25	AE10	126
MD	132	J16	54	AE10	139
MD	145	P1	80	AE10	269
MD	214	P1	187	AE10	302
PRH	43	P2	37	AE10	323
D	6	P3	27	AE10	385
MF	195	P3	176	AE10	503
SAA	352	P3	45	AE10	657
SAA	391	P5	176	AE10	778
SAA	468	P5	234	AE10	838
SAA	507	P5	240	AE10	844
SAA	1115	P5	246	AE10	854
PDG	47	P5	252	AE10	881
EDG	3	M1	98	AE10	1044
EDG	9	M1	109	AE11	19
RL	62	M1	112	AE11	57
RL	112	M1	113	AE11	83
RL	195	M1	119	AE11	163
RL	215	M1	180	AE11	185
RL	221	M1	329	AE11	269
RL	247	M1	433	AE11	523
RL	313	M1	491	AE11	532
RL	365	M1	532	AE11	576
RL	394	M1	543	AE11	644
RL	434	M1	553	AE11	707
OE	36	M9	5	AE11	911
AT	97	M9	84	AE11	940
AT	107	M9	199	AE11	1045
PD	32	M9	204	AE11	1241
PD	44	M13	161	AE12	197
EC	27	HI	49	AE12	322
EC	35	HI	164	AE12	353
EC	38	PLT	7	AE12	802
EC	42	PLT	54	AE12	929
L2	16	GK	29	AE12	1359
L3	1	GK	36	OAL	112
L3	24	GK	144	OAL	317
L3	43	DHP	12	OAL	529
L3	49	DHP	13	OAL	574
L3	61	VP1	64	OAL	679
L3	147	VP3	29	OAL	696
L3	271	VP3	78	OAL	749
L3	288	VP5	77	OAL	793
L3	319	VP6	62	OAL	810
L4	82	G1	564	OAE2	15
L4	210	G2	406	KT1	361
T18	20	G2	698	KT1	490
T27	49	G3	805	KT1	494
H3	35	G4	366	KT1	529
H29	65	G4	602	KT1	591
H29	74	G4	643	KT2	70
TA	434	G4	647	KT2	99
TA	449	G4	715	KT2	139
PAA	34	AE1	1	KT2	141
EAA	7	AE1	14	KT2	287
AK	70	AE1	217	KT2	338
HH	2	AE1	868	KT2	378
HAP	118	AE2	1	KT2	446
HAP	195	AE2	84	KT3	16
HAP	247	AE2	130	KT3	228
HAP	257	AE2	166	KT3	277
HAP	274	AE2	717	KT3	399
HAP	679	AE2	948	KT3	432
HAP	695	AE3	459	KT3	739
HAP	707	AE3	610	KT3	742
HAP	814	AE3	773	KT3	883
HAP	1198	AE4	16	KT3	1048
HAP	1637	AE4	27	KT3	1066
HAP	1686	AE4	389	KT3	1072
HAP	2200	AE4	439	TJD	23
HAP	2232	AE4	519	TJD	95
SSC	15	AE4	608	M8	53
EL	168	AE4	858	M8	170
OD	12	AE5	528	B	163
ODA	36	AE5	1123	B	317
EH	31	AE6	37	B	323
J1	9	AE6	507	B	326
J1	126	AE6	608	B	426
J1	199	AE6	709	B	481
J3	136	AE6	746	B	502
J3	253	AE6	1103	B	511
J3	268	AE6	1125	B	526
J3	269	AE7	59	B	536
J6	40	AE7	375	B	579
J6	77	AE7	429	B	729
J6	81	AE7	591	BP	11
J6	149	AE7	598	BP	43

Word	Ref	No.
MAN	BP	166
	CAM	42
	CAM	52
	HIF	198
	HIF	236
	HIF	279
	HIF	406
	HIF	485
	HIF	525
	HIF	568
	HIF	750
	C	197
	C	309
	C	323
	C	336
	C	401
	C	420
	C	446
	C	460
	C	517
	C	520
	C	537
	C	544
	C	549
	C	558
	C	633
	C	797
	TH	383
	M11	328
	M11	454
	FL	290
	FL	296
	M12	286
	M12	467
	M12	530
	M12	531
	M12	581
	M12	604
	M12	629
	M12	634
	M12	666
	M12	662
	M12	663
	M12	669
	M12	702
	M12	816
	AU	79
	AU	88
	AU	97
	AU	192
	AU	226
	AU	235
	AU	284
	AU	367
	AU	381
	AU	419
	AU	446
	AU	473
	AU	498
	AU	565
	AU	567
	WB	78
	WB	290
	WB	297
	WB	320
	WB	340
	WB	349
	WB	414
	WB	431
	WB	461
	WB	544
	M15	26
	M15	77
	M15	146
	M15	149
	M15	153
	M15	242
	M15	309
	M15	325
	M15	328
	M15	574
	M15	679
	GP	2
	GP	45
	GP	66
	CI	124
	CI	234
	CI	260
	CI	463
	CI	556
	PTP	24
	ETP	44
	STP	4
	STP	21
	STP	29
	AS	31
MAN	AS	63
MANAGE	AM	674
	POE	19
	AA	895
	AK	90
	HAP	517
	J10	537
	P4	31
	AU	584
MANAGED	AA	77
	L1	46
	EL	66
	G3	301
	AT	111
	AE10	262
MANAGEMENT	ETG	22
	HAP	1473
	HAP	2267
	KT3	426
MANAGES	PM	24
	J6	638
	AU	415
	M15	346
MANAGING	PCG2	15
	AE11	1090
MAN-BEAST	CI	147
MAN-CHILD	CI	216
MANDATE	SAA	917
	HAP	1975
	AE1	195
MANDATES	AE7	603
	TJD	186
MANE	SAA	837
	HAP	1564
	M13	159
	G3	134
	G3	146
	AE5	459
	AE9	1075
	AE10	1021
	AE11	750
	AE12	14
	OAL	611
MANES	AM	790
	P1	74
	HI	69
	G4	787
	AE5	106
	AE6	681
	AE6	1006
	AE11	145
	AE12	135
MANFULLY	SAA	815
MANGER	WB	386
MANGLED	MF	99
	M1	300
	M13	22
	G3	424
	G4	759
	AE3	319
	AE3	811
	AE6	255
	AE8	261
	AE8	395
	AE9	278
	MG	28
	TH	329
MANGOES	PR	28
MANHOOD	TA	463
	HAP	73
	PTS	10
	P5	47
	VP4	45
	AE9	338
	M10	100
	AU	270
	AU	471
	M15	604
MANHOOD'S	AA	833
MANIFEST	AA	204
	BR	94
	J6	386
	AE4	513
	AE8	49
	OAE2	52
	KT2	623
	HIF	473
	M11	401
	AU	483
MANIFESTLY	AE2	415
	AE12	44
MANIUS	P6	132
MAN-KILLERS	M15	153
MAN-KILLING	P3	167
MANKIND	PFD	13
	ECD	14
MANKIND	HP	99
	AA	772
	RL	157
	RL	296
	RL	364
	L1	43
	L3	260
	SKA1	8
	ESH	10
	EH	17
	J6	719
	J6	819
	P2	13
	P5	133
	M1	183
	M1	322
	M1	494
	M1	513
	SFL	24
	VP4	21
	AE6	1174
	AE11	570
	AE12	1203
	OAL	243
	DO	72
	KT2	509
	TJD	84
	CAM	37
	C	282
	WB	484
	M15	660
	CI	490
	SMP	64
	EMKG	17
	ESK	5
MANKIND'S	AM	642
	AA	318
	AA	546
	SAA	492
	RL	450
MANLIEST	POE	10
MANLIUS	AE8	867
MANLY	AR	56
	AM	353
	PTC	14
	AA	22
	AA	382
	AA	889
	AA	948
	ER	25
	T18	41
	TA	130
	TA	323
	TA	509
	BR	14
	BR	105
	BR	221
	OD	6
	PSH	35
	J6	437
	J10	552
	P1	190
	P1	202
	M1	553
	M9	196
	M9	67
	M13	153
	MC	30
	G2	70
	G3	755
	AE1	694
	AE1	833
	AE2	376
	AE4	215
	AE5	410
	AE6	1181
	AE7	902
	AE8	675
	AE8	828
	AE8	905
	AE9	417
	AE9	698
	AE10	906
	AE11	55
	AE11	480
	AE11	738
	AE11	983
	AE11	1088
	AE12	166
	AE12	934
	AE12	1295
	AE12	1363
	OAL	686
	OAE1	11
	MM	47
	MFL	34

Word	Code	No.	Word	Code	No.	Word	Code	No.
MANLY	KT1	150	MANSION	VHH	6	MARBLES	AE1	254
	KT3	40		AK	36	MARCELLUS	MO	23
	KT3	295		HAP	643		AE6	1180
	KT3	510		M1	778		AE6	1190
	KT3	712		M1	1085		AE6	1221
	KT3	854		G2	319	MARCH	GK	87
	KT3	916		G4	23		G3	370
	M8	349		AE10	1163		G4	86
	C	137		KT2	529		AE1	570
	TH	126		M11	270		AE4	582
	FL	551	MANSIONS	HI	73		AE5	768
	M12	285		G4	691		AE7	953
	M12	741	MANSLAUGHTER	J6	774		AE7	963
	AU	270	MANTLE	RH	101		AE8	735
	AU	407		MF	216		AE8	772
	SMP	50		T23	76		AE8	962
MANNA	SMA	24		T27	124		AE8	971
	E	25		J6	768		AE9	29
	PUF	17		M1	312		AE11	137
	MD	131		M1	361		AE11	1158
	SAA	6		AE3	718		KT3	454
	SAA	700		AE8	947		C	446
	TA	426		AE9	650		CI	403
	BR	65		AE12	1281	MARCHED	VHH	44
	EL	21		OAE2	62		PM	9
	TJD	49		OAE2	64		L3	245
MANNED	AE3	42		KT3	70		J6	169
	AE5	201		WB	255		AE2	681
	M8	49	MANTLES	FL	228		AE7	235
	HIF	274		FL	348		AE11	975
	M12	9	MANTLING	BR	129		KT1	121
	CI	554	MANTO	AE10	287		KT1	163
MANNER	AR	130	MANTUA	VP1	30		KT3	939
	AE6	766		G2	273		FL	340
	KT3	163		G3	18		AU	442
	M8	248	MANTUAN	VP6	2	MARCHES	G3	538
	B	92		VP9	33		AE7	865
MANNERLY	EMM	7		AE10	288	MARCHING	AM	947
	HAP	556		AE10	292		HAP	867
MANNERS	ECD	8	MANUFACTURE	EUO	35		J6	547
	ECD	10		PTW	4		AE5	725
	PUO1	21		EH	4		AE7	963
	EUO2	21	MANUFACTURED	BP	14		AE11	116
	SAA	345	MANUFACTURES	HAP	1136		AE11	218
	SAA	961	MANUMIZED	P3	210		AE11	687
	PD	7	MANURE	HAP	2286		AE11	1050
	HAP	1242		M1	567		KT1	40
	BR	279		G2	475		KT3	530
	MS	22		AE10	212		FL	285
	J1	35	MANURED	TA	363	MARCUS	P5	111
	J3	53		MC	7		P5	113
	J6	338		G1	121		P5	114
	J6	415	MANURES	SAA	327		P5	117
	J10	461	MANY-HEADED	TA	464	MARE	J6	435
	P2	112	MANY-TWISTED	AE4	834		G3	203
	P6	42	MAP	PCD	26		G3	328
	PLT	43		GE	2		G3	392
	ELT	1	MAPLE	P5	217		G3	419
	MC	9		AE8	238		OAL	316
	MC	33		C	17		CAM	44
	G4	6		C	771		EMKG	19
	AE5	957		M12	356	MAREOTIC	G2	131
	AE8	420		M8	110	MARES	L4	196
	OAL	869	MAPLE'S	AE9	99		M9	100
	OAE2	39	MAPLES	HS	54		VP8	38
	CI	32	MAPS	PLN	36		G3	430
	CI	163	MARABARAH	UDH	108		AE7	389
	CI	218	MARBLE	DA	207		AE11	855
	PWR	20		EPF	1	MARGIN	M13	45
MANNISH	J1	30		L3	75		VP2	32
MAN'S	J6	350		TA	7		AE3	501
	AR	165		J3	31		AE6	423
	SCG3	4		J3	353		AE10	428
	EAL	31		J10	230		AE11	500
	AA	651		M1	542		M11	438
	SAA	1050		VP6	102		M12	271
	RL	442		VP7	51		M15	71
	L4	209		G3	54		M15	334
	HAP	1251		AE1	596		CI	91
	HAP	1681		AE1	628	MARGINS	J1	7
	HAP	1722		AE1	831	MARICA	AE7	71
	EDS	5		AE3	173	MARIGOLDS	VP2	68
	J1	3		AE4	663	MARII	G2	235
	J3	471		AE6	1170	MARINER	HP	200
	J6	64		AE8	134		G3	488
	J6	310		AE11	892		OAL	627
	J10	37		AE11	1234	MARINERS	HS	70
	P1	22		OAL	117		AM	257
	P2	129		OAL	542		G1	40
	VCS	37		OAL	543		AE3	736
	G2	467		MFL	1		AE5	171
	G3	377		KT2	448		AE5	1000
	G4	450		BP	161		AE10	152
	AE4	531		M15	474		AE12	1115
	AE4	735		CI	608	MARIUS	J10	424
MANS	AE8	110	MARBLES	G1	360	MARK	PW	20

Word	Code	No.	Word	Code	No.	Word	Code	No.
MARK	EEL	2	MARKS	M1	71	MARS	J1	11
	PNH	44		M9	173		J3	118
	PCB	41		P5	231		J6	84
	PUO4	9		G1	193		J6	738
	AA	786		G4	120		J10	204
	AA	803		AE2	612		J10	486
	PLB	3		AE6	690		J16	8
	PPC	11		AE6	1062		VP9	23
	SAA	519		AE7	234		G1	688
	SAA	1122		AE9	736		G2	384
	EDGA	12		KT3	87		G4	489
	H9	35		AE11	507		G4	667
	HAP	176		AE12	261		AE1	372
	HAP	677		M8	158		AE7	422
	HAP	794		GP	92		AE7	840
	HAP	1473	MARKSMAN	M8	188		AE8	571
	HAP	1897	MARKSMEN	EDGA	34		AE8	835
	HAP	2556	MARLING	AM	589		AE8	929
	J3	433	MARO'S	RH	58		OAL	231
	ETS	13		TJD	85		OAE1	16
	J10	68		C	633		KT1	500
	J10	410	MARRED	HIF	779		KT2	104
	P1	92	MARRIAGE	EWG	3		KT2	231
	P1	113		SM1	1		KT2	308
	P3	117		SM1	7		KT2	462
	HI	167		CM	119		KT2	604
	OAL	438		HP	4		KT2	612
	DHP	1		PD	45		KT2	524
	G1	272		PD	52		KT2	545
	G1	354		T27	43		KT2	555
	G1	486		T27	45		KT2	592
	G1	547		HAP	353		KT2	596
	G2	45		HAP	367		KT3	66
	G2	362		HAP	1497		KT3	165
	G3	237		EDS	21		KT3	276
	AE2	744		EKA	27		KT3	291
	AE3	263		J6	33		KT3	314
	AE3	498		J6	36		KT3	369
	AE4	355		J6	52		KT3	390
	AE5	27		J6	59		KT3	395
	AE5	171		J6	67		KT3	421
	AE5	209		J6	287		KT3	425
	AE5	220		J6	388		KT3	440
	AE5	222		J10	520		KT3	668
	AE5	240		P2	127		C	751
	AE5	634		M1	653		M12	121
	AE5	651		M9	210		WB	164
	AE5	693		ELT	17		WB	401
	AE5	847		G4	755		SMP	51
	AE11	326		AE3	427		SMP	75
	AE11	957		OAL	46		VP2	68
	AE11	1237		AE4	23	MARSH	HI	90
	AE12	3		AE4	80	MARSHAL	KT2	259
	AE12	248		AE4	249	MARSHALED	L2	47
	AE12	405		AE7	442		HAP	731
	AE12	1334		OAL	522		J10	19
	M8	109		MFL	20		G2	376
	DO	70		KT3	1120		AE5	1079
	M8	169		B	15		KT3	541
	M8	188		B	25	MARSHALING	EL	199
	B	186		B	415	MARSHES	G2	156
	M10	34		B	487		AE10	1001
	HIF	117		BP	166		OAL	622
	HIF	271		CAM	221	MARSHY	M1	824
	M12	172		HIF	732		VP1	67
	EWR	19		C	76		G3	278
MARKED	HS	33		WB	339		G3	605
	SAA	168		CI	445		AE7	1046
	HAP	1934		AS	21		AE12	1078
	M1	998		J1	29		M8	95
	M13	36	MARRIAGE-BED				WB	185
	G4	150	MARRIAGE-			MARSIAN	G2	230
	AE5	430	OFFERINGS	HAP	1874		AE7	1039
	AE5	549	MARRIAGES	AE3	188	MARSIANS	P3	142
	AE6	524	MARRIED	EWG	2	MART	HAP	1144
	AE10	478		EKK	11		AE1	585
	AE10	670		SAA	360		M12	70
	KT3	897		TJD	34	MARTIAL	AR	198
	M11	41		BP	33		SMA	108
	FL	177		WB	335		AM	47
	WB	6		WB	489		AM	613
MARKET	RL	380		ETP	40		MD	26
	AT	85		P1	45		TA	509
	HAP	1522	MARROW	G3	215		TA	466
	EH	23		G3	428		AK	128
	VP1	30		AE8	515		BR	333
	WB	50		CAM	343		J16	19
	G3	614		M15	574		G4	99
MARKETS	P5	201	MARRUBIANS	AE7	1032		AE1	376
	AA	503	MARRY	EKK	4		AE4	195
	VP1	45		PD	51		AE4	337
	G2	741		T27	61		AE5	526
MARKS	AR	255		EDS	28		AE5	753
	AA	444		J10	522		AE6	253
	HAP	1092		STP	21		AE6	1110
	HAP	1148	MARS	HS	78		AE7	143
				AM	697			
				ETS	31			

MARTIAL	AE7	219
	AE8	836
	AE9	163
	AE9	616
	AE9	702
	AE9	804
	AE9	850
	AE10	252
	AE10	298
	AE11	971
	OAL	131
	KT3	465
	M12	229
	M12	240
	SMP	49
	EP	2
MARTIAN	AE6	1206
	AE9	793
MARTIN	HAP	1755
	HAP	1807
	HAP	1821
	HAP	1835
	HAP	1884
	HAP	1888
	HAP	1926
	HAP	1928
MARTIN'S	HAP	1859
	HAP	1874
	HAP	1921
	HAP	1938
MARTINS	HAP	1759
	HAP	1948
MARTLET	AM	439
MARTS	PKK	15
MARTYR	L3	150
	C	373
	AS	50
MARTYRDOM	SCG2	24
	AA	643
	RL	145
	TA	413
	HAP	631
MARTYRED	HAP	22
MARTYR'S	EPF	18
	AS	25
	AS	74
MARTYRS	AM	407
	EMK	6
	MF	101
	C	479
	AS	40
MARTYRS'	AR	186
	BR	160
MARY	BR	295
MARYBONE	EDGA	8
MARY-BONES	WB	192
MASCULINE	J6	168
MASHED	J3	415
MASKING	PCG2	27
	PM	33
MASKS	ELT	15
	ELT	28
MASON'S	J3	316
MASQUERADE	PM	31
	AA	752
	SAA	269
	HAP	386
MASS	EOE	4
	AA	113
	ELB	18
	SAA	464
	L3	51
	L3	191
	L4	251
	HAP	318
	P2	120
	P5	14
	M1	10
	M1	89
	G4	58
	G4	250
	G4	324
	G4	438
	AE6	985
	AE6	1168
	AE7	499
	AE8	595
	AE12	137
	KT3	1053
	DO	116
	M10	86
	B	502
	BP	14
	C	42
	M12	388
	M15	327

MASS	CI	119
MASSACRE	PUO3	30
MASSACRES	DO	68
MASSIC	AE7	1004
MASSICUS	AE10	245
MASSY	J10	63
	G4	38
	AE1	903
	AE3	751
	AE5	350
	AE9	55
	AE10	1100
	AE12	250
MASSYLIAN	AE4	187
	AE4	698
MAST	SCD2	20
	H29	91
	P6	71
	M13	55
	VP10	29
	G1	10
	G1	222
	G1	410
	G2	755
	AE4	642
	AE5	713
	AE5	648
	AE5	668
	AE10	1001
	HIF	598
	M11	199
MASTER	LC	55
	PNH	30
	HP	108
	AM	55
	AA	594
	AA	938
	SAA	361
	SAA	454
	PDG	47
	T27	82
	HAP	2270
	HAP	2352
	HAP	2395
	J1	94
	J3	259
	J6	91
	J6	544
	P3	32
	P3	88
	P3	210
	P5	181
	P6	5
	VP3	21
	VP5	76
	VP6	110
	G4	404
	G4	709
	AE5	1077
	AE5	1087
	AE8	605
	AE10	684
	AE10	807
	AE10	1059
	AE10	1238
	OAL	6
	OAL	353
	AF	69
	AF	93
	KT2	367
	KT2	455
	KT2	630
	BP	37
	HIF	755
	M11	101
	M11	115
	FL	78
	AU	2
	CI	335
	CI	362
	CI	464
MASTERED	AM	375
	MD	129
	J10	151
	AE6	460
	M12	669
MASTERING	C	776
MASTERPIECE	PA	6
	TA	445
	C	470
MASTER'S	AR	92
	ML	54
	AA	822
	SAA	1095
	EL	53
	J6	504

MASTER'S	J6	617
	VP3	6
	G3	294
	AE3	419
	AE5	1008
	AE7	683
	AE7	1067
	AE10	331
	KT1	576
	KT1	584
	FL	233
MASTERS	AM	767
	SAA	369
	EK	26
	EDG	13
	HAP	194
	J10	141
	PPS	15
	P5	101
	GK	141
	G3	187
	AE10	391
	AE11	937
	AE11	1296
	AE12	514
MASTERS'	G3	424
	SAA	814
	OAL	660
	BP	136
	FL	353
MASTERSHIP	M1	599
	KT2	318
MASTER-SKILL	AE8	580
MASTER-STREET	KT3	940
MASTER-STROKES	PTC	14
MASTERY	FL	434
MASTFUL	G2	20
	G2	98
MASTIFFS	TH	113
	TH	305
	TH	328
MASTIFFS'	G3	417
	G3	617
	TH	268
MASTLESS	KT3	208
MASTS	AM	259
	AM	571
	AM	590
	DA	190
	M1	412
	AE5	1084
	PAZ	20
MATCH	HAP	1562
	VP3	31
	VP3	65
	VP5	2
	MM	51
	AE5	491
	AE5	501
	AE7	87
	AE7	541
	AE7	654
	AE7	665
	AE11	268
	AE11	439
	KT3	57
	KT3	62
	M10	96
	HIF	246
	M12	597
	AU	428
MATCHED	AM	758
	PAR	2
	L4	260
	MC	27
	AE12	133
	AE12	1031
	KT3	567
	TJD	21
	WB	369
	WB	381
	DO	5
MATCHLESS	AM	482
	AA	840
	SAA	1097
	RL	228
	M1	965
	FS4	11
	AK	136
	EL	10
	GK	48
	GK	137
	HIF	396
	AE1	1055
	AE5	507
	AE6	1218

Word	Ref	Num
MATCHLESS	AE8	385
	AE8	682
	AE11	579
	AU	139
	AU	474
MATE	HAP	449
	ODA	69
	M1	911
	G3	371
	AE3	385
	AE12	831
	OAL	134
	KT3	229
	B	489
	M15	638
MATERIAL	G2	149
	CI	135
MATERIALS	OD	14
	AE11	499
	DO	120
MATERNAL	EL	218
MATES	SCD2	5
	SAA	926
	T18	23
	M1	429
	M9	103
	VP6	110
	VP7	17
	G2	20
	G2	93
	AE5	21
	AE5	243
	AE8	252
	AE8	281
	OAL	769
	FL	569
MATHO	J1	46
MATIN	HAP	368
	C	45
MATINS	HAP	2304
MATRIMONIAL	T27	42
	OAL	126
	WB	171
	WB	521
MATRIMONY	EH	16
	B	165
MATRON	L4	240
	T18	64
	HAP	719
	HAP	973
	HAP	1362
	HAP	1571
	HAP	1714
	HAP	1964
	HAP	2186
	J6	186
	J6	758
	AE7	1
	AE9	287
MATRONS	AM	202
	HP	209
	H2	61
	J3	221
	J3	347
	J6	12
	J6	72
	J6	399
	J6	432
	J6	673
	J6	783
	G4	683
	G4	754
	AE2	669
	AE2	1043
	AE2	1084
	AE3	90
	AE5	795
	AE5	809
	AE5	840
	AE5	850
	AE5	857
	AE5	876
	AE7	539
	AE8	736
	AE8	882
	AE10	55
	AE11	50
	AE11	220
	AE11	329
	AE11	692
	AE11	722
	AE11	871
	AE11	1271
	OAL	70
	OAL	382
	OAL	705

Word	Ref	Num
MATRONS	KT3	867
	M8	367
	CAM	239
	C	621
	C	712
MATTED	H2	37
	PSH	6
	J16	49
	VP4	36
	G4	24
	KT3	44
	CI	89
MATTER	SAA	464
	AT	103
	L3	20
	L3	30
	L3	33
	L3	169
	HAP	317
	HAP	616
	HAP	694
	PDS	18
	J1	232
	J10	338
	G3	455
	AE9	267
	OAL	164
	OAL	260
	OAL	487
	OAL	547
	KT3	1031
	KT3	1053
	C	523
	M15	237
	M15	526
MATTERS	POE	19
	P6	114
	C	408
MATTRESS	L2	41
	J6	128
	P5	214
MATURE	MF	16
	HAP	2403
	VP4	58
	M15	314
MATURELY	HAP	2527
MATURER	G3	79
MATURING	MO	20
MAUDLIN	PRL	34
	PLB	21
	OAL	270
MAUL	PO	22
MAULED	J16	46
MAURUS	TJD	83
	TJD	87
	PTP	16
MAUSOLEUMS	UDH	107
MAW	J1	214
	G3	654
	AE3	828
	AE10	1024
	M12	32
	M15	136
MAWKISH	L3	307
MAWS	M15	115
MAXIM	MD	214
	KT2	373
MAXIMINS	MF	78
MAY	AR	285
	KT1	169
	KT1	172
	KT1	175
	KT1	176
	KT1	190
	KT2	10
	KT2	44
	KT2	52
	KT2	224
	KT3	429
	FL	218
	FL	440
	FL	470
	FL	489
	FL	582
	FL	602
	FL	612
	HAP	1588
MAY-BE	MS	13
MAYBE	MHD	4
MAYDENHEAD	AR	212
MAY-GAME	P3	164
MAY-LADY	LS	2
MAYOR	H29	40
	J10	163
MAZE	RL	38
	L2	11

Word	Ref	Num
MAZE	J1	82
	AE6	39
MAZES	G1	267
	AE9	532
	FL	56
MAZY	G3	182
MEAD	L1	12
	H2	26
	VP2	63
	KT3	195
	FL	202
MEADOW	G4	391
	FL	287
MEADOWS	T18	66
	M1	138
	VP1	69
	G1	364
	AE2	1063
	AE6	920
	AE12	1097
	M8	21
	M15	118
	HAP	1851
MEADS	BR	171
	M1	405
	M13	68
	VP7	15
	VP9	54
	VP10	43
	G1	385
	G2	662
	G3	229
	G3	521
	G3	743
	G3	779
	G4	75
	G4	266
	G4	433
	AE6	915
	M15	422
MEAGER	SAA	281
	L4	127
	H3	42
	HAP	181
	G1	120
	G2	250
	G2	336
	AE3	772
	AE3	856
	OAL	831
	TJD	134
	TH	305
	PMQw	22
	PLG	26
MEAL	MD	227
	L3	191
	HAP	1327
	J1	145
	J1	209
	P3	162
	P4	70
	G3	613
	AE3	305
	AE7	157
	AE12	260
	C	18
	M15	196
	M15	680
	PA	38
MEALS	M15	138
	M15	361
MEAN	EWG	13
	AM	858
	PCG2	4
	ECG2	7
	SCG2	3
	PNH	7
	HP	70
	HP	122
	PR	11
	AA	366
	AA	582
	SAA	185
	AT	58
	PD	13
	L3	123
	T18	20
	T27	18
	T27	28
	T27	90
	TA	250
	HAP	658
	HAP	1006
	HAP	1155
	HAP	1283
	HAP	1502

MEAN	HAP	2092	MEANS	PSH	34	MEANTIME	AE1	670
	HAP	2218		J3	246		AE1	975
	PTS	30		M9	114		AE2	75
	STS2	8		PLT	22		AE2	328
	ESH	6		ELT	5		AE3	606
	J6	479		G4	727		AE4	123
	J6	680		AE2	110		AE4	231
	J10	261		AE2	476		AE4	419
	J10	294		AE4	395		AE5	1
	J10	499		AE4	413		AE5	44
	P1	91		AE4	690		AE5	1018
	P1	241		AE4	906		AE6	306
	P4	54		AE9	998		AE6	702
	P6	113		AE12	1319		AE7	215
	ELT	13		OAL	261		AE8	279
	VP2	82		OAL	417		AE8	369
	VP9	42		OAL	780		AE8	807
	G1	62		KT3	163		AE9	622
	G1	257		KT3	499		AE10	178
	G3	455		KT3	752		AE10	217
	AE1	954		TJD	40		AE10	402
	AE4	340		B	73		AE10	618
	AE4	396		B	100		AE10	854
	AE4	598		B	126		AE10	933
	AE5	84		B	450		AE10	974
	AE6	1108		B	622		AE10	1185
	AE7	315		B	669		AE11	33
	AE8	135		TH	47		AE11	618
	AE8	477		CI	456		AE11	805
	AE11	576		CI	477		AE11	1293
	AE12	908		CI	507		AE12	204
	AE12	1359		CI	533		AE12	520
	OAE1	23	MEANT	LCA	35		AE12	598
	KT2	98		VHH	42		AE12	1145
	B	311		ELN	19		OAL	554
	B	350		PKK	22		KT3	717
	M10	28		PTC	15		M8	151
	HIF	246		PCB	8		BP	122
	HIF	335		SAA	432		CAM	354
	C	792		RL	218		HIF	429
	TH	29		RL	420		HIF	594
	WB	368		PD	29		HIF	661
	WB	454		NS	6		M11	151
	CI	21		NS	17		M11	232
MEANER	HS	94		NS	28		FL	433
	RH	27		TA	265		M12	429
	VP1	41		PAA	10		M12	766
	AE10	206		HAP	603		CI	368
	M11	338		HAP	1068		CI	445
MEANING	MF	19		HAP	2343	MEANWHILE	SAA	79
	SAA	416		HAP	2498		HAP	1320
	PDG	45		J6	77		J6	549
	RL	252		P3	27		J6	651
	HAP	673		CM	81		J6	665
	HAP	959		EMW	16		KT3	749
	HAP	1250		AA	130		CI	625
	EKA	6		EDG	3	MEASURE	HS	104
	M1	526		GK	93		LC	150
	AE10	884		AE2	172		SSF	21
	OAL	755		AE5	579		SDG	7
	C	419		AE6	236		RL	412
	FL	599		AE6	437		HAP	2460
	PWR	20		AE9	155		HAP	2535
MEANINGS	CI	20		AE11	1090		G1	356
MEANLY	HAP	436		KT2	26		G3	212
	HAP	508		M10	69		G3	302
	BR	115		B	672		AE12	179
	PTS	24		CAM	120		AE12	326
	M9	6		C	30		AE12	537
	AE6	709		C	596		M8	257
	AE10	108		ERL	1		B	523
	B	557	MEANTIME	AM	257		FL	81
MEANS	LC	70		AM	325		AS	34
	AM	3		AM	929		EWR	17
	ET	15		AM	1041	MEASURED	L3	95
	PEL	33		PAR	23		VP1	33
	DA	63		PTW	13		AE12	1333
	AA	80		EAZ	24		B	219
	AA	434		ELB	37		C	450
	AA	567		L1	41		CI	34
	EPC	31		L3	236		C-I	327
	MD	64		L4	170	MEASURES	SAA	673
	MD	205		AK	165		SAA	783
	SAA	426		HAP	1529		EL	265
	SAA	668		J1	204		J6	761
	SAA	781		J3	125		J10	165
	RL	49		J3	418		AE6	876
	RL	117		J6	215		AE9	1065
	TA	171		J6	594		AE10	932
	HAP	115		M1	819		OAE1	2
	HAP	116		GK	164		AF	97
	HAP	2002		G3	67		DO	25
	HAP	2136		G3	485		B	693
	HAP	2177		G3	564		FL	181
	HAP	2379		AE1	176		FL	309
	PMS	33		AE1	420		FL	332

Word	Ref	No.
MEASUREST	P2	98
MEASURING	AE10	1093
MEAT	EWGR	12
	PCG1	16
	SAA	552
	PDG	9
	AT	74
	L4	53
	GE	60
	HAP	621
	J3	473
	J6	827
	J10	319
	J10	326
	P3	205
	P3	227
	P6	170
	AE1	299
	AE1	1012
	AE3	295
	AE3	306
	AE6	821
	AE7	168
	AE7	240
	AE8	395
	KT1	527
	HIF	642
	C	22
	M15	360
MEATS	M15	136
MECCAN	HAP	2392
MECHANIC	HS	127
	ECG2	3
	PUO2	12
	AE6	899
	AU	338
MEDAL	PCD	28
	MD	3
MEDALS	MD	143
MEDE	OAL	259
MEDEA	HP	224
	OAL	378
MEDEA'S	AT	116
	KT2	505
	WB	367
	J6	838
MEDES	G2	185
MEDIA	G4	306
MEDIAN	G2	175
	G2	187
MEDIANS	P3	104
MEDICINABLE	B	707
MEDICINAL	TA	111
	TA	170
	AE12	620
MEDICINALLY	MD	150
MEDICINE	SCG3	11
	HAP	1377
	J1	106
	M1	701
	G2	167
	G3	685
	AE12	73
	TJD	110
MEDICINES	UDH	96
	CM	47
	TA	160
	CAM	175
MEDITATE	J6	849
	AE10	639
MEDITATED	DO	144
MEDITATES	AA	446
	G3	361
	AE12	162
	B	244
	M15	640
MEDITATING	AE8	640
MEDLAR	FL	103
	FL	446
MEDLEY	AE9	427
	C	327
	M12	338
MEDON	AE6	651
	M12	419
MEEK	G4	483
	M15	169
MEET	UDH	3
	UDH	87
	AR	253
	AR	283
	RH	16
	AM	268
	AM	308
	AM	335
	AM	444
	AM	475
MEET	AM	741
	AM	775
	AM	802
	AM	856
	AM	908
	AM	988
	AM	1068
	AM	1192
	AM	1201
	EWGR	5
	SCG1	5
	SCG3	30
	PW	4
	A	4
	PTC	26
	EMP	3
	MF	96
	SAA	23
	SAA	490
	SAA	927
	RL	61
	T18	30
	T23	64
	H29	3
	HAP	699
	HAP	801
	HAP	1035
	HAP	2197
	EKA	16
	J3	436
	J6	537
	J6	854
	H1	31
	G1	346
	G1	510
	G1	532
	G2	380
	G3	366
	G4	115
	AE1	241
	AE1	497
	AE1	530
	AE2	348
	AE2	423
	AE2	535
	AE2	631
	AE2	973
	AE2	1006
	AE3	109
	AE5	761
	AE6	27
	AE7	651
	AE8	601
	AE8	759
	AE10	312
	AE8	917
	AE10	388
	AE10	526
	AE11	219
	AE11	551
	AE11	569
	AE11	639
	AE11	763
	AE11	810
	AE11	916
	AE11	1241
	AE12	8
	AE12	231
	AE12	420
	AE12	684
	AE12	1036
	AE12	1044
	OAL	188
	KT1	50
	KT1	558
	KT2	190
	KT3	79
	KT3	628
	KT3	1063
	M8	147
	B	92
	B	98
	B	672
	M11	154
	M11	239
	M11	488
	FL	56
	FL	310
	M12	12
	M12	93
	M12	784
	AU	506
	CI	105
	CI	564
	EIE	1
MEETING	J1	42
MEETING	B	73
MEETS	AR	233
	AM	246
	AM	439
	AM	1036
	PMM	1
	ESF	17
	PTC	25
	AA	260
	PPC	6
	T23	68
	HAP	1108
	HAP	2482
	J3	383
	GK	9
	AE6	930
	AE8	608
	TJD	66
MEGARA'S	AE3	905
MELAMPUS	M15	489
MELANCHOLY	PUO4	12
	L3	98
	HAP	368
	HAP	512
	HAP	1806
	HAP	2271
	J1	164
	G4	747
	KT3	403
	C	174
	C	408
	M12	422
MELANEUS	AE6	646
MELEAGER'S	M8	192
MELEAGROS	M8	44
	M8	155
	M8	227
MELEAGRUS	M8	2
MELFOIL	G4	87
MELIORATE	G2	88
MELL	EM	20
MELLA	G4	398
MELLOW	P1	72
	GK	178
	VP2	45
	G1	99
	G2	357
	M12	218
MELLOWED	G2	758
	M15	108
MELLOWS	MO	21
MELODIOUS	AT	89
	G4	697
	OAL	15
	GP	22
MELODY	SAA	413
	FL	125
MELT	AA	66
	MD	228
	HAP	1483
	AE9	393
	AE12	1363
	OAL	423
	KT2	331
	SDG	25
	SDG	30
	AE9	799
	FL	200
MELTED	SMA	55
	AM	1118
	DOD	16
	P5	15
MELTING	G3	215
	AE8	531
	AE11	57
	T23	60
	BR	312
	P2	120
	AF	96
	GP	37
MELTS	AS	68
	EKK	8
	RL	407
	J3	87
	VP9	43
MEMBER	PRL	28
	AM	279
	L4	229
	HAP	663
MEMBERS	HAP	1035
	HAP	1191
	J10	369
	M1	247
	M1	317
	M13	22
	G3	424

Word	Ref	No.	Word	Ref	No.	Word	Ref	No.
MEN	HIF	100	MEND	TJD	95	MERCY	AA	939
	HIF	134		TJD	134		AA	1004
	HIF	152		B	60		PLB	30
	HIF	375		B	414		SAA	734
	HIF	389		HIF	632		RL	106
	HIF	465		C	630		RL	188
	HIF	495		FL	577		RL	196
	HIF	555		WB	367		RL	403
	HIF	605		CI	595		TA	86
	HIF	683		ETP	35		TA	294
	HIF	733		SMP	1		HAP	259
	C	99		SMP	19		HAP	261
	C	199	MENDED	PRL	5		HAP	289
	C	394		HAP	573		HAP	1075
	C	734		GK	105		HAP	2097
	TH	37		G2	324		BR	257
	TH	278		KT1	36		BR	272
	TH	386		B	657		SKA2	23
	TH	398		BP	87		EL	59
	M11	121	MENDING	ETG	19		EL	119
	M11	336	MENDS	AM	489		EL	373
	FL	534		J6	330		J3	16
	FL	564		J10	34		J6	295
	M12	294		AE8	607		SFL	18
	M12	525		AE11	823		AE1	849
	M12	630		AE12	10		AE12	1351
	M12	699		OAL	711		KT1	281
	M12	827		TH	215		TJD	84
	AU	405		WB	480		CAM	332
	AU	504	MENELAS	M12	826		C	282
	WB	121	MENELAUS	T18	4		TH	116
	WB	149		AE2	344		TH	292
	WB	388		AU	329		WB	74
	M15	131		AU	548		M15	689
	M15	202	MENIAL	H2	92		GP	29
	M15	310		AE8	605		GP	36
	M15	443		KT1	601	MERE	PEL	24
	M15	482	MENOETES	AE5	213		PCG2	2
	M15	531		AE12	752		PUO1	36
	M15	675		M12	160		EMK	9
	CI	550		M12	175		PR	35
	ETP	40	MEN'S	EM	15		AA	535
	ESK	4		EAL	22		AA	572
	PMK	13		AA	239		SAA	47
	PMK	25		EDG	35		SAA	442
	EWR	15		J10	26		SAA	527
MENACE	AE9	38		P6	85		EDGA	36
	AE10	985		AE12	498		HAP	498
	HIF	271		HIF	382		P1	79
MENACED	KT3	917	MENTAL	J6	389		P3	158
	AU	146		EMKG	31		KT3	231
	M15	36	MENTION	J16	16	MERIDIAN	AR	289
MENACES	AE11	532		G2	221		AM	634
	KT2	573		KT1	201		M1	806
MENACING	AE4	327	MENTIONED	GE	51		B	5
	AE12	1105		KT1	37		M15	288
MENAGE	CI	484	MEPHIBOSHETH	SAA	405	MERIONES	HI	97
MENALCAS	T27	82	MERCENARIES	HAP	862	MERIT	UDH	9
	ODA	10	MERCHANDISE	ELB	39		RH	103
	VP2	17	MERCHANT	AM	1197		PWG	6
	VP3	86		H29	92		LCA	15
	VP9	13		HAP	143		ENH	25
	VP9	20		HAP	1639		ML	25
	VP9	76		J6	224		HP	195
	VP9	93		VP4	38		DA	191
	VP10	29		OAL	478		DA	192
MEN-BOYS	J1	21	MERCHANT'S	J10	482		MD	310
MEND	PWG	56	MERCHANTS	AR	305		SAA	1012
	PC2	12		AM	4		SAA	1138
	EKK	14		AM	806		GE	15
	PR	21		PKA	25		HAP	1381
	AA	808		P5	69		HAP	1417
	ELB	40		C	298		EL	32
	PRH	30	MERCHANTS'	H2	12		J1	55
	AK	38	MERCIA'S	C	360		P1	14
	HAP	2138	MERCIES	ESH	23		MC	77
	HAP	2350	MERCIFUL	TA	206		VP5	9
	SSC	47		EWR	11		AE9	401
	BR	38	MERCILESS	J10	295		AE11	580
	ETS	32		J10	395		OAL	695
	ODA	79	MERCURY	PR	17		M8	327
	J3	219		MD	263		B	481
	P3	176		AE8	182		TH	171
	DHP	31		C	322		AU	242
	G3	113	MERCY	AR	265		AU	380
	G4	196		LC	50		CI	491
	G4	341		LC	58	MERITED	AM	962
	AE4	871		AM	172		PUO3	30
	AE5	297		AM	1055		AE5	465
	AE5	456		AM	1056		CAM	26
	AE7	157		AM	1118	MERITS	PNH	45
	AE8	289		EEL	39		SAA	1014
	MM	10		PUO1	8		RL	195
	KT2	658		AA	146		B	409
	KT3	768		AA	326		HIF	167
	KT3	1125		AA	359		HIF	317

Word	Src	No.	Word	Src	No.	Word	Src	No.
MERITS	AU	165	MESSENGER	DO	101	METHINKS	SA	391
	AU	561		KT2	37		EK	11
MERLIN'S	HAP	1840		B	649		T27	102
MERMAID	C	578	MESSENGERS	HIF	483		GE	5
	WB	436	MESSENIA'S	M12	724		HAP	237
MERMEROS	M12	420	MESSIAH	AA	728		HAP	620
MEROE'S	J6	681		HAP	1470		HAP	1668
	M1	1092		AM	454		HAP	2060
	VP10	97		RL	174		BR	96
MEROPES	AE9	951	MESSIAH'S				EKA	8
MERRIER	HAP	369	MESSIEURS	PAR	11		P3	169
	C	578	MET	AM	81		P6	121
MERRILY	SKA4	5		AM	302		VP10	84
	SKA4	8		EMP	4		G3	33
MERRY	AR	226		SAA	550		AE9	251
	RH	2		EC	2		C	123
	SCD2	5		L3	258		M12	577
	EPC	29		TA	56	METHOD	AR	90
	H29	101		TA	124		PMQ	34
	HAP	1729		HAP	733		SAA	554
	P1	177		HAP	1319		SAA	863
	C	622		HAP	1344		EL	61
	AE4	211		HAP	1810		P1	227
	AE5	1000		HAP	1898		G3	269
	OAL	130		BR	3		G4	778
	OAL	405		G4	655		M15	602
	OAL	411		J10	134	METHODIZE	B	258
	KT2	44		P1	141	METHODS	EAZ	17
	C	42		M1	458		MD	237
	C	329		M1	935		SAA	755
	C	346		AE2	1008		G2	90
	FL	111		AE2	1028		AE5	788
	FL	352		AE6	459		AE7	581
	FL	612		AE6	646		AE7	816
	WB	25		AE6	854		AU	15
	WB	26		AE9	944		M15	689
	M15	344		AE10	533	METHOUGHT	SCG1	24
	CI	612		AE10	1034		DA	109
	PTP	39		AE11	435		FL	58
	SMP	39		AE11	978		FL	126
	SMP	43		AE12	528		FL	136
MERRY-ANDREW	PSH	11		HI	29		FL	182
MERRY-ANDREWS	EUO	11		DO	51	METISCUS	AE12	690
MESHES	RH	27		KT1	355		AE12	1070
	H2	52		KT2	256	METISCUS'	AE12	1135
MESS	PMK	3		KT3	619	METIUS	AE8	853
MESSAGE	AE1	415		B	64	METROPOLIS	PFD	23
	AE4	333		B	389		J3	317
	AE4	511		CAM	349	METTLE	PAL	11
	AE4	632		HIF	718		G3	209
	AE5	682		TH	172		M15	344
	AE8	158		FL	294	METTLED	AE11	915
	AE9	248		FL	612	MEWED	J1	186
	AE9	298		AU	138		CAM	320
	AE9	631		AU	289	MEWS	P6	71
	AE9	1001		AU	367	MEZENTIUS	AE7	895
	AE10	684		AU	384		AE8	10
	AE10	1196		WB	120		AE8	630
	AE11	179	METABUS	AE11	815		AE8	658
	AE11	271	METAL	PSF	10		AE8	752
	AE11	1242		AA	310		AE9	691
	AE11	1256		AA	634		AE10	223
	DO	74		HAP	2029		AE10	293
	B	626		P5	155		AE10	974
	B	632		M1	163		AE10	1016
	HIF	330		G4	247		AE10	1026
	TH	412		AE6	216		AE10	1037
MESSAGES	PRH	38		AE6	220		AE10	1081
	AE4	649		AE11	736		AE10	1092
	AE9	418		AE12	138		AE10	1096
MESSAPUS	AE7	955		M15	401		AE10	1257
	AE8	9	METALS	PNH	33		AE10	1292
	AE9	31		HAP	1482		AE11	9
	AE9	150		AE6	1169		AE11	25
	AE9	199		AE8	531	MICE	J3	340
	AE9	472		AE8	699	MICHAEL	BR	146
	AE9	608		KT2	331	MICHAL	AA	11
	AE9	693	METAMORPHOSED	M1	112		SAA	51
	AE10	1056		M12	2		SAA	52
	AE11	661	METAPHOR	RH	11		SAA	60
	AE11	705		EMK	9		SAA	67
	AE11	784	METEMPSUCHOSIS	UDH	72	MICON	VP7	43
	AE11	787	METEOR	CI	328	MICON'S	VP3	16
	AE11	903	METEORS	G1	657	MID-AIR	AK	178
	AE12	195		AE2	156	MIDAS	P1	240
	AE12	435		AE5	694		WB	157
	AE12	709	METER	SAA	402		WB	165
	AE12	808		SAA	488	MIDDAY	L3	261
	AE12	960		PK	38	MIDDLE	EDG	39
MESSAPUS'	AE9	497	METHEGLIN	G4	156		PD	58
MESSENGER	CM	109	METHINKS	AR	276		H29	57
	HAP	1232		AM	1169		HAP	342
	M1	921		PUO1	5		HAP	843
	AE3	321		ESF	10		EL	83
	AE4	822		PTC	3		J6	65
	AE7	223		PLG	13		J6	755
				MF	43			

Word	Ref	Num
MIDDLE	P2	63
	M1	55
	VP7	5
	G1	446
	G2	471
	G3	371
	G4	625
	AE6	200
	AE6	862
	AE8	130
	AE8	539
	AE8	608
	AE8	929
	AE10	481
	AE11	833
	AE11	907
	AE11	1066
	AE12	420
	AE12	785
	AE12	1063
	DO	139
	KT3	586
	B	360
	CAM	332
	M11	154
	FL	202
	FL	287
MIDLAND	AM	684
MIDMOST	AM	742
	J10	395
	AE10	568
	AE10	1083
	AE12	411
	KT3	536
	KT3	766
MIDNIGHT	ENH	19
	SAA	458
	AT	42
	L3	261
	T23	54
	HAP	214
	HAP	367
	HAP	1808
	HAP	2304
	J6	418
	J6	577
	P3	105
	WB	36
	M15	282
MIDNIGHT-MAGISTRATE	SAA	536
MID-PART	P1	183
MIDWAY	B	389
MIDWIFE	SAA	476
	T27	53
	KT2	562
	CAM	366
MIDWINTER	VP10	95
MIEN	G1	319
	HS	71
	DC	50
	ECD	15
	HAP	33
	HAP	2323
	SLT2	15
	AE1	435
	AE1	453
	AE1	703
	AE2	460
	AE3	778
	AE4	215
	AE4	804
	AE5	847
	AE7	84
	AE7	583
	AE7	902
	AE8	208
	AE9	891
	AE10	629
	AE10	906
	AE11	755
	AE12	341
	AE12	689
	B	539
	M11	330
	FL	176
	AU	269
	CI	56
	CI	219
MIGHT	AA	337
	AA	780
	AA	1023
	L1	5
	HAP	97
	HAP	266
	M13	180
	HI	55

Word	Ref	Num
MIGHT	G1	649
	G3	363
	AE6	624
	AE8	314
	AE9	590
	AE9	1070
	AE11	439
	AE12	230
	AE12	1189
	OAL	726
	KT2	247
	KT2	389
	KT3	14
	KT3	155
	KT3	642
	KT3	1135
	TJD	185
	B	105
	B	282
	HIF	336
	C	749
	C	770
	C	784
	M12	617
	AU	139
	AU	537
	M15	123
	M15	537
MIGHTIER	HIF	396
MIGHTIEST	EOE	10
MIGHTILY	PWGR	5
	RL	376
MIGHTY	RH	9
	SMA	125
	LC	109
	DC	56
	EIE	5
	AM	17
	AM	50
	AM	124
	AM	153
	AM	192
	AM	279
	AM	290
	AM	321
	AM	361
	AM	481
	AM	609
	AM	618
	AM	670
	AM	854
	AM	873
	AM	941
	AM	998
	AM	1173
	PNH	13
	PNH	45
	E	15
	ML	25
	ETC	19
	HP	56
	EMW	15
	AA	303
	AA	445
	AA	1029
	D	23
	MF	88
	MF	121
	RL	43
	ER	76
	L3	227
	L3	240
	T18	95
	T23	25
	T23	72
	FS1	8
	TA	2
	TA	31
	TA	316
	AK	31
	AK	90
	GE	13
	HH	3
	HAP	48
	HAP	283
	HAP	638
	HAP	965
	HAP	1283
	HAP	1591
	BR	247
	BR	25
	BR	33
	PDS	22
	EL	283
	OD	13
	OD	22

Word	Ref	Num
MIGHTY	J1	111
	J3	21
	J10	66
	J10	112
	J10	172
	J10	280
	J10	300
	J10	403
	J16	2
	PPS	6
	P2	9
	P2	17
	P5	7
	P6	111
	M1	71
	M1	412
	M1	517
	M1	528
	M1	773
	M13	211
	GK	120
	VP4	7
	VP6	51
	VP8	141
	VP8	88
	G1	466
	G1	667
	G2	171
	G2	237
	G3	23
	G3	109
	G3	236
	G3	369
	G3	551
	G3	569
	G3	808
	G4	5
	G4	97
	G4	124
	G4	684
	G4	809
	AE1	268
	AE1	596
	AE1	720
	AE1	756
	AE1	937
	AE2	661
	AE3	134
	AE3	217
	AE3	557
	AE3	846
	AE3	923
	AE4	52
	AE4	135
	AE4	321
	AE4	922
	AE5	205
	AE5	491
	AE5	562
	AE5	1044
	AE6	195
	AE6	425
	AE6	533
	AE6	556
	AE6	815
	AE6	893
	AE6	985
	AE6	1053
	AE6	1075
	AE7	225
	AE7	603
	AE7	887
	AE7	983
	AE8	90
	AE8	383
	AE8	464
	AE8	620
	AE8	754
	AE8	895
	AE9	34
	AE9	722
	AE9	989
	AE10	333
	AE10	465
	AE10	515
	AE10	534
	AE10	662
	AE10	792
	AE10	1066
	AE11	187
	AE11	266
	AE11	346
	AE11	576
	AE11	916
	AE11	953
	AE11	1069

Word	Ref	No.	Word	Ref	No.	Word	Ref	No.
MIGHTY	AE12	802	MILK	AT	34	MIND	PMQW	20
	AE12	876		PD	26		PLN	26
	AE12	929		PAA	18		PUO2	2
	AE12	1031		HAP	274		PUO2	16
	AE12	1298		J6	605		EUO2	4
	OAL	6		M1	142		PAL	12
	OAL	519		M13	131		CM	15
	OAL	638		VP2	27		CM	89
	OAE1	1		VP3	152		HP	83
	AF	27		VP5	106		HP	248
	AF	93		VP7	47		DA	143
	DO	69		G1	472		DA	191
	KT1	1		G3	604		AA	364
	KT1	137		G3	612		AA	423
	KT2	660		G3	704		AA	849
	KT2	504		AE3	93		AA	865
	KT2	524		AE4	660		AA	1000
	KT3	23		AE5	102		PPC	3
	KT3	63		AE11	855		MF	171
	KT3	605		OAL	395		MF	173
	M8	124		KT3	946		MF	189
	B	557		C	33		SAA	962
	HIF	198		M12	589		SAA	1097
	HIF	351		M15	172		EK	33
	C	633	MILKER'S	G2	764		EDG	16
	M11	433	MILKEST	VP3	7		RL	66
	FL	226	MILKMAID	VP3	153		RL	213
	FL	534	MILKMAIDS	PMK	7		OE	7
	M12	280	MILKS	PLB	21		L2	45
	M12	281	MILK-WHITE	AT	80		L2	64
	M12	460		AT	81		L3	10
	M12	718		HAP	1		L3	34
	M12	816		J10	99		L3	53
	WB	393		M1	900		L3	94
	M15	210		AE3	164		L3	212
	M15	635		AE4	83		L3	231
MILBOURNE	TJD	87		KT3	47		L3	256
MILD	AR	135		BP	116		L3	267
	LC	57		M10	59		L3	272
	AM	1134	MILKY	BR	210		L4	9
	AA	325		EL	144		L4	19
	AA	478		M1	219		L4	62
	MF	204		M13	128		L4	117
	SAA	902		VP3	50		L4	138
	SAA	991		VP5	87		T23	19
	SAA	1052		VP6	84		T27	40
	TA	88		G1	18		H2	56
	HAP	286		G1	426		FS3	8
	HAP	2353		G3	482		TA	247
	BR	221		G3	600		TA	280
	BR	305		G3	607		TA	323
	AE7	68		AE1	897		TA	501
	AE8	431		DO	154		TA	335
	AE10	1217		M15	300		EAA	10
	CAM	364	MILLENARY	DO	81		AK	23
	HIF	324	MILLET	G1	305		AK	34
	HIF	363	MILLION	EHC	39		AK	107
	GP	16	MILLIONS	AA	323		AK	131
MILDER	UDH	53		HAP	1073		HH	27
	SMA	90		M1	440		HAP	240
	AK	41		AE4	263		HAP	263
	VP5	96		OAL	70		HAP	1251
	G1	469	MILLS	G2	757		HAP	1363
	GP	36	MILO-LIKE	M15	351		HAP	1389
MILDEWS	G1	224	MIMALLONIAN	P1	194		HAP	1410
MILDLY	HAP	1377		OAL	608		HAP	1757
	HAP	2565	MIMAS	AE10	994		HAP	1842
MILDNESS	AR	258		AE10	995		HAP	1899
	AA	77		AE10	999		HAP	2219
	AA	327	MIMIC	J3	162		HAP	2326
	AA	381		J3	289		HAP	2388
	SAA	57		J6	437		HAP	2524
	TA	204		GK	38		BR	333
	TA	324		VP5	116		PTS	33
	HAP	2398		AE6	790		EL	27
	BR	218		C	326		EL	42
MILE	PSF	15		M11	330		EL	222
	J6	749	MIMICKED	HAP	40		EL	233
	KT2	441	MIMICKING	PAA	7		EL	238
	C	738	MINCE	PWR	20		EL	256
	TH	89	MINCIUS	VP7	15		EL	270
MILES	TH	56		G3	20		EL	281
MILESIAN	G4	476		AE10	294		EL	365
MILITANT	TA	254		AE10	295		OD	5
MILITARY	MD	179	MIND	AR	261		ODA	22
	GK	51		SMA	108		ESH	9
	AE5	725		LC	46		ESH	2
	AE5	766		LC	109		EH	21
	AE7	849		LC	134		J1	230
	KT3	102		AM	41		J3	105
	C	751		AM	163		J6	287
MILITIA	J6	570		AM	662		J6	293
	CI	400		SCG2	2		J6	797
MILK	AM	1036		SCG2	12		J10	81
	SAA	395		SCG2	26		J10	266
	SAA	879					J10	273

Word	Ref	No.		Word	Ref	No.		Word	Ref	No.
MIND	J 10	549		MIND	A E 5	888		MIND	B	561
	P 1	15			A E 5	927			B	583
	P 1	53			A E 5	933			B	606
	P 1	161			A E 5	943			B	617
	P 1	262			A E 5	1068			B	666
	P 2	133			A E 5	1083			B	729
	P 3	40			A E 6	116			B P	121
	P 3	114			A E 6	151			M 10	35
	P 3	127			A E 6	271			C A M	39
	P 3	233			A E 6	390			C A M	96
	P 4	47			A E 6	538			C A M	51
	P 5	35			A E 6	631			C A M	79
	P 5	66			A E 6	972			C A M	127
	P 5	124			A E 6	976			C A M	138
	P 5	130			A E 6	984			C A M	174
	P 5	142			A E 6	995			C A M	187
	M 1	510			A E 6	1230			C A M	230
	M 1	863			A E 7	52			C A M	260
	M 1	983			A E 7	282			H I F	311
	M 9	9			A E 7	347			H I F	443
	M 9	24			A E 7	1051			H I F	459
	M 9	76			A E 8	30			H I F	561
	M 13	65			A E 8	209			H I F	592
	V C S	3			A E 8	490			C	263
	H I	114			A E 9	239			C	334
	H I	50			A E 9	255			C	368
	E L T	15			A E 9	837			C	423
	E L T	34			A E 10	9			C	556
	S L T 1	11			A E 10	62			T H	11
	S L T 1	21			A E 10	384			T H	29
	S L T 1	30			A E 10	1202			T H	46
	M C	21			A E 10	1224			T H	76
	G K	2			A E 10	1254			T H	126
	G K	86			A E 11	568			T H	321
	V P 2	106			A E 11	1206			T H	339
	V P 3	103			A E 12	70			T H	349
	V P 7	11			A E 12	244			T H	360
	V P 9	48			A E 12	305			T H	370
	V P 9	75			A E 12	571			T H	380
	V P 9	91			A E 12	708			M 11	21
	G 1	54			A E 12	819			M 11	29
	G 2	72			A E 12	895			M 11	186
	G 2	700			A E 12	904			M 11	217
	G 2	704			A E 12	968			M 11	310
	G 4	290			A E 12	1067			M 11	445
	G 4	671			A E 12	1287			F L	160
	G 4	709			A E 12	1295			F L	432
	A E 1	36			O A L	13			F L	462
	A E 1	43			O A L	17			F L	474
	A E 1	485			O A L	42			M 12	257
	A E 1	652			O A L	125			M 12	315
	A E 1	812			O A L	169			M 12	539
	A E 1	849			O A L	301			M 12	608
	A E 1	859			O A L	412			M 12	626
	A E 1	876			O A L	504			A U	311
	A E 1	950			O A L	623			A U	448
	A E 1	1010			O A L	680			A U	558
	A E 2	46			O A L	810			A U	567
	A E 2	72			O A L	853			A U	582
	A E 2	229			O A L	869			W B	123
	A E 2	520			O A E 1	4			W B	133
	A E 2	710			A F	96			W B	232
	A E 2	766			M F L	4			W B	360
	A E 2	810			M F L	21			W B	384
	A E 2	999			M F L	34			W B	392
	A E 3	121			D O	131			W B	396
	A E 3	137			D O	144			W B	417
	A E 3	207			K T 1	91			W B	466
	A E 3	218			K T 1	281			W B	493
	A E 3	245			K T 1	455			M 15	8
	A E 3	327			K T 1	565			M 15	82
	A E 3	507			K T 2	318			M 15	259
	A E 3	558			K T 2	325			M 15	480
	A E 3	587			K T 2	330			G P	91
	A E 3	632			K T 2	355			C I	28
	A E 4	340			K T 3	482			C I	41
	A E 4	396			K T 3	498			C I	53
	A E 4	406			K T 3	817			C I	58
	A E 4	411			K T 3	885			C I	74
	A E 4	421			K T 3	893			C I	139
	A E 4	435			K T 3	1013			C I	322
	A E 4	18			K T 3	1035			C I	366
	A E 4	160			K T 3	1134			C I	201
	A E 4	460			T J D	16			C I	213
	A E 4	485			M 8	281			C I	230
	A E 4	529			B	21			C I	238
	A E 4	564			B	34			C I	259
	A E 4	611			B	44			C I	495
	A E 4	705			B	140			C I	498
	A E 4	724			B	341			C I	534
	A E 4	770			B	377			S M P	49
	A E 4	773			B	395			E S K	29
	A E 4	791			B	402			E M K G	16
	A E 4	905			B	519		MINDED	C	692
	A E 5	5			B	539		MINDFUL	J 3	500
	A E 5	250			B	545			G 2	485

Word	Ref	No.	Word	Ref	No.	Word	Ref	No.
MINDFUL	G3	492	MINGLED	AA	654	MIRACLE	PC1	18
	G4	230		L2	6		HAP	588
	AE8	607		L4	281		HAP	1827
	AE10	394		HAP	1295		HAP	2225
	AE12	650		BR	270		EL	35
MINDLESS	AE1	1006		M1	576		M1	536
	AE5	225		M1	792		M9	4
	AE5	434		M9	67		AE5	702
MIND'S	AE12	91		AE2	398		DO	141
	AU	568		AE2	750		KT3	685
MINDS	AM	767		AE5	549		M10	91
	AM	1146		AE5	602		M11	489
	PUO1	23		AE5	763		CI	259
	AA	303		AE5	860		AS	12
	MD	253		AE8	176	MIRACLES	AR	14
	MF	82		AE8	910		AR	241
	AT	109		AE9	966		AM	545
	L2	22		AE10	486		HP	130
	L4	131		AE10	503		RL	148
	HAP	1323		AE10	586		TA	90
	BR	96		AE10	1287		TA	293
	EL	204		AE11	736		TA	414
	EL	251		AE11	940		TA	427
	EH	15		AE11	1033		AK	52
	J6	653		AE11	1274		HAP	107
	P2	111		AE12	466		HAP	1490
	P6	42		AE12	920		HAP	1516
	M13	5		AE12	1183		OD	45
	VCS	26		B	253		M1	2
	G1	567		HIF	338		G4	638
	G2	119		C	684		KT2	353
	G3	5		TH	268	MIRACULOUSLY	AA	650
	G3	276		M11	114	MIRE	M1	504
	AE1	17		M12	335		G2	320
	AE1	302		WB	430		AE2	749
	AE2	153	MINGLES	AE4	271	MIRROR	L4	112
	AE2	193		AE6	985		AE6	1214
	AE2	265		AE11	694		OAL	344
	AE2	351	MINGLING	JH	20		KT1	561
	AE3	895		HS	95		KT2	559
	AE4	332		L4	46	MIRRORS	AK	113
	AE4	756		M1	818	MIRTH	PT	11
	AE5	272		M13	217		SAA	492
	AE5	835		AE3	913		SAA	525
	AE5	957	MINIO'S	AE10	265		SAA	918
	AE6	174	MINISTER	AM	1085		SAA	1106
	AE6	1015		MD	227		L3	98
	AE10	513		HAP	1368		H2	95
	AE10	557		BR	175		HAP	386
	AE11	347		J10	145		P1	177
	AE11	388		M1	1079		AE3	456
	AE11	619		G3	280		OAL	274
	AE12	339		G3	498		OAL	408
	AE12	473		AE5	836		KT1	534
	AE12	1232		AE7	636		KT3	428
	OAL	186		AE9	267		HIF	779
	OAL	863		M8	4		HIF	800
	KT2	332	MINISTERED	TH	300		WB	340
	TJD	21		TH	62		ESK	26
	BP	9	MINISTERIAL	HAP	712		EMKG	41
	HIF	642	MINISTERS	LC	86	MIRY	AE6	561
	FL	393		EK	1	MISAPPLIED	HAP	276
	AU	365		GE	44	MISBEGOTTEN	CAM	354
	GP	32		AE8	571	MISCALL	MG	24
	CI	465		AE12	1231	MISCHANCE	HAP	1715
MINE	HS	123		KT2	210		HAP	1716
MINED	TA	169		HIF	447	MISCHIEF	PWG	40
MINERS	KT3	415		M12	50		SAA	353
MINERVA	T18	59		AU	493		SAA	426
	AE11	402	MINISTRY	AE7	856		SAA	526
MINERVA'S	BR	211		HIF	805		SAA	532
	J10	204	MINOIAN	HP	190		T27	18
	HI	15	MINOS	AE6	582		HH	32
	G2	4		OAL	339		J1	111
	AE2	19		OAL	348		J6	849
	AE2	217	MINOTAUR	KT1	116		P2	10
	AE2	253	MINSTRELS	J3	62		M1	71
	AE2	545		KT2	492		M1	179
	AE3	696		FL	352		VP3	20
	OAE1	10		FL	433		VP8	138
	M8	9		CI	539		AE4	922
	M15	533	MINT	AR	162		AE5	803
MINERVAS	ER	72		BP	88		AE7	672
MINES	HS	92	MINTS	WB	19		AE8	23
	LC	66	MINUTE	SCG2	26		AE10	139
	AM	553		SCD1	11		AE12	830
	J3	486		AA	465		KT3	383
	AE10	254		EL	286		KT3	516
	KT3	415		EL	347		HIF	110
MINGLE	SAA	482		SSH	9		C	349
	EWGR	31		AE9	320		C	555
	L4	254		KT2	251		C	673
	M11	156	MINUTES	T23	60		M11	35
	M12	80		GE	42	MISCHIEFS	AM	854
MINGLED	PMQ	5		M15	272		AM	875
	AA	126		M15	273		ECD	7

MISCHIEFS	AA	757
	SAA	756
	L3	227
	J6	818
	B	613
MISCHIEVOUS	J10	304
MISCHIEVOUSLY	AA	778
	MD	62
	AK	158
MISCONSTRUE	SAA	185
MISCREANT	AE2	85
MISDEED	AE3	335
MISDEEDS	RL	109
	G4	655
	AE10	1217
MISDOUBTING	HP	144
	WB	116
MISEMPLOY	L4	105
MISENUS	AE3	313
	AE6	242
	AE6	307
	AE6	316
MISENUS'	AE6	278
MISER	P6	177
	WB	468
MISERABLE	L3	83
	HI	56
	AE6	507
	AE7	275
	OAL	842
	CAM	32
MISERIES	M1	510
	M1	1013
	AE1	311
	AE10	1076
MISER'S	P2	68
	KT3	174
MISERS	MF	91
MISERY	LC	121
	P1	177
	AE2	101
	KT1	506
MISFORTUNE	ELT	18
	AE6	513
	KT2	580
	CAM	160
MISFORTUNES	LCA	4
	L3	41
	L3	42
	AE5	443
	AE12	1011
MISGUIDE	AA	911
	AE4	149
MISGUIDED	SAA	105
MISIMPLOY	AA	613
MISJOINS	HAP	714
MISLAID	AE6	702
MISLEAD	SAA	27
MISLED	RH	86
	AM	1054
	DA	114
	M1	662
	RL	64
	HAP	73
	HAP	1683
	AE9	522
	AE12	220
	OAL	848
	HIF	477
MISS	SMM2	28
	ETC	6
	SAA	189
	HAP	149
	HAP	2483
	P3	162
	OAL	390
	OAE2	71
	TJD	200
	B	220
	C	452
	M12	114
MISSED	AM	343
	SAA	832
	AE5	674
	AE5	675
	AE8	281
	AE9	528
	AE12	405
	KT2	121
	M8	109
	M8	145
MISSES	ECG1	7
	EDGA	12
	L4	159
	ESH	18
	ELT	15
MISSES	ELT	28
	C	56
	ETP	21
MISSHAPEN	HAP	2348
	AE3	549
	AE7	455
MISSING	PPC	31
MISSIONER	GE	13
MISSIONERS	HAP	1137
MISSIONS	AR	193
MISSIVE	AE9	677
	AE12	429
	AE12	848
	CI	624
MISSPENT	L4	115
MIST	L2	16
	BR	129
	P5	82
	M1	821
	G1	546
	AE10	1050
	AE11	1193
	KT2	334
	HIF	499
	M12	50
MISTAKE	PIE	21
	AM	812
	SEL4	8
	EM	22
	ESF	8
	HP	50
	HP	86
	AA	911
	HAP	1712
	HAP	1955
	P5	145
	MC	49
	AE2	506
	AE10	549
	CI	60
MISTAKEN	AR	149
	AM	144
	SLN	17
	AA	497
	EL	350
	J10	305
	M1	828
	AE2	557
	AE2	580
	AE9	321
	KT2	630
	M15	218
MISTAKES	AR	108
	RH	79
	PWG	55
	EAZ	17
	HAP	902
MISTAKING	PLG	18
	HAP	713
	SSC	54
	CAM	120
MISTLETOE	AE6	298
MISTOOK	TA	323
	HAP	387
	C	621
	AS	15
	HS	29
	SMA	99
MISTRESS	AM	1191
	EEL	40
	ECG1	5
	SCG1	31
	EM	22
	PAZ	8
	PAL	16
	PAL	18
	EDG	24
	HAP	393
	ELW	2
	EH	2
	EH	8
	EH	15
	J6	149
	J10	475
	M1	754
	M1	834
	M1	851
	M13	194
	HI	177
	VP1	48
	VP3	103
	G3	333
	AE4	566
	AE6	142
	AE8	939
	AE10	867
MISTRESS	AE11	1256
	AE12	1207
	OAL	101
	OAL	124
	OAL	279
	OAL	416
	OAL	436
	OAL	449
	OAL	846
	OAE1	24
	KT1	571
	M8	182
	M10	72
	WB	79
MISTRESS'	PRL	33
MISTRESSES	LC	8
	PM	19
	PP	15
	J6	468
	WB	282
MISTRUSTFUL	SMA	115
MISTRUSTLESS	AE4	722
MISTS	HS	23
	RH	92
	TA	410
	HAP	2015
	P5	10
	M1	362
	M1	773
	VP6	57
	G1	591
	AE1	571
	AE1	823
	AE2	820
	AE3	684
	AE6	1198
	AE12	974
MISTY	G2	478
	AE3	766
	AE3	892
MISUNDERSTOOD	HAP	276
MITE	HAP	1407
	PMK	29
MITER	HAP	395
	J3	117
	M9	35
	AE2	581
MITERED	PLB	36
	GE	47
	HAP	202
	HAP	2027
	HAP	2301
	J6	665
MITHRIDATES'	J10	421
MITIGATE	AE9	784
	B	724
MIX	AR	125
	SAA	980
	HAP	836
	EL	251
	J6	576
	P5	145
	M1	575
	G1	472
	G3	447
	G3	685
	G3	704
	G4	89
	G4	359
	G4	387
	AE3	306
	AE4	156
	AE11	293
	AE11	329
	AE12	805
	OAL	682
	OAE2	66
	OAE2	70
	KT3	997
	B	344
	FL	332
	M12	299
	M15	315
MIXED	AR	208
	SMA	63
	HAP	21
	HAP	259
	HAP	333
	HAP	1075
	HAP	1915
	EL	159
	J6	455
	T27	46
	M1	24
	M1	106
	M1	201

Word	Ref	No.	Word	Ref	No.	Word	Ref	No.
MIXED	VP10	60	MNESTHEUS	AE5	241	MODEST	PA	27
	VP10	81		AE5	272		EM	23
	G3	773		AE5	282		ELN	16
	AE1	126		AE5	288		HP	32
	AE1	614		AE5	337		HP	209
	AE1	685		AE5	342		PRH	16
	AE2	422		AE5	657		SAA	79
	AE2	533		AE5	672		RL	295
	AE2	570		AE9	216		EC	16
	AE2	1084		AE9	410		HAP	2022
	AE3	134		AE9	1050		J1	96
	AE3	442		AE9	1054		J6	186
	AE4	208		AE9	1097		J10	465
	AE4	594		AE10	195		J10	503
	AE4	821		AE10	214		P4	84
	AE5	384		AE12	194		G4	288
	AE5	809		AE12	567		AE1	788
	AE5	969		AE12	654		AE3	414
	AE5	1033		AE12	806		AE8	882
	AE6	436	MNESTHEUS'	AE12	677		M8	76
	AE6	568	MOAB'S	SAA	834		C	664
	AE6	696	MOAN	ETG	13		TH	110
	AE6	1035		DOD	6	MODESTLY	ER	30
	AE6	1223		VP2	4		HAP	973
	AE7	799		VP6	115		J6	459
	AE7	992		VP10	77		ETP	21
	AE7	1098		G3	694	MODESTY	SEL3	10
	AE9	87		G4	504		EUO2	26
	AE9	847		G4	739		PAZ	3
	AE10	147		AE11	421		EPC	19
	AE10	289		KT1	79		HAP	2488
	AE10	512		KT1	445		OD	5
	AE10	557		KT1	532		M1	164
	AE10	608		C	98		AE1	833
	AE11	49	MOANS	T23	54		OAL	808
	AE11	203		G3	755		B	39
	AE11	221		AE6	600		M10	16
	AE11	488		AE11	329		CAM	113
	AE11	581	MOAT	M1	128		CAM	298
	AE11	1214		KT2	443		TH	418
	AE12	409	MOATS	AE10	35	MODESTY'S	J6	426
	AE12	970		AE11	1284	MODICUM	HAP	2295
	AE12	1216		M11	284	MODIFIED	HAP	989
	MFL	6	MOB	PSH	11	MODIFIES	KT3	501
	DO	116		J10	27	MODISH	ESH	14
	KT1	534		J10	112	MOERIS	VP8	137
	KT2	16		J10	113		VP9	1
	KT3	87		J10	116		VP9	21
	KT3	289		P5	257	MOIL	J10	495
	KT3	720		C	277	MOIST	SSC	8
	KT3	913		C	328		P3	38
	KT3	946		WB	269		M1	378
	B	489	MOCK	SAA	378		G1	146
	CAM	244		TA	168		G2	109
	HIF	331		HAP	498		G2	339
	C	808		J10	54		M8	95
	TH	326		M11	298	MOISTEN	L4	191
	M11	121	MOCKS	M1	640	MOISTENED	G3	652
	FL	75		AE4	644	MOISTENING	B	504
	FL	242		AE12	1311	MOISTURE	L4	254
	FL	295		KT3	750		P4	80
	FL	339	MODE	PRL	22		M1	547
	M12	86		EWGR	43		M1	559
	M12	440		PCG1	39		M1	573
	M12	546		PM	36		VP3	172
	M12	791		PLN	22		G1	105
	AU	42		PNH	9		G1	161
	M15	374		PPC	7		G1	387
	M15	383		PDG	16		G1	426
	M15	673		PAA	32		G2	256
	CI	119		PA	6		G2	298
	CI	579		POE	12		G2	449
MIXES	BR	213		MF	157		G2	472
	AE4	745		OD	14		G2	555
MIXING	HAP	507	MODELED	J3	20		OAL	734
	G2	179	MODERATE	UMR	5		M15	311
	G2	442		AA	75		AS	69
	AE4	961		BR	51	MOLD	AM	287
	AE5	197		BR	299		AM	1170
	AE7	262		EL	354		PA	11
	AE7	538		P6	147		AA	368
	AE7	915		AU	546		MD	33
	WB	414		M15	494		MO	4
	ETP	13		TJD	182		L3	30
MIXTURE	L4	209		BP	17		L4	230
	L4	266	MODERATELY	EL	110		TA	432
	BR	220	MODERATION	AR	242		HAP	11
	P2	115	MODERN	AM	1184		HAP	81
	G1	611		ESF	1		HAP	247
	AE6	993		AA	965		HAP	1483
	AE8	569		J6	8		ODA	60
	AE12	618		AE12	1302		J6	13
	AE12	907		C	203		P3	40
	CAM	84		C	639		G2	31
	M12	633	MODES	PNH	26		G2	299
MNESTHEUS	AE5	154		ESF	21		AE6	50

Word	Ref	No.
MOLD	AE6	1168
	AE7	877
	AE8	829
	AE9	351
	MFL	4
	DO	142
	KT3	757
	B	424
	B	502
	FL	483
	M12	330
	WB	90
	M15	265
	M15	663
MOLDED	M1	43
	AE9	111
	M15	327
MOLDER	L4	297
MOLDERING	L3	50
	OD	18
	J10	171
	AE3	535
	AE6	816
	J3	339
MOLDINESS		
MOLDS	AE1	1008
	KT2	355
MOLDY	AA	302
	P1	151
	P3	147
MOLE	VP8	115
	G1	266
	AE1	594
	AE4	126
	AE9	961
	M11	470
MOLEHILLS	OAL	104
MOLEST	SAA	827
	L3	58
	HAP	2305
MOLESTS	L4	19
MOLLIFIED	OAL	13
MOLLIFIES	L4	46
MOLLIFY	HAP	845
	EL	355
	AE3	558
	AU	498
MOLOCH	HAP	2476
MOLOSSIAN	M1	297
MOLTED	AM	570
MOLTEN	G3	686
	AE8	585
MOLTING	HAP	2577
MOLUCCAN	FL	327
MOMENT	L1	56
	L3	297
	L3	316
	L5	6
	T23	45
	T23	69
	BR	143
	SKA6	23
	EL	308
	ODA	71
	J6	751
	M1	929
	VP10	107
	G3	823
	AE2	878
	AE4	253
	AE6	769
	AE8	739
	AE8	764
	AE10	775
	AE11	1150
	AE12	623
	AE12	1362
	KT1	254
	KT1	324
	KT2	194
	KT2	215
	KT3	254
	KT3	553
	KT3	562
	KT3	595
	B	175
	B	220
	B	239
	HIF	213
	HIF	296
	TH	416
	M15	276
	CI	372
MOMENTARY	L4	80
	J6	279
	M11	350
MOMENT'S	KT3	820
MOMENTS	BR	237
	EL	287
MOMUS	SMP	22
MONARCH	AR	250
	AR	323
	LC	17
	LC	27
	LC	79
	LC	84
	AM	557
	AM	593
	SCG2	21
	PKK	12
	PUF	25
	AA	7
	AA	64
	AA	385
	AA	602
	MD	251
	MF	27
	SAA	29
	SAA	600
	SAA	738
	SAA	764
	SAA	882
	L3	246
	TA	205
	TA	253
	TA	446
	BR	324
	PDS	22
	EL	1
	J10	151
	M1	389
	G4	138
	AE1	84
	AE1	480
	AE7	191
	AE7	808
	OAL	129
	OAL	341
	AF	38
	AF	43
	KT2	665
	KT3	62
	KT3	478
	KT3	546
	KT3	1014
	KT3	1058
	B	282
	CAM	252
	CAM	282
	HIF	535
	C	61
	C	326
	M11	344
	FL	226
	M12	765
	M15	715
MONARCHIES	PCD	21
MONARCH-LIKE	PT	7
MONARCH'S	AM	75
	AA	146
	AA	946
	MD	322
	SAA	188
	SAA	576
	SAA	644
	SAA	664
	SAA	778
	PDG	32
	HAP	393
	HAP	1985
	HAP	2169
	G4	310
	KT2	369
	ETP	29
	HS	35
MONARCHS	AR	301
	AM	50
	AM	966
	SEL1	6
	PNH	21
	E	31
	PAZ	38
	AA	758
	AA	790
	PLB	1
	MD	114
	MD	199
	MF	2
	SAA	8
	SAA	748
	L3	240
	GE	40
	J6	162
MONARCHS	J10	78
	G4	109
	G4	198
	AE2	761
	AE7	235
	AE11	507
	MG	13
	B	557
	CAM	28
	WB	70
MONARCHS'	AR	77
	BR	213
	WB	160
MONARCHY	AM	794
	AA	496
	SAA	904
	MN	9
	HAP	203
	HAP	438
	J10	411
MONASTERIES	WB	64
MONDE	PAA	39
MONEY	AM	151
	PMQ	42
	PMQ	56
	PAZ	24
	PSF	9
	ELB	38
	PPC	31
	EK	48
	RL	382
	EC	14
	H2	99
	PP	11
	PKA	3
	PKA	36
	EKA	35
	J1	73
	J1	160
	J10	17
	J10	471
	R2	93
	P5	160
	PLT	2
	EHC	32
	OAL	39
	WB	281
MONEY-BAG	ELT	24
MONEY'S	J1	170
MONEYS	J6	705
MONK	AR	151
	RH	95
	C	639
MONKISH	ER	16
MONS	POE	25
MONSIEUR	PEL	12
MONSIEURS	EUO	8
MONSIEURS'	ENH	39
	EAZ	20
MONSTER	AM	871
	PLN	31
	EUO	20
	MD	4
	SAA	965
	HAP	537
	HAP	2345
	MS	11
	J6	119
	M1	322
	M9	108
	AE2	45
	AE5	120
	AE5	1077
	AE5	1107
	AE6	41
	AE6	46
	AE7	457
	AE8	258
	AE8	289
	AE8	329
	AE8	343
	AE8	390
	AE8	642
	AE9	959
	MG	22
	M8	137
	CAM	13
	M11	334
	M12	326
	M12	499
	M12	513
	M12	635
	M12	652
MONSTER'S	TH	324
MONSTERS	MD	173
	H3	25

MORN	C	306
	C	685
	WB	45
	M15	283
	M15	468
	CI	405
	AS	67
MORNING	RH	90
	AM	406
	ENH	20
	E	30
	AA	733
	MF	50
	SAA	194
	DOD	4
	DOD	19
	T18	45
	T18	91
	H2	11
	TA	40
	TA	380
	AK	85
	AK	192
	HAP	1916
	HAP	2306
	SKA2	4
	OD	26
	ODA	31
	J1	192
	P1	273
	P2	1
	P2	103
	HI	39
	VP1	110
	VP8	20
	VP8	24
	VP8	55
	VP9	29
	VP10	43
	G1	384
	G1	548
	G3	506
	G3	612
	AE8	106
	AE11	1
	AE11	319
	DO	154
	KT1	182
	KT1	206
	KT2	37
	KT2	38
	HIF	499
	HIF	674
	C	103
	C	205
	C	261
	TH	63
	TH	72
	M11	437
MORNING'S	P5	190
MORNINGS	G4	786
	G4	797
MORNS	SAA	57
MORPHEUS	M11	326
	M11	327
	M11	343
MORROW	P5	91
	B	297
MORROW'S	KT2	164
	KT3	337
MORSEL	J6	825
	OAE2	42
	C	19
MORSELS	AM	1007
	H2	80
	BR	276
	P5	7
	M1	300
	AE3	829
	AE10	1025
	HIF	639
	M15	131
	M15	361
	WB	340
MORT		
MORTAL	AR	15
	SMA	92
	AM	532
	PUO2	15
	MD	275
	MF	113
	SAA	707
	EC	42
	L3	9
	L3	29
	L3	124
	L3	254

MORTAL	L3	301
	L3	318
	H29	11
	TA	115
	AK	16
	AK	48
	AK	151
	GE	44
	HAP	81
	HAP	494
	SSC	28
	EL	135
	EL	237
	EL	336
	EL	352
	J6	243
	J6	634
	J6	693
	J10	134
	M1	436
	M1	536
	M1	733
	M1	912
	M1	294
	GK	174
	G1	185
	G1	643
	G1	668
	G2	406
	G4	115
	G4	319
	G4	600
	G4	643
	AE1	452
	AE1	495
	AE1	853
	AE2	193
	AE2	387
	AE2	820
	AE2	853
	AE3	771
	AE3	815
	AE3	849
	AE3	895
	AE4	486
	AE4	556
	AE4	686
	AE4	721
	AE4	895
	AE4	937
	AE5	361
	AE5	847
	AE6	77
	AE6	91
	AE6	526
	AE6	718
	AE6	977
	AE6	991
	AE6	1020
	AE6	1138
	AE7	138
	AE7	287
	AE7	390
	AE7	429
	AE7	643
	AE7	915
	AE8	42
	AE9	111
	AE9	133
	AE9	887
	AE10	42
	AE10	216
	AE10	526
	AE10	564
	AE10	589
	AE10	657
	AE10	838
	AE10	854
	AE11	426
	AE11	811
	AE12	632
	AE12	687
	AE12	805
	AE12	924
	AE12	1098
	AE12	1182
	AE12	1232
	OAL	297
	OAE1	30
	AF	169
	AF	179
	KT1	68
	KT1	253
	KT1	353
	KT1	420
	KT2	68

MORTAL	KT2	98
	KT2	140
	KT2	185
	KT2	243
	KT2	274
	KT2	294
	KT3	639
	KT3	782
	KT3	814
	KT3	1051
	BP	24
	CAM	135
	HIF	555
	HIF	665
	C	316
	C	681
	TH	96
	TH	178
	FL	82
	FL	100
	FL	478
	FL	499
	M12	124
	M12	466
	M12	562
	M12	791
	WB	388
	M15	202
	CI	450
MORTALITY	UDH	6
	L3	239
	VP7	32
	KT3	176
	TJD	162
MORTALS	AM	68
	AM	125
	RL	133
	H29	49
	HAP	1576
	OD	38
	ODA	40
	P3	25
	M1	65
	M1	126
	M1	154
	M1	174
	M1	219
	M1	422
	G1	631
	G3	108
	AE1	459
	AE8	566
	AE10	698
	KT2	218
	M10	63
	HIF	773
	C	512
	AU	105
	M15	101
	M15	218
	M15	684
	ESK	31
MORTAL-TEMPERED	AE12	1073
MORTGAGED	PCD	2
	P6	152
	J6	471
MORTGAGES	L4	96
MORTIFIED	KT3	712
	GP	52
MORTIFY	J10	66
MOSES	AR	262
	VHH	29
	AA	234
	SAA	1035
	HAP	704
	HAP	965
	BR	69
	MM	4
MOSES'	AA	628
	AA	649
	SAA	1024
	HAP	186
	HAP	781
	HAP	887
	BR	297
MOSES-LIKE	GP	103
MOSS	HAP	1270
	M1	157
	M1	504
	VP6	90
	G4	24
MOSSY	SKK	5
	J6	7
	M1	378
	VP7	66
	VP7	67

MOSSY	G3	233
	G4	472
	AE1	235
	AE6	914
	AE8	835
MOTES	WB	29
MOTHER	UDH	99
	SIE	9
	PWGR	1
	HP	230
	DA	36
	DA	115
	AA	1013
	SAA	383
	SAA	393
	SAA	429
	RL	284
	RL	319
	RL	376
	L2	41
	T18	69
	T27	105
	HAP	21
	HAP	352
	HAP	451
	HAP	505
	HAP	582
	HAP	1069
	HAP	1302
	HAP	1439
	HAP	1909
	BR	275
	EDS	8
	EDS	11
	PMS	25
	SKA2	1
	LS	11
	EL	161
	EL	215
	EL	231
	ODA	42
	EH	20
	J6	271
	J6	326
	J6	340
	J6	732
	J6	823
	J10	368
	J10	444
	J16	7
	P3	147
	M1	108
	M1	528
	M1	1045
	M1	1056
	M1	1057
	M1	1088
	M9	56
	M9	169
	M9	189
	M13	92
	HI	76
	HI	120
	HI	150
	HI	168
	VP4	73
	VP4	74
	VP8	64
	VP8	66
	G1	669
	G2	116
	G2	543
	G3	87
	G3	381
	G4	455
	G4	456
	G4	466
	G4	473
	G4	494
	G4	504
	G4	537
	G4	547
	G4	743
	AE1	434
	AE1	528
	AE1	821
	AE1	826
	AE1	919
	AE1	939
	AE2	801
	AE2	1071
	AE2	901
	AE3	127
	AE3	152
	AE4	45
	AE5	51

MOTHER	AE5	598
	AE5	1018
	AE6	187
	AE6	299
	AE6	501
	AE6	1067
	AE7	71
	AE7	186
	AE7	190
	AE7	562
	AE7	614
	AE7	1044
	AE8	115
	AE8	444
	AE8	504
	AE8	692
	AE8	708
	AE8	807
	AE9	110
	AE9	127
	AE9	224
	AE9	378
	AE9	398
	AE9	405
	AE9	666
	AE9	860
	AE9	917
	AE10	333
	AE10	354
	AE10	438
	AE10	768
	AE10	780
	AE10	1161
	AE11	102
	AE11	515
	AE11	722
	AE11	819
	AE11	934
	AE12	82
	AE12	114
	AE12	313
	AE12	607
	AE12	1126
	AE12	1226
	OAL	140
	OAL	150
	OAL	778
	AF	166
	AF	176
	KT2	104
	KT2	520
	KT2	638
	KT3	224
	KT3	960
	M8	268
	M8	283
	M8	312
	M8	356
	M8	322
	M8	373
	CAM	44
	CAM	89
	CAM	182
	CAM	221
	CAM	358
	HIF	490
	HIF	569
	HIF	776
	HIF	800
	C	610
	TH	248
	TH	421
	M12	20
	M12	268
	M12	370
	M12	523
	AU	468
	WB	237
	WB	401
	WB	420
	M15	129
	M15	373
	M15	561
	EMKG	27
MOTHER-BED	HAP	1121
MOTHERED	G3	683
MOTHER-FIRE	AM	935
MOTHER'S	CM	129
	DA	152
	AA	368
	PD	23
	PD	24
	L3	79
	L4	210
	L4	214
	L4	232

MOTHER'S	BR	111
	BR	131
	BR	252
	ODA	29
	ODA	51
	J3	290
	J6	805
	J10	456
	P6	127
	M1	517
	M1	1051
	M1	1084
	HI	14
	HI	172
	VP4	11
	VP5	30
	VP5	96
	G1	94
	G1	466
	G2	26
	G3	443
	G4	518
	G4	791
	AE1	967
	AE1	1006
	AE2	824
	AE2	839
	AE3	439
	AE4	475
	AE4	683
	AE4	747
	AE5	807
	AE6	282
	AE8	673
	AE9	95
	AE9	283
	AE9	631
	AE9	847
	AE10	457
	DO	168
	KT2	658
	KT3	1071
	TJD	110
	M8	291
	CAM	87
	CAM	389
	HIF	771
	C	59
	AU	237
	AU	311
	M15	330
MOTHERS	AM	903
	CM	136
	AA	13
	SAA	710
	HAP	1753
	HAP	1866
	HAP	1878
	J6	253
	VP6	84
	AE6	577
	AE7	722
	AE7	800
	AE9	72
MOTHERS'	VP3	9
MOTHER-STRUMPETS	MF	72
MOTHER-UNIVERSITY	PUO4	36
MOTHS	G4	360
MOTION	HS	134
	AR	168
	AR	252
	RH	24
	LC	112
	LC	118
	AM	1033
	PRH	32
	SAA	1122
	L3	21
	FS3	8
	TA	64
	HAP	317
	HAP	560
	EL	151
	P5	171
	M13	233
	AE5	572
	AE5	593
	AE5	892
	AE10	499
	AE10	806
	KT3	1024
	AU	174
	M15	264
	M15	518
	CI	30
	CI	34

Word	Code	No.
MOTION	ETP	25
MOTIONS	UDH	29
	LC	106
	LC	152
	AA	29
	AA	254
	SAA	166
	L3	40
	L4	279
	HAP	533
	J6	93
	J6	367
	P3	41
	P3	127
	M13	192
	G1	448
	G3	105
	G3	122
	G4	85
	AE1	214
	AE1	867
	AE1	993
	AE2	460
	AE3	635
	AE4	429
	AE5	751
	AE6	289
	AE8	208
	AE12	345
	KT1	514
	KT2	645
	FL	180
MOTIVE	HAP	109
	HAP	1410
MOTIVES	HAP	1679
MOTLEY	EWGR	42
	P1	154
	KT2	485
MOUND	M1	128
	G2	222
	G2	353
	AE11	1232
	FL	68
MOUNDS	J10	243
	VP10	83
	AE4	127
	AE11	745
MOUNSIEUR	ET	5
	EEL	13
MOUNSIRE	HS	90
MOUNT	AM	916
	PA	24
	EEL	31
	PUO2	37
	EOE	10
	DA	129
	AA	629
	L3	205
	L3	209
	FS3	12
	HAP	861
	HAP	1036
	HAP	1511
	J1	29
	J6	283
	J6	646
	J10	18
	J10	390
	P1	39
	P1	131
	M1	534
	VP1	95
	G2	491
	G3	328
	G3	435
	G4	331
	G4	625
	AE1	149
	AE2	404
	AE2	603
	AE2	625
	AE3	540
	AE3	727
	AE4	328
	AE4	961
	AE5	693
	AE6	1230
	AE7	381
	AE7	738
	AE7	920
	AE8	121
	AE8	672
	AE8	728
	AE9	93
	AE11	326
	AE11	571

Word	Code	No.
MOUNT	AE11	704
	AE11	725
	AE12	205
	AE12	221
	AE12	519
	AE12	1292
	KT2	498
	KT3	145
	KT3	546
	KT3	890
	B	102
	HIF	239
	M11	171
	M12	207
MOUNTAIN	LC	135
	CM	100
	DA	98
	J6	6
	J10	477
	M1	123
	M1	424
	M1	434
	M1	592
	HI	70
	VP5	97
	VP6	100
	VP9	11
	VP10	89
	G1	66
	G2	293
	G3	330
	G3	621
	G4	170
	AE1	92
	AE1	120
	AE1	856
	AE2	846
	AE4	218
	AE4	640
	AE4	709
	AE7	1027
	AE8	297
	AE9	917
	AE10	1087
	AE11	206
	AE11	795
	AE11	987
	AE12	138
	AE12	991
	KT2	542
	M12	477
	AU	500
	M15	407
	M15	461
MOUNTAIN-ASH	KT3	960
MOUNTAIN-BELLY	MF	193
MOUNTAINEERS	AE7	984
MOUNTAIN'S	L3	72
	H9	1
	VP1	107
	G1	159
	G3	372
	G4	603
	AE1	255
	AE1	429
	AE3	515
	AE3	697
	AE3	862
	AE4	236
	AE6	918
	AE7	934
	AE8	308
	AE10	193
	AE12	173
	M8	84
	B	115
	BP	145
	M15	461
MOUNTAINS	SKK	7
	PRH	7
	AT	2
	L1	23
	T18	50
	HAP	46
	J10	241
	M1	51
	M1	194
	M13	138
	VP2	4
	VP6	59
	VP6	60
	VP7	77
	VP10	80
	G1	12
	G1	22
	G1	375

Word	Code	No.
MOUNTAINS	G1	454
	G1	449
	G1	492
	G3	395
	G4	665
	AE1	83
	AE1	125
	AE1	192
	AE3	845
	AE3	888
	AE5	374
	AE5	912
	AE6	268
	AE7	551
	AE7	718
	AE8	917
	AE10	1000
	AE11	489
	AE11	1307
	OAL	252
	B	283
	M12	669
	M12	679
MOUNTAINS'	AE10	758
MOUNTAIN-TOPS	SKA2	5
	AE3	270
	AE3	293
MOUNTEBANK	PO	6
	PTP	38
MOUNTED	HS	63
	H29	29
	HAP	1830
	BR	234
	J1	241
	J6	807
	AE10	1227
	AE12	1016
	KT3	447
	KT3	992
	TH	366
	FL	255
	M15	288
MOUNTING	RH	13
	AM	238
	AM	610
	AM	1174
	SMQ	16
	AA	367
	MD	13
	H3	24
	AK	192
	P5	61
	G1	499
	G3	369
	AE3	750
	AE5	4
	AE5	1033
	AE6	486
	TH	335
MOUNTS	LC	141
	AM	591
	AA	851
	SAA	26
	SAA	337
	H9	2
	TA	118
	HAP	2026
	ODA	68
	M1	429
	EHC	1
	G2	159
	AE1	711
	AE2	311
	AE4	351
	AE4	928
	AE4	984
	AE5	855
	AE5	896
	AE5	1120
	AE6	894
	AE7	779
	AE12	964
	AE12	1098
	KT3	181
	KT3	1014
	B	711
	HIF	330
	HIF	719
	C	179
	M11	200
	M15	368
MOURN	AM	134
	PCG1	43
	ECG1	2
	PFD	16
	A	6

MOURN	A A	339
	A A	698
	P R H	35
	T 18	69
	H 29	64
	P P	25
	L S	11
	J 3	174
	J 3	347
	M 1	330
	M 13	1
	V P 1	48
	V P 1	54
	V P 1	91
	V P 5	15
	G 3	46
	G 4	374
	A E 1	785
	A E 1	847
	A E 2	495
	A E 7	24
	A E 9	247
	A E 9	277
	A E 9	346
	A E 10	1076
	A E 11	419
	O A L	81
	O A L	208
	D O	92
	K T 1	405
	K T 1	502
	K T 3	1103
	B	669
	H I F	255
	H I F	356
	M 11	374
	M 12	46
	M 12	776
	C I	204
MOURNED	A A	823
	A A	832
	D	6
	S A A	710
	S A A	794
	S A A	823
	S A A	1140
	B R	255
	E L W	10
	E L	184
	J 10	400
	J 10	407
	H I	191
	V P 10	45
	G 4	752
	A E 1	943
	A E 2	121
	A E 4	570
	A E 4	798
	A E 6	738
	A E 9	609
	A E 10	655
	A E 11	89
	A E 11	147
	A E 11	249
	D O	125
	K T 3	717
	K T 3	1004
	B	717
	H I F	695
MOURNER	J 10	380
	K T 3	961
MOURNERS	P 3	207
MOURNFUL	D A	2
	L 4	242
	T A	60
	H A P	1079
	B R	253
	E L	2
	O D	46
	O D A	44
	J 6	374
	J 10	215
	M 1	735
	M 1	898
	M 1	979
	M 9	169
	H I	8
	H I	29
	H I	73
	V P 8	1
	V P 8	6
	V P 10	4
	G 3	754
	G 3	775
	G 4	494
	G 4	495

MOURNFUL	G 4	671
	G 4	746
	A E 2	380
	A E 3	90
	A E 3	388
	A E 3	442
	A E 4	10
	A E 4	475
	A E 4	632
	A E 4	691
	A E 6	31
	A E 6	596
	A E 9	544
	A E 9	631
	A E 10	694
	A E 10	1198
	A E 11	293
	A E 11	1221
	A F	73
	K T 1	89
	K T 3	1013
	T H	80
	M 11	231
	M 11	493
	A S	46
MOURNING	A M	1060
	E L	349
	J 3	253
	P 6	100
	M 1	778
	V P 6	89
	G 4	455
	A E 11	50
	A E 11	221
	A E 11	530
	A E 12	586
	K T 1	41
	K T 1	55
	K T 1	134
	K T 3	927
	K T 3	942
	K T 3	979
	B	693
	C A M	189
MOURNS	S K K	9
	T A	372
	M 1	190
	M 9	149
	V P 6	68
	A E 1	304
	A E 2	853
	A E 6	257
	K T 1	381
	K T 1	508
	K T 2	2
	J 6	458
MOUSE	E L T	36
	G 1	265
	U D H	19
	D A	72
	R L	272
MOUTH	T 23	17
	T 27	7
	T 27	31
	A K	51
	J 10	321
	P 1	201
	P 1	203
	P 3	230
	M 13	59
	M 13	199
	V P 5	8
	G 1	636
	G 3	596
	G 4	49
	G 4	607
	A E 1	19
	A E 1	1032
	A E 3	479
	A E 3	705
	A E 3	904
	A E 4	113
	A E 4	264
	A E 4	333
	A E 5	625
	A E 6	68
	A E 6	113
	A E 6	339
	A E 7	607
	A E 8	301
	A E 8	305
	A E 8	335
	A E 8	354
	A E 9	592
	A E 10	1024
	O A E 2	37

MOUTH	O A E 2	49
	K T 2	578
	M 8	29
	M 8	108
	B	139
	B	689
	H I F	158
	H I F	364
	C	801
	M 11	104
	M 11	217
	M 12	353
	M 12	408
	M 12	587
	M 12	683
	A U	370
	M 15	70
	C I	108
	E M K G	15
MOUTHED	A A	528
	P 1	226
MOUTHFUL	J 3	499
MOUTHING	P 5	12
MOUTHS	A M	610
	H A P	1475
	P 1	43
	P 5	2
	G 2	62
	G 3	439
	G 3	611
	G 4	292
	A E 4	263
	A E 6	570
	A E 6	821
	A E 6	851
	A E 8	544
	A E 10	795
	A E 11	726
	O A L	496
	K T 3	58
	T H	307
	M 15	138
	C I	401
MOVABLES	E S H	12
MOVE	U D H	28
	H S	127
	A M	61
	A M	226
	A M	353
	A M	731
	S L N	13
	P C 2	19
	M L	33
	E A L	22
	E O E	12
	C M	23
	H P	66
	H P	97
	D A	143
	D A	191
	A A	884
	D	41
	S A A	722
	E K	33
	E D G A	21
	A T	89
	L 1	26
	L 1	53
	L 3	14
	L 4	190
	T 23	30
	T 23	89
	T 23	102
	H A P	790
	H A P	1912
	H A P	2092
	S S C	56
	P S H	35
	J 6	93
	J 6	157
	J 6	287
	J 10	535
	M 1	63
	M 1	193
	M 1	510
	M 1	728
	M 9	24
	H I	18
	M C	33
	V P 4	58
	V P 8	149
	G 1	53
	G 2	380
	G 2	487
	G 3	54
	G 3	155

Word	Code	No.	Word	Code	No.	Word	Code	No.
MOVE	G3	387	MOVED	KT2	342	MUCH	PW	9
	G4	733		KT3	482		PMQW	2
	AE1	285		M10	14		EMQW	17
	AE1	544		TH	127		EMQW	27
	AE2	193		M11	54		PLN	17
	AE2	197		M11	453		PCD	20
	AE2	944		FL	180		PCD	34
	AE3	254		FL	393		SCD1	10
	AE4	247		M12	535		ENH	6
	AE4	160		M12	802		PAZ	2
	AE4	421		AU	326		EAZ	17
	AE4	294		WB	71		ML	29
	AE4	340		CI	223		ML	42
	AE4	396		CI	244		ML	46
	AE4	443	MOVER	KT3	1032		PAL	13
	AE4	636	MOVES	EIE	17		PAL	35
	AE5	8		AM	384		EAL	17
	AE6	631		HP	73		EMK	2
	AE6	1186		J6	548		EMK	7
	AE7	523		J10	57		PTW	5
	AE7	1051		G3	366		POE	20
	AE8	490		AE1	225		EOE	8
	AE9	35		AE4	919		EOE	18
	AE10	513		AE5	876		HP	112
	AE11	427		AE6	606		HP	234
	AE12	1295		AE6	1181		DA	176
	OAL	3		AE9	1079		PUO4	1
	OAL	44		AE11	684		PUO4	8
	OAL	269		AE12	332		PUO5	17
	OAL	311		AE12	626		AA	27
	OAL	406		AE12	684		AA	308
	OAL	526		MM	50		AA	496
	OAL	534		KT1	178		AA	506
	OAL	559		KT1	260		AA	534
	OAL	835		KT2	58		AA	887
	OAE1	10		B	494		AA	942
	OAE2	83		HIF	715		AA	972
	AF	95	MOVING	VHH	47		AA	988
	DO	25		AM	312		PPC	3
	KT1	91		AA	739		EPC	25
	KT1	280		RL	17		EPC	30
	KT1	500		L2	G		MD	7
	KT2	220		L2	47		MF	65
	KT2	606		L3	113		MF	102
	KT3	167		P5	149		SAA	56
	KT3	398		M1	928		SAA	264
	B	474		M9	39		SAA	304
	M10	16		VP5	89		SAA	379
	M10	35		G4	438		SAA	573
	CAM	174		AE1	160		SAA	786
	HIF	543		AE1	209		SAA	1002
	TH	22		AE1	755		PK	11
	M11	21		AE3	928		PDG	26
	M11	39		AE4	59		PDG	33
	FL	134		AE8	913		EDG	1
	FL	214		AE9	672		RL	191
	M12	542		AE12	660		RL	225
	AU	311		OAL	528		RL	247
	WB	253		KT3	983		RL	253
	WB	370		M11	487		RL	295
	M15	81		M15	274		RL	425
	M15	100	MOW	G1	385		RL	444
	M15	139		AE12	964		OE	60
	CI	228	MOWED	SKA4	1		AT	15
	CI	458		M12	802		AT	18
	CI	595	MOWN	AR	110		EC	13
	STP	25	MOWS	TA	361		EC	17
	ESK	15		M13	29		ER	41
	AR	62		AE2	407		ER	42
	LC	116		AE10	775		MO	18
	SAA	202	MR.	EAL	17		L2	7
	AK	9		ESH	22		L3	319
MOVED	HAP	1618	MUCH	AR	86		L4	167
	P1	163		AR	243		L4	265
	P1	175		RH	71		T18	85
	M1	303		SMA	73		T27	78
	M1	1070		LC	4		T27	110
	MC	21		PWG	8		H29	85
	G4	509		PWG	30		TA	269
	G4	739		PWG	50		TA	323
	AE2	44		PRL	1		GE	3
	AE2	129		EIE	19		GE	16
	AE2	559		VHH	11		GE	36
	AE4	618		AM	548		HAP	24
	AE4	761		AM	960		HAP	307
	AE5	526		AM	1139		HAP	560
	AE5	1035		PMQ	43		HAP	702
	AE6	43		PWGR	19		HAP	945
	AE7	62		EWGR	27		HAP	1042
	AE7	344		PMM	7		HAP	1150
	AE9	393		ET	10		HAP	1295
	AE10	539		PA	38		HAP	1382
	AE10	793		EEL	33		HAP	1431
	AE10	969		PCG1	25		HAP	1445
	AE12	607		ECG1	37		HAP	1481
	OAL	694		SCG2	22		HAP	1759

MURDERED	KT1	494	MURTHER	MD	204	MUSE	P1	104
	KT1	529		EDGA	7		P1	235
	KT2	584		J1	4		P5	8
	TJD	85		J6	858		P6	5
MURDERER	AM	873		J10	193		MC	70
	DA	141		AE11	1122		GK	87
	M12	780		C	271		GK	95
	M15	171		C	285		VP1	2
MURDERER'S	DA	123		C	362		VP3	90
	AE2	129		C	371		VP3	93
	AE10	1302		M15	146		VP3	136
MURDERERS	AM	739	MURTHERED	ELB	17		VP4	1
	C	241		J3	200		VP4	3
	C	498		G4	658		VP4	69
MURDERESS	KT2	638		AE4	664		VP6	2
MURDERING	AM	103		AE6	709		VP6	9
	AM	219		AE10	1236		VP6	19
	SAA	769		AE10	1260		VP7	37
	PTS	31		C	272		VP8	1
	MG	24		C	279		VP8	6
MURDEROUS	TJD	57	MURTHERER	SAA	148		VP8	18
	C	114		HAP	279		VP9	23
	C	749		HAP	1554		VP10	4
	M15	194	MURTHERERS	SAA	389		G2	2
MURDERS	M1	187	MURTHERERS'	MD	218		G3	79
	M1	299	MURTHERING	MD	202		G3	457
MURMUR	SKK	6	MURTHERS	J6	841		G3	524
	L4	74		P4	123		G4	449
	TA	425		AE8	634		AE1	11
	HAP	1538		AE8	753		AE10	267
	BR	66	MUSAEUS	AE6	908		OAL	299
	OD	44	MUSCLES	AR	166		OAE1	3
	P5	16		M1	545		OAE1	23
	M1	257		KT3	479		OAE1	28
	AE6	915	MUSCOVITE	MS	11		AF	73
	AE11	454	MUSE	RH	11		MM	30
	AE11	461		RH	24		DO	150
	AE12	325		RH	64		KT2	80
	AE12	363		RH	93		KT3	117
	M8	221		LCA	5		TJD	85
	HIF	210		LCA	52		TJD	107
	AU	197		PIE	15		HIF	1
MURMURED	HP	85		AM	697		C	633
MURMURING	SIE	14		PA	22		C	695
	AM	906		PEL	4		CI	24
	TA	283		EEL	12		ERL	8
	AA	45		EEL	39	MUSED	AM	396
	SAA	375		PTL	19		AE7	347
	SAA	1082		ECG1	21		FL	102
	DOD	17		PC1	16	MUSEFUL	AE3	572
	M9	187		ML	46		KT1	541
	VP1	73		EOE	5	MUSE'S	EUO2	2
	VP5	130		PLG	25		VP6	93
	G1	492		PR	7	MUSES	HS	10
	G4	95		PUO4	26		LC	5
	AE1	238		PUO5	1		LC	23
	AE2	798		PUO5	27		AM	357
	AE4	760		AA	854		ET	4
	AE10	305		AA	828		PA	29
	AE11	370		AA	878		PUO2	24
	AE11	1210		AA	898		EUO2	20
	KT3	358		D	30		EUO2	30
	HIF	251		MF	83		EUF	11
	TH	88		MF	183		D	3
	M11	225		MF	198		SAA	818
MURMURS	SKA5	9		SAA	410		SAA	984
	EL	2		SAA	447		ER	9
	J6	280		SAA	518		TA	370
	P2	11		SAA	606		PP	35
	M1	266		SAA	959		J3	28
	VP9	51		SAA	935		PPS	4
	G4	276		SAA	1037		GK	49
	G4	382		SAA	1103		VP3	88
	AE1	416		ER	67		VP3	133
	AE4	594		L1	39		VP6	16
	AE5	197		H3	7		VP6	97
	AE5	602		TA	71		VP7	27
	AE7	794		TA	246		VP8	87
	AE10	9		TA	333		VP9	42
	AE10	147		TA	372		VP10	17
	AE10	408		AK	16		VP10	75
	AE12	906		AK	58		VP10	100
	KT1	538		AK	81		G2	615
	M8	366		AK	83		G2	673
	CAM	151		HAP	310		AE7	888
	M11	285		HAP	1297		AE9	88
	M12	86		BR	223		AE9	1045
	CI	331		EL	134		TJD	201
MURRANUS	AE12	776		EL	360		HIF	809
	AE12	928		J1	18		M15	720
MURREY-COLORED	J6	669		J1	28	MUSES'	ECD	2
MURTHER	CM	96		J1	85		PUO1	43
	PSF	45		J1	225		AA	877
	AA	39		J1	255		SAA	818
	AA	676		P1	9		ER	28
	AA	790		P1	97		PDS	42

Word	Ref	Num
MUSES'	MM	5
MUSHROOM	J6	812
MUSIC	RH	1
	SMA	53
	SMA	58
	AM	688
	FS2	7
	AK	49
	SSC	16
	SSC	24
	SSC	63
	BR	323
	EKA	40
	J6	434
	J10	336
	M1	981
	DHP	8
	DHP	24
	G4	671
	G4	747
	AE7	969
	OAE1	20
	AF	108
	KT2	492
	TH	62
	TH	80
	FL	49
	FL	149
	FL	200
	FL	338
	GP	22
	ESK	15
MUSICIAN	M1	938
	AF	47
	FL	444
MUSICIAN'S	G4	680
MUSIC'S	D	43
	SSC	10
MUSING	C	487
MUSK	EL	156
MUSKET	HAP	2413
MUSS	PTW	20
MUSSULMAN	HAP	377
MUST	J10	392
	G1	393
	G2	12
	BP	111
MUSTERED	G4	626
	AE6	922
	AE8	650
MUSTERS	KT3	575
MUTE	RL	315
	T18	58
	TA	52
	HAP	254
	HAP	931
	HAP	2509
	J6	568
	M1	107
	M1	334
	M1	518
	AE1	648
	AE2	176
	AE3	40
	AE4	405
	AE6	551
	AE11	182
	AE11	767
	AE12	1045
	OAL	93
	AF	157
	B	593
	B	685
	CAM	162
	HIF	689
	HIF	764
	TH	326
	M12	219
	M12	824
	AU	368
	CI	111
MUTELY	HAP	535
MUTES	HAP	159
MUTINY	J16	27
MUTIUS	P1	225
MUTTER	EAZ	25
MUTTERED	AT	75
	P2	67
	AE10	765
	B	165
MUTTEREST	P5	266
MUTTERING	CM	81
	P3	156
	C	261
MUTTERS	EAZ	26
	J6	558
MUTTERS	P3	13
	AE12	334
MUTTON	J16	45
	PAA	15
MUTUAL	ML	5
	HP	176
	MD	211
	L4	200
	T27	121
	HAP	1345
	M1	904
	M9	79
	M9	210
	M13	5
	DHP	7
	AE7	62
	AE7	422
	AE7	469
	AE8	220
	AE10	494
	AE12	123
	AE12	424
	AE12	1041
	OAL	644
	KT3	1150
	B	72
	B	231
MUTUSCANS	AE7	980
MUZZLE	SAA	273
	OAL	582
MUZZLED	HAP	159
	PTP	2
MUZZLES	G3	611
	KT3	58
MYCALE	M12	370
MYCENAE	AE2	446
	AE2	257
	AE7	302
	M15	635
MYRIADS	AK	30
	AE9	163
MYRMIDONS	J1	248
	HIF	270
MYRRH	VP3	138
	M15	595
MYRRHA	OAL	321
	CAM	19
	CAM	35
	CAM	126
	CAM	168
	CAM	203
	CAM	214
	CAM	228
	CAM	253
	CAM	258
	CAM	266
	CAM	274
	CAM	334
MYRRHA'S	CAM	69
	CAM	138
MYRTLE	SCG1	1
	SAA	1105
	VP2	75
	VP7	87
	VP7	90
	VP10	61
	G1	37
	G2	627
	AE1	973
	AE3	53
	AE5	93
	AE6	599
	AE7	1112
	OAL	299
	OAE1	33
	KT2	461
	KT3	87
	KT3	913
MYRTLES	LS	17
	VP7	7
	G1	412
	G2	90
	G2	159
	G4	185
	AE3	33
	AF	7
	KT2	518
MYSCELOS	M15	26
MYSIA	G1	149
MYSTERIES	M15	210
MYSTERIOUS	AM	645
	SAA	270
	T27	123
	HAP	96
	HAP	120
MYSTERIOUS	HAP	1296
	J10	279
	M1	522
	G4	409
	AE6	151
	AE8	829
	KT3	203
	M15	89
	M15	231
MYSTERY	P1	241
MYSTIC	SAA	1021
	BR	32
	J6	662
	P3	156
	AE1	357
	AE3	577
	AE6	377
	FL	283
	FL	460
	FL	601
MYSUS	M15	424
NADAB	AA	575
NAEVES	UDH	55
NAIL	MF	44
	BP	73
NAILED	AE9	787
	M8	191
	FL	257
	M12	450
NAILS	P1	205
	AE9	488
	OAL	584
	KT3	461
	C	53
NATS	VP6	33
	AE12	215
NAKED	AM	410
	EAZ	16
	HP	115
	AA	280
	AA	400
	EK	19
	L5	3
	T18	40
	T27	105
	H2	47
	HAP	264
	HAP	1147
	HAP	1305
	HAP	1589
	BR	262
	EL	47
	J1	128
	J1	168
	J3	344
	J3	354
	J6	347
	J6	787
	P3	218
	P4	77
	P5	35
	P6	67
	M1	638
	M13	139
	G1	88
	G1	401
	G2	562
	G3	679
	G3	683
	G3	718
	AE1	69
	AE3	364
	AE5	178
	AE5	1136
	AE7	492
	AE7	948
	AE7	953
	AE8	880
	AE9	468
	AE10	436
	AE11	10
	AE11	1103
	AE11	1157
	AE12	470
	AE12	794
	OAL	183
	OAL	597
	OAL	706
	KT2	628
	KT3	1000

NAKED	KT3	1064	NAME	T18	75	NAME	G4	508
	M10	30		T18	79		G4	561
	M10	50		T23	83		G4	646
	CAM	377		T27	71		AE1	23
	C	244		T27	72		AE1	48
	TH	111		T27	73		AE1	338
	TH	122		T27	118		AE1	451
	TH	273		TA	37		AE1	459
	M12	126		TA	77		AE1	461
	M12	651		TA	245		AE1	518
	M12	679		TA	327		AE1	521
	AU	170		TA	381		AE1	751
	M15	534		EAA	15		AE1	794
	ETP	22		AK	124		AE1	857
NAKEDLY	AT	9		HAP	50		AE1	1022
NAKEDNESS	SAA	385		HAP	142		AE2	100
NAME	UDH	76		HAP	156		AE2	103
	HS	7		HAP	325		AE2	114
	HS	135		HAP	354		AE2	118
	HS	146		HAP	1146		AE2	139
	AR	94		HAP	1450		AE2	169
	AR	98		HAP	1550		AE2	245
	AR	99		HAP	1629		AE2	385
	AR	191		HAP	1992		AE2	429
	AR	231		HAP	2107		AE2	445
	AR	265		HAP	2118		AE2	1045
	AR	286		HAP	2200		AE3	21
	RH	95		HAP	2201		AE3	142
	SMA	36		HAP	2265		AE3	183
	SMA	51		HAP	2458		AE3	184
	SMA	58		HAP	2479		AE3	224
	DC	15		BR	141		AE3	372
	DC	31		BR	193		AE3	381
	AM	687		BR	199		AE3	392
	AM	1171		BR	205		AE3	450
	SEL4	6		BR	211		AE3	505
	ECG1	3		BR	333		AE3	555
	SCG1	23		BR	339		AE3	657
	PFD	10		BR	342		AE3	800
	ELN	15		ETS	13		AE3	805
	ELN	17		EKA	20		AE3	915
	PCD	21		EL	48		AE4	52
	PNH	32		EL	199		AE4	249
	EUO2	17		EL	292		AE4	274
	PAZ	14		EH	5		AE4	319
	ESF	18		EH	21		AE4	401
	ML	2		J1	71		AE4	343
	ML	23		J1	230		AE4	468
	PAL	16		J3	349		AE4	485
	EMK	10		J6	358		AE4	490
	PTC	17		J6	394		AE4	554
	PCB	9		J6	624		AE4	857
	CM	69		J6	626		AE4	869
	HP	88		J10	216		AE4	896
	HP	214		J10	423		AE4	939
	DA	102		P1	39		AE4	968
	DA	180		P1	188		AE5	76
	PUO4	35		P1	225		AE5	141
	AA	39		P5	111		AE5	397
	AA	151		P5	117		AE5	521
	AA	179		P5	225		AE5	658
	AA	243		M1	219		AE5	737
	AA	419		M1	428		AE5	782
	AA	435		M1	551		AE5	807
	AA	573		M1	609		AE5	941
	AA	681		M1	642		AE5	980
	AA	707		M1	894		AE6	55
	AA	816		M1	897		AE6	184
	AA	830		M1	955		AE6	335
	AA	846		M1	987		AE6	347
	AA	965		M1	1053		AE6	353
	ELB	7		M1	1072		AE6	518
	MD	233		M9	60		AE6	520
	MD	260		M9	64		AE6	528
	MD	317		M9	151		AE6	682
	MF	34		M13	233		AE6	814
	MF	69		VCS	35		AE6	1035
	MF	162		HI	40		AE6	1041
	MF	172		HI	134		AE6	1044
	SAA	173		HI	167		AE6	1054
	SAA	295		VP2	81		AE6	1146
	SAA	941		VP3	61		AE6	1165
	EK	22		VP6	13		AE6	1194
	PDG	13		VP6	16		AE7	2
	RL	108		VP6	67		AE7	6
	RL	173		VP9	32		AE7	71
	RL	191		VP10	25		AE7	226
	RL	192		VP10	78		AE7	270
	AT	108		G1	208		AE7	373
	PD	34		G2	148		AE7	447
	L3	247		G2	191		AE7	465
	L4	16		G2	213		AE7	558
	L4	144		G2	236		AE7	562
	L4	159		G3	13		AE7	576
	L4	239		G3	442		AE7	778
	T18	70		G4	398		AE7	840

NAME	AE7	931	NAME	B	51	NAMES	PDS	35
	AE7	1001		B	340		J6	9
	AE7	1048		B	516		J10	93
	AE8	22		M10	100		J10	348
	AE8	66		CAM	123		J10	371
	AE8	87		CAM	184		P5	103
	AE8	73		CAM	205		PLT	55
	AE8	160		CAM	251		GK	120
	AE8	432		CAM	271		VP3	164
	AE8	436		CAM	353		AE2	798
	AE8	440		HIF	197		AE3	434
	AE8	447		HIF	386		AE3	566
	AE8	470		HIF	556		AE4	740
	AE8	551		C	204		AE5	393
	AE8	627		TH	10		AE5	654
	AE8	686		TH	152		AE6	30
	AE9	89		TH	154		AE6	109
	AE9	171		TH	357		AE6	927
	AE9	240		M11	243		AE6	1027
	AE9	283		FL	510		AE7	199
	AE9	379		M12	3		AE8	976
	AE9	399		M12	203		AE10	244
	AE9	525		M12	283		AE12	301
	AE9	877		M12	299		AE12	1100
	AE9	884		M12	624		OAL	251
	AE9	901		M12	721		OAL	257
	AE10	71		M12	805		LMC	3
	AE10	193		M12	827		KT2	504
	AE10	213		AU	27		KT3	12
	AE10	221		AU	44		KT3	573
	AE10	267		AU	48		CAM	88
	AE10	288		AU	62		CAM	106
	AE10	516		AU	95		CAM	303
	AE10	632		AU	245		HIF	162
	AE10	874		AU	435		M11	215
	AE10	1215		AU	546		M11	216
	AE10	1251		AU	613		M11	223
	AE11	117		WB	273		M11	432
	AE11	187		WB	275		FL	518
	AE11	314		WB	282		M12	613
	AE11	335		WB	364	NAMESAKE'S	SAA	323
	AE11	346		WB	390	NAMING	AA	816
	AE11	382		WB	404		HAP	309
	AE11	392		M15	12		HAP	1815
	AE11	408		M15	24		HAP	2520
	AE11	411		M15	223		OAL	418
	AE11	572		M15	233	NAMUR	TJD	152
	AE11	592		M15	249	NAN	EDG	21
	AE11	664		M15	378	NAP	P5	190
	AE11	677		M15	426	NAPAEAN	G4	776
	AE11	1017		M15	498	NAPLES	G4	815
	AE11	1075		M15	636	NAR	AE7	720
	AE11	1078		GP	115	NARCISSUS	ETG	6
	AE11	1228		CI	66		VP2	65
	AE12	207		CI	68		G4	184
	AE12	291		CI	184		G4	236
	AE12	522		CI	243		KT2	502
	AE12	702		CI	435	NARD	M15	592
	AE12	931		PTP	47	NARROW	UDH	22
	AE12	943		AS	16		AM	215
	AE12	983		PWR	21		AM	877
	AE12	1015	NAMED	HAP	810		AM	942
	AE12	1196		HAP	1687		AM	1105
	AE12	1200		HAP	1741		AA	838
	AE12	1210		HAP	2514		HAP	373
	AE12	1214		PKA	22		HAP	701
	OAL	40		J3	269		BR	205
	OAL	52		J6	430		EL	244
	OAL	289		M1	12		EL	271
	OAL	324		AE1	748		J1	69
	OAL	642		AE3	28		J3	155
	OAL	657		AE5	986		J3	384
	OAL	758		AE11	378		J6	3
	OAL	821		KT1	318		J6	250
	OAL	845		KT2	49		J10	62
	LMC	1		TH	117		J10	154
	LMC	5		M11	336		J10	276
	DO	18		M12	712		P3	110
	DO	55	NAMELESS	AT	9		M1	453
	KT1	2		J6	785		G1	523
	KT1	54		AE2	346		G2	106
	KT1	73		AE2	763		G4	49
	KT1	313		KT3	966		G4	124
	KT2	101	NAMES	AR	312		G4	418
	KT2	133		EWG	16		AE2	448
	KT2	272		AA	569		AE2	485
	KT2	280		AA	577		AE2	598
	KT3	19		AA	691		AE3	705
	KT3	23		AA	748		AE4	60
	KT3	63		SAA	518		AE4	311
	KT3	224		SAA	637		AE4	586
	KT3	245		PD	31		AE5	675
	KT3	993		T27	55		AE7	49
	M8	51		HAP	1545		AE8	475
	M8	393		HAP	1553		AE8	617
	M8	394		HAP	1640		AE9	884

NARROW	AE10	658
	AE11	793
	AE12	1333
	OAL	99
	AF	164
	AF	174
	B	674
	C	227
	C	422
	C	629
	FL	13
	FL	56
	AU	71
	M15	331
	M15	444
NARROWED	HAP	577
NARROWER	RL	390
	HAP	1702
	M1	318
	GK	124
	AE11	1026
	AE12	703
NARROWLY	J6	730
NARROW-SOULED	CI	35
NARYCIAN	G2	614
NASEBY	AR	230
NASTINESS	L4	182
	J3	185
NASTY	PDG	13
	MS	7
	J3	466
	J6	174
	J6	429
	J10	306
	P2	66
	P6	38
	OAL	585
	OAE2	40
NATION	AR	296
	AM	680
	AM	843
	EM	1
	ECD	9
	EUO	32
	PTW	4
	POE	18
	PO	9
	EUF	28
	AA	414
	AA	416
	AA	523
	AA	715
	EPC	21
	MD	266
	SAA	200
	SAA	374
	SAA	283
	SAA	630
	PK	2
	PDG	7
	PDG	13
	RL	316
	PD	20
	PAA	3
	GE	69
	HH	11
	HAP	548
	HAP	2159
	PDS	7
	PKA	4
	SKA5	5
	EL	12
	J3	136
	J3	169
	J3	351
	J10	107
	J10	216
	G3	714
	G4	73
	G4	238
	AE1	385
	AE2	84
	AE2	137
	AE3	308
	AE6	491
	AE6	958
	AE10	571
	AE12	1195
	AE12	1218
	DO	76
	C	63
	M12	662
	M15	716
	ETP	29
	PMK	41
	EMKG	30

NATION	PWR	12
	PWR	18
NATIONAL	HAP	942
NATION'S	UDH	49
	AR	204
	SMA	35
	LC	27
	AM	187
	AA	108
	AA	240
	AA	905
	AA	954
	MD	295
	SAA	760
	TA	295
	TJD	148
NATIONS	UDH	19
	AR	115
	AR	239
	VHH	20
	AM	25
	AM	153
	AM	167
	AM	228
	AM	358
	AM	494
	AM	644
	E	22
	PCB	27
	PUO4	30
	AA	635
	AA	1031
	PLB	37
	MF	34
	MF	96
	SAA	566
	ER	11
	ER	50
	AK	179
	HAP	244
	HAP	1233
	HAP	1971
	BR	280
	EL	275
	M1	222
	M1	261
	M1	587
	GK	56
	GK	130
	VP4	20
	G3	806
	AE1	32
	AE1	74
	AE1	360
	AE1	1023
	AE2	493
	AE2	737
	AE3	217
	AE4	898
	AE5	601
	AE6	139
	AE7	149
	AE7	762
	AE8	21
	AE8	175
	AE8	508
	AE8	620
	AE8	962
	AE12	732
	AE12	1024
	DO	16
	KT2	214
	KT3	5
	KT3	24
	CAM	58
	M15	626
	CI	38
	SMA	133
NATIONS'	SAA	718
NATIVE	UDH	21
	RH	5
	LCA	45
	ECG2	24
	E	2
	HP	221
	DA	18
	AA	87
	AA	300
	AA	354
	AA	760
	AA	891
	AA	939
	AA	949
	MD	72
	MD	120
	SAA	598

NATIVE	SAA	648
	ER	51
	MO	14
	L1	17
	T27	14
	H2	43
	FS1	10
	TA	69
	TA	152
	TA	326
	EAA	27
	HAP	15
	HAP	200
	HAP	204
	HAP	237
	HAP	238
	HAP	294
	HAP	863
	HAP	1186
	HAP	2023
	HAP	2446
	BR	162
	BR	265
	BR	307
	J3	36
	J3	125
	J3	205
	J3	483
	J10	128
	J10	207
	J10	259
	P1	135
	P3	31
	P6	15
	M1	115
	M1	127
	M1	201
	M1	559
	M1	831
	M1	1006
	M1	1035
	M13	227
	HI	79
	MC	61
	GK	125
	VP1	4
	VP4	53
	VP10	70
	G2	69
	G2	77
	G2	319
	G2	651
	G3	17
	G3	349
	G3	814
	G4	30
	AE1	575
	AE1	794
	AE2	127
	AE2	188
	AE3	15
	AE3	300
	AE3	326
	AE3	804
	AE4	206
	AE4	786
	AE5	377
	AE6	684
	AE6	997
	AE7	187
	AE7	370
	AE7	430
	AE8	441
	AE8	660
	AE8	674
	AE8	860
	AE10	101
	AE10	115
	AE10	285
	AE10	488
	AE10	615
	AE10	780
	AE10	972
	AE11	382
	AE11	892
	AE12	21
	AE12	359
	DO	1
	KT1	452
	KT2	358
	KT3	408
	TJD	139
	M8	69
	B	458
	B	538
	CAM	12

NATIVE	CAM	77	NATURE	ER	34	NATURE	AE6	1126		
	HIF	30		MO	13		AE7	503		
	HIF	52		L1	13		AE8	40		
	HIF	269		L1	20		AE9	295		
	C	686		L1	34		AE9	706		
	M11	192		L2	19		AE11	244		
	FL	131		L2	20		AE11	792		
	M12	263		L2	66		OAL	739		
	M12	625		L3	148		OAL	801		
	M12	779		L3	155		LMC	4		
	M15	30		L3	163		KT2	310		
	M15	78		L3	168		KT2	592		
	GP	33		L3	296		KT2	656		
	CI	118		L4	11		KT3	143		
	CI	394		L4	30		KT3	767		
	ETP	19		L4	49		KT3	1044		
NATIVES	AM	822		L4	53		TJD	115		
	PFD	6		L4	85		B	48		
	PRH	3		L4	197		B	251		
	SAA	945		L5	10		B	326		
	PK	13		AK	72		B	350		
	ODA	77		AK	123		B	357		
	AE3	222		HAP	76		B	361		
	AE7	992		HAP	244		B	444		
	AE10	8		HAP	1324		M10	8		
	AE12	1213		HAP	1829		CAM	11		
NATIVES'	DA	125		HAP	2272		CAM	40		
	AE7	199		HAP	2442		CAM	53		
	M12	152		HAP	2537		CAM	97		
NATIVITY	AA	230		SSC	3		C	452		
	SAA	481		EMI	5		C	456		
NATURAL	AR	164		BR	221		C	550		
	AM	1129		PDS	32		C	585		
	AA	28		PKA	18		TH	6		
	AA	219		EKA	39		TH	95		
	ELB	5		SKA2	13		TH	110		
	RL	70		SKA3	7		TH	337		
	RL	83		ODA	21		M11	278		
	RL	209		ODA	35		FL	32		
	L2	25		J1	121		FL	76		
	HAP	2586		J10	243		M12	189		
	M1	823		J10	463		AU	225		
NATURALLY	HS	74		J10	466		WB	413		
NATURE	UDH	25		J16	39		M15	9		
	HS	99		P4	121		M15	84		
	HS	114		P5	67		M15	103		
	AR	16		P5	142		M15	262		
	SMA	8		P6	7		M15	372		
	LC	24		M1	9		M15	414		
	LC	72		M1	25		M15	557		
	LC	136		M1	92		M15	694		
	DC	16		M1	102		CI	68		
	DC	27		M1	134		CI	72		
	PWG	46		M1	385		CI	107		
	SIE	9		M1	421		SMP	74		
	AM	617		M1	471		AS	1		
	AM	658		M1	551		AS	19		
	AM	864		M1	555	NATURE'S	LC	113		
	PT	8		M9	98		LCA	28		
	SCG1	17		M9	104		AM	617		
	PAR	26		M9	137		ESF	13		
	PLN	42		GK	3		CM	50		
	ECD	8		GK	8		AA	339		
	PUO1	35		GK	108		AA	424		
	EUO	19		GK	113		AA	794		
	PUO2	3		VP3	84		AA	458		
	PAZ	10		VP4	60		RL	13		
	ML	35		VP5	99		RL	151		
	PUO4	21		VP7	76		RL	159		
	AA	5		VP8	70		RL	204		
	AA	79		VP8	78		RL	246		
	AA	478		G1	92		ER	6		
	AA	692		G1	633		L3	121		
	AA	883		G2	13		L3	170		
	AA	960		G2	27		L3	296		
	MD	6		G2	47		L5	18		
	MD	71		G2	156		H3	28		
	D	29		G2	247		TA	13		
	MF	13		G2	283		HAP	57		
	MF	166		G2	445		HAP	448		
	MF	176		G2	600		HAP	2228		
	SAA	245		G2	665		BR	107		
	SAA	949		G2	687		EDS	19		
	SAA	992		G3	231		EL	334		
	SDG	15		G3	259		J1	59		
	SDG	17		G3	450		J6	1		
	RL	52		G3	724		J10	551		
	RL	165		G3	732		P1	20		
	RL	190		G4	143		P1	261		
	RL	201		G4	220		P6	143		
	RL	326		G4	417		M1	6		
	DOD	13		AE2	737		M1	577		
	DOD	23		AE3	78		M13	104		
	PD	11		AE3	535		M13	166		
	PD	53		AE4	926		GK	143		
	ER	6		AE4	996		VP6	49		

NATURE'S	G1	92	NAVY	AE2	39	NEAR	G4	505
	G1	288		AE2	240		G4	706
	G2	73		AE2	361		AE1	618
	G2	641		AE2	628		AE1	1005
	G2	698		AE3	266		AE2	701
	AE2	183		AE3	494		AE2	896
	AE2	727		AE3	603		AE2	961
	AE3	787		AE4	63		AE2	992
	AE4	767		AE5	790		AE3	7
	AE6	926		AE5	851		AE3	176
	AE9	926		AE5	1088		AE3	501
	AF	166		AE5	1124		AE3	549
	AF	176		AE6	499		AE3	660
	MG	3		AE6	946		AE4	377
	KT1	330		AE7	104		AE4	605
	KT1	416		AE7	150		AE4	807
	KT2	56		AE8	652		AE5	219
	KT2	337		AE9	79		AE6	159
	KT3	82		AE10	326		AE6	247
	KT3	757		M12	36		AE6	524
	B	322	NAXOS	AE3	171		AE6	657
	B	418	NEAERA	VP3	4		AE7	12
	B	518	NEAERA'S	VP5	135		AE7	124
	C	464	NEALCES'	AE10	1069		AE7	439
	TH	219	NEAR	HS	134		AE7	1089
	WB	426		AR	311		AE8	270
	M15	90		PWG	26		AE8	853
	M15	125		AM	499		AE8	909
	M15	150		AM	585		AE9	647
	M15	326		AM	737		AE10	747
	M15	387		AM	747		AE10	1181
	M15	590		AM	905		AE11	515
	CI	58		AM	953		AE11	945
NATURES	ETL	7		AM	1020		AE12	82
	HAP	2195		AM	1034		AE12	224
	J10	71		ET	14		AE12	600
NAUGHTY	EPC	12		SEL3	7		AE12	691
	T18	20		SEL3	19		OAL	75
	T27	23		EUO	2		OAL	88
	ESH	3		ML	38		OAL	295
	OAL	749		HP	175		KT1	38
NAUSEATES	PTC	27		AA	163		KT1	609
	J6	555		AA	685		KT2	23
NAUSEOUS	ENH	32		MF	74		KT2	64
	ESF	3		MF	97		KT3	5
	ELB	18		SAA	588		KT3	799
	SAA	826		SAA	831		M8	3
	T27	37		PDG	39		M8	136
	H29	14		AT	86		M8	184
	EH	16		MO	3		B	101
	J6	140		L3	113		BP	192
	J6	265		T27	15		CAM	238
	P1	42		NS	24		HIF	740
	P2	82		TA	35		C	60
	P4	126		TA	166		C	168
	EHC	25		TA	169		C	474
	VP4	75		TA	362		TH	105
	OAE2	5		AK	93		M11	175
	TJD	93		AK	117		M11	190
	C	133		HAP	179		M11	268
	WB	498		HAP	1711		FL	205
NAUSEOUSLY	OE	3		HAP	2155		FL	308
NAUTES	AE5	922		HAP	2240		FL	317
NAVAL	AM	1084		HAP	2251		FL	382
	AE2	332		EDS	6		FL	427
	AE5	319		PTS	7		M12	85
	AE5	657		EL	267		M12	361
	AE8	905		EL	300		M12	383
	OAL	198		J6	655		M12	770
	TJD	148		J6	729		AU	123
	CI	620		J10	341		WB	43
NAVEL	M13	225		P3	12		WB	185
	M12	520		P5	99		M15	451
NAVEL-STRING	J6	489		P6	94		M15	685
	P2	70		M1	63		GP	111
NAVIES	VHH	13		M1	717		CI	377
	J10	283		M9	27	NEARER	AM	128
NAVIES'	AM	570		SLT1	23		PM	27
NAVIGABLE	AE1	309		GK	19		EPF	16
NAVIGATION	AM	633		VP1	35		RL	340
NAVY	AM	206		VP3	146		HAP	541
	AM	215		VP5	36		HAP	578
	AM	311		VP7	68		HAP	1663
	AM	398		G1	46		HAP	1666
	AM	419		G1	488		PKA	33
	AM	483		G2	690		M1	731
	AM	498		G3	287		GK	170
	AM	706		G3	633		AE1	581
	AM	777		G4	23		AE3	395
	AM	805		G4	68		AE6	501
	AM	1201		G4	175		AE6	521
	TA	511		G4	181		AE10	671
	AE1	61		G4	282		AE10	1007
	AE1	272		G4	397		AE12	328
	AE1	783		G4	453		KT1	219
	AE1	1063					KT3	549

Entry	Code	No.
NEARER	CAM	73
	CAM	285
	TH	279
	M11	450
	M11	459
	M11	461
NEAREST	VHH	27
	AM	89
	AM	267
	RL	454
	AE1	227
	AE6	1030
	M8	201
	C	97
NEARLY	SAA	1101
NEAT	H29	25
NEATHERDS	VP10	28
NECESSARY	EMQW	10
	AA	83
	AA	405
	AA	623
	AA	1003
	HAP	1022
	HAP	1046
	HAP	1058
	G1	362
NECESSITATE	KT2	221
NECESSITY	HAP	1054
	HAP	2130
	EL	72
	EL	229
	AE2	610
	AE11	466
	KT3	1085
	TJD	68
	C	528
	C	529
	WB	191
	WB	423
	M15	152
NECK	SM2	3
	AA	596
	SAA	211
	SAA	487
	SAA	496
	T23	93
	J3	122
	J3	155
	J6	59
	J6	294
	P1	197
	M1	638
	M1	650
	M1	669
	M1	889
	M1	890
	M1	900
	M1	1022
	M1	1069
	HI	145
	G3	266
	G3	783
	AE1	557
	AE1	667
	AE2	513
	AE2	1077
	AE3	867
	AE6	950
	AE7	494
	AE7	680
	AE8	344
	AE9	445
	AE9	581
	AE9	1040
	AE10	640
	AE10	745
	AE11	18
	AE11	954
	AE12	541
	AE12	882
	OAE2	43
	DO	52
	M8	23
	M8	211
	M10	46
	CAM	149
	CAM	348
	C	89
	C	626
	C	667
	M11	467
	M12	532
	M12	649
	M12	755
	M15	182
	M15	183
NECKED	G3	88
	G3	125
NECKLACE	AE1	922
NECKS	AM	934
	MD	299
	SAA	24
	H2	91
	J10	175
	VP6	75
	G1	530
	AE1	32
	AE8	876
	KT3	59
	FL	236
NECTAR	M1	142
	VP5	110
	G4	240
	G4	599
	AE1	1030
	HIF	785
NEDYMNUS	M12	473
NEED	UDH	65
	LC	56
	PNH	31
	ENH	40
	EUO2	27
	E	7
	PC1	2
	ML	48
	PAL	24
	PTW	23
	HP	54
	ELB	39
	PRH	19
	SAA	20
	SAA	106
	SAA	299
	PK	9
	RL	433
	ER	35
	L4	287
	T27	20
	H2	38
	AK	80
	GE	55
	HH	15
	HAP	92
	HAP	861
	HAP	1314
	HAP	1433
	HAP	1687
	HAP	1802
	HAP	1887
	HAP	2029
	HAP	2131
	HAP	2329
	HAP	2441
	BR	142
	ETS	31
	EL	19
	EL	50
	MS	6
	PSH	13
	ESH	15
	J6	775
	J6	862
	P1	83
	P3	45
	P5	141
	P6	130
	M1	737
	MC	64
	G1	203
	G1	218
	G2	588
	G2	617
	G4	646
	AE1	239
	AE2	771
	AE6	708
	AE8	177
	AE9	818
	AE10	16
	AE10	390
	AE11	476
	AE11	498
	AE11	586
	AE12	121
	AE12	218
	OAL	160
	OAL	253
	OAL	689
	OAL	713
	AF	80
	KT1	123
	TJD	139
NEED	TJD	142
	B	33
	B	127
	HIF	260
	C	582
	M12	121
	M12	671
	AU	19
	AU	93
	AU	191
	AU	476
	WB	42
	WB	357
	WB	476
	CI	404
	PMK	33
NEEDED	AM	305
	PTC	11
	ODA	19
	B	172
	B	631
	TH	296
	TH	357
	WB	253
	WB	535
	M15	45
	M15	141
NEEDEST	SAA	571
	P2	8
	OAL	72
	B	427
	M11	22
NEEDFUL	AA	166
	PLB	41
	SAA	80
	SAA	156
	J6	152
	SAA	577
	RL	300
	RL	307
	RL	409
	RL	369
	ER	32
	HAP	668
	HAP	681
	HAP	716
	HAP	717
	HAP	913
	HAP	921
	HAP	1050
	BR	59
	SAA	161
	EHC	5
	VP8	5
	G1	14
	G2	54
	G3	480
	G4	465
	AE1	554
	AE1	946
	AE3	104
	AE4	63
	AE4	538
	AE4	807
	AE6	550
	AE6	686
	AE7	431
	AE8	265
	AE8	502
	AE9	196
	AE9	215
	AE9	655
	OAL	841
	KT2	160
	KT3	109
	KT3	1138
	CAM	323
	HIF	814
NEEDLE	HAP	1143
	DO	160
NEEDLES	T18	7
NEEDLESS	PUF	7
	PLB	16
	TA	427
	HAP	717
	HAP	2141
	HAP	2169
	J1	37
	M1	118
	AE9	135
	AE10	135
	AE10	622
	AE11	66
	AE11	391
	AE12	55
NEEDLESSLY	PK	22

Word	Ref	No.
NEEDLEWORK	AE5	327
	AE11	1142
NEEDS	RH	85
	PMQ	52
	PAZ	35
	EAZ	2
	PTW	32
	POE	33
	AA	120
	SAA	394
	SAA	423
	RL	121
	RL	126
	MO	15
	L2	19
	TA	330
	TA	475
	HAP	34
	HAP	1054
	HAP	1615
	HAP	1762
	PMS	6
	PKA	45
	EL	41
	EL	310
	PSH	37
	J6	392
	M1	381
	AE5	640
	AE9	185
	AE11	522
	AE12	737
	OAL	440
	LMC	2
	TJD	6
	TJD	130
	B	83
	WB	425
	M15	111
	GP	140
	CI	21
NEEDY	PCD	1
	SAA	954
	RL	382
	EL	36
NEGLECT	HAP	905
	J6	685
	P1	81
	AE2	808
	AE4	50
	AE9	312
	AE12	33
	AE12	912
	OAL	574
	OAL	838
	FL	152
NEGLECTED	PAR	23
	MF	100
	M1	335
	VP2	21
	AE4	127
	M8	83
	B	123
NEGLECTING	SAA	59
NEGLECTS	SAA	511
	P6	80
NEGLIGENCE	P3	31
	KT2	437
	KT3	73
	M8	71
	C	811
NEGLIGENT	AA	388
NEGOTIATION	GE	70
NEGROMANCER	VP8	141
NEIGH	AE11	1314
NEIGHBOR	AA	600
	HAP	2159
	J3	324
	J6	585
	J6	654
	P2	27
	VP3	79
	G4	66
	C	317
	C	613
	C	725
	M15	476
NEIGHBORHOOD	ELB	23
	HAP	1665
	P4	109
	M1	776
	M9	7
	VP1	15
	AE7	701
	AE8	352
	BP	141
NEIGHBORHOOD	BP	193
NEIGHBORING	SCD2	12
	AR	127
	AR	216
	PT	15
	T23	91
	AK	6
	HAP	1845
	HAP	523
	HAP	1905
	J10	78
	P6	31
	M1	306
	M1	724
	M13	190
	M13	204
	VP1	66
	VP1	75
	VP2	73
	VP3	149
	VP6	33
	VP7	14
	VP9	34
	G1	368
	G1	687
	G3	150
	G4	33
	G4	804
	AE3	337
	AE3	885
	AE5	374
	AE6	206
	AE7	81
	AE7	149
	AE7	762
	AE8	175
	AE9	514
	AE10	263
	AE10	569
	AE10	1142
	AE11	311
	AE12	60
	AE12	107
	AE12	215
	AE12	764
	AE12	822
	AE12	1301
	OAL	447
	MG	38
	BP	16
	CAM	28
	C	486
	C	771
	TH	60
	M11	470
	FL	412
	M12	725
NEIGHBOR'S	PC2	26
	M9	73
	OAL	394
NEIGHBORS	AR	81
	AM	655
	AM	887
	PNH	23
	PAZ	37
	POE	17
	PUO5	15
	HAP	2305
	TJD	7
	FL	43
NEIGHBORS'	AM	176
	DA	130
	HAP	2382
	J6	540
	P5	238
	BP	156
NEIGHING	TA	474
	AE7	885
	AE8	5
	AE8	789
	AE11	909
	AE12	129
	OAL	316
	KT3	443
	FL	211
	M12	336
NEIGHINGS	G3	150
NEIGHS	AE11	751
NELEIDES	M12	252
NELEUS	M12	728
NELL	EMQ	16
NELLY	ETL	4
	ETL	18
	ETL	29
NEPHEW	AE12	652
	M12	773
NEPHEW'S	AE1	931
	AE6	1092
NEPHEWS	M11	499
NEPTUNE	VHH	15
	AM	733
	SAA	923
	J10	291
	M1	446
	G1	42
	G4	567
	AE1	176
	AE2	827
	AE3	100
	AE3	162
	AE5	1019
	AE5	1069
	AE7	30
	AE7	955
	AE8	920
	AE8	926
	AE10	491
	M12	37
	M12	117
	M12	122
	M12	186
	M15	444
NEPTUNE'S	G3	193
	AE2	267
	AE5	473
	AE5	836
	AE5	1045
	AE5	1122
	AE9	693
	AE10	53
	AE10	820
	AE10	1062
NEPTUNIAN	M12	101
NEREID	SAA	622
NEREIDS	D	14
	M1	410
	AE1	236
	AE5	1081
	AE10	312
	DO	45
NEREUS	G4	564
	AE2	569
NERITOS	AE3	352
NERIUS	P2	27
NERO	J10	474
	C	713
NERO'S	PNH	6
	J1	93
	J10	23
NERVE	TA	473
	J6	285
	J10	328
	P4	108
NERVES	AR	166
	L4	22
	L4	84
	P2	75
	G3	297
	G3	728
	AE5	553
	AE12	1317
	TJD	89
	M8	131
	M12	665
	AU	445
	M15	343
NERVOUS	AE5	488
	HIF	631
NESSUS	M12	426
	M12	606
NEST	JH	11
	AR	181
	HAP	1730
	HAP	2358
	M13	137
	VP3	106
	G3	667
	G4	744
	AE12	694
	KT3	123
	C	566
	M11	495
	M12	18
	M15	587
NESTLE	HAP	2251
NESTOR	J6	443
	M8	60
	M8	133
	HIF	403
	M12	234
	M12	706
	M12	761

Word	Code	No.
NESTOR	A U	92
	A U	90
NESTS	J 3	331
	G 1	562
	G 2	292
	A E 8	310
NET	R H	26
	A M	723
	L 4	133
	J 10	486
	K T 3	320
NETHER	T A	33
	H A P	502
	E L	94
	V P 6	108
	G 1	333
	G 1	442
	A E 3	497
	A E 4	35
	A E 6	214
	A E 6	337
	A E 7	776
	A E 8	326
	A E 8	888
	A E 11	796
	A E 12	309
	A E 12	997
	K T 3	217
	C	605
	M 11	136
	M 12	634
NETS	A M	717
	A M	808
	L 4	81
	H 2	50
	V P 3	117
	G 1	213
	A E 4	186
	A E 12	755
	O A L	876
	M 15	697
NETTINGS	S C D 2	4
NETTLES	P 6	166
NEUTER	C I	537
NEUTERS	E D G	39
NEUTRAL	H A P	1958
NEUTRALITY	H A P	38
NEVER-CHANGING	L 3	299
NEVER-ERRING	M 8	55
NEVER-FADING	V P 4	67
NEVER-OPENING	T 23	53
NEW	U D H	46
	U D H	101
	H S	54
	H S	131
	S M A	24
	S M A	26
	S M A	112
	L C	148
	D C	44
	P W G	45
	L C A	52
	P I E	8
	E I E	8
	S I E	4
	V H H	28
	V H H	49
	A M	72
	A M	287
	A M	454
	A M	469
	A M	480
	A M	577
	A M	591
	A M	600
	A M	807
	A M	875
	A M	936
	A M	1179
	E M Q	5
	E W G R	16
	P T	2
	P T	4
	P E L	14
	E E L	13
	E E L	35
	S E L 3	12
	P C G 2	23
	S C G 2	24
	P F D	21
	P F D	30
	P A R	2
	P A R	4
	P M Q W	10
	P M	36
	S M 2	18

Word	Code	No.
NEW	E C D	11
	P U O 1	17
	P N H	41
	P N H	53
	E N H	2
	E S F	22
	P K K	19
	P L G	21
	P O	10
	D A	12
	D A	19
	D A	20
	D A	203
	P R	15
	P U O 3	23
	P U F	4
	P U F	14
	A A	393
	A A	554
	A A	576
	A A	1028
	P P C	29
	M D	17
	M D	111
	M D	119
	M F	43
	M F	146
	M F	188
	S A A	153
	S A A	155
	S A A	219
	S A A	562
	S A A	705
	S A A	868
	P K	12
	P K	17
	P K	30
	E K	1
	P D G	23
	E D G A	24
	R L	179
	R L	257
	R L	291
	O E	10
	L 1	29
	L 1	13
	L 3	144
	L 3	166
	L 3	169
	L 3	310
	L 4	86
	T 27	97
	H 9	2
	H 29	38
	H 29	40
	F S 1	4
	T A	90
	A K	3
	A K	40
	A K	175
	A K	192
	H A P	60
	H A P	75
	H A P	350
	H A P	673
	H A P	786
	H A P	1129
	H A P	1161
	H A P	1163
	H A P	1166
	H A P	1169
	H A P	1176
	H A P	1467
	H A P	1470
	H A P	1797
	H A P	1840
	H A P	1847
	H A P	1869
	H A P	1880
	H A P	2019
	H A P	2191
	H A P	2277
	H A P	2389
	B R	50
	B R	256
	E D S	29
	P P	13
	P T S	42
	E T S	18
	P K A	45
	E J G	3
	E J G	4
	E L	206
	E L	312
	E L	131
	O D A	58

Word	Code	No.
NEW	P S H	14
	J 1	101
	J 3	184
	J 3	426
	J 3	503
	J 6	9
	J 6	69
	J 6	95
	J 6	317
	J 6	494
	J 10	334
	J 16	68
	P 1	152
	P 2	4
	P 6	72
	M 1	94
	M 1	95
	M 1	103
	M 1	113
	M 1	125
	M 1	167
	M 1	203
	M 1	339
	M 1	368
	M 1	386
	M 1	492
	M 1	523
	M 1	531
	M 1	582
	M 1	584
	M 1	587
	M 1	593
	M 1	610
	M 1	855
	M 1	939
	M 1	965
	M 1	976
	M 1	981
	M 9	108
	M 9	111
	M 9	154
	M 13	76
	M 13	131
	M 13	221
	H I	188
	E H C	8
	E H C	35
	E H C	37
	V P 2	27
	V P 2	70
	V P 3	163
	V P 4	41
	V P 6	56
	V P 6	104
	G 1	67
	G 1	131
	G 1	133
	G 1	142
	G 1	417
	G 2	57
	G 2	88
	G 2	186
	G 2	452
	G 2	460
	G 2	468
	G 2	493
	G 2	548
	G 3	13
	G 3	398
	G 3	460
	G 3	476
	G 4	30
	G 4	156
	G 4	233
	G 4	246
	G 4	437
	G 4	733
	A E 1	104
	A E 1	356
	A E 1	484
	A E 1	506
	A E 1	736
	A E 1	928
	A E 2	133
	A E 2	250
	A E 2	364
	A E 2	375
	A E 2	421
	A E 2	496
	A E 2	521
	A E 2	593
	A E 2	644
	A E 2	977
	A E 3	188
	A E 3	298
	A E 3	315

Headword	Ref	No.
NEW	AE2	835
	AE3	387
	AE3	496
	AE3	605
	AE3	618
	AE3	895
	AE4	11
	AE4	254
	AE4	383
	AE4	458
	AE4	805
	AE4	963
	AE5	131
	AE5	737
	AE5	788
	AE5	850
	AE5	987
	AE5	1008
	AE5	1057
	AE6	136
	AE6	156
	AE6	576
	AE6	581
	AE6	707
	AE6	847
	AE6	924
	AE6	1107
	AE6	1221
	AE7	94
	AE7	115
	AE7	484
	AE7	537
	AE7	581
	AE7	599
	AE7	609
	AE7	630
	AE7	662
	AE7	868
	AE7	881
	AE8	75
	AE8	413
	AE8	487
	AE8	584
	AE8	529
	AE8	841
	AE9	267
	AE9	618
	AE9	872
	AE9	974
	AE9	1002
	AE9	1031
	AE9	1036
	AE9	1085
	AE10	41
	AE10	58
	AE10	1103
	AE10	1120
	AE10	1125
	AE11	44
	AE11	100
	AE11	259
	AE11	287
	AE11	307
	AE11	353
	AE11	674
	AE11	717
	AE11	813
	AE12	239
	AE12	365
	AE12	371
	AE12	472
	AE12	521
	AE12	912
	AE12	1147
	OAL	112
	OAL	257
	OAL	261
	OAL	266
	DO	29
	DO	79
	DO	102
	KT1	36
	KT1	172
	KT1	179
	KT1	221
	KT1	257
	KT3	769
	KT3	618
	KT3	999
	KT3	1029
	TJD	149
	M8	138
	M8	275
	M8	306
	B	375
	BP	185
NEW	HIF	728
	HIF	805
	TH	232
	M11	11
	M11	235
	M11	302
	FL	44
	FL	65
	FL	94
	FL	203
	FL	220
	FL	332
	FL	338
	FL	444
	M12	159
	M12	275
	M12	739
	M12	821
	M15	13
	M15	229
	M15	238
	M15	247
	M15	265
	M15	274
	M15	389
	M15	538
	CI	110
	CI	188
	ETP	20
	SMP	91
	SMP	97
	ESK	9
	ESK	21
	PMK	23
	AS	49
	AS	52
	AS	69
	P2	4
NEW-ADDED	VP5	100
NEW-ADMITTED	AE6	462
	AE8	322
NEW-BEGOTTEN	L4	212
NEW-BORN	UDH	80
	SMA	8
	AM	70
	AM	476
	EUO	20
	M15	642
	CI	163
NEWBORN	LC	100
	VHH	52
	CM	78
	TA	364
	BR	27
	P2	61
	G2	501
	AE4	746
	AE9	820
	KT2	590
	M8	260
NEW-BUDDING	SEL3	2
NEW-BUILT	PFD	20
	DA	133
	PKA	21
NEW-CAST	AM	594
NEW-CHOSEN	HAP	449
NEW-CLOSING	LC	101
NEW-COME	ODA	72
NEW-DEIFIED	AM	1178
NEW-DRAWN	M12	573
NEW-DRESSED	M11	239
NEW-ELECTED	AE7	212
NEW ENGLANDS	PK	9
NEWER	M9	2
	FL	546
NEWEST	J6	535
NEW-FALLEN	AE5	1010
NEW-FASHIONED	J1	47
NEW-FOUND	PSF	46
	AE1	427
NEW-INVENTED	AE6	900
NEW-LAID	AM	1168
	BP	97
NEWLY	PDG	16
	TA	38
	J3	407
	AE2	501
	AE5	429
	AE12	1080
	KT1	186
	KT3	975
	BP	88
	FL	68
NEW-MADE	HAP	1371
	L3	24
	HAP	274
NEW-MADE	M11	474
	M12	290
NEWMARKET	PMK	17
NEW-RAISED	AE10	430
NEW-RISING	J10	451
NEWS	AM	286
	ETL	3
	PCB	20
	PCB	24
	HP	259
	MD	158
	SAA	1077
	RL	366
	TA	19
	TA	49
	TA	119
	HAP	1233
	HAP	1879
	BR	222
	EL	4
	EL	11
	ODA	30
	J6	525
	J6	535
	P1	105
	P6	96
	VP9	14
	AE2	95
	AE3	239
	AE4	269
	AE4	284
	AE4	420
	AE4	428
	AE4	561
	AE4	609
	AE5	866
	AE8	188
	AE8	727
	AE8	768
	AE9	939
	AE10	711
	AE11	209
	AE11	280
	AE11	349
	AE11	686
	AE11	779
	AE12	119
	AE12	883
	M8	242
	CAM	258
	HIF	467
	M12	68
	M12	79
	WB	266
	CI	451
NEWS-BOOK	PKA	30
NEW-STRUNG	TA	473
NEW-YEAR	LC	152
NEXT	SMA	45
	AM	901
	EEL	8
	EEL	22
	PC2	28
	PAL	32
	PKK	10
	PKK	23
	ETC	15
	AA	401
	AA	441
	AA	501
	AA	511
	AA	721
	AA	876
	PLB	18
	PLB	40
	PPC	29
	MD	30
	MD	122
	SAA	192
	SAA	259
	SAA	261
	SAA	298
	SAA	309
	SAA	310
	SAA	614
	SAA	867
	SAA	985
	SAA	1013
	SAA	1136
	EK	29
	RL	339
	OE	11
	T23	102
	TA	28
	TA	261
	AK	92

Word	Ref	Num		Word	Ref	Num		Word	Ref	Num
NEXT	AK	146		NEXT	AE7	955		NICE	G3	450
	GE	70			AE7	990			AE10	550
	HAP	39			AE7	1026			HIF	296
	HAP	327			AE8	69			FL	69
	HAP	791			AE8	351		NICELY	ESF	7
	HAP	934			AE8	724			RL	245
	HAP	1741			AE8	774			HAP	1246
	HAP	1749			AE9	442			J6	125
	HAP	1764			AE9	539			P5	153
	EMI	4			AE9	950		NICENE	HAP	728
	BR	18			AE9	1042		NICENESS	HP	16
	ETS	26			AE10	249			J6	8
	ETS	29			AE10	285			G4	67
	EL	90			AE10	437			PUO4	17
	EL	200			AE10	447		NICER	M1	961
	EL	308			AE10	490		NICEST	G2	358
	MS	31			AE10	725			KT3	570
	PSH	22			AE10	783			PMQ	57
	ESH	11			AE11	129		NICK	L4	175
	ESH	22			AE11	997		NIGGARD	AA	369
	J1	56			AE12	1222			B	49
	J1	104			OAL	162		NIGH	AM	406
	J3	330			OAL	249			AM	1002
	J6	32			OAL	610			DA	1
	J6	525			OAL	860			AA	162
	J6	539			OAE2	17			T27	101
	J6	614			AF	94			H29	36
	J6	641			KT1	391			TA	10
	J10	88			KT2	22			HAP	532
	J10	388			KT2	29			HAP	2299
	P1	4			KT2	564			HAP	2410
	P1	38			KT2	625			VP7	19
	P2	60			KT3	27			G1	617
	P5	275			KT3	290			AE2	970
	P6	25			KT3	464			AE2	996
	P6	58			KT3	538			AE3	489
	M1	30			KT3	548			AE3	678
	M1	34			KT3	592			AE4	696
	M1	62			KT3	596			AE9	221
	M1	160			KT3	694			KT1	71
	M1	176			KT3	908			KT2	35
	M1	546			KT3	926			KT2	230
	M9	159			KT3	937			B	132
	VP5	78			M8	97			B	585
	VP8	116			M8	113			B	676
	G1	379			M8	128			B	745
	G1	583			B	13			CAM	73
	G2	213			B	77			C	725
	G2	219			B	411			C	764
	G2	309			BP	58			TH	95
	G2	313			BP	92			M11	278
	G2	368			BP	100			FL	103
	G2	400			M10	78			FL	387
	G2	435			CAM	158			AU	251
	G2	511			HIF	75		NIGHER	EMKG	7
	G2	688			HIF	404		NIGHT	AR	94
	G3	45			HIF	431			RH	85
	G3	469			HIF	631			PRL	32
	G3	670			C	487			AM	140
	G4	220			C	493			AM	269
	G4	374			TH	30			AM	389
	G4	577			TH	34			AM	405
	AE1	580			TH	246			AM	476
	AE1	657			TH	270			AM	479
	AE1	980			TH	304			AM	740
	AE1	984			TH	376			AM	900
	AE1	1033			M11	281			AM	955
	AE2	285			FL	240			AM	1010
	AE2	419			FL	250			AM	1013
	AE2	968			FL	602			AM	1043
	AE3	352			M12	410			AM	1086
	AE3	476			M12	440			PA	19
	AE3	914			M12	641			PEL	29
	AE4	164			AU	43			EEL	22
	AE4	696			WB	37			SEL2	2
	AE4	716			WB	94			EMQW	23
	AE4	741			WB	200			SLN	4
	AE4	750			WB	301			SLN	10
	AE5	389			M15	163			SLN	18
	AE5	407			M15	336			SCD1	8
	AE5	420			M15	345			SCD1	11
	AE5	442			GP	111			STC	4
	AE5	656			GP	120			PCB	25
	AE5	659			CI	212			PLG	3
	AE5	976			CI	522			CM	51
	AE6	29			CI	602			HP	198
	AE6	365		NIBBLE	HAP	1443			DA	109
	AE6	586		NICANDER'S	MF	179			PUO3	8
	AE6	1077		NICE	HAP	55			PLB	18
	AE6	1109			HAP	408			MF	23
	AE6	1117			HAP	1523			RL	182
	AE6	1131			HAP	2466			OE	11
	AE7	156			J6	639			OE	22
	AE7	197			J10	513			AT	115
	AE7	900			P6	54			DOD	5
	AE7	907			VP3	167			DOD	20

Ref	No.	Ref	No.	Ref	No.
NIGHT		NIGHT		NIGHT	
MO	25	AE1	129	AE9	514
L4	108	AE1	420	AE9	545
T18	25	AE1	486	AE10	360
T18	44	AE1	935	AE10	380
T27	47	AE1	1049	AE10	694
T27	89	AE2	11	AE10	909
H29	47	AE2	16	AE10	996
TA	157	AE2	185	AE10	1015
HAP	1231	AE2	329	AE10	1051
HAP	1243	AE2	334	AE11	281
HAP	1275	AE2	350	AE11	306
HAP	1311	AE2	382	AE11	320
HAP	1748	AE2	480	AE11	423
HAP	1900	AE2	487	AE11	1083
HAP	1901	AE2	488	AE11	1318
HAP	1954	AE2	496	AE12	1265
EDS	27	AE2	841	AE12	1225
EDS	30	AE2	912	AE12	1244
EKA	21	AE2	1001	AE12	1313
SKA2	3	AE2	1022	OAL	248
SKA2	8	AE2	1025	OAL	285
EL	16	AE2	1047	OAL	840
EL	78	AE2	1081	OAE2	75
EL	328	AE3	201	OAE2	87
J1	237	AE3	230	KT1	121
J3	11	AE3	257	KT1	177
J3	181	AE3	265	KT1	186
J3	319	AE3	663	KT1	375
J3	390	AE3	668	KT1	405
J3	429	AE3	761	KT1	505
J3	441	AE3	850	KT1	506
J6	72	AE4	12	KT2	13
J6	165	AE4	36	KT2	21
J6	189	AE4	107	KT2	27
J6	291	AE4	173	KT2	159
J6	402	AE4	504	KT2	277
J6	426	AE4	674	KT2	465
J6	545	AE4	739	KT2	493
J6	546	AE4	744	KT3	109
J6	686	AE4	757	KT3	119
J10	372	AE4	801	KT3	257
J10	524	AE4	816	KT3	346
P1	179	AE4	821	KT3	425
P2	34	AE4	992	KT3	431
P4	53	AE5	17	KT3	882
P4	122	AE5	28	KT3	998
M1	283	AE5	944	KT3	1143
M1	357	AE5	967	TJD	19
M1	816	AE5	1089	M8	14
M1	830	AE6	170	B	135
M1	866	AE6	192	B	174
M1	1001	AE6	199	B	213
M9	29	AE6	208	B	260
M9	48	AE6	356	B	288
SLT1	24	AE6	375	B	592
DHP	5	AE6	380	B	716
VP1	113	AE6	495	CAM	124
VP6	125	AE6	529	CAM	264
VP7	56	AE6	614	CAM	273
VP7	59	AE6	626	CAM	278
VP8	19	AE6	638	CAM	306
VP8	43	AE6	675	CAM	314
VP8	125	AE6	692	HIF	4
VP9	60	AE6	725	HIF	71
VP9	87	AE6	730	HIF	50
G1	343	AE6	750	HIF	647
G1	338	AE6	1136	HIF	807
G1	386	AE6	1199	C	48
G1	383	AE7	9	C	129
G1	390	AE7	16	C	229
G1	445	AE7	22	C	232
G1	503	AE7	30	C	262
G1	574	AE7	147	C	283
G1	616	AE7	188	C	338
G1	631	AE7	460	C	392
G1	642	AE7	478	C	421
G1	653	AE7	579	C	434
G2	287	AE7	685	TH	63
G2	603	AE7	771	M11	158
G2	664	AE8	34	M11	194
G2	761	AE8	40	M11	197
G3	248	AE8	117	M11	229
G3	318	AE8	127	M11	259
G3	405	AE8	309	M11	288
G3	492	AE8	327	FL	21
G3	528	AE8	337	FL	452
G3	612	AE8	484	FL	485
G3	788	AE8	539	FL	490
G3	793	AE8	546	FL	495
G4	264	AE8	559	FL	614
G4	275	AE8	646	M12	70
G4	675	AE8	874	M12	188
G4	681	AE9	188	M12	221
G4	718	AE9	196	M12	705
G4	746	AE9	210	AU	158
AE1	105	AE9	386	AU	159

Word	Ref	No.	Word	Ref	No.	Word	Ref	No.
NIGHT	AU	170	NIGHTS	AE8	953	NISUS	AE9	358
	AU	383		AE10	651		AE9	428
	AU	397		OAL	80		AE9	475
	AU	511		B	414		AE9	523
	AU	524		CAM	242		AE9	586
	AU	533		M11	233		AE9	619
	WB	9	NILE	AA	332		OAL	374
	WB	43		MD	168	NISUS'	AE6	1099
	WB	213		MD	171		AE9	222
	WB	361		ER	1	NITER	G1	281
	M15	37		HAP	2098		M15	96
	M15	279		J1	34	NOAH	BR	101
	M15	500		M1	565	NOAH'S	AA	302
	M15	625		M1	1010		HAP	191
	GP	65		M9	37	NOBILITY	VHH	46
	GP	72		M9	167		HAP	2514
	CI	118		G3	43		J1	153
	CI	173		G4	409		B	561
	CI	332		AE6	1091		WB	439
	CI	486		AE9	36		WB	445
	CI	546		OAL	732		WB	382
	CI	566		AS	92		WB	391
	SMP	81	NILUS	AM	183	NOBLE	UDH	1
	ESK	26		J10	238		UDH	13
	AS	6		AE8	945		SMA	75
NIGHTCAP	OAL	837	NIMBLE	DC	35		SMA	98
NIGHT-HAGS	AM	990		MD	45		LC	70
NIGHTINGAL	SEL3	4		AT	100		DC	27
NIGHTINGALE	VP6	114		G4	103		LCA	24
	G4	743		AE2	278		AM	348
	FL	115	NIMBLER	J6	802		PMQ	21
NIGHTINGALES	D	28		OAL	142		A	8
	VP9	53	NIMBLY	AM	229		SCD2	1
NIGHTLY	DA	28		AT	24		SCD2	23
	RL	8	NIMRODS	HAP	2568		EUO2	16
	J3	321	NINE	ECG1	32		AA	41
	J6	48		CM	52		AA	195
	J6	789		EUF	11		AA	616
	P5	83		L3	193		AA	867
	P5	238		AK	88		EPC	8
	M1	664		GE	30		RL	19
	VP3	124		EDS	30		AT	91
	VP5	93		J6	776		ER	3
	G1	535		PPS	6		MO	17
	G2	278		G4	689		T18	1
	G3	619		G4	786		T27	114
	G3	801		G4	797		TA	130
	G4	630		AE1	335		TA	161
	AE1	658		AE5	82		TA	444
	AE2	815		AE5	995		PAA	25
	AE4	437		AE6	595		AK	75
	AE6	177		AE6	807		HAP	250
	AE7	128		AE9	696		HAP	1153
	AE8	59		AE12	408		HAP	1324
	AE9	66		OAL	731		HAP	1762
	AE9	200		CAM	242		HAP	2044
	AE9	297		CAM	320		HAP	2219
	AE9	457		HIF	77		HAP	2415
	AE9	652		HIF	78		PTS	4
	AE10	217		FL	254		J1	79
	AE10	309		FL	300		J1	230
	AE12	524		FL	527		J3	39
	AE12	1249		FL	535		J3	336
	M11	277		M12	30		J6	238
	FL	319		M12	128		J6	784
	FL	477		M12	768		J6	861
	WB	18		AU	335		J16	92
NIGHT-MURTHERERS	PSF	44		M15	533		P1	53
NIGHT-PERFORMANCE	J1	55	NINTH	G1	382		P1	63
NIGHT-ROBBERS	AM	910		AU	431		P1	116
NIGHT'S	AM	863	NIOBE	TA	7		P5	121
	SAA	1081		J6	254		P5	212
	AE1	959	NIOBE'S	KT3	221		P6	4
NIGHTS	AM	1110	NIPHAEUS	AE10	803		P6	74
	SMM2	7	NIPHATES	G3	45		M1	599
	ETL	12	NISA	VP8	46		HI	26
	ENH	28		VP8	51		HI	101
	CM	30	NISAEA	G4	484		PLT	35
	HP	177	NISA'S	VP8	26		GK	24
	SAA	1106		VP8	37		GK	166
	H2	64	NISUS	MO	9		AE1	141
	PTS	39		G1	549		AE1	864
	SKA6	15		G1	552		AE1	886
	J6	595		G1	553		AE3	365
	J6	691		AE5	385		AE3	624
	J10	457		AE5	388		AE4	523
	P5	56		AE5	418		AE5	658
	G1	299		AE5	427		AE5	722
	G1	420		AE5	461		AE7	976
	G1	581		AE5	464		AE7	1079
	G2	684		AE5	474		AE9	223
	G3	582		AE9	235		AE9	254
	AE1	1046		AE9	257		AE9	414
	AE3	266		AE9	266		AE10	1125
	AE4	279		AE9	304		AE11	515
	AE6	484		AE9	309		AE12	39

Word	Ref	No.
NOBLE	AE12	593
	OAL	524
	OAL	769
	DO	35
	KT1	289
	KT1	588
	KT2	511
	KT3	13
	KT3	711
	KT3	746
	KT3	824
	TJD	185
	B	54
	B	322
	B	513
	B	520
	CAM	103
	C	40
	C	104
	C	643
	C	785
	TH	9
	TH	125
	TH	217
	M12	778
	AU	285
	WB	384
	WB	404
	WB	451
	WB	456
	CI	185
	CI	497
	PTP	39
NOBLEMAN	WB	384
NOBLER	UDH	103
	HS	115
	AR	232
	LCA	27
	AM	223
	AM	702
	AM	848
	AM	937
	AM	1150
	PFD	10
	AA	299
	AA	900
	MD	176
	SAA	1007
	RL	67
	RL	232
	ER	40
	ER	51
	HAP	1375
	HAP	1669
	J10	327
	PPS	8
	P1	187
	M1	224
	M1	248
	GK	63
	GK	109
	G2	91
	G3	80
	G4	142
	AE1	768
	AE4	228
	AE5	325
	AE5	643
	AE7	1097
	OAL	782
	KT2	450
	FL	185
	M12	453
	M15	117
NOBLES	AR	29
	AA	572
	MD	299
	SAA	342
	SAA	608
	SAA	1013
	J1	51
	J3	347
	J10	70
	J10	174
	P1	42
	P1	95
	OAL	303
NOBLEST	VHH	8
	AM	256
	POE	10
	AA	827
	SAA	633
	SAA	642
	SAA	961
	SAA	977
	T18	70

Word	Ref	No.
NOBLEST	TA	338
	HAP	327
	J6	218
	VP8	136
	DO	18
	KT3	937
NOBLY	PA	11
	SAA	803
	ER	55
	P4	40
	AE5	954
	CI	418
NOBODY	SEL3	19
	T27	101
NOCTURNAL	HAP	301
	HAP	1227
	HAP	1259
	G3	234
	G4	756
	AE1	1016
	AE3	672
	AE6	364
	AE6	695
	AE7	564
	AE9	478
	AU	395
	AA	801
NOD	H9	17
	HAP	1665
	J3	305
	J3	410
	J10	149
	P1	72
	P2	56
	M1	232
	VP5	99
	G1	449
	G4	245
	AE9	124
	AE9	927
	AE10	154
	AE10	175
	AE12	297
	AF	40
	AF	45
	KT2	352
	M11	259
NODDED	HAP	1349
	M9	183
	HI	149
	AE8	312
	M8	284
NODDING	AA	1026
	MF	127
	T23	106
	M1	514
	VP4	61
	VP6	45
	VP10	38
	G4	691
	AE2	850
	AE9	291
	AE9	358
	AE10	1245
	KT3	370
	HIF	706
	M11	286
	M12	775
NODDLE	PDS	25
NODS	AM	888
	L3	265
	L4	85
	AE2	384
	AE11	1207
	OAL	161
	CAM	137
	M12	688
	AU	403
NOEMON	OAL	746
NOINT	HS	44
NOISE	LC	107
	AM	227
	AM	364
	AM	436
	AM	897
	PCG2	19
	ENH	17
	EAZ	4
	PLG	14
	CM	89
	EPC	4
	EK	14
	PDG	34
	L3	200
	H29	18
	H2	65

Word	Ref	No.
NOISE	EL	317
	J1	18
	J3	379
	J6	547
	P1	33
	P5	29
	M1	877
	PLT	44
	G2	636
	G2	659
	G4	381
	G4	801
	AE1	218
	AE1	585
	AE2	51
	AE2	399
	AE2	994
	AE3	74
	AE3	884
	AE6	743
	AE9	533
	AE9	670
	AE12	599
	AE12	605
	KT3	554
	B	293
	B	685
	TH	105
	TH	277
	TH	359
	M11	277
	M11	478
	M12	72
	M12	435
	WB	147
	EMKG	41
NOISED	J6	79
NOISEFUL	AM	159
	AM	861
	EUO2	5
NOISELESS	H29	56
NOISES	AM	906
	G3	125
NOISOME	G3	841
	AE3	191
	AE10	263
	AE12	455
NOISY	EK	7
	PDG	30
	EDGA	2
	L2	17
	J3	4
	J6	101
	J10	109
	GK	83
	VP2	35
	G4	816
	AE7	814
	AE10	447
	AE11	600
	OAL	89
	FL	358
	AU	13
	AU	520
	ESK	12
NOKES	PCG1	7
	MS	18
NOM	EH	6
NOMAEA	T27	76
NOMENTUM	AE6	1051
NONACRINE	M8	213
NONAGE	G2	497
NON-POPERY	HAP	1034
NON-PLUSED	J6	567
NONPLUSED	OAL	92
NONRESISTANCE	HAP	1957
NONSENSE	PCG1	26
	PLN	18
	PUO1	37
	PLG	21
	ELB	18
	MF	6
	SAA	415
	SAA	499
	SAA	529
	HAP	429
	P5	18
	VP3	21
	MG	25
	PW	7
NOOK	UDH	44
NOON	PCB	25
	AT	115
	T27	86
	G4	615
	AE3	669

Word	Ref	No.
NOON	AE4	744
	KT3	119
	TH	86
	M11	271
	FL	372
	WB	213
	M15	468
NOONTIDE	E	30
	P3	3
	G3	233
NOOSE	SAA	496
	L4	204
	T23	93
	J6	44
	J6	59
	AE12	881
	CAM	149
NORMAN	PNH	41
	B	1
.ORTH	VHH	45
	AM	636
	AM	1112
	CM	13
	HAP	207
	J6	606
	M1	80
	G1	509
	G1	623
	G2	364
	G3	310
	G3	436
	GE3	902
	KT2	463
	KT3	297
NORTHERN	SMA	89
	AM	845
	AM	1199
	PAZ	33
	DA	185
	MF	170
	BR	6
	M1	355
	M1	442
	GK	47
	G1	210
	G1	308
	G1	340
	G1	618
	G2	158
	G2	454
	AE12	133
	DO	102
	KT2	552
	KT2	624
	CAM	265
	AS	1
NORTH'S	AM	99
NORTHWARD	D	10
NORWAY	AM	571
NORWAY'S	AM	98
NORWICH	MF	33
NOSE	PUO5	6
	EK	20
	EC	28
	J1	90
	J6	140
	J6	555
	J10	341
	P1	71
	G4	67
	AE6	669
	KT3	74
	M12	353
	M12	434
	M12	587
	CI	150
NOSEGAYS	VP2	76
NOSES	SAA	457
	J6	420
NOSTRADAME	PP	1
NOSTRADAMUS	PKK	23
	HAP	1814
NOSTRILS	J10	321
	M1	1031
	G2	193
	G3	139
	G3	431
	G3	759
	G4	423
	AE5	574
	AE5	625
	AE7	387
	AE7	668
	AE8	335
	AE12	16
	AE12	157

Word	Ref	No.
NOSTRILS	AE12	176
	OAL	585
	HIF	131
	M8	121
NOTARIES	J10	517
NOTCHED	PSF	21
NOTE	AT	88
	MO	5
	PAA	42
	HAP	1525
	HAP	1854
	HAP	1986
	J1	9
	P1	70
	P3	14
	P5	16
	P5	279
	G3	162
	G3	252
	G3	443
	GE4	671
	OAE2	24
	B	80
	C	90
	C	271
	C	630
	C	669
	M11	481
	FL	111
	FL	118
	FL	137
	FL	199
	WB	315
	M9	176
NOTED	FL	207
NOTES	HS	5
	RH	2
	RH	83
	SMA	4
	SMA	54
	SIE	7
	AM	592
	AM	892
	PAL	4
	PAA	5
	HAP	369
	SSC	14
	SSC	27
	SSC	34
	SSC	45
	SSC	46
	J1	98
	J6	95
	J6	664
	J10	190
	PPS	12
	M1	698
	DHP	2
	DHP	23
	VP9	73
	G1	558
	G4	733
	AE3	464
	AE3	674
	AE3	566
	AE6	664
	AE6	880
	AE7	968
	AE8	407
	AF	23
	KT3	1118
	C	42
	TH	106
	FL	450
NOTHING	RH	52
	LC	31
	SIE	8
	EWGR	14
	SMM2	5
	EEL	19
	PAR	19
	EM	12
	PCD	24
	EMK	19
	HP	24
	ETG	15
	PUO5	29
	AA	33
	AA	117
	AA	343
	AA	532
	AA	548
	AA	560
	SAA	432
	SAA	462
	SAA	655

Word	Ref	No.
NOTHING	L1	29
	L1	55
	L3	110
	L3	116
	L3	144
	L3	216
	L4	61
	L4	69
	L4	152
	AK	142
	HAP	641
	HAP	1208
	HAP	1322
	HAP	1407
	HAP	1585
	HAP	1587
	HAP	1589
	HAP	1797
	EL	131
	OD	18
	OD	33
	J3	187
	J3	342
	J3	343
	J6	141
	J6	300
	J6	395
	J6	440
	J10	108
	J10	184
	J10	249
	J10	555
	P1	5
	P1	58
	P1	94
	P1	105
	P1	242
	P3	159
	P3	160
	P3	188
	P3	189
	P5	94
	P5	208
	P5	225
	M1	1034
	M9	106
	PLT	21
	PLT	22
	PLT	38
	ELT	1
	GK	17
	EHC	25
	VP10	17
	G1	242
	G3	70
	G4	572
	AE2	51
	AE2	894
	AE3	796
	AE4	455
	AE12	1276
	OAL	177
	OAE2	16
	DO	166
	KT1	296
	KT1	417
	B	154
	TH	15
	FL	26
	M12	599
	AU	362
	AU	520
	WB	320
	M15	239
	M15	388
	M15	398
	GP	12
	GP	14
	GP	56
	ETP	28
	SMP	88
	SMP	94
	EMKG	4
	EMKG	8
	EMKG	16
	EMKG	17
NOTICE	EL	324
	AE8	277
NOTIONS	AA	171
	SAA	419
	RL	65
	P5	131
NOTORIOUS	ESH	33
	J6	58
NOTWITHSTANDING	POE	32
NOUN	J6	584

Word	Ref	No.
NOUN	J 10	181
NOURISH	M 15	709
	AS	82
NOURISHED	SMA	78
	PAA	12
	OAL	332
NOURISHES	G 2	208
NOURISHMENT	PLG	24
	PR	28
	HAP	137
	J 6	753
	M 15	306
	M 1	548
	G 1	131
	G 2	590
	KT 1	525
NOVELTY	EUO	10
	M 12	242
NOVICE	OAL	56
	KT 3	325
	C I	110
NOVICES	HAP	417
NOWADAYS	PD	1
NOXIOUS	G 3	445
	C	143
	M 15	707
NUISANCE	EK	25
NULL	J 1	87
NUMA	UDH	70
	J 3	20
	J 3	232
	AE 10	786
	M 15	5
	M 15	712
NUMANUS	AE 9	806
	AE 9	868
NUMA'S	TA	465
	P 2	107
	J 3	232
NUMBER	AM	214
	AM	301
	CM	18
	AA	350
	MF	55
	SAA	513
	HAP	308
	J 16	89
	VP 3	50
	G 1	355
	G 2	152
	AE 2	1083
	AE 11	309
	AE 11	501
	AE 11	664
	KT 3	4
	KT 3	597
	C	44
	FL	250
	FL	547
NUMBERED	TA	211
	TA	422
	J 10	391
	AE 9	125
	M 12	613
	AS	43
NUMBERING	EL	198
	C	453
NUMBERLESS	TA	315
	EL	294
NUMBERS	RH	7
	RH	72
	SMA	105
	AM	304
	AM	339
	AM	348
	AM	688
	MF	197
	ER	8
	MO	14
	L 4	246
	FS 2	3
	HAP	1266
	HAP	1882
	J 10	382
	PPS	11
	P 1	32
	P 1	120
	P 1	180
	P 1	228
	P 1	269
	M 1	3
	M 1	698
	M 13	123
	VP 3	87
	VP 6	45
	VP 6	104
NUMBERS	VP 7	28
	VP 7	33
	VP 8	12
	VP 8	13
	VP 8	105
	VP 10	4
	G 1	13
	AE 2	24
	AE 4	882
	AE 8	404
	AE 9	604
	AE 10	244
	AE 11	482
	AE 12	349
	AE 12	725
	AE 12	963
	OAL	237
	KT 3	474
	C	188
	M 11	235
	G 1	402
NUMBS	VHH	55
NUMEROUS	AM	217
	AM	303
	AM	678
	AM	728
	EAL	29
	AA	17
	AA	529
	AA	533
	AA	730
	AA	919
	MD	177
	SAA	193
	TA	297
	TA	366
	HAP	20
	HAP	655
	OD	52
	J 6	255
	M 1	36
	M 1	789
	VP 6	42
	AE 1	697
	AE 2	52
	AE 2	509
	AE 3	445
	AE 5	380
	AE 5	842
	AE 5	935
	AE 6	649
	AE 7	948
	AE 7	973
	AE 8	21
	AE 8	650
	AE 9	1059
	AE 12	200
	AE 12	654
	M 11	327
	FL	229
	C I	47
NUMEROUSLY	SAA	689
	OAL	105
NUMICIAN	AE 7	1089
NUMICUS	AE 7	201
	AE 7	332
NUMIDIAN	AE 8	965
NUMIDIANS	AE 4	57
NUMITOR	AE 6	1042
	AE 10	475
NUN	ELN	4
	EDS	4
	ELN	7
NUNS	ELN	20
	HAP	1234
NUNTIUS	CM	117
NUPTIAL	EPC	28
	T 18	6
	T 27	125
	HAP	181
	HAP	1869
	EL	327
	J 6	32
	J 6	288
	M 1	648
	M 1	1023
	M 9	208
	VP 8	43
	G 3	100
	G 3	194
	G 4	289
	G 4	749
	AE 2	685
	AE 4	80
	AE 4	276
	AE 4	458
NUPTIAL	AE 4	735
	AE 4	873
	AE 7	81
	AE 7	436
	AE 7	558
	AE 8	548
	AE 12	1193
	OAL	633
	KT 2	477
	KT 3	227
	KT 3	862
	KT 3	1143
	M 8	355
	B	16
	CAM	242
	HIF	172
	M 11	252
	M 12	295
	WB	65
	WB	339
	WB	527
	C I	421
	C I	446
	C I	541
NUPTIALS	DA	98
	L 4	255
	AE 4	177
	AE 4	490
	AE 4	624
	AE 7	484
	B	35
	B	45
	M 12	558
	AS	28
NURSE	AS	55
	CM	33
	CM	45
	CM	56
	CM	79
	CM	85
	PD	24
	PD	30
	L 5	12
	HAP	1685
	P 2	71
	M 9	58
	H I	25
	H I	37
	G 4	238
	AE 4	907
	AE 4	919
	AE 5	842
	AE 7	4
	M 10	5
	CAM	150
	CAM	169
	CAM	186
	CAM	232
	CAM	289
	C	364
	M 11	395
NURSED	ER	4
	ER	47
	HAP	55
	HAP	597
	HAP	882
	EL	22
	EL	81
	J 6	465
	M 1	205
	G 3	290
	G 3	469
	AE 7	1046
	KT 1	315
	B	67
	FL	565
NURSERIES	HAP	2292
NURSERY	MF	74
	SAA	325
	G 2	359
NURSE'S	H I	145
	CAM	215
	C	335
NURSES	PD	21
	J 6	767
	KT 2	590
NURSIA	AE 7	1027
NURSIANS	AE 7	991
NURSING	AE 6	805
	EWR	30
NURSLING	P 2	75
	G 2	500
NUT	PAA	8
NUT-BROWN	PCG 2	16
	AT	82
	M 13	131

Word	Code	No.
NUTMEGS	GE	21
NUTRIMENT	AA	1014
NUTS	VP8	42
	BP	113
NYMPH	MHD	5
	SCG1	33
	SCG3	18
	SM2	20
	E	7
	SKK	9
	PUO3	10
	D	12
	SDG	3
	AT	6
	AT	37
	AT	89
	PD	12
	T18	54
	T23	2
	T23	35
	T23	107
	T27	24
	H9	36
	ETS	7
	SKA2	22
	SKA5	14
	MS	9
	J3	21
	J6	85
	J6	131
	M1	632
	M1	680
	M1	733
	M1	745
	M1	945
	M1	951
	M1	965
	M1	1024
	M13	2
	M13	144
	M13	173
	M13	183
	VP6	41
	VP10	56
	G4	768
	AE1	514
	AE7	117
	AE7	1015
	AE8	444
	AE9	141
	AE10	768
	AE11	811
	AE11	847
	AE11	893
	AE12	216
	AE12	235
	AE12	244
	AE12	1139
	OAL	575
	OAL	629
	OAL	637
	DO	13
	M8	74
	M8	212
	B	217
	CAM	257
	FL	462
	M12	276
	M15	487
	EMKG	22
NYMPHS	E	29
	HP	120
	HP	141
	DA	98
	AK	116
	LS	3
	J6	9
	M1	250
	M1	434
	M1	973
	HI	70
	VP2	60
	VP3	14
	VP5	27
	VP5	92
	VP5	117
	VP6	81
	VP9	24
	VP10	13
	VP10	81
	VP10	91
	G1	12
	G3	68
	G4	539
	G4	551
	G4	772

Word	Code	No.
NYMPHS	AE1	206
	AE1	702
	AE4	244
	AE5	312
	AE5	1081
	AE7	187
	AE8	97
	AE8	418
	AE9	118
	AE10	314
	OAL	729
	OAL	815
	OAL	835
	KT2	621
	KT3	966
	CAM	370
	FL	478
	FL	561
	M12	304
	M12	541
	CI	93
OAF	EWGR	24
	PTW	17
OAFS	ETC	21
OAK	UDH	79
	SMA	129
	AM	243
	AM	572
	DA	37
	H3	14
	H2	36
	HAP	1769
	HAP	1929
	P5	80
	M1	143
	M13	82
	VP1	24
	VP3	17
	VP7	17
	VP9	12
	VP9	19
	G1	238
	G1	410
	G2	21
	G2	93
	G3	514
	G3	638
	AE4	640
	AE5	170
	AE6	266
	AE6	298
	AE7	711
	AE8	61
	AE8	286
	AE8	419
	AE8	818
	AE10	597
	AE10	1188
	AE11	6
	AE11	206
	AE11	832
	KT2	246
	KT3	208
	KT3	961
	KT3	1058
	M8	187
	BP	18
	BP	192
	FL	230
	FL	279
	FL	284
	FL	503
	M12	462
	M12	446
	WB	226
	M15	28
OAKEN	M1	602
	G1	200
	G1	480
	AE6	1049
	AE11	95
	FL	253
	M15	587
	MF	27
	J6	19
OAKS	M1	412
	VP3	139
	VP4	35
	VP8	72
	G1	221

Word	Code	No.
OAKS	G2	101
	G2	634
	G3	580
	G4	119
	AE2	411
	AE4	576
	AE6	309
	AE9	924
	AE11	1233
	KT3	905
	FL	39
OAKUM	AM	582
OAR	AE3	896
	AE5	157
	AE5	246
	AE5	357
	AE6	333
	AE8	122
	AE10	417
	C	533
	CI	387
OARS	AM	628
	MF	39
	AE1	50
	AE1	150
	AE1	226
	AE1	777
	AE3	177
	AE3	272
	AE3	375
	AE3	493
	AE3	605
	AE3	841
	AE3	877
	AE4	71
	AE4	576
	AE4	838
	AE5	21
	AE5	35
	AE5	204
	AE5	172
	AE5	180
	AE5	185
	AE5	188
	AE5	267
	AE5	271
	AE5	274
	AE5	287
	AE5	301
	AE5	368
	AE5	865
	AE5	983
	AE7	39
	AE8	110
	AE8	913
	AE10	297
	AE10	404
	AE10	411
	AE10	424
	HIF	430
	HIF	597
	HIF	652
	M11	73
	M11	92
	M11	107
	CI	613
	CI	626
OATES	PAA	6
	HAP	2013
	ETP	47
OATH	SM1	8
	AA	589
	AA	643
	EKA	12
	J3	200
	M1	1025
	AE9	402
	AE12	1186
	KT1	291
	KT2	128
	KT2	279
	CAM	237
	C	481
	C	796
	WB	174
	WB	180
	WB	250
	WB	300
	WB	305
OATHS	EMQW	12
	AA	111
	PPC	14
	MD	85
	MD	153
	TA	489
	ELT	30

OBSCURED	M11	229	OBTAIN	G1	51	OCEAN	M13	204
OBSCURELY	AM	858		AE3	794		VP6	55
	AE10	80		AE6	986		G3	553
OBSCURES	MC	2		AE9	356		G3	834
	AE4	504		AE12	1207		G4	550
	AE4	816		KT1	305		AE1	161
	AE11	908		KT1	424		AE1	196
OBSCUREST	RL	411		KT3	1142		AE1	325
OBSCURITY	HAP	918		CAM	337		AE1	391
OBSEQUIES	HS	140		HIF	589		AE2	329
	AE6	307		C	81		AE3	143
	AE9	648	OBTAINED	HP	118		AE3	531
	KT1	132		SAA	126		AE5	186
	KT3	928		SAA	723		AE5	208
OBSEQUIOUS	KT3	486		AE11	382		AE5	1074
	HIF	771		OAL	366		AE5	1127
OBSERVANCE	KT1	175		OAL	773		AE6	167
	KT2	44		KT2	391		AE6	1066
	KT3	179		HIF	179		AE7	737
OBSERVANT	AA	319		TH	18		AE9	965
	SAA	953		TH	48		AE10	321
	AE1	769		FL	553		AE12	273
	AE2	578		M12	605		AE12	668
	AE6	751	OBTAINS	TA	431		DO	84
	CAM	100		AE5	317		KT2	513
OBSERVATION	HAP	1237		AE5	406		M11	37
OBSERVATOR	J10	502	OBTEND	AE10	126		M11	152
OBSERVE	PIE	8	OBTENDING	HIF	161		M12	53
	HAP	1517	OBTEST	AE11	151		M12	272
	G1	294	OBTRUDE	AR	175		AU	589
	G1	348	OBVIATE	HAP	1054		M15	405
	G1	459		AE9	709	OCEAN'S	SAA	687
	G1	571		AE12	422		G4	325
	G3	163	OBVIOUS	MD	88		AE5	17
	G4	368		T23	21		HIF	497
	AE2	573		HAP	669		AU	455
	AE6	1029	OCCASION	EWG	11		M15	622
	AE6	1196		HP	82	OCEANS	PP	12
	OAL	184		HP	172		M1	49
	TJD	150		AA	78		M1	125
OBSERVED	PLN	20		AA	208		AE5	799
	EAL	11		AA	461		AE6	938
	AK	137		OE	16		AE10	285
	HAP	1770		HAP	566	OCNUS	BR	21
	J1	150		HAP	1413	OCTAVE	M12	578
	P4	82		EL	165	ODD	AA	123
	VP3	13		J1	38	ODDS	SAA	540
	AE5	32		J1	50		AE2	575
	AE6	523		M1	781		AE5	1058
	AE6	925		VP1	36		AE9	542
	AE7	158		G4	631		KT3	641
	AE7	833		AE3	801		HIF	282
	AE9	475		AE9	82		M12	703
	OAE2	13		AE9	430	ODES	RH	41
	KT3	211		AE11	697		P6	12
	BP	123		AE12	819		C	660
	HIF	768		OAL	166	ODIOUS	AA	288
	FL	209		OAL	402		HAP	766
	M15	85		OAL	811		HAP	1545
OBSERVES	PIE	16		KT2	377		G4	463
	SAA	1032		B	695		AE3	305
	AE3	674		B	720		AE4	906
	AE4	748		CAM	248		AE7	465
	AE10	406		HIF	101		KT1	313
	M11	234		TH	414		B	169
OBSERVING	PMM	9		HAP	911		B	235
	J10	154	OCCASIONAL	RL	416		HIF	757
	AE5	589	OCCASIONED	EH	2		M15	315
	AE6	289	OCCASIONS	PWG	10		GP	115
	AE9	428		SAA	424	ODOR	EL	304
	AE9	465		OE	56		G3	628
	OAL	182		J3	185		M12	212
OBSOLETE	P1	157		AE4	69	ODOROUS	P4	89
OBSTINATE	HAP	1699	OCCUPATION	SAA	282		G1	86
	AE4	812	OCCUPATIONS	SAA	78		G1	273
	AE5	298	OCEAN	HS	137		G2	164
	OAL	7		AR	303		AE8	884
	MG	11		DC	26		AE12	617
	B	584		AM	61		OAL	323
	M11	48		AM	88		KT3	194
	CI	280		AM	124		KT3	368
OBSTINATELY	L4	136		AM	129		M10	43
	TA	498		AM	335		CAM	20
	HAP	2381		AM	402		M11	241
	G4	127		AM	603	ODORS	AR	271
	AE2	79		AM	647		AM	114
OBTAIN	UDH	26		AM	654		P6	82
	EWG	23		AM	710		G4	383
	LCA	4		AM	1206		G4	601
	STC	12		SAA	1019		AE11	72
	HP	28		L1	10		KT3	976
	SSF	18		TA	514		FL	97
	SAA	247		HAP	207		FL	326
	L2	22		HAP	1121		M15	599
	J10	218		HAP	2125	OEBALUS	AE7	1014
	VP3	5		J6	131			

OECHALIAN	AE8	386	OFFENSE	HAP	1316	OFFERED	M8	8
OEDIPUS	POE	7		HAP	2274		B	391
OENEUS	M8	5		P6	117		B	696
	M8	303		G4	771		CAM	171
OENIDES'	KT2	635		AE1	13		HIF	94
OENONE	HP	193		AE1	318		HIF	439
OENONE'S	VP2	88		AE2	998		C	702
OENOTRIANS	AE1	750		AE3	44		TH	22
	AE3	223		AE7	425		M11	255
OESTROS	G3	238		AE7	817		M12	135
OFFAL	UDH	83		AE10	943		M12	351
OFFALS	L3	54		OAE2	48		M12	651
OFFEND	PC2	26		KT1	241		AU	49
	CM	126		KT1	376		M15	714
	HP	67		KT2	303	OFFERING	AR	120
	PR	20		KT2	335		AM	83
	PRH	31		KT2	336		AM	790
	RL	93		B	278		RL	92
	T27	24		B	314		TA	102
	HAP	331		B	353		EL	7
	PTS	6		B	387		P2	55
	J6	141		B	480		AE3	343
	P1	103		B	484		AE3	689
	G1	257		B	573		AE4	1007
	G4	67		B	752		AE5	134
	AE6	99		CAM	351		AE6	181
	AE9	177		HIF	94		AE6	406
	AE9	575		HIF	118		AE6	552
	OAL	675		HIF	266		AE7	134
	OAE2	27		HIF	462		AE7	240
	KT3	784		C	275		AE9	858
	HIF	770		C	294		AE10	754
	C	591		C	792		AE12	1372
	C	778		TH	131		M8	308
	FL	475		AU	289		BP	197
	WB	358		WB	362		M10	61
OFFENDED	AM	161		M15	45		CAM	241
	PUO2	27		M15	167		GP	44
	RL	108		CI	9	OFFERINGS	HS	77
	J6	636		CI	114		RL	128
	J10	136		CI	367		T27	100
	J10	484	OFFENSES	BR	189		J3	311
	G4	788	OFFENSIVE	PR	37		P2	134
	AE2	245		J6	213		VP4	24
	AE2	305		J10	323		AE1	75
	AE3	280		AE11	797		AE4	301
	AE3	340	OFFER	HS	7		AE4	897
	AE4	410		AM	998		AE4	911
	AE6	516		SCG2	16		AE6	26
	CAM	178		CM	135		AE7	127
	CAM	179		SAA	293		AE8	139
	M12	48		ELW	6		AE8	402
	WB	89		P2	126		AE9	548
OFFENDER	HAP	479		P5	241		AE11	117
	SKA6	20		GK	103		AE11	1085
	WB	75		VP2	79		AE12	256
	WB	276		VP2	80		AE12	1219
	M15	161		AE5	642		KT3	349
	GP	76		AE8	228		GP	48
	CI	367		AE8	376	OFFERS	PDS	37
OFFENDER'S	RL	108		OAL	413		P2	124
OFFENDERS	AA	944		KT1	190		M1	890
	HIF	609		M8	380		VP3	101
	C	295		BP	170		VP7	43
OFFENDERS'	KT2	327		WB	254		G4	631
OFFENDING	AR	128	OFFERED	EM	12		AE6	358
	AA	359		HP	117		AE8	722
	AA	941		DA	12		AE9	430
	SAA	1050		DA	113		AE10	877
	H3	44		AT	83		AE12	819
	HAP	323		HAP	1654		OAE2	40
	P4	27		HAP	2091	OFFICE	EEL	32
	AE1	62		HAP	2476		AA	148
	KT2	386		J6	514		AA	597
	TH	303		J16	62		MF	119
OFFENDS	AM	485		M9	205		SAA	236
	AM	520		VP5	104		H29	75
	HAP	1404		G2	546		HH	5
	HAP	1953		AE1	460		HAP	1021
	AE10	129		AE1	577		HAP	2040
	KT3	1110		AE1	893		AE7	761
	HIF	123		AE1	1033		AE7	852
OFFENSE	PKK	22		AE2	305		AE9	291
	PLN	6		AE3	763		AE11	322
	PTW	16		AE4	660		AE12	911
	HP	95		AE5	103		OAL	398
	AA	184		AE5	137		DO	28
	ELB	16		AE5	309		KT3	981
	SAA	450		AE5	964		B	214
	RL	52		AE6	1026		B	694
	RL	87		AE8	197		CAM	218
	RL	111		AE9	28		M12	5
	AK	97		AE10	257		AU	310
	GE	55		AE11	302		AU	600
	HAP	241		DO	130		CI	455
	HAP	539		KT3	491	OFFICERS	AA	766

OFFICERS	J16	23	OIL	P6	164	OLD	PK	41		
	AE4	188		VP5	106		RL	221		
OFFICES	L4	97		G1	23		RL	237		
	HAP	1352		G1	281		RL	256		
	EL	130		G1	368		RL	335		
	J3	216		G1	412		AT	57		
	J6	301		G2	530		L3	151		
	J10	126		G2	654		L3	166		
	P3	132		G2	775		T27	68		
	P6	60		G3	453		H29	63		
	AE1	772		G3	683		GE	9		
	AE1	840		AE3	364		HAP	351		
	M8	376		AE4	317		HAP	459		
	FL	497		AE5	178		HAP	546		
OFFICIOUS	HS	1		AE6	321		HAP	736		
	SMA	42		AE6	362		HAP	752		
	AM	735		AE12	156		HAP	786		
	SAA	145		OAL	867		HAP	809		
	SAA	827		KT3	1000		HAP	1071		
	TA	370		M15	537		HAP	1157		
	J3	351	OILED	PLN	29		HAP	1160		
	G4	539	OILS	J6	600		HAP	1166		
	AE4	919		AE6	315		HAP	1175		
	AE10	1241	OILY	G1	538		HAP	1177		
	AE11	73	OINT	G3	683		HAP	1503		
	AE12	134	OINTED	AE6	363		HAP	1949		
	AE12	260		AE10	208		HAP	2374		
	OAL	176	OINTMENT	L4	99		HAP	2429		
	OAE2	34		P2	115		EDS	5		
	KT3	785		FL	419		EDS	7		
	B	194	OLD	UDH	81		ETS	23		
	BP	46		UDH	67		PMS	32		
	CAM	247		HS	117		SKA4	25		
	FL	439		AR	302		SKA4	26		
OFFICIOUSLY	LC	1		SMA	23		SKA4	27		
	G3	469		SMA	129		SKA4	28		
	M11	106		LCA	44		SKA4	29		
OFFSPRING	AR	302		PWG	46		EL	319		
	CM	131		PIE	5		ESH	14		
	DA	35		AM	243		ESH	16		
	PRH	9		AM	245		J1	58		
	HAP	22		AM	582		J1	80		
	HAP	1386		AM	602		J1	101		
	HAP	1651		AM	685		J1	117		
	HAP	1862		AM	691		J1	123		
	J6	255		AM	876		J1	146		
	J10	544		AM	925		J1	153		
	M1	79		AM	989		J1	200		
	M1	161		AM	1157		J3	48		
	VP4	9		PMQ	41		J3	118		
	G1	167		SMM1	10		J3	286		
	G1	685		PT	3		J3	463		
	G2	234		PT	25		J6	30		
	AE3	504		PCG1	27		J6	55		
	AE5	59		ECG1	14		J6	84		
	AE6	441		PFD	21		J6	116		
	AE6	1072		PFD	30		J6	163		
	AE6	1242		PAR	1		J6	186		
	AE7	404		PAR	4		J6	226		
	AE8	51		PW	6		J6	276		
	AE8	113		PMQW	9		J6	426		
	AE8	971		EMQW	11		J6	443		
	AE9	878		PNH	40		J6	640		
	AE12	298		ENH	15		J6	703		
	AE12	1140		PAL	9		J6	813		
	OAL	379		EMK	24		J10	108		
	M12	772		ETC	5		J10	281		
OFTENTIMES	WB	127		PCB	14		J10	303		
OFT-REPEATED	TA	414		HP	232		J10	305		
	AE2	849		DA	162		J10	311		
OFT-TOLD	RL	348		DA	173		J10	337		
OG	SAA	408		PSF	31		J10	400		
	SAA	459		ETG	23		J10	417		
	SAA	462		PR	21		J10	462		
OGLE	PP	45		PUO3	13		J10	493		
	ESH	26		PUO5	13		J16	20		
	OAL	564		AA	82		J16	86		
OGLEBY	MF	102		AA	85		P1	56		
	MF	174		AA	239		P1	101		
OGLING	EDGA	26		AA	262		P1	156		
	L4	120		AA	439		P1	223		
	P1	41		AA	513		P2	60		
OGULNIA	J6	469		AA	522		P3	49		
OIL	SMA	59		AA	530		P3	178		
	AA	265		AA	710		P4	3		
	MF	185		AA	971		P4	39		
	H29	7		PLB	29		P5	87		
	J3	122		PLB	31		P5	225		
	J3	422		MF	60		P5	258		
	J6	347		MF	70		P6	16		
	P2	114		SAA	107		P6	141		
	P3	85		SAA	156		M1	489		
	P4	78		SAA	471		M1	656		
	P4	89		SAA	659		M1	786		
	P6	91		SAA	844		PLT	28		
	P6	119		PK	28		PLT	54		

OLD	MC	39	OLD	AE8	448	OLIVE	G4	26
	GK	46		AE8	740		AE5	405
	GK	87		AE9	151		AE5	1013
	VP1	64		AE9	325		AE6	328
	VP4	37		AE9	349		AE6	1104
	VP6	99		AE9	381		AE7	208
	VP7	17		AE9	664		AE7	588
	VP8	70		AE9	888		AE8	153
	VP8	137		AE10	923		AE11	150
	VP9	19		AE11	83		AE11	505
	VP9	62		AE11	386		AE12	1111
	G1	455		AE11	401		OAL	828
	G1	581		AE11	693		BP	91
	G2	22		AE11	711		AS	61
	G2	89		AE11	816	OLIVE-BEARING	AE7	980
	G2	146		AE11	975	OLIVE'S	G2	196
	G2	227		AE12	201	OLIVES	LC	104
	G2	246		AE12	1354		PUO1	5
	G2	525		OAL	392		H2	81
	G2	781		OAL	276		G2	39
	G2	791		OAL	771		G2	124
	G3	190		OAL	880		G2	301
	G4	156		AF	167		G2	414
	G4	188		AF	177		G2	586
	G4	404		MG	13		G2	594
	G4	421		LMC	3		G2	757
	AE1	172		DO	8		AE7	1034
	AE1	647		DO	161		M8	9
	AE1	683		KT1	1		M8	38
	AE1	748		KT1	81		AF	30
	AE2	5		KT2	434	OLYMPIA	G3	288
	AE2	173		KT2	536	OLYMPIAN	C	668
	AE2	591		KT3	17	OLYMPIC	LC	145
	AE2	683		KT3	47	OLYMPUS'	HIF	68
	AE2	717		KT3	174		DA	68
	AE2	789		KT3	211	OMEN	T18	29
	AE2	845		KT3	769		PAA	44
	AE2	864		KT3	871		HAP	799
	AE2	872		KT3	877		HAP	1771
	AE2	935		KT3	943		BR	327
	AE2	948		M8	60		J6	781
	AE2	1084		B	298		M9	156
	AE3	7		BP	11		HI	178
	AE3	13		BP	34		PLT	56
	AE3	71		BP	63		G3	410
	AE3	130		BP	80		G4	555
	AE3	142		BP	82		AE1	619
	AE3	148		BP	181		AE2	254
	AE3	221		BP	183		AE2	264
	AE3	238		CAM	222		AE3	467
	AE3	279		HIF	497		AE5	701
	AE3	343		HIF	525		AE7	160
	AE3	610		HIF	728		AE8	66
	AE3	733		C	2		AE8	123
	AE3	910		C	78		AE8	710
	AE4	77		C	140		AE10	431
	AE4	675		C	365		AE11	28
	AE5	95		C	366		AE12	394
	AE5	314		M12	711		AE12	1257
	AE5	396		M12	761		OAL	232
	AE5	705		M12	808		OAL	241
	AE5	769		AU	97		DO	76
	AE5	805		WB	1		KT3	185
	AE5	922		WB	126		KT3	261
	AE5	934		WB	323		KT3	367
	AE5	936		WB	331		CAM	275
	AE6	327		WB	346		M11	454
	AE6	847		WB	487		FL	53
	AE6	881		WB	497	OMENS	AM	422
	AE6	921		M15	53		MF	133
	AE6	1080		M15	237		HAP	1858
	AE7	68		M15	264		ODA	9
	AE7	76		M15	364		J6	672
	AE7	166		M15	645		M9	188
	AE7	243		GP	66		AE2	239
	AE7	267		CI	1		AE2	935
	AE7	338		SMP	23		AE2	954
	AE7	571		SMP	90		AE3	5
	AE7	589		SMP	96		AE3	25
	AE7	609		ESK	22		AE3	48
	AE7	697		PMK	3		AE3	346
	AE7	741		EMKG	1		AE3	708
	AE7	747		EMKG	36		AE4	949
	AE7	833	OLD-CAST	PIE	7		AE7	806
	AE7	851	OLDEST	PAA	34		AE8	309
	AE7	874	OLIVE	CM	80		AE9	23
	AE7	881		PUF	8		AE10	352
	AE7	979		T27	15		AE10	357
	AE7	1008		VP5	21		AE12	115
	AE7	1015		VP8	21		OAL	469
	AE7	1022		G2	52	OMER	SAA	333
	AE7	1049		G2	89	OMINOUS	HAP	1891
	AE7	1085		G2	122	OMISSIONS	EL	332
	AE8	54		G2	254	OMIT	G2	358
	AE8	74		G2	427		AE6	1158
	AE8	379		G3	32	OMITTED	RL	266

Entry	Ref	No.
OMITTED	OAL	761
OMITTING	AE11	394
OMNIPOTENCE	RL	112
	TA	438
	HAP	84
	HAP	102
	HIF	763
	C	545
OMNIPOTENT	HAP	1086
	J1	234
OMNISCIENT	RL	282
	KT3	1054
ONE-EYED	J10	255
	AE3	890
ONESIMUS	M8	129
ONION	P4	73
ONSET	AA	1019
	AE9	190
ONSETS	SAA	821
	M12	99
ONYTHES	AE12	747
OOZE	AM	927
	G2	260
	G4	623
	AE2	570
	AE6	411
OOZED	G3	730
OOZY	TA	513
	M1	96
	AE6	1246
	AE9	152
OPE	T23	67
	T23	96
	AE1	409
	AE5	189
	AE6	127
	CAM	281
OPED	G3	762
	AE2	337
	AE4	990
	AE6	569
	AE9	6
	DO	73
	M10	94
OPEN	HS	80
	LC	31
	AM	91
	AM	486
	AM	637
	AM	859
	AM	878
	PUO4	21
	MD	37
	MD	242
	SAA	180
	SAA	862
	L1	51
	L3	282
	T27	28
	AK	99
	HAP	99
	HAP	272
	HAP	1207
	HAP	1212
	HAP	1250
	HAP	1365
	HAP	1619
	HAP	1930
	HAP	2046
	HAP	2172
	BR	116
	EKA	20
	EL	32
	J1	100
	J6	26
	P1	46
	P4	37
	M1	221
	M1	225
	M1	384
	M1	1063
	GK	60
	G1	98
	G1	173
	G1	627
	G2	51
	G2	76
	G2	261
	G2	456
	G2	464
	G2	499
	G2	589
	G3	74
	G3	407
	G3	499
	G3	502
OPEN	G3	513
	G3	635
	G3	662
	G4	138
	AE1	824
	AE2	88
	AE2	168
	AE2	416
	AE2	721
	AE3	541
	AE3	700
	AE4	222
	AE5	331
	AE5	480
	AE5	534
	AE5	721
	AE5	1086
	AE6	82
	AE6	160
	AE6	192
	AE6	391
	AE6	930
	AE6	1123
	AE7	627
	AE7	888
	AE8	329
	AE8	350
	AE9	49
	AE9	190
	AE9	569
	AE9	813
	AE9	929
	AE10	241
	AE10	433
	AE11	850
	AE11	1309
	AE12	673
	AE12	1181
	AE12	1278
	OAL	407
	OAL	433
	KT2	240
	KT3	107
	KT3	361
	B	388
	B	742
	BP	119
	HIF	358
	C	284
	C	339
	C	348
	C	590
	C	801
	TH	68
	TH	389
	FL	36
	FL	311
	M12	70
	M12	597
	AU	276
	WB	144
	M15	212
	ETP	6
	ETP	28
OPENED	SMA	30
	AM	513
	AM	1141
	DA	120
	PUF	11
	AA	30
	HAP	949
	J6	603
	J10	364
	P6	70
	AE6	808
	AE8	772
	AE10	435
	AE11	1204
	B	182
	TH	183
	CI	188
	CI	561
OPENING	AM	1106
	AM	1180
	SAA	562
	HAP	188
	BR	108
	OD	3
	P6	18
	M1	997
	G2	375
	AE4	263
	AE12	1086
	B	235
	FL	105
	AU	370
OPENING	M15	701
OPENS	AM	930
	ER	77
	VP8	156
	G3	472
	AE7	786
	AE8	945
	AE10	1022
	KT3	134
OPERA	J6	95
	GK	150
OPERAS	PNH	36
	PAA	35
OPERATION	WB	428
OPERATIONS	PUO2	12
OPES	AE1	209
	AE3	525
	AE7	332
	M15	414
	RH	53
OPINION	J10	206
	B	484
	C	656
OPINIONS	AA	547
	RL	451
OPIS	G4	483
	AE11	807
	AE11	1236
OPIUM	SAA	482
	KT2	17
OPPOSE	LCA	9
	AA	279
	SAA	4
	SAA	150
	SAA	265
	SAA	586
	SAA	1090
	RL	158
	RL	223
	TA	392
	TA	459
	AK	148
	BR	201
	J3	103
	AE1	328
	AE1	694
	AE1	819
	AE2	425
	AE2	596
	AE4	516
	AE4	881
	AE5	507
	AE6	144
	AE6	594
	AE6	1218
	AE7	405
	AE8	928
	HIF	351
	M12	179
OPPOSED	AM	538
	AA	143
	HAP	1106
	HAP	1188
	BR	91
	P6	42
	M1	659
	M13	223
	G4	420
	AE4	903
	AE5	89
	AE5	760
	AE7	416
	AE8	298
	AE8	896
	AE8	907
	AE9	134
	AE10	983
	AE10	1003
	AE11	613
	AE11	902
	AE11	916
	KT2	462
	KT2	490
	KT3	577
	C	682
	FL	291
	M12	11
	M12	566
	M15	125
	M15	465
	M15	520
OPPOSING	SAA	1112
	HAP	97
	HAP	699
	G4	528
	AE11	879

Word	Ref	No.
OPPOSITE	P6	49
	G2	586
	AE3	725
	AE5	480
	AE8	945
	AE10	792
	M8	278
	KT2	414
	KT2	449
	C	586
	FL	129
OPPOSITION	SAA	250
	BR	58
OPPRESS	AM	1080
	AA	727
	SAA	614
	H9	4
	H29	74
	HAP	2530
	J3	56
	HI	55
	AE1	839
	AE9	1016
	AE9	1071
	AE10	525
	AE12	916
	AE12	1172
	OAL	726
	M15	123
OPPRESSED	AM	39
	ML	30
	PLG	22
	CM	44
	AA	195
	AA	338
	AA	353
	AA	933
	RL	161
	L3	74
	L3	81
	L3	147
	L3	197
	FS2	5
	TA	461
	HH	3
	HAP	183
	HAP	2170
	HAP	2537
	HAP	2581
	ODA	42
	J3	271
	J10	16
	J10	59
	J10	119
	P3	217
	P5	159
	P5	188
	M1	118
	M1	191
	M1	292
	M1	421
	HI	139
	VP5	71
	G4	362
	AE1	92
	AE1	183
	AE1	670
	AE2	347
	AE2	539
	AE2	575
	AE2	772
	AE4	882
	AE6	238
	AE6	141
	AE6	699
	AE8	43
	AE8	438
	AE9	464
	AE9	493
	AE9	542
	AE9	582
	AE9	953
	AE10	1036
	AE10	1120
	AE10	1187
	AE10	1249
	AE11	772
	AE11	1109
	AE12	5
	AE12	235
	AE12	467
	AE12	746
	AE12	970
	OAL	46
	OAL	665
	AF	114
OPPRESSED	AF	121
	KT1	74
	KT1	142
	KT1	270
	KT1	502
	KT3	762
	KT3	856
	KT3	1038
	B	496
	CAM	214
	CAM	322
	CAM	358
	HIF	475
	HIF	666
	C	159
	C	689
	TH	217
	M11	379
	M12	451
	M12	763
	CI	450
OPPRESSION	AA	784
	SAA	772
	TJD	194
OPPRESSOR	HAP	2004
OPPRESSOR'S	M1	274
OPPRESSORS	RL	91
OPPROBRIOUS	HIF	38
	HIF	524
	AU	121
OPTIC	ESK	1
OPTICS	HAP	57
	EL	268
ORACLE	EAL	13
	MD	164
	J1	126
	AE4	496
ORACLES	SMA	131
	RL	75
	L4	246
	J6	718
	M1	435
	M1	498
	M1	662
	M9	177
	VP6	103
	AE6	111
	AE6	1090
	AE7	368
	AE9	164
	AU	292
	M15	212
ORACULOUSLY	G2	22
ORAISONS	EL	114
ORAL	RL	271
	HAP	752
ORANGE	AM	802
	PAZ	34
ORANGES	GE	22
ORANGE-WENCH	OE	41
ORANGE-WENCHES	EDGA	10
	PSH	7
ORATOR	AE11	591
ORATORIES	KT2	467
ORATORS	J10	186
ORATORY	MF	168
ORB	UDH	27
	CM	52
	EL	273
	VP4	8
	AE10	1139
	AE10	1269
	KT3	168
	M11	64
	FL	5
	AU	179
	SMP	85
ORBITS	AE12	1076
ORBS	LC	38
	LC	114
	AE8	589
ORCHARD	G2	126
ORCHARDS	M13	115
	G4	266
	M15	104
ORCHITS	G2	124
ORDAIN	AR	165
	LC	24
	PM	17
	PUF	25
	AA	729
	SAA	192
	ER	39
	H9	38
	FS2	6
	TA	173
ORDAIN	HAP	1030
	HAP	1786
	M1	340
	VP5	45
	VP5	60
	G1	189
	G2	27
	G2	156
	G4	329
	AE1	592
	AE1	780
	AE2	242
	AE2	251
	AE2	468
	AE2	893
	AE2	1055
	AE3	215
	AE4	878
	AE5	255
	AE6	119
	AE6	1107
	AE7	665
	AE11	1231
	AE12	1194
	AF	55
	KT2	360
	KT3	964
	KT3	1115
	HIF	573
	C	513
	TH	186
	WB	110
	M15	718
ORDAINED	SMA	119
	AA	963
	RL	167
	AK	60
	ODA	49
	P3	131
	G3	31
	G3	732
	AE2	169
	AE2	327
	AE4	290
	AE5	79
	AE5	342
	AE6	643
	AE6	923
	AE6	1166
	AE6	1231
	AE7	977
	AE8	357
	AE8	428
	AE11	289
	KT3	1084
	HIF	708
	TH	255
	TH	276
	FL	423
	CI	446
ORDAINS	EIE	11
	MF	68
	G3	245
	AE2	98
	AE4	207
	AE5	747
	AE5	989
	AE7	227
	AE8	56
	KT3	1056
	CAM	59
	M15	54
ORDER	HS	19
	AR	156
	LC	15
	AM	226
	PUO1	34
	AA	531
	L3	36
	L3	117
	H2	67
	SSC	9
	EL	200
	EL	313
	P1	35
	P5	262
	P6	107
	VP2	69
	G1	217
	G1	329
	G2	376
	G4	251
	AE1	544
	AE1	638
	AE1	924
	AE1	980

Word	Ref	No.
ORDER	AE1	984
	AE2	1043
	AE3	391
	AE3	533
	AE3	567
	AE3	574
	AE4	195
	AE4	734
	AE4	761
	AE5	133
	AE5	383
	AE5	743
	AE5	756
	AE5	767
	AE6	926
	AE6	978
	AE6	1034
	AE7	239
	AE7	963
	AE8	833
	AE9	474
	AE10	259
	AE10	338
	AE11	1308
	AE12	186
	AE12	197
	AE12	525
	AE12	1028
	DO	18
	KT3	464
	M8	97
	M8	163
	B	93
	B	590
	BP	92
	HIF	612
	M11	73
	FL	38
	FL	214
	FL	546
	AU	260
	WB	516
	M15	163
ORDERED	HAP	1823
	J16	20
	G2	579
	AE4	802
	AE5	703
	AE6	331
	B	495
	AU	346
	WB	277
ORDERING	AE2	980
	AE9	308
ORDERLY	TA	509
ORDERS	AM	970
	SAA	11
	SAA	178
	VP3	49
	AE4	830
	AE5	646
	KT3	495
	KT3	531
	GP	138
	EMKG	5
ORDINATION	HAP	711
	HAP	1029
ORDINATIONS	HAP	1479
ORDURE	AE3	283
	C	252
ORDURES	MD	188
	AK	65
	HAP	2456
	AE3	306
ORE	SMA	125
	LC	66
	DC	39
	AM	555
	PUO4	5
	AK	35
	HAP	2030
	BR	97
	P2	119
	P5	15
	M1	175
	G2	228
	G2	728
ORESTES	P3	242
	AE3	428
	AE4	683
ORESTES'	J1	6
ORGAN	SSC	52
	C	622
ORGAN-PIPE	PO	28
ORGAN'S	SSC	44
ORGANS	HAP	88
ORGANS	HAP	1307
	EL	216
	AE6	125
	AF	157
	KT3	762
	KT3	1048
	C	42
ORGIES	G4	756
	AE6	695
	AE7	564
ORIENT	P2	118
	M13	71
	AE1	922
	KT3	68
	M10	39
	C	52
	FL	237
ORIGINAL	UDH	101
	PO	20
	SAA	108
	RL	278
	RL	294
	EC	38
	HAP	1626
	EL	300
	OD	30
	M1	207
	M1	241
	GK	31
	G1	91
	AE1	1042
	TJD	199
	M15	90
ORIGINALLY	TA	495
ORINDA	AK	162
ORION	AE3	677
	AE7	995
	AE10	1084
	OAL	834
ORION'S	AU	457
ORLANDO	PUO5	2
ORMISDA	CI	433
	CI	442
	CI	515
	CI	602
ORMOND	DO	7
	DO	166
	CI	39
ORMOND'S	DO	62
ORMONDS	DO	143
ORNAMENT	PNH	32
	HAP	821
	J3	297
	AE3	599
	AE4	387
	AE5	343
	AE8	665
	AE8	240
	AE10	1228
	AE11	105
	M8	69
	BP	102
	FL	313
	FL	548
	M12	118
	M12	813
ORNAMENTS	EMW	16
	AE1	597
ORNEUS	M12	418
ORNITHUS	AE11	1003
ORODES	AE10	1031
	AE10	1036
ORONTES	J3	110
	AE1	305
	AE1	820
ORONTES'	AE1	162
ORPHAN	EL	345
	P2	40
	HI	51
	AE12	313
	EWR	27
ORPHANS	AM	1093
	SAA	64
	M1	274
	G2	180
	AE11	330
ORPHEUS	SSC	48
	DHP	16
	VP3	69
	VP4	66
	VP8	76
	G4	748
	AE6	178
	C	605
ORPHEUS'	G4	656
ORSES	AE10	1054
ORSILOCHUS	AE11	945
	AE11	1019
	AE11	1024
ORTYGIA	M15	504
ORTYGIAN	AE3	909
ORTYGIUS	AE9	778
ORYTHIA	AE12	130
ORYUS	M12	369
ORYUS'	M12	370
OSCA'S	AE7	1008
OSIER	G2	328
	G4	37
	AE11	835
	AE12	148
OSIERS	T18	54
	M1	157
	VP10	103
	G2	15
	G2	608
	G3	267
	G4	48
	M8	96
OSINIUS	AE10	923
OSIRIS	M9	37
	AE12	674
OSTENT	AE7	121
	M12	24
	EL	28
OSTENTATION	P1	158
OTHERWISE	AE1	552
	AE4	220
	AE10	1010
	KT2	360
	HIF	573
	M12	136
	M12	691
	AU	81
OTHNIEL'S	SAA	994
OTHO	J6	723
	AR	67
OTHRYS	M8	139
	M12	239
	M12	678
OTHRYS'	AT	104
OTTER'S	ECG2	6
OTTOBUONI	PKA	37
OUGHT	VHH	20
	PC2	32
	HP	129
	AA	384
	SAA	346
	SAA	442
	HAP	1417
	HAP	2408
	PSH	35
	M1	493
	M9	123
	OAL	322
	B	531
	HIF	174
	KT3	1107
OUNCE	J1	60
OUTBALANCE	AU	397
OUTBIDS	J10	494
OUTBOUND	AM	816
OUTCASTS	AE11	399
OUTDOES	ER	62
OUTDONE	AA	518
	EL	293
OUTFACE	J6	387
OUTFLIES	AE5	288
OUT-FLY	AM	1068
OUTGO	MD	203
OUTGOES	J6	710
	HI	167
OUTGROWS	ML	29
OUT-LAUGH	PAR	17
OUTLAWS	MD	242
OUTLET	B	113
OUTLETS	AM	878
	M15	516
OUTLINES	PUO4	23
	GK	31
OUTLIVED	L3	152
OUTMOST	P3	56
OUT-OF-FASHION	ETL	22
	PSF	39
OUT-PRAYS	AM	1042
OUTRAGE	AE10	38
OUTRAGEOUS	J6	623
	P3	241
	M13	92
	AE4	521
	OAE2	80
	KT1	445
	C	69

Word	Ref	No.	Word	Ref	No.	Word	Ref	No.
OUTRAN	MD	45	OVERFLOWING	EL	13	OVERSPREAD	VP5	8
OUTRIDDEN	KT3	388	OVERFLOWS	J6	554		G2	254
OUTRIDES	AE4	224		VP2	28		TH	92
OUTRUN	SAA	404		G2	10		AE4	840
	KT3	388		C	150		AE5	14
OUTRUNS	AA	344		AE9	607		AE6	85
OUTSHINE	L2	14	OVERFLY	P4	53		AE7	641
OUTSIDE	P4	32	OVERFORCE	M8	112		AE8	483
	B	159	OVER-GROWN	L4	157		AE9	611
OUTSTRIP	SAA	22	OVERGROWN	PRH	30		AE10	1164
	J3	220		RL	370		AE11	864
OUTSTRIPPED	AE1	442		P4	92		AE12	101
	AE5	200		P5	270	OVER-SOLD	AE9	265
	AE7	1100		B	113	OVERSTAND	AT	85
	AE10	350	OVERHEAD	TH	258	OVER-STOCKED	PKA	4
OUTSTRIPS	AE5	153	OVERHEARD	CAM	151	OVERSTOCKED	MD	102
	AE12	519	OVER-INFORMED	AA	158		HAP	2288
OUT-VIED	J1	32	OVERJOYED	M10	90		EMKG	4
OUT-WEEPS	AM	1042		FL	205	OVERSTOCKS	PTW	5
OUTWEIGHED	HS	90		CI	532	OVER-STRAINING	PEL	26
	P3	72	OVER-LABORED	L4	104	OVERTAKE	CM	138
OUTWRIT	PT	13		AE10	1274		H2	76
OUT-WRITE	PCG1	12	OVERLABORED	H2	68		HAP	268
OVERAWED	AE12	1024		G2	793		M8	302
	KT3	1135	OVERLAID	M1	88		C	286
OVERBALLASTED	P3	155		AE10	1286	OVERTAKES	AM	836
OVERBEAR	KT3	552		KT2	590		B	338
OVERBLOWN	G1	561		KT3	641	OVER-THREW	HI	64
	STP	16	OVERLEAP	H3	32	OVERTHREW	AM	372
	AE10	1144	OVERLEAPS	AE9	457		PNH	52
OVERBOARD	AE5	228		AE11	745		AE8	386
	M11	199		PTP	33		AE12	751
OVERBORNE	AE1	164	OVERLOOK	AE2	61		CI	287
	M8	126	OVERLOOKED	HAP	2213	OVER-THROW	J3	411
	TH	422		M8	85	OVERTHROW	AA	403
	CI	412		AE5	378		SAA	138
OVERBURDENED	H2	25		AE7	232		SAA	926
OVERBUYS	TJD	138		KT2	543		HAP	243
OVERCAME	AR	56		KT3	50		OAL	238
	VHH	41		HIF	785		KT2	99
	L3	246		M15	444		AU	281
	AE10	1065	OVERLOOKS	AM	887		AU	602
	BP	85		HAP	2126	OVERTHROWN	AE2	869
OVER-CARE	PTL	13		J6	660		AE11	1295
	P2	81		M13	49		AE11	623
OVERCARE	PLB	48		G1	426	OVERTHROWS	G2	403
	CAM	54		AE7	663		AE10	1027
OVERCAST	AR	294	OVER-LOUD	PUO4	12	OVERTOOK	MD	320
	BR	229	OVER-MASTED	AE5	202		C	349
	G4	583	OVERMATCH	PTS	41		M11	366
OVERCHARGED	AE9	584		MM	51	OVERTOP	M1	393
OVER-CIVIL	AA	557	OVERMATCHED	AM	423	OVERTOPS	SAA	493
OVERCLOUDS	AE11	1193		MC	27		G1	168
OVER-COME	AE11	1163		AE10	953		AE1	702
OVERCOME	PWG	59		AE12	230	OVERTURES	OAL	190
	VHH	7		AE12	323	OVERTURN	AE1	387
	LCA	36	OVERNIGHT	J6	612		AE7	467
	AM	319		J16	72	OVERTURNED	HAP	2024
	AM	536	OVERPAID	SAA	807		M1	303
	J10	258	OVERPASS	AE7	419		AE3	1
	MC	38	OVERPASSED	AE5	418		AE12	425
	VP9	81		AE5	872		M12	195
	G2	748	OVERPLUS	EKA	29		AU	138
	G3	61	OVERPOISE	TJD	180	OVER-VIOLENT	AA	557
	G3	493	OVERPOWERED	KT3	650	OVERWATCHED	M11	344
	G3	538		KT3	740	OVERWHELM	TA	33
	AE2	907		FL	120		AE9	1096
	AE6	1133	OVERPOWERING	KT1	235		AE9	710
	AE10	1074	OVERPRESSED	AE9	926	OVERWHELMED	PUO3	2
	OAL	229	OVERRAN	FL	302		J3	497
	OAL	234		SAA	73		AE6	694
	OAL	339	OVERRATE	PNH	50		AE9	1090
	OAL	525	OVERRULED	L3	241		AE10	1146
	M8	337	OVERRUN	J10	248	OVERWORKS	L3	288
	CAM	257		M1	821	OVERWORN	AE6	699
	AU	584		G1	103	OVID	WB	156
OVERCOMES	HP	43	OVERRUNS	M1	722	OVID'S	ER	59
OVER-COST	DO	135	OVERSEE	H2	65	OWE	HS	38
OVERDO	PLN	22		B	490		HS	111
OVERFEEDS	L2	18	OVER-SEEN	PMQ	12		AR	146
OVERFILLED	B	689	OVERSET	C	351		RH	71
OVERFLOATS	AE10	34		AE6	460		SMA	109
OVERFLOW	MD	172		AE9	105		DC	23
	SKA6	18		G2	568		AM	468
	P2	5	OVER-SHADE	G1	276		AM	1107
	G1	394	OVERSHADE	AE12	383		EUO2	18
	G2	265		M12	297		DA	46
	AE8	741	OVERSHADOWED	M15	29		PPC	16
	AE11	590	OVER-SNOWED	AE5	553		MF	90
	AE12	307	OVERSPENT	VP2	10		L1	43
	TJD	174		AE9	381		HAP	2079
	TJD	177		AE10	1187		J1	114
OVERFLOWED	HAP	2097	OVER-SPREAD	MF	126		P5	32
	BR	170		VP1	115		P5	134
	G2	308	OVERSPREAD	HI	148		M9	179
OVERFLOWING	UDH	91		VP1	66		VP8	132

OWE	G2	13	OWNING	KT2	303	PACE	AE3	668			
	AE6	1225	OWNS	AR	286		AE4	924			
	AE9	338		PUO1	40		AE5	47			
	AE9	878		L4	187		AE5	191			
	AE11	75		HAP	475		AE5	297			
	AE11	102		HAP	1056		AE5	585			
	AE12	480		VP3	1		AE6	373			
	OAL	221		VP10	17		AE6	407			
	DO	166		AE12	878		AE6	453			
	TJD	199		KT3	666		AE6	1190			
	HIF	231		M12	820		AE7	211			
	HIF	277	OX	J10	416		AE7	526			
	AU	280		G2	203		AE8	289			
OWED	VP10	101		G3	733		AE8	607			
	AE4	401		AE2	293		AE10	634			
	AE6	967		AE5	630		AE10	921			
	AE8	498		M12	351		AE11	125			
	AE10	718		M15	176		AE11	133			
	AE10	1218	OX-CHEEKS	J3	463		AE11	225			
OWES	HS	65	OXEN	AM	278		AE11	701			
	AR	120		RL	89		AE11	823			
	AR	308		H2	8		AE12	10			
	SAA	370		H2	90		AE12	126			
	HAP	1935		P2	83		AE12	452			
	P5	253		M1	159		AE12	1079			
	G2	9		HI	75		AE12	1092			
	AE1	837		VP4	49		OAL	711			
	HIF	193		VP5	54		KT1	435			
	AU	559		G1	3		KT3	398			
	M15	655		G1	300		KT3	939			
OWEST	P3	136		G1	380		B	657			
	M1	646		G1	644		TH	215			
OWING	J10	426		G2	322		TH	372			
	AE11	276		G3	567		FL	248			
OWL	AE4	672		G3	637		WB	53			
	CAM	276		G3	796		M15	316			
	WB	336		G3	829		CI	595			
OWLS	MF	129		G4	406		SMP	1			
	VP8	75		AE1	895	PACED	OAE1	32			
	G1	547		AE3	286		FL	465			
	AE8	309		AE3	324	PACES	M13	190			
OWN	HS	87		AE5	135		AE2	985			
	AR	238		AE5	429		AE9	1065			
	PCD	21		AE7	750		KT2	445			
	PNH	31		AE8	274	PACHYNUS	AE3	548			
	EUO2	30		AE8	421		AE3	918			
	PTW	30		AE8	474	PACHYNUS'	AE7	395			
	SAA	381		AE9	526	PACIFIED	HAP	1292			
	TA	443		AE9	833	PACING	J1	36			
	HAP	2107		KT1	26	PACK	AA	527			
	HAP	2506		HIF	62		PPC	10			
	J6	193		HIF	630		MD	45			
	J16	9		C	223		HAP	1447			
	AE1	384		AE2	410		J3	258			
	AE3	790		M15	117		J6	212			
	AE4	484	OXFORD	PUO1	28		P5	206			
	AE5	311		PO	18		VP9	6			
	AE6	997		PUO3	36		AE7	667			
	AE7	270		PUO4	35		SMP	14			
	AE7	609		ESK	5	PACKED	AA	607			
	AE10	95		ESK	7	PACKING	EH	16			
	AE10	292	OX'S	AE11	1006		J3	18			
	AE11	1015		C	234	PACKS	TH	379			
	KT2	285	OYSTER-BREEDING	G1	297	PACTOLUS	AE10	211			
	KT3	666	OYSTERS	H2	73	PADDERS	PA	19			
	B	396		J6	419		EKK	20			
	B	398					J3	14			
	B	438					J3	482			
	CAM	59					J6	429			
	CI	506				PADDLE	G3	812			
	CI	633				PADDOCKS	AE1	336			
OWNED	HS	125				PADUA'S	AE9	924			
	AR	46	PACE	AM	489	PADUS'	HAP	1622			
	MD	207		EEL	12	PAEAN	J6	251			
	MF	5		PTL	22		J6	253			
	HAP	611		ML	43		AE10	1040			
	HAP	969		MD	44	PAEANS	HIF	648			
	AE9	97		SAA	404	PAESTAN	G4	179			
	AE11	714		TA	215	PAGAN	ETS	30			
	KT1	321		EAA	3		KT3	201			
	KT3	667		AK	9		KT3	293			
	B	387		ODA	10		KT3	952			
	BP	141		J3	219	PAGANS	FL	536			
	M15	236		J3	392	PAGASAEAN	M12	549			
OWNER	HAP	1276		J6	167	PAGASUS	AE11	991			
	HAP	2246		J6	523	PAGE	RH	84			
	HAP	2522		J10	34		PO	5			
	HAP	2563		M1	731		MD	158			
	G2	657		M1	974		SAA	1053			
	AE10	552		M13	44		EK	42			
OWNER'S	PA	24		HI	30		RL	137			
OWNERS'	J10	356		G1	691		RL	328			
OWNERS'	AM	1005		G2	380		RL	336			
	LMC	4		G3	708		RL	404			
OWNING	BR	127		G4	341		ER	19			
	AE5	396		AE1	976		ER	76			

PAGE	TA	494
	HAP	1126
	BR	108
	EL	296
	OD	3
	J1	5
	J3	307
	J6	486
	J6	616
	J10	475
	P1	22
	P1	190
	P5	28
	VP6	17
	B	52
	C	297
	CI	19
PAGEANT	AA	751
	PLB	23
	PAA	25
	SSC	60
	KT1	48
PAGEANTRIES	L2	56
PAGEANTRY	MD	1
	H29	19
	P3	53
	P6	105
PAGEANTS	G3	34
	B	437
PAGES	PP	32
	J6	219
	BP	103
PAID	DC	15
	AM	587
	ML	22
	SAA	930
	PK	16
	RL	113
	RL	116
	RL	385
	FS2	12
	HAP	42
	HAP	171
	HAP	1354
	HAP	1524
	HAP	1605
	HAP	2256
	HAP	2282
	EL	25
	J1	62
	J10	180
	J10	519
	M1	270
	M9	59
	M9	204
	PLT	3
	MC	56
	G1	556
	G2	524
	G4	551
	AE1	820
	AE2	22
	AE2	304
	AE2	385
	AE3	29
	AE3	161
	AE3	720
	AE6	641
	AE6	685
	AE6	848
	AE7	7
	AE7	90
	AE8	139
	AE8	360
	AE9	176
	AE10	1169
	AE11	1223
	AE12	1113
	OAL	488
	KT3	690
	KT3	952
	KT3	1016
	M8	309
	M8	338
	BP	39
	CAM	61
	HIF	687
	C	10
	TH	235
	FL	328
	FL	363
	M12	209
	M12	627
	GP	42
PAIL	VP3	43
	G2	764
PAIL	G3	283
	G3	484
	BP	72
PAILS	VP2	28
	M15	109
PAIN	HS	46
	RH	20
	AM	127
	SMQ	7
	SMM2	15
	PEL	9
	SEL2	4
	SEL2	6
	SEL2	14
	SCG1	35
	SCG3	5
	SM1	15
	SKK	3
	SKK	16
	STC	10
	CM	37
	CM	54
	CM	58
	SSF	8
	SSF	10
	SSF	24
	SAA	32
	EK	20
	RL	162
	AT	16
	AT	118
	L2	3
	L2	23
	L2	26
	L3	3
	L3	11
	L3	57
	L3	91
	L3	150
	L3	210
	L4	22
	L4	32
	L4	46
	T23	25
	T23	45
	T27	50
	H3	35
	NS	26
	TA	174
	HAP	138
	HAP	1378
	HAP	1505
	SKA3	3
	SKA6	1
	PSH	39
	SSH	10
	J3	442
	J6	64
	J6	766
	J10	525
	J10	553
	P4	97
	M1	485
	M9	139
	M13	186
	R	6
	R	12
	R	18
	R	24
	SLT1	15
	VP2	77
	VP2	102
	VP8	51
	VP8	58
	VP10	55
	G1	147
	G1	286
	G2	552
	G2	556
	G3	421
	G3	603
	G3	699
	G3	803
	G4	172
	G4	230
	G4	356
	G4	424
	AE2	698
	AE2	1054
	AE2	1081
	AE3	934
	AE4	97
	AE4	629
	AE4	925
	AE4	994
	AE5	233
PAIN	AE5	848
	AE5	1134
	AE6	835
	AE6	1019
	AE7	402
	AE7	699
	AE8	306
	AE8	761
	AE9	68
	AE10	1279
	AE11	1196
	AE12	13
	AE12	73
	AE12	594
	OAL	857
	OAE2	21
	AF	60
	AF	65
	AF	109
	AF	116
	KT1	56
	KT1	285
	KT1	306
	KT1	476
	KT1	489
	KT1	519
	KT2	118
	KT2	253
	KT2	383
	KT2	658
	KT3	152
	KT3	329
	KT3	881
	TJD	27
	M8	372
	M8	380
	M10	87
	CAM	358
	HIF	505
	HIF	572
	C	102
	C	287
	TH	44
	TH	161
	TH	175
	TH	187
	TH	198
	TH	367
	M11	59
	M11	324
	FL	23
	M12	415
	M12	686
	M12	768
	WB	23
	WB	199
	WB	236
	CI	190
	CI	361
PAINED	HAP	1427
	AE2	1012
	AE10	1127
	KT2	6
	C	627
	C	669
	AU	72
PAINFUL	AA	854
	SAA	897
	SAA	1102
	L3	68
	TA	154
	G2	356
	G2	549
	G3	356
	G3	637
	G4	464
	AE2	1060
	AE6	944
	AE7	865
	AE12	669
	AE12	758
PAINFULLY	SAA	601
PAINS	AR	176
	LC	108
	PIE	19
	PMQ	1
	SMQ	2
	EEL	30
	STL	3
	STL	5
	SCG3	7
	ESF	12
	PC2	16
	STC	6
	HP	74
	AA	757

Word	Ref	No.
PALAMEDE	AU	478
PALAMEDES	EM	10
	AE2	104
PALAMON	DO	35
	DO	39
	KT1	156
	KT1	207
	KT1	251
	KT1	274
	KT1	282
	KT1	286
	KT1	311
	KT1	397
	KT1	443
	KT1	502
	KT1	508
	KT2	2
	KT2	14
	KT2	21
	KT2	65
	KT2	76
	KT2	106
	KT2	121
	KT2	140
	KT2	162
	KT2	169
	KT2	203
	KT2	242
	KT2	261
	KT2	286
	KT2	356
	KT2	426
	KT3	19
	KT3	22
	KT3	38
	KT3	124
	KT3	185
	KT3	394
	KT3	562
	KT3	641
	KT3	654
	KT3	776
	KT3	807
	KT3	827
	KT3	835
	KT3	854
	KT3	899
	KT3	922
	KT3	947
	KT3	1005
	KT3	1011
	KT3	1119
PALATE	P3	231
	G3	597
	G3	758
	TH	308
PALATES	EOE	31
PALE	HS	70
	AM	737
	SKK	2
	MF	57
	SAA	75
	RL	10
	BR	82
	J3	323
	J6	514
	J10	509
	PPS	5
	P1	249
	P3	71
	P3	161
	P5	83
	M1	733
	M1	999
	VP2	64
	VP5	22
	VP8	95
	G1	373
	G1	596
	G1	642
	G3	60
	G3	821
	G4	185
	AE2	1049
	AE4	709
	AE6	386
	AE6	648
	AE6	773
	AE7	995
	AE8	942
	AE10	383
	AE10	635
	AE11	99
	OAL	840
	KT1	529
	KT1	530

Word	Ref	No.
PALE	KT2	122
	KT2	190
	M8	246
	M8	271
	C	244
	C	457
	C	493
	TH	306
	M11	317
	M11	353
	M11	405
	AU	112
PALE-FACED	CM	51
PALENESS	AE4	721
	AE8	290
	AE10	1164
	OAL	835
	KT1	467
PALER	AM	408
	PRH	6
	AE4	115
PALES	P4	65
	VP5	53
	G3	1
	G3	461
	DO	65
	M8	8
	C	37
	PMK	8
PALFREYS	KT3	459
PALICUS	AE9	794
PALINURUS	AE3	264
	AE3	671
	AE3	737
	AE5	18
	AE5	1093
	AE6	461
	AE6	518
PALINURUS'	AE11	718
PALISADE	AE7	214
PALISADES	AE9	694
PALL	OE	25
	L3	104
	KT3	943
PALLADIAN	G2	252
PALLADIUM	EPF	5
	AE2	250
	AE9	189
PALLANTEAN	AE11	140
PALLANTEUM	AE8	72
PALLAS	LC	100
	PUO1	3
	HP	134
	L4	147
	T18	56
	J1	165
	J3	357
	VP2	89
	G1	23
	G2	594
	AE1	60
	AE2	41
	AE2	227
	AE2	242
	AE2	297
	AE2	302
	AE2	833
	AE3	715
	AE5	660
	AE5	923
	AE6	1155
	AE7	1097
	AE8	146
	AE8	73
	AE8	409
	AE8	576
	AE8	609
	AE8	672
	AE8	776
	AE8	926
	AE10	237
	AE10	510
	AE10	559
	AE10	593
	AE10	613
	AE10	624
	AE10	627
	AE10	644
	AE10	667
	AE10	718
	AE10	723
	AE10	741
	AE11	44
	AE11	55
	AE11	84
	AE11	135

Word	Ref	No.
PALLAS	AE11	145
	AE11	211
	AE11	230
	AE11	245
	AE11	252
	AE11	267
	AE11	280
	AE12	1367
	AE12	1373
	OAL	706
	OAL	782
	OAE1	11
	BP	90
	HIF	296
	HIF	551
	M12	485
	AU	162
	AU	517
PALLAS'	AE1	671
	AE2	576
	AE8	751
	AE10	575
	AE11	273
	AE11	725
PALLED	PMQ	39
	J10	326
	KT3	686
	TH	232
PALLENIAN	G4	561
PALLIARDS	HAP	1135
PALLID	KT2	563
	M11	484
PALLING	AM	835
PALLS	J6	49
PALM	AT	64
	HAP	786
	J6	757
	G2	94
	G3	748
	AE5	145
	AE5	253
	AE5	453
	AE5	514
	AE5	630
	AE8	95
	DO	4
	KT3	338
	KT3	396
	TJD	152
	FL	284
	M12	406
	M12	453
	M15	588
PALMS	HS	57
	AK	3
	M1	892
	G1	90
	G3	18
	G3	153
	G4	26
	AE7	908
	KT3	737
PALMUS	AE10	987
	AE10	990
PALMY	AE3	926
	CAM	319
PALSY	J10	317
PALTRY	EAZ	20
	PD	63
	J1	149
	J3	63
	J10	30
	J10	163
	P1	6
PAMPER	SAA	471
	G3	197
PAMPERED	AA	47
	SAA	7
	SAA	48
	HAP	374
	HAP	2291
	BR	274
	EL	19
	P6	171
	G3	323
	TJD	90
PAMPERING	J1	205
	P3	108
PAMPHLET	SAA	491
PAMPHLETEERS	EUF	18
PAN	T27	62
	HAP	284
	HAP	1283
	LS	6
	LS	7
	LS	12

Word	Ref	No.	Word	Ref	No.	Word	Ref	No.
PAN	LS	18	PANTHER'S	HAP	800	PARCELLED	RL	377
	P4	65		HAP	1647	PARCHED	H29	33
	M1	964		HAP	1939		P5	70
	M1	980		AE8	604		VP7	79
	VP2	40		M12	553		G1	385
	VP2	41	PANTHERS	HAP	1298		G3	751
	VP2	42	PANTHEUS	AE2	429		AE3	193
	VP4	70		AE2	433		M15	412
	VP5	92		AE2	435	PARCHING	G2	520
	VP10	39		AE2	581		G3	844
	G1	20	PANTING	J3	393		G4	579
	G3	601		J6	335	PARCHMENT	AM	1064
	AE8	454		G3	167		P3	17
	M8	8		AM	392	PARDELIS	HAP	1961
PANACEE	AE12	617		L1	49	PARDON	PWGR	22
PANCHAEA	CAM	318		L4	190		PLN	26
PANDARUS	AE5	659		NS	9		PUO2	31
	AE9	977		NS	20		PKK	22
	AE9	993		NS	31		CM	102
	AE9	914		HAP	25		AA	959
PANDER	MD	256		HAP	1559		SAA	112
PANDER'S	J3	262		M1	675		SAA	858
PANDERS	HAP	1135		VP3	111		SAA	861
	J6	304		AE4	88		SAA	1128
PANDORA'S	UDH	54		AE5	180		L4	188
PANE	HAP	1844		AE6	488		TA	262
PANEGYRIC	J3	183		AE7	694		TA	271
PANGS	SEL2	1		AE8	306		HAP	16
	CM	69		AE8	522		HAP	1138
	MF	148		AE8	942		J3	472
	AT	53		AE10	1023		G4	704
	L4	125		AE10	1187		AE3	342
	HAP	1581		AE12	1061		AE3	474
	SSC	38		B	230		AE6	835
	BR	161		M12	197		AE12	834
	AE3	895		CI	379		CAM	148
	AE4	591	PANTON	MF	84	PARDONED	AA	147
	AE5	641	PANTS	AM	523		AA	323
	AE11	1253		SCD1	15		TA	183
	KT1	501		AE7	785	PARDONS	SAA	288
	B	371		AE11	1205	PARDS	KT3	57
	CAM	136		M12	680	PARED	OAL	584
	M15	455	PAP	P3	28	PARENT	L1	2
PANIC	SAA	907		AE11	1175		J10	470
	HAP	1899	PAPAL	MD	87		M13	206
	AE10	602	PAPER	CM	4		HI	156
	AE11	619		J1	25		VP4	68
	AE11	1077		ESK	4		VP5	31
	C	731	PAPERS	MF	52		G2	242
	M12	86		P3	18		G3	432
PANOPEA	AE5	313	PAPHIAN	G2	90		G4	467
PANOPES	AE5	394		AE5	991		AE1	534
PANS	J3	403		OAL	263		AE2	740
	J10	97	PAPHOS	AE1	575		AE2	892
PANSIES	VP2	66		M10	100		AE2	1072
PANT	P1	44		M10	101		AE6	286
	AE2	540	PAPIST	HAP	2039		AE6	947
	AE9	459	PAPISTS	RL	356		AE9	284
PANTAGIAS	AE3	903		PDS	41		AE10	1133
PANTALOONS	PMQW	9	PAPS	AM	1035		OAL	225
PANTED	M1	749		G3	840		B	234
	AE9	332		CI	102		B	352
PANTHER	T23	13	PARABLE	HAP	1951		B	358
	HAP	326		P3	213		CAM	371
	HAP	327	PARABLES	C	816		HIF	491
	HAP	392	PARACLETE	BR	20		HIF	502
	HAP	468		VCS	39		AU	303
	HAP	497	PARACLITE	VCS	8		CI	299
	HAP	524	PARADISE	AA	30		M15	602
	HAP	538		SAA	1056		M15	580
	HAP	549		TA	363	PARENTAGE	AR	257
	HAP	553		TA	380		SAA	354
	HAP	573		AK	3		J6	125
	HAP	612		HAP	383		M1	1087
	HAP	632		HAP	697		AE11	516
	HAP	709		BR	106	PARENTHESIS	MC	52
	HAP	740		EL	172	PARENT'S	SAA	173
	HAP	748		DO	155		L4	213
	HAP	785		KT1	402		BR	218
	HAP	822		TJD	22		HI	50
	HAP	869		TJD	179		AE2	725
	HAP	971		C	558		AE7	503
	HAP	1263		FL	121		AE12	71
	HAP	1314	PARAGRAPHS	RL	266	PARENTS	AM	1032
	HAP	1334	PARALLEL	MD	171		DA	81
	HAP	1349		PDG	1		DA	178
	HAP	1425		MN	3		AA	958
	HAP	1485		P3	166		OD	46
	HAP	1635		TH	357		J10	457
	HAP	1704	PARALLELS	EP	6		M9	129
	HAP	2050	PARAPHRASE	CI	21		M9	136
	HAP	2120	PARASITE	HAP	2450		M9	202
	HAP	2178		B	554		HI	62
	HAP	2184	PARASITES	SAA	520		HI	83
	HAP	2194		J1	210		GK	122
	HAP	2584	PARCEL	MD	301		G3	412

PARENTS	G4	685	PART	LC	150	PART	GK	63
	AE1	138		PWG	23		G1	51
	AE1	853		VHH	12		G1	96
	AE5	750		AM	122		G1	679
	AE6	31		AM	757		G2	55
	AE6	825		AM	985		G2	73
	AE6	1225		AM	987		G4	3
	AE10	1176		AM	1210		G4	636
	B	413		ET	11		AE1	574
	AU	238		PA	33		AE1	584
	M15	257		EEL	1		AE2	8
	M15	543		SEL1	5		AE2	40
PARENTS'	AM	132		PCG2	23		AE3	433
	UMR	1		EMQW	5		AE3	590
	ODA	21		PLN	43		AE4	115
	M13	3		PAL	39		AE4	612
	AE10	548		EKK	5		AE4	710
	B	309		PTW	21		AE4	714
PARIAN	J3	354		ETC	4		AE4	772
	VP6	102		HP	24		AE5	143
	VP7	45		HP	121		AE5	590
	G3	19		HP	215		AE5	852
	G3	54		DA	150		AE5	926
	AE1	831		PR	5		AE5	986
	AE8	959		PR	38		AE6	37
	OAL	117		AA	69		AE6	47
PARIS	HP	34		AA	368		AE6	62
	T27	1		AA	977		AE6	91
	PKA	33		AA	994		AE6	312
	J10	409		PLB	22		AE7	867
	VP2	87		PLB	32		AE7	914
	AE1	39		ELB	11		AE8	32
	AE2	817		EPC	7		AE8	813
	AE4	314		MD	170		AE9	785
	AE5	491		MD	308		AE9	831
	AE7	447		MF	175		AE9	895
	AE10	997		MF	216		AE10	13
	AE10	998		SAA	329		AE10	504
	OAL	59		RL	51		AE11	22
	OAL	283		RL	359		AE11	310
	M12	5		RL	395		AE11	311
	M12	792		ER	55		AE11	491
	AU	326		L3	27		AE11	833
	CI	319		L3	56		AE11	956
PARISH	PTW	32		L3	177		AE12	223
	C	641		L4	5		AE12	589
	WB	35		L4	193		AE12	622
	GP	1		L4	264		AE12	857
	GP	42		H3	11		OAL	148
	GP	60		H2	34		OAL	197
PARISHES	TJD	83		TA	112		OAL	360
PARK	PWGR	8		PAA	37		OAL	497
	L4	108		AK	129		OAL	759
	J6	88		HAP	12		OAL	800
	PMK	8		HAP	337		OAL	887
PARLEY	TA	172		HAP	396		OAE2	37
PARLIAMENT	J10	109		HAP	500		OAE2	75
	KT3	1007		HAP	536		MM	27
	KT3	1122		HAP	1343		KT1	153
	TJD	175		HAP	1820		KT1	437
	WB	83		HAP	1839		KT2	188
PARLIAMENTS	EUF	8		HAP	1941		KT2	285
	TJD	189		HAP	2091		KT2	436
PARLOR	C	15		HAP	2144		KT3	421
	C	93		HAP	2243		KT3	688
	FL	84		EDS	22		KT3	778
PARLOUS	WB	168		STS2	12		KT3	889
PARNASSUS	J1	124		SKA6	4		KT3	902
	PPS	1		EL	119		KT3	1044
	M1	428		EL	156		KT3	1051
	VP10	16		EL	158		TJD	39
PARNASSUS'	M1	625		EL	168		TJD	131
PAROS'	AE3	173		EL	191		TJD	132
PARRICIDE	AU	235		EL	336		M8	27
	AU	241		EL	357		M8	181
PARROT	EWGR	32		ODA	55		M8	215
	SAA	426		PSH	38		B	17
	PPS	12		J1	253		B	75
PARROTS	J6	109		J6	796		B	611
	M10	41		J10	463		B	635
PARSIMONY	G3	281		J10	490		B	700
	OAL	474		J16	92		B	732
PARSLEY	AT	51		PPS	6		CAM	211
	G4	181		P1	84		HIF	502
PARSON	PLB	34		P3	86		C	221
	NS	15		P3	169		TH	303
	SKA4	10		P3	219		M11	8
	EHC	3		P4	84		M11	50
	EHC	11		P4	105		M11	89
	EHC	16		P5	242		M11	169
	WB	36		P6	12		M11	249
	ETP	1		M1	48		M11	376
PART	UDH	102		M1	301		M11	416
	AR	188		M1	749		FL	455
	SMA	34		ELT	6		M12	213
	LC	82		MC	49		M12	528

Word	Code	No.
PART	M12	580
	M12	705
	M12	787
	AU	168
	AU	239
	AU	412
	AU	421
	AU	542
	AU	568
	WB	322
	M15	321
	M15	556
	CI	156
	STP	29
	ERL	3
	ESK	30
	PWR	21
PARTAKE	HAP	423
	HAP	1881
	J6	529
	VP5	98
	AE4	767
	AE7	359
	HIF	566
	M15	394
	M15	502
PARTAKER	PD	14
PARTAKES	M1	59
PARTED	HP	30
	PSF	42
	G1	193
	AE3	523
	KT2	164
	FL	610
PARTERRES	KT1	222
PARTES	GE	14
PARTHENIUS	AE10	1055
PARTHIAN	P5	5
	VP1	81
	VP10	85
	G4	445
	AE12	1240
	OAL	259
	KT3	953
PARTHIANS	G3	48
	AE7	838
	OAL	207
	OAL	240
PARTHIANS'	OAL	238
PARTIAL	HP	11
	HP	123
	RL	48
	RL	356
	AT	19
	J3	215
	AE1	39
	AE2	336
	AE2	836
	AE5	195
	AE10	21
	AE12	1296
	KT3	162
	KT3	482
	HIF	701
	AU	417
	AU	594
PARTICIPLE	J6	584
PARTICLES	HAP	1728
	M1	101
	G4	323
	B	514
	C	462
	M15	290
PARTIES	HS	42
	AR	312
	AM	939
	AA	493
	AA	564
	J6	391
	AE2	447
	AE2	537
	AE2	973
	AE7	732
	AE11	219
	KT3	386
	TJD	143
	CI	635
PARTING	STL	14
	SLN	12
	SAA	606
	SAA	615
	TA	249
	EDS	26
	MS	24
	VP3	122
	AE1	562
PARTING	AE3	296
	AE3	608
	AE3	622
	AE5	1002
	AE9	383
	AE10	347
	AE10	1263
	AE11	67
	AE11	1202
	KT3	285
	KT3	544
	HIF	590
	M11	69
	M11	443
	M15	260
	CI	196
PARTITION	AE9	179
	KT1	204
PARTITIONS	AA	164
	FL	69
PARTLET	HAP	2318
	C	68
	C	97
	C	358
	C	409
	C	436
	C	455
	C	574
	C	704
PARTLY	M1	947
PARTNER	M1	485
	M1	888
	M1	982
	HI	52
	AE4	159
	AE11	240
	C	102
	AU	535
PARTNER'S	MD	43
PARTNERS	AM	192
	AE3	289
PARTNERSHIP	M8	209
	C	299
PARTRIDGE	C	413
PARTS	UDH	21
	UDH	32
	HS	20
	AM	1180
	ECG1	27
	PCG2	4
	PUO2	1
	ETG	11
	PUO5	9
	AA	808
	AA	836
	AA	1008
	PPC	34
	MD	176
	D	43
	SAA	531
	SAA	633
	EK	7
	RL	141
	RL	180
	RL	315
	RL	334
	PD	32
	L4	69
	L4	250
	L4	253
	TA	332
	TA	337
	HAP	95
	HAP	1375
	HAP	1461
	PTS	43
	EL	12
	EL	164
	OD	52
	OD	53
	J1	57
	J3	283
	J6	103
	J6	277
	J6	351
	J6	412
	J6	861
	P4	10
	P4	94
	P6	111
	M1	41
	M1	62
	M1	248
	M1	546
	M9	198
	VCS	20
PARTS	GK	71
	GK	168
	VP6	108
	AE2	51
	AE2	498
	AE3	511
	AE3	545
	AE5	366
	AE5	758
	AE6	899
	AE6	993
	AE7	104
	AE7	105
	AE7	198
	AE7	525
	AE8	569
	AE9	12
	AE11	479
	OAL	529
	OAL	667
	DO	165
	KT2	197
	KT3	711
	KT3	745
	KT3	1042
	B	527
	C	91
	TH	109
	M15	526
	CI	31
	CI	149
	CI	231
	CI	499
	CI	617
	ESK	13
	PMK	5
	EMKG	5
PARTY	SAA	365
	EDG	7
	LC	21
	AA	285
	ELB	34
	L4	218
	VP6	32
	AE2	460
	AE9	601
	AE11	343
	KT2	417
	FL	431
PARTY-COLORED	L4	148
	G4	482
	AE4	763
	AE7	265
	KT1	195
	BP	91
PASCHAL	AA	576
PASIMOND	CI	353
	CI	383
	CI	250
	CI	298
	CI	421
	CI	431
	CI	445
	CI	511
	CI	516
	CI	597
PASIPHAE	AE6	604
PASQUINS	HH	2
PASS	PRL	2
	AM	209
	AM	1073
	PMM	5
	ET	8
	PA	2
	ECG2	16
	PNH	33
	ESF	3
	HP	82
	AA	246
	AA	408
	AA	632
	ELB	19
	MD	146
	SAA	442
	SAA	528
	PD	33
	ER	78
	L3	166
	T27	12
	H3	33
	HAP	188
	HAP	701
	HAP	1018
	HAP	1540
	HAP	2032
	HAP	2549

PASS	HAP	2565	PASS	ESK	2	PASSED	T 27	133
	BR	272	PASSAGE	AM	240		TA	127
	PDS	19		AM	316		PAA	25
	EL	275		AM	365		HAP	29
	EL	332		AM	449		HAP	100
	ODA	3		AM	624		HAP	516
	J 6	250		AM	985		HAP	561
	J 6	611		CM	77		HAP	1182
	J 6	782		D	15		EL	32
	P 1	118		SAA	163		EL	282
	P 5	155		L 3	181		EL	307
	P 6	26		T 23	95		EL	312
	M 1	70		H 3	13		J 10	242
	M 1	90		TA	281		J 10	297
	M 1	537		HAP	1754		J 10	527
	M 1	760		HAP	1796		M 9	57
	M 1	944		J 3	427		H I	24
	M 13	126		J 6	133		H I	28
	M 13	230		J 10	245		G 3	82
	H I	100		J 10	276		G 4	696
	GK	86		M 1	391		AE 1	615
	GK	101		M 1	998		AE 2	430
	VP 2	20		G 1	16		AE 2	1075
	G 1	239		G 3	219		AE 2	1081
	G 1	665		G 4	36		AE 3	456
	G 2	148		G 4	346		AE 3	926
	G 2	645		AE 1	102		AE 4	378
	G 3	124		AE 1	572		AE 4	801
	G 3	415		AE 1	650		AE 4	927
	G 3	583		AE 2	153		AE 5	121
	G 4	815		AE 2	162		AE 5	222
	AE 1	333		AE 2	652		AE 5	284
	AE 1	957		AE 2	839		AE 6	372
	AE 1	994		AE 2	917		AE 6	575
	AE 2	248		AE 2	1023		AE 6	691
	AE 2	613		AE 3	158		AE 6	861
	AE 2	625		AE 3	332		AE 6	926
	AE 2	795		AE 3	530		AE 6	935
	AE 2	1034		AE 3	559		AE 6	938
	AE 3	172		AE 3	661		AE 6	1239
	AE 3	174		AE 3	693		AE 8	410
	AE 3	497		AE 3	906		AE 9	1
	AE 3	761		AE 3	911		AE 9	167
	AE 3	904		AE 4	32		AE 9	420
	AE 3	916		AE 4	809		AE 9	501
	AE 3	922		AE 5	1006		AE 9	524
	AE 5	115		AE 5	1043		AE 10	677
	AE 5	995		AE 6	400		AE 10	828
	AE 6	205		AE 6	432		AE 10	928
	AE 6	720		AE 6	503		AE 10	941
	AE 6	751		AE 6	523		AE 10	1115
	AE 6	796		AE 6	532		AE 11	373
	AE 6	916		AE 6	547		AE 12	556
	AE 6	1026		AE 8	77		AE 12	989
	AE 6	1238		AE 9	65		MFL	30
	AE 8	127		AE 9	76		KT 1	356
	AE 9	210		AE 9	252		KT 1	589
	AE 9	933		AE 9	316		KT 2	378
	AE 9	1059		AE 9	433		KT 3	102
	AE 10	86		AE 9	922		KT 3	1008
	AE 10	596		AE 9	929		B	296
	AE 11	804		AE 9	947		CAM	318
	AE 11	887		AE 10	425		H I F	158
	AE 11	1301		AE 10	483		C	19
	AE 12	799		AE 10	523		C	486
	AE 12	1078		AE 10	529		TH	30
	AE 12	1324		AE 11	229		TH	173
	OAL	151		AE 11	781		TH	348
	DO	119		AE 11	1206		FL	36
	KT 1	14		AE 12	412		FL	88
	KT 1	168		OAL	409		FL	108
	KT 1	472		OAL	499		FL	136
	KT 2	196		KT 1	272		FL	372
	KT 3	111		TJD	36		FL	428
	KT 3	1004		M 8	201		FL	566
	KT 3	1037		B	107		M 12	127
	KT 3	1052		C	250		M 12	272
	B	192		C	347		M 12	517
	H I F	213		M 15	651		AU	333
	C	285		C I	597		AU	400
	C	564	PASSAGES	J 3	384		C I	283
	M 11	373		G 2	330	PASSENGER	RH	92
	FL	21		AE 9	515		T 18	74
	FL	68	PASSED	HS	49		J 10	29
	FL	157		AR	283		AE 10	1141
	FL	392		VHH	18	PASSENGERS	PFD	1
	M 12	717		AM	130		DA	184
	M 12	727		AM	229		MD	244
	M 12	778		AM	405		T 23	87
	AU	524		AM	727		AE 6	560
	AU	525		MD	264		M 15	450
	WB	17		D	16	PASSES	AA	453
	WB	339		SAA	554		MD	279
	M 15	225		SAA	1057		P 1	234
	PTP	13		L 3	133		PKA	3
	ETP	27		T 23	100			

Word	Code	Num
PASSES	AE4	278
	AE7	1105
	AE11	707
	KT1	341
PASSING	J3	442
	LC	65
	AM	202
	AM	510
	AM	511
	PMQw	1
	SCD2	16
	PC2	13
	EK	44
	T23	67
	H9	21
	J10	283
	VP6	109
	G1	323
	G3	34
	G4	679
	AE1	710
	AE6	955
	AE6	1179
	OAE2	18
	KT3	486
	KT3	532
	KT3	695
	HIF	183
	C	67
	C	71
	TH	112
	M11	289
	WB	168
PASSION	AM	111
	AM	433
	AM	495
	SEL1	15
	SEL3	17
	SEL4	6
	ECG1	39
	SM1	4
	PAZ	9
	ETC	1
	SSF	17
	AA	903
	L3	198
	FS3	15
	SSC	16
	SSC	24
	SSC	40
	SKA5	7
	SKA6	7
	EL	185
	J6	99
	M9	91
	M9	111
	M9	121
	M9	149
	M13	11
	M13	186
	HI	36
	ELT	30
	VP2	23
	VP6	83
	AE4	6
	AE4	312
	AE4	918
	AE12	974
	OAL	314
	OAL	318
	OAL	699
	MFL	33
	KT1	315
	KT1	321
	KT2	6
	KT2	334
	KT2	349
	B	71
	B	401
	CAM	251
	CI	238
	EWR	13
PASSIONS	EMQw	24
	PUO1	26
	EAZ	7
	ML	33
	HP	189
	SAA	585
	L4	125
	TA	136
	HAP	1681
	PSH	35
	J1	131
	J10	541
	P3	234
	P5	187
PASSIONS	AE2	92
	AE5	8
	B	476
	HIF	373
PASSIVE	AM	564
	HAP	1428
	HAP	1959
	HAP	2355
	HAP	2555
	AE2	471
	C	73
	CI	424
PASSIVELY	HAP	2242
PASSPORT	ODA	75
	ODA	76
PAST	HS	3
	HS	77
	AR	280
	SIE	1
	AM	351
	SMA	72
	AM	524
	AM	1161
	EMM	16
	PEL	5
	ECG1	2
	SCD1	10
	EUO2	13
	PAL	37
	ETC	13
	D	25
	SAA	314
	SAA	861
	SAA	867
	SAA	1101
	RL	180
	L3	32
	L3	175
	L3	178
	L4	224
	T23	58
	H29	71
	FS2	14
	TA	80
	TA	270
	MN	3
	HAP	927
	HAP	1157
	HAP	1329
	HAP	2187
	BR	267
	STS3	18
	PSH	42
	SSH	6
	J1	255
	J6	486
	P5	43
	P5	82
	M9	134
	MC	2
	VP10	47
	G1	675
	G3	210
	AE1	278
	AE1	284
	AE1	293
	AE1	600
	AE1	912
	AE2	993
	AE2	1060
	AE3	357
	AE3	799
	AE4	766
	AE6	488
	AE6	707
	AE6	969
	AE6	1013
	AE6	1018
	AE7	55
	AE7	311
	AE8	213
	AE9	98
	AE11	432
	AE11	1197
	OAL	128
	DO	91
	DO	105
	DO	111
	KT1	266
	KT2	57
	KT3	119
	KT3	773
	KT3	1111
	KT3	1131
	M8	318
	B	381
PAST	B	431
	BP	180
	CAM	381
	HIF	103
	HIF	357
	HIF	627
	C	677
	TH	384
	M11	218
	M11	444
	FL	609
	AU	263
	M15	197
	CI	254
	SMP	46
	SMP	72
	ERL	9
	ESK	24
	EMKG	43
PASTE	M1	105
	AE2	750
	B	503
PASTED	AE9	1099
PASTERNS	G3	121
	WB	52
PASTIME	PW	9
PASTIMES	P1	21
PASTOR	HAP	288
	VP6	98
	G3	485
	AE10	573
PASTORAL	BR	254
	VP6	9
PASTORS	HAP	882
	HAP	2128
PASTURAGE	G2	317
PASTURE	AM	60
	M1	918
	VP3	154
	G1	683
	G2	304
	G3	592
	G3	816
	AE8	280
PASTURES	AT	4
	T27	58
	HAP	389
	M1	813
	VP1	102
	VP9	29
	G3	2
	G3	258
	AE7	749
	AE7	967
	OAL	338
	TJD	62
	M8	20
PATAREIAN	M1	694
PATCH	AA	802
	KT3	769
PATCHED	PCG1	39
PATCHES	J3	254
PATE	P3	10
PATENT	HAP	496
PATERNAL	SMA	96
	CM	140
	AA	961
	H2	9
	TA	365
	HAP	1109
	BR	37
	M1	736
	VP1	102
	VP4	21
	G4	505
	AE1	909
	AE5	107
PATH	RL	224
	J1	27
	J1	79
	J10	558
	G3	449
	G4	814
	AE1	555
	AE1	569
	AE2	946
	AE6	185
	AE6	526
	AE6	862
	AE6	917
	AE8	677
	AE10	522
	DO	40
	B	140
	FL	55
	FL	59

PATHLESS	AM	798	PATROCLUS	HIF	428	PAUSES		B	176
	VP6	77		HIF	470	PAUSIA		G2	125
PATHS	AM	648		HIF	482	PAUSING		AE7	116
	SAA	701		AU	423			AE11	125
	SAA	799	PATROCLUS'	AM	253			B	640
	RL	187	PATRON	AM	788	PAVED		AM	1172
	T18	66		AM	1045			AE3	811
	HAP	383		TA	387	PAVEMENT		T23	108
	HAP	2451		HAP	2376			M1	507
	AE6	45		HAP	2473			AE3	822
	AE6	726		HAP	2520			AE7	529
	AE6	1102		BR	148			AE8	38
	AE9	315		J1	194			AE8	260
	AE9	520		VP3	133			BP	161
	AE11	365		G1	33			M15	474
PATIENCE	SMA	92		AE3	361			CI	583
	PEL	27		AE5	390	PAVEMENTS		KT3	448
	PR	18		AE5	391			KT3	942
	AA	935		AE9	899	PAVILION		TH	257
	MD	160		AE11	1153	PAVILIONS		AE9	421
	SAA	169		AE12	596	PAVING		KT3	1062
	SAA	725		AE12	597	PAW		AM	387
	SAA	1111		KT2	308			AE9	459
	RL	163		KT3	561			AE12	783
	TA	109		M8	114	PAWED		KT3	457
	HAP	1933		HIF	526	PAWN		VP3	54
	HAP	2133		C	680			KT2	165
	PP	48	PATRONAGE	EUO2	15	PAWNED		AA	406
	J16	65	PATRONESS	AE11	729			J6	472
	P2	45		AU	528	PAWNS		J10	497
	P5	130	PATRON'S	AA	859			VP8	132
	M13	97		SAA	984	PAWS		AA	450
	G2	65		HAP	533			HAP	1290
	AE1	513		HAP	1228			HAP	1564
	AE5	929		HAP	1252			PDS	10
	AE8	69		HAP	1361			G3	133
	AE8	641		HAP	2393			G3	749
	AE9	852		HAP	2497			AE4	192
	AE10	1153		J3	77			AE5	459
	AE12	40		J3	182			AE8	733
	KT1	28		J3	207			AE9	71
	KT1	243		J10	506			AE9	1075
	M8	349		MC	49			AE10	1023
	B	286		AE2	118			KT3	633
	C	7		KT2	421			M15	149
	WB	480		KT3	324	PAY		HS	108
	GP	44	PATRONS	J3	132			AR	138
	GP	91		J3	306			AR	146
PATIENT	AR	171		OAL	97			AR	319
	AA	1005	PATTERING	AE9	910			AM	415
	OE	49	PATTERN	PAL	14			PMQ	39
	AT	14		EL	175			EWGR	39
	L2	40		KT2	311			EEL	35
	ODA	57		TJD	16			PAR	19
	J3	134		M10	10			A	14
	P3	123	PATTERNS	EMW	15			ML	4
	P4	87		GP	81			EMK	26
	M1	196	PAUL	HAP	916			POE	34
	G2	666		HAP	1513			EOE	25
	G3	755	PAUL'S	AM	1097			PLB	27
	AE7	681		GP	69			SAA	826
	AE9	682	PAUNCH	SAA	469			PDG	36
	AE9	827		HAP	1462			EDGA	14
	AE12	1157		J1	47			RL	51
	MFL	36		J1	205			RL	103
	M15	170		P1	108			TA	423
PATIENT'S	G3	763		P6	176			GE	61
PATIENTS	J10	350		M12	459			HAP	144
PATRIARCH	PUF	3		M12	592			HAP	1471
	SAA	384	PAUNCHES	ECD	16			HAP	1530
	KT3	1058		HAP	374			HAP	2213
	C	383		AE3	283			BR	303
PATRIARCH'S	BR	42	PAUPERIS	HAP	2055			BR	316
PATRICIAN	J1	163	PAUSE	L3	25			PDS	46
	J6	116		L3	38			PP	18
	P1	118		L3	47			PP	35
PATRIMONIAL	PSF	27		L3	120			PMS	21
	HAP	1856		L4	85			SKA5	13
	M1	373		AE3	414			OD	41
PATRIMONIES	AM	502		AE4	627			SSH	6
	J1	137		DO	92			J1	58
PATRIMONY	G3	534	PAUSED	MF	144			J3	94
PATRIOT	AA	968		AA	347			J3	226
	AA	973		HAP	1555			J3	310
	SAA	334		VP10	46			J6	174
	G2	730		AE3	782			J6	673
	TJD	171		AE4	480			J6	684
	TJD	195		AE4	933			J16	64
PATRIOT'S	AA	179		AE6	1178			P1	213
	AA	965		AE9	332			P4	65
PATRIOTS	AA	497		KT2	328			M1	782
	SAA	749		B	276			M9	201
	AE6	895		M11	458			PLT	16
	TJD	184		AU	200			GK	156
PATRIOTS'	SAA	751	PAUSES	ER	17			VP5	117
PATROCLUS	OAL	848		AE12	1325			VP5	123

Word	Ref	Num
PAY	VP6	40
	G1	461
	G1	586
	G3	129
	AE3	360
	AE3	556
	AE4	77
	AE4	915
	AE5	785
	AE6	229
	AE6	307
	AE6	320
	AE6	734
	AE6	934
	AE7	827
	AE8	147
	AE8	80
	AE8	402
	AE8	714
	AE8	797
	AE8	883
	AE9	270
	AE9	566
	AE10	734
	AE12	1218
	OAL	154
	OAL	494
	DO	127
	KT1	376
	KT1	380
	KT2	43
	KT2	278
	KT2	369
	KT3	680
	M8	330
	M8	393
	B	596
	B	664
	B	670
	M10	58
	HIF	319
	FL	269
	FL	570
	AU	305
	WB	21
	WB	242
	WB	244
	PTP	6
	EWR	30
PAYING	AR	319
	M8	296
PAYMENT	ELB	22
	SAA	316
	ELT	25
	EHC	31
PAYS	RH	93
	SAA	322
	AK	167
	GE	50
	J3	26
	J3	98
	J10	383
	G2	768
	AE4	310
	AE10	876
	KT3	330
	M8	243
	M10	91
	M15	63
PEACE	HS	61
	HS	81
	AR	1
	AR	12
	AR	15
	AR	139
	AR	313
	RH	66
	SMA	57
	SMA	136
	SMA	122
	LC	107
	LC	105
	LC	118
	AM	21
	AM	23
	PM	6
	EUO2	12
	E	24
	E	25
	DA	52
	DA	174
	PUF	6
	AA	25
	AA	752
	MD	116
	MD	230
PEACE	MF	7
	MF	117
	SAA	145
	SAA	269
	SAA	589
	SAA	800
	SAA	1100
	SAA	1139
	EDGA	5
	RL	94
	RL	448
	L1	42
	L1	57
	H9	18
	H2	56
	TA	230
	TA	289
	TA	290
	TA	291
	TA	302
	TA	483
	HAP	1040
	HAP	1315
	HAP	1672
	HAP	1968
	HAP	2011
	HAP	2023
	HAP	2053
	HAP	2060
	HAP	2560
	HAP	2590
	PDS	34
	PTS	36
	PMS	35
	EL	16
	J1	172
	J6	406
	J10	9
	J10	558
	J16	30
	P6	112
	VCS	27
	HI	163
	VP4	20
	G2	240
	G2	593
	G2	714
	G3	153
	G3	345
	G3	781
	G4	812
	AE1	225
	AE1	397
	AE1	417
	AE1	466
	AE1	1029
	AE3	342
	AE3	590
	AE3	714
	AE4	140
	AE4	762
	AE4	889
	AE5	168
	AE5	343
	AE5	616
	AE5	802
	AE5	890
	AE6	234
	AE6	1114
	AE6	1175
	AE7	144
	AE7	209
	AE7	322
	AE7	362
	AE7	364
	AE7	394
	AE7	401
	AE7	437
	AE7	464
	AE7	474
	AE7	621
	AE7	648
	AE7	653
	AE7	747
	AE7	758
	AE7	805
	AE7	824
	AE7	854
	AE8	57
	AE8	151
	AE8	159
	AE8	431
	AE8	757
	AE8	848
	AE9	370
	AE10	12
PEACE	AE10	23
	AE10	123
	AE10	1228
	AE11	145
	AE11	178
	AE11	194
	AE11	354
	AE11	387
	AE11	449
	AE11	503
	AE11	541
	AE11	553
	AE11	555
	AE11	563
	AE11	640
	AE11	671
	AE11	699
	AE11	973
	AE12	63
	AE12	172
	AE12	191
	AE12	279
	AE12	289
	AE12	297
	AE12	316
	AE12	423
	AE12	435
	AE12	474
	AE12	721
	AE12	839
	AE12	854
	AE12	857
	AE12	919
	AE12	1004
	AE12	1193
	AE12	1222
	OAL	153
	MG	14
	DO	78
	KT1	459
	KT1	608
	KT2	405
	KT2	418
	KT3	235
	KT3	1027
	TJD	3
	TJD	15
	TJD	141
	TJD	142
	TJD	143
	TJD	155
	TJD	159
	TJD	170
	TJD	181
	TJD	184
	CAM	51
	HIF	150
	HIF	339
	HIF	609
	C	805
	C	806
	M11	277
	M11	310
	M12	256
	M12	492
	M12	760
	WB	519
	M15	142
	M15	716
	CI	38
	CI	305
	CI	402
	CI	636
	SMP	52
	SMP	53
	SMP	57
	ESK	11
	AS	61
PEACEFUL	HS	145
	LC	104
	AM	47
	E	21
	AA	70
	AA	321
	AA	991
	MF	206
	ER	71
	L3	109
	TA	346
	TA	465
	HAP	1177
	HAP	1277
	HAP	1387
	HAP	2066
	J3	100
	P5	20

Word	Ref	No.
PEACEFUL	M1	298
	M1	451
	VP5	96
	G1	191
	G1	198
	G1	681
	G2	429
	G2	577
	G2	660
	G2	787
	G4	815
	AE4	266
	AE4	546
	AE4	881
	AE6	500
	AE6	928
	AE6	1107
	AE7	65
	AE7	76
	AE7	203
	AE7	481
	AE7	861
	AE7	1034
	AE7	1047
	AE8	120
	AE8	169
	AE9	458
	AE10	61
	AE12	191
	AE12	245
	AE12	752
	M15	6
	M15	142
	CI	575
PEACHES	PAL	38
	VP2	72
PEACHING	EMQ	5
PEACOCK	J1	215
	P6	24
	M13	90
	OAL	708
PEACOCK'S	M1	1003
PEAKING	EC	15
PEAL	AE2	941
	AF	126
PEALS	AA	1027
	HAP	1613
	M1	365
	G1	655
	G2	790
	G4	713
	AE1	131
	AE1	1047
	AE1	1048
	AE2	397
	AE3	261
	AE5	440
	AE5	749
	AE8	696
	AE8	788
	AE9	621
	AE10	258
	AE10	1041
PEAR	H2	30
	G4	214
PEARL	L4	106
PEARLS	PAL	26
	EUF	26
	ODA	2
	VP10	20
	KT3	68
	KT3	977
	M10	39
	M10	46
	FL	164
	FL	237
PEARLY	SKA2	11
	EL	207
	G1	387
	G2	279
	G3	505
	AE3	769
	AE8	780
PEARS	VP1	100
	G2	43
	G2	99
	G2	127
	OAL	855
PEASANT	EUO	1
	G1	137
	G1	191
	G1	286
	G1	681
	G2	738
	AE2	510
PEASANT'S	G1	72
PEASANT'S	G1	147
	G2	556
	AE2	410
PEASANTS	M1	569
	G2	329
	G2	358
	G3	612
	KT3	904
	KT3	1062
	M12	640
PEBBLE	H2	39
PEBBLES	VP5	132
	M11	284
PECCADILLOS	ETP	27
PECCANT	J10	490
	C	166
PECK	HAP	2364
PECKED	C	100
PECKERS'	G4	18
PECKING	C	84
	FL	108
PECULIAR	AR	287
	RH	100
	HP	93
	AA	559
	AA	674
	SAA	14
	TA	432
	HH	20
	HAP	827
	J3	152
	P4	13
	G1	33
	G2	6
	AE7	617
	AE9	136
	AE11	470
	KT2	625
	BP	198
	CI	144
PEDAGOGUE	J10	355
PEDANT	J3	138
	J6	566
	J10	181
	PTP	49
PEDANTIC	J1	20
PEDANTS	J10	467
PEDESTAL	T23	105
PEDESTALS	J1	16
	G2	647
PEDIGREE	PTW	18
	AA	101
	T23	37
	HAP	174
	HAP	1447
	HAP	2065
	P3	48
	P4	41
	P6	7
	P6	137
	M1	840
	M1	1052
	AU	231
PEDIGREES	T27	83
PEDIUS	P1	165
PEEL	HIF	343
PEELED	P4	73
PEEP	JH	14
	EMM	8
	EUF	2
	EDGA	16
	HH	6
	HAP	2587
	J1	189
	G4	271
	M11	223
	AM	1101
PEEPED	ETG	6
PEEPING	HAP	1844
PEEPS	AM	1135
	PM	22
	M1	463
	G3	550
PEER	SAA	81
	SAA	297
	ER	60
	AE10	822
	C	39
	C	609
	C	631
PEERAGE	MD	312
	SAA	295
	HAP	2077
PEERLESS	AK	138
PEERS	AA	876
	HAP	2023
PEERS	HAP	2176
	AE3	83
	AE4	188
	AE9	296
	AF	6
	FL	543
	M15	342
	PMQ	25
	P3	20
	HIF	750
PEEVISH	RH	38
PEGASUS	PA	24
	PDS	44
PELAGIUS	RL	346
PELAGON	M8	127
PELEUS	J10	400
	M12	266
	M12	492
	M12	519
	AU	251
PELEUS'	HIF	1
PELF	AA	599
	H2	100
	PMS	17
	P5	252
	WB	319
PELIAS	AE2	592
PELIDES	AE2	354
	HIF	108
	HIF	391
	HIF	704
	M12	233
	M12	782
	AU	267
	AU	287
	AU	437
PELIDES'	AE6	249
	M12	112
PELION	M12	678
PELLETS	P3	119
PELLMELL	POE	23
PELOPS'	G3	10
PELORUS	AE3	525
PELORUS'	AE3	902
PELT	PO	22
PELTED	VP3	97
PELTS	G3	672
PEN	RH	49
	RH	100
	DC	41
	PT	14
	ET	16
	PUO1	30
	PNH	37
	ETC	22
	PCB	1
	CM	3
	HP	140
	HP	257
	DA	197
	EUF	36
	MF	91
	MF	143
	MF	202
	SAA	386
	SAA	481
	SAA	483
	ER	29
	TA	248
	MN	13
	J1	251
	P3	19
	P3	30
	GK	52
	VP6	7
	VP10	54
	OAL	499
	OAL	592
	PTP	20
	EWR	19
PENAL	SAA	216
	HAP	2123
PENALTY	EK	9
PENANCE	PAL	36
	HAP	364
	EL	310
	AE6	452
	AE6	734
	AE6	1014
PENANCES	AE6	1002
PENCE	PLB	10
	PDG	28
	PD	40
PENCIL	PNH	37
	TA	248
	AK	106

PENCIL	GK	9		PEOPLE	EWG	6		PEOPLE	KT3	419
	GK	52			VHH	18			KT3	492
	GK	104			AM	47			KT3	665
	GK	127			AM	204			KT3	1122
	GK	166			AM	299			TJD	136
	GK	176			AM	1141			TJD	181
	KT2	56			PT	26			B	553
	KT2	656			ESF	18			HIF	343
PENCILS	AR	157			DA	17			HIF	398
PENDANTS	M10	46			PUF	12			C	652
PENDULUM	P4	119			AA	47			M12	16
PENEIAN	KT2	631			AA	88			M12	24
PENELEUS	AE2	576			AA	215			WB	161
PENELOPE	OAL	545			AA	245			M15	628
	DO	158			AA	277			M15	714
PENETRABLE	M12	787			AA	341			GP	85
PENETRATE	EL	252			AA	271			CI	66
	KT1	568			AA	329			CI	615
	M15	83			AA	383		PEOPLED	AK	126
PENETRATES	VP8	97			AA	387			HAP	1297
PENETRATING	HAP	95			AA	409			HI	10
	M12	454			AA	415			AE2	7
PENEUS	M1	609			AA	459		PEOPLE'S	CI	37
	M1	771			AA	759			SMA	61
PENEUS'	G4	453			AA	795			AM	1050
PENITENCE	AR	255			AA	928			CM	12
	RL	53			MD	87			AA	183
	RL	88			MF	144			AA	206
	TJD	20			RL	260			AA	238
	CAM	327			AK	46			AA	444
PENITENT	PSF	37			HAP	1883			AA	726.
	KT2	347			BR	103			AA	739
	HIF	609			EJG	3			AA	743
	GP	75			PSH	13			AA	776
PENITENTS	CAM	336			J1	240			AA	781
PENMEN	HAP	874			J10	121			AA	814
PENNED	RH	41			J10	450			AA	967
PENNON	KT1	115			P1	112			AA	974
PENNSYLVANIA'S	PK	4			P3	53			MD	256
PENNY	PLB	19			P4	14			D	38
	SAA	491			P4	110			SAA	168
	PK	2			P6	119			SAA	664
	EH	26			M1	95			SAA	740
	P5	202			M1	287			SAA	768
	WB	23			M1	339			SAA	864
PENNY'S	P6	45			M1	492			HAP	1940
PENNYWORTH	PLG	9			M1	513			HAP	2183
	OAL	484			HI	119			P1	127
	EH	26			HI	161			G2	706
	J10	300			G4	7			AE2	117
PENNYWORTHS	ML	7			G4	36			AE2	1041
	POE	33			G4	163			AE4	274
PENS	EDGA	20			G4	386			AE8	107
	H2	69			G4	411			AE8	641
	KT1	473			G4	650			AE10	1307
PENSION	SAA	92			G4	812			AE11	618
	TA	382			AE1	21			KT3	565
	PDS	4			AE1	28			TJD	184
	ETS	10			AE1	377			B	22
PENSIONED	SAA	46			AE1	389			B	317
PENSIONERS	AA	398			AE1	416			HIF	175
	SAA	690			AE1	466			HIF	478
PENSION-					AE1	623			GP	121
PARLIAMENT	ELB	25			AE1	712			ESK	27
PENSION-PURSE	SAA	321			AE1	808		PEOPLES	D	33
PENSIVE	AM	38			AE2	165			TJD	83
	PM	22			AE3	21		PEPPER	P5	71
	HAP	25			AE3	347			P5	199
	AE3	868			AE3	584			P6	48
	AE10	1193			AE4	156			P6	89
	AE12	585			AE4	896			C	24
	KT1	379			AE5	140		PERCEIVE	PPC	31
	HIF	458			AE5	470			SAA	909
	TH	76			AE5	656			HAP	91
PENT	AR	59			AE5	671			AU	462
	EUF	14			AE5	988		PERCEIVED	HP	75
	L4	123			AE6	438			G4	663
	BR	241			AE6	848			AE12	628
	EL	244			AE6	965			BP	135
	G4	435			AE6	1233		PERCEIVES	SAA	121
	G4	520			AE7	61			SAA	855
	AE3	70			AE7	69			AE4	425
	AE3	767			AE7	425		PERCEIVEST	M15	296
	AE5	374			AE7	439		PERCEIVING	L3	255
	AE8	323			AE8	510			SSH	12
	AE9	986			AE8	629		PERCH	C	422
	AE10	401			AE8	661		PERCHED	AE6	296
	KT1	383			AE8	666			FL	319
	B	62			AE10	136			FL	448
	AU	71			AE10	1218			EMKG	14
	M15	331			AE11	213		PERCHING	C	93
	M15	438			AE11	443		PEREGRINE	PWG	37
PENTHEUS	AE4	681			AE12	833		PERFECT	HS	60
PENTHISILEA	AE1	688			AE12	1209			DC	42
	AE11	979			OAL	526			AM	562
PENTHOUSE	AE9	681			MM	20			PT	36
PENURY	TA	500								

Word	Ref	No.	Word	Ref	No.	Word	Ref	No.
PERFECT	POE	16	PERFORMED	HIF	220	PERHAPS	C	183
	HP	141		HIF	536		M12	266
	AA	839		M11	376		WB	235
	MF	15		FL	331		WB	338
	RL	352		M12	228		M15	198
	EL	308		AU	373		CI	235
	ESH	10		AU	388		CI	239
	SLT1	13		AU	580		ETP	1
	GK	71		WB	248	PERICLES	PC10	16
	AE3	232		GP	66		P4	5
	AE3	237		CI	522	PERICLYMENOS	M12	732
	AE4	162	PERFORMS	G4	791	PERIDIA	AE12	748
	KT2	311		AE1	415	PERIL	SAA	171
	KT3	1046		AE12	589		AE10	1121
	HIF	438	PERFUME	PCB	37		AE11	373
PERFECTION	SMA	88		H29	7		KT1	380
	SAA	205		EL	302		C	173
	SAA	638	PERFUMED	AM	101		WB	107
	ER	53		AE4	317		WB	251
	TA	437	PERFUMES	LC	74		WB	284
	PTS	33		EL	154	PERILLUS	OAL	737
	EL	232		FL	147	PERILS	AE6	935
	EL	272		M15	305		AE7	311
	J6	266	PERGAMUS	AE3	183		AE10	86
	J6	488		AE3	434		AE10	1225
	J6	858		AE10	89		AE11	233
	KT3	1049		HIF	232		M11	246
	WB	476	PERHAPS	AM	621	PERIOD	HAP	1178
	M15	380		AM	851	PERIODS	P1	167
	M15	685		PA	45		DO	23
PERFECTIONS	PD	41		PEL	13		KT3	1063
	EL	234		EAZ	10	PERIPHANTAS	M12	600
PERFECTLY	AK	101		PC1	28	PERIPHANTES	AE5	715
PERFIDIOUS	VP8	126		HP	11	PERIPHAS	AE2	649
	G1	688		HP	251	PERISH	AM	354
	AE2	260		DA	149		DA	151
	AE4	439		DA	161		DA	152
	AE4	608		PUO3	23		SAA	142
	AE10	144		AA	384		HAP	23
PERFORM	CM	140		AA	439		SKA1	8
	CM	146		AA	468		J1	84
	L4	264		MD	228		M1	422
	T18	91		PRH	26		HI	115
	TA	112		SAA	156		G3	566
	LS	14		AT	87		AE5	1067
	P1	255		L4	116		AE9	275
	P3	133		L4	119		AE10	872
	P4	121		FS2	9		AE12	1199
	VP5	76		TA	276		KT1	256
	VP5	113		HH	4		KT3	1083
	VP8	41		HAP	192		TJD	86
	AE5	23		HAP	1296		M8	319
	AE5	73		HAP	1423		M8	320
	AE5	558		HAP	1711		BP	142
	AE6	258		HAP	1807		HIF	82
	AE8	84		HAP	1943		HIF	476
	AE10	502		HAP	1986		WB	412
	AE11	322		HAP	2075	PERISHABLE	KT3	1033
	DO	28		PDS	30	PERISHED	AM	1140
	KT3	421		EL	7		RL	422
	TJD	204		EL	79		M1	371
PERFORMANCE	HAP	2215		OD	39		M1	433
	MM	32		EH	30		M1	492
	FL	114		J1	225		VP8	58
	WB	300		J6	39		G4	650
PERFORMED	PAZ	11		J6	114		AE2	815
	MO	10		J6	296		AE9	181
	TA	187		J16	69		M8	397
	GE	35		P1	264		M11	261
	AE1	574		P3	227		M11	362
	AE1	950		P4	9		M11	374
	AE2	296		P6	41		M11	422
	AE2	584		M1	691		M12	730
	AE3	721		M9	1		M15	633
	AE6	109		GK	30		AS	18
	AE6	336		GK	115	PERISHING	H3	12
	AE6	867		VP2	40		TA	28
	AE7	184		VP6	83	PERITHOUS	AE6	814
	AE8	408		AE1	773		OAL	851
	AE8	813		AE2	691		KT1	358
	AE11	5		AE5	302		KT1	366
	AE11	22		AE6	722		KT1	377
	AE11	372		AE11	71		KT1	392
	AE11	479		AE12	41		M8	50
	AE12	318		OAL	546		M8	179
	MM	22		OAL	550		M12	292
	KT1	103		OAL	760		M12	322
	KT3	202		OAE2	72		M12	450
	KT3	929		MM	36	PERITHOUS'	ESF	25
	B	167		KT3	200	PERIWIG	DA	69
	B	577		TJD	19	PERJURED	DA	144
	B	604		TJD	29		SSF	2
	B	700		M8	356		PR	16
	M10	17		CAM	300		PPC	24
	M10	53		HIF	149		MN	7
	CAM	256					HAP	16

Word	Src	No.	Word	Src	No.	Word	Src	No.
PERJURED	HAP	1554	PERSECUTE	HAP	2510	PERVIOUS	EL	343
	J1	68		G1	416		M8	146
	M1	1082		AE1	14	PEST	SAA	69
	VP8	26	PERSECUTED	AE12	1087		SAA	1035
	AE4	553		BP	137		J6	670
	AE4	850	PERSECUTES	HAP	240		AE5	916
	AE4	902		G2	562		AE12	1239
	AE8	717		KT1	499		M12	384
	AE8	852	PERSECUTING	HAP	287	PESTERED	J6	578
	AE12	837		HAP	1724	PESTILENCE	KT3	418
	KT1	310		HAP	1940		HIF	624
	KT2	279		HAP	1981	PESTILENTIAL	HAP	233
	KT2	339	PERSECUTION	HAP	282		G3	636
PERJURIA	PPC	19		C	737		AE3	195
PERJURIES	OAL	715	PERSEUS	OAL	59	PET	SMM2	19
	KT2	479	PERSEVERE	B	475	PETER	HAP	1513
PERJURY	J3	245		FL	571		HAP	2300
	KT2	149	PERSIA	AF	1		BR	258
PERKS	PCG2	15	PERSIAN	MF	98	PETER'S	PSF	13
PERMANENT	AE6	1205		H29	27		HAP	587
PERMISSION	HAP	523		P6	122		GP	99
	G1	363		G2	648	PETILIA	AE3	515
PERMIT	HAP	1637		AF	144	PETITION	AA	981
	BR	93		TJD	160		PLB	9
	P5	23		FL	226		FS4	13
	AE1	538		M1	75		GE	63
	AE1	776	PERSIANS				HAP	2426
	AE2	1056	PERSIST	AE2	883		J10	261
	AE5	509		HIF	145		G2	676
	AE6	376		AU	119		AE10	122
	AE7	369	PERSISTING	SAA	262		HIF	692
	AE7	621		HAP	2188		M11	250
	AE9	389	PERSISTS	M9	23	PETITIONERS	AA	986
	AE11	576		AE2	885		T23	28
	AE12	78	PERSON	EWG	13		TA	100
	OAL	165		AM	593	PETITIONS	PLB	7
	M11	373		DA	136		PLB	52
PERMITS	PRH	43		PUO3	11		EPC	17
	AE5	1071		AA	475		PDS	27
	AE10	602		AA	673		M9	11
	AE10	665		AA	687		G4	733
	OAL	561		PDG	39		AE1	713
PERMITTED	AM	1006		T23	6	PETRAEUS'	M12	445
	HAP	1608		HAP	1643	PETRARCH	ER	21
	AE2	151		HAP	1978	PETRIFIED	BR	238
	AE5	108		BR	34	PETRIFY	TA	8
	AE10	21		ESH	27		M15	472
	AE10	116		AE1	108	PETTICOAT	OAE2	54
	B	497		AE4	520		FL	344
	CI	475		AE4	855	PETTY	AR	301
PERNICIOUS	AA	929		AE8	216		AM	851
	SAA	122		KT1	609		PAL	22
	SAA	752		KT2	390		AA	709
	AE3	80		KT3	729		HAP	1062
	C	813		B	527		GK	148
PEROGATIVE	HIF	510		B	577		AU	165
PERPETRATE	AE2	191		M10	45	PEW	PLN	3
	C	498		HIF	133	PHAEACIA	AE3	376
PERPETRATED	AE8	452		HIF	452	PHAEACIAN	M13	115
PERPETRATION	P2	52		C	785	PHAEDRA	OAL	381
PERPETUAL	LC	136		C	792		OAL	851
	DA	27		M15	42	PHAEDRA'S	AE6	605
	L3	305	PERSON'S	SAA	167		OAL	576
	BR	187	PERSONS	HAP	1815	PHAEDRIA	P5	234
	EL	123		J1	185	PHAEOCOMES	M12	577
	EH	11		J1	258	PHAESTUS	M9	5
	P4	59		J3	27	PHAETON	M1	1047
	M1	5		AE1	571		AE10	273
	M1	57		FL	87	PHALARIS	AE9	1027
	M1	379	PERSPECTIVE	RH	77		OAL	737
	M1	766		EL	196	PHALEG	SAA	330
	M1	775		GK	37		SAA	340
	M1	1001		GK	39		SAA	350
	HI	60	PERSPECTIVES	AK	115	PHANAEUS	G2	140
	G1	338	PERSUADE	PC2	18	PHANTASUS	M11	337
	G2	204		AA	125	PHANTOM	AE3	407
	G2	276		AA	614		AE4	260
	G3	564		MF	62		AE10	902
	G4	540		HAP	492		AE10	913
	AE4	895		G3	271		AE10	935
	AE5	961		AE10	104	PHANTOMS	L4	17
	AE6	884		AE11	199		L4	67
	AE11	1078		KT3	326		AE6	408
	M11	273		KT3	1138	PHARAOH	EUF	9
	AU	362		HIF	353		AA	331
	M15	266		WB	363		AA	843
PERPLEX	HP	248	PERSUASIONS	J10	470		SAA	672
	PPC	3	PERSUASIVE	AU	497		SAA	717
PERPLEXED	HAP	671	PERTAINS	KT2	596		EL	71
	B	143	PERTAKE	SAA	689	PHARAOH'S	AA	281
	M11	2	PERVERSE	HAP	2342		AA	286
PERPLEXING	AE11	794		CAM	230		AA	398
PERQUISITES	EH	29		WB	140		SAA	229
	J16	56	PERVERSENESS	CAM	70		SAA	264
PERSECUTE	HAP	2148	PERVERT	KT3	206		SAA	556
	HAP	2273		C	556		SAA	1006
			PERVERTING	CI	10			

Term	Ref	No.
PHARIAN	M1	565
	M1	1009
	M9	166
PHARISEES	SAA	788
PHAROS	J6	118
	AE10	447
	M15	438
PHASIS	H2	79
	G4	524
PHEASANT	SAA	472
PHEGEUS	AE12	550
PHENEOS	M15	497
PHENEUS	AE8	222
PHERES	AE10	580
PHILEMON	BP	32
	BP	63
	BP	168
	BP	181
	BP	183
PHILEUS	M8	56
PHILIP	PSF	28
PHILIP'S	AM	790
	AF	2
PHILISTINES	HAP	574
	BR	287
PHILLIPPIC	J10	196
PHILOCTETES	AE3	516
	AU	63
	AU	484
	AU	503
PHILOMEL	DHP	6
	VP6	111
	FL	439
	KT1	199
	FL	50
PHILOSOPHERS	HAP	646
	WB	464
PHILOSOPHIC	HAP	685
	J6	576
PHILOSOPHY	HAP	1805
PHILOSTRATUS	KT1	590
	KT2	102
	KT2	282
PHILTERS	J6	795
PHLEGETHON	AE6	741
PHLEGETHON'S	AE9	122
PHLEGM	EM	4
	P2	102
	P3	199
PHLEGME	ML	42
PHLEGYAN	M11	5
PHLEGYAS	AE6	842
PHLEGYS	AE9	1030
PHOBETOR	M11	336
PHOCION	MD	96
PHOCAE	G3	808
PHOCUS'	M8	58
PHOEBE	M1	637
	M1	959
	VP8	95
	AE10	309
	AE11	805
	OAL	768
	M12	41
	M12	52
	WB	8
PHOEBEAN	AE12	584
PHOEBE'S	M1	959
	G1	385
	AE3	206
	AE4	115
	AE4	743
PHOEBUS	PIE	20
	EIE	2
	EIE	9
	EIE	22
	HAP	2113
	M1	590
	M1	604
	M1	621
	M1	622
	M1	747
	M1	765
	VP3	93
	VP3	162
	VP4	69
	VP5	12
	VP5	54
	VP5	103
	VP6	16
	VP6	47
	VP6	101
	VP7	30
	VP7	85
	VP9	18
	G4	9
PHOEBUS	AE2	582
	AE3	101
	AE3	133
	AE3	250
	AE3	328
	AE3	461
	AE3	476
	AE3	508
	AE3	552
	AE3	616
	AE6	12
	AE6	23
	AE6	58
	AE6	469
	AE7	474
	AE7	997
	AE10	439
	AE11	1154
	AE12	751
	OAL	372
	OAE1	8
	OAE1	15
	M8	114
	M8	377
	HIF	67
	HIF	104
	HIF	128
	HIF	163
	HIF	222
	HIF	608
	M12	25
	M12	794
	WB	158
	M15	284
PHOEBUS'	VP3	166
	G4	458
	AE1	797
PHOENICIAN	AE1	469
	AE6	610
PHOENICIAN'S	AE1	947
PHOENIX	UDH	80
	VHH	52
	AM	602
	TA	364
	AK	134
	AE2	38
	AE2	1036
	OAL	380
	M8	56
	M15	579
	M15	600
PHOLOE	AE5	371
PHOLON	M12	585
PHOLUS	AE12	514
	M12	422
PHORBAS	AE5	1096
	M12	439
PHORCUS	AE5	312
PHOSPHOR	AE2	1090
	KT3	120
PHRYGIA	HAP	1301
PHRYGIAN	PDS	15
	HP	58
	HP	222
	AE1	795
	AE1	527
	AE2	361
	AE2	791
	AE3	248
	AE3	626
	AE3	718
	AE4	859
	AE6	1069
	AE7	284
	AE7	404
	AE7	443
	AE7	615
	AE7	655
	AE8	509
	AE10	607
	AE10	998
	AE11	261
	AE11	617
	AE11	732
	AE11	984
	AE11	1132
	BP	15
	BP	20
	HIF	369
	AU	510
PHRYGIANS	AE9	845
	AE9	870
	AE10	358
PHRYGIANS'	AE8	154
	AE10	686
PHTHIA	HIF	254
	AU	254
PHYLACTERIES	HAP	399
PHYLLIS	SCG1	4
	SCG1	32
	SCG2	2
	SCG2	3
	SCG2	7
	SCG2	8
	SCG2	11
	SCG2	13
	SCG2	18
	SCG2	19
	SCG2	27
	SCG3	2
	SCG3	22
	SLN	1
	LS	4
	LS	5
	P1	70
	VP3	97
	VP3	119
	VP3	121
	VP3	166
	VP5	14
	VP7	20
	VP7	81
	VP7	88
	VP10	55
	VP10	57
	VP10	61
	STP	14
	STP	15
	STP	20
PHYLLIS'	ETC	20
PHYLLODOCE	G4	478
PHYSIC	UDH	86
	EAZ	12
	AA	810
	PAA	11
	HAP	222
	P5	146
	M1	707
	G3	817
	KT3	768
	KT3	774
	TJD	116
PHYSICIAN	EDG	30
	J3	139
	P3	168
	P3	184
	P3	196
	M1	703
	M1	707
	AE12	587
	C	402
PHYSICIAN'S	SEL4	18
PHYSICIANS	HAP	908
	TJD	73
	TJD	101
PICK	AM	581
	PUO3	33
	SAA	359
	P3	20
PICKED	SCD1	4
	OAL	584
PICKING	P3	231
PICKING-WORK	SAA	418
PICKLE	PCD	10
	PR	29
PICKLED	BP	93
PICTS	POE	18
PICTURE	RH	78
	AM	1014
	SAA	372
	EL	365
	J10	253
	GK	36
	AE1	652
	MFL	12
	TJD	197
PICTURES	PCD	27
	PTW	29
	J6	459
	GK	7
	GK	11
	GK	72
	AE1	169
	LMC	3
PICUS	AE7	72
	AE7	229
	AE7	256
PIE	PMM	12
	PPS	13
	P6	172
	AE7	265

PIEBALD	AE9	54	PIERCED	AE12	556	PILE	AE6	259
PIECE	RH	29		AE12	608		AE6	308
	PAR	9		AE12	773		AE6	319
	POE	21		AE12	789		AE6	747
	EOE	3		AE12	1342		AE6	1207
	EMP	9		KT1	150		AE7	232
	EPF	15		KT1	255		AE7	1073
	MD	25		KT2	111		AE9	965
	TA	329		KT3	626		KT3	950
	AK	119		C	244		KT3	953
	HAP	1813		M12	115		KT3	990
	HAP	2339		M12	161		M8	293
	PMS	8		M12	384		M12	693
	PKA	11		M12	520		M12	814
	EL	62		M12	561		M15	590
	EL	164		M12	592		M15	598
	EL	298		CI	118	PILED	M1	194
	J3	184	PIERCES	L4	253		G1	375
	J6	472		P1	45		AE5	66
	J10	443	PIERCING	AA	882		M15	470
	P1	123		L4	184	PILES	RL	82
	P5	155		H29	4		HAP	733
	GK	38		AE4	262		M1	398
	GK	109		AE4	951		G1	664
	GK	153		AE6	266		G4	685
	C	340		AE8	201		AE7	922
	CI	59		AE9	76		AE11	203
	SMP	86		MFL	14		AE11	284
	SMP	92		HIF	529		AE11	288
	EMKG	37		TH	302		AE11	304
PIECED	AA	661		FL	272		AE11	309
PIECEMEAL	P5	80		M12	153		AE12	1248
	AE2	636	PIES	MF	101	PILGRIM	C	270
	AE3	752		PPS	18		GP	1
	AE4	861		P6	119		CI	172
PIECES	GK	18	PIETY	HS	148	PILGRIMAGE	AR	54
	J10	448		AA	419		J6	681
	M1	199		SAA	67		C	212
	M1	999		AK	153	PILGRIM'S	C	263
	AE12	1062		HAP	1142	PILGRIMS	GK	103
PIERCE	AM	952		HAP	1206		KT3	887
	DA	34		HAP	2168	PILLAGED	SAA	541
	L4	78		BR	309	PILLAGERS	KT1	139
	M1	685		J3	236	PILLAR	AA	233
	M13	105		M1	190		MF	109
	G1	134		AE2	938		AE12	145
	AE1	333		AE6	546		KT2	558
	AE7	870		AE6	685		KT3	517
	AE9	661		AE9	395		KT3	614
	AE11	869		AE12	719		KT3	651
	AE12	11		LMC	2		C	723
	AE12	152		CAM	45	PILLARED	KT3	416
	OAL	744		CAM	61	PILLARS	AM	368
	HIF	65		M15	254		AM	954
	C	627		PWR	18		AA	176
	TH	183	PIG				AA	874
	M12	787	PIGEON	AE5	669		AA	953
	CI	157		AE5	711		MC	17
	CI	161	PIGEON-HALL	HAP	2345		G3	44
	SMP	33	PIGEON-HOUSE	HAP	2328		AE2	604
	SMP	35		HAP	2418		AE6	747
PIERCED	SAA	1102	PIGEON'S	J6	709		AE7	230
	M1	700	PIGEONS	HAP	2291	PILLED	J1	72
	G3	673		HAP	2391	PILLOW	DOD	2
	G4	617		HAP	2489		KT3	777
	AE1	266		HAP	2494		M10	56
	AE2	66		HAP	2502		M11	89
	AE2	73		HAP	2515		EUF	33
	AE2	576		J3	330	PILLOWS	J6	7
	AE2	849	PIGEONS'	HAP	2193		C	400
	AE3	428		HAP	2422	PILLS	AM	139
	AE5	639		HAP	2549	PILOT	AA	159
	AE5	713		HAP	2574		SAA	844
	AE6	91	PIGMIES	PAL	28		HAP	132
	AE7	402	PIGMY	AA	157		AE1	165
	AE7	694		MD	27		AE5	18
	AE7	742		J6	648		AE5	211
	AE9	468		AE4	255		AE5	231
	AE9	555		J6	257		AE5	289
	AE9	578	PIGS	AE11	138		AE5	1087
	AE9	592	PIKES	PNH	34		AE5	1102
	AE9	787	PILE	CM	122		AE5	1112
	AE9	800		MF	69	PILOT'S	P5	148
	AE9	947		MF	88		AE5	1121
	AE10	436		AE2	40		AE5	1131
	AE10	467		AE2	41	PILOTS	AE3	605
	AE10	473		AE2	155	PILUMNUS	AE10	875
	AE10	482		AE2	202		AE12	131
	AE10	584		AE2	752	PIMP	PMS	23
	AE10	600		AE4	713		B	554
	AE10	678		AE4	727	PIMPING	OE	60
	AE10	828		AE4	871	PIMPLE	UDH	59
	AE10	1130		AE4	928	PIMPS	AA	81
	AE11	300		AE4	971		SAA	521
	AE11	951		AE4	978		J6	304
	AE12	445		AE4	984		ETP	13
				AE5	838			

Word	Ref	No.
PINARIAN	AE8	358
PINCERS	P4	93
	AE12	595
PINCH	J6	105
	J6	634
	P4	24
	AE12	1095
PINCHED	HAP	305
	J6	403
	C	11
	TH	115
	AU	72
	GP	48
PINCHING	G4	348
PINDARIC	MD	94
PINDAR'S	P6	12
	C	634
PINDUS	M1	772
	VP6	47
	VP10	15
	M11	203
PINE	M1	124
	M1	407
	M1	966
	M13	54
	VP7	34
	G2	536
	AE2	21
	AE3	866
	AE5	599
	AE7	556
	AE9	106
	AE9	692
	AE11	1155
	KT1	450
	CAM	134
	TH	129
	M12	374
	M12	482
PINED	VP1	49
	AE5	848
	AE8	639
	KT2	502
	HIF	593
	HIF	661
	C	440
	TH	351
	WB	177
PINES	AM	259
	T18	50
	VP1	55
	VP7	92
	VP7	96
	VP8	31
	VP10	21
	G2	623
	G4	170
	G4	209
	AE4	729
	AE6	264
	AE6	309
	AE9	86
	AE9	139
	TH	78
PIN-FEATHERED	P1	130
PINING	G3	335
	G3	778
	AE6	600
	WB	470
PINION	M12	746
PINIONED	AE2	1042
	AE10	474
	AE11	115
	WB	60
PINIONS	AM	432
	AA	855
	SAA	1037
	M1	928
	G4	40
	G4	264
	G4	442
	AE1	545
	AE3	320
	AE4	254
	AE4	350
	AE6	19
	AE11	212
	AE11	422
	AE11	1116
	AE12	375
	OAL	269
	OAE1	22
	M15	538
	M15	605
PINIONS'	M12	697
PINK	EAL	14
PINNACE	H29	99
PINTO	GE	20
PINY	M1	281
	AE4	364
PIOUS	UDH	71
	VHH	23
	AM	255
	AM	425
	AM	958
	AM	1090
	CM	142
	DA	108
	EPF	24
	AA	1
	AA	593
	AA	983
	SAA	51
	TA	36
	TA	71
	TA	93
	TA	178
	TA	206
	TA	304
	TA	386
	HAP	288
	HAP	1218
	HAP	1773
	HAP	2290
	BR	310
	PP	35
	EL	40
	EL	110
	EL	205
	EL	223
	EL	297
	ESH	9
	J1	175
	J6	696
	J6	850
	J10	546
	M1	269
	M1	261
	M1	496
	M9	65
	VCS	3
	VP5	31
	AE1	146
	AE1	217
	AE1	275
	AE1	317
	AE1	524
	AE1	743
	AE1	840
	AE1	860
	AE2	285
	AE2	766
	AE3	60
	AE3	235
	AE3	347
	AE3	522
	AE3	720
	AE3	775
	AE4	89
	AE4	404
	AE4	550
	AE4	632
	AE4	823
	AE4	858
	AE5	125
	AE5	899
	AE6	11
	AE6	43
	AE6	174
	AE6	229
	AE6	270
	AE6	349
	AE6	641
	AE6	934
	AE6	1125
	AE7	28
	AE7	203
	AE7	813
	AE9	284
	AE9	384
	AE9	547
	AE10	873
	AE10	1111
	AE10	1131
	AE10	1151
	AE10	1165
	AE11	3
	AE11	57
	AE11	141
	AE11	294
	AE11	308
	AE11	448
PIOUS	AE12	265
	AE12	415
	AE12	482
	AE12	581
	AE12	850
	AE12	1130
	AE12	1216
	MFL	28
	DO	165
	M8	287
	M8	322
	M8	388
	B	669
	BP	6
	BP	197
	CAM	120
	CAM	122
	CAM	240
	HIF	222
	HIF	607
	C	370
	C	484
	M11	1
	M11	245
	M12	5
	AU	298
	AU	437
	AU	468
	AU	469
	M15	6
	M15	608
	CI	350
	PMK	28
	AS	22
PIOUSLY	AM	613
	PKA	42
	EWR	14
PIPE	PO	30
	T27	21
	T27	23
	J6	432
	M1	945
	M13	59
	VP1	12
	VP1	112
	VP2	39
	VP2	43
	VP2	45
	VP3	34
	VP5	133
	VP6	98
	VP7	34
	FL	358
PIPED	M1	936
	M1	988
PIPES	AM	915
	VP3	39
	G4	385
	MG	25
	EWR	8
PIPING	T27	133
	VP5	75
PIQUE	HAP	1695
PIRATE	HS	117
	AE7	507
	AE10	1097
	AE11	617
PIRATE'S	AE11	731
PIRATES	AM	1208
	HAP	1640
	PWR	6
PIRATES'	AR	304
PISANS	AE10	260
PISA'S	G3	287
PISO	AR	70
PISS	HAP	1453
	J6	370
	J16	72
PISSED	J1	198
PISSES	J6	92
PISSEST	P1	109
PISSING	MF	47
PISSING-PLACE	P1	218
PISSPOT	J3	439
PISSPOTS	J10	97
PIT	PRL	24
	PMQ	22
	EEL	4
	PCG2	13
	PW	11
	PLN	3
	PLN	32
	PUO1	6
	PUO2	32
	PC2	20
	PAL	15

PIT	EAL	3
	EKK	13
	ETC	7
	PLG	8
	PSF	1
	PSF	40
	ETG	20
	PR	7
	PUO3	27
	PUO4	3
	PUO4	17
	ELB	24
	MF	153
	EK	5
	PAA	37
	MS	3
	MS	13
	J3	293
	ELT	20
	EHC	2
	EHC	31
	G2	312
	AE8	843
	MG	21
	M15	541
	PWR	6
	EWR	10
PIT-A-PAT	ETG	12
PITCH	AM	585
	L3	229
	PKA	7
	J6	140
	P1	114
	G1	370
	G2	338
	G2	349
	G2	614
	G3	540
	G3	687
	G4	57
	G4	237
	AE4	168
	AE6	264
	AE6	309
	AE7	666
	AE9	121
	AE9	201
	OAL	661
	HIF	660
PITCHED	HAP	575
	ODA	6
	AE8	124
	AE9	421
	AE12	1090
	KT1	136
	HIF	798
	TH	59
PITCHER	J1	249
	BP	100
PITCHERS	J3	334
PITCHES	G3	572
PITCHING	AE10	1285
	AE12	442
	KT3	703
PITCHY	AE3	748
	AE4	170
	M11	147
PITEOUS	M1	473
	M1	892
	C	98
	C	256
	EMKG	39
PITH	CAM	343
	M15	576
PITHY	HAP	2428
PITIED	SEL3	18
	SCG3	25
	AA	961
	SAA	898
	J10	43
	G1	629
	AE2	740
	TH	43
	TH	356
PITIES	PLB	23
	J6	564
	AE1	419
PITIFUL	OAL	698
PITIFULLY	G3	575
PITILESS	T23	80
PITTANCE	P6	75
PITTHEUS	BP	19
PITY	LCA	16
	AM	353
	AM	960
	AM	999

PITY	AM	1156
	SEL2	4
	ECG1	29
	ECG1	31
	SCG3	7
	EM	31
	SM2	13
	S	6
	A	5
	SLN	17
	PNH	16
	PC2	15
	EKK	7
	EOE	9
	DA	33
	DA	77
	DA	175
	SSF	10
	AA	695
	AA	725
	PLB	31
	SAA	445
	EDG	25
	RL	190
	AT	26
	AT	120
	NS	24
	FS2	10
	FS3	4
	FS3	17
	HAP	236
	HAP	288
	HAP	1076
	STS3	21
	SKA1	8
	J1	190
	J10	511
	P1	175
	P3	180
	M1	212
	M1	329
	M1	509
	M1	967
	HI	50
	VP10	3
	VP10	47
	G1	61
	G2	714
	G4	460
	G4	538
	G4	739
	AE1	649
	AE1	891
	AE2	92
	AE2	193
	AE2	197
	AE3	785
	AE4	462
	AE4	569
	AE4	630
	AE4	791
	AE5	457
	AE5	798
	AE5	903
	AE5	1023
	AE6	179
	AE7	504
	AE7	699
	AE8	754
	AE9	657
	AE10	969
	AE10	1304
	AE11	401
	AE11	560
	AE12	71
	AE12	366
	AE12	608
	AE12	1126
	AE12	1353
	OAL	567
	OAL	835
	AF	74
	AF	96
	KT1	63
	KT1	92
	KT2	312
	KT2	325
	KT2	332
	KT2	473
	KT3	148
	KT3	313
	KT3	336
	KT3	835
	KT3	1133
	TJD	75
	M8	271

PITY	M8	282
	CAM	148
	HIF	492
	TH	411
	M12	43
	M15	51
PITYING	AM	1117
	T23	98
	SFL	8
	AE2	873
	AE6	641
	AE10	956
	HIF	762
PLACE	AR	184
	RH	75
	LC	47
	DC	55
	PIE	16
	AM	74
	AM	384
	AM	954
	AM	1010
	AM	1023
	AM	1070
	AM	1125
	AM	1143
	PMQ	4
	ET	7
	PAR	12
	EUO	11
	PNH	40
	PAZ	36
	ML	18
	PTC	26
	PCB	14
	CM	120
	HP	57
	DA	30
	DA	97
	PUO3	36
	PUO4	25
	AA	154
	AA	579
	AA	668
	AA	736
	AA	772
	AA	864
	AA	971
	MD	11
	PRH	15
	MF	85
	SAA	235
	SAA	298
	SAA	396
	SAA	796
	SAA	974
	SAA	1014
	EK	1
	RL	211
	RL	411
	PD	23
	MO	9
	L3	119
	L3	278
	L4	54
	L4	252
	T23	75
	T27	28
	T27	95
	TA	204
	AK	12
	HAP	45
	HAP	101
	HAP	529
	HAP	641
	HAP	658
	HAP	666
	HAP	706
	HAP	1128
	HAP	1201
	HAP	1274
	HAP	1282
	HAP	1418
	HAP	1494
	HAP	2023
	HAP	2045
	HAP	2074
	HAP	2236
	HAP	2456
	HAP	2556
	HAP	2567
	SSC	49
	PDS	5
	EL	260
	EL	266
	EL	274

PLACE

EL	371
ODA	77
EH	23
J1	55
J1	197
J3	27
J3	50
J3	115
J3	272
J3	260
J3	391
J3	426
J6	178
J6	483
J6	504
J10	33
J10	55
J10	338
P4	71
M1	29
M1	69
M1	91
M1	226
M1	409
M1	594
M1	835
M1	976
M1	1033
MC	59
GK	33
GK	73
GK	95
GK	116
GK	125
GK	167
EHC	5
VP1	58
VP3	81
VP6	61
G1	658
G2	33
G2	311
G2	331
G2	696
G3	17
G3	133
G3	628
G4	23
G4	65
G4	417
AE1	627
AE1	632
AE1	761
AE1	794
AE1	889
AE1	987
AE1	1033
AE2	7
AE2	322
AE2	669
AE2	690
AE2	727
AE2	800
AE2	827
AE2	923
AE2	952
AE3	10
AE3	114
AE3	135
AE4	461
AE4	476
AE4	498
AE4	503
AE4	781
AE4	884
AE4	927
AE4	969
AE5	38
AE5	136
AE5	144
AE5	161
AE5	174
AE5	240
AE5	390
AE5	586
AE5	743
AE5	901
AE6	64
AE6	96
AE6	104
AE6	292
AE6	518
AE6	586
AE6	682
AE6	759
AE6	766

PLACE

AE6	913
AE6	970
AE6	1034
AE6	1067
AE6	1155
AE7	3
AE7	161
AE7	165
AE7	167
AE7	174
AE7	185
AE7	213
AE7	246
AE7	527
AE7	626
AE7	880
AE8	52
AE8	279
AE8	450
AE8	470
AE8	577
AE8	627
AE8	964
AE9	326
AE9	388
AE9	706
AE9	940
AE10	64
AE10	488
AE10	964
AE10	1154
AE11	326
AE11	374
AE11	702
AE11	782
AE11	1126
AE11	1233
AE12	181
AE12	197
AE12	223
AE12	253
AE12	742
AE12	812
AE12	840
AE12	888
AE12	932
AE12	980
AE12	1107
OAL	98
OAL	106
OAL	159
OAL	289
OAL	437
OAL	652
OAE2	68
MM	33
DO	23
DO	27
DO	124
DO	167
KT1	434
KT1	498
KT1	595
KT2	64
KT2	125
KT2	177
KT2	235
KT2	252
KT2	305
KT2	326
KT2	349
KT2	421
KT2	431
KT2	443
KT2	575
KT2	626
KT3	38
KT3	132
KT3	281
KT3	322
KT3	397
KT3	744
KT3	887
KT3	894
KT3	920
M8	169
M8	257
B	28
B	78
B	92
B	117
B	376
BP	19
BP	100
HIF	212
HIF	590

PLACE

HIF	613
HIF	668
HIF	719
C	277
C	290
C	541
TH	7
TH	81
TH	169
TH	201
TH	216
TH	255
TH	259
TH	276
TH	299
TH	398
TH	411
M11	408
M11	439
M11	445
FL	62
FL	101
FL	141
M12	57
M12	305
AU	358
AU	526
WB	32
WB	125
WB	379
M15	14
M15	22
M15	74
M15	253
M15	371
GP	96
CI	302
CI	261
CI	569
CI	586
PTP	46
ESK	11
EMKG	36
AS	24

PLACED

PWG	26
EIE	6
AM	155
CM	11
AA	482
MF	121
SAA	967
HAP	219
HAP	297
ODA	26
J3	335
J3	144
J6	725
P5	262
M1	228
M9	33
SFL	17
G2	373
AE1	711
AE2	717
AE3	697
AE4	716
AE4	736
AE5	455
AE6	29
AE6	706
AE6	816
AE7	214
AE7	242
AE7	256
AE8	71
AE8	818
AE8	951
AE10	6
AE11	7
AE11	17
AE11	904
AE12	146
AE12	958
AF	6
AF	20
MM	25
DO	156
KT1	333
KT2	446
KT2	600
KT3	464
KT3	477
KT3	518
KT3	549
KT3	557
KT3	658

PLACED	KT3	694
	KT3	1014
	KT3	1032
	TJD	69
	TJD	96
	B	190
	B	320
	B	484
	B	526
	C	646
	TH	263
	FL	87
	FL	89
	FL	170
	FL	244
	FL	427
	M12	51
	M12	62
	M12	128
	M12	814
	AU	185
	AU	257
	AU	512
	M15	609
	CI	573
PLACE'S	AE5	127
PLACES	PUO2	26
	ELB	34
	SAA	516
	EC	11
	HAP	103
	HAP	2036
	J6	670
	J10	72
	M1	165
	G1	93
	G1	176
	AE5	802
	AE7	874
	AE9	1
	AE11	310
	M15	402
	CI	103
PLACING	HS	95
PLAGUE	AM	1163
	PLB	5
	MD	188
	SAA	1036
	HAP	1114
	HAP	2166
	G3	237
	G3	722
	G4	774
	AE3	815
	AE4	265
	AE5	893
	AE7	486
	AE8	262
	AE9	714
	AE11	1163
	AE12	1237
	HIF	90
	HIF	752
	M12	781
	WB	545
PLAGUES	EUO	6
	BR	154
	J1	18
	J6	560
	AE10	383
PLAIN	AM	381
	AM	429
	AM	523
	AM	989
	PNH	10
	PAL	17
	PAL	33
	PCB	34
	HP	226
	PUF	12
	MD	206
	MD	243
	MF	27
	SAA	834
	SAA	921
	PK	19
	EDGA	28
	RL	204
	RL	274
	RL	311
	RL	316
	RL	369
	RL	409
	RL	432
	L1	23
	L2	44

PLAIN	L3	211
	L4	138
	T23	2
	H29	25
	TA	367
	EAA	4
	EAA	5
	EAA	28
	HAP	100
	HAP	140
	HAP	460
	HAP	645
	HAP	669
	HAP	680
	HAP	716
	HAP	734
	HAP	783
	HAP	806
	HAP	890
	HAP	913
	HAP	952
	HAP	959
	HAP	1247
	HAP	1325
	HAP	1563
	HAP	1845
	HAP	1991
	HAP	2017
	HAP	2200
	HAP	2201
	PTS	12
	J3	292
	J6	415
	J10	83
	J10	318
	J10	462
	P1	103
	P2	89
	P5	250
	M1	169
	M1	217
	M1	392
	M1	814
	R	2
	HI	8
	HI	34
	HI	85
	VP1	11
	VP2	12
	VP2	21
	VP2	26
	VP3	128
	VP3	172
	VP4	2
	VP5	54
	VP5	59
	VP6	100
	VP6	122
	VP7	81
	VP8	139
	VP10	56
	G1	174
	G1	168
	G1	235
	G1	512
	G1	515
	G1	546
	G1	683
	G1	691
	G2	35
	G2	201
	G2	369
	G2	427
	G2	553
	G3	150
	G3	382
	G3	706
	G4	118
	G4	147
	G4	171
	G4	534
	G4	579
	AE1	141
	AE1	259
	AE1	267
	AE1	655
	AE1	685
	AE2	276
	AE2	355
	AE2	855
	AE3	444
	AE4	170
	AE4	221
	AE4	679
	AE5	99
	AE5	347

PLAIN	AE5	374
	AE5	428
	AE5	438
	AE5	610
	AE5	721
	AE5	754
	AE5	912
	AE5	1052
	AE6	281
	AE6	891
	AE6	660
	AE6	929
	AE6	1141
	AE7	219
	AE7	406
	AE7	599
	AE7	604
	AE7	666
	AE7	726
	AE7	839
	AE7	895
	AE7	1100
	AE8	804
	AE8	898
	AE9	29
	AE9	74
	AE9	314
	AE9	423
	AE9	583
	AE9	593
	AE9	778
	AE9	801
	AE9	835
	AE9	936
	AE10	31
	AE10	286
	AE10	464
	AE10	546
	AE10	559
	AE10	608
	AE10	778
	AE10	817
	AE10	835
	AE10	898
	AE10	947
	AE10	999
	AE10	1020
	AE10	1045
	AE10	1053
	AE10	1082
	AE10	1190
	AE10	1258
	AE11	27
	AE11	112
	AE11	151
	AE11	301
	AE11	653
	AE11	749
	AE11	887
	AE11	998
	AE11	1047
	AE11	1064
	AE11	1072
	AE11	1178
	AE11	1203
	AE11	1217
	AE11	1230
	AE11	1298
	AE11	1302
	AE11	1307
	AE12	28
	AE12	487
	AE12	509
	AE12	551
	AE12	560
	AE12	653
	AE12	666
	AE12	685
	AE12	724
	AE12	815
	AE12	832
	AE12	835
	AE12	925
	OAL	614
	OAE2	53
	AF	140
	KT1	90
	KT1	136
	KT1	299
	KT2	415
	KT2	639
	KT3	514
	KT3	559
	KT3	653
	KT3	848
	KT3	968

Word	Ref	No.
PLAIN	M8	132
	HIF	600
	C	810
	C	818
	TH	379
	FL	90
	FL	166
	FL	187
	FL	216
	FL	241
	FL	306
	FL	312
	FL	425
	FL	530
	FL	609
	M12	102
	M12	157
	M12	592
	M12	426
	AU	92
	AU	341
	WB	47
	WB	285
	WB	411
	GP	101
	CI	18
	CI	88
	PMK	4
	EMKG	32
	EWR	25
PLAIN-BUILT	PNH	1
PLAIN-DEALING	HAP	2229
PLAINER	BR	128
PLAINLIEST	RL	331
PLAINLY	PAA	5
	HAP	1784
	HAP	1951
	B	93
	C	202
	C	398
	WB	444
PLAINNESS	PNH	29
	HAP	2222
PLAINS	AM	223
	D	5
	H2	88
	FS1	5
	AK	109
	HAP	152
	HAP	1906
	SKA2	11
	J6	26
	M1	51
	M1	94
	M1	306
	M1	953
	M13	20
	M13	61
	M13	232
	HI	89
	VP1	66
	VP5	52
	VP5	67
	VP6	2
	VP6	84
	VP7	2
	VP7	79
	VP7	94
	VP8	62
	VP8	68
	VP9	33
	VP10	63
	VP10	97
	G1	7
	G1	12
	G1	18
	G1	388
	G1	663
	G1	659
	G2	166
	G2	409
	G2	625
	G2	695
	G3	4
	G3	308
	G3	315
	G3	435
	G3	525
	G3	531
	G3	662
	G3	719
	G4	74
	G4	266
	G4	552
	G4	747
	AE1	223
PLAINS	AE1	599
	AE1	666
	AE2	408
	AE3	144
	AE3	685
	AE5	71
	AE5	962
	AE6	681
	AE6	868
	AE6	1099
	AE7	5
	AE7	284
	AE7	303
	AE7	864
	AE7	908
	AE7	940
	AE8	787
	AE9	166
	AE9	362
	AE9	525
	AE10	19
	AE10	810
	AE11	527
	AE11	565
	AE11	744
	AE11	1097
	AE12	537
	AE12	661
	AE12	695
	AE12	900
	KT2	47
	KT3	399
	TJD	62
	M8	85
	M8	317
	B	283
	BP	153
	CAM	134
	CAM	319
	HIF	86
	TH	58
	M11	289
	WB	308
PLAINTIFF		
PLAINTIFF'S	HAP	2054
PLAINTIFFS	J6	342
PLAINTIVE	G4	473
	AE7	500
	HIF	500
PLAINTS	AE2	498
PLAISTER	G4	63
PLAISTERED	J6	608
PLAN	MD	201
	M15	589
PLANE	T18	73
	KT3	962
PLANES	M13	74
	G2	97
	G4	216
PLANET	AM	1167
	AA	231
	SAA	932
	SAA	999
	HAP	2134
	HAP	2150
	HAP	2224
	P5	59
	M1	1075
	GK	133
	HIF	576
	C	680
PLANETARY	HAP	1766
	J6	750
	G3	444
	AE7	25
	KT2	483
	KT3	290
PLANETS	AK	41
	MS	2
	J3	79
	G4	332
	AE4	754
	AE9	22
	KT1	252
	AU	455
	M15	94
PLANETS'	J6	731
PLANK	AE10	924
	AE10	928
PLANKED	AE2	21
PLANKS	AM	240
	AM	572
	AE1	171
	AE1	777
	AE2	66
	AE4	71
	AE5	915
PLANKS	AE9	715
	AE10	424
	M11	27
	M11	147
	M11	208
PLANT	PAZ	31
	PR	22
	PUF	8
	ER	3
	HAP	24
	HAP	361
	HAP	1883
	M1	706
	GK	121
	VP1	97
	VP10	78
	G1	380
	G2	30
	G2	70
	G2	81
	G2	116
	G2	154
	G2	181
	G2	252
	G2	362
	G2	371
	G2	411
	G2	434
	G2	479
	G2	594
	G3	638
	G4	25
	G4	171
	AE3	36
	AE3	42
	AE4	644
	AE6	209
	AE7	92
	AE12	1129
	TJD	99
	CAM	21
	CAM	371
	CI	130
PLANTAGENET	DO	14
	DO	30
PLANTATION	PTW	8
	PK	3
	PK	12
	G2	360
	PWR	13
PLANTATIONS	HAP	1174
	G2	372
PLANTED	HAP	881
	HI	71
	VP2	71
	VP8	55
	G2	395
	AE5	994
	AE8	2
	AE8	71
	AE8	313
	FL	41
	FL	103
	M15	104
	M15	619
PLANTER	AE7	247
PLANTERS	PSH	14
PLANTING	G2	14
	G2	27
	G2	352
PLANTS	CM	45
	PSF	24
	SAA	562
	T18	78
	HAP	232
	BR	72
	VP4	29
	VP8	135
	G1	79
	G2	89
	G2	103
	G2	348
	G2	367
	G2	393
	G2	397
	G2	425
	G2	449
	G2	475
	G2	482
	G2	579
	G2	606
	G2	622
	AE10	568
	AE12	583
	KT3	1048
	M11	288

PLASTER	J3	255
PLASTRON	J6	349
PLATE	L2	31
	J1	114
	J1	208
	J3	336
	J3	419
	J6	472
	J10	30
	J10	269
	P2	94
	AE1	903
	AE9	482
PLATED	AE2	687
	AE7	878
	AE8	828
	AE10	436
	AE12	556
	AE12	795
PLATES	AE1	629
	AE3	336
	AE5	345
	AE7	159
	AE10	467
	AE10	676
	AE10	1112
	KT1	473
	KT2	557
	KT3	35
PLATO	RL	74
PLATONIC	UDH	97
	DO	29
PLATONISTS	HAP	341
PLATTER	J3	419
PLAUDIT	PUO1	39
	OAL	127
PLAUSIBLE	MD	111
	AE4	417
PLAUSIBLY	HAP	2071
PLAUSTRIS	PO	4
PLAY	AR	172
	LC	141
	PWG	2
	PWG	12
	PWG	27
	PWG	37
	PWG	52
	EWG	8
	EWG	9
	EWG	21
	LCA	42
	PRL	10
	PRL	18
	PIE	4
	PIE	11
	PIE	23
	VHH	30
	AM	394
	AM	511
	AM	576
	AM	915
	PMQ	3
	PMQ	9
	PMQ	25
	PMQ	40
	PMQ	46
	PMQ	51
	PMQ	56
	EMQ	13
	EWGR	16
	EWGR	30
	EWGR	45
	PMM	2
	EMM	5
	PT	4
	PT	32
	PT	35
	ET	11
	PA	29
	EEL	2
	ETL	10
	ETL	22
	ETL	23
	PCG1	9
	PCG1	13
	PCG1	15
	ECG1	27
	ECG1	38
	PCG2	12
	PCG2	22
	ECG2	9
	ECG2	14
	PAR	8
	PAR	20
	PM	33
	PM	38

PLAY	EM	8
	PLN	39
	PLN	45
	ELN	2
	ELN	14
	ELN	19
	PCD	26
	ECD	4
	PUO1	33
	EUO	20
	PNH	44
	ENH	35
	PAZ	4
	PAZ	24
	PAZ	40
	EAZ	16
	EAZ	23
	PC1	18
	PC2	31
	ML	2
	ML	6
	ML	25
	PAL	3
	EAL	25
	PKK	25
	POE	33
	POE	36
	EOE	10
	EOE	26
	PTC	13
	ETC	25
	PO	14
	PSF	36
	ETG	2
	PR	9
	EUF	31
	ELB	2
	ELB	6
	ELB	15
	ELB	20
	PPC	4
	EPC	15
	EPC	23
	EPC	29
	MF	182
	MF	188
	EK	8
	EK	28
	PDG	16
	PDG	1
	EDG	1
	EDGA	1
	RL	321
	PD	37
	T18	23
	T27	19
	T27	22
	T27	127
	EAA	2
	GE	53
	GE	67
	GE	73
	HH	38
	HAP	1015
	PDS	16
	PDS	18
	PP	3
	PP	42
	PMS	2
	PMS	11
	PMS	21
	PMS	23
	PKA	21
	EKA	40
	EL	217
	ODA	68
	PSH	4
	EH	14
	J1	3
	J1	137
	J3	163
	J6	372
	J6	470
	J6	525
	J6	791
	J10	257
	P1	222
	P3	96
	P3	153
	M1	941
	M13	143
	PLT	19
	PLT	33
	PLT	55
	ELT	2
	ELT	18

PLAY	GK	151
	GK	152
	EHC	14
	EHC	19
	VP2	54
	VP5	129
	VP8	154
	G1	157
	G1	507
	G3	582
	G4	157
	G4	432
	G4	621
	AE1	1001
	AE5	121
	AE5	694
	AE5	773
	AE5	1077
	AE7	987
	AE8	38
	AE8	892
	AE9	210
	AE9	454
	AE11	966
	AE12	247
	OAL	563
	OAL	567
	OAE2	30
	OAE2	46
	MG	26
	KT2	492
	KT3	98
	KT3	428
	KT3	889
	B	81
	B	251
	C	69
	C	337
	C	437
	C	622
	M11	342
	FL	364
	FL	373
	M12	69
	M12	550
	GP	36
	GP	120
	CI	538
	PTP	5
	PTP	46
	ERL	5
	PMK	3
	PWR	37
	EWR	12
PLAYED	EWG	1
	PWGR	20
	EUO	23
	MD	234
	MF	111
	PK	35
	PDG	7
	OE	10
	TA	164
	AK	84
	HAP	127
	J1	65
	M1	198
	M1	879
	M13	198
	GK	43
	VP3	12
	VP5	134
	VP6	98
	G1	377
	G4	818
	AE9	508
	AE12	1109
	KT3	999
	B	247
	TH	79
	FL	352
	FL	433
	WB	10
	WB	26
	PTP	19
PLAYER	M11	375
PLAYERS	PLG	33
	J3	364
	J6	124
	MG	18
PLAYERS'	J6	103
PLAYHOUSE	PCG2	3
	PM	16
	PNH	35
	PAZ	35
	PTC	25

Word	Ref	No.	Word	Ref	No.	Word	Ref	No.
PLAYHOUSE	EUF	13	PLEAD	AE11	153	PLEASE	HAP	154
	PK	15		KT1	347		HAP	828
	EK	29		KT2	153		PDS	17
	EH	23		KT3	377		EDS	32
	J3	364		C	782		PTS	6
	J6	88		AU	126		SKA6	13
	J6	124		AU	230		ESH	12
	OAL	98		AU	249		SSH	13
	OAL	117		AU	306		J1	95
	OAL	562		AU	321		J3	168
	OAL	563		AU	572		J3	180
	EMKG	1		CI	520		J3	306
PLAYING	ELN	11	PLEADED	J10	507		J6	214
	M1	937		KT1	343		J6	754
PLAY'S	EC	1	PLEADING	AA	960		J10	272
	EMM	10		J1	46		P1	166
PLAYS	PWG	35		J6	110		P1	189
	PWG	53		AE6	1126		P1	212
	PWG	55	PLEADINGS	J3	348		P2	20
	PRL	6		P1	273		P2	113
	PRL	22	PLEADS	J6	833		P3	47
	PRL	26		MF	13		P4	29
	EIE	10		AE4	542		P4	124
	AM	932		AE5	447		P5	120
	PMQ	10		M8	335		M1	123
	PMM	7		M8	336		M13	177
	PA	16	PLEAS	HAP	2325		M13	178
	PTL	2		J6	344		MC	22
	PTL	4		CI	302		GK	131
	PCG1	44	PLEASANT	RH	86		VP1	111
	PAR	4		EWGR	9		VP2	66
	PW	19		ELN	8		VP5	5
	PM	22		HP	64		VP8	105
	PLN	2		L2	5		G2	51
	PLN	27		L2	1		G2	533
	PNH	35		L3	126		G4	199
	ENH	31		AK	115		AE2	141
	EAL	16		HH	2		AE2	893
	EMK	6		KT2	15		AE3	164
	PTC	34		KT3	142		AE3	861
	PLG	12		KT3	195		AE5	38
	PSF	12		FL	427		AE7	358
	PSF	16		ER	33		AE7	361
	D	32	PLEASANTLY				AE10	723
	MF	62	PLEASANT-				AE11	493
	MF	205	SOUNDING	T27	72		AE12	902
	PK	28	PLEASE	RH	4		OAL	68
	PK	30		SMA	100		OAL	348
	PD	2		LC	51		OAL	353
	L4	108		EWG	6		OAL	363
	PKA	2		PRL	21		OAL	669
	MS	1		PIE	19		OAL	864
	ESH	24		AM	458		KT1	516
	J3	66		EWGR	14		KT2	406
	J3	286		EWGR	37		KT3	386
	J10	135		PA	44		KT3	682
	PLT	14		EEL	41		M8	288
	PLT	36		ECG1	22		B	42
	PLT	40		ECG2	34		B	463
	GK	69		PMQW	12		BP	121
	G2	528		PLN	25		HIF	211
	AE6	955		PLN	41		HIF	219
	AE8	955		ELN	9		HIF	272
	OAL	111		PNH	47		HIF	601
	OAL	264		EMQW	20		C	624
	MG	18		EMQW	25		TH	76
	MG	24		ENH	37		M11	114
	M11	331		PUO2	32		M12	808
	FL	566		PAZ	2		WB	68
	PWR	1		EAZ	2		WB	124
PLEA	HAP	1652		EAL	18		WB	244
	HAP	2080		EAL	31		WB	252
	HAP	2151		PKK	10		WB	517
	AU	30		POE	15		WB	528
	M15	162		EOE	18		M15	114
	GP	117		EOE	34		M15	191
PLEAD	ENH	25		PCB	2		M15	255
	AA	875		HP	128		CI	31
	MD	157		DA	82		CI	222
	SAA	28		PUO4	20		CI	500
	RL	197		AA	28		EWR	20
	RL	204		AA	48		EWR	22
	L3	145		AA	115	PLEASED	RH	43
	TA	86		AA	167		VHH	57
	HAP	727		AA	228		AM	331
	HAP	950		AA	748		PWGR	3
	HAP	1043		AA	791		PA	1
	HAP	1440		AA	925		ECG1	40
	HAP	1644		PLB	17		PLN	38
	HAP	2065		MD	108		PNH	31
	PDS	2		MD	163		EAZ	14
	PSH	26		EK	2		POE	9
	AE6	1171		EK	4		PTC	35
	AE7	503		EK	28		EPF	21
	AE9	288		L3	138		ETG	21
	AE11	30		FS1	12		AA	160
				PAA	31			
				HH	34			

PLEASED			PLEASED			PLEASURE		
	SAA	533		CI	76		SEL2	7
	SAA	695		CI	190		SEL2	8
	EDGA	2		CI	311		SEL2	14
	RL	98		CI	429		SCG3	16
	OE	14		CI	480		SCG3	24
	AT	59		CI	557		SM1	7
	AT	60		EMKG	33		SM1	8
	ER	59					SM2	4
	H29	76	PLEASES				EAZ	13
	H2	89		PIE	25		PC1	5
	GE	66		PEL	17		STC	13
	HAP	1565		PSF	2		CM	26
	HAP	2344		P2	113		HP	97
	HAP	2415		KT1	32		UMR	2
	BR	178					SSF	5
	EL	56	PLEASING				SSF	23
	EL	197		SMA	44		AA	776
	EL	293		SMQ	3		EK	47
	MS	13		STL	3		SDG	8
	J6	316		HP	87		RL	33
	J6	391		AA	474		EC	43
	J10	127		D	37		L3	80
	J10	450		ER	23		L3	129
	P1	162		L1	8		L4	32
	P3	90		L1	48		L4	46
	P4	110		L1	52		L4	207
	M1	78		L2	4		T23	71
	M1	493		L2	32		NS	3
	M1	767		L4	11		HAP	496
	M1	980		L4	17		PTS	9
	M9	62		T23	22		SKA6	16
	GK	4		H9	29		LS	9
	DHP	30		H9	33		SSH	11
	G3	459		H2	58		EH	13
	AE1	867		H2	80		J3	96
	AE1	1012		HAP	1226		J3	73
	AE2	179		HAP	1329		J6	49
	AE2	242		HAP	1388		J6	357
	AE2	939		SKA3	3		J6	482
	AE3	366		P6	19		J6	693
	AE3	636		M1	770		J10	494
	AE4	936		M13	73		J10	529
	AE5	79		M13	104		P1	44
	AE5	370		VP1	4		P1	271
	AE5	671		VP1	76		P2	97
	AE5	749		VP3	170		P4	88
	AE5	837		G1	467		P5	226
	AE6	520		G2	391		M1	837
	AE6	531		G2	611		M1	938
	AE6	848		G2	616		M13	3
	AE7	1037		G3	4		VP2	102
	AE8	203		G3	206		VP3	128
	AE8	216		G3	354		VP7	24
	AE10	573		G3	397		G1	406
	AE10	598		G3	449		G3	107
	AE10	1174		G4	338		G3	258
	AE11	963		G4	430		AE1	118
	AE12	1220		AE1	954		AE1	283
	OAL	164		AE1	970		AE1	1003
	OAL	338		AE2	799		AE1	1036
	OAL	361		AE3	140		AE4	323
	OAL	704		AE3	239		AE4	397
	OAL	710		AE3	270		AE4	341
	OAL	805		AE3	299		AE4	424
	OAE2	29		AE3	580		AE4	946
	DO	119		AE3	681		AE6	868
	KT1	119		AE4	53		AE12	336
	KT1	453		AE4	460		OAL	262
	KT2	118		AE4	561		OAL	311
	KT2	428		AE5	1098		OAL	406
	KT2	665		AE6	571		OAL	857
	KT3	185		AE7	269		OAE2	85
	KT3	367		AE7	1038		AF	57
	KT3	421		AE8	50		AF	59
	KT3	424		AE8	78		AF	60
	KT3	748		AE8	411		AF	62
	KT3	805		AE8	490		AF	64
	KT3	1054		AE8	538		AF	65
	M8	242		AE10	323		KT1	534
	B	180		AE10	868		KT3	428
	B	454		AE10	1167		TJD	68
	B	617		AE11	385		M8	219
	M10	4		AE12	190		B	188
	M10	11		KT1	219		B	250
	CAM	107		KT2	512		B	451
	CAM	256		KT3	93		CAM	7
	C	305		B	192		CAM	50
	C	606		BP	71		CAM	117
	C	651		M10	83		HIF	259
	TH	247		C	817		HIF	773
	FL	113		TH	58		C	459
	M12	275		M11	309		C	789
	M12	315		FL	121		C	820
	WB	9		FL	314		FL	101
	WB	129		M12	221		FL	372
	M15	213		GP	15		FL	594
				ESK	26			
			PLEASURE	AM	487			
				SMM2	14			
				SEL2	3			

PLEASURE	M12	735	PLENTEOUS	P6	36	PLIGHTED	AE7	513		
	CI	45		P6	164		AE10	720		
	PTP	12		M13	152		AE11	80		
	SMP	53		VCS	13		AE11	230		
	SMP	57		VP3	154		AE12	52		
	SMP	82		G1	1		AE12	1174		
	EWR	18		G2	187		KT1	291		
PLEASURES	SMA	98		G2	747		KT2	165		
	SMA	110		G3	604		HIF	127		
	LC	45		G3	744		FL	523		
	STL	6		AE1	294		WB	173		
	PM	27		AE5	54		WB	322		
	SM1	9		AE8	103		CI	587		
	L2	36		AE10	210	PLIGHTS	EAA	31		
	L3	28		KT3	195	PLODS	RL	323		
	H9	21		KT3	354	PLOT	PWG	43		
	H29	14		M15	179		PRL	14		
	H29	21	PLENTEOUSLY	TA	279		PRL	19		
	HAP	367	PLENTIFUL	ETP	10		PIE	13		
	STS1	4	PLENTY	AM	184		PMQ	8		
	SKA3	9		AM	1142		EMQ	2		
	SKA3	18		PTW	10		EWGR	41		
	SKA5	2		HP	218		ET	5		
	J1	131		MD	126		EEL	11		
	J6	165		D	25		PCG1	10		
	P3	162		SAA	32		EM	26		
	P4	75		PDG	38		PCD	31		
	VP9	51		TA	298		EOE	24		
	VP10	63		GE	31		ETC	28		
	G2	658		G1	184		PO	16		
	G4	30		G1	476		PSF	48		
	AE3	453		G2	593		AA	82		
	AE4	458		G2	657		AA	108		
	AE4	793		AE8	431		AA	134		
	AE6	57		OAL	108		AA	208		
	AE6	390		MM	37		AA	275		
	OAL	38		M8	5		AA	490		
	AF	98		C	385		AA	517		
	KT1	52		SMP	53		AA	631		
	KT1	485		SMP	57		AA	671		
	KT3	323	PLEXIPPUS'	M8	237		AA	751		
	TJD	61	PLIANT	L4	190		AA	922		
	B	438		HAP	269		AA	930		
	CAM	249		EL	220		AA	1013		
	CAM	263		J10	95		MD	220		
	FL	95		P3	38		SAA	90		
	FL	143		M1	104		SAA	96		
	FL	144		VP10	60		SAA	109		
	FL	331		G1	153		SAA	121		
	M12	555		G2	367		SAA	534		
	WB	137		AE1	1007		EC	29		
	CI	6		AE5	194		EC	32		
PLEBEIAN	BR	213		AE5	570		EC	34		
	M12	793		M10	85		HAP	563		
	B	489	PLIED	AM	497		HAP	2013		
	HIF	340		G4	475		ESH	21		
PLEDGE	UDH	51		AE5	422		MG	20		
	PUF	6		AE6	263		KT2	562		
	H3	9		AE10	579		C	491		
	HAP	1228		HIF	170		PMK	26		
	BR	150		HIF	597		EMKG	3		
	BR	290		M12	470		EWR	1		
	HI	143	PLIES	AU	357	PLOTS	LCA	41		
	AE4	474		AM	751		EEL	29		
	AE5	706		M1	945		PCG2	23		
	AE8	190		VP3	97		PUO3	1		
	AE11	555		G1	535		AA	83		
	KT1	459		G4	248		AA	393		
	DO	54		G4	266		AA	466		
	B	610		AE2	671		AA	651		
	B	747		AE4	376		AA	985		
	M12	492		AE8	334		ELB	37		
	M15	661		AE10	1267		SAA	867		
PLEDGE'S	WB	107		AE11	1114		SAA	860		
PLEDGES	EL	346		AE12	691		EDGA	37		
	VP8	130		M8	199		EC	6		
	AE2	811		M11	474		BR	157		
	AE2	923		M12	399		M13	79		
	AE4	936	PLIGHT	DA	20		G3	802		
	DO	164		HAP	2360		AE4	972		
PLEIADES	G4	338		AE8	220	PLOTTED	MS	15		
PLEIADS	AK	175		AE8	848		MM	22		
	G1	210		AE9	344	PLOTTING	PO	10		
	AE3	675		KT3	834		MD	201		
	AU	456		HIF	112		SAA	96		
PLEMMYRIUM'S	AE3	908		WB	247		C	775		
PLENIPO	GE	12		WB	254	PLOW	J3	488		
PLENTEOUS	AM	566	PLIGHTED	DA	20		J10	417		
	PAL	37		DA	121		P1	145		
	SAA	63		AA	470		M1	132		
	L3	130		MD	259		VP2	97		
	TA	374		TA	232		VP4	38		
	AK	94		AE1	345		VP4	50		
	HAP	1680		AE3	111		G1	24		
	HAP	2254		AE4	37		G1	69		
	P3	76		AE4	444		G1	220		

Word	Ref	No.
PLOW	G1	243
	G1	250
	G1	401
	G2	262
	G2	280
	G2	304
	G2	310
	G2	324
	G2	489
	G2	591
	G2	666
	G3	85
	G3	102
	G3	227
	G3	256
	G3	771
	G4	464
	AE3	642
	AE3	681
	AE4	311
	AE5	984
	AE7	944
	AE7	1086
	AE9	118
	AE9	833
	OAL	456
	KT1	26
	HIF	235
	HIF	435
	WB	451
	M15	693
PLOWED	MD	23
	H2	8
	TA	357
	M1	169
	G1	664
	AE5	221
	AE7	8
	AE7	1030
	AE12	759
	AU	411
	M15	181
PLOWING	G2	282
	AE1	53
PLOWMAN	P5	147
	G1	159
	G1	177
	G1	294
	G2	289
	AE6	1163
	AE10	1141
PLOWMAN'S	G1	24
	G1	61
PLOWMEN	G1	247
	OAL	455
	OAL	826
PLOWS	M1	158
	M1	403
	G1	141
	G2	617
	G2	739
	AE2	240
	AE9	829
	AE10	931
	CI	325
PLOWSHARE	L4	283
	P1	140
	OAL	540
PLOWSHARES	J3	488
PLOW-TAIL	G1	254
PLUCK	OE	32
	VP3	144
PLUCKED	AK	3
	C	766
PLUCKEST	OAE1	22
PLUCKING	J6	804
PLUM	VP2	72
	G2	44
PLUME	PAR	10
	ENH	8
	PUO3	19
	AA	920
	PP	23
	J6	361
	HI	149
	AE3	601
	AE12	716
PLUMES	AE3	318
	AE4	261
	AE7	265
	AE7	880
	AE7	1073
	AE10	277
	AE11	1067
	M11	293
	FL	107

Word	Ref	No.
PLUMP	VP9	16
	AE12	374
	TH	316
	CI	155
PLUMS	M13	113
	G4	215
	BP	113
PLUMY	AE1	966
	AE2	530
	AE10	903
	AE11	14
	AE11	1207
	KT3	452
	M10	56
PLUNDER	PA	18
	SKA1	14
	AE8	271
	AE9	840
PLUNDERED	AK	159
	HAP	1639
	AE4	585
PLUNDERING	AE7	1029
PLUNDERS	J16	85
PLUNGE	AA	394
	MD	133
	AT	59
	J6	675
	VP8	84
	G4	343
	AE1	954
	AE9	146
	AE10	423
	AE11	828
	AE12	868
	OAL	79
	M11	472
PLUNGED	L1	52
	T23	4
	H3	51
	J3	276
	P3	4
	M13	204
	G4	766
	AE2	101
	AE4	371
	AE4	999
	AE5	1116
	AE6	1004
	AE7	639
	AE8	91
	AE8	640
	AE9	1103
	AE10	542
	AE12	144
	AE12	459
	AE12	535
	AE12	1282
	M8	237
	BP	68
	HIF	329
	C	710
	TH	163
	M11	224
	M12	654
	CI	344
PLUNGES	G3	682
	AE8	339
PLUNGING	AE5	231
	AE9	885
PLUS	PAA	39
PLUTARCH	RL	79
	BR	336
	EP	1
PLUTO	G1	373
	AE7	455
	AE7	785
	KT3	700
	G4	753
PLUTO'S	AE5	958
	AE6	360
	AE6	727
	AE6	856
	AE6	866
PLY	PW	14
	SCD2	10
	AA	393
	AE1	226
	AE1	587
	AE2	657
	AE3	177
	AE3	272
	AE3	374
	AE4	590
	AE5	274
	AE8	545
	AE8	598

Word	Ref	No.
PLY	AE9	244
	AE10	411
	AE11	1024
	M11	111
	AU	131
	CI	336
	CI	613
PLYMOUTH	AM	681
PO	VP6	92
	G4	529
	AE6	893
POACHED	PLG	29
POCKET	OE	50
	J16	42
POCKETS	PMS	16
PODALIRIAN	AE2	343
PODALIRIUS	AE12	460
POEM	AM	702
	POE	15
	EOE	9
	ER	31
	EL	374
	P1	62
	M1	756
	M13	65
	VP6	40
	G2	56
POEMATA	PO	4
POEMS	JH	8
	PUO1	32
	PUO4	8
	P1	192
	P1	205
	VP6	12
	M15	225
POESY	RH	45
	AK	19
	AK	57
POET	RH	88
	PWG	1
	PWG	7
	PWG	44
	EWG	5
	PIE	22
	VHH	56
	PMQ	15
	PMQ	23
	PMQ	44
	EMQ	12
	EWGR	7
	EWGR	20
	EWGR	37
	PMM	13
	EWGR	45
	PA	23
	PEL	1
	PEL	29
	EEL	23
	PTL	7
	PTL	16
	ETL	17
	ETL	28
	PCG1	3
	ECG1	2
	ECG1	13
	PCG2	11
	PCG2	27
	ECG2	18
	ECG2	28
	ECG2	22
	EM	11
	PLN	4
	PLN	26
	PLN	34
	PLN	39
	ELN	10
	ELN	19
	ECD	1
	ECD	3
	PUO1	38
	EUO2	1
	EAZ	11
	EAZ	31
	PC1	2
	PC1	20
	EOE	17
	PCB	6
	PSF	5
	ETG	4
	PR	1
	PUO5	25
	PLB	11
	ELB	1
	SAA	475
	SAA	495
	SAA	942

POET	AT	102
	GE	65
	PDS	11
	PDS	24
	PMS	8
	PMS	27
	PKA	13
	ESH	1
	J1	246
	J10	288
	P1	128
	P1	146
	P1	239
	M1	756
	PLT	5
	ELT	9
	ELT	2
	EHC	2
	EHC	7
	EHC	18
	VP5	69
	VP7	35
	VP10	25
	G2	56
	AE6	912
	AE9	697
	OAL	592
	OAE1	28
	MG	1
	MG	26
	MM	55
	TJD	202
	FL	125
	PTP	11
	ERL	1
	ERL	8
POETARUM	EDGA	18
POETESS	AK	47
POETIC	PRL	8
	PUO1	4
	EUO	3
	PTW	11
	MO	4
	J3	340
	PPS	18
	PLT	49
POETICAL	PR	35
POETRY	JH	2
	LCA	49
	PA	33
	ECG1	20
	PUO1	28
	EUO	25
	POE	31
	PCB	5
	AK	98
	P1	109
	P1	153
	MC	47
	GK	50
	VP9	72
	KT2	492
POET'S	LCA	40
	PIE	29
	AM	1099
	PMQ	27
	PCG1	22
	ECG1	17
	ELN	2
	PAL	39
	PTC	18
	PUO4	5
	D	38
	PSH	37
	J3	14
	J6	109
	J6	240
	J6	469
	PLT	28
	EHC	15
	G1	61
	G2	25
	G2	676
	AE7	52
	PTP	20
POETS	AR	93
	DC	18
	PWG	46
	LCA	17
	LCA	44
	LCA	46
	PRL	7
	EMQ	15
	EWGR	29
	PMM	3
	PMM	9

POETS	ET	3
	ET	7
	PA	36
	PEL	15
	EEL	26
	PTL	2
	PTL	12
	PCG1	40
	ECG2	26
	EM	5
	PLN	7
	PLN	13
	PLN	19
	PUO1	12
	PUO1	18
	PUO1	45
	PUO2	1
	PUO2	23
	PUO2	32
	PAZ	25
	ML	50
	PAL	5
	PAL	19
	EAL	1
	EKK	7
	EOE	2
	EOE	30
	PTC	5
	ETC	7
	ETC	12
	ETC	18
	PCB	12
	PLG	16
	PO	8
	PO	17
	PSF	18
	PUO4	24
	PUO4	29
	PUO5	9
	PLB	1
	ELB	16
	MD	287
	MF	99
	SAA	319
	PK	42
	PDG	44
	EDG	4
	EDGA	1
	PD	3
	MO	18
	L3	183
	H3	8
	TA	433
	PAA	3
	AK	31
	AK	100
	AK	188
	EMI	1
	B.R	71
	PDS	3
	PP	38
	PPS	8
	P1	96
	P1	118
	P4	127
	P5	1
	P5	9
	P6	146
	M1	758
	GK	124
	G2	66
	G3	12
	G3	141
	AE6	898
	MM	2
	DO	12
	KT2	661
	C	659
	WB	66
	WB	464
	PTP	5
	ETP	11
	ETP	18
	PWR	2
POETS'	AM	1100
	SAA	495
	ENH	33
	G4	787
POINT	HS	76
	EWGR	8
	MF	128
	SAA	279
	L4	106
	HAP	681
	HAP	1178
	HAP	1821

POINT	PSH	38
	J6	639
	P1	260
	GK	41
	AE3	263
	AE3	902
	AE4	842
	AE7	868
	AE10	670
	AE11	1104
	AE11	1191
	AE11	1252
	AE12	939
	OAL	547
	AF	144
	DO	24
	KT2	408
	KT3	511
	KT3	820
	KT3	1116
	CAM	188
	C	363
	C	543
	M12	145
	M12	498
	M12	574
	M12	643
	M12	748
	AU	604
	WB	117
	CI	603
	ETP	1
POINT-BLANK	HAP	734
POINTED	AM	480
	POE	26
	CM	20
	H9	32
	H2	49
	P1	113
	P3	77
	M1	628
	VP7	10
	G3	576
	G4	107
	G4	152
	G4	440
	AE1	145
	AE1	431
	AE1	690
	AE3	775
	AE5	50
	AE5	468
	AE6	532
	AE6	662
	AE6	791
	AE7	923
	AE7	1084
	AE8	307
	AE8	827
	AE8	919
	AE9	44
	AE9	543
	AE9	620
	AE9	744
	AE9	777
	AE9	834
	AE9	1028
	AE10	672
	AE10	805
	AE10	1243
	AE11	356
	AE12	11
	AE12	187
	AE12	199
	AE12	614
	AE12	710
	AE12	1143
	KT1	115
	KT2	138
	KT2	602
	KT3	584
	M8	200
	B	537
	FL	577
	GP	94
	CI	157
POINTEST	AU	535
POINTING	TA	81
	P1	61
	P3	209
POINTLESS	HAP	992
	AE8	563
	M12	603
POINTS	RL	307
	RL	331
	RL	443

POINTS	RL	449	POLE	M1	365	POLYCLETE	J3	355		
	HAP	410		G1	334	POLYDORE	AE3	65		
	HAP	668		AE4	232		AE3	72		
	HAP	716		AE5	911		AE3	87		
	HAP	721		AE6	418		AE3	94		
	HAP	1009		AE7	143	POLYGAMY	AA	2		
	HAP	2420		AE9	670	POLYGNOTUS'	P3	103		
	J10	294		M11	123	POLYPHEME	AE3	842		
	P1	167	POLEAX	KT3	32		HIF	378		
	P4	28	POLES	M1	56	POLYPHEMUS	M13	9		
	P6	17		G1	330	POMETIA	AE6	1051		
	AE12	1320		G2	34	POMMEL	KT3	702		
	KT3	599		G2	492	POMP	AR	285		
	M8	209		AE1	131		SMA	7		
POISE	HS	42		AE5	270		SMA	34		
	AR	297		AE7	923		AM	205		
	AM	48		AE9	677		PEL	25		
	EDG	38		AE10	175		PNH	3		
	G1	46		AE11	1289		PNH	16		
	TJD	124	POLESTAR	AM	636		HP	218		
POISED	HAP	345	POLICIES	SAA	205		DA	202		
	M1	16	POLICY	AR	260		AA	740		
	AE4	369		SAA	674		PLB	28		
	AE5	544		PKA	32		SAA	59		
	AE8	119	POLISH	MD	3		SAA	179		
	AE9	15		MD	15		SAA	1006		
	AE9	552		HAP	979		L2	53		
	AE10	672	POLISHED	PAZ	17		TA	51		
	AE10	1092		AT	40		GE	64		
	AE11	836		ER	19		HAP	1284		
	AE12	403		J6	605		HAP	1680		
	AE12	1304		P1	123		HAP	2067		
	M12	752		P5	54		BR	20		
POISES	AE8	821		GK	36		BR	111		
POISING	G2	344		AE1	830		PP	22		
	G4	286		AE3	595		EL	261		
POISON	PCB	34		AE5	403		EL	277		
	MD	294		AE6	1236		J1	36		
	SAA	1070		AE6	1238		J1	48		
	EH	34		AE8	35		J10	516		
	J3	207		AE10	205		P1	33		
	J6	827		KT2	559		P2	82		
	J10	38		KT3	451		P6	85		
	J10	269		KT3	931		HI	153		
	M1	188		BP	161		G2	383		
	VP7	40		FL	272		G2	767		
	G2	652		CI	32		G4	5		
	G3	669		PWR	14		G4	373		
	G3	742	POLITES	AE2	718		G4	411		
	AE1	932	POLITIC	PA	38		G4	559		
	AE9	1043	POLITICIAN	SAA	210		AE1	698		
	AE10	209	POLITICIAN'S	AA	967		AE2	268		
	DO	89	POLITICIANS	LC	67		AE2	1041		
	KT1	279		AA	223		AE3	90		
	KT2	91	POLITICS	SAA	347		AE3	445		
	C	404		SAA	899		AE4	105		
	TH	21	POLL	PTW	12		AE4	970		
POISONED	HS	27	POLLED	HAP	1925		AE6	819		
	AM	1067		J3	268		AE6	1069		
	G3	813	POLLIO	J6	507		AE6	1208		
	AE7	525		J6	508		AE7	827		
	KT3	404		VP3	132		AE7	925		
POISONER	J6	819		VP3	134		AE7	957		
POISONING	PSF	46		VP3	136		AE8	883		
	PDG	15		VP8	7		AE11	73		
	J1	108	POLLIO'S	VP3	137		AE11	131		
	J6	810		VP4	14		AE11	261		
	G3	725	POLLS	J3	308		AE11	328		
	ETO	2	POLLUTE	HAP	1558		AE11	971		
	KT3	412		BR	183		AE12	245		
POISONOUS	HAP	2373		AE2	570		AE12	373		
	J1	239		AE3	60		KT1	14		
	VP4	29		KT1	52		KT1	39		
	VP8	135		KT2	91		KT3	61		
	G2	209		M15	138		KT3	532		
	G3	447	POLLUTED	AR	181		KT3	718		
	G3	838		MF	71		KT3	949		
	G4	66		T23	101		B	607		
	AE2	645		AE2	223		B	608		
	AE7	487		AE3	87		HIF	216		
	AE12	1242		AE6	38		TH	17		
	HIF	576		AE6	759		M11	69		
	FL	375		AE7	648		FL	165		
POISONS	L3	228		AE10	451		FL	187		
	L4	111		AE12	840		GP	88		
	HAP	229		BP	172		GP	101		
	SKA5	7	POLLUTERS	AE11	416	POMPEY	HS	32		
	J6	190	POLLUTES	AE6	228		J10	435		
	J6	859		CI	6	POMPEY'S	J10	172		
POLAR	AE5	33	POLLUTIONS	AK	64		OAL	73		
POLE	UDH	28		HAP	45	POMPOUS	T18	3		
	AA	851		J6	452		VP4	54		
	GE	6		G3	142		G3	664		
	HAP	1124	POLLUX	AE6	181		AE1	687		
	J3	396	POLONIAN	HAP	152		AE4	46		
	P6	178	POLTRON	HIF	413		AE12	756		

POMPOUS	TH	51
POMPS	AA	242
	J6	166
	J10	386
	M1	760
	G3	34
	AE11	33
	KT3	894
	HIF	442
POMPTINA	AE7	1093
PONDERED	RL	245
	M1	522
	AE1	33
	AE1	789
	KT3	498
	HIF	404
	CI	485
PONDERING	MF	11
	AE1	311
	AE7	345
	KT2	340
PONDEROUS	AM	750
	EOE	4
	HAP	1081
	M1	37
	M1	86
	G3	90
	AE2	558
	AE3	867
	AE4	588
	AE5	345
	AE5	459
	AE5	534
	AE5	544
	AE6	121
	AE9	681
	AE9	1016
	AE11	1098
	AE12	149
	AE12	386
	OAL	788
	M11	204
	AU	177
	AU	446
	SMP	85
PONIARD	AE12	459
PONIARDS	OAL	79
	KT3	507
PONTIC	VP8	137
PONTUS	G1	87
POOL	AE4	764
	CI	30
POOLS	DC	29
	VP8	123
	G1	528
	G3	655
	G3	725
	AE12	1078
	FL	30
POOP	P6	67
	AE10	299
	AE10	364
	AE10	931
	M11	76
POOR	HS	127
	PIE	11
	AM	642
	AM	997
	AM	1096
	AM	1142
	EMQ	12
	EWGR	39
	EMM	10
	ET	10
	SEL3	14
	ETL	4
	SCG2	17
	SCG2	26
	PFD	14
	PW	2
	EMQW	29
	PM	22
	EM	30
	PLN	7
	SLN	6
	EUO	1
	PAL	32
	PAL	39
	EAL	15
	PTW	13
	EOE	14
	STC	11
	PCB	12
	CM	125
	HP	221
	DA	7

POOR	DA	160
	EUF	5
	EUF	16
	AA	275
	AA	390
	AA	961
	PLB	23
	PLB	38
	ELB	30
	PPC	13
	PPC	23
	MD	126
	MD	158
	MF	208
	SAA	402
	SAA	469
	SAA	474
	SAA	550
	EK	39
	PDG	27
	EDG	1
	EDGA	6
	RL	93
	RL	381
	OE	35
	PD	56
	EC	18
	L2	40
	H29	21
	H2	72
	HAP	1251
	HAP	1279
	HAP	1406
	HAP	1589
	HAP	2233
	HAP	2259
	HAP	2289
	EDS	4
	PTS	13
	STS3	32
	STS3	38
	EKA	19
	EL	14
	EL	33
	EL	45
	ESH	4
	ESH	32
	SSH	1
	EH	19
	EH	27
	J1	51
	J1	146
	J1	163
	J1	167
	J1	178
	J3	18
	J3	56
	J3	129
	J3	215
	J3	227
	J3	244
	J3	245
	J3	249
	J3	266
	J3	269
	J3	271
	J3	299
	J3	325
	J3	342
	J3	343
	J3	379
	J3	424
	J3	454
	J3	471
	J6	104
	J6	170
	J6	309
	J6	381
	J6	398
	J6	469
	J6	591
	J6	766
	J10	37
	J10	163
	J10	297
	J10	330
	J16	95
	P1	105
	P1	168
	P1	259
	P3	139
	P4	55
	P5	243
	P6	73
	P6	132
	P6	155

POOR	M13	205
	EHC	20
	VP2	77
	G2	251
	G2	337
	G2	714
	G3	321
	AE1	843
	AE2	109
	AE2	619
	AE2	717
	AE2	870
	AE3	806
	AE4	142
	AE6	829
	AE8	135
	AE8	472
	AE8	479
	AE8	869
	AE10	734
	AE10	1169
	AE10	1309
	AE12	758
	OAL	273
	OAL	505
	OAL	603
	OAE2	3
	TJD	37
	B	521
	B	547
	B	653
	BP	36
	C	2
	C	613
	C	733
	M11	456
	FL	226
	AU	77
	WB	294
	WB	323
	WB	470
	GP	5
	GP	49
	GP	57
	GP	134
	PTP	25
	ETP	42
POORER	GP	53
POOREST	J6	762
POORLY	AM	1155
	HAP	1357
POPE	EOE	34
	PCB	42
	PLG	11
	PO	22
	PLB	38
	RL	255
	HAP	653
	HAP	666
	HAP	678
	PKA	35
POPERY	EPC	32
	MD	105
	HAP	597
	HAP	766
POPISH	PO	16
	RL	250
	HAP	1459
	PMK	32
POPLAR	L2	34
	H2	19
	HAP	440
	M1	785
	VP7	54
	VP7	84
	G2	18
	G2	94
	G4	742
	AE5	176
	AE8	45
	AE8	378
	AE10	274
	AE11	206
POPLARS	VP7	92
	VP7	96
	VP9	55
	AE8	366
POPPIES	MF	126
	G1	115
	M11	286
POPPITS	HAP	2074
POPPY	G1	302
	G4	196
	G4	786
	AE4	702
	AE9	583

POPPY-LEAF	AT	64	PORTENT	AE12	1238	POSSESS	KT1	458
POPPY'S	VP2	64		C	109		KT2	301
POPULAR	MD	80	PORTENTS	VP1	22		KT3	178
	MD	249		AE2	154		KT3	1114
	SAA	614		AE4	655		CAM	231
	PDG	30		AE5	924		M11	23
	L3	203		AE7	87		M11	248
	HAP	2386		AE7	351		CI	467
	G2	730	PORTER	EKA	4	POSSESSED	AM	194
	AE6	1116		AE6	563		SEL1	11
	OAL	152		AE6	535		HP	167
	KT3	739		AE7	246		AA	355
POPULARITY	SAA	180		AE8	393		SAA	516
POPULARLY	AA	336		TJD	36		SAA	854
	AA	490	PORTHOLE	AM	751		AT	116
	AA	689	PORTICO	OAL	73		EC	11
	SAA	191		OAL	76		L2	61
	J3	68		OAL	558		L3	253
	KT3	689	PORTICOES	AE3	452		L3	264
POPULONIA	AE10	251	PORTION	AR	28		L3	309
PORCELAIN	AM	115		PFD	14		H9	30
	DO	121		AM	937		H29	70
PORCH	J3	467		MF	217		HAP	803
	P3	101		SAA	817		HAP	1345
	AE2	775		PD	49		HAP	1452
	AE2	1035		HAP	251		HAP	1502
	AE6	865		EH	28		HAP	1729
	AE8	959		J6	203		HAP	2023
	M15	611		J10	223		HAP	2202
PORE	J6	70		J10	519		HAP	2264
	P1	147		MC	61		HAP	2356
	G2	12		AE1	295		STS1	4
	AE9	1098		AE5	484		EL	184
PORES	M1	143		AE9	363		J1	23
	G1	129		AE10	601		J10	7
	ETO	2		AE11	74		P2	36
PORKET	AE12	257		KT1	463		M1	852
PORPOISE	AE10	303		KT3	171		M9	92
PORRIDGE	PA	40		M8	179		VP2	103
	AA	576		BP	66		VP6	71
PORSENA	AE8	857		AU	166		G4	501
PORT	AM	139		M1	42		AE1	427
	AM	107	PORTIONS	G3	561		AE1	474
	AM	235		G4	322		AE2	55
	HP	202		AE1	274		AE2	383
	DA	128		AE1	715		AE2	516
	SAA	47	PORTLY	HAP	2435		AE2	1035
	P6	21	PORTRAIT	HS	59		AE3	478
	G1	586	PORTRAITURES	KT2	468		AE3	511
	G4	561	PORTRAYED	AK	134		AE4	141
	AE1	230	PORTRESS	KT2	501		AE4	284
	AE1	270	PORTS	AM	89		AE4	724
	AE1	553		AM	813		AE5	1036
	AE1	952		G2	221		AE6	74
	AE3	285		AE1	409		AE6	86
	AE3	332		AE1	809		AE6	701
	AE3	386		AE3	170		AE6	865
	AE3	378		AE7	276		AE7	68
	AE3	693	PORTUGAL	MF	36		AE7	334
	AE3	704	PORTUNUS	AR	121		AE7	524
	AE3	746		AE5	314		AE7	696
	AE3	930		DO	48		AE7	722
	AE5	43	PORY	G4	536		AE7	767
	AE5	317	PO'S	G2	633		AE8	259
	AE5	367	POSITIVE	HAP	649		AE8	460
	AE5	790		KT1	329		AE8	537
	AE7	295		EWR	5		AE8	766
	AE7	826	POSSE	EDGA	18		AE9	494
	DO	60	POSSESS	SMA	71		AE11	388
	B	524		SMA	135		AE11	485
	HIF	273		AM	1048		AE11	804
	HIF	596		EUO2	10		AE11	1302
	HIF	658		HP	96		B	7
	M11	437		AA	200		B	370
	M12	55		AA	476		M10	55
	AU	291		MD	124		HIF	413
	AU	365		L4	55		TH	32
	CI	371		HAP	1672		TH	380
	CI	554		HAP	2133		M12	320
	PWR	4		HAP	2144		M12	418
PORTAL	ODA	73		HAP	2529		M12	539
	G4	375		STS3	16		AU	207
	AE7	241		J6	41		WB	360
PORTEND	HS	70		P2	24		CI	345
	HS	110		M1	803	POSSESSING	STC	2
	P3	83		AE1	302		STC	8
	AE3	465		AE2	690		STC	10
	TH	223		AE5	342		DA	181
	M12	30		AE6	200		SSF	5
PORTENDS	EUF	12		AE6	994		SDG	4
	G1	606		AE10	64		SDG	10
PORTENDING	H3	20		AE11	68		SDG	22
PORTENT	AE2	264		AE11	177		SDG	27
	AE2	322		AE11	575		FS4	10
	AE5	689		AE12	536		STS1	9
	AE7	115		KT1	339		STS1	11

Word	Ref	No.
POSSESSING	SKA3	16
	SKA6	31
	G2	700
POSSESSION	PA	18
	AA	685
	MD	218
	SAA	662
	L4	51
	HAP	809
	HAP	2062
	HAP	2210
	BR	46
	AE3	424
	AE8	74
	AE9	367
	KT3	164
	KT3	632
	FL	141
	WB	484
POSSESSIONS	SAA	332
POSSET	C	24
POSSETS	UDH	86
POSSIBLE	J6	81
POST	AM	836
	J6	348
	P6	109
	HI	88
	MC	64
	AE2	1091
	AE6	777
	AE9	65
	AE9	199
	AE11	578
	AE11	705
POSTED	AE12	659
	B	152
POSTERITY	LCA	39
	AA	426
	AA	770
	SAA	1043
	TA	307
	TA	308
	J10	129
	G2	82
	AE3	659
	AE10	1126
POSTERN	AE2	619
	B	152
POSTHASTE	P5	201
POSTING	AE7	223
	FL	491
	WB	36
POSTPONE	HAP	2142
POSTS	M1	761
	AE2	447
	AE2	604
	AE2	658
	AE2	670
	AE2	687
	AE7	252
	AE9	716
	KT3	104
	CI	561
POSTURE	CM	5
	L4	271
	L4	277
	HH	10
	GK	37
	GK	158
	OAL	601
	B	688
POSTURES	J6	409
	GK	66
POT	ET	6
	PO	15
	H2	82
	SKA4	19
	SKA4	20
	SKA4	21
	SKA4	22
	SKA4	23
	J6	370
	OAE2	66
	BP	68
POTENT	AR	290
	MF	121
	SAA	671
	HAP	2408
	AE11	591
POTENTATE	GE	49
	HAP	2424
POTHER	EDGA	25
	PWR	16
POT-HERBS	G4	192
POTION	J6	796
	J6	816
POTITIUS	AE8	357
	AE8	371
POTSHERDS	J3	431
POTTED	P3	145
POTTER'S	P3	39
POTTERS'	G2	482
POT-VALOR	OAL	664
POULTRY	HAP	2289
	HAP	2362
	C	703
	M15	692
POUNCED	HAP	2411
POUNCES	AE11	1067
	M12	740
POUND	PD	40
	PDS	44
	J3	412
	J6	196
	J10	165
	G4	87
POUNDED	G2	125
	G4	389
	AE2	636
	AE5	626
POUNDER	G2	127
POUNDERS	J6	488
POUNDS	ELN	6
	J10	235
	G1	138
	M11	392
POUR	PRH	34
	J6	412
	P6	164
	M1	353
	M1	374
	VCS	4
	VP5	110
	G2	266
	G4	444
	G4	784
	AE2	554
	AE3	93
	AE6	324
	AE7	179
	AE9	676
	AE11	801
	KT2	189
	HIF	636
	HIF	645
POURED	T23	32
	TA	294
	HAP	1914
	VP6	109
	G1	655
	G2	144
	G4	548
	AE5	101
	AE5	131
	AE5	625
	AE5	897
	AE5	1015
	AE6	314
	AE7	302
	AE12	72
	KT3	990
	B	366
	B	683
	HIF	61
	FL	216
	FL	384
	WB	536
	M15	59
	M15	445
	CI	604
POURING	P2	91
	M1	366
	G1	439
	G4	413
	AE4	298
	AE9	910
	AE10	19
	AE10	576
	AE12	666
	B	707
POURS	AA	375
	J10	247
	M1	359
	G1	174
	G2	440
	AE4	84
	AE4	233
	AE4	658
	AE6	350
	AE6	362
	AE6	559
	AE8	936
POURS	AE9	470
	AE12	593
	AE12	619
POUT	L4	160
POUTING	G3	421
POVERTY	RL	103
	H29	23
	H29	86
	H2	2
	HAP	1277
	HAP	1287
	J3	42
	J3	276
	J6	410
	J6	474
	P1	258
	AE3	807
	AE6	592
	AE6	1161
	KT2	587
	B	548
	B	638
	BP	35
	C	29
	WB	458
	WB	463
	WB	465
	WB	485
	GP	91
POWDER	AM	595
	AM	977
	EDGA	36
POWDERED	FL	237
POWER	AR	32
	AR	133
	AR	202
	AR	266
	SMA	96
	LC	58
	LC	85
	LCA	29
	PIE	3
	EIE	25
	AM	152
	AM	158
	AM	185
	AM	413
	AM	524
	AM	796
	AM	838
	AM	856
	AM	960
	SMM2	2
	PT	24
	SCG2	23
	SCG2	28
	PUO2	38
	E	11
	ML	48
	EAL	22
	EOE	29
	CM	70
	DA	54
	ETG	18
	AA	143
	AA	148
	AA	155
	AA	226
	AA	298
	AA	305
	AA	411
	AA	417
	AA	496
	AA	531
	AA	612
	AA	712
	AA	718
	AA	777
	AA	838
	AA	864
	AA	896
	AA	984
	AA	993
	AA	996
	AA	999
	AA	1024
	MD	50
	MD	82
	MD	90
	MD	92
	MD	115
	MD	128
	MD	134
	MD	138
	MD	204
	MD	213

POWER	MD	223	POWER	G3	500	POWER	TJD	182
	MD	230		AE1	59		M8	116
	MD	235		AE1	74		B	95
	MD	244		AE1	80		B	105
	MD	273		AE1	98		B	279
	MD	300		AE1	199		B	413
	MD	303		AE1	317		B	420
	PRH	28		AE1	382		B	430
	SAA	93		AE1	579		B	493
	SAA	129		AE1	937		B	505
	SAA	169		AE1	1022		B	559
	SAA	234		AE2	101		B	581
	SAA	264		AE2	102		B	599
	SAA	741		AE2	239		B	622
	SAA	778		AE3	76		BP	13
	SAA	790		AE3	467		BP	14
	SAA	801		AE3	488		CAM	245
	SAA	875		AE4	79		HIF	9
	SAA	881		AE4	302		HIF	66
	PK	23		AE4	355		HIF	115
	EK	4		AE4	422		HIF	120
	PDG	33		AE4	755		HIF	143
	RL	379		AE4	813		HIF	183
	RL	99		AE4	829		HIF	282
	RL	430		AE5	810		HIF	342
	AT	28		AE5	1041		HIF	393
	AT	109		AE5	1112		HIF	398
	EC	14		AE6	88		HIF	410
	L1	3		AE6	158		HIF	453
	L1	29		AE6	176		HIF	542
	L1	36		AE6	275		HIF	548
	L2	13		AE6	467		HIF	653
	L2	43		AE6	473		HIF	686
	L3	206		AE6	1076		HIF	701
	T23	8		AE6	1082		HIF	736
	H9	22		AE7	24		HIF	780
	H29	51		AE7	234		HIF	793
	H29	71		AE7	430		C	519
	TA	57		AE7	433		C	544
	TA	231		AE7	610		C	683
	TA	412		AE7	761		M11	145
	AK	120		AE7	815		FL	97
	HAP	28		AE8	80		FL	403
	HAP	114		AE8	195		M12	48
	HAP	467		AE8	425		M12	61
	HAP	484		AE8	442		M12	272
	HAP	492		AE8	503		M12	642
	HAP	499		AE8	521		M12	776
	HAP	510		AE8	550		AU	302
	HAP	526		AE8	631		AU	347
	HAP	577		AE8	657		WB	76
	HAP	674		AE9	19		WB	92
	HAP	1165		AE9	88		WB	322
	HAP	1822		AE10	26		WB	356
	HAP	1968		AE10	51		WB	379
	HAP	2140		AE10	868		M15	49
	HAP	2182		AE10	879		M15	153
	HAP	2278		AE10	895		M15	209
	HAP	2516		AE11	366		GP	98
	HAP	2531		AE11	566		GP	122
	HAP	2564		AE11	1154		CI	2
	SSC	10		AE11	1159		CI	455
	SSC	55		AE12	289		CI	456
	BR	341		AE12	583		CI	461
	BR	345		AE12	926	POWERFUL	AR	309
	PSH	42		AE12	1170		SMA	15
	J1	171		OAL	669		VHH	24
	J3	61		AF	27		AM	24
	J6	314		DO	8		AM	943
	J6	770		DO	89		AM	1201
	J10	85		DO	92		PM	15
	J10	125		DO	146		CM	46
	J10	159		KT1	73		HP	51
	J10	176		KT1	270		HP	61
	P1	265		KT1	318		AA	917
	M1	87		KT1	329		MD	68
	M1	295		KT1	408		SAA	539
	M1	552		KT1	480		SAA	1000
	M1	809		KT2	166		MN	13
	M9	134		KT2	210		HAP	303
	M9	151		KT2	214		P2	56
	M9	181		KT2	350		M1	993
	M13	16		KT2	363		VP2	82
	SFL	17		KT2	470		VP8	139
	VCS	16		KT2	508		G1	36
	HI	125		KT2	636		AE4	410
	HI	179		KT3	128		AE6	353
	MC	21		KT3	129		AE6	568
	DHP	20		KT3	267		AE7	262
	VP1	27		KT3	291		AE7	1037
	VP7	44		KT3	293		AE8	661
	VP8	151		KT3	300		OAL	787
	G1	41		KT3	308		KT3	273
	G1	471		KT3	790		KT3	317
	G3	423		KT3	813		M10	36
	G3	445		KT3	1054		CAM	177

POWERFUL	CAM	367	POWERS	KT2	219	PRAISE	HS	9
	HIF	384		KT2	482		HS	16
	M15	491		KT3	264		SMA	54
POWERS	AR	101		KT3	671		SMA	106
	AR	195		M8	11		LC	82
	EMQW	18		B	397		LCA	17
	SLN	11		BP	3		AM	190
	HP	137		BP	137		AM	659
	PUF	13		M10	62		AM	660
	SAA	229		CAM	326		AM	772
	SAA	1087		HIF	25		AM	774
	L3	188		HIF	105		AM	1038
	L4	237		HIF	109		AM	1098
	HAP	1573		HIF	272		PCG1	33
	HAP	2117		HIF	327		ECG2	33
	HAP	2137		HIF	475		PLN	44
	HAP	2303		HIF	670		PUO1	42
	OD	39		HIF	715		PUO2	36
	J3	490		C	200		PC1	25
	J6	515		M11	244		PC2	23
	J10	536		M11	309		ML	26
	P2	15		M12	12		ML	33
	P2	98		M12	29		ML	45
	P2	125		WB	430		EOE	28
	P3	179		M15	190		PCB	5
	M1	381		CI	361		HP	125
	M1	508		CI	489		PUO4	14
	M1	702		CI	565		PUO5	30
	M1	764		STP	23		AA	187
	M1	957	POX	PMQ	43		AA	247
	M9	51		EEL	17		AA	297
	HI	93		PCG2	20		AA	303
	HI	157		PC1	22		AA	312
	M1	235		PPC	18		AA	440
	VP5	80		SAA	407		AA	816
	VP5	123		PAA	38		AA	899
	VP8	27		PMK	18		MD	169
	VP9	32		EMKG	1		MF	173
	G1	9	POXED	MD	266		SAA	942
	G1	145	POYNANT	C	21		SAA	971
	G1	672	PRACTICE	HS	128		SAA	984
	G2	703		AR	92		SAA	1054
	G2	768		PUO2	11		SAA	1059
	G4	292		ETG	17		SAA	1100
	G4	775		EPC	16		RL	50
	G4	783		SAA	1018		RL	83
	G4	798		PD	37		RL	452
	AE1	803		AK	18		PD	19
	AE1	870		HAP	433		ER	56
	AE2	207		HAP	1480		L4	143
	AE2	332		HAP	1632		T18	61
	AE2	470		HAP	1967		TA	304
	AE2	542		BR	293		TA	332
	AE2	561		ETS	28		TA	382
	AE2	1058		J6	111		AK	16
	AE3	30		J6	713		HAP	331
	AE3	210		P2	131		HAP	388
	AE3	648		VCS	31		HAP	1355
	AE3	689		G1	122		HAP	2466
	AE3	786		AE11	1057		SSC	44
	AE4	66		OAL	742		SSC	57
	AE4	547		MM	26		BR	4
	AE4	738		LMC	6		BR	343
	AE4	876		LMC	10		EL	29
	AE4	978		HIF	160		EL	125
	AE5	304		C	171		EL	129
	AE5	1079		M15	205		EL	367
	AE6	81		GP	77		J3	77
	AE6	98		ETP	26		J3	155
	AE6	119	PRACTICED	PCB	39		J3	159
	AE6	621		AA	825		J3	186
	AE6	711		MF	124		J6	263
	AE7	132		EL	126		J10	41
	AE7	354		J1	107		J10	226
	AE7	726		OAE2	58		P1	12
	AE7	871		HIF	266		P1	51
	AE7	981		C	788		P1	74
	AE8	1	PRACTICES	SAA	115		P1	88
	AE8	96		AE5	287		P1	136
	AE8	417	PRAENESTE	AE7	943		P4	109
	AE8	492	PRAENESTE'S	AE7	938		M13	125
	AE9	28		AE8	743		PLT	38
	AE9	880	PRAESCIOUS	AE11	242		MC	20
	AE10	14	PRAETOR	J3	219		MC	58
	AE10	524		J3	348		GK	27
	AE11	76		J10	54		GK	77
	AE11	427		P5	126		VP2	50
	AE11	504		P5	253		VP4	32
	AE11	663		CI	476		VP4	64
	AE12	208	PRAETORIAN	PUO1	40		VP5	13
	AE12	273	PRAETOR'S	P5	132		VP5	64
	AE12	295		P5	182		VP5	78
	AE12	301	PRAETORS'	J1	155		VP6	18
	AE12	721	PRAISE	UDH	15		VP7	33
	AE12	796		JH	22		VP7	37
	OAL	638		HS	7		VP9	26

Word	Ref	No.
PRAISE	VP9	45
	G1	481
	G2	136
	G2	221
	G2	535
	G2	543
	G2	706
	G2	730
	G3	81
	G3	176
	G3	188
	G3	293
	G4	8
	G4	314
	G4	816
	AE1	857
	AE1	1047
	AE4	341
	AE4	397
	AE5	296
	AE6	1164
	AE8	381
	AE8	954
	AE9	254
	AE9	896
	AE11	699
	AE11	772
	AE11	1229
	AE12	79
	AE12	583
	OAL	677
	OAL	703
	OAL	708
	OAL	846
	AF	47
	KT1	51
	TJD	206
	M8	45
	M8	215
	B	4
	B	533
	B	550
	M10	90
	M12	713
	M12	721
	M12	722
	M12	758
	AU	377
	AU	388
	AU	389
	AU	537
	AU	561
	CI	14
	CI	149
	EP	1
	EWR	20
PRAISED	SMM2	11
	PA	35
	ECG2	22
	EUO	36
	PAZ	29
	HP	164
	AA	41
	J1	113
	J16	35
	P1	171
	P3	88
	M13	90
	VP5	83
	AE1	884
	AE2	179
	KT1	119
	KT1	599
	M8	156
	CAM	121
	CAM	252
	CAM	375
	GP	49
PRAISES	LCA	48
	PUO4	3
	SAA	501
	HAP	2451
	EL	64
	EL	363
	J6	358
	P4	126
	M1	676
	VP6	8
	G4	471
	AE4	134
	AE10	707
	AE10	1169
	OAL	704
	MM	6
	TJD	206
	M8	159

Word	Ref	No.
PRAISEWORTHY	TJD	205
PRAISING	AA	555
	EL	129
PRANCE	J6	661
	G3	300
	M12	619
PRANCES	AE11	744
PRANCING	G3	122
	AE5	871
	KT2	47
	FL	241
PRANKS	PCB	41
	WB	26
PRATE	EMK	15
	P6	28
	VP3	21
	WB	143
PRATING	SKA4	18
	J6	566
PRATTLERS	EK	5
PRATTLING	L3	77
	L4	261
PRAY	EWG	22
	VHH	23
	PWGR	22
	ELN	7
	PKK	22
	POE	25
	EMW	7
	AA	592
	AA	983
	EPC	20
	SAA	358
	PDG	24
	PDG	33
	EDG	27
	EDGA	8
	RL	50
	OE	55
	H29	94
	PAA	28
	HAP	1458
	HAP	1710
	HAP	2312
	HAP	2319
	BR	4
	PKA	39
	PKA	43
	ELW	7
	EL	19
	J10	167
	J10	450
	P2	7
	P3	134
	M1	287
	G1	40
	AE1	74
	AE2	882
	AE3	716
	AE3	830
	AE5	74
	AE5	75
	AE6	711
	AE7	824
	AE10	774
	OAL	501
	MFL	31
	KT1	424
	KT1	426
	KT1	431
	KT3	126
	KT3	154
	KT3	295
	B	171
	B	571
	M11	243
	AU	353
	CI	81
	EMKG	29
PRAYED	MD	34
	TA	45
	TA	93
	TA	163
	HAP	1753
	HAP	1836
	HAP	2235
	BR	254
	EL	115
	J6	509
	J10	299
	AE6	188
	AE6	282
	AE10	353
	AE10	727
	AE12	596
	AE12	1125

Word	Ref	No.
PRAYED	AE12	1348
	KT2	162
	KT3	285
	M10	66
	CAM	170
	CAM	325
	CAM	360
	HIF	67
	HIF	526
	M11	248
	WB	74
	M15	48
	CI	313
PRAYER	AR	142
	PO	14
	DA	6
	AA	238
	PLB	49
	SAA	55
	PDG	25
	RL	414
	RL	83
	L4	245
	HAP	367
	HAP	1400
	HAP	2322
	HAP	2503
	BR	2
	EL	112
	EL	117
	EL	125
	ESH	26
	J3	427
	J6	513
	J6	542
	J6	628
	J10	300
	J10	444
	J16	61
	P2	46
	P2	54
	P2	67
	P2	71
	P2	82
	P6	65
	M1	1018
	M1	1071
	M9	134
	M9	161
	VP1	59
	G4	783
	G4	792
	AE1	577
	AE1	675
	AE1	1006
	AE4	85
	AE4	621
	AE5	697
	AE6	107
	AE6	287
	AE6	517
	AE7	237
	AE7	326
	AE10	227
	AE10	598
	AE10	841
	AE11	352
	AE11	1165
	AE12	94
	AE12	269
	AE12	1130
	OAL	314
	MFL	29
	KT3	175
	KT3	249
	KT3	306
	M8	118
	BP	128
	BP	197
	M10	68
	CAM	327
	HIF	57
	HIF	149
	HIF	216
	HIF	353
	HIF	606
	HIF	619
	HIF	627
	C	483
	M11	215
	M11	250
	M12	277
	AU	205
	M15	194
PRAYERS	SCD1	20
	CM	81

PRAYERS	EDGA	21
	T23	66
	TA	98
	TA	105
	HAP	1392
	HAP	2169
	BR	35
	BR	247
	BR	248
	PKA	41
	EL	64
	J6	695
	J10	177
	J10	436
	P2	7
	P5	266
	M1	496
	M1	509
	M1	973
	M1	1044
	HI	19
	G1	63
	G3	696
	G4	573
	G4	656
	G4	775
	G4	797
	AE1	95
	AE2	238
	AE2	470
	AE2	886
	AE2	938
	AE3	45
	AE3	120
	AE3	339
	AE3	558
	AE4	299
	AE4	335
	AE4	461
	AE4	598
	AE4	636
	AE4	893
	AE5	901
	AE5	1022
	AE6	82
	AE6	174
	AE6	632
	AE9	416
	AE10	512
	AE11	546
	AE11	726
	AE12	265
	AE12	334
	OAL	400
	OAL	502
	OAL	816
	LMC	7
	KT2	346
	KT2	385
	KT2	473
	KT3	128
	M10	62
	CAM	179
	CAM	336
	HIF	14
	HIF	45
	HIF	142
	HIF	402
	HIF	492
	TH	22
	M11	182
	M11	219
	WB	24
	CI	350
PRAYING	PLB	50
	NS	7
	NS	18
	NS	29
PRAYS	EAL	15
	J10	184
	P2	73
	M9	51
	G4	727
PRAYTHEE	P2	35
	P6	135
PREACH	MD	157
	MD	269
	SAA	703
	GE	17
	HAP	1203
	P5	276
	EHC	12
	OAL	530
PREACHED	HAP	878
	HAP	1510
	AE7	747

PREACHED	MM	20
	GP	27
	GP	128
PREACHER	GP	18
	PTP	49
PREACHERS	L3	103
	GP	54
PREACHERS'	SAA	303
PREACHES	MD	82
PREACHING	ETC	24
	PO	13
	HAP	907
	HAP	914
	HAP	1028
	GP	77
PREASE	J3	392
	AE8	933
	AE12	436
	HIF	338
PRECARIOUS	DA	160
	HAP	510
	J1	154
	M11	44
PRECEDE	CI	638
PRECEDENT	AA	53
	J6	811
PRECEDING	RL	347
PRECEPT	AM	1055
	HAP	2331
	AE3	553
	MM	26
	C	77
	GP	18
PRECEPTS	PUO1	18
	P5	55
	G1	256
	G3	276
	G4	403
	OAL	44
	M15	205
	M15	711
PRECIOUS	LC	97
	AM	10
	AM	79
	AM	95
	AM	1170
	EK	29
	OE	38
	EKA	24
	EL	287
	EL	301
	J6	216
	J6	228
	J6	600
	P5	198
	M1	175
	PLT	49
	AE1	169
	AE1	913
	AE3	627
	AE5	833
	AE6	299
	AE8	733
	AE8	894
	AE9	483
	DO	142
	KT3	977
	B	610
	B	636
	B	747
	CAM	17
	CAM	353
	C	671
	FL	262
	FL	566
	M12	344
	AU	177
	M15	661
	GP	83
PRECIOUSLY	AM	115
PRECIPICE	TH	403
PRECIPICE'S	AM	979
PRECIPICES	AM	43
	AM	281
	G1	67
PRECIPITATE	EL	134
	AE11	1284
	AE12	767
PRECIPITATED	AE4	371
PRECIPITATES	M1	829
	G4	614
	AE8	560
	AE9	976
	TH	212
PRECIPITOUS	MD	66

PREDECESSOR	BR	194
	WB	348
	M15	273
PREDESTINATING	HAP	165
PREDESTINATION	C	508
PREDESTINED	AE11	1246
PREDICAMENT	AA	680
PREDICTED	M15	74
PREDICTION	AE12	46
PREDOMINANT	HAP	1681
PREËXISTING	AK	29
PREFACE	G2	66
PREFER	HAP	474
	HAP	2437
	PDS	27
	J10	261
	J10	556
	J16	8
	P2	37
	M9	11
	M13	175
	G3	595
	AE3	342
	AE11	644
	OAL	403
	OAL	418
	OAL	640
	OAL	768
	OAL	798
	B	525
	CAM	107
	HIF	209
PREFERENCE	HAP	2261
PREFERMENT	EMK	16
	AA	510
	SAA	436
	SAA	881
	HAP	1533
	EHC	22
	GP	70
PREFERMENT'S	J1	57
PREFERMENTS	ELB	33
	J1	110
	P5	75
	P5	255
PREFERRED	HAP	2037
	HAP	2075
	J1	156
	J6	165
	VP2	88
	VP7	24
	G3	254
	AE2	936
	AE4	320
	AE12	583
	OAL	707
	KT3	214
	B	272
	HIF	142
	HIF	168
	HIF	620
	TH	388
	AU	432
	CI	442
PREFERRING	AE4	79
PREFERS	AA	199
	J6	305
	G1	58
	AE10	65
	BP	168
	M15	194
PREFIXED	AR	147
	AE1	364
	AE9	126
	AE12	799
	WB	106
PREGNANT	AA	882
	J6	531
	G1	156
	AE6	694
	AE7	572
	M15	96
PRE-INGAGED	CI	246
PREJUDGE	AE12	115
PRELACY	MD	301
	GP	88
PRELATE	AM	145
	GP	87
PRELUDE	MF	37
	BR	187
	G3	359
	AE11	237
PRELUDES	TA	462
	AE12	160
	M15	283
PRELUDING	CAM	220

PRESENCE	L2	54	PRESENT	AE6	287	PRESERVE	HAP	1484
	HAP	414		AE6	548		EL	376
	HAP	604		AE7	55		M1	597
	HAP	612		AE7	182		M9	94
	HAP	1273		AE7	392		M9	105
	PP	42		AE8	107		M13	65
	PMS	34		AE9	489		VP9	33
	M9	207		AE10	719		G3	467
	VP8	10		AE11	144		G4	349
	AE2	816		AE11	345		AE2	214
	AE4	215		AE11	634		MFL	3
	AE8	265		AE12	233		C	165
	AE8	950		AE12	370	PRESERVED	RH	95
	AE9	84		OAL	533		SMA	48
	AE9	346		OAL	724		SMA	62
	KT1	387		AF	35		LCA	42
	KT3	78		AF	36		DA	80
	B	82		KT3	286		PR	29
	B	169		KT3	1096		RL	259
	C	416		M8	116		L3	71
PRESENT	LC	11		B	88		BR	101
	DC	24		B	580		EL	174
	AM	87		B	608		VP1	28
	AM	613		B	614		AE1	530
	PT	30		B	628		AE3	612
	PEL	29		B	640		AE4	859
	PFD	7		B	647		AE6	112
	CM	7		M10	68		AE10	1210
	CM	116		M10	96		MM	33
	HP	71		HIF	103		DO	142
	HP	110		C	289		M8	264
	DA	70		TH	38		M8	329
	PUF	24		TH	360		BP	93
	AA	718		TH	414		AU	425
	AA	755		M11	51		M15	62
	AA	980		M11	262	PRESERVES	HAP	1040
	SAA	172		M11	371		AE12	635
	SAA	261		M11	489		TJD	172
	SAA	316		FL	569		TJD	209
	SAA	386		M12	491	PRESERVING	AE10	1209
	SAA	578		M12	709	PRESIDE	G1	34
	RL	363		GP	119		G4	232
	L3	156		CI	324		M15	720
	T27	123		CI	354	PRESIDENT	SAA	946
	H9	20		ETP	36	PRESIDES	EUO2	15
	H29	50	PRESENTED	PLN	9		G4	313
	TA	306		CM	112		AE3	537
	HAP	467		M12	316	PRESIDING	G3	179
	HAP	566	PRESENTING	AE1	836		AE3	690
	HAP	1658	PRESENTS	SMA	125	PRESS	AM	1035
	HAP	1772		LC	3		EWGR	22
	HAP	1968		PP	4		SEL2	8
	HAP	2135		J1	53		ENH	13
	HAP	2146		J3	84		HP	80
	BR	61		J10	469		EUF	17
	BR	286		PPS	18		PRH	19
	STS2	9		P2	125		SAA	310
	J1	214		P5	255		SAA	767
	J1	221		M13	141		SAA	826
	J6	457		M13	145		L4	74
	J10	140		VP2	60		HAP	2504
	J10	524		VP2	82		VP10	54
	P2	56		AE1	115		G1	412
	P2	94		AE1	674		G2	482
	M1	863		AE1	931		G3	612
	M9	170		AE1	952		G4	152
	PLT	6		AE1	999		AE1	693
	MC	2		AE2	63		AE2	82
	VP1	59		AE4	715		AE2	444
	VP3	104		AE7	210		AE5	263
	VP3	109		AE7	333		AE6	432
	VP3	165		AE7	357		AE7	795
	VP5	127		AE8	731		AE9	207
	VP5	140		AE8	960		AE9	972
	VP6	97		AE11	352		AE10	199
	VP8	85		AE11	380		AE11	24
	G2	177		AE11	433		AE11	690
	G3	715		AE11	505		AE11	799
	AE1	134		AE11	536		AE11	899
	AE1	278		AE11	726		AE11	945
	AE1	289		OAL	472		AE11	1119
	AE1	727		M8	216		AE11	1230
	AE1	859		HIF	14		AE12	28
	AE1	908		HIF	142		OAL	185
	AE1	919		HIF	606		OAL	215
	AE1	1027		TH	321		KT3	399
	AE2	47	PRESERVATION	BR	106		KT3	492
	AE3	113	PRESERVE	AM	334		M8	390
	AE3	125		PAR	12		B	232
	AE3	800		CM	67		HIF	656
	AE3	624		DA	64		HIF	740
	AE3	631		EMW	10		C	597
	AE4	179		PUF	28		M12	589
	AE4	979		AA	985		M12	658
	AE5	90		SAA	537		CI	283
	AE6	213		SAA	577	PRESSED	HS	135

PRESSED	AM	507
	AM	707
	SEL3	15
	SCG1	7
	SM2	1
	CM	66
	SAA	147
	SAA	570
	SAA	584
	SAA	759
	SAA	763
	SAA	853
	SAA	1101
	TA	229
	TA	453
	J6	133
	HI	46
	HI	173
	G1	681
	G2	318
	G3	733
	G4	106
	G4	124
	AE1	864
	AE2	511
	AE4	118
	AE5	598
	AE5	608
	AE5	1051
	AE6	123
	AE6	461
	AE6	571
	AE6	627
	AE6	743
	AE6	1193
	AE8	475
	AE8	605
	AE9	54
	AE9	357
	AE9	589
	AE9	959
	AE10	336
	AE10	541
	AE10	611
	AE11	844
	AE11	857
	AE11	965
	AE11	969
	AE11	1098
	AE11	1133
	AE12	458
	OAL	131
	AF	30
	KT1	149
	KT3	711
	M8	180
	BP	111
	CAM	164
	M11	204
	M11	90
	FL	57
	FL	293
	M12	19
	M12	196
	M12	328
	M12	467
	M12	680
	M15	336
	CI	445
PRESSES	L4	40
	AE9	1076
	AE12	593
	M10	89
	M11	164
	M12	190
PRESSING	HP	179
	SAA	25
	SAA	164
	SAA	600
	L3	272
	EL	283
	AE1	83
	AE5	424
	AE6	559
	AE9	645
	AE10	771
	AE11	1273
	AE12	402
	AE12	533
	AE12	1001
	AE12	1082
PRESUME	SAA	490
	PCG1	33
	PAR	9
	PMQW	2
	EMQW	22

PRESUME	PM	29
	ENH	34
	EMK	15
	PUO3	33
	PRH	41
	PD	21
	PAA	33
	AK	39
	HAP	1036
	J16	16
	G1	52
	AE6	627
	AE9	389
	AE9	757
	AE10	130
	AE10	622
	AE11	24
	AE11	1120
	KT2	257
	HIF	132
	C	564
	FL	475
	AU	259
PRESUMED	AM	86
	SAA	159
	RL	401
	HAP	388
	BR	340
	VP7	31
	AE1	63
	AE10	329
	AE11	427
	M8	86
	C	562
	M12	826
	PTP	51
PRESUMER	PK	32
PRESUMES	PAZ	12
	PUO4	28
	HAP	1805
	AE6	343
	AE10	1007
PRESUMEST	AE6	527
PRESUMING	EAZ	42
	HAP	679
	J10	15
	VP5	11
	AE5	503
	AE9	918
	M8	184
PRESUMPTION	SAA	177
	EL	372
PRESUMPTUOUS	CI	363
PRETENCE	OE	13
PRETEND	AR	193
	LC	69
	AM	21
	PMQW	3
	ML	15
	CM	125
	DA	135
	PR	30
	AA	955
	PLB	5
	MD	308
	EK	6
	RL	290
	GE	71
	HAP	481
	HAP	1034
	BR	346
	ELT	9
	AE2	23
	AE4	974
	AE10	123
	AE12	1370
	KT1	317
	B	378
	HIF	198
	AU	544
	ETP	33
	SSF	17
PRETENDED	AA	919
	MD	224
	SAA	209
	SAA	693
	HAP	1456
	HAP	2550
	HAP	2555
	AE2	106
	AE4	489
	AE9	189
	B	393
	HIF	280
	AU	268
PRETENDER	M1	1053

PRETENDER'S	SAA	868
PRETENDERS	HAP	946
	G4	93
PRETENDING	AA	504
	HAP	835
	P2	65
	TJD	155
	M11	249
PRETENDS	HAP	952
	J6	334
	P3	151
	PLT	53
PRETENSE	UDH	13
	PFD	9
	PKK	20
	PR	13
	AA	315
	AA	362
	AA	428
	AA	463
	AA	745
	ELB	28
	MD	50
	MF	19
	MF	193
	SAA	34
	SAA	106
	SAA	154
	SAA	582
	SAA	647
	AK	96
	HAP	347
	HAP	677
	HAP	726
	HAP	2040
	AE1	484
	AE2	1092
	AE4	417
	AE7	463
	OAL	178
	KT1	306
	KT1	375
	KT3	409
	WB	183
	WB	361
	M15	168
	EMKG	24
PRETENSION	PDS	3
PRETENSIONS	HAP	1061
	AU	256
	AU	550
PRETHEE	CAM	204
PRETTY	SMM2	15
	EAZ	1
	ESF	10
	EC	39
	L4	156
	T27	55
	T27	72
	T27	73
	T27	92
	HAP	1715
	EKA	22
	J3	371
	J6	757
	M13	141
	VP3	104
	OAE2	46
	C	733
PREVAIL	HP	198
	AA	461
	AA	724
	MD	69
	MD	290
	MF	24
	SAA	892
	PDG	17
	RL	349
	RL	376
	L3	207
	L4	231
	FS2	4
	HAP	62
	HAP	466
	HAP	630
	HAP	1194
	HAP	1266
	HAP	1678
	HAP	1719
	HAP	2333
	BR	295
	EL	110
	PSH	21
	J10	471
	P1	13
	P1	172

PREVAIL	P4	25
	VP9	15
	G2	453
	G2	681
	AE6	548
	AE7	430
	AE10	735
	AE12	280
	OAL	700
	KT1	481
	KT3	311
	KT3	755
	M8	278
	CAM	5
	HIF	687
	M11	47
	AU	502
	WB	535
	ETP	17
PREVAILED	RL	250
	HAP	2428
	BR	246
	PMS	29
	EL	163
	J6	460
	SAA	1135
	M1	849
	AE7	815
	AE9	941
	AE10	430
	AE12	741
	KT3	648
	KT3	670
	CAM	232
	TH	375
	TH	393
	M12	43
	AU	297
	AU	592
	CI	463
PREVAILING	SAA	167
	L4	208
	H2	100
	HAP	1688
	J1	77
	J6	236
	AE11	817
	AE12	927
	M8	273
PREVAILS	MD	132
	L4	210
	HAP	1665
	G4	129
	AE5	896
	AE10	1062
	AE12	860
	M11	66
	M12	626
	WB	432
PREVALENT	L4	236
PREVENT	HS	15
	HS	131
	AR	67
	LCA	34
	EMQ	10
	SMQ	9
	EMQw	26
	S	6
	A	6
	AA	699
	L3	79
	L4	128
	FS3	17
	AK	153
	HAP	937
	HAP	1213
	EL	69
	J10	434
	P2	65
	P4	10
	M1	832
	M1	856
	G1	303
	G2	751
	G3	115
	AE1	946
	AE1	957
	AE2	107
	AE2	844
	AE4	816
	AE5	915
	AE9	504
	AE9	942
	AE10	400
	AE10	1195
	AE12	751
PREVENT	OAL	214
	HIF	125
	HIF	537
	TH	27
	M12	491
	AU	172
	CI	193
	CI	255
	CI	597
	ESK	24
PREVENTED	PD	30
	EL	74
	ODA	38
	J1	181
	AE10	458
PREVENTING	AR	282
	BR	3
	BR	274
	G3	736
	AE4	446
	AE10	361
	AE10	477
	KT3	124
	FL	36
PREVENTION	HAP	1145
PREVENTS	AA	344
	HAP	1968
	J6	860
	G1	384
	AE4	440
	AE10	540
	AE10	1133
	AE10	1182
	M8	175
	M12	407
	CI	337
PREY	SMA	39
	AM	44
	AM	101
	AM	121
	AM	328
	AM	426
	AM	525
	AM	810
	AM	885
	AM	940
	AM	996
	AM	1089
	AM	1106
	PA	19
	PC1	9
	PAL	2
	CM	100
	HP	22
	HP	114
	DA	139
	AA	448
	AA	701
	PLB	15
	MD	192
	MD	297
	SAA	1
	RL	402
	H3	51
	H2	53
	AK	94
	HAP	155
	HAP	246
	HAP	304
	HAP	330
	HAP	1566
	HAP	1920
	HAP	2298
	HAP	2408
	BR	53
	ODA	4
	J6	328
	M1	280
	M1	315
	M1	636
	M1	721
	VP3	27
	VP3	117
	G1	552
	G2	84
	G2	515
	G3	74
	G3	621
	G3	713
	G3	844
	G4	16
	G4	168
	AE1	744
	AE2	77
	AE2	296
	AE2	412
PREY	AE2	904
	AE2	1036
	AE3	3
	AE3	288
	AE3	319
	AE4	227
	AE4	585
	AE5	332
	AE5	1093
	AE6	491
	AE8	342
	AE8	349
	AE8	846
	AE9	71
	AE9	159
	AE9	485
	AE9	499
	AE9	521
	AE9	601
	AE9	646
	AE9	686
	AE9	753
	AE9	763
	AE9	803
	AE9	840
	AE10	781
	AE10	1023
	AE11	1067
	AE11	1098
	AE11	1107
	AE11	1174
	AE12	386
	AE12	399
	AE12	1094
	OAL	377
	AF	149
	AF	153
	DO	114
	KT2	237
	KT3	247
	KT3	633
	KT3	697
	TJD	80
	M8	19
	M8	83
	M8	344
	B	62
	B	244
	B	266
	HIF	5
	HIF	248
	HIF	449
	C	339
	C	762
	TH	132
	TH	137
	TH	207
	TH	214
	TH	287
	TH	305
	TH	324
	TH	362
	M11	142
	M11	168
	M12	406
	AU	12
	AU	162
	AU	441
	AU	530
	WB	413
	M15	17
	M15	124
	M15	148
	GP	73
	CI	318
	CI	326
	CI	284
	CI	530
	CI	550
	CI	587
PREYED	SAA	1035
PREYING	L3	198
PREYS	HS	115
	AM	31
PRIAM	HP	208
	J10	402
	HI	119
	AE1	642
	AE1	647
	AE1	678
	AE1	1051
	AE2	622
	AE2	683
	AE2	713
	AE2	726
	AE2	758

PRIAM	AE2	789
	AE3	71
	AE5	734
	AE7	338
	AE8	210
	AE9	349
	AE9	1001
	AE11	401
	OAL	502
	HIF	232
	C	702
	M12	1
	M12	808
	AU	325
PRIAM'S	HP	58
	HP	203
	HI	17
	VP2	88
	AE1	921
	AE2	28
	AE2	74
	AE2	385
	AE2	463
	AE2	691
	AE2	718
	AE2	898
	AE2	1032
	AE3	2
	AE3	382
	AE3	415
	AE4	451
	AE4	495
	AE5	389
	AE5	842
	AE6	653
	AE6	666
	AE8	216
	AE8	498
	AE9	378
	M12	96
PRIAPUS	H2	33
	J6	494
	VP7	48
PRICE	AR	140
	STL	17
	EUO	37
	DA	157
	PUO5	24
	MD	49
	SAA	143
	RL	113
	RL	116
	RL	145
	AT	84
	HAP	1142
	HAP	1524
	HAP	1772
	PMS	22
	SSH	6
	J3	228
	J3	366
	J6	106
	J6	259
	AE12	89
	OAL	481
	M8	309
	HIF	18
	HIF	45
	HIF	514
	FL	269
	M12	627
	WB	244
PRICKED	OAL	446
	HIF	633
PRICKING	C	118
	WB	47
PRICKLES	MD	148
PRICKLY	VP1	108
	G2	572
	G3	358
	KT2	535
	TH	112
PRICKS	T23	14
	HAP	165
	G3	132
PRIDE	UDH	57
	LC	122
	AM	86
	AM	367
	AM	463
	AM	506
	AM	676
	AM	823
	AM	1184
	PNH	28
	PAZ	13

PRIDE	EMK	11
	AA	480
	MD	298
	D	18
	MF	40
	SAA	356
	SAA	556
	SAA	818
	SAA	843
	SAA	901
	SAA	956
	SAA	1007
	SAA	1077
	SAA	1125
	RL	306
	RL	428
	DOD	13
	T18	52
	TA	130
	AK	157
	HAP	75
	HAP	277
	HAP	1366
	HAP	1581
	HAP	1680
	HAP	1718
	HAP	2059
	HAP	2175
	HAP	2514
	HAP	2534
	BR	281
	EL	204
	J6	411
	J6	589
	J10	56
	J10	66
	J10	174
	P3	47
	P3	90
	P6	105
	M1	610
	M1	953
	HI	153
	GK	92
	VP5	140
	VP6	5
	G1	452
	G2	652
	G2	661
	G3	300
	G3	663
	AE1	966
	AE3	422
	AE3	627
	AE4	574
	AE4	775
	AE5	111
	AE5	516
	AE5	725
	AE5	1020
	AE6	264
	AE6	647
	AE7	880
	AE8	82
	AE8	629
	AE9	843
	AE10	479
	AE10	1063
	AE11	524
	AE11	745
	AE12	12
	AE12	136
	AE12	216
	OAL	816
	AF	11
	AF	72
	MM	28
	KT1	39
	KT2	257
	KT2	321
	KT3	102
	KT3	231
	KT3	452
	KT3	688
	KT3	770
	B	39
	B	458
	B	463
	B	482
	B	545
	B	737
	B	751
	BP	102
	HIF	13
	HIF	183
	HIF	356

PRIDE	HIF	451
	HIF	655
	C	83
	C	391
	TH	27
	TH	169
	TH	374
	TH	375
	TH	391
	FL	106
	M12	631
	M12	553
	AU	436
	WB	392
	M15	343
	CI	363
PRIED	J3	83
	FL	123
PRIEST	PLN	4
	AA	523
	AA	864
	MF	119
	RL	253
	NS	15
	HAP	1026
	HAP	1685
	HAP	1822
	HAP	1857
	J6	674
	J6	680
	P2	122
	P6	47
	G2	675
	AE2	267
	AE2	288
	AE2	429
	AE3	106
	AE3	592
	AE5	993
	AE6	652
	AE7	127
	AE7	1032
	AE8	242
	AE10	747
	AE10	753
	AE11	1131
	AE12	255
	AE12	450
	OAL	360
	KT2	461
	M8	114
	B	96
	B	151
	B	406
	HIF	12
	HIF	53
	HIF	66
	HIF	107
	HIF	140
	HIF	164
	HIF	513
	HIF	523
	HIF	538
	HIF	622
	HIF	635
	C	641
	AU	162
	M15	161
	M15	194
	GP	1
	GP	49
	GP	110
	GP	118
PRIESTCRAFT	AA	1
PRIESTESS	AE1	371
	AE3	582
	AE4	698
	AE4	719
	AE4	737
	AE6	55
	AE6	177
	AE6	240
	AE6	350
	AE6	1022
	AE6	1057
	AE7	921
PRIESTHOOD	PT	25
	AA	98
	MD	283
	SAA	2
	J6	696
PRIESTLY	HAP	580
	J6	667
	AE4	89
	AE12	430
	HIF	156

PRIESTLY	HIF	203
	CI	8
PRIEST'S	RL	383
	RL	391
	J6	700
	EHC	22
PRIESTS	AM	831
	PLN	5
	AA	50
	AA	99
	AA	128
	MD	268
	SAA	319
	SAA	357
	SAA	1029
	RL	373
	ETS	23
	J6	657
	J6	684
	J10	546
	P2	106
	P5	270
	M1	1041
	VP5	105
	G1	654
	G2	266
	AE2	181
	AE2	1041
	AE3	391
	AE3	518
	AE4	85
	AE4	290
	AE6	115
	AE6	326
	AE6	354
	AE6	897
	AE8	358
	AE8	371
	AE8	879
	AE12	47
	AE12	182
	OAL	296
	C	638
	C	642
	M12	16
	M12	45
	AU	528
	WB	24
	M15	201
	GP	54
	GP	81
	CI	564
PRIME	ETL	19
	AA	217
	AA	833
	SAA	963
	MO	19
	T23	58
	T27	12
	HAP	1830
	G2	459
	G4	430
	AE5	529
	AE5	530
	KT3	82
	KT3	103
	KT3	543
	B	25
	HIF	47
	C	438
	TH	60
	M12	253
	WB	135
	SMP	37
	SMP	41
	EMKG	43
PRIMITIVE	SAA	387
	HAP	928
	J3	119
	GP	128
PRIMROSE	C	457
PRINCE	HS	125
	HS	138
	AR	139
	AR	248
	AR	318
	SMA	73
	SMA	95
	LC	21
	AM	175
	AM	193
	AM	421
	AM	433
	AM	505
	AM	529
	AM	855

PRINCE	AM	963
	PC1	17
	DA	18
	EMW	5
	AA	205
	AA	230
	AA	273
	AA	441
	AA	476
	AA	516
	AA	672
	AA	746
	AA	823
	AA	879
	AA	966
	PLB	11
	MD	29
	MD	52
	MD	212
	PRH	37
	MF	7
	MF	51
	MF	88
	MF	106
	MF	124
	MF	179
	SAA	81
	SAA	165
	SAA	174
	SAA	182
	SAA	265
	SAA	288
	SAA	381
	SAA	572
	SAA	591
	SAA	616
	SAA	636
	SAA	663
	SAA	677
	SAA	683
	SAA	694
	SAA	702
	SAA	722
	SAA	739
	SAA	824
	SAA	889
	SAA	999
	EDG	6
	ER	69
	L2	53
	TA	21
	TA	234
	TA	237
	TA	429
	TA	430
	TA	437
	TA	481
	EAA	16
	HAP	183
	HAP	217
	HAP	361
	HAP	664
	HAP	863
	HAP	1317
	HAP	1822
	HAP	1974
	HAP	2041
	HAP	2435
	HAP	2490
	HAP	2515
	BR	135
	BR	143
	BR	144
	BR	145
	BR	146
	BR	328
	J10	107
	J10	136
	J10	150
	J10	528
	G4	27
	G4	145
	AE1	146
	AE1	562
	AE1	582
	AE1	695
	AE1	767
	AE1	778
	AE1	837
	AE1	723
	AE4	109
	AE4	214
	AE4	239
	AE4	286
	AE4	382
	AE4	404

PRINCE	AE4	823
	AE4	896
	AE5	41
	AE5	125
	AE5	320
	AE5	369
	AE5	454
	AE5	477
	AE5	506
	AE5	614
	AE5	698
	AE5	984
	AE6	11
	AE6	61
	AE6	86
	AE6	188
	AE6	269
	AE6	336
	AE6	373
	AE6	467
	AE6	735
	AE6	863
	AE6	1057
	AE6	1110
	AE6	1233
	AE7	7
	AE7	76
	AE7	103
	AE7	207
	AE7	211
	AE7	224
	AE7	333
	AE7	349
	AE7	392
	AE7	464
	AE7	502
	AE7	612
	AE7	813
	AE8	138
	AE8	165
	AE8	482
	AE8	613
	AE9	9
	AE9	103
	AE9	217
	AE9	247
	AE9	1036
	AE10	433
	AE10	459
	AE10	540
	AE10	576
	AE10	753
	AE10	769
	AE10	851
	AE10	1089
	AE10	1153
	AE10	1165
	AE11	51
	AE11	187
	AE11	218
	AE11	348
	AE11	404
	AE11	511
	AE11	609
	AE11	753
	AE12	45
	AE12	438
	AE12	482
	AE12	528
	AE12	566
	AE12	671
	AE12	683
	AE12	711
	AE12	719
	AE12	786
	AE12	825
	AE12	852
	AE12	918
	AE12	1099
	AE12	1137
	AE12	1340
	OAL	204
	AF	109
	AF	116
	DO	107
	KT1	2
	KT1	37
	KT1	93
	KT1	368
	KT1	393
	KT2	302
	KT2	344
	KT3	408
	KT3	419
	KT3	493
	KT3	526

Word	Ref	No.
PRINCE	T J D	175
	T J D	181
	M 8	232
	B	2
	B	7
	B	104
	B	269
	B	313
	B	352
	B	603
	B	753
	CAM	3
	H I F	182
	H I F	362
	H I F	486
	H I F	620
	H I F	623
	C	759
	C	790
	M 11	1
	F L	549
	M 12	713
	A U	288
	W B	68
	W B	74
	W B	182
	M 15	6
	G P	101
	G P	110
PRINCELY	A R	234
	D C	50
	SAA	1084
	SAA	1125
	A E 1	979
	A E 4	183
	A E 4	318
	K T 3	731
	K T 3	928
	C	108
PRINCE'S	R H	54
	A M	442
	A M	449
	A M	518
	A A	639
	PRH	29
	SAA	901
	T A	382
	B R	337
	J 10	119
	T J D	189
	B	744
	F L	269
PRINCES	L C	81
	PUO1	17
	H P	163
	A A	495
	A A	543
	SAA	765
	T 18	28
	G 4	121
	A E 3	139
	A E 4	50
	A E 7	61
	A E 7	81
	A E 7	851
	A E 11	161
	A E 11	364
	A E 11	663
	A F	146
	M G	11
	D O	15
	K T 2	661
	T J D	67
	H I F	24
	H I F	520
	C	659
	B	550
PRINCESS	E T L	30
	E P C	23
	HAP	1602
	A E 4	175
	A E 4	295
	A E 11	567
	K T 2	396
	B	30
	B	253
	M 12	263
PRINCESSES	P D	43
PRINCIPAL	O D	22
	P 6	159
PRINCIPIO	C	417
PRINCIPLE	A A	1015
	M D	42
	R L	14
	H H	22
	HAP	634
PRINCIPLE	HAP	1102
	HAP	1435
	HAP	1669
	W B	429
PRINCIPLES	A A	154
	A A	508
	HAP	432
	HAP	686
	M 1	111
	M 1	340
	G 2	17
	OAL	45
	B	500
	M 15	120
	M 15	365
PRINT	A M	1146
	T 27	130
	PSH	6
	G 1	101
	MFL	27
	M 10	81
	M 11	485
PRINTED	A E 8	275
	M 11	412
	F L	55
PRINTER'S	EUF	17
PRINTING	L 4	174
PRINTS	HAP	215
	M 1	897
	G 2	672
	G 3	308
	K T 2	46
PRISCIAN'S	J 6	586
PRISON	A M	874
	A M	1166
	G 4	435
	K T 1	383
	K T 1	402
	K T 1	426
	K T 1	440
	K T 1	450
	K T 1	461
	K T 1	508
	K T 2	2
	K T 2	6
	K T 2	14
	K T 3	1106
	B	62
	B	656
	C	769
	M 15	332
	C I	527
PRISONER	A E 9	566
	A E 11	1108
	K T 1	207
	K T 1	378
	K T 2	290
	K T 2	337
	B	268
	B	287
	H I F	221
	H I F	486
	H I F	522
	C	769
	A U	162
	C I	486
	C I	557
PRISONERS	K T 1	160
	K T 3	517
	C I	397
PRISONS	L 3	228
	J 6	220
	J 10	293
	A E 1	81
	K T 1	478
PRIVATE	H S	33
	L C	50
	P W	4
	P C 2	31
	M L	9
	POE	30
	H P	252
	A A	181
	A A	779
	SAA	113
	SAA	208
	SAA	758
	R L	396
	R L	415
	R L	447
	HAP	63
	HAP	478
	HAP	695
	HAP	824
	HAP	836
	HAP	1643
PRIVATE	HAP	1700
	HAP	2278
	HAP	2554
	J 1	22
	J 1	145
	J 6	161
	J 6	280
	J 6	392
	P 2	17
	P 6	29
	A E 1	714
	A E 2	121
	A E 7	797
	A E 12	892
	T J D	117
	B	302
	H I F	174
	H I F	371
PRIVATEER	PSH	16
PRIVATION	L 2	27
PRIVATIONS	GK	14
PRIVERNUM	A E 11	816
PRIVERNUS	A E 9	782
PRIVILEGE	E I E	22
	PAR	13
	A A	674
	SAA	14
	SAA	207
	SAA	766
	EAA	30
	HAP	1309
	HAP	2546
	J 3	149
	J 3	451
	J 6	204
	J 6	304
	J 10	551
	P 5	102
	A E 9	734
	T J D	172
	B	193
PRIVILEGED	HAP	1721
	HAP	2043
	HAP	2248
	PTS	28
	J 3	263
	A E 12	1272
	H I F	744
	F L	487
	C I	471
PRIVILEGES	J 16	10
PRIVY	K T 3	412
PRIZE	H S	61
	H S	124
	A R	34
	A R	210
	A R	217
	LCA	18
	A M	117
	A M	300
	A M	756
	EWGR	18
	PMM	4
	EEL	29
	PCG2	17
	E	26
	H P	72
	H P	116
	EUF	31
	A A	260
	M D	3
	SAA	189
	SAA	997
	FS3	1
	HAP	1583
	HAP	1642
	PTS	30
	PSH	17
	J 1	65
	J 6	372
	J 6	439
	J 6	507
	P 1	91
	P 5	280
	M 1	601
	M 1	755
	GK	5
	V P 3	12
	V P 3	31
	V P 3	168
	V P 5	136
	G 2	142
	G 2	772
	G 3	83
	G 3	163
	G 3	286

PRIZE	AE5	269	PRIZES	HIF	186	PROCLAIM	AE10	961
	AE5	289	PROBABILITY	RL	345		AU	171
	AE5	302	PROBABLE	SAA	45		WB	272
	AE5	317	PROBABLY	OAL	260		GP	40
	AE5	338	PROBATIONER	AK	21	PROCLAIMED	AM	1070
	AE5	382	PROBE	HAP	1374		AA	60
	AE5	439	PROBED	P1	232		SAA	802
	AE5	447	PROCAS	AE6	1041		HAP	1315
	AE5	450	AR	88		HAP	1854
	AE5	455	PROCEED	POE	27		EL	159
	AE5	464		SAA	975		P5	44
	AE5	504		L4	247		AE1	893
	AE5	512		HAP	990		AE1	1020
	AE5	519		J6	397		AE5	709
	AE5	532		P3	165		DO	79
	AE5	632		M9	52		M12	264
	AE5	686		MC	65	PROCLAIMS	HAP	361
	AE5	703		VP6	19		VP5	100
	AE5	710		G2	680		AE2	301
	AE6	305		G3	193		AE4	739
	AE6	874		G3	224		AE5	149
	AE7	594		G4	440		AE5	318
	AE8	269		G4	467		AE7	797
	AE8	897		AE1	1041		AE12	600
	AE9	492		AE6	735		KT3	572
	AE9	894		AE11	618	PROCLAMATION	C	736
	AE10	652		KT3	541	PROCLAMED	AM	406
	AE11	397		C	635	PROCRIS	AE6	602
	AE11	681		FL	573	PROCURE	SKA6	22
	AE11	1118		M12	122		P2	56
	AE11	1145		M15	208		G2	180
	AE12	80		CI	473		AE7	210
	AE12	935	PROCEEDED	AE3	479		AE12	64
	AE12	1109		AE12	919		OAL	397
	OAL	173		FL	306		CAM	180
	OAL	192	PROCEEDING	VCS	17		C	680
	OAL	284		AE3	448		M15	689
	OAL	296		AE3	668	PROCURED	SAA	224
	OAL	393		AE7	215		AE8	388
	AF	167		AE12	42		AE10	142
	AF	177		M15	308		B	451
	MG	11	PROCEEDS	PWGR	12		B	622
	DO	15		M1	692	PROCURES	J10	481
	KT1	345		G1	569	PROCURING	J1	86
	KT1	460		G3	86	PRODIGAL	AA	168
	KT2	416		G3	359		AA	599
	KT2	635		G4	244		EPC	7
	KT3	166		AE1	609		SAA	594
	KT3	657		AE1	710		HAP	1145
	KT3	680		AE8	596		MC	62
	M8	213		KT3	750		G4	135
	M8	225		M12	159		AE2	586
	M8	228		WB	445		AE6	896
	B	88		WB	477		B	37
	B	268	PROCESS	J6	343		M15	114
	HIF	165		G3	753		ETP	41
	HIF	178		AE6	837	PRODIGALITY	EMK	22
	HIF	200		AE7	790	PRODIGALLY	L4	29
	HIF	209		KT1	123		AE6	587
	HIF	244		M15	44	PRODIGIES	TA	145
	HIF	391		M15	296		G1	634
	HIF	418	PROCESSION	AA	1029		AE2	154
	HIF	511		AK	8		AE3	84
	HIF	684		HAP	1625		AE4	273
	C	668		BR	28		AE7	369
	C	759		EL	278		AE10	257
	TH	18		J6	658		M11	1
	M12	311		J16	61	PRODIGIOUS	AM	857
	M12	825		M1	760		PCB	18
	AU	9		M9	39		AA	377
	AU	23		HI	15		AA	638
	AU	166		G1	474		L3	191
	AU	194		AE1	671		TA	149
	AU	217		AE6	1024		J1	212
	AU	243		AE8	372		M9	92
	AU	453		AE11	141		M13	58
	AU	591		AE11	721		AE1	613
	CI	504		CAM	240		AE8	566
	CI	555	PROCHYTA	J3	8	PRODIGY	G4	799
	CI	592		AE9	968		AE3	37
	CI	610	PROCLAIM	AR	264		AE7	96
PRIZED	AR	47		SMA	35		AE8	704
	RH	82		AA	242		BP	193
	T23	5		AA	357	PRODUCE	HS	126
	HAP	1357		AA	386		RH	32
	B	323		AA	464		CM	45
	GP	87		HAP	1613		AA	50
PRIZE-GOODS	EEL	32		SSC	37		MF	92
PRIZES	AM	808		EL	10		SAA	338
	EWGR	17		P6	101		SAA	352
	PUO1	4		G1	558		L2	4
	ML	43		G3	368		L4	209
	J3	63		G4	95		L4	224
	G2	528		AE2	1044		L4	268
	AE5	482		AE4	651		L4	294
	AE7	219		AE4	895		H9	9

PRODUCE	H2	70	PROFANE	AE6	368	PROFOUND	G4	527
	HAP	321		AE10	330		AE6	730
	HAP	458		OAL	730		HIF	714
	HAP	806		KT3	203		M11	423
	HAP	964		CAM	99	PROFOUNDLY	CAM	185
	HAP	1114		CAM	330	PROFUSE	EL	65
	BR	137		HIF	422	PROFUSION	EL	87
	J1	39		C	599		OD	17
	J1	187		M15	102		J1	135
	J3	231		ETP	13	PROGENITOR	L4	221
	J16	44	PROFANED	AM	1103	PROGENITORS	WB	398
	M1	824		ESF	26	PROGENY	UDH	104
	M9	17		AK	57		AA	17
	G1	69		HAP	2267		L1	21
	G1	252		VP3	35		J1	174
	G2	34		AE2	223		M1	911
	G2	124		AE6	849		HI	19
	G2	128		AE12	839		VP4	10
	G2	133		AE12	854		G2	3
	G2	175		AE12	1129		G2	413
	G2	264		HIF	164		G3	250
	G2	367	PROFANELY	MM	15		AE1	322
	G2	609		DO	124		AE2	686
	G3	202	PROFANENESS	J6	460		AE6	36
	G3	273	PROFANES	J1	197		AE6	1024
	G3	502		CAM	296		AE6	1074
	G4	57	PROFESS	HAP	1967		AE10	45
	G4	433	PROFESSED	EUO	25		AE10	730
	AE2	266		HAP	38		AU	252
	AE12	240		HAP	1346	PROGNE	VP6	115
	DO	83		HAP	1422		G4	19
	TJD	118		HAP	1500	PROGNE'S	P5	11
	M15	105		HAP	1548	PROGNOSTICATE	J3	81
	M15	493		HAP	2087	PROGRESS	VHH	54
PRODUCED	AR	215		HAP	2409		AA	729
	PDG	4		J10	520		AA	444
	RL	155		AE11	184		SAA	168
	RL	392		OAL	697		SAA	192
	HAP	283		KT2	193		SAA	228
	J10	410		KT3	158		SAA	681
	M1	558		B	733		TA	367
	M1	583		TH	389		AK	148
	M9	108		ETP	15		HAP	1183
	G2	209	PROFESSING	BP	36		BR	6
	G3	468	PROFESSOR	PO	1		EL	257
	AE2	168	PROFFER	VP3	54		AE7	550
	AE4	258		TH	135		AE12	660
	AE5	471	PROFFERED	HP	133		FL	63
	AE7	389		HAP	1081		CI	230
	AE10	997		HAP	2060	PROHIBITED	PTW	13
	AE11	439		AE4	472	PROJECT	AM	212
	OAL	866		AE7	464		AE4	75
	M8	265		AE11	170		AE4	181
	BP	77		AE12	73		AE8	284
	CAM	1		AE12	579	PROJECTED	L4	250
	AU	83		KT2	281		AE8	842
	AU	276		HIF	514		DO	52
	AU	609		FL	597	PROJECTS	SAA	50
PRODUCES	PK	8		AU	268		G1	622
	HAP	901		WB	104	PROLE	HAP	1707
	PTS	20		WB	317	PROLIFIC	L1	5
	OD	27		CI	196		L4	260
	G2	339	PROFFERING	HAP	557		G3	439
PRODUCING	AU	348		J6	498		G4	414
PRODUCT	AR	169		KT1	579		M15	311
	SAA	341	PROFFERS	J6	498		M15	365
	RL	66		P3	125	PROLIXLY	HAP	1339
	L4	124		VP3	71	PROLOGUE	PRL	9
	HAP	1395		AE9	996		PIE	7
	BR	266	PROFICIENT	JH	3		PMQ	37
	J6	113	PROFIT	SAA	397		EMQ	1
	J6	189		SAA	1009		ENH	1
	M13	119		HAP	2146		ETC	17
	VP4	48		HAP	2372		ELT	3
	G1	113		HAP	2445		ERL	2
	G1	398		J3	41	PROLOGUES	PRL	2
	G2	4		P2	121		PRL	6
	G4	207		P5	87		PMQ	36
	M12	482		G1	137		PLN	1
	M15	197		G3	477		PD	4
	PWR	3		OAL	431	PROLONG	SAA	68
PRODUCTION	L4	238		FL	600		L3	148
PRODUCTIONS	HAP	2035		AU	558		T18	78
PRODUCTIVE	L1	33		WB	517		H2	44
PRODUCTS	P1	98		M15	166		TA	418
PROETIDES	M15	490	PROFITABLE	HAP	1657		ODA	52
PROFANATION	M1	288		P4	19		VP4	64
PROFANE	PUO2	26	PROFITED	PLT	32		AE3	620
	HP	4	PROFITS	AE10	84		AE10	895
	MD	290		OAL	820		AE11	1102
	H3	30		KT3	764		KT1	505
	PDS	35	PROFLIGATE	AK	58		KT3	810
	PTS	37	PROFOUND	SAA	679		WB	81
	G2	670		PD	39	PROLONGED	HS	46
	AE2	252		G2	400		UMR	5
	AE4	618		G3	806		AE1	1049

PROLONGED	AE12	798	PROMISED	OE	21	PROMISES	AE6	817
	M8	372		RL	261		OAL	400
	M12	221		H9	32		OAL	510
	WB	9		TA	187		OAL	519
PROLONGS	M1	914		TA	408		AU	521
	VP1	76		TA	428	PROMONTORY	AM	809
	M12	686		HAP	71		J6	153
PROMETHEUS	H3	38		BR	30		M13	48
	M1	105		BR	70	PROMOTE	PNH	23
	GK	22		BR	250		AE3	188
PROMETHEUS'	VP6	65		OD	10	PROMOTES	H29	79
PROMETHEUS-LIKE	JH	7		ODA	34		J6	792
PROMINENT	AE5	351		ODA	50	PROMOTING	TJD	17
	KT3	477		J1	184	PROMOTION	AK	2
PROMISCUOUS	AA	6		VCS	8		OAL	296
	M1	605		MC	1	PROMPT	HAP	1076
	VP8	40		VP5	25		HAP	2477
	AE11	318		VP6	31		BR	283
	AE12	201		VP6	40		M1	161
	AE12	1002		VP8	130		AE12	1139
	KT3	551		G1	74	PROMPTED	A	5
PROMISE	SMA	73		G1	248		AA	5
	PIE	12		G1	440	PROMPTS	RL	58
	HP	219		G1	532		P4	121
	PR	9		G1	586		AE2	454
	AA	585		G1	594	PRONE	HP	188
	MD	280		G3	133		P4	87
	TA	487		G3	225		G4	344
	EAA	32		G4	281		AE2	260
	HAP	2247		AE1	322		AE6	1110
	HAP	2497		AE1	343		AE9	964
	HAP	2539		AE2	481		AE10	136
	BR	16		AE3	180		AE10	825
	BR	293		AE3	333		AE12	994
	ODA	16		AE3	429	PRONG	AE11	1009
	M9	48		AE3	440		BP	63
	MC	55		AE3	486	PRONGS	G2	487
	MC	56		AE3	735	PRONOUNCE	AR	176
	VP1	21		AE4	335		AA	404
	VP5	82		AE4	399		AE11	731
	G2	341		AE4	128		KT2	305
	G4	461		AE4	498		M8	336
	AE1	287		AE4	549	PRONOUNCED	AR	268
	AE2	686		AE4	625		MD	14
	AE3	679		AE4	857		HAP	970
	AE5	25		AE5	109		HAP	2527
	AE5	39		AE5	450		AE2	177
	AE7	609		AE5	504		AE3	686
	AE7	754		AE5	532		AE10	12
	AE7	798		AE5	921		KT3	278
	AE8	108		AE5	1006		KT3	372
	AE8	530		AE6	102		KT3	716
	AE8	703		AE6	1076		TJD	78
	AE8	814		AE6	1079		WB	334
	AE10	50		AE6	1230	PRONOUNCES	EMM	12
	AE10	517		AE7	401	PRONOUNCING	KT3	660
	AE11	742		AE8	52	PROOF	AA	430
	AE11	761		AE8	607		RL	126
	AE11	764		AE8	663		RL	342
	AE12	129		AE8	707		HAP	644
	OAL	505		AE9	167		HAP	2535
	OAL	712		AE10	81		J10	554
	DO	63		AE10	121		P5	114
	KT1	212		AE10	142		EHC	26
	KT1	378		AE10	726		AE3	317
	KT2	162		AE11	65		KT2	156
	KT3	682		AE11	170		B	275
	M8	174		AE11	425		BP	15
	CAM	213		AE11	716		TH	190
	HIF	193		AE12	4		TH	385
	C	370		AE12	51		M12	513
	M11	66		AE12	170		AU	83
	M12	268		OAL	504		GP	134
	M12	729		KT2	290		CI	501
	AU	494		KT3	121	PROOFS	HAP	806
	WB	303		KT3	394		HAP	1831
	WB	325		M8	34		J6	310
	M15	179		B	147		KT3	847
	M15	325		B	585		AU	407
	CI	128		CAM	170	PROP	AA	954
	CI	329		M11	236		G4	263
	CI	251		M12	770		AE9	638
	CI	433		AU	395		AE11	994
PROMISED	AM	136		WB	112		AE12	91
	AM	324		WB	525		AU	436
	AM	1136		M15	70	PROPAGATE	AA	424
	HP	118		GP	13		L4	268
	HP	133	PROMISES	E	28		HAP	111
	AA	235		HP	63		HAP	839
	AA	732		HAP	584		HI	135
	MF	182		HAP	675		G3	114
	SAA	30		HAP	1065	PROPAGATED	AE6	520
	SAA	329		P6	58		AE6	1083
	SAA	599		VP4	23		KT3	1057
	SAA	712		G3	364	PROPAGATES	G3	78
	SAA	1114		G4	538		G3	433

PROPAGATES	CI	7	PROPHET	G4	634	PROPOSE	AE11	483
PROPAGATION	G2	91		AE3	473		AE11	535
	C	692		AE3	608		KT3	1119
PROPER	EIE	20		AE3	936		CI	532
	AM	404		AE9	438	PROPOSED	HAP	2145
	PC2	15		HIF	135		P3	115
	PTC	26		M12	607		AE10	222
	AA	193		AU	510		TH	47
	SAA	371	PROPHETESS	PP	2	PROPOSING	CI	467
	SAA	810		AE2	543	PROPOUND	HAP	1075
	HAP	1203		AE6	190	PROPOUNDED	CI	636
	HAP	2490		AE6	506	PROPOUNDING	PP	46
	HAP	2491	PROPHETIC	MF	138	PROPOUNDS	G2	772
	PP	32		SAA	477	PROPPED	AM	248
	P4	20		AT	63		AA	842
	P4	22		HAP	1932		SAA	757
	M1	29		BR	223		AE7	583
	M1	614		AE2	464		AE7	811
	M1	778		AE3	552		AE12	145
	GK	68		AE3	563		AE12	585
	VP3	81		AE6	116		HIF	678
	G1	409		AE8	448		FL	591
	G2	317		KT2	496		WB	227
	G2	631		M11	46		CI	179
	AE8	964		M11	414	PROPPING	M11	345
	AE10	165	PROPHETICALLY	HI	47	PROPS	J3	315
	AE12	197	PROPHET'S	MF	216		G2	565
	OAL	683		SAA	629	PROSE	EAL	6
	OAL	867	PROPHETS	SAA	326		POE	6
	KT3	429		SAA	703		MF	5
	M8	234		HAP	974		MF	164
	HIF	212		HAP	1003		SAA	491
	HIF	567		BR	71		RL	454
	M11	352		G1	515		ER	13
	GP	140		HIF	91		J10	189
	PWR	21	PROPHETS'	AA	237		P1	31
	EWR	7		AA	870		P1	32
PROPERTY	AA	499		SAA	967		MM	6
	AA	536		SAA	1045	PROSECUTE	AA	490
	AA	777	PROPITIATE	G4	788		G3	619
	MD	117		AE6	516		AE5	857
	MD	312	PROPITIOUS	SMA	131		AE11	790
	SAA	220		HP	160	PROSECUTES	AE5	1028
	SAA	335		SAA	617		M11	396
	SAA	696		L1	2	PROSECUTION	J3	481
	SAA	874		AK	177	PROSELYTE	HAP	977
	PK	15		BR	135		HAP	2440
	L3	174		BR	304	PROSELYTES	HAP	379
	TA	298		PP	42		HAP	1467
	AE4	390		J10	201		HAP	1674
PROPHECIES	HP	232		M9	129		HAP	1707
	HAP	1813		HI	156	PROSE-PROPHET	SAA	368
	HAP	1838		GK	133	PROSERPINE	G1	56
	HAP	2551		VP5	101		AE4	1001
	AE4	675		G1	11		AE6	176
	C	379		G1	59		AE6	213
PROPHECY	MD	165		G3	1		AE6	359
	MN	6		AE2	542	PROSERPINE'S	G4	701
	HAP	1736		AE3	159	PROSPECT	SMA	3
	ODA	59		AE4	62		LC	31
	AE2	325		AE4	300		SAA	1055
	AE3	346		AE5	620		L3	291
	AE3	461		AE6	88		HAP	1659
	AE7	116		AE6	275		P6	19
	AE7	123		AE7	30		M1	123
	M15	25		AE7	355		M9	98
PROPHESIED	MF	87		AE8	118		G2	391
	BR	336		AE8	403		G2	611
	M13	41		AE8	503		AE1	256
	AE7	102		AE8	904		AE3	851
	AE7	166		AE11	730		AE4	374
	AE10	1043		AE11	1159		AE5	12
PROPHESIES	J6	702		AE12	269		AE8	691
PROPHESY	RH	102		AE12	1130		OAL	120
	PCG2	21		OAL	626		C	534
	PNH	49		KT3	286	PROSPECTIVE	PP	3
	HAP	1710		CAM	326	PROSPECTS	HAP	1673
	MC	51		HIF	64	PROSPER	P2	12
	VP3	74		HIF	98		M9	131
	OAL	234	PROPITIOUSLY	AA	363		M9	132
PROPHET	RH	88	PROPONENT	HAP	121		G2	348
	AA	655	PROPORTION	AR	91		AE4	832
	MF	30		AM	420	PROSPEROUS	AR	41
	AT	102		RL	113		AR	95
	TA	144		L4	217		LC	81
	TA	288		EL	92		AM	357
	HAP	378		EL	159		L4	124
	HAP	703		KT3	956		TA	289
	HAP	893		FL	80		TA	507
	HAP	2392		CI	52		HAP	1390
	HAP	2440	PROPORTIONED	M1	985		HAP	2226
	BR	250		M13	59		G2	202
	EL	187		M12	534		AE1	102
	J6	665	PROPORTIONS	PCD	23		AE1	502
	M13	34		P1	91		AE1	619
	G4	558	PROPOSE	AE5	482		AE3	97

Word	Ref	No.	Word	Ref	No.	Word	Ref	No.
PROSPEROUS	AE3	466	PROTESTANT	HAP	1625	PROUD	AE8	819
	AE3	692	PROTESTANTS	ELB	40		AE8	857
	AE3	916	PROTESTATION	M1	244		AE8	970
	AE5	74	PROTESTING	SAA	308		AE9	357
	AE8	903	PROTEUS	AM	59		AE9	421
	AE11	64		HAP	2112		AE9	499
	OAL	232		G4	561		AE9	808
	HIF	594		G4	569		AE10	28
	M15	64		G4	619		AE10	211
	ESK	10		G4	647		AE10	223
PROSTITUTE	AK	58		G4	765		AE10	262
	H29	84		OAL	871		AE10	596
	P1	48	PROTOGENES	J3	203		AE10	653
	HIF	726	PROTRACT	AE9	289		AE10	717
PROSTITUTED	J1	54	PROTRACTED	HAP	1677		AE10	750
PROSTITUTES	EAZ	37		AE7	437		AE10	778
PROSTRATE	AM	1114		AE10	11		AE10	984
	AA	453		AE11	444		AE10	1017
	HAP	1563	PROTRACTING	B	334		AE10	1026
	M1	287	PROTRACTIVE	HAP	2397		AE10	1044
	M1	506	PROUD	HS	118		AE10	1081
	AE1	385		AR	81		AE10	1292
	AE3	125		AR	248		AE11	9
	AE3	716		AM	137		AE11	198
	AE10	773		AM	535		AE11	413
	AE11	1217		AM	753		AE11	1134
	AE12	28		AM	997		AE12	192
	AE12	458		AM	1191		AE12	1348
	AE12	533		EMQW	3		OAL	74
	DO	53		PNH	29		OAL	708
	KT2	326		PUO4	16		OAE1	31
	KT3	294		DA	139		KT1	14
	M8	370		AA	283		KT1	453
	CAM	198		AA	647		KT2	242
PROTECT	PC2	34		MD	134		KT2	347
	AA	611		SAA	815		KT3	15
	SAA	38		L2	30		KT3	61
	HAP	2540		L3	245		KT3	110
	VCS	29		H29	75		KT3	177
	G1	7		HAP	183		KT3	558
	AE2	546		HAP	828		KT3	569
	AE2	809		HAP	1699		KT3	809
	AE4	831		HAP	2494		M8	165
	AE6	175		EL	29		M8	237
	AE7	601		EL	203		B	101
	AE10	1308		EH	3		HIF	65
	HIF	314		J1	68		HIF	215
	TH	282		J6	246		HIF	279
	M11	246		J6	625		HIF	320
	M15	51		J10	181		HIF	406
PROTECTED	AE2	298		J10	449		HIF	510
	AE11	1157		P4	107		HIF	567
	FL	391		P5	254		C	319
	AU	538		M13	90		C	475
PROTECTING	HS	139		M13	111		C	614
	AE2	470		HI	105		C	652
	AE2	816		GK	76		TH	13
	AE5	1041		VP2	16		TH	65
	AU	122		VP10	3		TH	158
PROTECTION	PWG	44		G1	233		TH	257
	HAP	290		G3	38		TH	319
	HAP	1317		G3	142		TH	351
	M9	180		G3	164		M11	201
	G4	343		G3	348		FL	217
	AE2	949		G3	544		FL	241
	AE10	27		G4	27		FL	496
	AE10	47		G4	105		M12	111
PROTECTOR	EUO2	28		G4	483		M12	280
PROTECTORS	PSH	29		AE1	947		M12	620
	FL	549		AE2	130		M12	714
PROTECTRESS	AE3	915		AE2	443		M12	782
PROTECTS	SMA	116		AE2	553		M15	427
	AM	1096		AE2	649		GP	75
	MN	10		AE2	688		CI	324
	HAP	2140		AE2	833		CI	343
	HAP	2170		AE2	1069		PTP	7
	BR	95		AE3	525		ETP	12
	G2	409		AE4	192	PROUDER	T23	3
	AE1	419		AE4	553		AE5	632
	AE3	483		AE5	209		AE9	499
	AE10	599		AE5	502	PROUDEST	WB	245
	AE10	1133		AE5	512	PROUDLY	PAZ	37
	KT3	276		AE5	632		RL	430
PROTENDED	AE2	299		AE5	1051		TA	511
	AE10	770		AE6	91		HAP	2126
	AE10	1256		AE6	299		M1	386
	M8	104		AE6	653		VP4	54
PROTENDS	AE10	825		AE6	1068		AE4	472
	M12	504		AE6	1176		AE6	1116
PROTESILAUS	M12	94		AE7	229		AE11	1314
PROTEST	PMQ	19		AE7	873		AE12	129
	HAP	1013		AE7	909		AE12	160
PROTESTANT	PDG	18		AE7	1032		C	493
	EC	4		AE7	1088	PROVE	UDH	42
	NS	15		AE8	519		UDH	5
	HAP	1511		AE8	752		LC	3

Word	Code	No.
PROVE	LC	9
	LC	155
	AM	20
	SMM2	5
	ET	17
	ETL	17
	STL	3
	ECG1	17
	PCG2	30
	SCG1	30
	SCG2	24
	ENH	19
	EUO2	2
	PC1	10
	PO	3
	HP	38
	HP	55
	DA	53
	DA	179
	ETG	8
	AA	996
	MD	220
	SAA	102
	SAA	134
	SAA	374
	SAA	378
	SAA	383
	SAA	656
	SAA	721
	RL	147
	RL	150
	RL	217
	RL	311
	AT	67
	L1	47
	L4	91
	L4	125
	T23	49
	TA	456
	HAP	117
	HAP	859
	HAP	1169
	HAP	1185
	HAP	1188
	HAP	1458
	HAP	2030
	HAP	2192
	BR	127
	SKA5	12
	SKA5	14
	J6	69
	J10	185
	M1	276
	M1	290
	M1	293
	M1	657
	PLT	15
	PLT	55
	ELT	30
	ELT	35
	SLT1	12
	VP3	169
	G3	211
	G3	814
	G4	105
	AE5	143
	AE7	610
	AE12	577
	OAL	388
	OAL	512
	KT1	293
	KT1	325
	KT2	403
	M8	209
	TH	149
	FL	600
	M12	645
	M12	785
	WB	399
	CI	277
	CI	491
PROVED	PLN	8
	PO	30
	AA	648
	EPC	29
	SAA	86
	SAA	203
	SAA	988
	RL	274
	HAP	782
	HAP	949
	HAP	1153
	HAP	1159
	HAP	1162
	HAP	1500
	HAP	1617

Word	Code	No.
PROVED	HAP	2093
	EDS	6
	EDS	15
	PKA	35
	J6	313
	P5	116
	OAL	823
	KT2	169
	M12	96
	M12	646
PROVERB	HP	163
	HAP	2241
	KT2	364
	C	642
	PTP	25
PROVES	AR	63
	EIE	17
	AA	44
	AA	180
	AA	213
	AA	974
	SAA	387
	SAA	759
	L4	116
	EAA	11
	HAP	1666
	HAP	2152
	J6	227
	J6	436
	C	475
PROVIDE	SMA	85
	SMA	91
	SMA	123
	AM	800
	PCB	20
	ELB	15
	RL	49
	AT	80
	L3	164
	T23	81
	H9	12
	H2	64
	TA	458
	HAP	64
	HAP	290
	HAP	586
	HAP	818
	HAP	871
	HAP	906
	HAP	918
	HAP	1293
	HAP	1475
	HAP	1927
	PP	22
	EH	28
	J1	203
	J6	36
	J6	190
	J6	392
	J6	478
	J10	488
	P6	129
	P6	167
	M1	339
	M13	112
	G2	218
	G2	328
	G3	231
	G3	250
	G3	606
	G4	233
	G4	789
	AE2	980
	AE2	1064
	AE3	309
	AE5	467
	AE10	1047
	AE10	1309
	AE11	541
	AE12	1212
	OAL	43
	OAL	162
	AF	106
	MFL	17
	KT2	159
	KT2	435
	KT3	21
	KT3	461
	B	566
	CAM	341
	HIF	327
	C	310
	M12	134
	WB	516
	CI	493
	CI	278

Word	Code	No.
PROVIDE	AS	83
PROVIDED	HAP	743
	EL	72
	PLT	9
	PLT	11
	PLT	13
	KT3	34
	B	145
	TH	52
	AU	243
	AU	343
PROVIDENCE	AR	151
	AR	238
	RH	34
	AM	768
	EUF	4
	AA	625
	RL	24
	RL	54
	RL	187
	TA	410
	BR	95
	M9	93
	MC	69
	G3	774
	KT1	421
	KT2	212
	HIF	587
	HIF	686
	TH	242
	TH	290
	GP	117
	AS	33
	AS	79
	AS	80
PROVIDENCE'S	AA	834
PROVIDENT	KT3	527
PROVIDENTLY	AA	81
PROVIDES	AM	144
	AM	807
	AM	849
	L4	53
	SFL	5
	G1	271
	G2	294
	G2	624
	G2	756
	G3	644
	G4	229
	AE1	430
	AE1	496
	AE2	610
	M11	236
	AU	554
	M15	112
	M15	129
PROVIDING	TA	216
	OAL	115
PROVINCE	MF	187
	MF	206
	SAA	943
	SAA	1011
	L1	34
	AK	94
	J1	72
	J1	77
	P5	132
	G2	368
	MM	30
	KT3	143
	AU	159
	AU	555
PROVINCES	J10	352
PROVINCIAL	PNH	22
	PUO4	32
PROVING	MD	220
PROVISION	UMR	4
	PUO5	16
	RL	178
	HAP	1866
	J6	793
	J16	22
	P3	142
	G3	497
	G4	80
PROVISIONS	PFD	11
	HAP	1825
PROVOCATIVES	J6	284
	J6	421
PROVOKE	PMQW	14
	PLB	24
	MD	303
	RL	346
	ER	58
	L4	286
	TA	482

Word	Ref	No.	Word	Ref	No.	Word	Ref	No.
PROVOKE	PP	13	PRUDENT	AE6	566	PUBLIC	P3	34
	J10	92		BP	85		P3	164
	G2	771		AU	553		P5	141
	G4	630		WB	168		P6	112
	G4	642	PRUDENTLY	AM	35		P6	118
	AE5	569		HAP	919		M1	1044
	AE7	141	PRUNE	VP1	100		M1	1059
	AE7	532		G2	413		M1	1079
	AE7	616		MM	7		HI	169
	AE7	622	PRUNED	VP2	104		G1	630
	AE7	712	PRUNER'S	VP1	76		G2	731
	AE10	123	PRUNES	EAL	13		G3	33
	AE10	136		J3	148		G4	232
	OAE2	56	PRUNING	VP4	50		AE2	170
	KT2	250		G2	502		AE2	486
	HIF	778		G2	563		AE2	663
	M11	275		G2	577		AE5	144
	FL	414		AE7	248		AE6	1124
	M12	762	PRUNING-HOOK	H2	20		AE7	527
	CI	539	PRY	AM	656		AE7	805
PROVOKED	AM	778	PRYING	HAP	995		AE8	844
	HH	34		G4	744		AE10	122
	J1	19		HIF	754		AE11	64
	J10	328	PRYTANIS	AE9	1032		AE11	143
	P1	26		AU	402		AE11	553
	G4	345	PSALM	SAA	489		AE11	586
	AE1	12	PSALMS	SAA	403		AE11	671
	AE4	463		PTP	34		AE12	3
	AE8	155	PSECAS	J6	631		AE12	316
	AE9	49		J6	635		AE12	330
	AE10	793	PSYCHE	MF	125		AE12	888
	AE12	73		J6	278		AE12	892
	HIF	9	PSYCHE'S	MF	180		OAL	165
	HIF	111		MF	54		OAL	248
	HIF	163	PSYCHES	MF	90		OAL	461
	HIF	266	PSYTHIAN	G2	132		OAL	107
	TH	284		G4	388		MM	31
	M12	138	PTISAN	PAA	16		KT1	225
PROVOKES	SAA	840	PTOLOMEE	DO	134		KT3	6
	L4	58	PTOLEMIES	C	62		KT3	315
	L4	198	PTOLEMY	UDH	39		KT3	919
	P4	120		PWG	34		TJD	118
	M1	631		HAP	2341		TJD	130
	G3	94		J6	754		B	19
	G3	338	PUBLIC	HS	6		B	71
	AE1	246		HS	127		B	106
	AE1	693		LC	49		B	358
	AE6	252		AM	175		B	408
	AE10	1182		EWGR	6		B	457
	M8	198		EWGR	23		B	533
PROW	AM	261		PLG	6		B	741
	AM	620		AA	148		HIF	173
	AE1	151		AA	176		HIF	256
	AE3	358		AA	181		HIF	392
	AE5	188		AA	275		C	295
	AE5	259		AA	293		TH	67
	AE5	1096		AA	316		AU	431
	AE10	255		AA	400		M15	2
	AE10	929		AA	421		M15	4
	CI	274		AA	488		GP	56
PROWESS	J16	82		AA	504		GP	69
	AE6	676		AA	640		CI	65
	KT2	508		AA	788		CI	453
	M12	156		AA	889		CI	487
PROWLED	G3	801		AA	953		CI	617
PROWLING	G3	620		MD	76		ESK	7
	G4	630		MD	231		ESK	23
	GP	73		SAA	154	PUBLISHED	MF	94
PROWLS	VP5	93		SAA	820		RL	219
PROWS	AE3	698		SAA	894	PUDDING	SKA4	19
	AE8	913		EK	3		SKA4	22
	AE9	146		RL	448		P4	71
PROXIMITY	AU	249		T23	82	PUDDLE	HAP	205
PRUCE	KT3	31		EAA	19		AE5	431
PRUDENCE	AM	676		HAP	63	PUFF	CM	87
	AM	799		HAP	1116		AA	278
	HAP	1540		HAP	1142		H29	84
	HAP	1737		HAP	1331		M1	443
	HAP	2324		HAP	1577		G1	623
	PTS	40		HAP	1644		WB	392
	P1	91		HAP	1899	PUFFED	AA	480
	P3	133		HAP	2338		MD	298
	P4	10		EL	11		L3	118
	G3	115		EL	274		AE9	453
	AE2	891		J3	66	PUFFING	J3	420
	AE2	980		J3	92		G4	248
	AE5	929		J3	115	PUGS	EKK	18
	OAL	71		J3	391	PULING	M9	15
	M12	245		J6	281	PULL	SEL1	10
	AU	580		J10	85		PLB	13
	WB	479		J10	436		SAA	496
PRUDENT	PKK	14		J10	483		PDG	47
	AA	796		J10	517		EDGA	9
	MD	102		P1	6		L4	69
	J16	92		P1	30		T27	93
	M1	176		P2	16		H3	55

Word	Code	No.
PULL	H2	30
	P2	58
	G2	708
	AE9	673
	OAE2	28
	TJD	30
PULL-BACK	EEL	14
PULLED	AA	519
	RL	268
	AE3	36
	AE8	305
	AE11	846
	AE12	1132
	OAL	374
	CAM	291
	C	100
	C	317
	M12	481
PULLS	AM	844
	AE12	910
	OAL	709
	HIF	478
PULPIT	AR	22
	EHC	1
	MM	20
PULPITS	HAP	1476
PULSE	L4	123
	TA	64
	P3	171
	P3	215
	G1	110
	KT1	154
	M10	89
	M15	103
PUMICE	OAL	571
PUMICES	G4	61
PUN	PKK	7
PUNCTUAL	B	93
PUNIC	AM	20
	L3	4
	J10	251
	AE1	409
	AE1	473
	AE5	4
	AE6	1184
	C	709
PUNISH	AA	167
	AA	610
	AA	996
	BR	347
	P3	69
	P4	27
	AE2	213
	OAL	718
	OAL	721
	MM	28
	M8	297
	B	353
	HIF	243
	C	275
	C	520
	CI	472
PUNISHED	SEL2	6
	BR	228
	AE2	797
	AE4	941
	AE6	730
	AE8	886
	AE9	174
	KT2	640
	M8	374
	B	751
	TH	169
	CI	363
PUNISHES	AA	44
	KT2	97
PUNISHING	HAP	243
PUNISHMENT	LC	94
	SAA	735
	RL	61
	L3	233
	HAP	488
	HAP	1603
	HAP	1677
	J1	214
	J10	143
	J16	13
	M1	116
	M1	258
	M1	321
	M1	328
	M1	352
	M1	657
	M9	96
	M9	179
	G1	555
PUNISHMENT	G3	244
	G4	773
	G4	777
	AE3	281
	AE4	560
	AE6	586
	AE8	649
	B	679
	CAM	10
	CAM	329
	TH	203
	TH	276
	CI	352
PUNISHMENTS	AE6	854
	AE6	1014
	AE10	1217
PUNK	PM	22
	ENH	23
	EMK	13
	EKK	3
	PTW	31
	PLB	28
	PD	60
	PD	63
	ELN	16
	MF	77
	J3	262
PUNNED	J10	189
PUNY	PMQ	26
	MD	303
	P2	100
	M1	809
	EHC	7
	HIF	670
PUPIL	J3	198
	P1	24
	P2	23
	P4	5
	AE3	838
PUPILAGE	J10	150
	OAL	10
PUPIL'S	AE11	123
PUPPET	SAA	454
	J10	131
PURBLIND	HAP	1953
PURCELL	DHP	10
PURCELL'S	DHP	30
PURCHASE	AR	86
	EMK	21
	DA	50
	DA	158
	MF	203
	PDG	23
	J3	102
	J3	116
	J3	129
	J3	381
	AE9	265
	AE9	609
	AE9	795
	OAL	482
	KT1	382
	KT3	18
	FL	225
	FL	616
	D	21
PURCHASED	HAP	1575
	J3	365
	KT1	605
	CI	592
PURE	JH	24
	AA	508
	MF	83
	T27	35
	EAA	11
	HAP	320
	HAP	785
	HAP	890
	HAP	1120
	HAP	1189
	PKA	18
	EL	310
	OD	29
	J6	92
	P2	133
	G1	616
	G3	739
	G4	154
	AE6	321
	AE6	1012
	MM	45
	DO	121
	KT2	175
	AU	257
	WB	191
	M15	290
PURE	M15	369
PURELY	PDS	25
PURER	SMA	102
	DA	26
	L1	11
	L4	33
	FL	235
PUREST	TA	375
	G3	593
	AE12	182
PURFLED	FL	163
PURGE	MD	188
	AK	35
	J6	672
	P4	34
	M1	443
	VCS	20
	G1	619
	G4	239
	AE2	821
	AE10	144
	AE10	965
	C	166
	C	175
	C	189
	C	403
	FL	17
	CI	499
PURGED	AM	1104
	AA	38
	HAP	1167
	BR	156
	P2	102
	M1	86
	AE6	1004
PURGES	MD	254
PURGING	HAP	858
	AE12	840
	TJD	89
PURIFIED	G4	541
PURIFY	HIF	437
	MD	202
PURITAN	MHD	6
PURITY	P1	155
	MC	29
	BR	157
PURJURED	TH	55
PURLIEUS	HAP	1864
PURLING	VP9	54
	CI	106
PURLOIN	MF	183
	HAP	1661
	G4	353
PURLOINED	OAE1	5
PURPLE	AR	35
	EAL	14
	L2	55
	T18	45
	H2	31
	BR	133
	ODA	66
	J1	162
	J3	145
	J3	298
	P1	68
	P3	51
	M1	1095
	M13	108
	M13	217
	VP2	62
	VP4	53
	VP5	91
	VP7	46
	VP8	73
	VP9	52
	G1	556
	G1	615
	G2	135
	G2	652
	G2	705
	G4	46
	G4	76
	G4	346
	AE1	464
	AE1	900
	AE2	364
	AE2	1040
	AE3	107
	AE3	519
	AE3	822
	AE4	7
	AE4	165
	AE4	192
	AE4	384
	AE4	658
	AE4	659

PURPLE	AE4	817
	AE4	951
	AE5	103
	AE5	326
	AE5	354
	AE5	625
	AE5	748
	AE5	1015
	AE6	134
	AE6	317
	AE6	870
	AE6	1100
	AE6	1223
	AE7	36
	AE7	340
	AE7	382
	AE7	1108
	AE8	94
	AE8	920
	AE9	446
	AE9	471
	AE9	580
	AE9	791
	AE9	841
	AE10	750
	AE10	1017
	AE10	1160
	AE11	56
	AE11	104
	AE11	506
	AE11	989
	AE11	1176
	AE12	106
	AE12	193
	AE12	262
	AE12	437
	AE12	612
	AE12	880
	AE12	1090
	OAL	118
	OAL	267
	OAL	374
	OAL	642
	AF	51
	M10	52
	TH	144
	M12	116
	M12	387
	AU	610
	M15	124
	M15	192
	M15	702
	GP	95
	CI	96
	CI	604
PURPLED	KT1	187
	HIF	651
PURPOSE	SMM2	8
	HAP	2516
	J3	192
	G2	311
	AE4	433
	AE4	652
	AE5	978
	AE7	356
	OAE1	27
	MFL	4
	B	97
	B	109
	M11	55
	WB	151
PURPOSED	AE2	861
	AE7	87
PURPOSES	M11	3
PURSE	PUO3	33
	SAA	512
	J3	96
	J3	296
	J6	298
	P2	93
	OAL	473
	C	132
PURSES	PC2	21
	PDG	24
PURSEVANTS	FL	250
PURSUE	AR	134
	AR	159
	SIE	5
	VHH	38
	AM	269
	AM	380
	AM	424
	AM	538
	HP	239
	DA	118
	PUO4	33

PURSUE	PUF	13
	AA	806
	MD	124
	SAA	69
	SAA	214
	SAA	522
	SAA	716
	SAA	869
	L2	53
	H3	41
	HAP	963
	EL	311
	J1	79
	J6	843
	J10	2
	P5	143
	M1	115
	M1	499
	M1	713
	MC	74
	VP3	117
	VP3	122
	VP8	71
	VP10	90
	G3	67
	G3	74
	G3	269
	G3	449
	G3	622
	G4	336
	AE1	185
	AE1	554
	AE1	779
	AE2	552
	AE2	967
	AE3	350
	AE3	362
	AE3	590
	AE4	75
	AE4	625
	AE4	784
	AE4	851
	AE4	902
	AE4	949
	AE5	330
	AE5	336
	AE5	931
	AE6	515
	AE6	855
	AE6	1101
	AE6	1130
	AE6	1138
	AE8	191
	AE8	677
	AE8	787
	AE9	283
	AE9	757
	AE9	1025
	AE10	325
	AE11	29
	AE11	233
	AE11	824
	AE11	924
	AE11	1181
	AE12	95
	AE12	381
	AE12	602
	AE12	683
	AE12	1149
	AE12	1355
	OAL	613
	OAL	818
	KT1	34
	KT1	365
	KT1	485
	KT2	92
	KT2	113
	KT2	295
	KT2	434
	KT2	629
	M8	45
	M8	83
	M8	339
	HIF	455
	HIF	560
	C	727
	C	744
	TH	192
	TH	214
	TH	378
	FL	331
	FL	491
	FL	563
	FL	608
	M12	676
	WB	488

PURSUE	WB	545
	CI	621
	PWR	19
PURSUED	AM	901
	AA	522
	SAA	111
	SAA	208
	SAA	281
	ER	24
	T23	2
	HAP	756
	HAP	760
	HAP	1592
	HAP	1897
	HAP	1965
	HAP	2452
	J10	42
	J10	224
	M1	717
	M1	813
	M1	955
	M9	182
	VP6	62
	AE1	448
	AE1	547
	AE1	562
	AE1	655
	AE2	147
	AE2	719
	AE4	653
	AE5	201
	AE5	348
	AE6	97
	AE6	373
	AE6	1025
	AE7	63
	AE7	415
	AE9	536
	AE9	718
	AE10	511
	AE10	921
	AE10	1031
	AE11	1273
	AE11	1284
	AE12	460
	AE12	532
	AE12	794
	AE12	1122
	MM	19
	KT2	226
	KT2	622
	KT3	186
	KT3	814
	TJD	155
	M8	399
	B	650
	B	699
	BP	134
	CAM	188
	CAM	262
	HIF	673
	HIF	786
	C	674
	TH	71
	TH	113
	TH	120
	TH	174
	TH	256
	TH	280
	TH	353
	FL	181
	M12	113
	M12	141
	M12	315
	M12	403
	M12	702
	M12	740
	AU	344
PURSUERS	SAA	836
	AE11	1273
PURSUES	RH	23
	AM	177
	SCD1	19
	OE	36
	HAP	1723
	J1	214
	J6	513
	J6	713
	J10	86
	M1	186
	M1	634
	M1	721
	M9	102
	VP2	91
	VP6	123
	VP8	122

Word	Ref	No.	Word	Ref	No.	Word	Ref	No.
PURSUES	G1	552	PUT	J3	235	PYRRHUS	AE2	722
	G1	555		J3	254		AE2	746
	G3	314		J6	294		AE2	897
	G4	1		J16	43		AE3	383
	G4	471		J16	77		AE3	423
	G4	654		P2	41		AE3	600
	G4	814		P2	109		C	701
	AE1	329		P3	96		AU	252
	AE1	839		P5	116	PYRRHUS'	AE3	412
	AE2	722		P5	235		AE3	431
	AE4	218		P6	159	PYTHAGORAS	P6	25
	AE5	241		P6	187	PYTHAGOREAN	J3	373
	AE5	291		M1	26	PYTHIAN	M1	598
	AE9	1081		M1	238	PYTHON	M1	586
	AE11	1027		AE1	501		M1	598
	AE12	118		AE3	170		M1	616
	AE12	1082		AE3	348			
	AE12	1105		AE3	596			
	OAL	612		AE5	698			
	OAE1	27		AE6	1167			
	KT2	255		AE8	121			
	CAM	274		AE12	61			
	C	288		OAL	57	QUACK	PTP	49
	M15	602		OAL	357		PTP	16
	CI	511		OAL	463	QUAFF	HIF	585
	CI	605		OAL	649	QUAFFING	SMP	40
PURSUEST	P3	118		KT3	790		SMP	44
PURSUING	DA	85		TJD	27	QUAFFS	P6	51
	M1	683		TJD	160		AE3	817
	AE5	764		M8	125		B	710
	AE10	511		B	95	QUAIL	SAA	472
	B	132		B	241	QUAIL-PIPE	J6	107
	C	731		B	381		J6	500
	M12	141		HIF	215	QUAILS	MD	131
PURSUIT	PD	43		HIF	770		TA	426
	L2	15		HIF	786	QUAINT	AE11	698
	M1	686		C	311		KT3	454
	AE2	175		C	347	QUAKE	AE6	1087
	KT1	294		C	545	QUAKED	EDS	1
	KT2	26		C	781	QUAKERS	PK	4
	TH	48		C	785	QUAKES	EHC	3
	TH	238		TH	375		AE12	641
PURVEYED	HAP	2234		TH	409	QUAKING	AA	515
PUSH	AM	530		AU	125		HAP	37
	PDG	28		AU	286	QUALIFIED	AA	75
	J6	349		WB	111		HAP	1021
	G3	343		M15	254	QUALITIES	J3	161
	AE1	589	PUTREFACTION	HAP	226		FL	560
	AE2	632	PUTRID	G2	281		M15	465
	AE5	929		G2	355	QUALITY	G3	237
	AE6	1234		G4	406	QUALM	EPC	1
	AE12	810		AE3	811		KT2	119
	AE12	1049		AE4	659	QUALMISH	PCB	15
	OAL	420		AE9	629	QUALMS	VP4	75
	KT3	511		M15	542	QUANTITIES	P1	132
	AU	336	PUTS	AM	551		G2	141
PUSHED	HAP	605		SCD1	22	QUANTITY	P5	145
	AE5	315		T23	45	QUARREL	HS	43
	AE9	1025		HAP	1495		AM	262
	AE10	348		J6	566		SEL4	4
	AE10	971		J6	790		PAL	21
	AE12	1168		G2	38		EAL	7
	KT3	414		AE3	683		HP	247
	M12	195		AE6	554		ER	51
	M12	511		OAL	195		L4	177
	M12	704	PUZZLE	AA	115		HAP	773
PUSHES	AE12	163	PYGMALION	AE1	477		HAP	1415
	CAM	357		AE4	61		HAP	2581
PUSHING	AM	729		AE4	941		J3	449
	G3	343		M10	1		P3	20
	AE10	805		M10	61		G4	318
	OAL	756		WB	534		AE2	565
	M15	332	PYGMALION'S	AE1	500		AE4	638
PUSS	EK	16		AE4	470		AE8	21
	ELT	32		OAL	850		AE11	174
PUT	PRL	2	PYLADES	J10	388		AE12	124
	SEL4	20	PYLIAN	HIF	362		KT2	155
	PAZ	35		M12	713		KT3	15
	EKK	14	PYLUS	AT	104		TJD	163
	ETC	1		M12	725		HIF	787
	HP	173	PYRACHMUS	M12	611		AU	206
	ETG	11	PYRAMID	AM	1121		WB	527
	PR	15	PYRE	J10	396	QUARRELED	G2	638
	EUF	34	PYRENAEANS	J10	242	QUARRELS	AR	15
	RL	395	PYRENE	PPS	5		SEL4	16
	RL	400	PYRETUS	M12	600		G2	659
	L4	145	PYRGI	AE10	265		AE10	146
	H9	22	PYRGO	AE5	841		AE11	162
	H29	51		AE5	842		OAL	663
	H2	102	PYRRHA	M1	474		WB	147
	HAP	317		M1	519	QUARRIES	AM	10
	HAP	1819		T23	38		G2	227
	HAP	1992	PYRRHUS	AE2	342		G2	467
	HAP	1995		AE2	639		AE1	596
	HAP	2325		AE2	671		AE3	173
	PP	34		AE2	719		KT2	555

QUARRY
AM	343
AM	1124
OE	36
H3	37
HAP	104
HAP	593
P1	55
M1	593
AE1	294
AE12	1246
OAL	55
OAL	99
B	423

QUARTER
AE3	304
AE4	639
AE9	129
AE9	938
AE11	709
B	141
C	10

QUARTERED
G1	208
AE9	472
HIF	456

QUARTERS
PDS	14
G1	349
G2	363
G4	357
AE2	37
AE2	572
AE8	891

QUARTERSTAFF
CI	82

QUARTIL
KT1	500

QUASHED
SAA	216
EC	25

QUEAN
J10	500

QUEANS
L4	181

QUEASY
EDS	16
PMK	2

QUEEN
RH	45
SMA	119
VHH	53
AM	1185
EMQ	2
HP	20
PLB	18
D	2
L1	2
T18	87
T27	35
H3	1
AK	134
AK	141
HAP	498
HAP	1304
BR	304
LS	4
EH	2
EH	3
J10	418
J10	506
P6	98
M1	850
M9	165
M13	141
HI	95
VP6	77
VP6	68
VP7	87
VP10	27
G3	148
G3	795
AE1	13
AE1	55
AE1	95
AE1	112
AE1	371
AE1	411
AE1	418
AE1	436
AE1	496
AE1	539
AE1	561
AE1	634
AE1	704
AE1	732
AE1	735
AE1	772
AE1	788
AE1	836
AE1	866
AE1	908
AE1	953
AE1	977
AE1	1002
AE1	1018
AE1	1049

QUEEN
AE2	3
AE2	624
AE2	664
AE2	682
AE2	708
AE3	329
AE3	388
AE3	557
AE3	622
AE3	942
AE4	1
AE4	49
AE4	81
AE4	166
AE4	180
AE4	189
AE4	194
AE4	239
AE4	247
AE4	385
AE4	410
AE4	425
AE4	445
AE4	472
AE4	480
AE4	483
AE4	516
AE4	653
AE4	733
AE4	747
AE4	769
AE4	841
AE4	985
AE5	746
AE5	991
AE5	1020
AE6	34
AE6	207
AE6	274
AE6	542
AE6	552
AE6	618
AE6	820
AE7	85
AE7	190
AE7	445
AE7	534
AE7	555
AE7	560
AE7	857
AE8	81
AE8	703
AE8	921
AE8	926
AE8	948
AE9	503
AE9	546
AE10	129
AE10	855
AE10	997
AE11	346
AE11	428
AE11	722
AE11	756
AE11	978
AE11	1231
AE12	84
AE12	112
AE12	204
AE12	268
AE12	869
AE12	958
AE12	1138
AE12	1147
OAL	330
OAL	340
OAL	350
OAL	706
OAE1	9
OAE1	11
KT1	7
KT1	18
KT1	21
KT1	66
KT1	76
KT1	107
KT1	261
KT2	92
KT2	227
KT2	310
KT2	459
KT2	465
KT2	639
KT2	645
KT3	217
KT3	233

QUEEN
KT3	276
KT3	376
KT3	547
KT3	668
KT3	694
KT3	1154
M8	14
B	78
CAM	1
CAM	69
CAM	244
CAM	388
HIF	298
HIF	722
HIF	764
M10	49
M11	75
M11	317
M11	360
M11	496
FL	51
FL	177
FL	397
FL	401
FL	442
FL	455
FL	470
FL	509
FL	560
M12	7
M12	811
WB	3
WB	75
WB	83
WB	196
WB	208
WB	270
WB	292
WB	332

QUEEN'S
AE4	867
AE7	480
AE11	973
HIF	79
M11	257
M11	354

QUEENS
MF	75
SAA	53
PD	43

QUELL
AM	301
ELB	13
SSC	16
SSC	24

QUELLED
AE12	2
TH	391

QUELLING
PK	20

QUENCH
SAA	132
L4	64
T23	52
HAP	527
VP2	105
VP5	74
VP8	124
G3	470
G4	250
AE2	934
AE7	690
AE11	748
AE12	1208
KT3	236
AU	328

QUENCHED
SMA	79
AM	390
HAP	1320
M8	262
B	246

QUENCHES
AE1	220

QUENDA
C	372

QUERCENS
AE9	930

QUEST
AE1	810
AE12	816

QUESTION
PWG	23
EPC	11
AA	944
SAA	302
RL	321
T27	56
HAP	84
HAP	540
HAP	600
HAP	1819
HAP	1990
HAP	2497
EDS	15
J3	235
J10	111

QUESTION	P4	20
	P5	210
	OAL	425
	B	351
	WB	96
QUESTIONED	TA	417
	AE12	4
	AU	29
QUESTIONS	RL	435
	AE12	278
QUICK	AM	649
	SM2	20
	EUO	8
	SAA	406
	L3	88
	TA	343
	HAP	1275
	HAP	2215
	J3	237
	J3	464
	G3	105
	G3	673
	AE4	430
	KT1	234
	KT3	626
	M8	202
	C	347
	CI	191
	CI	451
	CI	587
QUICKENED	PMQ	40
	HAP	208
	M1	562
	G4	328
QUICKER	SEL4	15
QUICKLY	SIE	1
	SLN	5
	T23	58
	PDS	36
	G4	301
	WB	266
QUICKNESS	MO	20
QUICK-WITTED	J3	133
QUIET	AR	3
	AM	865
	SMQ	11
	PEL	4
	PM	1
	EUO2	4
	EKK	12
	DA	210
	EPF	2
	AA	139
	SAA	666
	RL	450
	EC	27
	L1	58
	L3	179
	H29	54
	H2	3
	TA	285
	TA	303
	HH	27
	HAP	2305
	J3	3
	J6	326
	J6	402
	J6	581
	J10	179
	J10	218
	G1	616
	G2	655
	G2	700
	G4	10
	AE1	339
	AE1	549
	AE2	1065
	AE3	641
	AE3	916
	AE4	13
	AE4	765
	AE4	770
	AE6	456
	AE9	595
	AE10	23
	AE10	109
	AE12	818
	B	716
	CAM	96
	M11	281
	ESK	11
QUIETLY	ET	11
	EAL	19
	H29	85
QUILL	MF	169
	P3	21

QUILL	AE6	879
QUILLS	HAP	2517
QUILTED	AE5	561
	B	210
QUINCES	G2	43
QUINSY	KT3	406
QUINTIUS	P1	139
QUIRINUS	AE1	400
QUIT	AM	91
	AM	542
	PAZ	16
	PUF	16
	SAA	256
	L3	91
	HAP	744
	HAP	1380
	HAP	1526
	HAP	1610
	HAP	1653
	HAP	2264
	SKA1	9
	J1	1
	J3	50
	J6	159
	J6	357
	P5	147
	G4	200
	AE1	654
	AE2	296
	AE4	788
	AE8	938
	AE10	1072
	AE11	611
	AE11	935
	AE11	1081
	AE11	1257
	AE12	487
	AE12	735
	AE12	1264
	OAL	346
	OAE1	15
	HIF	205
	HIF	321
	M12	140
QUITS	SAA	62
	SAA	599
	RL	106
	HAP	809
	AE9	942
	AE11	702
	AE11	969
	M12	187
QUITTING	L3	91
	TA	394
	G2	73
QUIVER	M1	595
	M1	626
	G3	536
	G4	487
	AE1	264
	AE1	439
	AE1	446
	AE1	703
	AE1	966
	AE4	197
	AE4	214
	AE5	408
	AE5	665
	AE7	1113
	AE8	224
	AE11	859
	AE11	883
	AE11	965
	AE11	1140
	AE11	1245
	KT2	522
	KT2	648
	KT3	936
	M8	72
	HIF	69
	HIF	144
QUIVER-BEARING	H29	43
QUIVERED	KT3	704
	M12	496
QUIVERING	T23	97
	AE1	121
	AE11	1186
	TH	79
	AU	124
	WB	347
QUIVERS	AE1	463
	AE5	729
	AE9	560
	AE9	658
	AE10	248
QUOIT	M1	600

QUONDAM	J10	357
QUORUM	J16	70
QUOTATIONS	RL	243
QUOTE	HAP	1661
QUOTED	HAP	1760
	P1	65
	C	196
QUOTES	J6	563
QUOTH	C	126
	C	195
	C	795
	WB	247
	WB	519
RABBIN	SAA	1021
RABBINICAL	AA	658
RABBINS	AA	104
RABBINS'	RL	237
RABBLE	AR	43
	AA	579
	AA	931
	SAA	118
	SAA	522
	SAA	546
	RL	403
	HAP	1304
	HAP	1924
	M8	42
RABBLE'S	J3	67
RABID	M15	258
RABSHEKA	SAA	298
RACE	DC	56
	AM	76
	PTL	23
	PNH	41
	ML	44
	PCB	26
	HP	54
	HP	58
	UMR	4
	PUF	12
	AA	45
	AA	525
	AA	642
	AA	771
	AA	837
	AA	900
	PRH	14
	SAA	743
	SAA	1085
	RL	422
	MO	10
	L1	28
	L3	258
	L3	271
	L4	212
	T18	39
	T18	51
	T18	86
	T23	35
	H3	43
	TA	447
	EAA	4
	AK	7
	HAP	22
	HAP	46
	HAP	56
	HAP	160
	HAP	175
	HAP	255
	HAP	283
	HAP	640
	HAP	705
	HAP	854
	HAP	1129
	HAP	1281
	HAP	1456
	HAP	1586
	HAP	1921
	HAP	2022
	HAP	2044
	HAP	2095
	HAP	2348
	HAP	2407
	HAP	2455
	HAP	2568
	SSC	48
	BR	216
	EPN	3
	EL	198
	OD	10

RACE	OD	52
	ODA	34
	ODA	62
	J1	195
	J3	220
	J6	450
	J6	782
	J10	404
	P2	100
	P5	237
	P6	143
	M1	238
	M1	249
	M1	341
	M1	356
	M1	554
	MC	5
	GK	47
	GK	76
	GK	96
	VP1	90
	VP4	15
	VP5	50
	VP6	60
	VP10	81
	G1	90
	G1	521
	G1	584
	G1	589
	G1	603
	G1	690
	G2	34
	G2	148
	G2	230
	G2	467
	G2	697
	G2	781
	G3	28
	G3	30
	G3	58
	G3	84
	G3	116
	G3	144
	G3	167
	G3	178
	G3	193
	G3	205
	G3	309
	G3	377
	G3	586
	G3	618
	G3	629
	G4	137
	G4	145
	G4	224
	G4	301
	G4	344
	G4	776
	AE1	9
	AE1	29
	AE1	101
	AE1	346
	AE1	363
	AE1	689
	AE1	743
	AE1	760
	AE1	795
	AE2	597
	AE2	953
	AE2	1071
	AE3	115
	AE3	129
	AE3	138
	AE3	214
	AE3	240
	AE3	415
	AE3	522
	AE3	670
	AE3	860
	AE3	925
	AE4	300
	AE4	337
	AE4	347
	AE4	360
	AE4	367
	AE4	462
	AE4	502
	AE4	782
	AE4	880
	AE5	46
	AE5	59
	AE5	78
	AE5	85
	AE5	97
	AE5	160
	AE5	190
RACE	AE5	239
	AE5	256
	AE5	298
	AE5	389
	AE5	425
	AE5	476
	AE5	736
	AE5	776
	AE5	842
	AE5	902
	AE5	1105
	AE6	97
	AE6	105
	AE6	197
	AE6	646
	AE6	672
	AE6	721
	AE6	758
	AE6	782
	AE6	881
	AE6	922
	AE6	931
	AE6	971
	AE6	1033
	AE6	1040
	AE6	1063
	AE6	1068
	AE6	1074
	AE6	1153
	AE7	144
	AE7	160
	AE7	175
	AE7	186
	AE7	351
	AE7	373
	AE7	415
	AE7	435
	AE7	455
	AE7	521
	AE7	299
	AE7	976
	AE7	977
	AE8	51
	AE8	63
	AE8	129
	AE8	192
	AE8	401
	AE8	449
	AE8	501
	AE8	507
	AE8	539
	AE8	626
	AE8	635
	AE8	833
	AE8	965
	AE8	977
	AE9	62
	AE9	135
	AE9	169
	AE9	327
	AE9	378
	AE9	879
	AE10	65
	AE10	83
	AE10	138
	AE10	309
	AE10	394
	AE10	487
	AE10	589
	AE11	77
	AE11	386
	AE11	458
	AE11	471
	AE11	620
	AE11	1014
	AE11	1026
	AE12	127
	AE12	254
	AE12	777
	AE12	1216
	OAL	116
	OAL	158
	OAL	212
	OAL	710
	DO	21
	DO	30
	DO	168
	KT1	269
	KT1	456
	KT1	474
	KT1	499
	KT2	30
	KT2	92
	KT2	105
	KT2	251
	KT2	288
RACE	KT2	393
	KT3	131
	KT3	585
	KT3	1130
	TJD	50
	TJD	90
	TJD	202
	M8	396
	B	337
	B	521
	B	540
	BP	177
	HIF	191
	HIF	375
	HIF	667
	C	540
	C	635
	TH	85
	M11	493
	FL	499
	M12	294
	M12	420
	M12	541
	M12	615
	M12	664
	WB	89
	WB	333
	WB	368
	WB	378
	WB	401
	WB	455
	M15	23
	M15	288
	M15	348
	M15	531
	M15	553
	M15	633
	M15	655
	CI	8
	CI	167
	CI	185
	SMP	4
	AS	25
	AS	38
	AS	52
RACK	MD	156
	PRH	33
	G1	435
	G1	619
	G3	606
	G3	698
	G3	744
	AE10	498
	AE12	544
	KT3	407
RACKED	HAP	2211
RACKING	AE4	361
RACKS	L3	228
	TA	185
RADIANT	AT	41
	M13	165
	VP4	8
	AE1	832
	AE1	855
	AE1	992
	AE2	802
	AE3	662
	AE4	513
	AE6	211
	AE6	982
	AE8	778
	AE8	818
	AE8	822
	AE9	16
	AE9	109
	AE9	206
	AE9	885
	AE10	377
	AF	29
	FL	168
	FL	507
	M15	94
	M15	382
	CI	121
	STP	10
	SMP	3
RADII	G2	124
RADISHES	P3	232
	BP	95
RAETHEAN	G2	136
RAFTER	J3	396
	BP	64
RAFTERS	AM	918
	AE1	630
	AE2	609
	AE2	631

RAIL	SAA	378	RAISE	PAZ	26	RAISED	AM	925
	SAA	447		EAL	29		SMM2	12
	EDGA	22		HP	126		ECG2	21
	HH	4		PUO4	13		EUO	37
	HAP	1977		PUO5	29		EAZ	7
	P3	165		AA	84		PTW	12
	PLT	11		MD	271		PTW	15
	GK	82		MF	174		CM	69
	EWR	4		MF	207		HP	165
RAILED	EPC	5		SAA	109		DA	106
	PRH	24		SAA	983		DA	129
	AU	369		RL	82		AA	110
RAILING	AA	555		TA	306		AA	148
	SAA	298		PAA	43		AA	364
	SAA	441		AK	179		AA	338
	PD	16		HAP	1062		AA	962
	P1	213		HAP	1129		MD	154
	CI	14		HAP	2108		D	14
RAILS	EAL	15		HAP	2301		MF	66
RAIMENT	J1	180		HAP	2389		SAA	556
	M15	174		SSC	16		T23	91
RAIN	AM	438		SSC	24		TA	349
	AM	1134		BR	264		HAP	1525
	STL	24		PP	7		HAP	2235
	PLN	29		PP	13		SSC	51
	L4	298		J3	311		BR	55
	H3	20		J6	138		BR	180
	H29	69		J6	283		ELW	3
	TA	426		P1	231		EL	89
	HAP	1915		P3	9		J1	124
	BR	259		P5	218		J1	170
	ODA	15		M13	144		J6	7
	ODA	33		MC	21		J6	434
	M1	57		GK	26		J10	67
	M1	82		VP4	31		J10	127
	M1	361		VP5	63		J10	170
	M1	369		VP5	80		J10	351
	VP7	83		VP9	36		P3	89
	G1	29		G1	4		HI	70
	G1	173		G2	243		GK	45
	G1	236		G2	492		VP5	82
	G1	301		G3	14		VP6	42
	G1	350		G3	19		G2	212
	G1	423		G3	39		G4	555
	G1	437		G3	272		AE1	406
	G1	511		G3	454		AE1	634
	G1	532		G3	608		AE1	812
	G1	578		G4	317		AE1	885
	G1	593		AE1	105		AE1	1032
	G1	612		AE1	118		AE2	41
	G2	483		AE1	125		AE2	60
	G3	673		AE1	192		AE2	144
	G4	119		AE1	804		AE2	155
	G4	281		AE2	150		AE2	202
	AE3	256		AE2	882		AE2	246
	AE4	171		AE3	258		AE2	314
	AE5	913		AE3	591		AE2	646
	AE7	995		AE4	59		AE3	390
	AE8	567		AE4	238		AE3	802
	AE9	584		AE4	261		AE4	940
	AE9	911		AE4	978		AE5	181
	OAL	732		AE4	988		AE5	299
	KT3	533		AE5	603		AE5	1032
	M8	94		AE5	1084		AE6	664
	B	684		AE6	517		AE6	744
	M11	151		AE6	1052		AE6	1204
	M11	155		AE6	1197		AE7	353
	FL	384		AE7	204		AE7	569
	FL	390		AE7	468		AE7	650
	FL	408		AE8	727		AE8	188
RAINBOW	G1	524		AE9	12		AE8	238
	AE9	16		AE9	674		AE8	359
	DO	77		AE11	51		AE8	553
RAINED	TJD	47		AE11	90		AE9	436
RAINS	SAA	1118		AE11	219		AE9	510
	HAP	1162		AE11	284		AE9	620
	G1	387		AE11	326		AE9	962
	G1	456		AE11	692		AE10	60
	G1	484		AE11	718		AE10	1222
	G1	566		AE11	927		AE10	1280
	G2	585		AE12	775		AE11	1
	AE1	1043		AE12	1303		AE11	658
	AE4	237		OAL	415		AE11	827
	AE11	827		OAL	847		AE12	8
	KT3	863		KT2	482		AE12	657
	FL	10		B	554		AE12	978
RAINY	HH	37		BP	47		AE12	1058
	H3	437		C	253		AE12	1374
RAISE	UDH	16		C	623		OAL	421
	HS	14		C	669		AF	128
	AM	192		M11	476		AF	169
	AM	843		FL	97		AF	179
	AM	899		M12	14		KT1	43
	AM	1100		M12	774		KT1	600
	PAR	4		CI	428		KT2	52
	PNH	34		EP	2		KT2	348

Word	Ref	Num
RAISED	KT2	445
	KT2	458
	KT2	663
	KT3	295
	KT3	375
	KT3	777
	M8	155
	M8	256
	M8	391
	B	498
	B	698
	M10	51
	CAM	214
	CAM	373
	C	263
	C	390
	C	659
	C	682
	TH	107
	M11	73
	M11	292
	M11	304
	M11	471
	M11	487
	FL	194
	M12	86
	M12	302
	M12	675
	AU	201
	M15	556
	M15	666
RAISES	EUO	29
	SAA	337
	G4	793
	AE5	649
	B	283
RAISING	AE4	383
	AE9	151
	KT1	98
	B	642
RAISINS	T27	14
	G4	388
RAKE	SAA	504
	J1	234
	P2	21
	G1	154
	G1	390
	G1	665
	G3	797
	AE11	323
RAKED	AA	127
	HIF	119
RAKES	J3	69
	J6	711
	P2	119
	M13	27
	G1	138
	G1	233
	G2	487
	G2	588
	AE5	973
	BP	48
RAKING	AM	326
RALLIES	AE9	1050
RALLY	SKA1	6
	AE2	561
RALLYING	AE5	765
RAM	HAP	1830
	G3	476
	G3	594
	AE7	240
	AE11	718
	OAL	587
	CAM	45
	C	179
	FL	2
RAMMED	PLN	33
RAMPANT	EKK	19
RAMPARTS	AE2	44
	AE4	383
RAMPIRE	AE7	213
	AE9	39
	HIF	401
RAMPIRES	AE9	63
	AE9	212
	AE9	634
	AE9	1056
	AE11	710
	AE11	1270
RAMS	M11	140
RAN	AM	921
	AM	1066
	EUO	16
	AA	1029
	SAA	551
	AT	36

Word	Ref	Num
RAN	AT	91
	L3	140
	TA	54
	TA	312
	TA	448
	HAP	194
	HAP	571
	HAP	596
	HAP	829
	BR	254
	SSC	14
	OD	31
	J1	92
	J6	155
	J6	238
	J6	806
	M1	417
	VP3	25
	G1	645
	G1	657
	G2	526
	G3	149
	G4	601
	AE2	53
	AE2	165
	AE2	364
	AE2	616
	AE3	53
	AE3	63
	AE3	450
	AE3	783
	AE4	40
	AE4	959
	AE5	47
	AE5	299
	AE5	808
	AE6	708
	AE10	783
	AE10	1122
	AE10	1134
	AE10	1194
	AE11	939
	AE12	17
	AE12	344
	AE12	662
	AE12	1305
	OAL	609
	KT1	237
	KT2	313
	KT3	56
	KT3	691
	KT3	968
	M8	52
	B	304
	BP	125
	BP	134
	CAM	111
	CAM	268
	C	725
	C	728
	C	730
	TH	116
	TH	274
	M11	9
	M11	198
	M11	390
	FL	297
	M12	152
	M12	421
	M12	468
	M12	633
	AU	111
	AU	355
	AU	438
	WB	186
	M15	575
	AE11	1184
	M8	140
RANCHED		
RANCOR	HAP	2353
RANDOM	AA	67
	PD	9
	AE4	96
	KT1	255
	TJD	26
	TJD	105
RANGE	HP	189
	PSF	16
	PRH	4
	HAP	152
	HAP	1706
	J6	317
	VP1	80
	VP5	138
	VP6	77
	G1	687
	G3	230

Word	Ref	Num
RANGE	AE9	823
RANGED	EK	13
	HAP	2
	HAP	25
	J6	14
	AE8	907
	KT3	572
	HIF	71
	HIF	531
	FL	289
RANGER	AE7	676
RANGES	AE9	74
RANK	AA	544
	SAA	510
	SAA	973
	EDG	24
	L3	190
	TA	354
	AK	141
	HAP	213
	HAP	596
	HAP	2271
	J1	117
	J3	188
	J6	58
	J6	432
	J6	633
	P3	130
	P4	96
	G2	340
	G3	592
	G3	628
	G4	213
	AE2	1042
	AE7	900
	AE7	1026
	KT1	66
	KT3	310
	KT3	470
	KT3	537
	B	558
	TH	259
	FL	249
	FL	254
	FL	538
	CI	261
	CI	406
	CI	602
RANKED	HS	31
	J6	438
	P6	107
	AE2	270
	AE11	141
	KT3	343
	KT3	965
	CAM	240
	HIF	638
RANKEST	J6	175
	G3	279
RANKLES	AE4	100
RANKLING	L4	118
RANKNESS	AA	194
	MC	8
	G3	218
RANKS	VHH	17
	H3	26
	VP4	63
	G2	86
	G2	375
	G2	508
	G4	514
	G4	606
	AE7	242
	AE8	966
	AE10	1083
	AE11	1073
	AE12	192
	AE12	344
	AE12	666
	AE12	805
	M12	103
	M12	619
RANSACKED	J1	206
	AE2	1038
	HIF	507
RANSOM	AM	415
	AE10	734
	AE10	1209
	KT1	161
	HIF	31
	HIF	180
	FL	269
	AU	305
	CI	305
RANSOMED	KT1	340
RANSOM-FREE	HIF	147

RAVES	AE1	334	RAYS	VP9	65	REACHED	CAM	366		
	AE7	526		G1	45		C	36		
	AE12	157		G1	421		TH	143		
	AE12	879		G1	615		FL	436		
	M11	224		AE4	165		M12	632		
RAVING	AE2	1014		AE5	846		M12	719		
	AE4	94		AE6	791		M12	745		
RAVISH	AR	259		AE7	735	REACHES	AM	931		
	HIF	280		AE8	567		J3	391		
RAVISHED	AR	143		KT2	41		J6	824		
	VHH	40		KT3	476		AE2	723		
	EMP	8		B	64		AE5	452		
	SSH	3		CAM	176		AE12	495		
	J3	168		HIF	576	REACHING	VP3	108		
	VP5	70		C	683	READ	DC	28		
	VP6	111	RAZED	AE11	379		ETC	2		
	G2	674		AE12	557		CM	2		
	G4	719		HIF	506		HP	87		
	AE1	40	RAZOR	J1	33		SAA	358		
	AE1	130		KT3	353		SAA	440		
	AE1	867	RAZOR-EDGE	HAP	1982		SAA	505		
	AE1	955	REACH	AR	39		RL	227		
	AE3	260		AR	59		RL	375		
	AE4	286		AR	92		AT	61		
	AE5	518		PTL	15		EC	5		
	AE7	511		EOE	22		AK	79		
	AE8	203		SAA	141		AK	80		
	AE8	349		SAA	189		HAP	399		
	AE9	173		RL	40		HAP	682		
	AE10	654		H3	54		HAP	713		
	AE12	1269		HH	9		HAP	895		
	OAL	803		HAP	1837		HAP	949		
	AF	37		HAP	2578		HAP	1459		
	AF	42		SSC	43		HAP	1543		
	KT2	427		PKA	12		HAP	2172		
	HIF	418		J10	340		BR	63		
	HIF	684		J10	528		BR	227		
	C	654		P3	64		EKA	5		
	FL	118		P5	99		EKA	7		
	AU	210		GK	115		OD	2		
	WB	348		VP9	86		MS	26		
	CI	260		G1	201		J1	71		
	CI	481		G4	720		J3	16		
	CI	512		AE3	459		J3	389		
RAVISHER	AE3	430		AE3	879		J6	832		
	OAL	769		AE5	35		J6	850		
	OAL	799		AE5	109		J10	472		
	M12	275		AE5	240		P1	3		
	M12	333		AE5	426		P1	20		
	AU	324		AE6	132		P1	192		
	WB	72		AE6	947		P1	254		
	CI	584		AE9	274		P3	102		
RAVISHERS	AE2	551		AE9	752		VP3	132		
	M15	356		AE10	88		VP4	76		
	CI	570		AE10	340		VP6	11		
	CI	590		AE10	1094		VP9	31		
	CI	606		AE11	223		G4	3		
	CI	625		M8	117		AE5	655		
RAVISHING	STC	9		M8	208		AE6	53		
RAW	PWGR	1		C	124		AE11	121		
	HAP	1259		M15	97		OAL	522		
	J1	215		PT	9		OAL	536		
	J6	270	REACHED	CM	89		OAL	643		
	J16	4		SAA	196		OAL	840		
	P1	130		T23	91		OAE2	19		
	P1	180		T23	110		MFL	27		
	M1	167		TA	48		C	140		
	EHC	1		HAP	1235		C	144		
	G3	673		M1	275		C	297		
	G4	32		M13	210		C	375		
	AE3	829		GK	145		C	380		
	AE7	728		VP5	30		WB	233		
	AE7	954		AE1	558		M15	15		
	AE10	105		AE3	870		CI	16		
	AE10	430		AE4	216		EWR	21		
	AE11	235		AE5	209	READER	JH	23		
	CI	400		AE5	682		EMW	7		
RAW-HEAD	P5	24		AE6	2		P1	119		
RAY	UDH	43		AE6	132		P1	129		
	AM	400		AE6	472		PLT	49		
	MF	23		AE9	467		G3	8		
	RL	5		AE9	754		WB	338		
	MG	35		AE10	457	READERS	SAA	457		
	CI	118		AE10	467		PTS	22		
RAYMOND	MF	93		AE10	469		MS	19		
RAYS	JH	9		AE10	678	READIER	AE12	573		
	AR	95		AE10	929	READIEST	TH	130		
	E	30		AE10	1101	READILY	HAP	1755		
	L2	65		AE11	245	READINESS	EL	322		
	HAP	504		AE11	374	READING	PUO1	31		
	HAP	1089		AE11	994		RL	227		
	J6	739		AE12	555		TA	345		
	P3	3		AE12	737		HAP	380		
	M1	54		M8	119		P1	257		
	M1	581		B	108		VP6	11		
	M1	806		B	657		OAL	2		

Word	Code	No.
READING	OAL	643
	OAL	771
READINGS	RL	242
READS	SAA	347
	SAA	505
	OAL	548
READY	SMA	43
	PMQ	56
	SMM1	1
	PAZ	24
	CM	4
	HP	46
	DA	163
	PUO4	19
	AA	591
	PPC	31
	L5	3
	H29	5
	TA	111
	HH	6
	HAP	1213
	HAP	2067
	HAP	2214
	ETS	31
	EL	20
	EL	290
	J3	17
	J3	182
	J6	778
	P1	77
	P5	196
	M1	239
	M1	391
	PLT	2
	GK	176
	VP4	58
	VP7	25
	VP8	8
	G1	49
	G2	763
	G3	699
	AE1	208
	AE1	499
	AE1	604
	AE1	650
	AE3	523
	AE4	185
	AE4	935
	AE5	717
	AE5	835
	AE6	354
	AE7	379
	AE8	677
	AE8	787
	AE9	83
	AE9	203
	AE9	500
	AE10	924
	AE12	134
	AE12	339
	AE12	492
	AE12	588
	AE12	1231
	OAL	57
	OAL	131
	OAL	486
	DO	45
	KT1	272
	KT2	56
	B	152
	B	209
	B	226
	B	265
	B	602
	B	681
	CAM	370
	HIF	291
	C	249
	TH	27
	M15	243
	CI	180
	CI	547
REAL	AR	152
	ML	34
	SAA	724
	SAA	829
	L3	135
	L4	64
	FS4	17
	HAP	414
	HAP	604
	HAP	614
	HAP	618
	M11	357
REALM	D	31
	SAA	138

Word	Code	No.
REALM	SAA	794
	PDG	42
	AK	92
	HAP	1706
	G1	264
	G2	660
	AE1	6
	AE3	23
	AE3	215
	AE6	529
	AE6	1080
	AE7	64
	AE7	317
	AE9	808
	AE11	195
	AE12	1102
	KT3	168
	MF	116
	BR	187
REALM'S	AR	84
REALMS	AM	176
	AM	552
	MF	6
	SAA	3
	BR	31
	M1	75
	M1	83
	G4	667
	AE1	196
	AE1	286
	AE1	310
	AE5	305
	AE5	965
	AE6	374
	AE6	621
	AE6	658
	AE6	763
	AE6	1136
	AE7	296
	AE7	467
	AE8	426
	AE10	120
	AE11	559
	AE12	1234
	BP	20
	CAM	333
	HIF	714
	FL	4
REAP	AM	446
	MD	292
	SAA	686
	HAP	1395
	BR	164
	VP3	64
	G1	204
	G1	345
	G1	398
	G2	567
	G3	279
	G4	207
	OAL	454
	KT2	359
REAPED	AE4	744
	SKA4	1
	CI	289
REAPER	G1	429
REAR	AM	325
	AM	363
	H2	48
	J3	404
	J6	767
	G1	25
	G3	668
	G4	782
	AE2	572
	AE3	89
	AE4	391
	AE4	727
	AE6	106
	AE6	259
	AE6	308
	AE6	564
	AE6	663
	AE6	1050
	AE7	835
	AE7	991
	AE8	775
	AE9	31
	AE10	611
	AE11	53
	AE11	96
	AE11	116
	AE11	142
	AE11	924
	AE12	180
	AE12	569

Word	Code	No.
REAR	AE12	602
	AE12	846
	AF	133
	KT3	481
	M8	32
	BP	98
	FL	465
	M12	392
	AU	51
	CI	593
REARED	AM	1090
	MF	107
	VP2	30
	VP6	76
	AE1	179
	AE2	19
	AE2	935
	AE4	971
	AE6	748
	OAL	330
	KT2	445
	KT3	707
	KT3	909
	BP	87
	HIF	498
	M12	47
	M15	593
REARING	PR	23
	G3	129
REARS	H2	29
	TA	514
	HAP	164
	M1	462
	G4	526
	AE1	222
	AE5	231
	AE6	822
	AE7	631
	M11	75
	M12	501
REASON	DC	3
	HP	49
	HP	62
	AA	903
	MD	88
	MD	93
	SAA	433
	SAA	468
	PDG	11
	RL	3
	RL	10
	RL	40
	RL	58
	RL	69
	RL	78
	RL	117
	RL	164
	RL	185
	RL	446
	RL	447
	OE	60
	L2	57
	L2	66
	HAP	63
	HAP	85
	HAP	104
	HAP	119
	HAP	126
	HAP	259
	HAP	261
	HAP	706
	HAP	820
	HAP	831
	HAP	838
	HAP	1692
	HAP	2203
	HAP	2376
	EL	219
	J6	287
	J6	308
	J6	315
	J6	337
	J6	844
	J10	3
	P2	78
	P4	18
	P5	53
	P5	138
	P5	139
	M1	114
	M9	122
	AE11	715
	AE12	973
	KT1	542
	KT2	349
	KT3	473

REASON	CAM	229
	HIF	288
	HIF	312
	C	207
	C	237
	C	326
	M15	221
	CI	123
	CI	236
REASONABLE	PLG	2
	C	330
	WB	314
	AS	31
REASONING	SAA	703
	HIF	363
REASON'S	DC	21
	RL	5
	RL	208
	SAA	745
	L3	208
	B	443
	WB	363
REASONS	EAL	1
	SAA	234
	PDS	30
	RL	196
	HAP	2014
	P4	24
	AE2	885
	AE5	942
	AE7	522
	AE8	523
	KT2	333
	KT3	1076
	M11	47
	M11	54
	AU	313
REASSURED	AE8	146
REBATE	KT3	502
	M12	231
REBECCA'S	TJD	43
REBEL	AR	24
	AA	78
	AA	215
	AA	336
	AA	627
	AA	873
	AA	974
	ELB	12
	MD	28
	MD	127
	SAA	16
	SAA	378
	SAA	435
	SAA	473
	SAA	884
	RL	96
	FS1	14
	HAP	86
	HAP	518
	HAP	730
	HAP	903
	HAP	1582
	HAP	1960
	STS3	28
	G2	785
	AE1	189
	DO	117
	KT3	408
	KT3	1086
	FL	156
	AU	342
REBELLED	TA	275
	HAP	851
REBEL-LIKE	UDH	61
REBELLING	PK	21
	HAP	278
	PWR	40
REBELLION	AR	33
	AM	792
	PKK	11
	PUO3	23
	EMW	2
	AA	460
	AA	582
	MD	221
	MD	281
	SAA	291
	SAA	387
	SAA	401
	TA	350
	HAP	47
	HAP	215
	HAP	456
	HAP	483
	HAP	987

REBELLION	BR	152
	BR	236
	M1	241
	AE5	1035
	MM	19
REBELLIONS	SAA	314
REBELLIOUS	AA	789
	MD	292
	SAA	65
	SAA	148
	TA	264
	HAP	1437
	HAP	2024
	VCS	24
REBELLOW	AE5	1128
	AE11	460
	AE12	1051
	KT3	140
REBELLOWED	AE6	149
REBELLOWING	AE7	18
REBELLOWS	G1	686
	AE4	708
REBEL-RACE	HAP	196
REBEL'S	EC	24
REBELS	PLG	15
	PUO3	4
	AA	147
	AA	806
	AA	819
	AA	992
	PRH	27
	SAA	730
	PD	47
	TA	182
	TA	460
	HAP	357
	HAP	461
	PP	26
	P1	28
	AE10	1039
REBELS'	SAA	108
	SAA	321
REBOUND	L2	33
	SKA1	2
	M13	201
	VP6	119
	VP10	11
	G1	443
	G3	77
	G3	342
	G3	523
	G4	70
	G4	668
	AE2	319
	AE3	687
	AE3	730
	AE5	198
	AE6	67
	AE8	407
	AE10	455
	AE12	998
	AF	36
	M12	171
REBOUNDS	G4	100
	AE3	318
	AE9	670
	CI	580
REBUFFED	AE3	319
REBUILD	AM	1160
	J3	353
REBUILT	M15	665
REBUKE	MS	25
	HIF	766
	GP	76
REBUKED	AE1	188
RECALL	AM	1076
	SMM2	23
	ENH	21
	MD	100
	SAA	939
	OD	21
	SFL	22
	A,E2	810
	AE8	207
	AE8	742
	KT3	1108
	HIF	561
	M12	565
RECALLED	UDH	52
	G4	90
	TJD	166
	B	124
	B	335
RECALLS	D	32
	AE11	1075
	HIF	505

RECANT	PTS	40
RECANTING	SAA	856
RECEDE	G2	206
	KT3	378
RECEDES	AE9	1079
	M11	79
RECEDING	M12	74
RECEIPT	J3	114
RECEIPTS	AR	175
	G3	690
RECEIVE	SMA	128
	AM	163
	AM	513
	AM	1188
	SMM1	4
	HP	184
	HP	243
	AA	391
	MD	136
	RL	303
	OE	3
	L4	274
	L4	296
	FS3	1
	TA	341
	TA	386
	HAP	422
	HAP	614
	HAP	1590
	HAP	1693
	BR	43
	J1	152
	J1	161
	J6	670
	J6	696
	J6	759
	J10	535
	P2	117
	P4	87
	P4	111
	P5	119
	P6	147
	M1	549
	VCS	30
	VP5	133
	VP6	97
	G1	49
	G2	411
	G4	704
	AE1	604
	AE1	742
	AE1	842
	AE2	88
	AE2	908
	AE4	937
	AE4	946
	AE5	414
	AE5	653
	AE5	706
	AE5	952
	AE6	206
	AE6	355
	AE7	316
	AE7	357
	AE8	66
	AE8	99
	AE8	197
	AE8	348
	AE8	402
	AE9	335
	AE10	45
	AE10	69
	AE10	367
	AE10	918
	AE10	952
	AE10	1263
	AE11	180
	AE11	207
	AE11	927
	AE11	1202
	AE12	942
	OAL	809
	OAE2	47
	DO	73
	KT2	273
	KT2	431
	KT3	761
	KT3	991
	TJD	186
	M8	290
	CAM	292
	CAM	370
	HIF	31
	HIF	251
	TH	68
	M12	64

RECEIVE	M15	320
	M15	578
	CI	492
RECEIVED	LC	93
	EIE	10
	PT	25
	ML	4
	SAA	616
	RL	354
	L4	54
	AK	105
	HH	22
	HAP	419
	HAP	879
	HAP	1225
	HAP	1280
	HAP	2290
	HAP	2461
	EL	132
	J3	108
	J16	24
	M1	390
	M1	558
	M1	581
	M1	1043
	GK	34
	VP3	19
	G4	517
	AE1	801
	AE2	555
	AE3	930
	AE4	780
	AE5	781
	AE7	147
	AE7	234
	AE8	239
	AE8	478
	AE9	1006
	AE10	447
	AE10	449
	AE10	598
	AE11	84
	AE12	1014
	AE12	1127
	OAL	12
	OAL	193
	OAL	774
	KT2	10
	M8	78
	M8	218
	M8	241
	B	70
	B	274
	B	318
	CAM	201
	HIF	524
	HIF	611
	HIF	718
	HIF	799
	C	335
	C	663
	TH	412
	FL	48
	FL	390
	FL	410
	M12	454
	M12	564
	M12	571
	WB	63
	GP	132
	CI	189
	CI	205
	CI	451
	ETP	4
RECEIVES	AR	233
	AM	242
	CM	117
	AA	735
	HAP	501
	HAP	1280
	HAP	2171
	HAP	2465
	J6	652
	J6	753
	M13	161
	G1	151
	G2	96
	G2	418
	G2	439
	G2	627
	G2	629
	G2	641
	G3	476
	AE1	248
	AE2	293
	AE3	446

RECEIVES	AE6	556
	AE10	990
	OAL	22
	KT1	530
	M11	197
	M12	458
	M15	59
	M15	280
	M15	247
	M15	306
	M15	562
	M15	616
RECEIVING	G2	71
RECEPTACLE	FL	61
RECEPTION	HP	206
	DA	16
	MF	81
	HAP	647
RECESS	J3	6
	G2	682
	G4	604
	AE1	228
	AE2	59
	AE5	772
	AE6	147
	B	136
	B	203
	C	598
	FL	85
	M12	296
RECESSES	P2	133
	AE1	433
	AE3	303
	AE4	611
	AE10	134
	AE10	79
	DO	163
	CI	87
RECHABITE	AA	617
RECHARGE	AM	265
RECHLESS	KT3	1074
RECIPE	TJD	105
RECIPROCATING	G4	249
RECITE	EL	143
	KT1	16
	KT1	372
	M15	624
RECITES	P1	69
RECKON	CM	18
	AU	258
	PMK	24
RECKONING	J6	322
RECLAIM	AR	316
	EWG	3
	G2	86
	AE5	873
	HIF	385
RECLAIMED	ER	43
	AE3	712
	AE4	132
	AE4	703
	OAL	21
	KT3	89
	HIF	289
RECLINED	MD	322
	SAA	621
	ODA	43
	M13	64
	G3	134
	AE3	564
	AE9	303
	AE12	1165
	B	210
	CAM	215
	HIF	458
RECLINES	AE7	248
RECLINING	AE9	581
	HI	145
	AE12	198
	KT3	270
RECOGNISE	TA	515
RECOILS	L3	211
RECOLLECT	M9	122
RECOLLECTED	AE1	869
RECOMMEND	PM	33
	PTC	24
	HP	156
	MD	255
	P5	4
	KT1	596
RECOMMENDED	AA	119
	TA	225
	B	534
	M15	5
RECOMMENDING	J16	7
RECOMMENDS	AE5	1007

RECOMMENDS	HIF	607
RECOMPENSE	AM	1054
	EMW	6
	AE5	370
	AE8	251
	AE9	250
	AE9	334
	AE12	529
	AE12	1269
	DO	69
	KT1	396
	HIF	327
	M12	281
	M15	188
RECONCILE	L5	12
	AE1	672
	AE2	243
	HIF	97
	HIF	148
	HIF	431
	TH	411
RECONCILED	MD	52
	HI	154
	G4	91
	AE12	269
	KT3	745
	M12	42
	M12	52
	CI	38
RECONCILER	HIF	802
RECONCILES	BR	151
RECORD	POE	35
	AA	218
	MD	143
	RL	393
	T18	61
	VP5	64
	AE7	893
	AE11	1229
	AE12	218
	AE12	274
	KT2	115
	KT2	304
	TJD	204
RECORDED	RH	96
	MF	125
	GK	162
	C	640
RECORDING	AA	828
RECORDS	AM	782
	PTC	37
	PUOS	3
	RL	123
	VP9	62
	AE7	73
	AE7	1049
	AE8	381
RECOUNT	SAA	226
RECOURSE	MD	219
	RL	254
	AT	70
	M9	161
	AE12	926
	OAL	320
	B	415
RECOVER	SM2	18
	PDG	29
RECOVERED	HAP	1158
	PMS	19
	AE2	615
	AE10	1294
	KT1	57
	KT2	261
	KT3	982
	C	108
	TH	337
	M11	75
	AU	368
	PMK	2
RECOVERING	AR	85
	P3	176
	AE3	399
	AE10	837
	AE12	275
	AE12	1348
	KT2	415
	C	128
RECREANT	M12	795
RECREATION	PP	47
	C	691
RECRUIT	G1	404
	G2	218
	G3	113
	G4	364
	PMK	37
RECRUITED	L4	86

Word	Code	No.
RECRUITED	G3	766
RECRUITS	ENH	38
	AE3	603
	AE7	727
	AE11	648
RED	MHD	3
	LCA	45
	PM	10
	DA	73
	EDG	40
	HAP	1241
	M1	198
	M13	110
	G1	343
	G1	377
	G1	605
	G1	610
	G1	657
	G2	601
	G3	840
	G4	67
	AE2	977
	AE4	924
	AE6	324
	AE6	801
	AE10	35
	AE12	102
	DO	152
	KT1	111
	KT1	195
	KT1	467
	KT2	518
	KT2	524
	KT2	563
	KT2	611
	KT3	42
	KT3	560
	M8	122
	M8	259
	C	117
	C	151
	C	152
	C	413
	FL	347
	FL	351
	FL	355
	M12	152
	M15	287
	M15	623
	SMP	51
REDCOAT	J10	32
REDDEN	M10	76
REDDENED	J10	509
	G3	741
REDDENING	AE8	698
REDEEM	LC	126
	AM	666
	DA	103
	HAP	1072
	HAP	2138
	J6	572
	M1	1067
	G2	40
	G3	365
	AE2	170
	AE3	429
	AE4	346
	AE5	257
	AE6	180
	AE6	498
	AE6	707
	AE11,	1072
	AE12	401
	OAL	226
	DO	145
	KT1	364
	AU	195
	WB	267
	CI	519
	CI	587
REDEEMED	AM	1132
	DC	38
	HI	78
	AE3	204
	AE5	823
	AE6	1133
	AE8	350
	AE10	939
	HIF	688
	AU	12
	AU	441
	WB	243
	GP	73
REDEEMER	HAP	883
	GP	7
	AS	23
REDEEMING	J6	851
REDEEMS	M12	325
REDEMPTION	VCS	37
	AE10	1211
RED-HOT	M12	390
REDOLENT	M15	110
REDOUBLE	SKK	8
	G1	456
REDOUBLED	AA	1023
	HAP	626
	G2	732
	AE3	261
	AE4	959
	AE5	511
	AE5	608
	M8	199
	M12	329
	M12	399
REDOUBTS	AE9	79
REDRESS	AM	966
	AA	190
	AA	747
	EK	48
	FS2	14
	HH	12
	HAP	1645
	HI	138
	AE1	838
	AE5	771
	AE12	722
	KT1	59
	HIF	240
	HIF	357
REDRESSED	HAP	198
	HAP	568
REDUCE	HAP	2398
	M10	85
REDUCED	AM	501
	HAP	1539
	HAP	2553
	J1	163
	J6	473
	J10	130
	J10	412
	AE3	336
	MG	18
	TH	242
	AU	365
	AU	576
REDUNDANT	G1	129
REED	HAP	2089
	VP5	2
	VP6	6
	WB	194
REEDEN	G4	385
REEDS	J6	5
	P1	239
	M1	939
	M1	949
	M1	976
	M1	985
	M13	58
	M13	221
	M13	227
	VP2	41
	VP7	16
	VP8	34
	G2	491
	G2	573
	G3	22
	G4	686
	AE8	48
	AE8	458
	AE10	295
	OAL	255
	OAL	622
	M8	98
	BP	31
REEKING	HAP	2507
	G2	269
	AE1	297
	AE2	898
	AE4	864
	AE4	951
	AE5	1014
	AE9	469
	AE9	607
	AE11	952
	C	280
	TH	304
	M12	211
	M12	573
	M15	182
	M8	35
REEKS	RH	36
REEL		
REEL	G4	493
REELED	M12	520
REELING	VP5	46
	G2	526
REELS	AE6	573
	M15	495
REFECTORIES	HAP	1824
REFERS	M15	550
REFINE	AR	272
	EMK	24
	AA	616
	VCS	20
	SLT1	13
REFINED	ECG2	24
	PUO1	14
	ESF	11
	PCB	35
	EAA	9
	OD	54
	MM	44
	B	130
	B	426
	GP	10
	CI	231
	CI	239
REFINES	EWG	20
	SEL4	13
	HAP	1983
REFINING	SDG	24
	SDG	29
	PD	52
REFIT	AE3	298
REFITTED	AE1	777
REFLECT	L4	213
	HP	210
	J3	182
	AE2	646
REFLECTED	L2	31
	AE2	1006
	M15	355
REFLECTING	HAP	503
	OD	13
	KT1	224
	TH	225
	GP	103
REFLECTION	LC	48
	LCA	25
	SAA	373
	EL	78
	EL	137
	AE9	508
	TH	383
	CI	142
REFLECTIVE	AM	1012
REFORM	PLB	4
	HH	14
	HAP	460
	HAP	461
	HAP	2324
	G2	605
	MM	23
REFORMATION	EM	2
	PO	10
	HAP	372
	HAP	473
	HAP	1007
	HAP	1507
	HAP	1618
REFORMATIONS	SAA	905
REFORMED	AR	209
	PM	1
	POE	12
	HAP	362
	HAP	409
	HAP	701
	HAP	1003
	HAP	1028
	HAP	1032
	HAP	1849
	HAP	1947
REFORMERS	HAP	359
	HAP	1008
	HAP	2022
REFORMERS'	HAP	1987
REFORMING	PRL	7
	P5	52
	ETP	33
REFORMS	SAA	283
	G2	563
	M8	273
REFRAIN	CM	96
	AA	587
	HAP	2168
	J1	44
	G3	100
	OAL	362

Word	Ref	Num
REFRAIN	C	393
	C	537
	M11	58
REFRAINING	M9	89
REFRAINS	SAA	600
REFRESH	HAP	1865
	J6	102
	G1	388
	AE8	575
	AE9	197
	MFL	26
REFRESHED	SMA	22
	VP8	20
	AE8	540
	AE8	806
	FL	417
	FL	613
	AS	97
REFRESHING	H29	36
	VP5	72
	G4	174
	FL	404
REFUGE	DC	57
	EUO	4
	EAL	2
	J10	260
	AE1	492
	AE1	838
	AE8	453
	AE10	1309
	B	346
REFUGED	AE2	782
	AE4	779
REFUGEES	J3	129
REFULGENT	M1	628
	G4	396
	AE1	557
	AE2	834
	AE6	660
	AE8	697
	AE11	1238
	AE12	637
REFUND	PA	46
REFUSE	AM	531
	EWGR	45
	STL	15
	EOE	6
	AA	166
	AA	485
	AA	899
	SAA	13
	AT	84
	AT	90
	AT	100
	T18	17
	TA	332
	HAP	221
	HAP	407
	HAP	1027
	HAP	1219
	EL	359
	MS	23
	J6	106
	J10	523
	J16	64
	P2	78
	P3	29
	P4	111
	P5	112
	P5	227
	P5	249
	P5	266
	P6	82
	M1	846
	ELT	8
	GK	23
	VP2	58
	VP4	29
	VP5	142
	VP8	5
	VP10	5
	AE2	542
	AE2	1010
	AE4	152
	AE5	554
	AE6	828
	AE7	19
	AE8	671
	AE8	726
	AE10	1305
	AE11	660
	AE12	94
	AE12	1081
	OAL	841
	CAM	105
	AU	394
REFUSE	AU	586
	WB	484
	M15	116
REFUSED	E	4
	TA	262
	HAP	2274
	STS1	7
	LS	5
	EL	43
	J6	111
	J16	29
	M1	519
	M9	140
	VP8	48
	G2	210
	G4	755
	AE2	227
	AE2	862
	AE4	635
	AE5	542
	AE6	440
	AE7	261
	AE7	852
	AE11	60
	AE11	351
	AE11	452
	AE11	672
	AE12	597
	KT1	62
	KT1	586
	KT3	675
	TJD	161
	HIF	14
	HIF	142
	AU	107
REFUSES	P3	203
	M9	138
REFUSING	CI	202
REGAIN	PTC	39
	DA	4
	ER	49
	AE7	838
	KT3	515
	CI	528
REGAINED	AE3	431
REGAL	AA	920
	MD	11
	MD	229
	SAA	129
	SAA	739
	TA	318
	TA	429
	HAP	1962
	HAP	2026
	HAP	2111
	BR	220
	BR	313
	G4	137
	G4	294
	AE2	692
	AE6	819
	AE6	1181
	AE7	228
	AE8	665
	AE12	438
	EWGR	12
	PMM	2
	AM	1147
	HP	123
	J1	108
	J10	222
	P6	48
	VP6	48
	G2	160
	AE2	783
	AE3	630
	AE4	398
	KT1	213
	KT2	372
	KT2	661
	KT3	696
	B	66
	B	549
	C	663
	CI	188
REGARDFUL	HIF	225
REGARDING	B	284
REGARDLESS	AR	13
	T23	99
	G3	382
	AE4	346
	AE10	927
	AE11	1149
	AE12	571
	TH	348
	P1	193
REGARDS		
REGARDS	M1	1014
	VP8	51
	G1	140
	AE1	345
	AE6	635
	GP	15
REGENCY	PP	51
REGENT	J6	67
REGIMENT	J16	27
REGION	AK	12
	GE	28
	GK	137
	VP3	163
	G1	50
	G3	371
	G4	415
	AE1	427
	AE1	752
	AE1	880
	AE3	116
	AE6	728
	KT2	528
	KT3	766
	CAM	318
	M11	272
	FL	337
REGIONS	AM	96
	AM	650
	ML	38
	AA	820
	PRH	1
	L1	6
	L1	26
	TA	365
	HAP	291
	HAP	502
	M1	52
	M1	74
	G1	333
	G3	437
	AE1	77
	AE6	162
	AE6	198
	AE6	233
	AE6	375
	AE6	625
	AE9	123
	AE10	174
	AE12	1224
	B	678
	WB	28
	SAA	978
REGISTER	B	186
REGORGE	AR	72
REGRET	AR	222
	TA	152
	MG	5
REGULAR	UDH	29
	EEL	18
	EPF	14
	AK	8
	MC	58
	MM	41
REGULARLY	P3	215
REGULATE	PLB	3
	HIF	736
REHEARSAL	GE	77
REHEARSALS	P1	43
REHEARSE	AA	569
	SAA	408
	SAA	937
	EK	7
	AK	16
	P1	66
	P5	55
	P6	7
	VP6	103
	VP8	13
	VP8	87
	VP9	24
	G3	1
	DO	3
	C	337
REHEARSED	VP7	26
	FL	452
REIGN	AR	87
	EIE	27
	EM	148
	AM	194
	EM	863
	SCG2	21
	PNH	36
	PUF	26
	AA	70
	AA	321
	AA	331

Word	Ref	Num
REIGN	AA	245
	AA	378
	AA	525
	AA	721
	MD	249
	MD	302
	D	34
	MF	12
	MF	28
	MF	88
	MF	139
	SAA	6
	SAA	68
	SAA	263
	SAA	583
	SAA	652
	SAA	700
	SAA	714
	SAA	903
	OE	23
	ER	29
	L1	25
	L2	63
	L3	317
	TA	180
	TA	211
	TA	230
	TA	289
	TA	507
	TA	346
	TA	373
	TA	418
	TA	465
	PAA	44
	HAP	1522
	HAP	1917
	HAP	1177
	HAP	2142
	HAP	2169
	HAP	2396
	HAP	2550
	BR	42
	BR	99
	BR	163
	BR	217
	ETS	11
	EJG	2
	EL	8
	MS	2
	J6	1
	J6	840
	HI	35
	HI	160
	GK	155
	VP2	16
	VP2	89
	VP6	15
	VP6	64
	VP8	78
	G1	38
	G1	52
	G1	190
	G1	274
	G2	28
	G2	157
	G2	368
	G2	405
	G3	462
	G3	475
	G4	129
	G4	136
	AE1	52
	AE1	57
	AE1	178
	AE1	194
	AE1	200
	AE1	365
	AE1	738
	AE3	95
	AE3	131
	AE3	216
	AE3	277
	AE3	326
	AE4	305
	AE4	315
	AE4	451
	AE4	509
	AE5	1035
	AE5	1045
	AE6	129
	AE6	177
	AE7	280
	AE7	435
	AE7	575
	AE8	501
	AE9	355
REIGN	AE10	53
	AE10	602
	AE10	790
	AE12	282
	AE12	1201
	OAE1	19
	MG	4
	KT2	57
	KT2	167
	KT3	837
	KT3	1075
	M8	315
	B	336
	HIF	234
	HIF	697
	HIF	743
	C	501
	FL	490
	FL	542
	AU	91
	AU	159
	WB	46
	M15	604
	M15	660
	M15	667
	GP	100
REIGNED	AA	42
	M1	138
	MC	42
	AE3	265
	AE3	382
	AE3	453
	AE7	1016
	AE9	349
	AE11	371
	B	1
	AU	290
REIGNING	SAA	580
	HAP	506
	BR	168
REIGNS	PA	13
	PTL	3
	EUO	29
	PLG	21
	J1	139
	J6	316
	M1	317
	MC	48
	VP4	12
	VP5	95
	VP6	113
	VP7	100
	G2	783
	G3	246
	G3	720
	G4	303
	AE1	945
	AE2	54
	AE4	92
	AE5	41
	AE7	941
	AE8	459
	B	282
	HIF	549
REIN	G3	324
	G3	422
	AE7	220
	AE10	834
	AE11	1063
	AE11	1204
	AE12	552
	AE12	723
	AE7	1070
REINED	AE10	356
RE-INFLAME	VP8	92
REINFORCED	AM	473
	AE7	732
REINS	PTL	19
	SCD1	6
	P5	48
	P5	136
	M1	383
	G1	692
	G3	169
	G3	307
	AE1	224
	AE1	665
	AE5	748
	AE5	863
	AE5	1071
	AE6	654
	AE6	1100
	AE9	426
	AE9	755
	AE10	811
	AE10	1240
REINS	AE11	743
	AE11	992
	AE11	1052
	AE12	492
	AE12	502
	AE12	696
	AE12	910
	DO	59
	KT2	48
	HIF	416
REINSPIRED	TH	330
REJECT	HAP	766
	HAP	2035
	P1	80
	P4	126
	G3	598
	AE4	51
	AE4	619
	AE12	957
	OAE2	41
REJECTED	VP8	2
	AE4	319
	AE6	445
	AE10	83
	KT3	239
REJECTING	J10	521
REJECTS	BR	212
	AE8	31
	C	320
	WB	319
REJOICE	AM	297
	AM	890
	PUO4	9
	MD	15
	SAA	1061
	HAP	1384
	HAP	2184
	P1	46
	HI	168
	DHP	28
	VP5	97
	VP9	93
	G1	570
	G2	371
	G2	589
	AE4	694
	AE12	954
	OAL	206
	KT1	198
	HIF	391
	C	649
	M15	664
	CI	204
REJOINED	HAP	719
	HIF	310
RELAPSE	M1	855
RELAPSING	HAP	1058
RELATE	SAA	935
	J6	720
	J10	348
	J10	420
	PLT	27
	G3	432
	AE1	11
	AE1	283
	AE1	513
	AE1	613
	AE1	648
	AE1	1058
	AE2	3
	AE2	747
	AE2	930
	AE3	36
	AE3	84
	AE3	209
	AE3	244
	AE3	329
	AE3	323
	AE3	582
	AE3	589
	AE4	109
	AE4	333
	AE4	657
	AE6	119
	AE6	376
	AE6	713
	AE7	54
	AE7	109
	AE8	387
	AE11	191
	AE11	271
	AE11	369
	KT1	327
	KT3	111
	KT3	844
	KT3	860

Word	Code	Ref
RELATE	BP	179
	HIF	9
	M11	371
	M12	243
	M12	717
	M12	732
	AU	21
	M15	464
RELATES	AE4	271
	AE12	169
	C	210
	C	376
	TH	189
	M12	278
RELATION	HAP	1440
	AE1	912
	AU	247
RELATIONS	HP	241
	EL	357
	G4	374
	TJD	48
RELATIONS'	EDS	12
RELAX	PRH	42
RELEASE	G3	101
	G3	346
	AE1	83
	AE2	32
	AE3	49
	AE11	547
	KT1	304
	KT2	417
	CI	304
	HIF	200
	HIF	397
RELEASED	VHH	3
	HAP	2511
	EL	118
	AE5	677
	AE6	976
	B	683
	CI	418
RELENT	AE2	638
	AE7	413
	OAL	422
	M10	79
	HIF	222
	M15	524
RELENTING	M12	49
RELENTLESS	SAA	887
	T23	97
	M1	325
	VP8	64
	G2	467
	AE2	897
	AE10	740
	HIF	145
	TH	20
	TH	353
RELENTS	M8	281
RELIC	AK	161
	AE2	953
RELICS	EPF	1
	MF	101
	EL	373
	P6	66
	M1	521
	G1	667
	AE1	841
	AE2	396
	AE2	431
	AE2	974
	AE3	115
	AE4	494
	AE4	718
	AE5	905
	AE6	325
	AE6	1000
	AE8	509
	AE11	146
	AE11	325
	DO	72
	AU	440
RELICTS	SAA	544
RELIED	HAP	2089
	AE10	141
RELIEF	AM	974
	AM	1043
	SCG3	6
	S	2
	A	2
	AA	563
	AA	811
	SAA	725
	RL	118
	RL	443
	L3	88

Word	Code	Ref
RELIEF	L3	282
	L4	48
	T23	27
	FS2	6
	TA	5
	TA	54
	TA	158
	TA	272
	HH	37
	HAP	1959
	M1	435
	M1	485
	M1	498
	M1	894
	M1	912
	M1	973
	M9	86
	HI	176
	VP3	25
	VP10	47
	G3	618
	G4	416
	G4	538
	AE1	136
	AE2	1053
	AE2	1092
	AE4	689
	AE6	44
	AE6	628
	AE7	126
	AE8	44
	AE8	159
	AE8	755
	AE9	157
	AE9	299
	AE9	1049
	AE10	183
	AE10	221
	AE10	276
	AE10	307
	AE10	619
	AE10	950
	AE10	1122
	AE11	94
	AE12	74
	AE12	225
	AE12	608
	AE12	613
	AE12	949
	AE12	1139
	KT1	53
	KT1	64
	KT1	417
	KT3	150
	KT3	876
	KT3	1094
	TJD	102
	M8	1
	B	696
	B	723
	CAM	163
	CAM	191
	C	245
	TH	31
	TH	135
	M11	177
	M11	318
	FL	404
	M12	46
	M12	686
	AU	438
	WB	471
	GP	58
	CI	451
RELIES	HAP	656
	G2	452
	AE1	940
	AE5	570
	AE5	591
	AE5	1122
	TJD	139
RELIEVE	AA	415
	L2	45
	BR	44
	EL	68
	P6	73
	M9	168
	HI	151
	AE1	605
	AE1	843
	AE6	89
	AE9	220
	AE10	956
	AE11	1201
	AE12	1166
	KT1	74

Word	Code	Ref
RELIEVE	B	199
	GP	57
RELIEVED	HH	23
	J16	25
	AE4	779
	AE5	927
	AE9	292
	AE10	714
	B	341
	M12	225
	GP	131
RELIEVES	ENH	27
	SLT1	15
RELIGION	LC	18
	PCD	8
	PCD	14
	PCD	15
	PCD	18
	EUO2	25
	PO	23
	PSF	13
	PUO4	34
	AA	292
	AA	747
	AA	969
	MD	152
	MD	263
	MD	286
	SAA	245
	SAA	582
	SAA	658
	SAA	754
	PDG	22
	RL	68
	HAP	370
	HAP	1139
	HAP	1491
	HAP	1548
	HAP	2162
	HAP	2323
	BR	279
	PDS	16
	AE2	251
	AE2	972
	AE3	24
	AE8	791
	LMC	1
	M15	717
RELIGION'S	AR	191
	PCD	21
	MD	103
	SAA	785
	RL	10
	RL	173
RELIGIONS	AA	99
	SFL	15
RELIGIOUS	SAA	649
	SAA	650
	SAA	915
	J6	461
	J6	519
	P2	108
	AE1	769
	AE2	202
	AE3	465
	AE3	477
	AE7	841
	AE9	101
	AE12	181
	AE12	286
	AE12	1128
	AE12	1186
	WB	212
	GP	2
RELINQUISH	M1	845
RELISH	EOE	31
	J10	327
	P3	144
	BP	109
	C	22
RELUCTANCY	M9	19
RELUCTANT	AE4	786
	HIF	329
RELY	POE	30
	PTC	11
	HAP	120
	HAP	757
	HAP	1141
	HAP	2217
	AE3	841
	AE8	76
	AE8	184
	AE11	761
	AE11	1260
	CAM	140
	CAM	193

RELY	HIF	127
	HIF	705
RELYING	B	532
REMAIN	RH	14
	PWG	40
	ENH	17
	DA	174
	AA	264
	PLB	54
	SAA	67
	SAA	103
	SAA	132
	SAA	713
	SAA	971
	L3	55
	HAP	888
	HAP	1668
	OD	9
	OD	18
	J3	414
	J10	461
	J16	55
	M1	184
	M1	479
	M1	484
	M1	494
	HI	86
	GK	161
	VP2	22
	VP4	37
	G2	574
	G2	582
	G3	705
	G4	377
	AE2	187
	AE2	894
	AE2	922
	AE5	630
	AE5	799
	AE5	824
	AE5	903
	AE5	935
	AE6	115
	AE6	130
	AE6	542
	AE6	834
	AE10	1044
	AE10	1174
	AE11	321
	AE11	554
	AE12	29
	AE12	283
	AE12	1202
	OAL	43
	OAL	142
	AF	139
	KT2	290
	KT3	280
	KT3	812
	HIF	574
	M11	169
	WB	410
	WB	499
	M15	699
	CI	590
REMAINDER	M1	423
REMAINDERS	HAP	1896
	AE1	242
	AE1	529
	AE5	877
REMAINED	AA	41
	SAA	950
	OD	33
	ODA	50
	M1	850
	VP1	57
	AE1	38
	AE3	321
	AE3	432
	AE5	662
	AE6	645
	B	138
	B	516
	B	661
	TH	338
	TH	391
	TH	417
	AU	59
	WB	224
	CI	288
	CI	443
	CI	456
	CI	503
REMAINING	HAP	1087
	BR	119
	BR	185

REMAINING	OD	49
	J3	473
	J6	472
	AE2	870
	AE5	982
	OAL	205
	B	399
	B	563
	B	731
	CAM	202
	M12	614
REMAINS	AA	396
	AA	542
	AA	990
	MD	265
	MF	69
	SAA	1066
	PK	25
	RL	289
	RL	427
	L3	53
	L3	66
	L3	254
	L4	293
	PAA	5
	AK	68
	HAP	153
	HAP	1055
	HAP	1600
	ODA	60
	J6	22
	J10	533
	J16	80
	P5	179
	M1	272
	M1	316
	M1	544
	M1	746
	M9	90
	MC	72
	VP1	64
	G2	474
	G2	742
	G3	154
	G3	676
	G3	718
	G4	71
	G4	274
	G4	304
	AE1	73
	AE1	404
	AE2	87
	AE2	889
	AE3	405
	AE4	117
	AE4	409
	AE4	468
	AE4	652
	AE5	72
	AE5	290
	AE5	528
	AE5	635
	AE5	685
	AE5	960
	AE5	1029
	AE5	1040
	AE6	813
	AE6	999
	AE6	1012
	AE7	6
	AE7	334
	AE7	774
	AE8	67
	AE8	469
	AE9	167
	AE9	198
	AE9	654
	AE10	985
	AE10	1309
	AE11	430
	AE11	564
	AE11	596
	AE11	642
	AE11	661
	AE11	1191
	AE12	573
	AE12	802
	AE12	964
	AE12	1276
	OAL	270
	DO	106
	KT2	105
	KT2	285
	KT3	400
	KT3	754
	KT3	1057

REMAINS	KT3	1111
	M8	383
	B	351
	B	650
	BP	154
	CAM	135
	CAM	180
	HIF	85
	HIF	493
	HIF	578
	M11	430
	FL	559
	M12	671
	M12	816
	AU	579
	M15	53
	GP	1/21
	ETP	46
	EWR	24
REMARKS	AR	82
REMEDIES	PUO1	23
	M1	705
	KT3	756
	TJD	103
REMEDY	UDH	96
	T23	49
	TA	161
	J16	31
	G3	701
	DO	132
	KT1	411
	TH	25
	TH	400
	FL	422
	WB	376
REMEMBER	HAP	590
	HAP	715
	HAP	1312
	HAP	1996
	PPS	3
	M1	329
	AE7	172
	AE9	703
	B	429
	TH	154
	M12	255
	M12	613
	M12	627
	WB	353
	M15	233
	CI	2
REMEMBERED	T27	11
	J10	325
	HI	165
	M11	432
REMEMBERING	HAP	1330
	M1	347
REMEMBRANCE	AM	757
	SAA	68
	SAA	706
	L3	37
	ETS	19
	J16	87
	AE2	4
	AE3	412
	AE6	679
	AE10	703
	AE11	1053
	KT1	180
	KT2	385
	HIF	546
REMIT	G4	777
REMITS	M15	515
REMITTED	B	287
REMNANT	P5	223
	AE1	743
	KT1	27
REMNANTS	AM	405
	AM	1032
	HAP	510
	HAP	1570
	M1	78
	G3	474
	AE1	45
	ESK	22
REMONSTRANCE	PLB	9
REMORSE	AM	1075
	RL	85
	RL	115
	L4	113
	AE10	743
	KT2	345
	CAM	286
	TH	374
	TH	375
REMORSES	EDS	23

Word	Code	No.
REMOTE	AM	67
	AM	152
	AM	364
	AM	813
	AM	907
	SAA	171
	RL	97
	L4	221
	EL	80
	AE1	492
	AE1	797
	AE9	12
	AE9	301
	AE11	495
	AE12	1032
	HIF	233
	M12	59
	M15	81
REMOTELY	PUO4	4
REMOTER	TA	510
	GK	43
REMOTEST	AM	650
REMOUNT	HAP	1894
	AE2	540
REMOUNTS	TH	215
	CI	600
REMOVAL	SAA	203
REMOVE	SMQ	4
	PW	7
	E	6
	EMK	14
	PLG	8
	AA	25
	AA	487
	AA	995
	SAA	655
	L4	17
	L4	59
	HAP	1986
	HAP	1087
	HAP	1737
	HAP	1972
	HAP	2552
	SKA5	6
	EL	326
	J6	698
	P2	18
	M1	387
	VP2	99
	G1	57
	AE3	815
	AE5	1023
	AE8	533
	OAL	476
	OAE1	31
	KT2	7
	KT3	236
	B	588
	CAM	79
	CAM	299
	HIF	96
	TH	237
	M12	831
	AU	346
	CI	71
	CI	109
	CI	357
	CI	639
REMOVED	SMA	25
	DA	124
	AA	921
	SAA	1107
	HAP	1160
	HAP	1503
	PDS	1
	J3	324
	J6	604
	G1	201
	AE1	343
	AE1	1012
	AE8	235
	AE8	885
	AE9	439
	B	629
	HIF	583
	TH	385
	AU	574
	ESK	12
	PMK	26
REMOVES	SAA	261
	M1	682
REMULUS	AE9	490
	AE11	946
REMURMUR	AE6	963
REMURMURED	G4	667
	AE7	1042

Word	Code	No.
REMURMURING	AE11	695
REMUS	G2	778
	AE1	400
	AE9	441
REND	PD	54
	J1	51
	M1	70
	VP10	109
	G1	557
	AE1	83
	AE1	673
	AE2	653
	AE2	668
	AE3	58
	AE4	32
	AE4	641
	AE5	184
	AE5	602
	AE5	671
	AE6	219
	AE7	554
	AE8	324
	AE8	751
	AE10	1288
	AE11	52
	AE11	1272
	AE12	154
	AE12	681
	AE12	1344
	OAL	138
	AF	107
	KT3	665
	M8	230
RENDER	AM	30
	SAA	1039
	G3	744
	G4	69
	AE3	346
RENDERED	UDH	38
	HS	8
	HAP	2011
	HIF	146
RENDERS	AE5	684
RENDEZVOUS	PW	6
	HAP	1742
RENDS	J10	447
	G3	422
	AE4	967
	AE5	899
	AE9	635
	AE11	128
	AE11	221
	AE12	885
	KT2	347
RENEGADES	PUO3	25
RENEGADO	MD	268
RENEGADOES	SAA	366
RENEW	AR	214
	AR	290
	SCG3	29
	PUO1	2
	SAA	715
	H2	94
	FS1	6
	TA	427
	AK	53
	HAP	1830
	M1	14
	VP5	122
	VP10	49
	VP10	106
	G1	117
	G1	521
	G2	279
	G2	445
	G3	448
	G4	737
	AE1	132
	AE1	657
	AE1	778
	AE1	787
	AE2	562
	AE2	630
	AE3	338
	AE3	363
	AE3	694
	AE3	847
	AE4	76
	AE4	107
	AE5	74
	AE5	238
	AE5	481
	AE5	749
	AE5	765
	AE5	825
	AE5	983

Word	Code	No.
RENEW	AE7	194
	AE8	576
	AE9	209
	AE9	282
	AE10	181
	AE10	267
	AE10	555
	AE10	1145
	AE12	24
	AE12	312
	KT3	601
	B	449
	M10	83
	M11	22
	M11	311
	FL	540
	M12	232
	M12	716
	M15	134
RENEWED	AR	285
	AM	1175
	PUO2	22
	AA	32
	L4	88
	HAP	22
	HAP	56
	HAP	967
	HAP	973
	M1	141
	M1	554
	VP1	12
	VP1	61
	VP6	63
	G3	663
	G4	406
	G4	430
	AE1	338
	AE1	1065
	AE2	146
	AE2	615
	AE2	641
	AE3	56
	AE3	67
	AE3	246
	AE5	126
	AE5	1083
	AE6	52
	AE6	1179
	AE8	242
	AE8	750
	AE10	39
	AE10	372
	AE10	977
	AE11	319
	AE11	1212
	AE12	631
	AE12	680
	KT1	352
	KT1	519
	KT3	253
	KT3	1117
	TJD	169
	B	642
	HIF	690
	HIF	787
	TH	176
	TH	343
	TH	352
	M11	90
	FL	450
	M12	402
	AU	343
	CI	374
	CI	578
	AS	18
RENEWING	AE10	359
	KT3	136
RENEWS	AA	217
	J6	593
	VP4	6
	G1	287
	G2	438
	G2	479
	G3	509
	G3	521
	G4	813
	AE2	4
	AE2	723
	AE3	268
	AE4	87
	AE4	207
	AE5	63
	AE5	798
	AE5	973
	AE5	1025
	AE6	1119

RENEWS	AE7	116
	AE8	612
	AE8	781
	AE9	1080
	AE10	757
	AE11	1076
	KT2	41
	M10	75
	C	777
	M11	69
	M11	481
	M12	177
	M15	603
	CI	606
RENOUNCE	EKA	11
	PSH	25
	J6	626
	G2	326
	AE1	543
	AE5	269
	AE5	645
	AE12	277
	KT2	136
	KT2	146
	KT2	288
	KT3	657
	WB	331
RENOUNCED	AE5	542
RENOUNCES	HAP	1437
	G3	748
RENOUNCING	PPC	34
	TA	94
	AE9	1060
RENOWN	PWGR	7
	PM	7
	EUO	29
	HP	135
	AA	23
	AA	684
	MF	31
	MF	94
	AT	96
	HAP	2416
	P5	19
	J1	21
	J6	729
	J10	162
	M1	601
	M1	755
	M1	1046
	HI	112
	HI	120
	HI	160
	G2	55
	G2	722
	G3	26
	AE1	637
	AE2	462
	AE5	77
	AE5	517
	AE7	874
	AE7	979
	AE8	174
	AE8	625
	AE9	829
	AE11	312
	AE11	765
	AE12	1199
	OAE1	21
	MG	19
	KT1	37
	KT1	58
	C	712
	WB	61
	WB	439
	M15	4
	PMK	26
RENOWNED	DC	33
	RL	75
	SKA5	16
	J6	195
	J6	642
	J10	186
	P1	64
	VP5	66
	AE1	811
	AE2	29
	AE2	458
	AE3	724
	AE3	925
	AE4	699
	AE5	388
	AE6	243
	AE6	1045
	AE6	1156
	AE7	123

RENOWNED	AE7	144
	AE7	322
	AE7	372
	AE7	1004
	AE8	88
	AE10	254
	AE10	603
	AE11	387
	AE11	412
	AE12	217
	KT1	165
	KT2	317
	KT2	420
	KT3	17
	TH	2
	FL	513
	M12	420
	CI	436
RENT	CM	64
	SAA	585
	HAP	1098
	HAP	2211
	HAP	2579
	J3	58
	J3	87
	J6	652
	J10	245
	M1	199
	ELT	24
	VP5	34
	G1	455
	G1	640
	G4	309
	AE1	148
	AE2	5
	AE2	826
	AE2	845
	AE2	846
	AE6	215
	AE6	304
	AE6	757
	AE8	932
	AE9	760
	AE12	759
	AE12	1259
	KT1	157
	KT1	604
	KT3	262
	KT3	525
	C	10
	C	352
	TH	281
RENT-CHARGE	PFD	15
	MC	69
RENTS	EUF	7
	J1	161
	J3	240
	J6	340
REPAID	TA	47
	HAP	2286
	M8	299
	FL	597
	FL	554
REPAIR	SMA	101
	AM	89
	AM	427
	AM	567
	AM	880
	AM	1017
	PSF	33
	SAA	25
	HAP	554
	HAP	1742
	HAP	1862
	HAP	2576
	PSH	14
	J3	498
	J6	756
	M1	96
	G1	22
	G1	561
	G2	5
	G3	355
	G3	430
	G3	634
	G3	652
	G4	91
	G4	102
	G4	790
	AE2	1026
	AE3	278
	AE4	71
	AE4	415
	AE6	352
	AE6	1007
	AE7	238

REPAIR	AE7	312
	AE7	771
	AE8	571
	OAL	104
	KT2	406
	KT2	531
	KT3	144
	TJD	115
	TJD	149
	M8	402
	HIF	278
	TH	239
	FL	16
	FL	32
	M12	558
	AU	489
	M15	332
	M15	514
	CI	200
	SMP	75
REPAIRED	PWG	50
	VP7	1
	AE1	801
	AE4	432
	KT3	969
	M15	21
REPAIRER	M11	310
REPAIRING	P1	200
REPAIRS	G4	798
	AE2	350
	AE7	495
REPASSED	M12	444
REPASSING	G1	323
REPAST	HAP	1244
	G2	756
	TH	86
	TH	249
REPAY	STC	7
	AE1	394
REPAYS	SKA6	16
REPEAL	HAP	2148
	HAP	2176
REPEALED	AE6	847
REPEALING	HAP	1991
REPEAT	SMA	11
	AM	1028
	DA	158
	AA	651
	TA	441
	HAP	620
	EL	290
	HAP	1687
	J1	80
	VP5	17
	AE3	305
	AE3	554
	AE4	483
	AE4	540
	AE6	853
	C	382
	FL	366
	M12	82
REPEATED	AR	142
	SAA	71
	TA	270
	VP6	67
	G1	454
	AE1	245
	AE2	656
	AE2	880
	AE6	704
	AE8	337
	AE8	788
	AE8	696
	AE10	1252
	DO	75
	FL	10
	M12	69
	M12	187
	M12	470
REPEATING	FL	466
REPEATS	AA	691
	J6	376
	M12	178
	M15	229
REPEL	LCA	32
	CM	50
	BR	282
	M1	627
	HI	91
	AE2	426
	AE5	1109
	AE7	600
	AE11	1201
	M11	103
	M15	557

REPELLED	AM	883	REPLIED	HAP	1716	REPLY		HIF	751
	P5	64		M1	337	REPORT		MF	96
	AE10	977		M1	620			HAP	341
	AE11	938		M1	899			HAP	1429
	AE12	521		M13	40			HAP	1529
	AE12	719		HI	101			HAP	2483
	HIF	643		G4	764			M9	4
	M11	254		AE1	449			G3	601
	M12	646		AE1	461			AE4	251
	AU	333		AE4	150			AE4	282
	AU	425		AE5	36			AE4	431
	WB	450		AE6	190			AE11	453
REPELLING	MF	137		AE6	473			B	530
REPELS	AE4	707		AE6	685			C	661
REPENT	AR	68		AE6	758			M11	139
	HP	33		AE6	912			M11	316
	HP	34		AE6	1200	REPORTED		AE6	619
	AA	957		AE7	547	REPORTS		EC	6
	MD	97		AE7	613			J6	536
	L4	129		AE9	108			J10	527
	ODA	27		AE9	372			AE3	910
	P5	81		AE10	153			AE7	571
	M13	102		AE10	737			AE7	939
	G4	776		AE10	878			AE11	619
	AE1	772		AE10	1046			M11	370
	AE6	132		AE11	160			M12	64
	AE12	367		AE12	30			M12	274
	AE12	834		OAL	735	REPOSE		HS	143
	OAL	423		KT1	312			RH	63
	C	786		KT2	302			SMA	41
	TH	415		KT3	662			AM	909
	CI	351		B	280			AM	1013
REPENTANCE	PRH	26		CAM	253			PUO2	4
	EDS	21		HIF	53			DA	167
	AE6	590		HIF	182			SAA	242
	KT3	813		HIF	411			L1	43
REPENTED	HAP	2384		HIF	569			L3	291
	HAP	2561		TH	150			TA	238
	ODA	48		FL	115			HAP	1901
	TA	83		FL	198			HAP	2586
	EDS	18		FL	480			PTS	36
	HIF	357		M12	326			EL	243
REPENTING	SMA	86		WB	511			J3	3
	AM	122		WB	374			J3	319
	AM	789		CI	536			P5	57
	AA	259	REPLIES	AA	375			M1	948
	EDS	30		SAA	157			M1	1018
	R	21		SAA	182			M9	46
	B	754		SAA	204			G2	664
	CI	251		SAA	1033			G4	275
REPENTS	KT1	382		J6	312			G4	624
	M8	282		P5	106			AE1	244
	M8	335		P5	172			AE3	10
	CAM	287		P5	240			AE4	758
REPINE	PTC	40		HI	188			AE5	1100
	AA	361		AE1	349			AE7	161
	MD	126		AE1	512			AE10	1108
	SAA	903		AE1	789			AE12	91
	PDS	22		AE4	41			KT3	1151
	MS	18		AE4	482			CAM	125
	J10	393		AE5	293			CAM	126
	P6	31		AE6	942			M11	280
	P6	45		AE7	162			CI	106
	AE8	327		AE7	630	REPOSED		P5	49
	M15	315		AE8	161			AE5	1135
REPINED	SAA	1098		AE10	25	REPOSSESS		HAP	1856
	HAP	2260		AE10	863	REPRESENT		EMQW	14
REPINES	L3	64		AE10	1294			AA	907
	G2	318		AE11	520			L4	227
	G3	774		AE12	113			AK	101
REPINING	BR	61		AE12	912			GE	40
	J6	183		AE12	1203			OAL	198
	AE6	588		KT1	282			OAL	693
	AE6	386		B	726	REPRESENTATIVES	PUO5	19
REPLACE	AE8	634		BP	5			HAP	663
REPLACED	AE8	236		HIF	224	REPRESENTED		AA	109
REPLENISHED	UDH	47		C	378	REPRESENTERS		SAA	573
	SAA	399		M11	396	REPRESENTS		ESF	16
REPLETE	C	181		M15	14			M11	339
	M15	310	REPLY	SCD2	8			ESK	5
REPLETION	L4	56		P4	117	REPRESSED		HAP	305
	C	141		P6	84			M1	1055
REPLETIONS	J1	217		AE2	377			AE4	935
REPLIED	AA	315		AE3	404			AE6	453
	HAP	612		AE7	290			AE8	244
	HAP	632		AE10	367			AE10	970
	HAP	785		AE11	220			AE12	1297
	HAP	788		AE11	693			AE12	1361
	HAP	1485		AE11	770			M8	267
	HAP	1512		AE12	1294			HIF	373
	HAP	1670		AE12	1345	REPRIEVE		FS3	18
	HAP	1961		KT3	581			TA	105
	HAP	2050		B	744			J10	437
	HAP	2080		CAM	230			AE10	890
	HAP	2196		HIF	126			AE10	881
	HAP	1714		HIF	691			KT1	388

Word	Ref	No.
REPRISAL	PA	47
	ER	49
REPRISE	HAP	2156
	M12	319
REPRISES	BR	231
REPROACH	PMQw	16
	G2	546
	AE6	498
	AE9	851
	AE9	1062
	AE10	97
	AE10	946
	AU	324
REPROACHED	BR	344
	AE5	515
	AE10	976
	CAM	226
REPROACHES	SAA	289
REPROACHFUL	AE10	1290
REPROBATES	ETC	13
REPRODUCE	BR	217
REPROOF	SAA	181
	SAA	1054
REPTILE	M12	22
REPUBLIC	MD	301
	HAP	2545
REPUBLICS	MD	247
REPULSE	M13	175
	G3	620
REPULSED	J10	262
	AE9	932
	AE11	934
	BP	41
	M12	660
REPULSES	SKA5	11
REPUTATION	DA	103
REPUTE	HAP	1840
	M12	245
REPUTED	SAA	533
REQUEST	PIE	20
	T23	66
	HAP	2512
	J10	8
	J10	35
	J10	83
	P2	35
	M1	654
	GK	162
	VP5	142
	VP9	91
	AE1	539
	AE1	729
	AE1	787
	AE2	936
	AE4	607
	AE4	630
	AE5	557
	AE7	333
	AE7	366
	AE9	96
	AE9	271
	AE10	654
	AE10	889
	AE11	157
	AE11	537
	KT1	54
	KT1	370
	KT3	214
	B	391
	B	735
	BP	168
	CAM	337
	M12	288
	AU	215
	WB	121
	WB	221
	WB	295
	WB	515
	GP	62
	CI	207
	CI	417
REQUESTS	PCB	23
	AU	601
REQUIRE	AM	1022
	EMP	3
	AA	343
	AA	624
	AA	1006
	SAA	127
	SAA	590
	RL	300
	L4	196
	L5	4
	H29	38
	HAP	649
	HAP	988
REQUIRE	HAP	1634
	HAP	2586
	BR	38
	BR	160
	EL	92
	J10	9
	P3	135
	SLT1	4
	VP2	106
	G1	386
	G2	37
	G2	587
	AE2	190
	AE3	84
	AE4	719
	AE7	209
	AE7	375
	AE8	161
	AE8	581
	AE8	649
	AE8	667
	AE11	522
	AE11	1300
	AE12	318
	AE12	526
	AE12	1007
	KT1	422
	KT2	260
	KT3	193
	TJD	130
	M8	328
	B	83
	M10	64
	TH	243
	AU	339
	WB	96
	M15	661
	EMKG	5
REQUIRED	RL	201
	RL	216
	RL	246
	T23	40
	HAP	1022
	HAP	1170
	HAP	1885
	EL	50
	J6	152
	M1	172
	M13	55
	VP7	4
	G2	85
	G2	548
	G2	471
	G3	186
	AE1	48
	AE1	417
	AE1	1056
	AE2	43
	AE4	569
	AE5	925
	AE6	866
	AE7	135
	AE7	324
	AE8	525
	AE9	707
	AE12	393
	AE12	899
	DO	132
	KT1	227
	KT2	246
	KT3	201
	TJD	134
	B	19
	B	472
	CAM	75
	TH	38
	WB	274
	WB	314
	CI	209
	CI	454
	CI	559
REQUIRES	AA	82
	L2	24
	J1	104
	M1	382
	VP3	94
	VP9	92
	G2	399
	G3	116
	G3	160
	G3	695
	G4	658
	AE6	1183
	AE11	586
	AE12	490
	AE12	828
REQUIRES	AE12	839
	OAL	552
	TJD	137
	M8	339
	B	433
	B	443
	HIF	176
	M15	515
REQUIRING	M15	300
REQUISITE	HP	183
	AA	978
	P3	137
REQUITAL	DA	88
REQUITE	VP4	75
	AE1	851
	AE2	729
	PTP	52
REQUITES	VP1	65
RESCIND	HAP	2077
RESCUE	AM	463
	AE12	401
RESCUED	HS	65
	AE1	524
RESEMBLANCE	L4	211
	L4	234
	TA	87
	TA	247
	GK	108
	GK	161
	G3	96
	G4	532
	AE1	968
RESEMBLE	ESF	6
	PLG	13
RESEMBLED	AE3	773
RESEMBLES	MF	14
	AE3	393
	TJD	198
RESEMBLING	SMA	78
	HAP	1455
	M1	546
	G2	283
	G3	56
	AE3	408
	M11	261
	M15	298
RESENT	SAA	129
	SAA	175
	J16	12
RESENTING	HIF	591
RESENTMENT	AE1	17
	AE10	1219
RESENTMENTS	SAA	731
	M12	10
RESENTS	G3	350
RESERVATION	J6	389
	EMKG	31
RESERVE	G3	253
	AE1	290
	AE8	756
	M8	80
RESERVED	AR	321
	ENH	35
	ETC	12
	AA	378
	AT	25
	FS3	2
	BR	196
	J6	862
	J10	439
	M13	109
	M13	132
	VP8	11
	G3	31
	AE5	812
	DO	86
	KT3	354
	B	131
	B	325
	AU	275
	AU	471
	GP	14
	AS	62
RESERVES	SAA	92
	BR	99
RESERVING	KT3	1010
	WB	92
RESIDE	LC	121
	HAP	653
	G4	292
	AE5	919
	AE6	913
	AE7	1089
	AS	80
RESIDENCE	HAP	644
RESIDES	HAP	674

RESIDES	SFL	6	RESOLVE	SCD2	13	RESOLVED	CI	535
	G4	610		AA	456		CI	570
	AE7	207		RL	285	RESOLVES	M1	354
	CI	631		HAP	2215		AE11	831
RESIGN	SCG3	23		M1	533		CAM	130
	L3	162		M1	1069		CI	526
	PPS	5		VP6	31	RESOLVING	HAP	813
	M1	333		G4	330	RESORT	VHH	46
	VP7	33		AE2	883		PCB	22
	G1	42		AE7	517		RL	357
	AE4	830		AE8	150		T18	3
	AE5	557		AE9	246		HAP	516
	AE5	559		B	564		HAP	2114
	AE5	645		HIF	204		J6	87
	AE9	850		CI	519		J10	146
	AE10	80	RESOLVED	AR	66		M1	781
	AE10	663		AM	53		HI	17
	AE10	1208		AM	356		G2	720
	AE11	655		AM	549		G4	562
	AE12	287		PCD	11		AE2	1032
	OAE2	49		POE	34		AE4	432
	MG	5		DA	7		AE4	167
	KT3	274		AA	174		AE6	139
	KT3	802		MF	13		AE7	807
	M8	326		SAA	997		AE8	471
	HIF	45		L4	131		KT1	578
	HIF	176		H2	97		HIF	715
	HIF	199		HAP	446		AU	320
	HIF	271		PTS	8		AU	366
	WB	512		EL	229		WB	30
	WB	522		P5	206		M15	478
	CI	294		M1	295		CI	43
	CI	509		AE2	150		CI	94
RESIGNED	VHH	1		AE2	465	RESORTS	AM	799
	H29	85		AE2	483		AE4	206
	TA	217		AE2	484	RESOUND	MF	48
	HAP	441		AE2	424		M1	365
	ODA	56		AE2	784		M13	61
	P5	40		AE2	888		VP5	90
	G1	124		AE2	1087		VP6	67
	G2	701		AE3	357		G1	679
	AE1	1009		AE4	22		G2	543
	AE2	957		AE4	73		G3	826
	AE3	426		AE4	571		AE1	1014
	AE5	928		AE4	690		AE2	498
	AE10	164		AE4	801		AE3	853
	AE10	484		AE4	922		AE4	169
	AE11	1263		AE5	42		AE5	578
	AE12	1189		AE5	297		AE5	726
	MFL	36		AE6	157		AE5	1001
	KT2	586		AE9	543		AE7	15
	B	562		AE9	743		AE8	954
	HIF	483		AE10	189		AE9	722
	M15	161		AE10	646		AE9	907
	GP	112		AE10	963		AE11	205
RESIGNS	LC	47		AE10	1131		AE11	984
	PUO1	44		AE10	1224		AE12	1053
	G1	616		AE10	1275		KT2	622
	CI	545		AE11	464		KT3	684
RESIST	M1	364		AE11	940		KT3	993
	AE2	452		AE12	116		M8	366
	AE12	927		AE12	571		HIF	1
	OAL	309		AE12	811		M12	300
	HIF	139		AE12	821	RESOUNDED	SAA	831
	HIF	211		AE12	1144	RESOUNDING	AE6	797
	AU	274		KT1	350	RESOUNDS	AM	273
	M15	508		KT2	43		M9	4
	CI	556		KT2	249		AE2	848
RESISTANCE	OAL	747		KT3	904		AE6	743
RESISTED	P5	230		M8	274		AE8	843
	OAL	145		B	41		AE12	504
	CI	365		B	99		AE12	1037
RESISTING	T27	113		B	254		KT3	582
	AE6	148		B	347		M11	173
	TJD	185		B	382		M12	318
RESISTLESS	HS	49		B	587		M15	434
	BR	349		CAM	142	RESOURCE	AE10	512
	M1	70		CAM	231		AE11	477
	M1	616		HIF	690	RESPECT	HS	143
	AE5	494		C	73		AM	251
	AE8	391		C	306		SEL4	7
	AE8	442		TH	26		POE	27
	AE10	1115		TH	59		MD	311
	AE11	962		TH	128		SAA	392
	AE11	1297		TH	227		L2	55
	AE12	546		TH	250		HAP	521
	KT2	213		TH	399		HAP	548
	TH	424		M11	7		HAP	2521
	FL	302		M11	254		HAP	2539
RESISTS	G1	154		M11	324		J6	684
	AE11	1109		M12	311		AE11	35
	M10	25		AU	336		AE12	32
RESOLUTE	AE2	862		M15	375		AE12	1154
RESOLUTION	PR	5		CI	264		AE12	1218
RESOLUTIONS	SAA	854		CI	447		M8	223
RESOLVE	PWG	23		CI	476		HIF	231

Word	Ref	No.
RESPECT	HIF	315
	FL	467
	AU	587
RESPECTED	TH	386
RESPECTING	HIF	32
RESPECTS	SAA	635
	SAA	826
RESPIRE	FL	379
RESPIRED	HIF	626
RESPIRES	M12	687
RESPITE	HAP	1676
	AE12	745
	M12	192
REST	HS	104
	HS	145
	AR	2
	AR	297
	RH	53
	SMA	76
	LC	112
	LC	115
	LC	118
	DC	51
	PIE	29
	VHH	6
	AM	154
	AM	297
	AM	377
	AM	487
	AM	505
	AM	575
	AM	832
	AM	864
	AM	899
	AM	950
	AM	1120
	PMQ	20
	EWGR	31
	EEL	9
	SCG2	10
	PAR	17
	EMQW	17
	EUO2	7
	ML	28
	ML	29
	PLG	4
	HP	44
	DA	94
	DA	212
	EMP	7
	AA	13
	AA	166
	AA	349
	AA	477
	AA	572
	AA	630
	PPC	10
	MD	321
	PRH	22
	MF	19
	SAA	331
	SAA	531
	SAA	571
	SAA	621
	SAA	682
	SAA	760
	SAA	828
	SAA	937
	SAA	1130
	OE	62
	AT	117
	ER	25
	L3	131
	L3	199
	L4	161
	T18	48
	T18	88
	T23	84
	H9	29
	FS1	2
	TA	38
	TA	74
	TA	128
	TA	142
	TA	307
	AK	5
	AK	176
	HAP	146
	HAP	160
	HAP	257
	HAP	308
	HAP	400
	HAP	528
	HAP	534
	HAP	570
	HAP	928

Word	Ref	No.
REST	HAP	978
	HAP	986
	HAP	1008
	HAP	1018
	HAP	1037
	HAP	1043
	HAP	1249
	HAP	1274
	HAP	1379
	HAP	1478
	HAP	1501
	HAP	1687
	HAP	1721
	HAP	1887
	HAP	1919
	HAP	1946
	HAP	1961
	HAP	2235
	HAP	2256
	HAP	2306
	HAP	2403
	HAP	2414
	HAP	2488
	HAP	2535
	HAP	2590
	BR	70
	BR	158
	BR	187
	PDS	25
	PKA	38
	EL	119
	EL	213
	EL	247
	EL	269
	EL	298
	EL	337
	ELW	8
	ELW	3
	ODA	18
	MS	19
	J1	25
	J3	100
	J3	272
	J3	381
	J3	441
	J6	100
	J6	152
	J6	639
	J6	673
	J6	737
	J10	36
	J10	548
	P2	2
	P5	238
	P6	139
	P6	162
	M1	22
	M1	100
	M1	136
	M1	480
	M1	549
	M1	557
	M1	676
	M1	861
	M1	993
	M1	1023
	M13	121
	M13	132
	HI	102
	SLT2	12
	GK	175
	VP1	89
	VP3	169
	VP5	72
	VP8	114
	VP9	69
	VP9	85
	G1	116
	G1	121
	G1	587
	G1	682
	G2	88
	G2	148
	G2	397
	G3	11
	G3	257
	G3	334
	G3	419
	G3	793
	G4	240
	AE1	236
	AE1	304
	AE1	538
	AE1	705
	AE1	730
	AE1	757

Word	Ref	No.
REST	AE1	821
	AE1	865
	AE1	889
	AE1	980
	AE1	989
	AE1	996
	AE2	12
	AE2	46
	AE2	308
	AE2	573
	AE2	773
	AE3	196
	AE3	487
	AE3	498
	AE3	521
	AE3	555
	AE3	600
	AE3	667
	AE3	778
	AE3	944
	AE4	202
	AE4	67
	AE4	106
	AE4	468
	AE4	541
	AE4	800
	AE5	124
	AE5	174
	AE5	200
	AE5	324
	AE5	474
	AE5	611
	AE5	700
	AE5	747
	AE5	821
	AE6	53
	AE6	269
	AE6	152
	AE6	434
	AE6	645
	AE6	651
	AE6	686
	AE6	700
	AE6	877
	AE6	906
	AE7	5
	AE7	82
	AE7	136
	AE7	167
	AE7	255
	AE7	550
	AE7	650
	AE7	659
	AE7	746
	AE7	793
	AE7	1072
	AE8	33
	AE8	146
	AE8	217
	AE8	368
	AE8	404
	AE8	437
	AE8	538
	AE8	575
	AE8	700
	AE8	730
	AE8	776
	AE9	34
	AE9	53
	AE9	196
	AE9	238
	AE9	337
	AE9	416
	AE9	452
	AE9	497
	AE9	605
	AE9	790
	AE9	982
	AE10	80
	AE10	318
	AE10	351
	AE10	457
	AE10	688
	AE10	1077
	AE10	1177
	AE10	1239
	AE11	59
	AE11	136
	AE11	200
	AE11	314
	AE11	389
	AE11	538
	AE11	632
	AE11	644
	AE11	666
	AE11	680

REST

AE11	708
AE11	998
AE11	1010
AE11	1166
AE12	202
AE12	434
AE12	468
AE12	641
AE12	655
AE12	747
AE12	886
AE12	1279
OAL	78
OAL	83
OAL	388
OAL	756
OAL	888
OAL	841
OAE2	43
DO	72
DO	103
KT1	78
KT1	141
KT1	185
KT1	476
KT2	109
KT2	114
KT2	135
KT2	310
KT2	516
KT2	641
KT3	21
KT3	38
KT3	108
KT3	162
KT3	173
KT3	205
KT3	269
KT3	356
KT3	583
KT3	731
KT3	851
KT3	922
KT3	965
KT3	1004
TJD	153
TJD	163
M8	65
M8	168
M8	220
B	123
B	153
B	276
B	291
B	365
B	487
B	516
B	528
B	540
B	632
B	646
B	713
B	747
BP	9
BP	45
BP	110
M10	56
CAM	323
HIF	23
HIF	246
HIF	509
HIF	519
HIF	639
HIF	673
HIF	676
HIF	813
C	120
C	210
C	235
C	262
C	305
C	610
TH	5
TH	14
TH	31
TH	252
TH	259
TH	363
TH	388
TH	405
TH	425
M11	166
M11	244
M11	251
M11	287
M11	308

REST

M11	342
FL	24
FL	140
FL	174
FL	185
FL	227
FL	292
M12	160
M12	192
M12	213
M12	267
M12	452
M12	711
M12	727
M12	731
M12	764
M12	778
AU	266
AU	489
AU	505
WB	13
WB	175
WB	245
M15	21
M15	121
M15	548
M15	676
GP	23
GP	81
GP	138
CI	46
CI	51
CI	94
CI	154
CI	167
CI	209
CI	435
CI	545
CI	618

RESTED

AE4	370
AE10	1038
AE10	1192
B	469
M11	96
CI	427

RESTIFF

TA	472
HAP	2320
G3	324
AE7	864
OAL	539
HIF	416

RESTING

G4	40
AE3	114

RESTITUTION
RESTLESS

HAP	1634
AR	9
LC	106
AM	405
AM	938
AA	154
PRH	32
SAA	719
L3	279
L3	281
L4	7
L4	36
J10	275
M13	191
AE1	77
AE7	482
AE10	1194
KT1	208
KT3	457
KT3	1075
B	174
AU	38
WB	344
M15	381

RESTORATION
RESTORE

TA	292
HS	62
AR	157
SMA	43
LCA	12
VHH	34
AM	171
AM	258
AM	390
AM	572
PKK	12
DA	31
DA	104
PUO5	24
SAA	569
RL	288
DOD	21
L1	58
L3	21

RESTORE

T23	79
H3	9
HH	35
HAP	1233
HAP	1632
HAP	2077
HAP	2176
BR	103
STS3	36
EL	189
P1	169
P6	69
M1	512
SFL	21
HI	194
ELT	22
DHP	16
VP4	16
VP7	55
VP8	119
VP8	93
VP8	99
VP8	106
VP8	109
VP8	127
VP8	134
VP8	145
G2	364
G3	608
G4	134
G4	650
G4	671
AE1	299
AE2	128
AE2	911
AE2	955
AE2	1066
AE3	104
AE4	495
AE6	1055
AE6	1081
AE7	653
AE8	56
AE8	494
AE8	858
AE9	269
AE10	92
AE11	178
AE11	298
AE11	547
AE12	1158
OAL	226
OAE2	41
DO	103
TJD	156
M8	228
M8	331
B	179
CAM	78
HIF	187
HIF	194
AU	444
CI	630
AS	95
AR	81
SMA	48
LC	23
DC	58
AM	122
AM	358
HP	31
PUO5	6
AA	516
AA	1030
D	31
SAA	970
SAA	973
SAA	1071
SAA	1139
ER	20
ER	28
L1	52
MN	5
BR	248
BR	265
J1	126
J6	603
M1	469
M1	1027
HI	172
VP1	63
VP4	62
G4	212
G4	752
AE1	7
AE1	204

RESTORED

Word	Code	Number
RESTORED	AE1	422
	AE1	878
	AE2	338
	AE2	374
	AE2	645
	AE3	384
	AE3	410
	AE4	8
	AE4	451
	AE5	56
	AE5	132
	AE6	1046
	AE6	1118
	AE7	1057
	AE8	54
	AE8	236
	AE8	282
	AE10	706
	AE11	282
	AE11	409
	AE12	627
	AE12	1136
	DO	27
	DO	71
	DO	78
	DO	146
	KT1	127
	KT1	371
	KT3	1106
	B	28
	HIF	147
	HIF	173
	HIF	534
	HIF	605
	HIF	803
	M15	652
	CI	307
	CI	506
	CI	507
RESTORER	SAA	995
RESTORES	RH	50
	TA	516
	M1	831
	AE4	359
	AE6	128
	AE10	341
	AE10	973
	AE11	1076
	KT3	592
	C	338
RESTORING	PAA	45
	G4	399
	AE11	282
	CI	295
RESTRAIN	DA	11
	AA	340
	L3	243
	L4	21
	L4	45
	H3	34
	HAP	1028
	J3	491
	M1	265
	VP3	171
	G1	351
	G1	361
	G1	488
	G2	685
	G3	213
	G3	145
	G3	611
	G3	393
	G4	159
	G4	203
	AE1	99
	AE1	193
	AE1	401
	AE1	737
	AE2	15
	AE9	664
	AE10	157
	DO	109
	B	727
	C	321
	M15	717
RESTRAINED	G3	275
	ETC	21
	CM	59
	SAA	610
	SAA	1049
	HAP	27
	HAP	545
	J6	71
	M1	1062
	AE5	663
	AE6	48
RESTRAINED	AE11	148
	DO	51
	TJD	59
	B	271
	CI	162
RESTRAINING	CI	460
RESTRAINS	M1	50
	VP3	161
	AE2	1073
	AE4	198
	AE5	804
	AE8	655
	AE11	826
RESTRICTION	AE12	1187
RESTS	AM	712
	PUO2	6
	EUO2	23
	EMW	5
	B	701
	CAM	142
	HIF	181
	AU	581
RESTY	AT	76
RESULT	EL	157
RESULTING	KT3	405
	KT3	1117
RESULTS	M1	574
	AE11	694
RESUME	P5	168
	P5	251
	AE1	282
	AE7	516
	DO	23
	HIF	190
	HIF	312
	M12	734
RESUMED	AA	412
	AA	521
	TA	468
	HAP	1572
	M1	266
	G4	640
	AE5	784
	AE12	974
	KT2	349
	TH	336
RESUMES	D	30
	AE3	572
RESUMING	AA	767
	AE4	389
	HIF	135
RESURRECTION	AS	17
RETAIL	RL	377
RETAIN	LC	63
	SAA	657
	SAA	1005
	L4	183
	HAP	623
	P5	165
	M1	319
	M1	551
	M1	987
	M9	176
	VP9	61
	AE7	281
	AE12	1196
	KT3	245
	CAM	353
	M12	156
	AU	349
	M15	663
RETAINED	M1	104
	M1	931
	AE6	479
	AE7	1069
	AE12	553
	OAL	546
	KT2	282
	TJD	193
	M11	404
	M12	35
	M12	397
RETAINING	M12	617
RETAINS	SAA	1065
	M13	233
	AE6	682
	AE8	470
	M15	461
RETARD	VP10	15
	G4	166
	KT2	215
	AU	184
RETARDS	P5	208
	AE12	1080
RETINUE	TA	507
	AE9	441
RETINUE	KT3	453
RETIRE	AM	608
	AM	787
	AM	902
	AM	979
	AM	995
	AM	1027
	AM	1112
	AM	1155
	PW	18
	PNH	15
	PAZ	21
	EAZ	8
	AA	1021
	PLB	25
	L3	283
	H29	37
	BR	37
	BR	155
	J1	202
	J3	233
	M1	452
	M1	35
	GK	16
	G1	202
	G2	319
	G3	578
	AE2	360
	AE2	857
	AE2	1093
	AE6	733
	AE8	408
	AE8	744
	AE10	588
	AE10	623
	AE11	608
	AE11	1059
	AE12	763
	AE12	1006
	OAL	612
	DO	123
	CAM	4
	CAM	288
	TH	66
	AU	426
RETIRED	AM	87
	SAA	981
	SAA	1091
	H2	98
	HAP	966
	J3	21
	J3	474
	J6	181
	P6	15
	DHP	14
	G4	620
	G4	723
	AE3	531
	AE3	944
	AE5	124
	AE7	136
	AE8	810
	AE9	5
	AE9	452
	AE10	626
	KT3	202
	KT3	578
	KT3	748
	B	87
	B	207
	B	218
	B	256
	CAM	267
	HIF	427
	M12	557
	M12	742
	AU	388
	CI	557
RETIREMENT	EL	260
	M13	47
RETIRES	HP	181
	L1	47
	TA	4
	J6	319
	J6	458
	G3	348
	G3	643
	AE8	721
	AE9	1074
	AE11	287
	AE11	1125
	AE11	1210
	AE12	1221
	CI	593
RETIRING	PAL	35
	M10	27

Word	Ref	No.
RETORT	HAP	811
RETOSSED	CI	370
RETOUCH	GK	177
RETRACE	AE7	520
RETRACT	CI	252
RETRACTS	CAM	132
RETREAT	AM	371
	AM	380
	PUO2	5
	EUO2	2
	HAP	1283
	SSC	32
	J3	46
	J3	265
	J3	472
	P6	2
	M1	559
	G1	55
	G2	615
	G2	655
	G2	697
	G4	31
	G4	216
	G4	354
	G4	582
	AE1	337
	AE1	430
	AE2	538
	AE3	5
	AE3	665
	AE4	217
	AE7	452
	AE7	689
	AE10	832
	AE10	1306
	AE11	798
	AE12	10
	AE12	602
	TJD	120
	B	112
	TH	56
	FL	314
	FL	322
	CI	290
	CI	572
RETREATED	SAA	346
RETREATING	M15	404
RETREATS	L3	201
	AE6	718
	FL	583
RETRENCH	PCB	28
RETRENCHING	M15	464
RETRIEVE	M1	491
	AE6	590
RETRIEVED	G4	402
RETROGRADE	KT2	616
RETURN	VHH	37
	AM	136
	AM	926
	AM	1056
	PUO1	19
	EUO2	13
	EUO2	31
	PCB	32
	HP	155
	AA	276
	SAA	178
	L3	119
	T18	68
	T18	64
	T23	64
	T23	111
	T27	117
	TA	369
	TA	422
	AK	38
	AK	167
	HAP	1356
	PP	26
	SKA1	15
	LS	12
	LS	18
	ODA	14
	EH	20
	J3	92
	J3	171
	J3	274
	J3	429
	J10	289
	P5	248
	M1	1032
	M9	98
	M13	214
	HI	183
	VP1	55
	VP1	49
RETURN	VP1	92
	VP5	55
	VP7	56
	VP8	125
	G1	112
	G2	565
	G2	746
	G2	761
	G3	37
	G4	12
	G4	372
	AE1	398
	AE1	784
	AE1	846
	AE2	22
	AE2	68
	AE2	163
	AE2	258
	AE2	1082
	AE3	226
	AE3	302
	AE5	311
	AE6	194
	AE6	975
	AE7	394
	AE7	401
	AE7	625
	AE7	968
	AE8	757
	AE9	248
	AE9	345
	AE9	870
	AE9	998
	AE10	138
	AE10	946
	AE10	1145
	AE11	63
	AE11	71
	AE11	348
	AE11	386
	AE11	433
	AE11	685
	AE11	1164
	AE11	1167
	AE12	380
	AE12	774
	AE12	1049
	OAL	207
	OAE2	83
	DO	93
	KT1	23
	KT1	70
	KT1	314
	KT1	503
	KT2	191
	KT3	811
	TJD	9
	TJD	24
	B	286
	B	558
	B	648
	M10	26
	HIF	34
	HIF	254
	HIF	649
	C	716
	M11	65
	M11	365
	AU	121
	AU	151
	WB	105
	WB	111
	WB	200
	WB	356
	CI	203
RETURNED	AM	549
	AM	1071
	AA	824
	D	12
	SAA	184
	SAA	341
	SAA	349
	SAA	793
	SAA	824
	HAP	1267
	BR	246
	BR	256
	ELW	9
	EL	182
	J3	69
	J6	722
	J10	296
	HI	190
	MC	6
	VP1	47
	VP10	46
RETURNED	G4	729
	G4	768
	AE1	270
	AE2	358
	AE2	370
	AE3	742
	AE5	605
	AE5	774
	AE7	791
	AE8	749
	AE9	469
	AE10	823
	AE11	148
	AE11	248
	AE11	441
	AE11	769
	AE11	981
	DO	100
	KT1	137
	KT1	518
	KT2	171
	KT2	278
	KT3	288
	KT3	374
	KT3	718
	KT3	1005
	B	253
	HIF	38
	HIF	332
	HIF	586
	HIF	696
	TH	363
	TH	367
	M11	15
	M12	172
	M12	280
	M12	606
	M12	643
	AU	144
	AU	392
	CI	599
RETURNEST	AE8	83
RETURNING	M11	469
	AR	248
	AR	274
	EUO2	8
	SKK	13
	EPF	10
	DOD	5
	DOD	20
	H2	88
	HAP	1880
	EL	17
	EL	133
	P1	141
	M1	759
	M1	799
	M9	30
	VP5	105
	VP7	81
	G1	369
	G1	540
	G4	41
	G4	197
	G4	628
	AE1	550
	AE2	190
	AE5	53
	AE6	365
	AE9	403
	AE10	695
	OAL	97
	DO	70
	KT1	122
	KT2	132
	KT2	407
	KT3	290
	KT3	709
	KT3	999
	M10	72
	M11	239
	M11	321
	FL	310
	FL	602
	WB	17
	WB	267
	ETP	6
	PMK	7
RETURNS	AR	254
	SAA	289
	L3	281
	L3	290
	L4	87
	H9	18
	TA	140
	TA	159

Word	Ref	No.
RETURNS	HAP	2462
	J3	287
	P3	37
	M1	191
	M1	664
	G2	433
	G2	478
	G2	642
	G3	429
	AE2	643
	AE6	15
	AE10	796
	AE12	12
	DO	26
	DO	109
	KT1	509
	TJD	208
	CAM	132
	C	240
	EMKG	35
REVEAL	RL	120
	HAP	940
	P2	13
	AE2	212
	AE6	767
	KT3	200
	WB	152
	WB	172
REVEALE	MHD	7
REVEALED	RL	68
	RL	123
	RL	173
	RL	206
	RL	331
	HAP	69
	BR	198
	P1	59
	M9	171
	M9	198
	VP6	112
	AE2	662
	AE2	801
	AE3	768
	AE3	936
	AE4	661
	AE5	977
	AE6	152
	AE8	321
	AE9	613
	AE12	47
	MFL	11
	TH	109
	TH	409
	AU	273
	AU	483
	WB	160
	CI	177
	ETP	22
REVEALER	CAM	310
REVEALS	G1	624
	G2	432
	AE1	490
	AE8	229
	KT3	134
	C	284
REVEILLE	SMP	60
REVELATION	RL	71
	HAP	92
	HAP	1779
REVELED	WB	15
REVELS	VP5	46
	HIF	584
REVENGE	AR	261
	LC	122
	AM	331
	AM	471
	AM	490
	AM	699
	PCG2	2
	SCG1	18
	PLN	11
	PCB	7
	HP	236
	AA	40
	AA	324
	AA	446
	AA	716
	AA	940
	PLB	24
	SAA	108
	PDG	35
	ER	43
	T23	110
	HH	25
	HAP	489
	HAP	1368

Word	Ref	No.
REVENGE	HAP	1593
	HAP	2149
	HAP	2490
	HAP	2491
	BR	283
	J1	254
	J6	408
	J6	843
	M1	1004
	G3	709
	G4	344
	G4	660
	AE1	388
	AE1	766
	AE2	137
	AE2	428
	AE2	618
	AE4	812
	AE5	788
	AE6	1152
	AE8	648
	AE8	658
	AE8	845
	AE9	565
	AE9	852
	AE9	1052
	AE10	540
	AE10	625
	AE10	760
	AE10	965
	AE10	980
	AE10	1011
	AE10	1235
	AE11	405
	AE11	630
	AE11	884
	AE12	110
	AE12	416
	AE12	931
	AE12	1355
	OAL	28
	OAL	223
	OAL	378
	OAL	413
	OAL	776
	AF	131
	M8	239
	B	241
	B	258
	B	593
	B	607
	HIF	43
	HIF	64
	HIF	119
	C	246
	TH	124
	TH	139
	TH	204
	M12	319
	M12	495
	AU	289
	CI	512
	CI	605
REVENGED	EPF	20
	HH	26
	AE9	596
	KT1	102
	CAM	389
REVENGEFUL	AM	789
	J10	487
	M13	94
	AE1	60
	AE1	941
	AE4	257
	AE6	28
	AE6	385
	OAL	382
	HIF	592
	TH	322
REVENGER	AE11	413
REVENGES	J6	831
	AE4	756
REVENGING	M8	295
	TH	256
REVENUE	J16	79
REVENUES	SAA	669
	HAP	1442
	P6	123
REVERENCE	UDH	23
	PIE	3
	STL	13
	PTC	26
	EUO2	17
	AA	707
	PRH	41
	SAA	95

Word	Ref	No.
REVERENCE	SAA	474
	AK	128
	HAP	588
	HAP	923
	HAP	1000
	M1	268
	GK	75
	AE7	233
	AE10	156
	AE11	448
	KT1	73
	KT3	489
	KT3	1017
	C	478
	HIF	718
	WB	292
REVERENCED	HI	69
	AE5	841
	AE11	366
	HIF	604
REVEREND	AM	925
	MF	129
	RL	337
	TA	514
	HAP	399
	AE6	171
	AE6	320
	AE12	255
	HIF	107
	M12	258
	GP	2
REVERENT	AE8	459
REVERENTLY	AM	91
REVERSE	A	15
	MD	12
	HAP	2453
	AE2	258
	AE7	506
REVERSED	HAP	58
	AE1	326
	AE1	355
	AE12	561
	KT3	344
REVERSION	HAP	1673
REVERSIONS	ML	20
REVIEW	HAP	1333
	AE2	787
	AE4	494
	AE6	580
	AE8	724
REVIEWED	AE5	107
	AE6	922
REVIEWS	AE4	572
REVILE	HIF	410
REVILED	HAP	1601
REVILES	HAP	2557
REVIVE	PTC	6
	SAA	1029
	AT	43
	G2	40
	G2	89
	AE7	407
	MG	6
	KT3	877
REVIVED	LC	25
	AA	82
	TA	348
	PP	50
	AE1	633
	AE3	381
	KT3	279
	M11	486
	M15	665
REVIVES	D	32
	GK	70
	VP7	82
	AE3	245
	KT1	179
REVIVING	PT	4
	SAA	64
	ER	15
	MG	24
REVOKE	AM	1077
REVOKES	SAA	603
REVOLUTION	AA	253
	J6	56
	VP9	4
	AS	53
REVOLVE	L3	19
	AE9	245
REVOLVED	AE7	348
	AE10	962
REVOLVING	AA	549
	AA	934
	SAA	847
	L3	266

Headword	Code	No.
REVOLVING	HAP	512
	HAP	1275
	BR	136
	ODA	22
	M1	209
	G1	371
	G1	572
	G1	584
	AE1	386
	AE1	959
	AE3	137
	AE4	406
	AE4	564
	AE5	60
	AE5	814
	AE6	271
	AE6	454
	AE6	511
	AE10	236
	AE12	968
	AF	85
	AF	89
	KT2	9
	KT2	611
	HIF	459
	HIF	592
	TH	208
	M15	23
	M15	25
	SMP	4
REWARD	AM	1145
	HP	124
	AA	593
	SAA	640
	RL	61
	HAP	1393
	BR	181
	BR	347
	PTS	35
	J3	93
	J6	49
	J10	223
	J16	93
	P1	88
	R	10
	R	14
	HI	104
	VP2	5
	G4	655
	AE1	393
	AE2	688
	AE2	784
	AE5	91
	AE5	296
	AE5	322
	AE5	349
	AE5	452
	OAL	721
	MM	28
	KT1	104
	KT1	413
	KT2	273
	KT2	373
	KT2	662
	KT3	539
	KT3	1132
	B	273
	B	550
	HIF	728
	C	521
	AU	68
	AU	569
	WB	23
	CI	484
	CI	494
REWARDED	AM	1158
	HP	9
	EMW	5
	MD	48
	MD	54
	HAP	1385
	VP6	41
	AE5	353
	AE12	538
REWARDS	HS	39
	HS	40
	LC	94
	VHH	40
	SMQ	12
	SAA	1060
	H2	33
	G1	72
	G1	147
	AE1	344
	AE5	371
	AE5	462

Headword	Code	No.
REWARDS	AE5	465
	AE5	476
	AE9	377
	MM	43
	KT2	367
	KT3	731
	AS	38
REYNARD	HAP	53
	C	492
	C	581
	C	599
	C	662
	C	670
	C	721
	C	768
	C	794
	C	805
REYNARD'S	PRH	14
RHADAMANTHUS	AE6	764
RHAMNES	AE9	435
	AE9	486
	AE9	605
RHEA	AE7	921
RHENISH	GE	45
RHESUS	AE1	657
RHETORIC	MF	165
	J6	387
	OAL	689
RHETORICIAN	J1	66
	J3	137
RHEUMATISMS	KT3	407
RHEUMS	UDH	82
	J10	307
	C	159
RHEUMY	M1	360
RHINE	AM	1193
	P6	99
	G1	686
	AE8	969
RHINOCEROS	AM	236
RHODES	CI	382
	CI	272
	CI	541
	CI	619
	CI	627
RHODIAN	G2	143
	M12	757
	CI	389
	CI	250
	CI	286
	CI	292
	CI	434
	CI	437
	CI	631
RHODIANS	CI	278
	CI	614
RHODOPHILS	EM	9
RHOEBUS	AE10	1231
RHOESUS	AU	390
RHOETEAN	AE3	148
RHOETEUS	AE10	558
	AE10	561
RHOETUS	AE9	463
	AE9	465
	M12	380
	M12	397
	M12	407
RHYME	EIE	8
	EIE	16
	PMQ	6
	EMQw	6
	ENH	32
	PAZ	8
	EAZ	6
	PAL	7
	ETC	18
	PTC	21
	PLG	29
	PUO3	15
	MF	54
	SAA	403
	SAA	485
	SAA	486
	PD	13
	ER	19
	ER	22
	MO	21
	HAP	1781
	PMS	2
	PMS	6
	J1	256
	J3	15
	P1	69
	P1	106
	P1	182
	P1	217

Headword	Code	No.
RHYME	GK	50
	VP3	75
	VP7	25
	VP9	35
	VP9	70
	C	693
	CI	33
RHYMED	SAA	420
RHYMER	VP3	77
RHYMES	PRL	11
	PUO5	1
	EUF	26
	PKK	3
	SAA	411
	SAA	505
	PK	24
	RL	456
	ER	12
	HAP	1816
	J3	77
	J10	194
	P1	213
	P4	127
	M1	5
	VP4	5
	VP7	97
	VP9	14
	G2	532
	C	640
	PTP	34
	ET	5
	PA	31
	AA	551
	PTS	26
RHYMING	M13	209
	AE8	295
RIB	HAP	1935
RIBALD	KT1	184
RIBAND	ENH	14
RIBBONDS	G3	734
RIBBONS	AE7	679
	H3	15
RIBS	AE9	680
	AE12	736
RICE	EWGR	11
RICH	UDH	69
	HS	103
	AR	218
	AR	271
	RH	28
	SMA	125
	LC	78
	LC	74
	DC	39
	AM	101
	AM	157
	AM	554
	AM	569
	AM	603
	AM	663
	AM	873
	AM	997
	AM	1171
	PCD	2
	PAL	31
	EMK	20
	PTC	12
	MD	218
	SAA	314
	SAA	469
	SAA	512
	SAA	1059
	RL	90
	RL	429
	H29	22
	H2	2
	TA	365
	AK	5
	AK	28
	AK	35
	AK	73
	HAP	1442
	BR	162
	PP	26
	PTS	13
	EL	44
	EL	157
	OD	14
	ESH	29
	J1	58
	J3	65
	J3	224
	J3	248
	J3	267
	J3	271
	J3	359

RICH	J3	380	RICHER	HAP	1093	RIDES	AE3	531
	J6	55		J10	36		AE5	863
	J6	106		G2	130		AE6	946
	J6	125		G2	189		AE7	494
	J6	225	RICHES	AM	18		AE9	64
	J6	235		AM	94		AE10	572
	J6	592		P6	33		AE10	1266
	J6	599		P6	62		AE11	1073
	J6	707		AE5	807		M11	134
	J6	758		KT1	424		M15	341
	J6	763		TJD	38		CI	340
	J6	768		WB	466		PTP	44
	J10	26		GP	57	RIDET	PPC	19
	J10	421	RICHEST	RH	56	RIDGE	M1	39
	J10	493	RICHLY	AE1	902	RIDGELING	AT	5
	J10	497		AE5	351	RIDGES	G1	168
	P2	68		M10	49		G3	149
	P2	95		FL	167		AE5	1056
	P2	115	RICKETS	P2	25	RIDGIL'S	VP9	30
	P5	71	RICKS	G2	748	RIDGY	G1	599
	P6	170	RID	J3	325		AE3	739
	M9	6		C	173		AE5	167
	VCS	14		M11	324	RIDICULE	J3	257
	GK	102	RIDDEN	PDS	41		PTP	31
	VP2	80	RIDDLE	RH	16	RIDICULOUS	ELN	5
	G2	218		HAP	140		J3	444
	G2	337		J3	135	RIDING	AE3	386
	G2	657	RIDE	AR	223		AE5	115
	G2	713		SMA	103	RIDS	P2	28
	G2	726		AM	233	RIFT	AM	582
	G3	789		AM	991		B	115
	AE1	674		ECD	13	RIGGED	AE1	499
	AE1	916		DA	43		AE4	541
	AE1	995		PPC	29		CI	264
	AE3	593		MD	299	RIGGING	AM	242
	AE5	344		P6	71		AM	258
	AE6	1181		SAA	44		PCG2	18
	AE6	1149		J10	65		PP	18
	AE7	5		J10	355	RIGHT	HS	93
	AE7	13		M1	410		AR	86
	AE7	111		G2	212		AR	99
	AE7	392		G2	496		AR	241
	AE7	746		G3	44		RH	102
	AE7	996		G3	288		AM	78
	AE7	1086		G4	109		AM	172
	AE8	226		G4	411		AM	539
	AE8	911		AE1	230		AM	584
	AE9	30		AE1	551		AM	667
	AE9	361		AE2	289		AM	700
	AE9	441		AE2	628		AM	746
	AE9	485		AE3	739		PMQ	28
	AE9	489		AE4	235		PEL	30
	AE9	841		AE4	575		SEL1	8
	AE10	212		AE5	1081		SCG3	4
	AE11	72		AE6	1147		PMQW	14
	AE11	512		AE9	112		ECD	2
	AE11	1145		AE10	1016		PUO1	41
	AE12	449		AE11	972		EAZ	19
	OAL	505		AE12	192		PC1	8
	AF	58		OAL	244		HP	115
	AF	63		OAL	291		AA	87
	KT1	181		OAL	636		AA	317
	KT2	452		KT1	11		AA	330
	KT2	468		KT3	459		AA	342
	KT3	29		KT3	536		AA	354
	KT3	104		KT3	545		AA	405
	KT3	977		KT3	992		AA	409
	KT3	986		C	422		AA	420
	KT3	1077		FL	537		AA	540
	TJD	118		WB	209		AA	713
	B	609		WB	260		AA	763
	M10	45		M15	443		AA	779
	TH	4	RIDER	G3	140		AA	794
	TH	384		G3	184		AA	944
	FL	160		AE4	191		AA	980
	FL	187		AE10	1283		AA	1017
	FL	244		AE11	1136		MD	114
	FL	265		KT3	610		MD	138
	FL	341		M12	472		MD	213
	WB	30	RIDERS	AE5	724		MD	245
	M15	584		AE8	6		MF	108
	GP	5		KT3	600		MF	116
	GP	76		KT3	933		MF	122
	CI	211	RIDERS'	AE9	534		SAA	681
RICHARD	C	694	RIDES	AM	515		SAA	736
	GP	108		AM	604		SAA	741
	GP	112		AM	706		SAA	790
	GP	114		AM	805		SAA	986
RICHARD'S	ET	9		PLB	24		EDG	8
	BR	217		HAP	1122		EDG	13
RICHER	UDH	64		J3	394		RL	208
	AR	247		G1	689		RL	362
	SMA	64		G3	458		AT	86
	AM	52		G4	559		ER	49
	SAA	544		AE1	211		L2	66
	PDG	25		AE2	646		L3	95

Word	Ref	No.
RIGHT	TA	227
	MN	5
	AK	98
	AK	135
	HAP	458
	HAP	859
	HAP	953
	HAP	1094
	HAP	1466
	HAP	2005
	HAP	2208
	PP	3
	J1	158
	J6	366
	J10	69
	J10	391
	J16	5
	J16	80
	P3	169
	P4	18
	P4	21
	P5	52
	M1	170
	M1	223
	M1	1067
	M9	61
	VP3	19
	G1	324
	G1	678
	G3	134
	G4	134
	AE1	690
	AE1	769
	AE1	862
	AE2	578
	AE2	606
	AE2	753
	AE3	536
	AE3	908
	AE4	455
	AE5	559
	AE5	1080
	AE6	727
	AE6	1124
	AE7	462
	AE7	562
	AE7	954
	AE8	228
	AE8	313
	AE8	804
	AE9	303
	AE9	386
	AE9	625
	AE9	773
	AE9	921
	AE9	1038
	AE10	80
	AE10	320
	AE10	358
	AE10	473
	AE10	518
	AE10	624
	AE10	745
	AE10	797
	AE10	1095
	AE11	17
	AE11	173
	AE11	543
	AE11	550
	AE11	568
	AE11	799
	AE11	1198
	AE12	27
	AE12	478
	OAL	220
	OAL	725
	OAL	765
	OAE2	22
	DO	34
	DO	107
	KT1	309
	KT1	343
	KT2	154
	KT2	338
	KT2	390
	KT3	324
	KT3	377
	KT3	424
	KT3	772
	KT3	808
	KT3	820
	KT3	822
	KT3	914
	KT3	943
	KT3	1124
	TJD	184

Word	Ref	No.
RIGHT	M8	15
	M8	126
	M8	231
	B	219
	CAM	100
	HIF	176
	HIF	200
	HIF	206
	HIF	262
	HIF	280
	HIF	704
	C	47
	C	450
	TH	282
	M12	281
	M12	382
	AU	15
	AU	57
	AU	175
	AU	191
	AU	230
	AU	255
	AU	396
	AU	544
	WB	70
	WB	311
	M15	221
	M15	706
	GP	117
	GP	121
	CI	360
	CI	520
	CI	523
	ESK	27
	AS	24
RIGHTEOUS	RL	206
	AA	811
	MD	141
	MF	124
	SAA	36
	SAA	585
	M1	508
	AE1	401
	KT2	300
	TH	355
RIGHTEOUSLY	AA	1010
	MD	95
	MD	97
RIGHTEOUSNESS	JH	16
	RL	110
	AE6	844
RIGHTFUL	AR	75
	AA	89
	MD	322
	AE12	839
	OAL	739
	KT2	268
	KT3	669
	HIF	684
	TH	149
	CI	296
RIGHTLY	PTL	1
	EAL	7
	SAA	438
	G3	301
	B	543
RIGHTS	SMA	17
	PMQ	49
	HP	4
	AA	920
	MD	229
	PRH	42
	SAA	13
	SAA	233
	SAA	576
	SAA	648
	SAA	650
	SAA	684
	SAA	696
	PDG	32
	HAP	1920
	HAP	2530
	J10	128
	J16	55
	M1	184
	AE1	765
	AE8	860
	AE11	547
	OAL	224
	KT1	333
	HIF	397
RIGID	AR	268
	MD	302
	HAP	376
	J3	198
	J10	461

Word	Ref	No.
RIGID	AE1	418
	AE10	18
RIGOR	PRH	28
	SAA	733
	TA	178
	HAP	1977
	HAP	2511
	M1	538
	G2	510
	AE4	238
RILLS	T18	74
RIND	M1	743
	M1	751
	VP10	78
	VP10	79
	G2	108
	G2	135
	G2	176
	AE6	211
	AE6	301
	AE9	1004
	BP	186
	CAM	345
	CAM	356
RINDS	G2	104
	G2	416
	BP	190
RING	AM	951
	PLB	39
	MD	229
	J6	39
	J6	227
	G3	182
	G4	539
	AE2	593
	AE6	876
	AE7	998
	AE9	1091
	AE10	316
	AE10	1040
	AE10	1266
	AE11	1026
	AE12	703
	AE12	1060
	AE12	1097
	OAL	195
	OAL	493
	KT2	120
	KT3	437
	M8	103
	FL	203
	M12	621
RINGING	PAA	39
	AE10	1134
RINGLETS	KT3	72
	AE7	1110
	AE10	202
RING'S	J10	269
RINGS	AM	710
	P3	7
	AE1	551
	AE5	278
	AE12	887
	OAE2	30
	KT1	447
	KT2	207
	KT3	359
	KT3	582
	M10	47
	WB	15
	CI	399
	B	708
RINSED	PLN	18
RIOT	J6	407
	P3	108
	AE4	331
	OAL	666
	M15	669
RIOTED	B	183
RIOTOUS	AM	205
	TH	253
	CI	8
RIOTS	HAP	363
	P1	127
RIPE	AM	446
	AM	853
	PO	27
	EMP	2
	AA	251
	MO	11
	ODA	37
	J6	433
	P3	99
	G2	134
	AE1	353
	KT3	1069

RIPE	B	15	RISE	EL	2	RISE	KT3	365
	CAM	355		EL	150		KT3	514
	M12	769		PSH	23		M8	289
RIPEN	HAP	2149		J1	75		M8	360
	AE8	564		J3	217		B	198
RIPENED	AR	89		J3	258		B	332
	H2	30		J3	275		BP	17
	TA	446		J3	459		BP	160
	M1	564		J6	371		CAM	338
	VP4	45		J6	533		HIF	417
	KT1	361		J6	650		M11	207
	KT2	562		J10	32		M11	372
	B	467		J10	328		M11	374
RIPENING	AM	10		J16	15		M12	318
	BR	163		J16	27		M12	764
	GK	177		P1	129		AU	258
	VP9	66		P2	121		M15	637
	G1	478		P3	105		M15	682
	G2	585		P3	236		AS	12
	AE1	386		P4	14		PWR	14
RIPENS	M15	309		P5	196	RISEN	TA	38
RIPER	PUO4	38		M1	428		J16	48
	L2	60		M13	226		AE4	182
	AE12	649		HI	99		OAL	681
	OAL	66		GK	59	RISES	PFD	20
	CAM	387		EHC	17		ESF	30
	AU	471		VP3	162		HAP	213
RIPHAEAN	G3	586		VP5	103		J3	41
RIPHEUS	AE2	457		VP8	34		J3	369
	AE2	531		VP8	154		J6	322
	AE2	577		VP9	16		G1	102
	M12	476		VP10	107		G1	341
RIPPED	J3	254		VP10	110		G3	95
	AE10	438		G1	79		G3	823
RIPS	M8	176		G1	242		AE3	145
RISE	HS	23		G1	295		AE7	1075
	AR	149		G1	330		AE8	739
	SMA	16		G1	589		AE11	1029
	LC	14		G2	21		OAL	569
	LC	142		G2	36		CAM	143
	PRL	16		G2	92		WB	419
	AM	51		G2	315		M15	591
	AM	64		G2	425	RISING	UDH	60
	AM	183		G2	467		SMA	3
	AM	198		G3	400		AM	94
	AM	220		G3	722		AM	588
	AM	260		G4	437		AM	796
	AM	324		G4	496		ML	37
	AM	397		AE1	148		CM	44
	AM	399		AE1	213		DA	11
	AM	508		AE1	249		EPF	17
	AM	848		AE1	288		AA	819
	AM	857		AE1	390		ELB	13
	AM	906		AE1	506		MF	24
	AM	1178		AE1	610		SAA	158
	ETL	2		AE2	569		ER	41
	PMQW	22		AE3	227		L1	12
	SCD1	1		AE3	496		L3	209
	SCD1	14		AE3	670		T18	45
	PTC	1		AE4	64		TA	368
	PSF	5		AE4	481		HAP	506
	AA	143		AE4	901		HAP	1385
	AA	269		AE5	185		HAP	1775
	AA	636		AE5	463		HAP	2126
	AA	1023		AE5	601		BR	317
	MD	224		AE6	1172		J16	90
	MF	70		AE7	34		P2	96
	SAA	309		AE7	629		P5	62
	SAA	265		AE7	645		P5	70
	EDG	19		AE7	669		M1	39
	RL	421		AE7	736		M1	73
	AT	60		AE7	745		M1	391
	L3	131		AE7	996		M1	545
	L3	171		AE8	101		M1	976
	T18	90		AE8	134		M13	67
	AK	4		AE8	370		M13	89
	HAP	792		AE8	543		VP4	27
	HAP	936		AE8	600		VP5	56
	HAP	1183		AE9	39		VP6	59
	HAP	1206		AE9	917		VP6	91
	HAP	1531		AE10	147		VP6	95
	HAP	1582		AE10	176		G1	166
	HAP	1874		AE10	377		G1	182
	HAP	1882		AE10	380		G1	305
	HAP	2036		AE11	659		G1	442
	HAP	2098		AE12	407		G1	489
	HAP	2308		OAL	75		G1	525
	BR	54		OAL	111		G1	617
	BR	76		OAL	174		G1	649
	BR	202		OAL	569		G2	23
	PP	10		OAL	615		G2	121
	PP	16		OAE2	50		G2	260
	PP	37		OAE2	56		G2	353
	PP	51		AF	69		G2	373
	ETS	29		MG	12		G2	479
	PKA	30		KT2	513		G2	539

RISING	G3	436
	G3	520
	G3	613
	G3	840
	G4	393
	G4	515
	AE1	323
	AE1	467
	AE1	636
	AE2	454
	AE2	513
	AE2	960
	AE3	30
	AE3	32
	AE3	182
	AE3	190
	AE3	269
	AE3	434
	AE3	533
	AE3	682
	AE3	732
	AE3	768
	AE4	103
	AE4	123
	AE4	138
	AE4	164
	AE4	398
	AE4	696
	AE5	58
	AE5	63
	AE5	119
	AE5	139
	AE5	156
	AE5	226
	AE5	377
	AE5	533
	AE5	588
	AE5	821
	AE5	991
	AE5	999
	AE6	32
	AE6	1023
	AE6	1059
	AE6	1209
	AE7	31
	AE7	67
	AE7	231
	AE7	810
	AE7	831
	AE8	131
	AE8	149
	AE8	487
	AE8	718
	AE8	801
	AE8	830
	AE9	323
	AE9	678
	AE9	738
	AE9	1012
	AE10	233
	AE10	1021
	AE11	7
	AE11	375
	AE11	511
	AE12	258
	AE12	291
	AE12	324
	AE12	363
	AE12	975
	AE12	1334
	OAL	130
	KT1	4
	KT2	22
	KT2	51
	KT2	205
	KT3	479
	KT3	563
	KT3	957
	KT3	1059
	TJD	66
	M8	148
	M8	217
	BP	186
	CAM	346
	C	142
	TH	91
	M11	83
	M11	96
	M11	153
	M11	270
	FL	91
	M12	110
	M12	331
	AU	178
	AU	371
	WB	84

RISING	M15	24
	M15	653
	CI	152
	CI	194
	CI	382
RITE	J10	519
	P2	108
RITES	HS	3
	RH	63
	A	14
	PUO1	3
	CM	81
	AA	118
	AA	706
	SAA	655
	RL	128
	HAP	2283
	HAP	2303
	J6	451
	J6	461
	P6	47
	M1	958
	M9	145
	M9	208
	HI	67
	VP5	45
	VP5	60
	VP5	113
	VP5	117
	VP8	41
	G2	670
	G3	100
	G3	383
	G4	289
	G4	548
	G4	755
	AE1	7
	AE1	341
	AE1	394
	AE1	843
	AE1	1022
	AE3	88
	AE3	154
	AE3	465
	AE3	521
	AE3	720
	AE4	89
	AE4	179
	AE4	291
	AE4	723
	AE4	748
	AE4	910
	AE5	92
	AE5	129
	AE5	786
	AE5	849
	AE6	60
	AE6	108
	AE6	219
	AE6	228
	AE6	320
	AE6	336
	AE6	686
	AE6	867
	AE7	7
	AE7	90
	AE7	135
	AE7	542
	AE7	564
	AE7	851
	AE8	147
	AE8	232
	AE8	242
	AE8	246
	AE8	355
	AE8	408
	AE8	454
	AE8	719
	AE9	279
	AE9	342
	AE9	847
	AE10	650
	AE10	876
	AE11	33
	AE11	153
	AE11	180
	AE11	325
	AE12	24
	AE12	181
	AE12	286
	AE12	318
	AE12	722
	AE12	854
	AE12	1212
	OAL	81
	OAL	358

RITES	OAL	590
	KT1	83
	KT1	129
	KT2	260
	KT3	193
	KT3	203
	KT3	211
	KT3	293
	KT3	952
	B	415
	BP	170
	M10	53
	CAM	245
	HIF	163
	HIF	627
	FL	331
	FL	535
	WB	33
	M15	7
	ETP	24
RIVAL	HS	82
	SCG2	15
	AA	487
	SAA	250
	OE	40
	T18	28
	HAP	2048
	J6	172
	M1	838
	M1	1046
	DHP	2
	DHP	10
	VP7	100
	VP10	35
	G3	28
	AE2	565
	AE5	207
	AE5	264
	AE5	383
	AE5	652
	AE6	798
	AE11	410
	AE11	742
	AE11	872
	AE12	768
	AE12	1142
	OAL	412
	OAL	847
	OAL	858
	DO	16
	KT1	324
	KT1	353
	KT1	444
	KT1	451
	KT1	503
	KT2	167
	KT2	299
	CAM	87
	M11	249
	FL	398
	AU	24
	AU	91
	CI	272
	CI	297
	CI	444
RIVAL'S	CI	511
	SAA	832
	M1	1005
	AE5	436
	AE12	915
	OAL	359
	KT3	657
	CI	601
RIVALS	SMA	123
	HP	104
	DA	135
	J3	206
	J6	307
	M1	637
	VP5	10
	G3	338
	G3	416
	AE6	782
	AE7	57
	AE12	1048
	OAL	347
	KT3	3
	KT3	117
	KT3	235
	KT3	536
	KT3	619
	M12	828
	AU	549
RIVELED	PAL	40
	G4	616
	FL	378

RIVEN	J3	313	ROAR	MF	46	ROARS	AE10	1021
	VP1	24		SAA	478		AE11	458
	AE11	1031		SAA	568		AE11	1032
RIVER	AM	922		SAA	839		AE12	13
	OD	31		EK	23		KT3	631
	J10	88		AT	112		M12	138
	M1	972		PD	63	ROAST	SAA	928
	M13	215		L2	2		G4	67
	G4	181		H3	18		HIF	638
	G4	563		H29	100		C	36
	G4	764		TA	141	ROASTED	BP	98
	AE8	119		TA	192		M12	214
	AE11	687		HAP	306	ROASTS	M1	301
	AE12	1084		HAP	530	ROB	AM	1208
	M15	425		SKA4	5		PA	28
RIVER'S	AM	1182		SKA4	8		PA	17
	M1	773		P1	146		PA	20
	M13	221		P3	232		AK	161
	G1	520		M1	38		SKA6	14
	G4	662		M1	459		J10	546
	AE8	799		M13	201		G4	20
	AE8	810		VP5	42		G4	312
	C	802		VP9	57		AE8	272
RIVERS	RH	9		G1	458		AE11	773
	AM	991		G1	489	ROBBED	AM	950
	AM	1195		G3	313		SM2	8
	HAP	1865		G3	343		L3	199
	EL	242		G3	369		P1	168
	J10	285		G4	520		AE5	296
	P2	119		G4	590		AE8	426
	M1	47		G4	608		AE9	189
	M1	780		AE1	126		TJD	85
	VP3	150		AE1	756		M12	342
	VP7	78		AE3	699		AU	58
	VP8	4		AE3	887		CI	297
	G1	202		AE5	159	ROBBER	AE8	347
	G1	442		AE5	165		AU	172
	G2	573		AE6	569	ROBBER'S	H3	41
	G3	554		AE6	636		AE8	256
	G3	825		AE6	775	ROBBERS	HAP	1345
	G4	203		AE7	33		J3	478
	AE1	854		AE7	971		G3	621
	AE6	963		AE8	557		KT1	425
	OAL	252		AE10	408		M8	233
	KT3	1064		AE10	498		C	265
	C	159		AE11	929		M11	5
	M15	156		KT2	550	ROBBING	AE4	747
	M15	267		HIF	655	ROBE	PTC	29
	M15	501		M12	73		MF	214
RIVET	P1	123		PTP	6		HAP	2368
RIVETED	AR	104		STP	6		P1	144
RIVETS	FL	257	ROARED	AE3	882		P5	40
RIVULET	AM	624		AE7	417		M1	361
	AE3	450		AE8	284		M1	449
RIVULETS	H29	36		AE9	151		AE1	915
ROAD	AM	600		AE9	956		AE3	625
	AM	820		KT1	523		AE4	199
	PA	26		M8	285		AE5	899
	PLN	23		HIF	488		AE7	337
	ENH	29		AU	109		AE8	47
	HAP	1348	ROARING	AA	450		AE11	506
	J3	6		PAA	46		AE11	822
	M1	220		PDS	10		AE11	863
	G2	274		J3	477		AE11	1136
	G3	459		PLT	43		OAE2	59
	AE5	359		G1	441		PTP	24
	AE6	159		G4	637		SMP	29
	AE6	394		AE2	292	ROBES	RH	70
	OAL	432		AE3	261		J3	298
	M11	5		AE3	529		VP4	55
	WB	230		AE3	537		AE4	933
ROADS	AM	813		AE8	392		AE6	1120
	EKK	20		AE10	641		AE7	848
ROAM	J6	521		AE10	983		AE8	911
	M1	1007		AE12	1051		AE12	587
	VP1	3		OAL	874		KT3	911
	G3	805		KT3	139		M8	247
	OAL	338		C	277		BP	80
	KT1	432		M11	124		M10	45
ROAMING	C	435		M11	149		M11	237
ROAMS	L4	7		M12	336		M11	264
	AE6	962		M12	415		M12	45
	AE9	66		AM	383		WB	50
ROAR	HS	116	ROARS	TA	512	ROBS	SMA	76
	AR	123		VP6	80		AU	420
	AM	219		G2	152	ROCK	HP	136
	AM	447		G2	224		SAA	486
	AM	495		G3	364		SAA	1063
	AM	923		AE2	678		SAA	1080
	PT	16		AE5	20		AT	56
	SCD2	11		AE5	1127		L3	186
	ENH	24		AE6	127		L3	228
	PTW	25		AE7	19		H29	35
	CM	92		AE7	738		TA	167
	HP	228		AE7	1007		HAP	493
	DA	185		AE9	968		HAP	1748

Word	Code	No.	Word	Code	No.	Word	Code	No.
ROCK	J6	225	ROCKS	AE3	705	RODS	J10	50
	M1	996		AE3	730		AE6	1119
	M13	103		AE3	735		AE7	236
	M13	209		AE3	742	ROGUE	EEL	15
	M13	222		AE3	751		PPC	7
	VP1	75		AE3	851		PPC	21
	VP3	149		AE3	928		MD	155
	VP10	22		AE4	645		SAA	373
	G3	66		AE5	817		SAA	425
	G3	357		AE5	1128		SAA	463
	G3	780		AE6	636		EC	2
	G4	493		AE6	743		EKA	36
	G4	611		AE6	963		ESH	4
	G4	627		AE7	15		EH	17
	AE1	69		AE7	717		J1	99
	AE3	297		AE7	946		J1	167
	AE3	564		AE8	282		J3	225
	AE4	219		AE8	553		J10	115
	AE4	524		AE9	680		J16	57
	AE5	165		AE10	18		P2	16
	AE5	173		AE11	404		P5	109
	AE5	264		AE11	931	ROGUE'S	PC1	8
	AE5	355		AE12	767	ROGUES	PCB	33
	AE6	816		AE12	1097		PK	1
	AE7	809		C	588		EDGA	26
	AE8	252		M11	340		EC	14
	AE8	295		AU	65		EC	23
	AE8	307		SMP	32		EC	41
	AE8	315	ROCKY	SAA	943		J1	234
	AE8	454		M1	51		J3	15
	AE8	457		M1	777	ROGUESHIP	J3	467
	AE8	867		G2	157	ROGUE-SOLDIER	J3	398
	AE8	887		G3	370	ROI	PAA	39
	AE9	773		AE1	757	ROLL	LC	111
	AE10	281		AE3	352		AM	938
	AE10	982		AE3	377		ENH	11
	AE10	1091		AE3	904		RL	36
	AE12	861		AE3	919		AK	31
	M8	257		AE5	217		HAP	1125
	C	352		AE5	276		P3	47
	C	551		AE5	285		P3	204
	TH	20		AE6	339		P5	45
	M11	283		AE6	483		P6	23
	M12	171		AE6	1052		M1	378
	M12	461		AE8	276		M13	215
	M12	648		AE9	963		SLT2	8
ROCKED	CM	75		AE11	460		VP4	7
	SAA	622		AE12	994		VP9	78
	TH	91		KT2	588		AE1	88
	M11	279		CI	376		AE1	127
ROCKER	C	228		T18	16		AE2	941
ROCK'S	DA	37	ROD	HAP	1984		AE2	961
ROCKS	AM	32		HAP	2321		AE3	732
	AM	82		HAP	2554		AE3	913
	AM	102		J1	26		AE4	233
	AM	105		M1	931		AE6	78
	AM	1003		M1	993		AE6	268
	H3	27		G4	654		AE6	783
	H29	63		AE1	415		AE6	838
	AK	109		AE6	551		AE8	578
	HAP	2543		AE8	934		AE9	557
	J10	245		OAL	12		AE9	680
	P1	54		KT1	550		AE9	967
	M13	60		BP	25		AE11	129
	M13	88		CI	61		AE12	111
	VP1	20		EUO	15		AE12	766
	VP5	97		SAA	620		AE12	980
	VP10	77		TA	134		AE12	1045
	VP10	84		AE2	39		OAL	581
	G1	161		AE5	210		TJD	132
	G1	443		AE5	745		M8	122
	G1	455		AE7	900		M11	124
	G1	636		AE7	1072		M11	337
	G2	259		AE8	539		CI	334
	G2	520		AE8	774		BR	21
	G2	618	ROLLED	AE9	148		BR	230
	G3	149		AE10	315		M1	343
	G3	234		AE10	819		G3	780
	G3	342		AE10	1268		G4	652
	G3	394		AE11	962	ROLLED	AE1	180
	G3	430		AF	29		AE2	86
	G4	69		KT1	106		AE2	232
	G4	202		KT2	45		AE2	286
	G4	297		KT2	227		AE2	328
	G4	528		KT2	237		AE5	113
	G4	739		KT3	99		AE7	45
	G4	764		KT3	538		AE7	341
	AE1	156		KT3	933		AE7	557
	AE1	207		FL	217		AE7	1082
	AE1	233		FL	249		AE8	119
	AE1	279		M12	621		AE8	302
	AE1	428		WB	49		AE8	347
	AE3	543		WB	57		AE8	586
	AE3	573		GP	69		AE8	819
	AE3	660		CI	223		AE9	773
	AE3	701	RODRIGUEZ'	HAP	1627		AE10	284

ROLLED		AE10	564	ROLLING				ROMANS,		
		AE10	776	ROLLS		AA	256	ROMANS'		
		AE10	829			AA	302	ROMANTIC		
		AE10	1113			RL	353			
		AE10	1250			L3	211	ROME		
		AE11	976			HAP	372		WB	449
		AE12	551			M13	31		AM	691
		AE12	1299			M13	232		DA	83
		AE12	1362			VP8	124		J10	287
		OAL	173			G2	557		HS	118
		MFL	15			G3	544		RH	96
		DO	22			G3	649		AM	19
		KT3	41			G3	658		AM	251
		KT3	533			G3	665		AM	776
		CAM	127			G3	754		EOE	13
		HIF	223			AE1	143		ETC	24
		TH	266			AE1	357		PUO4	30
		FL	243			AE2	407		MD	105
		M12	151			AE2	647		MF	113
		AU	5			AE3	748		RL	81
		WB	345			AE5	1074		ER	7
		CI	122			AE6	584		ER	26
		CI	426			AE7	331		L1	2
ROLLER		G1	260			AE8	832		H29	18
ROLLERS		PCG1	30			AE9	108		AK	120
ROLLEST		AK	7			AE11	455		HAP	639
ROLLING		LC	144			AE11	920		HAP	2508
		AM	447			AE12	495		BR	199
		ESF	20			AE12	545		PKA	34
		AM	655			AE12	815		P1	42
		SAA	459			AE12	900		P1	63
		SAA	964			OAL	40		P1	142
		RL	4			KT3	611		P1	202
		L1	4			AU	38		P2	9
		L2	2			M15	31		P6	89
		H3	25	ROMAN		UDH	76		P6	97
		H29	60			L3	248		P6	131
		H2	76			EL	198		J1	168
		TA	139			J3	20		J1	196
		HAP	1313			J3	322		J3	4
		HAP	1568			J10	93		J3	12
		EL	149			J10	174		J3	39
		J3	322			J10	251		J3	75
		J10	55			J10	430		J3	106
		J10	246			J10	520		J3	114
		P5	17			P1	17		J3	127
		M1	772			P1	155		J3	150
		VP1	92			P1	172		J3	215
		VP5	89			P1	201		J3	277
		G1	349			P3	91		J3	344
		G1	418			P5	6		J3	381
		G1	453			P5	26		J3	471
		G1	651			P5	103		J3	484
		G2	188			P6	3		J3	492
		G2	259			M1	757		J3	503
		G3	66			GK	61		J6	270
		G3	367			G1	660		J10	190
		G3	408			G1	661		J10	427
		G3	717			G1	671		M1	260
		G4	622			G2	246		MC	37
		AE1	229			G2	531		GK	45
		AE1	334			AE1	48		GK	139
		AE1	366			AE6	1074		VP1	29
		AE1	828			AE6	1106		VP1	36
		AE1	854			AE6	1151		VP6	1
		AE2	513			AE6	1204		VP8	7
		AE4	238			AE6	1212		G1	629
		AE4	367			AE7	847		G2	239
		AE4	924			AE8	46		G2	781
		AE4	964			AE8	134		G3	537
		AE5	116			AE8	416		AE1	10
		AE6	134			AE8	446		AE1	377
		AE6	1013			AE8	830		AE5	781
		AE6	1085			AE8	860		AE6	1064
		AE8	63			AE9	600		AE6	1065
		AE8	87			AE12	252		AE6	1107
		AE8	141			OAL	63		AE6	1118
		AE9	42			OAL	203		AE6	1173
		AE9	64			OAL	206		AE7	978
		AE9	195	ROMANIAN		TH	1		AE8	90
		AE9	1083	ROMANO		MC	39		AE8	841
		AE10	192	ROMANS		HS	3		AE8	857
		AE11	134			AR	57		AE8	869
		AE11	395			PAZ	15		AE8	950
		AE11	1269			J3	104		AE9	878
		AE11	1297			J3	201		AE10	17
		AE12	59			J6	371		OAL	60
		AE12	950			P6	20		OAL	201
		AE12	966			G3	15		OAL	205
		AE12	995			AE1	323		OAL	230
		CAM	127			AE1	377		OAL	461
		HIF	154			AE4	343		OAL	524
		M11	99			AE7	834		MG	36
		M12	76			AE8	846		KT2	451
		M15	267			AE8	900		C	637
		M15	339			OAL	468		M15	637
									M15	644
									M15	659
									M15	713
									EP	2
								ROME'S	PSF	13

Word	Code	Num		Word	Code	Num		Word	Code	Num
ROME'S	MF	109		ROOM	ESK	1		ROSE	HAP	1937
	G1	33			EMKG	20			ODA	5
	AE1	384		ROOMS	P1	30			J6	164
	AE4	401			AE2	661			M13	189
	AE8	450			B	153			GK	61
	AE8	473		ROOMY	AM	609			VP5	22
	AE12	254			G2	388			G2	230
	AE12	1202			AE5	275			G2	779
	OAL	199			AE9	954			G4	7
ROMULUS	MF	130		ROOST	C	46			AE1	157
	J3	118		ROOT	PT	1			AE1	423
	P1	139			EL	94			AE1	628
	G1	669			P3	49			AE2	125
	AE1	375			P4	96			AE2	339
	AE6	1055			G1	433			AE2	595
	AE8	452			G2	23			AE2	602
	OAL	111			G2	37			AE2	1051
	OAL	152			G2	414			AE3	38
	M15	3			G2	431			AE3	69
ROOF	PWG	30			G2	486			AE3	671
	AM	578			G3	56			AE5	437
	HAP	1269			G4	393			AE5	605
	EL	56			G4	399			AE5	972
	G4	554			G4	468			AE8	93
	AE2	654			AE12	1118			AE8	145
	AE2	944			AE12	1141			AE8	550
	AE7	715			M8	148			AE9	100
	AE8	481			M8	368			AE9	468
	KT3	266			M12	446			AE9	610
	KT3	342			M12	483			AE11	438
	BP	30		ROOTED	TA	358			AE11	517
	FL	84			G2	31			AE11	1151
	CI	580			G2	505			AE12	107
ROOFED	AE6	17			AE3	38			OAL	327
	AE8	458			AE3	102			DO	151
	AE8	870			AE8	916			KT1	193
ROOFS	PNH	15			AE10	507			KT1	361
	L2	33			M11	38			KT2	41
	M1	504			M12	352			KT2	456
	G1	599			M12	674			KT3	190
	G4	61		ROOTING	M15	157			KT3	435
	G4	536			M15	508			KT3	1016
	AE1	1015		ROOTS	T18	77			B	252
	AE2	611			J1	203			B	294
	AE2	1031			VP8	143			BP	11
	AE9	550			G2	75			M10	82
	AF	36			G2	92			HIF	425
	BP	41			G2	402			HIF	499
	M12	300			G2	792			TH	99
ROOFY	G3	634			AE2	848			TH	331
ROOKS	G1	525			AE2	854			FL	81
ROOM	UDH	48			AE3	856			FL	613
	UDH	84			AE5	601			M12	535
	LC	41			AE10	1087			M12	683
	AM	869			AE12	993			M12	828
	AM	1022			BP	185			AU	129
	PM	37			CAM	340			WB	6
	PNH	8			PLG	10			WB	73
	CM	77		ROPE	J10	100			WB	448
	P'D	46			G2	333			M15	33
	L5	7			EMKG	9			CI	105
	H29	26		ROPES	AM	589		ROSE-BUDS	UDH	58
	TA	4			J3	139		ROSEMARY	G4	45
	TA	60		ROPY	J6	188			M12	547
	HAP	2047			J10	307		ROSES	SMQ	8
	BR	119			G3	759			SAA	1105
	EL	217		ROSAMOND	EH	6			T27	13
	EL	284		ROSCIAN	J3	266			T27	125
	EL	327		ROSCOMMON	ER	66			P1	76
	J3	201			ER	68			VP4	30
	J6	174			ER	70			G4	179
	J6	175		ROSCOMMON'S	ER	29			G4	201
	J6	399		ROSE	SMA	104			G4	389
	HI	129			LC	104			AE5	104
	MC	46			AM	321			AE6	1223
	GK	94			AM	868			AF	7
	G1	391			AM	1111			KT2	461
	G2	394			ECG2	10			KT2	518
	G3	219			EMW	14			CAM	373
	G4	331			PUO3	13			M12	546
	AE5	1101			SAA	58		ROSY	AT	52
	AE6	216			SAA	151			H29	5
	AE6	708			RL	222			SKA2	4
	AE11	799			T23	57			VP6	24
	OAL	789			T27	129			VP7	57
	B	108			TA	25			G3	552
	B	674			TA	223			AE2	807
	C	217			TA	360			AE2	1090
	FL	13			TA	390			AE3	682
	FL	119			TA	455			AE4	182
	FL	574			TA	461			AE4	842
	M12	51			AK	147			AE5	82
	AU	26			HAP	282			AE5	139
	M15	331			HAP	1083			AE7	34
	M15	341			HAP	1236			AE7	197
	PTP	34			HAP	1749			AE8	780

Word	Ref	No.	Word	Ref	No.	Word	Ref	No.
ROSY	AE9	6	ROUND	G3	300	ROW	AE8	966
	AE10	341		G3	821		KT3	907
	AE11	1		AE3	90		KT3	974
	AE11	1194		AE5	763		C	575
	AE12	174		AE5	772		M11	92
	AE12	886		AE6	1069	ROWED	AE5	252
	OAL	274		AE8	589	ROWELS	AE11	1054
	KT1	173		AE9	216		KT2	250
	KT3	189		KT3	46		FL	577
	HIF	650		KT3	68	ROWERS	AE5	151
ROSY-CHEEKED	HIF	512		TJD	63		AE5	268
ROSY-COLORED	T18	52		CAM	111		AE5	1090
	HAP	370		FL	493	ROWS	J3	399
	AE1	992		AU	178		G4	45
ROT	ET	4		WB	5		G4	213
	AA	251		WB	215		AE1	233
	PLB	5		WB	352		AE5	326
	L3	50		M15	644		OAL	121
	L3	171		CI	155		AU	560
	VP1	70	ROUND-BELLIED	HAP	1758	ROYAL	AR	78
	G2	357	ROUNDELAY	KT2	78		AR	223
ROTE	J1	13		FL	192		SMA	9
ROTTEN	SAA	407	ROUNDS	HAP	212		SMA	113
	J3	148		HAP	792		SMA	129
	J3	338	ROUSE	AM	759		LC	55
	P4	106		HP	240		DC	55
	G1	304		OE	51		AM	76
	G4	62		L3	114		AM	573
	AE11	1268		G3	624		AM	661
	BP	55		AE6	246		AM	964
	FL	413		AE7	451		AM	1011
ROTS	P5	80		AE7	591		AM	1145
	P6	30		AE9	668		AM	1159
	M1	82		AE12	111		PNH	30
ROUGH	RH	73		AF	126		PUF	9
	SMA	89		KT2	237		AA	11
	DA	39		AS	11		AA	231
	PRH	11	ROUSED	AR	117		AA	250
	SAA	781		AM	382		AA	285
	SAA	844		EAZ	23		AA	294
	OE	22		MF	96		AA	355
	HAP	164		TA	473		AA	936
	HAP	1259		J1	78		MF	39
	J6	14		P3	106		SAA	204
	J10	307		AE4	824		SAA	223
	M1	447		AE5	140		SAA	233
	M13	88		AE5	277		SAA	240
	VP7	60		AE6	698		SAA	579
	G2	569		AE7	64		SAA	595
	G3	92		AE8	5		SAA	601
	G3	357		AE12	7		SAA	611
	G3	758		AE12	1368		SAA	645
	AE1	466		KT3	440		SAA	766
	AE4	525		M8	99		SAA	814
	AE5	49		C	235		SAA	862
	AE5	704		TH	126		SAA	917
	AE5	957	ROUSES	SEL4	21		SAA	932
	AE5	1006		HAP	1562		SAA	987
	AE6	339	ROUSING	SAA	547		SAA	990
	AE7	1009	ROUT	EMM	4		SAA	1066
	AE9	1004		ELN	3		SAA	1099
	AE11	850		AA	513		SAA	1127
	AE11	1307		AA	785		T18	4
	AE12	611		PD	61		TA	150
	OAL	576		BR	118		TA	280
	B	102		BR	296		TA	501
	B	609		J1	148		TA	335
	M12	331		J3	131		TA	356
	M12	438		J6	353		TA	398
	AU	177		J6	519		BR	22
	AU	330		G4	314		BR	104
	WB	257		AE7	531		BR	164
ROUGH-DRAWN	PTC	13		AE7	807		BR	277
ROUGHLY	M8	217		AE7	948		BR	329
ROUGHNESS	P4	94		AE11	998		EDS	1
	M1	544		OAL	101		J10	405
ROUND	HS	19		KT3	304		HI	38
	AM	71		C	742		HI	65
	AM	990	ROUTED	AE6	663		HI	76
	SAA	460		AF	68		G4	140
	L3	140	ROVE	M15	140		G4	150
	L3	305	ROVED	SAA	987		AE1	195
	GE	45	ROVERS	HIF	77		AE1	374
	HAP	1313	ROVES	VP6	79		AE1	996
	HAP	1808		AE4	94		AE2	385
	BR	74		AE4	435		AE2	543
	EL	273	ROW	M1	404		AE2	560
	M1	43		M1	666		AE2	752
	M13	164		G2	490		AE2	1065
	VP3	160		G4	252		AE2	1071
	G1	35		AE4	852		AE3	79
	G1	260		AE5	187		AE3	458
	G2	124		AE5	207		AE3	942
	G2	740		AE5	258		AE4	270
	G3	136		AE5	287		AE4	280
	G3	182		AE5	305		AE4	644

ROYAL	AE5	79
	AE5	389
	AE5	738
	AE5	874
	AE5	976
	AE6	1039
	AE6	1059
	AE6	1120
	AE7	79
	AE7	291
	AE7	337
	AE7	365
	AE7	508
	AE7	568
	AE8	65
	AE8	204
	AE8	245
	AE8	731
	AE9	293
	AE9	378
	AE9	731
	AE9	808
	AE11	178
	AE11	379
	AE11	506
	AE11	575
	AE11	634
	AE11	676
	AE11	822
	AE11	1109
	AE12	310
	AE12	382
	AE12	777
	AE12	853
	AE12	874
	AE12	1173
	AE12	1358
	OAL	337
	OAL	346
	OAL	789
	AF	1
	KT1	108
	KT1	145
	KT1	596
	KT2	105
	KT2	230
	KT2	259
	KT2	317
	KT2	393
	KT2	410
	KT2	439
	KT3	111
	KT3	125
	KT3	283
	KT3	538
	KT3	658
	KT3	663
	KT3	732
	KT3	944
	KT3	1017
	KT3	1130
	B	66
	B	120
	B	255
	B	301
	B	343
	B	619
	B	756
	M10	51
	CAM	246
	HIF	48
	HIF	427
	HIF	442
	HIF	538
	C	433
	FL	244
	FL	254
	M12	47
	AU	393
	WB	175
	WB	198
	M15	607
ROYALTIES	HAP	1062
ROYALTY	AA	362
	AA	990
	HAP	1097
	AE2	612
RUB	HAP	2029
	J3	178
	G4	542
	OAL	745
	M8	384
RUBBED	HAP	1426
	BP	88
RUBBERS	J3	421
RUBBISH	AM	1119

RUBBISH	AM	1174
	TA	358
	AE8	253
	KT3	173
	M15	462
RUBICON	HAP	2549
RUBIES	KT3	54
	KT3	71
	FL	166
	FL	245
	FL	345
RUBRIC-MARTYRS	RL	211
RUBS	PKA	11
	J16	73
	P3	10
	G3	401
RUBY	CI	150
RUDDER	AM	620
	TA	395
	P5	148
	AE1	165
	AE5	1101
	AE5	1108
	AE5	1117
	AE6	482
	AE10	311
	M11	199
RUDDY	AT	21
	VP3	107
	VP8	54
	G2	44
	G2	599
	G3	553
	G4	141
	AE4	84
	AE5	310
	AE6	301
	AE9	610
	KT3	75
	KT3	946
	HIF	62
	HIF	636
	C	397
	FL	186
	M12	443
RUDDY-COLORED	FL	45
RUDE	AR	226
	AM	633
	AM	1183
	HP	27
	HP	138
	RL	417
	ER	13
	TA	100
	J3	287
	J6	7
	J6	131
	P1	201
	M1	10
	M1	111
	M1	543
	M1	570
	MC	9
	GK	31
	GK	47
	GK	55
	G2	532
	G2	780
	G3	588
	AE1	466
	AE3	273
	AE6	437
	AE7	724
	AE7	1028
	AE8	460
	AE10	609
	OAL	577
	OAL	666
	DO	127
	KT3	551
	M10	34
	HIF	803
	M11	41
	WB	453
	CI	74
	CI	117
	CI	400
	CI	585
	PWR	15
RUDELY	AM	622
	TA	246
	P1	144
	P6	68
	M1	168
	M13	62
	OAE2	46

RUDIMENTS	AM	558
	HAP	199
	EL	219
	M1	541
	GK	28
	OAL	2
	OAL	221
RUE	AR	81
RUED	MM	20
RUEFUL	HAP	514
	AE2	91
	KT1	43
RUEFULLY	SAA	929
RUFFIAN	J3	478
	M13	62
RUFFIANS	J6	306
RUFFLE	ENH	23
RUFFLED	T27	96
	G1	619
	KT2	514
	KT3	364
RUFFLES	G3	135
RUFFLING	AM	605
	AE3	258
	AE5	999
RUFUS'	RH	96
RUG	PW	10
RUGGED	RL	453
	MO	16
	BR	305
	J10	271
	PPS	11
	M1	312
	M1	1028
	M13	27
	HI	110
	G3	394
	G3	430
	G3	490
	G3	751
	G3	785
	G4	146
	OAL	18
	OAL	432
RUIN	AR	11
	AR	200
	SMA	48
	SIE	2
	AM	828
	AM	868
	AM	1000
	AM	1026
	AM	1108
	PLN	19
	PCD	6
	DA	95
	PUO3	2
	AA	65
	AA	84
	AA	174
	AA	808
	AA	848
	AA	930
	SAA	224
	SAA	697
	SAA	871
	SAA	885
	SAA	1001
	SAA	1083
	AT	39
	L3	172
	L4	136
	H3	26
	HAP	248
	HAP	441
	HAP	2387
	BR	78
	J3	209
	J3	410
	J10	149
	M1	320
	HI	87
	HI	117
	GK	49
	G1	378
	G1	600
	G2	425
	G4	311
	G4	469
	AE1	30
	AE1	920
	AE2	41
	AE2	125
	AE2	558
	AE2	825
	AE2	855

RUIN

AE2	884
AE4	617
AE4	717
AE4	964
AE6	268
AE7	441
AE7	467
AE8	254
AE9	173
AE9	327
AE9	685
AE9	727
AE9	961
AE10	713
AE12	994
AE12	1102
M8	301
M8	396
HIF	537
M12	348
M12	491

RUINED

AR	30
LC	122
AM	198
ECG1	33
PAZ	38
L4	98
HAP	1072
J10	8
J10	173
J10	425
G2	531
AE1	73
AE1	327
AE2	634
AE2	693
AE2	759
AE2	894
AE2	955
AE2	969
AE2	992
AE2	1013
AE3	3
AE4	495
AE4	541
AE10	72
AE11	430
AE12	1248
KT2	104
KT2	594
EMKG	37

RUINS

SMA	25
DC	53
AM	842
AM	1147
AM	1152
MF	70
SAA	230
SAA	556
AK	119
HAP	363
EL	344
G2	291
G4	263
AE1	914
AE3	438
AE5	813
AE8	467
AE9	760
AE12	441
M8	364
M11	150
AU	446
M15	355
ESK	20

RULE

HS	104
AR	84
AR	90
DC	52
AM	662
EEL	19
EUO2	20
EAZ	2
EAZ	41
CM	15
AA	53
AA	174
AA	291
AA	333
AA	946
MF	14
MF	123
SAA	138
SAA	1131
RL	132
RL	202
RL	203
RL	206
RL	315
RL	402
FS1	7
HAP	89
HAP	261
HAP	719
HAP	750
HAP	759
HAP	775
HAP	783
HAP	929
HAP	997
BR	168
BR	305
J3	202
J3	264
P1	27
P1	133
P4	25
P5	51
P5	228
M1	100
M1	114
ELT	11
GK	156
VP1	96
VP4	21
G1	8
G1	145
G4	552
AE4	337
AE6	375
AE6	621
AE6	1174
AE7	1028
AE9	889
AE11	550
AE12	1047
OAL	5
OAL	879
KT1	471
KT3	168
KT3	1074
FL	81
WB	286
WB	363
M15	659
PTP	30
PTP	43
VHH	21
HP	255

RULED

AA	231
AA	902
PLB	1
L3	241
HAP	168
HAP	509
HAP	696
AE2	113
AE6	150
AE6	1080
DO	16
KT1	247
CI	437
SMP	81

RULER

AA	910
AE5	1044

RULES

AR	260
PWG	24
PMQ	3
PA	14
PTW	11
SAA	674
RL	46
RL	339
ER	32
ER	35
ER	39
H3	3
PAA	32
HAP	509
HAP	1609
EL	106
MS	3
P5	146
M1	810
M13	150
PLT	50
MC	8
VP3	49
G2	74
G2	350
G3	183
G3	262
G4	530
AE1	339
AE1	469
AE3	47
AE4	755
AE6	413
AE6	764
AE6	1234
AE7	298
AE8	503
AE10	740
OAL	45
OAL	57
OAL	689
KT2	345
KT2	352
M11	259
M15	487
GP	79
AS	34

RULING

AE11	1154
KT2	610
CI	61

RUMBLED

WB	178

RUMBLING

AE8	323
HIF	334
M15	456
PTP	42

RUMINATES

CAM	128

RUMMAGE

AM	829
P1	148

RUMMAGING

M1	174

RUMMERS

GE	45

RUMOR

HP	145
TA	48
VP5	30
AE1	27
AE2	165
AE3	166
AE4	957
AE6	619
AE7	193
AE7	763
AE12	888

RUMORS

HAP	571
AE2	131
M12	86

RUMPLE

J10	455

RUN

AR	64
AR	293
RH	37
VHH	48
AM	279
AM	726
AM	907
AM	914
AM	971
AM	1026
EMQ	16
EMM	2
EMM	4
EEL	36
PTL	19
EM	11
ELN	3
SCD2	19
PKK	6
POE	26
PCB	26
HP	74
EUF	24
AA	336
AA	783
AA	837
MD	2
MD	99
PRH	7
SAA	7
PK	7
AT	81
AT	96
L3	140
L4	188
L4	194
T18	94
TA	354
HAP	349
HAP	446
HAP	1144
HAP	1482
HAP	1593
BR	6
BR	59
BR	241
BR	318

RUN

SKA1	14
EPN	3
EL	150
J3	35
J3	189
J3	217
J3	224
J3	279
J3	406
J6	65
J6	503
J6	776
J16	36
P1	273
P3	2
P3	109
P5	69
P5	236
P6	144
M1	75
M1	600
M9	68
M13	100
VP4	8
VP4	57
VP8	155
G1	67
G1	260
G1	491
G1	497
G1	584
G2	260
G2	333
G2	736
G3	182
G3	214
G3	226
G3	258
G3	300
G3	437
G4	301
AE1	363
AE1	515
AE1	854
AE2	423
AE2	433
AE2	455
AE2	594
AE2	650
AE2	669
AE2	1020
AE2	1088
AE3	238
AE3	472
AE3	745
AE3	859
AE3	874
AE3	899
AE3	907
AE4	697
AE4	836
AE5	85
AE5	117
AE5	168
AE5	294
AE5	763
AE5	814
AE6	483
AE7	12
AE8	63
AE8	726
AE9	62
AE9	622
AE9	904
AE9	1056
AE9	1077
AE10	309
AE10	418
AE10	514
AE10	589
AE11	77
AE11	134
AE11	527
AE12	104
AE12	416
AE12	434
AE12	512
AE12	696
AE12	765
AE12	863
AE12	1314
OAL	109
OAL	370
OAL	886
DO	62
KT1	580

RUN

KT2	9
KT2	408
KT3	72
KT3	683
KT3	1079
KT3	1098
M8	42
B	337
BP	177
HIF	667
C	107
C	330
C	448
C	472
C	553
TH	85
TH	312
M11	40
M11	95
M11	174
FL	2
FL	382
AU	356
AU	499
WB	28
M15	156
M15	266
M15	272
M15	669
CI	327
STP	17
SMP	3
EMKG	10
AS	4

RUNG

P1	199
G2	790
AE10	989
KT3	360
B	228
C	45
C	746
TH	314
FL	117
M12	301
M12	471
AU	589

RUNNERS

AE5	383

RUNNEST

KT3	131

RUNNING

H29	52
H29	101
HAP	1875
BR	49
J3	406
P5	201
M1	46
M13	78
VP3	147
VP5	32
VP5	37
VP5	62
VP7	78
VP8	4
VP8	89
G1	90
G3	84
G3	791
G4	35
G4	180
G4	203
G4	637
AE2	284
AE2	933
AE6	1168
AE8	423
AE10	1033
AE12	272
AE12	881
OAL	711
OAL	873
C	444
M11	340
M15	501

RUNS

CI	117
AM	722
STL	24
ETG	24
AA	733
AA	786
EDGA	20
RL	446
L4	65
L4	96
H2	17
HAP	223
HAP	2482
J6	688

RUNS

J10	237
M1	456
VP8	160
G2	556
G3	745
G4	534
AE2	719
AE2	865
AE4	969
AE5	261
AE5	603
AE7	526
AE9	634
AE9	748
AE9	943
AE10	641
AE10	1021
AE10	1024
AE11	224
AE11	500
AE11	627
AE11	720
AE12	59
AE12	363
AE12	703
KT2	332
TJD	63
M15	344
M15	421
M15	429
M15	474

RUPERT

AM	417
AM	466
AM	474
AM	704
AM	764

RURAL

M1	637
M1	957
VP1	12
VP1	75
VP1	95
VP1	111
VP3	132
VP5	79
VP6	12
G1	11
G1	27
G1	264
G2	387
G2	658
G2	703
G2	768
G3	260
G3	462
AE5	867
AE11	97
M8	10
FL	125

RUSH

EUO	15
J10	31
VP10	85
G1	155
G3	167
G3	379
G4	272
AE1	122
AE2	456
AE2	652
AE2	675
AE2	915
AE4	836
AE4	849
AE7	936
AE8	8
AE9	541
AE9	1083
AE10	643
AE10	1149
AE11	911
AE11	1276
AE12	997
M8	178
B	231
C	334
M11	150

RUSHED

CM	95
G1	650
AE2	329
AE2	483
AE2	1080
AE3	124
AE9	569
AE10	486
AE10	1082
AE12	469
KT3	362

Word	Ref	No.
RUSHED	KT3	551
	M8	147
	C	670
	FL	299
	M12	523
	AU	440
	AU	608
RUSHES	AM	996
	VP1	66
	VP8	124
	AE6	725
	AE10	1026
	OAL	119
	M8	126
	C	16
	C	739
	M11	144
RUSHING	TA	33
	M1	394
	G1	639
	G3	106
	G3	309
	G3	621
	G4	633
	AE1	171
	AE2	756
	AE3	531
	AE3	888
	AE4	858
	AE5	626
	AE6	36
	AE6	79
	AE6	127
	AE6	165
	AE6	422
	AE8	348
	AE9	672
	AE9	767
	AE9	930
	AE10	506
	AE10	1313
	AE11	213
	AE11	1127
	AE12	638
	AE12	667
	AE12	1035
	AE12	1377
	B	266
	B	433
	TH	269
	M11	434
	M12	658
	M15	441
	CI	581
RUSSET	WB	50
RUST	RL	370
	G1	190
	AE6	1005
	AE6	1114
	GP	86
RUSTIC	G2	767
	AE1	216
	AE7	879
	AE8	596
	OAL	123
	OAL	685
	CI	56
	CI	74
	CI	195
RUSTICALLY	P1	142
RUSTLES	AE12	549
RUSTLING	G1	418
	KT2	183
	KT3	445
RUSTS	G2	299
RUSTY	TA	467
	G1	664
	AE7	867
	M15	407
RUT	CAM	46
RUTHLESS	AE6	179
RUTILA	J10	454
RUTULI	AE7	656
RUTULIAN	AE7	443
	AE7	1086
	AE9	137
	AE9	203
	AE9	657
	AE10	959
	AE12	122
	AE12	177
	AE12	734
RUTULIANS	AE8	191
	AE10	28
	AE10	167
	AE10	1288

Word	Ref	No.
RUTULIANS	AE11	487
	AE12	66
	AE12	322
	AE12	346
	AE12	1006
SABAEAN	P5	199
	G2	164
	AE4	86
	CAM	323
SABAEANS	AE8	938
SABAN	AE8	378
SABBATH	AM	892
	AA	588
	AA	913
	BR	19
	BR	186
	EL	116
	GK	58
	G1	107
	OAL	466
	TJD	134
SABBATHS	EL	122
	P5	267
	OAL	83
	WB	14
SABELLIAN	G2	230
SABER	HAP	984
SABINE	H2	61
	P6	2
	AE7	125
	AE7	974
	AE8	673
	AE8	842
	AE8	845
	AE10	479
	OAL	115
	M15	7
SABINE'S	J10	462
SABINES	J6	236
	P4	51
	G2	777
	M15	712
SABINUS	AE7	247
SABLE	HAP	1488
	EHC	21
	G1	576
	AE1	129
	AE3	257
	AE4	586
	AE5	130
	AE6	201
	AE6	230
	AE6	348
	AE6	357
	AE6	1199
	AE7	188
	AE8	485
	AE10	206
	AE11	1318
	KT3	923
	CAM	273
	TH	272
	TH	335
	M15	58
	M15	279
SACK	HIF	193
SACKED	AE9	350
	KT1	126
SACKS	G1	356
	AS	96
SACRAMENT	HAP	604
	HAP	615
SACRAMENTS	HAP	2469
SACRANA	AE7	1087
SACRATOR	AE10	1053
SACRED	HS	4
	AR	35
	AR	119
	AR	183
	RH	58
	RH	84
	SMA	17
	SMA	45
	SMA	46
	SMA	59
	SMA	132
	DC	53
	AM	956
	AM	1098
	AM	1102

Word	Ref	No.
SACRED	PT	24
	PUO1	6
	PNH	32
	ENH	14
	PUO2	26
	PAZ	14
	ESF	25
	EPF	1
	PUO4	25
	AA	182
	AA	237
	AA	465
	AA	706
	MF	118
	SAA	534
	SAA	637
	SAA	650
	SAA	655
	SAA	696
	SAA	736
	RL	125
	RL	166
	RL	328
	RL	353
	RL	418
	RL	455
	ER	76
	T18	77
	T23	103
	H3	4
	TA	65
	TA	282
	AK	114
	AK	139
	AK	188
	HAP	18
	HAP	45
	HAP	258
	HAP	312
	HAP	680
	HAP	714
	HAP	777
	HAP	874
	HAP	925
	HAP	1048
	HAP	1074
	HAP	1126
	HAP	1282
	HAP	1342
	HAP	1781
	HAP	1831
	HAP	2236
	HAP	2284
	HAP	2303
	HAP	2313
	HAP	2471
	HAP	2528
	SSC	44
	SSC	55
	BR	29
	BR	43
	BR	85
	BR	183
	BR	197
	PDS	35
	ELW	6
	EL	121
	J1	166
	J3	22
	J3	27
	J3	187
	J3	272
	J6	162
	J6	231
	J6	451
	J6	632
	J16	60
	PPS	2
	P1	270
	M1	498
	M1	762
	M9	38
	M9	177
	VCS	11
	VP4	5
	VP4	28
	VP4	57
	VP6	94
	VP6	120
	VP7	34
	VP8	91
	VP8	104
	VP8	115
	VP8	132
	VP9	23
	VP10	1

SACRED

	VP10	100
	G2	143
	G2	245
	G2	673
	G2	692
	G3	461
	G4	280
	G4	533
	G4	545
	G4	551
	G4	757
	AE1	340
	AE1	395
	AE1	482
	AE1	698
	AE1	1022
	AE2	209
	AE2	303
	AE2	316
	AE2	395
	AE2	429
	AE2	545
	AE2	752
	AE2	757
	AE2	934
	AE3	8
	AE3	80
	AE3	142
	AE3	198
	AE3	236
	AE3	391
	AE3	582
	AE3	715
	AE3	913
	AE4	211
	AE4	298
	AE4	490
	AE4	664
	AE4	736
	AE4	829
	AE4	914
	AE4	1002
	AE5	120
	AE5	435
	AE5	783
	AE6	11
	AE6	60
	AE6	71
	AE6	100
	AE6	112
	AE6	166
	AE6	236
	AE6	285
	AE6	298
	AE6	354
	AE6	443
	AE6	652
	AE6	731
	AE6	912
	AE6	943
	AE7	110
	AE7	238
	AE7	589
	AE7	719
	AE7	781
	AE7	846
	AE7	854
	AE8	98
	AE8	139
	AE8	359
	AE8	447
	AE8	453
	AE8	462
	AE8	551
	AE8	796
	AE9	100
	AE9	106
	AE9	120
	AE9	139
	AE9	402
	AE9	696
	AE10	79
	AE10	134
	AE10	172
	AE10	241
	AE10	439
	AE10	595
	AE10	1175
	AE11	12
	AE11	371
	AE11	727
	AE11	1225
	AE11	1233
	AE12	180
	AE12	185
	AE12	300

SACRED

	AE12	1112
	OAL	84
	AF	163
	AF	173
	MM	3
	MFL	3
	DO	50
	KT2	128
	KT2	459
	KT3	180
	KT3	206
	KT3	265
	B	394
	BP	169
	M10	60
	CAM	36
	CAM	88
	CAM	96
	HIF	57
	HIF	102
	HIF	166
	HIF	214
	HIF	498
	HIF	534
	HIF	617
	HIF	710
	C	254
	C	274
	C	792
	M11	242
	M11	277
	M11	308
	FL	61
	FL	330
	M12	362
	AU	526
	WB	174
	M15	610
	AS	33

SACRIFICE

	AM	832
	SMQ	10
	PC1	27
	RL	53
	T18	91
	HAP	1584
	HAP	2283
	J6	708
	J10	415
	P2	54
	P2	83
	P5	173
	P5	241
	M1	1044
	VP5	104
	G2	786
	G3	36
	G3	254
	G3	740
	G4	779
	G4	797
	AE2	172
	AE3	343
	AE3	473
	AE3	520
	AE4	76
	AE4	87
	AE4	658
	AE4	910
	AE5	643
	AE5	909
	AE5	1015
	AE6	57
	AE6	349
	AE6	364
	AE7	134
	AE7	289
	AE7	336
	AE7	490
	AE8	81
	AE8	851
	AE8	957
	AE10	724
	AE11	26
	AE12	259
	AE12	426
	AE12	447
	OAL	358
	OAL	736
	KT3	366
	M8	290
	B	594
	BP	132
	HIF	148
	HIF	216
	HIF	432
	HIF	629

SACRIFICE	M12	15
	M12	213
	M15	718
SACRIFICED	PUO5	23
	AE2	268
	M15	168
SACRIFICER	HAP	2067
	M12	350
SACRIFICER'S	AA	124
	G3	736
SACRIFICERS	SAA	40
	G3	36
SACRIFICES	HAP	581
	AE3	160
	HIF	595
SACRILEGE	PTC	16
	AK	160
	HAP	355
	M1	527
	VP6	39
	HIF	187
SACRILEGIOUS	DA	147
	MD	203
	HAP	2010
	AE2	546
	AE7	822
	M15	710
	AS	77
SACRISTY	M12	345
SAD	UDH	50
	SMA	25
	LC	91
	AM	1032
	ECG1	2
	SCG2	12
	PM	9
	PM	12
	PLN	3
	PAL	9
	CM	110
	MD	285
	D	4
	SAA	83
	SAA	556
	SAA	704
	OE	34
	DOD	3
	T23	48
	T23	68
	T23	85
	NS	24
	TA	4
	TA	67
	HAP	1715
	HAP	1735
	EL	349
	EL	3
	ODA	24
	EH	1
	J10	386
	P2	53
	VP5	17
	VP10	50
	G4	451
	G4	485
	G4	748
	AE1	680
	AE2	4
	AE2	549
	AE2	916
	AE3	115
	AE4	731
	AE4	954
	AE5	64
	AE6	235
	AE6	1209
	AE7	23
	AE8	945
	AE9	387
	AE9	630
	AE10	704
	AE10	712
	AE11	40
	AE11	58
	AE11	66
	AE11	96
	AE11	322
	AE11	349
	AE11	368
	AE11	721
	AE11	1177
	AE11	1221
	AE12	87
	AE12	244
	AE12	504
	AE12	747

SAD	AE12	885	SAFE	OAL	246	SAFETY	C	504
	AE12	1372		OAL	433		M11	116
	KT3	859		DO	50		M11	218
	KT3	922		DO	93		AU	559
	CAM	142		KT2	26		M15	61
	CAM	168		KT3	483		CI	592
	C	329		TJD	146		CI	629
	TH	352		B	112	SAFFRON	G1	84
	M11	71		CAM	369		G4	165
	M11	263		HIF	574		G4	268
	CI	349		C	311		AE4	839
SADDEN	AE10	381		C	355		AE7	35
SADDENED	HIF	768		C	772	SAGACIOUS	AA	153
SADDLE	KT3	69		M11	247		HAP	577
	KT3	621		M11	280		C	752
	KT3	735		M12	638		WB	169
SADDLEBOW	KT3	32		M12	742	SAGAN	AA	866
	KT3	695		AU	414	SAGAR	AE9	781
	KT3	711		CI	197	SAGE	KT3	728
SADDLED	P5	207		CI	294		M8	62
SADLY	AM	1041		CI	391		M15	711
	AM	1107		PMK	27	SAGES	J10	41
	AM	1147	SAFEGUARD	KT2	296		AE12	945
	PFD	8	SAFELY	SAA	718		M15	656
	ENH	1		L2	1	SAGITTARY	PWG	29
	MD	137		H3	10	SAHEM	PLN	36
	RL	119		TA	238	SAIL	AM	629
	HAP	1329		TA	396		AM	649
	PP	5		HAP	130		AM	705
	SKA6	2		HAP	297		PKK	26
	ELW	4		HAP	1399		DA	187
	M1	903		HAP	2139		MD	79
	G4	505		BR	121		MF	43
	AE10	1167		EL	33		H3	49
	M11	441		J3	484		H29	99
	WB	470		G3	837		H29	89
SADNESS	EDS	28		AE2	127		HAP	1144
	PMS	20		AE3	499		HAP	1391
	ODA	47		AE5	1065		HAP	1749
	CI	309		AE9	252		J10	21
SAFE	AR	178		AE10	1006		P1	250
	SMA	116		AE11	1130		M13	33
	AM	348		OAL	677		G1	246
	AM	367		C	617		G1	529
	PTL	15		M12	427		G2	274
	PCG2	11		M15	139		G4	176
	PUO2	9		AS	44		AE1	527
	ESF	33	SAFER	PLB	49		AE1	802
	DA	188		HAP	831		AE2	785
	AA	182		AE2	538		AE3	18
	AA	913		AE3	547		AE3	88
	PLB	17		HIF	290		AE3	172
	ELB	27		HIF	344		AE3	896
	MD	215		FL	446		AE4	801
	SAA	164		AU	13		AE4	817
	SAA	621	SAFEST	LCA	36		AE4	852
	EDGA	15		RL	435		AE5	800
	RL	295	SAFETY	HS	65		AE5	1005
	L4	27		AM	351		AE5	1086
	H3	53		AM	356		AE5	1099
	HAP	676		AM	444		AE10	230
	HAP	938		AM	467		AE10	325
	EKA	10		DA	63		OAL	58
	J6	748		AA	176		OAL	817
	P5	73		AA	983		DO	47
	M1	122		SAA	80		HIF	214
	M1	192		SAA	246		HIF	598
	M1	396		SAA	1098		HIF	653
	G4	343		RL	269		C	306
	G4	517		L5	15		C	347
	G4	608		H29	102		M11	48
	AE1	92		EAA	19		M12	9
	AE1	430		HAP	1772		M15	261
	AE1	778		M1	720		CI	269
	AE2	163		H1	21		CI	524
	AE2	334		VP3	14	SAILED	J10	282
	AE3	275		G4	697		AE2	186
	AE3	332		AE1	771		AE2	238
	AE3	360		AE1	817		AE3	366
	AE3	560		AE2	186		AE5	1130
	AE3	665		AE2	546		AE6	20
	AE6	166		AE2	719		M8	49
	AE7	855		AE2	741	SAILER	VP4	46
	AE7	1065		AE3	212	SAILING	HAP	1130
	AE8	429		AE4	430		P4	52
	AE9	318		AE5	35		M13	55
	AE9	345		AE6	145		AE4	844
	AE9	625		AE6	481		AE12	243
	AE9	998		AE9	107		OAL	3
	AE9	1107		AE9	113	SAILOR	SAA	1077
	AE10	924		AE11	534		L5	1
	AE10	1143		AE11	553		P1	174
	AE11	63		AE12	92		AE3	356
	AE11	798		KT2	357		C	588
	AE11	1059		HIF	87	SAILORS	AM	512
	AE11	1167		C	310		DA	41

SAILORS
SAA 609
M1 167
G1 208
G1 296
G1 407
G1 513
G1 586
G4 285
AE1 156
AE3 176
AE3 272
AE3 666
AE4 593
AE5 158
AE5 184
AE5 1126
AE6 460
OAL 455
OAL 824
M11 92
M11 174
CI 336
CI 385

SAILORS'
AE1 128
AE1 899
AE7 21

SAILS
AR 64
AR 224
VHH 19
AM 221
AM 238
AM 258
AM 303
AM 419
AM 490
AM 512
AM 711
AM 732
HP 199
DA 9
DA 190
SAA 213
SAA 461
SAA 618
SAA 1067
H3 5
AK 170
HAP 829
HAP 1804
J1 224
J6 121
M1 125
M1 166
G1 516
G2 58
AE1 50
AE1 147
AE1 553
AE1 658
AE2 32
AE3 253
AE3 350
AE3 457
AE3 581
AE3 606
AE3 692
AE3 698
AE3 721
AE4 784
AE4 809
AE4 826
AE5 22
AE5 38
AE5 368
AE5 895
AE5 1121
AE6 1
AE6 558
AE7 8
AE8 939
AE10 311
OAL 118
OAL 870
C 300
M11 57
M11 84
M11 85
M11 93
M11 103
M11 109
M11 155
M12 37
AU 315
CI 276
CI 330
CI 368

SAILS
CI 626

SAINT
STP 11
JH 19
AM 788
AM 1042
ETL 30
SCD2 7
PSF 13
AA 609
AA 974
MD 38
MD 155
MF 53
SAA 285
SAA 300
SAA 390
EC 3
EAA 23
AK 193
GE 73
HAP 684
HAP 916
HAP 1513
HAP 1859
HAP 2300
EL 359
M1 507
GK 91
MFL 19
C 492
C 648
C 796
M15 719
GP 99
GP 102
STP 11
STP 13
AS 5
EWR 14

SAINTED
SAINTLIKE
HAP 2347
AA 648
EPC 27
P5 167

SAINTS
MD 33
AR 153
AA 529
PLB 50
MD 41
MD 284
SAA 381
SAA 553
PK 7
TA 412
BR 79
BR 147
BR 165
BR 240
EL 291
MM 21
DO 79
C 628
FL 150
CI 350
ETP 25
TA 419

SAINTS'
SAKE
PMQ 53
PC2 28
CM 144
HP 74
HP 85
SAA 100
RL 254
HAP 1334
PP 39
J6 530
P5 109
G3 416
AE2 858
AE3 630
AE6 167
AE6 514
AE6 910
AE9 547
AE12 1354
OAL 449
OAL 568
OAL 718
OAE2 86
KT2 298
M8 219
C 648
PWG 54
VHH 1
PAR 25
PC2 11
CM 67

SAKES

SAKES
EDGA 10
HAP 1828
OAL 698
BP 67
HIF 177
J10 493
G3 199
G3 481
CAM 46

SALACIOUS
HAP 1321
P3 226
BP 94

SALAD
P6 90

SALADS
P6 165
FL 421

SALAMANCA EMKG 7
SALAMIS AE1 877
SALENTINIAN AE3 514
SALERNO B 1
SALIAN B 101
SALII AE8 879
SALIUS AE8 377
AE5 390
AE5 392
AE5 421
AE5 437
AE5 438
AE5 444
AE5 453
AE5 460
AE10 1067
AE12 219

SALLIES L4 145
SALLOW T23 19
VP1 71
VP5 22
G1 358
G2 155
BP 78

SALLOW'S VP3 130
SALLOWS VP10 59
G2 573
AE7 876

SALLY HP 246
SALMACIS M15 481
SALMONEUS AE6 788
SALT AM 587
HAP 1752
HAP 2245
HAP 2286
J10 349
P4 92
VP8 115
G2 323
G2 518
G3 606
G3 609
G3 615
AE12 260
BP 69

SALTED HIF 628
SALUTATIONS H2 17
J1 192
KT3 690
TH 235

SALUTE AM 442
AA 734
PRH 39
J1 174
J6 73
VP6 95
G1 596
AE2 716
AE8 102
AE12 388
HIF 461

SALUTED FL 15
TA 127
KT2 38

SALUTES T18 46
T18 93
J3 465
P5 256
P6 98
VP5 100
AE3 696
AE8 599
AE9 892

SALUTING SAA 195
TH 347
FL 398

SALVAGE AR 46
DC 20
PMQ 47
PRH 9
L1 18

Word	Ref	No.	Word	Ref	No.	Word	Ref	No.
SALVAGE	HAP	156	SAND	G3	362	SANHEDRINS	AA	787
	HAP	507		G3	390		AA	920
	HAP	548		G3	544		AA	976
	HAP	794		G4	516	SAP	AE12	307
	HAP	1316		AE1	160		CAM	343
	HAP	1716		AE1	755		FL	583
	HAP	1652		AE2	570	SAPLESS	L4	264
	M13	135		AE3	732		J1	29
	VP8	3		AE3	928		M15	349
	VP8	61		AE4	59		KT1	531
	G2	24		AE4	892	SAPLIN	TH	129
	G2	72		AE5	89	SAPLING	M12	448
	G2	84		AE5	212	SAPLINGS	AE5	860
	G2	465		AE5	495	SAPPED	M1	396
	AE3	155		AE7	44		AE12	993
	AE3	512		AE9	141	SAPPHIRE	ODA	73
	AE3	855		AE10	426	SAPPHIRES	FL	245
	AE4	217		AE10	640		FL	166
	AE4	796		AE10	776	SAPPHO	AK	33
	AE6	262		AE11	932	SAPPHO'S	P6	11
	AE7	684		AE11	936	SAPPY	M1	546
	AE7	925		AE11	996	SARCENET	J6	364
	AE8	418		AE12	164	SARDINIAN	VP7	61
	AE11	856		AE12	199	SARNUS	AE7	1019
	AE11	876		AE12	1074	SARPEDON	AE1	142
	KT2	642		OAL	175		AE10	661
	M8	196		DO	49	SARPEDON'S	AE9	946
	HIF	382		C	575		AE10	187
	TH	82	SANDALS	AE8	602	SAT	AA	188
	M15	716	SANDS	AM	726		SAA	75
SALVAGES	EWGR	13		AA	162		HAP	1116
	POE	16		SAA	1084		HAP	1751
SALVATION	RL	192		HAP	1161		HAP	2084
	RL	303		M1	1092		M13	63
	RL	381		G1	534		KT2	501
SALVE	TA	243		G2	150		KT2	580
	HH	36		G3	374		KT3	692
SALVES	KT3	726		G4	187		KT3	921
SALVO	HAP	606		G4	414		BP	46
SAMIAN	AE1	24		AE1	209		BP	70
	M15	711		AE4	378		TH	339
	P3	109		AE4	552		FL	132
SAMOS	J3	126		AE5	67		FL	146
	AE7	285		AE5	563		FL	429
	M15	77		AE5	795	SATCHEL	J10	183
SAMOTHRACIA	AE7	285		AE5	817	SATE	AM	893
SAMPLE	EM	24		AE6	93		AM	1182
SAMPLES	EKA	15		AE9	862		SEL3	5
SAMSON	AA	955		AE9	966		CM	63
	MD	73		AE10	212		CM	76
	KT2	503		AE10	957		HP	84
	KT3	416		AE11	960		MD	18
SAMSON'S	RH	16		AE12	966		MF	108
SAMUEL	AA	677		HIF	487		TA	70
SANCHOS	ELT	20		M11	127		HAP	1071
SANCTIFIED	HAP	1282		M11	220		PP	44
	HAP	2265		M11	299		ODA	47
SANCTIFIES	BR	185		M11	466		M1	267
SANCTIFY	AR	184		M15	411		M1	919
	VCS	12		M15	428		M13	52
	EL	239	SANDY	AM	381		G3	179
	AE4	250		HAP	677		G4	735
	TJD	39		G3	742		G4	738
	B	164		G4	285		AE1	977
SANCTIFYING	CAM	243		AE5	189		AE1	980
SANCTION	KT1	330		AE5	754		AE2	664
	TJD	15		AE7	864		AE2	777
	M12	259		AE7	1053		AE2	1004
SANCTIONS	SAA	1018		M12	271		AE3	234
	P5	141	SANGUINARY	HAP	1973		AE3	322
	AE7	805	SANGUINE	AR	36		AE5	379
	AE12	475		AM	606		AE5	515
	CAM	97		HAP	17		AE7	38
	HIF	399		BR	159		AE7	154
SANCTITY	HAP	44		AE2	757		AE7	258
	HAP	1104		AE3	43		AE7	267
	C	480		AE6	750		AE7	896
	WB	43		AE10	381		AE9	296
	GP	15		AE11	594		AE10	235
SANCTUARY	DO	126		AE11	960		AE10	635
SAND	RH	14		AE12	1003		AE12	967
	AM	95		KT1	114		OAL	121
	AM	821		KT3	260		AF	4
	AM	449		C	158		AF	10
	AM	736		M12	139		AF	84
	AA	270	SANHEDRIM	SAA	719		KT3	112
	SAA	598		HAP	183		KT3	486
	SAA	687	SANHEDRIMS	SAA	251		HIF	557
	SAA	711		SAA	572		HIF	720
	ER	67		SAA	584		HIF	764
	J6	681		SAA	670		HIF	151
	P5	149		SAA	750		HIF	360
	M1	897	SANHEDRIN	AA	390		FL	128
	G1	104		AA	523		FL	443
	G2	188		AA	902		M12	298
	G3	173	SANHEDRIN'S	AA	878		M12	824

SATE WB 270
M15 3

SATED PP 14

SATHAN HAP 735
HAP 2475

SATIATE AE10 574
M8 399

SATICULANS AE7 1009

SATIN FL 342

SATIRE PAR 25
EM 17
ELN 2
PKK 6
ETC 3
PUO5 30
PLB 8
SAA 421
SAA 501
SAA 525
SAA 1049
MO 15
PAA 11
HH 1
HH 13
HAP 1128
HAP 1558
PDS 33
PTS 3
PTS 18
EL 366
J1 224
J6 828
P1 126
MC 30
GK 94

SATIRE-PROOF HAP 2481

SATIRE'S J1 26

SATIRES MF 200
PDG 44
EDGA 30
J3 502
P1 3
P1 209

SATIRICAL J1 132

SATISFACTION AM 543
EUF 37
RL 98
J10 219

SATISFIED ETC 14
AA 241
L2 27
L4 55
HAP 2053
P3 216
M9 190
VP10 42
KT2 424
KT3 678
KT3 891
FL 77
WB 246

SATISFIES L4 68

SATISFY PLG 4
HAP 273
AE11 484
FL 462

SATURN PWG 26
AM 629
J6 738
M1 144
VP6 64
G1 460
G3 145
AE6 1080
AE7 73
AE7 75
AE7 243
AE8 425
KT1 246
KT1 498
KT3 381
KT3 677
C 681

SATURNIA AE7 774
AE9 1031
AE12 237

SATURNIAN G2 241
G2 532
VP4 6
AE5 786
AE5 1069
AE7 789
AE7 944
AE8 469

SATURNIA'S AE10 94
AE10 929

SATURN'S J6 1
P2 107
P5 64
G2 785
AE7 280
AE8 436
AE12 1205
KT3 700

SATYR HIF 192
PD 12

SATYRS L4 159
AK 117
VP5 116
VP6 19
VP6 43
OAL 609

SAUCE OAL 615
T27 46
GE 60
P5 265

SAUCILY C 21

SAUCY SAA 343
J6 211
J10 467
PK 27

SAUL PD 9
AA 57
AA 417

SAUNTERING AA 677

SAVAGE OAL 558
L5 9
T23 16
SSC 48
J6 14
VP5 119
VP6 44
VP6 60
VP6 99
VP10 81
G3 587
G4 758
AE9 550
AE9 803
AE10 781
AE10 1000
AE11 1014
M8 119

SAVAGES AA 56

SAVE DC 31
EIE 25
AM 695
PMQ 44
PCG1 23
PTW 1
CM 133
AA 986
PLB 40
PLB 47
ELB 17
SAA 82
SAA 780
PDG 37
RL 242
RL 379
L3 303
H3 11
HAP 421
HAP 583
HAP 624
HAP 695
HAP 704
HAP 1452
HAP 2434
HAP 2491
EDS 23
PMS 1
PSH 5
J3 481
J6 314
J6 853
J10 438
P1 159
P4 57
M9 44
M13 212
G1 673
G4 351
G4 363
AE1 841
AE2 215
AE2 474
AE2 867
AE2 870
AE6 1166
AE7 320

SAVE AE9 128
AE9 327
AE9 1052
AE10 77
AE10 130
AE10 885
AE10 1128
AE11 484
AE11 509
AE11 922
AE11 1018
AE11 1225
AE12 581
AE12 1184
AE12 1261
AE12 1354
OAL 808
DO 138
KT3 91
KT3 764
KT3 851
TJD 11
TJD 82
B 580
B 587
B 671
CAM 86
HIF 113
HIF 175
C 170
C 618
TH 46
AU 150
AU 418
WB 76
WB 317
M15 707
CI 280
ETP 44
EMKG 21
EMKG 30

SAVED EWR 12
PC2 16
AA 539
PLB 43
PPC 24
SAA 211
SAA 852
RL 320
RL 397
HAP 710
ETS 14
M9 181
VP9 13
AE1 835
AE2 582
AE3 438
AE3 935
AE4 537
AE5 369
AE5 636
AE5 950
AE8 250
AE8 872
AE9 729
AE11 817
AE12 228
AE12 1115
OAL 376
B 339
BP 140
TH 188
AU 148
AU 152
WB 303
WB 353
CI 384

SAVER ESK 22

SAVES HAP 1638
BR 257
STP 15

SAVIN J6 775

SAVING AA 999
SAA 211
RL 308
HAP 588
P4 72
HAP 873
B 381

SAVIOR HAP 131
HAP 735
HAP 878
HAP 969
HAP 1053
HAP 1066
HAP 1510

SAVIOR	HAP	1599	SAW	AE2	682	SAW	C	581
	HAP	2009		AE2	692		C	587
	BR	127		AE2	726		TH	107
	J10	107		AE2	844		TH	207
	VCS	36		AE3	76		TH	218
	GP	89		AE3	108		M11	8
SAVIOR'S	HAP	948		AE3	231		M11	27
	HAP	1591		AE3	312		M11	401
	EL	299		AE3	678		FL	103
SAVIOUR	AA	240		AE3	743		FL	106
SAVOR	J6	555		AE3	858		FL	213
	G3	609		AE3	863		FL	361
	G3	836		AE3	889		FL	392
	M10	93		AE4	130		FL	459
SAVORILY	PWR	25		AE4	511		FL	481
SAVORLY	PKA	2		AE4	592		FL	506
SAVORS	G4	88		AE4	682		M12	445
SAVORY	AA	120		AE4	842		M12	455
	AT	83		AE4	932		M12	584
	H29	24		AE4	954		M12	657
	P5	265		AE5	11		M12	692
	G4	43		AE5	218		M12	694
	G4	171		AE5	234		M12	770
	C	16		AE5	516		AU	356
	BP	109		AE5	614		AU	400
	HIF	441		AE5	793		AU	437
	HIF	642		AE5	829		WB	215
SAW	HS	99		AE5	1032		WB	348
	RH	90		AE6	455		WB	531
	SMA	44		AE6	522		M15	71
	VHH	13		AE6	604		GP	104
	AM	37		AE6	784		GP	106
	AM	88		AE6	1192		CI	192
	AM	252		AE7	398		CI	381
	AM	893		AE7	522	SAWEST	AE9	357
	AM	1093		AE7	1058	SAWS	G1	215
	AM	1101		AE8	136		M15	645
	AM	1119		AE8	143	SAWTRY	FL	358
	EEL	4		AE8	215	SAXON	BR	216
	SEL3	22		AE8	289	SAXONS	DC	46
	PTL	22		AE8	463		SKA1	9
	SM2	6		AE8	467	SCABBARD	AE9	409
	SCD2	1		AE8	924		SMP	63
	PUF	3		AE9	39	SCABBY	G3	672
	AA	72		AE9	506	SCABS	G3	468
	AA	517		AE9	627	SCAEAN	HI	89
	AA	923		AE10	376		AE2	831
	SAA	607		AE10	469		AE3	451
	RL	69		AE10	644	SCAFFOLD	P1	40
	RL	183		AE11	359	SCAFFOLDING	HAP	125
	RL	394		AE11	608	SCALDED	CAM	111
	AT	100		AE11	711	SCALDING	G4	32
	T23	97		AE12	1		KT2	476
	NS	5		AE12	487		FL	445
	NS	24		AE12	550	SCALE	HS	91
	TA	60		AE12	586		SAA	201
	EAA	3		AE12	663		SAA	936
	HAP	966		AE12	713		HAP	63
	HAP	1118		AE12	869		HAP	1196
	HAP	1230		AE12	976		HAP	1679
	HAP	1559		AE12	1139		BR	294
	HAP	1652		AE12	1300		J10	20
	HAP	1846		OAL	32		P1	14
	HAP	1939		OAL	125		P4	23
	HAP	2397		OAE1	4		DHP	24
	BR	19		AF	69		G1	376
	EL	33		DO	140		AE9	674
	EL	36		KT1	41		AE9	695
	ODA	10		KT1	122		AE10	736
	J10	397		KT1	214		AE11	1111
	J16	45		KT1	320		AE12	1054
	J16	46		KT1	563		AE12	1057
	P3	242		KT2	242		KT3	26
	M1	1095		KT2	341		M11	125
	M9	31		KT2	451		AU	526
	M9	171		KT2	560		M15	215
	M9	172		KT2	576	SCALED	AR	37
	M13	195		KT2	604		AE9	1033
	MC	35		KT3	322		AE10	434
	VP3	105		KT3	841	SCALES	HAP	226
	VP8	58		KT3	970		HAP	1799
	G2	464		TJD	154		EL	108
	G2	718		B	69		G3	813
	AE1	182		B	163		G4	141
	AE1	312		B	259		AE5	365
	AE1	638		B	276		AE7	751
	AE1	651		B	368		AE9	958
	AE1	653		BP	19		AE11	1135
	AE1	663		BP	184		M8	283
	AE1	684		BP	195	SCALING	AE2	603
	AE1	818		CAM	112		AE12	845
	AE1	1037		CAM	155	SCALP	AE9	1018
	AE2	8		HIF	258		M15	318
	AE2	172		HIF	460	SCALY	AM	59
	AE2	465		C	114		SAA	982
	AE2	628		C	270		G3	806

SCALY	G4	568
	AE5	114
	AE8	575
	AE11	734
SCAMANDRIUS	HI	40
SCAN	AA	1004
	MD	213
	PDG	45
	AU	191
	AS	32
SCANDAL	ELN	19
	EUF	28
	MD	40
	SAA	109
	SAA	1086
	HAP	1116
	J10	195
	MM	13
	KT3	204
	C	57
	FL	607
	PTP	7
	ETP	20
SCANDALIZE	SAA	295
SCANDALOUS	PLG	19
SCANDALS	HAP	1950
SCANDALUM	J1	231
SCANNED	CI	236
SCANT	HAP	1322
	G3	219
	B	549
SCANTED	AA	369
	AA	839
SCANTIER	HAP	657
SCANTY	TA	334
	EL	105
	J10	165
	P1	266
	P2	90
	G2	59
	G3	212
	AE7	157
	AE9	202
	AE10	527
	AE11	457
	AE12	810
	KT1	230
	M8	257
	B	365
	AS	92
SCAPE	AR	180
	PO	19
	SAA	1095
	HAP	589
	J6	485
	J10	486
	P1	217
	PLT	17
	P4	101
	G4	639
	G4	659
	AE2	856
	AE3	194
	AE4	442
	AE7	407
	AE9	728
	AE9	757
	AE10	84
	AE10	817
	AE12	790
	AE12	1088
	OAL	445
	OAL	760
	OAL	872
	KT1	265
	CI	467
SCAPED	EMQ	12
	ETC	26
	HP	26
	SAA	210
	HAP	172
	HAP	579
	J6	61
	J10	441
	AE2	430
	AE8	866
	FL	447
	WB	350
SCAPES	AM	877
	J1	72
	J3	191
	M1	724
	TJD	115
SCAR	G1	100
	M12	595
SCARAMOUCHA	EUO	15

SCARCE	AR	130
	DC	6
	PRL	6
	EIE	18
	AM	3
	AM	215
	AM	311
	AM	339
	AM	995
	PA	16
	PA	21
	PFD	3
	ML	18
	PAL	11
	PAL	30
	PTC	20
	CM	96
	CM	110
	DA	132
	AA	374
	PLB	54
	EPC	14
	PRH	15
	SAA	56
	SAA	130
	SAA	197
	SAA	600
	SAA	950
	SAA	1082
	SAA	1096
	RL	135
	RL	380
	AT	118
	AT	126
	ER	39
	H3	52
	TA	27
	TA	406
	GE	74
	HAP	318
	HAP	545
	EL	331
	J1	230
	J3	380
	J3	404
	J3	487
	J3	492
	J6	104
	J6	244
	J6	591
	J10	180
	PPS	10
	P2	90
	P3	8
	P4	53
	M1	87
	M1	741
	M9	89
	M13	59
	EHC	10
	EHC	38
	VP3	36
	VP5	76
	VP8	19
	VP8	20
	VP8	56
	G1	16.4
	G1	493
	G1	599
	G2	294
	G2	389
	G3	129
	G3	272
	G3	569
	G4	97
	G4	464
	G4	632
	AE1	50
	AE1	529
	AE1	600
	AE1	822
	AE2	435
	AE2	451
	AE2	666
	AE2	697
	AE2	940
	AE3	11
	AE3	54
	AE3	122
	AE3	175
	AE3	399
	AE3	708
	AE3	768
	AE3	769
	AE3	773
	AE3	862

SCARCE	AE3	873
	AE4	587
	AE4	785
	AE4	844
	AE5	111
	AE5	346
	AE5	528
	AE5	910
	AE5	1114
	AE6	279
	AE6	506
	AE8	688
	AE9	231
	AE9	755
	AE9	971
	AE10	33
	AE10	538
	AE10	802
	AE10	929
	AE10	1086
	AE10	1126
	AE10	1294
	AE11	1
	AE11	908
	AE11	1303
	AE12	58
	AE12	132
	AE12	353
	OAL	127
	OAL	362
	OAL	385
	MG	26
	MFL	25
	KT1	57
	KT1	233
	KT1	468
	KT1	564
	KT2	261
	KT3	16
	KT3	436
	KT3	550
	M8	208
	B	259
	B	263
	B	348
	BP	65
	BP	157
	C	755
	TH	413
	M11	319
	M11	348
	M12	233
	AU	327
	CI	327
SCARCE-COVERED	VP5	132
SCARCELY	AM	412
	SEL3	6
	ENH	30
	EUO2	18
	MF	211
	HAP	702
	HAP	1846
	EL	97
	EL	142
	EL	305
	J1	125
	J3	315
	J6	320
	J10	253
	M9	28
	VP1	19
	VP9	79
	G3	167
	G3	308
	G3	741
	AE6	466
	AE6	558
	AE6	670
	AE8	122
	AE9	246
	AE11	858
	AE12	174
	AE12	625
	AE12	1306
	DO	61
	KT2	4
	KT2	46
	B	324
	C	442
	FL	55
	FL	379
	M12	817
	CI	102
	SMP	80
SCARCE-RECOVERED	KT1	557
SCARECROW	T27	44

Word	Ref	No.
SCARF	PP	23
	AE4	384
	M12	552
SCARFS	CAM	372
SCARLET	AR	35
	HAP	1387
	KT2	600
	C	413
	M12	139
SCARS	AA	73
	SAA	705
	J6	151
	G2	522
	AU	410
SCATTER	ETC	10
	VP8	42
	AE9	551
SCATTERED	UDH	34
	AM	244
	EEL	4
	EAZ	38
	CM	141
	AA	10
	AA	278
	MF	99
	SAA	836
	SAA	927
	T27	125
	ER	32
	L3	118
	H29	64
	HAP	1398
	M13	182
	G2	416
	G3	525
	G3	719
	G4	131
	AE1	47
	AE1	242
	AE1	541
	AE1	722
	AE1	847
	AE3	174
	AE3	259
	AE3	573
	AE4	862
	AE8	466
	AE9	242
	AE9	477
	AE9	717
	AE9	965
	AE10	509
	AE10	575
	AE10	851
	AE10	954
	AE10	1190
	AE11	609
	AE12	547
	AE12	988
	M8	368
	M11	161
	M11	208
SCATTEREST	L1	27
SCATTERING	AE1	547
	PC2	20
	AM	503
	AM	867
	G4	192
	AE9	86
	AE12	443
SCATTERS	AE7	117
	AE11	1080
SCENE	AR	153
	EWG	14
	ECG2	8
	EM	19
	PUO2	9
	PTC	37
	PUO3	11
	PUO4	13
	PUF	4
	PUF	18
	SAA	136
	SAA	606
	SAA	715
	EK	14
	L1	13
	L3	142
	TA	13
	TA	78
	AK	127
	MS	17
	J3	10
	VP5	5
	G3	38
	AE1	233

Word	Ref	No.
SCENE	AE7	66
	AE11	328
	AE11	657
	OAL	157
	KT2	619
	KT3	866
	TH	204
	TH	276
	TH	326
	M15	389
	ETP	39
	SMP	24
	EMKG	20
SCENE-ROOM	EK	35
SCENES	SMA	30
	PRL	11
	PIE	5
	PMQ	5
	PAR	3
	PW	23
	PM	28
	ELN	21
	EUO	24
	EUO	36
	PNH	36
	PNH	50
	EAZ	4
	PLG	28
	MF	71
	MF	183
	PD	42
	L4	182
	AK	108
	PSH	33
	EH	22
	PLT	21
	ELT	6
	VP8	14
	AE1	597
	AE3	34
	OAL	120
	MG	31
	KT3	882
	M11	341
	PWR	14
	PWR	36
SCENT	AM	101
	EMQ	11
	PAL	5
	AA	527
	L4	168
	T18	77
	HAP	2254
	EL	155
	MS	7
	G2	182
	G3	391
	G3	626
	AE7	668
	AE12	455
	KT2	532
	KT3	365
	BP	89
	FL	17
SCENTS	SMA	60
	G2	654
	AE1	559
SCEPTER	AA	769
	MF	123
	H29	2
	TA	466
	HAP	1094
	HAP	2064
	HAP	2552
	J10	413
	M1	230
	M1	694
	M9	166
	HI	76
	AE1	85
	AE1	477
	AE1	921
	AE2	760
	AE4	149
	AE4	400
	AE6	1108
	AE7	69
	AE7	338
	AE7	344
	AE7	350
	AE7	596
	AE11	547
	AE12	310
	AE12	311
	KT3	296

Word	Ref	No.
SCEPTER	HIF	22
	HIF	42
	HIF	80
	HIF	348
	HIF	359
	HIF	518
	M11	210
	FL	189
SCEPTERED	HIF	258
SCEPTERS	AR	97
	SAA	898
	DA	19
	AE1	344
	AE11	409
	HIF	394
SCHEME	PWG	11
	J6	747
	C	686
SCHEMES	HAP	1766
	J3	79
	J10	155
SCHEVELINE'S	AR	219
SCHILLING	P5	281
SCHISM	HAP	355
	HAP	1098
	HAP	1172
	HAP	1192
	HAP	1498
	HAP	2579
SCHOLAR	MC	40
SCHOOL	ESF	13
	EPC	28
	SAA	967
	HAP	1600
	J6	582
	J10	183
	J10	272
	P1	57
	P1	132
	P3	85
	M9	78
	G3	261
	OAL	1
	OAL	6
	OAL	304
	C	204
SCHOOLBOYS	PTS	21
SCHOOL-FELLOW	PWGR	9
SCHOOLFELLOWS	G3	270
SCHOOLMEN	TA	242
SCHOOLS	PUO1	24
	PD	33
	EL	107
	J1	20
	J3	197
	J10	204
	P3	158
	PLT	49
SCIENCE	PUO1	27
	EUO2	16
	SAA	77
	ER	2
	TA	349
	P1	59
	P1	268
	G4	449
	DO	139
	TJD	77
SCIENCES	HAP	147
SCIPIO	AM	197
	L3	249
	MC	35
	C	377
	G2	236
SCIPIO'S	AE6	1159
SCIPIOS'	J6	461
SCOFFERS	J6	273
SCOLD	M12	344
SCONCE	L2	28
SCONCES	AE9	26
SCOOPED	PTL	17
SCOPE	MD	40
	M9	25
	AM	933
SCORCH	EL	111
SCORCHED	VP10	96
	G2	516
	G4	581
	G4	616
	AE9	717
	FL	381
SCORCHES	SKA6	11
SCORCHING	M1	806
	VP1	86
	VP2	11
	G1	136

SCORCHING	M8	30	SCORNING	R	13	SCRIPTURE	RL	440
	B	202		AE4	312		HAP	472
	FL	323		FL	34		HAP	482
	FL	408	SCORNS	PAL	21		HAP	696
SCORE	PRL	25		SKK	11		HAP	729
	AM	180		J10	522		HAP	745
	PSF	19		VP2	17		HAP	754
	AA	542	SCORPIO	HAP	1462		HAP	755
	SAA	785	SCORPION	HAP	1984		HAP	759
	RL	106		G1	48		HAP	762
	HAP	1605		G1	49		HAP	763
	PMS	23		G4	341		HAP	769
	J1	1		M15	548		HAP	779
	P6	184	SCOT	PO	25		HAP	826
	PLT	15	SCOTCH	PUO3	24		HAP	935
	EMKG	10		PUO3	4		HAP	945
SCORN	AR	195	SCOTLAND	PUO3	9	SCRIPTURES	JH	18
	LCA	36		HS	66		RL	181
	PRL	33		EJG	5		RL	297
	EWGR	43	SCOTS	EJG	1		HAP	381
	PA	19	SCOUR	MD	243		HAP	727
	PEL	28		MN	12		HAP	784
	SCG1	34		J3	419		HAP	997
	PFD	17		G1	691	SCRITCH-OWL	PPC	22
	PM	35		G2	625	SCRIVENER	H2	5
	PNH	7		G4	103	SCRIVENERS	PCG2	10
	EOE	16		AE2	448	SCRIVENERS'	PCD	1
	AA	275		AE2	480	SCROLL	AE5	655
	AA	400		AE4	221	SCRUBBING	J6	484
	AA	578		AE6	1114	SCRUBS	J10	312
	SAA	231		AE7	867		P3	10
	PDG	9		AE8	5	SCRUPLES	J6	138
	OE	4		AE10	307		AE4	73
	OE	46		AE10	810	SCUD	AE5	43
	AT	14		AE11	776		AE5	1086
	T23	23		KT3	600	SCUDDING	AE9	513
	T23	82		EMKG	20		AE8	944
	T23	110	SCOURED	P1	36		OAL	609
	H29	20		M12	102		FL	195
	HAP	767	SCOUREST	P4	122	SCULLER	G4	735
	J1	218	SCOURGE	AM	850	SCULPTOR	G3	58
	J3	256		MF	89	SCULPTOR'S	M12	529
	J3	273		J6	545	SCULPTURE	AE6	33
	J3	280		AE10	1080		BP	162
	J6	271	SCOURGED	AM	1162		M10	6
	J10	195		AE6	1123	SCULPTURES	AU	454
	P1	28	SCOURING	PSF	39		J3	107
	M13	145		PD	51	SCUM	G3	686
	HI	104		J3	440	SCURF	HAP	226
	VP2	23	SCOURINGS	ENH	19		AE6	1010
	VP2	43	SCOURS	HAP	2481		KT2	534
	VP8	127		M1	306	SCUTCHEON	FL	251
	G4	467		G3	307	SCUTCHEONS	FL	236
	AE3	421		G3	382		FL	244
	AE4	51		AE12	502	SCYLACAEAN	AE3	726
	AE4	975	SCOUT	T23	14	SCYLLA	G1	550
	AE7	613		AE12	528		G1	551
	AE7	896	SCOUTS	AE7	198		G1	554
	AE9	869		AE11	684		AE1	279
	AE10	1152		AE11	779		AE3	536
	OAL	19	SCRAMBLE	P5	257		AE3	541
	KT1	225	SCRAMBLING	VP8	42		AE3	549
	HIF	256	SCRAPS	PLT	40		AE3	899
	HIF	523	SCRATCH	T27	29		AE5	162
	C	722		AE12	384		AE5	220
	WB	104	SCRATCHED	OE	40		AE5	290
	WB	319		G3	797		AE5	295
	CI	595	SCREAMED	CI	320	SCYLLA'S	VP6	105
SCORNED	AA	518	SCREAMING	AE11	692	SCYLLAS	AE7	418
	SAA	348		AE12	1257	SCYRIAN	AE2	651
	PD	35		TH	100	SCYROS	AU	254
	T23	12	SCREAMS	AE12	1267		AU	282
	HAP	1358	SCREECH	AE4	672	SCYTHE	M13	28
	HAP	2214	SCREEN	GK	53		AE7	243
	VP8	49		B	211		AE7	879
	AE2	90		B	457		KT2	599
	AE4	472	SCREENS	J3	357	SCYTHES	G1	684
	KT2	279	SCRIBBLE	PDG	44	SCYTHIA	KT1	7
	C	434		GE	79	SCYTHIAN	HAP	6
	TH	14	SCRIBBLED	EUF	29		J3	142
	TH	161	SCRIBBLER	J1	15		VP1	88
	CI	65	SCRIBBLERS	P1	6		G1	331
SCORNER	FL	34		P1	116		G2	161
SCORNFUL	T23	96	SCRIBBLING	EAL	11		G3	306
	HAP	1704		ETC	20		G3	541
	P1	196	SCRIBES	AA	218		G3	587
	M1	635		SAA	1030		G3	701
	M13	40		PK	2		AE7	837
	AE10	830	SCRIPTURE	MD	156		AE8	287
	AE11	702		RL	124		KT3	298
	AE12	446		RL	258		M15	535
	OAL	362		RL	278	SCYTHIANS	AE4	208
	C	319		RL	308		AE8	967
	M11	200		RL	311	SE	EDG	12
	M12	135		RL	313	SEA	HS	85
SCORNING	R	9		RL	380		HS	144

SEA			SEA						
	AR	44		AE9	271	SEAL		WB	524
	AR	299		AE5	275	SEALE		MHD	8
	SMA	114		AE5	282	SEALED		DC	8
	VHH	16		AE5	797			AM	70
	VHH	43		AE5	818			HAP	435
	AM	35		AE5	1048			AE10	1051
	AM	60		AE5	1056			AE12	468
	AM	123		AE5	1073			OAL	536
	AM	265		AE5	1086			B	214
	AM	404		AE5	1116			B	726
	AM	587		AE6	4			AU	370
	AM	608		AE6	252			CI	178
	AM	637		AE6	715	SEALS		L4	211
	AM	684		AE6	945			AE1	970
	ML	27		AE6	1244			AE4	358
	CM	91		AE6	1247			AE12	297
	DA	45		AE7	11			M15	247
	DA	127		AE7	38			M15	415
	DA	156		AE7	45	SEAM		AM	582
	PUF	19		AE7	307			AE7	867
	AA	840		AE7	352	SEAMAN		PEL	32
	SAA	878		AE7	507	SEAMAN'S		AE6	333
	L1	3		AE7	1019	SEA-MARKS		HS	34
	L1	20		AE8	196	SEAMEN		RH	91
	L1	41		AE8	891			LCA	1
	H3	12		AE9	119			AM	55
	H29	89		AE9	138			AM	452
	TA	139		AE9	316			AM	709
	MN	10		AE10	128			AM	751
	HAP	2157		AE10	240			AM	829
	HAP	2206		AE10	246			EWGR	22
	J1	206		AE10	314			AE3	374
	J3	98		AE10	327			AE5	172
	J6	137		AE10	423			OAL	3
	J10	124		AE10	428	SEAMEN'S		AR	226
	J10	290		AE10	528	SEAMLESS		HAP	1192
	P5	206		AE10	782	SEAMS		AM	586
	P5	213		AE10	919			AA	72
	M1	388		AE10	931			AE1	174
	M1	447		AE10	838			AE5	890
	M1	487		AE10	964			FL	162
	VP8	10		AE11	627	SEAR		KT3	905
	VP8	80		AE11	934			KT3	974
	VP10	35		AE11	1316			FL	413
	G1	42		AE12	175			M12	386
	G1	297		AE12	398	SEARCH		RH	83
	G1	337		AE12	766			AM	658
	G1	495		OAL	200			PAL	26
	G1	585		OAL	376			DA	161
	G2	223		OAL	456			SAA	538
	G3	378		OAL	463			RL	390
	G3	806		OAL	854			RL	438
	G4	622		DO	52			L2	15
	AE1	4		TJD	147			L3	278
	AE1	20		BP	13			L3	295
	AE1	102		HIF	504			H29	49
	AE1	124		HIF	669			J3	194
	AE1	171		HIF	748			J6	383
	AE1	198		C	311			P3	47
	AE1	203		C	578			P5	90
	AE1	212		M11	26			VP1	38
	AE1	229		M11	99			VP2	71
	AE1	501		M11	153			VP6	85
	AE1	527		M11	438			VP9	62
	AE1	740		M12	9			G1	530
	AE1	756		M12	123			G3	596
	AE1	1062		M12	202			G4	170
	AE2	87		M12	271			AE2	1033
	AE2	269		M15	403			AE3	228
	AE2	1059		M15	445			AE3	642
	AE2	1088		M15	504			AE5	819
	AE3	13		CI	325			AE6	8
	AE3	170		CI	379			AE7	177
	AE3	348		CI	613			AE11	495
	AE3	526		CI	619			KT1	567
	AE3	527	SEA-BORN	DA	61			KT2	406
	AE3	547		AE7	964			KT3	845
	AE3	722		AE12	808			TJD	76
	AE3	735	SEA-BUILT	AM	226			M8	89
	AE3	874	SEA-DOGS	OAL	375			B	499
	AE3	919	SEA-FIGHT	SCD2	2			HIF	743
	AE4	61		SCD2	24			M11	267
	AE4	448	SEA-GODS	AR	120			M11	391
	AE4	573	SEA-GREEN	AM	82			AU	527
	AE4	601		G4	474	SEARCHED		PCG1	41
	AE4	604		AE1	205			VP2	63
	AE4	623		AE5	162			AE1	357
	AE4	814		AE10	299			KT2	77
	AE4	826		OAL	256			B	136
	AE4	843	SEAL	PA	47			B	145
	AE5	2		J1	103			FL	123
	AE5	26		AE9	120	SEARCHER		AE8	278
	AE5	29		KT2	307	SEARCHER'S		DA	10
	AE5	164		HIF	709	SEARCHING		AM	1072
	AE5	213		WB	171			G3	674
	AE5	260		WB	250			G3	690

Word	Ref	No.	Word	Ref	No.	Word	Ref	No.
SEARCHING	AE6	899	SEAS	AE3	255	SEASON	PCD	3
SEARCLOTH	AM	590		AE3	275		SAA	232
SEA'S	M13	35		AE3	369		H9	31
SEAS	AR	237		AE3	491		HAP	1712
	AR	303		AE3	580		M1	149
	SMA	99		AE3	642		G1	112
	DC	17		AE3	690		G1	303
	VHH	2		AE3	872		G2	434
	AM	120		AE3	883		G2	457
	AM	215		AE4	352		G2	749
	AM	666		AE4	372		G4	112
	S	9		AE4	378		AE1	358
	A	9		AE4	788		OAL	308
	EAZ	8		AE4	838		OAL	455
	CM	92		AE4	903		OAL	738
	HP	6		AE5	12		TJD	60
	DA	39		AE5	37		FL	20
	DA	80		AE5	68		M15	310
	DA	90		AE5	85		PMK	11
	AA	235		AE5	303	SEASONED	AM	566
	MD	71		AE5	937		AE9	715
	SAA	595		AE5	998	SEASONING	G3	615
	SAA	605		AE5	1010	SEASONS	DA	183
	SAA	616		AE5	1017		AA	911
	SAA	802		AE5	1135		L3	215
	SAA	816		AE6	93		BR	17
	SAA	839		AE6	459		J10	392
	SAA	981		AE6	472		VP3	62
	L3	13		AE7	8		VP9	63
	H29	62		AE7	274		G1	8
	TA	24		AE7	409		G1	34
	AK	165		AE7	415		G1	76
	HAP	1788		AE7	1102		G1	344
	BR	170		AE8	443		G3	101
	EL	242		AE8	778		G4	152
	J6	223		AE9	142		OAL	453
	J6	722		AE9	161		DO	94
	J6	761		AE9	165		KT3	413
	J6	847		AE9	286		C	453
	J10	274		AE9	656		M15	297
	J10	283		AE9	962		M15	466
	P5	197		AE10	86		AS	10
	M1	7		AE10	282	SEAT	HS	64
	M1	17		AE10	334		AR	168
	M1	27		AE10	374		LC	87
	M1	68		AE10	982		EUO2	1
	M1	124		AE11	494		AA	908
	M1	232		AE11	1168		L3	205
	M1	344		AE12	306		H29	12
	M1	375		AE12	1171		TA	318
	M1	400		OAL	627		TA	455
	M1	463		DO	46		HAP	640
	M1	480		KT2	351		HAP	1036
	M1	810		KT2	514		HAP	1277
	M13	49		KT3	216		HAP	1730
	M13	167		KT3	297		HAP	2066
	VP1	79		KT3	555		BR	87
	VP4	41		M8	49		SKA5	2
	VP4	46		M8	280		J3	2
	VP4	62		HIF	214		J3	266
	VP6	50		HIF	435		J10	335
	VP6	54		HIF	489		P1	156
	VP9	50		HIF	552		P3	42
	VP10	7		HIF	714		P6	1
	VP10	98		M11	32		VP7	5
	G1	207		M11	36		G1	56
	G1	407		M11	57		G1	134
	G1	443		M11	110		G2	291
	G1	490		M11	113		G2	782
	G1	528		M11	122		G3	221
	G1	634		M11	131		G3	641
	G2	217		M11	145		G3	697
	G2	720		M11	196		G4	294
	G3	689		M11	204		G4	355
	G3	711		M11	223		G4	580
	G4	339		M11	247		AE1	26
	G4	558		M11	424		AE1	287
	AE1	88		M11	456		AE1	336
	AE1	181		M11	477		AE1	367
	AE1	190		M11	499		AE2	1007
	AE1	222		FL	30		AE3	6
	AE1	256		M12	88		AE3	116
	AE1	309		M12	757		AE3	149
	AE1	315		AU	295		AE3	242
	AE1	320		AU	457		AE3	252
	AE1	381		M15	64		AE3	219
	AE1	519		M15	156		AE3	641
	AE1	763		M15	261		AE4	216
	AE1	854		M15	404		AE6	730
	AE2	152		M15	438		AE6	1039
	AE2	270		M15	441		AE6	1062
	AE2	273		CI	384		AE7	212
	AE2	419		CI	552		AE7	228
	AE3	165		CI	553		AE7	267
	AE3	175	SEASICK	J6	142		AE7	451
	AE3	213	SEASON	SMA	26		AE8	89

SEAT	AE8	233	SECOND	BR	217	SECRET	PAZ	13
	AE8	393		PP	14		CM	26
	AE8	417		PTS	20		HP	258
	AE8	611		EL	170		AA	31
	AE9	300		J10	197		AA	466
	AE10	812		P3	146		AA	693
	AE10	833		P4	6		PPC	3
	AE11	797		P5	76		SAA	225
	AE11	1192		M1	512		SAA	981
	AE12	690		M1	483		RL	13
	AE12	830		PLT	30		RL	187
	OAL	162		MC	14		RL	252
	OAL	652		MC	48		RL	43
	KT3	838		VP5	78		L3	53
	B	654		G2	144		L3	80
	BP	47		AE1	109		L4	92
	HIF	84		AE2	616		T27	18
	HIF	362		AE4	24		HAP	30
	TH	57		AE4	788		HAP	551
	M11	172		AE5	337		HAP	567
	FL	446		AE5	338		HAP	685
	M12	61		AE5	640		HAP	1779
	M12	534		AE5	707		HAP	2057
	AU	199		AE5	712		HAP	2474
	AU	393		AE5	742		HAP	2560
	GP	33		AE5	757		ETS	15
	ESK	11		AE6	215		J6	171
SEATED	AA	778		AE6	1043		J6	682
	J10	54		AE7	447		J10	152
	P5	39		AE7	448		J10	376
	MC	53		AE7	901		P1	231
	G1	46		AE7	1069		P4	47
	G4	627		AE8	375		P4	83
	AE1	20		AE8	966		M9	102
	AE10	3		AE9	56		M9	160
	AE11	1215		AE9	175		HI	192
	OAL	637		AE9	559		VP3	145
	KT1	498		AE9	786		VP6	49
	KT3	550		AE9	812		VP8	82
	B	221		AE10	40		G1	127
	HIF	457		AE10	89		G1	134
SEATS	HAP	2027		AE10	104		G1	522
	PP	43		AE10	471		G1	560
	PSH	6		AE12	254		G2	699
	J1	143		AE12	353		G3	376
	J3	365		AE12	737		G3	645
	M1	228		AE12	1159		G3	662
	G1	327		OAE1	5		G3	693
	G4	496		MG	18		G4	77
	AE1	235		DO	80		G4	221
	AE5	179		KT2	626		G4	360
	AE5	832		KT3	974		G4	519
	AE6	555		TJD	41		G4	522
	AE6	719		M8	194		G4	570
	AE6	871		M8	242		G4	580
	AE8	885		M8	300		G4	778
	AE11	495		B	35		AE1	37
	AE12	1102		B	68		AE1	155
	AE12	1151		B	413		AE1	490
	AF	26		BP	112		AE1	706
	KT3	549		CAM	18		AE2	59
	KT3	597		CAM	237		AE2	540
	KT3	969		CAM	271		AE2	664
	FL	426		HIF	622		AE3	154
	M15	230		C	454		AE3	911
	M15	257		C	541		AE3	928
SEAWARD	AE4	843		TH	187		AE4	4
SEA-WASP	AM	612		TH	296		AE4	163
SEAWEED	DA	186		FL	33		AE4	248
	VP7	59		FL	270		AE4	418
SEAWEEDS	AE7	812		M12	260		AE4	427
SEBASTIAN	EDS	14		M12	359		AE4	488
SECOND	JH	5		M12	519		AE4	552
	AR	281		M15	371		AE4	712
	RH	42		M15	421		AE4	723
	SMA	118		CI	530		AE4	728
	LC	16		CI	531		AE4	773
	AM	20		CI	573		AE5	8
	AM	561		AS	21		AE5	214
	PCG2	23	SECONDED	G1	633		AE6	599
	HP	22		AE4	792		AE6	733
	HP	232		OAL	656		AE6	738
	ETG	25		M12	464		AE6	953
	PUO3	30	SECONDS	AE4	633		AE7	1062
	AA	234		AE8	903		AE8	520
	D	34	SECRECY	PMQW	2		AE8	611
	SAA	952		J3	102		AE9	4
	OE	30		M9	55		AE10	95
	TA	110		CAM	170		AE10	884
	TA	438		WB	150		AE10	1248
	TA	494	SECRET	AR	77		AE11	1304
	AK	66		AM	31		AE12	110
	HAP	137		AM	162		OAL	311
	HAP	349		AM	450		OAL	332
	HAP	832		PWGR	4		OAL	399
	BR	88		PT	1		OAL	442

Word	Code	Num	Word	Code	Num	Word	Code	Num
SECRET	OAL	680	SECTS	HAP	699	SECURE	AE3	746
	KT1	322		HAP	756		AE4	92
	KT2	65		HAP	843		AE4	866
	KT2	392		HAP	974		AE5	790
	KT2	560		HAP	994		AE5	1043
	KT3	199		HAP	1088		AE5	1124
	KT3	760		HAP	1100		AE6	143
	KT3	1068		HAP	1176		AE6	281
	M8	263		HAP	1478		AE6	472
	B	36		HAP	2037		AE6	969
	B	46		HAP	2090		AE7	420
	B	59		BR	94		AE7	580
	B	97		EDS	29		AE7	956
	B	123		PTP	40		AE8	800
	B	134		HS	53		AE8	815
	B	178	SECURE	AR	115		AE8	839
	B	216		AR	236		AE9	46
	B	257		AR	259		AE9	161
	B	265		RH	103		AE9	166
	B	369		SMA	12		AE9	241
	B	457		LC	80		AE9	301
	B	499		LC	124		AE9	745
	B	590		AM	458		AE10	1239
	B	736		AM	667		AE10	1296
	CAM	34		ML	10		AE11	345
	CAM	116		EOE	30		AE11	589
	CAM	123		CM	49		AE11	680
	CAM	167		HP	161		AE11	759
	CAM	194		DA	167		AE11	956
	CAM	245		PUF	24		AE11	1306
	CAM	290		AA	354		AE12	818
	HIF	106		AA	475		AE12	1288
	HIF	661		AA	578		OAL	343
	C	132		AA	635		OAL	388
	C	368		AA	779		OAE2	74
	TH	102		AA	984		DO	72
	TH	351		MD	116		KT2	19
	TH	406		MD	251		KT3	374
	FL	204		SAA	247		KT3	1151
	FL	308		SAA	275		TJD	144
	FL	436		SAA	848		TJD	145
	FL	460		SAA	865		M8	43
	FL	599		RL	285		M8	174
	AU	514		OE	23		M8	208
	WB	173		H9	25		B	106
	WB	188		H29	67		B	183
	WB	201		H29	97		B	223
	WB	238		H29	98		B	249
	WB	330		TA	230		B	586
	CI	206		HAP	493		B	626
	CI	257		HAP	705		B	678
	CI	266		BR	46		BP	150
	CI	422		BR	85		CAM	96
	CI	487		BR	298		CAM	277
	ETP	25		PTS	9		HIF	55
SECRETLY	HP	150		EL	17		HIF	124
	KT1	603		EL	95		HIF	322
SECRETS	HS	128		MS	19		HIF	580
	EL	248		J3	4		HIF	650
	J3	91		J3	319		TH	406
	J3	194		J3	379		M11	53
	J6	273		J3	451		M12	125
	J6	430		J6	90		AU	319
	P5	30		P3	42		AU	378
	G1	624		P6	27		M15	256
	G4	512		P6	28		M15	508
	AE2	212		M1	763		CI	325
	AE4	612		M1	856		CI	379
	AE5	933		M1	1023		CI	477
	KT3	845		HI	100		CI	576
	HIF	743		GK	86		ESK	18
	C	598		DHP	29		PWR	30
SECT	WB	155		VP4	26	SECURED	DA	181
	MD	197		G1	427		MD	116
	MD	264		G2	225		SAA	92
	SAA	393		G2	240		SAA	225
	RL	309		G2	474		SAA	822
	RL	310		G2	597		RL	270
	HAP	547		G2	655		HAP	2546
	HAP	999		G2	689		PKA	12
	HAP	1020		G3	579		P1	30
	HAP	2538		G3	726		G3	793
	HAP	2033		G4	610		G4	210
SECTARIAN	SMA	81		G4	612		AE5	1061
SECTS	MD	165		AE1	230		AE5	1062
	MD	203		AE1	263		AE9	1021
	MD	294		AE1	333		AE10	766
	MD	303		AE1	337		KT3	1091
	SAA	277		AE1	817		CAM	315
	SAA	325		AE2	186		AU	341
	RL	310		AE2	330	SECURELY	UDH	14
	RL	421		AE2	602		AM	656
	HAP	40		AE2	861		AM	1215
	HAP	52		AE2	993		FS1	1
	HAP	60		AE3	116		TA	15
	HAP	686		AE3	299		EAA	23

Word	Ref	No.	Word	Ref	No.	Word	Ref	No.
SECURELY	HAP	1294	SEE	AM	354	SEE	AT	59
	EL	247		AM	398		ER	21
	J3	475		AM	542		L2	12
	J10	535		AM	640		L4	141
	J10	550		AM	1170		L4	212
	P3	79		PMQ	25		T18	74
	M1	253		PMQ	40		T27	84
	M13	33		EWGR	17		T27	86
	M13	53		EWGR	19		T27	113
	M13	198		EMM	8		H29	104
	VP10	7		PT	36		H2	87
	G1	469		PTL	5		FS1	14
	G2	38		PTL	11		FS3	3
	G2	396		PCG1	23		TA	504
	G2	450		ECG1	19		TA	411
	G3	458		SCG1	21		TA	492
	AE1	394		SCG2	8		HAP	443
	AE3	667		PFD	9		HAP	636
	AE4	765		PAR	9		HAP	648
	AE5	1099		PAR	16		HAP	761
	AE6	232		PW	21		HAP	866
	AE7	826		EMQW	3		HAP	975
	AE9	73		EMQW	16		HAP	986
	AE9	178		PM	10		HAP	1211
	AE9	311		PM	28		HAP	1286
	AE9	432		PM	34		HAP	1384
	AE9	985		E'M	8		HAP	1408
	AE10	414		S	15		HAP	1446
	AE10	870		PLN	33		HAP	1951
	AE11	1116		ELN	4		HAP	2299
	KT1	570		ELN	13		HAP	2377
	TJD	144		SLN	20		HAP	2395
	B	709		PCD	25		BR	52
	B	747		SCD1	1		BR	95
	M12	438		PUO1	5		BR	110
	M15	140		PUO1	9		BR	114
	M15	676		EUO	14		PDS	6
SECURER	M1	352		PUO2	17		PP	45
SECURES	SAA	326		PUO2	27		PP	49
	HAP	1277		E	27		ETS	29
	BR	151		PAZ	40		PMS	7
	VP6	18		PC1	18		EKA	36
	AE9	81		PTW	29		SKA2	4
SECURITY	TA	484		POE	23		SKA2	12
	J16	51		PTC	1		SKA2	17
SEDANS	J1	186		PTC	35		EL	21
SEDATE	AE9	999		PLG	11		EL	140
SEDATELY	AE12	30		CM	8		EL	240
SEDGE	G3	46		CM	10		EL	293
SEDGY	AM	927		CM	105		EL	344
SEDITION	MD	175		HP	19		EL	350
	D	39		HP	101		ODA	32
	SAA	7		HP	204		ODA	57
	SAA	296		DA	23		PSH	33
	SAA	528		PR	16		SSH	5
	SAA	798		AA	36		J1	143
	SAA	916		AA	271		J1	169
	M12	85		AA	860		J1	243
SEDITION'S	SMA	79		AA	863		J3	61
	SAA	931		ELB	31		J3	107
	SAA	1132		ELB	37		J3	223
SEDITIOUS	SAA	1030		EPC	27		J3	255
SEDLEY	MF	163		MD	2		J3	293
SEDUCE	MF	171		MD	137		J3	400
	L3	201		MD	145		J6	369
	HAP	2495		MD	147		J6	372
SEDUCED	AA	498		MD	222		J6	470
	MD	78		PRH	8		J6	689
	SAA	699		MF	43		J10	131
	EDS	2		SAA	369		J10	339
	G2	428		SAA	484		J10	410
	AE4	791		SAA	524		J10	450
	AE12	897		SAA	747		J16	10
	FL	156		SAA	751		J16	47
SEDUCER	HAP	1689		SAA	807		P1	60
	G3	337		SAA	872		P1	112
SEDUCERS	HAP	903		SAA	887		P1	130
SEE	AR	24		SAA	910		P1	150
	AR	130		SAA	993		P1	176
	AR	155		SAA	1071		P1	271
	AR	164		SAA	1113		P2	30
	AR	276		SAA	1125		P3	71
	RH	21		EK	11		P3	90
	RH	73		EDG	26		P3	190
	RH	77		RL	21		P4	48
	SMA	9		RL	72		P5	277
	LC	14		RL	101		P6	33
	LC	119		RL	107		P6	42
	LCA	19		RL	109		P6	176
	PRL	24		RL	115		P6	180
	EIE	10		RL	210		M1	696
	SIE	6		RL	248		M1	838
	AM	29		RL	301		M1	914
	AM	61		RL	328		M1	1082
	AM	183		RL	439		M9	172
	AM	323		AT	3		M13	120

SEE		SEE		SEE	
M13	200	AE10	674	M12	673
VCS	32	AE10	729	M12	702
HI	1	AE10	733	AU	19
HI	124	AE10	804	AU	356
HI	148	AE10	948	AU	409
HI	164	AE10	959	AU	445
MC	28	AE10	1135	WB	18
GK	13	AE10	1208	WB	93
GK	166	AE11	81	WB	142
VP1	19	AE11	86	WB	418
VP1	48	AE11	476	WB	493
VP1	52	AE11	483	M15	278
VP1	94	AE11	1035	M15	653
VP1	107	AE12	26	GP	14
VP1	117	AE12	98	GP	53
VP2	35	AE12	925	GP	80
VP2	95	AE12	936	GP	135
VP3	23	OAL	95	CI	72
VP3	148	OAL	109	CI	160
VP4	19	OAL	121	CI	197
VP4	60	OAL	183	STP	1
VP4	62	OAL	250	STP	7
VP6	13	OAL	543	SMP	24
VP7	17	OAL	720	EMKG	14
VP8	39	OAL	819	AS	27
VP8	153	OAE2	4	AS	70
VP9	3	OAE2	5	AA	16
VP9	28	AF	93	AA	195
VP9	52	AF	132	AA	306
VP9	54	AF	133	SAA	16
VP9	64	MG	17	L4	8
VP10	63	MG	39	L4	211
G2	41	MM	21	L4	215
G2	216	MM	34	L4	222
G2	616	DO	38	L4	228
G2	704	DO	104	L4	233
G2	247	DO	149	L4	243
G3	29	KT1	103	L4	248
G3	718	KT1	119	L4	256
G4	562	KT1	329	L4	265
AE1	29	KT1	341	H3	2
AE1	258	KT1	396	H3	39
AE1	467	KT1	510	HAP	17
AE1	647	KT1	520	HAP	837
AE1	682	KT1	571	BR	30
AE1	758	KT2	40	M1	158
AE2	82	KT2	84	M1	204
AE2	188	KT2	278	M1	562
AE2	365	KT2	320	VP4	59
AE2	469	KT2	366	G1	151
AE2	559	KT2	467	G1	280
AE2	821	KT2	447	G1	285
AE2	833	KT2	631	G2	81
AE2	835	KT3	94	G2	208
AE2	904	KT3	492	G2	284
AE2	910	KT3	586	G2	439
AE3	387	KT3	796	G3	157
AE3	448	TJD	197	G3	222
AE3	645	M8	133	G3	798
AE3	851	M8	157	AE1	873
AE3	920	B	316	AE6	6
AE4	230	B	495	AE6	961
AE4	453	B	527	AE7	140
AE4	557	B	543	AE12	195
AE4	857	B	730	OAL	368
AE4	886	BP	126	M8	397
AE5	236	CAM	77	B	442
AE5	513	CAM	90	M12	117
AE5	836	CAM	308	M12	667
AE6	100	HIF	220	M12	707
AE6	217	HIF	281	AU	45
AE6	442	HIF	790	WB	414
AE6	551	HIF	804	WB	425
AE6	776	C	123	M15	158
AE6	804	C	296	AM	141
AE6	1023	C	331	AM	866
AE6	1055	C	397	MD	113
AE6	1073	C	455	ER	2
AE6	1134	C	459	L1	27
AE6	1160	C	563	L3	35
AE6	1180	C	614	L3	112
AE6	1208	C	753	H29	47
AE7	159	C	760	H2	6
AE7	218	C	764	M1	12
AE8	154	C	803	M1	37
AE8	207	C	810	M1	240
AE8	252	M11	138	M1	582
AE8	756	M11	183	VP6	49
AE9	21	M11	193	G1	28
AE9	318	M11	367	G1	29
AE9	394	FL	146	G1	79
AE9	477	FL	205	G1	120
AE9	604	FL	428	G1	206
AE9	928	FL	537	G2	19
AE10	346	M12	16	G2	443
AE10	527	M12	577	AE1	37

SEED

SEEDS

SEEDS			SEEK			SEEM		
	AE4	702		AE8	661		HAP	1653
	AE7	472		AE8	659		J3	355
	AE7	766		AE8	815		M1	933
	OAL	213		AE9	9		VP3	67
	KT3	1027		AE9	829		VP9	44
	HIF	10		AE9	967		G3	39
	HIF	110		AE11	196		G3	54
	FL	414		AE11	521		G3	172
	M15	522		AE11	599		G3	304
	CI	495		AE11	934		G3	484
	ETP	6		OAL	41		G4	589
SEEING	AA	241		OAL	348		G4	691
	L4	68		OAL	349		AE1	454
	T27	85		OAE1	21		AE2	273
	EL	58		KT1	250		AE3	175
	KT1	325		KT1	436		AE7	59
	KT2	628		KT2	62		AE12	191
	WB	53		KT2	128		AE12	365
SEEK	UDH	45		TJD	51		AE12	1314
	SMA	41		B	601		OAL	254
	SIE	4		B	739		OAL	534
	AM	146		HIF	87		OAL	555
	AM	256		C	711		OAL	565
	AM	1004		TH	179		OAL	746
	S	5		TH	214		OAL	764
	PUO2	4		M11	3		DO	94
	DA	10		M12	596		M12	668
	DA	13		AU	41		CI	575
	DA	19		M15	253	SEEMED	HS	131
	DA	49		GP	33		AR	13
	PRH	11		CI	371		AM	8
	RL	430		CI	596		AM	13
	L4	48		CI	628		AM	186
	H29	102		DA	159		AM	312
	HAP	970	SEEKEST				AM	315
	HAP	1150	SEEKING	AT	62		AM	479
	HAP	1738		AE4	93		AM	672
	EL	241		AE12	947		AM	733
	EL	243	SEEKS	AM	164		AM	1111
	J6	268		L3	287		ESF	2
	J6	682		H29	36		AA	26
	J6	820		H2	48		AA	545
	P1	16		J6	186		AA	740
	P6	2		M1	81		MD	7
	HI	54		M1	566		MF	127
	M1	498		M1	661		SAA	112
	VP7	14		M1	1056		SAA	215
	G1	450		VP8	123		SAA	756
	G1	526		G3	553		TA	81
	G2	272		G4	533		PAA	4
	G2	722		G4	810		AK	76
	G3	514		AE4	98		HAP	1427
	G4	365		AE4	121		HAP	1778
	G4	624		AE4	689		HAP	2436
	AE1	244		AE6	12		HAP	2586
	AE1	492		AE6	1092		J6	609
	AE1	510		AE7	570		J10	274
	AE1	549		AE7	696		M1	878
	AE1	800		AE7	1019		M1	1017
	AE1	834		AE8	606		M9	41
	AE2	137		AE9	587		AE1	440
	AE2	915		AE10	593		AE2	232
	AE2	1021		AE10	760		AE2	353
	AE3	6		AE10	933		AE2	556
	AE3	127		AE11	340		AE2	743
	AE3	157		AE11	747		AE2	943
	AE3	197		AE11	1127		AE3	203
	AE3	330		AE11	1149		AE3	394
	AE3	618		AE12	686		AE3	774
	AE4	236		AE12	702		AE4	128
	AE4	373		AE12	816		AE5	115
	AE4	503		AE12	1326		AE6	76
	AE4	549		OAL	828		AE7	343
	AE4	614		KT3	739		AE7	590
	AE4	680		TJD	68		AE10	283
	AE4	783		M10	35		AE10	377
	AE5	173		HIF	714		AE10	901
	AE5	253		M11	72		AE10	913
	AE5	959		M11	192		AE10	1230
	AE6	172		M11	391		AE12	1360
	AE6	499		M11	476		KT1	112
	AE6	545		M12	563		KT1	145
	AE6	836	SEEM	M15	610		KT1	551
	AE6	973		UDH	17		KT2	47
	AE6	1121		UDH	66		KT2	246
	AE6	1200		HS	24		KT2	473
	AE7	140		LC	25		KT2	512
	AE7	272		LC	125		KT2	547
	AE7	324		AM	606		KT3	8
	AE7	328		EMM	7		KT3	380
	AE7	431		PAR	18		KT3	957
	AE7	551		PUO4	23		KT3	1136
	AE7	598		AA	472		M8	111
	AE7	689		SAA	221		M8	218
	AE7	972		SAA	1019		M8	343
	AE8	523		HAP	159		B	81
				HAP	982			

SEEMED	B	104	SEEMS	AE8	623	SEEN	G1	642		
	B	440		AE8	915		G2	199		
	B	688		AE10	300		G2	613		
	M10	80		AE10	639		G3	147		
	C	748		AE10	910		G3	236		
	TH	96		AE11	570		G3	264		
	TH	414		AE11	741		G3	794		
	M11	448		AE11	1025		G3	808		
	FL	56		AE12	1158		G4	598		
	FL	76		AF	41		AE1	168		
	FL	150		AF	46		AE1	370		
	FL	200		KT2	427		AE1	443		
	FL	212		KT3	13		AE1	450		
	FL	330		BP	158		AE1	906		
	M12	639		M10	21		AE2	156		
	M12	690		C	197		AE2	234		
	AU	212		C	323		AE2	665		
	AU	335		M12	584		AE2	869		
	AU	424		AU	216		AE4	214		
	WB	216		AU	230		AE4	580		
	GP	8		CI	17		AE5	546		
	CI	166		CI	471		AE5	732		
	CI	221		ESK	6		AE5	846		
SEEMING	SMA	92	SEEN	AR	26		AE6	33		
	AM	66		AR	219		AE6	420		
	AM	760		AR	281		AE6	553		
	PUF	15		RH	51		AE7	274		
	AA	466		DC	27		AE8	275		
	PRH	12		DC	49		AE8	885		
	SAA	271		PWG	3		AE8	935		
	L4	259		VHH	52		AE9	322		
	HAP	1773		AM	341		AE9	1035		
	HAP	2116		AM	377		AE11	15		
	HAP	2570		AM	521		AE11	129		
	P1	233		AM	1109		AE11	407		
	PLT	26		EMQ	1		AE11	721		
	G1	502		PFD	8		AE11	908		
	AE5	890		EMK	1		AE11	977		
	OAL	670		PKK	1		AE11	1044		
	OAL	790		PTW	16		AE11	1309		
	KT2	651		HP	105		AE12	690		
	B	46		PUO3	26		AE12	890		
	B	86		SAA	40		AE12	1357		
	B	286		SAA	919		OAL	31		
	C	480		SAA	1109		OAL	109		
	C	791		SAA	1122		OAL	626		
	M11	357		L3	36		OAL	885		
	CI	309		L3	216		MFL	16		
	CI	407		T27	17		KT1	22		
SEEMINGLY	HIF	118		TA	53		KT1	75		
	C	781		TA	145		KT1	170		
SEEMLY	KT3	462		AK	125		KT1	233		
SEEMS	SMA	27		AK	140		KT1	220		
	LC	32		AK	151		KT1	394		
	LC	115		HAP	34		KT2	4		
	LC	148		HAP	171		KT2	471		
	AM	34		HAP	212		KT2	507		
	AM	57		HAP	552		KT2	517		
	AM	612		HAP	1216		KT2	644		
	AM	1175		HAP	1752		KT3	76		
	HP	45		HAP	1850		KT3	216		
	PLB	6		HAP	2226		KT3	232		
	PRH	42		HAP	2349		KT3	821		
	MF	26		BR	11		KT3	869		
	SAA	30		PDS	26		B	77		
	EK	32		PKA	9		B	274		
	RL	254		EL	284		BP	21		
	HAP	753		MS	26		BP	90		
	HAP	346		EH	1		BP	181		
	HAP	602		J3	47		M10	13		
	HAP	2422		J6	151		HIF	635		
	BR	27		J6	491		HIF	721		
	BR	177		J6	608		C	318		
	ODA	52		J10	65		C	495		
	J1	174		P1	39		M11	85		
	J3	173		P3	23		M11	101		
	J6	647		P3	163		FL	44		
	P1	178		P4	11		FL	63		
	M1	959		M1	218		FL	66		
	GK	8		M1	542		FL	88		
	GK	146		M1	851		FL	175		
	GK	159		M1	1034		FL	273		
	G2	156		M13	7		FL	341		
	G2	251		M13	71		FL	348		
	G2	615		M13	140		FL	395		
	G4	694		HI	94		M12	182		
	AE1	700		MC	51		M12	236		
	AE3	489		GK	54		M12	273		
	AE3	707		GK	141		AU	292		
	AE4	191		VP1	23		WB	35		
	AE4	677		VP3	45		WB	540		
	AE5	205		VP3	99		M15	418		
	AE5	330		VP4	19		GP	84		
	AE6	1031		VP9	74		CI	169		
	AE7	912		G1	330		SMP	55		
	AE7	1078		G1	431		EMKG	9		

Word	Ref	No.
SEER	BR	253
	G4	651
	AE2	173
	AE2	245
	AE3	458
	AE3	734
	AE7	115
	KT2	605
	M8	63
	HIF	102
	HIF	532
	M12	40
SEERS	AE6	1089
SEES	LC	144
	AM	131
	AM	244
	AM	346
	AM	973
	PM	23
	PUO1	26
	EUO2	7
	AA	443
	SAA	17
	SAA	958
	L3	233
	L4	121
	PAA	35
	BR	78
	J1	99
	J6	91
	J6	557
	J6	708
	J6	799
	J10	32
	J10	33
	J10	285
	J10	538
	P3	62
	M1	611
	M1	676
	M1	1078
	G2	204
	G3	8
	G4	522
	G4	566
	AE1	582
	AE1	705
	AE1	718
	AE2	413
	AE4	119
	AE4	210
	AE4	362
	AE4	655
	AE5	4
	AE5	461
	AE6	614
	AE6	615
	AE6	953
	AE7	128
	AE7	1020
	AE10	1002
	AE10	1016
	AE11	1218
	AE11	1278
	AE11	1311
	AE12	38
	AE12	1332
	OAL	352
	OAL	359
	KT1	513
	KT2	183
	CAM	102
	TH	324
	M11	463
	M12	87
	M15	200
	M15	351
	M15	495
	CI	148
SEE'ST	L3	179
	AE9	241
	KT1	403
SEEST	P2	88
	P3	222
	P4	24
	G3	705
	G4	83
	G4	383
	AE4	304
	AE10	28
	KT1	78
SEETHER	BP	57
SEGMENT	M11	265
SEINE	AM	1195
SEIZE	MD	162
	HAP	267
SEIZE	HAP	302
	SSH	14
	J3	204
	J10	25
	G4	333
	AE1	499
	AE2	606
	AE6	537
	AE7	600
	AE8	874
	OAL	134
	HIF	121
	HIF	207
	HIF	244
	C	790
	TH	137
	M11	143
	CI	280
	CI	457
	CI	530
	CI	549
	CI	584
	ESK	14
SEIZED	AR	22
	AA	178
	MD	175
	SAA	84
	SAA	907
	SAA	922
	SAA	1085
	HAP	1363
	HAP	1817
	P3	201
	GK	96
	VP6	23
	VP6	70
	G1	560
	G3	241
	G4	509
	G4	714
	AE1	68
	AE1	421
	AE1	495
	AE2	423
	AE2	710
	AE2	990
	AE3	819
	AE3	874
	AE4	1
	AE4	404
	AE5	229
	AE5	348
	AE5	417
	AE5	506
	AE5	537
	AE5	619
	AE5	850
	AE5	856
	AE5	884
	AE6	303
	AE6	405
	AE6	477
	AE6	488
	AE7	498
	AE7	550
	AE8	148
	AE8	395
	AE9	213
	AE10	465
	AE10	744
	AE10	834
	AE10	1279
	AE11	136
	AE11	926
	AE11	1063
	AE11	1077
	AE11	1091
	AE12	456
	AE12	552
	AE12	687
	AF	147
	AF	151
	KT1	45
	KT1	233
	KT2	309
	KT3	701
	M8	160
	M8	220
	B	205
	B	266
	B	746
	BP	63
	BP	126
	HIF	510
	HIF	540
	HIF	804
SEIZED	C	290
	TH	93
	TH	301
	FL	64
	M12	274
	M12	23
	M12	313
	M12	455
	M12	572
	AU	134
	AU	276
	WB	60
	WB	533
	CI	318
SEIZES	AM	387
	AM	974
	G1	451
	AE2	300
	AE5	865
	AE9	765
	KT2	188
SEJANUS	J10	93
	J10	94
	J10	100
	J10	117
	J10	166
SEJANUS'	J10	143
SELDOM	HS	108
	AR	133
	AM	754
	PEL	32
	ECG1	28
	ECG2	10
	PM	29
	EM	30
	ENH	3
	ETC	3
	AA	723
	MD	56
	PK	21
	PD	7
	MO	17
	H29	76
	HAP	915
	HAP	1278
	HAP	1980
	HAP	2226
	J6	768
	J10	28
	P4	11
	G1	514
	OAL	471
	KT2	84
	KT3	384
	C	403
	WB	131
	WB	403
	CI	392
	PTP	43
SELECT	G3	593
	G4	779
SELECTED	AE2	24
	KT3	20
SELECTS	AE7	205
	M12	381
	AU	381
SELF	SAA	36
	SAA	253
	TA	261
	HAP	591
	HAP	628
	BR	355
	EL	241
	M1	959
	VP3	166
	G3	160
	KT2	511
	KT3	562
	HIF	169
SELF-BANISHED	M15	78
SELF-BORN	M15	580
SELF-CONCEIT	OAL	807
SELF-CONSCIOUS	AE8	174
SELF-DEFENSE	AA	458
	WB	184
	M15	151
SELF-DISCOVERED	CM	88
SELFE	MHD	2
	MHD	3
SELF-KINDLED	KT3	253
SELF-LOVE	PTL	1
SELF-MURTHER	UDH	12
SELF-PRESERVING	HAP	295
SELF-RESTRAINED	HIF	398
SELFSAME	L3	142
	HAP	592

SELFSAME	HAP	1126	SEND	AE11	74	SENSE	AA	868
	J10	317		AE11	434		AA	905
	J10	530		AE11	535		AA	965
	P6	154		AE11	551		ELB	17
SELINUS	AE3	926		AE12	631		ELB	29
SELL	PKK	8		AE12	649		MD	163
	PTW	6		OAL	490		MD	288
	AA	502		DO	97		MF	20
	AA	897		KT3	6		MF	55
	SAA	317		KT3	407		MF	89
	EDG	10		KT3	775		MF	117
	HAP	1146		KT3	954		MF	156
	J3	60		M11	315		MF	194
	J6	300		AU	195		SAA	33
	J10	123		AU	254		SAA	42
	P6	177		AU	497		SAA	50
	CI	299		WB	542		SAA	99
SELLING	PP	46		AS	59		SAA	105
SELLS	PR	33	SENDER	AE4	514		SAA	123
	J3	310	SENDEST	MN	12		SAA	173
	TJD	108		P3	66		SAA	270
SEMETHIS	AE7	1015	SENDS	EIE	2		SAA	409
SENATE	TA	492		AM	293		SAA	415
	HAP	664		ET	13		SAA	449
	HAP	1319		CM	111		SAA	529
	PDS	26		CM	113		SAA	1021
	J10	137		L4	5		SAA	1069
	P6	98		L4	48		PK	19
	VP6	95		HAP	488		PK	37
	AE4	981		J3	353		EDGA	13
	AE5	988		J10	446		RL	149
	AE7	846		P3	177		RL	157
	AE10	6		M1	94		RL	160
	AE10	155		G1	87		RL	186
	AE10	176		G1	165		RL	266
	AE11	363		G1	428		RL	332
	OAL	526		AE1	895		RL	357
	KT3	1016		AE3	209		PD	3
	HIF	331		AE3	603		EC	19
	WB	268		AE3	869		ER	62
SENATE'S	PUO1	41		AE4	327		L2	27
	HAP	845		AE5	687		L3	11
	G2	718		AE5	787		L3	40
SENATES	PUO5	13		AE7	391		L3	55
	SAA	262		AE7	329		L3	113
	SAA	755		AE7	602		L3	114
	SAA	761		AE7	943		L4	185
	SAA	782		AE7	988		T27	121
	TA	319		AE9	2		PAA	17
	AE1	593		AE9	1107		PAA	21
	AE6	928		AE10	387		HH	11
	KT3	411		AE10	402		HAP	83
	TJD	121		AE10	934		HAP	94
	CAM	54		AE11	776		HAP	107
	ESK	31		AE11	970		HAP	108
SENATORS	J1	176		AE11	1072		HAP	119
	J3	204		AE12	171		HAP	126
	P4	11		AE12	497		HAP	147
	AE7	238		AE12	634		HAP	379
	AE11	503		OAL	536		HAP	428
	OAL	96		KT2	209		HAP	462
	TJD	135		TJD	121		HAP	540
SEND	AM	326		M8	26		HAP	613
	AM	566		B	615		HAP	656
	AM	814		CAM	178		HAP	669
	STL	16		CAM	362		HAP	773
	PAR	12		M11	478		HAP	777
	PMQW	18	SENECA	UDH	70		HAP	779
	PNH	2		RL	79		HAP	935
	PSF	48	SENECA'S	EOE	5		HAP	957
	ELB	38	SENIOR	M15	14		HAP	1014
	ELB	40	SENNIGHT	C	78		HAP	1958
	HAP	909	SENSE	AR	168		HAP	2313
	HAP	2100		LC	110		PTS	14
	J1	54		PRL	12		PKA	6
	J3	500		EIE	6		MS	4
	P2	26		EIE	18		PSH	2
	P3	142		AM	1146		PSH	20
	M9	44		PTL	14		J3	434
	VP3	110		PCG1	25		J6	354
	VP3	119		EM	5		P1	34
	G3	503		PKK	3		P1	121
	AE2	939		PKK	21		P1	148
	AE5	661		PTC	22		P1	160
	AE5	909		ETC	13		P3	150
	AE7	362		PLG	15		P4	45
	AE8	13		CM	115		P6	49
	AE8	573		HP	253		M1	523
	AE8	616		DA	17		VP3	142
	AE9	227		PSF	8		G3	220
	AE9	259		PSF	12		AE1	796
	AE9	660		PUO4	9		AE2	428
	AE10	197		EUF	3		AE2	999
	AE10	685		PUO5	3		AE4	132
	AE10	729		PUO5	10		AE4	247
	AE11	40		AA	134		AE4	275

Word	Code	No.
SENSE	AE7	518
	AE8	250
	AE9	1054
	AE10	556
	AE10	940
	AE10	1178
	AE11	520
	AE11	759
	OAL	618
	MG	25
	MM	11
	KT2	334
	KT2	575
	KT3	808
	KT3	839
	TJD	124
	B	311
	B	424
	B	455
	B	732
	BP	9
	M10	55
	M10	88
	CAM	233
	CAM	307
	CAM	350
	HIF	326
	C	201
	C	818
	AU	218
	AU	497
	M15	396
	M15	572
	GP	10
	CI	10
	CI	113
	CI	127
	CI	168
	CI	224
	CI	366
	AS	34
	EWR	18
SENSELESS	ETL	18
	L3	67
	TA	65
	SKA6	19
	PSH	26
	J3	208
	P1	70
	P3	62
	GK	150
	GK	159
	GP	117
	PTP	37
SENSES	L3	160
	HAP	91
	HAP	366
	J10	334
	J10	379
	VCS	23
	AE7	498
	KT2	19
	KT2	120
	B	749
	C	108
	FL	139
SENSIBLE	HP	92
	M1	1061
	AE10	1230
	B	270
SENSUAL	KT3	231
SENT	UDH	63
	HS	115
	HS	137
	SMA	51
	SMA	62
	LC	93
	LC	125
	PWG	9
	VHH	27
	AM	124
	AM	411
	AM	569
	AM	834
	AM	836
	AM	918
	AM	1095
	AM	1158
	PMQ	20
	PCG1	38
	PLN	38
	PCD	3
	PUF	5
	MF	32
	MF	213
	SAA	229

Word	Code	No.
SENT	SAA	345
	PDG	6
	OE	12
	L4	217
	L4	235
	T18	29
	TA	208
	TA	266
	GE	19
	HAP	206
	HAP	1209
	HAP	1886
	HAP	2166
	HAP	2427
	HAP	2451
	BR	4
	BR	27
	BR	64
	BR	251
	BR	254
	PKA	20
	EL	339
	ODA	13
	EH	16
	J6	606
	J6	721
	J6	815
	J10	25
	J10	28
	J10	108
	J10	204
	J10	435
	M1	73
	M1	297
	M9	95
	M13	208
	HI	68
	DHP	19
	VP3	109
	VP10	67
	G2	465
	G4	233
	G4	774
	AE1	408
	AE1	730
	AE2	159
	AE2	637
	AE2	741
	AE3	72
	AE3	73
	AE3	129
	AE3	280
	AE3	436
	AE3	598
	AE3	806
	AE4	394
	AE4	514
	AE4	995
	AE5	875
	AE5	914
	AE5	976
	AE6	27
	AE6	475
	AE6	545
	AE6	625
	AE6	1034
	AE6	1080
	AE7	424
	AE7	1027
	AE7	1033
	AE8	188
	AE8	230
	AE8	622
	AE8	664
	AE8	748
	AE9	20
	AE9	156
	AE9	225
	AE9	503
	AE9	512
	AE9	570
	AE9	644
	AE9	665
	AE9	699
	AE9	726
	AE9	733
	AE9	795
	AE9	829
	AE9	1002
	AE9	1086
	AE10	54
	AE10	251
	AE10	260
	AE10	264
	AE10	472
	AE10	489

Word	Code	No.
SENT	AE10	560
	AE10	708
	AE10	754
	AE10	848
	AE10	1067
	AE10	1111
	AE10	1196
	AE10	1264
	AE11	68
	AE11	149
	AE11	168
	AE11	257
	AE11	839
	AE11	995
	AE11	1243
	AE12	130
	AE12	152
	AE12	524
	AE12	750
	AE12	923
	AE12	947
	AE12	1147
	AE12	1237
	OAL	209
	OAL	239
	OAL	472
	DO	36
	KT1	143
	KT1	160
	KT1	603
	KT3	19
	KT3	360
	KT3	488
	KT3	622
	KT3	700
	KT3	1027
	KT3	1153
	M8	192
	M8	401
	B	153
	B	613
	B	719
	BP	19
	BP	107
	CAM	328
	HIF	4
	HIF	74
	HIF	93
	HIF	221
	HIF	180
	HIF	313
	HIF	538
	HIF	606
	C	376
	C	700
	TH	233
	TH	320
	M12	115
	M12	130
	M12	389
	M12	358
	M12	483
	M12	492
	M12	561
	AU	33
	AU	277
	AU	284
	AU	344
	AU	384
	AU	522
	WB	170
	WB	329
	M15	715
	GP	74
	CI	254
	CI	271
	CI	317
	CI	486
	CI	487
	CI	571
	CI	591
	AS	79
	AS	94
	EWR	5
SENTENCE	AM	1074
	AM	1075
	PO	19
	HP	122
	SAA	581
	AE2	179
	AE6	581
	TH	173
SENTENCED	SAA	438
	AE2	106
SENTRIES	G4	607
	AE1	660

SENTRIES	AE2	330
	AE6	777
SENTRY	AE6	389
	BP	131
SEPARATE	MD	170
	SAA	643
	HAP	2571
	AE6	954
SEPARATES	CI	148
SEPARATION	PPC	23
	EDS	2
SEPULCHER	P1	77
	M1	521
	AE2	875
	AE5	104
	AE5	128
	B	755
	BP	176
	M11	429
	M15	607
	M15	634
SEPULCHERS	J10	232
	AE4	552
	AE6	446
	AE12	1250
SEQUACIOUS	SSC	50
SEQUEL	AE3	54
SEQUESTRATIONS	SAA	313
SERAPHIMS	AK	11
SERAPHS	BR	44
SERENADE	EUO	18
	P5	239
SERENE	D	26
	SAA	29
	SAA	948
	SAA	1121
	L1	11
	L2	23
	L3	182
	TA	9
	J10	552
	AE1	180
	AE1	347
	AE2	157
	AE8	697
	AE12	1204
	KT2	348
	TJD	16
	BP	163
SERENELY	TA	240
	EL	307
	M1	444
	AE1	708
	AE1	825
	AE7	10
	KT3	167
SERENER	G1	540
SERES	G2	169
SERESTHUS	AE9	216
	AE9	1051
	AE10	755
	AE12	806
SERESTUS	AE1	863
SERGESTHUS	AE5	160
	AE5	240
	AE5	263
	AE5	284
	AE5	355
SERGESTHUS'	AE5	648
SERGESTUS	AE1	719
SERGIAN	AE5	160
SERGIUS	J10	442
SERIES	AR	292
	AA	1028
	TA	508
	AE1	1057
SERIOUS	EWGR	41
	PAR	9
	PSF	37
	KT3	471
	TJD	60
SERMON	EMM	1
	HAP	1511
	WB	509
	GP	78
SERMONS	PSF	21
	HAP	912
SERPENT	AM	491
	AA	634
	M1	596
	G1	269
	AE5	112
	AE7	491
	AE11	1106
	KT1	492
	C	563
SERPENT	M12	32
SERPENTINE	MD	257
SERPENT'S	HAP	1937
	VP4	28
SERPENTS	SAA	452
	P1	219
	G2	194
	G2	211
	G2	433
	AE2	270
	AE2	296
	AE7	911
	AE7	1036
	AE8	384
	AE12	1228
	CAM	93
SERRANUS	AE9	451
	AE9	605
SERVANT	PP	44
	ETS	8
	KT1	429
	KT3	157
	KT3	229
	BP	37
	TH	233
	EMKG	23
SERVANT'S	AM	1056
	L1	46
	EL	55
SERVANTS	HS	30
	PRL	33
	AM	378
	ECG1	31
	EM	29
	AA	102
	AA	626
	AA	998
	PDG	37
	EL	49
	J3	240
	J3	419
	J6	378
	J6	614
	J6	656
	P4	69
	HI	16
	AE2	968
	AE5	346
	AE6	60
	AE8	770
	KT1	601
	B	272
	FL	504
	WB	283
	J3	278
	J10	371
SERVANTS'	FL	179
SERVE	JH	26
	SMA	110
	EWGR	26
	PW	23
	EMW	12
	AA	192
	AA	494
	AA	504
	AA	611
	D	46
	SAA	812
	RL	45
	RL	456
	L4	179
	PAA	21
	HAP	320
	HAP	863
	HAP	2147
	HAP	2158
	PP	15
	PSH	11
	P3	150
	SLT1	13
	VP3	142
	G3	106
	AE1	987
	AE7	316
	AE8	681
	AE11	339
	AE11	1155
	KT1	396
	KT2	98
	KT2	150
	KT2	370
	KT2	396
	B	84
	BP	169
	HIF	327
	C	401
SERVE	WB	234
	WB	320
	M15	177
	GP	63
	ETP	12
SERVED	AR	145
	AR	192
	EUO2	20
	ETC	11
	AA	121
	ELB	1
	MD	53
	PDG	9
	HAP	1359
	HAP	2268
	J1	157
	M1	1041
	M9	47
	M13	131
	VP3	68
	AE4	977
	AE6	247
	AE8	241
	AE11	46
	KT1	231
	KT1	582
	KT2	381
	KT3	1091
	B	132
	B	555
	BP	92
	BP	99
	BP	109
	HIF	641
	HIF	680
	C	690
	TH	157
	TH	262
	WB	8
	CI	315
SERVES	H2	32
	HAP	1692
	PDS	20
	J3	209
	M1	301
	OAL	664
	KT2	232
	TJD	171
SERVICE	HS	97
	SAA	952
	SAA	989
	RL	45
	HAP	860
	J6	171
	OAL	186
	OAL	413
	OAL	650
	KT1	579
	KT2	281
	KT3	781
	KT3	1131
	KT3	951
	KT3	979
	HIF	728
	FL	440
	FL	597
	AU	190
	CI	196
SERVICES	J3	211
	J10	376
	G2	144
	G4	221
	OAE2	35
SERVILE	AA	332
	SAA	24
	H2	17
	EL	118
	J3	131
	J6	24
	J10	147
	P1	236
	P5	185
	G4	307
	G4	314
	AE2	1068
	AE6	795
	AE12	358
	HIF	191
	HIF	611
	M15	80
SERVILELY	PTL	14
SERVITUDE	P5	231
	G3	268
SERVIUS	WB	448
SESSIONS	AE10	176
SESTIAN	G3	414

Word	Code	Number
SET	UDH	56
	HS	34
	AR	205
	SMA	87
	DC	12
	PWG	29
	VHH	3
	AM	47
	AM	378
	PEL	1
	PCG1	37
	EMQW	19
	EM	28
	ECD	11
	PUO2	13
	PC1	8
	POE	16
	PSF	40
	PUO5	6
	AA	98
	AA	479
	D	22
	MF	210
	SAA	523
	SAA	533
	PDG	47
	PK	15
	RL	276
	RL	305
	OE	44
	AT	11
	AT	88
	MO	8
	T27	44
	TA	223
	TA	412
	PAA	33
	PAA	41
	EAA	3
	EAA	30
	MN	13
	HAP	87
	HAP	364
	HAP	479
	HAP	732
	HAP	750
	HAP	819
	HAP	854
	HAP	1096
	HAP	1142
	HAP	1300
	HAP	1749
	HAP	1982
	PDS	39
	PP	3
	PKA	38
	EKA	31
	J1	236
	J6	587
	J10	56
	J10	561
	P3	69
	P3	71
	P3	226
	P4	21
	P5	47
	P5	51
	P5	135
	P6	75
	M1	923
	VCS	5
	SLT1	17
	SLT1	23
	VP2	67
	VP3	72
	VP4	15
	VP9	7
	G1	413
	G1	485
	G2	386
	G2	605
	G2	708
	G2	794
	G3	249
	G3	261
	G4	43
	G4	45
	G4	400
	G4	607
	AE1	273
	AE1	617
	AE1	920
	AE1	924
	AE2	142
	AE2	797
	AE4	588

Word	Code	Number
SET	AE4	852
	AE4	864
	AE4	963
	AE6	820
	AE6	971
	AE7	239
	AE7	507
	AE8	237
	AE8	579
	AE8	583
	AE8	648
	AE8	745
	AE9	929
	AE10	205
	AE10	230
	AE10	503
	AE10	657
	AE10	958
	AE11	245
	AE11	496
	AE11	526
	MG	22
	DO	13
	DO	124
	KT2	134
	KT2	266
	KT3	54
	KT3	69
	KT3	77
	KT3	682
	KT3	744
	TJD	194
	B	50
	B	63
	B	263
	B	401
	B	675
	BP	74
	BP	114
	HIF	36
	HIF	433
	HIF	497
	HIF	522
	HIF	642
	C	442
	TH	260
	FL	86
	FL	162
	FL	167
	FL	239
	FL	261
	FL	292
	FL	437
	M12	215
	M12	545
	AU	1
	WB	95
	WB	206
	M15	275
	SMP	49
SETS	HS	105
	LCA	38
	AM	852
	PMQ	54
	SEL4	13
	PCG2	16
	HP	35
	AA	688
	MD	87
	PD	42
	PKA	33
	J6	331
	J6	791
	P5	257
	M9	139
	AE1	965
	AE3	574
	AE7	995
	AE8	603
	AE12	1054
	BP	56
	BP	83
	WB	40
SETTEST	MF	199
SETTING	LC	87
	AA	268
	L2	26
	GE	64
	HAP	678
	HAP	2588
	P6	104
	M1	866
	VP6	121
	G1	77
	G1	547
	G1	601

Word	Code	Number
SETTING	G2	411
	G4	674
	AE2	12
	AE8	79
	MG	35
	KT1	4
	TJD	66
	B	338
	HIF	797
	M11	271
SETTLE	MF	10
	HAP	1872
	J6	53
	AE11	493
	BP	44
SETTLED	AA	796
	J3	261
	J3	435
	G1	558
	G3	781
	AE1	8
	AE3	679
	HIF	97
SETTLEMENT	PR	8
	T27	59
	ELT	31
SETTLES	BR	244
SETTLING	M9	70
	AE1	124
SEVEN	AM	107
	EUF	10
	EM	26
	DA	90
	SAA	399
	HAP	1202
	HAP	2469
	BR	185
	J1	145
	J6	263
	J6	837
	HI	72
	GK	132
	VP2	45
	G2	783
	G3	548
	G4	302
	G4	736
	AE1	46
	AE1	107
	AE1	241
	AE1	268
	AE1	269
	AE1	529
	AE1	1064
	AE5	113
	AE5	538
	AE5	814
	AE6	27
	AE6	58
	AE6	59
	AE6	361
	AE6	880
	AE8	589
	AE9	203
	AE9	204
	AE10	453
	AE10	455
	KT2	368
	C	365
	C	444
	M11	495
SEVENFOLD	MN	11
	M9	167
	VCS	14
	G4	409
	AE6	1091
	AE12	1340
	AU	2
	AU	532
SEVENTH	EL	72
	G1	379
SEVENTY	PLB	29
SEVERAL	AM	763
	AM	818
	AM	819
	PMM	12
	PEL	15
	AA	13
	AA	14
	AA	140
	AA	494
	ELB	4
	MD	294
	SAA	213
	RL	141
	RL	309

SEVERAL			SEX			SHADE		
SEVERAL	RL	425	SEX	PT	34	SHADE	M13	8
	HAP	683		EUO2	26		M13	73
	HAP	690		PC1	5		M13	104
	HAP	1025		EAL	21		MC	75
	HAP	2540		EMK	10		GK	37
	EL	164		HP	41		VP1	1
	J6	361		HP	185		VP1	117
	J10	42		HP	249		VP2	3
	M1	564		ELB	13		VP2	8
	M1	583		EPC	20		VP2	68
	VP2	94		PPC	4		VP3	81
	G1	78		M1	441		VP4	2
	G1	321		M9	61		VP5	3
	G1	527		EDGA	28		VP5	72
	G1	687		L3	221		VP5	112
	G2	47		T27	33		VP8	21
	G2	53		PTS	28		G1	235
	G2	119		PTS	32		G2	52
	G2	162		PTS	41		G2	80
	G2	247		STS3	11		G2	409
	G2	749		EL	175		G2	609
	G4	228		J6	193		G2	614
	G4	523		J6	355		G3	517
	AE2	37		J6	446		G3	662
	AE2	572		J6	458		G4	33
	AE2	447		J6	467		G4	210
	AE3	259		J6	674		G4	217
	AE4	590		J6	762		G4	552
	AE5	397		J6	845		G4	684
	AE5	985		ELT	16		G4	726
	AE6	10		VP6	88		G4	817
	AE7	198		AE6	609		AE2	703
	AE10	290		AE9	177		AE2	751
	OAL	878		AE12	201		AE3	35
	KT3	24		OAL	475		AE3	299
	KT3	748		OAL	762		AE3	402
	CI	149		OAL	779		AE3	577
	PMK	5		OAL	790		AE4	560
	TH	201		OAL	804		AE5	177
SEVERALLY	HAP	897		KT3	157		AE5	945
SEVERE	EWG	12		KT3	228		AE5	959
	PRL	35		KT3	861		AE6	12
	S	3		KT3	984		AE6	172
	A	3		B	32		AE6	616
	PUO2	24		C	130		AE6	642
	E	18		C	561		AE6	686
	PC1	1		C	572		AE6	947
	AA	441		TH	415		AE6	893
	SAA	165		M12	241		AE6	1066
	RL	233		M12	248		AE7	51
	ER	33		M12	628		AE7	776
	TA	235		WB	97		AE8	214
	HAP	295		WB	129		AE8	359
	HAP	2323		WB	153		AE8	791
	EKA	9		WB	234		AE9	4
	J6	259		WB	279		AE9	231
	M1	327		WB	285		AE9	506
	M1	922		CI	44		AE9	699
	G4	701		C1	368		AE9	849
	AE3	2		EMKG	17		AE10	235
	AE4	394		EMKG	40		AE10	728
	AE6	1119	SEXANGULAR	M15	563		AE10	901
	AE6	1162	SEXES	EMQW	20		AE10	921
	AE6	1220		EMQW	24		AE11	1293
	AE11	42		EM	18		AE12	1112
	AE11	161		PR	32		AE12	1153
	AF	76		L4	247		OAL	118
	KT2	540		J10	478		DO	106
	KT3	501		M9	105		B	703
	KT3	917		OAL	311		C	702
	B	361		KT3	867		TH	102
	B	596		M15	614		TH	108
	B	627	SEX'S	TH	397		M11	349
	HIF	316		WB	135		M11	377
	AU	209	SFORZA	AR	201		FL	85
	AU	292	SHACKLES	J3	487		FL	204
	WB	108	SHADE	HS	60		FL	259
	GP	12		RH	65		FL	314
	GP	79		LC	138		FL	320
	CI	4		AM	234		FL	330
SEVERED	AM	505		SCG1	1		FL	343
	AE6	645		SCG1	17		FL	351
	M15	441		HP	142		FL	382
SEVERELY	AM	208		AA	635		FL	441
	EM	15		MF	27		FL	461
	J1	149		AT	31		M12	678
	P3	101		L2	34		WB	212
	AE3	334		T27	86		CI	80
	AE6	779		TA	256		LC	104
	AE7	927	SHADED	TA	291	SHADED	SCG1	10
SEVERER	P1	22		HAP	352		AE2	329
SEVEREST	J10	488		HAP	511		AE5	375
SEVERITY	ETS	26		J6	3		AE11	955
SEVERUS	AE7	984		J10	403		AE12	184
SEW	OAL	780		M1	281		MFL	13
SEX	LCA	43		M1	942		KT2	238

SHADED			SHADOW			SHAFT			SHAFT	AE5	681

SHADED
M8 85
FL 278
CI 100

SHADES
RH 3
AM 514
AM 1063
SCG1 19
PUO2 4
EUO2 6
PTC 4
RL 182
T18 14
T23 48
T27 15
H29 37
H29 38
AK 114
HAP 231
HAP 2337
EL 141
J1 15
J3 22
J3 501
J10 178
P3 3
M1 50
M1 805
M1 814
M9 29
M13 110
GK 69
VP6 79
VP7 16
VP7 67
VP8 19
VP10 111
G1 467
G2 427
G2 692
G3 603
G3 631
G3 706
G3 778
G4 579
G4 718
G4 742
AE1 229
AE1 420
AE1 856
AE2 841
AE2 995
AE2 1047
AE3 663
AE4 505
AE4 1002
AE5 969
AE6 378
AE6 180
AE6 203
AE6 425
AE6 599
AE6 613
AE6 638
AE6 861
AE6 1022
AE6 1199
AE7 41
AE7 123
AE7 566
AE7 1062
AE8 128
AE9 521
AE9 538
AE9 660
AE10 275
AE10 754
AE10 934
AE11 281
AE11 346
AE11 874
AE11 1243
AE12 763
AE12 1043
KT2 620
M8 311
M8 316
B 247
CAM 348
HIF 4
FL 71
FL 485
M12 188
M12 360
M12 476
AU 37

SHADOW
AR 192

SHADOW
AM 604
TA 107
HAP 621
J10 22
J10 31
GK 30
AE2 990
AE5 528
AE6 285
AE6 466
AE6 951
AE10 742
AE10 925
M15 167

SHADOWS
AM 504
AA 269
L2 62
HAP 1222
BR 318
M1 830
GK 14
VP2 98
VP5 6
G1 181
G4 679
AE4 8
AE5 14
AE6 297
AE6 733
AE6 738
AE8 45
AE10 360
AE10 832
AE10 1177
AE11 36
AE11 320
KT2 27
M15 452

SHADWELL
MF 15
MF 17
MF 20
MF 47
MF 48
MF 103
MF 114
J1 122

SHADWELL'S
MF 23
MF 86
MF 95
RL 456

SHADY
DC 12
AM 382
AT 7
STS3 2
J6 702
M1 768
M13 154
VP1 6
VP5 119
VP8 82
VP9 55
VP10 59
G2 3
G2 649
G2 663
G4 74
G4 624
G4 785
AE1 267
AE1 429
AE1 810
AE3 500
AE3 761
AE4 167
AE6 262
AE6 523
AE6 639
AE6 660
AE6 1036
AE6 1136
AE7 151
AE7 666
AE8 48
AE8 270
AE9 99
OAL 32
OAL 73
OAL 325
KT1 222
KT1 259
B 202
M12 557
WB 44

SHAFT
M1 594
AE4 96
AE5 316

SHAFT
AE5 681
AE5 687
AE9 786
AE11 1246
AE12 946
OAE1 27
KT1 255
KT3 954
M8 152
M12 753
M12 804

SHAFTS
MN 12
HAP 6
M1 616
M1 621
M1 626
VP3 18
G2 627
G3 571
AE9 227
AE10 248
AE11 1138
AE12 604
AE12 1002
HIF 65
HIF 96
HIF 529
M12 796
AU 74

SHAGGED
G4 371
AE8 353

SHAGGY
AK 117
VP8 49
G3 452
AE3 776
AE5 459
AE7 926
AE8 240

SHAKE
AM 26
ESF 30
AA 203
AA 796
AA 956
L2 62
L3 113
L3 289
ESH 18
J3 176
J10 47
G1 238
G3 819
G4 271
AE2 235
AE3 854
AE4 438
AE5 259
AE5 888
AE6 122
AE7 472
AE7 721
AE8 790
AE9 871
AE11 1268
AE12 305
OAE1 12
AF 41
AF 46
CAM 93
M15 353

SHAKEN
CM 91
M1 358
M1 978
G4 119
AE3 82
AE4 645
AE5 29
AE9 830
HIF 712
FL 580

SHAKES
AR 109
AM 588
AM 1174
H29 83
TA 473
HAP 2455
J1 16
J6 694
J10 31
P5 76
P5 77
G2 683
G3 138
G3 312
AE1 85
AE1 1045
AE3 883

SHAKES	AE3	760
	AE5	277
	AE5	912
	AE6	392
	AE6	654
	AE6	771
	AE6	817
	AE7	485
	AE7	632
	AE7	999
	AE7	1112
	AE8	780
	AE8	827
	AE8	934
	AE9	83
	AE9	632
	AE9	970
	AE9	1075
	AE10	154
	AE10	1009
	AE10	1021
	AE10	1079
	AE11	1037
	AE12	375
	AE12	640
	AE12	1023
	OAL	25
	OAL	269
	OAL	516
	M8	101
	M12	685
	WB	22
	M15	422
	M15	517
	M15	602
SHAKESPEARE	PT	5
	PT	27
	PTC	1
	PMS	27
	GK	73
	MC	63
SHAKESPEARE'S	PT	3
	PT	14
	PT	16
	PT	19
	PT	24
	PUO2	21
	PAZ	14
	PC1	16
	PMS	29
	PLT	47
SHAKING	L3	290
	J16	86
	AE2	728
	AE6	802
	M11	77
SHALLOW	AK	110
	J3	369
	P3	56
	VP3	151
	G1	213
	G2	396
	G3	809
	G3	798
	AM	715
SHALLOWS	AE1	160
SHAM	T27	48
	EMKG	32
SHAME	AR	206
	AR	230
	AM	758
	PMQ	15
	PCG1	3
	ECG1	4
	EM	25
	PAZ	13
	ML	24
	HP	24
	HP	205
	DA	149
	EUF	34
	PLB	32
	SAA	294
	SAA	370
	OE	59
	L4	240
	T27	30
	TA	344
	HAP	51
	HAP	77
	HAP	164
	HAP	1147
	HAP	1577
	HAP	1696
	HAP	2108
	HAP	2151

SHAME	J3	103
	J3	265
	J6	354
	J6	474
	J10	509
	J10	511
	P2	14
	P5	151
	M1	164
	M1	844
	M1	1054
	M1	1055
	M1	1062
	M9	179
	HI	135
	VP7	64
	G3	40
	AE2	1068
	AE4	29
	AE4	250
	AE4	275
	AE4	324
	AE4	132
	AE4	466
	AE4	870
	AE5	606
	AE5	618
	AE5	884
	AE6	690
	AE9	811
	AE9	1061
	AE10	215
	AE10	556
	AE10	939
	AE10	1248
	AE11	926
	AE11	1018
	AE11	1077
	AE12	346
	AE12	890
	AE12	937
	AE12	942
	AE12	970
	OAL	808
	KT2	100
	KT2	623
	KT3	319
	KT3	733
	KT3	1090
	KT3	1095
	B	339
	B	457
	B	587
	M10	66
	CAM	122
	CAM	185
	CAM	204
	CAM	215
	CAM	277
	CAM	307
	HIF	494
	C	126
	C	773
	C	774
	FL	615
	M12	282
	M12	623
	M12	662
	AU	61
	AU	96
	AU	362
	CI	65
	CI	133
SHAMED	EMKG	25
	ER	44
	HAP	1544
	TJD	194
	AU	80
	AU	310
SHAME-FACED	HP	183
SHAMEFACED	SLN	6
SHAMEFUL	CM	37
	MD	206
	P4	94
	AE10	509
	AE10	976
	AE11	86
	AE12	933
	OAL	759
	KT3	304
	FL	301
	M12	704
	AU	350
	SAA	503
SHAMEFULLY		
SHAMELESS	J6	512
SHAMES	RH	6

SHAMING	ETC	13
SHAMMED	PK	33
SHAPE	E	2
	HP	47
	AA	49
	OE	29
	L4	163
	L4	229
	T23	22
	NS	23
	AK	102
	AK	136
	AK	150
	HAP	269
	J10	314
	P4	32
	M1	277
	M1	1027
	M9	115
	M13	157
	G1	680
	G2	128
	G3	145
	G4	598
	G4	640
	AE1	929
	AE1	958
	AE1	993
	AE2	822
	AE4	389
	AE4	804
	AE5	805
	AE10	547
	AE12	344
	AE12	689
	AE12	1136
	AE12	1290
	OAL	288
	OAL	871
	KT1	264
	KT3	232
	CAM	350
	C	120
	M11	314
	M11	328
	M12	735
	M15	298
	M15	327
	M15	561
	CI	51
SHAPED	G4	139
SHAPELESS	AA	172
	G3	385
SHAPES	SMA	44
	EMQw	16
	L3	34
	L4	62
	M1	542
	G2	123
	AE1	565
	AE2	499
	AE6	399
	AE7	27
	AE7	129
	AE9	846
	KT2	585
	M11	334
	M11	490
	FL	482
	M12	528
	H2	82
SHARDS	HAP	321
SHARE	LC	44
	LC	46
	LC	118
	LC	150
	AM	996
	AM	1207
	PCD	23
	EUO2	10
	PTW	30
	AA	789
	AA	956
	MF	176
	SAA	114
	SAA	248
	SAA	763
	RL	395
	L4	163
	L4	192
	TA	378
	HAP	297
	HAP	338
	HAP	457
	HAP	900
	HAP	2064

Headword	Code	Ref
SHARE	EL	113
	EL	209
	ESH	25
	J1	151
	J1	178
	J1	188
	J3	439
	J16	84
	PPS	5
	P5	261
	P6	52
	P6	155
	M1	94
	M1	173
	M9	16
	VP3	118
	G1	71
	G1	101
	G1	187
	G1	243
	G1	253
	G1	354
	G2	455
	G3	777
	G4	230
	G4	356
	G4	366
	G4	698
	AE1	269
	AE1	294
	AE2	115
	AE2	921
	AE2	965
	AE3	786
	AE4	163
	AE5	81
	AE5	1005
	AE7	350
	AE7	879
	AE7	978
	AE7	1050
	AE8	106
	AE8	421
	AE9	59
	AE9	217
	AE9	258
	AE9	295
	AE9	359
	AE9	405
	AE9	582
	AE9	700
	AE9	734
	AE10	519
	AE11	48
	AE11	62
	AE11	93
	AE11	168
	AE11	264
	AE11	331
	AE11	492
	AE11	577
	AE11	680
	AE11	873
	AE11	1286
	AE12	56
	AE12	288
	AE12	353
	AE12	886
	AE12	924
	DO	82
	KT1	497
	KT2	400
	KT3	1049
	TJD	42
	TJD	170
	TJD	180
	M8	224
	B	17
	B	331
	B	678
	BP	199
	HIF	380
	HIF	502
	HIF	730
	C	265
	M11	50
	M11	171
	M11	249
	M12	5
	AU	155
	AU	166
	AU	329
	AU	421
	AU	473
	AU	536
	WB	504
SHARE	WB	525
	M15	189
SHARED	AR	41
	SMA	18
	L4	207
	BR	33
	BR	338
	AE1	274
	AE2	758
	AE4	796
	AE5	302
	AE5	338
	AE5	350
	AE9	233
	AE9	1019
	AE12	730
	KT3	291
	HIF	509
	M12	710
	CI	508
	EP	3
SHARES	RH	106
	LC	44
	AM	485
	EKK	14
	L4	221
	BR	218
	M1	1045
	VP4	40
	G1	220
	G3	274
	AE3	202
	KT1	534
	KT3	565
SHAREST	TJD	196
SHARING	MD	307
SHARON	SAA	58
SHARP	AM	757
	AM	1133
	DA	199
	MD	189
	PD	5
	L4	113
	HAP	1327
	HAP	1581
	HAP	2442
	SSC	37
	PTS	1
	J10	285
	P3	41
	P5	21
	M1	633
	M1	687
	M13	91
	SLT1	12
	G3	234
	G3	358
	G4	107
	G4	397
	AE3	33
	AE6	1219
	AE9	75
	AE9	711
	MG	19
	HIF	317
	HIF	638
	C	402
	TH	165
	M11	446
	M12	377
SHARPEN	M12	498
SHARPENED	M12	574
	G1	357
	HAP	1290
	VP4	40
	G1	542
	G1	582
	G2	33
	AE2	283
	AE3	847
	AE10	1155
	AE11	1289
	DO	82
	KT2	571
	KT2	599
	TJD	103
	M8	138
	M10	98
	M11	80
	M12	413
	M12	459
	M15	147
	M13	48
	KT3	442
SHARPENING	J6	327
SHARPENS	G1	391
SHARPER	OE	11
	PD	39
	G3	803
	OAL	383
	C	121
	M12	514
SHARPERS	EDS	35
SHARP-EYED	M15	619
SHARP-GRINDED	KT3	513
SHARP-HEADED	G3	126
SHARPING	PKA	38
	EKA	18
SHARP-JUDGING	AA	877
SHARP-KEELED	AM	627
SHARPLY	HAP	1303
	HAP	1489
	HAP	2050
	J3	204
	OAL	100
	OAL	551
	B	482
SHARPNESS	B	69
	WB	478
SHARP-TASTED	G2	175
SHARP-WITTED	L4	154
SHATTER	AE4	641
	AE10	415
SHATTERED	AM	89
	AM	115
	AM	258
	HAP	1100
	P6	71
	G2	621
	G3	44
	AE1	226
	AE4	71
	AE5	356
	AE5	287
	AE5	648
	AE9	685
	M12	458
	J3	308
SHAVE	AA	277
SHEAF	HAP	2296
	KT3	282
	G1	430
SHEAFS	M8	7
SHEAR	T27	67
	VP3	143
	G3	679
	G3	837
SHEARING	P4	64
	VP3	120
	G3	680
SHEARS	AT	70
	H2	25
	G3	485
	AE10	1155
	AE12	257
SHEATH	CAM	313
	HIF	329
SHEATHE	BR	177
	PDS	33
	J6	159
	AE2	1018
	AE5	536
	AE7	954
	AE8	602
	KT2	271
	HIF	323
SHEATHED	AE9	409
	AE10	746
	AE12	137
	KT2	613
	HIF	295
SHEATHES	HAP	1564
SHEAVES	M9	34
SHED	PIE	10
	STL	9
	PFD	28
	MF	135
	T18	14
	TA	347
	HAP	1269
	BR	12
	EL	351
	J3	59
	SAA	646
	M1	796
	VP8	65
	G2	558
	G3	440
	AE1	932
	AE4	457
	AE4	528
	AE7	1067

SHED
AE8	484
AE9	672
AE12	100
OAL	324
M8	39
B	687
B	697
BP	30
BP	157
CAM	111
FL	592
M11	378
WB	11
M15	620

SHEDDEST AE11 270

SHEDDING
HAP	1733
M11	357

SHEDS
AA	229
M1	156
G3	520
AE3	447
AE4	380
AE6	1129
AE7	315
AE8	132
AE12	262
CAM	352
HIF	576
M11	289

SHEEP
RL	89
T27	67
H29	61
H2	25
HAP	286
HAP	1005
HAP	1420
J1	164
J3	239
J6	4
J6	217
P2	90
P6	30
M1	414
M13	161
HI	75
VP1	110
VP2	8
VP3	1
VP3	3
VP3	95
VP3	146
VP5	36
VP7	2
VP7	56
VP10	24
VP10	54
VP10	97
G1	3
G1	354
G1	366
G1	644
G2	203
G2	277
G2	464
G2	607
G3	464
G3	478
G3	637
G3	680
G3	705
G3	829
G4	190
G4	464
G4	579
AE3	844
AE4	911
AE5	129
AE6	230
AE7	134
AE8	722
AE11	303
AE12	996
KT1	477
M8	8
M8	40
FL	320
M15	117
M15	168
M15	696

SHEEPFOLDS G4 469

SHEEPHOOK VP5 137

SHEEPHOOKS LS 16

SHEET
UDH	4
AM	986

SHEETS
AR	232
AM	222

SHEETS
AM	448
T18	33
J6	280
J6	375
G1	437
G1	513
AE1	148
AE2	1030
AE5	914
AE5	1084
AE10	574
CAM	296
M11	151

SHE-JOCKEYS ETG 20

SHEKEL
AA	391
SAA	930

SHEKELS SAA 359

SHELF
PLN	13
PD	17
H2	101
HAP	829
OD	19

SHELFS AE5 1132

SHELFY AE5 230

SHELL
AE5	1125
SSC	17
SSC	22
M1	453
AE10	300
KT3	1069

SHELLS
P2	118
M13	71
G2	476
M10	38
M15	406

SHELTER
AM	245
AM	346
PCG1	4
SCG1	20
HP	5
DA	96
HAP	1922
M1	155
M1	305
M1	725
G1	526
G3	811
G4	620
AE1	776
AE2	705
AE2	714
AE2	1001
AE3	500
AE4	174
AE4	503
AE7	320
AE9	538
AE10	925
AE10	1142
C	672
C	764
FL	315
FL	382
FL	387

SHELTERED
DC	53
DA	128
G2	26

SHELVES
CI	394
SAA	846
SAA	1088
RL	425
AE1	155
AE5	214
AE7	12
AE10	957
M10	38

SHELVINGS AE5 219

SHENT
G2	621
C	110

SHEPHERD
SEL3	22
SM2	20
AA	431
SAA	742
T27	1
H29	34
H2	87
HAP	1005
M13	53
M13	62
VP2	1
VP2	103
VP3	1
VP5	11
VP7	55
VP7	65
VP10	24

SHEPHERD
VP10	56
G2	607
G3	3
G3	442
G3	533
G3	541
G3	638
G3	694
G4	558
G4	621
AE2	413
AE3	863
AE4	95
AE7	941
AE10	567
AE12	461

SHEPHERDESS
AM	1181
J3	163

SHEPHERD'S
AT	55
AT	110
STS3	4
M1	690
M1	933
VP5	65
G4	627
AE11	854
AE11	1184

SHEPHERDS
PLB	15
LS	3
J6	4
VP2	42
VP3	95
VP5	59
VP5	92
VP9	44
G3	680
G3	701
G4	397
G4	818
AE2	75
AE4	380
AE7	716
AE12	996
M8	41

SHEPHERDS'
G1	19
G3	720
AE1	583
AE8	132

SHE-PRIVATEERS PWR 8

SHERD BP 86

SHERDS G2 482

SHERIFFS
ET	13
PK	42
PDG	3

SHE-TYRANT J6 316

SHEVA SAA 1025

SHEW
UDH	30
AR	194
AR	256
RH	14
AM	483
AM	756
PMQ	52
EMQ	8
HP	59
HP	120
AA	556
AA	751
AA	950
AA	1006
MF	154
SAA	377
SAA	401
SAA	531
AT	26
HAP	90
HAP	1095
HAP	1164
HAP	1192
HAP	2229
EKA	7
EKA	32
J6	119
G3	40
AE5	766
AE6	290
AE7	510
AE8	676
AE8	784
AE9	299
OAL	61
OAL	667
KT1	269
KT1	573
KT3	85.5
B	395

Headword	Ref	No.
SHEW	CAM	167
	HIF	443
	M12	629
	GP	138
	CI	51
	CI	533
SHEWED	HS	19
	HS	59
	RH	76
	PUO2	14
	AA	431
	AA	924
	AK	113
	SAA	385
	EC	4
	MO	20
	HAP	397
	HAP	548
	BR	130
	EKA	15
	VP3	62
	M9	66
	AE2	919
	AE5	779
	AE6	549
	AE8	445
	AE9	428
	AE10	225
	KT2	126
	M8	68
	B	234
	M10	50
	C	255
	C	434
	M12	800
	GP	134
	CI	10
SHEWING	J6	277
SHEWN	EUO	20
	M9	206
	M12	676
SHEWS	RH	92
	AM	1127
	PCD	26
	ML	54
	AA	235
	MD	81
	RL	119
	RL	132
	L4	42
	HAP	1445
	J1	196
	P6	70
	M9	98
	AE2	951
	AE4	268
	AE6	919
	AE8	451
	AE8	811
	AF	52
	B	344
SHIBBOLETH	HAP	2370
SHIELD	PMQ	30
	PCG1	4
	TA	442
	TA	468
	MN	11
	HAP	1487
	P5	44
	M13	164
	HI	161
	VP9	33
	G3	234
	G3	488
	G3	517
	AE1	691
	AE2	235
	AE2	745
	AE2	914
	AE3	371
	AE3	396
	AE3	837
	AE5	471
	AE6	1048
	AE6	1217
	AE7	642
	AE7	876
	AE7	884
	AE7	910
	AE7	1077
	AE8	465
	AE8	576
	AE8	587
	AE8	878
	AE8	929
	AE8	973
SHIELD	AE9	359
	AE9	735
	AE9	784
	AE9	814
	AE9	960
	AE9	1089
	AE9	1094
	AE10	262
	AE10	344
	AE10	366
	AE10	379
	AE10	436
	AE10	456
	AE10	599
	AE10	676
	AE10	705
	AE10	710
	AE10	761
	AE10	762
	AE10	820
	AE10	905
	AE10	1101
	AE10	1112
	AE10	1135
	AE10	1158
	AE10	1199
	AE10	1267
	AE11	36
	AE11	438
	AE11	675
	AE11	691
	AE11	1023
	AE11	1050
	AE11	1081
	AE11	1265
	AE12	501
	AE12	558
	AE12	630
	AE12	639
	AE12	647
	AE12	795
	AE12	1072
	AE12	1253
	AE12	1332
	AE12	1340
	OAL	784
	OAL	797
	OAE1	16
	KT1	111
	KT3	49
	KT3	92
	KT3	308
	KT3	445
	KT3	599
	KT3	933
	FL	275
	FL	281
	M12	129
	M12	179
	M12	503
	M12	800
	M12	813
	M12	823
	AU	2
	AU	116
	AU	122
	AU	128
	AU	152
	AU	176
	AU	180
	AU	187
	AU	195
	AU	254
	AU	414
	AU	454
	AU	532
	AU	549
	M15	236
	CI	283
SHIELD'S	AE8	829
SHIELDS	J6	348
	AE1	143
	AE2	526
	AE7	253
	AE7	733
	AE7	867
	AE7	1084
	AE7	1088
	AE8	6
	AE8	126
	AE8	506
	AE8	715
	AE8	745
	AE8	785
	AE9	302
	AE9	671
SHIELDS	AE9	685
	AE9	907
	AE10	798
	AE11	669
	AE11	900
	AE11	922
	AE11	983
	AE12	198
	AE12	1053
	KT1	148
	KT3	31
	KT3	461
	KT3	987
	KT3	996
	SAA	554
	SAA	850
SHIFT	AT	93
	EH	28
	AE5	38
	AE11	899
	OAL	476
	OAL	870
	OAE2	60
SHIFTED	SAA	213
	G4	639
	M15	389
SHIFTING	AE5	27
	CI	329
SHIFTS	MD	79
	HAP	2217
	J6	473
	G3	133
	AE5	586
	AE8	279
	AE9	971
	AE11	657
	AE11	1126
SHILLING	EK	44
SHILLINGS	EDGA	14
SHILLINGS	PC2	22
SHILOH	HAP	2552
SHIMEI	AA	585
	AA	599
	AA	603
	AA	932
	SAA	1134
	HAP	1602
SHINE	HS	69
	DC	19
	E	30
	EKK	17
	HP	44
	HP	78
	AA	248
	AA	637
	MO	15
	H29	69
	TA	289
	AK	42
	HAP	503
	BR	326
	J1	172
	J3	298
	P2	131
	M1	1083
	VP4	51
	VP10	104
	G1	421
	G1	541
	G1	582
	AE1	705
	AE1	827
	AE1	903
	AE2	420
	AE5	178
	AE5	724
	AE6	1134
	AE6	1189
	AE7	118
	AE8	206
	AE9	20
	AE9	241
	AE9	312
	AE9	841
	AE11	317
	AE11	1147
	AE11	1156
	KT1	403
	KT3	132
	KT3	350
	B	527
	FL	528
	WB	407
	WB	442
SHINES	LC	48
	L2	30

Word	Ref	Num
SHINES	L4	103
	T18	48
	AK	177
	EL	266
	G1	469
	G4	140
	G4	396
	AE2	641
	AE4	202
	AE8	826
	AE10	204
	AE12	454
	M15	289
	GP	140
SHINING	AM	924
	AM	986
	PNH	6
	SDG	24
	SDG	29
	HAP	1099
	HAP	1560
	BR	131
	ODA	74
	PSH	38
	P1	140
	M1	216
	M9	34
	VP2	68
	VP5	88
	G1	187
	G1	230
	G1	253
	G1	354
	G3	93
	G3	274
	G4	150
	AE1	978
	AE2	800
	AE2	997
	AE2	1018
	AE3	318
	AE3	396
	AE5	11
	AE5	61
	AE5	175
	AE6	197
	AE6	303
	AE6	404
	AE6	549
	AE6	886
	AE6	919
	AE6	1032
	AE7	379
	AE7	734
	AE7	884
	AE8	215
	AE8	421
	AE8	785
	AE8	871
	AE8	929
	AE8	953
	AE9	30
	AE9	205
	AE9	407
	AE9	507
	AE9	922
	AE10	31
	AE10	668
	AE10	691
	AE10	746
	AE10	904
	AE11	296
	AE11	653
	AE11	977
	AE12	264
	AE12	534
	AE12	1146
	AE12	1375
	KT2	175
	KT3	207
	KT3	456
	KT3	931
	B	53
	BP	104
	HIF	257
	FL	164
	FL	183
	FL	351
	FL	476
	M15	214
	M15	279
	M15	477
	CI	575
	CI	588
SHINS	J16	39
SHINY	VHH	31

Word	Ref	Num
SHINY	AE5	693
SHIP	AM	57
	AM	247
	AM	273
	AM	420
	AM	696
	AM	763
	L2	2
	H3	4
	TA	192
	AE1	64
	AE1	166
	AE3	597
	AE4	416
	AE5	80
	AE5	289
	AE5	1121
	AE6	460
	AE6	483
	AE10	317
	AE10	350
	AE10	922
	AE10	930
	M8	49
	M8	276
	HIF	214
	HIF	275
	HIF	595
	HIF	649
	M11	67
	M11	74
	M11	92
	M11	198
	M11	205
	AU	34
	AU	559
	CI	254
	CI	266
	CI	271
	CI	339
	CI	376
	CI	390
	CI	554
	STP	7
	STP	15
	PKK	24
SHIPPED		
SHIPPING	AM	619
	AM	625
	G2	623
	AE1	741
	AE7	276
SHIP'S	AE5	322
SHIPS	VHH	34
	AM	17
	AM	89
	AM	107
	AM	131
	AM	287
	AM	407
	AM	502
	AM	506
	AM	568
	AM	598
	AM	633
	AM	649
	AM	816
	AM	986
	CM	91
	HP	228
	DA	55
	H3	30
	HAP	1130
	M1	169
	M13	33
	M13	55
	G2	625
	G3	44
	G3	557
	G4	608
	AE1	154
	AE1	174
	AE1	230
	AE1	241
	AE1	269
	AE1	537
	AE1	552
	AE1	728
	AE1	776
	AE1	802
	AE1	895
	AE1	911
	AE2	30
	AE2	262
	AE2	504
	AE2	538
	AE3	186

Word	Ref	Num
SHIPS	AE3	420
	AE3	858
	AE4	432
	AE4	603
	AE4	814
	AE4	844
	AE5	831
	AE5	861
	AE5	916
	AE5	935
	AE5	1038
	AE5	1099
	AE5	1126
	AE6	663
	AE6	1243
	AE7	254
	AE7	328
	AE7	606
	AE8	121
	AE8	126
	AE8	136
	AE8	143
	AE8	724
	AE9	116
	AE9	128
	AE9	136
	AE9	144
	AE9	184
	AE10	128
	AE10	306
	AE10	375
	AE10	415
	AE10	418
	OAL	5
	OAL	291
	KT2	588
	TJD	149
	HIF	574
	HIF	580
	C	354
	M12	9
	AU	150
	AU	341
	AU	538
	M15	443
	CI	620
SHIPWRACK	AM	138
	BR	97
	AE12	1115
SHIPWRACKED	AR	124
	LCA	1
	AM	8
	AM	282
	AM	1003
	PFD	1
	SAA	198
	LS	2
	P1	174
	AE1	871
	AE4	537
	AE10	958
SHIPWRECK	AE1	759
	AE1	835
	KT3	401
SHIPWRECKED	P6	61
	G3	807
	AE1	842
	M11	400
	M11	454
	CI	384
SHIPWRECKS	AE3	727
SHIRE	ESF	16
SHIRLEY	MF	29
	MF	102
SHIRTS	KT3	27
SHIVER	J3	176
SHIVERED	AE3	752
	AE4	926
	AE5	267
	AE11	16
	AE11	301
	AE12	1074
SHIVERING	PRH	3
	HAP	1751
	BR	174
	P3	201
	P6	63
	M1	154
	G3	488
	G4	735
	AE1	150
	AE3	68
	AE3	234
	AE6	71
	AE6	431
	AE12	1309

SHIVERING	KT3	403	SHOOK	M1	231	SHOOTS	AE4	646
	C	236		M1	768		AE5	281
	M11	9		M9	183		AE6	383
	M15	532		G1	200		AE7	450
SHIVERS	M12	649		G1	641		AE7	735
SHOAL	HIF	670		AE3	122		AE10	930
SHOALS	ETC	19		AE4	685		AE11	1112
	J3	127		AE4	922		AE12	994
	AE1	210		AE4	955		MG	35
	AE5	285		AE5	1034		KT1	492
SHOALY	AE5	1130		AE6	149		KT3	1059
	AE7	1007		AE7	192		M8	23
SHOCK	EEL	19		AE7	305		M8	363
	SAA	674		AE7	402		BP	159
	AE2	989		AE7	556		M11	473
	AE5	266		AE8	285		FL	374
	AE5	356		AE8	691		M15	299
	AE5	939		AE9	124		CI	341
	AE8	316		AE9	543	SHOP	PLN	31
	AE9	153		AE10	172		PPC	27
	AE10	419		AE12	250		EKA	25
	AE10	609		AE12	1294		J10	203
	AE10	836		OAL	621		G4	26
	AE10	1092		KT1	194	SHOPMAN	TJD	108
	AE11	916		KT2	342	SHOPMEN	PK	36
	AE12	439		KT3	184	SHOPS	MD	192
	AE12	673		KT3	265		MF	100
	AE12	998		KT3	282	SHORE	AR	124
	AE12	1146		M8	180		AR	216
	KT3	589		BP	5		AR	219
SHOCKED	AR	101		CAM	222		AR	279
SHOCKING	G4	115		HIF	710		LC	74
SHOD	AE4	751		TH	265		LCA	1
SHOE	J3	254		M11	78		AM	16
	P1	260		M11	306		AM	132
SHOES	L4	100		FL	206		AM	169
	J3	398		M12	110		AM	282
	J16	37		M12	391		AM	293
	OAL	581		AU	272		AM	392
	WB	22		M15	93		AM	493
SHOG	ESF	28		PT	2		AM	779
SHOLE	J3	395	SHOOT	EDGA	36		AM	921
SHONE	UDH	43		EL	93		AM	1198
	UDH	36		P1	55		AM	1216
	AR	288		M1	90		PT	15
	AM	393		M1	593		PFD	4
	AM	636		M1	929		HP	222
	AM	1012		M9	199		HP	229
	EPF	16		GK	15		DA	186
	RL	12		VP8	73		PUO4	6
	AK	144		VP9	67		PUF	1
	EL	231		G2	485		MF	45
	P5	59		G2	499		SAA	602
	M1	673		AE3	67		SAA	616
	M9	196		AE8	901		SAA	802
	HI	152		AE9	711		SAA	845
	AE1	1017		AE9	803		OE	32
	AE2	946		AE10	381		AT	59
	AE7	10		AE12	312		ER	1
	AE8	712		AE12	864		L2	1
	AE8	776		OAL	213		T18	30
	AE9	790		KT2	647		H3	10
	AE9	931		FL	595		H3	19
	AE10	749		M15	549		TA	140
	AE12	1074		STP	14		TA	191
	MFL	12	SHOOTER	HIF	431		TA	396
	DO	104		HIF	601		HAP	132
	KT2	552	SHOOTING	AM	1086		HAP	155
	KT2	559		BR	236		HAP	1751
	KT3	73		G1	503		BR	138
	KT3	250		G2	105		BR	332
	KT3	267		G4	439		LS	7
	KT3	363		AE5	653		J3	57
	BP	57		AE5	687		J10	284
	HIF	295		CAM	347		M1	39
	C	51	SHOOTINGS	CM	54		M1	127
	M12	385	SHOOTS	AM	431		M1	460
	M12	302		ML	30		M1	1009
	M12	536		AA	452		VP1	80
	GP	102		SAA	1032		VP4	42
	CI	121		AT	120		VP5	41
	STP	13		L4	113		VP5	130
SHOOK	AR	104		J6	253		VP7	59
	AR	227		VP3	145		VP9	52
	DC	9		G1	230		VP9	58
	AM	199		G1	392		VP9	78
	PTC	16		G1	591		G1	17
	AA	176		G2	26		G1	457
	AA	1027		G2	30		G1	490
	MF	134		G2	81		G1	544
	SAA	732		G2	113		G1	614
	TA	59		G2	254		G2	58
	TA	318		G2	427		G2	64
	HAP	1789		G2	451		G3	53
	BR	244		G3	552		G3	314
	J10	200		AE2	971		G3	370

SHORE	G3	414	SHORE	AE6	522	SHORES	P6	15
	G3	809		AE6	529		M1	17
	G4	609		AE6	561		M1	68
	G4	731		AE6	1247		M13	71
	AE1	3		AE7	2		VP6	67
	AE1	24		AE7	32		G2	153
	AE1	127		AE7	142		G2	159
	AE1	321		AE7	168		G2	171
	AE1	414		AE7	200		G3	523
	AE1	425		AE7	284		G4	668
	AE1	537		AE7	399		AE1	51
	AE1	541		AE7	510		AE1	227
	AE1	739		AE7	615		AE1	272
	AE1	757		AE7	652		AE1	309
	AE1	762		AE7	762		AE1	776
	AE1	783		AE7	820		AE1	798
	AE1	809		AE7	861		AE1	871
	AE1	842		AE7	972		AE2	161
	AE1	875		AE7	1046		AE2	241
	AE1	1053		AE7	1053		AE2	333
	AE2	127		AE8	111		AE3	98
	AE2	224		AE8	121		AE3	148
	AE2	275		AE8	136		AE3	176
	AE2	538		AE8	748		AE3	330
	AE2	762		AE9	115		AE3	331
	AE2	832		AE9	121		AE3	363
	AE2	1061		AE9	425		AE3	492
	AE3	15		AE10	103		AE3	512
	AE3	26		AE10	330		AE3	588
	AE3	64		AE10	375		AE3	642
	AE3	86		AE10	409		AE3	745
	AE3	108		AE10	415		AE4	150
	AE3	157		AE10	527		AE4	903
	AE3	181		AE10	809		AE4	837
	AE3	197		AE10	922		AE5	11
	AE3	311		AE10	958		AE5	34
	AE3	349		AE10	967		AE5	71
	AE3	353		AE11	256		AE5	109
	AE3	486		AE11	306		AE5	173
	AE3	489		AE11	930		AE5	270
	AE3	517		AE11	935		AE5	816
	AE3	527		AE12	60		AE5	1001
	AE3	616		AE12	123		AE5	1128
	AE3	650		AE12	545		AE5	1136
	AE3	661		AE12	667		AE6	939
	AE3	666		AE12	749		AE6	973
	AE3	681		OAL	258		AE7	12
	AE3	698		OAL	594		AE7	103
	AE3	707		OAL	605		AE7	294
	AE3	775		DO	44		AE7	420
	AE3	789		CAM	14		AE7	1006
	AE3	864		CAM	76		AE8	162
	AE3	870		HIF	54		AE9	967
	AE3	888		HIF	455		AE10	88
	AE3	915		HIF	474		AE10	385
	AE3	919		HIF	486		AE10	972
	AE3	929		HIF	565		AE11	460
	AE4	60		HIF	652		AE12	307
	AE4	345		HIF	660		KT2	588
	AE4	493		C	311		M11	97
	AE4	537		C	534	SHORN	CM	135
	AE4	579		TH	212		MD	74
	AE4	592		M11	36		P3	105
	AE4	625		M11	86		G2	602
	AE4	786		M11	91		G3	676
	AE4	815		M11	192		AE9	887
	AE4	859		M11	299	SHORT	LC	142
	AE4	943		M11	475		DC	45
	AE5	4		M12	14		PWG	27
	AE5	39		M12	54		PWG	31
	AE5	142		M12	74		AM	1019
	AE5	164		M12	92		EMM	6
	AE5	199		M12	99		SMM2	18
	AE5	212		AU	6		ECG2	28
	AE5	217		M15	68		PMQW	22
	AE5	235		M15	78		PM	38
	AE5	308		M15	260		EM	28
	AE5	341		M15	404		EUO	9
	AE5	358		M15	441		PC1	13
	AE5	623		CI	268		PAL	14
	AE5	649		CI	376		CM	30
	AE5	794		CI	383		DA	209
	AE5	1065		CI	388		UMR	4
	AE6	2		CI	394		PSF	14
	AE6	18		CI	572		SSF	7
	AE6	32		CI	592		AA	817
	AE6	242		CI	629		AA	837
	AE6	252		STP	8		AA	847
	AE6	331		PWR	2		MD	302
	AE6	434	SHORES	AM	1001		SAA	669
	AE6	438		SAA	625		SAA	1108
	AE6	451		TA	510		EK	45
	AE6	464		HAP	1123		RL	34
	AE6	472		HAP	1130		OE	43
	AE6	487		J3	111		MO	23
	AE6	505		P1	218		L3	102

Word	Ref	No.
SHORT	L4	252
	H29	23
	TA	159
	TA	188
	HAP	1031
	HAP	1244
	HAP	1873
	HAP	1980
	HAP	2096
	HAP	2516
	SKA3	15
	EL	263
	EL	287
	EL	295
	EL	304
	OD	45
	J1	140
	J3	142
	J3	332
	J3	333
	J6	221
	P4	70
	P5	56
	M1	571
	M9	12
	MC	52
	VP2	65
	VP3	161
	VP4	74
	G1	544
	G1	572
	G2	114
	G3	474
	G3	679
	G4	283
	G4	302
	G4	438
	AE1	247
	AE1	472
	AE2	928
	AE4	128
	AE4	626
	AE4	906
	AE5	230
	AE7	248
	AE7	1012
	AE7	1017
	AE8	528
	AE8	690
	AE9	11
	AE9	558
	AE9	755
	AE10	657
	AE10	844
	AE10	890
	AE10	1034
	AE11	210
	AE11	228
	AE11	424
	AE11	701
	AE11	731
	AE11	1063
	AE11	1205
	AE11	1268
	AE12	1294
	AE12	338
	AE12	1310
	OAL	588
	OAE2	74
	LMC	7
	KT2	21
	KT2	57
	KT3	123
	KT3	642
	KT3	505
	KT3	833
	TJD	20
	B	25
	B	185
	HIF	204
	HIF	411
	HIF	577
	C	340
	TH	54
	TH	166
	TH	364
	M11	62
	M11	66
	M11	475
	FL	114
	M12	686
	WB	54
	M15	554
	CI	194
	CI	217
	CI	407
SHORT	CI	624
	CI	638
	ETP	43
SHORTEN	H3	47
	EL	112
	KT3	1036
SHORT-ENDURING	KT2	481
SHORTENED	VP9	27
	AE6	669
	AE11	1099
	KT1	505
	KT3	509
	BP	71
	AS	2
	MD	91
SHORTENEST		
SHORTENS	G1	420
	G2	684
	AE1	1046
SHORTER	AE1	976
	AE9	1100
SHORTEST	UMR	8
	AE3	661
	B	176
SHORTHAND	PSF	20
SHORT-LIVED	PTC	19
	TA	119
	HAP	1347
	AE10	885
	HIF	491
	FL	588
SHORTLY	EUO	24
	AE10	663
	AE10	878
	AE12	733
	MG	17
SHORT-WAISTED	J6	649
SHORT-WINGED	HAP	1767
SHOT	LC	88
	AM	238
	AM	517
	AM	699
	AM	749
	SCD2	10
	EDGA	33
	L4	13
	T23	10
	HAP	97
	HAP	1223
	G2	173
	AE2	942
	AE5	120
	AE5	418
	AE5	674
	AE7	857
	AE9	130
	AE9	885
	AE9	988
	AE12	1244
	OAL	239
	KT2	245
	B	66
	CAM	25
	HIF	154
	WB	214
	M15	458
	CI	118
	J10	359
	P4	104
	G3	10
	G3	134
	AE8	604
	AE10	669
	AE10	1286
	AE11	750
	AE11	965
	AE11	968
	AE11	1140
	KT3	924
	M8	72
	M12	170
	M12	654
SHOULDER	AE12	1000
	M12	414
	AM	708
	EOE	6
	J3	155
	J6	243
	J6	631
	J10	48
	J10	60
	M1	314
	M1	638
	M1	670
SHOULDERING	M13	154
SHOULDER'S	HI	131
SHOULDERS	VP9	90
SHOULDERS	G3	402
	G3	800
	G4	317
	G4	760
	AE1	558
	AE2	963
	AE2	657
	AE2	697
	AE2	981
	AE4	366
	AE4	588
	AE5	178
	AE5	340
	AE5	565
	AE5	424
	AE6	1086
	AE7	913
	AE7	926
	AE7	1109
	AE9	980
	AE9	1018
	AE10	202
	AE10	755
	AE10	993
	AE10	1086
	AE11	96
	AE11	865
	AE11	958
	AE11	1266
	AE12	442
	KT1	183
	KT3	70
	KT3	938
	BP	187
	HIF	69
	M12	527
	M12	681
	AU	443
	AU	444
SHOUT	AR	226
	AM	709
	AA	60
	J10	117
	G4	317
	AE5	235
	AE5	656
	AE9	1070
	AE10	1006
	AE11	1211
	AE11	1281
	OAL	633
	AF	35
	KT1	117
	M8	103
	M8	161
	C	743
	M11	170
	AU	198
SHOUTED	POE	9
	KT3	994
SHOUTING	SCD2	8
	L4	202
	G1	474
	AE4	603
	AE5	670
	AE6	1197
	AE9	872
	AE11	909
	KT3	439
	M8	161
	C	344
	SMP	33
	SMP	35
SHOUTINGS	AE7	554
SHOUTS	SMA	35
	AA	734
	SAA	195
	J10	433
	G3	33
	G3	131
	G4	98
	G4	111
	G4	633
	AE1	52
	AE1	1047
	AE2	75
	AE2	397
	AE2	653
	AE3	176
	AE4	593
	AE5	184
	AE5	196
	AE5	292
	AE5	293
	AE5	294
	AE5	726

SHOUTS	AE5	749	SHOW	HAP	1413	SHOWERS	AE4	234		
	AE5	602		HAP	1827		AE9	67		
	AE7	849		HAP	1932		M11	155		
	AE8	123		HAP	2158		FL	5		
	AE8	788		PDS	7		FL	315		
	AE8	954		PTS	10		FL	386		
	AE9	45		STS3	17	SHOWERY	L4	243		
	AE9	61		PMS	11		G1	171		
	AE9	621		EL	335		AE9	909		
	AE9	669		MS	10	SHOWEST	T23	37		
	AE9	904		PSH	10	SHOWING	ECD	4		
	AE10	367		J3	62		PTC	34		
	AE10	1041		J3	297	SHOWN	HS	54		
	AE10	1134		J3	493		HS	94		
	AE10	1287		J6	747		AR	36		
	AE11	824		J10	51		AR	83		
	AE11	984		J10	131		SMA	20		
	AE11	1095		J10	138		LC	99		
	AE12	388		J10	558		DC	57		
	AE12	407		P3	242		EWG	7		
	AE12	606		P5	167		EWG	9		
	AE12	681		G1	473		AM	68		
	AE12	906		G1	610		AM	331		
	AE12	1060		G2	348		AM	643		
	DO	79		G4	805		EMQ	5		
	KT1	15		AE1	17		PCG2	29		
	KT2	601		AE2	272		ECG2	19		
	M8	204		AE2	556		SCG2	9		
	HIF	35		AE3	584		EM	15		
	HIF	521		AE4	211		PLN	7		
	C	734		AE4	374		ELN	10		
	CI	612		AE5	687		ELN	20		
	M12	518		AE12	941		PUO1	20		
SHOVED	AM	736		AE12	982		EUO	33		
SHOVEL-BOARD	PKA	10		OAL	781		PUO2	29		
SHOVING	AE12	1000		TJD	173		EUO2	29		
SHOW	MHD	2		TJD	200		ESF	1		
	HS	126		M8	157		PTW	7		
	HS	146		CAM	376		EOE	27		
	AR	145		M11	128		CM	103		
	LC	69		FL	104		CM	130		
	LCA	33		FL	187		HP	16		
	PRL	3		FL	460		HP	204		
	PIE	12		FL	481		AA	379		
	VHH	51		FL	599		AA	725		
	AM	162		AU	521		MD	5		
	AM	202		AU	601		SAA	803		
	AM	263		M15	389		SAA	851		
	AM	502		M15	449		SAA	1025		
	AM	543		GP	89		RL	123		
	AM	680		CI	638		TA	92		
	AM	1063		SMP	23		EAA	1		
	AM	1181		AS	39		HAP	1542		
	PMQ	14		AS	40		HAP	1977		
	SMQ	6		PWR	24		EL	279		
	EWGR	33	SHOWED	EPC	23		OD	45		
	PCG1	29		NS	25		J3	165		
	ECG2	3		BR	32		J6	487		
	PAR	16		AE1	158		P3	53		
	PW	16		AE2	37		PLT	9		
	PM	32		AE5	468		VP6	17		
	PCD	28		KT3	595		G4	470		
	PNH	31		M8	222		AE3	906		
	PUO2	17		C	60		AE4	856		
	EUO2	11		AU	410		AE6	145		
	EAZ	15		AU	588		AE6	1203		
	PAL	24		WB	444		AE6	1229		
	PKK	2	SHOWER	LC	127		AE7	793		
	EOE	32		AM	958		AE8	361		
	PCB	33		PRH	35		AE9	811		
	CM	114		SAA	6		AE11	1040		
	CM	136		SAA	789		AE12	44		
	DA	63		TA	280		AE12	1351		
	AA	688		G1	533		KT2	637		
	MD	246		AE11	802		B	122		
	PRH	21		B	684		BP	17		
	PLB	21		FL	447		M11	489		
	SAA	190	SHOWERED	TA	297		M12	222		
	SAA	454		KT3	1147		PTP	12		
	PDG	26	SHOWERS	UDH	90		PTP	18		
	L4	280		AM	52	SHOWS	LC	137		
	T18	65		PLN	28		AM	486		
	T23	19		OE	28		PWGR	24		
	TA	74		SKA6	10		PM	28		
	TA	277		P2	91		PNH	50		
	PAA	16		M1	360		EPC	8		
	PAA	24		M1	366		SAA	931		
	PAA	40		VP3	129		L4	23		
	EAA	7		VP3	139		HAP	288		
	AK	194		VP4	35		HAP	370		
	GE	11		VP7	83		HAP	1049		
	GE	43		G1	134		HAP	1379		
	HAP	216		G1	539		HAP	1669		
	HAP	295		G2	441		HAP	2221		
	HAP	390		G2	454		EL	75		
	HAP	1382		G4	119		ODA	75		

SHOWS	VP5	21
	G2	428
	G3	119
	AE1	494
	AE1	926
	AE2	476
	AE2	522
	AE4	105
	AE5	498
	AE6	501
	AE9	619
	AE10	302
	AE12	105
	AE12	698
	AE12	1020
	OAL	165
	OAL	261
	OAL	461
	BP	191
	M15	130
	M15	613
	M15	632
SHRED	J3	459
SHREW	T23	20
SHREWD	PAZ	32
	EKA	6
SHREWDLY	PD	2
	HAP	1427
SHRIEK	AE5	858
	OAL	139
	CI	586
SHRIEKED	OAL	600
	KT1	89
	KT3	856
	CAM	276
	C	714
	TH	278
SHRIEKS	AM	952
	AE2	668
	AE4	960
	AE6	427
	AE6	436
	AE7	554
	AE7	794
	AE8	843
	AE9	661
	AE11	220
	AE11	1272
	AE12	887
	KT3	262
	CAM	156
	C	705
	C	735
	M11	180
	M11	464
	M12	318
SHRIEVAL	AA	618
	MD	14
SHRIEVES	EDGA	3
SHRILL	AM	709
	L4	153
	SSC	27
	G3	150
	AE11	1086
	AE12	1060
	FL	116
SHRINE	AK	161
	ELW	6
	J6	231
	PPS	11
	P2	99
	GK	103
	VP7	43
	AE1	395
	AE1	626
	AE1	711
	AE2	545
	AE3	113
	AE3	478
	AE4	657
	AE8	356
	AE8	453
	AE10	877
	AE11	727
	AE11	840
	KT3	127
	KT3	184
	KT3	209
	KT3	265
	M8	9
	BP	169
	M10	61
	HIF	61
	GP	135
	ETP	23
SHRINES	LC	20
SHRINES	HAP	2347
	AE6	112
SHRINK	AM	1064
	EWGR	22
	STL	22
	HAP	1061
	G2	682
	AE9	687
SHRINKING	AE8	940
SHRINKS	SCD1	19
	SAA	806
	M11	346
SHRIVELED	G1	158
	M12	385
SHRIVELS	M8	31
SHROUD	G2	121
	AE2	353
	AE10	124
	AE10	935
	AE12	82
SHROUD-LIKE	G1	25
SHROUDS	UDH	49
	AM	591
	G1	444
	G1	575
	AE1	570
	AE3	268
	M11	121
SHROVETIDE	PLG	7
	C	106
SHRUB	VP5	21
	VP10	20
	TH	403
SHRUBS	GK	121
	VP1	108
	VP4	2
	VP5	98
	VP10	44
	G2	28
	G2	166
	G2	572
	G2	602
	G3	489
	G3	510
SHRUNK	AM	928
	TA	214
	G3	728
	AE3	41
	AE8	319
	AE11	1119
	M8	345
	CAM	269
	M12	253
SHUDDERING	TH	312
SHUFFLED	HAP	190
	AE11	1166
SHUN	HS	34
	AM	504
	AM	780
	AM	1028
	AM	1067
	PUO2	17
	PUO2	25
	CM	119
	DA	13
	DA	49
	DA	76
	UMR	7
	AA	267
	MD	215
	SAA	407
	SAA	871
	EK	9
	L3	289
	L4	18
	L4	130
	T23	15
	HAP	1064
	HAP	1819
	BR	120
	BR	200
	J1	130
	J6	484
	J6	741
	P3	3
	P3	94
	P3	110
	P4	76
	M1	805
	M9	55
	M13	99
	HI	103
	VP9	20
	VP10	70
	G1	372
SHUN	G2	410
	G3	245
	G4	354
	G4	591
	G4	661
	AE1	470
	AE1	565
	AE2	1021
	AE3	471
	AE3	485
	AE3	707
	AE3	860
	AE3	898
	AE3	927
	AE4	453
	AE4	620
	AE5	217
	AE5	520
	AE5	764
	AE6	294
	AE6	637
	AE6	947
	AE7	419
	AE9	63
	AE9	903
	AE9	1010
	AE9	1057
	AE10	519
	AE11	647
	AE11	1000
	AE11	1084
	AE12	117
	AE12	782
	AE12	865
	AE12	933
	OAL	82
	OAL	158
	OAL	373
	OAL	885
	KT1	250
	KT2	26
	KT2	533
	KT3	574
	TJD	33
	TJD	34
	B	202
	CAM	242
	HIF	703
	C	676
	TH	227
	M11	25
	FL	445
	M12	486
	M15	204
	M15	710
	CI	447
	CI	487
SHUNAMMITE	BR	249
SHUNNED	AM	302
	SLN	2
	AA	617
	HAP	51
	BR	343
	J10	504
	VP6	73
	AE2	508
	AE5	594
	AE5	1004
	AE10	726
	AE11	513
	AE11	853
	AE11	878
	AE12	714
	AE12	753
	TJD	34
	B	454
	M10	3
	C	588
	FL	323
	AU	49
	AU	56
	CI	81
	M1	684
SHUNNEST		
SHUNNING	AA	864
	HAP	636
	G3	631
	HI	146
	KT1	105
	KT2	68
	TJD	3
SHUNS	AR	162
	AM	164
	H2	15
	HAP	1724
	G1	554
	M1	635

SHUNS	M1	643	SICK	P5	268	SIDE	HAP	1732
	AE4	563		G4	375		HAP	1962
	AE4	685		AE4	93		HAP	2051
	AE5	1132		AE9	1098		HAP	2111
	AE12	700		OAL	833		J6	164
	TJD	122		KT3	730		J6	391
	C	588		C	24		J6	577
	M11	312		C	401		P2	97
SHUT	SAA	223		TH	313		P3	17
	TA	157		GP	63		P6	17
	EL	262		ERL	8		P6	70
	P1	125	SICKEN	AM	499		P6	128
	VP6	54		AE8	328		M13	50
	G2	223	SICKENED	BR	124		M13	113
	G4	240		AE4	991		G1	252
	AE1	321	SICK-FEATHERED	HAP	1908		G2	217
	AE1	762	SICKLE	AR	110		G2	364
	AE3	844		G3	279		G2	375
	AE7	830	SICKLES	G1	478		G2	540
	AE7	1038		AE4	744		G3	43
	AE9	45	SICKLY	SMA	28		G3	230
	AE9	982		AM	1111		G3	757
	KT3	469		ECG1	30		G4	110
	C	628		PAR	1		G4	513
	ETP	31		L3	266		G4	662
SHUTS	SCD1	24		L4	34		G4	680
	J1	199		HAP	1751		AE1	120
	J6	223		M1	470		AE1	151
	G3	399		VP5	55		AE1	231
	G4	717		G1	596		AE1	980
	AE3	702		G3	550		AE2	23
	AE5	265		G3	721		AE2	457
	AE9	161		G4	384		AE2	694
SHUTTERS	J3	390		G4	400		AE2	709
SHUTTLE	G1	392		AE1	731		AE3	704
SIBYL	J3	5		AE12	91		AE3	900
	AE3	563		AE12	1313		AE4	55
	AE6	14		KT2	119		AE4	100
	AE6	147		C	657		AE4	169
	AE6	236		FL	377		AE4	236
	AE6	369		FL	592		AE4	387
	AE6	442		M12	188		AE4	580
	AE6	407		CI	381		AE4	950
	AE6	538	SICKNESS	M9	155		AE5	196
	AE6	566		G3	110		AE5	410
	AE6	724		G3	671		AE5	423
	AE6	905		G4	367		AE5	726
SIBYLLA	AE5	963		ECG1	28		AE5	1080
SIBYL'S	PUO5	22		ECG1	32		AE6	54
	HAP	1783		H9	28		AE6	238
	AE6	67		TA	22		AE6	536
	AE6	128		MFL	36		AE6	740
	AE6	277		DO	102		AE6	808
	AE6	305		DO	122		AE6	1193
SICANIAN	AE7	1085		KT1	569		AE7	48
SICANIANS	AE8	435		KT3	1095		AE7	730
SICE	P3	93		M15	241		AE7	779
SICHAEUS	AE1	472		EWR	8		AE7	886
	AE4	26	SICKNESSES	J10	347		AE7	1079
	AE4	726	SICYON	J3	126		AE8	37
	AE6	639	SIDE	HS	87		AE8	187
SICHAEUS'	DA	207		AR	18		AE8	196
	AE4	907		VHH	25		AE8	317
SICILIA	AE5	34		AM	27		AE8	468
SICILIAN	J6	626		AM	229		AE8	603
	P3	73		AM	332		AE8	618
	VP4	1		AM	486		AE8	773
	VP4	3		AM	628		AE8	799
	VP6	1		AM	753		AE9	81
	AE1	51		AM	932		AE9	468
	AE1	774		AM	934		AE9	731
	AE3	492		AM	1182		AE9	787
	AE5	39		PMQ	11		AE9	971
	AE5	52		PW	13		AE9	1027
	AE5	384		ELN	12		AE9	1067
	AE5	393		DA	44		AE9	1083
	M8	21		PR	27		AE10	216
SICILIANS	AE5	696		AA	76		AE10	237
SICILIA'S	AE3	528		AA	689		AE10	436
	AE8	552		AA	885		AE10	500
SICILY	AE3	524		MD	10		AE10	1009
	AE5	919		MD	109		AE10	1104
	AE9	285		MD	155		AE10	1146
	AE9	380		MF	191		AE10	1310
SICK	AM	364		EDG	37		AE11	359
	AM	580		AT	81		AE11	687
	PLG	26		H3	15		AE11	723
	RL	119		AK	145		AE11	737
	RL	120		HAP	585		AE11	845
	J1	185		HAP	1057		AE11	913
	J6	139		HAP	1294		AE11	961
	J6	334		HAP	1432		AE11	964
	J6	510		HAP	1471		AE11	971
	J10	303		HAP	1474		AE11	988
	J16	70		HAP	1486		AE11	1023
	P3	168		HAP	1671		AE11	1184

Word	Ref	No.
SIDE	AE11	1248
	AE12	11
	AE12	134
	AE12	140
	AE12	227
	AE12	253
	AE12	302
	AE12	317
	AE12	326
	AE12	568
	AE12	727
	AE12	962
	AE12	1056
	AE12	1060
	AE12	1173
	AE12	1365
	OAL	147
	OAL	163
	OAL	168
	OAL	245
	OAL	561
	OAL	637
	OAL	791
	OAE2	62
	AF	9
	DO	36
	KT1	13
	KT2	103
	KT2	490
	KT2	569
	KT3	101
	KT3	230
	KT3	273
	KT3	460
	KT3	472
	KT3	492
	KT3	520
	KT3	537
	KT3	571
	KT3	616
	KT3	737
	KT3	783
	KT3	926
	KT3	943
	KT3	1144
	M8	284
	B	23
	B	161
	B	363
	B	416
	B	742
	BP	103
	M10	54
	CAM	138
	HIF	290
	HIF	497
	HIF	815
	C	59
	C	84
	C	97
	C	239
	C	302
	C	309
	C	421
	TH	75
	TH	115
	TH	143
	TH	183
	TH	365
	M11	150
	M11	459
	FL	22
	FL	107
	FL	128
	FL	289
	FL	325
	FL	433
	M12	135
	M12	223
	M12	362
	M12	303
	M12	498
	M12	552
	M12	559
	M12	575
	M12	632
	M12	645
	M12	646
	M12	651
	CI	279
	CI	306
	CI	396
	M12	752
	AU	237
	WB	210
	WB	261

Word	Ref	No.
SIDE	WB	346
	WB	370
	SMP	69
SIDEBOARDS	AE1	903
SIDELONG	P3	224
	M11	143
SIDES	AM	513
	AM	581
	AM	1106
	HP	228
	EL8	32
	J3	393
	J10	48
	VP3	60
	G1	687
	G2	293
	G3	91
	G3	320
	G3	344
	G3	401
	G3	646
	G4	144
	G4	802
	AE1	429
	AE1	906
	AE2	21
	AE2	49
	AE2	68
	AE2	609
	AE2	645
	AE3	33
	AE3	101
	AE3	759
	AE3	873
	AE4	225
	AE5	260
	AE5	375
	AE5	578
	AE6	64
	AE6	311
	AE6	559
	AE6	820
	AE7	694
	AE7	811
	AE9	578
	AE9	1019
	AE10	14
	AE10	422
	AE11	1054
	AE12	14
	AE12	761
	AE12	1023
	AE12	1050
	KT2	471
	KT2	525
	KT2	620
	KT3	467
	KT3	848
	HIF	432
	HIF	634
	HIF	656
	M11	107
	M11	140
	M11	146
	FL	73
	FL	84
	M12	467
	AU	336
	M15	534
	M15	696
	CI	462
	PMK	40
SIDE-WIND	AM	941
SIDICINIAN	AE7	1006
SIDONIAN	AE1	624
	AE11	106
	M10	52
SIEGE	EPF	8
	TA	172
	AE1	882
	AE2	262
	AE2	150
	AE9	261
	AE9	679
	AE10	40
	AE10	178
	AE11	444
	OAL	410
	HIF	27
	HIF	565
	TH	33
	AU	332
	AT	70
SIEVE	AT	76
	L3	129
SIEVES	WB	155

Word	Ref	No.
SIFTED	M11	127
SIFTING	RL	236
SIGAEAN	M12	99
SIGH	SMQ	7
	SMM2	9
	SEL2	13
	SCG2	14
	SCG3	2
	SM2	7
	S	16
	A	15
	STC	13
	CM	29
	HP	79
	SDG	2
	OE	55
	L3	125
	FS2	9
	PP	43
	SKA2	25
	EL	309
	SSH	5
	J6	183
	M1	899
	SFL	10
	AE4	933
	AE11	809
	AE11	1209
	AE11	1221
	AE12	1297
	AF	87
	AF	91
	KT2	87
	TJD	70
	M8	356
	B	366
	CAM	220
	C	256
	WB	91
SIGHED	AR	17
	AM	291
	AM	895
	SEL2	2
	EM	27
	MD	34
	AT	100
	DOD	3
	M1	212
	M1	1016
	HI	47
	VP5	33
	VP10	22
	G4	673
	AE2	91
	AE2	547
	AE4	528
	AE7	403
	AE10	1122
	AF	112
	AF	113
	AF	119
	AF	120
	KT1	95
	KT1	216
	KT1	276
	KT3	843
	KT3	1022
	M8	81
	M8	285
	CAM	110
	CAM	168
	CAM	185
	HIF	570
	C	95
	M11	71
	M11	380
	M11	413
	M12	714
	AU	211
	WB	313
	WB	509
	CI	256
SIGHING	SCD1	21
	AA	347
	NS	6
	NS	10
	NS	11
	NS	17
	NS	21
	NS	22
	NS	28
	NS	32
	NS	33
	LS	5
	ODA	8
	J10	215

Word	Ref	No.
SILENT	VP8	86
	VP9	78
	G1	56
	G1	644
	G4	609
	G4	612
	AE1	706
	AE2	123
	AE2	334
	AE2	1045
	AE3	668
	AE3	875
	AE3	939
	AE4	98
	AE4	416
	AE4	712
	AE4	761
	AE5	893
	AE5	1074
	AE6	377
	AE6	957
	AE6	1235
	AE7	147
	AE7	497
	AE7	972
	AE8	44
	AE8	689
	AE9	35
	AE9	196
	AE9	300
	AE9	458
	AE9	513
	AE10	155
	AE10	790
	AE11	227
	AE12	583
	AE12	754
	AE12	890
	AE12	1028
	OAL	709
	KT2	79
	KT2	328
	KT3	116
	KT3	855
	KT3	1019
	CAM	108
	CAM	200
	HIF	55
	HIF	428
	M11	267
	M11	289
	FL	394
	AU	22
	M15	87
	CI	187
	AM	168
SILENTLY	SMQ	8
	HP	2
	HAP	1532
	J3	172
	OAE2	19
	PMK	15
SILENUS	VP6	20
	VP6	119
	OAL	610
SILIUS	J10	512
SILK	J6	218
	J6	604
SILKEN	HAP	1256
	G1	468
	AE1	983
	AE7	680
	AE8	939
	KT3	535
SILKS	J6	364
SILK-WEAVERS	EAZ	21
SILKWORN	FL	235
SILLY	HAP	1708
	HAP	1765
	PKA	2
	J10	304
	AE4	136
SILVANUS	VP10	37
	AE8	796
SILVER	AM	394
	AM	943
	AM	1172
	AM	1189
	D	37
	MF	38
	ER	20
	T18	76
	PP	24
	J6	35
	J6	413
	P2	99

Word	Ref	No.
SILVER	M1	146
	VP7	52
	VP10	6
	G1	529
	G1	576
	G2	228
	G2	274
	G3	230
	G3	520
	G3	686
	AE3	597
	AE5	147
	AE5	323
	AE5	350
	AE7	11
	AE7	878
	AE7	1082
	AE8	484
	AE8	585
	AE8	699
	AE8	871
	AE8	892
	AE9	348
	AE9	735
	AE9	761
	AE10	270
	AE10	732
	AE12	377
	AE12	894
	OAL	15
	KT2	232
	KT2	621
	KT2	647
	KT3	85
	KT3	218
	M10	42
	HIF	58
	HIF	616
	C	53
	C	619
	FL	242
	WB	7
	WB	23
	M15	400
	SMP	26
SILVER-FOOTED	HIF	722
	HIF	747
SILVER-STUDDED	AE5	404
SILVIA	AE7	677
	AE7	700
SILVIUS	AE6	1033
	AE6	1043
	AE6	1044
SIMAGRES	M13	31
SIMAR	AE4	196
	CI	100
SIMARS	FL	341
SIMKIN	MF	81
SIMOEIS	AM	926
SIMOÏS	AE1	143
	AE3	394
	AE3	645
	AE5	826
	AE5	1050
	AE6	135
	AE11	395
	AE10	92
SIMOÏS'		
SIMON	EUO	30
SIMPLE	AM	822
	STL	18
	J6	415
	M1	117
	G3	790
	OAL	530
	OAL	885
	M8	70
	C	7
	C	529
	FL	618
	M15	177
SIMPLER	HAP	736
SIMPLES	M1	701
	AE4	743
	AE12	592
	B	624
	M11	287
	M15	491
SIMPLICITY	HAP	1325
	J3	292
	OAL	276
	M15	144
	PLT	25
SIMPLY	UDH	49
	AR	184
	SMA	2
	AM	373

Word	Ref	No.
SIN	PCD	23
	CM	128
	PR	10
	EDG	12
	RL	85
	RL	90
	RL	160
	RL	182
	AA	2
	AA	79
	AA	183
	AA	372
	AA	613
	PPC	16
	HAP	4
	ETS	11
	ETS	27
	EL	88
	EL	173
	OD	27
	J1	116
	J1	120
	J6	31
	J6	185
	J6	193
	J6	232
	J6	634
	J6	849
	P5	46
	P5	171
	P5	203
	P5	272
	VCS	5
	AE6	1001
	OAL	466
	OAL	727
	OAL	805
	OAL	856
	DO	155
	KT3	813
	TJD	76
	B	166
	B	180
	B	340
	CAM	10
	CAM	39
	CAM	40
	CAM	51
	CAM	128
	CAM	286
	CAM	303
	CAM	307
	CAM	315
	C	64
	C	483
	C	516
	C	528
	C	550
	C	560
	TH	168
	TH	323
	WB	132
	WB	457
	M15	152
	M15	684
	M15	707
	GP	11
	ETP	19
	ETP	20
	PMK	36
	STL	16
SINCERE	HP	38
	MD	57
	SAA	1017
	HAP	822
	BR	181
	J6	381
	J6	446
	M1	117
	M1	437
	AE2	98
	KT3	884
	B	477
	M10	93
	M12	133
	M15	142
	GP	13
	CI	48
SINCERELY	AA	43
	EAA	28
	ESH	5
	AE12	43
SINECURES	GP	71
SINEW	M12	747
SINEWS	RL	349
	AK	186

Word	Ref	Num		Word	Ref	Num		Word	Ref	Num
SINEWS	AE3	41		SING	AE7	963		SINGLE	AE10	637
	AE5	571			AE8	377			AE10	736
	AE7	222			AE9	208			AE10	1064
	AE9	974			AE9	698			AE11	670
	AE12	327			AE9	849			AE12	25
	KT1	585			AE10	242			AE12	124
	KT3	45			AE10	1125			AE12	347
	KT3	763			OAL	37			AE12	700
	M12	253			OAL	238			AE12	1031
	M15	351			OAL	301			OAL	102
SINFUL	EDS	8			OAL	307			KT2	400
SING	SMA	105			OAL	633			KT3	649
	AM	359			OAL	667			M8	51
	AM	892			OAE1	16			M10	3
	AM	1038			OAE1	34			FL	142
	SEL3	4			KT1	199			M12	506
	PSF	32			KT2	666			M12	702
	AA	856			KT3	118			AU	140
	D	28			KT3	123			AU	152
	MF	210			KT3	427		SINGLED	EMQ	13
	SAA	64			CAM	5			AE11	1011
	SAA	1046			C	87		SINGLES	SMA	39
	ER	40			C	92		SINGLETON	MF	57
	L1	35			C	361		SINGLY	AE8	148
	T18	6			C	428			AE11	613
	T27	73			C	458			AU	538
	PAA	42			C	625		SINGS	VHH	56
	HAP	1853			C	647			ESF	9
	AK	192			C	696			DA	2
	BR	172			C	800			PAA	37
	BR	322			FL	47			EL	377
	PP	38			FL	52			J10	33
	EL	363			FL	440			J10	288
	ODA	69			FL	452			VP6	10
	ODA	78			WB	464			VP6	18
	ODA	80			M15	210			VP7	30
	J6	190		SINGE	AE5	116			VP8	50
	J6	522			AE9	139			VP10	111
	J10	473		SINGED	P6	166			G1	396
	PPS	19			M1	200			G4	3
	P1	76			AE6	783			G4	492
	P1	131			AE8	342			AE3	565
	P1	174			C	34			AE12	1250
	P1	187		SINGER	J6	96			C	665
	P5	5			J6	453			WB	472
	P6	5		SINGER'S	J6	499		SINGULAR	EIE	1
	M1	1			VP10	111		SINISTER	MF	120
	SFL	3		SINGING	PAA	40			HAP	1786
	VCS	12			RH	7			AE10	382
	DHP	1			PK	38		SINK	AM	1126
	VP1	5			DOD	6			DA	80
	VP2	39			PAA	46			PPC	33
	VP3	34			J6	507			TA	30
	VP3	81			J6	522			EAA	26
	VP3	83			VP3	30			M1	314
	VP3	88			VP3	44			M13	128
	VP4	64			VP3	167			GK	158
	VP6	15			VP5	75			G1	253
	VP6	101			VP7	23			G2	312
	VP6	105			VP9	84			G3	206
	VP7	4			AE9	702			G3	214
	VP8	6			C	41			G4	298
	VP8	12			C	616			AE1	106
	VP9	24			FL	201			AE4	850
	VP9	38		SINGING-BIRDS	M10	42			AE10	415
	VP9	53		SINGING-BOY	J6	105			AE11	717
	VP9	76		SINGLE	HS	101			AE12	996
	VP9	90			PTW	30			MM	6
	VP10	2			PUO3	11			KT1	526
	VP10	8			SAA	200			KT3	177
	VP10	9			SAA	359			M8	360
	VP10	76			EDG	5			C	159
	VP10	48			HAP	101			C	748
	G1	6			HAP	2296			M11	206
	G1	14			EL	77			M12	703
	G1	419			EL	160			AU	437
	G2	2			EL	289		SINKING	AM	1164
	G2	53			EL	307			CM	44
	G2	246			EL	358			AA	822
	G2	457			MS	10			MF	214
	G2	580			J3	136			SAA	757
	G2	594			J6	819			TA	388
	G3	2			P5	247			BR	258
	G3	70			M1	320			J6	480
	G3	462			M13	163			G1	673
	G4	178			HI	55			G3	519
	G4	407			GK	153			G4	363
	G4	677			VP4	73			AE2	474
	G4	740			G1	534			AE3	542
	AE1	1			G3	705			AE4	688
	AE2	313			G3	713			AE5	813
	AE3	12			AE5	341			AE6	1166
	AE6	875			AE6	676			AE8	497
	AE7	60			AE6	1185			AE9	583
	AE7	889			AE8	746			AE11	509
	AE7	968			AE9	1058			AE11	561

Word	Ref	No.
SINKING	AE12	91
	AE12	228
	AE12	582
	AE12	1115
	AE12	1315
	AE12	1353
	TH	239
	M11	305
	M15	647
SINKS	SCD2	22
	MF	186
	P3	23
	M1	36
	G1	263
	G3	655
	AE5	260
	AE7	449
	AE9	1015
	AE10	571
	AE10	1062
	AE11	126
	M11	205
	WB	418
	M15	347
	M15	385
	PTP	29
SINLESS	CAM	99
SINNED	AR	207
	AM	1061
	RL	111
	BR	285
	BR	292
	EDS	18
	EL	331
	PMK	8
SINNER	PWGR	26
	HAP	1096
	J3	227
	J6	438
	AE6	773
	GP	28
	GP	34
SINNERS	PMQ	41
	ESH	17
SINNING	UDH	85
	SAA	376
SINON	AE2	100
	AE2	336
	AE2	443
	C	500
SIN-POLLUTED	HIF	437
SIN'S	UDH	7
SINS	AR	316
	EUO	5
	AA	587
	MD	39
	EDGA	27
	HAP	340
	HAP	1135
	HAP	1409
	HAP	2471
	BR	39
	J6	691
	P3	62
	P4	83
	M1	288
	CAM	278
	CAM	329
	C	520
	TH	156
SINTHIANS	HIF	799
SION	AA	42
	SAA	1046
SION'S	SAA	805
	SAA	1063
	SAA	1080
SIP	HAP	1361
	VP1	110
	G3	505
	G4	76
SIPPETS	PLG	28
SIPPING	AE1	1033
SIPS	G4	268
SIR	SMA	9
	SMA	135
	PA	22
	E	15
	ESF	7
	ESF	15
	PUO3	10
	PLB	20
	MF	169
	MF	168
	SAA	1099
	EDG	27
	EDG	31

Word	Ref	No.
SIR	HAP	1821
	EDS	32
	J1	190
	P3	186
	P3	189
	P5	250
	C	103
	C	185
	C	595
	C	804
	WB	86
	WB	229
	EMKG	30
SIRE	UDH	95
	DA	115
	MF	60
	MF	113
	MF	134
	T27	74
	HAP	789
	HAP	2006
	BR	26
	BR	40
	J6	21
	J6	690
	J10	203
	J10	412
	J16	86
	P6	142
	M1	609
	M1	656
	M1	1048
	HI	150
	VP3	49
	VP6	20
	VP6	123
	G1	183
	G3	104
	G3	204
	G3	252
	G4	582
	AE1	313
	AE1	683
	AE2	189
	AE2	735
	AE2	748
	AE2	838
	AE2	900
	AE2	919
	AE2	1017
	AE2	1094
	AE3	17
	AE3	108
	AE3	227
	AE3	238
	AE3	602
	AE3	606
	AE3	688
	AE4	288
	AE4	299
	AE4	864
	AE5	52
	AE5	705
	AE5	707
	AE6	497
	AE6	545
	AE6	966
	AE6	1025
	AE6	1058
	AE6	1061
	AE7	108
	AE7	190
	AE7	334
	AE7	388
	AE7	517
	AE7	900
	AE7	905
	AE7	955
	AE7	1044
	AE7	1081
	AE8	182
	AE8	262
	AE8	409
	AE9	350
	AE9	889
	AE10	7
	AE10	85
	AE10	294
	AE10	516
	AE10	587
	AE10	662
	AE10	685
	AE10	707
	AE10	730
	AE10	768
	AE10	997

Word	Ref	No.
SIRE	AE10	1260
	AE11	81
	AE11	839
	AE11	1060
	AE11	1277
	AE12	142
	AE12	343
	AE12	582
	AE12	1233
	AE12	1353
	OAL	216
	OAL	369
	OAL	612
	OAL	613
	MG	30
	KT3	418
	M8	320
	M8	354
	B	38
	B	233
	B	270
	B	606
	B	620
	B	751
	BP	163
	CAM	2
	CAM	3
	CAM	26
	CAM	112
	CAM	235
	CAM	295
	CAM	304
	HIF	34
	HIF	146
	HIF	154
	HIF	513
	HIF	557
	HIF	588
	HIF	603
	HIF	679
	HIF	733
	HIF	777
	C	59
	C	608
	TH	153
	M11	30
	M11	496
	M12	124
	M12	202
	M12	266
	M12	493
	M12	718
	M12	765
	AU	31
	AU	233
	AU	241
	AU	245
	AU	251
	WB	329
	CI	210
	CI	240
	CI	250
	CI	431
SIREN	AE5	1106
SIRENS'	AM	82
SIRENS'	AE5	1125
SIRE'S	KT1	551
SIRES	UDH	73
	AR	27
	EOE	16
	PSF	25
	J3	413
	J6	21
	MC	3
	VP1	32
	G3	282
	AE5	755
	AE5	779
	AE10	392
	AE11	330
	AE12	130
	TJD	71
	CAM	60
	CAM	67
	M15	674
SIRIUS	AE3	194
	AE10	382
	FL	374
SIRS	EMQW	1
	ENH	7
	EK	7
	EK	27
	ETS	16
	PMS	1
	J10	110
	EHC	24

Word	Ref	No.	Word	Ref	No.	Word	Ref	No.
SIRS	PWR	24	SIT	LCA	19	SIZE	M13	149
SISTER	ELN	11		AM	1021		G4	139
	CM	68		PMQ	51		AE3	812
	DA	205		ETL	23		AE4	255
	AK	103		PW	12		AE5	571
	HAP	2318		PW	17		AE8	353
	EDS	9		PUO1	5		AE9	916
	J10	395		ENH	9		AE9	951
	J10	451		E	24		AE10	547
	M1	475		E	27		AE12	327
	GK	57		PAZ	39		M12	17
	G4	501		PC2	21		M15	302
	AE1	71		EKK	11	SIZED	KT3	569
	AE1	454		POE	3	SKELETONS	SAA	338
	AE1	485		PTC	35		AK	186
	AE4	9		D	35	SKEWERS	HIF	633
	AE4	41		MD	281	SKIES	AR	5
	AE4	72		SAA	524		AR	62
	AE4	662		H2	93		AR	113
	AE4	691		HAP	781		AR	143
	AE4	791		J3	263		AR	227
	AE4	909		J16	18		DC	19
	AE4	966		VP5	3		AM	62
	AE4	975		VP5	25		AA	268
	AE4	976		VP7	12		AA	637
	AE7	456		AE1	117		L1	4
	AE7	677		AE3	297		T18	47
	AE9	807		AE6	827		TA	102
	AE10	275		AE10	23		AK	1
	AE10	856		OAL	123		HAP	219
	AE12	212		OAL	164		HAP	793
	AE12	918		OAL	562		HAP	1223
	AE12	981		OAL	569		HAP	1239
	AE12	1158		OAE2	17		HAP	1609
	AE12	1237		M15	507		HAP	1731
	AE12	1261		EWR	9		HAP	1914
	OAL	768	SITHONIAN	VP10	95		HAP	2341
	MFL	35	SITS	LC	49		BR	37
	KT1	10		LC	131		BR	125
	KT1	107		PLB	33		BR	195
	KT2	397		J6	562		ETS	6
	KT3	284		J10	214		ODA	71
	KT3	1127		J10	312		J6	815
	M8	268		J10	339		J10	561
	M8	283		J10	516		M1	110
	M8	296		P5	76		M1	218
	CAM	89		VP3	101		M1	239
	CAM	383		AE1	407		M1	365
	FL	402		AE4	118		M1	429
	WB	308		AE7	886		M1	443
	M15	475		AE7	1108		M1	774
SISTER'S	CM	24		AE8	958		M1	825
	AK	172		AE11	368		M1	858
	J6	733		AE11	723		M1	1075
	VP6	112		AE11	737		M13	150
	AE1	184		OAL	184		VP1	79
	AE4	633		OAL	250		VP2	86
	AE8	210		OAL	569		VP5	87
	AE12	234		OAL	714		VP6	120
	M8	284		AF	105		VP7	17
	M8	290		C	463		VP9	17
	M8	311		M11	44		VP9	64
	C	373		M11	495		G1	294
SISTERS	CM	123		M12	83		G1	331
	PUO3	6		M12	87		G1	322
	J6	29		WB	470		G1	353
	P6	126		STP	11		G1	374
	GK	89	SITTING	J1	140		G1	397
	VP6	89		P3	76		G1	432
	G1	310		P5	258		G1	439
	G4	474		M1	722		G1	417
	G4	492		FL	133		G1	500
	G4	551		FL	294		G1	502
	AE1	444	SITUATE	C	302		G1	515
	AE1	450	SIX	MF	131		G1	536
	AE3	46		J1	100		G1	565
	AE4	1000		J3	334		G1	588
	AE6	773		J3	448		G1	596
	AE7	452		P5	219		G1	638
	AE10	241		G3	101		G2	20
	OAL	31		AE10	251		G2	93
	KT3	172		OAE1	3		G2	115
	M8	255		KT2	3		G2	400
	M8	295		C	56		G2	451
	M8	400		M12	579		G2	466
	M8	354	SIXPENCE	P5	281		G2	785
	C	59	SIXTEEN	M13	7		G3	248
	C	440	SIXTH	KT2	9		G3	310
	C	575	SIXTY	KT2	445		G3	552
SISTERS'	G4	495		GP	8		G3	565
	KT1	155		GP	9		G3	721
	M8	380	SIXTY-SEVEN	ET	2		G3	824
SISYPHIAN	AU	45	SIZE	AM	705		G4	73
SISYPHUS	L3	200		AM	749		G4	84
	G3	65		AA	49		G4	447
	AU	37		P6	106		G4	461

SKIES	AE1	105	SKIES	KT3	665	SKIMMED	AE6	1244			
	AE1	129		BP	159		AE7	1102			
	AE1	149		CAM	273		C	33			
	AE1	181		HIF	543	SKIMMING	G1	497			
	AE1	250		HIF	651	SKIMS	G1	393			
	AE1	287		HIF	742		G1	520			
	AE1	348		C	627		AE1	223			
	AE1	391		M11	125		AE4	372			
	AE1	413		M11	183		AE7	491			
	AE1	551		M11	230		AE12	693			
	AE2	295		M11	265	SKIN	UDH	58			
	AE2	570		FL	3		UDH	63			
	AE2	653		FL	17		PC2	28			
	AE2	668		FL	491		EDG	10			
	AE3	255		M12	57		L4	145			
	AE3	320		M12	88		J6	210			
	AE3	497		M12	693		J10	308			
	AE3	683		M15	212		P3	56			
	AE3	813		M15	638		P3	122			
	AE4	231		M15	671		P3	183			
	AE4	256	SKIFF	J10	297		P3	191			
	AE4	353		M1	431		P5	273			
	AE4	363	SKILFUL	UDH	95		M1	746			
	AE4	504		AR	66		M1	836			
	AE4	535		RH	91		M1	1035			
	AE4	816		PMQ	14		M9	192			
	AE4	842		J10	310		M13	70			
	AE4	961		P5	54		VP3	157			
	AE5	12		AE7	903		G3	674			
	AE5	28		OAL	583		G4	426			
	AE5	83	SKILL	UDH	41		G4	800			
	AE5	138		HS	94		AE1	295			
	AE5	184		AR	178		AE3	317			
	AE5	208		LC	69		AE7	926			
	AE5	279		AM	143		AE12	557			
	AE5	294		PMQ	26		KT3	77			
	AE5	335		ECG2	32		CAM	345			
	AE5	602		AA	254		M12	183			
	AE5	671		AA	909		CI	151			
	AE5	678		MD	25	SKINKER	HIF	803			
	AE5	694		SAA	91	SKINS	G2	530			
	AE5	711		SAA	182		G3	588			
	AE5	945		SAA	779		AE7	127			
	AE6	345		SAA	956		AE7	552			
	AE6	382		SAA	960		AE8	372			
	AE6	194		RL	318		KT3	27			
	AE6	214		TA	163		FL	420			
	AE6	781		HAP	1943		M15	459			
	AE6	997		P3	173	SKIPPET	AE10	926			
	AE6	1061		P5	33	SKIRTS	G4	410			
	AE6	1171		P5	152	SKITTISH	OAL	822			
	AE7	35		M1	341	SKULK	J3	484			
	AE7	288		MC	12	SKULKED	AA	207			
	AE7	569		GK	7		VP3	28			
	AE7	670		GK	113		AE10	926			
	AE7	738		VP2	44		C	497			
	AE7	754		VP3	39		AU	334			
	AE7	788		VP8	75	SKULL	SAA	476			
	AE7	850		AE1	543		J10	318			
	AE7	997		AE3	938		AE5	639			
	AE8	93		AE5	143		HIF	799			
	AE8	102		AE8	495		M12	401			
	AE8	141		AE8	530		M12	586			
	AE8	369		AE10	345	SKY	HS	2			
	AE8	518		AE12	391		AR	37			
	AE8	564		AE12	1291		AR	196			
	AE8	698		OAL	309		AR	295			
	AE9	40		OAL	439		RH	12			
	AE9	124		OAL	476		LC	32			
	AE9	314		B	508		AM	408			
	AE9	560		M10	6		AM	439			
	AE9	611		C	590		AM	654			
	AE9	866		M11	119		AM	1116			
	AE10	177		WB	103		SEL3	1			
	AE10	371		M15	536		AA	231			
	AE10	381	SKILLED	J6	760		SAA	559			
	AE10	850		AE3	463		RL	4			
	AE10	897		AE8	654		T18	13			
	AE10	1288		AE9	227		H29	32			
	AE10	1293		AE9	1043		TA	11			
	AE11	805		AE10	252		AK	46			
	AE11	1169		AE10	587		AK	185			
	AE12	174		AE12	46		HAP	346			
	AE12	210		HIF	106		HAP	558			
	AE12	406	SKIM	AM	451		HAP	968			
	AE12	1098		HAP	1863		HAP	1226			
	AE12	1241		G4	76		HAP	1768			
	AF	107		AE1	123		HAP	1802			
	AF	169		AE1	549		HAP	1856			
	AF	179		AE5	212		HAP	1908			
	MFL	19		AE7	32		HAP	2115			
	DO	77		AE11	424		SSC	63			
	KT2	514		M11	477		BR	235			
	KT3	217		WB	21		EL	80			
	KT3	222		WB	216		EL	89			
	KT3	262	SKIMMED	AE3	377		EL	202			

Word	Ref	No.
SLAUGHTERED	SAA	712
	SAA	1091
	HAP	13
	J10	298
	G4	117
	AE3	816
	AE3	839
	AE6	678
	AE9	480
	AE9	1049
	AE10	934
	AE11	257
	AE12	494
	AE12	724
	OAL	734
	KT1	143
	M10	60
	HIF	530
	M12	610
	AU	399
	M15	541
SLAUGHTERS	SAA	140
	EC	6
	M1	310
SLAVE	AM	166
	SMM2	2
	PUF	22
	AA	879
	MD	130
	MD	185
	SAA	81
	SAA	237
	L3	250
	H29	74
	J1	159
	J6	308
	J6	312
	J6	425
	J10	64
	J10	65
	J10	290
	J10	439
	P5	169
	P5	188
	P5	229
	P5	254
	P6	92
	HI	126
	AE5	371
	AE6	1176
	AE9	945
	AE12	62
	AE12	98
	KT3	157
	B	316
	CAM	52
	HIF	146
	HIF	165
	HIF	180
	HIF	495
	HIF	534
	HIF	595
	WB	65
	CI	317
	CI	459
SLAVERED	EMKG	15
SLAVERING	CI	179
	J6	813
SLAVERY	TA	303
	G2	705
SLAVES	VHH	39
	AM	200
	EWGR	15
	AA	9
	AA	15
	AA	56
	AA	775
	SAA	402
	AT	38
	L3	8
	HAP	220
	HAP	857
	J1	100
	J3	402
	J6	220
	J6	449
	J10	140
	P3	210
	P4	60
	P5	105
	P5	206
	P6	53
	P6	182
	G4	164
	AE1	101
	AE2	761

Word	Ref	No.
SLAVES	AE3	427
	AE9	360
	AE9	440
	AE11	571
	AE12	833
	OAL	116
	OAL	245
	OAL	246
	KT1	586
	B	596
	HIF	228
	HIF	258
	HIF	415
	C	533
	WB	286
	CI	92
	CI	178
	CI	591
SLAY	AA	130
	B	580
SLAYER	KT2	576
SLED	G1	245
SLEEK	P4	89
	M13	70
SLEEKS	M13	28
SLEEP	AR	105
	SMA	113
	LC	45
	AM	284
	AM	1031
	AM	1126
	ETL	14
	PCB	16
	EPF	2
	PSF	28
	AA	448
	MF	73
	MF	198
	SAA	308
	AT	123
	L3	90
	L3	108
	L3	111
	L3	182
	L3	264
	L3	300
	L4	66
	T18	20
	T18	22
	T18	88
	T18	89
	H2	11
	H2	38
	H2	44
	AK	183
	HAP	1902
	HAP	1988
	HAP	2308
	HAP	2588
	J1	118
	J1	190
	J3	26
	J3	320
	J3	376
	J3	380
	J3	390
	J3	445
	J3	475
	J6	128
	J6	402
	J6	550
	J6	613
	P3	25
	P3	80
	P3	112
	P5	74
	M1	292
	M1	862
	HI	139
	GK	57
	VP1	74
	VP2	101
	VP7	66
	G2	609
	G2	663
	G3	661
	G4	270
	G4	279
	AE1	421
	AE1	954
	AE2	331
	AE2	347
	AE2	350
	AE3	667
	AE3	680
	AE4	116

Word	Ref	No.
SLEEP	AE4	358
	AE4	559
	AE4	678
	AE4	703
	AE4	801
	AE4	758
	AE4	769
	AE4	770
	AE5	829
	AE5	1091
	AE5	1095
	AE5	1109
	AE6	388
	AE6	396
	AE6	477
	AE6	572
	AE6	701
	AE6	1235
	AE7	580
	AE7	1038
	AE8	92
	AE9	242
	AE9	295
	AE9	311
	AE9	464
	AE11	424
	AE12	467
	AE12	1312
	AF	125
	KT1	177
	KT1	527
	KT3	434
	KT3	784
	B	196
	B	199
	B	208
	B	214
	B	243
	HIF	814
	C	152
	C	331
	C	339
	TH	368
	M11	88
	M11	258
	M11	267
	M11	291
	M11	309
	M11	320
	M11	346
	FL	21
	FL	34
	FL	613
	M12	441
	M15	32
	M15	38
	M15	484
	CI	153
	CI	178
SLEEP-COMPELLING	KT1	550
SLEEPER	AU	161
SLEEPEST	P3	112
	AE4	806
SLEEPING	GE	58
	J10	263
	VP6	39
	G4	643
	AE2	221
	AE6	688
	AE6	943
	AE8	720
	AE9	433
	AE9	440
	B	233
	M11	380
	AU	372
	CI	92
SLEEP-PROCURING	M1	932
SLEEPS	AM	1019
	AT	115
	J1	90
	VP6	79
	G1	468
	AE10	324
	C	326
	M11	285
	CI	342
SLEEPY	G1	115
	G3	399
	G4	277
	AE9	668
	AE12	864
	KT2	18
	M11	288
	M11	326
	CI	29

Word	Src	No.	Word	Src	No.	Word	Src	No.
SLEEPY	CI	193	SLIDES	RL	52	SLOTHFUL	FL	562
SLEET	AM	743		CAM	272	SLOUGH	G3	664
	G3	564	SLIDING	EAZ	6		AE2	643
SLEEVE	KT3	37		T23	92	SLOVENLY	MD	285
SLEEVES	AE9	843		M13	83	SLOW	AM	207
	FL	163		VP3	62		SM2	20
SLENDER	PC1	20		AE3	674		SLN	12
	L4	156		AE11	1203		EAZ	32
	T18	49		KT3	131		AA	697
	G1	424	SLIGHT	AR	157		TA	22
	G2	170		AM	460		AK	158
	AE11	861		PWGR	27		HAP	698
	OAL	622		AA	943		HAP	1362
	AF	32		SAA	133		HAP	1667
	KT2	603		SAA	1007		HAP	1682
	M10	48		PK	29		HAP	2215
	C	18		HAP	2004		BR	245
	C	657		BR	141		STS3	19
	M11	478		J3	208		EL	49
SLEPT	SCG1	3		M1	846		P1	121
	AA	139		G4	8		P3	238
	SAA	844		AE9	179		M1	465
	TA	15		AE9	735		GK	35
	EL	16		AE9	783		VP1	37
	M1	131		AU	157		G1	291
	AE2	642		CI	100		G1	318
	AE10	97	SLIGHTED	PRL	34		G2	4
	B	288		PC1	15		G2	206
	C	228		L1	18		G3	20
	TH	365		AE1	75		G3	736
	M11	295	SLIGHTLY	AE10	670		G4	689
	M11	323		M12	753		AE4	189
	M12	438	SLIGHTS	TJD	138		AE4	421
SLEW	SAA	70	SLILY	HAP	1778		AE5	377
	RL	86	SLIM	SAA	340		AE5	572
	J3	198	SLIME	MD	174		AE5	892
	P1	195		M1	580		AE6	294
	M1	995		G1	175		AE9	35
	HI	65		G4	414		AE9	1065
	HI	66		M15	553		AE10	539
	G3	724	SLIMY	P1	47		AE10	642
	AE1	660		G3	441		AE10	1129
	AE1	677	SLIMY-BORN	HAP	311		AE11	1088
	AE2	221	SLING	VP3	150		AE11	1205
	AE2	898		AE7	1024		AE12	973
	AE3	163		AE9	797		AE12	1239
	AE3	430		AE11	867		OAL	142
	AE5	129		AE11	922		KT2	331
	AE6	1094		M8	123		KT3	1059
	AE8	746	SLINGS	G1	415		M8	151
	AE9	440		AE7	951		M8	238
	AE9	451		AE9	690		TH	36
	AE9	463		AE9	905		FL	248
	AE9	593		KT3	507		M12	91
	AE9	725	SLINKED	AE9	466		M12	427
	AE9	775	SLIP	SAA	859		M15	338
	AE9	946		PD	7		CI	596
	AE9	1039		PD	25	SLOW-CREEPING	G3	843
	AE10	487		HAP	1057	SLOWER	AE9	504
	AE10	605		G2	112	SLOWEST	ML	43
	AE10	994	SLIPPED	EL	286	SLOWLY	AM	384
	AE10	1056		M1	718		AM	794
	AE11	991		AE5	428		AM	946
	AE11	1012		AE5	594		SM2	13
	AE11	1019		AE6	951		ENH	15
	AE12	516		M11	408		DA	112
	AE12	540		AS	7		EL	9
	AE12	738	SLIPPERY	AM	67		G2	165
	AE12	745		SMA	6		G3	645
	AF	68		MO	9		AE1	262
	KT2	630		TA	400		AE5	367
	KT3	416		G4	586		AE6	558
	M8	190		AE10	225		AE12	332
	HIF	630		AE12	1003		OAL	559
	M12	369		TJD	69		KT2	58
	M12	593	SLIPPING	AE5	428	SLOWNESS	AE10	831
	M12	727	SLIPS	HAP	477	SLUBBER	OAE2	86
	M12	404		G2	38	SLUGGARD	KT1	177
	M12	423		G4	170		J6	163
	AU	284		AE5	1011		P5	194
	AU	391	SLIT	G2	106	SLUICES	G3	407
	AU	611	SLOES	G4	215	SLUICY	G1	437
SLICE	BP	65	SLOPING	VP9	11	SLUMBER	L3	96
SLICED	P4	73		G1	328		T18	19
SLICK	M1	836	SLOPS	J6	772		H2	40
SLID	AE7	497	SLOTH	PSF	27		TA	70
SLIDDERING	AE2	749		MD	185		M1	860
SLIDE	AA	198		P3	4		M1	990
	EL	312		P3	31		G4	583
	SSH	12		P5	74		G4	717
	G4	594		G1	190		AE1	970
	AE2	341		G2	604		AE3	202
	AE10	409		G4	205		AE7	128
	M15	476		AE9	842		AE7	137
SLIDES	PLB	8		TJD	74		AE8	44
	MD	250	SLOTHFUL	AE4	331		AE8	540

Word	Ref	No.
SLUMBER	KT2	20
	B	197
	B	205
	C	318
	M11	386
	FL	27
	CI	98
	CI	160
SLUMBERING	AM	276
	AM	894
	AA	447
	MD	74
	SAA	834
	SAA	1045
	TA	472
	M9	29
	AE1	660
	AE4	349
	AE5	944
	KT1	545
SLUMBERS	SMA	42
	SIE	16
	CM	30
	SAA	1108
	HAP	2591
	P3	106
	M9	41
	AE1	935
	AE2	403
	AE4	267
	KT2	472
	CAM	124
	TH	364
	M15	281
SLURS	P1	167
SLUT	L4	146
SLY	ETG	20
	HAP	1689
	P1	229
	AE9	818
	AE11	1150
SLYLY	M1	935
	OAE2	20
SMACK	P4	69
SMACKINGS	PEL	10
SMALL	UDH	74
	AR	155
	SMA	3
	LC	140
	PWG	10
	AM	618
	AM	878
	EMQ	15
	EEL	1
	PTL	4
	PLN	28
	SCD2	10
	PNH	15
	PAL	23
	PKK	20
	HP	243
	AA	906
	AA	914
	AA	990
	ELB	31
	SAA	516
	SAA	1007
	EDG	3
	RL	374
	RL	449
	H29	99
	H2	9
	HAP	144
	HAP	204
	HAP	1530
	HAP	1896
	HAP	2246
	HAP	2344
	HAP	2416
	HAP	2559
	PMS	36
	ESH	25
	EH	29
	J1	102
	J3	24
	J3	260
	J3	368
	J3	374
	J6	80
	J6	264
	J6	705
	J10	162
	J10	182
	J10	280
	P2	26
	P2	35

Word	Ref	No.
SMALL	M1	381
	M1	423
	M1	654
	G1	137
	G2	592
	G4	8
	AE2	793
	AE2	1027
	AE4	252
	AE7	334
	AE9	162
	AE9	198
	AE10	222
	AE10	601
	AE12	941
	KT3	171
	KT3	1138
	M8	179
	B	399
	BP	59
	HIF	493
	C	369
	FL	199
	M12	640
	M12	816
	AU	219
	WB	535
	ETP	14
	PMK	30
	PWR	40
SMALL-CRAFT	J3	147
SMALLEST	J6	134
	J6	193
	KT3	778
SMALLPOX	UDH	53
SMALL-TIMBERED	PEL	21
SMART	PMQ	36
	SMQ	3
	SMM2	17
	STL	10
	L3	28
	L4	11
	L4	44
	L4	263
	HAP	1376
	SSH	2
	J1	254
	M13	188
	AE1	292
	AE4	6
	AE9	784
	AE10	95
	AE10	468
	AE12	571
	AE12	623
	KT1	233
	KT2	123
	KT3	148
	KT3	336
	B	373
	HIF	501
	M11	90
	M12	635
	CI	190
SMARTER	G1	541
SMEAR	J6	347
SMEARED	J1	236
	VP8	139
	AE5	469
	AE7	476
	AE9	628
	AE12	156
	M15	537
SMEARS	G2	775
SMELL	HAP	2049
	VP2	66
	G4	44
	C	16
	FL	77
	FL	138
SMELLING	PCB	37
	KT3	366
	B	317
SMELLS	EC	35
	MS	8
SMILE	LCA	18
	AM	276
	AM	830
	AM	842
	SMM2	21
	PT	17
	SEL3	11
	SCG1	25
	SAA	64
	SAA	157
	SAA	158

Word	Ref	No.
SMILE	AT	43
	L4	122
	HH	19
	HAP	1704
	HAP	1994
	HAP	2460
	BR	149
	BR	359
	SSH	7
	J6	329
	J6	689
	P1	251
	M9	165
	HI	44
	GK	133
	VP4	73
	VP4	76
	VP6	36
	AE2	28
	AE4	557
	AE8	403
	AE12	446
	OAL	714
	DO	84
	CI	488
SMILED	EOE	13
	HP	158
	HAP	740
	HAP	2395
	ODA	35
	P1	234
	HI	150
	AE2	518
	AE5	470
	AF	93
	KT2	303
	KT3	288
	KT3	432
	KT3	490
	KT3	743
	KT3	1141
	B	627
	HIF	284
	HIF	800
	C	319
	FL	604
	M12	53
SMILERS	EEL	5
SMILES	AR	158
	LC	52
	LC	136
	AA	912
	MF	198
	L1	10
	H2	87
	FS1	9
	TA	121
	HAP	2582
	BR	114
	EL	215
	P1	11
	HI	173
	AE1	292
	AE4	180
	AE5	1104
	AE8	520
	AE10	1144
	OAL	94
	KT3	136
SMILING	AM	376
	HP	118
	SAA	992
	H29	50
	HAP	760
	J6	787
	GK	5
	VP7	9
	AE1	347
	AE5	698
	AE5	1082
	AE7	158
	AE8	676
	AE10	1046
	KT2	512
	KT2	565
	KT3	167
	M8	118
	HIF	801
	M12	26
	WB	346
	CI	153
SMINTHEUS	HIF	61
SMITH	HAP	253
	J1	83
	J10	91
	G4	248

Word	Code	Count
SMITH	AE8	831
	KT2	598
	HIF	768
SMITHFIELD	EKK	22
SMITHS	HAP	2562
	KT3	459
SMITHY	AE8	591
	M12	390
SMOCK-FACED	J10	491
SMOKE	LC	19
	AM	329
	AM	366
	AM	953
	SAA	524
	L3	229
	H29	18
	H2	90
	HAP	1612
	HAP	1726
	J3	400
	P2	11
	M1	335
	VP1	118
	VP2	95
	G1	255
	G3	274
	G3	626
	G3	740
	G4	336
	G4	545
	G4	710
	G4	723
	AE1	578
	AE3	271
	AE3	760
	AE4	86
	AE5	574
	AE6	802
	AE7	109
	AE8	141
	AE8	336
	AE8	378
	AE9	313
	AE11	286
	AE11	908
	AE12	16
	AE12	862
	AE12	976
	KT3	181
	KT3	186
	KT3	587
	HIF	426
	M12	362
	WB	442
	CI	565
SMOKED	KT2	474
	KT3	197
SMOKES	L3	211
	J3	326
	AE7	909
	BP	52
SMOKING	G2	794
	AE3	161
	AE3	375
	AE5	861
	AE8	553
	AE9	516
	AE9	760
	AE10	72
	AE11	1312
	AE12	510
	AE12	696
	KT3	347
	BP	107
	CI	583
SMOKY	G2	421
	AE2	418
	AE3	728
	AE5	185
	AE8	558
SMOLDERING	G3	740
	AE5	891
	AE7	638
	AE11	286
	KT3	980
	C	708
SMOOTH	AR	246
	DA	57
	DA	82
	AA	256
	AA	745
	T18	74
	EL	337
	J6	604
	J10	491
	P1	122
SMOOTH	P4	94
	VP2	45
	VP6	76
	G1	39
	G1	261
	G3	256
	G3	785
	AE1	100
	AE3	693
	AE5	1074
	AE6	193
	AE7	529
	AE7	1109
	OAL	18
	OAL	409
	DO	46
	M10	22
	AU	18
SMOOTHED	AE1	203
	AE8	118
	KT2	514
	CI	508
SMOOTHER	JH	14
	P3	17
	VP9	25
	G2	110
	AE5	281
SMOOTH-GRAINED	G2	631
SMOOTHLY	AR	293
	LC	111
	ER	33
	VP4	57
	AE2	271
	AE7	379
	AE10	409
SMOOTHNESS	P1	153
	M1	746
	AE5	998
SMOOTHS	L1	10
	M1	447
	G1	138
	M11	499
SMOTHER	PTS	18
	AE2	827
SMOTHERED	VP8	150
	M12	768
SMOULDERING	AM	870
	G2	418
SMUT	J6	188
SMYRNA	AM	686
SNAFFLE	G3	296
SNAG	AE11	10
SNAKE	ESF	24
	J1	64
	M13	94
	VP3	145
	VP8	98
	G3	647
	G3	812
	G4	663
	AE2	511
	AE2	641
	AE5	359
	AE7	524
	AE8	398
	KT1	494
	M12	17
	M12	35
	M15	577
SNAKES	L3	222
	TA	453
	TA	458
	BR	56
	G2	295
	G3	62
	G3	632
	G4	693
	AE6	393
	AE6	565
	AE6	772
	AE6	822
	AE7	486
	AE7	458
	AE7	626
	AE7	631
	AE8	575
	AE8	924
	AE10	1080
	OAL	215
	AF	133
	CAM	91
SNAKY	SAA	806
	M1	927
	AE2	833
	AE4	685
	KT1	552
SNAP	HAP	1708
	VP3	24
SNARE	HAP	579
	G1	365
	G1	413
	OAL	445
	KT2	36
	KT2	509
	KT3	328
	TJD	33
	TH	227
	AU	53
SNARES	AM	716
	G4	591
	KT2	383
	M15	697
SNARL	HAP	1464
	P1	212
	GK	83
	G4	692
SNARY	G4	361
SNATCH	PAL	34
	H9	21
	BR	290
	AE3	295
	AE4	836
	AE5	858
	AE9	13
	AE9	320
	AE10	870
	AE12	238
	OAE2	36
	M8	231
SNATCHED	AA	833
	L3	76
	OD	42
	H3	51
	ODA	39
	J3	234
	M1	484
	AE1	914
	AE6	1203
	AE7	78
	AE7	335
	AE7	674
	AE8	536
	AE10	691
	AE11	817
	AE11	1118
	AE12	238
	AE12	1068
	KT1	345
	KT2	656
	M12	332
	AU	127
	AU	436
SNATCHES	AE6	821
	AE9	750
SNATCHING	AU	597
SNEAK	PAZ	23
SNEAKED	VP3	28
SNEAKING	EPC	13
	OE	45
	EKA	19
	J1	116
SNEEZED	T18	28
SNIP	ETP	14
SNORE	L3	286
	J6	163
	P3	4
	AE9	424
	HIF	650
	KT2	19
	C	229
SNORED	OAE2	67
SNORES	P3	111
SNOREST	P5	191
SNORING	VP6	22
	AE3	828
	M12	436
SNORTING	KT3	458
SNORTS	G3	392
	AE11	751
SNOUT	J10	103
	P1	240
	C	121
	M15	157
SNOW	PAZ	34
	ETG	6
	PRH	4
	T23	60
	H9	2
	HAP	1915
	HAP	1918
	J3	177
	M1	153

SNOW	VP10	71	SOBER	HAP	534	SOFT		VP8	114
	VP10	95		HAP	590			VP10	62
	G1	641		EDS	28			G1	86
	G3	495		PMS	20			G1	491
	G3	548		J6	40			G1	685
	G3	564		J10	464			G2	457
	G3	568		P1	191			G2	593
	G3	575		P3	6			G2	664
	AE3	504		G2	380			G2	689
	OAL	326		AE1	219			G3	266
	M8	382		AE1	1032			G3	296
	FL	161		OAL	282			G3	337
	FL	584		KT3	939			G3	611
	AS	68		B	684			G4	379
SNOWBALL	ESF	20		BP	12			G4	776
SNOWS	HAP	2565		HIF	612			AE3	151
	J6	223		C	7			AE4	92
	M13	67		FL	178			AE4	613
	VP10	72		FL	248			AE4	628
	G1	66		FL	604			AE4	758
	G1	325		M12	304			AE5	962
	AE4	366		AU	203			AE5	1091
	AE12	132		M15	312			AE6	1008
	AE12	1021		M15	492			AE7	865
	FL	586		CI	488			AE8	514
	M15	91		RL	396			AE8	882
SNOW-WHITE	AE5	308	SOBERLY	AE9	558			AE8	938
	AE9	859	SOBS	AE11	228			AE9	1006
SNOWY	STS3	5		AE12	75			AE10	134
	G2	203		AE12	338			AE10	863
	G3	594		AE12	1283			AE11	385
	AE4	666		OAL	800			OAL	542
	AE5	740	SOCIETY	AE11	853			OAL	543
	AE7	965	SOCINIAN	RL	312			OAL	751
	AE8	512	SOCINUS	HAP	55			AF	74
	AE9	581		HAP	722			AF	160
	AE10	277	SOCKET	G1	253			DO	46
	AE10	319	SOCKETS	AM	1164			DO	101
	AE12	249		G1	538			DO	163
	AF	31		AE8	346			KT1	548
	KT3	55		KT1	526			KT2	565
	FL	234		CAM	269			KT3	116
	CI	151	SOCKS	MF	80			KT3	901
SNUFF	PUO5	14	SOCRATES	POE	3			KT3	1018
	G3	431		MD	96			KT3	1134
	AE6	1031		RL	210			M10	22
	AE7	667		HAP	2374			M10	84
	KT3	141		P4	3			CAM	125
SNUFF-BOX	PCB	38		P5	50			HIF	289
SNUFFED	PUO5	6	SODDEN	P6	166			C	598
SNUFFLING	P1	71		G4	387			TH	12
SNUFFS	G1	519	SODOM	WB	434			M11	285
	G3	362	SODOM'S	SAA	980			M11	312
	G3	391		SAA	1073			M11	348
	AE11	746	SODS	AE8	237			M11	436
SNUG	HAP	2308		AE12	180			FL	10
	VP3	24		FL	70			FL	85
SOAK	P4	80	SOFT	AR	67			FL	314
SOAKED	L3	70		AR	293			FL	359
	AE5	429		RH	7			AU	18
SOAKING	G1	134		SMA	29			AU	203
SOAKS	G3	677		SMA	51			M15	67
	G4	187		LC	50			M15	327
SOAP	P4	97		VHH	6			M15	534
SOAR	RL	62		SMM2	15			M15	622
	RL	437		DA	167			M15	629
	G1	500		PPC	26			M15	716
	AE8	558		SAA	618			ESK	15
	M8	360		SAA	1104	SOFTEN		E	20
	M15	377		L1	43			PRH	35
SOARED	PUO5	5		L3	201			TA	23
	SAA	557		T18	35			AE6	1170
	B	515		H3	6			M15	482
	M12	696		TA	286	SOFTENED		AT	40
	M12	737		TA	350			J1	127
SOARING	M1	624		GE	42			M1	656
	VP9	36		HAP	346			AE1	397
	AE5	335		HAP	1482			KT3	316
	AE11	869		SSC	33			M15	247
	OAE1	21		SKA5	11			GP	26
SOARS	G2	172		SKA6	23			CI	36
	AE5	864		LS	9	SOFTENING		AE12	592
	AE9	764		EL	2	SOFTENS		M15	628
	AE11	1116		EL	224	SOFTER		AR	269
SOB	L3	125		J3	6			HAP	247
SOBBED	PM	13		J6	280			M13	75
	VP5	33		J6	483			G1	255
	AE4	528		P1	121			AE11	820
	B	290		P1	192			OAL	17
SOBBING	G3	755		P5	19			KT3	963
SOBER	RH	54		M1	24			B	375
	AM	1130		M1	131			B	424
	PUO5	10		VP1	73			B	425
	ENH	24		VP2	67			BP	18
	AA	69		VP5	85			WB	90
	H2	74		VP5	128				

Word	Code	Ref
SOFTER	CI	44
SOFTEST	AE4	419
	KT2	331
SOFTLY	LC	96
	AM	1118
	SEL3	19
	SCD1	21
	EL	315
	J6	98
	M1	1038
	VP5	62
	G4	484
	AE1	974
	AE4	567
	AE8	770
	AE9	434
	OAL	556
	AF	97
	KT1	158
	KT2	315
	KT2	343
	KT3	555
	M8	285
	CAM	145
	CAM	190
	HIF	210
	FL	465
SOFTNESS	AM	826
	ER	62
	HAP	270
	M1	539
	M13	26
	AE12	895
	MFL	34
	M12	625
	M15	593
SOFTNESSE	MHD	6
SOIL	UDH	21
	UDH	55
	RH	57
	AA	12
	AA	194
	SAA	1065
	RL	32
	RL	159
	BR	162
	P4	96
	MC	7
	VP1	68
	VP4	48
	VP6	53
	VP10	70
	G1	2
	G1	71
	G1	80
	G1	100
	G1	117
	G1	144
	G1	151
	G1	186
	G1	304
	G2	38
	G2	88
	G2	154
	G2	241
	G2	251
	G2	253
	G2	256
	G2	283
	G2	297
	G2	305
	G2	316
	G2	337
	G2	346
	G2	357
	G2	359
	G2	361
	G2	529
	G2	583
	G2	590
	G3	785
	G4	414
	AE1	623
	AE1	749
	AE2	188
	AE3	129
	AE3	222
	AE3	804
	AE5	136
	AE7	1004
	AE7	1031
	AE10	413
	AE10	494
	AE11	382
	AE12	155
	AE12	266
SOIL	AE12	1037
	OAL	866
	MG	37
	MM	42
	DO	82
	KT2	358
	TJD	134
	HIF	60
	HIF	234
	M15	30
	ETP	9
	PWR	32
SOILING	T27	96
SOILS	MD	247
	G1	104
	G1	106
	G1	120
	G2	53
	G2	130
	G2	247
	G2	309
SOJOURNER	HAP	1276
SOLA	C	90
SOLACE	AE3	869
	AE3	934
	C	55
	C	423
SOLAR	TA	353
	AE6	1084
	C	652
SOLD	EMK	17
	AA	406
	MF	181
	SAA	697
	RL	378
	HAP	1220
	HAP	1520
	HAP	1528
	HAP	2009
	J1	86
	J3	301
	J6	360
	J6	723
	VP1	87
	G2	735
	G3	480
	AE1	679
	AE2	739
	AE6	826
	AE6	832
	AE6	845
	KT2	454
	KT3	18
	C	386
	GP	71
	CI	317
SOLDIER	PMQW	17
	SAA	636
	J10	415
	J16	6
	J16	12
	G2	377
	G3	487
	AE2	793
	B	597
	HIF	188
	M11	162
SOLDIER-LIKE	PMQ	17
SOLDIER'S	EPF	18
	ER	58
	J16	23
	J16	45
	P3	149
	AE6	333
	AF	57
	AF	62
	KT2	586
SOLDIERS	AM	216
	AM	469
	SAA	1124
	J3	479
	J16	21
	HI	90
	G4	32
	G4	117
	AE2	24
	AE2	665
	AE4	581
	AE7	892
	AE8	237
	AE8	922
	AE9	219
	AE9	700
	AE10	342
	AE10	361
	AE10	423
SOLDIERS	AE11	4
	AE11	1259
	OAL	113
	OAL	131
	OAL	206
	KT1	117
	AU	1
	AU	349
SOLDIERS'	AE6	647
	AE9	669
	KT2	601
	FL	211
SOLE	SAA	589
	SAA	612
	RL	84
	TA	301
	TA	477
	J1	207
	J10	191
	J10	376
	AE9	96
	AE11	765
	KT2	539
	TJD	156
	TJD	183
	HIF	487
	CI	542
SOLEMN	SMA	7
	SMA	50
	PRH	21
	MF	28
	HAP	2283
	BR	19
	EKA	12
	M1	505
	VP3	31
	G2	143
	G3	786
	AE1	577
	AE1	624
	AE1	1022
	AE2	268
	AE2	321
	AE4	910
	AE5	84
	AE5	380
	AE6	107
	AE6	517
	AE7	339
	AE7	798
	AE7	833
	AE8	137
	AE8	231
	AE8	403
	AE8	719
	AE8	883
	AE11	328
	AE12	24
	AE12	317
	AE12	898
	OAL	151
	AF	165
	AF	175
	DO	79
	KT3	919
	B	96
	B	685
	M10	53
	M10	57
	CAM	238
	HIF	584
	HIF	627
	M12	15
SOLEMNITY	HAP	2433
	AE6	1209
SOLEMNIZED	AK	55
	AE3	389
SOLEMNLY	J6	513
	KT1	99
	HIF	348
	WB	14
	AE11	1157
SOLICIT	AM	308
	HP	111
	AE6	140
	AE11	390
	OAL	815
	B	383
SOLICITING	AE12	590
SOLICITOR	P4	118
SOLICITOUS	HI	20
SOLICITS	AE10	57
SOLID	AA	298
	H9	6
	HAP	493
	HAP	619

SOLID	HAP	1099	SOMETIMES	H2	36	SON	HI	166
	J6	485		AK	83		HI	173
	J10	218		HAP	821		MC	43
	P1	160		HAP	1836		VP4	18
	P5	34		BR	269		VP4	59
	M1	398		EL	52		VP9	23
	M1	549		J16	95		G2	785
	MC	17		ELT	27		G4	461
	G1	640		GK	157		G4	466
	G2	112		G4	195		G4	471
	G2	312		AE10	966		G4	503
	G2	683		OAL	560		G4	510
	G3	138		OAL	613		G4	535
	G3	561		OAL	696		G4	556
	AE1	1045		OAL	820		G4	599
	AE2	829		M8	285		G4	613
	AE3	760		C	333		G4	768
	AE3	854		C	337		AE1	317
	AE7	811		M15	191		AE1	358
	AE7	999	SOMNUS	T18	16		AE1	449
	AE8	314	SON	AM	129		AE1	512
	AE8	790		EEL	18		AE1	564
	AE10	982		DA	36		AE1	679
	AE10	1113		DA	77		AE1	937
	AE12	307		DA	173		AE1	941
	OAL	573		AA	32		AE2	261
	KT1	455		AA	170		AE2	750
	KT3	606		AA	433		AE2	808
	TJD	124		AA	469		AE2	837
	CAM	342		AA	639		AE2	881
	M11	340		AA	703		AE2	899
	M12	648		AA	836		AE2	905
	M15	403		AA	881		AE2	919
	M15	405		AA	960		AE2	928
SOLITARY	AM	412		MD	100		AE2	950
	PTS	39		MD	216		AE2	966
	J3	2		MF	139		AE2	996
	G2	696		MF	145		AE2	1009
	G3	516		SAA	385		AE2	1017
	AE4	672		SAA	405		AE3	17
	AE6	1038		SAA	958		AE3	243
	AE11	854		EK	10		AE3	382
	KT1	532		RL	195		AE3	619
	AU	65		T18	32		AE3	624
SOLITUDE	AE6	599		HAP	117		AE4	135
	TH	77		HAP	789		AE4	335
SOLOMON	AM	171		HAP	1082		AE4	342
	MN	4		HAP	1209		AE4	863
	MM	4		HAP	1592		AE5	715
	KT2	503		HAP	1604		AE5	948
SOLON	J10	422		HAP	1627		AE5	1041
	P3	153		HAP	1660		AE6	49
SOLUS	C	90		HAP	1867		AE6	175
SOLUTION	M1	531		HAP	2436		AE6	243
	WB	96		BR	35		AE6	441
SOLVE	WB	205		BR	50		AE6	497
SOLYMAEAN	AA	513		BR	60		AE6	604
SOMETHING	PEL	14		BR	249		AE6	666
	PCG2	28		B.R	251		AE6	948
	PW	19		ETS	20		AE6	979
	ESF	5		EPN	4		AE6	1022
	AA	554		LS	18		AE6	1194
	PPC	2		OD	28		AE6	1229
	PPC	8		ODA	56		AE7	142
	PPC	33		J3	191		AE7	515
	AT	111		J3	223		AE7	799
	T27	6		J6	53		AE7	905
	T27	16		J6	510		AE7	912
	NS	3		J6	528		AE7	920
	HAP	1777		J6	777		AE7	924
	HAP	2056		J10	380		AE7	939
	PMS	2		J10	396		AE7	1043
	PMS	19		J10	545		AE7	1069
	J3	166		J16	85		AE8	64
	PLT	39		P2	19		AE8	78
	C	104		P6	134		AE8	140
	EMKG	25		P6	158		AE8	400
	CI	469		P6	180		AE8	430
	LC	139		M1	188		AE8	449
	LC	141		M1	189		AE8	486
	PWG	10		M1	620		AE8	504
	PRL	12		M1	647		AE8	673
	AM	333		M1	922		AE8	678
	SMM2	19		M1	1042		AE8	686
	ECG1	39		M1	1043		AE8	727
	SCG2	12		M1	1050		AE8	757
	E	12		M1	1058		AE8	809
	HP	79		M1	1065		AE8	817
	MF	51		M9	12		AE9	94
	SAA	62		M9	59		AE9	108
	PK	23		M9	70		AE9	401
	EDGA	11		VCS	33		AE9	642
	L4	220		VCS	36		AE9	693
	L4	221		HI	4		AE9	731
SOMETIME	H29	22		HI	87		AE9	790
SOMETIMES	H29	53		HI	158		AE9	893

SON

AE9	946
AE10	77
AE10	84
AE10	98
AE10	124
AE10	131
AE10	196
AE10	279
AE10	287
AE10	491
AE10	590
AE10	650
AE10	685
AE10	742
AE10	788
AE10	1062
AE10	1135
AE10	1208
AE10	1260
AE10	1301
AE11	46
AE11	78
AE11	82
AE11	158
AE11	249
AE11	274
AE11	277
AE11	356
AE11	1278
AE12	47
AE12	99
AE12	169
AE12	343
AE12	522
AE12	642
AE12	644
AE12	652
AE12	813
AE12	957
AE12	1127
AE12	1352
OAL	192
OAL	369
AF	2
DO	166
KT2	625
KT2	638
KT3	877
TJD	41
TJD	163
M8	58
M8	288
M8	304
M8	319
M8	324
M8	339
BP	3
CAM	89
HIF	1
HIF	8
HIF	11
HIF	192
HIF	401
HIF	491
HIF	500
HIF	542
HIF	671
C	194
C	360
C	609
C	641
M12	2
M12	96
M12	186
M12	292
M12	766
M12	828
AU	199
AU	234
AU	450
AU	469
WB	399
WB	418
M15	27
M15	62
M15	646
GP	114
CI	431
AS	54

SONG

PWG	38
EIE	14
AM	687
AM	1099
EAZ	15
EOE	32
ETC	16
AA	197
SAA	1042
SAA	1048
SAA	1058
SAA	1064
ER	6
L1	32
T18	12
H2	42
PAA	16
PAA	36
AK	13
J3	287
J6	96
PPS	8
M1	992
GK	150
VP1	111
VP4	65
VP5	85
VP5	114
VP6	31
VP6	43
VP6	62
VP6	111
VP6	125
VP7	4
VP7	28
VP7	40
VP9	13
VP9	59
VP9	80
VP9	88
VP9	92
VP10	50
VP10	104
G1	22
G2	5
G2	59
G4	1
G4	177
AE1	1047
AE6	892
AE7	544
AE7	558
AE8	106
AE8	380
AE10	276
OAL	128
OAL	633
AF	25
DO	2
KT2	38
CAM	4
CAM	7
C	602
C	603
C	631
FL	18
FL	133
FL	198
FL	208
FL	367
FL	466
FL	224
WB	339
M15	624
PTP	41
EIE	8

SONGS

AM	1100
ESF	31
MF	210
L1	17
ODA	67
J6	499
VP1	75
VP3	92
VP3	94
VP5	79
VP6	117
VP9	14
VP10	52
VP10	91
AE4	674
AE7	15
AE7	49
AE8	596
AE8	600
AE8	955
AE12	1250
KT1	15
KT1	535
HIF	646
FL	332
FL	488

SONGSTER

FL	449

SON-IN-LAW

T18	80
M1	186
AE7	371
AE7	440

SONNETTEER

SON'S

EIE	13
SAA	131
SAA	996
RL	193
HAP	723
J1	118
AE1	927
AE2	733
AE2	769
AE2	925
AE4	885
AE8	227
M8	244
M8	332
HIF	685
CI	203

SONS

EIE	3
EIE	5
EAZ	28
AA	14
AA	598
AA	720
AA	760
AA	870
PRH	20
MF	11
MF	17
SAA	710
PD	62
TA	160
HAP	414
HAP	798
HAP	924
HAP	1319
HAP	1356
HAP	1436
HAP	1438
HAP	1454
HAP	1481
HAP	1487
HAP	1523
HAP	1529
HAP	1574
HAP	1622
HAP	1636
HAP	1650
HAP	1672
HAP	1707
HAP	1739
HAP	1939
HAP	1945
HAP	1956
HAP	1962
HAP	1967
HAP	2123
BR	238
EL	202
J1	222
J3	262
J3	413
J6	17
J6	253
J6	835
J6	836
J10	445
P1	151
P6	140
M1	203
M1	911
HI	17
GK	122
G1	374
G4	226
AE1	388
AE2	718
AE5	780
AE6	652
AE6	1121
AE6	1143
AE6	1201
AE7	78
AE8	579
AE9	32
AE9	817
AE10	392
AE10	489
AE10	659
AE10	721
AE11	330
AE11	872
AE12	361
AE12	410

Word	Ref	No.
SONS	AE12	516
	AE12	1215
	KT1	155
	TJD	90
	M8	52
	HIF	25
	C	642
	FL	156
	AU	37
	GP	97
SONS'	SAA	709
	HAP	1213
SONS-IN-LAW	J6	820
SOON	JH	11
	HS	4
	HS	27
	HS	79
	AM	23
	AM	58
	AM	477
	AM	765
	AM	859
	AM	905
	AM	919
	AM	1058
	PEL	21
	PEL	26
	ECG1	6
	ECG1	7
	EAZ	31
	PTW	16
	CM	90
	CM	138
	HP	239
	ETG	7
	AA	137
	AA	252
	AA	287
	SAA	43
	EK	40
	L2	40
	L4	249
	T18	15
	T23	43
	T23	59
	T27	5
	T27	87
	H29	49
	H2	101
	FS2	14
	TA	48
	TA	119
	TA	154
	TA	157
	AK	169
	HAP	499
	HAP	562
	HAP	983
	HAP	1288
	HAP	1923
	HAP	1954
	HAP	2116
	HAP	2421
	HAP	2430
	BR	252
	BR	265
	BR	294
	BR	319
	STS3	12
	SKA6	17
	EL	4
	EL	188
	EL	303
	OD	21
	OD	44
	ODA	5
	ODA	27
	J1	148
	J3	130
	J3	241
	J3	329
	J6	211
	M1	924
	M1	992
	M1	1056
	M1	1089
	M9	75
	HI	80
	DHP	14
	VP2	20
	VP6	42
	G1	223
	G2	150
	G3	326
	G4	131
	G4	776
SOON	AE1	277
	AE1	414
	AE2	129
	AE2	241
	AE2	506
	AE2	897
	AE3	285
	AE3	350
	AE3	376
	AE3	781
	AE3	784
	AE3	870
	AE4	255
	AE4	425
	AE4	574
	AE4	814
	AE5	14
	AE5	284
	AE5	664
	AE5	784
	AE5	872
	AE5	874
	AE5	1113
	AE6	241
	AE6	564
	AE7	156
	AE7	193
	AE7	507
	AE7	692
	AE8	236
	AE8	514
	AE9	630
	AE9	932
	AE9	971
	AE10	230
	AE10	430
	AE10	549
	AE10	800
	AE10	900
	AE11	51
	AE11	200
	AE11	245
	AE11	753
	AE11	1011
	AE11	1062
	AE11	1230
	AE11	1238
	AE11	1315
	AE12	398
	AE12	883
	AE12	897
	AE12	1016
	AE12	1245
	OAL	101
	OAL	346
	OAL	421
	AF	98
	KT1	557
	KT1	577
	KT2	39
	KT2	122
	KT2	252
	KT2	330
	KT2	649
	KT3	725
	KT3	763
	KT3	1103
	TJD	86
	M8	232
	B	85
	B	168
	B	214
	B	332
	B	657
	CAM	214
	HIF	83
	HIF	121
	HIF	294
	HIF	463
	HIF	481
	TH	99
	TH	166
	TH	412
	M11	67
	M11	101
	FL	213
	FL	372
	FL	406
	FL	592
	M12	89
	M12	199
	M12	273
	M12	678
	AU	297
	WB	51
	WB	268
SOON	WB	364
	WB	376
	M15	381
	M15	683
	CI	134
	CI	281
	CI	306
	CI	363
	CI	381
	CI	507
	CI	600
	SMP	29
SOONER	HS	89
	AM	770
	PTW	19
	PPC	28
	L3	285
	EDS	32
	PKA	22
	J6	78
	J6	698
	J6	853
	J10	348
	P5	245
	VP10	43
	AE1	516
	AE6	562
	AE7	137
	AE9	143
	OAL	854
	C	45
	FL	114
	AU	467
	STP	34
SOONEST	SMA	16
	MO	8
	KT2	332
SOOTH	HAP	1763
SOOTHE	PCG2	26
	G3	293
	AE1	485
	AE1	535
	AE2	1052
	AE10	275
	AE10	656
	AE12	136
	OAL	17
	CAM	125
	HIF	500
	C	800
	M11	59
SOOTHED	SAA	1104
	AE4	703
	AE5	618
	AE6	519
	OAL	148
	AF	66
	AF	98
	KT3	392
	CAM	190
	FL	113
	FL	371
SOOTHES	AA	304
	M1	651
	AE1	219
	CAM	209
SOOTHING	AE4	133
	AE10	1229
	KT3	327
SOOTY	VP10	113
	BP	64
SOP	PDG	40
	AE6	567
SOPHISTER	EHC	1
SOPHISTICATE	DC	6
SOPHISTICATED	EMK	21
	RL	237
SOPHISTRY	MD	219
SOPHOCLES	POE	3
	EOE	1
	EOE	27
	VP8	15
SORACTE'S	AE11	1153
SORCERERS	HAP	1110
SORCERIES	BR	200
	KT2	482
SORDID	J1	177
	J1	211
	J3	69
	J10	333
	G1	118
	AE6	414
	AE12	894
SORE	MD	151
	L4	92
	HH	36

SORE	HAP	305
	HAP	1119
	HAP	1426
	HAP	1463
	ESH	2
	J6	609
	P3	231
	G3	360
	G3	691
	KT1	274
	TJD	167
	C	99
	C	584
	WB	372
	WB	509
SORELY	KT3	724
SORES	HAP	939
	J10	347
SORROW	UDH	89
	AR	222
	AR	255
	UMR	2
	PSF	6
	H9	26
	HAP	1128
	EL	354
	ODA	46
	HI	60
	VCS	5
	VP3	122
	AE1	511
	AE5	618
	AE8	50
	AE10	656
	AE11	48
	AE11	125
	AE11	228
	AE11	331
	AE11	355
	AE11	1227
	AE12	87
	AE12	886
	AE12	970
	AE12	1298
	OAL	634
	KT1	524
	KT2	309
	KT3	150
	KT3	686
	KT3	857
	KT3	860
	KT3	921
	KT3	1109
	M8	370
	B	315
	B	371
	B	685
	B	728
	HIF	577
	C	560
	C	773
	C	774
	TH	326
	TH	351
SORROWS	AR	52
	AM	292
	AM	957
	AM	1031
	SMM2	8
	DA	200
	L3	92
	STS3	18
	M1	740
	HI	136
	HI	176
	VP10	102
	G4	737
	AE1	284
	AE1	307
	AE2	489
	AE2	738
	AE4	48
	AE4	629
	AE6	385
	AE6	1201
	AE12	924
	KT1	463
	KT3	289
	KT3	1115
	HIF	500
	C	416
	TH	161
	WB	330
SORRY	C	218
SORT	EMM	3
	AA	75

SORT	AA	682
	EK	5
	RL	238
	EC	15
	EC	21
	HAP	342
	HAP	1135
	HAP	1363
	HAP	1791
	HAP	2240
	J6	47
	J6	755
	J10	264
	P1	151
	M1	224
	G2	162
	OAL	70
	OAE2	83
	C	530
	WB	352
SORTED	M10	44
	CI	186
SORTS	AM	596
	AA	289
	M1	583
	M13	136
	G1	527
	G2	122
SOT	PTW	31
	OE	4
	L3	151
	SKA4	18
	J6	813
	P3	197
	P5	108
	KT1	433
	CI	187
SOTS	GK	160
	KT1	432
SOTTED	J6	798
SOUGHT	HS	42
	AR	32
	AR	69
	SMA	130
	AM	245
	AM	642
	AM	754
	AM	927
	EUO2	4
	HP	99
	HP	104
	DA	96
	AA	161
	AA	501
	AA	563
	MD	128
	SAA	513
	SAA	825
	SAA	880
	SAA	998
	L4	110
	TA	403
	HAP	511
	HAP	536
	HAP	935
	HAP	1624
	BR	91
	STS3	4
	EL	245
	J3	272
	J6	108
	M1	155
	M1	523
	M1	640
	M1	797
	M1	825
	M1	902
	M9	37
	M13	46
	HI	9
	PLT	29
	VP1	43
	VP6	74
	G4	671
	AE1	77
	AE1	535
	AE1	878
	AE1	1002
	AE2	132
	AE2	161
	AE2	333
	AE2	588
	AE2	705
	AE2	1001
	AE3	425
	AE4	9

SOUGHT	AE4	990
	AE5	215
	AE5	501
	AE5	1062
	AE6	94
	AE6	164
	AE6	537
	AE6	639
	AE6	683
	AE6	795
	AE6	911
	AE7	56
	AE7	123
	AE7	203
	AE7	284
	AE7	294
	AE7	480
	AE7	510
	AE7	597
	AE7	630
	AE7	684
	AE7	776
	AE7	799
	AE7	1050
	AE7	1099
	AE8	221
	AE8	443
	AE9	4
	AE9	505
	AE9	594
	AE9	992
	AE10	103
	AE10	219
	AE10	332
	AE10	451
	AE10	552
	AE10	919
	AE10	1108
	AE10	1128
	AE10	1193
	AE11	164
	AE11	333
	AE11	353
	AE11	397
	AE11	534
	AE11	876
	AE11	961
	AE12	127
	AE12	610
	OAL	49
	OAL	321
	OAL	378
	OAL	849
	AF	31
	MFL	19
	KT2	22
	KT2	50
	KT2	173
	KT2	338
	KT3	3
	KT3	231
	KT3	386
	TJD	99
	M8	1
	M8	92
	B	200
	B	256
	B	716
	CAM	299
	C	222
	C	668
	C	672
	TH	35
	TH	77
	TH	270
	M11	59
	M11	88
	M11	194
	M11	439
	FL	21
	FL	37
	FL	115
	FL	314
	FL	417
	FL	421
	M12	104
	M12	266
	AU	428
	M15	1
	M15	19
	M15	456
	GP	48
	CI	84
	CI	201
	CI	214
	CI	293

SOUGHT	CI	479	SOUL	ODA	29	SOUL	AE12	942		
	AS	85		ODA	37		AE12	970		
SOUL	UDH	27		ODA	53		AE12	1164		
	UDH	35		J3	416		AE12	1265		
	UDH	64		J3	417		AE12	1322		
	UDH	98		J10	280		AE12	1363		
	JH	1		J10	335		AE12	1372		
	HS	125		J10	433		AE12	1377		
	AR	273		J10	464		OAL	16		
	SMA	97		J10	550		OAL	27		
	LC	27		P2	5		AF	85		
	LC	116		P2	130		AF	89		
	LCA	23		P3	46		AF	98		
	AM	31		P3	60		AF	160		
	SMM2	13		P3	205		LMC	2		
	PW	2		P3	221		MFL	10		
	SM2	5		P4	31		MFL	32		
	ENH	12		P4	128		DO	119		
	PTC	35		P5	175		KT1	276		
	PO	28		P5	244		KT1	293		
	CM	34		P6	22		KT1	464		
	EPF	4		P6	177		KT1	521		
	AA	156		M1	102		KT2	266		
	AA	171		M1	117		KT2	579		
	AA	365		M13	11		KT3	373		
	AA	370		VCS	23		KT3	430		
	AA	445		SLT2	7		KT3	843		
	AA	467		GK	23		KT3	844		
	AA	850		GK	77		KT3	852		
	AA	857		VP2	103		KT3	1043		
	AA	867		VP5	82		TJD	16		
	AA	964		VP7	55		TJD	87		
	PPC	17		VP8	113		TJD	197		
	MD	257		VP9	70		TJD	208		
	MD	53		G2	674		M8	203		
	SAA	433		G2	686		M8	250		
	SAA	643		G4	734		M8	363		
	SAA	820		AE1	89		M8	373		
	SAA	1004		AE1	421		B	370		
	RL	3		AE1	1034		B	375		
	RL	16		AE2	797		B	568		
	RL	37		AE2	1073		B	652		
	RL	137		AE3	82		CAM	34		
	AT	11		AE3	94		CAM	36		
	AT	46		AE4	4		CAM	95		
	L2	23		AE4	12		CAM	99		
	L2	67		AE4	141		HIF	128		
	L3	16		AE4	507		HIF	206		
	L3	160		AE4	597		HIF	323		
	L3	265		AE4	606		HIF	340		
	L4	13		AE4	628		HIF	415		
	L4	149		AE4	656		C	173		
	L4	193		AE4	937		C	330		
	T27	26		AE4	1009		C	412		
	H29	21		AE5	525		C	547		
	H29	86		AE5	960		C	596		
	FS1	8		AE6	79		C	806		
	FS4	6		AE6	125		TH	97		
	TA	4		AE6	143		TH	195		
	TA	114		AE6	154		TH	377		
	TA	138		AE6	202		M11	24		
	TA	150		AE6	970		M11	338		
	TA	322		AE6	982		M11	379		
	TA	456		AE6	989		FL	95		
	EAA	11		AE6	999		FL	113		
	AK	25		AE6	1012		FL	371		
	AK	29		AE6	1020		M12	199		
	AK	36		AE7	53		M12	443		
	AK	106		AE7	403		M12	497		
	AK	131		AE7	882		M12	672		
	AK	145		AE8	670		M12	756		
	HAP	146		AE8	749		AU	303		
	HAP	1285		AE8	768		AU	439		
	HAP	1367		AE9	84		AU	452		
	HAP	1708		AE9	367		WB	477		
	HAP	1728		AE9	387		M15	227		
	HAP	2133		AE9	471		M15	246		
	HAP	2474		AE9	789		M15	252		
	HAP	2514		AE9	838		M15	664		
	BR	86		AE9	999		M15	672		
	BR	112		AE10	484		M15	681		
	BR	215		AE10	680		GP	5		
	BR	256		AE10	736		GP	10		
	EL	29		AE10	849		GP	33		
	EL	85		AE10	893		CI	3		
	EL	191		AE10	1177		CI	29		
	EL	210		AE10	1249		CI	54		
	EL	217		AE10	1313		CI	123		
	EL	240		AE11	241		CI	135		
	EL	244		AE11	632		CI	186		
	EL	318		AE11	678		CI	228		
	EL	340		AE11	759		CI	422		
	EL	375		AE11	1209		EWR	12		
	OD	6		AE12	8	SOULED	HIF	185		
	OD	16		AE12	489	SOUL'S	SAA	146		
	ODA	23		AE12	841		OAL	148		

Word	Ref	No.
SOUND	M12	697
	AU	89
	AU	136
	GP	41
	CI	56
	CI	125
	SMP	58
	SMP	62
	SMP	60
SOUNDED	AE9	865
	KT1	56
SOUNDER	AE2	46
	C	201
SOUNDING	HAP	439
	VP5	130
	VP10	85
	VP10	91
	G1	215
	G2	788
	G4	252
	AE1	81
	AE2	275
	AE3	562
	AE3	731
	AE4	234
	AE4	955
	AE5	140
	AE5	179
	AE5	193
	AE5	277
	AE5	1128
	AE6	263
	AE6	753
	AE6	772
	AE7	32
	AE7	775
	AE7	812
	AE7	848
	AE7	882
	AE8	325
	AE11	843
	AE11	894
	AE11	1251
	AE12	375
	AE12	1023
	AE12	1096
	AE12	1267
	OAL	605
	AF	159
	KT3	906
	M8	72
	M8	86
	FL	212
SOUNDLY	M1	292
SOUNDS	ELB	9
	RL	271
	L2	52
	FS2	7
	M1	451
	M1	776
	GK	12
	G2	732
	G3	290
	G3	563
	G4	95
	G4	101
	G4	279
	G4	379
	AE2	405
	AE2	842
	AE3	313
	AE3	762
	AE3	916
	AE4	214
	AE5	757
	AE6	775
	AE9	133
	AE9	669
	AE10	258
	AE11	655
	AE11	1086
	AE11	1140
	AE11	1210
	AE12	1051
	AF	165
	AF	175
	KT3	581
	CAM	152
	HIF	666
	C	751
	TH	308
	M12	68
	M12	72
	M12	81
	CI	579
SOUR	PR	27
SOUR	T27	46
	GE	60
	HAP	213
	J6	555
	P3	112
	AE7	896
	AE9	1086
	AE12	10
	M15	317
SOURCE	AM	865
	M1	388
	RL	70
	HAP	1186
	HAP	2361
	VCS	7
	VP10	16
	G1	625
	G4	522
	AE7	332
	AE8	186
	AE12	830
	B	651
	HIF	57
	HIF	399
	HIF	533
	WB	70
SOURCES	J3	382
SOURED	HAP	277
SOUR-HEADED	G3	88
SOURLY	AE9	52
	AE10	1046
	KT2	303
	HIF	284
SOURNESS	G2	186
	G4	215
SOUSE	AE8	931
SOUSING	VP9	17
	AE5	332
	AE9	762
	TH	318
SOUTH	CM	13
	M1	357
	G1	622
	G2	364
	G3	472
	AE1	126
	AE1	756
	AE2	567
	AE3	457
	AE5	997
	AE5	1106
	AE10	371
	M11	366
SOUTHERN	HS	122
	DC	19
	VHH	44
	AM	95
	PAZ	29
	AA	231
	P6	30
	M1	81
	VP2	84
	VP5	128
	G1	337
	G1	487
	G1	593
	G2	261
	G2	454
	G3	651
	AE1	154
	AE2	152
	AE3	96
	AE3	621
	AE5	910
	AE6	484
	AE7	575
	AE8	568
	AE11	1168
	KT3	542
	M12	674
SOUTHERNE'S	MC	29
SOUTHING	G4	577
	AE5	33
SOUTHWARD	G3	437
SOUTHWARDS	HAP	1747
SOUTHWARK'S	PUO5	11
SOVEREIGN	HS	76
	SMA	95
	LC	14
	DC	51
	AM	57
	E	11
	AA	780
	AA	896
	MD	77
	MD	117
SOVEREIGN	MD	213
	PRH	42
	SAA	736
	SAA	790
	RL	57
	L3	205
	FS1	8
	TA	75
	HAP	28
	HAP	186
	HAP	531
	HAP	1599
	HAP	1997
	HAP	2026
	HAP	2078
	HAP	2100
	HAP	2378
	HAP	2425
	HAP	2513
	BR	329
	J6	314
	M1	451
	G1	485
	G4	120
	AE1	31
	AE1	222
	AE1	361
	AE4	355
	AE4	422
	AE7	234
	AE7	321
	AE7	851
	AE8	677
	AE10	6
	AE10	177
	AE10	864
	AE10	878
	AE12	288
	AE12	592
	AF	33
	KT1	66
	KT2	267
	KT2	381
	KT2	388
	KT2	529
	KT3	498
	KT3	728
	KT3	1011
	HIF	6
	HIF	165
	HIF	206
	HIF	227
	HIF	312
	HIF	389
	HIF	457
	HIF	553
	HIF	674
	C	68
	C	171
	C	420
	C	637
	C	705
	FL	177
	FL	422
	FL	508
	FL	550
	WB	70
	GP	55
	CI	619
SOVEREIGN'S	AM	1037
	PUO2	2
	SAA	11
	TA	41
	TA	268
	HAP	2458
	G3	81
	G4	318
	AE1	116
	AE6	536
	HIF	716
	HIF	767
	AU	300
	GP	84
SOVEREIGNS	PSF	6
	B	273
	HIF	116
SOVEREIGNS'	DHP	18
SOVEREIGNTY	HP	133
	HAP	985
	G2	398
	WB	279
SOW	PUO1	13
	L4	30
	J6	256
	VP1	97
	VP3	64

Word	Code	No.	Word	Code	No.	Word	Code	No.
SOW	G1	2	SPACE	AE2	598	SPAIN	AR	14
	G1	219		AE2	666		AR	308
	G1	300		AE2	689		PWG	41
	G1	304		AE2	928		PWG	51
	G1	316		AE3	239		AM	32
	G1	345		AE4	311		AM	788
	G1	401		AE4	361		ETC	24
	G2	303		AE5	13		PSF	9
	G2	323		AE5	60		HAP	291
	G2	605		AE5	424		HAP	1626
	G4	190		AE5	539		J10	242
	AE3	502		AE5	733		AE7	917
	AE8	61		AE6	200		AE8	266
	AE8	851		AE6	372		TH	52
	AE12	359		AE6	783		M15	17
	OAL	454		AE6	807	SPAKE	AM	292
	OAE1	13		AE6	984		HAP	2076
	KT1	25		AE8	64		M9	42
	M15	157		AE8	130		M8	185
SOWED	TA	357		AE8	608		M11	378
	GE	33		AE10	481	SPAN	L2	18
	HAP	1394		AE10	585		HAP	1702
	HAP	1937		AE10	626		HAP	2104
	M1	403		AE10	880		AE9	755
	AE6	300		AE10	1094		AE10	658
	AE7	766		AE11	457		AE10	880
	TJD	46		AE11	834		B	327
	HIF	10		AE11	907	SPANGLES	FL	92
	FL	91		AE11	1310	SPANIARDS	PIE	6
	M15	324		AE12	179		PSF	27
	CI	495		AE12	196		G1	88
SOWING	G1	319		AE12	420	SPANIEL	EPC	13
SOWN	HS	56		AE12	785	SPANISH	PWG	43
	PMM	7		AE12	810		ET	5
	H29	47		AE12	979		MS	9
	H2	6		AE12	1111	SPANISH-LEATHER	J6	362
	EL	145		DO	22	SPARE	EWG	24
	P5	86		KT1	259		SIE	8
	G1	242		KT2	451		PMQ	47
	G1	314		KT3	252		PCD	16
	G2	195		KT3	586		PAL	20
	MM	36		KT3	705		EMK	20
	HIF	110		KT3	842		POE	21
SOW'S	P6	166		B	27		EK	29
SOWS	G1	545		B	658		PDG	24
	B	442		BP	178		RL	263
	C	13		C	276		L3	293
SPACE	AA	839		FL	42		PAA	9
	L3	31		FL	498		HAP	1399
	L3	38		FL	587		EL	235
	L3	120		M12	56		OD	22
	L4	53		M12	742		J6	755
	L4	59		AU	571		J16	91
	TA	27		M15	139		P3	137
	AK	13		M15	252		P5	158
	HAP	256		M15	370		PLT	13
	HAP	272		M15	462		EHC	9
	HAP	282		M15	554		VP10	72
	HAP	657		M15	632		G2	500
	HAP	665		CI	627		AE1	743
	HAP	1200	SPACES	AE4	730		AE3	59
	HAP	1569		AE9	675		AE3	60
	HAP	1617	SPACIOUS	AM	402		AE5	905
	HAP	1873		H29	26		AE7	313
	HAP	2073		AK	88		AE8	422
	HAP	2139		HAP	575		AE9	275
	EL	271		J1	226		AE9	652
	OD	9		P2	80		AE10	67
	ODA	52		P4	79		AE10	729
	M1	31		M1	43		AE10	840
	M1	84		M13	104		MFL	28
	M1	318		G2	219		DO	98
	M1	552		G2	571		KT1	131
	M1	563		AE1	78		KT3	171
	M1	588		AE1	158		KT3	499
	M1	1032		AE1	898		B	99
	M13	219		AE2	306		B	587
	MC	18		AE3	19		CAM	204
	GK	124		AE3	454		C	196
	G1	47		AE3	818		TH	418
	G1	657		AE6	62		M12	119
	G2	59		AE6	573		M15	680
	G2	106		AE7	207		GP	50
	G2	114		AE8	589	SPARED	PFD	19
	G2	381		AE8	804		EM	25
	G2	388		AE9	466		PUO5	28
	G3	117		AE10	1266		EUF	10
	G3	531		AE11	957		L3	247
	G4	218		AE12	1013		EL	70
	G4	302		KT1	25		G4	758
	G4	516		KT3	553		AE1	660
	AE1	88		CAM	316		KT3	619
	AE1	181		WB	15		GP	67
	AE1	507	SPADE	J16	49		CI	417
	AE1	855	SPAIN	HS	86	SPARES	AA	453
	AE1	959					HAP	2458

SPARES	J6	817	SPARTAN	G3	618	SPEAKER'S	AE4	113		
	M15	346		AE1	440		M11	104		
	C	57		AE4	187	SPEAKEST	J6	281		
	AU	477		AE7	510		KT1	284		
SPARING	HAP	2212		AE10	142	SPEAKING	SAA	474		
	BR	273		M12	7		GE	57		
	P6	48		AU	288		PKA	44		
	KT3	383		CI	319		AE4	402		
	C	23	SPARTANS	ECD	1		AE5	218		
SPARINGLY	G3	614	SPARTA'S	M15	234		KT3	1140		
SPARK	AA	308	SPAWL	P2	63		M11	444		
	EDGA	11	SPAWN	J1	34	SPEAKS	UDH	15		
	PD	42	SPEAK	UDH	19		AM	92		
	PKA	48		UDH	24		PLN	26		
	P3	167		AR	284		PRH	17		
	AE5	903		AM	478		SAA	1021		
SPARKLE	L4	100		PMQ	20		RL	153		
	T23	18		ETL	2		RL	368		
	J10	40		ECG2	25		L3	149		
	P2	6		PAZ	37		M1	1039		
	M1	318		PUO4	5		GK	127		
SPARKLED	G4	652		AA	630		AE3	372		
	AE2	232		AA	905		AE3	400		
	AE3	634		PPC	7		AE7	633		
	DO	10		MD	163		AE7	755		
SPARKLES	H29	8		FS3	10		AE9	577		
	TA	436		HAP	335		AE11	227		
	AK	176		HAP	553		AE11	229		
	HAP	75		HAP	598		AE11	1196		
	HAP	1100		HAP	803		OAL	275		
	OD	51		HAP	842	SPEAR	LC	102		
	AE1	248		PMS	2		H2	49		
	AE2	672		ODA	18		TA	473		
	AE2	959		PSH	7		VP5	44		
	AE4	31		J1	228		AE1	121		
	AE5	186		J3	105		AE1	145		
	AE5	869		J6	272		AE1	668		
	AE8	340		J6	557		AE2	65		
	AE9	86		J10	164		AE2	299		
	AE12	158		P1	26		AE4	438		
	OAL	277		P1	41		AE5	728		
	AF	135		P1	106		AE6	248		
	HIF	154		P1	265		AE6	532		
SPARKLING	J3	406		P4	12		AE6	654		
	P3	240		P5	226		AE6	662		
	P5	264		M1	482		AE6	1032		
	M9	196		M1	876		AE8	827		
	VP5	108		ELT	15		AE9	226		
	G1	472		GK	10		AE9	303		
	G1	537		GK	125		AE9	543		
	G2	415		AE1	567		AE9	552		
	AE1	828		AE2	119		AE9	754		
	AE1	1013		AE2	807		AE9	1044		
	AE3	455		AE2	1075		AE10	465		
	AE4	303		AE4	487		AE10	471		
	AE4	519		AE4	106		AE10	476		
	AE5	102		AE7	761		AE10	481		
	AE5	411		AE9	143		AE10	535		
	AE5	503		AE11	392		AE10	560		
	AE6	78		AE11	522		AE10	579		
	AE8	363		AE12	40		AE10	592		
	AE9	988		AE12	1197		AE10	667		
	KT3	54		OAL	236		AE10	672		
	KT3	71		OAL	254		AE10	675		
	KT3	95		OAL	556		AE10	726		
	M10	40		OAL	557		AE10	814		
	HIF	306		OAL	671		AE10	823		
	FL	162		OAL	688		AE10	912		
	CI	192		OAL	810		AE10	1082		
SPARKS	JH	9		OAL	883		AE10	1094		
	AM	867		OAE2	19		AE10	1100		
	AM	956		KT3	152		AE10	1129		
	EAL	30		KT3	805		AE10	1256		
	EPC	5		B	162		AE10	1277		
	SAA	132		B	362		AE11	836		
	EK	13		B	368		AE11	842		
	EDG	21		BP	164		AE11	846		
	ESH	14		HIF	128		AE11	946		
	M1	346		HIF	129		AE11	987		
	PLT	23		C	92		AE11	1021		
	ELT	6		C	396		AE11	1099		
	PWR	10		C	616		AE12	444		
SPARROW	M12	19		C	651		AE12	570		
SPARROW'S	J6	11		C	813		AE12	787		
SPARTA	J10	409		M11	12		AE12	1121		
	M15	635		FL	474		AE12	1188		
SPARTAN	HP	202		AU	4		AE12	1284		
	T18	1		AU	19		AE12	1332		
	T18	30		AU	192		OAL	781		
	T18	39		WB	16		KT2	181		
	T27	1		WB	496		KT3	25		
	PSH	34		CI	12		KT3	270		
	HI	95		CI	182		KT3	480		
	VP6	118		CI	526		KT3	513		
	G2	693		EWR	25		KT3	960		
	G3	142	SPEAKER	WB	84		M11	144		

Word	Ref	No.
SPEAR	FL	271
	FL	275
	M12	112
	M12	132
	M12	144
	M12	161
	M12	454
	M12	496
	M12	514
	M12	632
	AU	279
	AU	548
SPEARS	G3	576
	AE7	252
	AE7	1084
	AE8	877
	AE9	43
	AE9	620
	AE9	744
	AE9	1072
	AE10	259
	AE10	460
	AE11	900
	AE11	906
	AE12	187
	AE12	250
	AE12	770
	AE12	1002
	AE12	1036
	KT3	461
	KT3	599
	M8	25
	M8	104
	M8	146
	M8	192
	M8	208
	FL	296
SPECIAL	HIF	729
SPECIES	HAP	193
	M1	479
	M9	103
	EHC	36
	G1	567
	G2	119
	G3	830
	AE8	36
	KT3	1057
	M15	624
	ESK	2
SPECIOUS	AA	39
	AA	746
	SAA	695
	SAA	955
	HAP	354
	HAP	2014
	AE4	249
	HIF	162
SPECK	AE6	1011
SPECKLED	G3	663
	AE2	274
	AE5	111
	AE7	458
	AE11	1106
SPECKS	G4	140
SPECTACLE	HI	128
	OAL	197
	OAL	250
	M12	807
SPECTATOR	POE	9
	KT3	79
SPECTATORS	SMA	37
	AE5	749
	AE10	712
SPECTER	AE1	487
	AE2	377
	AE2	1049
	AE10	900
	AE10	910
	KT1	529
	TH	150
	TH	197
	M11	317
	M11	410
SPECTERS	AM	890
	G1	642
	AE6	398
	AE11	423
SPECULATION	EL	107
	P2	131
SPED	AM	941
	ECG2	11
	T27	108
	T27	131
	M1	924
	AE5	315
	AE5	681
SPED	AE7	31
	AE11	1061
	AE12	788
	M8	18
	HIF	54
	HIF	529
	HIF	629
	C	25
	FL	610
	M12	398
	M12	506
	WB	263
	CI	157
SPEECH	PLG	5
	HAP	1349
	HAP	2428
	OD	24
	P1	103
	P1	151
	P5	31
	M1	266
	M1	907
	AE1	789
	AE2	477
	AE2	574
	AE3	442
	AE4	565
	AE4	720
	AE4	41
	AE6	905
	AE6	1179
	AE7	160
	AE8	490
	AE10	416
	AE11	523
	OAL	692
	B	71
	B	642
	CAM	312
	HIF	384
	HIF	464
	M11	104
	M15	98
SPEECHES	M1	679
	G2	731
SPEECHLESS	FS2	15
SPEED	AR	200
	AT	99
	AT	101
	HAP	1232
	HAP	1535
	M1	688
	M1	720
	M1	721
	M9	152
	VP4	11
	VP4	25
	VP7	44
	G1	152
	G3	75
	G3	135
	G3	191
	G3	305
	AE4	348
	AE4	920
	AE5	691
	AE5	716
	AE7	211
	AE7	771
	AE7	883
	AE7	1100
	AE8	304
	AE8	582
	AE9	103
	AE10	284
	AE10	352
	AE10	932
	AE11	497
	AE11	601
	AE11	684
	AE11	923
	AE11	1000
	AE11	1047
	AE11	1052
	AE11	1199
	AE11	1245
	AE11	1260
	AE12	510
	AE12	828
	AE12	944
	OAL	688
	KT2	250
	KT3	585
	KT3	691
	BP	144
SPEED	CAM	366
	TH	142
	TH	180
	TH	273
	M12	468
	AU	132
	WB	219
	CI	253
SPEEDIER	EAA	3
	C	287
SPEEDIEST	S	8
SPEEDING	AE2	755
	AE11	1187
	AU	358
SPEEDS	AE1	709
SPEEDY	AM	565
	AM	1068
	SAA	404
	M1	974
	AE4	172
	AE4	828
	AE5	153
	AE5	206
	AE9	515
	AE10	892
	AE11	701
	AE12	126
	M15	44
	CI	264
SPELL	PLN	34
	PUO1	31
	RL	375
	FS1	13
SPELLED	G3	445
SPELLS	BR	200
	VP8	145
	AE10	765
	CAM	367
SPEND	AR	203
	PRL	8
	PLN	19
	J6	481
	P1	275
	P3	137
	P3	143
	P6	56
	P6	162
	TJD	118
	M8	108
	M12	796
SPENDS	PTW	9
	L2	18
	J3	236
	G1	406
	AE7	16
SPENT	UDH	85
	AR	28
	AR	79
	PWG	49
	AM	409
	AM	571
	AM	1009
	ECG1	15
	PKK	17
	DA	190
	RL	236
	H2	94
	TA	255
	GE	38
	HAP	820
	HAP	2212
	OD	17
	J6	651
	P5	82
	P6	154
	M1	594
	M1	734
	VP1	46
	G1	108
	G2	750
	G4	274
	AE1	243
	AE2	772
	AE2	907
	AE3	933
	AE5	426
	AE5	617
	AE6	722
	AE7	277
	AE7	412
	AE7	522
	AE9	906
	AE9	1088
	AE10	1116
	M8	395
	BP	150

SPENT	AU	343	SPIN	KT3	169	SPITE	J1	24
	M15	523		M12	629		J1	157
	CI	378	SPINE	M15	575		J10	509
	CI	620	SPINNING	AE7	16		P1	96
	ERL	2		AE7	1096		P4	54
SPERCHAEUS	M1	785	SPINS	KT3	604		P5	179
SPET	G4	148		M8	202		DHP	7
SPETTLE	P1	206	SPIO	G4	477		VP3	20
	P2	62	SPIRES	G3	642		G4	470
SPEW	G1	176		AE2	646		AE1	18
SPEWED	SAA	465		AF	29		AE7	459
	AE11	936		KT1	215		AE10	830
SPEWING	AE8	343		BP	162		AE11	341
SPEWS	G2	298		M12	34		AE12	3
	G3	772	SPIRIT	RH	36		AE12	110
	J6	145		AM	353		AE12	717
	J6	553		POE	30		OAL	28
	J6	556		AA	657		KT3	754
	M11	129		ELB	12		M8	230
SPHERE	UDH	34		SAA	300		HIF	581
	UDH	30		RL	406		AU	79
	LC	111		RL	415	SPITEFUL	SAA	421
	EIE	16		HAP	824	SPLAYMOUTHS	P1	112
	PUO2	14		HAP	836	SPLEEN	PUO5	29
	TA	152		BR	300		SAA	158
	BR	7		OD	26		HH	39
	BR	305		J10	77		J1	45
	EL	37		P1	121		J10	47
	J6	760		VCS	1		P1	2
	M1	81		VCS	17		P1	27
	DHP	21		G2	447		P3	164
	VP3	61		AE2	466		AE1	60
	VP5	88		AE6	73		AE7	413
	G1	308		AE6	1021		M8	223
	G1	340		KT3	345		B	257
	OAL	63		KT3	787		C	30
	DO	28		B	676		AU	503
	KT1	597		CAM	325	SPLEENFUL	AM	470
	KT3	218		M12	163	SPLENDID	HAP	2489
	C	605		M15	229		HAP	2427
	M12	371		M15	240		AE1	901
	M15	213		M15	329	SPLENDIDLY	J3	238
	CI	121	SPIRITS	SMA	64	SPLENDOR	AM	1199
SPHERES	AK	49		AR	167		PNH	24
	SSC	56		LC	29		VP5	49
	AE9	22		AA	340		AE2	420
	AE10	765		AA	367		AE11	217
	AE12	308		SAA	310		M15	283
	AF	41		L4	29	SPLINTERS	AM	116
	AF	46		L4	86	SPLIT	AM	1002
	GP	22		L4	123		PLN	13
SPICE	CAM	56		HAP	342		MD	38
SPICES	AM	99		J6	51		PD	17
	AM	113		M1	330		H29	91
	ML	39		VP4	65		H2	101
	P5	72		G3	155		OD	19
	P6	81		AE5	552		P1	55
SPICY	AM	12		AE6	461		G4	202
	AM	1216		AE6	923		KT3	907
SPIDER	AM	717		AE6	1179	SPLITS	P2	49
SPIDERS	PKA	28		OAL	271		VP8	98
	G4	361		KT1	536		G2	520
SPIED	CM	84		KT1	548	SPLITTING	AE10	957
	AE2	269		M12	565		C	551
	AE2	775		M15	520	SPOIL	PTL	13
	AE9	316		M15	676		AA	704
	AE9	501		CI	630		MD	193
	AE9	796	SPIRITUAL	AA	626		SAA	775
	AE11	1005		MD	298		RL	92
	AE12	1364		HAP	1097		T27	54
	KT1	561		HAP	1190		HAP	53
	KT2	627	SPIRT	G4	622		HAP	169
	M12	18	SPIRY	G1	334		HAP	457
	CI	102		G2	212		VP3	144
SPIES	PIE	18	SPIT	PA	40		G1	411
	J1	52		EUF	18		G1	428
	J6	331	SPITE	AR	103		AE1	295
	AE1	642		AR	271		AE2	472
	AE2	512		PTL	5		AE4	318
	AE4	270		PCG2	2		AE4	589
	AE9	78		PAZ	13		AE5	135
	AE9	440		ML	13		AE5	523
	AE10	638		EUF	22		AE12	149
	AE12	374		PRL	31		MG	34
	AE12	1065		AA	353		KT1	140
SPIKES	M8	33		AA	565		C	265
	CAM	241		MD	157		M12	591
	M12	459		SAA	108		M15	158
SPILL	L3	220		SAA	287		M15	189
SPILT	AR	274		SAA	411		M15	591
	SAA	149		SAA	451	SPOILED	PWGR	26
	G1	674		T27	30		EEL	16
	AE2	979		H29	70		J10	352
SPIN	J3	49		GE	32		EHC	22
	G2	169		HH	19		AE6	669
	OAL	780		HH	32		CAM	57

Word	Ref	No.
SPOILED	M12	616
SPOILERS	KT1	157
SPOILING	T27	97
SPOILS	HS	136
	AM	256
	AM	1008
	PAZ	28
	AA	524
	MD	307
	SAA	718
	ER	8
	T18	95
	HAP	267
	HAP	2560
	PP	27
	SKA1	16
	EL	275
	J1	51
	J6	298
	J10	208
	P4	123
	P6	108
	VP5	93
	G3	17
	G3	589
	G4	268
	G4	810
	AE1	392
	AE2	359
	AE2	503
	AE2	529
	AE2	687
	AE2	874
	AE2	982
	AE2	1038
	AE4	287
	AE4	715
	AE4	734
	AE5	49
	AE5	458
	AE6	1149
	AE6	1181
	AE6	1187
	AE7	952
	AE8	952
	AE9	319
	AE9	356
	AE9	484
	AE9	495
	AE9	550
	AE10	597
	AE10	654
	AE10	697
	AE11	8
	AE11	111
	AE11	263
	AE11	295
	AE11	415
	AE11	876
	AE11	1161
	AE11	1174
	AE12	448
	AE12	1366
	OAL	218
	OAL	447
	KT2	452
	KT3	341
	M8	224
	HIF	99
	HIF	508
	M12	554
SPOKE	RH	61
	PIE	9
	SCG1	24
	CM	29
	CM	70
	AA	655
	AA	695
	AA	937
	SAA	732
	RL	347
	T23	12
	T23	20
	T23	34
	HAP	624
	HAP	1221
	SSC	23
	M1	307
	M1	474
	M1	876
	M1	893
	M1	1021
	M1	1059
	M9	9
	M9	182
	HI	47
SPOKE	HI	155
	G1	644
	G2	22
	G4	641
	AE1	203
	AE1	291
	AE1	786
	AE1	833
	AE1	936
	AE1	1020
	AE3	207
	AE3	442
	AE4	402
	AE4	518
	AE4	935
	AE4	1008
	AE4	21
	AE5	218
	AE5	637
	AE5	946
	AE6	77
	AE6	80
	AE6	147
	AE7	139
	AE7	341
	AE7	353
	AE7	623
	AE8	91
	AE8	154
	AE8	201
	AE8	245
	AE8	445
	AE8	535
	AE9	253
	AE9	332
	AE9	406
	AE9	434
	AE9	591
	AE10	322
	AE10	347
	AE10	842
	AE10	917
	AE10	1043
	AE10	1230
	AE10	1255
	AE11	43
	AE11	384
	AE12	481
	AE12	944
	AE12	1145
	AE12	1197
	AE12	1369
	KT1	57
	KT1	270
	KT1	561
	KT2	121
	KT2	262
	KT2	350
	KT2	473
	KT3	84
	KT3	482
	KT3	982
	M8	292
	B	389
	B	583
	B	715
	CAM	338
	CAM	367
	HIF	85
	HIF	100
	HIF	384
	HIF	404
	HIF	570
	HIF	724
	C	344
	C	768
	C	816
	TH	197
	TH	209
	M11	385
	M11	409
	M12	168
	M12	284
	M12	714
	M12	761
	AU	202
	WB	187
	WB	316
	M15	98
	GP	26
	GP	125
	CI	113
	CI	253
	CI	318
	CI	426
SPOKEN	J1	228
SPOKEN	AE1	822
	OAL	275
	PWR	23
SPOKES	G2	624
	AE6	839
SPONGY	AM	826
	ODA	15
	G1	438
SPONTANEITY	C	532
SPOOMS	HAP	1390
SPOON-MEAT	P3	28
SPORT	PWGR	3
	EM	27
	PO	7
	RL	239
	AT	38
	HAP	1792
	J10	101
	M1	1073
	G3	197
	G3	211
	AE6	117
	AE7	528
	AE7	1029
	OAL	71
	OAL	427
	OAL	447
	OAL	684
	OAE2	84
	KT1	189
	M8	316
	B	81
	WB	128
	CI	93
SPORTFUL	G1	497
	AE5	882
	OAL	299
SPORTING	P6	9
SPORTS	T18	24
	H9	29
	VP10	86
	AE4	207
	AE5	78
	AE5	84
	AE5	663
	AE5	783
	AE6	873
	AE9	825
	KT2	466
	TJD	51
	TJD	60
	FL	477
	FL	566
SPORUS	J10	476
SPOT	EOE	14
	HP	14
	J3	371
	G2	49
	G4	191
	AE1	590
	AE4	54
	AE9	162
	AE10	68
	AE12	803
	OAL	327
	KT2	201
	KT3	897
	BP	59
	TH	206
	M11	439
	FL	93
	FL	145
SPOTLESS	SCG1	23
	M1	653
	M9	50
	AE1	476
	KT3	209
	KT3	245
	FL	510
	GP	139
SPOTS	UDH	55
	G1	590
	G1	609
	AE1	447
	AE4	923
	AE6	1001
SPOTTED	AM	1066
	HAP	328
	HAP	572
	HAP	1651
	J1	109
	P1	199
	G3	415
	G3	650
	M12	553
SPOUSALS	KT1	21

Word	Code	No.
SPOUSALS	CI	538
SPOUSE	UDH	94
	EM	1
	EKK	12
	PD	56
	HAP	1091
	EH	19
	J1	188
	J6	286
	J6	429
	J10	476
	P2	27
	ELT	35
	AE2	838
	AE10	1015
	BP	189
	M11	185
	CI	249
	CI	319
	CI	563
	ETP	42
SPOUSE'S	UDH	108
SPOUSES	WB	142
SPOUTING	AE3	822
	AE4	953
	AE11	989
	AU	608
SPOUTS	AE3	539
SPRAG	AM	693
SPRANG	G1	653
	AE7	477
SPRAWLING	M8	149
SPRAWLS	AE5	641
SPRAY	FL	47
	FL	127
SPRAYS	H2	41
SPREAD	RH	26
	SMA	60
	VHH	42
	AM	605
	AM	628
	AM	717
	AM	732
	AM	860
	AM	973
	SCG1	9
	PC1	21
	MF	28
	MF	98
	SAA	797
	SAA	805
	RL	182
	T23	76
	T27	124
	H2	31
	TA	19
	TA	119
	TA	511
	AK	186
	HAP	899
	HAP	1120
	HAP	1189
	HAP	1240
	HAP	1270
	HAP	1910
	HAP	1911
	BR	162
	J1	224
	J6	5
	J6	85
	J6	416
	J6	434
	J6	768
	J10	61
	J16	69
	M1	64
	M1	125
	M1	166
	M1	711
	M9	199
	M13	151
	VP10	22
	G1	213
	G1	347
	G2	417
	G2	455
	G2	497
	G2	618
	G3	407
	G3	465
	G3	710
	G4	361
	G4	422
	G4	767
	AE1	559
	AE2	131

Word	Code	No.
SPREAD	AE2	800
	AE2	931
	AE3	166
	AE3	253
	AE3	291
	AE4	56
	AE4	64
	AE4	642
	AE4	561
	AE4	602
	AE4	734
	AE4	826
	AE4	931
	AE4	957
	AE5	77
	AE5	416
	AE5	539
	AE5	1060
	AE6	1
	AE6	397
	AE6	1064
	AE6	1198
	AE7	113
	AE7	151
	AE7	567
	AE8	22
	AE8	47
	AE8	240
	AE8	542
	AE9	600
	AE9	650
	AE9	716
	AE10	325
	AE10	1087
	AE10	1204
	AE11	107
	AE11	206
	AE11	685
	AE11	1007
	AE11	1233
	AE12	174
	AE12	443
	OAL	118
	KT2	525
	KT3	104
	KT3	207
	KT3	534
	KT3	913
	KT3	941
	M8	88
	M8	217
	BP	79
	M10	52
	CAM	219
	CAM	372
	HIF	15
	TH	257
	TH	315
	M11	482
	FL	72
	FL	316
	M12	374
	M12	509
	M12	582
	WB	255
	WB	266
	CI	578
	SMP	6
	AS	86
SPREADING	AM	1137
	L3	193
	AK	4
	G1	182
	G2	596
	G4	216
	G4	443
	AE2	165
	AE12	888
	KT2	509
	BP	192
	CAM	340
	TH	78
	FL	104
	FL	312
	M12	68
	M12	297
	M12	679
SPREADS	AM	434
	HP	145
	AA	261
	SAA	26
	H2	50
	HAP	1879
	EL	4
	J3	370
	J6	538

Word	Code	No.
SPREADS	J6	788
	M1	1003
	AE1	209
	AE2	855
	AE4	193
	AE4	269
	AE4	282
	AE6	418
	AE8	734
	AE8	947
	AE10	568
	OAL	708
	KT3	1059
	BP	49
	FL	18
	M15	378
SPRIG	UDH	79
SPRIGHTLY	L4	8
	H9	10
	G3	131
	G3	157
	AE1	930
	AE4	200
	AE5	96
	AE5	387
	AE5	751
	AE8	3
	AE8	730
	AE11	898
	KT1	175
	KT1	176
	KT2	481
	KT3	429
	TJD	124
	B	428
	BP	182
	M12	528
	SMP	54
	SMP	56
SPRIGS	KT3	87
	M12	547
SPRING	UDH	78
	SMA	29
	SMA	93
	HS	109
	LC	136
	LCA	24
	AM	100
	SEL3	2
	AA	262
	D	29
	SAA	63
	SAA	691
	SAA	905
	SAA	1119
	RL	44
	RL	340
	L1	12
	L1	29
	L2	37
	T18	46
	T18	86
	TA	259
	HAP	1854
	HAP	2101
	BR	12
	BR	171
	SKA6	9
	LS	1
	ODA	17
	MS	29
	J6	682
	P1	77
	P6	6
	M1	2
	M1	139
	M1	149
	SFL	1
	SFL	6
	DHP	4
	VP2	62
	VP2	84
	VP3	84
	VP3	144
	VP4	23
	VP5	91
	VP8	40
	VP9	52
	VP10	108
	G1	171
	G1	64
	G1	423
	G1	464
	G1	477
	G2	204
	G2	245

Word	Ref	No.
SPRING	G2	438
	G2	432
	G2	459
	G2	471
	G2	592
	G3	429
	G4	30
	G4	112
	G4	179
	G4	201
	G4	205
	G4	211
	G4	408
	G4	431
	G4	458
	G4	540
	G4	751
	AE1	1065
	AE2	643
	AE3	11
	AE4	912
	AE6	1092
	AE6	1223
	AE8	247
	AE9	146
	AE10	241
	AE10	1282
	AE11	437
	OAL	308
	KT1	200
	KT3	121
	KT3	134
	KT3	429
	KT3	436
	KT3	1024
	KT3	1083
	B	653
	C	88
	C	427
	C	457
	C	769
	TH	60
	FL	19
	FL	46
	FL	53
	FL	591
	M12	123
	WB	238
	M15	110
	M15	185
	M15	299
	M15	417
	M15	492
	M15	544
	AS	9
	AS	50
SPRINGAL	J10	479
SPRINGES	VP5	94
	M15	697
SPRINGEST	P3	35
SPRINGING	LC	101
	HAP	214
	G2	498
	G2	751
	G4	339
	AE11	949
SPRING'S	G3	428
	KT1	221
SPRINGS	HS	112
	AR	168
	RH	22
	PT	4
	EAZ	33
	AA	499
	L1	6
	HAP	1618
	HAP	1864
	P4	98
	M1	46
	VP1	54
	VP3	163
	VP7	66
	G2	277
	G2	450
	G3	299
	G3	651
	AE3	754
	AE5	8
	AE5	280
	AE5	439
	AE7	521
	AE7	960
	AE8	291
	AE9	749
	AE10	1132
	AE12	776
SPRINGS	AE12	1018
	AE12	1095
	AE12	1240
	OAL	252
	KT3	1065
	B	494
	B	499
	CAM	153
	TH	187
	M11	144
	M11	472
	WB	163
	M15	465
	M15	579
	M15	600
SPRING-TIDES	STL	19
SPRINKLE	M1	502
	G1	118
	AE11	118
SPRINKLED	G4	335
	G4	553
	AE6	329
	AE6	863
	AE8	368
	AE10	1203
	KT3	76
	WB	27
	CI	607
SPRINKLES	P6	48
	AE4	741
SPRINKLING	G1	531
	AE1	1031
	AE4	912
SPRITE	SCD2	5
	HAP	1225
	AE3	771
	C	104
	TH	283
	TH	371
SPRITES	ETL	7
	ETL	11
	P5	269
SPROUT	UDH	57
SPROUTING	LC	103
	AA	542
	BP	182
	BP	184
SPROUTS	P4	98
SPRUNG	AM	572
	CM	72
	HP	231
	AA	306
	MF	125
	SAA	215
	RL	69
	AK	40
	EL	126
	M1	204
	M1	241
	M1	842
	G2	16
	G2	75
	AE4	523
	AE5	200
	AE7	1015
	AE8	179
	AE9	129
	AE12	1209
	KT3	266
	KT3	699
	M8	99
	M8	262
	C	85
	C	350
	TH	118
	TH	370
	FL	34
	AU	130
	G3	368
SPUMY	VP4	56
SPUN	M15	381
SPUR	SEL4	23
	AE9	516
	AE9	834
	AE11	1053
	AE11	1262
	EMKG	19
SPURGE	C	190
SPURN	J10	139
	G4	339
	AE11	996
SPURNED	G3	174
	AE9	801
	AE10	565
	AE10	690
	C	435
SPURNING	T23	94
	VP3	135
	AE9	448
	AE10	640
	C	85
SPURNS	ER	67
	G3	336
	AE5	641
	AE9	862
	AE10	1028
	AE12	164
	M12	755
SPURRED	AR	280
	SAA	414
	AE2	427
	AE10	1246
	AE12	436
	KT2	249
	TH	335
	TH	345
SPURRING	G3	49
	AE5	872
	AE9	60
	AE11	923
	AE11	1188
	KT3	586
	KT3	691
SPURS	MD	119
	L3	284
	AE4	224
	AE6	1219
	AE11	1089
	FL	576
	M12	468
SPUTTERED	AE2	279
SPUTTERING	EK	15
	G1	537
	AE12	762
	HIF	162
	M12	359
SPY	EWGR	4
	SMM1	9
	AE1	257
	AE3	727
	AE3	671
	AE12	524
	OAL	451
	KT1	583
	B	255
	HIF	752
	C	412
	C	597
	AU	161
	AU	384
	AU	395
	M15	356
SQUADRON	AM	681
	AM	819
	AM	941
	AE2	564
	AE5	742
	AE11	668
	AE11	757
	M8	221
	CI	609
SQUADRONS	AM	333
	AM	731
	AM	741
	AM	817
	MD	243
	HAP	731
	G4	4
	G4	115
	G4	448
	AE10	1016
	AE11	609
	AE11	897
	AE11	921
	AE12	209
	AE12	547
	AE12	809
	AE12	1000
	KT3	992
	FL	289
SQUALID	G4	686
	AE11	423
	KT1	539
SQUALLING	EPC	4
	PMK	30
SQUANDER	AM	266
	L3	134
SQUANDERED	RL	231
	L4	29
	AE2	571
SQUANDEREST	P6	79
SQUANDERING	EPC	8

Word	Ref	No.	Word	Ref	No.	Word	Ref	No.
SQUANDERING	AA	559	STAGE	PR	4	STAINED	G4	19
SQUARE	J1	97		PUO3	2		AE6	492
	J3	179		PLB	1		AE9	580
	HAP	750		MF	151		AE10	544
	AE2	486		SAA	455		AE12	853
	KT1	205		PK	33		M12	100
SQUARED	GP	79		EK	38		M12	793
SQUAT	J10	312		EDGA	6	STAINS	HAP	329
SQUEAK	J6	664		L3	162		AE6	998
	PPS	19		PAA	1		AE6	1011
	C	732		AK	65		AE11	1160
SQUEAKING	MD	35		PP	25	STAIRS	EK	23
SQUEAKS	MF	46		PP	50		AE8	293
SQUEASY	OE	26		PMS	31		B	111
SQUEEZE	L4	75		EKA	38		B	135
	G4	208		J3	41		CI	574
SQUEEZED	J1	105		J3	162		CI	596
	M1	364		J3	293	STAIUS	P2	38
	AE8	344		J6	353		P2	41
	OAL	745		J6	829	STAKE	AR	239
	FL	419		P5	4		AA	457
SQUIBS	PMS	16		P5	23		SAA	275
SQUILLS	G3	689		PLT	5		PDG	37
SQUINTIFEGO	P5	271		PLT	34		TA	165
SQUINTING	HIF	753		MC	9		HAP	695
SQUIRE	PWGR	1		MC	25		J1	235
	AE9	888		MC	67		J6	644
	KT1	575		EHC	34		VP3	40
	B	52		AE4	686		VP3	44
	M12	489		OAL	119		VP3	72
	CI	76		MG	16		OAL	195
SQUIRES	EWGR	34		MG	20		M12	413
	PSH	27		MM	2	STAKES	AM	494
	KT3	453		MM	21		AM	535
STAB	PMQ	25		KT3	1079		PKA	42
	P4	100		KT3	976		P3	94
	KT3	509		WB	68		G1	357
STABBING	EM	17		M15	344		G2	32
STABLE	KT3	1046		CI	20		G2	89
STABLES	G3	292		PTP	2	STALE	AA	249
	AE7	378		ETP	4		OAL	392
STABS	J10	489		ETP	14	STALK	G2	494
STACKS	G3	499		ETP	36		AE3	846
STAFF	HH	29		EMKG	21		AE3	863
	BR	254		EMKG	38		KT1	194
	M13	56		PWR	39	STALKED	BR	232
	AE3	866	STAGERS	HAP	1791		AE10	906
	AE7	583		PKA	22	STALKING	M13	44
	AE8	678	STAGE'S	PTS	16		VP8	142
	BP	148	STAGGER	RL	185		G1	413
	WB	227	STAGGERED	AE5	627		AE5	487
	CI	111		AE10	468		AE6	776
	CI	179		AE10	1223		AE10	1084
STAFFORD'S	AS	36		KT3	644		FL	567
STAG	M1	417	STAGGERING	AA	373	STALKS	P5	222
	M9	102		G2	133		G1	111
	VP7	41		AE9	593		G1	534
	G3	418		AE10	396		G2	31
	G3	804		AE11	860		G3	383
	AE7	669		AE12	1305		BP	60
	AE9	741		TH	372		M15	307
	AE10	1020		M12	563	STALL	M1	868
	AE12	1083	STAGGERS	AE5	573		G3	331
	AE12	1095		AE9	555		G3	545
	KT2	627		AE11	1192		G4	228
	M15	701		AE12	955		C	223
	SMP	31		KT1	435		C	234
STAGE	EWGR	26	STAGIRITE	DC	3		C	258
	PCG1	20		RL	21	STALLED	AE9	526
	PCG1	27	STAG'S	M12	375	STALLION	J6	335
	PCG1	34	STAGS	VP1	80		G3	118
	PCG2	5		VP5	94		G3	190
	ECG2	1		G1	414		G3	391
	PFD	7		G3	569		G3	433
	PFD	18		G3	625		OAL	316
	PLN	9		AE1	260	STALLS	G3	464
	ELN	20		AE4	220		G3	566
	PUO1	10		KT3	56		G3	627
	EUO	12	STAIN	AR	88		G3	630
	EUO	21		CM	1	STAMMERING	AA	243
	EUO	28		CM	95		G2	133
	PNH	7		HP	17	STAMMERS	L4	151
	PNH	22		AA	69	STAMP	PNH	33
	PAZ	16		SAA	709		MD	144
	EMK	5		L4	241		HAP	278
	PTW	2		TA	489		BR	30
	POE	12		P2	117		HIF	709
	PTC	8		AE2	684	STAMPED	PUO3	32
	PTC	20		AE6	1144		EAA	8
	ETC	15		OAL	849		M13	45
	PCB	33		CAM	331		AF	33
	PLG	12	STAINED	AR	289	STAMPS	EAA	10
	PLG	33		AM	1196		J6	368
	PO	6		AA	480		KT1	446
	PSF	19		SAA	708		KT2	355
	ETG	3		G3	742	STANCH	HS	48

Word	Ref	No.	Word	Ref	No.	Word	Ref	No.
STANCH	AE4	987	STAND	AE4	141	STANDING	G1	169
	OAL	474		AE4	195		G1	528
STANCHED	AE12	624		AE4	826		G3	653
STAND	HS	57		AE5	21		G3	725
	HS	119		AE5	44		G4	35
	SMA	43		AE5	88		G4	37
	LC	23		AE5	211		G4	695
	DC	51		AE5	383		AE2	407
	AM	154		AE5	481		AE9	781
	AM	978		AE5	490		OAL	873
	AM	1078		AE5	566		KT2	541
	AM	1188		AE5	938		KT3	672
	PMQ	28		AE6	31		M12	802
	SMM1	2		AE6	111		M15	501
	PA	22		AE6	256		CI	274
	PA	35		AE6	527		ETP	23
	EEL	40		AE6	1073	STANDINGS	SMA	38
	SEL2	5		AE7	382	STANDS	HS	146
	PFD	2		AE7	662		AM	244
	PM	8		AE7	842		AM	546
	ML	5		AE7	998		AM	593
	ML	17		AE8	152		DA	107
	EAL	21		AE8	849		DA	126
	ETC	6		AE9	203		AA	355
	HP	79		AE9	425		AA	1025
	PUO4	31		AE9	430		MF	18
	AA	198		AE9	511		SAA	20
	AA	544		AE9	559		SAA	854
	AA	635		AE9	921		RL	42
	AA	776		AE9	1063		L1	13
	AA	915		AE10	155		L4	171
	AA	1022		AE10	165		L4	199
	ELB	34		AE10	184		AK	138
	PPC	27		AE10	259		HAP	334
	MD	171		AE10	396		HAP	473
	MD	239		AE10	527		HAP	493
	MF	155		AE10	641		HAP	809
	SAA	144		AE10	713		HAP	1162
	SAA	220		AE10	1191		HAP	1213
	SAA	1063		AE11	213		HAP	2067
	SAA	1127		AE11	595		HAP	2173
	EDG	22		AE12	19		HAP	2470
	RL	441		AE12	134		PTS	14
	OE	38		AE12	351		J1	253
	ER	65		AE12	823		J3	456
	L3	146		AE12	1230		J6	366
	TA	3		AE12	1360		J6	512
	TA	116		OAL	100		J6	760
	MN	9		DO	58		J10	362
	HH	6		KT1	191		P6	63
	HAP	306		KT1	355		M1	424
	HAP	309		KT3	299		M1	889
	HAP	816		KT3	332		VP10	19
	HAP	831		KT3	470		G2	407
	HAP	981		KT3	495		G3	363
	HAP	1009		TJD	27		G3	694
	HAP	1052		TJD	146		G4	186
	HAP	1110		TJD	175		G4	505
	HAP	1514		BP	17		AE1	84
	HAP	1994		BP	143		AE1	208
	HAP	2007		HIF	168		AE1	647
	SKA4	24		HIF	422		AE1	675
	PSH	8		TH	311		AE1	723
	PSH	28		M11	317		AE2	256
	J1	223		FL	9		AE2	830
	J3	456		AU	57		AE2	969
	J6	427		AU	132		AE2	1043
	J6	520		AU	358		AE3	515
	J10	548		AU	499		AE3	725
	P1	77		M15	67		AE4	81
	P3	104		M15	87		AE4	750
	P6	47		M15	386		AE4	952
	M1	518		PTP	3		AE5	156
	M13	110	STANDARD	AA	785		AE5	165
	GK	162		HAP	1175		AE5	543
	GK	176		BR	85		AE5	562
	VP7	45		MS	28		AE5	583
	G1	498		J1	59		AE5	668
	G2	376		G4	102		AE5	1012
	G2	597		AE7	835		AE6	207
	G2	763		AE8	2		AE6	400
	G3	23		KT1	113		AE6	413
	G3	499	STANDARDS	AE6	1133		AE6	431
	G3	567	STANDART	AR	225		AE6	778
	G4	515	STANDERS-BY	OAL	556		AE6	857
	AE1	251		KT2	309		AE6	878
	AE1	351	STANDEST	P3	231		AE7	104
	AE1	604	STANDING	AM	448		AE7	201
	AE2	434		AM	1139		AE7	811
	AE2	957		AA	137		AE7	961
	AE3	144		AK	117		AE7	1078
	AE3	391		J3	385		AE7	1093
	AE3	526		J16	56		AE8	255
	AE3	533		M1	46		AE8	321
	AE3	721		VP8	143		AE8	333
	AE4	123					AE8	624

STANDS	AE8	792
	AE9	343
	AE9	861
	AE9	1030
	AE10	499
	AE10	664
	AE10	773
	AE11	623
	AE11	725
	AE11	795
	AE11	1190
	AE11	1271
	AE12	293
	AE12	332
	AE12	617
	AE12	624
	AE12	849
	AE12	1026
	AE12	1028
	AE12	1045
	AE12	1331
	OAL	76
	OAL	141
	KT2	181
	M8	25
	M8	304
	M8	332
	CAM	207
	HIF	683
	TH	2
	M11	116
	M11	355
	M11	438
	M12	57
	M15	349
	M15	429
	M15	451
	CI	174
	ERL	9
STAPLE	AM	828
	EWGR	48
	E'UO	34
	PKK	15
STAR	UDH	46
	AR	113
	AR	288
	AM	67
	AM	400
	AM	1086
	AM	1199
	AA	733
	SAA	194
	SAA	241
	L3	261
	H29	30
	AK	6
	AK	175
	HAP	504
	HAP	1470
	ETS	20
	EL	264
	P5	65
	P6	41
	M9	206
	HI	39
	VP5	35
	VP8	24
	VP9	65
	G1	209
	G3	97
	AE2	803
	AE2	949
	AE3	764
	AE5	740
	AE8	370
	AE8	779
	AE8	902
	OAL	625
	KT2	611
	KT2	624
	KT3	406
	M11	157
	M12	305
	AU	457
STARBOARD	AE3	527
STARE	EAZ	24
	DA	71
	P2	43
	G4	370
	AE5	696
	AE5	840
	AE7	722
	AE10	808
	AE11	215
	KT3	43
	AU	452

STARED	AE2	86
	AE12	1323
	TH	306
STARES	VP6	34
	G4	592
	AE1	487
	AE3	813
	AE11	1037
	AE12	873
	AF	130
	KT1	446
STARING	T23	33
	J6	798
	P5	213
	VP8	22
	G3	813
	AE6	78
	AE10	1293
	TH	150
	M11	359
	P5	213
STARK	AE3	266
STARLESS	BR	311
STARLIGHT	G1	548
	FL	454
STARLIKE	M11	54
STARRY	AA	851
	M1	917
	VP5	87
	VP9	60
	G1	459
	G1	574
	AE4	363
	AE5	184
	AE6	981
	AE6	1084
	AE8	181
	AE11	307
	M15	568
STARS	UDH	33
	HS	56
	HS	69
	HS	106
	HS	122
	AR	19
	AR	154
	LC	86
	DC	19
	LCA	25
	AM	529
	AM	1111
	AM	1161
	SMM1	6
	DA	119
	PRH	6
	SAA	934
	SAA	969
	SAA	1062
	RL	1
	T18	13
	H3	2
	H29	102
	HAP	1903
	HAP	2588
	BR	83
	EL	145
	EL	149
	J6	29
	J6	754
	J16	5
	P5	149
	M1	88
	M1	220
	M1	275
	M1	858
	GK	136
	VP6	124
	VP9	63
	G1	348
	G1	419
	G1	502
	G1	541
	G1	658
	G2	466
	G2	677
	G3	248
	AE1	1044
	AE1	1056
	AE2	12
	AE3	263
	AE3	460
	AE3	674
	AE3	683
	AE3	743
	AE3	767
	AE4	116

STARS	AE4	505
	AE4	707
	AE4	761
	AE5	33
	AE5	56
	AE6	463
	AE6	476
	AE6	872
	AE6	1172
	AE7	10
	AE7	188
	AE7	293
	AE8	79
	AE9	109
	AE9	574
	AE10	239
	AE10	256
	AE11	1211
	OAL	62
	DO	21
	KT1	248
	KT3	95
	KT3	238
	KT3	442
	KT3	738
	M8	46
	M8	141
	CAM	268
	FL	476
	AU	22
	WB	447
	M15	214
	AS	6
STARS'	SAA	1086
START	AM	739
	G3	165
	AE5	183
	AE10	808
	KT1	555
	C	235
	C	583
STARTED	T27	132
	AE3	233
	KT1	236
	CAM	184
	TH	361
	FL	461
STARTING	TA	513
	G1	690
	G3	137
	G4	496
	M1	882
	AE5	415
	AE7	640
	AE11	1151
	AE12	782
	KT1	565
	KT2	125
	C	720
	M11	386
STARTLE	RL	185
STARTLING	KT3	701
STARTS	EEL	13
	PCG2	3
	EUF	1
	AA	548
	HAP	1595
	P3	80
	M13	225
	AE2	143
	AE2	512
	M15	422
	CAM	153
STARVE	PC8	6
	EUF	19
	AA	245
	PL8	11
	SAA	255
	EC	20
	HAP	1468
	P5	204
	G3	216
	KT1	441
	TH	37
	ETP	11
STARVED	DA	91
	HAP	366
	HAP	1468
	HAP	2269
STARVES	VP7	65
	G2	79
	WB	468
STARVING	SAA	106
	RL	145
	VP3	9
	G3	566

STARVING	OAL	511	STATE	J3	285	STATE	AE7	367
STATE	AR	21		J3	401		AE7	467
	AR	41		J6	32		AE7	767
	LC	15		J6	248		AE8	19
	LC	26		J6	548		AE8	56
	LC	134		J10	77		AE8	446
	DC	5		J10	145		AE8	618
	AM	83		J10	200		AE8	872
	PCG1	36		J10	430		AE9	297
	PCD	19		J10	440		AE10	163
	ECD	14		J10	516		AE10	225
	E	5		J16	69		AE11	131
	POE	1		P1	145		AE11	162
	PTC	32		P1	263		AE11	192
	CM	75		P2	47		AE11	224
	DA	62		P3	208		AE11	246
	UMR	6		P4	2		AE11	313
	EMW	13		P4	14		AE11	368
	PUF	28		P5	75		AE11	509
	EUF	15		P6	27		AE11	550
	AA	66		M1	237		AE11	587
	AA	174		M1	268		AE11	634
	AA	402		M1	297		AE11	712
	AA	501		M1	659		AE12	228
	AA	794		M1	691		AE12	1010
	AA	799		M1	1040		AE12	1033
	AA	821		SLT1	1		AE12	1156
	AA	879		MC	45		AE12	1271
	AA	930		GK	51		AF	3
	AA	953		G1	30		KT3	192
	PLB	4		G2	102		KT3	227
	D	40		G2	639		KT3	487
	MF	10		G2	700		KT3	768
	MF	28		G3	180		KT3	845
	MF	109		G3	786		KT3	862
	SAA	73		G4	80		KT3	867
	SAA	80		G4	229		KT3	880
	SAA	84		G4	260		KT3	919
	SAA	211		G4	296		KT3	1061
	SAA	219		G4	351		TJD	34
	SAA	537		G4	367		TJD	176
	SAA	577		AE1	35		B	129
	SAA	601		AE1	70		B	191
	SAA	644		AE1	289		B	358
	SAA	693		AE1	305		B	418
	SAA	723		AE1	356		B	488
	SAA	757		AE1	387		B	679
	SAA	847		AE1	411		B	756
	SAA	895		AE1	469		CAM	332
	SAA	951		AE1	497		HIF	116
	PK	18		AE1	624		HIF	347
	RL	23		AE1	707		HIF	407
	RL	58		AE1	727		C	675
	ER	77		AE1	791		TH	223
	L2	30		AE1	978		TH	423
	L2	39		AE2	123		FL	547
	L3	16		AE2	170		M12	725
	L3	179		AE2	212		AU	82
	L3	240		AE2	321		AU	493
	L3	298		AE2	389		WB	166
	L3	299		AE2	439		WB	209
	H29	48		AE2	469		M15	1
	H2	15		AE2	612		M15	219
	FS4	1		AE2	663		M15	647
	TA	57		AE2	759		CI	437
	TA	218		AE2	788		PMK	25
	TA	388		AE3	1		AS	22
	TA	429		AE3	591	STATECRAFT	SAA	238
	TA	485		AE3	639	STATELY	SMA	107
	GE	10		AE3	800		PNH	34
	HH	3		AE3	825		H29	26
	HAP	12		AE4	188		J6	259
	HAP	198		AE4	308		G3	195
	HAP	360		AE4	400		G4	186
	HAP	434		AE4	464		AE1	262
	HAP	496		AE4	546		AE1	582
	HAP	616		AE5	380		AE5	406
	HAP	844		AE5	813		AE6	259
	HAP	1063		AE5	928		AE6	332
	HAP	1072		AE6	103		AE7	393
	HAP	1190		AE6	222		AE7	673
	HAP	1330		AE6	258		AE8	468
	HAP	1709		AE6	377		BP	159
	HAP	1940		AE6	443	STATE'S	G4	229
	HAP	2024		AE6	588	STATES	DC	28
	HAP	2038		AE6	622		AM	772
	HAP	2529		AE6	714		PCD	22
	HAP	2592		AE6	764		ML	10
	BR	61		AE6	1166		EOE	29
	BR	345		AE6	1204		AA	24
	BR	357		AE6	1232		AE8	137
	EJG	7		AE7	55		AE10	143
	EL	188		AE7	79	STATESMAN	AA	187
	EL	250		AE7	120		AA	550
	ODA	72		AE7	235		SAA	157
	J3	20		AE7	266		SAA	860

Word	Source	No.		Word	Source	No.		Word	Source	No.
STATESMAN'S	SAA	182		STAY	EDGA	15		STAYED	AE9	287
STATESMEN	SAA	207			RL	168			KT2	125
STATION	PK	11			AT	95			KT3	939
	M1	861			L3	133			HIF	639
	G4	10			L4	27			C	221
	G4	608			L4	250			TH	332
	AE6	1030			T23	69			WB	11
	CAM	272			H29	11		STAYING	CAM	204
	M15	263			H29	83			AU	488
STATIONERS	MF	104			FS1	15		STAYS	SMA	105
STATIONS	AM	306			FS3	12			AM	985
	SSC	9			TA	142			J6	748
	OAL	453			HAP	124			VP3	16
STATIUS	RH	69			HAP	556			G1	381
	KT3	212			HAP	609			G2	320
STATUE	DA	107			HAP	842			AE1	725
	J6	426			HAP	1253			AE5	611
	J10	87			HAP	1522			KT3	1060
	VP7	45			HAP	1820			M10	77
	VP7	51			HAP	1888		STEAD	H2	22
	AE2	222			HAP	2454			BR	14
	AE2	244			BR	12			J10	374
	AE10	250			BR	51			AE1	931
	KT3	184			BR	140			AE5	642
	KT3	370			PTS	26			KT1	466
	M10	31			EPN	1			BP	78
	M10	65			EL	56			M11	293
	M10	74			EL	287			AS	89
	AU	588			ESH	20		STEADFAST	H3	23
	WB	534			ESH	31			HAP	434
	EP	2			J3	495			AE12	305
STATUES	AK	121			J6	138			M15	93
	J1	16			P3	85			M15	263
	J1	195			P6	131		STEADFASTNESS	AA	889
	J3	354			M1	679		STEADS	G2	726
	PPS	7			M1	680		STEADY	AA	909
	P2	101			M1	916			SAA	643
	G1	647			M1	1029			SAA	820
	G2	647			M13	101			EDG	36
	G3	55			HI	26			TA	395
	AE2	394			HI	188			HAP	32
	AE3	203			SLT2	9			BR	360
	OAL	172			G2	575			P1	124
STATURE	DC	50			G3	173			G2	63
	HAP	2437			G4	164			G2	431
	M13	149			AE1	572			G2	505
	M13	228			AE1	803			G4	287
	AE7	225			AE2	403			KT3	880
	KT3	569			AE3	578		STEAL	PA	44
	FL	177			AE3	620			PA	48
	M15	302			AE4	69			EEL	29
STATUTABLE	PMM	6			AE4	447			MD	195
STATUTE	SAA	440			AE4	670			MD	243
	HAP	2365			AE6	629			T18	15
	J16	19			AE6	723			AE5	1100
STATUTES	AA	581			AE8	193			AU	528
	ELB	22			AE8	211			GP	58
	HAP	840			AE9	158		STEALS	AR	127
	HAP	2086			AE9	484		STEALTH	G4	352
	PDS	38			AE10	605			G4	745
	AE1	737			AE11	275			AE1	481
	AE6	847			AE11	766			AE11	1163
	CAM	85			AE12	103			AE12	221
STAVES	C	727			OAL	455			B	179
STAY	SMA	13			OAL	506		STEAM	J6	187
	PIE	10			OAL	799			AE12	158
	AM	296			OAL	819			KT3	197
	AM	379			KT3	591			KT3	348
	AM	413			M8	181		STEAMING	AK	65
	AM	579			M8	358			G2	479
	AM	549			B	306			G4	68
	AM	834			CAM	81			AE2	947
	AM	1151			C	312			AE6	345
	PMQ	24			C	321		STEED	BR	173
	EMM	3			C	595			M13	159
	EMM	9			C	675			G3	141
	ECG1	33			TH	59			G3	181
	ECG2	10			M11	66			G3	185
	PM	19			M11	383			G3	195
	SM2	4			M11	417			G3	285
	EUO	8			M12	601			AE2	20
	PNH	1			AU	354			AE2	54
	HP	152			M15	36			AE2	304
	DA	51			M15	268			AE5	406
	DA	76			STP	30			AE5	738
	DA	169		STAYED	AR	68			AE5	745
	DA	188			AM	677			AE5	871
	DA	193			DA	85			AE7	377
	EMP	4			SAA	228			AE9	54
	MD	46			SAA	1036			AE9	486
	MD	93			TA	254			AE10	1230
	PRH	12			M1	970			AE10	1246
	PRH	19			PLT	4			AE10	1280
	D	9			AE3	807			AE11	131
	EK	11			AE6	71			AE11	756
	PDG	39			AE8	293			AE11	918

STEED	AE11	948	STEEL	AE10	440	STEER	SAA	186
	AE11	993		AE10	538		SAA	241
	AE11	1003		AE10	669		PSH	15
	AE11	1133		AE11	296		G1	69
	AE12	945		AE11	734		G1	177
	KT1	97		AE11	947		G2	63
	KT2	45		AE11	1031		G2	551
	KT2	174		AE12	13		G3	770
	KT2	249		AE12	427		G3	778
	KT3	66		AE12	573		G4	421
	KT3	609		AE12	614		G4	447
	KT3	701		AE12	625		AE1	103
	KT3	930		AE12	1073		AE2	268
	M8	47		AE12	1128		AE2	274
	M8	146		AE12	1133		AE3	352
	TH	120		AE12	1157		AE3	494
	TH	141		OAL	541		AE4	409
	TH	272		KT2	124		AE4	498
	TH	335		KT2	175		AE5	173
	TH	345		KT2	546		AE6	343
	FL	255		KT2	592		AE9	859
	FL	291		KT2	597		AE11	587
	AU	94		KT3	35		OAL	538
	M15	117		KT3	353		DO	139
	M15	545		KT3	451		TJD	128
STEEDS	T18	51		KT3	628		B	360
	TA	474		KT3	931		M15	180
	M1	600		M8	105		M15	541
	G1	90		M8	241		ESK	30
	AE1	661		M8	373		AS	35
	AE1	1054		FL	272	STEERAGE	AE4	376
	AE3	709		M12	231		AE6	24
	AE3	711		M12	153		M11	351
	AE3	925		M12	289	STEERED	AM	455
	AE5	724		M12	500		AM	631
	AE5	1089		AU	320		SAA	213
	AE6	887		M15	147		HAP	753
	AE7	382	STEELY	AE11	1191		AE3	738
	AE7	393	STEEP	MD	122		AE5	215
	AE7	864		RL	33		AE5	230
	AE7	885		L4	65		AE7	30
	AE7	909		H3	24		AE9	816
	AE7	1070		H2	23		AE10	410
	AE8	5		EL	91		DO	50
	AE8	728		P3	110		M15	505
	AE8	854		M1	860		CI	272
	AE9	516		G1	280	STEERING	EDG	39
	AE10	811		G1	365		AE5	211
	AE10	818		G1	602		AE6	463
	AE10	831		G2	94	STEERS	AM	419
	AE12	246		G3	614		DA	155
	AE12	782		G4	278		J6	597
	AE12	1066		AE1	152		P1	250
	KT2	326		AE1	334		VP2	96
	KT3	299		AE1	412		G2	489
	KT3	598		AE3	846		G4	287
	KT3	600		AE4	702		AE5	80
	FL	217		AE6	1017		AE5	130
	FL	260		AE7	1037		AE5	321
	FL	304		AE8	457		AE5	1087
	FL	456		AE11	777		AE5	1132
	M12	107		AE12	995		AE6	418
	AU	394		AE12	1089		AE12	697
STEEL	SAA	709		OAL	634		AE12	1086
	TA	326		M11	266		AU	560
	M1	162		AU	526		M15	693
	M1	178	STEEPED	AE6	567		CI	326
	M1	181	STEEPLE-HIGH	AM	248	STEM	AM	627
	HI	148	STEEPLE'S	HAP	1739		AA	867
	G1	88	STEEPLES	HAP	1488		SAA	1132
	G2	508		HAP	1525		RL	428
	G2	632		HAP	2543		BR	263
	G4	255		AA	860		G1	163
	AE1	481		AT	104		G1	290
	AE4	226		J10	243		G1	424
	AE4	789		M1	279		G1	532
	AE4	951		HI	5		G2	184
	AE5	403		VP1	105		G2	342
	AE6	224		VP10	15		G3	427
	AE6	404		VP10	84		G4	45
	AE6	748	STEEPY	G1	376		G4	393
	AE7	840		G2	215		AE1	164
	AE7	923		G3	427		AE3	493
	AE7	956		AE3	670		AE5	26
	AE8	556		AE6	267		AE8	126
	AE8	586		AE7	662		AE11	102
	AE8	591		AE9	729		AE12	611
	AE8	711		AE9	770		FL	280
	AE8	824		AE11	795		FL	589
	AE9	591		AE11	881		AU	610
	AE9	834		M12	456		M15	302
	AE9	867	STEER	AM	140		AS	45
	AE9	922		AM	311	STEMMED	AE5	251
	AE9	1011		AA	162		AE8	143
	AE9	1018		MD	30		AE8	864
	AE10	254				STEMMMED	AE11	844

Word	Ref	No.
STEMS	EL	362
	G1	158
	G2	633
	AE6	558
	M15	592
STENCH	HAP	1132
	HAP	2456
	G3	836
	G4	68
	AE2	947
	AE3	296
	AE6	294
	AE8	638
	HIF	441
STENCHES	AE6	344
STEP	EIE	15
	OD	10
	VCS	28
	AE5	423
	AE9	1069
	B	158
	CAM	284
	TH	371
	FL	181
STEPDAM	J6	528
	AE7	1050
STEPDAME	M1	188
	VP3	48
STEPDAMES	J6	820
	G3	446
STEPDAM'S	G2	178
	AE10	544
STEPHEN	AA	643
STEPPED	AM	1057
	TA	214
STEPPING	AE10	1063
STEPS	AR	282
	AA	242
	ER	24
	L2	7
	TA	125
	J3	29
	J3	436
	P3	109
	P5	178
	M1	687
	M13	46
	M13	56
	VP3	122
	G2	672
	G4	612
	AE1	262
	AE1	432
	AE1	628
	AE2	967
	AE3	213
	AE3	476
	AE3	650
	AE3	866
	AE5	963
	AE6	276
	AE6	373
	AE6	629
	AE6	737
	AE6	1240
	AE8	609
	AE8	933
	AE9	993
	AE11	124
	AE11	793
	AE11	860
	AE11	1124
	AE11	1240
	AE12	655
	KT2	65
	KT3	191
	KT3	292
	KT3	785
	BP	26
	HIF	54
	M12	191
	M12	563
	WB	8
	AU	527
STERN	AM	543
	HAP	1078
	J3	443
	P1	23
	P3	88
	HI	63
	AE1	164
	AE1	397
	AE1	675
	AE2	10
	AE3	889
	AE4	406

Word	Ref	No.
STERN	AE4	676
	AE5	218
	AE5	547
	AE5	956
	AE5	1117
	AE8	152
	AE8	899
	AE10	232
	AE10	250
	AE10	280
	AE10	320
	AE10	627
	AE10	843
	AE12	1284
	KT2	302
	KT3	339
	KT3	390
	B	379
	HIF	10
	HIF	126
	HIF	259
	HIF	751
	TH	193
	M12	235
	CI	386
STERNHOLD'S	RL	456
STERNLY	HAP	794
	G3	383
	AE2	231
	AE5	637
	AE10	737
	KT2	166
	B	634
	B	726
	TH	341
STERNS	AM	326
	AE5	864
	AE6	4
	AE6	1247
STERVE	PUO3	36
	TA	501
	HAP	2043
	P1	214
STERVES	J1	113
STEWARD	J1	138
	J6	211
	AS	83
STEWARDS	GP	55
STEWED	PC1	24
STEWS	AA	127
	SAA	301
	HAP	1132
	HAP	2507
STHENELUS	AE2	340
	AE12	515
STICK	PPC	11
	HAP	1474
	HAP	1987
	PMS	4
	PLT	1
	G3	672
	AE6	311
	M15	341
	PMK	22
STICKING	AE1	668
	AE5	285
STICKLE	PD	63
STICKLERS	HS	41
STICKS	EAZ	23
	P6	70
	AE4	100
	AE6	57
	AR	65
	RH	74
	PRL	20
	EM	5
	AA	547
	G3	559
	G3	838
STIFF	AE1	915
	AE5	572
	AE8	824
	AE9	67
	CAM	223
	C	292
	M15	347
	M15	605
	CI	387
	CI	634
STIFFEN	HAP	444
	BP	186
STIFFENED	P4	78
	AE2	362
	AE2	1051
	AE6	315
	AE7	624

Word	Ref	No.
STIFFENING	VP6	53
STIFFENS	AE11	1111
STIFFER	B	375
	M11	98
STIFFNESS	AM	592
STIFF-STRETCHED	AM	483
STIFLE	SCG2	9
STIFLED	G4	381
	AE8	342
	AE10	655
	M8	286
	M12	568
	AU	198
	M15	333
STIGMATIZED	HAP	401
STILL	AM	472
	SAA	1083
	L3	150
	L3	181
	TA	288
	HAP	535
	EL	318
	P3	174
	VP2	33
	AE3	782
	AE3	917
	KT3	677
STILLBORN	TH	308
STILLER	GP	41
STILLING	J3	122
STILL-MISTAKING	HAP	1698
STILLNESS	AR	7
STILLS	OAL	323
STIMICHON	VP5	84
STING	L3	53
	L4	113
	HH	28
	PTS	1
	VP3	145
	KT1	492
	B	36
	TH	349
	M15	549
STINGS	EDGA	32
	P1	126
	G3	239
	G3	326
	G4	107
	G4	347
	G4	440
	AE12	864
STINGY	J10	499
STINK	PCD	24
	EC	35
	PSH	28
	P6	37
STINKING	SAA	551
	G3	627
STINKS	L4	167
	P3	146
	P5	216
STINT	PMQ	53
	J6	475
	KT3	393
STINTED	SAA	169
STINTS	L2	20
STIPENDS	SAA	318
STIR	AM	1025
	EEL	9
	EEL	17
	HAP	2519
	G1	75
	G2	429
	CI	173
	EMKG	18
STIRRED	L4	195
	HAP	1171
	G4	380
	M10	15
STIRRUPS	TH	284
STIRS	PLG	7
	AE8	590
	M12	689
STITCH-FALLEN	J10	309
STOCK	EEL	37
	PNH	15
	PC2	17
	ETC	5
	AA	101
	SAA	564
	SAA	994
	AK	25
	HAP	388
	EL	66
	VP1	102
	VP3	47

Word	Ref	Num		Word	Ref	Num		Word	Ref	Num
STOCK	G2	426		STONE	FL	239		STOOD	MC	6
	G2	465			M12	34			VP1	48
	G3	599			M12	192			VP2	31
	G3	715			M12	393			VP3	108
	G4	227			M12	366			VP6	102
	G4	400			M12	460			VP8	3
	AE1	390			AU	38			VP8	4
	AE5	493		STONEHENGE	DC	47			G1	110
	MM	54		STONES	DC	44			G1	633
	B	696			L4	298			G2	290
	AU	45			T23	53			G4	453
	AS	81			J1	127			G4	678
STOCKDOVES	VP1	77			P3	119			AE1	25
	VP3	105			M1	387			AE1	263
STOCKED	HAP	1299			M1	528			AE1	434
	HAP	2503			M1	535			AE1	616
	G4	405			M1	536			AE1	812
STOCKINGED	J3	397			VP2	30			AE1	866
STOCKS	AM	600			G1	87			AE1	869
	HAP	2347			G1	666			AE2	67
	G2	46			G2	250			AE2	74
	G2	264			G2	295			AE2	85
	G2	522			G2	481			AE2	176
	EMKG	22			G3	640			AE2	362
STOIC	J3	198			G4	38			AE2	399
	P1	19			G4	286			AE2	639
	P3	101			AE1	215			AE2	683
	P5	84			AE1	589			AE2	700
	P5	122			AE2	553			AE2	765
STOICS	RH	19			AE2	608			AE2	801
STOLE	AR	129			AE2	826			AE2	847
	EEL	10			AE3	820			AE2	880
	SAA	541			AE7	784			AE2	1051
	H3	39			AE7	1024			AE3	16
	HAP	1632			AE8	334			AE3	32
	M1	935			AE9	710			AE3	40
	VP3	16			AE9	964			AE3	205
	AE7	388			AE10	198			AE3	669
	AF	87			AE10	507			AE3	743
	AF	91			AE11	456			AE3	782
	AU	180			AE11	718			AE4	405
STOLEN	PW	10			AE11	936			AE4	564
	J10	521			AE12	1337			AE4	576
	AE2	244			KT3	977			AE4	663
STOLES	CAM	239			M10	40			AE4	827
STOMACH	AR	173			M15	55			AE4	1005
	J3	459			M15	60			AE5	162
	J6	139			M15	473			AE5	220
	J6	553		STONY	VP1	68			AE5	376
	P3	108			G2	467			AE5	599
	G3	322			AE3	741			AE5	679
	C	148			AE9	1092			AE5	926
STOMACHS	PLG	22			AE11	802			AE5	1056
	PR	31			M12	35			AE6	74
	OE	26		STOOD	AM	17			AE6	171
	J3	378			AM	248			AE6	422
	G3	584			AM	310			AE6	551
	HIF	639			AM	377			AE6	610
	PMK	2			AM	395			AE6	754
	PWR	24			AM	472			AE6	964
STONE	PO	21			AM	733			AE7	41
	AA	101			AM	772			AE7	88
	L3	209			HP	154			AE7	108
	T23	37			EMW	1			AE7	230
	T23	90			AA	205			AE7	237
	HAP	685			MF	67			AE7	242
	HAP	1978			MF	104			AE7	379
	HAP	2031			MF	136			AE7	480
	J3	36			SAA	679			AE7	743
	J3	354			T23	31			AE7	751
	J3	433			T23	105			AE7	813
	P2	2			TA	193			AE8	119
	M1	544			HAP	99			AE8	133
	M13	210			HAP	434			AE8	312
	M13	216			HAP	535			AE8	447
	M13	220			HAP	600			AE8	467
	VP7	45			HAP	1084			AE8	700
	VP10	23			HAP	1365			AE8	750
	G3	19			HAP	1435			AE8	863
	G4	536			HAP	2202			AE8	867
	AE1	78			HAP	2381			AE9	25
	AE2	133			HAP	2404			AE9	98
	AE6	838			HAP	2475			AE9	149
	AE8	257			SSC	18			AE9	228
	AE8	314			BR	128			AE9	253
	AE8	959			EL	21			AE9	518
	AE10	192			EL	290			AE9	527
	AE10	534			ODA	8			AE9	624
	AE10	583			ODA	44			AE9	704
	AE10	988			J6	154			AE9	740
	AE12	779			J10	404			AE9	855
	AE12	1300			P3	193			AE9	948
	AE12	1310			M1	471			AE9	1012
	OAL	493			M13	225			AE10	186
	M8	124			HI	12			AE10	280
	C	742			HI	45			AE10	328

Word	Ref	No.
STOOD	AE10	420
	AE10	462
	AE10	578
	AE10	753
	AE10	775
	AE10	792
	AE10	799
	AE10	1083
	AE10	1092
	AE10	1093
	AE10	1185
	AE10	1278
	AE11	265
	AE11	182
	AE11	767
	AE11	1175
	AE11	1232
	AE12	408
	AE12	585
	AE12	1111
	AE12	1255
	OAL	11
	OAL	410
	OAL	598
	OAL	608
	KT1	224
	KT1	235
	KT1	245
	KT2	79
	KT2	126
	KT2	198
	KT2	234
	KT2	328
	KT2	460
	KT2	520
	KT2	542
	KT2	545
	KT2	564
	KT2	569
	KT2	612
	KT2	623
	KT2	653
	KT3	49
	KT3	254
	KT3	270
	KT3	283
	KT3	362
	TJD	29
	M8	84
	M8	93
	M8	97
	M8	104
	M8	153
	M8	173
	M8	187
	M8	194
	M8	240
	M8	252
	B	5
	B	101
	B	152
	B	226
	B	240
	B	681
	B	691
	BP	104
	BP	183
	CAM	108
	CAM	164
	CAM	224
	CAM	228
	CAM	231
	CAM	364
	HIF	19
	HIF	55
	HIF	287
	HIF	295
	HIF	300
	HIF	381
	HIF	515
	HIF	614
	HIF	674
	HIF	676
	HIF	717
	C	3
	C	223
	C	309
	C	625
	C	666
	C	679
	TH	27
	TH	33
	TH	74
	TH	88
	TH	98
	TH	103
STOOD	TH	145
	TH	217
	TH	328
	TH	337
	TH	404
	TH	409
	M11	409
	M11	441
	FL	38
	FL	60
	FL	119
	FL	130
	FL	312
	FL	392
	M12	34
	M12	133
	M12	143
	M12	330
	M12	449
	M12	501
	M12	650
	M12	661
	M12	745
	M12	792
	AU	114
	AU	327
	AU	607
	WB	211
	M15	39
	M15	72
	GP	114
	CI	90
	CI	107
	CI	111
	CI	171
	CI	180
	CI	187
	CI	345
	CI	406
	CI	443
	CI	602
STOOL	PTP	44
STOOP	SMA	27
	EEL	14
	PUO2	32
	ML	48
	HAP	1865
	G3	169
STOOPED	AE1	545
	AM	19
	AE4	379
	AE10	725
	AE12	1120
STOOPING	ER	78
	M1	516
	G3	340
	G4	75
	AE2	1070
	AE6	295
	AE8	475
	AE10	535
	AE12	376
	AE12	713
	BP	42
	M11	466
	M12	591
STOOPS	AM	342
	AM	429
	HAP	1108
	AE11	1105
	AE12	543
STOP	AM	1052
	PMQ	50
	CM	29
	AA	854
	SAA	457
	TA	89
	HAP	844
	HAP	937
	BR	159
	PSH	21
	P2	81
	VP3	26
	VP7	57
	G3	173
	G3	183
	G3	572
	G4	25
	G4	56
	G4	423
	G4	726
	AE2	872
	AE5	916
	AE6	1167
	AE10	808
	AE11	456
STOP	AE11	910
	AE12	704
	AE12	1148
	AE12	1324
	OAL	458
	BP	150
	TH	136
	M11	107
	M15	416
	M15	691
	CI	473
	ETP	39
STOPPED	AM	6
	PKK	5
	AA	843
	MF	60
	SAA	798
	RL	267
	AT	99
	ER	7
	T23	95
	J3	19
	M1	345
	M1	387
	M1	625
	M1	972
	VP8	4
	AE1	644
	AE2	916
	AE4	41
	AE4	637
	AE6	288
	AE6	407
	AE7	744
	AE10	448
	AE10	453
	AE10	483
	AE10	1101
	AE11	142
	KT2	79
	CI	274
	B	238
	B	749
	CAM	217
	M11	369
	M11	435
	M12	49
	M12	193
STOPPING	B	366
STOPS	LC	132
	AM	431
	HAP	1980
	BR	177
	J3	392
	AE4	562
	AE4	706
	AE5	611
	AE9	65
	AE10	320
	AE11	830
	AE12	910
	KT3	559
	CAM	132
	M11	226
	CI	342
STORE	AR	278
	SMA	21
	SMA	65
	AM	14
	AM	97
	AM	1000
	AM	1032
	SEL1	14
	SM1	10
	PTC	9
	DA	59
	SAA	223
	SAA	549
	SAA	669
	SAA	924
	SAA	949
	SAA	1038
	PK	8
	RL	105
	MO	11
	L2	43
	L3	138
	L3	153
	L3	216
	T18	84
	H29	16
	H2	70
	TA	14
	TA	309
	HAP	520
	HAP	700

STORE		
HAP	1155
HAP	1407
HAP	1877
HAP	2232
HAP	2391
BR	325
BR	330
EL	69
OD	13
OD	49
SSH	9
J3	248
J3	324
J3	360
J6	475
J10	168
J10	301
P1	136
P2	57
P2	124
P3	138
P3	150
P4	54
P5	218
P6	56
P6	72
P6	150
P6	183
M1	174
M1	383
M1	594
M9	107
M13	123
M13	133
MC	61
VP2	79
VP3	43
VP3	109
G1	176
G1	204
G1	271
G1	279
G1	356
G1	403
G2	486
G2	713
G2	729
G3	482
G3	690
G3	837
G4	519
G4	795
AE1	603
AE2	504
AE5	54
AE8	568
AE9	1085
AE10	1170
AE11	648
OAL	60
AF	163
AF	173
DO	83
KT2	16
KT2	523
B	683
BP	34
BP	66
BP	113
FL	164
FL	225
M12	254
AU	83
WB	468
M15	112
M15	270
M15	511
GP	56
CI	620
AS	87
AS	97
PWR	1

STORED		
AM	1084
PD	27
G3	615
AE3	597
AE4	541
AE12	37
BP	100
CI	266

STORES		
AM	409
AM	469
AM	566
AM	1142
SAA	981
AK	74

STORES		
J10	20
J10	46
M1	133
VP2	25
VP7	76
G1	160
G1	475
G2	190
G2	218
G4	55
G4	333
AE3	604
AE8	101
AE8	109
AE11	502
TJD	44
TJD	148
HIF	429
M15	130

STORIES		
DA	82
T27	48
PP	16
KT1	363

STORK		
J1	173

STORM		
AM	713
AM	743
AM	1120
PT	15
CM	73
DA	67
DA	96
D	14
SAA	558
H29	104
TA	393
HAP	629
HAP	1330
BR	259
P1	33
P4	120
VP9	88
G1	303
G1	431
G1	517
G1	536
G2	422
AE1	170
AE1	758
AE1	806
AE1	819
AE2	179
AE4	648
AE5	16
AE5	69
AE5	579
AE5	869
AE5	1032
AE7	739
AE7	831
AE8	16
AE9	830
AE9	908
AE10	897
AE10	1137
AE10	1147
AE11	712
AE12	814
KT1	23
KT1	125
KT3	362
M11	261
M11	314
M11	497
FL	384
FL	394
FL	568
M12	53
WB	536
GP	35
CI	329
STP	16

STORMED		
AR	143
EEL	26
SAA	841
SAA	849
AE4	216
HIF	535

STORMS		
HS	70
AR	123
LCA	5
AM	122
AM	1213
DA	61
AA	161
AA	889
PRH	34

STORMS		
SAA	605
SAA	820
SAA	1104
H3	27
H9	15
H29	90
M1	64
SFL	4
VP3	125
VP3	127
G1	40
G1	198
G1	561
G1	598
G1	612
G1	617
G2	558
G2	620
G3	711
G4	342
G4	443
G4	681
AE1	47
AE1	77
AE1	240
AE1	530
AE2	553
AE3	95
AE3	436
AE3	702
AE3	932
AE4	70
AE5	166
AE5	419
AE5	612
AE5	910
AE6	939
AE7	421
AE9	116
AE10	152
AE10	850
AE11	403
AE12	427
KT3	135
M8	272
M11	425
FL	590
M12	674
CI	379
SMP	72
AS	57

STORMY		
CM	11
CM	86
DA	45
SAA	878
G1	297
G1	407
G1	419
G1	622
G2	184
G3	549
G4	281
AE1	183
AE2	480
AE3	165
AE3	275
AE5	7
AE5	818
AE5	1010
AE7	416
AE7	574
AE7	825
AE9	912
AE10	371
AE10	966
AE11	844
AE11	895
OAL	464
KT3	1081
HIF	71
HIF	235
HIF	489
M11	26
M11	212
M11	366
M11	456
CI	257
CI	386

STORY		
AR	108
AM	783
PMM	6
ELN	4
HP	45
PUO5	7
EK	18
EDG	23

Word	Code	No.
STORY	RL	147
	HAP	1615
	HAP	1831
	J3	326
	P3	166
	M1	873
	PLT	13
	PLT	27
	AE1	471
	AE1	793
	AE4	114
	OAL	334
	LMC	4
	KT1	35
	KT2	1
	KT3	212
	C	665
	C	716
	TH	154
	M12	1
	M12	700
	PWR	38
STORY'S	KT3	1003
STOUT	EUO	15
	J16	86
	P3	149
	G2	231
	G3	322
	AE1	22
	HIF	208
	CI	403
	CI	600
STOUTEST	AE1	170
STOUT-HEARTED	HAP	1842
STOW	PMM	12
	M11	107
STOWED	HAP	191
	J3	148
	HIF	432
STRAGGLE	AM	939
	G2	377
STRAGGLED	SAA	1124
STRAGGLER	J6	633
STRAGGLERS	G2	503
STRAGGLING	G1	358
	G1	592
	AE2	537
	AE12	901
	MM	8
	GP	61
STRAIGHT	AR	174
	AM	213
	AM	261
	AM	344
	AM	860
	AM	931
	AM	982
	AM	1136
	EWGR	21
	SMM2	21
	SEL3	11
	PCG2	14
	SCG1	3
	SCG1	29
	PLN	10
	PSF	36
	EPC	11
	L3	114
	L3	281
	L4	177
	L5	7
	T18	49
	TA	360
	AK	191
	HAP	868
	SSC	53
	J6	403
	P2	41
	P3	20
	P5	51
	P5	196
	M1	87
	M1	960
	M13	216
	VP8	107
	G3	121
	G4	90
	G4	710
	G4	802
	AE6	570
	AE6	771
	AE6	1243
	AE8	512
	AE10	1241
	AE10	1264
	AE12	699

Word	Code	No.
STRAIGHT	OAL	356
	C	267
	FL	38
	WB	52
STRAIGHTENED	AR	245
	G1	684
STRAIN	PEL	8
	MF	180
	SAA	977
	OE	15
	ER	40
	PAA	43
	L4	69
	AK	27
	BR	216
	J6	285
	J10	207
	J10	460
	P5	15
	P5	164
	M1	975
	DHP	3
	VP1	12
	VP1	73
	VP2	39
	VP2	55
	VP4	1
	VP5	20
	VP6	12
	VP6	123
	VP8	30
	VP8	35
	VP8	45
	VP8	52
	VP8	59
	VP8	79
	VP8	86
	G2	330
	G3	461
	G4	596
	G4	726
	AE7	723
	AE8	767
	AE9	54
	AE10	553
	AE10	1292
	AF	124
	M8	205
STRAINED	PLN	24
	GK	32
	AE5	699
	AE8	741
	AE11	1062
	AE12	642
	AE12	1132
	M10	23
	M11	407
STRAINING	PKA	14
	M10	31
	CAM	57
STRAINS	SMA	55
	SAA	1045
	SAA	1059
	L4	39
	VP6	1
	VP8	63
	VP8	69
	G4	746
	AE4	672
	AE5	291
	AE7	536
STRAIT	RL	324
	J10	278
	G2	330
	KT2	548
STRAITENED	EL	280
	G4	218
STRAITER	RL	324
STRAITS	AM	682
	PCD	9
	L4	133
	G1	297
	AE3	524
	AE3	532
	AE11	1303
	M15	506
STRAND	AR	276
	AA	272
	P6	61
	VP6	94
	VP8	137
	G1	497
	G3	543
	AE2	276
	AE3	186
	AE3	731

Word	Code	No.
STRAND	AE3	908
	AE3	927
	AE6	5
	AE6	255
	AE6	547
	AE8	164
	AE8	650
	AE10	397
	AE10	404
	AE10	552
	AE11	284
	AE11	594
	AE12	163
	AE12	1090
	HIF	41
	HIF	659
	M12	94
	CI	389
STRANDED	AM	1002
	G3	809
	AE10	420
STRANDS	AE3	726
	M15	406
STRANGE	RH	17
	PWG	1
	ETL	3
	RL	292
	AK	125
	HAP	1656
	EDS	34
	J6	56
	J6	414
	VP1	69
	VP9	4
	G3	727
	G4	288
	AE2	930
	AE3	37
	AE3	410
	AE4	14
	AE4	657
	AE4	668
	AE6	139
	AE7	109
	AE9	145
	KT3	13
	KT3	879
	FL	59
	M12	242
	M12	578
	M12	695
	M15	453
STRANGELY	HS	147
	LC	105
STRANGER	AR	69
	HP	3
	HP	10
	HP	212
	HAP	535
	HAP	1243
	HAP	1286
	EPN	1
	J6	123
	M1	949
	G4	502
	AE1	457
	AE3	876
	AE4	500
	AE8	165
	AE8	412
	KT3	972
	B	568
	M11	455
	M15	479
STRANGER'S	AM	149
STRANGERS	HP	188
	DA	93
	RL	191
	HAP	2063
	VP6	61
	AE1	443
	AE1	510
	AE1	845
	AE8	150
	AE12	99
STRANGLED	AE8	384
	KT2	589
	M12	199
STRANGLING	B	592
STRATAGEM	AE11	775
	OAL	878
	C	490
STRATAGEMS	AE1	1059
	AE11	1058
STRATOCLES	J3	167
STRAW	VP3	37

STRAW	G1	279	STREAM	AE12	1282	STREAMS	TH	144		
	G3	465		OAL	873		M11	340		
	AE8	870		KT2	627		M12	151		
	KT3	956		KT3	141		M12	550		
	KT3	973		KT3	198		AU	608		
	BP	31		TJD	26		M15	268		
	Br	47		M15	471		M15	412		
	C.	742		M15	497		M15	417		
	WB	349	STREAMED	AE2	364		M15	436		
STRAWBERRIES	M1	135	STREAMER	J10	211		M15	479		
	M13	110		AE7	35		M15	485		
STRAWS	PAL	25	STREAMERS	AR	225		CI	106		
STRAY	RH	85		AM	418	STREET	UDH	88		
	AT	2		AM	606		AM	906		
	M13	78		SAA	26		AM	1066		
	G3	526		AK	166		EWGR	6		
	G4	158		AE1	258		ELN	3		
	G4	280	STREAMING	CM	1		MF	97		
	AE2	986		HAP	1222		SAA	928		
	OAE2	45		G4	784		HAP	2196		
	CAM	64		AE1	511		EKA	2		
	CI	173		AE2	942		EKA	17		
STRAYED	M1	795		AE3	817		PSH	5		
	VP2	51		AE4	953		J1	167		
	G2	507		AE4	987		J3	9		
	AE1	445		AE6	356		J3	437		
	AE3	287		AE11	960		J6	538		
	AE8	273		AE12	1376		J6	688		
	KT2	63		KT2	320		J6	855		
	TJD	26		KT3	604		P3	52		
	TH	78		M12	566		P5	46		
STRAYS	G3	20	STREAMS	UDH	92		HI	28		
	AE3	266		JH	20		AE2	536		
STREAK	RH	89		LC	66		AE2	1023		
	AE6	357		DC	29		AE2	1045		
STREAKED	G1	610		SAA	315		AE4	94		
	AE5	114		H9	5		AE4	849		
	KT3	189		H29	38		KT3	447		
STREAKS	AM	271		HAP	1420		KT3	1062		
	AT	21		J3	35	STREETS	AM	859		
	T18	55		J3	370		AM	913		
	G2	650		M1	106		AM	931		
	G4	150		M1	359		AM	1034		
	AE2	277		M1	391		AM	1105		
	AE9	477		M1	464		AM	1139		
STREAKY	HAP	2587		M1	736		AM	1179		
	FL	586		M1	872		ENH	28		
STREAM	AM	626		M13	78		SAA	805		
	SAA	980		M13	83		HAP	2481		
	L2	35		VP2	83		J1	69		
	T18	60		VP3	147		J1	94		
	H29	52		VP5	131		J1	237		
	H2	39		VP7	73		J3	344		
	AK	68		VP9	54		J3	384		
	AK	87		VP10	6		J6	281		
	HAP	1186		VP10	26		J6	523		
	HAP	1775		G1	67		J6	658		
	HAP	1809		G1	156		J10	430		
	J6	675		G1	592		P4	122		
	J10	13		G1	645		VP3	36		
	PPS	2		G2	216		G2	526		
	P3	200		G2	259		AE1	584		
	M1	500		G2	276		AE2	400		
	M13	30		G2	662		AE2	448		
	M13	216		G3	21		AE2	491		
	M13	231		G3	396		AE8	880		
	HI	130		G3	470		AE8	954		
	VP5	74		G3	809		AE11	721		
	G1	291		G4	180		KT1	432		
	G1	335		G4	514		KT3	104		
	G1	532		G4	594		KT3	437		
	G3	231		G4	637		KT3	462		
	G3	682		G4	689		M15	632		
	G4	23		G4	738		GP	61		
	G4	35		AE1	175		CI	560		
	G4	46		AE1	232	STRENGTH	RH	15		
	G4	397		AE1	238		LC	53		
	G4	454		AE2	757		AM	295		
	G4	505		AE4	367		AM	595		
	AE1	549		AE5	826		AM	609		
	AE2	978		AE6	595		CM	28		
	AE6	443		AE6	915		HP	242		
	AE6	965		AE7	1089		AA	279		
	AE7	689		AE8	77		AA	744		
	AE8	126		AE8	97		MD	72		
	AE8	726		AE8	186		SAA	252		
	AE9	323		AE8	318		SAA	914		
	AE9	470		AE8	792		SDG	9		
	AE9	580		AE10	381		RL	62		
	AE9	821		AE10	1160		L4	94		
	AE10	287		AE12	564		HAP	1083		
	AE10	595		AE12	1003		HAP	1337		
	AE10	1312		OAL	292		HAP	2528		
	AE11	585		OAL	701		BR	202		
	AE11	828		M8	378		OD	5		
	AE11	989		M8	379		J1	226		

STRENGTH	P1	191
	P4	33
	M9	194
	VCS	15
	MC	12
	MC	16
	MC	19
	MC	22
	MC	30
	VP8	145
	G1	127
	G2	248
	G2	407
	G3	325
	G3	355
	G3	765
	G4	155
	G4	291
	AE1	299
	AE1	746
	AE1	937
	AE2	660
	AE3	51
	AE3	399
	AE3	591
	AE4	900
	AE5	250
	AE5	622
	AE5	897
	AE5	1115
	AE6	169
	AE6	224
	AE6	487
	AE6	1232
	AE8	580
	AE8	742
	AE9	560
	AE9	707
	AE9	1085
	AE10	222
	AE10	443
	AE10	525
	AE10	575
	AE10	610
	AE10	799
	AE10	1054
	AE10	1091
	AE11	268
	AE11	481
	AE11	620
	AE11	741
	AE11	868
	AE11	1041
	AE11	1247
	AE11	1260
	AE12	399
	AE12	1317
	OAL	147
	OAL	757
	DO	108
	KT1	28
	KT1	144
	KT3	333
	KT3	510
	KT3	568
	TJD	139
	CAM	172
	CAM	321
	HIF	267
	HIF	409
	C	625
	TH	286
	FL	544
	M12	96
	M12	238
	M12	653
	AU	132
	AU	147
	AU	336
	AU	391
	AU	543
	AU	566
	M15	82
	M15	346
	CI	304
	CI	385
	PMK	2
STRENGTHEN	HAP	1774
STRENGTHENED	MM	47
STRENGTHENS	BP	54
STRENGTH'S	SAA	1038
STRESS	AE1	503
	AE7	273
	AE11	845
STRETCH	AA	46
	MF	143

STRETCH	L3	286
	HAP	2104
	PDS	40
	J6	107
	P3	15
	P4	51
	GK	60
	G1	381
	G4	682
	AE3	177
	AE3	721
	AE3	581
	AE3	783
	AE5	21
	AE5	172
	AE5	247
	AE5	259
	AE8	195
	AE9	751
	AE9	853
	AE9	1012
	AE10	658
	AE10	967
	AE12	1058
	B	327
	HIF	389
	M11	482
	M15	551
STRETCHED	AM	132
	AM	278
	AM	523
	SAA	1105
	AT	8
	AK	92
	BR	7
	BR	255
	J3	409
	J10	275
	P3	209
	M1	1074
	VP1	5
	VP6	20
	VP7	32
	VP8	21
	G3	643
	AE1	298
	AE3	320
	AE3	820
	AE3	831
	AE4	765
	AE5	495
	AE7	1018
	AE8	804
	AE8	853
	AE9	207
	AE10	1028
	AE10	1168
	AE11	993
	AE12	1092
	KT3	122
	M8	173
	M8	245
	M8	391
	C	270
	C	626
	C	667
	C	770
	M11	381
	FL	43
	M12	749
	WB	316
	M15	152
	GP	127
	ETP	1
STRETCHER	AE10	417
STRETCHES	DA	127
	BR	257
	GK	126
STRETCHEST	P5	192
STRETCHING	G1	496
	G1	530
	G2	408
	AE10	297
	AE10	836
	AE11	486
	AE12	850
	AE12	1004
	C	89
	AU	7
STREW	A	16
	G2	255
	G4	88
	AE2	536
	AE6	310
	AE9	723
	AE9	906

STREW	AE9	913
	M12	180
STREWED	HS	55
	GE	31
	P5	262
	G4	759
	AE11	98
	C	16
	M12	100
	AU	399
	M15	593
STREWEST	G1	36
STREWS	AE12	259
STRICT	AM	465
	S	3
	EUO2	29
	M1	975
	G2	381
	AE2	968
	AE5	48
	AE6	582
	AE9	51
	B	160
	C	528
	C	529
	M11	407
	WB	172
STRICTER	G4	596
STRICTEST	SAA	1053
STRICTLY	TA	328
	TA	423
	HAP	2239
	BR	355
STRIDE	PW	14
	M9	191
	AE9	809
	M8	167
STRIDED	AE3	880
STRIDES	BR	232
	AE3	846
	AE3	872
	AE5	487
	AE7	929
	AE8	930
	KT2	24
STRIDING	AE9	434
	AE12	126
	AE12	653
	AE12	989
STRIDOR	AE12	1258
STRIFE	UDH	61
	UDH	67
	AM	414
	PUO2	7
	D	18
	SAA	142
	AT	91
	L2	17
	L3	157
	L3	200
	L3	269
	L3	302
	L4	94
	L4	114
	T23	43
	H29	79
	H2	4
	TA	154
	TA	188
	HAP	1654
	BR	193
	EH	11
	J6	234
	J6	440
	J6	654
	J10	481
	P5	135
	GK	19
	VP7	23
	G2	688
	AE1	479
	AE2	585
	AE4	995
	AE5	560
	AE5	647
	AE5	1025
	AE6	392
	AE7	490
	AE8	911
	AE9	172
	AE9	268
	AE9	542
	AE9	804
	AE10	857
	AE10	1075
	AE11	1102

Word	Code	Num
STRIFE	AE11	1224
	AE12	85
	AE12	96
	AE12	354
	AE12	1110
	AE12	1183
	AE12	1260
	AE12	1359
	KT1	352
	KT1	462
	KT2	254
	KT3	339
	KT3	375
	KT3	380
	KT3	393
	KT3	504
	KT3	521
	KT3	539
	KT3	815
	KT3	1149
	TJD	2
	TJD	17
	BP	172
	CAM	356
	HIF	7
	HIF	419
	C	111
	M12	250
	M12	821
	AU	119
	AU	193
	AU	323
	WB	98
	WB	519
	CI	133
STRIKE	HS	44
	AR	32
	AM	903
	PUO1	6
	EUO	21
	E	30
	PLG	15
	MF	22
	SAA	908
	PD	62
	MO	5
	L3	306
	TA	436
	HAP	241
	HAP	323
	HAP	742
	HAP	1184
	HAP	2343
	PDS	36
	OE	46
	J16	12
	G4	176
	G4	254
	G4	419
	AE2	140
	AE5	575
	AE6	6
	AE6	880
	AE8	35
	AE9	1009
	AE11	520
	AE12	770
	AE12	810
	AE12	1361
	OAL	817
	AF	123
	KT3	511
	M11	102
	CI	276
STRIKES	OE	33
	J6	817
	G3	827
	AE2	569
	AE5	683
	AE12	562
	KT1	278
	M12	458
STRING	EOE	7
	J3	72
	J16	15
	P5	137
	OAE1	15
STRINGS	T18	58
	PAA	22
	J6	503
	P6	4
	G1	133
	OAL	15
STRIP	AM	221
	PA	28
	AT	55

Word	Code	Num
STRIP	G2	11
	G2	504
	AE1	295
	AE2	532
	AE12	448
	KT1	140
	M12	200
STRIPES	L3	229
STRIPLING	J1	93
	J10	505
	M1	611
	M13	177
	OAE1	25
STRIPLINGS	AE7	528
STRIPPED	EM	14
	J6	616
	G2	775
	G4	204
	AE5	561
	AE11	133
	KT2	539
	BP	60
	TH	109
	PTP	24
STRIVE	UDH	26
	AM	230
	PNH	17
	PAZ	19
	EAZ	36
	PTW	18
	PTC	5
	DA	172
	AA	387
	MD	6
	SAA	1030
	SAA	1111
	L3	207
	L4	17
	L4	79
	L4	203
	EAA	29
	HAP	1067
	HAP	2228
	M1	599
	GK	46
	GK	132
	VP8	76
	VP10	68
	G1	43
	G1	292
	G3	28
	G3	574
	G4	93
	AE3	655
	AE3	898
	AE5	37
	AE5	326
	AE7	831
	AE10	1136
	AE12	57
	OAL	42
	OAL	363
	KT2	196
	KT3	634
	M11	425
	M11	427
	M12	477
	WB	390
	M15	649
	P3	20
	L4	44
	HAP	412
	M1	724
	M9	154
	GK	69
	G4	423
	OAL	24
	OAL	802
	M15	642
STRIVES		
STRIVING	PAR	17
	SAA	123
	AE1	637
	AE6	670
	C	629
STRODE	J6	167
	M13	44
	M13	189
	HI	189
	AE5	496
	AE10	531
	M11	470
STROKE	AM	1079
	SAA	735
	L3	259
	L4	276
	L4	281

Word	Code	Num
STROKE	L4	296
	TA	5
	ODA	48
	J3	152
	J10	91
	M1	889
	M1	995
	G3	639
	AE3	838
	AE4	954
	AE4	979
	AE5	193
	AE5	494
	AE5	582
	AE5	596
	AE5	639
	AE6	265
	AE7	533
	AE7	710
	AE9	1040
	AE10	554
	AE10	740
	AE10	1095
	AE10	1229
	AE10	1277
	AE11	241
	AE12	136
	AE12	1063
	KT3	625
	CAM	135
	M12	108
	M12	464
	M12	639
	M12	647
STROKED	OAL	337
	CAM	115
STROKES	TA	441
	J1	246
	AE1	245
	AE2	656
	AE2	847
	AE3	273
	AE5	159
	AE5	187
	AE5	247
	AE5	579
	AE5	612
	AE5	1016
	AE8	556
	AE10	1270
	KT2	176
	M8	199
	M12	399
	M12	470
STROKING	M1	890
STROLLERS	PUO3	33
STROLLS	J6	704
STRONG	RH	35
	VHH	45
	AM	19
	AM	22
	AM	423
	AM	590
	AM	871
	AM	935
	ENH	6
	EOE	5
	EOE	19
	PLG	23
	CM	49
	DA	114
	DA	196
	ETG	8
	AA	88
	AA	149
	AA	215
	AA	487
	SAA	380
	SAA	481
	RL	99
	L4	2
	L4	295
	TA	158
	TA	494
	PAA	17
	HAP	729
	HAP	870
	HAP	1670
	J6	17
	J6	442
	J6	677
	J10	315
	P3	171
	MC	3
	G2	264
	G2	366

Word	Code	No.
STRONG	G2	595
	G4	702
	AE1	140
	AE1	719
	AE1	948
	AE2	657
	AE3	77
	AE3	314
	AE5	88
	AE5	251
	AE6	533
	AE6	740
	AE6	1050
	AE7	916
	AE8	629
	AE9	79
	AE9	450
	AE9	819
	AE9	955
	AE9	1030
	AE9	1040
	AE10	252
	AE10	442
	AE10	786
	AE10	970
	AE10	1054
	AE10	1095
	AE11	589
	AE11	946
	AE11	1016
	AE11	1067
	AE11	1092
	AE11	1118
	AE11	1249
	AE12	377
	AE12	567
	AE12	674
	AE12	1302
	AE12	1338
	KT1	203
	KT1	316
	KT1	585
	KT2	245
	KT2	557
	KT3	45
	KT3	62
	KT3	296
	KT3	303
	KT3	473
	KT3	640
	KT3	787
	KT3	809
	KT3	847
	M8	59
	M8	183
	M8	211
	B	432
	B	445
	B	455
	CAM	174
	TH	222
	M12	413
	M12	429
	M12	460
	M12	645
	AU	134
	AU	283
	AU	401
	WB	423
	CI	265
STRONG-BACKED	J6	450
STRONG-BONED	M15	343
STRONG-BUILT	AE5	588
STRONGER	AM	760
	L4	204
	HAP	246
	J3	457
	J6	132
	M1	849
	M9	137
	G2	494
	AE1	250
	HIF	557
	M12	612
	M15	123
STRONGER-PINIONED	VP9	35
STRONGEST	L4	235
	P4	95
	AE12	791
	M12	666
STRONG-LIMBED	BR	173
	G2	231
STRONGLY	RL	245
	M1	398
	G2	68
	G3	88

Word	Code	No.
STRONGLY	G4	254
	AE1	68
STRONG-POUNCED	M15	570
STRONG-SCENTED	G4	390
STRONG-SINEWED	AE10	194
STROOK	AR	171
	L1	19
	AK	128
	AE6	803
	KT2	245
	TH	286
	M12	637
	AE3	274
STROPHADES		
STROVE	UDH	95
	HS	88
	AM	153
	AM	195
	AM	228
	AM	355
	AM	964
	AM	1124
	CM	69
	T23	26
	HAP	1117
	HAP	1324
	HAP	1376
	HAP	2389
	HAP	2398
	HAP	2525
	J1	21
	J1	94
	M1	212
	M1	876
	G1	375
	AE2	588
	AE2	1076
	AE5	436
	AE6	122
	AE7	86
	AE7	629
	AE9	537
	AE10	791
	AE10	1160
	AE12	1135
	KT1	7
	KT1	173
	KT2	374
	M8	28
	M8	323
	B	456
	M10	15
	CAM	216
	CAM	297
	TH	23
	M11	484
	M12	565
	AU	416
STROW	ETC	9
	HAP	1733
	VP5	59
	VP8	90
	G4	37
	AE6	428
	AE6	1224
	HIF	355
STROWED	SCG1	6
	VP2	69
	G1	659
	G4	428
	AE4	861
	AE5	104
	AE10	800
	AE11	941
	OAL	119
	KT3	596
	KT3	956
	M8	38
STROWS	AR	119
	VP7	76
	M8	265
STRUCK	UDH	43
	AR	95
	LC	102
	ML	31
	DA	87
	AT	65
	AT	66
	L4	6
	HAP	75
	HAP	254
	HAP	1674
	SSC	17
	BR	233
	J16	12
	M1	389

Word	Code	No.
STRUCK	DHP	12
	VP8	66
	G1	15
	AE1	135
	AE2	318
	AE2	1050
	AE4	846
	AE4	950
	AE5	266
	AE5	856
	AE7	1060
	AE8	160
	AE8	700
	AE9	254
	AE9	567
	AE10	485
	AE10	585
	AE10	629
	AE11	1211
	AE12	414
	AE12	482
	OAL	139
	OAL	196
	OAL	875
	KT1	235
	KT1	277
	KT3	642
	KT3	646
	CAM	196
	C	644
	C	743
STRUCTURE	G2	224
STRUCTURES	AM	1090
STRUGGLE	SMM2	24
	DA	194
	L4	133
	G1	291
	TJD	33
STRUGGLED	AA	314
	OAL	794
STRUGGLES	G4	424
	AE11	1101
	AE12	229
	OAL	750
	KT3	1070
	M11	212
STRUGGLING	AM	224
	AM	720
	CM	59
	HAP	580
	HAP	1919
	J6	19
	J10	275
	P5	232
	AE1	80
	AE3	493
	AE4	1009
	AE5	35
	AE5	1118
	AE6	120
	AE7	39
	AE10	77
	AE10	1293
	AE11	1209
	OAL	24
	KT3	328
	CAM	365
	TH	50
	M12	684
	J6	181
	J10	545
	P1	271
STRUMPET	AE2	783
	B	407
	M12	623
	ETP	24
STRUMPET'S	HP	214
STRUMPETS	L4	280
	PMK	18
STRUNG	AA	196
	MF	35
	AK	45
	P2	75
	AE9	974
	AE10	674
	TJD	89
	B	375
	M15	343
STRUT	PMQW	6
	EMQW	2
	PUO3	15
	J6	523
	PM	31
STRUTS	SAA	334
	T18	93
	J6	492

Word	Ref	No.
STRUTS	J6	829
STRUTTED	HIF	654
STRUTTING	PSH	8
	J6	365
	P1	108
	VP4	25
	VP7	22
	C	432
	C	460
STRYMONIAN	G1	179
STRYMONIUS	AE10	582
STRYMON'S	G4	738
STUBBLE	J6	156
	M1	663
	M13	29
	G1	124
	G1	385
	G1	434
	G3	159
	KT3	980
	M12	386
STUBBORN	AR	117
	VHH	45
	AA	327
	SAA	678
	SAA	743
	RL	163
	TA	185
	J10	174
	P4	98
	M1	163
	M13	29
	M13	82
	MC	7
	G1	111
	G1	144
	G2	627
	G3	265
	G3	638
	G4	247
	AE3	713
	AE4	28
	AE6	224
	AE6	266
	AE7	221
	AE8	419
	AE9	826
	AE11	1247
	AE12	1133
	OAL	8
	OAL	23
	OAL	541
	KT3	27
	KT3	316
	M8	373
	TH	159
	GP	34
STUBBORNNESS	TJD	185
STUBS	KT2	535
STUCK	UDH	58
	PSF	24
	HAP	2341
	J6	596
	AE9	714
	AE9	726
	AE10	421
	AE10	537
	AE10	1060
	AE11	947
	KT3	599
	M8	110
	C	15
	M12	129
	M12	377
	M12	415
	M12	483
	M12	501
	M12	604
STUD	AE3	175
STUDDED	G3	555
	AE8	733
STUDENT	P3	6
STUDIED	AA	228
	AE11	1087
	M10	90
	M15	41
	CI	215
	CI	451
STUDIES	AM	1043
	PUO1	25
	EUO2	7
	MO	7
	J6	742
	P5	58
	P5	83
	G3	285

Word	Ref	No.
STUDIES	G4	816
STUDIEST	MN	14
STUDIOUS	AA	325
	HH	40
	HAP	1969
	P1	166
	P5	85
	G1	203
	G3	83
	G3	771
	G4	258
	AE1	22
	AE4	578
	AE6	925
	AE7	863
	AE12	200
	AE12	581
	CI	31
STUDIOUSLY	AE7	249
STUDY	UDH	12
	RL	263
	RL	328
	RL	413
	L3	296
	MN	14
	HAP	1690
	P3	92
	P3	130
	P3	161
	MC	25
	OAL	840
	M15	7
STUDYING	PA	37
	G2	698
	TJD	3
STUFF	EM	24
	ENH	31
	PKK	10
	PTC	30
	PPC	19
	PK	34
	J1	122
	P1	8
	P1	50
	P1	172
	P1	186
	P4	125
	P5	273
	P5	9
	P6	39
	EHC	29
	AE2	26
	C	568
	PTP	22
	PWR	31
STUFFED	J3	460
	BP	47
	M11	293
STUFFING	AE8	483
STUM	MD	270
STUMBLE	PMS	7
	OAL	662
STUMBLED	CAM	275
STUMBLES	PTL	20
	KT3	609
STUMBLING	AM	907
STUMP	M8	137
	M12	583
STUMPS	G2	39
	AE2	849
STUN	AE7	21
	KT3	33
STUNG	AM	429
	L1	22
	L4	43
	VP8	122
	G2	445
	G3	381
	G4	243
	AE1	608
	AE2	1014
	AE4	845
	AE10	940
	KT1	234
	M12	635
STUNNED	J1	2
	AE12	998
	HIF	698
	M12	186
	M12	571
	CI	341
STUPENDOUS	L3	243
	M1	424
	G2	214
	AE2	155
	AE9	705

Word	Ref	No.
STUPID	HAP	1842
	J10	337
	P1	87
	P3	60
	GK	51
	VP3	37
	VP6	34
	G3	781
	AE7	1104
	AE12	467
	AE12	967
	KT1	524
	HIF	305
	TH	218
	M11	116
	M11	179
	AU	217
	AU	452
	CI	57
	CI	107
STUPIDITY	MF	18
STUPIDLY	CI	145
STUPIFIES	J6	797
STURBRIDGE	PKK	16
STURDY	PMQ	23
	HAP	1923
	G1	69
	G2	489
	G2	551
	G3	85
	G3	639
	AE2	847
	AE5	159
	AE9	819
	MM	46
	DO	58
	CI	75
	CI	591
STYGIAN	HAP	1281
	J3	424
	AE3	497
	AE4	357
	AE4	915
	AE5	1111
	AE6	207
	AE6	222
	AE6	442
	AE6	503
	AE6	521
	AE6	529
	AE6	547
	AE6	563
	AE6	594
	AE6	714
	AE7	450
	AE7	477
	AE7	661
	AE7	782
	AE8	393
	AE8	711
	AE8	748
	AE8	885
	AE9	699
	AE10	56
	AE10	847
	AE11	1210
	AE12	144
	AE12	1185
	OAL	716
	M11	130
	M11	373
	M12	440
STYLE	ML	47
	PLG	16
	AA	616
	MD	22
	RL	152
	RL	172
	HAP	2199
	HAP	2459
	MS	28
	J6	330
	P1	154
	P1	252
	P5	19
	AE1	452
	OAL	532
	KT2	34
	HIF	409
	C	146
	FL	618
	GP	40
STYLED	SAA	1051
STYLES	HH	21
	EKA	7
STYPHELUS	M12	612

Word	Code	No.
STYX	M1	1024
	G4	688
	AE9	120
	AE10	173
SUAREZ	PO	25
SUBDUE	HS	50
	HS	68
	AR	160
	VHH	11
	AM	370
	MD	244
	RL	256
	TA	463
	MN	7
	G1	228
	AE1	118
	AE5	930
	AE7	352
	AE8	389
	M12	8
SUBDUED	ECD	22
	G4	247
	AE1	362
	AE9	870
	OAL	750
	TJD	152
	HIF	383
SUBDUING	HIF	326
SUBJECT	SMA	106
	LC	63
	EAZ	33
	PTW	26
	HP	41
	EMW	13
	AA	809
	AA	836
	MD	130
	MF	1
	SAA	636
	HAP	932
	HAP	955
	HAP	2041
	BR	358
	G1	257
	G2	60
	G3	454
	G4	8
	AE1	384
	AE6	991
	OAL	230
	OAL	675
	OAE1	2
	OAE1	28
	DO	107
	KT3	1047
	B	44
	B	559
	HIF	789
	M12	87
	M12	222
	AU	300
	AU	347
	CI	24
SUBJECTED	HI	125
	AE4	596
	AE11	786
	B	316
	CI	310
SUBJECT-GRIEF	TA	74
SUBJECT-HUSBAND	J6	318
SUBJECTING	HIF	387
SUBJECTION	DO	58
SUBJECT'S	SAA	996
	TA	301
	TA	502
	KT3	336
SUBJECTS	SMA	133
	LC	83
	DC	49
	SIE	12
	VHH	53
	AM	46
	AM	170
	AM	173
	AM	564
	AM	952
	AM	966
	PT	7
	PUO2	1
	CM	86
	DA	23
	EMW	11
	PUO3	20
	AA	384
	AA	951
	AA	983
SUBJECTS	PLB	17
	PRH	15
	SAA	335
	SAA	642
	SAA	646
	PAA	40
	EAA	17
	HAP	245
	HAP	515
	HAP	2087
	BR	114
	EL	181
	GK	155
	AE1	201
	AE4	680
	AE4	885
	AE7	519
	AE11	521
	AE11	665
	AE12	56
	OAL	112
	OAL	298
	OAE1	7
	HIF	390
	C	790
SUBJECTS'	LC	81
	LC	92
	AM	181
	SAA	737
	HAP	2378
	G4	313
	AE8	633
SUBJECT-SERVANT	WB	518
SUBLIME	UDH	27
	RL	76
	ODA	37
	G1	332
	AE1	354
	AE1	574
	AE6	748
	AE6	974
	AE7	393
	AE7	478
	AE8	450
	AE8	958
	AE10	936
	AF	29
	KT3	487
	M11	134
	GP	33
SUBLIMELY	AK	4
	AE10	3
SUBMISSION	HAP	486
	HAP	989
	HAP	1013
	KT2	346
SUBMISSIONS	AE4	598
SUBMISSIVE	HIF	782
SUBMISSIVELY	HAP	1081
	AE10	863
SUBMIT	AR	266
	PMQ	23
	AM	735
	PNH	42
	AA	93
	EK	47
	HAP	924
	HAP	976
	PTS	40
	VCS	23
	MC	26
	G3	104
	AE3	712
	AE4	492
	AE7	608
	AE8	77
	AE8	651
	OAL	314
	OAL	538
	MG	4
	MM	10
	KT2	508
SUBMITS	LC	139
	J6	183
	AE8	969
SUBMITTED	AR	249
	PC2	33
	AA	422
	HAP	500
	AE3	422
	GP	116
SUBMITTING	G3	26
	RL	319
SUBORDINATE	HAP	1191
SUBORDINATION	HAP	943
SUBORN	KT3	1039
SUBORN	CI	552
SUBORNED	AE6	589
	B	151
	B	718
SUBORNING	AE12	959
SUBSCRIBED	P5	117
SUBSERVIENT	HAP	88
SUBSIDE	AE12	1213
SUBSIDES	AE1	212
	AE5	1073
	M15	373
SUBSIDING	HIF	711
SUBSIDY	TA	305
SUBSISTENCE	HAP	1539
	J1	179
SUBSISTS	SAA	741
SUBSTANCE	AR	192
	RH	82
	AM	462
	PUF	15
	HAP	411
	HAP	413
	HAP	427
	HAP	619
	HAP	622
	G2	78
	M15	397
	M15	636
SUBSTANTIAL	ESF	4
	M15	306
SUBSTITUTE	G3	599
SUBSTITUTING	AE7	389
SUBTERFUGE	AE12	1286
SUBTERRANEAN	MF	215
	HAP	639
	G3	578
	G4	522
SUBTILE	AM	673
	EMK	12
	SAA	268
	H2	50
	G2	297
	G4	723
	M15	377
	M15	520
SUBTLE	PA	7
	SAA	554
	J6	859
SUBURB	OAL	75
	OAL	295
SUBURBIAN	MF	83
SUBURBS	G4	353
SUBVERT	G4	312
	AE4	27
SUBVERTER	AE12	797
	C	501
SUCCEED	AM	936
	AM	1168
	ENH	39
	HP	34
	HP	53
	AA	529
	AA	874
	MD	273
	SAA	19
	HAP	1064
	HAP	2372
	HAP	2429
	HAP	2560
	ETS	30
	MS	5
	J1	88
	P1	85
	GK	122
	VP5	7
	G1	217
	G3	632
	AE1	109
	AE1	330
	AE2	346
	AE2	617
	AE2	637
	AE3	714
	AE7	77
	AE9	669
	AE9	857
	AE11	228
	AE11	1051
	AE11	1200
	AE11	1304
	OAL	537
	KT3	239
	HIF	27
	FL	254
	AU	213
	PMK	34

Headword	Ref	No.
SUCCEEDED	ECG2	1
	EL	315
	J10	119
	M1	162
	G4	771
	AE3	383
	AE8	434
SUCCEEDING	AM	396
	PWGR	7
	AA	116
	AA	151
	PLB	44
	SAA	410
	L4	14
	HAP	797
	HAP	882
	HAP	2073
	M1	146
	G1	99
	AE3	575
	AE4	246
	AE5	349
	AE5	780
	AE8	117
	AE8	953
	AE10	975
	AE12	206
	AE12	357
	KT1	466
SUCCEEDS	AM	389
	AM	700
	MD	255
	HAP	225
	HAP	1614
	J1	254
	J6	179
	M1	34
	G2	262
	G3	758
	AE1	247
	AE3	838
	AE6	1109
	AE7	1083
	AE8	325
	AE8	843
	AE9	1098
	AE10	491
	KT3	346
	TJD	20
	BP	112
	M12	188
	M12	204
	M15	312
	GP	41
SUCCESS	HS	131
	LCA	7
	LCA	39
	AM	73
	AM	558
	AM	671
	AM	680
	AM	968
	ECG1	1
	PRH	18
	MF	147
	SAA	276
	SAA	809
	AT	62
	L4	255
	TA	184
	BR	85
	PTS	22
	PMS	31
	M1	610
	M1	977
	G1	284
	G3	760
	AE1	540
	AE2	520
	AE2	699
	AE5	262
	AE5	273
	AE5	299
	AE5	575
	AE7	400
	AE7	806
	AE8	68
	AE8	679
	AE9	404
	AE9	934
	AE10	48
	AE10	505
	AE10	631
	AE10	1227
	AE11	21
	AE11	62
SUCCESS	AE11	193
	AE11	369
	AE11	1120
	AE11	1239
	AE12	55
	AE12	903
	AE12	917
	AE12	1221
	KT1	60
	KT3	374
	KT3	752
	KT3	1155
	TJD	140
	TJD	154
	TJD	169
	M12	167
	M12	411
	M12	657
	AU	509
	CI	470
SUCCESSES	AM	837
SUCCESSFUL	HS	79
	RH	49
	AA	266
	AA	289
	MD	208
	T·A	508
	HAP	2192
	PTS	42
	G3	364
	AE1	359
	AE1	881
	AE6	928
	AE8	519
	MG	13
	MG	31
	M8	158
SUCCESSION	DA	18
	AA	16
	AA	413
	MD	116
	MD	289
	MF	10
	SAA	260
	SAA	773
	TA	311
	HAP	712
	HAP	1187
	HAP	1999
	J6	724
	G4	78
	G4	303
	AE1	8
	AE1	369
	AE4	158
	AE7	346
	DO	147
	KT3	1055
	M8	251
SUCCESSIVE	AA	301
	MD	84
	HAP	1202
	AE12	34
	M15	272
SUCCESSLESS	L4	91
	AE12	1131
	KT2	587
SUCCESSOR	AA	401
	AA	921
	PRH	10
	SAA	110
	SAA	656
	GP	99
SUCCESSOR'S	AA	721
SUCCESSORS	PTC	17
	HAP	933
	FL	556
SUCCOR	VHH	27
	AM	290
	DA	93
	AA	281
	HAP	1610
	HAP	1909
	BR	59
	VP10	1
	G1	14
	G2	54
	G2	251
	AE1	940
	AE4	774
	AE4	884
	AE5	304
	AE7	431
	AE7	701
	AE7	945
	AE8	495
SUCCOR	AE11	66
	AE12	227
	AE12	400
	TH	381
	M11	175
	AU	107
	GP	63
	CI	589
SUCCORS	AM	970
	HAP	2171
	AE8	616
	AE8	690
	AE9	11
	AE9	1036
SUCCORY	G1	182
	G4	180
	BP	95
SUCK	AA	1014
	HAP	1845
	J6	13
	P4	80
	P5	10
	G1	105
	G2	555
	G3	222
	AE4	525
	AE6	961
	OAE2	38
	TJD	110
SUCKED	AM	375
	G1	438
	AE1	171
	AE8	839
	C	484
	FL	109
SUCKEST	J6	382
SUCKING	MD	150
	PD	27
	J10	270
	M1	581
	AE3	503
SUCKLES	VP3	41
SUCKS	L1	51
	L4	209
	J6	99
	AE3	538
	KT3	629
	M15	515
SUCRO	AE12	734
SUDDEN	AR	228
	CM	54
	AA	452
	SAA	1117
	TA	6
	BR	130
	BR	228
	BR	259
	M13	196
	VP6	125
	G1	431
	G3	540
	G3	554
	AE2	1047
	AE3	874
	AE4	404
	AE6	405
	AE7	38
	AE8	515
	AE11	921
	AE12	372
	AE12	454
	AE12	472
	AE12	1243
	KT1	233
	KT1	565
	KT2	79
	KT3	251
	KT3	265
	KT3	701
	KT3	972
	M8	236
	M8	246
	M8	100
	B	233
	B	266
	BP	182
	C	583
	TH	93
	TH	330
	M11	303
	M11	386
	FL	210
	FL	315
	FL	426
	FL	595
	M12	313

Word	Code	No.	Word	Code	No.	Word	Code	No.
SUDDEN	M12	455	SUFFERED	T23	55	SUFFERS	KT1	512
	WB	219		TA	179		FL	581
	CI	273		TA	180	SUFFICE	EL	359
	CI	582		HAP	1334		G3	451
SUDDENLY	LC	103		HAP	2025		AE2	872
	AM	737		HAP	2205		AE9	893
	TA	16		HAP	2397		AE9	1085
	EL	337		EL	317		B	251
	ODA	32		J10	122		C	398
	AE9	535		M1	865	SUFFICED	J10	273
	AE9	939		VP8	34		HIF	653
	OAL	423		G1	190		TH	194
	FL	148		AE2	105		FL	110
SUE	PFD	29		AE2	584	SUFFICES	G2	252
	E	7		AE3	409		AE8	104
	EAL	19		AE4	19	SUFFICIENT	EWGR	26
	PRH	27		AE4	481		SAA	676
	AE1	456		AE5	618		RL	167
	AE1	731		AE10	240		RL	299
	AE3	793		AE11	396		L3	196
	AE4	884		AE12	257		HAP	808
	AE7	326		B	320		HAP	1551
	AE10	1303		B	752		J1	226
	OAL	814		M11	314		J3	99
	KT1	61		M11	397		J10	74
	HIF	320		M11	416		VP1	65
SUED	PUO4	30		FL	402		AE8	588
	HAP	2055		AU	188	SUFFISED	HAP	554
	AE8	221		AU	479	SUFFOCATED	M12	690
	GP	43		M15	48	SUFFOCATING	L3	229
SUES	AA	322		CI	504		AE12	862
	P5	248		AS	37	SUFFRAGATING	PUO4	31
	VP2	57	SUFFERER	LC	92	SUFFRAGE	PUO1	46
	AE1	678	SUFFEREST	CM	128		PC2	32
	AE11	1032	SUFFERING	ETC	28		HI	169
SUFFER	AR	50		SCG1	18		MC	37
	AR	87		PR	5		HIF	179
	RH	20		AA	609		HIF	245
	AM	138		SAA	613		HIF	541
	SMQ	11		SAA	793	SUFFRAGES	M15	54
	SCG3	21		RL	108	SUFFUSED	KT2	487
	E	16		HAP	1356		M8	22
	HP	185		HAP	1432	SUFFUSION	M15	287
	DA	188		HAP	1598	SUGAR	PD	26
	DA	195		HAP	1671	SUGGEST	HAP	2499
	EUF	17		HAP	1979	SUGGESTED	HAP	2390
	AA	416		HAP	2524	SUGGESTION	J3	208
	AA	798		PTS	5	SUIT	PNH	10
	SAA	432		SSH	1		PUO2	16
	HAP	1200		M1	948		PC1	3
	PTS	27		VP10	101		PKK	19
	J6	406		AE5	930		PUO3	16
	J6	521		AE6	788		AA	327
	J10	490		AE7	554		AA	982
	AE4	422		AE10	130		MF	209
	AE4	465		KT3	833		SAA	722
	AE6	157		M8	32		EDG	29
	AE6	1020		HIF	487		RL	314
	AE7	466		HIF	495		GE	52
	AE12	645		C	565		HAP	2272
	AE12	985		TH	140		HAP	2430
	OAL	741		M11	113		BR	333
	OAL	805		FL	395		EL	204
	DO	108	SUFFERINGS	AR	72		J6	567
	KT1	385		AR	210		J10	59
	KT1	481		SCG3	20		J10	459
	KT1	491		EMW	3		J16	9
	KT2	96		EMW	14		J16	74
	KT2	114		AA	797		P1	101
	KT2	316		SAA	664		AE1	96
	KT2	362		SAA	768		AE4	619
	KT3	779		SAA	807		AE8	502
	TJD	55		SAA	823		AE11	159
	M8	214		SAA	1101		AE11	758
	HIF	177		SAA	1130		OAL	92
	C	688		AT	38		OAL	169
	TH	175		TA	270		OAL	403
	TH	331		STS3	13		OAL	418
	M11	51		M1	920		OAL	424
	M12	282		VP10	52		OAL	458
	M12	623		VP10	86		OAL	282
	M15	256		AE5	1021		OAL	565
	M15	532		AE8	633		OAL	640
	M15	672		KT1	443		OAL	798
	CI	423		KT2	118		OAE1	2
	AS	37		KT3	151		KT1	348
SUFFERED	AR	42		AU	66		KT3	155
	AR	68	SUFFERINGS'	SAA	1068		BP	177
	AR	205	SUFFERS	AM	1041		CAM	164
	LC	18		RL	56		HIF	23
	ML	14		GE	8		HIF	519
	STC	12		J6	617		HIF	579
	PUO3	3		AE6	56		HIF	608
	AA	824		AE5	961		HIF	677
	D	20		MG	28		HIF	690
	L3	15		KT1	443		HIF	706

Word	Code	No.	Word	Code	No.	Word	Code	No.
SUIT	TH	24	SULTRY	M1	152	SUMMONED	AE4	753
	FL	533		G3	246		AE4	976
	FL	618		G3	509		AE5	338
	M12	244		G4	615		KT3	1011
	WB	314		AE7	309		B	216
	CI	68		KT2	58		HIF	81
	CI	210		FL	373		TH	86
	CI	244	SUM	D	23		TH	97
SUITED	AA	478		HAP	1591		M12	298
	AA	662		J3	229		CI	541
	SAA	18		J6	323	SUMMONS	AM	58
	SAA	47		P5	112		DA	111
	SAA	284		AE1	472		MF	2
	B	350		HIF	123		L3	257
	CAM	301	SUMMED	EK	45		TA	198
	CI	74		HAP	1950		M1	460
SUITING	G1	78	SUMMER	UDH	78		AE2	908
	OAL	125		SMA	101		AE5	318
	B	44		EUO	5		AE7	725
	BP	110		PKK	23		AE10	1
	TH	81		SAA	57		AE11	362
SUITORS	AM	1186		HAP	1723		HIF	717
	M1	640		HAP	1730		CI	276
	CAM	103		BR	14	SUMPTERS	HIF	74
SUITS	J6	361		J1	143	SUMPTUOUS	AE1	901
	J16	57		P3	3	SUMS	LCA	48
	G1	81		P5	55		EEL	36
	AE7	1109		M1	148		PNH	13
	AE9	496		M13	73		AA	405
	OAL	47		VP2	28		AA	709
	OAL	758		VP5	112		MD	32
	KT1	285		VP7	68		HAP	144
	KT1	286		G1	146		ESH	33
	KT2	173		G1	262		J10	18
	TJD	12		G2	206		AE1	678
	CI	14		G2	470		AE2	738
SULLEN	AR	4		G2	516		AE3	597
	E	13		G2	684		AE5	323
	MD	284		G3	503		AE10	733
	D	20		G3	665		AE10	738
	T23	23		G4	443		AE11	508
	HAP	313		AE1	600		KT1	602
	ODA	6		AE1	1046	SUN	JH	16
	J3	30		AE10	566		HS	23
	J6	253		OAL	308		AR	61
	P3	29		OAL	72		LC	47
	P4	107		C	88		LC	87
	SFL	1		FL	85		LC	154
	G1	591		FL	593		DC	18
	G1	611		M15	309		VHH	49
	G1	656	SUMMER-RINGS	J1	40		AM	13
	G2	81	SUMMER'S	AM	574		AM	66
	G2	318		SKA2	7		AM	69
	G4	144		J1	4		AM	94
	AE6	385		VP9	71		AM	397
	AE6	466		G1	477		AM	472
	AE6	616		G3	246		AM	499
	AE7	775		G3	512		AM	640
	AE7	900		G4	51		AM	1109
	AE11	133		G4	217		SCD1	5
	AE11	217		G4	231		ENH	11
	KT2	579		AE6	960		ML	38
	KT3	371		AE8	127		AA	732
	M8	220		FL	224		MD	13
	B	288		M12	221		PRH	8
	B	606		CI	79		D	11
	CAM	164		AS	7		SAA	982
	HIF	720	SUMMERS	PRH	1		L3	261
	M11	312		M13	7		T18	64
	FL	98		G1	45		T18	65
	GP	14		DO	95		T27	15
	ESK	28		C	486		H29	29
SULLENLY	HS	106	SUMMETS	G1	641		TA	107
	AM	490		AE3	924		HAP	90
SULLIED	J3	252	SUMMING	ELW	4		HAP	447
SULLIES	MFL	20	SUMMIT	M1	430		HAP	1621
SULLY	BR	183		AE9	100		HAP	1723
SULMO	AE9	554		AE10	984		HAP	1799
	AE10	721		M11	135		HAP	1828
SULPHER	VP8	117		M12	18		HAP	1892
SULPHUR	AE2	947		M12	62		BR	5
	AE3	753		M13	35		BR	9
	AE6	345	SUMMITS	SMP	32		BR	121
	AE7	624	SUMMON	AM	738		BR	229
	OAL	292		H2	10		BR	317
	KT3	958		AE4	669		SKA6	9
	WB	433	SUMMONED	SAA	1124		EL	136
	M15	510		HAP	1739		EL	137
	M15	523		J6	639		OD	26
	M15	525		M1	215		J1	193
SULPHUREOUS	AE7	720		M1	867		J3	494
	M15	509		VP2	30		J6	21
SULPHUROUS	AE7	124		AE1	186		P3	1
SULPHURS	G3	684		AE3	13		P4	37
SULPHURY	AE4	555		AE3	580		P4	77
SULTRY	H29	32		AE3	621		P5	70

SUN		
	P5	258
	M1	13
	M1	54
	M1	76
	M1	150
	M1	457
	M1	806
	M1	822
	M1	866
	M1	1048
	M1	1080
	M9	109
	M13	165
	VP2	11
	VP2	98
	VP6	56
	VP6	121
	VP8	44
	VP9	71
	G1	66
	G1	73
	G1	102
	G1	323
	G1	384
	G1	399
	G1	469
	G1	560
	G1	547
	G1	571
	G1	587
	G1	601
	G1	620
	G1	624
	G1	633
	G2	261
	G2	411
	G2	437
	G2	452
	G2	464
	G2	680
	G2	737
	G3	215
	G3	247
	G3	436
	G3	476
	G3	504
	G3	513
	G3	519
	G3	550
	G3	635
	G4	39
	G4	577
	G4	617
	G4	674
	AE1	362
	AE1	422
	AE1	601
	AE1	855
	AE1	1041
	AE1	1064
	AE2	646
	AE3	368
	AE3	662
	AE3	744
	AE3	768
	AE4	164
	AE4	696
	AE4	872
	AE5	60
	AE5	118
	AE5	169
	AE6	365
	AE6	721
	AE7	13
	AE7	146
	AE7	297
	AE7	309
	AE7	735
	AE8	34
	AE8	129
	AE8	229
	AE8	259
	AE8	328
	AE8	369
	AE9	195
	AE9	612
	AE10	308
	AE10	345
	AE11	1316
	AE12	258
	AE12	266
	OAL	824
	MG	35
	MFL	13
	DO	42
	DO	63

SUN		
	KT1	4
	KT1	341
	KT1	403
	KT1	504
	KT2	10
	KT2	22
	KT2	39
	KT2	57
	KT2	241
	KT2	407
	KT3	73
	KT3	121
	KT3	146
	KT3	131
	KT3	190
	KT3	563
	KT3	638
	KT3	796
	KT3	972
	TJD	66
	B	338
	HIF	95
	HIF	797
	C	178
	C	213
	C	447
	C	574
	C	679
	M11	96
	M11	270
	FL	1
	FL	15
	FL	373
	FL	408
	FL	437
	AU	20
	AU	398
	WB	29
	WB	407
	M15	94
	CI	121
	CI	328
	CI	560
	SMP	2
	AS	3
SUN-BEAT	J10	239
SUN-BEGOTTEN	HAP	311
SUNBURNT	H2	63
	G4	411
	OAL	829
	FL	420
SUNDAY	KT3	103
	WB	37
SUNDERED	M1	31
	G4	133
	M12	488
	M15	121
SUNDRY	L3	34
	L4	224
	HAP	1009
	HAP	1504
	G1	93
	G1	264
	G2	122
	G2	123
	G3	187
	AE2	499
	OAL	863
	OAL	872
	LCA	43
SUNG	SKK	15
	POE	6
	PO	2
	MF	36
	MF	130
	TA	372
	TA	379
	GE	30
	GE	35
	HAP	2196
	SSC	57
	EL	127
	EL	128
	M1	936
	M1	988
	GK	90
	DHP	11
	DHP	26
	VP2	29
	VP5	19
	VP5	135
	VP6	4
	VP6	49
	VP6	87
	VP6	93
	VP6	119

SUNG		
	VP9	60
	VP9	71
	VP10	62
	VP10	102
	G2	693
	G4	673
	G4	807
	AE1	1039
	AE6	20
	AE7	558
	AE8	178
	AE8	404
	AE9	1046
	AE10	274
	OAL	300
	AF	75
	AF	47
	AF	99
	DO	6
	KT1	197
	KT2	78
	KT2	85
	KT3	979
	M8	259
	HIF	809
	C	46
	C	578
	C	605
	C	633
	TH	265
	FL	33
	FL	116
	FL	126
	FL	192
	FL	194
	FL	308
	FL	365
	GP	24
	AM	374
SUNK	PKK	7
	AA	646
	MD	130
	TA	273
	GE	49
	HAP	2564
	M1	28
	G3	735
	AE2	844
	AE7	586
	AE8	538
	AE8	769
	AE9	959
	AE10	776
	AE11	355
	AE11	1203
	AF	115
	AF	122
	DO	49
	KT2	86
	KT2	443
	KT3	257
	KT3	372
	KT3	857
	KT3	981
	KT3	1080
	M8	370
	B	488
	CAM	349
	C	122
	C	355
	TH	295
	M11	304
	M15	448
	CI	64
	CI	328
SUNLESS	AE3	267
SUNNY	HAP	1850
	BR	306
	VP1	117
	G1	544
SUN'S	AR	289
	AM	360
	M1	560
	G3	509
	AE3	105
	AE3	356
	AE3	837
	OAL	287
	M15	610
SUNS	M13	73
	G1	99
	G1	136
	G1	157
	G1	421
	G1	540
	G2	206

Word	Code	Num		Word	Code	Num		Word	Code	Num
SUNS	G2	516		SUPPED	J10	372		SUPPLIED	BP	148
	G4	71			G3	786			C	300
	AE4	682			G4	197			C	758
	AE6	872		SUPPER	J1	203			TH	61
	M15	279			J10	364			M11	436
SUNSET	HIF	649			P1	100			FL	456
SUNSHINE	LC	128			P5	58			M12	364
	PA	20			OAE2	2			AS	89
	SCG1	11			KT1	33			AS	98
	L2	65		SUPPERS	L2	29		SUPPLIES	AM	181
	HAP	1953		SUPPLANT	AA	966			AM	287
	G1	566			SAA	776			AM	597
	G2	754		SUPPLE	P3	183			AA	718
	G3	473			G3	266			SAA	253
	FL	487		SUPPLED	P4	97			L1	3
	WB	539			M1	539			L5	18
SUP	J3	434		SUPPLER	B	425			HAP	467
	J6	551		SUPPLIANT	HS	81			EL	78
	P5	216			AM	997			J3	352
	OAL	647			E	31			J10	320
SUPERCILIOUS	J6	246			DA	125			M9	101
	P5	184			J6	512			G2	590
SUPEREROGATION	EPC	22			P5	256			G4	746
SUPERFICE	G2	316			M1	120			AE2	835
SUPERFLUOUS	G2	510			M9	169			AE3	605
	G4	769			HI	171			AE4	900
SUPERIOR	AA	1024			G4	775			AE5	301
	AK	10			AE1	95			AE5	789
	HAP	87			AE1	456			AE5	837
	HAP	2182			AE2	948			AE5	1123
	EL	178			AE4	775			AE6	216
	J1	52			AE8	504			AE8	230
	M1	254			AE11	624			AE9	1031
	M1	268			AE11	840			AE10	311
	M1	691			KT1	98			CAM	172
	AE5	621			BP	139			HIF	430
	AE5	1115			HIF	19			M11	67
	AE6	123			HIF	515			M11	81
	AE6	716			HIF	588			M15	174
	AE11	1069			WB	311			M15	270
	AE12	621			M15	51			M15	527
	AE12	1189		SUPPLIANT'S	AE10	841		SUPPLING	P4	78
	OAL	147		SUPPLIANTS	AM	1188		SUPPLY	VHH	35
	KT3	490			HAP	1216			AM	280
	B	491			VP5	126			AM	517
	HIF	304			AE11	149			PEL	11
	HIF	658			OAE2	31			STL	21
	HIF	791		SUPPLICATING	HIF	543			PTC	12
	TH	142		SUPPLICATION	AE11	728			AA	395
	M11	138		SUPPLIED	DC	5			SAA	574
	FL	468			PWG	51			SAA	1038
	M12	788			AM	14			SAA	1080
	AU	566			AM	469			RL	422
	CI	98			AM	652			AT	126
SUPERIORS	HAP	459			AM	677			L3	139
	TJD	113			AM	1044			L3	196
SUPERNATURAL	PT	23			AM	1143			AK	72
	RL	11			PTW	24			HAP	367
	RL	169			DA	212			HAP	1053
	TA	412			AA	892			HAP	1249
SUPERSCRIPTION	EKA	22			RL	105			HAP	1307
SUPERSEDE	HAP	1646			PD	23			J1	141
SUPERSTIOUS	RL	127			L2	8			J6	773
	HAP	983			L4	262			P6	152
	G2	711			HAP	907			M1	92
	AE7	91			HAP	1870			M1	368
	OAL	467			HAP	2099			VP6	58
SUPERSTITION	SAA	651			EL	67			VP7	20
	HAP	1765			EL	14			G1	28
	P5	261			J6	402			G2	259
	AE8	247			J10	46			G2	502
	AE8	459			J10	366			G2	597
SUPERSTITIONS	P2	59			G1	221			G3	212
SUPERSTITIOUS	OD	40			G2	61			G3	320
SUPINE	AR	107			G2	741			AE1	216
	TA	14			G3	756			AE1	856
	J3	326			G4	454			AE1	982
	P2	47			AE3	457			AE2	527
	P3	4			AE3	594			AE3	765
	G2	373			AE4	701			AE3	835
	AE3	827			AE5	409			AE4	476
	AE5	1113			AE5	564			AE5	1101
	AE9	242			AE5	829			AE6	1071
	AE12	934			AE6	169			AE7	17
	OAL	723			AE6	811			AE7	433
	C	229			AE7	32			AE8	543
	M11	295			AE8	424			AE9	281
	M12	163			AE9	1082			AE10	459
SUPINELY	MF	28			AE10	970			AE10	647
	L1	49			KT2	172			AE12	233
	L3	109			KT2	523			AE12	1103
	L4	278			TJD	136			OAL	113
	HAP	2307			M8	73			OAL	732
	GK	58			M8	275			M11	297
	AE9	424			B	74			M11	329
	AE12	443			B	460			BP	94

Word	Code	No.		Word	Code	No.		Word	Code	No.
SUPPLY	FL	26		SUPREME	TA	417		SURE	EL	38
	FL	437			HAP	674			EL	52
	M12	339			EL	162			ODA	28
	M15	111			AE1	191			MS	1
	PWR	1			AE4	890			J3	244
SUPPLYING	DOD	23			AE7	327			J6	81
	H3	6			AE11	366			J6	375
	HAP	526			AE11	786			J6	516
	M1	548			KT3	1061			J6	614
SUPPORT	PNH	19			HIF	104			J6	724
	AA	284			AU	347			J16	38
	SAA	737			CI	78			P4	13
	AT	118		SUPREMELY	AA	376			P5	59
	HAP	1962		SURCEASE	AE12	1024			P5	93
	PP	24		SURCHARGED	KT1	490			P5	140
	EJG	7		SURCOAT	KT3	51			P5	202
	J1	41			KT3	67			M1	621
	J3	39		SURCOATS	KT1	148			M1	699
	J3	336			FL	258			M1	849
	J6	243		SURE	RH	29			M1	1066
	G4	316			AM	703			M9	95
	AE1	493			ETL	26			M13	37
	AE2	112			ECG2	31			HI	114
	AE2	120			EM	25			GK	133
	AE2	367			PLN	34			G1	122
	AE7	876			ELN	21			G1	372
	AE9	390			PCD	28			G2	327
	AE11	343			PNH	47			G3	119
	MG	16			ENH	40			G4	303
	TJD	127			PUO2	15			G4	416
	HIF	292			ESF	32			G4	565
	M11	320			PC1	22			AE1	8
	M15	2			EAL	2			AE1	816
SUPPORTED	AE7	230			ETC	27			AE1	948
	AE11	124			HP	24			AE2	62
	AE12	570			HP	35			AE2	730
	M11	473			AA	163			AE2	868
SUPPORTER	D	8			AA	360			AE2	999
SUPPORTERS	PO	26			AA	623			AE3	679
SUPPORTING	H2	19			AA	647			AE4	158
SUPPORTS	HAP	1816			PPC	22			AE4	780
	HAP	2247			MD	200			AE5	36
	AE4	363			MF	196			AE5	747
	AE10	857			SAA	3			AE5	892
	M15	216			SAA	885			AE5	1131
SUPPOSE	RH	10			SAA	979			AE7	351
	PA	9			EDG	36			AE8	68
	DA	15			EDGA	2			AE9	270
	AA	385			RL	119			AE9	335
	AT	98			RL	284			AE9	379
	L2	46			RL	293			AE10	48
	L3	15			RL	307			AE10	1171
	L3	121			PD	34			AE11	21
	L3	141			ER	3			AE12	281
	HH	29			MO	3			AE12	613
	HAP	489			L3	8			AE12	1242
	HAP	642			L3	164			OAL	396
	HAP	768			L3	275			OAL	441
	HAP	945			L4	79			OAE2	15
	HAP	961			L4	152			OAE2	70
	HAP	1198			H3	13			DO	33
	HAP	2004			TA	2			DO	41
	PDS	11			TA	36			DO	131
	EDS	14			TA	483			KT1	559
	PKA	42			AK	41			KT2	218
	J6	234			GE	15			KT2	378
	J6	240			HAP	102			KT3	331
	J6	385			HAP	116			KT3	850
	J10	379			HAP	316			KT3	1041
	J10	460			HAP	327			TJD	82
	J10	463			HAP	388			TJD	170
	P2	37			HAP	431			CAM	181
	P2	79			HAP	495			C	48
	EHC	24			HAP	699			C	60
	AE4	449			HAP	730			C	144
	KT1	323			HAP	742			C	208
	CAM	98			HAP	784			C	817
	M15	571			HAP	884			M11	489
	CI	9			HAP	922			FL	31
	STP	30			HAP	1049			AU	104
SUPPOSES	SAA	433			HAP	1197			AU	380
SUPPOSITION	L2	50			HAP	1410			AU	429
SUPPRESSED	PO	23			HAP	1512			AU	572
	CM	56			HAP	1649			WB	174
	HP	187			HAP	1747			M15	76
	HAP	1555			HAP	1776			M15	539
	M1	817			HAP	2109			ETP	5
	M1	992			HAP	2184			STP	28
SUPREMACY	HAP	195			HAP	2224			PWR	13
SUPREME	POE	4			HAP	2255			EWR	6
	AA	409			HAP	2330		SURELY	HS	64
	AA	437			PDS	42			AA	431
	EK	4			PMS	6			SAA	489
	RL	44			PKA	1			AT	119
	TA	228			PKA	40			EC	44
	TA	394			EL	20			TA	503

SURELY	G4	585	SURPRISE	AE8	352	SURVEY	EL	344
	PWR	24		AE8	413		ODA	8
SURER	HAP	124		AE8	862		ODA	40
	HAP	585		AE10	99		P4	128
SUREST	AA	527		AE11	767		P6	31
	MD	183		AE11	792		M1	1090
	OE	33		AE11	1096		M13	149
	G1	581		AE12	371		HI	6
	M15	572		KT3	78		HI	22
SURETIES	WB	105		KT3	115		VP5	118
SURETY	P5	113		M8	206		G1	601
	KT2	147		B	347		AE1	423
	WB	88		B	633		AE2	35
SURFACE	PAL	25		M10	95		AE2	404
	M1	63		CAM	108		AE2	574
	M1	579		C	123		AE3	918
	G1	101		CI	108		AE6	1025
	G1	133		CI	187		AE7	216
	G1	261		HIF	305		AE8	410
	G2	553	SURPRISED	AM	855		AE10	1075
	G4	182		SAA	542		KT2	651
	AE4	377		L2	59		B	142
	M11	477		VP6	125		HIF	616
SURFEITED	J1	215		AE1	723		M15	217
	G3	789		AE2	514		CI	380
SURFEITS	BR	274		AE4	686	SURVEYED	AM	49
SURGEON	EK	18		AE5	125		HAP	536
	J6	65		AE5	359		HAP	1845
SURGEONS	AM	568		AE7	233		EL	202
	KT3	725		AE9	149		M1	820
SURGES	SAA	1132		AE10	1279		M1	880
	H3	24		AE12	1075		G2	578
	VP9	58		B	65		AE4	520
	G1	39		CAM	152		AE8	301
	G3	314		HIF	550		AE10	628
	AE1	124		TH	145		AE12	208
	AE7	33		M12	442		B	65
	AE8	892		AU	511		B	248
	AE9	962		WB	100		B	529
	AE11	929	SURPRISING	TA	34		M12	143
	HIF	235		M1	980		M12	260
SURLINESS	KT2	192		OAL	247	SURVEYING	M1	438
SURLY	MD	311	SURRENDERING	HAP	2006		G3	450
	PRH	9	SURROUND	H3	44		AE11	796
	HAP	551		M1	61	SURVEYS	AA	732
	HAP	2120		VP6	81		MD	12
	J10	262		VP10	24		D	31
	VP7	36		G1	212		H29	17
	VP9	5		G1	264		BR	76
	G1	154		AE1	429		J6	621
	G2	289		AE1	591		G3	354
	AE1	416		AE3	830		G4	313
	AE3	729		AE9	163		G4	340
	AE6	433		AE9	606		G4	628
	AE6	522		AE12	506		AE1	308
	KT1	355		AE12	611		AE1	726
	KT3	39		AE12	1077		AE7	146
	KT3	231		AE12	1324		AE7	249
	HIF	328		KT3	59		AE8	897
	HIF	655		KT3	649		AE9	76
	M15	183		TJD	52		AE10	3
SURMISE	KT2	486		M8	392		AE11	1070
	B	171		BP	116		AE11	1216
SURMISED	CAM	187	SURROUNDED	AA	682		HIF	60
	M11	451		SAA	188	SURVIVE	L3	62
SURPASS	PFD	23		AE6	877		EJG	6
	M1	952		AE6	906		P2	30
	C	41		AE7	228		AE2	812
	FL	140		AE9	625		AE6	890
SURPASSED	ECG2	33		AE12	962		AE8	614
	ER	25		TH	75		AE10	735
	L3	260	SURROUNDING	AE5	375		M11	426
	AK	107		AE9	588	SURVIVED	J10	418
	HAP	24		AE11	739		M1	441
	EMI	3		AU	529		VP9	21
	VP5	68	SURROUNDS	G4	410		M12	730
	FL	184		AE6	161	SURVIVES	HAP	1554
	CI	217		AE6	201		G2	138
SURPASSES	SSF	6		AE6	741		G4	308
SURPASSING	AE10	789		AE8	618		CAM	182
	TH	219		AE9	741		M12	819
SURPRISE	LC	100		AE11	468	SURVIVING	BR	102
	PRL	15		AE11	1139		AE6	1037
	ETL	14		M10	48	SURVIVORS	SAA	713
	CM	36	SURTOUT	J3	250	SUSANNA	MN	8
	HP	144	SURVEY	HS	101	SUSPECT	PC2	27
	AA	686		AM	563		POE	20
	L4	120		AM	781		HP	129
	HAP	167		AM	887		HP	211
	HAP	937		PUO2	5		HP	226
	G4	574		SAA	914		AA	664
	G4	728		ER	30		PPC	21
	AE1	696		L1	34		SAA	96
	AE2	449		T23	70		OE	40
	AE7	1104		TA	365		HAP	830
	AE8	202		PP	43		ESH	16

SUSPECT	J10	333	SUSTAIN	AE9	663	SWAIN	VP2	90		
	VP3	53		AE9	1051		VP3	1		
	G1	593		AE9	1089		VP3	3		
	AE1	945		AE10	38		VP3	63		
	AE4	137		AE10	470		VP3	104		
	KT2	375		AE10	1189		VP5	19		
	C	779		AE10	1220		VP5	71		
	CI	124		AE11	1177		VP6	121		
SUSPECTED	PWGR	16		AE12	232		VP7	62		
	RL	441		AE12	385		VP8	44		
	J3	361		AE12	795		VP8	85		
	AE3	722		AE12	924		VP10	21		
	KT2	76		OAL	784		G1	106		
SUSPECTING	MD	315		KT3	1087		G1	223		
	M1	827		TJD	28		G1	362		
	M13	198		M8	131		G1	401		
	B	718		HIF	233		G1	422		
SUSPECTS	SMA	115		HIF	249		G1	471		
SUSPEND	SMA	134		HIF	256		G1	487		
	VP10	17		HIF	698		G2	640		
	G2	463		HIF	767		G3	796		
	AE10	501		M11	19		G4	188		
SUSPENDED	HAP	1289		FL	590		G4	259		
	M1	15		M12	750		G4	737		
	AE8	712		M12	823		AE12	861		
	AE12	244		AU	174		WB	16		
	HIF	287		AU	300	SWAINS	H2	86		
	M12	205		AU	445		M1	954		
	M12	745		AU	595		VP5	36		
SUSPENDS	SAA	218		WB	337		VP5	68		
	AE1	418		M15	135		VP5	122		
	AE11	144		M15	605		VP7	1		
	AE12	955	SUSTAINED	SAA	638		VP7	23		
SUSPENSE	AE12	1360		J10	64		VP7	35		
SUSPICION	SAA	694		MC	41		VP7	99		
	HAP	1463		G3	555		VP8	1		
	C	263		AE1	439		VP8	6		
	M12	85		AE3	421		VP10	28		
SUSPICIONS	KT2	486		AE5	550		VP10	48		
SUSPICIOUS	B	104		AE5	1061		G1	11		
	HIF	756		AE6	676		G1	145		
SUSTAIN	AM	187		AE6	939		G1	314		
	AM	761		AE7	814		G1	403		
	DA	55		AE7	1099		G1	428		
	DA	148		AE9	1084		G1	662		
	AA	954		AE10	905		G3	524		
	MD	248		AE10	1139		G4	206		
	SAA	222		AE11	763		G4	277		
	TA	175		AE11	905		G4	616		
	EL	135		AE12	267		AE1	745		
	EL	354		AE12	361		AE7	942		
	SSH	2		OAL	367		AE8	460		
	J6	148		MFL	14		AE9	12		
	J10	552		KT2	603		AE12	9		
	P3	203		KT3	311		KT3	635		
	P4	33		TH	199		CI	76		
	M1	168	SUSTAINING	AE12	639	SWALLOW	AM	811		
	M1	486	SUSTAINS	G1	17		PDG	40		
	M1	1037		G1	73		HAP	1721		
	M9	15		AE1	691		HAP	1763		
	VP2	15		AE2	914		HAP	1841		
	VP3	86		AE4	199		HAP	1860		
	VP4	60		AE8	181		HAP	2373		
	VP6	86		AE8	185		J10	367		
	G1	164		AE8	878		P6	55		
	G1	178		AE9	653		G1	520		
	G2	514		AE10	858		AE11	936		
	G2	743		AE11	1098		AE12	691		
	G3	99		AE12	911	SWALLOWED	AR	302		
	G3	256		TJD	74		AA	113		
	G4	82		M15	582		J1	209		
	G4	365	SUSTENANCE	EL	34		M1	48		
	AE1	150		KT2	160		M1	480		
	AE1	400	SWABBERS	P5	215		AE1	781		
	AE2	673	SWAGE	SAA	781		AE1	819		
	AE2	697	SWAGGER	EMQW	6		KT2	18		
	AE2	854		PUO3	15		M15	418		
	AE2	864	SWAGGERED	C	443	SWALLOWS	HAP	1944		
	AE3	132	SWAIN	SSF	2		J6	552		
	AE4	590		SAA	560		G4	434		
	AE4	628		SAA	922	SWALLOWS'	HAP	1713		
	AE4	993		T23	1	SWAM	AM	621		
	AE4	788		NS	23		G1	207		
	AE5	346		FS2	1		AE7	689		
	AE5	480		STS3	1		DO	45		
	AE5	800		SKA5	13		M15	507		
	AE6	747		ODA	14	SWAN	SKK	15		
	AE6	1048		M1	690		DA	2		
	AE6	1108		M1	936		J6	241		
	AE6	1121		R	10		VP7	53		
	AE7	461		R	14		AE9	761		
	AE7	592		VP1	42		AE10	270		
	AE7	727		VP1	74		AE11	869		
	AE8	497		VP2	1		AE12	377		
	AE8	588		VP2	77		C	634		
	AE8	760		VP2	81	SWAN-LIKE	VP9	47		

Word	Ref	Num	Word	Ref	Num	Word	Ref	Num
SWANS	AM	263	SWAY	J10	77	SWEAR	ESH	17
	M13	75		J10	150		ESH	22
	VP8	75		M1	394		J3	76
	VP9	35		M1	694		J3	178
	G1	529		M13	16		J3	243
	G2	274		G1	329		J6	24
	AE1	544		G1	651		J6	207
	AE7	965		G4	120		J6	569
	AE11	695		AE1	31		J16	52
SWARM	AM	575		AE1	86		PPS	19
	PKK	27		AE1	93		P3	13
	RL	418		AE1	709		P3	243
	AK	50		AE2	679		P5	202
	J3	127		AE5	666		P5	204
	G4	28		AE6	1083		P5	246
	G4	163		AE6	1173		M1	1024
	AE7	97		AE7	352		M1	1080
	AE7	129		AE7	937		AE6	480
	AE9	1082		AE7	1018		AE7	321
	AE11	709		AE8	134		AE9	386
	AE12	202		AE8	194		AE9	402
	OAL	107		AE8	430		AE12	299
SWARMING	HAP	60		AE8	438		OAL	419
	VP7	18		AE8	671		OAL	712
	G4	83		AE8	677		KT2	425
	AE1	712		AE10	62		HIF	130
	AE2	35		AE10	292		HIF	348
	FL	219		AE10	1157		C	409
	WB	58		AE11	340		C	582
SWARMS	AR	216		AE11	507		M11	63
	PCB	9		AE11	816		PTP	9
	SAA	1123		AE11	1030		PWR	30
	H3	44		AE11	1235	SWEARERS	SAA	98
	HAP	1112		AE12	270		PMK	34
	VP9	39		AE12	288	SWEARING	EMKG	29
	G3	236		AE12	974	SWEARS	EAL	10
	G4	157		OAL	23		PR	23
	G4	802		OAL	318		AA	132
	AE4	581		OAE1	6		PD	20
	AE6	1022		DO	41		AE6	635
	AE8	652		KT2	212		OAL	310
	C	741		KT2	652	SWEAT	RH	18
	CI	400		KT3	80		AM	11
SWARTHY	L4	145		TJD	180		ETG	24
	H2	63		BP	7		MD	271
	TA	361		HIF	227		AT	122
	G3	596		HIF	286		L4	104
	AE1	686		HIF	312		T27	128
	AE1	1052		HIF	389		TA	439
	AE10	1028		HIF	397		BR	174
	OAL	824		HIF	406		J1	40
	TH	119		HIF	617		J1	81
SWATHED	CM	79		M11	167		J1	253
	AE8	383		FL	298		J3	178
	CAM	372		WB	285		J6	364
SWAY	HS	33		M15	640		J6	380
	AR	77		GP	119		P1	143
	AR	297	SWAYED	DC	1		P2	97
	RH	98		AA	939		VP4	54
	SMA	96		SAA	29		G1	648
	AM	850		H29	2		G3	676
	AM	1149		AK	103		G3	750
	ECD	15		J10	200		G3	841
	EOE	9		HI	76		AE2	233
	AA	22		AE1	477		AE3	233
	AA	330		AE2	760		AE5	261
	AA	760		AE7	889		AE6	85
	AA	780		TJD	183		AE7	641
	AA	991		HIF	383		AE9	1098
	MD	78	SWAYEST	M9	166		AE9	1105
	MD	117	SWAYS	M13	167		KT1	449
	MD	249		AE4	393		KT3	260
	MD	314		KT3	296		KT3	337
	PRH	42	SWEAR	EWG	4		B	553
	MF	123		EMQW	13		BP	76
	MF	131		EMQW	28		C	27
	SAA	37		PTW	25		C	107
	SAA	214		PR	14		C	124
	SAA	290		AA	1012		M12	188
	SAA	747		PPC	15	SWEATING	H2	90
	SAA	739		SAA	478		J6	694
	SAA	803		SAA	100		J10	64
	SAA	893		EDGA	9		P6	90
	SAA	901		PD	29		M1	143
	SAA	1010		T27	8		VP2	96
	PDG	34		T27	29		M15	159
	L3	8		T27	34	SWEATS	AM	279
	TA	146		T27	60		L3	205
	AK	92		T27	62		J6	548
	HAP	186		T27	93		J6	599
	HAP	245		HAP	38	SWEATY	H2	68
	HAP	455		PDS	36		AE5	177
	HAP	2084		STS2	7	SWEDE	AR	9
	HAP	2127		PMS	13	SWEDEN	AM	586
	HAP	2425		EKA	11	SWEEP	AM	992
	EL	178		EKA	30		EDGA	37

Word	Code	No.
SWEEP	AK	156
	HAP	1112
	HAP	2128
	J3	388
	P6	100
	G1	432
	G3	715
	AE1	87
	AE1	124
	AE2	271
	AE2	409
	AE9	147
	AE10	296
	AE10	314
	OAL	180
	KT3	173
	M11	33
SWEEPING	AM	1190
	PP	7
	HI	105
	G1	504
	AE1	560
	AE3	375
	AE3	605
	AE5	582
	AE6	1071
	AE7	39
	AE9	843
	AE12	665
	KT1	336
	CI	626
SWEEPS	L3	84
	J6	220
	G3	98
	G3	310
	G4	84
	AE2	680
	KT3	419
	TJD	83
	M11	167
SWEEPY	M1	394
	M13	127
	G1	651
	AE7	937
SWEET	UDH	36
	AR	261
	RH	15
	SIE	7
	SMM2	21
	SEL3	4
	ETL	5
	ETL	13
	STL	1
	PCG2	26
	SCG1	7
	PW	9
	PMQW	9
	SLN	15
	PUO2	5
	EMP	1
	PR	27
	AA	697
	OE	16
	DOD	21
	PD	14
	ER	59
	L1	37
	L2	7
	L4	16
	T18	35
	T23	58
	FS3	1
	FS3	15
	AK	51
	AK	193
	GE	60
	HAP	383
	HAP	800
	PP	11
	ETS	2
	ETS	7
	SKA2	3
	SKA2	10
	SKA3	4
	SKA5	9
	EL	158
	EL	260
	EL	304
	J3	122
	J3	128
	J3	365
	J3	499
	P1	181
	P5	20
	M1	674
	M1	698
SWEET	M13	7
	SLT1	15
	GK	2
	VP2	66
	VP5	70
	VP5	85
	VP7	53
	VP8	30
	VP8	35
	VP8	45
	VP8	52
	VP8	59
	VP8	63
	VP8	69
	VP8	79
	VP8	86
	VP9	59
	VP10	25
	VP10	58
	G1	116
	G2	192
	G2	241
	G2	325
	G2	593
	G2	736
	G3	376
	G3	744
	G4	44
	G4	52
	G4	154
	G4	165
	G4	239
	G4	428
	G4	478
	G4	680
	G4	488
	G4	721
	AE1	388
	AE1	752
	AE1	930
	AE1	956
	AE1	963
	AE1	968
	AE5	1082
	AE5	1100
	AE6	505
	AE7	296
	AE10	1163
	OAL	526
	OAL	568
	OAL	702
	OAL	854
	OAE2	37
	OAE2	49
	AF	47
	AF	59
	AF	60
	AF	64
	AF	65
	AF	97
	AF	163
	AF	173
	DO	118
	KT1	455
	KT2	53
	KT3	321
	KT3	366
	KT3	696
	KT3	806
	KT3	1143
	M8	71
	B	66
	B	203
	CAM	16
	HIF	30
	HIF	52
	HIF	364
	C	632
	C	648
	M11	156
	M11	287
	M11	309
	FL	20
	FL	101
	FL	112
	FL	116
	FL	141
	FL	199
	FL	367
	FL	368
	FL	400
	FL	432
	FL	435
	M12	568
	M15	436
	M15	583
SWEET	GP	15
	CI	42
	CI	134
	CI	579
	EMKG	17
	EMKG	23
SWEETBREADS	HIF	633
SWEETENS	STC	6
SWEETER	STL	5
	HP	247
	T27	4
	BR	323
	M13	76
	VP2	29
	G1	468
	AE9	230
	FL	93
SWEETHEART	J6	708
SWEETLY	AT	46
	SSC	23
	C	620
	GP	26
SWEETMEATS	J6	289
SWEETNESS	RH	5
	SMA	56
	LC	76
	LCA	23
	ER	25
	T27	13
	HAP	2306
	M1	1029
	MC	33
	VP5	24
	G2	654
	OAL	65
	C	600
SWEETS	AR	53
	MO	21
	L4	110
	L4	189
	HAP	1361
	VP2	75
	VP3	170
	G4	300
	AE7	760
	AE11	417
	M11	20
	FL	16
	FL	109
	FL	131
	EWR	16
SWELL	AM	15
	ECD	16
	SAA	1077
	SAA	911
	SAA	609
	SAA	472
	L3	190
	HAP	2375
	BR	281
	EH	34
	P3	46
	P3	190
	P5	28
	P6	184
	VP9	66
	G1	29
	G1	156
	G1	283
	G3	484
	G3	607
	AE1	100
	AE10	409
	AF	160
	KT3	759
	FL	13
SWELLED	UDH	57
	RH	11
	AM	837
	EAZ	8
	MF	40
	SAA	983
	J1	215
	P2	10
	M1	540
	M1	562
	M1	610
	VP5	53
	G1	198
	G1	425
	G3	730
	AE2	792
	AE5	261
	AE10	94
	AE11	607
	DO	47

Headword	Ref	No.
SWELLED	M11	152
SWELLEST	P5	13
SWELLING	VHH	2
	AM	730
	AM	853
	CM	43
	HP	6
	MD	294
	SAA	923
	L4	22
	EL	242
	P5	273
	M1	386
	M1	540
	M13	77
	M13	127
	VP3	129
	VP7	69
	VP10	54
	G1	269
	G2	105
	G2	763
	G3	218
	G3	493
	G4	514
	AE2	271
	AE3	457
	AE3	350
	AE3	581
	AE3	692
	AE5	15
	AE5	22
	AE7	33
	AE7	482
	AE7	1019
	AE8	120
	AE8	837
	AE8	969
	AE10	374
	AE10	971
	AE11	929
	AE12	1298
	OAL	395
	CAM	356
	HIF	323
	HIF	535
SWELLS	LC	134
	STL	20
	MD	267
	SAA	729
	J6	665
	P1	108
	G1	174
	KT1	445
SWEPT	AM	18
	PM	5
	EUO	7
	MF	180
	P3	94
	M1	363
	AE2	946
	AE7	1102
	AE11	863
	FL	166
SWERVE	RL	455
	AE2	604
SWERVED	AT	24
	M1	752
	M11	322
SWERVING	G2	453
	G2	494
SWIFT	HS	49
	AM	420
	AM	796
	PTL	22
	CM	85
	HP	155
	PSF	14
	AA	191
	AA	242
	AA	837
	MD	133
	SAA	640
	H2	62
	TA	34
	TA	110
	BR	225
	BR	230
	EL	278
	M1	678
	M1	969
	M13	79
	G1	552
	G3	554
	G4	525
	AE1	553
SWIFT	AE3	903
	AE4	187
	AE4	253
	AE4	259
	AE4	329
	AE5	191
	AE5	316
	AE5	394
	AE5	418
	AE6	89
	AE8	230
	AE8	287
	AE8	517
	AE8	931
	AE9	299
	AE9	504
	AE9	786
	AE10	375
	AE10	619
	AE10	806
	AE10	832
	AE10	898
	AE11	1004
	AE11	1088
	AE12	1240
	AE12	1338
	OAL	256
	OAL	617
	M8	18
	CAM	382
	HIF	15
	HIF	298
	M11	322
	M11	349
	FL	595
	M12	171
	M12	319
	AS	55
SWIFTER	SAA	23
	AE2	633
	AE9	747
SWIFTEST	SAA	23
SWIFTLY	AM	386
	AM	1083
	AM	1105
	TA	448
	M1	624
	M1	728
	M1	729
	M9	68
	HI	24
	G3	157
	AE2	840
	AE3	179
	AE4	813
	AE4	852
	AE4	927
	AE5	299
	AE5	791
	AE6	80
	AE9	865
	AE12	462
	OAL	632
	M8	52
	C	673
	FL	136
	M12	535
SWIFTNESS	LC	109
	LC	113
	M13	95
	M13	98
	AE5	86
	AE12	1288
SWIFTS	HAP	1841
SWIFT-SURE	AR	235
SWIG	AE9	73
SWILLED	AE1	1036
SWILLING	HAP	1418
	P3	182
	OAL	265
SWILLS	L4	66
SWIM	AM	338
	AM	603
	P3	63
	G1	528
	G3	228
	G3	378
	AE4	764
	AE5	776
	AE9	142
	AE10	529
	AE10	966
	AE12	374
	C	803
	M11	209
	M15	556
SWIMMING	J6	422
	G4	717
	AE5	1113
	AE9	594
	AE10	1050
	KT3	962
	HIF	814
SWIMS	M1	414
	M1	417
	G3	682
	G3	686
	AE3	822
	AE11	749
	AE11	1197
	M12	189
SWINE	PLN	12
	J6	232
	VP3	143
	G2	100
	G2	756
	G3	745
	AE5	130
	AE8	111
	C	733
SWING	PTL	17
	T23	94
	J10	529
	AE11	933
	AE12	1335
SWINGE	EMQ	2
SWINGEING	J6	552
SWINGS	AM	386
	AE11	1029
	HAP	1471
	HAP	1843
SWITCH	PMK	17
SWITCHING	EMKG	18
SWIZZERS	EMK	26
SWOLLEN	UDH	76
SWOLN	G1	607
	AE2	356
	AE2	520
	AE6	251
	AE11	1239
	KT3	751
	HIF	13
	HIF	591
SWOON	T27	93
SWOONING	AE8	769
	KT3	859
	M11	71
SWOONS	OAL	606
SWORD	AM	1082
	AM	1088
	ESF	23
	ML	8
	EOE	20
	CM	3
	CM	20
	CM	112
	HP	239
	DA	198
	DA	204
	DA	211
	EPF	11
	AA	456
	AA	515
	AA	761
	AA	1002
	MD	306
	MF	58
	SAA	769
	PDG	22
	TA	325
	TA	467
	TA	482
	HAP	993
	HAP	1172
	HAP	1485
	HAP	1979
	HAP	1996
	HAP	2208
	PKA	49
	J6	117
	J6	159
	J6	349
	J6	816
	J10	148
	J10	413
	P1	196
	P3	77
	HI	126
	VP1	14
	VP8	66
	G2	385
	G2	788

SWORD	G3	576	SWORD	KT3	509	SWORN	KT1	290
	G4	168		KT3	914		KT1	308
	AE1	659		M8	237		KT2	391
	AE1	768		CAM	313		AU	69
	AE1	879		HIF	90		EMKG	30
	AE2	585		HIF	291	SWOUND	KT1	537
	AE2	709		HIF	317		KT3	982
	AE2	780		HIF	323	SYBARIS	AE12	540
	AE2	907		HIF	329		M15	67
	AE2	913		TH	122		M15	475
	AE2	318		TH	165	SYCAMORE	FL	75
	AE3	318		TH	182	SYCAMORES	FL	72
	AE4	386		TH	273	SYLLA	J1	22
	AE4	734		TH	334	SYLVAN	AK	108
	AE4	833		M12	183		HAP	515
	AE4	902		M12	360		VP1	2
	AE4	929		M12	508		VP5	5
	AE4	977		M12	646		VP5	72
	AE5	485		M12	654		VP6	15
	AE5	629		M12	801		VP6	44
	AE6	371		M12	822		G1	274
	AE6	662		AU	148		G2	28
	AE6	703		AU	548		G3	67
	AE6	1113		AU	599		AE1	233
	AE6	1117		M15	146		AE3	34
	AE6	1217		M15	651		AE4	167
	AE7	607		CI	283		AE5	379
	AE7	642		CI	537		AE7	566
	AE8	510		CI	603		AE8	417
	AE8	603		SMP	63		AE9	549
	AE8	823	SWORDFISH	AM	314		AE11	874
	AE9	169	SWORDMAN	J6	115		KT2	466
	AE9	407	SWORDPLAY	OAL	191		KT2	619
	AE9	435	SWORDS	ENH	22		KT3	226
	AE9	445		J10	192		TJD	51
	AE9	461		J10	267		M12	555
	AE9	567		M1	130	SYLVANS	H29	37
	AE9	577		HI	106		M1	955
	AE9	590		G1	684		G2	703
	AE9	735		AE2	430		AE12	763
	AE9	1038		AE2	454	SYLVANUS	H2	34
	AE9	1058		AE2	629	SYLVESTER	BR	84
	AE10	343		AE2	720	SYLVIA	SEL3	13
	AE10	435		AE2	997		NS	1
	AE10	452		AE3	314	SYMETHIS	M13	2
	AE10	549		AE6	688	SYMMETRY	MFL	11
	AE10	715		AE7	409	SYMPHONY	KT3	529
	AE10	814		AE7	733		FL	210
	AE10	848		AE7	880		M12	219
	AE10	904		AE7	949	SYMPTOM	L4	23
	AE10	911		AE7	1012	SYMPTOMS	G3	752
	AE10	964		AE7	1023		G4	368
	AE10	968		AE7	1084		AE4	529
	AE10	1095		AE8	715		KT3	710
	AE10	1132		AE9	571		C	146
	AE10	1156		AE10	113	SYNOD	SMA	83
	AE10	1173		AE10	391		HAP	1035
	AE10	1289		AE10	797		M1	257
	AE10	1311		AE11	296		HI	157
	AE11	18		AE11	586	SYRIAN	H29	7
	AE11	231		AE11	957		H29	30
	AE11	390		AE12	124		VP4	30
	AE11	513		AE12	434	SYRIAN'S	SAA	549
	AE11	691		AE12	770	SYRIANS	J3	109
	AE11	1049		AE12	1029	SYRINX	LS	7
	AE11	1081		AE12	1033		LS	12
	AE11	1207		AE12	1053		LS	18
	AE12	264		KT1	148		M1	955
	AE12	418		KT3	523	SYRTES	AE4	59
	AE12	460		FL	411		AE7	418
	AE12	480		M12	237	SYRTES'	AE5	252
	AE12	501		AU	150	SYSTEM	RL	82
	AE12	534		AU	327			
	AE12	630		CI	588			
	AE12	782	SWORE	EEL	26			
	AE12	793		PM	13			
	AE12	916		DA	60			
	AE12	1062		MF	114			
	AE12	1069		AT	77	TABLE	SAA	340
	AE12	1101		HAP	627		HAP	2268
	AE12	1137		LS	14		J1	218
	AE12	1143		VP8	27		J6	562
	AE12	1159		AE4	617		P6	77
	AE12	1375		AE5	223		M1	303
	OAL	781		AE9	120		VP3	68
	OAE1	16		OAL	716		AE7	152
	KT1	111		KT1	99		DO	130
	KT2	138		M12	286		BP	83
	KT2	142		WB	299		BP	84
	KT2	195		WB	324		BP	107
	KT2	253		WB	355		TH	327
	KT2	271	SWORN	CM	71		M12	764
	KT2	425		MF	113		WB	352
	KT2	602		M1	323		CI	578
	KT3	25		AE12	317		AS	86
	KT3	308		AE12	367	TABLE-BOOK	J1	97

Word	Ref	No.		Word	Ref	No.		Word	Ref	No.
TABLE'S	BP	102		TAKE	PW	4		TAKE	EL	249
TABLES	J1	208			EMQW	12			EL	367
	J6	423			PM	27			PSH	18
	M9	203			EM	31			EH	13
	G4	543			PCD	20			J1	9
	AE2	1040			SCD1	14			J1	224
	AE3	291			PUO2	34			J1	233
	AE3	454			E	16			J3	175
	AE7	239			PC2	22			J3	222
	AE8	375			ML	48			J3	298
	TH	257			PAL	39			J3	304
	M15	99			EKK	2			J3	329
	CI	582			EKK	7			J3	345
TABLETS	P1	82			POE	28			J3	423
	GK	34			ETC	18			J3	499
	AE12	1114			PLG	1			J6	240
	BP	196			PLG	9			J6	627
TABORS	J6	571			PLG	12			J6	643
TABURNUS,	G2	52			PLG	19			J6	764
TABURNUS'	AE12	1043			CM	120			J10	161
TACK	AM	229			HP	73			J10	228
	AM	325			HP	81			J10	529
	AM	337			HP	199			J10	530
	PUO3	16			HP	236			J16	50
	AE3	526			PSF	10			J16	60
TACKED	P5	125			PSF	31			P2	8
TACKING	AE3	901			PR	25			P3	40
TACKLE	AE5	21			PUO4	8			P3	196
TACKLINGS	SCD2	20			AA	316			P4	91
TADIUS	P6	153			AA	464			P4	110
TADPOLE	MD	304			AA	717			P5	148
TAGGED	P1	182			AA	757			P5	190
	AE3	777			AA	772			P5	199
TAGUS	AM	1193			AA	860			P5	227
	J3	97			AA	791			P5	250
	AE9	561			AA	984			P6	52
	AE12	746			AA	1020			P6	117
TAIL	AR	117			PLB	31			P6	130
	AM	386			ELB	16			P6	148
	AM	620			ELB	23			P6	149
	PWGR	28			EPC	18			M1	29
	PUO3	18			MD	121			M1	409
	HAP	163			MD	160			M1	618
	HAP	1292			MF	133			M1	837
	J6	70			SAA	196			M1	948
	J6	417			SAA	540			M1	1033
	P1	173			SAA	681			M13	207
	P4	92			SAA	733			HI	130
	M1	1003			SAA	778			HI	180
	G3	98			PK	2			ELT	7
	G3	105			PK	31			ELT	12
	G3	644			EDGA	8			ELT	23
	AE10	303			RL	97			ELT	25
	AE11	1112			RL	382			SLT2	5
	AE11	1186			OE	13			MC	76
	C	118			OE	20			VP2	60
	M12	537			OE	52			VP3	29
	M15	549			AT	120			VP3	106
	ETP	18			PD	57			VP5	5
TAILOR	J6	765			L3	131			VP8	85
	EHC	29			L4	226			VP8	87
TAIL'S	AE3	544			T23	42			G1	664
TAILS	EDGA	32			T23	75			G2	107
	P5	265			T27	58			G2	355
	AE2	274			T27	89			G2	431
	AE8	893			TA	143			G3	209
TAINT	OD	28			AK	135			G3	211
	M15	102			HH	39			G3	434
TAINTED	M1	248			HAP	32			G3	459
	VP1	70			HAP	70			G3	527
	G3	834			HAP	125			G3	638
	G4	435			HAP	141			G3	709
	M11	130			HAP	427			G4	159
	M11	254			HAP	595			G4	219
	ETP	14			HAP	706			G4	282
TAINTS	WB	402			HAP	833			G4	329
TAKE	UDH	40			HAP	994			G4	421
	UDH	45			HAP	1418			AE1	540
	AR	238			HAP	1477			AE1	950
	AR	270			HAP	1483			AE1	958
	RH	101			HAP	1941			AE2	13
	SMA	83			HAP	2003			AE2	77
	SMA	102			HAP	2199			AE2	192
	PWG	30			HAP	2274			AE2	280
	PIE	19			BR	72			AE2	496
	PIE	28			PDS	17			AE2	874
	AM	34			PTS	3			AE2	875
	AM	174			STS3	27			AE2	921
	AM	832			STS3	35			AE2	983
	AM	933			PMS	3			AE3	313
	AM	1060			PMS	36			AE3	614
	EWGR	36			PKA	24			AE3	788
	SEL1	5			EKA	12			AE3	897
	PTL	24			LS	16			AE4	172
	PCG2	6			EL	139			AE4	776
	SCG3	24			EL	238			AE4	790

Word	Ref	No.
TAKE	AE5	179
	AE5	644
	AE5	801
	AE5	885
	AE5	1005
	AE5	1101
	AE6	232
	AE6	370
	AE6	410
	AE6	513
	AE7	828
	AE8	233
	AE8	920
	AE9	367
	AE9	500
	AE9	531
	AE9	872
	AE10	115
	AE10	396
	AE10	846
	AE10	882
	AE10	1242
	AE11	674
	AE11	688
	AE11	881
	AE11	921
	AE11	928
	AE11	933
	AE11	1264
	AE11	1306
	AE12	22
	AE12	76
	AE12	394
	AE12	655
	AE12	768
	AE12	1186
	AE12	1274
	OAL	1
	OAL	69
	OAL	181
	OAL	465
	OAL	646
	OAL	748
	OAE1	11
	OAE2	13
	OAE2	32
	OAE2	55
	OAE2	68
	OAE2	85
	AF	106
	KT1	30
	KT2	306
	KT2	421
	KT3	243
	KT3	530
	KT3	542
	KT3	571
	KT3	618
	KT3	800
	KT3	1086
	KT3	1112
	KT3	1128
	TJD	105
	M8	111
	M8	218
	M8	306
	M8	307
	B	83
	B	391
	B	569
	BP	8
	BP	188
	M10	10
	CAM	379
	HIF	28
	HIF	36
	HIF	251
	HIF	417
	HIF	522
	HIF	586
	C	164
	C	187
	C	249
	C	416
	C	595
	C	738
	C	786
	C	797
	C	821
	TH	138
	TH	288
	TH	293
	M11	130
	M12	270
	M12	440
	AU	258

Word	Ref	No.
TAKE	AU	260
	AU	346
	AU	419
	AU	514
	WB	93
	WB	250
	WB	254
	WB	304
	WB	332
	WB	408
	WB	504
	WB	518
	M15	24
	M15	534
	M15	555
	M15	675
	M15	705
	CI	302
	SMP	76
	SMP	78
	PMK	31
	EMKG	5
	EMKG	33
	PWR	33
	PWG	33
	PM	30
TAKEN	MD	210
	SAA	698
	EK	38
	RL	412
	OE	56
	J6	385
	J10	425
	M13	137
	GK	30
	VP8	47
	G3	762
	AE2	77
	AE2	796
	AE7	407
	AE9	384
	AE9	537
	AE11	295
	AE12	1016
	OAL	553
	KT3	516
	B	370
	HIF	201
	HIF	507
	M12	317
	AU	161
	AU	578
	WB	114
	WB	480
	CI	418
TAKER	EMK	23
TAKES	AR	309
	PWG	8
	AM	162
	AM	533
	AM	1121
	PCD	4
	PKK	14
	PKK	20
	AA	208
	AA	257
	AA	667
	PLB	32
	SAA	1083
	RL	70
	L3	168
	L4	32
	L4	289
	TA	364
	BR	1
	BR	113
	J3	441
	J6	54
	J6	173
	J6	178
	J6	225
	J6	329
	J6	536
	J6	596
	J6	712
	J6	752
	J10	515
	P1	119
	P2	61
	P2	114
	P2	118
	P3	18
	P3	81
	P5	193
	M1	453
	M1	771

Word	Ref	No.
TAKES	M1	1002
	GK	181
	VP3	51
	G1	131
	G1	508
	G1	553
	G4	626
	AE1	256
	AE1	713
	AE1	968
	AE4	318
	AE5	240
	AE5	1094
	AE5	1131
	AE6	773
	AE6	1023
	AE7	127
	AE7	457
	AE7	583
	AE7	662
	AE7	986
	AE8	115
	AE9	82
	AE9	157
	AE9	291
	AE9	1100
	AE10	107
	AE10	798
	AE11	367
	AE11	697
	AE11	778
	AE12	546
	AE12	822
	OAL	186
	KT1	379
	KT2	466
	M8	165
	CAM	139
	C	403
	M11	354
	M11	437
	M12	790
	M15	427
	CI	45
TAKEST	P4	75
	P4	88
	M1	1051
	AE2	732
	B	480
TAKING	EEL	31
	ETL	13
	PCG1	2
	EM	20
	PLN	24
	STC	6
	PSF	32
	EPC	14
	STS2	8
	EH	15
	J16	24
TALBOT	C	728
TALE	PCG1	15
	PAL	8
	PCB	18
	DA	83
	RL	348
	T27	68
	HAP	1720
	HAP	1934
	HAP	2199
	MS	14
	J1	80
	J10	281
	J10	508
	P5	225
	M1	988
	VP3	51
	VP9	10
	G4	212
	AE1	484
	AE1	516
	AE2	143
	AE2	204
	AE5	1097
	AE6	922
	AE7	282
	OAL	771
	KT1	27
	KT1	32
	KT1	365
	KT2	141
	KT3	576
	CAM	6
	C	5
	C	67
	C	210

Word	Ref	No.
TALE	C	359
	C	374
	C	474
	C	552
	C	573
	C	815
	M12	706
	WB	154
	WB	156
	WB	203
	CI	26
TALENT	RH	100
	PO	9
	SAA	493
	PK	19
	P5	27
	AU	219
	CI	496
TALENTS	PCB	17
	MF	209
	SAA	293
	EL	24
	MC	24
	EHC	5
	AE9	352
	HIF	344
TALES	ELN	5
	EPC	28
	L3	183
	T27	103
	HAP	587
	G3	12
	AE10	774
	OAL	443
	C	342
TALK	PFD	28
	PLG	20
	AA	534
	SAA	351
	SAA	509
	SAA	531
	EDG	14
	RL	315
	HAP	558
	HAP	571
	HAP	1328
	J1	218
	J3	196
	M13	192
	VP3	22
	AE1	1049
	AE4	272
	AE6	720
	AE8	411
	AE8	612
	OAL	260
	OAL	559
	OAL	881
	OAL	884
	KT3	471
	CAM	82
	C	135
	M12	225
	AU	16
	CI	523
	PWR	25
TALKED	EEL	6
	AE6	239
	AE10	845
	HIF	729
	M12	225
TALKING	MD	162
	T27	17
	OAL	160
TALKS	ESF	9
	SAA	334
	J6	425
	J6	573
	J6	620
TALL	AM	571
	T18	49
	M1	960
	VP5	21
	VP7	54
	G2	93
	G2	453
	G3	557
	AE1	429
	AE9	148
	AE9	924
	AE10	315
	AE10	1084
	KT3	56
	M12	465
	CI	52
TALLER	M13	228

Word	Ref	No.
TALLER	G2	93
TALLEST	AE3	894
TALLY	EL	256
TALMUD	J6	701
TALONS	AE5	333
	AE6	809
	AE9	763
	AE11	1107
	AE12	377
TALTHYBIUS	HIF	446
TAMARISK	VP8	74
TAME	EWG	2
	EWG	4
	AA	385
	AA	455
	SAA	1049
	HAP	157
	BR	219
	J3	330
	M1	787
	G2	85
	G2	510
	G3	836
	G3	724
	G4	215
	AE1	360
	AE6	1176
	AE7	674
	KT3	97
	BP	69
	M11	278
TAMED	MC	9
	G2	324
	G3	142
	G3	803
	AE8	968
	HIF	304
	M15	108
	GP	75
TAMELY	HS	83
	PNH	42
	SAA	1092
	AE5	518
	AE11	654
	HIF	199
	HIF	414
TAMES	G1	144
TAMING	G3	227
TAMPERING	AA	809
TANAGRUS	G3	242
TANAÏS	AE12	746
TANCRED	B	1
	B	52
	B	189
	B	298
	B	390
	B	421
	B	482
	B	635
	B	719
	B	727
TANGLED	L4	81
TANKARD	ECG2	6
	J3	335
TANNED	OAL	825
TANTALIZED	L3	158
TANTALUS	L3	185
	G3	64
TAPER	M1	675
	M1	1033
	VP7	54
	OAL	703
	CAM	310
TAPERED	M10	47
TAPERS	AM	64
	DA	26
	RL	8
	HAP	90
	J6	423
	G1	343
	AE8	373
	OAL	281
	M11	390
	M12	345
TAPESTRY	AE9	436
	KT3	104
	KT3	535
	J6	140
TAR	AE8	664
TARCHON	AE8	801
	AE10	228
	AE10	406
	AE11	1071
	AE11	1097
	AE11	1118
TARCHON'S	AE10	219

Word	Ref	No.
TARCHON'S	AE10	420
TARDIER	M15	107
TARDY	AM	778
	L4	225
	J3	222
	VP10	28
	AE2	832
	AE5	894
	AE9	194
	AE9	1079
	AE12	1100
	KT3	185
	KT3	398
	BP	147
	HIF	40
	C	247
	C	286
	M11	304
	M12	252
	M12	421
	AU	94
	M15	316
	M15	566
	CI	255
	CI	539
	M11	393
TARE	G4	186
TARENTUM	M15	65
	G2	272
TARENTUM'S	AE3	723
TARES	G1	110
TARGET	EAZ	18
	AE11	297
TARGETS	AE2	601
	AE8	881
TARNISH	AA	249
TARNISHED	PNH	11
TARPAULING	AM	590
TARPEIA	AE11	972
TARPEIAN	L3	228
	AE8	457
TARQUIN	AE6	1117
	AE8	857
TARQUITUS	AE10	767
TART	ETL	20
TARTAR	PK	23
TARTARUS	AE6	729
TASK	AR	163
	EAZ	1
	ETC	23
	AA	895
	SAA	134
	SAA	939
	SAA	986
	L4	161
	HAP	78
	HAP	1836
	J6	629
	P5	26
	P5	97
	HI	184
	G2	582
	G3	206
	G4	161
	G4	219
	AE5	23
	AE5	854
	AE6	195
	AE8	534
	AE12	820
	OAL	887
	B	169
	M10	83
	CAM	257
	HIF	51
	TH	247
	AU	312
	AU	388
	AU	507
	AU	523
	AU	579
	WB	248
	CI	522
TASKS	SAA	1109
	G2	322
	AE1	715
	AE2	296
	AE4	590
	AE8	579
TASTE	AR	53
	AR	188
	AM	835
	EWGR	14
	EMM	6
	PAZ	6
	PAL	38

Word	Code	No.
TASTE	AA	119
	AT	35
	T27	14
	H9	27
	H29	21
	GE	52
	HAP	86
	HAP	1245
	BR	210
	J10	326
	PPS	2
	P3	144
	P6	54
	M1	295
	M13	76
	VP3	142
	G2	129
	G2	326
	G2	334
	G3	507
	G3	608
	G4	44
	G4	397
	AE1	662
	AE5	122
	AE6	968
	AE9	824
	AE10	801
	OAE2	40
	KT3	138
	TJD	97
	B	426
	C	473
	C	490
	C	788
	M15	99
	M15	255
	M15	437
	M15	472
	M15	710
	PMK	3
TASTED	AM	576
	EC	42
	HAP	2574
	AE7	760
	B	448
	C	31
TASTER	J6	826
TASTES	TJD	61
TASTING	STS1	11
TATTERED	AM	534
	DA	190
	J3	250
	P1	260
	AE3	774
TAUGHT	HS	116
	AR	31
	AR	180
	AR	318
	RH	4
	AM	644
	AM	1053
	AM	1184
	EMQ	7
	EWGR	32
	EWGR	43
	SMM2	30
	PT	5
	PT	16
	PLN	45
	PUO1	11
	PUO1	19
	ESF	22
	PSF	28
	AA	243
	AA	883
	AA	932
	AA	976
	D	28
	RL	151
	RL	327
	RL	392
	AT	35
	PD	29
	PD	32
	MO	14
	T23	17
	HAP	417
	HAP	471
	HAP	676
	HAP	880
	HAP	903
	HAP	915
	HAP	924
	HAP	933
	HAP	2085

Word	Code	No.
TAUGHT	HAP	2328
	EL	73
	EL	179
	J1	89
	J6	38
	J6	333
	PPS	12
	PPS	15
	P3	158
	P4	26
	P5	177
	PLT	31
	ELT	16
	MC	40
	MC	60
	DHP	26
	VP2	41
	VP2	43
	VP5	43
	VP6	118
	G1	219
	G2	200
	G3	181
	G3	295
	G4	321
	G4	449
	AE1	194
	AE1	1039
	AE3	154
	AE3	249
	AE3	461
	AE4	702
	AE5	522
	AE5	777
	AE6	762
	AE8	428
	AE9	260
	AE9	679
	AE12	518
	OAL	14
	OAL	489
	OAL	293
	OAL	737
	DO	134
	DO	161
	KT3	385
	B	126
	HIF	104
	C	356
	M11	105
	M12	25
	WB	276
	WB	295
	M15	204
	M15	711
	GP	30
	GP	78
	GP	93
	GP	133
	CI	133
	CI	134
	CI	163
	CI	303
	OAL	362
TAUNT	G2	533
TAUNTS	FL	4
TAURUS	MF	30
TAUTOLOGY	MF	56
TAVERN	HH	38
	J3	279
	J3	477
TAVERNS	EWGR	34
TAWDRY	ECG1	7
	J3	120
TAWNY	AE1	374
	AE4	230
	KT2	488
TAX	HS	108
	AM	876
	EWGR	39
	PD	3
	HAP	436
	HAP	1420
	HAP	1521
	PP	7
	M1	1017
TAXED	HAP	1489
	M1	1054
	AU	103
	AU	369
TAXES	AA	95
	PLB	10
	PDS	46
	GK	156
	G2	723
	AU	466

Word	Code	No.
TAYGETUS	G3	74
TEACH	AM	147
	PAR	20
	PUO1	11
	EOE	21
	AA	992
	MF	34
	MF	147
	SAA	345
	SAA	704
	ER	63
	HAP	68
	HAP	2275
	SSC	42
	BR	280
	EL	108
	PSH	35
	ESH	4
	J3	59
	J6	338
	J6	345
	J16	39
	P1	150
	P2	78
	P5	133
	VP3	76
	G2	309
	G2	490
	G2	679
	G3	300
	G4	178
	AE3	485
	AE3	588
	OAL	17
	MM	14
	MM	24
	M15	221
	M15	717
TEACHER	B	126
TEACHERS	AA	126
	HAP	1699
	MM	24
TEACHES	OAL	28
	CI	19
TEACHING	EUO2	11
TEAGUE	PP	27
TEAM	T23	90
	G1	97
	G3	775
	AE1	548
	AE5	1069
	AE7	965
	M12	392
	M12	583
TEAMS	J3	385
	J3	488
	G2	286
	G2	322
TEAR	UDH	59
	AM	1007
	AM	1036
	SMQ	7
	S	12
	EAZ	27
	CM	10
	CM	143
	DA	67
	AA	1013
	PPC	14
	D	40
	AT	49
	T23	74
	T27	104
	T27	106
	FS2	9
	TA	52
	HAP	1332
	PTS	8
	EPN	1
	J6	382
	J6	663
	P1	271
	M1	520
	VP8	143
	VP10	73
	G2	707
	G3	678
	G4	297
	G4	665
	AE2	10
	AE4	528
	AE10	121
	AE10	850
	AE12	153
	AE12	1174
	OAL	375

Word	Ref	No.
TEAR	KT3	634
	KT3	872
	M8	367
	B	579
	C	157
	TH	184
	FL	212
	M15	353
TEARS	UDH	90
	AR	274
	AM	388
	AM	958
	STL	9
	CM	60
	CM	97
	DA	199
	AA	454
	AA	717
	AA	959
	MD	67
	SAA	837
	SAA	592
	SAA	600
	SAA	609
	L3	94
	T23	28
	T23	29
	TA	3
	TA	5
	HAP	1585
	SKA6	18
	ODA	46
	ODA	80
	J1	254
	J3	59
	J6	380
	J6	11
	J10	80
	J10	385
	J10	406
	J16	42
	M1	495
	M1	796
	M1	895
	M9	21
	M9	89
	M9	182
	R	2
	HI	60
	HI	173
	ELT	30
	VP5	29
	VP6	92
	VP10	19
	VP10	42
	G1	86
	G3	422
	G3	505
	G4	454
	AE1	313
	AE1	650
	AE2	15
	AE2	197
	AE2	263
	AE2	353
	AE2	886
	AE2	1053
	AE3	15
	AE3	61
	AE3	443
	AE3	447
	AE3	637
	AE3	785
	AE3	794
	AE4	40
	AE4	46
	AE4	457
	AE4	633
	AE4	651
	AE4	935
	AE5	449
	AE5	796
	AE5	1019
	AE6	31
	AE6	512
	AE6	616
	AE6	632
	AE6	641
	AE6	722
	AE6	930
	AE6	949
	AE6	1200
	AE7	504
	AE8	736
	AE8	741
	AE9	282

Word	Ref	No.
TEARS	AE9	330
	AE9	393
	AE9	458
	AE9	664
	AE11	57
	AE11	134
	AE11	148
	AE11	222
	AE11	270
	AE11	292
	AE11	328
	AE11	361
	AE11	530
	AE11	1115
	AE12	88
	AE12	100
	AE12	114
	AE12	211
	AE12	237
	AE12	880
	AE12	891
	OAL	323
	OAL	599
	OAL	743
	OAL	744
	OAL	745
	OAL	798
	AF	88
	AF	92
	DO	67
	DO	159
	KT1	74
	KT1	93
	KT1	131
	KT1	448
	KT1	525
	KT2	314
	KT2	341
	KT2	344
	KT2	476
	KT3	674
	KT3	855
	KT3	868
	KT3	923
	KT3	1100
	KT3	1108
	M8	252
	M8	274
	M8	275
	M8	325
	M8	393
	M8	394
	B	304
	B	367
	B	373
	B	669
	B	675
	B	687
	B	697
	B	708
	B	727
	BP	174
	CAM	17
	CAM	20
	CAM	111
	CAM	158
	CAM	216
	CAM	351
	CAM	352
	CAM	363
	CAM	371
	HIF	581
	TH	22
	M11	11
	M11	69
	M11	229
	M11	357
	M11	378
	M11	436
	M11	465
	WB	71
	WB	313
	M15	585
	CI	312
	AS	46
TEASE	OE	7
	PTS	5
	ETS	17
TEASES	J6	377
TEAT	VP3	153
TECKELITES	EC	22
TECKELY	EC	31
TEDIOUS	PMQ	33
	AA	569
	PRH	5
	HH	38

Word	Ref	No.
TEDIOUS	HAP	559
	SKA2	3
	J3	442
	J6	72
	J10	268
	J10	384
	J16	74
	P3	206
	P4	70
	VP9	27
	G1	396
	G3	539
	G3	583
	G4	748
	AE1	514
	AE2	18
	AE2	237
	AE3	761
	AE8	411
	AE8	847
	AE12	365
	B	296
	PWR	16
TEEM	HAP	1877
TEEMING	CM	131
	HP	230
	L1	14
	J1	183
	J6	19
	M1	132
	M1	557
	VP1	69
	VP3	130
	VP5	53
	G1	4
	G1	15
	G1	156
	G1	598
	G2	443
	G3	225
	G4	412
	AE8	466
	M15	106
TEEMLESS	HAP	228
TEEMS	SAA	1054
TEETH	EM	28
	MD	121
	EDG	44
	OE	14
	HAP	199
	HAP	1937
	PDS	39
	J3	473
	J16	14
	P3	204
	M13	27
	G2	194
	G2	487
	G3	766
	G4	653
	AE3	872
	AE5	626
	AE6	779
	AE7	384
	AE7	927
	AE8	303
	AE9	69
	AE10	682
	OAL	580
	KT2	60
	TH	146
	M12	359
	M15	132
	M15	358
	CI	622
TEG	PUO3	27
TEINT	GK	178
TELAMON	M8	56
	M8	147
	M12	829
	AU	31
	AU	35
TELEBOAN	AE7	1016
TELEBOAS	M12	593
TELEMUS	M13	34
TELEPHUS	J1	5
	M12	153
	AU	279
TELETHUSA	M9	23
	M9	153
	M9	161
TELL	AM	130
	AM	135
	AM	303
	AM	358
	EMQ	1

Word	Ref	No.
TELL	ETL	3
	ETL	15
	EM	19
	SLN	9
	EMK	11
	PKK	10
	PTC	37
	CM	37
	PUF	13
	AA	856
	AA	857
	MD	20
	SAA	384
	EDG	23
	SDG	1
	RL	287
	EC	36
	L3	177
	L3	183
	L3	218
	T23	56
	T27	68
	FS2	1
	FS2	11
	FS2	13
	HAP	587
	HAP	610
	HAP	1639
	HAP	1714
	HAP	1720
	STS3	30
	PMS	4
	PMS	32
	EH	7
	EH	32
	J3	103
	J6	273
	J6	529
	J10	144
	J10	235
	P1	102
	P1	105
	P1	209
	P1	239
	P2	35
	P2	122
	P3	165
	P3	225
	P4	5
	P5	37
	P5	152
	P5	259
	P6	78
	P6	157
	M1	512
	EHC	10
	VP1	27
	VP1	77
	VP3	162
	VP3	163
	G2	150
	G2	169
	G4	646
	AE1	457
	AE1	573
	AE2	10
	AE2	15
	AE2	94
	AE2	201
	AE2	488
	AE2	1002
	AE3	54
	AE3	239
	AE3	439
	AE3	488
	AE3	552
	AE3	799
	AE4	273
	AE5	925
	AE5	1030
	AE6	528
	AE6	717
	AE7	270
	AE7	362
	AE7	365
	AE7	614
	AE7	618
	AE7	634
	AE8	112
	AE8	461
	AE9	90
	AE9	145
	AE9	703
	AE9	1002
	AE10	52
	AE10	687
	AE10	1179
TELL	AE11	177
	AE11	272
	AE11	383
	AE12	725
	OAL	186
	OAL	334
	OAL	443
	OAL	450
	OAL	496
	OAL	645
	OAL	702
	DO	116
	KT1	47
	KT1	123
	KT1	363
	KT1	406
	KT1	516
	KT3	149
	KT3	153
	KT3	1002
	M8	247
	B	432
	B	635
	CAM	210
	HIF	114
	HIF	451
	HIF	693
	C	1
	C	136
	C	409
	C	552
	TH	395
	M11	16
	FL	82
	FL	155
	FL	223
	FL	477
	M12	226
	M12	246
	M12	599
	AU	331
	AU	387
	WB	154
	WB	195
	WB	202
	WB	236
	WB	240
	WB	262
	WB	298
	WB	362
	M15	453
	P3	195
TELLEST		
TELLING	EPC	28
	T27	103
	J6	704
	ELT	26
	HIF	505
TELLS	EMM	16
	PKK	23
	M1	895
	G4	537
	G4	572
	AE1	489
	AE3	209
	AE4	111
	AE6	1231
	AE8	455
	OAL	315
	OAL	344
	ETP	3
TELON	AE7	1015
TEMISES	M15	66
TEMPE	G2	695
	G4	451
TEMPER	SMA	85
	CM	12
	AA	662
	HAP	1445
	HAP	2088
	HAP	2525
	J10	81
	P3	233
	M1	59
	M1	574
	G1	88
	G1	565
	G2	471
	AE2	482
	AE9	413
	AE11	714
	KT3	1139
TEMPERATE	DC	10
	MD	248
	P3	215
	OAL	317
TEMPERED	L4	215
	HH	18
	M1	105
	G1	259
	AE4	628
	AE7	881
	AE8	699
	AE8	824
	AE9	1011
	AE12	137
	GP	26
TEMPERING	G1	162
	AE12	618
TEMPERS	HS	97
	AM	459
	AA	948
	M1	811
TEMPE'S	M1	770
TEMPEST	AR	8
	LC	127
	PT	16
	SM2	5
	DA	40
	DA	51
	MD	254
	SAA	144
	L2	2
	L5	1
	TA	25
	TA	192
	TA	390
	BR	263
	G1	577
	G3	409
	G4	447
	AE1	721
	AE3	678
	AE5	20
	AE5	30
	AE5	613
	AE6	1089
	AE7	302
	AE7	810
	AE7	860
	AE8	29
	KT2	538
	M8	280
	B	174
	M11	43
	M11	118
	M11	158
	M11	198
	CI	337
	CI	375
TEMPESTS	AR	122
	AR	269
	LC	144
	AM	117
	AM	243
	AM	1004
	PNH	53
	CM	92
	HP	228
	DA	184
	L1	7
	H2	76
	BR	351
	M13	96
	G1	445
	G1	585
	G1	606
	G4	608
	AE1	81
	AE1	98
	AE1	118
	AE1	320
	AE1	457
	AE1	519
	AE1	799
	AE1	834
	AE4	448
	AE5	1075
	AE6	459
	AE7	417
	AE7	971
	AE8	466
	AE10	52
	AE11	1168
	AE12	992
	OAL	621
	M11	279
	ESK	17
TEMPESTUOUS	UDH	90
	CM	15
	CM	76
	PUF	19

Word	Ref	No.	Word	Ref	No.	Word	Ref	No.
TEMPESTUOUS	H29	54	TEMPLES	VP10	40	TEMPTS	VP10	35
	M1	72		G1	480		G4	750
	G1	501		G4	542	TEN	VHH	45
	G2	220		AE1	104		ELN	6
	AE4	171		AE1	399		EKK	16
	M11	194		AE1	827		DA	58
	GP	65		AE2	472		AA	123
TEMPLE	SMA	45		AE2	492		AA	552
	DC	47		AE2	932		MF	208
	DC	57		AE4	287		AT	20
	SAA	398		AE4	302		AT	25
	SAA	146		AE4	965		T18	62
	EKA	3		AE4	986		GE	81
	EL	302		AE5	75		HAP	2591
	J10	447		AE5	97		SKA4	11
	M1	503		AE5	177		SKA4	12
	M9	184		AE5	354		SKA4	13
	M9	202		AE5	580		SKA4	14
	SFL	19		AE5	995		SKA4	15
	HI	18		AE5	1110		SKA4	16
	MC	14		AE6	904		SKA4	17
	G3	19		AE6	1070		J6	196
	G3	35		AE7	130		P6	185
	G4	782		AE7	303		VP3	107
	G4	792		AE7	588		VP4	75
	AE1	578		AE7	1038		G3	100
	AE1	625		AE8	366		AE1	527
	AE1	635		AE8	901		AE1	895
	AE2	220		AE8	951		AE2	262
	AE2	776		AE9	561		AE7	471
	AE2	969		AE9	800		AE9	679
	AE3	105		AE9	867		AE11	497
	AE3	112		AE9	1091		AE12	1107
	AE3	356		AE10	1276		OAL	496
	AE3	696		AE11	867		OAL	545
	AE3	706		AE12	247		KT3	55
	AE3	717		AE12	787		KT3	649
	AE4	663		OAL	653		TJD	91
	AE4	700		AF	145		M8	323
	AE5	991		KT1	214		M10	98
	AE6	17		KT3	86		M15	630
	AE6	61		M8	243		PTP	13
	AE6	106		M11	241		EMKG	28
	AE6	149		FL	243	TENACIOUS	G2	184
	AE7	266		FL	263		G4	58
	AE7	620		FL	354		AE12	1121
	AE7	842		FL	540		TJD	190
	AE7	961		M12	185		HIF	184
	AE7	1066		M12	383		FL	280
	AE8	868		M15	196		CI	282
	AE8	952	TEMPT	AM	456	TENANT'S	PAL	32
	AE11	725		HP	97	TENANTS	AA	776
	AE11	1146		DA	56		HAP	2211
	OAL	80		AA	625	TEND	AM	580
	OAL	84		AA	916		AT	3
	OAL	94		AA	1009		T27	9
	DO	123		OE	41		HAP	60
	KT1	71		L1	19		HAP	1606
	KT2	116		HAP	735		P3	116
	KT2	459		P5	213		M1	108
	KT2	471		M1	807		VP5	16
	KT2	526		M13	113		VP9	28
	KT2	545		HI	85		G2	402
	KT2	548		G3	123		G4	176
	KT2	618		G3	581		AE1	82
	KT3	197		AE2	616		AE7	826
	KT3	266		AE4	105		AE10	163
	KT3	292		AE4	452		AE12	1167
	KT3	350		AE5	920		KT3	636
	BP	159		AE5	955		KT3	887
	BP	180		AE6	214		CAM	35
TEMPLE'S	AE2	553		AE8	865		M15	367
	AE3	370		AE9	48	TENDER	AM	550
	AE8	868		AE9	897		AM	879
TEMPLES	HS	25		AE11	231		AM	952
	RH	58		AE11	390		AM	983
	LC	22		KT3	141		AM	1135
	AM	860		TJD	168		PWGR	1
	SCG1	10		HIF	86		PC2	14
	PFD	19		HIF	575		PLG	27
	MF	126		HIF	780		CM	136
	AT	122		CI	386		HP	257
	L4	99	TEMPTATION	ELN	7		DA	87
	T18	19		EDS	34		ETG	13
	EJG	4	TEMPTATIONS	WB	505		D	42
	J1	170	TEMPTED	H3	17		MF	16
	J3	309		HAP	2575		MF	77
	J10	62	TEMPTER	GP	106		SAA	1050
	P2	10	TEMPTING	AM	692		RL	404
	P2	64		MD	111		AT	8
	P2	106		P3	222		AT	35
	M1	1045		P3	223		T23	29
	M9	34		B	172		HAP	382
	M13	226		GP	64		HAP	440
	VCS	6	TEMPTS	AM	151		HAP	1257
	VP6	35		J6	692		HAP	1753

Word	Ref	No.
TENDER	HAP	2518
	BR	202
	PTS	28
	EL	166
	EL	220
	EL	346
	ODA	38
	SSH	5
	J6	131
	J6	278
	M1	406
	M1	650
	M1	685
	M1	901
	M1	978
	M13	129
	HI	45
	VP1	9
	VP1	31
	VP3	16
	VP3	130
	VP3	159
	VP6	3
	VP6	53
	VP9	67
	VP10	9
	VP10	72
	G1	114
	G1	597
	G1	180
	G2	18
	G2	104
	G2	363
	G2	367
	G2	451
	G2	468
	G2	497
	G2	513
	G2	576
	G2	743
	G3	250
	G3	297
	G3	464
	G3	496
	G3	501
	G3	707
	G4	210
	G4	297
	G4	442
	G4	502
	AE1	534
	AE2	189
	AE2	282
	AE2	432
	AE2	548
	AE2	919
	AE2	954
	AE4	421
	AE4	591
	AE4	606
	AE4	751
	AE5	449
	AE5	1019
	AE6	577
	AE7	680
	AE8	840
	AE9	266
	AE9	578
	AE9	765
	AE10	150
	AE10	730
	AE10	1150
	AE11	818
	AE11	867
	AE12	169
	AE12	625
	AE12	647
	AE12	1265
	OAL	9
	OAL	149
	OAE2	44
	OAE2	55
	KT1	94
	KT2	59
	KT2	312
	KT2	330
	KT3	147
	KT3	225
	KT3	984
	M8	31
	M8	269
	B	436
	CAM	112
	CAM	345
	C	421
	TH	115
TENDER	TH	183
	FL	7
	FL	594
	WB	500
	M15	585
	M15	601
TENDERNESS	AA	947
	SAA	150
	TA	249
	B	645
	EWR	16
TENDING	GK	173
	M15	314
TENDRILS	KT2	60
	M15	164
TENDS	AM	1020
	L4	6
	EL	152
	P4	35
	P5	171
	G3	541
	AE5	367
	AE6	728
	AE7	330
	M11	152
	M1	693
	AE2	27
	AE2	333
	HIF	59
	HIF	618
	M12	150
	AU	281
TENEDOS	AA	158
	M15	245
TENEMENT	AE5	985
TENEMENTS	J6	357
TENFOLD	HAP	537
TEN-HORNED	PO	8
TENNIS	RL	330
TENOR	M1	5
	G2	276
	G2	461
	AE1	96
	AE12	305
	KT3	1148
	BP	178
	AE2	741
TENT	AE9	293
	AE9	505
	AE9	666
	AE10	219
	AE12	569
	KT1	158
	HIF	279
	HIF	428
	HIF	482
	TH	234
	TH	275
	AU	84
TENTH	G1	379
	AE9	194
	HIF	79
	M11	166
	FL	225
	M12	31
TENTS	M12	106
	SAA	718
	G3	487
	AE1	657
	AE8	800
	AE11	375
	AE12	598
	HIF	72
	HIF	660
	TH	59
	AU	510
TEPID	AE3	93
	KT2	41
	M15	312
TERENCE	MS	15
TEREUS	P5	25
	VP6	113
	AE11	999
	M12	477
TERM	ETL	20
	TA	250
	HAP	1959
	HAP	2117
	AE1	379
	AE2	891
	AE6	511
	AE11	201
	AE12	303
	CI	639
	AE12	168
	KT3	504
TERMINATE		
TERMINATE	TJD	10
TERMINATED	AE4	499
TERMS	AM	501
	PMQ	17
	HP	29
	AA	677
	RL	94
	RL	262
	ER	75
	TA	72
	HAP	412
	HAP	1084
	HAP	2060
	J16	65
	P6	124
	AE4	947
	AE4	320
	AE6	152
	AE9	810
	AE9	935
	AE10	222
	AE10	1232
	AE11	492
	AE11	1043
	AE12	476
	CAM	236
	WB	110
	M15	603
	CI	275
	EMKG	32
	EWR	25
TERRACE	AE2	404
TERRESTRIAL	M1	7
	AE6	975
	AE6	993
	HIF	556
TERRIBLE	L2	48
	AE6	389
	AE9	691
	AE11	668
	AE9	667
TERRIBLY	AE10	1244
TERRIFIES	AE12	1236
TERROR	EOE	9
	AA	1009
	SAA	567
	SAA	231
	SAA	73
	BR	139
	P3	67
	M13	19
	AE3	40
	AE6	155
	AE8	292
	AE8	392
	AE9	618
	AE11	1282
	AE12	505
	AE12	603
	KT3	93
	KT3	302
	CAM	207
	HIF	711
	C	735
	M12	812
TERRORS	AE5	844
TERSE	GE	76
	P1	181
TERTIAN	C	182
TEST	EAZ	34
	MD	103
	RL	338
	TA	502
	AK	81
	HAP	602
	HAP	1992
	HAP	2029
	HAP	2032
	HAP	2047
	HAP	2076
	HAP	2086
	HAP	2124
	HAP	2176
	HAP	2486
	BR	157
	P1	15
	P2	7
TESTAMENT	HAP	948
	HAP	953
	J6	305
TESTAMENTS	RL	283
TESTATOR	PLT	39
TESTICLES	J6	663
TESTIFIED	B	373
	CI	108
TESTIMONY	AE2	583

THETIS'	AE2	261
	HIF	8
THICK	HS	56
	RH	75
	AM	311
	AM	478
	AM	497
	AM	953
	ETC	6
	MF	110
	SAA	414
	SAA	476
	SAA	711
	L4	123
	L4	267
	HAP	1873
	HAP	2341
	EL	145
	J1	15
	J1	182
	P3	21
	M1	37
	M1	64
	M13	227
	PLT	2
	VP8	49
	G2	329
	G2	371
	G3	134
	G4	682
	AE1	617
	AE4	432
	AE4	581
	AE4	649
	AE6	208
	AE6	411
	AE6	428
	AE6	431
	AE6	959
	AE7	41
	AE7	780
	AE7	1025
	AE8	141
	AE9	518
	AE10	521
	AE10	1140
	AE11	614
	AE11	908
	AE11	1268
	AE12	427
	AE12	1038
	MM	36
	KT1	230
	KT1	578
	KT3	71
	KT3	624
	B	102
	B	161
	FL	67
	FL	86
	FL	218
	FL	345
	WB	29
	WB	536
	M15	632
THICKEN	AE9	1063
THICKENED	G4	387
THICKENING	AE9	40
	AE12	338
	AE12	383
THICKENS	AE9	908
	AE11	1298
THICKER	PMM	7
	CM	55
	G4	118
	AE7	994
	AE7	996
	CAM	363
THICKEST	HS	133
	AE6	165
	AE8	340
	AE9	684
	AE9	746
	AE10	532
	OAE2	70
	M12	368
THICKET	TH	103
	TH	261
THICKETS	VP10	83
	G3	426
	KT1	495
	M8	145
THICKSET	M13	156
	M8	23
THICK-SKULLED	P1	162
THICK-SPREAD	KT2	23

THIEF	JH	7
	PC2	13
	PLB	34
	VP3	26
	G3	619
	KT1	493
	KT1	494
	AU	38
	WB	472
	GP	59
THIEFS	G4	168
THIEVES	PRL	27
	HAP	1135
	HAP	1641
	J6	27
	J10	34
THIGH	AE8	828
	AE10	478
	AE10	1116
	AE10	1130
	AE12	1343
	M8	130
THIGHS	L4	72
	P5	6
	M1	712
	G3	90
	G3	782
	G4	267
	G4	438
	AE11	735
	AE11	1141
	AE11	1186
	AE12	637
	OAL	183
	OAE2	55
	CAM	339
	HIF	63
	HIF	631
	M15	566
THIN	DC	39
	AM	503
	PLG	24
	EUF	15
	AA	164
	AA	443
	SAA	414
	L4	62
	L4	267
	H29	64
	J6	22
	J6	156
	P3	22
	P4	102
	M1	461
	VP3	156
	G2	544
	G2	554
	G3	718
	AE1	73
	AE1	242
	AE1	529
	AE3	772
	AE4	425
	AE6	419
	AE7	129
	AE8	133
	AE9	179
	AE9	555
	AE9	676
	AE10	184
	AE10	1160
	AE11	1058
	M8	316
	FL	390
	M15	319
	M15	616
	PMK	22
THING	AM	79
	ELN	15
	CM	32
	HP	98
	PUO3	22
	AA	170
	PPC	6
	MD	195
	L1	28
	L3	24
	L3	86
	L3	124
	L4	49
	T27	72
	HAP	420
	HAP	422
	HAP	645
	HAP	956
	PDS	31

THING	J6	2
	J10	112
	J10	389
	J10	530
	P1	130
	P3	156
	P4	41
	P5	138
	M13	178
	AE2	763
	AE3	774
	AE4	819
	AE9	264
	B	323
	M10	12
	CAM	384
	AU	217
	WB	179
	WB	275
	WB	465
	M15	222
	M15	391
	M15	393
	M15	617
THINGS	RH	99
	SMA	116
	LC	97
	LC	133
	LCA	38
	AM	618
	EWGR	29
	EWGR	35
	EMM	16
	PT	23
	PCG1	21
	PMQW	13
	PMQW	20
	EUO	7
	PLG	14
	HP	76
	HP	84
	AA	83
	AA	532
	AA	656
	AA	935
	EPC	12
	MD	85
	MF	1
	SAA	882
	EDG	33
	EDG	36
	RL	300
	RL	369
	RL	432
	L3	35
	L3	142
	L3	156
	L3	166
	L3	169
	L3	171
	H2	67
	TA	399
	AK	160
	HAP	120
	HAP	321
	HAP	768
	HAP	884
	HAP	1823
	BR	198
	STS2	7
	PMS	14
	EKA	37
	J1	61
	J1	222
	J3	140
	J3	300
	J10	9
	J10	84
	J10	207
	J10	287
	J10	499
	J10	555
	M1	726
	M9	15
	M9	113
	M9	131
	M9	132
	VP9	70
	G3	194
	G4	5
	G4	256
	AE1	133
	AE2	119
	AE2	976
	AE2	1024
	AE3	244

THINGS

AE3	380
AE3	484
AE4	271
AE4	802
AE6	101
AE6	1239
AE7	55
AE7	345
AE8	414
AE9	215
AE10	1178
AE12	41
AE12	1167
OAL	254
OAL	257
OAL	406
OAL	453
OAL	533
OAL	549
OAL	839
OAL	866
OAE2	53
KT1	24
KT1	327
KT1	423
KT1	431
KT3	206
KT3	636
KT3	865
KT3	886
M8	62
B	500
CAM	226
HIF	103
HIF	123
HIF	213
C	154
C	206
C	327
C	333
C	531
TH	218
M11	297
M11	338
FL	594
M12	59
M12	80
M12	226
M12	343
WB	413
WB	475
WB	516
M15	97
M15	220
M15	239
M15	274
M15	359
M15	374
M15	388
M15	706
M15	503
M15	578
CI	12
CI	168
SMP	70

THINK

LC	16
LC	123
EWG	3
PIE	25
AM	296
AM	1040
PMQ	35
PMQ	49
PA	43
EEL	37
PTL	6
ECG1	25
PCG2	28
ECG2	17
PFD	18
EMQW	1
A	7
A	12
PCD	30
PUO1	45
ENH	5
PUO2	3
PAZ	30
ML	12
ML	41
PAL	24
POE	18
POE	24
EOE	25
EOE	27
PCB	4
CM	5
CM	144
HP	12
HP	39
HP	62
HP	120
HP	124
HP	142
DA	16
DA	71
PR	26
AA	106
AA	534
AA	759
PLB	49
MD	101
MD	236
MD	238
SAA	423
SAA	552
SAA	807
PK	27
EK	23
EK	30
EK	31
EK	34
PDG	11
EDG	27
SDG	7
RL	65
RL	218
RL	271
RL	318
EC	34
EC	22
MO	2
L3	308
L4	125
L4	241
T23	69
T27	97
PAA	20
HAP	242
HAP	315
HAP	316
HAP	925
HAP	975
HAP	1000
HAP	1197
HAP	1210
HAP	1423
HAP	1467
HAP	1528
HAP	1656
HAP	1690
HAP	1711
HAP	1808
HAP	1866
HAP	1994
HAP	2129
HAP	2498
BR	98
BR	101
BR	109
BR	261
PP	44
STS2	10
SKA6	5
LS	15
EL	59
EL	314
OD	11
OD	55
PSH	1
PSH	36
J3	156
J3	215
J3	438
J3	474
J6	232
J6	266
J6	386
J6	424
J6	482
J6	828
J10	480
J16	40
J16	48
P1	148
P1	192
P2	113
P5	151
P5	230
P6	145
M1	689
M13	155
HI	179
PLT	38
GK	13
GK	25
GK	72
GK	159
VP3	33
G1	563
G4	320
AE2	56
AE3	578
AE4	46
AE7	512
AE7	513
AE7	562
AE7	970
AE8	534
AE9	265
AE10	112
AE10	141
AE10	857
AE11	194
AE11	432
AE11	556
AE11	637
AE11	1013
AE12	97
AE12	225
AE12	1351
OAL	459
OAL	466
OAL	495
OAL	535
OAL	695
OAE2	25
AF	104
KT1	595
KT2	287
KT2	371
KT3	205
M8	43
TJD	70
TJD	201
M8	224
BP	8
M10	28
HIF	386
HIF	422
C	572
C	783
TH	49
M11	370
AU	153
WB	163
WB	496
M15	207
M15	222
M15	574
CI	15
PWR	34

THINKEST

RL	71
J6	77
J6	381
P1	242
P2	45
P2	87
P3	32
P4	81
VP10	42
AE6	508
AE9	258
OAL	354

THINKING

PSF	37
AA	552
SAA	422
PD	35
HAP	601
ETS	1
J6	145
KT1	228
B	247
CAM	188
C	239

THINKS

EIE	13
AM	548
PWGR	4
PWGR	18
PTL	7
PCG1	36
PCG2	14
PCB	8
PR	38
SAA	337
RL	42
PD	39
L3	62

Word	Code	No.	Word	Code	No.	Word	Code	No.
THINKS	L3	104	THIRST	HIF	294	THOUGHT	AA	65
	L3	280		AU	328		AA	91
	L4	121		CI	86		AA	130
	J6	590	THIRSTS	G4	578		AA	142
	J10	137	THIRSTY	AM	437		AA	433
	J10	498		P4	69		AA	460
	P1	268		VP5	38		AA	496
	VP5	12		VP6	58		AA	505
	VP8	51		G1	105		AA	510
	AE6	615		G1	162		AA	882
	AE8	31		G2	484		AA	972
	AE10	1110		G3	727		EPC	6
	AE11	830		G4	146		MF	150
	AE12	1094		AE1	1034		SAA	22
	OAL	679		AE4	58		SAA	46
	OAL	806	THIRTEEN	M9	68		SAA	52
	OAL	833	THIRTIETH	EL	296		SAA	135
	OAL	884	THIRTY	J6	257		SAA	516
	OAE2	39		AE1	366		SAA	948
	OAE2	80		AE3	503		EK	10
	MG	27		AE8	62		EK	20
	KT2	185		AE8	63		PDG	10
	KT2	187		AE8	114		RL	29
	M10	76		AE10	306		RL	391
	M11	187	THISTLES	MD	146		RL	416
	WB	338		G1	225		OE	28
THIN-LEAVED	G2	96		G3	591		L3	58
THINLY	AE9	312		AE2	342		L3	97
	MM	41	THOAS,	AE10	584		L3	104
THINNER	SMP	67	THOAS'				L3	105
	SMP	71	THONG	AE9	798		L4	28
THINNESS	HAP	2569	THONGS	AE2	356		TA	333
THINNEST	KT2	197		AE7	1011		TA	415
THINS	HAP	815		KT3	461		TA	438
THIRD	HAP	1153		M12	579		AK	89
	EMI	6	THORN	ODA	2		HAP	112
	BR	244		M1	685		HAP	512
	EL	339		VP3	138		HAP	539
	J3	326		VP4	34		HAP	566
	J6	95		G2	167		HAP	597
	P2	27		G2	572		HAP	1242
	EHC	13		AE9	519		HAP	1726
	G4	459		TH	112		HAP	2056
	AE3	159		WB	44		HAP	2100
	AE5	349		GP	94		HAP	2109
	AE5	412	THORNS	TA	358		HAP	2276
	AE5	443		HAP	382		HAP	2295
	AE5	658		VP5	58		HAP	2339
	AE5	713		AE3	777		HAP	2376
	AE6	1187		AE11	794		HAP	2513
	AE7	74		KT1	192		SSC	21
	AE9	870		B	143		EMI	3
	AE10	255		B	150		BR	98
	AE11	939	THORNY	RL	32		BR	196
	KT2	618		G3	490		BR	286
	KT3	456		AE2	642		EL	102
	KT3	935		AE11	777		EL	331
	KT3	975		M8	23		J6	109
	BP	94	THORO'	AE8	349		J6	848
	HIF	366	THOROUGHFARE	M12	79		P3	11
	C	243	THOUGHT	AR	27		M1	99
	C	454		AR	89		M1	253
	M11	337		AR	184		M1	975
	FL	271		AR	199		M9	31
	M12	132		RH	27		M9	69
	M12	259		RH	97		M9	84
	AU	40		DC	29		M9	124
	WB	419		DC	47		M13	18
	M15	347		PWG	56		HI	10
	CI	327		EWG	17		PLT	30
THIRD-DAYS	EUF	15		EIE	26		GK	10
THIRST	SAA	1110		AM	379		GK	72
	L3	106		AM	1037		VP1	29
	L3	311		AM	1104		VP9	3
	L4	55		PMQ	1		G1	660
	L4	64		PWGR	15		G4	322
	HAP	527		EMM	12		AE1	1004
	J10	220		ETL	24		AE2	31
	M9	144		PCG1	24		AE2	136
	M13	32		ECG1	35		AE2	501
	VP5	74		SCG1	4		AE2	556
	VP8	39		EM	23		AE2	579
	VP8	124		PLN	40		AE2	768
	G1	53		ELN	14		AE3	50
	G2	734		EUO	5		AE3	247
	G3	176		PAZ	25		AE4	10
	G3	201		EAZ	3		AE4	414
	G3	470		EAZ	9		AE4	605
	G3	509		ML	3		AE4	669
	G3	608		PTC	16		AE4	724
	G3	659		HP	22		AE6	925
	AE2	140		HP	169		AE7	182
	AE8	424		DA	98		AE7	621
	AE9	476		DA	99		AE8	463
	AE11	566		PUO3	34		AE8	975
	AE11	748		AA	56		AE9	3

Word	Ref	No.
THOUGHT	AE9	176
	AE9	246
	AE10	886
	AE10	914
	AE10	966
	AE10	1032
	AE10	764
	AE10	1167
	AE10	1194
	AE10	1248
	AE11	190
	AE11	362
	AE11	772
	AE11	1051
	AE12	971
	OAL	266
	OAL	294
	OAL	529
	OAL	577
	OAL	794
	OAL	799
	OAL	823
	OAE1	1
	MM	47
	MFL	15
	MFL	18
	DO	12
	KT1	438
	KT1	565
	KT2	66
	KT2	75
	KT2	324
	KT2	376
	KT2	512
	KT2	561
	KT2	660
	KT3	1021
	KT3	1152
	M8	91
	M8	136
	B	12
	B	94
	B	223
	B	308
	B	384
	B	467
	B	486
	B	536
	B	584
	M10	15
	M10	23
	M10	28
	M10	77
	CAM	142
	CAM	254
	HIF	546
	HIF	680
	C	266
	C	309
	C	599
	C	622
	C	758
	C	778
	TH	320
	TH	344
	TH	362
	M11	349
	M11	377
	FL	119
	M12	38
	AU	38
	AU	423
	AU	427
	AU	523
	WB	78
	WB	135
	WB	167
	WB	296
	WB	475
	WB	502
	M15	499
	GP	125
	CI	12
	CI	85
	CI	162
	CI	321
	CI	478
	PTP	26
THOUGHTFUL	SAA	526
	RL	235
	AE7	347
	OAE1	33
THOUGHTLESS	MF	26
	MF	27
	SAA	480
	TA	320
THOUGHTLESS	HAP	72
	G3	668
	AE3	825
	AE4	305
	AE7	606
	AE9	524
	MG	19
	B	245
THOUGHTS	HS	28
	AR	71
	AR	280
	SMA	100
	VHH	36
	AM	550
	HP	70
	HP	78
	HP	250
	AA	25
	SAA	60
	SAA	125
	SAA	159
	SAA	627
	SAA	667
	SAA	792
	SAA	847
	RL	36
	RL	226
	L2	49
	L3	199
	L3	236
	L3	266
	L4	114
	AK	132
	HAP	315
	HAP	1206
	HAP	1795
	EL	311
	MS	16
	P2	36
	P6	29
	M1	352
	M1	853
	HI	137
	HI	183
	GK	68
	VP10	90
	AE1	747
	AE1	935
	AE4	799
	AE4	921
	AE5	20
	AE5	399
	AE5	918
	AE6	454
	AE12	1322
	OAL	532
	OAL	686
	OAE1	23
	MFL	29
	KT2	33
	KT2	392
	B	35
	B	170
	B	172
	B	296
	B	541
	CAM	33
	CAM	51
	CAM	65
	CAM	79
	CAM	99
	HIF	226
	HIF	459
	HIF	592
	HIF	756
	C	149
	M11	184
	M11	338
	M11	444
	ESK	23
THOUGHTS'	DA	27
THOUSAND	VHH	45
	EOE	23
	HP	76
	HP	104
	DA	58
	DA	135
	EPF	22
	AA	552
	PLB	42
	PLB	54
	MF	208
	RL	211
	RL	421
	RL	422
	L3	193
THOUSAND	L3	321
	T18	62
	FS3	5
	HAP	1816
	HAP	2591
	ETS	22
	SKA6	13
	EL	79
	J3	239
	J3	14
	J6	196
	P3	50
	P6	185
	VP2	26
	AE1	579
	AE1	693
	AE2	262
	AE2	445
	AE3	935
	AE4	1004
	AE6	40
	AE6	164
	AE6	1013
	AE7	471
	AE7	904
	AE7	1003
	AE8	387
	AE9	184
	AE10	245
	AE10	259
	AE11	91
	AE12	1290
	AE12	1322
	OAL	385
	KT2	585
	KT2	608
	M8	64
	BP	27
	BP	28
	M12	9
	M12	63
	M12	65
	M12	147
	M12	237
	AU	150
THOUSANDS	AM	464
	AM	701
	AE5	99
	KT3	1078
THRACE	J6	527
	G3	143
	G3	542
	AE10	489
	KT2	527
	KT3	39
	KT3	67
THRACIA	AE3	21
	AE3	72
THRACIAN	J3	142
	VP4	66
	VP6	46
	VP10	93
	G4	754
	AE1	442
	AE3	47
	AE5	409
	AE5	705
	AE5	738
	AE6	877
	AE9	54
	AE11	975
	AE12	127
	AE12	132
	KT2	181
	KT3	47
	CAM	14
	AU	390
THRACIANS	AE8	966
	M15	471
THRACIA'S	G3	702
	KT3	298
THRASH	J10	194
	VP2	73
	G1	400
	G1	409
THRASHING	G1	258
	G1	278
THREAD	AM	719
	L3	318
	OAL	786
	KT2	603
THREADBARE	EAL	9
	P1	101
THREAT	AM	241
	AM	457
	AA	141

Word	Ref	No.	Word	Ref	No.	Word	Ref	No.
THREAT	AA	801	THREE	AM	424	THREE	FL	264
	SAA	862		AM	471		FL	536
	BR	57		AM	519		M12	58
	VP4	17		PWGR	20		WB	403
	AE2	232		ENH	32		CI	571
	AE4	70		PCB	27		PTP	19
	AE4	128		HP	116	THREEFOLD	AE4	740
	AE8	643		EUF	8	THREE-LEGGED	UDH	81
	AE9	815		AA	601	THREE-MOUTHED	G4	692
	KT2	255		PRH	25	THREE-PENCE	PUO3	9
	M12	324		D	22	THREESCORE	EC	43
THREATEN	AM	104		GE	47		J6	276
	MD	280		HAP	79		TJD	91
	H29	91		HAP	1148	THRESHING	MF	52
	J3	410		HAP	1233		P6	57
	J16	29		HAP	1488	THRESHING-FLOOR	M8	36
	G2	647		HAP	1525		BR	176
	AE10	554		HAP	2202	THRESHOLD	L4	173
	AU	353		EMI	1		T23	34
THREATENED	EWG	5		BR	31		T23	54
	SAA	66		BR	231		J10	386
	L3	244		BR	232		VP8	131
	AE2	126		PP	16		VP8	155
	AE2	180		PMS	10		G3	493
	AE3	507		J1	75		AE1	628
	AE3	710		J1	238		AE2	917
	AE3	890		J6	209		AE7	481
	AE6	1182		J6	276		AE11	415
	AE9	89		J10	248		M12	393
	AE10	1256		J10	392	THRESHOLDS	AE2	670
	AE12	784		P1	4	THREW	SMM2	4
	KT2	551		P1	253		PEL	28
	TH	96		P3	175		EDG	4
	M12	394		P3	192		AT	94
	CI	376		P5	178		TA	378
THREATENEST	HIF	242		P5	274		HAP	2015
THREATENING	AM	155		EHC	5		M1	553
	AM	888		VP3	161		M1	900
	DA	71		VP8	102		AE2	64
	SAA	557		VP8	107		AE2	742
	T23	105		G4	712		AE3	758
	TA	10		G4	713		AE5	228
	HAP	2155		AE1	154		AE5	533
	G1	692		AE1	159		AE5	839
	AE2	135		AE1	260		AE5	1110
	AE2	639		AE1	370		AE6	950
	AE3	678		AE3	266		AE7	487
	AE4	605		AE3	267		AE8	293
	AE5	16		AE3	847		AE8	513
	AE6	1090		AE4	415		AE9	60
	AE7	650		AE4	741		AE9	692
	AE8	311		AE5	157		AE9	777
	AE9	861		AE5	158		AE9	798
	AE9	952		AE5	321		AE9	1003
	AE10	281		AE5	405		AE9	1029
	AE10	380		AE5	731		AE10	465
	AE10	1148		AE5	732		AE10	476
	AE11	927		AE5	758		AE10	559
	AE11	1112		AE5	1009		AE10	667
	AE12	558		AE6	484		AE10	672
	AE12	714		AE6	570		AE10	725
	KT2	543		AE7	378		AE10	807
	KT2	602		AE8	567		AE10	1059
	CAM	136		AE8	747		AE10	1099
	AU	263		AE8	951		AE11	842
	M15	39		AE8	953		AE11	952
THREATENINGS	AE4	636		AE9	502		AE11	1152
	AE10	512		AE10	253		AE12	403
THREATENS	J6	534		AE10	264		AE12	541
	AE4	61		AE10	290		AE12	712
	AE9	994		AE10	487		AE12	739
THREATINGS	AM	1077		AE10	488		AE12	744
THREATS	SCD1	20		AE10	1114		AE12	1307
	G3	660		AE12	295		AE12	1334
	AE1	407		AE12	744		OAL	630
	AE2	315		AE12	1225		OAE2	9
	AE2	398		OAL	44		KT3	180
	AE2	851		OAL	283		KT3	987
	AE4	521		DO	15		M8	109
	AE5	592		DO	67		M8	113
	AE6	745		DO	164		M8	185
	AE9	1075		KT1	607		M8	189
	AE10	815		KT3	540		CAM	198
	AE10	1262		KT3	732		HIF	69
	AE11	1129		KT3	1060		HIF	359
	AE12	1101		KT3	1061		HIF	795
	AE12	1295		KT3	1077		M12	127
	CAM	209		M8	294		M12	168
	HIF	337		M8	305		M12	211
	M15	430		C	13		M12	347
	GP	34		C	14		M12	495
THREE	UDH	82		C	187		M12	515
	AR	239		C	486		M12	585
	PWG	39		TH	56		M12	594
	AM	129		M11	341		M12	659
	AM	167		FL	139		M12	675

Word	Ref	No.
THREW	AU	476
THRICE	UDH	41
	PEL	33
	DA	110
	PSF	43
	T23	83
	T23	84
	J1	62
	P2	33
	VCS	9
	VP8	103
	VP8	104
	G1	375
	G1	377
	G1	557
	G2	550
	G4	553
	G4	554
	AE1	137
	AE1	166
	AE1	363
	AE1	610
	AE1	676
	AE2	234
	AE2	1077
	AE2	1078
	AE3	94
	AE3	392
	AE3	599
	AE3	741
	AE3	742
	AE3	743
	AE4	738
	AE4	988
	AE4	989
	AE4	990
	AE6	327
	AE6	329
	AE6	681
	AE6	950
	AE6	951
	AE7	191
	AE7	192
	AE8	268
	AE8	303
	AE8	305
	AE8	306
	AE8	693
	AE8	694
	AE8	695
	AE8	748
	AE9	798
	AE10	968
	AE10	970
	AE10	1251
	AE10	1268
	AE11	240
	AE11	288
	AE11	290
	AE11	291
	AE11	319
	AE11	320
	AE12	236
	OAL	619
	OAL	620
	AF	68
	KT3	496
	KT3	732
	KT3	992
	KT3	993
	KT3	994
	KT3	995
	M8	267
	M8	293
	M8	294
	M8	352
	B	155
	B	227
	B	306
	M10	71
	CAM	275
	CAM	276
	HIF	372
	C	245
	M11	12
	M15	467
THRICE-DEVOTED	VP8	103
THRICE-REPEATED	B	226
THRID	HAP	1572
	VP10	83
THRIDS	KT1	495
THRIFT	EL	75
	P6	50
	TH	239
THRIFTY	AA	390
THRIVE	AR	24
THRIVE	PAZ	27
	PTC	23
	EUF	19
	MD	184
	PK	3
	EC	19
	ER	54
	TA	300
	TA	373
	HAP	232
	HAP	2043
	HAP	2229
	HAP	2449
	PLT	42
	G1	79
	G2	91
	G2	601
	OAL	153
	TJD	136
	M15	127
	EWR	6
THRIVED	HS	58
THRIVEN	G3	743
THRIVES	PTW	5
	RL	162
	HAP	1552
	J1	106
	OAL	191
	M15	641
	ETP	7
THRIVING	AM	1
	VP3	41
	G4	774
	MG	23
	ETP	17
THROAT	L3	131
	PAA	41
	J1	212
	P1	71
	P3	15
	P3	199
	P5	15
	P5	278
	G3	642
	AE2	287
	AE4	672
	AE7	743
	AE8	344
	AE10	482
	AE10	583
	AE10	1311
	AE11	954
	AE11	1103
	OAL	586
	B	709
	C	19
	C	89
	C	270
	C	629
	C	670
	FL	110
	FL	200
	M12	444
	WB	316
THROATS	PDG	31
	J6	663
	P1	38
	DHP	3
	AE6	665
	AE6	852
	AE7	49
	C	458
	FL	449
THROB	P2	96
THROBBING	L4	197
	P6	173
THROES	CM	55
	M9	13
	M9	52
	AE1	372
	KT2	653
	M8	254
	CAM	355
	CAM	366
	M15	330
THRONE	AR	22
	AR	75
	AR	104
	AR	321
	RH	105
	DC	9
	DC	48
	DC	58
	PO	12
	CM	11
	AA	147
THRONE	AA	322
	AA	351
	AA	380
	AA	483
	AA	503
	AA	796
	AA	892
	AA	925
	AA	936
	AA	975
	D	8
	MF	86
	MF	107
	MF	142
	SAA	10
	SAA	133
	SAA	683
	SAA	789
	SAA	804
	SAA	1063
	PDG	32
	L3	253
	TA	90
	TA	101
	TA	217
	TA	446
	HAP	66
	HAP	1019
	HAP	1070
	HAP	1107
	HAP	2251
	HAP	2572
	BR	116
	EJG	4
	EL	267
	J6	215
	J10	153
	M1	229
	M13	17
	MC	44
	MC	53
	VP1	95
	G4	316
	AE1	79
	AE1	343
	AE1	369
	AE1	375
	AE1	473
	AE1	711
	AE1	836
	AE1	938
	AE2	387
	AE2	622
	AE3	2
	AE3	383
	AE3	651
	AE4	159
	AE4	276
	AE4	539
	AE4	855
	AE5	379
	AE5	987
	AE6	825
	AE6	1230
	AE7	188
	AE7	514
	AE7	906
	AE8	238
	AE8	672
	AE8	718
	AE8	958
	AE9	855
	AE10	1216
	AE11	367
	AE11	461
	AE11	515
	AE11	542
	AE11	571
	AE12	34
	AE12	45
	AE12	93
	AE12	98
	AE12	1230
	OAL	129
	OAL	226
	AF	5
	DO	19
	KT3	381
	KT3	487
	KT3	546
	KT3	692
	KT3	890
	KT3	1010
	KT3	1014
	KT3	1075
	KT3	1134

THRONE	B	601	THROW	PKA	10	THROWS	AE9	745
	HIF	152		J1	241		AE10	593
	HIF	159		J3	225		AE10	1275
	HIF	239		P1	144		KT1	334
	HIF	258		P1	259		KT3	610
	HIF	394		P3	93		B	709
	HIF	558		M1	517		M11	87
	HIF	579		M1	665		M12	376
	HIF	719		G3	374		M12	472
	HIF	740		AE1	63		GP	37
	M11	44		AE2	607	THRUMS	AA	439
	M12	788		AE3	795	THRUSH	P6	55
	WB	1		AE5	761		C	428
	M15	3		AE5	908	THRUST	MD	317
	M15	49		AE6	321		SAA	519
	M15	714		AE6	587		EDGA	11
	GP	112		AE7	1010		J6	59
THRONES	AM	1114		AE9	711		J6	368
	OAL	723		AE9	770		J6	420
	TJD	69		AE10	197		M13	39
THRONG	LC	113		AE10	281		AE2	356
	SCD1	4		AE10	368		AE2	755
	AA	509		AE10	534		AE9	985
	MF	49		AE10	1069		AE12	737
	MF	132		AE11	294		OAE2	51
	TA	103		AE11	437		KT1	192
	EL	283		AE11	1289		HIF	338
	ODA	74		AE12	417		M12	506
	J6	679		AE12	1026		M12	643
	J10	101		AE12	1188		M12	654
	J10	198		KT3	1039		CI	598
	M1	789		M8	143	THRUSTS	EUF	30
	M1	36		HIF	781		HAP	2480
	HI	27		C	570		AE2	723
	VP6	42		M12	110		KT3	607
	AE1	261		M12	167		BP	86
	AE1	547		M12	393		M12	324
	AE1	588		M12	669		M12	644
	AE1	614	THROWING	AM	494	THULE	G1	41
	AE1	720	THROWN	LCA	6	THUMB	MF	45
	AE1	1048		PTW	19	THUMBS	J3	68
	AE2	34		AA	144		J3	461
	AE4	102		MD	50	THUMPS	AE5	578
	AE5	497		MD	217	THUNDER	AR	6
	AE5	627		SAA	109		LC	143
	AE6	830		SAA	629		VHH	31
	AE6	925		RL	124		AM	92
	AE6	966		L3	132		AM	156
	AE6	1025		T23	38		AM	744
	AE7	538		AK	143		SCD2	11
	AE7	545		HAP	1804		EUO	23
	AE7	557		J1	135		E	23
	AE7	814		J3	432		DA	73
	AE8	775		J6	671		AA	1027
	AE8	944		P6	68		MD	215
	AE9	684		M1	17		SAA	627
	AE9	717		M1	1057		H3	55
	AE10	532		AE1	532		HAP	1109
	AE11	225		AE3	751		P2	49
	AE11	1010		AE5	310		P5	17
	AE11	1275		AE7	740		M1	197
	AE12	200		AE8	919		M1	343
	AE12	810		AE9	784		M1	763
	AE12	859		AE9	969		M1	811
	OAL	105		AE10	455		M13	18
	OAL	632		AE10	507		M13	171
	KT3	468		AE10	668		G1	377
	KT3	553		AE10	782		G1	453
	KT3	607		AE10	981		G1	508
	FL	197		AE11	1006		G1	655
THRONGED	AM	913		AE12	760		G3	408
	EKK	20		AE12	778		G4	246
	AA	271		AE12	870		G4	713
	PRH	14		OAL	495		AE1	131
	J10	386		KT3	735		AE1	315
	KT3	11		M8	123		AE2	634
	C	277		M8	163		AE2	941
	M12	368		M8	342		AE3	261
	CI	560		M12	352		AE4	171
THRONGING	SAA	1123		M12	461		AE4	305
	AE6	438		AU	141		AE4	533
	M8	162		M15	469		AE5	419
THROTTLED	P3	199		CI	583		AE5	908
THROTTLING	KT3	406	THROWS	L4	283		AE5	1073
THROUGHLY	EAA	14		T23	92		AE6	148
THROW	PMQ	54		J1	89		AE6	790
	PNH	35		P6	132		AE6	798
	PSF	35		G1	453		AE8	517
	EUF	36		G4	325		AE8	563
	L4	29		AE1	692		AE9	956
	T27	95		AE2	443		AE10	258
	HAP	592		AE2	851		AE10	798
	HAP	767		AE5	499		AE12	297
	HAP	1419		AE5	899		AE12	1336
	HAP	1978		AE8	604		OAL	210
	HAP	2122		AE9	27		AF	126

Word	Code	No.	Word	Code	No.	Word	Code	No.
THUNDER	M8	29	THYRSIS	SDG	12	TIDE	AE10	499
	BP	25		STS3	3		AE10	971
	TH	266		VP7	26		AE11	844
	M12	75		VP7	98		AE12	860
	M15	95	TIARA	AE7	337		OAL	817
	GP	38	TIBER	AM	631		B	432
THUNDERBOLT	L3	249		DA	159		HIF	596
THUNDERBOLTS	HAP	1568		P2	33		TH	422
	AE6	1159		G4	526		M11	149
	AE9	914		AE2	1062		M11	458
THUNDERCLAP	TA	16		AE6	134		M12	64
	CAM	196		AE6	1208		CI	270
THUNDERED	EAL	3		AE7	42	TIDED	P6	67
	AE7	191		AE7	201	TIDES	AM	15
	AE8	693		AE7	331		AM	451
	AE9	864		AE7	986		AM	645
	AU	293		AE8	87		AM	708
THUNDERER	J6	808		AE8	98		AM	923
	M1	262		AE8	118		EAZ	8
	M1	1025		AE8	320		MD	172
	AE1	938		AE8	617		SAA	25
	AE4	321		AE8	715		RL	428
	AE6	786		AE9	151		L4	84
	AE7	426		AE10	594		HAP	1123
	AE8	464		AE11	486		HAP	506
	AE10	171		AE11	607		J3	98
	AE12	1175	TIBER'S	MF	130		M1	566
	AE12	1222		J3	111		VP9	51
	HIF	751		G1	671		G2	644
	HIF	765		AE1	19		G2	681
THUNDERER'S	AR	42		AE3	650		G3	834
	BR	204		AE5	110		G4	382
	P2	19		AE7	420		AE2	81
	M1	221		AE7	607		AE3	102
	KT3	277		AE7	919		AE3	529
	HIF	579		AE7	1090		AE3	538
THUNDERING	SAA	1107		AE8	43		AE4	760
	HAP	1613		AE8	96		AE5	261
	SSC	30		AE8	270		AE5	1074
	EDS	36		AE8	439		AE6	558
	SKA1	4		AE9	1066		AE7	812
	G4	809		AE10	1186		AE8	969
	AE2	397		M15	638		AE10	305
	AE3	747	TIBRIS	AE10	191		AE10	321
	AE3	853	TIBUR	AE7	872		AE10	426
	AE4	834		AE7	930		KT3	466
	AE5	522		AE11	785		KT3	627
	AE6	662	TIBURS	AE7	931		B	186
	AE6	823	TICK	PMQ	58		HIF	286
	AE9	712	TICKLE	PCG2	26		FL	298
	AE9	1015		P1	173		M12	74
	AE10	1246		P1	232		CI	339
	AE11	929		VP3	37	TIDINGS	HAP	1232
	AE12	452	TICKLED	EHC	28		AE3	227
	AE12	709	TICKLES	SMM2	16		AE11	1294
	AE12	1327	TICKLING	P1	28	TIE	AA	149
	HIF	812		CI	190		AA	769
	HIF	558	TIDE	SMA	111		SAA	244
	TH	133		VHH	24		HAP	437
	TH	294		AM	730		HAP	1341
	TH	362		AM	938		M1	653
	AU	352		STL	21		G1	358
THUNDER'S	AR	198		SAA	43		AE5	650
	M1	65		SAA	610		KT2	148
THUNDERS	AM	411		SAA	844		B	413
	AM	447		SAA	1073		CAM	72
	T18	32		SAA	1126		SMP	30
	HAP	1017		L4	28	TIED	AR	260
	AE2	157		H29	52		LC	64
	AE4	233		TA	134		AM	755
	AE12	1098		HAP	2100		EDG	17
	M11	124		EL	243		L4	201
	CI	334		J1	192		HAP	662
THUNDERSTRUCK	AE9	660		VP6	25		HAP	1580
THURINE	M15	66		VP8	80		HAP	1871
THWARTED	AE5	1024		VP10	6		HAP	2069
THWARTING	C	684		G2	226		HAP	2112
THYESTEAN	M15	680		G2	633		HAP	2174
THYESTES	P5	25		G3	607		PTS	11
THYESTES'	P5	11		G4	412		OD	47
THYMBRAEUS	AE3	114		G4	605		J6	198
	AE12	674		AE1	615		M1	868
THYMBRUS	AE10	546		AE2	224		AE2	548
THYMBRUS'	AE10	551		AE2	271		AE2	1076
THYME	VP1	105		AE2	590		AE3	232
	VP2	9		AE3	732		AE5	97
	VP5	121		AE8	865		AE5	411
	G4	43		AE8	894		AE5	483
	G4	171		AE8	946		AE5	565
	G4	267		AE9	80		AE6	535
	G4	350		AE9	113		AE7	679
	G4	390		AE9	928		AE7	885
	G4	429		AE9	1066		AE8	638
THYMOETES	AE2	42		AE10	217		AE9	474
	AE10	190		AE10	238		AE9	844
THYRSIS	SDG	1		AE10	405		AE11	18

TIED	AE11	540
	AE12	139
	AE12	316
	AE12	881
	AE12	1211
	KT2	171
	M8	70
	M8	72
	B	45
	B	238
	B	406
	M11	492
	M12	199
	M12	268
	WB	180
	WB	184
	WB	343
	WB	393
	M15	363
	M15	442
	CI	316
	CI	433
	CI	517
	AS	71
TIES	HP	221
	AE4	79
	AE6	496
	AE9	491
	AE10	720
	AE12	53
	KT2	477
	CAM	144
	WB	65
	CI	246
TIGER	G4	592
	AE9	986
	AE10	246
	KT2	202
	KT3	629
TIGERS	AT	34
	VP5	43
	VP8	61
	G2	207
	G3	387
	G4	741
	AE4	525
	AE6	1098
	AE10	356
	OAL	617
	OAL	629
	M15	119
TIGER'S	AE11	864
TIGHT	L4	156
TIGRESS	DA	38
	T23	36
TIGRIS	VP1	82
	OAL	256
TILED	G4	418
TILES	J3	13
	J3	330
	G1	599
	BP	162
	M12	638
TILL	AE3	187
	AE7	962
	AE7	1004
	AE9	833
	AE11	487
TILLAGE	G1	240
	G2	1
	G3	771
	AE3	22
TILLED	TA	357
	HAP	1394
	P5	85
	G2	257
	AE7	750
	M15	180
TILLER	J6	384
TILLER'S	AA	12
TILLS	G2	739
TILT	EUO	16
TILTING	PSF	40
TILTS	EDGA	6
	KT1	22
	TH	18
TIMAVUS	VP8	9
	AE1	334
TIMBER	AM	566
	AE3	8
	AE5	893
	AE9	93
	AE9	715
	AE11	204
	KT3	975
TIMBER-TREES	J3	408

TIMBREL	P5	271
	M9	187
TIMBREL'S	M9	175
TIMBRELS	J6	662
	M9	40
	G4	222
	AE9	132
TIME	HS	1
	AR	79
	AR	109
	AR	302
	SMA	27
	SMA	68
	LC	7
	LC	9
	LC	147
	LC	149
	DC	13
	EIE	7
	AM	1
	AM	162
	AM	193
	AM	422
	AM	555
	AM	559
	AM	847
	AM	1176
	PMQ	4
	PA	26
	PEL	34
	EEL	1
	ETL	20
	STL	13
	ECG1	21
	EMQW	5
	EUO	9
	PNH	46
	ENH	40
	PAZ	7
	EAZ	5
	EAZ	28
	PC1	20
	PAL	6
	PKK	18
	PTW	17
	ETC	17
	PLG	28
	CM	21
	HP	250
	HP	255
	DA	187
	DA	194
	ETG	22
	PUO3	14
	AA	407
	AA	451
	AA	459
	AA	598
	AA	612
	AA	837
	AA	902
	AA	950
	AA	1028
	MD	107
	MD	238
	MF	53
	MF	128
	SAA	733
	SAA	778
	SAA	859
	SAA	964
	EDG	1
	EDG	19
	RL	134
	RL	263
	RL	270
	AT	121
	DOD	10
	MO	20
	L2	14
	L3	21
	L3	30
	L3	94
	L3	171
	L4	164
	L4	175
	L4	297
	T23	25
	T23	57
	T23	62
	T27	11
	H9	27
	H9	30
	TA	314
	PAA	36
	AK	14

TIME	HAP	32
	HAP	626
	HAP	861
	HAP	940
	HAP	1158
	HAP	1178
	HAP	1313
	HAP	1318
	HAP	1648
	HAP	1711
	HAP	1732
	HAP	1780
	HAP	1785
	HAP	1795
	HAP	1882
	HAP	2017
	HAP	2135
	HAP	2419
	HAP	2495
	BR	11
	BR	202
	PDS	13
	ETS	2
	PMS	19
	PKA	23
	SKA3	14
	EL	299
	ODA	38
	PSH	25
	SSH	14
	SSH	15
	J1	123
	J1	255
	J3	43
	J3	50
	J6	216
	J6	447
	J6	611
	J6	618
	J6	692
	J10	23
	J10	399
	J16	73
	J16	76
	P1	68
	P1	107
	P2	28
	P2	51
	P2	69
	P3	31
	P3	121
	P4	29
	M1	131
	M1	196
	M1	347
	M1	467
	M1	715
	M1	944
	M9	8
	M9	27
	M9	69
	M9	159
	MC	59
	GK	57
	GK	167
	GK	176
	GK	179
	VP3	76
	VP3	120
	VP7	14
	VP9	3
	VP9	69
	G1	409
	G1	662
	G2	264
	G2	794
	G3	79
	G3	194
	G3	267
	G3	273
	G3	301
	G3	448
	G4	403
	AE1	48
	AE1	364
	AE1	372
	AE2	218
	AE2	616
	AE2	962
	AE3	534
	AE3	578
	AE4	162
	AE4	245
	AE4	690
	AE5	187
	AE5	398

TIME			TIME			TIMES		
	AE5	553		C	162		RL	386
	AE5	833		C	285		ER	11
	AE5	1023		C	372		TA	264
	AE6	56		C	467		HH	16
	AE6	69		C	497		HAP	573
	AE6	723		C	774		HAP	797
	AE6	766		TH	162		HAP	1415
	AE6	970		TH	262		HAP	1815
	AE6	1009		TH	296		HAP	1833
	AE7	161		TH	402		HAP	2315
	AE7	194		M11	236		HAP	2476
	AE7	280		FL	136		HAP	2577
	AE7	282		M12	252		PDS	37
	AE7	318		M12	596		EKA	32
	AE7	505		AU	223		J1	220
	AE7	618		AU	556		J3	78
	AE7	634		WB	106		J3	89
	AE7	682		WB	459		J6	34
	AE8	67		WB	357		J6	398
	AE8	264		WB	529		J6	840
	AE8	541		M15	25		J10	43
	AE8	593		M15	75		J10	120
	AE9	90		M15	228		J10	142
	AE9	175		M15	241		J10	195
	AE9	375		M15	268		J10	226
	AE9	812		M15	324		P1	166
	AE9	836		M15	342		P1	223
	AE10	15		M15	358		P3	66
	AE10	20		M15	503		P4	126
	AE10	145		M15	512		P5	260
	AE10	396		M15	529		M1	6
	AE10	700		M15	565		M1	146
	AE10	1213		M15	628		M1	322
	AE11	640		M15	638		HI	165
	AE11	713		M15	668		GK	118
	AE12	303		GP	108		GK	147
	AE12	833		CI	217		VP4	6
	AE12	993		CI	258		VP9	15
	AE12	1134		ETP	27		G1	32
	OAL	78		SMP	23		AE1	29
	OAL	102		SMP	40		AE1	137
	OAL	290		SMP	44		AE1	324
	OAL	402		SMP	91		AE1	1064
	OAL	404		SMP	97		AE2	105
	OAL	420		PMK	32		AE2	318
	OAL	465		EMKG	42		AE2	712
	OAL	489		AS	15		AE5	736
	OAL	537		EWR	1		AE6	67
	OAL	538	TIMELY	AR	190		AE6	882
	OAL	539		PIE	4		AE6	936
	OAL	541		AM	30		AE6	1063
	OAL	548		AM	775		AE7	894
	OAL	559		HAP	1719		AE7	977
	OAL	568		BR	15		AE8	89
	OAL	604		BR	266		AE8	432
	OAL	683		EL	326		AE8	451
	OAL	888		J3	331		AE8	632
	OAE2	68		G1	352		AE11	517
	MG	33		G3	762		AE12	1107
	MM	33		G4	160		OAL	454
	MFL	28		AE2	381		OAL	491
	DO	38		AE2	860		DO	167
	KT1	30		AE4	856		KT2	495
	KT1	130		AE11	1200		CAM	320
	KT1	472		AE12	400		C	70
	KT2	115		OAL	687		C	438
	KT2	177		TH	242		C	453
	KT2	562	TIME'S	UDH	83		C	565
	KT3	377		AR	292		C	639
	KT3	398		HAP	772		TH	3
	KT3	637		J10	233		M11	43
	KT3	747		G3	753		FL	490
	KT3	820		M15	23		WB	16
	KT3	860	TIMES	AR	320		M15	266
	KT3	1034		LC	59		M15	533
	KT3	1088		LC	91		CI	404
	KT3	1125		PCG1	2		SMP	2
	TJD	139		PMQW	8		SMP	19
	M8	46		PCB	12	TIMOROUS	HAP	37
	M8	340		CM	52		AE9	761
	B	26		EMW	1		M15	140
	B	41		EMW	7	TIMOTHEUS	AF	20
	B	73		EPF	23		AF	131
	B	92		EUF	27		AF	158
	B	114		AA	1		AF	167
	B	219		AA	116		AF	177
	B	250		AA	180	TINCTURE	LC	66
	B	399		AA	644		L4	235
	B	592		AA	662	TINE	HIF	635
	BP	70		AA	789	TINKER'S	P5	155
	CAM	94		MD	101	TINKLED	ER	14
	CAM	246		PRH	25		AE2	745
	CAM	380		SAA	410		TH	94
	HIF	46		SAA	18	TINKLING	G4	89
	HIF	212		SAA	282		G4	222
	HIF	682		RL	370		AE3	153

TINSEL	EMQW	13	TITLE	HAP	1151	TOE	OAL	682	
	EAZ	39		HAP	2007	TOES	CAM	340	
TIP	P4	116		BR	344		C	666	
	PWR	17		J6	324	TOGETHER	UDH	3	
TIPHYS	VP4	41		P3	43		HS	72	
	M15	260		AE8	20		RH	31	
	M15	505		KT1	325		AM	201	
TIPPED	EDG	22		M8	226		AM	466	
	M1	630		M8	328		SEL4	30	
	G1	576		B	2		PK	42	
	C	118		B	512		T27	23	
TIPPLES	P4	73		CAM	301		H29	61	
TIPS	J6	202		M12	3		AK	184	
TIPTOE	AE5	566		AU	30		HAP	2570	
	M8	173		AU	250		PDS	39	
	C	625		AU	572		PTS	8	
TIPTOES	J6	650		WB	163		J10	161	
	VP3	108		M15	427		M9	78	
TIRE	AA	631		GP	114		M9	194	
	HAP	1611	TITLES	AA	569		PLT	25	
	P2	76		AA	580		ELT	10	
	P5	37		HH	41		VP5	1	
	G2	65		HAP	771		VP7	2	
	KT1	28		HAP	950		AE2	650	
TIRED	SMA	114		BR	330		AE2	1085	
	AM	277		J1	197		AE5	768	
	AM	522		J10	87		AE7	100	
	PUO2	3		J10	230		AE8	471	
	PAL	31		G1	666		AE10	586	
	HP	257		AE10	497		AE10	762	
	PSF	19		AE11	121		AE11	943	
	AA	935		AE11	360		AE11	996	
	MD	25		AE12	1033		LMC	6	
	TA	184		OAL	222		KT2	256	
	PMS	32		DO	152		B	64	
	J6	185		KT2	153		BP	26	
	J6	369		KT3	541		BP	31	
	J6	519		M8	269		C	212	
	J6	623		WB	393		C	307	
	P5	200	TITMOUSE	G4	18		C	430	
	M1	972	TITS	EK	39		C	569	
	G2	549		M9	14		TH	234	
	AE2	148	TITTLE	EK	43		M11	53	
	AE2	175	TITYRUS	AT	3		M11	420	
	AE6	489		VP1	2		FL	300	
	AE6	677		VP1	27		M12	367	
	AE6	1164		VP1	53		M12	557	
	AE7	412		VP5	16		M12	579	
	AE8	641		VP8	76		M12	658	
	AE10	1107		VP9	28		PWR	18	
	AE10	1153	TITYUS	L3	189	TOIL	RH	18	
	AE12	364		L3	197		PUF	14	
	AE12	1190		AE6	804		AA	169	
	OAL	545		M12	707		MD	271	
	KT1	228	TLEPOLEMUS	AE9	930		MF	150	
	KT2	617	TMARUS	G1	84		SAA	686	
	M11	218	TMOLUS	J1	105		SAA	869	
	M11	253	TOAD	J3	83		SAA	1115	
	M11	391		G1	269		RL	31	
	AU	94		MD	304		RL	235	
	AU	340	TOADS	MF	50		ER	58	
	CI	93	TOAST	EWR	8		H3	34	
	EMKG	1	TOBACCO	PTP	31		H2	94	
TIRES	RL	162	TOBIT	HAP	2048		TA	165	
TIRING	G4	597	TOBY'S	EWG	7		TA	439	
TIRING-ROOM	PM	11	TO-DAY	PRL	32		HAP	456	
TISIPHONE	G3	820		AM	297		HAP	1705	
	AE6	749		EMQ	12		BR	161	
TISSUE	AE1	915		ET	12		PTS	36	
	AE3	625		PEL	35		EL	118	
	KT3	534		EEL	1		J6	185	
	TH	258		ECG1	37		J6	346	
TITAN	ER	74		PCG2	11		P2	76	
	AE6	782		PCG2	21		P3	120	
	KT3	669		PM	32		M1	1011	
TITANIAN	AE4	258		ELN	1		VP2	10	
TITHES	GP	42		PAL	1		G1	24	
TITHON	G3	82		PSF	7		G1	70	
TITHON'S	AE9	610		PR	2		G1	116	
TITIAN	ML	52		ELB	1		G1	185	
TITIAN'S	GK	64		MD	109		G1	305	
TITLE	HS	16		EDGA	2		G1	367	
	RH	66		L3	320		G2	282	
	EIE	3		H9	24		G2	356	
	ELN	14		H29	66		G2	750	
	DA	208		H29	68		G3	10	
	AA	224		EAA	1		G3	784	
	AA	301		STS3	35		G4	270	
	AA	408		EKA	1		G4	313	
	AA	462		EKA	41		G4	581	
	AA	901		EH	33		AE1	48	
	MD	10		P5	91		AE1	598	
	EK	22		VP9	74		AE2	772	
	RL	394		TH	188		AE3	365	
	GE	55		M15	322		AE4	590	
	HAP	458		ERL	6		AE5	617	

Word	Ref	No.
TOIL	AE6	204
	AE7	592
	AE12	267
	OAL	829
	AF	99
	MG	33
	MM	43
	KT1	586
	KT2	359
	TJD	89
	TJD	133
	B	555
	HIF	238
	HIF	383
	M11	218
	AU	441
	AU	537
	M15	188
TOILED	TA	409
	AE7	428
	AE10	446
TOILING	G1	422
	G2	286
	G2	329
	AE1	586
	M15	176
TOILS	HS	61
	AM	389
	AM	665
	AA	349
	AA	913
	SAA	1130
	L3	205
	T23	15
	TA	450
	HAP	575
	HAP	591
	J10	556
	HI	186
	VP5	94
	VP6	81
	VP10	68
	G1	211
	G1	414
	G2	581
	G3	572
	G3	625
	G4	711
	AE1	243
	AE1	393
	AE2	351
	AE2	358
	AE2	372
	AE2	688
	AE2	859
	AE2	1064
	AE3	472
	AE3	935
	AE3	943
	AE4	168
	AE4	125
	AE4	186
	AE5	948
	AE6	388
	AE6	1112
	AE6	1150
	AE6	1180
	AE7	599
	AE7	666
	AE7	1099
	AE8	584
	AE9	549
	AE9	831
	AE10	1002
	AE10	1107
	AE10	1145
	AE11	21
	AE11	282
	AE11	774
	AE12	650
	AE12	1084
	AE12	1190
	M8	89
	HIF	98
	HIF	345
	HIF	507
	M11	144
TOILSOME	G2	664
	BP	26
TOKEN	EKA	21
TOLD	EEL	8
	EEL	24
	ECG2	17
	EAZ	1
	PAL	8
	EPC	25

Word	Ref	No.
TOLD	SAA	87
	EK	18
	AT	71
	ER	33
	T27	110
	HAP	1505
	HAP	1774
	HAP	2199
	HAP	2404
	BR	231
	ESH	13
	M1	873
	M1	894
	M1	988
	M1	1059
	R	16
	R	20
	ELT	3
	VP9	10
	G3	670
	AE1	727
	AE2	125
	AE6	408
	AE7	283
	AE8	873
	AE10	221
	AE11	69
	OAL	497
	LMC	4
	KT1	306
	KT3	212
	B	427
	B	631
	CAM	106
	C	364
	C	374
	C	451
	C	479
	TH	293
	M12	706
	WB	156
	WB	170
	WB	171
	WB	181
	M15	531
	M15	662
TOLDEST	DA	87
TOLERABLE	J6	591
TOLL	PLN	1
	SCD2	15
	G4	277
TOLLED	PCB	19
TOLLS	PTC	22
TOLUMNIUS	AE11	662
	AE12	390
TOM	PO	25
	EK	24
	MC	48
	RL	456
	PTP	3
TOMB	SMA	2
	SMA	55
	AM	404
	CM	132
	CM	135
	EPF	24
	L3	74
	T23	85
	AK	189
	HAP	1543
	ELW	3
	J10	227
	J10	278
	HI	70
	VP9	82
	AE3	55
	AE3	89
	AE3	417
	AE4	668
	AE4	977
	AE5	100
	AE5	112
	AE5	124
	AE5	134
	AE6	332
	AE6	517
	AE6	680
	AE8	456
	AE9	281
	AE10	779
	AE11	892
	AE11	1234
	AE12	1279
	MFL	3
	M8	308
	M8	391

Word	Ref	No.
TOMB	M8	392
	M8	402
	B	640
	B	660
	B	675
	M12	4
	M15	72
	M15	577
TOMBS	AR	186
	SFL	21
	VP8	142
	AE12	1249
	M11	28
	M15	633
TOMBSTONE	J6	324
TO-MORROW	EMM	15
	PEL	35
	PSF	7
	MD	109
	AT	25
	L3	313
	H9	19
	H29	68
	STS3	36
	P5	90
	P5	93
	VP3	110
	OAE2	88
	KT2	152
	TH	188
	M15	323
	CI	513
	CI	517
TO-MORROW'S	T18	64
	T18	65
	AE7	176
	AE8	229
	AE10	345
	AE12	120
	WB	239
TO-MORROWS	P5	96
TOMS	PA	25
TONE	HAP	1350
	HAP	2120
	J6	623
	P6	157
	M9	197
	VP9	5
	AE3	413
	AE10	863
	KT1	283
	KT2	255
	HIF	724
	TH	134
	TH	294
	M12	285
	AU	203
	CI	116
TONGS	G4	255
	AE8	595
TONGUE	UDH	19
	UDH	91
	AM	525
	SMQ	6
	SEL2	10
	CM	29
	CM	98
	PUF	33
	AA	510
	SAA	1024
	SAA	632
	EDG	14
	ER	5
	ER	53
	MO	14
	MO	23
	HAP	602
	HAP	610
	HAP	2448
	J6	198
	J6	271
	J6	274
	J6	568
	J6	574
	J10	199
	J10	317
	P3	172
	P4	12
	M1	308
	M1	905
	M1	1038
	M1	1062
	GK	4
	GK	127
	VP7	39
	G2	543

Word	Ref	No.
TONGUE	G3	596
	G3	666
	G3	758
	G4	762
	AE2	488
	AE2	648
	AE2	1010
	AE2	1076
	AE3	68
	AE3	400
	AE4	106
	AE4	264
	AE4	405
	AE5	122
	AE5	364
	AE8	394
	AE8	838
	AE8	963
	AE10	889
	AE11	600
	AE11	605
	AE11	1112
	AE12	1210
	AE12	1318
	OAL	399
	OAL	662
	MM	53
	MM	44
	DO	1
	KT3	786
	B	238
	B	271
	BP	194
	M10	41
	CAM	218
	HIF	123
	HIF	155
	HIF	699
	HIF	723
	HIF	760
	TH	309
	M11	13
	M11	435
	FL	82
	M12	264
	M12	761
	AU	18
	AU	352
	WB	145
	WB	184
	GP	17
	CI	219
	EMKG	27
TONGUE-DEBATE	AE11	588
TONGUES	UDH	16
	UDH	24
	HP	36
	MD	267
	L4	75
	L4	201
	TA	123
	AK	61
	HAP	594
	HAP	598
	HAP	1343
	HAP	1598
	BR	57
	BR	203
	J3	133
	P1	114
	P5	2
	P5	37
	VCS	18
	G2	62
	G2	133
	G4	741
	AE1	214
	AE2	278
	AE6	851
	AE8	910
	OAL	496
	OAL	645
	OAL	767
	M8	375
	M8	379
	FL	607
TONGUE-VALIANT	AE11	514
	HIF	336
	AU	147
TONIES	PAL	15
TO-NIGHT	SMM1	1
	J3	458
	C	145
TOOK	JH	12
	AR	57
	AR	141
TOOK	AR	144
	RH	70
	LC	96
	LCA	47
	AM	463
	AM	1167
	SCD1	6
	PUO1	44
	EUO	11
	ESF	12
	ESF	32
	ML	32
	UMR	8
	AA	128
	MD	19
	MD	48
	MF	131
	SAA	364
	SAA	368
	SAA	373
	SAA	546
	EDG	5
	RL	381
	OE	16
	AT	101
	AT	110
	T23	94
	T23	99
	TA	17
	TA	110
	TA	116
	TA	120
	TA	125
	TA	198
	TA	212
	TA	229
	AK	139
	AK	157
	HH	14
	HAP	256
	HAP	621
	HAP	736
	HAP	1268
	HAP	1571
	HAP	2210
	EL	321
	J10	291
	P1	169
	P3	175
	P5	53
	M1	33
	M1	165
	M1	196
	M1	279
	M1	503
	M1	541
	M1	564
	M1	594
	M1	842
	M1	891
	M1	932
	M1	968
	M9	115
	M13	142
	HI	13
	HI	46
	HI	73
	HI	110
	HI	142
	HI	154
	HI	173
	VP5	51
	VP7	5
	G1	658
	G2	671
	G3	405
	G4	662
	G4	676
	G4	795
	AE1	264
	AE1	569
	AE1	661
	AE1	1002
	AE1	1030
	AE1	1035
	AE2	167
	AE2	1000
	AE2	1091
	AE3	373
	AE3	637
	AE4	402
	AE4	539
	AE4	820
	AE4	1003
	AE5	161
	AE5	390
TOOK	AE5	673
	AE5	870
	AE5	969
	AE6	290
	AE6	536
	AE6	575
	AE6	643
	AE6	804
	AE6	867
	AE6	922
	AE6	1243
	AE7	42
	AE7	44
	AE7	98
	AE7	162
	AE7	479
	AE7	396
	AE7	931
	AE8	11
	AE8	95
	AE8	148
	AE8	152
	AE8	212
	AE8	418
	AE8	465
	AE9	325
	AE9	331
	AE9	420
	AE9	434
	AE9	797
	AE9	807
	AE9	888
	AE10	480
	AE10	722
	AE10	964
	AE10	1103
	AE11	43
	AE11	510
	AE11	517
	AE11	803
	AE12	52
	AE12	253
	AE12	340
	AE12	1134
	OAL	114
	OAL	797
	DO	42
	DO	48
	DO	76
	KT1	188
	KT1	206
	KT1	211
	KT2	14
	KT2	24
	KT2	233
	KT2	433
	KT3	60
	KT3	125
	KT3	185
	KT3	491
	KT3	626
	KT3	747
	KT3	1001
	KT3	1012
	M8	167
	M8	357
	B	85
	B	173
	B	188
	B	348
	B	439
	B	465
	B	529
	B	628
	BP	58
	CAM	248
	HIF	101
	HIF	434
	HIF	614
	HIF	801
	HIF	719
	HIF	533
	C	256
	C	267
	C	345
	C	439
	C	721
	TH	58
	TH	205
	TH	231
	TH	334
	TH	363
	TH	395
	M11	70
	M11	78
	M11	416

Word	Code	Num	Word	Code	Num	Word	Code	Num
TOOK	M11	454	TOPS	AE4	362	TORN	AE2	636
	FL	54		AE6	960		AE4	861
	FL	283		AE8	132		AE4	885
	FL	287		AE12	203		AE5	601
	FL	398		AE12	870		AE6	212
	FL	406		KT3	941		AE6	577
	FL	413		M15	588		AE7	1053
	M12	194	TOPSAIL	M11	102		AE8	626
	M12	285	TOPSY-TURVY	PK	18		AE8	856
	M12	305	TORCH	DC	4		AE10	438
	M12	316		CM	120		AE10	992
	M12	356		P6	144		AE10	1097
	M12	382		M1	618		AE11	1183
	AU	298		M9	147		AE12	320
	AU	337		AE6	697		AE12	991
	AU	491		AE6	794		KT3	273
	WB	50		AE6	823		B	23
	WB	387		AE7	470		B	595
	M15	11		AE7	638		HIF	350
	M15	16		OAL	25		TH	111
	GP	42		OAE1	12		TH	325
	GP	108		AF	137		M12	346
	CI	80	TORCHES	P3	206		M15	201
	CI	194		M1	665	TORQUATUS	AE6	1130
	CI	198		VP7	71	TORRENT	AR	279
	CI	308		G1	391		J10	199
	PTP	16		G2	603		J10	246
	ETP	16		AE4	684		M13	218
	AS	42		AE5	861		M13	219
TOOL	AA	967		AF	143		AE5	26
	SAA	362		CAM	91		AE10	506
TOOLS	PEL	15		CI	546		AE11	455
	AA	541		CI	567	TORRENTS	G1	160
	SAA	267	TORE	M13	209		G3	396
	EC	15		VP5	34		AE4	238
	HIF	237		G1	650		AE4	706
TOOTH	P3	229		AE4	591		AE10	850
TOOTHED	G1	215		AE4	846		AE12	764
TOOTHLESS	J6	345		AE4	986		AE12	992
	AE7	586		AE5	224	TORRID	DC	10
TOP	LC	145		AE5	340		G1	322
	SMM2	12		AE5	1117	TORTOISE	AE2	601
	MF	167		AE8	346	TORTURE	MF	208
	AT	104		AE10	696	TORTURED	ECD	4
	AT	115		AE11	1093		HAP	691
	L3	72		AE12	236		J1	12
	AK	111		AE12	715		J10	441
	J1	12		AE12	781		M8	196
	P3	97		AE12	1366		C	293
	G2	420		KT1	523		M15	517
	G3	489		B	654	TORTURES	HAP	610
	AE2	635		TH	304		P3	73
	AE3	355		M11	198		AE6	756
	AE4	673		M11	202		AE6	762
	AE5	650		M12	741		KT2	658
	AE5	990	TORIES	EDG	14	TORY	ELB	3
	AE6	260		EDG	41		ELB	11
	AE6	332	TORMENT	SCG2	26		EDG	24
	AE6	1099		STC	5		EDG	44
	AE7	528		ETS	17		EC	8
	AE8	183		STS1	2		NS	14
	AE9	916		SKA6	24	TOSS	ESF	22
	AE11	797		AE2	265		H9	14
	BP	149	TORMENTED	SLN	1		HAP	2047
	EMKG	12		AE8	556		SKA4	24
TOPE	GE	59	TORMENTORS	RL	162		J3	74
	PSH	30		HAP	1369		J6	435
	OAE2	65		J6	619		AE10	463
TOP-HEAVY	J10	170	TORMENTS	SMQ	1		AE12	128
	P3	154		L3	195		AE12	846
TOPICS	J6	344		SLT1	26		AE12	1188
TOPMOST	AT	23		AE6	719		AF	143
	HAP	793		OAL	697		C	157
	J3	74	TORN	AM	511		AU	175
	VP9	79		CM	64		M15	521
	G2	401		DA	39	TOSSED	AR	9
	G2	412		AA	399		AR	51
	AE3	873		AA	881		LCA	5
	AE4	714		L3	68		AM	129
	AE4	1000		L3	189		PUF	19
	AE6	312		H29	42		MF	42
	AE7	99		HAP	201		SAA	1104
	AE10	1086		EL	298		L3	14
TOPPLES	OAL	614		J1	159		L3	33
TOPS	PUF	3		J3	250		HAP	430
	M1	404		J3	407		HAP	1330
	M1	467		J6	846		M1	342
	VP5	97		J10	211		M1	407
	VP6	115		P6	67		M13	42
	VP10	89		M13	181		G1	494
	G1	149		G1	433		G1	545
	G2	36		G1	637		AE1	47
	G2	496		G4	760		AE1	64
	G4	434		AE1	165		AE1	166
	AE1	856		AE1	755		AE1	320
	AE3	845		AE2	568		AE1	457

TOSSED	AE1	519	TOUCH	WB	498	TOWERING	AE2	289
	AE1	721		PWR	12		AE3	705
	AE1	739	TOUCHED	AM	374		AE3	893
	AE1	834		AM	1118		AE4	370
	AE1	1063		SAA	1128		AE4	646
	AE3	436		T23	101		AE5	156
	AE3	931		HAP	2031		AE5	563
	AE4	684		HAP	2467		AE6	264
	AE4	868		HAP	2557		AE6	907
	AE5	816		M1	1009		AE10	629
	AE5	839		AE2	230		AE10	1083
	AE5	948		AE3	870		AE11	595
	AE6	493		AE3	873	TOWERS	DA	11
	AE8	286		AE4	460		DA	21
	AE8	443		AE4	547		OE	27
	AE8	922		AE4	943		J10	251
	AE9	712		AE11	378		VP2	90
	AE9	770		AE11	1249		VP9	33
	AE10	581		AE12	625		G1	671
	AE11	402		AF	22		G4	186
	AE11	436		KT1	93		AE1	30
	AE11	867		KT3	147		AE1	376
	AE11	1166		KT3	839		AE1	582
	AE12	150		HIF	809		AE1	612
	AE12	952	TOUCHES	AM	1198		AE1	804
	AE12	1171		ELT	14		AE2	74
	M8	256		AE12	589		AE2	607
	M8	316		M8	14		AE3	4
	B	82		M10	21		AE3	150
	C	701		M15	473		AE3	647
	M11	114		M15	620		AE3	726
	M11	204	TOUCHING	NS	4		AE4	123
	M12	332		FL	359		AE4	268
	WB	344	TOUGH	HAP	2230		AE4	381
	M15	245		P2	76		AE4	391
	M15	522		G1	225		AE4	501
	M15	549		G2	322		AE6	1052
	CI	370		AE5	539		AE6	1065
	ESK	17		AE9	854		AE7	216
TOSSES	G3	94		AE9	1003		AE7	872
TOSSING	PO	8		AE10	677		AE7	1021
	AE1	149		AE12	148		AE8	2
	AE5	1130		AE12	1141		AE8	131
	AE6	823		KT2	557		AE8	416
	AE6	945		KT3	513		AE8	493
	STP	8		M12	132		AE9	34
TOTAL	J6	323	TOUGHER	J3	463		AE9	626
	M1	862		G2	628		AE10	78
TOTTERING	M12	775	TOUGHEST	G2	173		AE10	133
	AU	173	TOUGHNESS	TA	326		AE10	184
	AU	577		AE12	1071		AE10	368
TOTTERS	AE2	384	TOW	AE5	891		AE10	948
TOUCH	AR	157	TOWELS	G4	542		AE11	140
	AM	723		AE1	983		AE11	375
	AM	750		BP	76		AE11	1286
	SEL2	7	TOWER	AM	945		AE12	209
	PLN	36		MD	12		AE12	291
	ECD	18		J6	646		AE12	797
	ENH	4		J10	170		AE12	831
	ESF	26		HI	5		KT1	574
	PTC	6		HI	21		KT3	1063
	PTC	16		HI	86		M12	724
	DA	145		AE2	244		AU	577
	PUO4	6		AE2	297		CI	382
	AA	804		AE2	322	TOWN	EWG	10
	MF	202		AE2	625		PRL	1
	T23	101		AE2	834		PRL	30
	T27	91		AE4	592		EIE	4
	EAA	12		AE4	841		AM	937
	HAP	86		AE6	740		AM	1149
	EL	38		AE6	748		AM	1162
	J6	283		AE7	106		AM	1171
	M13	75		AE9	214		AM	1203
	VP3	35		AE9	704		EMQ	15
	G1	478		AE9	724		PWGR	8
	G3	172		AE11	740		PWGR	17
	G3	839		AE12	977		PMM	5
	G4	403		KT1	166		EMM	12
	AE1	849		KT1	201		ECG1	5
	AE6	822		KT1	211		PMQW	3
	AE7	29		KT1	447		PM	5
	AE9	657		KT2	600		PM	8
	AE12	300		HIF	781		PM	39
	OAL	178		M11	146		EM	31
	OAL	179		M12	62		PLN	10
	OAL	565	TOWERED	AE11	1010		ELN	9
	OAL	649		M12	742		EUO	4
	OAE2	4	TOWERING	PP	16		EUO	30
	OAE2	26		J3	11		PAZ	36
	OAE2	33		M13	149		EKK	21
	MM	45		VP7	91		PTW	5
	KT2	427		VP7	95		PTW	20
	M10	84		G1	181		PTC	27
	HIF	133		G1	243		HP	146
	HIF	421		G1	549		DA	23
	M11	486		G2	602		PUO5	8

Word	Code	No.
TRACTS	AE12	372
TRADE	HS	45
	AR	218
	AR	304
	PRL	28
	AM	5
	AM	157
	AM	828
	AM	1204
	AM	1207
	PMQ	50
	EWGR	48
	PCG2	10
	PM	30
	PCD	9
	PUO1	29
	PNH	13
	PC2	19
	EMK	13
	PTC	11
	PTC	23
	PCB	39
	PSF	31
	PSF	44
	PUO4	5
	AA	124
	AA	615
	AA	620
	AA	667
	AA	705
	ELB	37
	MD	41
	MF	119
	SAA	2
	SAA	78
	SAA	284
	SAA	355
	SAA	389
	SAA	428
	SAA	493
	SAA	672
	SAA	822
	PK	36
	RL	249
	RL	371
	RL	408
	HAP	796
	HAP	1139
	HAP	1867
	T27	53
	PP	24
	PTS	17
	ETS	3
	PKA	29
	J6	159
	J6	685
	J6	810
	J10	97
	P3	167
	VP3	63
	VP9	43
	G2	631
	G3	260
	G3	535
	AE1	22
	AE7	1029
	AE9	850
	AE12	430
	OAL	825
	OAE1	29
	KT3	325
	TJD	74
	TJD	132
	TJD	144
	HIF	160
	HIF	340
	C	406
	M12	66
	M12	364
	AU	338
	ETP	39
	EMKG	2
	PWR	2
TRADERS	SKA1	15
TRADES	EKK	9
	AM	861
	MD	193
	KT2	597
TRADESMAN	P5	205
TRADESMEN	EWGR	46
TRADE-WIND	AM	1215
TRADING	G4	20
	C	301
	PWR	10
TRADITION	POE	29
	RL	276
TRADITION	RL	281
	RL	305
	RL	350
	HAP	742
	HAP	746
	HAP	755
	HAP	761
	HAP	776
	HAP	805
	HAP	881
	HAP	785
	HAP	1169
	J3	288
	M1	537
	M15	76
TRADITIONARY	J10	460
TRADITION'S	HAP	754
	HAP	470
	HAP	739
	HAP	749
	RL	255
	RL	334
TRADITIONS	RL	256
	RL	267
	RL	342
	HAP	812
	HAP	819
	HAP	833
	HAP	858
TRADITIVE	HAP	768
TRADUCED	M1	1073
	PTP	52
TRADUCTION	AK	23
TRAFFIC	AM	1196
	PCG2	9
	HAP	1140
	PTS	16
	G4	227
TRAGEDIAN'S	P5	3
TRAGEDIANS	J6	108
TRAGEDIES	PK	37
TRAGEDY	ETL	16
	PAZ	40
	PKK	5
	PLG	26
	MG	28
	MM	22
TRAGIC	VP8	14
	MF	198
	SAA	136
	PSH	33
	J6	829
	AE4	114
	MM	30
TRAIL	M1	998
	G4	184
	AE5	692
	AE5	1092
	AE7	113
	AE10	1200
	AE11	138
	FL	262
	WB	441
TRAILED	PCB	1
	AE5	628
TRAILING	AE2	945
	AE11	863
	KT3	186
TRAILS	AM	492
	G1	504
	AE5	366
TRAIN	SMA	39
	VHH	55
	AM	205
	AM	440
	AM	1190
	EUO	3
	ENH	18
	PUF	11
	AA	332
	AA	730
	AA	876
	AA	938
	MD	35
	MD	304
	SAA	193
	SAA	807
	SAA	833
	D	13
	EK	21
	L4	139
	H3	40
	TA	120
	TA	366
	TA	509
	AK	140
TRAIN	HAP	99
	HAP	192
	HAP	470
	HAP	514
	HAP	1787
	HAP	2018
	HAP	2431
	BR	22
	BR	83
	EL	53
	EL	149
	J3	450
	J6	170
	J6	219
	J6	247
	J6	607
	J10	298
	M1	216
	M1	589
	M1	791
	M9	32
	M9	174
	M13	160
	HI	14
	VP5	46
	VP6	99
	VP8	140
	G2	65
	G2	200
	G2	637
	G2	669
	G2	744
	G3	37
	G4	146
	G4	342
	AE1	46
	AE1	108
	AE1	139
	AE1	205
	AE1	260
	AE1	455
	AE1	515
	AE1	560
	AE1	684
	AE1	697
	AE1	844
	AE1	971
	AE1	988
	AE2	531
	AE2	704
	AE3	445
	AE4	46
	AE4	172
	AE4	183
	AE4	220
	AE4	314
	AE4	589
	AE4	725
	AE4	779
	AE4	824
	AE4	835
	AE4	972
	AE5	98
	AE5	209
	AE5	348
	AE5	380
	AE5	629
	AE5	753
	AE5	883
	AE5	905
	AE5	934
	AE5	953
	AE5	1003
	AE5	1053
	AE6	114
	AE6	541
	AE6	649
	AE6	659
	AE6	795
	AE6	830
	AE6	1071
	AE7	205
	AE7	215
	AE7	268
	AE7	50
	AE7	320
	AE7	398
	AE7	573
	AE7	605
	AE7	664
	AE7	728
	AE7	748
	AE7	958
	AE8	215
	AE8	408
	AE8	805

TRAIN	AE8	928	TRAITOR	AE11	1150	TRANSGRESSING	TH	219
	AE9	30		AE11	1237	TRANSIENT	EL	353
	AE9	719		AE11	1252		AE1	132
	AE9	1050		AE12	1062		OAE2	74
	AE10	30		AE12	1370	TRANSLATE	PCG1	35
	AE10	285		OAL	602		ER	63
	AE10	298		KT1	299		AK	163
	AE10	306		KT2	127		J6	580
	AE10	789		KT2	283		M11	490
	AE10	852		KT2	640	TRANSLATED	SAA	403
	AE10	1191		HIF	344		ER	3
	AE11	811		HIF	550		ER	48
	AE11	877		C	500		BR	304
	AE11	886		C	597		M13	187
	AE11	1011		C	772		G2	361
	AE11	1048		AU	483		M15	396
	AE11	1056	TRAITOR-FRIEND	KT2	568	TRANSLATING	RL	229
	AE11	1195	TRAITOROUS	MD	205		HAP	1628
	AE11	1219	TRAITOR'S	G3	709	TRANSLATION	ER	7
	AE12	191		KT1	313		ER	35
	AE12	376		KT2	561		ER	54
	AE12	415	TRAITORS	AM	889		EL	338
	AE12	488		PK	6	TRANSLATIONS	RL	242
	AE12	542		PDG	43	TRANSLATOR'S	RL	249
	AE12	654		HAP	218	TRANSLATORS	ER	63
	AE12	665		HAP	2001	TRANSMIGRATING	P6	23
	AE12	676		M1	259	TRANSMITS	HAP	483
	AE12	843		AE6	579		ESK	2
	OAL	179	TRALINEATE	WB	396	TRANSMITTED	RL	272
	OAL	708	TRAMPLE	HAP	358	TRANSPARENT	AE6	1236
	KT1	55		EDS	19		AE6	1237
	KT1	89		G2	314		MFL	17
	KT2	382		G4	15	TRANSPIERCED	AE2	68
	KT2	478	TRAMPLED	HAP	201		AE10	1116
	KT3	192		AE10	689		AE11	988
	KT3	244		AE12	783	TRANSPLANTED	J3	107
	KT3	558		M12	503		G2	72
	KT3	723	TRAMPLES	M8	33		G2	76
	KT3	948	TRAMPLING	AE2	994	TRANSPORT	SAA	1069
	KT3	967		AE3	854		TA	133
	TJD	104		AE7	999		BR	222
	M8	100		AE9	534		AE5	955
	B	47		HIF	407		AE6	449
	B	201	TRANCE	ER	15		AE10	306
	B	253		T27	132	TRANSPORTED	SAA	60
	CAM	240		AE2	366		AE2	1031
	TH	51	TRANSACT	HAP	1308		M12	276
	TH	233		HIF	739	TRANSPORTING	FL	65
	TH	311	TRANSCEND	TA	75	TRANSPORTS	SAA	829
	M11	327		VP4	66	TRANSPROSE	SAA	444
	FL	155		AE11	188	TRAP	MF	212
	FL	165		MFL	23		P1	178
	FL	215	TRANSCENDED			TRAPPED	KT3	931
	FL	240	TRANSCENDENT	AE10	1170		AU	340
	FL	305	TRANSCENDING	RL	165	TRAPPINGS	PO	24
	FL	407		RL	194		TA	330
	FL	426	TRANSCENDS	UDH	41		P3	54
	FL	457		PUO2	38		AE4	192
	FL	512	TRANSCRIBE	UDH	101		AE5	407
	FL	529	TRANSFER	DA	165		AE7	383
	M12	83		AE1	367		AE11	113
	M12	425	TRANSFERRED	GK	6		AE11	133
	M12	797		VP6	1		AE11	1134
	M12	807		M12	833		KT3	65
	AU	342		M15	713		FL	260
	WB	18	TRANSFERS	AE2	439		M12	582
	WB	48		AE7	597	TRASH	PCG1	33
	M15	568	TRANSFIX	L4	2	TRAVAIL	HAP	1705
	M15	629	TRANSFIXED	P5	5		BR	53
	GP	1		M1	200	TRAVAILING	HAP	385
	PTP	38		M1	633	TRAVEL	J6	749
TRAINBANDS	EWGR	25		HI	81		M1	1094
	EDGA	36		G3	404		VP4	75
TRAINED	AR	97		AE1	69		G1	382
	AT	37		AE2	724		AE10	1145
	AE6	886		AE3	755		BP	150
	AE7	970		AE5	711		CAM	76
	AE9	361		AE9	788		CAM	321
	B	436		AE10	1278		WB	232
	FL	565		AE11	959		M15	214
TRAINING	G3	321		AE12	1343	TRAVELED	ESF	11
TRAINS	L2	51		M12	439		SAA	89
	PP	32		M12	454		M1	277
	J1	69		M12	507		G4	147
	HI	105	TRANSFORM	AT	28		AE5	1089
	AE5	1076		M15	536		AE10	1105
TRAITOR	SSF	1	TRANSFORMATION	PT	31		OAE1	32
	PPC	9	TRANSFORMED	PT	34	TRAVELER	VP5	73
	TA	183		VP6	106		KT1	493
	J10	440		AE11	420	TRAVELERS	RL	2
	AE4	539	TRANSFORMS	M1	834		M1	664
	AE4	557	TRANSFUSE	MF	184		AE6	380
	AE4	847	TRANSFUSED	MF	185	TRAVELING	SAA	342
	AE5	1097		AK	26		HAP	1260
	AE8	853	TRANSGRESS	KT1	337	TRAVELOUR	AR	148
	AE8	887		M15	669	TRAVELS	AR	82
			TRANSGRESSING	HAP	490			

Headword	Ref	No.
TREE		
TREES	M15	606
	LC	138
	DC	12
	AM	503
	PAZ	34
	OE	32
	T27	103
	H29	60
	PAA	8
	AK	114
	HAP	1733
	HAP	2347
	SSC	49
	M1	123
	M1	168
	M1	467
	M1	869
	VP1	71
	VP3	82
	VP4	2
	VP5	29
	VP5	47
	VP5	129
	VP6	59
	VP7	67
	VP9	41
	VP9	84
	G1	82
	G1	222
	G1	355
	G2	13
	G2	28
	G2	52
	G2	67
	G2	75
	G2	85
	G2	89
	G2	104
	G2	107
	G2	117
	G2	122
	G2	162
	G2	168
	G2	171
	G2	205
	G2	349
	G2	534
	G2	576
	G2	595
	G2	600
	G2	603
	G2	611
	G2	618
	G2	716
	G4	26
	G4	33
	G4	48
	G4	62
	G4	170
	G4	173
	G4	211
	G4	468
	G4	740
	G4	807
	AE1	429
	AE1	617
	AE1	856
	AE2	412
	AE3	192
	AE3	300
	AE6	8
	AE6	264
	AE6	267
	AE6	309
	AE6	366
	AE6	955
	AE7	42
	AE7	1021
	AE8	419
	AE8	424
	AE10	507
	AE12	670
	KT2	184
	KT2	535
	KT3	959
	KT3	1058
	M8	86
	M8	101
	BP	16
	BP	55
	CAM	17
	TH	80
	M11	279
	M11	298
	M12	297
	M15	353
TREMBLE	AR	115
	HP	142
	L2	60
	HAP	306
	G1	449
	G4	108
	AE7	718
	AE10	419
	AE11	689
	HIF	761
TREMBLED	CM	94
	EDS	5
	M1	261
	AE2	769
	AE3	783
	AE5	670
	AE7	11
	AE7	623
	AE8	396
	AE10	175
	AE12	148
	KT2	123
	KT3	184
	CAM	297
	HIF	711
	FL	222
	AU	116
TREMBLES	SCD1	15
	TA	118
	EHC	2
	G3	392
	AE9	968
	AE11	1129
TREMBLING	HS	119
	AM	387
	AM	527
	AM	719
	SEL2	11
	SEL2	12
	CM	112
	DA	41
	MF	44
	SAA	560
	SAA	628
	T23	31
	J3	234
	J6	279
	J6	632
	J10	362
	P1	141
	P2	97
	P3	81
	P3	170
	P4	66
	M1	390
	M1	592
	M1	681
	M1	751
	M9	163
	M9	187
	HI	127
	VP5	129
	VP8	71
	VP9	16
	G1	554
	G1	693
	G3	124
	G3	132
	G3	298
	G3	653
	G4	21
	G4	96
	G4	677
	G4	762
	AE1	66
	AE1	165
	AE1	296
	AE1	654
	AE2	67
	AE2	85
	AE2	146
	AE2	627
	AE2	665
	AE2	708
	AE2	748
	AE2	783
	AE2	838
	AE3	476
	AE3	823
	AE3	885
	AE4	220
	AE4	241
	AE4	269
	AE4	846
	AE4	934
	AE5	227
TREMBLING	AE5	268
	AE5	329
	AE5	501
	AE5	697
	AE5	1003
	AE5	1053
	AE6	75
	AE6	84
	AE6	203
	AE6	536
	AE6	664
	AE6	761
	AE7	583
	AE8	7
	AE8	35
	AE8	291
	AE8	320
	AE8	535
	AE8	700
	AE8	782
	AE8	937
	AE9	154
	AE9	459
	AE9	552
	AE9	719
	AE9	759
	AE9	1016
	AE10	152
	AE10	553
	AE10	925
	AE11	23
	AE11	1014
	AE11	1066
	AE11	1179
	AE11	1271
	AE12	17
	AE12	320
	AE12	333
	AE12	658
	AE12	1037
	AE12	1081
	AE12	1188
	AE12	1327
	OAL	11
	OAL	144
	OAL	619
	OAE1	15
	AF	23
	M8	98
	M8	144
	B	628
	BP	52
	CAM	156
	CAM	207
	C	717
	TH	317
	TH	344
	M11	68
	M11	467
	M12	127
	M12	193
	AU	112
	M15	33
	M15	220
	M15	411
	M15	588
	M15	701
	CI	170
	CI	336
	FL	359
TREMELLIUS	RL	241
TRENCH	J16	21
	AE7	173
	AE12	604
	KT2	443
	M8	24
TRENCHERS	AE7	156
	AE7	169
TRENCHES	AE7	214
	AE9	420
	AE9	623
	AE9	692
	AE9	694
	AE10	32
	AE10	530
	AE11	717
	HIF	479
	M12	207
TRENDINGS	AE7	200
TRESPASS	PO	3
	J6	821
TRESSES	AE6	393
	OAL	138
	KT1	184
TRIAL	UDH	39
	VP3	38

TRIAL	B	477	TRIDENT	VHH	16	TRIED	CI	385		
	M12	159		AM	736		CI	494		
TRIALS	BR	267		G1	15		CI	501		
TRIBE	PUO3	26		AE1	198	TRIES	H3	36		
	AA	645		AE1	208		J6	794		
	ELB	21		AE1	222		J10	414		
	SAA	312		M12	785		P3	19		
	SAA	977					M1	1038		
	HH	40	TRIED	AM	471		G3	355		
	HAP	311		AM	679		G3	360		
	HAP	2124		PCG1	2		G4	637		
	J6	230		SCG3	11		G4	727		
	J6	688		EMQW	12		AE1	928		
	P5	103		CM	47		AE4	412		
	G3	252		SSF	15		AE5	590		
	TJD	109		AA	46		AE9	65		
	B	516		AA	49		AE12	161		
	C	406		AA	427		AE12	703		
	AS	101		AA	884		M10	88		
TRIBES	PUO4	31		MD	96		C	237		
	AA	906		MD	127		C	777		
	MD	177		SAA	744		M11	475		
	MF	93		RL	224		M12	682		
	SAA	22		RL	355		M15	689		
	SAA	82		AT	63	TRIFLE	PAZ	4		
	SAA	181		H3	13		GE	67		
	SAA	224		TA	160	TRIFLES	P5	28		
	SAA	264		TA	201		P6	88		
	SAA	678		TA	445		AE3	630		
	SAA	712		TA	457	TRIFLING	P1	94		
	SAA	776		HAP	476		P1	160		
	HAP	1473		HAP	729	TRIM	AM	601		
	J10	71		HAP	754		PCG2	18		
	P5	256		HAP	776		HAP	1795		
	AE10	290		HAP	944		EL	323		
TRIBUNAL	LC	51		HAP	959		J6	502		
	AE7	237		HAP	1579		J6	589		
	KT3	658		HAP	1926		P3	58		
TRIBUNE	J10	50		HAP	1963		VP2	70		
TRIBUNE'S	J3	226		HAP	2031		G4	285		
TRIBUNES'	J1	166		HAP	2088		KT1	540		
TRIBUNES'	J1	155		HAP	2110		HIF	215		
TRIBUNITIAL	J3	490		HAP	2379	TRIMMED	G3	734		
TRIBUTARY	J3	98		HAP	2533	TRIMMER	EDG	23		
	J3	310		J1	33		EC	8		
TRIBUTE	HS	137		J6	341		EC	38		
	AM	123		J10	277		NS	14		
	SAA	1039		J10	354	TRIMMERS	EDG	33		
	HAP	171		J10	365		EDG	38		
	HAP	2465		J10	442		EC	29		
	EL	360		J10	487		EC	37		
	OD	38		P1	134	TRIMS	HAP	1960		
	MC	76		M1	246	TRINACRIAN	AE1	272		
	VP6	9		M1	591	TRINE	AK	43		
	B	662		M1	643		BR	33		
	C	86		M13	57		BR	327		
	M15	173		VP5	139	TRINED	KT3	389		
TRIBUTES	SAA	13		VP6	3	TRINES	AM	1165		
TRICE	P4	26		G2	327	TRINITY	BR	25		
	M1	834		AE1	279	TRINKETS	J6	212		
	C	278		AE1	664		C	406		
	WB	223		AE4	988	TRIP	PTL	24		
	CI	158		AE5	466		J3	394		
TRICK	EMQ	5		AE6	167		G2	776		
	PKK	7		AE6	809		KT1	189		
	EKK	7		AE7	581	TRIPE	SAA	473		
	PCB	38		AE7	731	TRIPLE	PO	26		
	PSF	46		AE8	580		AA	175		
	AA	424		AE9	413		MD	65		
	PDG	7		AE11	360		SAA	226		
	OE	10		AE11	612		BR	33		
	L4	287		AE11	637		AE6	402		
	HAP	2216		AE12	31		AE6	563		
	J1	184		AE12	567		AE7	917		
	J6	333		AE12	1319		AE7	1073		
	J16	76		OAL	33		AE8	393		
TRICKING	MG	23		OAL	87		KT3	232		
TRICKLED	CM	60		KT3	579		M12	58		
TRICKLES	G2	165		KT3	830	TRIPLED	MM	35		
TRICKLING	STL	10		M8	183	TRIPOD	HAP	2113		
	L4	194		B	135		AE3	462		
	AE3	443		B	196	TRIPODS	AE5	146		
	AE11	292		CAM	217		AE9	351		
	M8	154		C	207	TRIPOS	AE3	124		
	B	304		TH	172	TRIPPED	HAP	31		
	CAM	363		FL	114		AE2	985		
TRICKS	ETL	10		M12	132	TRIPPING	VP3	98		
	PKK	17		M12	641		VP5	115		
	T27	32		M12	735		VP6	43		
	HAP	825		AU	8		HIF	748		
	HAP	844		AU	248		WB	9		
	PKA	45		AU	336	TRIPS	M1	681		
	AE11	1058		AU	405	TRIPTOLEMUS	GE	30		
	OAL	878		AU	481	TRISTRAM	C	477		
	EMKG	11		AU	599		FL	526		
	EWR	29		M15	163	TRITON	M1	448		
				GP	116					

Word	Ref	No.	Word	Ref	No.	Word	Ref	No.
TRITON	AE1	205	TRIUMPHANT	AE8	950	TROJAN	AE1	29
	AE6	253		AE10	31		AE1	35
	AE10	298		AE10	1098		AE1	45
	DO	44		AE11	623		AE1	50
TRITONS	AE5	1078		AE11	981		AE1	135
TRIUMPH	SMA	10		DO	66		AE1	182
	LCA	13		KT1	110		AE1	288
	AM	536		KT3	718		AE1	323
	AM	724		M8	315		AE1	383
	MF	58		HIF	564		AE1	410
	MF	151		C	722		AE1	518
	SAA	17		PTP	44		AE1	645
	SAA	890	TRIUMPHANTLY	HAP	1122		AE1	649
	SAA	1076	TRIUMPHED	VHH	41		AE1	670
	SAA	1094	TRIUMPHS	HS	110		AE1	676
	PD	49		HS	132		AE1	695
	L3	250		SMA	18		AE1	720
	TA	134		LCA	43		AE1	775
	TA	372		AM	1206		AE1	786
	TA	488		E	21		AE1	812
	AK	105		ML	35		AE1	824
	HAP	1711		PLB	39		AE1	882
	PP	27		SAA	634		AE1	978
	LS	12		SAA	802		AE1	990
	EL	276		SAA	831		AE1	1024
	J1	239		RL	56		AE1	1048
	J3	263		ER	71		AE1	1053
	J10	210		T18	94		AE2	43
	P6	71		TA	346		AE2	75
	P6	176		HAP	1226		AE2	161
	M1	169		HAP	1860		AE2	256
	M1	759		EL	364		AE2	317
	HI	53		J6	247		AE2	420
	HI	163		J6	298		AE2	439
	VP2	97		J10	80		AE2	504
	VP4	14		M1	603		AE2	531
	VP6	27		VP8	36		AE2	583
	VP8	8		G2	202		AE2	780
	G1	689		AE6	1112		AE2	790
	G2	240		AE8	830		AE2	953
	G3	15		AE11	63		AE2	1066
	G3	40		AE11	79		AE3	1
	G3	47		AE11	212		AE3	63
	AE1	211		AE11	577		AE3	83
	AE2	289		AE12	565		AE3	115
	AE2	495	TRIUMVIRS	KT2	606		AE3	138
	AE4	471	TRIVET	BP	84		AE3	146
	AE5	210	TRIVIA	AE7	719		AE3	150
	AE5	473		AE7	1062		AE3	183
	AE5	519	TRIVIAL	MD	195		AE3	243
	AE5	1076		SAA	175		AE3	363
	AE6	1147		HAP	2420		AE3	381
	AE6	1186		P1	134		AE3	385
	AE7	918		AE12	1109		AE3	396
	AE8	267		KT1	29		AE3	426
	AE10	572	TRIVIA'S	AE6	16		AE3	623
	AE10	767		AE7	1066		AE3	591
	AE11	10	TROD	PO	6		AE4	14
	AE11	1094		SAA	701		AE4	101
	AE11	1161		EAA	23		AE4	110
	AE12	486		J1	27		AE4	143
	AE12	1367		J1	64		AE4	157
	OAL	235		J1	167		AE4	175
	OAL	244		AE6	185		AE4	201
	OAL	636		AE9	1069		AE4	313
	OAL	774		AE10	767		AE4	330
	AF	49		KT2	46		AE4	382
	KT1	9		KT2	649		AE4	493
	KT1	50		B	150		AE4	579
	KT3	614		BP	26		AE4	648
	HIF	238		C	438		AE4	714
	TH	204		FL	182		AE4	777
	AU	530		M12	191		AE4	781
	AS	61		M12	522		AE4	800
TRIUMPHAL	P6	109		WB	218		AE4	831
TRIUMPHANT	AR	284	TRODDEN	AM	491		AE4	868
	AM	815		M13	94		AE4	917
	PW	16		AE5	362		AE4	929
	D	13	TRODE	KT2	515		AE4	943
	SAA	620	TROEZEN	M15	451		AE4	948
	TA	253	TROILUS	AE1	663		AE5	1
	MN	9	TROJAN	AM	254		AE5	41
	BR	315		PTC	38		AE5	57
	SKA1	16		ETC	5		AE5	78
	J10	433		HP	157		AE5	97
	P1	145		HP	203		AE5	141
	PLT	56		HP	220		AE5	163
	G2	496		HP	231		AE5	341
	G2	783		DA	198		AE5	348
	AE1	270		HAP	2068		AE5	373
	AE2	359		J1	153		AE5	610
	AE2	785		J1	245		AE5	617
	AE4	533		J10	406		AE5	773
	AE5	864		HI	129		AE5	782
	AE6	1098		VP4	44		AE5	795
	AE7	421		AE1	3		AE5	825

TROJAN

AE5	905
AE5	932
AE5	1051
AE5	1105
AE6	105
AE6	188
AE6	269
AE6	306
AE6	370
AE6	453
AE6	465
AE6	543
AE6	612
AE6	649
AE6	681
AE6	696
AE6	754
AE6	953
AE6	1028
AE6	1041
AE6	1152
AE6	1212
AE7	40
AE7	56
AE7	150
AE7	160
AE7	268
AE7	398
AE7	435
AE7	381
AE7	484
AE7	509
AE7	541
AE7	594
AE7	605
AE7	651
AE7	759
AE7	770
AE8	28
AE8	42
AE8	56
AE8	136
AE8	187
AE8	192
AE8	205
AE8	239
AE8	386
AE8	410
AE8	476
AE8	493
AE8	614
AE8	723
AE8	728
AE8	774
AE8	805
AE9	10
AE9	89
AE9	103
AE9	135
AE9	229
AE9	296
AE9	327
AE9	975
AE9	1003
AE9	1048
AE10	33
AE10	65
AE10	137
AE10	145
AE10	179
AE10	229
AE10	317
AE10	340
AE10	373
AE10	402
AE10	452
AE10	476
AE10	530
AE10	606
AE10	751
AE10	799
AE10	817
AE10	822
AE10	852
AE10	914
AE10	1062
AE10	1089
AE10	1097
AE10	1111
AE10	1118
AE10	1138
AE10	1234
AE10	1240
AE11	105
AE11	139
AE11	250

TROJAN

AE11	260
AE11	283
AE11	338
AE11	434
AE11	443
AE11	490
AE11	536
AE11	622
AE11	628
AE11	706
AE11	775
AE11	886
AE11	896
AE11	1002
AE11	1020
AE11	1147
AE11	1213
AE11	1304
AE12	22
AE12	99
AE12	119
AE12	122
AE12	152
AE12	165
AE12	177
AE12	189
AE12	208
AE12	350
AE12	487
AE12	530
AE12	680
AE12	729
AE12	744
AE12	778
AE12	797
AE12	807
AE12	826
AE12	1014
AE12	1077
AE12	1101
AE12	1119
AE12	1360
HIF	230
HIF	658
C	700
M12	97
M12	103
M12	206
M12	223
M12	596
M12	807
M12	812
AU	32
AU	145
AU	583
M15	232
AE5	516
HP	197
DA	171
HI	23
HI	42
HI	104
HI	163
AE1	57
AE1	226
AE1	243
AE1	251
AE1	337
AE1	419
AE1	654
AE1	739
AE1	790
AE1	885
AE2	6
AE2	33
AE2	81
AE2	196
AE2	367
AE2	494
AE2	607
AE2	626
AE3	781
AE3	788
AE4	538
AE4	601
AE5	10
AE5	157
AE5	384
AE5	696
AE6	84
AE6	263
AE7	170
AE7	213
AE7	270
AE7	463
AE7	393

TROJAN'S
TROJANS

TROJANS

AE7	661
AE8	121
AE8	158
AE9	37
AE9	202
AE9	211
AE9	414
AE9	622
AE9	678
AE9	684
AE9	709
AE9	718
AE9	723
AE9	810
AE9	871
AE9	899
AE9	937
AE9	991
AE9	1020
AE9	1096
AE10	113
AE10	160
AE10	167
AE10	234
AE10	858
AE10	873
AE10	1288
AE11	49
AE11	202
AE11	316
AE11	606
AE11	612
AE11	686
AE11	1201
AE11	1223
AE11	1313
AE12	276
AE12	282
AE12	421
AE12	473
AE12	521
AE12	565
AE12	735
AE12	1071
AE12	1116
AE12	1199
AE12	1211
OAL	775
HIF	702
M12	91
M12	791
AU	426

TROJANS'

AE2	525
AE4	432
AE7	28
AE9	155
AE9	661
AE11	597

TROOP

PAR	6
EUO	7
ENH	39
PR	16
PUO3	34
SAA	281
SAA	310
J10	25
M1	937
AE4	203
AE5	717
AE5	757
AE5	760
AE5	782
AE7	224
AE7	381
AE9	741
AE9	1051
AE11	49
AE11	218
AE11	304
KT2	428
KT3	577
KT3	720
TH	317
FL	161
FL	205
FL	229
FL	252
FL	338
FL	352
FL	369
M12	697
WB	5
CI	558
CI	575
CI	582
CI	593

TROY	M12	779	TRUE	AA	530	TRUE	MS	16
	AU	74		AA	781		PSH	19
	AU	317		AA	879		J1	167
	AU	387		AA	921		J3	32
	AU	495		AA	981		J3	342
	AU	501		PLB	39		J3	444
	AU	515		PLB	52		J6	129
	AU	518		ELB	11		J10	446
	AU	533		ELB	40		P1	125
	AU	534		EPC	15		P3	68
	AU	577		EPC	23		P3	220
	M15	630		EPC	31		P4	40
	M15	650		MD	106		P5	109
	M15	652		MD	107		P5	118
	M15	665		MD	112		P5	123
TROY'S	AE1	318		MD	179		P5	133
	AE2	14		MD	289		P6	151
	AE3	449		PRH	20		M1	537
	AE5	811		PRH	26		ELT	31
	AE7	320		PRH	29		SLT2	6
	AE7	1001		MF	90		GK	3
	AE10	307		MF	115		GK	39
	AE11	393		SAA	102		GK	65
	HIF	28		SAA	165		GK	108
	HIF	105		SAA	238		VP2	33
	HIF	564		SAA	372		VP2	55
	AU	69		SAA	870		VP10	65
TRUANT	G3	708		SAA	1010		G3	479
	EMKG	35		SAA	1062		G4	598
TRUANTS	G4	160		PDG	15		G4	736
	AE2	505		PDG	18		AE1	432
TRUCE	MF	117		EDG	6		AE2	197
	AE11	150		EDG	43		AE2	793
	AE11	165		EDGA	33		AE3	552
	AE11	200		SDG	16		AE3	724
	AE11	452		SDG	18		AE3	790
	AE12	24		SDG	19		AE4	780
	AE12	232		SDG	20		AE6	278
	AE12	239		RL	147		AE6	469
	AE12	471		RL	169		AE6	619
	AE12	679		RL	186		AE6	936
	AE12	1009		RL	292		AE6	1237
	C	808		RL	398		AE7	73
	M12	204		DOD	12		AE8	610
	CI	636		EC	4		AE9	869
TRUCK	P6	178		EC	41		AE10	1126
TRUDGE	PSH	5		ER	69		AE11	629
	P6	178		L3	86		AE11	1038
TRUDGED	J1	168		L3	208		AE12	354
	CI	84		L4	186		AE12	960
TRUDGES	PM	25		L5	8		AE12	1183
TRUE	HS	66		T18	78		OAL	116
	HS	73		T27	78		OAL	334
	AR	54		TA	327		OAL	344
	AR	222		TA	343		OAL	675
	RH	60		EAA	14		OAL	699
	LC	90		HAP	31		OAL	848
	PWG	3		HAP	432		DO	30
	EWG	16		HAP	451		KT1	35
	LCA	17		HAP	579		KT3	1141
	SMM1	5		HAP	634		KT3	1155
	PA	26		HAP	657		TJD	195
	EEL	27		HAP	709		M8	235
	ETL	15		HAP	749		B	219
	ECG2	27		HAP	762		B	561
	SCG1	30		HAP	917		M10	25
	SCG3	28		HAP	1067		HIF	112
	PFD	8		HAP	1101		HIF	537
	PMQW	5		HAP	1244		C	197
	PM	13		HAP	1353		C	414
	SLN	17		HAP	1548		C	417
	PCD	17		HAP	1656		C	476
	ECD	17		HAP	1791		C	691
	ENH	1		HAP	1796		M11	388
	ENH	10		HAP	1817		M11	414
	E	19		HAP	1956		M11	451
	PAZ	1		HAP	2013		FL	28
	EAZ	20		HAP	2046		FL	526
	EAZ	28		HAP	2162		FL	550
	ESF	13		HAP	2216		M12	233
	ML	54		HAP	2242		AU	60
	PAL	18		HAP	2337		AU	418
	EMK	7		HAP	2416		AU	488
	PKK	1		HAP	2515		WB	445
	PO	3		BR	121		WB	391
	PTC	37		BR	199		GP	54
	DA	117		BR	277		ETP	19
	EMW	8		PP	20		ERL	1
	PR	24		STS1	18		PWR	38
	PUO4	22		ELW	1	TRUE-BORN	POE	24
	PUO4	24		EL	264	TRUER	PCD	26
	PUO5	7		EL	166		OAL	624
	PUF	15		EL	187	TRULY	HS	18
	AA	16		EL	222		AM	661
	AA	83		EL	253		A	5
	AA	383		ODA	24		RL	289

Headword	Ref	No.
TRULY	TA	222
	GE	68
	HAP	1834
	EL	273
	J10	144
	J10	407
	P1	189
	P5	162
	AE2	201
	AE4	457
	TJD	137
	C	451
	AS	32
TRUMP	PPC	35
	AK	178
	J10	113
TRUMPERY	L3	224
	J6	191
TRUMPET	LCA	18
	AM	575
	AM	1015
	MD	162
	TA	475
	SSC	61
	P1	40
	M1	450
	AE5	182
	AE6	244
	AE6	248
	AE6	332
	AE7	882
	AE8	3
	AE11	655
	KT3	85
	KT3	581
	FL	231
	SMP	58
	SMP	62
TRUMPET-CHEEKS	J3	64
TRUMPET'S	SSC	25
	M1	129
	M1	459
	AE5	149
	AE7	870
TRUMPETS	SCD2	15
	H2	10
	SKA1	1
	SKA1	10
	J6	571
	J10	69
	J10	340
	P3	206
	G2	790
	G3	131
	G3	290
	AE2	422
	AE7	850
	AE8	695
	AE9	667
	AE10	429
	AE11	137
	AE11	293
	AE11	719
	KT3	464
	KT3	528
	KT3	662
	AF	50
	C	750
	FL	228
	FL	246
TRUMPETS'	G4	101
	AE5	708
	AE8	574
	FL	285
TRUMPS	FL	212
TRUNCHEON	KT3	612
	FL	267
TRUNCHEONS	AE11	16
TRUNK	G2	418
	AE3	866
	AE7	89
	AE9	447
	AE9	654
	AE10	775
	AE11	7
	AE11	266
	AE12	564
	CAM	341
	FL	326
	M12	448
	M12	483
TRUNK-BREECHES	P3	104
TRUNKS	H29	60
	G2	171
	G2	595
	G3	580

Headword	Ref	No.
TRUNKS	G4	62
	AE6	267
	AE8	419
	AE11	207
	AE12	742
	M15	565
TRUSS	AE9	763
TRUSSED	AE12	377
TRUSSES	AE11	1066
TRUST	UDH	51
	SMA	81
	LCA	47
	EIE	8
	AM	149
	AM	1179
	ETL	28
	EPF	3
	ETG	14
	AA	411
	AA	766
	AA	849
	MD	55
	MD	313
	MF	166
	SAA	77
	SAA	174
	SAA	237
	SAA	242
	SAA	572
	SAA	604
	SAA	619
	SAA	702
	SAA	736
	SAA	814
	SAA	864
	SAA	953
	TA	233
	EAA	17
	EAA	21
	EAA	32
	HAP	83
	HAP	141
	HAP	1048
	HAP	1743
	HAP	2144
	HAP	2180
	HAP	2214
	HAP	2360
	HAP	2372
	HAP	2412
	EKA	39
	EL	34
	J3	298
	J6	171
	J6	497
	J10	126
	P2	16
	M9	46
	M13	125
	ELT	36
	VP2	19
	G1	312
	G2	456
	G3	601
	G3	817
	AE2	63
	AE2	1074
	AE4	280
	AE4	467
	AE5	934
	AE5	1041
	AE5	1103
	AE9	178
	AE9	270
	AE9	326
	AE9	514
	AE10	104
	AE10	520
	AE11	46
	AE11	849
	AE11	1041
	AE11	1162
	AE12	25
	OAL	142
	OAL	281
	OAL	344
	OAL	659
	OAL	690
	OAL	846
	MFL	3
	DO	101
	KT1	302
	KT3	420
	TJD	87
	M8	228
	B	94

Headword	Ref	No.
TRUST	B	531
	HIF	447
	C	313
	M11	29
	GP	68
	GP	85
	CI	453
TRUSTED	HP	170
	SAA	470
	EAA	22
	HAP	2180
	AE4	612
	AE4	700
	AE10	231
	AE11	1196
	KT1	428
	KT2	283
	B	273
	B	531
	B	613
	WB	167
TRUSTEES	HAP	2183
TRUSTIER	P2	40
TRUSTING	HP	191
	HAP	583
	STS3	10
	G2	598
	TJD	35
	M8	139
TRUSTS	SAA	893
	HAP	791
	AE12	1143
TRUSTY	PW	7
	PUO3	14
	PKA	35
	J3	335
	J6	765
	P1	238
	P3	178
	P6	159
	M1	857
	G3	536
	G4	110
	AE1	264
	AE3	598
	AE5	664
	AE7	886
	AE8	603
	AE9	413
	AE12	1101
	B	262
	BP	148
	TH	233
	AU	599
	WB	227
TRUTH	DC	5
	PAZ	7
	ETC	24
	EUF	20
	AA	114
	AA	357
	AA	891
	PRH	16
	PRH	17
	SAA	47
	SAA	131
	SAA	996
	SAA	908
	SAA	955
	PK	7
	RL	214
	RL	233
	RL	281
	RL	285
	RL	337
	RL	345
	RL	349
	RL	455
	OE	34
	ER	33
	TA	334
	TA	486
	EAA	8
	EAA	29
	MN	4
	HAP	33
	HAP	681
	HAP	739
	HAP	880
	HAP	1173
	HAP	1194
	HAP	1201
	HAP	1335
	HAP	1690
	HAP	1806
	HAP	1816

TRUTH	HAP	2018	TRY	MF	77	TUG	C	533	
	HAP	2205		SAA	868	TUGGED	AE3	51	
	BR	120		SAA	1037		AE8	314	
	PMS	32		AT	58		AE12	1120	
	ESH	21		L1	56	TUGGING	EOE	3	
	J3	55		L3	313	TUGS	VP3	153	
	J10	279		L4	91		AE10	679	
	J10	462		L4	246		AE12	572	
	J16	47		L4	276		AE12	595	
	J16	54		H29	22	TULLA	AE11	972	
	P1	18		HH	12	TULLIA	J6	425	
	P1	19		HAP	141	TULLIUS	WB	448	
	P1	103		HAP	452	TULLUS	AE6	1109	
	P4	102		HAP	755	TULLUS'	AE8	855	
	P5	86		HAP	1743	TULLY	J10	185	
	P5	115		HAP	2218	TUMBLED	KT3	653	
	P6	10		EDS	24		FL	296	
	M1	164		PP	48		M12	592	
	M1	1056		J6	347		WB	344	
	M9	65		J6	473	TUMBLING	AA	274	
	ELT	13		J16	18		EDGA	39	
	ELT	30		PPS	12		NS	4	
	SLT2	14		P1	152		HAP	1809	
	GK	104		P3	225		J3	11	
	EHC	10		P3	228		J3	431	
	EHC	31		P5	144		AE2	611	
	VP1	83		M1	289		AE3	756	
	G2	327		M1	341		AE5	1057	
	G3	716		M1	533		AE8	317	
	AE2	195		M13	30		AE9	801	
	AE2	204		VP1	69		AE9	963	
	AE3	78		VP1	88		AE11	658	
	AE4	271		VP5	20		AE11	1068	
	AE4	536		G2	95	TUMBRIL	G1	245	
	AE6	1215		G2	379		C	251	
	AE8	67		G4	441	TUMOR	ECD	18	
	AE9	375		G4	586		PK	31	
	AE9	574		AE2	484	TUMULT	J6	548	
	AE10	102		AE2	565		AE2	595	
	AE10	893		AE2	887		AE2	600	
	OAL	33		AE3	42		AE3	134	
	OAL	65		AE3	673		AE6	436	
	OAL	260		AE4	608		AE11	222	
	OAL	335		AE4	638		AE12	505	
	OAL	844		AE4	711		AE12	1098	
	KT3	825		AE5	87		M12	435	
	KT3	1150		AE5	788	TUMULTS	G1	627	
	B	239		AE5	956		G2	710	
	B	394		AE7	222		AE1	213	
	C	653		AE7	865		AE2	498	
	C	664		AE8	827		AE3	74	
	C	815		AE9	1000		AE6	719	
	TH	408		AE10	150		AE8	487	
	FL	601		AE10	497		AE12	239	
	M12	80		AE10	646	TUMULTUOUS	CM	41	
	M12	720		AE11	171		L4	80	
	WB	117		AE12	234		TA	284	
	WB	131		AE12	865		HAP	2580	
	WB	150		AE12	985		VP9	57	
	WB	254		AE12	1033		AE1	998	
	WB	285		AE12	1144		AE12	407	
	WB	506		AE12	1185		M12	77	
	AS	39		OAL	878	TUN	MF	195	
	AS	75		KT1	350		SAA	458	
	DC	37		KT2	260		KT2	558	
	ECG2	17		KT3	655		C	473	
TRUTHS	AA	654		CAM	130	TUNE	EIE	8	
	MD	94		TH	399		T27	21	
	RL	66		M12	653		VP4	69	
	RL	72		M12	786		VP9	61	
	RL	142		AU	414		G2	542	
	RL	409		WB	529		OAE1	1	
	HAP	876		M15	471		ESK	16	
	HAP	925		GP	107	TUNED	AK	45	
	J1	228		CI	623		HAP	369	
	J6	205	TRYING	ETC	25		DHP	21	
	VCS	30		AE11	1129		DO	2	
	AE6	152		B	307		FL	111	
	AE11	519	TUB	PO	13	TUNEFUL	AM	1116	
	OAL	275	TUBE	PP	5		AA	196	
	TJD	76	TUCK	SMP	29		ER	5	
	HIF	114	TUCKED	PM	11		L1	32	
	C	207		J6	367		FS2	3	
	C	335		OAE2	76		AK	27	
	M15	211		WB	37		SSC	6	
	M15	231	TUCKING	BP	82		PP	37	
	GP	78	TUCKS	AE12	587		M1	945	
TRY.	AM	591	TUFT	FL	360		DHP	27	
	AM	595	TUFTED	AE3	300		VP1	112	
	SM2	17	TUFTS	G4	24		VP3	87	
	E	7	TUG	AE3	896		VP3	88	
	PSF	34		AE5	157		VP5	2	
	AA	171		AE5	246		VP5	133	
	AA	462		AE5	258		VP6	123	
	AA	744		AE9	759		VP9	43	
	EPC	31		AE10	417		VP9	80	

Word	Code	No.		Word	Code	No.		Word	Code	No.
TUNEFUL	VP10	11		TURN	M1	569		TURNED	M1	547
	G2	243			M1	722			M13	76
	G3	522			M13	101			M13	205
	G4	670			M13	113			HI	144
	AE7	49			VP3	87			VP3	55
	AE12	580			VP8	148			VP7	51
	AF	21			G1	1			G2	194
	KT2	229			G1	97			AE1	556
	KT3	122			G1	330			AE1	860
	KT3	137			G1	360			AE4	659
	HIF	808			G1	567			AE5	230
TUNES	PAA	35			G1	663			AE5	701
TUNNELS	AE8	558			G2	552			AE5	774
TUNNY'S	P5	265			G2	583			AE6	80
TURBANTS	AM	824			G3	255			AE6	319
	AE9	844			G3	260			AE6	737
TURBET	H2	75			G3	302			AE6	1247
TURBOTS	P6	53			G3	769			AE7	1052
TURBULENCE	HIF	311			G3	785			AE8	136
TURBULENT	AA	153			G4	255			AE9	1007
	J10	266			G4	492			AE9	1038
	M1	787			AE2	254			AE10	127
	HIF	724			AE2	494			AE10	458
TURF	AM	554			AE3	698			AE10	843
	J3	35			AE4	776			AE10	1269
	J3	285			AE5	529			AE11	1111
	P1	75			AE5	653			AE11	1170
	VP10	51			AE5	697			AE12	557
	G1	98			AE5	879			AE12	975
	G1	465			AE6	4			KT1	164
	G2	194			AE6	713			KT1	216
	G3	138			AE8	595			KT1	400
	AE1	298			AE9	571			KT2	48
	AE3	390			AE10	736			KT2	51
	AE7	152			AE10	846			KT2	506
	AE7	999			AE11	928			KT2	624
	AE8	237			AE11	938			KT3	253
	AE11	326			AE11	1095			KT3	261
	OAL	121			AE11	1241			KT3	645
	KT2	46			AE11	1264			KT3	995
	FL	66			OAL	877			KT3	996
	FL	222			MG	14			M8	258
TURFS	G1	192			MM	12			M8	382
	G1	663			DO	48			B	3
	AE6	231			KT1	30			B	156
TURK	HAP	693			KT1	191			B	666
	EDS	9			KT2	34			BP	98
TURKISH	AM	823			KT3	204			CAM	168
	EPF	9			KT3	237			HIF	304
TURK'S	MD	104			KT3	397			HIF	638
TURKS	AR	187			KT3	427			TH	21
	AM	982			BP	151			TH	365
	EWGR	11			C	754			M11	291
	SCD2	8			M12	652			FL	22
	EC	37			WB	320			FL	180
	HAP	706			WB	362			FL	191
TURMOILED	AE3	243			WB	371			FL	290
TURMOILS	AE1	381			M15	404			M12	34
TURN	LC	111			M15	409			M12	203
	PWGR	28			M15	483			M12	287
	PCG2	2			CI	386			M12	417
	PCG2	6			CI	420			WB	520
	EKK	18			CI	606			WB	533
	POE	31			EMKG	3			CI	603
	PLG	33		TURNAMENTS	KT2	493			PTP	31
	PSF	14			TH	18			AS	47
	PUOS	30		TURNED	HS	91		TURNER'S	G2	631
	AA	336			SEL1	13		TURNEY	KT3	512
	AA	964			SCD2	12			FL	288
	SAA	297			POE	18		TURNEYS	KT1	22
	SAA	366			AA	403		TURNING	AR	153
	PDG	37			AA	886			J3	55
	EDGA	8			AA	930			J3	252
	EDGA	22			MD	51			P5	105
	AT	119			D	5			AE5	797
	EC	44			SAA	383			AE6	633
	L4	106			SAA	201			AE6	1097
	T27	108			SAA	936			AE9	527
	H9	14			PK	18			AE10	1034
	TA	81			OE	29			AE11	701
	HAP	1359			EC	8			AE11	1063
	HAP	1679			HH	5			AE12	118
	BR	11			HAP	1328			KT3	642
	PP	5			HAP	1732			KT3	1137
	PTS	15			HAP	2523			M8	259
	EL	44			OD	7			HIF	629
	EL	150			EL	88			C	455
	PSH	32			EL	228			FL	1
	J3	329			J3	120			WB	54
	J3	375			J3	200		TURNS	AM	261
	J6	346			J3	257			AM	386
	J6	641			J6	467			ECG1	12
	P3	150			J6	613			SCD2	22
	P5	110			J10	398			PUO2	8
	P5	202			J10	508			MD	110
	M1	350			P3	160			SAA	988

TURNS	RL	420	TURNUS	AE7	795	TURNUS	AE12	785
	OE	26		AE7	823		AE12	816
	L1	52		AE7	901		AE12	836
	H29	48		AE7	1072		AE12	872
	TA	118		AE8	1		AE12	900
	HAP	434		AE8	27		AE12	926
	HAP	466		AE8	714		AE12	947
	HAP	1007		AE8	816		AE12	948
	HAP	1041		AE9	3		AE12	999
	HAP	2467		AE9	8		AE12	1058
	BR	44		AE9	34		AE12	1066
	PTS	2		AE9	53		AE12	1110
	J6	797		AE9	74		AE12	1125
	P1	249		AE9	153		AE12	1152
	P5	228		AE9	168		AE12	1178
	M1	311		AE9	357		AE12	1252
	M1	848		AE9	438		AE12	1286
	M1	860		AE9	503		AE12	1319
	VP3	88		AE9	614		AE12	1366
	VP8	87		AE9	698	TURNUS'	AE7	558
	G2	78		AE9	712		AE7	898
	G2	540		AE9	753		AE7	942
	G3	138		AE9	768		AE7	1002
	G3	353		AE9	779		AE7	1033
	G4	367		AE9	938		AE8	647
	G4	597		AE9	984		AE9	807
	G4	613		AE9	1000		AE10	869
	AE1	151		AE9	1009		AE11	552
	AE1	865		AE9	1064		AE12	84
	AE3	748		AE9	1078		AE12	63
	AE3	749		AE10	30		AE12	212
	AE3	759		AE10	116		AE12	249
	AE4	375		AE10	215		AE12	790
	AE4	411		AE10	224	TURRET	H29	17
	AE4	562		AE10	328		KT2	463
	AE4	853		AE10	372	TURRET'S	AE4	673
	AE5	181		AE10	384	TURRETS	AM	1186
	AE6	183		AE10	427		EL	91
	AE6	994		AE10	636		J3	322
	AE6	1085		AE10	642		M1	404
	AE7	999		AE10	653		VP2	30
	AE8	30		AE10	663		AE1	506
	AE8	593		AE10	671		AE2	602
	AE8	594		AE10	683		AE6	1070
	AE8	821		AE10	696		AE8	782
	AE9	220		AE10	700		AE9	323
	AE9	331		AE10	717		AE9	770
	AE9	523		AE10	739		AE10	355
	AE9	748		AE10	784		OAL	75
	AE9	849		AE10	882	TURTLES	M13	137
	AE9	979		AE10	891		VP1	77
	AE9	1074		AE10	912		KT2	519
	AE10	1004		AE10	914	TUSCAN	H29	2
	AE10	1072		AE10	927		J1	31
	AE11	657		AE10	937		P3	49
	AE11	1124		AE10	962		G1	671
	AE11	1195		AE10	975		G2	268
	AE12	102		AE11	27		AE1	102
	AE12	258		AE11	171		AE7	286
	AE12	462		AE11	184		AE7	331
	AE12	700		AE11	195		AE7	600
	AE12	1088		AE11	265		AE7	919
	AE12	1247		AE11	275		AE8	657
	OAL	270		AE11	336		AE8	664
	AF	86		AE11	343		AE8	753
	AF	90		AE11	518		AE8	792
	KT1	467		AE11	556		AE8	800
	KT1	530		AE11	575		AE8	861
	KT2	1		AE11	677		AE9	12
	KT3	623		AE11	697		AE9	796
	TJD	180		AE11	733		AE10	109
	M8	196		AE11	767		AE10	229
	M8	279		AE11	803		AE10	242
	C	439		AE11	1199		AE10	287
	TH	408		AE11	1258		AE10	292
	M11	159		AE11	1293		AE10	332
	FL	299		AE11	1313		AE10	423
	M12	225		AE12	1		AE10	594
	WB	438		AE12	15		AE10	978
	M15	627		AE12	88		AE10	1065
	CI	635		AE12	150		AE11	262
	SMP	34		AE12	275		AE11	283
	SMP	36		AE12	330		AE11	783
	ESK	10		AE12	354		AE11	871
TURNUS	J1	245		AE12	480		AE11	896
	AE7	83		AE12	487		AE11	924
	AE7	84		AE12	509		AE11	953
	AE7	483		AE12	530		AE11	1073
	AE7	513		AE12	546		AE12	189
	AE7	520		AE12	555		AE12	351
	AE7	570		AE12	659		AE12	409
	AE7	578		AE12	685		AE12	438
	AE7	592		AE12	718		AE12	807
	AE7	610		AE12	729	TUSCANS	AE8	626
	AE7	623		AE12	738		AE8	648
	AE7	660		AE12	749		AE9	186

Word	Ref	Num
TUSCANS	AE11	928
	AE11	937
	AE11	1213
	AE12	421
TUSK	M8	137
TUSKS	HAP	50
	G3	387
	G3	398
	G4	589
	AE10	1004
	KT2	206
	M8	28
	M8	106
TUSKY	H2	48
	VP7	41
	VP10	89
	AE1	448
	AE4	229
	AE7	424
	M8	216
TUTELARY	G1	19
	AU	574
TUTOR	J6	826
	P2	40
	AE5	715
	CI	214
TUTOR'S	CI	129
TUTORS	J10	467
	P1	23
TUZZES	P4	90
TWAIN	G4	202
	C	717
TWANGED	HIF	70
TWANGING	AE5	87
	AE5	688
	AE9	804
	AE9	900
	AE11	1251
TWEED	PUO3	5
	HAP	209
TWELFTH	PWG	26
	PWG	41
TWELVE	PLG	9
	MF	129
	PK	26
	T18	1
	TA	421
	TA	422
	J1	75
	J6	263
	J6	746
	G1	320
	G1	329
	AE1	544
	AE5	733
	AE9	360
	AE11	201
	AE12	247
	AE12	1302
	HIF	584
	HIF	667
	C	448
	FL	543
	M12	727
TWELVEMONTHS	EC	43
TWELVEPENCE	J3	268
TWELVESCORE	T18	39
TWENTY	PWGR	2
	AA	218
	SAA	448
	PD	45
	PAA	1
	J6	630
	AE9	56
	KT3	955
	TJD	157
	HIF	430
	C	438
	C	738
	FL	249
TWICE	AR	182
	AM	129
	AM	398
	AM	683
	ETL	23
	POE	23
	PSF	43
	MF	131
	PDG	7
	PDG	21
	AT	85
	TA	183
	TA	422
	HAP	2468
	VP3	7
	VP3	41
TWICE	VP3	42
	VP3	50
	G1	73
	G1	661
	G2	205
	G2	568
	G2	569
	G3	482
	G4	732
	AE1	107
	AE1	527
	AE1	895
	AE1	986
	AE2	173
	AE2	286
	AE2	287
	AE2	869
	AE3	612
	AE4	334
	AE4	822
	AE6	49
	AE6	50
	AE6	203
	AE6	205
	AE6	781
	AE8	511
	AE9	203
	AE9	204
	AE9	870
	AE9	1080
	AE9	1081
	AE11	497
	AE11	498
	AE11	937
	AE11	938
	AE12	57
	AE12	835
	AE12	854
	DO	99
	KT3	649
	M8	60
	CAM	217
	HIF	557
	C	798
	M12	153
	M12	551
	M15	41
	M15	357
TWICE-CONQUERED	AE9	811
	AE11	620
TWICE-FIRED	AM	695
TWIG	G2	451
TWIGS	VP2	107
	G1	358
	G2	329
	G2	626
	AE6	310
	AE11	95
	AE11	835
TWILIGHT	PRH	5
	EDG	43
	T18	14
	B	118
	C	214
	M11	273
TWILLET	PD	50
TWIN	H3	2
	AE6	107
	AE7	930
TWINE	L4	72
	HAP	440
	P3	78
	VP8	17
	G1	357
	G2	170
	G2	329
	AE7	876
	OAL	785
	KT2	603
	KT3	171
	FL	263
TWINED	AE8	365
	FL	130
TWINES	G2	302
TWINING	L4	41
	NS	8
	NS	19
	NS	30
	M1	157
	FL	80
TWINKLE	SMM1	6
	SEL2	14
	WB	29
TWINKLED	HAP	1469
TWINKLES	L4	101
TWINKLING	H2	51
TWINKLING	AE4	505
	M15	704
TWINS	T27	119
	P5	61
	P6	42
	GK	89
	AE5	372
	AE6	784
	AE8	836
	AE10	545
	KT2	10
	M8	46
	M8	141
TWIN-STARS	SAA	611
TWIRLS	ESF	24
TWIST	AE11	95
	AE11	561
	M12	198
TWISTED	G4	48
	AE2	754
	AE7	631
	AE12	185
	B	64
TWITCHING	TH	371
TWITTER	G4	434
TWO	SMA	127
	PRL	15
	VHH	13
	AM	25
	AM	64
	AM	185
	AM	186
	AM	335
	AM	506
	AM	746
	AM	762
	AM	1162
	PCG1	19
	SCG1	31
	ECD	18
	EUO	14
	E	29
	PAZ	21
	EKK	21
	EOE	3
	EOE	8
	EOE	12
	EOE	23
	HP	237
	ETG	12
	AA	601
	AA	748
	ELB	30
	MD	182
	SAA	409
	SAA	814
	PK	9
	EK	17
	EDGA	1
	EDGA	3
	AT	81
	ER	50
	T18	33
	HH	21
	HAP	101
	HAP	1662
	HAP	1826
	HAP	1831
	HAP	2195
	HAP	2572
	EMI	6
	BR	17
	EDS	2
	EDS	14
	ETS	22
	PMS	20
	EKA	15
	EL	109
	J3	428
	J6	488
	J6	835
	J6	836
	J10	526
	J16	34
	P1	4
	P1	219
	P1	253
	P2	39
	P3	192
	P3	243
	P6	115
	M1	56
	M1	58
	M1	359
	M1	433
	M1	441

Word	Ref	No.
TWO	M1	479
	M1	626
	M1	860
	M1	1037
	M9	11
	M9	105
	M9	112
	M9	148
	M13	43
	M13	138
	HI	94
	SLT1	3
	VP2	51
	VP2	53
	VP3	41
	VP3	55
	VP3	60
	VP3	65
	VP3	105
	VP5	103
	VP5	106
	VP5	108
	VP6	19
	VP7	1
	VP8	1
	VP8	6
	VP9	8
	G1	327
	G1	330
	G1	360
	G3	51
	G3	270
	G3	333
	G4	93
	G4	121
	G4	337
	G4	421
	G4	515
	G4	531
	G4	547
	AE1	233
	AE1	373
	AE1	431
	AE2	270
	AE3	427
	AE3	456
	AE3	705
	AE3	819
	AE4	136
	AE4	682
	AE4	77
	AE5	80
	AE5	102
	AE5	103
	AE5	346
	AE5	350
	AE5	352
	AE5	393
	AE5	403
	AE5	443
	AE5	482
	AE5	534
	AE6	230
	AE6	280
	AE6	537
	AE6	1059
	AE6	1131
	AE6	1235
	AE7	631
	AE7	673
	AE7	840
	AE7	930
	AE8	109
	AE8	226
	AE8	467
	AE8	468
	AE8	684
	AE8	605
	AE8	895
	AE9	315
	AE9	347
	AE9	351
	AE9	352
	AE9	730
	AE9	775
	AE9	916
	AE9	924
	AE9	957
	AE9	1014
	AE10	187
	AE10	233
	AE10	784
	AE10	811
	AE10	1077
	AE11	103
	AE11	439
TWO	AE12	249
	AE12	250
	AE12	710
	AE12	732
	AE12	738
	AE12	749
	AE12	764
	AE12	801
	AE12	1031
	AE12	1042
	MM	38
	ETO	3
	DO	10
	KT1	42
	KT1	94
	KT1	142
	KT1	155
	KT2	173
	KT2	176
	KT2	198
	KT2	204
	KT2	234
	KT2	317
	KT2	400
	KT2	614
	KT3	275
	KT3	488
	KT3	567
	KT3	595
	KT3	1115
	TJD	24
	TJD	30
	TJD	203
	M8	192
	M8	269
	M8	304
	B	132
	B	262
	BP	16
	BP	38
	BP	47
	BP	157
	HIF	286
	HIF	365
	C	11
	C	35
	C	171
	C	186
	C	191
	C	211
	C	298
	C	460
	TH	113
	TH	379
	M11	64
	FL	286
	FL	306
	M12	323
	M12	507
	M12	508
	M12	510
	M12	586
	M12	666
	M12	828
	AU	85
	AU	458
	WB	495
	M15	366
	M15	367
	M15	446
	CI	60
	CI	102
	CI	515
	CI	591
	CI	600
	PTP	13
	PTP	52
	PMK	30
	PMK	32
	EMKG	13
TWOFOLD	G2	217
TWO-HANDED	L4	150
	J1	30
	J6	456
TWO-LEGGED	AA	170
	J10	389
TWOPENCE	PDG	25
	AT	74
TYANAEAN	BP	191
TYBRIS	AE8	437
TYBURN	PLB	34
TYCHO	UDH	43
TYDEUS	AE6	646
TYDIDES	AE1	139
	AU	536
TYMPANY	MF	194
TYPE	TA	258
	P3	68
TYPES	MF	29
TYPHOEUS	AR	37
	AE8	398
	AE9	969
TYRANNIC	AT	37
	HAP	245
	HAP	2164
	AE11	816
TYRANNIES	HAP	239
TYRANNY	DC	1
	AA	784
	SAA	85
	SAA	667
	HAP	853
	HAP	1974
	KT1	86
	KT3	671
TYRANT	AM	166
	PTL	18
	AA	337
	MD	283
	MD	303
	L3	198
	PDG	23
	TA	136
	HAP	219
	HAP	2459
	HAP	2582
	J10	295
	J10	472
	P3	67
	P5	193
	M1	287
	M1	305
	M1	377
	SLT1	10
	SLT1	11
	SLT1	20
	SLT1	21
	SLT1	29
	SLT1	30
	G4	164
	AE1	79
	AE1	498
	AE4	597
	AE6	1121
	AE8	859
	AE10	1011
	KT1	270
	KT3	228
	B	3
	B	108
	B	131
	B	288
	HIF	139
	HIF	523
	HIF	567
	HIF	742
	C	713
	CAM	41
	M15	178
TYRANT'S	PRH	28
	SAA	714
	J10	263
	AE3	75
	AE4	463
	AE8	440
	AE8	659
	AE8	633
	B	119
	B	595
	HIF	416
	HIF	476
	HIF	511
	HIF	664
	C	606
TYRANTS	H3	21
	BR	342
	J6	626
	AE6	845
	KT2	168
	M11	114
	M15	79
TYRE	PC1	17
	SAA	71
	SAA	178
	SAA	230
	SAA	597
	SAA	625
	AE1	470
	AE1	1028
	AE4	788
	AE4	962
	M15	438

Word	Ref	Num
TYRE'S	SAA	556
	SAA	815
TYRES	AE10	562
TYRIAN	ER	1
	H29	27
	J1	36
	P2	117
	M1	449
	VP4	55
	G2	727
	G3	25
	G3	479
	AE1	21
	AE1	463
	AE1	468
	AE1	477
	AE1	804
	AE1	866
	AE1	902
	AE1	962
	AE1	988
	AE1	1019
	AE1	1024
	AE4	50
	AE4	103
	AE4	143
	AE4	157
	AE4	166
	AE4	188
	AE4	199
	AE4	295
	AE4	348
	AE4	391
	AE4	433
	AE4	464
	AE4	500
	AE5	148
	AE5	175
	AE5	746
	AE11	1136
	SMP	56
TYRIANS	AA	842
	BR	130
	AE1	586
	AE1	618
	AE1	796
	AE1	933
	AE1	1047
	AE4	867
	AE4	894
TYRIANS'	AE1	649
TYRRHENE	G2	226
	AE6	459
	AE6	945
	AE7	8
	AE7	64
	AE7	1019
	AE8	695
	AE8	729
	AE8	803
	AE10	219
	AE11	764
	AE11	1119
TYRRHENUS	AE11	914
TYRRHEUS	AE7	675
	AE7	676
	AE7	708
	AE9	32
TYRRHEUS'	AE7	741
TYRRHIDAE	AE7	673
TYRUS	AA	705
TYSANDER	AE2	340
TYTHES	SAA	661
UCALEGON	AE2	419
UDDER	G3	284
UDDERS	VP2	53
	VP7	22
	G2	763
	G3	483
	AE8	113
	OAL	395
	M15	109
	M15	695
UFENS	AE7	1026
	AE7	1092
	AE8	9
	AE10	721
	AE12	675
	AE12	932
UGLINESS	C	66

Word	Ref	Num
UGLINESS	WB	366
	WB	491
UGLY	AA	73
	HAP	2348
	PKA	17
	J10	475
	WB	126
	WB	323
	WB	487
ULCER	P3	230
	P4	103
ULTIMATE	P1	90
ULYSSEAN	AU	100
ULYSSES	AE2	10
	AE2	116
	AE2	167
	AE2	172
	AE2	219
	AE2	341
	AE2	1036
	AE3	354
	AE3	806
	AE3	824
	AE6	710
	AE9	818
	AE11	406
	HIF	208
	HIF	434
	HIF	594
	HIF	603
	AU	9
	AU	87
	AU	135
	AU	598
ULYSSES'	J10	401
	M13	38
	VP8	96
	AE2	57
	AU	76
UMBRIAN	P3	140
	AE12	1088
UMBRITIUS	J3	37
UMBRO	AE7	1032
	AE10	758
UMPIRE	SMA	83
	VP7	5
	KT2	209
UMPIRES	TJD	170
UNABLE	PNH	19
	AA	699
	EL	245
	J1	41
	J6	795
	M9	15
	G2	514
	AE6	768
	AF	109
	AF	116
	CAM	230
	M11	320
	AU	4
	M15	353
UNACCOMPLISHED	HIF	560
UNACQUAINTED	AR	25
UNACTIVE	M1	35
UNAFFECTED	KT3	921
UNAIDED	AE12	27
UNALTERED	TA	215
	KT3	1041
UNANIMOUS	AE10	266
UNANSWERED	VP2	105
	OAL	546
	B	696
UNAPPALLED	AE10	1224
	AE11	963
	M11	143
UNARMED	PAL	7
	J10	319
	AE2	85
	AE10	201
	AE11	954
	KT2	137
	M8	120
	TH	128
	TA	54
UNARRAYED	OAL	65
UNARTFUL	RL	144
UNASKED	M1	141
	VP3	100
	VP5	143
	G3	492
	AE10	688
	KT2	259
UNASSISTED	AE9	259
UNASSISTING	HIF	381
UNATTENDED	HAP	1901

Word	Ref	Num
UNAUSPICIOUS	AE11	238
	AE11	524
UNAUTHORIZED	AE1	191
UNAVAILING	H1	140
	G4	489
	G4	753
	AE2	626
	AE6	1226
	AE11	18
	AE11	239
	B	728
	CAM	356
UNAWARE	KT1	258
	KT1	492
	KT2	18
	AU	611
UNAWARES	J1	64
	AE11	1184
UNAWED	M1	116
UNBAR	AE2	34
	AE2	349
	AE7	853
	AE9	918
UNBARRED	AE8	348
	C	431
	AU	573
UNBARS	AE7	848
UNBATHED	AE7	1103
	CI	599
UNBEARDED	BR	260
UNBEARING	H2	21
UNBELIEVED	B	314
UNBELIEVERS	SAA	94
UNBELIEVING	C	745
UNBELOVED	AE1	536
UNBEND	PUO2	2
	GE	42
UNBENDS	SMA	97
UNBENEFICED	HAP	1478
UNBENT	AE6	143
	HIF	626
UNBESPOKEN	AA	242
UNBIASED	SAA	783
UNBID	HIF	784
UNBIDDEN	VP4	22
	G1	83
	G1	227
	DO	83
	TH	275
	WB	6
	CI	542
	CI	543
UNBIND	M1	534
	AE2	198
	AE4	704
	AE7	563
	AE12	304
UNBINDS	G1	64
	AE3	475
UNBLAMED	AA	479
	FL	513
UNBLEMISHED	SAA	131
	HAP	806
	J3	231
	J6	235
	AE6	897
	AE10	1215
	PMK	9
	EMM	4
UNBLEST	HAP	1931
	G1	229
UNBODIED	M15	240
UNBORN	SMA	120
	DA	151
	EL	236
	KT2	497
	M8	255
	M12	598
UNBORROWED	VP4	53
	G1	542
	WB	385
UNBOSOM	EL	248
UNBOUGHT	H2	72
	TJD	92
	TH	62
UNBOUND	G1	98
	AE3	92
	AE4	737
	AE11	847
	KT3	708
	M8	90
	M8	150
UNBOUNDED	AA	762
	TA	62
	HAP	2096
	BR	351

UNBRACE	J6	210	UNCONCERNED	TA	12	UNDAUNTED	AE10	1147
UNBRACED	AE12	1317		M1	126		AE10	1296
UNBRED	AE7	1096		AE10	166		AE11	480
UNBRIBED	AA	190		AE10	865		AE11	645
	EL	30		AE12	26		AE12	352
UNBROKEN	PMQ	5		TH	211		AE12	806
	ETG	21		M11	20		B	389
	G1	75	UNCONCERNEDLY	TA	199		HIF	85
	G4	426		G2	589	UNDEBAUCHED	PUO2	10
	AE10	1102	UNCONDITIONAL	AM	1074		J6	17
	HIF	366	UNCONFINED	CM	16	UNDECAYED	AE10	860
	PWR	22		P3	234	UNDECEIVED	KT3	1151
UNBUILT	DA	13		P5	41	UNDECEIVES	SAA	1034
UNBURIED	AE4	892		M1	810	UNDECIDED	G4	132
	AE6	227		OAL	37	UNDEFENDED	HAP	1920
	AE11	4	UNCONFINEDLY	HAP	1189	UNDEFILED	AK	69
	AF	139	UNCONQUERED	AR	55	UNDEPLORED	M11	372
	KT1	85		AA	844	UNDEPRIVED	GP	126
UNBURNED	AE11	324		AE5	247	UNDERGO	SIE	12
	KT1	85		AE8	389		HP	110
UNCALLED	HAP	2473		AE8	971		DA	193
	CAM	364		AE9	824		EPF	4
	AU	48		AE11	471		G3	539
UNCANCELED	B	519		AE12	283		AE3	586
UNCASED	HAP	2021		FL	527		AE9	682
UNCAUTIOUS	KT2	75		M12	814		OAL	298
UNCENSURED	P1	215	UNCONQUERING	SAA	1092		KT1	243
UNCERTAIN	VHH	19	UNCONSCIONABLE	P2	77		HIF	368
	SAA	565	UNCONSCIONABLY	J3	301	UNDERGROUND	G3	832
	PDG	17	UNCONSTANT	DA	53	UNDERMINED	RL	161
	L3	8		H29	77		G4	355
	L3	269	UNCONSTRAINED	G4	572		OAL	701
	L3	276		GP	112		AU	303
	HAP	1702	UNCONSUMMATE	AE10	1015		AU	386
	PP	6	UNCONTENDED	AE5	510	UNDERPRAISING	MM	52
	M1	796	UNCONTROLLED	L1	25	UNDERSONG	VP3	86
	HI	98		KT1	514	UNDERSTAND	AR	91
	VP5	6		HIF	466		RH	71
	G1	172		WB	138		AM	646
	G1	344	UNCORRUPT	RL	299		PAR	22
	G2	514	UNCORRUPTED	M1	114		PC1	5
	AE1	305		AE8	548		HP	256
	AE3	9	UNCOUPLED	L3	10		MF	178
	AE6	615		KT2	236		SAA	777
	AE7	692	UNCOUTH	J3	426		RL	401
	AE8	338		HI	147		OE	51
	AE9	113		G1	482		L4	181
	AE10	426		AE7	226		HAP	126
	AE10	711		KT3	200		J10	342
	KT1	434		TH	82		P5	181
	TJD	169	UNCOUTHLY	ECD	13		M1	526
	FL	588	UNCOVERED	AE2	700		M1	896
	M12	560	UNCREATED	VCS	7		G3	293
UNCERTAINLY	AM	126	UNCROWN	AE12	449		OAL	161
UNCHANGED	HAP	1	UNCTION	MF	118		OAL	416
	KT3	272		VCS	11		C	383
	CAM	229	UNCTUOUS	AM	65		AU	459
	FL	550		AM	984		WB	513
UNCHARMING	HAP	1503		G2	123		PWR	27
UNCHASTE	HP	13		G2	416	UNDERSTANDS	PIE	28
UNCHAWED	P5	8		G2	603		CAM	133
UNCHECKED	HAP	1593		AE6	309		M15	195
UNCHEWED	AA	113		AE11	1155	UNDERSTOOD	AM	150
	AE10	1025		KT3	959		AM	770
UNCIVIL	HAP	2304		M15	526		PTL	1
	T27	90	UNCULTIVATED	TA	352		PCG1	32
UNCLE	MF	174		G2	601		PAR	18
	J6	707		AE1	425		PNH	47
	P2	18	UNCUMBERED	TJD	18		EAL	7
UNCLEAN	J3	116	UNCURL	G4	693		PTC	33
	G1	545		AE5	167		CM	101
	AE3	283	UNCURLED	OAL	575		RL	121
	AE6	415	UNCURLS	HAP	1564		L4	215
	GP	83	UNDAMS	G1	160		HAP	424
UNCLE'S	J6	733	UNDAUNTED	SMA	103		HAP	429
	P6	128		AM	696		HAP	1002
	M12	789		EPF	4		HAP	1761
	AU	245		PUO5	27		HAP	2200
	AU	255		SAA	593		J6	431
UNCLES	J1	238		TA	176		J10	160
	P1	23		HAP	442		P1	149
UNCLOGGED	M15	370		BR	112		GK	141
UNCLOSE	SAA	745		ODA	53		G2	288
UNCLOSED	AE9	1022		G2	234		AE1	882
	CI	177		G4	113		AE6	1127
UNCLOUDED	G2	687		AE1	84		OAL	469
	G4	112		AE2	80		KT1	439
	AE5	83		AE2	456		B	97
UNCOMBED	G3	562		AE2	614		B	421
	AE6	415		AE3	127		WB	474
	OAL	575		AE6	1215		CI	63
	KT1	539		AE8	170		ERL	4
	KT3	207		AE8	613	UNDERTAKE	AM	106
UNCONCERNED	PAZ	39		AE9	153		SEL1	9
	MD	281		AE9	903		EAZ	2
	H3	23		AE10	384		EOE	1

UNDERTAKE	PP	40	UNDOUBTED	AE8	51	UNERRING	M12	169	
	P4	8		AE8	400	UNESPIED	PMQ	12	
	AE2	859		AE11	531		AE9	786	
	AE6	204		AE11	578		AE11	1122	
	AE6	502		AU	252		WB	57	
	C	476	UNDRAINED	AE3	921	UNEVEN	M1	687	
	AU	507	UNDRESS	HAP	2325	UNEXACTED	G1	196	
UNDERTAKEN	M12	224	UNDRESSED	SCG1	5	UNEXAMPLED	AE8	844	
UNDERTAKER	PD	15		VP2	104	UNEXERCISED	AE7	958	
UNDERTAKES	J10	483	UNDRIED	AE11	361		AU	412	
UNDERTOOK	AE5	492	UNDRIVEN	AE10	499	UNEXHAUSTED	EL	234	
	AE10	1090	UNDULATING	M12	60		AE10	254	
	AU	301	UNDUTEOUS	AE8	430	UNEXPECTED	AM	738	
UNDERWENT	TA	176	UNEASY	AM	1019		TA	26	
	HAP	1084		PLN	40		AE1	718	
	G2	581		E	5		AE2	441	
	AE2	6		MD	60		AE9	57	
	AE2	740		L3	277		AE11	656	
	AE9	727		HAP	385		KT3	645	
	AE10	1068		SKA6	4		KT3	686	
	B	21		J6	28		CI	549	
	AU	309		J10	249	UNEXPERIENCED	AE7	728	
UNDERWOOD	M13	156		P5	235	UNEXPLORED	AE4	600	
UNDERWRITE	EOE	18		AE11	458		B	678	
UNDESERVED	HAP	2463		HIF	758	UNEXTINGUISHED	AE6	601	
	AE11	1244		M11	323		B	732	
	CI	470	UNEMPLOYED	EL	286	UNFADED	AE11	101	
UNDESERVING	J3	77		DO	65	UNFADING	M1	764	
	AE8	763	UNENJOYED	KT3	772	UNFAILING	HAP	585	
	OAL	357	UNENVIED	AE12	223		HAP	652	
	M8	190	UNEQUAL	AR	232		HAP	667	
UNDESIRED	AE2	902		AM	106		HAP	1056	
UNDESIRING	P5	161		AM	236		HAP	1063	
UNDETERMINED	G1	30		AM	323		HIF	322	
UNDIGESTED	J3	327		AA	834	UNFAITHFUL	H29	89	
	J3	377		AA	910		HAP	764	
	P3	5		T23	25		HAP	2032	
	G3	787		TA	188	UNFAITHFULLY	SM2	9	
UNDIMINISHED	J10	443		HAP	9	UNFASHIONED	M1	11	
UNDIPPED	AU	457		J10	394	UNFATHOMED	SAA	43	
UNDISCERNED	AE5	767		P3	171		AE6	783	
	AE5	792		P3	233		C	544	
UNDISCOVERED	LC	78		M1	42	UNFEATHERED	AA	170	
	PA	43		M1	986		G4	745	
	DA	162		M9	81	UNFEATURED	J10	308	
	AE4	442		HI	54	UNFED	RL	159	
	CAM	380		VP2	41		HAP	1489	
UNDISGUISED	KT1	264		VP8	105		HAP	1515	
UNDISTINGUISHED	AM	141		G1	261		AE11	101	
	SAA	140		G3	435	UNFELT	AA	693	
	EL	145		G3	573		L2	4	
	J3	291		G4	359		AE7	491	
	P5	16		AE1	664		M12	442	
	AE2	412		AE1	716	UNFINISHED	AM	766	
	AE12	334		AE2	452		PCG2	12	
	AE12	605		AE2	486		HP	201	
	M12	354		AE2	508		P1	180	
	M12	569		AE2	577		M1	570	
UNDISTURBED	EPF	2		AE2	985		M1	749	
	AA	42		AE4	882		VP6	125	
	MF	73		AE5	1059		VP9	31	
	SAA	657		AE9	542		G3	777	
	L2	21		AE9	683		AE2	143	
	G2	659		AE9	848		AE2	911	
	AE7	862		AE10	408		AE4	126	
UNDIVIDED	HAP	1103		AE10	643		AE8	145	
UNDO	PAR	5		AE10	1274		AE10	106	
	OAL	110		AE11	469		AE12	814	
UNDONE	HS	36		AE11	1070		CAM	163	
	S	3		AE12	229		TH	327	
	HP	225		AE12	354		M11	13	
	PUO3	1		AE12	1260		M15	564	
	AA	470		OAE1	34	UNFIRM	AE10	397	
	AA	702		C	188	UNFIT	AA	161	
	SAA	8		M15	292		HAP	1767	
	SAA	307	UNEQUALLY	GK	46		G3	102	
	SAA	872	UNERRING	RL	277		G4	190	
	SAA	886		HAP	65		AE8	669	
	HH	43		HAP	1051		KT1	26	
	HAP	445		HAP	1255		CI	1	
	HAP	1208		HAP	1717	UNFIXED	AM	228	
	PTS	16		J10	538		AA	154	
	STS3	10		M1	615		CAM	141	
	SSH	8		M1	699	UNFLEDGED	MF	76	
	J10	6		G1	620		J1	119	
	AE4	136		G3	403		AE5	753	
	OAL	110		G4	565		AE10	149	
	KT2	504		AE3	461		KT2	521	
	TJD	13		AE6	173		C	461	
	TJD	164		AE6	473		M12	20	
UNDOUBTED	HAP	656		AE9	227	UNFLETCHED	PWGR	14	
	HAP	751		AE9	591	UNFOLD	AM	692	
	HAP	935		AE10	1277		TA	491	
	M1	294		AE12	580		P2	41	
	G2	253		AE12	712		AE10	1	
	AE6	931		M8	186		ESK	21	

UNFOLDED	LC	98
	BR	109
	G3	643
UNFOLDS	J10	279
	AE6	393
	AE6	774
	AE10	24
UNFORCED	M1	116
	GK	66
	AE11	466
	AE11	654
	AU	382
UNFORDED	G3	396
UNFORESEEN	AE11	656
	KT2	74
	B	314
	CAM	160
	CI	337
UNFORGIVING	M15	160
UNFORTUNATELY	AA	821
	B	630
UNFOUGHT	AE9	159
UNFOUND	HAP	2032
	CI	138
UNFRAMED	M1	11
UNFREQUENTED	RH	3
UNFRIENDED	AM	1047
UNGATHERED	VP1	51
	M8	39
UNGENTLE	M1	875
UNGILDED	PNH	7
UNGIRT	AE8	965
UNGIVING	EUF	8
UNGODDED	HAP	2036
UNGODLY	MD	42
	M1	322
	M15	136
	ETP	16
UNGORGED	TH	213
UNGOVERNABLE	BR	224
UNGOVERNED	SAA	761
	AE2	1044
	AE7	724
	AE12	878
	M11	118
	CI	13
	CI	358
UNGRACIOUS	HAP	1441
	J10	545
UNGRANTED	AE9	377
UNGRATEFUL	PEL	6
	DA	29
	SSF	1
	AA	12
	AA	149
	RL	144
	L3	123
	T23	47
	T23	107
	TA	266
	HAP	1569
	HAP	2455
	BR	118
	J3	41
	M1	987
	M1	1015
	M13	183
	MC	67
	VP6	85
	G2	262
	G2	427
	AE2	211
	AE4	441
	AE4	467
	AE4	529
	AE4	777
	AE4	847
	AE4	879
	AE5	1063
	AE12	119
	OAL	354
	KT3	413
	TJD	109
	HIF	114
	HIF	472
	TH	140
	TH	291
	M15	181
	CI	71
UNGUARDED	AE12	817
	AE12	1059
	M11	290
	CI	604
UNGUIDED	ER	38
UNHALLOWED	J3	233
	HIF	133

UNHALLOWED	M12	346
UNHAND	T27	29
UNHAPPY	LC	90
	SCG3	1
	SCG3	17
	PCB	1
	CM	57
	CM	83
	CM	131
	DA	175
	DA	210
	SAA	885
	HAP	230
	ODA	14
	J10	399
	P5	89
	M1	739
	HI	52
	HI	81
	HI	121
	VP2	1
	VP2	77
	VP3	3
	VP5	134
	VP8	50
	VP8	65
	G1	106
	G1	228
	G1	339
	G1	555
	G1	663
	G2	308
	G2	424
	G3	108
	G4	462
	G4	669
	G4	689
	G4	715
	G4	751
	G4	772
	AE1	46
	AE1	487
	AE1	639
	AE1	647
	AE1	742
	AE1	914
	AE1	1004
	AE1	1049
	AE2	88
	AE2	323
	AE2	682
	AE2	786
	AE2	867
	AE2	903
	AE3	59
	AE3	420
	AE3	438
	AE3	789
	AE3	825
	AE3	840
	AE3	930
	AE4	617
	AE4	768
	AE4	973
	AE5	370
	AE5	547
	AE5	624
	AE5	735
	AE5	811
	AE5	827
	AE5	877
	AE6	226
	AE6	342
	AE6	445
	AE6	598
	AE6	607
	AE6	618
	AE6	694
	AE6	700
	AE6	728
	AE6	840
	AE6	1125
	AE7	320
	AE7	560
	AE7	1001
	AE7	1054
	AE7	1061
	AE8	494
	AE9	277
	AE9	530
	AE9	576
	AE9	1026
	AE10	273
	AE10	704
	AE10	1027
	AE11	39

UNHAPPY	AE11	59
	AE11	81
	AE11	116
	AE11	269
	AE11	332
	AE11	379
	AE11	1172
	AE11	1224
	AE11	1294
	AE12	680
	AE12	1252
	KT1	252
	KT2	106
	KT2	286
	KT3	243
	B	346
	B	644
	CAM	227
	CAM	236
	HIF	491
	C	503
	TH	164
	TH	383
	M11	361
	M11	457
	WB	355
	CI	256
UNHARMED	HAP	299
	M1	763
UNHARMFUL	HAP	299
UNHARNASSED	VP2	96
	AE9	425
UNHEARD	AT	53
	HAP	2198
	M1	979
	VP2	6
	KT3	783
UNHEEDED	AR	127
	AT	39
	M8	71
	B	242
	HIF	815
	C	674
UNHONORED	M8	16
	AE11	314
	DO	65
UNHOPED	AR	140
	AE5	262
	AE7	400
	AE10	99
	AE12	489
	HIF	318
	C	314
	M12	657
UNHOPED-FOR	AE9	939
UNHORSED	KT3	514
	KT3	601
	KT3	623
UNHOSPITABLE	L5	5
	HAP	1906
	M1	284
	AE3	64
	AE6	492
UNHURT	HP	26
	G2	454
UNIMPAIRED	LC	147
UNINFORMED	RH	1
UNINSPIRED	RL	247
	VP6	10
	BR	224
UNINTELLIGIBLE	AU	453
UNINTOMBED	AE6	508
UNION	L4	202
	HAP	1034
	HAP	1347
	HAP	1371
	BR	32
	AE4	65
	AE12	303
UNIT	BR	326
UNITE	DC	40
	AM	165
	AA	285
	MD	197
	HAP	686
	HAP	2068
	AE2	561
	AE9	14
	AE10	575
	AE12	733
	AE12	804
	DO	151
	CAM	74
	M11	161
	ESK	13
UNITED	AR	296

Word	Code	No.	Word	Code	No.	Word	Code	No.
UNITED	AA	916	UNKIND	VP2	5	UNKNOWN	KT1	578
	BR	31		AE1	564		KT2	155
	G4	241		WB	359		KT3	313
	AE1	548	UNKINDLY	E	3		M8	242
	AE1	606		AA	128		B	114
	AE2	852		HAP	994		B	464
	AE4	145		J10	291		B	494
	AE10	143		P5	242		CAM	288
	AE10	454		M9	97		M11	16
	AE11	481		KT3	413		M11	232
	AE11	613	UNKINDNESS	SEL2	5		M11	452
	AE11	897		STS1	17		FL	143
	AE12	381		M1	1017		M12	1
	AE12	399	UNKNOWING	AM	384		M12	96
	KT2	214		PUO4	37		AU	605
	M12	12		SAA	715		WB	175
	M12	665		ER	38		M15	277
	AS	73		J3	418		M15	412
UNITES	AA	491		M1	908		CI	137
	AE6	985		VP1	49		CI	380
UNITIES	PMQ	4		G4	126		CI	391
	GK	167		G4	796	UNLABORED	L5	17
UNITY	HAP	1024		AE2	145		VP4	33
	HAP	1102		AE2	516	UNLACED	M12	198
	MM	35		AE4	725	UNLADE	AM	1200
UNIVERSAL	UDH	72		AE6	236	UNLATCHED	AE6	704
	DC	4		AE10	323	UNLAWFUL	PCG1	44
	AA	421		AE10	351		KT3	200
	RL	15		AE11	472	UNLEARNED	PUO1	30
	RL	354		AE12	621		RL	417
	L1	42		AE12	773	UNLED	M13	52
	HAP	1063		AE12	1029	UNLESS	PA	44
	SSC	2		KT2	629		PLG	27
	SSC	12		KT3	309		PSF	20
	BR	87		KT3	1012		PSF	46
	ODA	45		KT3	1068		AA	590
	J6	445		CAM	295		RL	217
	P1	7		TH	83		RL	291
	M1	237		WB	100		RL	439
	HI	117		CI	84		L2	46
	G3	827	UNKNOWINGLY	AE11	1306		FS3	14
	AE8	194		KT1	278		HAP	765
	AE11	331	UNKNOWN	SMA	89		HAP	820
	M11	173		LCA	2		BR	348
UNIVERSALS	HAP	651		VHH	27		EL	332
UNIVERSE	AM	651		AM	641		J3	435
	AE4	266		AM	703		J6	667
UNIVERSITIES	PTP	17		AM	865		J6	860
UNIVERSITY	AA	659		SCG2	5		P5	208
UNJUDGED	SAA	581		CM	47		P5	274
UNJUST	HS	83		AA	659		GK	155
	SAA	134		T23	18		G1	231
	SAA	236		HAP	1298		G1	235
	SAA	587		BR	192		G1	286
	SAA	863		J6	409		AE1	759
	TA	322		J6	518		AE7	608
	HAP	1198		J6	782		AE10	345
	HAP	1990		HI	146		AE10	529
	HAP	2130		VP1	85		AE10	714
	HAP	2143		G2	116		AE11	494
	EL	105		G2	210		AE11	600
	VP1	93		G3	124		AE12	833
	AE9	271		G3	532		KT3	331
	AE10	97		AE1	890		KT3	333
	AE10	114		AE1	427		AU	42
	AE11	169		AE1	522		WB	94
	AE11	549		AE1	531		WB	240
	KT1	497		AE1	566		ERL	3
	KT2	96		AE2	104		PMK	36
	B	480		AE2	535	UNLETTERED	RL	322
	HIF	190		AE2	777	UNLICKED	SAA	502
	HIF	242		AE2	998		HAP	36
	M12	327		AE3	44	UNLIGHTED	M8	253
	AU	479		AE4	450	UNLIKE	EEL	27
UNJUSTLY	AM	529		AE4	678		L4	255
	PA	14		AE5	5		HAP	2342
	DA	138		AE5	1136		J6	8
	HAP	2537		AE7	98		J6	609
	AE8	156		AE7	187		P1	227
	AE11	333		AE7	226		M1	341
	KT1	488		AE7	271		G2	127
	M8	337		AE7	1063		G4	149
	AU	478		AE8	976		AE2	358
UNKEMBED	J3	121		AE10	76		AE9	640
UNKENNEL	SMP	31		AE10	960		AE12	508
UNKENNELED	HAP	152		AE11	390		KT1	540
UNKIND	SCG2	7		AE11	516		C	119
	SCG2	27		AE11	1005		M11	228
	SM2	9		AE12	484		M15	493
	SLN	19		AE12	1065	UNLIMITED	SAA	234
	L4	116		OAL	254	UNLOAD	G2	554
	T23	47		OAL	257		AE12	1165
	HAP	337		AF	166	UNLOADED	BR	263
	PP	25		AF	176	UNLOCK	L1	15
	J10	437		KT1	409		G2	245
	SLT1	14		KT1	571	UNLOCKED	HAP	258

Word	Code	No.
UNLOCKED	AE2	337
	B	229
UNLOCKS	AM	1134
	CAM	154
UNLUCKY	T27	116
	HAP	1944
	HAP	2450
	J6	672
	J10	205
	RL	17
UNMADE		
UNMAN	AE9	662
UNMANLY	J6	664
	P3	235
	P4	93
	AE2	810
	AE8	332
UNMANNERED	PFD	17
	J6	543
UNMARKED	AE1	614
	FL	62
UNMARRIED	G4	683
	AE6	424
	AE12	39
	OAL	113
UNMASKED	MD	221
UNMASTERED	AU	595
UNMATCHED	VHH	14
UNMEANT	AE10	561
UNMINDFUL	VP8	125
	G4	635
	AE1	293
	AE5	46
	AE12	481
	HIF	671
UNMIXED	L2	22
	AK	69
	VP10	7
UNMOOR	AE4	573
UNMOVED	AM	457
	CM	10
	RL	17
	AT	14
	VP10	45
	G1	670
	G2	404
	G2	704
	G3	630
	AE1	675
	AE3	569
	AE4	480
	AE4	644
	AE5	516
	AE5	526
	AE6	634
	AE7	809
	AE7	813
	AE10	985
	AE11	352
	AE11	1217
	AE12	586
	B	673
	M11	340
	M11	356
UNNAMED	PTC	3
	BR	192
UNNATURAL	PLN	24
	HAP	2322
	HAP	2380
UNNAVIGABLE	J10	13
	M1	20
	AE6	341
UNNECESSARY	M1	338
UNNERVED	ETG	24
UNNUMBERED	AE6	398
	AE8	398
UNOBSERVED	SAA	116
	AE2	619
	AE2	1034
UNOFFENDING	CM	133
	AE11	163
UNOPPOSED	AM	940
UNPAID	J3	479
	HIF	136
	CI	618
UNPALATABLE	MD	148
UNPARDONING	KT2	344
UNPAYING	EK	26
UNPEOPLED	VP6	61
	G3	719
UNPERCEIVED	VP6	124
UNPERFORMING	ECG1	38
UNPERPLEXED	RL	264
UNPITIED	AT	53
	HAP	1541
	VP2	6
	VP10	14
UNPITIED	AE7	406
	AE10	778
	HIF	476
	M12	779
UNPLEASED	AA	155
	AE12	205
	OAL	164
	KT1	379
UNPLEASING	GK	101
	AE11	686
	HIF	467
	SAA	502
UNPOINTED		
UNPOLISHED	RL	453
	J6	12
	CI	130
UNPOLLUTED	HAP	339
UNPRACTICED	AR	211
	PTC	7
	HP	140
	HAP	1908
	KT3	326
UNPRAISED	AE1	994
	CI	469
UNPREPARED	TA	17
	KT2	74
	CI	551
UNPRINCIPLED	HAP	1196
UNPROFANED	AE11	890
UNPROFITABLE	T23	32
	J10	417
	AE6	827
	AE12	922
	C	775
UNPROFITABLY	MC	68
UNPROPPED	M8	132
UNPROVED	J6	313
UNPROVIDED	TA	6
	AE12	843
UNPROVOKED	M1	133
UNPUNISHABLE	OAL	38
UNPUNISHED	AA	845
	RL	100
	J1	4
	P2	58
	AE6	1216
	AE8	752
	AE9	1059
	AE10	29
	AE10	1044
	AE11	887
	KT2	570
	M8	305
	M8	314
	HIF	292
	C	285
	M12	372
UNPURSUED	SAA	187
UNQUESTIONED	HS	117
	CM	82
	AA	317
	AA	764
	KT1	578
	KT2	139
UNRAISED	GK	55
UNREAD	HAP	1703
UNREADY	AM	1016
UNREASONABLE	PLG	14
UNRECLAIMED	M13	81
UNREGARDED	HAP	1017
	J3	427
	AE12	432
	TH	238
UNRELENTING	M13	24
	AE1	2
	AE6	763
	KT2	88
UNRELIEVED	HIF	82
UNREMEMBERING	AE6	1019
UNREPENTING	HAP	1586
	AE6	770
	TH	168
UNRESISTED	AA	1020
	L4	4
	HAP	2127
	AE1	86
	AE2	660
	AE2	679
	AE6	387
	AE6	624
	AE9	680
	AE12	270
	AE12	766
	AE12	1170
	KT2	352
	B	282
	HIF	120
UNRESISTING	M15	169
UNRESOLVED	HP	154
	AE9	1078
	AE12	62
UNRESOLVING	AE8	513
UNREST	L3	273
UNRESTRAINED	HAP	2103
	HAP	2298
	B	438
UNREVEALED	AE6	374
UNREVENGED	G3	352
	AE2	789
	AE2	910
	AE3	824
	AE4	945
	AE11	1226
	M8	17
UNREWARDED	AA	560
UNRIGGED	CI	620
UNRIGHTEOUS	PA	13
	HAP	2007
	HAP	2160
	CI	474
UNRIGHTEOUSLY	HAP	2371
UNRIPE	AM	553
	HP	254
	PR	25
	AE9	246
	B	254
	M10	26
UNRIVALED	HAP	1070
	J10	492
UNROOT	AE2	411
UNROOTED	SSC	49
UNROUNDED	GK	55
UNRUFFLE	AE1	212
UNRUFFLED	AE12	1204
UNRULY	M1	38
	G3	396
	AE7	748
UNSAFE	PUO1	23
	MD	66
	J3	331
	AE3	928
	HIF	777
	M11	5
UNSAFELY	EL	368
UNSAID	C	468
UNSATED	J6	185
UNSATIATE	AA	987
UNSATISFIED	L3	155
	J1	7
	L4	176
UNSAVORY	OAL	586
	OAE2	42
UNSEAL	P6	37
	C	247
UNSEALED	M11	303
UNSEASONABLY	P4	30
UNSEEN	LC	85
	AM	839
	HAP	52
	P4	81
	M1	677
	M13	195
	AE1	572
	AE1	615
	AE1	723
	AE1	957
	AE2	623
	AE2	1075
	AE4	2
	AE4	821
	AE7	491
	AE11	913
	AE11	1130
	AE12	617
	AE12	1243
	OAL	211
	KT3	589
	KT3	783
	B	212
	B	256
	TH	96
	FL	501
	FL	567
	AU	21
	WB	291
	M15	155
UNSEIZED	AA	258
UNSETTLED	AE1	791
UNSHAKEN	HAP	1336
UNSHAMED	KT3	741
UNSHEATHE	AE6	371
UNSHEATHED	AE6	404
	AE12	264

Word	Code	No.
UNSHEATHED	KT2	142
	KT2	253
UNSHEATHES	AE4	929
UNSHIELDED	M12	135
UNSHORN	M1	765
	VP5	97
	AE9	925
	AE11	852
	FL	39
	FL	266
UNSINCERE	AM	833
	L3	52
	L4	42
	G2	584
	CAM	259
UNSINEWED	P6	89
UNSINGED	AE11	1158
UNSINGLED	AE4	221
UNSKILFUL	RL	225
UNSKILLED	PAZ	17
	DA	134
	RL	140
	J3	79
	P3	63
	P5	144
	SLT2	1
	AE7	1096
	AE11	775
UNSLAIN	HIF	136
UNSLUICE	M8	365
UNSOILED	RL	341
	AK	68
UNSOLD	M8	63
UNSOLID	M15	307
UNSOUGHT	HS	39
	AA	190
	MF	169
	HAP	1533
	B	206
	B	727
UNSOULED	L4	251
UNSOUND	AE5	366
UNSOURED	H9	26
UNSOWN	M1	138
UNSPELLED	SAA	117
UNSPENT	DC	36
UNSPOILED	AE11	890
UNSPOTTED	HP	114
	HAP	3
	HAP	1091
	AE6	59
	AE11	729
UNSTABLE	M1	19
	SAA	855
	HAP	1161
UNSTAINED	FL	552
UNSTAYED	AE10	675
UNSTOPPED	AE5	862
UNSTRING	VP6	29
UNSTRUNG	AE5	553
	M12	748
UNSUCCESSFUL	AE2	149
	AE7	427
UNSUITING	L3	161
UNSULLIED	AE12	942
UNSUNG	AE7	1014
UNSUPPLIED	B	38
	CAM	321
	M12	751
UNSUSPECTED	RL	436
	HAP	2222
UNSUSTAINED	AE11	1258
UNSWEATING	J3	178
UNTAINTED	SMA	19
	EUO2	21
	EMW	1
	RL	264
UNTAKEN	AE10	1173
UNTAMED	HAP	1314
	J10	266
	AE4	880
	HIF	288
	TH	37
UNTASTED	G3	532
	AE6	821
UNTAUGHT	PTC	7
	HP	139
	AM	626
	AE6	348
	AE8	832
UNTEACH	BR	284
UNTHANKED	AM	766
	KT1	388
UNTHINKING	L3	52
	P3	197
	AE10	999
UNTHINKING	SMP	40
	SMP	44
UNTHRIFT	HAP	1590
	P5	237
UNTHRIFTY	G1	226
UNTIE	HAP	2116
UNTIED	KT3	782
UNTIMELY	EL	236
	AE4	26
	AE4	887
	AE4	891
	AE7	1041
	KT3	868
	KT3	1104
	C	184
UNTIRED	G3	318
	AE6	1180
UNTOLD	J6	560
	G1	239
	AE10	731
	KT3	965
UNTOUCHED	ENH	14
	HP	31
	G3	68
	AE10	701
	AE10	1173
	OAL	766
	M12	648
UNTRIED	HAP	199
	HAP	1535
	VP7	42
	G3	298
	G4	781
	AE4	599
	M15	261
UNTRODDEN	AE8	280
UNTRODE	AE11	793
UNTRUE	FL	564
	SMP	89
	SMP	95
UNTRUTHS	HAP	610
UNTUNE	SSC	63
	VP9	70
UNTURNED	AE2	133
UNTWIST	M15	381
UNUSEFUL	J3	88
	J6	813
UNUSUAL	HP	80
	G3	241
	AE1	135
	AE8	319
	AE11	827
	AE11	1096
	AE12	378
	B	342
UNUSED	HAP	1246
	EHC	3
	G4	34
	AE10	508
	AE10	815
	AE11	673
	TH	97
UNUSEFUL	HAP	125
UNVANQUISHED	AE5	290
	AU	144
UNVEIL	AE3	121
	M15	212
UNVEXED	G2	659
	TJD	2
UNWARILY	AA	311
UNWARLIKE	G2	239
	G3	587
	M15	629
UNWARMED	AE11	30
UNWARY	G2	415
	G4	662
	G4	708
	AE2	265
	AE2	449
	AE2	511
	AE12	463
	OAL	521
	KT3	643
	B	263
	HIF	121
UNWASHED	G3	677
UNWEARIED	LC	117
	AM	1049
	HAP	1705
	VP6	123
	AE6	656
UNWELCOME	AE4	284
	AE11	496
	KT1	388
UNWEPT	AE11	573
UNWET	B	673
UNWHOLESOME	HAP	1236
	M1	82
	VP10	112
	FL	17
UNWIELDILY	G4	623
UNWIELDY	AM	498
	L4	251
	H9	28
	J3	408
	J10	18
	M1	37
	G1	164
	G1	244
	G3	783
	AE1	589
	AE2	309
	AE5	265
	AE10	1284
	AE12	779
	AE12	1307
UNWILLING	AM	285
	AM	294
	HP	27
	DA	48
	H3	55
	HAP	1207
	HAP	2136
	HAP	2137
	EL	9
	P3	19
	P5	194
	M1	837
	G1	144
	G1	589
	AE6	89
	AE6	622
	AE7	776
	AE9	51
	AE12	576
	AE12	1178
	KT3	274
	KT3	380
	TJD	119
	M8	341
	HIF	454
	M12	468
UNWILLINGLY	AM	975
	M1	585
	AE2	1093
	AE10	331
	HIF	158
UNWIND	LC	71
UNWISE	M13	102
	G1	514
UNWONTED	AE10	1279
UNWORTHY	DA	179
	AA	846
	SAA	1085
	T23	39
	G2	517
	G3	55
	G3	6
	AE6	226
	AE7	905
	AE9	257
	AE9	262
	AE11	573
	AE12	1156
	KT2	316
	B	498
	HIF	419
	HIF	553
	TH	127
UNWOUNDED	AU	434
UNWROUGHT	P3	39
UNYIELDED	KT3	651
UNYOKED	AE6	58
UPBRAID	HP	194
	HP	216
	L4	115
	PSH	31
	HI	134
	AE3	575
	AE11	250
	HIF	701
	CI	354
UPBRAIDED	EMP	7
	J6	262
	HIF	490
	WB	458
UPBRAIDING	G4	507
UPBRAIDS	PRL	33
	HAP	1544
	AE10	777
	AE10	830
	AE12	852

Word	Ref	No.
UPBRAIDS	AE12	1285
	B	549
UPHELD	VHH	29
	SAA	559
	HAP	739
	HAP	1386
	M1	874
	KT1	91
	HIF	615
UPHOLD	AA	595
	HAP	770
UPLIFTED	L4	275
	TA	82
	M15	199
UPRIGHT	AM	872
	J3	48
	J3	405
	M1	436
	G3	121
	AE4	405
	AE10	1280
	KT3	49
	CAM	224
	C	617
	TH	146
	FL	271
	AU	173
	WB	227
UPRIGHTLY	KT3	850
UPROARS	HIF	265
UPSILON	P3	109
UPSTAIRS	PCB	26
UPSTART	HAP	175
UPSTARTED	TH	210
	AU	3
UPSTARTING	HIF	152
UPSTARTS	WB	291
URANIA'S	SAA	1100
URGE	AM	839
	ENH	26
	CM	8
	HP	112
	AA	419
	AA	1022
	MD	187
	SAA	156
	SAA	721
	SAA	785
	RL	168
	HI	49
	VP4	44
	G3	787
	AE4	624
	AE5	273
	AE5	301
	AE6	138
	AE6	60
	AE6	628
	AE6	1219
	AE7	39
	AE8	27
	AE8	597
	AE10	181
	AE10	866
	AE11	925
	AE12	121
	AE12	913
	HIF	547
	FL	575
	AU	119
	AU	322
	AU	354
	M15	273
URGED	CM	58
	AA	684
	AA	749
	SAA	41
	SAA	105
	SAA	758
	SAA	764
	AT	123
	L3	210
	TA	92
	HAP	106
	HAP	804
	HAP	931
	HAP	1168
	M1	728
	M1	729
	G1	218
	G2	637
	AE1	814
	AE2	887
	AE4	828
	AE5	660
	AE6	944
URGED	AE7	703
	AE8	496
	AE9	84
	AE10	108
	AE10	1274
	AE12	50
	OAE2	8
	TJD	119
	B	455
	CAM	169
	HIF	67
	HIF	229
	HIF	534
	TH	273
	M12	109
	M12	429
	AU	544
	M15	10
URGES	AM	516
	RL	313
	G3	75
	AE4	162
	AE5	446
	AE6	270
	AE7	660
	AE9	239
	AE10	613
	AE11	1052
	AE12	424
	AE12	511
URGING	M1	327
	M1	1094
	AE2	722
	AE2	832
	AE10	619
	AE12	945
	OAL	77
	M11	164
URINE	P1	220
	M15	620
URN	HS	145
	AM	928
	CM	142
	DA	206
	TA	368
	J3	36
	P6	80
	M13	215
	G3	45
	AE6	29
	AE6	326
	AE6	584
	AE7	1082
	AE8	103
	OAL	206
	M8	388
	M8	389
	B	638
	M11	430
	M12	817
	M15	55
	M15	57
URNS	J10	382
	P2	108
	M1	379
	M1	790
	AE12	1248
URSIDIUS	J6	52
USAGE	HP	8
	HP	32
	J10	292
	TH	127
USE	AR	44
	LC	39
	LC	67
	LCA	29
	AM	664
	EWGR	23
	PA	21
	STL	13
	SCG1	28
	PM	17
	SCD1	20
	CM	114
	HP	49
	HP	141
	HP	172
	PUO3	12
	AA	6
	AA	281
	AA	720
	SAA	300
	RL	167
	RL	232
	RL	387
	RL	409
USE	RL	424
	RL	449
	L3	174
	L4	139
	L4	293
	T27	12
	TA	72
	AK	59
	HAP	39
	HAP	222
	HAP	806
	HAP	1130
	HAP	2288
	HAP	2378
	SKA3	15
	OD	21
	MS	22
	J3	96
	J6	274
	J6	495
	J6	770
	J6	810
	P2	77
	P5	1
	P6	52
	P6	160
	M1	547
	M9	18
	GK	33
	VP2	22
	VP8	135
	G1	63
	G2	366
	G2	608
	G2	622
	G2	630
	G3	6
	G3	101
	G3	480
	G3	703
	G3	732
	G4	154
	G4	231
	G4	383
	AE2	541
	AE2	711
	AE3	599
	AE4	125
	AE4	387
	AE5	555
	AE7	359
	AE7	1022
	AE9	901
	AE10	71
	AE10	474
	AE10	1300
	AE11	1082
	AE12	592
	AE12	1350
	OAL	540
	OAE2	31
	KT3	30
	KT3	47
	KT3	201
	TJD	84
	TJD	117
	B	100
	B	119
	B	209
	B	384
	M10	86
	C	498
	C	628
	M12	118
	M12	365
	AU	226
	AU	551
	M15	125
	M15	494
	AM	637
USED	PMQ	35
	EEL	28
	E	3
	PO	17
	PSF	23
	PR	14
	AA	124
	AA	677
	MD	159
	SAA	122
	AT	72
	L4	25
	T27	56
	PAA	31
	HAP	693
	HAP	1170

USED	HAP	2309	USURPER	HAP	2573	VAIN	SCG2	16		
	HAP	2392		VP8	62		SCG3	2		
	J6	110		VP8	68		SCG3	11		
	M9	64	USURPER'S	MD	31		S	2		
	VP2	74	USURPERS	AM	40		PLN	28		
	G3	760		PC2	29		PNH	50		
	AE1	265		HAP	517		E	1		
	AE1	1019		HAP	1019		ML	19		
	AE2	736		J10	178		SKK	4		
	AE5	490	USURPING	AR	133		SKK	17		
	AE6	320		MD	129		PTW	7		
	AE6	439		AE8	430		EOE	27		
	AE7	682		AE10	53		PTC	40		
	AE7	687		KT3	670		ETC	23		
	AE7	851	USURPS	J10	561		HP	3		
	AE9	403		AE6	125		HP	18		
	AE10	512		KT1	82		DA	3		
	AE10	1300		LC	33		DA	12		
	MM	4	UTMOST	DC	17		SSF	12		
	KT1	588		AM	1161		PUF	13		
	KT3	752		PUO4	32		AA	265		
	FL	409		MD	239		AA	322		
	M12	477		L4	35		AA	377		
	AU	222		TA	163		AA	428		
	AU	385		HAP	2090		AA	763		
	CI	81		HAP	2484		PLB	30		
	CI	452		J6	473		MD	219		
USEFUL	AM	634		P4	36		MF	114		
	PUO1	10		VP8	151		SAA	5		
	TA	338		G1	41		SAA	41		
	G1	203		G2	579		SAA	59		
	G2	574		AE3	316		SAA	484		
	G4	449		AE9	221		SAA	671		
	M15	170		AE9	1012		SAA	703		
USELESS	AR	190		AE10	1099		SAA	744		
	AM	222		AE11	1104		SAA	1029		
	AM	622		AE12	510		SAA	1030		
	PEL	27		AE12	712		EDGA	25		
	HP	55		AE12	828		RL	38		
	AA	505		AE12	958		RL	64		
	AA	615		AE12	1167		RL	267		
	D	4		AF	80		RL	431		
	SAA	77		KT1	39		L2	12		
	RL	334		KT1	438		L2	50		
	L2	44		KT2	389		L2	62		
	J3	297		KT3	308		L3	89		
	J10	84		KT3	620		L3	107		
	M1	665		CAM	377		L3	123		
	G3	833		TH	400		L3	157		
	AE1	406		M11	446		L3	188		
	AE2	696		AU	93		L3	205		
	AE2	871	UXORIOUSLY	J6	292		L3	224		
	AE3	620	UZ	PTP	24		L3	244		
	AE5	934	UZZA	SAA	407		L4	70		
	AE10	1127					L4	77		
	OAL	572					L4	87		
	B	565					L4	109		
	HIF	548					L4	184		
USES	PD	10					L4	204		
	B	667					L4	237		
USHER	SEL2	12	VACANT	HAP	1476		L4	245		
	FL	489		EL	347		T23	26		
USQUEBAUGH	PP	28		M1	93		T23	41		
USUAL	AA	555		AE9	388		T23	73		
	TA	40		CAM	246		H3	28		
	HAP	1798		ESK	25		FS3	16		
	BR	77	VACATION	PM	20		TA	168		
	M9	96		EUF	6		TA	186		
	G2	41		J6	100		TA	232		
	G4	635		HIF	583		AK	167		
	AE12	1317	VAILS	J1	177		HAP	72		
	B	196		J3	311		HAP	123		
	B	297	VAIN	UDH	25		HAP	513		
	TH	73		UDH	95		HAP	875		
	TH	235		AR	175		HAP	1029		
	M12	148		AR	213		HAP	1150		
USURER	SAA	285		SMA	53		HAP	1479		
USURP	EPC	21		LC	58		HAP	1811		
	HAP	89		PWG	56		HAP	2090		
	HAP	1201		LCA	3		HAP	2395		
	J1	151		LCA	19		PTS	38		
	AE6	825		AM	30		STS3	3		
	AE7	595		AM	125		SKA3	5		
	HIF	247		AM	132		SKA3	10		
USURPED	AA	179		AM	146		SKA3	11		
	HAP	1629		AM	207		SKA6	19		
	HAP	2157		AM	399		EL	7		
	ETS	13		AM	510		EL	101		
	M1	1052		AM	641		OD	17		
	G2	785		AM	755		MS	1		
	AE5	514		AM	800		PSH	40		
	AE11	334		AM	917		J1	76		
	AE12	99		AM	974		J1	94		
	B	419		AM	1026		J3	211		
USURPER	AM	849		SEL2	2		J3	217		
	SAA	153		SCG1	34		J6	246		

VAIN				VAIN				VAIN		
	J6	284			AE5	254			AE12	921
	J6	331			AE5	286			AE12	1072
	J10	80			AE5	334			AE12	1122
	J10	206			AE5	363			AE12	1134
	J10	319			AE5	517			AE12	1208
	J10	328			AE5	530			AE12	1311
	J10	547			AE5	590			AE12	1316
	J16	88			AE5	819			AE12	1326
	P1	1			AE5	823			OAL	26
	P1	268			AE5	904			OAL	140
	P3	59			AE5	1119			OAL	180
	P3	123			AE6	83			OAL	391
	P4	32			AE6	120			OAL	474
	P4	101			AE6	176			OAL	503
	P5	192			AE6	224			OAL	506
	P5	232			AE6	403			OAL	516
	P6	86			AE6	631			OAL	530
	M1	372			AE6	746			AF	66
	M1	418			AE6	794			DO	125
	M1	523			AE6	1116			KT1	420
	M1	723			AE7	260			KT1	567
	M1	797			AE7	410			KT2	605
	M1	815			AE7	417			KT3	634
	M9	126			AE7	428			KT3	652
	M9	140			AE7	506			KT3	794
	M9	149			AE7	562			KT3	1086
	M9	177			AE7	593			TJD	78
	M13	41			AE7	747			TJD	79
	M13	44			AE7	1039			M8	34
	M13	189			AE8	32			M8	36
	R	4			AE8	247			M8	336
	R	8			AE8	268			M8	379
	R	16			AE8	284			B	133
	R	20			AE8	305			B	280
	HI	9			AE8	496			B	294
	PLT	38			AE8	927			B	696
	GK	83			AE9	69			B	724
	GK	160			AE9	164			BP	194
	VP2	2			AE9	288			CAM	98
	VP2	11			AE9	377			CAM	228
	VP2	56			AE9	496			CAM	299
	VP2	101			AE9	537			CAM	336
	VP3	4			AE9	766			CAM	352
	VP3	73			AE9	836			CAM	359
	VP3	153			AE9	869			HIF	142
	VP7	98			AE9	1030			HIF	211
	VP8	28			AE9	1037			HIF	622
	VP8	34			AE9	1076			HIF	744
	VP8	50			AE9	1101			HIF	754
	G1	278			AE10	182			C	233
	G1	531			AE10	345			C	242
	G2	390			AE10	443			C	357
	G2	406			AE10	463			C	394
	G3	66			AE10	469			C	514
	G3	159			AE10	554			TH	43
	G3	394			AE10	607			TH	135
	G3	409			AE10	654			TH	174
	G3	574			AE10	679			TH	289
	G3	696			AE10	700			TH	238
	G3	816			AE10	766			M11	34
	G4	53			AE10	774			M11	119
	G4	423			AE10	816			M11	213
	G4	578			AE10	832			M11	253
	G4	588			AE10	853			M11	318
	G4	720			AE10	887			M11	357
	G4	725			AE10	915			M11	365
	G4	727			AE10	1197			FL	22
	G4	752			AE10	1257			FL	54
	AE1	407			AE11	73			FL	392
	AE1	456			AE11	232			FL	434
	AE1	818			AE11	239			M12	84
	AE2	285			AE11	270			M12	131
	AE2	452			AE11	300			M12	141
	AE2	464			AE11	408			M12	155
	AE2	467			AE11	475			M12	184
	AE2	515			AE11	520			M12	307
	AE2	705			AE11	555			M12	326
	AE2	713			AE11	812			M12	424
	AE2	886			AE11	1013			M12	487
	AE2	1078			AE11	1032			M12	644
	AE3	317			AE11	1037			M12	749
	AE3	346			AE11	1055			M12	767
	AE3	644			AE11	1227			M12	776
	AE3	703			AE11	1240			M12	796
	AE3	880			AE11	1301			AU	26
	AE3	935			AE12	72			AU	313
	AE4	111			AE12	150			AU	350
	AE4	181			AE12	497			AU	438
	AE4	304			AE12	559			AU	531
	AE4	344			AE12	595			WB	17
	AE4	532			AE12	686			WB	19
	AE4	634			AE12	708			WB	22
	AE4	680			AE12	791			WB	204
	AE4	887			AE12	816			WB	313
	AE5	37			AE12	865			WB	317
	AE5	107			AE12	873			M15	225
									M15	456

Word	Code	No.
VAIN	M15	567
	M15	690
	C1	62
	C1	302
	C1	323
	C1	335
	C1	336
	C1	362
	C1	385
	C1	523
	C1	529
	C1	589
	C1	623
	ERL	7
VAINER	J10	80
	OAL	26
	TH	31
	TH	289
	M11	119
VAINLY	AR	185
	LC	144
	PFD	27
	L3	280
	L4	66
	HAP	1017
	HAP	1111
	HAP	1168
	HAP	2102
	HAP	2498
	BR	57
	BR	286
	EL	268
	P2	92
	P4	81
	VP9	58
	AE3	890
	AE4	557
	AE5	452
	AE7	33
	AE7	618
	AE7	831
	AE10	822
	AE10	1267
	KT1	250
VALE	J3	29
	P5	35
	VP9	11
	AE4	224
	AE6	921
	AE6	953
	AE7	663
	AE8	809
	AE9	322
	AE11	795
	OAL	325
	WB	211
VALERUS	AE10	1065
VALES	DC	12
	H2	24
	M1	420
	VP5	57
	VP6	119
	VP10	11
	G1	517
	G2	258
	AE3	151
	AE8	406
	AE8	407
VALIANT	AM	667
	AM	1068
	SAA	1074
	SAA	1078
	EAA	14
	AE2	317
	AE6	1242
	AE8	205
	AE9	182
	AE11	528
	AE11	1285
	AE12	1289
	AF	6
	AF	142
	KT1	2
	KT1	156
	KT1	407
	KT3	522
	M8	2
	AU	543
	C1	287
VALLANCY	ENH	8
VALLEY	AK	180
	M1	770
	VP2	51
	VP5	131
	G2	662
	G2	691
VALLEY	G3	20
	G3	512
	AE5	376
	AE11	791
	M8	93
VALLEYS	M1	142
	M1	50
	M13	121
	G2	216
	G2	370
	G2	539
	AE4	643
	AE6	9
	AE12	1345
	FL	117
	M15	409
VALOR	HS	148
	AR	73
	AR	145
	PWG	59
	VHH	4
	AM	74
	AM	119
	AM	159
	AM	211
	AM	317
	AM	410
	AM	460
	AM	532
	PWGR	11
	A	10
	PTC	38
	HP	117
	EPF	8
	EPC	10
	TA	488
	EAA	13
	J1	172
	J16	93
	HI	121
	AE1	795
	AE1	884
	AE2	458
	AE2	541
	AE4	3
	AE5	507
	AE9	869
	AE10	444
	AE10	859
	AE11	64
	AE12	31
	AE12	735
	OAL	781
	KT2	416
	KT2	635
	KT3	824
	M8	159
	M8	235
	B	530
	HIF	125
	FL	545
	M12	222
	M12	608
	AU	29
	C1	493
VALOR'S	PTS	35
VALUE	PUO2	20
	EUO2	12
	AA	70
	L4	140
	J3	261
	KT3	780
	HIF	568
VALUED	HP	59
	PDS	44
	AE4	47
VALUES	AE11	538
VALUEST	P4	41
VAN	AM	741
	AE9	31
	AE10	784
VANDAL	ER	16
	PTP	35
VANDALS	HAP	2508
	GK	47
VANISH	SMA	16
	PNH	40
	G4	575
	AE5	695
	AE5	967
	KT3	585
VANISHED	AM	602
	PT	15
	UMR	2
	MF	82
	RL	28
VANISHED	DOD	8
	L3	87
	HAP	514
	EL	303
	EL	305
	AE1	318
	AE2	840
	AE2	945
	AE4	403
	AE5	238
	AE9	898
	AE10	936
	AE12	1276
	KT3	281
	M8	261
	C	315
	TH	216
	M11	14
	M11	388
	M11	408
	M12	201
	M15	636
	WB	223
VANISHES	J6	602
VANISHING	KT3	794
VANITIES	P2	120
VANITY	AM	675
	EMK	11
	P1	92
	AE11	630
VANQUISH	VHH	37
	AM	1212
	FS1	12
	AE3	472
	AE11	176
	OAL	220
	KT3	160
VANQUISHED	LC	21
	LCA	10
	LCA	12
	AM	119
	AM	1125
	AM	1156
	ER	10
	PDS	8
	PP	26
	SKA1	16
	J1	66
	J6	249
	J6	408
	P3	89
	M13	193
	VP7	98
	G3	346
	AE1	56
	AE1	104
	AE1	747
	AE2	495
	AE3	371
	AE5	402
	AE5	441
	AE5	462
	AE5	1025
	AE5	1061
	AE5	1112
	AE7	410
	AE8	962
	AE10	1042
	AE10	1073
	AE10	1135
	AE11	477
	AE11	1281
	AE12	57
	AE12	386
	AE12	497
	AE12	835
	AE12	981
	AE12	1104
	AF	115
	AF	122
	DO	96
	KT2	417
	CAM	229
	FL	431
	M12	191
	M12	737
	C1	396
VANQUISHER	P3	89
VANS	M12	749
	M12	750
VANTAGE	AE11	1042
VAPOR	EUF	13
	J6	807
VAPORS	SMA	15
	AM	51
	AM	330
	AM	984

Word	Ref	No.
VAPORS	AA	269
	AA	637
	AK	85
	HAP	1236
	BR	241
	J6	422
	M1	444
	M1	816
	AE3	190
	AE3	570
	AE4	365
	AE7	647
	AE8	323
	AE9	87
	AE9	313
	AE12	866
	OAL	266
	C	30
	TH	366
	M11	272
	M15	454
	STP	26
VARE	AA	595
VARIED	EL	121
	G1	609
	AE1	447
	AE1	1054
	OAL	871
	M12	735
	M15	238
VARIES	HAP	608
	G4	595
VARIOUS	SMA	4
	AM	817
	EEL	2
	PUO2	8
	ESF	21
	AA	545
	MD	25
	MD	252
	MD	297
	D	43
	SAA	277
	SAA	511
	SAA	854
	RL	18
	RL	129
	RL	242
	RL	244
	L1	21
	H29	77
	HAP	434
	HAP	770
	EL	143
	P5	67
	M1	1
	M1	367
	M1	558
	GK	71
	GK	169
	VP5	91
	VP6	55
	G1	76
	G1	217
	G1	604
	G2	102
	G2	118
	G2	126
	G2	622
	G2	679
	G4	587
	G4	610
	AE1	134
	AE1	285
	AE1	320
	AE1	519
	AE1	1040
	AE4	819
	AE4	1003
	AE5	117
	AE5	787
	AE5	948
	AE6	398
	AE6	1002
	AE6	1239
	AE7	428
	AE7	311
	AE8	414
	AE8	963
	AE9	2
	AE10	236
	AE10	962
	AE10	1073
	AE12	70
	AE12	190
	AE12	697
VARIOUS	AE12	708
	AE12	726
	AE12	968
	AE12	1322
	OAL	864
	OAL	865
	AF	86
	AF	90
	KT1	408
	KT2	619
	KT2	641
	KT3	878
	M8	193
	M10	40
	CAM	260
	HIF	170
	M11	133
	M11	264
	M11	297
	FL	356
VARIOUSLY	AM	817
	AA	8
	RL	55
	L3	33
	FL	116
VARLET	VP3	6
VARLETS	HAP	995
VARNISHED	TA	132
VARRO	AM	775
VARUS	VP6	8
	VP6	13
	VP9	31
	VP9	32
VARUS'	VP9	46
VARY	L3	215
	AE12	1290
	FL	76
	CI	567
VARYING	TA	79
	AE6	52
	AE12	102
	M15	614
	J6	226
VASES	AE1	904
VASSALS	PNH	43
	SAA	881
	AE11	641
	KT2	389
	B	20
VAST	AR	101
	LC	61
	AM	28
	AM	227
	AM	280
	AM	706
	PNH	19
	PNH	25
	PTW	15
	PCB	22
	MF	72
	SAA	687
	RL	360
	TA	73
	AK	11
	GE	41
	PP	4
	EL	304
	ESH	33
	J3	416
	J3	483
	J10	22
	J16	1
	P1	7
	P2	22
	P4	8
	P6	180
	M1	589
	M13	54
	G2	174
	G2	211
	G2	222
	G3	531
	AE1	49
	AE1	1050
	AE3	22
	AE3	835
	AE3	842
	AE4	260
	AE4	290
	AE5	155
	AE5	495
	AE6	626
	AE6	830
	AE7	229
	AE7	1107
	AE8	202
VAST	AE8	215
	AE8	820
	AE8	962
	AE9	606
	AE9	701
	AE9	760
	AE9	883
	AE9	960
	AE9	965
	AE11	1096
	AE12	1302
	OAL	202
	KT2	438
	KT2	451
	KT2	664
	KT3	525
	KT3	665
	M8	206
	B	103
	TH	241
	M11	423
	M12	829
	AU	166
	WB	393
	CI	401
	EMKG	15
VASTEST	AR	155
VASTLY	PWG	49
	J3	359
VAT	G2	10
VATS	G2	265
VAULT	G4	361
	AE12	433
	KT2	541
	KT3	797
VAULTED	L2	33
	J10	447
	M1	33
	G4	61
	G4	536
	G4	554
	AE2	668
	AE4	961
	AE5	671
	AE11	221
	AE12	1344
	AF	36
	KT3	266
	KT3	524
	KT3	582
	M8	134
	CI	580
VAUNTED	HAP	964
	AE2	735
	AE4	857
VAUNTER	HIF	336
VAUNTING	AE9	809
	AE10	907
	AE11	1060
	AE12	520
VAUNTS	AE10	30
	AE10	630
	AE10	822
	AE10	1257
	AE10	1291
	AE11	1015
	M15	342
	P4	50
VECTIDIUS	AE3	495
VEER	AE3	527
VEERED	SAA	212
	AE3	737
VEERS	AE5	1088
VEGETABLE	G2	118
	G4	178
	M15	709
VEGETIVE	M1	750
	KT3	1076
VEHICLE	ELB	19
VEHICLES	HAP	1400
VEIL	UDH	49
	LC	71
	SCG1	9
	MD	81
	L4	144
	FS3	16
	HAP	134
	HAP	135
	HAP	2071
	M1	515
	AE1	994
	AE3	519
	AE4	250
	AE10	820
	MFL	17
	CAM	219

Word	Code	Num		Word	Code	Num		Word	Code	Num
VEILED	HAP	2394		VENGEANCE	AR	199		VENT	MD	295
	J6	459			DA	59			SAA	451
	J6	511			AA	452			L3	66
	M1	535			MD	320			EL	245
	AE3	718			MD	187			J3	43
VEIN	HS	48			SAA	149			J6	526
	SMM2	16			SAA	170			M1	453
	STL	20			HAP	51			G3	421
	MF	179			HAP	1318			AE1	55
	AK	28			HAP	1573			AE3	703
	J1	227			HAP	1597			AE7	667
	J6	65			PDS	8			AE10	849
	P1	253			J1	6			AE11	142
	P6	173			P2	51			AE12	866
	M1	550			M1	374			AE12	986
	G3	700			VP6	109			KT3	150
	AE2	865			AE1	43			M8	223
	OAL	684			AE2	128			B	271
	KT1	284			AE2	781			HIF	334
	KT3	709			AE2	796			HIF	444
	M10	89			AE3	307			HIF	581
	PTP	39			AE3	839			AU	81
VEINS	DC	39			AE4	870			WB	178
	AM	553			AE6	98			WB	190
	PC2	17			AE6	515			M15	457
	L4	197			AE7	760			M15	518
	J1	67			AE8	643		VENTS	HI	192
	J6	239			AE9	585			G4	56
	J6	806			AE9	993			AE12	75
	J10	344			AE10	223		VENTURE	RH	102
	M1	142			AE10	1308			AM	980
	M1	545			AE11	274			SEL2	11
	VP8	99			AE12	1170			PAL	36
	G1	133			OAL	417			HP	102
	G1	205			AF	141			HP	168
	G2	165			KT2	637			PM	23
	G2	228			KT3	220			T27	22
	G3	677			M8	334			HAP	149
	G4	346			B	254			G1	613
	AE1	932			B	589			MG	9
	AE1	964			HIF	12		VENTURED	AR	239
	AE3	63			HIF	138			VHH	33
	AE3	398			HIF	150		VENTURES	PMQ	55
	AE4	2			HIF	294			AE9	531
	AE4	91			HIF	309			PWR	11
	AE4	131			HIF	427		VENTUROUS	AM	1197
	AE5	527			HIF	443			G4	28
	AE8	668			HIF	526			KT3	735
	AE11	643			HIF	536		VENULUS	AE8	13
	AE12	662			HIF	664			AE11	370
	KT1	468			C	273			AE11	453
	KT2	189			TH	136			AE11	1093
	KT3	755			TH	288		VENUS	UDH	55
	M8	348			M12	759			PWG	36
	CAM	25			M12	798			HP	124
	FL	11			M15	165			HP	235
	M15	511		VENGEFUL	AE10	777			DA	61
	STP	24			AE11	403			D	16
VELIN	AE6	499			AE12	1181			AT	110
VELINE	AE7	720		VENIAL	J6	821			L4	162
VELINUM'S	AE7	982			OAL	727			L4	204
VELVET	ENH	4			ETP	29			T18	82
	OAE2	28		VENICE	GK	139			T27	24
	FL	161		VENISON	M13	136			T27	100
	FL	252			AE1	274			T27	115
	FL	266		VENOM	EUF	18			HAP	2358
VENAL	MD	32			AA	229			BR	211
	J3	480			ELB	26			SKA5	3
VENERABLE	BR	110			MD	265			J6	739
	J6	659			MF	201			J10	444
	P6	10			EDGA	20			J16	8
	GK	175			EDGA	32			P2	126
	G2	668			L4	24			M1	620
	G3	517			PTS	7			M9	207
	AE1	617			J3	503			M13	15
	AE2	206			G1	197			G3	423
	AE2	394			AE1	964			G4	289
	AE2	971			AE2	291			G4	749
	AE5	806			AE4	131			AE1	312
	AE6	13			AE7	497			AE1	449
	AE6	553			AE7	567			AE1	570
	AE7	89			DO	87			AE1	874
	AE12	893			KT3	763			AE1	927
	AE12	1112			CAM	116			AE3	29
	DO	55			CI	11			AE3	611
	M8	87		VENOMED	G2	522			AE4	133
	HIF	17			G3	629			AE4	148
	C	374			AE7	1036			AE4	334
	FL	39			KT2	60			AE5	1045
	GP	3			CAM	25			AE8	78
VENERABLY	J6	31			M15	360			AE8	511
VENERATE	FL	330		VENOMOUS	PWR	8			AE8	974
VENERATION	P2	104		VENOMOUSLY	HAP	2466			AE9	165
VENEREAL	J6	440		VENOMS	MD	297			AE10	25
	L4	94		VENT	AA	589			AE10	200
VENETIANS	ECD	13			ELB	26			AE10	1078

Word	Code	No.	Word	Code	No.	Word	Code	No.
VENUS	AE12	615	VERSE	P1	31	VESSEL	HIF	429
	OAL	34		P1	67		HIF	599
	OAL	94		P1	93		C	346
	OAL	174		P1	106		C	472
	OAL	192		P1	120		M11	95
	OAL	577		P1	180		M11	133
	OAL	688		P1	187		M11	206
	OAL	707		P1	210		CI	265
	OAL	772		P5	12		CI	294
	DO	63		P6	8		CI	369
	KT1	262		VP3	132		CI	393
	KT1	500		VP4	31		CI	610
	KT2	83		VP4	70	VESSEL'S	PWR	11
	KT2	499		VP5	17	VESSELS	AM	16
	KT3	126		VP5	69		AM	216
	KT3	129		VP5	127		AM	263
	KT3	315		VP6	104		AM	455
	KT3	379		VP8	14		AM	565
	KT3	389		VP8	32		AM	779
	KT3	425		VP8	88		AM	1190
	KT3	433		VP8	93		RL	35
	KT3	563		VP8	95		L3	220
	KT3	673		VP8	97		L3	221
	KT3	1141		VP8	99		G1	408
	M10	57		VP8	149		AE1	207
	C	687		VP9	25		AE1	239
	FL	5		VP10	5		AE1	259
	CI	42		VP10	101		AE1	501
	ETP	22		G2	246		AE1	755
	SMP	77		G3	2		AE3	97
VENUS'	HP	131		AE3	372		AE3	879
	DA	35		AE3	573		AE4	553
	AE10	820		AE6	875		AE4	573
	AE10	857		AE9	597		AE5	29
	OAL	80		OAL	235		AE5	207
	KT2	471		OAL	236		AE5	906
VERB	J6	584		OAE1	3		AE6	3
VERDANT	AE6	869		OAE1	5		AE8	124
VERDICT	PMQ	28		OAE1	32		AE9	111
	EMM	11		OAE1	34		AE9	148
	HAP	2051		DO	4		AE10	315
VERGE	AM	455		TJD	31		AE10	418
	AM	653		TJD	209		AE11	402
	D	10		CAM	177		OAL	3
	BR	70		FL	616		KT3	758
	AE10	664		CI	33		CI	279
	M15	349	VERSED	J6	701	VEST	J3	250
VERIER	P4	61		AE2	935		J6	669
VERIEST	P3	153		AE5	924		J10	60
VERIFIED	L3	184		AE12	390		G3	839
VERJUICE	P4	73		TH	189		AE1	916
VERMILION	AA	649		AU	338		AE1	994
	VP10	40	VERSES	L1	40		AE2	529
VERMIN	ETC	9		VP9	49		AE3	626
	MD	31		AE9	1047		AE4	714
	HAP	593		DO	127		AE5	175
	HAP	1112	VERSES'	PMS	7		AE5	325
	G1	268	VERSIFY	J1	24		AE6	549
VERNAL	C	178	VERVAIN	VP8	90		AE6	878
	C	447		G4	194		AE7	344
VERNISHED	BP	105		AE4	731		AE8	225
VERRES	J3	95		AE12	185		AE8	777
	J3	96	VESPASIAN	DO	125		AE9	791
VERSE	RH	5	VESPER	G1	343		AE11	107
	RH	87		FL	437		AE12	880
	AM	688	VESSEL	AR	124		AE12	935
	EWGR	41		AM	818		M8	67
	PLN	2		AM	1002		M11	466
	PAZ	11		DA	67		M12	581
	PAZ	20		HAP	131		AU	55
	EAL	6		PKA	21		AU	265
	POE	6		EL	208		M15	238
	AA	570		J3	147		CI	96
	AA	858		P3	36	VESTA	AE2	395
	MF	5		P5	197		AE5	974
	SAA	409		P6	70	VESTAL	HS	136
	SAA	428		M9	26		AM	1025
	SAA	444		G1	494		AK	67
	SAA	490		G2	63		P2	108
	SAA	502		G2	331		G4	553
	SAA	938		AE1	149		AE1	399
	SAA	1047		AE1	170	VESTALS	OAL	35
	PK	31		AE3	542	VESTA'S	J6	506
	RL	453		AE5	266		AE2	776
	ER	5		AE5	321		AE9	342
	ER	12		AE5	1130	VESTED	AE6	870
	AK	17		AE6	449	VESTMENTS	M1	515
	AK	75		AE6	557		AE6	1105
	HH	12		AE7	832	VESTRY	M12	342
	HAP	1543		AE10	348	VESTS	EWGR	44
	HAP	1633		AE10	412		M1	535
	EL	376		AE10	931		G2	649
	J1	247		AE10	957		AE1	674
	J3	341		AE10	971		AE2	1040
	J10	231		DO	50		AE5	148
	PPS	9		HIF	273		AE7	340

VESTS	AE8	877
	AE9	841
	AE9	843
	AE11	103
	AE12	193
	AE12	1114
	KT3	193
	CI	575
VESUVIUS	G2	306
VETCHES	G1	110
	G1	316
VEX	AM	125
	D	40
	L3	202
	HAP	2303
	VP4	40
	G1	278
	G4	255
	AE6	541
	OAL	412
	DO	82
VEXATIOUS	J16	57
VEXED	AM	825
	EEL	21
	EUO2	11
	MD	252
	G1	191
	G2	220
	AE5	186
	AE12	386
VEXING	AE12	156
VEXISSE	PO	4
VIAL	B	705
VIANDS	RL	418
VICAR	ELN	6
	C	726
	C	760
VICARS	EMM	1
VICE	PUO1	26
	PUO2	10
	PTW	4
	PSF	20
	PSF	45
	AA	784
	SAA	83
	RL	56
	RL	115
	RL	231
	H2	6
	HAP	2334
	HAP	2467
	EL	86
	EL	364
	EL	370
	J1	223
	J3	227
	J3	300
	J6	195
	P1	126
	P1	231
	P3	61
	P3	110
	P4	27
	P5	22
	P5	169
	P5	175
	M13	98
	VCS	22
	G1	128
	G3	693
	AE6	1000
	WB	463
	M15	683
	ETP	6
	ETP	7
	ETP	32
VICEGERENT	P3	68
VICEROY	HAP	549
VICES	PAZ	29
	PSF	22
	PUO5	28
	ELB	31
	BR	308
	EL	228
	J1	133
	WB	160
VICIOUS	HP	33
	AA	305
	J3	306
	P5	136
	G3	721
	WB	67
	CI	27
VICISSITUDE	H29	23
	AE5	1082
	KT3	1112

VICISSITUDES	EL	124
	G1	116
	KT3	879
VICTIM	RL	87
	J6	711
	SFL	24
	VP1	44
	G2	203
	G3	733
	AE2	170
	AE2	752
	AE4	293
	AE12	319
	TH	301
	M12	47
	M15	190
VICTIMS	EPF	22
	VP1	61
	VP5	118
	G1	654
	G4	784
	AE1	460
	AE4	303
	AE5	964
	AE6	322
	AE10	722
	HIF	94
VICTIMS'	L4	241
VICTOR	LCA	10
	SAA	891
	M1	602
	HI	77
	G3	747
	AE5	286
	AE5	325
	AE5	337
	AE5	402
	AE5	430
	AE5	441
	AE5	709
	AE5	1120
	AE8	194
	AE8	949
	AE9	356
	AE9	779
	AE9	875
	AE9	1021
	AE10	538
	AE10	777
	AE10	1030
	AE10	1068
	AE11	136
	AE11	249
	AE11	847
	AE11	1113
	AE12	125
	AE12	446
	AE12	497
	AE12	561
	AE12	1046
	AE12	1348
	AF	84
	AF	115
	AF	122
	KT1	126
	KT1	135
	KT2	637
	KT3	254
	KT3	687
	KT3	738
	M8	205
	M12	190
	M12	209
	M12	441
	AU	392
VICTORIA	SKA1	12
VICTORIES	HS	133
	AM	207
	G3	164
	AE7	595
	TJD	164
VICTORIOUS	AM	73
	AM	398
	FS1	4
	FS3	2
	HAP	206
	HAP	1281
	BR	134
	J6	408
	J10	248
	P6	99
	G2	237
	G2	420
	AE5	898
	AE8	83
	AE9	882

VICTORIOUS	AE10	714
	AE11	1125
	KT1	13
	C	759
	FL	518
VICTOR'S	HI	125
	G3	351
	AE2	688
	AE2	1070
	AE3	421
	AE5	320
	AE5	1060
	AE9	495
	AE11	5
	AE11	117
	AE11	641
	AE12	935
	FL	541
	M12	767
	CI	291
VICTORS	M1	758
	AE2	495
	AE5	91
	AE5	210
	AE10	977
	AE10	1073
	AE11	1281
	TJD	164
	FL	304
	FL	431
	CI	396
	CI	610
VICTORS'	AE5	145
VICTORY	HS	52
	VHH	38
	AM	763
	AM	786
	PK	25
	HAP	967
	HAP	1227
	SKA1	13
	J10	213
	AE5	238
	AE5	514
	AE7	221
	AE8	757
	AE8	960
	AE10	460
	AE10	573
	AE10	1035
	AE10	1298
	AE11	255
	AE11	651
	AE11	673
	AE11	1015
	AE12	129
	OAL	384
	KT1	58
	KT1	118
	KT1	399
	KT2	412
	KT3	334
	KT3	355
	KT3	372
	FL	545
	WB	521
	CI	290
VIE	SAA	537
	M1	226
	VP2	34
	AE5	1016
	AE6	869
	AE11	316
VIED	AE11	871
	FL	434
VIES	BR	194
VIEW	UDH	29
	JH	21
	AR	252
	RH	72
	SMA	37
	LC	33
	LC	77
	AM	399
	AM	654
	AM	743
	AM	1139
	PFD	7
	PCD	29
	PUO2	8
	ESF	5
	HP	203
	PUO4	21
	PUF	5
	SAA	196
	SAA	940

VIEW

SAA	1053
RL	146
L3	32
L3	226
L4	185
T18	73
T18	95
T23	72
H3	24
H2	90
FS3	11
TA	191
TA	515
TA	504
TA	329
TA	428
TA	446
HAP	129
HAP	542
HAP	748
HAP	758
HAP	964
HAP	1148
HAP	1176
HAP	1300
HAP	2083
HAP	2338
HAP	2345
BR	9
BR	49
BR	88
BR	112
PP	5
SKA2	10
EL	138
EL	196
EL	340
EL	353
OD	1
J1	44
J1	100
J3	31
J3	196
J3	302
P1	124
P6	16
M1	13
M1	469
M1	536
M1	674
M1	712
M13	146
GK	40
GK	170
VP8	53
VP10	3
VP10	107
G2	258
G3	36
G3	450
G4	243
G4	512
AE1	157
AE1	163
AE1	259
AE1	506
AE1	555
AE1	581
AE1	597
AE1	608
AE1	658
AE1	991
AE2	700
AE2	899
AE3	32
AE3	232
AE3	269
AE3	497
AE3	549
AE3	561
AE3	617
AE3	695
AE3	723
AE3	776
AE3	780
AE3	815
AE3	848
AE4	201
AE4	222
AE4	519
AE4	948
AE5	144
AE5	331
AE5	417
AE5	480
AE5	534

VIEW (continued)

AE5	750
AE5	826
AE5	874
AE6	41
AE6	133
AE6	155
AE6	194
AE6	203
AE6	222
AE6	292
AE6	389
AE6	465
AE6	509
AE6	593
AE6	613
AE6	718
AE6	856
AE6	1026
AE6	1102
AE6	1117
AE6	1131
AE7	150
AE7	869
AE8	682
AE9	37
AE9	268
AE9	569
AE9	626
AE9	691
AE9	874
AE9	898
AE10	625
AE10	653
AE11	64
AE11	78
AE11	270
AE11	401
AE11	739
AE11	1096
AE12	316
AE12	350
AE12	731
AE12	1035
AE12	1245
AE12	1333
OAL	345
DO	32
KT1	217
KT3	451
KT3	656
M8	261
M8	295
B	235
B	742
HIF	102
HIF	303
HIF	309
HIF	358
HIF	422
C	152
C	410
C	612
M11	79
M11	83
M11	234
M11	387
M11	401
FL	349
FL	609
M12	21
M12	24
M12	174
M12	405
WB	59
WB	223
M15	664
CI	26
CI	50
CI	101
CI	169
CI	382
CI	487
CI	622
STP	9
SMP	87
SMP	93
ESK	20
SCD2	2

VIEWED

AA	31
AA	917
SAA	166
SAA	824
AT	22
HAP	21
HAP	57
HAP	58
HAP	974
J1	128
P3	77
M1	669
M1	673
M1	674
VP1	60
VP8	53
AE1	611
AE1	1064
AE3	669
AE3	706
AE4	931
AE5	125
AE5	547
AE6	51
AE6	463
AE6	649
AE6	1178
AE7	688
AE8	202
AE8	473
AE8	702
AE9	535
AE10	364
AE10	373
AE10	510
AE10	1030
AE10	1121
AE11	54
AE11	1133
AE12	336
AE12	530
AE12	661
KT1	223
KT1	353
KT2	488
B	88
B	640
B	649
BP	133
M10	95
TH	342
TH	354
M12	59
M12	272
CI	154
CI	373
FL	180
P5	35

VIEWEST

AE4	872

VIEWING

AR	77
AM	617
AE8	413
M12	696

VIEWLESS

AR	167

VIEWS

PCG2	17
AT	57
H2	24
J6	514
VP5	87
G4	519
AE4	88
AE4	227
AE4	534
AE5	589
AE5	786
AE5	803
AE6	299
AE6	1209
AE7	115
AE11	1313
AE12	817
AE12	1327
OAL	461
M11	68
M15	198

VIGILANT

HAP	303

VIGILS

KT1	177
KT3	118
FL	614

VIGOR

DC	44
VHH	28
AM	1160
ECG1	15
ML	46
CM	50
L4	35
L4	194
T18	83
TA	479
AK	75
AK	191
GE	12
BR	265
PTS	4

Word	Ref	No.
VIGOR	J10	14
	P1	53
	M1	615
	M9	196
	G2	69
	G2	174
	G2	393
	G3	112
	G3	223
	G4	600
	AE1	829
	AE4	254
	AE4	693
	AE5	246
	AE5	291
	AE5	664
	AE6	421
	AE6	988
	AE8	675
	AE9	838
	AE9	872
	AE11	1104
	AE12	7
	AE12	627
	AE12	640
	AE12	712
	AE12	828
	AE12	1106
	AE12	1311
	OAL	266
	KT3	954
	M8	138
	M12	155
	AU	568
	WB	432
	CI	29
VIGOROUS	AM	751
	AA	8
	J6	442
	P2	132
	G1	281
	G3	764
	KT3	476
VIGOROUSLY	AM	507
	AE6	1047
VILE	ML	50
	EPC	17
	SAA	145
	SAA	318
	PK	34
	PSH	9
	J1	35
	P5	239
	M1	273
	GK	161
	G1	316
	G2	602
	AE11	632
	AE11	1014
	OAL	852
	OAL	886
	C	501
VILER	SAA	103
	SAA	523
	SAA	1133
VILLA	L3	283
VILLAGE	AM	851
	J3	316
	J6	80
	G2	285
	C	760
	WB	40
VILLAGES	G2	527
VILLAIN	MD	49
	SAA	86
	SAA	363
	SAA	519
	J6	313
	AE2	147
	TH	132
VILLAINIES	J1	78
VILLAIN'S	SAA	145
	HAP	2008
	C	273
VILLAINS	PCB	31
	PPC	24
	SAA	874
	HH	3
	J1	257
	J3	51
	J3	487
VILLAINY	MD	242
	HAP	2523
	P1	249
	P2	44
VILLANAGE	WB	443

Word	Ref	No.
VILLANIZE	WB	405
VILLERIUS	MF	59
VINDICATE	AM	1204
	DA	62
	M1	1060
	AE6	1154
	AE12	1008
	KT1	332
	KT1	457
	HIF	453
VINDICATES	HAP	1109
	TJD	80
	CAM	23
VINE	H2	18
	HAP	439
	M1	406
	M13	86
	VP1	100
	VP4	50
	VP5	109
	VP7	86
	VP10	54
	VP10	59
	G1	4
	G1	358
	G1	380
	G1	597
	G2	7
	G2	372
	G2	537
	G2	555
	G2	562
	G2	569
	G2	753
	MM	7
	M15	164
	J3	461
VINEGAR	VP3	16
VINES	VP5	8
	VP5	47
	VP7	69
	VP7	80
	VP9	56
	G2	2
	G2	35
	G2	91
	G2	128
	G2	130
	G2	159
	G2	196
	G2	264
	G2	301
	G2	310
	G2	317
	G2	351
	G2	386
	G2	396
	G2	434
	G2	453
	G2	490
	G2	505
	G2	548
	G2	559
	G2	566
	G2	575
	G2	577
	G4	190
	G4	210
	G4	388
	AE6	1100
	AE7	247
	M15	106
	M15	619
VINEYARD	MD	217
	SAA	561
	VP2	104
	G2	351
	G2	410
	G2	424
	G2	538
	G2	551
VINEYARD'S	G2	368
VINEYARDS	SAA	878
	SAA	1118
	J6	218
	G2	355
	G2	571
	G2	574
	G4	469
VINTAGE	M13	77
	VP5	109
	VP7	80
	G2	139
	G2	567
	AE3	171
	MG	38

Word	Ref	No.
VIOLATE	HP	1
	SAA	576
	J3	100
	M1	1024
	AE2	252
	AE2	303
	AE6	444
	AE10	329
	AE11	428
	AE12	239
	AE12	474
	B	203
	B	291
	HIF	132
	M12	289
	M15	677
	CI	360
VIOLATED	AR	40
	DA	101
	AE2	751
	AE3	53
	AE4	875
	AE6	1155
	AE8	327
	AE10	46
	AE12	221
	AE12	423
	AE12	721
	OAL	776
	B	753
	HIF	12
	AU	322
VIOLATING	HAP	1291
VIOLENCE	AR	144
	SAA	222
	L4	87
	BR	35
	J16	59
	M1	319
	C	791
VIOLENT	EMK	8
	AA	931
	SAA	364
	M13	89
	AE1	948
	AE10	224
	KT2	585
VIOLENTLY	M1	345
	G1	136
VIOLET	T18	2
	T23	58
	C	457
VIOLET-PURPLE	G4	394
VIOLETS	VP2	64
	VP5	57
	VP10	58
	G4	46
	G4	269
	M12	546
VIOLINS	SSC	37
VIPER	L4	26
	J6	836
	G3	810
VIPER-LIKE	AA	1013
VIPER'S	G1	197
	G3	629
	AE7	1035
	TJD	109
VIPERS	CAM	25
VIRAGO	AE3	716
	AE7	1098
	AE11	768
VIRAGOES	T18	39
	J6	346
VIRBIUS	AE7	1048
	AE7	1064
	AE7	1069
VIRELAY	FL	365
VIRGIL	EUO2	18
	ER	40
	J6	563
	P1	188
VIRGIL'S	ER	76
	GK	64
	GK	152
	DO	4
VIRGIN	MHD	3
	AR	20
	AM	578
	SCD1	13
	HP	104
	ELB	1
	T18	34
	T27	117
	H2	27
	NS	16

Word	Code	No.
VIRGIN	AK	152
	HAP	1894
	G1	535
	AE1	440
	AE1	451
	AE2	222
	AE2	560
	AE3	282
	AE3	544
	AE5	313
	AE7	460
	AE7	508
	AE7	543
	AE7	546
	AE11	100
	AE11	178
	AE11	754
	AE11	813
	AE11	980
	AE11	1133
	AE11	1172
	MFL	19
	KT3	198
	KT3	223
	KT3	244
	KT3	283
	KT3	696
	KT3	927
	M8	151
	M10	13
	CAM	184
	CAM	197
	CAM	271
	HIF	307
	TH	209
	M11	300
	FL	173
	M12	41
	M12	274
	AS	60
	AS	68
VIRGIN-DAUGHTER	AK	1
VIRGINIA	PSH	15
	J10	453
	PWR	13
VIRGINIAN	PWR	3
VIRGINITY	M1	641
	AE11	874
	FL	513
VIRGIN'S	RH	70
	AE2	162
	M12	41
	M12	51
VIRGINS	ECG1	29
	SAA	1046
	T18	1
	L3	219
	ELW	5
	J1	128
	G1	43
	AE1	463
	AE1	986
	AE2	313
	AE11	1285
	WB	63
VIRGIN-WIDOW	UDH	93
VIRTUE	UDH	5
	UDH	9
	UDH	100
	HS	27
	HS	105
	AR	58
	LC	56
	DC	41
	LCA	9
	LCA	32
	AM	414
	AM	461
	AM	759
	S	3
	A	3
	PUO1	13
	PUO1	26
	EUO2	29
	ML	29
	ML	47
	PTC	29
	HP	33
	HP	97
	HP	169
	EPF	16
	EPC	19
	AA	355
	AA	374
	AA	380
	AA	622

Word	Code	No.
VIRTUE	SAA	83
	SAA	111
	SAA	127
	SAA	590
	SAA	808
	SAA	810
	SAA	947
	SAA	968
	SAA	1000
	RL	31
	RL	56
	H29	87
	HAP	614
	HAP	708
	HAP	1390
	HAP	1557
	HAP	1633
	HAP	2467
	BR	221
	BR	338
	BR	343
	BR	357
	EL	101
	EL	146
	EL	160
	EL	225
	EL	364
	J1	113
	J1	172
	J3	40
	J6	135
	J6	439
	J10	24
	J10	222
	J10	458
	J10	558
	P1	268
	P2	66
	P2	132
	P3	69
	P3	88
	P5	51
	P5	175
	M1	927
	VP4	16
	G2	779
	AE5	607
	AE8	175
	AE8	361
	AE9	1062
	AE12	25
	OAL	685
	DO	149
	KT1	482
	KT2	313
	KT3	758
	KT3	824
	KT3	1052
	KT3	1085
	B	310
	B	404
	B	510
	B	524
	CAM	233
	C	82
	C	510
	M11	288
	M12	148
	AU	372
	WB	404
	WB	440
	WB	457
	WB	395
	M15	486
	CI	493
VIRTUE'S	UDH	28
	AM	180
	AA	199
	AA	247
	AA	311
	SAA	1086
	L2	8
	EL	230
	J3	275
	P3	110
	AE10	658
VIRTUES	UDH	31
	HS	101
	AR	69
	SMA	89
	LC	37
	EKK	17
	UMR	3
	AA	193
	AA	403
	AA	483

Word	Code	No.
VIRTUES	SAA	1052
	RL	130
	OE	8
	PD	38
	TA	501
	TA	335
	HH	21
	HAP	333
	HAP	2447
	HAP	2487
	BR	308
	ELW	7
	EL	83
	EL	89
	EL	143
	EL	282
	EL	146
	EL	294
	J3	85
	J6	242
	J6	262
	P5	162
	VP4	21
	G2	53
	G3	162
	AE10	1214
	KT1	598
	KT1	610
	B	530
	WB	449
	WB	474
	WB	399
	M15	479
	M15	492
	M15	502
	GP	137
	AS	72
VIRTUOSOS	MF	149
VIRTUOUS	UDH	71
	AR	206
	P1	258
	P6	10
	HI	2
	AE6	1161
	M8	160
	B	520
	HIF	383
	C	521
	FL	418
	CI	28
VISAGE	HAP	514
	J10	307
	M1	462
	M1	881
	AE1	825
	AE9	890
	AE9	1019
	OAL	836
	KT3	916
VISIBLE	HAP	418
	MFL	15
VISION	EUF	11
	AA	239
	MD	287
	EL	209
	AE5	977
	AE6	1202
	AE7	139
	AE8	59
	LMC	9
	C	242
	C	315
	C	369
	C	376
	C	381
	C	390
	TH	216
	TH	222
	TH	320
	M11	388
VISIONARY	AA	656
	AE2	365
	AE3	576
	C	149
	TH	280
	FL	614
VISION'S	SCG1	8
VISIONS	DC	56
	ET	9
	HAP	2592
	P2	102
	AE3	230
	AE3	644
	AE4	12
	AE6	1237
	AE7	128

VISIONS	AE10	909	VOCATION	HAP	712	VOICE	AE8	176
	C	242	VOGUE	PPC	20		AE9	133
	C	296		J6	721		AE9	510
	C	357	VOICE	HS	6		AE9	534
	C	434		AR	227		AE9	570
	M11	259		AR	264		AE10	318
	M11	296		AM	175		AE10	907
VISIT	EUO	6		AM	892		AE10	1252
	HAP	909		CM	93		AE12	947
	VCS	3		CM	102		AE12	1255
	VP7	94		CM	107		AE12	1345
	AE1	575		HP	105		OAL	107
	AE6	510		HP	131		OAL	618
	AE6	975		DA	110		OAL	667
	AE8	211		PUO4	10		MM	31
	TH	52		AA	646		KT1	536
VISITANTS	G2	644		AA	982		KT1	599
VISITED	AE4	667		MD	14		KT2	52
	B	298		RL	351		KT3	6
	HIF	662		L3	121		KT3	84
VISITORS	J6	620		L4	153		KT3	115
VISITS	J3	222		L4	228		KT3	295
	G4	792		FS2	3		KT3	662
	OAL	462		TA	20		M8	156
	KT3	729		TA	288		M8	357
	M11	271		TA	477		B	408
VITAL	LC	28		PAA	38		B	533
	SAA	339		AK	18		CAM	361
	L1	3		HAP	971		HIF	392
	HAP	298		HAP	2185		C	600
	J1	127		SSC	6		C	623
	M1	562		SSC	43		C	627
	G2	555		PP	37		C	650
	G3	500		EL	4		M11	15
	G3	698		EL	318		M11	360
	G3	728		ODA	13		M11	376
	G4	699		ODA	79		M11	402
	AE1	770		EH	24		M11	433
	AE2	338		J1	155		M11	479
	AE3	397		J3	157		FL	52
	AE3	787		J6	107		FL	111
	AE4	42		J6	499		FL	194
	AE4	486		J6	716		FL	370
	AE5	946		J10	123		M12	71
	AE6	593		J10	336		M12	113
	AE6	769		AT	89		AU	269
	AE6	1031		T23	109		AU	431
	AE6	1075		PPS	13		M15	4
	AE7	525		P1	47		M15	95
	AE7	744		P5	184		CI	56
	AE7	1059		M1	65		CI	195
	AE9	555		M1	258	VOICES	MF	77
	AE9	949		M1	265		L2	33
	AE10	680		M1	308		PAA	45
	AE12	876		M1	905		BR	320
	AE12	1309		M1	992		P5	36
	OAL	607		M9	42		VP3	39
	KT3	345		M9	197		G1	643
	TJD	116		M13	203		AE3	229
	M8	258		HI	169		AE4	668
	B	653		GK	11		AE6	66
	M10	55		DHP	27		AE10	150
	HIF	131		VP1	76		FL	152
	M11	486		VP2	13		CI	579
	FL	147		VP4	69	VOID	AM	999
	FL	583		VP5	2		DA	17
VITRUVIUS	MC	15		VP5	10		ELB	22
VIZARD	AR	179		VP5	12		SAA	50
	PM	4		VP5	20		L2	23
	ENH	23		VP5	23		H2	4
VIZARD-MASK	PCG2	13		VP5	98		TA	61
	PW	14		VP6	3		TA	198
	EK	11		VP6	42		BR	262
	EK	19		VP6	119		OD	9
VIZARD-MASKS	PCG2	25		VP9	73		SSH	11
	PWR	7		VP9	94		J10	3
VIZARDS	G2	534		VP10	11		P2	47
VIZORS	KT3	583		VP10	75		M1	19
VOCAL	HAP	15		VP10	111		M1	92
	SSC	52		G1	443		M1	130
	T18	58		G1	569		M1	505
	M1	939		G3	523		EHC	7
	VP4	4		G4	70		VP6	51
	VP6	14		G4	502		G1	585
	VP8	31		G4	763		G1	47
	VP10	10		AE1	453		G2	688
	G2	21		AE1	593		G4	676
	AF	162		AE1	734		AE2	599
	AF	172		AE1	993		AE3	201
	HIF	808		AE3	592		AE4	843
	FL	149		AE3	814		AE6	162
	M12	571		AE3	853		AE6	342
	SMP	45		AE5	847		AE6	625
VOCATION	PTW	3		AE5	875		AE7	932
	ETC	16		AE6	128		AE9	329
	PK	10		AE6	665		AE9	675

Word	Ref	No.
VOID	AE9	1054
	AE10	634
	AE10	1255
	AE11	156
	AE11	914
	AE12	994
	AE12	1224
	AE12	1321
	AE12	1356
	OAE2	51
	KT3	758
	KT3	767
	TJD	2
	C	217
	FL	23
	M12	678
	AU	77
	M15	369
VOLLEYS	AE1	215
VOLPONE	PC1	12
VOLSCENS	AE9	502
	AE9	509
	AE9	563
	AE9	587
	AE10	788
VOLSCIAN	AE11	666
	AE11	703
	AE11	1122
	KT2	639
VOLSCIANS	G2	233
	AE7	1094
	AE9	671
	AE9	682
	AE11	754
	AE11	783
	AE11	1257
	AE11	1295
VOLUME	AM	492
	RL	166
	BR	109
	OD	7
	G2	212
VOLUMES	PUO5	24
	AE2	286
	AE5	113
	AE7	496
	AE11	1110
VOLUNTARY	AU	48
	AS	76
VOLUNTEERING	PKA	47
VOLUPTUOUSNESS	P5	209
VOLUSUS	AE11	703
VOMIT	C	175
	M12	443
VOMITING	M15	509
VOMIT'S	KT3	765
VOMITS	P3	205
	AE5	894
	AE6	403
	AE8	822
	M12	334
VORACIOUS	HAP	2244
VOTARY	M9	43
VOTARY'S	AE11	1227
VOTE	PRL	2
	EOE	23
	DA	18
	EK	48
	HAP	977
	HAP	1740
	HAP	2078
	M1	258
	AE2	304
	AE3	86
	AE9	298
	AU	590
VOTES	EAZ	43
	DA	137
	PUO5	11
	PUO5	14
	AA	993
	AA	994
	ELB	24
	SAA	551
	SAA	762
	PDG	30
	HAP	655
	EDS	36
	MC	37
	AE7	846
	M15	58
VOTIVE	M9	203
	M12	375
VOTRESS	KT3	225
VOUCH	HAP	951
	J16	54

Word	Ref	No.
VOUCH	AU	22
	AU	101
VOUCHED	ELN	6
VOUCHERS	ML	5
VOUCHSAFE	VP1	40
	M9	10
	DO	7
	DO	97
	TJD	197
	FL	477
VOUCHSAFED	HS	81
	SAA	1087
VOUCHSAFES	VP3	132
VOW	SM1	1
	ESF	10
	MF	114
	ER	64
	L3	276
	TA	386
	J6	388
	J6	515
	J10	446
	J10	452
	VP5	126
	G1	586
	AE2	22
	AE4	550
	AE4	873
	AE5	307
	AE5	313
	AE6	620
	AE9	120
	AE12	479
	OAL	151
	OAL	522
	DO	130
	KT1	298
	KT2	132
	BP	132
	HIF	732
	CAM	132
	C	76
	FL	522
	WB	328
VOWED	EEL	27
	PUF	2
	MF	59
	TA	93
	HAP	435
	J6	506
	P6	115
	M1	641
	AE5	1063
	AE7	95
	AE7	543
	AE8	796
	AE8	960
	AE9	365
	AE9	490
	AE9	585
	AE9	852
	AE9	993
	AE11	874
	AE12	1355
	OAL	776
	KT3	830
	KT3	925
	B	54
	HIF	43
	HIF	150
	HIF	536
	TH	124
	M12	495
	CI	605
VOWELS	HAP	958
VOWS	AR	319
	SMA	131
	VHH	24
	AM	203
	PMQ	51
	DA	9
	DA	20
	DA	60
	DA	69
	AA	111
	AA	240
	AA	470
	PPC	5
	PPC	26
	PD	12
	TA	40
	TA	46
	TA	232
	TA	505
	AK	167
	BR	1

Word	Ref	No.
VOWS	PDS	34
	PP	35
	ELW	9
	LS	11
	EL	7
	J10	35
	J10	83
	P2	12
	P2	77
	M1	1020
	M9	59
	M9	201
	M9	205
	M13	93
	VP1	55
	VP1	62
	VP10	8
	G1	236
	G4	775
	AE1	577
	AE1	1028
	AE2	304
	AE2	937
	AE3	29
	AE3	45
	AE3	113
	AE3	342
	AE3	360
	AE3	518
	AE3	556
	AE3	649
	AE4	38
	AE4	50
	AE4	90
	AE4	320
	AE4	444
	AE4	454
	AE4	499
	AE4	915
	AE5	81
	AE5	900
	AE6	87
	AE6	107
	AE6	274
	AE6	517
	AE6	629
	AE7	184
	AE8	84
	AE8	106
	AE8	357
	AE8	883
	AE9	7
	AE9	28
	AE9	270
	AE9	416
	AE10	594
	AE11	5
	AE11	239
	AE11	847
	AE11	1152
	AE11	1231
	AE12	304
	AE12	317
	AE12	393
	AE12	1113
	AE12	1131
	KT1	190
	KT1	427
	KT2	63
	KT3	114
	KT3	375
	KT3	834
	KT3	1126
	M8	355
	B	96
	B	406
	B	413
	BP	196
	HIF	27
	HIF	136
	HIF	622
	TH	22
	TH	160
	TH	390
	M11	182
	M11	245
	M11	365
	M12	209
	M12	767
	AU	143
	AU	392
	WB	63
	M15	63
	CI	248
	CI	317
	CI	362

Word	Code	No.	Word	Code	No.	Word	Code	No.
VOWS	CI	517	WADE	AE3	881	WAIT	HAP	2591
VOYAGE	AR	240		DO	105		BR	28
	AM	816	WADES	AM	931		J1	166
	DA	153		AE8	341		J1	183
	J6	141	WADING	B	135		J1	194
	P5	208	WAFT	SMA	29		J3	402
	AE1	752		H2	77		J6	249
	AE3	466		AK	169		J6	535
	AE3	482		G4	731		J10	262
	AE5	2		AE6	504		J10	349
	AE5	74		HIF	275		J10	517
	AE5	792	WAFTED	HP	229		P3	210
	AE5	815		AE6	452		M1	761
	AE6	855		AE6	560		M1	1041
	AE7	171		AE9	114		VP3	79
	AE7	825		M11	220		VP5	27
	AE10	107		M11	450		AE1	108
	CAM	317	WAFTING	M1	431		AE1	402
	C	343	WAFTS	AE9	1106		AE2	962
	C	738	WAG	T27	19		AE4	185
	TH	53		P1	173		AE4	189
	M11	7		P5	170		AE4	623
	M11	58		P5	172		AE4	865
	M11	247	WAGE	MF	12		AE5	91
	AU	490		AE1	359		AE5	179
VULCAN	AM	1008		AE3	308		AE5	508
	J6	570		AE8	529		AE6	924
	J10	203		AE11	169		AE8	663
	AE5	863		AE11	469		AE8	729
	AE8	262		AE11	549		AE9	52
	AE8	579		M11	113		AE9	414
	AE8	974	WAGED	AE1	34		AE10	43
	AE9	185		AE7	427		AE10	177
	AE10	343		AE10	216		AE11	92
	AE10	572		AE11	481		AE11	132
	KT3	320		AE12	54		AE11	754
VULCANIAN	G3	835		B	598		AE12	824
	AE8	710		ETP	2		AE12	836
	AE10	757	WAGER	AT	106		AE12	1046
	AE10	1139		VP3	47		OAL	78
	AE11	675	WAGER-HALL	PKA	31		OAL	127
	AE12	1072	WAGERS	PCG2	19		OAL	457
	KT3	908		PKA	23		OAL	817
VULCAN'S	SAA	921		PKA	44		KT1	70
	J1	10		KT3	474		KT1	580
	G4	489	WAGES	UDH	7		KT3	785
	AE2	960	WAGGED	AT	76		TJD	8
	AE8	551	WAGING	MF	84		M8	307
	AE8	814		GE	39		C	324
	HIF	800	WAGON	M1	80		M11	181
VULGAR	AR	33	WAGONER	J3	495		M12	494
	RH	81		G1	318		CI	372
	VHH	48	WAGONERS	J3	385	WAITED	SAA	964
	EMM	4	WAGON'S	G3	800		AE7	683
	PT	22	WAGONS	J3	408		AE8	610
	PCG1	43		G1	244		AU	316
	PC2	34		G3	317		KT1	71
	EOE	11		G3	556		M11	389
	PTC	5	WAIL	UDH	60	WAITER	OAE2	35
	AA	353	WAIN	HAP	1397	WAITING	AR	223
	AA	453		CAM	265		AM	819
	SAA	647		G2	624		ECG1	34
	RL	400		AE11	208		M9	36
	ER	64	WAINS	EM	14		HIF	717
	AK	52		AE2	286		C	300
	EL	360		AE4	385		CI	269
	J10	79		AE5	917	WAITING-MAN	SAA	342
	J10	90		AE10	302	WAITS	SMA	46
	P1	126		AE11	1092		AM	711
	P4	112		OAL	630		AA	448
	P6	28		AF	32		MD	241
	GK	26		M10	48		SAA	725
	VP9	49		M12	580		SAA	885
	G3	2		M12	488		L4	172
	G4	94	WAIST-BELT	PCG1	10		HAP	2582
	G4	653	WAISTCOAT	T27	96		J10	366
	AE1	266	WAISTCOATS	PM	10		J10	416
	AE2	50	WAIT	AR	177		AE3	523
	AE5	358		SMA	120		AE6	1075
	AE6	212		SMA	127		AE7	845
	AE12	5		LCA	34		AE12	1330
	OAL	304		VHH	39		OAL	812
	B	311		AM	380	WAIVE	SAA	724
	M11	488		AM	454		AE12	95
VULTURE	L3	59		AM	1005		C	551
	AE6	808		PFD	5	WAIVES	AU	256
VULTURE'S	AE8	856		PAL	2	WAIVING	LCA	41
VULTURES	PAL	2		HP	197		SAA	392
	MF	131		DA	61		RL	427
	L3	189		SAA	79	WAKE	AM	284
	HIF	5		TA	451		SCG2	13
VULTURNUS	AE7	1007		HAP	110		SAA	733
				HAP	374		SAA	871
				HAP	557		L3	90
				HAP	1261		AK	183
				HAP	1532		EDS	28

Word	Ref	No.	Word	Ref	No.	Word	Ref	No.
WAKE	J3	386	WALK	GK	15	WALL	AE9	1033
	J6	618		VP6	81		AE11	468
	AE4	349		G2	493		AE11	707
	AE8	78		AE1	70		AE11	1283
	AE8	574		AE1	561		AE12	842
	AE9	823		AE3	90		AE12	914
	C	620		AE4	259		KT1	204
	TH	220		AE6	16		KT2	464
	TH	368		AE9	216		KT2	474
WAKED	SCG1	29		OAL	82		KT2	494
	AE7	640		OAL	558		C	50
	AE8	720		KT1	188		M12	149
	KT1	174		KT3	470		M12	774
	KT3	484		CAM	240	WALLED	G4	418
	KT3	715		TH	74		AE1	508
	FL	122		M11	329		AE7	92
	M15	33		WB	43		M10	100
	CI	162		M15	213		M15	73
	CI	193		M15	336	WALLOW	ESF	22
	CI	232	WALKED	AM	872		BR	281
	CI	540		EAA	23		G4	623
WAKEFUL	SAA	1026		HAP	513	WALLOWED	M1	596
	SKA6	15		HAP	2016	WALL'S	AE2	828
	J1	90		M13	138	WALLS	HS	63
	AE1	659		TJD	98		AM	1100
	AE3	671		C	84		HP	178
	AE4	185		TH	76		HP	246
	AE4	267		FL	58		DA	13
	AE4	289		FL	62		DA	129
	AE4	358		WB	52		DA	133
	AE4	701		M15	443		EPF	6
	AE4	841	WALKING	HAP	1848		MF	64
	AE9	210		P5	269		L2	28
	AE9	244		AE3	852		HAP	1273
	AE9	296		AE4	210		HAP	2316
	AE9	465		AE6	239		J3	193
	KT3	124		AE8	445		J3	492
	B	197		KT1	228		J6	400
	BP	131		KT1	354		P3	103
	M11	276		B	289		M1	128
WAKEN	AM	905	WALKS	HS	116		HI	64
	SMP	27		AM	72		VP4	39
WAKENED	AM	923		AM	929		G2	648
	M10	94		PMM	9		G3	59
	HIF	673		L3	279		G3	567
	C	100		HAP	237		G3	626
	C	235		HAP	1566		G4	282
	C	316		BR	74		G4	351
WAKENING	AE9	614		BR	306		AE1	138
WAKES	LC	45		J1	164		AE1	237
	PO	2		J3	394		AE1	352
	SAA	834		J6	143		AE1	610
	TA	470		M1	1036		AE1	648
	P5	194		G1	212		AE1	676
	M9	49		G3	121		AE1	696
	AE9	290		G3	384		AE1	900
	KT3	998		AE1	704		AE2	33
	C	326		AE1	708		AE2	61
	WB	37		AE1	967		AE2	256
WAKING	AM	898		AE7	773		AE2	311
	AM	1035		AE7	1080		AE2	391
	ETL	14		AE11	134		AE2	456
	SCG1	4		KT1	222		AE2	790
	SCG1	35		KT1	259		AE2	969
	STC	4		KT1	533		AE2	1020
	EL	311		KT3	1072		AE3	217
	J3	437		B	202		AE3	333
	VP8	154		C	802		AE3	434
	AE4	511		TH	63		AE3	923
	AE4	559		FL	493		AE4	102
	AE10	908		WB	34		AE4	127
	KT3	784		M15	340		AE4	391
	C	116		SMP	28		AE4	501
WALES	BR	135		SMP	55		AE4	515
WALK	AM	283	WALL	AA	802		AE5	248
	AM	1024		TA	31		AE5	821
	PT	20		HAP	205		AE5	825
	ET	7		HAP	605		AE5	1053
	ETL	15		J3	313		AE6	705
	EMQW	4		M1	399		AE6	741
	TA	353		HI	41		AE6	856
	PAA	22		HI	43		AE6	1050
	GE	45		GK	30		AE7	217
	HAP	15		G4	262		AE7	829
	HAP	166		AE1	587		AE8	38
	HAP	559		AE1	638		AE8	71
	HAP	1808		AE2	383		AE8	90
	J3	48		AE2	634		AE8	386
	J3	401		AE3	27		AE8	619
	J3	405		AE8	743		AE8	782
	J3	451		AE9	178		AE8	874
	J6	575		AE9	220		AE9	42
	J6	854		AE9	720		AE9	80
	P4	79		AE9	781		AE9	200
	M13	51		AE9	904		AE9	623
	M13	191		AE9	963		AE9	675

WALLS	AE9	713	WANDERING	L4	36	WANT	EK	20
	AE9	749		L4	291		RL	122
	AE9	760		AK	7		RL	211
	AE9	814		HAP	73		RL	372
	AE9	981		HAP	338		PD	3
	AE9	995		HAP	1225		EC	20
	AE9	1066		J1	82		L2	57
	AE10	33		J3	424		L3	87
	AE10	106		VP6	82		L3	106
	AE10	179		VP8	122		L5	11
	AE10	660		G1	209		H29	39
	AE11	220		G2	677		TA	236
	AE11	376		G4	166		AK	72
	AE11	589		AE1	46		AK	96
	AE11	599		AE1	101		GE	25
	AE11	700		AE1	807		GE	42
	AE11	719		AE1	844		HAP	526
	AE11	848		AE1	995		HAP	872
	AE11	898		AE1	1040		HAP	962
	AE11	923		AE2	392		HAP	1049
	AE11	1270		AE2	774		HAP	1051
	AE12	58		AE2	1058		HAP	1323
	AE12	179		AE3	943		HAP	1509
	AE12	203		AE4	63		HAP	1717
	AE12	906		AE4	105		HAP	2501
	AE12	1001		AE4	277		PP	38
	AE12	1016		AE4	308		STS1	8
	AE12	1324		AE5	770		PKA	47
	AE12	1337		AE5	818		EL	32
	KT1	125		AE5	831		EL	48
	KT2	434		AE6	97		MS	18
	KT2	549		AE6	104		J1	70
	KT2	595		AE6	498		J1	216
	M8	42		AE6	540		J3	85
	BP	16		AE6	686		J3	256
	HIF	506		AE7	175		J3	376
	M11	168		AE7	293		J3	434
	M12	65		AE7	502		J6	266
	M12	206		AE7	540		J6	403
	AU	32		AE7	773		J6	478
	WB	31		AE9	1008		J6	775
	WB	450		AE10	69		J10	159
	M15	450		AE10	107		J10	538
	M15	665		AE10	234		PPS	14
	CI	608		AE10	256		PPS	15
	ESK	6		AE10	688		P6	152
WAN	J1	63		AE12	219		M1	423
	P3	186		KT1	153		M1	886
	AE3	772		KT2	61		MC	13
	OAL	831		TJD	64		GK	164
	KT1	239		TJD	100		VP6	28
	KT1	528		CAM	316		VP8	93
	FL	389		HIF	87		G2	251
WAND	AA	234		FL	58		G2	394
	HAP	1111		M12	565		G2	597
	P5	182		AU	527		G3	796
	M1	927		WB	204		AE1	774
	M1	932		M15	218		AE2	527
	AE4	355		CI	369		AE2	712
	AE7	257	WANDERINGS	AE1	1061		AE3	594
	AE7	1035	WANDERS	M1	415		AE6	110
	AE12	148		G4	73		AE6	387
	KT1	552	WANDS	HS	75		AE6	580
	KT2	461		G2	491		AE7	278
WANDER	AM	312	WANE	KT2	649		AE7	313
	AM	798	WANES	M15	294		AE7	828
	L4	70	WANING	AM	499		AE8	199
	BR	68		M11	234		AE9	399
	VP2	26		M15	293		AE10	647
	G3	329		M15	470		AE10	861
	G3	529	WANT	PRL	36		AE11	585
	AE1	533		AM	295		AE12	34
	AE3	262		AM	1039		AE12	225
	AE4	678		AM	1044		AE12	914
	AE6	380		PWGR	13		AE12	1311
	AE6	451		PWGR	22		OAL	484
	OAL	56		PT	28		OAE1	24
	FL	485		PA	34		KT1	347
	WB	102		PEL	11		KT2	437
WANDERED	D	10		PTL	25		KT3	327
	HAP	26		PMQW	17		KT3	813
	VP7	8		EMQW	17		KT3	983
	AE2	1004		EM	21		TJD	137
	OAL	594		PNH	28		TJD	143
	OAL	834		ETC	17		TJD	189
	TH	83		ETC	19		M8	159
WANDERER	SAA	987		PO	21		B	38
WANDEREST	L3	270		HP	98		BP	35
WANDERING	RH	65		DA	24		M10	4
	AM	1018		PUO4	2		M10	63
	PTW	27		EUF	16		CAM	172
	HP	189		AA	134		HIF	94
	DA	90		MD	11		HIF	261
	RL	2		MF	156		HIF	352
	L2	58		SAA	161		FL	32
	L3	40		SAA	362		M12	515

WANT	AU	154	WANTON	AM	920	WAR	PM	3		
	AU	407		HP	78		PCD	7		
	AU	445		HAP	1453		PCD	15		
	WB	143		J6	405		E	24		
	WB	231		P1	153		PAZ	28		
	WB	473		P6	11		PAZ	38		
	WB	486		M1	77		EAL	8		
	M15	530		M13	70		DA	134		
	GP	58		VP2	92		AA	25		
	GP	91		VP3	98		AA	284		
	CI	85		VP7	15		AA	394		
	CI	114		G2	216		AA	752		
	CI	126		G2	765		AA	841		
	CI	127		G3	277		MD	27		
WANTED	AM	63		G4	159		MD	113		
	AM	838		G4	291		MD	230		
	AA	52		AE3	287		MD	307		
	AA	197		AE7	553		MF	12		
	SAA	34		AE7	678		MF	84		
	AK	71		AE7	987		SAA	137		
	HAP	1255		AE11	744		SAA	144		
	HAP	1307		AE12	219		SAA	269		
	M9	107		KT3	564		SAA	774		
	AE9	346		C	437		L1	45		
	AE10	58		WB	128		L2	6		
	AE10	182		CI	22		L3	249		
	AE10	907		PTP	51		L5	16		
	AE12	937	WANTONED	AE1	438		H2	10		
	KT1	525		AE6	302		TA	104		
	KT3	196		KT1	185		TA	170		
	KT3	369	WANTONLY	P1	66		HAP	732		
	KT3	876	WANTONNESS	OAL	408		HAP	1278		
	B	60	WANTS	AM	158		HAP	2419		
	B	71		AM	856		PP	22		
	B	154		PR	5		PTS	28		
	B	372		AA	220		PTS	36		
	B	682		SAA	258		J10	208		
	BP	149		SAA	294		J10	268		
	HIF	808		PDG	38		J10	483		
	C	752		L4	31		J16	2		
	FL	26		L5	4		J16	54		
	FL	53		L5	18		J16	90		
	FL	432		HAP	453		HI	103		
	M12	300		HAP	906		HI	108		
	M12	307		BR	51		HI	153		
	M12	825		BR	329		HI	162		
	AU	107		EL	361		HI	186		
	M15	566		J3	428		VP10	36		
	EMKG	37		J3	447		VP10	68		
WANTEST	WB	103		J6	222		G1	88		
WANTING	PIE	13		J10	512		G1	232		
	AM	1093		P6	13		G1	612		
	SEL4	7		MC	23		G1	639		
	AA	892		GK	10		G2	202		
	MD	295		VP2	106		G2	383		
	SAA	10		G1	676		G2	627		
	L2	26		G2	643		G2	710		
	L3	110		AE1	16		G3	42		
	HAP	1053		AE1	818		G3	131		
	PTS	14		AE1	839		G3	183		
	PMS	7		AE4	583		G3	345		
	EL	23		AE5	368		G3	359		
	EL	103		AE7	1009		G3	368		
	M1	98		AE11	343		G3	535		
	M1	791		OAL	756		G3	571		
	M1	895		MFL	2		G3	641		
	M9	126		KT1	422		G4	7		
	M13	116		B	74		G4	95		
	GK	146		CAM	361		G4	113		
	EHC	5		AU	64		G4	606		
	G2	277		WB	39		G4	630		
	G2	668		WB	471		G4	810		
	AE2	912		AS	83		AE1	5		
	AE2	1008	WAR	HS	41		AE1	22		
	AE4	431		HS	45		AE1	34		
	AE6	135		HS	62		AE1	270		
	AE6	829		AR	4		AE1	327		
	AE7	938		AR	140		AE1	359		
	AE9	375		LC	108		AE1	396		
	AE10	207		AM	20		AE1	466		
	MM	54		AM	27		AE1	881		
	KT1	525		AM	46		AE1	1057		
	TJD	125		AM	96		AE1	1060		
	TJD	127		AM	106		AE2	18		
	B	420		AM	177		AE2	111		
	CAM	303		AM	208		AE2	149		
	TH	25		AM	242		AE2	237		
	FL	403		AM	291		AE2	359		
	M12	727		AM	315		AE2	372		
	AU	351		AM	665		AE2	398		
	AU	583		AM	667		AE2	414		
	M15	219		AM	674		AE2	527		
	M15	301		AM	1051		AE2	600		
	CI	49		AM	1103		AE2	815		
WANTON	AR	271		AM	1209		AE2	850		
	RH	46		SEL1	12		AE2	977		

Word	Code	No.
WAR	AE3	21
	AE3	74
	AE3	308
	AE3	325
	AE3	339
	AE3	710
	AE3	714
	AE3	890
	AE4	594
	AE4	888
	AE5	343
	AE5	569
	AE5	762
	AE5	955
	AE5	1006
	AE6	886
	AE6	928
	AE6	1090
	AE6	1097
	AE6	1112
	AE6	1159
	AE6	1166
	AE6	1175
	AE7	58
	AE7	120
	AE7	304
	AE7	322
	AE7	372
	AE7	427
	AE7	441
	AE7	475
	AE7	500
	AE7	568
	AE7	616
	AE7	621
	AE7	637
	AE7	643
	AE7	657
	AE7	707
	AE7	721
	AE7	742
	AE7	756
	AE7	764
	AE7	766
	AE7	790
	AE7	803
	AE7	818
	AE7	822
	AE7	837
	AE7	854
	AE7	860
	AE7	866
	AE7	880
	AE7	970
	AE8	4
	AE8	8
	AE8	27
	AE8	57
	AE8	75
	AE8	83
	AE8	151
	AE8	156
	AE8	199
	AE8	334
	AE8	572
	AE8	574
	AE8	588
	AE8	681
	AE8	691
	AE8	706
	AE8	709
	AE8	738
	AE8	785
	AE8	843
	AE8	847
	AE8	910
	AE9	24
	AE9	38
	AE9	48
	AE9	61
	AE9	184
	AE9	198
	AE9	233
	AE9	273
	AE9	371
	AE9	427
	AE9	634
	AE9	668
	AE9	678
	AE9	701
	AE9	707
	AE9	733
	AE9	748
	AE9	815
	AE9	825
	AE9	831
WAR	AE9	850
	AE9	883
	AE9	897
	AE9	914
	AE9	919
	AE9	984
	AE10	4
	AE10	11
	AE10	15
	AE10	74
	AE10	87
	AE10	93
	AE10	99
	AE10	123
	AE10	136
	AE10	140
	AE10	164
	AE10	207
	AE10	216
	AE10	243
	AE10	363
	AE10	391
	AE10	445
	AE10	489
	AE10	591
	AE10	601
	AE10	609
	AE10	639
	AE10	706
	AE10	740
	AE10	793
	AE10	950
	AE10	1004
	AE10	1013
	AE10	1090
	AE10	1106
	AE10	1139
	AE10	1246
	AE11	12
	AE11	26
	AE11	34
	AE11	74
	AE11	79
	AE11	143
	AE11	156
	AE11	164
	AE11	204
	AE11	235
	AE11	238
	AE11	332
	AE11	351
	AE11	389
	AE11	431
	AE11	444
	AE11	450
	AE11	469
	AE11	481
	AE11	524
	AE11	552
	AE11	562
	AE11	616
	AE11	681
	AE11	742
	AE11	787
	AE11	798
	AE11	806
	AE11	901
	AE11	962
	AE11	974
	AE11	981
	AE11	1132
	AE11	1216
	AE12	25
	AE12	33
	AE12	54
	AE12	70
	AE12	95
	AE12	115
	AE12	131
	AE12	270
	AE12	289
	AE12	365
	AE12	434
	AE12	476
	AE12	507
	AE12	514
	AE12	598
	AE12	631
	AE12	644
	AE12	650
	AE12	660
	AE12	818
	AE12	830
	AE12	838
	AE12	857
	AE12	1017
WAR	AE12	1035
	AE12	1067
	AE12	1236
	AE12	1291
	OAL	153
	OAL	411
	OAL	778
	AF	99
	KT1	109
	KT1	123
	KT1	160
	KT1	362
	KT2	31
	KT2	193
	KT2	377
	KT2	420
	KT2	570
	KT3	6
	KT3	90
	KT3	101
	KT3	339
	KT3	376
	KT3	423
	KT3	427
	KT3	509
	KT3	557
	KT3	575
	KT3	594
	KT3	660
	TJD	150
	TJD	157
	TJD	181
	M8	179
	M8	209
	M8	225
	HIF	237
	HIF	339
	HIF	345
	HIF	379
	HIF	496
	HIF	772
	TH	134
	M11	100
	M11	172
	FL	210
	FL	321
	M12	6
	M12	76
	M12	120
	M12	139
	M12	177
	M12	490
	M12	508
	M12	559
	M12	596
	M12	630
	M12	781
	M12	799
	AU	14
	AU	50
	AU	54
	AU	70
	AU	262
	AU	278
	AU	330
	AU	335
	AU	440
	AU	474
	AU	490
	AU	512
	AU	535
	AU	542
	AU	554
	AU	570
	WB	430
	M15	232
	M15	629
	CI	265
	CI	277
	CI	402
	CI	413
	CI	623
	CI	633
	ETP	2
	STP	5
WARBLED	FL	110
WARBLES	J6	98
WARBLING	MF	35
	SSC	36
	SFL	3
	DHP	3
	VP6	114
	C	89
WARD	P1	24
	AE1	691
	AE5	575

Word	Ref	No.
WARD	AE6	749
	AE10	662
	AE12	1330
	OAL	859
	KT3	620
	M8	239
	M12	206
	M12	515
WARDERS	AE2	451
WARDING	AE7	1013
	AE10	541
WARDROBE	HAP	1090
	J3	251
WARDS	OE	46
	L3	44
	J1	70
	AE5	584
WARE	AM	828
	EMK	21
	PKK	15
	RL	127
	RL	237
	OE	38
	J3	432
	J6	226
	J6	491
	P5	72
	VP4	47
WARES	DC	7
	PCG1	37
	EUO	33
	PTW	7
	P6	178
	OAL	479
	AU	268
WARLIKE	LC	102
	AM	505
	AM	611
	AM	731
	ENH	21
	AA	221
	EK	33
	TA	429
	MN	10
	AK	131
	AK	165
	M1	161
	HI	46
	G3	144
	G3	285
	AE3	604
	AE3	711
	AE3	925
	AE4	55
	AE5	773
	AE6	1150
	AE7	202
	AE7	250
	AE7	964
	AE7	990
	AE7	1026
	AE7	1095
	AE8	362
	AE8	629
	AE8	685
	AE8	805
	AE9	222
	AE9	693
	AE9	894
	AE10	259
	AE11	32
	AE11	70
	AE11	92
	OAL	14
	AF	2
	DO	110
	KT1	14
	KT1	163
	KT1	366
	KT3	529
	KT3	998
	KT3	915
	C	154
	FL	305
	M12	219
	AU	272
	M15	545
WARM	SMA	51
	AM	496
	AM	526
	AM	554
	AM	573
	AM	933
	AM	1023
	EEL	13
	ENH	11
WARM	ML	36
	ML	37
	AA	37
	AA	459
	SAA	418
	RL	417
	L2	37
	H29	87
	TA	476
	EL	64
	P6	2
	M1	540
	M9	211
	M13	86
	M13	129
	GK	25
	GK	110
	G1	302
	G1	397
	G3	487
	AE2	865
	AE5	551
	AE6	313
	AE7	657
	AE11	323
	AE12	59
	AE12	466
	OAL	743
	KT3	795
	M10	77
	C	280
	WB	534
	M15	171
	M15	468
WARMED	AR	34
	SMA	14
	CM	40
	LS	9
	EL	111
	J10	345
	M1	567
	G1	127
	AE9	84
	AE9	949
	AE10	975
	KT3	335
	K_3	1145
	B	514
	BP	74
	FL	416
WARMER	M1'	329
	HA	1738
	P6	13
WARMING	SL	16
WARMLY	AE	562
WARMS	SM	80
	S	2
	AE7	957
	AE8	922
	AE12	166
	OAL	271
	B	76
WARMTH	AM	210
	AA	8
	SAA	339
	L1	30
	NS	2
	HAP	2565
	AK	86
	BR	256
	M1	748
	VP3	94
	G1	130
	G2	435
	G2	455
	G2	472
	G3	199
	G3	429
	AE1	1043
	AE8	515
	AE9	236
	KT1	178
	C	576
WARN	AR	187
	PP	9
	ELT	6
	AE4	546
	AE10	323
	AE10	1197
	OAL	843
WARNED	CM	124
	AA	753
	T23	111
	HAP	1604
	HAP	1737
	HAP	2300
WARNED	J6	618
	J6	676
	M13	44
	ELT	28
	VP6	121
	VP9	18
	G3	831
	AE2	245
	AE3	5
	AE3	65
	AE4	822
	AE8	444
	AE9	45
	AE10	226
	AE10	363
	AE11	69
	AE11	232
	OAL	778
	B	565
	CAM	200
	C	245
	C	310
	C	362
	C	393
	C	394
	C	799
	TH	296
	TH	425
	M11	25
	M12	485
	M15	41
	M15	205
	GP	28
	CI	278
WARNING	PIE	4
	GE	81
	HAP	1719
	EL	326
	AE2	380
	AE6	843
WARNS	AM	534
	AE1	491
	AE6	842
	AE10	618
	AE11	787
WARP	TA	322
WARPED	HAP	1693
	B	402
WARPING	M13	85
	AE5	584
WARRANT	PLT	7
	PLT	9
	EHC	22
	WB	251
WARRANTED	B	440
WARRANTS	J10	133
	PLT	2
WARRING	G1	432
	AE1	753
	AE11	1223
	CI	38
WARRIOR	AA	828
	TA	474
	HAP	1386
	G2	200
	AE1	768
	AE4	349
	AE6	244
	AE6	645
	AE7	1070
	AE7	1095
	AE8	140
	AE9	973
	AE10	1276
	AE11	756
	AE11	1016
	KT1	7
	KT2	529
	KT2	615
	KT3	723
	M8	100
	M8	170
	HIF	307
	FL	215
	FL	255
	M12	290
	M12	391
	M12	677
	M12	811
	M15	546
	SMP	61
WARRIOR-HORSES	AE9	474
WARRIOR'S	AE1	648
	AE9	1053
	KT3	165
	KT3	988

WATER	HAP	2294		WATERS	M1	788		WATERY	AE3	550
	EL	136			VP5	37			AE3	675
	J6	683			VP5	62			AE3	908
	P3	22			VP9	25			AE4	594
	M1	18			VP9	29			AE5	1
	M1	439			G1	169			AE5	85
	M1	738			G1	507			AE5	152
	M1	973			G2	225			AE5	304
	M9	144			G3	373			AE5	776
	M13	50			G4	174			AE5	1035
	M13	223			G4	432			AE5	1078
	VP5	39			G4	540			AE6	129
	VP8	89			G4	761			AE7	310
	G1	10			AE1	232			AE7	967
	G2	332			AE3	273			AE7	1081
	G2	477			AE3	699			AE8	101
	G3	200			AE5	168			AE8	118
	G3	655			AE6	313			AE8	898
	G3	812			AE6	342			AE8	938
	G4	37			AE6	981			AE9	118
	G4	65			AE6	1004			AE10	239
	G4	335			AE7	645			AE10	261
	AE1	982			AE7	690			AE10	286
	AE2	933			AE7	987			AE10	325
	AE4	377			AE8	125			AE10	348
	AE4	982			AE8	396			AE11	2
	AE5	914			AE8	557			AE12	1223
	AE6	559			AE9	152			KT3	401
	AE6	863			AE9	1103			TJD	132
	AE7	314			AE11	752			B	683
	AE7	1093			AE12	183			BP	153
	AE8	85			AE12	765			HIF	86
	AE8	95			OAL	294			C	314
	AE8	914			M8	94			M11	25
	AE9	26			M11	130			M11	100
	AE10	407			M11	149			AU	455
	OAL	542			M11	152		WATLING	MF	97
	OAL	543			M11	156		WAULING	EK	15
	OAE2	66			M11	487		WAVE	S	13
	KT1	414			M12	440			DA	57
	KT1	469			M12	549			HAP	430
	KT1	580			M15	413			P1	184
	KT1	587			M15	433			AE6	486
	BP	74			M15	482			M11	201
	M11	126			M15	494			M15	271
	M11	160			PMK	12		WAVED	G4	513
	M11	358		WATER-SPANIEL	ESF	30			AE6	794
	WB	27		WATERY	HS	138			AE7	35
	M15	198			AM	14			AE7	257
	M15	372			AM	53			AE10	813
	M15	449			AM	201			AE10	1289
WATERED	HAP	1123			AM	542			KT1	108
	TJD	179			AM	1093			KT3	564
WATERFALLS	G1	366			L4	248		WAVERING	AR	225
WATERFOWL	AE4	373			L4	249		WAVES	SMA	104
WATERING	AT	4			TA	141			VHH	17
	HAP	529			EL	139			AM	85
	VP7	14			M1	63			AM	264
	G3	511			M1	169			AM	375
	G3	518			M1	353			AM	391
	G4	282			M1	377			AM	587
	AE11	747			M1	383			AM	612
WATERISH	G3	730			M1	399			DA	44
WATERMEN	PLG	32			M1	791			PUF	5
	J6	450			M13	61			AA	160
WATER'S	MF	185			M13	147			MD	69
	P3	64			M13	168			SAA	596
	G3	22			G1	38			SAA	622
	M1	20			G1	43			SAA	727
	OAL	598			G1	104			SAA	1082
	WB	193			G1	160			SAA	1122
WATERS	SMA	113			G1	176			AT	57
	SIE	13			G1	498			L3	243
	AM	390			G1	520			EAA	23
	AM	621			G1	527			HAP	1125
	AM	707			G1	608			BR	258
	AM	734			G2	16			P5	150
	AM	924			G2	155			P6	68
	AM	928			G2	274			M1	168
	AM	1122			G2	625			M1	376
	RL	341			G3	368			M1	443
	H3	29			G3	405			M1	449
	HAP	1775			G4	341			M1	452
	J3	371			G4	518			M13	145
	J10	239			G4	549			VP4	47
	M1	38			G4	552			VP9	78
	M1	45			G4	559			G1	44
	M1	242			G4	568			G1	457
	M1	250			G4	606			G2	202
	M1	392			AE1	52			G3	368
	M1	401			AE1	178			G4	499
	M1	427			AE2	48			G4	619
	M1	459			AE2	240			G4	767
	M1	466			AE2	414			AE1	100
	M1	501			AE3	100			AE1	153
	M1	776			AE3	350			AE1	164

WAY			WAY			WAY		
	AE1	528		AE9	516		CAM	137
	AE1	573		AE9	522		CAM	280
	AE1	717		AE9	531		CAM	281
	AE1	814		AE9	561		CAM	349
	AE1	822		AE9	685		HIF	287
	AE2	280		AE9	739		HIF	318
	AE2	297		AE9	754		HIF	448
	AE2	522		AE9	764		HIF	455
	AE2	621		AE9	867		HIF	657
	AE2	774		AE9	880		HIF	670
	AE2	896		AE9	1092		C	249
	AE2	916		AE10	171		C	267
	AE2	951		AE10	239		C	314
	AE2	987		AE10	339		C	349
	AE3	171		AE10	349		C	492
	AE3	250		AE10	422		C	621
	AE3	350		AE10	460		C	673
	AE3	361		AE10	514		C	817
	AE3	508		AE10	520		TH	41
	AE3	525		AE10	523		TH	58
	AE3	714		AE10	716		TH	131
	AE3	717		AE10	932		TH	138
	AE3	904		AE10	1112		TH	231
	AE4	68		AE10	1158		TH	288
	AE4	228		AE10	1278		TH	361
	AE4	411		AE11	43		M11	15
	AE4	640		AE11	177		M11	25
	AE4	831		AE11	255		M11	106
	AE5	1		AE11	526		M11	141
	AE5	30		AE11	615		M11	154
	AE5	274		AE11	782		M11	163
	AE5	283		AE11	803		M11	321
	AE5	373		AE11	933		M11	354
	AE5	430		AE11	967		M11	384
	AE5	667		AE11	1031		M11	418
	AE5	693		AE11	1108		M11	437
	AE5	774		AE11	1123		FL	37
	AE5	789		AE11	1129		FL	54
	AE5	853		AE11	1306		FL	361
	AE5	865		AE12	387		FL	457
	AE5	891		AE12	395		FL	575
	AE5	964		AE12	573		FL	589
	AE5	1055		AE12	590		FL	610
	AE5	1057		AE12	982		M12	11
	AE5	1078		AE12	988		M12	114
	AE5	1094		AE12	1093		M12	193
	AE6	193		AE12	1307		M12	270
	AE6	232		OAL	57		M12	447
	AE6	337		OAL	153		M12	671
	AE6	370		OAL	409		AU	529
	AE6	410		OAL	433		AU	605
	AE6	501		OAL	448		WB	50
	AE6	575		OAL	500		WB	114
	AE6	643		OAL	507		WB	190
	AE6	710		OAL	509		WB	257
	AE6	717		AF	148		WB	259
	AE6	726		AF	152		WB	264
	AE6	751		DO	42		WB	276
	AE6	859		DO	51		WB	362
	AE6	867		DO	113		M15	16
	AE6	909		DO	154		M15	218
	AE6	935		KT1	15		M15	269
	AE6	1084		KT1	42		M15	421
	AE6	1175		KT1	106		M15	424
	AE6	1243		KT1	188		M15	444
	AE7	39		KT1	211		M15	520
	AE7	44		KT1	379		M15	639
	AE7	198		KT2	24		GP	136
	AE7	215		KT2	213		CI	10
	AE7	277		KT2	226		CI	80
	AE7	292		KT2	233		CI	127
	AE7	409		KT2	434		CI	172
	AE7	423		KT2	539		CI	285
	AE7	646		KT3	60		CI	465
	AE7	703		KT3	97		CI	531
	AE7	936		KT3	117		STP	20
	AE7	986		KT3	125		EL	144
	AE8	30		KT3	382	WAYLAID	AM	98
	AE8	118		KT3	530	WAYLAYS	AM	806
	AE8	148		KT3	542	WAYS	AM	1047
	AE8	212		KT3	698		AA	311
	AE8	316		KT3	1012		MF	208
	AE8	341		M8	82		RL	60
	AE8	411		B	61		L4	91
	AE8	676		B	107		TA	173
	AE8	787		B	125		HAP	476
	AE9	24		B	131		HAP	690
	AE9	70		B	134		SSC	46
	AE9	118		B	160		BR	75
	AE9	252		B	181		BR	299
	AE9	317		B	196		SKA6	13
	AE9	321		B	307		J10	42
	AE9	420		B	460		P1	152
	AE9	431		B	663		M1	687
	AE9	434		B	704		M1	1011
	AE9	500		BP	144		G2	27

WAYS	G2	102	WEAKNESS	SAA	692	WEALTHY	AA	738
	G2	527		RL	257		MD	183
	G2	677		PKA	12		SAA	10
	G3	13	WEAL	C	206		L2	43
	G3	187	WEALTH	AR	239		T18	84
	AE2	1000		RH	80		T27	39
	AE2	1058		PWG	51		HAP	1123
	AE3	259		LCA	2		J1	102
	AE4	678		VHH	20		J3	104
	AE5	576		AM	7		J3	225
	AE5	770		AM	43		J3	256
	AE6	40		AM	98		J3	344
	AE6	272		AM	126		J3	387
	AE7	203		AM	807		P2	18
	AE7	471		AM	1154		P2	124
	AE7	540		AM	1202		P3	141
	AE12	769		AM	1213		P5	113
	OAL	865		HP	203		ELT	12
	KT1	409		HP	220		VP2	81
	TJD	64		DA	122		KT3	986
	B	73		DA	163		TJD	37
	C	284		AA	165		TJD	127
WAYWARD	G4	582		AA	559		WB	28
	KT3	385		AA	591		CI	47
WEAK	RH	89		AA	826	WEAN	AE4	341
	LC	127		MD	172		AE4	397
	AM	160		SAA	470	WEANING	VP7	21
	AM	363		SAA	687		G3	295
	PWGR	27		SAA	881	WEANS	P3	108
	EOE	29		RL	105	WEAPON	PMQW	17
	EOE	30		L2	15		SAA	539
	PTC	19		H29	18		HAP	1560
	PLG	22		H29	96		HAP	1995
	HP	111		H2	57		AE4	952
	HP	178		TA	44		AE5	668
	DA	114		HAP	1251		AE5	684
	AA	214		HAP	1278		AE6	406
	AA	288		HAP	1287		AE7	743
	AA	388		HAP	2529		AE7	886
	RL	97		HAP	2560		AE9	553
	TA	158		EDS	33		AE9	1008
	TA	278		PP	10		AE10	542
	PAA	14		J1	32		AE10	673
	HAP	870		J3	23		AE10	1049
	HAP	1061		J3	111		AE11	995
	HAP	1245		J6	204		AE11	1031
	HAP	1664		J10	18		AE11	1175
	HAP	1692		J10	24		AE11	1190
	HAP	2163		P2	84		AE12	81
	HAP	2413		P3	125		AE12	404
	PDS	30		P4	113		AE12	574
	PKA	10		P5	161		AE12	641
	EL	268		P6	79		AE12	715
	PSH	31		P6	112		AE12	788
	J3	314		P6	183		AE12	1068
	J6	677		VP2	24		AE12	1123
	J6	844		VP2	88		AE12	1141
	P1	262		G4	198		AE12	1335
	P5	244		G4	353		M8	186
	M9	15		AE1	473		TH	130
	G3	190		AE1	480		M12	114
	G3	551		AE1	805		M12	127
	AE2	872		AE2	29		M12	169
	AE6	665		AE2	1037		M12	415
	AE9	1030		AE3	79		AU	606
	AE9	1037		AE4	103	WEAPONS	EMQW	8
	AE11	94		AE8	629		PTS	31
	AE11	1044		AE10	731		M1	182
	AE11	1113		AE10	789		M1	618
	AE12	1262		AE12	34		AE3	288
	OAL	273		KT1	425		AE3	310
	DO	120		KT2	372		AE9	677
	KT1	154		KT2	393		AE9	1091
	KT2	144		KT2	480		AE10	461
	KT3	473		KT2	507		AE10	612
	M8	225		B	552		AE11	247
	FL	590		B	556		AE11	841
	AU	496		BP	36		AE11	1082
	M15	123		TH	7		AE12	429
	CI	287		M11	187		AE12	498
	CI	402		WB	125		AE12	655
WEAKEN	AM	27		WB	321		M8	105
WEAKENED	AA	92		WB	379		CI	291
	L3	256		WB	466		CI	624
WEAKER	RH	36		WB	485	WEAR	AR	179
	AM	884		M15	42		AM	774
	PMQ	11		CI	617		AM	822
	HAP	246	WEALTHIER	AM	830		E	17
	AE3	77		AM	1193		PTW	28
	AE9	81	WEALTHY	AR	304		AA	11
	AE9	1067		AM	19		EK	40
	TJD	28		AM	995		EDGA	31
WEAKLY	SAA	916		AM	1002		OE	61
	B	393		AM	1193		AT	50
WEAKNESS	AM	540		AM	1208		HAP	2396
	ECG1	39		PNH	12		PTS	31

Word	Ref	No.	Word	Ref	No.	Word	Ref	No.
WEAR	LS	6	WEARY	AM	489	WEAVER	AM	607
	J3	284		AM	909	WEAVER'S	AA	639
	J6	481		AM	1010	WEAVERS	G1	381
	J6	575		E	3	WEAVING	VP2	107
	P1	36		PAZ	8	WEAZON	AE9	592
	M9	203		HP	197	WEAZON'S	M12	756
	MC	54		DA	189	WEB	VP4	56
	VP4	30		AA	200		G3	839
	VP7	89		AA	898		AE9	633
	G1	26		RL	2		HIF	50
	G2	619		L1	58		FL	235
	G2	675		L3	288		M15	381
	G3	87		L4	245	WEBS	G4	361
	G3	546		TA	154	WED	UDH	97
	G3	588		HAP	310		AR	20
	G3	839		J3	495		AM	78
	AE1	366		J10	367		CM	123
	AE1	464		M13	46		H2	19
	AE4	399		HI	131		HAP	1499
	AE5	727		VP5	71		EDS	31
	AE6	1000		VP7	6		J6	75
	AE6	1120		VP9	85		J6	245
	AE7	594		G4	36		J10	223
	AE7	949		G4	264		J10	513
	AE7	1012		G4	278		J10	542
	AE8	876		G4	562		AE3	425
	AE9	922		G4	581		AE11	357
	AE11	507		G4	619		B	466
	AE12	185		G4	632		M10	3
	AE12	1198		AE1	226		CAM	47
	OAL	36		AE2	18		WB	127
	OAL	540		AE2	331		WB	333
	OAL	579		AE2	618		WB	543
	OAL	837		AE2	1004		CI	249
	DO	168		AE3	104		CI	448
	KT2	53		AE3	200		CI	632
	M8	394		AE3	218	WEDDING	UDH	4
	CAM	239		AE3	759		T27	64
	M11	237		AE3	929		HAP	1091
	FL	521		AE4	757		BR	278
	M12	823		AE5	771		J6	39
	AU	156		AE6	701		J6	320
	AU	196		AE7	170		J10	521
	AU	451		AE8	40		ELT	19
	AU	459		AE8	482		OAL	666
	M15	80		AE9	287		WB	361
	M15	298		AE9	971	WEDDING-NIGHT	PEL	2
	M15	560		AE10	1271	WEDGE	M13	49
WEARIED	AR	313		AE11	823		AE7	711
	LC	129		AE12	285		AE12	842
	VHH	28		AE12	1279	WEDGED	AE5	285
	MD	321		KT3	1038		AE11	1190
	J1	100		TJD	161	WEDGES	G1	216
	J1	200		BP	45		AE6	266
	M1	1011		CAM	321		AE11	208
	AE2	149		CAM	348	WEDLOCK	J6	62
	AE2	371		C	228		G3	203
	AE3	745		FL	22		WB	136
	AE6	477		FL	32	WEDS	HAP	353
	AE8	806		M12	410		ELT	32
	AE8	847		AU	489		VP8	36
	OAL	497		M15	21		AS	74
	TH	25		M15	378	WEED	AA	305
	M11	88		SMP	7		HAP	2373
	M15	281	WEASEL	G1	270		G3	278
WEARIES	J10	238	WEATHER	SEL4	27	WEEDS	TA	354
	P6	65		DA	45		P4	96
	G4	638		PUF	20		VP4	29
	CI	350		PK	40		G1	103
WEARINESS	M12	763		TA	393		G1	181
WEARS	AR	254		HAP	1239		G1	226
	LC	145		HAP	1768		G1	263
	PCB	27		HAP	1801		G2	179
	PRH	5		PLT	26		G3	445
	T27	62		G1	77		G4	687
	HAP	163		G1	172		AE6	561
	PDS	6		G1	350		KT1	50
	J3	295		G1	397	WEEDY	VP8	123
	J10	346		G1	514		AE2	185
	M1	449		G1	588		AE4	764
	EHC	27		G1	608	WEEK	HAP	1894
	G1	436		AE1	503	WEEKLY	SAA	1033
	G4	138		AE2	30		J10	351
	G4	531		AE5	19		TJD	72
	AE4	804		AE7	273	WEEP	UDH	92
	AE5	1096		FL	388		SAA	608
	AE7	925	WEATHER-BEATEN	OAL	827		SAA	1079
	AE9	498	WEATHER-COCK	HAP	465		T18	68
	AE9	891	WEATHERED	CM	73		HAP	1214
	KT3	1031	WEAVE	RL	142		J3	172
	KT3	1062		VP1	116		VP4	35
	WB	197		G1	359		AE1	673
WEARY	AR	150	WEAVED	VP9	56		AE2	489
	LC	47		VP10	103		AE2	1067
	AM	278		AE7	340		AE4	557
	AM	391		AE11	1141		AE6	257

Word	Ref	No.
WEEP	AE9	648
	AE11	305
	KT3	420
	B	578
	B	671
	B	672
	B	682
	M11	178
WEEPER'S	J10	46
WEEPING	CM	134
	D	26
	TA	275
	BR	171
	J10	398
	HI	45
	G1	647
	G3	412
	AE1	644
	AE5	797
	AE6	306
	AE9	406
	AE10	888
	AE11	43
	AE12	568
	OAL	149
	KT3	674
	KT3	938
	M8	400
	B	662
	BP	155
	BP	175
	CAM	159
	M12	45
WEEPS	PAL	13
	EPN	2
	G1	86
	AE11	229
	CAM	352
	M11	177
WEFT	G1	381
WEIGH	SMA	133
	PWG	6
	PMQ	8
	ECG2	13
	HAP	241
	BR	294
	J10	235
	P1	14
	G3	161
	AE3	374
	AE3	680
	AE4	602
	AE4	825
	AE8	25
	AE12	33
	AE12	70
	KT1	287
	HIF	776
	WB	507
	CI	612
WEIGHED	AM	709
	AA	112
	SAA	200
	RL	114
	TA	236
	HAP	2527
	J1	61
	G2	344
	AE7	67
	DO	115
	KT3	275
	TJD	189
	B	619
	M11	443
	M12	36
	CI	462
WEIGHING	HAP	1265
WEIGHS	SAA	847
	J6	563
	J10	555
	G1	419
	AE4	905
	AE5	1011
	AE12	1055
WEIGHT	AR	235
	RH	17
	RH	37
	LC	151
	AM	708
	PEL	27
	ECG2	16
	EOE	5
	CM	44
	AA	565
	AA	887
	AA	954
WEIGHT	EDG	37
	L3	272
	H9	3
	TA	30
	HAP	62
	HAP	1064
	HAP	1085
	HAP	1811
	HAP	2227
	J1	41
	J6	33
	J6	243
	J10	64
	J10	171
	P2	95
	P4	22
	P5	198
	M1	88
	M9	53
	M13	127
	G1	164
	G1	244
	G2	197
	G2	343
	G3	372
	G3	561
	G3	800
	G4	286
	AE2	697
	AE5	346
	AE5	543
	AE5	555
	AE6	478
	AE6	557
	AE7	345
	AE9	15
	AE9	680
	AE9	774
	AE9	972
	AE9	980
	AE9	1071
	AE10	534
	AE10	1242
	AE10	1284
	AE11	836
	AE12	779
	AE12	1303
	AE12	1307
	B	232
	B	365
	M12	344
	M12	394
	M12	457
	M12	487
	M12	682
	M12	754
	AU	174
	AU	177
	WB	226
	WB	424
	M15	2
	M15	216
	M15	369
	CI	412
	CI	427
	SMP	7
	SMP	80
WEIGHTLESS	LC	155
WEIGHTS	HS	57
	AR	155
	RH	36
	AM	1167
	HAP	1195
	HAP	1607
	J10	165
	P1	266
	M12	590
	M12	673
WEIGHTY	HS	135
	LC	132
	AA	868
	RL	234
	T23	90
	TA	331
	GE	39
	HAP	721
	G1	260
	G3	782
	AE2	914
	AE4	587
	AE5	488
	AE5	598
	AE6	838
	AE6	1048
	AE7	1024
	AE9	710
WEIGHTY	AE10	988
	AE12	1284
	M15	372
WELCOME	AR	250
	AR	277
	PRL	17
	VHH	48
	AM	732
	PMM	15
	PMM	16
	S	8
	PTW	2
	PRH	36
	SAA	1129
	RL	366
	L1	16
	L3	258
	AK	20
	HAP	1248
	HAP	1272
	HAP	1276
	HAP	1577
	HAP	2430
	P6	103
	M1	302
	DHP	4
	G2	761
	AE1	244
	AE1	816
	AE1	887
	AE2	983
	AE3	288
	AE3	447
	AE6	931
	AE8	163
	AE8	211
	AE8	234
	AE9	1104
	AE10	566
	AE11	1256
	AE12	1015
	KT1	15
	KT1	49
	KT1	200
	KT1	365
	KT2	52
	B	204
	B	713
	BP	43
	BP	119
	CAM	258
	TH	412
	FL	15
	CI	181
	CI	375
	PMK	5
	PMK	9
	PMK	13
	PMK	14
	PMK	20
WELCOMED	VP6	94
WELCOMES	AE5	53
WELFARE	EK	3
	TA	238
	AE9	339
WELKIN	ODA	6
	C	746
WELL	RL	34
	J3	369
	KT2	82
	M15	486
WELL-BECOMING	AE11	94
WELL-BOILED	AE11	832
WELL-BORN	AE2	453
	TJD	127
WELL-BREATHED	AA	631
	G3	315
	TJD	52
WELL-BRED	HAP	569
WELL-BUILT	HIF	613
WELL-CALKED	AE4	575
WELL-CHOSEN	AE8	685
	M12	132
WELL-COZENED	AR	128
WELL-DEFENDED	AE9	933
WELL-DESERVING	G3	784
	AE3	876
	M15	206
WELL-DISPUTED	AE8	897
WELL-DISSEMBLED	AE3	394
	AE5	762
WELL-DRAWN	SMA	108
WELL-DRESSED	P4	43
WELLED	AE10	1184
WELL-FASHIONED	OAL	579
WELL-FED	P2	55

WELL-FED	AE8	113
WELL-FILLED	J1	136
WELL-FLESHED	EPF	11
WELL-GROWN	AE7	669
	AE11	499
	M12	446
WELL-HEAPED	H9	7
WELL-HUMORED	L4	290
WELL-HUNG	AA	574
WELL-INVENTED	AE2	204
WELL-KNOWN	G3	391
	AE2	333
	AE6	661
	AE11	747
	AE11	803
WELL-LABORED	L4	244
WELL-LUNGED	P5	3
WELL-MANAGED	AE10	1226
WELL-MATCHED	HAP	356
WELL-MEANERS	KT3	205
WELL-MEANING	PAL	12
	RL	225
	TA	100
WELL-MOUTHED	H2	49
	AE10	1226
WELL-NATURED	PAL	18
	H29	9
WELL-PISSING	J3	186
WELL-PLEASING	AE10	856
WELL-PROPORTIONED	AK	150
	M1	960
	CI	150
WELL-PURGED	P5	86
WELL-RIGGED	HIF	273
WELL-RIPENED	AR	170
WELLS	HI	130
	G1	653
	KT1	587
WELL-SCOURGED	PDG	5
WELL-SHARPENED	MF	45
WELL-SKILLED	AE10	1069
WELL-STORED	AM	910
WELL-TEMPERED	TA	325
	AE11	734
WELL-TIMED	MF	39
WELL-TUNED	L2	32
WELL-TURNED	M1	669
WELL-UNITED	FL	70
WELL-VERSED	AA	513
WELL-VOWELED	ER	17
WELL-WATERED	BP	59
WELL-WINNOWED	TA	375
WELL-WROUGHT	LMC	3
WELTERING	AE2	906
	AE11	1218
	AF	79
WELTERS	AE9	447
WEN	J6	153
WENCH	EEL	22
	L4	155
	J6	170
	OAL	448
WENCHES	PWGR	20
	EM	20
WENCHES'	PMK	6
WENT	HS	129
	HS	139
	AR	189
	LC	17
	PWG	48
	AM	84
	AM	630
	AM	693
	AM	870
	AM	920
	AM	1089
	AM	1160
	EEL	7
	EEL	23
	SEL3	3
	CM	82
	CM	107
	AA	160
	AA	560
	AA	644
	AA	742
	MD	98
	MD	101
	SAA	344
	RL	380
	AT	75
	TA	107
	TA	253
	AK	105
	GE	20
	HAP	525

WENT	HAP	1888
	PDS	29
	EL	190
	EL	337
	OD	44
	J6	455
	J10	166
	J10	244
	M1	257
	M1	887
	M9	189
	HI	1
	HI	25
	VP1	47
	VP9	27
	AE2	916
	AE3	34
	AE3	112
	AE5	413
	AE6	234
	AE6	338
	AE6	378
	AE7	122
	AE7	1026
	AE9	292
	AE9	414
	AE9	603
	AE9	643
	AE10	218
	AE10	926
	AE10	1112
	AE10	1265
	AE12	131
	OAL	59
	KT1	364
	KT1	573
	KT2	538
	KT3	844
	KT3	852
	KT3	1018
	M8	221
	B	149
	B	171
	BP	122
	CAM	276
	HIF	379
	HIF	802
	C	26
	C	84
	C	212
	C	261
	C	305
	C	346
	C	353
	C	432
	TH	23
	TH	50
	TH	56
	TH	83
	TH	352
	M11	321
	FL	396
	M12	200
	M12	312
	AU	382
	AU	434
	WB	114
	WB	119
	WB	169
	WB	189
	WB	342
	GP	23
	GP	135
	CI	75
	CI	85
	CI	232
	CI	267
	AS	78
WEPT	AR	158
	AM	961
	MF	60
	AT	77
	T23	98
	M1	474
	M1	794
	M1	901
	M1	1016
	VP10	23
	AE2	365
	AE6	1
	AE10	1122
	AE10	1166
	OAL	600
	KT2	312
	KT3	855
	KT3	944

WEPT	B	290
	B	694
	CAM	351
	HIF	484
	HIF	593
	M11	380
	M11	455
	M12	4
	M15	354
	CI	312
WEST	AM	1187
	AA	731
	HAP	1122
	M1	458
	G1	509
	G3	438
	G3	549
	AE1	126
	AE2	567
	AE5	27
	AE9	195
	AE9	877
	AE11	486
	KT3	545
	KT3	566
	KT3	638
	M11	123
	FL	337
WESTERN	SMA	29
	DC	17
	AA	268
	AA	738
	AA	868
	MF	140
	L1	15
	HAP	1240
	M1	139
	G1	65
	G2	151
	G2	447
	G3	217
	G3	431
	G3	500
	G4	205
	G4	432
	AE1	186
	AE3	164
	AE4	328
	AE4	351
	AE4	808
	AE5	42
	KT2	449
	KT3	556
	C	249
	C	267
WESTWARD	AM	711
	M1	77
	AE9	909
	AE11	1316
	DO	42
WET	AM	440
	PCG1	30
	ODA	2
	ODA	11
	J1	103
	VP8	55
	VP10	29
	G1	514
	G1	608
	G4	506
	AE1	251
	AE5	233
	AE9	67
	OAL	268
	M11	356
	M11	405
	FL	389
	FL	416
WEXING	KT2	649
	M15	293
	SMP	30
WHALE	AM	314
	PCB	19
	J10	22
WHALES	AE5	1077
WHEAT	HAP	2276
	BR	234
	VP3	125
	G1	309
	G1	478
WHEEDLED	PCD	15
WHEEDLING	J10	205
WHEEL	LC	132
	SCD2	21
	SAA	337
	J3	74

Word	Ref	No.
WHEEL	J 10	89
	P 3	41
	G 1	535
	G 3	66
	G 3	271
	G 4	492
	G 4	695
	AE 5	761
	AE 11	297
	AE 11	926
	KT 2	533
	KT 2	593
	M 8	258
	C I	426
WHEEL-BROAD	PCG 1	42
WHEELED	AE 10	806
	AE 10	913
	AE 10	1268
	AE 12	1076
	FL	286
	M 12	749
WHEELING	G 4	803
	AE 5	222
	AE 12	699
	KT 3	545
WHEELS	P 5	98
	G 2	624
	G 3	179
	G 3	287
	G 3	555
	AE 2	307
	AE 5	194
	AE 5	361
	AE 6	839
	AE 9	426
	AE 9	443
	AE 10	825
	AE 11	1126
	AE 12	780
	AE 12	980
	M 8	200
	PTP	42
WHEEZING	G 3	745
WHELMED	AE 6	455
	AE 9	725
	KT 3	1081
	M 15	448
WHELMING	VP 8	80
WHELMS	M 11	227
WHELP	C	120
WHELPED	HAP	182
	M 15	560
WHELPS	AT	36
	VP 1	32
	AE 2	481
WHEREWITHAL	J 6	104
	J 6	197
	P 6	174
WHET	PR	31
	AA	670
	MD	240
	T 27	88
	J 3	458
	G 1	354
	G 3	387
	G 4	107
	AE 7	712
WHETS	AE 10	1004
	AE 12	167
WHETSTONE	OE	31
WHETSTONE'S	PWGR	8
WHETTED	J 10	365
	G 1	188
WHEY	G 3	617
	M 12	589
WHIFF	L 4	176
WHIG	PLB	7
	PLB	13
	ELB	3
	ELB	35
	PRH	30
	PK	42
	PDG	2
	NS	14
WHIGGISH	EDG	44
WHIGS	PLB	2
	PLB	4
	PLB	11
	ELB	16
	PK	15
	PDG	35
	EDG	14
	EDG	25
	EDG	41
	EDGA	2
	EDGA	22
WHIGS	EC	11
	PAA	42
WHILOM	PCB	23
	MF	35
WHINE	OE	55
	L 3	101
WHINING	L 4	171
	NS	7
	NS	18
	NS	29
WHIP	PTS	21
	P 3	97
	P 5	186
	AE 6	772
	AE 7	528
	AE 7	632
WHIPPED	PMQ	42
	J 10	290
	P 1	132
WHIPS	J 3	496
	G 3	292
WHIP-STITCH	MF	181
WHIRL	PSF	18
	AE 7	951
	AE 9	905
	M 11	196
WHIRLED	HAP	690
	J 1	94
	VP 8	144
	G 1	332
	G 1	434
	G 1	505
	AE 6	412
	AE 6	637
	AE 9	590
	AE 9	798
	AE 9	956
	AE 9	1005
	M 8	123
	M 12	412
WHIRLING	P 3	97
	AE 3	273
	AE 10	1264
	AE 11	436
	AE 12	1239
	FL	3
	M 12	381
WHIRLPOOL	AE 3	538
WHIRLPOOLS	AE 7	43
WHIRLS	AE 7	784
	AE 7	530
	AE 10	715
WHIRLWIND	CM	85
	BR	235
	AE 2	568
	AE 6	127
	AE 12	667
	AE 12	1338
	TH	99
WHIRLWINDS	AE 1	64
WHISK	PWR	29
WHISKS	AE 11	1112
WHISPER	PPC	2
	T 27	16
	H 9	33
	HAP	1079
	HAP	2393
	P 6	95
	AE 4	759
	BP	167
	CAM	302
WHISPERED	SEL 3	19
	SSC	36
	EL	318
	AE 5	716
	AE 12	324
	HIF	289
WHISPERING	EEL	10
	CM	66
	T 27	102
	P 5	139
	VP 1	55
	HIF	722
	TH	90
WHISPERS	HP	146
	AA	371
	TA	286
	HAP	2474
	EL	2
	J 6	699
	J 10	142
	VP 5	128
	G 1	491
	G 4	379
	AE 6	955
	AE 10	150
WHISPERS	KT 3	554
	KT 3	1018
WHISTLE	M 13	57
	G 1	492
	AE 3	867
	C	428
	M 11	32
WHISTLED	AM	341
	KT 3	258
	C I	85
WHISTLES	H 2	41
WHISTLING	AM	430
	VP 5	6
	G 4	287
	AE 5	500
	AE 9	927
	AE 12	404
	M 12	384
WHITE	MHD	1
	AR	127
	AR	254
	LCA	45
	PCG 2	16
	SCG 1	10
	ENH	8
	MD	62
	PRH	12
	T 23	59
	HAP	343
	HAP	1651
	HAP	2366
	LS	3
	EL	330
	PSH	18
	J 3	55
	J 3	294
	J 3	354
	J 6	224
	J 6	687
	J 10	70
	P 1	36
	P 2	2
	P 2	3
	P 2	73
	P 5	44
	M 1	1041
	M 13	111
	VP 2	21
	VP 2	55
	VP 2	61
	G 1	85
	G 2	99
	G 2	346
	G 2	433
	G 2	651
	G 3	93
	G 3	129
	G 3	593
	G 3	600
	G 3	734
	G 4	195
	AE 1	658
	AE 3	173
	AE 3	504
	AE 3	709
	AE 4	660
	AE 5	739
	AE 5	1127
	AE 6	357
	AE 7	737
	AE 8	62
	AE 8	114
	AE 8	366
	AE 8	876
	AE 9	583
	AE 10	811
	AE 11	459
	AE 12	102
	AE 12	132
	AE 12	182
	AE 12	255
	AE 12	1021
	OAL	326
	OAL	244
	MFL	19
	DO	152
	KT 1	195
	KT 1	221
	KT 2	448
	KT 2	464
	KT 3	565
	KT 3	912
	M 8	142
	M 10	75
	CAM	239
	C	32

Word	Ref	No.
WHITE	C	53
	FL	228
	FL	252
	FL	258
	FL	266
	FL	342
	FL	347
	FL	351
	FL	355
	FL	391
	FL	397
	FL	409
	FL	430
	FL	442
	FL	464
	FL	502
	FL	507
	M11	99
	M11	131
	FL	161
	M12	210
	M12	537
	M12	618
	M15	55
	M15	573
	M15	622
	CI	155
WHITE-ARMED	HIF	298
WHITEHALL	PLB	47
	EKA	3
	PRH	21
	ETP	22
WHITE-MANED	M12	107
WHITENED	HAP	44
	AS	48
WHITENESS	P1	36
	M1	1035
	M9	192
	KT3	77
WHITER	VP7	53
	AR	292
	T23	60
	M13	66
WHITE-WIG	PM	4
WHIZZED	AE10	673
	AE11	1169
	M8	112
WHIZZING	AE5	667
	AE11	1250
	M12	114
WHOLE	UDH	38
	AM	54
	AM	113
	AM	242
	AM	464
	AM	814
	PA	16
	PTL	4
	PTL	10
	ECG1	32
	PCG2	19
	EOE	9
	PSF	21
	AA	541
	AA	808
	AA	994
	PLB	51
	MD	47
	MF	93
	MF	184
	SAA	224
	EDG	7
	RL	330
	RL	359
	AK	98
	AK	126
	GE	48
	HAP	500
	HAP	720
	HAP	1023
	HAP	1080
	BR	38
	EKA	33
	EL	231
	J1	137
	J1	179
	J1	191
	J1	209
	J1	212
	J3	189
	J6	219
	J6	268
	J6	376
	J6	570
	J6	617
	J6	651

Word	Ref	No.
WHOLE	J6	679
	J10	7
	J10	97
	J16	37
	M1	41
	HI	68
	PLT	37
	GK	71
	GK	168
	G1	437
	G3	529
	G3	568
	G3	828
	G4	324
	AE2	564
	AE2	1030
	AE4	278
	AE5	914
	AE6	983
	AE6	1015
	AE8	127
	AE8	745
	AE10	709
	AE11	257
	AE11	302
	AE11	1155
	MFL	9
	KT1	111
	KT2	428
	KT2	441
	KT2	596
	KT3	1042
	KT3	1045
	KT3	1147
	TJD	39
	TJD	83
	TJD	86
	M8	301
	HIF	253
	TH	98
	FL	50
	M12	669
	AU	567
	M15	323
	M15	673
	CI	148
	PTP	33
	PWR	18
WHOLESOME	EIE	12
	H2	95
	HAP	2199
	P5	86
	P5	203
	G1	366
	G2	332
	G3	791
	G4	196
	AE3	190
	AE5	952
	AE10	227
	OAL	292
	KT1	210
	BP	89
	M15	105
	M15	432
	M15	499
	PWR	35
WHOLLY	AM	121
	POE	29
	MD	175
	MD	228
	EK	38
	HAP	334
	HAP	857
	HAP	1573
	HAP	1653
	J3	205
	J6	356
	J10	547
	P5	176
	M1	750
	VP6	10
	G1	584
	G4	401
	AE4	479
	AE5	714
	AE5	814
	AE6	998
	AE9	366
	AE10	1074
	OAL	589
	DO	105
	KT1	151
	KT1	544
	TJD	104

Word	Ref	No.
WHOLLY	CAM	335
	C	173
	C	542
	ETP	20
WHORE	EEL	18
	PTW	26
	PO	24
	PCB	8
	EUF	6
	PLB	31
	ELB	9
	MD	153
	SAA	382
	SAA	429
	EK	34
	OE	1
	OE	31
	PD	8
	L4	150
	GE	53
	J1	30
	J3	163
	J3	228
	J6	69
	J6	164
	J6	365
	J6	378
	J6	467
	J10	377
	J16	94
	OAL	84
	PMK	28
WHORED	MD	258
WHOREMASTER	J6	58
WHORES	PD	62
	J3	112
	J6	35
	J6	615
	P6	140
	P6	174
	OAL	154
WHORESONS	J6	449
WHORING	PSF	38
	MD	40
	PD	52
	EH	14
	J6	30
WHORLBAT	G3	30
WICKED	EUO	22
	ENH	3
	EUF	3
	AA	498
	AA	567
	AA	600
	MD	64
	SAA	552
	L5	16
	H2	57
	H2	97
	HAP	1423
	HAP	2373
	ESH	6
	EH	13
	J3	229
	P2	46
	P2	109
	P4	96
	G1	103
	G2	179
	AE7	26
	AE7	856
	C	74
	C	488
	C	724
	WB	34
WICKEDLY	P2	32
WICKEDNESS	PWGR	22
	SAA	34
WICKER	J6	348
	G1	359
	AE7	478
WICKET	B	182
WICKHAM'S	ESH	32
WIDE	AR	300
	AM	62
	AM	88
	AM	710
	AM	887
	AM	930
	AM	1141
	CM	14
	AA	9
	SAA	557
	EDGA	11
	ER	77
	HAP	661

WIDE	J10	278
	J10	364
	M1	225
	M1	456
	M13	199
	VP1	3
	G2	374
	G3	431
	G3	660
	AE1	114
	AE2	448
	AE2	896
	AE3	131
	AE6	339
	AE6	744
	AE7	663
	AE7	786
	AE8	772
	AE8	945
	AE9	592
	AE9	877
	AE10	67
	AE10	435
	AE10	955
	AE10	1022
	AE12	16
	AE12	157
	OAL	581
	KT2	222
	KT2	320
	KT2	406
	KT2	530
	KT3	397
	CAM	340
	M12	63
	AU	370
	GP	60
WIDELY	AM	426
	AM	1106
	GK	126
	G4	767
	AE1	559
	AE1	722
	AE3	927
	AE4	282
WIDENESS	M1	1031
WIDENING	AM	1179
	M15	639
WIDER	HAP	1911
	G2	381
	AE3	525
WIDOW	EPF	24
	HAP	1870
	J6	531
	HI	59
	AE1	491
	KT3	927
	B	46
	C	2
	C	431
	C	717
	M11	372
	WB	252
	WB	287
WIDOWED	EL	345
	DO	159
	B	414
	C	703
	M11	89
	M11	457
WIDOWHOOD	J6	204
WIDOW'S	AE9	282
	B	662
	BP	174
	WB	127
	AS	46
WIDOWS	SAA	64
	AE11	329
	KT1	335
	WB	543
WIDOWS'	KT1	74
	KT1	131
WIDTH	G2	388
WIELD	SAA	769
	TA	466
	HAP	1996
	G1	239
	AE1	690
	AE2	234
	AE2	913
	AE5	488
	AE5	535
	AE5	555
	AE6	1047
	AE7	949
	AE7	1023
WIELD	AE8	877
	AE9	1088
	AE10	343
	AE10	611
	AE10	904
	AE11	1082
	OAL	783
	HIF	354
	M12	801
	M12	822
	AU	179
WIELDED	HAP	395
	M13	56
	AE5	551
	M12	144
WIELDEST	MF	52
WIELDS	AE10	797
WIFE	AM	134
	PWGR	16
	PAL	16
	PAL	18
	EKK	6
	EKK	22
	CM	68
	HP	171
	DA	24
	DA	84
	DA	111
	DA	142
	DA	179
	DA	207
	AA	750
	PLB	22
	SAA	53
	OE	37
	OE	41
	OE	53
	AT	93
	EC	28
	L3	77
	L3	84
	L4	244
	T27	49
	H2	58
	TA	76
	HAP	384
	HAP	442
	HAP	2236
	BR	250
	ELW	2
	ELW	7
	EL	161
	EL	166
	MS	22
	EH	8
	EH	12
	J1	86
	J1	118
	J3	163
	J3	190
	J3	232
	J6	41
	J6	87
	J6	112
	J6	206
	J6	208
	J6	233
	J6	242
	J6	252
	J6	263
	J6	299
	J6	303
	J6	312
	J6	521
	J6	558
	J6	561
	J6	582
	J6	592
	J6	653
	J6	731
	J6	794
	J6	811
	J6	833
	J6	850
	J6	856
	J10	322
	J10	381
	J10	482
	J10	504
	J10	513
	P1	141
	P2	29
	P3	81
	M1	187
	M1	432
	M1	475
WIFE	M1	554
	M9	8
	M9	62
	HI	2
	HI	30
	HI	32
	HI	45
	HI	87
	HI	133
	HI	177
	ELT	34
	G1	389
	G2	743
	G4	658
	G4	672
	G4	752
	AE1	71
	AE1	941
	AE2	622
	AE2	768
	AE2	876
	AE2	881
	AE2	905
	AE2	925
	AE2	1048
	AE3	408
	AE3	631
	AE4	45
	AE5	806
	AE5	1024
	AE6	180
	AE6	687
	AE6	702
	AE6	1037
	AE8	912
	AE9	173
	AE9	807
	AE10	59
	AE10	856
	AE10	868
	AE11	413
	AE11	418
	AE11	575
	AE12	50
	AE12	1358
	OAL	370
	OAL	377
	KT1	76
	KT1	429
	KT2	32
	KT2	567
	KT3	224
	KT3	394
	KT3	379
	KT3	538
	KT3	1107
	TJD	18
	TJD	98
	M8	63
	B	447
	M10	2
	CAM	87
	HIF	297
	HIF	731
	HIF	735
	HIF	788
	C	56
	C	366
	C	391
	C	554
	C	570
	C	607
	C	706
	M11	19
	M11	49
	M11	57
	M11	190
	M11	361
	M11	457
	M11	469
	AU	324
	AU	469
	WB	148
	WB	166
	WB	180
	WB	252
	WB	280
	WB	287
	WB	304
	WB	326
	WB	346
	WB	354
	WB	363
	WB	490
	WB	500
	WB	511

Word	Ref	No.	Word	Ref	No.	Word	Ref	No.
WIFE	WB	520	WILDS	M1	644	WILL	AE7	714
	CI	512		VP10	74		AE10	356
WIFE'S	J3	333		G2	465		AE10	867
	J6	360		G3	532		AE12	878
	J6	690		AE1	810		OAL	93
	P5	225		AE3	848		OAL	631
	M11	213		AE7	540		KT1	486
WIFES	AE10	393		AE7	801		KT2	221
WIG	PCG2	16		OAL	351		KT3	246
	ENH	8		KT2	226		KT3	675
WIGHT	HAP	637		CI	75		KT3	678
	C	690	WILE	G4	593		KT3	1023
WIGHTS	EC	21		KT2	131		KT3	1036
WIGS	PMQW	11	WILES	AR	202		KT3	1056
WILD	AR	45		SAA	108		TJD	40
	AR	112		SAA	845		B	22
	RH	2		AE2	83		B	279
	SMA	1		AE4	181		B	430
	EWG	1		AE8	519		B	507
	AM	375		OAL	95		B	604
	PWGR	14	WILFUL	HAP	1287		B	682
	HP	78		KT3	405		CAM	120
	AA	55	WILFULLY	L4	137		CAM	172
	AA	198	WILL	SMA	82		CAM	229
	EPC	5		EIE	24		CAM	261
	MD	321		AM	149		HIF	6
	SAA	926		AM	470		HIF	325
	RL	38		AM	1055		HIF	408
	AT	36		CM	146		HIF	680
	L3	243		HP	111		HIF	708
	L4	37		PRH	44		HIF	789
	TA	61		MF	192		C	74
	HAP	157		AA	183		C	511
	HAP	166		AA	255		C	531
	HAP	194		AA	379		C	539
	HAP	430		AA	567		C	589
	HAP	690		MD	24		TH	193
	HAP	2542		MD	134		TH	420
	BR	68		SAA	532		AU	603
	EL	313		SAA	780		WB	87
	EL	362		RL	101		WB	102
	J6	317		RL	121		WB	424
	J10	228		RL	123		CI	206
	P1	54		RL	392		CI	240
	P4	43		RL	423		CI	310
	P5	45		RL	442	WILLED	PNH	30
	P6	68		L3	288		TA	85
	M9	91		L4	95		KT3	106
	M9	118		H3	33	WILLING	AR	224
	HI	24		TA	325		AM	259
	HI	36		HAP	340		HP	42
	HI	92		HAP	560		AA	941
	GK	113		HAP	622		AA	1031
	VP2	9		HAP	949		EK	39
	VP9	58		HAP	1077		H9	34
	G2	86		HAP	1369		T18	54
	G2	99		HAP	1697		TA	516
	G2	157		HAP	2008		J6	293
	G2	254		ESH	11		VP8	36
	G2	414		ESH	32		VP9	41
	G2	427		J1	101		G2	716
	G2	665		J1	131		G4	812
	G3	386		J3	67		AE2	963
	G4	26		J6	305		AE2	1087
	G4	43		J6	315		AE3	253
	G4	171		J6	379		AE3	583
	AE1	425		J6	731		AE5	273
	AE1	738		J6	821		AE5	909
	AE4	436		J6	844		AE6	220
	AE5	614		J10	159		AE7	294
	AE7	1053		J10	325		AE8	536
	AE9	978		J10	374		AE12	631
	OAL	7		J10	533		BP	121
	KT3	302		J16	81		C	300
	M15	115		J16	87		C	533
	SMP	32		P5	68		C	710
WILDER	AR	279		P5	116		M15	104
	M13	19		P6	120		M15	714
WILDERED	HAP	1254		M1	380		CI	318
	CI	172		GK	8		CI	632
WILDERNESS	PTW	27		GK	114	WILLINGLY	SAA	349
WILDING	G4	269		AE1	112	WILLOW	DOD	1
WILDINGS	AT	20		AE1	331		M13	85
	M1	135		AE2	302		VP2	107
	M13	117		AE2	824		G4	269
	VP3	107		AE2	938	WILLOWS	EUF	32
	VP8	54		AE3	480		G2	17
WILDLY	MD	30		AE4	571		G2	120
	VP8	22		AE4	832		G2	626
	AE5	696		AE4	893	WILL'S	HAP	1692
	AE5	840		AE5	70	WILLS	PUF	20
	AE7	722		AE5	923		T18	83
	AE10	1293		AE5	979		TA	495
	AE11	215		AE5	1064		G1	185
WILDNESS	G2	73		AE6	732		KT3	504
WILDS	D	5		AE7	279		HIF	408

WILLS	ESK	13	WIND	G3	305	WINDING	HAP	1270
WILY	AM	453		G3	362		J1	82
	CM	33		G3	432		J3	384
	G4	571		G3	513		PPS	7
	TJD	54		G4	11		M1	47
	C	496		G4	342		M1	225
	GP	74		G4	575		M13	121
WIMBLE	P4	68		G4	605		VP5	131
WIN	AM	982		AE1	200		VP8	98
	PCG1	5		AE1	438		G1	267
	SCG3	12		AE2	30		G1	335
	AT	92		AE2	282		G2	216
	HAP	855		AE2	406		G2	296
	HAP	2187		AE2	785		G2	691
	HAP	2227		AE2	1080		G3	22
	HAP	2320		AE3	97		G3	642
	J6	507		AE3	253		G3	649
	VP3	74		AE3	366		G4	184
	VP8	56		AE3	523		AE1	809
	G4	127		AE3	569		AE1	918
	AE2	462		AE3	692		AE2	286
	AE3	339		AE3	746		AE2	1000
	AE7	594		AE4	604		AE3	886
	AE8	862		AE5	22		AE3	905
	AE10	493		AE5	37		AE5	770
	OAL	171		AE5	42		AE6	40
	OAL	441		AE5	153		AE7	549
	MG	11		AE5	241		AE8	809
	KT1	33		AE5	316		AE8	947
	KT2	394		AE5	595		AE9	324
	KT3	331		AE5	695		AE9	517
	HIF	690		AE5	1086		AE11	284
	M12	825		AE6	302		AE11	782
	WB	131		AE6	117		AE11	791
WINCH	HAP	1427		AE6	920		AE11	1123
WIND	AR	64		AE6	1003		OAL	50
	VHH	2		AE7	820		KT2	382
	VHH	24		AE7	1113		B	107
	AM	120		AE9	286		TH	408
	AM	230		AE9	756		M12	63
	AM	344		AE10	86		CI	377
	AM	485		AE10	350	WINDOW	S	14
	AM	591		AE10	483		A	14
	AM	605		AE10	917		DO	73
	AM	615		AE10	931		KT1	229
	AM	744		AE10	1140		C	15
	AM	819		AE10	1282	WINDOWS	PWGR	10
	AM	917		AE11	32		OE	40
	AM	946		AE11	584		HAP	2504
	AM	985		AE12	243		J3	432
	AM	1191		AE12	404		J3	437
	ESF	26		AE12	503		P5	263
	PKK	27		AE12	519		G4	419
	HP	6		AE12	549		KT2	553
	HP	197		AE12	905		KT3	533
	PSF	14		AE12	989	WIND'S	G1	484
	AA	258		AE12	1096	WINDS	HS	144
	AA	278		OAL	14		AR	44
	PRH	33		OAL	824		AR	224
	MF	215		OAL	870		AR	242
	SAA	212		OAE1	14		AR	269
	H3	3		KT1	108		SMA	29
	H29	39		KT1	185		LC	75
	H29	82		KT1	469		VHH	17
	H2	41		KT3	358		AM	218
	HAP	465		KT3	364		AM	510
	HAP	113		KT3	592		AM	511
	HAP	447		C	304		AM	879
	HAP	1750		C	351		AM	881
	HAP	1796		TH	90		CM	9
	HAP	1801		M11	30		CM	91
	ODA	7		M11	94		HP	160
	J6	121		M11	216		HP	229
	P5	29		M11	497		DA	40
	P5	34		FL	232		DA	44
	P5	150		FL	280		DA	52
	M1	83		FL	357		MD	27
	M1	166		M12	751		MD	252
	M1	442		AU	520		SAA	559
	M1	678		WB	161		SAA	595
	M1	710		M15	65		SAA	1067
	M1	978		M15	456		SAA	1082
	M9	184		M15	508		SAA	1121
	M13	60		CI	104		H9	16
	M13	96		CI	105		H29	64
	GK	88		CI	106		H29	95
	VP3	127		CI	369		AK	166
	VP5	128		CI	387		AK	169
	VP7	12		CI	524		HAP	629
	VP8	101	WIND-BOUND	M12	36		HAP	1125
	G1	125	WINDBOUND	AU	291		HAP	1162
	G1	519	WINDING	UDH	4		HAP	1912
	G2	151		SAA	182		HAP	1932
	G2	541		AT	30		J1	11
	G3	120		H29	103		J1	224
	G3	135		HAP	476		J10	290

WINDS	P6	30	WINDS	AE9	714	WINE	AE1	271
	M1	44		AE9	748		AE1	299
	M1	66		AE9	927		AE1	898
	M1	139		AE10	149		AE1	987
	M1	153		AE10	157		AE1	1013
	M1	356		AE10	238		AE1	1018
	VP2	33		AE10	496		AE2	347
	VP2	84		AE10	566		AE3	455
	VP3	113		AE10	956		AE3	688
	VP5	6		AE10	983		AE3	817
	VP7	15		AE11	895		AE3	826
	VP7	72		AE11	1166		AE4	84
	VP9	79		AE12	133		AE4	298
	G1	65		AE12	163		AE4	303
	G1	77		AE12	761		AE4	658
	G1	432		AE12	952		AE4	659
	G1	456		AE12	1292		AE5	102
	G1	489		KT3	133		AE5	131
	G1	501		KT3	404		AE5	310
	G1	568		KT3	555		AE5	322
	G1	580		KT3	564		AE5	1015
	G1	606		M8	276		AE6	324
	G1	612		M8	316		AE6	350
	G1	617		HIF	653		AE7	1004
	G2	184		C	300		AE8	241
	G2	354		C	313		AE8	368
	G2	403		TH	79		AE9	311
	G2	417		M11	103		AE9	424
	G2	422		M11	112		AE9	452
	G2	463		M11	134		AE9	470
	G2	495		M11	145		AE12	262
	G3	217		M11	251		OAL	262
	G3	500		FL	394		OAL	268
	G4	12		FL	581		OAL	271
	G4	42		M12	11		OAL	278
	G4	205		M12	13		OAL	280
	G4	287		M15	92		OAL	616
	G4	380		M15	452		OAL	639
	G4	420		M15	519		OAL	665
	G4	432		M15	524		OAL	674
	AE1	80		CI	333		OAL	867
	AE1	105		CI	339		OAE2	24
	AE1	98		STP	5		AF	114
	AE1	122		STP	16		AF	121
	AE1	183	WINDS'	H3	18		MM	8
	AE1	188		G4	25		KT2	16
	AE1	502	WINDY	PUO5	10		KT3	946
	AE1	542		J3	460		KT3	989
	AE1	753		J6	15		M8	7
	AE2	152		J10	219		BP	93
	AE2	565		G3	585		BP	109
	AE2	846	WINE	AE12	1227		BP	110
	AE2	960		AR	273		BP	127
	AE2	1030		AA	617		CAM	249
	AE3	103		SAA	466		CAM	254
	AE3	157		H9	9		HIF	62
	AE3	164		H29	3		HIF	636
	AE3	191		H29	8		HIF	644
	AE3	258		H2	71		C	31
	AE3	574		GE	53		M12	309
	AE3	691		HAP	417		M12	335
	AE3	702		PDS	23		M12	341
	AE3	744		J1	105		M12	436
	AE4	70		J3	327		M12	763
	AE4	328		J3	446		M15	166
	AE4	351		J6	218		M15	485
	AE4	365		J6	289		M15	495
	AE4	447		J6	417		CI	551
	AE4	623		J10	40		AS'	96
	AE4	638		J10	326	WINES	P5	198
	AE4	759		J10	392		G1	470
	AE5	27		P1	67		G2	567
	AE5	74		P3	5		G4	387
	AE5	273		P3	181		AE7	249
	AE5	416		P5	216		M15	460
	AE5	789		P6	37		CI	630
	AE5	999		VP5	108	WING	AM	345
	AE5	1098		VP6	25		AM	426
	AE6	2		G1	10		AM	896
	AE6	243		G1	202		SAA	139
	AE6	480		G1	393		AK	191
	AE6	493		G1	472		SSC	46
	AE6	715		G2	12		G1	496
	AE6	952		G2	137		G3	14
	AE7	37		G2	330		G3	378
	AE7	292		G2	535		G4	29
	AE7	553		G2	636		AE5	789
	AE7	1100		G2	637		AE6	430
	AE8	287		G2	638		KT1	153
	AE8	568		G3	560		KT3	122
	AE8	784		G3	760		M8	125
	AE8	944		G3	789		FL	318
	AE9	105		G4	155		M12	748
	AE9	419		G4	399		SMP	6
	AE9	533		G4	547	WINGED	AR	6
	AE9	656		G4	553		DA	61

Word	Ref	No.
WINGED	EUO	1
	L4	5
	TA	49
	HAP	6
	HAP	72
	HAP	1224
	HAP	2411
	BR	52
	J1	83
	M1	624
	G1	508
	G3	236
	G4	73
	G4	448
	AE1	936
	AE2	943
	AE3	278
	AE3	463
	AE4	259
	AE4	388
	AE4	803
	AE5	316
	AE5	416
	AE5	681
	AE6	295
	AE6	962
	AE8	304
	AE8	310
	AE8	568
	AE8	936
	AE10	278
	AE10	466
	AE10	673
	AE11	1175
	AE11	1246
	AE12	243
	AE12	404
	AE12	482
	B	515
	C	771
	FL	441
WINGS	HS	52
	AR	109
	SMA	28
	SMA	52
	LC	75
	VHH	57
	AM	218
	AM	255
	AM	440
	AM	570
	AM	712
	AM	912
	AM	930
	AM	1085
	MF	207
	EDG	44
	H3	49
	H29	83
	HAP	322
	HAP	1360
	HAP	1743
	HAP	1803
	HAP	1857
	HAP	1865
	HAP	1910
	HAP	2302
	EL	58
	J3	45
	J6	789
	J10	367
	P6	146
	M1	66
	M1	77
	M1	153
	M1	358
	M1	418
	M1	710
	M1	926
	M1	931
	VP3	113
	VP9	35
	G4	108
	G4	120
	G4	161
	G4	271
	G4	297
	G4	439
	AE1	413
	AE1	550
	AE2	1030
	AE3	294
	AE3	312
	AE4	254
	AE4	369
	AE4	376

Word	Ref	No.
(WINGS cont.)	AE4	379
	AE4	762
	AE5	277
	AE5	281
	AE5	678
	AE5	855
	AE6	24
	AE7	478
	AE7	569
	AE7	775
	AE7	966
	AE8	292
	AE8	485
	AE9	15
	AE9	764
	AE10	270
	AE11	1255
	AE11	1318
	AE12	387
	AE12	863
	AE12	1227
	AE12	1249
	AE12	1258
	AE12	1266
	AE12	1292
	OAL	267
	OAE1	21
	KT1	549
	KT2	521
	M8	400
	HIF	318
	C	46
	C	155
	C	429
	C	666
	TH	54
	M11	274
	M11	348
	M11	351
	M11	473
	M11	482
	FL	450
	M12	804
	M15	368
	M15	566
	M15	601
	M15	700
WINK	AR	185
	PA	44
	AA	184
	PPC	32
	MD	282
	EDG	22
	RL	100
	J3	475
	J6	202
	P4	116
	PWR	17
WINKED	C	667
WINKING	HAP	90
	M1	989
	AE8	545
	B	289
	C	630
	C	800
WINNER	SMP	69
WINNING	L1	57
	AF	103
WINNOW	HAP	112
	G1	400
WINNOWED	AA	112
	BR	234
	G3	217
WINS	AR	317
	TA	140
	G3	316
	AU	27
	AU	196
	CI	635
	UDH	77
	HS	58
	SMA	103
	AM	100
	AM	598
	AM	682
	ENH	28
	PAL	40
	DA	45
	L5	13
	T18	44
	H2	45
	H2	64
WINTER	HAP	1735
	HAP	1745
	HAP	1825
	HAP	1928

Word	Ref	No.
WINTER	PDS	14
	J3	175
	J6	223
	P5	56
	P6	1
	P6	14
	M1	57
	M1	66
	M1	148
	M13	73
	SFL	4
	VP2	27
	VP3	127
	VP5	111
	VP10	29
	VP10	68
	G1	96
	G1	146
	G1	147
	G1	300
	G1	390
	G1	402
	G1	403
	G1	436
	G2	354
	G2	430
	G2	437
	G2	470
	G2	684
	G2	755
	G2	758
	G3	463
	G3	471
	G3	495
	G3	499
	G3	615
	G3	711
	G4	72
	G4	202
	G4	342
	G4	348
	G4	357
	AE1	600
	AE1	1046
	AE1	1065
	AE2	642
	AE4	70
	AE4	279
	AE4	583
	AE6	429
	AE9	656
	AE9	822
	AE9	913
	KT3	135
	C	620
	M11	112
	M11	490
	FL	581
	FL	593
	M15	316
	M15	452
	M15	696
	PMK	24
	AS	9
	AS	20
WINTER'S	H9	3
	G1	463
	G2	403
	G2	515
	G3	475
	G4	231
WINTERS	DA	90
WINTERY	AE4	205
WINTRY	VP7	72
	G1	271
	G2	463
	G3	567
	AE1	183
	AE2	152
	AE4	234
	AE4	447
	AE6	298
	AE7	292
	AE7	995
	AE10	496
	KT3	298
	BP	113
	M11	496
	FL	1
	FL	321
	FL	388
WIPE	T27	7
	T27	8
	OAL	181
	OAL	182
	KT1	74

Word	Code	No.	Word	Code	No.	Word	Code	No.
WIPED	AA	717	WISE	P5	174	WISH	MD	132
	T27	128		P5	176		EDG	25
	P1	143		M1	105		RL	282
	AE9	1105		M1	932		OE	58
	DO	67		G1	271		L3	87
	B	698		AE1	925		L3	134
	AU	211		AE5	922		L3	276
	CI	312		AE6	843		L3	310
WIPING	HI	175		AE9	47		T18	68
WIRE	P2	75		AE11	467		T23	73
	AE1	915		OAL	870		T27	109
WIRES	AE6	839		MM	13		H2	74
WISDOM	E	19		KT2	73		AK	168
	POE	4		KT2	354		HH	24
	POE	5		KT2	364		HAP	944
	MD	185		KT3	385		HAP	1441
	RL	75		TJD	7		HAP	2425
	RL	104		TJD	94		BR	145
	RL	188		TJD	137		BR	324
	L2	8		B	30		ELW	9
	SKA6	26		CAM	58		EL	371
	J6	642		HIF	405		ODA	59
	J10	538		HIF	776		J1	222
	TJD	32		C	132		J6	451
	WB	236		C	162		J10	6
	M15	219		C	197		J10	158
WISDOM'S	G2	428		C	200		J10	167
	ESK	30		C	474		J10	534
WISE	AR	114		C	753		J10	543
	AR	125		AU	460		P2	79
	AR	170		WB	141		P5	2
	AR	175		WB	512		M1	657
	AM	533		CI	47		M9	129
	AM	659		CI	247		ELT	27
	AM	674		CI	466		GK	123
	E	6		PMK	25		GK	161
	E	18		EWR	4		VP2	101
	PAZ	39	WISELY	LC	64		VP8	157
	PC1	1		SEL4	17		AE1	109
	POE	22		AA	493		AE3	639
	HP	249		AA	587		AE5	254
	EUF	30		L2	20		AE6	272
	AA	71		T27	12		AE6	591
	AA	105		H29	45		AE6	674
	AA	115		H2	15		AE7	866
	AA	142		HAP	525		AE8	163
	AA	376		HAP	582		AE10	182
	AA	441		HAP	906		AE10	701
	AA	566		HAP	1265		AE10	702
	AA	738		HAP	1604		AE10	894
	PLB	20		HAP	1724		AE11	85
	MD	90		HAP	2052		AE11	463
	MD	98		HAP	2469		AE11	563
	MD	183		ETS	15		AE11	875
	SAA	92		EL	66		AE12	1292
	SAA	165		EL	254		OAL	171
	SAA	242		J3	125		OAL	329
	SAA	512		J10	422		OAL	406
	SAA	546		P3	185		OAL	795
	SAA	639		G4	198		OAE2	32
	EDG	18		AE12	757		OAE2	85
	L4	152		MG	14		DO	110
	L4	187		KT2	371		KT3	176
	T23	111		B	328		KT3	1092
	H3	28		M15	121		KT3	1101
	H29	20		CI	182		B	572
	TA	389	WISER	ECG1	13		CAM	146
	PAA	24		RL	31		C	467
	GE	70		PD	5		M12	167
	HH	8		L4	21		M12	720
	HAP	823		HAP	1004		M12	784
	HAP	883		HAP	1791		M12	810
	HAP	1237		P6	84		AU	67
	HAP	2016		KT2	503		AU	77
	HAP	2106		AU	266		AU	349
	HAP	2401		AU	325		AU	506
	PP	9	WISEST	EKA	38		WB	127
	PKA	27		FL	596		WB	139
	SKA3	14		WB	134		WB	373
	EL	98	WISH	HS	36		CI	164
	PSH	30		AM	472		ESK	10
	J3	271		SMM2	27		EMKG	28
	J6	496		SEL1	4		PWR	10
	J10	124		SCG3	12	WISHED	HS	119
	J10	560		PAR	25		PWG	54
	J16	22		SLN	2		SCD1	3
	J16	38		SCD1	10		SCD1	9
	P2	39		PUO1	39		PUO1	9
	P2	72		EUO2	3		EUO2	1
	P3	106		EOE	16		AA	208
	P3	124		HP	102		AA	222
	P3	131		HP	109		SAA	517
	P3	241		DA	15		TA	46
	P4	30		AA	554		HAP	2190
	P5	49		AA	721		J1	50
	P5	163		ELB	8		J10	169

WISHED

M1	732
M13	100
AE1	244
AE1	352
AE1	725
AE3	613
AE5	971
AE7	361
AE9	82
AE10	161
AE10	387
AE10	540
AE10	980
AE11	193
AE12	419
KT1	226
KT1	357
KT3	322
B	464
B	638
BP	67
HIF	275
HIF	665
C	304
TH	220
TH	413
FL	135
FL	605
M12	306
AU	142
WB	126
CI	161

WISHES

SMA	65
AM	496
EM	29
A	16
SCD1	16
AA	33
AA	344
AA	471
SAA	1067
HAP	801
HAP	1391
HAP	1954
J6	336
J10	160
P2	32
P4	38
M1	127
M9	25
M9	124
M9	126
PLT	51
PLT	54
VP3	99
VP7	31
VP8	158
AE3	490
AE4	160
AE5	294
AE11	60
AE12	225
OAL	575
OAL	803
KT1	409
KT2	8
KT3	474
B	40
CAM	35
CAM	129
CAM	288
M11	190
M11	191
M11	219
M11	235
M12	307
AU	67
AU	350
CI	269

WISHING

L1	55
L3	154
NS	9
NS	20
NS	31
HAP	1719
HAP	2150
HAP	2589
J10	534
AE4	228
FL	470

WISP

J3	24

WIT

AR	200
AR	202
RH	34
LC	18
PWG	47

WIT

PWG	58
PRL	4
PRL	10
PRL	20
PRL	36
PIE	18
EIE	15
EIE	21
EIE	27
AM	642
PMQ	8
PMQ	21
PMQ	52
EMQ	7
EMQ	9
EWGR	1
EWGR	10
EWGR	30
PMM	14
PT	6
PA	3
PA	17
PEL	17
EEL	3
SEL4	18
PTL	8
PTL	25
PCG1	14
PCG1	15
PCG1	37
ECG1	34
PCG2	4
PCG2	9
PCG2	14
ECG2	23
ECG2	25
PFD	14
PFD	25
PLN	21
PCD	33
PUO1	46
EUO	6
EUO	13
EUO	23
EUO	32
EUO	35
PNH	43
ENH	10
PUO2	4
PUO2	20
PUO2	33
E	20
PAZ	6
PAZ	26
PAZ	30
PAZ	33
PAZ	40
ESF	8
PC2	22
ML	17
PAL	23
EAL	4
EAL	16
PKK	1
PKK	12
PKK	21
EKK	14
PTW	13
POE	4
POE	5
POE	20
POE	27
EOE	18
ETC	8
ETC	24
PCB	16
PLG	9
PLG	23
PO	23
UMR	3
EMP	2
PSF	2
PSF	39
ETG	3
ETG	21
PR	8
PUO3	28
PUO3	36
PUO4	4
PUO4	5
PUO4	18
PUO4	27
PUO5	3
PUO5	8
EUF	16
EUF	19

WIT

AA	153
AA	162
AA	386
AA	648
AA	653
AA	882
ELB	25
MD	32
MD	45
MD	49
MD	92
MF	12
MF	21
MF	89
MF	117
MF	150
MF	154
MF	161
MF	164
MF	177
MF	196
SAA	319
SAA	532
SAA	851
SAA	1057
EK	6
EDGA	34
RL	65
RL	76
RL	118
RL	325
RL	333
OE	44
PD	9
ER	26
ER	75
MO	15
L2	13
L3	260
H9	10
TA	337
PAA	11
PAA	19
AK	70
AK	153
GE	74
GE	76
HAP	123
HAP	747
HAP	891
HAP	1295
HAP	1717
HAP	1837
HAP	1983
HAP	2444
HAP	2465
PDS	4
PTS	12
PTS	41
PKA	1
OD	5
MS	4
MS	9
MS	14
MS	29
PSH	2
PSH	12
J3	153
J3	257
J3	288
J3	447
J6	573
J10	75
PPS	10
P1	243
P2	6
P3	149
P4	9
M9	117
PLT	12
PLT	45
ELT	10
ELT	12
MC	2
MC	4
MC	10
MC	27
MC	30
MC	53
EHC	9
EHC	23
EHC	30
EHC	32
OAL	280
OAL	383
OAL	535

Word	Code	No.	Word	Code	No.	Word	Code	No.
WIT	AF	166	WITHERS	ODA	41	WITS	PMQ	32
	AF	176		KT1	528		EMM	9
	MG	3		KT3	303		PT	22
	MM	39	WITHHELD	AM	881		PEL	16
	MFL	21		VP10	12		PEL	21
	KT2	507		AE9	612		PCG1	17
	KT3	983	WITHHOLD	JH	23		ECG1	14
	TJD	124		AE9	957		PCG2	21
	M8	375	WITHSTAND	AM	28		PW	22
	M8	379		AM	587		PM	2
	B	33		E	10		EM	17
	B	76		AA	845		PLN	44
	B	128		HAP	2125		ENH	25
	B	460		AE5	821		ENH	34
	AU	221		AE5	898		ESF	1
	AU	474		AE5	1042		PAL	10
	AU	496		AE7	87		EAL	30
	AU	502		AE10	230		PO	15
	AU	566		AE10	424		PSF	15
	WB	99		AE11	671		AA	163
	WB	143		AE12	1191		AA	571
	WB	168		HIF	43		PK	30
	WB	400		AU	593		RL	80
	WB	478		WB	109		L3	97
	M1.5	225	WITHSTANDS	AE10	616		L3	252
	CI	3	WITHSTOOD	PM	15		HH	1
	CI	126		AA	819		PTS	15
	CI	476		SAA	815		PMS	32
	PTP	18		HAP	1970		PKA	31
	PMS	14		HAP	2131		EKA	2
	ERL	2		AE2	153		PSH	41
	EMKG	10		AE2	173		PSH	42
	PWR	5		AE2	302		P6	563
WITCH	AT	71		AE2	678		PLT	8
	WB	331		AE8	391		PLT	10
WITCHCRAFT	EUO	29		AE10	969		AE6	899
	P2	65		AE10	1269		C	569
	MM	19		AE12	48	WITTOL	OE	48
WITCHES	MD	62		HIF	174	WITTY	PMQ	27
WITHDRAW	AR	133		HIF	423		PP	47
	AM	250		AU	250		J3	249
	AM	715		M15	630		PPS	14
	AM	1125		GP	110		OAL	691
	HAP	2379		CI	164		CI	11
	J16	30		CI	387	WIVES	PEL	11
	AE10	47	WITLINGS	PPS	17		PAR	24
	AE11	559	WITNESS	HP	137		EM	10
	KT3	840		AA	631		EM	20
	M12	764		AA	655		EM	29
WITHDRAWING	AM	391		AA	668		AA	9
	EMM	7		AA	681		EPC	31
WITHDRAWN	AA	912		RL	234		EK	30
	AE3	662		HAP	62		L4	259
	AE5	721		HAP	1262		L4	275
WITHDRAWS	HAP	1410		HAP	1384		L4	280
	AE4	116		HAP	2137		L4	287
	KT3	1052		J3	231		L4	290
	CAM	270		J16	47		GE	11
WITHDREW	AM	271		J16	52		J1	54
	AM	765		M1	601		J1	107
	HAP	2589		M9	19		J1	187
	J3	272		VP5	29		J6	373
	J6	29		VP8	27		J10	544
	M9	195		AE2	587		AE2	683
	VP8	19		AE4	710		AE6	424
	AE6	291		AE5	1031		AE8	782
	AE12	757		AE7	817		OAL	36
	AE12	1178		AE9	574		KT1	335
	HIF	559		AE11	361		C	94
	HIF	813		AE11	402		C	430
	TH	346		B	397		C	444
	M12	422		C	787		WB	546
	CI	381		TH	203		M15	535
WITHERED	PTC	6		M11	368		ETP	8
	HAP	1769		M12	157		PMK	13
	G2	40		WB	156	WIZARD	J6	727
	G2	426		M15	45		G4	571
	AE1	247		PMK	26	WIZARD'S	SAA	405
	AE5	644		EMKG	3	WIZARDS	J10	155
	B	290	WITNESSED	CM	36	WOE	DA	194
	BP	175		AE5	868		PUO3	3
	CAM	165		AE11	605		MD	67
	HIF	47		CI	112		SAA	738
	TH	286	WITNESSES	AA	922		SAA	1076
	FL	568		AA	1012		AT	77
	WB	226		MD	149		L3	43
	WB	490		VP8	28		L3	233
	M15	352		HIF	471		TA	2
WITHERING	AT	68		AU	20		TA	73
	T23	61	WITNESSES'	AA	642		TA	278
	H9	27	WIT'S	EMK	14		HAP	1607
	VP7	80		CI	62		BR	238
	VP10	113	WITS	RH	46		P1	174
	G1	158		EWG	10		HI	192
	MG	4		PIE	14		G3	389
	KT3	795		EIE	19		G4	771

Word	Ref	No.	Word	Ref	No.	Word	Ref	No.
WOE	AE1	18	WOLF	M1	316	WOMAN	WB	181
	AE1	670		M1	414		WB	201
	AE2	13		M1	682		WB	297
	AE2	6		VP2	91		WB	431
	AE3	506		VP2	92		CI	311
	AE3	585		VP3	124		ETP	44
	AE4	46		VP5	93		EWR	21
	AE4	627		VP8	71	WOMANHOOD	KT2	311
	AE4	970		VP8	140	WOMANISH	TA	278
	AE9	659		G3	620		CI	349
	AE10	1235		G3	801	WOMAN-KIND	OAL	390
	KT1	208		G4	630	WOMANKIND	PT	34
	KT1	490		AE1	374		PSH	26
	KT1	497		AE8	836		J6	136
	KT1	554		AE9	66		J6	479
	KT2	270		AE9	765		HI	185
	KT3	866		AE11	1007		G4	291
	C	206		AE11	1183		AE5	7
	C	471		GP	73		AE12	896
	C	557	WOLFISH	HAP	160		OAL	700
	FL	402		HAP	235		B	419
	M12	48	WOLFS	G1	653		M10	2
	WB	108	WOLVES	CM	100		WB	146
	WB	238		SAA	698		CI	424
	WB	345		SAA	742	WOMAN-MAN	M12	663
WOES	AR	49		AT	125	WOMAN'S	EM	13
	AM	1109		HAP	1298		HP	111
	CM	90		M13	20		DA	82
	MD	262		VP3	127		EDGA	19
	SAA	715		VP7	73		L4	95
	T23	27		VP9	74		L4	208
	TA	26		G1	199		AE4	390
	HAP	1912		AE2	479		AE4	426
	SSC	35		AE3	550		AE5	804
	P3	83		AE7	21		AE11	1079
	M1	914		AE7	952		OAL	380
	M1	1019		OAL	135		KT3	1134
	G4	570		M15	119		B	372
	AE1	243	WOLVES'	G3	417		B	376
	AE1	278	WOMAN	PMQ	38		B	460
	AE1	515		PT	38		C	557
	AE1	523		EMK	12		AU	264
	AE1	645		HP	258		WB	174
	AE1	793		DA	134	WOMB	AR	132
	AE1	891		ETG	3		SMA	119
	AE1	1061		PUO3	13		CM	43
	AE2	124		ELB	11		CM	131
	AE2	694		SAA	437		HP	231
	AE2	740		PD	32		DA	37
	AE3	199		EC	39		DA	150
	AE3	936		L4	180		AA	987
	AE4	44		L4	289		L4	240
	AE4	246		T27	61		L4	254
	AE6	143		T27	75		BR	165
	AE7	454		EL	167		M1	561
	AE7	830		J3	165		M13	222
	AE8	105		J6	77		G1	126
	AE10	93		J6	295		G2	109
	AE11	144		J6	395		G2	439
	AE11	818		J6	640		G3	158
	AE12	892		J6	741		G3	218
	OAE1	34		J6	810		G4	603
	B	658		P4	39		AE3	54
	B	710		M1	437		AE12	1278
	HIF	89		M1	531		CAM	305
	HIF	106		M9	49		CAM	322
	M12	715		VP6	70		CAM	346
WOFUL	PLB	20		AE1	502		CAM	357
	PK	38		AE2	794	WOMBS	M1	568
	EK	18		AE4	49		AE3	282
	L3	84		AE4	136		AE7	390
	J1	122		AE4	308		M15	415
	J10	43		AE4	819	WOMEN	AM	403
	P1	97		AE6	608		PT	30
	T27	43		AE7	915		ECG1	26
	M1	873		AE11	1016		PMQw	1
	KT1	131		AE11	1044		EMQw	9
	KT1	167		KT1	320		EMQw	21
	C	111		KT2	653		EMQw	28
	C	700		KT3	675		PM	13
	C	718		TJD	23		PC2	18
WOLF	PMQ	48		M8	53		EMK	25
	L3	59		M8	170		HP	64
	L3	217		M8	225		AA	551
	HAP	153		B	323		EPC	3
	HAP	293		B	452		EK	37
	HAP	338		BP	165		EDG	26
	HAP	466		CAM	222		PD	53
	HAP	538		CAM	360		L4	166
	HAP	551		HIF	418		L4	256
	HAP	801		C	128		L4	257
	HAP	818		C	420		PP	30
	HAP	1414		TH	409		EL	98
	HAP	1424		M12	241		J6	142
	HAP	1460		M12	283		J6	342
	HAP	2189		M12	626		J6	393

WOMEN	J6	455	WON	AE10	1259	WONDERING	SMA	112
	J6	464		AE11	24		DC	49
	J6	465		AE11	256		VHH	51
	J6	474		AE12	48		AM	924
	VP8	114		OAL	187		D	14
	AE2	668		OAL	305		SAA	969
	AE4	961		AF	1		TA	143
	AE5	884		AF	108		TA	492
	AE5	953		KT1	5		HAP	264
	AE5	980		KT1	125		HAP	564
	AE5	1003		KT2	32		SSC	19
	AE7	1104		KT2	161		J6	118
	AE9	846		KT3	387		J10	450
	OAL	115		KT3	661		M1	411
	OAL	305		KT3	664		M1	586
	OAL	309		KT3	1099		VP5	86
	OAL	312		TJD	12		VP10	30
	OAL	318		TJD	157		G4	519
	OAL	386		TJD	165		AE1	635
	OAL	421		HIF	492		AE2	40
	OAL	530		HIF	541		AE6	51
	OAL	695		M11	61		AE6	435
	OAL	741		FL	299		AE6	964
	OAL	806		M12	95		AE6	1178
	OAL	863		M12	249		AE6	1192
	KT1	61		M12	293		AE7	1105
	KT3	202		M12	603		AE8	352
	KT3	697		AU	308		AE8	802
	KT3	872		AU	591		AE10	628
	KT3	997		M15	61		AE12	1030
	B	33		M15	205		KT1	199
	B	127		M15	380		KT1	563
	B	384		CI	414		BP	155
	B	466	WONDER	AR	154		M12	230
	B	578		EUO2	9		M15	356
	HIF	735		EAL	5		M15	413
	C	555		DA	130		M15	450
	C	734		PUO4	13	WONDERMENTS	HAP	1792
	TH	278		MD	69	WONDERS	AM	360
	TH	420		D	38		AA	320
	WB	42		SAA	1043		AA	378
	WB	97		EC	34		SAA	49
	WB	122		L4	141		TA	144
	WB	141		TA	347		HAP	114
	WB	220		AK	24		BR	99
	WB	240		AK	122		M1	939
	WB	269		HAP	1552		M9	2
	WB	275		HAP	1667		EHC	4
	WB	290		SSC	51		AE6	377
	WB	298		EL	240		AE6	979
	WB	307		EL	295		AE12	369
	M15	482		OD	7		M15	463
	EMKG	41		J10	45	WONDERSTRUCK	AE9	394
	EWR	17		J10	198	WONDROUS	AM	1047
WOMEN-HATERS	EDGA	29		M1	518		PAL	13
WOMEN-KIND	OAL	868		VP1	52		AA	661
WOMEN'S	ETC	8		AE1	582		MF	187
	AA	472		AE1	696		SAA	374
	J6	380		AE1	723		EDG	18
	GK	84		AE1	990		RL	358
	KT2	341		AE5	497		L1	36
WON	AM	638		AE5	537		L4	132
	PUO1	4		AE5	545		TA	78
	POE	25		AE5	697		TA	91
	HP	23		AE7	115		TA	367
	HP	136		AE7	163		GE	15
	HP	224		AE8	125		HAP	637
	AA	23		AE8	218		HAP	700
	AA	169		AE8	975		BR	21
	AA	835		AE9	149		BR	75
	AA	959		AE9	603		EL	26
	SAA	957		AE9	972		J10	264
	OE	15		AE11	374		P1	62
	MO	10		AE12	378		P6	103
	T18	95		OAE2	7		M1	340
	TA	165		MM	50		M9	71
	EAA	4		DO	9		M13	224
	SKA1	13		KT2	247		GK	140
	J3	190		KT3	1019		G2	32
	J10	242		B	439		G3	432
	P6	111		B	490		G4	437
	VP3	30		BP	17		AE2	246
	VP3	168		C	365		AE3	380
	VP5	136		FL	64		AE5	123
	G3	281		AU	109		AE5	472
	AE1	5		AU	476		AE6	39
	AE2	263		WB	370		AE6	210
	AE4	134		M15	612		AE7	345
	AE4	334		CI	112		AE8	112
	AE5	425	WONDERED	EUO2	3		AE10	547
	AE6	174		AA	63		AE11	103
	AE6	496		M1	821		MFL	31
	AE8	505		VP1	50		KT2	216
	AE9	694		AE10	372		C	284
	AE9	894		FL	28		C	382
	AE10	515		CI	203		TH	218

WONDROUS	M12	732	WOOD	AE7	241	WOODLAND	KT3	215
	M15	537		AE7	684		KT3	967
WONDROUSLY	HAP	100		AE7	781		M12	476
	HAP	2329		AE7	1056		SMP	28
WONT	AE5	535		AE8	45		SMP	55
	AE9	803		AE8	144	WOODS	AA	55
	AE10	445		AE8	392		H9	4
	KT2	239		AE9	99		H29	64
WONTED	AM	1022		AE9	224		H2	47
	PW	6		AE9	517		AK	113
	AT	101		AE9	533		HAP	158
	BR	170		AE9	556		HAP	196
	G4	386		AE9	823		HAP	235
	G4	620		AE9	1072		HAP	2542
	AE6	661		AE10	313		BR	172
	AE8	516		AE10	329		J3	482
	AE10	1242		AE10	679		P1	200
	AE12	151		AE10	1270		M1	50
	B	232		AE11	13		M1	250
	HIF	352		AE11	266		M1	644
	C	672		AE11	286		M9	102
	TH	214		AE11	499		M13	19
	M11	15		AE11	1191		M13	121
	M12	156		AE12	1051		VP2	4
	AU	221		AE12	1112		VP2	86
	CI	559		KT1	588		VP3	98
WOO	RH	43		KT2	183		VP4	4
	LC	12		KT2	226		VP5	40
	PR	36		KT2	233		VP5	90
	L4	165		KT2	239		VP5	119
	ELT	10		KT2	543		VP6	114
	OAL	386		KT3	139		VP7	71
	OAL	806		KT3	255		VP7	74
WOOD	AM	312		KT3	269		VP7	82
	AM	345		KT3	284		VP7	91
	AA	97		KT3	630		VP7	95
	AT	36		KT3	905		VP8	76
	T27	58		KT3	934		VP8	82
	T27	112		KT3	957		VP10	12
	H3	16		KT3	974		VP10	64
	HAP	14		KT3	990		VP10	85
	HAP	521		TJD	52		VP10	91
	J1	181		M8	23		G1	458
	J6	14		M8	98		G1	491
	M1	775		B	102		G1	650
	M13	117		B	143		G2	118
	M13	190		BP	184		G2	187
	VP3	55		CAM	342		G2	398
	VP3	66		CAM	365		G2	438
	VP3	107		HIF	636		G2	572
	VP6	77		C	4		G2	614
	VP6	101		C	486		G2	665
	G1	111		C	613		G3	3
	G1	216		C	672		G3	339
	G1	272		C	764		G3	386
	G1	276		TH	75		G3	522
	G1	409		TH	84		G3	647
	G1	417		TH	89		G3	778
	G1	526		TH	104		G4	86
	G2	23		TH	269		G4	380
	G2	112		FL	39		G4	521
	G2	168		FL	61		G4	790
	G2	289		FL	271		AE1	777
	G2	421		FL	313		AE1	810
	G2	691		FL	413		AE2	568
	G3	124		FL	611		AE3	46
	G3	229		M12	386		AE3	153
	G3	240		M12	450		AE3	351
	G3	329		M12	746		AE3	761
	G3	426		WB	212		AE3	770
	G4	394		M15	469		AE3	848
	G4	785		M15	476		AE4	97
	AE1	433		CI	88		AE4	167
	AE1	617		CI	165		AE4	759
	AE2	66	WOODALLS	EKK	13		AE4	764
	AE2	73	WOODBIND	KT2	50		AE4	862
	AE2	303		FL	282		AE5	198
	AE2	400	WOODBINE	FL	171		AE5	885
	AE3	61		FL	521		AE6	8
	AE3	393		FL	525		AE6	208
	AE3	500	WOODCOCKS	PMM	10		AE6	380
	AE3	562	WOODEN	AE7	530		AE6	428
	AE3	855		AE9	191		AE6	760
	AE4	577		AE9	713		AE6	894
	AE5	375		AE12	977		AE7	540
	AE5	403		M8	150		AE7	717
	AE5	600		OAL	367		AE7	801
	AE6	217		CAM	357		AE7	936
	AE6	261		M12	144		AE7	1041
	AE6	523		M12	681		AE8	125
	AE6	956		M1	957		AE8	406
	AE6	1036	WOODLAND	VP10	81		AE8	417
	AE7	40		G2	3		AE9	102
	AE7	46		G4	552		AE9	514
	AE7	89		G4	783		AE9	803
	AE7	231		AE7	687		AE10	149

Word	Ref	Num	Word	Ref	Num	Word	Ref	Num
WOODS	AE11	203	WORD	PMS	20	WORDS	J10	193
	AE11	696		EL	331		P1	33
	AE11	821		J3	500		P5	8
	AE11	838		J6	240		P5	35
	AE11	1013		J6	566		M1	117
	AE11	1155		M1	842		M1	522
	AE11	1301		M1	1026		M1	895
	AE12	760		M1	1051		M1	901
	AE12	1345		ELT	7		M1	904
	OAL	351		AE1	769		M9	176
	OAL	834		AE2	578		M9	182
	OAE1	14		AE2	892		HI	168
	KT2	72		AE5	533		GK	10
	KT2	536		AE5	801		VP3	10
	KT2	622		AE7	162		VP3	114
	KT3	226		AE7	512		VP9	61
	M8	66		AE7	883		VP10	46
	M12	670		AE9	325		G2	179
	WB	17		AE9	406		G3	445
WOOD-SIDE	AM	989		AE10	1290		G3	456
WOODY	HI	34		AE11	89		G4	556
	G3	603		AE11	230		AE1	219
	AE7	703		AE11	510		AE1	276
WOOED	PR	36		AE12	22		AE1	291
	T27	39		AE12	1374		AE1	563
	HAP	2186		OAL	132		AE2	98
	AE11	545		OAL	401		AE2	199
WOOF	M11	237		OAL	553		AE2	263
WOOING	SEL4	27		OAL	671		AE2	380
WOOL	AM	825		OAL	690		AE3	57
	DA	107		OAE2	27		AE3	404
	J6	217		KT1	439		AE3	479
	P2	117		KT2	121		AE3	583
	M13	161		KT2	145		AE3	609
	VP4	51		KT2	305		AE3	620
	G2	651		KT3	372		AE4	5
	G3	590		KT3	716		AE4	72
	G3	679		M8	18		AE4	133
	G4	476		M8	236		AE4	388
	AE6	357		B	715		AE4	515
	AE8	881		CAM	122		AE4	650
	KT3	170		HIF	322		AE5	400
WOOLEN	POE	36		HIF	328		AE5	809
	VP8	102		HIF	533		AE5	927
WOOLLY	M13	25		HIF	545		AE6	67
	VP1	9		HIF	731		AE6	151
	VP3	158		HIF	770		AE6	240
	G1	366		HIF	782		AE6	722
	G2	168		C	276		AE7	26
	G3	452		C	382		AE7	326
	G3	478		C	768		AE7	603
	G4	493		M11	68		AE7	622
	AE3	844		M12	653		AE7	1035
	AE3	868		WB	187		AE8	50
	AE7	135		WB	188		AE8	489
	AE11	303		WB	502		AE8	632
	AE12	611		GP	54		AE8	655
	OAL	785	WORDS	DC	8		AE8	662
	M15	171		PMQW	5		AE9	154
WORCESTER	AR	74		EM	5		AE10	323
WORCESTER'S	DC	54		EAZ	6		AE10	627
WORD	PA	16		CM	70		AE10	1295
	ETL	21		CM	115		AE11	190
	ECG2	14		HP	88		AE11	199
	ELN	17		HP	182		AE11	476
	CM	111		HP	243		AE11	519
	PLB	35		HP	253		AE11	581
	PPC	20		DA	4		AE11	585
	MD	14		DA	68		AE11	771
	MF	208		AA	229		AE11	1199
	SAA	417		AA	675		AE11	1221
	PK	24		AA	690		AE12	72
	RL	383		AA	696		AE12	362
	RL	392		AA	869		OAL	93
	EC	26		MF	84		OAL	438
	L4	117		MF	211		OAL	498
	T23	12		SAA	185		OAL	526
	T27	43		SAA	427		OAL	534
	T27	83		RL	154		OAL	640
	TA	251		RL	270		OAL	693
	TA	484		ER	17		OAL	749
	EAA	20		L5	13		OAL	882
	EAA	33		FS2	4		MM	12
	EAA	34		TA	203		MM	54
	HAP	465		HAP	139		KT1	548
	HAP	618		HAP	462		KT3	92
	HAP	716		HAP	669		KT3	149
	HAP	758		HAP	773		KT3	891
	HAP	871		HAP	951		KT3	983
	HAP	877		HAP	970		B	271
	HAP	894		HAP	1307		B	307
	HAP	929		HAP	1616		B	394
	HAP	1268		HAP	2147		B	614
	HAP	1826		ESH	30		M10	66
	HAP	1958		J6	278		CAM	151
	HAP	2360		J6	282			

Headword	Ref	Num
WORDS	CAM	299
	HIF	38
	HIF	316
	HIF	364
	HIF	405
	HIF	412
	HIF	524
	C	468
	C	571
	TH	236
	TH	307
	M11	329
	M11	378
	M11	434
	FL	596
	M12	326
	M12	570
	AU	14
	AU	89
	AU	191
	AU	204
	AU	351
	AU	363
	AU	409
	WB	252
	WB	253
	CI	114
	CI	126
	ERL	6
	PMK	31
	PWR	23
	PWR	33
WORE	RH	58
	LC	54
	PIE	6
	PA	10
	PUO3	24
	AK	32
	HAP	395
	HAP	2368
	M1	859
	M1	966
	M9	35
	AE1	447
	AE1	922
	AE1	1052
	AE4	196
	AE4	385
	AE4	932
	AE5	49
	AE5	1027
	AE6	1056
	AE7	337
	AE10	249
	AE10	697
	AE10	764
	AE10	903
	AE11	1136
	AE11	1141
	AE12	146
	AE12	716
	AE12	1070
	AE12	1198
	AE12	1367
	KT2	476
	KT2	648
	KT3	26
	KT3	28
	KT3	36
	FL	168
	FL	236
	FL	266
	FL	346
	FL	354
	GP	94
WORK	AR	275
	RH	25
	RH	73
	RH	103
	LC	30
	LC	70
	DC	43
	AM	562
	AM	563
	AM	573
	PEL	15
	PEL	20
	ESF	13
	PC2	12
	EAL	31
	EOE	2
	AA	141
	AA	806
	EPC	22
	SAA	374
	SAA	458
WORK	RL	19
	RL	228
	RL	244
	RL	330
	OE	44
	AT	75
	ER	30
	L3	254
	T27	99
	TA	444
	EAA	7
	AK	158
	GE	15
	HAP	310
	HAP	1210
	HAP	1627
	HAP	2395
	PTS	2
	PMS	8
	PKA	23
	EL	59
	ODA	49
	J3	132
	J3	355
	J6	785
	J10	481
	P1	252
	P5	89
	P5	143
	P6	8
	M1	4
	M9	152
	GK	4
	GK	24
	GK	107
	GK	110
	GK	149
	GK	152
	VP3	59
	G1	13
	G1	352
	G1	390
	G2	296
	G4	81
	G4	244
	G4	273
	G4	475
	G4	808
	AE1	113
	AE1	609
	AE1	906
	AE2	671
	AE3	535
	AE3	877
	AE4	307
	AE5	891
	AE6	261
	AE7	67
	AE7	714
	AE7	765
	AE8	583
	AE8	596
	AE8	733
	AE8	820
	AE9	828
	AE10	658
	AE11	103
	AE11	198
	AE12	632
	AE12	1012
	OAL	33
	OAL	44
	OAL	306
	OAL	463
	DO	137
	KT2	457
	KT3	767
	KT3	945
	TJD	95
	B	104
	B	167
	M10	9
	CAM	291
	C	25
	C	74
	C	407
	C	534
	C	535
	C	589
	C	692
	TH	23
	M11	111
	FL	83
	AU	517
	WB	134
	WB	426
WORK	GP	105
	CI	74
	CI	559
	ETP	34
	ETP	46
	STP	32
	EMKG	39
WORKING	AM	683
	AA	156
	MD	223
	G1	490
	AE1	36
	BP	111
	M15	639
WORKMAN	J10	498
	FL	78
WORKMAN'S	HS	59
WORKMANSHIP	P2	95
WORK'S	P1	90
WORKS	DC	40
	AM	211
	AM	660
	AM	1092
	AM	1168
	PT	23
	SEL4	15
	MD	253
	SAA	455
	H9	19
	HAP	371
	HAP	925
	HAP	2327
	EL	119
	EL	373
	J6	796
	P1	97
	M1	199
	M9	91
	HI	185
	VP3	141
	G1	267
	G1	362
	G1	378
	G1	383
	AE1	1007
	AE4	127
	AE9	43
	AE9	205
	AE9	214
	AE12	1016
	DO	161
	KT3	774
	C	464
	WB	430
	CI	465
WORLD	HS	15
	AR	1
	AR	2
	AR	323
	RH	32
	RH	98
	SMA	1
	LC	8
	LC	78
	LC	76
	DC	23
	PRL	5
	VHH	14
	AM	7
	AM	18
	AM	656
	AM	876
	AM	1204
	ETL	8
	ELN	17
	PUO2	13
	EUO2	7
	EUO2	11
	EAL	23
	POE	2
	POE	14
	PCB	21
	EMP	9
	AA	358
	AA	809
	MD	102
	MD	278
	SAA	62
	SAA	682
	EDG	13
	RL	135
	EC	10
	ER	10
	L1	42
	L1	58
	L3	6

Word	Code	Num
WORLD	L3	241
	L3	294
	L5	2
	T18	47
	H9	14
	TA	238
	EAA	34
	GE	43
	HH	23
	HH	30
	HAP	82
	HAP	133
	HAP	275
	HAP	671
	HAP	691
	HAP	898
	HAP	1423
	HAP	2311
	HAP	2320
	HAP	2479
	J1	23
	J3	213
	J6	16
	J6	408
	J6	738
	J10	1
	J10	151
	J10	273
	P1	104
	P2	18
	M1	13
	M1	70
	M1	145
	M1	164
	M1	278
	M1	333
	M1	382
	M1	401
	M1	456
	M1	469
	M1	586
	M1	797
	M1	903
	M1	1007
	M1	1083
	M1	1090
	M9	70
	M9	117
	HI	58
	GK	132
	VP1	3
	VP1	90
	VP1	112
	VP3	131
	VP4	17
	VP6	56
	VP6	63
	VP8	15
	VP8	19
	G1	33
	G1	94
	G1	333
	G1	677
	G1	689
	G2	458
	G2	784
	G3	264
	AE1	87
	AE1	324
	AE1	384
	AE1	407
	AE1	640
	AE1	847
	AE1	920
	AE3	131
	AE3	216
	AE4	149
	AE4	165
	AE4	339
	AE4	393
	AE4	872
	AE5	1027
	AE6	337
	AE6	842
	AE6	843
	AE6	1076
	AE6	1174
	AE7	352
	AE7	374
	AE9	613
	AE9	883
	AE10	5
	AE10	17
	AE10	144
	AE10	308
	AE12	757

Word	Code	Num
WORLD	AE12	1236
	OAL	61
	OAL	201
	OAL	844
	AF	33
	AF	103
	MG	19
	MG	39
	DO	100
	KT1	60
	KT1	471
	KT1	567
	KT2	201
	KT2	263
	KT2	406
	KT2	607
	KT3	3
	KT3	21
	KT3	144
	KT3	433
	KT3	566
	KT3	826
	KT3	878
	KT3	888
	KT3	1100
	M8	87
	B	501
	B	658
	CAM	30
	C	445
	C	658
	C	678
	C	690
	FL	143
	FL	518
	FL	558
	M12	719
	AU	178
	WB	462
	M15	226
	M15	291
	M15	334
	M15	364
	M15	644
	M15	655
	GP	90
	CI	15
	CI	37
	PTP	10
	SMP	9
	SMP	16
	SMP	46
	SMP	59
	SMP	65
	SMP	79
	ESK	9
	ESK	21
WORLDLING	M11	186
WORLDLY	GE	64
	HAP	1578
	HAP	2267
	WB	493
	GP	88
WORLD'S	LCA	14
	AM	847
	PLG	33
	BR	361
	J3	317
	J10	168
	VCS	2
	M15	90
	ESK	3
WORLDS	MF	91
	RL	179
	EL	79
	M1	349
WORM	RL	93
WORMS	G4	354
	C	187
	M15	551
WORN	PMQ	41
	PCG1	20
	PCG1	38
	PAR	3
	ENH	31
	EUF	29
	AA	92
	MF	9
	PDG	5
	L3	167
	J3	282
	J6	501
	J6	744
	P1	140
	M1	604
	M1	758

Word	Code	Num
WORN	M1	1011
	MC	66
	VP6	26
	VP7	84
	G3	6
	G3	151
	AE1	243
	AE2	351
	AE6	1010
	AE7	282
	AE9	520
	AE10	1098
	AE11	9
	AE11	400
	MG	37
	TJD	133
	TH	36
	FL	555
	M12	118
	AU	156
	AU	190
	M15	408
WORRY	HH	17
WORSE	AM	828
	ETL	19
	PCG1	25
	ECG2	30
	PW	8
	EMQW	8
	ECD	5
	PAZ	5
	PLG	11
	CM	105
	PSF	30
	PUO3	34
	AA	109
	AA	583
	AA	810
	AA	885
	AA	931
	EPC	6
	MD	220
	SAA	96
	SAA	521
	SAA	713
	EDGA	17
	EDGA	23
	AT	67
	PAA	31
	HAP	693
	HAP	1602
	HAP	1801
	HAP	1976
	HAP	2351
	HAP	2383
	BR	158
	PDS	29
	STS2	8
	EKA	35
	J3	13
	J3	277
	J6	299
	J6	539
	J10	322
	J10	370
	J10	488
	J16	31
	P3	33
	P3	195
	P4	75
	M1	904
	M1	1064
	PLT	48
	G1	289
	G2	517
	G2	731
	AE1	330
	AE2	264
	AE4	526
	AE4	530
	AE4	726
	AE5	1081
	AE10	697
	OAL	471
	MM	19
	KT1	286
	KT1	482
	KT1	484
	KT1	520
	KT3	656
	KT3	750
	KT3	890
	KT3	1110
	M8	129
	CAM	27
	HIF	368

Word	Code	No.
WORSE	HIF	759
	C	133
	C	500
	C	518
	WB	415
	WB	432
	M15	319
	GP	124
	CI	425
	PTP	5
	PWR	34
WORSER	AR	3
WORSHIP	AR	291
	PIE	2
	PCD	19
	DA	147
	AA	121
	MD	106
	SAA	652
	SAA	915
	RL	46
	RL	50
	RL	70
	RL	83
	RL	169
	T18	75
	HAP	281
	HAP	2313
	SSC	20
	ETS	25
	J10	357
	M1	336
	G4	315
	AE4	39
	AE6	795
	AE8	356
	KT1	318
	FL	531
WORSHIPED	ETS	4
	J3	195
	J10	560
	AE7	841
	AE9	101
	B	31
WORSHIPPED	EUO	28
	PUO2	24
WORSHIP'S	P5	111
WORST	PCG1	37
	PO	18
	AA	815
	SAA	76
	SAA	275
	SAA	633
	L3	95
	L3	105
	T27	48
	H29	68
	TA	182
	HAP	240
	HAP	598
	HAP	1456
	EL	82
	J1	17
	J10	480
	P2	38
	M1	827
	PLT	41
	ELT	33
	VP3	77
	AE3	937
	AE4	974
	AE6	850
	AE8	761
	AE9	392
	KT1	289
	KT2	157
	C	61
	WB	140
	CI	22
	STP	31
WORTH	UDH	15
	UDH	100
	HS	98
	AR	141
	DC	22
	AM	460
	PCG2	28
	EUO	34
	E	26
	PC2	22
	ML	16
	ML	31
	ML	52
	EKK	21
	EOE	28
	ETC	10
WORTH	ETC	25
	STC	2
	PLG	28
	HP	8
	DA	5
	DA	76
	PR	23
	PUO5	22
	AA	578
	AA	840
	AA	901
	EPC	14
	SAA	631
	SAA	648
	SAA	809
	SAA	819
	SAA	957
	SAA	1000
	SAA	1003
	SAA	1051
	EK	32
	PDG	10
	RL	134
	RL	283
	OE	28
	L2	57
	L3	294
	H9	12
	H29	11
	HAP	1385
	HAP	1398
	HAP	2198
	PKA	36
	EL	103
	J6	610
	J10	207
	J10	525
	P1	58
	P2	135
	P5	108
	P6	20
	M9	14
	PLT	20
	VP3	72
	VP5	127
	G3	86
	G4	105
	AE1	851
	AE4	15
	AE4	446
	AE6	197
	AE6	901
	AE6	1159
	AE6	1215
	AE8	174
	AE9	328
	AE9	336
	AE10	1171
	AE10	1249
	AE11	760
	AE12	48
	AE12	650
	AE12	971
	OAL	771
	AF	103
	AF	104
	MFL	23
	DO	141
	KT3	330
	B	374
	B	550
	B	659
	CAM	66
	HIF	402
	HIF	412
	TH	147
	FL	158
	FL	558
	M12	713
	M12	825
	AU	563
	WB	385
	PTP	20
WORTHIER	AA	348
	B	638
WORTHIES	AA	915
	FL	535
WORTHIEST	AM	186
	M12	822
WORTHILY	P5	38
WORTHY	RH	99
	AM	972
	PTC	36
	SAA	186
	SAA	946
	L1	40
WORTHY	BR	198
	J6	233
	J10	498
	J16	32
	P1	82
	M1	251
	M1	802
	VCS	6
	VP4	65
	VP5	83
	VP8	12
	VP10	50
	AE4	135
	AE6	702
	AE6	898
	AE6	1177
	AE7	546
	AE7	547
	AE7	906
	AE9	893
	AE11	633
	AE12	1269
	OAL	41
	OAL	784
	KT1	49
	KT1	359
	KT1	595
	KT2	161
	KT3	827
	B	44
	B	498
	BP	165
	C	197
	C	615
	C	686
	M12	533
	AU	536
	CI	49
	CI	492
	AS	70
WOUND	LC	101
	AM	436
	S	11
	S	15
	CM	25
	CM	34
	CM	108
	CM	144
	AA	500
	AA	924
	SAA	135
	L4	26
	L4	44
	NS	24
	TA	295
	HAP	224
	HAP	1374
	SKA6	6
	P1	232
	P3	220
	P4	99
	P4	104
	M1	390
	M1	928
	VP2	37
	G2	587
	G3	397
	G4	116
	G4	426
	AE1	668
	AE1	68
	AE1	122
	AE2	69
	AE2	293
	AE2	756
	AE3	38
	AE4	434
	AE4	952
	AE4	982
	AE5	361
	AE5	584
	AE5	640
	AE5	661
	AE5	684
	AE6	603
	AE6	611
	AE6	667
	AE7	1040
	AE8	768
	AE9	470
	AE9	564
	AE9	579
	AE9	783
	AE9	948
	AE9	1006
	AE9	1017

Word	Ref	No.
WOUND	AE10	43
	AE10	180
	AE10	412
	AE10	486
	AE10	564
	AE10	828
	AE10	990
	AE10	1007
	AE10	1029
	AE10	1032
	AE10	1049
	AE10	1109
	AE10	1117
	AE10	1127
	AE10	1184
	AE10	1199
	AE10	1213
	AE10	1223
	AE10	1313
	AE11	54
	AE11	84
	AE11	646
	AE11	948
	AE11	958
	AE11	970
	AE11	989
	AE11	1100
	AE12	465
	AE12	486
	AE12	574
	AE12	588
	AE12	620
	AE12	628
	AE12	774
	AE12	929
	AE12	1049
	AE12	1080
	AE12	1156
	AE12	1342
	AE12	1377
	OAL	693
	OAE1	30
	KT1	150
	KT1	257
	KT1	273
	KT2	199
	KT2	206
	KT3	400
	KT3	603
	KT3	613
	KT3	644
	M8	140
	M8	154
	M8	177
	M8	189
	M8	197
	M8	351
	HIF	799
	C	280
	TH	195
	TH	210
	M12	154
	M12	174
	M12	182
	M12	257
	M12	354
	M12	387
	M12	414
	M12	421
	M12	473
	M12	519
	M12	562
	M12	716
	M12	747
	M12	756
	AU	130
	AU	407
WOUNDED	AM	245
	AM	293
	AM	492
	SMM2	6
	SMM2	28
	CM	143
	J3	255
	G2	108
	G4	116
	AE1	475
	AE2	592
	AE3	55
	AE3	61
	AE9	785
	AE10	1280
	AE12	566
	AE12	613
	AE12	946
	OAL	293
	KT1	274
WOUNDED	KT2	199
	KT3	724
	M12	391
	M12	419
	M12	575
	M12	595
	AU	94
	AU	123
	AU	485
WOUND'S	M8	198
WOUNDS	AR	57
	AM	295
	CM	10
	DA	203
	AA	72
	T27	52
	HAP	6
	SFL	12
	G1	142
	G3	350
	G3	570
	AE2	363
	AE2	375
	AE2	849
	AE2	1019
	AE3	317
	AE4	96
	AE5	615
	AE6	1139
	AE7	251
	AE7	1036
	AE9	134
	AE9	648
	AE10	1186
	AE11	428
	AE11	1137
	AE11	1264
	OAL	25
	OAL	27
	OAL	193
	OAL	301
	OAL	302
	KT2	320
	KT3	505
	KT3	626
	TJD	167
	M8	107
	HIF	665
	C	244
	C	255
	M12	614
	M12	656
	M12	673
	AU	72
	AU	413
	M15	435
WOVE	AT	50
	AE3	629
	AE9	651
	AE10	1161
	KT1	196
	FL	74
WOVEN	AE11	104
WRACK	J6	614
	P6	66
	P6	76
WRACKED	DA	56
WRAP	AR	204
WRAPPED	SMA	51
	LC	19
	LC	97
	L3	108
	AE5	840
	AE11	108
	AE11	822
	AE12	1281
	GP	35
WRAPS	AE8	948
WRASTLER'S	J6	346
WRASTLERS'	AE3	365
WRATH	AM	1070
	AA	324
	RL	91
	L3	188
	HAP	2492
	HAP	2524
	BR	175
	J1	78
	J6	843
	M1	213
	G4	651
	AE1	342
	AE5	616
	AE6	168
	AE6	514
	AE6	525
WRATH	AE7	423
	AE10	1247
	AE11	358
	AE11	584
	AE12	505
	AE12	1170
	AE12	1231
	AE12	1368
	KT1	268
	KT1	445
	KT1	499
	KT3	264
	M8	4
	M8	14
	HIF	1
	HIF	11
	HIF	125
	HIF	608
	HIF	624
	M12	49
	AU	295
WRATHFUL	T23	104
	AE2	178
	G4	344
	AE2	438
	AE8	81
	AE8	339
	AE9	461
	AE12	74
WREAK	HAP	1262
	HAP	2412
	AE12	1233
	B	589
	M12	338
WREAKS	M1	1005
WREATH	PUO1	43
	SAA	1040
	AT	51
	T18	71
	H29	5
	VP6	24
	VP7	89
	G3	50
	AE1	973
	AE4	731
	AE7	588
	AE8	48
	AE8	365
	KT2	518
	KT3	913
WREATHED	DA	107
	M1	761
	AE10	745
	KT3	86
	FL	540
WREATHES	AE7	549
WREATHING	VP4	22
	VP9	84
WREATHS	PTC	5
	T18	2
	M13	227
	VP7	36
	VP10	61
	G1	480
	AE2	396
	AE4	212
	AE5	145
	AE5	176
	AE5	405
	AE5	727
	AE6	1049
	AE7	208
	AE7	678
	AE10	295
	AE12	185
	OAL	122
	OAE1	33
	FL	172
	FL	528
	FL	555
WREATHY	AE4	438
WRECK	SAA	486
	SAA	852
	SAA	1002
	RL	426
	L3	244
	H29	91
	M11	316
	M11	371
WRECKED	AK	171
	G4	42
WRECKS	J6	537
WRENCH	AE10	1273
	M12	499
WRENCHED	AE11	1189
	AE12	534

Word	Code	No.
WRENCHED	AE12	1132
	TH	129
	M12	130
	M12	447
	M12	500
WRENCHES	AE12	13
WRENCHING	P5	6
	AE2	630
WREST	RL	309
	HAP	186
	WB	307
WRESTLED	KT3	1000
WRESTLER'S	AE6	874
WRESTLERS	TJD	30
WRESTLING	G2	775
WRETCH	AM	724
	ET	10
	EAL	15
	AA	584
	AA	669
	MD	51
	L3	83
	L3	123
	L3	147
	L3	292
	T23	70
	T23	86
	H3	44
	FS2	15
	PDS	9
	J1	48
	J3	251
	P2	92
	P2	124
	P3	24
	P3	59
	P3	63
	P3	76
	P4	50
	P6	141
	M1	291
	M1	739
	G2	728
	AE1	67
	AE2	169
	AE2	196
	AE2	898
	AE4	718
	AE4	879
	AE6	504
	AE6	767
	AE6	793
	AE8	299
	AE9	529
	AE10	773
	AE10	956
	AE10	1031
	AE11	1187
	AE11	1228
	AE12	1160
	KT1	450
	M8	287
	M8	314
	HIF	121
	M11	182
	M11	456
	FL	495
	AU	181
	WB	294
	M15	46
	M15	143
WRETCHED	EWG	8
	PIE	18
	AM	959
	ECG1	20
	SCG3	19
	ML	35
	EUF	9
	AA	190
	SAA	888
	RL	64
	L2	16
	L4	205
	T23	1
	HAP	468
	HAP	510
	AK	62
	J1	178
	J3	324
	J6	557
	J10	139
	P1	106
	P3	24
	M1	65
	M1	180
	M1	481

Word	Code	No.
WRETCHED	M1	486
	M1	898
	M1	899
	R	4
	R	8
	VP1	15
	VP1	91
	VP5	31
	VP6	70
	VP6	77
	G4	466
	G4	737
	G4	752
	AE1	459
	AE1	739
	AE1	846
	AE2	54
	AE2	89
	AE2	108
	AE2	284
	AE2	725
	AE2	736
	AE2	1009
	AE2	1042
	AE2	1085
	AE3	407
	AE4	653
	AE5	810
	AE5	812
	AE6	842
	AE6	588
	AE10	438
	AE10	449
	AE10	690
	AE10	837
	AE10	1260
	AE11	77
	AE11	400
	AE11	1277
	OAL	350
	KT1	61
	KT1	75
	KT1	96
	KT1	482
	KT2	264
	KT3	1108
	M8	369
	B	756
	CAM	86
	CAM	126
	CAM	334
	HIF	571
	M11	316
	M11	372
	M11	427
	PTP	1
WRETCHES	J3	403
	P3	127
	AE3	816
	AE3	840
	AE8	639
WRETCH'S	KT1	417
WRIGGLED	WB	345
WRIGGLING	MD	31
WRING	AE11	1272
WRINKLE	TA	11
	P6	34
WRINKLED	AE9	890
	BP	114
WRINKLES	EAL	27
	J6	209
	J10	310
	AE7	585
	OAL	272
WRISTS	AE5	565
WRIT	LC	146
	PRL	3
	PRL	18
	PRL	26
	PMQ	1
	EMQ	4
	PWGR	14
	EWGR	38
	PT	26
	PA	4
	PCG1	13
	ECG1	33
	ECG2	26
	ECG2	32
	EM	3
	PCD	32
	PUO2	19
	PAZ	5
	ESF	7
	EAL	19
	AA	665

Word	Code	No.
WRIT	MF	149
	MF	195
	SAA	95
	GE	81
	HAP	746
	HAP	777
	HAP	886
	HAP	910
	HAP	915
	HAP	917
	HAP	923
	HAP	1296
	HAP	1784
	HAP	2039
	PMS	13
	OD	2
	MS	15
	J1	7
	J6	325
	J10	110
	P1	221
	P1	244
	P1	252
	PLT	46
	MC	3
	VP5	18
	VP5	19
	OAL	521
	OAE2	24
	MM	15
	B	89
	B	93
	C	380
	PTP	19
WRITE	RH	99
	PRL	21
	EIE	8
	AM	357
	AM	698
	PMQ	54
	PMQ	57
	PA	16
	PA	48
	PEL	1
	PEL	9
	EEL	34
	PTL	6
	ETL	28
	PCG1	9
	PCG1	29
	PCG1	40
	PCG2	1
	ECG2	13
	PLN	16
	ESF	32
	PC1	12
	PC1	29
	ML	14
	PLG	2
	PLG	16
	ETC	14
	CM	5
	HP	90
	HP	139
	HP	143
	PSF	21
	ETG	17
	PUO4	15
	MF	167
	MF	199
	SAA	444
	SAA	452
	SAA	479
	SAA	509
	SAA	941
	PK	30
	EDGA	22
	RL	291
	MO	21
	TA	333
	GE	67
	HAP	175
	HAP	1649
	PDS	3
	PMS	26
	PKA	6
	MS	2
	J1	43
	J1	122
	J3	389
	J3	503
	J6	343
	J6	831
	P1	29
	P1	86
	P1	95

Word	Code	No.
WRITE	P5	11
	P5	254
	GK	74
	GK	77
	GK	94
	EHC	12
	VP6	8
	G3	6
	AE3	583
	AE6	119
	OAL	489
	OAL	518
	OAL	533
	OAL	551
	OAL	642
	MM	1
	KT1	472
	KT2	662
	FL	613
	CI	7
	CI	15
	CI	25
	PTP	1
	PTP	21
	PTP	51
	EP	5
	EWR	18
WRITER	PUO1	22
	CM	2
	PSF	5
	PR	30
WRITER'S	MF	154
WRITERS	PMQ	57
	RL	139
WRITES	PIE	25
	PTL	8
	ECG2	28
	EAZ	31
	EAZ	40
	PD	9
	ER	66
	PKA	8
	J6	201
	P3	21
	VP3	134
	OAL	550
	PTP	9
	PTP	42
WRITEST	P1	109
WRITHED	T23	17
	AE8	344
	AE10	448
	M12	655
WRITHEN	M1	453
	AE6	802
	AE8	567
WRITHES	AE11	1102
	CAM	359
WRITING	PRL	29
	PMQ	33
	EWGR	1
	PEL	12
	ECG2	30
	EAZ	35
	AA	614
	MF	205
	SAA	395
	SAA	497
	GE	57
	PDS	46
	PMS	30
	EKA	11
	J1	23
	PLT	37
	OAL	487
WRITINGS	MF	191
	HAP	1513
WRITTEN	RL	139
	RL	202
	RL	270
	RL	350
	RL	392
	HAP	877
	HAP	890
	HAP	894
	M1	118
	M1	119
	C	677
	EP	4
WRONG	PWG	30
	PMM	15
	SM1	11
	HP	240
	DA	113
	AA	89
	AA	414
WRONG	AA	547
	MD	135
	MD	138
	MD	245
	SAA	681
	EDG	13
	RL	100
	OE	50
	TA	419
	HAP	1732
	HAP	2042
	HAP	2071
	HAP	2532
	EKA	36
	ESH	16
	J10	384
	J16	13
	P5	122
	M1	1061
	G1	678
	AE7	515
	MM	52
	KT3	808
	KT3	811
	B	270
	B	333
	HIF	233
	HIF	357
	HIF	700
	C	593
	M12	322
	WB	146
	WB	338
	GP	44
WRONGED	DA	70
	EUF	35
	AA	321
	HI	95
WRONGFUL	AE6	581
WRONGFULLY	AE5	447
WRONGS	HP	35
	HP	184
	AA	726
	AA	940
	SAA	111
	SAA	767
	HAP	2014
	HAP	2412
	J3	134
	J16	24
	HI	138
	G4	740
	AE1	471
	AE2	732
	AE4	534
	KT1	102
	HIF	241
	HIF	308
	HIF	351
	M12	280
	AU	309
WROTE	SAA	421
	PTP	22
WROTH	AE5	1110
WROUGHT	AM	316
	AM	356
	PMQ	3
	PUO2	12
	SAA	136
	RL	245
	T18	7
	TA	293
	TA	416
	TA	442
	HAP	114
	HAP	914
	HAP	2315
	HAP	2329
	BR	100
	BR	152
	MC	59
	GK	71
	G2	329
	G3	296
	G3	764
	AE1	902
	AE1	918
	AE2	135
	AE3	212
	AE3	625
	AE5	328
	AE5	351
	AE5	472
	AE5	702
	AE6	271
	AE8	831
WROUGHT	AE8	973
	AE9	348
	AE10	1247
	AE11	106
	AE12	972
	DO	11
	DO	162
	KT2	175
	KT2	325
	KT2	454
	KT2	511
	KT2	560
	TJD	40
	B	468
	BP	103
	HIF	545
	C	757
	M11	58
	M11	106
	FL	59
	GP	77
	CI	259
WRUNG	ODA	12
WRY	EDG	26
WYCHERLEY	MS	29
	MC	30
	MM	39
WYCLIFFE'S	HAP	176
XANTHE	G4	477
XANTHIAN	AE1	662
	AE2	791
XANTHUS	AE3	450
	AE4	205
	AE5	1050
	AE5	1055
	AE6	135
	AU	499
XENOPHON	AM	371
YARD	SCD2	20
	HAP	2377
	J3	369
	G2	766
	OAL	88
	KT3	466
	C	37
	C	114
	C	172
	C	192
	C	225
	C	435
	C	602
	C	719
	C	784
	M11	108
YARD-LONG	ESF	24
YARDS	M11	93
YARN	KT3	174
YAWN	L3	286
YAWNED	M11	307
YAWNEST	P5	192
YAWNING	PCB	15
	HAP	2059
	P3	8
	M13	220
	G1	646
	AE4	32
	AE4	708
	AE5	1102
	AE8	544
	AE9	579
	AE10	1199
	CAM	385
	M11	148
	EMKG	14
YAWNINGS	HAP	2585
YAWNS	J10	366
YEANING	VP1	20
	G2	751
YEAR	SMA	10
	SMA	19
	SMA	32
	LC	2
	PIE	6
	AM	13

YEAR

AM	639
EMM	16
ET	2
PEL	33
STL	17
ECG1	30
ELN	6
ML	37
PSF	9
ETG	5
PR	22
ELB	38
MD	16
PRH	2
PRH	10
SAA	290
SAA	456
SAA	1131
L1	15
L5	14
T18	26
T18	45
H2	28
H2	46
AK	15
HAP	170
HAP	1275
HAP	1712
HAP	1732
HAP	1849
HAP	1880
HAP	2314
BR	8
BR	16
BR	169
BR	183
BR	266
BR	306
LS	2
MS	12
EH	19
J3	277
J3	320
J3	367
J6	25
J6	619
J6	666
J6	672
P2	4
P6	168
M1	82
M1	149
M1	372
M13	119
SFL	4
EHC	37
VP3	62
VP5	89
VP5	105
VP7	63
G1	8
G1	27
G1	35
G1	68
G1	113
G1	178
G1	307
G1	321
G1	349
G1	398
G1	420
G1	428
G1	572
G2	8
G2	432
G2	459
G2	461
G2	469
G2	514
G2	550
G2	557
G2	561
G2	568
G2	740
G2	751
G3	669
G4	72
G4	337
AE2	267
AE2	409
AE3	191
AE5	61
AE5	63
AE6	1084
AE9	194
AE12	1047

YEAR

OAL	491
DO	29
DO	81
KT1	168
KT1	543
KT1	589
KT2	9
KT2	54
KT2	91
KT2	456
KT3	134
KT3	217
KT3	1004
TJD	19
TJD	134
M8	33
C	12
C	31
C	456
FL	9
FL	486
FL	605
M12	106
M12	771
WB	15
WB	102
WB	204
M15	179
M15	214
M15	296
M15	304
M15	308
CI	122
SMP	11
AS	2
AS	11

YEARLY

EEL	36
EUO2	10
TA	297
J3	236
J3	289
VP7	48
G1	475
G3	112
G3	113
AE5	77
AE6	27
MG	12
M8	402

YEARNS

PRH	29

YEAR'S

ECG1	25

YEARS

SMA	27
LC	146
AM	26
AM	71
ECG1	17
EAZ	31
PC1	3
PTW	28
EOE	23
PO	11
DA	156
PSF	23
AA	218
AA	818
AA	985
AA	1029
PLB	29
MD	59
D	22
MF	16
MF	149
RL	235
AT	35
L2	60
L3	141
L3	215
L3	321
T18	38
H9	28
TA	43
TA	210
TA	508
TA	421
PAA	1
HAP	1444
HAP	1504
HAP	1586
HAP	1588
BR	68
BR	136
ETS	22
ODA	38
J6	10
J6	276
J6	323

YEARS

J10	387
J10	391
P3	99
P4	1
P5	82
M1	140
M1	189
M1	786
M1	1046
M9	68
HI	61
VP1	92
VP4	7
VP4	58
VP5	9
G1	107
G1	284
G3	151
G3	299
G3	717
G4	302
G4	421
AE1	46
AE1	72
AE1	366
AE1	379
AE2	767
AE2	1060
AE3	440
AE3	636
AE4	43
AE4	77
AE5	232
AE5	386
AE5	814
AE6	420
AE6	451
AE6	511
AE6	734
AE6	882
AE6	1013
AE6	1018
AE6	1201
AE7	311
AE7	577
AE8	63
AE8	385
AE9	266
AE9	310
AE9	364
AE9	417
AE9	638
AE9	892
AE10	766
AE10	895
AE11	268
AE11	366
AE11	814
AE11	868
AE12	649
OAL	485
OAL	214
OAL	545
OAL	731
KT1	55
KT1	68
KT1	607
KT2	3
KT2	71
KT2	217
KT2	368
KT3	225
KT3	1131
TJD	59
TJD	91
TJD	157
M8	324
CAM	18
CAM	159
CAM	252
CAM	301
CAM	382
CAM	387
HIF	372
C	365
C	385
TH	200
M12	30
M12	617
M12	768
AU	335
M15	343
M15	614
M15	630
GP	8
AS	47

Word	Code	No.	Word	Code	No.	Word	Code	No.
YEARS	AS	48	YIELD	L3	262	YIELDS	AE7	1087
YEARS'	GE	81		HAP	730		AU	596
	J10	301		HAP	813	YOKE	AA	177
	AE2	262		BR	331		AA	332
	AE9	679		SKA2	2		MD	302
YELL	AE3	550		J1	225		SAA	227
	AE4	958		M13	193		SAA	678
	M15	121		HI	23		T27	42
YELLED	DA	100		HI	108		H2	91
YELLING	AE3	887		SLT2	2		J6	294
	C	271		VP2	80		J10	175
YELLOW	ER	67		VP7	80		M1	159
	HAP	1734		VP7	95		M1	642
	P3	191		VP10	99		M13	81
	M1	415		G1	115		VP2	96
	M9	34		G1	161		VP3	143
	VP5	48		G1	169		VP5	43
	G1	84		G1	181		G1	69
	G2	745		G1	363		G1	254
	G3	544		G2	746		G1	300
	G4	187		G3	163		G1	380
	G4	267		AE1	56		G3	88
	AE2	409		AE1	653		G3	94
	AE2	982		AE2	660		G3	227
	AE3	186		AE2	951		G3	273
	AE4	585		AE2	1093		G3	770
	AE4	967		AE3	218		G4	781
	AE5	89		AE4	25		G4	796
	AE5	495		AE5	644		AE1	31
	AE7	45		AE6	1207		AE3	155
	AE7	952		AE8	699		AE4	22
	AE7	986		AE8	937		AE6	348
	AE8	85		AE9	159		AE7	140
	AE8	875		AE9	258		AE7	750
	AE9	862		AE9	1064		AE12	249
	AE9	1104		AE10	500		AE12	433
	AE10	1186		AE10	752		OAL	357
	AE11	109		AE10	1054		OAL	538
	AE11	955		AE10	1074		M12	107
	AE11	1105		AE11	472		M15	182
	AE12	164		AE11	654	YOKED	OAL	21
	AE12	885		AE11	682		KT3	48
	OAL	580		AE11	1258	YOKES	VP6	75
	KT1	530		AE12	275		G3	799
	KT3	42		AE12	565		AE3	713
	KT3	83		AE12	773	YOLK	M15	573
	KT3	351		OAL	310	YOLKS	PMM	8
	M8	32		OAL	395	YON	AT	57
	CAM	241		AF	167		T27	20
	HIF	302		AF	177		T27	86
	C	117		MG	7		H9	1
	C	148		KT3	160		ODA	66
	C	174		KT3	309		M1	805
	M11	127		KT3	771		HI	92
	M12	385		TH	33		VP1	24
	M12	692		M11	148		VP1	71
	M15	428		AU	143		VP1	117
YELLOW-LOCKED	AE10	786		AU	151		VP3	17
YELLS	AE6	755		AU	550		VP7	17
	AE8	332		WB	208		VP8	84
YEOMAN	KT3	462		M15	184		AE2	825
	B	262	YIELDED	AM	120		AE4	608
YEOMEN	MF	104		EL	221		AE6	494
YESTERDAY	J6	801		AE12	1359		AE6	505
	P5	93		KT3	318		AE6	916
	P5	94		KT3	521		AE8	252
	B	335		HIF	450		AE9	251
	HIF	582	YIELDING	AM	240		AE10	521
	M15	322		MD	253		KT1	259
YEW	VP9	39		HAP	1482	YONDER	AU	577
	G2	158		STS3	9	YORE	MF	67
	G2	349		G1	216		HAP	2392
	G2	628		G4	29		OAL	770
	G4	66		G4	666		C	1
	AE4	731		AE1	413		C	91
	AE6	311		AE2	66	YORK	AR	234
	AE9	854		AE2	295		AM	73
	AE11	1247		AE3	893	YOUNG	UDH	23
	AE12	1241		AE5	678		UDH	74
	KT3	961		AE7	850		UDH	80
YIELD	HS	78		AE9	1006		JH	11
	AM	446		M12	43		HS	29
	AM	544		PWG	53		LC	53
	PNH	18	YIELDS	EWGR	45		LC	136
	PAZ	18		SAA	739		LCA	44
	EOE	8		H2	79		AM	432
	HP	43		HAP	2541		AM	580
	HP	49		VP1	68		AM	697
	HP	66		G1	50		PWGR	25
	HP	251		G2	190		PEL	2
	SAA	661		G2	306		SEL1	6
	SAA	707		G2	753		STL	2
	SAA	835		G3	482		PCG1	21
	SAA	1055		AE2	852		ECG1	12
	SAA	1087		AE5	289		ECG1	18
	ER	10		AE7	945		PC1	8

YOUTH

Ref	Num
VP1	84
VP4	31
VP5	141
VP8	83
G2	531
G2	666
G3	83
G3	103
G3	108
G3	191
G3	263
G3	269
G3	275
G3	403
G3	537
G3	664
G4	265
G4	511
G4	631
G4	642
G4	645
G4	702
G4	725
G4	754
G4	817
AE1	465
AE1	602
AE2	93
AE2	641
AE2	724
AE3	79
AE3	187
AE3	364
AE3	629
AE4	201
AE5	388
AE5	570
AE5	874
AE5	954
AE6	668
AE6	1029
AE6	1077
AE6	1189
AE6	1202
AE6	1210
AE6	1211
AE6	1214
AE7	78
AE7	218
AE7	260
AE7	849
AE7	1017
AE7	1046
AE7	1087
AE8	7
AE8	161
AE8	657
AE8	723
AE8	742
AE8	860
AE9	262
AE9	276
AE9	329
AE9	366
AE9	374
AE9	452
AE9	530
AE9	573
AE9	579
AE9	737
AE9	745
AE9	801
AE9	827
AE9	876
AE9	895
AE9	902
AE9	1024
AE10	141
AE10	194
AE10	479
AE10	518
AE10	588
AE10	614
AE10	679
AE10	885
AE10	892
AE10	1123
AE10	1131
AE10	1152
AE10	1169
AE10	1191
AE11	45
AE11	59
AE11	690
AE11	745
AE11	1051

YOUTH (continued)

Ref	Num
AE12	31
AE12	65
AE12	74
AE12	414
AE12	578
AE12	581
AE12	874
OAL	46
OAL	64
OAL	209
OAL	259
OAL	524
OAL	828
AF	11
MG	4
KT1	176
KT1	418
KT1	419
KT1	454
KT2	480
KT2	506
KT3	387
KT3	771
TJD	4
TJD	58
TJD	61
M8	79
M8	103
B	26
B	34
B	57
B	138
B	252
B	276
B	433
B	434
B	568
B	752
M10	72
CAM	386
HIF	4
HIF	324
HIF	427
HIF	637
C	184
TH	9
TH	217
M12	111
M12	251
AU	470
WB	505
WB	532
M15	478
CI	50
CI	292
CI	467

YOUTHFUL

Ref	Num
STL	20
PC1	2
ML	46
DA	173
AA	32
RL	230
L4	71
HAP	1862
HAP	1870
BR	264
J3	446
M1	1047
VP6	23
VP6	74
VP7	35
G1	672
G2	669
G3	155
G3	166
G3	185
G3	329
G4	27
G4	259
G4	491
AE1	829
AE2	519
AE4	124
AE4	804
AE5	604
AE5	663
AE6	421
AE7	612
AE7	664
AE7	727
AE7	899
AE7	1003
AE8	218
AE8	766
AE11	233
AE11	582

YOUTHFUL (continued)

Ref	Num
OAL	96
OAL	791
KT1	142
KT1	534
KT2	222
KT3	82
KT3	861
HIF	373
FL	23
M12	617
WB	55
M15	342
AS	10

YOUTH'S

Ref	Num
AR	53
SAA	22

YOUTHS

Ref	Num
PT	29
PAA	19
HAP	1441
M1	599
G4	685
AE1	986
AE2	1042
AE3	127
AE5	393
AE5	722
AE5	782
AE5	882
AE6	27
AE6	426
AE6	831
AE7	205
AE8	236
AE8	362
AE9	916
AE10	245
OAL	200
OAL	289
OAL	293
KT2	317
M12	729

ZACYNTHIAN — AE3 351
ZADOC — AA 864
ZAKEN — SAA 555
ZANCLE — M15 442

ZEAL

Ref	Num
SMA	80
AA	181
AA	489
AA	586
AA	672
AA	674
PLB	46
MD	38
PRH	20
D	39
SAA	106
SAA	113
SAA	299
SAA	809
SAA	855
SAA	918
SAA	951
SAA	1005
SAA	1025
RL	216
RL	416
PAA	27
EAA	3
GE	26
HH	19
HAP	228
HAP	233
HAP	1137
HAP	1697
EL	49
EL	111
J10	138
P1	248
G4	300
AE2	320
AE4	835
AE5	126
AE5	972
AE8	249
AE11	1287
AE12	771
AF	147
AF	151
KT1	317
BP	133
HIF	436

ZEAL	TH	419
	GP	28
	CI	13
ZEALOTS	PFD	17
	MD	238
ZEALOUS	AR	193
	ELN	3
	PO	21
	AA	521
	HAP	2394
ZEBEDEE	GP	97
ZENO	P3	102
ZENOS	P5	280
ZEPHYR	M1	77
ZILOAH	SAA	1131
ZILOAH'S	SAA	1135
ZIMRI	AA	544
ZIPH	SAA	1134
ZODIAC	EL	150
ZOE	J6	278
ZONE	DC	10
	M1	55
	G1	322
	VP1	86
	M10	48
	CAM	144
	CAM	156
ZONES	M1	52
	M1	516
ZUINGLIUS	HAP	180
	HAP	688